P9-BJR-797

FOR REFERENCE

Do Not Take From This Room

WEST'S LEGAL
DESK REFERENCE

WEST'S LEGAL DESK REFERENCE

William P. Statsky
Bruce L. Hussey
Michael R. Diamond
Richard H. Nakamura

WEST PUBLISHING COMPANY
St. Paul • *New York*
Los Angeles • *San Francisco*

Riverside Community College
Library
4800 Magnolia Avenue
Riverside, California 92506
OCT '91

R

REF KF 387 .W49 1991

West's legal desk reference

Composition: Parkwood Composition Service, Inc.

COPYRIGHT ©   By WEST PUBLISHING COMPANY
                   50 W. Kellogg Boulevard
                   P.O. Box 64526
                   St. Paul, MN 55164-0526

All rights reserved

Printed in the United States of America

98 97 96 95 94 93 92 91   8 7 6 5 4 3 2 1 0

West's legal desk reference / William P. Statsky ... [et al.].
        p.   cm.
    Includes index.
    ISBN 0-314-48146-X (hard). — ISBN 0-314-79997-4 (soft)
    1. Law—United States. 2. Law students—United States—Handbooks, manuals, etc. I. West Publishing Company.
  II. Title: Legal desk reference.
  KF387.W49 1991
  349.73—dc20
  [347.3]   90-45651
                                                                         CIP

For:

Pat, Jess & Gabe
—WPS

Jodette Hussey
—BLH

Rebecca Caleff, Irene
and Mitchell Diamond
—MRD

Don
—RHN

CONTENTS

LEGAL DICTIONARY

Abaction 1. Carrying away by violence. **2.** Stealing animals.

Abandon To surrender totally and intentionally.

Abandonee A person to whom something is abandoned.

Abandonment The total and intentional surrender of property, persons, or rights.

Abandonment of actions, in general Failure to prosecute or bring action within statutorily prescribed period; failure to object or submit jury instructions; failure to demand jury trial.

Abandonment of children Desertion, willful forsaking, or foregoing parental duties.

Abandonment of property Relinquishment of all title, possession, or claim; a virtual intentional throwing away of property.

Abatable nuisance A nuisance that can be diminished or eliminated. A nonpermanent interference with the use of land or with a right that is common to the public.

Abate 1. To eliminate (abate a nuisance). **2.** To diminish (the wind abated).

Abatement 1. Termination (abatement of a lawsuit; abatement of a nuisance). **2.** Reduction (abatement of taxes; abatement of a legacy because of inadequate funds available).

Abatement of action An entire overthrow or destruction of the suit so that it is quashed and ended.

Abatement of a nuisance The removal, stoppage, or destruction of that which causes a nuisance, whether by breaking or pulling it down, or otherwise removing or destroying it.

Abatement of taxes Diminution or decrease in the amount of tax imposed.

Abator 1. Someone who illegally takes possession of land upon the death of the owner before the heir or devisee can take legal possession. **2.** Someone who abates a nuisance.

Abbacy The government of a religious house, and the revenues thereof, subject to an abbot.

Abdicate To voluntarily renounce.

Abdication The voluntary renunciation of a privilege or an office.

Abduct To take away a child, wife, ward, or servant unlawfully.

Abduction The unlawful taking away of a child, wife, ward, or servant.

Abearance Behavior.

Aberemurder Plain or notorious murder.

Abesse In the civil law, to be absent.

Abet To encourage someone to commit a crime.

Abetment The incitement of someone to commit a crime.

Abettor A person who encourages or incites another to commit a crime.

Abeyance Not finally settled; not being in force or use for a time.

Abide 1. To accept the consequences of. **2.** To obey.

Ability 1. The power to do something (the court's ability to enforce the order). **2.** The competence to do something (the ability to make decisions).

1

Ab initio From the beginning (the marriage was void ab initio).

Ab intestato In the civil law, from an intestate.

Abishering or **abishersing** Quit of amercements. It originally signified a forfeiture or amercement.

Abjudicate To deprive one of something as a result of a judgment.

Abjudicatio In old English law, the depriving of a thing by the judgment of a court.

Abjuration Formally giving up rights; a renunciation given under oath.

Abjure To give something up formally; to renounce under oath.

Able See ability.

Able-bodied Capable of performing the regular and ordinary duties of a job.

Ablocatio A letting out to hire, or leasing for money.

Abnegate To renounce.

Abnormal Considerably irregular.

Abnormally dangerous Extrahazardous.

ABO The system of human blood typing that produces the blood types A, B, AB, and O.

Abode Home, residence.

Abogado An advocate (Spanish).

Abolish To eliminate completely.

Abolition A complete elimination.

Aboriginal Relating to natives.

Abortifacient Drug or medicine used for producing abortion.

Abortion The knowing destruction of the life of an unborn child or the intentional expulsion or removal of an unborn child from the womb other than for the principal purpose of producing a live birth or removing a dead fetus.

Aboutissement An abuttal or abutment.

About Near in quantity or amount.

Above 1. Mentioned earlier (the above discussion). **2** Superior status (the court above). **3.** In excess of (above forty pages).

Abridge 1. To diminish (the order abridged the mayor's power). **2.** Condensed (an abridged edition).

Abridgment 1. Reduction. **2.** Summary.

Abrogate To annul, cancel, or destroy.

Abrogation The destruction or annulling of a former law, by an act of the legislative power, by constitutional authority, or by usage.

Abscond To flee in order to avoid legal process; to run away and hide in order to escape the consequences of something.

Absent without leave (AWOL) Not present at one's military position or assignment when there is no permission to be away, but without the intent to stay away permanently or to desert.

Absentee A person who is not present; pertaining to one who is not present.

Absentee landlord Lessor of real property (often the owner) who does not live on the premises.

Absentee voting Participation (usually by mail) in elections by qualified voters who, because of serious illness, military service, or absence from home for business or other reasons, are unable to appear at the polls in person on election day.

Absente reo The defendant being absent.

Absoile See assoil.

Absolute 1. Unconditional (absolute authority). **2.** Complete (absolute nullity).

Absolute delivery An absolute delivery, as distinguished from conditional delivery or delivery in escrow, is one that is complete upon the actual transfer of the instrument from the possession of the grantor.

Absolute disability A disability that originates with a particular person, but extends also to his or her descendants or successors.

Absolute estate An absolute estate is a full and complete estate, or an estate in lands not subject to be defeated upon any condition.

Absolute gift An absolute gift, or gift inter vivos, as distinguished from a testamentary gift, or one made in contemplation of death, is one by which the donee becomes in the lifetime of the donor the absolute owner of the thing given.

Absolute interest That which is so completely vested in an individual that no contingency can deprive him or her of it without his or her consent.

Absolute law The true and proper law of nature, immutable in theory, but not in application; very often the object, the reason, situation, and other circumstances may vary its exercise and obligation.

Absolute legacy One given without condition and intended to vest immediately.

Absolute liability Responsibility without fault or negligence.

Absolution 1. In the civil law, a sentence whereby a party accused is declared innocent of the crime. **2.** In French law, the dismissal of an accusation. **3.** In canon law, a juridical act whereby the clergy declare that sins are remitted.

Absolutism A system of government in which public power is vested in some person or persons, unchecked and uncontrolled by any law, institution, constitutional device, or coordinate body.

Absolve To set free or release, as from an obligation, debt, or responsibility.

Absorción Take-over (Spanish). Term used in business law to denote that one enterprise assumes control over another one.

Absorption Term used in collective bargaining agreements to provide seniority for union members if the employer's business is merged with another.

Abstention doctrine Doctrine providing that a federal court, in the exercise of its discretion, can relinquish jurisdiction where necessary to avoid needless conflict with the administration by a state of its own affairs.

Abstract 1. A lesser quantity containing the essential qualities and force of a greater quantity. **2.** An abridgment.

Abstraction Taking with intent to injure or defraud.

Abstract of record A complete history in short, abbreviated form of the case as found in the record, complete enough to show that the questions presented for review have been properly reserved. Abbreviated accurate and authentic history of proceedings.

Abstract of title A condensed history of the title to land, consisting of a summary of all the conveyances that affect the land, or any estate or interest therein, together with a statement of all liens, charges, or liabilities to which the land may be subject, and of which it is in any way material for purchasers to be apprised.

Absurdity Obviously and flatly opposed to the manifest truth; inconsistent with the plain dictates of common sense; logically contradictory.

Abuse 1. Departure from reasonable use; immoderate or improper use. Physical or mental maltreatment. **2.** To wrong in speech, to disparage and malign. **3.** To make excessive or improper use of a thing, or to employ it in a manner contrary to the natural or legal rules for its use.

Abused and neglected children Those who are suffering serious physical or emotional injury inflicted on them.

Abuse of discretion A decision that is manifestly unreasonable, arbitrary, biased, illogical, inconsistent, not supported by the evidence, or beyond the power of the decision maker. A decision that is clearly erroneous or unjust.

Abuse of process A tort that exists when there has been (a) a use of civil or criminal proceedings, (b) for an improper or ulterior purpose, (c) resulting in actual damage. Example: You have someone arrested in order to pressure him or her to repay a loan or to marry your child. The purpose of the criminal law is not to collect debts or to encourage marriage.

Abusive Tending to deceive; practicing abuse; prone to ill-treat by insulting words or harmful acts.

Abut To reach; to touch at one end; be contiguous; join at a border or boundary.

Abutment That which abuts or borders on something.

Abuttals End lines of land.

Abutter One whose property abuts, is contiguous, or joins at a border or boundary where no other land, road, or street intervenes.

Accede 1. To give one's agreement (accede to the request). **2.** To attain an office or position; to take control of (accede to the throne).

Accelerate To cause something to happen sooner.

Accelerated depreciation Depreciating property in such a way that the deductions are greater during the early years of the life of the asset. Methods of this kind of depreciation include double declining balance and sum of the years' digits.

Acceleration The shortening of the time for the vesting in possession of an expectant interest.

Acceleration clause A clause in a contract (e.g., mortgage, promissory note) stating that if a certain event happens, the payment schedule under the contract is advanced. For example, a mortgage might provide that the entire loan must be repaid immediately if a single payment is missed or if the mortgaged property is transferred.

Accept 1. To receive with approval or with the intent to retain. **2.** To assent.

Acceptance 1. Compliance with the terms and conditions of an offer. **2.** The act of a person to whom a thing is offered or tendered by another, whereby he or she receives the thing with the intention of retaining it.

Acceptance credit Arrangement whereby a bank authorizes a credit receiver to draw upon the amount requested. The one who receives the credit may then discount the draft or note.

Acceptance in blank Drawee's signed engagement to honor a draft in which the amount is unstated. Signature of the drawee is sufficient acceptance, and must be written on the instrument.

Acceptance of check The signed engagement of the drawee (usually a bank) to honor a draft (a document for the transfer of money) as presented.

Acceptance of deed Acts, conduct, or words that manifest an intent to take title to the property described in the deed.

Acceptance of goods There are three ways a buyer can accept goods: (a) by signifying to the seller that the goods are conforming or that the buyer will accept them in spite of their nonconformity, (b) by failing to make an effective rejection, and (c) by doing an act inconsistent with the seller's ownership.

Acceptance of offer The assent by the person to whom an offer has been made (offeree) to enter into a binding agreement with the person making the offer (offeror) according to the terms of the offer.

Acceptilation Release made by a creditor to his or her debtor without receiving any consideration.

Acceptor One who engages to pay the draft according to its tenor at the time of his or her engagement or as completed pursuant to authority on incomplete instruments.

Acceptor supra protest One who accepts a bill that has been protested, for the honor of the drawer or any one of the indorsers.

Access 1. Opportunity to reach or communicate with. **2.** The availability of contact for a designated purpose.

Accessary See accessory.

Access, easement of The right an abutting owner has of ingress to and egress from his or her premises, in addition to the public easement in the street.

Accession 1. Increase, addition. **2.** A country's acceptance of a treaty. **3.** Taking control or possession of something.

Accessory 1. Someone who, without being present, helps another to commit a crime (accessory before or after the fact). **2.** Something added or joined; a subordinate part; an incident (computer accessories).

Accessory after the fact A person, knowing that a crime has been committed, who receives, harbors, or conceals the offender (the principal) in order to assist the latter to escape arrest or punishment.

Accessory before the fact Someone who procures, counsels, commands, abets, or encourages another (the principal) to commit a crime. The accessory before the fact is not present at the time and place of the crime.

Accessory building A structure that is detached from the main building on the land. An outbuilding; a subordinate structure.

Accessory contract A subsidiary contract (e.g., mortgage, suretyship) made to assure performance of another contract.

Accessory during the fact One who stands by without giving such help as may be in his or her power to prevent the commission of a criminal offense.

Accessory obligation An obligation that is incidental to another or principal obligation (e.g., the obligation of a surety).

Accessory use In zoning law, the use of land in a way that is customarily incidental or subsidiary to the principal use of the land. For example, in a residential area, it may be an accessory use of land to park a commercial vehicle in the driveway of one's home if the vehicle is used to travel to and from work.

Accident 1. An unexpected occurrence (discovery by accident). **2.** An unexpected misfortune (motor vehicle accident).

Accidental 1. Happening unexpectedly, happening by chance. **2.** Nonessential.

Accidental cause A causal entity that could not have been foreseen.

Accidental death benefit (in insurance policy) An additional benefit that is paid when death is caused by sudden, unexpected, external force. Also called double indemnity.

Accidental means (in insurance policy) Something that happens by chance or fortuitously without intention or design and which is unexpected, unusual, and unforeseen.

Accidental killing Killing resulting from an act that is lawful and lawfully done under a reasonable belief that no harm is possible; distinguished from involuntary manslaughter, which is the result of an unlawful act, or of a lawful act done in an unlawful way.

Accident arising out of employment (worker's compensation) An occurrence that is neither expected, designed, nor intentionally caused by the worker. A causal connection exists, however, between the occurrence and the job. There are four basic categories of accidents in the Worker's Compensation Act: (a) a sudden, unexpected traumatic event such as a fall or blow, (b) an unusual exertion in the course of work causing an unexpected and sudden injury, (c) an unusual pathological result of an ordinary condition of work, and (d) a sudden and unexpected injury caused by failure of an employer to furnish medical care to an employee.

Accident-prone Having a tendency to become involved in accidents.

Accola In civil law, one who inhabits or occupies land near a place, such as one who dwells by a river.

Accomenda In maritime law, a contract between the owner of goods and the master of a ship, by which the former entrusts the property to the latter to be sold on their joint account.

Accommodated party One to whom the credit of the accommodation party (see this phrase) is loaned.

Accommodation 1. A favor done for someone, usually without payment or consideration (e.g., signing a note to help someone secure a loan). **2.** An adjustment or settlement (reach an accommodation). **3.** Lodging.

Accommodation bill See accommodation paper.

Accommodation indorser See accommodation party.

Accommodation lands Land bought by a builder or speculator, who erects houses theron, and then leases portions thereof upon an improved ground-rent.

Accommodation loan Loan furnished as an act of friendship or assistance without tangible consideration.

Accommodation maker Someone who signs a promissory note or other instrument as a surety to lend his or her credit to another.

Accommodation note See accommodation paper.

Accommodation paper A promissory note or bill of exchange that is signed by a person in order to help someone else secure credit or a loan. The person signing is the accommodation party.

Accommodation party Someone who signs commercial paper (see this phrase) as maker, acceptor, drawer, or indorser for the purpose of lending his or her name to another party on the paper.

Accommodation road A road opened for the benefit of certain individuals to go from and to their homes, for service of their lands, and for use of some estates exclusively.

Accompany To go with or attend as a companion or associate; to occur in association with.

Accomplice A person who knowingly, voluntarily, and intentionally participates with someone else in the promotion, facilitation, or commission of a crime.

Accord An agreement or contract to settle an existing dispute, barring all actions based thereon; both sides agree to accept something other than what was originally claimed to be due.

Accordance Agreement, conformity.

Accord and satisfaction An agreement or contract to settle an existing dispute whereby both sides agree to accept something other than what they initially claimed was due. See accord. The accord is the agreement. The satisfaction is the execution or performance of the agreement which in effect eliminates the original dispute. The initial debt or claim is extinguished.

Accordant Agreeing; concurring.

Accouchement The act of a woman in giving birth to a child.

Account 1. A financial record or statement of debts, credits, transactions, etc. **2.** Any right to payment for goods sold or leased or for services rendered that is not evidenced by an instrument or chattel paper. **3.** A form of action at common law against a person who by reason of some fiduciary relation (as guardian, bailiff, receiver, etc.) was bound to render an account to another, but refused to do so. See account render.

Accountability State of being responsible or answerable.

Accountable Subject to pay; responsible; liable.

Accountable receipt A written acknowledgment that something (e.g., money) has been received and that a duty therefore arises under the agreement to respond (e.g., by delivering goods, by making payment).

Account annexed A simple method of pleading a common account; a pleading in account form (e.g., of goods sold and delivered).

Accountant A person who is skilled in keeping financial records and accounts.

Accountants, chartered Persons skilled in the keeping and examination of accounts who are employed for the purpose of examining and certifying to the correctness of accounts. The British Commonwealth equivalent of a Certified Public Accountant.

Account balance Difference between debit and credit sides of an account.

Account book A book kept by a merchant, trader, mechanic, or other person, in which are entered from time to time the transactions of the trade or business.

Account current An open or running account; an account that is periodically settled.

Account debtor The person who has obligations on an account.

Accounting 1. A bookkeeping system for recording

business transactions, balancing debits and credits, settling accounts, maintaining internal control, etc. **2.** A statement or report on the financial condition of an enterprise. **3.** A settling of an account with a determination of what is owed. **4.** The payment of profits made from the unfair use by the defendant of the plaintiff's trademark or trade name.

Accounting identity A statement that two numerical things are equal by accepted definition (e.g., "assets equal liabilities plus stockholder's equity").

Accounting period The period of time, usually a year, used by a taxpayer for the determination of tax liability.

Account in trust Account established by an individual to be held in trust for the benefit of another.

Account payable A regular business debt not yet paid; a debt owed by a business, usually on open account.

Account receivable A regular business debt not yet collected; a debt owed to a business, usually an open account.

Account render An action at common law when a person fails to make an accounting (e.g., if an administrator of an estate fails to render an account of expenses and payments, etc.).

Account rendered A statement of debts presented to the debtor by the creditor.

Account sales An account rendered by a sales agent, consignee, factor, or broker stating the sales of goods, the prices, the commissions, the expenses, and balance due the consignor or constituent.

Account stated An account that has been accepted as correct by the debtor and creditor; an agreement on the accuracy of the account stating the balance due.

Accouple To join, unite, marry.

Accredit 1. To acknowledge or recognize officially; to recognize as having met designated institutional standards. **2.** To accept the credentials of a foreign envoy. **3.** To send an envoy to a foreign country with credentials. **4.** To attribute.

Accredited representative A representative having general authority to act.

Accretion 1. Growth in size by accumulation or addition. **2.** A growing together. **3.** The gradual and imperceptible addition of soil to the shore of waterfront property. **4.** The incorporation of employees to an already existing bargaining unit when there is such a community of interest among the entire group that the additional employees have no separate unit identity.

Accroach 1. To exercise power without authority; to infringe. **2.** To attract; to acquire.

Accrocher To delay; retard; put off.

Accrual Something that is accrued; something that comes into existence or that grows in amount.

Accrual basis A method of accounting that shows expenses incurred and income earned for a given period (e.g., a year), although such expenses and income may not have actually been paid or received during this period. For example, an amount is included in gross income when a right to receive it exists regardless of whether the amount has actually been received. See cash basis.

Accrual method of accounting See accrual basis.

Accrual of cause of action The time at which the right to bring the action or suit arises (e.g., when the breach of contract occurs, when the last act necessary to complete the tort occurs, when the injury occurs, when the plaintiff discovers the error that caused the injury).

Accrue 1. To grow in amount. **2.** To come into existence; to vest.

Accrued alimony and child support payments Payments for alimony and child support that are due but not yet paid.

Accrued assets Assets arising from revenues earned but not yet due.

Accrued compensation Awarded compensation, due and payable, but not yet paid.

Accrued depreciation Amount reserved each year in the accounting system for replacement of assets. Portion of useful service life that has expired.

Accrued dividend A share of net earnings declared but not yet paid as a dividend.

Accrued expense An expense that has been incurred but not yet paid.

Accrued interest Interest that has been earned but is not yet paid or payable.

Accrued liability An expense that is recognized or chargeable but not yet payable.

Accrued right A matured cause of action.

Accrued taxes Taxes that are properly chargeable in a given accounting period but not yet payable.

Accruer (or accrual), clause of An express clause, frequently occurring in the case of gifts by deed or will to persons as tenants in common, providing that upon the death of one or more of the beneficiaries, his, her, or their shares go to the survivor or survivors. The share of the decedent is then said to accrue to the others.

Accruing In the early stages; developing; inchoate.

Accruing costs Costs and expenses incurred after judgment.

Accruing interest Running or accumulating interest, as distinguished from accrued or matured interest. Interest daily accumulating on the principal debt but not yet due and payable.

Accumulated dividend Dividend due a shareholder that has not been paid.

Accumulated earnings tax A tax imposed on corporations that accumulate their earnings beyond the reasonable needs of the business rather than distribute them as dividends to the stockholders.

Accumulated interest Interest on bonds and other debts that is due or overdue but not yet paid.

Accumulated legacy That part of an estate that has not yet been paid to the beneficiaries.

Accumulated profits Earned surplus or undivided profits.

Accumulated surplus The fund a company has in excess of its capital and liabilities.

Accumulation 1. Increase by additions. **2.** An accumulation of a fund by an executor or trustee occurs when he or she amasses rents, dividends, and other income received, treats it as capital, invests it, makes new capital of the income derived therefrom, and then invests that capital. The capital and income procured in this way constitute accumulations. **3.** The separate property of a wife while living separately from her husband in a community property state.

Accumulation trust A trust in which the income is collected or accumulated for a period of time before being distributed to beneficiaries.

Accumulative Resulting from additions or accumulations.

Accumulative dividend A dividend on preferred stock that is to be paid before any distribution to holders of common stock. The dividend is accumulated before distribution to holders of common stock. See cumulative preferred dividend.

Accumulative judgment A second sentence that is to be added to the first. When the sentence imposed by the first judgment has been served, the defendant begins serving the sentence imposed by the second judgment. See consecutive sentences.

Accumulative legacy An additional gift of personal property in a will.

Accumulative sentence A sentence, additional to others, imposed on a defendant who has been convicted upon an indictment containing several counts, each of such counts charging a distinct offense, or who is under conviction at the same time for several distinct offenses; one of such sentences to begin at the expiration of another.

Accurate Precise, free from errors, conforming to a standard.

Accusation A formal charge that a person has committed a crime or other misconduct.

Accusatory body An entity that determines whether enough evidence exists to accuse someone of a crime (e.g., grand jury).

Accusatory part The accusatory part of an indictment is that part where the offense is named.

Accusatory stage The stage of a criminal investigation during which the focus is on an individual who has been taken into custody and from whom a confession or incriminating statements are being sought.

Accuse To bring formal charges against someone for a crime or other misconduct.

Accused The person against whom criminal proceedings are instigated; the defendant in a criminal case; the target of a criminal investigation.

Accuser A person who claims that a specific individual has committed a crime.

Accustomed Habitual, often used, usual or customary.

AC/DC Bisexual.

Ac etiam (And also.) The introduction of the statement of the real cause of action, used formerly in those cases where it was necessary to allege a fictitious cause of action to give the court jurisdiction, and also the real cause in compliance with the statutes. It is sometimes written acetiam.

Acidhead A frequent user of LSD.

Acid test Method of financial analysis; ratio of cash and receivables to current liabilities. Sum of cash, marketable securities, and receivables divided by current liabilities. Also called the quick ratio.

Acknowledge To own or admit; to confess; to recognize one's acts, and assume the responsibility therefor.

Acknowledgment 1. An affirmation that something is genuine; an admission or declaration. **2.** Recognition or acceptance.

Acknowledgment of paternity An admission that the child is one's own. Recognition of a parental relation, either by a written agreement, verbal declarations or statements, by the life, acts, and conduct of the parties, or any other satisfactory evidence that the relation was recognized and admitted.

Acknowledgment of receipt A written affirmation

that the buyer has taken physical possession of the goods.

A coelo usque ad centrum From the sky to the center of the earth (describing the extent of one's ownership of land).

Acquainted Having personal, familiar knowledge of a person, event, or thing.

Acquereur In French and Canadian law, one who acquires title, particularly to immovable property, by purchase.

Acquest An estate acquired newly or by purchase.

Acquêts Property that has been acquired by purchase or gift, not by succession.

Acquiesce To consent passively or without enthusiasm; to consent by implication, e.g., through silence.

Acquiescence Passive consent or submission; implied consent through the failure to object; conduct that would lead others to conclude that you consent or that you have waived your rights.

Acquire To obtain; to gain ownership of; to secure by one's own efforts.

Acquired allegiance Allegiance that binds a naturalized citizen.

Acquired surplus The surplus that exists in one company that is purchased or taken over by another.

Acquisition Obtaining ownership or possession; the thing obtained is also referred to as the acquisition.

Acquisitive Grasping or greedy (an acquisitive offense is a crime against ownership or possession).

Acquit 1. To release someone from an obligation. **2.** To declare that the accused is innocent of the crime.

Acquittal 1. A discharge or release from an obligation (e.g., a contract debt). **2.** A formal declaration or certification of innocence of a crime.

Acquittal contract A release, absolution, or discharge from an obligation, liability, or engagement.

Acquittals in fact Those that take place when the jury, upon trial, finds a verdict of not guilty.

Acquittals in law Those that take place by mere operation of law; as where a person has been charged merely as an accessory, and the principal has been acquitted.

Acquittance A written discharge from an obligation.

Acre A quantity of land; 4,840 square yards or 43,560 square feet or 160 square rods.

Acre foot 325,850 gallons, or the amount of water which will cover one acre one foot in depth.

Acre right The share of a citizen of a New England town in the common lands.

Act 1. Something done voluntarily as opposed to convulsive movements or in reaction to coercive outside forces; an external manifestation of the will (the act of pulling the trigger). **2.** A law passed by the legislature (Social Security Act).

Acta publica Things of general knowledge and concern.

Acting Temporarily functioning as or substituting for (acting director).

Acting within scope of employment See scope of employment.

Act in pais Something done out of court without being a part of the court's official proceedings.

Actio damni injuria Action for damages due to negligent or other wrongful acts.

Actio ex contractu A contract action.

Actio ex delicto A tort action.

Action A proceeding in a court of law in which one seeks the redress of an alleged wrong.

Actionable Pertaining to that which can become the basis of a lawsuit; pertaining to that which can be remedied by a court action.

Actional fraud Deception practiced in order to induce another to part with property or to surrender some legal right.

Actionable negligence The breach or nonperformance of a legal duty, through neglect or carelessness, resulting in damage or injury to another.

Actionable per se Pertaining to words that are defamatory in themselves. Pertaining to defamation that can be established without pleading and proving special damages. Words that are actionable per se fall into four categories: Statements that (a) accuse plaintiff of a crime, (b) adversely affect the plaintiff's trade, calling, or profession, (c) accuse the plaintiff of having a loathsome disease, and (d) accuse the plaintiff of unchastity.

Actionable tort A wrong that fits within all of the elements of one of the available torts.

Actionable words In law of libel and slander, such words as naturally imply damage.

Actionary A foreign commercial term for the proprietor of an action or share of a public company's stock; a stockholder.

Action at common law An action governed by the common law rather than an action based on a statute, equitable remedies, or continental (civil) law.

Action at law A judicial proceeding to redress an alleged wrong, usually involving the right to a jury trial.

Action ex contractu An action for the breach of a promise in a contract.

Action ex delicto An action of tort; an action arising out of fault, misconduct, or malfeasance; an action arising from a breach of duty growing out of a contract.

Action for accounting An action in equity particularly applicable to mutual and complicated accounts and where a confidential or fiduciary relationship exists. An action to adjust mutual accounts and to strike a balance.

Action for poinding An action by a creditor to obtain a sequestration of the rents of land and the goods of the debtor for the satisfaction of the debt, or to enforce a distress.

Action in equity An action seeking equitable remedy or relief.

Action in personam See in personam.

Action in rem See in rem.

Action malum in se See malum in se.

Action malum prohibitum See malum prohibitum.

Action of assumpsit See assumpsit.

Action of book debt A form of common law action for the recovery of claims, such as are usually evidenced by a book-account.

Action non datur non damnificato There is no action given to one who is not injured.

Action on the case Also called trespass on the case or cases. An action on the case is an action to recover for injuries that were caused in a variety of ways: (a) where the injury resulted indirectly and consequentially, not directly or immediately; (b) where the injury resulted from acts that were not committed with force (or if force was used, the matter involved was not tangible); or (c) where the injury resulted from nonfeasance, negligence, or the failure to use proper skill in the performance of a contract. An action on the case was created to cover those injuries that could not be handled by a straight trespass action. For example, if someone threw a log on the road, the person hit by the log as it fell could sue in trespass (direct injury), but the person who later ran his or her car into the log would bring an action on the case (indirect injury).

Action quasi in rem See quasi in rem.

Action to quiet title An action in which the plaintiff asserts his or her title or interest in land and that the defendant's claim in the land is invalid; an action compelling an adverse claimant either to establish his or her claim or be forever estopped from asserting it.

Actio personalis moritur cum persona A personal action dies with the person.

Active In action; demanding action; the opposite of passive.

Active debt A debt due a person.

Active negligence Negligence resulting from positive, affirmative acts or conduct, not from mere inaction or passiveness.

Active trust A trust in which the trustee is under a duty to take active steps in the carrying out of the trust (e.g., invest assets, distribute profits).

Act malum in se See malum in se.

Act malum prohibitum See malum prohibitum.

Act of attainder See bill of attainder, attainder.

Act of bankruptcy Conduct of a debtor that could force him or her into involuntary bankruptcy (e.g., transferring property, while insolvent, to creditors in order to prefer them over other creditors).

Act of dominion See dominion.

Act of God An unusual event caused exclusively by nature; the cause of an injury exclusively due to nature, which could not have been avoided or prevented by the use of reasonable care. Examples: flood, tornado.

Act of honor When a bill has been protested, and a third person wishes to take it up, or accept it, for the "honor" (credit) of one or more of the parties, the notary draws up an instrument, evidencing the transaction, which is called an act of honor.

Act of insolvency 1. Conduct that demonstrates that a bank is unable to meet its liabilities. **2.** Conduct of a debtor that would justify the filing of invountary bankruptcy proceedings against him or her.

Act of law The operation of fixed legal rules upon given facts or occurrences, producing consequences independent of the design or will of the parties concerned; as distinguished from "act of parties." Also an act performed by judicial authority that prevents or precludes a party from fulfilling a contract or other engagement.

Act of nature See act of God.

Act of parliament A statute; a law made by the British sovereign, with the advice and consent of the lords and the commons, in parliament assembled.

Act of providence An accident against which ordinary skill and foresight could not guard. An act of God.

Act of sale An official record of a sale of property,

made by a notary who writes down the agreement of the parties as stated by them, and which is then signed by the parties and attested by witnesses.

Act of state doctrine Courts of this country are precluded from inquiring into the validity of governmental acts of foreign governments that take place within their own territory.

Act of supremacy An act of 26 Hen. VIII, c. 1, and also 1 Eliz., c. 1, which recognized the king as the only supreme head on earth of the Church of England having full power to correct all errors, heresies, abuses, offenses, contempts and enormities. The oath, taken under the act, denies to the Pope any other authority than that of the Bishop of Rome.

Act of uniformity The English statute of 13 & 14 Car. II, c. 4, enacting that the book of common prayer, as then recently revised, should be used in every parish church and other place of public worship, and otherwise ordaining a uniformity in religious services, etc.

Actor 1. Plaintiff, litigant. **2.** Agent. **3.** A person who acts.

Actrix Female actor (e.g., female litigant, female agent).

Acts and Resolutions; Acts and Resolves The session laws of a state legislature, printed chronologically.

Acts of court Legal memoranda made in the admiralty courts in England, in the nature of pleas.

Actual Real; existing presently in act.

Actual authority In the law of agency, such authority as a principal intentionally confers on the agent, or intentionally or by want of ordinary care allows the agent to believe himself or herself to possess.

Actual cash value Fair market value as measured by what a willing buyer would offer and what a willing seller would accept in a cash sale in an open and free market—not at a forced sale. In some contexts, actual cash value may also mean the cost of restoration or the replacement costs less depreciation.

Actual controversy A concrete dispute in which the underlying issues are not moot or premature, the interests of the parties are real and adverse, and the controversy is ripe for judicial determination; a justiciable controversy.

Actual damages Compensatory damages for actual loss or injury; damages in satisfaction of, or in recompense for, loss or injury actually sustained; all damages other than punitive or exemplary damages.

Actual loss One resulting from the real and substantial destruction of the property insured.

Actual malice 1. For purposes of an award of punitive damages, actual malice is ill will, the intent to injure, or a reckless disregard of another's rights. **2.** For purposes of a defamation action involving constitutional issues, actual malice is knowledge of falsity or a reckless disregard as to truth or falsity.

Actual market value The price at which merchandise is freely offered for sale to all purchasers in the ordinary course of trade.

Actual notice Such notice as is positively proved to have been given to a person directly and personally, or notice the person is presumed to have received personally because the evidence within the person's knowledge was sufficient to put him or her upon inquiry.

Actual seisin Actual possession of the freehold as distinguished from constructive possession or possession in law.

Actual tare The weight of the box, bag or other receptacle containing goods after they have been unpacked and removed.

Actual value The price that would probably result from negotiations between a willing seller and a willing buyer.

Actuarial Pertaining to the calculation of statistical risks, premiums, estate values, etc., for insurance purposes.

Actuary A person skilled in mathematical calculations to determine insurance risks, premiums, etc. A statistician.

Actum Something done; a deed.

Actus reus The wrongful deed or act. When the actus reus is combined with the mens rea (guilty mind), a crime has been committed. For the crime of murder, for example, the actus reus is the homicide, and the mens rea is the malice aforethought.

Ad At, by, for, near, on account of, to, until, upon, concerning.

Adapted Capable of use, made suitable, made fit by alteration.

Ad colligendum bona defuncti For collecting the goods of the deceased.

Ad curiam At a court; before the court.

Ad damnum A clause (usually in the complaint) stating the amount of money that is claimed as damages for the alleged wrong committed.

Addendum Something added, e.g., charts added at the end of an appellate brief.

Addict Any individual who habitually uses any narcotic drug so as to endanger the public morals, or who has lost the power of self-control with reference to the addiction.

Ad diem At a day, at the day.

Addition 1. Something added. **2.** In insurance law, coverage for "additions" includes buildings added, joined, or appurtenant to other buildings. **3.** A title or description added to someone's name (Mary Jones, painter).

Additionales In the law of contracts, additional terms or propositions to be added to a former agreement.

Additional servitude A new and additional servitude or easement on land taken by eminent domain for which additional compensation is required.

Additur The court's power to increase the amount of a jury award. The process often works as follows: (a) the plaintiff wins a jury award that is deemed inadequate, (b) the plaintiff moves for a new trial, (c) the judge tells the defendant that a new trial will be ordered unless the defendant agrees to increase the verdict by a designated amount. The denial of the new trial is conditioned on the defendant's consent to the increase.

Add on clause A clause in an installment contract making earlier purchases security for new purchases.

Addone Given to.

Address 1. Place of residence or business where a person can usually be reached by mail, phone, visit. **2.** That portion of a bill in equity describing the court where the bill is filed.

Adduce To present or introduce.

Adeem To take away; to revoke the bequest of a legacy.

Ademption A revocation or satisfaction of a gift in a will; this result is implied by the law from the acts of the person making the will (testator) before the death of the latter. From these acts, the law presumes an intent to revoke or satisfy. For example: Mary leaves Bill a specific horse in her will. Before Mary dies, she gives the horse to Bill, she sells it to Bob, or the horse dies. The legacy of the horse is ademed. When Mary dies, Bill does not get a substitute for the horse.

Adequate Sufficient, commensurate, satisfactory.

Adequate cause Sufficient cause for a particular purpose.

Adequate consideration Consideration that is equal to or reasonably proportioned to the value of that for which it is given; consideration that is not so grossly disproportionate to value as to offend against fair dealing.

Adequate remedy at law Adequacy is determined by comparing the remedy available at law with the remedy being sought in equity. The remedy at law is adequate if it is as plain, as complete, and as efficient to the prompt administration of justice as the remedy being sought in equity. If there is an adequate remedy at law, then the equitable remedy (e.g., injunction) will be denied.

Ad fidem In allegiance.

Ad fin., Ad finem To the end.

Ad gravamen To the grievance or injury.

Adhering Joining, leagued with, cleaving to. Giving to the country the loyalty due from a citizen.

Adhesion 1. Adherence. **2.** The combining of bodily tissues. **3.** A country's agreement to accept part of a treaty.

Adhesion contract A contract that often has the following characteristics: (a) a standardized, form contract, (b) covering consumer goods and services, (c) the seller is in a superior bargaining position, (d) the buyer has no realistic opportunity to bargain over terms—the contract is offered on a "take it or leave it" basis, (e) the buyer has no realistic opportunity to shop elsewhere for a more favorable contract.

Ad hoc For this; for this special case or purpose only (an ad hoc committee).

Ad hominem To the person; appealing to the prejudices of a person; a personal attack.

Ad int., Ad interim In the meantime; temporary.

Adjacent Lying near or close by (adjacent objects may or may not be in contact with each other).

Adjective law The rules of practice and procedure; remedial laws; the rules by which the substantive law is administered; the legal machinery by which substantive rights and duties are enforced or made effective. Example: the service of process rules.

Adjoining Touching; contiguous.

Adjourn To postpone or suspend until another time.

Adjourned summons A summons taken out in the chambers of a judge, and afterwards taken into court to be argued by counsel.

Adjournment A putting off or postponing of a session until another time or place.

Adjournment day in error In English practice, a day appointed some days before the end of the term at which matters left undone on the affirmance day are finished.

Adjournment sine die An adjournment without setting a time for another meeting or session.

Adjudge To decide judicially; to settle, or decree; to sentence or condemn.

Adjudicataire In Canadian law, a purchaser at a sheriff's sale.

Adjudicate To judge; to determine finally.

Adjudicatee In French and civil law, the purchaser at the judicial sale.

Adjudication A formal determination or judgment by a court of law.

Adjudicative facts Facts (in a dispute before an administrative agency) about the parties, their activities, business, and property. Adjudicative facts usually answer the questions of who did what, where, when, how, why, and with what motive and intent. Legislative facts, on the other hand, do not usually concern the immediate parties but are general facts that help the tribunal decide questions of law, policy, and discretion.

Adjudicatory proceeding A method of resolving factual disputes, usually within an administrative agency.

Adjunct Something secondary or subordinate that is added.

Adjunction Adding or attaching one thing to another. In civil law, the permanent attachment or union of a thing belonging to one person to that belonging to another.

Adjuration A solemn statement, a sworn statement, an entreaty.

Adjust 1. To settle or arrange; to remove differences or discrepancies. **2.** To pay a liquidated claim.

Adjusted basis The cost of other basis of property (a) reduced for depreciation, depletion, and any item that represents a return of capital, and (b) increased by capital improvements, purchase commissions, zoning costs, legal fees in defending title, etc.

Adjusted gross estate The gross estate less deductions for administration expenses, funeral expenses, debts of the decedent, etc.

Adjusted gross income Gross income of an individual less certain deductions (e.g., business expenses, long-term capital gain deductions).

Adjuster One who makes any adjustment or settlement, or who determines the amount of a claim.

Adjustment Settlement of a claim; a determination of the accuracy of a claim, whether it should be reduced, etc.

Adjustment bond A bond that is issued as part of a corporate reorganization.

Adjustment securities Stocks, bonds, and other securities issued as part of a corporate reorganization.

Ad legem At the law.

Ad libitum At will; as one pleases.

Ad litem For the suit, for purposes of this litigation (guardian ad litem).

Ad majus For the larger or greater.

Admanuensis A person who swore or took oath by laying his or her hands on the book.

Admeasurement Apportionment; assignment of shares.

Admeasurement of dower 1. A writ brought by an heir (upon reaching majority) to rectify an assignment of dower made during minority by which the doweress received more than that to which she was entitled. **2.** The settlement of a widow's dower right.

Admeasurement of homestead The identification at an execution sale of the portion of land to which a homestead exemption applies.

Adminicle 1. Aid, support. **2.** Evidence used to support other evidence; corroboration.

Adminicular Auxiliary; subordinate to; corroborative.

Adminiculate To give adminicular evidence.

Adminiculator A church officer who administered to the wants of widows, orphans, and afflicted persons.

Administer 1. To manage, carry out, or execute. **2.** To settle and distribute the estate of a dead person. **3.** To give or cause to be taken.

Administration 1. The management of something (e.g., a government agency, a business, an estate). **2.** The executive department of the government. **3.** The management and settlement of the estate of a decedent.

Administration ad colligendum The right to manage an estate which is granted for the purpose of collecting and preserving the goods of the deceased that are about to perish (bona peritura).

Administration cum testamento annexo (CTA) Administration of an estate where no executor is named in the will, or where one is named but is unable to serve. Administration with the will annexed.

Administration de bonis non (DBN) Administration of that portion of an estate which was not administered by a prior executor or administrator, e.g., because of the death of the latter.

Administration letters The document that authorizes a person to manage the estate of someone who has died without leaving a valid will.

Administration of estate The management and settlement of an estate involving the collection of assets, the payment of debts and claims against the estate, the payment of estate taxes, and the distribution of the remainder of the estate to those entitled to receive it. The decedent is an intestate (someone who dies without leaving a valid will) or a testate (someone who dies leaving a valid will) where no executor is available.

Administration pendente lite Administration of an estate pending the resolution of a controversy over the will (e.g., its validity).

Administrative Pertaining to administration by managing, conducting, directing, or superintending the execution, application, or conduct of persons or things.

Administrative act A routine, ministerial, clerical, or necessary act that carries out something else.

Administrative agency A governmental body that carries out or adminsters the law, particularly the law passed by the legislature. Examples: City Sanitation Division, the FBI.

Administrative authority The power of an agency or its head to carry out the terms of the law creating the agency as well as to make regulations for the conduct of business before the agency; distinguishable from legislative authority to make laws.

Administrative board An administrative agency, often one with quasi-judicial powers.

Administrative discretion The power of an administrative agency to choose among alternative courses of action based on beliefs, perceptions, inclinations, and preferences that are usually not susceptible of proof or disproof.

Administrative law 1. The law governing the conduct, powers, and procedures of administrative agencies. **2.** The laws created by administrative agencies.

Administrative Law Judge (ALJ) A hearing officer within an administrative agency; someone who presides over administrative hearings pursuant to an agency's quasi-judicial power.

Administrative order A resolution of a dispute before an administrative agency; a final disposition following an administrative hearing.

Administrative Procedure Act (APA) 1. A federal statute governing procedures before federal administrative agencies, e.g., participation in rule

making, the conduct of hearings. **2.** A state statute with the same name, serving the same function for state administrative agencies.

Administrative remedy A procedure within an administrative agency for allowing someone to assert a right; a nonjudicial remedy provided by the agency itself. Generally, such remedies must be exhausted before the case can be taken to court.

Administrative rule-making The power of an administrative agency to make rules and regulations for proceedings before it.

Administrative tribunal An administrative agency that holds hearings and renders decisions on controversies within the agency.

Administrator 1. A manager. **2.** A person appointed by the court to manage or administer the estate of a decedent.

Administrator ad litem A special administrator appointed by the court to represent the estate of a decedent in a court proceeding.

Administrator cum testamento annexo (CTA) See administration cum testamento annexo.

Administrator DBN See administration de bonis non.

Administrator de bonis non (DBN) See administration de bonis non.

Administrator of estate See administration of estate.

Administrator pendente lite See administration pendente lite.

Administrator with will annexed See administration cum testamento annexo.

Administratrix A woman who administers the estate of the deceased. See administration of estate.

Admiralty The law of the sea, the law pertaining to navigable waters, maritime law, e.g., contract and tort actions that arise out of commerce on the seas.

Admiralty Court A court exercising jurisdiction over all maritime contracts, torts, injuries, or offenses.

Admissible Pertaining to that which can be allowed because it is relevant or pertinent to the matter at hand and should be considered (admissible evidence). Whether it is true or false will be determined separately.

Admission 1. A statement (or conduct) of a party that is inconsistent with a position the party is taking in the litigation. **2.** A voluntary concession or confession (admission of guilt). **3.** Entrance (restricted admission).

Admission against interest A statement made by one of the parties to an action that amounts to a prior acknowledgment that one of the material facts relevant to the issues is not as he or she now claims.

Admit 1. To accept as true or valid. **2.** To give access to.

Admittance In English law, the act of giving possession of a copyhold estate.

Admixture A mixture; something formed by mixing.

Admonish 1. To warn or caution. **2.** To criticize or censure.

Admonition 1. A warning. **2.** A reprimand.

Admonitio trina The threefold warning given to a prisoner who stood mute.

Admortization In feudal customs, the reduction of property of lands or tenements to mortmain.

Adolescence The time between puberty and the age of majority.

Adopt 1. To go through a formal process of establishing a relationship of parent and child between persons who are not so related by nature. **2.** To follow.

Adoptee The person adopted.

Adoption by estoppel A child acquires the status of an adopted child when others are prevented from denying this status. No formal (statutory) adoption procedures are followed, but conduct or promises made by a person make it inequitable for this person (or his or her estate) to claim that the child does not have the status of an adopted child. An equitable adoption.

Adoptive parent Someone who adopts another person.

Ad perpetuam In perpetuity.

Ad quod damnum 1. To what damage or injury; how will others be prejudiced. **2.** A writ to complain of an assessment of condemnation damages.

Adult A person who has reached the age of majority (e.g., 21, 18). The age may differ depending on what the person is trying to do (e.g., vote, marry, administer an estate).

Adulterant That which makes something else inferior or impure.

Adulterate To make inferior or impure; to contaminate.

Adulterator Corrupter, counterfeiter.

Adulterer A man who commits adultery.

Adulteress A woman who commits adultery.

Adulterine Begotten in an adulterous intercourse.

Adulterium A fine anciently imposed for the commission of adultery.

Adultery Voluntary sexual intercourse by a married person with someone other than his or her spouse.

Ad valorem duty A duty laid in the form of a percentage on the value of property.

Ad valorem freight tariffs Freight rates that are computed on the basis of the value of the goods conveyed and are usually expressed as a percentage of that value.

Ad valorem tax A tax calculated on the basis of the value of the property to be taxed.

Advance 1. To prepay; to fulfill an obligation before it is due. **2.** To loan; to supply on credit. **3.** To move ahead. **4.** To improve. **5.** To increase. **6.** To offer.

Advancement 1. An irrevocable gift from a parent (while living) to his or her child which anticipates what the child would inherit upon the death of this parent. The intention of the parent is to have this gift deducted from what the child would have inherited. **2.** Improvement.

Advance payment Payments made in anticipation of a contingent or fixed future liability.

Advance sheets 1. Unbound reporters containing court opinions that are printed in advance of the bound reporter volumes. When the bound volume comes out, the advance sheets are usually thrown away. **2.** The most recent pamphlet of Shepard's Citations giving the latest shepardizing data.

Adventitious Accidental, occurring fortuitously.

Adventure 1. A hazardous enterprise. **2.** Peril (as used in marine insurance). **3.** A shipment of goods in charge of an agent to be sold for the best price available.

Adversary Opponent.

Adversary hearing A hearing when both parties are present arguing their respective positions.

Adversary proceeding One having opposing parties; contested, as distinguished from an ex parte hearing or proceeding.

Adversary system A system of justice or a legal system where an impartial judge presides over a proceeding in which opponents present their case in the best light possible. The judge does not act as prosecutor as in an inquisitional system of justice.

Adverse 1. Opposed, in opposition, having opposite interests, against. **2.** Unfavorable.

Adverse claim 1. An alleged right of one person asserted against the interest of another person. **2.** A claim to possession of land that is contrary to the rights of the title holder. **3.** A claim asserted against a trustee in bankruptcy.

Adverse enjoyment The possession or exercise of an

easement under a claim of right against the owner of the land out of which such easement is derived.

Adverse interest Goals, needs, or claims of one person or group that are different from or opposed to those of another person or group.

Adverse party A party to an action whose interests are opposed to or opposite of the interests of another party to the action.

Adverse possession A method of acquiring title to land without buying or paying for it in the traditional sense. The following is required: (a) actual possession or occupancy of the land that is (b) hostile to the current owner, (c) visible, open, and notorious, (d) exclusive, (e) continuous for a statutorily defined number of years, and (f) maintained under a claim of right as against everyone else.

Adverse title A title set up in opposition to or defeasance of another title; one acquired or claimed by adverse possession.

Adverse use Use without license or permission.

Adverse witness 1. A hostile witness. **2.** A witness who gives evidence that is prejudicial to the party that produced the witness (which allows the party to impeach the witness).

adversus bonos mores In civil law, against good morals.

Advertise To make known to; to announce publicly.

Advertisement Notice given in a manner designed to attract public attention.

Advice 1. An opinion or viewpoint offered as guidance. **2.** Information, notification. **3.** The instruction usually given by one merchant or banker to another by letter informing him of shipments made to him, or of bills or drafts drawn on him, with particulars of date, or sight, the sum, and the payee.

Advice of shipment The instruction given by one merchant to another by letter informing him that goods have been shipped to him.

Advise 1. To recommend a course of action. **2.** To inform.

Advise and consent The constitutional power and right of the U.S. Senate to advise the president on treaties and major presidential appointments and to approve or disapprove them.

Advisedly With deliberation; intentionally.

Advisement 1. Careful consideration. **2.** The act of a judge in taking time to deliberate before making a decision (take under advisement).

Advising bank A bank that gives notification of the issuance of a credit by another bank.

Advisory 1. Giving nonbinding advice or counsel (advisory opinion). **2.** A report giving information (small craft advisory).

Advisory jury A jury whose verdict is not binding on the court. A jury used in a federal court when a right to a jury does not exist.

Advisory opinion An opinion of a court that is not binding. Unlike the normal opinion, which arises out of adversarial proceedings, the advisory opinion is usually requested by the legislature or by the chief executive.

Advocacy Speaking, writing, or otherwise acting in support of or in opposition to something.

Advocate 1. Someone who assists or argues for another. **2.** To support or argue for.

Advocator One who called on or vouched another to warrant a title.

Advocatus diaboli In ecclesiastical law, the devil's advocate; the advocate who argues against the canonization of a saint.

Advoutrer An adulterer.

Advoutry or **advowtry** Adultery between parties, both of whom were married. Or the offense by an adulteress of continuing to live with the man with whom she committed the adultery.

Advowson In ecclesiastical law, the right of presentation to a church or ecclesiastical benefice; the right of presenting a fit person to the bishop, to be by him admitted and instituted to a certain benefice within the diocese, which has become vacant.

Advowtry See advoutry.

Aequitas sequitur legem Equity follows the law.

Affair 1. What a person does. **2.** A sexual liaison, usually brief. **3.** A lawsuit.

Affaire Business transaction. Settlement, either judicial or out of court.

Affect 1. To act on (upon); to influence. **2.** To feign.

Affected class 1. Persons who suffer the present effects of past job discrimination. **2.** Persons who constitute a class for purposes of bringing a class action.

Affecting commerce 1. In commerce. **2.** Having led or tending to lead to a labor dispute burdening or obstructing commerce or the free flow of commerce.

Affection 1. The making over, pawning, or mortgaging of a thing to assure the payment of a sum of money, or the discharge of some other duty or service. **2.** An abnormal bodily condition.

Affectus Disposition, intention.

Affeer To assess, liquidate, appraise, fix in amount.

Affiance 1. To pledge, promise. **2.** To agree to marry; to engage.

Affiant Someone who makes and files an affidavit.

Affidavit A written or printed declaration or statement of facts made voluntarily and confirmed under oath or affirmation before a person authorized to administer the oath or affirmation.

Affidavit of defense An affidavit stating that the defendant has a good defense to the plaintiff's action on the merits.

Affidavit of merits An affidavit stating that the defendant has a sound defense; an affidavit of defense.

Affidavit of service A sworn statement that a document (e.g., summons) has been exhibited or delivered to a designated person.

Affile A term employed in old practice, signifying to put on file. In modern usage it is spelled *file*.

Affiliate 1. A branch; a company controlled by another company. **2.** To join. **3.** To determine the paternity of an illegitimate child.

Affiliation 1. Being associated with a group or organization but not necessarily as a member thereof. See association. **2.** Determining the paternity of an illegitimate child and the obligation to support it; a bastardy proceeding.

Affinitas affinitatis Remote relationship by marriage.

Affinity The relationship that exists between a wife and her husband's blood relatives, or between a husband and his wife's blood relatives. Relationship by marriage, not by blood.

Affirm 1. To declare that a judgment, decree, or order of a lower tribunal is valid and must stand as rendered (the appellate court affirmed the judgment below). **2.** To approve or ratify (she affirmed the agent's contract). **3.** To declare or assert (affirm his innocence).

Affirmance 1. A declaration that a judgment, decree, or order of a lower tribunal is valid and must stand as rendered. **2.** The ratification or confirmation of a voidable or unauthorized act or contract by a party who is to be bound thereby.

Affirmant Someone who testifies on affirmation, or who affirms instead of taking an oath.

Affirmation 1. A solemn assertion or declaration which can be a substitute for an oath. **2.** Testimony, certification.

Affirmative 1. Pertaining to that which establishes or declares something positively (an affirmative response). **2.** Yes; assent.

Affirmative action 1. Steps and programs that are designed to eliminate existing and continuing discrimination, to remedy the lingering effects of past discrimination, and to create systems and procedures to prevent future discrimination. **2.** Action taken by the National Labor Relations Board to correct wrongs that have been committed—remedial action, not merely punitive or disciplinary.

Affirmative charge An instruction to the jury that the defendant cannot be convicted under a designated count; removing an issue from the jury's consideration.

Affirmative condition A condition consisting of doing a thing (e.g., pay rent).

Affirmative covenant Covenant in which the party binds himself or herself to the existence of a present state of facts as represented, or to the future performance of some act.

Affirmative defense A defense that raises matters not covered in the plaintiff's complaint and that will defeat the plaintiff's claim even if the plaintiff is able to prove all of the allegations in its complaint. Examples: contributory negligence, accord and satisfaction.

Affirmative easement An easement involving the giving of rights to use the land burdened with the easement when this use would otherwise be unlawful.

Affirmative plea In equity pleading, a plea that sets up a single fact, not appearing in the bill, or sets up a number of circumstances all tending to establish a single fact, which fact, if existing, destroys the complainant's case.

Affirmative pregnant An allegation in a pleading that implies a negative in favor of one's opponent.

Affirmative relief Relief, benefit, or compensation that may be due and granted to defendant.

Affirmative statute A statute couched in affirmative or mandatory terms. One that directs the doing of an act, or declares what shall be done.

Affirmative warranty An insurance warranty that asserts the existence of a fact at the time the policy is entered into. A promissory warranty, on the other hand, is an agreement that the insurer's duties shall be conditional on the future existence of certain facts.

Affix To attach physically; to attach securely and permanently.

Afforce To add to or strengthen.

Afforce the assize In old English practice, a method of securing a verdict, where the jury disagreed, either by confirming them without meat and drink, or, more anciently, by adding other jurors to the panel, to a limited extent, until twelve could be found who were unanimous.

Afforestation The turning of a part of a country into forest or woodland or subjecting it to forest law.

Affranchise To set free from obligations.

Affray The fighting of two or more persons in a public place.

Affreightment A contract to transport goods by ship.

Affretement In French law, the hiring of a vessel.

A force et armis With force and arms.

Aforementioned See aforesaid.

Aforesaid Mentioned earlier in the statute, contract, or other document (the aforesaid clause).

Aforethought Thought of beforehand for any length of time, however short; deliberate, planned (malice aforethought).

A fortiori With greater force, with stronger reason, all the more so (if the earlier case is invalid, then a fortiori the later case is invalid).

Aft At or near the stern of a ship.

After Later, succeeding, subsequent to, inferior in point of time or of priority or preference.

After-acquired Acquired after a particular date or event.

Afterbirth The placenta and fetal membranes expelled after childbirth.

Afternoon May mean the whole time from noon to midnight, or it may mean the earlier part of that time as distinguished from evening, or may mean that part of day between noon and evening.

After sight This term as used in a bill payable so many days after sight, means after legal sight; that is, after legal presentment for acceptance. The mere fact of having seen the bill or known of its existence does not constitute legal "sight."

Afterward, afterwards Subsequent in point of time, thereafter.

Against 1. Contrary (against my wishes). **2.** Facing (against the wall).

Against the form of the statute Technical words used in framing an indictment for a breach of the statute prohibiting the act complained of.

Against the manifest weight of the evidence An opposite conclusion is clearly evident, or the verdict is palpably erroneous and wholly unwarranted.

Age 1. The length of time during which a person has lived. **2.** The time at which one attains full personal rights and capacities.

Agency 1. A relationship in which one person acts for another or represents another by the latter's authority (e.g., principal and agent, master and servant). **2.** A governmental body that carries out or administers the law. **3.** A business that acts on behalf of others. **4.** The means by which something is accomplished.

Agency by estoppel An agency that arises when the principal's negligence allows others to believe that the agent possesses authority, which in fact does not exist.

Agency by operation of law An agency created by the law and not by agreement of the principal and agent. An agency by estoppel.

Agency in fact An agency created by agreement of principal and agent and not by operation of law.

Agency of the United States A department, division, or administration within the federal government.

Agency shop A union security device whereby to continue employment any nonunion employee is required to pay to the union sums equivalent to those paid by union members, either in an amount equal to both union dues and initiation fees or in an amount equal to dues alone.

Agenda Memoranda of things to be done, as items of business or discussion to be brought up at a meeting; a program consisting of such items.

Agent 1. A person authorized to act for another; someone who conducts the business of another (a lawyer is the agent of the client). **2.** That which produces an effect; a power (agent of destruction).

Agent provocateur A spy; a secret agent hired to penetrate an organization to gather evidence against its members or to incite trouble.

Age of consent 1. The age at which people can marry without parental consent. See majority. **2.** The age at which a female can consent to sexual intercourse so that the male can avoid the charge of statutory rape.

Age of majority 1. Age of 18 or 21, depending on what the person is trying to do, the intent of the parties, the intent of the statute, etc. **2.** The age at which a person can no longer disaffirm a contract. **3.** The age at which one can vote, enter a will, etc. **4.** The age at which the right to be supported by parents often ends.

Age of reason The age at which a child is deemed capable of acting responsibly (often 7 years of age). Below age 7, a child is conclusively presumed to be incapable of committing a crime.

Aggravated assault 1. Often, an assault with a deadly weapon or with the intent to kill, rob, or rape. **2.** An attempt to cause serious bodily injury to another or causing such bodily injury knowingly or recklessly under circumstances manifesting extreme indifference to the value of human life.

Aggravated battery An unlawful act of violent injury to the person of another, accompanied by circumstances of aggravation, such as the use of a deadly weapon, great disparity between the ages and physical conditions of the parties, or the purposeful infliction of shame and disgrace.

Aggravated robbery A robbery committed by a person who is armed with a dangerous weapon or who inflicts bodily harm upon any person in the course of such robbery.

Aggravation Circumstances that increase the enormity of a crime or tort, adding to its injurious consequences; the circumstances go beyond the essential elements of the crime or tort itself.

Aggravation of damages 1. Special circumstances that warrant an increase in the damage award, e.g., malice of the wrongdoer. **2.** An increase in the damages suffered in connection with a pre-existing injury.

Aggregate 1. Total amount. **2.** To bring together.

Aggregate theory of partnership A partnership is the totality of persons engaged in a business and not an entity in itself as in the case of a corporation.

Aggregatio mentium The meeting of minds. The moment when a contract is complete.

Aggregation The combination of two or more elements in patent claims, each of which is unrelated and each of which performs separately and without cooperation, where the combination does not define a composite integrated mechanism.

Aggregation doctrine A rule that precludes a totaling of claims in order to reach the jurisdictional amount necessary to sue in a federal court.

Aggressor The person who initiates the use of force; the person who provokes, invites, or seeks trouble.

Aggrieved Having been injured; having been deprived of legal rights (aggrieved minority).

Aggrieved party Someone who suffers a substantial grievance; someone whose legal right is invaded; someone whose personal or property rights or interests are directly affected by a decree, order or judgment.

Aging; aging of accounts Classifying the accounts receivable according to the time that has elapsed since the date of billing or the due date (e.g., 30 days, 60 days).

Agio In commercial law, a term used to express the difference in point of value between metallic and paper money, or between one sort of metallic money and another.

Agiotage A speculation on the rise and fall of the public debt, or the public funds. The speculator is called agioteur.

Agitator Someone who stirs up or disturbs things.

Agnate Having a common source; descended from the male side.

Agnation Kinship by the father's side.

Agnomination A surname; an additional name or title.

Agrarian laws In Roman law, laws for the distribution among the people of the lands constituting the public domain, usually territory conquered from an enemy. In common parlance the term is frequently applied to laws which have for their object the more equal division or distribution of landed property; laws for subdividing large properties and increasing the number of landholders.

Agrarium A tax upon or tribute payable out of land.

Agree 1. To come to an agreement. **2.** To accept. **3.** To come into harmony.

Agreed case A written statement of facts agreed to by the parties and submitted to the court so that a trial on these facts will not be needed. The court will then rule on the questions of law. The facts agreed upon are the ultimate, material facts of the case.

Agreed statement of facts A statement of facts, agreed on by the parties as true and correct, to be submitted to a court for a ruling on the law of the case.

Agreement 1. A manifestation of mutual assent by two or more persons to one another; a meeting of the minds (agreement to sell). **2.** Harmony; the absence of dissension (agreement between the accounts).

Agreement of sale A contract in which a seller agrees to sell and a buyer agrees to buy, under specific terms and conditions spelled out in writing and signed by both parties. Also called a contract of purchase, a purchase agreement, or a sales agreement.

Agribusiness Agriculture operating as big business.

Agricultural lien A statutory lien to secure money or supplies advanced to an agriculturist to be expended or employed in the making of a crop and attaching to that crop only.

Agriculture Raising crops and livestock.

Aid 1. To assist; to supplement the efforts of others. **2.** Assistance. **3.** Assistant.

Aid and abet Assist, counsel, or incite someone to commit a crime.

Aid and comfort Help, support, assist, counsel, encourage.

Aid bond Local government bonds that aid private industry engaged in a project that will benefit the public.

Aider and abettor One who assists another in the accomplishment of a common design or purpose.

Aider by verdict The curing or healing, by the verdict rendered, of a defect or error in the pleading that might have been objected to before the verdict. The facts that the jury logically needed to reach the verdict are assumed to have been properly alleged.

Air bill of lading A negotiable instrument used in shipment of goods by air.

Air tramping Inland, coastwise, or intercontinental transportation of cargo by air which does not follow a regular airline route or schedule.

Ajournement In French law, the document pursuant to which an action or suit is commenced.

Akin 1. Related by blood. **2.** Comparable.

Aktiengesellschaft (AG) Stock corporation as defined by the German stock corporation code.

Albacea In Spanish law, an executor or administrator.

Alcoholism The pathological effect (as distinguished from physiological effect) of excessive indulgence in intoxicating liquors.

Alderman A member of the local legislative body.

Aleatory contract A mutual agreement in which the advantages and losses depend on an uncertain event, e.g., an insurance contract. Performance depends on uncertain contingencies.

Aler sans jour In old practice, the final dismissal of a case from court without continuance. "To go without day."

Alia Other things.

Alia enormia Other wrongs.

Aliamenta In old English law, a liberty of passage, open way, watercourse, etc., for the tenant's accommodation.

Alia False name; also known as (a.k.a.).

Alias execution A second writ of execution after the

first one was returned without being successful in satisfying the judgment.

Alias summons A new summons issued when the original has not produced its effect because of a defect in the form or manner of service.

Alias writ A second or further writ that takes the place of an earlier writ that has not been effective.

Alibi A defense alleging that the defendant was "elsewhere" at the time of the crime and therefore could not have committed it.

Alien 1. A foreign-born person who has not qualified as a U.S. citizen. **2.** To convey; to transfer title.

Alienability The quality or attribute of being transferable.

Alienable Legally capable of being transferred to the ownership of another.

Alienage The condition or status of an alien.

Alien amy A subject of a foreign state at peace with our own.

Alien and Sedition Acts Federal statutes of 1798 punishing those who criticized or defamed the government, giving the president the power to deport undesirable aliens, lengthening residency requirements to become a citizen, etc.

Alienate To transfer; to transfer title.

Alienation 1. The transfer of property by conveyance, by will, etc. **2.** Rupture, schism, bitterness. **3.** Mental derangement; insanity.

Alienation clause A clause in an insurance policy that voids the policy if the property being insured is sold.

Alienation of affections A tort consisting of (a) the intent of a third person to diminish the marital relationship between a husband and wife, (b) affirmative conduct in carrying out this intent, (c) affections (e.g., society, assistance, sexual relations) between the spouses are in fact alienated, and (d) the alienation was caused by the third person.

Alien corporation A corporation organized under the laws of a foreign power.

Alienee A person to whom property is conveyed or transferred.

Alien enemy In international law, an alien who is the subject or citizen of some hostile nation or power.

Alien friend A subject of a foreign state at peace with our own.

Alieni juris Under the control, or subject to the authority, of another person.

Alienism The state, condition, or character of an alien.

Alienist A doctor specializing in mental diseases; a doctor who is an expert on the mental competence of witnesses.

Alien nee A person who has been born an alien.

Alienor A person who transfers or conveys property.

Alignment, alinement 1. An adjustment to a line. **2.** The plan for a road.

Alike Similar.

Alimony Support that one spouse pays another after they have been separated or divorced.

Alimony in gross A single, definite, and determined sum of alimony not subject to change or modification. The amount, however, may be payable over a set period of time in installments.

Alimony pendente lite Alimony that is provided pending the outcome of the suit for divorce, legal separation, or separate maintenance. Temporary alimony.

Aliquot 1. Contained in something else an exact number of times. **2.** Fractional; any definite interest.

Aliter Otherwise; as otherwise held or decided.

Aliunde From another source; from elsewhere; from outside.

Alive As respects birth, it means that a child has independent life of its own for some period, even momentarily, after birth; evidenced by respiration or other indications of life, such as beating of heart and pulsation of arteries (Hydrostatic test); or heart tones in response to artificial respiration, or pulsation of umbilical cord after being severed.

All The entire amount of something; the whole; all the individual components without exception.

All and singular All without exception. A comprehensive term often used in conveyances and wills which includes the aggregate or whole and also each of the separate items or components.

Allegation A statement of fact that one expects to prove.

Allegation of faculties A wife's statement on the property of her husband in reference to an alimony claim.

Allege To state facts you expect to prove.

Alleged Supposed, represented, declared, or affirmed.

Allegiance The obligation of fidelity and obedience to the government in return for protection.

Allegiare To defend and clear one's self.

Allen charge A supplementary instruction to a jury having difficulty reaching a decision, in which the judge tells the jurors that they should carefully listen to and be deferential toward each other's views. Also called a "dynamite" charge, a "shotgun" instruction, a "third-degree" instruction, and a "nitroglycerine" charge.

Alleviare In old records, to levy or pay an accustomed fine or composition; to redeem by such payment.

All faults A sale of goods with "all faults" covers, in the absence of fraud on the part of the vendor, all such faults and defects as are not inconsistent with the identity of the goods as described.

All fours Two cases or decisions which are alike in all material respects are said to be on "all fours."

Alliance 1. Union through intermarriage; affinity. **2.** An association of states or nations. **3.** Treaty.

Allision The running of one vessel into or against another.

Allocable Distributable. In analyzing accounts, the breaking down of a lump sum charged or credited to one account into several parts to be charged or credited to other accounts.

Allocate To assign or distribute.

Allocation Assignment or allotment.

Allocation of income 1. In trust accounting, the process by which income is distributed between principal and income. **2.** When two or more businesses are controlled by the same interests, the IRS may allocate or distribute income to prevent tax evasion.

Allocatur It is allowed.

Allocution A formal inquiry by the judge of the defendant who has just been convicted of a crime as to whether the latter has any cause to show why sentence should not be imposed. The right to make a statement before sentence is imposed.

Allodarii Owners of allodial lands. Owners of estates as large as a subject may have.

Allodial Free; not holden of any lord or superior; owned without obligation of vassalage or fealty; the opposite of feudal.

Allodium Absolute ownership of land; land not subject to any rent, service, or other tenurial right of an overlord.

Allograph A writing or signature made for a person by another; the opposite of autograph.

Allonge A piece of paper annexed to a bill of exchange or promissory note. Endorsements are written on this attached paper when no room is available on the instrument itself.

Allot To divide, apportion, or distribute; to apportion shares, debentures, etc., to those who have applied for them.

Allotment 1. A share, portion, or partition. **2.** Land acquired by or awarded to individual Indians.

Allotment certificate A document issued to an

applicant for shares in a company or public loan announcing the number of shares allotted or assigned and the amounts and due dates of the calls or different payments to be made on the same.

Allotment note In English law, a writing by a seaman, made on an approved form, whereby he makes an assignment of part of his wages in favor of his wife, father or mother, grandfather or grandmother, brother, or sister.

Allottee A person who receives a share under an allotment.

Allow 1. To confer, give, or allocate. **2.** To approve, to authorize.

Allowance 1. Portion assigned or bestowed. **2.** Acceptance, admission, or authorization. **3.** Tolerance. **4.** Family support. **5.** Deduction, exemption.

Allowance pendente lite The court-ordered provision for a spouse and children during the pendency of a divorce or separate support proceeding.

All risks policy An insurance policy that insures against exposure to loss occasioned by many different kinds of disasters, such as fire, theft, and earthquake, as opposed to a specific policy for fire insurance or theft insurance.

Alluvion Accretion; the process of gradual and imperceptible increase of the earth on the shore due to the movements of the water.

Ally 1. One nation that has joined an alliance with another. **2.** A citizen or subject of one of two or more allied nations.

Almoin Alms; a tenure of lands by divine service.

Almoner One charged with the distribution of alms.

Alms Charitable donations.

Almshouse A house for the publicly or privately supported paupers of a city or county.

Alta proditio High treason.

Altarage In ecclesiastical law, offerings made on the altar; all profits that accrue to the priest by means of the altar.

Alter To make a change in; to change partially; to modify without changing its identity.

Alteration 1. Making a thing different from what it was before without destroying its identity. **2.** Writing or erasing on a document or instrument that changes its language or meaning.

Alternate legacy One by which the testator gives one of two or more things without designating which.

Alternative Choice between two things, courses, or propositions; the option that may be selected.

Alternative contract A contract whose terms allow performance by the doing of one of several acts at the election of the party from whom performance is due.

Alternative judgment One that by its terms might be satisfied by doing either of several acts at the election of the party or parties against whom the judgment is rendered and from whom performance is by the judgment required.

Alternative obligation An obligation allowing the obligor to choose which of two things he or she will do, the performance of either of which will satisfy the instrument.

Alternative pleading Alleging facts in a pleading (e.g., complaint) that are not necessarily consistent. Pleading statements in the alternative, any one of which would be sufficient independently.

Alternative remainders Remainders in which disposition of the property is made in the alternative, one to take effect only if the other does not, and in substitution of it.

Alternative writ A common law writ commanding the person against whom it is issued to do a specified thing, or show cause to the court why he or she should not be compelled to do it.

Altius non tollendi In the civil law, a servitude due by the owner of a house, by which he or she is restrained from building beyond a certain height.

Altius tollendi In the civil law, a servitude consisting of the right to build a house as high as desired.

Alto et basso High and low. This phrase is applied to an agreement made between two contending parties to submit all matters in dispute, alto et basso, to arbitration.

Altum mare The high sea, or seas.

Amalgamation 1. Consolidation, combining. **2.** The union or merger of two or more corporations into one corporate body.

Amalphitan code or **table** A collection of sea laws, compiled about the end of the eleventh century, by the people of Amalphi.

Ambassador A public officer clothed with high diplomatic powers, commissioned by a government to transact the international matters of his or her government with a foreign government.

Ambassadors extraordinary Public officers who are sent to conduct special business or to remain for an indeterminate period.

Ambidexter 1. Able to use both hands. **2.** An attorney who is paid by both sides. **3.** A juror who is paid by both sides.

Ambiguity That which is doubtful or uncertain.

Ambiguity upon the factum An ambiguity as to the foundation of the document itself as opposed to doubt on the meaning of a certain clause in it.

Ambiguous Doubtful or capable of more than one meaning.

Ambit Boundary; the limits of a power.

Ambulance chasing Soliciting business by or for an attorney, e.g., seeking out people who have been recently injured in order to offer attorney services.

Ambulatory 1. Revocable (ambulatory will). **2.** Walking, moving (ambulatory exercise).

Ambulatory courts The court of king's bench in England was formerly called an ambulatory court because it followed the king's person, and was held sometimes in one place and sometimes in another.

Ambulatory will A changeable will.

Ameliorating waste Waste committed by the tenant that in fact improves the land.

Amelioration 1. Improvement. **2.** Mitigation.

Amenable Subject to answer to the law; accountable; responsible; liable to punishment.

Amend 1. To improve. **2.** To change.

Amende honorable An apology.

Amendment 1. An improvement. **2.** A change. **3.** A proposed change to a rule or law; an enacted change to a rule or law. **4.** An attachment.

Amends Payment of satisfaction for a wrong.

Amenity, amenities 1. Features of property that make it agreeable or pleasant. **2.** A negative easement that restrains the owner of property from doing on or with the land that which would otherwise be lawful.

A mensa et thoro See divorce a mensa et thoro.

Amentia Insanity; idiocy.

Amerce To punish by fine or penalty.

Amercement A fine or punishment.

American clause In marine insurance, if any subsequent insurance is obtained, the insurer shall nevertheless be answerable for the full extent of the sum subscribed by it, without right to claim contribution from subsequent underwriters.

American rule The winning party in litigation cannot obtain the costs of attorney fees from the losing party unless authorized by statute or unless the losing party acted in bad faith, vexatiously, wantonly, or for oppressive reasons.

Ami or **amy** A friend.

Amicable Mutually agreed to by the parties; friendly.

Amicable action An action brought and carried on by the mutual consent and arrangement of the parties to obtain a judgment of a court on a doubtful question of law, the facts being usually settled by agreement.

Amicable compounders In Louisiana, arbitrators authorized to abate some of the strictness of the law in favor of natural equity.

Amicus curiae Friend of the court. A nonparty who advises or makes suggestions to the court. An amicus curiae brief is the document containing this advice that is submitted to an appellate court.

Amittere curiam To lose the court; to be deprived of the privilege of attending the court.

Amnesia Loss of memory as a result of organic trauma, delirium lesions of the diencephalon area of the brain, hysteria or epilepsy.

Amnesty A collective or general pardon from the state.

Amortization The liquidation of a debt by installments or by payments into a sinking fund. The allocation (and charge to expense) of the cost or other basis of an intangible asset to the periods benefited. Examples of amortizable intangibles include patents, copyrights, and leasehold interests. Intangible assets with an indefinite life (e.g., goodwill) are not amortizable. Reduction of a debt or fund, discharge, liquidating a debt or claim.

Amortized loan One that calls for periodic payments that are applied first to interest and then to principal as provided by the terms of the note.

Amortized mortgage Repayment of a mortgage over regular specified time intervals, with equal payments. This would reduce the principal, after any monies owing for interest are applied.

Amotio In the civil law, a moving or taking away.

Amotion Removing something or someone from a position or office.

Amount in controversy The amount sued for; the amount claimed; the value of the right asserted by the plaintiff. The amount needed to establish diversity jurisdiction in a federal court.

Amount realized The amount realized by a taxpayer on the sale or exchange of property. The measure of this amount is the sum of the cash and the fair market value of any property or services received.

Amount to To reach in the aggregate.

Amove To remove from a post or station.

Ampere The rate that electricity flows through electric wires. A unit of electric current.

Ampliation In civil law, a deferring of judgment until

a cause be further examined. An order for the rehearing of a cause on a day appointed, for the sake of more ample information.

Amusement tax A government levy imposed on tickets sold to places of amusement, sporting events, etc.

Anacrisis In the civil law, an investigation of truth, interrogation of witnesses, and inquiry made into any fact, especially by torture.

Analogous Sufficiently similar to lend support. Bearing some resemblance or likeness.

Analogy Alikeness; partial similarity.

Anarchist Someone who believes in the absence of government and in the overthrow of government by force.

Anarchy The absence of government, lawlessness, mob rule.

Anathema An ecclesiastical punishment by which a person is separated from the body of the church, and forbidden all intercourse with the members of the same.

Anathematize To pronounce anathema upon; to pronounce accursed by ecclesiastical authority.

Anatocism In the civil law, repeated or doubled interest; compound interest; usury.

Ancestor One from whom a person lineally descended or may be descended; a progenitor. A former possessor; the person last seised. A deceased person from whom another has inherited land. Embraces both collaterals and lineals.

Ancestral Relating to ancestors, or to what has been done by them.

Ancestral debt A debt of an ancestor the law compels the heir to pay.

Ancestral estates Realty transmitted by descent, and not by purchase; or such as are acquired either by descent or by operation of law.

Ancestry The persons within one's line of descent.

Anchorage A duty paid by the owners of ships for the use of the port or harbor where they cast anchor.

Ancient Old; that which has existed from an indefinitely early period, or which by age alone has acquired certain rights or privileges.

Ancient deed A deed 30 (or 20) years old and shown to come from a proper custody and having nothing suspicious about it.

Ancient demesne Manors that in the time of William the Conqueror were in the hands of the crown, and are so recorded in the Domesday Book. Also, in old English law, a species of copyhold.

Ancient documents Deeds, wills, and other writings more than 30 years old (20 years under Fed. Rules); they are presumed to be genuine without express proof, when coming from the proper custody.

Ancient house One that has stood long enough to acquire an easement of support against the adjoining land or building.

Ancient lights Windows that have had outside light for over a given length of time (e.g., 20 years) cannot be blocked off by an adjoining landowner in some states. Both the windows and the rule about blocking them are called ancient lights.

Ancients In England, gentlemen of the inns of court and chancery. In Gray's Inn the society consists of benchers, ancients, barristers, and students under the bar. The ancients are of the oldest barristers. In the Middle Temple, those who had passed their readings used to be termed "ancients." The Inns of Chancery consist of ancients and students or clerks; from the ancients a principal or treasurer is chosen yearly.

Ancient wall A wall built to be used, and in fact used, as a party-wall, for more than 20 years by the express permission and continuous acquiescence of the owners of the land on which it stands.

Ancient water course A water course is "ancient" if the channel through which it naturally runs has existed from time immemorial, independent of the quantity of water it discharges.

Ancient writings or documents A document that is more than 30 years old (or 20 years in some states) with nothing suspicious about it. The document is presumed genuine if it has come from a proper place of custody.

Ancienty Eldership; seniority.

Ancillary Auxiliary, aiding.

Ancillary administration A proceeding in a state where a decedent had property, but which is different from the state where that person lived and had his or her main estate administered.

Ancillary attachment One sued out in aid of an action already brought; its only office being to hold the property attached under it for the satisfaction of the plaintiff's demand.

Ancillary bill or **suit** One growing out of and auxiliary to another action or suit, either at law or in equity, such as a bill for discovery, or a proceeding for the enforcement of a judgment, or to set aside fraudulent transfers of property.

Ancillary jurisdiction Once federal jurisdiction

properly attaches to the primary case before the federal court, the latter also has jurisdiction over certain subsidiary or subordinate disputes, even though it might not independently be able to proceed to adjudicate them.

Ancillary proceeding One growing out of or auxiliary to another action or suit, or which is subordinate to or in aid of a primary action, either at law or in equity.

Ancillary receiver One appointed in aid of, and in subordination to, a foreign reciever for the purpose of collecting and taking charge of assets in the jurisdiction where he or she is appointed.

Ancipitis usus In international law, of doubtful use; the use of which is doubtful.

And Added to, together with, joined with, as well as, including. Sometimes, however, construed as "or."

An et jour Year and day; a year and a day.

Anew Over again, de novo.

Angaria A forced or compulsory service exacted by the government for public purposes; in particular, the right of a public officer to require the service of vehicles or ships.

Angary, right of The right of a belligerent to appropriate, for use or destruction, neutral property temporarily located in its own territory or in that of the other belligerent.

Angel An ancient English coin, of the value of ten shillings sterling.

Angel dust An illegal hallucinogen; phencyclidine.

Angild In Saxon law, the single value of a man or other thing; a single weregild; the compensation of a thing according to its single value or estimation.

Anglice A term formerly used in pleading when a thing is described both in Latin and English.

Anguish Extreme distress; great mental or physical suffering.

Angylde In Saxon law, the rate fixed by law at which certain injuries to person or property were to be paid for.

Aniens; anient Null, void, of no force or effect.

Animal Any living organism with the power of voluntary motion. Often, however, the word is meant to exclude humans.

Animals of a base nature Animals in which a right of property may be acquired by reclaiming them from the wildness, but which, at common law, by reason of their base nature, are not regarded as possible subjects of a larceny.

Animo With intention, disposition, design, will.

Animus 1. Intention (the offense must contain a separate animus). **2.** Animosity (antilabor animus).

Animus furandi The intent to steal.

Animus lucrandi The intention to make a gain or profit.

Annates In ecclesiastical law, first-fruits paid out of spiritual benefices to the Pope, so called because the value of one year's profit was taken as their rate.

Annex 1. To join together. **2.** To take over. **3.** An extension.

Annexation 1. Merging or attaching one thing to another. **2.** The takeover of something (e.g., territory).

Anniented Abrogated, frustrated, or brought to nothing.

Anniversary An annual day, recurring each year on the same date.

Annotation A remark, note, case summary, or commentary on some passage of a book, statutory provision, or the like, intended to illustrate or explain its meaning.

Annoyance Exasperation, discomfort.

Annual Of or pertaining to a year.

Annual depreciation The annual loss, not restored by current maintenance, due to all the factors causing the ultimate retirement of the property. These factors embrace wear and tear, decay, inadequacy, and obsolescence.

Annual percentage rate The true cost of borrowing money expressed in a standardized, yearly way to allow the consumer to understand the credit terms and to "shop" for credit.

Annual report A report for stockholders and other interested parties prepared once a year; includes a balance sheet, an income statement, etc.

Annual value The net yearly income derivable from a given piece of property. Its fair rental value for one year, deducting costs and expenses; the value of its use for a year.

Annuitant One who receives an annuity.

Annuity A fixed sum payable to a person at specified intervals for a specific period of time or for life.

Annuity bond A bond without a maturity date, that is, perpetually paying interest.

Annuity certain An annuity payable for a specified period no matter when the annuitant dies.

Annul To obliterate or nullify.

Annulment 1. A declaration that a marriage never existed; a declaration that an attempted marriage is invalid or void. **2.** Nullification.

Annus luctus The year of mourning.

Anomalous Deviating from common rule, method, or type.

Anomalous indorser A stranger to a note, who indorses it after its execution and delivery but before maturity, and before it has been indorsed by the payee.

Anomalous plea One which is partly affirmative and partly negative.

Anonymous Namely, unknown source.

Answer 1. A pleading in which a response is made to the claim of another party (file an answer). **2.** An acknowledgment (it took ten days to receive the answer). **3.** The solution (the only answer is to pay the debt). **4.** To take responsibility for (she will answer for his debts). **5.** To respond (I have not answered the charge). **6.** To be sufficient (the qualifications of the witness answer the requirements).

Ante Before, prior to.

Antecedent Prior in point of time.

Antecedent debt A debt that is prior in time to another transaction. In contract law, this earlier debt may furnish consideration for a new contract to pay.

Antecessor An ancestor.

Antedate 1. To place a date on a document that is earlier than the date the document was written (to antedate a check). **2.** To precede (Justice Story antedates Justice Holmes).

Ante natus Born before.

Antenuptial Made before marriage. An antenuptial agreement or settlement is a contract made by people about to be married which settles matters such as support and property division in the event of death of one of the parties or the dissolution of the marriage.

Anthropometry The science of measuring the human body.

Antichresis In the civil law, a species of mortgage, or pledge of immovables. An agreement by which the debtor gives to the creditor the income from the property pledged, in lieu of the interest on the debt.

Anticipate To foresee.

Anticipation 1. The act of doing a thing before its proper time or simply doing it before something else. **2.** The right to pay off a mortgage before it comes due without paying a "prepayment penalty." **3.** The right under some contracts to deduct some money (usually equal to the current interest rate) when paying early. **4.** In patent law, a person is anticipated if someone else has already patented substantially the same thing.

Anticipatory breach of contract A repudiation of a contract duty before the time fixed in the contract for the performance of that duty.

Antidumping law Legislation prohibiting the sale of imported merchandise in quantity at a very low price, without regard to price, or at less than the market price in the country where the merchandise was produced, if such imports are determined to be injurious to domestic sales of like products.

Antidumping tariff A tariff calculated to prevent the dumping or unloading of imported goods below cost by fixing the tariff at the difference between the price at which the goods commonly sell in the country of origin and the price at which it is to be sold in the importing country.

Antigraphy A copy or counterpart of a deed.

Anti-lapse statute Prevents a lapse (termination) of a clause in a will which would otherwise occur if the person who was to receive property under the clause dies before the testator (the one who wrote the will).

Antinomy A term used in logic and law to denote a real or apparent inconsistency or conflict between two authorities or propositions.

Antitrust Concerning the prevention or regulation of monopolies, price fixing, and other unlawful restraints on trade and commerce.

Antitrust acts Federal and state statutes to protect trade and commerce from unlawful restraints, price discriminations, price fixing, and monopolies. Most states have mini-antitrust acts patterned on the federal acts. The principal federal antitrust acts are: Sherman Act, 15 U.S.C.A. § 1 et seq.; Clayton Act, 15 U.S.C.A. § 12 et seq.; Federal Trade Commission Act, 15 U.S.C.A. § 41 et seq.; Robinson-Patman Act, 15 U.S.C.A. § 13 et seq.

Anxiety Apprehension, tension, or uneasiness that stems from the anticipation of impending danger or the fear of the unknown.

Apartheid Sanctioned or mandated racial segregation.

Apartment house A building arranged in several suites of connecting rooms, each suite designed for independent housekeeping, but with certain mechanical conveniences, such as heat, light, or elevator services, in common to all families occupying the building.

Apex juris The summit of the law; a legal subtlety; a

nice or cunning point of law; close technicality.

Aphasia Loss of the faculty or power of articulate speech.

Apographia In civil law, an examination and enumeration of things possessed; an inventory.

Apoplexy A sudden loss of consciousness, sensation, and voluntary action due to an escape of blood or serum into the brain or spinal cord.

Apostasy A renunciation of principles.

A posteriori From the effect to the cause (a posteriori reasoning).

Apostles In admiralty practice, letters granted to a party who appeals from an inferior to a superior court, embodying a statement of the case and a declaration that the record will be transmitted.

Apostoli In civil law, certificates of the inferior judge from whom a cause is removed, directed to the superior.

Apostolus A messenger; an ambassador, legate, or nuncio.

Apparator A furnisher or provider.

Apparent 1. Capable of being clearly seen or understood. **2.** Seeming.

Apparent authority Authority of an agent that exists because the principal knowingly or negligently permits the agent to exercise it, or because the principal holds the agent out as possessing it.

Apparent defects 1. Those defects in goods that can be discovered by simple inspection. **2.** Title defects that appear on the record.

Apparent easement One capable of being seen or known on inspection.

Apparent heir One whose right of inheritance is indefeasible, provided he or she outlives the ancestor.

Apparitor In the civil law, an officer who waited upon and executed the commands of a magistrate or superior officer.

Apparlement Resemblance; likelihood.

Appeal Asking a higher tribunal to review the decision of an inferior tribunal.

Appeal bond A bond submitted by the person bringing an appeal which will cover the costs of the opponent if a determination is made that the appeal had no merit or that it was not prosecuted with effect.

Appear To come formally and properly before a tribunal.

Appearance 1. Formally and properly coming before a tribunal. **2.** Coming into view. **3.** External look.

Appearance by attorney An act of an attorney in prosecuting an action on behalf of his or her client. The document filed in court in which the attorney states that he or she is representing a party to the action.

Appearance docket A docket kept by the clerk of the court in which appearances are entered, containing also a brief abstract of all the proceedings in the cause.

Appellant The person or party who brings the appeal.

Appellate Concerning appeals.

Appellate court A court having jurisdiction of appeal and review.

Appellate jurisdiction The power of an appellate court to review the decision of an inferior tribunal to determine whether this tribunal made any errors of law.

Appellate review The process by which a higher court determines whether a lower tribunal has committed any errors of law in a particular case. A review of the decisions made below.

Appellator An old term for appellant.

Appellee The person against whom an appeal is brought; respondent.

Appellor A criminal who accused his or her accomplices, or who challenged a jury.

Append To add or affix.

Appendage Something added as a supporting component.

Appendant 1. Attached; attachment. **2.** That which beyond memory has belonged to something more important or worthy.

Appenditia The appendages or appurtenances of an estate or house, dwelling, etc.

Appendix Something added; supplementary materials added to a document.

Appensura Payment of money by weight instead of by court.

Appertain To belong to.

Appertaining Connected with in use or occupancy.

Applicable Capable of being applied (an applicable holding).

Applicant Someone who applies for something.

Application 1. A petition; a request for something. **2.** Relevance. **3.** Diligent attention.

Apply 1. To make a formal request. **2.** To have relevance (the case does not apply). **3.** To persevere. **4.** To put into practice.

Appoint To designate, prescribe, or nominate.

Appointee The person selected.

Appointment 1. The selection of a person to carry out a responsibility. **2.** Position. **3.** Engagement.

Appointor The person who appoints, or executes a power of appointment.

Apport A tax, tribute, payment, or charge.

Apportion To divide and distribute proportionally.

Apportionment 1. Dividing and assigning in just proportion. **2.** The process of allocating legislators or representatives among several areas or political subdivisions. **3.** The allocation of a charge or cost (e.g., taxes) among several parties. **4.** The distribution of legal responsibility for a transaction or tort.

Apportum The revenue, profit, or emolument a thing brings to the owner.

Appostille An addition or annotation made in the margin of a writing.

Appraisal A valuation or an estimation of value of property as of a given date by disinterested persons of suitable qualifications.

Appraise To fix a price for something.

Appraisement A valuation or estimation of the value of property. A just and true valuation of property.

Appraiser Someone who evaluates (appraises) property.

Appreciable Capable of being perceived.

Appreciate 1. To increase in value. **2.** To understand. **3.** To value.

Appreciation surplus Surplus that results from the revaluation of the assets of a business.

Apprehend 1. To be aware of; to have knowledge of. **2.** To arrest. **3.** To fear.

Apprehension 1. Knowledge or belief. **2.** Seizure or arrest. **3.** Fear.

Apprendre A fee or profit taken or received.

Apprenticeship The term during which an apprentice is to serve; the status of an apprentice; the relation subsisting between an apprentice and his master.

Apprise To give notice.

Approach 1. To come nearer in place or time. **2.** An access, street, or way.

Approach, right of In international maritime law, the right of a ship of war, upon the high sea, to draw near to another vessel for the purpose of ascertaining the nationality of the latter.

Approbation Praise, approval.

Appropriate 1. To make something your own, to exercise dominion over. **2.** To designate money for a particular purpose. **3.** Fit and proper.

Appropriated surplus In accounting, the portion of surplus set aside for a specific purpose other than for existing liability.

Appropriation 1. The act of taking something over, of making it your own; seizure. **2.** The designation of money for a specific purpose.

Appropriation of land The act of selecting, devoting, or setting apart land for a particular use or purpose, as where land is appropriated for public buildings, military reservations, or other public uses. Taking private property for public use in the exercise of the power of eminent domain.

Appropriation of payments The application of a payment to the discharge of a particular debt.

Appropriator One who makes an appropriation.

Approval The act of confirming, ratifying, sanctioning, or consenting to some act or thing done by another.

Approval sale An agreement that passes title when the buyer indicates that the goods are acceptable.

Approve To consider acceptable; to sanction.

Approvement 1. The improvement or partial inclosure of a common. The profits arising from the improvement of land approved. **2.** In old English law, a practice of criminal prosecutions by which a person accused of treason or felony was permitted to exonerate himself or herself by accusing others.

Approver To approve or prove; to vouch (French).

Approximate 1. To estimate. **2.** To come close to. **3.** More or less.

Approximation 1. When the terms of a charitable trust have become impossible or impractical to observe, a court can alter the terms to fulfill the donor's general charitable intent. **2.** An estimate.

Appruare To take to one's use or profit.

Appurtenance That which belongs to something else; something physically secondary to a primary part but serving a useful or necessary function in connection with the primary part (the light fixtures were appurtenances).

Appurtenant Belonging to.

Appurtenant easement An incorporeal right that is attached to a superior right and inheres in land to which it is attached and is in the nature of a covenant running with the land. An easement interest that attaches to the land and passes with it.

A prendre To take; to seize.

A priori From what goes before; prior to investigation.

Apron 1. A paved area. **2.** A platform at the entrance to a dock.

Apt 1. Suitable, appropriate. **2.** Inclined. **3.** Gifted. **4.** Having the requisite qualifications.

Apta viro Fit for a husband; a woman who has reached marriageable years.

Apud acta Among the acts; among the recorded proceedings.

Aquae ductus In the civil law, a servitude that consists of the right to carry water by means of pipes or conduits over or through the estate of another.

Aquae haustus In the civil law, a servitude that consists of the right to draw water from the fountain, pool, or spring of another.

Aquatic rights Rights that individuals have to the use of the sea and rivers for the purpose of fishing and navigation, and also to the soil in the sea and rivers.

Arable Fit for cultivation.

Araho In feudal law, to make an oath in the church or some other holy place.

Arbeiter Worker (German).

Arbiter A referee, someone chosen to resolve a dispute.

Arbitrage The simultaneous purchase and sale of the same or an equivalent security or commodity in different markets in order to profit from price discrepancies.

Arbitrament The decision of an arbitrator.

Arbitrament and award A plea to an action brought for the same cause that had been submitted to arbitration and on which an award has been made.

Arbitrary 1. Capricious, subjective, at pleasure. **2.** Absolute.

Arbitrate 1. To submit a dispute to arbitration. **2.** To render a decision as an arbitrator. **3.** Reconcile.

Arbitration 1. The submission of a dispute to an impartial third party as an alternative to traditional litigation in court. The disputants agree in advance to abide by the decision of the arbitrator. **2.** The decision of an arbitrator.

Arbitration and award An affirmative defense to the effect that the subject matter of the action has been settled by a prior arbitration.

Arbitration board A panel of arbitrators appointed to hear and decide a dispute according to the rules of arbitration.

Arbitration clause A clause inserted in a contract providing for compulsory arbitration in case of dispute as to rights or liabilities under the contract.

Arbitrator Someone to whom matters in dispute between two or more parties are submitted for final determination.

Arbitrium The decision of an arbiter, or arbitrator; an award; a judgment.

Arbitrium est judicium An award is a judgment.

Arbor consanguinitatis A table, formed in the shape of a tree, showing the geneaology of a family.

Arbor finalis A tree used for making a boundary line.

Arcarius A treasurer; a keeper of public money.

Archives 1. Place where old documents are stored. **2.** Documents that are stored.

Archivist Custodian of archives.

Ardent spirits Intoxicating liquors; distilled liquors.

Ardour An arsonist.

Area 1. A particular territory or surface. **2.** In the civil law, a vacant space in a city; a place not built upon.

A render To render, to yield. That which is to be rendered, yielded, or paid.

Argentum album Bullion; uncoined silver; common silver coin.

Argentum dei Money given as earnest in making a bargain; (God's money).

Arguendo In arguing; in the course of the argument.

Argument An effort to establish belief by a course of reasoning.

Argumentative 1. Quarrelsome; given to debate or dispute; containing conclusions as well as facts. **2.** A pleading is argumentative when it contains arguments as well as statements of fact.

Arise 1. To spring up, originate, to come into being or notice. **2.** A case "arises" under the Constitution or a law of the United States, so as to be within the jurisdiction of a federal court, whenever its correct decision depends on the construction of either. **3.** A cause of action or suit "arises" at the time and place when the act is unlawfully omitted or committed.

Aristocracy 1. A government in which a class of people, believed to be superior, rule. **2.** A privileged class of the people.

Aristo-democracy A form of government where the power is divided between the nobles (or the more powerful) and the people.

Armed Equipped with weapons and with whatever is needed for the occasion.

Armed neutrality An attitude of neutrality between belligerents which the neutral state is prepared to maintain by armed force if necessary.

Armed robbery Taking another's property by force while armed with a deadly weapon.

Armistice A suspension of fighting.

Armory A place where arms are stored.

Arms Weapons; that which is used to defend oneself.

Arm's length At a distance; as between two strangers

who are looking out for their individual self-interests.

Army Armed forces of a nation intended for military service on land.

Arpen, arpent, arpennus A civil and French measure of land equal to about an acre.

Arpentator A measurer or surveyor of land.

Arra In the civil law, earnest; earnest-money; evidence of a completed bargain.

Arraign To bring an accused before a court to hear the criminal charges and to enter a plea of guilty, not guilty, etc.

Arraignment Bringing the accused before a court to hear the criminal charges and to enter a plea of guilty, not guilty, etc.

Arrangement with creditors A plan whereby the debtor settles with his or her creditors or obtains more time to repay debts. Under the Bankruptcy Act, the court can supervise such plans.

Array 1. A group of persons summoned to be jurors; the list of jurors impaneled. **2.** Collection. **3.** To place in order.

Arrearages, arrears 1. Unpaid debts. **2.** Cumulative preferred stock dividends that have not been declared on time.

Arrest To deprive a person of his or her liberty by legal authority. Taking someone into custody. Arrest involves the authoroity to arrest, the assertion of that authority with the intention to affect an arrest, and restraint of the person to be arrested.

Arrest of judgment A court's refusal to render a judgment; a court's decision to stay a judgment because of errors that have been discovered in the record.

Arrest warrant A written order signed by a judge or magistrate that commands a law enforcement officer to arrest a person and bring him or her before the court in order to answer the charges made in a complaint.

Arret A judgment, sentence, or decree of a court of competent jurisdiction.

Arretted Convened before a judge and charged with a crime.

Arrhae In the civil law, money or other valuable things given by the buyer to the seller, for the purpose of evidencing the contract; earnest money.

Arriere vassal In feudal law, the vassal of a vassal.

Arrogation 1. Claiming or seizing something without authority or right. **2.** The adoption of an adult.

Arsenal 1. A place to store arms. **2.** A collection of weapons.

Arson The malicious burning of the house of another. Starting a fire or explosion with the purpose of destroying a building or an occupied structure of another, or damaging any property (even one's own) in order to collect insurance. Incendiarism, pyromania, destroying property by fire.

Art 1. The systematic application of knowledge and skill in producing a desired result. **2.** In patent law, the process or method used to produce a useful result.

Article A clause or provision in a document.

Articled Bound by agreement.

Articled clerk In English law, a clerk bound to serve in the office of a solicitor in consideration of being instructed in the profession. Also applicable to other trades and professions.

Articles A connected series of propositions; a system of rules. The subdivisions of a document, code, book, etc.

Articles of agreement A written memorandum of the terms of an agreement.

Articles of apprenticeship Written agreement between master and minor under which the minor agrees to work for the master for stated period of time in return for instruction in a trade by the master.

Articles of Confederation The name of the instrument embodying the compact made among the thirteen original states of the Union, operative from March 1, 1781 to March 4, 1789, before the adoptiond of the present Constitution.

Articles of incorporation A certificate of incorporation. The document that establishes (incorporates) a corporation when it is filed with the appropriate governmental agency.

Articles of the Navy Articles (statutes) for the government of the Navy.

Article III courts See constitutional court.

Artifice Contrivance, trick, or fraud.

Artificer 1. One who buys goods in order to reduce them, by his or her own art or industry, into other forms, and then to sell them. **2.** One who is actually and personally engaged or employed to do work of a mechanical or physical character.

Artificial 1. Not natural; created by humans. **2.** Not based on reality; forced.

Artificial insemination Injecting semen into a woman by a method other than sexual intercourse.

Artisan Someone skilled in a trade, craft, or art.

Artisan's lien The statutory right of an artisan to keep possession of the object that he or she has worked on until paid for such labor.

Art, words of Words used in a technical sense.

Ascendant A person with whom one is related in the ascending line: parent, grandparent, great-grandparent, etc.

Ascent 1. Passage upward. **2.** The transmission of an estate from the ancestor to the heir in the ascending line.

Ascertain 1. To fix; to render certain or definite. **2.** To find out by investigation, no warranty given.

As is In its present condition; no warranty given.

Ask 1. To inquire. **2.** To petition.

As per In accordance with.

Aspersion 1. Damaging statement. **2.** Criticism.

Asportation Carrying away or removing something.

Asportavit He carried away.

Assailant A person who attacks.

Assassination The murder of someone, often a public figure. Slaying, homicide, execution, killing, elimination, annihilation, silencing, massacre, slaughter.

Assault A tort with the following elements: (a) an act, (b) an intent to cause a harmful or offensive contact, or an intent to cause an apprehension of a harmful or offensive contact, (c) the apprehension of imminent harmful or offensive contact to the plaintiff's own person, and (d) causation of the apprehension. A reasonable apprehension of an imminent battery. Assault can also be a crime. The word "assault" sometimes means actual physical contact with the victim, so that under this meaning, the word is synonymous with battery.

Assay An examination or trial to test the quality and quantity of metals.

Assayer One whose business it is to make assays of the precious metals.

Assecurator In maritime law, an insurer.

Assemblage 1. A collection of persons. **2.** The act of coming together. **3.** Public address upon public grounds. **4.** Combining of adjoining lots into single large lot.

Assembly 1. A gathering or meeting of people. **2.** One of the houses of the legislature in many states.

Assemblyman Member of state Assembly.

Assembly, right of Right guaranteed by First Amendment, U.S. Constitution, allowing people to meet for any purpose connected with government; it encompasses meeting to protest governmental policies and actions and the promotion of ideas.

Assent 1. Agreement, consent, approval. **2.** To approve, ratify, confirm.

Assented stock Stock an owner deposits with a third person in accordance with an agreement by which the owner voluntarily accepts a change in the securities of the corporation.

Assert To declare; to state as true.

Assertion A declaration or positive statement.

Assertory covenant One affirming that a particular state of facts exists; an affirming promise under seal.

Assertory oath One relating to a past or present fact as distinguished from a "promissory" oath which relates to future conduct.

Asservation An affirmation; a positive assertion.

Assess 1. To fix the value of something. **2.** To charge with one's share.

Assessable policy A policy under which a policyholder may be held liable for losses of the insurance company beyond its reserves.

Assessable security A security on which a charge or assessment for the obligations of the issuing company may be made. In many instances, bank and insurance company stocks are assessable.

Assessable stock Stock where the stockholder may have to pay more than his or her original investment if corporate affairs so require.

Assessed Imposed, appraised.

Assessed valuation Value on each unit of which a prescribed amount must be paid as property taxes.

Assessment 1. A determination of the value of something. **2.** A determination of the share that is due from someone; an amount assessed.

Assessment company In life insurance, a company in which a death loss is met by levying an assessment on the surviving members of the association.

Assessment contract One wherein the payment of the benefit is in any manner or degree dependent on the collection of an assessment levied on persons holding similar contracts.

Assessment district In taxation, any subdivision of territory, whether the whole or part of any municipality, in which a separate assessment of taxable property is made by the officers elected or appointed therefor.

Assessment fund The assessment fund of a mutual benefit association is the balance of the assessments, less expenses, out of which beneficiaries are paid.

Assessment insurance A species of mutual insurance in which the policyholders are assessed as losses are incurred. A contract by which payments to insured are not unalterably fixed, but are dependent on collection of assessments necessary to pay amounts insured.

Assessment list The list furnished by the assessor to the board of equalization or board of assessment.

Assessment roll In taxation, the list or roll of taxable persons and property, completed, verified, and deposited by the assessors.

Assessor A person who assesses or appraises the value of things.

Asset Anything of value; property.

Assets entre mains Assets in hand; assets in the hands of executors or administrators, applicable for the payment of debts.

Assets per descent That portion of the ancestor's estate that descends to the heir that is sufficient to charge him, as far as it goes, with the specialty debts of his ancestors.

Asseveration A solemn declaration.

Assign 1. To transfer ownership or rights. **2.** To apportion or distribute.

Assignable Pertaining to that which can be transferred or negotiated.

Assignation house A house of prostitution.

Assigned account A debt owed to a company that the company uses as security for its own debt to a bank. Also called pledged accounts receivable.

Assigned counsel An attorney appointed by the court to represent a poor person.

Assigned risk A risk that an insurer would not take on its own. The government requires the insurer to provide coverage in such situations, usually involving automobile insurance.

Assignee The person to whom property or rights are transferred (Smith assigns his contract to Jones. Jones is the assignee; Smith is the assignor).

Assignee in fact One to whom an assignment has been made in fact by the party having the right.

Assignee in law One in whom the law vests the right as an executor or administrator.

Assignment 1. The transfer of ownership or rights. **2.** Allotment, distribution.

Assignment for benefit of creditors A general assignment for benefit of creditors is a transfer of all or substantially all of debtor's property to another person in trust to collect any money owed to the debtor, to sell property, to distribute the proceeds to the creditors and to return the surplus, if any, to the debtor.

Assignment of errors A specification of the errors upon which the appellant will rely in seeking to have the judgment of the lower court reversed, vacated, modified, or a new trial ordered.

Assignment with preferences An assignment for the benefit of creditors, with directions to the assignee to prefer a specified creditor or class of creditors, by paying their claims in full before the others receive any dividend, or in some other manner.

Assignor The person who transfers property or rights (Smith assigns his cause of action to Jones. Smith is the assignor; Jones is the assignee).

Assigns Assignees; persons to whom property or rights are transferred or assigned.

Assise or assize 1. An ancient court. **2.** An old writ (e.g., assise of nuisance). **3.** A verdict or finding of jurors pursuant to a writ of assise.

Assise of nuisance A writ of assise which lay where a nuisance had been committed to the complainant's freehold, either for abatement of the nuisance or for damages.

Assiser An assessor; an officer who has the care and oversight of weights and measures.

Assist To help, benefit, or serve.

Assistance 1. Service or help provided. **2.** Financial support.

Assistant A helper or deputy.

Assize See assise.

Associate 1. To combine or join together. **2.** A colleague or subordinate.

Associate justices Judges of courts, other than the presiding or chief justice.

Association 1. An organization of people joined for a common purpose. **2.** An unincorporated society; a body of persons united and acting together without a charter.

Assoil, assoile, absoile, or assoilyie 1. To pardon; to deliver from excommunication. **2.** To absolve; acquit.

Assume 1. To take upon oneself, to undertake. **2.** To suppose, to speculate. **3.** To seize, to confiscate. **4.** To imitate, to pretend.

Assumed name An alias, a false name.

Assumpsit 1. A promise or agreement. **2.** An action to recover damages for the nonperformance of a contract.

Assumption 1. The act of taking something upon oneself. **2.** A conjecture. **3.** Seizure.

Assumption clause A provision in an instrument of

transfer in which the transferee agrees to assume an obligation of the transferor.

Assumption of mortgage An obligation undertaken by the purchaser of property to be personally liable for payment of an existing mortgage. In an assumption, the purchaser is substituted for the original mortgagor in the mortgage instrument and the original mortgagor is released from further liability under the mortgage. Since the mortgagor is to be released from further liability in the assumption, the mortgagee's consent is usually required. An "Assumption of Mortgage" is often confused with "purchasing subject to a mortgage." When one purchases subject to a mortgage, the purchaser agrees to make the monthly mortgage payments on an existing mortgage, but the original mortgagor remains personally liable if the purchaser fails to make the monthly payments. Since the original mortgagor remains liable in the event of default, the mortgagee's consent is not required to a sale subject to a mortgage.

Assumption of the risk A defense to a damage action. Elements: (a) The injured person knew of and appreciated the danger—there was an understanding of the risks, and (b) the injured person voluntarily chose to be exposed to the danger.

Assurance 1. A declaration tending to inspire confidence; the act of assuring. **2.** The deed or document that conveys real property. **3.** Insurance.

Assure 1. To state with certainty. **2.** To make secure.

Assured 1. A person who has been insured. **2.** Occasionally, the beneficiary under an insurance policy (the named assured). **3.** Secure.

Assurer An insurer against certain perils and dangers; an underwriter.

Astipulation 1. A mutual agreement, assent, and consent between parties. **2.** A witness or record.

Astitution An arraignment.

Asylum 1. An institution for the care of unfortunates. **2.** A sanctuary or hiding place.

At arm's length See arm's length.

Atavunculus The brother of a great-grandfather's grandmother, or a great-great-great-grandfather's brother.

Atavus The male ascendant in the fifth degree. The great-grandfather's or great-grandmother's grandfather; a fourth grandfather.

At bar Before the court (the case at bar).

At issue A case is at issue when the answer has been filed and no futher pleadings are necessary, or at the point at which there has been an affirmation

and a denial.

At large 1. Free; not limited to any specific place. **2.** An entire area rather than a designated district of the area (at large elections).

At par Said of a bond or preferred stock issued or selling at its face value.

Atrocity Outrageous conduct.

Atrophy Degeneration of the body; wasting away.

Attach Seizure of property under a writ of attachment.

Attaché A person assigned to a diplomatic office.

Attached Seized through a writ of attachment or other court order.

Attachment The seizure of persons or property so that they will come under the custody and control of the court.

Attachment bond Money that is put up to free property that has been attached. The bond substitutes for the property and guarantees that if the person who attached it wins in court, money will be available to pay the claim.

Attachment execution A name given in some states to a process of garnishment for the satisfaction of a judgment.

Attachment of risk Used to describe a point in time, generally when title passes, when the risk of loss for destruction of property which is the subject of sale passes to buyer from seller.

Attain To arrive at or accomplish.

Attainder The loss of civil rights that occurs when a defendant receives the death sentence (e.g., a forfeiting of property). See bill of attainder.

Attaint 1. Disgrace. **2.** A writ to determine whether the jury has rendered a false verdict. **3.** To condemn to attainder.

Attempt 1. A crime consisting of the following elements: (a) an intent to commit the crime, (b) an overt act toward its commission, (c) the failure to complete the crime, and (d) the apparent possibility of commmitting it. **2.** An effort to do something.

Attendant 1. A person who assists someone else. **2.** Resulting as a consequence (attendant hardships).

Attendant circumstances Facts surrounding an event.

Attest To bear witness; to affirm to be true or genuine.

Attestation The act of witnessing the actual execution (making) of a document and subscribing (signing) one's name as a witness to that fact (the attestation of a will).

Attestation clause That clause (e.g., at the end of a will) wherein witnesses certify to the facts and circumstances attending the execution of a will.

Attesting witness Someone who signs a document for the purpose of proving and identifying it.

Attestor A person who attests; an attesting witness.

At the market Order to broker to buy or sell a stock at the current market price, rather than at a specified price.

Attorn To transfer or turn over to another, to agree to become the tenant of the new owner.

Attorney 1. A lawyer. **2.** A person who is authorized to act in place of another.

Attorney ad hoc One appointed for a special purpose, generally to represent the client or infant in the particular action in which the appointment is made.

Attorney at large An attorney who practiced in all the courts.

Attorney at law A person admitted to practice law in his or her respective state.

Attorney-client privilege An evidentiary rule that confidential communications in the course of professional employment between attorney and client may not be divulged by the attorney without the consent of the client.

Attorney General The chief attorney for the government. He or she is often called the corporation counsel in local governments.

Attorney in fact Someone who is given authority through a power of attorney to do a particular nonlegal act. An "attorney in fact" need not be a member of the legal profession.

Attorney of record Attorney whose name must appear somewhere in permanent records or files of the case, or on the pleadings or some instrument filed in the case, or on an appearance docket.

Attorney's lien The right of an attorney at law to retain possession of money or property of a client until his or her proper charges have been adjusted and paid.

Attornment See attorn.

Attractive nuisance doctrine A duty of reasonable care is owed to prevent injury (a) to a trespassing child unable to appreciate the danger (b) from an artificial condition or activity on land (c) to which the child can be expected to be attracted.

Attribution 1. The act of ascribing or attributing. **2.** Assigning to one taxpayer the ownership interest of another taxpayer.

Attrition Gradual and natural decrease.

Auction A public sale of property to the highest bidder by one licensed and authorized for that purpose.

Audit A formal or official examination and verification of books of account by an auditor.

Auditor Someone who is trained to examine financial records and accounts and to verify the accuracy of statements therein.

Augmentation The increase of the crown's revenues from the suppression of religious houses and the appropriation of their lands and revenues.

Aula In old English law, a hall or court; the court of a baron, or manor; a court baron.

Aula ecclesiae A nave or body of a church where temporal courts were anciently held.

Aula regis The chief court of England in early Norman times.

Australian ballot A system for voting in elections in which the names of candidates are printed and the vote of each citizen is secret.

Authentic Trustworthy, real.

Authentic act In the civil law, an act which has been executed before a notary or public officer authorized to execute such functions, or which is testified by a public seal, or has been rendered public by the authority of a competent magistrate, or which is certified as being a copy of a public register.

Authenticate To confirm the correctness, truth, or authenticity of a writing by affidavit, oath, or deposition.

Authentication The process of establishing the genuineness and authenticity of a writing; the process of establishing that an item of evidence is what it purports to be.

Authenticum In the civil law, an original instrument or writing.

Author A writer; someone who writes an original literary composition.

Authority 1. The power or right to act, to make decisions, to enforce decisions, to control. **2.** A source relied upon for a legal argument.

Authorize 1. To empower. **2.** To sanction, to approve.

Authorized capital The legal capital stock of a corporation.

Autocracy Government by one person, the autocrat.

Autograph One's handwriting; written with one's own hand.

Automatic premium loan A clause in a life insurance policy which provides that any premium not paid by the end of the grace period (e.g. a month) will be automatically paid by a policy loan if sufficient cash value remains in the policy.

Automatism Behavior in a state of mental unconsciousness or dissociation without full awareness.

Autonomy Self-government.

Autopsy An examination of a dead body to determine the cause of death.

Autoptic evidence An exhibit of a thing offered before a jury as evidence to be seen through the jury's own eyes.

Autre action pendant In common law pleading, another action pending.

Autre droit In right of another.

Autrefois At another time.

Autre vie Another's life. See estate pur autre vie.

Auxiliary Aiding, subsidiary.

Auxiliary covenant A covenant that does not relate directly to the principal matter of the contract between the parties, but to something connected with it.

Available Ready for immediate use.

Aval 1. In French law, the guaranty of a bill of exchange. **2.** In Canadian law, the act of subscribing one's signature at the bottom of a promissory note or of a bill of exchange; an act of suretyship.

Avanture Chance; hazard; mischance.

Aventure, adventure A mischance or accident causing the death of a person.

Aver In pleading, to declare or assert; to set out distinctly and formally; to allege.

Average 1. The mean between two or more quantities (average salary). **2.** Typical (average ability).

Average clause A clause providing that similar items in one location or at several locations that are covered by one insurance policy shall each be covered in the proportion that the value in each bears to the value in all.

Averment In pleading, to allege or assert positively.

Averment of notice The statement in a pleading that notice has been given.

Aversio In the civil law, an averting or turning away.

A vinculo matrimonii See divorce a vinculo matrimonii.

Avocat Advocate (French).

Avocation Side interest; hobby.

Avoid 1. To annul or cancel. **2.** To escape.

Avoidable consequences The damages that the injured party could have minimized. See mitigation of damages.

Avoidance 1. In pleading, avoidance is a statement admitting the facts in a pleading by the other side, but showing how these facts could not have their ordinary legal effect (confession and avoidance). **2.** Escaping or evading. **3.** Cancellation.

Avoirdupois The name of a system of weights (sixteen ounces to the pound) used in weighing articles other than medicines, metals, and precious stones; so named in distinction from the Troy weight.

Avoué In French and Canadian law, a barrister, advocate, solicitor, or attorney.

Avow In pleading, to acknowledge and justify an act done.

Avowal An open declaration.

Avowant One who makes an avowry.

Avowry A common law pleading in the action of replevin by which the defendant avows, that is, acknowledges and justifies the taking of the distress or property complained of.

Avowterer In English law, an adulterer with whom a married woman continues in adultery.

Avowtry In old English law, adultery.

Avulsion 1. The sudden and perceptible loss or addition to land by the action of water, or a sudden change in the bed or course of a stream. **2.** A tearing away.

Avunculus In the civil law, a mother's brother.

Avunculus magnus In the civil law, a great-uncle.

Award 1. The decision of a body or entity such as an arbitration board. **2.** Prize.

Away-going crop A crop sown before the expiration of a tenancy, which cannot ripen until after its expiration to which, however, the tenant is entitled.

Ayant cause In French law, and also in Louisiana, this term signifies one to whom a right has been assigned; an assignee.

Back 1. To assume financial responsibility for; to endorse. **2.** Delayed, deferred.

Backbond A bond of indemnification given to a surety.

Backdating Dating a document prior to the date it was prepared or drawn.

Backwardation (also called **Backadation**) Money paid to postpone the delivery of stock that has been purchased.

Baculus A rod, staff, or wand, used in old English practice in making livery of seisin where no building stood on the land.

Bad 1. Defective. **2.** Evil.

Bad check A check that is dishonored on presentation for payment because of no, or insufficient, funds.

Bad debt A debt that is uncollectible.

Bad faith Conscious doing of wrong; dishonest purpose.

Badge A distinctive mark.

Badge of fraud A fact tending to throw suspicion upon a questioned transaction, raising an inference that it is fraudulent.

Bad title One that conveys no property to the purchaser of the estate. One so defective it is not marketable.

Bail 1. The amount of money or property that is presented to the court by or on behalf of someone accused of a crime in order to allow him or her to be released from jail and to secure his or her appearance in court as the case proceeds. **2.** The person who furnishes the money or property that enables an accused to be released until the next court appearance. **3.** To obtain the release of someone by being responsible (security) for his or her appearance in court as the case proceeds.

Bailable offense An offense for which an accused can be admitted to or be eligible for bail.

Bail bond A three-party contract that involves the state, the accused, and a surety under which the surety guarantees the state that the accused will appear in court as the case proceeds. If the accused does not appear, the surety must pay the state the amount of the bond.

Bail dock Formerly at the Old Bailey, in London, a small room taken from one of the corners of the court, and left open at the top, in which certain malefactors were placed during trial.

Bailee The person to whom personal property is entrusted under a contract of bailment (Bob leaves his car with the XYZ Parking Garage while he shops. The Garage is the bailee; Bob is the bailor).

Bailee's lien Bailee's right (usually statutory) to retain bailed goods for payment of services.

Bailiff 1. A court officer who keeps order while the court is in session, watches over the jury and prisoners, etc. **2.** A person to whom some authority, care, guardianship, or jurisdiction is delivered, committed or entrusted.

Bailiff-errant A bailiff's deputy.

Bail in error Bail given by a defendant who intends to bring a writ of error on the judgment and desires a stay of execution in the meantime.

Bailivia A bailiff's jurisdiction.

Bailiwick 1. The area within which someone has authority or skill. **2.** The territory over which a bailiff or sheriff has jurisdiction.

Bailment A delivery of personal property to someone under an express or implied contract whereby the property is accepted and later redelivered after the purpose of the contract is fulfilled. (Sue stores her furniture at a warehouse. Their transaction is a bailment. Sue is the bailor; the warehouse is the bailee.)

Bailment for hire A bailment contract in which the bailor agrees to compensate the bailee.

Bailor The person who delivers personal property to another under a contract of bailment. (Jim borrows Bill's book. Bill is the bailor; Jim is the bailee).

Bait and switch A deceptive sales practice in which an offer is made not to sell the advertised product at the advertised price, but to draw a customer to the store to sell him or her a similar product that is more profitable to the advertiser-seller.

Balance 1. What is left over. **2.** The difference between the debit and credit sides of an account; an equality between the total of the two sides of an account. **3.** To determine whether a difference exists between the debit and credit sides of an account; to equalize both sides.

Balance of payments The difference between all payments made by one nation to all other nations in the world and the payments made to that nation by all other nations.

Balance of power In international law, a distribution and an opposition of forces, forming one system, so that no nation or country shall be in a position, either alone or united with others, to impose its will on any other nation or country or interfere with its independence.

Balance of trade Part of the balance of payments. It shows the net figure for the value of all the goods imported and exported by one nation. An excess of imports over exports constitutes a trade deficit.

Balance sheet A statement of financial position of any economic unit disclosing its assets (at cost, depreciated cost, or other indicated value) its liabilities, and the equity of the owners in conformity with generally accepted accounting principles.

Ban 1. A prohibition. **2.** To prohibit. **3.** An announcement.

Banc Bench. En banc is the full bench or the full court as opposed to a smaller number of judges on the bench.

Banco 1. a seat or bench of justice. **2.** A bank.

Banishment Punishment by exile.

Bank 1. A financial institution that receives money on deposit, cashes checks or drafts, makes loans, discounts commercial paper, and performs similar functions. **2.** A mound, elevation of earth, slope, etc.

Bank acceptance Draft drawn on and accepted by bank.

Bank debit Total of checks and other commercial paper charged to deposit accounts.

Bank draft A check, draft, or other order for payment of money drawn by an authorized officer of a bank upon either the officer's own bank or some other bank in which funds of the officer's bank are deposited.

Banker's acceptance A bill of exchange draft payable at maturity that is drawn by a creditor against his or her debtor.

Bank note A promissory note issued by a bank or banker authorized to do so, payable to bearer on demand, and intended to circulate as money.

Bank of discount One that lends money on collateral or by means of discounts of commercial paper.

Bank overdraft A loan granted by a bank on a current account that reduces the account balance below zero, often used to finance short-term business needs.

Bank post bill An instrument that both orders and authorizes a bank to pay a sum certain to a party named therein, for the account of the party who ordered the payment.

Bankrupt Being unable to pay debts as they are due; a debtor undergoing a federal bankruptcy proceeding.

Bankruptcy The inability to pay debts as they are due; the condition of being bankrupt.

Bankruptcy, act of See act of bankruptcy.

Bankruptcy discharge The release of a bankrupt from all of his or her debts that are provable in bankruptcy, other than those excepted by the Bankruptcy Act.

Bankruptcy trustee One appointed by a Bankruptcy Court to take charge of the bankruptcy estate, to collect assets, to bring suit on the bankrupt's claims, and to defend actions against it; he or she has power to examine the bankrupt, to initiate actions to set aside preferences, etc.

Banns Public announcement

Bar 1. The court (the case at bar). **2.** Members of the legal profession. **3.** An impediment. **4.** To prohibit. **5.** To obstruct.

Bar association An association of members of the legal profession.

Bar docket A bar docket is an unofficial paper consisting of a transcript of the docket for a term of court, printed for distribution to members of the bar.

Bare licensee or **mere licensee** One whose presence on premises is merely tolerated; while a "licensee" or "invitee" is one who is on the premises by invitation.

Bareboat charter A document under which one who charters or leases a boat becomes for the period of the charter the owner for all practical purposes.

Bare owner The person who has mere legal title to property without the right to enjoy it.

Bare trustee One whose trust is to convey, and the time has arrived for a conveyance by him or her; the trustee of a dry trust.

Bar examiners Persons appointed to test individuals and determine their qualifications to practice law.

Bargain 1. An agreement. **2.** To negotiate an agreement.

Bargain and sale A contract or bargain by the owner of property to sell it to another person for a consideration, whereupon a use arises in the latter; a contract to convey.

Bargainee The grantee of an estate in a deed of a bargain and sale.

Bargaining unit A group of employees who have banded together to improve their working conditions; a labor union authorized to engage in collective bargaining.

Barnard's inn An inn of chancery.

Baron et feme Man and woman; husband and wife.

Barony of land In England, a quantity of land amounting to 15 acres. In Ireland, a subdivision of a county.

Barrator One who commits barratry.

Barratrous Fraudulent; having the character of barratry.

Barratry 1. The offense of stirring up quarrels or litigation. See also champerty. **2.** An act committed by the master or mariners of a vessel for some fraudulent or unlawful purpose contrary to their duty to the owner, resulting in injury to the owner.

Barrel A measure of capacity, equal (in England) to 36 imperial gallons. The standard United States measure, except as to barrels of petroleum, equals $31\frac{1}{2}$ gallons.

Barren money In the civil law, a debt that bears no interest.

Barretor See barrator.

Barretry See barratry.

Barrister An English attorney with special skills and rights as a trial or litigation attorney.

Barter To exchange goods or services without the use of money.

Bas Low, inferior, subordinate.

Base 1. Inferior. **2.** Sordid, corrupt. **3.** The locality on which a military or naval force relies for supplies or from which it initiates operations.

Base bullion Base silver bullion is silver in bars mixed to a greater or less extent with alloys or base materials.

Base coin Debased, adulterated, or alloyed coin (e.g., copper, nickel) as distinguished from silver or gold.

Base court In old English law, an inferior court, that is, not of record, as the court baron.

Base fee A fee that may last forever if the contingency does not happen, but debased because its duration depends upon collateral circumstances which qualify it; sometimes called a conditional, determinable, or qualified fee.

Base line Survey line used in the government survey to establish township lines. Horizontal elevation line used as centerline in a highway survey.

Base pay Wages, exclusive of overtime, bonuses, etc.

Base tenants Tenants who held at the will of the lord, as distinguished from frank tenants, or free-holders.

Base tenure A tenure by villenage, or other customary service, as distinguished from tenure by military service or tenure by free service.

Basileus A greek word meaning king.

Basis 1. The foundation of something. **2.** The amount assigned to an asset for income tax purposes (capital improvements will increase the basis of your house).

Bastard A child born before its parents were married or born from those who never married.

Bastardize To give evidence that would tend to establish the illegitimacy of a child.

Bastardy proceeding A court proceeding to determine paternity and to compel support.

Batable-ground Land that is in controversy.

Batonnier The chief of the French bar in its various centres, who presides in the council of discipline.

Battel Trial by combat.

Battery A tort with the following elements: (a) an act, (b) the intent to cause a harmful or offensive contact, (c) a harmful or offensive contact with the plaintiff's person, and (d) causation of the harmful or offensive contact. Battery can also be a crime.

Bawd One who procures opportunities for persons to cohabit in an illicit manner.

Bawdyhouse A house of prostitution.

Beams and balance Instruments for weighing goods and merchandise.

Bear 1. To produce or yield. **2.** One who believes stock prices will decline; opposite of a "bull."

Bearer Someone in possession of a document (the check was payable to bearer).

Bearer bond A bond payable to the person who has possession of the bond. Endorsement is not necessary to transfer ownership.

Bearer paper Commercial paper payable to bearer or the order of bearer, or any other order that does not designate a specific payee. The person in possession can present it for payment.

Bearing wall A wall that supports a floor or roof of a building.

Beat In some of the southern states (e.g., Alabama, Mississippi, South Carolina) the principal legal subdivision of a county, corresponding to towns or townships in other states; a voting precinct.

Beget To procreate as the father.

Behalf In the interest of.

Behavior Conduct; the manner in which a person acts and reacts.

Behoof Advantage, benefit.

Belief 1. A persuasion of the truth or an assent of the mind to the truth of a declaration, proposition, or alleged fact. **2.** Accepted principle.

Belligerency 1. The status of de facto statehood attributed to a body of insurgents by which their hostilities are legalized. **2.** Warfare.

Belligerent 1. As a noun, it designates either of two nations that are actually in a state of war with each other, as well as their allies actively co-operating, as distinguished from a nation that takes no part in the war and maintains a strict indifference as between the contending parties, called a "neutral." **2.** One who is overly assertive, hostile, or combative.

Belongings Effects, possessions.

Below 1. At a lower rank. **2.** A lower court. **3.** Under. **4.** Infra.

Below par At a discount. A value that is below the arbitrary value set as the face amount of a security.

Bench The seat where the judges sit; the court.

Bench conference A meeting at the judge's bench between the judge and the attorneys out of the hearing of the jury.

Benchers In England, the principal officers of each inn of court.

Bench warrant A process issued by the court for the attachment or arrest of a person to compel his or her attendance before the court.

Benefice 1. Ecclesiastical preferments to which rank or public office is attached. **2.** A permanent stipendiary estate, or an estate held by feudal tenure.

Bénéfice In French law, a benefit or advantage.

Beneficial Tending to the benefit of a person.

Beneficial enjoyment The enjoyment that a person has in an estate in his or her own right and not as a trustee for another.

Beneficial estate The person takes this type of estate solely for his or her own use and benefit and not as the mere holder of the title for the use of another.

Beneficial interest 1. Profit, benefit, or advantage resulting from a contract, or the ownership of an estate as distinct from the legal ownership or control of the estate. **2.** The interest of a devisee, legatee, or donee that is taken for his or her own use or benefit.

Beneficial owner 1. One who does not have title to property but has those rights in the property that are the normal incidents of owning the property. **2.** The cestui que trust who enjoys ownership of the trust but not legal title.

Beneficial power A power that has for its object the donee of the power, and that is to be executed solely for his or her benefit.

Beneficial use 1. The right to use and enjoy property to one's liking as distinguished from a mere right of occupancy. **2.** Such right to the enjoyment of property where the legal title to the property is in one person while the right to its enjoyment is in another.

Beneficiary One who benefits from the act of another. An instrument such as trust can also be a beneficiary.

Beneficiary heir One who has accepted the succession under the benefit of an inventory regularly made (Louisiana).

Beneficium 1. In feudal law, a benefice; a permanent stipendiary estate. **2.** In the civil law, a benefit or favor.

Benefit An advantage. The receiving as the exchange for a promise some performance or forbearance which one was not previously entitled to receive.

Benefit certificate 1. A written obligation to pay the person therein named the amount specified upon the conditions therein stipulated. **2.** A term usually applied to policies issued by fraternal and beneficiary societies.

Benefit of clergy 1. An exemption for members of the clergy that allowed them to avoid being subject to the jurisdiction of certain secular courts. **2.** An exemption from capital punishment. **3.** Married, not merely living together.

Benefit of discussion In the civil law, the right of a surety to cause the property of the principal debtor to be applied in satisfaction of the obligation in the first instance.

Benefit society A corporation that exists to receive periodic payments from members and to hold the payments as a fund to be loaned or given to members needing financial help.

Benelux Economic and customs union between Belgium, Luxembourg, and the Netherlands that has as its goal the free movement of workers, capital, goods, and services among these countries.

Benevolence Doing helping things for others that one is not under an obligation to do.

Benevolent Loving others and being actively desirous of their well-being; philanthropic.

Benevolent association (or corporation) An organization having a charitable, philanthropic, nonprofit purpose (e.g., to promote the mental, physical, or spiritual welfare of people).

Benny Amphetamine tablet used as a stimulant.

Bequeath 1. To give personal property to another through a will (I bequeath the car to my sister). **2.** To hand down; to endow (he bequeathed a tradition of integrity).

Bequest A gift of personal property by will.

Bertillon system A method of anthropometry once used for the identification of criminals and other persons, consisting of taking numerous, minute, and uniform measurements of various parts of the human body.

Besot To stupefy, to make dull or senseless.

Best Of the highest quality.

Best evidence rule A rule of evidence requiring that a party produce the most reliable proof of a fact that is available. For example, if a painting is available as evidence, a photograph of the painting will not do.

Bestiality 1. Sexual relations between a human and an

animal. **2.** Savage or bestial behavior.

Bestow To give or confer.

Bet 1. A contract by which two or more parties agree that a sum of money or other thing shall be paid or delivered to one of them on the happening or not happening of an uncertain event. **2.** To wager or risk something.

Betray 1. Act of delivering up to an enemy something of value. **2.** To divulge a matter in breach of a confidence.

Betrothal, betrothment A mutual promise of marriage.

Betterment 1. An improvement on property that increases its value more than mere repairs, maintenance, or replacements. **2.** Making something better.

Betterment acts Statutes providing that a bona fide occupant of real estate making lasting improvements in good faith shall have a lien upon the estate recovered by the real owner to the extent that his or her improvements have increased the value of the land. Also called occupying claimant acts.

Betting The act of placing a bet or wager.

Beyond a reasonable doubt The measure of proof needed for conviction in a criminal case: The factfinder must be convinced or satisfied to a moral certainty. Absolute certainty is not required. On the other hand, reasonable doubt means more than a vague suspicion.

B.F. Bonum factum; a good or proper act, deed, or decree; approved.

BFP See bona fide purchaser.

Biannually Twice a year.

Bias A predisposition to decide a question in a certain way.

Bicameral Having two chambers or houses in the legislature.

Bid An offer by a prospective purchaser to pay a designated price for property that is about to be sold at auction. An offer to perform a contract for a designated price.

Bid and asked Price quotation for securities that are not frequently traded. The bid quotation is the highest price a prospective buyer is willing to pay; the asked quotation is the lowest price the seller is willing to sell for.

Bid bond Type of bond required in public construction projects that must be filed at the time of the bid that protects the public agency in the event that the bidder refuses to enter into a contract after the award to it or withdraws its bid

before the award. A type of indemnity bond.

Bid in Property sold at auction is said to be "bid in" in by the owner or an incumbrancer or someone else who is interested in it, when he or she attends the sale and makes the successful bid.

Bienes In Spanish law, goods, property of every description.

Bienes gananciales A species of community in property enjoyed by husband and wife, the property being divisible equally between them on the dissolution of the marriage (Spanish).

Biennial Occurring every 2 years; lasting 2 years.

Biennium A 2-year period.

Biens In old English law, property of every description, except estates of freehold and inheritance.

Bifurcate To divide into two parts.

Bifurcated trial A case in which certain issues are tried separately (e.g., guilt and punishment; liability and damages).

Bigamy Knowingly entering a second marriage when the first marriage still exists. Bigamy is a crime and a ground for an annulment.

Bilan A book in which bankers, merchants, and traders write a statement of all they owe and all that is due them; a balance sheet (Louisiana).

Bilateral Having or involving two sides.

Bilateral contract A contract in which both contracting parties are bound to fulfill obligations reciprocally toward each other; a contract with rights and duties on both sides; a contract with mutual promises between the parties.

Bilingual Pertaining to expression in two languages.

Bill 1. A proposed law. **2.** An invoice. **3.** A written statement of the terms of a contract.

Bill after date A promissory obligation for the payment of money that is payable on the expiration of a certain period after the date specified in the document.

Bill after sight A promissory obligation for the payment of money that is payable a specified number of days, weeks or months after presentment.

Bill broker Middleman who negotiates the purchase or sale of commercial paper.

Billet 1. The soldier's quarters in a civilian's house. **2.** A ticket that authorizes the soldier to occupy a civilian's house.

Bill-head A printed form on which merchants and traders make out their bills and render accounts to their customers.

Bill obligatory A bond absolute for the payment of money.

Bill of attainder A legislative act that applies either to named individuals or to easily identifiable members of a group in such a way as to inflict punishment on them without a judicial trial. If the punishment is death, the act is a bill of attainer. If the punishment is less than death, the act is a bill of pains and penalties.

Bill of conformity One filed by an executor or administrator who finds the affairs of the deceased so involved that he or she cannot safely administer the estate except under the direction of a court of chancery.

Bill of credit A bill or promissory note issued by the government, upon its faith and credit, designed to circulate in the community as money.

Bill of entry A form filled out by an importer for the use of a customs officer; it describes goods, their value, etc.

Bill of exceptions A formal statement in writing of the objections or exceptions to a judge's rulings taken by a party during a trial.

Bill of exchange A three-party document in which the first party draws an order for the payment of a sum certain on a second party for payment to a third party at a definite future time. A draft.

Bill of indemnity A law under which a public official is protected from liability in the performance of his or her official acts.

Bill of indictment A formal written document from a grand jury accusing a named person or persons of having committed a felony or misdemeanor.

Bill of interpleader See interpleader.

Bill of lading A document evidencing receipt of goods for shipment issued by a person engaged in the business of transporting and forwarding goods (including airbills).

Bill of pains and penalties Statutory provision for punishment without judicial determination of guilt similar to bill of attainder except that punishment is less severe.

Bill of particulars A more detailed or specific statement of the claims brought by one party against another (civil case), or of the charges brought by the prosecutor against the defendant (criminal case).

Bill of revivor One brought to continue a suit that has abated before its final consummation as, for example, by death, or marriage of a female plaintiff.

Bill of rights The first ten amendments to the U.S. Constitution.

Bill of sale A legal document that conveys title from seller to buyer.

Bill quia timet A bill invoking the aid of equity "because he fears," that is, because the complainant apprehends an injury to its property rights or interests from the fault or neglect of another.

Bill receivable In a merchant's accounts, all notes, drafts, checks, etc., payable to him or of which he is to receive the proceeds at a future date.

Bill rendered A bill of items rendered by a creditor to its debtor; an "account rendered," as distinguished from "an account stated."

Bill single A written promise to pay to a named person or persons a stated sum at a stated time, without any condition.

Bill to order A negotiable instrument in which it is stated that goods are to be cosigned or money is to be paid to the order of any person named therein.

Bi-metallic Pertaining to, or consisting of, two metals used as money at a fixed relative value.

Bimonthly Happening every two months.

Bind To obligate.

Binder 1. A statement of the major terms of an insurance contract that gives temporary protection to the insured until a formal policy is issued. **2.** A deposit to secure the right to purchase property.

Bind out To place one under a legal obligation to serve another.

Bioethics The study of the ethical implications of medical and biological developments.

Bipartisan Supported by both parties.

Bipartite Consisting of or divisible into two parts.

Birretum, birretus A cap or coif used formerly in England by judges and serjeants at law.

Birth The act of being born.

Bissextile The day added every fourth year (leap-year) to the month of February, in order to make the year agree with the course of the sun.

Black acre A fictitious name that teachers and writers use to indicate a parcel of land. Also: white acre.

Black Book of the Exchequer The name of an ancient book kept in the English exchequer, containing a collection of treaties, conventions, charters, etc.

Black cap In England, the head-dress worn by the judge in pronouncing the sentence of death.

Black code Laws of southern states regulating slavery.

Blackleg A person who makes a living by frequenting race-courses and places where games of chance are played, getting the best odds, and giving the

least he or she can, but not necessarily cheating.

Blacklist A list of persons marked out for special avoidance or enmity.

Blackmail An unlawful demand of money or property under a threat to do bodily harm, to damage property, to accuse of a crime, or to expose someone.

Black maria A closed vehicle or van in which prisoners are carried to and from the jail, or between the court and the jail.

Black market Illegal buying and selling; a business operating independent of government regulation.

Black rents In old English law, rents reserved in work, grain, provisions, or baser money than silver, in contradistinction to those which were reserved in white money or silver, which were termed "white rents" (reditus albi), or blanch farms.

Blame Responsibility for a fault or wrong.

Blanche firme White rent; a rent reserved, payable in silver.

Blank acceptance An acceptance of a bill of exchange written on the paper before the bill is made, and delivered by the acceptor.

Blank bill A bill of exchange with the payee's name left blank.

Blank check A check signed by the drawer but left blank as to the payee and/or the amount.

Blanket bond Any bond used for multiple purposes.

Blanket mortgage Covers two or more assets or properties that are pledged to support the given debt.

Blank indorsement The indorsement of a bill of exchange or promissory note without mentioning any person to whom the bill or note is to be paid.

Blasphemy Contempt or reproach in written or oral form directed against God or sacred matters.

Block 1. A square or portion of a city or town surrounded on at least three sides by streets. **2.** Large amount of stock or bonds sold as a unit.

Blockade Action taken against an enemy nation so as to prevent supplies and people from entering or leaving the nation.

Blockage A recognition in tax law that in some instances a large block of stock cannot be marketed and turned into cash as readily and as advantageously as a few shares. This is taken into consideration in determining the value of the stock.

Block policy An insurance policy covering all the property of the insured against most perils.

Block to block rule The "block to block rule" for assessing the benefits for the opening of a new street is the assessment against the lots in each block of the cost of acquiring the lands in that block.

Blood grouping test A test to determine who could not possibly be the father of a child.

Blood relations Kindred; consanguinity; family relationship; relation by descent from a common blood ancestor.

Bludgeon 1. A heavy club or stick, often weighted at one end by metal, used as a weapon. **2.** To inflict injury with a heavy club or stick.

Blue laws Laws regulating Sunday entertainment activities, work, and commerce.

Blue notes Notes accepted by a life insurance company for the amount of premiums on the policy that provide for the continuance of the policy in force until the due date of the notes.

Blue sky laws State statutes that regulate offerings and sales of securities.

Board 1. A group of persons with managerial, supervisory, or investigatory functions and powers. **2.** Meals (room and board).

Boarder One who is provided with regular meals, with or without lodging.

Board of appeals A non-judicial administrative tribunal that reviews the decisions made by the hearing officer or by the head of the agency.

Board of directors The governing body of a corporation elected by the stockholders.

Board of examiners A state agency or board appointed to examine the qualifications of applicants for a license to practice a trade or profession.

Board of Patent Appeals A tribunal that reviews adverse decisions of examiners on applications for patents.

Board of regents A body of officials appointed to direct and supervise an educational institution or, in some states, the educational system of a state.

Board of review Board authorized to review administrative agency decisions and rulings.

Board of supervisors An organized committee, or body of officials, constituting part of the county government, with special charge of county revenues.

Boc In Saxon law, a book or writing; a deed or charter.

Boc land In Saxon law, allodial lands held by deed or other written evidence of title.

Bodily Pertaining to or concerning the body; of or belonging to the body or the physical constitution; not mental but corporeal.

Bodily heirs Heirs begotten or borne by the person referred to; lineal descendants.

Body 1. The main part (the body of the memo). **2.** A person. The person can be natural (a human) or artificial (a corporation). **3.** A group of persons or things considered as a whole (governing body; a body of laws).

Body excution The seizure of a person by order of the court.

Body politic, body corporate 1. A social compact by which the whole people covenants with each citizen, and each citizen with the whole people, that all shall be governed by certain laws for the common good. **2.** A municipal corporation, school district, county, or city. **3.** State or nation. **4.** Public associations.

Bogus Counterfeit, sham.

Bolting In English practice, a term formerly used in the English inns of court, but more particularly at Gray's Inn, signifying the private arguing of cases, as distinguished from mooting, which was a more formal and public mode of argument.

Bona Goods, property, possessions.

Bona confiscata Goods confiscated or forfeited to the imperial fisc or treasury.

Bona fide In good faith.

Bona fide holder for value An innocent or "bona fide holder for value" of negotiable paper is one who has taken it in good faith for a valuable consideration in the ordinary course of business and when it was not overdue.

Bona fide purchaser (BFP) One who has purchased property for value without any notice of defects in the title of the seller.

Bona mobilia Movables.

Bona vacantia Unclaimed property.

Bond 1. A certificate of evidence of a debt in which the entity that issues the bond (a company or a governmental body) promises (a) to pay the bondholders a specified amount of interest for a specified amount of time and (b) to repay the loan on the expiration date. **2.** An obligation to pay a designated amount of money if a certain act is not done.

Bondage Slavery; involuntary personal servitude.

Bond coupon Part of a bond that is cut and surrendered for payment of one of successive payments of interest.

Bond creditor A creditor whose debt is secured by a bond.

Bond dividend A type of dividend distribution in which the shareholder receives bonds instead of scrip, property, or money.

Bonded Secured by a bond (a bonded employee).

Bonded warehouse Special type of private warehouse used to store products on which a federal tax must be paid before they can be sold.

Bond rating System of appraising and rating the investment value of individual bond issues. Triple A bonds (AAA) have the highest rating.

Bond redemption Retirement of bonds upon payment.

Bondsman A person who has entered into a bond as surety; one who furnishes a bond.

Bonification A waiving of taxes, especially on export goods.

Bonis cedere In the civil law, to make a transfer or surrender of property.

Bonus Something extra; a consideration or premium paid in addition to what is strictly due.

Bonus stock 1. Stock given as a premium in connection with (and to encourage) the sale of another class of securities. **2.** Shares issued for no lawful consideration. The term commonly used interchangeably with watered stock and discount stock.

Boodle The money paid as a bribe for corrupt official action.

Boodling Corrupt legislative practices and corrupt influences affecting legislation.

Book 1. To enter charges against someone. **2.** Bound sheets of paper with writing on them.

Booking The step taken after an arrested person is brought to the police station, which may involve entering relevant facts on the police "blotter," fingerprinting, etc.

Bookkeeper A person who records the financial accounts and transactions of a business.

Bookmaker Someone who makes or collects bets for others.

Books of account Books in which merchants and traders generally keep their accounts.

Book value The going-concern value for a company, which is arrived at by adding all assets, deducting all liabilities, and dividing that sum by the number of shares of outstanding common stock. The valuation at which assets are carried on the books.

Boot Cash or other consideration used to balance an equal exchange of two properties.

Bootlegger Someone who makes, stores, or transports alcoholic beverages for sale in violation of the law.

Bootstrap sale 1. Using the assets or cash of a business to acquire that business. **2.** Converting

ordinary income from a business into capital gain from the sale of corporate stock.

Booty Property captured from the enemy at war.

Born 1. Being delivered or expelled from a mother's body; brought into life.

Borough A town or township with a municipal charter. A political subdivision of a state.

Borough English A custom prevalent in some parts of England, by which the youngest son inherits the estate in preference to his older brothers.

Borrow To solicit and receive money or other property from another with the intention and promise to repay or return it.

Bote, bot In old English law, a recompense, compensation, or profit.

Bottomage Bottomry.

Bottomry A contract by which the owner of a ship borrows money for equipment or for repairs of the ship. The ship becomes the security for the loan.

Bound The term denotes a limit or boundary, or a line inclosing or marking off a tract of land.

Boundary The separation that marks the division between two things (e.g., two adjoining properties).

Bound over 1. The act by which a court requires a person to promise to appear for trial or to furnish bail. **2.** Transferring a case to a grand jury after finding probable cause that the accused committed the crime.

Bounds External or limiting lines of any object or space.

Bounty An additional benefit.

Bourg In old English law, a borough, a village.

Bourse An exchange; a stock exchange (French).

Boycott A concerted refusal to do business with a particular person or business in order to obtain concessions or to express displeasure with certain practices of the person or business.

Bozero In Spanish law, an advocate.

Bracery The English statute of 32 Hen. VIII, c. 9, to prevent the buying and selling of pretended rights or titles.

Brain death (a) Unreceptivity and unresponsiveness to externally applied stimuli and internal needs, (b) no spontaneous movements or breathing, (c) no reflex activity, and (d) a flat electroencephalograph reading after a 24-hour period of observation.

Branch A subdivision, member, or department.

Brand A mark used to identify a product or service.

Brandeis brief An appellate brief in which economic and social studies are included along with legal principles.

Brassage Government charge for coining metals.

Brawl A noisy quarrel in a public place leading to the disturbance of the peace.

Breach The breaking or violation of an obligation or a law.

Breach of close The unlawful entry on another's soil, land, or close.

Breach of contract The failure, without legal excuse, to perform any promise one is contractually obligated to perform.

Breach of the peace A violation or disturbance of the public tranquility and order.

Breach of trust Any act done by a trustee contrary to the terms of the trust, or in excess of his or her authority and to the detriment of the trust; or the wrongful omission by a trustee of any act required by the terms of the trust.

Breach of warranty The failure or falsehood of an affirmative promise or statement; the nonperformance of an executory stipulation.

Breakage 1. Allowance given by a manufacturer to a buyer for breakage damage caused while in transit or storage. **2.** Fractional amounts (e.g., pennies) due either party as, for example, in computing interest on loan or deposits.

Breaking Forcibly separating, parting, disintegrating, or piercing any solid substance. Using any act of force to gain entry with a criminal intent.

Breaking a close Unlawful entry upon land.

Breaking and entry Common-law burglary: Breaking and entering the dwelling of another with the intent to commit a felony therein. Statutes have modified this definition in many states.

Breaking bulk The offense committed by a bailee (particularly a carrier) in opening or unpacking the chest, parcel, or case containing goods intrusted to its care, and removing the goods and converting them to its own use.

Breast of the court The conscience, discretion, or recollection of the judge.

Breathalyzer test A test to determine the content of alcohol in someone suspected of operating a motor vehicle under the influence of liquor.

Breve A writ.

Brevet 1. The promotion of an officer without an increase in pay. **2.** In French law, a privilege or warrant granted by the government to a private person, authorizing him or her to take a special benefit or to exercise an exclusive privilege. Thus a brevet d'invention is a patent for an invention.

Brevia Writs.

Breviate **1.** A brief statement, epitome, or abstract. **2.** A short statement of contents, accompanying a bill in parliament.

Bribe A gift of money or of something else of value given to influence the conduct of the receiver.

Bribery The offering, giving, receiving, or soliciting of anything of value to influence the action of an official in discharge of a legal or public duty.

Bribour A thief.

Bridewell In England, a house of corrections.

Brief **1.** A written statement or argument prepared by counsel concerning a case in court (appellate brief; trial brief). **2.** A summary of something (a brief of a case).

British thermal unit (BTU) The amount of heat required to raise a pound of water one degree Fahrenheit.

Broken Financially ruined.

Broken lot Odd lot; less than the usual unit of measurement or unit of sale.

Broken stowage In maritime law, that space in a ship that is not filled by its cargo.

Broker An agent who arranges contracts for a fee (real estate broker; insurance broker).

Brokerage **1.** The business or occupation of a broker. **2.** The wages or commissions of a broker.

Brothel House of prostitution.

Bubble An extravagant or unsubstantial project for extensive operations in business or commerce, generally founded on a fictitious or exaggerated prospectus.

Bucket shop An office or place (other than a regularly incorporated or licensed exchange) where persons engage in pretended buying and selling of securities or commodities.

Budget **1.** A plan for the coordination of resources and expenditures. **2.** The amount of money set aside for a specific purpose.

Buffed Slang for a person who is visibly heavier and more muscular because of the use of steroids.

Bug, bugging A form of electronic surveillance by which conversations may be secretly overheard and recorded.

Buggery Sodomy.

Building and loan association An organization for the purpose of accumulating a fund by subscriptions and savings of its members to assist them in building or purchasing for themselves dwellings or real estate by loaning them the requisite money.

Building line Distances from the ends and/or sides of the lot beyond which construction may not extend. The building line may be established by a filed plat of subdivision, by restrictive covenants in deeds, or leases, by building codes, or by zoning ordinances. Often referred to as the "setback" requirement.

Bulk goods Goods that are not divided into parts or packaged in separate units; the aggregate forms the unit, as in grain, sand, or coal.

Bulk sale The sale of all or a substantial part of the seller's materials, supplies, merchandise, other inventory, or in some cases, equipment not in the ordinary course of business.

Bull A person who buys commodities or securities in anticipation of a rise in prices in order to sell later at a profit. Also one who tries by speculative purchases to effectuate such a rise.

Bulletin An official publication or notice; an ongoing publication.

Bulletin des lois In France, the official sheet that publishes the laws and decrees; this publication constitutes the promulgation of the law or decree.

Bullion Uncoined gold or silver.

Bullpen A place of close confinement in a jail or prison. A place for temporary detention.

Bull position Bull account. Position of a stock market investor who has entered into a contract to buy, anticipating that the stock market will rise.

Bunco game A swindling game or scheme.

Bundesanzeiger A German federal publication used to inform the public of administrative decrees, ordinances, and directives.

Bundesgerichtshof (BGH) Federal Supreme Court of Germany.

Bundesgesetzblatt (BGBl) German federal legal gazette used for the publication of federal, state, or regional legislation as well as ordinances and decrees.

Bundesverfassungsgericht Federal Constitutional Court (German).

Burden **1.** The onus or responsibility. **2.** A restrictive or onerous load.

Burden of evidence See burden of going forward.

Burden of going forward The responsibility of a party during the trial to present evidence on an issue in order to make or meet a prima facie showing on that issue. The burden of evidence. See burden of producing evidence.

Burden of persuasion The responsibility of a party with the burden of proof to convince the trier of fact (judge or jury) of all of the elements of its case.

Burden of producing evidence The obligation of a

party to introduce evidence sufficient to avoid a ruling against him or her on the issue. This burden is met when the party with the burden of proof has introduced sufficient evidence to make out a prima facie case.

Burden of proof The duty of affirmatively proving a fact or facts in dispute on an issue. The duty of establishing a fact or facts by the requisite amount of proof (e.g., preponderance of the evidence, clear and convincing evidence).

Bureau A division of the government or other organization.

Bureaucracy An organization consisting of a chain of command, specialty departments, regulations, red tape, etc.

Burgage A name given to a dwelling house in a borough town.

Burgess An inhabitant or freeman of a borough or town.

Burgh-breche A fine imposed on the community of a town.

Burghmote In Saxon law, a court of justice held semiannually by the bishop or lord in a burg, which the thanes were bound to attend without summons.

Burglar A person who commits burglary.

Burglary Breaking and entering the dwelling house of another in the nighttime with the intent to commit a felony therein. Statutes have modified this definition in many states (e.g., breaking may not be required, any kind of structure can be burglarized at any time of day).

Burking, burkism Murder committed with the object of selling the cadaver for purposes of dissection.

Burning in the hand In old English criminal law, laymen, upon being accorded the benefit of clergy, were burned with a hot iron in the brawn of the left thumb, in order that, being thus marked, they could not again claim their clergy.

Bursar A treasurer of a college.

Buscarl In Saxon and old English law, seamen or marines.

Bushel Unit of measurement: 32 quarts; 4 pecks; 35.24 liters; 2,150.42 cubic inches.

Business Employment, occupation, profession, or commercial activity engaged in for gain or livelihood.

Business agent One employed by union members to represent them in relations with the business-employer.

Business entry rule An exception to the hearsay rule allowing the introduction into evidence of entries made in the usual course of business even if the person who made the entries is ... n court.

Business guest One who is impliecily or expressly invited to the premises for transacting business and to whom a duty of care is owed.

Business invitee One who is impliedly or expressly invited to the premises for transacting business and to whom a duty of care is owed.

Business purpose A justifiable business reason (not mere tax avoidance) for carrying out a transaction.

Business records exception An exception to the hearsay rule allowing original, routine records (whether or not part of a business) to be used as evidence even though they are hearsay.

Business trust A form of business organization in which the property is placed in the hands of trustees who manage and deal with it for the benefit and use of beneficiaries.

Business visitor One who is invited or permitted to enter or remain on the premises of another for a purpose directly or indirectly connected with the business dealings between them.

"But for" test A test for causation in tort law. "But for" what the defendant did or failed to do, would the plaintiff have been injured?

Butts and bounds A phrase used in conveyancing to describe the end lines or circumscribing lines of a certain piece of land.

Buy To acquire the ownership of property by giving the agreed price or consideration or by agreeing to do so.

Buy and sell agreement An agreement among partners or owners of a company that if one dies or withdraws from the business, his or her share will be bought by the others or disposed of according to a prearranged plan.

Buy in, buying in Buying property at auction, at a tax sale, or at a mortgage foreclosure sale by the original owner or by someone with an interest in the property.

Buying on margin The purchase of security paying part in cash and part by a loan. Normally, the loan is made by the broker.

By-bidder Someone employed by the seller to bid on property, not to become a purchaser but to stimulate others to make bids.

By estimation In conveyancing, a term used to indicate that the quantity of land as stated is estimated only, not exactly measured.

Bylaws Regulations or rules adopted by organizations for their own government.

By operation of law Effected or brought about by some positive legal rule.

Bystander One who stands near; someone who is not directly concerned or involved.

Cabal A small association formed for the purpose of intrigue.

Cabalist In French commercial law, a factor or broker.

Cabinet An advisory board or counsel of a chief executive.

Cabotage In international law, navigating and trading along the coast between the ports thereof.

Cadaver A dead body.

Cadena perpetua Life imprisonment.

Cadena temporal Imprisonment for a term less than life.

Cadi A Turkish civil magistrate.

Caduca 1. In the civil law, property of an inheritable quality. **2.** The lapse of a testamentary disposition or legacy. **3.** Escheated property.

Caeterorum When a limited administration has been granted, and all the property cannot be administered under it, administration caeterorum (as to the residue) may be granted.

Calaboose A jail or prison.

Calculated Intended by design to produce a certain effect or result.

Calendar 1. A list of cases awaiting trial or other action by the court. **2.** A system of dividing time into years, months, weeks, and days.

Calendar year The period from January 1 to December 31 inclusive.

Call 1. To make a request or demand (called to testify). **2.** To demand payment (to call a note). **3.** An option to buy a specified number of shares of stock. **4.** A visible, natural object or landmark designated in a conveyance of land that is a limit or boundary to that land. **5.** A demand by a company for persons to fulfill their promise to buy stock.

Callable Subject to be called and paid for before maturity.

Callable bonds Bonds that may be called for payment before their maturity.

Callable preferred stock Preferred stock that may be called by the issuing corporation at a prestated price.

Called meeting A special meeting assembled in pursuance of a "call" or summons from some officer, committee, or group of stockholders.

Call loan Loan that is callable by the lender at any time.

Call option An option permitting its holder (who has paid a fee for the option) to call for a certain commodity or security at a fixed price in a stated quantity within a stated period.

Call price Price paid a corporation for the redemption of securities.

Calumniator In the civil law, one who brought a false accusation.

Calumny Defamation, false accusation of a crime or offense.

Cambiator In old English law, a money-changer.

Cambium In the civil law, change or exchange.

Camera A judge's chamber.

Camera stellata The star chamber.

Campers A champertor's share; a champertous division or sharing of land.

Cancel To obliterate, cross out, or invalidate.

Cancellaria Chancery; the court of chancery.

Cancellation Destruction of the force, effectiveness, or validity of something.

Cancelled check A check that bears the notation of cancellation of the drawee bank as having been paid and charged to the drawer.

Canfara A trial by hot iron.

Canon 1. A rule or law (canons of professional responsibility). **2.** Principle, standard.

Canonical disability Incurable physical impotency or incapacity for copulation.

Canon law Ecclesiastical law; Roman church jurisprudence.

Canons of construction Rules, principles, or guidelines that can be of help in interpreting statutes, regulations, wills, and other written documents.

Cant In the civil law, a method of dividing property held in common by two or more joint owners.

Canvass 1. To examine and count the votes cast in an election in order to determine authenticity. **2.** To solicit votes, contributions, opinions, etc.

Capable 1. Having the capacity or ability. **2.** Competent, skillful.

Capacity 1. Legal qualification or competency to do something; the ability to understand the nature and effects of one's acts (capacity to contract; capacity to sue). **2.** Skill (a judge of formidable capacity). **3.** Occupation or function (the judge spoke in her capacity as chairperson).

Capax doli Capable of committing a crime, or capable of criminal intent.

Capias "That you take." A name for a category of writs that requires an officer to take the body of the defendant into custody.

Capias ad respondendum A judicial writ that commands the sheriff to take the defendant and bring him or her to court in order to answer the charges of the plaintiff.

Capias ad satisfaciendum A writ of execution that commands the sheriff to take and hold a judgment debtor until the latter satisfies its judgment debt.

Capita head, person, body.

Capital 1. Accumulated assets used for the production of profit. **2.** An owner's equity in a business. **3.** The sum total of corporate stock.

Capital account In accounting, the account that represents the contributions of the proprietors, partners or stockholders to which creditors may look and from which no dividends should be paid.

Capital case, crime, or offense One for which death is the possible punishment.

Capital expenditure Expenditure for long-term betterments or additions that is chargeable to the capital asset account and is added to the basis of the property improved.

Capital gain Profit (gain) realized on the sale or exchange of a capital asset.

Capitalis debitor The chief or principal debtor, as distinguished from a surety.

Capitalization The total amount of the various securities issued by a corporation.

Capitalize 1. To supply with investment funds. **2.** To convert a periodical payment into an equivalent capital sum. To compute the present value of an income extended over a period of time. **3.** To use to one's advantage.

Capital punishment Punishment by death.

Capital stock All shares representing ownership of a business, including preferred stock and common stock. The amount fixed by the charter to be subscribed and paid in or secured to be paid in by the shareholders.

Capital surplus Property paid into a corporation by the shareholders in excess of capital stock liability.

Capitation tax A tax or imposition upon the person. A per capita tax.

Capite By the head.

Capitulary A systematic collection or code of laws.

Capitulation The act or agreement of surrendering upon negotiated or stipulated terms.

Caprice The disposition to change one's mind impulsively; a sudden change of mind; an illogical notion.

Capricious Impulsive; not based on standards.

Captation In French law, the act of one who controls the will of another.

Captator A person who obtains a gift or legacy through artifice.

Captio A taking or seizure.

Caption The heading or introductory part of a pleading, court opinion, memo, or other document that identifies what it is, who is involved, the court or agency, etc.

Captor In international law, one who takes or seizes property in time of war.

Capture The taking of property or persons by force, threats, or strategy.

Carat A measure of weight for precious stones equivalent to 3 1/6 grains Troy, or 200 milligrams.

Carcan In French law, an instrument of punishment, resembling a pillory.

Carcer A place of detention.

Care Watchful attention; the manner in which a reasonable person will act in the face of risks.

Careless Absence of care, negligent.

Carence In French law, a lack of assets; insolvency.

Caretaker One who takes care of a person, property, or an estate.

Carga In Spanish law, an incumbrance; a charge.

Cargo Goods transported on a truck, train, ship, or other carrier.

Carnal Pertaining to the bodily passions.

Carnal abuse An act of assault or debauchery of the female sexual organs via the genital organs of the male, short of penetration.

Carnaliter In old criminal law, carnally. Carnaliter cognovit, carnally knew.

Carnal knowledge Sexual intercourse.

Carriage Transportation of goods, freight, or passengers.

Carrier An individual or company engaged in transporting passengers or goods for hire.

Carry 1. To bear; to transport. **2.** To possess or hold.

Carry-back A provision in the tax law that permits a taxpayer to apply the net operating loss in one year to recompute the tax owed in several preceding years.

Carrying away The act of removal by which the crime of larceny is completed and which is essential to it.

Carrying charge Charge made by the creditor, in

addition to interest, for providing installment credit.

Carry-over Net operating loss for one year that may be used or applied in following years.

Carta A charter or deed (Magna Carta).

Carte blanche 1. A blank sheet of paper that is signed. **2.** Unlimited authority.

Cartel 1. A combination of producers of any product joined together to control the production, sale, and price of the product in order to obtain a monopoly. **2.** An agreement between enemies while the hostilities continue.

Cartulary A place where papers or records are kept.

Case 1. An action or lawsuit. **2.** See action on the case. **3.** A statement of arguments.

Case agreed on See agreed case.

Case and controversy Claims or contentions of litigants brought before the court for adjudication by regular proceedings established for the protection or enforcement of rights, or for the prevention, redress, or punishment of wrongs. If the judicial power is capable of acting on the claim or contention of a party, it is a case or controversy. See actual controversy, justiciable.

Case in chief That part of a trial in which the party with the initial burden of proof presents its evidence and then rests.

Case law The aggregate of reported cases.

Case of actual controversy A controversy of justiciable nature, excluding an advisory decree on hypothetical facts.

Case of first impression See first impression.

Cash Money or its equivalent.

Cash account A bookkeeping record of moneys received and expended.

Cash basis A system of accounting that treats as income only that which is actually received and as an expense only that which is actually paid out.

Cash flow The cash generated from property. The amount of cash left over after all payments are made.

Cashier 1. To dismiss with dishonor. **2.** One who collects and records payments.

Cashier's check A check drawn by a bank upon itself and issued by an authorized officer of the bank, directed to another person evidencing the fact that the payee is authorized to demand and receive from the bank, upon presentation, the amount of money represented by the check.

Cash market value See fair market value.

Cash surrender value The cash amount available upon surrender of an insurance policy before it becomes payable in the normal course (e.g. at death).

Cash value The price in ready money (no deferred payments) that property would bring at a private sale, not at a forced or auction sale.

Cassation In French law, annulling.

Cassation, court of (cour de cassation,) The highest court in France; so termed from possessing the power to quash (casser) the decrees of inferior courts.

Cassetur breve That the writ be quashed.

Cast 1. To deposit formally. **2.** To discard.

Castigatory An engine used to punish women who had been convicted of being common scolds.

Casual 1. Unexpected (casual meeting). **2.** Irregular (casual employment). **3.** Indifferent, perfunctory (casual inspection).

Casual condition In civil law, that which depends on chance, and is in no way in the power either of the creditor or of the debtor.

Casualty 1. A serious or fatal accident; an accident that occurs by chance or without design. **2.** A person or thing lost, injured, or destroyed.

Casualty loss The complete or partial destruction of property resulting from an identifiable event of a sudden, unexpected, or unusual nature (e.g., flood, car accident).

Casus belli An occurrence giving rise to or justifying war.

Casus omissus An event or contingency for which no provision is made; a case omitted.

Catalla Chattels.

Catastrophe A disaster.

Catching bargain A bargain by which money is loaned, at an extortionate or extravagant rate, to an heir or any one who has an estate in reversion or expectancy, to be repaid on the vesting of his or her interest.

Catchpoll A name formerly given to an officer whose duty was to arrest persons.

Categorical question One inviting a distinct and positive statement of fact; one that can be answered by "yes" or "no."

Cater cousin A cousin in the fourth degree; hence any distant or remote relative.

Caucus A meeting of the members of a particular group.

Causa A cause, reason, occasion, motive, or inducement.

Causa causans The immediate cause; the last link in the chain of causation.

Causa mortis In contemplation of approaching death.

Causation The fact of being the cause of something. The act by which an effect is produced.

Causator 1. A litigant. **2.** One who manages or litigates another's cause.

Cause 1. Something that precedes and brings about or helps to bring about an effect or result. **2.** A lawsuit.

Cause in fact An actual cause of something. That without which an event would not have occurred.

Cause of action The facts that give a person a right to judicial relief. A legally acceptable reason for suing.

Causeway A raised road or path through low lands, wet ground, or water.

Cautio In the civil and French law, security given for performance.

Caution 1. To give notice of danger. **2.** Prudence, carefulness.

Cautionary instruction That part of a judge's charge in which he or she instructs the jury to consider certain evidence only for a specific purpose.

Caveat A formal notice or warning. "Let him beware."

Caveat actor Let the doer or actor beware.

Caveat emptor Let the buyer beware. A buyer must examine and judge the product on his or her own.

Caveator One who files a caveat.

Caveat venditor Let the seller beware.

Ceap In English law, a bargain; anything for sale.

Cease To come to an end; to become extinct.

Cease and desist order An order of an administrative agency or court prohibiting a person or business from continuing a particular course of conduct.

Cede To surrender or yield.

Celation Concealment of pregnancy or delivery.

Celebration Solemnization, going through the necessary formalities.

Celibacy 1. The condition of being unmarried. **2.** Refraining from intercourse.

Censor A person who examines material in order to identify what is objectionable.

Censorship Reviewing publications in order to identify and remove objectionable material.

Censure An official reprimand.

Census An official counting of people.

Centena A hundred. A district or division containing originally a hundred freemen.

Centralize To concentrate power and authority in a central location or body; to unite.

Century One hundred years.

Cepit "He took."

Ceremonial marriage A marriage that follows all of the statutory requirements of blood tests, license, waiting period, and that has been solemnized by a person (religious or civil) authorized to preside at a marriage.

Certain Definite, ascertained, free from doubt.

Certainty Inevitability, absence of doubt.

Certificate A written assurance or official representation that some act has or has not been done.

Certificate creditor A creditor of a municipal corporation who receives a certificate of indebtedness for the amount of its claim, there being no funds available for repayment.

Certificate into chancery In English practice, a document containing the opinion of the common-law judges on a question of law submitted to them for their decision by the chancery court.

Certificate of authority Document issued by a state corporation authority (e.g., Secretary of State) on application of a foreign corporation granting it a right to do business in state.

Certificate of deposit A written acknowledgment by a bank of a deposit with a promise to pay a depositor, to his order, or to some other person or to his order. A document evidencing existence of a time deposit.

Certificate of occupancy A document certifying that the premises comply with zoning or building ordinances.

Certificate of participation A certificate issued instead of shares of stock to show a proportionate interest in an unincorporated business or in the ownership of debt of a corporation.

Certificate of registry In maritime law, a certificate of the registration of a vessel according to the registry acts, for the purpose of giving it a national character.

Certificate of title A certificate issued by a title company or a written opinion rendered by an attorney that the seller has good marketable and insurable title to the property which he or she is offering for sale. A certificate of title offers no protection against any hidden defects in the title which an examination of the records could not reveal. The issuer of a certificate of title is liable only for damages due to negligence. The protection offered a homeowner under a certificate of title is not as great as that offered in a title insurance policy.

Certification 1. A formal assertion, usually in writing, of some fact. **2.** Formal designation by the NLRB that a labor organization represents a majority of employees in a particular bargaining unit.

Certification of a check See certified check.

Certification of assize A writ granted for the re-examination or retrial of a matter passed by assize before justices.

Certification of record on appeal Formal acknowledgment of questions for appellate review, commonly signed by a lower court.

Certificats de coutume In French law, certificates given by a foreign lawyer, establishing the law of the country to which he or she belongs upon one or more fixed points.

Certified check A check whose payment will be guaranteed by the bank on which it is drawn. The acceptance of the check by the bank is a warranty that funds are available to cover it.

Certified copy A copy of a document or record, signed and certified as a true copy by the officer to whose custody the original is intrusted.

Certified Public Accountant (CPA) An accountant who has satisfied the statutory and administrative requirements of his or her jurisdiction to be registered or licensed as a public accountant.

Certify To state formally that something is true or genuine.

Certiorari "To be informed of." A higher court, in a case in which it has discretion to hear an appeal, asks a lower court to send up a certified copy of the record in the case so that the higher court can determine whether any irregularities have occurred in the proceedings. A writ of certiorari.

Cesset processus The formal order for a stay of proceedings.

Cessio bonorum A bankrupt's assignment of property to be distributed among his or her creditors.

Cession A surrender or yielding up.

C'est le crime qui fait la honte, et non pas l'echafaud It is the offense which causes the shame, and not the scaffold.

Cestui que trust Beneficiary of a trust. One who has a right to a beneficial interest in an estate, the legal title to which is vested in a trustee.

Cestui que vie The person whose life measures the duration of a trust, gift, estate, or insurance contract.

Cf. Compare or confer. Refers to contrasted, analogous, or explanatory views or statements.

Chaffery Traffic; the practice of buying and selling.

Chain As regards land measure, 66 feet, 100 links, or 4 rods.

Chain of title Successive conveyances or other transactions that affect a particular parcel of land, arranged consecutively from the original title holder to the present holder.

Chairman The presiding officer.

Challenge To put in question; to render doubtful.

Challenge for cause A request from a party that a certain prospective juror not be allowed to sit on the jury because of specified causes or reasons (e.g., bias).

Chamber 1. A room or office that is usually private. **2.** A legislative body.

Champerty An illegal bargain between one person (called a champertor) and a party to a lawsuit whereby the champertor carries on the litigation at his or her own expense and shares whatever is recovered. The bargain is called a champertous agreement.

Chance 1. A risk. **2.** Accident, fate.

Chancellor 1. Judge in a court of equity. **2.** Prime minister. **3.** Chief executive officer.

Chancer To adjust according to principles of equity.

Chancery Equity; the system of jurisprudence administered in courts of equity (as opposed to courts of law).

Chance verdict A verdict determined by hazard or lot and not by careful deliberation.

Change An alteration.

Change of venue The removal of a suit begun in one court to another court, usually in a different county or district.

Channel 1. The bed in which the main stream of a river flows. **2.** A generic term applicable to any water course, whether a river, creek, slough, or canal.

Chapman An itinerant vendor of small wares.

Chapter A division or local branch of an organization.

Character The aggregate of moral qualities that belong to and distinguish an individual.

Charge 1. To impose a burden or obligation (the board was charged with the task of reconciling the figures). **2.** To instruct or command (the judge charged the jury on the law of libel). **3.** To accuse (the police charged her with armed robbery). **4.** To defer payment (he charged a new shirt). **5.** To hold financially responsible (the store charged her for extra linen). **6.** A claim or encumbrance (any advancements made will constitute a charge against commissions that are due). **7.** Supervision (the infant was in the charge of the agency).

Chargeable 1. Subject to be charged (the offense was chargeable under state law). **2.** Attributable (the tax was chargeable to the estate).

Chargé d'affaires A diplomatic representative of an inferior rank.

Charge-off To treat as a loss or expense an amount originally recorded as an asset.

Charge-sheet A record kept at a police station in which you will find the names of the persons taken into custody, the nature of the accusation, and the name of the accuser in each case.

Charge to the jury A final address to the jury in which the judge instructs the jurors on the rules that they are to apply in reaching a verdict.

Charging lien An attorney's lien on the fund or judgment the client has recovered by means of the attorney's professional services. The lien protects the attorney in the event that the client does not pay agreed-upon fees and costs.

Charitable Having the character or purpose of a charity; philanthropic, eleemosynary.

Charitable bequest A bequest or gift where the aim or accomplishment is religious, educational, political, or of general social interest to mankind, and the ultimate recipients are either the community as a whole or an indefinite and unascertainable portion thereof.

Charitable contribution A contribution made for tax purposes to a qualified, nonprofit charitable organization.

Charitable corporation A nonprofit corporation organized for charitable purposes (e.g., promoting the community's welfare).

Charitable immunity doctrine A charity is not liable for the torts it commits. The doctrine has been modified or abolished in many states.

Charitable trust A fiduciary relationship with respect to property arising as a result of a manifestation of an intent to create it, and subjecting the person by whom the property is held to equitable duties to deal with the property for charitable purposes.

Charitable use Uses of religious, educational, political, or general social interest to mankind. Uses for the relief of poverty, advancement of education or religion, or beneficial to the general community.

Charity 1. A gift. **2.** An institution engaged in public benevolent purposes. **3.** The attempt to benefit and advance mankind in general, or those specifically in need, spiritually, socially, economically, physically, or intellectually without expectation of gain or profit to the donor.

Charlatan One who pretends to have more knowledge and skill than he or she possesses.

Charta A charter, deed, or formal instrument, especially from the sovereign (e.g., Magna Charta).

Charter 1. A document from the state legislature or sovereign power that grants rights, liberties, or powers. **2.** A document created by an organization that states the fundamental purposes and powers of the organization. **3.** To rent for temporary use.

Chase To pursue or follow rapidly with the intention of catching or driving away.

Chaste 1. Never having had unlawful sexual intercourse. **2.** Never having experienced any sexual intercourse. **3.** Virtuous.

Chattel 1. An article of personal property (e.g., car, rug, dog) as opposed to real property (e.g., land, house). Movable property.

Chattel lien A lien in personal property in favor of persons who have expended labor, services, or materials on the property at the request of the rightful owner or possessor.

Chattel mortgage A mortgage on personal property. A security interest is taken in the property.

Chattel paper A document or documents that evidence both a monetary obligation and a security interest in or a lease of personal property.

Cheat To deceive and defraud.

Cheaters, escheators In old English law, officers appointed to look after the king's escheats, a duty that gave them great opportunities of fraud.

Check 1. to hold within bounds. **2.** To examine for accuracy. **3.** A draft drawn upon a bank and payable on demand, signed by the maker or drawer, containing an unconditional promise to pay a sum certain in money to the order of the payee (paid by check).

Check kiting The practice of writing a check against a bank account in which funds are insufficient to cover it, with the hope that before the check is deposited, the necessary funds will have been deposited.

Checkoff system A procedure whereby the employer deducts union dues directly from the pay of the employees and gives them to the union.

Check only for account A draft on which the restrictive endorsement "account payee" is written to specify that the instrument may only be paid to a current account.

Chief Justice The presiding, most senior, or principal judge of a court.

Child, children Offspring of a human.

Chilling Seriously discouraging.

Chippingavel A tax upon trade.

Chirograph In civil and canon law, an instrument written out and subscribed by the hand of the party who made it.

Chiropractic(s) A system of therapeutic treatment

that removes pressure on the nerves by the adjustment of the spinal vertebrae and other structures.

Choate Pertaining to that which has become perfected or ripened.

Choate lien A lien that is perfected so that nothing more need be done to make it enforceable.

Choice of law The determination of what law should govern when a conflict of law issue is present in the case.

Chose A thing; an article of personal property.

Chose in action A right to recover something through a lawsuit.

Chose in possession A personal thing of which one has possession.

Chose transitory A thing that is movable.

Christian name The name given after birth or at baptism as distinct from the surname.

Church A religious society following Christian doctrine and observing Christian ritual.

Churning An abuse of a customer's confidence by a broker by making excessive transactions for personal gain, (e.g., increased commissions).

Cipher 1. Secret writing unintelligible to someone without the key. **2.** Someone of no importance.

Circa Approximately (he was born circa 1789).

Circuit A district or area traveled by a judge or minister.

Circuit courts of appeals Former name for federal intermediate appellate courts, changed in 1948 to United States Courts of Appeals.

Circuity of action A complex, indirect, or roundabout course of legal proceeding, making two or more lawsuits necessary when a more direct approach would have required only one lawsuit.

Circular note or letter of credit A writing that authorizes one person (or entity) to pay money or extend credit to another person (or entity) on the credit of the writer.

Circulate To pass from place to place.

Circulation Transmission from person to person or from place to place.

Circumstances Accompanying facts, events, or conditions.

Circumstantial Indirect, inferential.

Circumstantial evidence Indirect evidence. The proof of certain facts in a case from which the jury may infer other connected facts that usually and reasonably follow according to common experience.

Circumvent To evade, to go around.

Citación In Spanish law, a citation or summons.

Citation 1. A notice or order to appear in court at a later date (the police issued the driver a citation). **2.** The reference to or quotation of authority (the citations in the brief were incomplete). **3.** Award.

Citator A research book containing lists of references or cites (e.g., Shepard's Citations) that serves two main functions: first and foremost, to help you assess the current validity of a case, statute or other law; and secondarily, to provide you with leads to additional laws.

Cite 1. To notify someone to appear in a proceeding; to accuse. **2.** A reference to or quotation of an authority. **3.** To refer to.

Citizen A person born or naturalized in a country to which he or she owes allegiance, and who is entitled to full civil rights.

Citizen's arrest A private citizen making an arrest, usually for a crime that constitutes a breach of the peace.

City A municipal corporation.

City council The principal governmental body of a municipal corporation with power to pass ordinances, levy taxes, appropriate funds, and generally administer city government.

Civic Pertaining to a city or to citizenship.

Civil 1. Relating to private rights and remedies sought by civil actions (civil proceeding). **2.** Pertaining to the state or its citizenry (civil authorities). **3.** Courteous.

Civil action An action to enforce private rights. A lawsuit involving either (a) one private party suing another private party, or (b) a private party suing or being sued by the government, which does not directly involve criminal prosecution.

Civil arrest 1. The apprehension of a person by virtue of a lawful authority to answer the demand against him or her in a civil action. **2.** Arrest of a ship or cargo in maritime in rem actions.

Civil code The code containing the civil law of France.

Civil commitment Confinement, through a process other than criminal prosecution, of individuals who are insane, alcoholic, drug addicted, etc., who cannot care for themselves and/or who pose a danger to themselves or to society.

Civil conspiracy A combination of two or more persons who, by concerted action, seek to accomplish an unlawful purpose or to accomplish a lawful purpose by unlawful means.

Civil contempt A contempt of court that does not involve a serious affront to the authority of the court. A serious affront would be a criminal contempt. Example of civil contempt: failure to comply with an injunction.

Civil death All rights and privileges (e.g., the right to vote or to enter a contract) are forfeited once a person is convicted of a serious crime.

Civil disabilities Those rights or privileges that are lost when a person is convicted of a serious crime (e.g., the right to vote, to hold public office, to obtain certain licenses).

Civil disobedience Breaking the law in order to demonstrate the injustice or unfairness of the law and to focus public attention on it.

Civilian Pertaining to private citizens; nonmilitary, nonpolice.

Civilization Progressive and improved conditions of a society under an organized government.

Civil law 1. Law that originated from ancient Rome rather than from the common law or from canon law. **2.** The law governing private rights and remedies as opposed to criminal law, military law, international law, natural law, etc.

Civil liberties Personal rights guaranteed by the Constitution (e.g., freedom of speech, press, religion).

Civil possession In civil law and in Louisiana, possession that exists when a person ceases to reside on the land that he or she occupied, or to detain the movable that he or she possessed, but without intending to abandon the possession.

Civil procedure The body of law concerning the methods, procedures, and practices in civil litigation.

Civil rights See civil liberties.

Civil service Employment in federal, state, city, or town government, often obtained through merit and competitive exams rather than through political connections.

Civil side Litigation on civil matters in a court that can hear both civil and criminal cases.

Civil war Armed conflict between opposing factions within the same country.

Claflin trust A type of trust in which the donor or settlor makes specific provisions for the termination of the trust. Courts respect these provisions by denying the beneficiary the right to terminate.

Claim 1. To demand as one's own or as one's right (the complaint claimed $750 in damages). **2.** A cause of action (a negligence claim). **3.** To assert (she claimed that the room was wired).

Claim adjustor An independent agent or employee of an insurance company who negotiates and settles claims against the insurer.

Claim and delivery An action at law for the recovery of specific personal chattels wrongfully taken and detained.

Claimant One who asserts a right, demand, or claim.

Clandestine Concealed, often for an illegal or illicit purpose.

Class A group of persons, things, qualities, or activities having common characteristics or attributes.

Class action A device by which a suit can be instituted by or against numerous persons whose interests are sufficiently common that the dispute involving all of them can be litigated in one action without joining everyone. One member of the class (the named representative) represents everyone. Before a class action is allowed, the court must be convinced that the class, although ascertainable, contains so many persons that it would be impracticable to bring them all before the court. It must also be clear that there is a well-defined commonality of interest among the group in the questions of law and fact involved in the dispute. Finally, the named representative must demonstrate that he or she will fairly and adequately represent everyone.

Class gift A gift of an aggregate sum to a body of persons whose number is uncertain at the time of the gift. The number of persons will be ascertained at a later time. Each is to receive a definite proportion or share of the gift in an amount that will be dependent on the ultimate number in the group.

Classification An arrangement into groups or categories on the basis of established criteria.

Clause A single sentence, paragraph, or other subdivision of a pleading, contract, will, statute, or other document.

Clausum fregit "He broke the close." Pertaining to a trespass action (e.g., stepping over a boundary line).

Clayton Act A 1914 statute dealing with antitrust regulations and unfair trade practices. It prohibited price discrimination, tying, exclusive dealing contracts, etc.

Clean Free from fraud or other wrongdoing.

Clean acceptance An unconditional engagement signed on a bill of exchange or draft by the drawee to honor the instrument as presented.

Clean bill Bill of exchange without documents attached.

Clean hands doctrine Equity will not grant relief to a party who seeks to use the courts and obtain a remedy when that party has engaged in some prior unlawful or inequitable conduct in connection with the matter in litigation.

Clear 1. Obvious plain. **2.** Free from encumbrance (clear title). **3.** To vindicate.

Clearance 1. The act of a ship in clearing or leaving a port. **2.** In a contract for the exhibition of motion pictures, the interval of time between the conclusion of an exhibition in one theater and the commencement of one at another. **3.** Approval or permission.

Clearance certificate One issued to a ship's captain showing that customs requirements have been met.

Clear and convincing evidence That degree of evidence that will produce in the mind of the trier of fact a firm belief or conviction as to the truth of an allegation. Highly likely, more than a preponderance but less than beyond all reasonable doubt, highly probable.

Clear and present danger Imminent danger. Danger that is approaching, forthcoming, close at hand.

Clearing account An account containing amounts to be transferred to another account(s) before the end of the accounting period.

Clearinghouse An association or place where banks exchange checks and drafts drawn on each other, and settle daily balances.

Clearly erroneous Based on substantial error, a misapplication of law, the lack of substantial evidence; induced by an erroneous view of the law, or unsupported by substantial evidence.

Clear title Title that is free from any encumbrance, obstruction, burden, or limitation that presents a doubtful or even a reasonable question of law or fact. Good title, marketable title, a title free from palpable defects.

Clear view doctrine See plain view doctrine.

Clemency Mercy; treatment with less rigor than one's authority permits.

Clergy Ministers of religion.

Clerical 1. Pertaining to the clergy. **2.** Pertaining to the office or labor of a clerk.

Clerical error Generally, a mistake in writing or copying a document (e.g., an omission).

Clerk 1. An officer of the court who receives and files pleadings, motions, judgments, etc., issues process, and keeps records of court proceedings.

Clerkship 1. The period that a law student spends in the office of a practicing attorney before being admitted to the bar. Apprenticeship. **2.** Employment of a law student or attorney with a judge. **3.** Employment of a law student at a law firm.

Client 1. A person who employs or retains an attorney for advice and representation on legal matters. A client may also include someone who discloses confidential information to an attorney while seeking assistance, whether or not the attorney is actually hired. **2.** A person who uses the services—often professional—of someone else; a customer.

Clifford trust A grantor trust whereby the grantor (i.e., creator) of the trust retains the right to possess again the property transferred in trust upon the occurrence of an event (e.g, the death of the beneficiary) or the expiration of a period of time. The grantor retains a reversionary interest.

Close 1. To terminate; to wind up. **2.** To bar access to; to obstruct. **3.** A portion of land enclosed by a hedge, fence, or other visible enclosure, or by an invisible boundary based on one's title (breaking the close).

Close corporation A corporation whose shares (or at least whose voting shares) are held by a single shareholder or by a closely knit group of shareholders.

Closed-end borrowing A mortgage that does not permit additional borrowing.

Closed shop The practice whereby a worker must be a member of a union as a condition of employment.

Closing The final steps in a transaction for the sale of real estate (e.g., payment is made, mortgage is secured, taxes are allocated, etc.).

Closing argument The final statements by the attorneys to the jury or to the court, summarizing the evidence that they think they have established and that the other side has failed to establish during the trial.

Closing costs Expenses in the sale of real estate in addition to the purchase price (e.g., fees for title examination, commission, insurance, appraisal, deed preparation, settlement statement, escrows for future payments of taxes or insurance, etc.).

Closing day The day on which the formalities of a real estate sale are concluded. The certificate of title, abstract, and deed are generally prepared for the closing by an attorney and this cost charged to the buyer. The buyer signs the mortgage, and closing costs are paid. The final closing merely confirms the original agreement reached in the agreement of sale.

Closing entries In accounting, the entries that accomplish the transfer of balances in temporary accounts to the related balance sheet accounts.

Cloture A legislative procedure whereby extended and unreasonable debate is ended to allow a vote on the measure.

Cloud on title An outstanding claim or encumbrance which, if valid, would affect or impair the title of the owner of a particular estate but which can be shown to be invalid or inapplicable to the estate in question.

Club A voluntary, incorporated or unincorporated association of persons who have common purposes.

Coadjutor Helper or ally.

Coadventurer One who takes part with others in an adventure, in a venture, or in a business undertaking containing risks.

Co-assignee One of two or more assignees of the same subject matter.

Coaster A vessel plying exclusively between domestic ports, and usually engaged in domestic trade, not including pleasure yachts.

Co-conspirator One who engages in an illegal alliance with others.

Code A collection of laws, rules, or regulations organized by subject matter.

Code Civil The code that embodies the civil law of France. The name was later changed to Code Napoleon. It is the basis of some of the Louisiana Civil Code today.

Co-defendant One of two or more defendants being sued in the same litigation or being charged with the same crime.

Code Napoleon See Code Civil.

Code of Federal Regulations (C.F.R.) An annual accumulation of some federal agency regulations.

Code of Military Justice The substantive and procedural law governing military justice and its administration in all of the armed forces of the United States.

Code of Professional Responsibility Rules of conduct governing the legal profession written by the American Bar Association and adopted by many states.

Code pleading A system of pleading that replaced common-law pleading. In code pleading, the ultimate facts had to be stated as the basis for the cause of action or defense.

Codex A code or collection of laws.

Codicil A supplement or addition to a will.

Codification The process of collecting and systematically arranging by subject matter, the laws, rules, or regulations of a particular geographic location (e.g., a state), or of a certain area of the law (e.g.,

criminal law statutes).

Codify To collect and arrange laws, rules, and regulations by subject matter.

Co-emption The act of purchasing the whole quantity of any commodity.

Coequal The same in rank, value, or degree.

Coercion Compelling something by force, arms, or threats.

Co-executor One who is a joint executor with one or more others.

Cognate Related; similar (cognate offenses).

Cognates Relations by the mother's side or by females.

Cognitor In the Roman law, an advocate.

Cognizable Capable of being tried or examined before a designated tribunal; within the jurisdiction of the court to adjudicate.

Cognizance 1. The exercise of jurisdiction; the power to hear a case. **2.** Judicial notice or knowledge.

Cognomen A surname.

Cognovit note A written statement that the debtor owes money and "confesses judgment," or allows the creditor to obtain a judgment in court for the money whenever the creditor wishes or whenever a particular event takes place (such as a failure to make a payment).

Cohabitation The act of living together as husband and wife whether or not the parties are married.

Co-heir One of several heirs to whom an inheritance passes or descends.

Coif A hat or cap worn by sergeants at law. A title given to sergeants at law. See Order of the Coif.

Coin 1. Metal money; pieces of gold, silver, or other metal in a prescribed form authorized by the government to circulate as money. **2.** To fashion pieces of metal into a prescribed form to circulate as money on the authority of the government.

Coinage 1. The process or function of coining metallic money. **2.** The great mass of metallic money in circulation.

Coinsurance Insurance risks shared jointly (e.g., by two or more insurers, by the insurer and the insured).

Coitus Sexual intercourse.

Cold turkey Complete and immediate termination or withdrawal from that to which one is addicted.

Collaboration The act of working together in a joint project.

Collapsible corporation A corporation set up under a prearranged plan to fold or liquidate before it realizes substantial taxable income from its property.

Collateral 1. Property that is pledged as security for the satisfaction of a debt. **2.** Subordinate. **3.** By the side; additional; confirming.

Collateral affinity That which subsists between the husband and the relations of his wife's relations.

Collateral ancestor A phrase sometimes used to designate uncles, aunts, and other collateral "ancestors" who, strictly speaking, are not ancestors.

Collateral attack An attack against a judgment in an incidental proceeding. The attack is not brought in the original proceeding; it is brought in a proceeding other than the one that resulted in the judgment now being attacked.

Collateral consanguinity Persons are related collaterally when they have a common ancestor.

Collateral estoppel doctrine When an issue of law or fact has been litigated in one action (and when the determination of the issue was essential to the judgment), it cannot be relitigated in another action even if the two suits did not involve the same cause of action.

Collateral facts Facts that are not directly connected with the principal issue in the dispute.

Collateral heir An heir who is not of the direct line of the deceased, but comes from a collateral line—a brother, aunt, nephew, or cousin of the deceased.

Collateral issues Issues that are not directly involved in the case.

Collateral kinsmen Those who descend from the same common ancestor but not from one another.

Collateral line A line of descent connecting persons who are not directly related to each other as ascendants or descendants, but whose relationship consists in a common descent from the same ancestor.

Collateral mortgage A mortgage that is designed not directly to secure an existing debt, but to secure a mortgage note pledged as collateral security for a debt or succession of debts.

Collateral negligence The negligence attributable to a contractor employed by a principal for which the principal is not responsible. The principal would be responsible if his or her servant had committed the negligence.

Collateral proceeding One in which the particular question may arise or be involved incidentally, but which is not instituted for the very purpose of deciding such question.

Collateral relatives Next of kin (e.g., a cousin) who are not in the direct line of inheritance.

Collateral security A security given in addition to the direct security and subordinate to it. The creditor goes after the collateral security if the direct security fails.

Collateral source rule If an injured person receives compensation for his or her injuries from a source that is independent of the wrongdoer, the compensation is not deducted from the damages that the latter must pay.

Collateral warranty A warranty given by a third party (not the seller). This warranty does not run with the land; only the buyer (covenantee) can enforce it.

Collation 1. The comparison of a copy with its original to determine its correctness. **2.** Taking into account money or property already given to children (as an advance on an inheritance) by the deceased in order to equalize the shares when dividing the assets of the deceased.

Collect 1. To bring scattered things into one mass or fund.

Collectible Obligations, debts, demands, and liabilities that one could be forced to pay by means of the legal process.

Collective bargaining A procedure designed to achieve collective work agreements between employers and their accredited representative, the union.

Collective bargaining unit All of the employees of a single employer except for the employees of a particular department or division who have voted otherwise.

Collective mark A trademark or service mark used by members of a cooperative, an association, or other collective group.

Collegatary A co-legatee; a person who has a legacy left to him or her in common with other persons.

Collegia In the civil law, the guild of a trade.

Collegialiter In a corporate capacity.

Collision insurance Type of coverage that protects insured for damage to his or her own property in an accident as contrasted with liability insurance that protects him or her in an action or claim for loss to another's property.

Collistrigium The pillory.

Colloquium 1. That part of a complaint for defamation which alleges that the defamatory matter was published of and concerning the plaintiff. **2.** A conference.

Collusion 1. An agreement between two or more persons to defraud someone of his or her rights by the forms of law, or to obtain an object forbidden by law. **2.** An agreement between a husband and wife in a divorce proceeding that one of them will lie to the court in order to facilitate the obtaining of the divorce.

Collusive Pertaining to an agreement to defraud someone of his or her rights by the forms of the law, or to obtain an object forbidden by law.

Collusive action An action that is not founded on an actual controversy between the parties, but is brought for the purpose of securing a decision on a point of law out of curiosity or to settle the rights of third persons who are not parties.

Color A deceptive appearance (the seizure was carried out under color of law).

Colorable 1. Having only the appearance of truth (a colorable transaction). **2.** Plausible.

Color of authority The semblance or ßpresumption of authority of a public officer derived from his or her apparent title to office or from a writ or other apparently valid process in his or her hands.

Color of law 1. The appearance of legal right but without the substance. **2.** The misuse of power possessed by virtue of state law and made possible only because the wrongdoer is clothed with the authority of the state.

Color of office The pretense of an official right to do an act by someone who has no such right.

Color of title Apparent title. The appearance or semblance of title but not the reality.

Combat A forcible encounter between two or more persons.

Combination The union or association of two or more entities for the attainment of some common end.

Combination in restraint of trade An agreement or understanding between two or more persons, in the form of a contract, trust, pool, holding company, or other form of association, for the purpose of unduly restricting competition, monopolizing trade in a certain commodity, controlling its production, distribution, and price, or otherwise interfering with freedom of trade without statutory authority.

Comfort Consolation or benefit.

Comity 1. The courts of one jurisdiction will give effect to the laws and judicial decisions of another state as a matter of deference and mutual respect even if no obligation exists to do so. **2.** A willingness to grant a privilege.

Command 1. An order. **2.** Power to dominate and control. **3.** To direct.

Commanditaires Special partners.

Commence To initiate by performing the first act.

Commendatio In the civil law, commendation, praise, or recommendation.

Comment A statement that explains, criticizes, illustrates, etc. The mere assertion of a fact, however, is not a "comment."

Commerce Buying, selling or exchanging property or services.

Commercia belli Contracts between nations at war.

Commercial Related to trade, traffic, or commerce in general.

Commercial agency An office for the collection of debts for clients; also an agency for gathering credit information.

Commercial bank An institution authorized to receive both demand and time deposits, to make loans of various types, to engage in trust services and other fiduciary funds, to issue letters of credit, to accept and pay drafts, to rent safety deposit boxes, and to engage in many similar activities.

Commercial loan Generally a short term loan for 30 to 90 days given by financial institutions.

Commercial paper Bills of exchange (drafts), promissory notes, bank checks, and other negotiable instruments for the payment of money, which, by their form and on their face, purport to be such instruments.

Commercial traveler A drummer; a traveling salesperson.

Commingle To put together in one mass.

Commingling of funds The act of a fiduciary in mingling funds of a beneficiary, client, employer, or ward with his or her own funds. Such act is generally considered to be a breach of the fiduciary relationship.

Commissaire In French law, a person who receives special authority to conduct an inquiry or investigation.

Commissary 1. One who is sent or delegated to execute some office or duty as the representative of his or her superior **2.** An establishment that sells food.

Commission 1. The authority or instructions under which one person transacts business or negotiates for another. **2.** A group of persons appointed or elected to perform a function. **3.** Compensation or fee, often based on a percentage of designated amounts involved in the transaction(s). **4.** The performance of something. **5.** To empower.

Commissioners of deeds Officers empowered by the government of one state to reside in another state, and there take acknowledgments of deeds and other papers that are to be used as evidence or placed on record in the former state.

Commission merchant One whose business is to receive and sell goods for a commission, being intrusted with the possession of the goods to be sold. A factor.

Commit 1. To place into the custody of another. **2.** To perform an act. **3.** To pledge.

Commitment 1. A warrant, order, or process by which a court directs an officer to institutionalize a person. **2.** An agreement or pledge to do something. **3.** An obligation. **4.** An investment.

Committitur An order or minute, setting forth that the person named in it is committed to the custody of the sheriff.

Commixtio or **commixtion** In the civil law, the mixing together or confusion of things, dry or solid, belonging to different owners, as distinguished from confusio, which refers to liquids.

Commodatum A gratuitous loan of goods to be temporarily used by the bailee, and returned in specie.

Commodities arbitrage Simultaneous buying of commodities contracts in one market and selling them in another market at a higher price.

Commodity Something that is useful or serviceable as an article of merchandise.

Commodity future A contract to purchase a fixed amount of a commodity at a future date for a fixed price.

Commodity loan One secured by a commodity such as cotton or wool in the form of a warehouse receipt or other negotiable instrument.

Commodity paper Commercial paper representing loans secured by bills of lading or warehouse receipts covering commodities.

Common 1. An incorporeal hereditament that consists in a profit that one person has in connection with one or more others in the land of another. **2.** A tract of land set apart by a city or town for use by the general public; shared among several. **3.** Familiar by reason of frequency.

Commonalty The great body of citizens; the mass of the people, excluding the nobility. The body of people composing a municipal corporation, excluding the corporate officers.

Common appurtenant A right of feeding one's beasts on the land of another.

Common bench The ancient name for the English court of common pleas that handled the causes of common persons (i.e., causes between subject and subject, in which the crown had no interest).

Common carrier Any carrier required by law to transport passengers or freight without refusal if the approved fare or charge is paid.

Common counts Certain general counts or forms inserted in a declaration in an action to recover a money debt, not founded on the circumstances of the individual case, but intended to guard against a possible variance, and to enable the plaintiff to take advantage of any ground of liability that the proof may disclose, within the general scope of the action.

Common disaster A case in which two people with shared interests appear to die simultaneously, with no clear evidence of who died first.

Common intendment The plain meaning of any writing as apparent on its face.

Common knowledge Knowledge that every intelligent person has; it includes matters of learning, experience, history, and facts of which judicial notice may be taken.

Common law 1. Judge-made law (based on ancient customs, mores, usages, and principles handed down through the ages) in the absence of controlling statutory or other enacted law. **2.** All the statutory and case law of England and the American colonies before the American Revolution.

Common-law action An action (litigation) governed by the common law rather than by statutory, equitable, or civil law.

Common-law crime One punishable by the force of the common law, as distinguished from crimes created by statute.

Common-law marriage A nonceremonial marriage created by agreement and followed by cohabitation. Elements: (a) legal capacity to marry, (b) present agreement to be married, (c) living together as husband and wife, (d) open-ness—holding themselves out to the world as married.

Common-law trust A business trust in which trustees hold the property and manage the business; the shareholders are the trust beneficiaries. Massachusetts Trust.

Common market See European Economic Community.

Common pleas In common law pleading, common causes of suits; civil actions brought and prosecuted between subjects or citizens, as distinguished from criminal cases.

Common sense Sound practical judgment; that degree of intelligence and reason as exercised by the generality of the populace.

Common stock A class of corporate stock that represents the ownership of the corporation. The holders of this equity stock receive dividends after the holders of preferred stock.

Common tenancy A type of tenancy in which tenants hold property in common without right of survivorship.

Common traverse A simple and direct denial of the material allegations of the opposite pleading.

Common weal The public or common good or welfare.

Commonwealth 1. The public or common weal or welfare. **2.** The corporate entity, or the government, of a jural society (or state) possessing powers of self-government in respect of its immediate concerns, but forming an integral part of a larger government (or nation). In this latter sense, it is the official title of several of the United States (as Pennsylvania, Massachusetts, Virginia, and Kentucky).

Commorancy In English law, dwelling as an inhabitant. In American law, a temporary residence.

Commorientes Several persons who perish at the same time in the same calamity.

Commotion A condition of turmoil or civil unrest.

Commune A small community of people; a self-governing town or village.

Communia Common things, res communes, (e.g., running water, the air, the sea, and sea shores).

Communicate To make known.

Communication 1. The sharing of knowledge by one with another. **2.** A message.

Communism A system of social organization in which property is held in common—the opposite of the system of private property ownership.

Community 1. Locality, neighborhood. **2.** The citizenry. **3.** Identity; similar character (a community of interests).

Community debt One chargeable to the community (of husband and wife) rather than to either of the parties individually.

Community property Property owned in common by a husband and wife, with each having an undivided one-half interest in the property by reason of their marital status. For example, the earnings of one spouse during the marriage do not belong solely to that spouse; the earnings are community property.

Commutation 1. A change of punishment to one that is less severe. **2.** A substitution of one form of payment for another. **3.** A change or alteration.

Commutative contract In civil law, one in which each of the contracting parties gives and receives an equivalent.

Compact 1. An agreement or contract between persons, states, or nations. **2.** Closely or firmly united or packed. **3.** Concise.

Companage All kinds of food, except bread and drink.

Company A combination or association of persons to carry on a commercial or industrial enterprise.

Comparative negligence 1. The measurement of negligence by percentage. **2.** The damages allowed shall be diminished in proportion to the amount of negligence attributable to the victim. **3.** The victim's damages are reduced proportionately, provided his or her fault was less than that of the defendant.

Comparative rectitude In a divorce action, relief will be granted to the party least in fault when both have established grounds for the divorce.

Compatibility Capable of functioning together in harmony.

Compel To urge forcefully; to use extreme pressure to achieve a result.

Compelling state interest The test used to uphold state action in the face of an Equal Protection or First Amendment attack. A substantial or serious need for the state to act.

Compendium A comprehensive summary.

Compensable Entitled to compensation.

Compensate To make satisfactory payment.

Compensatio criminis Set-off of crime or guilt. **1.** The set-off of one crime against another. **2.** The plea or defense of recrimination in a suit for a divorce; that is, that the complainant is guilty of the same kind of offense with which the respondent is charged.

Compensation 1. Renumeration for services rendered. **2.** Indemnification.

Compensatory Involving payment or reparation.

Compensatory damages Damages that will compensate the injured party for the injury sustained and nothing more. Damages that will make good or replace the loss caused by the wrong or injury. Includes out-of-pocket expenses, pain and suffering.

Compete To strive for something that someone else is also seeking.

Competence 1. Having sufficient skill. **2.** Having a sound mind.

Competency The presence of those characteristics that render a witness legally fit to give testimony in a court.

Competent 1. Duly qualified; meeting all the requirements. **2.** Skillful.

Competent court A court with lawful jurisdiction.

Competition A contest between rivals. The efforts of two or more parties, acting independently, to secure the business of a third party by the offer of the most favorable terms.

Competitive 1. Opposing, contending. **2.** Unrestricted, open.

Competitive bidding Requires that all bidders be placed on a plane of equality, and that they bid upon the same terms and conditions.

Compilation 1. A bringing together of statutes that already exist and, in the process, removing repealed statutes, adding amendments, arranging the text in a convenient order, etc. **2.** An organized collection.

Compiled statutes A collection of the statutes existing and in force in a given state arranged by subject matter.

Complainant One who applies to the courts for legal redress by filing a complaint; one who instigates a criminal prosecution.

Complaint The original or initial pleading that sets forth the plaintiff's claim for relief.

Complete 1. To accomplish that which one starts out to do. **2.** Entire; including all elements without omissions or deficiencies. **3.** Perfect; not lacking in any element or particular.

Completion Finishing or accomplishing something in full.

Compliance Submission, obedience.

Complice One who is united with others in an ill design.

Complicity The state of being an accomplice; participation in guilt.

Comply To accept or yield.

Composition deed An agreement embodying the terms of a composition between debtor and creditors.

Composition with creditors An agreement, founded on sufficient consideration, between a debtor and his or her creditors whereby the latter agree to accept a lesser payment, to be distributed pro rata among the creditors, in discharge of the entire debt.

Compound 1. A combination of two or more elements or things, often as a result of human intervention. **2.** To compromise; to effect a composition with a creditor.

Compounder In Louisiana, the maker of a composition, generally called the "amicable compounder."

Compounding crime Elements of this offense: (a) the agreement not to prosecute or not to inform against someone who has committed a crime, (b) the knowledge of the actual commission of a crime, and (c) the receipt of property or other consideration in exchange for the agreement.

Compound interest Interest on interest; the interest that is earned generates further interest on this earning.

Compound larceny Larceny or theft accomplished by taking the thing stolen either from one's person or from his or her house.

Comprint A surreptitious printing of another bookseller's copy of a work, to make gain thereby.

Comprise To include.

Compromise 1. The settlement of a dispute through mutual concessions. **2.** To endanger.

Compromise and settlement An agreement by which a controversy is terminated. The consideration for the agreement is mutual concessions by the disputants.

Compromise verdict A verdict that is reached when one or more jurors surrender their conscientiously held positions on an issue in the case in exchange for the surrender of similarly held positions by other jurors on other issues.

Compromissarius In the civil law, an arbitrator.

Comptroller An officer whose job is to examine and audit accounts, to keep records, and report the financial situation from time to time.

Comptroller General Government official (head of G.A.O.) whose main function is to audit governmental agencies.

Comptroller of currency The administrator responsible for the execution of laws relating to national banks.

Compulsion 1. Forcible inducement to the commission of an act. **2.** An overpowering impulse.

Compulsory Obligatory by agreement or by law.

Compulsory counterclaim The counterclaim is logically related to the original claim and arises out of the same subject matter on which the original claim is based.

Compulsory nonsuit An involuntary termination of an action ordered by the court when the plaintiff totally fails to substantiate its claim by evidence.

Compulsory process Compelling the attendance of a person in court through subpoena, arrest warrant, attachment, etc.

Compurgation Exoneration through the testimony of others on innocence.

Computation The act of numbering or estimating.

Computus A writ to compel a guardian, bailiff, receiver, or accountant to yield up his or her accounts.

Con buena fe In Spanish law, with (or in) good faith.

Conceal To withhold from the knowledge of others.

Concealment 1. A withholding of something that one knows and which, in duty, ought to be revealed. **2.** Hiding.

Conception The beginning of pregnancy. The fecundation of the female ovum by the male spermatozoon, resulting in human life capable of survival under normal conditions.

Concern 1. To have reference to. **2.** A business.

Concert Acting with another to bring about a preconceived result.

Concerted Planned or arranged by parties who have agreed to act together pursuant to a design or scheme.

Concession 1. A grant or authorization. **2.** A yielding to a claim or demand.

Conciliatory Having an inclination to adjust and settle a dispute in an unantagonistic manner.

Conclusion 1. The termination. **2.** The final decision.

Conclusion of fact An inference or fact drawn from other facts.

Conclusion of law A statement by the court of the law that applies to the facts found by the jury or by the trial judge if no jury is present.

Conclusive Final; shutting out all further evidence.

Conclusive presumption A presumption that requires the trier of fact to find a fact as it is conclusively presumed. Evidence to the contrary is inadmissible.

Concomitant Occurring together.

Concord An agreement settling differences.

Concordance An alphabetical index of key words in a book or set of books.

Concordat A formal agreement or treaty.

Concubinage 1. Living together without being legally married. **2.** The state of being a concubine.

Concubine A woman who cohabits with a man with whom she is not married.

Concur to agree.

Concurator In the civil law, a joint or co-curator or guardian.

Concurrence 1. A meeting of the mind. **2.** A simultaneous occurrence.

Concurrent 1. Running together. **2.** In agreement.

Concurrent causes Causes acting roughly contemporaneously, and together causing an injury.

Concurrent estates Ownership or possession of property by two or more persons at the same time (e.g. joint tenancy, tenancy in common).

Concurrent jurisdiction The jurisdiction of several different tribunals, each authorized to adjudicate the same subject matter at the choice of the petitioner.

Concurrent negligence The negligence of two or more persons concurring in producing a single indivisible injury. The persons need not have acted at the same time.

Concurrent power The power of either Congress or the state legislatures, each acting independently of the other, to make laws on the same subject matter.

Concurrent resolution A statement of Congress passed in the form of a resolution of one house, the other house concurring, that expresses the sense of Congress on a particular subject.

Concurrent sentences Two or more terms of imprisonment, all or a part of each to be served simultaneously. The prisoner is entitled to be discharged at the expiration of the longest term specified.

Concurring opinion A separate opinion delivered by one or more judges on a case that agrees with the result of the majority opinion but provides separate reasons for reaching that result.

Concussion In the civil law, the unlawful forcing of another by threats of violence to give something of value.

Condemn 1. To find or adjudge guilty and impose a sentence. **2.** To set apart or expropriate for public use in the exercise of the power of eminent domain. **3.** To censure.

Condemnation The taking of private property for public use by a government unit, against the will of the owner, but with payment of just compensation under the government's power of eminent domain. Condemnation may also be a determination by a governmental agency that a particular building is unsafe or unfit for use.

Condictio In Roman law, a general term for actions of a personal nature, founded upon an obligation to give or do a certain and defined thing or service.

Conditio A condition.

Condition A future and uncertain event on which an obligation is dependent.

Conditional Pertaining to that which is dependent on a condition.

Conditional fee An estate restrained to some particular heirs, exclusive of others.

Conditional indorsement One by which the indorser annexes some condition (other than the failure of prior parties to pay) to his or her liability.

Conditional judgment One whose force depends upon the performance of certain acts to be done in the future by one of the parties.

Conditional sales contract The seller reserves title until the buyer pays for the goods, at which time title passes to the buyer.

Condition collateral One requiring the performance of a collateral act having no necessary relation to the main subject of the agreement.

Condition precedent A condition that must happen or be performed before some right dependent thereon accrues or some act dependent thereon is performed.

Conditions concurrent In contract law, conditions that must be performed by each party simultaneously.

Condition subsequent A condition referring to a future event, upon the happening of which an obligation no longer becomes binding on the other party at the option of the latter. A condition subsequent divests liability that has already attached.

Condominium A system of separate ownership of individual units in a multiple-unit building. The owner also has an individual interest in the common areas and facilities that serve the project.

Condonación In Spanish law, the remission of a debt.

Condonation 1. A voluntary forgiveness of an offense. **2.** Voluntary forgiveness by one spouse of the marital wrong of the other, barring the former from a divorce action on the basis of the wrong.

Condone To overlook or accept without protest.

Conduce To contribute to as a result.

Conduct 1. Personal behavior. **2.** To manage.

Conduct money In English practice, money paid to a witness who has been subpoenaed on a trial, sufficient to defray the reasonable expenses of going to, staying at, and returning from the place of trial.

Confederacy 1. The association or banding together of two or more persons to commit an act or to further an enterprise that is forbidden by law, or which, through lawful in itself, becomes unlawful when carried out through the confederacy.

Confederation A league or compact for mutual support.

Confess To admit the truth of a charge or accusation.

Confession A voluntary statement acknowledging guilt or responsibility for the offense charged.

Confession and avoidance A plea in which one admits (expressly or by implication) the truth of the allegations of fact in the complaint, but then proceeds to allege new matter that tends to neutralize or avoid the legal consequence of the allegations in the complaint.

Confession of judgment A written confession of the action by the defendant by virtue of which the plaintiff enters judgment. Allowing a judgment to be entered against someone without legal proceedings. See cognovit note.

Confide To place something in the confidence of another.

Confidence 1. Trust, reliance. **2.** A secret; privileged information (the attorney must not reveal the confidences of a client).

Confidence game Obtaining money or other property by trick. Elements: (a) intentional false representation to the victim concerning a present fact, (b) known to be false, (c) with the intent that the victim rely on the information, (d) the representation is made to obtain the victim's confidence and thereafter his or her money or other property, and (e) the defendant abuses this confidence.

Confidential Pertaining to that which is done in confidence with the expectation of privacy.

Confidential communication Privileged statements or communications between designated individuals (e.g., attorney and client, doctor and patient, confessor and penitent). The speaker must have clearly intended the statement to be heard only by the person in whom confidence was placed. The latter cannot be forced to disclose the statement.

Confidentiality The state or quality of being confidential.

Confidential relation A fiduciary relationship such as exists between attorney and client, husband and wife, principal and agent, etc. The relationship calls for the utmost degree of good faith in all transactions between the parties; they cannot deal with each other at arm's length.

Confinement State of being confined, detained, or locked up.

Confirm 1. To verify or make certain. **2.** To approve.

Confirmation 1. The giving of formal approval. **2.** Substantiation.

Confiscable Capable of being confiscated.

Confiscate To seize or take private property.

Confitens reus An accused person who admits guilt.

Conflict of interest A clash of loyalties (it would be a conflict of interest for the lawyer to represent both sides in the dispute).

Conflict of laws A branch of jurisprudence based on an inconsistency or difference among the laws of different states or countries that are involved in a controversy between the parties (e.g., a contract dispute in which the contract was signed in Ohio for the delivery of goods in New York, and the contract law of these two states is different; the conflict-of-law problem is to determine whether the contract law of Ohio or of New York applies to the case).

Conformed copy An exact copy of a document on which explanations of things have been written that could not be or were not copied.

Conforming In accordance with the contract or the law (conforming goods).

Conforming use The use of a structure that is in conformity with the uses permitted by zoning and land use planning laws.

Conformity Correspondence in form, manner, or use.

Confrontation Allowing an accused a face-to-face opportunity to cross-examine adverse witnesses.

Confusio In the civil law, the inseparable intermixture of property belonging to different owners.

Confusion In the civil law, a blending or inter-mingling.

Confute To prove to be false, defective, or invalid.

Congeable Lawful, permissible.

Congildones In Saxon law, fellow-members of a guild.

Congius An ancient measure containing about a gallon and a pint.

Conglomerate A corporation that has diversified its operations, usually by acquiring enterprises in widely varied industries.

Congregate To come together.

Congregation A gathering or assembly.

Congregationalism Self-governing local church congregations.

Congress 1. The federal legislature. **2.** A formal meeting of delegates or representatives.

Conjecture An idea or surmise inducing a slight degree of belief founded on some possible or perhaps probable fact as to which no positive evidence exists.

Conjoint Joined together; involving more than one in combination.

Conjoints Persons married to each other.

Conjudex In old English law, an associate judge.

Conjugal Of or belonging to marriage or to the married state.

Conjugal rights The rights that a wife and husband have to each other's society, support, and affection.

Conjunctive Connecting in a manner denoting union.

Conjunctive denial Where several material facts are stated conjunctively in the complaint, an answer that undertakes to deny their averments as a whole, conjunctively stated, is called a conjunctive denial.

Conjuration A plot or compact made by persons combining by oath to do any public harm.

Connivance A secret or indirect consent or permission to allow another to commit an unlawful act.

Connive To cooperate secretly with; to look upon with secret favor.

Connoissement In French law, an instrument similar to a bill of lading signed by the master of a ship.

Connotation An implied association or meaning.

Connubium In the civil law, marriage.

Conocimiento In Spanish law, a bill of lading.

Conpessessio In civil law, a joint possession.

Conquêts In French law, the name given to every acquisition that the husband and wife, jointly or severally, make during the conjugal community.

Consanguinity The relation of persons descended from the same stock or common ancestor.

Conscience The faculty of judging the moral quality of actions or of discriminating between right and wrong.

Conscientious objector One who by reason of religious training and belief is sincerely opposed to war in any form.

Conscript To draft.

Conscription Compulsory enrollment and induction into military service.

Consecutive Succeeding one another in regular order.

Consecutive sentences One sentence of imprisonment begins after another sentence of imprisonment ends.

Conseil d'état Council of state (France) that decides or advises upon state questions and measures proposed for legislation, submitted to it by the President of the Republic, by the members of the Cabinet, and by Parliament.

Consensual Coming into existence through consent.

Consensus Collective agreement.

Consensus ad idem An agreement of parties to the same thing; a meeting of minds.

Consent 1. To agree or approve. **2.** A voluntary agreement by a person, in the possession and exercise of sufficient mental capacity, to make an intelligent choice to do something proposed by another.

Consent degree Agreement by the defendant to cease activities that the government asserts are illegal.

When the court approves the agreement, the government's action against the defendant is dropped.

Consent dividend For purposes of avoiding or reducing the penalty tax on the unreasonable accumulation of earnings or the personal holding company tax, a corporation may declare a consent dividend. No cash or property is distributed to the shareholders although the corporation obtains a dividends paid deduction. The consent dividend is taxed to the shareholders and increases the basis in their stock investment.

Consent judgment A judgment whose terms are settled and agreed to by the parties to the action.

Consequence That which follows from an earlier occurrence.

Consequential damages Damages, losses, or injuries that do not directly and immediately flow from the act of the defendant. They result from special circumstances that are not ordinarily predictable.

Conservator Someone appointed by the court to manage the affairs of an incompetent person, to liquidate a business, etc.

Consider To fix the mind on something in order to examine it carefully.

Consideration That which induces someone to enter a contract, e.g., a right, interest, benefit, or profit accruing to one party; or a forbearance, detriment, loss, or responsibility assumed by the other party.

Consign To entrust goods; to deliver goods to a merchant for sale.

Consignee One to whom a consignment is made. A person to whom goods are shipped for sale. A person named in a bill of lading to whom or to whose order the bill promises delivery.

Consignment The commitment of property for sale by the consignee for the consignor. A bailment for sale, the transportation of consigned goods, agency for sale.

Consignor One who sends or makes a consignment. one who ships goods. The person named in a bill of lading as the person from whom the goods have been received for shipment.

Consiliarius In the civil law, a counsellor, as distinguished from a pleader or advocate. An assistant judge. One who participates in the decisions.

Consilium A day appointed to hear the counsel of both parties. A case set down for argument.

Consistent 1. Being in agreement with itself or with something else. **2.** Regular.

Consistor A magistrate.

Consistory courts In England, the courts of diocesan bishops for the trial of all ecclesiastical causes and for granting probates and administrations.

Consolation Comfort, pleasure, ease.

Consolidate 1. To unify into one mass or body. **2.** To solidify or strengthen.

Consolidated laws A compilation of all the laws of a state in force, arranged according to subject matter.

Consolidation The combination of two or more corporations into a newly created corporation. The old corporations are extinguished, and the new one takes over the assets and liabilities of the old.

Consolidation of actions Uniting several suits or actions into one trial where they all involve the same parties in the same court and have substantially similar subject matters, issues, and defenses.

Consonant statement A prior hearsay declaration of a witness whose credibility has been impeached, which the court will allow to be proved by the person to whom the declaration was made in order to support the credibility of the witness.

Consortium 1. The society, affection, assistance, conjugal fellowship, and sexual relations that one spouse has a right to expect from another. **2.** A coalition of companies or groups.

Conspiracy A combination or confederacy between two or more persons formed for the purpose of joining efforts to commit some unlawful or criminal act.

Conspire To engage in a conspiracy.

Constable An officer (often elected) of a municipality who has duties similar to that of a sheriff (e.g., preserve the peace, execute process, serve writs, maintain custody of juries).

Constat It is clear or evident.

Constating instruments Instruments of a corporation that include its charter, organic law, or the grant of powers to it.

Constituency 1. The inhabitants of an electoral district. **2.** Supporters.

Constituent 1. A voter in a certain district. **2.** Component. **3.** With the authority to make law (constituent assembly).

Constituted authorities Properly appointed officers.

Constitution 1. The fundamental law of a nation or state that establishes the branches and powers of the government and the basic principles for the regulation of society to which officials, citizens, and all other laws must conform. **2.** The physical structure of something.

Constitutional Consistent with the constitution.

Constitutional court A court expressly named or established by the U.S. Constitution. An Article III court.

Constitutional officer A governmental official whose tenure and term of office are fixed and defined by the constitution, as distinguished from the incumbents of offices created by the legislature.

Constitutional right A right guaranteed to the citizens by the Constitution, with which the legislature or others must not interfere.

Constitutional tort When a person subjects another to a deprivation of any rights, privileges, or immunities secured by the Constitution and laws while acting under color of any statute, ordinance, regulation, custom, or usage of a state or territory, that person shall be liable to the injured party in an action at law, suit in equity, or other proper proceeding for redress.

Constraint 1. Coercion. **2.** Confinement.

Construction 1. The process of determining the sense, real meaning, or proper explanation of obscure or ambiguous terms in a statute, contract, will, etc. **2.** Building.

Construction contract A contract in which the plans and specifications for construction (e.g., of a building) are made a part of the contract itself. The contract is often secured by performance and payment bonds.

Constructive True legally even if not factually.

Constructive authority Authority inferred or assumed to have been given because of the grant of some other prior authority.

Constructive contract An obligation created by law for reasons of justice without regard to expressions of assent by either words or acts.

Constructive delivery Those acts that are equivalent to acts of real delivery. A constructive delivery of personalty takes place when the goods are set apart and notice is given to the person to whom they are to be delivered, or when, without actual transfer of the goods or their symbol, the conduct of the parties is such as to be inconsistent with any other supposition than that there has been a change in the nature of the holding.

Constructive desertion Arises when one spouse, through misconduct, forces the other to abandon the marital abode. The former spouse is the deserting party in the eyes of the law.

Constructive eviction Occurs when the landlord makes the rented premises uninhabitable or unfit for the tenant. If the tenant leaves because of this condition, the landlord has evicted him or her.

Constructive knowledge Knowledge of a fact that the law presumes a person has if, in the exercise of reasonable care, he or she would have known

it (e.g., knowledge of a matter of public record).

Constructive notice Notice that the law presumes a person has by reason of the obvious or notorious nature of the subject of the notice.

Constructive possession Possession that one has the power and the intent to control even though not actually possessing it. Hence, you can be in possession of your apartment even if you are not in it at a given time.

Constructive service of process Form of service of process other than actual service (e.g., publication in newspaper).

Constructive taking An act not amounting to an actual taking of personal property but shows an intent to convert it to one's own use.

Constructive trust A trust created by operation of law against one who has improperly obtained possession of or legal rights to property through fraud, duress, abuse of confidence, or other unconscionable conduct.

Construe To determine the meaning of language.

Constuprate To ravish or rape.

Consul An officer appointed by a country to watch over commercial and tourist interests and its citizens in foreign countries.

Consular courts Courts held by the consuls of one country, within the territory of another, under authority given by treaty, for the settlement of civil cases.

Consulate The residence or headquarters of a foreign consul.

Consul general Consular officer of highest grade.

Consultation 1. Seeking advice. **2.** A conference.

Consumer A person who purchases, uses, keeps, and disposes of goods and services.

Consumer credit sale Any sale in which consumer credit (loan) is extended to or arranged by the seller.

Consumer Price Index (CPI) A price index computed and printed monthly by the U.S. Bureau of Labor Statistics, which tracks the price level of a group of goods and services purchased by the average consumer.

Consumers' cooperative A corporation or association owned and often managed by its members who, along with nonmembers, buy goods and services through the organization to secure price and quality advantages through bulk purchases and quantity discounts, and whose members share in the resulting profits.

Consummation The completion of a thing; the completion of a marriage by sexual intercourse between spouses.

Consumption 1. Using up something; waste. **2.** Tuberculosis.

Contact Touching.

Contaminate To make impure by mixture or contact with a foreign substance.

Contemplate 1. To view or consider with continued attention. **2.** To anticipate.

Contemplation Consideration of an event or state of facts with the expectation that it will happen.

Contemplation of death The apprehension or expectation of approaching death due to present sickness or impending danger.

Contemporaneous Occurring at the same time.

Contempt A willful disregard or disobedience of a public authority.

Contempt of court An act that is calculated to embarrass, hinder, or obstruct the court in the administration of justice, or that is calculated to lessen the court's authority or dignity.

Contentious 1. Quarrelsome. **2.** Contested, in opposition.

Contentious jurisdiction That part of the jurisdiction of a court that is concerned with contested matters, as opposed to voluntary, undisputed matters.

Conterminous Having a common boundary.

Contest 1. To raise a defense to an adverse claim. **2.** A competition.

Context That which surrounds words or sentences and helps to determine their meaning.

Contiguous 1. Touching, sharing a boundary. **2.** In close proximity.

Continental Congress The first national legislative assembly in the United States. It met in 1774.

Contingency An event that may or may not occur.

Contingency reserve In accounting, a fund created in anticipation of unforeseen expenditures.

Contingency with double aspect A remainder is said to be "in a contingency with double aspect" when there is another remainder limited on the same estate, not in derogation of the first, but as a substitute for it in case it should fail.

Contingent Possible but not assured, conditional.

Contingent beneficiary A person who may or will receive a benefit, but only if the primary beneficiary becomes disqualified for the benefit (e.g., by death).

Contingent estate, interest, or right An estate, interest, or right that depends for its effect on an event that may or may not happen.

Contingent fee A contractual arrangement whereby an attorney agrees to represent the client with the compensation to be a percentage of the amount recovered for the client.

Contingent remainder A remnant of an estate that is either (a) limited to a person not in being or not certain or ascertained, or (b) limited to a certain person when his or her right to the estate depends on some uncertain event in the future.

Continuance The adjournment or postponement of a session, hearing, trial, or other proceeding to a later day or time.

Continuando A form of allegation in which the wrongful act complained of is charged to have been committed on a specified day and to have "continued" to the present time.

Continuing Enduring, subsisting; not terminated by one act or occurrence.

Continuing jurisdiction A court that once acquired jurisdiction on a case continues to possess it in order to modify its orders.

Continuing offense At crime committed over a span of time as, for example, a conspiracy.

Continuous Uninterrupted.

Continuous offense A crime that is committed over a span of time. The last act of the offense controls for purposes of the beginning of the statute of limitations.

Contra Against, opposite to, on the contrary.

Contra accounts In accounting, those accounts that are related to and should be shown with their cognate accounts (e.g., reserve for depreciation should be shown with the asset being depreciated).

Contraband Property that is unlawful to produce, possess, transport, or import.

Contra bonos mores Against good morals.

Contracausator A criminal; one prosecuted for a crime.

Contract A legally binding agreement that creates an obligation to do or not to do a particular thing. There must be mutuality of agreement and obligation, legal consideration, and competent parties.

Contract clause U.S. Const., Art. I, Sec. 10, providing that no state shall pass a law impairing the obligation of contract.

Contract for deed An agreement by a seller to deliver the deed to the property when certain conditions have been met (e.g., completion of the payments by the buyer).

Contraction Abbreviation; abridgment or shortening of a word by omitting a letter or letters.

Contract of sale An agreement under which the seller agrees to convey title to property upon payment by the buyer under the terms of the contract.

Contractor See independent contractor. In the construction industry, a contractor is one who contracts to erect buildings or portions of them. There can be contractors for each phase of construction: heating, electrical, plumbing, air conditioning, roads, bridges, etc.

Contract system The labor of prisoners utilized by private persons or contractors.

Contradict To deny; to prove the contrary.

Contradictory judgment A judgment that has been given after the parties have been heard. Used in Louisiana to distinguish such judgments from those rendered by default.

Contraindicate To suggest or show that an approach or treatment is not recommended or warranted.

Contrainte par corps In French law, the civil process of arrest of the person.

Contra pacem Against the peace.

Contra proferentem An ambiguous provision is construed most strongly against the person who in a written document selected the language.

Contravene To violate or go against.

Contravening equity A right or equity, in another person, that is inconsistent with and opposed to the equity sought to be enforced or recognized.

Contribute 1. To help produce or bring about. **2.** To lend assistance to or aid a common purpose.

Contributing cause Any factor that contributes to a result.

Contribution A tortfeasor against whom a judgment is rendered is entitled to recover proportional shares of the judgment from other joint tortfeasors whose negligence contributed to the injury and who are also liable to the plaintiff.

Contributory 1. Lending assistance to or having a part in bringing about a given result. **2.** A person liable to contribute to the assets of a company which is being wound up, as being a member or a past member thereof.

Contributory negligence An unreasonable act or omission on the part of the complaining party that, concurring with the defendant's negligence, is the proximate cause of the injury.

Contrite Remorseful.

Contrivance Any device that has been arranged to deceive.

Control 1. To exercise a directing influence over something. **2.** To restrain. **3.** Power to regulate.

Controversy 1. A concrete case admitting of an immediate and definitive determination of legal rights of parties in an adversary proceeding upon facts alleged. Claims based merely on assumed potential invasions of rights are not enough. **2.** A dispute.

Controvert To take issue with.

Contumacious Rebellious, disobedient.

Contumacy The refusal or intentional failure to appear in court as required, or to obey a court order.

Contumax One accused of a crime who refuses to appear and answer the charge.

Contusion Wound or bruise.

Conusance Cognizance or jurisdiction.

Conusant Cognizant; having actual knowledge.

Convalescence Gradual recovery of health.

Convenable Suitable; agreeable.

Convene 1. To call together. **2.** In the civil law, to bring an action.

Convenient Suitable; easy to use.

Conventicle A private assembly or meeting for the exercise of religion.

Convention 1. An agreement (Geneva Convention). **2.** A formal meeting (Democratic Convention). **3.** A custom (wigs are not a U.S. Court convention).

Conventional 1. Conforming to generally accepted practices. **2.** Arising from the mutual agreement of the parties rather than created by operation of law.

Conventional mortgage A mortgage loan not insured by the Department of Housing and Urban Development or guaranteed by the Veterans' Administration. It is subject to rates and other conditions established by the lending institution and state statutes.

Conversant Familiar.

Conversation 1. Talk or discussion. **2.** Manner of living. See Criminal Conversation.

Conversion The unauthorized exercise of dominion or control over someone's personal property (chattel). Elements: (a) a chattel; (b) the plaintiff is in possession of the chattel or is entitled to immediate possession of the chattel; (c) the defendant intends to exercise dominion or control over the chattel; (d) there is a serious interference with the plaintiff's possession; (e) that is caused by the defendant.

Convert 1. To misappropriate. **2.** To change the character or function of something. **3.** To make an equivalent exchange.

Convertible Capable of being changed.

Convertible bond A bond that can, at the option of the holder, be converted into stock.

Convertible securities A bond, debenture, or preferred share that may be exchanged by the owner for common stock or another security, usually of the same company, in accordance with the terms of the issue.

Convertible term insurance Term insurance that offers the policyholder the option of exchanging it for a permanent plan of insurance without evidence of insurability.

Convey To transfer or deliver to another.

Conveyance The transfer of an interest in land (e.g., title, mortgage, lease, assignment).

Conveyancer One whose business is to prepare deeds and mortgages, examine title, and perform other functions relating to the transfer of real estate.

Conveyancing Performing the various functions relating to the transfer of real property.

Convict 1. To find a person guilty of a criminal charge. **2.** A person in prison serving a sentence.

Conviction 1. A judgment of guilty following a verdict or finding of guilt, a plea of guilty, or a plea of nolo contendere. **2.** A firm belief.

Convincing proof Proof that is sufficient to establish the proposition in question beyond hesitation, ambiguity, or reasonable doubt in an unprejudiced mind.

Convocation In ecclesiastical law, the general assembly of the clergy.

Convoy An escort for protection.

Co-obligor Someone bound jointly with another (or others) in a bond or obligation.

Cool blood In the law of homicide, the absence of passion; calmness, in possession of one's faculties.

Cooling-off period A period of time in which no action of a particular sort may be taken by either side in a dispute.

Cooperate To act jointly or concurrently toward a common end.

Cooperation The association of persons for a common benefit.

Cooperative 1. A business owned by its customers. A corporation or association organized for the purpose of rendering economic services (without gain to itself) to shareholders or members who own and control it. **2.** Accommodating.

Cooperative federalism The distribution of power between (a) the national government and (b) the local or state governments, with each recognizing the powers of the other.

Cooperative housing An apartment building or a group of dwellings owned by a corporation, the stockholders of which are the residents of the dwellings. It is operated for their benefit by their elected board of directors. In a cooperative, the corporation or association owns title to the real estate. A resident purchases stock in the corporation which entitles him or her to occupy a unit in the building or property owned by the cooperative. While the resident does not own a unit, he or she has an absolute right to occupy his or her unit for as long as he or she owns the stock.

Cooperative insurance A type of non-stock mutual insurance in which the policyholders are the owners.

Co-optation The election, by the members of a close corporation, of a person to fill a vacancy.

Coordinate 1. To adjust or bring together for integrated action. **2.** Of the same or equal order, rank, degree, or importance.

Coordinate jurisdiction Jurisdiction possessed by courts of equal rank or authority to deal with the matter in question. Concurrent jurisdiction.

Cop a plea To plead guilty.

Coparcenary An estate that arises when several persons inherit property (from the same ancestor) to share as if they were one person or one heir.

Coparceners Persons to whom an estate of inheritance descends jointly, and by whom it is held as an entire estate.

Copartner A member of a partnership.

Copesmate A merchant; a partner in merchandise.

Coprincipal 1. One of two or more participants in a crime who actually perpetrates the crime or who is present, aiding and abetting the persons who commit it. **2.** One of two or more persons who has appointed agents whom he or she has the right to control.

Copy A reproduction of the original.

Copyhold An old form of holding land at the will of the lord. Records of this estate were often kept in court rolls according to local custom.

Copyright The intangible right or privilege of an author (or other originator) to control for a limited period the copying, publication, and sale of books, articles, movies, records, or other original works of authorship fixed in any tangible medium of expression. Copyright is a limited monopoly or franchise granted by statute or by common law.

Coram nobis In our presence; before us. A writ of coram nobis asks a court to reform its own judgment due to an error or mistake of fact that did not appear on the face of the record because of fraud, duress, or excusable neglect (e.g., the petition did not present certain facts during the trial because the other side fraudulently prevented the petitioner from discovering them). If the facts had been known, the same judgment allegedly would not have been rendered.

Coram vobis Before you. A writ of error (to correct an error of fact) directed by a court of review to the court that tried the case.

Cord A measure of wood containing 128 cubic feet, otherwise expressed as a pile of wood 8 feet long, 4 feet high, and 4 feet wide.

Co-respondent A person summoned with another to answer a bill, petition, or libel (he was charged with adultery as the co-respondent in their divorce case).

Corner A combination among dealers in a specific commodity to buy up most of that commodity and hold it back from sale until the price rises.

Corollary An obvious or easily drawn deduction or inference.

Coroner A public official who has the duty to make inquiry into the causes and circumstances of any death that occurs through violence or suddenly and with marks of suspicion (i.e., an unnatural death). A medical examiner.

Corporal Physical; relating to the human body.

Corporal imbecility Physical inability to perform completely the act of sexual intercourse.

Corporal punishment Punishment of or inflicted on the body. Physical punishment. Depending on the context, the phrase may or may not include imprisonment itself.

Corporate Pertaining to a corporation.

Corporate bonds A written promise by a corporation to pay a fixed sum of money at a future time with stated interest payable at a fixed time or at intervals, given in return for money or its equivalent received by the corporation.

Corporate charter A document issued by a state agency (e.g., secretary of state), granting a proposed corporation its legal existence and right to function as a corporation.

Corporate veil See piercing the corporate veil.

Corporation 1. An organization that is an artificial person or legal entity created by or under the authority of the government. The corporation has an existence that is distinct from its members (shareholders).

Corporation de facto A corporation that has been defectively formed but in good faith.

Corporation de jure A corporation that exists by reason of full compliance by the incorporators

with the requirements of existing law.

Corporeal Perceptible by the senses.

Corporeal hereditaments Substantial permanent objects that may be inherited.

Corpse The dead body of a human being.

Corpus 1. Body, aggregate, collection. **2.** Principal sum as opposed to interest or income.

Corpus delicti The body of a crime. The material substance upon which a crime has been committed (e.g., the charred remains of a house that has been burned).

Corpus Juris 1. A body of law; collections of law. **2.** The first edition of a legal encyclopedia by West Publishing Company.

Corpus Juris Civilis The body of the civil law. The system of Roman jurisprudence compiled and codified under the direction of Emperor Justinian in A.D. 528–534, consisting of the Institutes, Digest (or Pandects), Code, and Novels.

Corpus Juris Secundum (C.J.S.) The second edition of a legal encyclopedia by West Publishing Company.

Correction 1. The act or system of imposing discipline and treatment for offenders (Board of Corrections). **2.** That which is presented as a substitute for an error.

Correspondent A securities firm, bank, or other financial organization that regularly performs services for another in a place or market to which the other does not have direct access.

Corroborate To add weight or credibility to a thing by additional and confirming facts or evidence.

Corroborating evidence Evidence supplementary to that already given, which tends to strengthen or confirm it. Additional evidence of a different character to the same point.

Corrupt 1. Spoiled; morally degenerate. **2.** To change one's morals and principles from good to bad.

Corruption An act done with the intent to give some advantage that is inconsistent with an official or fiduciary duty and the rights of others.

Cosa juzgada In Spanish law, a cause or matter adjudged (res judicata).

Cosas comunes In Spanish law, things open to the common enjoyment of all persons such as the air, the sea, and the water of running streams.

Cosign To sign an instrument or document with another.

Cosignatory One who cosigns.

Cost 1. The sum (or equivalent) expended, paid or charged for something. **2.** A loss or detriment.

Cost and freight (C & F) The quoted sales price

includes the cost of goods and freight but not insurance or other special charges.

Cost bond A bond given by a party to an action to secure the eventual payment of such costs as may be awarded against him or her.

Costing The assignment of a monetary value to each clause in a given contract to assess the total cost of the contract. A system used to calculate actual losses during production.

Cost of living clause A contract clause (often in union, pension, and retirement agreements) providing an automatic wage or benefit increase that is tied to cost-of-living rises in the economy as measured by indicators such as the Consumer Price Index (CPI).

Cost of living rider A live insurance option that permits the policyholder to purchase increasing term insurance coverage. The death proceeds increase by a stated amount each year, to coincide with an estimated increase in the cost of living.

Cost-plus contract A contract that fixes the amount to be paid to a contractor based on the cost of the material and labor plus an agreed percentage thereof as profit.

Costs A monetary allowance made to the successful party in litigation (and recoverable from the losing party) for the expenses incurred in bringing or defending the action (e.g., filing and service expenses). Attorney fees are usually not included. Costs are entirely separate from what is sought or won in the litigation itself.

Costs, insurance and freight (C.I.F.) The quoted sales price includes the cost of goods, freight and insurance.

Co-sureties Two or more sureties to the same obligation.

Cotenancy An interest in property whereby two or more persons have an undivided right to possession (e.g., tenancy in common, joint tenancy).

Coterie An exclusive association of persons.

Cotuchans A term used in Domesday for peasants.

Coulisse The stockbrokers' curb market in Paris.

Council A group of people who convene to advise, assist, or legislate.

Council of the bar A body composed of members of the English bar that hears complaints against barristers and reports its findings with recommendations to the benchers of the Inn of Court of which the barrister is a member.

Counsel 1. An attorney. **2.** Advice and assistance given by one person to another.

Counsel of record An attorney who has filed a notice of appearance for a party in court.

Count In pleading, a separate and independent claim or charge (Count I, Count II, etc.).

Countenance 1. To give approval or encouragement. **2.** Face, expression.

Counter To oppose; adverse.

Counter-bond A bond that indemnifies a surety.

Counterclaim A cause of action or claim asserted by one or more defendants against one or more plaintiffs in the same action.

Counter-deed A secret writing, either before a notary or under a private seal, that destroys, invalidates, or alters a public one.

Counterfeit 1. To copy without authority in order to deceive by passing off the copy as genuine. **2.** Fake.

Counter-letter A species of instrument of defeasance common in the civil law. It is executed by a party who has taken a deed of property, absolute on its face, but intended as security for a loan of money, and by it he or she agrees to reconvey the property on payment of a specified sum. The two instruments, taken together, constitute what is known in Louisiana as an antichresis.

Countermand To change or revoke instructions or authority previously issued.

Counteroffer A statement by the offeree that has the legal effect of rejecting the offer and of proposing a new offer to the offeror.

Counterpart In conveyancing, the corresponding part of an instrument; a duplicate or copy.

Countersign 1. To sign in addition to the signature of another in order to attest authenticity. **2.** To underwrite.

Countervailing equity A contrary and balancing equity; an equity or right opposed to that which is sought to be enforced or recognized, and which ought not to be sacrificed or subordinated to the latter, because it is of equal strength and justice, and equally deserving of consideration.

Counter wills Another name for "double," "mutual," or "reciprocal" wills.

Country 1. The territory occupied by an independent nation or people. **2.** Pertaining to a rural or farm area.

County the largest territorial division of a local government in many states.

County commissioners Officers of a county, charged with the management of the affairs of the county. In some states they are called supervisors.

Coupon An interest or dividend certificate in detachable form.

Coupon bond A bond with interest coupons attached. The coupons are clipped as they come due and are presented by the holder for payment of interest.

Course 1. The path or direction that something takes; the typical or normal manner of proceeding. **2.** In surveying, the direction of a line with reference to a meridian.

Course of business What is usually and normally done in the management of a trade or business.

Course of dealing A sequence of previous acts and conduct between the parties to a particular transaction, which fairly establishes a common basis of understanding for interpreting their communications and other conduct.

Course of employment As a worker's compensation term: A worker is in the course of employment when, within the time covered by the employment, he or she is doing something at a proper place, which he or she might reasonably do while so employed. See scope of employment.

Court A unit of the judicial branch of government that applies the law to disputes and administers justice.

Court above The court to which a case is appealed.

Court below The court from which a case is appealed (normally the trial court).

Court-martial A military or naval court, operating under the Code of Military Justice, for trying and punishing offenses committed by members of the armed forces.

Court of Admiralty A court having jurisdiction of admiralty and maritime matters.

Court of Appeals for the Federal Circuit A federal court that reviews decisions of the United States Claims Court and the Court of International Trade.

Court of Chancery A court administering equity; a court that proceeds according to the forms and principles of equity; a court of equity as distinguished from a common-law court.

Court of Claims A court that hears designated claims of individuals against the government (e.g., breach-of-contract claims).

Court of Customs and Patent Appeals See Court of Appeals for the Federal Circuit.

Court of Equity See Court of Chancery.

Court of Error A court of last resort with the power to review the decision of lower courts.

Court of first instance A court of original or primary jurisdiction (e.g., a trial court).

Court of general jurisdiction A court having unlimited trial jurisdiction, both civil and criminal.

Court of General Sessions The name given in some states to a court of general, original jurisdiction in criminal cases.

Court of King's (or Queen's) Bench In English law, the supreme court of common law in the kingdom.

Court of last resort A court whose decision is final.

Court of law 1. Any duly constituted tribunal administering the laws of the state or nation. **2.** A court proceeding according to the common law as contrasted with a court of equity.

Court of limited jurisdiction A court with jurisdiction over only certain types of matters (e.g., probate).

Court of Military Appeals An appellate tribunal that reviews court-martial convictions in the armed services.

Court of Nisi Prius A trial court with a jury and one presiding judge; any court of general, original jurisdiction in civil cases.

Court of Orphans A probate or surrogates court with general jurisdiction over matters of probate, estate administration, orphans, wards, and guardians.

Court of Oyer and Terminer and General Gaol (or Jail) Delivery Formerly, a court of criminal jurisdiction in Pennsylvania.

Court of record A court that is required to keep a record of its proceedings and that may fine or imprison.

Court of Sessions A court of criminal jurisdiction.

Court packing An attempt to restructure a court so that people who agree with the appointing chief executive's views are chosen.

Court reporter 1. A person who transcribes testimony by shorthand (or who takes it down stenographically) during court proceedings or during trial-related proceedings such as depositions. **2.** The person responsible for the publications of the opinions of the court; the Reporter of Decisions.

Court rules Regulations with the force of law, governing practice and procedure in various courts (e.g., the Federal Rules of Civil Procedure).

Cousin The male or female child of the brother or sister of one's father or mother; kindred in the fourth degree.

Covenable Convenient or suitable (French).

Covenant An agreement, convention, or promise of two or more parties, by deed in writing, signed and delivered, by which one of the parties (a) pledges to the other that something is done, shall be done, or shall not be done, or (b) stipulates the truth of certain facts.

Covenant against incumbrances A covenant that there are no incumbrances on the land conveyed.

Covenantee The party to whom a covenant is made.

Covenant for further assurance An undertaking, in the form of a covenant, on the part of the vendor of real estate to do such further acts for the purpose of perfecting the purchaser's title as the latter may reasonably require.

Covenant for quiet enjoyment An assurance against the consequence of a defective title and of any disturbances by hostile claimants.

Covenant in gross One that does not run with the land.

Covenant of seisin An assurance to the purchaser that the grantor has the very estate in quantity and quality the latter purports to convey.

Conventor The party who makes a covenant.

Covenant running with the land A covenant that goes with the land and cannot be separated from it. The land cannot be transferred without the covenant. Hence, future buyers of the land are bound by it.

Cover 1. To protect by means of insurance. **2.** To conceal. **3.** To include. **4.** The right of a buyer, after breach by a seller, to purchase goods in substitution for those due from the seller if such purchase is made in good faith and without unreasonable delay.

Coverage The amount and extent of risk covered by an insurer.

Cover note A written statement by an insurance agent that coverage is in effect. Distinguished from the binder that is prepared by the company.

Covert Concealed.

Coverture The condition or state of a married woman.

Covin A secret conspiracy or agreement between two or more persons to injure or defraud another.

Convinous Deceitful.

Craft 1. A trade or occupation requiring skill and training, particularly manual skill, combined with a knowledge of the principles of the art. **2.** Deception.

Craft union A labor union whose members do the same kind of work for different employers and industries.

Create To bring into being.

Credentials Documentary evidence of a person's authority or capacity.

Credibility Worthiness of belief.

Credible Worthy of belief.

Credit The right to delay payment; the ability of a business or person to borrow money or to obtain goods on time, as a result of the favorable opinion that the lender has of the borrower's solvency and reliability.

Credit bureau Establishments that make a business of collecting information relating to the credit, character, and reputation of businesses and individuals in order to furnish the information as credit reports to subscribers (e.g., merchants, banks).

Credit line The limit of money that may be borrowed or merchandise purchased on credit.

Creditor A person to whom a debt is owed by another; one who has the right to require the fulfillment of an obligation or contract.

Creditor's bill or **suit** An equitable proceeding brought to enforce payment of a debt out of the property or other interest of the debtor that cannot be reached by execution at law.

Credit rating The evaluation of a person's or a business's ability and past performance in paying debts.

Creditrix A female creditor.

Credit union A cooperative association that uses money deposited by a defined group of persons (e.g., fellow employees) and lends it out again to persons within this group at favorable interest rates.

Crier An officer of the court who makes proclamations (e.g., announces the opening of the court, calls the names of jurors, witnesses, and parties).

Crime A positive or negative act that violates the penal law of the state or federal government; any act done in violation of those duties that an individual owes to the community and for the breach of which the law has decided that the offender shall make satisfaction to the public.

Crimen Crime (crimen furti—crime of theft).

Criminal One who has been convicted of a crime.

Criminal contempt A crime involving the obstruction of judicial duty; conduct directed against the dignity and authority of the court, often in the presence of a judge.

Criminal Conversation (Crim. Con.) A tort against the marriage bed: The defendant has sexual relations with the plaintiff's spouse.

Criminal libel Criminal libel is the malicious publication of durable defamation.

Criminal negligence The failure to use the degree of care required to avoid criminal consequences. Negligence for which the law imposes a criminal penalty.

Criminal nonsupport The willful and unreasonable failure to support those whom one is legally obligated to support.

Criminal syndicalism Any doctrine or precept advocating, teaching, or aiding the commission of the crime of sabotage or unlawful acts of violence or terrorism as a means of achieving industrial or political change.

Criminal trespass An offense that is committed when one, without license or privilege, enters or surreptitiously remains in a building or on the property of another. The person does so knowingly, intentionally, or recklessly when he or she has notice that this conduct is not allowed.

Criminate To charge one with a crime; implicate.

Criminology The science that studies the causes, prevention, and punishment of crimes.

Crop Products of the soil annually grown, raised, and harvested.

Cross-action An independent suit brought by a defendant against a plaintiff or a co-defendant.

Cross appeal An appeal by the appellee.

Cross-claim A related claim by one party against a co-party.

Cross-complaint A pleading filed by the defendant, stating any related cause of action the defendant has against a party who filed the complaint against the defendant, or against a person alleged to be liable thereon whether or not this person is currently a party.

Cross-demand When a person against whom a demand is made by another in turn makes a demand against that other, these mutual demands are called cross-demands (e.g., a set-off).

Cross-examination The examination of a witness (at a trial, hearing, or deposition) by the other side after the direct examination of the witness by the side that initially called the witness.

Cross-remainder Property that is given to several persons as a group. As each person dies, the others share that person's interest.

Crown The sovereign power and position of a monarch.

Crown cases In English law, criminal prosecutions on behalf of the crown representing the public; causes in the criminal courts.

Cruel Causing suffering intentionally or recklessly; being indifferent to suffering.

Cruel and unusual punishment Such punishment that would amount to torture or barbarity; any degrading punishment not known to the common law; punishment that is so disproportionate to the offense as to shock the moral sense of the community; uncivilized and inhumane punishment.

Cruelty The intentional and malicious infliction of physical or mental suffering on living creatures.

Cuckold A man whose wife is unfaithful.

Cui bono For whose use or benefit.

Cul-de-sac A blind alley; a street open at one end only; an impasse.

Culpa Fault.

Culpability Blameworthiness.

Culpable Pertaining to that which is deserving of moral blame.

Cum With.

Cum dividend When a share of stock is sold after a dividend is declared, the buyer has the right to the dividend.

Cum testamento annexo With the will annexed. See administration cum testamento annex.

Cumulative Involving the addition of things together.

Cumulative evidence Addition or corroborative evidence to the same point.

Cumulative legacies Legacies given in addition to a prior legacy.

Cumulative preferred dividend A dividend on preferred stock which, if declared at the end of a particular year, must be paid before any common stock dividend is paid.

Cumulative sentence A sentence that is to take effect after the expiration of a prior sentence.

Cumulative stock A type of stock on which unpaid dividends accumulate until paid.

Cumulative voting A type of voting in which the number of members of the board of directors to be elected is multiplied by the total number of voting shares a shareholder has. The result equals the number of votes a shareholder has. This total can be cast for one or more nominees for director.

Cunnilingus A sexual act in which the mouth or lips come into contact with the female sexual organs.

Cura Care; guardianship.

Curateur In French law, a person charged with supervising the administration of the affairs of an emancipated minor.

Curatio In the civil law, the power or duty of managing the property of an incompetent.

Curative Tending to cure; avoiding the ordinary legal consequences of defects or errors.

Curator 1. A temporary guardian or conservator appointed by the court to care for the property or person of an incompetent, a spendthrift, or a minor. **2.** The manager of a museum or collection.

Curator ad litem Guardian for the suit or action.

Cure To correct or heal (the motion cured the defect).

Curfew A rule on when individuals must be off the streets.

Curia A court of justice.

Curia regis The king's court.

Curing title Removing those defects from the title to land that make it unmarketable; removing any clouds on the title.

Currency Authorized money (i.e., coin and paper money) that circulates from hand to hand as the medium of exchange.

Current Present existence.

Current market value The present value of an asset that may be realized in an arm's length transaction between a willing buyer and a willing seller.

Cursory examination An inspection for defects visible or ascertainable by ordinary examination; contrasted with a thorough examination.

Curtesy A husband's right to a life estate in the property left by his deceased wife.

Curtesy consummate The husband's curtesy interest in the estate of his wife after she dies if children were born of the marriage capable of inheriting.

Curtesy initiate The husband's curtesy interest in his wife's estate before she dies and after the birth of children capable of inheriting. An interest in expectancy.

Curtilage The enclosed space of ground and buildings immediately surrounding a dwelling-house.

Custodes In Roman law, guardians; inspectors.

Custodial interrogation Questioning initiated by law enforcement officers after a person has been taken into custody or otherwise deprived of his or her freedom in any significant way.

Custodian Someone who has charge or custody of property, papers, etc.

Custody 1. The care and control of a thing or person. **2.** Physical confinement.

Custom, customs 1. An established practice or habit. **2.** A tax on the importation and exportation of commodities.

Custom and usage A habitual or customary practice, more or less widespread, which prevails within a geographical or sociological area. By repetition and uninterrupted acquiescence, the practice acquires the force of a tacit and common consent.

Customary Founded on, growing out of, or dependent on a custom.

Customer One who makes purchases from or has other commercial dealings with a business.

Cut-over land Land that has been logged, from which desired timber has been removed.

Cutpurse One who steals by cutting purses (when men wore their purses at their girdles).

Cy In French law, here. Also as, so.

Cy-pres As near as possible. The intention of the author of an instrument (e.g., will, trust) will be carried out as near as can be, when giving the instrument its literal effect is impossible.

Daily 1. Every day in the week. **2.** Commonplace.

Damage 1. An injury or loss to person, property, or rights. **2.** To cause an injury or loss to person, property, or rights.

Damages Monetary compensation that may be recovered in court by someone who has suffered injury or loss to person, to property, or to rights through an unlawful act or omission of another.

Damna Damages.

Damnum absque injuria A loss that does not give rise to an action for damages against the person causing it.

Danelage A system of laws, introduced by the Danes on their invasion and conquest of England.

Danger Exposure to loss or injury, peril.

Dangerous Hazardous, attended with risk.

Dangerous instrumentality Anything that has the inherent capacity (by itself or through careless use) to place people in peril.

Dangerous per se A thing that may inflict injury without the immediate application of human aid or instrumentality.

Danism The act of lending money or usury.

Darrein Last.

Data Organized information often collected for a specific purpose (e.g., to make a decision).

Date 1. A specific point in time—day, month, year. **2.** To determine the time of something.

Date of issue An arbitrary date fixed or agreed upon as the beginning or effective date of a document, which may be later than the date the parties prepared the document.

Date of maturity The day on which a debt falls due.

Dative A word derived from the Roman law, signifying "appointed by public authority."

Day bill A promissory obligation for the payment of money that is payable on a certain date stated in the document.

Day loan One made to a broker on a day-to-day basis to finance his or her daily transactions.

Dead freight When a vessel is chartered, dead freight is the amount paid for the portion of the vessel that is contracted for but not used.

Deadly force Force, whether reasonable or unreasonable, that is likely or intended to cause death or great bodily harm.

Dead man's statute An evidential disqualification that renders inadmissible oral promises or declarations of a dead person when offered in support of claims against the estate of the dead person.

Deal 1. An arrangement to obtain a desired result by a combination of interested parties. **2.** To transact business.

Dealer One who buys goods for resale to final customers.

Dealer's talk The puffing of goods to induce their sale.

Dealings Transactions in the course of trade or business.

De arbitratione facta (Of arbitration had.) A writ used when an action is brought for a cause that has been settled by arbitration.

Death Permanent cessation of all vital functions and signs. See brain death. States have enacted laws that determine the moment of death for various purposes (e.g., discontinuation of life support systems).

Debasement Reducing the weight of gold and silver in coins or increasing the amount of alloy in such coins which has the effect of reducing their intrinsic value.

Debauchery Sexual immorality or excesses.

De bene esse Conditionally, provisionally.

Debenture A promissory note or bond backed by the general credit of a corporation and usually not secured by a mortgage or lien on any specific property.

Debet et detinet He owes and detains, words used in a writ on a debt.

De biens le mort Of the goods of the deceased.

Debit A sum due or owing; an entry made on the asset (left) side of a ledger or account.

Debit balance An accounting condition where there is an excess of debit over credit entries.

Debitor A debtor.

Debitrix A female debtor.

Debitum Something due, or owing, a debt.

De bone memorie Of good memory, of sound mind.

De bonis asportatis For taking away goods; for goods taken away (trespass de bonis asportatis).

De bonis non administratis Of the goods not administered. When an administrator is appointed to succeed another administrator who left the estate partially unsettled, the successor is granted administration de bonis non, that is, of the goods not already administered.

De bonis propiis Of his own goods.

Debt An amount of money that is due.

Debt adjusting Engaging in the business of entering contracts with the debtor, whereby the debtor agrees to pay a certain amount of money periodically to a person in the debt-adjusting business, who then distributes the money among certain creditors.

Debtee A person to whom a debt is due, a creditor.

Debt financing Funds raised by issuing bonds or notes—unlike equity financing by issuing stocks.

Debtor One who owes a debt.

Debt pooling An arrangement by which the debtor adjusts many debts by distributing his or her assets among several creditors who may or may not agree to take less than what is owed. An arrangement by which the debtor agrees to pay a sum of money in regular installments to one creditor who agrees to discharge all his or her debts.

Debt service The interest and charges currently payable on a debt, including principal payments.

Deceased A dead person.

Decedent A dead person.

Decedent's estate Real and personal property that a person possesses at the time of death.

Deceit A fraudulent and deceptive misrepresentation, artifice, or device used to deceive and trick another, who is ignorant of the true facts, to the prejudice and damage of the party imposed upon.

Decency Propriety of action, speech, manners, etc.

Decennial Concerning a 10-year period.

Deception Intentional misleading by spoken or acted falsehood.

Decessus In the civil law, death; departure.

Decide To arrive at the determination.

Decision A determination arrived at after a consideration of relevant factors (e.g., the facts and the law).

Declarant A person who makes a declaration.

Declaration 1. A formal statement. **2.** In common-law pleading, the first of the pleadings on the part of the plaintiff in an action at law.

Declaration against interest A statement that at the time made (a) conflicts with the pecuniary or proprietary interest of the person making it, or (b) tends to subject him or her to civil or criminal liability, or (c) tends to render invalid his or her claim against someone else.

Declaration of state of mind A statement concerning a person's state of mind (e.g., "I'm furious").

Declaration of trust The act by which the person who holds the legal title to property acknowledges that he or she holds it in trust to the use of another person or for certain specified purposes.

Declaratory Designed to fix or elucidate what has been uncertain or doubtful.

Declaratory covenant A covenant that serves to limit or direct uses.

Declaratory judgment A binding adjudication of the rights and status of the litigants in a justiciable controversy without granting any coercive relief (e.g., no damages are awarded, no injunction is issued).

Declaratory statute A statute enacted for the purpose of removing doubts or of putting an end to conflicting decisions as to what the law is in relation to a particular matter.

Declare To make known or to announce.

Declassify To make available; to remove security classification.

Declination 1. A document filed in court by a fiduciary who chooses not to serve in his or her named capacity. **2.** A plea to the court's jurisdiction on the ground that the judge is personally interested in the suit.

Decline 1. To refuse or reject. **2.** A decrease; a falling off or downward tendency.

Decoctor In the Roman law, a bankrupt; a spendthrift.

De computo Writ of account. A writ commanding a defendant to render a reasonable account to the plaintiff.

Decoy To lure, to entice by deception.

Decree The judgment of a court of equity or chancery.

Decree nisi A provisional decree that upon motion will be made absolute unless cause is shown against it.

Decree of nullity A decree adjudging the marriage to have been null and void ab initio.

Decree pro confesso A decree entered in a court of equity in favor of the complainant where the defendant has made no answer to the bill; the allegations are consequently taken "as confessed."

Decreet absolvitor A decree dismissing a claim, or acquitting a defendant.

Decreet arbitral An award of arbitrators.

Decrement The act of decreasing.

Decrepit 1. Disabled; weakened by defects. **2.** Dilapidated.

Decretal order A preliminary order that does not determine any question on the merits.

Decretals Letters of the pope determining some point or question in ecclesiastical law. The decretals form part of the body of canon law.

Decriminalization Officially declaring (through a new law) that acts or omissions that were once criminal are no longer criminal.

Decry To deprecate, disparage, or belittle.

Dedicate To appropriate and set apart one's private property to some public use.

Dedication 1. The appropriation of land, or an easement therein, by the owner for the use of the public and accepted for such use by or on behalf of the public. **2.** The first publication of a work, without having secured a copyright, is a dedication of it to the public.

De die in diem From day to day.

Dedimus potestatem (We have given power.) A writ or commission issuing out of chancery, empowering the person named therein to perform certain acts (e.g., a commission to take testimony).

Dedition The act of yielding up.

Deductible Capable of being taken away or subtracted.

Deduction 1. That which is deducted; the part taken away. **2.** In the civil law, a portion or thing that an heir has a right to take from the mass of the succession before any partition takes place.

Deed A conveyance of real property transferring title from the grantor to the grantee.

Deed indented, indenture In common-law conveyancing, a deed executed or purporting to be executed in parts, between two or more parties, and distinguished by having the edge of the paper or parchment on which it is written indented or cut at the top in a particular manner.

Deed in fee A deed conveying the title to land in fee simple with the usual covenants.

Deed of agency A revocable and voluntary trust for the payment of debts.

Deed of gift A deed executed and delivered without consideration.

Deed of separation An instrument by which, through the medium of some third person acting as trustee, provision is made by a husband for separation from his wife and for her separate maintenance.

Deed of trust An instrument used in some states, taking the place and serving the functions of a mortgage. Like a mortgage, a deed of trust is a security instrument whereby real property is given as security for a debt. However, in a deed of trust there are three parties to the instrument: the borrower, the trustee, and the lender (or beneficiary). In such a transaction, the borrower transfers the legal title for the property to the trustee who holds the property in trust as security for the payment of the debt to the lender or beneficiary. If the borrower pays the debt as agreed, the deed of trust becomes void. If, however, he or she defaults in the payment of the debt, the trustee may sell the property at a public sale, under the terms of the deed of trust. In most jurisdictions where the deed of trust is in force, the borrower is subject to having his or her property sold without benefit of legal proceedings. A few states have begun in recent years to treat the deed of trust like a mortgage.

Deed poll A deed made by one party only.

Deep pocket The defendant who has resources with which to pay a judgment if rendered.

Deface To mar or destroy the physical appearance of something.

De facto In fact.

De facto government A government that maintains itself by force against the will of the rightful legal government.

De facto officer An officer who is in actual possession of the office, but is not holding it in the manner prescribed by law.

De facto segregation Segregation that is inadvertent and without the active assistance of the government. It is caused by social, economic, and other factors rather than by state action.

Defalcate To embezzle.

Defalcation Misappropriation of funds.

Defalk To set off one claim against another.

Defamacast Defamation by broadcast.

Defamation Libel and slander, the two defamation torts. Generally, the elements of both torts are as follows: (a) a defamatory statement by the defendant, (b) of and concerning the plaintiff, (c) that is published, (d) causing damages.

Defamatory Injurious to reputation.

Defamatory per quod Those words that require an allegation of facts, aside from the words themselves, to show how the words were used to libel the plaintiff.

Defamatory per se Words that by themselves injure the reputation of the plaintiff. No external proof is needed.

Defamatory statement A statement of fact that in the eyes of at least a substantial and respectable minority of people would tend to harm the reputation of another by lowering him or her in the estimation of those people or by deterring them from associating with him or her.

Defame To injure someone's reputation.

Default An omission of that which ought to be done; the failure to carry out a duty.

Default judgment A judgment rendered against a party from whom affirmative relief was sought because the party failed to file an answer or otherwise defend the action.

Defeasance An instrument that defeats the force or operation of some other deed or estate.

Defeasance clause A provision in a mortgage that assures the revesting of title in the mortgagor when all of the terms and conditions of the mortgage have been met (e.g., making all the payments).

Defeasible Subject to being revoked or terminated upon the happening of specified conditions.

Defeat To prevent, frustrate, or circumvent.

Defect The lack of something required.

Defective Lacking in some particular that is essential to completeness, safety, or legal sufficiency.

Defend 1. To protect. **2.** To contest or oppose.

Defendant The person defending or denying; the person against whom relief or recovery is sought.

Defendemus We will defend.

Defendour A defendant (French).

Defeneration The act of lending money on usury.

Defense 1. Allegations of fact or legal theories offered to offset or defeat claims or demands. **2.** Protection.

Defense of property The use of force that is reasonable under the circumstances to protect one's property. Such force can be a defense to a tort or criminal action (e.g., assault).

Defensum An inclosure of land.

Defer To delay or postpone.

Deferred bonds Bonds carrying a provision that interest payments are postponed for a certain period of time.

Deferred compensation Compensation that will be taxed when received or upon the removal of certain restrictions on its receipt. It will not be taxed when earned.

Deferred stock The payment of dividends upon this type of stock is expressly postponed until some other class of stock has received a dividend, or until a certain liability or obligation of the corporation is discharged.

Deficiency A shortage or insufficiency.

Deficiency decree In a mortgage foreclosure suit, a decree for the balance of the indebtedness after applying the proceeds of a sale of the mortgaged property to such indebtedness.

Deficiency judgment A judgment for an unpaid balance after the creditor has used up all available secured property of the debtor.

Deficiency notice A notice of tax deficiency (90 day letter) which is a prerequisite to the jurisdiction of Tax Court.

Deficit An excess of expenditures over revenues.

Defile To corrupt or debase.

Define 1. To explain or state the exact meaning of words or phrases. **2.** To set the limits of something.

Definite Clearly defined.

Definite sentence A sentence of imprisonment for a specified number of years.

Definition An explanation of the meaning of language.

Definitive Complete, clear, final.

Deflation A decrease in price levels, currency, and available credit.

Defloration Seduction of, debauching.

Deforce To withhold wrongfully.

Deforciant One who wrongfully keeps the owner of lands and tenements out of the possession of them.

Deforciato The seizure of goods for satisfaction of a lawful debt.

Deformity A deformed or misshapen condition.

Defossion The punishment of being buried alive.

Defraud See deceit, fraud.

Defunct Having ceased to exist.

Degradation Moral or intellectual decadence.

Degrading Exposing someone to disgrace.

Degree 1. The measure or scope of something. **2.** Formal recognition from a school. **3.** A step in the line of descent.

Degrees of kindred The relationship between a deceased and his or her survivors.

Dehors Beyond, out of.

De injuria Of (his own) wrong.

Deinstitutionalize To let out of an institution.

Dejeration A taking of a solemn oath.

De jure Sanctioned by law; in compliance with the law.

De jure segregation Segregation directly intended or mandated by the law.

Delay 1. To postpone. **2.** To set up obstacles.

Del credere An agreement by which a factor, when he or she sells goods on credit, for an additional commission (called a "del credere commission"), guaranties the solvency and the performance of the purchaser.

Delectus personae Choice of the person.

Delegate 1. To give a duty, responsibility, or power to another. **2.** A person who is authorized or commissioned to act for another.

Delegation 1. The transfer of authority by one person to another. **2.** A body of delegates. **3.** In civil law, a species of novation consisting of the change of one debtor for another.

Delegatus non potest delegare An agent cannot delegate his functions to a subagent without the knowledge or consent of the principal.

Delete To erase, remove, or strike out.

Deliberate 1. To weigh or examine. **2.** Carefully considered; willful.

Deliberately Willfully; with premeditation; in cold blood.

Deliberation The act of weighing and examining the reasons for and against a contemplated act.

Delict, Delictum A tort, wrong, injury, or offense.

Delimit To mark or lay out the limits or boundaries.

Delinquency 1. A violation of duty. **2.** An offense or misconduct; unruly or immoral behavior.

Delinquency charges Additional money assessed against the borrower solely because of the failure to make timely payments.

Delinquent 1. Pertaining to that which is still due (delinquent payments). **2.** Failing to abide by the law or to conform to moral standards (delinquent minor). **3.** Someone who has committed a crime, offense, violation of duty, or other misconduct (juvenile delinquent).

Delinquent child A person below a designated age (e.g., 16) who has violated criminal laws or who engages in disobedient, indecent, or immoral conduct and who is in need of treatment, rehabilitation, and supervision. An infant who is beyond the control of parents or other guardian because of habitual truancy, defiance of other school rules, continuous law breaking, running away from home, etc.

Delirium tremens (DTs) Sickness or delirium caused by alcohol poisoning.

Delivered weight The actual weight of goods after they are unloaded from a ship or other form of transport upon reaching their destination.

Delivery The act by which something is placed within the possession or control of another.

Delusion A belief that is contrary to fact but adhered to in spite of tangible evidence that it is false.

Demand 1. To claim as one's right. **2.** The assertion of a legal right.

Demandant A plaintiff.

Demand deposits Any bank deposit that the depositor may demand (withdraw) at any time, in contrast to a time deposit that requires the depositor to wait the specified time before withdrawing, or pay a penalty for early withdrawal.

Demand note A note that expressly states it is payable on demand, on presentation, or on sight.

Demeanor Physical appearance.

Demease Death.

Demens One whose mental faculties are enfeebled.

Demented Of unsound mind.

Dementia A form of mental disorder in which cognitive and intellectual functions of the mind are affected (e.g., impairment of memory).

Dementia praecox Schizophrenia.

Demesne Domain; held in one's own right.

De minimis Very small; trifling.

Demise 1. A conveyance of an estate to another for life, for years, or at will. **2.** To convey or create an estate for years or for life. **3.** Death.

Demise charter The hiring of a vessel, transferring possession and control for a limited purpose; title does not pass.

Demised premises The property or portion of property that is leased to a tenant.

Demonetization The disuse of a particular metal for purposes of coinage.

Demonstrate 1. To prove by reasoning or evidence. **2.** To describe by illustrations or examples. **3.** To participate in a public display over an issue or a person.

Demonstrative bequest A testamentary gift that by its terms must be paid from a specific fund.

Demonstrative evidence Evidence addressed directly to the senses, apart from the testimony of witnesses; real evidence (e.g., gun, map, photo).

Demonstrative legacy A bequest of a certain sum of money with the direction that it be paid out of a particular fund.

Demotion A reduction to a lower rank, grade, or type of position.

Demur 1. To state a demurrer. **2.** To take exception.

Demurrable A pleading is demurrable when it does not state such facts as support the asserted claim, prayer, or defense.

Demurrage The money paid to the owner of a ship or railroad car by a person who holds or uses it beyond the contract time.

Demurrant One who demurs.

Demurrer An admission, for the sale of argument, of the allegations of fact made by the other party in order to show that even if they are true, they are insufficient to entitle this party to relief (i.e., the facts do not state a cause of action).

Denationalization As applied to a person, the act of depriving him or her of national rights or status. As applied to an industry or function or other state-owned thing, the act of returning it to private ownership and control after a period of national or sovereign ownership and control.

Denial 1. A declaration that something is not true. **2.** Refusing to do something.

Denization Conferring the privileges of citizenship upon an alien born.

Denizen A dweller; a stranger admitted to certain rights in a foreign country or one who lives habitually in a country but is not a native-born citizen.

Denomination 1. A designation. **2.** A society of individuals.

Denounce To condemn openly.

Denouncement An application to the authorities for a grant of the right to work a mine, based on new discovery, or on forfeiture of the rights of a former owner.

De novo Anew.

De novo trial Trying a case again as if the first trial had not taken place.

Denumeration The act of present payment.

Deny 1. To contradict. **2.** To refuse to grant or accept.

Deodand A chattel that caused the death of a person is forfeited to the crown.

Depart 1. To go away from. **2.** To deviate.

Department 1. A separate unit within the executive branch of the government or within another organization. **2.** One of the territorial divisions of a country (France).

Departure 1. Deviation from a standard. **2.** Leaving.

Depeculation Embezzling the public treasure.

Dependence The state of looking to another for support, care, maintenance, comfort, etc.

Dependency A geographically separate territory under the jurisdiction of another country or sovereign.

Dependent 1. One who derives his or her main support from another. **2.** Contingent.

Dependent covenant Covenants are dependent where performance by one party is conditioned on and subject to performance by the other.

Dependent relative revocation When a person revokes a will with the objective of creating a new one, some courts will assume that he or she intended the revocation of the old will to be dependent on the validity of the new will. If for any reason the later will fails, the court will presume that the person would not have revoked the earlier will, which can now be admitted to probate.

Deplete To reduce or lessen through use, exhaustion, waste, etc.

Depletion 1. An emptying, exhausting, or wasting of assets. **2.** A reduction during the taxable year of oil, gas, or other mineral deposits and reserves as a result of production. An allowance for this reduction through a tax deduction represents a return of capital.

Deponent A person who gives testimony under oath (e.g., at a deposition).

Deportation Banishment to a foreign country; the transfer of an alien out of the country.

Deportee One who has been deported.

Depose 1. To make a deposition; to give sworn testimony; to take sworn testimony. **2.** To remove a head of state from office against his or her will.

Deposit 1. To place for safekeeping. **2.** Money given as security for the performance of a contract that is forfeited upon nonperformance.

Depositary The party or institution (e.g., bank) receiving a deposit for safekeeping.

Deposition A pretrial discovery device by which one party questions the other party or a witness for the other party. It usually takes place in the office of one of the lawyers, in the presence of a stenographer or court reporter who transcribes what is said. For most depositions, questions are asked and answered orally. Occasionally, the questions are submitted in writing and answered orally.

Depositor Someone who makes a deposit.

Depository The place where a deposit is placed and kept for safekeeping.

Depraved Having an inherent deficiency of moral sense and rectitude; malicious.

Depreciable life The time period over which the depreciable cost of an asset is to be allocated.

Depreciation A decline in the value of property that is caused by wear or obsolescence. Depreciation is usually measured by a set formula that reflects these factors over a given period of the property's useful life.

Depredation Plundering or robbing.

Depression 1. Feelings of dejection, self-depreciation, inadequacy, guilt, etc. **2.** A period of severe economic stress, often accompanied by poor business conditions, high unemployment, etc.

Deprivation A taking away or confiscation.

Deputize To empower someone to act on behalf of another.

Deputy A person duly authorized to act on behalf of another.

Deraign To prove; to vindicate.

Deranged Mentally deficient.

Derecho In Spanish law, a law or right.

Deregulate To remove or minimize regulatory restrictions.

Derelict 1. Abandoned. **2.** Delinquent. **3.** A vagrant.

Dereliction 1. Neglect. **2.** The gaining of land from the water as a result of the sea's shrinking back below the usual watermark.

Derivative Coming from another; secondary.

Derivative action A suit by a shareholder to enforce a corporate cause of action.

Derivative contraband Property not otherwise illegal but subject to forfeiture because of the use to which it is placed.

Derivative evidence Evidence that is inadmissible because it is derived or spawned from other evidence that was illegally obtained.

Derivative tort Tort liability imposed on one person (e.g., a principal) because of a wrong committed by someone else (e.g., an agent).

Derive To receive from a specified source or origin.

Dermal Pertaining to the skin.

Derogation A partial repeal or abolishing of a law, as by a subsequent act that limits its scope or impairs its ability and force.

Derogatory Belittling, disparaging.

De sa vie Of his or her own life (French).

Descend 1. To pass by succession, as when an estate immediately vests by operation of law in the heirs upon the death of the ancestor. **2.** To go to, to belong to.

Descendant Those persons who are in the bloodline of an ancestor (e.g., children, grandchildren, great-grandchildren).

Descent 1. Succession to the ownership of an estate by inheritance. **2.** Hereditary derivation.

Descent cast The devolving of realty upon the heir on the death of the ancestor intestate.

Desegregation The elimination of segregation on the basis of unacceptable classifications (e.g., race, sex).

Desert To leave or quit with the intention to cause a permanent separation.

Desertion 1. Abandonment. **2.** A ground for divorce. Elements: (a) voluntary separation of the spouses; (b) for an uninterrupted statutory period of time; (c) with the intent not to return; (d) the separation was without the consent of the other spouse; and (e) there was no justification for the separation. **3.** Criminal desertion is the abandonment of a spouse or the willful failure without just cause to provide for the care, protection, or support of a spouse in need. **4.** Without authority, remaining absent from one's military unit or place of duty with the intent to remain away permanently.

Deshonra In Spanish law, dishonor; injury, slander.

Design 1. The plan or scheme conceived in the mind and intended for subsequent execution. **2.** In patent law, the drawing or depiction of an original plan or conception for a novel pattern, model, shape, or configuration, to be used in the manufacturing or textile arts or the fine arts, and chiefly of a decorative or ornamental character.

Designate To appoint or select.

Designation 1. A distinctive title or association added to one's name (e.g., Mary Jones, president-elect). **2.** An appointment. **3.** Pointing out something.

Designee Appointee, nominee.

Desist To stop.

Desistement The name of a doctrine under which the court, in construing a foreign will, applies the law of the forum.

De son tort Of his own wrong.

Despoil To plunder.

Desponsation The act of betrothing persons to each other.

Despotism That abuse of government where the sovereign power is in the hands of a single person.

Destination 1. The purpose for which something is set up. **2.** The place to which someone or something is going.

Destination contract A contract between the buyer and seller according to which the risk of loss passes to the buyer upon the seller's tender of the goods at the destination.

Destitute Not having the necessities of life.

Destroy To ruin, injure, or mutilate beyond possibility of use.

Desuetude Discontinuation of use.

Detain 1. To restrain from proceeding. **2.** To hold in custody.

Detainee One who is detained or confined.

Detainer 1. Illegally withholding possession of land or goods from a person; restraint of a person's liberty against his or her will. **2.** A notification filed with an institution in which a prisoner is serving a sentence advising the institution that the prisoner is wanted in connection with criminal charges in another jurisdiction.

De temps dont memorie ne court From time whereof memory runneth not.

Detention Keeping back or withholding a person or thing; confinement.

Deter To discourage or stop by fear.

Deterioration Degeneration in the substance of a thing.

Determinable 1. Capable of coming to an end upon the happening of a certain contingency. **2.** Susceptible of being determined or settled.

Determinable fee An estate that may last forever is a "fee," but if it may end on the happening of a merely possible event, it is a "determinable," or "qualified fee."

Determinant A decisive or determining factor.

Determinate Capable of being fixed or ascertained.

Determinate sentence A sentence to confinement for a fixed period as specified by statute.

Determination 1. The decision of a court or administrative agency. **2.** The ending or expiration of an estate or interest in property, or of a right, power, or authority. **3.** An estimate after weighing the facts.

Deterrent Anything that impedes or has a tendency to prevent.

Detinet He detains. A species of action of debt for the recovery of goods, under a contract to deliver them.

Detinue An action for the recovery of personal property from one who acquired it lawfully but has kept it without right. The plaintiff also seeks damages for the detention.

Detour A temporary turning aside from the usual or regular route, course, task, or procedure.

Detraction The removal of property from one state to another upon a transfer of the title to it by will or inheritance.

Detriment Any loss or harm suffered to person or property.

Detrimental reliance A loss, disadvantage, or injury suffered by a promisee because of his or her reliance on the promise of the promisor.

Devadiatus or **divadiatus** An offender without sureties or pledges.

Devaluation A reduction in the value of a currency or of a standard monetary unit.

Devastation Wasteful use of the property of a deceased person.

Devest To take away or withdraw.

Deviant 1. Not following accepted norms of society. **2.** Someone who violates conventional social and moral standards, often in the area of sexuality.

Deviation Departure from established or usual conduct or ideology.

Deviation doctrine A doctrine that allows a variation in the terms of a will or trust where the purposes of the document would be defeated if the variation is not allowed.

Device 1. An invention, gadget, or contrivance. **2.** A scheme to trick or deceive.

Devisable Capable of being devised.

Devisavit vel non An issue as to whether a document is the will of the testator.

Devise 1. The gift of land (and sometimes personal property) through a will (a devise of all my lands). **2.** To dispose of land or personal property by will (he devised his property to his son).

Devisee The person to whom real property is devised or given in a will.

Devisor The person who devises or gives real property in a will.

Devolution The transfer or transition of a right, title, estate, or office from one person to another.

Devolve To pass or be transferred from one person to another.

Devy Dies (French).

Dicta See dictum, which is the singular form of dicta.

Dictum An observation made by a judge in an opinion that is not essential to the determination of the case; comments that go beyond the facts before the court.

Die To cease to live.

Dies A day; days.

Dies ad quem The day to which a period of time is computed.

Dies a quo The day from which a transaction begins.

Dies non juridicus A day on which courts are not open for business.

Diet The name of the legislature in some countries.

Dieta 1. A day's work. **2.** A day's expenses.

Digama, digamy Second marriage; marriage to a second wife after the death of the first.

Digest 1. An organized summary or abridgment (a digest of the discovery documents). **2.** A set of volumes that contain small-paragraph summaries of court opinions, arranged by subject matter (Federal Practice Digest, 3d).

Dijudication Judicial determination.

Dilapidated The condition of ruin or decay.

Dilatory Tending or intended to cause delay, to gain time, or to put off a decision.

Diligence 1. Persistent activity. **2.** Prudence, carefulness.

Diligent Attentive and persistent in doing something.

Diminished capacity or responsibility The lack of capacity to achieve the state of mind needed for the commission of a crime; partial insanity.

Diminution 1. The act or process of taking away or diminishing. **2.** Incompleteness.

Diminution of record Incompleteness of the record sent up on appeal.

Dinarchy A government of two persons.

Diplomatic immunity Exemption from legal process given to designated diplomats in foreign countries.

Dipsomania A mental disease characterized by an uncontrollable desire for intoxicating liquor.

Direct 1. To command, regulate, or manage. **2.** To aim or cause to move in a certain direction. **3.** Without interruption; immediate (direct cause). **4.** Personal (direct confrontation). **5.** Honest, straightforward.

Direct attack To seek to have a judgment or decree corrected, vacated, or enjoined in a proceeding instituted for this specific purpose (e.g., an appeal).

Direct cause That which sets in motion a chain of events that brings about a result without the intervention of any actively operating force from a new or independent source; that without which the injury would not have happened.

Direct contempt A contempt committed in the presence of the court or so near the court as to interrupt its proceedings.

Direct damages Damages that follow immediately upon the act done. Damages that arise naturally or ordinarily from breach of contract.

Directed verdict In a case in which the party with the burden of proof has failed to present a prima facie case, the trial judge may order the entry of a verdict without allowing the jury to consider it.

Direct estoppel A form of estoppel by judgment where the issue has actually been litigated and determined in an action between the same parties based on the same cause of action.

Direct evidence Evidence that, if believed, proves the existence of the fact in issue without using any inferences or presumptions; testimony from a witness who actually saw, heard, or touched the matter in question.

Direct examination The first interrogation or questioning of a witness by the party who has called the witness.

Direct line A line of descent traced through those persons who are related to each other directly as descendants or ascendants.

Direct loss A loss resulting immediately and proximately from the occurrence and not remotely from some of the consequences or effects thereof.

Director One who directs, regulates, guides, or orders.

Directory Pertaining to a provision in a statute that does not relate to the essence of the statute. Noncompliance with a directory provision does not invalidate a transaction or action if there is compliance with the other parts of the statute.

Directory trust One that is not completely and finally settled by the instrument creating it, but only defined in its general purpose and to be carried into detail according to later specific directions.

Direct tax A tax that is imposed directly on property.

Direct trust An express trust, as distinguished from a constructive or implied trust.

Diriment impediments In the civil law, impediments that render a marriage void.

Dirty bill of lading A bill of lading showing on its face that the goods were damaged or that there was a shortage at the time of shipment.

Disability 1. The lack of legal capacity to perform an act. **2.** A disabled condition; handicap.

Disable To render incapable of effective action.

Disadvocare To deny a thing.

Disaffirm To repudiate; to revoke consent.

Disaffirmance The refusal to accept the legal consequences of one's acts.

Disallow To refuse to allow, to deny.

Disavow To repudiate; to deny responsibility.

Disbar To revoke an attorney's license to practice law.

Disbarment See disbar.

Disbursement The act of paying out money; expenditure.

Discharge 1. To relieve of an obligation (discharge them of the debt). **2.** To fulfill an obligation (she discharged her responsibilities under the contract). **3.** To liberate (she was discharged from prison). **4.** To shoot (he discharged the gun). **5.** To release from employment or service (discharged for insubordination).

Dischargeable claim A claim against the bankrupt that, if properly scheduled, is barred when the latter receives an adjudication of bankruptcy.

Discharge in bankruptcy The release of a bankrupt from all nonexcepted debts that are provable in a bankruptcy proceeding.

Disciplinary proceedings Proceedings brought against an attorney to secure his or her censure, suspension, or disbarment.

Discipline 1. Strict training. **2.** Self-control. **3.** Punishment.

Disclaimer The repudiation of a claim, power, or obligation.

Disclose To bring into view by uncovering, to expose.

Disclosure The act of revealing that which is secret or not fully understood.

Discontinuance Ending; causing to cease.

Discount An allowance or deduction from the original price or debt.

Discount rate A percentage of the face amount of commercial paper (e.g., note) that a holder pays when he or she transfers the paper to a financial institution for cash or credit; the rate charged for discounting a loan.

Discovered peril doctrine An exception to the rule of contributory negligence. Elements: (a) an exposed condition brought about by the negligence of the plaintiff, (b) the actual discovery by the defendant of the plaintiff's perilous situation in time to have averted the injury by the use of means commensurate with the defendant's own safety, (c) the failure to use such means.

Discovert Not married.

Discovery 1. Pretrial devices that can be used by a party to obtain information about a suit from the other side in order to assist in preparing for the trial (e.g., interrogatories, deposition). **2.** The ascertainment of that which was previously unknown.

Discovery rule A cause of action for medical malpractice will not accrue until the patient knows, or in the exercise of reasonable diligence should have known, of the alleged malpractice.

Discredit To destroy or impair the credibility of a person.

Discrepancy A difference between two things that ought to be identical.

Discretion 1. The power or right to act according to the dictates of one's own judgment and conscience. **2.** Good judgment; diplomacy.

Discriminate To make decisions on the basis of prejudice.

Discrimination Unfair and unreasonable treatment or denial of privileges to persons because of their sex, age, race, nationality, or religion.

Discussion In the civil law, a proceeding, at the instance of a surety, by which the creditor is obliged to exhaust the property of the principal debtor, towards the satisfaction of the debt, before having recourse to the surety. This right of the surety is termed the "benefit of discussion."

Disease Deviation from the healthy or normal condition of any of the functions or tissues of the body.

Disfigurement Impairment of or injury to the beauty, symmetry, or appearance of a person or thing so as to render the external form unsightly, misshapen, or imperfect.

Disfranchise To deprive of the rights and privileges of a free citizen.

Disherison Disinheritance.

Dishonor 1. To refuse to accept or pay a draft or to refuse to pay a promissory note when duly presented. **2.** Shame, disgrace. **3.** To degrade or defile.

Disincarcerate To set at liberty.

Disinherison In the civil law, the act of depriving a forced heir of the inheritance which the law gives him or her.

Disinter To take a body out of the grave.

Disinterested Having nothing to gain or lose as a result of the transaction or proceeding.

Disjunctive Designating a conjunction (such as "or," "either," "neither," "nor," "but," "although") that denotes an alternative, contrast, or opposition between the ideas it connects (e.g., a disjunctive allegation that the defendant stole the car or caused it to be stolen).

Dismiss 1. To dispose of an action, suit, or motion without a trial on the issues involved. **2.** To discharge. **3.** To send away.

Dismissal 1. An order or judgment disposing of an action, suit, or motion without a trial of the issues involved. **2.** A discharge.

Dismissal without prejudice A dismissal without prejudice to the right of the complainant to sue again on the same cause of action.

Dismissal with prejudice An adjudication on the merits; a final disposition barring the right to bring an action on the same cause of action.

Dismortgage To redeem from mortgage.

Disorder 1. Turbulent or riotous behavior. **2.** A physical or mental health impairment.

Disorderly Violative of the public peace, good order, or good behavior.

Disorderly conduct Behavior that tends to disturb the public peace, to scandalize the community, or to shock the public sense of morality. Engaging in the following activities with the purpose of causing (or recklessly causing) a public annoyance: fighting, threatening, making unreasonable noise, using abusive language, creating offensive displays, creating unnecessarily hazardous conditions.

Disorderly house A house or place where acts are performed that tend to corrupt the morals of the community, promote breaches of the peace, or become a nuisance to the neighborhood (e.g., house of prostitution, gambling house).

Disparage To discredit one's person or property.

Disparagement A tort with the following elements: (a) false statements of fact, (b) disparaging the plaintiff's business, property, or title to property, (c) publication of the statements, (d) intent or malice, (e) causation, (f) special damages. Disparagement of title; disparagement of goods; injurious falsehood; conduct that adversely influences the public's dealings with the plaintiff (e.g., causes the public not to buy from the plaintiff).

Disparity A marked difference in quantity or quality between two things or among many things.

Dispassionate Impartial.

Dispatch In maritime law, diligence or proper speed in the discharge of a cargo.

Dispauper To lose the right to sue as a pauper (in forma pauperis).

Dispensary A place where medicine is prepared or distributed.

Dispensation An exemption from a law.

Dispense 1. To give, distribute, or administer. **2.** To do without.

Displaced person A person left homeless in his or her own country because of war.

Disposable 1. Available for use. **2.** Capable of being discarded or disposed of after use.

Disposal 1. The sale, consumption, or other disposition of a thing. **2.** Capable of being discarded or disposed of after use.

Dispose 1. To transfer property. **2.** To finalize. **3.** To discard.

Disposing capacity or **mind** Sound mind.

Disposition 1. The transferring of property. **2.** The final arrangement or decision.

Disposition hearing A judicial proceeding in which a criminal or juvenile defendant is sentenced or otherwise handled as a result of what has been adjudicated on the substance of the case.

Dispositive facts Those facts that are critical to the resolution of an issue.

Dispossess To oust or eject from land.

Dispossession An ouster.

Dispute A conflict or controversy, the subject of litigation.

Disqualify To render ineligible or unfit.

Disrate In maritime law, to deprive a seaman or petty officer of his rating or rank.

Disregard 1. To treat as unworthy of regard or notice. **2.** Neglect or violation.

Disrepute Loss of reputation, discredit.

Dissection The anatomical examination of a dead body by cutting one or more parts or organs.

Disseise To deprive or dispossess.

Disseisee One who is wrongfully put out of possession of his or her lands.

Disseisin Dispossession; a wrongful invasion of the possession of another.

Disseisor One who wrongfully dispossesses another of his or her lands.

Dissemble To conceal by assuming a false appearance.

Dissentiente Dissenting.

Dissenting opinion A dissenting opinion disagrees with the result and the reasoning of the majority opinion.

Dissignare To break open a seal.

Dissipate To destroy or waste.

Dissolution The act or process of dissolving; termination.

Dissolving bond A bond given to obtain the dissolution of a legal writ or process, particularly an attachment or an injunction, and conditioned to indemnify the opposite party or to abide the judgment to be given.

Distinguish To point out an essential difference; to demonstrate a cited case to be inapplicable.

Distrain To take and hold the personal property of another until the latter performs an obligation.

Distrainee A person who has been distrained.

Distrainer or **distrainor** One who seizes property under a distress.

Distraint Seizure of personal property to enforce a right; the act of distraining or making a distress.

Distress 1. A common-law right of the landlord, now regulated by statute, to seize a tenant's goods and chattels in a nonjudicial proceedings to satisfy a debt for past rent. **2.** The taking of goods and chattels out of the possession of a wrongdoer into the custody of the party injured, to procure the satisfaction of a wrong committed.

Distressed property Property that must be sold because of a mortgage foreclosure or on probate of an insolvent estate.

Distress warrant A writ authorizing an officer to make a distraint.

Distribute To deal or divide out in proportion or in shares.

Distributee A person entitled to share in the distribution of an estate.

Distribution The apportionment and division of something.

Distributive Pertaining to a distribution.

Distributive finding of the issue A finding in part for the plaintiff, and in part for the defendent.

Distributive share The share or portion that is given to a person upon the distribution of a fund (e.g., an estate, the assets of a dissolved partnership, the remaining assets of an insolvent).

Distributor An individual or organization that stands between the manufacturer and the retail seller in purchases, consignments, or contracts for sale of consumer goods.

District One of the geographic or territorial areas into which an entire state, country, county, municipality, or other political subdivision is divided for judicial, political, electoral, or administrative purposes.

District attorney The prosecutor for the government in criminal cases for a certain area or district.

Disturbance of the peace An interruption of the peace, quiet, and good order of a neighborhood or community; an affray or public disturbance.

Divers Various, several.

Diversion A turning aside or altering the natural course or route of a thing.

Diversion program An alternative to incarceration; the disposition of a criminal defendant (before or after a finding of guilt), in which the court directs the defendant to participate in a work or educational program in the community.

Diversity of citizenship One of the ways a federal court acquires jurisdiction: the case is between citizens of different states and the controversy between them involves the minimum monetary requirement.

Divert To alter the course of things; to misdirect.

Divest To deprive someone of rights, duties, or possessions.

Divestiture In antitrust law, the order of a court to a defendant to divest itself of property, securities, or other assets.

Divestment In property law, the cutting short of an interest prior to its normal termination.

Dividend The payment designated by the board of directors of a corporation to be distributed pro rata among the outstanding shares.

Divisible Capable of being divided.

Divisible divorce A divorce decree is divisible when only part of it is enforceable in another state. The part that dissolves the divorce may be enforceable, but, due to a lack of personal jurisdiction, not the part that awards alimony, child support, and a property settlement.

Divisible offense An offense that includes one or more offenses of lower grade.

Divorce The termination of a marital relationship by a court judgment or decree. The word divorce sometimes refers to a legal separation—a limited divorce, or a divorce from bed and board—which allows the parties to live separate and apart but does not dissolve the marriage.

Divorce a mensa et thoro A judicially approved separation; the spouses remain married but no longer cohabitate. A separation from bed and board, a limited divorce, a partial divorce, a qualified divorce, a legal separation.

Divorce a vinculo matrimonii An absolute divorce in which the marital relationship is dissolved.

Divulge To make known.

Dock 1. The cage or enclosed space in a criminal court where prisoners stand when brought in for trial. **2.** A landing place for boats. **3.** To curtail or diminish.

Dockage A pecuniary compensation for the use of a dock.

Docket 1. A list or calendar of cases to be tried at a specified term of the court. **2.** A minute, abstract, or brief entry; the book containing such entries; a formal record, entered in brief, of the proceedings in a court of justice.

Docket fee An attorney's fee, of a fixed sum, chargeable with or as a part of the costs of the action, for the attorney of the successful party.

Doctor 1. A licensed practitioner of medicine. **2.** Someone who holds the highest degree in designated areas. **3.** To prescribe or treat medically. **4.** To falsify.

Doctor-patient privilege In the law of evidence, the right of the patient to exclude from evidence (by refusing to divulge or by preventing the doctor from divulging) confidential communications made by the patient to the doctor.

Doctrine A rule or principle.

Document 1. Any physical embodiment of information or ideas (e.g., letter, contract, map, X-ray plate, blueprint). **2.** To support with documentary evidence or with authorities.

Documentary evidence Evidence that is furnished by written instruments, inscriptions, and documents of all kinds; tangible or material objects that are symbols of ideas.

Documentary stamp A state tax, in the forms of stamps, required on deeds and mortgages when real estate title passes from one owner to another. The amount of stamps required varies in each state.

Documentation The production of supporting documents, other evidence, or authorities.

Document of title A document that is accepted in the trade as proof that the person possessing it has the right to receive and dispose of goods covered by the document (e.g., a bill of lading, a warehouse receipt).

Dogma Authoritative and formal principles or doctrines.

Doing business Carrying on, conducting, or managing a business; the exercise of the ordinary functions for which the business was organized.

Doli capax Capable of criminal intention.

Doli incapax Incapable of criminal intention.

Dolo In Spanish law, a bad or mischievous design.

Dolus In the civil law, deceitfulness.

Domain Land that is owned; the complete and absolute ownership of land.

Dome-book A Saxon book or code containing maxims of the common law, penalties for misdemeanors, and the forms of judicial proceedings.

Domesday, domesday-book An ancient record made in the time of William the Conqueror, containing minute and accurate surveys of the lands in England.

Domesmen In old English law, an inferior kind of judge.

Domestic Pertaining, belonging, or related to a home, a domicile, the place of birth, or the place of origin.

Domestic animals Tamed animals; those that are habituated to live in or around the habitations of humans (e.g., dogs, sheep, horses).

Domestic corporation When a corporation is organized and chartered in a particular state, it is considered a domestic corporation of that state; all others are foreign corporations.

Domestic relations Family law (e.g., the law governing marriage, divorce, adoption, custody).

Domicile The place (a) where someone has physically been present (b) with the intention to make that place a permanent home; the place to which one would intend to return when away. The word "residence" is sometimes used interchangeably with "domicile," but there is a distinction. A residence is a temporary place of abode. A person can have many residences but only one domicile.

Domicile of choice The domicile that an individual has the power to select through intent and physical presence. A child does not have this choice. A child automatically acquires the domicile of his or her parents, which is referred to as a *domicile of origin* or a domicile by operation of law.

Domiciliary Someone who is physically present in a place with the intent to remain there indefinitely.

Domiciliary administration The administration of an estate in the state where the decedent was domiciled at the time of death.

Domiciliate To establish one's domicile.

Dominant estate The parcel of land that is benefited from an easement on a servient estate.

Dominion The exercise of the right of ownership; control over the disposition of something.

Dominium directum In the civil law, strict ownership.

Dominus litis The master of the suit (i.e., the person who is really and directly interested in the suit as a party).

Donated surplus Contribution of assets to a corporation generally in the form of stock from its stockholders.

Donative intent The intent of the donor that title to the subject matter of the gift be irrevocably and presently transferred.

Donee One to whom a gift is given; one who is invested with a power of appointment.

Donee beneficiary In a third-party contract, the person who receives the benefit of the contract. He or she is not one of the contracting parties.

Donor One who makes a gift, confers a power, or creates a trust.

Doomsday-book See domesday.

Dope An opium derivative; any narcotic.

Dorks Slang for someone who uses steroids indiscriminately without knowledge about the drugs or the source.

Dormant In abeyance; sleeping.

Dormant corporation An inactive but legal corporation that is capable of being activated.

Dormant judgment An unsatisfied judgment that has remained unexecuted for so long that it needs to be revived before execution can be issued on it.

Dormant partner One whose name is not known or whose name does not appear as a partner, but who nevertheless is a silent partner and shares in the profits.

Dos In Roman law, a wife's dowry.

Dossier A group of papers on a person or event.

Dotage Feebleness of the mental faculties proceeding from old age.

Dotal Relating to the dos or portion of a woman; constituting her portion.

Dotal property Property that the wife brings to the husband to assist him in bearing the expenses of the marriage establishment.

Dote In Spanish law, property the wife gives to the husband on account of marriage.

Double entry A system of bookkeeping in which the entries are posted twice in the ledger—once as a credit and once as a debit.

Double hearsay An out-of-court statement is introduced into evidence, and this statement contains another out-of-court statement by someone else, e.g., an officer makes a report (statement # 1) of what a motorist says (statement # 2) at the scene of the accident.

Double indemnity Payment of twice the basic benefit in the event of loss resulting from specified causes or under specified circumstances (e.g., a life insurance policy provides twice the face amount of the policy in the event of death by accidental means).

Double jeopardy A second prosecution after the first trial for the same offense.

Double taxation Taxing the same thing twice for the same purpose by the same taxing authority during identical taxing periods.

Double use In patent law, an application of a principle or process, previously known and applied, to some new use, but which does not lead to a new result or the production of a new article.

Double will A will in which two persons join, each leaving everything to the other, so that the survivor takes the whole.

Doubt Uncertainty of mind; the absence of a settled opinion or conviction.

Doubtful title A title that raises such doubts as to its validity that it could reasonably invite or expose the party holding it to litigation.

Dowable Subject to be charged with dower.

Dowager A widow who holds property from her deceased husband.

Dower The provision that the law makes for a widow out of the lands or tenements of her deceased husband. It has been abolished or replaced in most states. At common law, it consisted of a life estate in one-third of the lands of which the husband was seised in fee at any time during the marriage and that could have been inherited by her issue.

Down payment An amount of money paid by the buyer to the seller at the time of sale, which represents only a part of the total cost.

Dowry Property that a woman brings to her husband upon marriage.

Draft A written order by the first party (called the drawer) instructing a second party (called the drawee, e.g., a bank) to pay a third party (called the payee); an order to pay a sum certain in money, signed by the drawer, payable on demand or at a definite time to order or to bearer.

Dragnet clause A provision in a mortgage in which

the mortgagor gives security for past and future advances as well as for present indebtedness.

Drainage rights A landowner may not obstruct or divert the natural flow of a watercourse or natural drainage course to the injury of another.

Dram A drink of some substance containing alcohol; something that can produce intoxication.

Dram Shop Act A civil liability act in many states that imposes liability on the seller of intoxicating liquor (which may or may not include beer) when a third party is injured as a result of the intoxication of the buyer, where the sale has caused or contributed to the intoxication. In some states, the Act also applies to gifts of intoxicating liquor.

Draw 1. To prepare a legal document. **2.** To withdraw money. **3.** To advance money periodically on a construction loan agreement. **4.** To select a jury.

Drawback A refund of taxes or duties on imported goods when they are exported rather than sold here.

Drawee The person on whom a bill or draft is drawn; the one who is requested to pay the amount mentioned in the bill of exchange or draft (the drawee of a check is the bank on which it is drawn).

Drawer The person who draws a bill, draft, or order for the payment of money (the drawer of a check is the person who signs it).

Drawing account A fund of money from which employees may draw in anticipation of earnings or commissions.

Drayage A charge for the local transportation of property.

Droit A legal right; a body of law (French).

Drop-letter A letter addressed for delivery in the same city or district in which it is posted.

Drop shipment delivery Shipment of goods directly from a manufacturer to a dealer or consumer rather than first to the wholesaler, though the wholesaler still earns the profit because it placed the order.

Drug 1. An article intended for use in the diagnosis, treatment, or prevention of disease in humans and in animals; any substance used as a medicine. **2.** A narcotic.

Drug abuse A state of chronic or periodic intoxication detrimental to the individual and to society, produced by repeated consumption of a natural or synthetic drug.

Drummer Traveling salesperson.

Drunk Intoxicated; so far under the influence of intoxicating liquor as to be impaired in judgment, sense perceptions, muscular coordination, continuity of thought, or speech.

Drunkard One who is habitually intoxicated.

Dry Without imposing any duty or responsibility; without bringing any profit or advantage; nominal.

Dry mortgage One that creates a lien on land for the payment of money, but does not impose any personal liability upon the mortgagor, collateral to or over and above the value of the premises.

Dry trust A passive trust; a trust that requires no action on the part of the trustee beyond turning over money or property to the cestui que trust.

Dual citizenship Pertaining to persons who are citizens of the United States and of a particular state.

Dual-purpose doctrine If the work of an employee creates a necessity for travel, he or she is in the course of employment while doing that work even though at the same time he or she is serving a purpose of his or her own. An injury on a trip that serves both business and personal purposes is within the course of employment if the trip involves service for the employer that would have caused the trip to have been taken by someone even if it had not coincided with a personal purpose.

Dubitatur It is doubted.

Duces tecum Bring with you. See subpoena duces tecum.

Due 1. Payable. **2.** Proper; just, regular, sufficient. **3.** Caused by.

Due care Just, proper, and sufficient care under the circumstances; that care which an ordinary prudent person would have exercised under the same or similar circumstances. Reasonable care.

Due course holder See holder in due course.

Due diligence The prudence and effort that is ordinarily used by a reasonable person under the circumstances.

Due notice Notice that is reasonably intended to reach and that has the likelihood of reaching the particular target or public; sufficient, legally prescribed notice.

Due process of law 1. Fundamental fairness; substantial justice. **2.** Law in its regular course of administration through the courts of justice.

Duly In due and proper form or manner.

Dum bene se gesserit During good behavior.

Dummy 1. One who purchases property and holds the legal title for someone else, usually to conceal the identity of the real owner. **2.** Sham, imitation.

Dummy corporation A corporation formed for sham purposes and not for the conduct of legitimate business (e.g., formed solely to avoid paying certain creditors).

Dumping 1. Selling in quantity at a very low price.

2. Selling goods abroad at less than the market price at home—at less than its fair value.

Dun To make persistent demands; a demand for payment.

Duopoly A condition in the market in which there are only two producers or sellers of a given product.

Duplicate A counterpart produced by the same impression as the original, or by photography, electronic re-recording, etc.; that which exactly resembles or corresponds to something else.

Duplicatio In the civil law, the defendant's answer to the plaintiff's replication, corresponding to the rejoinder of the common law.

Duplicitous 1. Characterized by deception. **2.** The technical fault in common-law pleading of uniting two or more causes of action in one count in a writ, or two or more grounds of defense in one plea. **3.** Charging several distinct, unrelated crimes in one indictment.

Duress 1. Coercion; acting under the pressure of an unlawful act or threat. **2.** Illegal confinement or imprisonment.

Duress of goods A tortious seizure or detention of property from the person entitled to it and requiring some act before it is surrendered.

Duress per minas Duress by threats.

Durham rule The irresistible impulse test of criminal responsibility. Under the Durham rule, to find a defendant not guilty by reason of insanity or mental irresponsibility, the jury must find (a) that the accused was suffering from a diseased or defective mental condition at the time of the commission of the act charged, and (b) that there was a causal relation between this disease or defective condition and the act. Durham v. United States, 214 F.2d 862 (D.C.Cir. 1954).

Dutch auction A method of sale by auction that consists in the public offer of the property at a price beyond its value, and then gradually lowering the price until someone becomes the purchaser.

Duties Taxes on imported or exported goods.

Duty 1. A legal or moral obligation. **2.** A tax on imports or exports.

Dying declaration Statements made by a person who is at the point of death and is conscious of his or her approaching death, concerning the circumstances leading up to the injury or death (e.g., who caused it).

Dying without issue Dying without a child either before or after the decedent's death.

Dynamite instruction See Allen charge.

Dysnomy Bad legislation.

Earmark 1. To place a mark on a thing to distinguish it from another. **2.** To set aside.

Earn 1. To acquire by labor, service, or performance. **2.** To merit or deserve.

Earned income Income (e.g., wages, salary, fees) derived from labor, professional service, or entrepreneurship, as opposed to income derived from invested capital (e.g., rents, dividends, interest).

Earned surplus The surplus that has been generated from profits as opposed to a paid-in surplus.

Earnest Earnest money. The payment of a part of the price by the buyer at the time of entering the contract to indicate the intention and ability of the buyer to carry out the contract.

Earning capacity The capability of a worker to sell his or her labor or services in any reasonably accessible market, taking into consideration his or her age, prior earnings, education and training, prior work experience, physical health, mental health, and other responsibilities.

Earnings That which is earned; money earned from the performance of labor, services, or the sale of goods.

Earnings and profits A tax concept peculiar to corporate taxpayers, which measures economic capacity to make a distribution to shareholders that is not a return of capital.

Earth Soil of all kinds, including gravel, clay, loam, and the like, in distinction from the firm rock.

Easement A right-of-way granted to a person or company authorizing access to or over the owner's land. An electric company obtaining a right-of-way across private property is a common example. A right to use the land of another for a special and limited purpose not inconsistent with a general property in the owner.

Easement appurtenant An easement interest that attaches to the land and passes with it.

Easement by implication An easement that the law imposes by inferring that the parties to a transaction intended it even though they did not express it.

Easement by necessity An easement that arises by operation of law when land conveyed is completely shut off from access to any road by the land retained by the grantor or by the land of the grantor and that of a stranger.

Easement by prescription An easement created by the open, notorious, hostile, adverse, uninterrupted, exclusive, and continuous use of the land for a designated period of time.

Easement in gross An easement that is a purely personal right to use the land of another and usually ends with the death of the grantee.

Easement of access The right that an abutting owner has of ingress and egress to and from his or her premises and to have the premises accessible to patrons.

Eavesdrop Knowingly and without lawful authority or consent (a) to enter into a private place with the intent to listen surreptitiously to private conversations, or (b) to install or use outside a private place any device for hearing, recording, amplifying, or broadcasting sounds originating in such place when such sounds would not ordinarily be audible or comprehensible outside, or (c) to install or use any device or equipment for the interception of any telephone, telegraph, or other wire communication.

Ecclesiastical Pertaining to the church.

Ecology The study or science of the relationships between organisms and their environments; study of the environment.

Econometrics The application of statistics to the study of economics.

Economic Pertaining to the production, distribution, and management of the wealth, goods, and services within a unit (e.g., home, state, country).

Economy 1. The economic status or structure of an area. **2.** Prudent expenditure of money or use of resources.

Edict A formal decree, command, or proclamation.

Education Acquisition of all knowledge tending to train and develop the individual.

Effect 1. That which is produced. **2.** To bring about.

Effects The personal estate of someone.

Efficient Properly producing a desired effect; adequate in performance.

Efficient cause The cause that produces the effect or result; the procuring cause; the immediate agent in the production of an event.

Efficient intervening cause A new and independent force that breaks the causal connection between the original wrong and the injury; a new and independent force that so interrupts the chain of events as to become the proximate cause of the injury.

Effigy An image, model, or representation of a person.

Effluent Treated sewage from a septic tank or sewage treatment plant.

Efflux The running as of a prescribed period of time to its end.

Effraction A breach or breaking by the use of force.

Egress The means or act of going out.

Eject To throw out.

Ejectment An action for the recovery of the possession of land and for damages for its unlawful detention. The action was used as a method of establishing the title to the land.

Ejuration Renouncing or resigning.

Ejusdem generis Of the same kind, class, or nature. In a written document (e.g., statute, contract), general words sometimes follow a list of specific items (e.g., dogs, cats, *and other animals*). When the meaning of the general language at the end is in doubt, it is to be interpreted as being limited by the kind, class, or nature of the items in the specific list unless it is otherwise clear that the general language was intended to have a broader meaning.

Election The act of choosing or selecting one or more from a greater number of persons, things, courses, or rights.

Election against the will See election by spouse.

Election at large An election in which a public official is selected from a major election district (e.g., the entire city), rather than from a subdivision within the larger unit.

Election by spouse The right provided by statute allowing a surviving spouse to take what her husband provided for her in his will, *or* to take the share of his estate designated by the statute even if it is more than the will provided. If she elects against the will, the statute often gives her what she would have received if her husband had died intestate.

Election of remedies A choice between two inconsistent remedies by a party. Today, most courts allow a party to plead inconsistent remedies. There was a time, however, when a choice had to be made and the party was bound by the choice.

Elective Dependent on choice.

Elective share The statutory share selected by a widow against the will. See election by spouse.

Elector A duly qualified voter.

Electoral college A body of electors from each state who are chosen to elect the president and vice-president. Each state legislature determines how the electors are appointed. The number of electors from a state is equal to the total number of representatives and senators of the state in Congress.

Eleemosynary Having to do with charity.

Eleemosynary corporation A private corporation created for charitable and benevolent purposes.

Elegit "He has chosen." A writ of execution chosen by the plaintiff by which the debtor's goods and chattels were delivered to the plaintiff in satisfaction of the debt. The debtor's land was also held by the plaintiff if further satisfaction was needed. During this period, the plaintiff's interest in the debtor's land was called an "estate by elegit."

Element A constituent party.

Eligible Fit and proper to be chosen.

Ellipsis The omission of words or clauses from something that is quoted (use dots [...] or asterisks [* * *] to indicate ellipsis).

Elogium In the civil law, a will or testament.

Eloign To remove in order to conceal.

Emancipation The express or implied consent of a parent to relinquish his or her control and authority over a child. The parent no longer supports the child, and the latter no longer must turn over his or her earnings to nor perform services for the parent.

Embargo A proclamation or order of the government prohibiting the departure of ships or goods from some or all ports until further order; a government order prohibiting commercial trade with individuals or businesses of other countries.

Embassy The mission, headquarters, or official residence of an ambassador; the body of diplomatic representatives headed by the ambassador.

Embezzle To willfully take or convert to one's own use the money or property of another, which the wrongdoer initially acquired lawfully because of a position of trust.

Emblements The crops annually produced by the labor of the tenant to which the latter is entitled.

Embraceor or **embracer** A person guilty of embracery.

Embracery The crime of corruptly trying to influence a jury by promises, entertainments, etc.

Emergency A sudden unexpected happening.

Emergency doctrine When a person is confronted with a sudden peril requiring instinctive action, he or she is not held to the exercise of the same degree of care as when there is time for mature reflection. There may be no liability for negligence if this person injures someone while responding to the peril if he or she used due care to avoid getting into the emergency and responded as prudently as possible under these unusual circumstances.

Emigrant One who leaves his or her country with the intention to reside elsewhere and not return.

Emigration The act of moving from one country to another with the intention of not returning.

Émigré One who leaves a country for political reasons.

Eminent domain The power of government to take private property for public use upon the payment of just compensation.

Emissary A person sent on a mission as the agent of another.

Emission The discharge of something.

Emit 1. To place in circulation. **2.** To put forth or send out.

Emolument Compensation for services or for an occupation.

Empire The territory ruled over by one country; supreme dominion.

Empirical Based on experience, experiment, or observation.

Emplead To indict, to prefer a charge against.

Employ To engage in one's service; to use as an agent or substitute in transacting business.

Employee A person in the service of another under an express or implied, oral or written contract of hire, in which the employer has the power and the right to control and direct the employee in the material details of how the work is to be performed.

Employer One who employs the services of others for wages or other compensation, with the right and power to control and direct them in the material details of how the work is to be performed.

Employment The activity in which a person is engaged or is employed, usually on a day-to-day basis.

Empower To grant authority.

Emptor A buyer or purchaser. See caveat emptor.

Enable To give power to do something.

Enabling cause That portion of a statute or constitution giving to governmental officials the right to put it into effect and to enforce it.

Enact To establish by law.

Enacting clause A clause at the beginning of a statute, which states the authority by which it is made (e.g., "Be it enacted by the people of the state of Illinois represented in general assembly").

Enactment The method or process by which a bill in the legislature becomes a law; the law itself that is enacted.

En autre droit In the right of another.

En banc A session of the court in which the full membership of the court, rather than a smaller grouping or panel of the judges, will participate in the decision (the court sitting en banc).

Enclose 1. To surround or fence. **2.** To insert.

Enclosure Land surrounded by visible obstruction; that which is enclosed.

Encroach To enter by gradual steps or stealth into the possession or rights of another.

Encroachment An obstruction, building, or part of a building that intrudes beyond a legal boundary onto neighboring private or public land, or a building extending beyond the building line.

Encumber To burden, hinder, or obligate.

Encumbrance Any right to or interest in land that may subsist in another, resulting in a diminution in the value of the land; a claim, lien, charge, impediment, or liability attached to and binding real property (e.g., mortgage, mechanics' lien, judgment lien, tax lien, security interest, easement).

Endorsee See indorsee.

Endorsement See indorsement.

Endorser See indorser.

Endow 1. To bestow upon, to fund. **2.** To give a dower.

Endowment A transfer, usually by gift, of property or money to an institution for a particular purpose.

Enemy alien An alien residing or traveling in a country that is at war with the country of which he or she is a national.

Enfeoff To invest with an estate; to place someone in possession of an estate in fee.

Enforce To make effective; to put into execution.

Enforcement The act of putting something into effect.

Enfranchisement The act of giving freedom or a franchise to someone.

Engage 1. To employ. **2.** To participate. **3.** To pledge oneself.

Engrossment 1. The drafting of a resolution or bill in the legislature just prior to the final vote. **2.** Buying up or securing enough of a commodity in order to obtain a monopoly. **3.** Preparing a deed for execution.

Enjoin To require a person to perform or to abstain from some act.

Enjoy To have, possess, and use something.

Enjoyment 1. The exercise of a right or privilege. **2.** Comfort, pleasure.

Enlisted man One who has enlisted in the military without an officer's commission.

Enlistment Voluntary entry into one of the armed services by one other than a commissioned officer.

En masse In bulk; all together.

Enoc Arden doctrine When a spouse leaves under such circumstances and for such a period of time as to allow the other spouse to believe that the missing spouse is dead, the law will presume that death has occurred. States differ, however, as to what happens if the spouse in fact returns.

Enrolled bill The final copy of a bill or joint resolution that has been passed by both houses of the legislature and is ready for signature; a bill that has gone through all the steps necessary to make it a law.

Enschedule To insert in a list, account, or writing.

Enseal To affix a seal.

Entail 1. To impose a limitation on who can inherit real property. **2.** A fee estate that is limited as to who can inherit it; it does not descend to all the heirs of the owner.

Enter 1. To place anything before a court or on the court records in a formal way. **2.** To cause to go into or be received into.

Enter a judgment To record the judgment formally on the rolls or records (e.g., the civil docket) of the court, which is necessary before bringing an appeal or an action on the judgment. In some states the judgment is entered merely by filing the judgment with the clerk.

Enterprise A venture or undertaking often involving a financial commitment.

Entice To solicit wrongfully.

Enticement of a child A tort with the following elements: (a) an intent to interfere with the parent's custody over the child; (b) affirmative conduct to force or encourage the child to leave its parents and/or to stay away; (c) the child in fact leaves the custody of the parent; (d) the defendant causes this.

Entire Whole; without division, separation, or diminution.

Entirety The whole. See tenancy by the entirety.

Entitle To give a right, claim, or legal title to.

Entitlement The right to benefits, income, or other property, which cannot be abridged without due process.

Entity A real and distinct being or organization.

Entrap To induce a person to commit a crime that he or she is not contemplating in order to arrest and prosecute him or her for that crime; to originate an idea for a crime and then induce someone to commit it when the latter is not already disposed to do so.

Entrepreneur One who initiates and assumes the financial and management responsibility for a new enterprise.

Entrust To give something to another after a relationship of trust has been established.

Entrusting The transfer of possession of goods to a merchant who deals in goods of that type and who may in turn transfer such goods and all rights therein to a purchaser in the ordinary course of business.

Entry 1. The act of making and entering a record; placing something before the court in writing; the record itself. **2.** For purposes of burglary, an entry with the whole body, or any part of the body, or with any instrument or weapon introduced for the purpose of committing a felony is sufficient to complete the offense.

Entry in the regular course of business A record of a fact made by someone in the ordinary and regular course of one's business, employment, office, or profession when it is the duty of this person to make the record in such manner, or when the record is commonly or regularly made, or when it is convenient to make the record in the conduct of the business to which it pertains.

Entry of judgment See enter a judgment.

Entry, writ of See writ of entry.

Enumerated Mentioned specifically (e.g., the enumerated powers of Congress in the Constitution).

Enure To operate or take effect. To serve to the use, benefit, or advantage of a person.

En ventre sa mere In its mother's womb; an unborn child.

En vie In life; alive.

Environment The totality of physical, economic, cultural, and social circumstances or factors that surround and affect the qualify of life and the value of property.

Envoy A diplomat of the rank of minister or ambassador sent by a country to the government of a foreign country to execute a special mission or to serve as a permanent diplomatic representative.

Epilepsy An occasional, periodic, excessive, and disorderly discharge of nerve cells in the brain; a disruption of the normal rhythm of the brain, manifesting itself in seizures.

Episcopacy A form of church government by bishops; the office of a bishop.

Equal 1. On the same plane or level with respect to efficiency, worth, value, amount, or rights. **2.** Identical.

Equal degree Persons are related to a decedent "in equal degree" when they are all removed by an equal number of steps or degrees from the common ancestor.

Equality The condition of possessing substantially the same rights, privileges, and immunities, and being subject to substantially the same duties.

Equalization The act or process of making equal or bringing about conformity to a common standard.

Equal protection of the law A constitutional guarantee that no person or class of persons shall be denied the same protection of the laws concerning life, liberty, property, and pursuit of happiness that is enjoyed by other persons or other classes in like circumstances; all persons similarly situated shall be treated alike.

Equal Rights Amendment Proposed constitutional amendment: "Equality of rights under the law shall not be denied or abridged by the United States or by any State on account of sex."

Equip To supply whatever is necessary for the efficient operation of something.

Equipment Furnishings or what is needed for the required purposes.

Equitable 1. Just; conformable to the principles of justice and right. **2.** Existing under equity; available or sustainable in equity or under the principles of equity.

Equitable abstention doctrine A court may refrain from exercising jurisdiction that it possesses in the interests of comity between courts and between states.

Equitable action An action seeking an equitable remedy of relief (e.g., an injunction).

Equitable adjustment theory In the settlement of federal contract disputes, the contracting officer should make a fair adjustment within a reasonable time before the contractor is required to settle with its subcontractors, suppliers, and other creditors.

Equitable adoption For some purposes (e.g., determining heirship), a child will be considered the adopted child of a person who has made a contract to adopt the child even though the statutory adoption procedures were not followed, if the contract was otherwise performed.

Equitable assignment An assignment that, though invalid at law, will be recognized and enforced in equity.

Equitable conversion An "equitable conversion" takes place when a contract for the sale of real property becomes binding on the parties. Thenceforth, the buyer is deemed the equitable owner of the land, and the seller is the owner of the purchase price. For a limited purpose, there is a constructive alteration in the nature of the property; the real estate is considered personalty and the personal estate is considered realty.

Equitable distribution Following a divorce, the equitable (but not necessarily equal) division between the former spouses of all property legally and beneficially acquired during the marriage by either party regardless of which party holds legal title.

Equitable election The obligation imposed upon a party to choose between two inconsistent or alternative rights or claims in cases where there is a clear intention that this party should not enjoy both (e.g., a party cannot accept the benefits of a will and at the same time refuse to recognize the validity of the will in other respects).

Equitable estoppel The voluntary conduct of a person will preclude him or her from asserting rights against another who has justifiably relied on the conduct and who would suffer damage or injury if the person is now allowed to repudiate the conduct. Such a repudiation would be against equity and good conscience.

Equitable interest The interest of a beneficiary under a trust is considered equitable as contrasted with the legal interest of the trustee who holds legal title to the trust property.

Equitable lien A right to have specific property applied in whole or in part to the payment of a particular debt or class of debts.

Equitable mortgage An agreement to post certain property as security before the security agreement .is formalized.

Equitable owner The person who is recognized in equity as the owner of the property even though bare legal title to the property is in someone else.

Equitable recoupment A rule of law that diminishes the right of a party to recover a debt to the extent that the party holds money or property of the debtor to which the party has no moral right.

Equitable relief The kind of relief sought in a court with equity powers (e.g., injunction, specific performance of a contract).

Equitable restraint doctrine A federal court will not intervene to enjoin a pending state criminal prosecution without a strong showing of bad faith and irreparable injury.

Equitable servitude A restriction on the use of land, enforceable in a court of equity.

Equity 1. Justice administered according to fairness in a particular case, as contrasted with the strictly formalized rules of the old common-law courts. This kind of justice was available in Courts of Equity or Courts of Chancery. Since the merger of law and equity, however, equitable principles or doctrines are applied in most courts today. **2.** Fairness, justice, and right. **3.** The monetary value of the property in excess of what is owed on it. The value of a homeowner's unencumbered interest in real estate. Equity is computed by subtracting from the property's fair market value the total of the unpaid mortgage balance and any outstanding liens or other debts against the property. A homeowner's equity increases as the mortgage is paid off or as the property appreciates in value. When the mortgage and all other debts against the property are paid in full the homeowner has 100% equity in his or her property.

Equity financing Raising capital by a corporation by issuing (i.e., selling) stock, as opposed to debt financing, which is raising capital by issuing bonds or by borrowing money.

Equity jurisdiction Those cases that are proper subjects for the application of equitable principles. Before law and equity were merged in the same court, "equity jurisdiction" referred to the power of a separate Court of Equity to hear the case.

Equity of a statute A rule of statutory construction that includes within the scope of a statute those situations that are neither expressly included nor excluded but which are clearly within the spirit and general meaning of the statute. The statute is treated as a declaration of policy which serves as precedent in analogous situations not expressly covered by the statute itself.

Equity of redemption The right of a mortgagor upon payment of the debt plus interest and costs to redeem mortgaged property after it has been forfeited by a breach of a condition of the mortgage.

Equity ratio A stockholders' equity divided by total assets.

Equity shares Shares of any class of stock, whether or not preferred as to dividends or assets, having unlimited dividend rights.

Equivalent Equal in value, force, measure, volume, power, or effect.

Equivocal Having more than one meaning or sense.

Erase To obliterate words or marks from a written instrument by rubbing, scraping, or scratching them out.

Erie v. Tompkins The landmark case holding that in an action in a federal court, the law to be applied is the law of the state in which the federal court is situated, except as to matters governed by the U.S.

Constitution and acts of Congress. 304 U.S. 64, 58 S.Ct. 817, 82 L.Ed.2d 1188 (1938).

Erosion Wearing away by the action of water, wind, or other elements.

Errant Wandering.

Erratum Error.

Erroneous Involving error; deviating from the law.

Error A mistaken judgment or incorrect belief as to the existence or the consequences of a fact; a false or mistaken conception or application of the law.

Error coram nobis See coram nobis.

Error coram vobis See coram vobis.

Error in fact Error in fact occurs when, by reason of some fact unknown to the court and not apparent on the record (e.g., infancy, or death of one of the parties), it renders a judgment void or voidable.

Error nominis Error of name. A mistake of detail in the name of a person.

Escalator clause In a union contract: A clause that wages will rise or fall depending on a standard such as the cost-of-living index. In a lease: A clause that the rent may be increased to reflect increases in operating costs or increases allowed by new rent-control regulations. In a construction contract: A clause authorizing the contractor to increase the contract price if the costs of labor and materials increase.

Escape 1. To flee from or avoid. **2.** The voluntary departure from lawful custody by a prisoner with the intent to evade the due course of justice. **3.** To leak or flow from an enclosure.

Escape clause A provision in a contract or other document allowing the parties to avoid liability or performance under certain conditions.

Escapium That which comes by chance or accident.

Escheat A reversion of property to the state when no individual is available who qualifies to inherit it.

Escobedo rule An accused has been denied assistance of counsel when the following circumstances occur: A police investigation has begun to focus on a particular suspect, the suspect is in custody, the suspect requests and is denied counsel, and the police have not warned him or her of the right to remain silent. No statement elicited during such interrogation may be used in a criminal trial.

Escrow Property (e.g., money, stock, deed) delivered by one person (called the grantor, promisor, or obligor) into the hands of another person (e.g., bank, escrow agent) to be held by the latter until a designated condition or contingency occurs, at which time the property is delivered to the grantee, promisee, or obligee.

Escrow account A bank account generally held in the name of the depositor and an escrow agent, which is returnable to the depositor or payable to a third person on the fulfillment of the escrow condition. In FHA mortgage transactions, an escrow account usually refers to the funds a mortgagor pays the lender at the time of the periodic mortgage payments. The money is held in a trust fund, provided by the lender for the buyer. Such funds should be adequate to cover yearly anticipated expenditures for mortgage insurance premiums, taxes, hazard insurance premiums, and special assessments.

Espionage Gathering, transmitting, or losing information on national defense with the intent or with reason to believe that the information will be used to the injury of the United States or to the advantage of any foreign nation.

Esquire The title given to an attorney.

Essence 1. The gist or substance of something. **2.** That which is indispensable.

Essential Required for the continued existence of a thing.

Essoin To present or offer an excuse for not appearing in court on an appointed day in obedience to a summons.

Establish 1. To make or form. **2.** To place beyond doubt or dispute. **3.** To make secure.

Establishment 1. A business or institution. **2.** The act of creating, building or establishing. **3.** Providing governmental sponsorship, aid, or preference of one religion over another (Establishment Clause). **4.** The people or institutions that dominate a society.

Estate 1. An interest in real or personal property; the extent of one's interest in real or personal property. **2.** The total property of whatever kind that is owned by a decedent prior to the distribution of that property according to the terms of a will or according to the laws of inheritance if the decedent dies intestate; all of the property of a bankrupt, incompetent person, insane person, ward, etc. **3.** A large amount of property on which someone lives. **4.** The social, civil, or political condition or standing of a person.

Estate at sufferance The interest that someone has in land when he or she comes into possession of it by permission of the owner, but who continues to occupy the land after the permission has ended.

Estate at will The interest that a person has in land that is held at the will of the lessor.

Estate by elegit See elegit.

Estate by purchase An estate acquired by a method other than descent (e.g., through a sale).

Estate by the entirety See tenancy by the entirety.

Estate for life See life estate.

Estate for years An estate for a fixed and determinate period of time (e.g., a lease of land for 3 years).

Estate from year to year 1. An estate for which the parties have agreed to renewal for successive 1-year periods. **2.** An estate that arises after a tenant has been allowed to hold over after the expiration of his or her term; an estate that arises when no term has been set by the parties.

Estate in common See tenancy in common.

Estate in coparcenary See coparcenary.

Estate in expectancy An estate that is not yet in possession; the enjoyment of the estate will begin at a future time.

Estate in severalty An estate held by a person in his or her right only, without any other person being joined or connected in point of interest during his or her estate.

Estate in tail An estate of inheritance that, instead of descending to heirs generally, goes to the heirs of the donee's body—the donee's lawful issue, the donee's children, and through them to the donee's grandchildren and on in a direct line.

Estate of inheritance An estate that may descend to heirs.

Estate planning The branch of the law that arranges a person's property and estate, taking into account the law of wills, taxes, insurance, property, and trusts so as to gain maximum benefit of all laws and to carry out the person's wishes for the disposition of his or her property upon death.

Estate pur autre vie An estate that is held during the period of someone else's life (i.e., someone other than the holder).

Estate tail female When lands are given to a person and the female heirs of his or her body. The male heirs are not capable of inheriting it.

Estate tail male When certain lands are given to a person and the male heirs of his or her body. The female heirs are not capable of inheriting it.

Estate tax A tax imposed on the right to transfer property at death; the tax is imposed on the decedent's estate and not on the recipients of the property. The latter pay an inheritance tax.

Estate upon condition An estate in lands having a qualification annexed to it by which it may be created, enlarged, or destroyed upon the happening of a particular event.

Estimate An attempt to value or rate something without actually measuring, weighing, etc.

Estimated tax A tax that is initially computed without fully accurate and complete information, filed as a preliminary matter, to be followed by a final tax return.

Estimated useful life The period over which an asset will be used by a particular taxpayer.

Estop To stop or bar.

Estoppel Prevention of a party, due to his or her own conduct, from claiming a right to the detriment of another party when the latter was entitled to rely and did in fact rely on this conduct.

Estoppel by deed A grantor in a warranty deed who did not have title at the time of the conveyance but who subsequently acquires title, is estopped from denying that he or she had title at the time of the transfer. Such after-acquired title inures to the benefit of the grantee and his or her successors.

Estoppel by election An estoppel that arises by a voluntary and intelligent choice between inconsistent positions; the party so choosing cannot afterward reverse his or her election and dispute the state of affairs or rights of others resulting from his or her original choice.

Estoppel by judgment When a fact has been agreed upon or decided in a court of record, neither party shall be allowed to call it into question or have it tried over again at any time thereafter so long as the judgment or decree stands unreversed; a final adjudication of a material issue by a court of competent jurisdiction binds the parties in any subsequent proceeding between or among them, irrespective of any difference in the forms or causes of action.

Estoppel by verdict Under the doctrine of estoppel by verdict or collateral estoppel, when a particular issue is actually or necessarily finally determined by a court of competent jurisdiction and then is put into issue in a subsequent suit on the same or on a different cause of action between the same parties or those in privity with them, the former adjudication of the issue is held to bind the parties or their privies in the subsequent suit.

Estoppel in pais A person may be precluded by his or her act, conduct, or silence (when there is a duty to speak) from asserting a right that he or she otherwise would have had. A prohibition imposed due to action or inaction on the part of one against whom estoppel is asserted, which induces reliance thereon by another to the detriment of the latter.

Estrepe To commit waste upon an estate.

Ethical Conforming to standards of professional conduct.

Ethics Standards of professional conduct.

European Economic Community (EEC) Common Market. An economic union to stimulate free trade, and to standardize economic and social conditions among member nations.

Euthanasia The act or practice of painlessly putting to death those persons who are suffering from incurable and distressing diseases.

Evasion The act of eluding or avoiding something by artifice.

Evasive Tending or seeking to evade.

Evasive answer Refusing either to admit or to deny a matter in a direct, straightforward manner on a matter the person is necessarily presumed to have knowledge.

Evening The closing part of the day and early night before bedtime.

Evict To dispossess.

Eviction The act of depriving a person of land or rental property that he or she has held or leased; dispossession by process of law.

Evidence Anything offered to establish the existence or nonexistence of a fact in dispute (e.g., testimony, writings, other material objects, demonstrations).

Evidence aliunde Evidence from outside.

Evident Clear to the understanding; apparent to observation.

Evidentiary facts Those facts that are necessary for a determination of the ultimate facts; the premises upon which conclusions of ultimate facts are based.

Evidentiary harpoon Deliberately placing improper evidence by the prosecution before the jury (e.g., evidence of prior arrests), where such evidence would not be admissible.

Exaction Taking that which is not due; the wrongful act of an officer or other person in compelling payment of a fee or reward for his or her services under color of his or her official authority, where no payment is due.

Exactor In the civil law, a gatherer or receiver of money; a collector of taxes.

Examination An inspection or interrogation.

Examination de bene esse A provisional examination of a witness; an examination of a witness whose testimony is important and might be lost.

Examination in chief The first examination of a witness by the party who produces the witness.

Examined copy A copy of a record, public book, or register that has been compared with the original.

Examinee The person being examined.

Examiner An officer or other person authorized to conduct an examination or appointed by the court to take the testimony of witnesses.

Except 1. To leave out. **2.** Other than.

Exceptio An exception, plea, or objection.

Exception 1. An objection to an order or ruling of a hearing officer or judge. **2.** The act of excluding or separating something out; that which is not included. **3.** A deviation.

Excess Pertaining to an act or amount that goes beyond what is usual, proper, or necessary.

Excessive Greater than what is usual or proper; going beyond a just measure or amount.

Excessive bail A sum that is more than will be reasonably sufficient to prevent evasion of the law by flight or concealment; bail that is per se unreasonably great and clearly disproportionate to the offense involved or shown to be so by the special circumstances of a particular case.

Excessive damages Damages awarded by a jury that are grossly in excess of the amount warranted by law on the facts and circumstances of the case; unreasonable or outrageous damages.

Excessive force That amount of force which is beyond the need and circumstances of the particular event or which is not justified in the light of all the circumstances (e.g., the use of deadly force to protect property when life or limb is not in jeopardy).

Excess profits tax A tax levied on profits that are beyond the normal profits of a business; a tax on corporations that accumulate an unreasonable surplus of profits rather than paying them out as dividends.

Exchange 1. To barter, transfer, or give. **2.** The act of giving or taking one thing for another; a transaction in which one piece of property is given in return for another piece of property. **3.** An organization that provides a marketplace or facilities for bringing together buyers and sellers of securities (New York Stock Exchange).

Exchange broker One who negotiates bills of exchange drawn on foreign countries or on other places in the same country; one who makes and concludes bargains for others in matters of money or merchandise.

Exchange rate The value of one country's money in terms of the value of another country's money (e.g., the dollar vs. the pound).

Exchequer The department in the government of England in charge of collecting national revenue; the Treasury Department.

Excise 1. A tax imposed on the performance of an act, engaging in an occupation, or the enjoyment of a privilege. **2.** To remove or cut away.

Excited utterance A statement relating to a startling event or condition, made while the declarant was under the stress of excitement caused by the event or condition. Such statements are exceptions to the hearsay rule.

Exclusion Denial of entry or admittance.

Exclusionary rule Where evidence has been obtained in violation of the U.S. Constitution (e.g., evidence obtained through an illegal search and seizure), the evidence will be excluded from the trial. Exceptions to this rule now exist.

Exclusionary zoning Any form of zoning ordinance that tends to exclude specific classes of persons or businesses from designated districts or areas.

Exclusive Not allowing others to participate; belonging to one person or group.

Exclusive agency A grant to an agent of the exclusive right to sell within a particular market or area.

Exclusive agency listing An agreement between a property owner and a real estate broker whereby the owner agrees to pay a fee or commission to the broker if the property is sold during the listing period, regardless of whether the broker is responsible for the sale.

Exclusive jurisdiction The power of a court or other tribunal over an action or person, to the exclusion of all other courts or tribunals.

Ex contractu From or out of a contract (an action arising ex contractu).

Exculpate To free from guilt or blame.

Exculpatory Clearing or tending to clear from alleged fault or guilt.

Exculpatory statement A statement that tends to justify, excuse, or clear the defendant from alleged fault or guilt.

Excusable Capable of being forgiven; implying the existence of a legal excuse.

Excusable neglect The failure to take the proper steps at the proper time, not because of carelessness, inattention, or recklessness but because of (a) some unexpected or unavoidable hindrance or accident, (b) reliance on the care and vigilance of one's attorney, or (c) reliance on promises made by an adverse party.

Excusatio In the civil law, an excuse or reason that exempts from some duty or obligation.

Excuse 1. A reason alleged for doing or not doing something; a reason for relief or exemption from some duty or obligation **2.** To grant forgiveness.

Excussio In civil law, a diligent prosecution of a remedy against a debtor.

Ex delicto From a tort, fault, crime, malfeasance, or delict.

Ex dividend Without dividend. When stock is sold ex dividend, the seller, not the buyer, has the right to the next dividend that has been declared but not paid.

Exeat See ne exeat.

Execute 1. To complete or carry into full effect. **2.** To put to death.

Executed Carried out according to its terms.

Executed consideration A consideration that is wholly performed.

Executed remainder A remainder that vests a present interest in the tenant, though the enjoyment is postponed to the future.

Execution 1. Carrying out some act or course of conduct to its completion. **2.** The process of carrying into effect the decisions in a decree or judgment; a court officer (e.g., sheriff) is commanded to take the property of the losing litigant in order to satisfy the judgment debt. **3.** Capital punishment.

Execution creditor A creditor who has obtained a judgment against a debtor and has caused an execution to be issued on the judgment.

Execution lien A lien created when execution is levied.

Execution of an instrument The performance of all acts necessary to render an instrument (e.g., a will) complete, to make it valid, or to carry it into effect (e.g., signing it, delivering it).

Execution sale A sale of a debtor's property under the authority of a writ of execution by a sheriff or other ministerial officer.

Executive 1. Pertaining to that branch of government that is charged with carrying the laws into effect. **2.** A managing official.

Executive agreement An agreement with another country, in which the president may bind the country without seeking the approval of the Senate.

Executive clemency The power of the president or a governor to pardon or commute a criminal sentence (e.g., reduce a death sentence to life imprisonment).

Executive order An order or regulation issued by the president for the purpose of interpreting, implementing, or giving administrative effect to a constitutional provision, statute, or treaty.

Executive privilege The privilege, based on the separation of powers, that exempts the chief executive from disclosing information and documents where the exemption is necessary to the discharge of highly important executive responsibilities and the frank expression necessary in intragovernmental advisory and deliberative communications.

Executive session A meeting of a board or governmental unit that is closed to the public.

Executor A person appointed by a testator to carry out the directions in his or her will (e.g., dispose of the testator's property as provided in the will).

Executory Yet to be executed or performed; remaining to be carried into operation or effect; dependent on a future performance or event.

Executory accord An agreement for the future discharge of an existing claim by a substituted performance; a compromise agreement; an accord that has not been fully performed.

Executory bequest A bequest of a future, deferred, or contingent interest in personal property.

Executory contract A contract that has not yet been fully completed or performed.

Executory devise The disposition of a future estate in a will.

Executory interest A future interest created in someone other than the grantor, which is not a remainder and vests upon the happening of a condition or event; an estate in futuro.

Executory process An extraordinary procedure, summary in nature, designed to expedite the satisfaction of delinquent negotiable paper and make it more acceptable in commerce.

Executory remainder A contingent remainder; one that exists where the estate is limited to take effect either to a dubious and uncertain person or upon a dubious and uncertain event.

Executory sale A sale whose terms have been agreed upon but which has not yet been carried into full effect in some of its terms or details.

Executory trust A trust in which a further conveyance or settlement is to be made by the trustee.

Executrix A female executor; a woman appointed by a will to carry it out.

Exemplars Nontestimonial identification evidence taken from the defendant (e.g., fingerprints, blood sample, lineup identification, voiceprints, handwriting sample).

Exemplary 1. Serving as a warning. **2.** Serving as a model.

Exemplary damages Punitive damages; increased damages awarded to the plaintiff over and above what will compensate for his or her loss to person or property, where the wrong was aggravated by circumstances of violence, oppression, malice, fraud, or wanton conduct of the defendant.

Exemplification An official transcript of a document from public records, made in a form to be used as evidence, authenticated or certified as a true copy.

Exemplified copy A copy of a document that has been authenticated.

Exempt 1. To release from liability. **2.** Freed from a duty.

Exemption 1. Freedom from a general duty or service. **2.** A privilege allowed by law to a judgment debtor by which he or she may hold designated property free from all liability to levy and sale on execution or attachment; property exempt in bankruptcy proceedings. **3.** An amount to be subtracted from gross income to determine taxable income.

Exempt security Those securities that need not be registered under provisions of the Securities Act of 1933.

Exercise 1. To make use of. **2.** To fulfill or perform.

Ex gratia Out of grace; as a matter of grace.

Ex gratia payment Payment made by one who recognizes no legal obligation to pay but who makes payment to avoid greater expense. A payment without legal consideration.

Exhaustion of administrative remedies A party must first seek relief by trying all available administrative remedies before going to a court to ask for judicial action.

Exhibit 1. To show; to offer for inspection. **2.** A paper, document, chart, or other thing that is shown to a judge, jury, hearing officer, auditor, arbitrator, etc., and upon being received, is marked for identification and made a part of the case or proceeding.

Exhibitionism Indecent exposure of sexual organs.

Exhume To remove from the earth something that was buried.

Exigency (exigence) Something arising suddenly, calling for immediate action.

Exigent Pressing, requiring a prompt response.

Exigent circumstances The emergency-like demands of the occasion call for immediate police response (e.g., the presence of weapons in a car stopped on the road). Such circumstances may justify a warrantless search and seizure.

Exigent list A list of cases set down for hearing upon various incidental and ancillary motions and rules.

Exile 1. Banishment. **2.** A person who is banished.

Ex-interest A bond or other interest-bearing security is said to be sold "ex-interest" when the seller reserves to itself the interest already accrued and payable (if any), or the interest accruing up to the next interest day.

Exist 1. To live or have life; to be in present force, activity, or effect at a given time. **2.** To occur.

Ex officio By virtue of the office; because of holding a particular office; implied by reason of the office.

Exonerate To free from guilt.

Exoneration 1. The removal of a burden, charge, responsibility, or duty. **2.** The right to be reimbursed by reason of having paid that which another should be compelled to pay.

Exorbitant Deviating from the normal or customary course; going beyond the rule of established limits of right or propriety.

Exordium The beginning or introductory part of a speech or document.

Ex parte In behalf of or on application of one party only; with only one side present.

Ex parte divorce A divorce proceeding in which only one spouse participates; the other spouse does not appear.

Ex parte hearing, or **proceeding** A hearing in which the court or tribunal hears only one side of the controversy.

Expatriation 1. The voluntary act of abandoning one's country and becoming a citizen or subject of another. **2.** Sending someone into exile.

Expect 1. To look forward to something intended, promised, or likely to happen. **2.** To require.

Expectancy That which is expected or hoped for; the condition of being deferred to a future time; the condition of being dependent on an expected event.

Expectant Contingent as to possession or enjoyment.

Expectant right A right that is contingent, not vested; one that is dependent on an event or condition that may not happen.

Expedient Whatever is suitable and appropriate to a particular end.

Expedite To hasten; to make haste.

Expediter Someone who sees to it that materials are always available for production.

Expedition 1. An important journey or excursion. **2.** The persons making the important journey or excursion.

Expeditious Performed with speed and efficiency.

Expel To drive out, often by the use of force.

Expend 1. To pay out. **2.** To consume.

Expenditure The act of spending or paying out money.

Expense An outlay, cost, or price.

Expense ratio Proportion or ratio of expenses to income.

Experience The skill, facility, or practical wisdom gained by personal knowledge, feeling, and action.

Experience rating A method of determining insurance rates by using the loss experience of the insured over a period of time.

Experiment A special test or observation made to confirm or disprove something doubtful.

Expert One who is knowledgeable, through experience or education, in a specialized field.

Expert testimony The opinion evidence of a person who possesses special skill or knowledge in some science, profession, or business that is not common to the average person.

Expert witness A person who by reason of education or specialized experience possesses superior knowledge on a subject about which persons of no particular training are incapable of forming an accurate opinion or deducting correct conclusions.

Expiration Cessation. Coming to a close from the mere lapse of time.

Explicit Clear in understanding; not obscure or ambiguous.

Exploit 1. To take unjust advantage of another for one's own advantage or profit. **2.** To make use of.

Exploration Discovery efforts directed at the unknown; the examination and investigation of land, which may contain valuable minerals, by drilling, boring, sinking shafts, driving tunnels, etc.

Export 1. To carry or send abroad. **2.** A thing or commodity that is exported.

Export-Import Bank An independent agency of the federal government whose function is to aid in financing exports and imports.

Expose 1. To offer for public view. **2.** To submit to danger or harm.

Exposition An explanation or interpretation.

Expository statute A statute enacted to explain the meaning of a previously enacted statute.

Ex post facto After the fact.

Ex post facto law A law passed after the occurrence of a fact or the commission of an act, which retroactively changes the legal consequences of this fact or act.

Exposure The act or state of exposing or being exposed.

Express Definite; unambiguous and not left to inference.

Express active trust A trust where the will confers general authority upon the executor to manage the property of the estate and to pay over net income to devisees or legatees.

Express authority Authority delegated to an agent by words that expressly, plainly, and directly authorize him or her to perform a delegated act.

Express contract An actual oral or written agreement of the parties, the terms of which are openly uttered or declared at the time the agreement is made.

Expressio unius est exclusio alterius A maxim or canon of statutory construction: When the legislature expressly mentioned one thing in a statute, we can assume that it intended to exclude other things (e.g., if the statute says "teachers" must register, the implication is that police officers do not have to register under this statute).

Express malice Actual malice; malice in fact; ill will or wrongful motive; a deliberate intention to commit an injury; knowing falsehood or a reckless disregard for truth or falsity.

Express private passive trust A trust where land is conveyed to or held by one person in trust for another without any power being expressly or impliedly given to the trustee to take actual possession of the land or to exercise acts of ownership over it except by direction of the beneficiary.

Express trust A trust created or declared in express terms for specific purposes and usually in writing.

Express warranty An affirmation of fact or a promise made by the seller to the buyer, which relates to the goods and becomes part of the basis of the bargain, and creates an express warranty that the goods shall conform to the affirmation. Any description of the goods and any sample or model that is made part of the basis of the bargain creates an express warranty that all of the goods shall conform to the description, sample, or model.

Expromissio In the civil law, a species of novation by which a creditor accepts a new debtor, who becomes bound instead of the old debtor.

Expropriate To take private property for public purposes.

Expulsion A putting or driving out; a permanent cutting off from the privileges of an institution or society.

Expunge To erase or eliminate.

Expungement of record The process by which the record of (a) a criminal conviction, (b) an arrest, or (c) an adjudication of delinquency is destroyed or sealed after the expiration of a designated period of time.

Expurgate To purge or cleanse.

Expurgator A censor; someone who expurgates.

Ex quay Onto the dock.

Ex rel. Upon relation or information (State ex rel. Doe v. Roe). Legal proceedings that are instituted by the attorney general, or other proper person, in the name of the state but on the information and at the instigation of an individual who has a private interest in the matter are said to be taken "on the relation" (ex rel.—the abbreviation for ex relatione) of such person, who is called the relator.

Ex relatione See ex rel.

Ex rights Without certain rights.

Extend 1. To enlarge; to carry or draw out further than the original limit. **2.** To give or offer.

Extended term insurance A non-forfeiture provision in most policies that continues the existing amount of life insurance for as long a period of time as the contract's cash value will purchase term coverage.

Extension 1. An increase in the length of time (extension of the lease). **2.** An addition or enlargement to a structure.

Extenuating Tending to lessen or mitigate; making something less heinous or reprehensible than it would otherwise be.

Extenuation That which renders a crime or tort less heinous or offensive.

External 1. Outward. **2.** Acting from without.

Exterritoriality An exemption from a foreign country's local laws, enjoyed by ambassadors and many subordinates when living in that country.

Extinct No longer in existence or use.

Extinguish To bring an end to.

Extinguishment The destruction or cancellation of a right, power, contract, or estate.

Extinguishment of legacy This occurs if the identical thing bequeathed is not in existence, or has been disposed of so that it does not form part of the testator's estate at the time of death.

Extort To compel or coerce; to gain by wrongful methods.

Extortion Obtaining property from another through the wrongful use of actual or threatened force, violence, or fear. This includes a threat to cause public officials to take designated action (i.e., a threat that is made under color of official right).

Extra 1. Additional. **2.** Beyond.

Extract 1. To draw out or forth; to pull out from a fixed position. **2.** A portion or segment of a writing.

Extradition The surrender of one state or country to

another of an individual accused or convicted of an offense outside its own territory and within the territorial jurisdiction of the other, which, being competent to try and punish the individual, demands the surrender.

Extra-dotal property In Louisiana, property that does not form part of the dowry of a woman, also called paraphernal property.

Extrahazardous Concerning conditions of special and unusual danger.

Extrajudicial Done, given, or effected outside the course of regular judicial proceedings; unconnected with an action in a court of law.

Extrajudicial confession A confession made out of court; one that is not made in the course of a judicial examination or investigation.

Extranational Beyond the territorial and governing limits of a country.

Extraneous 1. Irrelevant. **2.** Foreign, of external origin.

Extraneous evidence As to a document (e.g., contract, will), extraneous evidence is evidence not furnished by the document itself but derived from outside sources.

Extraordinary Exceeding the usual, average, or normal measure or degree.

Extraordinary dividend A dividend of a corporation that is nonrepetitive and generally paid at an irregular time because of some unusual corporate event.

Extraterritoriality The operation of laws to persons who are physically beyond the limits of the enacting state or nation but still amenable to its authority.

Extraterritorial jurisdiction Judicial power that extends beyond the physical limits of a particular state or country.

Extra vires Beyond powers.

Extreme 1. Intense, abnormal. **2.** Concerning the most remote in a direction.

Extreme case A case in which the facts, the law, or both reach the outer limits of probability; a desperate case.

Extremis, in In the last illness.

Extremity 1. A limb of the body. **2.** The farthest point, section, or part.

Extrinsic 1. From outside sources. **2.** Not essential.

Extrinsic evidence External evidence; evidence that is not contained in the body of an agreement or other document; evidence outside of the writing.

Extrinsic fraud Fraud that is collateral to the issues tried in the case where the judgment is rendered; the type of deceit that may form the basis for setting aside a judgment.

Eyewitness A person who saw the act, fact, or transaction to which he or she is giving testimony.

Fabricate To invent or make up.

Fabricated evidence Evidence manufactured or arranged after the fact; it is either wholly false or distorted by contrivance with an evil intent.

Face 1. That which is apparent to a spectator. **2.** To confront.

Face amount The amount shown on the document or instrument, not including accrued interest.

Face of the instrument That which is shown by the language used by the document without any explanation, modification, or addition from extrinsic facts or evidence.

Facere To do, to make.

Face value The value expressly stated in the security, policy, or other document.

Facias That you cause.

Facilitation In criminal law, the act of making it easier for another to commit a crime.

Facsimile 1. An exact copy of the original. **2.** Transmitting printed text or pictures by electronic means. For example, two "fax" machines connected by regular telephone lines can send a page of an appellate brief to each other in seconds.

Facsimile signature One that has been reproduced by some mechanical or photographic process.

Fact That which is ascertained by the senses or by the testimony of witnesses describing what they perceived; an actual thing, event, action, circumstance, or occurrence.

Factio testamenti In the civil law, the right, power, or capacity of making a will.

Factor 1. A circumstance or influence that brings about or contributes to a result. **2.** A commercial agent employed by a principal to take custody of and sell merchandise consigned to him or her on behalf of the principal.

Factorage 1. The wages, allowance, or commission paid to a factor. **2.** The business of a factor.

Factoring The sale of a firm's accounts receivable to a factor at a discounted price.

Factorizing process A process by which the effects of a debtor are attached in the hands of a third person.

Fact question See issue of fact.

Factum 1. The fact; the existence; the doing. **2.** A statement of facts. **3.** The execution of a will.

Factum probandum The fact to be proved.

Faculties 1. Abilities, powers, capabilities. **2.** The capability of a husband to provide his wife with alimony. **3.** The teaching staff of a school.

Failing circumstances The lack of sufficient assets to pay one's debts.

Failure 1. The lack of success. **2.** An omission or neglect.

Failure of consideration The consideration, although originally existing and good, has since become worthless, has ceased to exist, or has been partially or entirely extinguished.

Failure of issue Dying without children.

Failure to state a cause of action The failure of the plaintiff to allege enough facts in the complaint to warrant the granting of relief even if the plaintiff could prove all of the facts alleged.

Fair Free from prejudice and favoritism; evenhanded.

Fair comment Statements made on a matter of public concern in the honest belief of their truth.

Fair hearing A hearing that is conducted according to fundamental principles of justice; a hearing that provides procedural due process of law (e.g., the right to an impartial decision maker, the right to present evidence, the right to have the decision based on the evidence presented).

Fair Labor Standards Act A federal statute that sets the minimum standard wage (periodically increased by later statutes) and a maximum work week for industries engaged in interstate commerce. The statute also regulates child labor and established the Wage and Hour Division in the Department of Labor.

Fairly 1. Equitably, honestly. **2.** Somewhat.

Fair market value The amount at which property would change hands between a willing buyer and a willing seller, neither being under any compulsion to buy or sell and both having reasonable knowledge of the relevant facts.

Fairness Justice, balance.

Fairness doctrine The affirmative responsibility of a broadcaster to provide coverage of issues of public importance that is adequate and that fairly reflects differing viewpoints. Major advocates of both sides of political and public issues should be given fair or equal opportunity to broadcast their viewpoints.

Fair preponderance of the evidence Evidence that outweighs that which is offered to oppose it; the more convincing evidence.

Fair trade laws Statutes that permitted manufacturers or distributors of brand goods to fix minimum retail prices.

Fair use doctrine The privilege of someone other than the owner of copyrighted material to use the latter in a reasonable manner without consent.

Fair value The present market value; the price a seller, willing but not compelled to sell, would take, and a buyer, willing but not compelled to buy, would pay.

Fait accompli That which is done and cannot be changed.

Faith 1. Purpose, intent, design (good faith, bad faith). **2.** Confidence, reliance, trust. **3.** One's religious beliefs. **4.** Loyalty.

Faithfully Diligently, conscientiously.

Fake 1. To falsify. **2.** A counterfeit.

Fallacious Logically inconsistent.

Fallopian tube An essential part of the female reproductive system consisting of a narrow conduit, about 4 inches in length, which extends on each side of a woman's body from the base of the womb to the ovary upon that side; the tubes carry the egg cells to the uterus.

Fallow Barren.

False Not true. Knowingly, negligently, or innocently untrue.

False arrest An unlawful restraint of an individual's personal liberty or freedom of locomotion; an arrest without proper legal authority.

Falsehood A statement or assertion known to be untrue and intended to deceive.

False imprisonment A tort with the following elements: (a) An act that completely confines the plaintiff within fixed boundaries set by the defendant; (b) intent to confine the plaintiff or a third person; (c) causation of the confinement; (d) the plaintiff either was conscious of the confinement or was harmed by it.

False light See invasion of privacy.

False personation The criminal offense of falsely representing some other person and acting in the character thus unlawfully assumed, in order to deceive others, and thereby gain some advantage, or enjoy some privilege belonging to the one so personated, or subject him or her to some expense, charge, or liability.

False return A return of a writ of process in which the officer falsely reports that he or she served it or makes some other false or incorrect statement, whereby injury results to a person.

False pretenses A statutory crime. The elements are often as follows: (a) A false representation of a material present or past fact, (b) which causes the victim to pass title to his or her property to the wrongdoer, (c) who knows the representation is false and intends thereby to defraud the victim.

False representation Elements: (a) A statement of fact that is untrue; (b) the defendant knew it was false or made it without knowledge as a positive statement of known fact; (c) the plaintiff believed the statement to be true; (d) relied and acted on it; (e) and was injured thereby.

False swearing Knowingly making a false statement under oath or affirmation.

False token A false document or sign of the existence of a fact, used for the purpose of fraud.

Falsi crimen Fraudulent subornation or concealment.

Falsify To give a false appearance to something.

Family Parents and children; a group of blood relatives; a collective body of persons who live in one house and under one head or management.

Family allowance A certain amount of decedent's property allocated for the support of the widow and children during the period of estate administration.

Family purpose (automobile) doctrine When a car is maintained by its owner for the general use and convenience of his or her family, the owner is liable for the negligence of a member of the family (who has general authority to drive the car) while the car is being used for the pleasure or convenience of a member of the family.

Family settlement An agreement among members of a family settling the distribution of family property among them. An arrangement among heirs of a deceased person, by which they agree on distribution or management of the estate without administration by a court.

Fannie Mae See Federal National Mortgage Association.

Farm A track of land devoted to agriculture, stock raising, and the like.

Farm Credit Administration An independent agency that supervises and coordinates the activities of the cooperative Farm Credit System, which is comprised of federal land banks, federal land bank associations, federal intermediate credit banks and production credit associations, and banks for cooperatives.

Farmer One engaged in agricultural pursuits as a livelihood or business.

Farmer's cooperative An organization whose major function is to market the combined crops, produce, or livestock of its farmer-owners.

Farm out 1. To lease for a term at a stated rental. **2.** To exhaust farm land by the continuous raising of a single crop.

FAS See free alongside.

Fatal Causing death.

Fatal error Errors that may reasonably be held to have worked substantial injury or prejudice to the complaining party; harmful error, reversible error.

Fatal variance A variance between the pleading and the proof that misleads the defendant in making a defense.

Fault An error or defect of judgment or conduct to which blame and culpability attaches.

Faux In French law, a falsification or fraudulent alteration.

Favor 1. An act of kindness and generosity. **2.** Partiality. **3.** To show partiality or unfair bias toward. **4.** To support.

Favored nation See most favored nation clause.

Favoritism Invidious preference and selection based on friendship and factors other than merit.

Fax See facsimile.

FCC See Federal Communications Commission.

FCIC Federal Crop Insurance Corporation, which sponsors insurance coverage against financial loss due to destruction of agricultural products resulting from the elements of nature.

FDIC See Federal Deposit Insurance Corporation.

Fealty Fidelity; allegiance to the feudal law of the manor.

Fear Apprehension of harm; consciousness of approaching danger.

Feasance A performance; the doing of an act.

Featherbedding An employee practice designed to create or spread employment by unnecessarily maintaining or increasing the number of employees used or the amount of time consumed to work on a particular job (e.g., encouraging make-work and minimum crew regulations).

FECA See Federal Employees' Compensation Act.

Federal Pertaining to the national government of the United States.

Federal Aviation Administration (FAA) The FAA, within the Department of Transportation, regulates air traffic to foster safety, operates a common system of air traffic control, etc.

Federal Communications Commission (FCC) The FCC regulates interstate and foreign communications by radio and television broadcasting; telephone, telegraph, and cable operations; two-way radio operators; and satellite communication.

Federal courts The courts of the United States as created either by Art. III of U.S. Const., or by Congress.

Federal Deposit Insurance Corporation (FDIC) An independent federal agency that insures a designated amount of deposits in national banks and in state banks that meet prescribed qualifications.

Federal Employees' Compensation Act (FECA) A type of workers' compensation plan for federal employees by which payments are made for death or disability sustained in performance of employment duties.

Federal Employer's Liability Act (FELA) A federal workers' compensation law that protects employees of railroads engaged in interstate and foreign commerce, who are injured in the performance of employment duties.

Federal Home Loan Bank Board The board that charters and regulates federal savings and loan associations, and controls the system of Federal Home Loan Banks.

Federal Home Loan Banks Banks created for the purpose of keeping a permanent supply of money available for home financing. Savings and loan associations, insurance companies, and similar companies making long-term mortgage loans may become members of the Federal Home Loan Bank System and thus may borrow from one of the twelve regional banks throughout the country.

Federal Home Loan Mortgage Corporation (Freddie Mac) A federal agency that purchases first mortgages (both conventional and federally insured) from members of the Federal Reserve System and the Federal Home Loan Bank System.

Federal Housing Administration (FHA) A federal agency that insures mortgage loans made by FHA-approved lenders on homes that meet FHA standards in order to make mortgages more desirable investments for lenders.

Federal Insurance Contributions Act (FICA) A federal statute imposing social security taxes on employers, employees, and the self-employed.

Federalism The interrelations between the states and the federal government and among the states.

Federalist Papers A series of essays by Alexander Hamilton, James Madison, and John Jay, expounding and advocating the adoption of the Constitution of the United States.

Federal jurisdiction The powers of the federal courts based on Article III of the U.S. Constitution and specific acts of Congress.

Federal Land Banks Regional banks established by Congress to provide mortgage loans to farmers.

Federal Maritime Commission The federal agency that regulates waterborne foreign and domestic offshore commerce of the United States, assures that U.S. international trade is open to all nations on fair and equitable terms, and guards against unauthorized monopoly in the waterborne commerce of the United States.

Federal Mediation and Conciliation Service A federal agency that helps prevent disruptions in the flow of interstate commerce caused by labor-management disputes by providing mediators to assist disputing parties in the resolution of their differences.

Federal National Mortgage Association (Fannie Mae) A federal agency that provides a secondary market for the purchase and sale of mortgages guaranteed by the Veterans Administration and those insured under the Federal Housing Administration.

Federal Power Commission (FPC) A federal agency that issues permits and licenses for nonfederal hydroelectric power projects, regulates interstate wholesale transactions in electric and natural gas, issues certificates for interstate gas sales and the construction of interstate pipeline facilities, conducts investigations of power industries, etc.

Federal pre-emption See pre-emption.

Federal question A legal issue in a case arising under and involving the interpretation and application of the U.S. Constitution, acts of Congress, or treaties; a case within the jurisdiction of the federal courts.

Federal Register A daily publication that makes available to the public federal agency regulations and other legal documents of the executive branch. It includes proposed changes in rules, regulations, and standards on which the public is invited to submit commentary before final adoption.

Federal regulations See Code of Federal Regulations.

Federal Reporter (F., F.2d) A reporter that publishes opinions of designated federal courts, primarily the U.S. Courts of Appeals.

Federal Reserve Act The federal statute that created the Federal Reserve Banks, which act as agents in maintaining money reserves, issuing money in the form of bank notes, lending money to banks, and supervising banks.

Federal Reserve Board of Governors The seven-member board appointed by the president and confirmed by the Senate, which sets reserve requirements for member banks, reviews and approves the discount-rate actions of regional Federal Reserve Banks, sets ceilings on the rate of interest that banks can pay on time and savings deposits, and issues regulations.

Federal reserve notes A form of currency issued by Federal Reserve Banks in the likeness of noninterest-bearing promissory notes payable to bearer on demand (e.g., the one-dollar bill).

Federal reserve system A network of twelve central banks to which most national banks belong and to which state-chartered banks may also belong. Membership rules require investment of stock and minimum reserves. The system was designed to give the country an elastic currency, provide facilities for discounting commercial paper, and improve the supervision of banking.

Federal Rules Decisions (F.R.D.) A reporter that publishes some federal court decisions that construe or apply the Federal Rules of Civil, Criminal, and Appellate Procedure as well as the Federal Rules of Evidence.

Federal Rules of Appellate Procedure The rules governing procedure in appeals to United States Courts of Appeals from lower federal courts, and procedure in proceedings in the Courts of Appeals involving the review or enforcement of orders of federal agencies, boards, or commissions.

Federal Rules of Civil Procedure Procedural rules that govern civil actions in United States District Courts.

Federal Rules of Evidence Rules that govern the admissibility of evidence at trials in federal courts and before United States magistrates.

Federal Supplement (F.Supp.) A reporter that publishes some opinions of designated federal courts, primarily the United States District Courts.

Federal Torts Claims Act The federal statute that gave the government's consent to be sued in tort in designated kinds of cases (e.g., a negligence action arising out of acts or omissions of a federal employee at the ministerial level where no discretion at the planning level is involved).

Federal Trade Commission (FTC) A federal agency that promotes free and fair competition in interstate commerce through prevention of general trade restraints such as price-fixing agreements, false advertising, boycotts, illegal combinations of competitors, and other unfair methods of competition.

Federation A joining together of states or nations in a league or association; the league itself.

Fee 1. Payment for a service. **2.** An estate of inheritance without condition; an estate in which the owner has full powers of disposition.

Fee simple absolute An estate in which the owner is entitled to the entire property with unconditional power of disposition during his or her life; if the owner dies intestate, the property descends to his or her heirs and legal representatives.

Fee simple conditional A fee that is limited or restrained to particular heirs exclusive of others.

Fee simple defeasible A fee estate that may end upon the happening of a specified event.

Fee simple determinable A fee simple with a provision for automatic expiration of the estate on occurence of a stated event.

Fee splitting 1. Receiving part of the fee as a result of making a referral of the client. **2.** A single bill to a client covering the fee of two or more lawyers who are not in the same law firm.

Fee tail An estate of inheritance that, instead of descending to heirs generally, goes to the heirs of the body of the grantee or devisee and through them, to his or her grandchildren in a direct line.

Feigned Pretended, fictitious.

FELA See Federal Employers' Liability Act.

Fellatio A sexual act in which the mouth or lips come into contact with the penis.

Fellow Concerning a companion.

Fellow servant rule At common law, in an action for damages brought against an employer by an injured employee, the employer may reduce or extinguish its liability by proving that the negligence of another employee was partly or wholly responsible for the accident resulting in the injury.

Felo de se Killing of self; suicide.

Felon A person who has committed a felony.

Felonious Done with the intent to commit a crime.

Felonious assault A criminal assault that amounts to a felony; aggravated assault.

Felonious entry A type of statutory burglary.

Felonious intent An act of the will in which one forms a desire to commit a felony.

Feloniously Proceeding from an evil heart or purpose; done with the deliberate intent to commit a crime; pertaining to a felony.

Felonious taking Taking with the intent to steal. See larceny, seizure, felony.

Felony Any offense punishable by death or imprisonment for a term exceeding a year; a crime more serious than a misdemeanor.

Felony murder rule At common law, one whose conduct brought about an unintended death in the commission or attempted commission of a felony was guilty of murder.

Feme covert A married woman.

Feme sole A single woman.

Fence 1. An enclosure about a field or other space. **2.** A receiver of stolen property.

Fencing patents Patents procured in an effort to broaden the scope of the invention beyond the article or process intended to be manufactured or licensed.

Feneration Usury; the gain of interest.

Feoffee One to whom a fee is conveyed.

Feoffment The grant of a fee (i.e., full ownership of an estate); the grant of a corporeal hereditament where seisin is passed by investiture or by livery of seisin.

Feoffor The person making a feoffment.

Ferae naturae Of a wild nature or disposition.

Feral Pertaining to wild animals.

Ferine Untamed.

Ferry To transport people or property across a body of water commercially.

Festinum remedium A speedy remedy.

Fetal Pertaining to an unborn child.

Feticide The destruction of a fetus.

Fetter Chain or shackle.

Fetus Unborn offspring. In humans, the unborn offspring in the postembryonic period after major structures have been outlined—from 7 or 8 weeks after fertilization until birth.

Feud 1. Bitter strife between individuals or groups. **2.** An inheritable right to the use and occupation of land, held on condition of rendering services to the lord or proprietor who retained the property in the land.

Feudal Pertaining to a feud or fee; growing out of feudalism based on the relationship between the vassal and the lord.

Fiat An authoritative order or decree; "let it be done."

Fiat money Paper currency not backed by gold or silver; also called "flat money."

Fiction of law An assumption or supposition of law that a state of facts exists that has never really taken place. An assumption, for purposes of achieving justice, that a fact is true even though it may not be true (e.g., an assumption that you are in possession of your home even though you may not be actually in it all the time).

Fictitious Based on a fiction, pretended, counterfeit.

Fictitious person or **payee** A person, who, though named as payee in a check has no right to it or its proceeds because the drawer of it so intended.

Fidei-commissum In the civil law, a gift of property (usually by will) to a person, accompanied by a request or direction of the donor that the recipient will transfer the property to another, the latter being a person not capable of taking directly under the will or gift.

Fidelity bond or insurance A contract whereby the insurer agrees to indemnify the insured against loss resulting from the dishonesty or default of a designated person.

Fides Faith, honesty, veracity.

Fiduciary A person or institution that manages money or property for another; someone in whom another has a right to place great trust and to expect great loyalty.

Fiduciary bond A type of surety bond that the court requires of persons who serve as trustees, administrators, executors, guardians, and conservators to assure proper performance of their duties.

Fiduciary capacity Acting on behalf of another in a relationship that necessitates great confidence, trust, and good faith.

Fiduciary money Money, the face value of which is measured by the full faith and credit backing of the issuing government, as opposed to being backed by any measure of real value such as gold or silver.

Fiduciary or confidential relation A relationship founded on trust, reliance, dependence, or confidence, reposed by one person in the integrity and fidelity of another who is in a position of relative dominance and influence (e.g., the attorney-client relationship).

Fief An estate in fee; feud; land held by a vassal.

Field An open area of land commonly used for cultivation or pasturage.

Field audit An audit conducted on the business premises of the taxpayer.

Field book A description of the courses and distances of the lines, and of the corners of the lots of the town as they were surveyed, and as they appear by number and division on the town plan.

Field Code The original New York Code created by David Dudley Field in 1848, calling for the simplification of civil procedure.

Field warehousing An arrangement whereby a wholesaler, manufacturer, or merchant finances its business through a pledge of goods remaining on its premises.

Fieri facias You "cause [it] to be done." A writ of execution commanding the sheriff to levy and make the amount of a judgment from the goods and chattels of the judgment debtor.

FIFO First in, first out; an inventory flow assumption by which ending inventory cost is determined from the most recent purchases, and the cost of goods sold is determined from the oldest purchases, including the beginning inventory.

Fifth degree of kinship The degree of kinship between a deceased intestate and the children of the deceased's first cousin.

Fighting words Words that would have a tendency to cause acts of violence by the person to whom they are addressed.

Filch To steal something, usually of small value.

File 1. A record; the place where records are kept. **2.** To deposit in the custody or among the records of another. **3.** To arrange something in a particular order.

File wrapper estoppel If, to obtain a patent, an inventor restricts what is claimed, he or she is thereafter bound by that surrender, which may readily be ascertained by an examination of the file wrapper. The latter is the written record of the preliminary negotiations between the applicant and the Patent Office for a patent monopoly. One cannot recapture in an infringement action the breadth of a patent previously abandoned in the patent office.

Filial Relating to or befitting a child.

Filiate To assign or determine paternity.

Filiation A judicial determination of paternity.

Filiation proceeding A statutory proceeding, criminal in form but in the nature of a civil action, to establish paternity and to enforce the duty to support the child.

Filibuster A tactic designed to obstruct and delay legislation by prolonged and often irrelevant speeches on the floor of the legislature.

Filius nullius The son or child of nobody; an illegitimate child.

Final 1. Conclusive. **2.** Last.

Final judgment A judgment is final when it determines the rights of the parties and disposes of all the issues involved so that no future action by the court will be necessary in order to settle and determine the entire controversy.

Finance 1. To supply with funds through the issuance of stocks, notes, etc.; to provide with capital or loan money for a business. **2.** The management of money, credit, investments, etc.; the acquisition and valuation of financial resources.

Finance bill A draft or bill of exchange in the nature of an advance issued by a bank to draw funds from another bank, often secured only by the full faith and credit of the drawee bank.

Finance charge The extra cost imposed for the privilege of deferring payment of the purchase price.

Financial Responsibility Acts State statutes that require owners of motor vehicles to produce proof of financial accountability (through personal assets or insurance) as a condition of acquiring a license and registration so that judgments rendered against them arising out of the operation of the vehicles may be satisfied.

Financial statement Any report summarizing the financial condition of an organization on any date or for any period.

Find 1. To come upon by effort or by chance. **2.** To make a determination of what the facts are.

Finder Someone who finds or locates something for another (e.g., someone who secures mortgage financing for a borrower).

Finding The result of the deliberations of a jury, referee, arbitrator, court, agency, or other entity conducting an inquiry.

Fine 1. To sentence a person convicted of an offense to pay a penalty in money. **2.** A monetary punishment imposed on someone convicted of an offense.

Firearm An instrument used in the propulsion of shot, shell, or bullets by the action of gunpowder exploded within it.

Firm 1. A business or professional entity. **2.** Fixed, binding.

Firma The name under which a person does business (German).

Firm bid or **offer** An offer that by its terms will remain open and binding until accepted or rejected.

First Preceding all others; entitled to preference or priority above others.

First cousins The children of one's uncle or aunt.

First-degree murder Killing someone (a) with malice aforethought—premeditation—or (b) with extreme cruelty or atrocity, or (c) in the commission or attempted commission of a crime punishable by death or life imprisonment.

First impression, case of A case that presents the court with an entirely new or novel question of law.

First in, first out See FIFO.

First lien A lien that takes priority and must be satisfied before all other charges or encumbrances upon the same property.

First mortgage A senior mortgage that has a priority right of payment on default over all junior encumbrances.

Fisc The treasury of a governmental body.

Fiscal Having to do with financial matters (e.g., revenue, taxes).

Fiscal year A period of 12 consecutive months chosen by a business as the accounting period for annual reports (e.g., 7/1 to 6/30, or 1/1 to 12/31).

Fishing expedition A loose, vague, or unfocused questioning or investigation; an overly broad use of the discovery process.

Fit Suitable, appropriate.

Fitness Suitability.

Fitness for a particular purpose, warranty of Where the seller at the time of contracting has reason to know any particular purpose for which the goods are required and that the buyer is relying on the seller's skill or judgment to select or furnish goods that are suitable, there is, unless excluded or modified, an implied warranty that the goods shall be good for that purpose.

Fix 1. To determine. **2.** To fasten. **3.** To repair. **4.** To assign. **5.** To prearrange something dishonestly.

Fixed assets Plant assets (e.g., machinery, land, buildings).

Fixed capital The amount of money that is permanently invested in the business.

Fixed charges Expenses that must be borne regardless of the condition of the business (e.g., interest and tax payments).

Fixed income Income that does not fluctuate over a period of time (e.g., interest on a bond).

Fixed opinion A bias or prejudgment as to guilt or liability.

Fixed trust A non-discretionary trust in which the trustee may not exercise his or her own judgment.

Fixture Something so attached to land as to be deemed a part of it; something attached to land by roots, embedded in it, permanently resting on it, or connected by cement, plaster, bolts, etc.

Flagrante delicto In the very act of committing the crime.

Flagrant necessity A case of urgency, rendering lawful an otherwise illegal act.

Flat bond A bond that includes accrued interest in the price.

Flat money See fiat money.

Fleet policy A blanket insurance policy that covers a number of vehicles owned by the same insured.

Float, floating 1. The time between the deposit of a check in one bank and its subtraction from an account in another bank; checks and other items in the process of collection. **2.** To allow a given currency to freely establish its own value as against other currencies by the law of supply and demand.

Floater policy An insurance policy that is issued to cover items that have no fixed location (e.g., jewelry that is worn).

Floating debt Liabilities, other than bonds, that are payable on demand or at an early date (e.g., accounts payable).

Floating easement An easement for a right-of-way that is not limited to any specific area on the land to which the easement attaches.

Floating interest rate A rate of interest that is not fixed but which varies depending on the existing rate in the money market.

Floating lien A security interest under which the borrower pledges security for present and future advances. Such security is not only in inventory or accounts of the debtor in existence at the time of the original loan but also in its after-acquired inventory or accounts.

Floating stock The process by which stock is issued and sold.

Floating zone A special detailed use district of undetermined location in which the proposed kind, size, and form of structures must be preapproved.

Flogging Thrashing or beating with a whip or lash.

Floor 1. The lower limit. **2.** The part of the legislature in which members sit and cast their votes. **3.** The right of someone to address the assembly.

Floor plan financing A loan to a retail seller that is secured by the items to be sold and that is paid off as each item sells.

Flotsam, flotsan Goods that float on the sea when cast overboard for the safety of the ship or when the ship is sunk.

Fluctuating clause A type of escalator clause that is inserted in some long-term contracts to allow for an increase in costs during the contract period.

Flume A stream, river, or artificial channel.

Fly-power A written assignment in blank, whereby, on being attached to a stock certificate, the stock may be transferred.

FOB See free on board.

Follow 1. To accept as authority. **2.** To go or come after.

Food and Drug Administration A federal agency within the Department of Health and Human Services, established to set safety and quality standards for foods, drugs, cosmetics, and other consumer products.

Forbearance The act by which a creditor waits for payment of a debt after it becomes due from the debtor; refraining from taking action, especially to enforce one's rights.

For cause A reason that is relevant to ability and fitness to perform one's duty.

Force 1. Strength directed to an end. **2.** Physical coercion. **3.** Legal validity.

Force and arms Done with violence.

Forced heir Persons whom the testator or donor cannot deprive of the portion of his or her estate reserved for them by law unless a just cause exists to disinherit them.

Forced sale A sale of property pursuant to an execution of a judgment (e.g., to satisfy a mortgage or tax debt).

Force majeure An unexpected event; an irresistible and superior force.

Forcible detainer A summary, speedy, and adequate statutory remedy to obtain possession of premises to which one is entitled. The remedy exists against a person who originally had rightful possession of the realty but who refused to surrender it when his or her right ended.

Forcible entry Taking possession of lands or tenements with force and arms, against the will of those entitled to possession, and without lawful authority.

Forcible trespass Taking or seizing the personal property of another by force, violence, or intimidation, or by forcibly damaging it.

For collection A form of indorsement on a note or check where it is not intended to transfer title to it or to give it credit or currency, but merely to authorize the transferee to collect the amount of it.

Foreclose 1. To initiate a procedure by which mortgaged property is sold in satisfaction of the mortgage debt upon default of the mortgagor; to destroy an equity of redemption. **2.** To exclude.

Foreign 1. Belonging to another nation or country. **2.** Relating to or rendered in another state. **3.** Unfamiliar.

Foreign agent A person who acts as a lobbyist representing the interests (e.g., trade, foreign aid) of a foreign nation or corporation.

Foreign corporation A corporation doing business in one state but chartered or incorporated in another state or in another country.

Foreigner A person who is not a citizen of the state or country in which he or she is present.

Foreign exchange Conversion of the money of one country into its equal of another country. The process by which the money of one country is used to pay balances due in another.

Foreign judgment A judgment of a sister state or of a foreign nation.

Foreign jurisdiction The jurisdiction of a sister state or of a foreign nation. The exercise by a state or nation of jurisdiction beyond its own territory.

Foreign substance A substance in any part of the body or organism where it is not normally found, usually introduced from without.

Foreman 1. The presiding member and spokesperson of a jury. **2.** A superintendent.

Forensic 1. Belonging to courts of justice. **2.** Concerning argumentation.

Forensic medicine The science of applying medical knowledge to the purposes of the law.

Foresee To see or know in advance.

Foreseeability The ability to see or know in advance; the extent to which something can be known in advance; reasonable anticipation of something.

Foresight Reasonable anticipation of the consequences of certain acts or omissions; prudence.

Forestall To intercept or obstruct.

Forestalling the market Securing control of commodities such as by buying or contracting for merchandise on its way to market, with the intention of selling it again at a higher price; or dissuading persons from bringing their goods or provisions there; or persuading them to enhance the price when there.

Forfeit To lose the right or privilege to something because of error, default, or crime.

Forfeiture A deprivation or destruction of a right or privilege due to neglect, crime, nonperformance of a condition, etc.; that which is forfeited.

Forge 1. To fabricate by false imitation. **2.** To give shape to.

Forgery 1. Making a false document or altering a real one with the intent to commit a fraud. **2.** The document or thing that is forged.

Forgive To cancel.

Form 1. Technical matters of style and format not involving the merits or substance of something. **2.** A document, usually preprinted, to be filled in and adapted to one's needs.

Formal 1. Following accepted procedures or regulations. **2.** Pertaining to matters of form.

Formality The conditions required by the law to use a legal proceeding (e.g., civil action) or to make an instrument (e.g., contract, conveyance) in order to ensure the regularity and validity of the proceeding or instrument.

Forma pauperis See in forma pauperis.

Former adjudication A final determination of questions of fact or rights in a former action.

Former jeopardy Double jeopardy: A person cannot be tried for the same offense more than once.

Form of the statute The words, language, or frame of a statute, and hence the inhibition or command it may contain; used in the phrase (in criminal pleading) "against the form of the statute in that case made and provided."

Forms of action The procedural devices or remedies (e.g., trespass on the case) that were used to take advantage of common-law theories of liability.

Formula 1. A fixed way of doing something. **2.** A set form of words used in judicial proceedings at common law.

Formula instruction An instruction that advises the jury that under certain facts hypothesized in the instruction, the jury should reach a verdict for one of the parties: "If you find that ..., then your verdict should be for...."

Fornication Unlawful sexual intercourse between two unmarried persons.

Forswear 1. To give up something completely. **2.** To make an oath on what one knows to be untrue.

Forthcoming bond A bond conditioned on the forthcoming of property to answer such judgment as may be entered.

Forthwith Without delay.

Fortiori See a fortiori.

Fortuitous Happening by chance or accident.

Forum 1. The court; the court where the litigation is brought. **2.** A setting or place for public discussion.

Forum contractus The place where a contract is made.

Forum non conveniens The discretionary power of a court to decline the exercise of the jurisdiction that it has when the convenience of the parties and the ends of justice would be better served if the action were brought and tried in another forum.

Forum originis The place of a person's birth.

Forum rei gestae The place where an act is done.

Forum rei sitae The place where the subject matter in controversy is situated.

Forum shopping An attempt by a party to find a particular court to try the case where he or she believes the chances are greatest for a favorable decision—assuming more than one jurisdiction is available to take the case.

Forwarder A person or firm in the business of receiving goods for further handling by way of warehousing, packing, carload shipping, delivery, etc.

Foster home A home where substitute family care can be provided for a child when its own family cannot care for it for a temporary or extended period and adoption is neither desirable nor possible at the present time.

Foundation A permanent fund established and maintained for charitable, educational, religious, or other benevolent purpose.

Foundling A deserted or abandoned child.

Four corners The face of a written document.

Fourth estate The press.

Frais de justice In French and Canadian law, costs incurred incidental to an action.

Franchise 1. A privilege that is granted or sold. **2.** The right to vote.

Franchise clause A provision in a casualty insurance policy to the effect that the insurer will pay those claims only over a stated amount and that the insured is responsible for all damage under the agreed amount. Once the claim exceeds the agreed amount, the insurer pays the entire claim.

Franchise tax A tax on the right and privilege of a company to engage in business.

Franking privilege The privilege of sending certain matter through the mail without paying postage.

Fraternal benefit association or **society** A nonprofit association of persons of similar calling or background who aid and assist one another and promote worthy causes. The organization has a representative form of self-government, a lodge system, and ritualistic practices.

Fratriage A younger brother's inheritance.

Fratricide The killing of one's brother or sister.

Fraud A harmfully false and deceptive statement of fact. Elements of this tort (also called deceit): (a) a statement of past or present fact, or a concealment of past or present fact, or a nondisclosure of past or present fact where there is a duty to disclose; (b) the statement is false; (c) scienter, the intent to deceive—in some states this element is met by negligently misleading the victim; (d) the defendant intends to have the victim rely on the statement or has reason to believe that the victim will rely on it; (e) the victim actually relies on it; (f) the victim's reliance is justifiable; (g) the victim suffers actual damages.

Fraud in law Constructive or presumed fraud.

Fraud in the factum Fraud that goes to the nature of the document itself.

Fraud in the inducement Fraud that induces the

transaction by the misrepresentation of motivating factors such as value and usefulness.

Frauds, statute of See statute of frauds.

Fraudulent Performed with the purpose of carrying out a fraud.

Fraudulent concealment The hiding or suppressing of a material fact or circumstance that one is legally or morally bound to disclose.

Fraudulent conveyance or **transfer** A conveyance or transfer of property made with the goal of defrauding, hindering, or delaying a creditor by placing the property beyond the reach of the creditor.

Freddie Mac See Federal Home Loan Mortgage Corporation.

Free Not subject to the legal constraint of another.

Free alongside (FAS) In price quotations, the price includes all costs of transportation and delivery of the goods alongside of the ship.

Freedom of Information Act (FOIA) A federal statute making information held by federal agencies available to the public unless it falls within categories that are exempt from public disclosure.

Freehold An estate for life or in fee; an estate in real property of uncertain duration.

Free on board (FOB) In a sales price quotation, the seller assumes all responsibilities and costs up to the point of delivery, including insurance, transportation, etc.

Free port An area or section of a port set aside for handling foreign goods without entering customs.

Freeze-out The use of corporate control vested in the statutory majority of shareholders or the board of directors to eliminate minority shareholders from the enterprise or to reduce to relevant insignificance their voting power or claims on corporate assets.

Freight Goods transported by carrier. The price paid for transported goods. The transportation itself.

Freight forwarder One who in the ordinary course of business assembles and consolidates small shipments into a single lot and assumes responsibility for transportation of such property from point of receipt to point of destination.

Fremdenrecht Legal status of aliens or foreigners (German).

Fresh Following without any material interval.

Fresh pursuit Hot pursuit. The common-law right of a police officer, engaged in a continuous and uninterrupted pursuit, to cross geographic or jurisdictional lines to arrest a felon.

Friendly Pertaining to someone who is favorably disposed.

Friendly fire A fire burning in a place where it is intended to burn.

Friendly suit A suit instituted by agreement between the plaintiff and the defendant in order to obtain the opinion of the court on a question in which both are interested.

Friend of the court See amicus curiae.

Fringe benefits Side benefits that accompany or are in addition to a person's regular compensation (e.g., paid insurance, paid holidays and vacations).

Frisk To conduct a pat-down search of a suspect in order to discover weapons.

Frivolous Clearly insufficient on its face; of little weight or importance.

Frivolous appeal An appeal raising no justiciable issue and devoid of merit in that the prospect of its success is very small.

Frontage The front part of property between the building and the street; the line of property on a public street.

Frontier That portion of the territory of any country that lies close along the border line of another country and hence "fronts" or faces it.

Front wages or **pay** Prospective payments made to a victim of job discrimination who cannot yet be given the job to which he or she is entitled. These payments, given until the job comes through, make up the difference between money earned now and money that would be made now if the new position were immediately available.

Frozen account An account in which no activity is permitted until a court order is lifted.

Fruit The effect or consequence of an act or operation.

Fruit of the poisonous tree doctrine An unlawful search taints not only the evidence obtained at the search but also facts discovered by the process initiated by the unlawful search.

Frustration of contract The duty to perform a promise in a contract is discharged in the following circumstances: The parties expressly agree or impliedly understand that a specific thing is necessary for the performance of the promise and the thing is no longer in existence at the time for performance.

Frustration of purpose A promisor is excused from performance when the objectives of the contract have been utterly defeated by circumstances arising after the formation of the agreement even if performance is still technically possible.

Fugitive One who flees; someone who escapes from the law.

Full blood Children of the full blood, whole blood, or entire blood have the same mother and father.

Full court A court en banc; a bench with all the judges present.

Full faith and credit The states must recognize (give full faith and credit to) the legislative acts, public records, and judicial decisions of sister states. U.S. Const., Art. IV, Sec. 1.

Full indorsement One by which the indorser orders the money to be paid to some particular person by name; it differs from a blank indorsement which consists merely in the name of the indorser written on the back of the instrument.

Functionary Someone who serves a special function; a public officer or employee.

Functus officio A task performed.

Fundamental error An error that goes to the merits of the plaintiff's cause of action; error of such character as to render the judgment void.

Funded debt A debt that has resources earmarked for the payment of interest and principal as they become due (e.g., a special fund, future taxation).

Fundi patrimoniales Lands of inheritance.

Fundi publici Public lands.

Fundus Land.

Fungibles Goods consisting of identical and interchangeable particles or components (e.g., grain, oil).

Furandi animus An intention of stealing.

Furlong One-eighth of a mile.

Furlough A leave of absence.

Furtherance An act of helping forward.

Fusion Complete takeover of a business either by terminating the legal existence of the firm taken over or by continuing its legal existence under the control of the acquiring firm.

Future Pertaining to what is still to come or to a later time.

Future advances Money lent after a security interest has attached, and secured by the original security agreement.

Future interests Interests in land or in other things in which the privilege of possession or other enjoyment is future and not present.

Futures Items sold or bought to be delivered in the future.

Futures contract A present right to receive at a future date a specific quantity of a given commodity for a fixed price.

Gabel An excise or tax.

Gag order An order by the court (a) to bound and gag an unruly defendant to prevent further interruptions of the trial, or (b) to stop attorneys and witnesses from discussing the case with the media, or (c) to stop the media from reporting aspects of the trial.

Gain Profits; winnings; increments of value; differences between receipts and expenditures.

Gainful Advantageous, profitable.

Gallon A liquid measure containing 231 cubic inches, four quarts, 3.785 liters.

Gallows Scaffold.

Gambler One who practices games of chance with the expectation of winning something.

Gambling The dealing, operating, carrying on, or maintaining any game for pay involving chance and the possibility of a reward.

Gambling device An apparatus or device used and employed for gambling where money is staked, wagered, lost, or won as a direct result of its employment or operation.

Game laws Laws for the preservation of wild birds and beasts.

Game of chance A game in which success or failure depends less on skill and experience than on purely fortuitous or accidental circumstances not under the control of the player.

Gaming Playing games of chance. An agreement between two or more persons to play together at a game of chance for a stake or wager, which becomes the property of the winner and to which all contribute.

Gaol A prison for temporary confinement.

Garnishee A person against whom the process of garnishment is issued; a person who has property of the judgment debtor that is being reached or attached (garnished) by another.

Garnishment A statutory proceeding whereby a person's property or credits in the possession or under the control of another are applied to the former's debt to a third person; the satisfaction of an indebtedness out of property or credits of the debtor in the possession of or owed by another.

GATT General Agreement on Tariffs and Trade. A multilateral international agreement that requires foreign products to be accorded no less favorable treatment under the law than that accorded domestic products.

Gay Attracted to the same sex, homosexual, homophile, lesbian.

Gazette The official publication of the English government.

Geld In Saxon law, money or tribute.

Genealogy The summary history or table of a family, showing how the persons listed are related to each other; an examination of descent from an ancestor.

General Accounting Office (GAO) An independent nonpolitical agency in the legislative branch of the federal government. The GAO assists Congress in carrying out its legislative and oversight functions (e.g., by conducting audits and other accountability investigations of federal programs). See audit.

General administration An unrestricted grant of authority to administer the entire estate of the decedent.

General appearance The defendant submits his or her person to the jurisdiction of the court by coming to the court in person or through a duly authorized representative; a consent to the jurisdiction of the court.

General Assembly A legislative body in many states.

General assignment for the benefit of creditors A transfer of legal and equitable title to all of the debtor's property to a trustee, who will have the authority to liquidate the debtor's affairs and distribute the proceeds to creditors.

General bequest A gift payable out of the general assets of the estate, not a gift of a particular item.

General contractor One who contracts to construct an entire building or project rather than a portion of it; a prime contractor who hires subcontractors, coordinates the work, etc.

General Court The name of the legislature in Massachusetts and in New Hampshire.

General damages Damages the law implies or presumes to have accrued from the wrong for the reason that they are its immediate, direct, and proximate result; damages that necessarily result from the injury; damages that did in fact result from the wrong, directly and proximately, and without reference to the special character, condition, or circumstances of the plaintiff.

General denial A response by a party that controverts all of the allegations in the preceding pleading.

General Digest One of the units of the American Digest System. The General Digest gives small paragraph summaries of published opinions for every court during the period of time since the last Decennial Digest was published.

General indorsement An indorsement without mentioning the name of an indorsee.

General jurisdiction Jurisdiction that extends to all controversies that may be brought before a court.

General mortgage Mortgages are sometimes classified as general and special. A general mortgage binds all property, present and future, of the debtor (sometimes called a "blanket" mortgage). A special mortgage is limited to particular and specified property.

General partner One of two or more persons who associate to carry on a business as co-owners for profit and who are personally liable for all the debts of the partnership.

General power of appointment One exercisable in favor of any person the donee may select.

General Services Administration (GSA) The federal agency that manages government property and records. The GSA supervises building construction and operation, supply procurement, communication systems, etc.

General strike Cessation of work by employees throughout an entire industry or country.

General verdict A verdict whereby the jury finds either for the plaintiff or for the defendant in general terms; the ordinary form of a verdict—distinguished from a special verdict, in which the jury finds facts only.

General warranty deed A deed that conveys not only all the grantor's interests in and title to the property to the grantee, but also warrants that if the title is defective or has a "cloud" on it (such as mortgage claims, tax liens, title claims, judgments, or mechanic's liens against it), the grantee may hold the grantor liable.

General welfare The government's concern for the health, peace, morals, and safety of its citizens.

Generation A single succession of living beings in natural descent; a degree of removal in computing descents; individuals born around the same time period; the average span of time between the birth of parents and that of their offspring.

Generic Relating to or characteristic of an entire group or class.

Genetics The study of heredity.

Geneva Convention An 1864 international agreement for the conduct of nations at war, providing that a belligerent shall give proper care to enemy sick or wounded, that Red Cross personnel shall be respected, etc.

Genitals Reproductive organs.

Genoese lottery The numerical lottery. Out of ninety consecutive numbers, five are to be selected or drawn by lot; the players wager that one, two, or more of their selected numbers will be drawn among the five or that they will appear in a certain order.

Gentleman's agreement An agreement reached without formalities; an agreement based on honor.

Gentrification The process by which deteriorated or slum neighborhoods are renovated by those with financial resources.

Genuine A document or other item is genuine when it is what it purports to be.

Genuine issue An issue that can be sustained by substantial evidence; a real issue; a triable issue where sufficient evidence exists to warrant a jury determination.

Geriatrics The study of old age.

Gerrymander Dividing a geographic area into voting districts or divisions in order to provide an unfair advantage to one political party.

Gestation The time during which a woman carries a fetus in her womb from conception to birth.

Gestor In the civil law, one who acts for another.

Get Under Hebraic law, evidence of the granting of a divorce.

Gibbet A gallows; the post on which malefactors are hanged.

Gift A gratuitous transfer of property to another. Elements: (a) There must be a delivery of the property; (b) the transfer must be voluntary; (c) the donor must have legal capacity to make a gift; (d) the donor must intend to divest him or herself of title and control of what is given; (e) the donor must intend that the gift take effect immediately; (f) there must be no consideration (e.g., payment) from the donee; (g) the donee must accept the gift.

Gift causa mortis A gift of personal property made in the expectation of the donor's death and on condition that the donor die as anticipated.

Gift inter vivos A gift between the living; a gift that is perfected during the lifetime of the donor and the donee.

Gifts to Minors Act A Uniform Act adopted by most states to provide a method of transferring property to a minor. An adult custodian receives the property, invests it, and makes the income available for the support of the minor.

Gift tax A tax imposed on the transfer of property by gift, which is paid by the donor.

Gild In Saxon law, a tax or tribute.

Gill One-fourth of a pint.

Ginnie Mae See Government National Mortgage Association.

Gist 1. The essential point. **2.** The essential ground or object in point of law, without which no cause of action would exist.

Give To make a gratuitous transfer of property to another.

Giving in payment In Louisiana, the delivery and acceptance of real or personal property in satisfaction of a debt, instead of a payment in money.

Gloss An interpretation of a text.

GNP See gross national product.

Going and coming rule While an employee is going to or coming from work, he or she is generally not considered to be within the scope of employment for purposes of workers' compensation benefits and respondeat superior.

Going concern An existing solvent business operating in its ordinary and regular manner.

Going private Delisting a class of equity securities from a national securities exchange; removing the authorization to quote a class of equity securities in an interdealer quotation system of a registered national securities exchange.

Going public Issuing stock for public purchase for the first time; becoming a public corporation.

Golden rule 1. A canon of statutory interpretation in which we presume that the legislature did not intend an interpretation that would lead to absurd or ridiculous consequences **2.** In the golden rule argument, the jurors are urged by counsel to place themselves in the position of the injured party or victim.

Good 1. Sufficient in law. **2.** Orderly; conformable to law.

Good cause A cause that affords a legal excuse; sufficient reason; legally sufficient ground or reason.

Good faith A state of mind characterized by honest belief, absence of malice or intent to defraud, absence of a design to seek an unconscionable advantage or of knowledge that such an advantage is likely to occur.

Good faith purchaser Someone who buys without notice of circumstances that would place a person of ordinary prudence on inquiry as to whether the seller has title to what he or she is trying to sell.

Goods Movable things other than money, securities, or intangible rights.

Good Samaritan Someone who unselfishly comes to the assistance of another.

Goodtime allowance A credit for good conduct that reduces the time a prisoner must spend in prison.

Good title A title that is free from reasonable doubt; one that is valid in fact and could be sold to a reasonable purchaser or mortgaged to a person of reasonable prudence.

Goodwill The reputation of a company that generates additional customers; the ability of a business to generate income in excess of what is normal because of superior management skills, market position, new product technology; the custom or patronage of any established trade or business.

Go to protest Commercial paper is said to "go to protest" when it is dishonored by non-payment or non-acceptance.

Govern To direct or control by authority.

Government The process of governing; the framework of political institutions by which the executive, legislative, and judicial functions of the state are carried on.

Governmental functions The functions of a municipality that are essential to its existence; functions that can be performed adequately only by the government (e.g., operation of the courts).

Governmental immunity A government cannot be sued in tort except for those categories of cases where it has consented to be sued.

Governmental instrumentality A government agency created by the constitution or by the legislature.

Government de facto A government not established according to its constitution but nevertheless operating in fact as the government.

Government de jure A government of right established according to its constitution.

Government instrumentality doctrine The doctrine that governmental instrumentalities are tax exempt.

Government National Mortgage Association (Ginnie Mae) The federal agency within the Department of Housing and Urban Development that makes a market for higher risk loans by acquiring the loans from lenders who otherwise would not make such mortgage loans.

Government Printing Office (GPO) The federal office that prints and publishes laws, regulations, forms, and other documents.

Government survey system A type of legal description whereby the United States is generally divided into checks or tracts of ground, which are further broken down by smaller descriptions such as metes and bounds.

Governor A chief executive official.

Grace A favor or indulgence.

Grace period A designated period beyond the due date of a premium on an insurance policy, during which the insurance is continued in force. If the premium is paid during this period, the policy will be kept in good standing.

Grade 1. To bring property to the level of an abutting highway; to establish a level by mathematical points and lines and then bring the surface of a street or highway to the level by the elevation or depression of the natural surface to the line fixed. **2.** The line of the street's inclination from the horizontal; a part of a street inclined from the horizontal. **3.** A unit or degree in a scale.

Grade crossing A place where a railroad is crossed at grade by a public or private road, or by another railroad, or where one highway crosses another.

Graduated lease A lease arrangement that provides that the rent will vary depending on future contingencies such as the amount of gross income produced.

Graduated tax A tax that is structured so that the rate increases as the amount of income of the taxpayer increases.

Graft Money, advantage, or personal gain unlawfully received because of one's position of public trust.

Grain 1. In Troy weight, the twenty-fourth part of a pennyweight. **2.** Any kind of corn sown in the ground.

Grandchild Descendant of the second degree; the child of one's child.

Grandfather clause An exception to a restriction that allows all those already doing something to continue doing it in spite of the restriction; a special exemption for those already doing that which is now prohibited.

Grand Jury A jury of inquiry that receives complaints and accusations in criminal cases, hears the evidence of the prosecutor, and issues indictments in those cases in which the jury is satisfied that a trial should be held.

Grand larceny Taking and carrying away personal property of another valued in excess of a statutorily set amount (e.g., $100) with the intent to feloniously deprive the owner or possessor of it permanently.

Grange A farm furnished with barns, granaries, stables, and all conveniences for husbandry.

Grant 1. To bestow or confer on another with or

without compensation. **2.** A transfer of title to real or personal property by deed or other instrument.

Grantee The person to whom a grant is made. The party in the deed who is the buyer or recipient.

Grant-in-aid A sum of money given by a governmental agency to a person or institution for a specific purpose such as education or research.

Granting clause That portion of a deed or instrument of conveyance that contains the words of transfer of a present interest.

Grantor The person who makes the grant; the transferor. The party in the deed who is the seller or giver.

Grantor-Grantee Index A master index to all recorded instruments, containing the volume and page number where the specific instrument can be located in the record books.

Grantor trust A trust in which the grantor retains control over the income or corpus, or both, to such an extent that the grantor will be treated as the owner of the property and its income for income tax purposes.

Grass The street name for marijuana.

Gratis Without reward or consideration.

Gratis dictum A voluntary assertion; a statement a party is not legally bound to make.

Gratuitous 1. Given or granted free, without consideration. **2.** Unwarranted.

Gratuitous bailee A person to whom possession of personal property is transferred and who furnishes no consideration for such transfer.

Gratuitous guest or **passenger** A person riding in an automobile at the invitation of the owner or authorized agent but without paying any consideration or fare.

Gratuitous licensee A person who has permission (though not an invitation) to come on the property of another and who has furnished no consideration for such permission.

Gratuitous promise A promise made by one who has received no consideration for it.

Gratuity 1. Something acquired without bargain or inducement. **2.** A bribe.

Gravamen The material part of a grievance; the gist of a charge.

Gravatio An accusation or impeachment.

Gree Satisfaction for an offense committed or injury done.

Greenback United States paper currency.

Grievance 1. An injury or wrong that gives ground for a complaint. **2.** A charge or complaint.

Gross 1. Glaring, reprehensible. **2.** Total; before or without diminution or deduction.

Gross alimony See alimony in gross.

Gross average More commonly called "general average." Where loss or damage occurs to a vessel or its cargo at sea, average is the adjustment and apportionment of such loss between the owner, the freight, and the cargo, in proportion to their respective interests and losses.

Gross earnings The total receipts of a person or business before deductions and expenses.

Gross estate The property owned or previously transferred by a decedent that will be subject to the federal death tax.

Gross income All income from whatever source derived (e.g., compensation, fees, commissions; gains from dealings in property; business income; interest, rents, royalties, dividends, annuities; alimony received, etc.).

Gross interest Total interest payment by borrower including administrative, service, and insurance charges.

Gross lease A lease in which the lessee pays a flat sum for rent, out of which the lessor is required to pay all expenses such as taxes, water, utilities, insurance, etc.

Gross margin The difference between the amount of sales after returns and allowances and the cost of goods sold.

Gross misdemeanor Classification of a type of crime which, while not a felony, is ranked as a serious misdemeanor.

Gross national product (GNP) The market value within a nation of all goods and services produced, as measured by final sales of goods and services to individuals, businesses, and governments, plus the excess of exports over imports.

Gross neglect Serious failure to attend to one's duties; substantial nonfeasance.

Gross negligence The intentional failure to perform a manifest duty in reckless disregard of the consequences to the life or property of another; aggravated carelessness; conduct that is highly culpable although less serious than willful and intentional conduct.

Gross receipts The total amount of money or the value of other consideration received from selling property or from performing services.

Gross up To add back to the value of the property or income received the amount of the tax that has been deducted.

Ground 1. Foundation; points relied on. **2.** The earth's surface.

Ground rent Rent paid to the owner for the use of the land, usually to construct a building on it.

Group legal services Legal advice and representation given to members of an organization, who pay for the services in advance, in a manner similar to group health insurance programs.

Group libel The holding up of a group to ridicule, scorn, or contempt to a respectable and considerable part of the community.

Guarantee 1. An assurance that a particular outcome will occur; a contract of guaranty; the obligation of a guarantor. **2.** To assume the obligations of a guarantor.

Guaranteed insurability An option that permits the policyholder to buy additional stated amounts of life insurance at stated times in the future without evidence of insurability.

Guarantor One who makes a guaranty; one who becomes secondarily liable for another's debt or performance.

Guaranty 1. A collateral agreement by a guarantor for the performance of another's undertaking or promise—the principal obligor; if the latter fails to perform, the guarantor will do so. **2.** To undertake collaterally to answer for the payment of another's debt or performance.

Guardian A person who lawfully has the power and duty to care for the person, property, or rights of another who is incapable of managing his or her ßaffairs (e.g., a minor, an insane person).

Guardian ad litem A special guardian appointed by the court to defend or bring a suit on behalf of an infant or incompetent.

Guardianship The office, duty, or authority of a guardian; the relationship that exists between guardian and ward.

Guest 1. One who receives lodging for payment at an inn, hotel, or motel. **2.** One who is received and entertained at another's home, club, etc., other than a regular member; one who takes a ride in an automobile driven by another without providing any funds or benefits for the driver.

Guest statute Operators of automobiles shall be liable for injuries to guests only if caused by gross or willful negligence. A guest is a recipient of voluntary and gratuitous hospitality of the driver or owner of the car.

Guild A voluntary association of persons pursuing the same trade, art, profession, or business.

Guilt 1. Criminal responsibility for an offense. **2.** A feeling of remorse for wrongdoing.

Guilty 1. Having committed a crime or tort. **2.** Fraudulent, corrupt.

Gym pusher Slang for someone who sells steroids out of a gym bag around weight machines.

Habeas corpus "You have the body." A writ designed to bring a party before a court in order to test the legality of his or her detention or imprisonment (e.g., a prisoner in the custody of a warden, a child in the custody of a relative).

Habendum clause The portion of a deed beginning with the words, "to have and to hold," which describes the ownership rights being transferred (i.e., the estate or interest being granted).

Habit A disposition or condition of the body or mind, acquired by custom or repetition of the same act or function.

Habitability The condition of the premises that permits an inhabitant to live free of serious defects that endanger health and safety.

Habitable Suitable for living.

Habitancy A fixed place of abode to which one intends to return when away; a fixed and permanent residence.

Habitation Place of abode; occupancy.

Habitual Customary, usual, regular.

Habitual criminal Someone who can be subjected to more severe punishment after having been convicted of crimes a designated number of times (e.g., three); repeat offenders on whom greater sentences can be imposed.

Habitual drunkenness or intoxication Repeated and excessive indulgence in intoxicating liquor so as to acquire a fixed habit and an involuntary tendency to become inebriated as often as the temptation is presented.

Half blood (half brother, half sister) The degree of relationship that exists between persons who have the same father or the same mother but not both.

Halfway house A house in the community that helps individuals make the adjustment from prison or other institutionalization to normal life.

Halifax law A synonym for lynch law.

Hallucination An apparently real sensory perception,

auditory or visual, without any real external stimuli to cause it.

Hammer Metaphorically, a forced sale, or sale at public auction.

Hammurabi, Code of One of the oldest compilations of law in history, prepared by the Babylonian king 1792–1750 B.C. (circa).

Handbill A written or printed notice displayed, handed out, or posted to provide information.

Hand money Money paid in hand to bind a bargain; earnest money, when it is in cash.

Handwriting The cast or form of writing peculiar to a person—the size, shape, and style of letters, etc.

Handwriting exemplars Samples of one's handwriting for purposes of comparison.

Harbor 1. To shelter or protect; to receive clandestinely and without lawful authority. **2.** A place of retreat or shelter. **3.** A port for ships.

Hardship Privation, suffering.

Harm 1. Loss or detriment to a person. **2.** To injure.

Harmful Likely to cause damage or illness.

Harmless Not causing any damage.

Harmless error An error committed that was trivial, formal, and not prejudicial to the substantial rights of the party alleging it.

Harter Act A statute of Congress governing attempts to limit liability by vessel owners and operators (46 U.S.C. § 190 ff.).

Hashish A drug that is formed of resin scraped from the flowering top of the cannabis plant.

Hatch Act A federal statute that prohibits federal, state, and local employees from partaking in certain types of political activities.

Hawker A traveling salesperson who carries goods in order to sell or "hawk" them.

Hazard 1. A risk or danger lurking in a situation which by chance or fortuity could become an active agent of harm. **2.** To speculate.

Hazardous Exposed to or involving danger.

Hazardous employment High-risk and extra-perilous work.

H.B. House Bill. A proposed statute being considered by the House of Reppresentatives.

Headnote A small paragraph summary of a portion of a court opinion. The headnotes are placed before the beginning of the opinion.

Head of household An individual in one household who actually supports and maintains one or more individuals who are closely connected with him or her by blood, marriage, or adoption, and whose right to exercise family control and provide for dependent members is based on some moral or legal obligation.

Head tax A tax of a flat amount per person.

Health Freedom from pain and sickness; being whole in body and mind.

Healthy Freedom from or not being peculiarly susceptible to disease, injury, or ailment.

Hearing A proceeding with definite issues of fact or law to be resolved in which witnesses are heard, the parties confront each other, and an impartial officer presides.

Hearing de novo A second hearing; trying the matter anew as if it had not previously been heard.

Hearing examiner or **officer** See Administrative Law Judge.

Hearsay Testimony in court of a statement made by another out of court when the statement is being offered to assert the truth of the matter in the statement. The value of such a statement depends on the credibility of the out-of-court asserter.

Heart Balm Statute A law abolishing the right to sue for breach of promise to marry, alienation of affections, criminal conversation, and the seduction of a nonminor.

Heat of passion A state of violent and uncontrollable rage engendered by provocation; an emotional state of mind that is so intense that reason is overcome to the extent that the person could not form a deliberate purpose and fully control his or her actions.

Hedging Safeguarding oneself from loss on a bet, bargain, or speculation by making compensatory arrangements on the other side.

Hegemony The leadership or predominant influence of one independent state over others.

Heir One whom the state designates to receive the estate of a person who has died without leaving a valid will.

Heir apparent One who will receive the inheritance if he or she survives the ancestor; one next in line of succession.

Heir at law Lineal descendant; one who has the right to inherit the estate of his or her ancestor if the latter dies without leaving a valid will; one who has a right to the real property of his or her intestate ancestor.

Heir beneficiary In the civil law, one who has accepted the succession under the benefit of an inventory regularly made.

Heir collateral One who is not lineally related to the decedent but is of collateral kin (e.g., uncle, cousin, brother, nephew).

Heir general An heir at law.

Heir of the blood One who inherits because of consanguinity (relationship by blood) with the decedent in the ascending or descending line, including illegitimate children, but excluding husbands, wives, and adopted children.

Heir of the body An heir begotten or borne by the person referred to, or a child of such heir; any lineal descendant of the decedent, excluding a surviving spouse, adopted children, and collateral relations.

Heir unconditional In the civil law and in Louisiana, one who inherits without any reservation, or without making an inventory.

Held Decided.

Hereditament Anything that can be inherited.

Hereditary 1. Capable of being inherited. **2.** Genetically transmitted or transmittable from parent to offspring.

Heritable Capable of being inherited.

Heritage Property that can be or has been inherited; that which can be passed down to future generations.

Hermeneutics, legal The science or art of interpreting or construing legal documents.

Heroin A narcotic drug that is a derivative of opium; diacetyl-morphine.

Hidden defect A deficiency in property that is not discoverable by reasonable inspection and for which a lessor or seller is generally liable if such defect causes harm to a user.

Hierarchy An institution organized into ranks or degrees of position, power and authority.

High 1. Extreme. **2.** Superior. **3.** Intoxicated; under the influence of drugs.

High seas That portion of the ocean that is beyond the territorial jurisdiction of any country.

High-water line or **mark** The line on the shore to which high tide rises under normal weather conditions.

Highway A public roadway that everyone has the right to use.

Hijack To rob goods or vehicles while they are in transit; to seize a vehicle and force it to go in another direction.

Hire 1. To purchase the temporary use of a thing; to engage the labor of another for a fee. **2.** Compensation for labor, services, or the use of a thing.

Hiring at will Employment that can be ended at any time by either side; a general and indefinite hiring.

Hiring hall An agency or office operated by a union (or by both union and management) to place applicants for work.

Hold 1. To possess something by virtue of a lawful title (the deed gave the land to John "to have and to hold"). **2.** To occupy a position. **3.** To adjudge or decide (the court did not hold the statute invalid). **4.** To restrain or control.

Holder The person who has possession of something; the person who has legally acquired possession of an instrument (e.g., a check, a promissory note) and who is entitled to receive payment of the instrument.

Holder for value Someone who has given valuable consideration for the document of title, instrument, or investment security in his or her possession.

Holder in due course A holder who takes an instrument for value, in good faith, and without notice that it is overdue, that it has been dishonored, or that there is any defense against it or claim to it by any person.

Hold harmless To assume any liability in a situation or transaction and thereby relieve from responsibility the party who is being held harmless.

Holding 1. A court's answer to or resolution of the legal issue before it. **2.** Property owned by a person or an organization.

Holding company A company that confines its activities to owning stock in and supervising the management of other companies.

Holdover tenant A tenant who retains possession after the expiration of a lease or after a tenancy at will has been terminated.

Holiday A day set apart for commemorating an important event in history; a day of exemption from labor.

Holographic Pertaining to a will or deed written entirely by the testator or grantor in his or her own handwriting and not witnessed or attested (holographic will).

Homage In feudal law, the service that a tenant was bound to perform for his lord; the ceremony for rendering such service.

Home 1. One's dwelling place. **2.** An institution for the special care of individuals in need.

Homeowner policy A multiperil insurance policy covering fire, burglary, water, and liability.

Homeowners warranty (HOW) A warranty and insurance protection program offered by many home builders, providing protection for 10 years against major structural defects.

Home port doctrine A vessel engaged in interstate and foreign commerce is taxable only at its home port (e.g., where it is registered or enrolled).

Home rule A designated amount of self-government exercised by local cities and towns.

Homestead The dwelling house and adjoining land where the head of the family dwells; the home farm.

Homestead exemption laws Laws that allow a householder or head of a family to designate a house and land as his or her homestead, which is exempted from execution or attachment for his or her general debts.

Homicide The killing of one human being by the act, procurement, or omission of another. It is a crime only if done knowingly, purposefully, recklessly, or negligently and without justification.

Homologate In civil law, to approve; to confirm.

Honor To pay, or to accept and pay.

Honorable discharge An authoritative declaration by the government that a soldier has left the service in a status of honor.

Honorarium A fee for services or a special reward.

Honorary Referring to a title or office given as a mark of honor and esteem without duties or compensation.

Hope To desire; to expect. As used in a will, this word is usually precatory rather than mandatory.

Horizontal merger The acquisition of one company by another company producing the same or a similar product and selling it in the same geographic market.

Horizontal price fixing Agreements between producers, wholesalers, or retailers as to sale or retail prices.

Horizontal restraint An agreement between competitors at the same level of market structure.

Hornbook A book explaining the basics or fundamentals of a topic.

Hospital An institution for the treatment and care of sick, wounded, infirm, or aged persons.

Hostage An innocent person held captive by one who threatens to kill or harm the person if certain demands are not met by others.

Hostile Having the character of an enemy; opposing, unfriendly.

Hostile fire A fire that breaks out or spreads to an unexpected area.

Hostile or adverse witness A witness who manifests so much hostility or prejudice under examination that he or she can be treated as though called by the other side (i.e., the witness can be cross-examined by the side that called him or her).

Hostile possession The person in possession asserts that all other claims to possession are invalid.

Hostility A state of enmity between individuals or nations.

Hot 1. Close behind. **2.** Excited.

Hot blood The condition of one whose passions have been aroused to an uncontrollable degree, causing the homicide charge to be reduced from murder to manslaughter.

Hot cargo 1. Goods produced or handled by an employer with whom a union has a dispute. **2.** Stolen goods.

Hotchpot The blending and mixing of property belonging to different persons in order to divide it equally.

Hot pursuit See fresh pursuit.

House 1. A structure that serves as the living quarters for one or more persons or families. **2.** A business firm.

House arrest The confinement of an individual in his or her home rather than in an institution.

Housebreaking Breaking and entering a dwelling-house with the intent to commit any felony therein.

House counsel A lawyer who is an attorney-employee of a business or organization. He or she works for a salary, unlike an independent attorney who works for a fee.

Household 1. Belonging or pertaining to the house and family. **2.** A family living together.

House of Commons One of the constituent houses of the British parliament, composed of representatives of the counties, cities, and boroughs.

House of Delegates The lower branch of the legislative assembly of several states (e.g., Maryland, Virginia).

House of ill fame A brothel.

House of Lords The upper chamber of the British parliament. It is the court of final appeals in most civil cases, and has jurisdiction over impeachment.

House of prostitution A brothel.

House of Representatives The lower house of the U.S. Congress, consisting of 435 members elected to 2-year terms.

Housing Code Laws concerning fitness for habitation, setting forth standards and requirements for construction, maintenance, operation, use, or appearance of buildings, premises, and dwelling units.

Huckster A peddler, a petty merchant.

Humanitarian Concerned with social welfare and social reform.

Humanitarian doctrine See last clear chance doctrine.

Hung jury A jury so irreconcilably divided in opinion that a verdict cannot be agreed upon.

Huntley hearing A separate proceeding in a criminal case wherein the admissibility of the accused's extrajudicial statements is determined.

Husbandry Operating land to raise crops and livestock.

Husband-wife privilege See marital communications privilege.

Hush money Payment to secure silence; a bribe to hinder the release of information.

Hybrid security A security in the form of a debenture containing elements of indebtedness and elements of equity stock.

Hypothecate To pledge property as security or collateral for a debt; the pledged property is usually not physically transferred to the lender.

Hypothesis An assumption or theory to be proven or disproved.

Hypothetical Based on conjecture; theoretical.

Hypothetical question A form of question calling for an opinion from an expert based on stated fact assumptions; the expert is asked to give an opinion on the assumption that the facts are true.

Ibid In the same place; in the work previously cited or mentioned; in the same book.

Identification The act of identifying something; proof of identity; the proving that a person, subject, or article before the court is as it is alleged to be.

Identity of interests Closely related in business operations or in other activities.

Idiocy Mental retardation; subnormal intellectual ability.

Ignominy Public disgrace.

Ignorance The absence of knowledge.

Ignorantia legis neminem excusat Ignorance of the law excuses no one.

Illegal Against the law; not authorized by the law.

Illegal entry Unauthorized entry; an alien is guilty of illegal entry is he or she (a) enters at the wrong time or place in the country, or (b) eludes an examination by the immigration officers, or (c) obtains entry by fraud.

Illegality That which is contrary to the principles of the law.

Illegal per se Illegal in and of itself.

Illegitimate 1. Born out of wedlock. **2.** Contrary to law.

Ill fame Evil repute; notorious bad character.

Illicit Not permitted.

Illicit cohabitation Two unmarried persons living together as man and wife.

Illusory Deceiving by false appearances.

Illusory appointment A nominal, overly restrictive, or conditional transfer of property under a power of appointment; lacking in substantial existence.

Illusory promise A supposed promise that leaves the promisor's performance optional or entirely within the discretion of the promisor.

Illusory trust A "trust" where the creator (settlor) has retained so much control over the "trust" property that he or she clearly did not intend to reliquish any rights in the "trust" property; an invalid trust.

Imbecility A condition of mental deficiency or feeble-mindedness.

Immaterial Not material, essential, or necessary.

Immaterial evidence Evidence offered to prove a proposition that is not in issue.

Immaterial variance A discrepancy between the pleading and the proof that is so slight that a party cannot claim to have been misled thereby.

Immediate 1. At once; not deferred by any interval of time. **2.** Not separated by the intervention of any intermediate object, cause, or relation.

Immediate cause The last of a series or chain of causes tending to a given result, and which, of itself and without the intervention of any further cause, directly produces the result or event.

Immemorial Beyond human memory.

Immigrant A foreigner who comes into a country with the intention to live there permanently.

Immigration The entry of foreigners into a country for purposes of permanent residence.

Immigration and Naturalization Service (INS) A federal agency responsible for administering the immigration and naturalization laws relating to the admission, exclusion, deportation, and naturalization of aliens.

Imminent Near at hand; threatening.

Imminently dangerous article An article that is reasonably certain to place life or limb in peril.

Imminent peril Such position of danger to the plaintiff that if existing circumstances remain unchanged, injury to the plaintiff is reasonably certain.

Immoral Contrary to good morals; inimical to public welfare according to the standards of a given community as expressed through laws and otherwise.

Immovables Land and those things so firmly attached to it as to be regarded as part of it; property that cannot be moved.

Immunity Exemption or freedom from a duty, penalty, or liability.

Impacted area An area whose school district has been burdened because of attendance by the children of a large number of federal employees and which may be losing tax revenues because of the U.S. government's immunity from land taxes.

Impair To weaken or otherwise affect in an injurious manner.

Impaired capital Condition of a business when the surplus account shows a negative balance, and hence the capital is reduced below its value from when the stock was issued.

Impair the obligation of contracts To render the contract less valuable or less enforceable by changing its terms or the availability of remedies for its enforcement; to nullify or materially change existing contract obligations.

Impanel To make a list of jurors who have been selected for the trial of a particular case.

Impartial Favoring neither side; not prejudging the merits of the case.

Impeach To attack; to accuse; to challenge the credibility of.

Impeachment 1. An attack because of impropriety or lack of veracity. **2.** A procedure against a public officer before a quasi-political court (e.g., a legislative body), instituted by written accusations called articles of impeachment.

Impediment Disability or hindrance to the making of a contract.

Impediment to marriage A legal obstacle to contracting a valid marriage (e.g., being under age).

Imperfect title One that requires a further exercise of the granting power to pass the fee in land, or that does not convey full and absolute dominion.

Imperfect trust An executory trust.

Impersonate To pretend or represent oneself to be another.

Implead To bring a new party into the action on the ground that the new party is or may be liable for all or part of the current claim to the party bringing him or her in.

Implication An inference of something not directly said but arising from what is admitted or expressed.

Implied Gathered by implication or deduction from the circumstances.

Implied authority Actual power given by a principal to his or her agent, which necessarily follows from the express authority that is given; authority that is necessary, usual, and proper to accomplish the main authority that is expressly conferred.

Implied consent Signs, actions, facts, inaction, or silence that raise a presumption that consent has been given.

Implied contract A contract not created or evidenced by the explicit agreement of the parties but inferred as a matter of reason and justice from their conduct and the surrounding circumstances; a contract that exists by the tacit understanding of the parties.

Implied partnership Not a real partnership but one recognized by the court as such because of the conduct of the parties; in effect, the parties are estopped from denying the existence of a partnership.

Implied powers Such as are necessary to carry into effect those powers that are expressly granted and must therefore be presumed to have been within the intention of the constitutional or legislative grant.

Implied promise A fiction that the law creates to render one liable on a contract theory in order to avoid fraud or unjust enrichment.

Implied reservation An easement created by a grantor for the benefit of land retained by him or her and not included in the conveyance.

Implied warranty A warranty imposed by operation of law regardless of the intent of the parties; a warranty that is based on the apparent intentions of the parties.

Import To bring goods into a country from a foreign country.

Import duties Taxes payable upon goods and merchandise brought into a country from a foreign country.

Impose To inflict, thrust, or levy.

Imposition An unreasonable request or burden; a tax or impost; the act of imposing.

Impossibility That which no person in the course of nature or the law can do or perform; that which can be done only at an excessive and unreasonable cost.

Impossibility of performance Strict impossibility or impracticality because of extreme and unreasonable difficulty, expense, or loss.

Imposts Taxes, duties, or impositions that are levied.

Impotence The organic, mental, or functional inability to perform the act of sexual intercourse.

Impound To seize and take into custody of the law.

Imprimatur Let it be printed; authorization, license, or sanction.

Imprison To place in confinement.

Improper Not in accordance with fact, truth, procedure, or good taste.

Improved land Real estate whose value has been increased by the addition of sewers, roads, utilities, etc.

Improvement A valuable addition made to property or an amelioration of its condition, costing labor and capital and intended to enhance its value, utility, or beauty, or to adapt it for new or further purposes; permanent addition to or betterment of property that enhances its capital value beyond mere repairs or replacement.

Improvident Lacking in care and foresight.

Impulse A sudden urge or thrusting force within a person.

Impunity Exemption or protection from penalty or punishment.

Impute To charge or attribute.

Imputed Attributed vicariously; making one person responsible for the actions, omissions, or knowledge of another because of that person's relationship with the other.

Imputed income A value or monetary worth that is assigned to certain property, transactions, or situations for tax purposes (e.g., the value of a home provided by an employer for an employee).

Imputed knowledge Implied notice; knowledge attributed or charged to a person because the facts in question were open to his or her inspection, and his or her duty was to be aware of them.

Imputed negligence One person responsible for the negligence of another because of the relationship between them (e.g., the negligence of an employee within the scope of employment is imputed to the employer).

Inadequate Lacking in effectiveness; nonconformity to a prescribed standard or measure.

Inadequate remedy at law An ineffective legal remedy; the remedy in its nature and character is unfitted or not adapted to the end sought (e.g., collecting damages would be an inadequate remedy to force the defendant to stop poisoning the plaintiff's prize dogs; only an injunction will be adequate).

Inadmissible Pertaining to evidence that cannot be received and considered.

In adversum Against an unwilling party.

Inadvertent Careless, accidental.

Inalienable Incapable of being bought, sold, or transferred.

In arbitrium judicis At the pleasure of the judge.

Inauguration The act and ceremony of installing or inducting into office.

In banc See en banc.

In being In existence.

In bonis Among the goods or property.

In camera In private with the judge; in chambers; without spectators.

Incapacitated person A person who is impaired by reason of mental illness, mental deficiency, physical illness or disability, advanced age, or drug or alcohol addiction, to the extent of lacking sufficient understanding or capacity to make or communicate responsible decisions concerning his or her affairs.

Incapacity The absence of legal power or ability to act; the existence of an impediment preventing action.

Incarcerate To imprison or confine.

Incendiary 1. Causing fire. **2.** Provocative. **3.** One who maliciously and willfully sets fire to the buildings of others.

Incest Sexual intercourse between a man and woman who are related to each other within prohibited degrees (e.g., brother and sister).

In chief Principal; directly obtained; a term applied to the evidence obtained from a witness upon his or her examination by the party that called the witness, i.e., the direct examination of the witness (examination in chief).

Inchoate Begun but not completed; partial.

Inchoate crime A crime in its early stage, which generally leads to another crime (e.g., assault is an inchoate battery).

Inchoate dower A wife's interest in the land of her husband's during his life; a possibility of acquiring dower.

Inchoate instrument If an instrument must be registered, it is inchoate prior to its registration.

Inchoate interest An interest in land that is not a present interest but which can ripen into a vested interest if not barred, extinguished, or divested.

Inchoate lien The lien of a judgment.

Incident 1. Connected with or inherent in something else (a search incident to an arrest). **2.** An occurrence.

Incidental Depending upon and secondary to something else.

Incidental beneficiary Someone who benefits from the performance of a contract though not a party thereto.

Incidental powers Such powers as are directly and immediately appropriate to the execution of the powers expressly granted.

Incidental use In zoning, the use of premises that is dependent on or affiliated with the principal use of such premises.

Incident of ownership Ownership rights; a measure of control.

Incipitur It is begun; it begins.

Incite To urge; to instigate another to commit a crime.

Inclose To surround; to fence in on all sides.

Inclosure Land surrounded by some visible obstruction. An artificial fence around one's estate.

Include To contain; to place within.

Included offense A crime that is part of another crime (e.g., an assault and battery is included within murder).

Inclusive 1. Including the two extremes as well as what falls in between (twelve to fifteen inclusive). **2.** Comprehensive.

Income The financial return or gain derived from one's business, labor, or invested capital.

Income averaging A method of computing income taxes by an individual who has unusually large income in the current taxable year as compared with the four prior years, whereby the taxpayer elects to have the excess taxed as if it had been received ratably over a 5-year period.

Income basis A method of computing the rate of return on a security based on the dividend or interest and on the price paid rather than on its face or par value.

Income bond A bond that pays interest only when earned and after payment of interest upon prior mortgages.

Income tax A tax on the yearly profits arising from property, business pursuits, professions, trades, etc.

Incommunicado Without a way of communicating with others.

Incompatible 1. Disagreeing; characterized by deep and irreconcilable conflicts in personalities or temperaments so that it is impossible to live together normally. **2.** Mutually exclusive.

Incompetent 1. Without ability, legal qualification, or fitness. **2.** Inefficient.

Incompetent evidence Evidence that is not admissible under the rules of evidence.

Inconclusive Not final; capable of being disproved or rebutted.

Inconsistent Mutually repugnant in the sense that acceptance of one implies the abandonment of the other.

In contemplation of death With a view toward death. Certain transfers made within 3 years of the decedent's death are deemed to be made in contemplation of death for federal estate tax purposes, resulting in the inclusion of the value of the property in the decedent's estate.

Incontestability clause A clause in an insurance policy providing that after the policy has been in effect a certain length of time (e.g., 2 years), the insurer cannot contest it as to statements made in the application.

Incontestable Incapable of being disputed.

Incontinent 1. Lacking moderation; unchaste. **2.** Not being able to control urination or defecation.

Incorporate 1. To create a corporation. **2.** To unite or fuse.

Incorporation by reference The method of making one document a part of another separate document by referring to the former in the latter and declaring that the former shall be considered part of the latter.

Incorporator A person who joins with others to form a corporation.

Incorporeal Not of a material nature; intangible.

Incorporeal chattels A class of incorporeal rights growing out of or incident to things personal, such as patent rights and copyrights.

Incorporeal hereditament A right growing out of or concerning a corporeal thing (e.g., the right to dispose of water onto the property of another).

Incorporeal right Rights to intangibles such as legal actions rather than rights to property.

Incorrigible Incapable of being corrected.

Incriminate To charge with a crime; to involve oneself in the possibility of criminal prosecution. See self-incrimination.

Incriminating evidence Evidence that tends to establish guilt or from which an inference of guilt can be drawn.

Incriminatory Having a tendency to incriminate.

Incriminatory statement A statement that tends to establish the guilt of the accused or from which guilt can be inferred; a statement that tends to disprove a defense to a crime.

Incroachment An unlawful gaining upon the right or possession of another.

Inculpate To impute blame or guilt; to involve in guilt or crime.

Inculpatory Tending or intending to establish guilt.

Incumbent 1. A person who is presently in possession of an office. **2.** Obligatory.

Incumbrance See encumbrance.

Incur To become liable or subject to; to bring down upon oneself.

Indebtedness The state of being in debt; an obligation.

Indecent Obscene, vulgar.

Indecent exposure Exposing the private parts of the body in a lewd or indecent manner in a public place where he or she knows or should know that the act will be open to the observation of others.

Indefeasible Not capable of being defeated, revoked, or made void.

Indefinite Not definite; no fixed boundaries.

Indefinite failure of issue A failure of issue whenever it shall happen, sooner or later.

Indefinite legacy A legacy that passes property by a general or collective term without enumeration of number or quantity (e.g., a bequest of all the decedent's goods or of the bank account).

Indemnify To secure someone against loss or damage; to restore the victim of a loss by payment, repair, or replacement.

Indemnitee A person who is protected by another through a contract of indemnity.

Indemnitor A person who is bound by an indemnity contract to indemnify or protect another.

Indemnity 1. A right to receive compensation (or the compensation itself) to make one person whole from a loss that has already been sustained but which in justice ought to be sustained by the person from whom indemnity is sought; the obligation or duty resting on one person to make good 100% of the loss or damage another has incurred while the latter was acting at the request or for the benefit of the former. **2.** An agreement to protect another against loss suffered by the latter.

Indent 1. A certificate or indented certificate issued by the government of the United States at the close of the Revolution for the principal or interest of the public debt. **2.** To cut in a serrated or wavy line. In old conveyancing, if a deed was made by more than one party, it was usual to make as many copies of it as there were parties, and each was cut or indented (either in acute angles, like the teeth of a saw, or in a wavy line) at the top or side, to tally or correspond with the others, and the deed so made was called an indenture.

Indenture 1. A written agreement under which bonds and debentures are issued; the agreement sets forth terms such as the maturity date and the interest rate. See indent. **2.** A mortgage, deed of trust, or similar instrument in which there is a lien or other security interest. **3.** An apprenticeship agreement.

Independent Not subject to control, restriction, modification, or limitation from a given outside source.

Independent contractor A contractor who carries on an independent business and contracts to do a piece of work according to his or her own methods without being subject to the control of the employer except as to the product or result of the work.

Indeterminate Uncertain or not designated with particularity.

Indeterminate sentence A sentence to imprisonment for the maximum period defined by law, subject to termination by the parole board or other agency after the service of a minimum designated period.

Indexing Linking the level of payments on bonds, pensions, or benefits to an index such as the Consumer Price Index.

Indian Claims Commission An agency that hears and determines claims against the United States by American Indians.

Indicia Circumstances that point to the existence of a given fact as probable but not certain.

Indicia of ownership Evidence of control or title.

Indict To accuse formally of a crime through an indictment.

Indictable Subject to being indicted.

Indicted Charged in an indictment with a criminal offense.

Indictee A person indicted.

Indictment A sworn accusation of crime against one or more persons, made by a grand jury; a true bill.

Indifferent Impartial, disinterested, neutral.

Indigent Being needy and poor.

Indirect tax A tax upon some right, privilege, or franchise rather than a tax directly on property according to its value.

Indispensable evidence That without which a particular fact cannot be proved.

Indispensable party A necessary party whose absence should force the court to dismiss the action. A party is indispensable if a case cannot be decided on its merits without prejudicing the rights of that party.

Individual Retirement Account (IRA) An individual retirement trust account in which qualified persons can set aside a certain amount of income each year. The amount can be deducted, and will be subject to income tax only upon withdrawal as specified in the regulations governing the account.

Indivisible Not susceptible of division or apportionment.

Indorsee The person to whom a negotiable instrument, promissory note, bill of lading, etc., is assigned by indorsement.

Indorsement 1. The act of a payee, drawee, accommodation indorser, or holder of a negotiable instrument (e.g., note, bill, check) in writing his or her name on the back of the instrument, with or without further words, whereby the ownership or property in the instrument is assigned and transferred to another. **2.** The giving of approval.

Indorser One who indorses; the payee or holder who writes his or her name on the back of a negotiable instrument.

Inducement 1. In contracts, the benefit or advantage that the promisor is to receive from a contract is the inducement for making it. **2.** The act of influencing, bringing on, or causing.

Induct To place in possession or enjoyment; to enter formally.

Industrial development bonds Bonds issued by a municipality as a means of attracting private business.

Industrial disease A physical disorder that is caused by or is incident to a particular occupation.

Industrial relations The relationship between employer and employee (on matters such as collective bargaining and safety on the job).

Industry An art, occupation, or business conducted as a means of livelihood or for profit, especially one that is a distinct branch of trade.

Inebriated Intoxicated.

Inescapable Being helpless to avoid a consequence by oneself; inevitable.

In esse In being, actually existing.

Inevitable Incapable of being avoided; transcending human power to prevent.

Inevitable accident An unavoidable accident; one produced by an irresistible physical cause; one that cannot be prevented by human skill or care.

Inexcusable neglect Such neglect that will preclude setting aside a default judgment; neglect that is due to more than unintentional inadvertence or common frailty.

In extremis In the last illness.

Infamous Having a notorious reputation; shameful.

Infamous crime A crime punishable by death or by imprisonment in a prison or penitentiary; a crime that brings shame and disgrace on the person who commits it.

Infamy The condition of being infamous, shameful, and notorious.

Infancy Under the age of legal majority; at common law, under 21; today, usually under 18.

Infanticide The murder or killing of an infant soon after its birth.

Infeoffment The act or instrument of feoffment. See feoffment.

Inference A process of reasoning by which a fact or proposition sought to be established is deduced from other facts; the deductions or conclusions reached by this process.

Inferior 1. Having less authority and power in relationship to others. **2.** Poor quality.

Inferior court Any court that is subordinate to the highest court within its judicial system; a special court whose judgments are not given presumptive jurisdictional validity.

Infidelity Unfaithfulness in marriage; usually involving adultery.

Infirm Lacking health or moral character.

Infirmative Having the tendency to weaken or to render infirm.

Infirmity Disability, feebleness.

Informal Not observing formal regulations; deficient in legal form; casual.

Informal proceedings Proceedings that are less formal (usually considerably so) than a normal court trial (e.g., an agency hearing in which the technical rules of evidence do not apply).

Informant See informer.

In forma pauperis In the character or manner of a pauper; permission given to a poor person to proceed without having to pay court fees or costs.

Information 1. A formal accusation of a criminal offense other than through an indictment; a written accusation from a prosecutor rather than from a grand jury. **2.** Knowledge or facts that have been acquired.

Information and belief Good faith belief as to the truth of an allegation, not based on firsthand knowledge.

Informed consent A person's agreement to allow something to happen based on a full disclosure of the facts needed to make the decision intelligently.

Informer A person who informs or brings an accusation against another on the basis of a suspicion that the latter has committed a crime; the identity of the informer is usually undisclosed, and he or she volunteers the information confidentially.

Infra Below; later in the text.

Infraction A breach, violation, or infringement of a law, agreement, right, or duty.

Infringement An invasion of a right; a violation of a law or duty.

Infringement of copyright The unauthorized use of copyrighted material.

Infringement of patent The unauthorized making, using, or selling (for practical use or profit) of an invention covered by a valid claim of patent during the life of the patent.

Infringement of trademark The unauthorized use or colorable imitation of a mark already appropriated by another on goods of a similar class.

In futuro At a future time.

Ingress The act or right of entering.

In gross In a large sum or quantity; without deduction or division.

Ingrossing See engrossment.

Inhabit To dwell or live.

Inherent Existing as a permanent or essential component.

Inherently dangerous A danger inhering in the instrumentality or condition itself at all times so as to require special precautions to prevent injury; dangerous per se without requiring human intervention to produce the harmful effects.

Inherent power An authority that is not derived from another; a power in the nature of the organization or person.

Inherit To take by inheritance on the death of an ancestor.

Inheritance Property that descends to an heir when an ancestor dies without leaving a valid will (i.e., intestate).

Inheritance tax A tax imposed on the privilege of receiving property from a decedent at death; a tax on the right to acquire property gratuitously by descent or will.

In hoc In this; in respect to this.

Inhuman treatment As a ground for divorce: Such mental or physical cruelty as to endanger the life or health of the party to whom it is addressed, or as to create a well-founded apprehension of such danger.

In invitum Against an unwilling party.

Initial surplus A surplus that appears on the financial statement at the commencement of an accounting period that does not reflect the operations for the period covered by the statement.

Initiative An electoral process whereby designated percentages of the electorate may initiate legislative or constitutional changes through the filing of formal petitions to be acted on by the legislature or by the total electorate; the power of the people to propose laws and to enact or reject them at the polls independent of the legislative assembly.

Injunction A prohibitive, equitable remedy issued by a court to forbid someone to do an act that he or she is threatening to do or to restrain him or her from continuing the act; a court order requiring a person to do or to refrain from doing a particular thing.

Injure To violate the legal right of another or to inflict an actionable wrong; to impair the soundness of.

Injuria absque damno A wrong done, but from which no loss or damage results, will not sustain an action.

Injurious falsehood A tort with the following elements: (a) a false statement of fact; (b) publication of the statement; (c) intent to make the statement; (d) the statement is harmful to the interests of the plaintiff—special damages; (e) causation.

Injury Any wrong or damage done to another; an invasion of a legally protected interest of another.

Injustice The denial of justice; the act, fault, or omission of a court in a particular case.

In jus vocare To call, cite, or summon to court.

In kind Of the same species or category.

Inland Pertaining to the interior part of a land mass; within a country, state, or territory.

Inland bill of exchange A bill that is drawn and payable within the same state or country.

In lieu of In place of.

In limine On or at the threshold, at the beginning.

In loco parentis In the place of a parent; assuming the duties of a parent without adoption.

Inmate 1. A person confined in a jail, prison, state hospital, etc., convict, captive. **2.** A person who dwells in the same house with another, occupying different rooms but using the same door for passing in and out of the house.

Inn A public lodging establishment; a restaurant or bar.

Innocence The absence of guilt.

Innocent 1. Free from guilt. **2.** Harmless.

Innocent purchaser One who purchases without notice, actual or constructive, of any infirmity, pays valuable consideration, and acts in good faith.

Innocent trespasser One who enters another's land

unlawfully but inadvertently and unintentionally, or in the honest and reasonable belief in his or her right to do so.

Innominate In the civil law, belonging to no specific class.

Inns of Court Private associations or societies in London (e.g., Gray's Inn, the Middle Temple) that have the exclusive privilege of calling men and women to the bar (i.e., conferring on them the rank or degree of barrister—a trial or litigation attorney).

Innuendo 1. In a defamation action, the innuendo is that portion of a complaint which seeks to explain the derogatory meaning of language (or its application to the plaintiff) that otherwise might be considered innocuous or so ambiguous that the defamatory sense is not revealed. **2.** An indirect derogatory comment or suggestion.

Inofficious testament A will not in accordance with the testator's natural affection and moral duties.

In pais Done informally or without legal proceedings; not arising from a deed, record, or written contract.

In pari delicto In equal fault; equally culpable or criminal.

In pari materia Upon the same matter or subject. Statutes in pari materia are to be construed together; even though they may have been enacted at different times, a court will attempt to interpret such statutes as consistent with each other if possible.

In perpetuity Forever.

In personam Against the person. In personam jurisdiction is the power that a court has over the defendant himself or herself as distinguished from the more limited power a court has over his or her interest in property (quasi in rem) or over the property itself (in rem).

In praesenti At the present time.

Inquest An inquiry by a coroner or medical examiner, sometimes with the aid of a jury, to determine the cause of death of a person who appears to have died suddenly or by violence.

Inquiry 1. A careful examination of a matter. **2.** A question.

Inquisitor A person (e.g., coroner, sheriff) who has the power to inquire into certain matters.

In re In the matter of; a way of designating a court case in which there are no adversary parties in the traditional sense but merely some "res" concerning which a judicial determination must be made (e.g., a bankrupt's estate, an estate in probate court, a proposed public highway).

In rem Designating a proceeding or action binding the whole world which determines rights in specific property or the status of a specific subject matter.

Insane delusion The conception of a disordered mind that imagines facts to exist for which there is no evidence.

Insanity 1. That degree of mental illness that negates the individual's legal responsibility or capacity. **2.** Restatement test: A person is not responsible for criminal conduct if, at the time of such conduct as a result of mental disease or defect, he or she lacks substantial capacity either to appreciate the criminality (wrongfulness) of his or her conduct or to conform his or her conduct to the requirements of the law. **3.** Durham test: An accused is not criminally responsible if his or her unlawful act was the product of mental disease or mental defect **4.** M'Naghton test: At the time of committing the act, the accused was laboring under such a defect of reason, from disease of the mind, as not to know the nature and quality of the act the accused was doing, or if the accused did know it, he or she did not know that it was wrong.

Inscribe To enter on a list; to write in or mark on.

Inscription 1. Anything written or engraved on a solid substance intended for great durability. **2.** The entry of a mortgage, lien, or other document in a book of public records.

Insider Someone who has knowledge of facts not available to the general public.

Insider trading Buying and selling corporate shares by officers, directors, and shareholders who own more than 10% of the stock of a corporation listed on a national exchange.

Insignia Distinctive mark.

Insinuation An indirect comment or suggestion.

Insinuation of a will In the civil law, the first production of a will for probate.

Insolvency The condition of being unable to pay one's debts as they fall due or in the usual course of trade and business.

In specie In kind; in the same or like form.

Inspectator A prosecutor or adversary.

Inspection An examination to determine the quality, quantity, authenticity, or condition of something.

Inspector Officers whose duty is to inspect things over which they have jurisdiction.

Install To place in an office.

Installment Partial payment of a debt; a portion of a debt payable at successive periods; a part of something coming out or issued in stages.

Installment credit A commercial arrangement in which the buyer undertakes to pay in more than one payment, and the seller agrees to sell on this basis, for which a finance charge may be imposed.

Installment loan A loan to be repaid in specified, and often equal, amounts over a designated number of months.

Installment method A method of accounting enabling a taxpayer to spread the recognition of gain on the sale of property over the payout period.

Installment sale A commercial arrangement by which a buyer makes an initial down payment and signs a contract for the payment of the balance in installments over a period of time.

Instant Now under consideration.

In statu quo In the condition in which it was.

Instigate To stimulate or goad to an action.

In stirpes See per stirpes.

Institute 1. To inaugurate; to commence. **2.** An organization that studies or promotes a particular area. **3.** Textbooks containing elementary principles of jurisprudence (e.g., Institutes of Justinian).

Instruction to the jury A statement given by a judge to the members of the jury informing them of the law applicable to the case.

Instrument A written document.

Instrumental Helpful to achieve an end.

Instrumentality A means or agency.

Instrumentality rule The corporate existence of a subsidiary will be disregarded when it is so organized and controlled in its affairs by its parent corporation that it is really an adjunct and instrument of the latter. The corporate veil will be pierced, making the parent liable for the obligations of the subsidiary.

Insubordination Disobedience to constituted authority; a willful or intentional disregard of the lawful and reasonable instructions of an employer.

Insufficient Inadequate to meet a need, purpose, or use.

Insular Pertaining to an island or its inhabitants.

Insurable Capable of being insured against loss, damage, death, etc.

Insurable interest A relationship to the subject of the insurance that will necessarily entail pecuniary loss in case of its injury or destruction; an interest that furnishes a reasonable expectation of pecuniary benefit from the continued existence of the subject of the insurance.

Insurance A contract to provide compensation for a loss on a specified subject by specified perils.

Insurance agent Someone who represents a particular insurance company in dealing with the public on insurance matters.

Insurance broker An intermediary or middleman between the public and an insurer on insurance matters. A broker, unlike an agent, is not tied to a particular insurance company.

Insurance policy An instrument in writing by which one party (insurer) engages for the consideration of a premium to indemnify another (insured) against a contingent loss by providing compensation if a designated event occurs, resulting in the loss.

Insurance premium The consideration paid by an insured to an insurer for insurance protection.

Insurance rating The process by which the premium for a policy is set after considering the risks involved.

Insurance trust An agreement between an insured and a trustee, whereby the proceeds of a policy are paid directly to the trustee for investment and distribution to designated beneficiaries as provided in the trust agreement.

Insure To engage to indemnify a person against pecuniary loss from specified perils or possible liability.

Insured The person covered by insurance.

Insurer The underwriter or insurance company with whom a contract of insurance is made.

Insurgent One who participates in an insurrection.

Insurrection A rising of citizens or subjects in revolt against their government.

Intangible 1. Not capable of being perceived by the senses. **2.** Property that is a "right" rather than a physical object even though the right may be evidenced by a physical piece of paper (e.g., patent, stock, trademark, copyright, goodwill, chose in action). **3.** Incapable of being readily defined.

Integrated 1. Open to different groups without restriction. **2.** Unified into a whole.

Integrated bar A bar association to which all lawyers must belong if they want to practice law in the geographic area covered by the association. The highest court in this area has supervisory control over the association.

Integrated contract A contract that contains within its four corners the entire agreement of the parties and is the final expression of their agreement.

Integration 1. Bringing together different groups as equals. **2.** The act or process of making whole or entire.

Intend To plan for, design, or expect a certain result.

Intendment The true meaning of something.

Intent, intention 1. The design or aim of a person in

acting; the desire to cause the consequences of one's acts or the knowledge with substantial certainty that the consequences will follow from what one does. **2.** The meaning or sense of something.

Intentional Done on purpose; planned.

Inter alia Among other things.

Intercept To interfere; to seize; to acquire the contents of a wire or oral communication through the use of any electronic, mechanical, or other device.

Interdict To forbid, prevent, restrict.

Interest 1. A right, claim, title, or legal share in something; a right to have the advantage accruing from something. **2.** A charge that is paid to borrow or use money.

Interested Involved, nonobjective.

Interest equalization tax A tax imposed on each acquisition by a U.S. person of the stock of a foreign issuer or of a debt obligation of a foreign obligor if such obligation has a period remaining to maturity of a year or more.

Interest rate The percentage of an amount of money that is paid for its use for a specified time.

Interim 1. Intervening time. **2.** Temporary.

Interim financing A short-term loan usually obtained to pay for the construction costs of a building or house, with the final financing to be covered by a mortgage.

Interior Department A federal agency overseeing Indian affairs, mining, fish and wildlife, geologic research, land management, national parks and monuments, flood control, conservation, etc.

Interlineation The act of writing between the lines of an instrument; that which is written between the lines.

Interlining The practice whereby a carrier, whose certified routes do not reach a particular shipment destination, transfers the shipment to another carrier for delivery.

Interlocking Closely joined or fitted together.

Interlocking directorate A board of directors of one corporation linked with the board of another corporation by having some of the same people serving on both boards so that the businesses of the two companies are to some degree under one control.

Interlotory Not final; interim.

Interlocutory appeal An appeal of an issue or matter that is taken before the trial court reaches its final judgment.

Interloper A person who meddles in the affairs of others, to which he or she has no right or responsibility.

Intermeddle To interfere wrongly with the property or affairs of another.

Intermediary One who tries to resolve a matter or problem between two or more persons or groups.

Intermediary bank Any bank to which an item is transferred in the course of collection except the depositary or payor bank.

Intermediate Occurring or lying between the beginning and end.

Intermediate courts Courts with general jurisdiction (trial, appellate, or both) that are below the court of last resort in the jurisdiction.

Intermediate order A nonappealable order made between the commencement of an action and its final determination on an incidental or ancillary matter that does not finally resolve the case.

Intermittent Starting and stopping at intervals.

Intermittent easement One that is usable or used only at times, and not continuously.

Intermixture of goods Confusion of goods; commingling.

Intern 1. To restrict or confine a person or group. **2.** A graduate student obtaining practical experience and training outside the classroom; an assistant resident doctor.

Internal 1. Relating to the interior or the inside. **2.** Relating to the domestic affairs of a country.

Internal revenue Government tax revenue from internal sources as contrasted with revenue from customs and foreign sources.

Internal Revenue Code (I.R.C.) The federal statute in title 26 of the U.S. Code that codifies federal tax laws including income, estate, stamp, gift, excise, and other taxes.

Internal Revenue Service (I.R.S.) The federal agency responsible for enforcing the internal revenue laws except those relating to alcohol, tobacco, firearms, explosives, and wagering.

Internal security Laws and government activity dealing with measures to protect the country from subversive activities.

International Concerning two or more countries.

International Court of Justice The judicial arm of the United Nations with jurisdiction to give advisory opinions on matters of law and treaty construction, and to settle legal disputes voluntarily submitted to it by the parties.

International Monetary Fund (IMF) An agency of the United Nations established to stabilize international exchange and to promote balanced international trade.

Internist A specialist in internal medicine.

Internment The detainment or confinement of enemy aliens or persons suspected of disloyalty.

Internuncius A messenger between two parties; a go-between.

Interpellation 1. In the civil law, the act by which, in consequence of an agreement, the party bound declares that he or she will not be bound beyond a certain time. **2.** An intermittent inquiry in proceedings before civil law courts or a formal inquiry in continental European parliamentary practice.

Interpleader A procedure to determine the rights of rival claimants to property held by a third party (called the stakeholder) when the latter has no interest in the property. For example, an insurance company is willing to pay out on a policy, but is faced with several persons who say they are separately entitled to the funds. To avoid possible multiple liability, the stakeholder uses interpleader to force the rivals to resolve their dispute in one action.

Interpol International Criminal Police Organization; a coordinating group for international law enforcement.

Interpolate To insert additional or false words in a complete instrument or document, and thus alter its meaning.

Interposition The doctrine that a state in the exercise of its sovereignty can reject a law or mandate of the federal government that the state deems to be unconstitutional or beyond the powers delegated to the federal government in the U.S. Constitution.

Interpret To seek out the meaning of language.

Interregnum An interval or vacancy between reigns or governments.

Interrogation A methodical process of questioning.

Interrogatories A discovery device consisting of written questions about the case submitted by one side of a lawsuit to the other.

In terrorem clause A provision in a document such as a lease or will that is a warning designed to frighten a beneficiary or lessee into doing or not doing something (e.g., a clause in a will stating that a gift will be forfeited if a beneficiary contests the validity of the will).

Inter se or **inter sese** Among or between themselves.

Intersection A space occupied by more than one street, road, track, etc., at the point where they cross each other.

Interspousal Relating to husband and wife.

Interspousal immunity A prohibition against tort actions between husband and wife. The immunity has been abolished or limited by most states (e.g., allowing property tort actions such as conversion).

Interstate Between or affecting two or more states; between places or persons in different states.

Interstate commerce Traffic, intercourse, commercial trading, or transportation of persons or property between or among the states of the United States.

Interstate Commerce Commission (ICC) A federal regulatory agency with jurisdiction over carriers (railroads, trucks, buses, etc.) engaged in transportation in interstate commerce and in foreign commerce to the extent that it takes place within the United States. The ICC assures that the carriers it regulates will provide the public with rates and services that are fair and reasonable.

Interstate compact An agreement between two or more states that is designed to meet common problems (e.g., flood control, boundary disputes).

Interval ownership Ownership of property for a portion of a year (e.g., 2 weeks).

Intervening Coming or occurring between two times or events.

Intervening cause A cause that comes between an antecedent and a consequence; a new force that breaks the causal connection between the original conduct and the injury; an independent cause that intervenes between the original act or omission and the injury, turning aside the natural sequence of events and producing a result that would not otherwise have followed and which could not have been reasonably anticipated.

Intervenor One who voluntarily enters (becomes a party in) a lawsuit between other persons.

Intervention The procedure by which a third person, not originally a party but claiming an interest in the subject matter of the suit, is allowed to come into the case to protect his or her own interests.

Inter vivos From one living person to another (a gift inter vivos). Between the living.

Inter vivos gift A gift that is made and that takes effect when the donor is living.

Intestable One who lacks testamentary capacity (e.g., an infant).

Intestacy Dying without a valid will.

Intestate Without making a valid will; the person who dies without making a valid will.

Intestate succession The transfer of property to the relatives of a decedent who has died without leaving a valid will. In most states, a statute will specify which relatives receive intestate shares and in what amount.

In testimonium In witness; in evidence whereof.

Intimidate To coerce unlawfully.

Intoxication A condition of an individual who does not have the normal use of his or her physical or mental faculties as a result of drinking intoxicants; a greatly lessened ability to function normally, caused by alcohol or drugs.

Intra Within.

Intramural Existing within; within the walls.

In transitu In transit.

Intrastate commerce Commerce that occurs within a state; business carried on entirely in one state.

Intra vires Within the power; within lawful authority.

Intrinsic Pertaining to the essential nature of a thing.

Intrinsic fraud Fraud that occurs within the framework of the actual conduct of a trial and affects the determination of issues therein (e.g., perjured testimony, forged documents, concealment or misrepresentation of evidence).

Intrinsic value The true, inherent, and essential value of a thing, not depending upon accident, place, or person, but being the same everywhere and to everyone.

Intruder One who enters upon land without either the right to possession or color of title.

Intrusion 1. The act of wrongfully entering upon or taking possession of the property of another. **2.** See invasion of privacy.

Intrust See entrust.

Inure 1. To come to the benefit of a person; to take effect. **2.** To cause to withstand or endure.

Invalid 1. Not of binding force or legal efficacy. **2.** A disabled person.

Invasion An encroachment on the rights of others.

Invasion of corpus Making payments from the principal rather than from the income.

Invasion of privacy Four separate torts. (a) Appropriation: The unauthorized use of a person's name, likeness, or personality for the benefit of another. (b) False light: Unreasonably offensive publicity placing the plaintiff in a false light. (c) Intrusion: An unreasonably offensive intrusion into someone's private affairs or concerns. (d) Public disclosure of a private fact: Unreasonably offensive publicity concerning the private life of a person.

Invent To produce something not previously known or in existence by the exercise of independent investigation and experiment.

Inventory 1. A detailed list of property. **2.** The property or goods themselves.

Inverse condemnation A cause of action for the taking of private property for public use without formal condemnation proceedings and without just compensation.

Invest To use money to acquire property or other assets in order to produce revenue.

Investitive fact The fact by means of which a right comes into existence, e.g., a grant of a monopoly, the death of one's ancestor.

Investiture The ceremony by which land is transferred, authority is conferred, or an office is entered.

Investment An expenditure to acquire property or other assets in order to produce revenue.

Investment bill A type of bill of exchange purchased at a discount and intended to be held to maturity in the form of an investment.

Investment company A company or trust that uses its capital to invest in other companies.

Investment contract A contract, transaction, or scheme whereby one invests money in a common enterprise and is led to expect profits solely from the efforts of the promoter or a third party.

Investment tax credit A credit against taxes, consisting of a percentage of the purchase price of capital goods and equipment.

Inviolability The condition of being safe from trespass, assault, or violation.

Invitation An express or implied request for someone to be present or involved; the act of one who solicits or entices others to enter upon, remain in, or make use of his or her property; the act of inducing others to believe that they should enter upon, remain in, or use the property.

Invitee Someone who is present on land with the express or implied invitation of the occupier of the land, and uses it for a purpose for which it is open to the public or to pursue the business of the occupier.

Invoice A document itemizing the details of a sale or purchase transaction.

Involuntary Without will or power of choice; performed under duress, force, or coercion.

Involuntary bailment One arising by the accidental leaving of personal property in the possession of any person, without negligence on the part of its owner.

Involuntary confession A confession that is not the product of an essentially free and unrestrained choice of its maker; a confession that is extracted by a threat of violence, or obtained by improper promises or other influences.

Involuntary conversion The loss or destruction of property through theft, casualty, or condemnation.

Involuntary manslaughter The unlawful killing of a human being without malice, without premeditation and deliberation, and without the intention to kill or to inflict serious bodily injury; the unlawful killing of a human being during the commission of an unlawful act not amounting to a felony; death from negligence that is gross, wanton, willful, or criminal, indicating a culpable indifference to the safety of others.

Involuntary nonsuit The dismissal of an action when the plaintiff is called but neglects to appear, or gives no evidence on which a jury could find a verdict, or is put out of court by some adverse ruling precluding a recovery.

Involuntary servitude The condition of a person who is compelled to labor for another by force, coercion, imprisonment, and against his or her will, whether or not payment is made for the labor.

Involuntary trust An implied trust imposed by law.

Ipse dixit He himself said it; a bare assertion resting on the authority of the individual.

Ipso facto By the mere fact; by the fact itself.

Ipso jure By the law itself; by the mere operation of law.

Irrational Illogical, lacking reason.

Irrebuttable presumption In evidence, a conclusive presumption that requires a finding of the presumed fact once the underlying evidence is introduced. Evidence tending to rebut it is not admissible.

Irreconcilable Not capable of being harmonized or compromised.

Irreconcilable differences A no-fault ground of divorce: Discord or conflict between spouses that destroys the legitimate ends of the marriage and prevents any reasonable expectation of reconciliation.

Irrecusable Pertaining to a contract obligation imposed on a person without his or her consent or own act; not subject to challenge, refusal, or rejection.

Irregular Not according to rule; departing from the norm.

Irrelevant Not relating or applicable to the matter in issue; not tending to prove or disprove any issue of fact involved in the case.

Irreparable Not capable of being repaired or restored.

Irreparable harm or injury As a standard for granting injunctive relief: An injury that cannot be adequately redressed by an award of monetary damages; a wrong of a repeated and continuing nature.

Irresistible impulse An urge to commit an act that cannot be resisted or overcome because mental disease or derangement has destroyed the freedom of will, the power of self-control, and the ability to choose. See insanity.

Irretrievable breakdown See irreconcilable differences.

Irrevocable Not capable of being revoked or recalled.

Irrigation The supply of water by pipes, channels, streams, etc.

Isolated sale A sale that occurs only once or very infrequently within the ordinary course of business.

Issuable Capable of producing an issue for debate or for litigation.

Issuable plea At common law, a plea to the merits.

Issue 1. To send forth or promulgate. **2.** Sending forth, promulgation. **3.** A matter in controversy. **4.** All persons who have descended from a common ancestor.

Issue of fact A question at a trial or hearing that concerns facts or events, whether such occurred, and how they occurred, as contrasted with the law governing these facts or events; the controversy that exists when one party asserts a fact that is disputed by the other side.

Issue of law The question that arises in litigation when the facts are not in dispute either because the evidence is undisputed or because the facts are assumed upon a demurrer; a question that involves the application or interpretation of a law.

Issue preclusion No relitigation of an issue.

Itemize To set down or list by item.

Itinerant Wandering or traveling from place to place.

Jactitation False boasting; false claims.

Jail A place of confinement, usually for persons awaiting trial or serving sentences for minor crimes.

Jailhouse lawyer A prisoner who studies law on his or her own in prison and provides legal assistance and advice to other prisoners.

Jehovah's Witnesses A Christian sect that is opposed to war and government interference in matters of conscience. It also believes in the imminent end of the world.

Jencks rule A criminal defendant in federal court is entitled to access to government documents for use in the cross-examination of witnesses.

Jeopardy Legal jeopardy: The danger of conviction and punishment once a criminal defendant has been placed on trial before the trier of fact in a court of competent jurisdiction acting on an indictment or information that is sufficient in form and substance to sustain a conviction.

Jeopardy assessment If the collection of a tax appears to be in question, the IRS may assess and collect the tax immediately without going through the usual formalities.

Jetsam Goods that the owner voluntarily throws overboard in an emergency in order to lighten the ship.

Jettison 1. To discard, to throw overboard. **2.** The thing or things cast out.

Jetty A projection of stone or other material, serving as a protection against the waves.

Jobber One who buys and sells goods for others; a dealer in securities.

Joinder Uniting two or more into a single transaction or proceeding.

Joinder of issue The assertion of a fact by a party in a pleading and its denial by the opposing party; the filing of an answer.

Joinder of offenses Charging an accused with two or more crimes as multiple counts in a single indictment or information.

Joinder of parties The act of joining parties to an action as co-plaintiffs or as co-defendants.

Joint Shared by or between two or more; coupled together in interest or liability.

Joint adventure See joint venture.

Joint and several liability The liability that exists when a creditor has the option of suing one liable party separately or all liable parties together. Each wrongdoer is individually responsible for the entire judgment, and the person who has been wronged can collect from one wrongdoer or from all of them together until the judgment is satisfied.

Joint bank account An account in the names of two or more persons who have equal right to it, generally with the right of survivorship.

Joint enterprise An express or implied agreement among members of a group to carry out a common purpose, in which the members have a community of pecuniary interest and an equal right to a voice in the control and direction of the enterprise.

Jointly Combined or joined together in unity of interest or liability.

Joint tax return A federal, state, or local tax return filed by a husband and wife together.

Joint tenancy Property (an estate) held by two or more persons jointly (called cotenants or joint tenants) in undivided equal shares with the right of survivorship (when a cotenant dies, his or her share automatically passes to the surviving cotenants). The joint tenants have one and the same interest; accruing by one and the same conveyance, instrument, or act; commencing at one and the same time; with one and the same undivided possession.

Joint tort-feasors Two or more persons who are jointly and severally liable in tort for the same injury to person or property; persons who have acted in concert in committing a tort.

Jointure A freehold estate in lands or tenements secured to the wife, and to take effect on the decease of the husband, and to continue during her life. Property provision for a wife, made prior to marriage, in lieu of dower.

Joint venture An association of persons who jointly undertake some commercial enterprise. There must be a community of interest in the performance of the enterprise, an equal right to direct and govern policy in connection with the enterprise, and a sharing in the resulting profits and losses.

Joint will A single testamentary instrument that contains the will of, and is executed by, more than one person.

Journal A book in which entries are made, often on a regular basis.

Journeyman A person who has progressed through an apprenticeship in a craft or trade and is now qualified to work for another.

Joy rider Slang for someone who uses steroids solely to improve personal appearance.

Joyriding Temporarily taking an automobile without authorization but without the intent to deprive the owner of it permanently.

Judex A judge.

Judge 1. A public officer appointed or elected to preside over and to administer the law in a court of justice or similar tribunal. **2.** To resolve a dispute authoritatively.

Judge Advocate A legal officer on the staff of a military commander.

Judgment The official decision of a court in a case brought before it; a judicial determination of the rights and duties of parties growing out of litigation before a court.

Judgment book The book in which the clerk enters

the judgments that are rendered; a judgment docket; a civil or criminal docket.

Judgment creditor A person in whose favor a money judgment is entered or who becomes entitled to enforce it.

Judgment debtor A person who has yet to satisfy a judgment that has been rendered against him or her.

Judgment execution The formal or written evidence of the judgment that commands an officer to seize the property of the judgment debtor in order to satisfy the judgment.

Judgment in personam See in personam.

Judgment in rem See in rem.

Judgment lien A lien binding the real estate of a judgment debtor in favor of the judgment creditor, giving the latter the right to levy on the real estate to satisfy the judgment.

Judgment note A promissory note (also called cognovit note) embodying an authorization to an attorney, or to a designated attorney, or to the holder, or the clerk of the court, to enter an appearance for the maker of the note and confess a judgment against him or her for a sum therein named, upon default of payment of the note.

Judgment notwithstanding the verdict (JNOV) A judgment of the court that is opposite to the verdict reached by the jury; a ruling by the judge that the jury was not reasonable in reaching its verdict because there was not sufficient evidence of all the essential elements on which to base the verdict.

Judgment on the merits A judgment, rendered after evidentiary inquiry and argument, determining which party is in the right, as opposed to a judgment based solely on a matter of form, a technical point, or a procedural error.

Judgment proof A person who has no available resources out of which a judgment can be satisfied.

Judgment quasi in rem See quasi in rem.

Judgment roll The papers filed by the clerk on a case after entry of the judgment (e.g., summons, pleadings, admissions, jury instructions, verdict, findings, orders, the judgment).

Judicare Publicly funded legal services delivered by private practitioners (rather than by full-time "poverty lawyers") to low-income persons.

Judicature The judiciary; the administration of justice; a court of justice; the jurisdiction of a court.

Judicial Pertaining to the office of a judge.

Judicial bonds Generic term for bonds required by a court for appeals, costs, attachment, injunction, etc.

Judicial estoppel A party who by pleadings, statements or contentions, under oath, has assumed a particular position in a judicial proceeding is estopped to assume an inconsistent position in a subsequent action.

Judicial immunity The absolute protection of all judges from civil liability arising out of the discharge of judicial functions.

Judicial notice The recognition of certain facts (usually matters of common knowledge) that a court may take into consideration without requiring evidence to be introduced to establish the facts.

Judicial review 1. The power of a court to interpret statutes and to declare them unconstitutional when they violate the constitution. **2.** A form of appeal from an administrative body to the courts for a review of the agency's findings of fact or law.

Judicial sale A sale based on a decree of a court directing the sale.

Judiciary The branch of government vested with the judicial power; the system of courts in a country; the body of judges; the bench.

Juice Slang for steroids.

Junior creditor One whose claim ranks below other creditors in rights to the debtor's property.

Junior mortgage A mortgage that is subordinate to the priority or prior mortgage.

Junket A trip or tour taken at public expense; an arrangement to go to a gambling casino hotel, in which the hotel pays part of the expenses.

Jural Pertaining to law, rights, and obligations.

Jurat A certificate of a person before whom a writing was sworn; the clause on an affidavit as to where, when, and before whom it was sworn.

Juration The act of swearing; the administration of an oath.

Jure By the law; by right.

Juridical Relating to the administration of justice or to the office of a judge.

Juris Of law; of right.

Jurisdiction 1. The power of a court to decide a matter in controversy (a challenge to the jurisdiction of the court). **2.** The geographic area over which a particular court has authority (the matter has not been decided in this jurisdiction).

Jurisdictional amount The amount involved in the particular case; the value of the object sought to be attained in the litigation.

Jurisdictional dispute The competing claims made to an employer by different unions that their respective members are entitled to perform certain work.

Jurisdictional facts Those facts that must exist before the court can properly take jurisdiction of the particular case (e.g., the amount in controversy, service of process).

Jurisdiction in personam See in personam.

Jurisdiction in rem See in rem.

Jurisdiction of the subject matter See subject matter jurisdiction.

Jurisdiction quasi in rem See quasi in rem.

Juris Doctor (J.D.) Doctor of laws. The degree received by lawyers, replacing the LL.B. degree.

Juris et de jure Of law and of right.

Jurisprudence The philosophy of law; the science that seeks to ascertain the principles on which legal rules are based; the science of positive law and legal relations.

Juris publici Of common right; of common or public use (e.g., highways).

Jurist A legal scholar.

Juror A member of a jury.

Jury A group of men and women selected and sworn to inquire into matters of fact and to declare the truth on the basis of the evidence to be presented before it.

Jury instructions A direction given by the trial judge to the jury concerning the law of the case that they will need to know in order to reach a verdict.

Jury panel A group of prospective jurors who are summoned to appear on a stated day and from which a grand jury or a petit jury is chosen.

Jury trial The trial of a matter before a judge and jury as opposed to a trial solely before a judge.

Jury wheel A physical device or electronic system for the storage and random selection of the names or identifying numbers of prospective jurors.

Jus Law; system of law; right; power; privilege; authority.

Jus civile The system of law peculiar to one state or people; civil law.

Jus civitatus The right of citizenship.

Jus gentium The law of nations.

Jus publicum Public law; the law relating to the Constitution and functions of government and its officers.

Just Conforming to or consonant with what is legal or lawful.

Just cause Such reasons as will suffice in law to justify the action taken.

Just compensation Compensation that is fair to both the owner and the public when property is taken for public use through eminent domain; adequate compensation; fair market value at the time of taking.

Jus tertii The right of a third person; defending what one has done or proposes to do on the basis of

rights (e.g., ownership) in third persons.

Justice 1. A judge, usually of a higher court. **2.** The proper administration of the law; the resolution of legal matters or disputes so that all receive their due.

Justice Department A federal agency headed by the attorney general. The agency enforces federal laws, gives legal advice to other agencies, represents the government in court cases, etc.

Justice of the Peace A judicial magistrate of inferior rank with very limited jurisdiction.

Justiciable Referring to a matter appropriate for court review (justiciable controversy).

Justifiable Warranted or sanctioned by law.

Justifiable homicide Killing another when permitted by law (e.g., in self-defense when faced with the danger of death or with serious bodily injury).

Justification A just or lawful reason to act or to fail to act.

Justify 1. To prove to be correct or valid. **2.** To absolve.

Justness Conformity to truth, propriety, or accuracy.

Just value In taxation, the fair, honest, and reasonable value of property, without exaggeration or depreciation; its actual market value.

Juvenile A young person who has not yet reached the age at which he or she should be treated as an adult for purposes of the criminal law; in some states, a person under 18.

Juvenile delinquent See delinquent child.

Juxtapose To place side by side for comparison.

Juzgado In Spanish law, a court of law.

Kangaroo court A sham legal proceeding in which a person's rights are totally disregarded and in which the result is a foregone conclusion because of the bias of the court or tribunal.

Kartell Cartel (Germany).

Keeper One who has the care, custody, or management of something.

Keogh plan A retirement plan for self-employed tax-payers—the contributions to which are tax deductible up to a certain amount each year; an H.R. 10 plan.

Key number; key topic and number Part of the subject-matter classification system for the digests of West Publishing Company (e.g., under the key topic of "Libel & Slander," key number 8 ( 8) summarizes court opinions on an aspect of this area of the law).

Kickback A payment back by the seller of a portion of the purchase price to the buyer or to a public official in order to induce the purchase or to influence future business transactions.

Kidnapping The taking and carrying away of a human being by force, fraud, threats, or intimidation against the victim's will and without lawful authority.

Kill To destroy the life of a person or animal.

Kilogram 2.2046 pounds or 1,000 grams.

Kilometer .62137 mile.

Kilowatt 1,000 watts.

Kin Family, kindred.

Kind Generic class; type.

Kindred Family, relatives.

King's Bench (K.B.) One of the superior courts of common law in England.

Kiting Writing checks against a bank account in which the funds are insufficient to cover them, with the hope that the necessary funds will be deposited before the checks are presented.

Klan See Ku Klux Klan.

Kleptomania An irresistible propensity to steal.

Knock down Property is said to be "knocked down" when the auctioneer, by the fall of the hammer, or by any other audible or visible announcement, signifies to the bidder that he or she is entitled to the property on paying the amount of his bid, according to the terms of the sale.

Knowingly With knowledge; intentionally.

Knowledge Acquaintance with fact, truth, or understanding.

Known Understood, discovered.

Ku Klux Klan An organization that supports segregation and white supremacy.

Labor Mental or physical exertion, usually for a wage.

Laches An equitable defense to the assertion of a right when there has been a delay of such duration and character as to render the enforcement of the right inequitable; such neglect or omission to assert a right over a period of time which, when taken with other circumstances causing prejudice to the party asserting the defense, operates to bar relief in equity.

Laissez-faire A political-economic philosophy of government that allows the marketplace to operate relatively free of restrictions and intervention.

Laity People not part of the clergy.

Lake A considerable body of standing water in a depression of land or in an expanded part of a river.

Lame duck 1. An elected official during the time when he or she is waiting to be succeeded by a replacement. **2.** A speculator in stock who has overbought and cannot meet his commitments.

Lame duck session A legislative session conducted after the election of new members but before they are installed.

Land Any ground, soil, or surface of the planet.

Land Bank A federally created bank under the Federal Farm Loan Act organized to make loans on farm security at low interest rates.

Land Court A Massachusetts court with exclusive original jurisdiction of all applications for registration of title to land within the state.

Landed Owning land; having an estate in land; consisting of real estate or land.

Landed securities Mortgages or other encumbrances affecting land.

Land grant A donation of public land to an individual, corporation, or subordinate government.

Landing A place on a river or other navigable water for loading and unloading goods or passengers.

Landlocked Referring to land belonging to one person that is surrounded by land belonging to other persons so that it cannot be approached except over their land.

Landlord The owner who leases land, buildings, or apartments to another.

Landmark 1. A feature of the land, a monument, or other marker set up on the boundary line of two adjoining estates to fix such boundary. **2.** Historically important.

Land patent A document or instrument conveying a grant of public land; the land so conveyed.

Lapse 1. To end because of a failure to use or a failure to fulfill a condition; to fail to vest because of the death of the prospective beneficiary before the death of the donor. **2.** To deteriorate. **3.** A mistake or error. **4.** A period of time.

Lapsed Expired.

Lapsed devise A devise that fails because of the death of the devisee before the testator.

Lapsed legacy Where the legatee dies before the testator, or before the legacy is payable, the bequest is said to lapse.

Lapsed Policy A policy terminated at the end of the grace period because of non-payment of premiums.

Larcenous Having the character of or contemplating larceny.

Larceny The unlawful stealing, taking and carrying, or driving away another's personal property with the intent to convert it to one's own use, to deprive the owner of it, or otherwise to deal with it in a manner inconsistent with the owner's rights.

Lascivious Tending to incite lust.

Last antecedent rule A canon of statutory construction that qualifying words are to be applied only to the immediately preceding words unless the qualifying words were clearly intended to apply to other language in the statute as well.

Last clear chance doctrine Even though a plaintiff has been contributorily negligent in placing himself or herself in a position of peril, he or she can still recover if the negligent defendant had the last clear chance to avoid the accident and failed to do so. Humanitarian doctrine.

Last in, first out (LIFO) A method of identifying and valuing inventories which assumes that the last goods purchased are the first ones sold and therefore the goods left in inventory at the end of the year are assumed to be those first purchased.

Last resort Refers to a court from which there is no further appeal.

Latent Concealed, dormant.

Latent deed A deed kept for 20 years or more in a strongbox or other secret place.

Lateral support The right of lateral and subjacent support is the right to have land supported by the adjoining land or the soil beneath.

Law A rule of action or conduct prescribed by a controlling authority and having binding force; that which must be obeyed.

Law courts Courts that have no equitable powers, but administer justice according to the rules and practice of the common law, and award money damages.

Lawful Legal, authorized.

Lawful cause Legitimate reason for acting, based on the law or on the evidence in a particular case as contrasted with acting on a whim or out of prejudice, or for a reason not recognized by the law.

Lawless 1. Not observing the rules and forms of the law. **2.** Uncontrolled.

Law list A publication containing the names and addresses of practicing attorneys and information of interest to the legal profession (e.g., court calendars, attorneys practicing in certain specialties).

Law merchant Commercial law; mercantile law; the law applicable to the rights and relations of persons engaged in commerce, trade, or mercantile pursuits.

Law of the case doctrine Once a court has decided a point in a case, that point becomes and remains settled unless and until it is reversed or modified; the law applied on the first appeal of a case is binding on the second appeal; the initial determination of an issue governs the case throughout subsequent stages unless compelling circumstances call for a redetermination.

Law reports, law reporters Volumes containing decisions and opinions of state and federal courts.

Law review A student-edited journal published by a law school, containing articles, notes, studies, book reviews, etc.

Laws 1. See law, regulation, statute. **2.** The statutes or session laws of the legislature.

Lawsuit An action, suit, or cause.

Lawyer An attorney.

Lay 1. Nonprofessional; nonecclesiastical. **2.** Pertaining to a person with no particular expertise. **3.** To state or allege in a pleading. **4.** A share of the profits of a fishing voyage.

Lay advocate A nonlawyer or paralegal who acts as an advocate for clients in tribunals where authorized to do so (e.g., administrative agencies).

Layaway Pertaining to an agreement by a retail seller with a consumer to hold consumer goods for sale to the consumer at a later date at a specified price.

Layoff A temporary or permanent termination of employment at the will of the employer.

Lead counsel The attorney who is managing and directing the litigation for a party represented by more than one attorney.

Leading case An opinion that has had an important influence in the development of the law on a particular point.

Leading question A question that suggests the answer because of the way that it is asked (e.g., "You were speeding, isn't that correct?").

League An association of people, groups, or countries for a common purpose.

Lease 1. A contract for the exclusive possession of lands or tenements for a determinate period; a contract by which the lessor grants the lessee the exclusive right to possess and use personal property of the lessor for a specified period. **2.** To let, rent, demise, engage, sublease, sublet, subrent, convey, grant.

Leaseback A transaction whereby a party sells property and later leases it back.

Leasehold An estate in real property held under a lease; property held by a lease.

Leave 1. To give. **2.** To withdraw. **3.** To allow or cause to remain or stay the same. **4.** Permission to do something. **5.** Authorization to be absent.

Leave of absence Temporary absence from employment or duty with the intention to return.

Leave of court Permission of the court to take some action.

Ledger A book of account in which a record of transactions is made.

Legacy 1. A disposition of personal property by a will. **2.** Something handed down.

Legal Required, permitted, or involving the law.

Legal acumen The doctrine of legal acumen is that if a defect in a claim to land is such as to require legal acumen to discover it, a court of equity may remove the cloud created by such defect.

Legal age The age at which a person acquires the capacity to make contracts or to enter legal relations. The age may differ depending on what the person wants to do (e.g., vote, buy liquor, marry). For most situations, however, the legal age is 18.

Legal aid A system of providing legal services to people who cannot afford counsel.

Legal capital The par or stated value of issued capital stock; the amount of contributed capital that must be kept in the firm as protection for creditors; property sufficient to balance capital stock liability.

Legal cause Proximate cause; substantial factor in bringing about the harm; the causal sequence by which a person's tortious conduct resulted in an invasion of a legally protected interest of another, so that the law holds the person responsible for the harm.

Legal conclusion A statement of a legal duty without stating the facts from which the duty arises.

Legal death See death, brain death, civil death.

Legal description A description of real property by government survey, metes and bounds, or lot numbers of a recorded plat, including a description of portions subject to any easements or other restrictions.

Legal detriment The giving up or the doing of some-

thing that the promisee, immediately prior thereto, was privileged to retain or to refrain from doing; a change of position or an assumption of a duty or liability that did not exist earlier.

Legal entity Legal existence; an entity other than a natural person (e.g., a corporation) that can function legally, sue, be sued, act through agents etc.

Legalese See term of art.

Legal ethics Usages, customs, and rules among members of the legal profession involving their moral and professional duties toward one another, toward clients, and toward the courts (e.g., client confidentiality).

Legal fiction See fiction of law.

Legal impossibility 1. The defendant's intended acts, even if completed, would not amount to a crime. **2.** See impossibility of performance.

Legal investments Those investments, sometimes called legal lists, in which banks and other financial institutions may invest.

Legal issue 1. A legal question. **2.** Descendants.

Legality Lawfulness; the state of being legal.

Legalization The act of making something legal or lawful.

Legal jeopardy See jeopardy.

Legal list See legal investments.

Legal malpractice The failure of a lawyer to use such skill, prudence, and diligence as lawyers of ordinary skill and capacity commonly possess and exercise.

Legal memory An ancient usage, custom, supposed grant (as a foundation for prescription) and the like, are said to be immemorial when they are really or fictitiously of such an ancient date that "the memory of man runneth not to the contrary," or "beyond legal memory." In America, by statute, the time of legal memory is generally fixed at a period corresponding to that prescribed for actions for the recovery of real property, usually 20 years.

Legal newspaper A newspaper containing summaries of important decisions, notices of local court proceedings, and news of general interest to the legal profession.

Legal remedy A remedy available in a court of law, as distinguished from a remedy available only in equity.

Legal representative One who stands in the place of and represents another; one who oversees the legal affairs of another.

Legal reserve 1. Liquid assets that life insurance companies are required by statute to set aside and maintain to assure payment of claims and benefits. **2.** In banking, the percentage of bank deposits that must be maintained in cash or equally liquid assets to meet the demands of depositors.

Legal residence The place of domicile or permanent abode as opposed to a temporary residence.

Legal separation A court order allowing a married couple to live separately and establishing their rights and duties while separated.

Legal Service Corporation (LSC) A federal government agency that provides funds for legal services to the poor in noncriminal cases.

Legal tender All coins and currencies of the United States that can be used to pay debts.

Legal title A title that is recognizable and enforceable in a court of law; a title that provides the right of ownership but no beneficial interest in the property, which exists in another.

Legatee The person to whom personal property (and sometimes real property) is given by will.

Legation A diplomatic mission below the rank of an embassy; the staff and premises of such a mission.

Legem, leges Law; laws.

Legislate To enact laws or pass resolutions through legislation.

Legislation 1. The enactment of laws by the legislature. **2.** Law or laws passed by the legislature.

Legislative Pertaining to the enactment of laws by the legislature.

Legislative apportionment See apportionment; gerrymander.

Legislative counsel The person or office that assists legislators in tasks of research, drafting, etc.

Legislative court A court created by the legislature as opposed to one created by the Constitution.

Legislative divorce A divorce granted to a couple by an act of the legislature rather than by a court decree.

Legislative history The background of events leading up to the enactment of a law (e.g., the text of the proposed law, amendments considered, committee reports, committee hearings, floor debate).

Legislative immunity An immunity from civil suit enjoyed by a member of Congress while engaged in legislative functions (e.g., voting, giving a speech on legislation, making reports, engaging in debates).

Legislative veto Legislative disappproval of an action taken or contemplated by the executive branch of government, the effect of which is to require the executive to act or to refrain from acting in a particular way. The disapproval does not take the form of a traditional statute which is passed by the House and Senate, and signed by the President. A single committee of the House or Senate might announce the disapproval. It could also come in a joint resolution.

Legislator A member of a legislative body.

Legislature The assembly or body of persons that makes statutory laws for a state or nation.

Legitimacy 1. The condition of being born in wedlock. **2.** The condition of being in compliance with the law or with established standards.

Legitimate 1. Lawful, valid, or genuine. **2.** Born to married parents. **3.** To make lawful; to confer legitimacy.

Legitimation Making legitimate or lawful that which was not originally so; the statutory procedure for legitimating the status of an illegitimate child.

Lend To provide money to another for a period of time, usually for an interest charge; to give something of value to another for a fixed or indefinite time, with or without compensation, with the expectation that it will be returned.

Lender One from whom money or some other thing is borrowed.

Lesbian A female who is sexually attracted to other females.

Lesion A wound.

Lessee A person who rents property from another.

Lesser included offense Another offense that is necessarily established by proof of the greater offense in that it is impossible to commit the greater offense without having committed the lesser offense; an uncharged offense that does not require the proof of any additional elements beyond those required by the greater offense that was charged (e.g., larceny is a lesser included offense within the offense of robbery). All of the elements of the lesser crime are also elements of the greater crime, but not vice versa.

Lessor A person who rents property to another.

Lethal Deadly

Letter 1. A message sent from one person to another usually in a sealed envelope. **2.** A commission, patent, or written instrument containing or attesting the grant of some power, authority, or right.

Letter of advice Drawer's communication to the drawee that a described draft has been drawn.

Letter of attorney A power of attorney.

Letter of credence In international law, the document that accredits an ambassador, minister, or envoy to the courts or government to which he or she is sent.

Letter of credit A written instrument addressed by one person to another requesting the latter to give credit to the person in whose favor it is drawn. The drafter of the letter promises to repay the person making the advance.

Letters of administration A formal document issued by the probate court, appointing an administrator of an estate. On the kinds of administrators that can be appointed, see administration and the entries that follow it.

Letters patent A document issued by the government to a patentee that grants or confirms the right to the exclusive possession and enjoyment of land or of a new invention or discovery.

Letters rogatory A request by one court to a court in another jurisdiction to take the testimony of a witness residing in the latter jurisdiction or to otherwise assist the requesting court in a pending case.

Letters testamentary A formal document issued by a court that empowers a person to act as an executor of a will.

Leverage 1. Added power or influence (the leverage of her inside contacts). **2.** The ability to control an investment by a small outlay such as a down payment; the use of a smaller investment to generate a larger rate of return through borrowing; the effect on common stockholders of the requirement to pay bond interest and preferred stock dividends before the payment of common stock dividends.

Levy 1. To assess or impose. **2.** To conscript. **3.** To seize in order to satisfy a claim. **4.** To wage or carry on. **5.** A tax or charge. **6.** The obtaining of money by legal process through the seizure and sale of the property.

Lewd Indecent, lascivious, obscene.

Lewdness Gross and wanton indecency in sexual matters.

Lex Law or a collection of laws.

Lex contractus The law of the place where the contract was formed.

Lex domicilii The law of the domicile.

Lex fori The law of the forum where the suit is brought.

Lexis A computerized legal research system.

Lex loci actus The law of the place where the act was done.

Lex loci delictus The law of the place where the wrong or crime took place.

Lex situs The law of the place where the property is situated.

Liability The condition of being responsible for a possible or actual loss, penalty, evil, expense, or burden; a legal obligation.

Liability in solido Either of the debtors may be required to discharge the obligation in full at the creditor's election.

Liability insurance The insurer pays the covered damages that the insured is obligated to pay to a third person. The insurer agrees to indemnify the insured against the loss from specified causes.

Liable 1. Bound or obligated in law or equity.

Libel A defamatory statement expressed by print, writing, pictures, or signs. See defamation.

Libelant The complainant in an admiralty action.

Libelee The defendant in an admiralty action.

Libelous Defamatory; constituting or involving libel.

Libelous per quod Extrinsic proof is needed to show the defamatory nature of the statement; the statement is not obviously defamatory or defamatory on its face.

Libelous per se The statement is defamatory on its face without the need of extrinsic proof; the statement is so obviously and naturally hurtful to the aggrieved person that proof of its character is unnecessary.

Liberal 1. Not literal; not restricted or restrained. **2.** Pertaining to a political philosophy that tends to favor the use of government to promote social reforms, civil liberties, and economic regulation.

Liberal construction An expansive interpretation of the meaning of a statute or other law to include facts or cases that are within the spirit and reason of the law, or are within the mischief that the law was designed to remedy. Reasonable doubts are resolved in favor of the applicability of the law unless an intent to the contrary is clear.

Liberate To release.

Liberty Exemption from extraneous control; freedom regulated by law; the enjoyment of personal rights.

License Permission to do that which otherwise would be illegal, a trespass, or a tort.

Licensee A person acting for his or her own purposes who has a privilege to enter or remain on land due to the express or implied consent of the possessor of the land (e.g., someone soliciting money for charity).

Licensor The person who gives or grants a license.

Licentious 1. Lascivious, prurient, obscene. **2.** Acting with disregard for ethics, law, or the rights of others.

Licitation In the civil law, an offering for sale to the highest bidder.

Lie 1. The uttering or acting of that which is false for the purpose of deceiving. **2.** To make a false statement intentionally. **3.** To exist; to be sustainable (an action lies).

Lie detector A machine that records (by a needle on a graph) the varying emotional disturbances that occur when answering questions truthfully or falsely, due to fluctuating blood pressure, respiration, perspiration, etc. A polygraph.

Liege A feudal lord; bound by feudal tenure and allegiance.

Lien A charge, security, or encumbrance on property; a claim or charge on property for the payment of a debt, obligation, or duty.

Lien creditor One whose debt or claim is secured by a lien on particular property.

Lienee One whose property is subject to a lien.

Lienor One who has a lien on the property of another.

Lieu See in lieu of.

Life estate An estate or interest in property whose duration is limited to the life of the party holding the estate or of some other person.

Life in being The remaining length of time in the life of a person who is in existence at the time that a deed or will takes effect.

Life insurance A contract for the payment of a specified amount to a designated beneficiary upon the death of the insured.

Life tenancy An estate in real property in which the tenant has a freehold interest for his or her life or for the life of another.

LIFO See last in, first out.

Ligament Tissue that connects bones or cartilages. Tissue that supports organs.

Limine See motion in limine.

Limitation 1. Restriction. **2.** A certain time allowed by statute for bringing an action at the risk of losing it. See statute of limitation.

Limited 1. Restricted in duration, extent, or scope. **2.** "Ltd." A designation indicating that a business is a corporation with limited liability (Times Chemical Co. Ltd.).

Limited divorce See legal separation.

Limited partnership A type of partnership comprised of one or more general partners who manage the business and who are personally liable for partnership debts, and one or more limited partners who take no part in running the business and who incur no liability for partnership obligations beyond the contribution they invested in the partnership.

Lineage Line of descent from an ancestor.

Lineal Proceeding in a direct or unbroken line.

Lineal descendant A person in the direct line of descent, such as a child or grandchild, as contrasted with a collateral descendant such as a niece.

Lineal descent Descent in a direct or right line as from father or grandfather to son or grandson.

Lineal heir One who inherits in a line either ascending or descending from a common source, as distinguished from a collateral heir.

Line of credit The maximum borrowing power (credit limit) of one person from another or from a financial institution.

Line-up A police identification procedure by which the suspect in a crime is exhibited before the victim or a witness to determine whether the suspect can be identified as the one who committed the crime.

Liquid Consisting of cash or capable of being easily converted into cash.

Liquidate 1. To pay and settle. **2.** To wind up the affairs of a business by identifying assets, converting them into cash, and paying off liabilities.

Liquidated claim A claim whose amount has been agreed upon by the parties, has been fixed by operation of law, or is capable of ascertainment by mathematical computation.

Liquidated damages The amount of the damages has been stipulated by the parties or has been ascertained by a judgment.

Liquid debt A debt immediately and unconditionally due.

Liquidity The condition of a person or business in terms of an ability to convert assets into cash.

Liquor Alcoholic beverage made by distillation, as opposed to wine which is made by fermentation.

Lis pendens A pending suit; notice of the pendency of an action affecting title to real property; confirmation of the power or jurisdiction of the court over property pending the outcome of legal proceedings.

Listed security A security listed for trading on one of the stock exchanges or with the Securities and Exchange Commission.

Listing 1. An agreement between an owner of real property and a real estate agent, whereby the latter agrees to secure a buyer or tenant under specified terms in return for a fee or commission. **2.** A contract between a firm and a stock exchange, covering the trading of that firm's securities on the stock exchange **3.** Making a schedule or inventory.

List price The published or advertised price of goods.

Lite pendente Pending the suit.

Literal According to the exact language; adhering closely to the words.

Literal construction The interpretation of a document according to its words alone without any consideration of the intent of the drafter(s).

Literary Pertaining to literature; connected with authors, books, and writings.

Literary property The exclusive right that entitles an author and his or her assigns to the use and profit of his or her composition.

Literary work Under the copyright law: Any work (except audiovisual works) expressed in words, numbers, or symbols regardless of its physical form.

Literate Able to read and write; knowledgeable and educated.

Litigant A party in litigation.

Litigate To resolve a dispute or seek relief in a court of law.

Litigation A legal action including all the proceedings therein.

Litigious Prone to engage in disputes and litigation.

Littoral Concerning or belonging to the shore.

Livery of seisin A ceremony for transferring possession of land (e.g., the parties went on the land where a twig, as a symbol of the whole land, was delivered by the grantor to the grantee).

Livestock Domestic animals used or raised on a farm, especially those kept for profit; all domestic animals.

Living 1. Existing. **2.** The financial means for maintaining life. **3.** Having life.

Living separate and apart A ground for divorce: Spouses live separately for a statutorily designated period, with no present intention of resuming marital relations.

Living trust An inter vivos trust; a trust that is active during the life of the creator of the trust—the settlor.

Living will A will specifying the conditions under which a person suffering from a terminal illness does not wish to be kept alive by life-support instruments.

LL.B.; LL.M.; LL.D. Law degrees: bachelor (LL.B.), master (LL.M.), doctor (LL.D.)

Loading 1. That portion of the insurance premium used for meeting selling and administrative expenses beyond the portion required to meet the liability reserve. **2.** Filling; placing in or on a structure.

Loan Anything furnished for temporary use with or without compensation on the condition that it or its equivalent in kind be returned.

Loaned servant doctrine When an employer lends its employee to another for the performance of some special service, the employee becomes the employee of the party to whom he or she has been loaned with respect to that special service.

Loan ratio The ratio, expressed as a percentage, of the amount of a loan to the value or selling price of the real property.

Loansharking Lending money at excessive and usurious rates with the threat or actual use of force to obtain repayment.

Lobbying All attempts, including personal solicitation, to induce legislators to vote in a certain way or to introduce legislation.

Lobbyist One who makes it a business to procure the passage or defeat of bills pending before a legislative body.

Lobotomy A surgical operation in which designated nerve connections in the brain are cut.

Local action An action or lawsuit wherein all the principal facts on which it is founded are of a local nature; an action that must be brought in the jurisdiction where the act occurred or where the subject matter is located.

Local agent A person who takes care of a company's business in a particular area; an agent at a given place or within a definite district.

Local government City, county, or other governing body at a level smaller than a state.

Locality A definite region in any part of space; geographical position.

Localization The doctrine that concerns the amount and nature of local activity of a foreign corporation sufficient to subject it to the laws of the state in which it operates.

Local law A local law is one that operates over a particular locality instead of over the whole territory of the state.

Locative calls The description of land in a deed or other document by using landmarks, natural objects, and the like, by which the land is located and identified.

Lockout Withholding work from employees; temporarily closing down a business during a labor dispute; employer work stoppage.

Lockup A place of detention in a police station, court, or other facility used for persons awaiting trial or court appearance.

Loco parentis See in loco parentis.

Locus A place; a place where a thing is done (e.g., locus delicti—the place where the wrong or offense was committed).

Lodger An occupant who has the use of property without exclusive possession.

Logical Internally consistent; concerning logic.

Logrolling A strategy of obtaining approval of a proposal, which the voters (or legislators) would probably not accept if voted upon independently, by combining it with one or more other proposals on different topics that they are more likely to accept; trading political favors.

Loiter To stand idly around; to move around slowly.

Long arm statute A statutory method of obtaining personal jurisdiction by substituted service of process over a nonresident defendant who has sufficient purposeful contact with a state so that it is fair and reasonable for the state to adjudicate the dispute involving the defendant.

Long position The status of one who owns securities held in expectation of a rise in the market or for income as contrasted with one who goes in and out of the market on a short point spread.

Longshoreman A maritime laborer who works about the wharves of a port; one who loads and unloads ships.

Long-term capital gain The gain (profit) realized on the sale or exchange of a capital asset held for more than 12 months.

Long ton A measure of weight equivalent to 2,240 pounds.

Lookout Keeping watch; one who keeps watch.

Loose-leaf service Texts with pages that are easily removable, often through three-ringed binders.

Lord Campbell Act A statutory remedy for wrongful death; a statute that creates a new cause of action for wrongful death in favor of the decedent's personal representative for the benefit of designated persons.

Lord High Chancellor The highest judicial functionary in England.

Lord Mansfield's Rule The testimony of either spouse is inadmissible on the question of whether the husband had access to the wife at the time of conception, since such evidence would tend to "bastardize" the child.

Loss leader An item sold by a merchant at a very low price (perhaps even below cost) in order to attract people to come into the store.

Loss of consortium See consortium.

Loss reserve That portion of an insurance company's assets set aside for payment of losses that will probably arise or that have arisen but have not been paid.

Lost property Property that the owner has involuntarily parted with and does not know where to find or recover. Lost property is distinguishable from mislaid property, which has deliberately been placed somewhere and forgotten.

Lot 1. One of several parcels into which real property is divided (lot and block number). **2.** A number of associated persons or things taken collectively.

Lottery A chance for a prize, for which a price is paid; a device whereby anything of value is, for a consideration, distributed by lot or by chance.

Loyalty 1. Adherence to law. **2.** Faithfulness.

LSAT Law School Admission Test: A standardized test on reasoning, general academic ability, and command of written English. Law schools consider performance on the test in making a decision on admission.

Ltd. Limited.

Lucid interval A temporary restoration to sanity; a period during which an insane person has sufficient intelligence, judgment, and will to enter contractual relationships.

Lucrative title In the civil law, title acquired without giving anything in exchange for it.

Lucrum cessans A ceasing gain. The element of contract damages covering lost profits.

Lump-sum payment A single amount instead of in installments.

Lunacy A major mental disorder; an impairment of one or more faculties of the mind.

Lunatic 1. Pertaining to insanity. See insanity. **2.** Senseless.

Luxury 1. An expensive item that is not a necessity but that gives comfort or pleasure. **2.** Lavishness.

Lynch law The action of unofficial persons, bands, or mobs who seize persons suspected of crimes and summarily punish them without legal trial or authority.

Mace 1. A chemical liquid which, when sprayed in the face of a person, causes dizziness and immobilization. **2.** A war club. **3.** An ornamented staff used as an emblem of authority.

Machination The act of planning or contriving a scheme to execute a purpose that is often evil.

Magistrate 1. A federal judicial officer appointed by judges of federal district courts, having some but not all the powers of a judge. **2.** A public civic officer with executive or judicial power.

Magna Charta The great charter, considered the foundation of English constitutional liberty. In 1215, King John granted the charter to the barons at Runnymade. Its provisions regulated the administration of justice, defined ecclesiastical jurisdiction, secured personal liberty and rights of property, defined limits on taxation, etc.

Mailed Something is mailed when it is properly addressed, stamped with the correct amount of postage, and deposited in a proper place for the receipt of mail.

Maim To inflict an injury upon a person, which deprives him or her of the use of any limb or member of the body, or renders him or her lame or defective in bodily vigor.

"Mainline" To take drugs directly into a vein.

Main purpose doctrine Under the statute of frauds, contracts to answer for the debt, default, or misdoing of another must be in writing unless the main purpose of the promisor's undertaking is his or her own benefit or protection.

Maintain 1. To make repairs or perform other acts to prevent a decline from the present state or condition. **2.** To bear the expenses for the support of. **3.** To declare or affirm. **4.** To carry forward; to institute.

Maintenance 1. Support or assistance (the spouse's action for maintenance). **2.** Keeping something in working order.

Major general An officer next in rank above a brigadier general and next below a lieutenant general.

Majority 1. The age at which a person is entitled to the management of his or her own affairs and to the enjoyment of civil rights (e.g., voting). **2.** The greater number; greater than half of any total.

Majority opinion The opinion of an appellate court in which a majority of its members joined.

Maker One who makes or executes; one who signs a note to borrow; one who signs a check.

Mala fides Bad faith.

Mala in se Wrongs in themselves; morally wrong acts; offenses against conscience.

Malapportionment An improper or unconstitutional apportionment of legislative districts.

Mala prohibita Acts that are made offenses by positive laws that prohibit them—they are not wrongs in themselves.

Malefactor One who is guilty or has been convicted of a crime or offense.

Malfeasance Doing an act that a person ought not do. Compare with misfeasance—the improper performance of an act that a person has a right to do; and nonfeasance—the failure to do an act that a person ought to do.

Malice The intentional doing of a wrongful act without just cause or excuse, with an intent to inflict injury, or under circumstances that the law will imply an evil intent.

Malice aforethought The intentional doing of an unlawful act when the intent was formed before the act was executed; a predetermination to commit an act without justification or excuse.

Malice in fact Express or actual malice; the desire or intent to injure.

Malice in law Implied, inferred, or legal malice; malice that is presumed from tortious acts that are deliberately done without just cause and that are reasonably calculated to injure others.

Malicious Performed with wicked or mischievous intentions or motives; doing a wrongful act intentionally and without just cause or excuse.

Malicious abuse of process Willfully misapplying a court process to obtain an object not intended by the law; the malicious perversion of a regularly issued process to obtain an end that the process was not designed to accomplish.

Maliciously Involving a wish to vex, annoy, or injure another; involving an intent to do a wrongful act; involving a direct intention to injure or a reckless disregard of another's rights.

Malicious mischief Willful destruction of personal property from wantonness, ill will, or resentment toward its owner or possessor.

Malicious prosecution A tort with the following elements: (a) To initiate or procure the initiation of legal proceedings—civil or criminal; (b) without probable cause; (c) with malice; (d) the proceedings terminate in favor of the person against whom the proceedings were brought.

Malicious use of process The use of process for its ostensible purpose but maliciously and without probable cause; the wrongful initiation of a meritless suit with a malicious motive.

Malingerer One who pretends sickness or other disablement, especially for the purpose of escaping work.

Mallory rule A confession is inadmissible if it is given by one who has been detained an unreasonable time before being brought before a magistrate.

Malpractice Professional misconduct or unreasonable lack of skill; the failure to exercise that degree of skill and learning commonly applied under the circumstances in the community by an ordinary, prudent, and reputable member of the profession in good standing.

Malum in se A wrong in itself; an act that is inherently and essentially evil and immoral in its nature.

Malum prohibitum A prohibited wrong; an act that is wrong because it is expressly prohibited—the act is not inherently wrong, evil, or immoral.

Mandamus "We command." An order to a public official from a court to compel the performance of a ministerial act or a mandatory duty where there is a clear legal right in the plaintiff.

Mandate 1. A judicial command; the order issued upon a court decision. **2.** A territory administered under a commission of the United Nations until the territory is ready for self-government.

Mandatory Compulsory, obligatory.

Mandatory injunction That which requires a person to do some positive act.

Mandatory instruction An instruction to the jury that sets up a factual situation: If the jurors find that a certain set of facts exist, then they must find for one party and against the other.

Mandatory sentence A person convicted of a certain crime must be sent to a penal institution—the statute gives the sentencing judge no discretion.

Mandatory statute A provision in a statute on an essential matter that requires a course of action; the failure to comply renders the proceeding void to which it relates.

Mania Abnormal behavior; wild, excessive enthusiasm; insanity; manic-depressive psychosis.

Manifest 1. Evident to the senses, especially to sight. **2.** A list of cargo or passengers.

Manifest necessity As a ground for a mistrial: A sudden, unforeseeable, and overwhelming emergency beyond the control of the court (e.g., illness of the judge). The accused can be retried without violating double jeopardy rules.

Manifesto A formal written declaration that is made public.

Manipulation A series of transactions involving the buying or selling of a security for the purpose of creating a false or misleading appearance of active trading, or to raise or depress the price to induce the purchase or sale by others.

Mann Act The White Slave Traffic Act: A federal statute making it a crime to transport a woman or girl in interstate or foreign commerce for the purpose of prostitution, debauchery, or any other immoral purpose.

Manner A mode of proceeding in any case or situation.

Manslaughter The unlawful killing of another without express or implied malice; criminal homicide committed recklessly or under the influence of extreme mental or emotional disturbance for which there is a reasonable explanation or excuse from the perspective of the defendant.

Manticulate To pick pockets.

Manual 1. Made or performed with the hands. **2.** A book with basic practical information or procedures.

Manual labor Work done with the hands or by the exercise of physical force, with or without the use of tools or equipment; work whose effectiveness depends chiefly on personal muscular exertion rather than on skill, intelligence, or adroitness.

Manufacture To make products by hand or machinery, especially on a large scale.

Manufacturer One who by labor, art, or skill transforms raw material into a finished product or an article of trade.

Manumission The act of liberating a slave from bondage.

Manuscript An author's handwritten or typed work product.

Margin 1. The edge or border. **2.** An amount available beyond what is needed. **3.** In commercial transactions the difference between the purchase price paid by a middleman or retailer and his selling price.

Margin account A method that the securities industry uses to extend credit to customers: A broker lends the customer money to purchase securities; the customer advances only a portion of the purchase price and pays interest on the balance.

Marijuana, or **marihuana** A drug prepared from cannabis sativa; any part of the hemp plant or extracts therefrom that induce somatic and psychic changes in a person.

Marine Pertaining to the sea, naval.

Marine insurance A contract whereby one party indemnifies another against designated perils or sea risks to a ship, freight, or cargo during a cerain voyage or for a fixed period of time.

Mariner One engaged in navigating vessels upon the sea.

Marital Relating to the status of marriage.

Marital communications privilege A spouse has a privilege to refuse to disclose and to prevent others from disclosing private or confidential communications between the spouses during the marriage. The privilege does not apply to prosecutions for crimes committed by one spouse against the other or against the children.

Marital deduction A deduction allowed upon the transfer of property from one spouse to another: Under the federal gift tax for lifetime—inter vivos—transfers, and under the federal estate tax for testamentary transfers.

Maritime Pertaining to navigable waters and the commerce thereon.

Maritime Administration An agency within the Department of Commerce that promotes and regulates the activities of the U.S. merchant marine, establishes specifications for shipbuilding and design, determines routes, etc.

Mark 1. A token, evidence, proof. **2.** A substitute for the signature of a person who cannot write.

Market 1. A place of commercial activity in which tangible or intangible property is bought and sold. **2.** Trade and commerce. **3.** The geographical or economic extent of commercial demand.

Marketability The probability of selling property at a specific time and price.

Marketable Capable of attracting buyers.

Marketable title A title free from objectionable encumbrances and any reasonable doubt as to its validity; one that an informed business person would be willing to accept in the exercise of ordinary business prudence; one that would not expose the person who holds it to the hazards of litigation as to its validity.

Market price The price at which a seller is ready and willing to sell, and a buyer is ready and willing to buy in the ordinary course of trade; the price actually given in current market dealings.

Market share The percentage of a market that is controlled by a firm.

Market value The price that would be fixed by negotiation and agreement between a willing buyer (who is not forced to buy) and a willing seller (who is not forced to sell) in the ordinary course of business.

Marking up The process by which a legislative committee goes through a bill section by section, revising its language and amending it as desired.

Marriage The legal union of one man and one woman as husband and wife; the status of a couple united as husband and wife.

Marriage settlement An agreement before the parties marry in which they release or modify property rights that would otherwise arise from the marriage.

Marshal A federal court officer who executes all lawful writs, process, and orders. An officer similar to the sheriff or constable at the state and local level.

Marshaling Arranging, ranking, or disposing in order; an equitable doctrine that allows a court to arrange assets or claims so as to secure the proper application of the assets to the various claims and to allow all parties having interests therein to receive their due proportion. If claimant # 1 has two available funds of the debtor from which to satisfy a debt, and claimant # 2 can reach only one of these funds to satisfy its debt, then claimant # 2 can force claimant # 1 to use the fund that is not available to claimant # 2 in order to preserve the only fund available to the latter.

Mart A place of public traffic or sale.

Martial law The military authorities carry on the government or exercise varying degrees of control over civilian matters.

Martindale-Hubbell Law Directory A set of books that contain a state-by-state list of attorneys.

Mary Carter agreement An agreement between the plaintiff and some, but less than all, the defendants, whereby limitations are placed on the financial responsibility of the agreeing defendants, the amount of which is usually in inverse ratio to the amount of recovery that the plaintiff is able to make against the nonagreeing defendant(s).

Masochism Deriving increased sexual pleasure by being beaten and maltreated by someone else.

Massachusetts rule As regards sending out checks through banks for collection, the "Massachusetts rule" is that each bank that receives the item acts as an agent for the depositor; but in some other states, the "New York rule" prevails, under which only the bank first receiving the item is responsible to, or is the agent of, the depositor, the other banks being the agent of the bank, in the process of the collection.

Massachusetts Trust See business trust.

Master 1. A principal who hires others and who controls or has the right to control their physical conduct in the performance of their service. **2.** An officer appointed by the court to assist it in specific judicial duties (e.g., take testimony). **3.** One who has reached the summit of his or her trade, and who has the right to hire apprentices and journeymen. **4.** Main or central.

Master agreement The omnibus labor agreement reached between a union and the leaders of the industry or a trade association. It becomes the pattern for labor agreements between the union and individual employers.

Master and servant Employer-employee relationship that exists where the employer has the right to select the employee, the power to remove and discharge him or her, and the right to direct what work shall be done and the manner in which it shall be done.

Master in Chancery An officer of a court of chancery who acts as an assistant to the judge or chancellor (e.g., takes testimony, computes damages).

Master policy An insurance policy that covers a group of persons (e.g. health or life insurance written as group insurance). Generally, there is only one master policy and the participants have only certificates evidencing their participation.

Material 1. Having influence or effect. **2.** Pertaining to concrete, physical matter. **3.** A substance out of which something is made.

Material evidence Evidence that tends to influence the trier of fact because of its logical connection with the issue; evidence pertinent to the issue in dispute.

Material fact An influential fact; a fact that induced the action or inaction; an essential fact; a fact likely to affect the result.

Materialman One who furnishes materials and supplies for construction or repair work.

Material representation A representation of such character that if it had not been made, the contract or transaction would not have been entered into.

Material witness A person who can give testimony that no one else or few others can.

Maternal Pertaining to, belonging to, or coming from the mother.

Maternal line A line of descent or relationship between two persons, which is traced through the mother of the younger.

Matriculate To enroll in or be admitted to an organization (e.g., a college).

Matrix In civil law, the protocol or first draft of a legal instrument, from which all copies must be taken.

Matter in controversy, or **in dispute** The subject of litigation; the issue on which the court action is brought.

Matter in pais A matter of fact that is not in writing.

Mature To be developed, complete, ripe for payment.

Matured claim A claim that is unconditionally due and owing.

Maturity The date on which an obligation becomes due.

Maxim A principle; a general statement of a rule or a truth.

Maximum The highest or greatest amount, quality, value, or degree.

Mayhem Crime: depriving someone of a limb or member of the body; maliciously disabling, dismembering, or disfiguring.

McNabb-Mallory rule See Mallory rule.

McNaghten rule See M'Naghten rule, insanity.

M.D. Middle District (e.g., U.S. District Court for the Middle District of Ohio).

Mean 1. A middle between two extremes. **2.** To intend.

Meaning That which one intends to signify or denote by language or acts.

Means That which is used to attain an end.

Measure 1. That by which length, breadth, thickness, capacity, or amount is ascertained. **2.** A statute or legislative proposal. **3.** To ascertain the dimensions of something.

Mechanic's lien A security interest (in the nature of a mortgage) created by law on real property and the improvements thereon to secure those persons who have furnished labor or materials for the erection of structures or for the making of improvements on the real property.

Mediation The process by which a neutral third person assists and encourages parties in conflict to reach a settlement of the dispute that will be satisfactory to them all.

Mediation and Conciliation Service An agency of the federal government that tries to settle labor disputes through mediation.

Mediator One who tries to help disputing parties to reconcile or settle their differences.

Medicaid A form of public assistance sponsored jointly by the federal and state governments, providing medical aid for people whose income falls below a certain level.

Medical examiner A public officer with the responsibility of investigating all sudden, une..plained, unnatural, or suspicious deaths that are reported.

Medical malpractice Negligence by a doctor; injury caused by a doctor's failure to have and use the skill and learning commonly possessed by members of the profession in good standing.

Medicare A federal program that provides hospital and medical insurance for the aged under the Social Security Act.

Medicine 1. The science and art dealing with the prevention, alleviation, and cure of diseases. **2.** Substances used to treat a disease or injury.

Melancholia Mental unsoundness characterized by extreme depression of spirits, ill-grounded fears, delusions, and brooding; the depressed phase of manic-depressive psychosis.

Memorandum 1. A written statement or note that is often brief and informal. **2.** A written analysis of how the law applies to a given set of facts.

Memorandum decision The decision or ruling of a court with little or no statement of the reasons for it.

Memorial 1. A petition or statement of facts presented to the legislature or to the executive. **2.** Commemorative.

Memory The mental power to review and recollect the successive states of consciousness in their consecutive order; the ability to recollect past events; the recollection of past events.

Menace 1. Showing or threatening a determination to inflict harm on another. **2.** To threaten.

Mensa et thoro From bed and board.

Mens legis The mind of the law; that is, the purpose, spirit, or intention of a law.

Mens rea A guilty mind, wrongful purpose, criminal intent.

Mental 1. Relating to or existing in the mind. **2.** Involving a mental illness.

Mental anguish or suffering The mental sensation of pain and the accompanying feelings of distress, fright, and anxiety.

Mental capacity or competence The ability to understand the nature and effect of the act in which the person is engaged and the business he or she is transacting.

Mental cruelty A ground for divorce: A course of conduct that can endanger the mental and physical health and efficiency of another to the extent of rendering a continuation of the relationship intolerable.

Mental disease or defect A condition that results in a lack of substantial capacity either to appreciate the criminality (wrongfulness) of one's conduct or to conform his or her conduct to the requirements of the law. See insanity.

Mental reservation An unexpressed exception to the general words of a promise or agreement, often with the aim of having a dishonest excuse to evade the promise or agreement.

Mercantile Involving the business of merchants and commerce.

Mercantile paper See commercial paper, negotiable instrument.

Merchandise Goods that merchants usually buy and sell at wholesale or retail; the objects of trade and commerce.

Merchant A person who deals in the purchase and sale of goods.

Merchantability The article sold is of the general kind described and is reasonably fit for the general purpose for which it is sold.

Merchantable Fit for the ordinary purposes for which the goods are used; acceptable without objection in the trade under the contract description; conformable to ordinary standards of care; of average grade, quality, and value of similar goods sold under similar circumstances.

Merchantable title A good and marketable title that is acceptable to a knowledgeable buyer not under duress to purchase; a title that would be free from litigation, palpable defects, and grave doubts; a title that will enable the owner to hold it in peace and to sell it to a person of reasonable prudence; a readily transferable title in the market.

Merchant seaman One employed on a private vessel.

Mercy killing Euthanasia.

Mere licensee One who enters upon the land or property of another without objection or by the mere permission, sufferance, or acquiescence of the owner or occupier.

Meretricious Involving vulgarity, insincerity, or unlawful sexual relations.

Merger The fusion or absorption of one thing or right into another; the absorption of one company by another, with the latter retaining its own identity and name. The absorbed company ceases to exist as a separate business entity.

Meridians Imaginary north and south lines used in the Government Survey System which intersect the base line to form the starting point for the measurement of land.

Meritorious 1. Characterized by merit; deserving serious judicial inquiry; going to the heart or essence of the case. **2.** Deserving reward.

Merit system The system used for hiring and promoting government employees to civil service positions on the basis of competence rather than patronage.

Mesne Intermediate; intervening; occurring between two periods or ranks.

Metabolism The sum total of all processes of the human body by which food is transformed into chemicals, which are absorbed into the bloodstream and lymphatic system to nourish the body so that it can continue to function.

Mete To apportion or distribute.

Meter 1. An instrument of measurement. **2.** A metric unit of length equal to 3.28 feet.

Metes and bounds The boundary lines of land with their terminal points and angles; a way of describing land by listing the compass directions and distances of the boundaries.

Methadone A synthetic opiate of approximately the same strength as morphine, used in treating drug addiction.

Methamphetamine A synthetic drug closely related to amphetamines, producing prominent central stimulant reactions without peripheral effects.

Metric system A decimal system of weights and measures, based on the meter as the unit length and the kilogram as the unit mass.

Metropolitan Pertaining to a city and the surrounding towns.

Microfiche A photographic film (microfilm) containing a large amount of material in reduced form. Ultrafiche contains an even greater amount.

Middleman One who brings parties together.

Midwife A woman who assists at childbirth.

Migration Movement from one place to another; movement from one region or country to another.

Migratory divorce A divorce obtained by a spouse who travels (migrates) to another state or country for a temporary period in order to obtain the divorce, which is often procedurally easier to obtain than in the state of original domicile.

Mil One-thousandth of an inch.

Mileage Money for traveling expenses at a certain rate per mile.

Military law A system of laws governing the armed forces.

Militia Citizen army; a citizen military force used in emergencies.

Mill One-tenth of one cent.

Millimeter One-thousandth of a meter or .0394 inch.

Mine An excavation in the earth from which ores, coal, or other mineral substances are removed.

Mineral A lifeless substance formed or deposited through natural processes and found either in or upon the soil or in the rocks beneath the soil; a natural constituent of the crust of the earth, inorganic or fossil, homogeneous in structure, having a definite chemical composition and known crystallization.

Minimum fee schedules A bar association suggested list of fees to be charged by lawyers.

Minimum or **minimal contacts** A standard used to determine when a state can acquire personal jurisdiction over a nonresident defendant who is not served in the state: There must be a sufficient connection between the defendant and the state to make it fair to force him or her to defend the action in the state.

Minimum sentence The least severe sentence that a court may impose on a convicted defendant.

Minimum wage The amount set by federal statute that employees must be paid by employers engaged in businesses that affect interstate commerce.

Mining The process or business of extracting from the earth precious or valuable metals in their native state or in their ores.

Minister 1. A person ordained by a Christian church to preach and perform other religious functions. **2.** An administrator or person in charge of a department. **3.** To give attention or assistance to another.

Ministerial Involving obedience to instructions and no special discretion, judgment, or skill (ministerial act).

Ministry Religious ministers; the duties or functions of a religious minister.

Minor 1. A person under the legal age, usually under 18. **2.** Lesser in importance, seriousness, or size.

Minority 1. The status of being under the legal age—under the age of majority. **2.** The smaller number.

Minority opinion An opinion in a case written by less than a majority of the court. It can be a dissenting opinion (disagreeing with the result and with the reasoning of the majority) or a concurring opinion (agreeing with the result but disagreeing with the reasoning of the majority).

Mint 1. The place where bullion is coined into money under the authority of the government. **2.** To coin money.

Minutes A record of what occurred at a meeting; an account of the actions formally taken.

Miranda warnings Prior to any custodial interrogation, a person must be warned: (a) that he or she has a right to remain silent, (b) that any statement made can be used as evidence against him or her, (c) that he or she has the right to the presence of an attorney, and (d) that if he or she cannot afford an attorney, one will be appointed at government expense if desired.

Misadventure An accident or misfortune.

Misapplication The wrongful use of funds or other property.

Misappropriate To take wrongfully; to use someone else's property to one's own advantage.

Miscarriage 1. Poor management or administration, failure. **2.** Premature expulsion of a nonviable fetus.

Miscegenation Mixture of races; marriage between persons of different races.

Mischarge An erroneous charge to a jury.

Mischief 1. Conduct that causes harm intentionally, recklessly, or negligently. **2.** The evil or danger that a statute is intended to cure or avoid.

Misconduct A transgression of an established rule; willful impropriety.

Misdelivery Delivery of mail or goods to someone other than the specified or authorized recipient.

Misdemeanant A person convicted of a misdemeanor.

Misdemeanor A crime other than a felony; a crime punishable by fine or by detention in a jail or in an institution other than a penitentiary.

Misdirection An error made by the judge in the instruction given to the jury.

Misfeasance The improper performance of an act that is otherwise proper.

Misfortune An unforeseeable calamity arising by accident.

Misjoinder The improper joining together of parties; the improper joining together of causes of action.

Mislay To forget where one placed something.

Misleading Capable of leading one astray or into error.

Misprision Maladministration of public office; contempt against the courts or the state; failure to prevent or disclose a crime.

Misprision of felony Concealing a felony committed by another, without prior concert with or subsequent assistance to the felon.

Misrepresent To portray something inaccurately.

Misrepresentation 1. Any untrue statement of fact. **2.** An intentionally false statement of fact. See fraud.

Mistake An unintentional act, omission, or error arising from ignorance, surprise, imposition, or misplaced confidence.

Mistrial An erroneous, invalid, or nugatory trial.

Mitigate To render less painful or severe.

Mitigating Qualifying or extenuating.

Mitigating circumstances Circumstances surrounding the commission of an act, which in fairness can be considered as extenuating or reducing the severity or degree of moral culpability of the act, but do not serve to excuse or justify it.

Mitigation of damages A rule of avoidable consequences: An injured party has a duty to use reasonable diligence and ordinary care in attempting to minimize his or her damages after an injury has been inflicted.

Mittimus An order commanding that a person be conveyed to a prison and held there.

Mixed larceny Attended with circumstances of aggravation or violence to the person, or taking from a house. Also called compound or complicated larceny.

M'Naghten rule A test of insanity: An accused is not criminally responsible if, at the time of committing the act, he or she was laboring under such a defect of reason from a disease of the mind as not to know the nature and quality of the act, or if he or she did know this, he or she did not know that the act was wrong. The defendant must know and understand the nature and quality of the act and must be able to distinguish between right and wrong at the time of committing it.

Model A representation or pattern of something to be made or of something already made.

Model act A statute proposed to legislatures for adoption (e.g., the Model Probate Code proposed by the National Conference of Commissioners of Uniform State Laws).

Modem An instrument that converts data from one form into another.

Modification An alteration that does not change the general purpose and effect of that which is modified.

Modus Manner, means, way.

Modus operandi (MO) A method of doing things.

Modus vivendi A way of living.

Moiety 1. One-half (joint tenants hold by moieties). **2.** Portion.

Monarchy A government in which the supreme power is vested in a single person.

Monetary Having to do with coinage or currency—money.

Money Coins and paper currency used as the circulating medium of exchange.

Money market The financial machinery for dealing in short term paper such as notes and loans, in contrast to the capital market that furnishes long-term financing.

Money order A type of negotiable draft used by the purchaser as a substitute for a check; a form of credit instrument calling for the payment of money to a named payee.

Monition 1. A summons to appear in an admiralty case. **2.** A warning of danger.

Monogamy Being married to one person at a time.

Monopoly A form of market structure in which one or only a few firms dominate the total sales of a product; the power to fix prices, exclude competition, and control the market in a geographical area, coupled with policies designed to preserve that power.

Monopsony A condition of the market in which there is but one buyer for a particular commodity.

Month Calendar month. The period from any day in a month of the calendar to the corresponding day of the next month.

Monument 1. Anything by which the memory of a person, thing, idea, art, science, or event is preserved or perpetuated. **2.** Visible marks or indications left on natural or other objects (posts, stone markers, blazed trees, watercourse), indicating the lines and boundaries of a property survey.

Moonshine Intoxicating liquor illicitly produced or smuggled into a community for beverage purposes; spirituous liquor, illegally distilled or manufactured.

Mooring Anchoring or securing a vessel to a shore or dock.

Moot 1. Pertaining to a nonexistent controversy where the issues have ceased to exist from a practical point of view (the question is moot because the plaintiff received what he wanted before the trial began). **2.** A subject for argument.

Moot court A simulated court in a law school where a hypothetical case is argued for learning purposes.

Moral 1. Pertaining to conscience or to the general principles of right conduct. **2.** Demonstrating correct character or behavior.

Moral certainty That degree of assurance that induces a person of sound mind to act without doubt upon the conclusions to which it leads; a very high degree of probability although not demonstrable to a certainty.

Moral hazard In fire insurance: The risk or danger of the destruction of the insured property by fire.

Moral obligation A duty that rests on moral considerations alone and is not imposed or enforced by positive law; a duty binding in conscience but not in law.

Moral turpitude Acts or behavior that gravely violates accepted moral standards of the community; baseness or depravity in private or social duties that one person owes another or owes society in general.

Moratorium Temporary suspension of the obligations of a debtor and the right to use remedies against him or her; a period of permissive or obligatory delay.

Morgue A place where dead persons are kept for a limited time for identification purposes.

Mormon A member of the Church of the Latter-day Saints, organized by Joseph Smith in 1830 and headquartered in Salt Lake City, Utah.

Morning loan An unsecured loan to permit the borrower, generally a stockbroker, to carry on business for the day.

Mortal Exposing to death; destructive of life, fatal.

Mortality tables A means of ascertaining the probable number of years a male or female of a given age will live, assuming ordinary health.

Mortgage 1. An interest in land created by a written instrument providing security for the performance of a duty or the payment of a debt. A lien or claim against real property given by the buyer to the lender as security for money borrowed. See also assumption of mortgage. **2.** To make subject to a pledge.

Mortgage bond A bond for which real estate or personal property is pledged as security that the bond will be paid as stated in its terms.

Mortgage commitment A written notice from the bank or other lending institution saying it will advance mortgage funds in a specified amount to enable a buyer to purchase a house.

Mortgage company A firm engaged in the business of originating and closing mortgages, which are then assigned or sold to investors.

Mortgagee The person who takes, receives, and holds a mortgage; the person to whom property is mortgaged. The lender.

Mortgage insurance Insurance from which the benefits are used to pay off the balance of a mortgage upon the death or disability of the insured; insurance against loss to the mortgagees in the event of default and a failure of the mortgaged property to satisfy the balance owing plus the costs of foreclosure.

Mortgage lien A lien on the property of the mortgagor, which secures the debt obligation.

Mortgage note A written agreement to repay a loan. The agreement is secured by a mortgage, serves as proof of an indebtedness, and states the manner in which it shall be paid. The note states the actual amount of the debt that the mortgage secures and renders the mortgagor personally responsible for repayment.

Mortgage (open-ended) A mortgage with a provision that permits borrowing additional money in the future without refinancing the loan or paying additional financing charges. Open-end provisions often limit such borrowing to no more than would raise the balance to the original loan figure. At least the stated ratio of assets to the debt must usually be maintained.

Mortgagor The person who mortgages his or her property; the person who pledges property; the person who gives legal title or a lien to the mortgagee to secure the mortgage loan. The borrower.

Mortis causa By reason of death. See in contemplation of death.

Mortmain acts Statutes that are designed to prevent lands from permanently getting into the possession or control of institutions such as churches, which could not transfer them.

Mortuary An undertaking and embalming establishment; a funeral home.

Most favored nation clause A clause found in a treaty, providing that each side grants to the other the broadest rights and privileges that it accords to any other nation (any third nation) in treaties it has made or will make.

Motion An application made to a court or other decision-making body in order to obtain a favorable action or decision.

Motion for a directed verdict A request that the court order a verdict in favor of the moving party, on the ground that the other side has failed to produce sufficient evidence of facts that support its theory of the case as to which it had the burden of proof.

Motion for a judgment notwithstanding the verdict (JNOV) A request that the judge enter a verdict contrary to that reached by the jury, on the ground that the evidence is insufficient to support the jury's verdict.

Motion for a judgment on the pleadings A request that the judge make a decision on the basis of the pleadings alone without a trial, on the ground that the material facts are not in dispute and only questions of law remain.

Motion for a more definite statement A request that the court order the other side to make its pleading more definite, since it is so vague or ambiguous that one cannot reasonably frame a responsive pleading.

Motion for a new trial A request that the trial judge set aside the judgment and order a new trial, on the ground that the trial was improper or unfair due to specified prejudicial errors that occurred (e.g., jury misconduct).

Motion in limine A motion made before or after the beginning of a jury trial for a protective order against the potential use of prejudicial statements or questions by the other side.

Motion to dismiss A request, usually made before the trial begins, that the judge dismiss the case because of an insufficiency in the pleadings of the other side.

Motion to strike A request that the court remove from a pleading any insufficient defense or any redundant, immaterial, or scandalous matter.

Motion to suppress A request that the court eliminate from the trial any illegally secured evidence.

Motive The cause or reason that moves the will and induces action or inaction.

Movables Things that can be carried from one place to another.

Movant One who makes a motion or applies for a ruling or order.

Move To make an application for a certain action or decision.

Moving papers Papers or documents submitted in support of a motion.

Moving party The party making the motion.

Mulct 1. A penalty or punishment imposed on a person guilty of some offense or tort. **2.** To defraud a person of something.

Mulier puisné When a man has a bastard son, and afterwards marries the mother, and then has a legitimate son by her, the elder son is bastard eigné, and the younger son is mulier puisné.

Multidistrict litigation Civil actions involving one or more common questions of fact pending in several different federal district courts (e.g., antitrust cases, air crash cases). Such cases can be transferred to one district for coordinated and consolidated trial under a single judge.

Multifarious Diverse, varied, diversified.

Multifarious issue An issue that inquires about several different facts, when each fact should be inquired about in a separate issue.

Multifariousness In equity pleading, the misjoinder of causes of action in a bill.

Multilateral Involving many sides, persons, firms, or nations.

Multinational Having centers of operation in many countries.

Multipartite Divided into many or several parts.

Multiple access The defense of several men in a paternity case that more than one lover had access to the mother during the time of conception.

Multiple listing An arrangement between a number of real estate brokers in a given area whereby any member broker is authorized to sell the property listed with one broker. The latter shares the fee or commission with the broker who made the sale.

Multiplicity 1. A large number or variety of matters or particulars. **2.** The charging of a single offense in several counts.

Multiplicity of actions or suits Numerous and unnecessary attempts to litigate the same right against the same defendant.

Municipal 1. Pertaining to a city, town, or other local unit of government. **2.** Pertaining to a self-governing or independent state or nation.

Municipal corporation A body corporate created by the legislature for the purpose of local government, with a corporate name and continuous succession, consisting of the inhabitants of a designated area or portion of the state.

Municipality A legally incorporated or duly authorized association of inhabitants of a limited area of the state for local government or other public purposes.

Municipal securities The evidences of indebtedness issued by cities, towns, counties, townships, school districts, and other such territorial divisions of a state. They are of two general classes: (1) municipal warrants, orders, or certificates; (2) municipal bonds.

Muniments Documentary evidence of title; documents the owner can use to defend his or her title to land.

Murder The unlawful killing of a human being with malice aforethought.

Mutatis mutandis With the necessary changes in any of the details.

Mute Speechless; concerning one who cannot or will not speak.

Mutilate 1. To maim, to dismember, to disfigure. **2.** To alter or deface a document by cutting, tearing, burning, or erasing, without totally destroying it.

Mutinous Tending to incite or encourage mutiny.

Mutiny An insurrection of soldiers or seamen against the authority of their commanders.

Mutual Interchangeable, common to both parties.

Mutual combat A fight that both parties willingly enter. Two persons, upon a sudden quarrel and in hot blood, mutually fight on equal terms.

Mutual company A company in which the customers are also the owners and receive the profits in proportion to the business they do with the company.

Mutual fund An investment company that raises money by selling its own stock to the public and investing the proceeds in other securities.

Mutual insurance company An insurance company that has no capital stock and in which the policyholders are the owners.

Mutuality An action by each of two parties; reciprocation; both sides being bound.

Mutuality of obligation Unless both sides are bound by the contract, neither is bound.

Mutual mistake A mistake common to both contracting parties, where each is laboring under the same misconception as to a past or existing material fact. The agreement entered into by the parties does not in its written form express what the parties actually intended.

Mutual savings bank A banking institution that has no capital stock and in which the depositors are the owners.

Mutual wills 1. Separate wills made by two persons, which are reciprocal in their provisions. **2.** Wills executed pursuant to an agreement between two persons to dispose of their property in a particular manner, each in consideration of the other.

Naked possibility A bare chance or expectation of acquiring a property or succeeding to an estate in the future, but without any present right in or to it that the law would recognize as an estate or interest.

Naked promise One given without any consideration, equivalent, or reciprocal obligation, and for that reason not enforceable at law.

Naked trust A dry or passive trust; one that requires no action on the part of the trustee, beyond turning over money or property to the cestui que trust.

Named insured The person specifically mentioned in an insurance policy as the one protected.

"Narc" A law enforcement officer assigned to enforce the drug laws.

Narcotic Any drug that dulls the senses or induces sleep and which often becomes addictive after prolonged use.

Narrative evidence A descriptive account of a sequence of events.

Nation An aggregation of people united under one political system in a distinct portion of the globe, often with common traditions, customs, and history.

National 1. Pertaining to the nation as a whole. **2.** A citizen of a particular nation.

National bank A bank incorporated and doing business under the laws of the United States.

National Guard An organization that serves as a reserve of the Army and Air Force. Members of the Guard, serving on a statewide basis, are subject to being activated for federal service as well as for state emergencies.

Nationality The status that arises as a result of a person's belonging to a nation because of birth or naturalization.

Nationalization The acquisition and control of privately owned businesses by the government.

National Labor Relations Board (NLRB) An independent federal agency that seeks to prevent and remedy unfair labor practices, conducts employee elections in appropriate collective bargaining units, etc.

National Mediation Board An agency that mediates disputes between rail and air carriers, and the unions of their employees.

National origin The country where a person was born or from which his or her ancestors came.

Native A citizen by birth.

Natural 1. Based on moral considerations; proceeding from or determined by physical conditions as opposed to positive enactments of the law; attributed to the nature of humankind. **2.** Not artificial or manmade. **3.** Innate. **4.** Normal.

Natural affection The affection that naturally exists between near relatives.

Natural and probable consequences Those consequences that a person using prudent human foresight should be able to anticipate as likely to result from an act because they result so frequently from this act in the experience of humanity.

Natural domicile Domicile of origin or domicile by birth.

Natural guardian The father and mother of a child.

Natural heirs Heirs by consanguinity as distinguished from heirs by adoption and collateral heirs.

Naturalization The process by which a person acquires citizenship after birth.

Natural law A system of rules and principles (not created by human authority or enacted law) that can be discovered by the rational intelligence of a person as growing out of and conforming to the nature of men and women.

Natural obligation A natural obligation is one that cannot be enforced by action, but that is binding in conscience and according to natural justice.

Natural person A human being, in contrast to legal entities such as an association, a corporation, a foundation, an organization, or a state.

Natural resources Any material in its native state which, when extracted, has economic value (e.g., timberland, oil, gas).

Nautical Pertaining to ships, navigation, or the sea carriage business.

Nautical mile About 6,076 feet.

Navigable waters Any body of water that, by itself or by uniting with other waters, forms a continuous highway over which commerce can be carried on with other states or countries.

Navigation The art, science, or business of traveling the sea or other navigable waters in ships or vessels.

N.D. Northern District, e.g., U.S. District Court for the Northern District of New York (N.D.N.Y.).

Near money Liquid assets that are readily convertible into money.

Necessaries Those things that are indispensable or proper and useful for the sustenance of human life; those things that are suitable for the individual according to his or her circumstances and condition in life.

Necessary 1. Essential. **2.** Convenient or suitable.

Necessary and proper Appropriate and adapted to carrying a given object into effect.

Necessary party A party that must be joined in an action (as plaintiff or defendant) because complete relief cannot otherwise be obtained by the present parties; those persons who have such an interest in the controversy that a final judgment or decree cannot be made without either affecting their interests or leaving the controversy in such a condition that its final adjudication may be inconsistent with equity and good conscience.

Necessities See necessaries.

Necessitous Poverty-stricken.

Necessity 1. A power or impulse so great that it admits no choice of conduct. **2.** That which is indispensable.

Necropsy An autopsy or post-mortem examination of a human body.

Need The lack of something that is necessary or desired.

Ne exeat A writ that forbids a person from leaving the country, state, or jurisdiction of the court.

Negative Expressing or containing a denial or refusal.

Negative averment An allegation of some substantive fact that is really affirmative in substance although negative in form.

Negative covenant A clause in an employment

agreement or contract for the sale of a business, which prohibits the employee or seller from competing in the same area or market.

Negative easement An easement that restrains a landowner from making a certain use of his or her land that would otherwise be lawful; the right of the owner of the dominant tenement to restrict the owner of the servient tenement in the exercise of certain property rights.

Negative income tax Money given by the government to individuals with income below a designated level.

Negative plea In equity pleading, a plea that does not undertake to answer the various allegations of the bill, but specifically denies some particular fact or matter, the existence of which is essential to entitle the complainant to any relief.

Negative pregnant A negative statement that also implies an affirmative statement; a denial that admits important facts; a denial that is pregnant with an admission (e.g., "I deny that I owe $500" may be an admission that at least some amount is owed).

Neglect 1. To fail to do that which can be done and is required to be done. **2.** The failure to do what can be done and what is required to be done.

Neglected child A child who is abandoned by its parent, who lacks proper parental care by reason of the fault or habits of the parent, or whose parent neglects or refuses to provide proper or necessary subsistence, education, or other care necessary for the health, morals, and well-being of the child.

Negligence The failure to do what a reasonable person would have done under the same circumstances. A departure of the conduct that would be expected of a reasonably prudent person under like circumstances. A tort with the following elements: (a) a duty of reasonable care owed to the injured person, (b) a breach of this duty, (c) proximate cause, (d) actual damages.

Negligence per se Negligence as a matter of law; acts or omissions that can be declared negligent without any argument or proof as to the particular surrounding circumstances either because (a) they are in violation of a statute or ordinance, or (b) they are so palpably opposed to the dictates of common prudence that it can be said without hesitation or doubt that no careful person would have acted or failed to act in the same way.

Negligent See neglect, negligence.

Negligent homicide A criminal offense committed by one whose negligence is the proximate result of another's death; the death of a human being through the instrumentality of a motor vehicle operated on a highway in a negligent manner.

Negligent misrepresentation A false statement made by someone who has no reasonable grounds for believing it to be true, although he or she does not know it is untrue, but does know that another is expected to rely on the statement and that the latter would be damaged if it is false.

Negotiability The legal character of being negotiable.

Negotiable 1. Legally capable of being transferred by endorsement or delivery (e.g., checks, notes). **2.** Open to compromise and discussion.

Negotiable instrument An instrument (e.g., check, note, bill of exchange) that (a) is a writing signed by the maker or drawer, (b) contains an unconditional promise or order, (c) to pay a sum certain in money, (d) is payable on demand or at a definite time, (e) is payable to the bearer or to order, and (f) does not contain any other promise, order, obligation, or power given by the maker or drawer except as authorized by statute.

Negotiate To bargain with another concerning a sale, settlement, or matter in contention.

Negotiated plea The result of plea bargaining in which the accused agrees to plead guilty to the charge, or to a reduced charge, in return for a recommendation from the prosecutor for a less severe sentence.

Negotiation 1. The transfer of an instrument through delivery (if the instrument is payable to bearer), or through endorsement and delivery (if it is payable to order) in such form that the transferee becomes a holder. **2.** The process of submitting and considering offers until a satisfactory offer is made and accepted.

Neighbor One who lives in close proximity to another.

Neighborhood The immediate vicinity.

Nepotism Granting privileges, appointments, or other patronage to one's relatives by blood or marriage.

Net Pertaining to the amount that remains after all allowable deductions (e.g., charges, expenses, discounts, commissions, taxes).

Net assets A bookkeeping balance obtained by subtracting a company's liabilities from its gross assets.

Net earnings The excess of the gross earnings over the expenditures incurred in producing them.

Net estate The gross estate less deductions for funeral expenses, claims against the estate, unpaid mortgages or indebtedness on property that is included in the gross estate, etc.

Net income Income subject to taxation after allowable deductions and exemptions have been subtracted from gross or total income; what remains out of gross income after subtracting ordinary and necessary expenses incurred in efforts to obtain or keep it.

Net lease A lease in which the lessee pays not only rent, but also taxes, insurance, and maintenance charges.

Net operating loss Loss before interest and income taxes but after depreciation produced by operating assets; the excess of the deductions allowed over the gross income.

Net proceeds Gross receipts less charges that can be deducted.

Net profits Profits after deductions of all expenses.

Net weight The weight of an article after deducting from the gross weight the weight of the boxes, coverings, casks, etc.

Net worth The total assets of a person or business less the total liabilities.

Net worth method A method used by the IRS to reconstruct the income of a taxpayer who fails to keep adequate records: The gross income for the year is the increase in net worth of the taxpayer (i.e., assets in excess of liabilities) with appropriate adjustment for nontaxable receipts and nondeductible expenditures.

Net yield The return on an investment after deducting all costs, losses, and charges for management.

Neurology The branch of medicine dealing with the nervous system and its disorders.

Neutral Not taking an active part with either of the contending sides; disinterested, unbiased.

Neutrality The status of a nation that takes no part in a war between other nations.

Neutrality laws Acts of Congress that forbid equipping armed vessels or enlisting troops for the aid of either of two belligerent powers with which the United States is at peace.

Neutralization Erasure or cancellation.

Ne varietur It must not be altered.

Newly discovered evidence Evidence discovered after the trial and not discoverable before the trial by the exercise of due diligence.

New matter In pleading, a fact not previously alleged by either party in the pleadings.

New York Stock Exchange An unincorporated association of member firms that handle the purchase and sale of securities for themselves and for customers.

Next friend Someone specially appointed by the court to look after the interests of a person who cannot act on his or her own (e.g., a minor).

Next of kin 1. The nearest blood relatives of the decedent. **2.** Those who would inherit from the decedent if he or she died intestate, whether or not they are blood relatives.

Nient dedire To say nothing. To deny nothing; to suffer judgment by default.

Nighttime The period between sunset and sunrise when there is not enough daylight to discern a person's face; 30 minutes after sunset to 30 minutes before sunrise.

Nihil dicit He says nothing. The name of the judgment that may be taken as of course against a defendant who omits to plead or answer the plaintiff's declaration or complaint within the time limited.

Nihil est There is nothing. A form of return made by a sheriff when he or she has been unable to serve the writ.

Nihilist One who advocates the destruction of present political, religious, and social institutions.

Nihil obstat Official approval.

Nisi Unless.

Nisi decree See rule nisi.

Nitroglycerine charge See Allen charge.

No bill In the opinion of the grand jury, the evidence is insufficient to justify a formal charge or indictment.

No contest clause A provision in a will to the effect that the legacy or devise is given on condition that no action is taken to contest the will, and if such action is initiated, the legacy or devise is forfeited.

No fault 1. A type of automobile insurance in which each person's own insurance company pays for injury or damage up to a certain limit regardless of whether its insured was actually at fault. **2.** No fault also refers to a divorce granted on a ground other than the marital fault of either side.

Nolle prosequi (nol-pros) A formal entry in the record by the prosecuting officer that he or she will not prosecute the case further. The entry is also used to indicate that civil cases will not be pursued further.

No-load Sold without a commission—at net asset value.

Nolo contendere "I will not contest it." A type of plea in a criminal case in which the defendant does not admit or deny the charges. The effect of the plea, however, is similar to a plea of guilty in that the defendant can be sentenced to prison, fined, etc. The trial judge must consent to the defendant's use of the plea of nolo contendere.

Nol-pros See nolle prosequi.

Nominal 1. In name only; not real or substantial. **2.** Trifling.

Nominal consideration Consideration bearing no relation to the real value of the contract or article.

Nominal damages A trifling sum awarded to the plaintiff because there was no substantial loss or injury to be compensated, although a technical invasion of rights did occur.

Nominate To name or propose for an election or appointment.

Nominee 1. One who has been nominated or proposed for an office or appointment. **2.** One designated to act for another as a representative in a limited sense.

Nomography A treatise or description of laws.

Non-access A defense in a paternity case in which the alleged father asserts the absence of opportunities for sexual intercourse with the mother.

Nonacquiescence (non acqu.; NA) A disagreement by the IRS on the result reached by the U.S. Tax Court.

Nonage The status of being under legal age.

Nonappearance The failure to appear within the designated time limit.

Non bis in idem Not twice for the same; that is, a person shall not be twice tried for the same crime.

Noncombatant A person connected with the armed forces for a purpose other than fighting (e.g., chaplain, surgeon; conscientious objector, CO).

Noncommissioned officer An officer of the armed forces (e.g., sergeant) who holds his or her rank by appointment by a superior officer rather than by commission.

Non compos mentis Not sound of mind.

Nonconforming Not consistent or conforming with accepted customs, practices, or standards.

Nonconforming use A use that does not comply with present zoning provisions but which existed lawfully and was created in good faith prior to the enactment of the zoning provisions; a use permitted by zoning statutes or ordinances even though similar uses are not permitted in the same area.

Noncontestability clause See incontestability clause.

Noncontestable Pertaining to that which cannot be disputed.

Noncumulative dividends If dividends are not paid in a given year or period, they are gone forever or lost; there is no obligation to pay them when the next dividend is paid.

Nondisclosure The failure to reveal facts without necessarily concealing them.

Nondiscretionary trust A fixed trust under which the trustees may exercise no judgment or discretion at least as to distributions.

Nonfeasance Nonperformance of an act that should be performed; neglect of duty.

Nonjoinder The failure to join a person to a suit as plaintiff or defendant who ought to have been joined.

Nonleviable Exempt from seizure.

Nonmailable Pertaining to letters and parcels that by law are excluded from transportation in the U.S. mail because of size, obscene content, etc.

Nonmerchantable title See merchantable title.

Non-negotiable Not capable of passing title or property by indorsement and delivery.

Non obstante veredicto Notwithstanding the verdict. See judgment notwithstanding the verdict.

Nonpartisan Neutral, objective.

Nonperformance The neglect, failure, or refusal to perform an act one is under a contract to perform.

Nonprofit corporation A corporation that does not distribute any of its income to its members, directors, or officers; a corporation organized and operated exclusively for one or more of the following purposes: religious, charitable, scientific, testing for public safety, literary, educational, prevention of cruelty to children or animals, or fostering national or international sports.

Non prosequitur A judgment against a plaintiff who fails to appear.

Nonrecourse The status of a person who holds an instrument, which gives him or her no legal right against prior endorsers or the drawer to compel payment if the instrument is dishonored.

Nonresident One who does not reside in the jurisdiction; one who is not an inhabitant of the state of the forum.

Non sequitur A statement or conclusion that does not logically follow.

Nonsuit A termination or dismissal of an action when the plaintiff is unable to prove his or her case, defaults, fails to prosecute, etc.

Nonsupport The unreasonable failure or neglect to support those to whom an obligation of support is owed.

No-par Without par value. See par value.

No recourse No access to; no assumption of any liability whatsoever.

Normal 1. Conforming to a standard; not deviating from an established norm. **2.** Average. **3.** Without mental problems.

Normal school A school that trains teachers.

Norris-La Guardia Act A federal statute restricting the use of injunctions by federal courts in labor disputes.

Noscitur a sociis "It is known by its associates." A guide to interpreting written language: The meaning of questionable words or phrases may be determined by the context of the words or phrases associated with them in the text.

Notarial Performed or taken by a notary.

Notary public One whose function is to administer oaths, certify documents, take affidavits, attest to the authenticity of signatures, etc.

Note 1. A two-party instrument made by the maker and payable to the payee, which is negotiable if signed by the maker containing an unconditional promise to pay a sum certain in money on demand at a definite time, to order or to bearer. **2.** A formal commentary.

Not guilty A jury verdict acquitting the accused; a plea entered by the accused to a criminal charge.

Notice Knowledge of facts that would naturally lead an honest and prudent person to make inquiry —this does not necessarily mean knowledge of all the facts.

Notice of appeal A document filed with the appellate court and served on the opposing party, giving notice of an intention to appeal.

Notice of appearance A written notice filed by a party or by its attorney that it is making an appearance in an action.

Notice recording statute A statute providing that an unrecorded conveyance or other instrument is invalid as against a subsequent bona fide purchaser for value and without notice.

Notice to quit A written notice given by a landlord to the tenant stating that the landlord wishes to repossess the leased premises and that the tenant should leave at the end of the term or immediately if the tenancy is at will or by sufferance.

Notorious 1. Well-known or widely known, conspicuous. **2.** Infamous, shameful.

Notorious cohabitation Two persons openly living together while not being married to each other.

NOV See judgment notwithstanding the verdict.

Novation The substitution by mutual agreement of one debtor for another or of one creditor for another, whereby the old debt is extinguished; the substitution of a new contract, debt, or obligation for an existing one between the same or different parties.

Novelty That which has not been known before.

N.O.W. account Negotiable Order of Withdrawal; an interest-bearing checking account.

Nude Lacking an essential.

Nude pact A pact without consideration; an executory contract without consideration; a naked promise.

Nudum pactum A promise or undertaking made without any consideration for it; a voluntary promise without consideration other than mere goodwill or natural affection.

Nugatory Without force, validity, or vitality.

Nuisance An unreasonable interference with the use and enjoyment of land (see private nuisance); an unreasonable interference with a right that is common to the public (see public nuisance).

Nuisance per se An act, occurrence, or structure that is a nuisance at all times and under all circumstances regardless of location or surroundings.

Nulla bona No goods on which a writ of execution can be levied.

Null and void Pertaining to that which binds no one.

Nullification The state or condition of being without legal effect or status; the process of rendering something void.

Nullity That which can be treated as having absolutely no legal force or effect, as though it never took place.

Nullius filius The son of no one; an illegitimate child.

Numbers game The player wages that on a given day, a certain series of digits will appear or "come out." The winning number is determined by a set process (e.g., the last three digits of the pari-mutuel payoff totals of particular races at a designated racetrack).

Nunciatio In the civil law, a solemn declaration, usually in prohibition of a thing; a protest.

Nunc pro tunc Now for then; although a thing is done now, it will have the same force and effect as though it had been done when it should have been done; with retroactive effect.

Nuncupative will An oral will declared or dictated by the testator before witnesses; a will by verbal declaration.

Nuptial Pertaining to marriage.

Nurture To bring up or train.

Nymphomania Excessive sexual desires of a woman.

Oath An affirmation of the truth of a statement.

Oath of calumny In the civil law, an oath of good faith of the plaintiff that he or she had a good cause of action.

Obedience The performance of what is required or abstinence from what is prohibited by authority.

Obiter dictum Language in an opinion that is not necessary for the decision of the case; a remark of the court that does not directly bear on the issue before it and therefore is not binding as precedent.

Object 1. To express disapproval; to consider something improper or illegal and ask the court to take action accordingly. **2.** The end aimed at; the thing sought to be accomplished.

Objection That which is presented in opposition; the act of objecting.

Objective 1. Real; observable by the senses; existing outside the mind. **2.** Unbiased **3.** Goal.

Obligate To bind or place under an obligation.

Obligation 1. Any duty imposed by law, contract, morals, or social relations. **2.** A formal and binding agreement or acknowledgment of a liability to pay a certain sum or do a specific thing.

Obligation of contract The duty of performance including the means of enforcement.

Obligatory Compulsory, mandated.

Obligatory writing The technical name by which a bond is described in pleading.

Obligee The person to whom an obligation is owed; the party to whom a bond is given; a promisee.

Obligor The person obligated under a contract or bond; a promisor.

Obliterate To destroy or wipe out.

Obloquy Censure and reproach.

Obnoxious Highly objectionable, offensive.

Obrogation In the civil law, annulling a law, in whole or in part, by passing a law contrary to it.

Obscene Objectionable or offensive to accepted standards of decency. Test: whether, taken as a whole, the predominant appeal of the material is to prurient interest, that is, a shameful or morbid interest in nudity, sex, or excretion, and whether it goes substantially beyond customary limits of candor in describing or representing such matters.

Obscenity The character of being obscene; conduct tending to corrupt the public morals by its indecency or lewdness.

Observe To adhere to or abide by.

Obsignatory Ratifying and confirming.

Obsolescence Diminution in value caused by changes in taste or new technology, rendering the property less desirable on the market; the condition or process of falling into disuse.

Obsolescent Gradually going out of use.

Obsolete Pertaining to that which is no longer used.

Obstante Withstanding; hindering.

Obstetrician A doctor specializing in the treatment of women during pregnancy, birth, and recovery.

Obstriction Obligation; bond.

Obstruct 1. To hinder or prevent progress. **2.** To screen, to cut off from sight.

Obstructing justice The act by which a person prevents or attempts to prevent the execution of lawful process; impeding the administration of justice (e.g., hindering witnesses from appearing).

Obstruction A hindrance or barrier.

Obtain To get possession of.

Obvious Easily discovered.

Occasion 1. To cause or bring about by furnishing the condition or opportunity. **2.** That which produces an opportunity for a casual agency to act.

Occupancy Taking possession of property and using it; the period during which someone holds or uses property.

Occupant A person in possession.

Occupation 1. One's regular business or employment. **2.** Seizure, possession, control.

Occupational disease A disease resulting from exposure during employment to conditions or substances detrimental to health.

Occupational Safety and Health Administration (OSHA) A federal agency that develops occupational and health safety standards, and conducts investigations to determine compliance with the standards.

Occupation tax A form of excise tax imposed on persons for the privilege of carrying on a business, trade, or occupation.

Occupy 1. To take or hold possession for use. **2.** To seize by force.

Ocean The main or open sea that is not subject to the territorial jurisdiction or control of any country; the high sea.

Oculist A doctor specializing in diseases of the eye.

Odd lot doctrine A finding of total disability is possible where the claimant is not altogether incapacitated for any kind of work but is nevertheless so handicapped that he or she will not be able to obtain regular employment in any well-known branch of the competitive labor market, absent superhuman efforts, sympathetic employers or friends, a business boom, or temporary good luck.

Of age See adult, majority.

Of counsel An attorney who is assisting the attorney of record on a case; an associate.

Offender One who has committed a crime or offense.

Offense A violation of the criminal law.

Offensive Causing disagreeable sensations; objectionable, displeasing.

Offer 1. To present for acceptance or rejection. **2.** A proposal to do a thing or to pay an amount.

Offeree The person to whom an offer is made.

Offering An issue of securities offered for sale to the public or to a private group.

Offer of proof Telling the court what evidence a party proposes to present in order to obtain a ruling on admissibility.

Offeror The party who makes an offer.

Office A position of trust; a right and duty to exercise a public trust.

Officer A person holding a position of trust, command, or authority in organizations.

Official 1. An officer. **2.** Concerning that which is authorized; proceeding from, sanctioned by, or pertaining to an officer.

Official immunity doctrine Government officials of suitable rank cannot be subject to civil liability for activity falling within the scope of their authority that calls for the exercise of discretion.

Official record A record kept pursuant to the official duty of a particular officer whether or not required by statute.

Official reports or reporters A collection of court opinions whose printing is authorized by the government (e.g., by statute).

Officio, ex See ex officio.

Officious Meddlesome, interfering.

Officious will A will in which everything is left to the decedent's family.

Offset A contrary claim or demand by which a given claim may be lessened or canceled; a deduction.

Offspring Children, issue.

Of record Entered on the records; recorded.

Of right As a matter of legal right.

Old Age, Survivors', and Disability Insurance A Social Security program, providing for retirement, disability, and benefits for widows, widowers, and dependents.

Oligarchy Government power in the hands of a few persons.

Oligopoly A market climate dominated by a few sellers.

Ombudsman One who investigates grievances that people have against an organization.

Omission The intentional or unintentional failure to act.

Omnibus bill 1. A legislative bill that includes a number of different subjects in one measure. **2.** In equity pleading, a bill that embraces the whole of a complex subject by uniting all parties in interest having adverse or conflicting claims.

Omnibus clause 1. A clause in a will passing all property not specifically mentioned or known at the time. **2.** A clause extending liability insurance coverage to persons using the car with the express or implied permission of the named insured.

Omnium In mercantile law, the aggregate value of the different stock in which a loan is usually funded.

On account In part payment; in partial satisfaction.

On all fours The facts and issues in a client's case are the same as or substantially similar to the facts and issues covered in a particular court opinion.

On demand Payable on request; when demanded.

Onerous Unreasonably burdensome or one-sided.

Onomastic Concerning names; referring to the signature of an instrument, the body of which is in a different handwriting from that of the signature.

On point Germane, relevant.

On the juice Slang for taking steroids.

Open account An account that has not been finalized, settled, or closed, but is still running or open to future adjustment or liquidation; a type of credit extended by a seller, which permits a buyer to make purchases without a note or security.

Open bid An offer to perform a contract in which the bidder reserves the right to reduce the bid to compete with a lower bid.

Open-end credit Credit cards and "revolving charges," where one can pay a part of what is owed each month on several different purchases, with each new purchase representing an additional extension of credit.

Open-ended Not restricted by definite limits.

Open-end mortgage See mortgage (open-ended).

Open order An order to buy securities or commodities at or below or above a certain price. This order remains viable until canceled by the customer.

Open shop A business in which union and nonunion workers are employed indiscriminately; a business in which union membership is not a condition of employment.

Open verdict A verdict of a coroner's jury that the subject "came to his death by means to the jury unknown," or "came to his death at the hands of a person or persons to the jury unknown;" that is, one that leaves open the question of whether any crime was committed or the identity of the criminal.

Operating expenses Expenses required to keep a business running (e.g., rent, utilities).

Operating surplus The surplus transferred to earned surplus at the end of an accounting period.

Operation of law Legal consequences that apply because of rules of law and not because of the act or cooperation of the parties.

Operative 1. Producing effects; functioning effectively. **2.** A working person, especially in factories.

Operative words In a deed or lease, the words that carry into effect the transaction intended to be consummated by the instrument.

Ophthalmologist One who specializes in the treatment of diseases and disorders of the eye.

Opiate A narcotic containing opium or its derivatives; addiction-forming or addiction-sustaining, similar to morphine or being capable of conversion into a drug with this characteristic.

Opinion 1. A statement by an individual judge or by a court of its decision in a case and the reasons for it. **2.** A belief or conclusion not proven by complete or positive knowledge but appearing to the witness to be true, based on his or her own ideas and thinking.

Opinion evidence or testimony Evidence of what the witness thinks, believes, or infers in regard to facts in dispute as distinguished from his or her personal knowledge of the facts themselves.

Opinion letter A document prepared by an attorney for a client, containing the attorney's understanding of the law as applicable to facts submitted for this purpose.

Opium A drug consisting of the dried juice of the opium poppy.

Oppression An act of cruelty or excessive use of authority.

Opprobrium In the civil law, ignominy, infamy, shame.

Option 1. An agreement that gives the person to whom the option is granted (i.e., the optionee) the right and power within a limited time to accept an offer. **2.** An opportunity to choose.

Option to purchase A bilateral contract in which one party is given the right to buy the property within a period of time for a consideration paid to the seller.

Optometry Treatment of eye problems that do not require the attention of a doctor.

Oral argument A verbal presentation before an appellate court of the reasons why the lower court's decision should be affirmed, modified, or reversed.

Oral will A will by verbal declaration.

Oratrix A female petitioner; a female plaintiff in a bill of chancery.

Orbation Deprivation of one's parents or children, or privation in general.

Ordain 1. To institute or establish. **2.** To enact a law.

Ordeal An ancient form of trial in which the innocence of an accused person was determined by his or her ability to come away from an endurance test unharmed (e.g., hold a heavy, red-hot iron in the hand, plunge a bare arm in boiling water).

Order 1. An authoritative command (court order). **2.** To command (the court ordered her to remove the sign). **3.** The designation of the person to whom a bill of exchange or negotiable promissory note is to be paid (payable to order). **4.** The arrangement of something (placed in order). **5.** A scheme or logical system (a lower order). **6.** Harmony (maintain order). **7.** Functioning properly (out of order). **8.** A structured organization (religious order).

Order nisi A provisional or conditional order that will not be made final if a designated act is performed.

Order of the Coif An honorary organization of law students and lawyers, whose membership is based on excellence.

Order to show cause See show cause order.

Ordinance The enactment of the legislative body of a municipality (e.g., city council); a rule established by authority.

Ordinary 1. Regular, according to established order, usual, recurring. **2.** Average, unimpressive.

Ordinary care The degree of care that a reasonably prudent and competent person would exercise in similar circumstances; reasonable care.

Ordinary course of business That which transpires as a matter of daily custom in business; the transaction of business according to the usages and customs of the commercial world generally, of a particular community, or of a particular individual.

Ordinary income Income taxed at ordinary rates; reportable income not qualifying as capital gain.

Ordinary interest Interest computed entirely on the principal with no interest computed on the interest past due.

Ordinary negligence The failure to use that degree of care which the ordinary or reasonable person would have used under similar circumstances.

Ordinary repairs Repairs needed as a result of usual wear and tear in order to keep the property in good condition.

Organic 1. Inherent, fundamental. **2.** Pertaining to living things (organic substance). **3.** Interrelated.

Organic law The fundamental law or constitution of a state or nation; the system of laws or principles that establish and define the organization of government.

Organization Two or more persons joined in a common purpose.

Original 1. The first form, from which copies are made. **2.** First in order. **3.** Unusual or creative.

Original document rule The best evidence of the contents of a document is the original of that document; the party with the burden of proving the contents of a document is required to produce the original unless it is unavailable.

Original jurisdiction Jurisdiction in the first instance; the power of a court to hear a case at its inception.

Original package Unbroken and undivided; a package remaining in the same condition as when it left the shipper.

Orphan A minor who has lost both, or sometimes one, of his or her parents.

Orphan's Court A special court that handles probate, guardianship of minors and incompetents, etc.

Orthopedics Treatment of disorders of the bones, muscles, joints, etc.

Ostensible agency An agency based on estoppel; an implied or presumptive agency that exists where a person intentionally or negligently induces another to believe that a third person is his or her agent, though in fact the latter has not been hired as an agent.

Ostensible authority Such authority as a principal intentionally or negligently causes or allows a third person to believe that an agent possesses.

Osteopathy A complete system of medical practice based on the maintenance of proper relationships among the various parts of the body. Osteopathic physicians emphasize manipulative therapy but also use other accepted therapeutic methods.

Ounce The twelfth pound troy; the sixteenth pound avoirdupois.

Oust To remove; to deprive of possession.

Ouster A putting out, discharge.

Outbuilding A small building used in connection with the main building and usually separated from it (e.g., outhouse, storage shed).

Outhouse A smaller or subordinate building connected with and usually detached from a dwelling, used as a convenience or necessity and not to live in (e.g., shed, barn, privy, toolhouse, stable).

Outlaw To prohibit or make illegal.

Out-of-pocket expenses Expenditures usually paid for with cash; expenses incurred, paid, or disbursed.

Out-of-pocket rule The determination of damages for fraudulent misrepresentation, which permits recovery of the difference between the price paid and the actual value of the property acquired.

Output contract A contract in which one party agrees to sell his or her entire output and the other agrees to buy it.

Outside director A member of a board of directors who is not a corporate officer and does not participate in the corporation's day-to-day management.

Outstanding Uncollected, unpaid.

Outstanding security A security held by an investor that has not been redeemed or purchased back by the issuing corporation.

Overbreadth doctrine A law is invalid if it does not aim specifically at evils within the allowable area of government control, but sweeps within its ambit other activities that constitute an exercise of protected expression or association rights.

Overdraft A check written on an account containing less funds than the amount of the check.

Overdraw To draw upon a person or a bank in an amount in excess of the funds remaining to the drawer's credit with the drawee, or to an amount greater than what is due.

Overdue Pertaining to that which should have already been paid or done.

Overhead All administrative costs incident to the management of a business or other operation that cannot be precisely attributed to any one department or product (e.g., taxes, utilities).

Overissue To issue in excessive quantity; to issue in excess of the amount that is limited and prescribed by the charter.

Overlying right The right of an owner of land to take water from the ground underneath the land for use on the land.

Overplus The surplus or excess; what is left beyond a certain amount.

Overreaching Going too far; misconduct, outsmarting by deception.

Override 1. To set aside. **2.** A commission paid to managers on sales made by subordinates; a commission paid to a real estate agent when a landowner makes a sale on his or her own (after the listing agreement has expired) to a purchaser who was found by the agent.

Overrule To reject by subsequent action or decision; to deprive an earlier opinion of authority as precedent by rendering an opposite decision on the same question of law.

Overseer A superintendent or supervisor.

Oversubscription The existence of more orders or subscriptions for corporate stock than can be issued.

Overt act An open act in pursuance and manifestation of an intent or design; an outward act from which criminality may be implied.

Over-the-counter Sold or transferred independent of an exchange or without the need of a prescription.

Owelty Equality; an equalization charge.

Own To have a legal or rightful title to.

Owner The person in whom title, ownership, or dominion is vested.

Ownership The complete dominion, title, or proprietary right in something; a collection of rights to use and enjoy property, including the right to transmit it to others.

Oyer and terminer A commission to a judge to inquire into and hear criminal cases.

Oyez Hear ye; a call announcing the beginning of a court proceeding or a proclamation.

Pack To assemble with an improper purpose.

Package A parcel; a bundle that is ready for transportation or for commercial handling; that which is wrapped, bound, tied up, or boxed; that which is shipped.

Packing list A document that contains the contents, weight, and other information concerning a package to be shipped.

Pact A bargain; an agreement between two or more nations or states.

Pactions In international law, contracts between nations that are to be performed by a single act.

Paid-in capital Money or property paid to a corporation by its owners for its capital stock.

Paid-in surplus That portion of the surplus of a corporation not generated by profits but contributed by the stockholders.

Paid-up policy In life insurance, a policy on which no further annual premiums are to be made.

Paid-up stock Shares of stock for which full payment has been received by the corporation.

Pain Physical discomfort and distress.

Pain and suffering Physical discomfort and distress; mental and emotional trauma.

Pairing-off Two voting members of an organization agree to be absent on the day a vote is to be taken on an issue on which they would have voted differently if they had been present.

Palimony The word "palimony" is the creation of the media to describe payments sought by one nonmarital party from another after they cease living together. The word is intended to describe the rough equivalent of alimony following the breakup of a marital relationship. In fact, it is not the legal equivalent of alimony. Nonmarital parties do not have to make support or other payments to each other after their relationship is over unless the following conditions are met: (a) They entered an express or implied contract for such payments, (b) the contract does not involve payment for sexual services, and (c) they live in a state that will recognize the contract as enforceable or that is willing to fashion other remedies to prevent an injustice.

Palmarium In civil law, a conditional fee for professional services in addition to the lawful charge.

Palming off Deception in selling or passing off goods of one manufacturer as those of another.

Palmistry The practice of telling fortunes by an interpretation of the lines and marks on the hand; a trick with the hand.

Palpable Readily noticeable, manifest, apparent.

Pander 1. Panderer. One who caters to the lust of others; pimp, go-between. **2.** To cater to the gratification of the lust of another; to cater to the base desires of others.

Panel 1. A list of jurors to serve in a particular court or for the trial of a particular action **2.** A group of judges (smaller than the entire court) that decides a case; e.g., a nine member appellate court might be divided into three, three-member panels with each panel hearing and deciding cases.

Paper 1. A written or printed document; written or printed evidence of a debt. **2.** A product made by a general process of matting fibers.

Paper patent A discovery or invention that has never been put to commercial use nor recognized in the trade.

Paper profit An unrealized profit on a security or other investment that is still held.

Paper standard A money system based on pure paper that is not convertible into gold or other metal of intrinsic value.

Par 1. Equal; an equality between the actual selling value and the nominal or face value of a bill of exchange, share of stock, etc. **2.** An acceptable standard.

Parachronism Error in the computation of time.

Paralegal A person with legal skills who works under the supervision of a lawyer or who is otherwise authorized by law to use his or her skills; a person engaged in the delivery of legal services beyond the secretarial level who is not licensed to practice law in the state in which he or she works.

Parallel citation A reference to another set of books or reporters in which the same case—word for word—can be located.

Paramedic A trained assistant to a doctor.

Paramilitary Pertaining to a group that is organized similar to the armed forces.

Paramour A lover, often in an adulterous alliance.

Paranoid Concerning someone afflicted with paranoia—delusions of grandeur or persecution; excessive feelings of distrust or of self-importance.

Paraphernalia 1. Miscellaneous articles, equipment, or personal belongings. **2.** The separate property of a married woman, other than her dowry.

Paraprofessional One who assists a professional person though not a member of the profession himself or herself.

Parcel 1. To divide into portions. **2.** A small package or bundle. **3.** A part or portion of land; a contiguous quantity of land. **4.** A collection or group.

Parcener A joint heir; one who, with another, holds an estate in coparcenary.

Parchment The skin of a lamb, goat, young calf, or other animal prepared for writing on; stationery.

Pardon An act of grace from the governing power that exempts an individual from punishment for crime and from all civil disabilities that result therefrom.

Parens patriae The state's power to act as a guardian of persons who suffer disabilities (e.g., minors, insane persons).

Parent The lawful mother or father of a person.

Parentage The condition of being a parent; kindred in the direct ascending line.

Parent-child immunity In some states, a child cannot sue its parents for designated personal torts (e.g., battery).

Parent company A company owning more than 50% of the voting shares of another company; a corporation that controls its subsidiary corporations through stock ownership.

Parenticide One who murders a parent; also the crime so committed.

Paresis Progressive general paralysis, involving or leading to the form of insanity known as dementia paralytica.

Pari delicto See in pari delicto.

Pari materia See in pari materia.

Pari-mutuel betting A betting pool; a mutual stake or wager in which those that bet on the winner share the total stakes less a percentage for management.

Parish 1. A territorial government division in Louisiana. **2.** An ecclesiastical division of a city or town under the ministry of one pastor.

Par items Items that a drawee bank will remit to another bank without charge.

Parity Equality in amount or value; equivalence in the prices of goods or services in two different markets.

Park An enclosed pleasure ground in or near a city set apart for public recreation.

Parliament The supreme legislative assembly of Great Britain, consisting of the House of Lords and the House of Commons.

Parliamentary Pertaining to the legislature.

Parliamentary law The general body of rules (e.g., Roberts Rules of Order) and usages that govern the procedure of legislative assemblies and other deliberative bodies.

Parochial 1. Relating to a parish (e.g., parochial schools). **2.** Narrow in scope.

Parol Oral.

Parole Release from confinement after serving part of the sentence; conditional release from prison under the supervision of a parole officer, who has the authority to recommend a return to prison if the conditions of parole (e.g., not leaving the state without permission) are violated.

Parole Board The administrative body with the power (a) to determine whether a prisoner shall be conditionally released from prison before the expiration of his or her sentence, (b) to establish and modify the conditions of parole, and (c) to revoke parole after making a determination that the parolee has violated the conditions of parole.

Parolee An ex-prisoner who has been placed on parole.

Parol evidence rule When parties put their agreement in writing, all previous oral agreements merge in the writing, and the contract as written cannot be altered or changed by oral or verbal evidence, in the absence of mistake, duress, or fraud in the preparation of the writing.

Parricide Killing one's father or other close relative.

Particeps criminis A participant in a crime.

Participate To experience in common with others.

Participation mortgage A type of mortgage where the lender participates in the profits of the venture in addition to the normal interest rate.

Particularity Precision in providing details; carefulness.

Particulars The details.

Particulars, bill of See bill of particulars.

Parties See party.

Partition The dividing of land held by joint tenants, tenants in common, or coparceners into distinct portions, resulting in individual ownership.

Partner One who has united with others to form a partnership.

Partnership A voluntary contract between two or more competent persons to place their resources or services, or both, in a business or enterprise, with the understanding that there shall be a proportional sharing of the profits and losses.

Partnership association A type of business association that resembles a partnership and a joint stock company. Its salient feature is the limited liability of the members.

Partnership at will One that may be dissolved by any partner without prior notice.

Party 1. A person whose name is designated on record as bringing a legal action or as being litigated against in the action. **2.** One who is concerned with, has an interest in, or takes part in the performance of an act. **3.** A voluntary association of persons sponsoring certain ideas of government or maintaining certain political principles in public policies of government; a group organized for a common purpose.

Party wall A wall on a property boundary as a common support to structures on both sides, which have different owners.

Par value The face value of a share of stock; the value of a mortgage based on the balance owing without discount.

Pass 1. To utter or pronounce. **2.** To accept.

Passbook A bankbook; a document issued by a bank, in which a customer's transactions are recorded (e.g., withdrawals).

Passenger One who is being carried by another for hire; any occupant of a vehicle other than the operator.

Passion Any emotion that interferes with cool reflection of the mind.

Passive 1. Inactive. **2.** Submissive, unresisting.

Passive bond A bond that bears no interest.

Passive debt A debt upon which, by agreement between the debtor and creditor, no interest is payable.

Passive negligence The failure to do something that should have been done; permitting defects, obstacles, or pitfalls to exist on premises.

Passive restraint A safety device that provides protection automatically.

Passive trust A trust as to which the trustee has no responsibilities or discretionary duties to perform.

Passport A document that (a) identifies a citizen, (b) acts as evidence of permission from a sovereign to its citizen to travel to foreign countries, (c) acts as a request to foreign powers that the citizen be allowed to pass freely and safely.

Past recollection recorded A memorandum or record concerning a matter about which a witness once had knowledge but now has insufficient recollection to enable him or her to testify fully and accurately, shown to have been made or adopted by the witness when the matter was fresh in his or her memory and to reflect that knowledge correctly, is not excluded by the hearsay rule.

Patent 1. Open, obvious. **2.** A grant of a privilege, property, or authority to an individual by the government; a grant made by the government to an inventor, securing to him or her the exclusive right to make, use, and sell the invention for a term of years.

Patentable Suitable to be patented because the device embodies a new idea or principle not known before and constitutes a discovery as distinguished from mere technical skill or knowledge.

Patent and Trademark Office A federal agency in the Department of Commerce that examines patent and trademark applications, issues patents, registers trademarks, etc.

Patent defect 1. In sales of personal property, a defect that is plainly visible or that can be discovered by such an inspection as would be made in the exercise of ordinary care and prudence. **2.** A patent defect in a legal description is one that cannot be corrected on its face. A new description may be used.

Patentee A person to whom a patent is granted.

Patent pooling An arrangement in which a number of manufacturers agree to an interchange of patent licenses among the members of the pooling group.

Paterfamilias The father of a family.

Paternal line A line of descent or relationship between two persons, which is traced through the father.

Paternity The state or condition of being a father.

Paternity suit A civil action to prove that a person is the father of a child and to enforce the duty to support the child.

Pathology That part of medicine which examines the nature, causes, and symptoms of diseases.

Patient-physician privilege See doctor-patient privilege.

Patricide Killing one's father; a person who has killed his or her father.

Patrimony That which is inherited from a father or from the father's side; an estate that has descended in the same family.

Patronage 1. The practice of a public official in making appointments to non-civil service jobs and in conferring awards. **2.** The customers of a business. **3.** The assistance or encouragement received from a patron.

Pattern 1. A reliable sample of traits, acts, or other observable features characterizing an individual. **2.** A guide or model.

Pauper A person so poor that he or she must be supported at public expense.

Pawn 1. To deliver property to another in pledge or as security for a debt. **2.** A pledge of chattels as security for a debt.

Pawnbroker A person in the business of lending money on the security of property deposited with him or her.

Pawnee The person receiving a pawn or to whom goods are delivered by another in pledge.

Pawnor The person pawning goods or delivering goods to another in pledge.

Pay 1. Compensation. **2.** To discharge a debt by tender of payment due; to compensate for goods, services, or labor.

Payable Justly or legally due.

Payee The person to whom or to whose order a check, bill of exchange, or promissory note is made payable.

Payer or **payor** The person who makes or should make payment, particularly on a check, bill of exchange, or promissory note.

Payment The performance of a duty, promise, or obligation, or the discharge of a debt or liability by the tender and acceptance of money or some other valuable thing.

Payor See payer.

Payroll tax A tax based on and deducted from wages and salaries paid to employees.

Peace A sense of safety in the community; quiet, orderly behavior of individuals toward each other and the government.

Peaceable 1. Without force or violence. **2.** Gentle, calm.

Peace bond A type of surety bond that must be provided by someone who has threatened to breach the peace.

Peace officers A person designated by public authority to keep the peace, and to arrest persons suspected of crime.

Peculation The misappropriation of money or goods entrusted to one's care.

Peculiar 1. Distinctive, special. **2.** Unusual.

Pecuniary Relating to money or that which can be valued in money.

Pecuniary damages Any loss, deprivation, or injury that can be estimated in and compensated by money.

Pecuniary injury in wrongful death The deprivation of a reasonable expectation of a monetary advantage that would have resulted from a continuation of the life of the deceased.

Peddler A person who sells wares carried from place to place.

Pederasty In criminal law, the unnatural carnal copulation of male with male, particularly of a man with a boy; a form of sodomy.

Pedestrian A person traveling on foot.

Pediatrician A doctor specializing in the care of children.

Pedigree The line of ancestors from which a person descends.

Peeping Tom One who sneaks up to a window for the purpose of spying on or invading the privacy of the inhabitants, particularly women in the bedroom.

Peg To set or fix.

Penal Concerning or containing a penalty.

Penal institution A place for the confinement of those convicted of crimes.

Penal sum A sum agreed upon in a bond, to be forfeited if the condition of the bond is not fulfilled.

Penalty Punishment imposed by law.

Penalty clause A provision in a clause or law that calls for the imposition of a penalty instead of actual damages.

Pendency After something has begun but before its final disposition; while undecided.

Pendent Pertaining to matters that are additional, supplementary or complementary.

Pendente lite During the actual progress of the suit; pending the suit; during litigation.

Pendent jurisdiction doctrine A federal district court, in the exercise of jurisdiction over a federal law claim properly before it, has the discretion to extend its jurisdiction over a related state law claim where both claims arise from a common nucleus of operative facts.

Pending Begun but not yet completed; in the process of settlement or adjustment.

Penetration The insertion of the penis, however slight, into the vagina.

Penitentiary A place of confinement for convicted felons.

Penny stocks Low-priced issues often highly speculative, selling at less than $1 a share.

Pennyweight A Troy weight, equal to 24 grains, or one-twentieth of an ounce.

Penology The science of prison management, punishment, and the rehabilitation of criminals.

Pen register A device that records the numbers dialed on a telephone without overhearing the calls or determining whether they were actually completed.

Pension Regularly paid retirement benefits, often based on a person's length of employment and salary level.

Pension Benefit Guaranty Corporation An agency that guarantees the payment of insured benefits if a covered employee retirement plan terminates without sufficient assets to pay the benefits.

Pensioner A recipient or beneficiary of a pension plan.

Pension plan A plan established and maintained by an employer, primarily to pay determinable benefits to its employees or their beneficiaries over a period of years after retirement.

Penumbra doctrine The implied powers of the federal government predicated on the Necessary and Proper Clause of the U.S. Constitution permit one implied power to be engrafted on another implied power.

Peonage The condition of servitude, compelling persons to perform labor in order to pay off a debt.

People 1. The entire body of citizens of a state or nation. **2.** Human beings.

Perambulation To walk over the boundaries of land for the purpose of inspection or surveying.

Per annum Yearly.

Per autre vie For or during another's life.

Per capita According to the number of individuals.

Per cent 1. One part in every hundred; so many hundredths. **2.** Percentage.

Percentage A proportion or share.

Percentage lease A lease using a percentage of the gross or net sales to determine the rent.

Perception 1. Taking into possession. **2.** Counting out and payment of a debt. **3.** Seeing, noticing or otherwise comprehending.

Percolating water Water that passes through the ground beneath the surface of the earth without any definite channel and that does not form a part of the body or flow of any watercourse; water that oozes, seeps, or filters through the soil beneath the surface.

Per curiam By the court; an opinion of the whole court; an opinion written by the chief judge; a brief announcement of a decision without a written opinion.

Per diem By the day; an allowance or amount of so much per day.

Peremptory 1. Absolute. **2.** Imperative. **3.** Dogmatic.

Peremptory challenge The right to challenge and remove a prospective juror without giving any reasons.

Peremptory defense The plaintiff never had the right to institute the suit, or if he or she had, the original right is extinguished.

Peremptory exceptions In the civil law, any defense that entirely denies the ground of action.

Peremptory rule An absolute rule; a ruling without conditions.

Per eundem By the same.

Perfect 1. Complete, executed. **2.** Without defect. **3.** To finish, complete, or put in final form.

Perfected Completed, executed; brought to a state of perfection.

Perfection The act or process of making something complete.

Perfection of a security interest Taking the steps legally required to protect the secured party against other creditors of the debtor (e.g., filing with the secretary of state, taking possession of the collateral).

Perfect trust An executed trust.

Perfidy Violation of a promise, vow, or trust.

Perform To fulfill an obligation according to its terms.

Performance 1. The fulfillment of an obligation according to its terms. **2.** The manner in which something functions.

Performance bond A completion bond; a bond that guarantees that the contractor will perform the contract as awarded.

Peril That which may cause damage or injury.

Perils of the sea Natural accidents peculiar to the sea that do not happen by the intervention of humans and cannot be prevented by human prudence.

Per incuriam Through inadvertence.

Periodic Recurring at fixed intervals; now and then.

Periodic payment of alimony An alimony payment of either (a) a fixed amount (e.g., $50 a week) for an indefinite period (e.g., for life); or (b) an indefinite amount (e.g., 10% of yearly income) for either a fixed period or an indefinite period.

Periodic tenancy A tenancy that continues for successive periods (e.g., week to week) unless terminated at the end of a period by notice.

Perishable goods Goods that quickly decay if they are not put to their intended use within a short period of time.

Perjury A crime committed by a person if, in an official proceeding, he or she makes a false statement under oath, or an equivalent affirmation, when the statement is material and he or she does not believe it to be true.

Perks See perquisites.

Permanent Continuing in the same status without fundamental change; not temporary or transient.

Permanent disability A disability that will remain substantially the same during the remainder of the worker's life; a disability that causes impairment of earning capacity, impairment of the normal use of a member, or a competitive handicap in the open labor market.

Permanent employment Employment that will continue indefinitely until either party wishes to sever the relationship.

Permanent injury An injury that will last during the lifetime of the injured person; permanent disability.

Permanent nuisance One that cannot be readily abated at small expense.

Permission The authority to do something that would be unlawful without the authority.

Permissive 1. Allowable. **2.** Lenient.

Permissive counterclaim A counterclaim that does not arise out of the same transaction or occurrence that is the subject matter of the plaintiff's claim.

Permit 1. To expressly agree to the doing of an act; to acquiesce by failing to prevent. **2.** A document that grants a person the right to do something.

Permit card A document given by a union to a nonunion member, allowing the employer to hire him or her when not enough union members are available.

Permutation 1. An exchange of goods. **2.** A transformation.

Per my et per tout By the half and by the whole; a phrase descriptive of the mode in which joint tenants hold the joint estate.

Pernancy Taking; a taking or receiving, as of the profits of an estate.

Perpetration The commission of an act, often criminal in nature.

Perpetrator The person who commits wrongdoing or by whose immediate agency it occurs.

Perpetual Continuing without intermission.

Perpetuate To take steps to ensure that something will last and be available.

Perpetuity Continuing forever.

Per procuration (per proc., p.p.) By proxy; by one acting as an agent with special powers.

Perquisites Incidental profits or benefits attaching to an office or position.

Per quod Whereby; by means of which.

Per se In itself; referring to activities or omissions that are so blatant that there is no need to look into underlying reasonableness or propriety.

Person A natural person or human being, plus legal entities such as corporations, partnerships, unions, associations, firms, trustees, receivers, legal representatives, etc.

Person aggrieved The victim; the one who has actually suffered the injury.

Personal Pertaining or belonging to a particular individual.

Personal effects Articles associated with the person; movable or chattel property (e.g., clothing, car).

Personal jurisdiction See in personam.

Personal liability The kind of responsibility for the performance of an obligation that exposes the personal (not just business) assets of the person to the payment of the obligation.

Personal property Everything, other than real estate, that is the subject of ownership; any right or interest that one has in things movable; personalty.

Personal property tax A state or local tax on items of personal property such as household furniture, jewelry.

Personal recognizance Pretrial release without posting a bond, based on the defendant's promise that he or she will appear at all future court proceedings in the case and remain amenable to the orders and processes of the court.

Personalty Movable property, personal property.

Persona non grata An undesirable person.

Personate To pass oneself off as another in order to deceive others.

Person in loco parentis See in loco parentis.

Per stirpes Taking by class or representation; together the class takes the share to which their deceased ancestor would have been entitled.

Per totam curiam By the whole court.

Per tout et non per my By the whole, and not by the moiety.

Perverse verdict A verdict reached when the jury refuse to follow the direction of the judge on a point of law.

Petition A formal written request.

Petitioner One who presents a petition to a court or other body.

Petition in bankruptcy A paper filed in a court of bankruptcy by a debtor seeking the benefits of the bankruptcy act, or by creditors alleging the commission of an act of bankruptcy by the debtor and seeking an adjudication of bankruptcy against the debtor.

Petit jury An ordinary jury for the trial of a civil or criminal action.

Pettifogger A small-time lawyer; a dishonest lawyer.

Petty 1. Of less importance. **2.** Of little merit. **3.** Spiteful.

Petty cash A relatively small fund for current expenses.

Petty larceny The larceny of goods with a value below a statutorily set amount (e.g., $100).

Petty officer A noncommissioned naval officer.

Peyote A type of cactus called mescal, containing button-like tubercles that are dried and chewed as a hallucinatory drug. Mescaline is an alkaloid of it.

Phencyclidine See angel dust.

Physical Pertaining to the body or other material things.

Physical force Actual violence; force applied to a body.

Physical incapacity In the law of marriage and divorce, impotence, inability to accomplish sexual coition arising from physical imperfection or malformation.

Physician-patient privilege See doctor-patient privilege.

Physiotherapy The treatment of disease by physical remedies other than drugs; physical therapy.

Picket To patrol the entrance of a business in order to inform other employees and the public of a strike and to deter them from entering.

Pickpocket A thief who secretly steals money or other property from the person of another.

Piercing the corporate veil In certain cases (e.g., fraud) a court will disregard the principle of limited liability inherent in the corporate structure and impose personal liability on stockholders, officers, and directors.

Pignorative contract In the civil law, a contract of pledge, hypothecation, or mortgage of realty.

Pilfer To steal.

Pilferage Stealing small items; petty larceny.

Pillage The forcible taking of private property, usually in times of war.

Pillory A frame with holes and movable boards, through which the head and hands of an offender were placed.

Pimp One who obtains customers for a whore or prostitute.

Pin money Funds for incidental purchases; a small allowance set apart by a husband for the personal expenses of his wife.

Piracy Robbery and depredation on the high seas; stealing.

Piscary The right of fishing.

Placard 1. A sign, advertisement, or public announcement. **2.** A declaration, edict, manifesto.

Placement 1. Arranging or placing. **2.** Selling a new issue of securities. **3.** Arranging a loan or mortgage. **4.** Locating employment for someone.

Place of abode One's residence or domicile.

Placer A superficial deposit of sand, gravel, or disintegrated rock, carrying precious metals along the shore of the sea, along the course of a watercourse, or under the bed of a watercourse; ground, including valuable deposits that are in a loose state.

Placita See placitum.

Placitum 1. In civil law, an agreement of parties. **2.** A judicial decision; the judgment, decree, or sentence of a court.

Plagiarism Appropriating part or all of the composition or ideas of another and passing them off as the product of one's own mind.

Plain Clearly seen or understood.

Plainclothes man A police officer who wears civilian clothes.

Plain error rule Even though a party did not object to an error during the trial, an appellate court can still review the error if it is obvious, prejudicial, affects substantial rights, relates to the fundamental fairness of the trial, and which, if uncorrected, would be an affront to the integrity and reputation of the court.

Plaintiff The person who complains and brings an action.

Plaintiff in error The party who sues out a writ of error to review a judgment or other proceeding at law.

Plain view doctrine If an incriminating object falls within the plain view of an officer who has the right to be present, the object can be seized without a warrant and introduced into evidence.

Planned Unit Development (PUD) An area with a specified minimum contiguous acreage to be developed as a single entity according to a plan, containing one or more residential clusters or planned unit residential developments, and one or more public, quasi-public, commercial, or industrial areas. A device that has as its goal a self-contained mini-community built within a zoning district under density and use rules as to buildings and open space.

Plat, plot A map of a town, section, or subdivision showing the location and boundaries of individual parcels of land subdivided into lots, with streets, alleys, easements, etc., usually drawn to scale.

Platform A statement of principles and policies.

Plea The first pleading of the defendant.

Plea bargaining The process whereby the accused and the prosecutor work out a mutually satisfactory disposition of the case, subject to court approval (e.g., the defendant agrees to plead guilty to a lesser included offense or to one of the counts in a multicount indictment in exchange for a lighter sentence).

Plead To file a pleading or to argue a case in court.

Pleadings Formal allegations by the parties of their claims and defenses.

Plea in abatement A plea that, without disputing the justice of the plaintiff's claim, objects to the place, mode, or time of asserting it.

Plea of privilege A method of objecting to venue by which the pleader seeks to be sued in the county of the pleader's residence.

Plebiscite A vote of the people on a proposed law or policy submitted to them.

Pledge 1. The bailment or delivery of property as security for a debt, an engagement, or the performance of an act; a security interest in a chattel; a promise or agreement to do or forbear something. **2.** To deposit something as security; to give a solemn promise.

Pledgee The person to whom something is delivered in pledge; the one to whom a pledge is given.

Pledger or **pledgor** The person who pledges; the one who delivers goods in pledge.

Plenary Complete; fully attended.

Plenary powers Authority and power as broad as is required in a given case.

Plenary session A meeting of all the members of a deliberative body.

Plenipotentiary One who has full power to do a thing; a diplomatic minister.

Plenum dominium In the civil law, full ownership.

Plottage The additional value of city lots because they are contiguous. Vacant and unimproved parcels held in one ownership are more valuable because of their greater use adaptability as a single unit.

Plunder To take property from persons or places by open force; to take without right.

Plurality In an appellate case with more than one opinion, if no opinion commands a majority of the court, the decision is by plurality; in a case in which there are not enough agreeing justices to form a majority of the court, a plurality is the opinion in which more justices join than in any concurring opinion; the side that receives the greatest number of votes without receiving a majority; the excess of the votes cast for one side over those of any other; a large number or quantity.

Plutocracy A government controlled by the wealthy.

Pneumoconiosis Lung diseases caused by dust particles.

Poach To steal or destroy game on another's land; to hunt illegally.

Pocket veto Inaction on the part of the President when sent a bill just passed by Congress, which has the effect of vetoing it. While Presidential inaction for ten days normally results in the bill becoming law as if signed, inaction by the President results in nonapproval through a "pocket veto" if Congress adjourns, thereby preventing the bill's return within the ten-day period. At the state level, indirect vetoes of this kind are also possible in many states.

P.O.D. account Payable on death. An account payable to one person during life, and when he or she dies, payable to someone else who is designated.

Point 1. A distinct proposition or question of law arising or propounded in a case. **2.** A fee or charge equal to 1 percent of the principal amount of the loan, collected by the lender at the time the loan is made. **3.** For shares of stock, a point is $1; for bonds, a point is $10.

Poison A substance with inherent characteristics that are dangerous to life or bodily functions.

Poisonous tree doctrine See fruit of the poisonous tree.

Police A unit of the government with the responsibility for the preservation of public order and tranquility, the promotion of public safety and morals, and the prevention and investigation of crime.

Police Court An inferior court in some states with jurisdiction over minor offenses, city ordinances, etc.

Policy jury The governing body of Louisiana parishes. Parishes are comparable to counties in other states.

Police magistrate An inferior judicial officer having jurisdiction of minor criminal offenses, breaches of police regulations, etc.

Police power The power of government to place restraints on the personal freedom and property rights of persons for the protection and promotion of public safety, health, morals, convenience, and prosperity. An authority conferred by the Tenth Amendment of the U.S. Constitution on individual states, which in turn is delegated to local governments, under which police departments can be established and laws enacted to prevent crime and secure the comfort, safety, morals, health, and prosperity of the citizens.

Policy 1. The general principles by which an organization is guided and managed. **2.** An insurance contract. **3.** A kind of lottery or game of chance in which bettors select numbers to bet on.

Policyholder The person who owns the policy of insurance whether or not he or she is the insured.

Political Pertaining to the policy or administration of government; pertaining to the organization of people, parties, and interests that seek to control the management of government.

Political offenses Crimes that are incidental to and form a part of political disturbances; offenses committed in attacking the political order of things; offenses committed to obtain any political object.

Political question A question of a purely political character; a question whose determination would involve the judiciary in an encroachment upon executive or legislative powers.

Political rights Rights established or recognized by constitutions, which give citizens the power to participate directly or indirectly in the establishment or administration of government.

Political subdivision A division of the state, established by the constitutional authority of the state to carry out designated public functions.

Polity The system or form of government, state or organized society, body politic, civil constitution.

Poll 1. To single out one by one; to question each juror after a verdict to determine whether he or she assents to the verdict. **2.** An individual person; a list or register of persons who may vote in an election.

Poll tax A tax of a specific sum, levied upon everyone or upon each person within a certain class without reference to the amount of property owned by the person.

Pollute To contaminate the soil, air, water or environment in general by noxious substances or noises; to corrupt.

Polyandry A system permitting a woman to have more than one husband at the same time; a form of polygamy permitting a plurality of husbands.

Polygamy The offense of having more than one spouse at the same time.

Polygraph Lie detector apparatus and test: an electromechanical instrument that simultaneously measures and records certain physiological changes in the human body that are believed to be involuntarily caused by an examinee's conscious attempt to deceive the questioner.

Pond A body of stagnant water without an outlet, usually smaller than a lake.

Pool 1. To combine for a common purpose. **2.** A combination or agreement by persons or companies, which has the effect of eliminating competition, establishing a monopoly, or controlling prices. **3.** A sum of money made up of stakes contributed by bettors.

Pornographic Pertaining to material that the average person, applying contemporary community standards, would find appeals to the prurient interest; pertaining to material that depicts sexual conduct in a patently offensive way and that taken as a whole, lacks serious literary, artistic, political, or scientific value.

Port A place for the loading and unloading of vessels and for the collection of duties and customs on imports and exports.

Port authority A government agency that regulates and plans traffic through a port, encourages businesses to use the area served by the port, etc.

Portfolio 1. All the securities held by one person or institution. **2.** The office of a government minister.

Positive 1. Express, affirmative, or reliable. **2.** Actually enacted.

Positive evidence Evidence that, if believed, establishes the truth or falsity of a fact in issue without the need of a presumption; direct proof or evidence.

Positive law Law actually and specifically enacted or adopted by proper authority.

Positive servitude A positive servitude is one that obliges the owner of the servient estate to permit or suffer something to be done on his or her property by another.

Posse comitatus The power or force of the county; the entire population of a county, over the age of 15, which a sheriff could summon for assistance as an aid in keeping the peace, in apprehending felons, etc.

Possess To have in one's actual and physical control; to own or be entitled to.

Possession 1. The control or custody of property for one's use or enjoyment; the condition of being able to exercise control over a corporeal thing, to the exclusion of others. **2.** That which one holds or owns.

Possessor One who has possession.

Possessory Relating to, founded on, or claiming possession.

Possessory action An action that has for its immediate objective the actual possession of the subject matter.

Possessory interest The right to exert control over specific property to the exclusion of others; the right to possess land whether or not based on title.

Possessory lien The creditor has a right to hold possession of the specific property until the debt or obligation is satisfied.

Possibility An uncertain thing that may happen; a contingent interest in property.

Possible Capable of existing, happening, or being.

Post 1. Later, coming after. **2.** A military establishment. **3.** A position to which one is assigned. **4.** A solid material used as a marker or as support. **5.** To publish. **6.** The system of delivering mail; the mail delivered.

Postconviction remedies Remedies sought by a prisoner to challenge the legality of his or her conviction or sentence.

Postdate To date an instrument at a time later than it was actually made.

Posterity All the descendants of a person in a direct line to the remotest generation.

Post facto After the fact.

Posthumous Referring to events done after the death of a person.

Posthumous child A child born after the death of its father.

Posting 1. A form of service of process in which process is displayed in a prominent place (e.g., on the front door of the defendant's residence). **2.** The act of transferring an original entry to a ledger.

Postmortem 1. Pertaining to matters occurring after death. **2.** An autopsy or review of what occurred.

Post natus Born afterwards.

Postnuptial agreement An agreement after marriage between spouses who may or may not be contemplating divorce (e.g., separation agreement, property settlement, property division).

Post-obit An agreement to borrow money to be repaid at a high interest upon the death of a person from whom the borrower hopes to inherit.

Postpone 1. To delay. **2.** To set below something else, to subordinate.

Post-trial Pertaining to that which takes place after the trial.

"Pot" Marijuana.

Potable Suitable for drinking.

Potentate A person with great power or sway.

Potential 1. Naturally and probably expected to come into existence at some future time. **2.** Inherent abilities that can be developed.

Pour-over trust A provision in a will that directs the residue of the estate into a trust.

Poverty The state or condition of being poor.

Power The right, ability, authority, or faculty of doing something; the ability of a person to produce a change in a given legal relation by doing or not doing a given act.

Power coupled with an interest A right or power to do some act, together with an interest in the subject matter on which the power is to be executed.

Power of alienation The power to sell, transfer, assign, or otherwise dispose of property.

Power of appointment The power conferred on another (called the donee) to select the persons who are to receive a fund, an estate, or the income therefrom at a designated time.

Power of attorney A document that authorizes another to act as one's agent or attorney.

Practicable Feasible; pertaining to that which may be done, practiced, or accomplished.

Practice 1. A repeated or customary action; habitual performance. **2.** The act of carrying something out. **3.** Training. **4.** The exercise of a profession or occupation. **5.** A scheme.

Practitioner One engaged in the exercise or employment of an art or profession.

Praecipe 1. A formal request that a court clerk take some action. **2.** A writ ordering an action or a statement of the reasons why the action has not been taken.

Prayer A request that the court do something.

Prayer for relief The demand for relief; the portion of the complaint that sets forth the requested relief or damages that the pleader seeks in the civil action.

Preamble A clause at the beginning of a statute or constitution, explaining the reasons for its enactment and the objects sought to be accomplished.

Preappointed evidence The kind and degree of evidence prescribed in advance as required for the proof of certain facts.

Preaudience The right of being heard before another.

Precarious right The right that the owner of a thing transfers to another, to enjoy until it shall please the owner to revoke it.

Precatory Embodying a recommendation or advice rather than a positive command or direction.

Precatory words Words of wish, recommendation, or desire in a will, which are ineffective to dispose of property.

Precaution Care taken to prevent mischief or to secure the desired result.

Precedence The right of being placed first in order.

Precedent 1. A prior decision that serves as an example or authority for resolving an identical or similar case; a prior court opinion that interpreted and applied a rule to a set of facts that is similar to the rule and facts currently before the court. **2.** Preceding, prior.

Precedent condition See condition precedent.

Precept 1. A rule imposing a standard of conduct or action. **2.** A warrant, writ, or order.

Precinct A geographical unit of government; an election district.

Precipitate 1. To hasten the occurrence of something. **2.** Acting without careful deliberation. **3.** Unexpected.

Preclude Estop; to prohibit or prevent from doing something.

Precontract A contract that precludes a person from entering into another contract of the same nature.

Predatory Larcenous or preying.

Predecessor One who goes or who has gone before.

Predominant Something greater or superior in power and influence to others.

Pre-emption 1. A judicially created doctrine based on the Supremacy Clause of the U.S. Constitution, providing that federal laws take precedence over state laws on a matter that is national in character when Congress has completely taken over the matter or has otherwise explicitly or implicitly excluded state regulation in the area; a legislative intent to regulate an entire area. **2.** The right of first purchase.

Pre-emptive right The right of a stockholder to maintain a proportionate share of ownership by purchasing a proportionate share of any new stock issues.

Prefect A public official in charge of administrating the law in France and in other countries.

Prefer 1. To prosecute or try. **2.** To give advantage, priority, or privilege.

Preference Making a payment or a transfer by an insolvent debtor to one of the creditors, to the detriment of the other creditors; the choice of one over another; the choice made.

Preferential debts In bankruptcy, those debts that are payable in preference to all others (e.g., employee wages, administrative costs).

Preferential shop A place of employment in which union members are given preference over non-union members in matters of employment by agreement with the employer.

Preferred Having a priority, advantage, or privilege; having a prior or superior claim or right of payment as against another thing of the same kind or class (e.g., preferred security interest).

Preferred creditor A creditor with a prior right to payment over junior credtiors (e.g., a creditor with a perfected security interest).

Preferred dockets Lists of preference cases prepared by the clerks when the cases are set for trial.

Preferred stock Capital stock with a claim to income (dividends) or assets before common stock but after bondholders.

Pregnant negative See negative pregnant.

Prejudice 1. A leaning toward or against one side of a cause for a reason other than the merits of the case. **2.** To injure or impair.

Prejudicial error An error that substantially affects a litigant's rights; an error that affects or presumptively affects the final result of the trial.

Preliminary hearing A pretrial proceeding in which the court determines whether there is probable cause to believe that the accused committed the crime(s) charged and should be held for trial.

Preliminary injunction A temporary order designed to preserve the status quo pending a trial on the merits of the case.

Premeditated Pertaining to that which is deliberated in advance or thought of beforehand for any length of time.

Premises 1. The foregoing statements (in consideration of the premises). **2.** Lands and buildings (removed from the premises). **3.** Prior statements asserted or accepted as true, from which conclusions are drawn (a faulty premise).

Premium 1. A prize or bonus for an act done. **2.** Payment to an insurer as consideration for the insurance. **3.** Part of the rent that is capitalized and paid in a lump sum at the time the lease is granted. **4.** In high demand. **5.** Above the normal value.

Premium loan A loan made for the purpose of paying an insurance premium and secured by the policy.

Prenatal Pertaining to the time before birth.

Prender, prendre The power or right of taking a thing without waiting for it to be offered.

Prenuptial agreement See antenuptial.

Prepaid legal services A plan by which people pay premiums to cover future legal services either from an attorney of his or her choice (open-ended plan) or from a designated list of attorneys (closed-ended plan).

Preparation Taking preliminary steps for a particular purpose.

Prepayment Making payment in whole or in part before the due date or before maturity.

Prepayment penalty A penalty or extra payment that is imposed when a promissory note, mortgage, or deed of trust is paid before it is due.

Preponderance of evidence Evidence that is of greater weight or more convincing than the evidence offered in opposition to it; more probable than not; outweighing evidence.

Prerogative An exclusive or peculiar right or privilege.

Pres Near.

Presbyterianism A system of church administration or government through teaching or ruling elders.

Prescribable That to which a right may be acquired by prescription.

Prescription 1. A method of acquiring the right to use a way, water, light, or air by reason of continuous usage. **2.** A bar to bringing an action or using a remedy as to claims that have been unasserted for an extended period of time. **3.** A direction or a formula for the preparation and use of a medicine. **4.** A direction or order.

Prescriptive Arising or sanctioned by continuous usage.

Prescriptive easement A right to use another's property, which is acquired by usage that is open, notorious, exclusive, adverse, under claim of right, and continuous for the statutory period of time.

Present danger See clear and present danger.

Pre-sentence report A report, often prepared by a social worker or probation officer, based on an investigation of the background of a convicted offender designed to assist the judge in imposing a sentence.

Presenting bank Any bank presenting an item, except a payor bank.

Present interest An interest that entitles the owner to the immediate possession of the property.

Presentment 1. An accusation of crime initiated by a grand jury based on its own knowledge. **2.** Giving or producing a negotiable instrument to the drawee for its acceptance, or to the drawer or acceptor for payment; a demand for acceptance or payment made by or on behalf of the holder upon the maker, acceptor, drawee, or other payor.

Present recollection recorded The use of a document that helps a witness revive or jog his or her memory of a past event. The evidence is the testimony of the witness, not the document itself.

Present recollection revived The use by a witness of some writing or other object to refresh his or her recollection so that testimony can be given about past events from present recollection.

Presents This document; the present instrument (these presents).

Preservation Keeping safe from harm or decay.

Preside To exercise authority; to direct the proceedings.

President The chief executive officer.

Presidential elector See electoral college.

President pro tempore A senator who presides over the U.S. Senate in the absence of the vice-president.

Presumably By reasonable supposition or inference.

Presume To assume beforehand; to believe or accept upon probable evidence.

Presumed intent A person is presumed to intend the natural and probable consequences of his or her voluntary acts.

Presumption An assumption of fact that a rule of law requires to be assumed from another fact or group of facts that have been established.

Presumption of innocence The government has the burden of proving every element of the crime beyond a reasonable doubt. The defendant does not have the burden of proving his or her innocence.

Presumption of legitimacy When it is established that a child was born to a woman while she was married to a specified man, the party asserting the illegitimacy of the child has the burden of proving that the man was not the father of the child.

Presumptive Created by or arising out of a presumption.

Presumptive death Death that is presumed from a long absence (e.g., 7 years) during which the person is not heard from, and the absence is unexplained.

Presumptive evidence Prima facie evidence; evidence sufficient to establish a given fact and which, if not rebutted or contradicted, will remain sufficient.

Presumptive trust A trust raised by implication of law and presumed always to have been contemplated by the parties because of the nature of the transaction.

Prêt In French law, a loan.

Pretermission statute A law that makes provision for children and heirs who have been omitted from the will of the father or ancestor so that they will still be able to share in the estate.

Pretermit To pass by, omit, or disregard.

Pretermitted heir A child or other descendant omitted by a testator.

Pretrial conference A meeting of the lawyers and the judge before the trial to attempt to narrow the issues to be tried, to secure stipulations, and to make a final effort to settle the case without a trial.

Pretrial discovery Devices that can be used by parties to help them prepare for trial (e.g., depositions, interrogatories, requests for admissions).

Pretrial diversion The referral of a defendant in a criminal case to a community agency prior to trial, where he or she receives counseling, therapy, training, etc. If progress is made in this diversion program, the criminal charges are often dismissed.

Prevail 1. To be in general use or practice. **2.** To succeed.

Prevailing 1. Widespread, common, or current. **2.** Victorious.

Prevailing party The party in whose favor the decision or verdict is rendered and judgment is entered.

Prevarication The willful concealment or misrepresentation of the truth.

Prevent To keep from occurring.

Preventive Intended to prevent something.

Preventive detention Detaining accused persons to prevent them from engaging in future antisocial behavior; confinement imposed on a defendant in a criminal case who threatens to violate the law while awaiting trial or disposition; confinement of a mentally ill person who poses a danger to self or to others.

Preventive law Steps taken in anticipation of and in an effort to avoid legal problems; policies and practices designed to maximize advantages within the law before any legal disputes have arisen.

Price The consideration given for the purchase of something.

Price-earnings ratio The market value of a company's common stock per share divided by the earnings per common share for the past year.

Price fixing Agreements by competing firms on the setting of price levels or ranges; an agreement for the purpose of and with the effect of raising, depressing, fixing, pegging, or stabilizing the price of a commodity.

Price supports A device for keeping prices from falling below a predesignated level (e.g., loans, subsidies, government purchases, etc.).

Priest-penitent privilege A person can bar testimony as to the contents of a communication with his or her confessor.

Prima facie On the face of it; pertaining to a fact that is presumed to be true unless disproved by some evidence to the contrary.

Prima facie case A case as presented that will prevail until contradicted and overcome by contrary evidence; a case consisting of evidence that is sufficient to overcome a motion for a directed verdict and to get the case to the jury.

Prima facie evidence Evidence that is good and sufficient on its face; evidence that is sufficient to establish a given fact or group of facts and will remain sufficient unless rebutted or contradicted.

Prima facie tort The intentional infliction of harm without justification, resulting in special damages.

Primary 1. First in order of importance or intention. **2.** First in time.

Primary boycott Action by a union by which it tries to induce people not to use, handle, transport or purchase goods of an employer with which the union has a grievance.

Primary election A preliminary election for the nomination of candidates for office or of delegates to a party convention.

Primary jurisdiction doctrine Although a case is properly before a court, if there are issues requiring administrative discretion and expertise, the court can refrain from proceeding until the administrative agency acts.

Prime contractor General contractor; the party to a building contract who has responsibility for total construction and who enters into subcontracts for part of the work.

Prime rate The lowest rate of interest charged by a specific lender to its best customers for short-term, unsecured loans.

Primogeniture The status of being the first-born among several children of the same parents; the superior or exclusive right of the oldest son to succeed to the entire estate of his ancestor.

Principal 1. The amount of debt not including interest; the capital sum of a debt or obligation, as distinguished from interest or other additions to it. **2.** A superintendent. **3.** A chief actor or perpetrator of a crime, or an aider and abettor who is actually or constructively present at the commission of a crime. **4.** Someone who permits or directs an agent to act for his or her benefit, subject to his or her control. **5.** Greatest or foremost in importance or rank.

Principal in the first degree The one who actually commits the crime.

Principal in the second degree The one who is actually or constructively present and aids in the commission of the crime.

Prior inconsistent statements A basis for impeaching the credibility of a witness: prior statements made by the witness: that contradict statements of the latter on the stand.

Priority A legal preference or precedence.

Prior jeopardy See jeopardy.

Prior lien A first or superior lien, not necessarily antecedent in time.

Prior restraint The imposition of restrictions on a publication before it is published.

Prison An institution for the imprisonment of persons convicted of serious crimes; a place for the confinement of persons as punishment imposed by law or otherwise in the course of the administration of justice.

Privacy 1. See invasion of privacy. A person's right to be left alone; the right to restrict access to private information. **2.** Concealment or seclusion.

Private 1. Concerning or belonging to an individual; not official or public. **2.** An enlisted person of low rank in the military.

Private bill Legislation for the special benefit of an individual or of a small area of the state or nation.

Private easement One in which enjoyment is restricted to one or a few individuals.

Privateer A vessel, owned by a private individual, commissioned by a belligerent power to attack enemy ships.

Private international law A name used by some writers to indicate that branch of the law that is now more commonly called "Conflict of laws."

Private law The law governing the relations between private individuals.

Private nuisance A nuisance affecting a single individual or a definite small number of persons in the enjoyment of private rights that are not common to the public.

Private offering An issue of securities made to a limited number of persons who are so well informed concerning the affairs of the company that they do not require the protections afforded by the disclosure provisions of the Securities Act of 1933.

Private placement 1. A direct placement; the placement of a child for adoption by the parents or by their intermediaries and not through an adoption agency. **2.** The sale of corporate stock to private persons outside of a public offering.

Private ruling Advice from the Internal Revenue Service to an individual taxpayer on the tax consequences of a specific transaction that is contemplated or completed.

Privation The lack of basic necessities and comforts; a taking away or withdrawal.

Privies Those who are partakers or have an interest in any action or thing, or any relation to another.

Privilege A defense to a tort action that negates the tortious nature of the defendant's conduct (e.g., the privilege of self-defense); a special benefit or immunity enjoyed by a person, company, or class beyond the common advantages of other citizens; preferential treatment.

Privilege against self-incrimination The government must prove its criminal case without the aid of the defendant as a witness against himself or herself.

Privileged Possessing or enjoying a privilege; entitled to priority.

Privileged communications Statements made by persons within protected relationships (e.g., husband-wife, attorney-client, doctor-patient, priest-penitent), which the law protects from forced disclosure at the option of the person enjoying the privilege (e.g., spouse, client, patient, penitent).

Privileges and Immunities Clause Clauses in the U.S. Constitution that place the citizens of each state on the same footing with citizens of other states so far as the advantages resulting from citizenship are concerned. If a person from one state goes into another state, the person must be accorded the same privileges as citizens of the latter state.

Privity A close and direct relationship between two or more persons that gives rise to legal consequences that do not apply to persons outside the relationship; a mutual or successive relationship to the same rights of property; an identity or mutuality of interest between parties; a relationship between a party to a suit and a person who was not a party but whose interest in the suit was such that the latter will be bound by the final judgment as if he or she was a party.

Privity of contract The connection or relationship that exists between two or more contracting parties, e.g., X sells a car to Y, and Y then sells the car to Z. There is privity between X and Y and between Y and Z, but no privity between X and Z.

Privy 1. A person who is in privity with another; a party or partaker; one who has a part or interest in any action, matter, or thing. **2.** Participating in something private or secret.

Privy Council In England, the principal council of the sovereign. The Judicial Committee of the Privy Council acts as a court of ultimate appeal in various cases.

Prize A reward offered to a person who is the first to perform a condition or who performs it best.

Probability The likelihood of a proposition or hypothesis being true.

Probable Appearing to be founded in reason or experience; having more evidence for than against.

Probable cause A reasonable ground for a belief in the existence of supporting facts; the existence of circumstances that would lead a reasonably prudent person to believe that the accused person committed the crime charged.

Probate A court procedure by which a will is proved to be valid or invalid.

Probate Court A court with jurisdiction over the probate of wills, the administration of estates, and in some states, the appointment of guardians and the adoption of children.

Probation 1. The conditional release to the community of a person convicted of a crime so long as there is compliance with certain conditions of good behavior under the supervision of a probation officer. **2.** A trial or test period for a new, transferred, or promoted employee to determine competence and suitability for the position.

Probationer A convicted offender who is out on probation rather than in prison.

Probative Furnishing proof; serving to test.

Probative evidence Evidence that furnishes, establishes, or contributes toward proof.

Probative value Tending to prove an issue; carrying a quality of proof.

Pro bono For the good; work or services performed free of charge.

Pro bono publico For the public good; for the welfare of the whole.

Procedural Pertaining to the manner of proceeding or accomplishing something; pertaining to the manner in which rights are enforced, as distinguished from the law that gives or defines the rights.

Procedural due process Minimum standards of procedure such as notice, hearing, and the opportunity to respond before the government deprives an individual of life, liberty, or property. The standards may differ depending on factors such as the nature of the deprivation that is about to take place.

Procedural law A law that prescribes a method of enforcing rights or of obtaining redress for the invasion of rights.

Procedure A method or process by which legal rights are enforced, as distinguished from substantive law which gives or defines the rights; the machinery as distinguished from the product; the machinery for carrying on a suit.

Proceeding 1. The form or manner of conducting business before a court, agency, or other organization. **2.** A litigation. **3.** A sequence of events. **4.** A record of what takes place at a meeting.

Proceeds That which results or accrues from some possession or transaction.

Process 1. A series of actions, motions, or occurrences. **2.** The means used by a court to acquire or exercise its jurisdiction over a person or over specific property (service of process). **3.** To treat or handle.

Process agent A person authorized to accept service of process on behalf of another.

Process server A person authorized by law (e.g., a sheriff) to serve process papers on defendants.

Pro-choice Being in favor of the availability of abortion.

Prochronism An error in chronology, consisting of dating a thing before it happened.

Proclamation A formal and public declaration.

Proctor One appointed to manage the affairs of or to represent another.

Procuration The act of designating someone as an agent; doing something as the agent of another.

Procurator One who acts for another.

Procuratrix A female agent or attorney in fact.

Procurement The act of obtaining or acquiring something.

Procurer One who procures; a pimp.

Procuring cause The cause that originates a series of events that results in the accomplishment of the object without a break in their continuity.

Prodigal Extravagant or wasteful.

Produce 1. The product of natural growth, labor, or capital; articles produced or grown from or on the soil. **2.** To bring forward or exhibit.

Producer One who produces, generates, or brings forth; the person who raises agricultural products and puts them in condition for the market.

Producing cause An efficient, existing, or contributing cause which, in natural and continuous sequence, produces the damage, injury, or other impact; that without which the result would not have occurred.

Product Something produced by physical labor, intellectual effort, or natural processes.

Product liability The liability of a manufacturer, supplier, wholesaler, assembler, retail seller, or lessor of a defective product placed on the market, which causes damage or injury. Several causes of action can be used to impose such liability: negligence, strict liability in tort, deceit, breach of express warranty, breach of implied warranty of merchantability, breach of implied warranty of fitness for a particular purpose.

Profane 1. Showing disrespect for God or for other sacred things. **2.** Not involving religious matters.

Profanity Irreverence toward sacred things; blasphemous use of the name of God.

Profess To make an open declaration.

Profession 1. A vocation or occupation requiring special, often advanced, education and skill. **2.** A declaration.

Professional 1. Pertaining to or characteristic of a profession. **2.** A person with considerable skill in his or her field.

Professional corporation (P.C.) A corporation organized by those performing personal services to the public, of the type that requires a license or other legal authorization.

Professional responsibility, code of See Code of Professional Responsibility.

Profit The gross proceeds of a business transaction less the costs of the transaction; excess of revenue over expenses.

Profit and loss (P & L) Gain or loss arising from goods bought or sold or from carrying on any other business.

Profit à prendre The right to take from the land of another through mining, logging, drilling, fishing, grazing; an interest in the land of another conferring rights of use and removal.

Profiteering Taking advantage of unusual or exceptional circumstances to make excessive profits (e.g., selling scarce goods at inflated prices during a war).

Pro forma As a matter of form; done in a perfunctory manner.

Progressive tax A type of graduated tax that applies higher tax rates as one's income increases.

Pro hac vice (P.H.V.) For this particular occasion (e.g., a lawyer is given permission to practice law in the jurisdiction for this case only).

Prohibit To prevent; to forbid by law.

Prohibition 1. Suppression or interdiction. **2.** A law preventing the manufacture, sale, or transportation of intoxicating liquors except for medicinal purposes.

Prohibitive impediments In the civil law, impediments that do not render the marriage null, but subject the parties to a punishment.

Proletariat The class of unskilled laborers without property or capital; those with no place in the established order of society.

Pro-life In favor of restrictions on access to abortion; opposed to abortion.

Prolixity Unnecessary and superfluous statement of facts in pleading or in evidence.

Promise 1. A manifestation of an intention to act or to refrain from acting in a specified way so as to justify the promisee in understanding that a commitment has been made. **2.** To make a commitment.

Promisee One to whom a promise has been made.

Promisor One who makes a promise.

Promissory estoppel A promise (not supported by consideration) will be binding if (a) the promisor makes a promise that he or she should reasonably expect to induce action or forbearance of a definite and substantial character on the part of the promisee, (b) the promise does induce such action or forbearance, and (c) injustice can be avoided only by enforcement of the promise.

Promissory note A signed paper unconditionally promising to pay another a certain sum of money at a specified date or on demand.

Promote To contribute to the growth, enlargement, or prosperity of.

Promoter One who promotes, urges on, or encourages; one who takes the preliminary steps in the organization of a corporation.

Prompt Responding immediately.

Promulgate To announce officially.

Pronotary First notary. See prothonotary.

Pronounce To declare formally.

Proof The establishment of a fact by evidence; a logically sufficient reason for asserting the truth of a proposition.

Proof of claim A statement under oath filed in a bankruptcy proceeding by a creditor, in which the latter sets forth the amount owed and sufficient detail to identify the basis for the claim.

Proof of loss A formal statement given to an insurer by the policyholder concerning a loss suffered by the latter, providing enough information to enable the insurer to determine the extent of its liability under a policy or bond.

Proof of service Evidence submitted by a process server that he or she has made service on a defendant in an action. It is also called a return of service.

Proper Appropriate or correct; reasonably sufficient.

Proper party A party who has an interest in the subject matter of the litigation that may be conveniently settled therein; one who may be joined in the action but whose nonjoinder would not result in a dismissal.

Property 1. That which one can possess or own; every species of valuable right and interest; everything that is the subject of ownership, tangible or intangible, corporeal or incorporeal, real or personal. **2.** The quality or characteristic of a thing.

Property dividend A portion of corporate property paid to shareholders instead of cash or corporate stock.

Property right Any type of right to specific property whether it is personal property or real property, tangible (e.g., house, car) or intangible (e.g., the right to work and earn a living, the right of a professional baseball player in his name, photograph, and image).

Property settlement An agreement settling property rights between spouses incident to their separation or divorce.

Property tax A tax levied on real and personal property, the amount being dependent on the value of the property.

Propinquity 1. Kindred, parentage. **2.** Proximity.

Proponent The one who brings forth or propounds something.

Proportionate Being in proportion; adjusted to something else according to a certain rate of comparative relation.

Proposal A suggestion for examination; an offer.

Proposition 1. An offer to do a thing. **2.** An assumption or theory.

Propound To offer or propose for analysis.

Proprietary 1. Owned by a private person or company. **2.** Exclusively made or controlled by right. **3.** Pertaining to ownership. **4.** One who has exclusive title.

Proprietary function A function exercised by a municipal corporation for the peculiar or private benefit and advantage of the citizens of the municipality (e.g., operation of a public swimming pool); a function of a city that does not involve an exercise of sovereignty or in which the city is not acting as the agent or arm of the state in the exercise of sovereign powers; an activity that is commercial or chiefly for the private advantage of the community.

Proprietary rights Those rights an owner of property has by virtue of his or her ownership.

Proprietor One who has the legal right or exclusive title to anything; one who runs a small business.

Proprietorship A form of small business, often owned and controlled by one person.

Propriety 1. Conformity to standards and customs. **2.** Property.

Pro rata According to a certain rate, percentage, or proportion.

Pro rata clause An insurance company will be liable only for the proportion of the loss represented by the ratio between its policy limits and the total limits of all available insurance.

Prorate To divide, share, or distribute proportionally.

Prorogation Prolonging or putting off to another day. The discontinuation or termination of a session of the legislature.

Prorogue To suspend or terminate a legislative session.

Proscribe To prohibit or condemn.

Pro se In his own behalf; appearing for or representing oneself.

Prosecute To commence and carry an action through to its ultimate conclusion.

Prosecuting attorney See prosecutor.

Prosecution 1. In a criminal case, the judicial proceedings instituted to determine the guilt or innocence of a person accused of a crime. **2.** The prosecuting attorney or the government in a criminal case.

Prosecutor The person who initiates and conducts criminal cases on behalf of the government or the people.

Prosecutrix A female prosecutor.

Prosequi To follow up, pursue, or prosecute.

Prospective Looking forward; pertaining to the future.

Prospective damages Damages that have not yet accrued but which in the nature of things must necessarily or most probably will result from the acts or facts complained of; damages expected to follow.

Prospective law A law that applies only to cases that arise after the enactment of the law.

Prospectus A document published by a company or by its agent, setting forth the nature and objects of an issue of shares, debentures, or other securities created by the company, and inviting the public to subscribe to the issue; a document containing all material facts concerning a company and its operations, so that a prospective investor may make an informed decision as to the merits of an investment.

Prostitute A person who engages in sexual intercourse or other sexual acts for hire.

Prostitution Engaging in sexual activities for hire.

Pro tanto For so much; partial payment made on a claim.

Protection The act of defending or shielding from harm; a system of providing security.

Protective Intended to isolate, secure, or protect.

Protective custody Being held under force of law for one's own protection.

Protective order A court order or decree designed to protect a person from further harassment.

Protective tariff A law imposing duties on imports with the purpose and effect of discouraging the importation of designated foreign products and hence of stimulating and protecting competing domestic products.

Pro tempore (pro tem) For the time being.

Protest 1. A formal declaration of dissent or disapproval. **2.** A certificate of dishonor of a negotiable instrument.

Prothonotary A clerk of court.

Protocol 1. A brief summary of the text of a document; the first copy of a treaty. **2.** The etiquette of diplomacy and the ranking of officials.

Provable Susceptible of being proved.

Prove To establish a fact or position by sufficient evidence.

Province 1. A division of the state or country. **2.** A sphere of expertise or authority.

Provisional Temporary.

Provisional remedy A remedy provided for present need or for the immediate occasion.

Proviso A condition or stipulation in a document, agreement, or proposal.

Provocation Inciting another to do a particular deed.

Provoke To excite, to stimulate; to irritate or enrage.

Proximate Nearest; close in causal connection.

Proximate cause The defendant is the proximate cause of the plaintiff's injury (a) if it can be said that the defendant's acts or omissions were a sub-stantial factor in producing the injury, or that but for these acts or omissions, the injury would not have occurred, and (b) the injury was the foreseeable consequence of the original risk created by the defendant's acts or omissions. Proximate cause is that cause which, in natural and continuous sequence, unbroken by any efficient intervening cause, produces the injury and without which the injury would not have occurred.

Proximity 1. The quality or state of being next in time, place, causation, influence, etc. **2.** Kindred between two persons.

Proxy 1. A person who is substituted for another in order to represent and act for the latter. **2.** Written authorization that allows one to act for another.

Proxy marriage A valid marriage contracted or celebrated through agents acting on behalf of one or both absent parties.

Prudence Good judgment and carefulness.

Prudent Careful in adapting means to ends.

Prurient Pertaining to a shameful or morbid interest in nudity, sex, or excretion.

Psychosis A severe mental disorder in which the patient departs from the normal pattern of thinking, feeling, and acting—often losing contact with reality.

Psychosomatic Concerning the interrelationship of the mind and body.

Puberty The earliest age at which persons are capable of begetting or bearing children—about 14 for boys and 12 for girls.

Public 1. The community at large. **2.** Common to all or many; open to common use. **3.** Generally known.

Public assistance Welfare.

Publication 1. Making something known to people. **2.** Something that has been published.

Public convenience and necessity Reasonable necessity to meet the convenience of the public; that which is fitting or suited to the public need.

Public corporation An artificial person (e.g., municipality, government corporation) created for the administration of public affairs; an instrumentality of the government, founded and owned in the public interest, supported by public funds, and governed by those deriving their authority from the government.

Public defender An attorney appointed by a court or employed by a government agency, whose work consists primarily in defending indigent defendants in criminal cases.

Public disclosure of private fact See invasion of privacy.

Public domain Property that is not protected by copyright, ownership, or other restrictions.

Public figures Those who have assumed a role of special prominence in society; those who occupy positions of persuasive power, who have thrust themselves to the forefront of particular public controversies in order to influence the resolution of the issues involved.

Public interest Something in which the public, the community at large, has some pecuniary interest, or some interest by which their legal rights or liabilities are affected; an interest shared by citizens generally in affairs of local, state, or national government.

Publicist One versed in, or writing upon, public law, the science and principles of government, or international law.

Public Law (PL) A law or statute that applies generally to the people of a nation or of a state; the law concerned with the organization of the state, the relations between the state and the people, the responsibilities of public officers, and the relationship between states (e.g., constitutional law, administrative law, criminal law, international law).

Public nuisance An unreasonable interference with a right that is common to the general public; behavior that unreasonably endangers or interferes with the health, safety, peace, morals, comfort, or convenience of the general community.

Public official The holder of a public office that requires the exercise of some portion of the sovereign power. At the very least, public officials include those among the hierarchy of government employees who have, or appear to the public to have, substantial responsibility for or control over the conduct of governmental affairs.

Public prosecutor See prosecutor.

Public purpose Governmental purpose; pertaining to a public service or use that affects inhabitants as a community and not merely as individuals; pertaining to the promotion of the public health, safety, morals, prosperity, and contentment of all the residents of a given political division such as a state.

Public record Records that a government unit is required by law to keep or that are necessary to keep in the discharge of duties imposed by law.

Public security Bonds, notes, certificates of indebtedness, and other negotiable or transferable instruments evidencing the public debt of a government.

Public service commission A board or commission created by the legislature to exercise power of supervision or regulation over public utilities or public service corporations.

Public statute A statute enacting a universal rule regarding the whole community, as distinguished from one concerning only particular individuals and their private rights.

Public use 1. A use that confers some benefit or advantage to the public; public usefulness, utility, advantage, or what is productive of general benefit. **2.** Any nonsecret use of a completed and operative invention in its natural and intended way.

Public utility A business or service regularly supplying the public with some commodity or service that is of public consequence and need (e.g., electricity, gas, water, transportation, telephone); a privately owned and operated business whose services are provided to the public without discrimination and are so essential to the general public as to justify special franchises (e.g., the use of public property).

Public welfare The prosperity, well-being, or convenience of the public at large or of the whole community as distinguished from the advantage of an individual or limited class; that which pertains to the primary social interests of safety, order, morals, economics, politics, etc.

Publish To make known; to make public.

Publisher One who by himself or herself, or through an agent, makes something publicly known; one in the business of manufacturing and selling books, magazines, or other literary productions.

PUD See planned unit development.

Puffing 1. A seller's expression of opinion that is not made as a representation of fact; a seller's exaggeration concerning the quality of goods. **2.** Secret bidding at an auction by or on behalf of the seller.

Punishment Any fine, penalty, or confinement imposed by law for a crime, offense, or omission of a duty.

Punitive Having the characteristic of punishment or a penalty.

Punitive damages See exemplary damages.

Punitive statute One that imposes a penalty.

Pur autre vie For or during the life of another.

Purchase The acquisition of title to property by a means other than descent; the voluntary transmission of property for consideration from one person to another.

Purchase agreement See agreement of sale.

Purchase money mortgage A mortgage or security device taken back to secure the performance of an obligation incurred in the purchase of the property.

Purchase money resulting trust When one person furnishes the money for the purchase of property with the title being placed in the name of another, the former is the equitable owner under a purchase money resulting trust.

Purchase money security interest A security interest (a) taken or retained by the seller of the collateral to secure all or part of its price, or (b) taken by a person who by making advances or incurring an obligation gives value to enable the debtor to acquire rights in or the use of the collateral if such value is in fact so used.

Purchaser One who acquires property by buying it for a consideration; one who has contracted to purchase property.

Purchase subject to a mortgage See assumption of mortgage.

Pure Free from conditions or restrictions; absolute.

Pure accident An unavoidable accident; an unforeseeable event that is not due to carelessness or fault.

Purgation Cleansing or exonerating oneself of suspicion of guilt by denying the charge on oath or by ordeal.

Purge 1. To clear or exonerate from a charge or imputation of guilt. **2.** Elimination.

Purport The meaning, substance, or legal effect.

Purpose That which one seeks to accomplish; intent.

Purposely Intentionally, consciously, knowingly.

Purpresture An appropriation to private use of that which belongs to the public; an encroachment upon public rights and easements.

Pursuit of happiness An inalienable right that includes the right to follow one's individual employment preferences, liberty of conscience, freedom of contract, the privileges of family, and exemption from oppression and invidious discrimination.

Purview 1. The scope or extent of something. **2.** The body of a statute; that part of a statute commencing with the words "Be it enacted"; the design, purpose, or scope of the statute.

Pusher One who engages in the illegal sale of drugs; a dealer.

Put An option to sell a certain stock or commodity at a fixed price for a stated quantity within a stated period.

Putative Alleged or reputed.

Putative father The alleged father of an illegitimate child.

Putative marriage A marriage contracted in good faith and in ignorance (on one or both sides) of an impediment that renders the marriage unlawful.

Pyramiding A device for increasing holdings of a stock by financing new holdings out of the increased margin of those already owned; the use of a small amount of money or of "paper profits" to finance buying stock.

Qua In the character or capacity of.

Quack One who practices medicine without the qualifications.

Quadrant An angular measure of ninety degrees; a quarter of a circle; one of the quarters created by two intersecting roads or streets.

Quadripartite Divided into four parts.

Quaere A query or doubt. Question.

Qualification 1. Quality or circumstance that is legally or inherently necessary to perform a function. **2.** Restriction.

Qualified 1. Eligible; possessing legal power or capacity. **2.** Restricted or imperfect.

Qualified indorsement An indorsement that restrains, limits, qualifies, or enlarges the liability of the indorser.

Qualified pension plan An employer-sponsored plan that meets the requirements of the Internal Revenue Code. The employer can deduct the contributions in the year made, and the employee is not taxed on these contributions until they are distributed.

Qualified privilege Conditional privilege; a privilege that can prevent tort liability so long as there was no actual malice.

Qualify 1. To make oneself fit or prepared. **2.** To limit or restrict.

Quality A character or nature of something; that which describes.

Quantum meruit "As much as he deserves." A theory of recovery on a contract implied in law in the absence of a specific contract. Valuable services are rendered or materials furnished by the plaintiff, and accepted, used, or enjoyed by the defendant under such circumstances that the plaintiff reasonably expected to be paid. To avoid unjust enrichment, the implied promise is to pay what the services or materials are reasonably worth.

Quarantine Isolation of a person with a contagious disease; detention of a vessel coming from a place where a contagious or infectious disease is prevalent.

Quare clausum fregit See trespass quare clausum fregit.

Quart One-fourth of a gallon; two pints; .946 liter.

Quarter-day The four days in the year upon which, by law or custom, moneys payable in quarter-yearly installments are collectible (payable).

Quartering Furnishing living quarters to military personnel.

Quarter section The quarter of a section of land according to the divisions of the government survey, laid off by dividing the section into four equal parts by north-and-south and east-and-west lines, and containing 160 acres. A quarter of a square mile of land. The amount of land originally granted to a homesteader.

Quash To vacate or overthrow.

Quasi Somewhat the same, but different; as if.

Quasi contract An obligation created by the law to avoid unjust enrichment, in the absence of an agreement between the parties.

Quasi estoppel A party should be precluded from asserting, to another's disadvantage, a right or claim that is inconsistent with a position previously taken by the party.

Quasi in rem A court's power to reach a person's interest in property within the jurisdiction of the court. This is different from the court's power over the person of the defendant (in personam) or over the property or thing itself (in rem).

Quasi judicial A term applied to public administrative officers or bodies required to investigate facts, or ascertain the existence of facts, hold hearings, and draw conclusions from them, as a basis for their official action, and to exercise discretion of a judicial nature.

Queen's Bench (Q.B.) A high English common-law court during the reign of a queen.

Question of fact See issue of fact.

Question of law See issue of law.

Quia emptores A 1290 English statute that had the effect of facilitating the alienation of fee-simple estates; it ended subinfeudation, a process of carving out smaller estates by tenants ad infinitum.

Quick 1. Readily convertible into cash. **2.** Capable of moving within the mother's womb; capable of surviving the trauma of birth. **3.** Speedy.

Quick asset ratio Ratio of cash, accounts receivable and marketable securities to current liabilities. Also called the "acid test."

Quickening The first motion of the fetus in the womb felt by the mother, usually occurring about the middle of the term of pregnancy.

Quick with child Having conceived.

Quid pro quo Something for something; giving one valuable thing for another.

Quiet 1. Free from interference (quiet enjoyment). **2.** To render secure or unassailable (action to quiet title).

Quiet title action See action to quiet title.

Quietus 1. A final discharge or acquittance from a debt or obligation; that which silences claims. **2.** Demise, death.

Quit To surrender possession.

Quitclaim deed A deed of conveyance that passes any title, interest, or claim that the grantor may have, without any assurance or warranty that the title is valid.

Quorum The number of members who must be present in a deliberative body before business may be transacted.

Quota An assigned goal; a proportional part.

Quotation 1. A word-for-word reproduction from another source.

Quotient verdict A verdict resulting from an agreement as follows: each juror writes down an amount for damages; all the amounts are then added together, and divided by the number of jurors.

Quo warranto A remedy to challenge the continued exercise of unlawful authority; a remedy brought by or on behalf of the state against a usurpation of public office.

Race 1. A major division of mankind, having in common certain physical peculiarities constituting a comprehensive class appearing to be derived from a distinct primitive source.

Race-notice recording statute A state law that provides that an unrecorded conveyance is invalid as against a subsequent purchaser for value who records without knowledge of the prior unrecorded instrument. The first to record in the chain of title without notice of a prior unrecorded deed or mortgage has superior rights.

Race recording statute A state law that provides that the party who records an instrument of conveyance has the better claim regardless of notice of prior unrecorded instruments. The first to record regardless of notice of an unrecorded deed or mortgage earlier in time has superior rights.

Racketeering An organized conspiracy to commit the crimes of extortion or coercion; activities of organized criminals who extort money from legitimate businesses by violence or other forms of threats; organized illegal enterprises such as gambling, narcotics, traffic, or prostitution.

Raffle A kind of lottery in which each participant buys a ticket for an article put up as a prize, with the winner being determined by a random drawing.

Raised check A negotiable instrument payable on demand, with a face amount that has been increased without authorization.

Rake-off An illegal payoff or bribe; a skimming of profits; a share of profits demanded, paid, or otherwise illegally taken.

Ransom The release of illegally detained persons or property for money; the money, price, or consideration paid or demanded for the return of a kidnapped person.

Rape To have sexual intercourse with a person without consent.

Rapine Feloniously taking another's personal property by violence.

Rap sheet Police arrest record.

Ratable According to a measure with fixed proportions; proportional; capable of being rated or assessed; taxable.

Rate 1. Proportional or relative value, measure, or degree; the standard by which something is adjusted. **2.** Cost. **3.** To estimate value.

Rate base The fair value of a utility's property upon which a reasonable return is allowed.

Rate of exchange The price at which the money of one country may be exchanged for the money of another; the price at which a bill drawn in one country upon another country can be bought or obtained in the former country.

Rate of return The annual percentage of return on an investment.

Ratification The confirmation of a prior act, with the effect of becoming bound by it.

Ratify To make valid, to sanction, to approve.

Ratio Proportion; the number resulting when one number is divided by another.

Ratio decidendi The ground, reason, or principle that is the basis of the decision; the dispositive point.

Ravine A long, deep, and narrow hollow worn by a stream or torrent of water; a long, deep pass through the mountains.

Ravish To have carnal knowledge of a woman by force.

Raw land Unimproved land.

Raw materials Goods (e.g., wood, steel) used in the manufacture of a product.

Raze To tear down or erase.

Re In the matter of, concerning.

Readjustment A voluntary readjustment of a corporation in financial trouble by the shareholders themselves, without outside intervention.

Real 1. Pertaining to land. **2.** Authentic or genuine.

Real estate Land and anything permanently affixed to the land.

Real estate investment trust (REIT) A financial device in which investors purchase shares in a trust the res of which is invested in real estate ventures.

Real Estate Settlement Procedures Act (RESPA) A federal statute governing disclosure of settlement costs in the sale of residential (one to four-family) improved property that is to be financed by a federally insured lender.

Real evidence Evidence furnished by things themselves on view or inspection, as opposed to a description of them from the testimony of a witness.

Realize To convert property into money; to receive the returns from an investment.

Realized gain or loss The difference between the amount realized on the sale or other disposition of property and the adjusted basis of the property.

Real party in interest The party who has the legal right under the applicable substantive law to enforce the claim in question; the one who has the right to control and receive the fruits from the litigation.

Real property See real estate.

Realtor A real estate broker or agent who is a member of the National Association of Realtors.

Realty See real estate.

Reapportionment A realignment or change in legislative districts brought about by changes in population.

Reargument A rehearing in which a party seeks to show a misapprehension of the facts or that a controlling law has been overlooked.

Reason 1. An inducement, motive, or ground for action. **2.** The faculty of the mind that distinguishes truth from falsehood, good from evil, and which deduces inferences from facts or propositions. **3.** To argue or exercise analytical powers.

Reasonable Consistent with what an ordinary, prudent person would do. Suitable under the circumstances; rational.

Reasonable belief See probable cause.

Reasonable care That degree of care which a person of ordinary prudence would exercise in the same or similar circumstances; due care under the circumstances.

Reasonable cause for an arrest Such a state of facts as would lead someone of ordinary care and prudence to believe and conscientiously entertain an honest and strong suspicion that a person is guilty of a crime.

Reasonable certainty Reasonable probability; facts that take the issue out of the arena of speculation; evidence that lays some foundation enabling the fact-finder to make a fair and reasonable estimate.

Reasonable doubt Doubt that would cause prudent people to hesitate before acting in matters of importance to themselves; doubt based on reason arising from evidence or the lack of evidence.

Reasonable force That degree of force which is not excessive, and is appropriate in protecting oneself or one's property.

Reasonable grounds See probable cause.

Reasonable man (person) A fictitious person of ordinary prudence under the circumstances.

Rebate To deduct or return money for stated reasons (e.g., prompt payment).

Rebellion Organized resistance, by force and arms, to the laws or operations of the government, committed by a subject.

Rebut To refute or take away the effect of something.

Rebuttable presumption A presumption that holds good until evidence to the contrary is introduced; a presumption that can be overcome.

Rebuttal Refutation, retort, retaliation.

Rebuttal evidence Evidence given to explain, counteract, or disprove facts given in evidence by the other side.

Recall A method of removing a public official from office before the end of his or her term, by a vote of the people.

Recant To withdraw and repudiate something formally and publicly.

Recapitalization An arrangement whereby stock, bonds, or other securities of a corporation are adjusted as to type, amount, income, or priority; reshuffling an existing corporation's capital structure.

Receipt 1. Written acknowledgment of having received something. **2.** Taking physical possession.

Receivable Awaiting collection whether or not it is currently due; pertaining to that which is due and owing a person.

Receive 1. To accept into possession and control. **2.** To obtain information about. **3.** To allow entrance.

Receiver A person appointed by the court to manage property in litigation or the affairs of a bankrupt.

Receiver of stolen property A person who receives property, knowing that it has been stolen or otherwise unlawfully taken.

Receivership The condition of a company or individual over whom a receiver has been appointed for the protection of its assets and for ultimate sale and distribution to creditors.

Recess An interval during which a body suspends business but usually without adjourning.

Recession 1. The act of ceding or falling back. **2.** A slowdown or temporary setback in economic growth, less serious than a depression.

Recidivist A habitual criminal.

Reciprocal Given or owed mutually as between two persons.

Reciprocal Enforcement of Support Act See Uniform Reciprocal Enforcement of Support Act (URESA).

Reciprocal insurance A type of insurance plan administered by an exchange rather than an insurance company in which each insured is the insurer of the other members of the plan.

Reciprocal laws Laws of one state that extend rights and privileges to citizens of another state if the latter grants similar rights and privileges to the citizens of the first state.

Reciprocal wills Wills of two or more persons in which each person makes reciprocal testamentary provisions in favor of each other. This is done either in one will, in which case the will is both joint and reciprocal, or it is done by separate wills.

Reciprocity A mutual exchange of benefits or treatment between countries, states, companies, or individuals; the granting of a privilege on condition that a comparable privilege is returned (when the California lawyer moved to Texas she had to take the Texas bar exam, since there was no reciprocity between the states).

Recision The termination of a contract upon the occurrence of a certain kind of default by the other party.

Recital The formal statement or setting forth of some facts.

Reckless Consciously failing to exercise due care without intending the consequences; wantonly disregarding the consequences of one's acts or omissions.

Reckless disregard 1. Going ahead with the publication of a matter even though the defendant entertained serious doubts as to the truth of the matter, or when there were obvious reasons to doubt the veracity of the matter. **2.** Wanton disregard; conscious indifference to the safety of others; an "I don't care" attitude.

Reckless driving Gross negligence in driving; a conscious and intentional driving that the driver knows, or should know, creates an unreasonable risk of harm to others even though there is no intent to harm; driving in deliberate disregard for the safety of others.

Reckless homicide Death resulting from a willful and wanton disregard of the consequences of one's acts or omissions.

Reclamation Increasing the value of land by physically changing it (e.g., draining a swamp).

Reclusion Incarceration as a punishment for crime.

Recognition 1. Identification or comprehension. **2.** An acknowledgment or confirmation.

Recognizance An obligation entered into before a court or magistrate whereby the recognizor acknowledges that he or she will do some act required by law which is specified therein. See personal recognizance.

Recompense A reward for services; remuneration for goods or other property.

Reconciliation The voluntary resumption of full marital relations; the renewal of amicable relations between persons who had been at odds; a statement showing the consistency of financial documents.

Reconciliation statement In accounting, a statement prepared to bring two or more accounts which show a discrepancy into agreement.

Reconduction In the civil law, a renewing of a former lease.

Reconstruction expert One who recreates the events of an accident from given facts.

Reconvention In the civil law, an action by a defendant against a plaintiff.

Record 1. To make an official note of; to enter in a book. **2.** A written account of some act or event. **3.** The available facts.

Recordation The act or process of recording an instrument such as a deed or mortgage in a public registry.

Recorder 1. An officer appointed to record documents. **2.** A magistrate with limited jurisdiction in some states.

Recording statutes Statutes that govern the manner of recording documents (e.g., deeds, mortgages) and the effect of such recording on creditors, subsequent purchasers, etc. See race recording statute, race-notice recording statute, notice recording statute.

Record notice When an instrument of conveyance or a mortgage is recorded in the appropriate public office, it is constructive notice of its contents to the whole world.

Recoup 1. To replace or make up for. **2.** To set off or keep back.

Recoupment A reduction or rebate by the defendant of part of the plaintiff's claim because of a right in the defendant arising out of the same transaction; the right of the defendant to reduce or eliminate the plaintiff's demand either because the plaintiff has not complied with some cross obligation of the contract, which is the basis of the suit, or because the plaintiff has violated some duty imposed by law in making or performing that contract.

Recourse 1. Turning or appealing for help (recourse to the courts). **2.** The right of a holder of a negotiable instrument to recover against a prior indorser or other party who is secondarily liable (the indorser was not liable for payment, since she signed "without recourse").

Recovery That which is obtained by a court judgment.

Recrimination 1. A charge made by an accused person against the accuser. **2.** If the conduct of both husband and wife has been such as to furnish grounds for divorce, neither is entitled to relief.

Recusation The disqualification of a judge because of prejudice or interest.

Reddition A surrendering or restoring.

Redeem 1. To recover ownership or buy back by making payment of a debt. **2.** To pay off.

Redeemable Subject to redemption or repurchase.

Redeemable bond A bond that the issuer may call back for payment before its maturity date.

Redemption The realization of a right to have the title of property restored free and clear of a mortgage (or other encumbrance) once the obligation has been paid or performed; a buying back; a repurchase of notes, bonds, stock, bills, or other evidence of debt by paying their value to their holders.

Redemption period A time period, often provided by statute, during which a defaulted mortgage, land contract, deed of trust, etc., can be redeemed.

Redhibition Avoiding a sale because of a vice or defect in the thing sold.

Redirect examination The examination of a witness by the party that conducted the direct examination of this witness, after the other side has cross-examined him or her.

Redistribute To reallocate.

Red-light district An area containing brothels, "smut shops", etc.

Redlining A pattern of discrimination in which financial institutions refuse to make mortgage loans, regardless of the credit record of an applicant, on property in specified areas because of alleged deteriorating conditions therein.

Redraft A second note or bill drafted by the original drawer after the first draft has been dishonored and protested.

Redress Satisfaction for an injury; damages or equitable relief.

Reductio ad absurdum Disproving an argument by showing that it leads to an absurd consequence.

Reduction to practice Embodying an inventor's conception in such form as to render it capable of practical and successful use.

Redundancy Needless repetition; superfluous matter.

"Reefer" Marijuana.

Referee A person to whom a judge refers a case, to take testimony and to file a report with the court.

Referee in bankruptcy An officer appointed by a court to exercise administrative and judicial functions in bankruptcy cases.

Reference statute A statute that refers to other statutes and makes them applicable to the subject of the legislation; a statute that incorporates and adopts pre-existing statutes.

Referendum Seeking approval from the electorate of a change in the state constitution or of a statute passed by the legislature.

Refinance To pay off existing debts with funds secured from new debts. The process of the same mortgagor paying off one loan with the proceeds from another loan.

Reformation An equitable remedy to correct a writing so that it embodies the actual agreement between the parties.

Reformatory A penal institution for youthful offenders.

Refreshing the memory Using documents, memos, or books to bring more distinctly to mind the details of past events. See past recollection recorded, present recollection recorded, present recollection revived.

Refunding A type of refinancing in which the issuer of bonds replaces outstanding bonds with a new issue.

Regent A governor or master; one who administers the government in the name of the king during the latter's minority or disability.

Register 1. To record formally. **2.** A book containing official facts.

Registered Entered or recorded in some official register, record, or list.

Registrant The person who registers.

Registrar of deeds Recorder; a public official in charge of recorded instruments affecting land title.

Registration Inserting in an official record; formally applying.

Registration statement A statement disclosing financial data and other items of interest to potential investors, which must be filed by companies wishing to issue securities to the public or to trade securities in public markets.

Registry A book or document kept for recording or registering documents or facts.

Regress To go back or revert.

Regressive tax A tax whose rate decreases as the amount being taxed increases; a tax bearing more heavily on poorer taxpayers.

Regs. See regulation.

Regular 1. Pertaining to a steady or uniform course, practice, or occurrence. **2.** Conformable to law.

Regular course of business The customary operation of a business; one's habitual or regular occupation.

Regularly At fixed intervals; in accordance with some consistent or periodical rule or practice.

Regulate To adjust or control by rule, method, or principle.

Regulation 1. A rule; a rule of an administrative agency, designed to explain or carry out the statutes or executive orders that govern the agency. **2.** The act of controlling or managing.

Regulation Z A regulation of the Federal Reserve Board, implementing provisions of the Truth-in-Lending Act.

Rehabilitation Restoration to a former capacity.

Rehabilitative alimony Alimony for a limited time until the recipient ex-spouse can get back on his or her feet and become self-sufficient.

Rehearing A second consideration of a case for the purpose of calling to the attention of the court or agency any error, omission, or oversight in the first hearing.

Reinstate To place again in a former state, condition, or office.

Reinstatement To place a case, insurance policy, etc., in the same position it was in before it was dismissed, canceled, or lapsed.

Reinsurance A contract by which one insurance company agrees to indemnify another in whole or in part against loss or liability that the latter has incurred under a separate contract as the insurer of a third party.

Reinsured An insurer who is insured against loss under its policies.

Reinsurer An insurance company that insures other insurance companies.

Reissuable notes Bank notes that after having been once paid, may again be put into circulation.

REIT See real estate investment trust.

Rejoinder The second pleading of the defendant, responding to the plaintiff's reply.

Relation back An act done at one time is considered by a fiction of the law to have been done at a prior time.

Relator, relatrix The person upon whose complaint or at whose instance certain writs are issued. See ex rel.

Release 1. To set free; to discharge a claim that one has against another. **2.** To allow something to be communicated. **3.** The giving up of a right, claim, or privilege.

Release on own recognizance See personal recognizance.

Relevancy Applicability to the issue at hand; the logical tendency of evidence to prove or disprove a material fact.

Relevant Applying to the matter in question; having a logical tendency to prove or disprove a material fact; having the tendency of making the existence of a fact more probable or less probable than it would otherwise be.

Relevant market The area of effective competition.

Reliable Worthy of confidence, trustworthy, reputable.

Reliance A belief that motivates an act or an omission; dependence.

Relict A widow or widower.

Reliction An increase of the land by the permanent withdrawal or retrocession of the sea or river.

Relief 1. Deliverance from an injustice or wrong. **2.** Private or public assistance for the poor.

Relieve 1. To release from a position or duty. **2.** To improve or make less burdensome.

Religion Belief in the existence of a superior being; a system of faith and worship practiced by a church, sect, or denomination; belief in a deity or deities.

Religious Pertaining to religion.

Relinquish To give up or renounce.

Remainder 1. An estate that will take effect and be enjoyed after another estate is determined, spent, or terminated. **2.** That which is left after everything or everyone else has been satisfied; the remaining portions.

Remainderman The one who is entitled to the remainder of an estate after another estate has expired.

Remand 1. To send back for further action. **2.** To return to custody.

Remedial Intended to correct wrongs and abuses.

Remedial statute A statute that provides a remedy or a means to enforce a right; a statute designed to correct an existing law or to redress an existing grievance.

Remedy 1. The means by which a right is enforced; the steps by which the violation of a right is prevented, redressed, or compensated. **2.** To relieve, cure, or correct.

Remise To give up or release.

Remiss Neglectful or careless.

Remission 1. The release or relinquishment of a debt. **2.** A diminution or abatement of symptoms of a disease.

Remit 1. To send or forward. **2.** To cancel or excuse. **3.** To lessen.

Remittance Money sent.

Remitter The relation back of a later defective title to an earlier valid one.

Remitting bank Any payor or intermediary bank remitting for an item.

Remittitur Diminishing or subtracting from a verdict that is excessive; the ordering of a new trial unless the plaintiff agrees to reduce the verdict by a stated amount.

Remonstrance A statement of reasons against something.

Remote cause An improbable, indirect, or speculative cause; a cause whose effect is uncertain, vague, or indeterminate; a cause whose effect does not necessarily follow.

Remote damages Unusual and unexpected results not reasonably to be anticipated from the accident.

Removal 1. The transfer of a person or thing from one place to another; the transfer of a case from one court to another. **2.** An ouster. **3.** Elimination.

Remuneration Reward or salary.

Render 1. To pronounce or execute. **2.** To cause to become.

Render judgment The official announcement of a judgment, either orally or in open court or by memorandum filed with the clerk. After the judgment is rendered, it is entered in the record by the clerk.

Rendition The return of a fugitive to the state in which he or she is accused of having committed a crime.

Renegotiation Negotiating again; the review of government contracts after performance to determine whether excess profits were made.

Renewable term insurance A type of term life insurance in which the premiums are level during each term, but increase at each new term with the age of the insured.

Renounce To make an affirmative repudiation.

Rent Consideration paid for the use of property.

Rent control A government-imposed restriction or limitation upon the maximum rent that may be charged.

Rent strike An organized effort among tenants to withhold rent until conditions are improved, rent increases are lowered, etc.

Renunciation The abandonment of a right.

Reo absente In the absence of the defendant.

Reopen To allow new evidence to be introduced in a trial that was completed.

Reorganization The act or process of organizing again; a total adjustment made in the capital structure of a corporation, in which old securities and indebtedness are retired, and new securities and bonds issued.

Reparation Payment for an injury; redress for a wrong done.

Repatriation The return to one's country; the regaining of nationality.

Repeal The express or implied abrogation or annulling of a pre-existing law by the enactment of a later law.

Replacement insurance Insurance that provides that the loss will be measured by replacement of the property new. If the property is actually replaced, the measure is the difference between the depreciated value and the replacement cost.

Replevin A possessory action designed to permit the party entitled to possession of personal property to recover it from the one who has wrongfully taken or detained it.

Replevy To regain possession of personal property through an action of replevin.

Replication 1. A reply made by the plaintiff to the defendant. **2.** Reproduction.

Reply The plaintiff's response to the answer of the defendant.

Report 1. A formal account or descriptive statement. **2.** Rumor. **3.** A volume of court opinions. **4.** To recite or give an account.

Reporter 1. The person who reports the decisions of a court of record; one who takes down and transcribes proceedings (court reporter). **2.** A volume of court opinions (Federal Reporter 2d). **3.** A loose-leaf service on a particular area of the law (CCH Labor Reporter).

Reports 1. Volumes of court opinions (United States Reports; American Law Reports). **2.** Volumes of administrative decisions (ICC Reports).

Repossession The taking back of property.

Represent 1. To speak or act with authority on behalf of another person. **2.** To present or hold out as. **3.** To exemplify.

Representation 1. The act of representing or speaking on behalf of another. **2.** A statement; any conduct that constitutes a statement of fact.

Representative 1. One who stands in the place of and acts on behalf of another. **2.** A legislator. **3.** Acting as an example.

Reprieve Temporary relief or postponement in carrying out a sentence.

Reprimand To censure someone.

Reprisal Action taken in retaliation.

Republic A form of government in which the supreme authority lies with the voters who act through their elected representatives.

Repudiation Rejection; refusal to perform.

Repugnant condition Conditions that contradict, annul, or neutralize the main purpose of the contract. Repugnant conditions are also called insensible.

Reputable Having a good reputation; worthy of repute or distinction.

Reputation The estimation in which one is held; the sum total of how one is seen by others.

Reputed Popularly considered.

Request for admission Discovery device: A written statement of facts is submitted to an adverse party who must admit or deny them. Admitted facts need not be proven at the trial.

Requirement contract A contract in which the purchaser agrees to buy all of its needs for specified material from a particular supplier, and the latter agrees to fill all the purchaser's needs during the period of the contract.

Requisition 1. A formal demand. **2.** To insist upon.

Res The subject matter of a trust or will; a thing or object, a status, everything that is the object of a right.

Res adjudicata See res judicata.

Rescind To annul or cancel.

Rescission The undoing or cancellation of something.

Rescue doctrine Danger invites rescue: One who negligently endangers a person can be liable to third parties who are injured in an attempt to save the person in danger, so long as the attempt is not reckless.

Reservation 1. The holding back or retention of a right or interest; a right created and retained by the grantor. **2.** A tract of land to which an American Indian tribe retains the original title or which is set aside for its use. **3.** A doubt, misgiving, qualm.

Reserve 1. To keep back or retain. **2.** A fund set aside to cover future expenses, losses, or claims. **3.** Military personnel awaiting active duty in an emergency.

Reserve banks Member banks of the Federal Reserve System.

Reserve Board See Federal Reserve Board of Governors.

Reserve clause A clause in the contract of a professional athlete that gives the club a continuing and exclusive right to the services of the athlete.

Reserved Kept or set apart for a designated purpose or person.

Reserved powers Powers not delegated to the federal government by the U.S. Constitution nor prohibited by it to the states are reserved to the states or to the people.

Reservist A member of a military reserve.

Res gestae An exclamation or utterance is admissible as an exception to the hearsay rule if it (a) is made at or near the time of the occurrence (e.g., an accident), (b) is made spontaneously without time to deliberate, and (c) is so influenced by the occurrence itself as to become a part thereof.

Reside To be in residence; to occupy a fixed abode; to dwell permanently or continuously.

Residence Living or remaining in a particular locality without the intent to stay there indefinitely. If this intent existed, the place would be a domicile. In some situations, however, the law treats residence and domicile as synonymous.

Resident One who resides or dwells in a place; one who occupies a dwelling within the state and establishes an ongoing physical presence therein.

Resident agent A person in the jurisdiction who is authorized to accept service of process for another.

Resident alien A person who is not yet a citizen of this country, who has come here from another country with the intent to abandon his or her former citizenship and reside here.

Residential Pertaining to or suitable for residences; noncommercial.

Residual Pertaining to that which is left over.

Residuary Pertaining to the remainder of an estate after all debts, claims, and other testamentary gifts are satisfied.

Residuary clause A clause in a will disposing that part of the estate that remains after everything else is paid or satisfied (e.g., debts, expenses, all other legacies).

Residue That which remains of a testator's estate after all debts and particular legacies have been discharged.

Residuum See residue.

Resignation Formal relinquishment of a job or office.

Res ipsa loquitur "The thing speaks for itself." An inference or rebuttable presumption of the defendant's negligence (unreasonableness) arises in the following circumstances: (a) The event producing the harm was of a kind that ordinarily does not occur in the absence of someone's negligence, (b) the event was caused by an agency or instrumentality within the defendant's exclusive control, and (c) the event was not due to any voluntary action or contribution on the part of the plaintiff.

Resistance Standing against or obstructing.

Res judicata A final judgment rendered by a court of competent jurisdiction on the merits is conclusive as to the rights of the parties and their privies, and hence bars any subsequent action by them involving the same claim, demand, or cause of action.

Res nova A new matter; a question not before decided.

Res nullius The property of nobody.

Resolution 1. A decision or solution. **2.** A formal expression of the opinion or will of an official body without constituting a rule or law.

Resort 1. To go to or make use of. **2.** To go often. **3.** Recourse.

Resource 1. That to which one can turn to for help. **2.** Assets.

RESPA See Real Estate Settlement Procedures Act.

Respite A delay; the temporary suspension of the execution of a sentence.

Respondeat superior "Let the master answer." The master, employer, or principal in certain cases is liable for what the servant, employee, or agent does or fails to do. The former is liable for the torts of the latter when committed within the course of employment.

Respondent The party who answers a claim, allegation, or bill; the party against whom an appeal is brought.

Responsibility The state of being answerable for an obligation; the obligation to answer for an act or to make restitution for an injury.

Responsible 1. Legally accountable or answerable. **2.** Trustworthy. **3.** Rational, competent.

Responsive Constituting an answer; nonevasive.

Responsive pleading A pleading that joins issue and replies to a prior pleading of an opponent.

Rest To indicate to the court that a party has presented all of the evidence he or she intends to submit at this time.

Restatements A series of volumes authored by the American Law Institute (e.g., Restatement of Torts 2d). The books state the law in a given area, note emerging changes, and sometimes indicate changes in the law that the Institute would like to see.

Restitution The restoration of something to its rightful owner; making good or giving an equivalent value for any loss, damage, or injury.

Restraining order A form of injunction issued ex parte for the purpose of restraining the defendant from doing the threatened act, pending notice and hearing on an application for an injunction.

Restraint Restriction or prohibition.

Restraint of trade Contracts or combinations that tend to or are designed to eliminate or stifle competition, create a monopoly, artificially maintain prices, or otherwise hamper or obstruct the course of trade and commerce that would be carried on if left to the control of natural economic forces.

Restraint on alienation A provision in a deed or other instrument of conveyance that prohibits the grantee from selling or transferring the property.

Restrictive Tending to confine, qualifying.

Restrictive covenant 1. Private restrictions limiting the use of real property. Restrictive covenants are created by deed and may "run with the land," binding all subsequent purchasers of the land, or may be "personal," binding only between the original seller and buyer. Examples of restrictive covenants: those that limit the density of buildings per acre, regulate the size, style, or price range of buildings to be erected, prevent particular businesses from operating, etc. **2.** A clause in a contract limiting a party from performing similar work for a period of time in a certain geographic area after the termination of the contract.

Restrictive indorsement An indorsement that limits the further negotiability of the instrument.

Resulting trust A trust implied in law from the intention of the parties to a given transaction; a trust that arises when a person makes a disposition of property under circumstances that raise the inference that he or she did not intend the transfer of a beneficial interest to the person taking or holding the property.

Resulting use A use raised by equity for the benefit of one who has made a voluntary conveyance to uses without any declaration of the use.

Retail Pertaining to a sale directly to the consumer.

Retailer A person engaged in making sales of goods to the ultimate consumer or user who is not in the business of reselling them.

Retain 1. To engage the services of. **2.** To hold or preserve.

Retained income That portion of profits which has not been paid out as dividends; net income over the life of a corporation less all income distributions.

Retainer The act of employing an attorney; the fee paid by a client to an attorney when the latter is hired; the contract between the client and attorney, stating the nature of the services to be rendered and the cost thereof.

Retaining lien The right of an attorney to retain possession of the client's property acquired by the attorney within the scope of his or her employment until the client pays the balance owed for professional services.

Retaliatory eviction An eviction by a landlord because the tenant has complained to the housing authority about conditions in the leased premises, the tenant has participated in a tenant's organization, etc.

Retire 1. To terminate employment or service upon reaching the age of retirement. **2.** To take out of circulation.

Retorsion A form of retaliation by one government against another.

Retract To take something back; to recant.

Retribution Something given or demanded in payment.

Retroactive Applying to the time prior to enactment; affecting or acting on things that are past.

Return The act of a sheriff, constable, marshal, or other ministerial officer, in delivering back to the court a writ, notice, process or other paper, which he or she was required to serve, with a brief account of the time and mode of service or the failure to accomplish service.

Returnable Requiring a return; to be returned on a certain day.

Reus In civil and canon law, the defendant in an action or suit. A person judicially accused of a crime.

Revaluation The restoration of purchasing power to an inflated currency.

Revendication In civil law, to reclaim or to demand the restoration of.

Revenue Return or yield from an investment, venture, job, collection effort, etc.

Revenue bond A bond issued by a state or local government, repayable by the unit of government that issues it; a bond issued for and payable solely from a revenue-producing public project.

Revenue Ruling (Rev. Rul.) An IRS official interpretation of the tax law as applied to specific transactions.

Revenue stamp A stamp affixed on a deed or other instrument of conveyancing to show the amount of federal tax on the sale of real property.

Reversal The setting aside by an appellate court of a decision of a lower court.

Reverse discrimination Prejudice or bias exercised against a person or class for the purpose of correcting a pattern of discrimination against another person or class.

Reversible error Substantial error; error that reasonably might have prejudiced the party complaining about the error.

Reversion The estate left in the grantor during the continuance of a particular estate; an interest created by law when the owner of real estate conveys an interest in it less than his or her own; the residue left in the grantor or his or her heirs after the termination of a particular estate.

Reversionary interest The interest that a person has in the reversion of land or other property; a right to the future enjoyment of property that at present is being enjoyed by another; the property that reverts to the grantor after the expiration of an intervening interest.

Reversioner A person who is entitled to an estate in reversion.

Revert To turn back; to return to.

Review 1. To examine or go over a matter again (e.g., to review the decision of a lower court). **2.** A consideration for the purpose of correction (judicial review).

Revise To correct or update.

Revised Statutes (R.S.) A collection of statutes that have been revised, rearranged, and reenacted as a whole.

Revision A correction or updating following a reexamination.

Revival Renewing the legal force or effectiveness of something (e.g., a cause of action).

Revive To renew; to make oneself liable again.

Revocable Susceptible of being withdrawn or canceled.

Revocable trust A trust in which the maker or settlor reserves to himself or herself the right to revoke the trust.

Revocation The destruction or voiding of something; the recall of some power, authority, or thing granted.

Revoke To make void, to annul, or cancel.

Revolt An attempt to overthrow the government.

Revolution The act of overthrowing a government.

Revolutionary One who instigates or takes part in a revolution.

Revolving credit An arrangement that permits a buyer or borrower to purchase goods or to secure loans on a continuing basis so long as the outstanding balance in the account does not exceed a certain limit.

Rev. Rul. See Revenue Ruling.

Reward That which is given for some service or attainment.

Rider An amendment or addition.

Right 1. Morally correct; consonant with ethical principles or rules of positive law. **2.** Appropriate, favorable. **3.** A power, privilege, or immunity. **4.** To redress.

Right of action The right to bring a suit.

Right of privacy See invasion of privacy.

Right of way The right to pass over the land of another; an easement; a preference in asserting the right of passage at the same time and place as between two vehicles, or between a vehicle and a pedestrian.

Right-to-life See pro-life.

Right-to-work law A state law that employees are not required to join a union as a condition of receiving or retaining a job.

Right-wrong test See insanity.

Rigor mortis One of the tests of death: a rigidity or stiffening of the muscular tissue and joints of the body.

Ring An exclusive combination of persons who seek an illegitimate or selfish end.

Ringing up A custom among commission merchants and brokers by which they exchange contracts for sale against contracts for purchase, or reciprocally cancel such contracts, adjust differences of price between themselves, and surrender margins.

Riot An unlawful assembly that has developed to the stage of violence; a designated number of persons (e.g., three or more), unlawfully assembled together and disturbing the peace by acting in a violent or tumultuous manner.

Riparian rights Those rights incident to the ownership of land contiguous to and abutting flowing navigable waters such as streams or rivers; the rights of persons, through whose land a natural watercourse runs, to the benefit of the water as it passes through their land for all useful purposes to which it may be applied.

Ripe Prepared or suitable.

Ripeness doctrine The constitutional mandate of case and controversy requires an appellate court to consider whether a case has matured or ripened into a controversy worthy of adjudication before it will determine the case. To warrant the issuance of a declaratory judgment, there must be a substantial controversy between parties having adverse legal interests of sufficient immediacy and reality.

Risk 1. The danger or hazard of a loss or injury (assumption of the risk). **2.** To expose to danger (risk losing the cargo).

Risk capital Money or property invested in a business venture.

River A natural stream of water, of greater volume than a creek or rivulet, flowing in a more or less permanent bed or channel between defined banks or walls.

Road An open way or public passage.

Robbery Unlawfully taking an article of value from the person of another by the use of violence or fear.

Rod A lineal measure of 5 1/2 yards or 16 1/2 feet.

Rogatory letters See letters rogatory.

'Roider Slang for someone who takes steroids.

'Roids Slang for steroids.

'Roids rage Slang for an outburst caused by steroids.

Roll 1. The record of the proceedings of a court or public office. **2.** To rob by force.

Rolling over An extension or renewal of a short-term loan from one period to another.

Rollover paper Short-term notes that may be extended (rolled over) or converted to installment payments after the initial due date.

Rood of land The fourth part of an acre in square measure, or 1,210 square yards.

Roomer One who rents a room or rooms.

Root of title The conveyance that begins the chain of title to land.

ROR Release on own recognizance.

Rorschach test A method of detecting neurotic and psychotic traits by noting the patient's reaction to a set of ten cards containing standardized inkblots.

Round lot A unit of trading on the New York Stock Exchange. For stocks, it is 100 shares; for bonds, $1000 par value.

Royalty Compensation for the use of property, expressed as a percentage of the receipts or as an account per unit produced; a payment made to an author or composer by a licensee, copyright holder, or assignee for each copy of his or her work sold; a payment made to an inventor for each article sold under his or her patent.

R.S. See Revised Statutes.

Rubber check A check that has been returned by the drawee bank because of insufficient funds in the account of the drawer.

Rule 1. An established standard, guide, or regulation. **2.** The controlling authority. **3.** To govern or control. **4.** To settle or decide a point of law (the court ruled that the defense does not apply).

Rule absolute A rule that must be enforced forthwith.

Rule against perpetuities No interest in property is good unless it must vest, if at all, not later than 21 years, plus the period of gestation, after some life or lives in being at the time of the creation of the interest. A rule that fixes the time within which a future interest must vest. The estate must vest within a time limited by a life or lives then in being and 21 years thereafter, together with the period of gestation necessary to cover cases of posthumous birth.

Rule in Shelley's case When in the same instrument a life estate is given to a person, followed by a remainder to this person's heirs, the heirs take nothing and the holder of the life estate gets an estate in fee. Where a person takes an estate of freehold, legally or equitably, under a deed, will, or other writing, and in the same instrument there is a limitation by way of remainder, either with or without the interposition of another estate, of any interest of the same legal or equitable quality to his heirs, or heirs of his body, as a class of persons to take in succession from generation to generation, the limitation to the heirs entitles the ancestor to the whole estate.

Rulemaking power The power of certain appellate courts, usually the highest appellate court within a given judicial system, to prescribe rules of procedure to be followed by lower courts within that judicial system.

Rule nisi An ex parte order directing the other party to show cause why a temporary order should not become permanent; a rule that becomes final unless cause can be shown against it.

Rule of four A case is deserving of review if four United States Supreme Court justices find that the case raises a legal question of general importance.

Rule of law A legal principle of general application; an enforceable pronouncement of government that directly or indirectly establishes a standard of conduct.

Rule of lenity When the intention of the legislature is not clear from the act itself, and reasonable minds might differ as to its intention, the court will adopt the less harsh meaning.

Rule of necessity Even though a judge has an interest in a case, he or she should still hear the case if it cannot otherwise be heard. The normal rule of disqualification does not apply if there is no other judge available to hear and determine the matter.

Rule of reason The legality of restraints on trade is determined by weighing all the factors of the case (e.g., the history of the restraint, the evil believed to exist, the reason for adopting the particular remedy, and the purpose or end sought to be attained).

Rules of Appellate Procedure See Federal Rules of Appellate Procedure.

Rules of Civil Procedure See Federal Rules of Civil Procedure.

Rules of court Rules that regulate practice and procedure before a given court.

Rules of Criminal Procedure See Federal Rules of Criminal Procedure.

Rules of Decision Act The laws of the several states (except where the Constitution, treaties, or statutes of the United States otherwise require or provide) shall be regarded as rules of decision in trials at common law in the courts of the United States in cases where they apply.

Rules of Evidence See Federal Rules of Evidence.

Ruling A judicial or administrative interpretation of a statute, constitution, order, regulation, treaty, or ordinance; a determination on the admissibility of evidence, on the granting or denial of a motion, etc.

Run 1. To have legal effect during a period of time (the statute of limitations has run against the claim). **2.** To accompany, to go with (the covenant runs with the land).

Runaway shop An employer that moves its business to another location or that temporarily closes its business for anti-union purposes.

Runner 1. One who solicits business for an attorney from accident victims. An ambulance chaser. **2.** One who assists the bail bondsman in presenting the defendant in court when required.

Running account An open, unsettled account.

Running of the statute of limitations The time mentioned in the statute of limitations has passed, and hence the action is barred.

Running with the land Passing with the transfer of the land.

Rylands v. Fletcher The English case that helped establish the principle that a defendant is strictly liable for harm resulting from a non-natural or abnormal use of land which causes increased danger to persons or property.

Sabotage Willful destruction of property or interference with normal operations.

Sacrilege The desecration of anything considered holy.

Sadomasochism Pleasure derived from inflicting pain on others and on oneself.

Safe 1. A receptacle for the preservation of valuables. **2.** Secure from injury or damage. **3.** Conservative. **4.** Out of danger.

Safe deposit box A metal container kept by a customer in a bank in which he or she deposits papers, securities, and other valuable items. Generally, there are two keys required to open it, one retained by the bank and the other by the customer.

Said Before mentioned (the said agreement).

Salable Fit for sale in the usual course of trade.

Sale A contract in which the seller, in consideration of the payment or promise of payment of a certain price by the buyer, transfers title and possession of the thing sold to the buyer.

Sale in gross A sale by the tract, without regard to quantity.

Sale on approval A conditional sale that becomes absolute only if the buyer approves or is satisfied with the goods.

Sales agreement See agreement of sale.

Sales tax A tax imposed on the sale of goods, computed as a percentage of the purchase price.

Salvage 1. That portion of goods or property which has been saved or remains after a casualty; property that is no longer useful but which has scrap value. **2.** To rescue from loss.

Salvage value The value of an asset that remains after the useful life of an asset has expired.

Same evidence test Whether the facts alleged in the second indictment, if given in evidence, would have sustained a conviction under the first indictment; whether the same evidence would support a conviction in each case.

Same offense The same criminal act, transaction, or omission.

Sample 1. A small quantity of a commodity presented for inspection or examination as evidence of the quality of the whole. **2.** To test by examining a portion.

Sanction 1. To confirm or assent. **2.** Support or encouragement. **3.** A penalty for an infraction or violation.

Sane Of natural and normal mental condition; healthy in mind.

Sanitation Measures for promoting public health; removal or neutralization of elements injurious to public health.

Sanity Sound understanding; the normal condition of the human mind.

Satisfaction 1. The discharge of an obligation. **2.** Fulfillment.

Satisfactory Good enough, adequate.

Satisfy 1. To discharge a debt. **2.** To please. **3.** To convince.

Sauce Slang for steroids.

Save harmless clause A provision in a document by which one party agrees to indemnify another as to claims and suits that may be asserted against him or her.

Saving clause A restriction in a statute that preserves certain rights, remedies, or privileges; a provision in a statute that provides that if part of the statute is declared unconstitutional, the rest is to remain in force if it is self-sustaining.

Saving to suitors clause A suitor asserting an in personam admiralty claim may elect to sue in a common-law state court through an ordinary civil action. In such an action, the state court must apply the same substantive law as would be applied had the suit been instituted in admiralty in federal court.

Savings and Loan Association A bank chartered by the Federal Home Loan Bank Board and engaged primarily in making home loan mortgages from the savings accounts of the depositors.

Scab One who takes the job of a worker on strike; one who works for lower wages than, or under conditions contrary to, those prescribed by a trade union.

Scalper One who buys tickets and then sells them at an inflated price; a small-scale speculator; a small operator who takes profits on slight fluctuations in the securities market.

Scandal 1. Damage to reputation. **2.** Shameful or disgraceful conduct. **3.** Malicious gossip. **4.** Outrage over wrongdoing.

School board or committee An agency of municipal officers charged with the administration of the affairs of public schools.

Scienter Guilty knowledge; intent to deceive or manipulate.

Scintilla A minute amount.

Scire facias A judicial writ founded on a matter of record, requiring the person against whom it is brought to show cause why the party bringing the writ should not have advantage of the record or why the record should not be annulled and vacated.

Scope of employment Activities that fairly and reasonably may be said to be incident of the employment or logically and naturally connected with it; activities of an employee in furtherance of duties owed to the employer where the latter is exercising or could exercise control over what the employee does.

Scrip Something exchanged for money or a privilege; a document entitling the holder to something of value; temporary money.

Scrivener One who copies; one who prepares written instruments or documents.

Scroll 1. A rolled paper or parchment containing writing or painting. **2.** A mark intended to take the place of a seal.

Scutage A tax or payment given in lieu of military service.

S.D. Southern District (e.g., S.D.N.Y. is the United States District Court in the Southern District of New York).

Seal 1. An impression or sign to attest the execution of an instrument or to authenticate the document. **2.** To close.

Sealing of record Not allowing the record of a criminal or juvenile delinquent to be examined except by court order or by designated officials.

Search An examination of one's person, premises, vehicle, etc., for the purpose of discovering evidence of guilt.

Search warrant A written order issued by a judge or magistrate in the name of the government, directed to and authorizing a sheriff or other officer to search for and seize any property that constitutes evidence of a crime.

Seashore Land adjacent to the sea that is covered or left dry according to the movement of the tides.

Seasonable Done within the agreed-upon time, or within a reasonable time if no time was agreed upon.

Seasonal Carried on only at certain seasons or at fairly definite portions of the year.

Seat Headquarters; location of the principal government offices.

Seaworthy Pertaining to a vessel that is properly constructed, prepared, manned, equipped, and provided for the trip intended.

SEC See Securities and Exchange Commission.

Secession Withdrawing from membership.

Secondary affinity That which subsists between the husband and his wife's relations by marriage.

Secondary boycott A refusal to work for, purchase from, or handle the products of a secondary employer with whom the union has no dispute in order to force this employer to stop doing business with the primary employer with whom the union does have a dispute. A combination with the purpose and effect of coercing customers or suppliers, through fear of loss or bodily harm, to withhold or withdraw their business from the employer who is the primary subject of the attack.

Secondary creditor One whose claim is secondary to preferred creditor(s).

Secondary liability A liability that does not attach until or except upon the fulfillment of certain conditions.

Secondary meaning doctrine Protection given geographic or descriptive terms that the producer has used to such an extent as to lead the general public to identify the producer or the product with the mark or term. A geographic or descriptive mark receives protection against copying if consumers have come to associate it with a particular manufacturer or source.

Secondary parties In negotiable instruments, a drawer or endorser.

Second degree murder The unlawful taking of a human life with malice but without premeditation and deliberation.

Second mortgage A mortgage given on property that has a prior mortgage on it.

Secretary 1. The corporate officer in charge of keeping records, giving and receiving notices, etc. **2.** The administrator or director of the executive department of the government. **3.** A stenographer, typist, or scribe.

Secrete To hide away.

Sect A relatively small group having common beliefs or practices.

Sectarian 1. Promoting a particular sect or faith. **2.** Factional.

Secular Pertaining to the present, temporal world; not religious.

Secure To guaranty or make certain the payment of a debt or the discharge of an obligation.

Secured Supported or backed by security or collateral (secured debt).

Secured creditor A creditor who holds a special assurance of payment of his or her debt (e.g., via mortgage, collateral, lien).

Secured transaction A transaction founded on a security agreement that creates or provides for a security interest.

Securities Evidences of debts or of property; evidences of obligations to pay money or of rights to participate in earnings or the distribution of other corporate property.

Securities and Exchange Commission (SEC) A federal agency that regulates the exchange of securities.

Security 1. A pledge, mortgage, deposit, lien, etc., given by a debtor to assure payment or performance of the debt, which gives the creditor a resource to be used in case of failure of the principal obligation. **2.** Protection (national security).

Security agreement An agreement that creates or provides for a security interest.

Security deposit Money deposited by a tenant with the landlord as security for full and faithful performance of the lease.

Security interest An interest in property which provides that the property may be sold on default in order to satisfy the obligation for which the security interest is given. For example, a mortgage grants a security interest in real property.

Sedition A communication or agreement that has as its objective the stirring up of treason or certain lesser commotions; advocating the overthrow or reformation of the government by violence; defamation of the government.

Seditious Promoting sedition.

Seduce To induce someone to engage in sexual intercourse; to lead astray.

Segregation Separation (e.g., racial segregation).

Seisin or **seizin** Full and complete present ownership and possession of land; possession of real property under a claim of freehold estate.

Seize To put into possession; to take possession forcibly.

Seizure 1. To take possession of property. **2.** A sudden convulsion.

Selectman A municipal officer elected by towns to transact certain public business.

Self-dealing Acting out of self-interest when one should be acting in the interest of another.

Self-defense The protection of one's person against threatened injury from another; the use of force to repel impending peril to one's person or property.

Self-executing Immediately effective without the necessity of intervening action or legislation; requiring no affirmative action by a court.

Self-help Acting on one's own; acting independently of the courts.

Self-incrimination Acts or declarations by which one incriminates oneself in a crime; giving criminal evidence against oneself.

Self-insurance Setting aside a fund to meet losses instead of insuring against such losses by purchasing insurance.

Self-serving Serving one's own interests; tending to benefit oneself.

Sell To dispose of by sale.

Seller One who has contracted to sell.

Selling short The agreement to deliver at a future date a security or commodity the seller does not own but which he or she hopes to buy later at a lower price.

Semiannual Twice a year.

Senate The upper chamber of the legislative branch of government.

Send To deposit in the mail or deliver for transmission by other means, properly addressed and with postage or other cost of transmission.

Senile Suffering from a feebleness of mind and body because of old age.

Senior 1. Older. **2.** More experienced, or of higher rank.

Seniority Precedence or preference over others similarly situated; the length of continuous, unbroken service; more years of service and hence the last to be laid off, the first to be promoted, etc.

Senior mortgage A mortgage that is of superior priority, above junior mortgages.

Sentence 1. The judgment formally declaring the legal consequences of a determination of guilt in a criminal case. **2.** To impose a punishment.

Separability clause A clause providing that if one or more provisions of the contract are declared void, the balance of the contract remains in force (i.e., the invalid provisions are severable).

Separable Capable of being separated.

Separate and apart A ground for divorce. See living separate and apart.

Separate maintenance An allowance granted to a spouse, usually the wife, for her support and that of her children while no longer living with the other spouse.

Separate property Property owned by a married person in his or her own right during marriage.

Separate return A tax return filed by one spouse covering only his or her income.

Separation A decision by a court (a) that two people can live separately while still remaining husband and wife, and (b) declaring the rights and obligations of the parties while they are separated.

Separation agreement A contract between spouses who have separated or who are about to separate, concerning child custody, property division, child support, alimony, etc. The parties may or may not be contemplating a divorce or legal separation.

Separation of powers The constitutional requirement that the three branches of government—judicial, legislative, executive—not encroach upon or usurp each other's powers; no branch of government should exercise the functions exclusively committed to another branch.

Sequester 1. To separate or isolate (sequester the jury). **2.** To take and hold property pending litigation.

Sequestration The process by which property or funds are attached pending the outcome of the litigation.

Sergeant 1. A noncommissioned officer in the armed forces. **2.** An officer in the police force with rank below captain or lieutenant.

Serial Arranged in a series.

Serial bonds A number of bonds issued at the same time but with different maturity dates and usually with varying interest rates for each maturity date.

Seriatim One by one. One following after another, separately, individually, severally.

Series A related sequence of events or things.

Series bonds Groups of bonds (for example, series A, series B) usually issued at different times and with different maturities but under the authority of the same indenture.

Serrated Notched on the edge; cut in notches like the teeth of a saw. This was once the method of trimming the top or edge of a deed of indenture.

Servant 1. One employed to perform service, whose performance is controlled by or subject to the control of the master. **2.** One hired to perform household duties.

Service 1. Duty or labor to be rendered by one person to another. **2.** Helping hand. **3.** Ceremony. **4.** Armed forces. **5.** A branch of public employment (civil service). **6.** Delivery of legal process. See service of process. **7.** To keep repaired.

Service by publication The service of a summons or other process upon an absent or nonresident defendant by publishing the summons or other process as an advertisement in a designated newspaper.

Service charge An added cost for administration or handling.

Service mark A word, name, or symbol used in the sale or advertising of services to identify the services of one person and to distinguish them from the services of others. A trademark, on the other hand, is used to identify goods or products.

Service of process The delivery or other communication of writs, summonses, etc. The delivery or other acceptable communication of a formal notice to the defendant ordering him or her to appear in court in order to answer the allegations made by the plaintiff.

Servient Subject to a service or servitude.

Servient estate In the law of easements, a servient estate is the estate upon which the easement is imposed or against which it is enjoyed; an estate subjected to a burden or servitude for the benefit of another estate.

Servitude 1. The condition of being subjected to another person as a servant or slave. **2.** A charge or burden resting on one estate for the benefit of another estate, similar to an easement.

Session The sitting of a court, legislature, council, commission, etc., for the transaction of its business; the time during which such a body sits.

Session laws The laws enacted by the state legislature during one of its sessions. The laws are usually printed chronologically as they are enacted rather than by subject matter.

Set aside To reverse or cancel a judgment, order, etc.

Setback 1. A temporary or unexpected upset or loss. **2.** A distance from the curb, property line, or structure within which construction or building is prohibited.

Set down To enter in a calendar or docket.

Seti As used in mining laws, a lease.

Setoff A money demand by the defendant against the plaintiff based upon a debt that is independent of and unconnected with the plaintiff's cause of action. A defendant's remedy to discharge or reduce the plaintiff's demand by an opposite demand arising from a transaction that is extrinsic to the plaintiff's cause of action.

Set out To recite or narrate facts.

Settle 1. To make or arrange for final disposition; to adjust difficulties among disputants; to reach an agreement or compromise. **2.** To satisfy a debt. **3.** To establish a residence.

Settlement A payment, adjustment, or compromise agreed upon among parties; a resolution of difficulties in lieu of litigation.

Settler One who goes on land as a resident.

Settlor One who creates a trust; a trustor; the grantor or donor in a deed of settlement.

Severability clause A clause in a statute or contract, stating that if portions of the statute or contract are declared invalid, the remaining portions shall continue to be effective if they are self-sustaining.

Severable Susceptible to division into independent parts.

Several liability Liability that is separate and distinct from the liability of another.

Severally Apart from others.

Several tenancy A tenancy that is separate, and not held jointly with another person.

Severalty An estate in severalty is one held by a person in his or her own right without others being joined or connected.

Severance Partition or departure.

Severance damages An award made to the owner of land to compensate for the decrease in value of the remainder of his or her land due to a partial condemnation or taking.

Severance pay Payment by an employer to an employee beyond his or her wages upon termination of the employment.

Shakedown Extortion of money with threats of physical violence or arrest.

Shall Usually a word of command denoting obligation, although it is sometimes construed as permissive or directory.

Sham Deceptive, without substance, a hoax.

Shanghai To drug, intoxicate, trick, or otherwise force someone to become a sailor.

Share 1. To have a portion of. **2.** A portion of something owned by a number of persons. **3.** A unit of stock representing ownership in a corporation.

Share capital Capital stock. All shares representing ownership of a business, including preferred stock and common stock.

Sharecropper A tenant farmer who lives and works on the land of another. His or her compensation is a portion of the crops minus any advances for seed, tools, food, etc.

Sharp A "sharp" clause in a mortgage or other security is one that empowers the creditor to take prompt and summary action upon default in payment or breach of other conditions.

Shave 1. Obtaining the property of another by oppression or extortion. **2.** Buying notes and other securities for money at a discount.

Shelley's Case See Rule in Shelley's Case.

Sheriff's deed A deed given at a forced sale conducted by a sheriff in foreclosure of a mortgage.

Shield law A statute giving journalists the privilege to refuse to disclose information obtained while gathering news.

Shifting income Moving income to children and others in lower tax brackets.

Shifting trust An express trust that is so settled that it may operate in favor of beneficiaries additional to, or substituted for, those first named, upon specified contingencies.

Shill One who participates in a confidence game by pretending to be a bystander or one of the victims.

Shipment 1. The delivery of goods to a carrier and the issuance by the latter of a bill of lading therefor; the transportation of goods. **2.** Goods to be delivered.

Ship's papers The papers that must be carried by a vessel on a voyage, in order to furnish evidence of her national character, the nature and destination of the cargo, and of compliance with the navigation laws.

Shock The sudden agitation of the physical or mental sensibilities. A sudden depression of the vital forces of the entire body or a part of it, producing a profound impression upon the nervous system.

Shop book Records of customer accounts containing original entries.

Shop-book rule An exception to the hearsay rule, permitting the introduction into evidence of books of original entry made in the usual course of business.

Shoplifting Willfully taking possession of merchandise offered for sale in a store or business establishment, with the intent of converting the merchandise to the taker's own use without paying the purchase price.

Shop right rule The right of an employer to use an employee's invention in the employer's business without paying a royalty.

Shop steward A union official elected to represent members of a particular department.

Short sale The taxpayer sells borrowed property—usually stock—and repays the lender with substantially identical property either held on the date of the sale or purchased after the sale.

Short swing profits Profits made by an insider through the sale or other disposition of corporate stock within 6 months after purchase.

Short-term debt Debt evidenced by notes or drafts that are payable on demand or within a year of issuance.

Shotgun instruction See Allen charge.

Show cause order An order or decree to appear as directed and explain why the court should not take a proposed action.

Show-up A one-to-one confrontation between a suspect and the witness to or victim of a crime.

[sic] The error in the quotation was in the original (e.g., "the new atorney [sic] arrived late.").

Sick leave Period away from work allowed by an employer to an employee during the latter's sickness with or without pay but without loss of seniority.

Sicut alias As at another time, or heretofore. A second writ sent out when the first was not executed.

Side reports A term sometimes applied to unofficial volumes or series of reports, as contrasted with those prepared by the official reporter of the court, or to collections of cases omitted from the official reports.

Sight draft An instrument payable upon presentment.

Signatory The person who signs; the nation that signs.

Signature 1. One's name in writing. **2.** Trait.

Silent partner An investor in a firm who takes no active part in its management but who shares in its losses and profits; a dormant partner; a partner whose name does not appear in the firm but who has an interest in it and shares in its losses and profits.

Silicosis A condition of massive fibrosis of the lungs, marked by shortness of breath due to prolonged inhalation of silica dust.

Silver platter doctrine Evidence obtained illegally by state officials was formerly admissible in federal prosecutions if no federal officer had participated in the violation of the defendant's rights.

Simple 1. Not aggravated. **2.** Uncomplicated. **3.** Unpretentious, sincere.

Simple interest Interest paid on the initial amount invested and not on any earnings or interest thereon.

Simple larceny Felonious or wrongful taking and carrying away of personal goods of another with intent to steal, unattended by acts of violence.

Simple negligence The failure to exercise that degree of care and caution which an ordinary, prudent person would exercise under the circumstances.

Simplex dictum A mere assertion; an assertion without proof.

Simulate To give the appearance of something.

Simulated Contrived.

Simul cum Together with.

Simultaneous Pertaining to two or more occurrences or happenings taking place at the same time.

Simultaneous Death Act A Uniform State Law providing that if there is insufficient evidence that persons have died otherwise than simultaneously, the property of each person shall be disposed of as if he or she had survived unless the Act provides otherwise.

Sinecure A salaried position with little or no responsibility or work.

Sine die Without day; without assigning a day for a further meeting or hearing.

Sine qua non An indispensable requisite or condition; that without which a thing cannot be done.

Single publication rule A defendant can be sued only once for each mass publication of libel, but evidence of all sales can be introduced on the issue of damages.

Singular Unusual or distinctive.

Sinking fund Assets, and the earnings therefrom, that are earmarked for the retirement of bonds or other long-term obligations.

Sister corporations Two corporations that have common or substantially common ownership by the same shareholders.

Sit To hold a session; to be organized and proceeding with the transaction of business (the Court of Appeals sits every other week).

Sit-down strike A strike in which the workers stay in the plant but refuse to work.

Sitting in bank or **banc** A session of the court in which all judges or at least a quorum of judges sit and hear cases.

Situs The place where a thing happened, is located, or is considered (the situs of property).

Skeleton bill One drawn, indorsed, or accepted in blank.

Skill Knowledge of the principles and processes of an art, science, or trade, combined with an ability to apply them in practice in a proper and approved manner.

Skiptracing A service that assists creditors in locating delinquent debtors.

Slander 1. A tort with the following elements: (a) oral defamatory statement by the defendant, (b) of and concerning the plaintiff, (c) publication of the statement, (d) causing, (e) damages or harm to the plaintiff's reputation. See slander per se. If the statement is slander per se, the plaintiff does not have to prove special damages. **2.** To defame someone orally.

Slander of title A false and malicious oral or written statement made in disparagement of a person's title to real or personal property, or of some right that causes special damages.

Slander per se Slander in itself that does not require proof of special damages. Statements (a) accusing the plaintiff of a crime, (b) adversely affecting the plaintiff's trade, occupation, profession, or calling, (c) accusing the plaintiff of having an offensive or loathsome disease, or (d) accusing the plaintiff of unchastity.

Slavery The status of being totally subject to the power and control of another.

Sliding scale A payment schedule that varies according to another factor such as one's income.

Slip law A legislative enactment that is separately and promptly published in a pamphlet or single-sheet format after its passage.

Slip opinion An individual court opinion published separately soon after it is rendered.

Slot machine A gambling apparatus by which a person depositing money therein may, by chance, receive money or articles that are worth more or less than the money deposited.

Slowdown An organized effort by workers in a plant, by which production is slowed in order to bring pressure on the employer for better working conditions.

Slum A squalid, run-down section of a city, town, or village.

Slumlord The owner of deteriorating tenements in the slums.

Slush fund Money collected or spent for corrupt purposes.

Small Business Administration (SBA) A federal agency that assists small businesses by providing counseling, loans, help in obtaining government purchases or service contracts, etc.

Small-claims court A special court that provides expeditious, informal, and inexpensive adjudication of small claims.

Smart money Punitive damages; damages provided by way of punishment or example (e.g., for gross misconduct).

Smuggling Importing or exporting prohibited articles without paying the duties chargeable upon them.

Smut Obscene material.

Socage A species of tenure whereby the tenant held lands in consideration of certain inferior services of husbandry to be performed by him to the lord of the fee.

Social guest A person who goes on the property of another for companionship, diversion, and enjoyment of hospitality.

Social Security Administration (SSA) The Social Security Administration administers a national program of contributory social insurance whereby employees, employers, and the self-employed pay contributions which are pooled in special trust funds. When earnings stop or are reduced because the worker retires, dies, or becomes disabled, monthly cash benefits are paid to replace part of the earnings the person or family has lost. In addition to making social security payments, the SSA also administers cash assistance programs such as Aid to Families with Dependent Children (AFDC), and Supplementary Security Income (SSI).

Society 1. An association or company of persons united by mutual consent and acting jointly for a common purpose. **2.** The community at large.

Sodomy Oral or anal copulation between humans, or between humans and animals.

Soft currency A currency that is declining in value in relation to other currencies.

Soil bank A federal program of conservation under which farmers are paid for not growing crops, or for growing noncommercial vegetation in order to preserve the quality of the soil and to avoid surpluses.

Solatium Damages allowed for injury to feelings.

Soldier's will An informal, oral will that can dispose of the personal property of the testator.

Sole Individual or single.

Sole proprietorship A form of business in which one person owns all the assets.

Solicit 1. To appeal for something. **2.** To approach someone for sex.

Solicitation 1. The act of enticing, inviting, promoting, requesting, urging, or ordering someone to commit a crime. **2.** A request for something.

Solicitor 1. One who solicits. **2.** A lawyer for a city, town, or government agency. **3.** A British lawyer engaged in office work and litigation before some courts. For representation in other courts, particularly the higher courts, the solicitor refers the case to a barrister.

Solicitor General of the United States The lawyer in charge of representing the United States in the U.S. Supreme Court.

Solidary obligation In Louisiana, an obligation that binds each of the obligors for the whole debt, as distinguished from a "joint" obligation that binds the parties each for his or her separate proportion of the debt.

Solitary confinement The separate confinement of a prisoner, with little or no contact with other prisoners; complete isolation.

Solvent Able to pay debts as they mature.

Somnambulism Sleepwalking.

Sororicide The killing or murder of a sister.

Sound mind The faculties of perception and judgment are well-developed and not impaired by mental disorder. The ability to understand in a general way the nature and extent of the property to be disposed of, one's relationship to those who would naturally claim a substantial benefit from the will, and the practical effect of the will as executed.

Source 1. The person or thing that originates, sets in motion, or is the primary agency in producing a course of action or result. **2.** An informant.

Sovereign 1. Having supreme power. **2.** A person, body, or state in which independent and supreme authority is vested.

Sovereign immunity The sovereign (i.e., the state) cannot be sued without its consent.

Sovereignty The supreme and absolute power by which any independent state is governed;

supreme political authority; the power of self-government; the international independence of a state.

Speaker The president or chairperson of a legislative assembly (Speaker of the House).

Speaking demurrer A demurrer that is defective because it requires reference to facts that do not appear on the face of the pleading.

Special agent An agent delegated to do a single act.

Special appearance An appearance made in the litigation for the limited and sole purpose of testing the jurisdiction of the court.

Special assessment A special tax imposed on property, individual lots, or all property in the immediate area, for road construction, sidewalks, sewers, street lights, etc.

Special damages Damages that are peculiar to the particular plaintiff; damages that are the natural, but not the necessary, result of the injury complained of.

Special indorsement A special indorsement specifies the person to whom or to whose order it makes the instrument payable.

Special lien A lien that binds a specified piece of property, unlike a general lien, which is levied against all one's assets. It creates a right to retain something of value belonging to another person as compensation for labor, material, or money expended in that person's behalf. In some localities it is called "particular" lien or "specific" lien.

Specialist One who has extensively studied or has considerable experience in a particular area.

Special partner A member of a limited partnership, who furnishes certain funds, and whose liability extends no further than the funds furnished.

Specialty 1. An area or field that has been given special attention or study; a distinctive feature. **2.** A contract or obligation under seal. A writing that is sealed and delivered, containing an agreement. **3.** A structure that is uniquely adapted to the business conducted upon it and which cannot be converted to other uses without the expenditure of substantial sums of money.

Special verdict A jury's answers to specific factual questions.

Special warranty deed A deed in which the grantor conveys title to the grantee and agrees to protect the grantee against title defects or claims asserted by the grantor and by those persons whose right to assert a claim against the title arose during the period the grantor held title to the property. In a special warranty deed the grantor guarantees to the grantee that he or she has done nothing during the time he or she held title to the property which has, or which might in the future, impair the grantee's title.

Specie 1. Coined money; metallic money. **2.** Strictly, according to the exact terms. **3.** The thing itself; identity.

Species A type or category.

Specification A statement or listing of the particulars required or involved.

Specific bequest A testamentary gift of specific personal property that may be satisfied only by delivery of this particular property.

Specific performance The remedy of performance of a contract in the specific form in which it was made or according to the precise terms agreed upon. This remedy is granted when damages would be an inadequate compensation for a breach of the contract.

Specimen A part of something intended to exhibit the kind and quality of the whole.

Spectograph A machine used for voiceprint analysis.

Speculation 1. Buying or selling with the expectation of profiting by a rise or fall in price. **2.** Theorizing about a matter as to which the evidence is not sufficient for certain knowledge.

Speculative Based on conjecture or guessing.

Speculative damages Anticipated damages that are contingent, conjectural, or improbable.

Speech Talk, utterance, or oral expression.

Speedy trial A trial as soon as the prosecution can prepare for it with reasonable diligence. Factors considered: (a) length of the delay, (b) government's justification for the delay, (c) whether and how the defendant asserted the right to a speedy trial, and (d) prejudice caused by the delay.

Spendthrift One who spends money profusely and improvidently.

Spendthrift trust A trust created to provide a fund for the maintenance of a beneficiary, and at the same time to secure it against his or her improvidence by turning over only a certain portion of the total amount at any given time.

Spin-off A subsidiary organized by a parent corporation. Part of the assets of the parent is transferred to the subsidiary. The stock of the subsidiary is distributed to the shareholders of the parent without any surrender by them of their stock in the parent.

Spirit Underlying meaning or purpose.

Spite fence A fence of no beneficial use to the person

erecting it and maintained solely to annoy the occupant of adjoining land.

Split dollar insurance A type of insurance in which the insurer divides the premium dollar between life insurance protection and investment for the benefit of the insured.

Split income Allowing married couples to have their income taxed on a joint return at a rate equal to that which would apply if each spouse had one-half the amount and were taxed on a separate return.

Split-off A new corporation set up by a parent corporation. The shares of the new corporation go to the shareholders of the parent. In exchange, these shareholders surrender some of their stock in the parent corporation.

Split sentence A sentence that is active in part and suspended in part.

Splitting a cause of action Dividing a single or indivisible cause of action into several parts or claims and bringing several actions thereon; commencing an action for only part of the cause of action.

Split-up The process whereby a corporation divides into two or more separate new corporations, giving the shareholders the shares of these new corporations and then going out of business.

Spoliation The destruction of evidence; the destruction or meaningful alteration of a document.

Sponsions In international law, agreements or engagements made by certain public officers (e.g., generals or admirals in time of war) in behalf of their governments, either without authority or in excess of their authority.

Sponsor 1. One who makes a promise or gives security for another. **2.** To back or guarantee.

Spontaneous Arising on its own; unpremeditated.

Spontaneous declaration A spontaneous and unreflecting statement produced from a startling occurrence when there was no time to fabricate and the statement related to the circumstances of the occurrence.

Spontaneous exclamation A statement or exclamation made immediately after some exciting occurrence by a participant or spectator asserting the circumstances of the occurrence as observed by him or her.

Spot In commodity trading and in foreign exchange, immediate delivery in contrast to a future delivery.

Spot price The selling price of goods.

Spot zoning Granting a zoning classification to a piece of land that differs from that of the other land in the immediate area.

Spread 1. The difference between two amounts. **2.** To disperse or disseminate.

Sprinkling trust A trust that calls for distribution of income to various beneficiaries at different times.

Spurious Counterfeit or synthetic.

Spy 1. An undercover agent who attempts to obtain secrets from a rival. **2.** To watch or listen secretly.

Square 1. An open area surrounded by streets. **2.** An area measuring 24 x 24 miles.

Squat To settle.

Squatter One who settles on another's land without legal title or authority.

Squeeze-out A merger effected for no valid business purpose, resulting in the elimination of a minority shareholder.

Stacking Slang for using different kinds of steroids at the same time.

Stag To speculate in the stock market by oversubscribing to an issue, and selling as soon as possible to make a profit.

Stake 1. A deposit that shall be given to the one entitled to it upon the happening of a stated condition. **2.** A boundary marker used for land survey purposes.

Stakeholder A person who is or may be exposed to multiple liability as a result of adverse claims. One who holds assets in which he or she claims no interest and which are sought by rival claimants. A third party chosen by two or more persons to keep property or money on deposit and to deliver it to the one who eventually establishes the right to it.

Stale check A check that has been outstanding too long.

Stale claim or demand A claim or demand that has long remained unasserted.

Stamp A mark, design, or seal that indicates ownership or approval. An identifying or characterizing mark or impression.

Stamp tax The cost of stamps that must be affixed to legal documents such as deeds.

Stand 1. To remain in force (the award was allowed to stand). **2.** To submit to (stand trial).

Standard 1. A yardstick or point of reference. **2.** Customary.

Standard deduction A fixed deduction from taxable income, used by a taxpayer who does not wish to itemize deductions.

Standard of care That degree of care a reasonably prudent person should exercise under the same or similar circumstances. For professionals, the standard of care is the skill and learning commonly possessed by members of the profession in good standing, usually in the same or in a similar locality.

Standard of proof See beyond a reasonable doubt, preponderance of evidence, clear and convincing evidence.

Standing 1. As an aspect of justiciability, standing to sue is the legal right to set judicial machinery in motion. The requirement that a party in a lawsuit have sufficient personal interest in the outcome so that the case is fairly, fully, and vigorously litigated. **2.** One's place in the community in the estimation of others. **3.** Continuing or established.

Standing mute The defendant refuses to plead to the charge against him or her, usually resulting in the entry by the court of a plea of not guilty.

Standing orders Rules adopted by particular courts governing practice before them.

Starboard The right-hand side of a vessel when the observer faces forward.

Star Chamber An early English court that illegally extended its jurisdiction and acted secretly, arbitrarily, and harshly.

Stare decisis Similar cases should be decided in the same way unless there is good reason for a court to do otherwise. To abide by or adhere to decided cases.

Star page When reading a page from an opinion printed in an unofficial reporter, you may be told what the comparable page number is in the official reporter—by star paging.

State A body of people occupying a definite territory and organized under one government.

State action A sufficiently close involvement, sponsorship, interdependence, or nexus between the state and the challenged action so that the action may be fairly treated as that of the state itself.

Stated account An agreed balance between the parties to a settlement. They have agreed after an investigation of their accounts that a certain balance is due from one to the other.

Stated capital The amount of capital contributed by stockholders. The capital or equity of a corporation as it appears in the balance sheet.

Statement of account A report issued periodically by a bank or creditor to a customer, setting forth transactions, charges, payments, the balance due, etc.

Statement of confession Written authority of the debtor to enter a judgment against the debtor as stated therein. Also referred to as a "power of attorney," "cognovit note," or "confession of judgment."

State of mind A person's reasons and motives for acting or failing to act.

State's attorney An officer who represents the state in criminal cases.

State's evidence Testimony given by an accomplice or joint participant in the commission of a crime, which tends to incriminate the others.

State's rights A political philosophy favoring a limitation on federal power with corresponding increased autonomy for individual states.

Status crime or offense A crime or offense that consists not in proscribed action or inaction but in the accused's having a certain personal condition or being a person of a specified character.

Status quo The existing state of things at any given time. The present state of affairs, the existing condition, things as they were before the change.

Statute An act of the legislature declaring, commanding, or prohibiting something.

Statute of frauds No suit or action shall be maintained on certain classes of contracts or engagements unless there shall be a note or memorandum thereof in writing, signed by the party to be charged or by his or her authorized agent.

Statute of limitations No suit, action, or criminal prosecution shall be maintained unless brought within a specified period of time.

Statute of uses A statute that converted the purely equitable title of persons entitled to a use into a legal title or absolute ownership with the right of possession. The statute "executed" the use.

Statutes at Large An official compilation of the acts and resolutions of each session of Congress.

Statutory Relating to a statute; created or defined by a statute; conforming to a statute.

Statutory crime A crime created by statute.

Statutory rape The unlawful sexual intercourse with a female under the age of consent (e.g., 16). Her actual consent is not a defense to the crime.

Stay The suspension of a judicial proceeding or some phase of it by order of the court.

Stealing Taking the property of another without right; feloniously taking and carrying away the personal property of another with the intent to keep it.

Stealth Any secret, sly, or clandestine act.

Steering committee A committee that establishes or proposes an agenda for a larger body.

Step 1. Designates a relationship of affinity rather than blood. **2.** A grade or stage in a series.

Stepchild The child of one of the spouses by a former marriage.

Stepparent The "mother" or "father" of a child born during a previous marriage of the other parent and hence not the natural parent of such child.

Sterile 1. Incapable of reproducing. **2.** Unproductive or ineffective. **3.** Free from germs or bacteria.

Sterilization 1. The act or process by which one is rendered incapable of procreation (e.g., by tying the female Fallopian tubes, a vasectomy, castration). **2.** The act or process by which an article or instrument is rendered free of germs.

Steward 1. One who represents another. **2.** See shop steward.

Still A device used for separating alcoholic spirits from fermented substances.

Stillborn child A child born dead or in such an early stage of pregnancy as to be incapable of living.

Stipend A salary; fixed or settled pay.

Stipital "Stipital distribution" of property is distribution per stirpes; that is, by right of representation.

Stipulate To arrange or settle definitely.

Stipulation 1. A voluntary agreement between opposing counsel concerning the disposition of some relevant matter so that evidence on the matter does not have to be introduced at the trial. **2.** A requirement or prerequisite.

Stirpes The person from whom a family is descended; stock; a source of descent or title. See per stirpes.

Stock 1. An equity representing an ownership interest in a corporation; the capital or principal fund of a corporation formed by the contributions of subscribers or the sale of shares; all the wealth and resources of a corporation. **2.** The goods or wares of a merchant kept for sale; the entire property used in business. **3.** To supply.

Stockbroker One who buys or sells stock as the agent of another.

Stock dividend One paid in stock, that is, not in money, but in a proportional number of shares of the capital stock of the company.

Stock exchange The place at which shares of stock are bought and sold.

Stockholder A person who owns shares of stock in a corporation or joint-stock company.

Stockholder's derivative action See derivative action.

Stockholder's equity A stockholder's proportionate share in the corporation's capital stock and surplus.

Stock insurance company An insurance company whose shares are held by the public and which pays dividends, in contrast with a mutual insurance company, whose assets are owned by policyholders who receive dividends when available.

Stock in trade The inventory carried by a retail business for sale in the ordinary course of business. The tools and equipment owned and used by a tradesman.

Stockjobbing The buying and selling of stocks based on speculation.

Stock market An organized market or exchange where shares (stock) are traded (e.g., New York Stock Exchange).

Stock option The right to purchase a specified number of shares of stock at a specified price at specified times.

Stock redemption A partial or complete liquidation of corporate stock by the corporation. It generally consists of the purchase by the corporation of its own stock.

Stock rights The privilege to subscribe to new stock issues or to purchase stock.

Stock split One share is split into a larger number of shares. A reverse split or a split-down occurs when a number of shares are combined to form a smaller number of shares.

Stock swap In corporate reorganization, an exchange of stock in one corporation for the stock of another corporation.

Stock warrant A certificate evidencing the right to buy shares of stock, commonly attached to preferred stock and bonds.

Stop and frisk The temporary seizure and "patting down" of a person who behaves suspiciously and appears to be armed.

Stop-loss order An order given to a stockbroker to buy or sell certain securities when the market reaches a particular price.

Stop-payment order An order by the drawer of a draft (check) ordering the drawee not to make payment on it.

Storage Safekeeping of goods in a warehouse or other depository.

Stowage In maritime law, the storing, packing, or arranging of the cargo in a ship, in such a manner as to protect the goods from friction, bruising, or damage from leakage.

Straddle Having an option to purchase or sell; the privilege of both a "put" and a "call" on the same commodity at the same time.

Straight bill of lading One in which it is stated that goods are consigned to a specified person.

Straight-line depreciation The cost or other basis of the asset, less its estimated salvage value, if any, is determined first. Then this amount is distributed in equal amounts over the period of the estimated useful life of the asset.

Stratagem A dishonest scheme either by words or by action.

Stratocracy A military government.

Straw man A "front"; a nominal party; one who lends his or her name only to a transaction; a fictitious or bogus argument.

Stream A watercourse having banks and channels through which waters flow at least periodically.

Strict 1. Determined or governed by exact rules. **2.** Authoritarian.

Strict construction A close and rigid reading and interpretation of the law. A refusal to expand the law by implication. When there is doubt about whether the law should be read broadly or narrowly, the latter is generally preferred. When there is doubt as to whether language is more inclusive or less inclusive, the latter is generally preferred.

Strict foreclosure If the amount due under a mortgage is not paid within a certain time, title to the property vests absolutely in the mortgagee without any equity of redemption or sale of the property.

Strict liability See absolute liability.

Strict liability in tort Elements of this tort: (a) A seller or person engaged in the business of selling products for use or consumption, (b) a defective product that is unreasonably dangerous to person or property, (c) causes, (d) harm, (e) to a user or consumer. Some courts have extended the last element to include bystanders.

Strike The act of quitting or leaving work by a body of workers for the purpose of coercing the employer to accede to some demand that the workers have made, which has been rejected by the employer.

Strike off Signifying to a bidder at auction that the bid has been accepted.

Strike suit A shareholder derivative action begun with the hope of winning large attorney fees or private settlements, and with no intention of benefiting the corporation on behalf of which the suit is theoretically brought.

Structured settlement The resolution of a dispute (in lieu of litigation) whereby a series of future payments will be made in place of the more traditional lump-sum payment now.

Strumpet A whore.

Stultify To allege or prove one is insane and not legally responsible.

Stumpage The price paid for a license to cut and remove trees.

Suable Capable of being or liable to be sued.

Sua sponte On one's own motion; without prompting or suggestion; voluntarily.

Subagent An agent appointed by an agent; a substituted agent.

Subaltern 1. An inferior or subordinate officer. **2.** Subordinate.

Subchapter S corporation A small business corporation permitted to be taxed as if it were an individual proprietorship.

Subcontract A contract made under a prior contract. A subordinate contract made between one or more of the original contracting parties and a third party called the subcontractor.

Subcontractor One who takes a portion of a contract from the principal contractor or from another subcontractor. One who agrees with the contractor to perform part of the work that the contractor previously agreed to perform for another.

Subdivide To split a part into smaller parts.

Subdivision 1. The act of dividing into smaller parts. **2.** One of the parts that has been so divided. **3.** A type or category.

Subirrigate To irrigate below the surface.

Subjacent Underlying; located below or underneath; at a lower level but not directly beneath.

Subjacent support The right of land to be supported by the land that lies beneath it, distinguished from lateral or side support.

Subject 1. One who owes allegiance to a nation and is governed by its laws. **2.** The theme or topic acted upon. **3.** The recipient. **4.** To subjugate or dominate. **5.** To undergo. **6.** Susceptible. **7.** Conditioned.

Subjection Being under the dominion of another; domination by another.

Subject matter That which is presented for consideration; the thing in dispute.

Subject matter jurisdiction The court's power or competence to hear and determine this particular kind of case; judicial power over the nature of the action and the relief sought.

Sub judice Under judicial consideration; undetermined; before a court.

Sublease The grant by the tenant of an interest in the leased premises that is less than his or her own interest, or that reserves a reversionary interest.

Subletting A leasing by the lessee of a whole or a part of the premises during a portion of the unexpired balance of his or her term.

Submergence The disappearance of land under water and the formation of a more or less navigable body over it.

Submission 1. A yielding to authority. **2.** Offering something for consideration.

Submission bond The bond by which the parties agree to submit their matters to binding arbitration.

Submit 1. To commit to the discretion of another; to present for determination. **2.** Yield, acquiesce, defer.

Sub nomine Under the name; in the name of; under the title of.

Subordinate 1. One who works under or is dependent on another. **2.** Collateral, subservient, lesser.

Subordinated bonds or debentures Bonds or debentures with a lower priority in liquidation than other (senior) debt of a corporation. Such bonds or debentures are usually not subordinate to general creditors but only to debt owed to a financial institution.

Subordination The act or process by which a person's rights are ranked below the rights of others.

Subordination agreement An agreement by which the subordinating party agrees that its interests in property have a lower priority than the interest to which it is being subordinated.

Suborn To prepare, provide, or procure, usually in a secret or underhanded manner; to procure another to commit perjury; to procure another to commit a crime.

Subornation of perjury Procuring another to take a false oath that would be perjury.

Subpoena 1. A command to appear. **2.** To command one's presence.

Subpoena ad testificandum A subpoena to testify.

Subpoena duces tecum A process by which the court compels the production of documents or chattels.

Subrogation The substitution of a third party in place of the party having the claim, demand, or right against another party.

Subrogee The person who succeeds to the rights of another through subrogation; the one who is subrogated.

Sub rosa Secret; not for publication.

Subscribe 1. To sign at the end; to attest. **2.** To agree to purchase; to agree to pay. **3.** To support or lend approval.

Subscribed capital The total amount of stock or capital for which there are contracts of purchase or subscriptions.

Subscribed stock A stockholder's equity account showing the capital that will be contributed as the subscription price is collected.

Subscriber 1. One who writes his or her name on a document to authenticate or attest it, or to bind himself or herself by it. **2.** One who has agreed to purchase securities of a corporation, either bonds or stocks.

Subscribing witness One who witnesses or attests the signature of a party to a document, and in testimony thereof signs his or her own name to the document.

Subscription The act of writing one's name under a written instrument; affixing one's signature to any document.

Subscription rights The rights of existing stockholders to purchase additional stock, usually at a price under market and in an amount proportionate to their existing holdings.

Subsequent condition See condition subsequent.

Subservant The servant or agent of another servant or agent.

Subsidiary 1. Under another's control. **2.** A branch, division, or affiliate.

Subsidiary corporation One in which another corporation, the parent, owns at least a majority of the shares and thus has control.

Subsidize To support.

Subsidy A government grant to support a program or project that benefits the public.

Sub silentio Under silence; silently; without any notice being taken.

Subsistence 1. Means of support. **2.** Something that has real existence.

Substance 1. The material or essential part of a thing. **2.** Affluence or wealth. **3.** Element, ingredient, or matter. **4.** Reality.

Substantial 1. Actually existing; not seeming or imaginary; not elusive. **2.** Abundant. **3.** Strong.

Substantial compliance Compliance with the essential requirements.

Substantial damages Considerable in amount and intended as real compensation for a real injury.

Substantial evidence Such evidence that a reasonable mind might accept as adequate to support a conclusion.

Substantially Without material qualifications.

Substantial performance Honestly and faithfully performing the material and essential particulars, omitting technical and unimportant matters.

Substantiate To establish the existence or truth of something by true and competent evidence.

Substantive 1. Real, substantial, meritorious. **2.** Fundamental, essential.

Substantive due process Protection from arbitrary and unreasonable action.

Substantive evidence Evidence presented for the purpose of proving a fact in issue, as opposed to evidence that seeks to discredit or impeach a witness, or to corroborate the testimony of a witness.

Substantive law Law that creates, defines, and regulates rights, as opposed to adjective, procedural, or remedial law that provides a method of enforcing rights.

Substitute 1. To put in the place of another person or thing. **2.** One who stands in the place of another.

Substituted basis The basis of the value of an asset determined by reference to the basis in the hands of a transferor, donor, grantor, or by reference to other property held at any time by the person for whom the basis is to be determined.

Substituted service Service of process on the defendant in a manner other than personal service within the jurisdiction (e.g., by publication, by mail, by personal service in another state, etc.).

Substitution Serving in lieu of another; putting in place of.

Substitutional, substitutionary Pertaining to a clause in a will that provides for someone to take a gift in the event of the death of the original beneficiary before the period of disposition.

Subtenant One who leases all or part of the rented premises from the original lessee for a term less than that held by the latter.

Subterfuge A device for escape or concealment.

Subterranean 1. Existing beneath the surface of the earth. **2.** Clandestine, hidden.

Subversion 1. The act of overthrowing. **2.** Sabotage or disruption.

Subversive Pertaining to the overthrow of the government.

Succession 1. The devolution of title to property under the law of descent and distribution. The acquisition of rights upon the death of another. Persons who take by will or inheritance, as opposed to those who take by deed, grant, gift, purchase, or contract. **2.** Series or sequence. **3.** Promotion or induction.

Succession duty or tax See inheritance tax.

Successive Following one after another in a line or series.

Successor One who takes the place of another who has left; one who follows another by succession; another corporation which, through amalgamation, consolidation, or other legal succession, becomes invested with rights, and assumes the burdens of the first corporation.

Successor in interest One who follows another in ownership or control of property.

Successors Those persons, other than creditors, who are entitled to property of a decedent under a will or the probate code.

Successor trustee A trustee who follows or succeeds an earlier trustee.

Sudden emergency doctrine See emergency doctrine.

Sue To commence or continue legal proceedings; to proceed with an action.

Suffer 1. To feel pain. **2.** To allow or admit. **3.** To endure. **4.** To deteriorate.

Sufferance Negative authorization by not forbidding.

Suffering Anguish, anxiety, pain.

Sufficiency An adequate quality or quantity.

Sufficiency of the evidence Evidence that affords a substantial basis from which the fact in issue can reasonably be inferred; evidence that would warrant the conclusion reached; evidence that is substantial; some admissible evidence on each element that a reasonable jury could accept.

Sufficient Adequate, enough, as much as may be needed.

Sufficient cause 1. Reasonable or probable cause or that state of facts as would lead a person of ordinary caution to conscientiously entertain strong suspicion of the defendant's guilt. **2.** Legal cause; a reason of a substantial nature specifically relating to and affecting the administration of an office and the performance of one's duties.

Suffrage The right to vote.

Suicide The deliberate termination of one's life.

Sui generis Of its own kind or class; peculiar.

Sui juris In one's own right; not under any legal disability or guardianship.

Suit A lawsuit.

Suitable Fit and acceptable for the end in view.

Suitor One who sues, a litigant.

Summarily Without ceremony or delay.

Summary judgment, Motion for A request that the court conclude that there is no genuine issue as to any material fact and that a judgment be rendered without the need for a trial.

Summary jurisdiction The jurisdiction of a court to give a judgment or to make an order itself forthwith (e.g., to commit to prison for contempt). The power of a court to act promptly without having to comply with all the procedural requirements that govern regular proceedings.

Summation A summary or recapitulation of the evidence that a party (or its attorney) believes has been established or not established during the trial.

Summon To notify a defendant to appear in court and answer the case brought against him or her.

Summons A document used to commence a civil action or special proceeding, commanding a person to appear in order to answer the complaint or charge brought against him or her.

Sunday closing laws See blue laws.

Sunset law A statute that requires administrative bodies to justify their existence to the legislature periodically.

Sunshine law A law that requires open meetings of governmental agencies.

Superior 1. One who holds a higher rank with the power to command. **2.** Belonging to a higher grade.

Superior force In the law of bailments and of negligence, an uncontrollable and irresistible force, of human agency, producing results the person in question could not avoid.

Supersede To take the position of; to suspend or render unnecessary.

Supersedeas A writ containing a command to stay the proceedings at law; a suspension of a judgment's effectiveness.

Supersedeas bond A bond required of one who petitions to set aside a judgment or execution. If the action is unsuccessful, the other party may be made whole from the bond.

Superseding Replacing.

Superseding cause The act of a third person or other force that by its intervention prevents the actor from being liable for the harm or injury that the actor's antecedent conduct was a substantial factor in bringing about. An intervening cause that is so extraordinary that the defendant could not have reasonably anticipated that the cause would intervene.

Supervening cause A new effective cause which, operating independently of anything else, becomes the proximate cause of the accident.

Supervening negligence See last clear chance doctrine.

Supplemental Pertaining to that which is added.

Supplemental act A statute designed to improve an existing statute by adding something without changing the original text.

Supplemental pleading A new pleading containing facts that have arisen since the filing of the last pleading.

Supplementary proceedings New proceedings to help collect the judgment debt after an execution on the judgment has been issued (e.g., discovery of the judgment debtor's property from which to satisfy the judgment).

Supplicant One who makes a request; an aspirant.

Supplier One engaged in the business of making products available to consumers; all persons in the chain of production and distribution of a consumer product.

Support 1. To provide a means of livelihood; to subsidize. **2.** To champion, promote, or affirm. **3.** The means of livelihood. **4.** Verification.

Supposition A conjecture based upon the possibility or probability that a thing could or may have occurred, without proof that it did occur.

Suppress To put a stop to a thing actually existing; to keep something from being used.

Suppression hearing A pretrial proceeding in a criminal case, in which the defendant seeks to prevent the introduction of evidence alleged to have been seized illegally.

Supra Above; ante.

Supremacy The state of being in the highest position of power.

Supremacy Clause Federal laws made in pursuance of the U.S. Constitution, and treaties made under the authority of the United States have superiority over any conflicting provision of a state constitution or law.

Supreme Court An appellate court. In most states and in the federal judicial system, it is the highest court or court of last resort. In New York, it is a trial court with some appellate jurisdiction.

Supreme Court of Errors The former name of the highest appellate court in Connecticut.

Surcharge 1. The imposition of an additional tax, impost, or cost. Extra fee, penalty, burden. **2.** The imposition of personal liability on a fiduciary for willful or negligent misconduct in the administration of his or her fiduciary duties.

Surety One who promises to answer for the debt, default, or miscarriage of another; one who undertakes to pay money or to do any other act in the event that his or her principal fails to do so.

Surety bond Obligation of a guarantor to pay a second party upon default by a third party in the performance the third party owes to the second party.

Suretyship contract See surety, surety bond.

Surface waters Waters that diffuse over the surface of the ground, following no defined course or channel, and not gathering into or forming any more definite body of water than a mere bog or marsh.

Surgeon One whose profession or occupation is to cure diseases, defects, or injuries of the body by manual operation; one who specializes in surgery.

Surgeon General The chief medical officer of the U.S. Public Health Service.

Surgery The branch of medical science that uses mechanical or operative measures for healing diseases, deformities, or injuries; treatment by removal or repair of parts of the body.

Surmise 1. Conjecture; an idea based on weak evidence. **2.** To infer or guess.

Surname The family name.

Surplus That which remains of a fund appropriated for a particular purpose.

Surplusage Extraneous, impertinent, superfluous, or unnecessary matter.

Surrender 1. To give back or repudiate. **2.** To give in or capitulate. **3.** The act of giving up.

Surrogate 1. The judge or judicial officer with jurisdiction over probate, guardianship, etc. **2.** One who substitutes for another. **3.** Alternate.

Surrogate mother A woman who is artificially inseminated with the semen of a man who is not her husband, and who surrenders the baby at birth to the father and his wife.

Surrogate parent A nonparent who voluntarily assumes parental rights and responsibilities and hence stands in loco parentis to the child.

Surtax An additional tax on top of what has already been taxed. A tax on a tax.

Surveillance Observation, oversight.

Survey 1. To scrutinize or examine. **2.** To tabulate or poll. **3.** A map or plat made by a surveyor showing the results of measuring the land with its elevations, improvements, boundaries, and its relationship to surrounding tracts of land. A survey is often required by the lender to assure it that a building is actually on the land according to its legal description.

Surveyor One who makes surveys, determines the area of portions of the earth's surface, the length and direction of boundary lines, the contour of the surface.

Survival Continuation of life or existence.

Survival action An action or cause of action that does not become extinguished with the death of the injured party.

Survivorship 1. Living after another has died. **2.** Becoming entitled to property by reason of surviving the death of one of the joint tenants.

Susceptible Capable of experiencing something; easily stirred.

Suspect 1. A person who is believed to have committed a crime. **2.** To have a slight or vague idea of something. **3.** To be skeptical. **4.** Open to suspicion.

Suspect classification A classification based on race, religion, alienage, national origin, or sex.

Suspend 1. To cause to cease for a time; to hold in abeyance. **2.** To remove or displace for a time. **3.** To invalidate.

Suspended Postponed; temporarily inoperative; held in abeyance.

Suspended sentence A sentence that is formally given but not actually served at the time imposed.

Suspension 1. A temporary stop or delay. **2.** A disbarment or dismissal.

Suspensive condition A condition that depends either on a future or uncertain event or on an event that has actually taken place without its being yet known to the parties.

Suspicion A belief or opinion based upon facts or circumstances that do not amount to proof.

Sustain 1. To affirm. **2.** To support, to keep alive or nourish. **3.** To endure.

Swatch A small sample of cloth from which suits, etc., are to be ordered.

Swear To take or administer an oath.

Sweat equity Equity created through the labor of the owner in making improvements to his or her property.

Sweating Questioning an accused through harassment or threats.

Sweepstakes In horse racing, the sum of the stakes for which the subscribers agree to pay for each horse nominated.

Sweetheart contract A contract between a union and an employer, in which concessions are granted to one or the other for the purpose of keeping a rival union out.

Swindle To cheat and defraud with deliberate artifice; to exploit or victimize.

Swindler One who defrauds others.

Syllabus A brief statement summarizing the rulings of a court opinion.

Syllogism The full, logical form of a single argument consisting of two premises and the conclusion.

Symbol That which stands for something else.

Symbolic delivery The constructive delivery of the cumbersome or inaccessible subject matter of a sale or gift by the actual delivery of an article that is conventionally accepted as representative of the subject matter, or which renders access to it possible, or which is evidence of the purchaser's or donee's title to it.

Symbolic speech Conduct that expresses opinions or thoughts about a subject; actions that have as their primary purpose the expression of ideas (e.g., burning the U.S. flag).

Sympathetic 1. Approving. **2.** Compassionate.

Sympathetic strike A strike designed to show support for another strike by different employees.

Syndicalism The theory, plan, or practice of trade-union action that aims, by general strike and direct action, to establish control over the means and processes of production by local worker organizations. See criminal syndicalism.

Syndicate A grouping or organization of individuals formed for the purpose of conducting and carrying out some particular business transaction; a group of investment brokers who together underwrite and distribute securities.

Syndication The act or process of forming a syndicate.

Table 1. To suspend consideration of a pending matter. **2.** A listing or graph.

Table of cases An alphabetical list of opinions that will be covered or referred to in the body of the text.

Tacit Inferred or understood without being openly expressed or stated; inferred by silence.

Tack To annex some junior lien to a first lien, thereby acquiring priority over an intermediate one.

Tacking The process of obtaining title to land by adverse possession: The adverse possessor adds his or her period of possession to that of a prior adverse possessor in order to establish a continuous possession for the statutory period; joining or combining in order to avoid a bar or to fulfill a requirement.

Tail Limited, curtailed, or abridged (e.g., to a certain order of succession or to certain heirs). See fee tail.

Tail female When lands are given to a person and the female heirs of his or her body. The male heirs are not capable of inheriting it.

Tail male When lands are given to a person and the male heirs of his or her body. The female heirs are not capable of inheriting it.

Take effect To go into operation; to become operative or executed; to be in force.

Take over To assume control or management.

Taking Gaining possession; laying hold of something with or without removing it.

Talesman A person summoned to act as a juror from among the bystanders in the court.

Talmud A work that embodies the civil and canonical law of the Jewish people.

Tamper To meddle so as to change something, usually with illegal or unauthorized results.

Tampering with the jury See embracery.

Tandem One behind another.

Tangible Having or possessing physical form.

Tangible evidence Evidence consisting of something that can be seen or touched.

Tangible property Corporeal property; property that can be felt or touched.

Tapping The interception of a telephonic or telegraphic message by connecting a device to the lines that permits a person to overhear the message.

Tare An allowance or deduction for the weight of the carton, box, bag, or other container.

Tariff The custom or duty paid on articles imported into the United States; a list or schedule of articles subject to such a custom or duty.

Tautology Describing the same thing twice in one sentence in equivalent terms.

Tax 1. A pecuniary burden imposed on individuals, businesses, or property to support the government. **2.** To place a burden on.

Taxable Subject to taxation; liable to be assessed.

Taxable estate The gross estate of a decedent reduced by allowable deductions.

Taxable income The gross income of a business or the adjusted gross income of an individual minus deductions and exemptions.

Taxable year The calendar year or the fiscal year upon which net taxable income is computed; the annual accounting period of the taxpayer.

Tax audit An examination of books, vouchers, and records of a taxpayer conducted by agents of the Internal Revenue Service.

Tax avoidance The minimization of one's tax liability by taking advantage of legally available tax-planning opportunities.

Tax benefit rule If an amount deducted from gross income in one taxable year is recovered in a later year, the recovery is income in the later year.

Tax certificate An instrument issued to the buyer of property at a tax sale, which entitles the holder to the property thus purchased if it is not redeemed within the period provided by law.

Tax credit A subtraction from the taxes owed or paid.

Tax deduction A subtraction from revenues and gains to arrive at taxable income.

Tax deed Proof of ownership of land given to the purchaser by the government after the latter has taken the land from another person and has sold it for failure to pay taxes.

Tax evasion Illegally paying less taxes than the law permits.

Tax exemption Immunity from the obligation of paying taxes in whole or in part.

Tax lien A lien on real estate in favor of the government, which may be foreclosed for non-payment of taxes.

Tax roll The official record maintained by cities and towns listing the names of taxpayers and the assessed property.

Tax sale The sale of property for nonpayment of taxes.

Tax shelter A device used by taxpayers to reduce or to defer the payment of taxes.

Teamster A truck driver.

Technical error An error that has not prejudiced the complaining party and hence is not a ground for reversal.

Technicality A narrow or fine point; a matter of form or procedure; something that does not go to the heart or substance of the case.

Telegraph To send a message by means of a system using electrical impulses.

Teller One who receives and pays out money; one who counts.

Temporary Lasting for a limited time.

Temporary alimony An interim order of payment to a spouse pending the final outcome of the action for divorce.

Temporary disability A disability that lasts for a limited time while the worker is undergoing treatment; the healing period during which the claimant is totally or partially unable to work due to injury, which continues as long as recovery or last-ing improvement of the injured person's condition can reasonably be expected.

Temporary injunction A preliminary or provisional injunction; an injunction granted pendente lite.

Temporary restraining order (TRO) An emergency remedy of brief duration maintaining the status quo pending a hearing on the application for an injunction.

Tenancy 1. The interest in real property in one who holds it for temporary use and occupation; control and possession or occupancy of land under a lease. **2.** A form of ownership. See joint tenancy, tenancy by the entirety, tenancy in common.

Tenancy by the entirety A tenancy that is created between a husband and wife by which they together hold title to the whole property with the right of survivorship so that when one dies, the other takes the whole property to the exclusion of the heirs of the deceased. A joint tenancy between husband and wife.

Tenancy in common A form of ownership whereby each tenant (i.e., owner) holds an undivided interest in the property. Each tenant in common has a right to possession of the property, but the share in the property may not be equal. There is no right of survivorship. When one dies, his or her share passes to his or her heirs and not to the other tenant(s) in common (unless the latter happen to be heirs).

Tenant 1. One who pays rent to possess or hold another's property for temporary use and occupation (landlord-tenant relationship). **2.** One who has an ownership interest in land (tenant in common).

Tenant at sufferance One who after rightfully being in possession of leased premises continues after his or her right has terminated.

Tenant at will One who holds possession of premises by permission of the owner or landlord but without a fixed term.

Tenant by the entirety See tenancy by the entirety.

Tenant from year to year 1. A tenant paying an annual rent but without an agreed-upon time or term for the tenancy. **2.** A tenant who holds over by express or constructive consent of the landlord after the expiration of a term for years.

Tenant in common See tenancy in common.

Tender 1. To offer payment or other performance. **2.** That which is offered.

Tender offer A take-over bid. An offer to purchase shares made by one company direct to the stockholders of another company.

Tender years doctrine In custody disputes, some courts will award custody of very young children to the mother unless she is unfit.

Tenement 1. An apartment building. **2.** Everything that may be holden of a permanent nature.

Tenet 1. A doctrine or principle. **2.** He holds.

Tennessee Valley Authority (TVA) A government-owned corporation that conducts a program of resource development for the advancement of economic growth in the Tennessee Valley region. Its activities include flood control, navigation development, electric power development, etc.

Tentative 1. Provisional or experimental. **2.** Manifesting uncertainty or hesitancy.

Tentative trust See totten trust.

Tenure A status give a teacher upon completing a trial period, protecting him or her from summary dismissal. A right, term, or mode of holding or occupying something. The manner in which an office is held, especially as to time.

Term 1. A fixed period. **2.** A phrase or expression. **3.** A proviso, specification, or detail. **4.** To designate or label.

Terminable Capable of being terminated; ending upon the occurrence of a specified event.

Terminer To determine.

Term insurance A form of pure life insurance having no cash surrender value and generally furnishing insurance protection for only a specified or limited period of time, though it is usually renewable from term to term.

Terminus A limit either of space or time.

Term of art The vocabulary or terminology of a particular art or science. Words or phrases that have a special or technical meaning.

Termor One who holds lands or tenements for a term of years or life.

Terra Earth, soil, arable land.

Terra transit cum onere Land passes with the encumbrances.

Terrazzo Marble or stone flooring.

Terre-tenant One who is actually in possession of the land, as distinguished from an owner out of possession.

Territorial Having to do with a particular area or land.

Territorial jurisdiction The territory over which a government or a subdivision thereof has jurisdiction.

Territory 1. A part of a country. **2.** A portion of the United States not within the limits of any state, which has its own branches of government but has not yet been admitted as a state. **3.** A geographical area under the jurisdiction of another country or sovereign power.

Terror Apprehension of harm from some hostile or threatening event or manifestation.

Terrorist One who uses systematic violence, intimidation, or intense fear to obtain his or her goals.

Testable A person with the capacity to make a will.

Testacy The state or condition of leaving a valid will at one's death.

Testament 1. A statement of principle. **2.** A covenant or agreement. **3.** A document that diposes personal property at death.

Testamentary Pertaining to a will.

Testamentary capacity The mental ability that must be present in order to make a will: Your mind and memory must be such that you know in a general way the character and extent of your property, you understand your relationship to the objects of your bounty and those who ought to be on your mind on the occasion of making the will, and you understand the nature and effect of the testamentary act.

Testamentary disposition A disposition of property by way of gift, will, or deed, which is not to take effect unless the grantor dies or until that event.

Testamentary guardian A guardian appointed by the last will of a parent for the person and estate of a child until the latter becomes an adult.

Testamentary power A power of appointment that can only be exercised through a will (i.e., upon the death of the holder).

Testamentary trust A trust that is to take effect at the death of the settlor.

Testate 1. One who has died leaving a valid will. **2.** Having made a valid will.

Testation Witness; evidence.

Testator One who has died leaving a valid will.

Testatrix A female testator.

Testify To give evidence as a witness; to make a solemn declaration under oath.

Testimonial 1. In the nature of testimony; elicited from a witness. **2.** A statement of one's qualities; a recommendation.

Testimonial evidence Evidence elicited from a witness.

Testimonium clause In conveyancing, the concluding clause of a deed or instrument: "In witness whereof, the parties to these presents have hereunto set their hands and seals." A clause in the instrument reciting the date on which the instrument was executed and by whom.

Testimony Evidence given by a competent witness under oath or affirmation.

Test oath An oath taken by a person to fill a public office, particularly an oath of fidelity to the established government.

Test-paper A paper or instrument shown to a jury as evidence.

Test-tube baby A baby conceived outside the womb.

Theft The taking of property without the owner's consent. See larceny.

Theft of services Obtaining services from another by deception, threat, coercion, stealth, mechanical tampering, or the use of a false token or device.

Theocracy Government of a state by the assumed direction of a divinity.

Theory An explanation; systematic ideas or knowledge that explains facts.

Thief One who commits larceny or theft.

Thin capitalization When the debt owed by a corporation is large in relationship to its capital structure, the corporation may be seen as thinly capitalized.

Thing in action A right to recover money or other personal property by a judicial proceeding.

Third degree Securing information from a suspect by prolonged questioning, the use of threats, actual violence, etc.

Third-degree instruction See Allen charge.

Third-party beneficiary One for whose benefit a contract is made but who is not a party to the contract.

Third-party complaint A complaint filed by the defendant against someone who is not presently a party to the lawsuit.

Third-party practice A procedural device whereby the defendant may bring in additional parties.

Threat 1. A communicated intent to inflict harm; a declaration of intent to injure another. **2.** A risk or menace.

Threaten 1. To warn or terrorize. **2.** To be imminent.

Through bill of lading A bill of lading used when more than one carrier is required for shipping.

Through lot A lot that abuts upon a street at each end.

Throwback rule In a trust, the amount distributed in any tax year that is in excess of that year's distributable net income must be "thrown back" to the preceding year and treated as if it had then been distributed.

Ticket A paper entitling the holder to a right or privilege; a pass, voucher, or coupon.

Tideland The land between the lines of the ordinary high and low tides, covered and uncovered by the ebb and flow thereof.

Tidewater Water that falls and rises with the ebb and flow of the tide.

Tie 1. To fasten, secure, or bind. **2.** To restrict or restrain. **3.** A bond or connection. **4.** Each with the same number.

Tie-in arrangement The vendor will sell one product only on the condition that the buyer will also purchase another and different product.

Tillage Land under cultivation.

Time bill A bill of exchange that contains a definite or determinable date for payment, in contrast to a demand or sight bill.

Time draft One payable a certain number of days after sight or after presentation for acceptance.

Time immemorial An ancient time; time before legal records; time beyond memory; time long past.

Time is of the essence The failure to do what is required by the time specified is a breach of the contract.

Time note A note payable at a definite future time, as contrasted with a demand note.

Time-sharing Joint lease or ownership of property that is used individually for designated periods of time.

Tithe A tenth part of one's income contributed for charitable or religious purposes.

Title 1. The means whereby the owner of land has the just possession of his or her property. The union of all the elements that constitute ownership. The evidence of one's ownership interest in property. **2.** A unit or part of a statute, usually one of its major subdivisions. **3.** To label something. **4.** A designation by which something is known. **5.** One's position or status.

Title insurance Insurance against loss or damage resulting from defects in the title to land, or from the enforcement of liens existing against it at the time of the insurance. Title insurance may be issued to either the mortgagor, as an "owner's title policy," or to the mortgagee, as a "mortgagee's title policy."

Title retention A form of lien, in the nature of a chattel mortgage, to secure the purchase price.

Title search A check of the title records, generally at the local courthouse, to make sure the buyer is purchasing a house from the legal owner and that there are no liens, overdue special assessments, or other claims or outstanding restrictive convenants filed in the record, which would adversely affect the marketability or value of title.

To have and to hold The words in a conveyance that show the estate intended to be conveyed.

Token 1. See mark, badge. **2.** Superficial.

Toll 1. A sum of money paid for the use of something. **2.** To suspend or stop temporarily. **3.** Disruption.

Ton A measure of weight. In the United States, it is fixed at 2,000 pounds avoirdupois.

Ton mile In transportation, the measure equal to the transportation of one ton of freight one mile.

Tonnage The capacity of a vessel for carrying freight, calculated in tons.

Tontine A financial arrangement whereby the participants share in a fund, with each participant's share increasing upon the death or default of another until the final survivor receives everything.

Torpedo doctrine See attractive nuisance doctrine.

Torrens title system A system for registration of land under which, upon the landowner's application, a court issues a certificate of title that states the status of the title.

Tort A civil (as opposed to criminal) wrong (other than a breach of contract) that has caused harm to person or property.

Tortfeasor A person who has committed a tort.

Tortious Pertaining to an act that will subject the actor to tort liability.

Torture To inflict intense pain in order to punish, to extract information, or to derive sadistic pleasure.

Torturous Causing severe abuse or cruelty; excruciating.

Total disability A disability, whether temporary or permanent, that prevents the employee from doing the substantial and material acts required in his or her usual occupation.

Toties quoties As often as the occasion shall arise.

Totten trust A tentative trust during the grantor's lifetime, revocable at will. A deposit of a person's own money in his or her own name as trustee for another.

Tourniquet A device to control the flow of blood.

Towage 1. The towing of vehicles. **2.** The fee charged for towing.

To wit That is to say, namely.

Town A civil and political division of a state, usually part of a county.

Toxic Poisonous.

Toxicology The science of poisons.

Toxin Any diffusible alkaloidal substance; the poisonous products of pathogenic bacteria.

Trace 1. To make a copy or facsimile of an original by following its lines through a transparent medium. **2.** To follow. **3.** Clue, evidence.

Tract 1. A relatively large piece of land. **2.** A pamphlet.

Trade 1. Buying and selling for profit. **2.** What one does for a living; a job requiring manual skills. **3.** Exchange, barter.

Trade acceptance A draft drawn by a seller that is presented for signature (acceptance) to the buyer at the time goods are purchased, and that then becomes the equivalent of a note receivable of the seller and the note payable of the buyer.

Trade fixture Personal property supplied and used by tenants in business, which they have a right to remove.

Trade libel See disparagement, slander.

Trademark A distinctive mark, motto, device, or emblem that a manufacturer stamps, prints, or otherwise affixes to the goods it produces so that they may be identified in the market and distinguished from others.

Trade name A name used in trade to designate a particular business.

Trader One in the business of buying and selling goods for a profit.

Trade secret A business formula, pattern, device, or compilation of information known only by certain individuals in the business and used as an advantage over competitors.

Tradesman A mechanic, craftsman, or artificer of any kind whose livelihood depends primarily on manual labor.

Trade-union A combination of workers of the same trade or of several allied trades, for the purpose of securing by united action the most favorable conditions regarding wages, hours of labor, etc.

Tradition 1. Past customs and usages that influence or govern present acts or practices. **2.** Delivery.

Traditional Handed-down; historic. See conventional, common.

Traditionary evidence Evidence derived from tradition or reputation or the statements formerly made by persons since deceased, in regard to questions of pedigree, ancient boundaries, and the like, where no living witnesses can be produced having knowledge of the facts.

Traffic 1. The sale or exchange of merchandise, bills, money, etc. **2.** To transact business. **3.** The subjects of transportation on a route; the passage or flow of people, goods, vehicles, etc.

Trafficking Trading and dealing, usually in illegal goods.

Traitor One who betrays a trust; one who commits treason.

Tramp One who roams about from place to place begging or living without any visible means of support.

Trance Detachment from one's surroundings.

Transact To have dealings.

Transaction The act of conducting something; that which is done or conducted.

Transactional immunity Absolute protection against prosecution for any event or transaction about which a witness is compelled to give testimony or furnish evidence. Immunity from prosecution for offenses to which compelled testimony relates. See use and derivative use immunity.

Transcript That which has been written out or typed, such as from shorthand; a copy; a writing made from the original.

Transcription See transcript.

Transfer 1. To convey or remove from one place or person to another. **2.** A delivery or conveyance.

Transferable Pertaining to that which may pass with the rights of the original owner.

Transferee One to whom a transfer is made.

Transferor One who makes a transfer.

Transfer payments Payments made by the government to individuals for which no services are rendered in return (e.g., a Social Security check, an unemployment check).

Transferred intent 1. The defendant intends to commit acts that would constitute one intentional tort (e.g., assault), but in fact commits another intentional tort (e.g., battery). The law will conclude that the defendant had the intent to commit the latter tort. **2.** The defendant intended to commit an intentional tort against one person, but in fact the tort is committed against another person. The law will conclude that the defendant had the intent needed to commit the tort against the latter person.

Transfer tax A tax on the transfer of property (e.g., bonds, stock) between living persons.

Transient 1. Passing, momentary, or transitory. **2.** One who wanders from place to place.

Transit Movement from one location to another.

Transitory 1. Pertaining to that which may pass or be changed from one place to another. **2.** Ephemeral, momentary, transient, or fleeting.

Transitory action A lawsuit that may be brought in one of several places.

Translative fact A fact by means of which a right is transferred or passes from one person to another.

Transmission 1. The act of sending or conveying. **2.** A system in a car for transmitting power from the engine to the driving axle and wheels.

Transmit To send or transfer from one person or place to another.

Transsexual A person whose sex has been surgically changed; one who desires to become a member of the opposite sex.

Trauma A physical injury caused by a blow or fall; a psychologically damaging emotional experience.

Traumatic 1. Caused by or resulting from a wound or any external injury. **2.** Shocking.

Travail 1. Arduous work. **2.** The act of childbearing.

Traveler's check An instrument purchased from a bank, express company, etc., in various denominations, which can be used as cash upon the second signature by the purchaser.

Traverse 1. A denial of material facts stated in an adverse pleading. **2.** To reject or contest. **3.** To pass from point to point. **4.** To scrutinize.

Traverser In pleading, one who traverses or denies.

Treachery Deliberate and willful betrayal of trust and confidence.

Treason Attempting by overt acts to overthrow the government of the state to which the offender owes allegiance; betraying the state into the hands of a foreign power; rendering aid and comfort to the enemy.

Treasurer An officer of an organization with responsibility over the receipt, custody, and disbursement of moneys or funds.

Treasure-trove Money or precious metals found hidden in a private place.

Treasury 1. A place or building in which revenue or wealth is stored; the agency charged with the receipt, custody, and disbursement of revenue or funds. **2.** Money or resources.

Treasury bill Short-term obligations of the U.S. government.

Treasury bond 1. A bond issued by a corporation and then reacquired. **2.** A bond issued by the federal government as evidence of long-term indebtedness.

Treasury stock Stock issued as fully paid to stockholders, and reacquired by the corporation.

Treasury warrant An order in check form on the U.S. Treasury on which treasury (i.e., government) disbursements are paid.

Treatment All the steps taken to effect a cure of an injury or disease.

Treaty A compact made between two or more nations.

Treble damages Damages tripled in amount.

Trespass An unlawful interference with a person's property or rights. See trespass to land, trespass to chattels, infringement.

Trespass ab initio A trespass from the beginning even though the entry was initially lawful. A subsequent wrong relates back and makes a previously innocent act unlawful.

Trespass de bonis asportatis See de bonis asportatis.

Trespasser One who commits a trespass.

Trespass on the case See action on the case.

Trespass quare clausum fregit A common-law action for damages for an unlawful entry or trespass upon the plaintiff's land. "Trespass wherefore he broke the close."

Trespass to chattels A tort with the following elements: (a) personal property—chattel, (b) plaintiff is in possession of the chattel or is entitled to immediate possession, (c) intent to dispossess or to intermeddle with the chattel, (d) dispossession, impairment, or deprivation of use for a substantial time, (e) causation of the dispossession, impairment, or deprivation.

Trespass to land A tort with the following elements: (a) an act, (b) intrusion on land, (c) in possession of another, (d) intent to intrude, (e) causation of the intrusion. There are four kinds of intrusion covered: physically going on the land, remaining on the land, going to a prohibited part of the land, or failing to remove goods from the land.

Trespass vi et armis Trespass with force and arms. The common-law action for any injury committed by the defendant with direct and immediate force or violence against the person or property of the plaintiff.

Trial 1. A judicial examination and determination of issues between adverse parties. **2.** A test or evaluation. **3.** Misfortune.

Trial balance A listing of debit and credit balances of all ledger accounts.

Trial brief A collection of all the documents, arguments, and strategies that an attorney plans to use at trial. A trial manual or trial book.

Trial by fire See ordeal.

Trial court A court of original jurisdiction; the first court to consider the litigation.

Trial de novo A new trial where the whole case is retried as if no trial had taken place in the first instance.

Trial per pais A trial by one's peers.

Tribal lands Lands within the boundaries of an Indian reservation held in trust by the federal government for the Indian tribe as a community.

Tribunal The place where a judge administers justice.

Tributary Any stream flowing directly or indirectly into a river.

Tribute 1. Money paid by subjects to sustain the expenses of the estate. **2.** Praise or celebration.

Triens Dower or third.

Trier of fact The jury. If there is no jury, the trier of fact is the trial judge.

Trifurcated Divided into three parts.

Trimester Three-month periods; three academic semesters.

Trimonthly Occurring every three months.

Tripartite In three parts.

TRO See temporary restraining order.

Trover A common-law action for the recovery of damages against a person who wrongfully interferes with, detains, or converts the goods of another.

Troy weight A weight of twelve ounces to the pound.

Truant One who willfully and unjustifiedly fails to attend school as required.

Truce A suspension or temporary cessation of hostilities; a cease-fire.

True 1. Conformable to fact or to the actual state of things. **2.** Sincere and trustworthy.

True bill An endorsement made by a grand jury upon a bill of indictment when it is satisfied of the truth of the accusation and finds sufficient evidence to warrant a criminal charge.

True copy A true copy does not mean an absolutely exact copy but means that the copy shall be so true that anybody can understand it.

True value The market value of the property at a fair and bona fide sale at private contract; the value of property in exchange for money.

Trust 1. A right of property, real or personal, held by one party (the trustee) for the benefit of another (the beneficiary or cestui que trust). The creator of this right is the settlor. **2.** Reliance on the honesty or integrity of someone. **3.** An association of persons or companies having the intention and power, or the tendency to create a monopoly or otherwise to interfere with the free course of trade or transportation. **4.** Custody, care, and guardianship. **5.** Responsibility. **6.** To depend on.

Trust company A company formed for the purpose of accepting trusts committed to it and acting as trustee, executor, guardian, etc.

Trust deed The deed by which one creates a trust or transfers property to a trust.

Trustee The person or company holding property in trust. One who is given legal responsibility to hold property in the best interest of or "for the benefit of" another.

Trustee in bankruptcy A person in whom the property of a bankrupt is vested in trust for the creditors.

Trust ex maleficio A species of constructive trust arising out of some fraud, misconduct, or breach of faith on the part of the person to be charged as trustee, which renders it an equitable necessity that a trust should be implied.

Trust fund A fund that is devoted to a particular purpose and cannot or should not be diverted therefrom.

Trust fund theory The imposition of fiduciary obligations. Officers, directors, or stockholders of a corporation that is going out of business will be treated as holding in trust for the benefit of creditors those corporate assets that have been improperly distributed or appropriated.

Trust indenture The document that contains the terms and conditions that govern the conduct of the trustee and the rights of the beneficiaries.

Trust in invitum A constructive trust imposed by equity, contrary to the trustee's intention and will, upon property in his or her hands.

Trust legacy A bequest of personal property to trustees to be held upon trust.

Trustor See settlor.

Trust receipt A receipt stating that the wholesale buyer has possession of the goods for the benefit of the financier.

Trust territory A territory or colony placed under the administration of a country by the United Nations.

Trusty A prisoner who, because of good conduct, is given some measure of freedom in or around the prison, or responsibility over other inmates.

Truth Agreement of thought and reality; eventual verification.

Truthful Accurate, authentic, correct.

Truth-in-lending Meaningful information provided to the consumer on the cost or other terms of credit.

Try 1. To examine judicially. **2.** To undertake, put forth, or venture. **3.** An endeavor, turn, or effort.

Turnkey One who has responsibility over the keys in a prison or institution.

Turn-key contract A contract or job in which the contractor agrees to do all the work, assume all the risk, and turn over a finished product so that nothing further need be done except "turn the key" and unlock the building or other structure for use.

Turntable doctrine See attractive nuisance doctrine.

Turpitude Inherent baseness, vileness, or depravity. See moral turpitude.

Tutelage The state of being under a guardian; guardianship.

TVA See Tennessee Valley Authority.

Tying arrangement A person agrees to sell one product, the "tying product," only on the condition that the vendee also purchase another product, the "tied product."

Tyranny Autocratic or despotic government; reign of terror.

Tyrant A ruler, legitimate or otherwise, who uses his or her power unjustly and arbitrarily.

U.C.C. See Uniform Commercial Code.

U.C.C.C. See Uniform Consumer Credit Code.

U.C.M.J. See Uniform Code of Military Justice.

Ukase An official decree or proclamation.

Ulterior Beyond what is seen; intentionally kept secret.

Ultimate facts Facts essential to a cause of action or a defense; the facts on which the ultimate decision rests.

Ultimatum The final demand or proposal made by a negotiator.

Ultra Beyond, outside of, in excess of.

Ultrafiche See microfiche.

Ultrahazardous Extrahazardous, extremely dangerous.

Ultra vires Beyond the scope of the powers of a corporation, as defined by its charter or state law.

Umpirage The decision of an umpire or arbitrator.

Unable Without the power, skill, or credential.

Unaccrued Not become due.

Unalienable Incapable of being divided, separated, or transferred; inalienable.

Unambiguous Susceptible of but one meaning.

Unanimity Agreement of all persons concerned.

Unanimous All in agreement; no one voting in the negative.

Unauthorized Done without authority; wrongful, unjustified, or unconstitutional.

Unavailable Not available; dead, insane, or beyond reach of a summons.

Una voce Without dissent; with one voice.

Unavoidable Incapable of being prevented. See inevitable, inescapable.

Unavoidable accident An inevitable accident, an act of God.

Unbiased Dispassionate, neutral, fair.

Unborn Pertaining to human life in existence from fertilization till birth.

Unclean hands doctrine A court should not grant relief to a plaintiff who is a wrongdoer (e.g., through fraud, bad faith, or other misconduct) with respect to the subject matter in the suit.

Unconditional discharge A release without any terms or conditions attached.

Unconscionable So one-sided as to be oppressive and unfair.

Unconscious Unaware of one's acts; not possessed of mind.

Unconstitutional Contrary to the constitution.

Uncontrollable Incapable of being controlled; ungovernable.

Uncontrollable impulse See irresistible impulse, insanity.

Uncorroborated Baseless, inconclusive, frivolous.

Undercapitalization Inadequate property and assets to maintain profitable operations in a corporation.

Under color of law See color of law, color of office.

Undercover Operating in secret; underground.

Undercover agent See undisclosed agent, spy.

Under protest Waiving no rights; under duress.

Undersigned The person or persons who have signed at the end of the document or at the bottom of the page.

Understanding 1. A meeting of the minds. **2.** Realization or grasp. **3.** Acumen or intelligence. **4.** Point of view. **5.** The lack of prejudice; open-mindedness. **6.** Conciliatory, responsive.

Undertake To enter upon; to take upon oneself; to guarantee; to endeavor.

Undertaker One whose business is to prepare the dead for burial.

Undertaking A promise, engagement, or stipulation.

Under the influence See intoxication.

Underwrite To insure life or property; to agree to sell bonds or other securities to the public, or to furnish the necessary money for such securities and to buy those that cannot be sold.

Underwriter 1. Any person, banker, or syndicate that guarantees to furnish a definite sum of money by a definite date to a business or government in return for an issue of bonds or stock. **2.** In insurance, the one assuming a risk in return for the payment of a premium.

Undisclosed Operating in secret; unannounced.

Undisclosed agent A person who works as an agent without revealing his or her status as an agent.

Undisclosed principal One who acts through an agent at a time when a third party has no notice that the agent is acting for a principal.

Undisputed Uncontested; not questioned or challenged; stipulated; admitted.

Undistributed Accumulated, set aside, not distributed, not paid out as dividends.

Undistributed profits tax A tax imposed on the unreasonable accumulation of profits by a corporation that has sufficient surplus for expansion and other needs beyond the amount that it could but does not pay out in dividends.

Undivided profits Current undistributed earnings; profits not set aside as surplus or distributed as dividends.

Undue More than necessary; wrongful.

Undue influence Taking advantage of a person's weakness, infirmity, age, or distress in order to change that person's actions or decisions. Misuse of a position of confidence in order to take unfair advantage of another. Any unlawful or improper constraint that overpowers the will of another.

Unearned 1. Not acquired through or in exchange for labor or service. **2.** Undeserved.

Unearned income Income that has been received but not yet earned.

Unemployment insurance A form of taxation collected from business to fund unemployment payments and benefits.

Unequal 1. Discriminatory, biased, unjust. **2.** Disparate, variable, uneven, or not uniform.

Unequivocal Capable of being understood in only one way; unambiguous; categorical.

Unethical Disreputable or underhanded. In violation of standards of practice.

Unexceptionable Not subject to any objection or criticism.

Unexecuted See inchoate.

Unexpired term The remainder of a period prescribed by law after a portion of such time has passed.

Unfair One-sided, biased, unreasonable, inequitable.

Unfair competition Dishonest or fraudulent rivalry in trade and commerce (e.g., the imitation or simulation of the name, materials, or pattern used by another for the purpose of deceiving the public).

Unfair labor practice Interference by an employer with the right of employees to form or join a union, to bargain collectively, or to engage in concerted activities for their mutual aid and protection. Refusal of an employer to bargain collectively in good faith.

Unfair trade practices See unfair competition.

Unfit Not suitable or qualified.

Unforeseeable Not expected or foreseen.

Unified transfer tax A federal tax applicable to transfers by gift and death made after 1976.

Uniform 1. Without change; equally applicable. **2.** An official dress or outfit.

Uniform acts See uniform laws.

Uniform Code of Military Justice (U.C.M.J.) The body of law that governs persons in their conduct as military personnel.

Uniform Commercial Code (U.C.C.) A law adopted by almost all states, governing commercial transactions (e.g., sale of goods, commercial paper, bank deposits, secured transactions).

Uniform Consumer Credit Code (U.C.C.C.) A law adopted by some states governing consumer credit, usury, rate ceilings, unfair credit practices, etc.

Uniform Gifts to Minors Act See Gifts to Minors Act.

Uniform laws Laws prepared or sponsored by the National Conference of Commissioners on Uniform State Laws and then proposed to the various state legislatures, which may adopt, modify, or reject them.

Uniform Reciprocal Enforcement of Support Act (URESA) A law adopted by most states, by which a party can commence a support proceeding in one state against a party in another state who has the support obligation.

Unilateral Affecting only one side; obligating only one side.

Unilateral contract One party makes an express engagement or undertakes a performance without receiving in return any express engagement or promise of performance from the other.

Unilateral mistake A mistake or misunderstanding made by only one of the parties as to the terms or effect of a contract.

Unimproved Not improved, cultivated, or built upon to increase the value of something.

Unincorporated association A voluntary group of persons, without a charter, formed to promote a common enterprise or objective.

Uninsured motorist coverage Insurance protection for those who are injured by motorists who cannot pay damages because they do not carry liability insurance.

Union 1. An organization of workers formed to negotiate with employers on work issues. **2.** A league or federation.

Union certification The process by which a government body declares that a particular union has qualified as the bargaining representative of a group of workers by reason of a majority vote.

Union security clause The clause in a union contract that establishes the status of the union in a plant.

Union shop All workers are union members.

Unissued stock Stock of a corporation that has been authorized but is not outstanding.

Unit A single thing of any kind. The word is sometimes used in the sense of a share, as in an oil syndicate, or as the price of one share sold on a licensed stock exchange, ignoring all other facts regarding value.

United States Usually means the federal government centered in Washington, D.C. (agency of the United States).

United States Code (U.S.C.) An official collection of permanent and public federal statutes organized by subject matter. The collection also includes the U.S. Constitution.

United States Code Annotated (U.S.C.A.) An unofficial collection of permanent and public federal statutes organized by subject matter, published by West. The collection also includes the U.S. Constitution.

United States Code Service (U.S.C.S.) An unofficial collection of permanent and public federal statutes organized by subject matter, published by Lawyers Cooperative Publishing Co. The collection also includes the U.S. Constitution.

United States Reports (U.S.) The official collection of opinions of the U.S. Supreme Court.

Unity In the law of estates, a fourfold characteristic of an estate held by several in joint tenancy: unity of interest, unity of title, unity of time, and unity of possession. In other words, joint tenants have one and the same interest, accruing by one and the same conveyance, commencing at one and the same time, and held by one and the same undivided possession.

Unity of interest One of the essential characteristics of a joint tenancy requiring that interests accrue by one and the same conveyance. It also signifies that no one of the joint tenants can have a greater interest in the property than each of the others.

Unity of possession One of the essential characteristics of a joint tenancy requiring that the joint tenants must hold the same undivided possession of the whole and enjoy the same rights until the death of one.

Unity of time One of the essential characteristics of a joint tenancy requiring that the estates of the tenants be vested at one and the same period.

Unity of title One of the essential characteristics of a joint tenancy requiring that the joint tenants have their estate created by one and the same act.

Universal Pertaining to all without exception.

Universal agent One who is appointed to do all the acts that the principal can personally do.

Universal malice That depravity of the human heart which determines to take life upon slight or insufficient provocation, without knowing or caring who may be the victim.

University An institution of higher learning consisting of an assemblage of colleges under one governance.

Unjust Contrary to right and justice; violating the rights enjoyed by others.

Unjust enrichment A person has and retains a benefit that in equity and good conscience belongs to another.

Unlawful Pertaining to that which is contrary to the law.

Unlawful assembly The meeting together of a designated number of persons (e.g., three or more) to the disturbance of the public peace and with the intention of cooperating in the forcible execution of some unlawful private enterprise.

Unlawful detainer The unjustifiable retention of the possession of lands by one whose original entry was lawful.

Unliquidated Not determined; not ascertained in amount.

Unliquidated claim A claim that has not been finally determined or calculated.

Unliquidated damages Damages that have not yet been calculated or determined in amount.

Unlisted stock Stock not listed on one of the stock exchanges but traded over the counter or privately.

Unlivery The unloading of cargo of a vessel at the place where it is properly to be delivered.

Unmarketable title A title of such character as to expose the purchaser to the hazards of litigation where there are outstanding possible interests in third persons. An ordinary prudent person with knowledge of the facts would not accept the title in the ordinary course of business even if the title in fact is not bad.

Unnatural Against nature; strange; brutal.

Unnatural offense An infamous offense against nature (e.g., sodomy, buggery).

Unnecessary Not required by the circumstances of the case.

Unnecessary hardship A criterion for a variance if the property could be used for a permitted purpose only at a prohibitive expense, or if the restriction is so unreasonable as to constitute an arbitrary interference with the basic right of private property.

Unprofessional conduct Conduct that violates the ethical code of a profession, e.g., Code of Professional Responsibility.

Unreasonable Irrational, unwise; arbitrary. See negligence.

Unseaworthy Unable to withstand the perils of an ordinary voyage at sea.

Unsound mind An infirmity of mind that renders one incapable of managing oneself or one's affairs. See insanity.

Unusual punishment See cruel and unusual punishment.

Unwritten law The law observed and administered by the courts that has not been enacted or promulgated in the form of a statute or ordinance (e.g., unenacted portions of the common law, customs having the force of law, principles and maxims established by judicial precedents).

Upset price The price below which an item is not to be sold.

Urban renewal Redevelopment, slum clearance.

URESA See Uniform Reciprocal Enforcement of Support Act.

Urinalysis A chemical analysis of urine.

Usage A custom that is widely known or established; a uniform practice or course of conduct; a repetition of acts; handling or manipulation.

Usance The customary period for the payment of foreign bills of exchange.

U.S.C. See United States Code.

U.S.C.A. See United States Code Annotated.

U.S.C.S. See United States Code Service.

Use 1. To utilize or convert to one's service. **2.** The application or employment of something; usage, or the fact of being used or employed habitually. The enjoyment of property that consists in its employment, occupation, exercise, or practice. **3.** The right of one person, called the cestui que use, to take the profits from land of which another has legal title. Beneficial interest or ownership. An estate vested since the statute of uses. See statute of uses.

Use and derivative use immunity A witness is given immunity from the use of compelled testimony and the evidence derived therefrom; it cannot be used in a subsequent prosecution of the witness.

Useful life The period of time for which an asset is capable of being used for the production of income.

Use plaintiff In common law pleading, one for whose use (benefit) an action is brought in the name of another.

Use tax An ad valorem tax on the use, consumption, or storage of tangible property.

Use variance An authorization to use land for a purpose that is proscribed by the zoning regulations.

Usual According to custom or usage.

Usual course See regular course of business.

Usufruct The right to use and obtain the profits from something vested in another so long as it is not altered or damaged thereby.

Usurious Pertaining to usury; charging excessive interest.

Usurp To seize and hold any office by force and without right; to assume the functions, rights, or powers of another without authority to do so.

Usurpation See usurp.

Usury Laws on the charging of interest rates; lending money at an interest rate in excess of that authorized by law.

Uterine 1. Born of the same mother but with a different father. **2.** Pertaining to the uterus.

Utility 1. Usefulness; the capability of being applied in a practical, advantageous way. **2.** See public utility.

Utter 1. To put or send into circulation; to declare directly or indirectly by words or actions that an instrument is good; to offer a forged instrument and directly or indirectly claim that it is genuine. **2.** To express aloud. **3.** Total or entire.

Uxoricide The killing of one's wife.

V.A. See Veterans Administration.

Vacancy The condition or status of being empty, unfilled, or unoccupied.

Vacate 1. To annul or set aside. **2.** To move out, surrender, or evacuate.

Vacation of judgment The setting aside of a judgment on the ground that it was issued by mistake, inadvertence, surprise, excusable neglect, or fraud.

Vacatur "Let it be vacated."

Vadium Security by pledge of property.

Vagabond 1. A vagrant or homeless wanderer without means of honest livelihood. **2.** Traveling, homeless.

Vagrancy Going about from place to place without visible means of support, begging, etc.

Vagrant 1. An idle wanderer with no visible means of support. **2.** Roaming or nomadic.

Vague Not susceptible of being understood.

Vagueness Unclarity, obscurity, imprecision.

Vagueness doctrine A law that does not fairly inform a person of what is commanded or prohibited is unconstitutional.

Valid Having the force of law; legally sufficient.

Validate To make valid, confirm, or sanction.

Validity Truthfulness, accuracy, and effectiveness.

Valorization The assignment of an arbitrary value to a product or commodity by the government or by the producer; a form of price-fixing.

Valuable consideration Some right, interest, profit, or benefit accruing to one party, or some forbearance, detriment, loss, or responsibility given, suffered, or undertaken by the other.

Valuation Ascertaining the worth of a thing; the estimated worth of a thing.

Value 1. The usefulness or utility of something in satisfying a human need. **2.** Appraise, judge, assess.

Value-added tax (VAT) A tax on the increased value of goods at each stage as they move through production, manufacturing, and distribution to the marketplace.

Vandalism Willful or malicious destruction of property.

Variable Changeable, alterable, or varied.

Variance 1. Permission to depart from the literal requirements of a zoning ordinance. **2.** A difference of opinion. **3.** An inconsistency between two allegations or positions.

Vasectomy Resection of the ductus deferens. Sterilization of the male by surgical excision of part of the vas deferens.

Vassal A feudal tenant or grantee.

VAT See value-added tax.

Vehicle 1. A device used for transportation. **2.** A medium or method.

Vehicular homicide Homicide caused by the illegal operation of a motor vehicle.

Vein 1. A vessel carrying blood to the heart. **2.** A continuous body of mineral or mineralized rock, filling a seam or fissure in the earth's crust, within defined boundaries in the general mass of the mountain.

Vel non "Or not." See devisavit vel non.

Venal Capable of being bought; mercenary.

Vend Sell.

Vendee Buyer.

Vendetta A private blood feud.

Vendible Suitable for sale; merchantable.

Vendition Sale, the act of selling.

Vendor Seller.

Vendue An auction or public sale.

Venereal disease Diseases communicated through sexual intercourse.

Venire A list of people summoned to appear as prospective jurors.

Venireman A person summoned as a juror.

Venter The abdomen, belly, uterus, or womb. The maternal parentage of children.

Venture 1. An undertaking attended with risk; business speculation; a gamble or long shot. **2.** To take chances. **3.** To tender, put forward, or proffer.

Venue The county or geographical area in which a court with jurisdiction may hear and determine a case.

Veracity Accuracy, truthfulness.

Verbal Concerned with words; expressed orally.

Verbal act doctrine Where a declaration of an individual is so connected with his or her acts as to derive a degree of credit from this connection, independently of the declaration, the declaration becomes part of the transaction and is admissible.

Verdict The formal decision or finding of a jury, reported to the court.

Verge Margin or brink.

Verification Confirmation of correctness, truth, or authenticity, by affidavit, oath, or deposition.

Verified copy A copy of a document that is shown by independent evidence to be true. Successive witnesses trace the original into the hands of a witness who made or compared the copy.

Verify 1. To confirm by oath or affidavit. **2.** To test.

Verily In very truth, beyond doubt or question.

Verity Conformity to fact.

Versus (vs.) Against (e.g., Smith vs. Jones).

Vertical integration The control of the production and distribution of goods from raw material to their sale to the ultimate consumer.

Vertical merger A merger between two companies that have a buyer-seller relationship with each other (i.e., one produces a product that is then sold to the other).

Vertical price fixing An attempt to control retail prices; resale price maintenance.

Vertical union An industrial union organized along the lines of an industry and not a craft.

Vessel 1. A vehicle used in navigation on water. **2.** A container or tube.

Vest To give an immediate, fixed right of present or future enjoyment; to put into possession.

Vested Fixed; not subject to be defeated by a condition (vested pension rights).

Vested interest An interest in which there is a present fixed right either of present or of future enjoyment.

Vested remainder A remainder limited to a certain person at a certain time or upon the happening of a necessary event; an absolute right to become a possessory interest at the end of a prior particular estate.

Vested right An immediate or fixed right to present or future enjoyment, which is not dependent on an uncertain event.

Vestigial words Language remaining in a statute that has been rendered useless or meaningless by reason of later amendments.

Veteran 1. Any honorably discharged member of the military. **2.** An expert. **3.** Having considerable experience and skill.

Veterans Administration (V.A.) A federal agency that administers benefits to those who served in the armed forces and to their dependents (e.g., pension, health care).

Veterinarian One who practices the art of treating diseases and injuries of animals.

Veto 1. A chief executive's refusal to assent to a proposed law enacted by the legislature. **2.** To refuse to consent.

Vex To disquiet or annoy.

Vexation A source of irritation; an injury or damage suffered as a result of the tricks of another.

Vexatious 1. Without reasonable or probable cause or excuse (vexatious delay). **2.** Annoying.

Vexatious proceeding An action or proceeding instituted maliciously and without probable cause.

Via 1. Way or road. **2.** By way of, by means of.

Viability Capability of living. That stage of fetal development when the life of the unborn child may be continued indefinitely outside the womb by natural or artificial life-supporting systems.

Viable 1. Capable of living. **2.** Feasible.

Vicar One who performs the functions of another.

Vicarious Experienced, endured, or substituting for another.

Vicarious liability Being responsible because someone else is responsible; indirect legal responsibility (e.g., an employer is liable for the negligence of its employee).

Vice 1. In substitution for. **2.** Immoral conduct.

Vice consul A consular officer who is subordinate to and temporarily substitutes for a consul or consul general.

Vice principal An employee with authority to direct and supervise work, and authority to hire and discharge subordinate workers.

Vicinage 1. Neighborhood, vicinity. **2.** The county where a trial is had, a crime committed, etc.

Vicinity The state or quality of being near.

Victim The person who is the subject of a crime, tort, or other wrong.

Victimless crime A crime that involves only or primarily the criminal (e.g., illegal possession of drugs).

Viduity Widowhood.

Vie Life.

Vi et armis With force and arms.

Vigilance A proper degree of activity in pursuing one's rights and opportunities.

Vigilant Attentive to discover and avoid danger.

Vigilante A member of a group that takes the law into its own hands in the apprehension and punishment of criminals.

Vinculo matrimonii See divorce a vinculo matrimonii.

Vindex In the civil law, a defender.

Vindicate To clear of suspicion, blame, or doubt.

Vindicatio In the civil law, the claiming a thing as one's own.

Vindictive Characterized by desire for revenge.

Violation Breach of a duty, right, or law.

Violence The unjust and unwarranted use of force.

Violent Characterized by physical force; tempestuous.

Violent presumption In the law of evidence, proof of a fact by the proof of circumstances that necessarily attend it. Something more than a mere presumption.

Vires Powers or capabilities. See ultra vires.

Virtue 1. Integrity and character. **2.** On the grounds of.

Visa An official indorsement on a document, passbook, commercial book, etc., to certify that it has been examined and found correct or in due form; an indorsement on a passport giving the holder permission to enter or leave a country.

Vis-à-vis 1. In relation to. **2.** Face to face.

Visible Open or perceptible.

Visitation 1. Calling upon or being called upon (e.g., visitation rights of the noncustodial parent). **2.** Regulation or examination.

Vis major An irresistible force; a greater or superior force; pertaining to a loss that results immediately from a natural cause without human intervention and which could not have been prevented by the exercise of reasonable care.

Vital 1. Essential. **2.** Pertaining to life.

Vital statistics Public records kept by the government on births, deaths, marriages, etc.

Vitiate To destroy the legal efficacy and binding force of something.

Vitiligate To litigate vexatiously or from merely quarrelsome motives.

Vitium scriptoris A clerical error.

Viva voce By word of mouth, orally.

Vivisection The dissection of living animals for scientific reasons.

Viz Namely, that is to say, to wit.

Vocation One's regular occupation or business.

Voice exemplars A type of test in which one's voice is compared with the voice heard on a particular occasion.

Voiceprint A "print" of one's voice produced by a spectograph for use in comparing such readings with the actual voice of the person.

Void 1. Having no legal force or binding effect. **2.** To invalidate. **3.** Lacking.

Void ab initio Invalid from its inception or beginning.

Voidable Pertaining to that which may be avoided or declared invalid; pertaining to that which is defective but which remains effective until declared invalid (voidable contract).

Voidable marriage A marriage that can be annulled because of its invalidity but which remains valid until a court declares it invalid.

Voidable preference A preference given to a creditor of a bankrupt over other creditors in the same class.

Void for vagueness A law that is so obscure that a reasonable person could not determine what the law purports to command or prohibit.

Void judgment A judgment with no force or legal effect.

Void marriage A marriage that was void from its inception; a marriage that is invalid whether or not a court declares its invalidity.

Void on its face The invalidity of the document is relatively easy to determine upon inspection.

Voir dire Jury selection; a preliminary examination of prospective jurors or witnesses to inquire into their competence. "To speak the truth."

Volenti non fit injuria There is no cause of action for damages suffered by consent.

Voluntary Proceeding from the free and unconstrained will of a person.

Voluntary abandonment 1. As statutory ground for divorce, a final departure without consent of the other party, without sufficient reason, and without intent to return. **2.** As used in adoption statutes, the term "voluntarily abandoned" means a willful act or course of conduct such as would imply a conscious disregard or indifference in respect to the parental obligation owed to the child.

Voluntary manslaughter The intentional, unlawful killing of someone without malice or premeditation.

Voluntary nonsuit The plaintiff abandons his or her case and consents to the entry of a judgment against him or her.

Volunteer A person who provides services without any express or implied promise of remuneration.

Vote The formal expression of one's will or choice.

Voter A person who votes or who has the qualifications to vote.

Voting stock A type of stock that gives the holder the right to vote for directors and on other matters.

Voting trust An agreement between stockholders and a trustee whereby the rights to vote the stock are transferred to the trustee.

Vouch To give a personal assurance or to serve as a guarantee.

Voucher 1. A receipt or release that may serve as evidence of payment or that certifies the correctness of accounts. **2.** A document that serves to recognize a liability and to authorize the disbursement of cash.

Vouching-in A device by the defendant to bring another party into the litigation.

Vox populi Popular sentiment.

Voyeur A person who derives sexual satisfaction from observing the sexual organs or acts of others, usually from a secret vantage point.

Vs. See versus.

Wage Payments made to a hired person for his or her services.

Wage assignment A transfer to someone else of one's right to receive wages.

Wage earner's plan A type of partial bankruptcy in which a person keeps his or her property and pays off a court-established proportion of debt over a period of time under court supervision.

Wage garnishment See garnishment.

Wager A contract in which the parties agree that they will gain or lose upon the happening of an uncertain event in which they have no interest other than this possibility of gain or loss.

Waif That which nobody claims.

Waive To give up a right, claim, or privilege intentionally and voluntarily; to engage in conduct that warrants an inference that a right, claim, or inference is being relinquished.

Waiver The intentional and voluntary relinquishment of a known right or such a conduct as warrants an inference of the relinquishment of such a right.

Waiver of immunity See waive, immunity.

Waiver of premium A provision in an insurance policy that the premium is waived upon the disability of the insured.

Waiver of protest An agreement by the indorser of a note or bill to be bound in his or her character of indorser without the formality of a protest in case of nonpayment, or, in the case of paper that cannot or is not required to be protested, dispensing with the necessity of a demand and notice.

Waiver of tort An election by the plaintiff to treat the facts as establishing an implied contract and to sue on this theory rather than on a tort theory.

Walkout An organized withdrawal of employees from their place of employment because of a labor dispute.

Wall An upright structure of solid material, intended to enclose, provide privacy, or protect.

Want 1. Lack (e.g., want of consideration). **2.** Desire.

Wanton 1. Characterized by a conscious disregard of the consequences of one's acts or omissions; recklessly disregardful of the rights or safety of others. **2.** Lewd, obscene.

War Hostile contention by means of armed force carried on between nations, states, rulers, or among citizens in the same nation or state.

War crimes Crimes committed by countries in violation of international laws governing wars.

Ward 1. A person placed by the court under the care of a guardian. **2.** A division of a city or town. **3.** A unit of a hospital. **4.** To repel.

Warden A guardian; a person in charge of a prison; a turnkey.

Ward of the court An infant or person of unsound mind who has come under the protective jurisdiction of the court.

Warehouse A structure for the reception and storage of goods for compensation or profit.

Warehouseman's lien The right of a warehouseman to retain possession of the goods until storage charges have been paid.

Warehouse receipt A receipt issued by a warehouseman for goods received for storage in the warehouse.

Warning That which points out danger.

Warrant 1. To engage or promise that certain facts are as they are represented to be. **2.** To give sufficient reason for. **3.** An official order. **4.** An order by which the drawer authorizes one person to pay a particular sum of money. An option to purchase stock at a given price.

Warrantee A person to whom a warranty is made.

Warrant of arrest See arrest warrant.

Warranty A promise that a proposition of fact is true.

Warranty deed A deed in which the grantor promises a good clear title.

Warranty, express See express warranty.

Warranty, implied See implied warranty.

Warranty of fitness for a particular purpose See fitness for a particular purpose.

Warranty of habitability An implied promise by a landlord that the premises are fit for habitation at the time of letting and will remain so during the term of the tenancy.

Warranty of merchantability An implied promise that the goods are reasonably fit for the general purpose for which they were sold.

Warranty of title An implied promise that the seller owns the item offered for sale.

Warsaw Convention A 1929 treaty on rules for international air travel (e.g., a limitation on liability).

Wash sale The sale and purchase of the same or a similar asset within a short time period; a transaction involving no change in beneficial ownership; a fictitious kind of sale.

Waste 1. An abuse or destructive use of property by one in rightful possession. **2.** Useless material. **3.** To use or spend carelessly. **4.** To devastate.

Wasting asset An asset with a limited useful life (e.g., an oil well) and hence subject to amortization or depletion.

Wasting trust A trust, the res of which consists in whole or in part of property that is gradually being consumed.

Watercourse A natural stream fed from permanent or natural sources (e.g., rivers, creeks, runs, rivulets).

Watermark A mark indicating the highest point to which water rises or the lowest point to which it sinks.

Ways and Means Committee A legislative committee with jurisdiction over the methods and sources for raising revenue.

W.D. Western District (e.g., W.D. Ky. refers to the U.S. District Court for the Western District of Kentucky).

Weak Infirm or feeble.

Wealth Abundance of financial or material resources.

Weapon A device for combat.

Wear 1. To erode or impair. **2.** To carry on the body.

Wear and tear Deterioration and depreciation in value due to ordinary and reasonable use.

Wedlock The state of marriage.

Weight Influence, effectiveness, or power to influence judgment or conduct (weight of authority).

Weight of evidence The balance or preponderance of the evidence; the inclination of the greater amount of credible evidence to support one side of an issue rather than the other.

Welfare 1. The enjoyment of health and the common blessings of life. **2.** Public assistance, dole, financial aid.

Well 1. A hole sunk into the earth in order to obtain water, oil, or other fluids from a subterranean supply. **2.** Satisfactorily. **3.** Healthy.

Welshing A form of larceny: receiving money for a bet by falsely telling the depositor that the intention is to return it along with any winnings derived therefrom.

WESTLAW A system of computerized legal research.

Whack To divide into shares, apportion.

Wharf A structure on the shore or margin of navigable waters, alongside of which vessels can be brought for the sake of loading or unloading.

Wharfage A fee paid for landing goods upon or loading them from a wharf.

Wharton rule An agreement by two persons to commit a crime cannot be prosecuted as a conspiracy where the crime necessarily requires the participation of two persons.

Whenever At whatever time.

Whereas That being the case.

Whereby By means of which.

Whereupon Upon which; after which.

Wherewithal Means, property, wealth.

Whim Impulse or caprice.

Whiplash A snapping of the neck when a person has his or her head thrown forward or back, or from side to side. Whiplash can cause a sprain, fracture, dislocation, etc.

Whipping Punishment by thrashing or flogging.

White acre A fictitious name that teachers and writers use to indicate a parcel of land. Also: black acre.

White-collar crime A nonviolent crime committed by an individual or a company in the course of its business or occupation (e.g., embezzlement, price fixing).

White Slave Act A federal statute prohibiting the interstate and foreign transportation of women and girls for immoral purposes.

Whole 1. Entire or complete. **2.** In good health. **3.** Faultless.

Whole blood Kinship by descent from the same father and mother; the relationship of those who have both parents in common.

Whole life insurance Insurance for which premiums are collected as long as the insured may live. The amount of the premium remains the same, and the policy builds up cash reserves.

Wholesale 1. Pertaining to a sale in large quantity to one who intends to resell; a sale to retailers rather than to consumers. **2.** Widespread and indiscriminate.

Wholly Not partially.

Whore A woman who practices illicit sexual intercourse either for hire or to gratify a depraved passion.

Widow A woman who has lost her husband by death and who has not remarried.

Widower A man who has lost his wife by death and who has not remarried.

Widow's allowance The amount of money or property that a widow may claim from her husband's estate free from all claims.

Widow's election See election by spouse.

Wild 1. In a state of nature. **2.** Uncontrolled.

Wild animal An animal in the state of nature; an animal of an untamable disposition.

Wildcat strike A strike called without authorization from the union or in violation of a no-strike clause in the collective bargaining agreement.

Wild land Land in a state of nature, as distinguished from improved or cultivated land.

Will 1. An instrument by which a person makes a disposition of his or her property, which takes effect after his or her death but is revocable during his or her lifetime. **2.** Determination. **3.** Desire. **4.** The faculty of conscious and deliberate action. **5.** Shall or must.

Willful 1. Proceeding from a conscious motion of the will. **2.** Stubborn.

Willful misconduct of employee The intentional doing of something with knowledge that it is likely to result in serious injuries or with reckless disregard of its probable consequences. Mere incompetence or negligence is not enough to establish willful misconduct.

Willful neglect The intentional disregard of a plain or manifest duty without just cause or excuse.

Willful negligence Intentionally doing an act of an unreasonable character in disregard of a known risk, which makes it highly probable that harm will follow.

Willingly Of one's own free choice.

Will substitute Devices that try to achieve what a will is designed to accomplish (e.g., life insurance, joint ownership of property).

Windfall Unexpected gain.

Wind up To settle the accounts and liquidate the assets of a business, for the purpose of making a distribution and dissolving the concern.

Wiretap See eavesdrop.

Witchcraft Alleged intercourse with evil spirits.

With all faults As is, in its present condition, no warranty given.

Withdraw 1. To take away. **2.** To retreat. **3.** To cancel.

Withhold To retain or conceal.

Withholding tax Tax collected by deductions from wages as they are paid.

Within Inside the limits of.

Without notice In good faith.

Without prejudice No rights or privileges are waived or lost. A dismissal without prejudice allows a new suit to be brought later on the same cause of action.

Without recourse An indication by an indorser of a negotiable instrument that he or she declines to assume any responsibility for payment to subsequent holders. If the parties primarily liable refuse to pay, there can be no recourse to such an indorser.

Without reserve No minimum auction price.

With prejudice, dismissal The judgment is conclusive of the rights of the parties; a dismissal having the same effect as a final adjudication, barring the right to bring or maintain an action later on the same claim or cause.

With recourse An indication by the indorser of a negotiable instrument that he or she remains liable for the payment of the instrument.

Witness 1. To subscribe one's name to a deed, will, or other document for the purpose of attesting its authenticity and proving its execution. **2.** To see, hear, or experience something personally. **3.** One who, being present, personally sees or perceives a thing.

Woods Land covered with a large and thick collection of natural trees.

Word 1. A symbol indicating ideas; remark. **2.** An assurance or promise.

Words of art The vocabulary or terminology of a particular art or science.

Words of limitation In a conveyance or will, words that have the effect of marking the duration of an estate.

Words of purchase Words that denote the person who is to take the estate.

Work 1. To exert oneself for a purpose. **2.** To do something effectively, to function. **3.** Physical or mental exertion for the attainment of some object. **4.** An establishment for performing industrial labor. **5.** An achievement.

Worker 1. One who accomplishes things. **2.** Employee, laborer.

Workhouse A place for the confinement of persons convicted of lesser offenses.

Working Functioning.

Working capital Cash and other quick assets required to carry on operations; the difference between current assets and current liabilities.

Workman One who is employed in manual labor.

Workmen's compensation A state system of providing fixed benefits to employees or their dependents for employment-related accidents and diseases.

Work product rule The following material is protected against discovery: private memoranda of attorneys, and mental impressions or personal recollections prepared or formed by an attorney in anticipation of litigation or for trial. Some documents and tangible things prepared in anticipation of litigation or for trial are discoverable if it can be shown that the party seeking discovery has substantial need of the materials and is unable without undue hardship to obtain the substantial equivalent of the materials by other means. If this showing of need is made, the attorney is still entitled to have protected from disclosure his or her mental impressions, conclusions, opinions, or legal theories concerning the litigation.

Work release program A program that allows an inmate to leave the institution for employment during the day. The inmate returns to the prison each evening.

Work stoppage See strike.

World 1. Everyone. **2.** The earth.

World Court See International Court of Justice.

Worship A form of religious service showing reverence for a divine being; an assembly engaged in a religious exercise.

Worth 1. The quality of a thing that gives it value; the sum of valuable qualities. **2.** Wealth.

Worthless Having no value or use.

Worthy Possessing merit.

Wound 1. To inflict a cut or bruise. **2.** An injury to the body.

Wraparound mortgage A method of refinancing whereby a new mortgage to cover a new loan is placed in a secondary position to the existing mortgage on the original loan. The entire loan is treated as a single obligation.

Writ An order issued from a court requiring the performance of a specified act, or giving authority to have it done.

Write-off The removal of a worthless debt from the books of account.

Write-up To increase the valuation of an asset in a financial statement to reflect current value.

Writing 1. The expression of ideas by letters visible to the eye. **2.** A manuscript.

Writ of assistance A form of process used by an equity court to bring about a change in the possession of realty. The writ dispossesses the occupant and gives possession to the one adjudged entitled thereto by the court.

Writ of certiorari See certiorari.

Writ of entry An action to recover possession of land where the tenant or owner has been wrongfully dispossessed.

Writ of error A writ issued from a court of appellate jurisdiction, directed to the judge or judges of a court of record, requiring them to remit to the appellate court the record of an action before them, in which a final judgment has been entered, in order that examination may be made of certain errors alleged to have been committed.

Writ of error coram nobis See coram nobis.

Writ of execution See execution.

Writ of habeas corpus See habeas corpus.

Writ of mandamus See mandamus.

Writ of prohibition A device by which a court may restrain an inferior tribunal from exercising jurisdiction over matters not legally within its cognizance or from exceeding its jurisdiction in matters properly before it.

Wrong 1. A violation of the right of another. **2.** Illegal. **3.** Mistaken. **4.** To invade the right of someone.

Wrongdoer One who invades the right of another.

Wrongful death action A suit brought on behalf of a deceased person's beneficiaries, alleging that the death was attributable to the tortious or wrongful act of another. See Lord Campbell Act.

Wrongful life action A suit against a doctor whose malpractice has resulted in the birth of a child (e.g., unsuccessful sterilization operation, failure to diagnose pregnancy in time for an abortion, failure to perform an abortion successfully).

X-ray Radiograph.

Yard 1. Three feet, 36 inches, .914 meter. **2.** Grounds of a building.

Year Twelve calendar months. 365 or 366 days.

Yellow-dog contract As a condition of employment, the employer requires the employee to promise not to join a union.

Yellow journalism Distortion, exploitation, and sensationalism in reporting the news in order to increase profits.

Yield 1. To give up or relinquish. **2.** That which is produced.

Youth 1. Children and young persons of both sexes. **2.** The time between childhood and adulthood.

Youthful offender A youth who is treated as a delinquent in the juvenile or family courts, and not as a criminal.

Zone An area or region that has been set aside, and hence has distinctive characteristics.

Zoning The division of a city or community into districts in which regulations are imposed on the structure and architectural designs of buildings and the uses to which they may be put.

STYLE, GRAMMAR, AND USAGE: GUIDELINES AND EXAMPLES

a, an

The choice of "a" or "an" depends on sound. Use "a" before a consonant sound; use "an" before a vowel sound.

EX: a lawyer, a jury, an oral argumen; an hour

ability, capacity

Ability is the mental, physical, financial, or legal power to do something. Capacity is the ability to absorb, contain, or hold something.

EX: ability to communicate effectively, ability to pay; a courtroom filled to capacity

abjure, adjure

Abjure means to repudiate or renounce; adjure means to command something, often under oath.

EX: abjure the belief; adjure them to stop the picketing

about, around (see also *in connection with*)

Both of these words mean approximately. Use "about" in formal writing; limit "around" to speech.

above

Above is frequently used in the law to refer to material previously discussed.

EX: the doctrine discussed above; the above material

Make sure that the reference is clear. Will the reader know what you are referring to "above"? If not, avoid the word. Use a less vague reference.

EX: the doctrine discussed on page 24; the material in section C

absolutely See *definitely*.

accept, except

Accept means to receive with approval or to agree with. As a verb, except means to leave out; as a preposition, it means other than.

EX: accept the offer; excepted from the requirements; all the cases except the ones that were overruled

accident, mishap

An accident is an unexpected occurrence which may or may not be bad. A mishap is an unfortunate, usually minor, accident.

EX: money found by accident; suffer a mishap

accordance, in accordance with

Avoid such overly formal language.

SAY: as you requested

RATHER THAN: in accordance with your request

accredit, credit

To accredit means to acknowledge or recognize officially. To credit means to attribute.

EX: accredit the school; credit the theory to Holmes

acknowledge, admit, concede

These words mean to accept the existence or truth of something, often with some hesitation. When something is admitted, it is usually done much more reluctantly than when it is acknowledged. Concede means to yield.

EX: <u>acknowledge</u> the mistake; <u>admit</u> guilt; <u>concede</u> the argument

act, action

An act is a deed that is done; it is accomplished through an action. An action is the state or process of doing.

EX: child neglect is an unnatural <u>act</u> consisting of the <u>actions</u> of not feeding, clothing, or otherwise caring for the child

actual, real

Both words mean existing in fact. Real suggests something demonstrative or objectively present.

EX: <u>actual</u> intent; <u>real</u> evidence

actually

The word means in fact; avoid it in formal writing.

SAY: present

RATHER THAN: <u>actually</u> present

ad

Avoid this colloquial substitute for the word advertisement.

SAY: the lawyer's <u>advertisement</u>

RATHER THAN: the lawyer's <u>ad</u>

adapt, adopt, adept

To adapt means to make something suitable for use by adjustments. To adopt means to make something one's own. Adept is an adjective meaning very skilled.

EX: to <u>adapt</u> the standard form; to <u>adopt</u> the resolution; an <u>adept</u> litigator

adherence, coherence

Adherence means standing by or sticking to something; also, faithful attachment. Coherence is logical consistency.

EX: <u>adherence</u> to principle; a rambling brief that lacks <u>coherence</u>

adjacent, contiguous

Adjacent means lying near or close by; contiguous means touching or in actual contact.

EX: Maine and Rhode Island are <u>adjacent</u> states; Maine and New Hampshire are <u>contiguous</u> states

adjudge, judge

Adjudge means to adjudicate, to make a formal decision. Judge also means to consider and to rule, but it can be used in less formal settings.

EX: <u>adjudged</u> to be in contempt; <u>judge</u> of character

adjure See *abjure.*

admission, admittance

Admission is an earned or privileged entrance. It also means a voluntary concession or confession. Admittance is simply a physical entry.

EX: <u>admission</u> to the bar, <u>admission</u> of evidence, <u>admission</u> of guilt; <u>admittance</u> by the rear window

admit See *acknowledge.*

adopt See *adapt.*

adoptive, adopted

Adoptive means related by adoption. Adopted refers to the person accepted by others through the legal process of adoption.

EX: <u>adoptive</u> father; <u>adopted</u> child (don't say <u>adopted</u> father)

advance plans See *future plans.*

adverse, averse

Adverse means opposed or against one's interest. Averse means a feeling of distaste, a disinclination.

EX: <u>adverse</u> claim, <u>adverse</u> circumstances; <u>averse</u> to the settlement offer

advert, avert

Advert means to call attention to, or to refer. Avert means to avoid or prevent.

EX: <u>advert</u> to the problem; <u>avert</u> disaster

advice, advise

Advice is a noun meaning opinion, counsel, recommendation, or suggestion. Advise is a verb meaning to counsel or give advice to.

EX: the lawyer <u>advised</u> the client to accept the <u>advice</u> of the doctor

advise, notify, inform (see also *advice*)

Advise can be an overly formal way to say notify or inform.

SAY: <u>notify</u> us of the verdict

RATHER THAN: <u>advise</u> us of the verdict

a few See *few.*

affect, effect (see also *effect; impact*)

Affect is a verb meaning to have an influence on. As a verb, effect means to bring something about or to cause. As a noun, effect means the result.

EX: the ruling <u>affects</u> all contractors; the supervisor <u>effected</u> changes; the <u>effect</u> of the verdict

affective, effective

Affective means emotional. Effective means having the intended result.

EX: <u>affective</u> story; <u>effective</u> drug

afflict See *inflict.*

aforementioned, aforesaid

These words are verbose ways of saying mentioned earlier.

SAY: the theory discussed on page 5

RATHER THAN: the <u>aforementioned</u> theory, or the <u>aforesaid</u> theory

aggravate, irritate, annoy

Aggravate means to make something worse, to add to the problem. Avoid using it to mean to annoy or to provoke. Irritate means to vex, harass, or disturb. "Annoy" is a less severe form of "irritate."

EX: <u>aggravate</u> an injury; <u>irritate</u> the judge

ago, since

Both of these words refer to the past. Do not use them together.

SAY: it was ten days <u>ago</u> that I mailed the letter, or it has been ten days <u>since</u> I mailed the letter

RATHER THAN: it was ten days <u>ago</u> <u>since</u> I mailed the letter

a half a See *half.*

aid, aide

Aid means help or support. Aide is a person who provides help or support, an assistant.

EX: <u>aid</u> provided by the <u>aide</u>

alibi

Do not use this word to mean excuse or apology. Use it as the legal defense of being somewhere else at the time of the crime.

allege, contend

Allege means to state that something is true without proving it. Contend means to maintain or assert a position. Do not use contend unless disagreement exists. When it does not exist, "say" or "said" are preferable.

EX: the report <u>alleged</u> fraud; to respond to the report, she <u>contended</u> that there was no fraud

all of, all

Do not say "all of" unless this phrase is followed by a pronoun or a proper noun.

SAY: <u>all</u> the code volumes; <u>all</u> of them; <u>all</u> of Texas

RATHER THAN: <u>all</u> <u>of</u> the code volumes; <u>all</u> them; <u>all</u> Texas

allow, permit

Allow means to let happen, suggesting the absence of an affirmative prohibition. Permit is more forceful, suggesting an affirmative authorization.

EX: the animals were <u>allowed</u> to wander; the judge did <u>permit</u> the extension

all ready, already

All ready means fully prepared or completely ready. Already means earlier, previously, or before.

EX: they were <u>all</u> <u>ready</u>; <u>already</u> gone

all right, alright

All right is often misspelled as alright. Never use the latter word.

all the farther, as far as

Avoid the phrase "all the farther" in formal writing. Instead, use "as far as."

SAY: New York is as far as he would go

RATHER THAN: New York is <u>all</u> <u>the</u> <u>farther</u> he would go

all-time

Avoid this adjective in formal writing; it is colloquial.

SAY: one of the greatest judges

RATHER THAN: one of the <u>all-time</u> great judges

all together, altogether

All together means in agreement or present in one place. Altogether means completely or entirely.

EX: the lawyers were <u>all</u> <u>together</u> for a bench conference; the statement was not <u>altogether</u> true

allude, elude

Allude means to make an indirect reference to something. Elude means to escape or to avoid detection.

EX: she <u>alluded</u> to an undercurrent of opposition; <u>elude</u> the police

allude, refer

Use allude for an indirect reference, and refer for a direct or specific reference.

EX: the witness <u>alluded</u> to the problem; the lawyer <u>referred</u> to exhibit Z

allusion, illusion

Allusion is an indirect reference. Illusion is a false image or hallucination.

EX: an <u>allusion</u> that she was involved in organized crime; the <u>illusion</u> of grandeur

almost See *most.*

almost all See *most all.*

along this line

Avoid the phrase "along this line" or "along these lines."

SAY: the examiner continued with this theme in his questions

RATHER THAN: the examiner continued <u>along this line</u> in his questions

Similarly, do not use the phrase as a transition between sentences. Instead, say "consequently," "thus," or, "as a result."

SAY: the court might find for the other side on the issue. <u>Consequently</u>, we need to have the research available.

RATHER THAN: the court might find for the other side on the issue. <u>Along this line</u>, we need to have the research available.

a lot, a lot of, lots of

Avoid these colloquial phrases in formal writing. Instead, say "many."

SAY: object <u>many</u> times

RATHER THAN: object <u>a lot</u>

already See *all ready*.

alright See *all right*.

alternative, alternate

Alternative means one of two possibilities. An alternate is a substitute.

EX: the <u>alternative</u> of prison or probation; an <u>alternate</u> on the jury

Use alternative only when there is a choice between two options. If there are more than two, say "choice," "preference," "selection," "pick," etc.

SAY: three <u>choices</u>

RATHER THAN: three <u>alternatives</u>

although See *though; in spite of the fact that*.

altogether See *all together*.

alumnus, alumni, alumna, alumnae

Alumnus is a male graduate of a school. The plural is alumni. Alumna is a female graduate of a school. The plural is alumnae. At a coeducational school, alumni can refer to both male and female graduates.

a.m., am, A.M., AM; p.m., pm, P.M., PM

Use lower case with periods (a.m., p.m.). Do not use am, A.M., AM; pm, P.M., or PM. Do not spell out the time; use numerals. The colon and zeros are not needed when stating a time on the hour.

SAY: 3:45 a.m; 3 p.m.

RATHER THAN: 3:45 AM; 3:00 p.m.; three p.m.

ambiguous See *equivocal*.

ameliorate, mitigate

Ameliorate means to improve or make better. Mitigate means to make less severe.

EX: <u>ameliorate</u> his living conditions; <u>mitigate</u> the damages

amend See *emend*.

amiable, amicable

Both words mean friendly. Amiable suggests a sweetness, while amicable emphasizes the lack of bitterness or hostility.

EX: <u>amiable</u> personality; <u>amicable</u> settlement

among, between

Generally, use "among" when comparing more than two items, and "between" when comparing two items. Between can be used when more than two items are involved if each item is being considered individually or in relation to each other.

EX: listed <u>among</u> the wounded; divided <u>between</u> employee and employer, understanding <u>between</u> nations, <u>between</u> the lines

amoral, immoral, unmoral

Amoral means neither moral nor immoral; not to be judged by moral standards. Immoral means contrary to moral standards. Unmoral means unable to distinguish right from wrong. It has close to the same meaning as amoral. The same is true of nonmoral, meaning not connected with morality.

EX: animals are <u>amoral</u>; an <u>immoral</u> gambling contract; <u>unmoral</u> behavior of the mentally incompetent adult

amount, in the amount of

"In the amount of" is verbose. Use "for" whenever possible.

SAY: check <u>for</u> $100

RATHER THAN: check <u>in the amount of</u> $100

amount, number

Amount refers to things in the aggregate or in bulk. Number refers to things that can be counted one by one.

EX: <u>amount</u> of tension, <u>amount</u> of nitrogen; <u>number</u> of volumes

ampersand (&)

An ampersand (&) is the symbol for the word "and." Use it only if it is part of the official name of a company or firm. Do not use an ampersand or the plus sign (+) as shorthand.

SAY: reversed and remanded

RATHER THAN: reversed & remanded

an See *a, an*.

analyzation, analysis

Avoid analyzation as a substitute for analysis.
SAY: <u>analysis</u> of the problem
RATHER THAN: <u>analyzation</u> of the problem

and etc. See *etc.*

and/or

Avoid this phrase in formal writing; it can be ambiguous. When you mean "one or the other or both," say so explicitly.
SAY: the affidavit must be signed by the plaintiff, <u>or</u> her attorney, <u>or</u> <u>both</u>
RATHER THAN: the affidavit must be signed by the plaintiff <u>and/or</u> her attorney

and which

Use this phrase in a clause only if "which" appears in a preceding clause. If possible, rewrite to avoid using "which."
SAY: the first course <u>which</u> I took <u>and</u> <u>which</u> I passed
RATHER THAN: the first course I took <u>and</u> <u>which</u> I passed
EVEN BETTER: the first course I took and passed

and who

Use this phrase in a clause only if "who" appears in a preceding clause. If possible, rewrite to avoid overuse of "who."
SAY: a judge <u>who</u> has integrity <u>and</u> <u>who</u> is experienced
RATHER THAN: a judge with integrity <u>and</u> <u>who</u> is experienced
EVEN BETTER: a judge with integrity and experience

angle

In formal writing, do not use this word to mean point of view.
SAY: her <u>perspective</u> on the case
RATHER THAN: her <u>angle</u> on the case

angry See *mad.*

announce, annunciate

Both words mean to proclaim or declare. Announce is preferred.

annoy See *aggravate.*

ante, anti

Ante is a prefix that means before, prior, or in front of. Anti is a prefix that means opposed to or against. A hyphen is not needed unless anti precedes a proper name or the letter "i".

EX: <u>ante</u>nuptial agreement, <u>ante</u>room; <u>anti</u>discrimination ordinance, anti-American demonstration

anticipate, expect

Anticipate is an overly formal (and sometimes ambiguous) substitute for the word expect.
SAY: <u>expect</u> opposition; we <u>expect</u> the letter to go out today
RATHER THAN: <u>anticipate</u> opposition; we <u>anticipate</u> that the letter will go out today
Anticipate is proper when you mean to look forward to something occurring.
EX: <u>anticipate</u> the visit

anxious See *eager.*

any (see also *either*)

Do not use this word if it adds nothing to the sentence.
SAY: it does not help; are we nearer?
RATHER THAN: it does not help <u>any</u>; are we <u>any</u> nearer?

anybody, any body

Say "anybody" (one word) when you mean any person. Say "any body" (two words) when you are referring to corpses or focusing on specific items.
EX: anybody can answer; the police did not find <u>any</u> <u>body</u>
Anybody takes a singular verb.
EX: <u>anybody</u> is eligible

anyhow

This word means in any way whatever or in any case. Do not use it in formal writing

anymore, any more

Anymore means from now on, or at the moment. Any more means something additional.
EX: the court does not sit <u>anymore</u>; are there <u>any</u> <u>more</u> forms?

any one, anyone (see also *anybody*)

Say "any one" (two words) only when you are referring to any single person or thing. Say "anyone" when you are referring to persons or things in general.
EX: <u>any</u> <u>one</u> of the proposals is acceptable; <u>anyone</u> can come

anyplace

Avoid this colloquial substitute for anywhere.
SAY: sit <u>anywhere</u>
RATHER THAN: sit <u>anyplace</u>

anyways, anywheres

Do not use these colloquial words. Omit the "s" in each word.

a period of time See awhile; period of time.

apology, excuse

An apology is a request for forgiveness that implies an admission of wrongdoing. An excuse is a reason that tries to explain why something was done in the hope of avoiding a charge of wrongdoing.

EX: an apology for the discourtesy; an attempt to excuse herself from the requirement

a posteriori See *deduce*.

apparent, evident

Both words mean obvious and clear, but with different shades of meaning. Apparent suggests the use of reasoning, while evident suggests the presence of objective or external indications.

EX: it is apparent the theory will not succeed; evident defects

appear See *materialize; would seem*.

appraise, apprise

Appraise means to evaluate or to judge. Apprise means to give notice or to inform. Do not spell apprise with a "z" (apprize).

EX: appraise the furniture; apprise the suspect of her rights

apprehend, comprehend

Apprehend means to seize or capture. Comprehend means to grasp or understand.

EX: apprehend the suspect; comprehend the theory

approximately See *about*.

a priori See *deduce*.

apt, likely, prone, liable

All of these words can mean probably, having a tendency, or inclined. Use apt or prone when referring to a natural tendency or habit that is unpleasant or undesirable.

EX: apt to fall; prone to error; likely to succeed
The primary meaning of liable is legally responsible. Avoid using it to mean probability even in an unpleasant or undesirable context.

SAY: apt to overdrink and have an accident
RATHER THAN: liable to overdrink and have an accident

arbitrate, mediate

To arbitrate is to render a decision at the invitation of both parties. To mediate is to act as a go-between to encourage the parties to come to a mutually satisfactory resolution on their own.

around See *about; round*.

artless See *unsophisticated*.

as See *like*.

as, because, since (see also *because*)

Do not use "as" as a substitute for the other words listed.

SAY: he filed the claim because (or since) he qualified for it
RATHER THAN: he filed the claim as he qualified for it

as...as

When "as" is used in a comparison, complete the sentence in order to determine whether the pronoun that follows should be nominative or objective.

EX: she is as wise as I (the nominative "I" is used because if you completed the sentence, it would read: "she is as wise as I am.")
EX: the verdict shocked him as much as me (the objective "me" is used because if you completed the sentence, it would read: "the verdict shocked him as much as it shocked me.")

as far as See *all the farther*.

as if, as though

"As though" is preferable to "as if" in formal writing. Use a subjunctive verb after this phrase.

SAY: the witness acts as though he were knowledgeable
RATHER THAN: the witness acts as if he is knowledgeable

ask a question

The phrase is redundant; either of the two words alone is sufficient.

SAY: ask her; question her
RATHER THAN: ask her a question

as per, as regards, with regard to

Avoid these clumsy expressions.

SAY: as you instructed; concerning your letter; about your application
RATHER THAN: as per your instructions; as regards your letter; with regard to your application

assay See *essay*.

assert See *claim.*

as such
> Avoid this awkward phrase.
> SAY: the coins are rare and valuable.
> RATHER THAN: the coins are rare. <u>As such</u>, they are valuable.

assume, presume
> While often used interchangeably, assume suggests a reasoning process, while presume means to take for granted without proof.
> EX: from reading the transcript, I <u>assumed</u> that he was present; <u>presumed</u> to be innocent

assure, insure, ensure
> Assure means to convince or to guarantee, and to set one's mind at ease. Use it in reference to a person, not to property. Ensure and insure mean to guard against loss. Insure is the preferred spelling. Use it in reference to a person or to property.
> EX: <u>assure</u> the defendant that we will do our best; <u>insure</u> the spouse, with the child as beneficiary; <u>insure</u> the car against theft

as...than
> Do not omit the second "as" when making comparisons.
> SAY: <u>as</u> efficient <u>as</u>, or more efficient than
> RATHER THAN: <u>as</u> efficient or more efficient than

as though See *as if.*

as to
> Generally, this phrase should not be used as a substitute for "about."
> SAY: we are unsure <u>about</u> the trial date
> RATHER THAN: we are unsure <u>as to</u> the trial date

as to whether
> Avoid this awkward and wordy phrase.
> SAY: unsure <u>whether</u> to come
> RATHER THAN: unsure <u>as to whether</u> to come

as well as, both
> "As well as" and "both" do not need to be used together.
> SAY: <u>both</u> John and Jim
> RATHER THAN: <u>both</u> John <u>as well as</u> Jim

at See *in, at.*

at about
> Avoid this phrase.
> SAY: arrived <u>at</u> noon; arrived <u>about</u> noon
> RATHER THAN: arrived <u>at about</u> noon

at present
> Omit this phrase if it adds nothing to the sentence.

> SAY: we are preparing a handbook
> RATHER THAN: we are preparing a handbook <u>at present</u>

attached hereto
> The phrase is almost always redundant.
> SAY: the document is <u>attached</u>
> RATHER THAN: the document is <u>attached hereto</u>

attend, tend
> Attend means to take care of or wait upon. Tend means to be inclined.
> EX: <u>attend</u> the customer; <u>tend</u> to ramble

at this point in time
> A wordy way to say "now."

augment, supplement
> Augment means to increase. Supplement means to add to.
> EX: <u>augment</u> income; <u>supplement</u> the report

aural See *oral.*

author
> Avoid using this word as a verb. As a noun, use it for men and women; do not use the word authoress.
> SAY: <u>write</u> the memo; she is an <u>author</u>
> RATHER THAN: <u>author</u> the memo; she is an <u>authoress</u>

averse See *adverse.*

avert See *advert; divert.*

avocation, vocation
> Avocation: a hobby, something done in addition to one's regular work. Vocation: one's main source of livelihood.
> EX: his <u>avocation</u> was painting; his <u>vocation</u> was truck driver

avoid See *help but.*

await See *wait.*

awhile, a while
> "Awhile" is an adverb that means "for a short time." (Hence do not use the word "for" before awhile since it is already included in its meaning.) The word "while" is a noun meaning a period of time. "A while," therefore, means "a period of time." "For" can be used with this phrase.
> EX: wait <u>awhile</u> until I return; wait for <u>a while</u> before you decide to litigate

back down, back up, back out
Generally, these words are colloquial and should be avoided in formal writing.

back of, in back of, behind
"Behind" is preferable to "back of" or "in back of."
SAY: the digest volumes are <u>behind</u> the reporter volumes
RATHER THAN: the digest volumes are <u>in back of</u> (or <u>back of</u>) the reporter volumes.

backward, backwards
Both words are proper as adverbs. Only "backward" is proper as an adjective.
EX: move <u>backward</u>, move <u>backwards</u>; a <u>backward</u> move (not a <u>backwards</u> move)

bad, badly (see also *worse*)
"Bad" and "badly" are often misused with verbs such as look and feel.
SAY: I feel <u>bad</u>
RATHER THAN: I feel <u>badly</u> (unless you mean that your sense of touch is weak or impaired)
Use "badly" as an adverb.
EX: sung <u>badly</u>
Also, "badly" should not be used to mean "very much."

balance, remainder, rest
"Balance" should not be used as a substitute for "remainder" or "rest."
SAY: the <u>rest</u> of the week
RATHER THAN: the <u>balance</u> of the week
In accounting or bookkeeping, however, it is proper to refer to the balance in the account.

bank on, rely on, depend on
Avoid using "bank on" to mean to "rely on" or "depend on."
SAY: <u>rely</u> on her advice
RATHER THAN: <u>bank on</u> her advice

barely See *hardly.*

basis See *on the basis of.*

be advised that
Avoid this overly formal phrase.

SAY: you must appear
RATHER THAN: <u>be advised that</u> you must appear

bear See *born.*

because, as, for (see also *on account of; due to; due to the fact that*)
"As" and "for" are weak substitutes for "because" when you mean cause or a causal relationship.
SAY: lost the case <u>because</u> of a change in the law
RATHER THAN: lost the case, <u>as</u> the law changed; or lost the case, <u>for</u> the law changed

because, reason is because
"Because" means "for the reason that" or "since." Hence you do not need the phrase "reason is because."
SAY: he was fined <u>because</u> of the report
RATHER THAN: he was fined; the <u>reason is because</u> of the report
If you need to say the "reason is," say the "reason is that" rather than the "reason is because."
EX: the <u>reason</u> he succeeded <u>is that</u> he worked harder than the others

before See *preparatory to; in advance of.*

begin See *commence.*

begrudge See *envy.*

behind See *back of.*

being as
Avoid this phrase as a substitute for because.
SAY: <u>because</u> the jury was still out
RATHER THAN: <u>being as</u> the jury was still out

believe, feel (see also *expect*)
Use "believe" when you are emphasizing thinking or convictions. Use "feel" when you are emphasizing emotions.
EX: I <u>feel</u> at ease because the officer <u>believed</u> the story

beside, besides (see also *else but*)
Do not say "besides" when you mean "next to."
SAY: <u>beside</u> the lake
RATHER THAN: <u>besides</u> the lake
"Besides" is an adverb meaning "moreover." It can also mean "in addition," and except."

be sure and
Say "be sure to" rather than "be sure and."

between See *among.*

between you and I

The correct phrase is "between you and me." The preposition "between" takes the objective case.

biannual, biennial, semiannual

Biannual and semiannual mean occurring twice a year. Biennial means occurring once every two years or lasting two years.

EX: biannual conferences in March and November; semiannual conferences in March and November; biennial congress in 1990 and 1992

bilateral See *unilateral.*

bimonthly, semimonthly

Bimonthly: occurring every other month. Semimonthly: occurring twice a month.

EX: biweekly meetings in January, March, and May; semimonthly reports on the first and last week of each month

biweekly, semiweekly

Biweekly: occurring every two weeks. Semiweekly: occurring twice a week.

EX: biweekly meetings on the 1st and 15th of the month; semiweekly report every Monday and Friday

The word "regular" is redundant with biweekly, semiweekly, weekly, monthly, daily, yearly, etc.

SAY: a biweekly meeting; a monthly meeting

RATHER THAN: a regular biweekly meeting; a regular monthly meeting

black, blacks, white, whites

Do not capitalize these words when referring to race.

blame on

Rewrite in order to avoid this phrase.

SAY: he blamed Joe

RATHER THAN: he placed the blame on Joe

blank See *empty.*

blatant, flagrant

Blatant: offensively obvious. Flagrant: obviously wrongful or evil.

EX: to say it is raining is a blatant lie; to use company money for personal use is a flagrant violation

bloc, block

Bloc is a group united for a common purpose. Block is a solid piece of something. As a verb, block means to impede.

EX: bloc of nations; block of wood; block the vote

born, borne, bear

Born and borne are past participles of bear. Use born only with the verb to be. Borne can also be used with the verb to be, especially when followed by "by."

EX: a baby was born; she has borne five children; five children were borne by her

both See *as well as.*

both...and

Be sure that the elements linked by these words are parallel.

SAY: the judge instructed the jury both to follow the guidelines and to use their common sense

RATHER THAN: the judge instructed the jury both to follow the guidelines and use their common sense

brake, break

Brake is a device for stopping something. Break means to split or crack something.

EX: excessive pressure will break the truck's brake

breadth, breath, breathe

Breadth is a side-to-side measurement. Breath is air taken in and out in respiration. Breathe is the verb meaning to inhale and exhale air.

EX: three inches in breadth; her first breath after awaking; breathe slowly

break See *brake.*

bridegroom See *groom.*

bring, take

Use "bring" when moving toward something, and "take" when moving away from something.

EX: bring the code to the library; take the treatise out of the library

EX: bring the exhibits with you (they are somewhere else at the present time); take the exhibits with you (they are now here and can be removed)

Britain, Briton

Britain is the country; Briton is the person.

EX: a Briton who has always lived in Britain

broke

Broke is an unacceptable substitute for being without funds.

bunch, group

Avoid the word "bunch" when referring to people. Instead, use group, association, crowd, etc.

but also See *not only.*

but however See *however.*

but what, but that

Avoid these colloquial phrases.
SAY: I have no doubt <u>that</u> he is competent
RATHER THAN: I have no doubt <u>but</u> <u>that</u> (or <u>but</u> <u>what</u>) he is competent

but yet

This phrase is redundant.
SAY: we thought we understood torts, <u>but</u> we failed the exam
RATHER THAN: we thought we understood torts, <u>but</u> <u>yet</u> we failed the exam

by reason of

This phrase is usually too wordy unless you are quoting the term of art, "by reason of insanity."
SAY: rejected <u>due</u> <u>to</u> a failure to complete the application
RATHER THAN: rejected <u>by</u> <u>reason</u> <u>of</u> a failure to complete the application

calculate, figure, reckon

Do not use these words to mean "think," "suppose," or "anticipate."

can, may

"Can" indicates the ability or freedom to do something. "May" indicates permission.
EX: she <u>can</u> do legal research; she <u>may</u> use the law library.

cancel out

The "out" in this phrase is redundant.

cannot

Do not spell this as two words (can not) unless you are placing great emphasis on the word "not."

cannot but, can't but, cannot help but

Avoid these awkward phrases.
SAY: <u>cannot</u> help admiring
RATHER THAN: <u>cannot</u> <u>but</u> admire; <u>can't</u> <u>help</u> <u>but</u> admire

can't

Spell this word out in formal writing: "cannot."

can't hardly

A double negative.
SAY: <u>can</u> <u>hardly</u> hear
RATHER THAN: <u>can't</u> <u>hardly</u> hear
EVEN BETTER: does not hear very well

canvas, canvass

Canvas is the noun meaning a heavy piece of fabric. Canvass is the verb meaning to solicit or request.
EX: stand on the <u>canvas</u>; he <u>canvassed</u> the block for votes

capacity See *ability.*

capitol, capital

Capitol is a building, an edifice. Capital is a city, a form of wealth, etc.
EX: visiting the Senator at the <u>capitol</u> in Albany, the <u>capital</u> of New York

carat, karat, caret, carrot

Carat is a unit of weight. It is also spelled karat. Caret is a proofreader's mark (∧) indicating that an insertion must be made in the line. Carrot is a vegetable.

case of

This phrase is usually redundant.
SAY: in Johnson vs. Smith
RATHER THAN: in the <u>case</u> <u>of</u> Johnson vs. Smith

censor, censure, censer

A censor is someone who looks for objectionable material. To censure is to condemn. A censer is an incense vessel.
EX: he was <u>censured</u> by the <u>censor</u> for writing the passage

center around, center on

Avoid the phrase "center around." Instead say "center on" or "center in."
SAY: the brief <u>centered</u> <u>on</u> the estoppel theory
RATHER THAN: the brief <u>centered</u> <u>around</u> the estoppel theory

certainly, very

Both words are frequently overused. Try to avoid them.

chairman

Instead of this sexist word, say chair or chairperson.

SAY: the <u>chair</u> resigned
RATHER THAN: the <u>chairman</u> resigned

character, nature
Avoid using these words unnecessarily.
SAY: the argument is specious
RATHER THAN: the argument is of a specious <u>character</u>

cite, quote
Cite means to make reference to written material. Quote means to repeat verbatim what someone has said or written.
EX: <u>quote</u> from the statute after you <u>cite</u> it

cite, site, sight
Cite means to make reference to written material. A site is a place or location. Sight is the ability to see.
EX: <u>cite</u> the opinion; <u>site</u> of the accident; impaired <u>sight</u>

claim, assert, maintain
Use claim either to imply doubt or a legal right. Use assert or maintain to emphasize truth.
EX: a fraud <u>claim</u>; he <u>asserted</u> that he was not there; he <u>maintained</u> that he was not there

clean, cleanse
Clean refers to physical objects, while cleanse refers to intangible or moral matters.
EX: <u>clean</u> the floor; <u>cleanse</u> one's conscience

climatic, climactic
Climatic refers to atmospheric conditions, e.g., the temperature. Climactic refers to a culmination or high point.
EX: the trip was cancelled due to sudden <u>climatic</u> changes; the <u>climactic</u> moment of the trial was her testimony

close proximity
This phrase is redundant since proximity means close in place or time.
SAY: the car is <u>close</u> to the edge
RATHER THAN: the car is in <u>close</u> <u>proximity</u> to the edge

closure, cloture
Closure is the act of closing something; a conclusion. Cloture is a legislative procedure that terminates debate so that a vote can be taken.
EX: bring the matter to <u>closure</u>; <u>cloture</u> was invoked in order to end the filibuster

coherence See *adherence.*

college, university
Generally a college is one of the schools within a larger institution called the university.
EX: the <u>college</u> of arts and sciences at the state <u>university</u>

collusion, connivance
Collusion is an agreement to defraud, using the forms of the law. Connivance is an indirect consent or permission to allow another to commit an unlawful act.
EX: <u>collusion</u> by the husband and wife in pretending that grounds for divorce existed; <u>connivance</u> of the mayor in not notifying the police when she heard that the money was going to be embezzled

come and, try and, go and
Omit the "and" in these phrases. If you need **a** substitute, use the infinitive "to."
SAY: <u>come</u> <u>to</u> find out for yourself; <u>try</u> <u>to</u> find a case on point; <u>go</u> find the document
RATHER THAN: <u>come</u> <u>and</u> find out for yourself; <u>try</u> <u>and</u> find a case on point; <u>go</u> <u>and</u> find the document

commence, begin, initiate
For everyday events, use begin. For normal legal matters and other relatively important events, use commence. For very serious events, use initiate.
EX: <u>begin</u> work; <u>commence</u> litigation; <u>initiate</u> the investigation

committee is
Committee takes a singular verb when you are referring to the committee as a whole.
EX: the committee <u>is</u> scheduled to reconvene soon.

common See *mutual.*

common, ordinary
Common suggests what is shared by many. Ordinary suggests a lack of distinction.
EX: <u>common</u> knowledge; <u>ordinary</u> soldier

comparatively See *relatively.*

compare, contrast
When you compare, you emphasize similarities and differences. When you contrast, you emphasize differences.
EX: <u>compare</u> the two offers; <u>contrast</u> the civil law with the common law

compare and contrast

This phrase is redundant since "compare" means to point out similarities and differences.

compare to, compare with

"Compare to" suggests an existing similarity. "Compare with" suggests calling attention to differences and similarities.

EX: he was flattered when Jones compared him to the partner; compare the testimony with the prior statements

compel, impel

Compel suggests a greater degree of involuntariness and force than impel. Impel suggests the use of urging, persuasion, and moral pressure.

EX: the court compelled him to answer; the revelation impelled him to come forward

complement, compliment

Complement means to supplement, complete, or bring to a whole. Compliment means a flattering remark.

EX: the colors complement the design; an unexpected compliment

complete See *finalize.*

compose, comprise, include

Compose means to constitute or make up. Comprise means to consist of or to include. The parts compose the whole, the whole comprises the parts.

EX: the twelve counties compose the state; the state comprises twelve counties

When you say include, you are usually referring to less than all of the parts. When you say comprise, you are usually referring to all of the parts.

EX: the play comprises three acts; the play includes songs and dances

comprehend See *apprehend.*

comprise See *compose.*

concede See *acknowledge.*

concept, conception

Concept is a thought or general idea. Conception is one's understanding of something.

EX: the concept of equity; they had no conception of the magnitude of the loss

concerning See *in regard to.*

conclude See *finalize.*

concur with, concur in

Say "concur with" when the agreement is with a person. Say "concur in" when the agreement is with anything else.

EX: Judge Smith concurred with Judge Jones; I concur in the result

connection See *in connection with.*

connivance See *collusion.*

connotation, denotation

Connotation is the suggestive or secondary meaning of the word or phrase. Denotation is the literal meaning of the word or phrase.

EX: the connotation of widow is loneliness and grief; its denotation is a woman whose husband has died

consecutive, successive

Consecutive means following without interruption. Successive means following in logical order, which may or may not involve interruption.

EX: a consecutive sentence is served immediately after the prior sentence; successive defeats in 1982, 1985, and 1990

consensus of opinion

This phrase is redundant.

SAY: the consensus was to adjourn

RATHER THAN: the consensus of opinion was to adjourn

consider See *deem.*

consistently, constantly

Consistently means uniformly. Constantly means persistently, continually recurring.

EX: consistently wrong; constantly interrupting

constantly See *consistently.*

consul See *counsel.*

contact

Do not use this word to mean get in touch with.

SAY: telephone him, write to him, communicate with him

RATHER THAN: contact him

contagious, infectious

Contagious means transmitted by physical contact. Infectious means transmitted without actual contact, e.g., through disease-carrying organisms in water, air, etc.

contemptible, contemptuous
 Contemptible means deserving contempt. Contemptuous means showing contempt.
 EX: <u>contemptible</u> lie; he was <u>contemptuous</u> of the police officer

contend See *allege.*

contiguous See *adjacent.*

continual, continuous
 Continual means happening over and over, but with interruptions. Continuous means happening without interruption.
 EX: <u>continual</u> harassment; <u>continuous</u> weekend snow

continue on
 The word "on" is redundant.
 SAY: <u>continue</u> the project
 RATHER THAN: <u>continue on</u> the project

continuous See *continual.*

contrast See *compare.*

contributing factor See *factor.*

convince, persuade
 Convince means to cause someone to believe something. Persuade means to induce someone to act.
 EX: she <u>convinced</u> me that I had a cause of action; she <u>persuaded</u> me to litigate

cooperate together
 A redundant phrase.
 SAY: they <u>cooperated</u> on the project
 RATHER THAN: they <u>cooperated together</u> on the project

cooperation See *mutual cooperation.*

cope
 A somewhat informal word that means to contend. Use "with" when you use this word.
 SAY: he cannot <u>cope with</u> his job
 RATHER THAN: at his job he cannot <u>cope</u>
 EVEN BETTER: difficulty performing his job

controversial issue, noncontroversial issue
 An issue is a question about which there is disagreement. Therefore, to call an issue "controversial" is redundant, and to call it "noncontroversial" is a non sequitur. By definition, an issue must be controversial.

co-respondent, correspondent
 A co-respondent is someone with whom your spouse allegedly committed adultery. A correspondent is someone with whom you communicate in writing.
 EX: she was named as the <u>co-respondent</u> in the wife's divorce action against her husband; a <u>correspondent</u> in China

could of, should of, would of
 The "of" in these phrases should be "have."
 SAY: <u>could have</u> succeeded; <u>should have</u> succeeded; <u>would have</u> succeeded
 RATHER THAN: <u>could of</u> succeeded; <u>should of</u> succeeded; <u>would of</u> succeeded
Also avoid the contractions "could've," "should've," and "would've."

council See *counsel.*

councilor See *counselor.*

counsel, council, consul
 Counsel is a lawyer or a group of lawyers. Counsel also means the advice given by a respected or knowledgeable person. Council is an organized body set up to govern or to give advice. A consul is a government official who lives in another country in order to represent his or her country's commercial interests.
 EX: <u>counsel</u> for the corporation, wise <u>counsel</u> received from the accountant; rural county <u>council</u>; <u>council</u> of elders; trade problems handled by the <u>consul</u>

counselor, councilor
 A counselor is someone who gives advice. A councilor is a member of a council. The preferred spelling is with one "l" as indicated here.
 EX: <u>counselor</u> at law; an elected <u>councilor</u>

country, nation
 A country is a physical or geographic territory. A nation is a group of people with common customs, history, etc.
 EX: France is a <u>country</u> at war; America is a <u>nation</u> of immigrants

couple
 When referring to a man and woman, couple takes a plural or a singular verb so long as you are consistent. The plural is preferred.
 SAY: the <u>couple are</u> donating <u>their</u> time
 RATHER THAN: the <u>couple are</u> donating <u>its</u> time

course, in the course of
 The "in" phrase is redundant.
 SAY: <u>during</u> the trial
 RATHER THAN: <u>in the course of</u> the trial

courts-martial

This is the preferred plural spelling, rather than court-martials.

covet See *envy*.

credible, creditable, credulous

Credible means plausible, worthy of belief. Creditable means worthy of praise. Credulous means gullible, overly inclined to believe.

EX: a <u>credible</u> witness; he did a <u>creditable</u> job digesting the transcripts; he is unusually <u>credulous</u> for a person with so much education

credit See *accredit*.

criterion, criteria

Criterion is the singular of criteria. The preferred plural of criterion is criteria rather than criterions.

EX: the <u>criterion</u> used by the commission <u>is</u> efficiency; the <u>criteria</u> used by the commission <u>are</u> efficiency and experience

critique

Avoid this word as a verb.

SAY: <u>criticize</u> the presentation; <u>give</u> <u>a</u> <u>critique</u> of the presentation

RATHER THAN: <u>critique</u> the presentation

culmination See *final culmination*.

curious, inquisitive

Curious means being interested in having information. Inquisitive means being overly interested, sometimes to the point of prying.

EX: he was <u>curious</u> about the police report on his accident; they resented her <u>inquisitive</u> nature

currently

Omit this word if it adds nothing to the sentence.

SAY: we are preparing a handbook

RATHER THAN: we are <u>currently</u> preparing a handbook

customary, usual, habitual

Customary means commonly practiced. Usual means that which is normal and frequent. Habitual means acting by habit or constantly repeating a certain behavior.

EX: it was <u>customary</u> for the court to adjourn at noon; his <u>usual</u> hostility; <u>habitual</u> liar

cut See *laceration*.

data, datum

Datum means information. Data is the plural of datum and should, therefore, take a plural verb. Although some grammarians feel that data can also take a singular verb, in formal writing, use a plural verb.

SAY: the <u>data</u> <u>are</u> available

RATHER THAN: the <u>data</u> <u>is</u> available

dates See *from...to*.

dawn on

Avoid this phrase in formal writing.

SAY: it <u>occurred</u> <u>to</u> him

RATHER THAN: it <u>dawned</u> <u>on</u> him

dead end, dead-end

Dead end is a noun meaning the end of something such as a road. It also means a statement or impasse. The adjective form is dead-end.

EX: the negotiations reached a <u>dead</u> <u>end</u>; a <u>dead-end</u> job

deadly, deathly

Deadly means tending to cause, or causing death. Deathly means resembling death.

EX: <u>deadly</u> use of force; <u>deathly</u> apparition

deal

In formal writing, do not use this word to mean treatment or bargain.

SAY: a good <u>agreement</u>

RATHER THAN: a good <u>deal</u>

death See *demise*.

decided, decisive, incisive

Decided means definite, without doubt. Decisive means resolute or conclusive. Incisive means perceptive, sharp.

EX: a <u>decided</u> advantage; a <u>decisive</u> victory; an <u>incisive</u> remark

decimate

Literally, this word means to kill every tenth person (a Roman form of punishment). It also means to destroy a large part of something. If, however, you are referring to destruction in a proportion other than ten percent, do not use decimate.

SAY: <u>destroyed</u> half the population
RATHER THAN: <u>decimated</u> half the population

decisive See *decided*.

decline, refuse
    Decline means to say no politely. Refuse means to say no with a note of insistence or irritation.
    EX: <u>decline</u> the invitation; <u>refuse</u> to answer

deduce, deduct (see also *deduce, induce*)
    Deduce means to infer, to come to a position through reasoning (from the general to the specific). Deduct means to subtract something. The noun for both words is deduction.
    EX: the investigator <u>deduced</u> that the witness was not telling the truth; <u>deduct</u> business expenses

deduce, induce
    Deduce is to reason from the general facts to a specific conclusion, e.g., from cause to effect. This is known as "a priori" reasoning. Induce is to reason from specific facts to a general conclusion, e.g, from effect to cause. This is known as "a posteriori" reasoning.
    EX: since all employees we talked to had received the notice, we <u>deduced</u> that this employee received it; from the fact that workers had accidents at the machine on March 13th, March 26th, and July 31st, we <u>induced</u> that the machine was dangerous

deduct See *deduce*.

deem, consider, think
    Deem is an overly formal way to say consider or think.
    SAY: we <u>think</u> the matter is closed; we <u>consider</u> the matter closed
    RATHER THAN: we <u>deem</u> the matter closed

defective, deficient
    Defective means having a flaw. Deficient means insufficient, lacking in amount or degree.
    EX: <u>defective</u> computer; <u>deficient</u> in research skills

definite, definitive
    Definite means clearly defined. Definitive means decisive and authoritative.
    EX: <u>definite</u> plans; <u>definitive</u> ruling

definitely, absolutely, positively
    Avoid these words when you mean clearly or certainly.
    SAY: without doubt, I am going
    RATHER THAN: I am <u>definitely</u> going; I am <u>abso-</u>lutely going; I am <u>positively</u> going
    EVEN BETTER: I am going

definitive See *definite*.

delivery See *take delivery*.

delusion, illusion
    Both words mean a false image. A delusion is more permanent or fixed than an illusion.
    EX: he acted under the <u>delusion</u> that he was George Washington; his <u>illusion</u> of grandeur vanished when he lost the election

demise, death
    Demise is an overly formal word for death.
    SAY: an untimely <u>death</u>
    RATHER THAN: an untimely <u>demise</u>

democracy, republic
    When you use the word democracy, you are emphasizing the power of the people. When you use the word republic, you are emphasizing the power of the people through their elected representatives.

denotation See *connotation*.

deny See *rebut*.

dependent, dependant
    The preferred spelling is dependent as a noun or adjective.

depend on See *bank on*.

depository, depositary
    Depository is a place where something is kept or stored. Depositary is a person who has been entrusted with something. Occasionally, however, depositary is also used to refer to a place.
    EX: he placed the money in the <u>depository</u>; he gave the money to the <u>depositary</u>

desert, dessert
    Desert is a dry barren land. It also means to abandon. Dessert is part of a meal.

desire See *envy*.

dessert See *desert*.

device, devise
    A device is an invention or a product of some kind. A devise is a gift of real property (and sometimes personal property) by a will.
    EX: gambling <u>device</u>; a <u>devise</u> to his daughter

diagnosis, prognosis

Diagnosis is a process of studying something. It is also the opinion based on such a study. Prognosis is a prediction.

EX: a <u>diagnosis</u> of the illness; the <u>prognosis</u> for recovery

different

Avoid the redundant use of this word.

SAY: he will visit three cities

RATHER THAN: he will visit three <u>different</u> cities

different from, different than

Generally, "different from" is preferable to "different than."

EX: intent is <u>different</u> <u>from</u> apprehension

differ from, differ with

Use "differ from" when emphasizing dissimilarity between things. Use "differ with" when emphasizing differences between persons

EX: civil law <u>differs</u> <u>from</u> common law; he <u>differed</u> <u>with</u> the judge

dilemma, predicament

Dilemma involves a choice between two possibilities that are relatively equal in their undesirability. A predicament is a problem or an embarrassing situation.

EX: he faced the <u>dilemma</u> of accepting the forfeiture or the fine; the <u>predicament</u> of being without funds in a strange town

diminish, minimize

Diminish means to make something smaller. Minimize means to make something as small as possible.

EX: <u>diminish</u> the available assets; he tried to <u>minimize</u> his responsibility

disassociate See *dissociate.*

disburse, disperse

Disburse means to pay out. Disperse means to scatter or disseminate.

EX: <u>disburse</u> the surplus; <u>disperse</u> the crowd

disc, disk

The preferred spelling is disk except when referring to a phonograph record, which is spelled disc.

EX: computer <u>disk</u>; stereo <u>disc</u>

discharge See *fire.*

disclose, divulge, said (see also *indicate*)

Do not use "disclose" or "divulge" for "said" unless you mean that something is being revealed or uncovered rather than merely communicated.

SAY: he <u>said</u> that he was tired

RATHER THAN: he <u>disclosed</u> that he was tired; he <u>divulged</u> that he was tired (unless you mean that this information had some significance)

discomfit, discomfort

Both words are acceptable to mean "to make uneasy or uncomfortable." Discomfit also means to frustrate or to thwart.

discover, invent

Discover means to obtain knowledge of something that has existed but has been unknown. Invent means to produce or create something that has never existed.

EX: <u>discover</u> gold, <u>discover</u> rampant cheating; <u>invent</u> a more powerful computer

discreet, discrete

Discreet means being prudent, cautious. Discrete means separate, distinct.

EX: <u>discreet</u> about revealing the news; <u>discrete</u> sections of the brief

disfranchise, disenfranchise

Although the latter spelling is more commonly used in law, the former is preferred.

disinterested, uninterested

Disinterested means impartial, having no bias. Uninterested means indifferent.

EX: a <u>disinterested</u> witness; he was so <u>uninterested</u> that he fell asleep during the performance

disk See *disc.*

dismiss See *fire.*

disorganized, unorganized

Disorganized means disorder, usually in reference to that which was once organized. Unorganized means never having been organized.

EX: <u>disorganized</u> file after considerable use; <u>unorganized</u> notes at the beginning of her research

disperse See *disburse.*

disposal, disposition

Disposal means getting rid of something. Disposition means an arrangement of something, and also a final resolution or settlement of something.

EX: the <u>disposal</u> of the unwanted records; the court's <u>disposition</u> of the case

disposition, temperament

Disposition means one's usual frame of mind. Temperament is a more narrow word that refers to one's emotional outlook or traits.

EX: a <u>disposition</u> to accept things at face value; a volatile <u>temperament</u>

disqualified, unqualified

Disqualified means having lost the qualifications that you once had. Unqualified simply means not having the qualifications, whether or not you ever had them.

EX: the failure to register <u>disqualified</u> him from voting; he was <u>unqualified</u> because he did not have a scientific degree

Unqualified also means without limits.

EX: an <u>unqualified</u> success

dissatisfied See *unsatisfied*.

dissociate, disassociate

Both spellings are acceptable, but dissociate is preferred.

distinct, distinctive, distinguished

Distinct means separate, easily perceived. Distinctive means characteristic, allowing us to make a distinction. Distinguished means eminent, dignified.

EX: a <u>distinct</u> judicial system; the lawyer's <u>distinctive</u> thoroughness; the <u>distinguished</u> senator from Ohio

divert, avert

Divert means to distract or turn something off course. Avert means to turn away or prevent.

EX: <u>divert</u> their attention from the speaker; <u>avert</u> disaster

divide, separate

Divide means to partition or split something into parts according to a prior arrangement or plan. It is also used in the sense of splitting into opposing groups or camps. Separate means to partition or disconnect something by removing a component part or by keeping the parts away from each other.

EX: the judge must <u>divide</u> the assets; the issue will <u>divide</u> the community; the judge ordered the bailiff to <u>separate</u> the witnesses

divided into, composed of

"Divided into" means to partition or split something into its parts. "Composed of" means to constitute the parts of something.

EX: the profits were <u>divided</u> <u>into</u> four shares; the jury is <u>composed</u> <u>of</u> teachers, tellers, insurance agents, and housewives

divulge See *disclose*.

doesn't See *don't*.

dollars

Do not use this word if you also use the dollar sign.

SAY: he paid $200

RATHER THAN: he paid $200 <u>dollars</u>

dominant, predominant

Both words mean controlling or exercising the most control. "Predominant," however, suggests being overriding or uppermost at a particular time.

EX: the <u>dominant</u> forces seeking change; during the meeting, the shareholders were the <u>predominant</u> force

dominate, domineer

Dominate means to control by reason of power or authority. Domineer means to control or rule arbitrarily.

EX: the senior partner <u>dominated</u> the discussion; Stalin <u>domineered</u> for many years

don't, doesn't

Avoid contractions in formal writing unless you are quoting someone.

SAY: <u>do</u> <u>not</u> go; <u>does</u> <u>not</u> speak the language

RATHER THAN: <u>don't</u> go; <u>doesn't</u> speak the language

dope, drug, stupid

Do not use "dope" to mean a drug or a stupid person.

doubtful that, doubtful whether, doubtful if

Follow the guidelines under "doubt that, doubt whether, doubt if."

doubt that, doubt whether, doubt if

Use "doubt that" in a negative statement, in a question, and in a statement of unbelief. Use "doubt whether" to express uncertainty. Avoid "doubt if" since it is generally considered too informal.

EX: there is no <u>doubt</u> <u>that</u> the jury will convict; do you <u>doubt</u> <u>that</u> the jury will convict?; there is little <u>doubt</u> <u>that</u> the jury is biased; we <u>doubt</u> <u>whether</u> any hope of recovery exists

dreamed, dreamt

Both words are acceptable as the past tense and past participle of "dream."

drug See *dope*.

drunk, drunken

Use "drunk" as a predicate. Use "drunken" as an adjective.

EX: he is <u>drunk</u>; a <u>drunken</u> customer

due to See *on account of.*

due to, because of

"Due to" can be used as an adjective following a linking verb. Avoid using "due to" as a prepositional phrase.

SAY: his dismissal was <u>due to</u> inefficiency

RATHER THAN: he was dismissed <u>due to</u> inefficiency

"Because of" can be used as an adverb with a non-linking verb.

EX: he was dismissed <u>because of</u> inefficiency

due to the fact that, because

The "due to" phrase is a wordy way to say because.

SAY: he lost <u>because</u> he did not file

RATHER THAN: he lost <u>due to the fact that</u> he did not file

during the time that, during the course of

These are redundant phrases.

SAY: arrested <u>while</u> soliciting votes; arrested <u>during</u> the conference

RATHER THAN: arrested <u>during the time that</u> he was soliciting votes; arrested <u>during the course of</u> the conference

dying, dyeing

Dying means losing one's life. Dyeing is the coloring of material.

each

Each takes a singular verb when it is in front of the word it governs or refers to. This is so even if that word is plural in an "of" phrase. Each takes a plural verb when it comes after a plural subject.

EX: <u>each has</u> (not have) a supply. <u>Each</u> of the recruits <u>has</u> (not have) a supply. John and Mary <u>each have</u> (not has) their own supply.

each and every

This phrase is redundant.

SAY: <u>each</u> person must sign, or, <u>every</u> person must sign

RATHER THAN: <u>each and every</u> person must sign

each other, one another

The traditional view is that "each other" should be used only when referring to two people, and "one another" to more than two.

EX: the plaintiff and defendant would not look at <u>each other</u>; the five attorneys sent memos to <u>one another</u>

The possessive is 's rather than s'.

EX: Bob and Bill used each other's books; the three students used one another's books

eager, anxious

Eager means impatient and desirous. Anxious means worried or distressed.

EX: <u>eager</u> to leave the hospital; <u>anxious</u> about the doctor's report

early on

The phrase is redundant; "on" is unnecessary.

earth, Earth

Capitalize only when referring to the planet.

EX: dry <u>earth</u>; the satellite circles the <u>Earth</u>

East See *West.*

eatable, edible

These words, meaning fit to be eaten, are interchangeable.

ecology, environment

Ecology is a narrower word meaning the relationships between organisms and their surroundings. Environment means the total circumstances in a certain setting.

economic, economical

Economic refers to the production and management of wealth. Economical means prudent, not wasteful.

EX: <u>economic</u> forecast; an <u>economical</u> use of limited resources

ecstasy

Avoid the common misspelling "acy"

effect (see also *affect*)

Effect can be a noun (meaning the result), or a verb (meaning to bring something about or to cause). As a verb it is overly formal.

SAY: the administrator made changes
RATHER THAN: the administrator <u>effected</u> changes

effective See *affective*.

effective, efficient
Effective means producing the desired result. Efficient means producing the desired result without wasting effort or time.
EX: an <u>effective</u> remedy; an <u>efficient</u> management team

e.g., i.e.
E.g. (exempli gratia) means for example. I.e. (id est) means in other words, or, that is.
EX: the terms of the will, <u>i.e.</u>, what she wanted to do with her property; the terms of the will, <u>e.g.</u>, her husband receives the car, her son receives the stock, her daughter receives the business

egotist, egoist
An egotist is a selfish, conceited person. An egoist is one who follows self-interest as a matter of principle.

either, any
Use "either" when you are referring to two. Use "any" when referring to more than two.
EX: they will hire <u>either</u> John or Mary; I will read <u>any</u> of the three books

either, neither
Either takes a singular verb, even if followed by "of" and a plural. The same is true of neither.
EX: <u>either</u> theory <u>is</u> acceptable; <u>either</u> of the theories <u>is</u> acceptable
EX: <u>neither</u> theory <u>is</u> acceptable; <u>neither</u> of the theories <u>is</u> acceptable

either/or
Avoid this phrase in formal writing.

either...or, neither...nor
"Or" goes with "either." "Nor" goes with "neither."
SAY: <u>neither</u> the judge <u>nor</u> the jury
RATHER THAN: <u>neither</u> the judge <u>or</u> the jury
Use a singular verb unless one of the nouns joined is plural. If so, the verb should agree with the noun closest to the verb.
EX: <u>neither</u> the judge <u>nor</u> the jury <u>is</u> in the courtroom
EX: <u>neither</u> the jurors <u>nor</u> the judge <u>is</u> in the courtroom
EX: <u>neither</u> the judge <u>nor</u> the jurors <u>are</u> in the courtroom

elder (eldest), older (oldest)
Elder applies to persons. Older can apply to persons or to things. Older is preferable except when communicating the theme of seniority.
EX: <u>elder</u> brother; <u>older</u> document, <u>older</u> person

elemental, elementary
Use elemental when you are referring to the elements, e.g., air, wind. It also means essential or inherent in something. Use elementary when you mean introductory, simple, or fundamental.
EX: <u>elemental</u> force, <u>elemental</u> requirement; <u>elementary</u> research

elicit, illicit
Elicit means to bring out or to call forth. Illicit means illegal.
EX: <u>elicit</u> a response; <u>illicit</u> transaction

else but, else beside, else except
The word "else" can be redundant when used with "but," "besides," or "except."
SAY: no one <u>but</u> John came; no one <u>besides</u> John came; no one <u>except</u> John came.
RATHER THAN: no one <u>else</u> <u>but</u> John came; no one <u>else</u> <u>besides</u> John came; no one <u>else</u> <u>except</u> John came.

elude See *allude*.

emend, amend
Emend means to correct something by editing. Amend means to change something or to improve it.
EX: <u>emend</u> the draft; <u>amend</u> the law

emigrate, immigrate
Emigrate means to leave a country and settle elsewhere. The person who emigrates is an emigrant. Immigrate means to come into a country to settle. The person who immigrates is an immigrant.
EX: John <u>emigrated</u> from Poland. He is an <u>emigrant</u>. Mary <u>immigrated</u> to America. She is an <u>immigrant</u>.

eminent, imminent, immanent
Eminent means prominent or distinguished. Imminent means near at hand. Immanent means inherent.
EX: an <u>eminent</u> authority on torts; <u>imminent</u> threat; <u>immanent</u> in human nature

empathy, sympathy
Empathy means identifying with the emotions of another. It is a stronger word than sympathy which means understanding and compassion.
EX: <u>empathy</u> between the brothers; <u>sympathy</u> for the victim

employ, use

Employ is often an overly formal way to say use.
SAY: they <u>used</u> ingenuity
RATHER THAN: they <u>employed</u> ingenuity

empty, vacant, blank

Empty means containing nothing, usually over a period of time. Vacant means containing nothing, often momentarily. Blank means nothing meaningful on the surface.
EX: <u>empty</u> promises ; <u>vacant</u> lot; <u>blank</u> page

enclose, inclose

The preferred spelling is enclose.

enclosed herein, enclosed please find, please find enclosed

These phrases are redundant.
SAY: a copy <u>is</u> <u>enclosed</u>
RATHER THAN: <u>enclosed</u> <u>herein</u> is a copy; <u>enclosed</u> <u>please</u> <u>find</u> a copy

endemic, epidemic

Endemic means prevalent in a particular locality or people. Epidemic means spreading rapidly in an area.
EX: the disease is <u>endemic</u> to humid areas; emergency funds to combat an <u>epidemic</u> of smallpox

endorse, indorse

These words mean to place one's signature on something as part of a legal transfer. They also mean to approve of something. The preferred spelling is endorse.

enormity, enormousness

Enormity means excessively immoral. Do not use it to refer to size. Enormousness means very large in size.
EX: the <u>enormity</u> of the offense; the <u>enormousness</u> of the animal

enormous, immense

Enormous means extraordinary large. Immense means so large that the regular means of measurement are not adequate.
EX: an <u>enormous</u> box; the <u>immense</u> ocean floor

enquire, inquire

The preferred spelling is inquire.

ensure See *assure.*

enure See *inure.*

envelop, envelope

Envelop means to enclose. Envelope means a container for small objects or letters.
EX: he saw the smoke <u>envelop</u> the room; an unopened <u>envelope</u>

envious, jealous

Envious means feeling upset and resentful about what another has. Jealous means feeling fear or apprehension about being replaced.
EX: <u>envious</u> of her success; <u>jealous</u> of the time he spent with her

environment See *ecology.*

envision, envisage

Envision means to picture something in one's mind, to foresee. Envisage means to consider in a certain way.
EX: they <u>envisioned</u> considerable controversy; the order as <u>envisaged</u> by the chief justice

envy, begrudge, covet, desire

"Envy" and "begrudge" mean to be upset and resentful about what another has, but "begrudge" suggests a reluctance to accept the other's claim to it. "Covet" means to have a wrongful and often secret wish for what the other has. "Desire" is a broad**er** word meaning to crave or long for something.
EX: <u>envy</u> those who succeed; he <u>begrudged</u> him the honor; <u>covet</u> his neighbor's wife; <u>desire</u> to succeed

epicure See *gourmand.*

epidemic See *endemic.*

epilogue, prologue

An epilogue is a postscript, a concluding section at the end. A prologue is an introductory section.

episode, incident, event

All three words mean an occurrence. Episode suggests that the occurrence is part of a sequence or series of occurrences. An incident is a minor occurrence. An event is an important occurrence.
EX: another <u>episode</u> of violence in their feud; he thought nothing of the <u>incident</u>; all were present for the <u>event</u>

equable, equitable

Equable means steady, not extreme, serene. Equitable means fair, impartial, and just.
EX: an <u>equable</u> temper; an <u>equitable</u> division of the property

equal, perfect, unique

These are absolute words. Avoid using comparative language with them.

SAY: <u>equal</u> to; is <u>perfect</u>; is <u>unique</u>

RATHER THAN: <u>more</u> <u>equal</u> than; <u>most</u> <u>perfect</u> of; <u>less</u> <u>unique</u> than

equally as

This phrase is redundant.

SAY: <u>equally</u> guilty

RATHER THAN: <u>equally</u> <u>as</u> guilty

equitable See *equable.*

equivocal, ambiguous, obscure

Equivocal means intentionally unclear. Ambiguous means unclear because more than one meaning is possible. Obscure means not easily understood, often because it is almost hidden.

EX: an <u>equivocal</u> response; an <u>ambiguous</u> clause; an <u>obscure</u> reference

ergo

This word means therefore or consequently. Avoid it in formal writing.

esoteric, exotic

Esoteric means understood by a small group. Exotic means foreign, unusual, enticing.

EX: an <u>esoteric</u> formula; an <u>exotic</u> ceremony

especially, specially

Especially means particularly, exceptionally. Specially means in reference to a particular purpose.

EX: <u>especially</u> violent, <u>especially</u> now; <u>specially</u> trained

Esq.

If "Esq." is used after an attorney's name, do not use, Mr., Ms., etc., and, do not use the word attorney.

SAY: Mary Smith, Esq.

RATHER THAN: Ms. Mary Smith, Esq., Attorney at Law

essay, assay

Essay means to make an attempt. Assay means to subject to analysis.

EX: <u>essay</u> the project; <u>assay</u> the liquid

essential, necessary

Essential is stronger than necessary. When something is necessary, it is required and very important, but not necessarily indispensable. When something is essential, it is vital in the sense of continued existence or validity.

EX: an <u>essential</u> element of the tort; a <u>necessary</u> meeting

estimate, estimation

Estimate means a preliminary calculation or opinion. Estimation means the process of reaching an estimate.

EX: only an <u>estimate</u> could be provided; the <u>estimation</u> would take several weeks.

et al.

Et al. means "and other persons" (et alii). Avoid using it, even in case citations.

etc., and etc.

Etc. means "and others," or "and so forth". Hence "and etc." is redundant.

SAY: reporters, codes, regulations, <u>etc</u>.

RATHER THAN: reporters, codes, regulations, <u>and etc</u>.

etc., for example; etc., such as

Do not use "etc." when you introduce a list by "for example" or "such as." Etc. would be redundant.

SAY: for example, lawyers, paralegals, secretaries.

RATHER THAN: for example, lawyers, paralegals, secretaries, <u>etc</u>.

event See *episode.*

everyone, everybody

These words take singular verbs and singular pronouns.

SAY: <u>everyone</u> has <u>his</u> assignment; <u>everybody</u> performed <u>her</u> task

RATHER THAN: <u>everyone</u> have <u>their</u> assignment; <u>everybody</u> performed <u>their</u> task

EVEN BETTER: <u>they</u> have <u>their</u> assignment; <u>they</u> performed <u>their</u> task

every one, everyone

"Every one" means each individual person or thing. "Everyone" means every person.

EX: <u>every</u> <u>one</u> of the containers has been inspected; <u>everyone</u> must attend

everyplace, everywhere

Everywhere is more standard than everyplace.

everywhere that

"That" is superfluous.

SAY: <u>everywhere</u> I went

RATHER THAN: <u>everywhere</u> <u>that</u> I went

evidence, show

Do not use evidence to mean show.

SAY: their condition <u>showed</u> no weakness

RATHER THAN: their condition <u>evidenced</u> no weakness

evident See *apparent.*

exact replica The word "exact" is redundant.

except See *accept; else but; other than; save.*

except for See *inside of.*

except for the fact that
This can be shortened to "except that."

exceptionable, exceptional
Exceptionable means subject to objection. Exceptional means outstanding, uncommon.
EX: a punishment for <u>exceptionable</u> behavior; an award for <u>exceptional</u> skills

excess verbiage
The word "excess" is redundant since verbiage means excess words.

excuse See *apology.*

exhaustive, exhausting
Exhaustive means comprehensive. Exhausting means tiring, wearing oneself out.
EX: <u>exhaustive</u> study of the opinions; an <u>exhausting</u> performance

exotic See *esoteric.*

expect, suppose, believe, guess (see also *anticipate*)
Do not use "expect" when you mean suppose, believe, or guess.
SAY: I <u>believe</u> the jury will reach a verdict today
RATHER THAN: I <u>expect</u> the jury will reach a verdict today

explain See *expound.*

explicit, express
Both words mean clearly expressed. Explicit means defined, spelled out. Express is often used in reference to intention or a state of mind.
EX: <u>explicit</u> erotica; <u>express</u> offer

explicit, implicit
Explicit means clearly expressed. Implicit means implied, understood but not directly expressed.
EX: an <u>explicit</u> rejection by letter; an <u>implicit</u> rejection by silence

expound, explain
Expound is an overly technical, and often pompous, way to say explain.

express See *explicit.*

extant, extent
Extant means still in existence. Extent means the range or distance of something
EX: <u>extant</u> language; the <u>extent</u> of the damage

facilitate, help
Help or make easier is preferable to facilitate.
SAY: <u>help</u> the project
RATHER THAN: <u>facilitate</u> the project

facility, faculty
These words are close in meaning. A facility is an ease in doing something. Faculty suggests something more enduring; it is an inherent ability.
EX: a <u>facility</u> in driving; a <u>faculty</u> for analysis

fact, opinion
Do not say fact when you mean opinion. If the statement is a matter of judgment, it is an opinion no matter how strongly one feels it to be true. Facts must be capable of objective verification.
EX: fact: insurance rates have increased. Opinion: insurance rates are burdensome

fact, true fact, real fact
Since fact means something that is real, the phrase "true fact" or "real fact" is redundant.

factitious, fictitious
Factitious means artificial rather than natural. It also means not genuine. Fictitious means imaginary or invented.
EX: <u>factitious</u> smile; <u>fictitious</u> name

factor
A factor is that which contributes to a result. Hence the phrase "contributing factor" is redundant. Factor is a vague word. Avoid it when possible.
SAY: we must consider cost
RATHER THAN: cost is a <u>factor</u> we must consider

fact that
This phrase is often superfluous.
SAY: he admits he was there
RATHER THAN: he admits the <u>fact</u> <u>that</u> he was there

faculty See *facility*.

false illusion

The word false is redundant. All illusions are false.

famed, famous, noted, notable, noteworthy, notorious

Both famed and famous mean widely known. They also can mean well-regarded, but famous can be used in a negative sense as well. Noted means widely known either favorably or unfavorably. Notable and noteworthy mean valuable or worthy of notice. Notorious means widely known unfavorably.

EX: a <u>famed</u> physicist; <u>famous</u> for his blunders; a <u>noted</u> author; a <u>notable</u> record; a <u>noteworthy</u> case; a <u>notorious</u> criminal

fantasy, phantasy

The preferred spelling is fantasy.

farther, further

Farther means more distant physically. Further means more distant in degree, quantity, or time.

EX: they drove <u>farther</u> than expected; the judge would not tolerate <u>further</u> disruption

fatal, fateful

Fatal means causing or leading to death or destruction. Fateful means affecting one's destiny. It can also mean ominous.

EX: a <u>fatal</u> attack; a <u>fateful</u> decision

faze, phase

Faze means to disturb or bother. Phase means an aspect or a stage of something.

EX: the jury was not <u>fazed</u> by the revelation; the next <u>phase</u> of the project

feasible, possible

Feasible means capable of being done, often to a fair probability. Possible means capable of happening, however slight the odds may be.

EX: a <u>feasible</u> plan; a <u>possible</u> rejection

fee See *honorarium*.

feel See *believe*.

feel bad See *bad*.

female, woman, girl, lady, feminine

Some consider "female" to be objectionable except in scientific or research contexts. The preferable words are woman, girl, lady, and feminine.

SAY: the suspect is a <u>woman</u>; her <u>feminine</u> appeal
RATHER THAN: the suspect is a <u>female</u>; her <u>female</u> appeal

ferment, foment

As verbs, both words mean to excite or agitate. When used in a negative or disruptive sense, foment is more common.

EX: <u>foment</u> violence; <u>ferment</u> the passions

few See *limited*.

few, a few

"Few" and "a few" mean a small number, but with a potentially very different emphasis. "A few" can mean "at least some," while "few" can mean "hardly any."

EX: <u>a few</u> came forward; <u>few</u> came forward

fewer, less, smaller

Use "fewer" when referring to numbers, or items that can be counted. Use "less" with mass or collective nouns, and when the emphasis is on degree. Use smaller when referring to size.

EX: <u>fewer</u> applications; <u>less</u> hostility; <u>smaller</u> room

fiancé, fiancée

The first word is a man and the second is a woman engaged to be married. Note the acute accent above the e in the spelling of these words.

fictitious See *factitious*.

field

This word is overused and rarely adds anything to a sentence.

SAY: she studied law
RATHER THAN: she studied the <u>field</u> of law

fight with, fight along with, fight against

Avoid the phrase "fight with" when it is not clear whether the fight is "along with" or "against."

SAY: he <u>fought</u> <u>along</u> <u>with</u> the British; or, he <u>fought</u> <u>against</u> the British
RATHER THAN: he <u>fought</u> <u>with</u> the British

figuratively, literally

Figuratively means symbolically, or, in a manner of speaking. Literally means actually or really.

EX: he was <u>figuratively</u> on fire with rage; the bailiff <u>literally</u> lifted him out of the seat

figure See *calculate*.

final See *later*.

final culmination

The word "final" is redundant.

finalize, complete, conclude

Avoid the word finalize, meaning to put into final form. Acceptable substitutes: complete, conclude, etc.

finding, holding

A finding is a formal determination of what the facts are. The verb is find. A holding is a formal determination of how the law applies to the facts. The verb is hold.

EX: the court <u>found</u> that the defendant did not file the report, and <u>held</u> him in contempt

fine

Do not use "fine" to mean well or very well.
SAY: doing <u>well</u>
RATHER THAN: doing <u>fine</u>

fire, dismiss, discharge

Do not use "fire" to mean dismiss or discharge someone from employment. It is too informal.

first and foremost

A verbose phrase; drop "and foremost."

firstly, secondly, etc.

When presenting a list, it is preferable to say first, second, third, etc., rather than firstly, secondly, thirdly, etc. If you do use ly, be consistent. For example, do not say <u>first</u>..., <u>secondly</u>.

first of all

"Of all" is unnecessary.

fit, fitted

The past tense of fit is fit *or* fitted.
EX: the shoes <u>fit</u>; the shoes <u>fitted</u>
Use fitted, however, when you mean "to cause to fit" or "to make the right size".
EX: the seamstress <u>fitted</u> the dress

fit and proper

Select fit *or* proper. Both words are usually unnecessary.

fix

Use this word to mean to fasten securely or attach. Avoid the colloquial use of fix to mean arrange, repair, prepare, etc.

flagrant See *blatant.*

flair, flare

Flair means an aptitude or talent. Flare means to burn with a wavering light, or, to burst into flame.
EX: a <u>flair</u> for trial work; the candle <u>flared</u>

flammable, inflammable, nonflammable

Flammable and inflammable have the same meaning. They both mean easily ignited or likely to burn. Nonflammable means the opposite.

EX: gasoline is <u>flammable</u> (or <u>inflammable</u>); specially treated mattresses are <u>nonflammable</u>

flare See *flair.*

flaunt, flout

Flaunt means to brag or show off. Flout means to show contempt for or to defy openly.
EX: <u>flaunt</u> his wealth; <u>flout</u> the regulations

flier, flyer

Both words mean one who flies, and a handbill or circular. Flier is the preferred spelling.

flounder, founder

Flounder means to struggle or thrash about. Founder means to collapse or become disabled.
EX: he <u>floundered</u> through his answers; the horse <u>foundered</u> from exhaustion.

flout See *flaunt.*

flu

Do not use this shortened form of influenza.

flyer See *flier.*

foment See *ferment.*

for See *because.*

forbade See *forbid.*

forbear, forebear

As nouns, both words mean an ancestor, but forebear is the preferred spelling. As a verb, forbear (not forebear) means to resist or restrain.
EX: created by her <u>forebears</u>; <u>forbear</u> responding

forbid, forbade, forbad, forbidden

The past tense of forbid is forbade or forbad. Forbidden is an adjective and the past participle of forbid.
EX: <u>forbid</u> you to enter again; <u>forbade</u> (or <u>forbad</u>) you to enter yesterday; <u>forbidden</u> admission

forbid...from

Do not use this construction.
SAY: <u>forbid</u> you <u>to</u> enter
RATHER THAN: <u>forbid</u> you <u>from</u> entering

forced, forceful, forcible

Forced means involuntary or unnatural. Forceful means having strength or effectiveness. Forcible means brought about by physical force.
EX: <u>forced</u> landing; <u>forceful</u> argument; <u>forcible</u> entry

forebear See *forbear.*

forego, forgo

Both words mean to abstain from or give up; forgo is the preferred spelling. (Forego also means to go before, but the word is rarely used.)

EX: <u>forgo</u> force

forever See *indefinitely.*

foreword, preface, forward

A foreword is an introductory comment or note, usually written by someone other than the author. A preface is the author's introductory comment or note. Forward means bold, and at or close to the front.

EX: Senator Smith wrote a <u>foreword</u> for Jackson's book; Jackson's <u>preface</u> explained the purpose of the book; surprised by his <u>forward</u> manner; he fell <u>forward</u>

for example See *etc., for example.*

for free See *free gift.*

forgetful See *impervious.*

forgo See *forego.*

form See *formulate.*

formally, formerly

Formally means formal or in accordance with custom. Formerly means at an earlier time.

EX: dressed <u>formally</u>; <u>formerly</u> in charge of operations

former, latter

Use "former" when referring to the first of two items mentioned. Do not use it to refer to the first of three or more items. Use "latter" when referring to the last of two items mentioned. Do not use it to refer to the last of three or more items.

SAY: when Smith, Jones, and Davis objected, Smith spoke for the group. When Smith, Jones, and Davis objected, Davis resigned. When Davis resigned, he was replaced by the treasurer.

RATHER THAN: when Smith, Jones, and Davis objected, the <u>former</u> spoke for the group. When Smith, Jones, and Davis objected, the <u>latter</u> resigned. When Davis resigned, the <u>latter</u> was replaced by the treasurer.

formerly See *formally.*

formula, formulae, formulas

The plural of formula is formulae or formulas. The latter is more common.

formulate, form

Formulate is a wordy substitute for form or devise. Limit formulate to scientific settings.

SAY: <u>form</u> an opinion

RATHER THAN: <u>formulate</u> an opinion

for the purpose of

This phrase should be replaced by "to" when-ever possible.

SAY: came <u>to</u> negotiate

RATHER THAN: came <u>for</u> <u>the</u> <u>purpose</u> <u>of</u> negotiation

for the reason that

This phrase should be replaced by "because" whenever possible.

SAY: rejected <u>because</u> the report contained errors

RATHER THAN: rejected <u>for</u> <u>the</u> <u>reason</u> <u>that</u> the report contained errors

fortuitous, fortunate

Fortuitous means occurring by chance. What is fortuitous may be beneficial, negative, or neither. Fortunate means lucky.

EX: a <u>fortuitous</u> change of wind damaged the crop; a <u>fortunate</u> inheritance

fortunate See *fortuitous.*

forward, send (see also *foreword*)

When you mean send, do not use forward.

SAY: <u>send</u> the response

RATHER THAN: <u>forward</u> the response

for your information

This phrase adds nothing. Do not use it.

founder See *flounder.*

freak, freakish

These words refer to what is highly unusual or abnormal. Freak is a noun; freakish is an adjective. Do not use freak as an adjective.

EX: a <u>freak</u> of nature; a <u>freakish</u> occurrence (not a <u>freak</u> occurrence)

free gift, free pass, for free

By definition, gifts and passes are free. Free is redundant in such phrases. The word "for" is also unnecessary in the phrase "for free."

SAY: a <u>gift</u> of wine; a <u>pass</u> to the game; given to him <u>free</u>

RATHER THAN: a <u>free</u> <u>gift</u> of wine; a <u>free</u> <u>pass</u> to the game; given to him <u>for</u> <u>free</u>

free lance, free-lance

Free lance is the noun. Free-lance (with hyphen) is the verb and adjective.

frequently See *invariably.*

from...to

The following statement is ambiguous: "from March to April." Do you mean from the beginning of March to the beginning of April? From the end of March to the end of April? Be more precise.

EX: during March through April

fulfill, fulfil

The preferred spelling is fulfill, not fulfil or fullfill.

fulsome

Fulsome means offensive and excessive, not abundant.

EX: a <u>fulsome</u> manner

further See *farther*.

future plans

The word "future" usually adds nothing since most plans are for a later period. The same is true of the word "ahead" in the phrase "plan ahead," and the word "advance" in the phrase "advance plans."

gage See *gauge*.

gamut, gauntlet, gantlet

Gamut means the full range of something. Gauntlet is a protective glove. It has come to mean a challenge. Gantlet is a form of punishment in which a person is hit while running between lines of soldiers.

EX: the <u>gamut</u> of emotions; throw down the <u>gauntlet</u>; run the <u>gantlet</u>

gantlet See *gamut*.

garnish, garnishee

Both words are verbs meaning to attach a debtor's property in the possession of another. Garnishee is also a noun meaning the debtor against whom garnishment has been sought. Another meaning of garnish is to embellish, to add something for flavor or color.

EX: <u>garnish</u> his wages; <u>garnishee</u> his wages; the <u>garnishee</u> lost his job; <u>garnish</u> the salad

gauge, gage

Both words mean a standard or an instrument of measurement, but the preferred spelling is gauge. A less common meaning of gage is a challenge or pledge.

EX: pressure <u>gauge</u>

gauntlet See *gamut*.

gender, sex

Gender is a grammatical term that classifies words as masculine, feminine, or neuter. Do not use gender when you mean sex.

SAY: <u>sex</u> discrimination on the job
RATHER THAN: <u>gender</u> discrimination on the job

general consensus, general public

These are redundant phrases since "consensus" and "public" already incorporate the concept of "general."

get, got, gotten

Get means to acquire, to reach, to become, etc. Although this verb can be acceptable in formal writing, you should consider alternative language for the sake of simplicity and precision.

SAY: was arrested; must go; dressed for the trip; I have a headache; seek revenge; I must finish; we obtained the funds
RATHER THAN: <u>got</u> arrested; <u>got</u> to go; <u>get</u> dressed for the trip; I've <u>got</u> a headache; <u>get</u> back at him; I <u>have got</u> to finish; we <u>have gotten</u> the funds

There are times, however, when get seems more natural than substitutes.

COMPARE: <u>get</u> up in the morning; <u>get</u> a book
WITH: <u>arise</u> in the morning; <u>obtain</u> a book

gibe, jibe, jive

Gibe means a mocking remark or to mock someone. Jibe has the same meaning as gibe.

EX: trading <u>gibes</u>; trading <u>jibes</u>

Jibe also has additional meanings: to shift direction, and to be in agreement or accord. Do not confuse jibe with jive. The latter is slang for jazz, gibberish, or phony.

gift See *free gift*.

gipsy, gypsy

The preferred spelling is gypsy.

girl See *female*.

glamour, glamor; glamorize, glamourize

As an adjective, the preferred spelling is glamour. As a verb, however, the preferred spelling is glamorize.

glance, glimpse

A glance is a brief look. A glimpse is a brief, incomplete or partial look.

EX: a <u>glance</u> at her watch; a <u>glimpse</u> of the president in the car

glean, understand

Glean means to gather, bit by bit. It does not mean learn or understand.

EX: <u>glean</u> the evidence from the file

glimpse See *glance*.

glutton See *gourmand*.

go and See *come and*.

goes without saying

Do not use this trite phrase. It adds nothing.

good, well

Good is an adjective. Use it before nouns and with linking verbs such as be, seem, taste, appear, look, etc.

EX: a <u>good</u> response; the chances look <u>good</u>

Well is an adverb and an adjective. As an adjective, it refers to a person's health.

EX: spoke <u>well</u> (adverb); feel <u>well</u> (adjective)

In the last example (feel well), if you were referring to the sense of touch rather than to health, "well" would be an adverb.

good and sufficient reason

A vebose phrase unless you have distinct meanings in mind for "good" and for "sufficient." If you intend the same meaning for both, choose one.

goodwill, good will, good-will

The preferred spelling is good will.

got, gotten See *get*.

gourmand, gourmet, epicure, glutton

A gourmand is one who loves good food and wine, and may take in a lot of it. A gourmet is a connoisseur, an expert on good food and wine. Epicure is a synonym for gourmet. A glutton is one who eats and drinks to excess.

graduated from, was graduated from

The institution does the graduating; not the student. Hence, the traditional view is that the passive form (was graduated from) is needed. Today, however, both forms are acceptable. Be sure to include the preposition "from"

EX: she <u>graduated</u> <u>from</u> Duke; she <u>was</u> <u>graduated</u> <u>from</u> Duke

graffiti, graffito

Graffiti is plural—lots of drawings or marks; graffito is singular—one drawing or mark.

EX: the <u>graffiti</u> are obnoxious; the <u>graffito</u> is obnoxious

grateful, gratified

Grateful means appreciative. Gratified is the past tense of gratify, meaning to please or satisfy.

EX: <u>grateful</u> for your help; <u>gratified</u> by the verdict

gray, grey

The preferred spelling for this color is gray.

greatly minimize See *minimize*.

grievous, grievious

There is no such word as grievious. It is a common misspelling of grievous.

EX: <u>grievous</u> crime

grisly, grizzly

Grisly means gruesome. Grizzly means gray.

EX: a <u>grisly</u> crime; a <u>grizzly</u> bear

groom, bridegroom

Both words mean the man who is about to be married. Bridegroom is preferred by those who wish to use groom in its primary sense of one who takes care of horses.

group See *bunch*.

guerrilla, guerilla

The preferred spelling for this military person is guerrilla.

guess See *expect*.

guest See *invited guest*.

gypsy See *gipsy*.

habitable, inhabitable

Habitable means suitable to live in. Inhabitable means capable of living in.

EX: <u>habitable</u> dwelling; <u>inhabitable</u> region

habitual See *customary*.

hadn't ought See *ought*.

hail, hale

Hail means to greet or call out. Hail is also falling ice and hard snow. Hale means to force someone to go.

EX: <u>hail</u> a taxi; sudden <u>hail</u>; <u>haled</u> into court

half, a half a

Avoid the phrase "a half a" or "a half an."

SAY: a <u>half</u> hour

RATHER THAN: a <u>half</u> <u>an</u> hour

hangar, hanger

Airplanes are kept in hangars. Clothes are kept on hangers.

hanged, hung

The past tense and past participle of hang is hanged or hung. Use hanged when you mean put to death by hanging. Use hung in all other senses.

EX: <u>hanged</u> by the posse; <u>hung</u> the picture

hanged to death

This phrase is redundant. "Hanged" is sufficient.

happen, transpire, occur, take place (see also *materialize*)

For an accidental or chance event, use occur or happen; for a planned event, use take place.

EX: the accident <u>happened</u> at noon; the hearing will <u>take place</u> at noon

Transpire means to become known or to leak out. Do not use it to mean to happen or to take place.

SAY: they were surprised by what <u>occurred</u> at the scene

RATHER THAN: they were surprised by what <u>transpired</u> at the scene

hard and fast rule

Avoid this trite expression. Use a substitute.

SAY: a <u>firm</u> <u>rule</u>, or, a <u>final</u> <u>rule</u>, or, a <u>universal</u> <u>rule</u>

RATHER THAN: a <u>hard</u> <u>and</u> <u>fast</u> <u>rule</u>

hardly, scarcely, barely

These words are treated as negative. Do not use them with another negative.

SAY: he could <u>hardly</u> walk; with <u>scarcely</u> a nod

RATHER THAN: he <u>couldn't</u> <u>hardly</u> walk; <u>without</u> <u>scarcely</u> a nod

Do not use "than" with hardly or scarcely.

SAY: we <u>hardly</u> started <u>when</u> we were told to leave; we <u>scarcely</u> concluded <u>when</u> we asked to repeat it

RATHER THAN: we <u>hardly</u> started <u>than</u> we were told to leave; we <u>scarcely</u> concluded <u>than</u> we asked to repeat it

have got to, must, should

Avoid the phrase "have got to."

SAY: I <u>must</u> go, or, I <u>should</u> go

RATHER THAN: I <u>have</u> <u>got</u> <u>to</u> go

have lain See *lay*.

headquarters

This word usually takes a plural verb, but either the singular or the plural is proper.

EX: headquarters <u>are</u> located; or, headquarters <u>is</u> located

healthful, healthy

Healthful means conducive to health. Healthy means possessing good health.

EX: exercise is <u>healthful</u>; John is <u>healthy</u>

help See *facilitate*.

help but, avoid

Do not use "help but" to mean avoid or keep from.

SAY: I cannot <u>avoid</u> attending

RATHER THAN: I cannot <u>help</u> <u>but</u> attend

he or she

The phrase "he or she" is awkward. The use of "he" to refer to both sexes is considered offensive. Re-write the sentence to try to avoid the problem, e.g., use the plural pronoun, avoid pronouns altogether.

SAY: the rule applies to lawyers. <u>They</u> must be members of a bar association.

RATHER THAN: the rule applies to a lawyer. He or she must be a member of a bar association.

herein, hereto, herewith

Avoid these words. They are too formal and often redundant.

SAY: discussed in this letter

RATHER THAN: discussed <u>herein</u>

here is, here are

Here takes a singular or plural verb depending on the noun that follows the verb.

EX: here <u>is</u> the law library; here <u>are</u> the law libraries; here <u>are</u> Harvard and Yale

hereto, herewith See *herein*.

her's

To communicate ownership or possession, say hers; never say her's.

SAY: the research is <u>hers</u>

RATHER THAN: the research is <u>her's</u>

herself See *himself*.

hiccup, hiccough

Both spellings are correct, but hiccup is preferred.

himself, herself, myself, yourself, ourselves, themselves

These reflective pronouns can be useful to provide emphasis.

EX: he, <u>himself</u>, had no interest in the position

Avoid these pronouns, however, in compound subjects and objects.

SAY: he and <u>I</u> abstained; available to John and <u>her</u>

RATHER THAN: he and <u>myself</u> abstained; available to John and <u>herself</u>

historic, historical

Historic refers to what is significant in history. Historical refers to whatever has taken place in the past, whether significant or not. Historical means based on history.

EX: the <u>historic</u> Miranda decision; <u>historical</u> novel

hitherto

Use a less cumbersome substitute whenever possible.

SAY: <u>previously</u> unknown

RATHER THAN: <u>hitherto</u> unknown

hoard, horde

Hoard means a hidden supply of something. Horde means a large number of something.

EX: a <u>hoard</u> of food; a <u>horde</u> of shoppers

holding See *finding.*

honorarium, fee

If payment for services is expected, it is a fee. If it is not normally expected or specified, it is an honorarium.

hopefully

This word has two meanings: "with hope" (in a hopeful way) and "it is to be hoped" (I hope). The meanings are different. To avoid confusion, avoid the word.

SAY: I hope the court's decision will resolve the matter

RATHER THAN: the court's decision will <u>hopefully</u> resolve the matter

horde See *hoard.*

how come, why

"How come" is colloquial.

SAY: <u>why</u> were you absent?

RATHER THAN: <u>how come</u> you were absent?

however

There are a number of guidelines to keep in mind. Avoid "however" to start a sentence when you mean "nevertheless" or "yet." The phrase "but however" is redundant. Use one of these words, not both. Use a semicolon before "however" when it begins the second independent clause in a sentence.

EX: the lawyers are ready; however, the court is not

human, humane

Human means pertaining to man. Humane means compassionate. Avoid using human as a noun. It is an adjective.

EX: <u>human</u> remains; <u>humane</u> treatment

humankind, mankind

Use humankind rather than the sexist word, mankind.

hung See *hanged.*

I, me

"I" cannot be the object of a verb or preposition. Do not use "me" as the subject.

SAY: between you and <u>me</u>; Mary and <u>I</u> were elected; he has a longer record than <u>I</u>

RATHER THAN: between you and <u>I</u>; Mary and <u>me</u> were elected; he has a longer record than <u>me</u>

identical See *same identical.*

identical with, identical to

"Identical with" is preferred.

EX: your signature is <u>identical</u> <u>with</u> the one on the document

identify with

Use the reflexive pronoun with this phrase.

SAY: she <u>identified</u> <u>herself</u> with the character

RATHER THAN: she <u>identified</u> with the character

i.e. See *e.g.*

if See *in the event that.*

if, whether

"Whether" is preferable to "if" when introducing a clause that refers to alternatives.

SAY: let me know <u>whether</u> you can attend

RATHER THAN: let me know <u>if</u> you can attend

Note the ambiguity in the "if" clause. If the person *cannot* attend, there is no need to let you know? The "whether" clause makes clear that you want to know either way.

if and when See *when and if.*

if not

Avoid this phrase when it is not clear what you mean. The danger is that what follows "if not" may be incorrectly interpreted negatively.

SAY: the busiest <u>and</u> (or <u>and</u> <u>probably</u>); the most honest judge

RATHER THAN: the busiest, <u>if</u> <u>not</u> the most honest, judge (this sentence suggests that the judge was not honest)

if...then

Omit "then" when it adds nothing.

SAY: <u>if</u> he loses, he will resign

RATHER THAN: <u>if</u> he loses, <u>then</u> he will resign

ill See *worse.*

illegible, unreadable; legible, readable

Illegible and unreadable both mean difficult to read. Unreadable has the additional meaning of dull.

Similarly, legible and readable mean capable of being read. Readable has the additional meaning of interesting.

illicit See *elicit.*

illusion See *allusion; delusion; false illusion.*

immanent See *eminent.*

immense See *enormous.*

immigrate See *emigrate.*

imminent See *eminent.*

immoral See *amoral.*

impact, affect

As a verb, affect is preferable to impact.

SAY: the rule <u>affects</u> everyone

RATHER THAN: the rule <u>impacts</u> everyone

impassible, impassable

Impassible means unable to suffer. Impassable means unable to travel over.

impeach, remove

Someone who is impeached is <u>not</u> removed or dismissed. Impeach simply means accused, attacked, or discredited.

EX: a president is <u>impeached</u> when accused of high crimes and misdemeanors by the House; a president is <u>removed</u> from office when tried and convicted by the Senate

impel See *compel.*

impertinent See *impudent.*

impervious, oblivious, forgetful

Impervious means incapable of being affected; impenetrable. Oblivious means lacking memory, and being unaware. Forgetful means not remembering due to a problem or defect of memory.

EX: <u>impervious</u> to criticism; <u>oblivious</u> of the passage of time; <u>forgetful</u> as ever, he missed the appointment

implicit See *explicit.*

imply, infer

Imply means to signal or to hint at a meaning. Infer means to deduce something from the signal or the hint. It is the writer or speaker who implies. It is the reader or listener who infers.

EX: the director <u>implied</u> she was dissatisfied with the report; the staff <u>inferred</u> that the director wanted the report changed

importantly See *more importantly.*

impractical, practical; impracticable, practicable

Impractical means not prudent or sensible. Practical means wise or realistic. Impracticable means not capable of being carried out. Practicable means feasible, capable of being done.

EX: to read a book in a day may be <u>practicable</u> because you have done it before, but <u>impractical</u> because of the other things you must do today.

impudent, impertinent, imprudent

Impudent means brash and disrespectful. Impertinent is less strong. It means impolite, in bad taste. Imprudent means unwise.

EX: they were shocked by her <u>impudent</u> criticism; an <u>impertinent</u> question; an <u>imprudent</u> purchase

in See *within.*

in, at

Both words refer to a location. Use "at" when the focus is on a specific location. Use "in" when the focus is on more general boundaries.

EX: I live <u>in</u> Boston; I work <u>at</u> Smith, Jones & Jackson

in, into

"In" means inside of, within an area or space.

"Into" has the same meaning, but is used with motion or action verbs.

EX: the file is <u>in</u> her briefcase; she went <u>into</u> the court

in accordance with See *accordance*.

inadequate See *limited*.

in advance of, prior to, before

Before is preferable to "in advance of" and "prior to."

SAY: compliance <u>before</u> the hearing
RATHER THAN: compliance <u>in advance of</u> the hearing

in a position to

Avoid this wordy phrase.

SAY: we cannot accept the offer
RATHER THAN: we are <u>not in a position to</u> accept the offer

inasmuch as, insofar as

Whenever possible, substitute "since" or "because" for "inasmuch as" and "insofar as."

SAY: an extension was granted <u>because</u> of the delay
RATHER THAN: <u>inasmuch as</u> there was delay, an extension was granted

in back of See *back of*.

incident See *episode*.

incidentally, incidently

The correct spelling is incidentally.

incisive See *decided*.

inclose See *enclose*.

include See *compose*.

in connection with

When you mean "about" or "on" do not use this awkward phrase.

SAY: the Center prepared a report <u>on</u> the accident
RATHER THAN: the Center prepared a report <u>in connection with</u> the accident

incredible, incredulous

Incredible means implausible, not to be believed. Incredulous means skeptical, showing disbelief.

EX: he told an <u>incredible</u> story; we were <u>incredulous</u> of his story

incumbent See *present incumbent*.

indefinitely, forever

Indefinitely means "having no precise limits or boundaries." This is not the same as "a very long time." When you mean the latter, do not use indefinitely.

EX: a job that could end tomorrow or in twenty years is a job that will last <u>indefinitely</u>; housework is a job that lasts <u>forever</u>

index, indexes, indices

The preferred plural of index is indexes.

indicate, say, said, remark; state; insist (see also *allege*)

Say and said are preferred over more formal substitutes (e.g., indicate, remark) that do little more than provide variation for the sake of variation.

SAY: he <u>said</u> that he wanted the position; she would not <u>say</u> if the product was available
RATHER THAN: he <u>remarked</u> that he wanted the position; she would not <u>indicate</u> if the product was available

"State" is properly used when making a formal, full, or detailed declaration.

EX: for the record, he <u>stated</u> that he wanted to withdraw

"Insist" is properly used when someone is being very firm in a position.

EX: she <u>insisted</u> that she did not receive the funds

indices See *index*.

indiscreet, indiscrete

Indiscreet means lacking good judgment. Indiscrete means not divided into separate parts.

EX: an <u>indiscreet</u> disclosure of the confidence; an <u>indiscrete</u> unit

individual, person

Do not indiscriminately substitute individual (as a noun) for person. Say individual when you are emphasizing one from the group.

EX: an unknown <u>person</u> came forward; no one doubted the right of an <u>individual</u> to dissent from the party position

indorse See *endorse*.

induce, induction See *deduce*.

industry See *private industry*.

in excess of, over

"Over" is preferable to "in excess of."

SAY: <u>over</u> fifteen volumes
RATHER THAN: <u>in excess of</u> fifteen volumes

infectious See *contagious.*

infer See *imply.*

inferior to (than); superior to (than)
Use "to," not "than" with these words.
SAY: your library is inferior <u>to</u> mine; your school is superior <u>to</u> mine
RATHER THAN: your library is inferior <u>than</u> mine; your school is superior <u>than</u> mine

inflammable See *flammable.*

inflict, afflict
Inflict means to cause something burdensome to be endured. Afflict means to cause distress and suffering, to make miserable.
EX: <u>inflict</u> extra work on them; <u>afflicted</u> with the disease

inform See *this is to inform you that; advise.*

informant, informer
These words are interchangeable.

ingenious, ingenuous, naive
Ingenious means clever, imaginative. Ingenuous means straightforward and childlike. Naive means lacking insight or experience, and also foolishly simple.
EX: an <u>ingenious</u> plan; an <u>ingenuous</u> witness; a <u>naive</u> hope

inhabitable See *habitable.*

inhuman, inhumane, unhuman
Inhuman means cold and brutal. Inhumane means lacking compassion. Unhuman means other than human, not pertaining to a human being.
EX: <u>inhuman</u> punishment of those captured; <u>inhumane</u> care for the animals; an <u>unhuman</u> sound

initiate See *commence.*

in length, in size, in number
All of these phrases are often redundant.
SAY: the glass is five inches; the handle is small; he bought ten
RATHER THAN: the glass is five inches <u>in</u> <u>length</u>; the handle is small <u>in</u> <u>size</u>; he bought ten <u>in</u> <u>number</u>

innocent See *plead innocent.*

in number See *in length.*

in order to, in order that
These phrases often add nothing to a sentence.
SAY: file the pleading <u>to</u> start the case; delivered early <u>so</u> <u>that</u> they could prepare

RATHER THAN: file the pleading <u>in</u> <u>order</u> <u>to</u> start the case; delivered early <u>in</u> <u>order</u> <u>that</u> they could prepare

input
Avoid this word except when discussing science or computers.
SAY: your valuable <u>participation</u> in preparing the speech
RATHER THAN: your valuable <u>input</u> in preparing the speech

inquire See *enquire.*

inquisitive See *curious.*

in re See *re.*

in receipt of, received
Received is preferable to the awkward, "in receipt of."
SAY: we have <u>received</u> your application
RATHER THAN: we are <u>in</u> <u>receipt</u> of your application

in regard to, with regard to
Often erroneously spelled "in regards to" and "with regards to." Even when spelled properly, regarding or concerning is preferable to these phrases.
SAY: <u>in</u> <u>regard</u> <u>to</u> your application
RATHER THAN: <u>in</u> <u>regards</u> <u>to</u> your application
EVEN BETTER: <u>concerning</u> your application

insanitary See *unsanitary.*

inside of, inside; outside of, outside
Omit "of."
SAY: fell <u>inside</u> the elevator; the property <u>outside</u> city limits
RATHER THAN: fell <u>inside</u> of the elevator; the property <u>outside</u> of city limits
Also, "outside of" is not a good substitute for "except for."
SAY: <u>except</u> <u>for</u> the one error, the report was excellent
RATHER THAN: <u>outside</u> <u>of</u> the one error, the report was excellent

insidious, invidious
Insidious means spreading harm subtly and ready to entrap. Invidious means offensive, causing animosity.
EX: <u>insidious</u> plot; <u>invidious</u> discrimination

insist See *indicate.*

in size See *in length.*

insofar as See *inasmuch as.*

insoluble, insolvable, unsolvable

Insoluble means incapable of being dissolved. Insolvable and unsolvable means incapable of being solved.

EX: <u>insoluble</u> substance; <u>insolvable</u> crime

in spite of the fact that, although

Although is preferable to the wordy, "in spite...."

SAY: he went <u>although</u> he protested

RATHER THAN: he went <u>in spite of the fact that</u> he protested

instantaneously, instantly

Instantaneously means without perceptible delay. Instantly means at once.

EX: he responded <u>instantaneously</u>; died <u>instantly</u>

instinct, intuition

Instinct means unlearned behavior. Intuition means knowledge gained outside the normal process.

EX: an <u>instinct</u> for survival; an <u>intuition</u> that she was not being told everything

insure See *assure.*

intelligent, intellectual, intelligible

Intelligent means having intelligence, being mentally gifted. Intellectual means nonmaterial, and having above average intelligence. Intelligible means capable of being understood.

EX: an <u>intelligent</u> answer; an <u>intellectual</u> student; a barely <u>intelligible</u> message

intense, intensive

Intense means to an extreme degree. Intensive has the same meaning, but it often has the additional meaning of concentrated or very focused.

EX: <u>intense</u> hostility; <u>intensive</u> investigation

intentional, voluntary; unintentional, involuntary

An intentional act is one done with a particular intention, or one done deliberately. An unintentional act is one done without a certain intention, or one not done deliberately. Conduct is voluntary or involuntary depending on whether it is the product of a free will.

EX: his contact with her body was <u>intentional</u>; his driving into the wall was <u>unintentional</u>; his denunciation of his country was <u>voluntary</u>; his sneeze was <u>involuntary</u>

intents See *to all intents and purposes.*

interest See *intrigue.*

interesting

Avoid using this word. The reader will decide if what you have to say is interesting.

interment, internment

Interment means burial. Internment means imprisonment or confinement.

EX: <u>interment</u> will be on Monday morning; <u>internment</u> of those captured

in terms of

Avoid this phrase when it adds nothing.

SAY: there was confusion <u>about</u> the amount

RATHER THAN: there was confusion <u>in terms of</u> the amount

internment See *interment.*

interpersonal, personal

Avoid interpersonal if you mean nothing more than personal.

SAY: <u>personal</u> relationships

RATHER THAN: <u>interpersonal</u> relationships

interpretative, interpretive

The preferred spelling is interpretative.

interrelationship

Avoid interrelationship if you mean nothing more than relationship.

SAY: <u>relationship</u> between the two countries

RATHER THAN: <u>interrelationship</u> between the two countries

in that, since

"Since" is preferable to "in that."

SAY: they accepted the offer <u>since</u> the terms were sufficient

RATHER THAN: they accepted the offer <u>in that</u> the terms were sufficient

in the amount of See *amount.*

in the course of See *course.*

in the event that, if

Avoid the first phrase when "if" is adequate.

SAY: <u>if</u> you succeed

RATHER THAN: <u>in the event that</u> you succeed

in the immediate vicinity of

Avoid this phrase when all you mean is "near."

SAY: the accident occurred <u>near</u> the school

RATHER THAN: the accident occurred <u>in the immediate vicinity of</u> the school

in the light of

Avoid this cliché. If you use it, do not say "in light of." The "the" must be included.

into, in to (see also *in*, *into*)

"Into" and "in to" are distinct. Compare the following:
EX: she went <u>into</u> the court; she went <u>in</u> <u>to</u> obtain the file

intrigue, interest

As verbs, both words mean to arouse curiosity. Use intrigue, however, when you wish to include an element of suspense.
EX: the course <u>interested</u> her; the uncertainty <u>intrigued</u> her

intuition See *instinct.*

inure, enure

The preferred spelling of this word (meaning to take effect, and to become accustomed to something undesirable) is inure.

invariably, frequently

Invariably means not changing, constant. It does not mean often or frequently.
EX: he is <u>invariably</u> late (if you mean there has never been a time when he was not late); he is <u>frequently</u> late (if you mean he is often late)

invent See *discover.*

invidious See *insidious.*

in view of the fact that, since

"Since" is preferable to "in view of the fact that."
SAY: they accepted the offer <u>since</u> the terms were sufficient
RATHER THAN: they accepted the offer <u>in</u> <u>view</u> <u>of</u> <u>the</u> <u>fact</u> <u>that</u> the terms were sufficient

invited guest

The word "invited" is redundant since guest means one who is invited.

involuntary See *intentional.*

in which

Omit this phrase if it adds nothing.
SAY: the courteous way she was treated
RATHER THAN: the courteous way <u>in</u> <u>which</u> she was treated

irregardless, regardless

Never use "irregardless." Say "regardless."

irrelevant See *relevant.*

irritate See *aggravate.*

issue See *controversial issue.*

is when, is where

Avoid these phrases in your definitions.
SAY: impair means to weaken or to make worse
RATHER THAN: impair <u>is</u> <u>when</u> you weaken or make worse

it...it

Avoid the use of both the expletive "it" and the personal pronoun "it" in the same sentence.
SAY: <u>it</u> is our opinion that this matter requires more study
RATHER THAN: <u>it</u> is our opinion that <u>it</u> requires more study

its, it's

"It's" is a contraction for "it is." For the possessive, say "its," never "it's." If you cannot substitute "it is" for "it's," do not use the latter.
SAY: <u>it's</u> contagious; <u>its</u> product
RATHER THAN: <u>its</u> contagious; <u>it's</u> product
Even when correctly used, you should limit contractions to speaking. In formal writing, say "it is."
EX: <u>it</u> <u>is</u> contagious

I wish to state that

Avoid this verbose phrase.
SAY: the report is inadequate.
RATHER THAN: <u>I</u> <u>wish</u> <u>to</u> <u>state</u> <u>that</u> the report is inadequate.

jealous See *envious.*

jibe, jive See *gibe.*

join together

The phrase is redundant. Drop the "together" (even though the Bible cautions us not to put asunder what has been divinely "joined together.")
SAY: <u>join</u> the two factions
RATHER THAN: <u>join</u> the two factions <u>together</u>

judge See *adjudge; jurist.*

judgment, judgement

The preferred spelling is judgment.

judicial, judicious

Judicial means pertaining to the courts. Judicious

means demonstrating wise judgment.

EX: the volume contains <u>judicial</u> opinions; a <u>judicious</u> choice

jurist, judge, justice

Jurist does not mean judge. A jurist is someone skilled or versed in the law. This can include more than judges. The distinction between judge and justice depends on local custom. Members of the highest court in a judicial system are often called justices; others in that system, judges.

justice See *jurist*.

karat See *carat*.

kind, kind of a, this kind, these kinds; sort, sort of a, etc.

All of the following comments about "kind" apply to the same type of phrases using "sort."

Drop the "a" and "an" in the phrases, "kind of a" and "kind of an."

SAY: the <u>kind</u> of difficulty

RATHER THAN: the <u>kind</u> of <u>a</u> difficulty

Do not use "kind of" to mean somewhat or rather.

SAY: <u>somewhat</u> hostile; <u>rather</u> hostile

RATHER THAN: <u>kind</u> <u>of</u> hostile

Most careful writers prefer "this kind" and "these kinds." Do not use the plural "these" or "those" with the singular "kind."

SAY: <u>this</u> <u>kind</u> of binder; <u>these</u> <u>kinds</u> of binders

RATHER THAN: <u>these</u> <u>kind</u> of binders

knot

Knot is a nautical unit of speed. Do not add "per hour."

SAY: traveled twenty <u>knots</u>

RATHER THAN: traveled twenty <u>knots</u> <u>per</u> <u>hour</u>

know-how

Avoid this word in formal writing.

SAY: reputation for competence in management

RATHER THAN: reputation for management <u>know-how</u>

laceration, cut

Laceration is a verbose way to say "cut."

lady See *female*.

laid See *lay*.

lain See *lay*.

last See *later*.

last but not least

Avoid this cliché.

later, latest; latter, last

Later and latest pertain only to time. Latter and last pertain to succession or order of arrangement.

EX: the conference was postponed to a <u>later</u> date; this is not the <u>latest</u> report on their progress; both the report and the application have arrived, but the <u>latter</u> is incomplete; this is the <u>last</u> report he will ever prepare in this office

Avoid ambiguity in the word "last," e.g., the <u>last</u> case he tried. Do you mean the last case of his career (there were no more)? If so, say "final" or add language to make this clear.

EX: the <u>final</u> case he tried, or the <u>last</u> case he tried <u>before</u> <u>he</u> <u>resigned</u>

Or do you mean the most recent case that he tried (more are expected)?

EX: the <u>latest</u> case he tried, or the <u>most</u> <u>recent</u> case he tried

latter See *former, later*.

laudable, laudatory

Laudable means praiseworthy. Laudatory means giving praise.

EX: a <u>laudable</u> rescue effort; <u>laudatory</u> speech

lay, lie

Lay means to place; it must have an object. Lie means to rest or recline; it does not take an object.

EX: <u>lay</u> the pen on the desk; <u>lie</u> on the couch

Do not confuse the principal parts of these two verbs: *lay*: laid, laid, laying; *lie*: lay, lain, lying.

EX: <u>laid</u> a pen on the desk; caught <u>laying</u> the pen in his pocket; I <u>lay</u> there for two hours; I <u>have</u> <u>lain</u> there for hours; <u>lying</u> in bed

Lie also means to communicate a falsehood intentionally. The principal parts of this verb are: <u>lie</u>: lied, lied

laying See *lay*.

layman, layperson

The nonsexist word, layperson, is preferred.

lead, led

Lead means to show the way, to head. Led is the past tense and past participle of lead. Avoid the error of thinking that the past tense and past participle of lead is lead.

SAY: the evidence <u>led</u> him to the conclusion that ...

RATHER THAN: the evidence <u>lead</u> him to the conclusion that ...

A similar confusion can exist with the verb forms mislead, misled

leaped, leapt

The preferred spelling of the past tense of leap is leaped.

learn, teach

You learn yourself; you teach others.

SAY: <u>teach</u> them to read

RATHER THAN: <u>learn</u> them to read

learned, learnt

The preferred spelling of the past tense of learn is learned.

leave, let

Leave means to go out or away. Let means to allow or grant permission to.

EX: <u>leave</u> the court; <u>let</u> him enter

Avoid confusing these two verbs.

SAY: <u>let</u> her do it when she wants

RATHER THAN: <u>leave</u> her do it when she wants

"Leave alone" and "let alone" are equally acceptable, but they are slightly different: leave him alone (allow him to be in solitude) let him alone (do not interfere with him).

lectern, podium

When you speak, you place your notes on the <u>lectern</u> and you stand on the <u>podium</u>.

led See *lead*.

legal assistant See *paralegal*.

legitimate, legitimize

As a verb meaning to make lawful, legitimate is preferred.

EX: <u>legitimate</u> the child

lend, loan

When you need a verb, use lend. When you need a noun, use loan. While not improper, you should avoid the use of loan as a verb.

SAY: the bank <u>will</u> <u>lend</u> (or <u>lent</u>) him the money

RATHER THAN: the bank <u>loaned</u> him the money

length See *in length*.

lengthy, long

Both words mean extended. They also can mean boring or tedious, but lengthy is more common in this sense.

EX: a <u>lengthy</u> speech

lent See *lend*.

less See *fewer*.

let See *leave*.

let's, let us

Avoid the contraction "let's" in formal writing.

SAY: <u>let</u> <u>us</u> continue

RATHER THAN: <u>let's</u> continue

liable See *apt*.

lie See *lay*.

lied See *lay*.

lighted, lit

Both of these words are acceptable as the past tense and past participle of light.

EX: <u>lighted</u> the cigarette; <u>lit</u> the cigarette

lightening, lightning

Lightening means making something lighter or less heavy. Lightning means a flash in the sky.

EX: <u>lightening</u> of the load; fear of <u>lightning</u>

like, as

"Like" is often erroneously used for "as."

SAY: Winston tastes good <u>as</u> a cigarette should

RATHER THAN: Winston tastes good <u>like</u> a cigarette should

Use "like" as a preposition, not as a conjunction. "Like" should go with a noun or pronoun when a verb does not follow. Use "as" as a connective between clauses. "As" or "as if" should always be followed by a verb.

EX: the young lawyer examined the witness <u>like</u> a veteran; audit this return <u>as</u> you audited the others

like for

Avoid this phrase in formal writing.

SAY: the judge would <u>like</u> you to return

RATHER THAN: the judge would <u>like</u> <u>for</u> you to return

likely (see also *apt*)

When used as an adverb to mean probably, "likely" should be preceded by "very," "quite," and similar words.

SAY: the jury will <u>very</u> <u>likely</u> find for the plaintiff

RATHER THAN: the jury will <u>likely</u> find for the plaintiff

limited, small

Limited means within bounds, confined. Avoid using it to mean small, inadequate, few, or meager unless you are referring to something that is set within limits.

SAY: <u>meager</u> resources (when you mean few resources, rather than restricted resources)

RATHER THAN: <u>limited</u> resources

line See *along this line*.

lit See *lighted*.

literally See *figuratively*.

live See *reside*.

loan See *lend*.

loath, loathe

Loath means reluctant or unwilling. Loathe means to detest.

EX: she is <u>loath</u> to accept the position; she <u>loathes</u> the very idea of taking the position

long See *lengthy*.

loose, lose

Loose (as an adjective) means not fastened. Lose means to be unable to find, to be deprived of.

EX: a <u>loose</u> fitting; <u>lose</u> the case

lots of See *a lot*.

loud, loudly

Use loud as an adjective (a <u>loud</u> noise) rather than as an adverb. The adverb is loudly.

SAY: speak <u>loudly</u>

RATHER THAN: speak <u>loud</u>

luxuriant, luxurious

Luxuriant means abundant, flourishing. Luxurious means pertaining to luxury, very expensive.

EX: <u>luxuriant</u> hair; <u>luxurious</u> hotel

lying See *lay*.

mad, angry

Avoid using "mad" to mean "angry." In formal writing, use mad when you mean insane.

maintain See claim.

major

Use this word to mean important or significant only when it is clear that you are making a comparative statement or are viewing an event, object, or concept in relation to something else.

EX: a <u>major</u> announcement (as opposed to all other announcements)

Even when correctly used, major is overused. Consider alternatives such as principal, chief, etc.

majority, most of

Use majority when you are specifically comparing the majority with the minority. If you are simply referring to the larger number, "most" is preferable.

SAY: <u>most</u> of the agents approved

RATHER THAN: the <u>majority</u> of the agents approved (unless you specifically mean over 50%)

majority, plurality

Majority means more than half. Plurality means the largest number, but still less than half.

Assume there are seven justices on the bench. In a case, three justices write an opinion together, two others write a separate opinion, one justice writes an opinion by herself, and the seventh justice does not participate. There is no <u>majority</u> opinion since more than half of the justices (i.e., four or more) did not join together. The opinion in which the three justices joined is the <u>plurality</u> opinion.

In an election, plurality also means the number by which the winner exceeds the votes for his or her nearest rival.

major portion of, most of

Avoid "major portion of" when "most" is sufficient.

SAY: <u>most</u> of the applicants

RATHER THAN: the <u>major</u> <u>portion</u> of the applicants

male, man, boy, masculine

Use "male" only in scientific or research contexts. Otherwise, use man, boy, or masculine.

mankind See *humankind*.

manner
Replace this word by an adverb when possible.
SAY: written <u>clearly</u>; spoken <u>forcefully</u>
RATHER THAN: written <u>in a clear manner</u>; spoken <u>in a forceful manner</u>

manner, shape, or form
Avoid this cliché.
SAY: he totally refused to acknowledge his error
RATHER THAN: he refused to acknowledge his error <u>in any manner, shape, or form</u>

mantel, mantle
A mantel is a shelf over the fireplace. A mantle is a cloak or covering.

marijuana, marihuana
Either spelling is acceptable. Marijuana is more common.

marital, martial
Marital means pertaining to marriage. Martial means pertaining to the armed forces or war.
EX: <u>marital</u> discord; <u>martial</u> law

Masculine. See *male*.

masterful, masterly
Masterful means domineering, fit to command. Masterly means highly skillful.
EX; a <u>masterful</u> general; a <u>masterly</u> performance

material, materiel
Material is substance used to make something. Materiel is equipment and supplies.
EX: the <u>material</u> used in the drug; the navy's storage depot for its <u>materiel</u>
The preferred spelling of the latter word is materiel, not matériel.

materialize, happen, appear, take place
Materialize means to take a real form, to cause to become actual. Do not use it to mean happen, appear, or take place.
SAY: goals that did not <u>materialize</u>
RATHER THAN: the victory he sought never <u>materialized</u>

may, might (see also *can*)
May indicates permission or possibility. Might implies possibility.
EX: You <u>may</u> go if you wish (permission)
EX: We <u>may</u> go to the convention; we have not decided yet (possibility)

EX: We <u>might</u> go to the meeting if it is held on Friday (possibility)
"Might" is used in subordinate clauses when the verb in the main clause is in a tense indicating past time. "May" is used in the subordinate clause when the verb in the main clause is in the present or future tense.
EX: he <u>said</u> that I <u>might</u> borrow his book for a day or two; he <u>says</u> that I <u>may</u> borrow his book for a day or two.

maybe, may be
"Maybe" is an adverb; "may be" is a verb phrase.
EX: <u>maybe</u> the verdict will be favorable; it <u>may be</u> that the verdict will be favorable

may or may not
The phrase is redundant.
SAY: the jury <u>may</u> find for the plaintiff
RATHER THAN: the jury <u>may or may not</u> find for the plaintiff

me See *I*.

meager See *limited*.

media, medium
Media is the preferred plural of medium. While mediums is also acceptable, medias never is. Media takes a plural verb.
SAY: all the <u>media are</u> waiting for the interview; TV is a mass <u>medium</u>
RATHER THAN: all the <u>media is</u> waiting for the interview; TV is a mass <u>media</u>

mediate See *arbitrate*.

medium See *media*.

memorandum, memoranda, memorandums
The plural of memorandum is memorandums or memoranda. Either is acceptable.

meretricious, meritorious
Meretricious means involving vulgarity, insincerity, or unlawful sexual relations. Meritorious means having merit, deserving serious judicial inquiry, or going to the heart or essence of the case.
EX: a <u>meretricious</u> relationship; a <u>meritorious</u> defense

might See *may*.

minimize, greatly minimize (see also *diminish*)
The central meaning of minimize is to make something as small as possible. As such, minimize is an absolute term. The phrase "greatly minimize," therefore, is redundant.

Minimize also means to claim that something is less important. It is overused. Good substitutes include underestimate, disparage, and belittle.

mishap See *accident.*

mislead, misled See *lead, led.*

mitigate See *ameliorate.*

mobile, movable

Both words mean capable of being moved. The emphasis of mobile is that the thing can be moved with relative ease. The emphasis of movable is that the thing does move.

EX: mobile home; movable furniture

As a noun, movables are items of personal property.

money, moneys, monies

The preferred plural of money is moneys rather than monies.

moot

In the law, moot means no real controversy.

EX: the question is moot because the company has already received what it wanted

The word also means subject to debate or pertaining to debate.

EX: moot court

more importantly

The "ly" is unnecessary. Say, more important.

more preferable

This phrase is redundant. Say preferable.

more than one

This phrase is singular and takes a singular verb.

EX: more than one lawyer is present

most, almost

Do not use "most" to mean almost.

SAY: almost everyone accepted the proposal

RATHER THAN: most everyone accepted the proposal

most, mostly

Most means the greatest in number or degree. Mostly means almost entirely. Do not use mostly when you mean "for the most part."

SAY: the ones most angered were the clerks

RATHER THAN: the ones mostly angered were the clerks

most all, almost all

The phrase "most all" is colloquial. Avoid it in formal writing.

SAY: she checked almost all the volumes

RATHER THAN: she checked most all the volumes

most of See *majority; major portion of.*

most recent See *later.*

movable See *mobile.*

must See *have got to.*

mutual, common

The focus of mutual is the relationship with or between things. The focus of common is the relationship shared with a group.

EX: mutual respect between the rivals; the common concerns of the delegates

mutual cooperation

This phrase is redundant. Drop "mutual."

myself See *himself.*

naive See *ingenious.*

nation See *country.*

nature (see also *character*)

Avoid "nature" when you mean kind, type, or sort. In its place, be specific about what you mean.

SAY: the settlement is troublesome because of its failure to resolve every issue

RATHER THAN: the nature of the settlement is troublesome

nauseated, nauseous

Nauseated means suffering from nausea. Nauseous means causing nausea.

EX: the speech nauseated him; a nauseous infection

naval, navel

Naval means pertaining to ships. Navel means the groove in the abdomen.

near See *nowhere near, in the immediate vicinity of.*

necessaries, necessities

Both words mean that which is necessary. Use necessaries when referring to what is needed to sustain human life at a certain standard of living.

necessary See *essential.*

needless to say

Avoid this phrase. If what follows this phrase was really "needless to say," you would not have said it.

neither See *either.*

neither...nor See *either...or.*

no, or, nor

Use "or" when "no" begins a compound phrase.
SAY: no lawyers or paralegals
RATHER THAN: no lawyers nor paralegals

no doubt but

SAY: there is no doubt that the jury will convict her
RATHER THAN: there is no doubt but that the jury will convict her

noncontroversial issue See *controversial issue.*

none

None takes a singular verb if it goes with a singular noun. None takes a plural verb if it goes with a plural noun unless you want to emphasize "not one."
EX: none of the prior hostility was present;
none of the applicants were present;
none of the applicants was present (if you wanted to stress that "not one" of the applicants was present)

nonflammable See *flammable.*

nonmoral See *amoral.*

no question but that

Omit the "but" in this phrase.

nor See *no.*

North See *West.*

not

Avoid the ambiguous use of this word.
EX: all lawyers are not competent
Do you mean that all lawyers are incompetent? Or do you mean that not all lawyers are competent? Change the sentence to say what you mean.

notable See *famed.*

noted See *famed.*

noteworthy See *famed.*

notify See *advise.*

not only...but also

Follow the rules of parallelism when you use this construction. Be sure that what follows "not only" is of the same grammatical construction as what follows "but also."
SAY: the judge not only revoked the sale but also revoked the license
RATHER THAN: the judge not only revoked the sale but also the license was subjected to revocation
EVEN BETTER: the judge revoked both the sale and the license

notorious See *famed.*

now See *presently.*

no way

Avoid this colloquial phrase in formal writing.
SAY: he refused to accept
RATHER THAN: there was no way that he would accept

nowhere near

Avoid this colloquial phrase in formal writing.
SAY: the cost of the software was much more than (or much less than) the hardware
RATHER THAN: the cost of the software was nowhere near the cost of the hardware

nowheres

Never use this word in formal writing.

noxious, obnoxious

Noxious means harmful to health or morals. Use obnoxious when you mean disagreeable or offensive.
EX: noxious gas; obnoxious conduct

number (see also *amount; in length*)

The word "number" takes a plural verb when preceded by "a" and a singular verb when preceded by "the."
EX: a number of lawyers are available; the number of Ohio lawyers is decreasing

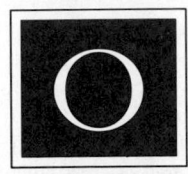

oblige, obligate

Both words mean to constrain or to bind, legally or morally. In legal contexts, obligated is more common.

EX: he is <u>obligated</u> by the contract to provide the service

Oblige also means to be grateful, or to acknowledge a favor.

EX: they were <u>obliged</u> to him for the hospitality

oblivious See *impervious.*

obnoxious See *noxious.*

obscure See *equivocal.*

obsolete, obsolescent

Obsolete means out of date, no longer in use. Obsolescent means becoming out of date.

EX: the quill pen is <u>obsolete</u>; the manual type-writer is <u>obsolescent</u>

obviate

Obviate means to make unnecessary. It does not mean remove or reduce.

SAY: <u>reduce</u> the pain

RATHER THAN: <u>obviate</u> the pain

occur See *happen.*

oculist See *ophthalmologist.*

odious, odorous

Odious means abhorrent. Odorous means having a certain odor.

EX: an <u>odious</u> attack; an <u>odorous</u> gas

of all See *first of all.*

official, officious

Official means authoritative, pertaining to an office. Officious means meddlesome, volunteering when not asked.

EX: an <u>official</u> answer; an <u>officious</u> clerk

off of, off from

The "of" and the "from" should not be used in these phrases.

SAY: keep <u>off</u> the platform; step <u>off</u> the platform

RATHER THAN: keep <u>off</u> <u>of</u> the platform; step <u>off</u> <u>from</u> the platform

oftentimes

Avoid this word when "often" is sufficient.

OK, okay

Avoid this word, under either spelling, in formal writing. It is colloquial.

older See *elder.*

on See *in connection with.*

on, onto

Both words convey the meaning of movement toward.

EX: fall <u>on</u> the rug; fall <u>onto</u> the rug

"Onto" suggests that the person or thing was once away from or outside the area indicated. In the first example, the person or thing was already on the rug before the fall.

When "on" is used as an adverb, the spelling is "on to."

EX: they moved <u>on</u> <u>to</u> the next assignment

on, upon

Whenever possible, say "on" rather that "upon."

SAY: there are few things <u>on</u> which they agreed

RATHER THAN: there are few things <u>upon</u> which they agreed

on account of, because of

"On account of" is colloquial. Use "because" or "due to."

SAY: he resigned <u>because</u> of the pressure

RATHER THAN: he resigned <u>on</u> <u>account</u> <u>of</u> the pressure

one See *more than one.*

one, one's

Avoid the stilted use of "one" as a substitute for a personal pronoun.

SAY: the property must be maintained; you should take care of your property; I must take care of my property; we must take care of our property

RATHER THAN: <u>one</u> must take care of <u>one's</u> property

one another See *each other.*

one of those...who

This construction takes a plural verb when "who" refers to a plural.

EX: he is <u>one</u> <u>of</u> <u>those</u> judges <u>who</u> <u>are</u> upset

(plural verb because "who" refers to a plural noun, judges)

When, however, you add "the only," "who" clearly refers to the singular "one" and takes a singular verb.

EX: he is the only one of those judges who is upset (singular verb because "who" refers to the singular "one")

oneself, one's self

While either spelling is proper, the less awkward "oneself" is preferred.

SAY: the task is difficult to do by oneself

RATHER THAN: the task is difficult to do by one's self

onetime, one-time

Onetime means former. One-time means only once.

EX: a onetime judge; a one-time chance to win

only

Place "only" as close as possible to the word it modifies to avoid confusion.

EX: the confusion can only be alleviated by a change in policy (if you mean that the confusion cannot be corrected entirely)

EX: the confusion can be alleviated only by a change in policy (if you mean that the confusion can be alleviated but there is just one way to do it —by a change in policy)

on the basis of

Rewrite the sentence to avoid this vague phrase.

SAY: the person who earned the most points won

RATHER THAN: the decision was made on the basis of points earned

on the ground that, on the ground of

Avoid these wordy phrases.

SAY: terminated because of incompetence

RATHER THAN: terminated on the ground of incompetence

on the part of

Avoid this wordy phrase.

SAY: discontent among the workers

RATHER THAN: discontent on the part of the workers

onto See *on.*

onward, onwards

As an adjective, the spelling is onward. As an adverb, the spelling is either onward or onwards—but onward is preferred.

EX: the onward march; they moved onward

opaque, transparent

Something is opaque if you cannot see through it, transparent if you can.

ophthalmologist, optician, optometrist

An ophthalmologist is a doctor who specializes in eye diseases. An optician is one who makes and sells eyeglasses, usually not a doctor. An optometrist is a non-doctor who can test for some eye defects and prescribe lenses. Another word for ophthalmologist is oculist.

opinion See *fact; reaction.*

optician See *ophthalmologist.*

optimistic, pessimistic

Avoid using optimistic to refer to specific events. Use it to convey a general sense of looking at things in their best light.

SAY: an optimistic attitude

RATHER THAN: an optimistic sign

Say "hopeful" when referring to specifics.

The same is true of pessimistic; apply it to a general outlook that the worst will probably happen. When referring to specifics, say ominous, discouraging, etc.

optometrist See *ophthalmologist.*

or See *no.*

oral, verbal, aural

Oral means spoken, and pertaining to the mouth. Verbal also means spoken, but in addition has a broader meaning of being associated with words. Aural means pertaining to the ear.

EX: oral hygiene, an oral contract; a verbal attack (can be spoken or written); aural examination

To avoid confusion, use oral when you mean spoken.

ordinance, ordnance

Ordinance means a law passed by a city or county government, usually the local legislature. Ordnance means military weapons or the weapons division of the military.

ordinary See *common.*

orient, orientate

These words have the same meaning. Orient is preferred.

other than

Avoid this phrase when "except" is adequate.

SAY: all counts were dismissed except the third

RATHER THAN: all counts were dismissed other than the third

ought, hadn't ought, shouldn't ought (see also
should)

When you want to express ought in the negative,
say "ought not to." Never say "hadn't ought" or
"shouldn't ought."

SAY: you <u>ought</u> <u>not</u> <u>to</u> stay
RATHER THAN: you <u>shouldn't</u> <u>ought</u> <u>to</u> stay
EVEN BETTER: you <u>should</u> <u>not</u> stay

ourselves See *himself.*

outside of See *inside of.*

over See *In excess of.*

overall

Avoid this vague, overused word whenever possible. Consider alternatives such as total, general,
aggregate, average, comprehensive, whole, complete.

SAY: the <u>complete</u> plan; the <u>comprehensive</u> plan
RATHER THAN: the <u>overall</u> plan

over with

The "with" is redundant.

SAY: the case is <u>over</u>
RATHER THAN: the case is <u>over</u> <u>with</u>
EVEN BETTER: the case is <u>finished</u>; the case is
<u>completed</u>

owing to

"Due to" or "because of" is preferable to "owing to."

SAY: <u>due</u> <u>to</u> the rain, the event was postponed
RATHER THAN: <u>owing</u> <u>to</u> the rain, the event was
postponed

paid, payed

The past tense and past participle of pay is paid.
Payed is a nautical term.

pair

Pair takes a single verb when the emphasis is on
oneness or the entire unit.

EX: this <u>pair</u> of shoes <u>is</u> defective
It takes a plural verb when the emphasis is on the individual members of the unit, or when the reference is
to people.

EX: the <u>pair</u> <u>were</u> unprepared for the news

panacea

A panacea is a remedy for all diseases or difficulties. Do not use it to refer to one disease or difficulty.

pander, panderer

Both words mean a go-between for sex. Pander is
the preferred spelling.

paralegal, legal assistant

These terms are interchangeable. They mean a
person with legal skills who works under the supervision of a lawyer or who is otherwise authorized by
law to use those skills.

parameter, perimeter

Parameter is a scientific word meaning an arbitrary
constant or variable. Do not use it to mean boundary,
limit, range, or scope.

SAY: stay within the <u>limits</u> of the budget
RATHER THAN: stay within the <u>parameters</u> of the
budget
Perimeter means boundary, or the outer limits of an area.

EX: the <u>perimeter</u> of the field

part and parcel

Avoid this cliché. Instead, say "part" or "essential
part."

SAY: the clause is an <u>essential</u> <u>part</u> of the contract
RATHER THAN: the clause is <u>part</u> <u>and</u> <u>parcel</u> of
the contract

partially, partly

When the emphasis is on a part of an object, use
partly. When you mean "to a certain degree," use partially.

EX: she is <u>partially</u> dependent on her uncle for
support; the memo is <u>partly</u> done

particular

This word often adds nothing to the sentence.

SAY: he was unable to attend at this time
RATHER THAN: he was unable to attend at this
<u>particular</u> time

partly See *partially.*

party, person

Other than in a legal context, do not refer to a
person as a party.

SAY: they took the wounded <u>person</u> to the hospital
RATHER THAN: they took the wounded <u>party</u> to
the hospital

pass See *free gift.*

pass, past, passed
The past tense and past participle of pass is "passed." Past is not a verb.
SAY: they <u>passed</u> the road
RATHER THAN: they <u>past</u> the road
Past can be an adjective or an adverb.
EX: a <u>past</u> president; they drove <u>past</u>

pass away
Say "die" rather than "pass away."

past See *pass.*

past history, past experience
The word "past" is redundant in these phrases.

payed See *paid.*

peaceful, peaceable
Peaceful means undisturbed. Peaceable means inclined toward or promoting peace.
EX: a <u>peaceful</u> setting; a <u>peaceable</u> way to resolve the dispute

pedal, peddle
A pedal is a lever. Peddle means to sell on the road.
EX: the bicycle <u>pedal</u>; they <u>peddled</u> vacuum cleaners

peer
Peer does not mean superior. It means equal.

pendant, pendent
Pendant, a noun, means something that hangs. Pendent, an adjective, means hanging or suspended.
EX: a <u>pendant</u> around her neck; <u>pendent</u> jurisdiction

people, persons
Use people when referring to a large number. Use persons when referring to relatively few, or when referring to them as individuals.
EX: the <u>people</u> in the stadium; the <u>persons</u> arrested

per See *as per.*

per cent, percent
The preferred spelling is "per cent." It takes a singular verb if the number is singular and a plural verb if the number is plural.
EX: ten per cent of the brief <u>is</u> done; ten per cent of the cases <u>are</u> frivolous

percentage
Percentage means a proportion or fraction.
EX: a <u>percentage</u> of registered voters

Do not use percentage if you simply mean some or few.
SAY: the teaching method is valuable in <u>some</u> of the classes
RATHER THAN: the teaching method is valuable in a <u>percentage</u> of the classes
Use the symbol (%) only in charts or tables, not is sentences.

perfect See *equal.*

perimeter See *parameter.*

period of
Omit this phrase if it adds nothing to the sentence.
SAY: he kept a record for two months
RATHER THAN: he kept a record for a <u>period of</u> two months

permit See *allow.*

perpetrate, perpetuate
Perpetrate means to perform or carry out. Perpetuate means to continue or prolong.
EX: <u>perpetrate</u> a crime; <u>perpetuate</u> her name

perquisite, prerequisite
Perquisite means an extra benefit. Prerequisite means a prior condition.
EX: the car was one of the <u>perquisites</u> of the job; passing the exam is a <u>prerequisite</u>

per se
This phrase means in itself, by itself, intrinsically. Unless you are referring to a specific legal doctrine (e.g., libelous per se), do not use this phrase in your writing. It usually adds little more than pomposity.

person See *individual, party, people.*

personal, personally (see also *interpersonal*)
Avoid using these words if they add nothing to the meaning of the sentence.
EX: a <u>personal</u> friend (as opposed to what other kind of friend?)
EX: his <u>personal</u> life (as opposed to what other kind of life?)
EX: she attended <u>personally</u> (how else could she attend?)
EX: <u>personally</u>, I disagree (how else could you disagree?)

personal, personnel
Personal means pertaining to an individual person. Personnel means a group or body of people, usually employees.

EX: the president's <u>personal</u> mail; the <u>personnel</u> office

Do not use personnel with a number.

SAY: three employees, or, three people
RATHER THAN: three <u>personnel</u>

persons See *people.*

persuade See *convince.*

peruse, perusal

These words are often pompous and stilted. Words such as read, study, and check are usually good substitutes.

SAY: <u>check</u> this request carefully; a careful <u>reading</u> (or <u>study</u>) of the plan
RATHER THAN: <u>peruse</u> this request carefully; a careful <u>perusal</u> of the plan

pessimistic See *optimistic.*

phantasy See *fantasy.*

phase See *faze.*

phenomenon, phenomena

Unless you are referring to a perceptible event that is remarkable or impressive in some way, avoid calling it a phenomenon.

The preferred plural of phenomenon is phenomena, not phenomenons.

phoney

Avoid this word in formal writing. Instead say false, deceptive, fraudulent, etc.

piteous, pitiable, pitiful

Piteous means arousing pity or compassion. Pitiable means deserving pity or compassion. Pitiful means so inadequate or insignificant as to be pathetic.

EX: a <u>piteous</u> call for help; the <u>pitiable</u> plight of the refugees; he gave a <u>pitiful</u> sum

plain See *plane.*

plan See *future plans.*

plan ahead See *future plans.*

plane, plain

Plane means a level of development or achievement. Plain means clear, simple, undecorated.

EX: research at a sophisticated <u>plane</u>; the <u>plain</u> meaning rule

plans and specifications

Unless you are making a clear distinction between that which is a "plan" and that which is a "specification," this phrase is redundant. Say "plans"

plan to, plan on

"Plan on" is colloquial. Say "plan to."

SAY: <u>plan to</u> attend.
RATHER THAN: <u>plan on</u> attending

pleaded, pled

Pleaded or pled can be used as the past tense and past participle of plead.

EX: yesterday he <u>pleaded</u> guilty, or, yesterday he <u>pled</u> guilty

plead innocent

Defendants plead not guilty. They do not plead innocent. There is no plea of innocence in court.

please find enclosed See *enclosed herein.*

pled See *pleaded.*

plurality See *majority.*

plus

Do not use "plus" to connect main clauses.

SAY: he failed the course <u>and</u> he left the city
RATHER THAN: he failed the course <u>plus</u> he left the city

Plus takes a singular verb unless a subject is plural. Plus is a preposition, not a conjunction. It does not affect the number of the verb.

EX: ten plus ten <u>is</u> twenty; their objections plus the error <u>are</u> recorded

pm See *a.m.*

podium See *lectern.*

point in time See *at this point in time.*

point of view, viewpoint, standpoint

Whenever possible, try to find substitutes for these words.

SAY:	RATHER THAN:
legally	from a legal <u>point</u> of <u>view</u>;
his opinion	his <u>point</u> of <u>view</u>;
her judgment	her <u>viewpoint</u>;
economcally	from an economic <u>standpoint</u>

politic, political

Politic means wise, judicious. Political means pertaining to politics.

EX: a <u>politic</u> decision; the <u>political</u> system

population, populace

Population means the people, the number of persons in a certain group or territory. Populace means the common people.

EX: the male <u>population</u> of the town; a land reform program acceptable to the <u>populace</u>

pore, pour

Pore means to examine carefully. Pour means to make something flow.

EX: they <u>pored</u> through the memorandum; <u>pour</u> the wine

position See *in a position to.*

positively See *definitely.*

possess

Unless you are referring to a legal doctrine, use simpler words such as have, has, and own.

SAY: he <u>has</u> a sense of humor

RATHER THAN: he <u>possesses</u> a sense of humor

possible See *feasible.*

pour See *pore.*

practicable See *impractical.*

practical See *impractical.*

practically, virtually

Practically means in a practical manner, and in all important respects. Do not use it to mean "almost." Virtually means in fact, although not formally.

EX: <u>practically</u> exonerated; <u>virtually</u> extinct

practice, practise

The American spelling is practice; the British spelling is practise.

precede, proceed

Precede means to come before. Proceed means to go on.

EX: Burger <u>preceded</u> Rehnquist; you may <u>proceed</u>

precedence, precedent

Precedence means going before, having priority. Precedent means something that happened in the past that can be helpful in similar situations in the future.

EX: whoever files first has <u>precedence</u>; the 1943 case is a clear <u>precedent</u>

precipitate, precipitous

Precipitate means happening suddenly, and often carelessly. Precipitous means very steep.

EX: he cautioned against <u>precipitate</u> action; a <u>precipitous</u> climb

predicament See *dilemma.*

predominant, predominate

Predominant, an adjective, means the most important. Predominate, a verb, means to dominate, to prevail.

EX: the <u>predominant</u> food of the country; he <u>predominates</u> over the others

preempt, pre-empt

The preferred spelling is preempt rather than pre-empt.

preface See *foreword.*

preferable See *more preferable.*

prefer...to

Use "prefer...to" rather than "prefer...than."

SAY: she <u>prefers</u> trial practice <u>to</u> corporate work

RATHER THAN: she <u>prefers</u> trial practice <u>than</u> corporate work

If the preference is between two infinitives, you must rewrite the sentence to avoid a "to to" construction.

SAY: he <u>prefers</u> research <u>to</u> investigation

RATHER THAN: he <u>prefers</u> to research <u>to</u> <u>to</u> investigate

premises

This word has two meanings: (a) a proposition or basis for reasoning, and (b) land and the buildings on it. In both senses, premises takes a plural verb.

EX: she claims that faulty <u>premises</u> <u>are</u> in the analysis; the <u>premises</u> <u>are</u> vacant

preparatory to

Avoid this phrase if all you mean is "before."

SAY: he proofread the brief <u>before</u> submitting it

RATHER THAN: he proofread the brief <u>preparatory</u> <u>to</u> submitting it

prepared

Prepared is not a substitute for "willing" or "ready."

SAY: he is not <u>ready</u> to acknowledge defeat

RATHER THAN: he is not <u>prepared</u> to acknowledge defeat

prerequisite See *perquisite.*

prescribe, proscribe

Prescribe means to provide rules or guidelines, and to recommend. Proscribe means to prohibit.

EX: she <u>prescribed</u> medication; the court <u>proscribed</u> picketing

present See *at present.*

presentiment, presentment

Presentiment means a premonition. A presentment is an accusation of crime initiated by a grand jury based on its own knowledge. It also means giving or producing a negotiable instrument to the drawee for its acceptance, or to the drawer or acceptor for payment.

present incumbent

The word "present" is redundant.

presently, now

Presently means forthwith or soon. Do not use presently to mean now.

SAY: we are <u>now</u> preparing a handbook

RATHER THAN: we are <u>presently</u> preparing a handbook

EVEN BETTER: we are preparing a handbook

presumably See *supposedly.*

presume See *assume.*

presumptive, presumptuous

Presumptive means warranting an inference, based on probability or presumption. Presumptuous means arrogant.

EX: an heir <u>presumptive</u>; it would be <u>presumptuous</u> of you to seek the position

pretty

Avoid this word in formal writing.

SAY: his guilt was rather obvious

RATHER THAN: his guilt was <u>pretty</u> obvious

preventive, preventative

The preferred spelling is preventive.

SAY: <u>preventive</u> measures taken

RATHER THAN: <u>preventative</u> measures taken

previous to, prior to

"Before" is preferable to either phrase.

SAY: she held the position before 1989

RATHER THAN: she held the position <u>previous</u> <u>to</u> 1989, or she held the position <u>prior</u> <u>to</u> 1989

principal, principle

Principal means the most important (adjective), the head of a school (noun), and money on which interest is earned (noun). Principle means a basic truth (noun).

EX: her <u>principal</u> argument in the brief; the <u>principle</u> of cause and effect

prior to See *previous to; in advance of.*

private industry

The word private is redundant.

probably See *likely.*

proceed See *precede.*

prognosis See *diagnosis.*

programing, programming

Either spelling is acceptable. One "m" is more common.

prologue See *epilogue.*

prone See *apt.*

prophecy, prophesy

Prophecy is the noun meaning a prediction or revelation through divine intervention. Prophesy is the verb meaning to predict or reveal by divine intervention.

EX: a <u>prophecy</u> that the city would be destroyed; she <u>prophesied</u> the destruction of the city

proportion

Use proportion when you mean a part in relationship to the whole. Do not use it if you simply mean some or few.

EX: a small <u>proportion</u> of the funds is used for expenses

proscribe See *prescribe.*

proselyte, proselytize

As verbs, both words mean to convert.

proved, proven

The past participle of prove is proved or proven. Proved is preferred.

EX: the lawyer has <u>proved</u> that the document is fraudulent.

Use proven only as an adjective.

EX: a <u>proven</u> winner

provided, providing

Use provided as a conjunction, meaning on condition that. Use providing as part of a verb form, not as a conjunction.

SAY: you may use this method <u>provided</u> you qualify

RATHER THAN: you may use this method <u>providing</u> you qualify

EVEN BETTER: you may use this method <u>if</u> you qualify

proximity See *close proximity.*

pseudo, quasi

Pseudo means false. Quasi means resembling, to some degree.

EX: <u>pseudo</u> doctor; <u>quasi</u>-legislation

purport

Purport means to give the appearance of something. Do not use this verb in the passive voice.

SAY: the documents <u>purport</u> to come from his office.

RATHER THAN: the documents <u>are</u> <u>purported</u> to come from his office

purpose See *with the purpose of.*

purposely, purposefully

Purposely means on purpose, intentionally. Purposefully means with a set purpose in mind, in a determined manner.

EX: he <u>purposely</u> missed the bus; he <u>purposefully</u> disrupted the meeting.

qualified expert

At a trial we speak of an expert who has been qualified, meaning that he or she has gone through a prescribed process in order to be allowed to testify. In any other context it is redundant to refer to a qualified expert. By definition, experts are qualified.

quasi See *pseudo.*

question of whether, question as to whether, question arises as to whether, question is whether

Pare down these phrases whenever possible.

SAY: the <u>question</u> <u>is</u> <u>whether</u> the contract is void

RATHER THAN: <u>the</u> <u>question</u> <u>arises</u> <u>as</u> <u>to</u> <u>whether</u> the contract is void

EVEN BETTER: is the contract void?

quick, quickly

Both words can be used as adverbs, but quickly is preferred.

EX: move <u>quickly</u>

quite See *likely.*

quote (see also *cite*)

Use quote as a verb when repeating someone else's words exactly as written or spoken. Do not use quote as a noun. Say quotation instead.

raise, rear

These words are interchangeable. At one time, however, animals were <u>raised,</u> and children were <u>reared.</u>

raise, rise

Raise takes an object; rise does not.

EX: <u>raise</u> the price; production costs <u>rise</u>

rare, scarce

If something is rare, it is seldom available. The same is true of that which is scarce, with the additional meaning that when it is available, the amount is often inadequate.

EX: a <u>rare</u> book; a <u>scarce</u> supply of water in the desert

rarely ever, seldom ever

The word "ever" in these phrases is redundant.

SAY: she <u>rarely</u> attends; he <u>seldom</u> participates

RATHER THAN: she <u>rarely</u> <u>ever</u> attends; he <u>seldom</u> <u>ever</u> participates

The following constructions, however, are proper: "rarely if ever" and "seldom if ever."

rate

Do not use this word to mean to deserve or to be entitled to.

SAY: she <u>was</u> <u>entitled</u> <u>to</u> a company car

RATHER THAN: she <u>rated</u> a company car

rational, rationale

Rational (an adjective) means reasonable or logical. Rationale (a noun) means the reason or explanation for something.

EX: a <u>rational</u> plan to solve the problem; the <u>rationale</u> of the court's decision

re, in re

The phrase "in re" means "in the matter of" or "concerning." The shorthand version is "re." Use them in the captions of memos and in legal citations. Avoid them otherwise.

reaction, opinion

Reaction means a response to a stimulus.

EX: his <u>reaction</u> to the drug

Do not use reaction to mean opinion, position, response, or feeling.

SAY: his <u>opinion</u> of the proposal
RATHER THAN: his <u>reaction</u> to the proposal, or his <u>feelings</u> about the proposal

read where See *see where.*

real See *actual.*

real fact See *fact.*

realize, realise
The American spelling is realize; the British spelling is realise.

realistic
Realistic means pertaining to what exists in fact. Do not use it to mean practical.
EX: the speech gave a <u>realistic</u> assessment of the farm crisis

Realtor
A Realtor is a real estate agent who belongs to the National Association of Realtors.

rear See *raise.*

reason See *simple reason.*

reason is because See *because.*

reason why
In place of this phrase, say "reason that," "reason," "because," etc.
SAY: laziness is the <u>reason</u> he failed
RATHER THAN: laziness is the <u>reason</u> <u>why</u> he failed
EVEN BETTER: he failed <u>because</u> of laziness

rebellion, revolt, revolution, riot
Rebellion: an organized uprising designed to overthrow the government (it usually fails; if it succeeds, it is a revolution).
Revolt: extensive opposition to a custom, law, authority, or government.
Revolution: the overthrow of a government and the substitution of a new government.
Riot: sudden violent disruption of public order.

rebut, refute, deny
To rebut a charge is to counter it by offering opposing evidence or arguments. To refute a charge is to counter it by offering other evidence that proves it is wrong. To deny a charge is simply to say that it is wrong.
EX: she <u>rebutted</u> Bill's claim that she was lazy by staying late that night to finish the report;
she <u>refuted</u> the claim that she did not pay for the

item by producing the sales receipt for it;
she <u>denied</u> that she was late

received See *in receipt of.*

recipient
Received is preferable to recipient.
SAY: she <u>received</u> a raise
RATHER THAN: she was the <u>recipient</u> of a raise

reckon See *calculate.*

recollect, re-collect
Recollect means to remember. Re-collect means to collect again.
EX: she could not <u>recollect</u> the incident; <u>re-collect</u> the items

recreate, re-create
Recreate means to amuse oneself. Re-create means to create anew.
EX: <u>recreate</u> in the country; <u>re-create</u> the jobs that had been eliminated

recur, reoccur
Both words mean to happen again. Recur is preferred. So too, say recurrence rather than reoccurrence.

re-enforce See *reinforce.*

refer See *allude.*

refer back
The word "back" is usually redundant even when discussing something that is earlier or that comes before.
SAY: <u>refer</u> to chapter one
RATHER THAN: <u>refer</u> <u>back</u> to chapter one

referendum, referendums, referenda
Referendums is the preferred plural of referendum.

refuse See *decline.*

refute See *rebut.*

regard See *in regard to.*

regardless See *irregardless.*

regretful, regrettable
Regretful means full of regret. Regrettable means producing or causing regret. People are regretful; occurrences or conditions are regrettable.
EX: he is <u>regretful</u> about the mistake; the mistake is <u>regrettable</u>

regular See *biweekly.*

regulations See *rules and regulations*.

reign, rein

Reign means the rule of a sovereign. Rein means control or guidance.

EX: the <u>reign</u> ended; tight <u>rein</u>

reinforce, re-enforce, reenforce

The preferred spelling is reinforce, meaning to strengthen.

relate

Do not use this word to mean to have rapport with.

SAY: John and Fred work well together

RATHER THAN: John and Fred <u>relate</u> well together

relations, relatives

Both of these words mean those related by blood or marriage. Relatives is more common.

relationship See *interrelationship*.

relatively, comparatively

These words are interchangeable. Be sure to use them when a comparison is expressed or implied. Do not use them to mean "somewhat," "rather," or "fairly."

SAY: <u>rather</u> tired

RATHER THAN: <u>relatively</u> tired

relevant, irrelevant

These words mean pertinent or not pertinent to something specific. Adding the word "to" will often make this relationship clear. When you call something relevant or irrelevant, your reader should not have to ask, "to what?"

SAY: the training is <u>irrelevant</u> <u>to</u> my current job

RATHER THAN: the training is <u>irrelevant</u>

rely on See *bank on*.

remainder See *balance*.

remark See *indicate*.

remediable, remedial

Remediable means that which can be corrected. Remedial means providing a remedy.

EX: the mistake is <u>remediable</u>; a <u>remedial</u> statute

remove See *impeach*.

remuneration

A less wordy substitute is "pay."

reoccur, reoccurrence See *recur*.

repairable, reparable

Both words mean that which can be restored or fixed. Use repairable when you are referring to concrete objects. Use reparable when you are referring to more abstract situations.

EX: the car is <u>repairable</u>; a <u>reparable</u> loss

repeat again

"Again" is often redundant.

SAY: <u>repeat</u> what he told you

RATHER THAN: <u>repeat</u> what he told you <u>again</u>

repel, repulse

Both of these words mean to drive back or ward off; and both can mean that this is done with rudeness. The difference is that repel includes the emotion of disgust and loathing.

EX: they were <u>repelled</u> by his appearance; she <u>repulsed</u> her attacker

The verb repulse is not associated with the adjective repulsive.

replete

Replete means fully supplied. It does not mean complete, equipped, or filled with.

SAY: an apartment <u>equipped</u> with air conditioning and wall-to-wall carpeting

RATHER THAN: an apartment <u>replete</u> with air conditioning and wall-to-wall carpeting

replica

Replica is a copy or reproduction of the original made by the original artist. Do not use replica to mean model or miniature.

SAY: he built a <u>model</u> of the White House to scale

RATHER THAN: he built a <u>replica</u> of the White House to scale

represent

Represent means "stands for." Do not use it as a substitute for "is."

SAY: this paycheck <u>is</u> the amount he received

RATHER THAN: this paycheck <u>represents</u> the amount he received

reproduction See *replica*.

republic See *democracy*.

repulse See *repel*.

reside, live

Unless you are using the legal definition of residence, say "live" rather than reside.

respect See *with respect to*.

respective, respectively

Respective means particular or regarded individually. Respectively means singly in the order mentioned.

EX: they returned to their <u>respective</u> cases; the awards went to Bob and Fred <u>respectively</u>

Both words are often unnecessary to the meaning of the sentence.

EX: they returned to their cases; the awards went to Bob and Fred

respite See *temporary*.

rest See *balance*.

restive, restless

Both words mean uneasy and nervous. A difference is that restive is used when the uneasiness comes from an outside pressure or restraint.

EX: a <u>restive</u> driver stalled in traffic; <u>restless</u> while waiting for the phone call

resume, résumé

Resume means to begin again. Résumé (note the accents) means a summary of past employment, education, etc.

return back, revert back

"Back" is redundant in these phrases.

SAY: <u>return</u> to your childhood memories; <u>revert</u> to your earlier behavior

RATHER THAN: <u>return</u> <u>back</u> to your childhood memories; <u>revert</u> <u>back</u> to your earlier behavior

revolt, revolution See *rebellion*.

rightly, rightfully

Rightly means correctly or accurately. Rightfully means morally, properly, or fairly.

EX: he <u>rightly</u> concluded that the document is missing; he <u>rightfully</u> claimed that he owned the document

riot See *rebellion*.

rise See *raise*.

rob

Persons and places are robbed; things are not.

EX: <u>rob</u> a stranger; <u>rob</u> a bank; <u>steal</u> the money

round, around

As an adverb, say around rather than round.

SAY: turn <u>around</u>

RATHER THAN: turn <u>round</u>

rules and regulations

Do not use this phrase unless you are sure that there is a clear distinction between a rule and a regulation. Often there is no such distinction.

Sabbath

Sabbath is not a synonym for Sunday. For Jews, the Sabbath is Saturday.

said (see also *indicate; disclose*)

Do not use "said" as an adjective to mean aforementioned.

SAY: this buyer; the XYZ Company

RATHER THAN: the <u>said</u> buyer; the <u>said</u> company

same

Do not use this word as a pronoun.

SAY: she completed the memo and filed it

RATHER THAN: she completed the memo and filed <u>same</u>

Also avoid the phrase "the same" when used as a substitute for "it."

same identical

This phrase is redundant. If two things are identical, they are the same.

sanction

Depending on context, this word can mean permission or penalty.

EX: they went on the trip after it received the <u>sanction</u> of the board; there are <u>sanctions</u> for the offense in the statute

sank See *sink*.

save, except

When you mean "other than," say except, not save.

SAY: all the workers except Paul are terminated

RATHER THAN: all the workers save Paul are terminated

savings

With the article "a," do not use the plural, "savings."

SAY: <u>a</u> <u>saving</u> of hundreds of dollars

RATHER THAN: <u>a</u> <u>savings</u> of hundreds of dollars

say See *indicate*.

scan

Avoid this word since it may not be clear which of the following two equally acceptable meanings you intend: to read very carefully, or to look over quickly.

scarce See *rare.*

scarcely See *hardly.*

seasonable, seasonal
Seasonable means within the agreed time, or appropriate to the season. Seasonal means that which depends on or is controlled by the seasons.
EX: <u>seasonable</u> acceptance of the offer; <u>seasonable</u> rain; <u>seasonal</u> employment

secondly See *firstly.*

second of all
"Of all" is unnecessary.

secular, sectarian
Secular means nonspiritual, worldly. Sectarian means pertaining to a particular religion or sect.
EX: <u>secular</u> music; <u>sectarian</u> education

seem See *would seem.*

see where, read where
Instead of these phrases, say "see that" and "read that."

seldom ever See *rarely ever.*

semiannual See *biannual.*

semimonthly See *bimonthly.*

semiweekly See *biweekly.*

send See *forward.*

sensual, sensuous
Both words mean pertaining to the senses. Sensual is often used in a physical or sexual context. Sensuous is often used in an aesthetic context.
EX: a <u>sensual</u> dress; a <u>sensuous</u> painting

sentiment, sentimentality
Both words refer to emotions or feelings. A sentiment is often sincere, while sentimentality is often affected or excessive.

separate See *divide.*

serve, service
As a verb, the primary meaning of service is to maintain and keep repaired.
EX: <u>service</u> the computer
Do not use service to mean to give services to, or to provide a general benefit. Instead, use serve.
SAY: the company <u>serves</u> the county

RATHER THAN: the company <u>services</u> the county
Two exceptions are debts (debts can be serviced) and breeding animals (animals can be serviced).

set, sit
Set usually takes an object. Sit usually does not.
EX: <u>set</u> the memo on the table; <u>sit</u> on the chair
There are a few common exceptions.
EX: the sun <u>sets</u>; <u>sit</u> the child down

sewage, sewerage
Both words mean waste material. Sewerage also means the system for the removal of this waste.
EX: <u>sewage</u> disposal; a <u>sewerage</u> fee

sex See *gender.*

shall, will
Use "shall" with the first person (I and we) to express a simple future action or willingness.
EX: I <u>shall</u> discuss the matter with the supervisor.
We <u>shall</u> be glad to file a response.
Use "will" with the second person (you) and with the third person (he, she, they, it).
EX: You <u>will</u> be chosen for the position.
He <u>will</u> be chosen for the position.
They <u>will</u> be chosen for the position.
It <u>will</u> be chosen for the position.
He <u>will</u> be glad to respond.
They <u>will</u> be glad to respond.
Reverse this order to show determination, obligation, or compulsion.
EX: I <u>will</u> have it ready on time (a promise).
We <u>will</u> have it ready on time (a promise).
You <u>shall</u> submit this report every day (an order).
They <u>shall</u> submit this report every day (an order).
It <u>shall</u> be submitted in two days (an obligation).
In practice, some of the above general rules have broken down. For example, "will" is considered proper for first, second, and third person.

she See *he or she.*

should, would (see also *have got to*)
Use "should" for the first, second, and third person to express obligation or duty (as a synonym for ought to).
EX: I know I <u>should</u> complete the memo
Use "should" for the first, second, and third person to express a condition.
EX: if the clerk <u>should</u> call, let me know immediately

Use "should" for the first, second, and third person to express an expectation.

EX: the letter <u>should</u> have reached him by now

Use "would" for the first, second, and third person to express habitual or customary action.

EX: each morning the clerk <u>would</u> follow the same ritual

Use "would" for the first, second, and third person to express insistence.

EX: he <u>would</u> constantly delay making decisions even though his supervisor advised him to change

shouldn't ought See *ought.*

should of See *could of.*

show See *evidence.*

shrink

Either shrank or shrunk is acceptable as the past tense of shrink.

siblings

This is a pretentious word for brothers or sisters.

sic [sic]

Use sic in brackets [sic] to indicate that any errors in a quote are in the original and hence are not copying mistakes of yours.

EX: "the wound did not heel [sic] in time"

sight See *cite.*

simple, simplified See *simplistic.*

simple reason

Avoid this phrase. "Because" is usually a preferable substitute.

SAY: he went <u>because</u> he was asked

RATHER THAN: he went for the <u>simple</u> <u>reason</u> that he was asked

simplistic

Simplistic means oversimplified. It does not mean simple. It also is not the same as simplified which means made less complex.

EX: a <u>simplistic</u> plan is naive; a <u>simple</u> plan can be very profound and effective; a <u>simplified</u> version of a plan may be so general that it is now simplistic

since See *ago; as; in that; in view of the fact that.*

sine qua non

Sine qua non ("without which not") means an essential condition or element. Plain English is preferable.

SAY: consideration is <u>essential</u> to a contract

RATHER THAN: consideration is a <u>sine</u> <u>qua</u> <u>non</u> of a contract

sink

The past tense of sink is sank or sunk. Sank is more common. Sunk is the past participle.

EX: the barge <u>sank</u>; they have <u>sunk</u> the barge

sit See *set.*

site See *cite.*

size See *in length.*

skillful, skilful

The preferred spelling is skillful.

slow

Slow is primarily an adjective, but it can function as an adverb. Nevertheless, when you need an adverb, slowly is preferred.

SAY: drive <u>slowly</u>

RATHER THAN: drive <u>slow</u>

small See *limited.*

smaller See *fewer.*

smell

Smell should be followed by an adjective rather than an adverb.

SAY: smell <u>bad</u>

RATHER THAN: smell <u>badly</u>

so

Do not use "so" as an intensifier.

SAY: very good; extremely warm

RATHER THAN: <u>so</u> good; <u>so</u> warm

"So" is usually a weak substitute for because, since, therefore, or consequently.

SAY: <u>since</u> the case was postponed, we went home

RATHER THAN: the case was postponed, <u>so</u> we went home

Say "so that" when "so" begins a purpose clause.

EX: he came <u>so</u> <u>that</u> he could participate

so-called

This word means often called or wrongly named. If quotation marks follow this word, the word is unnecessary.

SAY: he objected to the "improvement"

RATHER THAN: he objected to the <u>so-called</u> "improvement"

some, somewhat

Some (an adjective) means an undetermined

quantity. Somewhat (an adverb) means to some degree. Do not use "some" as an adverb.

SAY: his health has <u>somewhat</u> deteriorated
RATHER THAN: his health has deteriorated <u>some</u>

somebody, someone

These words are interchangeable. Do not use either to mean an important person.

someplace, somewhere, somewheres

Avoid using someplace. Use somewhere instead.

SAY: we will meet <u>somewhere</u> on Third Avenue
RATHER THAN: we will meet <u>someplace</u> on Third Avenue

Never use somewheres.

sometime, sometimes, some time

"Sometime" means at an indefinite time. "Sometimes" means now and then. Use "some time" (two words) when you want to emphasize a duration of time.

EX: the conference will be <u>sometime</u> this weekend; <u>sometimes</u> she becomes quite irritable; it took her <u>some time</u> to call

Sometime can also mean former.

EX: a <u>sometime</u> judge

Do not use sometime to mean occasional or on and off.

somewhat See *some*.

somewhere See *someplace*.

sort See *kind*.

so therefore

The "so" is unnecessary in this phrase.

SAY: he found no further cases; <u>therefore</u>, he submitted the memo as is
RATHER THAN: he found no further cases, <u>so therefore</u> he submitted the memo as is

South See *West*.

specially See *especially*.

specie, species

Specie means coined money. Species means a category or classification. The spelling is the same for the singular and the plural—species.

EX: payment in <u>specie</u>; this <u>species</u> is prevalent in Peru

specifications See *plans and specifications*.

spell out the details

"Spell out," meaning to give the particulars, is too informal. Also, the phrase "spell out the details" is redundant. When you spell something out, you give the details.

spoil, spoiled, spoilt

The past tense and past participle of spoil is spoiled or spoilt. Spoiled is more common.

spokesman

To avoid this sexist word, say spokesperson, representative, or agent.

spring, sprang, sprung

The past tense of spring is sprang or sprung. Sprang is more common. The past participle is sprung.

standpoint See *point of view*.

state See *indicate*.

stationary, stationery

Stationary means standing still. Stationery means writing paper.

EX: a <u>stationary</u> object; a <u>stationery</u> store

still

Do not join "still" and another adjective with a hyphen.

SAY: the still angry manager; the still climbing temperature
RATHER THAN: the still-angry manager; the still-climbing temperature

stimulant, stimulus

A stimulant is a temporary arousal or acceleration of activity. (The plural is stimulants.) A stimulus is anything that causes a response. (The plural is stimuli.)

EX: the drug acted as a <u>stimulant</u> so that she could stay awake; the <u>stimulus</u> of the rivalry

straight, strait

Straight means not curved. Strait means a water passage.

EX: a <u>straight</u> line; passage through the <u>strait</u>

strategy, tactics

Strategy is the overall plan to achieve a particular goal. Tactics are the means to implement the strategy. A strategy is a plan. A tactic is a technique.

EX: a conference to prepare <u>strategy</u> for the case; military <u>tactics</u>

stratum

The plural of stratum is strata or stratums. Strata is more common. The plural is not stratas.

structure

As a verb, this word is often used pretentiously.

SAY: create a place to work
RATHER THAN: <u>structure</u> an environment for work

stupid See *dope.*

subsequent, subsequently
"Later" is preferable to either of these words.
SAY: a <u>later</u> development; <u>later</u>, she resigned
RATHER THAN: a <u>subsequent</u> development; <u>subsequently</u>, she resigned

subsequent to
"After" is preferable.
SAY: he resigned <u>after</u> the release of the report
RATHER THAN: he resigned <u>subsequent</u> <u>to</u> the release of the report

successive See *consecutive.*

such
Do not use "such" as a substitute for it, them, any, these, etc.
SAY: the software will not be ordered; we no longer use it
RATHER THAN: the software will not be ordered; we no longer use <u>such</u>

such as See *etc., for example.*

suffer from
When you have a sickness or illness, you suffer <u>from</u> it, not <u>with</u> it.
SAY: suffer <u>from</u> tuberculosis
RATHER THAN: suffer <u>with</u> tuberculosis

sunk See *sink.*

superior to See *inferior to (than).*

supplement See *augment.*

suppose See *expect.*

supposedly, presumably
Supposedly refers to an assumption that is often questionable. Presumably refers to an assumption that is reasonable.

supra
Avoid "supra" to refer the reader to previously cited material. It is often cumbersome for the reader to go back to find the previous cite. Either repeat the full cite or give the cite in abbreviated form.

swap, swop
These words mean to trade or exchange. The preferred spelling is swap. Avoid the word, under either spelling, in formal writing.

sympathy See *empathy.*

systemize, systematize
Both words mean to formulate in a system. Systematize is more common.

tactics See *strategy.*

take See *bring.*

take delivery
A needlessly technical way to say receive.
SAY: expected to <u>receive</u> the goods on Tuesday
RATHER THAN: expected to <u>take</u> <u>delivery</u> of the goods on Tuesday

take place See *happen; materialize.*

target
Target means something you aim or fire at.
EX: an easy <u>target</u>; the <u>target</u> of criticism
It is overused in the sense of goal, purpose, or objective.
SAY: the <u>goal</u> of the program is to eliminate illiteracy
RATHER THAN: the <u>target</u> of the program is to eliminate illiteracy

tasteful, tasty
Tasteful means showing good taste. Tasty means having a good flavor.
EX: a <u>tasteful</u> presentation; a <u>tasty</u> meal

taunt, taut
Taunt means to mock or tease. Taut means tight, not slack.
EX: <u>taunt</u> the speaker; a <u>taut</u> rope
In addition, taut refers to discipline on a ship. The word tight also has this meaning.

teach See *learn.*

teen-age, teen-ager
Be sure to include the hyphen in the spelling of these words.

temperament See *disposition.*

temporal, temporary

Temporal means pertaining to nonspiritual matters. Temporary means for a limited time.

EX: the <u>temporal</u> concerns of the pastor; <u>temporary</u> employment

temporary respite

The word temporary is redundant.

tend to (see also *attend*)

Tend means to look after the needs of. "Tend to" is informal and should be avoided in formal writing.

SAY: <u>tend</u> the sick

RATHER THAN: <u>tend to</u> the sick

than

When "than" is used in a comparison, complete the sentence in order to determine whether the following pronoun should be nominative or objective.

EX: she is wiser <u>than</u> I (the nominative "I" is used because if you completed the sentence, it would read: "she is wiser <u>than</u> I am")

Complete the sentence and rewrite it, if necessary, to avoid ambiguity.

EX: she likes Paul better <u>than</u> <u>me</u> (the objective "me" is used if you mean: "she likes Paul better <u>than</u> she likes <u>me.</u>" The latter phrasing is clearer.)

EX: she likes Paul better <u>than</u> <u>I</u> (the nominative "I" is used if you mean: "she likes Paul better <u>than</u> <u>I</u> like him." The latter phrasing is clearer.)

thankfully

This word means "in a thankful way." Do not use it to mean "I am grateful that."

SAY: we prayed together <u>thankfully</u>

RATHER THAN: <u>thankfully</u>, we no longer pray together

that

When "that" is a conjunction, it can be omitted if it is not needed for clarity.

SAY: the court said he could have an extension

RATHER THAN: the court said <u>that</u> he could have an extension; But,

SAY: the court said <u>that</u> in 1989 we would have to file again

RATHER THAN: the court said in 1989 we would have to file again

The "that" is necessary to make clear that the court did not make the statement in 1989.

Also, do not repeat "that" needlessly.

SAY: the manager feels <u>that</u> when the case is over, there is no need to remain

RATHER THAN: the manager feels <u>that</u> when the case is over, <u>that</u> there is no need to remain

that, which

Use "that" to begin a restrictive clause. A restrictive clause is also called a limiting or defining clause. It modifies and defines. The meaning of a restrictive clause is essential to the sentence. Do not use commas to set off a restrictive clause.

EX: the opinion does not apply to sales <u>that</u> are paid by check (the clause is restrictive; it defines a certain category of sales)

Use "which" to begin a nonrestrictive clause. A nonrestrictive clause is also called a nonlimiting or nondefining clause. It modifies but does not define. It gives additional, nonessential information. The meaning of a restrictive clause is not essential to the sentence. If a clause can be dropped without changing the basic meaning of the sentence, it is a nonrestrictive clause. Commas are used to set off nonrestrictive clauses.

EX: the legal profession, which began centuries ago, has many different kinds of lawyers within it (the clause is nonrestrictive; it modifies the profession, but does not define or restrict it)

that, which, who

That is used to refer to persons, animals, or things. Which is used to refer to animals or things, and who is used to refer to persons only.

EX: the man <u>that</u> bought the car

the horse <u>that</u> won the race

the car <u>that</u> I own

the horse, <u>which</u> is a fine animal

the city, <u>which</u> I hope to visit one day

George, <u>who</u> is quite competent

the

Do not omit "the" where it obviously should go.

SAY: <u>The</u> Governor's Office issued a proposed revision.

RATHER THAN: Governor's Office issued a proposed revision.

theater, theatre

The preferred spelling is theater.

their's (see also *there*)

There is no such word as "their's." The possessive of they is theirs.

EX: the books are theirs

themselves See *himself.*

then See *if. . . then.*

there

The verb following "there" should be singular or plural depending on whether the true subject of that verb is singular or plural.

 EX: there <u>are</u> many mansions (plural verb "are" because the subject, mansions, is plural)

 EX: there <u>is</u> an error in the memo (singular verb "is" because the subject, error, is singular)

 EX: there <u>appears</u> to be a flaw (singular verb "appears" because the subject, flaw, is singular)

there, their, they're

 "There" is primarily an adverb. "Their" is the possessive of they. "They're" is a contraction of "they are."

 EX: the library is <u>there</u>; <u>their</u> responsibility; <u>they're</u> finished

In formal writing use "they are" rather than the contraction "they're."

thereafter, therein, therefrom, wherein

 Use less pompous substitutes for these words whenever possible, e.g., after that, then, from then on, in that place, in that way.

therefore, therefor

 Therefore means hence or consequently. Therefor means "for that," "for it," or "in return for that."

 EX: <u>therefore</u>, he resigned; he could not understand the reason <u>therefor</u>

Avoid the use of therefor.

therefrom See *thereafter*.

therein See *thereafter*.

the same See *same*.

these kind, these sort See *kind*.

the writer See *writer*.

they're See *there*.

thing

 Avoid this word.

 SAY: the part of the proposal that he objected to

 RATHER THAN: the <u>thing</u> about the proposal that he objected to

think See *deem*.

this

 Be sure the reader knows what "this" refers to. Avoid using "this" as a general reference to what precedes it.

 SAY: I want to enter the health field and to pursue my music education. <u>Both of these goals</u> will take considerable effort.

 RATHER THAN: I want to enter the health field and to pursue my music education. <u>This</u> will take considerable effort.

this is to inform you that

 Avoid this phrase.

 SAY: you are terminated

 RATHER THAN: <u>this is to inform you that</u> you are terminated

this kind, this sort See *kind*.

though, although As conjunctions, these words are interchangeable.

 EX: <u>although</u> closed to the general public, we were admitted; <u>though</u> closed to the general public, we were admitted

thrust

 Avoid this word when you mean general direction.

 SAY: the main theme of the plan

 RATHER THAN: the <u>thrust</u> of the plan

til, 'til, till, until

 Until and till are interchangeable. Never use til or 'til.

to, too, two

 "To" is a preposition. "Too" is an adverb. "Two" is a number.

 EX: go <u>to</u> the library; <u>too</u> difficult; <u>two</u> briefs

to all intents and purposes

 Avoid this phrase.

 SAY: the program is over; or, the program is practically over

 RATHER THAN: <u>to all intents and purposes</u>, the program is over

together See *join together*.

too See *to*.

tortuous, torturous, tortious

 Tortuous means twisting or winding. Torturous means painful. Tortious means pertaining to a tort.

 EX: a <u>tortuous</u> street; a <u>torturous</u> experience; a <u>tortious</u> interference

total

 Eliminate this word when it adds nothing.

 SAY: he purchased 233 volumes

 RATHER THAN: he purchased a <u>total</u> of 233 volumes

toward, towards

 Both spellings are correct, but toward is preferred.

track, tract

 A track is a mark, route, or course of action. A tract is land, a pamphlet, or a verse.

 EX: <u>track</u> and field; the distribution of the <u>tract</u>

trademark, trade name
The correct spelling is trademark, not trade-mark or tradename.

transitory, transient
Both words mean for a limited time. Use transitory when the emphasis is short-lived. Use transient when the emphasis is remaining a short time.
EX: transitory pain; transient guest

transparent See *opaque*.

transpire See *happen*.

treachery, treason
Treachery means any betrayal. Treason means a betrayal of one's country.

treble, triple
Both words can mean three times or threefold. Unless you are referring to a rule that uses treble (e.g., treble damages), you should use triple.

troubled
People or their faculties are troubled, not things or events.
SAY: troubled conscience
RATHER THAN: troubled company

true fact See *fact*.

try and See *come and*.

two See *to*.

type
When you mean kind or sort, you must say "type of."
SAY: that type of lawyer
RATHER THAN: that type lawyer

unaware, unawares
Unaware is the adjective. Unawares is the adverb.
EX: unaware of the error; caught unawares

undersigned
Do not use this word to refer to the signer(s) of a document.

understand See *glean*.

uneatable See *eatable*.

unedible See *eatable*.

unexceptional, unexceptionable
Unexceptional means usual or normal. Unexceptionable means not subject to objections.
EX: the unexceptional behavior of the animals observed; unexceptionable title

unhuman See *inhuman*.

unilateral, bilateral
Unilateral means involving one side only. Bilateral means involving both sides.
EX: a unilateral concession by Italy; a bilateral commitment of France and Italy

unintentional See *intentional*.

uninterested See *disinterested*.

unique See *equal*.

university See *college*.

unless and until
A redundant phrase. Substitutes: if, when, unless, until, etc.
SAY: he will not accept the offer unless the price is doubled
RATHER THAN: he will not accept the offer unless and until the price is doubled

unmoral See *amoral*.

unorganized See *disorganized*.

unqualified See *disqualified*.

unreadable See *illegible*.

unsanitary, insanitary
These words are interchangeable. Unsanitary is more common.

unsatisfied, dissatisfied
Unsatisfied means failure to meet standards or expectations. Dissatisfied means disappointed or upset.
EX: unsatisfied by your test scores; dissatisfied by your rudeness

unsolvable See *insoluble*.

unsophisticated, artless
Unsophisticated means naive, without worldly wisdom. Artless means without deceit.
EX: an unsophisticated attempt to solve the problem; an artless child

until See *unless and until; til*.

up

Avoid adding this word to a verb when it adds nothing.

SAY: finish the work; open the library

RATHER THAN: finish <u>up</u> the work; open <u>up</u> the library

upon See *on.*

upward, upwards

The preferred spelling is upward.

EX: move <u>upward</u>

urban, urbane

Urban means pertaining to the city. Urbane means elegant or sophisticated.

EX: <u>urban</u> renewal; an <u>urbane</u> manner

usable, useable

While these words are interchangeable, usable is preferred.

use See *employ; utilize.*

use, usage

Use means in operation or service. Usage means customary practice.

EX: the <u>use</u> of the computer; a common <u>usage</u> among Christians

useable See *usable.*

use to, used to

Say "use to" when "did" goes with the verb.

EX: she <u>did</u> not <u>use to</u> work overtime

Say "used to" with the past tense.

EX: we <u>used to</u> lock the door

usual See *customary.*

utilize, use

Use is preferable to the more pompous utilize.

SAY: <u>use</u> the library

RATHER THAN: <u>utilize</u> the library

vacant See *empty.*

valuable, valued

Valuable means worth money or of considerable importance. Valued means highly esteemed, whether or not a monetary value is attached.

EX: a <u>valuable</u> ring; a <u>valued</u> experience

venal, venial

Venal means corruptible. Venial means minor.

EX: a <u>venal</u> mayor; a <u>venial</u> offense

verbal See *oral.*

very (see also *certainly*)

This word is frequently overused. Either omit it or find a substitute.

SAY: the assignment is difficult; the assignment is unusually difficult

RATHER THAN: the assignment is <u>very</u> difficult

very, very much

Very should not modify a verb. What about modifying a past participle? If the past participle is generally accepted as an adjective, you can use "very" alone. If not, you should say "very much," "greatly," or just "much."

EX: he is <u>very</u> <u>interested</u> in the project; he was <u>very</u> <u>much</u> <u>disliked</u> by the public

very likely See *likely.*

via

Via is used in a geographic sense to mean "by way of." In formal writing do not use it to mean "by means of" or "through."

SAY: success came through hard work and competence

RATHER THAN: success came <u>via</u> hard work and competence

viable

This word means able to survive, and also practical. Avoid using the word unless it is very clear to the reader why you are saying something is survivable or practical.

SAY: the proposal is <u>viable</u> because it provides for adequate funding and competent staff

RATHER THAN: the proposal is <u>viable</u>

viewpoint See *point of view.*

virtually See *practically.*

virus

A virus is not a disease. It is an agent that causes a disease.

SAY: sick with the measles caused by a <u>virus</u>

RATHER THAN: sick with a <u>virus</u>

visit, visit with

Say "visit" rather than "visit with" in formal writing.

SAY: <u>visit</u> her neighbor

RATHER THAN: <u>visit</u> <u>with</u> her neighbor

vocation See *avocation*.

voiced

This word is often part of wordy phrases that should be avoided.

SAY: he <u>objected</u> <u>to</u> the resolution; she is <u>dissatisfied</u> <u>with</u> the plan

RATHER THAN: he <u>voiced</u> <u>objections</u> <u>to</u> the resolution; she <u>voiced</u> <u>dissatisfaction</u> <u>with</u> the plan

voluntary See *intentional*.

wait, await

These words are interchangeable. "Wait" is preferred.

wait for, wait on

Use "wait on" only in reference to providing service. Otherwise, say "wait for."

waive, wave

Waive means to give up. Wave means to move, usually with your hand.

EX: <u>waive</u> her rights; <u>wave</u> good-by

want for

Avoid the phrase "want for" to express a desire.

SAY: the president <u>wants</u> you to resign

RATHER THAN: the president <u>wants</u> <u>for</u> you to resign

was, were

To express conditions contrary to fact, use "were."

EX: if I <u>were</u> a judge; if she <u>were</u> elected

"Was" can be used when referring to the simple past that is not necessarily contrary to fact.

EX: if she <u>was</u> a member of the bar at the time, she was not in active practice

was graduated from See *graduated from*.

wave See *waive*.

weekly See *biweekly*.

well See *good*.

well-

Note the hyphen in the spelling of the following words when they precede the noun they modify:

well-being	well-known
well-defined	well-meaning
well-done	well-rounded
well-founded	well-thought-of

were See *was*.

West, East, South, North

Capitalize these words when referring to a region of the country.

what

Generally, you should try to avoid beginning a sentence with "what."

SAY: the weather bothered him

RATHER THAN: <u>what</u> bothered him was the weather

when See *if*.

when and if; if and when

Avoid these phrases in formal writing. Usually "if" or "when" will be sufficient.

SAY: you may enter <u>when</u> you pay the fee

RATHER THAN: you may enter <u>when</u> <u>and</u> <u>if</u> you pay the fee

whereabouts

This word can take a singular or a plural verb.

EX: his whereabouts <u>are</u> unknown; his whereabouts <u>is</u> unknown

whereas

An overused word in the law. Use a substitute when you can.

SAY: the plaintiff withdrew, while the defendant proceeded

RATHER THAN: the plaintiff withdrew, <u>whereas</u> the defendant proceeded

wherein See *thereafter*.

wherewithal

"Means" is preferable.

SAY: the <u>means</u> to survive

RATHER THAN: the <u>wherewithal</u> to survive

whether See *if*; *question of whether*.

whether or not

"Or not" is often redundant when a choice of alternatives is stated or implied. If you remove "and not" and the sentence still conveys your meaning, keep it out.

SAY: we did not know <u>whether</u> to go

RATHER THAN: we did not know <u>whether</u> <u>or</u> <u>not</u> to go

"Or not" is sometimes needed.

EX: you must leave school <u>whether</u> <u>or</u> <u>not</u> you can afford the tuition

which See *and which; that, which, who.*

while

While means "during the time that."

EX: he read <u>while</u> he waited

Do not use while to mean but, and, although, or whereas.

SAY: Mary is the attorney in charge <u>and</u> Paul is her assistant

RATHER THAN: Mary is the attorney in charge <u>while</u> Paul is her assistant

white See *black.*

who, whom (see also *and who; that, which, who*)

While there are general rules on when to use who and whom, the rules are often broken because the word "whom" has come into general disfavor.

Use "who" when it stands for the subject.

EX: the lawyer <u>who</u> argued the case (who is the subject of argued)

EX: the lawyer <u>who</u> I think argued the case (who is still the subject of argued)

EX: <u>who</u> do you think will win (who is the subject of will win)

Use "whom" when it stands for the object of a verb or preposition.

EX: the judge <u>whom</u> the lawyers hated has resigned (whom is the object of the verb hated)

EX: to <u>whom</u> will the honor go (whom is the object of the preposition to)

Widespread usage has produced some exceptions. The following examples are considered correct in spite of the above rules.

EX: <u>who</u> did you talk to? <u>who</u> did you see?

Except when used directly in front of a preposition (e.g., "to whom," "for whom"), whom is generally disfavored.

whoever, whomever

The guidelines above on "who" and "whom" also apply to "whoever" and "whomever."

whom See *who.*

who's, whose

"Who's" is the contraction for "who is." Avoid contractions in formal writing.

EX: <u>Who</u> <u>is</u> the officer in charge?

RATHER THAN: Who's the officer in charge?

Never use who's as the possessive. The possessive for who and which is whose.

SAY: <u>Whose</u> book is this?

RATHER THAN: <u>Who's</u> book is this?

Whose can refer to people or to things.

EX: the man <u>whose</u> car I borrowed; the flower <u>whose</u> fragrance I love

why See *how come; reason why.*

will See *shall.*

within, in

"In" is often a good substitute for "within."

SAY: he will stay <u>in</u> the building

RATHER THAN: he will stay <u>within</u> the building

without

Avoid this word when you mean "not within" the confines or boundaries of a particular principle.

SAY: the rule does not apply to your conduct

RATHER THAN: your conduct is <u>without</u> the reach of the rule

with regard to See *as per; in regard to.*

with respect to

Avoid using this wordy phrase.

SAY: we deny all of your allegations of negligence

RATHER THAN: <u>with</u> <u>respect</u> <u>to</u> your claim of negligence, we deny all of your allegations

with the purpose of

This phrase is often redundant unless you want to give emphasis to the state of mind.

SAY: he entered the library to study

RATHER THAN: he entered the library <u>with</u> <u>the</u> <u>purpose</u> <u>of</u> studying

witness

Do not use this word as a verb unless you are talking about evidence in a legal case.

SAY: we saw a play at the theater

RATHER THAN: we <u>witnessed</u> a play at the theater

woman See *female.*

won't, wont

"Won't" is a contraction that means "will not."

Avoid contractions in formal writing. "Wont" means used to or accustomed.

EX: he is <u>wont</u> to complain

worse, worst, bad

The comparative of bad is worse. The superlative of bad is worst.

worse, worst, ill

The comparative of ill is worse. The superlative of ill is worst.

would See *should.*

would of See *could have.*

would seem, would appear

Avoid such vague expressions.

SAY: I think the building is vacant

RATHER THAN: it <u>would</u> <u>appear</u> that the building is vacant

writer, the writer

Do not refer to yourself as "the writer" in your writing. Use a personal pronoun ("I") or find some other way to draw attention to yourself.

wrong, wrongly

Wrong is an adjective and an adverb.

EX: the <u>wrong</u> spelling; you spelled it <u>wrong</u>

Wrongly is also an adverb. Place it in front of the word it modifies.

EX: <u>wrongly</u> identified

xerox

Say "Xerox" when you are referring to a copy made by a Xerox machine. If not, say photocopy.

x-ray, X-ray, x ray, X ray

The preferred spelling is x-ray.

yourself, yourselves See *himself.*

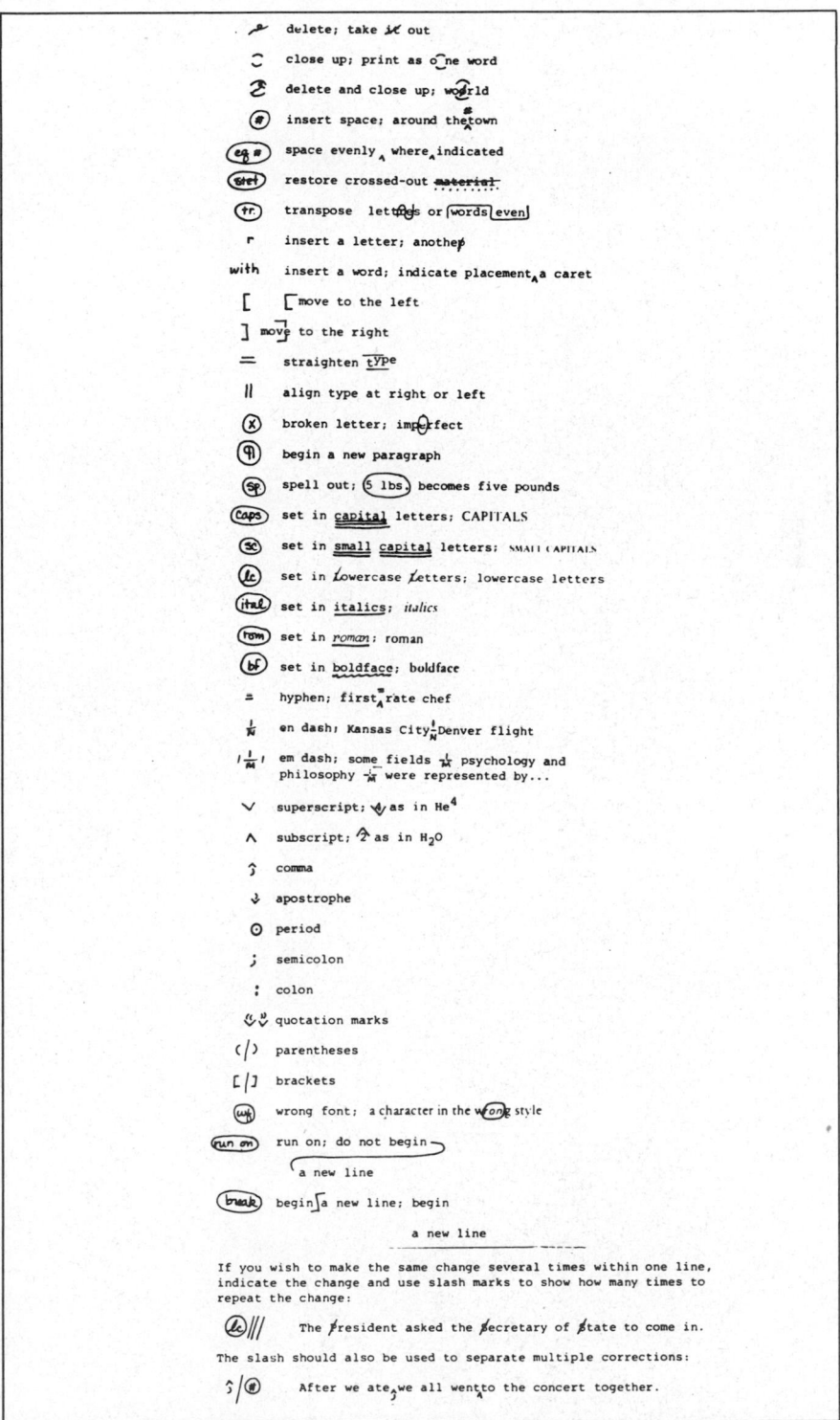

delete; take it out

close up; print as one word

delete and close up; world

insert space; around the town

space evenly where indicated

restore crossed-out material

transpose letters or words even

insert a letter; another

insert a word; indicate placement a caret

move to the left

move to the right

straighten type

align type at right or left

broken letter; imperfect

begin a new paragraph

spell out; 5 lbs. becomes five pounds

set in capital letters; CAPITALS

set in small capital letters; SMALL CAPITALS

set in lowercase letters; lowercase letters

set in italics; *italics*

set in roman; roman

set in boldface; **boldface**

hyphen; first rate chef

en dash; Kansas City Denver flight

em dash; some fields psychology and philosophy were represented by...

superscript; as in He^4

subscript; as in H_2O

comma

apostrophe

period

semicolon

colon

quotation marks

parentheses

brackets

wrong font; a character in the wrong style

run on; do not begin a new line

begin a new line; begin

a new line

If you wish to make the same change several times within one line, indicate the change and use slash marks to show how many times to repeat the change:

The President asked the Secretary of State to come in.

The slash should also be used to separate multiple corrections:

After we ate we all went to the concert together.

Proofreader's marks

RESEARCH BY SUBJECT

In this section you will find bibliographic leads to the law governing the following topics, countries, and states:

Abortion
Accounting
Administrative Law
Advertising
Afghanistan
Africa
Age
Agency
Agriculture
AIDS
Air & Aviation
Alabama
Alaska
Albania
Alcohol
Algeria
American Samoa
Andorra
Angola
Anguilla
Animals
Antarctica
Antigua & Barbuda
Antitrust Law & Trade
    Regulation
Architecture, Construction
    & Engineering
Argentina
Arizona
Arkansas
Art & Entertainment Law
Asia
Australia

Austria
Bahamas
Bahrain
Bangladesh
Banking Law
Bankruptcy
Barbados
Belgium
Belize
Benin
Bermuda
Bolivia
Bophuthatswana
Botswana
Brazil
British Virgin Islands
Brunei
Bulgaria
Burkina Faso
Burma
Burundi
Business Law
California
Cambodia
Cameroon
Canada
Canon Law
Caribbean
Cayman Islands
Central African Republic
Chad
Channel Islands
Chile

China
Church & State
Circuit Courts
Civil Law
Civil Rights
Civil Service
Colombia
Colorado
Commodities
Communism, Socialism &
    Eastern Europe
Community Property
Computers & the Law
Conflict of Law
Congo
Connecticut
Constitutional Law
Consumer Law
Contracts
Cook Islands
Corporate Law
Corrections, Probation &
    Parole
Costa Rica
Criminal Law &
    Procedure
Cuba
Customs
Cyprus
Czechoslovakia
Death
Delaware
Denmark

Dentistry
District of Columbia
Dominica
Dominican Republic
Economics & the Law
Ecuador
Education Law
Egypt
Election & Lobbying Law
El Salvador
Employee Benefits &
    Pension Law
Employment
    Discrimination &
    Wrongful Discharge
Energy
England
Environmental Law
Equatorial Guinea
Equity
Estate Planning &
    Probate
Ethiopia
Europe
European Economic
    Community
Falkland Islands
Family Law
Fiji
Finland
Florida
Food, Drugs &
    Cosmetics

Forensic Science
France
Franchise Law
Freedom of Information
Gabon
Gambia
Georgia
Germany (East)
Germany (West)
Ghana
Gibraltar
Government Contracts
Greece
Grenada
Guam
Guatemala
Guinea
Guinea-Bissau
Guyana
Haiti
Handicapped & the Law
Hawaii
Health & Medicine
Historic Preservation
Homosexuality
Honduras
Hong Kong
Human Experimentation,
     Genetics & Bioethics
Human Rights
Hungary
Iceland
Idaho
Illinois
Immigration Law
India
Indiana
Indians
Indonesia
Insurance
Intellectual Property
International Law
Iowa
Iran
Iraq
Ireland (Irish Republic)
Ireland, Northern
Islam
Isle of Man
Israel & Jewish Law
Italy
Ivory Coast
Jamaica

Japan
Jordan
Judicial Administration
Jurisprudence
Juvenile Law
Kansas
Kentucky
Kenya
Kiribati
Korea (North)
Korea (South)
Kuwait
Labor Law & Arbitration
Landlord-Tenant
Laos
Latin America
Law Office Management
Lebanon
Legal Education & Bar
     Admission
Legal History
Legal Research & Writing
Legislative History
Lesotho
Liberia
Libya
Liechtenstein
Louisiana
Luxembourg
Macao
Madagascar
Maine
Malawi
Malaysia
Maldives
Mali
Malta
Maritime Law
Maryland
Massachusetts
Mauritania
Mauritius
Media Law
Mediation
Mental Health
Mexico
Michigan
Micronesia
Middle East
Military Law
Minnesota
Mississippi
Missouri

Mongolia
Montana
Montserrat
Morocco
Mozambique
Namibia
Natural Resources, Mines
     & Mining
Nebraska
Nepal
Netherlands
Netherlands Antilles
Nevada
New Hampshire
New Jersey
New Mexico
New York
New Zealand
Nicaragua
Niger
Nigeria
Nonprofit Corporations
     & Associations
North Carolina
North Dakota
Norway
Notary Public
Nursing & the Law
Occupational Safety &
     Health
Ohio
Oil & Gas
Oklahoma
Oman
Ombudsman
Oregon
Pakistan
Palestine
Panama
Papua New Guinea
Paraguay
Paralegal
Partnership Law
Pennsylvania
Personal Property
Peru
Philippines
Poland
Portugal
Poverty Law
Professional
     Responsibility
Public Utilities

Puerto Rico
Qatar
Quebec
Real Estte
Rhode Island
Romania
Rwanda
Saudi Arabia
Scandinavian Law
Scotland
Sea, Law of the
Securities Law
Senegal
Seychelles
Singapore
Social Security
Solomon Islands
Somalia
South Africa
South Carolina
South Dakota
Soviet Union
Space
Spain
Sports Law
Sri Lanka
State & Local Government
Statistics
Statutes
St. Lucia
St. Vincent and the
     Grenadines
Sudan
Swaziland
Sweden
Switzerland
Syria
Tahiti
Taiwan
Tanzania
Taxation
Tennessee
Terrorism
Texas
Thailand
Togo
Tonga
Torts
Transportation
Trial & Appellate
     Practice
Trinidad & Tobago
Tunisia

Turkey	Uruguay	War	Yemen Arab Republic
Turks & Caicos Islands	Utah	Washington State	Yemen (People's
Uganda	Vanuatu	Water Law	Democratic
Unemployment	Venezuela	Western Samoa	Republic)
Compensation	Vermont	West Virginia	Yugoslavia
Uniform Commercial	Vietnam	Wisconsin	Zaire
Code	Virginia	Women & the Law	Zambia
United Arab Emirates	Virgin Islands (U.S.)	Workers' Compensation	Zimbabwe
United Nations	Wales	Wyoming	Zoning & Land Planning

ABA (AMERICAN BAR ASSOCIATION): See Computers, Professional Responsibility
ABANDONED PROPERTY: See Personal Property
ABANDONMENT: See Family Law, Juvenile Law, Maritime Law
ABDOMINAL INJURY: See Health & Medicine, Torts
ABDUCTION: See Criminal Law, Family Law
ABNORMALITY: See Health & Medicine, Mental Health

ABORTION

SEE ALSO: Constitutional Law, Criminal Law, Death, Family Law, Health & Medicine, Juvenile Law, Women & the Law

LOOSELEAFS: *Abortion Law Reporter* (Natl. Abortion Rights League & Antioch School of Law, 1976–).
Reporter on Human Reproduction and the Law (Boston: Legal-Med. Studies, 1971–).

TREATISES: *Abortion: A Case Study in Law and Morals* by F. Frochock (Greenwood Press, 1983).
Abortion and Infanticide by M. Tooley (Oxford: Clarendon Press, 1983).
Abortion and the Roman Catholic Perspective by J. Connery (Chicago: Loyola Univ. Press, 1977).
Abortion and the Status of the Fetus (Boston: Kluwer, 1983).
The Abortion Dispute and the American System (Wash. D.C.: Brookings Inst., 1983).
Abortion Laws: A Survey of Current World Legislation (World Health Org., 1971).
Abortion Laws in Commonwealth Countries by R. Cook (World Health Org., 1979).
Abortion, Medicine and the Law, 3d ed., J. Butler, ed. (Facts on File, Inc., 1986).
Abortion, Politics, and the Courts by E. Rubin (Greenwood Press, 1982).
Defining Human Life (Ann Arbor: AUPHA Press, 1983).
From Crime to Choice by N. Davis (Greenwood Press, 1985).
Induced Abortion: A World Review by C. Tietze (NY: Population Council, 1983).
The Law Giveth: Legal Aspects of Abortion Controversy by B. Milbauer (Atheneum, 1983).
The Law Governing Abortion, Contraception and Sterilization by I. Sloan (Oceana, 1988).
A Lawyer Looks at Abortion by L. Wardle (Brigham Young Univ. Press, 1982).
Legal Docket, L. Soto, ed. (NY: ACLU, Reproductive Freedom Project, 1984).
Restoring the Right to Life (Brigham Young Univ. Press, 1984).
The Sexual Rights of Adolescents by H. Rodman (Columbia Univ. Press, 1984).

MISCELLANEOUS: *Constitutional Amendments Relating to Abortion,* Hearings Before the Subcommittee on the Constitution, Senate Committee on the Judiciary, 97th Congress, 1st Session (GPO, 1981).

The Human Life Bill—S. 158, Senate, Committee on the Judiciary, Subcommittee on Separation of Powers (GPO, 1982).

Legal Ramifications of the Human Rights Amendment, Senate, Committee on the Judiciary, Subcommittee on the Constitution (GPO, 1983).

ENCYCLOPEDIAS:

AMERICAN JURISPRUDENCE 2D (Am Jur 2d)
Check the following topics in the *General Index* volumes for Am Jur 2d:

Abortion	Constitutional Law
Civil Rights	Miscarriage

CORPUS JURIS SECUNDUM (CJS)
Check the following topics in the *General Index* volumes for CJS:

Abortion	Constitutional Law
Birth	Miscarriage
Civil Rights	Pregnancy

DIGESTS:

CASE SEARCH IN WEST DIGESTS BY KEY TOPIC
In the *Descriptive Word Index* of the West digests (e.g., the Ninth Decennial or the Federal Practice Digest 3d), look for key topics and numbers under the subject headings listed below:

Abortion and Birth Control	Hospitals
	Infants
Civil Rights	Parent and Child
Constitutional Law	Social Security and
Criminal Law	Public Welfare

ALR:

ANNOTATIONS
Check the index volumes for ALR, ALR2d, ALR3d, ALR4th, and ALR Fed for annotations under the following subject headings:

Abortion	Pregnancy
Birth	Privacy

PERIODICALS:

CURRENT LAW INDEX (CLI) & LEGAL RESOURCE INDEX (LRI)
In the CLI and LRI, look for references to periodical literature under the following subject headings:

Abortion	Fertilization in Vitro
Abortion Counseling	Pregnancy
Birth Control	Unborn Children
Conception	

INDEX TO LEGAL PERIODICALS (ILP)
In the ILP, look for references to legal periodical literature under the following subject headings:

Abortion	Constitutional Law
Birth Control	Right of Privacy
Civil Rights	Sterilization

ABSENTEE BALLOT: See Election
ABSENTEEISM: See Labor Law
ABSOLUTE LIABILITY: See Torts
ABSTRACT OF TITLE: See Estate Planning, Real Estate

ABU DHABI: See United Arab Emirates
ABUSE: See Juvenile Law, Family Law
ABUSED WIVES: See Family Law, Women & the Law
ABUSE OF PROCESS: See Torts
ACADEMIC FREEDOM: See Education Law
ACCELERATION CLAUSE: See Contracts
ACCEPTANCE: See Contracts
ACCESSORY: See Criminal Law
ACCIDENT: See Insurance, Torts
ACCOMPLICE: See Criminal Law
ACCORD & SATISFACTION: See Contracts, Trial & Appellate Practice
ACCOUNT: See Accounting, Consumer Law, Estate Planning

ACCOUNTING

SEE ALSO: Bankruptcy, Business Law, Corporate Law, Employee Benefits, Estate Planning, Law Office Management, Securities Law, Taxation

JOURNALS, NEWSLETTERS & OTHER PERIODICALS:
Accounting & Auditing Update Service by A. Afterman (Warren, Gorham & Lamont).
Accounting Articles (CCH, 1965–).
Accounting for Law Firms (Leader Pubs.).
Attorney-CPA (Amer. Assn. of Attorney-CPA, 1963–).
Business Accounting for Lawyers Newsletter (Practicing Law Institute, 1984–).
Corporate Accounting (Warren, Gorham & Lamont).
Journal of Accountancy (American Institute of Certified Public Accountants).
Practical Accountant (Inst. for Cont. Prof. Development).
Real Estate Accounting and Taxation (Warren, Gorham & Lamont).
Taxation for Accountants (Warren, Gorham & Lamont, 1966–).
Tax Preparer Liability Service (Research Inst. of America, 1978–).

LOOSELEAFS:
Accountancy Law Reporter (CCH, 1938–).
Accountants SEC Practice Manual by M. Poloway & D. Charles (CCH, 1976–).
Accounting for Banks by J. Koltveit (Matthew Bender, 1982–).
Accounting for Government Contracts by L. Anderson (Matthew Bender, 1981–).
Accounting for Public Utilities by R. Hahne et al. (Matthew Bender, 1983–).
AICPA Audit and Accounting Manual (CCH, 1979–).
Applying GAPP and GASS by P. Munter & T. Ratcliffe (Matthew Bender, 1984–).
Attorney's Handbook of Accounting, 3d ed., H. Sellin, ed. (Matthew Bender, 1979–).
Cost Accounting Standards Guide (CCH, 1972–).
Federal Audit Guides (CCH, 1977–).
Financial Accounting Standards Practice Update, L. Collins, ed. (Shepard's, 1982–).
Income Taxation: Accounting Methods and Periods by G. Bauernfeind (Shepard's, 1983).
Managing Your Accounting and Consulting Practice by M. Altman & R. Weil (Matthew Bender, 1978–).
Modern Accounting and Auditing Checklists, M. Loscalzo & P. Wendell, eds. (Warren, Gorham & Lamont, 1983–).
Modern Accounting & Auditing Forms by P. Wendell (Warren, Gorham & Lamont, 1978–).
Tax Accounting by D. Alkire (Matthew Bender, 1982–).
Tax Fraud, Audits, Investigations, Prosecutions by R. Fink et al. (Matthew Bender, 1980–).

TREATISES:

Accountants' Cost Handbook: A Guide for Management Accounting, 3d ed. by J. Bulloch et al. (Wiley, 1983).

An Accountant's Guide to Malpractice Liability by D. Stern (Michie, 1979).

Accounting and Auditing Disclosure Manual, 1985 by A. Afterman (Warren, Gorham & Lamont, 1984).

Accounting and Law in a Nutshell by Faris (West, 1984).

Accounting for Lawyers, 4th ed. by E. Faris (Michie, 1982).

Accounting Standards, Financial Accounting Standards Board (McGraw-Hill).

Bankruptcy and Insolvency Accounting, 2d ed. by G. Newton (Wiley, 1981).

Codification of Statements on Accounting Standards, American Institute of Certified Public Accountants (CCH).

Duties and Liabilities of Public Accountants, rev. ed. by D. Causey (Dow Jones-Irwin, 1982).

Financial Accounting Standards: Explanation and Analysis, 7th ed. by B. Jarnagin & J. Booker (CCH, 1985).

Handbook of Accounting and Auditing by J. Burton et al. (Warren, Gorham & Lamont, 1981).

Handbook of EDP Auditing (Warren, Gorham & Lamont, 1985).

How to Find Negligence and Misrepresentations in Financial Statements by I. Kellogg (Shepard's, 1983).

The Law of Accountants and Auditors: Rights, Duties and Liabilities by J. Gormley (Warren, Gorham & Lamont, 1981).

Macmillan Dictionary of Accounting by R. Parker (Macmillan, 1984).

Practical Accounting for Lawyers by R. Berger (Wiley, 1981).

Real Estate Accounting and Reporting: A Guide for Developers, Investors, and Lenders, 2d ed. by J. Klink (Wiley, 1985).

Revocation of Professional Licenses by Government Agencies (Accountants by W. Morris (Michie, 1984).

Statement of Auditing Standards (American Institute of Certified Public Accountants, 1972).

ENCYCLOPEDIAS:

AMERICAN JURISPRUDENCE 2D (Am Jur 2d)
Check the following topics in the *General Index* volumes for Am Jur 2d

Accountants	Bookkeepers and
Account Books	Bookkeeping
Accounts and Accounting	Fraud and Deceit
Audits and Auditors	Records and Recording

CORPUS JURIS SECUNDUM (CJS)
Check the following topics in the *General Index* volumes for CJS:

Accountants	Confidential and Fiduciary
Accounts and Accounting	Relationship
Accounts Receivable	County Comptroller
Account Stated	Financial Statements
Audits and Auditors	Fraud
Book Account or Book	Income
Debt	Loss and Losses
Bookkeepers and	Records and Recordation
Bookkeeping	State Auditor
	State Comptroller

DIGESTS:

CASE SEARCH IN WEST DIGESTS BY KEY TOPIC
In the *Descriptive Word Index* of the West digests, look for key topics and numbers under the following subject headings:

Accountants	Accounts

Deposits and Escrows	Licenses
Executors and	Negligence
Administrators	Principal and Agent
Fraud	Taxation
Internal Revenue	

ALR:

ANNOTATIONS

Check the index volumes for ALR, ALR2d, ALR3d, ALR4th, and ALR Fed for annotations under the following subject headings:

Accountants	Books of Account
Accounts and Accounting	Checks and Drafts
Arrears	Fraud and Deceit

PERIODICALS:

CURRENT LAW INDEX (CLI) & LEGAL RESOURCE INDEX (LRI)

In the CLI and LRI, look for references to periodical literature under the following subject headings:

Accountants	Controllership
Accounting	Disclosure in Accounting
Accounts Receivable	Financial Statements
Auditing	Fraud
Auditors	Negligence
Bookkeeping	Tax Consultants
Confidential	
Communications	

INDEX TO LEGAL PERIODICALS (ILP)

In the ILP, look for references to legal periodical literature under the following subject headings:

Accountants and	Fraud
Accounting	Income Tax/Accounting
Auditors and Auditing	

ACCREDITATION: See Health & Medicine
ACCRETION: See Real Estate
ACID RAIN: See Environmental Law
ACQUISITIONS: See Animals, Business Law, Securities Law
ACQUITTAL: See Criminal Law
ACTING & ACTORS: See Art & Entertainment
ACTIONS: See Trial & Appellate Practice
ACT OF STATE: See International Law
ACTUARIES: See Insurance
ACUPUNCTURE: See Health & Medicine
ADEMPTION: See Estate Planning
ADJOINING LANDOWNER: See Real Estate
ADJOURNMENT: See Trial & Appellate Practice
ADJUSTERS: See Insurance
ADMINISTRATION: See Administrative Law, Law Office Management
ADMINISTRATION OF ESTATE: See Estate Planning
ADMINISTRATION OF JUSTICE: See Judicial Administration

ADMINISTRATIVE LAW

SEE ALSO:

Agriculture, Antitrust Law, Civil Service, Constitutional Law, Education Law, Election, Environmental Law, Fredom of Information, Immigration Law, Labor Law, Legal

Research, Occupational Safety, Public Utilities, Securities Law, Social Security, State & Local Government, Taxation, Transportation, Trial & Appellate Practice, Unemployment Compensation, Workers' Compensation

RESEARCH GUIDES & BIBLIOGRAPHIES:

Government Publications and Their Use, 2d rev. ed. by L. Schmeckebier & R. Eastin, (1969).

"Locating Presidential Proclamations and Executive Orders—A Guide to Sources" by D. Bennett & P. Yannarella, 5 *Legal Reference Services Quarterly 177 (1985).*

Locating United States Information: A Workbook Guide by E. Herman (Hein, 1983).

Research Essentials of Administrative Law by H. Jacobini et al. (Palisades Publishers, 1983).

REGULATIONS & EXECUTIVE ORDERS:

Code of Federal Regulations (Wash. D.C.: GPO).

A Compilation of the Messages and Papers of the President.

Federal Register (Wash. D.C.: GPO).

United States Code Congressional and Administrative News (West).

Weekly Compilation of Presidential Documents (Wash. D.C.: GPO, 1965–).

INDEXES:

CIS Federal Register Index (Congressional Information Service, 1984–).

Index to the Code of Federal Regulations (Congressional Information Service).

JOURNALS, NEWSLETTERS & OTHER PERIODICALS:

Administrative Law News (ABA Sect. of Admin. Law, 1971–).

Administrative Law Review (ABA Sect. of Admin. Law, 1949–).

Federal Regulatory Week (Prentice-Hall).

Yale Journal on Regulation (1983–).

LOOSELEAFS:

Administrative Law by B. Mezines (Matthew Bender, 1977–).

Administrative Law Service, 2d Series by J. Willis et al. (Pike and Fischer, Inc., 1950–).

BNA Administrative Practice Manual (BNA).

Federal Regulatory Process: Agency Practices and Procedures by G. Edles & J. Nelson (Law & Business, Inc., 1981).

TREATISES:

Administrative Law, 2d ed. by B. Schwartz (Little, Brown, 1984).

Administrative Law and Practice by C. Koch (West, 1985).

Administrative Law and Process by Pierce, Shapiro & Verkuil (Foundation Press, 1985).

Administrative Law and Process in a Nutshell, 2d ed. by E. Gellhorn & B. Boyer (West, 1981).

Administrative Law: Practice and Procedure by L. Mojeska (Lawyers Co-op., 1982).

Administrative Law Text, 3d ed. by K. Davis (West, 1972).

Administrative Law Treatise, 2d ed. by K. Davis (San Diego: Davis Pub. Co., 1984).

The Administrative Regulatory Process by F. Heffron (NY: Longman, 1983).

Administrative Rulemaking: Structuring, Opposing, and Defending Federal Agency Regulations by J. O'Reilly (Shepard's, 1983).

Bureaucratic Justice by J. Mashaw (1983).

Dismantling America: The Rush to Deregulate by S. & M. Tolchin (Oxford Univ. Press, 1985).

Federal Administrative Procedure Sourcebook by R. Berg (Admin. Conference of the U.S., 1985).

Federal Regulatory Process: Agency Practices and Procedures by G. Edles & J.
Nelson (Law & Business, Inc., 1981).
The Legislative Veto: Congressional Control of Regulation by B. Craig (Westview, 1983).
Manual for Administrative Law Judges (Admin. Conference of the U.S., 1981).
Administrative Rule Making by A. Bonfield (Little, Brown, 1986).
West's Federal Practice Manual, 2d ed. (West, 1970).

MISCELLANEOUS: *Code of Federal Regulations Citations* (Shepard's).
United States Administrative Law Citations (Shepard's).
United States Government Manual (Wash. D.C.: GPO).

ENCYCLOPEDIAS: AMERICAN JURISPRUDENCE 2D (AM Jur 2d)
Check the following topics in the *General Index* volumes for Am Jur 2d:

Administrative Law	Hearings
Civil Service	Licenses and Permits
Compliance	Mandamus
Constitutional Law	Municipal Corporations
Delegation of Powers	Quasi-Judicial Acts or
Exhaustion of Remedies	Officers
Federal Practice and	Statutes
Procedure	United States

CORPUS JURIS SECUNDUM (CJS)
Check the following topics in the *General Index* volumes for CJS:

Abuse of Discretion	Findings
Administrative Bodies	Government Agencies
Boards and Commissions	Hearings
Civil Service	Mandamus
Constitutional Law	Ministerial Acts
Delegation of Powers	Municipal Corporations
Discretion	Quasi Judicial Powers
Examination and	United States Board and
Examiners	Commissions

DIGESTS: CASE SEARCH IN WEST DIGESTS BY KEY TOPIC
In the *Descriptive Word Index* of the West digests, look for key topics and numbers
under the following subject headings:

Administrative Law	Mandamus
Constitutional Law	Municipal Corporations
Counties	Officers and Public
Federal Courts	Employees
Inspection	States
Licenses	United States

ALR: ANNOTATIONS
Check the index volumes for ALR, ALR2d, ALR3d, ALR4th, and ALR Fed for annotations
under the following subject headings:

Administrative Law	Exhaustion of Remedies
Arbitrary Acts	Freedom of Information
Boards and Commissions	Investigation
Delegation of Power	Licenses and Permits
Due Process of Law	

PERIODICALS

CURRENT LAW INDEX (CLI) & LEGAL RESOURCE INDEX (LIR)

In the CLI and LRI, look for references to periodical literature under the following subject headings:

Abuse of Administrative Power	Exhaustion of State Remedies
Administrative Agencies	Independent Regulatory Commission
Administrative Law	
Administrative Procedure	Judicial Review of Administrative Acts
Constitutional Law	
Delegation of Powers	Public Administration
Deregulation	Representation in Administrative Proceedings
Examiners	
Executive Orders	

INDEX TO LEGAL PERIODICALS (ILP)

In the ILP, look for references to legal periodical literature under the following subject headings:

Administrative Agencies	Delegation of Power
Administrative Evidence	Executive Power
Administrative Law	Judicial Review
Administrative Procedure	Public Administration
Constitutional Law	

ADMIRALTY: See Maritime Law

ADMISSIBLE: See Trial & Appellate Practice

ADMISSION (EVIDENCE): See Trial & Appellate Practice

ADMISSION TO THE BAR: See Legal Education, Professional Responsibility

ADOPTION: See Family Law, Juvenile Law

ADULTERY: See Family Law

AD VALOREM TAX: See Taxation

ADVANCEMENT: See Estate Planning

ADVERSARY SYSTEM: See Jurisprudence, Professional Responsibility, Trial & Appellate Practice

ADVERSE PARTIES: See Trial & Appellate Practice

ADVERSE POSSESSION: See Real Estate

ADVERTISING

SEE ALSO:

Business Law, Consumer Law, Media Law, Professional Responsibility

JOURNALS, NEWSLETTERS, & OTHER PERIODICALS:

Advertising Law and Practice (Frank Cass, 1984–).

Advertising Law Anthology (Bethesda, MD: Intl. Library, 1973–).

TREATISES & LOOSELEAFS:

Advertising Compliance Handbook by K. Plevan & M. Siroky (Practicing Law Institute, 1988).

Advertising Compliance Law by J. Lichtenberger (Quorum Books, 1986).

Advertising Compliance Service (Westport, CT: Meckler, 1981–).

Advertising Law and Practice by M. Schudson (Basic Books, 1984).

Corporate and Commercial Free Speech by E. Rome (Quorum Books, 1985).

Law and Business Aspects of the Advertising Industry (Practicing Law Institute, 1986).
The Law of Advertising by G. & P. Rosden (Matthew Bender, 1973–).
Legal and Business Aspects of the Advertising Industry (Practicing Law Institute, 1984).
Legal Problems in Advertising by F. Kent & D. Wood (Matthew Bender, 1984–).
Mass Media, Freedom of Speech, and Advertising by D. Rohrer (IA: Kendall/Hunt Pub. Co., 1979).
A Primer on the Law of Deceptive Practices by E. Kintner (Macmillan, 1978).
Selling and the Law: Advertising and Promotion by C. Smith (Callagham, 1987).

ENCYCLOPEDIAS: AMERICAN JURISPRUDENCE 2D (Am Jur 2d)
Check the following topics in the *General Index* volumes for Am Jur 2d:

Advertising	Markets and Marketing
Fraud and Deceit	

CORPUS JURIS SECUNDUM (CJS)
Check the following topics in the *General Index* volumes for CJS:

Advertisements	Marks, Brands and Labels
Fraud	Outdoor Advertising
Markets and Market Places	

DIGESTS: CASE SEARCH IN WEST DIGESTS BY KEY TOPIC
In the *Descriptive Word Index* of the West digests, look for key topics and numbers under the following subject headings:

Advertisements	Fraud
Advertising	Newspapers
Advertising Agencies	Trade Regulation

ALR: ANNOTATIONS
Check the index volumes for ALR, ALR2d, ALR3d, ALR4th, and ALR Fed for annotations under the following subject headings:

Advertising	Fraud and Deceit
Billboard	Magazines
Federal Trade Commission	Newspapers
	Outdoor Advertising

PERIODICALS: CURRENT LAW INDEX (CLI) & LEGAL RESOURCE INDEX (LRI)
In the CLI and LRI, look for references to periodical literature under the following subject headings:

Advertising	Public Relations
Marketing	

INDEX TO LEGAL PERIODICALS (ILP)
In the ILP, look for references to legal periodical literature under the following subject headings:

Advertising	Freedom of Speech
Agency	Zoning
Fraud	

ADVICE: See Professional Responsibility
ADVISORS: See Securities Law
ADVOCACY: See Administrative Law, Legal Research, Trial & Appellate Practice
AERONAUTICS: See Air & Aviation, Space

AFDC: See Poverty Law, Social Security
AFFIDAVITS: See Trial & Appellate Practice
AFFIRMATIVE ACTION: See Civil Rights, Employment Discrimination, Government
      Contracts, Women & the Law
AFFIRMATIVE DEFENSE: See Trial & Appellate Practice

AFGHANISTAN

SEE ALSO: Asia, Communism, Human Rights, International Law, Islam, Soviet Union, United
Nations

TREATISES: *A Dictionary of the Terminology of Pashtun's Tribal Customary Law and Usages* by I.
      Atayee, A. Shinwary, transl. (Kabul: Intl. Center for Pashte Studies, 1979).
Afghanistan: A Country Law Study by Gholam H. Vafai (Library of Congress, 1988).
Investment Laws of the World: The Developing Nations (Afghanistan) (Oceana, 1973–).
Law in Afghanistan by M. Kamali (Leiden: E.J. Brill, 1985).
Red Flag over Afghanistan by T. Hammond (Westview, 1984).
The Soviet Invasion of Afghanistan by J. Collins (Lexington Books, 1986).
Taxes and Investment in Asia and the Pacific (Afghanistan) (Amsterdam: Intl. Bureau
      of Fiscal Documentation, 1983–).
Tax Laws of the World–Afghanistan (FL: Foreign Tax Law Assn.).
Tears, Blood and Cries: Human Rights in Afghanistan Since the Invasion (NY:
      Helsinki Watch Committee, 1986).

ARTICLES: "Internationalized Non-International Armed Conflicts: Case Studies of Afghanistan,
      Kampuchea, and Lebanon" by H. Gasser, 33 *American University Law Review* 145
      (1983).
"Legal Education in Afghanistan Prior to Soviet Occupation" by R. Williams, 6 *Suffolk
      Transnational Law Journal* 247 (1982).
"Legal Elites in Afghan Society" by Weinbaum, 12 *International Journal of Middle
      East Studies* 39 (1980).
"The Modern Legal System of Afghanistan" by A. Sirat, 16 *American Journal of
      Comparative Law* 563 (1968–69).

AFRICA

SEE ALSO: Algeria, Angola, Benin, Botswana, Burkina Faso, Burundi, Cameroon, Central African
Republic, Chad, Congo, Egypt, Ethiopia, Gabon, Gambia, Ghana, Guinea, Guinea-
Bissau, International Law, Islam, Ivory Coast, Kenya, Lesotho, Liberia, Libya,
Madagascar, Malawi, Mauritania, Morocco, Mozambique, Niger, Nigeria, Rwanda,
Senegal, Somalia, South Africa, Sudan, Swaziland, Tanzania, Togo, Tunisia, Uganda,
United Nations, Zaire, Zambia, Zimbabwe

**RESEARCH GUIDES &
BIBLIOGRAPHIES:**   *African International Relations: An Annotated Bibliography* by M. DeLancey (West-
      view, 1981).
African Law Bibliography/Bibliograhie de Droit Africain (Brussels: Univ. of Brussels
      Press, 1972–).
"A Bibliographic Essay of Selected Secondary Sources on the Common Law and
      Customary Law of English-Speaking Sub-Saharan Africa" by C. Mwalimi, 80 *Law
      Library Journal* 241 (1988).

Colonial Law: A Bibliography with Special Reference to Native African System of Law and Land Tenure by C. Meek (Greenwood Press, 1978).

"Selected Bibliography on Law and Development in East Africa" by A. Blaustein, 6 *East African Law Journal* 229 (1970).

The United States and Sub-Saharan Africa: Guide to U.S. Official Documents and Government-Sponsored Publications, 1976–1980, J. Witherell, comp. (Library of Congress, 1984).

CONSTITUTIONS:

Constitutions of African States by the Secretariat of the Asian African Legal Consultative Committee (Oceana, 1972).

JOURNALS & OTHER PERIODICALS:

African Journal of International Law by the Intl. Society of African Lawyers (Gaunt, 1988–).

African Law Studies (Rothman, 1969–).

African Newspapers in the Library of Congress, 2d ed., J. Pluge, comp. (Lib. of Cong., 1984).

Annual Survey of African Law, N. Robin & E. Cotran, eds. (London: Frank Cass, 1970–).

Boston College Third World Law Journal.

East Africa Law Journal (Univ. of Nairobi, Kenya Institute of Administration, 1965–).

Easterm African Law Review.

Journal of African Law (Univ. of London, School of Oriental & African Studies).

TREATISES:

Africa and Law: Developing Legal Systems in African Commonwealth Nations, T. Hutchison, ed. (Univ. of Wisc. Press, 1968).

Africa and the International Law of the Sea by N. Rembe (Sijthoff, 1980).

Africa and the International Monetary Fund (IMF, 1986).

African Boundaries: A Legal and Diplomatic Encyclopedia by I. Brownlie (London: C. Hurst, 1979).

African Customary and Humanitarian Law by E. Bello (London: Oyez, 1980).

African Customs and Western Law by E. Mittlebeeler (N.Y.: African Publishing Co., 1976)

African Law: Adaptation and Development, H. & L. Kuper, eds. (Berkeley: Univ. of California Press, 1965).

African Law: New Law for New Nations, H. Badde, ed. (Oceana, 1963).

African Law South of the Sahara by C. Adei (Clayton, MO: Intl. Institute for Advanced Studies, 1981).

African Penal Systems, A. Milner, ed. (London: Routledge & Kegan Paul, 1969).

African Tax Systems by R. Hammond & M. van den Abeelen (Amsterdam: Intl. Bureau of Fiscal Documentation, 1980–).

Afrocommunism by D. & M. Ottaway (Holmes & Meier Publishers, 1981).

Basic Documents of African Regional Organizations, L. Sohn, ed. (Oceana, 1971–72).

Civil Service Laws in East Africa, 2d ed. by A. Kaipi (Nairobi: Kenya Literature Bureau, 1984).

Current Legal Aspects of Doing Business in Black Africa (ABA Intl. Law & Practice Section, 1975).

The Expropriation of Multinational Property in the Third World by A. Akinsanya (Praeger, 1980).

Ideas and Procedures in African Customary Law, M. Gluckman, ed. (Oxford Univ. Press, 1969).

International Jurisprudence in African Context by A. Sanders (Butterworths, 1979).

An Introduction to African Criminology by W. Clifford (Oxford Univ. Press, 1974).

An Introduction to Contract Procedures in the Near East & North Africa by C. Loustaunau & J. Cohen (Intl. Trade Admin., 1980).
An Introduction to the Law in French-Speaking Africa by J. Salacuse (Michie, 1969).
Islamic Law in Africa by J. Anderson (London: Totowa, NJ 1978).
Judicial and Legal Systems in Africa by S. Roberts (Butterworths, 1970).
Land in Africa: Its Administration, Law, Tenure, and Use by P. Ofori (Kraus, 1979).
Law and the Family in Africa, S. Roberts, ed. (The Hague: Mouton, 1977).
The Law of International Economic Institutions in Africa by S. Akintan (Sijthoff, 1977).
Lawyers in the Third World (Scandinavian Institute of African Studies, 1981).
Legal Aspects of Doing Business in Black Africa (Practicing Law Institute, 1981).
The Legal System of Africa Series, K. Redden, ed. (Michie).
Restatement of African Law (London: Sweet & Maxwell, 1972).
Rules and Processes: The Cultural Logic of Dispute in an African Context by J. Comaroff & S. Roberts (Univ. of Chicago Press, 1981).
Slaves and Slavery in Muslim Africa, J. Willis, ed. (Totowa, NJ: F. Cass, 1985).
Studies in African Native Law by J. Lewin (Univ. of Pa. Press, 1947).
Tax Systems of Africa, Asia, and the Middle East by C. Platt (Gower, 1982).
The West African Monetary Union: An Analytical Review by R. Bhatia (Intl. Monetary Fund, 1985).

ARTICLES:

"The African Development Bank's Role in Promoting Regional Integration in the Economic Community of West African States" by C. Barnes, 4 *Boston College Third World Law Journal* 151 (1984).
"African Patent Statutes and Technology Transfer" by M. Sklan, 10 *Case Western Reserve Journal of International Law* 55 (1978).
"Notes on Legal Literature in East Africa" by R. Martin, 10 *Case Western Reserve Journal of International Law* 123 (1978).
"The Urban Environment and the Law of Torts in Africa" by J. Cottrell, 6 *Urban Law and Policy* 5 (1983).

MISCELLANEOUS:

The African Law Reports Commercial Law Series (Oceana, 1964–78, 1978, 1984).

AFTER–ACQUIRED PROPERTY: See Estate Planning

AGE

SEE ALSO:

Employee Benefits, Employment Discrimination, Estate Planning, Health & Medicine, Social Security

RESEARCH GUIDES & BIBLIOGRAPHIES:

Elderly Neglect and Abuse: An Annotated Bibliography by T. Johnson (Greenwood Press, 1985).
"Gerontology and the Law: A Selected Bibliography" by J. Hasko, 56 *Southern California Law Review* 289 (1982). See also vol. 57, p. 631.
"Gerontology and the Law: A Selected Bibliography" by J. Mubarak et al., 73 *Law Library Journal* 255 (1980).
Summary of States' Issues on Aging by the General Accounting Office to the Chairman of the Select Committee on Aging, House of Rep. (GPO, 1985).

LEGISLATIVE HISTORY:

Legislative History of the Age Discrimination in Employment Act (Govt. Printing Office, 1981).

TREATISES: *Advocacy for the Aging* by J. Krauskopf (West, 1983).

Age and Sex Discrimination and Employment Benefit Plans by R. Blum (Tax Management Inc., 1984–).

Age Discrimination by H. Elgit (Shepard's 1981–).

Age Discrimination in Employment Act, ADEA (ABA; Natl. Council on the Aging, 1983).

Age Discrimination Problems in the Context of a Reduction in Work Force (Practicing Law Institute, 1983).

Estate and Financial Planning for the Aging or Incapacitated Client (Practicing Law Institute, 1989).

Estate Planning for the Elderly Client by S. Schlesinger (Wiley, 1983).

Federal Age Discrimination in Employment Law by C. Edelman & I. Siegler (Michie, 1978).

Geriatric Psychiatry: Clinical, Ethical, and Legal Issues, B. Stanley, ed. (Amer. Psychiatric Press, 1985).

The Law and Aging Resource Guide (ABA Comm. on Legal Problems of the Elderly, 1981–).

Law and the Elderly by R. Grimes (Longwood Pub. Group).

LCE Elderly Law Manual (Wash. D.C.: Legal Council for the Elderly, 1983–).

Litigating Age Discrimination Cases by A. Ruzicho (Callaghan, 1986–).

Mental Capacity: Medical and Legal Aspects of the Aging by J. Aker et al. (Shepard's, 1977).

Nursing Homes and the Law by S. Johnson (Harrison, 1985).

Older Americans Act: A Staff Summary by the Subcommittee on Human Services of the Select Committee on Aging, House of Rep. (GPO, 1985).

Public Benefit Checklists (Wash. D.C.: Legal Counsel for the Elderly, 1984).

Public Guardianship and the Elderly by W. Schmidt (Ballinger, 1981).

Tax, Estate and Financial Planning for the Elderly by J. Regan (Matthew Bender, 1985–).

ENCYCLOPEDIAS: AMERICAN JURISPRUDENCE 2D (Am Jur 2d)
Check the following topics in the *General Index* volumes for Am Jur 2d:

Civil Rights	Old Age
Discrimination	Pensions and Retirement

CORPUS JURIS SECUNDUM (CJS)
Check the following topics in the *General Index* volumes for CJS:

Aged Persons	Homes for the Aged
Civil Rights	Old Age Assistance
Discrimination	Retirement and Pensions

DIGESTS: CASE SEARCH IN WEST DIGESTS BY KEY TOPIC
In the *Descriptive Word Index* of the West digests, look for key topics and numbers under the following subject headings:

Age	Discrimination
Aged Persons	Health and Environment
Asylums	Retirement and Pensions
Civil Rights	Social Security
Constitutional Law	

ALR: ANNOTATIONS
Check the index volumes for ALR, ALR2d, ALR3d, ALR4th, and ALR Fed for annotations under the following subject headings:

Age	Pensions and Retirement
Aged Persons	Funds
Discrimination	

PERIODICALS:

CURRENT LAW INDEX (CLI) & LEGAL RESOURCE INDEX (LRI)
In the CLI and LRI, look for references to periodical literature under the following subject headings:

Age (Law)	Constitutional Law
Aged	Home Care Services
Age Discrimination	Old Age Pensions

INDEX TO LEGAL PERIODICALS (ILP)
In the ILP, look for references to legal periodical literature under the following subject headings:

Aged	Nursing Homes
Annuities	Old Age Insurance
Civil Rights	Pensions
Constitutional Law	Social Security
Discrimination/Age	

AGENCY

SEE ALSO:

Advertising, Business Law, Contracts, Corporate Law, Employee Benefits, Partnership Law, Real Estate, Securities Law, Torts

RESTATEMENT:

Restatement of the Law, Second, Agency (American Law Institute, 1958).

TREATISES:

Agency, Employment, and Partnership Law by M. Closen (Butterworths, 1984).
Agency-Partnership Law in a Nutshell by R. Steffen (West, 1977).
Handbook of the Law of Agency by W. Seavey (West, 1964).
A Hornbook on the Law of Agency, Partnership . . . by H. Reuschlein (West, 1979).
The Law of Agency by L. Lakin (Kendall/Hunt Pub. Co., 1984).
Law of Agency and Partnership by H. Gill (West, 1979).
Outline of the Law of Agency, 4th ed. by F. Mechem (Callaghan, 1952).

ENCYCLOPEDIAS:

AMERICAN JURISPRUDENCE 2D (Am Jur 2d)
Check the following topics in the *General Index* volumes for Am Jur 2d:

Agency	Independent Contractor
Apparent Authority	Insurance Agent
Authority	Master and Servant
Brokers	Ratification
Dealers	Respondeat Superior
Employment Agencies	Scope of Employment or
Factors	Authority
Implied Power	

CORPUS JURIS SECUNDUM (CJS)
Check the following topics in the *General Index* volumes for CJS:

Agents and Agency	Contract
Apparent Authority	Dealers
Authority	Delegation of Powers
Brokers	Deputies and Assistants
Collections	Employment Agencies
Commodities Brokers	Factors
Confidential and Fiduciary	Implied Powers
Relationship	Independent Contractors
Contractors	Insurance Adjusters

Power of Attorney   Salesman
Principal and Surety   Ticket Agents
Ratification   Undisclosed Principal
Respondeat Superior

DIGESTS:

CASE SEARCH IN WEST DIGESTS BY KEY TOPIC
In the *Descriptive Word Index* of the West digests, look for key topics and numbers under the following subject headings:

Agents	Hawkers and Peddlers
Apparent Agency	Implied Powers
Attorney and Client	Independent Contractors
Brokers	Insurance Agents
Commodities	Master and Servant
Confidential Relationship	Partnership
Contractors	Power of Attorney
Contracts	Principal and Agent
Credit Reporting Agencies	Ratification
Dealer	Respondeat Superior
Delegation of Authority or Power	Salesmen
	Securities Regulation
Deputies and Assistants	Torts
Employment Agencies	Undisclosed Agency
Factors	

ALR:

ANNOTATIONS
Check the index volumes for ALR, ALR2d, ALR3d, ALR4th, and ALR Fed for annotations under the following subject headings:

Adjusters	Fraud
Apparent Authority	Independent Contractors
Brokers	Insurance Agent
Collection Agency	Master and Servant
Corporate Officers	Principal and Agent
Dealers	Sales Representative
Employment Agencies	Stockbroker
Factors	

PERIODICALS:

CURRENT LAW INDEX (CLI) & LEGAL RESOURCE INDEX (LRI)
In the CLI and LRI, look for references to periodical literature under the following subject headings:

Agency (Law)	Master and Servant
Brokers	Power of Attorney
Business Agents	Proxy
Commercial Agents	Respondeat Superior
Consultants	Sports Agents
Independent Contractors	

INDEX TO LEGAL PERIODICALS (ILP)
In the ILP, look for references to legal periodical literature under the following subject headings:

Accomplices	Brokers
Agency	Collection Agencies
Architects and Engineers	Employer and Employee
Auctions and Auctioneers	Factors

Independent Contractors   Real Estate Agents
Powers

AGENCY, EMPLOYMENT: See Agency, Employee Benefits
AGENCY SHOPS: See Labor Law
AGENTS: See Agency, Business Law, Insurance, Real Estate, Sports Law
AGGRAVATED ASSAULT: See Criminal Law, Torts
AGGRESSION: See International Law, Terrorism, United Nations, War
AGRARIAN REFORM: See Algeria, Costa Rica, International Law
AGREEMENTS: See Business Law, Contracts, International Law

AGRICULTURE

SEE ALSO:

Animals, Commodities, Environmental Law, Estate Planning, Food, International Law, Natural Resources, Taxation, Water Law

JOURNALS, NEWSLETTERS & OTHER PERIODICALS:

Agricultural Law Journal (Callaghan, 1979–).
Agricultural Law Update (Skokie: Century Communications, 1983–).
Farmers Federal Tax Alert (NY: Research Inst. of Amer., 1979–)
Farmer's Legal Action Report (St. Paul: F.L.A.G.).
Farmer's Tax Report (NJ: Exec. Reports. Corp.).
Farmers Tax Watch (CCH, 1982–).
Journal of Agricultural Taxation & Law (Warren, Gorham & Lamont).
Midwest Agricultural Law Journal (St. Paul: Mason Pub. Co., 1983–).

ADMINISTRATIVE DECISIONS:

Agricultural Decisions (Secretary of Agriculture, 1942–).

TREATISES & LOOSELEAFS:

The ABC's of Farm Estate Planning by P. Levitt (St. Louis: Doane Agricultural Service, 1981).
Agricultural Estate, Tax & Business Planning by N. Harl (Matthew Bender, 1982–).
Agricultural Law, J. Davidson, ed. (Shepard's 1981).
Agricultural Law by J. Juergensmeyer & J. Wadley (Little, Brown, 1982).
Agricultural Law by N. Harl (Matthew Bender, 1980–).
Cattlemen's Tax Manual by T. Davis (Englewood, CO: Natl. Cattlemen's Assn., 1984–).
Estate Planning for Farmers and Ranchers by D. Kelley (Shepard's, 1980).
Farm and Ranch Real Estate Law by J. Cartwright (Lawyers Co-op., 1972).
Farm Estate & Business Planning by N. Harl (Skokie, IL: Agri Bus. Pub., 1983).
Farm Estate and Business Planning, 8th ed. by E. Neil (Skokie, IL: Agri Bus. Pub., 1983).
Farm Foreclosure Prevention and Reorganization by D. Peebles (Eau Claire, WI: Natl. Business Inst., 1983).
Farm Income Tax Manual, 7th ed. by J. O'Bryne & C. Davenport (Allen Smith, 1984).
Federal Taxation of Farmers and Ranchers by J. Kramer & T. Englebrecht (Tucson: Lawyers & Judges, 1980).
Handbook of Farm and Ranch Estate Planning by J. Polsen (Prentice-Hall, 1982).
Horse Owners and Breeders Tax Manual by T. Davis (Wash. D.C.: Amer. Horse Council, 1982–).
Horse Syndication Manual by K. Wood (Rancho Santa Fe, CA: Wood Pubs., 1983).
Law for the Horse Breeder by K. Wood (Rancho Santa Fe, CA: Wood Pubs., 1978).

ENCYCLOPEDIAS: AMERICAN JURISPRUDENCE 2D (Am Jur 2d)
Check the following topics in the *General Index* volumes for Am Jur 2d:

Agriculture	Horses
Animals	Irrigation
Commodities	Meat and Meat Products
Crops	Secretary of Agriculture
Dairy and Dairy Products	Stable or Livery
Eggs	Stockyards and
Food	Slaughterhouses
Fruit	Tobacco

CORPUS JURIS SECUNDUM (CJS)
Check the following topics in the *General Index* volumes for CJS:

Agricultural Lands	Nurseries and Nursery
Agriculture	Stock
Animals	Peanuts
Commodities	Perishable and Agricultural
Cotton	Commodities Act
Dairies	Poultry
Farm Credit	Share Croppers
Administration	Stockyards
Food	Sugar
Fruit	United States Department
Grain	of Agriculture
Inspection	Vegetables
Meat	

DIGESTS: CASE SEARCH IN WEST DIGESTS BY KEY TOPIC
In the *Descriptive Word Index* of the West digests, look for key topics and numbers under the following subject headings:

Agricultural Lands	Grain
Agriculture	Inspection
Animals	Meat
Commodities	Potato
Cotton	Poultry
Crops	Sharecroppers
Customs Duties	Stockyards
Dairies	Sugar
Farmers Home	Vegetables
Administration	Veterinarians
Food	Weights and Measures
Fruit	

ALR: ANNOTATIONS
Check the index volumes for ALR, ALR2d, ALR3d, ALR4th, and ALR Fed for annotations under the following subject headings:

Adulterated Food	Dairy
Agriculture	Food
Animals	Irrigation
Cigarettes	Livestock
Commodities	Migrant Labor
Co-operative Associations	Sharecroppers
Crops	Tobacco

PERIODICALS: CURRENT LAW INDEX (CLI) & LEGAL RESOURCE INDEX (LRI)
In the CLI and LRI, look for references to periodical literature under the following subject headings:

Agricultural Chemicals	Migrant Agricultural
Agricultural Credit	Workers
Agricultural Industries	Payment in Kind
Agriculture and State	Program
Animals	Rural Development
Cattle	Surplus Agricultural
Farmers	Commodities

INDEX TO LEGAL PERIODICALS (ILP)
In the ILP, look for references to legal periodical literature under the following subject headings:

Agriculture	Farm Tenancy
Animals	Migrant Labor
Anti-Dumping Duties	Pesticides

AIDING & ABETTING: See Criminal Law

AIDS

SEE ALSO: Death, Employment Discrimination, Health & Medicine, Insurance

**JOURNALS
& NEWSLETTERS:**   *AIDS and Public Policy Journal* (Frederick, MD: University Pub. Group, 1986–).
AIDS Policy and Law (Wash. D.C.: BNA; Buraff Pub., 1986–).

**TREATISES &
LOOSELEAFS:**   *AIDS and the Law,* Wm. Dornette, ed., (Wiley, 1987).
AIDS and the Law (ALI–ABA Comm. on Cont. Prof. Ed., 1986).
AIDS and the Law: A Guide for the Public by B. Dalton & the Yale AIDS Law Project
     (Yale Univ. Press, 1987).
AIDS and Patient Management: Legal, Ethical and Social Issues (Natl. Health Pub., 1986).
AIDS Law and Litigation Reporter (Univ. Publishing Group)
AIDS in the Workplace: Legal Questions and Practical Answers by W. Banta
     (Lexington Books, 1988).
AIDS Law: A Handbook on Providing Legal Services to Persons with AIDS and ARC
     (San Francisco: AIDS Legal Referral Panel, 1988).
AIDS Legal Guide: 2d ed. (NY: Lambda Legal Defense and Education Fund, 1987).
AIDS Practice Manual: A Legal and Educational Guide, 2d ed. (Nat'l Gay Rights
     Advocates and Nat'l Lawyers Guild AIDS Network, 1988).
Communicable Diseases in the Workplace (Practicing Law Institute, 1986).
*Employment Testing: A National Reporter on Polygraph, Drug, AIDS, and Genetic
     Testing* by S. Hurd (Univ. Pubs. of America, 1986–).
Employee Testing: Polygraphs and Urinalysis (Natl. Employment Law Project).

PERIODICALS: CURRENT LAW INDEX (CLI) & LEGAL RESOURCE INDEX (LRI)
In the CLI and LRI, look for references to periodical literature under the following subject headings:

AIDS (Disease)	Health, Diseases
AIDS Patients	Public Health

AID TO FAMILIES WITH DEPENDENT CHILDREN: See Poverty Law, Social Security

AIR & AVIATION

SEE ALSO: International Law, Space, Torts, Transportation, United Nations

RESEARCH GUIDES
& BIBLIOGRAPHIES: "Air and Space Law Research and Materials: A Bibliographic Essay" by K. Li, 5 *Annals of Air and Space Law* 720 (1980).
International Bibliograhy of Air Law, Supplement 1981–1984 by W. Heere (Kluwer, 1984).

TREATIES & OTHER
AGREEMENTS: *Air and Aviation Treaties of the World* by S. Lay (Oceana, 1984).
Provisions in U.S. International Air Transport Agreements (Wash. D.C.: Air Transport Assn. of America, 1985).

REPORTS: *Aviation Law Reports* (CCH, 1931–).
Reports (U.S. Civil Aeronautics Board, 1939–).
U.S. Aviation Reports, 1928–1982, C. Knauth, ed. (Oceana).

JOURNALS, NEWSLETTERS
& OTHER PERIODICALS: *The Air and Space Lawyer* (ABA, Forum Comm. on Air & Space Law, 1984–).
Air Law (Kluwer, 1976–).
Air Transportation and Antitrust Conference (Wash. D.C.: Federal Bar Assn., 1983).
Annals of Air and Space Law (McGill Univ., 1976–).
Journal of Air Law and Commerce (Southern Methodist Univ. Sch. of Law, 1939–).
Northrop University Law Journal of Aerospace, Business and Taxation (1985–).
Yearbook of Air and Space Law (McGill Univ., 1965–).

TREATISES &
LOOSELEAFS: *Air Cargo Regulation and Claims* by J. Madgelenat (Butterworths, 1983).
Aircrash Litigation Techniques by D. Cathcart (Michie, 1985).
Air Law, 4th ed. by C. Shawcross (Butterworths, 1983).
Airworthiness Inspector's Handbook (Dept. of Transp., FAA, 1985–).
Aviation Accident Law by L. Kreindler (Matthew Bender, 1963–).
Aviation: A Complete Legal Guide by C. Roberson (Blue Ridge Summit, PA: Tab Books, 1987).
Aviation Law: An Introduction, 3d ed. by F. Rollo (Maryland Historical Press, 1985).
Aviation Law Reporter (CCH).
Aviation Litigation Reporter (Andrews Pubs.)
Aviation Tort Law by S. Speiser (Lawyers Co-op., 1978).
Developments in Aviation Products Liability by I. Awford (Lloyds, 1984).
Dispute Resolution following Airplane Crashes by E. King (Rand Corp., 1988).
An Introduction to Air Law by I. Diedericks-Verschoor (Kluwer, 1983).
Law and Foreign Policy in International Aviation by P. Dempsey (Transnational Pub., 1987).
Liability of the International Air Carrier by R. Mankiewicz (Kluwer, 1981).
Litigating the Aviation Case, Juanita Madole, ed. (A.B.A., 1987).
Litigation and Trial of Air Crash Cases by J. Kennelly (Callaghan, 1968–).

Regulation of International Aviation by R. Rosenfield (Oceana, 1984–).
Shawcross and Beaumont on Air Law, 4th ed. (Butterworths, 1983).
Treatise on Air-Aeronautical Law, 3d ed. by N. Matte (McGill Univ.; Carswell, 1981).

ENCYCLOPEDIAS:

AMERICAN JURISPRUDENCE 2D (Am Jur 2d)
Check the following topics in the *General Index* volumes for Am Jur 2d:

Aviation	Space Law
Carriers	Transportation

CORPUS JURIS SECUNDUM (CJS)
Check the following topics in the *General Index* volumes for CJS:

Aeronautics and	Civil Aeronautics Board
Aerospace	Rates and Charges
Aircrafts	Pilots
Airports	Transportation
Carriers	Warsaw Convention

DIGESTS:

CASE SEARCH IN WEST DIGESTS BY KEY TOPIC
In the *Descriptive Word Index* of the West digests, look for key topics and numbers under the following subject headings:

Airports	Carriers
Air Traffic Controllers	Satellite
Aviation	Space

ALR:

ANNOTATIONS
Check the index volumes for ALR, ALR2d, ALR3d, ALR4th, and ALR Fed for annotations under the following subject headings:

Aviation	Federal Aviation
Carriers	Transportation
Civil Aeronautics Board	Warsaw Convention

PERIODICALS:

CURRENT LAW INDEX (CLI) & LEGAL RESOURCE INDEX (LRI)
In the CLI and LRI, look for references to periodical literature under the following subject headings:

Aeronautics	Space Law
Air Lines	Space Shuttles
Air Pilots	United States Civil
Airplanes	Aeronautics Boards
Airspace	United States Federal
Deregulation	Aviation Administration
Outer Space	

INDEX TO LEGAL PERIODICALS (ILP)
In the ILP, look for references to legal periodical literature under the following subject headings:

Accidents	Piracy
Air Laws	Rate Regulation
Airports	Space Law
Airspace	Transportation
Aviation	

AIRCRAFT: See Air & Aviation, Transportation
AIR CRASH: See Air & Aviation, Torts

AIR FORCE: See Military Law
AIR POLLUTION: See Environmental Law, Oil & Gas
AIRPORT: See Air & Aviation, Transportation
AIRSPACE: See Real Estate
AJMAN: See United Arab Emirates

ALABAMA

SEE ALSO:	Circuit Courts (Eleventh Circuit)
STATUTES:	*Acts of Alabama.* *Code of Alabama.*
STATE ADMINISTRATIVE CODE:	*Alabama Administrative Code* (Leg. Ref. Service, 1984–). *Alabama Administrative Monthly.*
CASES & OPINIONS:	*Alabama Reports* (1840–1976). *Alabama Appellate Court Reports* (1910–1976). *Southern Reporter* (1886–).
COURT RULES:	*Alabama Rules Annotated* (Michie, 1988). *Alabama Rules of Civil Procedure Annotated,* 2d ed. by C. Jones (West, 1986). *Alabama Rules of Court* (West). *Alabama Rules of Criminal Procedure* (Alabama Law Institute).
JURY INSTRUCTIONS:	*Alabama Jury Instructions with Forms* by W. Jones (West, 1953). *Alabama Pattern Jury Instructions: Civil* (Lawyers Co-op., 1974). *Pattern Jury Instructions: Criminal* (Alabama Bar, 1980).
ETHICS & PROFESSIONAL RESPONSIBILITY:	*Ethics Commission Advisory Opinions.*
OPINIONS OF THE ATTORNEY GENERAL:	*Attorney General Reports & Opinions.*
JOURNALS & OTHER PERIODICALS:	*Alabama Lawyer* (1940–). *Cumberland-Samford Law Review.*
SURVEY OF STATE LAW:	". . . Survey of Developments in Alabama Law," in the *Alabama Law Review.* See for example vol. 35, p. 571; vol. 36, p. 373.
TREATISES, LOOSELEAFS & OTHER MONOGRAPHS:	*Alabama Appellate Practice* (Alabama Bar, 1980). *Alabama Business Corporation Handbook* by J. Wilson (Alabama Bar, 1980). *Alabama Civil Practice Forms* by A. Howell (Michie, 1986). *Alabama Criminal Trial Practice,* 2d ed. by N. Chiarkas (Harrison, 1988). *Alabama Divorce, Alimony & Child Custody,* 2d ed. by R. McCurley & P. Davis (Harrison). *Alabama Evidence* by W. Schroeder et al. (Harrison, 1987). *Alabama Law of Damages,* 2d ed. by C. Gamble (Harrison, 1988).

Alabama Law Office Practice Deskbook by R. McCurley (Lawyers Educational Press, 1983).

Alabama Legal Forms Annotated by R. Smith (Harrison, 1967–).

Alabama Limitations of Actions and Notice Provisions by T. Hoff (Harrison, 1984).

Alabama Real Estate Handbook, 4th ed. by R. McCurley & P. Davis (Michie, 1984).

Alabama Torts Case Finder by A. Howell (Michie, 1988).

Alabama Trusts and Estates (Michie, 1984).

Alabama Workmen's Compensation by J. Wood (Harrison).

Basic Legal Skills (Alabama, 1982).

Double Taxation: Issues, Analysis and Alternatives for Alabama by J. Wilson (Auburn Univ., Office of Public Service and Research, 1984).

How to Administer Estates in Alabama, 2d ed. (Alabama Bar, 1988).

Legal Aspects of Real Estate Transactions (Alabama, 1971–).

Marital Law (Alabama Bar, 1976).

McElroy's Alabama Evidence, 3d ed. by C. Gamble (Birmingham: Samford University Press, 1987).

Real Estate Handbook: Land Laws of Alabama, 4th ed. by R. McCurley & P. Davis (Michie, 1984).

State and Local Taxes (Alabama) (Prentice-Hall).

State Tax Reports (Alabama) (CCH).

Williams' Alabama Evidence by R. Williams (Michie, 1967).

DIGESTS & CITATOR:

Alabama Advance Annotation Service (Michie, 1984–).

Alabama Digest (West).

Shepard's Alabama Citations.

Southern Digest (West)

ALASKA

SEE ALSO:

Circuit Courts (Ninth Circuit), Indians

**RESEARCH GUIDE
& BIBLIOGRAPHY:**

Alaska Legal and Law-Related Publications by A. Ruzicka (American Assn. of Law Libraries, 1986).

STATUTES:

Alaska Legislative Report (Legislative Reporting Service, 1958–).

Alaska Statutes (Michie, 1962–).

Alaska Session Laws.

**STATE ADMINISTRATIVE
CODE:**

Alaska Administrative Code.

**ADMINISTRATIVE
DECISIONS & REPORTS:**

Alaska Native Claims Appeal Board ANCAB Decisions (Dept. of Interior, 1974–).

Annual Report (Commn. on the Status of Women, 1979–).

Annual Report (Office of the Ombudsman, 1975–).

Decisions (Commercial Fisheries Entry Commn., 1975–).

Decisions (State Commn. for Human Rights, 1975–).

Rulings (Dept. of Revenue, 1973–).

CASES & OPINIONS:

Alaska Case Notes (Pleiades Research Group, 1983–).

Alaska Reporter (West, 1960–).

Alaska Reports (1884–1959).
Pacific Reporter (West, 1960–).

COURT RULES:
Alaska Court Rules (West).
Alaska Rules of Court (Seattle: Book Pub. Co., 1963–).

JURY INSTRUCTIONS:
Alaska Civil Pattern Jury Instructions (Alaska Bar Assn., 1984).
Alaska Pattern Jury Instructions (Criminal) (Alaska Court System, 1980).

ETHICS & PROFESSIONAL RESPONSIBILITY:
Ethics Opinions (Alaska Bar Assn., 1968–).

OPINIONS OF THE ATTORNEY GENERAL:
Informal Opinions of the Office of the Attorney General (Dept. of Law, 1973–).
Opinions of the Attorney General (Dept. of Law, 1959–).

DIRECTORY:
Alaska Directory of Attorneys (Todd Communications).

TREATISES, LOOSELEAFS & OTHER MONOGRAPHS:
Alaska Corporation Manual by W. Walker (Fairbanks: That New Pub. Co., 1977).
Alaska Mineral Development (Boulder: Rocky Mt. Mineral Law Foundation, 1978).
Attorneys' Handbook (Alaska Court of Appeals, 1983).
Attorneys' Handbook (Alaska Supreme Court, 1983).
A Citizen's Guide to the Constitution of the State of Alaska by G. Harrison (Univ. of Alaska, Inst. of Social & Economic Research, 1982).
Conflicts of Law: A Northwest Perspective (Alaska) by J. Nafziger (Butterworths, 1985).
Legal Status of the Alaska Natives (Alaska Statehood Commn.; Dept. of Law, 1982).
Legislative Handbook on Alaska State Government (Alaska Legislative Council, annual).
The Making of Alaska Law (Legislative Affairs Agency, 1975).
A Special Report on the Alaska Criminal Justice System (Div. of Legislative Audit, 1983).
Women's Legal Rights in Alaska (Alaska Women's Commn., (1984).

DIGESTS & CITATOR:
Alaska Advance Annotation Service (Michie, 1984).
Alaska Digest (West, 1869–).
Pacific Digest (West).
Shepard's Alaska Citations.

ALBANIA

SEE ALSO:
Communism, International Law, United Nations

RESEARCH GUIDE & BIBLIOGRAPHY:
The International Relations of Eastern Europe: A Guide to Information Sources (Albania) by R. Remington (Gale, 1978).

CONSTITUTION:
The Constitutions of the Communist World (Albania), W. Simons, ed. (Sijthoff & Noordhoff, 1980).
"The People's Republic of Albania, 1976–1980" by G. Flanz in *Constitutions of the Countries of the World* by A. Blaustein & G. Flanz (Oceana, 1981).

TREATISES:
Albania and China: A Study of an Unequal Alliance by E. Biberaj (Westview, 1986).
Albania: Political Imprisonment and the Law (London: Amnesty Intl. Pub., 1984).

The People's Republic of Albania by N. Pano (Johns Hopkins Press, 1968).
The Unwritten Law in Albania by M. Hasluck (Westport, CT: Hyperion Press, 1981).

ARTICLES: "Albania (Human Rights of the World)," *International Commission of Jurists Review* 5 (June, 1985).

ALBERTA: See Canada

ALCOHOL

SEE ALSO: Criminal Law, Employee Benefits, Employment Discrimination, Food, Forensic Science Health & Medicine, State & Local Government, Torts

**RESEARCH GUIDE &
BIBLIOGRAPHY:**   "Journal Articles Concerning the Legal Aspects of Alcohol and Alcoholism 1970–1982" by D. Hughes, 59 *North Dakota Law Review* 507 (1983).

**JOURNALS, NEWSLETTERS
& OTHER PERIODICALS:**   *DWI Journal* (CA: James Pub., 1986–).
Liquor Liability Journal (MN: Chandler Pub., 1984–).

**LOOSELEAFS &
TREATISES:**   *Alcohol and Drugs in the Workplace* (BNA, 1986).
Alcohol Problems in Employment (Croom Helm, 1983).
Alcohol-Related Misconduct by A. Koven (San Francisco: Coloracre, 1984).
Defending Drinking Drivers, 2d ed. by J. Tarantino (CA: James Pub., 1986–).
A Digest of State Alcohol-Highway Safety Related Legislation, 3d ed. (Dept. of Transp., Natl. Highway Traffic Safety Admin., GPO, 1985).
Digest of State Laws Relating to Driving under the Influence of Alcohol (NY: Amer. Insurance Assn., 1986).
Drinking/Driving Litigation, Criminal and Civil by D. Nichols (Callaghan, 1985–).
Drunk Driving by R. Joye (Kluwer, 1985–).
Drunk Driving Defense, 2d ed. by L. Taylor (Little, Brown, 1986).
Intoxication Test Evidence: Criminal and Civil by E. Fitzgerald (Lawyers Co-op., 1987)
Liquor Control Law Reports (CCH, 1934–).

ENCYCLOPEDIAS: AMERICAN JURISPRUDENCE 2D (Am Jur 2d)
Check the following topics in the *General Index* volumes for Am Jur 2d:

Alcohol	Habitual Intoxication
Beer	Intoxicating Liquors
Drugs and Narcotics	

CORPUS JURIS SECUNDUM (CJS)
Check the following topics in the *General Index* volumes for CJS:

Beverages	Drunkards
Drugs and Narcotics	Intoxicating Liquors

DIGESTS: CASE SEARCH IN WEST DIGESTS BY KEY TOPIC
In the *Descriptive Word Index* of the West digests, look for key topics and numbers under the folloiwng subject headings:

Alcohol	Drugs and Narcotics
Beverages	Drunkards
Criminal Law	Intoxicating Liquor

ALR: ANNOTATIONS
                           Check the index volumes for ALR, ALR2d, ALR3d, ALR4th, and ALR Fed for annota-
                           tions under the following subject headings:

Alcoholism	Driving While Intoxicated
Beverages	Habitual Drunkards
Blood Test	Intoxicating Liquors
Breath Analysis Test	Intoxication
Chemical Sobriety Test	

PERIODICALS: CURRENT LAW INDEX (CLI) & LEGAL RESOURCE INDEX (LRI)
                           In the CLI and LRI, look for references to periodical literature under the following
                           subject headings:

Addictive Beverages	Dram Shop Acts
Alcoholics	Drinking and Traffic
Alcohol in the Body	Accidents
Bars, Saloons	Drunkenness
Breathalyzers	

INDEX TO LEGAL PERIODICALS (ILP)
In the ILP, look for references to legal periodical literature under the following subject
headings:

Alcoholic Beverages	Criminal Law
Blood Tests	Intoxication

ALDERNEY: See Channel Islands

ALGERIA

SEE ALSO: Africa, Communism, International Law, Islam, United Nations

CONSTITUTION: "The Algerian Constitution," 4 *Middle East Journal* 446 (Autumn, 1963).
                           Constitutions of the Countries of the World (Algeria) by A. Almany & C. Flanz (Oceana,
                               1972).

TREATISES &
LOOSELEAFS: *African Tax Systems* (Algeria) by R. Hammond & M. van den Abeelen (Amsterdam:
                               Intl. Bureau of Fiscal Documentation, 1980–).
                           Agrarian Reform under State Capitalism in Algeria by K. Pfeifer (Westview, 1985).
                           Algeria: The Revolution Institutionalized by J. Entelis (Westview, 1986).
                           Bakaka and Bureaucracy: Algerian Muslim Judges and the Colonial State (1854–1892)
                               by A. Christelow (Ann Arbor: Univ. Microfilms, 1977) (no. 7804670).
                           Digest of Commercial Laws of the World (Algeria) by the Natl. Assn. of Credit Manage-
                               ment (Oceana, 1977–).
                           An Introduction to Law in French-Speaking Africa (Vol. II, Algeria) by J. Salacuse
                               (Michie, 1969).
                           Investment Codes of North Africa: Algeria, E. de Brauw, transl. (Amsterdam: Intl.
                               Bureau of Fiscal Documentation, 1979).
                           Muslim Law Courts and the French Colonial State in Algeria by A. Christelow
                               (Princeton Univ. Press, 1985).
                           Tax Laws of the World—Algeria (Fl: Foreign Tax Law Assn.).

ARTICLES: "The Evian Agreements on Algeria and the Lancaster Agreements on Zimbabwe: A

Comparative Analysis" by O. Musamirapamwe, 12 *Georgia Journal of International & Comparative Law* 153 (1982).

"Middle East Agency Law Survey" (Algeria) by F. Taylor, 14 *International Lawyer* 332 (1980).

"Setting Up a Liaison Office (Algeria)" by J. Andrieux, 6 *Middle E. Executive Rep.* 9 (1983).

"Socialism and the Law in Algeria" by J. Hazard, 7 *Review of Socialist Law* 243 (1981).

ALIBI: See Criminal Law
ALIENATION OF AFFECTIONS: See Torts
ALIENATION, RESTRAINTS ON: See Real Estate
ALIEN LABOR: See Labor Law, Immigration Law
ALIENS: See Civil Rights, Immigration Law, International Law
ALIMONY: See Family Law
ALLERGY: See Health & Medicine
ALLOCATION: See Estate Planning
ALTERATION OF INSTRUMENTS: See Contracts, Estate Planning
AMATEUR SPORTS: See Sports Law
AMBASSADORS: See International Law, United Nations
AMBULATORY SERVICES: See Health & Medicine
AMENDMENT OF CONSTITUTION: See Constitutional Law
AMENDMENT OF PLEADING: See Trial & Appellate Practice
AMERICAN BAR ASSOCIATION: See Computers, Professional Responsibility
AMERICAN INDIANS: See Indians
AMERICAN LAW: See Legal History
AMERICAN MARITIME COMMISSION: See Maritime Law
AMERICAN MEDICAL ASSOCIATION: See Health & Medicine

AMERICAN SAMOA

SEE ALSO: International Law, United Nations, Western Samoa

CONSTITUTION: "United States Territories" (American Samoa) in *Constitutions of the United States: National and State* (Oceana, 1982).

"United States Territories: American Samoa" by G. Chung in *Constitutions of Dependencies and Special Sovereignties* by A. & E. Blaustein (Oceana, 1981).

Statement of Robert B. Shanks . . . Before the Committee on Energy and Natural Resources, Subcommittee on Energy Conservation and Supply, United States Senate, Concerning Revised Constitution of American Samoa on May 8, 1984.

STATUTES: *American Samoa Code Annotated.*

ADMINISTRATIVE
REGULATIONS: *American Samoa Administrative Code.*

CASES: *American Samoa Reports* (Equity Pub. Corp., 1900–).
American Samoa Digest (Equity Pub. Corp.).

JOURNAL: *Samoan Pacific, L.J.*

ARTICLES: "American Samoa: Decline of a Culture" by A. Leibowitz, 10 *California Western International Law Journal* 220 (1980).

"The Application of the American Constitution to American Samoa" by M. McBride, 4 *Samoan Pacific. L.J.* 9 (August, 1977).
"The Chieftal System in Twentieth Century America: Legal Aspects of the Matai System in the Territory of American Samoa" by A. Lutali, 4 *Georgia Journal International and Comparative Law* 387 (1974).
"Land Tenure in American Samoa" by Stewart, 10 *Hawaii Bar Journal* 52 (1973).
"Ocean Boundaries in the South Pacific" by S. Border, 4 *University of Hawaii Law Review* 1 (1982).
"Possessions Corporation System of Taxation in American Samoa, Guam, and the Virgin Islands," 9 *International Tax Journal* 343 (1983).
"Some Observations on the Judiciary in American Samoa," 18 *U.C.L.A. Law Review* 581 (1971).

AMERICAN STOCK EXCHANGE: See Securities Law
AMERICAS: See Caribbean, Latin America
AMICUS CURIAE: See Trial & Appellate Practice
AMINOIL: See Kuwait
AMNESTY: See Criminal Law
AMORTIZATION: See Real Estate
AMUSEMENTS: See Art & Entertainment, Torts
ANALYSIS: See Jurisprudence, Legal Research
ANCIENT DOCUMENT RULE: See Trial & Appellate Practice
ANCILLARY PROCEEDING: See Estate Planning, Trial & Appellate Practice
ANCOM: See Peru
ANDEAN GROUP: See Bolivia, Caribbean, Chile, Colombia, Ecuador, Latin America, Peru, Venezuela

ANDORRA

SEE ALSO: Europe, France, International Law, Spain, United Nations

"Andorra in the Vise . . ." by A. MacDonald, 129 *Solicitor's Journal* 599 (1985).
"Corporate Reform in Andorra" by A. MacDonald, 128 *Solicitor's Journal* 425 (1984).

ANESTHESIOLOGY: See Health & Medicine

ANGOLA

SEE ALSO: Africa, Communism, Cuba, International Law, Portugal, United Nations

CONSTITUTION: "Angola" by K. Kerpen in *Constitutions of the Countries of the World* by A. Blaustein & G. Flanz (Oceana, 1981).

TREATISES: *Angola: A Country Study* (American Univ., Foreign Area Studies; Gov't. Printing Office).
The Angolan Revolution by J. Marcum (MIT Press, 1969–78).
Angola: The Road to Independence by F. Soremekun (Nigeria: Univ. of Ife Press, 1983).
Foreign Intervention in Civil War by C. Ebinger (Westview, 1986).
Tax Laws of the World—Angola (FL: Foreign Tax Law Assn.).

ARTICLES: "Portuguese Africa: A Brief History of United Nations Involvement," 4 *Denver Journal of International Law & Policy* 133 (1974).

ANGUILLA

SEE ALSO: Caribbean, International Law, United Nations

CONSTITUTION: "Anguilla" by S. Holt & N. Yell in *Constitutions of Dependencies and Special Sovereignties* by A. Balustein (Oceana, 1983).
West Indian Constitutions: Post Independence Reform (Anguilla) by F. Phillips (Oceana, 1985).

ARTICLES: "Anguilla Income Tax Law" by M. Chatzky, 7 *Common Market Lawyer* 1 (1982).

ANGUISH: See Mental Health, Torts

ANIMALS

SEE ALSO: Agriculture, Criminal Law, Environmental Law, Natural Resources, Torts

RESEARCH GUIDES & BIBLIOGRAPHIES: *A Bilbliography on Animal Rights and Related Matters* by C. Magel (Wash. D.C.: Univ. Press of America, 1981).
"Research Guide for Animal Welfare and Animal Rights" by R. Bennon, 4 *Legal Reference Service Quarterly* 3 (1984).

STATUTES: Animal Welfare Act, 7 U.S.C. 2131ff.
Bald Eagle Protection Act, 16 U.S.C. 668.
The Endangered Species Act, 16 U.S.C. 1531ff.
The Horse Protection Act, 16 U.S.C. 1821.
The Humane Methods of Slaughter Act, 7 U.S.C. 1901ff.
The Lacey Act, 18 U.S.C. 42.
Marine Mammal Protection Act of 1972, 16 U.S.C. 1361ff.
The Migratory Bird Conservation Act, 16 U.S.C. 715ff.
The Migratory Bird Treaty Act, 16 U.S.C. 701ff.
Tule Elk Preservation Act, 16 U.S.C. 673.
The Twenty-Eight Hour Law, 45 U.S.C. 71ff.
The Wild, Free-Roaming Horses and Burros Act, 16 U.S.C. 1331.

TREATISES & LOOSELEAFS: *All that Dwell Therein: Animal Rights and Environmental Ethics* by T. Regan (Univ. of CA Press, Berkeley, 1982).
Animal Law by D. Favre (Quorum Books, 1983).
Animal Liberation by P. Singer (NY: Review of Books, 1975).
Animal Rights by H. Salt (Clarks Summit, PA: Society for Animal Rights, 1980).
Animal Rights and Human Morality by B. Rollin (Prometheus Books, 1981).
Animal Rights and Human Objectives by T. Regan (Prentice-Hall, 1976).
The Case for Animal Rights by T. Regan (Univ. of CA Press, Berkeley, 1983).
In Defense of Animals, P. Singer, ed. (NY: Basil Blackwell, Inc., 1985).
Dog Law by M. Randolph (Nolo Press, 1989).

The Evolution of National Wildlife Law by M. Bean (Praeger, 1983).
Return to Eden: Animal Rights and Human Responsibility by M. Fox (Viking Press, 1980).

ENCYCLOPEDIAS: AMERICAN JURISPRUDENCE 2D (Am Jur 2d)
Check the following topics in the *General Index* volumes for Am Jur 2d:

Animals	Experimentation
Amusements and	Fish and Game
Exhibitions	Horses
Branding	Poultry
Cats	Racing
Chickens	Stockyards
Dairies	Veterinarians
Deer	Zoos
Dogs	

CORPUS JURIS SECUNDUM (CJS)
Check the following topics in the *General Index* volumes for CJS:

Animals	Horses
Auctions	Nuisance
Cats	Veterinarians
Horse Racing	

DIGESTS: CASE SEARCH IN WEST DIGESTS BY KEY TOPIC
In the *Descriptive Word Index* of the West digests, look for key topics and numbers under the following subject headings:

Animals	Horses
Auctions	Injunction
Cattle	Woods
Horse Racing	

ALR: ANNOTATIONS
Check the index volumes for ALR, ALR2d, ALR3d, ALR4th, and ALR Fed for annotations under the following subject headings:

Animals	Horses
Dogs	Livestock
Fish	Wildlife
Game	Veterinarian

PERIODICALS: CURRENT LAW INDEX (CLI) & LEGAL RESOURCE INDEX (LRI)
In the CLI and LRI, look for references to periodical literature under the following subject headings:

Animal Bites	Dogs
Animal Experimentation	Laboratory Animals
Animal Rights	Police Dogs
Animals	Wildlife Conservation
Animals, Treatment of	

INDEX TO LEGAL PERIODICALS (ILP)
In the ILP, look for references to legal periodical literature under the following subject headings:

Animals	Vivisection

ANNUAL REPORTS: See Securities Law
ANNUITIES: See Employee Benefits, Estate Planning, Insurance
ANNULMENT: See Canon Law, Family Law
ANSWER: See Trial & Appellate Practice

ANTARCTICA

SEE ALSO: Environmental Law, International Law, Natural Resources, Sea, United Nations

**TREATIES & RELATED
DOCUMENTS:**

Antarctica and International Law: A Collection of Inter-State and National Documents
(Oceana, 1982).
Basic Documents on Antarctica by W. Bush (Oceana, 1980).
"Antarctic Treaty Consultative Meeting," 20 *International Legal Materials* 1265 (1981).

TREATISES:

Antarctic Law and Politics by Auburn (Indiana Univ. Press, 1982).
Antarctic Mineral Exploitation: The Emerging Legal Framework by F. Orrego
(Cambridge Univ. Press, 1988).
Antarctic Resources Policy: Scientific, Legal, and Political Issues, F. Vicuna, ed.
(Cambridge Univ. Press, 1983).
The Antarctic Treaty Regime: Law, Environment and Resources, G. Triggs, ed.
(Cambrige Univ. Press, 1987).
The Antarctic Treaty System by J. Myhre (Westview, 1986).
International Law and Australian Sovereignty in Antarctica, G. Triggs, ed. (Sydney:
Legal Books, 1986).
A Pole Apart: The Emerging Issue of Antarctica by P. Quigg (McGraw-Hill, 1983).

ARTICLES:

"Antarctica and the Law of the Sea: An Introductory Overview" by C. Joyner, 13
Ocean Dev. & International Law Journal 277 (1983).
"The Exclusive Economic Zone and Antarctica" by C. Joyner, 21 *Virginia Journal of
International Law* 691 (1981).
"Iceberg Appropriation and the Antarctic's Gordian Knot" by E. Zuccaro, 9 *California
Western International Law Journal* 405 (1979).
"International Agreements: Antarctic Resources," 22 *Harvard International Law
Journal* 195 (1981), reprinted from 19 *International Legal Materials* 837 (1980).
"Sovereignty in Antarctica" by J. Bernhardt, 5 *California Western International Law
Journal* 297 (1975).
"The Soviet Union and the Antarctic Regime" by B. Boczek, 78 *American Journal of
International Law* 834 (1984).
"United States Criminal Jurisdiction in Antarctica: How Old is the Ice?" by C. Cosslett,
9 *Brooklyn Journal of International Law,* 67 (1983).

ANTENNAS: See Public Utilities
ANTENUPTIAL CONTRACTS: See Contracts, Family Law, Women & the Law
ANTHROPOLOGY: See Forensic Science, Jurisprudence
ANTICIPATORY BREACH: See Contracts
ANTIDUMPING: See Customs, International Law, Maritime Law, Taxation
ANTIFEDERALIST: See Legal History

ANTIGUA & BARBUDA

SEE ALSO: Caribbean, International Law, Latin America, United Nations

West Indian Constitutions: Post Independence Reform (Antigua) by F. Phillips (Oceana, 1985).

ANTITRUST LAW & TRADE REGULATION

SEE ALSO: Administrative Law, Air & Aviation, Business Law, Corporate Law, Criminal Law, Franchise Law, Intellectual Property, International Law, Media Law

RESEARCH GUIDES & BIBLIOGRAPHIES: "A Bibliography of Recent Antitrust Law Developments," 49 *Antitrust Law Journal* 1635 (1982).
"International Antitrust Law, 1976–1982; A Selected Annotated Bibliography" by K. Shimpock, 18 *Stanford Journal of International Law* 405 (1982).
Merger Law Bibliography: 1950–1980 (ABA Antitrust Law Section, 1982).

LEGISLATIVE HISTORY: *The Legislative History of the Federal Antitrust Laws and Related Statutes,* E. Kintner, ed. (Clark Boardman, 1978).

ADMINISTRATIVE DECISIONS: *Antitrust & Trade Regulation Report* (BNA, 1961–).
Decisions (Federal Trade Commn., 1914–).
Trade Regulation Reports (CCH, 1914–).

JOURNALS, ANNUALS, NEWSLETTERS & OTHER PERIODICALS: *Annual Advanced Antitrust Seminar* (Practicing Law Institute).
Annual Antitrust Law Institute (Practicing Law Institute).
Antitrust Bulletin (Federal Legal Publications, 1955–).
Antitrust Law and Economics Review (1968–).
Antitrust Law Journal (ABA Antitrust Law Section, 1952–).
Antitrust Law Symposium (NY State Bar Assn., Section of Antitrust Law).
Antitrust Newsletter (ABA Antitrust Law Section).
Business Competition Law Adviser by L. Altman (Callaghan).
Mergers & Acquisitions (McLean, VA: Information for Industry, Inc.).
New England Antitrust Conference (Mass. Cont. Legal Education).

LOOSELEAFS: *Acquisitions and Mergers: Negotiated and Contested Transactions* by S. Lorne (Warren, Gorham & Lamont, 1985–).
Acquisitions under the Hart-Scott-Rodino Antitrust Improvements Act by S. Axinn (Law Journal Seminars-Press, 1979–).
Antitrust and Restrictive Business Practices: International, Regional and National Regulation by J. Marke & N. Samie (Oceana, 1982–).
Antitrust: An Economic Approach by R. Givens (Law Journal Seminars-Press, 1983–).
Antitrust and Trade Regulation by S. Axinn et al. (N.Y. Law Pub. Co., 1988–).
Antitrust Basics by T. Vakerics (Law Journal Seminars-Press, 1985–).
Antitrust Counseling and Litigation Techniques, J. von Kalinowski, ed. (Matthew Bender, 1984–).

Antitrust Discovery Handbook (ABA, Section of Antitrust Law, 1981–).
Antitrust Division Manual (U.S. Dept. of Justice Manual, Antitrust Div., 1979–).
Antitrust Laws and Trade Regulation, J. von Kalinowski, ed. (Matthew Bender, 1984–).
Callmann's Unfair Competition, Trademarks and Monopolies, 4th ed. by R. Callmann, rev. by L. Altman (Callaghan, 1967–).
Competition Law in Western Europe and the United States, D. Gijlstra & F. Murphy, eds. (Rothman; Kluwer, 1976–).
Corporate Acquisitions and Mergers by B. & E. Fox (Matthew Bender, 1968–).
Federal Trade Commission: Regulatory Manual by S. Kanwit (Shepard's 1979–).
State Antitrust Law by W. Lifland (Law Journal Seminars-Press, 1984–).
State Antitrust Laws (ABA Section of Antitrust Law, 1974–).
Takeover and Freezeouts by M. Lipton & E. Steinberger (Law Journal Seminars-Press, 1978–).
United States, Common Market and International Anti-trust: A Comparative Guide by B. Hawk (Law & Business, Inc., 1979–).
World Law of Competition, J. von Kalinowski, ed. (Matthew Bender, 1978–).

TREATISES:

Acquisitions and Mergers (Practicing Law Institute, 1986).
Antitrust Adviser, 3d ed. by C. Hills (Shepard's, 1985).
Antitrust and American Business Aboard, 2d ed. by J. Atwood & K. Brewster (Shepard's, 1981).
Antitrust and Regulated Industries by D. Hjelmfelt (Wiley, 1985).
Antitrust Civil Jury Instructions (ABA, Section of Antitrust Law, 1980).
Antitrust Consent Decree Manual (ABA, Section of Antitrust Law, 1979).
Antitrust Law by L. Sullivan (West, 1977).
Antitrust Law: An Analysis of Antitrust Principles and Their Application by P. Areeda & D. Turner (Little, Brown, 1978).
Antitrust Law and Economics in a Nutshell, 3d ed. by E. Gellhorn (West, 1986).
Antitrust Law Developments (Second) (ABA Section of Antitrust Law, 1984).
Criminal Antitrust Litigation Manual (ABA Section of Antitrust Law, 1983).
The Deregulation of the Banking and Securities Industries by L. Goldberg & L. White (Heath, 1979).
Federal Antitrust Law by E. Kinter (Anderson).
Foreign Commerce and the Antitrust Laws, 3d ed. by W. Fugate (Little, Brown, 1982).
Handbook on Antitrust Grand Jury Investigations, 2d ed. (A.B.A., 1988).
Managing Antitrust and Other Complex Litigation by W. Schwarzer (Michie, 1982).
Mergers in the New Antitrust Era by T. Brunner et al. (BNA, 1985).
Merger Standards under the U.S. Antitrust Laws (ABA Section of Antitrust Law, 1981).
Pattern Discovery: Antitrust by D. Danner (Lawyers Co-op., 1981).
Pinner's World Unfair Competition Law: An Encyclopedia, H. Dawid, ed. (Sijthoff & Noordhoff, 1978).
Premerger Notification Practice Manual (ABA Section of Antitrust Law).
The Trial of an Antitrust Price-Fixing Case (ABA, 1981).
Understanding the Antitrust Laws, 9th ed. by J. Cise (Practicing Law Institute, 1986).

DIGEST:

Merger Case Digest (ABA Antitrust Law Section, 1984).

BRIEFS:

Antitrust Law: Major Briefs and Oral Arguments of the Supreme Court of the United States, P. Kurland & G. Casper, eds. (University Publications of America).

ENCYCLOPEDIAS:

AMERICAN JURISPRUDENCE 2D (Am Jur 2d)
Check the following topics in the *General Index* volumes for Am Jur 2d:
               Administrative Law   Corporations

Customs Duties and	Monopolies, Restraint
Import Regulations	of Trade
Fair Trade Laws	

CORPUS JURIS SECUNDUM (CJS)
Check the following topics in the *General Index* volumes for CJS:

Administrative Bodies	Merger or Consolidation
Competition	Monopolies
Corporations	Price Fixing
Federal Trade Commission	

DIGESTS: CASE SEARCH IN WEST DIGESTS BY KEY TOPIC
In the *Descriptive Word Index* of the West digests, look for key topics and numbers under the following subject headings:

Administrative Law	Merger
Conspiracy	Monopolies
Consumer Protection	Securities Regulation
Corporations	Trade Regulation
Joint-Stock Companies and Business Trusts	

ALR: ANNOTATIONS
Check the index volumes for ALR, ALR2d, ALR3d, ALR4th, and ALR Fed for annotations under the following subject headings:

Administrative Law	Federal Trade Commission
Competition	Price
Consolidation or Merger	Restraint of Trade and
Corporations	Monopolies
Double or Triple Damages	

PERIODICALS: CURRENT LAW INDEX (CLI) & LEGAL RESOURCE INDEX (LRI)
In the CLI and LRI, look for references to periodical literature under the following subject headings:

Antitrust Law	Non-Competition
Big Business	Agreements
Cartels	Oligopolies
Competition	Price
Conglomerate Corporation	Price Fixing
Consolidation and Merger	Restraint of Trade
Duopolies	State Action (Antitrust)
Economics	Trade Regulation
Industrial Competition	Trusts, Industrial
Market Share	United States Federal
Monopolies	Trade Commission

INDEX TO LEGAL PERIODICALS (ILP)
In the ILP, look for references to legal periodical literature under the following subject headings:

Administrative Law	Corporations/Consolidation
Antitrust Law	and Merger
Cartels	Prices
Commerce	Restraint of Trade
Conspiracy	Trade Regulation
	Unfair Competition

APACHE INDIANS: See Indians
APARTHEID: See South Africa
APARTMENTS: See Landlord-Tenant, Real Estate
APPEAL AND ERROR: See Trial & Appellate Practice
APPEARANCE: See Professional Responsibility, Trial & Appellate Practice
APPELLATE PRACTICE: See Trial & Appellate Practice
APPOINTMENT, POWER OF: See Estate Planning, Real Estate
APPORTIONMENT: See Estate Planning
APPRAISAL: See Business Law, Customs, Estate Planning, Real Estate
APPRENTICE: See Employee Benefits, Labor Law
APPURTENANCES: See Real Estate
ARAB: See Islam, Israel, Jordan, Libya, Middle East, Syria
ARABIAN GULF: See Islam, Middle East
ARBITRATION: See Architecture, Business Law, Contracts, Education Law,
    Government Contracts, International Law, Labor Law, Maritime Law, Mediation,
    Sports Law, Trial & Appellate Practice

ARCHITECTURE, CONSTRUCTION & ENGINEERING

SEE ALSO: Administrative Law, Contracts, Government Contracts, Historic Preservation, Insurance, Labor Law, Occupational Safety, Real Estate, Torts

JOURNALS, NEWSLETTERS & OTHER PERIODICALS:
The Construction Lawyer (ABA Forum Committee on the Construction Industry).
Yearbook of Construction Articles (Wash. D.C.: Federal Publications, 1983–).

LOOSELEAFS:
AIA Building Construction Legal Citator (IL: Charles D. Spenser & Associates, 1982–).
Construction and Design Law Digest by the Natl. Inst. of Construction Law (Michie, 1984–).
Construction Industry Litigation Reporter (PA: Andrews Pub., Inc., 1984–).
Construction Industry Standards and Interpretations (U.S. Dept. of Labor, OSHA, 1980–).
Construction Labor Report (BNA, 1955–).
Construction Law (Matthew Bender, 1986–).
Construction Litigation Reporter (CA: Litigation Research Group).
Forms and Agreements for Architects, Engineers and Contractors by A. Dib (Clark
    Boardman, 1976–).
Legal Handbook for Architects, Engieers and Contractors (Clark Boardman, 1985–).

DIRECTORY & DICTIONARIES:
Construction Glossary by J. Stein (Wiley, 1981).
Dictionary of Building, 3d ed. by J. Scott (Wiley, 1984).
Register of Expert Witnesses in the Construction Industry (ABA Sect. of Litigation,
    Comm. on Const. Litigation, 1984).

TREATISES:
Architect and Engineer Liability: Claims against Design Professional (Wiley, 1987).
Architects and Engineers, 2d ed. by J. Acret (Shepard's 1984).
The Architect's Guide to Law and Practice by B. Greenstreet (Van Nostrand Reinhold,
    1984).
The BOCA Basic/National Building Code, 9th ed. (IL: Building Officials and Code
    Administrators Intl., 1983).
Construction and Design Law by the Natl. Inst. of Construction Law (Michie, 1984).

Construction and Development Financing: Law, Practice, Forms by R. Harris (Warren, Gorham & Lamont, 1982).

Construction Claims (Practicing Law Institute, 1984).

Construction Claims and Liability by M. Simon (Wiley, 1989).

Construction Contract Documents for Private Work (ABA Forum Committee on the Construction Industry, 1981).

Construction Contracts (Practicing Law Institute, 1984).

Construction Engineer's Form Book by E. Fisk, (Wiley, 1981).

Construction Failures: Legal and Engineering Perspectives: Stouffer's Greenway Plaza Hotel (ABA Forum Committee on the Construction Industry, 1983).

Construction Industry Formbook by R. Cushman et al. (Shepard's, 1979).

Construction Industry Labor Relations 1982 (Practicing Law Institute, 1982).

Construction Law: Claims & Liability by M. Simon (Butler, NJ: Arlyse Enterprises).

Construction Litigation, R. Cushman, ed. (Practicing Law Institute, 1981).

Construction Litigation: Representing the Owner, R. Cushman, ed. (Wiley, 1984).

Construction Litigator: Representing the Contractor, R. Cushman, ed. (Wiley, 1986).

Construction Schedules by M. Callahan & H. Hohns (Michie, 1983).

Discovery in Construction Litigation 2d ed. by M. Callahan & B. Bramble (Michie, 1987).

Engineering Aspects of Product Liability by V. Colangelo (Metals Park, OH: American Society for Metals, 1981).

Engineering Evidence by M. Schwartz (Shepard's, 1981).

Engineering Law, Design Liability, and Professional Ethics by R. Morton (CA: Professional Pubs., 1983).

Handbook of Construction Law and Claims by I. Richter (Reston Pub., 1982).

Handbook of Construction Law, 2d, with Forms by S. Faber (Los Angeles: Legabooks, 1984).

McGraw-Hill Construction Business Handbook, 2d ed., R. Cushman, ed. (McGraw-Hill, 1985).

Revocation of Professional Licenses by Government Agencies (Architects) by W. Morris (Michie, 1984).

Selected Problems of Construction Law: International Approach (London: Sweet & Maxwell, 1983).

Uniform Building Code Standards (Whittier, CA: Int'n. Conf. of Building Officials, 1982).

ENCYCLOPEDIAS: AMERICAN JURISPRUDENCE 2D (Am Jur 2d)

Check the following topics in the *General Index* volumes for Am Jur 2d:

Architects	Engineers
Bids and Bidding	Fidelity Bonds
Building and Construction	Independent Contractor
Building Regulations	Plans and Specifications
Contractors' Bonds	Public Works
Contracts	Suretyship

CORPUS JURIS SECUNDUM (CJS)

Check the following topics in the *General Index* volumes for CJS:

Architects	Impossibility of
Bids and Bidding	Performance
Bonds	Mechanics' Liens
Building and Construction	Plans and Specifications
Contractors	Principal and Surety
Engineers	Public Works
	Subcontractors

DIGESTS: CASE SEARCH IN WEST DIGESTS BY KEY TOPIC
In the *Descriptive Word Index* of the West digests, look for key topics and numbers under the following subject headings:

Arbitration	Indemnity
Architects	Mechanics' Lien
Bids and Bidding	Plans
Bonds	Prinicpal and Surety
Building and Construction	Public Contracts
Contractors	Subcontractors
Engineers	Torts
Impossibility of Performance	

ALR: ANNOTATIONS
Check the index volumes for ALR, ALR2d, ALR3d, ALR4th, and ALR Fed for annotations under the following subject headings:

Architects	Engineers
Bids and Bidding	Plans and Designs
Building	Principal and Surety
Construction	Specific Performance
Contractor	Subcontractors

PERIODICALS: CURRENT LAW INDEX (CLI) & LEGAL RESOURCE INDEX (LRI)
In the CLI and LRI, look for references to periodical literature under the following subject headings:

Building	Specific Performance
Construction Industry	Subcontractors
Negligence	Suretyship and Guaranty

INDEX TO LEGAL PERIODICALS (ILP)
In the ILP, look for references to legal periodical literature under the following subject headings:

Agency	Bonds
Arbitration	Construction
Architects and Engineers	Suretyship

ARCHIVES: See Indians, Legal History

ARGENTINA

SEE ALSO: International Law, Latin America, United Nations

RESEARCH GUIDES & BIBLIOGRAPHIES: *A Guide to the Law and Literature of Argentina, 1917–1947* by H. Clagett (Library of Congress, 1948).
A Guide to the Official Publications of . . . Argentina (Library of Congress, 1944).

CONSTITUTION: "Argentina" by F. Roth in *Constitutions of the Countries of the World* by A. Blaustein & G. Flanz (Oceana, 1983).

TREATISES & LOOSELEAFS: *The Argentine Supreme Court: The Court of Constitutional Guarantees* by G. Bidart, W. Brisk, transl. (Rothman, 1982).

Business Operations in Argentina by A. Atchabahian, Tax Management Foreign
Income Portfolios, No. 253–3d (BNA, 1989–).

Capital Formation and Investment Incentives Around the World (Argentina) by
W. Diamond and D. Diamond (Matthew Bender, 1984–).

Digest of Commercial Laws of the World (Argentina), Natl. Assn. of Credit Management
(Oceana, 1977–).

Doing Business in Argentina (Price Waterhouse, 1980).

The Falkland Islands Dispute in International Law by R. Perl (Oceana, 1983).

Inflation and Indexation: Argentina, Brazil, and Israel by J. Williamson (MIT Press, 1985).

Investment Laws of the World (Argentina) (Oceana, 1981–).

Latin America . . . A Tax Tour (Argentina) (Arthur Anderson & Co., 1985).

Legal Aspects of Doing Business in Latin America (Argentina) (Practicing Law
Institute, 1980).

*Series of Statements of the Law of the OAS Member States in Matters Affecting Business:
Argentina* (Organization of American States, 1975).

Sovereignty Dispute over the Falkland Islands by L. Gustafson (Oxford Univ. Press, 1987).

Taxation in Argentina (Arthur Young Intl., 1980).

Taxation in Argentina (NY: Deloitte, Haskins & Sells, 1979).

Tax Laws of the World—Argentina (FL: Foreign Tax Law Assn.).

ARTICLES:

"Argentina: Divorce at Last?" by M. Bendersky, 26 *Journal of Family Law* 1 (1987–88).

"Argentina's System of Foreign Investments" by E. Dahl, 6 *Fordham International
Law Journal* 33 (1982).

"Argentine Compound Interest" by C. Onetto, 3 *International Financial Law Review*
28 (July, 1984).

"A Case Study in Third World Debt: Argentina" by A. De la Cruz, 22 *International
Lawyer* 643 (1988).

"Foreign Investment Under Contemporary Argentine Law" by R. Giacchino, 26
American Journal of Comparative Law 91 (1978).

"Judicial Review and Protection of Human Rights Under Military Government in Brazil
and Argentina" by M. Feinrider, 5 *Suffolk Transnational Law Journal* 171 (1981).

"Legal Memorandum: Argentina," 15 *Lawyer of the Americas* 185, 597 (1983, 1984).

"The New Argentine Antitrust Law" by G. Cabenellas, 17 *Journal of World Trade Law*
34 (1983).

"The New Technology Transfer System in Argentina" by I. Hajdenberg, 81 *Patent &
Trademark Review* 312 (1983).

"Sovereignty and Decolonization of the Malvinas (Falkland) Islands" by A. Hope, 6
Boston College International & Comparative Law Review 391 (1983).

"State of Siege and the Rule of Law in Argentina" by F. Snyder, 15 *Lawyer of the
Americas* 503 (1984).

"The Uruguayan-Argentinian Trade Co-Operation Agreement" by D. Ferrere, 18
Journal of World Trade Law 320 (1984).

ARGUMENTS OF COUNSEL: See Trial & Appellate Practice

ARIZONA

SEE ALSO: Circuit Courts (Ninth Circuit), Community Property

**RESEARCH GUIDE &
BIBLIOGRAPHY:** *Arizona Practice Materials: A Selective Annotated Bibliography* by A. Torres & C.
Elliott, 80 *Law Library Journal* 577 (1988).

Survey of Arizona State Legal and Law-Related Documents by R. Teenstra et al. (American Assn. of Law Libraries, 1984).

STATUTES & RELATED LEGISLATIVE MATERIAL:
Arizona Revised Statutes Annotated (West).
Session Laws, Arizona.
Arizona Legislative Service (West).
Arizona Capitol Times (Arizona News Service, 1982–).
Arizona Legislative Bill Drafting Manual (Legislative Council, 1983).

STATE ADMINISTRATIVE CODE:
Official Compilation Administrative Rules and Regulations.
Arizona Administrative Digest.

CASES & OPINIONS:
Arizona Reports (1866–).
Pacific Reporter (1866–).
Arizona Business Gazette (Phoenix Newspapers, 1880–).
Arizona Advance Sheets (Provo, Utah: Code Co. Law Publishers).

COURT RULES:
Arizona Rules of Court (West).

JURY INSTRUCTIONS:
Arizona Uniform Jury Instructions (Arizona State Bar, 1959).
Maricopa County Uniform Civil Jury Instructions (Arizona Weekly Gazette, 1974).
Recommended Arizona Jury Instructions (Civil and Criminal) (Arizona Supreme Court; State Bar of Arizona, 1974, 1980).

ETHICS & PROFESIONAL RESPONSIBILITY:
Ethics Opinions (State Bar of Arizona).

OPINIONS OF THE ATTORNEY GENERAL:
Opinions and Report of the Attorney General (1915–1977).
Summary of Attorney General Opinions (1980–).

JOURNALS & OTHER PERIODICALS:
Arizona Bar Briefs (1953–).
Arizona Bar Journal (1965–).

TREATISES, LOOSELEAFS & OTHER MONOGRAPHS:
Arizona Agency Handbook (Office of the Attorney General, 1981–).
Arizona Appellate Handbook by L. Haire & Ulrich (State Bar of Arizona, 1978–).
Arizona Civil Remedies by M. Clarke (State Bar of Arizona, 1982).
Arizona Civil Trial Manual, 7th ed. by C. Smith (Arizona Law Institute, 1983).
Arizona Civil Trial Practice by C. Smith (West, 1986).
Arizona Courtroom Evidence Manual, 2d ed. C. McClennen, ed. (State Bar of Arizona, 1988–).
Arizona Land Use Law by D. Jorden & M. House (State Bar of Arizona, 1988).
Arizona Law of Evidence, 2d ed. by M. Udall (West, 1982).
The Arizona Law of Medical Malpractice by R. Stephan (Phoenix: Medilex Co., 1983).
Arizona Legal Forms: Domestic Relations by J. Wolf (West, 1988).
Arizona Manual for Courts of Limited Jurisdiction by C. Smith (Administrative Director of Courts, 1981).

Arizona Practice Manual, D. Nix, ed. (State Bar of Arizona).
Arizona Probate by T. Wiley (Bancroft-Whitney, 1980–).
Arizona Probate Code Practice Manual by R. Effland (State Bar of Arizona, 1980).
Arizona Real Estate Practice, 2d ed., C. Rambo, ed. (State Bar of Arizona, 1982–).
Arizona State Tax Handbook (Joint Legislative Budget Committee, 1983).
Arizona Statutory Time Limitations (Butterworths, 1982–).
Arizona Will Drafting Manual, 3d ed. by C. Smith (Arizona Law Institute, 1982).
Constitutional Government in Arizona, 6th ed. by B. Mason (Cleber Pub. Co., 1979).
Secured Transactions in Arizona by W. Boyd (Arizona Law Institute, 1983).
Summary of Arizona Community Property Law, 6th ed., by C. Smith (Arizona Law Institute, 1981).

DIGESTS & CITATOR: *Pacific Digest* (West).
Arizona Digest (West).
Arizona Shepard's Citations.

ARKANSAS

SEE ALSO: Circuit Courts (Eighth Circuit)

LEGAL BIBLIOGRAPHY *Arkansas Legal Bibliography: Documents and Selected Commercial Titles* by L. Foster (American Association of Law Libraries, 1988).
"Arkansas Practice Materials: A Selective Annotated Bibliography" by K. Fitzhugh, 81 *Law Library Journal* 277 (1989).

STATUTES & RELATED
STATUTORY MATERIAL: *Acts of Arkansas.*
Arkansas Advance Legislative Service (Michie).
Arkansas Code of 1987 Annotated (Michie).
Arkansas Legislative Digest (1939–).
Arkansas Legislative Report (Leg. Reports, Inc., 1983–).
Interim Legislative Reporting Service (1980–).

STATE ADMINISTRATIVE
CODE: *Arkansas Register* (Secretary of State, 1977–).
Regulations, Bulletins, and Directives of the Arkansas Insurance Department (NY: Natl. Insurance Law Service, 1967–).

CASES & OPINIONS: *Arkansas Reports* (1837–).
South Western Reporter (1885–).
Arkansas Appellate Reports (1981–).

COURT RULES: *Arkansas Code of 1987 Annotated: Court Rules.*
Local Court Rules (Ark. Bar Assn., 1983–).

JURY INSTRUCTIONS: *Arkansas Model Criminal Jury Instructions,* (Michie, 1979–).
Arkansas Model Jury Instructions: Civil, 2d ed. (West, 1974).

OPINIONS OF THE
ATTORNEY GENERAL: *Arkansas Register* (1977–).
Digest of Decisions (Office of the Attorney General).

**JOURNALS, OTHER
PERIODICALS &
ANNUALS:**
Annual Arkansas Natural Resources Law Institute (Ark. Natural Resources Institute, 1976–).
Arkansas Bar Association Newsbulletin (1976–).
Arkansas Capitol Report (Chamber of Commerce).
Arkansas Law Letter (Ark. Law Letter, Inc., 1985–).
Arkansas Lawyer (Ark. Bar Assn., 1967–).
The ATLA Docket (Ark. Trial Lawyers Assn., 1982–).
Friends of the Court: Newsletter of the Arkansas Judicial Department (1982–).

**TREATISES, LOOSELEAFS
& OTHER MONOGRAPHS:**
Arkansas Civil Practice and Procedure by D. Newbern (Harrison, 1985).
Arkansas Corporation System (Ark. Bar Assn., 1988–).
Arkansas Debtor-Creditor Relations System, 2d ed. by G. Pasvogel (Ark. Bar Assn., 1988–).
Arkansas Domestic Relations System (Ark. Inst. Cont. Ed., 1981–).
Arkansas Form Book by R. Wright (Ark. Bar Assn., 1988–).
Arkansas Law of Damages by H. Brill (Harrison, 1984).
Arkansas, Louisiana and Mississippi Legal Directory (Los Angeles: Legal Directories
Publ. Co., 1955–).
Arkansas Probate System (Ark. Inst. Cont. Ed., 1977–).
Arkansas Rules of Evidence by M. Gitelman (M & M Press, 1988–).
Arkansas Senior Citizens' Handbook: A Legal Guide, 3d ed. (Ark. Bar Assn., 1984).
Arkansas Water Law by P. Mays (Ark. Soil and Water Conservation Comm'n., 1981).
Arkansas Wills and Trusts System by R. Wilkins (Ark. Bar Assn., 1978).
Arkansas Workers' Compensation (Ark. Inst. Cont. Ed., 1978–).
Arkansas Wrongful Death Actions by O. Harris (Harrison, 1984).
Criminal Law Handbook (Ark. Bar Assn., 1985–).
State and Local Taxes (Arkansas) (P–H).
A System for Advising Landowners, Farmers, Ranchers and Agribusiness by J. Looney
(Ark. Bar Assn., 1987).
Trial Handbook for Arkansas Lawyers by J. Hall (Lawyers Co–op., 1986).
*Unequal Laws unto a Savage Race: European Legal Traditions in Arkansas,
1686–1836* by M. Arnold (Univ. of Ark. Press, 1985).

DIGESTS & CITATOR:
Arkansas Advance Annotation Service (Michie, 1984–).
Arkansas Digest (West, 1937–).
South West Digest (West).
Shepard's Arkansas Citations.

ARMED CONFLICT: See War
ARMED FORCES: See Military Law
ARMENIAN GENOCIDE: See Turkey
ARMS CONTROL: See International Law, Military Law, War
ARMY: See Military Law
ARRAIGNMENT: See Criminal Law
ARREARS: See Family Law
ARREST: See Constitutional Law, Criminal Law, Immigration Law, Torts
ARSON: See Criminal Law, Insurance

ART & ENTERTAINMENT LAW

SEE ALSO:
Contracts, Employee Benefits, Intellectual Property, Labor Law, Media Law, Sports
Law

RESEARCH GUIDES &
BIBLIOGRAPHIES:

"Law and the Visual Artist: An Annotated Bibliography" by Berkowitz, 70 *Law Library Journal* 5 (1977).
"Music and the Law: A Comprehensive Bibliography" by G. Winson, 4 *Comm/Ent Law Journal* 489 (1982).
"Reference Sources for Art Law" by J. Minor 3 *Legal Reference Services Quarterly* 53 (1983).

JOURNALS, NEWSLETTERS
& OTHER PERIODICALS:

Art and the Law (Columbia Law Sch.; Volunteer Lawyers for the Arts, 1974–).
Cardozo Arts & Entertainment Law Journal (1982–).
Comm/Ent Law Journal (Hastings College of Law, 1977–).
Entertainment Law and Business by H. Orenstein & D. Guinn (Butterworth, 1989–).
The Entertainment and Sports Law Journal (Univ. of Miami School of Law; Darby Printing Co.).
The Entertainment and Sports Lawyer (ABA Forum Comm. on Entertainment).
Entertainment Law and Finance (New York Law Pub. Co., 1984–).
Entertainment Law Journal (Loyola Law School of Los Angeles).
The Journal of Arts Management and Law (Wash. D.C.)
Journal of Copyright, Entertainment & Sports Law (Tennessee Bar Assn.).
Law and the Arts (Columbia Univ. Sch. of Law, 1986–).
Loyola of Los Angeles Entertainment Law Journal (1981–).
Performing Arts Review (Law-Arts Publishers).
Publishing, Entertainment, Advertising and Allied Fields Law Quarterly (Pittsburgh, 1961/62–).
Rights Alert (White Plains).
The Working Arts (San Francisco: Bay Area Lawyers for the Arts, 1978–).

TREATISES &
LOOSELEAFS:

The Artist-Gallery Partnership by T. Crawford (NY: Amer. Council for the Arts, 1981).
Art Law by F. Feldman (Little, Brown, 1986).
Art Law in a Nutshell by L. Duboff (West, 1984).
Behind the Scenes: Practical Entertainment Law by M. Rudell (Law & Business, Inc., 1984).
Counseling Clients in the Entertainment Industry (Practicing Law Institute).
The Deskbook of Art Law by L. Duboff (Federal Pub., 1977).
Entertainment Law by T. Selz (Shepard's, 1983–).
Entertainment Law Reporter by L. Sobel (Santa Monica, CA).
Law, Ethics and the Visual Artist, J. Merryman, ed. (Matthew Bender, 1979–).
A Legal Primer on Managing Museum Collections by M. Malaro (Smithsonian Institution Press, 1985).
The Legal Representation Internationally of Clients in the Entertainment and Sports Industries (ABA Forum Comm. on Entertainment, 1986).
Lindey on Entertainment, Publishing and the Arts, 2d ed. by A. Lindey (Clark Boardman, 1980–).
Literary Rights Contracts by R. Wincor (Harcourt: Law & Business, Inc., 1980).
Museums and the Law by M. Phelan (Nashville: Amer. Assn. for State & Local History, 1982).
Museum Trusteeship by A. & P. Ullberg (Amer. Assn. of Museums, 1981).
The Performing Artist and the Law by D. Sharpe (New South Wales, Australia: Law Book Co., 1985).
Performing Arts Management and the Law by J. Taubman (Law-Arts Publishers, 1971–).
Representing Artists, Collectors, and Dealers (Practicing Law Institute, 1981).

Rights and Liabilities of Publishers, Broadcasters and Reporters by S. Metcalf (Shepard's, 1982–).

Tax Planning and Contract Negotiating Techniques for Creative Persons, Professional Athletes and Entertainers by G. Reed (Detroit: New National Publishing Co.).

The Visual Artist and the Law, H. Sandison, ed. (San Francisco: Bay Area Lawyers for the Arts, 1975).

The Writer's Legal and Business Guide (Beverly Hills Bar Assn., 1984).

ENCYCLOPEDIAS: AMERICAN JURISPRUDENCE 2D (Am Jur 2d)

Check the following topics in the *General Index* volumes for Am Jur 2d:

Art Galleries	Copyright
Art or Artist	Music and Musicians

CORPUS JURIS SECUNDUM (CJS)

Check the following topics in the *General Index* volumes for CJS:

Actors	Motion Pictures
Artists	Museums
Contracts	Music
Copyright	Theaters and Shows

DIGESTS: CASE SEARCH IN WEST DIGESTS BY KEY TOPIC

In the *Descriptive Word Index* of the West digests, look for key topics and numbers under the following subject headings:

Actors	Museums
Art	Music
Contracts	Photographs
Copyright	Theaters
Moving Pictures	

ALR: ANNOTATIONS

Check the index volumes for ALR, ALR2d, ALR3d, ALR4th, and ALR Fed for annotations under the following subject headings:

Actors and Performers	Freedom of Speech
Amusements, Exhibitions Shows	Literary and Artistic Property
Architects	Motion Pictures
Entertainers	Radio and Television

PERIODICALS: CURRENT LAW INDEX (CLI) & LEGAL RESOURCE INDEX (LRI)

In the CLI and LRI, look for references to periodical literature under the following subject headings:

Actors	Museums
Art	Performing Arts
Art Dealers	Privacy
Copyright	Publicity
Drama	Radio
Law and Literature	Theater
Motion Pictures	

INDEX TO LEGAL PERIODICALS (ILP)

In the ILP, look for references to legal periodical literature under the following subject headings:

Agency	Censorship
Authors	Contracts

Copyright   Motion Pictures
Entertainment   Museums
Freedom of Speech   Radio and Television
Law in Arts

ARTERIES: See Health & Medicine
ARTICLES OF INCORPORATION: See Corporate Law
ARTIFICIAL INSEMINATION: See Family Law, Women & the Law
ARTISTS: See Art & Entertainment, Intellectual Property
ASBESTOS: See Environmental Law, Torts
ASEAN: See Asia, Australia, Brunei, Indonesia, Malaysia, New Zealand, Philippines, Singapore, Thailand
ASHMORE AND CARTIER ISLANDS: See Australia

ASIA

SEE ALSO: Bangladesh, Brunei, Burma, Cambodia, China, Hong Kong, India, Indonesia, Japan, Korea, Laos, Malaysia, Mongolia, Nepal, Pakistan, Philippines, Singapore, Soviet Union, Sri Lanka, Taiwan, Thailand, Vietnam

RESEARCH GUIDE & BIBLIOGRAPHY: *ASEAN: A Bibliography,* P. Lim coordinator (Singapore: Institute of Southeast Asian Studies, 1984).

CONSTITUTIONS: *Constitutions of Asian Countries* by the Secretariat of the Asian African Legal Consultative Committee (India: N.M. Tripathi, Private, Ltd., 1968).
Constitutions of Nations (vol. 2, Asia), 4th ed. (Martinus Nijhoff, 1985).

TREATIES & RELATED DOCUMENTS: *Basic Documents of Asian Regional Organizations,* M. Hass (Oceana, 1974).

JOURNALS, NEWSLETTERS & OTHER PERIODICALS: *Asian Law Forum* (Northwestern Univ., Center for Urban Affairs, 1976–).
East Asian Executive Reports (Wash. D.C.: Intl. Executive Reports, Ltd., 1979–).
Far Eastern Law Review.
LAWASIA Human Rights Newsletter (Sydney, 1986–).
UCLA Pacific Basin Law Journal (UCLA School of Law, 1982–).

TREATISES & LOOSELEAFS: *Asia and the Pacific: A Tax Tour* (Arthur Anderson & Co., 1986).
A Concise Legal History of South-East Asia by M. Hooker (Clarendon Press, 1978).
Constitutionalism in Asia: Asian Views of the American Influence, L. Beer, ed. (Berkeley: Univ. of Cal. Press, 1979).
Corporate Taxation in Asia (NY: Deloitte, Haskins & Sells, 1986).
Current Legal Aspects of Doing Business in Japan and East Asia (ABA Intl. Law & Practice Sect., 1978).
Current Legal Aspects of Doing Business in the Far East (ABA Intl. Law & Practice Sect., 1972).
Digest of Commercial Laws of the World by the Natl. Assn. of Credit Management (Oceana, 1977–).
East Asia and the Law of the Sea by Choon-Ho Park (Seoul Natl. Univ. Press, 1983).

A Guide to Doing Business in the ASEAN Region: Brunei/Indonesia/Malaysia/
Philippines /Singapore/Thailand (U.S. Dept. of Commerce, Intl. Trade Admin.,
Office of Pacific Basin, 1985).

Human Rights in East Asia, by J. Hsiung (NY: Paragon House, 1985).

Introduction to the Energy Laws of Asia by G. McAfee (Hong Kong: Petroleum News
Southeast Asia; Houston: Gulf Pub. Co., 1985).

Investment Incentive Laws of the ASEAN Countries by Z Reyes (Philippines, 1978).

Law and Public Enterprise in Asia by the Intl. Law Center (Praeger, 1976).

Legal Aspects of Doing Business in Asia and the Pacific, D. Campbell, ed. (Kluwer;
West, 1985).

Legal Problems of Capital Investment and Secured Lending in the ASEAN Countries
(Practicing Law Institute, 1983).

Selected Writings on Asian Law by C. Kim (Rothman, 1982).

Taxes and Investment in Asia and the Pacific (Intl. Bureau of Fiscal Documentation,
1983–).

Tax Systems of Africa, Asia, and the Middle East by C. Platt (Gower, 1982).

ASSAULT & BATTERY: See Criminal Law, Torts

ASSEMBLY, RIGHT OF: See Civil Rights, Constitutional Law

ASSESSMENT: See Real Estate, Taxation

ASSETS: See Estate Planning

ASSIGNMENT: See Consumer Law, Contracts, Insurance

ASSIGNMENT FOR THE BENEFIT OF CREDITORS: See Bankruptcy

ASSISTANCE OF COUNSEL: See Constitutional Law, Professional Responsibility

ASSOCIATION, FREEDOM OF: See Civil Rights, Constitutional Law, Homosexuality

ASSOCIATIONS: See Corporate Law, Nonprofit Corporations, Real Estate

ASSUMPSIT: See Contracts

ASSUMPTION OF RISK: See Torts

ASTHMA: See Health & Medicine

ASTRONAUTICS: See Military Law

ASYLUM: See Health & Medicine, Immigration Law, International Law, Mental Health

ATHEIST: See Church & State

ATHLETICS: See Art & Entertainment, Sports Law

ATOMIC ENERGY: See Energy, Natural Resources, Oil & Gas, Public Utilities

ATOMIC WARFARE: See War

AT&T: See Public Utilities

ATTACHMENT: See Consumer Law, Employee Benefits, Personal Property, Trial &
Appellate Practice

ATTEMPT: See Criminal Law

ATTESTING WITNESSES: See Estate Planning

ATTORNEY: See Agency, Banking Law, Bankruptcy, Law Office Management, Legal
Education, Professional Responsibility, Trial & Appellate Practice

ATTORNEY-CLIENT PRIVILEGE: See Professional Responsibility, Trial & Appellate
Practice

ATTORNEY FEES: See Civil Rights, Professional Responsibility, Trial & Appellate
Practice

ATTRACTIVE NUISANCE: See Torts

AUCTIONS: See Animals, Contracts, Personal Property

AUDIT: See Accounting, Banking Law, Government Contracts, Taxation

AUSTRALASIA: See Bangladesh, Sri Lanka, Western Samoa

AUSTRALIA

SEE ALSO:	Antarctica, Asia, International Law, New Zealand, United Nations

**RESEARCH GUIDES &
BIBLIOGRAPHIES:**

Current Australian and New Zealand Legal Literature Index (Sydney: Law Book Co.,
   1974–).
Legal Research Materials and Methods, 2d ed. by E. Campbell (Sydney: Law Book Co.,
   1979).

CONSTITUTIONS:

The Constitution of the Commonwealth of Australia Annotated, 3d ed. by K. Ryan
   (Butterworths, 1981).
Constitutions of Dependencies and Special Sovereignties (Ashmore and Cartier
   Islands, Christmas Island, Cocos Islands, Coral Seas Islands, Norfolk Island) by A.
   Blaustein (Oceana, 1983).

**STATUTES & RELATED
LAWS:**

Acts of the Australian Parliament.
Commonwealth Acts.
Statutory Rules, Consolidation.

CASES:

Australian Argus Law Reports (1895–).
Australian Law Reports (1973–).
Australian Tax Cases (CCH).
Commonwealth Law Reports (1903–).
Federal Law Reports (1956–).

**TREATIES & RELATED
AGREEMENTS:**

Australia Treaty Series (Canberra: Dept. of External Affairs, (1948–).
"Australia-United States: Agreement Relating to Cooperation on Antitrust Matters," 21
   International Legal Materials 702 (1982).

**JOURNALS, NEWSLETTERS
& OTHER PERIODICALS:**

Australia and New Zealand Journal of Criminology.
Australian International Law News (1983–).
Australian Tax Review (1971–).
Banking Law Journal (1889–).
Law Institute Journal of Victoria (1927–).
Law Society Journal.
Melbourne University Law Review (1959–).
Sydney Law Review (1953–).
University of Tasmania Law Review (1958–).

DICTIONARY;

The Australian Legal Dictionary by S. Marantelli (Melbourne: Hargreen, 1980).

**TREATISES &
LOOSELEAFS:**

Aborigines and the Law: A Digest by J. McCorquodale (Canberra, Australia: Aboriginal
   Studies Press, 1987).
Australian and South Pacific Law: Structure and Legal Materials by I. Kavass (Hein,
   1983).
Australian Company Law Library (CCH, 1972–).

Australian Federal Tax Reports (CCH, 1969–).
Australian Income Tax Guide (CCH, 1969–).
Australian Income Tax Guide: Control Edition (CCH, 1981–).
Australian Patent Law by C. Bannon (Butterworths, 1984).
Australian Securities Law Reports (CCH, 1972–).
Australian Trade Practices Reports (CCH, 1974–).
Capital Formation and Investment Incentives Around the World (Australia) by W. Diamond & D. Diamond (Matthew Bender, 1984–).
Companies and Securities Leglislation Service (Victorian Govt. Bookshop, 1985–).
Copyright Law in Australia . . . by J. Sterling (Sydney: Legal Books, 1981).
Digest of Commercial Laws of the World (Australia) (Natl. Assn. of Credit Management; Oceana, 1977–).
Foreign Investment Law in Australia by D. Flint (Sydnew: Law Book Co., 1985).
Franchising in Australia, A Legal Guide by D. Shannon (Sydney: Law Book Co., 1982).
Guidebook to Environmental Planning Practice in New South Wales by W. Holt (CCH Australia, Ltd., 1980).
Information Guide: Doing Business in Australia (Price Waterhouse).
Labour Law in Australia by E. Sykes (Butterworths, 1980—).
Legal Aspects of Doing Business with Australia (Practicing Law Institute, 1984).
Meek's Australian Bankruptcy Law and Procedure by E. & H. McDonald (Sydney; Law Book Co., 1977).
Tax Laws of the World—Australia (FL: Foreign Tax Law Assn.).

ARTICLES:

"The Australian Constitution: The External Affairs Power and Federalism" by P. Van Son, 12 *Case Western International Law Journal* 46 (1982).
"Lawyers and Legal Culture in Australia" by R. Tomasic, 7 *International Journal of the Sociology of Law* 417 (1979).
"United States Investment in Australia" by J. Browne, 21 *International Lawyer* 71 (1987).

DIGESTS & CITATOR:

Australia Legal Monthly Digest (1947–).
Australian Case Citator (1983–).
Australian Current Digest.
Australian Digest (1825–).

AUSTRIA

SEE ALSO:

Europe, International Law, United Nations

**RESEARCH GUIDE &
BIBLIOGRAPHY:**

"A Guide to Austrian Legal Research" by J. Fox, 80 *Law Library Journal* 99 (1988).

**TREATISES &
LOOSELEAFS:**

The Austrian Banking System under the 1979 Statute (Library of Congress, 1980).
Austrian Business Law by K. Heller (Kluwer, 1984).
The Austrian Law on Companies with Limited Liability, J. Goldberg, ed. (Kluwer, 1985).
The Austrian Law on Extradition and Mutual Assistance in Criminal Matters, by E. Palmer (Library of Congress, 1983).
Business Operations in Austria by H. Kotrnoch, Tax Management Foreign Income Portfolios, No. 222–4th (BNA, 1977).
Capital Formation and Investment Incentives Around the World (Austria) by W. Diamond & D. Diamond (Matthew Bender, 1984–).
Digest of Commercial Laws of the World (Austria) by the Natl. Assn. of Credit Management (Oceana, 1977–).

A Guide to Commercial Arbitration in Austria by W. Melis (Vienna: Federal Economic Chamber, 1983).
Information Guide, Doing Business in Austria (Price Waterhouse).
Law and Taxation in Germany, Austria and Switzerland: Catalogue of a Basic Library (Munich: Schweitzer Sortiment, 1985).
An Outline of Austrian Constitutional Law by K. Heller (Vienna: Verfassungsgerichtshof, 1983).
Taxation of Intercompany Transactions in Selected Countries in Europe and USA (Kluwer, 1979).
Tax Laws of the World—Austria (FL: Foreign Tax Law Assn., 1983).

ARTICLES:
"Austria: Legal Education" by C. Schreuer, 5 *Comparative Law Yearbook* 17 (1981).
"The Austrian Codification of Conflicts Law" by E. Palmer, 28 *American Journal of Comparative Law* 197 (1980).
"The 1984 Law Amending the Austrian Patent Law" by O. Leberl, 25 *Ind. Prop.* 126 (1986).
"The 1986 Amendment to the Austrian Banking Act" by C. Dorda, 1 *Butterworths Journal of International Banking and Financial Law* 28 (no. 3, 1986).
"Review of Bankruptcy Laws . . . Austria" by L. Kaltenback, 8 *International Business Lawyer* 80 (1980).
"Service of Process Abroad (Austria)" by Baeck, 4 *International Lawyer* 55 (1970).

AUTHENTICATION: See Trial & Appellate Practice
AUTHORITY: See Agency, Contracts
AUTHORS: See Art & Entertainment, Intellectual Property, Media Law
AUTISTIC: See Handicapped & the Law
AUTOMOBILE: See Alcohol, Business Law, Consumer Law, Contracts, Criminal Law, Personal Property, Torts, Transportation
AUTOPSY: Death, Forensic Science, Health & Medicine
AVERAGE: See Maritime Law
AVIATION: See Air & Aviation, Torts, Transportation
AVOIDABLE CONSEQUENCES: See Torts
AWARD: See Labor Law, Trial & Appellate Practice

BACK PAY: See Employee Benefits, Labor Law
BAD FAITH: See Contracts, Equity, Insurance
BAGGAGE: See Personal Property

BAHAMAS

SEE ALSO: Caribbean, International Law, Latin America, United Nations

STATUTES: *The Bahamas Consolidated Index of Statutes. . .* by the Fac. of Law Lib., Univ. of the West Indies, Barbados (Gaunt, 1985).

TREATISES: *Caribbean Basin: A Tax Tour* (Bahamas) (Arthur Anderson & Co., 1985).
Information Guide, Doing Business in the Bahamas (Price Waterhouse).
The Monetary and Financial System of the Bahamas by R. Ramsaran (Jamaica: Univ. of the West Indies, 1984).

Tax Havens Encyclopedia by B. Spitz (Butterworths, 1975–).
West Indian Constitutions: Post Independence Reform (Bahamas) by F. Phillips
(Oceana, 1985).

ARTICLES: "Immovable Property Act, 1981 of the Bahamas" by J. Dyer, 19 *Comparative Journal
Review* 123 (1982).

BAHRAIN

SEE ALSO: International Law, Islam, Middle East, United Nations

**RESEARCH GUIDE
BIBLIOGRAPHY:**   *Bahrain* by P. Unwin (Clio Press, 1984).

**TREATISES &
LOOSELEAFS:**   *Capital Formation and Investment Incentives Around the World* (Bahrain) by W.
Diamond & D. Diamond (Matthew Bender, 1984–).
Commercial Laws of the Middle East (Bahrain) by A. Keesee (Oceana, 1980–).
Information Guide: Doing Business in Bahrain (Price Waterhouse).
Tax Laws of the World—Bahrain (FL: Foreign Tax Law Assn.).

BAIL: See Constitutional Law, Criminal Law
BAILMENT: See Consumer Law, Contracts, Personal Property
BALLOTS: See Education Law, Election, Labor Law

BANGLADESH

SEE ALSO: Asia, India, International Law, Islam, Pakistan, United Nations

CONSTITUTION: "Bangladesh" in *Constitutions of the Countries of the World* by A. Blaustein & G. Flanz
(Oceana, 1983).

**TREATISES &
LOOSELEAFS:**   *Asia and the Pacific: A Tax Tour* (Bangladesh) (Arthur Anderson & Co., 1986).
Bangladesh Public Administration and Policy by R. LaPorte (Bangladesh Books Intl.
Ltd.).
Copyright Law in Bangladesh by G. Rahman (Dacca: Natl. Book Centre, 1979).
Fiscal Policy and Tax Structure in Australasia (Bangladesh) (Amsterdam: Intl. Bureau
of Fiscal Documentation, 1978).
Income Taxation and Foreign Investment in Developing Countries (Bangladesh) by
M. Dominic (Amsterdam: Intl. Bureau of Fiscal Documentation, 1980).
Interpersonal Conflict of Laws in India, Pakistan and Bangladesh by D. Pearl
(London: Stevens, 1981).
Pre-Emption Laws in Bangladesh by S. Rahman (Dhaka: Ain-Grantha Prokashak, 1984).
*Principles of Muhammaden Law: With Exhaustive Up-to-date Caselaw of Bangladesh,
Pakistan, and India* (Dacca: Dacca Law Reports, 1984).
Summary of Taxation Rules in Bangladesh (Dacca: Metropolitan Chamber of
Commerce and Industry, 1982).
Taxes and Investment in Asia and the Pacific (Bangladesh) (Amsterdam: Intl. Bureau
of Fiscal Documentation, 1983–).

ARTICLES:
"Bangladesh (Human Rights in the World)," *International Commission of Jurists Review* 3 (Dec., 1986).
"Self-Determination Outside the Colonial Context: The Birth of Bangladesh in Retrospect" by V. Nanda, 1 *Houston Journal of International Law* 71 (1979).
"Tribals in the Chittagong Hill Tracts of Bangladesh," *International Commission of Jurists Review* 2 (Dec., 1985).

BANKING LAW

SEE ALSO:
Accounting, Antitrust Law, Bankruptcy, Cayman Islands, Consumer Law, Corporate Law, Economics, Estate Planning, International Law, Islam, Securities Law, Switzerland, Uniform Commercial Code

JOURNALS, NEWSLETTERS, & OTHER PERIODICALS:
The Banking Law Journal (Warren, Gorham & Lamont, 1889–).
The Banking Law Journal Digest (Warren, Gorham & Lamont, 1982–).
Banking Law Review (N.Y.: Faulkner and Gray, Inc., 1988–).
Bank Tax Report (Warren, Gorham & Lamont).
Butterworths Journal of International Banking and Financial Law.
Federal Home Loan Bank Board Journal.
Federal Reserve Bulletin (Board of Governors of the Federal Reserve System, 1915–).
Financial Services Law Report (Leader Pubs.).
Journal of International Banking (Oxford: ESC Pub., 1986–).

DIRECTORIES:
American Bank Attorneys (Capron Pub. Corp.).
Rand McNally International Bankers Directory (1968–).

LOOSELEAFS:
Accounting for Banks by J. Koltveit (Matthew Bender, 1982–).
Annotated Manual of Statutes and Regulations, 4th ed. (U.S. Fed. Home Loan Bank Board; GPO, 1980–).
Asset Based Financing, H. Ruda, ed. (Matthew Bender, 1985–).
Bank Holding Company Supervision Manual (Board of Governors of the Federal Reserve System, 1981–).
Banking Law by F. Solomon (Matthew Bender, 1981–).
Banking Law Manual by J. Norton (Matthew Bender, 1983–).
Bank Internal Auditing Manual by A. Ciliberti (Warren, Gorham & Lamont, 1984–).
Bank Officer's Handbook of Commercial Banking Law, 5th ed. by F. Beutel (Warren, Gorham & Lamont, 1982–).
Checks, Drafts and Notes by J. Reitman (Matthew Bender, 1984–).
Complying with Regulation E (WI: Professional Education Systems, Inc., 1980–).
Comptroller's Handbook for National Bank Examiners (U.S. Comptroller of the Currency, 1977–).
Comptroller's Handbook for National Trust Examiners (U.S. Comptroller of the Currency, 1976–).
Comptroller's Manual for National Banks (U.S. Comptroller of the Currency, 1979–).
Control of Banking (Prentice-Hall, 1962–).
Credit Union Guide (Prentice-Hall, 1971–).
Federal Bank Holding Company Law by P. Heller (Law Journal Seminars-Press, 1986–).
Federal Banking Law Reports (CCH, 1914–).
Federal Income Taxation of Banks and Financial Institutions, 5th ed. (Warren, Gorham & Lamont, 1978–).

Federal Regulation of Depository Institutions by M. Cobb (Warren, Gorham & Lamont, 1983–).

Federal Reserve Regulatory Service (Board of Governors of the Federal Reserve System).

Loan Documentation Handbook (Chicago: Continental Bank Educational Services Div., 1982–).

Manual of Laws Affecting Credit Unions (U.S. Natl. Credit Union Admin.; GPO, 1978–).

Modern Banking Checklists, 3d ed. by J. Cusnet (Warren, Gorham & Lamont, 1981–).

National Credit Union Administration Rules and Regulations (U.S. Natl. Credit Union Admin.; GPO, 1980–).

Regulation E: Comprehensive Compliance Manual by W. O'Connor (American Bankers Assn., 1982–).

Savings Institutions: Mergers, Acquisitions and Conversions by J. Williams (N.Y. Law Pub. Co., 1988–).

Taxation of Financial Institutions by H. Schmidt (Matthew Bender, 1983–).

Transnational Economic and Monetary Law by L. Lazar (Oceana, 1978–).

Washington Financial Reports (BNA, 1965–)

TREATISES:

Banking and Financial Institutions in a Nutshell by W. Lovett (West, 1988).

Brady on Bank Checks, 5th ed. by H. Bailey (Warren, Gorham & Lamont, 1979).

Encyclopedia of Banking and Finance, 8th ed. by G. Munn (Boston: Bankers Pub., 1983).

The Law of Bank Deposits, Collections and Credit Cards by B. Clark (Warren, Gorham & Lamont, 1985).

The Law of Electronic Fund Transfer Systems, 2nd ed. by D. Baker (Warren, Gorham & Lamont, 1988).

The Law of Letters of Credit by J. Dolan (Warren, Gorham & Lamont, 1984).

Michie on Banks and Banking (Michie, 1955).

Papers of the Federal Reserve System (Univ. Pubs. of America) (microfilm).

The Regulation of Money Managers by T. Frankel (Little, Brown, 1978).

Resource Materials: Banking and Commercial Lending Law (ALI–ABA Comm. on Cont. Prof. Ed., 1980).

ENCYCLOPEDIAS:

AMERICAN JURISPRUDENCE 2D (Am Jur 2d)

Check the following topics in the *General Index* volumes for Am Jur 2d:

Accommodation Party	Federal Savings and Loan
Banks	Associations
Bills and Notes	Indorsement
Cashiers' Checks	Interest and Usury
Certified Checks	Loans
Checks	National Banks
Federal Reserve Bank	

CORPUS JURIS SECUNDUM (CJS)

Check the following topics in the *General Index* volumes for CJS:

Accommodation Paper	Deposits
Banks and Banking	Federal Deposit Insurance
Bills and Notes	Act
Branch Banks	Federal Reserve Banks
Building and Loan	Federal Savings and Loan
Associations	Indorsements
Certificates of Deposit	Interest
Credit	Loans

Money
National Banks
Negotiable Instruments
Reserves

United States Comptroller
of the Currency
Usury

DIGESTS:

CASE SEARCH IN WEST DIGESTS BY KEY TOPIC
In the *Descriptive Word Index* of the West digests, look for key topics and numbers under the following subject headings:

Accommodation Paper
Account
Bankruptcy
Banks and Banking
Bills and Notes
Branch Banks
Building and Loan
    Associations
Certificates of Deposit
Consumer Protection
Credit
Debtor and Creditor
Deposits

Federal Deposit Insurance
    Act
Federal Reserve Banks
Federal Savings and Loan
Indorsements
Interest
Loans
Money
National Banks
Negotiable Instruments
Reserves
Signatures
Usury

ALR:

ANNOTATIONS
Check the index volumes for ALR, ALR2d, ALR3d, ALR4th, and ALR Fed for annotations under the following subject headings:

Banks and Banking
Bills and Notes
Bonds
Certificates of Deposit
Checks
Consumer Credit
Credit
Debtors and Creditors
Default
Escrow
Fraud

Holders
Indorsement
Interest
Joint Bank Accounts
Loans
Money
National Banks
Safety-Deposit Boxes
Savings Account
Truth in Lending
Usury

PERIODICALS:

CURRENT LAW INDEX (CLI) & LEGAL RESOURCE INDEX (LRI)
In the CLI and LRI, look for references to periodical literature under the following subject headings:

Bank Accounts
Banks and Banking
Building and Loan
    Associations
Checks
Credit
Debtor
Deposit Banking
Deregulation
Development Banks
Drafts

Finance Charges
Financial Institutions
Independent Retirement
    Accounts
Interest and Usury
Loans
Money
Mortgage Loans
NOW Accounts
Savings

INDEX TO LEGAL PERIODICALS (ILP)
In the ILP, look for references to legal periodical literature under the following subject headings:

Attachment	Fraud
Banks and Banking	Interest
Bonds	Letters of Credit
Checks	Loans
Credit	Mortgages
Debtor and Creditor	Negotiable Instruments
Electronic Funds Transfer	Trust and Trustees
Foreign Exchange	

BANKRUPTCY

SEE ALSO: Banking Law, Corporate Law, Consumer Law, Uniform Commercial Code

RESEARCH GUIDES &
BIBLIOGRAPHIES: "Bankruptcy Reform Act Bibliography Update" by C. Miller & M. Taylor, 87 *Commercial Law Journal* 38 (1982).
The Bankruptcy Reform Act of 1978: Analysis, Legislative History and Selected Bibliography by M. Voges & K. Shimpock (Austin: Univ. of Texas Tarlton Law Lib., 1981).
Doing Research in Federal Bankruptcy Law by J. Jagelski (Library of Congress, 1978).

CASES: *Bankruptcy Court Decisions,* N. Blair, ed. (Corporate Reorganization Reporter—CRR, 1974–).
Bankruptcy Law Reports (CCH, 1929–).
Collier Bankruptcy Cases, Second Series (Matthew Bender, 1979–).
National Bankruptcy Reporter (PA: Andrews Pubs., 1972–).
West's Bankruptcy Reporter (1980–).
West's Bankruptcy Digest (West, 1988–).

JOURNALS, NEWSLETTERS
& OTHER PERIODICALS: *American Bankruptcy Law Journal* (Natl. Conference of Bankruptcy Judges, 1927–).
Annual Survey of Bankruptcy Law, W. Norton, ed. (Callaghan, 1979–).
Bankruptcy Bar Bulletin (NY: Bankruptcy Lawyers Bar Assn.).
Bankruptcy Bar Letter (Warren, Gorham & Lamont).
Bankruptcy Developments Journal (Emory Univ. Sch. of Law, 1984–).
The Bankruptcy Strategist (Leader Pubs., 1986–).
Norton Bankruptcy Law Adviser, W. Norton, ed. (Callaghan, 1983–).

DIRECTORY: *The Directory of Bankruptcy Attorneys,* L. LoPucki, ed. (Prentice-Hall Law & Business, 1986).

LOOSELEAFS: *Bankruptcy* by J. Lee (Lawyers Co-op, 1981–).
Bankruptcy by R. Ginsberg (Prentice-Hall, 1985–).
Bankruptcy and Insolvency: Tax Aspects and Procedure by W. Tatlock (Tax Management, Inc., 1985–).
"Bankruptcy Fee Awards" in the *Attorney Fee Awards Reporter* (Prentice-Hall Law & Business).
Bankruptcy Law Fundamentals by R. Aaron (Clark Boardman, 1984–).

Bankruptcy Law Practice System by W. Scott (Michie, 1982–).
Bankruptcy Law Practice System for Federal Exemption States by S. Scott (Michie, 1982–).
Bankruptcy Practice for the General Practitioner by W. Drake & A. Mullins
    (Shepard's, 1980–).
Bankruptcy Practice Handbook by R. Williams (Callaghan, 1983–).
Bankruptcy Rules by J. Patchan (Clark Boardman, 1984–).
Bankruptcy Service, L.Ed., E. Barbre & J. Perovich, eds. (Lawyers Co-op., 1979–).
Capital Changes Reporter (CCH, 1963–).
Chapter 11 Reorganizations by J. Anderson (Shepard's, 1983–).
Chapter 13 Practice and Procedure by W. Drake & J. Morris (Shepard's, 1983–).
Collier Bankruptcy Exemption Guide, L. King, ed. (Matthew Bender, 1982–).
Collier Bankruptcy Manual, 3d ed by L. King et al. (Matthew Bender, 1979–).
Collier Bankruptcy Practice Guide, A. Herzog & L. King, eds. (Matthew Bender, 1981–).
Collier Forms Manual, 3d ed by A. King & A. Moller (Matthew Bender, 1979–).
Collier on Bankruptcy, 15th ed., L. King, ed. (Matthew Bender, 1979–).
Creditor's Rights in Bankruptcy by P. Murphy (Shepard's, 1980–).
Dalhuisen on International Insolvency and Bankruptcy by J. Dalhuisen (Matthew
    Bender, 1980–).
Federal Rules of Bankruptcy by J. Patchan (Clark Boardman, 1984–).
Federal Tax Aspects of Bankruptcy by C. McQueen & J. Crestol (Shepard's, 1984–).
Herzog's Bankruptcy Forms and Practice, 7th ed. by A. Herzog et al. (Clark
    Boardman, 1984–).
Norton Bankruptcy Law and Practice by W. Norton (Callaghan, 1981–).

TREATISES:

Bankruptcy and Insolvency Accounting by G. Newton (Wiley, 1981).
Bankruptcy in United States History by C. Warren (Harvard Univ. Press, 1935).
Bankruptcy Law Handbook by R. Aaron (Clark Boardman, 1985).
Bankruptcy Law Manual by B. Weintraub & A. Resnick (Warren, Gorham & Lamont,
    1980).
Bankruptcy Litigation Institute, Strategies for the New Law (Law & Business, Inc., 1981).
Bankruptcy Manual by J. Carr (Amer. Bankers Assn., 1980).
Bankruptcy Practice and Procedure (Practicing Law Institute, 1984).
Bankruptcy Reorganization (Law & Business, Inc. 1983).
Business Opportunities from Corporate Bankruptcies by R. Morrison (Wiley, 1985).
Business Reorganizations under the Bankruptcy Code (ALI-ABA Comm. on Cont.
    Prof. Ed., 1985).
Chapter 11 Business Reorganizations (Practicing Law Institute, 1983).
Chapter 13 Practice and Procedure by H. Drake & J. Morris (Shepard's, 1983).
Collier Handbook for Trustees and Debtors-in-Possession by I. Sulmeyer et al.
    (Matthew Bender, 1985).
Consumer Bankruptcy Law and Practice by H. Sommer (Boston: Natl. Consumer Law
    Center, 1982).
Consumer Bankruptcy Manual by A. Cohen & M. Miller (Warren, Gorham & Lamont,
    1985).
Cowans Bankruptcy Law and Practice by D. Cowans (West, 1986).
Debtor-Creditor Law in a Nutshell, 3d ed. by D. Epstein (West, 1985).
Debtors' and Creditors' Rights by J. Moore (Matthew Bender, 1979).
ERISA and Bankruptcy (Practicing Law Institute, 1983).
Purchase and Sale of Assets in Bankruptcy Cases by R. Tilton (Wiley, 1984).
Real Estate Bankruptcies and Workouts (ABA Section of Real Property, Probate, and
    Trust Law, 1983).
Strategies for Creditors in Bankruptcy Proceedings by L. LoPucki (Little, Brown,
    1985).

SHEPARD'S: *Shepard's Bankruptcy Citations.*

ENCYCLOPEDIAS: AMERICAN JURISPRUDENCE 2D (Am Jur 2d)
Check the following topics in the *General Index* volumes for Am Jur 2d:

Assignment for Benefit of Creditors	Debts
	Exemptions
Bankruptcy	Fraudulent Conveyances
Composition with Creditors	Insolvency
	Receivers
Creditors' Bills	

CORPUS JURIS SECUNDUM (CJS)
Check the following topics in the *General Index* volumes for CJS:

Assignment for Benefit of Creditors	Indebtedness
	Insolvency
Bankruptcy	Receivers
Composition with Creditors	Release
Creditors	Secured Transactions
Exemptions	Security
Fraudulent Conveyances	Vendor's Lien

DIGESTS: CASE SEARCH IN WEST DIGESTS BY KEY TOPIC
In the *Descriptive Word Index* of the West digests, look for key topics and numbers under the following subject headings:

Account	Fraudulent Conveyances
Assignment for Benefit of Creditors	Indebtedness
	Insolvency
Bankruptcy	Mortgages
Composition with Creditors	Receivers
	Release
Creditors	Secured Transactions
Exemptions	

ALR: ANNOTATIONS
Check the index volumes for ALR, ALR2d, ALR3d, ALR4th, and ALR Fed for annotations under the following subject headings:

Assets	Debtors and Creditors
Assignment for Benefit of Creditors	Fraud
	Receivers
Bankruptcy and Insolvency	

PERIODICALS: CURRENT LAW INDEX (CLI) & LEGAL RESOURCE INDEX (LRI)
In the CLI and LRI, look for references to periodical literature under the following subject headings:

Assignment for Benefit of Creditors	Extinguishment of Debts
	Fraudulent Conveyances
Bankruptcy	Homestead Law
Banks	Receivers
Debtor and Creditor	

INDEX TO LEGAL PERIODICALS (ILP)
In the ILP, look for references to legal periodical literature under the following subject headings:

Assignment for Benefit of Creditors	Debtor and Creditor Fraudulent Conveyances
Bankruptcy	Insolvency
Bonds	Receivers
Corporate Reorganization	Settlements

BAR ADMISSION: See Legal Education
BAR ASSOCIATION: See Law Office Management, Professional Responsibility

BARBADOS

SEE ALSO: Caribbean, International Law, Latin America, United Nations

STATUTES: *Barbados Consolidated Index of Statutes* by Fac. of Law Lib. (Barbados: Univ. of West Indies, 1986).

TREATISES & LOOSELEAFS:
Capital Formation and Investment Incentives Around the World (Barbados) by W. Diamond & D. Diamond (Matthew Bender, 1984–).
Caribbean Basin: A Tax Tour (Barbados) (Arthur Anderson & Co., 1985).
Commercial Laws of the World, Barbados (FL: Foreign Tax Law Assn., 1985–).
Contract of Service and the Worker by R. Chaudhary (Coles Printery, 1980).
Information Guide, Doing Business in Barbados (Price Waterhouse, 1980).
Investment Laws of the World (Barbados) (Oceana, 1981–).
Tax Laws of the World—Barbados (FL: Foreign Tax Law Assn.).
West Indian Constitutions: Post Independence Reform (Barbados) by F. Phillips (Oceana, 1985).

ARTICLES:
"Barbados as a Foreign Sales Corporation Jurisdiction" by B. Zagaris, 26 *Tax Notes* 71 (1985).
"Barbados Develops a Tax Law Jurisdiction" by B. Zagaris, 15 *International Lawyer* 673 (1981).
"Barbados . . . Renegotiating the Tax Treaty . . .," 33 *Tax Notes* 681 (1986).
"Investing in Barbados" by T. Hoyos, 33 *Canadian Tax Journal* 550, 559 (1985).
"U.S. Barbados Income Tax Treaty" by N. Freund, 14 *Tax Management International* 171 (1985).

BARBUDA: See Antigua
BAR EXAMINATIONS: See Legal Education
BARGAINING: See Civil Service, Education Law, Employee Benefits, Labor Law
BARGES: See Transportation
BARRISTERS: See England, Professional Responsibility
BASEBALL: See Sports Law
BASKETBALL: See Sports Law
BASTARD: See Estate Planning, Family Law
BATTERED WIVES, BATTERED WOMEN: See Family Law, Women & The Law
BATTERY: See Criminal Law, Torts
BEACHES: See State & Local Government, Torts

BEER: See Alcohol
BEHAVIOR MODIFICATION: See Corrections, Health & Medicine, Homosexuality,
   Juvenile Law, Mental Health
BEHAVIOR SCIENCES: See Mental Health
BEIJING: See China

BELGIUM

SEE ALSO: Europe, European Economic Community, International Law, United Nations

RESEARCH GUIDE &
BIBLIOGRAPHY: *Guide to Foreign Legal Materials, Belgium—Luxembourg—Netherlands* by P.
                          Graulich, et al. (Oceana, 1968).

CONSTITUTION: *The Constitution of Belgium and the Belgian Civil Code,* J. Crabb, transl. (Rothman,
                          1982).

TREATISES &
LOOSELEAFS: *Belgian Review of International Law* (Brussels: Societe Belge de Droit International,
                          1965–).
                          Belgium: A Country Study, S. Wickman, ed. (Amer. Univ., Foreign Area Studies, 1984).
                          Business Operations in Belgium by J. Malherbe, Tax Management Foreign Income
                          Portfolios, no 93–5th (BNA, 1979).
                          Capital Formation and Investment Incentives Around the World (Belgium) by
                          W. Diamond & D. Diamond (Matthew Bender, 1984–).
                          Digest of Commercial Laws of the World (Belgium) (Natl. Assn. of Credit Management;
                          Oceana, 1977–).
                          Information Guide, Doing Business in Belgium (Price Waterhouse).
                          International Handbook on Comparative Business Law (Belgium), D. Campbell, ed.
                          (Kluwer, 1979).
                          Litigation in Belgium: Trial Practice and Procedure Manual (ABA Litigation Section,
                          1980).
                          Recognition and Enforcement of Foreign Judgments in Various Foreign Countries
                          (Belgium) by G. Roman (Library of Congress, 1984).
                          Tax and Trade Guide to Belgium, 3d ed. (Arthur Anderson & Co.).
                          Taxation in Belgium (NY: Deloitte, Haskins & Sells, 1979).
                          Taxation of Intercompany Transactions in Selected Countries in Europe and USA
                          (Kluwer, 1979).
                          Tax Laws of the World—Belgium (FL: Foreign Tax Law Assn.).
                          World Law of Competition (Belgium), J. von Kalinowski, ed. (Matthew Bender, 1979–).

ARTICLES: "Astreinte in Belgian Law" by G. Glos, 13 *International Journal of Legal Information*
                          17 (1985).
                          "Bail, Probation and Parole in Belgian Law" by G. Glos, 14 *International Journal of
                          Legal Information* 100 (1986).
                          "Belgian System of Export Credit for Medium and Long-Term Financing" by T. Simms,
                          27 *International Lawyer* 391 (1983).
                          Belgium: Reforming Paternity" by M. Meulders-Klein, 25 *Journal of Family Law* 19
                          (1986–87).
                          "License or Research? Patent or Trade Secret? The Options in Belgium" by M. de
                          Brabanter, 78 *Patent and Trademark Review* 401, 502.

"Linguistic Legislation and Transnational Commercial Activity: France and Belgium"
by T. Carbonneau, 29 *American Journal of Comparative Law* 393 (1981).
"The Role of Shareholders, Managers and Directors in Belgian Company Law" by M.
von Sternberg, 10 *Brooklyn Journal of International Law* 303 (1984).
"Tax Planning Required in Establishing a European Headquarters Office in Belgium"
by J. Lagae, *Tax Management International Journal* 10 (Sept., 1979).

BELIZE

SEE ALSO: Caribbean, International Law, Latin America, United Nations

STATUTES: *Belize: Consolidated Index of Statutes* . . . by the Fac. of Law Lib., Univ. of West
                     Indies (Gaunt, 1985).

TREATISES: *Belize* by W. Bianchi (NY: Las Americas Pub. Co.).
                     Belize: A New Nation in Central America by O. Bolland (Westview, 1986).
                     Tax Laws of the World—Belize (FL: Foreign Tax Law Assn.).
                     West Indian Constitutions: Post Independence Reform (Belize) by F. Phillips (Oceana,
                     1985).

ARTICLES: "The Decolonization of Belize" by R. Maguire, 22 *Virginia Journal of International
                     Law* 849 (1982).
                     "Foreign Reserves Management in Belize: An Assessment of the Liquidity Constraints
                     in 1979," 30 *Social and Economic Studies* 187 (1981).

BENEFICIAL OWNER, BENEFICIAL TITLE: See Equity, Real Estate
BENEFICIARY: See Estate Planning
BENEFITS: See Employee Benefits, Insurance, Social Security, Unemployment
     Compensation, Workers' Compensation
BENEFITS REVIEW BOARD: See Maritime Law

BENIN

SEE ALSO: Africa, Communism, International Law, United Nations

CONSTITUTION: "People's Republic of Benin" by J. Salacuse in *Constitutions of the Countries of the
                     World* by A. Blaustein & G. Flanz (Oceana, 1982).

TREATISES: *African Tax Systems* (Benin) by R. Hammond (Amsterdam: Intl. Bureau of Fiscal
                     Documentation, 1980–).
                     An Introduction to Law in French-Speaking Africa (Dahomey) by J. Salacuse (Michie,
                     1969).

ARTICLES: "Law Collection in the University of Benin Library" by C. Ifebuzor, 15 *Law Librarian*
                     14 (1984).

BERMUDA

SEE ALSO: England, International Law, United Nations

**STATUTES &
RELATED LAWS:**   *Bermuda Consolidated Index of Statutes* . . . by the Fac. of Law Library, Univ. of West Indies, Barbados (Gaunt, 1986).

**TREATISES &
LOOSELEAFS:**   *Capital Formation and Investment Incentives Around the World* (Bermuda) by W. Diamond & D. Diamond (Matthew Bender, 1984–).
Information Guide, Doing Business in Bermuda (Price Waterhouse).
Tax Havens Encyclopedia by B. Spitz (Butterworths, 1975–).
West Indian Constitutions: Post Independence Reform (Bermuda) by F. Phillips (Oceana, 1985).

ARTICLES: "Baker Responds to Rostenkowski on Tax Policy of U.S.-Bermuda Tax Treaty," 32 *Tax Notes* 1186 (1986).
"Company Law in Bermuda" by D. Malcolm, 27 *Journal of the Law Society of Scotland* 467 (1982).
"New U.S.-Bermuda Pact" by E. Kracov, 32 *Tax Notes* 302 (1986).
"The United States-Bermuda Tax Convention" by J. Libin, 15 *Tax Management International Journal* 341 (1986).

BEST EVIDENCE: See Trial & Appellate Practice
BEVERAGE: See Alcohol
BIAS: See Trial & Appellate Practice
BIBLIOGRAPHIES: See Legal Research
BIDDING: See Contracts, Government Contracts
BIGAMY: See Criminal Law, Family Law, Women & the Law
BILL: See Legislative History
BILL DRAFTING: See Legal Research
BILL IN EQUITY: See Equity
BILL OF EXCHANGE: See Uniform Commercial Code
BILL OF LADING: See Maritime Law, Transportation, Uniform Commercial Code
BILL OF PARTICULARS: See Trial & Appellate Practice
BILL OF RIGHTS: See Civil Rights, Constitutional Law
BILLS & NOTES: See Consumer Law, Contracts, Uniform Commercial Code
BINDER: See Insurance
BIOCHEMISTRY: See Forensic Science
BIOETHICS: See Death, Health & Medicine, Human Experimentation
BIOLAW: See Health & Medicine, Human Experimentation
BIOLOGY: See Health & Medicine
BIOLOGY, MARINE: See Sea
BIOPSY: See Health & Medicine
BIOTECHNOLOGY: See Human Experimentation, Intellectual Property
BIRD: See Animals
BIRTH: See Abortion, Family Law, Health & Medicine, Torts, Women & the Law

BIRTH CONTROL: See Abortion, Family Law
BLACK LUNG: See Health & Medicine, Occupational Safety, Workers' Compensation
BLACKS: See Civil Rights
BLAME: See Criminal Law, Torts
BLASPHEMY: See Criminal Law, Media Law
BLEEDING: See Health & Medicine
BLINDNESS: See Handicapped & the Law
BLOCKADE: See International Law, War
BLOOD: See Forensic Science, Health & Medicine
BLOOD TEST: See Family Law, Health & Medicine
BLUE SKY: See Corporate Law, Securities Law
BOARD OF CONTRACT APPEALS: See Government Contracts
BOARD OF EDUCATION: See Education Law, State & Local Government
BOARD OF IMMIGRATION APPEALS: See Immigration Law
BOARD OF INDIAN APPEALS: See Indians
BOARDS & COMMISSIONS: See State & Local Government, Zoning & Land Planning
BOAT: See Maritime Law, Torts, Transportation
BODIES: See Forensic Science

BOLIVIA

SEE ALSO: International Law, Latin America, United Nations

RESEARCH GUIDES & BIBLIOGRAPHIES:
A Guide to the Law and Literature of Bolivia (Library of Congress, 1947; reprinted by Gordon Press, 1981).
A Guide to the Official Publications of . . . Bolivia (Library of Congress, 1945).
Nomenclature and Hierarchy: Basic Latin American Legal Sources (Brazil) by R. Medina (Govt. Printing Office, 1979).

TREATISES & LOOSELEAFS:
The Andean Legal Order (Bolivia) by F. Garcia-Amador (Oceana, 1978).
Business Operations in Brazil by S. Tozzini, Tax Management Foreign Income Portfolios, No. 430 (BNA, 1982).
Digest of Commercial Laws of the World (Bolivia) (Natl. Assn. of Credit Management; Oceana, 1977–).
External Debt in Bolivia by R. Devlin (Westview, 1987).
Fiscal Reform in Bolivia by R. Musgrave (Harvard Law School, Intl. Tax Program, 1981).
Human Rights in Bolivia (NY: Amnesty Intl. USA, 1984).
Information Guide, Doing Business in Bolivia (Price Waterhouse).
Latin America . . . A Tax Tour (Brazil) (Arthur Anderson & Co., 1985).
A Statement of the Laws of Bolivia in Matters Affecting Business, 4th ed. (Organization of American States, 1974).

ARTICLES:
"A Critical Evaluation of the American Transfer of Penal Sanctions Policy" by A. Abramovsky, 1980 *Wisconsin Law Review* 25.
"Latin American Tax Update: Bolivia" by M. Marti, 12 *Lawyer of the Americas* 633 (1980).
"Observations in Loco: Practice and Procedure of the Inter-American Commission on Human Rights" (Bolivia), 19 *Texas International Law Journal* 285, 305 (1984).

BONA FIDE PURCHASER: See Contracts, Real Estate, Uniform Commercial Code
BONDS: See Architecture, Banking Law, Bankruptcy, Insurance, Maritime Law, Real Estate, State & Local Government, Trial & Appellate Practice
BOOKKEEPING: See Accounting

BOPHUTHATSWANA

SEE ALSO: Africa, International Law, South Africa, United Nations

"Disputes, Rules and Method: The Tswana Way" by J. Bell, 3 *Oxford Journal of Legal Studies* 405 (1983).
Information Guide: Doing Business in Bophuthatswana (Price Waterhouse).

BORNEO: See Malaysia
BOSTON STOCK EXCHANGE: See Securities Law

BOTSWANA

SEE ALSO: Africa, International Law, United Nations

JOURNALS & OTHER PERIODICALS: *Botswana Notes and Records.*

TREATISES & LOOSELEAFS: *African Tax Systems* by R. Hammond & M. van den Abeelen (Botswana) (Amsterdam: Intl. Bureau of Fiscal Documentation, 1980–).
Botswana: Liberal Democracy and the Labor Reserve in Southern Africa by J. Parson (Westview, 1984).
"Contract in Tswana Law" by I. Schapera in *Ideas and Procedures in African Customary Law,* M. Gluckman, ed. (Oxford Univ. Press, 1969).
The Evolution of Modern Botswana, L. Picard, ed. (Univ. of Nebraska Press, 1985).
Information Guide, Doing Business in Botswana (Price Waterhouse).
Investment Laws of the World (Botswana) (Oceana, 1981–).
Law in Radically Different Countries (Botswana) by J. Barton (West, 1983).
Tax Laws of the World—Botswana (FL: Foreign Tax Law Assn.).

ARTICLES: "Human Rights in Africa . . . Botswana . . ." by S. Neff, 33 *The International and Comparative Law Quarterly* 331 (1984).
"Land Reform in the Making: Botswana," 24 *Journal of African Law* 1 (1980).
"Local Level Dispute Processes in Botswana" by A. Sutherland, 25 *Journal of African Law* 94 (1981).
"Notes on the Kwena Law of Marriage" by R. Stevens, 1 *Comparative and International Law Journal of South Africa* 100 (1968).
"The Parliaments of Botswana, Lesotho and Swaziland" by W. Macartney, 50 *Parliamentarian* 92 (1969).
"Sources of the Criminal Law of Botswana" by I. Brewer, 18 *Journal of African Law* 25 (1974).
"The Survival of Traditional Tswana Courts in the National Legal System of Botswana" by S. Roberts, 16 *Journal of African Law* 105 (1974).

BOUNDARIES: See Real Estate, Zoning & Land Planning
BOXING: See Sports Law
BOYCOTTS: See International Law, Labor Law
BRAIN: See Health & Medicine
BRAIN DEATH: See Death, Health & Medicine
BRANCH OFFICE: See Corporate Law, Law Office Management
BRANDS: See Intellectual Property

BRAZIL

SEE ALSO: International Law, Latin America, United Nations

**RESEARCH GUIDE &
BIBLIOGRAPHY:**   *A Guide to the Official Publication of Brazil* (Library of Congress, 1948).

CONSTITUTION: "Brazil 1975–1982" by G. Flanz in *Constitutions of the Countries of the World* by A. Blaustein & G. Flanz (Oceana, 1982).

**TREATISES &
LOOSELEAFS:**   *Capital Formation and Investment Incentives Around the World* (Brazil) by W. Diamond & D. Diamond (Matthew Bender, 1984–).

Digest of Commercial Laws of the World (Brazil) (Natl. Assn. of Credit Management; Oceana, 1977–).

Doing Business in Brazil, J. Neto, ed. (Matthew Bender, 1979–).

Inflation and Indexation: Argentina, Brazil, and Israel by J. Williamson (MIT Press, 1985).

Information Guide, Doing Business in Brazil (Price Waterhouse).

International Politics of the Sea: The Case of Brazil by M. Morris (Westview, 1979).

Investments in Brazil; Basic Legal Concepts by J. Araujo (Instituto de Desenuolumento Industrial, 1981).

Legal Aspects of Doing Business in Latin America (Brazil) (Practicing Law Institute, 1980).

Monetary Indexation in Brazil (Amsterdam: Intl. Bureau of Fiscal Documentation, 1983).

Prospects for Adjustment in Argentina, Brazil, and Mexico by J. Williamson (Wash. D.C.: Institute for Intl. Economics, 1983).

Statement of the Laws of Brazil in Matters Affecting Business (Organization of American States).

Tax and Trade Guide, Brazil, 2d ed. (Arthur Anderson & Co., 1978).

Taxation in Brazil (Arthur Young Intl., 1980).

The Taxation of Foreign Investment in Brazil by A. Xavier (Kluwer, 1980).

Tax Laws of the World—Brazil (FL: Foreign Tax Law Assn.).

ARTICLES: "Brazil: Improving the Law of Adoption" by J. Villela, 26 *Journal of Family Law* 21 (1987–88).

"Brazil: Petroleum Exploration, Evaluation, and Development under the Petrobras Risk Contract System" by U. Keener, 1 *Houston Journal of International Law* 95 (1979).

"Brazil's Technology Transfer Policies, 4 *Boston College Third World Law Journal* 99 (1983).

"Foreign Investment in Brazil" by W. Rowland, 14 *Journal of International Law and Economics* 39 (1979).

"Foreign Loans in Brazil: Theory and Practice" by T. Skola, 15 *International Lawyer* 73 (1981).

"Incentives for Investment in Brazil" by J. Neto, 13 *Case Western Reserve Journal of International Law* 123 (1981).

"Judicial Review and Protection of Human Rights Under Military Government in Brazil and Argentina" by M. Feinrider, 5 *Suffolk Transnational Law Journal* 171 (1981).

"Latin American Tax Update: Brazil" by M. Marti, 12 *Lawyer of the Americas* 636 (1980).

"Legal Memoranda: Brazil," 16 *University of Miami Inter-American Law Review* 701 (1985).

"Recent Highlights in Brazilian Banking Legislation" by T. Shola, 14 *Lawyer of the Americas* 121 (1982).

"Regulation of Foreign Investment in Brazil: A Critical Analysis" by K. Rosenn, 15 *Lawyer of the Americas* 307 (1983).

"Trademark Policy in Brazil . . .," 66 *Trademark Reporter* 173 (1976).

"U.S. Software Protection: Problems of Trade Secret Estoppel under International and Brazilian Technology Transfer Regimes" by J. Reidenberg, 23 *Columbia Journal of Transnational Law* 679 (1985).

BRAZZAVILLE: See Congo

BREACH OF CONTRACT: See Contracts, Government Contracts, Uniform Commercial Code

BREACH OF PROMISE TO MARRY: See Contracts, Family Law

BREACH OF THE PEACE: See Criminal Law

BRIBERY: See Criminal Law

BRIDGE: See State & Local Government, Torts

BRIEFS: See Constitutional Law, Legal Research, Trial & Appellate Practice

BRITAIN: See England, Ireland, Scotland, Wales

BRITISH COLUMBIA: See Canada

BRITISH HONDURAS: See Belize

BRITISH VIRGIN ISLANDS

SEE ALSO: Caribbean, England, International Law, Latin America, United Nations, Virgin Islands (U.S.)

CONSTITUTION: "British Dependent Territories: British Virgin Islands" by N. Yell in *Constitutions of Dependencies and Special Sovereignties* by A. Blaustein (Oceana, 1982).

STATUTES: *British Virgin Islands Consolidated Index of Statutes and Subsidiary Legislation to 1st January, 1985* (Gaunt, 1985).

TREATISES: *Caribbean Basin: A Tax Tour* (British Virgin Islands) (Arthur Anderson & Co., 1985).
Information Guide, Doing Business in British Virgin Islands (Price Waterhouse).
West Indian Constitutions: Post Independence Reform (British Virgin Islands) by F. Phillips (Oceana, 1985).

BROADCASTING: See Art & Entertainment, International Law, Media Law

BROKER: See Agency, Insurance, Real Estate, Securities Law

BROTHER: See Estate Planning, Family Law
BRUISE: See Health & Medicine

BRUNEI

SEE ALSO: Asia, International Law, Islam, United Nations

**TREATISES &
LOOSELEAFS:** *Asia and the Pacific: A Tax Tour* (Brunei) (Arthur Anderson & Co., 1986).
Brunei, 1839–1983: The Problems of Political Survival by D. Singh (Oxford Univ. Press, 1984).
A Guide to Doing Business in the ASEAN Region:Brunei/Indonesia/Malaysia/ Philippines/Singapore/Thailand (U.S. Dept. of Commerce, Intl. Trade Admin., Office of Pacific Basin, 1985).
Taxes and Investment in Asia and the Pacific (Brunei) (Amsterdam: Intl. Bureau of Fiscal Documentation, 1983–).
Tax Laws of the World—Brunei (FL: Foreign Tax Law Assn.).

BUDGETS: See Legislative History, State & Local Government
BUILDING: See Architecture, Historic Preservation, Real Estate, Zoning & Land Planning
BUILDING & LOAN ASSOCIATION: See Banking Law

BULGARIA

SEE ALSO: Communism, Europe, International Law, Soviet Union, United Nations

**RESEARCH GUIDES &
BIBLIOGRAPHIES:** "A Bibliographic Summary of United States-Bulgarian Diplomatic and Treaty Relations" by I. Sipkov, 5 *International Journal of Law Libraries* 212 (1977).
Legal Sources and Bibliography of Bulgaria by I. Sipkov (Praeger, 1956).

CONSTITUTIONS: *The Constitutions of the Communist World* (Bulgaria), W. Simons, ed. (Sijthoff & Noordhoff, 1980).

**STATUTES &
RELATED LAWS:** "Bulgaria: Amendments to the Regulation Implementing the Law on Passports," 23 *International Legal Materials* 442 (1984).
"Bulgaria: Law on Joint Ventures," 19 *International Legal Materials* 992 (1980).
Bylaws of the Bulgarian Communist Party, Sipkov, transl. (Library of Congress, 1980).

**TREATISES &
LOOSELEAFS:** *The Civil Aviation Law of Bulgaria* by I. Sipkov (Library of Congress, 1976).
Doing Business with Eastern Europe (NY: Business Intl. Corp., 1975–).
The First Consular Convention between the United States of America and Bulgaria by I. Sipkov (Library of Congress, 1976).
The Law on the People's Militia of the People's Republic of Bulgaria by I. Sipkov (Library of Congress, 1978).
Legal Aspects of Joint Ventures in Eastern Europe (Bulgaria), D. Campbell, ed. (Kluwer, 1981).

A New Conception of Labour Law and Labour Relations in Socialist Bulgaria by T. Zhivkov (Sofia Press, 1983).

Taxation in European Socialist Countries (vol. 5, Bulgaria) (Amsterdam: Intl. Bureau of Fiscal Documentation).

ARTICLES:

"Bulgaria: Law on Joint Ventures" by I. Sipkov, 8 *International Journal of Law Libraries* 154 (1980).

"Bulgarian Legislation for Legal Protection of Computer Software" by I. Eskenazi, 20 *Ind Prop.* 288 (1981).

"Joint Ventures in Eastern Europe" by P. Buzescu, 32 *American Journal of Comparative Law* 407 (1984).

"The Public International Law of Bulgaria" by I. Sipkov, 10 *International Journal of Legal Information* 326 (1982).

BULK TRANSFERS/SALES: See Business Law, Uniform Commercial Code
BURDEN OF PROOF: See Trial & Appellate Practice
BUREAU OF THE CENSUS: See Statistics
BURGLARY: See Criminal Law

BURKINA FASO (UPPER VOLTA)

SEE ALSO:

Africa, International Law, United Nations

An Introduction to Law in French Speaking Africa (Upper Volta) by J. Salacuse (Michie, 1969).

"Upper Volta" by M. Taratino in *Constitutions of the Countries of the World* by A. Blaustein & G. Flanz (Oceana, 1982).

BURMA

SEE ALSO:

Asia, Communism, International Law, United Nations

CONSTITUTION:

"Socialist Republic of the Union of Burma" by M. Wu in *Constitutions of the Countries of the World* by A. Blaustein & G. Flanz (Oceana, 1982).

TREATISES & LOOSELEAFS:

Burma: A Socialist Nation of Southeast Asia by D. Steinberg (Westview, 1982).

Law and Custom in Burma and the Burmese Family by M. Maung (Martinus Nijhoff, 1963).

Taxes and Investment in Asia and the Pacific (Burma) (Amsterdam: Intl. Bureau of Fiscal Documentation, 1983–).

Tax Laws of the World—Burma (FL: Foreign Tax Law Assn.).

ARTICLES:

"Burma: It Works, But is it Law?" by A. Huxley, 27 *Journal of Family Law* 23 (1988–89).

"New Regulation Prohibits Use of Local Representatives" (Burma) by P. Janssen, 8 *East Asian Executive Reports* 8(2) (July, 1986).

"Note, Lawyers and Legal Education in Burma" by M. Maung, 11 *International & Comparative Law Quarterly* 285 (1962).

BURN: See Health & Medicine, Torts

BURUNDI

SEE ALSO: Africa, International Law, United Nations

CONSTITUTION: "Burundi" by F. Jens in *Constitutions of the Countries of the World* by A. Blaustein & G. Flanz (Oceana, 1983).

TREATISES: *African Tax Systems* (Burundi) by R. Hammond & M. van den Abeelen (Amsterdam: Intl. Bureau of Fiscal Documentation, 1980–).
Area Handbook for Burundi by G. McDonald (American Univ. Foreign Area Studies, 1969).
Guide to the Text of the Criminal Law and Criminal Procedure Codes of Burundi, Rwanda, and Zaire by A. Wekerle (Library of Congress, 1975).
An Introduction to Law in French-Speaking Africa (Burundi) by J. Salacuse (Michie, 1969).
Investment Laws of the World: The Developing Nations (Burundi) (Oceana, 1972–).

BUS: See Transportation

BUSINESS LAW

SEE ALSO: Accounting, Agency, Antitrust Law, Architecture, Art & Entertainment, Banking Law, Bankruptcy, Commodities, Consumer Law, Contracts, Corporate Law, Economics, Employee Benefits, Employment Discrimination, Environmental Law, Food, Franchise Law, Government Contracts, Intellectual Property, International Law, Labor Law, Maritime Law, Nonprofit Corporations, Occupational Safety, Oil & Gas, Partnership Law, Real Estate, Securities Law, Sports Law, Taxation, Torts, Transportation, Unemployment Compensation, Uniform Commercial Code, Workers' Compensation, Zoning & Land Planning; see also entries under individual states and countries.

RESEARCH GUIDE &
BIBLIOGRAPHY: *Encyclopedia of Business Information Sources* (Gale, 1970–).

JOURNALS, NEWSLETTERS
& OTHER PERIODICALS: *The Business Lawyer* (ABA Section of Corp., Banking and Business Law, 1946–).
The Business Lawyer Update (ABA Section of Corp., Banking and Business Law, 1985–).
Business Periodicals Index (H. W. Wilson).
Commercial Damages Reporter (Matthew Bender, 1986–).
Commercial Law Bulletin (Commercial Law League of Amer., 1986–).
Commercial Law Journal (Commercial Law League of Amer.).
Journal of Business Law (Carswell, 1957–).
Journal of Law and Commerce (Univ. of Pittsburgh School of Law, 1981–).

LOOSELEAFS: *Basic Business Appraisal* by R. Miles (Wiley, 1984).
Basic Legal Forms by M. Hyman (Warren, Gorham & Lamont, 1981–).
Business Crime by S. Arkin (Matthew Bender, 1981–).

Business Organizations with Tax Planning by Z. Cavitch (Matthew Bender, 1963–).
Business Strategies by S. Kess (CCH, 1983–).
Commercial Arbitration Institutions by. L. Kos-Rabcewicz (Oceana, 1986).
Doing Business in the United States by J. Spires (Matthew Bender, 1978–).
Domke on Commercial Arbitration by M. Domke (Callaghan, 1984–).
Federal Business Laws by W. Hancock (Business Laws, Inc., 1970–).
The Law and Business of Licensing, R. Goldscheider, ed. (Clark Boardman, 1981–).
Licensing Law and Business Report (Clark Boardman).
Regulation of Business Enterprise in the U.S.A. by J. Norton (Oceana, 1983–).
Warren's Forms of Agreement (Matthew Bender, 1954–).

TREATISES:

Business Acquisitions, 2d ed. by J. Herz (Practicing Law Institute, 1981).
Business Contract Forms by R. English (Wiley).
Business Ethics by W. Hoffmann (McGraw-Hill, 1984).
Business Law Monographs (Matthew Bender).
Business Workouts Manual by D. Rome (Warren, Gorham & Lamont, 1985).
Commercial Arbitration with Forms by R. Rodman (West, 1984).
The Complete Guide for Your Small Business by P. Adams (Wiley, 1982).
The Complete Guide to Business Contracts by J. Howell (Prentice-Hall, 1981).
Credit Manual of Commercial Laws, 77th ed. (Natl. Assn. of Credit Management, 1985).
Defending Business and White Collar Crimes by F. Bailey (Lawyers Co-op., 1969).
How to Keep your Company Out of Court, P. Allen, ed. (Prentice-Hall, 1984).
Legal Aspects of Buying and Selling, P. Zeidman, ed. (Shepard's, 1983).
Legal Aspects of Government Regulation of Business by T. Dunfee (Wiley, 1984).
Legal Compliance Checkups: Business Clients by R. Hughs (Callaghan).
Modern Legal Forms (West, 1963).
Sales and Credit Transactions by T. Le (Shepard's, 1985).
Small Business Financing: Federal Assistance and Contracts by A. Chase (Shepard's, 1983).

ENCYCLOPEDIAS:

AMERICAN JURISPRUDENCE 2D (Am Jur 2d)
Check the following topics in the *General Index* volumes for Am Jur 2d:

Business	Industry
Commerce	Investment Companies
Commercial Code	Licenses and Permits
Contracts	Manufacturers
Corporations	Markets
Credit	Peddlers
Debts	Profit or Income
Factors	Sales
Franchises	Vendor and Purchaser

CORPUS JURIS SECUNDUM (CJS)
Check the following topics in the *General Index* volumes for CJS:

Accounts Receivable	Credit
Bills	Customers
Bulk Sales	Customs and Usages
Business Trusts	Dealers
Collections	Factors
Commerce	Financial Condition
Contracts	Goods
Corporations	Good Will

Income	Manufacturers
Inns	Principal and Surety
Licenses and Permits	Profits

DIGESTS: CASE SEARCH IN WEST DIGESTS BY KEY TOPIC
In the *Descriptive Word Index* of the West digests, look for key topics and numbers under the following subject headings:

Accounts	Goods
Bills & Notes	Good Will
Bulk Sales	Income
Business Trusts	Inns
Collections	Labor Relations
Commerce	Licenses
Contracts	Manufacturers
Corporations	Principal and Surety
Credit	Profits
Customers	Taxation
Customs and Usages	Torts
Dealers	Vendor
Factors	Wholesale
Financial Condition	Workers' Compensation
Food	

ALR: ANNOTATIONS
Check the index volumes for ALR, ALR2d, ALR3d, ALR4th, and ALR Fed for annotations under the following subject headings:

Accounts	Independent Contractors
Automobile Dealers	Industry
Business or Occupation	Inventory
Commerce	Leases
Commercial Property	Licenses
Customers	Manufacturers
Dealers	Merchandise
Franchises	Retailer
Good Will	Sales
Income or Profits	

PERIODICALS: CURRENT LAW INDEX (CLI) & LEGAL RESOURCE INDEX (LRI)
In the CLI and LRI, look for references to periodical literature under the following subject headings:

Arbitration	Interstate Commerce
Big Business	Joint Ventures
Branches	Labor Laws
Business	Manufacturers
Capital	Master and Servant
Commerce	Partnership
Debt	Sales
Entrepreneur	Small Business
Finance	Syndicates
Good Will	Taxation
Industry Laws	Vendors and Purchasers
International Business	

INDEX TO LEGAL PERIODICALS (ILP)
In the ILP, look for references to legal periodical literature under the following subject
headings:

Business	Good Will
Chambers of Commerce	Industrial Arbitration
Consumer Protection	International Trade
Contracts	Leases
Employee Ownership	Licenses
Equipment Leasing	Occupation Tax
Factories	Sales
Franchising	Taxation
Fraud	Trade Secrets

BUSINESS RECORDS: See Trial & Appellate Practice
BUSINESS TRUSTS: See Corporate Law
BUYOUTS: See Corporate Law, Securities Law
BYLAWS: See Corporate Law

CABLE: See Media Law
CALENDAR: See Judicial Administration, Law Office Management

CALIFORNIA

SEE ALSO: Circuit Courts (Ninth Circuit), Community Property

RESEARCH GUIDES &
BIBLIOGRAPHIES: *Legal Research Guide for California Practice* by T. Dabagh (Hein, 1985).
"California Current State Practice Materials: An Annotated Bibliography" by B. Ochal,
74 *Law Library Journal* 281 (1981).
California Law Guide, 2d ed. by D. Henke (Parker, 1976).
Research in California Law, 2d ed. by M. Fink (Dennis, 1964).

CONSTITUTION: *Bibliography on Constitution Revision Commission Publications* (Cal. State Library,
Law Library, 1971).
Constitutional Conventions and Commissions (CIS, 1849–).

STATUTES & RELATED
LEGISLATIVE MATERIALS: *Deering's Annotated California Code* (Bancroft-Whitney).
West's Annotated California Code (West).
Deering's California General Laws Annotated (compiles uncodified acts) (Bancroft-
Whitney).
Statutes of California (session laws).
California Legislative Service (West).
California Advance Legislative Service (Deering).
California Session Laws (Univ. Microfilm, 1849–).
LARMAC Consolidated Index to the Constitution and Laws of California (Parker, 1985).
Los Angeles Municipal Code, 4th ed. (Parker).

**MATERIALS ON
LEGISLATIVE HISTORY:**
"California Legislation: Sources Unlimited" by E. Steck, 6 *Pacific Law Journal* 536 (1975).
California Legislature and Legislative Intent Materials: A Selected Current Bibliography, V. Ford, comp. (So. Cal. Assn. of Law Libraries, 1976).
Hearings and Reports of Committees of the California Legislature, 1961– : A Listing (Cal. Legislature, Assembly, Office of Research).
Senate and Assembly Bills, Resolutions, and Constitutional Amendments (Cal. Legislature, 1849–).
Legislative Index (Cal. Legislature, 1959–).
Locating Legislative Intent by Extrinsic Aids by C. Kenyon (Cal. State Library, 1967).
Reports, Recommendations and Studies, Cal. Law Revision Commission (Stanford Law School, 1953–).

**CASES & RELATED
COURT MATERIALS:**
California Reports (Bancroft-Whitney, 1850–).
West's California Reporter (1959–).
Pacific Reporter (West, 1883–).
California Appellate Reports (Bancroft-Whitney, 1905–).
California Appellate Reports Supplement (1929–).
Reports of Cases Determined in the Supreme Court of the State of California (Bancroft-Whitney, 1850–).
Reports of Cases Determined in the Courts of Appeal of the State of California (Bancroft-Whitney, 1905–).
California Official Reports (Bancroft-Whitney, 1969–).
Advance California Reports and Advance California Appellate Reports (1940–).

JURY INSTRUCTIONS:
California Jury Instructions, Civil, 7th ed., BAJI—Book of Approved Jury Instructions (West, 1986).
California Jury Instructions, Criminal, 5th ed., CALJIC—California Jury Instructions Criminal (West, 1988).

**ETHICS & PROFESSIONAL
RESPONSIBILITY:**
California Compendium on Professional Responsibility, P. Vapnek, ed. (Cal. Cont. Ed. of the Bar, 1983–).

**REGULATIONS & RELATED
ADMINISTRATIVE
AGENCY MATERIALS:**
California Administrative Code (Cal. Office of Administrative Hearings, 1945–).
California Administrative Code (Univ. Microfilm, 1979–).
California Administrative Notice Register (Cal. Office of Administrative Hearings, 1945–).
State Administrative Manual (Cal. Dept. of Finance, 1955–).

**OPINIONS & REPORTS
OF THE ATTORNEY
GENERAL:**
Opinions, Cal. Attorney General (Matthew Bender, 1943–).
Report of the Attorney General of the State of California (Cal. Office of the Attorney General, 1850–).

**JOURNALS & OTHER
PERIODICALS:**
Index to California Legal Periodicals and Documents (Cal. State Law Library, 1964–).
Barclays California Law Monthly (Matthew Bender, 1984–).
Brief Case (Bar Assn. of San Francisco).
California Lawyer (Cal. Bar Assn., 1981–).
California Regulatory Law Reporter (1981–).
California State Publications (Cal. State Library, 1945/47–).

California Trial Lawyers Association Forum.
Journal of the Beverly Hills Bar Association.
Long Beach Bar Bulletin.
Los Angeles Bar Journal (1925–).
Los Angeles Daily Journal.
Orange County Bar Journal (1973–).
Santa Clara Lawyer.
Trial Bar News (San Diego Trial Lawyers Assn.).

DIRECTORIES:

Attorneys' Directory of Services and Information: Federal, California State and County Governments, E. Goldman, ed. (Cal. Cont. Ed. of the Bar, 1977–).
California Blue Book (Cal. Office of State Printing).
Membership Directory and Handbook (Los Angeles: Cal. Attys. for Criminal Justice, 1984).
Parker Directory of California Attorneys (Parker).
Roster: Federal, State, County, City and Township Officials: Directory of State Services of the State of California (Cal. Secretary of State) (annual).
Roster of the Judiciary of California (Cal. Dept. of Justice, 1966–).

LOOSELEAFS:

Attorney's Guide to Pension and Profit-Sharing Plans, 3d ed. by R. Gilbert (Cal. Cont. Ed. of the Bar, 1985–).
Ballentine & Sterling's California Corporation Laws, 4th ed., R. Clark, ed. (Parker, 1962–).
California Arbitration Practice Guide, 2d ed. by J. Toker (Lawpress, 1986–).
California Business Law Reporter (Cal. Cont. Ed. of the Bar).
California Business Practice by M. Ryder (Parker, 1981–).
California Civil Actions—Pleading and Practice (Matthew Bender, 1983–).
California Civil Litigation Forms Manual (Cal. Cont. Ed. of the Bar, 1980–).
California Civil Litigation Reporter (Cal. Cont. Ed. of the Bar).
California Civil Procedure Handbook by L. Mason (Parker, 1981–).
California Corporate Securities Law Notebook (Cal. Cont. Ed. of the Bar, 1973–).
California Courtroom Evidence, 2d ed. by F. Haight & J. Cotchett (Parker, 1981–).
California Criminal Defense Practice by R. Erwin et al. (Matthew Bender, 1981–).
California Damages: Law & Proof, 3d ed. by L. Johns (Parker, 1985–).
California Deposition and Discovery Practice by J. DeMeo et al. (Matthew Bender, 1971–).
California Eligible Securities List (CCH, 1971–).
California Family Law Practice, 6th ed. by S. Adams & N. Sevitch (San Francisco: Cal. Family Law Report, 1985–).
California Family Law–Practice and Procedures, C. Marke, ed. (Matthew Bender, 1978–).
California Family Tax Planning, 2d ed. by R. & T. Rice (Matthew Bender, 1966–).
California Forms of Pleading and Practice—Annotated (Matthew Bender, 1962–).
California Insurance Law (Matthew Bender, 1986–).
California Judicial Council Forms Manual (Cal. Cont. Ed. of the Bar, 1981–).
California Juvenile Court Deskbook, 2d ed. by H. Thompson (Cal. Cont. Ed. of the Bar, 1978–).
California Law of Employee Injuries and Workmen's Compensation, 2d ed. by W. Hanna (Matthew Bender, 1966–).
California Legal Forms—Transaction Guide by D. Badger et al. (Matthew Bender, 1968–).
California Mechanics' Lien and Construction Industry Practice, 4th ed. by M. Marsh (Parker, 1985–).
California Points and Authorities by P. Sallander (Matthew Bender, 1965–).
California Practice Guide—Civil Procedure Before Trial by R. Weil & I. Brown

(Rutter Group, 1983–).
California Practice Guide—Corporations by C. Friedman (Rutter Group, 1984–).
California Practice Guide—Enforcing Judgments by R. Schwartz (Rutter Group, 1984–).
California Practice Guide—Family Law by W. Hogoboom (Rutter Group, 1981–).
California Practice Guide—Personal Injury by W. Flahaven et al. (Rutter Group, 1984–).
California Practice Guide—Probate by B. Ross (Rutter Group, 1986–).
California Probate Procedure, 4th ed. by A. Marshall (Parker, 1979–).
California Probate Workflow Manual (Cal. Cont. Ed. of the Bar, 1980–).
California Products Liability Actions by J. Cotchett et al. (Matthew Bender, 1975–).
California Real Estate Law and Practice by D. Augustine et al. (Matthew Bender, 1973–).
California Ruling Law—Motor Vehicle Accidents by R. Magana & M. Donnelly (Matthew Bender, 1962–).
California Taxation by R. Peterson (Matthew Bender, 1983–).
California Workers' Compensation Law Practice, 3d ed. by S. Herlick (Parker, 1985–).
Commencing Civil Actions in California by K. Arnold (Matthew Bender, 1975–).
Estate Planning and California Probate Reporter (Cal. Cont. Ed. of the Bar).
Fair Employment & Housing Commission Precedential Decisions Service (Cal. Cont. Ed. of the Bar, 1982–).
Managing and Estate Planning Practice, 3d ed. by I. Kellogg (Cal. Cont. Ed. of the Bar, 1982–).
Marsh's California Corporation Law by H. Marsh (Law & Business, Inc., 1981–).
Owens California Forms and Procedure by W. Owens (Parker, 1982–).
Practice Under the California Corporate Securities Law by H. Marsh & R. Volk (Matthew Bender, 1972–).
Public Employee Reporter for California (Labor Relations Press, 1976–).
Real Property Law Reporter (Cal. Cont. Ed. of the Bar).

DIGESTS, ENCYCLOPEDIAS & INDEXES:

California Digest (West).
California Digest of Official Reports, 3d Series (Bancroft-Whitney, 1975).
California Jurisprudence 3d (Bancroft-Whitney, 1972–).
California Words, Phrases and Maxims (Bancroft-Whitney).
Index of the Spanish-Mexican Private Land Grant Records and Cases of California by J. Bowman (Bancroft-Whitney, 1958).
Pacific Digest (West).

CITATORS:

Shepard's California Case Names Citator.
Shepard's California Citations.
Shepard's California Reporter Citations.
California Citation Guide, Overruled and Disapproved Cases (Bancroft-Whitney).
Barclays California Advance Citator (Barclays Law Publishers, 1986–).

CAMBODIA (KAMPUCHEA)

SEE ALSO: Asia, Communism, International Law, United Nations

CONSTITUTION: *The Constitutions of the Communist World* (Kampuchea), W. Simons, ed. (Sijthoff & Noordhoff, 1980).

"People's Republic of Kampuchea" in *Constitutions of the Countries of the World* by A. Blaustein (Oceana, 1982).

TREATISES: *Human Rights in Cambodia* (NY: Lawyers Committee for Intl. Human Rights, 1985).
Kampuchea: After the Worst by F. Abrams (NY: Lawyers Committee for Human Rights, 1985).
Kampuchea: Decade of Genocide by K. Kiljunen (London: Zed, 1984).
Revolution and its Aftermath in Kampuchea, D. Chandler, ed. (Yale Univ. Southeast Asia Studies, 1983).
Tax Laws of the World—Cambodia (FL: Foreign Tax Law Assn.).

ARTICLES: "Humanitarian Intervention" (Cambodia) by R. Clark, 13 *Georgia Journal of International & Comparative Law* 211 (1983).
"Internationalized Non-International Armed Conflicts: Case Studies of Afghanistan, Kampuchea, and Lebanon" by H. Gasser, 33 *American University Law Review* 145 (1983).
"Kampuchea: Representation and Recognition" by C. Warbrick, 30 *International & Comparative Law Quarterly* 234 (1981).

CAMEROON

SEE ALSO: Africa, International Law, Islam, United Nations

TREATISES & LOOSELEAFS: *African Tax Systems* (Cameroon) by R. Hammond & M. van den Abeelen (Amsterdam: Intl. Bureau of Fiscal Documentation, 1980–).
Information Guide, Doing Business in Cameroon, Republic of (Price Waterhouse).
An Introduction to Law in French-Speaking Africa (Cameroon Federation) by J. Salacuse (Michie, 1969).
Investment Laws of the World (Cameroon) (Oceana, 1981–).
Tax Laws of the World—Cameroon (FL: Foreign Tax Law Assn.).

ARTICLES: "The Abiding Influence of English and French Criminal Law in . . . Cameroon" by P. Bringer, 25 *Journal of African Law* 1 (1981).
"The Dual Aspects of Doing Business in Cameroon" by D. Sams, 17 *International Lawyer* 489 (1983).
"Insurance Law and Practice in Cameroon" by A. Fonkam, 19 *Journal of World Trade Law* 136 (1985).
"The Legal Aspects of Doing Business in Cameroon" by D. Sams, 17 *International Lawyer* 489 (1983).
"Regulation of Business Activities of Petroleum Contractors in Cameroon, Congo, Gabon, and Ivory Coast" by M. Frilet, 30 *Oil and Gas Tax Quarterly* 485 (1982).

CAMPAIGNS: See Election

CANADA

SEE ALSO: International Law, Sea, Sports Law, United Nations

RESEARCH GUIDES & BIBLIOGRAPHIES: Marshall, D., "An Introduction to Canadian Legal Research," 81 *Law Library Journal* 465 (1989).

Canadian Bibliography of International Law by C. Witkor (Univ. of Toronto Press, 1984).

The Canadian Legal System, 2d ed. by G. Gall (Carswell, 1983).

Guide to Legal Citations: A Canadian Perspective in Common Law Provinces by C. Tang (Richard DeBoo Publishers, 1984).

Index to Canadian Legal Literature (Carswell, 1985–).

Index to Canadian Legal Periodical Literature (Canadian Legal Periodical Literature Publishers, 1963–).

Index to Current Legal Research in Canada (Ottawa: Dept. of Justice, 1972–).

An Introduction to Quebec Legal Bibliography (Montreal: Canadian Assn. of Law Libraries, 1980).

Law Library Guide for Alberta Practitioners, S. Beugin (Calgary: Canadian Bar Assn., 1979–).

Legal Research Handbook by D. MacEllven (Butterworths, 1980).

"The Quebec Legal System" by J. Goulet, 73 *Law Library Journal* 354 (1980).

Using a Law Library, 3d ed. by M. Banks (Carswell, 1980).

CONSTITUTIONAL LAW: *The Canadian Charter of Rights and Freedoms: Commentary,* W. Tarnopolsky, ed. (Carswell, 1982).

The Canadian Charter of Rights, Annotated (Canada Law Book).

A Consolidation of the Constitution Acts 1867 to 1982/Codification (Dept. of Justice; Carswell, 1983).

STATUTES: *Revised Statutes of Canada* (Govt. Printing Office; Carswell).

Statutes of Canada (Govt. Printing Office; Carswell).

Statutes of the Province of Canada.

Canada Statute Citator, R.S.C. (Canada Law Book).

Halsbury's Laws of England: Canadian Converter.

CASES: *All Canada Weekly Summaries* (Canada Law Book).

Canada: Supreme Court Reports (Govt. Printing Office; Carswell).

Canada Tax Cases (1985–).

Dominion Law Reports (Canada Law Book, 1912–).

Dominion Tax Cases (1920–).

Federal Court Reports (Carswell, 1971–).

CASE INDEXES, CITATORS & DIGESTS: *The Canadian Abridgment: Index to Canadian Legal Literature,* 2d ed. (Carswell, 1981–).

Canadian Current Law (Carswell, 1981–).

Canada Statute Annotations, R.S.C. (Canada Law Book).

REGULATIONS: *Consolidated Regulations of Canada* (Govt. Printing Office; Carswell).

Canada Gazette (Govt. Printing Office; Carswell).

Canada Regulations Index (Carswell).

JOURNALS, NEWSLETTERS & OTHER PERIODICALS: *Advocates Quarterly* (Canada Law Book).

Annual Review of Canadian Law (Carswell).

Canada-United States Law Journal (Cleveland: Case Western Reserve).

Canadian Association of Law Libraries Newsletter (Toronto, 1975–).

Canadian Bar Review (Canadian Bar Foundation).

Canadian Human Rights Yearbook (Univ. of Ottawa; Carswell, 1983–).

DIRECTORIES:

Alberta Legal Telephone Directory (Canada Law Book).

The American Bar, the Canadian Bar, the International Bar (CA: Reginald Bishop Forster and Associates, Inc.).

British Columbia Legal Telephone Directory (Canada Law Book).

Canadian Association of Law Teachers Directory (Carswell).

The Canadian Law List (Canada Law Book).

The Lawyer's Phone Book (Ontario) (Canada Law Book).

LOOSELEAFS:

Bankruptcy Law of Canada by L. Houlden & C. Morawetz (Carswell).

Canada Income Tax Guide (CCH, 1952–).

Canadian Commercial Law Guide (CCH, 1967–).

Canadian Corporations Law Reporter (CCH, 1949–).

Canadian Energy News (CCH, 1980–).

Canadian Energy Program Reporter (CCH, 1982–).

Canadian Estate Planning and Administration (CCH, 1979–).

Canadian Estate Planning and Administration Reporter (CCH, 1979–).

Canadian Family Law Guide (CCH, 1976–).

Canadian Government Programs and Services Guide (CCH, 1973–).

Canadian Income Tax Act, Regulations and Rulings (CCH, 1981–).

Canadian Income Tax Research Index (CCH, 1981–).

Canadian Securities Law Reports (CCH, 1966–).

Canadian Tax Reports (CCH, 1937–).

Doing Business in Canada, H. Strikeman & R. Elliot, eds. (Matthew Bender, 1984–).

Dominion Tax Cases (CCH, 1949–).

Foreign Investment in Canada by P. Hayden & J. Burns (Prentice-Hall, 1974–).

Income Taxation in Canada by W. MacDonald & G. Cronkwright (Prentice-Hall, 1977–).

YEARBOOK:

Canadian Yearbook of International Law (Univ. of British Columbia Press, 1963–).

DICTIONARIES:

Canadian Law Dictionary (Toronto: Law and Business Publications, 1980).

A Handbook of Canadian Legal Terminology by W. Flynn (Ontario: Gen. Pub. Co., 1981).

TREATISES:

Business Operations in Canada by R. Cowzin, Tax Management Foreign Income Portfolios, no. 43 (BNA, 1985).

Canadian Criminal Procedure, 4th ed. by J. Salhany (Canada Law Book, 1984).

Canadian Immigration Law and Procedure by C. Wydrzynski (Canada Law Book, 1983).

Corporate Law in Canada by B. Welling (Butterworths, 1984).

Customs and Excise by M. Prabhu (Carswell, 1983).

Extradition To and From Canada, 2d ed. by G. LaForest (Canada Law Book, 1977).

Foreign Investment Law in Canada by G. Hughes (Carswell, 1983).

Fraser's Handbook on Canadian Company Law, 7th ed. by W. Fraser (Carswell, 1985).

Information Guide, Doing Business in Canada (Price Waterhouse).

Law of Banking, 3d ed. by I. Baxter (Carswell, 1981).

The New Canada-United States Income Tax Treaty (Practicing Law Institute, 1984).

Taxation of Income of Foreign Affiliates by D. Ward (Carswell, 1983).

CANAL: See Transportation

CANAL ZONE: See Panama

CANCELLATION: See Contracts, Estate Planning, Real Estate
CANCER: See Health & Medicine

CANON LAW

SEE ALSO: Church & State, Constitutional Law, Family Law

RESEARCH GUIDES &
BIBLIOGRAPHIES:

An Annotated Bibliography of the Work of the Canon Law Society of America:
1965–1980 by R. Cunningham (Wash. D.C.: Catholic Univ. of America, Canon
Law Society of America, 1982).

Bibliography on Canon Law, 1965–1971 by L. Sheridan (Univ. of Texas, Tarlton Law
Library, 1971).

The Canon Law Collection of the Library of Congress by D. Ferreira-Ibarra (Library of
Congress, 1981).

"Canon Law, History, Sources and a Proposed Classification Scheme" by D. Gorecki
& A. Wajenberg, 75 *Law Library Journal* 381 (1982).

JOURNALS, NEWSLETTERS
& OTHER PERIODICALS:

Bulletin of Medieval Canon Law (Berkeley: Institute of Medieval Canon Law, 1971–).

Canon Law Abstracts (Scotland: Canon Law Society of Great Britain and Ireland,
1958–).

Canon Law Digest (Mundelein, IL: St. Mary of the Lake Seminary, 1917–).

The Jurist (Catholic Univ. of America, 1941–).

Studia Canonica (Ottawa: Saint Paul Univ., Faculty of Canon Law, 1967–).

TREATISES:

American Canon Law Due Process by M. McManus (Wash. D.C.: Law Research
Institute, 1971).

Annulments, 4th ed. by L. Wrenn (Catholic Univ. of America, Canon Law Society of
America, 1983).

The Art of Interpretation: Selected Studies on the Interpretation of Canon Law by J.
Coriden et al. (Catholic Univ. of America, Canon Law Society of America, 1983).

Canon Law: A Text and Commentary, 3d ed. by T. Bouscaren & A. Ellis (Milwaukee:
Bruce Pub. Co., 1957).

Canon Law in Pastoral Perspective: Principles for the Application of Law According to
Antonius of Florence by E. McDonough (Ann Arbor: University Microfilms Intl.,
1983).

The Canon Law of Medieval Papal Legation by R. Figueira (Ann Arbor: University
Microfilms Intl., 1980).

The Code of Canon Law: A Text and Commentary, J. Coriden et al., eds. (NJ: Paulist
Press).

Code of Canon Law: Latin-English Edition (Catholic Univ. of America, Canon Law
Society of America, 1983).

The Collection in Seventy-Four Titles: A Canon Law Manual of the Gregorian Reform
by J. Gilchrist (Toronto: Pontifical Institute of Medieval Studies, 1980).

A Dictionary of Canon Law by P. Trudel (St. Louis: B. Herder Book Co., 1919).

The Future of Canon Law (NY: Paulist Press, 1969).

Liturgical Law Today by T. Richstatter (Chicago: Franciscan Herald Press, 1977).

Matrimonial Jurisprudence United States, 1975–76 (Catholic Univ. of America, Canon
Law Society of America, 1977).

The New Canon Law (St. Louis: Catholic Health Assn. of the United States, 1983).

The Pastoral Companion: A Canon Law Handbook for Catholic Ministry by J. Huels

(Chicago: Franciscan Herald Press, 1986).
Readings, Cases, Materials in Canon Law by J. Hite (MN: Liturgical Press, 1980).
Roman Replies, W. Schumacher, ed. (Catholic Univ. of America, Canon Law Society of America, 1981, 82, 83).

ENCYCLOPEDIAS:

AMERICAN JURISPRUDENCE 2D (Am Jur 2d)
Check the following topics in the *General Index* volumes for Am Jur 2d:

Canon Law	Marriage
Clergymen	Religion and Religious
Divorce and Separation	Societies

CORPUS JURIS SECUNDUM (CJS)
Check the following topics in the *General Index* volumes for CJS:

Canon Law	Religious Societies
Marriage	

DIGESTS:

CASE SEARCH IN WEST DIGESTS BY KEY TOPIC
In the *Descriptive Word Index* of the West digests, look for key topics and numbers under the following subject headings:

Church	Religion
Clergymen	Religious Societies
Divorce	

ALR:

ANNOTATIONS
Check the index volumes for ALR, ALR2d, ALR3d, ALR4th, and ALR Fed for annotations under the following subject headings:

Clergy	Religion and Religious
Marriage	Societies

PERIODICALS:

CURRENT LAW INDEX (CLI) & LEGAL RESOURCE INDEX (LRI)
In the CLI and LRI, look for references to periodical literature under the following subject headings:

Canon Law	Ecclesiastical Law
Catholic Church	Marriage (Canon Law)
Church	Religion
Ecclesiastical Courts	

INDEX TO LEGAL PERIODICALS (ILP)
In the ILP, look for references to legal periodical literature under the following subject headings:

Churches	Marriage
Ecclesiastical Law	Religion

CAPACITY: See Contracts, Family Law, Mental Health
CAPITAL: See Corporate Law, International Law, Securities Law
CAPITAL GAIN OR LOSS: See Taxation
CAPITALIZATION: See Taxation
CAPITAL OFFENSE: See Criminal Law
CAPITAL PUNISHMENT: See Constitutional Law, Criminal Law
CAR: See Alcohol, Criminal Law, Personal Property, Torts, Transportation
CARE: See Health & Medicine, Mental Health, Nursing, Torts
CARGO: See Maritime Law, Transportation

CARIBBEAN

SEE ALSO: International Law, Latin America, United Nations

RESEARCH GUIDES &
BIBLIOGRAPHIES:
Business Information Sources on Latin America and the Caribbean (Organization of American States, 1982).
Commonwealth Caribbean Legal Literature: A Bibliography . . . by V. Newton (Univ. of the West Indies, Faculty of Law Library, 1987).
Legal Literature and Publishing in the Commonwealth Caribbean by V. Newton (Gaunt, 1979).
"Legal Materials from Latin America and the Caribbean: Some Ideas for Acquisition" by E. Schaffer, 12 *International Journal of Legal Information* 103 (1984).
"A Selected Guide to Law Related Publications of Latin America and the Caribbean" by E. Schaffer, 6 *International Journal of Law Libraries* 75 (1978).

JOURNALS & OTHER
PERIODICALS:
The Caribbean Law Librarian (Jamaica: Caribbean Assn. of Law Librarians, 1984–).
Caribbean Yearbook of International Relations (Sijthoff, 1975–).
West Indian Law Journal (Kingston, Jamaica: Council of Legal Education, 1977–).

TREATISES &
LOOSELEAFS:
Caribbean Basin: A Tax Tour (Arthur Anderson & Co., 1985).
Caribbean Basin Business Information Starter Kit (U.S. Dept. of Commerce, Intl. Trade Admin., 1984).
Caribbean Basin Trade and Investment Guide by K. Power (Wash. D.C.: Wash. Intl. Press, 1984).
The Caribbean in World Affairs by J. Braveboy-Wagner (Westview, 1987).
Commonwealth Caribbean Legal Systems: A Study of Small Jurisdictions by V. Newton (Barbados: Triumph Pubs., 1988).
Comparative Law Studies: Law and Legal Systems of the Commonwealth Caribbean States and the Other Members of the Organization of American States, rev. ed. (Wash. D.C.: General Secretariat, Secretariat for Legal Affairs, 1987).
Crime and Nation-Building in the Caribbean: The Legacy of Legal Barriers by C. Mahabir (Cambridge, MA: Schenkman Pub., 1985).
Instruments of Economic Integration in Latin America and in the Caribbean, F. Garcia-Amador, ed., Inter-American Institute of Intl. Legal Studies (Oceana, 1976).
Mining and Petroleum Legislation of Latin America and the Caribbean, Organization of American States (Oceana, 1978–).
A New Law of the Sea for the Caribbean, E. Gold, ed. (Springer, 1988).
The Soviet-Cuban Connection in Central America and the Caribbean (U.S. Dept. of State and Defense, 1985).
West Indian Constitutions: Post Independence Reform by F. Phillips (Oceana, 1985).

ARTICLES:
"The Caribbean Basin Economic Recovery Act and its Implications for Foreign Private Investment" by T. Clasen, 16 *New York University Journal of International Law and Politics* 715 (1984).
"A Caribbean Perspective of the Caribbean Basin Initiative" by Zagaris, 18 *International Lawyer* 563 (1984).
"Copyright and the Caribbean Basic Economic Recovery Act of 1983" by W. Patry, 31 *Journal of the Copyright Society of the U.S.A.* 264 (1983).

"An Historical Perspective of Law Reporting in English-Speaking Caribbean" by V. Newton, 7 *International Journal of Law Libraries* 1 (1979).

"Legal Aid Developments in the Caribbean" by W. McCalla, 12 *Lawyer of the Americas* 381 (1980).

"Legal Framework for Foreign Investment in the Caribbean and Central America" by Cherol, 18 *International Lawyer* 957 (1984).

"The Organization of Eastern Caribbean States" by P. Menon, 17 *University of Miami Inter American Law Review* 297 (1986).

"A Survey of Mental Health Legislation in the Eastern Caribbean" by N. Liverpool, 8 *International Journal of Law and Psychiatry* 119 (1986).

CARRIAGE: See Maritime Law
CARRIER: See Air & Aviation, Maritime Law, Public Utilities, Space, Torts, Transportation
CARTEL: See Antitrust Law, Corporate Law
CASUALTY: See Insurance
CATHOLIC CHURCH: See Abortion, Canon Law, Church & State
CATTLE: See Agriculture, Animals
CAUSA MORTIS GIFT: See Estate Planning
CAUSATION: See Torts
CAUSE OF ACTION: See Trial & Appellate Practice
CAVEAT EMPTOR: See Consumer Law

CAYMAN ISLANDS

SEE ALSO: Caribbean, England, International Law, Latin America, United Nations

INTERNATIONAL
AGREEMENTS: "United Kingdom-United States: Agreement Concerning Obtaining Evidence from Cayman Islands with Regard to Narcotics Activities," 24 *International Legal Materials* 1110 (1985). See also vol. 24, p. 937; vol. 26, p. 536.

STATUTES: *Cayman Islands: Consolidated Index of Statutes* . . . (Fac. of Law Library, Univ. of West Indies, Barbados, 1983).

TREATISES &
LOOSELEAFS: *Caribbean Basin: A Tax Tour* (Cayman Islands) (Arthur Anderson & Co., 1985).
Commercial Law of the Cayman Islands by I. Paget-Brown (Woodhead-Faulkner Publishers Ltd., 1981).
Information Guide: Doing Business in Cayman Islands (Price Waterhouse).
Tax Haven Encyclopedia (Cayman Islands) by B. Spitz (Butterworths, 1975–).
West Indian Constitutions: Post Independence Reform (Cayman Islands) by F. Phillips (Oceana, 1985).

ARTICLES: "Compelled Waiver of Bank Secrecy in the Cayman Islands" by E. Auwarter, 9 *Fordham International Law Review* 680 (1986).
"Getting to Grips with the Cayman Islands' Banking System" by D. Chaikin, 6 *The Company Lawyer* 93 (1985).
"Piercing Offshore Bank Secrecy Laws Used to Launder Illegal Narcotics Profits: The Cayman Islands Example" by J. Horowitz, 20 *Texas International Law Journal* 133 (1985).
"Why Bankers Love the Cayman Islands" by R. Miller, *Business and Society Review* 19 (Summer, 1981).

CEMETERIES: See State & Local Government
CENSORSHIP: See Civil Rights, Constitutional Law, Media Law
CENSUS: See Statistics

CENTRAL AFRICAN REPUBLIC

SEE ALSO: Africa, International Law, United Nations

CONSTITUTION: "Central African Republic" by J. Salacuse in *Constitutions of the Countries of the World* by A. Blaustein & G. Flanz (Oceana, 1981).

**TREATISES &
LOOSELEAFS:**   *African Tax Systems* by R. Hammond & M. van den Abeelen (Central African Republic) (Amsterdam: Intl. Bureau of Fiscal Documentation, 1980–).
The Central African Republic: The Continent's Hidden Heart by T. O'Toole (Westview, 1986).
An Introduction to Law in French-Speaking Africa (Central African Republic) by J. Salacuse (Michie, 1969).

CENTRAL AMERICA: See Belize, Caribbean, Costa Rica, Cuba, El Salvador, Guatemala, Honduras, Latin America, Mexico, Nicaragua, Panama
CENTRAL AMERICAN COMMON MARKET: See Costa Rica, El Salvador, Guatemala, Latin America, Nicaragua
CERTIFICATE OF PUBLIC CONVENIENCE: See Transportation
CERTIFIED LEGAL ASSISTANT: See Paralegal
CERTIFIED PUBLIC ACCOUNTANT: See Accounting
CERTIORARI: See Trial & Appellate Practice
CEYLON: See Sri Lanka

CHAD

SEE ALSO: Africa, International Law, United Nations

CONSTITUTION: "Chad" by M. Tarantino in *Constitution of the Countries of the World* by A. Blaustein & G. Flanz (Oceana, 1982).

TREATISES: *African Tax Systems* (Chad) by R. Hammond & M. van den Abeelen (Amsterdam: Intl. Bureau of Fiscal Documentation, 1980–).
An Introduction to Law in French-Speaking Africa (Chad) by J. Salacuse (Michie, 1969).
A State in Disarray: Conditions of Chad's Survival by M. Kelley (Westview, 1986).

ARTICLES: "UN Assistance to Chad" by U. Wasserman, 17 *Journal of World Trade Law* 170 (1983).

CHAMPERTY: See Professional Responsibility
CHANCERY: See Equity
CHANGE OF NAME: See Family Law, Trial & Appellate Practice, Women & the Law

CHANNEL ISLANDS

SEE ALSO: England, International Law, United Nations

**RESEARCH GUIDES &
BIBLIOGRAPHIES:** *A Bibliographic Guide to the Law of the United Kingdom, the Channel Islands and the Isle of Man,* 2d ed., A. Chloros, ed. (Univ. of London, Inst. of Advanced Legal Studies, 1973).

**TREATISES &
LOOSELEAFS:** *Channel Islands: Basic Business Information,* 2d ed. (NY: Deloitte, Haskins & Sells, 1980).
Information Guide: Doing Business in Jersey (Price Waterhouse).
Tax Havens Encyclopedia (Guernsey) by B. Spitz (Butterworths, 1975–).
Tax Laws of the World—Guernsey (FL: Foreign Tax Law Assn.).

ARTICLES: "Arbitration in the Channel Islands" by P. Redmond, 2 *Journal of International Arbitration* 45 (1985).
"Arbitration in the Channel Islands" by W. Moran & P. Redmond, *International Business Lawyer* 275 (June, 1985).
"Jersey: A Low Tax Area," 10 *Taxation* 566 (1983) (see also 1986 Conveyancer and Property Lawyer 146).
"Jersey," "Guernsey," "(Guernsey) Alderney," "(Guernsey) Fief of Sark" by N. Yell in *Constitutions of Dependencies and Special Sovereignties* by A. Blaustein (Oceana, 1981).
"Jersey's Housing Control Law," 128 *Solicitor's Journal* 749 (Nov., 1984).

CHARACTER & REPUTATION EVIDENCE: See Trial & Appellate Practice
CHARITABLE TRUSTS: See Estate Planning
CHARITY: See Estate Planning, Nonprofit Corporations
CHART: See Intellectual Property
CHARTER: See Corporate Law, State & Local Government
CHARTERING: See Maritime Law
CHATTEL MORTGAGE: See Personal Property, Uniform Commercial Code
CHECKS: See Banking Law, Uniform Commercial Code
CHEMICALS: See Environmental Law, Food, Natural Resources, Water Law
CHEMISTRY: See Forensic Science
CHICAGO BOARD OF TRADE: See Commodities
CHICAGO MERCANTILE EXCHANGE: See Commodities
CHICANOS: See Civil Rights
CHILD ABUSE: See Criminal Law, Family Law
CHILD CUSTODY: See Family Law, Mediation
CHILD LABOR: See Employee Benefits, Juvenile Law, Labor Law
CHILDREN: See Constitutional Law, Contracts, Education Law, Estate Planning, Family Law, Handicapped & the Law, Juvenile Law

CHILE

SEE ALSO: International Law, Latin America, United Nations

**RESEARCH GUIDES &
BIBLIOGRAPHIES:** *A Guide to the Law and Legal Literature of Chile, 1917–1946* (Library of Congress, 1947).

A Guide to the Official Publications of . . . Chile (Library of Congress, 1947).

INTERNATIONAL AGREEMENTS:

"Argentina-Chile: Negotiation and Conclusion of Border Dispute Agreement," 24 *International Legal Materials* 1 (1985).

TREATISES & LOOSELEAFS:

Capital Formation and Investment Incentives Around the World (Chile) by W. Diamond & D. Diamond (Matthew Bender, 1984–).

Digest of Commercial Laws of the World (Chile) (Natl. Assn. of Credit Management; Oceana, 1977–).

Four Failures: A Report of the U.N. Special Rapporteurs on Human Rights in Chile, Guatemala, Iran and Poland (NY: Americas Watch, 1986).

Information Guide, Doing Business in Chile (Price Waterhouse).

Latin America . . . A Tax Tour (Chile) (Arthur Anderson & Co., 1985).

Legal Aspects of Doing Business in Latin America (Chile) (Practicing Law Institute, 1980).

The Rise and Fall of Chilean Christian Democracy by M. Fleet (Princeton Univ. Press, 1985).

Series of Statements of the Law of the OAS Member States in Matters Affecting Business: Chile (Organization of American States, 1977).

Tax Laws of the World—Chile (FL: Foreign Tax Law Assn.).

ARTICLES:

"The Aviation Policy of Chile" by J. Langlois, 6 *Annals of Air and Space Law* 67 (1981).

"Chilean Antitrust Law" by D. Furnish, 19 *American Journal of Comparative Law* 464 (1971).

"Labor Relations Litigation: Chile, 1970–1972" by H. Ietswaart, 16 *Law & Society Review* 625 (1982).

"Latin American Tax Update: Chile" by M. Marti, 12 *Lawyer of the Americas* 643 (1980).

"Legal Memoranda: Chile," 17 *University of Miami Inter-American Law Review* 687 (1986).

"Married Women's Rights Under the Matrimonial Regime of Chile and Colombia, 7 *Harvard Women's Law Journal* 221 (1984).

"Stages of Repression and Legal Strategy for the Defense of Human Rights in Chile" by H. Fruhling, 5 *Human Rights Quarterly* 510 (1983).

CHINA

SEE ALSO:

Asia, Communism, International Law, Taiwan, United Nations

RESEARCH GUIDES & BIBLIOGRAPHIES:

"Annotated Bibliography," 22 *Colombia Journal of Transnational Law* 175 (1983).

"Annotated Bibliography of Selected English-Language Literature on Chinese Law," 6 *Legal Reference Services Quarterly* 95 (1986).

"Chinese Law in English: A Selected Bibliography" by J. Langevoort, 14 *International Journal of Legal Information* 111 (1986).

Chinese Law, Past and Present: A Bibliography of Enactments and Commentaries in English Text by F. Lin (NY: East Asian Institute, Columbia, 1966).

"Legal Aspects of U.S.-China Economic, Business, and Trade Relations: A Bibliography" in *International Legal Bibliography* (Oceana, 1984).

The People's Republic of China: A Bibliography of Selected English-Language Materials by J. Pinard (Library of Congress, 1985). (See also 11 *International Journal of Legal Information* 215 and 3 *China Law Reporter* 46).

"Selected Bibliography: Normalization of Relations with China" by H. Chiu, 5 *International Trade Law Journal* 196 (1979).

"Sources of Law in the People's Republic of China" by T. Hsia, 14 *International Lawyer* 25 (1980).

TREATIES & OTHER INTERNATIONAL AGREEMENTS:

Treaties of the People's Republic of China, 1949–1978: An Annotated Compilation by V. Li (Westview, 1978).

"U.S.-China Agreements," 80 *Department of State Bulletin* 1 (Nov., 1980).

U.S. Commercial Relations: A Compilation of Basic Documents (Wash. D.C.: Intl. Trade Admin., 1982).

CONSTITUTIONS:

The Chinese Communist Party Constitution of 1982: Deng Xiaoping's Program for Modernization by T. Hsia & C. Johnson (Library of Congress, Law Library, 1984).

"Constitution of the Communist Party of China," 25:38 *Beijing Review* 8 (1982).

"Constitution of the Communist Party of China," 9 *Review of Socialist Law* 183 (1982).

The Constitution of the People's Republic of China (Beijing: Foreign Language Press, 1983).

The Constitutions of the Communist World (China), W. Simons, ed. (Sijthoff & Noordhoff, 1980).

STATUTES & OTHER OFFICIAL DOCUMENTS:

The Laws of the People's Republic of China, 1979–1986 (Beijing: Foreign Languages Press, 1987).

Statutes and Regulations of the People's Republic of China (Carson, CA: R.E.O. Pubs., 1987–).

The T'ang Code, W. Johnson, transl. (Princeton Univ. Press, 1979).

The Chinese Criminal Procedure Code of the People's Republic of China and Related Documents, C. Kim, transl. (Rothman, 1985).

Criminal Code of the People's Republic of China, C. Kim, transl. (Rothman, 1982).

The Criminal Law and Criminal Procedure Law of the People's Republic of China (Beijing: Foreign Language Press, 1984).

Laws and Regulations of the People's Republic of China (Hong Kong Cultural Co., 1984).

The Official Chinese Customs Guide by the Chinese Office of the Customs General Admin. of the People's Republic of China (NY: Longman, 1985).

"Codification in Post-Mao China," 30 *American Journal of Comparative Law* 395 (1982).

ANNUALS, JOURNALS & OTHER PERIODICALS:

Annals (Chinese Society of Intl. Law).

Annual Report of China (Hong Kong: Kingsway Intl. Pubs., Ltd., 1983–).

Beijing Review (Beijing Rev. Pubs.).

China Law Reporter (ABA, Intl. Law & Prac. Section, 1982–).

China Law Review (1922–40).

Chinese Law and Government (1968–).

Chinese Yearbook of International Law and Affairs (Baltimore: Chinese Society of Intl. Law, 1982–).

Review of Socialist Law.

DICTIONARIES:

Dictionary of Chinese Law and Government by P. Bilancia (Stanford Univ. Press, 1981).

English-Chinese Law Dictionary by W. Hong (Hong Kong: Chinese Univ., 1972).

LOOSELEAFS: *Business Transactions with China, Japan, and South Korea,* P. Saney & H. Smit, eds. (Matthew Bender, 1983–).
China Hand: Investing, Licensing & Trading Conditions Today (NY: Business Intl. Corp., 1981–).
Digest of Commercial Laws of the World (Natl. Assn. of Credit Management; Oceana 1977–).
East Asian Executive Reports (Wash. D.C.: Intl. Executive Reports, Ltd., 1979–).

TREATISES: *Agreements and the People's Republic of China, 1949–1967* by D. Johnston & H. Chiu (Harvard Univ. Press, 1968).
China and the Law of the Sea, Air, and Environment by J. Greenfield (Sijthoff & Noordhoff, 1979).
China Laws for Foreign Business (CCH Australia, Ltd., 1985).
China's Boundary Treaties and Frontier Disputes by L. Chang (Oceana, 1982).
The Chinese Connection and Normalization (ABA, Standing Comm. on Law and Natl. Security, 1980).
Chinese Family Law and Social Change . . ., D. Buxbaum, ed. (Univ. of Wash. Press, 1978).
Commercial, Business, and Trade Laws: People's Republic of China (Oceana, 1982).
Criminal Justice in Post-Mao China by S. Leng & H. Chiu (Albany: State Univ. of N.Y. Press, 1985).
Doing Business in the People's Republic of China (Price Waterhouse).
Foreign Trade, Investment and the Law in the People's Republic of China, M. Moser, ed. (Oxford Univ. Press, 1984).
Fundamental Legal Documents of Communist China, A. Blaustein, ed. (Rothman, 1962).
Investment and Taxation in the People's Republic of China (Intl. Bureau of Fiscal Documentation).
Justice and Politics in People's China: Legal Order or Continuing Revolution by J. Brady (Academic Press, 1982).
Law Without Lawyers: A Comparative View of Law in China and the United States by V. Li, (Westview, 1978).
Legal Aspects of Doing Business in China (Practicing Law Institute, 1985).
The Legal System of the Chinese Soviet Republic, W. Butler, ed. (Transnational Publishers, 1983).
Sino-American Economic Exchanges: The Legal Contributions by G. Wang (Praeger, 1985).

ARTICLES: "China: Implementing Regulations under Trademark Law," 82 *Patent and Trademark Review* 120 (1984).
"China: Problems of Marriage and Divorce" by M. Palmer, 27 *Journal of Family Law* 57 (1988–89).
"China's Law of Civil Procedure" by Y. Cheng, 25:33 *Beijing Review* 20 (1982).
"China's New Joint Venture Law" by P. Brown, 4 *Boston College International and Comparative Law Review* 115 (1981).
"China's Offshore Petroleum Resources Law" by P. Yuan, 16 *International Lawyer* 647 (1982).
"A Comparative Study of Foreign Investment Laws in Taiwan and China" by T. Wan, 11 *California Western International Law Journal* 236 (1981).
"A Comparison of the Chinese and Soviet Codes of Criminal Law and Procedure" by H. Berman 73 *Journal of Criminal Law and Criminology* 238 (1982).
"Contract in China: Law, Practice, and Dispute Resolution" by R. Macneil, 38 *Stanford Law Review* 303 (1986).

"Copyright Relations Between the United States and the People's Republic of China" by R. Goldstein 10 *Brooklyn Journal of International Law* 403 (1984).

"The Criminal Law of the People's Republic of China," 73 *Journal of Criminal Law and Criminology* 138 (1982).

"Detailed Rules and Regulations for the Implementation of the Individual Income Tax Law," 3:3 *East Asian Executive Reports* 25 (1981).

"The Development of Inheritance Law in the Soviet Union and the People's Republic of China" by F. Foster-Simons, 33 *American Journal of Comparative Law* 33 (1985).

"Economic Contract Law," 2 *China Law Reporter* 61 (1982).

"Free Speech in China" by E. Eliasoph, 7 *Yale Journal of World Public Order* 287 (1981).

"Legal Analysis of the Sino-Soviet Frontier Disputes" by L. Chang, 3 *Hastings International and Comparative Law Review* 231 (1980).

"The New Legal Framework for Joint Ventures in China: Guidelines for Investors" by J. Swindler, 16 *Law and Policy in International Business* 1005 (1984).

"The People's Republic of China: New Marriage Regulations" by M. Palmer, 26 *Journal of Family Law* 39 (1987–88). See also 25 *Journal of Family Law* 41 (1986–87).

"Private Enterprise in China" by H. Chao & Y. Xiaoping, 19 *International Lawyer* 1215 (1985).

"Provisional Regulations on Lawyers," 1 *China Law Reporter* 217 (1981).

"Regulations for . . . Joint Ventures Using Chinese and Foreign Investment," 83 *Patent and Trademark Review* 131 (1985).

"Selected Documents (U.S.-China Policy)," 5 *International Trade Law Journal* 105 (1979).

"Tax Aspects of Doing Business with the People's Republic of China" by T. Gelatt, 22 *Columbia Journal of Transnational Law* 421 (1984).

"Technology Takes Command: The Policy of the People's Republic of China with Respect to Technology Transfer and Protection of Intellectual Property" by T. Chwang, 21 *International Lawyer* 129 (1987).

"The Trademark Law of the People's Republic of China," 2 *China Law Reporter* 111 (1982).

"Ventures in the China Trade: An Analysis of China's Emerging Legal Framework for the Regulation of Foreign Investment" by W. Alford & D. Birenbaum, 3 *Northwestern Journal of International Law and Business* 56 (1981).

MISCELLANEOUS:

"China: Economic Law," 22 *International Legal Materials* 330 (1983). See also vol. 24, p. 797.

"China-U.S.: Agreement for Cooperation Concerning Peaceful Uses of Nuclear Energy", 24 *International Legal Materials* 1393 (1985).

"China-U.S.: Agreement for the Avoidance of Double Taxation and the Prevention of Tax Evasion on Income," 23 *International Legal Materials* 677 (1984).

"People's Republic of China: Interim Regulations on Technology Transfer," 24 *International Legal Materials* 292 (1985).

"People's Republic of China: Patent Law," 24 *International Legal Materials* 295 (1985).

"People's Republic of China: Regulations on Implementing the Law of Chinese-Foreign Joint Ventures," 22 *International Legal Materials* 1033 (1985).

CHIPS: See Computers

CHIROPRACTOR: See Health & Medicine

CHOICE OF LAW: See Conflict of Law, Insurance

CHRISTIANITY: See Canon Law, Church & State

CHRISTMAS ISLAND: See Australia

CHURCH & STATE

SEE ALSO: Canon Law, Civil Rights, Constitutional Law, Education law, Nonprofit Corporations, Torts

RESEARCH GUIDES & BIBLIOGRAPHIES:

Law and Theology: An Annotated Bibliography (Oak Park, IL: Christian Legal Society, 1979–).

Religious Conflict in America: A Bibliography by A. Menendez (Garland, 1985).

JOURNALS, NEWSLETTERS & OTHER PERIODICALS:

Catholic Lawyer (St. John's Univ. Sch. of Law, 1955–).

CLS Quarterly (Christian Legal Society).

Journal of Christian Jurisprudence (O.W. Coburn Sch. of Law).

Journal of Church and State (Baylor Univ., J. M. Dawson Studies in Church and State, 1959–).

The Journal of Law and Religion (Hamline Univ., 1983–).

The Jurist (Catholic Univ. of America, 1941–).

Review of Religious Research (1959–).

TREATISES & LOOSELEAFS:

Ascending Liability in Religious and Other Nonprofit Organizations by E. Gaffney (Mercer Univ. Press).

On Being a Christian and a Lawyer by T. Shaffer (Brigham Young Univ. Press, 1981).

Clear and Present Danger: Church and State in Post-Christian America by W. Stanmeyer (Ann Arbor: Servant Books, 1983).

Clergy and Teacher Malpractice by R. McMenamin (Portland, OR: Jomac Pub., 1987).

Clergy Malpractice by R. McMenamin (Hein, 1986).

Constitutions of American Denominations by R. Schenck (Hein, 1984).

The First Freedoms: Church and State in America by T. Curry (Oxford Univ. Press, 1986).

Government Intervention in Religious Affairs by D. Kelley (Pilgrim Press, 1982).

Legal Aspects of Church Management, 3d ed. by R. Schmidt (CA: Intl. Church of the Foursquare Gospel, 1984).

Legal Aspects of Religious Instruction in Public Schools by R. Mize (Univ. Microfilms Intl., 1981).

Legal Problems of Religious and Private Schools by R. Mawdsley (Kansas: Natl. Org. on Legal Problems of Education, 1983).

Major Cases in First Amendment Law: Church and State, W. Marshall, ed. (Univ. Pubs. of America, 1984).

Pastor, Church & Law by R. Hammar (MO: Gospel Pub., 1983).

Private Churches and Public Money by P. Weber (Greenwood Press, 1981).

Religion in the Public Schools by R. McMillan (Mercer Univ. Press, 1984).

Religion, Law, and the Growth of Constitutional Thought, 1150–1650 by B. Tierney (Cambridge Univ. Press, 1982).

Religion, State and the Burger Court by L. Pfeffer (Prometheus Books, 1984).

State and Campus: State Regulation of Religiously Affiliated Higher Education by F. Dutile (Univ. of Notre Dame Press, 1984).

Toward Benevolent Neutrality: Church, State, and the Supreme Court by R. Miller (Waco, TX: Markham Press, 1982).

Trust Doctrines in Church Controversies by D. Oaks (Mercer Univ. Press).

Watson v. Jones: The Walnut Street Presbyterian Church and the First Amendment by R. Eades (Louisville: Archer Editions, 1982).

ENCYCLOPEDIAS: AMERICAN JURISPRUDENCE 2D (Am Jur 2d)
Check the following topics in the *General Index* volumes for Am Jur 2d:

Civil Rights	Freedom of Religion
Clergymen	Religion and Religious
Constitutional Law	Societies

CORPUS JURIS SECUNDUM (CJS)
Check the following topics in the *General Index* volumes for CJS:

Civil Rights	Jehovah's Witnesses
Clergymen	Religion
Constitutional Law	Religious Organizations
First Amendment	

DIGESTS: CASE SEARCH IN WEST DIGESTS BY KEY TOPIC
In the *Descriptive Word Index* of the West digests, look for key topics and numbers under the following subject headings:

Civil Rights	Religion
Clergymen	Religious Organizations
Constitutional Law	Sunday
First Amendment	

ALR: ANNOTATIONS
Check the index volumes for ALR, ALR2d, ALR3d, ALR4th, and ALR Fed for annotations under the following subject headings:

Atheists and Agnostics	Religion
Clergy	Religious Societies
Discrimination	

PERIODICALS: CURRENT LAW INDEX (CLI) & LEGAL RESOURCE INDEX (LRI)
In the CLI and LRI, look for references to periodical literature under the following subject headings:

Canon Law	Federal Aid to Private
Catholic Church	Schools
Christian Education	Marriage (Canon Law)
Church and Education	Monasticism
Church and State	Religion and Law
Church Schools	Religion and State
Constitutional Law	Religioous Liberty
Ecclesiastical Law	

INDEX TO LEGAL PERIODICALS (ILP)
In the ILP, look for references to legal periodical literature under the following subject headings:

Churches	Discrimination
Civil Rights	Ecclesiastical Law
Clergy	Establishment Clause
Conscientious Objectors	Freedom of Religion
Constitutional Law	Religion

CIGARETTES: See Agriculture, Environmental Law, Torts

CIRCUIT COURTS

SEE ALSO: Judicial Administration, Trial & Appellate Practice; and entries under individual states

ALL CIRCUITS:
Federal Circuit Court Rules Service (Rules Service Co., 1982–).
Federal Local Court Rules, Pike & Fischer, ed. (Callaghan, 1964–).
Federal Rules Citations (Shepard's).

FIRST CIRCUIT:
Federal Court Civil Litigation in the First Circuit (Massachusetts Cont. Legal Education, 1982).
Federal Procedure Rules Service. First Circuit (Lawyers Co-op., 1985–)

SURVEYS (example): "United States Court of Appeals for the First Circuit," 14 *Suffolk University Law Review* 199.

SECOND CIRCUIT:
Federal Procedure Rules Service. Second Circuit (Lawyers Co-op., 1985–).
New York Rules of Court: McKinney's State and Federal (West, 1965–).
Rules of the U.S. Courts in New York (Clark Boardman, 1984–).
Second Circuit Redbook (NY: Federal Bar Council, 1975/76–).

SURVEYS (example): "Second Circuit Review," 54 *Brooklyn Law Review* 321.

THIRD CIRCUIT:
Appeals to the Third Circuit by E. Wertheimer (Butterworths, 1986–).
Federal Procedure Rules Service. Third Circuit (Lawyers Co-op., 1985–).

SURVEYS (example): "Third Circuit Review," 33 *Villanova Law Review* 555.

FOURTH CIRCUIT:
Federal Procedure Rules Service. Fourth Circuit (Lawyers Co-op., 1985–).
Fourth Circuit Review (Louisville: Fourth Circuit Review).

SURVEYS (example): "Fourth Circuit Review," 44 *Washington and Lee Law Review* 507.

FIFTH CIRCUIT:
Appeals to the Fifth Circuit by G. Rahdert & L. Roth (Butterworths, 1977).
Federal Procedure Rules Service. Fifth Circuit (Lawyers Co-op., 1985–).
A Court Divided: The Fifth Circuit Court of Appeals and the Politics of Judicial Reform by D. Barrow & T. Walker (Yale Univ. Press, 1988).

SURVEYS (examples): "Fifth Circuit Symposium," 33 *Loyola Law Review* 533.
"Fifth Circuit Symposium," 19 *Texas Tech. Law Review* 223

SIXTH CIRCUIT:
Federal Procedure Rules Service. Sixth Circuit (Lawyers Co-op., 1985–).
Internal Operating Procedures (U.S. Court of Appeals for the Sixth Circuit, 1985).
Practitioner's Handbook for Appeals to the United States Court of Appeals for the Sixth Circuit (Committee on Federal Courts of the Cincinnati Chapter of the Federal Bar Assn., 1981).

SURVEYS (example): "Sixth Circuit Survey," 19 *University of Toledo Law Review* 217.

SEVENTH CIRCUIT:
Federal Procedure Rules Service. Seventh Circuit (Lawyers Co-op., 1985–).
The Attorney's Guide to the Seventh Circuit Court of Appeals (State Bar of WI, 1987–).
"Seventh Circuit Review," 62 *Chicago-Kent Law Review* 351.

SURVEYS (examples) "Seventh Circuit Review," 62 *Chicago-Kent Law Review* 351.
"Seventh Circuit Review," 54 *Notre Dame Lawyer* 341.

EIGHTH CIRCUIT:
Federal Procedure Rules Service. Eighth Circuit (Lawyers Co-op., 1985–).

NINTH CIRCUIT:
Federal Procedure Rules Service. Ninth Circuit (Lawyers Co-op., 1985–).
The United States Ninth Circuit Service (San Francisco: Barclay Law Publisher, 1985–)

SURVEYS (example): "Ninth Circuit Survey Notes," 18 *Golden Gate University Law Review* 1.

TENTH CIRCUIT: *Federal Procedure Rules Service. Tenth Circuit* (Lawyers Co-op., 1985–).
Practitioners' Guide to the United States Court of Appeals for the Tenth Circuit (Office of the Clerk, U.S. Court of Appeals for the 10th Circuit, 1982).
Tenth Circuit Newsletter (Denver: Tenth Circuit Newsletter, Inc.)

SURVEYS (example): "Annual Tenth Circuit Survey," 65 *Denver Law Journal* 357

ELEVENTH CIRCUIT: *Appeals to the Eleventh Circuit Manual* by L. Roth & G. Rahdert (Clearwater, FL: D&S Pub., 1984–).
Federal Procedure Rules Service. Eleventh Circuit (Lawyers Co-op., 1985–).

SURVEYS (example): "Eleventh Circuit Survey," 39 *Mercer Law Review* 1057.

DISTRICT OF COLUMBIA CIRCUIT: See District of Columbia

CIRCUMSTANTIAL EVIDENCE: See Trial & Appellate Practice
CITATION: See Legal Research
CITIZENS & CITIZENSHIP: See Civil Rights, Constitutional Law, Human Rights, Immigration Law, International Law, Soviet Union
CITY: See State & Local Government
CITY PLANNING: See Zoning & Land Planning
CIVIL AERONAUTICS BOARD: See Air & Aviation, Transportation
CIVIL ARREST: See Torts
CIVIL COMMITMENT: See Mental health
CIVIL DEATH: See Election
CIVIL DEFENSE: See Military Law

CIVIL LAW

SEE ALSO: Europe, France, International Law, Latin America, Louisiana, Quebec

JOURNALS & OTHER PERIODICALS: *Tulane Civil Law Forum* (1973–).

TREATISES: *Civil Law and the Anglo-American Lawyer* by H. DeVries (Oceana, 1976).
Civil Law in the Modern World, Yiannopoulos, ed. (Louisiana State Univ. Press, 1965).
The Civil Law System: An Introduction to the Comparative Study of Law, 2d ed. by von Mehren & Gordley (Little, Brown, 1977).
The Civil Law Tradition: An Introduction to Legal Systems of Western Europe and Latin America, 2d ed. by J. Merryman (Stanford Univ. Press, 1985).
A Common Law Lawyer Looks at Civil Law by F. Lawson (Univ. of Mich. Law Sch., 1955).
Drafting and Enforcing Contracts in Civil and Common Law Jurisdictions (Kluwer, 1986).

CIVIL PROCEDURE: See Trial & Appellate Practice

CIVIL RIGHTS

SEE ALSO: Constitutional Law, Election, Employment Discrimination, Human Rights, International Law, Legal History, Women & the Law

**JOURNALS, NEWSLETTERS
& OTHER PERIODICALS:**   *Bill of Rights Journal* (Natl. Civil Liberties Union).
Black Law Journal (UCLA Sch. of Law).
Chicano Law Review (1972–).
Civil Rights Developments (Rutgers Univ. Sch. of Law, Newark, 1985–).
Harvard Civil Rights—Civil Liberties Law Review (1966–).
Law & Inequality (Univ. of Minn. Law Sch., 1983–).
National Lawyers Guild Practitioner (1940–).
Perspectives: The Civil Rights Quarterly (U.S. Commn. on Civil Rights).
Race Relations Law Reporter (1956–).

**TREATISES &
LOOSELEAFS:**   *The Burden of Brown: Thirty Years of School Desegregation* by R. Wolters (Univ. of Tenn. Press, 1984).
Civil Rights Actions by J. Cook (Matthew Bender, 1983–).
Civil Rights and Civil Liberties Litigation: A Guide to Section 1983 by S. Nahmod (Shepard's, 1979).
Civil Rights—Discrimination by H. McCormick (Harnow Press).
Civil Rights Implications of the Education Block Grant Program (no. 83, 120–A; GPO, 1982).
Civil Rights Litigation and Attorney Fees Annual Handbook (Clark Boardman, 1985–).
The Criminal Justice System and Blacks by D. Georges-Abeyie (Clark Boardman, 1984).
The Eisenhower Administration and Black Civil Rights by R. Burk (Univ. of Tenn. Press, 1984).
Equal Opportunity in Housing (Prentice-Hall, 1973–).
Federal Civil Rights Acts—Civil Practice, 2d ed. by C. Antineau (Lawyers Co-op., 1980).
Police Misconduct and Civil Rights Law Report by Natl. Lawyers Guild (Clark Boardman).
Policy Guide of the American Civil Liberties Union (ACLU, 1981).
Recent Developments in Section 1983 Civil Rights Litigation (Practicing Law Institute, 1984).
Statistical Proof of Discrimination by D. Baldus (Shepard's, 1980).

ENCYCLOPEDIAS: AMERICAN JURISPRUDENCE 2D (Am Jur 2d)
Check the following topics in the *General Index* volumes for Am Jur 2d:

Civil Rights	Freedom of Religion
Constitutional Law	Freedom of Speech and
Discrimination	Press
Due Process	Negroes
Equal Protection	Race

CORPUS JURIS SECUNDUM (CJS)
Check the following topics in the *General Index* volumes for CJS:

Civil Rights	Political Rights
Discrimination	Race
Freedom of Speech	Right of Privacy

DIGESTS: CASE SEARCH IN WEST DIGESTS BY KEY TOPIC
In the *Descriptive Word Index* of the West digests, look for key topics and numbers under the following subject headings:

Aliens	Civil Rights
Citizens	Criminal Law

Discrimination	Political Rights
Freedom of Speech	Race
Liberty	Right of Privacy

ALR:
ANNOTATIONS
Check the index volumes for ALR, ALR2d, ALR3d, ALR4th, and ALR Fed for annotations under the following subject headings:

Civil Rights Attorney's Fees	Privacy
	Race or Color
Discrimination	Religion
Due Process of Law	Segregation
Equal Protection of Law	Sex Discrimination

PERIODICALS:
CURRENT LAW INDEX (CLI) & LEGAL RESOURCE INDEX (LRI)
In the CLI and LRI, look for references to periodical literature under the following subject headings:

Affirmative Action	Freedom of Association
Age Discrimination	Minorities
Assembly	Privacy
Blacks	Race Discrimination
Civil Rights	Racism
Constitutional Law	School Desegregation
Criminal Law	Sex Discrimination
Discrimination	Slavery

INDEX TO LEGAL PERIODICALS (ILP)
In the ILP, look for references to legal periodical literature under the following subject headings:

Censorship	Loyalty and Loyalty Oaths
Civil Rights	Minorities
Constitutional Law	Races
Discrimination	Right of Privacy
Elections	Segregation
Freedom	Women
Human Rights	

CIVIL SERVICE

SEE ALSO:
Employee Benefits, Employment Discrimination, Labor Law, State & Local Government

RESEARCH GUIDES & BIBLIOGRAPHIES:
Collective Bargaining for Public Employees: A Bibliography by M. Vance (Vance Bibliographies, 1981).
"Federal Labor Law and its Sources" by S. Pagel, 5 *Legal References Services Quarterly* 5 (1985).

LEGISLATION:
Civil Service Reform Act of 1978, 92 Stat. 1111 (1978).
Federal Employee's Compensation Act, 39 Stat. 742 (1916).
Longshoreman's and Harbor Worker's Compensation Act of 1927, 46 Stat. 1424 (1927).
Postal Reorganization Act of 1970, 84 Stat. 719 (1970).

LEGISLATIVE HISTORY: *Legislative History of the Civil Service Reform Act of 1978* (Govt. Printing Office, 1979).
Legislative History of the Federal Service Labor-Management Relations Statute, Title VII of the Civil Service Reform Act of 1978 (Govt. Printing Office, 1979).

ADMINISTRATIVE DECISIONS & RELATED MATERIALS: *Administrative Law Judge Decisions Report* (FLRA, 1981–).
Civil Service Laws, Executive Orders, Rules and Regulations (U.S. Civil Service Commission, 1978–).
Decisions (Employees Compensation Appeals Board, 1946–).
Decisions and Interpretations of the Federal Labor Relations Council (Govt. Printing Office, 1975–78).
Decisions of the Federal Labor Relations Authority (FLRA, 1981–).
Decisions of the United States Merit Protection Board (The Board, 1981–).
The Digest (U.S. Merit Systems Protection Board, 1980–).
Digests and Tables of Cases for Decisions of the Federal Labor Relations Authority (FLRA, 1980–).

ANNUAL REPORT: *Annual Report of the Federal Labor Relations Authority and the Federal Service Impasses Panel* (Govt. Printing Office, 1979–).

MICROFICHE: *Collective Bargaining Agreements,* Public Sector (Sanford, NC: Microfilming Corp. of America, 1981–).

JOURNALS & OTHER PERIODICALS: *Government Union Review* (VA: Public Service Research Foundation, 1980–).
Journal of Collective Negotiation in the Public Sector (Baywood Publishing Co.).
Labor Arbitration in Government (Amer. Arbitration Assn., 1971–).

LOOSELEAFS: *Federal Labor Relations Reporter* (Labor Relations Press, 1979–).
Federal Merit Systems Reporter (Labor Relations Press, 1981–).
Government Employee Relations Report (BNA, 1963–).
National Public Employment Reporter (Labor Relations Press, 1979–).
Public Employee Bargaining (CCH, 1977–).
Public Employee Bargaining Reporter (CCH, 1971–).
Public Personnel Administration: Labor-Management Relations (Prentice-Hall, 1973–).
Public Personnel Administration: Policies & Practices for Personnel (Prentice-Hall, 1973–).
United States Merit Systems Protection Board Digest (West, 1985–).
United States Merit Systems Protection Board Reporter (West, 1985–).

TREATISES: *Arbitration and the Federal Sector Advocate: A Practical Guide* by F. Loevi & R. Kaplan (Amer. Arbitration Assn., 1982).
Civilian Personnel Law Manual, 2d ed. (Gen. Accounting Off., Off. of the General Counsel, 1983).
Drug Testing Programs by Public Employees: Suggested Guidelines (A.B.A., 1988).
Federal Civil Service Law and Procedure: A Basic Guide, E. Bussey, ed. (BNA, 1984).
A Guide to Merit Systems Protection Board Law and Practice, 2d ed. by P. Broida (Wash. D.C.: Dewey Pubs., 1985).
Labor-Management Relations, Civil Service Reforms, and EEO in the Federal Service, A. Burnett, ed. (Federal Bar Assn., 1980).
Layoffs, RIFs, and EEO in the Public Sector (BNA, 1982).

Legislating Bureaucratic Change: The Civil Service Reform Act of 1978, P. Ingraham & C. Ban, eds. (Albany: State Univ. of N.Y. Press, 1984).

Merit Systems Protection Board: Rights and Remedies by R. Vaughn (Law Journal Seminars-Press, 1984).

Public Employee Organizing and the Law by M. Leibig & W. Kahn (BNA, 1987).

Public Sector Labor Relations by M. Levine & E. Hagburg (West, 1979).

The Right to Strike in Public Employment by G. Sterrett & A. Aboud (Cornell Univ., N.Y. State School of Ind. and Labor Relations, 1982).

ENCYCLOPEDIAS:

AMERICAN JURISPRUDENCE 2D (Am Jur 2d)
Check the following topics in the *General Index* volumes for Am Jur 2d:

Administrative Law	Public Officers and
Civil Service	Employees
Compensation	States
	United States

CORPUS JURIS SECUNDUM (CJS)
Check the following topics in the *General Index* volumes for CJS:

Civil Service	Officers
Compensation and	United States Officers
Salaries	and Employees

DIGESTS:

CASE SEARCH IN WEST DIGESTS BY KEY TOPIC
In the *Descriptive Word Index* of the West digests, look for key topics and numbers under the following subject headings:

Civil Service	Officers and Public
Compensation and	Employees
Salaries	Post Office
Labor Relations	States
Municipal Corporations	United States

ALR:

ANNOTATIONS
Check the index volumes for ALR, ALR2d, ALR3d, ALR4th, and ALR Fed for the annotations under the following subject headings:

Administrative Law	Hatch Act
Civil Service	

PERIODICALS:

CURRENT LAW INDEX (CLI) & LEGAL RESOURCE INDEX (LRI)
In the CLI and LRI, look for references to periodical literature under the following subject headings:

Bureaucracy	Public Service
Civil Service	Employment

INDEX TO LEGAL PERIODICALS (ILP)
In the ILP, look for references to legal periodical literature under the following subject headings:

Administrative Agencies	Labor Law/Public Sector
Arbitration and Award	Loyalty and Loyalty Oaths
Civil Service	Unions/Public Sector

CIVIL TRIAL: See Trial & Appellate Practice
CLAIMS: See Trial & Appellate Practice
CLAIMS COMMISSION: See Indians

CLASS ACTION: See Trial & Appellate Practice
CLEAN AIR ACT: See Environmental Law
CLEAN HANDS: See Equity
CLEAR & CONVINCING EVIDENCE: See Trial & Appellate Practice
CLEAR TITLE: See Real Estate
CLERGY: See Canon Law, Church & State
CLERKS OF COURT: See Judicial Administration, Trial & Appellate Practice
CLIFFORD TRUSTS: See Estate Planning
CLINICAL EDUCATION: See Legal Education
CLOSE CORPORATION: See Corporate Law
CLOSED SHOP: See Labor Law
CMEA: See Finland, Hungary
COAL: See Energy, Natural Resources, Oil & Gas, Water Law, West Virginia
COASTAL ZONE: See Natural Resources, Water Law
COAST GUARD: See Military Law
COCOS ISLANDS: See Australia
CODE OF PROFESSIONAL RESPONSIBILITY: See Professional Responsibility
COFFEE: See Agriculture, Commodities, Food
COHABITATION: See Family Law
COINSURANCE: See Insurance
COLLATERAL ATTACK: See Trial & Appellate Practice
COLLATERAL ESTOPPEL: See Trial & Appellate Practice
COLLECTION: See Agency, Banking Law, Business Law, Consumer Law, Trial &
    Appellate Practice
COLLECTIVE BARGAINING: See Civil Service, Employee Benefits, Labor Law,
    Women & the Law
COLLEGE: See Education Law
COLLEGE SPORTS: See Sports Law
COLLISION: See Maritime Law, Torts

COLOMBIA

SEE ALSO: International Law, Latin America, United Nations

RESEARCH GUIDE &
BIBLIOGRAPHY: *A Guide to the Official Publications of . . . Colombia* (Library of Congress, 1948).

CONSTITUTION: "Colombia" in *Constitutions of the Countries of the World* by A. Blaustein & G. Flanz
                      (Oceana, 1982).

STATUTES & RELATED
LAWS: *Colombia Penal Code,* P. Eder, transl. (Rothman, 1967).

TREATISES &
LOOSELEAFS: *The Andean Legal Order* (Colombia) by F. Garcia-Amador (Oceana, 1978).
                      Business Operations in Colombia by D. Perenzin, Tax Management Foreign Income
                          Portfolio, no. 260–3rd (1978).
                      Capital Formation and Investment Incentives Around the World (Colombia) by W.
                          Diamond & D. Diamond (Matthew Bender, 1984–).
                      The Central-Americanization of Colombia: Human Rights and the Peace Process (NY:
                          Americas Watch Committee, 1986).
                      Digest of Commercial Laws of the World (Colombia) (Natl. Assn. of Credit Manage-
                          ment; Oceana, 1977–).

Information Guide, Doing Business in Colombia (Price Waterhouse).
Intergovernmental Finance in Colombia (Harvard Law Sch., Intl. Tax Program, 1984).
Latin America . . . A Tax Tour (Colombia) (Arthur Anderson & Co., 1985).
Latin American Democracies: Colombia, Costa Rica, Venezuela by J. Peeler (Univ. of North Carolina Press, 1985).
Patent and Trademark Laws of Colombia by G. Cavelier (Bogotá: Edificio Siski, 1979).
Series of Statements of the Law of the OAS Member States in Matters Affecting Business: Colombia (Organization of American States).
Taxation and Development: Lessons from Colombia Experience by R. Bird (Harvard Univ. Press, 1970).
Tax Laws of the World—Colombia (FL: Foreign Tax Law Assn., 1985–).

ARTICLES:

"Colombia: Discriminating against Women" by M. Plata, 27 *Journal of Family Law* 81 (1988–89).
"Colombia Patent Sale Procedures . . ." by R. Campagna, 15 *International Lawyer* 262 (1981).
"Court Puts Foreign Loans in Danger" (Colombia) by J. Leavy, 5 *International Financial Law Review* 7 (1986).
"Latin American Tax Update: Colombia" by M. Marti, 12 *Lawyer of the Americas* 645 (1980).
"Lawyers in Colombia" by D. Lynch, 13 *Texas International Law Journal* 199 (1978).
"Legal Memorandum: Colombia" by M. Marti, 15 *Lawyer of the Americas* 421 (1983).
"Legal Memorandum: Colombia," 16 *University of Miami Inter-American Law Review* 239,452 (1984). See also vol. 17, pp. 387, 695.
"Married Women's Rights Under the Matrimonial Regime of Chile and Colombia, 7 *Harvard Women's Law Journal* 221 (1984).
"Observations in Loco: Practice and Procedure of the Inter-American Commission on Human Rights" (Colombia), 19 *Texas International Law Journal* 285, 301 (1984).
"Presidential Intervention in the Economy and the Rule of Law in Colombia" by R. Findley, 28 *American Journal of Comparative Law* 423 (1980).
"Transfer of Technology to Colombia" by R. Radway, 12 *Lawyer of the Americas* 321 (1980).

COLONIALISM: See Africa, Algeria, Bangladesh, Caribbean, International Law, Latin America, Mozambique, Somalia, Zambia
COLONY: See International Law

COLORADO

SEE ALSO: Circuit Courts (Tenth Circuit)

RESEARCH GUIDE: "Colorado Legal Source Materials—1981" by S. Weinstein, 10 *Colorado Lawyer* 1816 (August, 1981).

STATUTES: *Colorado Revised Statutes* (Bradford-Robinson Co.).
Session Laws of Colorado.

**ADMINISTRATIVE
REGULATIONS:**   *Code of Colorado Regulations* (Public Record Corp., 1977–).
Colorado Code of Regulations in the *Colorado Register.*

CASES & OPINIONS:
Colorado Court of Appeals Reports.
Colorado Reporter (West).
Colorado Reports (Golden Bell Press—up to vol. 200).
Pacific Reporter (West).

COURT RULES:
Colorado Civil Rules Annotated, 2d ed. by R. Hardaway (West, 1985).
Colorado Court Rules Annotated (Michie, 1984–)
Colorado Local Court Rules (Legal Publishing Co., 1978–).
Colorado Rules of Court (West).
Colorado Rules of Evidence Annotated, 2d ed. by E. Jacobson & A. Bucholtz
    (Colorado Legal Pub. Co., 1985–).

JURY INSTRUCTIONS:
Colorado Jury Instructions—Civil, 2d ed. (Lawyers Co-op., 1980–).
Colorado Jury Instructions, Criminal (West, 1983).

ETHICS & PROFESSIONAL RESPONSIBILITY:
Colorado Ethics Opinions, 2d ed. (Colo. Cont. Legal Ed., 1983–).
Colorado Ethics Opinions Deskbook, 3d ed. (Colo. Bar Assn. Ethics Committee; Cont.
    Legal Ed. in Colo., 1983).

OPINIONS OF THE ATTORNEY GENERAL:
Attorney General Reports and Opinions.

JOURNALS & OTHER PERIODICALS:
Colorado Lawyer (Colo. Bar Assn., 1971–).
Denver Bar Examiner.

TREATISES & LOOSELEAFS:
Closely Held Corporations by C. Krendl (Colo. Cont. Legal Ed., 1981–).
Colorado Corporate Forms by D. Erickson (Callaghan, 1984).
Colorado Estate Planning, 3d ed., Wm. Huff, ed. (Colo. Cont. Legal Ed., 1984–).
Colorado Estate Planning Forms Book, 3d ed. (Colo. Cont. Legal Ed., 1983–).
Colorado Estate Statutes: Wills, Estates, Trusts and Taxes (Colo. Cont. Legal Ed., 1980–).
Colorado Law Annotated by B. Pringle (Bancroft-Whitney, 1984).
Colorado Methods of Practice, 3d ed. by C. Krendl (West, 1983).
Colorado Taxation Reporter (CCH, 1952–).
Handbook of Colorado Family Law by S. Whicher (Colo. Cont. Legal Ed., 1982–).
Preservation Easements (Colo. Historical Society, 1984).
Quieting Title in Colorado by F. Williams (Courtright Pub., 1939) (Microfiche,
    Rothman).
Statutory Time Limitations: Colorado (Butterworths, 1981–).

DIGESTS, CITATOR & ENCYCLOPEDIA:
Colorado Advance Annotation Service (Michie, 1984–).
Colorado Digest (West).
Colorado Practice (West).
Pacific Digest (West).
Shepard's Colorado Citations.

COMEX: See Commodities
COMITY: See Trial & Appellate Practice
COMMENCEMENT OF ACTION: See Trial & Appellate Practice

COMMERCE: See Business Law, Constitutional Law, Maritime Law
COMMERCE DEPARTMENT: See Intellectual Property
COMMERCIAL ARBITRATION: See International Law, Labor Law
COMMERCIAL CODE: See Uniform Commercial Code
COMMERCIAL LAW: See Advertising, Business Law, Corporate Law, International
    Law
COMMERCIAL TORTS: See Torts
COMMINGLING OF FUNDS: See Professional Responsibility
COMMISSIONS: See State & Local Government, Zoning & Land Planning
COMMITTEES: See Legislative History

COMMODITIES

SEE ALSO: Agriculture, Business Law, European Economic Community, International Law, Securities Law

RULES & REGULATIONS: *By-Laws and Rules of the New York Mercantile Exchange* (NYME, 1977–).
COMEX By-Laws, Rules and Regulations (COMEX, 1978–).
Rules and Regulations of the Chicago Board of Trade (Chicago Board of Trade).
Rules and Regulations of the Chicago Mercantile Exchange (Chicago Mercantile Exchange).
Rules and Regulations of the Minneapolis Grain Exchange (Minn. Grain Exchange).

NEWSLETTER: *Commodities Law Letter* (NY: Commodities Law Press Associates, 1981–).

TREATISES &
LOOSELEAFS: *CFTC Administrative Reporter* (Washington Service Bureau, 1983–).
Coffee, Sugar and Cocoa Exchange Inc. Guide (CCH, 1979–).
Commodities Litigation Reporter (Andrews Pub., 1985–).
Commodities Regulation, 2d ed. by P. Johnson (Little, Brown, 1989).
Commodities Trading: The Essential Primer by R. Wasendorf (Dow Jones-Irwin, 1985).
Commodity Agreements and Price Stabilization by D. McNicol (Lexington Books, 1978).
Commodity Futures Law Reports (CCH, 1974–).
Commodity Market Controls: A Historical Review by C. Nappi (D.C. Heath & Co., 1979).
Commodity Trading Manual (Bruce Gold Publications, 1976–).
Handbook of Futures Markets: Commodity, Financial, Stock Index and Options by P. Kaufman (Wiley, 1984).
The Law and Organization of International Commodity Agreements by K. Khan (Martinus Nijhoff, 1982).
Law and Policy of Intergovernmental Primary Commodity Agreements, C. Johnston, ed. (Oceana, 1976–).
National Futures Association Manual (Prentice-Hall, 1983–).
Regulation of the Commodities Futures and Options Markets by T. Russo (Shepard's, 1983–).
Securities Fraud and Commodities Fraud by A. Bromberg & L. Lowenfels (Shepard's, 1967–).
Stabilizing World Commodity Markets, F. Adams & S. Klein, eds. (Lexington Books, 1978).
Winning in the Commodities Market: A Money-Making Guide to Commodity Futures Trading by G. Angel (Doubleday, 1979)

COMMON DISASTER: See Estate Planning

COMMON LAW: See Civil Law, Conflict of Law, Contracts, Criminal Law, Equity, Estate Planning, Family Law, Jurisprudence, Legal History, Lesotho, Panama, Papua New Guinea, Personal Property, Poverty Law, Real Estate, Statutes, Sudan, Torts, Trial & Appellate Practice, Turks & Caicos Islands, Uniform Commercial Code, Women & the Law, Workers' Compensation

COMMON MARKET: See Antitrust Law, European Economic Community, International Law, Peru

COMMONWEALTH: See Abortion, Antigua, Australia, England

COMMUNICABLE DISEASE: See AIDS, Health & Medicine

COMMUNICATIONS: See Media Law

COMMUNISM, SOCIALISM & EASTERN EUROPE

SEE ALSO: Albania, Benin, Bulgaria, Cambodia, China, Czechoslovakia, Germany (East), Guinea, Hungary, Korea (North), Laos, Madagascar, Mongolia, Mozambique, Poland, Romania, Somalia, Soviet Union, Vietnam, Yemen, Yugoslavia

RESEARCH GUIDES & BIBLIOGRAPHIES:
"Bibliography: Selected Soviet and Eastern European Periodicals of Special Interest to Lawyers" by I. Kavass, 10 *International Journal of Legal Information* 102 (1982).

The International Relations of Eastern Europe: A Guide to Information Sources, R. Remington, ed. (Gale, 1978).

"Judicial Reference Work and Its Means in the European Socialist Countries" by L. Nagy, 5 *International Journal of Law Libraries* 359 (1977).

"Socialist Law and its Legal Literature" by A. Liivak, 5 *International Journal of Law Libraries* 259 (1977).

A Source Book of Socialist International Organizations, W. Butler, ed. (Sijthoff & Noordhoff, 1978).

"United States Research of the Law of Communist-Ruled States of Europe" by I. Sipkov, 16 *Vanderbilt Journal of Transnational Law* 583 (1983).

CONSTITUTIONS:
The Constitutional Models of Socialist State Organization by O. Bihari, K. Bals, transl. (Budapest: Akad miai Kiad, 1979).

Constitutions of the Communist Party States, J. Triska, ed. (Stanford Univ., Hoover Inst. 1968).

The Constitutions of the Communist World, W. Simons, ed. (Sijthoff & Noordhoff, 1980).

STATUTES & RELATED LAWS:
The Codified Statutes on Private International Law of the East European Countries: A Comparative Study by I. Sipkov (Library of Congress, 1986).

The Party Statutes of the Communist World by W. Simons & S. White (Kluwer; Gaunt, 1984).

JOURNALS & OTHER PERIODICALS:
Journal of Communist Studies (London: Frank Cass, 1985–).

Review of Socialist Law (Sijthoff & Noordhoff, 1975–).

Yearbook on Socialist Legal Systems, W. Butler, ed. (Transnational Pub., 1986).

TREATISES & LOOSELEAFS:
The Communist Theory of Law by H. Kelsen (Praeger, 1955).

Doing Business with Eastern Europe (NY: Business Intl. Corp., 1975–).

East-West Joint Ventures: Economic, Business, Financial and Legal Aspects by the
Economic Commission for Europe (U.N., 1988).
East-West Trade, D. Loeber, ed. (Oceana, 1976).
*The International Payments and Monetary System in the Integration of the Socialist
Countries* by I. Vincze (Martinus Nijhoff, 1984).
Key to the Study of East European Law by P. Leideritz (Kluwer, 1978).
Legal Aspects of Joint Ventures in Eastern Europe, D. Campbell, ed. (Kluwer, 1981).
Legal Assistance within the Socialist Commonwealth of the East European Countries
by I. Sipkov (Library of Congress, 1987).
Manual on Trading with the Socialist Countries of Eastern Europe (United Nations,
1985).
Marx and Justice: The Radical Critique of Liberalism by A. Buchanan (Rowman &
Littlefield, 1982).
Marxism and Law by H. Collins (Clarendon Press, 1982).
Marxism and Law by P. Beirne & R. Quinney (Wiley, 1982).
A Socialist Approach to Comparative Law, I. Szabo & Z. Peteri, eds. (Sijthoff, 1977).
Taxation in European Socialist Countries (vol. 5), Guides to European Taxation
(Amsterdam: Intl. Bureau of Fiscal Documentation).
Trade Unions in Communist States, A. Pravda & B. Ruble, eds. (Allen & Unwin, 1986).
The Warsaw Pact: Alliance in Transition? by D. Halloway & J. Sharp (Cornell Univ.
Press, 1984).

ARTICLES:

"The Application of Foreign Law in Socialist States" by T. Erecinski, 5 *Comparative
Law Yearbook* 201 (1981).
"The Demographic Legislation of the Eastern Socialist Countries" by G. Litvinova, 20
Soviet Law and Government 71 (1981).
"Joint Ventures in Eastern Europe" by P. Buzescu, 32 *American Journal of
Comparative Law* 407 (1984).
"Legal Protection of Software in Poland and Other Socialist Countries" by B.
Czachorska, 2 *International Protection Ind. Property* 7 (1980).
"Marxism and the Law," 23 *Colombia Journal of Transnational Law* 217 (1985).
"Pursuing One's Rights Under Socialism" by I. Markovits, 38 *Stanford Law Review* 689
(1986).
"The Socialist Conception of Law" by Szab, 2 *International Encyclopedia of
Comparative Law* I–87 (1975).

COMMUNITY–BASED CORRECTIONS: See Corrections
COMMUNITY DEVELOPMENT: See State & Local Government, Zoning & Land
Planning
COMMUNITY HEALTH: See Health & Medicine, State & Local Government

COMMUNITY PROPERTY

SEE ALSO:

Arizona, California, Estate Planning, Family Law, Idaho, Louisiana, Nevada, New
Mexico, Real Estate, Taxation, Texas, Washington

**RESEARCH GUIDES &
BIBLIOGRAPHIES:**

"Community Property Bibliography" by L. Rodich, 19 *Gonzaga Law Review* 629
(1983/84).
Divorce, Support and Community Property by E. Cook (Monticello, IL: Vance
Bibliographies, 1985).

UNIFORM LAW: "Uniform Disposition of Community Property Rights at Death Act," 8A *Uniform Laws Annotated* 121 (West, 1986).

LOOSELEAFS & TREATISES: *Community Property: General Considerations* by J. Huston (Tax Management, 1974–).
Community Property in a Nutshell by R. Mennell (West, 1982).
Community Property in the United States by W. McClanahan (Lawyers Co-op., 1982).
Community Property in the United States, 2d ed. by W. Reppy (Michie, 1982).
Community Property Rights in Life Insurance by S. Scoville (Cincinnati: Natl. Insurance Co., 1969).
Community Property: The Migrant Client by S. Johanson (Tax Management, 1971–).
Comparative Studies in Community Property Law by J. Charmatz (Louisiana State Univ Press, 1955; Greenwood Press, 1977).
Principles of Community Property, 2d ed. by W. DeFuniak & M. Vaughn (Univ. of Arizona Press, 1971).

COMPACTS: See State & Local Government
COMPANY: See Business Law, Corporate Law, Securities Law
COMPARABLE WORTH: See Employee Benefits, Women & the Law
COMPARATIVE LAW: See International Law
COMPARATIVE NEGLIGENCE: See Torts
COMPENSATION: See Civil Service, Employee Benefits, Labor Law, Law Office Management, Paralegal, Taxation
COMPETENCE, COMPETENCY: See Juvenile Law, Mental Health, Professional Responsibility, Trial & Appellate Practice
COMPETITION: See Antitrust Law, Business Law, European Economic Community, Intellectual Property, International Law, Public Utilities
COMPLAINT: See Trial & Appellate Practice
COMPLEX LITIGATION: See Trial & Appellate Practice
COMPLIANCE: See Employee Benefits, Securities Law
COMPOSITION WITH CREDITORS: See Bankruptcy, Consumer Law, Contracts
COMPROMISE & SETTLEMENT: See Contracts, Estate Planning, Trial & Appellate Practice
COMPTROLLER: See Accounting, Banking Law, Government Contracts

COMPUTERS & THE LAW

SEE ALSO: Business Law, Contracts, Criminal Law, Intellectual Property, International Law, Law Office Management, Legal Research, Trial & Appellate Practice

RESEARCH GUIDES & BIBLIOGRAPHIES: *Annotated Bibliography on Software Maintenance* (C 13.10:500–141 S/N 003–003–02756–1) (Dept. of Commerce, 1986).
"Applications of Computers in the Legal Profession: A Selected Bibliography" by E. Day, 3 *Legal Reference Services Quarterly* 75 (1983).
Computers and Computing Information Resources Directory (Gale, 1985).
Lawyer's Microcomputing Sourcebook (Bowker, 1984).
LOCATE: A Directory of Law Office Computer Software (ABA).
"Survey of Online Legal and Law-Related Databases" by E. Fox, 5 *Legal Reference Services Quarterly* 87 (1985).

**JOURNALS, NEWSLETTERS
& OTHER PERIODICALS:**   *ABA Software Review* (ABA Press, 1985–).
Computer Law (Toronto, 1984–).
Computer Law and Practice (Frank Cass).
Computer Law and Tax Report (Warren, Gorham & Lamont, 1975–).
Computer Law Annual (Law & Business, Inc., 1985–).
Computer Law Developments (Computer Law Reporter, 1984–).
Computer/Law Journal (Univ. of So. Cal. Law Center, 1978–).
Computer Law Strategist (Leader Pubs., 1983–).
The Computer Lawyer (Law & Business, Inc., 1984–).
High Technology Law Journal (Berkeley: Univ. of Calif. Press, 1986–).
International Review of Computers, Technology and the Law (Sydney: Longman, 1985–).
Journal of Law and Technology (Georgetown Univ. Law Center, 1986–).
Jurimetrics Journal (ABA, 1959–).
Law/Technology (1968–).
Rutgers Computer & Technology Law Review (1970–).
Santa Clara Computer and High-Technology Law Journal (1985–).
Software Law Journal (CA: Center for Computer/Law, 1985–).
Software Law Journal (John Marshall Law School).
Software Protection (Manhattan Beach, CA: Law & Technology Press).
Yearbook of Law, Computers & Technology (Butterworths, 1985–).

LOOSELEAFS: *Bernacchi on Computer Law* by R. Bernacchi (Little, Brown, 1986–).
Computer Industry Litigation Reporter (Andrews Pub. Inc., 1983–).
Computer Law: Drafting and Negotiating Forms and Agreements by R. Raysman & P. Brown (Law Journal Seminars-Press, 1984–).
Computer Law: Evidence and Procedure by D. Bender (Matthew Bender, 1978–).
Computer Law Service (Callaghan).
Computers and Litigation Support by S. Haynes (Law & Business, Inc., 1981–).
Microworld: Software-Hardware Selection Guide (Auerbach).
The Software Legal Book by P. Hoffman (Carnegie Press, 1981–).
A User's Guide to Computer Contracting by L. Davis (Law & Business, Inc., 1984–).

TREATISES: *Advanced Legal Strategies for Buying and Selling Computers and Software* by D. Davidson (Wiley, 1986).
Computer Jurisprudence: Legal Responses to the Information Revolution by M. Rostoker (Oceana, 1986).
Computer Law by M. Scott (Wiley, 1985).
Computer Law, 3d ed. by C. Tapper (Longman, 1983).
Computer Law Forms Handbook by L. Schwartz (Clark Boardman, 1986).
Computer Law Institute (Practicing Law Institute).
Computer Litigation (Practicing Law Institute).
Computers and the Law, 3d ed., R. Bigelow, ed. (CCH, 1981).
Computer Software and Chips: Protection and Marketing (Practicing Law Institute).
Computer Technology and the Law by J. Soma (McGraw-Hill, 1983).
Criminal Justice Resource Manual on Computer Crime (1979).
From Yellow Pads to Computers: Transforming Your Law Office with a Computer, K. Braeman & F. Shellenberger, eds. (A.B.A., 1987).
International Computer Law by J. Keustermans (Matthew Bender, 1988).
The Law of Computer Technology by R. Nimmer (Warren, Gorham & Lamont, 1985).
Law Office Guide to Small Computers by F. Rhoads (Shepard's, 1984).
Legal Aspects of Computer Use by R. Wolk (Prentice-Hall, 1986).

Legal Protection of Computer Programs and Data by C. Millard (Carswell, 1985).

A Software Law Primer by F. Neitzke (Van Nostrand Reinhold).

The Software Legal Book: Forms by P. Hoffman (Croton-on-Hudson, NY: Shafer Books, 1989).

Wilmer, Cutler & Pickering Manual on Litigation Support Databases by D. Siemer (Wiley, 1987).

PERIODICALS:

CURRENT LAW INDEX (CLI) & LEGAL RESOURCE INDEX (LRI)

In the CLI and LRI, look for references to periodical literature under the following subject headings:

Computer Leases	Electronic Data Processing
Computer Literacy	High Technology
Computer Programs	Information Retrieval
Computers	Information Storage
Copyright	Microcomputers
Data Bases	On-Line Bibliographic
Data Programming	Searching
Data Transmission	Programming
Documentation	Software

INDEX TO LEGAL PERIODICALS (ILP)

In the ILP, look for references to legal periodical literature under the following subject headings:

Automation	Information Storage and
Computer Crimes	Retrieval Systems
Computers	Right of Privacy

CONCEPTION: See Abortion, Family Law, Health & Medicine

CONCILIATION: See Contracts, Labor Law, Mediation

CONDEMNATION: See Real Estate

CONDITIONAL GIFT: See Consumer Law, Contracts, Personal Property, Uniform Commercial Code

CONDOMINIUM: See Real Estate

CONFESSION: See Antitrust Law, Criminal Law

CONFESSION OF JUDGMENT: See Trial & Appellate Practice

CONFIDENTIALITY: See Banking Law, Freedom of Information, Health & Medicine, Partnership Law, Professional Responsibility

CONFINEMENT: See Corrections, Juvenile Law, Mental Health

CONFISCATION: See International Law

CONFLICT OF INTEREST: See Estate Planning, Professional Responsibility

CONFLICT OF LAW

SEE ALSO:
Contracts, Corporate Law, Insurance, International Law, Torts, Trial & Appellate Practice; see also entries under individual states and countries

RESTATEMENT:
Restatement of the Law, Second, Conflict of Laws (Amer. Law Inst., 1971).

UNIFORM LAW:
Uniform Conflict of Laws—Limitations Act, 12 *Uniform Laws Annotated* (West, 1986).

TREATISES & LOOSELEAFS:
American Conflicts Law, 4th ed. by R. Leflair (Michie, 1986).

Choice of Law, Selected Essays, 1933–1983 by D. Cavers (Duke Univ. Press, 1985).
Commentary on the Conflict of Laws, 3d ed. by R. Weintraub (Foundation Press, 1986).
Conflict of Laws by T. Schussler (Gould, 1982–).
Conflict of Laws by E. Scoles & P. Hay (West, 1982).
Conflict of Laws: A Northwest Perspective by J. Nafziger (Butterworths, 1985).
Conflict of Laws: Theory and Practice, 2d ed. by D. Vernon (Matthew Bender, 1982).
Conflicts in a Nutshell by D. Siegel (West, 1982).
Studies in Comparative Jurisprudence and the Conflict of Laws by G. Merrill (Little, Brown, 1886; reprint Rothman, 1985).
Studies in Modern Choice-of-Law: Torts, Insurance, Land Titles by M. Hancock (Hein, 1984).
Transnational Contracts: Applicable Law and Settlement in Disputes by G. Delaume (Oceana, 1979–).
A Treatise on the Conflict of Laws by A. Ehrenzweig (West, 1962).
Understanding Conflict of Laws by W. Richman (Matthew Bender, 1984).

ENCYCLOPEDIAS:

AMERICAN JURISPRUDENCE 2D (Am Jur 2d)
Check the following topics in the *General Index* volumes for Am Jur 2d:

Conflict of Laws　　　　Domicile or Residence

CORPUS JURIS SECUNDUM (CJS)
Check the following topics in the *General Index* volumes for CJS:

Common Law　　　　Domicile or Residence
Conflict of Laws

DIGESTS:

CASE SEARCH IN WEST DIGESTS BY KEY TOPIC
In the *Descriptive Word Index* of the West digests, look for key topics and numbers under the following subject headings:

Action　　　　Evidence
Conflict of Laws　　　　Federal Courts
Contracts　　　　Pleading
Death　　　　Torts
Domicile or Residence

ALR:

ANNOTATIONS
Check the index volumes for ALR, ALR2d, ALR3d, ALR4th, and ALR Fed for annotations under the following subject headings:

Conflict of Laws　　　　Multiple Residence

PERIODICALS:

CURRENT LAW INDEX (CLI) & LEGAL RESOURCE INDEX (LRI)
In the CLI and LRI, look for references to periodical literature under the following subject headings:

Conflict of Laws　　　　Jurisdiction

INDEX TO LEGAL PERIODICALS (ILP)
In the ILP, look for references to legal periodical literature under the following subject headings:

Actions and Defenses　　　　Conflict of Law
Appellate Procedure　　　　Contracts
Common Law　　　　Domicile and Residence
Comparative Law　　　　Foreign Law

Full Faith and Credit   Recognition of Foreign
Judgment

CONFLICT RESOLUTION: See International Law, Mediation, Trial & Appellate Practice
CONFRONTATION: See Criminal Law, Trial & Appellate Practice
CONFUCIAN STATE: See Korea (South)
CONGESTION: See Judicial Administration

CONGO

SEE ALSO: Africa, International Law, United Nations, Zaire

**TREATISES &
LOOSELEAFS:**   *African Tax Systems* (Brazzaville, Congo) by R. Hammond & M. van den Abeelen
(Amsterdam: Intl. Bureau of Fiscal Documentation, 1980–).
Historical Dictionary of the People's Republic of the Congo, 2d ed. by V. Thompson
(Scarecrow Press, 1984).
An Introduction to Law in French-Speaking Africa (Kinshasa, Congo) by J. Salacuse
(Michie, 1969).
The Legal System of Congo-Kinshasa by J. Crabb (Michie, 1970).

ARTICLES: "Regulation of Business Activities of Petroleum Contractors in Cameroon, Congo,
Cabon, and Ivory Coast" by M. Frilet, 30 *Oil and Gas Tax Quarterly* 485 (1982).
"The Rights of the Child in the People's Republic of Congo" by J. Tchilinda, 13
Columbia Human Rights Law Review 183 (1981).

CONGRESS: See Constitutional Law, Legislative History, Statutes, War
CONJUGAL VIOLENCE: See Criminal Law, Family Law

CONNECTICUT

SEE ALSO: Circuit Courts (Second Circuit)

**RESEARCH GUIDES &
BIBLIOGRAPHIES:**   *Checklist of Publications of Connecticut State Agencies* (State Library, 1964–).
"Connecticut Practice Materials" by M. Sullivan, 4 *Law Librarians of New England
News* 11 (1983).
Connecticut State Legal Documents: A Selective Bibliography by D. Voisinet et al.
(American Assn. of Law Libraries, 1985).
Sources of Connecticut Law by S. Bysiewicz (Butterworth, 1987).

**STATUTES & RELATED
LEGISLATIVE MATERIAL:**   *Connecticut General Statutes Annotated* (West).
Connecticut Legislative Service (West).
Ann. Report of the Connecticut Law Revision Commn. (1975–).
General Statutes of Connecticut.

**STATE ADMINISTRATIVE
CODE:**   *Regulations of Connecticut State Agencies* (1962–).

CASES & OPINIONS:	*Connecticut Reports* (1814–). *Connecticut Appellate Reports* (1983–). *Connecticut Supplement* (1935–). *Atlantic Reporter* (1885–).
COURT RULES & FORMS:	*Connecticut Rules of Court* (West). *Connecticut Superior Court Civil Rules* by M. Moller & W. Horton (West, 1979). *Connecticut Superior Court Criminal Rules* by L. Orland (West, 1986). *Connecticut Superior Court Forms* by J. Kaye & W. Effron (West, 1979). *Connecticut Supreme and Appellate Court Rules and Forms* by M. Moller & W. Horton (West, 1987). *Rules and Forms: Practice Book Annotated* (West).
JURY INSTRUCTIONS:	*Connecticut Criminal Jury Instructions* by D. Borland & L. Orland (West, 1986). *Connecticut Jury Instructions,* 3d ed. by D. Wright (Atlantic Law Book, 1981–).
ETHICS & PROFESSIONAL RESPONSIBILITY:	*Informal Opinions* (CT Bar Assn., Comm. on Prof. Ethics, 1982–). *Lawyers' Diary* (CT Bar Assn.).
JOURNALS & OTHER PERIODICALS:	*Connecticut Bar Journal* (1927–). *Connecticut Family Law Journal* (Butterworths, 1982–). *Connecticut Real Estate Law Journal* (Butterworths, 1982–). *The Defense Journal of the Connecticut Defense Lawyers Association* (1984–).
DIRECTORIES:	*Directory of Connecticut Bar Association* (CT Bar Assn.). *Juris Barmaster* (Judicial Info. Systems, 1978–).
TREATISES, LOOSELEAFS & OTHER MONOGRAPHS:	*Annual Tax Planning Institute* (CT Bar Assn., 1983–). *Basic Corporate Practice* (CT Bar Assn., 1980). *Connecticut Civil Procedure,* 2d ed. by E. Stephenson (Atlantic Law Book, 1970–). *Connecticut Estates Practice* by G. Wilhelm (Lawyers Co-op., 1971–79). *Connecticut Lawyers Basic Practice Manual* (CT Bar Assn., 1970–). *Connecticut Legal Forms* by W. Wright (Atlantic Law Book, 1959–). *Connecticut Real Property Law* by R. Anderson (Atlantic Law Book Co., 1984–). *Connecticut Tax Reporter, State and Local* (CCH, 1952–). *Connecticut Trial Practice* by J. Fitzgerald & R. Yules (West, 1987). *Connecticut Uniform Administrative Procedure Act* (CT Bar Assn., 1981). *Handbook of Connecticut Evidence,* 2d ed. by C. Tait (Little, Brown, 1988).
DIGEST & CITATORS:	*Connecticut Digest* (West, 1950–). *Shepard's Connecticut Citations.* *Connecticut Family Law Citations* (Butterworths, 1985).

CONNIVANCE: See Family Law
CONSANGUINITY: See Family Law
CONSCIENTIOUS OBJECTORS: See Church & State, Military Law
CONSCRIPTS: See Military Law
CONSENT: See Health & Medicine, Juvenile Law, Torts
CONSENT JUDGMENT: See Trial & Appellate Practice

CONSENT TO TREATMENT: See Health & Medicine, Mental Health, Nursing
CONSERVATION: See Energy, Environmental Law, Historic Preservation, Natural
    Resources, Oil & Gas, Water
CONSERVATORSHIP: See Age, Estate Planning, Juvenile Law, Mental Health
CONSIDERATION: See Contracts
CONSIGNMENT: See Contracts, Uniform Commercial Code
CONSOLIDATION: See Antitrust Law, Corporate Law
CONSOLIDATION OF JUDGMENT: See Trial and & Appellate Practice
CONSORTIUM, LOSS OF: See Family Law, Torts
CONSPIRACY: See Antitrust Law, Criminal Law

CONSTITUTIONAL LAW

SEE ALSO:

Abortion, Administrative Law, Church & State, Civil Rights, Corrections, Criminal Law, Education Law, Election, Employment Discrimination, Family Law, Handicapped & the Law, Immigration Law, International Law, Jurisprudence, Juvenile Law, Labor Law, Legal History, Media Law, State & Local Government, Trial & Appellate Practice, Women & the Law; see also entries under individual states and countries

**RESEARCH GUIDES &
BIBLIOGRAPHIES:**

Bibliography of Original Meaning of the United States Constitution (U.S. Dept. of
    Justice, 1988).
*Comprehensive Bibliography of American Constitutional and Legal History,
    1896–1979* by K. Hall (Kraus, 1984).
*State Constitutional Conventions, Commissions & Amendments: An Annotated
    Bibliography* (Congressional Information Service, 1959–).
State Constitutional Conventions, 1876–1959: A Bibliography by C. Browne & R.
    Leache (Greenwood Press, 1973).
*Supreme Court of the United States 1789–1980: An Index to Opinions Arranged by
    Justice,* L. Blandford & P. Evans, eds. (Kraus, 1983).
U.S. Constitution: A Guide to Information Sources by E. McCarrick (Gale Research
    Co., 1980).
The Writing and Ratification of the U.S. Constitution: A Bibliography by R. Wheeler
    (Federal Judicial Center, 1986).

**JOURNALS & OTHER
PERIODICALS:**

The Constitution (Wash. D.C.: Natl. Center for Constitutional Studies, 1985–).
Constitutional Commentary (Univ. of Minn. Law Sch., 1984–).
Constitutional Law Reporter (VA: Const. Law Center, 1985–).
Hastings Constitutional Law Quarterly (1974–).
Supreme Court Historical Society Yearbook (Butterworths).
Supreme Court Law Review (Butterworths, 1980–).
Supreme Court Review (Univ. of Chicago Press, 1960–).

**APPELLATE BRIEFS,
RECORDS & ORAL
ARGUMENTS:**

Complete Oral Arguments of the Supreme Court of the United States (Univ. Pubs. of
    America).
Records and Briefs (Denver Technological Center) (microcard edition).
Records and Briefs of the United States Supreme Court (Law Reprints, 1974–) (microform).
The Records and Briefs of the U.S. Supreme Court, 1832–1915 (Scholarly Resources,
    Inc.) (microfilm).

The Supreme Court Current: Complete Records and Briefs (Scholarly Resources, Inc.) (microfiche).

LOOSELEAFS: *Constitutions of the United States: National and State* by P. Grad & M. O'Connor (Oceana, 1976–).
United States Law Week (BNA, 1932–).
United States Supreme Court Bulletin (CCH, 1936–).

TREATISES: *American Constitutional Law, 2d ed.* by L. Tribe (Foundation Press, 1988).
Constitutional Construction by C. Antieau (Oceana, 1982).
Constitutional Litigation by K. Ripple (Michie, 1984).
The Constitution of the United States: Analysis and Interpretation by the Congressional Research Service (GPO, 1973).
Encyclopedia of the America Constitution by L. Levy et al. (Macmillan, 1986).
The Founder's Constitution, P. Kurland & R. Lerner, eds. (Univ. of Chicago Press, 1987).
Guide to the U.S. Supreme Court (Congressional Quarterly, 1979).
Joseph Story's "Commentaries on the Constitution" (1833) (Carolina Academic Press, 1987).
The Judicial Power of the United States: The Eleventh Amendment in American History by J. Orth (Oxford Univ. Press, 1986).
Modern Constitutional Law by C. Antieau (Lawyers Co-op., 1969).
State Constitutional Law in a Nutshell by T. Marks (West, 1988).
Supreme Court Practice, 6th ed. by R. Stern (BNA, 1986).
Treatise on Constitutional Law by R. Rotunda et al. (West, 1986).
United States Constitutional and Legal History, K. Hall, ed. (Garland).

ENCYCLOPEDIAS: AMERICAN JURISPRUDENCE 2D (Am Jur 2d)
Check the following topics in the *General Index* volumes for Am Jur 2d:

Administrative Law	Ex Post Facto Laws
Amendment of	Fourteenth Amendment
Constitution	Freedom of Religion
Children and Infants	Freedom of Speech and
Civil Rights	Press
Commerce	Full Faith and Credit
Constitutional Law	Impairment of Contracts
Criminal Law	Impeachment
Cruel and Unusual	Involuntary Servitude
Punishment	Police Power
Delegation of Powers	President of United States
Discrimination	Privileges and Immunities
Double Jeopardy	Statutes
Due Process	Supreme Court of United
Equal Protection of the	States
Law	

CORPUS JURIS SECUNDUM (CJS)
Check the following topics in the *General Index* volumes for CJS:

Administrative Bodies	Constitutional Law
and Procedure	Constitutions
Civil Rights	Crimes and Offenses
Color of Right	Cruel and Unusual
Commerce	Punishment
Congress	Delegation of Powers

Discrimination President of United States
Double Jeopardy Privileges and Immunities
First Amendment Right of Privacy
Freedom of Speech State
Impeachment Statutes
Legislative Powers United States Supreme
Police Power Court
Political Activities War

DIGESTS:

CASE SEARCH IN WEST DIGESTS BY KEY TOPIC
In the *Descriptive Word Index* of the West digests, look for key topics and numbers under the following subject headings:

Abortion Freedom of Speech
Administrative Law and Habeas Corpus
Procedure Impeachment
Arrest International Law
Bail Legislature
Citizens Obscenity
Civil Rights Police Power
Color of Right Political Activities
Commerce President of the United
Congress States
Constitutional Law Prisons
Constitutions Privacy
Criminal Law Privileges and Immunities
Cruel and Unusual Right of Privacy
Punishment Searches and Seizures
Delegation of Powers States
Discrimination Statutes
Double Jeopardy Treaties
Evidence United States
Federal Courts War
First Amendment

ALR:

ANNOTATIONS
Check the index volumes for ALR, ALR2d, ALR3d, ALR4th, and ALR Fed for annotations under the following subject headings:

Administrative Law Fourteenth Amendment
Assistance of Counsel Fourth Amendment
Criminal Law Freedom of Speech and
Cruel and Unusual Press
Punishment Impairment of Contract
Discrimination Privacy
Due Process of Law Privileges and Immunities
Equal Protection of Law Race or Color
Former Jeopardy Sex Discrimination

PERIODICALS:

CURRENT LAW INDEX (CLI) & LEGAL RESOURCE INDEX (LRI)
In the CLI and LRI, look for references to periodical literature under the following subject headings:

Administrative Law Constitutional Law
Assembly, Right of Criminal Procedure
Civil Rights Delegation of Powers

Discrimination
Double Jeopardy
Due Process of Law
Evidence
Executive Pover
Freedom
Freedom of Association
Free Press and Fair Trial
Habeas corpus
Impeachment
Implied Powers
Interstate Commerce
Legislation
Minorities
Police Power
Political Questions
Presidents

Prisons
Privacy
Privileges and Immunities
Race
Religious Liberty
Right to Counsel
School Integration
Segregation
Self-Incrimination
Separation of Powers
Sex Discrimination
State Action
United States
United States Supreme
   Court
War

INDEX TO LEGAL PERIODICALS (ILP)

In the ILP, look for references to legal periodical literature under the following subject headings:

Administrative Law
Bail
Capital Punishment
Censorship
Citizens
Civil Rights
Commerce Clause
Constitutional Law
Criminal Law
Cruel and Unusual
   Punishment
Diplomatic Privileges
Discrimination
Double Jeopardy
Due Process of Law
Equal Protection of Law
Establishment Clause
Executive Power
Fair Trial
Federalism
Federal Preemption
Full Faith and Credit

Freedom of Assembly
Freedom of Association
Freedom of Religion
Freedom of Speech
Human Rights
Interstate Commerce
Loyalty Oaths
Naturalization
Police Power
Races
Religion
Retroactive Laws
Right to Counsel
School Integration
Segregation
Self-Incrimination
Separation of Powers
Speedy Trial
States' Rights
Treaties
War and Emergency
   Powers

CONSTRUCTION: See Architecture, Government Contracts, Statutes
CONSTRUCTIVE NOTICE: See Real Estate, Torts
CONSTRUCTIVE POSSESSION: See Personal Property, Real Estate
CONSTRUCTIVE TRUST: See Equity, Estate Planning, Real Estate
CONSULS: See International Law
CONSULTANTS: See Agency

CONSUMER LAW

SEE ALSO:
Administrative Law, Antitrust Law, Banking Law, Bankruptcy, Business Law, Civil Rights, Constitutional Law, Contracts, Corporate Law, Employee Benefits, Energy, Environmental Law, Estate Planning, Family Law, Food, Franchise Law, Handicapped & the Law, Health & Medicine, International Law, Labor Law, Nonprofit Corporations, Occupational Safety, Ombudsman, Personal Property, Poverty Law, Public Utilities, State & Local Government, Taxation, Torts, Unemployment Compensation, Uniform Commercial Code, Workers' Compensation; see also entries under individual states

UNIFORM LAWS:
Uniform Consumer Credit Code, 7A *Uniform Laws Annotated* 1 (West, 1986).
Uniform Consumer Sales Practices Act, 7A *Uniform Laws Annotated* 231 (West, 1986).

JOURNALS, NEWSLETTERS & OTHER PERIODICALS:
Consumer Protection Reporting Service (George Wash. Univ. Natl. Law Center, 1983–).
NCLC Reports (Natl. Consumer Law Center).

LOOSELEAFS:
Consumer Credit Guide (CCH, 1969–).
Consumer Protection and the Law by D. Pridgen (Clark Boardman, 1986–).
Consumer Protection Reporting Service, D. Rothchild, ed. (Natl. Law Pub., 1974–).
Debtor-Creditor Law (Matthew Bender, 1982–).
Federal Consumer Protection: Laws, Rules and Regulations by B. Reams (Oceana, 1978–).
The Lemon Press (auto warranty) (Consumer Press, 1982–).

TREATISES:
Consumer Credit Compliance Manual, 2d ed. by J. Fonseca (Lawyers Co-op., 1984).
Consumer Protection in a Nutshell by D. Epstein (West, 1976).
The Consumer Protection Manual by A. Eiler (Facts on File, 1984).
Consumer Usury and Credit Overcharges (Natl. Consumer Law Center, 1982).
Creditor's Rights Handbook by D. Campbell (Clark Boardman, 1985).
Debtor-Creditor Law in a Nutshell, 3d ed. by D. Epstein (West, 1986).
Debtor-Creditor Law Manual by T. Crandell (Warren, Gorham & Lamont, 1985).
Debtor-Creditor Relations by L. Myers (Shepard's, 1986).
Debtors' and Creditors' Rights by A. Cohen (Michie, 1984)).
The Federal Truth-in-Lending Act and Regulation Z by D. Replansky (ALI–ABA Comm. on Cont. Prof. Ed., 1984).
Handling Automobile Warranty and Repossession Cases by R. Billings (Lawyers Co-op., 1984).
Handling Consumer Credit Cases, 2d ed. by J. Fonseca (Lawyers Co-op., 1980).
The Law of Truth in Lending by R. Rohner (Warren, Gorham & Lamont, 1984).
Repossessions (Natl. Consumer Law Center, 1982).
Unfair and Deceptive Acts and Practices (Natl. Consumer Law Center, 1984).

ENCYCLOPEDIAS:
AMERICAN JURISPRUDENCE 2D (Am Jur 2d)
Check the following topics in the *General Index* volumes for Am Jur 2d:

Bankruptcy	Duress or Coercion
Collection	Fraud
Commercial Code	Interest and Usury
Contracts	Loans
Credit	Moneylenders
Debts	Unconscionability
Defenses	Vendor and Purchaser
Discount or Rebate	

CORPUS JURIS SECUNDUM (CJS)
Check the following topics in the *General Index* volumes for CJS:

Bills and Notes	Duress
Caveat Emptor	Fraud
Collections	Garnishment
Conditional Sales	Indebtedness
Constitutional Law	Installment Payments
Contracts	Interest
Credit	Joint Debtors
Creditors	Loans
Debt	Unconscionable Contract
Defenses	Vendor and Purchaser

DIGESTS:

CASE SEARCH IN WEST DIGESTS BY KEY TOPIC
In the *Descriptive Word Index* of the West digests, look for key topics and numbers under the following subject headings:

Account	Debtor and Creditor
Administrative Law	Defenses
Attachment	Duress
Automobiles	Equity
Bailment	Fraud
Bills and Notes	Garnishment
Caveat Emptor	Indebtedness
Collections	Installment Payments
Conditional Sales	Interest
Constitutional Law	Joint Debtors
Consumer Credit	Loans
Consumer Protection	Product Liability
Contracts	Unconscionable Contract
Credit	Usury
Creditors	Vendor and Purchaser
Debt	

ALR:

ANNOTATIONS
Check the index volumes for ALR, ALR2d, ALR3d, ALR4th, and ALR Fed for annotations under the following subject headings:

Bankruptcy	Discrimination
Collections	Federal Trade Commission
Confession of Judgment	Fraud
Consumer Credit	Harassment
Consumers and	Loans
Consumer Protection	Truth in Lending
Credit	Uniform Consumer Credit
Debtors	Code
Default	

PERIODICALS:

CURRENT LAW INDEX (CLI) & LEGAL RESOURCE INDEX (LRI)
In the CLI and LRI, look for references to periodical literature under the following subject headings:

Assignments	Consumer Protection
Attachment and	Consumers
Garnishment	Contracts, Unconscionable
Consumer Credit	Loans

Debtor and Creditor	Fraud
Debts	Interest
Extinguishment of Debts	United States Federal
Finance Charges	Trade Commission

INDEX TO LEGAL PERIODICALS (ILP)

In the ILP, look for references to legal periodical literature under the following subject headings:

Administrative Agencies	Fraud
Advertising	Health
Assignments	Interest
Attachment and	Loans
Garnishment	Mistake
Bankruptcy	Motor Vehicles
Civil Rights	Prices
Collection Agencies	Products Liability
Conditional Sales	Safety Laws
Constitutional Law	Secured Transactions
Consumer Protection	Small Claims Court
Contracts	Undue Influence
Credit	Usury

CONSUMER PRODUCT SAFETY COMMISSION: See Torts
CONTAGIOUS DISEASE: See AIDS, Health & Medicine
CONTAMINATION: See Environmental Law
CONTEMPT: See Criminal Law, Trial & Appellate Practice
CONTINENTAL SHELF: See Oil & Gas, Sea, Water Law
CONTINGENT ESTATE: See Estate Planning
CONTINGENT FEES: See Professional Responsibility
CONTINUANCE: See Trial & Appellate Practice
CONTRACEPTION: See Abortion, Family Law, Women & the Law

CONTRACTS

SEE ALSO: Accounting, Air & Aviation, Antitrust Law, Architecture, Art & Entertainment, Banking Law, Bankruptcy, Business Law, Commodities, Computers, Conflict of Law, Corporate Law, Economics, Employee Benefits, Energy, Equity, Family Law, Franchise Law, Government Contracts, Insurance, Intellectual Property, International Law, Labor Law, Maritime Law, Oil & Gas, Personal Property, Public Utilities, Sports Law, Torts, Uniform Commercial Code; see also entries under individual states

RESTATEMENT: *Restatement of the Law, Restitution* (American Law Institute, 1937).
Restatement of the Law, Second, Contracts (American Law Institute, 1981).

LOOSELEAFS & TREATISES: *Attorney's Guide to Restitution* by G. Douthwaite (Allen Smith, 1977).
Contract Remedies in a Nutshell by J. Friedman (West, 1983).
Contracts by A. Farnsworth (Little, Brown, 1982).
Corbin on Contracts by A. Corbin (West, 1950).
The Death of Contract by G. Gilmore (Ohio State Univ. Press, 1974).
The Economics of Contract Law by A. Kronman (Little, Brown, 1979).
Handbook for the Trial of Contract Lawsuits by E. Imwinkelried (Prentice-Hall, 1982).

The Law of Contracts, 3d ed. by J. Calamari (West, 1987).
Modern Law of Contracts by H. Hunter (Warren, Gorham & Lamont, 1986).
Murray on Contracts by J. Murray (Michie, 1974).
Warren's Forms of Agreement by O. Warren (Matthew Bender, 1954–).
Willeston on Contracts, 3d ed. by W. Jaeger (Lawyers Co-op., 1957).

ENCYCLOPEDIAS:

AMERICAN JURISPRUDENCE 2D (Am Jur 2d)
Check the following topics in the *General Index* volumes for Am Jur 2d:

Acceptance	Impossibility
Accord and Satisfaction	Independent Contractor
Alteration of Instruments	Joint Ventures
Antenuptial Settlements	Legality
Anticipatory Breach	Market Value
Assignments	Mechanics' Lien
Assumpsit	Mental Capacity
Authority	Mistake
Bona Fide Purchaser	Mutuality
Cancellation	Notice or Knowledge
Capacity	Office
Children and Infants	Options
Commercial Code	Parol Acts or Agreement
Common Law	Part Performance
Compromise and	Payment
Settlement	Price
Conditions Precedent	Private Franchise
Consideration	Contracts
Consignment	Privity
Construction or	Promise
Interpretation	Promissory Estoppel
Contracts	Public Works and
Covenants	Contracts
Damages	Rescission
Default	Restitution and Implied
Defenses	Contracts
Delivery	Sales or Transfers
Demand or Request	Specific Performance
Duress	Statute of Frauds
Equity	Subrogation
Fraud	Suretyship
Fraudulent Conveyances	Tender
Gifts	Third Party Beneficiaries
Guaranty	Unconscionability
Impairment of Contracts	Undue Influence
Implied Warranty	Vendor and Purchaser

CORPUS JURIS SECUNDUM (CJS)
Check the following topics in the *General Index* volumes for CJS:

Acceptance	Assumpsit
Accord and Satisfaction	Breach of Contract
Alteration of Instruments	Cancellation of Instruments
Ambiguities	Capacity
Anticipatory Breach	Collateral Contract
Assignments	Common Law

Compromise and Settlement
Conditions
Consideration
Consignment
Contracts
Covenants
Credit
Customs and Usages
Damages
Default
Defenses
Delivery
Demand
Duress
Equity
Exchange of Property
Fraud
Frauds, Statute of
Fraudulent Conveyances
Gifts
Good Faith
Guaranty
Implied Contracts
Implied Warranties
Impossibility of Performance
Indemnity
Independent Contractor
Infants
Intent

Joint Adventures
Market Value or Price
Mechanics' Liens
Mistake
Notice
Offer
Options
Parol Contracts
Part Performance
Payment
Performance
Privity
Promise
Public Contracts
Public Works and Contracts
Rescission
Sales
Secured Transactions
Special Contracts
Subcontractors
Subrogation
Tender
Third Party Beneficiaries
Time
Unconscionable Contract
Undue Influence
Unilateral Contract
Value
Vendor and Purchaser
Waiver

DIGESTS:

CASE SEARCH IN WEST DIGESTS BY KEY TOPIC

In the *Descriptive Word Index* of the West digests, look for key topics and numbers under the following subject headings:

Acceptance
Accord and Satisfaction
Account, Action on
Alteration of Instruments
Ambiguities
Anticipatory Breach
Arbitration
Assignments
Assumpsit, Action of
Auctions
Automobiles
Bailment
Breach of Contract
Breach of Marriage Promise
Cancellation of Instruments
Capacity

Certainty
Collateral Contract
Common Law
Compromise and Settlement
Conditions
Consideration
Consignment
Contracts
Covenants
Credit
Customs and Usage
Damages
Default
Defenses
Delivery
Demand

Duress
Equity
Exchange of Property
Fraud
Frauds, Statute of
Fraudulent Conveyances
Gifts
Good Faith
Guaranty
Implied and Contructive
  Contracts
Implied Warranties
Impossibility of
  Performance
Indemnity
Independent Contractor
Infants
Intent
Joint Adventures
Market Value or Price
Master and Surety
Mechanics' Lien
Mistake
Notice
Offer
Options

Parol Contracts
Part Performance
Payment
Performance
Privity
Promise
Public Contracts
Public Works and
  Contracts
Rescission
Sales
Secured Transactions
Special Contracts
Subcontractors
Subrogation
Tender
Third Party Beneficiaries
Time
Unconscionable Contract
Undertakings
Undue Influence
Unilateral Contract
Value
Vendor and Purchaser
Waiver

ALR:

ANNOTATIONS

Check the index volumes for ALR, ALR2d, ALR3d, ALR4th, and ALR Fed for annotations under the following subject headings:

Acceptance
Assignments
Bids and Bidding
Bona Fide Purchasers
Capacity or Incapacity
Certainty and
  Definiteness
Coercion or Duress
Common Law
Competency
Conditional Sales
Conditions
Consideration
Contracts
Damages
Demand
Equity
Estoppel and Waiver
Fraud
Frauds, Statute of
Good Faith

Impairment of Contract
  Obligations
Implied Warranties
Inducement
Mistake
Parol Contracts
Privity
Promise
Promissory Estoppel
Quasi Contract
Reliance
Restitution
Sales
Specific Performance
Subcontractors
Third Party Beneficiaries
Time
Uniform Commercial
  Code
Vendor and Purchaser
Warranties

PERIODICALS: CURRENT LAW INDEX (CLI) & LEGAL RESOURCE INDEX (LRI)
In the CLI and LRI, look for references to periodical literature under the following subject headings:

Acceleration Clause	Immoral Contracts
Acceptances	Independent Contractors
Accord and Satisfaction	Offer and Acceptance
Antenuptial Contracts	Options (Contract)
Assignments	Performance
Breach of Contract	Public Contracts
Consideration (Law)	Quasi Contracts
Contractors	Repurchase Agreements
Contracts	Rescission
Covenants	Sales
Debtor and Creditor	Settlements
Discharge of Contracts	Specific Performance
Due on Sale Clauses	Subcontracting
Duress (Law)	Tortious Interference with
Equity	Contracts
Estoppel	Undue Influence
Forfeiture	Vendor and Purchaser
Fraud	Warranty
Good Faith	

INDEX TO LEGAL PERIODICALS (ILP)
In the ILP, look for references to legal periodical literature under the following subject headings:

Accord and Satisfaction	Duress
Agency	Independent Contractor
Antenuptial Contracts	Mistake
Arbitration and Award	Notice
Assignments	Quasi-Contracts
Auctions	Rescission
Authors and Publishers	Restitution
Bonds	Sales
Breach of Promise	Specific Performance
Common Law	Statute of Frauds
Conditional Sales	Subrogation
Conflict of Laws/Contracts	Unjust Enrichment
Contracts	Vendors and Purchasers
Government Contracts	Warranty

CONTRIBUTORY NEGLIGENCE: See Torts
CONTROLLED SUBSTANCE: See Criminal Law
CONVALESCENT HOME: See Age, Health & Medicine
CONVENTION/CONFERENCE ON LAW OF THE SEA: See Sea
CONVENTIONS (INTERNATIONAL): See International Law, Terrorism, United Nations
CONVENTIONS (STATE): See State & Local Government
CONVERSION: See Equity, Personal Property, Torts
CONVEYANCING: See Real Estate
CONVICTION: See Criminal Law
CONVICTS: See Corrections

COOK ISLANDS

SEE ALSO: Asia, International Law, United Nations

Taxes and Investment in Asia and the Pacific (Cook Islands) (Amsterdam: Intl. Bureau of Fiscal Documentation, 1983–).
"Avarua, Rarotonga: Will it Become the New Motion Picture Capital of the World for International Tax Planners?" by M. Chatzky, 7 *Common Law Lawyer* 1 (1982).

COOPERATIVES: See Real Estate
COPYRIGHT: See Art & Entertainment, Computers, Intellectual Property, Media Law, Personal Property
CORAL SEA ISLANDS: See Australia
CORAM NOBIS: See Criminal Law
CORONER: See Death, Forensic Science, Health & Medicine
CORPORAL PUNISHMENT: See Corrections, Education Law

CORPORATE LAW

SEE ALSO: Accounting, Administrative Law, Agency, Agriculture, Architecture, Art & Entertainment, Banking Law, Bankruptcy, Business Law, Commodities, Consumer Law, Economics, Employee Benefits, Employment Discrimination, Energy, Environmental Law, Food, Franchise law, Government Contracts, Health & Medicine, Insurance, Intellectual Property, International Law, Labor Law, Maritime Law, Media Law, Nonprofit Corporations, Occupational Safety, Oil & Gas, Partnership Law, Personal Property, Professional Responsibility, Public Utilities, Real Estate, Sports Law, State & Local Government, Taxation, Torts, Transportation, Unemployment Compensation, Uniform Commercial Code, Water Law, Workers' Compensation, Zoning & Land Planning; see also entries under individual states and countries

RESEARCH GUIDES &
BIBLIOGRAPHIES: *Bibliography of Multinational Corporations* by E. Browndorf (Oceana, 1978–).
Corporate Law Locator (R. R. Bowker, 1988).
Research Guide to Professional Corporation Law by P. Aitelli & D. Dietrich (Hein, 1985).

MODEL ACT: *Model Business Corporation Act Annotated* (ABA Sect. on Corp., Banking and Business Law) (West).

JOURNALS, NEWSLETTERS
& OTHER PERIODICALS: *Annual Institute for Corporate Counsel* (Practicing Law Institute).
BNA Corporate Counsel Weekly (BNA, 1986–).
Corporate Counsel Annual (Matthew Bender, 1966–).
The Corporate Counsellor (New York Law Pub. Co., 1986–).
Corporate Counsel Reporter (Warren, Gorham & Lamont, 1985–).
Corporation Law Adviser by W. Fletcher (Callaghan).
Corporation Law and Tax Report (Warren, Gorham & Lamont, 1985–).
Corporation Law Review (Warren, Gorham & Lamont, 1979–).
Delaware Journal of Corporate Law (1976–).
Journal of Comparative Corporate Law and Securities Regulation (Amsterdam: North-Holland Pub., 1977–).
Journal of Corporate Taxation (Warren, Gorham & Lamont).
Journal of Corporation Law (Univ. of Iowa).

DIRECTORIES: *Law & Business Directory of Corporate Counsel* (Law & Business, Inc.).
Standard & Poor's Register of Corporations, Directors and Executives.

LOOSELEAFS: *The Business Judgment Rule: Fiduciary Duties of Corporate Directors and Officers,* 2d ed. (Prentice-Hall, 1988–).
Close Corporations, 2d ed. by F. O'Neal (Callaghan, 1971–).
Closely Held Business (Prentice-Hall, 1976–).
The Consolidated Tax Return, 3d ed. by J. Crestol (Warren, Gorham & Lamont, 1980–).
Corporate Acquisitions and Mergers by B. & E. Fox (Matthew Bender, 1968–).
Corporate and Commercial Finance Agreements by S. Tomczak (Shepard's, 1984–).
The Corporate Counsellor's Deskbook, D. Block, ed. (Law & Business, Inc., 1982–).
Corporate Practice Series (BNA, 1978–).
Corporation (Prentice-Hall, 1930–).
Corporation Forms (Prentice-Hall, 1961–).
Corporation Law Guide (CCH, 1959–).
The Delaware Law of Corporations and Business Organizations by R. Balotti (Prentice-Hall, 1986–).
Encyclopedia of Corporate Meetings, Minutes, and Resolutions, 3d ed. (Prentice-Hall, 1986–).
Federal Income Taxation of Corporations Filing Consolidated Returns by H. Lerner (Matthew Bender, 1975–).
Mergers, Acquisitions and Leveraged Buyouts by M. Ginsburg (CCH, 1989–).
Model Business Corporations Act Annotated (Law & Business, Inc., 1985–).
Modern Corporation Checklists, 22d ed. by W. Sardell (Warren, Gorham & Lamont, 1982–).
Multinational Corporations Law, K. Simmonds, ed., (Oceana, 1979–).
Organizing Corporate and Other Business Enterprises, 5th ed. by C. Rohrlich (Matthew Bender, 1975–).
S Corporations (Prentice-Hall, 1983–).
S Corporations Guide (CCH, 1983–).
Shareholder Litigation by R. Magnuson (Callaghan, 1981–).
Tax Aspects of Buying and Selling Corporate Businesses by J. Fleming (Shepard's, 1984–).

TREATISES: *Attorney-Corporate Client Privilege* by J. Gergacz (Garland Law Pub., 1987).
Federal Income Taxation of Corporations, 5th ed. by H. Lidstone (ALI–ABA Comm. on Cont. Prof. Ed., 1983).
Fletcher Cyclopedia of Corporations by W. Fletcher (Callaghan, 1959).
Henn and Alexander's Hornbook on Laws of Corporations by H. Henn & R. Alexander (West, 1983).
How to Incorporate: A Handbook for Entrepreneurs and Professionals by M. Diamond & J. Williams (Wiley, 1987).
The Law of Corporations in a Nutshell, 2d ed. by R. Hamilton (West, 1987).
Liability of Corporate Officers and Directors, 4th ed. by W. Knepper & D. Bailey (Michie, 1988).

SHEPARD'S: *Corporation Law Citations* (Shepard's).

ENCYCLOPEDIAS: AMERICAN JURISPRUDENCE 2D (Am Jur 2d)
Check the following topics in the *General Index* volumes for Am Jur 2d:

Business Trusts	Parent and Subsidiary
Corporations	Corporations
Investment Securities	Professional Corporations
Joint Stock Companies	Profit or Income
Monopolies	Ultra Vires

CORPUS JURIS SECUNDUM (CJS)
Check the following topics in the *General Index* volumes for CJS:

Articles of Incorporation	Liquidation
Blue Sky Laws	Loans
Business Trusts	Merger or Consolidation
Corporations	Monopolies
De Facto Corporations	Nonprofit Corporations
Directors	Officers and Employees
Dissolution	Profits
Dividends	Quasi Corporations
Foreign Corporations	Recapitalization
Holding Companies	Stock and Stockholders
Incorporation and	Subsidiary Corporations
Organization	Ultra Vires
Joint Stock Companies	

DIGESTS:

CASE SEARCH IN WEST DIGESTS BY KEY TOPIC
In the *Descriptive Word Index* of the West digests, look for key topics and numbers under the following subject headings:

Articles of Incorporation	Joint Stock Companies
Banks and Banking	Liquidation
Blue Sky Laws	Loans
Business Trusts	Merger or Consolidation
Corporations	Monopolies
Criminal Law	Nonprofit Corporations
De Facto Corporations	Officers and Employees
Directors	Partnership
Dissolution	Profits
Dividends	Quasi Corporations
Foreign Corporations	Recapitalization
Holding Companies	Stocks and Stockholders
Incorporation and	Subsidiaries
Organization	Torts
International Law	Ultra Vires

ALR:

ANNOTATIONS
Check the index volumes for ALR, ALR2d, ALR3d, ALR4th, and ALR Fed for annotations under the following subject headings:

Bonds (Securities)	Foreign Corporation
Buy-Out Agreements	Incorporation
Bylaws	Liquidation or Dissolution
Capital Assets	Municipal Corporations
Charter	Personal Liability
Close Corporation	Professional Corporations
Consolidation or Merger	Promoters
Corporate Bonds	Restraint of Trade
Corporate Officers	Stockbrokers
Corporations	Subsidiary
Dividends	

PERIODICALS:

CURRENT LAW INDEX (CLI) & LEGAL RESOURCE INDEX (LRI)
In the CLI and LRI, look for references to periodical literature under the following subject headings:

Bonds	Close Corporations
Capital	Collapsible Corporations

Conglomerate Corporations	Partnership
Consolidation and Merger	Professional Corporations
Corporation Law	Proxy
Directors	Redemption (Law)
Domicile of Corporations	Securities
Holding Companies	Stock
Incorporation	Subsidiary Corporations
Liquidation	Taxation, Double
Minority Stockholders	Tort Liability of
Monopolies	Corporations
Municipal Corporation	Trade Secrets
Oligopolies	Ultra Vires

INDEX TO LEGAL PERIODICALS (ILP)
In the ILP, look for references to legal periodical literature under the following subject headings:

Antitrust Law	Franchising
Associations and Societies	Government Corporations
Business	Holding Companies
Cartels	Income Tax/Corporations
Commercial Law	Investment Companies
Conflict of Laws/	Municipal Corporations
Corporations	Professional Corporations
Corporate Liquidation	Public Utilities
Corporations	Stock Companies
Dividends	Stocks
Double Taxation	Taxation

CORPUS DELICTI: See Criminal Law

CORRECTIONS, PROBATION & PAROLE

SEE ALSO: Constitutional Law, Criminal Law, Juvenile Law, Mental Health, State & Local Government; see also entries under individual states and countries

RESEARCH GUIDES & BIBLIOGRAPHIES: *Corrections Law: An Updated Bibliography* (Amer. Correctional Assn., 1982).

JOURNALS, NEWSLETTERS & OTHER PERIODICALS: *American Journal of Correction* (1939–1966).
Federal Probation (Admin. Office of the U.S. Courts, 1937–).
International Journal of Offender Therapy & Comparative Criminology (England: APTO).
New England Journal of Prison Law (1974–).

TREATISES & LOOSELEAFS: *Community-Based Corrections* by J. Ortiz (Macmillan, 1981).
Community Corrections by S. Doeren (Anderson, 1982).
Constitutional Rights of Prisoners, 3d ed. by J. Palmer (Anderson, 1984).
Correctional Facility Design by D. Sechrest (U.S. Dept. of Justice, Natl. Institute of Justice, 1985).
Correctional Treatment by C. Bartollas (Prentice-Hall, 1985).
Criminal Corrections by J. Doig (Lexington Books, 1983).

A Jailhouse Lawyer's Manual, 2d ed. (Columbia Human Rights Law Review, 1985).

Law of Corrections and Prisoners' Rights in a Nutshell by S. Krantz (West, 1976).

The Law of Criminal Corrections by S. Rubin (West, 1963).

The Law of Probation and Parole by N. Cohen (Shepard's, 1983).

The Legal Dimensions of Private Incarceration by I. Robbins (A.B.A., 1988).

Manual for Prison Law Libraries by O. Werner (Assn. of American Law Libraries, 1976).

The Post-Conviction Litigation Self-Help Manual by D. Manville (Oceana, 1986).

Practical Law for Correctional Personnel (Amer. Correctional Assn., 1981).

Prisoner Litigation: The Paradox of the Jailhouse Lawyer by J. Thomas (Rowman & Littlefield, 1988).

Prisoners and the Law, I. Robbins, ed. (Clark Boardman, 1985).

Prisoner's Rights Sourcebook II, I. Robbins, ed. (Clark Boardman, 1980).

Probation, Parole, and Community Corrections, 3d ed., R. Carter, ed. (Wiley, 1984).

Procedures Manual (U.S. Parole Commn., 1983).

Rights of Prisoners by J. Gobert (Shepard's, 1981).

Standards for Criminal Justice: Legal Status of Prisoner (ABA Standing Comm. on Assn. Standards for Criminal Justice, 1983).

ENCYCLOPEDIAS:

AMERICAN JURISPRUDENCE 2D (Am Jur 2d)
Check the following topics in the *General Index* volumes for Am Jur 2d:

Administrative Law	Pardon and Parole
Civil Rights	Penal and Correctional
Constitutional Law	Institutions
Criminal Law	Probation
Cruel and Unusual	Sentence and Punishment
Punishment	

CORPUS JURIS SECUNDUM (CJS)
Check the following topics in the *General Index* volumes for CJS:

Administrative Bodies	Escape
Civil Rights	Federal Prisons
Constitutional Law	Pardons and Paroles
Convicts	Prisons
Crimes and Offenses	Probation
Cruel and Unusual	
Punishment	

DIGESTS:

CASE SEARCH IN WEST DIGESTS BY KEY TOPIC
In the *Descriptive Word Index* of the West digests, look for key topics and numbers under the following subject headings:

Administrative Bodies	Federal Prisons
Civil Rights	Pardons and Paroles
Constitutional Law	Prisons
Convicts	Probation
Criminal Law	Reformatories
Cruel and Unusual	Riot
Punishment	Sheriffs
Escape	States
Extradition and Detainers	United States Marshals

ALR:

ANNOTATIONS
Check the index volumes for ALR, ALR2d, ALR3d, ALR4th, and ALR Fed for annotations under the following subject headings:

Administrative Law	Corporal Punishment

Criminal Law
Cruel and Unusual
  Punishment
Detention
Due Process of Law

Pardon and Parole and
  Probation
Prisons and Convicts
Rehabilitation Institutions

PERIODICALS:

CURRENT LAW INDEX (CLI) & LEGAL RESOURCE INDEX (LRI)
In the CLI and LRI, look for references to periodical literature under the following subject headings:

Administrative Law
Civil Rights
Community-Based
  Connections
Constitutional Law
Convict Labor
Corporal Punishment
Correctional Institutions
Correctional Law
Corrections
Criminal Law

Ex-convicts
Habeas Corpus
Juvenile Corrections
Pardon
Parole
Prison
Probation
Punishment
Recidivism
Sentences

INDEX TO LEGAL PERIODICALS (ILP)
In the ILP, look for references to legal periodical literature under the following subject headings:

Administrative Law
Behavior Modification
Civil Rights
Constitutional Law
Corrections
Criminal Law
Criminology
Cruel and Unusual
  Punishment
Pardon

Parole
Post-Conviction Remedies
Prisons
Probation
Punishment
Recidivism
Rehabilitation of
  Offenders
Sentencing

CORROBORATION: See Criminal Law
CORRUPTION: See Criminal Law, Zoning & Land Planning
COSMETICS: See Food
COST ACCOUNTING: See Accounting, Government Contracts

COSTA RICA

SEE ALSO:

Caribbean, International Law, Latin America, United Nations

**RESEARCH GUIDE &
BIBLIOGRAPHY:**

A Guide to the Official Publications of . . . Costa Rica (Library of Congress, 1947).

CONSTITUTION:

"Costa Rica" by J. Gould in *Constitutions of the Countries of the World* by A. Blaustein & G. Flanz (Oceana, 1982).

**TREATISES &
LOOSELEAFS:**

Capital Formation and Investment Incentives Around the World (Costa Rica) by W. Diamond & D. Diamond (Matthew Bender, 1984–).

Caribbean Basin: A Tax Tour (Costa Rica) (Arthur Anderson & Co., 1985).

Digest of Commercial Laws of the World (Costa Rica) (Natl. Assn. of Credit Management; Oceana, 1977–).

Information Guide, Doing Business in Costa Rica (Price Waterhouse).

Latin American Democracies: Colombia, Costa Rica, Venezuela by J. Peeler (Univ. of North Carolina Press, 1985).

Law and Agrarian Reform in Costa Rica by J. Rowles (Westview, 1985).

Series of Statements of the Law of the OAS Member States in Matters Affecting Business: Costa Rica (Organization of American States, 1978).

Taxation in Costa Rica (NY: Deloitte, Haskins & Sells, 1979).

Tax Laws of the World—Costa Rica (FL: Foreign Tax Law Assn.).

ARTICLES:

"Constitutional Adjudication in Costa Rica" by R. Barker, 17 *University of Miami Inter-American Law Review* 249 (1986).

"Latin American Tax Update: Costa Rica" by M. Marti, 12 *Lawyer of the Americas* 648 (1980).

"Law and Agrarian Reform in Costa Rica" by J. Rowles, 14 *Lawyer of the Americas* 149, 399 (1982).

"Technology Transfer Patterns . . . Licensing in Costa Rica" by D. Grynspan, 36 *International Affairs* 29 (1981).

COST EFFECTIVENESS: See Accounting, Economics
COSTS: See Professional Responsibility, Trial & Appellate Practice
CO–TENANCY: See Real Estate
COUNCIL OF STATE GOVERNMENTS: See State & Local Government
COUNSEL: See Constitutional Law, Professional Responsibility
COUNSELORS: See Education Law
COUNTERCLAIM: See Trial & Appellate Practice
COUNTERFEITING: See Criminal Law
COUNTERVAILING DUTIES: See Customs, International Law
COUNTRIES: See International Law
COUNTY: See Election, State & Local Government
COUPLES: See Family Law
COURT: See Circuit Courts, Judicial Administration, Trial & Appellate Practice
COURT–MARTIAL: See Military Law
COURT OF CLAIMS: See Taxation
COURT OF MILITARY APPEALS: See Military Law
COURT RULES: See Circuit Courts, Trial & Appellate Practice
COVENANT: See Contracts, Equity, Estate Planning, Real Estate
CRASH: See Torts
CREDENTIALS: See Paralegal
CREDIT, CREDITORS: See Banking Law, Bankruptcy, Business Law, Consumer Law, Contracts, Securities Law, Uniform Commercial Code
CREDIT UNION: See Banking Law

CRIMINAL LAW & PROCEDURE

SEE ALSO:

Alcohol, Antitrust Law, Business Law, Civil Rights, Computers, Constitutional Law, Corrections, Forensic Science, International Law, Judicial Administration Juvenile Law, Legal History, Mental Health, Military Law, Securities Law, Trial & Appellate Practice

RESEARCH GUIDES &
BIBLIOGRAPHIES:

Bibliographic Guide for Prosecutors (Houston: Bates College of Law, Natl. College of District Attorneys, 1976–).

Crime and Justice: An Annual Review of Research, N. Morris & M. Tinry, eds. (Univ. of Chicago Press, 1979–).

Crime and Justice in America: A Historical Bibliography (ABC–Clio Press, 1983).

The Insanity Defense; A Bibliographic Research Guide by D. Picquet (Harrison, 1985).

"Recent Literature on Organized Crime" by J. Werner, 14 *International Journal of Legal Information* 155 (1986).

UNIFORM LAWS (from
Uniform Laws
Annotated):

Act on Status of Convicted Persons.

Act to Secure Attendance of Witnesses from Without a State in Criminal Proceedings.

Code of Military Justice.

Controlled Substances Act.

Crime Victims Reparations Act.

Criminal Extradition Act.

Criminal Statistics Act.

Extradition and Rendition Act.

Juvenile Court Act.

Mandatory Disposition of Detainers Act.

Model Insanity Defense and Post Trial Disposition Act.

Model Penal Code.

Model Sentencing and Corrections Act.

Motor Vehicle Certificate of Title and Anti-Theft Act.

Post Conviction and Procedure Act.

Rendition of Accused Persons Act.

Rendition of Prisoners Witnesses in Criminal Proceedings Act.

Rules of Criminal Procedure.

JOURNALS, INSTITUTES,
NEWSLETTERS &
OTHER PERIODICALS:

American Criminal Law Review (ABA, 1962–).

American Journal of Criminal Law (Univ. of Texas Sch. of Law).

American Justice (ABA).

Annual Institute on Defense of Criminal Cases (Georgetown Univ. Law Center, 1983–).

Crime and Delinquency (Natl. Council on Crime and Delinquency).

Crime and Justice: An Annual Review of Research (1979–).

Criminal Defense (1973–).

Criminal Justice Abstracts (Natl. Council on Crime and Delinquency, 1970–).

Criminal Justice and Behavior (Sage Pubs.)

Criminal Justice Bulletin (Warren, Gorham & Lamont).

Criminal Justice Journal (Western State Univ. College of Law, 1976–).

Criminal Justice Newsletter (Natl. Council on Crime & Delinquency).

The Criminal Justice Periodical Index (Univ. Microfilms Intl., 1975–).

Criminal Law Bulletin (Warren, Gorham & Lamont, 1965–).

Criminal Law Review (Clark Boardman, 1979–).

Death Penalty Reporter (Houston: Natl. College for Criminal Defense).

Drug Law Report (Clark Boardman).

Journal of Criminal Justice (Pergamon Press, 1973–).

Journal of Criminal Law and Criminology (Northwestern Univ. Sch. of Law, 1910–).

Journal of Police Science and Administration (Intl. Assn. of Chiefs of Police).

Journal of Research in Crime and Delinquency (1964–).

Legal and Law Enforcement Periodicals (NY: Facts on File, 1981).

National Journal of Criminal Defense (Houston: Natl. College for Criminal Defense, 1975–).

Police Law Quarterly (1971–).

Prosecutor, Journal of the National District Attorneys Association.

Research in Law, Deviance & Social Control (JAI Press).

Search and Seizure Law Report (Clark Boardman).

Victimology (Visage Press).

LOOSELEAFS:

ABA Standards for Criminal Justice, 2d ed. (Little, Brown, 1980–).

BNA Criminal Practice Manual (BNA, 1986–).

Business Crime by S. Arkin (Matthew Bender, 1981–).

Confession Standards by N. Sobel (Gould, 1966–).

Criminal Defense Ethics by J. Burkoff (Clark Boardman, 1986–).

Criminal Defense Techniques, M. Eisenstein, ed. (Matthew Bender, 1969–).

Criminal Law Advocacy by M. Kadish (Matthew Bender, 1982–).

The Criminal Law Reporter (BNA, 1967–).

Defense of Drunk Driving Cases, 3d ed. by R. Erwin (Matthew Bender, 1974–).

Defense of Narcotic Cases by D. Bernheim (Matthew Bender, 1972–).

Dictionary of Criminal Justice Terms (Gould, 1982–).

Drug Abuse and the Law Sourcebook by G. Uelman (Clark Boardman, 1983–).

Drug Testing Legal Manual by K. Zeese (Clark Boardman, 1988–).

Extradition Laws and Treaties by I. Kavass & A. Sprudzs (Hein, 1980–).

Eye-Witness Identification, 2d ed. by N. Sobel (Clark Boardman, 1981–).

Federal Jury Criminal Instructions by S. Saltzburg (Michie, 1985–).

Federal Rules of Criminal Procedure, 2d ed. by M. Hermann (Clark Boardman, 1980–).

Foreign Corrupt Practices Act Reporter (Business Laws, Inc., 1978–).

Identification and Police Line-Ups by W. Ringel (Gould, 1968–).

Plea Bargaining and Guilty Pleas, 2d ed. by J. Bond (Clark Boardman, 1982–).

Police Misconduct, 2d ed. by the Natl. Lawyers Guild (Clark Boardman, 1980–).

Prosecution and Defense of Criminal Conspiracy Cases by P. Marcus (Matthew Bender, 1978–).

Prosecution and Defense of Sex Crimes by A. Morosco (Matthew Bender, 1976–).

Prosecutorial Misconduct by B. Gershman (Clark Boardman, 1985–).

Proving Federal Crimes by the U.S. Dept. of Justice (GPO, 1980–).

Representation of Witnesses Before Federal Grand Juries, 3d ed. by the Natl. Lawyers Guild (Clark Boardman, 1984–).

Rules of Criminal Procedure by R. Cipes (Matthew Bender, 1965–).

Searches and Seizures, Arrests and Confessions, 2d ed. by W. Ringel (Clark Boardman, 1979–).

The Supreme Court and the Criminal Law by D. Nedrud (Decatur, MI: LE Pub., 1978–).

Trial Manual 5 for the Defense of Criminal Cases by A. Amsterdam (ALI–ABA Comm. on Cont. Prof. Ed., 1988–).

United States Attorneys' Manual by the U.S. Dept. of Justice (GPO, 1980–).

TREATISES:

Criminal and Tax Fraud by D. McGowen (Kluwer, 1986).

Criminal Law Defenses by P. Robinson (West, 1984).

Criminal Procedure by W. LaFave (West, 1984).

The Death Penalty in the Eighties: An Examination of the Modern System of Capital Punishment by W. White (Univ. of Mich. Press, 1987).

Eyewitness Identification by L. Taylor (Michie, 1982).

Federal Habeas Corpus, 2d ed. by R. Sokol (Michie, 1969).

Federal Habeas Corpus Practice and Procedure by J. Liebman (Michie, 1988).

Federal Jury Practice and Instructions: Civil and Criminal, 3d ed. by E. Devitt (West, 1977).

Investigation and Preparation of Criminal Cases by F. Bailey (Lawyers Co-op., 1970).

Limits of the Criminal Sanction by H. Packer (Stanford Univ. Press, 1968).

Major Cases in Capital Punishment, B. Winick, ed. (Univ. Pubs. of America, 1984).

Marijuana, Medicine and the Law by R. Randall (Galen Press, 1988).

Mental Disabilities and Criminal Responsibility by H. Fingarette (Berkeley: Univ. of CA Press, 1979).

Model Penal Code of Pre-Arraignment Procedure (American Law Institute, 1975).

Prostitution: Regulation and Control by J. Decker (Rothman, 1979).

Research Methods in Criminology and Criminal Justice by E. Johnson (Prentice-Hall, 1981).

Rethinking Criminal Law by G. Fletcher (Little, Brown, 1978).

Search and Seizure, 2d ed. by W. LaFave (West, 1987).

Sourcebook of Criminal Justice Statistics (U.S. Dept. of Justice).

Substantive Criminal Law by W. LaFave (West, 1986).

Wharton's Criminal Evidence, 13th ed. by C. Torcia (Lawyers Co-op., 1972).

Wharton's Criminal Law, 14th ed. by C. Torcia (Lawyers Co-op., 1978).

SHEPARD'S: *Shepard's Criminal Justice Citations.*

CROATIA: See Yugoslavia
CROP DUSTING: See Environmental Law
CROSS APPEAL: See Trial & Appellate Practice
CROSS COMPLAINT: See Trial & Appellate Practice
CROSS EXAMINATION: See Trial & Appellate Practice
CRUEL & UNUSUAL PUNISHMENT: See Constitutional Law, Corrections, Criminal Law
CRUELTY: See Family Law

CUBA

SEE ALSO: Caribbean, Communism, International Law, Latin America, United Nations

**RESEARCH GUIDES &
BIBLIOGRAPHIES:**   *A Guide to the Official Publications of . . . Cuba* (Library of Congress, 1945).

"A Selected Bibliography of the Cuban Legal System, 1959–1983" by B. Zagaris, 15 *Lawyer of the Americas* 545 (1984).

**STATUTES & RELATED
LAWS:**   "Cuba: Legislative Decree on Economic Association Between Cuban and Foreign Entities," 21 *International Legal Materials* 1106 (1982).

Cuban Commercial Code, 1978 (FL: Foreign Tax Law Assn., Inc.).

ARTICLES: "Cuban Enactment and Decrees Relevant to International Trade," 21 *International Legal Materials* 1107 (1982).

"The Cuban Popular Tribunals" by J. Berman, 69 *Columbia Law Review* 1317 (1969).

"Cuba's Joint Venture Law: New Rules for Foreign Investment" by J. Zorn, 21 *Columbia Journal of Transnational Law* 273 (1983).

"Cuba's 1976 Socialist Constitution . . ." by W. D'Zurilla, 55 *Tulane Law Review* 1223 (1981).

"Cuba's System of International Commercial Arbitration" by E. Dahl, 15 *Lawyer of the Americas* 441 (1984).

"Foreign Investment in Cuba," 15 *Law and Policy in International Business* 689 (1983).

"Foreign Investment Law (Cuba)" by S. Fiszman, 8 *Hastings International & Comparative Law Review* 147, 165 (1985).

"Impressions of Cuban Law" by H. Berman, 28 *American Journal of Comparative Law* 475 (1980).

"An Introduction to Cuban Socialist Law" by M. Azicri, 6 *Review of Socialist Law* 153 (1980).

"The Rights of Children in Cuba" by O. Finlay, 13 *Columbia Human Rights Review* 221 (1981).

CURTESY: See Estate Planning, Family Law, Real Estate
CUSTODIAN: See Personal Property
CUSTODY: See Family Law, Mediation
CUSTOM & USAGE: See Contracts
CUSTOMARY LAW: See Afghanistan, Africa, Botswana, Ghana, Hong Kong, International Law, Kenya, Papua New Guinea, Tanzania, Zimbabwe, Zambia

CUSTOMS

SEE ALSO: Agriculture, Food, International Law, Maritime Law, Taxation, Transportation

RESEARCH GUIDES & BIBLIOGRAPHIES:
"Research Tools in Customs Law" by M. Fisher, 33 *Business Lawyer* 89 (1977).
"The U.S. Law of Export Controls: A Selected Bibliography" by S. Boyd, 18 *International Lawyer* 483 (1984).

COURT RULES:
United States Court of International Trade: Rules (Invictus Pub. Corp., 1980–).
U.S. Court of International Trade Rules and Annotation Service (Rules Service Co., 1984–).

TREATISES & LOOSELEAFS:
Antidumpting and Countervailing Duty Laws by J. Pattison (Clark Boardman).
Customs Law and Administration by R. Sturm (Booklet 32) (Oceana).
Import Practice: Customs and International Trade Law by D. Serko (Practicing Law Institute, 1984).
U.S. Customs and International Trade Guide by P. Feller (Matthew Bender, 1979–).

ENCYCLOPEDIAS:
AMERICAN JURISPRUDENCE 2D (Am Jur 2d)
Check the following topics in the *General Index* volumes for Am Jur 2d:

Agriculture Court of	Exports
Customs	Food
Animals	Intoxicating Liquors
Court of Customs	Mines and Minerals
Customs Duties and	Money or Cash
Import Regulations	Smuggling
Embargo	Trademarks

CORPUS JURIS SECUNDUM (CJS)
Check the following topics in the *General Index* volumes for CJS:

Aeronautics	Drugs
Commerce	International Law
Customs Duties	Sales

DIGESTS:	CASE SEARCH IN WEST DIGESTS BY KEY TOPIC

In the *Descriptive Word Index* of the West digests, look for key topics and numbers under the following subject headings:

Aeronautics	Drugs
Antidumping	International Law
Commerce	Sales
Customs Duties	Searches

ALR: ANNOTATIONS

Check the index volumes for ALR, ALR2d, ALR3d, ALR4th, and ALR Fed for annotations under the following subject headings:

Customs & Patent	Custom Court
Appeals Court	Customs Duties

PERIODICALS: CURRENT LAW INDEX (CLI) & LEGAL RESOURCE INDEX (LRI)

In the CLI and LRI, look for references to periodical literature under the following subject headings:

Bonded Warehouses and Goods	Customs Appraisal
	Customs Courts
Customs Administration	Smuggling

INDEX TO LEGAL PERIODICALS (ILP)

In the ILP, look for references to legal periodical literature under the following subject headings:

Antidumping	Tariff and Customs Laws

CY PRES DOCTRINE: See Estate Planning

CYPRUS

SEE ALSO: Greece, International Law, Turkey, United Nations

STATUTES & RELATED LAWS: *Index to the Laws of the Republic of Cyprus* (Nicosia: Govt. Printing Office, 1971).

CASES: *Cyprus Law Reports* (Nicosia: Govt. Printing Office, 1965–).

JOURNALS & OTHER PERIODICALS: *Cyprus Law Review* (Nicosia: NST Bookservice Co., 1983–).

TREATISES & LOOSELEAFS:
Capital Formation and Investment Incentives Around the World (Cyprus) by W. Diamond & D. Diamond (Matthew Bender, 1984–).
Constitutional and Legal Problems in the Republic of Cyprus, 2d ed. by C. Tornaritis (Nicosiai Public Information Office, 1972).
Cyprus and its Constitutional and Other Legal Problems, 2d ed. by C. Tornaritis (Nicosia: Attorney General, 1980).
Cyprus in International Tax Planning by C. Demetriades (Kluwer, 1980).
Information Guide, Doing Business in Cyprus (Price Waterhouse, 1980).
Investment Laws of the World (Cyprus) (Oceana, 1981–).

Tax and Investment Profile: Cyprus (Touche Ross Intl., 1984).
Tax Laws of the World—Cyprus (FL: Foreign Tax Law Assn.).
The Turkish Republic of Northern Cyprus in Perspective by Z. Nejatigil (Nicosia: Tezel, 1985).

ARTICLES: "Constitutional Majority Rule and the Cyprus Constitution" by G. Swan, 5 *Boston College Third World Law Journal* 1 (1984).
"International Law and the Conflict in Cyprus" by R. Macdonald, 19 *Canadian Yearbook of International Law* 3 (1981).
"Some Legal and Tax Aspects of Foreign Investments in Cyprus" by K. Chrysostomides, *Worldlaw* 37 (Sept.–Oct., 1984).

CZECHOSLOVAKIA

SEE ALSO: Communism, Europe, International Law, Soviet Union, United Nations

**RESEARCH GUIDES &
BIBLIOGRAPHIES:**   *The International Relations of Eastern Europe: A Guide to Information Sources* (Czechoslovakia) by R. Remington (Gale, 1978).
Legal Sources and Bibliography of Czechoslovakia by A. Bohmer et al. (Praeger, 1959).

CONSTITUTIONS: *The Constitutions of the Communist World* (Czechoslovakia), W. Simons, ed. (Sijthoff & Noordhoff, 1980).

**JOURNALS & OTHER
PERIODICALS:**   *Bulletin Czechoslovak Law*.

**TREATISES &
LOOSELEAFS:**   *Commentary on the Czechoslovak Civil Code* by T. Vondracek (Nijhoff; Kluwer, 1988).
"Czechoslovakia: Law on Joint Ventures" by G. Glos, 17 *International Journal of Legal Information* 1 (1989).
The Czechoslovak Declaration of Independence: A History of the Document by G. Kovtun (Library of Congress, 1985).
Czechoslovak Private International Law by G. Glos (Library of Congress, 1983).
Digest of Commercial Laws of the World (Czechoslovakia) (Natl. Assn. of Credit Management; Oceana, 1977–).
Doing Business with Eastern Europe (NY: Business Intl. Corp., 1975–).
Employment and Wage Policies in Poland, Czechoslovakia, and Hungary Since 1950 by J. Adam (London: Macmillan, 1984).
The Law of Marital Property in Czechoslovakia and the Soviet Union by G. Glos (Library of Congress, 1981).
Legal Aspects of Joint Ventures in Eastern Europe (Czechoslovakia), D. Campbell, ed. (Kluwer, 1981).
Recognition and Enforcement of Foreign Judgments in Various Foreign Countries (Czechoslovakia) by G. Roman (Library of Congress, 1984).
Taxation in European Socialist Countries (vol. 5, Czechoslovakia) (Amsterdam: Intl. Bureau of Fiscal Documentation).

ARTICLES: "Czechoslovakia: Abortion and Social Security Reforms" by J. Haderka, 27 *Journal of Family Law* 91 (1988–89).

"Czechoslovakia: The Importance of Recent Changes" by J. Haderka, 25 *Journal of Family Law* 69 (1986–87).

"The Czechoslovak Law of Conflicts of Laws" by G. Glos, 9 *Review of Socialist Law* 261 (1983).

"The 1981 U.S.–Czechoslovak Claims Settlement Agreement" by Pechota, 76 *American Journal of International Law* 639 (1982).

"Violations of ILO Conventions by the USSR and Czechoslovakia" by T. Meron, 74 *American Journal of International Law* 206 (1980).

DAHOMEY: See Benin

DAMAGES: See Business Law, Contracts, Economics, Employment Discrimination, Environmental Law, Equity, Intellectual Property, Labor Law, Maritime Law, Personal Property, Real Estate, Torts, Trial & Appellate Practice

DAMS: See State & Local Government, Water Law

DANGER: See Occupational Safety, Torts

DATABASES: See Computers

DAY CARE: See Family Law, Women & the Law

DEAD BODIES: See Death, Health & Medicine

DEAD MAN STATUTES: See Estate Planning, Family Law

DEAF: See Handicapped & the Law

DEALER: See Agency, Securities Law

DEATH

SEE ALSO: Abortion, Age, AIDS, Air & Aviation, Alcohol, Community Property, Conflict of Law, Criminal Law, Estate Planning, Family Law, Forensic Science, Handicapped & the Law, Health & Medicine, Human Experimentation, Human Rights, Occupational Safety, Social Security, Torts, Workers' Compensation

RESEARCH GUIDES & BIBLIOGRAPHIES: "The Right to Die: Sources of Information" by K. Davenport, 5 *Legal Reference Services Quarterly* 47 (1985).

Abortion and Euthanasia: An Annotated Bibliography by K. Clouser & A. Zucker (Philadelphia: Society for Health and Human Values, 1974).

Bibliography of Bioethics, L. Walters, ed. (Gale Research).

Death: A Bibliographic Guide by A. Miller et al. (Scarecrow Press, 1977).

"Defining Death and Dying: A Bibliographic Overview" by K. Price, 71 *Law Library Journal* 49 (1978).

The Euthanasia Controversy, 1812–1974: A Bibliography with Selected Annotations by C. Triche (Troy, NY: Whitston, 1975).

UNIFORM STATUTES: Uniform Brain Death Act, 12 *Uniform Laws Annotated* (West, 1986).

Uniform Determination of Death Act, 12 *Uniform Laws Annotated* (West, 1986).

Uniform Rights of the Terminally Ill Act, 9A *Uniform Laws Annotated* (West, 1986).

JOURNALS, NEWSLETTERS & OTHER PERIODICALS: *Bioethics Quarterly* (Human Sciences Press).

Concern for Dying Newsletter (NY: Concern for Dying).

Ethics in Science and Medicine (Pergamon Press).

The Hastings Center Report (Institute of Society, Ethics, and Life Sciences).

Journal of Thanatology (Arno Press).

Omega: Journal of Death and Dying (Baywood Pub. Co.).

**TREATISES &
LOOSELEAFS:**

Catastrophic Diseases: Who Decides What? by J. Katz et al. (Russell Sage Foundation, 1975).

Death (Courtroom Medicine Series) by M. Houts et al. (Matthew Bender, 1966–).

Death, Dying and the Biological Revolution: Our Last Quest for Responsibility by R. Veatch (Yale Univ. Press, 1976).

Death Investigation: An Analysis of Laws and Policies of the United States . . . by P. Sheehan et al. (U.S. Dept. of HEW, Pub. Health Service, Health Services Admin., Bur. of Comm. Health Services, 1978) (HE20.5102:D34).

Deciding to Forego Life-Sustaining Treatment by the President's Commission for the Study of Ethical Problems in Medicine and Biomedical Research (GPO, 1983).

Defining Death by the President's Commn. for the Study of Ethical Problems in Medicine and Biomedical Research (GPO, 1981).

Ethics of Withdrawal of Life-Support Systems by D. Walton (Greenwood Press, 1983).

Good Life/Good Death: A Doctor's Case for Euthanasia and Suicide by C. Bernard (Prentice-Hall, 1980).

Killing and Letting Die by B. Steinbock (Prentice-Hall, 1980).

Legal Medicine, A. James, Jr., ed. (MD: Urban & Schwarzenberg, 1980).

Life and Death with Liberty and Justice: A Contribution to the Euthanasia Debate by B. Grisez & J. Boyle (Univ. of Notre Dame Press, 1979).

Making Healthcare Decisions by the President's Commission for the Study of Ethical Problems in Medicine and Biomedical Research (GPO, 1982).

Medico-Legal Implications of Death and Dying by D. Myers (Lawyers Co-op., 1981).

The Rights of the Critically Ill by J. Robertson (Ballinger, 1983).

Right to Die or Right to Live? Legal Aspects of Dying and Death by P. Riga (MD: Associated Faculty Press, 1981).

Sourcebook on Death and Dying, J. Fruehling, ed. (Chicago: Marquis Professional ., 1982).

Suicide and Euthanasia by S. Wallace (Univ. of Tenn. Press, 1981).

MISCELLANEOUS:

In the Matter of Karen Quinlan: The Complete Legal Briefs, Court Proceedings, and Decision in the Superior Court of New Jersey (Univ. Publications of America, 1975).

ENCYCLOPEDIAS:

AMERICAN JURISPRUDENCE 2D (Am Jur 2d)
Check the following topics in the *General Index* volumes for Am Jur 2d:

Abortion	Physicians and Surgeons
Criminal Law	Sickness or Illness
Death and Death Actions	Suicide

CORPUS JURIS SECUNDUM (CJS)
Check the following topics in the *General Index* volumes for CJS:

Abortion	Illness
Criminal Law	Physicians and Surgeons
Death	Suicide
Euthanasia	

DIGESTS:

CASE SEARCH IN WEST DIGESTS BY KEY TOPIC
In the *Descriptive Word Index* of the West digests, look for key topics and numbers under the following subject headings:

Criminal Law	Physicians and Surgeons
Death	Suicide

ALR:

ANNOTATIONS
Check the index volumes for ALR, ALR2d, ALR3d, ALR4th, and ALR Fed for annotations under the following subject headings:

Death	Hospitals
Euthanasia	Medical Research
Heath or Accident Insurance	Medical Treatment or Care
Homicide	Suicide

PERIODICALS:

CURRENT LAW INDEX (CLI) & LEGAL RESOURCE INDEX (LRI)
In the CLI and LRI, look for references to periodical literature under the following subject headings:

Bioethics	Right to Life
Criminal Law	Suicide
Death	Terminal Care
Euthanasia	Terminally Ill
Right to Die	

INDEX TO LEGAL PERIODICALS (ILP)
In the ILP, look for references to legal periodical literature under the following subject headings:

Euthanasia	Suicide
Right to Die	Wrongful Death

DEBT, DEBTORS: See Banking Law, Bankruptcy, Consumer Law, Contracts, Uniform Commercial Code
DECEDENT'S ESTATE: See Estate Planning
DECLARATION (EVIDENCE): See Trial & Appellate Practice
DECLARATORY JUDGMENT: See Trial & Appellate Practice
DECOLONIZATION: See Argentina, Belize, Mauritius, Puerto Rico
DEDUCTIONS: See Taxation
DEED: See Equity, Estate Planning, Real Estate
DEEP SEA: See Sea
DE FACTO CORPORATION: See Corporate Law
DEFAMATION: See Media Law, Torts
DEFAULT: See Contracts
DEFAULT JUDGMENT: See Trial & Appellate Practice
DEFECT: See Torts
DEFENDER: See Poverty Law
DEFENSE DEPARTMENT: See Government Contracts, International Law, Military Law
DEFENSES: See Criminal Law, Torts, Trial & Appellate Practice
DEFERRED COMPENSATION: See Employee Benefits, Taxation
DEINSTITUTIONALIZATION: See Mental Health

DELAWARE

SEE ALSO: Circuit Courts (Third Circuit), Corporate Law

STATUTES: *Delaware Code Annotated* (Michie).
Laws of Delaware.
Session Laws.

STATE ADMINISTRATIVE
REGULATIONS: *Register of Regulations* (1979–).
                        Delaware Documentation.

COURT OPINIONS: *Delaware Reports* (1920–1966).
                        Atlantic Reporter (1884–).
                        Delaware Reporter (West).

COURT RULES: *Court Rules* (Michie).

COURT
ADMINISTRATION: *Annual Reports of Delaware Judiciary* (Admin. Office of Court, 1977–).

JOURNALS & OTHER
PERIODICALS: *The Delaware Corporate Law Reporter* (Philadelphia: Packard Press Corp., 1985–).
                        Delaware Corporation Law Update (Corp. Law Center of Del., 1985–).
                        Delaware Journal of Corporation Law (1976–).
                        Delaware Lawyer.

TREATISES, LOOSELEAFS
& OTHER
MONOGRAPHS: *Delaware Business Kit for Starting and Existing Businesses* by L. Barrientos (Simon &
                            Schuster, 1983).
                        The Delaware Corporation by A. Sparks (BNA, 1978).
                        The Delaware General Corporation Law by E. Folk (Little, Brown, 1972).
                        Delaware Landlord-Tenant Handbook by D. Harris (Michie, 1980).
                        Delaware Law for Corporate Lawyers (Practicing Law Institute, 1985).
                        The Delaware Law of Corporations and Business Organizations by F. Balotti &
                            J. Finkelstein (Law & Business, Inc., 1985).

DIGESTS & CITATOR: *Atlantic Digest* (West).
                        Delaware Advance Annotation Service (Michie, 1984).
                        Delaware District Digest (Wilmington: 1984–).
                        Delaware Shepard's Citations.

DELAY: See Judicial Administration, Trial & Appellate Practice
DELEGATION OF POWERS: See Administrative Law, Constitutional Law
DELICT: See Scotland
DELINQUENCY: See Criminal Law, Family Law, Juvenile Law
DELINQUENT: See Taxation
DELIVERY: See Contracts, Personal Property
DEMAND: See Contracts
DEMOCRACY: See Jurisprudence
DEMOCRATIC EVIDENCE: See Trial & Appellate Practice
DEMURRER: See Trial & Appellate Practice

DENMARK

SEE ALSO: Europe, European Economic Community, International Law, Scandinavian Law

RESEARCH GUIDES &
BIBLIOGRAPHIES: *Bibliography of Danish Law with Contents and a Preface in English* by J. Sondergaard
                            (Copenhagen: Juristforbundets Forlag, 1976).

"Danish Legal Publications in English, French and German 1963–1974" by
J. Sondergaard, 20 *Scandinavian Studies in Law* 267 (1976).

**TREATISES &
LOOSELEAFS:**

Administrative Secrecy in Developed Countries (Denmark) by D. Rpwat (Columbia
Univ. Press, 1979).

Business Operations in Denmark by A. Spang-Hanssen, Tax Management Foreign
Income Portfolios, No. 181–2d (BNA, 1980).

Capital Formation and Investment Incentives Around the World (Denmark) by
W. Diamond & D. Diamond (Matthew Bender, 1984–).

Consumer Legislation in Denmark: A Study Prepared for the EC Commission by
B. Dahl (Van Nostrand Reinhold, 1981).

The Control of Police Discretion: The Danish Experience by T. Aaron (Thomas, 1966).

Danish and Norwegian Law: A General Survey (Copenhagen: Danish Committee on
Comparative Law; G.E.C. Gads Pub., 1963).

Danish Law: A General Survey by H. Gammeltoft-Hansen et al. (Copenhagen: The
Danish Committee on Comparative Law; G.E.C. Gads Pub., 1982).

Digest of Commercial Laws of the World (Denmark), Natl. Assn. of Credit
Management (Oceana, 1977–).

Information Guide, Doing Business in Denmark (Price Waterhouse).

International Handbook on Comparative Business Law (Denmark), D. Campbell, ed.
(Kluwer, 1979).

Tax Laws of the World—Denmark (FL: Foreign Tax Law Assn.).

World Law of Competition (Denmark), J. von Kalinowski, ed. (Matthew Bender, 1979–).

ARTICLES:

"Circumstances in Which Proceedings of Bankruptcy Winding-Up May be Initiated in
Denmark" by J. Lundregen, 10 *International Business Lawyer* 31 (1982).

"Comfort Letters Under Danish Law" by C. Wissum, 6 *International Financial Law
Review* 23 (1987).

"Denmark" (Issues Involving the EC) by H. Rasmussen, 9 *European Law Review* 66
(1984).

"Denmark: Legislation on Surrogate Maternity and Other Developments" by J.
Graversen, 26 *Journal of Family Law* 59 (1987–88). See also 25 *Journal of
Family Law* 81 (1986–87).

"The Impact of Consumer Law on the Law of Contracts in Denmark" by P. Madsen,
28 *Scandinavian Studies in Law* 83 (1984).

"International Arbitration in Denmark" by C. Pedersen, 14 *Case Western Reserve
Journal of International Law* 259 (1982).

"Structuring Business Opportunities in Denmark" by D. Lassila, 8 *International Tax
Journal* 256 (1982).

DENTISTRY

SEE ALSO:

Health & Medicine, Nursing, Torts

Dental Litigation, 2d ed. by W. Morris (Michie, 1977).
Dental Practice for Trial Lawyers by R. Pekarsky (Harrison, 1983).
Legal Considerations in Dentistry by S. Willig (Krieger, 1971; Williams & Wilkins, 1978).
Medical Malpractice: Handling Dental Cases by N. Schafler (Shepard's, 1985).
Revocation of Professional Licenses by Government Agencies (Dentists) by W. Morris
(Michie, 1984).

DENUCLEARIZATION: See Sea, War

DEPARTMENT OF STATE: See International Law

DEPENDENCIES: See American Samoa, International Law

DEPENDENTS: See Family Law, Juvenile Law, Military Law, Women & the Law

DEPLETION ALLOWANCE: See Natural Resources, Oil & Gas, Taxation

DEPORTATION: See Immigration Law, International Law

DEPOSIT: See Banking Law, Estate Planning, Personal Property, Real Estate, Uniform Commercial Code

DEPOSITION: See Trial & Appellate Practice

DERECOGNITION: See Taiwan

DEREGULATION: See Administrative Law, Media Law, Public Utilities, Securities Law, Transportation

DESCENT & DISTRIBUTION: See Estate Planning, Family Law, Real Estate

DESERTION: See Family Law

DESIGN: See Intellectual Property, Torts

DETAINER: See Corrections, Real Estate

DETENTION: See Corrections, Immigration Law, Juvenile Law

DETINUE: See Personal Property

DEUNIONIZING: See Labor Law

DEVELOPERS, DEVELOPMENT: See Architecture, Historic Preservation, State & Local Government, Zoning & Land Planning

DEVELOPING NATIONS: See International Law

DEVIANT BEHAVIOR: See Homosexuality, Mental Health

DIAGNOSIS: See Health & Medicine

DIAGRAM: See Intellectual Property

DIALYSIS: See Health & Medicine

DIE: See Death

DIPLOMACY, DIPLOMATIC OFFICES: See International Law

DIPLOMATIC PRIVELEGES: See Constitutional Law

DIRECTED VERDICT: See Trial & Appellate Practice

DIRECTOR: See Corporate Law

DISABILITY: See Handicapped & the Law, Health & Medicine, Insurance, Mental Health, Occupational Safety, State & Local Government, Workers' Compensation

DISARMAMENT: See International Law, War

DISCHARGE: See Employment Discrimination, Labor Law, Mental Health, Military Law

DISCIPLINE: See Education Law, Professional Responsibility

DISCLOSURE: See Labor Law, Securities Law

DISCOVERY: See Trial & Appellate Practice

DISCRETION: See Administrative Law, Trial & Appellate Practice

DISCRIMINATION: See Church & State, Civil Rights, Constitutional Law, Consumer Law, Education Law, Election, Employment Discrimination, Family Law, Handicapped & the Law, Homosexuality, Labor Law, Poverty Law, Real Estate, Women & the Law

DISEASE: See AIDS, Death, Health & Medicine, Occupational Safety, Workers' Compensation

DISMISSAL: See Civil Service, Employment Discrimination, Labor Law, Mental Health, Trial & Appellate Practice

DISORDERLY CONDUCT: See Criminal Law

DISPUTE RESOLUTION: See Labor Law, Mediation, Trial & Appellate Practice

DISTRESS: See Real Estate, Torts

DISTRIBUTION: See Estate Planning

DISTRICT ATTORNEY: See Criminal Law

DISTRICT OF COLUMBIA

**RESEARCH GUIDES &
BIBLIOGRAPHIES:**

"District of Columbia Courts" by Voorhes, 20 *Catholic University Law Review* 917 (1980).

Selected Information Sources for the District of Columbia, 2d ed. by C. Ahearn et al. (Amer. Assn. of Law Libraries, 1986).

"Separation of Powers in the District of Columbia under Home Rule" by J. Mckay, 27 *Catholic University Law Review* 515 (1978).

**STATUTES &
ADMINISTRATIVE
REGULATIONS:**

District of Columbia Code, 1973 ed. (Govt. Printing Office).

D.C. Code, 1981 ed. (Michie).

D.C. Code Advance Annotation Service (Michie).

D.C. Legislative Review.

D.C. Statutes at Large (D.C. Govt., 1975–).

D.C. Statutes at Large (Michie).

District of Columbia Register.

D.C. Rules and Regulations (D.C. Govt.).

D.C. Municipal Regulations (D.C. Govt.).

D.C. Code and D.C. Rules and Regulation Updater (D.C. Govt.).

CASES & OPINIONS:

Atlantic 2d.

Daily Washington Law Reporter.

Federal Reporter, Federal Reporter 2d.

U.S. Court of Appeals Reports, District of Columbia.

COURT RULES:

Rules for the D.C. Court of Appeals, U.S. District Court, U.S. Court of Appeals, and D.C. Superior Court (Rules Service Company).

D.C. Court Rules (Michie, 1985).

DCAA Internal Operating Procedures (D.C. Court of Appeals).

Civil and Criminal Rules of the District of Columbia (D.C. Institute for Continuing Education).

JURY INSTRUCTIONS:

Civil Jury Instructions by R. Jackson (Bar Assn. of the District of Columbia, 1985).

Criminal Jury Instructions for the District of Columbia, 4th ed. (Bar Assn. of the District of Columbia, 1981).

Standardized Civil Jury Instructions in the District of Columbia, rev. ed. (Bar Assn. of the District of Columbia, 1981).

**OPINIONS OF THE
ATTORNEY GENERAL:**

Opinions of the Corporation Counsel (D.C. Govt.).

**ETHICS AND
PROFESSIONAL
RESPONSIBILITY:**

Code of Professional Responsibility and Opinions for the D.C. Bar Legal Ethics Committee (D.C. Bar Assn., 1983).

Disciplinary Digest (Office of the Board of Prof. Resp., 1986).

JOURNALS & LEGAL NEWSPAPERS:

District Lawyer (D.C. Bar).
Legal Times of Washington.

DIRECTORIES:

Judicial Profiler: Federal Courts for the District of Columbia (Shepard's, 1981).
Lawyer Directory (D.C. Bar Assn.).

TREATISES, LOOSELEAFS & OTHER MONOGRAPHS:

Appellate Practice Manual for the District of Columbia Court of Appeals, C. Reischel, ed. (Bar Assn. of D.C., 1985).
D.C. Case Finder: Torts, 2d ed. by J. Stein (Callaghan, 1977).
D.C. Circuit Handbook (Law & Business, Inc., 1980–).
The D.C. Non-Profit Corporation Manual by J. Williams & M. Diamond (East Law Pub., 1975).
District of Columbia Administrative Procedure Manual (D.C. Law Revision Commn., 1982).
The District of Columbia Practice Manual (D.C. Bar Assn., 1987–).
District of Columbia Real Estate Reporter (Real Estate Reporter, Inc.).
Government of the District of Columbia Organization Handbook (Office of the Mayor).
Inheritance Estate and Gift Tax Reports (DC) (CCH).
Juvenile Law and Practice in the District of Columbia by W. Mlyniec & J. Copacino (D.C. Bar Assn., 1988).
Medical Malpractice and Health Care Law in the District of Columbia by J. Montedonico (Butterworths, 1988).
Probate Practice in the District of Columbia, 2d ed. by V. Mersch (Wash. Law Book Co.; West, 1952).
State and Local Taxes (DC) (Prentice-Hall).
State Tax Reports (DC) (CCH).
Trial Manual (Bar Assn. of the District of Columbia, 1982).
Will and Testamentary Trust Forms, 2d ed. (Bar Assn. of the District of Columbia, 1982).
Workers' Compensation Manual by E. May (D.C. Bar Assn.).

DIGESTS & CITATOR:

D.C. Citation Service (Rules Service Co., 1970–).
D.C. Digest (West, 1962–).
The District of Columbia Estates, Trusts and Probate Law Digest, N. Fax, ed. (D.C. Bar Assn., 1981–).
Shepard's District of Columbia Citations.

DOMINICA

SEE ALSO: Caribbean, International Law, Latin America, United Nations

West Indian Constitutions: Post Independence Reform by F. Phillips (Oceana, 1985).
Commonwealth of Dominica Consolidated Index of Statutes (Fac. of Law Library, Univ. of West Indies, Barbados, 1986).
Fisheries Development in Dominica by C. Mitchell (Canada: Dalhousie Ocean Studies Programme, 1983).

DOMINICAN REPUBLIC

SEE ALSO: Caribbean, International Law, Latin America, United Nations

RESEARCH GUIDE & BIBLIOGRAPHY: *A Guide to the Official Publications of . . . Dominican Republic* (Library of Congress, 1947).

TREATISES & LOOSELEAFS: *Business Operations in the Dominican Republic* by L. Bonetti, Tax Management Foreign Income Portfolios, No. 307–2nd (BNA, 1979).
Capital Formation and Investment Incentives Around the World (Dominican Republic) by W. Diamond & D. Diamond (Matthew Bender, 1984–).
Caribbean Basin: A Tax Tour (Dominican Republic) (Arthur Anderson & Co., 1985).
Dominican Republic: Divorce Law by A. Gonzalez (Library of Congress, 1986).
The Dominican Republic: A Caribbean Crucible by H. Wiarda (Westview, 1981).
The Dominican Republic: Politics and Development in an Unsovereign State by J. Black (Allen & Unwin, 1986).
Information Guide, Doing Business in Dominican Republic (Price Waterhouse).
Series of Statements of the Law of the OAS Member States in Matters Affecting Business: Dominican Republic (Organization of American States, 1964).
Tax Laws of the World—Dominican Republic (FL: Foreign Tax Law Assn.).

ARTICLES: "Dominican Republic's Investment Opportunities" by L. Beltr, 13 *Case Western Reserve Journal of International Law* 165 (1981).
"Latin American Tax Update: Dominican Republic" by M. Marti, 12 *Lawyer of the Americas* 650 (1980).

DONATION OF ORGANS: See Health & Medicine
DOUBLE JEOPARDY: See Constitutional Law, Criminal Law
DOUBLE TAXATION: See Constitutional Law, Taxation
DOWER: See Estate Planning, Family Law
DRAFTING: See Estate Planning, Legal Research, Statutes
DRAINS: See Real Estate, State & Local Government
DRAM SHOP: See Torts
DRG PAYMENTS: See Health & Medicine
DRILLING: See Environmental Law, Oil & Gas
DRINKING WATER: See Water Law
DRIVING: See Alcohol, Criminal Law, Transportation

DRUGGIST: See Food, Health & Medicine, Torts
DRUGS: Cayman Islands, Criminal Law, Environmental Law, Food, Forensic Science,
    Torts
DRUNK DRIVING: See Alcohol, Criminal Law
DRY TRUSTS: See Estate Planning
DUBAI: See United Arab Emirates
DUE CARE: See Torts
DUE PROCESS: See Administrative Law, Constitutional Law, Corrections, Criminal Law,
    Employee Benefits, Immigration Law, Military Law, Trial & Appellate Practice
DUMPING: See Customs, Environmental Law, International Law, Maritime Law, Poland,
    Taxation
DURESS: See Consumer Law, Contracts, Torts
DUTCH LAW: See Netherlands
DUTIES: See International Law, Taxation
DWELLING: See Real Estate
DYING: See Death, Health & Medicine
DYING DECLARATION: See Trial & Appellate Practice

EARTH: See Environmental Law, International Law, Natural Resources
EASEMENT: See Real Estate
EASTERN EUROPE: See Communism
EAVESDROPPING: See Criminal Law
ECCLESIASTICAL LAW: See Canon Law
ECOLOGY: See Energy, Environmental Law, Natural Resources, Water Law
ECONOMIC DEVELOPMENT: See Africa, Caribbean, International Law, Latin America,
    United Nations

ECONOMICS & THE LAW

SEE ALSO: Accounting, Antitrust Law, Banking Law, Business Law, Contracts, Corporate Law,
    Forensic Science, International Law, Jurisprudence, Law Office Management, Real
    Estate, Securities Law, Taxation, Zoning & Land Planning

**JOURNALS, NEWSLETTERS
& OTHER PERIODICALS:**   *Journal of Economic Literature* (1967–).
    Journal of International Law and Economics (1966–).
    Journal of Law and Economics (Univ. of Chicago, 1958–).
    Journal of Law, Economics, and Organization (Yale Univ. Press, 1985–).
    Research in Law and Economics (JAI Press, 1979–).
    The Supreme Court Economic Review (Collier Macmillan; Stockley Close, 1982–).

**TREATISES &
LOOSELEAFS:**   *Economic Analysis of Law* by R. Posner (Little, Brown, 1972).
    An Introduction to Law and Economics by M. Polinsky (Little, Brown, 1983).
    Law and Economics by J. Oliver (Allen & Unwin, 1979).
    Law and Economics: An Institutional Perspective, W. Samuels, ed. (Boston: Martinus
        Nijhoff, 1981).
    Law, Economics and Public Policy by N. Mercuto (JAI Press, 1984).
    Microeconomic Concepts for Attorneys by W. Curtis (Greenwood Press; Quorum
        Books, 1984).
    Sources and Uses of Social and Economic Data: A Manual for Lawyers (Bureau of
        Social Science Research, 1973).
    Statistical Concepts for Attorneys: A Reference Guide by W. Curtis (Greenwood Press;
        Quorum Books, 1983).

ENCYCLOPEDIA: AMERICAN JURISPRUDENCE 2D (Am Jur 2d)
Check the following topics in the *General Index* volumes for Am Jur 2d:

Damages	Economic Matters or
	Conditions

ALR: ANNOTATIONS
Check the index volumes for ALR, ALR2d, ALR3d, ALR4th, and ALR Fed for annotations under the following subject headings:

Damages	Economic Uncertainties
Economic Circumstances	Forensic Economics
Economic Loss	

PERIODICALS: CURRENT LAW INDEX (CLI) & LEGAL RESOURCE INDEX (LRI)
In the CLI and LRI, look for references to periodical literature under the following subject headings:

Antitrust, Economic	Economics
Aspects	Future Earnings Potential
Consumption (Economics)	Inflation
Cost Effectiveness	Mathematical Statistics
Economic Assistance	Regression Analysis
Economic Policy	Statistics

INDEX TO LEGAL PERIODICALS (ILP)
In the ILP, look for references to legal periodical literature under the following subject headings:

Antitrust Law	International Economic
Cost-Benefit Analysis	Relations
Economics	Money
Employee Ownership	Statistics

ECONOMIC TORT: See Tort

ECUADOR

SEE ALSO: International Law, Latin America, United Nations

RESEARCH GUIDES & BIBLIOGRAPHIES: *A Guide to the Law and Literature of Ecuador* (Library of Congress, 1947).
A Guide to the Official Publications of . . . Ecuador (Library of Congress, 1947).

CONSTITUTION: "Ecuador 1975–1981," *Constitutions of the Countries of the World* by A. Blaustein & G. Flanz (Oceana, 1981).

INTERNATIONAL AGREEMENTS: "Ecuador-United States: Investment Guaranty Agreement," 24 *International Legal Materials* 566 (1985).

TREATISES & LOOSELEAFS: *The Andean Legal Order* (Ecuador) by F. Garcia-Amador (Oceana, 1978).
Capital Formation and Investment Incentives Around the World (Ecuador) by W. Diamond & D. Diamond (Matthew Bender, 1984–).

Digest of Commercial Laws of the World (Ecuador) (Natl. Assn. of Credit Management; Oceana, 1977–).

Information Guide, Doing Business in Ecuador (Price Waterhouse).

Latin America . . . A Tax Tour (Ecuador) (Arthur Anderson & Co., 1985).

Series of Statements of the Law of the OAS Member States in Matters Affecting Business: Ecuador (Organization of American States, 1975).

Taxation in Ecuador (NY: Deloitte, Haskins & Sells, 1979).

Tax Laws of the World—Ecuador (FL: Foreign Tax Law Assn.).

ARTICLES:

"Latin American Tax Update: Ecuador" by M. Marti, 12 *Lawyer of the Americas* 651 (1980).

EDUCATION LAW

SEE ALSO:

Administrative Law, Church & State, Civil Rights, Constitutional Law, Handicapped & the Law, Labor Law, Nonprofit Corporations, Sports Law, State & Local Government, Torts

RESEARCH GUIDE & BIBLIOGRAPHY:

Legal Research for Educators by D. Lowe & A. Watters (Bloomington, IN: Phi Delta Kappa, 1984).

"Selected Survey of Educational Law and Policy Literature" by P. Piele, 12 *Journal of Law & Education* 175 (1983).

JOURNALS, NEWSLETTERS & OTHER PERIODICALS:

Journal of College and University Law (Natl. Assn. of College & Univ. Attorneys, 1973–).

Journal of Law and Education (Jefferson Law Book, 1972–).

School Law Bulletin (Univ. of North Carolina).

REPORTERS & DIGESTS:

The College Law Digest (Natl. Assn. of College & Univ. Attorneys, 1970–).

School Law Reporter (Arlington, VA: Capitol Pubs., Inc., 1977–).

School Law Update (Topeka, KS: Natl. Org. on Legal Problems of Education).

Specialty Law Digest: Education (BNA; Specialty Digest Pubs., 1981–).

West's Education Law Digest (1982–).

West's Education Law Reporter (1982–).

DIRECTORY:

Directory of Faculty Contracts and Bargaining Agents in Institutions of Higher Education (Natl. Center for the Study of Collective Bargaining in Higher Education and the Professions, Baruch College, City Univ. of NY, 1983).

TREATISES & LOOSELEAFS:

Ability Grouping of Public School Students: Legal Aspects of Tracking Methods by J. Bryson (Michie, 1980).

Academics in Court: The Consequences of Faculty Discrimination Litigation by G. LaNoue (Univ. of Mich. Press, 1987).

American Public School Law, 2d ed. by K. Alexander (West, 1985).

Clergy and Teacher Malpractice by R. McMenamin (Portland, OR: Jomac Pub., 1987).

College and University Law by K. Alexander (Michie, 1972).

Educational Malpractice by L. Freiheit (Univ. Microfilms Intl., 1985).

Education Law by J. Rapp (Matthew Bender, 1984–).

Education Law: Public and Private by W. Valente (West, 1985).

Educators, Children, and the Law, L. Sametz, ed. (C. C. Thomas, 1985).

The Fiscal, Legal, and Political Aspects of State Reform of Elementary and Secondary Education, V. Mueller, ed. (Ballinger, 1985).

Freedom of the High School Press by N. Kristof (Univ. Press of America, 1983).

Grievance Arbitration Procedure by R. Munro (Tarrytown, NY: Associated Faculty Press, 1982).

Law and the Shaping of Public Education, 1785–1954 by D. Tyack (Univ. of Wisc. Press, 1987).

The Law of Higher Education, 2d ed. by W. Kaplin (San Francisco: Jossey-Bass, 1985).

The Law of Schools, Students and Teachers in a Nutshell by K. Alexander (West, 1984).

Legal Deskbook for Administrators of Independent Colleges and Universities, K. Weeks, ed. (Notre Dame Law Sch., 1982–).

Legal Liability of School Board Members by E. Leverett (Alexandria, VA: Natl. School Boards Assn., Council of State Attorneys, 1985).

New Encyclopedic Dictionary of School Law by R. Gatti (NJ: Parker Pub. Co., 1983).

Resolving Faculty Disputes by J. McCarthy & I. Ladimer (Amer. Arbitration Assn., 1981).

The Rights of Teachers (ACLU; Bantam Books, 1983).

The School Attorney: A Practical Guide to Employing School District Legal Counsel, E. Bittle, ed. (Alexandria, VA: Natl. School Boards Assn., Council of School Attorneys, 1986).

School Grievance Arbitration by D. Brodie & P. Williams (Butterworths, 1982).

School Law for Counselors, Psychologists, and Social Workers by L. Fischer (Longman, 1985).

School Law for the Practitioner by R. O'Reilly (Greenwood Press, 1983).

The Scope of Faculty Collective Bargaining by R. Johnston (Greenwood Press, 1981).

Student Affairs and the Law, M. Barr, ed. (San Francisco: Jossey-Bass, 1983).

Teacher Liability in School-Shop Accidents by D. Kigin (Ann Arbor: Prakken, 1983).

Teachers Have Rights Too by L. Stelzer (Boulder: Social Science Education Consortium; Eugene: ERIC, 1980).

Teacher Strikes and the Courts by D. Colton & E. Graber (Lexington Books, 1982).

Unions and Public Schools by R. Eberts & J. Stone (Lexington Books, 1984).

University-Industry Research Partnerships by B. Reams (Greenwood Press, 1986).

ENCYCLOPEDIAS:

AMERICAN JURISPRUDENCE 2D (Am Jur 2d)

Check the following topics in the *General Index* volumes for Am Jur 2d:

Administrative Law	Colleges and Universities
Children	Equal Protection of Law
Civil Rights	

CORPUS JURIS SECUNDUM (CJS)

Check the following topics in the *General Index* volumes for CJS:

Administrative Bodies and Procedures	Independent School Districts
Civil Rights	Private Schools
Colleges and Universities	Scholarships
Education	Schools and School Districts
Education, Boards of	Teachers

DIGESTS:
CASE SEARCH IN WEST DIGESTS BY KEY TOPIC
In the *Descriptive Word Index* of the West digests, look for key topics and numbers under the following subject headings:

Administrative Bodies and Procedures	Labor Relations
	Municipal Corporations
Civil Rights	Private Schools
Colleges and Universities	Scholarships
Education	Schools
Education, Boards of	Teachers
Independent School Districts	

ALR:
ANNOTATIONS
Check the index volumes for ALR, ALR2d, ALR3d, ALR4th, and ALR Fed for annotations under the following subject headings:

Academic Freedom	Private School
Administrative Law	Schools
Colleges and Universities	School Teachers
Discrimination	Tuition

PERIODICALS:
CURRENT LAW INDEX (CLI) & LEGAL RESOURCE INDEX (LRI)
In the CLI and LRI, look for references to periodical literature under the following subject headings:

Administrative Law	High School
Christian Education	Junior Colleges
Church and Education	Religion in Private Schools
Church Schools	Right to Education
College	Schools
Community Colleges	Segregation and Education
Competency Based Education	Sex Discrimination in Education
Constitutional Law	State Aid
Curriculum	Student
Education	Teacher
Federal Aid to Private Schools	Universities and Colleges

INDEX TO LEGAL PERIODICALS (ILP)
In the ILP, look for references to legal periodical literature under the following subject headings:

Administrative Agencies	Education/Finance
Administrative Procedure	Loyalty and Loyalty Oaths
Civil Rights	School Integration
Colleges and Universities	Schools and School Districts
Education	Teachers and Teaching

EEC: See European Economic Community
EEOC: See Employment Discrimination, Handicapped & the Law

EGYPT

SEE ALSO:
International Law, Islam, Middle East, United Nations

CONSTITUTION: *Constitutions of Eastern Countries* by M. Ahmad (Karachi Pakistan, 1951).

**TREATISES &
LOOSELEAFS:**   *Business Law in Egypt* by M. Davies (Boston: Kluwer; Gaunt, 1984).

Business Laws of Egypt, M. Davies, ed.; N. Karam, transl. (London: Graham & Trotman, 1985–).

Capital Formation and Investment Incentives Around the World (Egypt) by W. Diamond & D. Diamond (Matthew Bender, 1984–).

Commercial Laws of the Middle East by A. Keesee (Oceana, 1980–).

Current Aspects of Doing Business in the Middle East—Saudi Arabia, Egypt and Iran, W. Wickersham & B. Fishburne, eds. (American Bar Assn., 1977).

Digest of Commercial Laws of the World (Egypt) (Natl. Assn. of Credit Management; Oceana, 1977–).

Information Guide, Doing Business in Egypt (Price Waterhouse).

Investment Laws of the World (Egypt) (Oceana, 1981–).

Law in Radically Different Cultures (Egypt) by J. Barton (West, 1980).

The Laws of Saudi Arabia, the UAE, Egypt, and Jordan: A Legal and Investment Guide for American Business (Wash. D.C.: American Arab Affairs Council, 1985).

The Mixed Courts of Egypt by J. Brinton (Yale Univ. Press, 1968).

Property Law in the Arab World: Real Rights in Egypt, Iraq, Jordan, Lebanon, Libya, Saudi Arabia and the Gulf States by F. Ziadeh (London: Graham & Trotman, 1979).

Taxes and Investment in the Middle East (Intl. Bureau of Fiscal Documentation).

Tax Laws of the World—Egypt (FL: Foreign Tax Law Assn.).

ARTICLES: "Back to Contract: Implications of Peace and Openness for Egypt's Legal System" by J. Salacuse, 28 *American Journal of Comparative Law* 315 (1980).

"Comparative Commercial Law of Egypt and the Arabian Gulf" by I. Edge, 34 *Cleveland State Law Review* 129 (1985).

"Foreign Investment Incentives in the Developing World: The Legislation of Greece, Egypt, Pakistan, Thailand, and the Republic of China" by P. Dempsey, 11 *Case Western Reserve Journal of International Law* 575 (1979).

"International Adjudication: Interpretation of WHO–Egypt Agreement," 22 *Harvard International Law Journal* 429 (1981).

"Law of Property in Egypt" by F. Ziadeh, 26 *American Journal of Comparative Law* 239 (1978).

"The Legal Framework of Foreign Investment in Egypt" by G. Nazer, 11 *Case Western Reserve Journal of International Law* 613 (1979).

"Middle East Agency Law Survey" by F. Taylor, 14 *International Lawyer* 335 (Egypt) (1980).

"Registration of the Egypt-Israel Peace Treaty" by M. Tabory, 32 *International & Comparative Law Quarterly* 981 (1983).

"The Rights of the Child in Egypt" by A. Azer, 13 *Columbia Human Rights Law Review* 315 (1981).

"The United States-Egypt Bilateral Investment Treaty" by Pattison, 16 *Cornell International Law Journal* 305 (1983).

EIGHTH CIRCUIT: See Circuit Courts
EJECTMENT: See Real Estate
EJUSDEM GENERIS: See Statutes
ELDERLY: See Age

ELECTION & LOBBYING LAW

SEE ALSO:
Administrative Law, Advertising, Civil Rights, Constitutional Law, Corporate Law, Criminal Law, Education, International Law, Media Law, Nonprofit Corporations, State & Local Government; see also entries under individual states and countries

RESEARCH GUIDES &
BIBLIOGRAPHIES:
Campaign Finance and Federal Elections: A Selected Bibliography with Annotations (Federal Election Commn.).
"The Federal Election Campaign Act and its Amendments: A Selected Legal Bibliography with Annotations" by F. Houdek & V. Ford, 72 *Law Library Journal* 194 (1979).

STATUTES:
Federal Election Campaign Laws (Federal Election Commn., 1986).

ADMINISTRATIVE
REGULATIONS &
RELATED GOVERNMENT
PUBLICATIONS:
11 *CFR.*
Advisory Opinion and Opinion of Counsel Index (Federal Election Commn., 1975–).
Campaign Guide for Corporations and Labor Organizations (Federal Election Commn., 1985).
Election Case Law (Federal Election Commn.).

JOURNALS, NEWSLETTERS
& OTHER PERIODICALS:
Campaign Practices Reports (Congressional Quarterly, 1980–).
Record (Federal Election Commn., 1975–).

TREATISES &
LOOSELEAFS:
Campaign Law Reporter (Sacramento: Pacific Communications Group).
Corporate Political Action Committee Guidelines (U.S. Chamber of Commerce, 1979).
The Corporation in Politics: PACs, Lobbying Laws, and Public Officials (Practicing Law Institute, 1982).
Executive's Handbook on Political Contributions by E. Bartz (Wash. D.C.: S&FA Reporting Services, 1976–).
Federal Election Campaign Financing Guide (CCH, 1976–).
Federal Regulation of Campaign Finance and Political Activity by T. Schwarz & A. Straus (Matthew Bender, 1981–).
The Law of Suffrage and Elections by N. Maar (Rothman, 1985).
Materials on Corporate Political Activity by W. Handcock (OH: Business Laws, 1980–).
State Lobbying Laws by E. Bartz (Wash. D.C.: S&FA Reporting Services, 1976–).
United States Federal Election Law by R. Bauer & D. Kafka (Oceana, 1982–).

ENCYCLOPEDIAS:
AMERICAN JURISPRUDENCE 2D (Am Jur 2d)
Check the following topics in the *General Index* volumes for Am Jur 2d:

Administrative Law	Lobbying
Ballots	Politics
Civil Death	Poll Taxes
Civil Rights	Public Officers and
Constitutional Law	Employees
Discrimination	Recall Election
Elections	Re-Election
Hatch Act	Voters and Voting
Initiative and Referendum	

CORPUS JURIS SECUNDUM (CJS)
Check the following topics in the *General Index* volumes for CJS:

Administrative Bodies	Elections
Ballots	Initiative and Referendum
Civil Death	Political Parties
Civil Rights	Poll Taxes
Constitutional Law	States
Counties	United States
Discrimination	

DIGESTS:

CASE SEARCH IN WEST DIGESTS BY KEY TOPIC
In the *Descriptive Word Index* of the West digests, look for key topics and numbers under the following subject headings:

Administrative Agencies	Elections
Ballots	Initiative and Referendum
Civil Death	Political Parties
Civil Rights	Poll Taxes
Constitutional Law	Schools
Counties	States
Discrimination	United States

ALR:

ANNOTATIONS
Check the index volumes for ALR, ALR2d, ALR3d, ALR4th, and ALR Fed for annotations under the following subject headings:

Absentee Voting	Election Campaign Act
Administrative Law	Elections
Ballots	Fraud
Campaign Expenses	Hatch Act
Discrimination	Voting

PERIODICALS:

CURRENT LAW INDEX (CLI) & LEGAL RESOURCE INDEX (LRI)
In the CLI and LRI, look for references to periodical literature under the following subject headings:

Advertising, Political	Political Action
Constitutional Law	Committees
Corruption	Political Crimes
Election Districts	Political Parties
Electioneering	Primaries
Election Law	Public Opinion Polls
Elections	Referendum
Initiative, Right of	Suffrage
Law and Politics	United States
Lobbying	Election Commission
Nominations	Voting

INDEX TO LEGAL PERIODICALS (ILP)
In the ILP, look for references to legal periodical literature under the following subject headings:

Administrative Law	Elections
Campaign Funds	Fraud
Civil Rights	Initiative and Referendum
Constitutional Law	Lobbying
Democracy	Recall
Discrimination	

ELECTION OF REMEDIES: See Equity, Estate Planning, Trial & Appellate Practice
ELECTRICITY: See Energy, Environmental Law, Natural Resources, Oil & Gas, Public Utilities, Water Law
ELECTRONIC DATA: See Computers
ELECTRONIC FUND TRANSFERS: See Banking Law, Uniform Commercial Code
ELECTRONIC PUBLISHING: See Media Law
ELEMENTARY EDUCATION: See Education Law
ELEVENTH CIRCUIT: See Circuit Courts

EL SALVADOR

SEE ALSO: Human Rights, International Law, Latin America, United Nations

RESEARCH GUIDE & BIBLIOGRAPHY: *A Guide to the Official Publications of . . . El Salvador* (Library of Congress, 1947).

TREATISES & LOOSELEAFS:
Digest of Commercial Laws of the World (El Salvador) (Natl. Assn. of Credit Management; Oceana, 1977–).
Free Fire: A Report on Human Rights in El Salvador (NY: Americas Watch Committee and the Lawyers Committee for Intl. Human Rights, 1984). (See also *The Continuing Terror*, 1985 and *Settling into Routine*, 1986).
Information Guide: Doing Business in El Salvador (Price Waterhouse).
Latin America . . . A Tax Tour (El Salvador) (Arthur Anderson & Co., 1985).
Series of Statements of the Law of the OAS Member States in Matters Affecting Business: El Salvador (Organization of American States, 1970).
Tax Laws of the World—El Salvador (FL: Foreign Tax Law Assn.).

ARTICLES:
"Dilemmas of Political Transition in El Salvador" by E. Baloyra, 38 *Journal of International Affairs* 221 (1985).
"Responding to the Crisis in El Salvador" by A. Caldeira, 8 *Yale Journal of World Public Order* 325 (1982)

EMANCIPATION: See Family Law, Juvenile Law, Women & the Law
EMBARGO: See Customs, International Law, Maritime Law, War
EMBEZZLEMENT: See Criminal Law
EMBRYOLOGY: See Health & Medicine
EMERGENCY LEGISLATION: See Statutes
EMERGENCY POWERS: See Constitutional Law
EMIGRATION: See Immigration Law
EMINENT DOMAIN: See Public Utilities, Real Estate, Zoning & Land Planning
EMOTIONAL DISTRESS: See Mental Health, Torts

EMPLOYEE BENEFITS

SEE ALSO: Accounting, Business Law, Civil Service, Corporate Law, Employment Discrimination, Labor Law, Social Security, Taxation, Unemployment Compensation, Worker's Compensation

JOURNALS, NEWSLETTERS
& OTHER
PERIODICALS: *Journal of Compensation and Benefits* (Warren, Gorham & Lamont).
Journal of Pension Planning and Compliance (1974–).
Pension and Profit-Sharing Tax Journal (Panel).
Tax Management Compensation Planning Journal (BNA).

LOOSELEAFS: *Benefits Today* (BNA, 1986–).
Compliance Guide for Plan Administrators (CCH, 1976–).
EBPR Research Reports (Chicago: Spencer & Associates, 1953–).
Employee Benefits Cases (BNA, 1981–).
Employee Benefits Compliance Coordinator (Research Institute of America, 1979–).
Employee Benefits Law by J. Mamorsky (Law Journal Seminars-Press, 1980–).
ERISA Qualified Plan Guide (Pension Pubs. of Denver, 1975–).
The ERISA Source Manual, L. Brown, ed. (Law Journal Seminars-Press, 1981–).
ERISA Update (Wash. Service Bureau, 1974–).
Executive Compensation and Taxation Coordinator (Research Institute of America, 1979–).
Federal Pension Law Service (Matthew Bender).
Forms and Workbook under ERISA by I. Schreiber & C. Scudere (Panel, 1973–).
Fringe Benefits Tax Guide (CCH, 1985–).
Individual Retirement Plans Guide—IRA, SEP, Keogh (CCH, 1982–).
International Benefits Information Service (Chicago: Spenser & Associates).
IRA Compliance Manual (Prentice-Hall, 1982–).
Modern Law of Employment Contracts: Formation, Operation and Remedies for Breach by C. Bakaly & J. Grossman (Law & Business, Inc., 1983–).
Pay Planning Program (Prentice-Hall, 1954–).
Payroll Guide (Prentice-Hall, 1943–).
Payroll Management Guide (Prentice-Hall, 1943–).
Pension & Annuity Withholding Service (Research Inst. of America, 1983–).
Pension and Profit-Sharing (Prentice-Hall, 1949–).
Pension and Profit-Sharing Forms (Prentice-Hall, 1960–).
Pension and Profit-Sharing Plans by S. Young (Matthew Bender, 1977–).
Pension and Profit-Sharing Plans for Small and Medium Size Businesses by C. Scudere & K. Moran (Panel, 1984).
Pension Plan Guide (CCH, 1953–).
Pension Reporter (BNA, 1974–).
Personnel Director's Legal Guide (Warren, Gorham & Lamont).
Personnel Management: Compensation (Prentice-Hall, 1977–).
Qualified Retirement Plans by R. Benner & L. Wellman (Natl. Law Pub., 1982–).
Spencer's Retirement Plan Service (Chicago: Spencer & Associates).
Wage-Hour Guide (Prentice-Hall, 1941–).
West's Legal Forms—Employment Agreements by Walzer (West).
Plan Administrator's Compliance Manual Prentice-Hall, 1977–).

TREATISES: *Basis Law of Pensions and Deferred Compensation* (ABA–ALI Comm. on Cont. Prof. Ed., 1985).
Collective Bargaining Implications of the FASB Proposals on Pension Accounting by K. Farney (WI: Intl. Foundation of Employee Benefit Plans).
The Collective Bargaining Process for Fringe Benefits in the Private Sector by K. Farney (WI: Intl. Foundation of Employee Benefit Plans).
Effective Collection of Employer Contributions—1985 (WI: Intl. Foundation of Employee Benefit Plans).

Employee Benefit Plans: A Glossary of Terms (WI: Intl. Foundation of Employee Benefit Plans).

Employee Benefit Plans in Corporate Acquisitions and Dispositions (ABA).

Employee Benefits Handbook by F. Foulkes (Warren, Gorham & Lamont, 1982).

Employee Benefits: Mergers and Acquisitions by F. Miller (Practicing Law Institute, 1984).

Employee Noncompetition Law by D. Aspelund & C. Eriksen (Clark Boardman, 1987).

ERISA: The Law and the Code, K. Gill, ed. (BNA, 1985).

Executive Compensation: A Survey of Laws and Regulations of Current Issues (ABA).

Executive Compensation: Planning Techniques and Strategies (Practicing Law Institute, 1986).

Fringe Benefits by J. Block (Prentice-Hall, 1988).

Guide to Pension and Profit Sharing Plans by D. Dunkle (Shepard's, 1984).

Guide to Professional Benefit Plan Management and Administration by L. Jost & C. Sutherland (WI: Intl. Foundation of Employee Benefit Plans).

Health and Life Insurance Benefit Plans (BNA, 1984).

Investment Policy Guidebook for Trustees, rev. ed. (WI: Intl. Foundation of Employee Benefit Plans).

The Law of Pensions and Profit-Sharing by R. Osgood (Little, Brown, 1984).

Pension and Profit-Sharing Plans Library. Series A: Kinds of Qualified Plans. Series B: Basic Concepts of Qualified Plans. Series C: Requirements for Qualifications of Plans, etc. (ABA–ALI Comm. on Cont. Prof. Ed.).

The Pension Answer Book, 3d ed. by S. Krass & R. Keschner (Panel, 1984).

"Plan Terminations and Mergers" by L. Laarman & D. Hildebrandt, *Tax Management Portfolios,* no. 357 (1983).

Primer on ERISA by B. Coleman (BNA, 1985).

Qualified Deferred Compensation Plans (Callaghan).

Qualified Retirement Plans by M. Canan (West, 1977).

Trustees Handbook, 3d ed. by C. Kordus (WI: Intl. Foundation of Employee Benefit Plans).

ENCYCLOPEDIAS:

AMERICAN JURISPRUDENCE 2D (Am Jur 2d)
Check the following topics in the *General Index* volumes for Am Jur 2d:

Attachment and Garnishment	Labor and Labor Relations
Civil Rights	Master and Servant
Civil Service	Pension and Retirement Funds
Compensation	Unemployment Insurance
Contracts	Work, Labor, and Services
Employment Agencies	Workmens' Compensation

CORPUS JURIS SECUNDUM (CJS)
Check the following topics in the *General Index* volumes for CJS:

Apprentices	Hours of Labor
Child Labor	Labor and Employment
Civil Rights	Occupation Taxes
Civil Service	Overtime
Compensation and Salaries	Retirement and Pensions
Constitutional Law	Severance Pay
Contracts	State Officers and Employees
Employment Agencies	
Fair Labor Standards Act	Work and Labor
Garnishment	Workmens Compensation

DIGESTS: CASE SEARCH IN WEST DIGESTS BY KEY TOPIC
In the *Descriptive Word Index* of the West digests, look for key topics and numbers under the following subject headings:

Apprentices	Labor Relations
Child Labor	Occupation Taxes
Civil Rights	Overtime
Civil Service	Partnership
Compensation and Salaries	Retirement and Pensions
Constitutional Law	Severance Pay
Contracts	Social Security
Employment Agencies	State Officers and
Fair Labor Standards Act	Employees
Fraud	Work and Labor
Garnishment	Workmens' Compensation
Hours of Labor	

ALR: ANNOTATIONS
Check the index volumes for ALR, ALR2d, ALR3d, ALR4th, and ALR Fed for annotations under the following subject headings:

Attachment and	Labor and Labor Unions
Garnishment	Pension and Retirementt
Back Pay	Funds
Bonus	Promotions
Civil Service	Scope of Employument
Compensation	Supervision
Due Process	Supervisors
Employment Agencies	Unemployment
Executive Officer	Compensation
Fair Labor Standards Act	Workmens' Compensation

PERIODICALS: CURRENT LAW INDEX (CLI) & LEGAL RESOURCE INDEX (LRI)
In the CLI and LRI, look for references to periodical literature under the following subject headings:

Employee Fringe Benefits	Personnel Management
Employee Ownership	Retirement Income
Employee Rights	Self-Employed
Equal Pay for Equal Work	Seniority
Hire	Sick Leave
Individual Retirement	Unemployed
Accounts	United States Pension
Old Age Pensions	Benefit Guaranty
Payroll Deductions	Corporation
Pensions	Wages

INDEX TO LEGAL PERIODICALS (ILP)
In the ILP, look for references to legal periodical literature under the following subject headings:

Administrative Law	Fraud
Annuities	Income Tax/Employee
Civil Rights	Benefits
Civil Service	Profit Sharing
Collective Bargaining	Unemployment
Contracts	Wages
Employer and Employee	Workers' Compensation

EMPLOYEE COMPENSATION APPEALS BOARD: See Civil Service
EMPLOYEE OWNERSHIP: See Economics, Employee Benefits, Labor Law
EMPLOYER LIABILITY: See Torts, Workers' Compensation
EMPLOYMENT: See Employee Benefits, Employment Discrimination, Paralegal,
    Partnership Law
EMPLOYMENT AGENCIES: See Agency, Employee Benefits
EMPLOYMENT AGREEMENTS: See Intellectual Property, Labor Law

EMPLOYMENT DISCRIMINATION & WRONGFUL DISCHARGE

SEE ALSO: Age, Civil Service, Civil Rights, Constitutional Law, Employee Benefits, Government Contracts, Handicapped & the Law, Labor Law, Women & the Law

**RESEARCH GUIDE &
BIBLIOGRAPHY:**   "Selected Materials on Employment-at-Will; Discharge-at Will," 40 *Record of the Bar Association of the City of New York* 276 (1985).

STATUTES: Civil Rights Act of 1964, 78 Stat. 241 (1964).
Comprehensive Employment and Training Act, 87 Stat. 839 (1973).
Employment Retirement Income Security Act of 1974 (ERISA), 88 Stat. 829 (1974).
Equal Employment Opportunity Act, 86 Stat. 103 (1972).
Equal Pay Act of 1963, 77 Stat. 56 (1963).

LEGISLATIVE HISTORY: "The Equal Employment Acts of 1964 and 1973: A Critical Analysis of the Legislative History and Administration of the Law," 2 *Industrial Relations Law Journal* 1 (1977).
The Equal Employment Opportunity Act of 1972 (BNA, 1973).
The Equal Employment Opportunity Act of 1972: Legislative History by P. Downing (Library of Congress, 1972).
Equal Employment Opportunity: Legislative History and Analysis of Title VII of the Civil Rights Act of 1964 by R. Celada (Library of Cong., Cong. Research Service, 1965).
Legislative History of the Equal Employment Opportunity Act of 1972 (Govt. Printing Office, 1972).

**JOURNALS & OTHER
PERIODICALS:**   "Annual Survey of Labor Relations and Employment Discrimination Law" in *Boston College Law Review.*
BNA Employee Relations Weekly (BNA, 1983–).
EEO Litigation 1982 (Practicing Law Institute, 1982).
Employee Relations Law Journal (NY: Executive Enterprises, 1975–).
Government Employee Relations Report (BNA, 1963–).
Labor and Employment Law Newsletter (Matthew Bender, 1984–).
Law and Employment Law (ABA, Section of Labor and Employment Law, 1968–).

LOOSELEAFS: *Affirmative Action Compliance Manual for Federal Contractors* (BNA, 1975–).
Drug Testing Legal Manual by K. Zeese (Clark Boardman, 1988–).
EEOC Compliance Manual (BNA, 1975–).
EEOC Compliance Manual (CCH, 1975–).
EEOC Compliance Manual (EEOC Office of Compliance).

Employment-at-Will Reporter (Boston: New England Legal Publishers, 1983–).

Employment Coordinator (Research Inst. of America).

Employment Discrimination by A. & L. Larson (Matthew Bender, 1975–).

Employment Practices Guide (CCH, 1972–).

Employment Testing: A National Reporter on Polygraph, Drug, AIDS, and Genetic Testing by S. Hurd (Univ. Pubs. of America, 1986–).

Equal Employment Compliance Manual by A. Ruzicho (Callaghan, 1977–).

Equal Employment Opportunity Compliance Manual (Prentice-Hall, 1979–).

Fair Employment Practice Cases in *Labor Relations Reporter* (BNA, 1969–).

Fair Employment Practice Service (BNA, 1964–).

Federal Contract Compliance Manual (Dept. of Labor, Office of Fed. Contract Compliance Programs, 1979–).

Federal Regulation of Employment Service (Lawyers Co-op., 1976–).

Human Resources Management (CCH, 1981–).

Individual Employment Rights (BNA, 1986–).

OFCCP Federal Contract Compliance Manual (CCH, 1979–).

A Practical Guide to Equal Employment Opportunity by W. & M. Connolly (Law Journal Seminars-Press, 1979–).

Unjust Dismissal by L. Larson & P. Borowsky (Matthew Bender, 1985–).

Use of Statistics in Equal Employment Opportunity Litigation by W. Connolly (Law Journal Seminars-Press, 1979–).

Wrongful Discharge Litigation Reporter (Andrews Pubs.).

TREATISES:

Abusive Discharge (Natl. Employment Law Project).

Annual Institute on Employment Law (Practicing Law Institute).

Avoiding and Defending Wrongful Discharge Claims by S. Pepe & S. Dunham (Callaghan, 1988).

Comparable Worth and Wage Discrimination by H. Remick (Temple Univ. Press, 1984).

The Comparable Worth Issue (BNA, 1981).

Creative Approaches in Wrongful Termination Cases (CA: Rutter Group).

Defending EEO Lawsuits Litigation Manual (CA: Natl. Employment Law Inst., 1985).

Defense of Equal Employment Claims by W. Diedrich & W. Gaus (Shepard's, 1982).

Drugs and Alcohol in the Workplace: Testing and Privacy by C. Cornish (Callaghan, 1988).

Employee Dismissal Law and Practice by H. Perritt (Wiley, 1984).

Employee Dismissal Law: Forms and Procedures by M. Dichter, et al. (Wiley, 1986).

Employee Testing: Polygraphs and Urinalysis (Natl. Employment Law Project).

Employment at Will and Unjust Dismissal (Research Institute of America).

Employment Discrimination, 2d ed. by C. Sullivan et al. (Little, Brown, 1988).

Employment Discrimination Law, 2d ed. by L. Modjeska (Lawyers Co-op., 1988).

Employment Discrimination Law, 2d ed. by B. Schlei & P. Grossman (BNA, 1983).

Employment Termination: Rights and Remedies by W. Holloway & M. Leech (BNA, 1985).

Equal Employment Audit Handbook by Z. Fasman (NY: Executive Enterprises Pubs., 1983).

Equal Employment Opportunity Manual for Managers and Supervisors (CCH, 1989).

Equal Employment Practice Guide (Federal Bar Assn., 1979, 1980).

Fair Employment Litigation: Proving and Defending a Title VII Case, 2d ed. by S. Agid (Practicing Law Institute, 1979).

Federal Law of Employment Discrimination in a Nutshell by M. Player (West, 1981).

Federal Statutory Law of Employment Discrimination by C. Sullivan et al. (Michie, 1980).

Handling Employment Discrimination Cases by L. Modjeska (Lawyers Co-op., 1980).
Hiring, Supervising, and Firing Employees: An Employer's Guide to Discrimination Laws by M. Greenwood (Callaghan, 1987).
The Law of the Workplace by J. Hunt (BNA, 1984).
Manual on Employment Discrimination and Civil Rights Actions in the Federal Courts by C. Richie (Kluwer, 1988).
Primer on Equal Employment Opportunity, 3d ed. by M. Levin-Epstein (BNA, 1984).
Punitive Damages in Wrongful Discharge Cases by J. McCarthy (Lawpress).
Recovery of Damages in Wrongful Discharge Cases by J. McCarthy (Lawpress, 1987).
Wrongful Discharge Claims: A Preventive Approach by P. Weiner (Practicing Law Institute, 1986).

ENCYCLOPEDIAS:　　AMERICAN JURISPRUDENCE 2D (Am Jur 2d)
Check the following topics in the *General Index* volumes for Am Jur 2d:

Civil Rights	Equal Protection of Law
Civil Service	Labor and Labor Relations
Constitutional Law	Removal or Discharge
Discrimination	from Employment

CORPUS JURIS SECUNDUM (CJS)
Check the following topics in the *General Index* volumes for CJS:

Civil Rights	Labor and Employment
Civil Service	Master and Servant
Constitutional Law	Sex Discrimination
Discrimination	Women
Insubordination	

DIGESTS:　　CASE SEARCH IN WEST DIGESTS BY KEY TOPIC
In the *Descriptive Word Index* of the West digests, look for key topics and numbers under the following subject headings:

Civil Rights	Insubordination
Civil Service	Labor Relations
Constitutional Law	Sex Discrimination
Discrimination	Women

ALR:　　ANNOTATIONS
Check the index volumes for ALR, ALR2d, ALR3d, ALR4th, and ALR Fed for annotations under the following subject headings:

Civil Service	Due Process of Law
Discharge from	Insubordination
Employment	Labor and Labor Unions
Discrimination	Supervisors

PERIODICALS;　　CURRENT LAW INDEX (CLI) & LEGAL RESOURCE INDEX (LRI)
In the CLI and LRI, look for references to periodical literature under the following subject headings:

Affirmative Action Program	Employee, Dismissal
Age and Employment	Employee Rights
Age Discrimination	Personnel Management
Constitutional Law	Reverse Discrimination
Discrimination in	Sex Discrimination
Employment	

INDEX TO LEGAL PERIODICALS (ILP)
In the ILP, look for references to legal periodical literature under the following subject headings:

Civil Rights	Employer and Employee
Civil Service	Loyalty and Loyalty Oaths
Collective Bargaining	Races
Constitutional Law	Segregation
Discrimination	

ENCUMBRANCES: See Real Estate
ENDOWMENT: See Estate Planning

ENERGY

SEE ALSO: Administrative Law, Environmental Law, International Law, Natural Resources, Oil & Gas, State & Local Government, Torts

RESEARCH GUIDES & BIBLIOGRAPHIES:

"How to Research Energy Law" by I. Lang, 3 *Journal of Energy Law and Policy* 243 (1983).

"A Plethora of Research Tools for Energy Lawyers" by S. Margeton, 1:39 *Legal Times of Washington* 8 (Feb., 1979).

"The Search for Energy and Environmental Information" by J. Coleman, 3 *Western New England Law Review* 635 (1981).

Solar Energy Legal Bibliography (U.S. Dept. of Energy; Solar Energy Research Institute, 1979).

JOURNALS, NEWSLETTERS, SYMPOSIA & OTHER PERIODICALS:

Annual Energy Litigation Institute (Law & Business, Inc.).

Atomic Energy Law Journal (Warren, Gorham & Lamont, 1959–).

Energy Law Journal (Wash. D.C.: Federal Energy Bar Assn., 1980–).

Journal of Energy Law and Policy (Univ. of Utah, 1980/81–).

Journal of Energy & Natural Resources Law (London: Sweet & Maxwell, 1983–).

Northrop University Law Journal of Aerospace, Energy and the Environment (1979–).

TREATISES & LOOSELEAFS:

Alternative Energy: The Federal Role by L. Buck (Shepard's, 1982–).

Coal Law and Regulation by T. Biddle (Matthew Bender, 1983–).

Encyclopedia of Energy, 2d ed. (McGraw-Hill, 1980).

Energy Law Service (Callaghan, 1978–).

Energy Management (CCH, 1973–).

Energy Resources Tax Reporter (CCH, 1983–).

Energy Users Report (BNA, 1973–).

Federal Energy Regulatory Commission Reports (CCH, 1979–).

Federal Lands: Energy and Mineral Development by T. Vanderver (MD: Govt Inst., 1981–).

Federal Power Service (Matthew Bender, 1974–).

Federal Regulation of Energy by W. Fox (Shepard's, 1983).

FERC Practice and Procedure Manual by S. Herman (Wash. D.C.: Federal Programs Advisory Service, 1982–).

Legal Aspects of Solar Energy, J. Minan, ed. (Lexington Books; Heath, 1981).

Model Energy Code (Council of American Building Officials, 1983).
The National Energy Act (Law Journal Seminars-Press, 1979).
Nuclear Litigation (Practicing Law Institute, 1982).
Nuclear Regulation Reports (CCH, 1975–).
Solar Law by S. Kraemer (Shepard's, 1978).
Solar Law Reporter (CO: Solar Energy Research Institute, 1979/80–).

SHEPARD'S: *Federal Energy Law Citations* (Shepard's).

ENFORCEMENT: See Antitrust Law, Consumer Law, Contracts, Criminal Law,
   Employment Discrimination, Environmental Law, Food, Immigration Law,
   Occupational Safety, Securities Law, Taxation
ENFORCEMENT OF JUDGMENT: See Trial & Appellate Practice
ENGINEERING: See Architecture, Torts
ENGINEERING, GENETICS: See Human Experimentation

ENGLAND

SEE ALSO: Europe, European Economic Community, International Law, Legal History, Scotland,
Wales, United Nations

**RESEARCH GUIDES &
BIBLIOGRAPHIES:**

*A Bibliographic Guide to the Law of the United Kingdom, the Channel Islands and the
   Isle of Man,* 2d ed., A Chloros, ed. (Univ. of London, Inst. of Advanced Legal
   Studies, 1973).
A Bibliography of British Industrial Relations by G. Bain & G. Woolven (Cambridge
   Univ. Press, 1980).
A Bibliography of Literature on British and Irish Labour Law by B. Hepple et al.
   (London: Mansell, 1975).
"British Legal Bibliography" by R. Logan, 81 *Law Library Journal* 691 (1989).
British Official Publications, rev. ed. by J. Pemberton (Pergamon Press, 1973).
Catalog of the Library of the Institute of Advanced Legal Studies, University of London
   (G. K. Hall, 1978).
Colored Minorities in Great Britain: A Comprehensive Bibliography by R. Madan
   (Greenwood Press, 1979).
*A Guide to Parliamentary Papers, What they Are, How to Find Them, How to Use
   Them,* 3d ed. by P. & G. Ford (Totowa, NJ: Rowman & Littlefield, 1972).
How to Use a Law Library by J. Dane & P. Thomass (Sweet & Maxwell, 1979).
"An Introduction to British Government Documents" by M. Banks, 5 *International
   Journal of Law Libraries* 191 (1977).
"Law Publishing and Legal Scholarship in the United Kingdom" by J. Uglow, 5
   International Journal of Law Libraries 292 (1977).
Lawyers' Law Books: A Practice Index to Legal Literature, 2d ed. by D. Raistrick
   (Professional Books, Ltd., 1985).
Manual of Legal Citation by G. Nokes (England: Institute of Advanced Legal Studies,
   1949–1960).
The Parliament of Great Britain: A Bibliography by R. Goehlert & F. Martin
   (Lexington Books, 1983).
Where to Look for Your Law by J. Dane & P. Thomas (Sweet & Maxwell, 1979).

**TREATIES & RELATED
MATERIALS:**

British and Foreign State Papers, 1841–1977 (London: H.M.S.O.).
British Year Book of International Law (Oxford Univ. Press, 1920–).

Bulletin of Legal Developments (British Institute of International and Comparative Law, 1966–).

An Index of British Treaties 1101–1968, C. Parry & C. Hopkins, eds. (London: H.M.S.O., 1970).

United Kingdom Treaty Series 1892–1972, W. Torrington, ed. (microfilm) (Trans-Media, 1977).

CONSTITUTIONAL LAW: *Constitutional and Administrative Law,* 10th ed. by E. Wade & A. Bradley (NY: Longman, 1985).

Multi-Party Politics and the Constitution by V. Bogdanor (Cambridge Univ. Press, 1983).

"British Dependent Territories: British Indian Ocean Territory" in *Constitutions of Dependencies and Special Sovereignties* by A. & P. Blaustein (Oceana, 1982).

Government and Law: An Introduction to the Working of the Constitution in Britain, 2d ed. by T. Hartley & J. Griffith (London: Weidenfeld & Nicolson, 1981).

STATUTES & RELATED LAWS: *Current Law Statutes Annotated.*
Halsbury's Statutes of England.
Halsbury's Statutory Instruments.
Law Report Statutes.
Statutes in Force (microfiche) (Pleasantville, NY: UNIFO Publishers, Ltd.).

CASES: *All England Law Reports* (1936–).
Annotated Tax Cases (1922–).
Court of Appeal Judgments (microfiche) (Pleasantville, NY: UNIFO Publishers, Ltd.).
English Reports—Full Reprint (1094–1865).
Law Reports—Appeal Cases (1875–).
Law Reports—Chancery (1891–).
Law Reports—Criminal Appeal Reports (1908–).
Law Reports—English and Irish Appeals (1866–1875).
Law Reports—Family (1972–).
Law Reports—Queen's and King's Bench (1952–).
Law Reports—Scotch and Divorce Appeals (1866–1875).
Weekly Law Reports (1953–).

JOURNALS & OTHER PERIODICALS: *The Anglo-American Law Review* (England: Justice of the Peace—Holding—Ltd., 1972–).
Annual Survey of Commonwealth Law (Clarendon).
Bracton Law Journal (Univ. of Exeter).
British Journal of Criminology (Rothman).
British Journal of Law and Society (Univ. of College Cardiff Press).
British Legal Developments (British Institute of Intl. & Comparative Law, 1966–).
British Tax Review (Carswell Co.).
British Yearbook of International Law (Oxford Univ. Press, 1920/21–).
The Cambrian Law Review (Aberystwyth: Univ. College of Wales Dept. of Law, 1970–).
City of London Law Review (City of London Polytechnic).
The Company Lawyer (Oyez Pub. Ltd., 1980–).
Corporate Legal Letter.
Criminal Law Review.
Current Index to Commonwealth Legal Periodicals (Halifax, Canada: Dalhousie Law School Library, 1974–).
Current Law Year Book (Sweet & Maxwell, 1947–).

Halsbury's Laws of England Monthly Review (Butterworths, 1973–).
International Legal Practitioner (London: Intl. Bar Assn., 1976–).
L.A.G. Bulletin.
Law and Justice (Edmund Plowden Trust).
Law & Policy (Basil Blackwell).
The Law Quarterly Review (Stevens, 1885–).
Liverpool Law Review.
Oxford Journal of Legal Studies.
Poly Law Review (Polytechnic of Central London).
Solicitor's Journal (Norwich House).
Union List of Periodicals: A Location Guide to Holdings of Legal Periodicals in the United Kingdom, 4th ed. (Univ. of London, Institute of Advanced Legal Studies, 1978).

DICTIONARIES:

Jowitt's Dictionary of English Law, 2d ed., J. Burke, ed. (Sweet & Maxwell; Carswell, 1977).
Osborne's Concise Law Dictionary, 6th ed. by J. Burke (Sweet & Maxwell, 1976).
Stroud's Judicial Dictionary of Words and Phrases, 4th ed. by J. James (Sweet & Maxwell).

ENCYCLOPEDIA:

Halsbury's Laws of England (Butterworths, 1973–).

LOOSELEAFS:

British Tax Cases (CCH, 1982–).
British Tax Guide (CCH, 1963–).
British Tax Legislation (CCH, 1982–).
Capital Formation and Investment Incentives Around the World (United Kingdom) by W. & D. Diamond (Matthew Bender, 1984–).
Digest of Commercial Laws of the World (England) by L. Nelson (Natl. Assn. of Credit Management, Inc.; Oceana, 1966–).
Doing Business in the United Kingdom by Clifford Turner (Matthew Bender, 1985–).
Encyclopedia of United Kingdom and European Patent Law by T. Blancoland et al. (Maxwell & Sweet, 1977–).
Insolvency Law and Practice (London: Frank Cass & Co., 1985–).

TREATISES:

Administrative Law by P. Craig (Sweet & Maxwell, 1983).
British Extradition Law and Procedure by V. Booth & P. Sells (Sijthoff & Noordhoff, 1980).
British Master Tax Guide (CCH, 1985/86).
The British Tax System by J. Kay & M. King (Oxford Univ. Press, 1978).
Business Operations in United Kingdom by D. Wilson, Tax Management Foreign Income Portfolios, No. 68–7th (BNA, 1981).
Byles on Bills of Exchange, 24th ed. by M. Megrah & F. Ryder (Sweet & Maxwell, 1979).
Charlesworth's Mercantile Law, 13th ed. by C. Schmitthoff & D. Sarre (Stevens, 1977).
Company Law in Great Britain by P. Meinhardt & N. Davis (Aldershot: Gower, 1982).
Doing Business in the United Kingdom (Price Waterhouse).
English Courts of Law, 5th ed. by D. Yardley (Oxford Univ. Press, 1979).
European Community Law in the United Kingdom, 2d ed. by L. Collins (Butterworths, 1980).
A History of English Law, 3d ed. by W. Holdsworth, 17 vols.
Information Guide: Doing Business in the United Kingdom (Price Waterhouse).
The Inns of Court and Chancery by W. Loftie (1893) (Reprint, Oceana, 1985).
Introduction to English Law, 10th ed. by P. James (Butterworths, 1979).

An Introduction to English Legal History, 2d ed. by J. Baker (Butterworths, 1979).
The Judicial Process: An Introductory Analysis of the Courts of the United States, England, and France, 4th ed. by H. Abraham (Oxford Univ. Press, 1980).
Law and Politics: The House of Lords as a Judicial Body, 1800–1976 by R. Stevens (Univ. of North Carolina Press, 1978; Weidenfeld & Nicholson, 1979).
Lawyers and Their Work: An Analysis of the Legal Profession in the United States and England by Q. Johnstone & D. Hopson (Bobbs-Merrill, 1967).
Learning the Law, 10th ed. by G. Williams (Stevens, 1978).
Litigation in England: Trial Practice and Procedure Manual (American Bar Assn., 1980).
Patent Law of Europe and the United Kingdom by A. Walton & H. Laddie (Butterworths, 1978).
Policy Arguments in Judicial Decisions by J. Bell (Clarendon, 1983).
System of Justice: An Introduction to the Criminal Justice System in England and Wales by M. Fitzgerald & J. Muncie (Basil Blackwell, 1983).
Taxation of Companies and Company Reconstructions, 3d ed. by R. Bramwell et al. (Sweet & Maxwell, 1985).
Tax Laws of the World—United Kingdom (Foreign Tax Law Assn.).
Trial Practice and Procedure Manual for England by L. Collins (CCH, 1975).
A User's Guide to Copyright, 2d ed. by M. Flint (Butterworths, 1985).
US/UK Double Tax Treaty on Income and Capital Gains by J. Newman (Butterworths).
The Winding-Up of Insolvent Companies in England and France by C. Livadas (Kluwer, 1983).

DIGESTS:

All E.R. Index & Noter-Up.
A British Digest of International Law, C. Perry, ed. (London: Stevens and Sons, ed. 1967; Canada: Carswell).
Current Law Citator.
English & Empire Digest (Butterworths, 1973–).
Mew's Digest.

ENJOYMENT: See Real Estate
ENTERTAINMENT: See Art & Entertainment, Sports Law
ENTIRETIES: See Estate Planning, Real Estate
ENTRAPMENT: See Criminal Law
ENTREPRENEUR: See Business Law, Corporate Law
ENTRY: See Real Estate

ENVIRONMENTAL LAW

SEE ALSO:

Administrative Law, Agriculture, Criminal Law, Energy, International Law, Natural Resources, Oil & Gas, State & Local Government, Torts, Water Law, Zoning & Land Planning

RESEARCH GUIDES & BIBLIOGRAPHIES:

Environmental Law: A Guide to Information Sources by M. Schwartz (Gale Research, 1977).
"Environmental Law and Land Use Planning" by F. Skillern in *Specialized Legal Research,* L. Chanin, ed. (Little, Brown, 1987).

STATUTES:

Clean Air Act, 42 U.S.C. 1857ff.
Environmental Quality Improvement Act of 1970, 42 U.S.C. 4371ff.

Environmental Statutes (MD: Govt. Inst., 1985).

Federal Environmental Pesticide Control Act of 1972, 7 U.S.C. 136–136y; 15 U.S.C. 1261, 1471; 21 U.S.C. 321, 346a.

Federal Water Pollution Control Act, 33 U.S.C. 1155, 1157, 1251ff, 1281ff, 1311ff.

The National Environmental Policy Act, 42 U.S.C. 4321, 4331–4335, 4341–4374.

Noise Control Act of 1972, 42 U.S.C. 4901ff; 49 U.S.C. 1431.

Rivers and Harbors Act of 1899, 33 U.S.C. 401ff.

Solid Waste Disposal Act, 42 U.S.C. 3251ff.

LEGISLATIVE HISTORY: *Legislative History of the Comprehensive Environmental Response, Compensation, and Liability Act of 1980 (Superfund), Public Law 95–510* by M. Reisch (GPO, 1983).

Superfund: A Legislative History, H. Needham & M. Menefee, eds. (Environmental Law Institute).

JOURNALS, NEWSLETTERS
& OTHER PERIODICALS: *Boston College Environmental Affairs Law Review.*

Columbia Journal of Environmental Law (1974/75–).

Earth Law Journal (Sijthoff, 1975–).

Ecology Law Quarterly (UC Berkeley School of Law, 1971–).

Environmental Law (Lewis and Clark, 1971–).

Environmental Law Quarterly (N.Y. Law School, 1982–).

Environmental Law Quarterly Newsletter (ABA)

Environmental Law Review (Clark Boardman).

Harvard Environmental Law Review (1976–).

Hazardous Waste and Toxic Torts: Law and Strategy (NY: Leader Pubs.).

Indoor Pollution Law Report (N.Y. Law Pub. Co.).

Journal of Environmental Systems (1971–).

Journal of Land Use and Environmental Law (Fla. State Univ. College of Law, 1985–).

Journal of Law and the Environment (USC Law Center, 1985–).

Journal of Planning and Environmental Law (Canada: Carswell, 1948–).

Land Use and Environmental Law Review (Clark Boardman).

Natural Resources and Environment (ABA Section of Natural Resources Law, 1985–) (old title: Natural Resources Lawyer).

Northrop University Law Journal of Aerospace, Energy and the Environment.

Outlook: Environmental Law Journal (Temple Univ. Sch. of Law, 1983–).

Sierra Club National News Report (San Francisco, 1981–).

Stanford Environmental Law Annual (1978–).

Temple Environmental Law & Technology Journal (1984–).

UCLA Journal of Environmental Law and Policy (1981–).

William Mitchell Environmental Law Journal (1983–).

DIRECTORIES &
DICTIONARIES: *Directory of State Environmental Agencies,* 2d ed., K. Hubler & T. Henderson, eds. (Environmental Law Institute).

Environmental Glossary, 2d ed., G. Frick, ed. (MD: Govt. Institutes, 1984).

LOOSELEAFS: *Air Pollution Control* (BNA, 1980–).

Air Pollution: Federal Law and Analysis by D. Currie (Callaghan, 1981–).

Asbestos: Federal & State Regulations (Arlington, VA: 1978–).

Chemical Regulation Reporter (BNA, 1977–).

Chemical Substances Control (BNA, 1980–).

Courtroom Toxicology: Environmental and Industrial Toxins and Drugs by M. Houts et al. (Matthew Bender, 1982–).

Environmental Law Reporter (Environmental Law Inst., 1971–).
Environmental Protection Agency Acquisition Regulation (EPA, 1985–).
Environmental Regulation of Real Property by N. Robinson (Law Journal Seminars-
    Press, 1982–).
Environment Reporter (BNA, 1970–).
Environment Reporter (BNA)
Federal Regulation of the Chemical Industry by T. O'Reilly et al. (BNA, 1980–).
Hazardous Materials Transportation (BNA, 1977–).
Hazardous Waste Management Guide (Neenah, WI: J. J. Keller & Associates, 1980–).
Hazardous Wastes Handbook, 4th ed. by T. Watson et al. (MD: Govt. Inst., 1982–).
Hofstra Environmental Law Digest (1984–).
Index to Governmental Regulation (BNA, 1979–).
International Environmental Law: Multilateral Treaties, W. Burhenne, ed. (Berlin: E.
    Schmidt, 1974–).
International Environment Reporter (BNA, 1978–).
International Hazardous Materials Transport Manual (BNA, 1983–).
Legal Practitioner's Guide to Hazardous Waste Management by M. Traylor (NJ:
    Carnegie Press, 1983–).
NEPA Law and Litigation by D. Mandelker (Callaghan, 1984–).
Noise Regulation Reporter (BNA, 1974–).
Pesticides Guide (Neenah, WI: J. J. Keller & Associates, 1979–).
Pollution Control Guide (CCH, 1973–).
Sewage Treatment Construction Grants Manual (BNA, 1976–).
Solid Waste Reference Service (MD: Business Publishers, 1970–).
Spill Reporting Procedures Guide by J. Leemann (BNA, 1984–).
Toxic Materials Reference Service (MD: Business Publishers, 1974–).
Toxics Law Reporter (BNA, 1986–).
Toxic Substances Control Guide (Neenah, WI: J. J. Keller & Associates, 1979–).
Water Pollution Control (BNA, 1979–).

TREATISES:

Beyond Dumping: New Strategies for Controlling Toxic Contamination, B. Piasecki,
    ed. (Quorum Books, 1984).
Deregulation and Environmental Quality by C. Reese (Quorum Books, 1983).
Environmental Dispute Resolution by L. Bacow & M. Wheeler (Plenum Press, 1984).
Environmental Health Law by S. Brown & T. Forrest (Praeger, 1984).
Environmental Law (ALI–ABA Committee on Cont. Prof. Ed., 1984).
Environmental Law, 3d ed. by F. Grad (Matthew Bender, 1985).
Environmental Law: Air and Water by W. Rodgers (West, 1986).
Environmental Law Handbook, 8th ed. by J. Arbuckle et al. (MD: Govt. Institutes,
    1985).
Environmental Law in a Nutshell, 2d ed. by R. Findley & D. Farber (West, 1988).
Environmental Litigation (ALI–ABA Comm. on Cont. Prof. Ed., 1985).
Environmental Protection: The Legal Framework (Shepard's, 1981).
Environmental Waste Litigation (Practicing Law Institute, 1984).
European Environmental Laws & Regulations (MD: Govt. Institutes).
Handbook for Implementing the National Environmental Policy Act (U.S. Dept. of
    Interior, Office of Surface Mining, 1981).
Hazardous Materials Transport Guide (BNA, 1984).
Hazardous Wastes Handbook, 5th ed. (MD: Govt. Institutes).
International Control of Marine Pollution by J. Timagenis (Oceana, 1980).
The International Law of Pollution by A. Springer (Quorum Books, 1983).
International Protection of the Environment Treaties and Related Documents, B.
    Ruster & B. Simma, eds. (Oceana, 1975).

Oil Pollution from Ships, 2d ed. by D. Abecassis & R. Jarashow (Carswell, 1985).
Pollution Control in European Communities (MD: Govt. Institutes).
Rodgers' Hornbook on Environmental Law by W. Rodgers (West, 1977).
Speer's Digest of Toxic Substances State Law, R. Speer & G. Bulanowski, eds. (CO: Strategic Assessments Inc., 1984).
Toxic Substances Controls Primer: Federal Regulation of Chemicals in the Environment by M. Worobec (BNA, 1984).
Toxic Tort Litigation (Practicing Law Institute, 1984).
Toxic Torts: Litigation of Hazardous Substance Cases by G. Nothstein (Shepard's, 1984).
Water Pollution and Water Quality: Legal Controls, 3d ed. by R. Beck (Michie, 1988).

ENCYCLOPEDIAS:

AMERICAN JURISPRUDENCE 2D (Am Jur 2d)
Check the following topics in the *General Index* volumes for Am Jur 2d:

Administrative Law	Fish and Game
Damages	Gas and Oil
Environment and Conservation	Pollution

CORPUS JURIS SECUNDUM (CJS)
Check the following topics in the *General Index* volumes for CJS:

Administrative Bodies	National Environmental Policy Act
Damages	
Fish and Game	Pollution
Gas	United States Secretary of Interior
Health and Environment	

DIGESTS:

CASE SEARCH IN WEST DIGESTS BY KEY TOPIC
In the *Descriptive Word Index* of the West digest, look for key topics and numbers under the following subject headings:

Administrative Law	Nuisance
Damages	Pollution
Fish and Game	Public Lands
Gas	Public Utilities
Health and Environment	United States Secretary of Interior
Mines and Minerals	
National Environmental Policy Act	Water
	Zoning

ALR:

ANNOTATIONS
Check the index volumes for ALR, ALR2d, ALR3d, ALR4th, and ALR Fed for annotations under the following subject headings:

Administrative Law	Insecticides, Pesticides, and Fumigants
Air Pollution	
Chemicals	Irrigation
Clean Air Act	Mines and Minerals
Crop Dusting	Oil Pollution
Environmental Law	Waste
	Water Pollution

PERIODICALS: .

CURRENT LAW INDEX (CLI) & LEGAL RESOURCE INDEX (LRI)
In the CLI and LRI, look for references to periodical literature under the following subject headings:

Acid Rain	Agricultural Chemicals
Administrative Law	Air Quality

Atomic Energy	Marine Pollution
Cigarette Smoke	Oil Pollution of the Sea
Environmental Health	Oil Well Drilling
Environmental Impact	Pesticides
Environmental Law	Pollution
Factory and Trade Waste	Strip Mining
Hazardous Substances	United States
Hazardous Waste	Environmental
Herbicides	Protection Agency
Liability for Environmental	Zoning
Damages	

INDEX TO LEGAL PERIODICALS (ILP)

In the ILP, look for references to legal periodical literature under the following subject headings:

Administrative Law	Nuclear Energy
Electricity	Pesticides
Environmental Law	Pollution
Forests	Water

EPA (ENVIRONMENTAL PROTECTION AGENCY): See Environmental Law

EQUAL EMPLOYMENT: See Employment Discrimination

EQUALITY: See Civil Rights, Women & the Law

EQUAL PAY: See Employment Discrimination, Women & the Law

EQUAL PROTECTION OF THE LAW: See Civil Rights, Constitutional Law, Education Law, Family Law, Handicapped & the Law, Homosexuality, Women & the Law

EQUAL RIGHTS AMENDMENT: See Women & the Law

EQUAL TIME: See Media Law

EQUATORIAL GUINEA

SEE ALSO: Africa, International Law, United Nations

CONSTITUTION: "Equatorial Guinea" by A. Rodriguez in *Constitutions of the Countries of the World* by A. Blaustein & G. Flanz (Oceana, 1983).

TREATISES: *Historical Dictionary of Equatorial Guinea* by M. Liniquer-Goumaz (Scarecrow Press, 1979).

ARTICLES: "Equatorial Guinea" *International Commission of Jurist Review* 29 (June, 1980).

"A Review of Regional Economic Integration in Africa with Particular Reference to Equatorial Guinea" by M. Marasinghe, 33 *International & Comparative Law Quarterly* 39 (1984).

EQUITABLE CONVERSION: See Equity, Personal Property

EQUITABLE DISTRIBUTION OF PROPERTY: See Equity, Family Law, Women & the Law

EQUITABLE LIEN: See Equity, Real Estate

EQUITABLE OWNER: See Equity, Real Estate

EQUITABLE REMEDIES: See Equity, Trial & Appellate Practice

EQUITY

SEE ALSO: Consumer Law, Contracts, Intellectual Property, Islam, Jurisprudence, Labor Law, Legal History, Personal Property, Torts, Trial & Appellate Practice, Uniform Commercial Code

RESTATEMENT: *Restatement of Restitution* (American Law Institute, 1937).

LOOSELEAFS &
TREATISES: *Attorney's Guide to Restitution* by G. Douthwaite (Michie, 1986).
Common Law and Equity under the Uniform Commercial Code by R. Hillman (Warren, Gorham & Lamont, 1985).
The Equitable Jurisdiction of the Court of Chancery by G. Spence (Hein, 1981).
Equity and the Constitution by G. McDowell (Univ. of Chicago Press, 1982).
Gibson's Suits in Chancery, 7th ed. by W. Inman (Michie, 1988).
Handbook of Modern Equity, 2d ed. by W. DeFuniak (Little, Brown, 1956).
Handbook of the Principles of Equity by H. McClintock (West, 1948).
Handbook on the Law of Remedies: Damages, Equity, Restitution by D. Dobbs (West, 1973).
Remedies, 7th ed. by J. Bauman (Harcourt Brace Jovanovich, 1985).
Remedies in a Nutshell, 2d ed. by J. O'Connell (West, 1984).
A Treatise on Equity Jurisprudence, 4th ed. (Lawyers Co-op., 1981).

ENCYCLOPEDIAS: AMERICAN JURISPRUDENCE 2D (Am Jur 2d)
Check the following topics in the *General Index* volumes for Am Jur 2d:

Adequacy of Relief	Equity
Clean Hands Doctrine	Estoppel and Waiver
Common Law	Fraud
Election of Remedies	Injunctions
Equitable Considerations	Laches or Delay
Equitable Conversion	Restitution and Implied
Equitable Interest or Title	Contracts
Equitable Liens	Specific Performance

CORPUS JURIS SECUNDUM (CJS)
Check the following topics in the *General Index* volumes for CJS:

Adequate Remedy at Law	Good Faith
Bills in Equity	Injunctions
Common Law	Laches
Constructive Trust	Mistake
Damages	Notice
Delay	Restitution
Election of Remedies	Resulting Trusts
Equity	Specific Performance
Estoppel	Undue Influence
Fraud	Unjust Enrichment

DIGESTS: CASE SEARCH IN WEST DIGESTS BY KEY TOPIC
In the *Descriptive Word Index* of the West digests, look for key topics and numbers under the following subject headings:

Adequate Remedy at Law	Common Law
Bills in Equity	Constructive Trust

Damages	Injunctions
Deeds	Laches
Delay	Liens
Election of Remedies	Mistake
Equity	Notice
Estoppel	Restitution
Fraud	Resulting Trusts
Good Faith	Specific Performance
Implied and Constructive	Undue Influence
Covenants	Unjust Enrichment

ALR: ANNOTATIONS

Check the index volumes for ALR, ALR2d, ALR3d, ALR4th, and ALR Fed for annotations under the following subject headings:

Beneficial or Equitable	Injunction
Title	Laches of Delay
Coercion or Duress	Mistake
Constructive Trust	Restitution and Implied
Contracts	Contracts
Correction	Specific Performance
Equity	Undue Influence
Fraud	

PERIODICALS: CURRENT LAW INDEX (CLI) & LEGAL RESOURCE INDEX (LRI)

In the CLI and LRI, look for references to periodical literature under the following subject headings:

Constructive Trusts	Ignorance
Equitable Remedies	Injunctions
Equity	Quasi Contracts
Equity Pleading	Remedies
Estoppel	Specific Performance
Fraud	

INDEX TO LEGAL PERIODICALS (ILP)

In the ILP, look for references to legal periodical literature under the following subject headings:

Common Law	Laches
Equitable Conversion	Mistake
Equitable Remedies	Quasi Contracts
Equitable Servitudes	Remedies
Equity	Restitution
Estoppel	Specific Performance
Fraud	Undue Influence
Implied Trusts	Unjust Enrichment
Injunctions	

ERA: See Women & the Law
ERIE v. TOMPKINS: See Trial & Appellate Practice
ERISA: See Bankruptcy, Employee Benefits
EROTIC LITERATURE: See Constitutional Law, Media Law
ESCAPE: See Corrections, Criminal Law
EXCHEAT: See Real Estate, State & Local Government
ESCROW: See Banking Law, Estate Planning, Real Estate

ESKIMOS: See Alaska, Indians
ESPIONAGE: See Criminal Law
ESTABLISHMENT CLAUSE: See Church & State, Constitutional Law

ESTATE PLANNING & PROBATE

SEE ALSO:
Age, Agriculture, Community Property, Death, Employee Benefits, Equity, Family Law, International Law, Real Estate, Taxation; see also entries under individual states and countries

UNIFORM LAWS:
Uniform Ancillary Administration of Estates Act.
Uniform Disposition of Community Property at Death Act.
Uniform Estate Tax Apportionment Act.
Uniform Fiduciary Act.
Uniform Probate Code.
Uniform Probate of Foreign Wills Act.
Uniform Simultaneous Death Act.
Uniform Trustees' Powers Act.

RESTATEMENT:
Restatement of the Law, Second, Trusts (American Law Institute, 1959).

JOURNALS, INSTITUTES, NEWSLETTERS & OTHER PERIODICALS:
Estate and Trusts Quarterly (Canada Law Book Co.).
Estate Planning (Warren, Gorham & Lamont, 1973–).
Estate Planning Institute (Univ. of Georgia School of Law).
Estates and Trusts Quarterly (1973/74–).
The Estates, Gifts and Trusts Journal (Tax Management, 1976–).
Federal Tax Articles: Income, Estate, Gift, Excise, Employment Taxes (CCH, 1967–).
Institute on Estate Planning (Matthew Bender, 1967–).
Notre Dame Estate Planning Institute.
Probate and Property (ABA).
Probate Lawyer (Amer. College of Probate Council, 1975–).
Real Property, Probate and Trust Journal (ABA).
Trusts and Estates (Communication Channels, Inc.).
University of Miami Law Center's Institute on Estate Planning (Matthew Bender, 1966–).

LOOSELEAFS:
Attorney Reference File: Will and Trust Forms (Citibank, 1983–).
Drafting Wills and Trust Agreements by R. Wilkins (Warren, Gorham & Lamont, 1980–).
Estate Management and Accounting by E. Biskind (Clark Boardman, 1969–).
Estate Planner's Complete Guide and Workbook (Panel, 1977–).
Estate Planning (Prentice-Hall, 1954–).
Estate Planning by G. Susman (Law Journal Seminars-Press, 1980–).
Estate Planning, 5th ed. by J. Casner (Little, Brown, 1983–).
Estate Planning and Taxation Coordinator (Research Institute of America, 1978–).
Estate Planning Law and Taxation by D. Westfall (Warren, Gorham & Lamont, 1981–).
Estate Planning Law Locator (R. R. Bowker, 1988).
Estate Planning Manual for Trust Officers by R. Adams (Amer. Bankers Assn., 1982–).
Estate Tax Techniques by J. K. Lasser Inst. (Matthew Bender, 1955–).
Federal Estate and Gift Taxation, 5th ed., R. Stephens, ed. (Warren, Gorham & Lamont, 1983–).
Federal Estate and Gift Tax Letter Rulings (Natl. Law Pub. Corp., 1977–).

Federal Estate and Gift Tax Reports (CCH, 1913–).
Federal Income, Gift and Estate Taxation by J. Rabkin (Matthew Bender, 1942–).
Federal Taxation of Income, Estates, and Gifts, 2d ed. by B. Bittker (Warren, Gorham & Lamont, 1989–).
Federal Taxation of Trusts, Grantors and Beneficiaries by L. Peschel (Warren, Gorham & Lamont, 1978–).
Financial and Estate Planning by S. Kess (CCH, 1980–).
How to Save Time and Taxes in Handling Estates, 2d ed. by J. Clark (Matthew Bender, 1979–).
Inheritance Estate and Gift Tax Reports (CCH, 1928–).
Law of Federal Estate and Gift Taxation: Analysis by D. Link (Callaghan, 1980–).
Modern Estate Planning (Matthew Bender, 1981–).
Modern Trust Forms and Checklists, 2d ed. by R. Parella (Warren, Gorham & Lamont, 1980–).
Murphy's Will Clauses by J. Murphy (Matthew Bender, 1960–).
Post Mortem Tax Planning by J. Kasner (Shepard's, 1982–).
State Inheritance Taxes (Prentice-Hall, 1925–).
Successful Estate Planning Ideas and Methods (Prentice-Hall, 1969–).
Tax Management: Estates, Gifts and Trusts Series (BNA, 1967–).
Trust Administration and Taxation, 2d ed. by W. Nossaman (Matthew Bender, 1966–).
Trust Department Administration and Operations by V. Whitney (Matthew Bender, 1981–).
Wills, Estates and Trusts (Prentice-Hall, 1928–).
Will Forms and Clauses by R. Lynn (Anderson, 1971–).
Wills Trusts Forms (Prentice-Hall, 1961–).

TREATISES:
A Compendium of State Statutes and International Treaties in Trust and Estate Law by M. Henner (Quorum Books, 1985).
Estate Planning Library (ALI–ABA Comm. on Cont. Prof. Ed.).
Estate Valuation Handbook by A. Averill (Wiley, 1983).
Family Estate Planning Guide by F. Hoops (Lawyers Co-op., 1982).
Hornbook on the Law of Trusts, 6th ed. by G. Bogert (West, 1987).
International Estate Planning by W. Newton (Shepard's, 1981).
The Law of Trusts, 4th ed. by A. Scott (Little, Brown, 1987).
Life Insurance in Estate Planning by J. Munch (Little, Brown, 1981).
Multistate and Multinational Estate Planning by J. Schoenblum (Little, Brown, 1982).
Revocable Trusts by G. Turner (Shepard's 1983).
Tax and Estate Planning with Closely Held Corporations by W. Rothenberg (Lawyers Co-op., 1981).
Trusts and Estates, 2d ed. by G. Bogert (West, 1965).

ESTOPPEL: See Contracts, Equity, Trial & Appellate Practice
ETHICS: See Business Law, Death, Health & Medicine, Human Experimentation, Jurisprudence, Nursing, Paralegal, Professional Responsibility

ETHIOPIA

SEE ALSO:
Africa, International Law, United Nations

JOURNALS & OTHER PERIODICALS:
Journal of Ethiopian Law (1965–).

TREATISES & **LOOSELEAFS**	*African Tax Systems* (Ethiopia) by R. Hammond (Amsterdam: Intl. Bureau of Fiscal Documentation, 1980–). *Ethiopia: A Country Study*, 3d ed. by H. Nelson (Wash. D.C.: American Univ., 1981). *Ethiopian Provincial and Municipal Government* by J. Cohen & P. Koehn (Mich. State Univ., African Studies Center, 1980). *Investment Laws of the World* (Ethiopia) (Oceana, 1981–). *Law, Development, and the Ethiopian Revolution* by P. Brietzke (Lewisburg: Bucknell Univ. Press, 1982). *The Legal System of Ethiopia* by K. Redden (Michie, 1968). *Tax Laws of the World—Ethiopia* (FL: Foreign Tax Law Assn.).
ARTICLES:	"Claims Settlement Agreements" (U.S.–Ethiopia) by M. Leich, 80 *American Journal of International Law* 344 (1986). "Highlights of Ethiopia's New Joint Venture Law" by F. Menghistu, 11 *Review of Socialist Law* 161 (1985). "Socialism and Law in the Ethiopian Revolution" by P. Brietzke, 7 *Review of Socialist Law* 261 (1981).

ETHYL ALCOHOL: See Forensic Science
EUGENICS: See Health & Medicine, Human Experimentation
EUROCOMMUNISM: See Communism, Italy

EUROPE

SEE ALSO:	Austria, Belgium, Bulgaria, Communism, Czechoslovakia, Denmark, England, European Economic Community, Finland, France, Germany (East), Germany (West), Greece, Hungary, Iceland, International Law, Ireland (Northern), Ireland (Irish Republic), Italy, Liechtenstein, Luxembourg, Netherlands, Norway, Poland, Portugal, Romania, Scotland, Soviet Union, Spain, Sweden, Switzerland, Turkey, United Nations, Wales, Yugoslavia
RESEARCH GUIDE & **BIBLIOGRAPHY:**	"Bibliography: Lawyers in Europe" by E. McNeill, 9 *International Journal of Law Libraries* 203 (1981).
JOURNALS & OTHER **PERIODICALS:**	*European Taxation* (Amsterdam: Intl. Bureau of Fiscal Documentation). *Tax News Service* (Amsterdam: Intl. Bureau of Fiscal Documentation).
YEARBOOKS:	*European Yearbook* (Martinus Nijhoff). *Yearbook of European Law* (Clarendon Press).
TREATISES & **LOOSELEAFS:**	*Business Law in Europe*, M. Ellis & P. Storm, eds. (Kluwer, 1982). *The Civil Law Tradition: An Introduction to Legal Systems of Western Europe and Latin America*, 2d ed. by J. Merryman (Stanford Univ. Press, 1985). *A Comparative Study of Inheritance and Gift Taxes in Europe* (Amsterdam: Intl. Bureau of Fiscal Documentation, 1984). *Digest of Commercial Laws of the World*, Natl. Assn. of Credit Management (Oceana, 1977–). *Discretionary Justice in Europe and America* by K. Davis (Univ. of Ill. Press, 1976).

Doing Business in Europe (CCH, 1972–).

European Environmental, Health & Safety Requirements Notebook, 2d ed., B. Biles & R. Denny, eds. (MD: Govt. Institutes, 1983).

European Insolvency Practitioners' Handbook (St. Martin's Press, 1984).

Guides to European Taxation (Amsterdam: Intl. Bureau of Fiscal Documentation).

A Guide to the Practice of the Legal Profession in Europe, D. Edward, ed. (Kluwer, 1979).

Investment Incentive Programs in Western Europe by R. Waldmann & B. Mansbach (Chamber of Commerce of the U.S., 1978).

Legal Aspects of Doing Business in Western Europe, D. Campbell, ed. (Kluwer; West, 1983).

Manual on Licensing Procedures in the Member Countries of the United Nations Economic Commission for Europe (Clark Boardman, 1984).

Pocket Guide to European Corporate Taxes (Arthur Anderson & Co., 1979).

Supplementary Service to European Taxation (Amsterdam: Intl. Bureau of Fiscal Documentation).

The Taxation of Companies in Europe (vol. 2), Guides to European Taxation (Amsterdam: Intl. Bureau of Fiscal Documentation).

The Taxation of Private Investment Income (vol. 3), Guides to European Taxation (Amsterdam: Intl. Bureau of Fiscal Documentation).

Tax Systems of Western Europe: A Guide for Business and the Professions, 2d ed. by C. Platt (England: Gower, 1983).

Value Added Tax in Europe (vol. 4), Guides to European Taxation (Amsterdam: Intl. Bureau of Fiscal Documentation).

EUROPEAN ECONOMIC COMMUNITY

SEE ALSO:

Belgium, Denmark, England, Europe, France, Germany (West), Greece, International Law, Ireland (Irish Republic), Italy, Luxembourg, Netherlands, Portugal, Spain

RESEARCH GUIDE & BIBLIOGRAPHY:

"An American Researcher's Guide to European Community Law and Legal Literature" by T. Kearly, 75 *Law Library Journal* 52 (1982).

EC Index: European Communities Index: An Abstracting and Indexing Guide to Publications and Documents of the European Communities (Europe Data; Congressional Info. Services, 1984–).

ELLIS: European Legal Literature Information Service (Europe Data; Congressional Info. Services, 1985–).

"European Communities" in "Bibliographic Notes," 15 *The Journal of International Law and Economics* 33, 307 (1981).

"European Community Law: A Selective Bibliography . . ." by C. Germain, 8 *International Journal of Law Libraries* 239 (1980).

A Guide to the Official Publications of the European Communities, 2d ed. by J. Jeffries (London: Mansell, 1981).

TREATIES:

European Conventions and Agreements (Council of Europe, 1971–).

European Treaty Series (Council of Europe, 1950–).

Sweet and Maxwell's European Community Treaties by K. Simmonds (Sweet & Maxwell, 1977).

Treaties Establishing the European Communities (European Communities Office for Official Publications).

STATUTES & RELATED LAWS:

European Parliament Working Documents.
Guide to EEC–Legislation (North-Holland; NY: Elsevier, 1978–).

CASES:

Digest of Cases before the Court of Justice (European Communities Office for Official Publications).
Guide to EC Court Decisions (North-Holland; NY: Elsevier, 1982–).
Reports of Cases before the Court of Justice (European Communities Office for Official Publications).

JOURNALS & OTHER PERIODICALS:

Common Market Law Reports (Sijthoff; Rothman, 1963–).
Common Market Law Review (Sijthoff & Noordhoff, 1963–).
Common Market Reporter (CCH, 1962–).
Common Market Reports Euromarket News (CCH, 1969–).
Eurolaw Commercial Intelligence (London: Common Law Reports, Ltd., 1972–).
European Competition Law Review (1980–).
European Law Letter (England: The Financial Times, Business Information Ltd.; NY: FT Publications Inc., 1977–).
European Law Review (Carswell; Sweet & Maxwell, 1975–).
Information Bulletin on Legal Activities (Strasbourg, France: Council of Europe, Directorate of Legal Affairs; NY: Manhattan Publishing Co., 1978–).
Journal of Common Market Studies (Basil Blackwell, 1962–).
Legal Issues of European Integration (Kluwer, 1974–).
Official Journal of the European Communities (1973–).
Yearbook of European Law (Oxford Univ. Press, 1981–).

TREATISES & LOOSELEAFS:

Antitrust and Trade Policies of the European Economic Community, B. Hawk, ed. (Matthew Bender, 1984).
Common Market Reports (CCH, 1962–).
The Customs Law of the European Economic Community by D. Lasok (Kluwer, 1983).
EEC Competition Law by U. Toepke (Wiley, 1982).
Encyclopedia of European Community Law, K. Simmonds, ed. (London: Sweet & Maxwell, 1973–).
The European Court of Justice: Practice and Procedure by K. Lasok (Butterworths, 1984).
European Court Practice by J. Usher (Oceana, 1983).
European Economic Community Competition Law Reporter by I. van Bael & J. Bellis (Matthew Bender, 1962–).
Europe Today, 3d ed. (Directorate-General for Research and Documentation, European Parliament, 1978).
A Guide to European Community Law by P. Mathijsen (London: Sweet & Maxwell, 1980).
Judicial Protection in the European Communities, 3d ed. by H. Schermers (Kluwer, 1983).
Law of the European Economic Community by H. Smit (Matthew Bender, 1976–).
Legal Issues of European Integration (Universiteit van Amsterdam, 1974–).
United States, Common Market and International Antitrust: A Comparative Guide by B. Hawk (Law & Business, Inc., 1979–).

EUTHANASIA: See Abortion, Criminal Law, Death, Health & Medicine, Human Experimentation
EVASION OF TAXES: See Taxation
EVICTION: See Real Estate

EVIDENCE: See Administrative Law, Conflict of Law, Constitutional Law, Criminal Law, Computers, Trial & Appellate Practice
EXAMINATIONS: See Health & Medicine, Legal Education, Mental Health
EXAMINERS: See Health & Medicine
EXCEPTIONAL CHILDREN: See Education Law, Handicapped & the Law
EXCESS PROFITS TAX: See Taxation
EXCHANGE: See Commodities, Securities Law
EXCHANGE OF PROPERTY: See Contracts, Real Estate
EXCISE TAXES: See State & Local Government, Taxation
EXECUTION: See Trial & Appellate Practice
EXECUTION SALE: See Real Estate
EXECUTIVE COMPENSATION: See Corporate Law, Employee Benefits
EXECUTIVE ORDER: See Administrative Law, Labor Law
EXECUTIVE POWER: See Constitutional Law
EXECUTOR: See Estate Planning, Real Estate
EXEMPLARY DAMAGES: See Torts
EXEMPTION: See Bankruptcy
EXEMPT ORGANIZATION: See Nonprofit Corporations
EXHAUSTION OF REMEDIES: See Administrative Law, Trial & Appellate Practice
EXHIBITS: See Trial & Appellate Practice
EX PARTE: See Trial & Appellate Practice
EXPATRIATION: See Immigration Law
EXPECTANCIES: See Estate Planning, Real Estate
EXPENSES: See Election, Taxation
EXPERT WITNESS: See Trial & Appellate Practice
EXPLORATION: See Environmental Law, Natural Resources, Oil & Gas, Water Law
EXPLOSION: See Torts
EXPORTS: See Customs, International Law, Maritime Law, Transportation
EX POST FACTO LAW: See Constitutional Law, Criminal Law
EXPROPRIATION: See Africa, International Law, Latin America
EXPUNGEMENT: See Juvenile Law
EXTORTION: See Criminal Law
EXTRADITION: See Austria, Canada, Corrections, Criminal Law, International Law, Ireland (Irish Republic)
EXTRATERRITORIALITY: See International Law
EYESIGHT: See Health & Medicine
EYEWITNESS: See Criminal Law, Trial & Appellate Practice

FACTORS: See Agency, Business Law
FACTORY: See Business Law, Environmental Law, Labor Law, Occupational Safety
FACTS: See Trial & Appellate Practice
FACULTY: See Education Law
FAIR EMPLOYMENT: See Employment Discrimination
FAIR HOUSING: See Constitutional Law, Real Estate
FAIR LABOR STANDARDS ACT: See Employee Benefits, Labor Law
FAIRNESS DOCTRINE: See Media Law
FAIR TRIAL: See Constitutional Law, Media Law
FAIR USE: See Intellectual Property

FALKLAND ISLANDS

SEE ALSO: Argentina, England, International Law, United Nations, War

"The Argentine Invasion of the Falklands and International Norms of Signalling" by M. Socarras, 10 *Yale Journal of International Law* 356 (1985).

"Dulce et Decorum Est: The Strategic Role of Legal Principles in the Falkland War" by T. Franck, 77 *American Journal of International Law* 109 (1983).

FALSE IMPRISONMENT: See Criminal Law, Torts
FALSE PRETENSES: See Criminal Law

FAMILY LAW

SEE ALSO: Abortion, Age, Canon Law, Civil Rights, Community Property, Constitutional Law, Criminal Law, Death, Estate Planning, Homosexuality, International Law, Juvenile Law, Mediation, Poverty Law, Social Security, Taxation, Women & the Law

RESEARCH GUIDE &
BIBLIOGRAPHY: *How and Where to Research and Find Information about Child Abuse* by R. Reed (Saratoga, CA: R&E Pub., 1983).

UNIFORM LAWS—*Uniform*
***Laws Annotated* (West):**   Uniform Child Custody Jurisdiction Act.
Uniform Divorce Recognition Act.
Uniform Marriage and Divorce Act.
Uniform Premarital Agreement Act.
Uniform Reciprocal Enforcement of Support Act (URESA).

JOURNALS, NEWSLETTERS
& OTHER
PERIODICALS: *Family Advocate* (ABA, 1978–).
Family Law Newsletter (ABA, 1960–).
Family Law Quarterly (ABA, 1967–).
Family Law Review (Canada: Jonah Pub., 1978–).
Journal of Family Law (Univ. of Louisville School of Law, 1961–).
Journal of Family Violence (Plenum Press, 1986–).
Journal of the American Academy of Matrimonial Lawyers (1985–).
The Matrimonial Strategist (Leader Pub.; Law Journal Seminars-Press).

LOOSELEAFS: *Child Custody and Visitation Law and Practice* by J. McCahey et al. (Matthew Bender, 1983–).
Disputed Paternity Proceedings, 4th ed. by S. Schatkin (Matthew Bender, 1975–).
Divorce, Separation and the Distribution of Property by T. Oldham (Law Journal Seminars-Press, 1987–).
Divorce Taxation by M. O'Connell (Prentice-Hall, 1981–).
Equitable Distribution Reporter (Panel Pub.).
Family Law Reporter (BNA, 1974–).
Family Law Tax Guide (Prentice-Hall).
Separation Agreements and Antenuptial Agreements, 2d ed. by A. Lindey (Matthew Bender, 1964–).
Tax Aspects of Separation and Divorce and Separation by R. Taft (Law Journal Seminars-Press, 1984–).
Valuation and Distribution of Marital Property (Matthew Bender, 1984–).

TREATISES: *Alimony: New Strategies for Pursuit and Defense* (A.B.A., 1988).
American Family Law in Transition by W. Weyrauch & S. Katz (BNA, 1983).

Beyond the Best Interests of the Child by J. Goldstein, et al. (Free Press, 1973).
Contemporary Family Law by L. Wardle et al. (Callaghan, 1988).
Divorce Taxation Guide by M. Vogel (Wiley, 1984).
Domestic Relations, 2d ed. by H. Clark (West, 1987).
Equitable Distribution of Property by L. Golden (Shepard's, 1983).
Family Law, 3d ed. by W. Statsky (West, 1990).
Fathers, Husbands, and Lovers (ABA, 1979).
Federal Regulation of Family Law by K. Redden (Michie, 1982).
Handling Child Custody Cases by A. Haralambie (Shepard's, 1983).
Joint Custody and Shared Parenting, J. Folberg, ed. (BNA, 1984).
The Law of Adoption and Surrogate Parenting by I. Sloan (Oceana, 1988).
The Law of Marriage and Marriage Alternatives by W. O'Donnell (Lexington Books, 1982).
Management of a Family Law Practice (ABA, 1981).
Marital and Family Law Agreements by S. Green & J. Long (Shepard's, 1984).
Mediate Your Divorce by J. Blades (Prentice-Hall, 1985).
Modern Child Custody Practice by J. Atkinson (Kluwer, 1986).
Separation Agreements and Marital Contracts by S. Schlissel (Michie, 1986).
Support Practice Handbook by N. Hurowitz (Michie, 1985).
Surrogate Motherhood by M. Field (Harvard Univ. Press, 1988).
Tax Planning in Divorce Settlements by R. McGee (Prentice-Hall, 1985).
Tax Strategies for Separation and Divorce by W. Brown (Shepard's, 1984).
Unmarried Couples and the Law by G. Douthwaite (Allen Smith, 1979).

FAR EAST: See Asia
FARM: See Agriculture
FATHERS: See Family Law
FAULT: See Torts
FCC: See Media Law
FDA: See Food
FDIC: See Banking Law, Insurance
FEDERAL AID: See Poverty Law, State & Local Government
FEDERAL COMMUNICATIONS COMMISSION: See Media Law
FEDERAL CONSUMER PRODUCT SAFETY ACT: See Torts
FEDERAL CONTRACT COMPLIANCE, OFFICE OF: See Government Contracts
FEDERAL COURTS: See Circuit Courts, Constitutional Law
FEDERAL DEPOSIT INSURANCE CORPORATION: See Banking Law, Insurance
FEDERAL ELECTION: See Election
FEDERAL EMPLOYERS LIABILITY: See Torts, Workers' Compensation
FEDERAL ENERGY REGULATORY COMMISSION: See Energy
FEDERAL GRANTS: See State & Local Government
FEDERAL HOME LOAN BANK: See Banking Law
FEDERALISM: See Constitutional Law, State & Local Government, War
FEDERALIST: See Legal History
FEDERAL LABOR RELATIONS AUTHORITY: See Civil Service, Labor Law
FEDERAL MARITIME COMMISSION: See Maritime Law
FEDERAL POWER COMMISSION: See Energy, Natural Resources
FEDERAL RESERVE SYSTEM: See Banking Law
FEDERAL RULES: See Circuit Courts, Trial & Appellate Practice
FEDERAL SAVINGS AND LOAN: See Banking Law
FEDERAL SECURITIES: See Securities Law
FEDERAL TAXATION: See Business Law, Computers, Corporate Law, Estate Planning, Family Law, Taxation

FEDERAL TORT CLAIMS ACT: See Torts
FEDERAL TRADE COMMISSION: See Antitrust Law, Consumer Law, Franchise Law
FEES: See Civil Rights, Professional Responsibility, Trial & Appellate Practice
FEE SIMPLE, FEE TAIL: See Estate Planning, Real Estate
FELLOW SERVANT: See Workers' Compensation
FELONIES: See Criminal Law
FEMALE EMANCIPATION: See Women & the Law
FENCE: Real Estate
FERRIES: See Maritime Law, Transportation
FERTILIZATION IN VITRO: See Family Law, Health & Medicine
FETUS: See Abortion, Health & Medicine
FIDUCIARY: See Accounting, Banking Law, Estate Planning, Partnership Law,
    Professional Responsibility, Real Estate
FIFTH CIRCUIT: See Circuit Courts

FIJI

SEE ALSO: Asia, International Law, United Nations

RESEARCH GUIDE &
BIBLIOGRAPHY: *Sources and Literature of the Law of Fiji* (Sydney: LAWASIA, 1986).

TREATISES &
LOOSELEAFS: *Financial Institutions and Markets in the Southwest Pacific: A Study of Australia, Fiji,*
    New Zealand, and Papua New Guinea, M. Skully, ed. (St. Martin's Press, 1985).
    Information Guide: Doing Business in Fiji (Price Waterhouse).
    Investment Laws of the World (Fiji) (Oceana, 1981–).
    Taxes and Investment in Asia and the Pacific (Fiji) (Amsterdam: Intl. Bureau of Fiscal
    Documentation, 1983–).

ARTICLES: "Ocean Boundaries in the South Pacific" by S. Border, 4 *University of Hawaii Law*
    Review 1 (1982).

FINAL JUDGMENT: See Trial & Appellate Practice
FINANCE: See Banking Law, Business Law, Corporate Law, Election, Intellectual
    Property, Uniform Commercial Code
FINANCE CHARGE: See Banking Law, Consumer Law
FINANCIAL SERVICES: See Banking Law
FINANCING: See Real Estate, Securities Law, State & Local Government
FINDINGS: See Trial & Appellate Practice
FINES: See Criminal Law, Trial & Appellate Practice

FINLAND

SEE ALSO: Europe, International Law, Scandinavian Law, United Nations

RESEARCH GUIDE &
BIBLIOGRAPHY: "Finnish Legal Publications in English, French and German 1957–77: A Bibliography"
    by H. Schauman, 24 *Scandinavian Studies in Law* 233 (1980).

CONSTITUTION: "Finland" by V. Saario in *Constitutions of the Countries of the World* by A. Blaustein
    & G. Flanz (Oceana, 1982).

**TREATISES &
LOOSELEAFS:**

Administrative Secrecy in Developed Countries (Finland) by D. Rpwat (Columbia Univ. Press, 1979).

Capital Formation and Investment Incentives Around the World (Finland) by W. Diamond & D. Diamond (Matthew Bender, 1984–).

Digest of Commercial Laws of the World (Finland) (Natl. Assn. of Credit Management; Oceana, 1977–).

Finland and the International Norms of Human Rights by K. Tornudd (Martinus Nijhoff, 1986).

The Finnish Legal System, 2d ed., J. Uotila, ed. (Helsinki: Finnish Lawyers Pub. Co., 1985).

Information Guide: Doing Business in Finland (Price Waterhouse).

The Ombudsman in Finland by M. Hiden (Univ. of Cal., Berkeley, Inst. of Govt. Studies, 1973).

Peace Research in Finnish and Soviet Scientific Literature, J. Berker, ed. (Finland: Tampere Peace Research Institute: 1983).

Tax Laws of the World—Finland (FL: Foreign Tax Law Assn.).

ARTICLES:

"Acquisitions in Finland" by T. Silbiger, 52 *Antitrust Law Journal* 1045 (1983).

"The Chancellor of Justice of Finland," 14 *Law Librarian* 24 (1983).

"Finland: More Rights for Children" by M. Savolainen, 25 *Journal of Family Law* 113 (1986–87).

"Finland: The New Marriage Act Enters into Force" by J. Rubellin-Devichi, 27 *Journal of Family Law* 143 (1988–89).

"The Law in Finnish Democracy" by L. Taxell, 20 *Scandinavian Studies in Law* 233 (1976).

"Recommended General Conditions for the Delivery of Goods Between Finland and the CMEA Countries" by R. Erma, 8 *Review of Socialist Law* 111 (1982).

"The Relations between the European Communities and Finland" by E. Wellenstein, 20 *Common Market Law Review* 713 (1983).

"The Role of Know-How Trade in Finland's Balance of Payments" by P. Miikkulaien, 54 *Bank Finland Mo. Bul.* 24 (1980).

"Suomen Asianajajaliitto: Private Legal Practice in Finland" by D. Reid, 28 *Journal of the Law Society of Scotland* 349 (1983).

FIRE: See Insurance, Torts

FIRE DEPARTMENT: See State & Local Government

FIRST AMENDMENT: See Church & State, Constitutional Law, Media Law

FIRST CIRCUIT: See Circuit Courts

FISH: See Environmental Law, International Law, Natural Resources, Water Law

FIXTURES: See Personal Property, Real Estate

FLEET: See Transportation

FLOOD CONTROL: See State & Local Government

FLOOD INSURANCE: See Insurance

FLORIDA

SEE ALSO:

Circuit Courts (Eleventh Circuit)

**BIBLIOGRAPHIES &
RESEARCH GUIDES:**

Guide to Florida Legal Research by R. Brown (Fla. Bar, 1980).

Research in Florida Law, 2d ed. by H. French (Oceana, 1965).

**STATUTES & OTHER
LEGISLATIVE MATERIALS:** *Florida Session Law Service* (West).
Florida Statutes (Law Book Distrib. Office).
Florida Statutes Annotated (Harrison).
Florida Statutes Annotated (West).
Laws of Florida.

**STATE ADMINISTRATIVE
REGULATIONS:** *Florida Administrative Code Annotated.*
Florida Administrative Weekly.

COURT OPINIONS: *Florida Reports* (1846–1948).
Southern Reporter (West, 1886–).
Florida Supplement (1948–).

COURT RULES: *Florida Rules of Court Service* (D&S Pub.).
Florida Rules of Court: State and Federal (West).

JURY INSTRUCTIONS: *Florida Jury Instructions* by J. Richardson (West, 1954).
Florida Standard Jury Instructions in Civil Cases (Fla. Bar, 1967–).
Florida Standard Jury Instructions in Criminal Cases, 2d ed. (Fla. Bar, 1981–).

**JOURNALS & OTHER
PERIODICALS:** *Florida Bar Journal* (1927–).
Florida Bar News.

**TREATISES, LOOSELEAFS
& OTHER MONOGRAPHS:** *Basic Estate Planning in Florida* (Fla. Bar, 1980).
Comparative Negligence and Contribution in Florida, 2d ed. (Fla. Bar, 1982).
Condominiums . . . by R. Boyer (Butterworths, 1986).
Environmental Regulation and Litigation in Florida (Fla. Bar, 1981).
Florida Administrative Practice Manual by A. England (D&S Pub., 1979–).
Florida Agricultural Law by J. Wershow (D&S Pub., 1981–).
Florida Appellate Practice Manual by A. England (D&S Pub., 1979–).
Florida Civil Trial Practice, 2d ed. (Fla. Bar, 1970–).
Florida Construction Law Manual by L. Leiby (Shepard's, 1981).
Florida Consumer Law Manual by T. Tennyson (D&S Pub., 1977–).
Florida Corporations by H. Ross (Lawyers Co-op., 1980).
Florida Corporation System by J. Martin (West, 1984).
Florida Criminal Procedure by T. Bratten (Lawyers Co-op., 1981).
Florida Damages by J. Alpert (Harrison, 1978).
Florida Dissolution of Marriage, 2d ed. (Fla. Bar, 1984–).
Florida Estate Practice Guide by T. Thomas (Matthew Bender, 1964–).
Florida Evidence, 2d ed. by C. Ehrhardt (West, 1984).
Florida Evidence, 2d ed. by S. Gard (Lawyers Co-op., 1979).
Florida Jury Forms Legal and Business (Lawyers Co-op., 1975).
Florida Jury Verdict Reporter (Fla. Legal Periodicals Inc., 1984–).
Florida Lawyer's Guide by W. Namack & W. Smiley (Callaghan, 1984).
Florida Real Estate by J. Alpert (Lawyers Co-op., 1982).
Florida Real Estate Handbook by J. Ballinger (Michie, 1979).
Florida Real Estate Transactions by R. Boyer (Matthew Bender, 1959–).
Florida Real Property Law by J. Van Doren (Harrison, 1984).

Florida Uniform Commercial Code Forms by J. Oeltjen (West, 1982).
Immigration Law and Practice in Florida (Fla. Bar, 1983).
State Tax Reporter (Florida) (CCH).
Trial Handbook for Florida Lawyers by W. Hicks (Lawyers Co-op., 1970).

DIGESTS, ENCYCLOPEDIA
& CITATOR:

Florida Bar Case Summary Service (1976–).
Florida Digest (West).
Florida Digestive-Index (Harrison).
Florida Jurisprudence 2d (Lawyers Co-op., 1985–).
Florida Law Finder (West, 1986).
Florida Supplement Digest (Lawyers Co-op., 1985).
Shepard's Florida Citations.

FM BROADCASTING: See Media Law
FOIA: See Freedom of Information

FOOD, DRUGS & COSMETICS

SEE ALSO:

Administrative Law, Advertising, Agriculture, AIDS, Alcohol, Animals, Business Law, Commodities, Consumer Law, Criminal Law, Franchise Law, Health & Medicine, Human Experimentation, International Law, Torts

JOURNALS, NEWSLETTERS
& OTHER PERIODICALS:

Drug Research Reports (The Blue Sheet) (F-D-C Reports, 1957–).
Food and Drug Letter (Wash. Business Info. Inc., 1976–).
Food Chemical News (Wash. D.C.: 1959–).
Food, Drug, Cosmetic Law Journal (CCH, 1946–).

TREATISES &
LOOSELEAFS:

Butterworths Law of Food and Drugs by A. Painter (Butterworths, 1980).
Drugs in Litigation (Allen Smith, 1982).
Drug Product Liability by M. Dixon (Matthew Bender, 1974–).
Fair Play in the Marketplace: The First Battle for Pure Food and Drugs by M. Okun
    (Northern Illinois Univ. Press, 1986).
FDA Compliance Policy Guides Manual (U.S. Dept. of Commerce, Natl. Technical
    Information Service, 1981–).
Food and Drug Administration: Regulatory Manual by J. O'Reilly (Shepard's 1979).
Food, Drug, Cosmetic Law Reports (CCH, 1938–).
HIMA Regulatory Manual (Health Industry Manufacturers Assn., 1983–).
Hunger in America: The Growing Epidemic (Boston: Physicians Task Force on
    Hunger, 1986).
The Law of Foods, Drugs, Cosmetics, 2d ed. by H. Toulmin (Anderson, 1963).
Pharmacy Law Digest (Harwal Pub. Co., 1971–).
Recall Manual (Health Industry Manufacturers Assn., 1981–).
Taking Your Medicine: Drug Regulation in the United States by P. Temlin (Harvard
    Univ. Press, 1980).
Survey of Pharmacy Law (Natl. Assn. of Boards of Pharmacy, 1967–).
A Treatise on the Law of Foods, Drugs and Cosmetics, 2d ed. by H. Toulmin
    (Anderson, 1963).
United States Food Laws, Regulations, and Standards, 2d ed. by Y. Hui (Wiley, 1986).

FORCE: See Criminal Law, Torts
FORCIBLE ENTRY: See Real Estate, Torts
FORECLOSURE: See Agriculture, Real Estate
FOREIGN CORPORATION: See Corporate Law
FOREIGN EXCHANGE: See International Law
FOREIGN JUDGMENT: See Trial & Appellate Practice
FOREIGN LAW: See Conflict of Law, International Law
FOREIGN LAWYERS: See Legal Education
FOREIGN RELATIONS: See International Law, Military Law, War
FOREIGN TAX CREDIT: See Taxation
FOREIGN WILLS: See Estate Planning
FORENSIC ECONOMICS: See Economics, Forensic Science

FORENSIC SCIENCE

SEE ALSO: Alcohol, Criminal Law, Death, Health & Medicine, Mental Health, International Law, Terrorism, Trial & Appellate Practice

RESEARCH GUIDE & BIBLIOGRAPHY: *A Bibliography on Ethyl Alcohol for Forensic Science and Medicine and Law* by R. Hollyhead (Forensic Science Society, 1979).

JOURNALS, NEWSLETTERS & OTHER PERIODICALS: *Advances in Forensic Psychology and Psychiatry* (Norwood, NJ: Ablex Pub. Corp., 1984–).
American Journal of Forensic Psychiatry (1978–).
Australian Journal of Forensic Science.
Forensic Science Abstracts (1975–).
Forensic Science International (Ireland, 1972–).
Journal of Forensic Medicine (1953–1971).
Journal of Forensic Sciences (Philadelphia).
Journal of the Canadian Society of Forensic Science (Ottawa, 1968–).
Journal of the Forensic Science Society (England, 1961–).

DIRECTORIES: *The Attorney's Directory of Forensic Psychiatrists* (Amer. College of Forensic Psychiatry, 1986–).
Forensic Science Directory (NJ: Natl. Forensic Center, 1984).

LOOSELEAFS & TREATISES: *A Clinician's Guide to Forensic Psychological Assessment* by M. Maloney (Free Press, 1985).
Courtroom Toxicology by M. Houts et al. (Matthew Bender, 1981–).
Essentials of Forensic Anthropology by T. Stewart (Thomas, 1979).
Essentials of Forensic Medicine, 4th ed. by C. Polson (Pergamon Press, 1985).
Forensic Accounting by F. Dykeman (Wiley).
Forensic Examination of Ink and Paper by R. Brunelle (Thomas, 1984).
Forensic Hypnosis: Clinical Tactics in the Courtroom by M. Kline (Thomas, 1983).
Forensic Medicine by C. Tedeschi et al. (Saunders, 1977).
Forensic Psychiatry and Legal Protection of the Insane by S. Pearlstein (Oceana, 1986).

Forensic Psychiatry: A Practical Guide for Lawyers and Psychiatrists, 2d ed. by R. Sadoff (Thomas, 1988).

Forensic Psychology by R. Green (Thomas, 1984).

Forensic Psychology by L. Haward (London: Batsford, 1981).

Forensic Science by P. DeForest (McGraw-Hill, 1983).

Forensic Science and the Police by J. Peterson (U.S. Dept. of Justice, Natl. Inst. of Justice, 1984).

Forensic Science: An Introduction to Criminalistics by P. DeForest (McGraw-Hill, 1983).

Forensic Science Handbook by R. Saferstein (Prentice-Hall, 1982).

Forensic Sciences by C. Wecht (Matthew Bender, 1981–).

Forensic Toxicology: Controlled Substances and Dangerous Drugs by W. Lowry & J. Garriott (NY: Plenum Press, 1979).

Handbook of Forensic Pathology by A. Fatteh (Lippincott, 1973).

Handbook of Legal Medicine by C. Hirsch (St. Louis: Mosby, 1979).

Introduction to Forensic Sciences, W. Eckert (St. Louis: Mosby, 1980).

Microscopic Diagnosis in Forensic Pathology (Thomas, 1980).

Psychology, Psychiatry, and the Law: A Clinical and Forensic Handbook, C. Ewig, ed. (Sarasota, FL: Professional Resource Exchange, 1985).

Selected Materials on Forensic Science: For Use by Criminal Defense Lawyers . . ., 3d ed. (Houston: Natl. College for Criminal Defense, 1982).

Sourcebook in Forensic Serology, Immunology, and Biochemistry by R. Gaensslen (U.S. Dept. of Justice, Natl. Inst. of Justice, 1983).

The Uses of Psychiatry in the Law: A Clinical View of Forensic Psychiatry by W. Bromberg (Greenwood Press, 1981).

ALR:

ANNOTATIONS

Check the index volumes for ALR, ALR2d, ALR3d, ALR4th, and ALR Fed for annotations under the following subject headings:

Forensic Economics   Forensic Science

PERIODICALS:

CURRENT LAW INDEX (CLI) & LEGAL RESOURCE INDEX (LRI)

In the CLI and LRI, look for references to periodical literature under the following subject headings:

Blood	Evidence
Chemistry, Forensic	Psychology, Forensic
Criminal Law	Trace Elements

INDEX TO LEGAL PERIODICALS (ILP)

In the ILP, look for references to legal periodical literature under the following subject headings:

Autopsy	Evidence
Dead Bodies	Medical Jurisprudence

FORESEEABILITY: See Torts

FOREST: See Environmental Law, Natural Resources, Water Law

FORFEITURE: See Banking Law, Contracts, Real Estate

FORGERY: See Criminal Law, Intellectual Property

FORMA PAUPERIS: See Poverty Law, Trial & Appellate Practice

FORMER JEOPARDY: See Constitutional Law, Criminal Law

FORUM NON CONVENIENS: See Trial & Appellate Practice

FORWARDER: See Transportation

FOSTER PARENT: See Family Law, Juvenile Law

FOUNDATIONS: See Nonprofit Corporations
FOURTEENTH AMENDMENT: See Constitutional Law
FOURTH AMENDMENT: See Constitutional Law
FOURTH CIRCUIT: See Circuit Courts
FRACTURE: See Health & Medicine, Torts

FRANCE

SEE ALSO: Europe, European Economic Community, Civil Law, International Law, United Nations

**RESEARCH GUIDES &
BIBLIOGRAPHIES:** "Current Research Sources in French Law" by C. Germain, 75 *Law Library Journal* 34 (1983).
Foreign Law Abbreviations: French by A. Sprudzs (Oceana, 1967).
"French Legal Bibliographies" by D. Combe, 7 *International Journal of Law Libraries* 23 (1979).
Guide to Foreign Legal Materials: French, 2d ed. by C. Szladits & C. Germain (Oceana, 1985).
Law of France, Cumulative Schedule and Index (Rothman, 1988–).
"Some Observations on the Acquisition of French Legal Materials" by T. Van Linh, 10 *International Journal of Legal Information* 3 (1982).

**STATUTES & RELATED
LAWS:** *French Law: Constitution and Selected Legislation* (Parker School of Foreign and Comparative Law; Matthew Bender, 1981–).
French Civil Code, J. Crabb, transl. (Rothman, 1977).
"International Arbitration Provisions of Decree Amending Code of Civil Procedure," 20 *International Legal Materials* 917 (1981).

DICTIONARIES: *Law and Commercial Dictionary in Five Languages* (English, German, Spanish, French, Italian) (West, 1985).

**TREATISES &
LOOSELEAFS:** *Business Operations in France* by C. Campbell, Tax Management Foreign Income Portfolios, no. 39–7th (BNA, 1985).
Capital Formation and Investment Incentives Around the World (France) by W. Diamond & D. Diamond (Matthew Bender, 1984–).
Digest of Commercial Laws of the World (France) (Natl. Assn. of Credit Management; Oceana, 1977–).
Doing Business in France by Sim on Moquet Borde & Associates (Matthew Bender, 1983).
French Administrative Law, 3d ed. by N. Brown & J. Garner (Butterworths, 1983).
French Business Enterprises: Basic Legislative Texts, J. Crabb, transl. (Rothman, 1979).
French Law of Arbitration by J. Robert & T. Carbonneau (Matthew Bender, 1983–).
French Law of Contract by B. Nichols (Butterworths, 1982).
The French Law of Marriage and the Conflict of Laws that Arises Therefrom by E. Kelly (Rothman, 1985).
Information Guide: Doing Business in France (Price Waterhouse).
Manual of French Law by J. Baker (London: Avebury Pub. Co., 1979).
A Sourcebook on French Law: System, Methods, Outlines of Contract, 2d ed. by O. Kahn-Freund (Oxford Univ. Press, 1980).
Tax Laws of the World—France (FL: Foreign Tax Law Assn.).

The Winding-Up of Insolvent Companies in England and France by C. Livadas (Kluwer, 1983).

World Law of Competition (France), J. von Kalinowski, ed. (Matthew Bender, 1979–).

ARTICLES:

"France: Legal Education" by J. Nagourney, 5 *Comparative Law Yearbook* 45 (1981).

"French Banking Law and the Continuation of Socialist Ideology" by C. Quinn, 18 *New York University Journal of International Law and Politics* 969 (1986).

"French Civil Law System Since 1804" by I. Bessette, 73 *Law Library Journal* 336 (1980).

"French Domestic Arbitration Law" by C. Seppala, 16 *International Lawyer* 749 (1982).

"The French Nationalizations" by J. Loyrette & L. Gaillot, 17 *George Washington Journal of International Law and Economics* 17 (1982).

"The French Response to the Extraterritorial Application of United States Antitrust Laws" by Toms, 15 *International Lawyer* 585 (1981).

"Legal Problems of United States Exporters Selling in France" by Baker, 14 *International Lawyer* 79 (1980).

"The New French Bankruptcy Statute" by Beardsley, 19 *International Lawyer* 973 (1985).

"New Opportunities for Financial Institutions in France" by T. Schoen, 2 *International Financial Law Review* 36 (1987).

FRANCHISE LAW

SEE ALSO:

Accounting, Agency, Antitrust Law, Business Law, Corporate Law, Food, Intellectual Property, International Law, Oil & Gas, Partnership Law, Taxation, Uniform Commercial Code

RESEARCH GUIDES & BIBLIOGRAPHIES:

Franchise Law Bibliography (American Bar Assn., Section of Antitrust Law, 1984).

"Selected Checklist on the Legal Aspects of Franchising" 24 *Record of the Association of the Bar of the City of New York* 262 (1969).

JOURNALS, ANNUALS & OTHER PERIODICALS:

Annual Franchise Law Seminar (Univ. of Missouri-Kansas City Law Center & Kansas City Bar Assn.).

Annual Legal and Government Affairs Symposium (Wash. D.C.: Intl. Franchise Assn.).

Antitrust & Trade Regulation Report (BNA).

Continental Franchise Review (Natl. Research Pub., Inc.).

Current Legal Digest (Wash. D.C.: Intl. Franchise Assn.).

Forum Committee on Franchising Annual Forum (ABA Forum Committee on Franchising, 1981–).

Franchise Annual, 1967, S. Misunas, ed. (Natl. Franchise Reports, 1967).

Franchising World (Wash. D.C.: Intl. Franchise Assn.).

Journal of the Forum Committee on Franchising (American Bar Assn.).

Journal of International Franchising and Distribution Law (London: Frank Cass; Gaunt, 1986–).

TREATISES & LOOSELEAFS:

Business Franchise Guide (CCH, 1980–).

The Franchise Boom by H. Kursh (Prentice-Hall, 1968).

Franchisee Rights by A. Hammond (Panel Publishers, 1979).

Franchise Law, Regulations & Rulings C. Zwisler, ed. (Wash. D.C.: Intl. Franchise Assn., 1981).

Franchise Operations and Antitrust by D. Thompson (D.C. Heath & Co., 1971).

Franchising by G. Glickman (Matthew Bender, 1969–).

Franchising by P. Zeidman (Federal Publications, 1982).

Franchising by W. Siegel (Wiley, 1983).

Franchising, 2d ed. by C. Vaughn (D.C. Heath & Co., 1979).

Franchising and Antitrust (Wash. D.C.: Intl. Franchising Assn).

Franchising and the Law by J. Fels (Wash. D.C.: Intl. Franchising Assn., 1978).

Franchising Law Institute (Minn. Cont. Legal Ed., 1984).

Franchising Realities and Remedies by H. Brown (Law Journal Seminars-Press, 1981–).

Franchising: Regulation of Buying and Selling a Franchise by P. Zeidman (BNA, 1983).

Franchising: Second Generation Problems (Practicing Law Institute, 1969).

Franchising: The Investors Complete Handbook by Dian & Gurnick (N.Y.: Hastings House, 1969).

Franchising: The Odds-on Favorite by J. Atkinson (Wash. D.C.: Intl. Franchising Assn., 1968).

Franchising Today, 1969, C. Vaughn, ed. (Farnsworth Pub., 1969).

Franchising: Trap for the Trusting by H. Brown (Little, Brown, 1969).

FTC Franchising Rule: The IFA Compliance Kit (Wash. D.C.: Intl. Franchising Assn., 1979).

The Guidebook: FTC Rule 436 (Johnstown, PA: Rudy Haupt & Co., 1979).

International Franchising, M. Mendelsohn (North-Holland; Elsevier, 1984).

The Law of Franchising by C. Rosenfield (Lawyers Co-op., 1970).

Modern Franchising Handbook by W. Stewart (Modern Franchising Magazine, 1969).

Partners for Profit: A Study of Franchising by J. Curry et al. (American Management Assn., 1966).

Regulation of Franchising and Other Methods of Distribution by P. Zeidman (Law Journal Seminars-Press, 1981).

Representing the Franchisor and Franchisee (Practicing Law Institute, 1979).

Seminar on Franchising Illinois Inst. for Cont. Ed., 1969).

Survey of Foreign Laws and Regulations Affecting International Franchising by R. Soloman (American Bar Assn., 1982).

A Woman's Guide to her Own Franchised Business by A. Small & R. Levy (NY: Pilot Books, 1967).

Workshop on Representing Franchisors (Practicing Law Institute, 1968)

FRAUD: See Banking Law, Bankruptcy, Commodities, Consumer Law, Contracts, Criminal Law, Election, Equity, Estate Planning, Family Law, Poverty Law, Real Estate, Securities Law, Taxation, Torts

FRAUD, STATUTE OF: See Estate Planning, Real Estate

FRAUDULENT CONVEYANCE: See Bankruptcy, Contracts, Estate Planning, Real Estate

FREEDOM OF ASSOCIATION: See Constitutional Law, Homosexuality

FREEDOM OF INFORMATION

SEE ALSO: Administrative Law, Trial & Appellate Practice

RESEARCH GUIDE &
BIBLIOGRAPHY: *The Freedom of Information: Comprehensive Bibliography of Law Related Materials* by F. Houdek (Austin: Univ. of Texas School of Law Tarlton Law Library, 1981).

STATUTES:	5 U.S.C. 552ff.
JOURNALS, NEWSLETTERS & OTHER PERIODICALS:	*Access Reports/Freedom of Information Newsletter and Reference File,* D. Drosnin, ed. (Wash. Monitor, Inc.). *FOIA Update* (Wash. D.C.: Dept. of Justice, 1979–).
TREATISES & LOOSELEAFS:	*Business Information: Protection and Disclosure—The Freedom of Information Act and Related Laws* by P. Hein (Law & Business, Inc., 1983–). *Federal Information Disclosure* by J. O'Reilly (Shepard's, 1977–). *Guidebook to the Freedom of Information and Privacy Acts,* 2d ed., J. Franklin & R. Bouchard, eds. (Clark Boardman, 1986). *Information Law: Freedom of Information, Privacy, Open Meetings, Other Access Laws* by B. Braverman & F. Chetwynd (Practicing Law Institute). *Your Right to Government Information* by C. Marwick (ACLU; Bantam, 1985).

FREEDOM OF RELIGION: See Church & State, Civil Rights, Constitutional Law
FREEDOM OF SPEECH: See Art & Entertainment, Civil Rights, Constitutional Law, Media Law
FREEDOM OF THE PRESS: See Constitutional Law, Media Law
FREEDOM OF THE SEAS: See Maritime Law, Sea
FREEHOLD: See Real Estate
FREE PRESS: See Constitutional Law, Media Law
FREEZEOUTS: See Securities Law
FREIGHT: See Maritime Law, Transportation
FRENCH POLYNESIA: See Tahiti
FRIVOLOUS CLAIM: See Trial & Appellate Practice
FRUIT: See Agriculture, Commodities
FUEL: See Energy, Environmental Law, Natural Resources, Oil & Gas, Public Utilities
FUEL TAXES: See Taxation
FUJAIRAH: See United Arab Emirates
FULL FAITH AND CREDIT: See Conflict of Law, Constitutional Law, Family Law, Trial & Appellate Practice
FUMIGANTS: See Environmental Law
FUTURE INTERESTS: See Estate Planning, Real Estate
FUTURES: See Commodities

GAAP: See Customs, International Law

GABON

SEE ALSO:	Africa, International Law, United Nations
TREATISES & LOOSELEAFS:	*African Tax Systems* by R. Hammond & M. van den Abeelen (Gabon) (Amsterdam: Intl. Bureau of Fiscal Documentation, 1980–).

Historical Dictionary of Gabon by D. Gardinier (Scarecrow Press, 1981).
An Introduction to Law in French-Speaking Africa by J. Salacuse (Michie, 1969).

ARTICLES: "Regulation of Business Activities of Petroleum Contractors in Cameroon, Congo, Gabon, and Ivory Coast" by M. Frilet, 30 *Oil and Gas Tax Quarterly* 485 (1982).

GAELIC LAW: See Ireland (Irish Republic)
GAIUS: See Legal History
GALLERY: See Art & Entertainment

GAMBIA

SEE ALSO: Africa, International Law, United Nations

CONSTITUTION: "Gambia" in *Constitutions of the Countries of the World* by A. Blaustein & G. Flanz (Oceana, 1983).

TREATIES: "Gambia-Senegal: Agreement and Protocols Concerning the Establishment of a Senegambian Confederation," 22 *International Legal Materials* 260 (1983) (see also vol. 21, p. 44).

TREATISES & LOOSELEAFS: *African Tax Systems* by R. Hammond & M. van den Abeelen (Gambia) (Amsterdam: Intl. Bur. of Fiscal Documentation, 1980–).
Investment Laws of the World (Gambia) (Oceana, 1981–).
Tax Laws of the World—Gambia (FL: Foreign Tax Law Assn.)

GAMBLING: See Criminal Law
GAME: See Animals, Environmental Law, Natural Resources, Water Law
GARNISHMENT: See Consumer Law, Employee Benefits, Personal Property, Trial & Appellate Practice
GAS: See Energy, Environmental Law, Natural Resources, Oil & Gas
GASOLINE: See Natural Resources, Oil & Gas, Taxation
GAY RIGHTS: See Homosexuality
GENERAL AVERAGE: See Maritime Law
GENERAL STRIKE: See Labor Law
GENETIC ENGINEERING & TESTING: See AIDS, Family Law, Health & Medicine, Human Experimentation
GENOCIDE: See Cambodia, Health & Medicine, Human Rights, International Law, Terrorism, United Nations
GEOLOGY: See Natural Resources

GEORGIA

SEE ALSO: Circuit Courts (Eleventh Circuit)

RESEARCH GUIDES & BIBLIOGRAPHIES: *Reference Guide to Georgia Legal History and Legal Research* by L. Chanin (Michie, 1980).
"A Selected Bibliography of Georgia Practice Materials" by S. Thorpe, 8 *Southeastern Law Librarian* 3 (no. 4) (Summer, 1983).

STATUTES:	*CCH Advance Session Laws, Georgia.* *Code of Georgia.* *Code of Georgia, Annotated.* *Georgia Laws.*
STATE ADMINISTRATIVE CODE:	*Official Compilation Rules & Regulations of the State of Georgia* (Ga. Sec. of State).
CASES & OPINIONS:	*Georgia Appellate Reporter* (Harrison, 1980–). *Georgia Cases* (West, 1938–). *Georgia Reports* (1846–). *Southeastern Reporter* (1887–). *Georgia Appeals Reports* (1907–).
COURT RULES:	*Georgia Court Rules, State and Federal* (West). *Georgia Rules of Court Annotated* (Michie).
JURY INSTRUCTIONS:	*Suggested Pattern Jury Instructions* (Civil), Council of Superior Court Judges of Georgia Committee (Univ. of Ga., Carl Vinson Inst. of Govt., 1984).
JOURNALS & OTHER PERIODICALS:	*Georgia Bar State Journal* (1926–).
SURVEY OF STATE LAW:	"Annual Survey of Georgia Law" in *Mercer Law Review*. See, for example, vol. 36, p. 1.
TREATISES & LOOSELEAFS:	*Additional Studies in Georgia Local Government Law* by R. Sentell (Michie, 1983). *Admissibility of Evidence in Civil Cases: A Manual for Georgia Lawyers* by R. Herman & M. McLaughlin (Harrison, 1984). *Bankruptcy: A Georgia Law Practice System* by W. Anderson & W. Scott (Michie, 1984). *CCH State Tax Reporter, Georgia.* *Cobb and Eldridge Georgia Law of Damages,* 2d ed. (Harrison, 1984). *Collections: A Georgia Law Practice System* by J. Glover & W. Anderson (Michie, 1984). *Criminal Offenses in Georgia* by P. Kurtz (Harrison, 1980). *Domestic Relations: A Georgia Law Practice System* by A. Smith (Michie, 1987). *Georgia Criminal Trial Practice,* 2d ed. by W. Daniel (Harrison, 1982). *Georgia Divorce* by B. McGough (Lawyers Co-op., 1981–). *Georgia Family Law Manual* by A. Butler (Butterworths, 1986). *Georgia Magistrate Court Handbook* by J. Warren (Harrison, 1984). *Georgia Probate* by R. Hall & B. Jackson (Lawyers Co-op., 1981–). *Georgia Probate Manual* by E. Hapner (Butterworths, 1986). *Georgia Real Estate Law and Procedure,* 2d ed. by G. Pindar (Harrison, 1979). *Georgia Water Law* by R. Katz (Univ. of Ga. School of Law, Inst. of Govt., 1969). *Georgia Will and Trust Forms* (First Natl. Bank of Atlanta, 1982). *Governmental Ethics and Conflicts of Interest in Georgia* by K. McVay et al. (Michie, 1980). *An Introduction to Law in Georgia* (Univ. of Ga., Carl Vinson Inst. of Govt., 1985). *Powers and Limits of State Government Under Georgia Law* by R. Stubbs (Univ. of Ga., Carl Vinson Inst. of Govt., 1980). *Real Estate: A Georgia Law Practice System* by W. Warren (Michie, 1983). *The Rule Against Perpetuities in Georgia* by V. Chaffin (Michie, 1984).

**ENCYCLOPEDIA, DIGESTS
& CITATOR:**
Encyclopedia of Georgia Law (Harrison).
Georgia Digest, 2d (West, 1985–).
Southeast Digest (West).
Georgia Advance Annotation Service (Michie).
Shepard's Georgia Citations.

GERMANY (EAST)

SEE ALSO:
Germany (West), Communism, Europe, International Law, Soviet Union, United Nations

**RESEARCH GUIDE &
BIBLIOGRAPHY:**
The International Relations of Eastern Europe: A Guide to Information Sources (East Germany) By R. Remington (Gale, 1978).

CONSTITUTION:
The Constitutions of the Communist World (East Germany), W. Simons, ed. (Sijthoff & Noordhoff, 1980).

TREATIES:
Aviation Laws and Treaties of . . . the German Democratic Republic, Hungary, the Democratic People's Republic of Korea, Laos, Poland, the USSR, Yugoslavia and the Republic of Vietnam (6 vols.) by J. Kneifel (Munich: J. Kneifel, 1985).
"Bulgaria . . . German Democratic Republic . . . Hungary . . . Mongolia . . . Agreement on the Establishment of the International Investment Bank and Statutes of the Bank", 23 *International Legal Materials* 641 (1984).

**TREATISES &
LOOSELEAFS:**
The Basic Treaty and the Evolution of East-West German Relations by E. Plock (Westview, 1986).
Digest of Commercial Laws of the World (East Germany) (Natl. Assn. of Credit Management; Oceana, 1977–).
Doing Business with Eastern Europe (NY: Business Intl. Corp., 1975–).
East Germany: A Country Study, 2d ed. by E. Keefe (GPO, 1982).
The Federal Republic of Germany and the German Democratic Republic in International Law, D. Doeker & J. Bruckner, eds. (Oceana, 1979).
Impressions of Law in East Germany: Legal Education and Legal System in the Germany Democratic Republic by D. Meador (Univ. Press of Va., 1986).
Law and Justice: The Legal System of the German Democratic Republic (Berlin: Panorama DDR, 1984).
Legal Aspects of Joint Ventures in Eastern Europe, D. Campbell, ed. (Kluwer, 1981).
Taxation in European Socialist Countries (vol. 5, German Democratic Republic) (Amsterdam: Intl. Bureau of Fiscal Documentation).

ARTICLES:
"Information and Documentation in the Copyright Law of the German Democratic Republic" by J. Straus, 8 *Review of Socialist Law* 5 (1982).
"The Supreme Control Organs in East Germany" by R. Szawlowski, 8 *Review of Socialist Law* 209 (1982).

GERMANY (WEST)

SEE ALSO: Germany (East), Europe, European Economic Community, International Law, United Nations

RESEARCH GUIDES &
BIBLIOGRAPHIES: *Basic Literature of Law: Federal Republic of Germany,* 3d ed. by R. Lansky (Transnational Pub., 1984).
Guide to Foreign Legal Materials: French, German, Swiss by C. Szladitz (Oceana, 1959).
"Important German Law Books" by J. Goedan, 11 *International Journal of Legal Information* 215 (1984).
"Legal Research in the Federal Republic of Germany" by R. Lansky, 16 *Vanderbilt Journal of Transnational Law* 537 (1983).
"Selective Bibliography of Recent Publications on the Law of the Federal Republic of Germany" by R. Lansky, 10 *International Journal of Legal Information* 209 (1982).

COMPUTER RESEARCH: German JURIS: Four data bases—case law, periodical articles, administrative regulations, and statutes.
"Legal Comparativists and Computerized Legal Information" by J. Goedan, 14 *International Journal of Legal Information* 1 (1986).

JOURNALS & OTHER
PERIODICALS: *German Yearbook of International Law.*

DICTIONARIES: *Dictionary of Legal and Commercial Terms,* 3d ed. by A. Romain (Butterworths, 1983).
Dictionary of Legal, Commercial and Political Terms by C. Dietl (Matthew Bender, 1979).
Law and Commercial Dictionary in Five Languages (English, German, Spanish, French, Italian) (West, 1985).

TREATISES &
LOOSELEAFS: *Banking and Finance in West Germany,* H. Francke & M. Hudson, eds. (St. Martin's Press, 1984).
Business Operations in West Germany by J. Killius, Tax Management Foreign Income Portfolios, no. 174–5th (BNA, 1985).
Business Transactions in Germany, B. Ruster, ed. (Matthew Bender, 1982–).
Capital Formation and Investment Incentives Around the World (Germany) by W. Diamond & D. Diamond (Matthew Bender, 1984–).
Commercial Arbitration in the Federal Republic of Germany by O. Glossner (Kluwer, 1984).
A Comparative Introduction to the German Law of Tort by B. Markesinis (Clarendon, 1986).
Digest of Commercial Laws of the World (West Germany) (Natl. Assn. of Credit Management; Oceana, 1977–).
German Administrative Law in Common Law Perspective by M. Singh (NY: Springer-Verlag, 1985).
The German Banking Systems, 4th ed. by H. Schneider (Frankfurt Am Main: Fritz Knopp Verlag, 1986).

German Insolvency Laws (Koln, O. Schmidt, 1975).

German Private and Commercial Law: An Introduction by N. Horn (Oxford; Clarendon Press, 1982).

Handbook of German Employment Law by J. Gres (Kluwer, 1983).

Handbook on the United States-German Tax Convention (Intl. Bureau of Fiscal Documentation, 1966–).

Information Guide: Doing Business in Germany, Federal Republic of (Price Waterhouse).

The Know-How Contract in Germany . . ., H. Stumpf, ed. (Kluwer, 1984).

Local Government in the German Federal System by A. Gunlicks (Duke Univ. Press, 1986).

Manual of German Law, 2d ed., E. Cohn, ed. (Oceana, 1968).

Policy and Politics in German and American Antitrust Law by J. Maxeiner (Praeger, 1986).

The Private Company in Germany, 2d ed. by M. Oliver (Kluwer, 1986).

Recognition and Enforcement of Foreign Judgments in Various Foreign Countries (Federal Republic of Germany) by G. Roman (Library of Congress, 1984).

Taxation in Germany (NY: Deloitte, Haskins & Sells, 1979).

Taxation in the Federal Republic of Germany, 2d ed. by H. Gumpel (CCH, 1969–).

Tax Laws of the World—West Germany (FL: Foreign Tax Law Assn.).

World Law of Competition (West Germany), J. von Kalinowski, ed. (Matthew Bender, 1979–).

World Tax Series: Germany (CCH, 1969–).

ARTICLES:

"Antitrust Sanctions and Remedies: A Comparative Study of German and Japanese Law" by J. Haley, 59 *Washington Law Review* 471 (1984).

"Arbitration between U.S. and West German Companies" by O. Sandrock, 9 *University of Pennsylvania International Business Law* 27 (1986).

"Federal Republic of Germany: Accommodating to Social Change After the Major Reforms" by R. Frank, 25 *Journal of Family Law* 103 (1986–87).

"German Tax Audits of Foreign Subsidiaries in Germany" by J. Strobl, *Tax Management International Journal* 28 (Sept., 1980).

"Germany, Federal Republic: Legal Education" by M. Braun, 5 *Comparative Law Yearbook* 69 (1981).

"The Extraterritorial Application of German Antitrust Laws" by D. Gerber, 77 *American Journal of International Law* 756 (1983).

"Obtaining Evidence in the Federal Republic of Germany" by Shemanski, 17 *The International Law* 465 (1983).

GERONTOLOGY: See Age

GHANA

SEE ALSO:

Africa, International Law, United Nations

CONSTITUTION:

"Ghana" by A. Kludze in *Constitutions of the Countries of the World* by A. Blaustein & G. Flanz (Oceana, 1982).

JOURNALS & OTHER PERIODICALS:

Review of Ghana Law (Gaunt, 1969–).

University of Ghana Law Journal (1963–).

TREATISES: *Africa and Law* (Ghana), T. Hutchison, ed. (Univ. of Wisc. Press, 1968).
African Law: New Law for New Nations (Ghana), H. Baade, ed. (Oceana, 1963).
African Tax Systems by R. Hammond & M. van den Abeelen (Ghana) (Amsterdam: Intl. Bureau of Fiscal Documentation, 1980–).
Capital Formation and Investment Incentives Around the World (Ghana) by W. Diamond & D. Diamond (Matthew Bender, 1984–).
Investment Laws of the World (Ghana) (Oceana, 1981–).
Law and Social Change in Ghana by W. Harvey (Princeton Univ. Press, 1966).
Tax Laws of the World—Ghana (FL: Foreign Tax Law Assn.).

ARTICLES: "Costs and Benefits from Foreign Direct Investment: A Study of Ghana" by K. Yelpaala, 2 *New York Journal of International and Comparative Law* 72 (1980).
"Foreign Investment in Ghana" by R. Bannerman, 5 *International Financial Law Review* 37 (1986).
"Ghana: Legislation for Today" by M. Freeman, 27 *Journal of Family Law* 159 (1988–89).
"Ghana's Wealth Tax," 40 *Bul. for Intl. Fiscal Documentation* 49, 165, 168 (1986).
"Interaction of the Judicial and Legislative Processes in Ghana Since Independence" by S. Gyandoh, 56 *Temple Law Quarterly* 351 (1983).
"Interests in Land in the Customary Law of Ghana" by S. Asante, 74 *Yale Law Journal* 848 (1965).
"Legal Aspects of Investing in Ghana" by M. Tyler, 7 *Loyola of Los Angeles International and Comparative Law Journal* 165 (1984).
"Timing Strategies for Reducing Tax Liabilities in Ghana" by A. Agyei, 8 *The International Tax Journal* 341 (1981–82).

GIBRALTAR

SEE ALSO: England, International Law, United Nations

TREATISES: *The Status of Gibraltar* by H. Levie (Westview, 1983).
The Straight of Gibraltar and the Mediterranean by S. Truver (Sijthoff & Noordhoff, 1982).
Tax Havens Encyclopedia (Gibraltar) by B. Spitz (Butterworths, 1975–).
Tax Laws of the World—Gibraltar (FL: Foreign Tax Law Assn.).

GIFT: See Contracts, Estate Planning, Family Law, Nonprofit Corporations, Personal Property, Real Estate, Taxation
GOING PUBLIC: See Securities Law
GOLD COAST: See Ghana
GOOD FAITH: See Contracts, Equity, Torts
GOODS: See Personal Property, Uniform Commercial Code
GOOD WILL: See Business Law
GOVERNMENT: See Ombudsman, State & Local Government

GOVERNMENT CONTRACTS

SEE ALSO: Accounting, Administrative Law, Agriculture, Architecture, Contracts, Employment Discrimination, Labor Law, Military Law, State & Local Government, Trial & Appellate Practice

RESEARCH GUIDE &
BIBLIOGRAPHY: "Techniques for Researching Public Contract Law" by Holmes, 10 *Public Contract Law Review* 54 (1978).

DECISIONS: *Comptroller General's Procurement Decisions* (Federal Publications, 1974–).
Contract Appeals Decisions (CCH, 1956–).
Decisions of the Comptroller General of the United States (Gen. Accounting Office, 1921–).
Extraordinary Contractual Relief Reporter (Federal Publications, 1974–).
Federal Contracts Report (BNA, 1964–).
Federal Court Procurement Decisions (Federal Publications, 1982–).
Government Contracts Reporter (CCH 1967–).

JOURNALS, NEWSLETTERS
& OTHER PERIODICALS: *IPC Report* (ABA, Pub. Contract Law Section, Intl. Procurement Committee).
Public Contract Law Journal (ABA, Pub. Contract Law Section, 1967–).
Public Contract Newsletter (ABA, Pub. Contract Law Section, 1965–).

LOOSELEAFS: *Accounting for Government Contracts* by L. Anderson (Matthew Bender, 1981–).
Affirmative Action Compliance Manual for Federal Contractors (BNA, 1979–).
Contract Audit Manual (U.S. Defense Contract Audit Agency, GPO, 1979–).
Cost Accounting Standards Guide (CCH, 1972–).
Encyclopedic Dictionary of Procurement Law, 2d ed. by W. Keyes (Oceana, 1982–).
Federal Contract Compliance Manual (Dept. of Labor, Office of Fed. Contract Compliance Programs, 1979–).
Federal Contract Management by N. Steiger (Matthew Bender, 1982–).
Federal Government Subcontract Forms by R. English (Callaghan, 1983–).
Government Contractor (Federal Publications, 1959–).
Government Contracts by J. McBride (Matthew Bender, 1963–).
Government Contracts Citator (Federal Publications, 1973–).
Government Contracts Guide (CCH, 1967–).
How to Conduct Foreign Military Sales: The U.S. Guide by W. Cullen (BNA, 1980–).
Navy Procurement Directives (GPO, 1974–).
OFCCP Federal Contract Compliance Manual by the Office of Federal Contract Compliance Programs (CCH, 1979–).

TREATISES: *Accounting Guide for Government Contracts,* 8th ed. by P. Trueger (CCH, 1985).
Federal Contracts, Grants and Assistance by D. Riley (Shepard's, 1984).
Federal Grant Law (ABA, Pub. Contract Law Section, 1982).
Government Contract Bidding (Federal Publications, 1981).
Government Contract Disputes by P. Latham (Federal Publications, 1980).
Government Contract Law Manual by G. Monroe (Michie, 1980).
Government Contracts under the Federal Acquisition Regulations by N. Keyes (West, 1986).
Manual of Practice before Boards of Contract Appeals (Wash. D.C.: Federal Bar Assn., 1981).
Personal Conflicts of Interest in Government Contracting (A.B.A., 1988).
Recommendations of the Commission on Government Procurement (Gen. Accounting Office, 1979).
Settling Claims under Government Contracts (ABA, 1981).

ENCYCLOPEDIA: CORPUS JURIS SECUNDUM (CJS)
Check the following topics in the *General Index* volumes for CJS:

Administrative Bodies	Public Contracts
Contracts	Public Works

DIGESTS:
CASE SEARCH IN WEST DIGESTS BY KEY TOPIC
In the *Descriptive Word Index* of the West digests, look for key topics and numbers under the following subject headings:

Administrative Law	Public Works
Contracts	States
Municipal Corporations	Turnpikes
Public Contracts	United States

ALR:
ANNOTATIONS
Check the index volumes for ALR, ALR2d, ALR3d, ALR4th, and ALR Fed for annotations under the following subject headings:

Administrative Law	Government
Contracts	United States

PERIODICALS:
CURRENT LAW INDEX (CLI) & LEGAL RESOURCE INDEX (LRI)
In the CLI and LRI, look for references to periodical literature under the following headings:

Contractors	Government Purchasing
Government Liability	Public Contracts

INDEX TO LEGAL PERIODICALS (ILP)
In the ILP, look for references to legal periodical literature under the following subject headings:

Administrative Agencies	Fraud
Arbitration and Award	Government Contracts
Contracts	

GOVERNMENT EMPLOYEE: See Civil Service, Employment Discrimination, Labor Law, State & Local Government
GOVERNMENT ETHICS: See Professional Responsibility
GOVERNMENT IMMUNITY: See International Law, State & Local Government, Torts
GOVERNMENT INFORMATION: See Freedom of Information
GOVERNOR: See State & Local Government
GRAMMAR: See Legal Research
GRANDCHILDREN: See Family Law
GRAND JURY: See Criminal Law
GRANTOR: See Estate Planning, Real Estate
GRANTS: See Government Contracts, Nonprofit Corporations, State & Local Government
GRATUITIES: See Personal Property

GREECE

SEE ALSO:
Communism, Cyprus, Europe, International Law, United Nations

RESEARCH GUIDE & BIBLIOGRAPHY:
"English, French, German and Italian Language Material Relating to Greek Law: A Selected Annotated Bibliography" by C. Spirou, 17 *International Journal of Legal Information* 10 (1989).

TREATISES & LOOSELEAFS:
Business Operations in Greece by D. Petracacos, Tax Management Foreign Income Portfolios, no. 194–4th (BNA, 1986).

Capital Formation and Investment Incentives Around the World (Greece) by
W. Diamond & D. Diamond (Matthew Bender, 1984–).

Digest of Commercial Laws of the World (Greece) (Natl. Assn. of Credit Management;
Oceana, 1977–).

The Greek Code of Private Maritime Law by T. Karatzas & N. Ready (Martinus Nijhoff,
1982).

Information Guide: Doing Business in Greece (Price Waterhouse).

Introduction to Greek Law, K. Kerameus, ed. (Kluwer, 1988).

Investment Laws of the World (Greece) (Oceana, 1981–).

Marriage and Marital Property under the New Greek Family Law by
T. Papademetriou (Library of Congress, 1985).

A Survey of the Greek Law of Inheritance by P. Tsilas (Library of Congress, 1979).

Tax Laws of the World—Greece (FL: Foreign Tax Law Assn.).

ARTICLES:
"Foreign Investment Incentives in the Developing World: The Legislation of Greece,
Egypt, Pakistan, Thailand, and the Republic of China" by P. Dempsey, 11 *Case
Western Reserve Journal of International Law* 575 (1979).

"Greece: Toward Freedom from Discrimination" by G. Koumantos, 25 *Journal of
Family Law* 137 (1986–87).

"Greek Copyright Law" by L. Kotsiris, 16 *International Review of Industrial Property
and Copyright Law* 734 (1985).

"Investment Legislation in Greece, Portugal, and Spain" by P. Artisien & P. Buckley,
17 *Journal of World Trade Law* 513 (1983).

"Marriage and Marital Property under the New Greek Family Law" by T.
Papademetriou, 13 *International Journal of Legal Information* 1 (June-August,
1985).

"Toward Establishing an International Tribunal for the Settlement of Cultural Property
Disputes: How to Keep Greece from Losing its Marbles," 72 *Georgetown Law
Journal* 1155 (1984).

GRENADA

SEE ALSO:
Caribbean, International Law, Latin America, United Nations

STATUTES:
Grenada Consolidated Index of Statutes and Subsidiary Legislation by the Faculty of
Law Library, University of the West Indies (Barbados: Gaunt, 1986).

TREATISES:
Documents on the Invasion of Grenada compiled by F. Lewis & D. Matthews
(Institute of Caribbean Studies, Univ. of Puerto Rico, 1984).

Grenada and Soviet/Cuban Policy by J. Valenta (Westview, 1986).

Tax Laws of the World—Grenada (FL: Foreign Tax Law Assn.).

West Indian Constitutions: Post Independence Reform (Grenada) by F. Phillips
(Oceana, 1985).

ARTICLES:
"The Grenada Intervention" by R. Dieguez, 16 *New York University Journal of
International Law & Policy* 1167 (1984).

"The Grenada Intervention: A Legal Analysis" by R. Riggs, 109 *Military Law Review* 1
(1985).

"Intervention in Grenada" by S. Maizel, 35 *Naval Law Review 47 (1986).*

"The Press and the Invasion of Grenada," 58 *Temple Law Quarterly* 873 (1985).
"The United States Action in Grenada," 78 *American Journal of International Law*
131 (1984).

GRENADINES: See St. Vincent
GRIEVANCE: See Civil Service, Education Law, Labor Law
GROSS NEGLIGENCE: See Torts
GROSS RECEIPTS TAX: See Taxation
GROUP INSURANCE: See Insurance
GROUP LEGAL SERVICES: See Professional Responsibility
GROUP PSYCHOTHERAPY: See Mental Health

GUAM

SEE ALSO: International Law, United Nations

CONSTITUTION: "United States Territories: Guam" in *Constitutions of the United States: National and State* (Oceana, 1982).

STATUTES & RELATED LAWS: *Guam Code Annotated.*
Administrative Rules & Regulations of the Government of Guam.
Guam Legislative Session Laws (Office of the Compiler of Laws).

CASES: *Federal Supplement* (1951–).
Guam Reports (Equity Pub. Corp., 1955–).

COURT RULES: *Guam Court Rules* (Guam Bar Assn.).

TREATISES: *Guam's Search for Commonwealth Status* by R. Rogers (Mangilao, Guam: Micronesian Area Research Center, Univ. of Guam, 1984).
Taxes and Investment in Asia and the Pacific (Guam) (Amsterdam: Intl. Bureau of Fiscal Documentation, 1983–).

ARTICLES: "The Application of Federal Law to Guam" by A. Leibowitz, 16 *Virginia Journal of International Law* 21 (1975).
"Coordination of Taxation between the United States and Guam" by B. Leiserowitz, 1 *International Tax and Business Lawyer* 218 (1983).
"Guam and Northern Mariana Islands Finance Companies After the New Temporary Regulations" by P. Lacy, 9 *International Tax and Business Lawyer* 218 (1983).
"Guam as a Foreign Sales Corporation Jurisdiction" by P. Faber, 26 *Tax Notes* 923 (1985).
"The Guam Constitutional Convention of 1977" by N. Solomon, 19 *Virginia Journal of International Law* 725 (1979).
"Possessions Corporation System of Taxation in American Samoa, Guam, and the Virgin Islands," 9 *International Tax Journal* 343 (1983).

GUARANTY: See Contracts
GUARDIAN AD LITEM: See Age, Family Law, Mental Health
GUARDIAN AND WARD: See Age, Estate Planning, Family Law, Handicapped & the Law, Juvenile Law, Mental Health

GUATEMALA

SEE ALSO: Caribbean, International Law, Latin American, United Nations

**RESEARCH GUIDE &
BIBLIOGRAPHY:** *A Guide to the Official Publications of Guatemala* (Library of Congress, 1947).

**TREATISES &
LOOSELEAFS:** *Caribbean Basin: A Tax Tour* (Guatemala) (Arthur Anderson & Co., 1985).
Civil Patrols in Guatemala (NY: Americas Watch Committee, 1986).
Digest of Commercial Laws of the World (Guatemala) (Natl. Assn. of Credit
   Management; Oceana, 1977–).
*Four Failures: A Report of the U.N. Special Rapporteurs on Human Rights in Chile,
   Guatemala, Iran and Poland* (NY: Americas Watch, 1986).
Information Guide: Doing Business in Guatemala (Price Waterhouse).
Little Hope: Human Rights in Guatemala (NY: Americas Watch Committee, 1985).
A Statement of the Laws of Guatemala in Matters Affecting Business, 3d ed.
   (Organization of American States, 1975).
Taxation in Guatemala (NY: Deloitte, Haskins & Sells, 1979).
Tax Laws of the World—Guatemala (FL: Foreign Tax Law Assn.).

ARTICLES: "Civil Servant Attitudes toward the U.N. in Guatemala, Norway, and the United
   States" by R. Riggs, 35 *International Organization* 395 (1981).
"Executions in Guatemala . . ." by C. Moyer, 6 *Human Rights Quarterly* 507 (1984)
   (see also p. 366).
"The Guatemala Family Court" by A. Goetting, 21 *Journal of Family Law* 53 (1982).
"Latin American Tax Update: Guatemala" by M. Marti, 12 *Lawyer of the Americas* 653
   (1980).
"Observations in Loco: Practice and Procedure of the Inter-American Commission on
   Human Rights" (Guatemala), 19 *Texas International Law Journal* 285, 297, 314
   (1984).
"The Undermining of the Legal Standards for Human Rights Violations in United
   States Foreign Policy: The Case of 'Improvement' in Guatemala" by P. Albert, 14
   Columbia Human Rights Law Review 231 (1982).

GUERNSEY: See Channel Islands
GUESTS: See Torts
GUILT: See Criminal Law

GUINEA

SEE ALSO: Africa, Guinea-Bissau, International Law, Papua New Guinea, United Nations

CONSTITUTION: "The Popular Revolutionary Republic of Guinea" in *Constitutions of the Countries of
   the World* by A. Blaustein & G. Flanz (Oceana, 1983).

**TREATISES &
LOOSELEAFS:** *African Tax Systems* (Guinea) by R. Hammond & M. van den Abeelen (Amsterdam:
   Intl. Bureau of Fiscal Documentation, 1980–).
Information Guide: Doing business in Guinea (Price Waterhouse).

An Introduction to Law in French-Speaking Africa (Guinea) by J. Salacuse (Michie, 1969).

ARTICLES: "Energy Development and Maritime Boundary Disputes: Two West African Examples" (Guinea) by D. Young, 19 *Texas International Law Journal* 435 (1984).

GUINEA–BISSAU

SEE ALSO: Africa, Guinea, International Law, United Nations

"Guinea-Bissau" by A. Ayuk Kima in *Constitutions of the Countries of the World* by A. Blaustein & G. Flanz (Oceana, 1982).
"Energy Development and Maritime Boundary Disputes: Two West African Examples" (Guinea-Bissau) by D. Young, 19 *Texas International Law Journal* 435 (1984).

GULF STATES: See Islam, Middle East

GUYANA

SEE ALSO: International Law, Latin America, United Nations

JOURNALS: *Guyana Law Journal* (Univ. of Guyana, Dept. of Political Science & Law; Gaunt, 1977–).

**TREATISES &
LOOSELEAFS:** *Industrial Relations* by A. Chase (Guyana Trade Union Congress, 1981).
Information Guide: Doing business in Guyana (Price Waterhouse).
Investment Laws of the World (Guyana) (Oceana, 1981–).
Law and the Political Environment in Guyana by R. James (Georgetown, Guyana: Institute of Govt. Studies, Univ. of Guyana, 1984).
The Legal System of Guyana by M. Shahabuddeen (Georgetown, Guyana, 1973).
Political Freedom in Guyana (NY: Americas Watch Committee, 1985).
Tax Laws of the World—Guyana (FL: Foreign Tax Law Assn.).
The Venezuela-Guyana Border Dispute by J. Braveboy-Wagner (Westview, 1985).
West Indian Constitutions: Post Independence Reform (Guyana) by F. Phillips (Oceana, 1985).

ARTICLES: "The State of Human Rights Enforcement in the Cooperative Republic of Guyana" by R. James, 7 *West Indian Law Journal* 14 (1983).

GYM: See Sports Law
GYN: See Health & Medicine, Torts

HABEAS CORPUS: See Constitutional Law, Corrections, Criminal Law, Trial & Appellate Practice
HABITABILITY: See Real Estate
HABITUAL CRIMINAL: See Criminal Law

H

HAITI

SEE ALSO:	Caribbean, International Law, Latin America, United Nations
RESEARCH GUIDES & BIBLIOGRAPHIES:	*A Guide to the Official Publications of . . . Haiti* (Library of Congress, 1947). *Nomenclature and Hierarchy: Basic Latin American Legal Sources* (Haiti) by R. Medina (Govt. Printing Office, 1979).
TREATISES & LOOSELEAFS:	*Caribbean Basin: A Tax Tour* (Haiti) (Arthur Anderson & Co., 1985). *Digest of Commercial Laws of the World* (Haiti) (Natl. Ass'n. of Credit Management; Oceana, 1977–). *Haiti: A Country Study* (GPO, 1985). *Series of Statements of the Law of the OAS Member States in Matters Affecting Business: Haiti* (Organization of American States, 1974). *Tax Laws of the World—Haiti* (FL: Foreign Tax Law Assn.). *Violations of Human Rights in Haiti* by Lawyers Comm. for Intl. Human Rights, 1984).
ARTICLES:	"Haiti" (Civil Rights), *International Commission of Jurists Review* 6–15 (1984).

HANDICAPPED & THE LAW

SEE ALSO:	Abortion, AIDS, Civil Rights, Education Law, Health & Medicine, Human Experimentation, Labor Law, Mental Health, Sports Law, State & Local Government, Torts
RESEARCH GUIDE & BIBLIOGRAPHY:	"Regulating Rehabilitation" by K. Carrick, 74 *Law Library Journal* 556 (1981).
STATUTES:	*A Compilation of Federal Laws for Disabled Children, Youth, and Adults* by the U.S. Senate, Subcommittee on the Handicapped of the Committee of Labor and Human Resources (GPO, 1985).
JOURNALS, NEWSLETTERS & OTHER PERIODICALS:	*AMICUS* (National Center for Law and the Handicapped, 1975–). *Disability Advocates Bulletin* (Boston Univ. Sch. of Law; Pike Institute for the Handicapped, 1985–).
LOOSELEAFS:	*Education for the Handicapped Law Reporter,* N. Blair, ed. (Alexandria, VA: CRR Pubs., Inc., 1979–). *Handicapped Requirements Handbook* by D. Fera (Wash. D.C.: Federal Programs Advisory Service, 1978–). *The Law of the Handicapped: Reporter and Commentator* (NY: R.M. Weiner, 1982–). *Mental and Physical Disability Law Reporter* (ABA, 1984–).
TREATISES:	*Children with Special Needs,* K. Bartlett, ed. (vol. 48 of Law and Contemporary Problems, 1985). *Civil Rights Issues of Handicapped Americans* (U.S. Commission on Civil Rights, 1981).

Clients and Lawyers: Securing the Rights of Disabled Persons by S. Olson (Greenwood Press, 1984).

Disabled Persons and the Law: State Legislative Issues by B. Sales (Plenum Press, 1982).

Discrimination on the Basis of Handicap (Boston Univ. Sch. of Law; Pike Institute for the Handicapped, 1986).

Employing Handicapped Persons: Meeting EEO Obligations by V. Grossman (BNA, 1980).

Employing the Handicapped: A Practical Compliance Manual by A. Zimmer (NY: Amacom, 1981).

Estate Planning for Families with Handicapped Dependents by R. Moore (MD Inst. for Cont. Prof. Ed. for Lawyers, 1983).

Legal and Educational Issues Facing Autistic Children by J. Myers (C.C. Thomas, 1986).

Legal Resources for the Mentally Disabled (ABA, 1983).

Legal Rights of Hearing-Impaired People (Gallaudet College Press, Natl. Center for Law and the Deaf, 1984).

The Principal's Guide to Educational Rights of Handicapped Students by J. Page (Reston, VA: Natl. Assn. of Secondary School Principals, 1986).

Progress in the Education of the Handicapped and Analysis of P.L. 98–199 by F. Weintraub (ERIC Clearinghouse on Handicapped and Gifted Children, Council for Exceptional Children, 1985).

Representing Learning Disabled Children by M. Bogin (ABA, Natl. Resource Center for Child Advocacy & Protection, 1985).

Representing the Handicapped Employee (Natl. Employment Law Project).

Rights of Physically Handicapped Persons by L. Rothstein (Shepard's, 1984).

The Right to Participate: The Law and Individuals with Handicapping Conditions in Physical Education and Sports by H. Appenzeller (Michie, 1983).

Selective Nontreatment of Handicapped Newborns by R. Weir (Oxford Univ. Press, 1984).

Special Education: A Manual for Advocates by D. Pullin (Cambridge: Center for Law and Education, 1982).

ENCYCLOPEDIAS:

AMERICAN JURISPRUDENCE 2D (Am Jur 2d)

Check the following topics in the *General Index* volumes for Am Jur 2d:

Blindness	Equal Protection of the
Civil Rights	Law
Constitutional Rights	Guardian and Ward
Deaf or Mute Persons	Physical Appearance or
Discrimination	Condition

CORPUS JURIS SECUNDUM (CJS)

Check the following topics in the *General Index* volumes for CJS:

Blind Persons	Discrimination
Civil Rights	Guardian Ad Litem
Constitutional Rights	Guardian and Ward
Deaf and Mute Persons	Handicapped Persons

DIGESTS:

CASE SEARCH IN WEST DIGESTS BY KEY TOPIC

In the *Descriptive Word Index* of the West digests, look for key topics and numbers under the following subject headings:

Blind Persons	Constitutional Rights
Civil Rights	Deaf and Mute Persons

Discrimination	Mental Health
Guardian Ad Litem	Physicians and Surgeons
Guardian and Ward	Schools
Handicapped Persons	Social Security and Public
Health	Welfare

ALR: ANNOTATIONS
Check the index volumes for ALR, ALR2d, ALR3d, ALR4th, and ALR Fed for annotations under the following subject headings:

Discrimination	Equal Protection of Law

PERIODICALS: CURRENT LAW INDEX (CLI) & LEGAL RESOURCE INDEX (LRI)
In the CLI and LRI, look for references to periodical literature under the following subject headings:

Exceptional Children	Mentally Handicapped
Handicapped	Vocational Rehabilitation
Intelligence Tests	

INDEX TO LEGAL PERIODICALS (ILP)
In the ILP, look for references to legal periodical literature under the following subject headings:

Administrative Agencies	Discrimination
Civil Rights	Handicapped
Constitutional Rights	

HARASSMENT: See Employment Discrimination, Women & the Law
HARBORS: See Environmental Law, Sea, Water Law
HARBOR WORKERS: See Consumer Law, Workers' Compensation
HARDWARE: See Computers
HARMLESS ERROR: See Trial & Appellate Practice
HARVARD LAW SCHOOL: See Legal Education
HATCH ACT: See Civil Service, Election
HAVENS, TAX: See International Law, Taxation

HAWAII

SEE ALSO: Circuit Courts (Ninth Circuit)

STATUTES & OTHER LEGISLATIVE MATERIALS: *Hawaii Revised Statutes.*
Session Laws of Hawaii.
Hawaii Legislative Manual (Univ. of Hawaii, Legislative Reference Bureau).
CCH Advance Session Laws Reporter. Hawaii.

CASES & OPINIONS: *Hawaii Reports* (1847–).
Pacific Reporter (1959–).
Hawaii Appellate Reports (1980–).

COURT RULES: *Hawaii Court Rules* (West).
Rules of Court (Supreme Court Library).

**JOURNALS & OTHER
PERIODICALS:** *Hawaii Bar Journal* (1959–).

**TREATISES, LOOSELEAFS
& OTHER MONOGRAPHS:** *Guide to Government in Hawaii,* 4th ed. by S. Claveria (Univ. of Hawaii, 1969).
Hawaii Collection Manual (Hawaii Inst. for Cont. Legal. Ed., 1979).
Hawaii Conveyance Manual (Hawaii Inst. for Cont. Legal Ed., 1980).
Hawaii Divorce Manual (Hawaii Inst. for Cont. Legal Ed., 1980).
Hawaii Probate Manual (Hawaii Inst. for Cont. Legal Ed., 1977–).
*Professional and Occupational Regulatory Boards and Commissions of the State of
Hawaii* by A. Miyagi (Univ. of Hawaii, Legislative Reference Bureau, 1970).
Regulating Paradise: Land Use Controls in Hawaii by D. Callies (Univ. Press of
Hawaii, 1979)
Sex Discrimination and the Law in Hawaii by J. Gething (Univ. Press of Hawaii, 1979).
State Tax Reporter (Hawaii) (CCH).
Taxes of Hawaii by R. Bock (Crossroads Press, 1977).
*Who Gets it When You Go: Wills, Probate, and Inheritance Taxes for the Hawaii
Resident* by D. Larson (Univ. Press of Hawaii, 1980).

DIGESTS & CITATORS: *Hawaii Digest.*
Pacific Digest.
Shepard's Hawaii Citations.

HAZARDOUS MATERIALS: See Energy, Environmental Law, Transportation
HAZARDOUS OCCUPATION: See Occupational Safety, Torts

HEALTH & MEDICINE

SEE ALSO: Abortion, Age, AIDS, Death, Employee Benefits, Handicapped & the Law, Human
Experimentation, Insurance, International Law, Mental Health, Nursing, Poverty Law,
Social Security, Torts, Trial & Appellate Practice

**RESEARCH GUIDES &
BIBLIOGRAPHIES:** *Bibliography of Bioethics,* L. Waters, ed. (Georgetown Institute of Ethics, 1985).
"Health Care Information Services: An Annotated Bibliography" by L. Baker, 3 *Legal
Reference Service Quarterly* 3 (1983).
Law, Medicine and Health Care: A Bibliography by J. Ziegenfuss (NY: Facts on File,
1983).
A Sourcebook for Research in Law and Medicine by S. Fiscina et al. (Natl. Health
Publishing, 1985).

**JOURNALS, NEWSLETTERS
& OTHER PERIODICALS:** *American Journal of Law and Medicine* (Amer. Society of Law & Medicine, 1975–).
Current Medicine for Attorneys.
Health Advocate (Natl. Health Law Program, 1969–).
Health Care Law Newsletter (BNA, 1986–).
Health Law Digest (Natl. Health Lawyers Assn., 1971–).
Health Law Vigil (Amer. Hospital Assn., 1984–).
The Health Lawyer (ABA, Forum Committee on Health Law, 1984–).
Index Medicus (1972–).
Issues in Law & Medicine (IN: Natl. Legal Center for the Medically Dependent and
Disabled, 1985–).

Journal of Bioethics (Human Sciences Press, 1983–).
Journal of Contemporary Health Law and Policy (Catholic Univ. Law School, 1985–).
Journal of Health, Politics, Policy & Law (Duke Univ.).
Journal of Law and Health (Cleveland-Marshall College of Law, 1985/86–).
Journal of Legal Medicine (Amer. College of Legal Medicine).
Journal of the American Medical Association.
Law, Medicine & Health Care (Amer. Society of Law & Medicine, 1973–).
Lawyers Medical Journal (Lawyers Co-op.).
Legal Aspects of Medical Practice (Pharmaceutical Communications, Inc.).
Legal Medical Quarterly (Jonah Pubs., 1977–).
Legal Medicine Annual (Prentice-Hall, 1969–).
McQuade's Medical Information Newsletter for Trial Lawyers (Callaghan).
Medical Trial Technique Quarterly (Callaghan).
Medicine, Science and the Law (England, 1960–).
Medico-Legal Journal (Carswell).
Specialty Law Digest: Health Care (BNA, 1979–).
Topics in Hospital Law (Aspen Systems Corp., 1985–).

LOOSELEAFS:
Ambulatory Services, M. Kander, ed. (Natl. Law Pub. Corp., 1979–).
Attorneys' Dictionary of Medicine by J. Schmidt (Matthew Bender, 1962–).
Attorneys Medical Deskbook, 2d ed. by D. Tennenhouse (Lawyers Co-op, 1983–).
Attorney's Textbook of Medicine, 3d ed. by R. Gray (Matthew Bender, 1950–).
Bender's Courtroom Medicine Series (Matthew Bender).
Bioethics Reporter by J. Childress (Univ. Pubs. of America, 1983–).
BioLaw: A Legal and Ethical Reporter (Univ. Pubs. of America).
Courtroom Medicine (Matthew Bender, 1965–).
Courtroon Toxicology: Environmental and Industrial Toxins and Drugs by M. Houts et al. (Matthew Bender, 1982–).
Health Administration, M. Kander, ed. (Natl. Law Pub. Corp., 1977–).
Health Care Labor Manual by M. Skoler (Aspen Systems Corp., 1974–).
Hospital Contracts Manual by Baker & Hostetler (Aspen Systems Corp., 1982–).
Hospital Cost Management by J. Steinle (Prentice-Hall, 1982–).
Hospital Law Manual, Attorney's Volumes (Aspen Systems Corp., 1959–).
Hospital Liability by J. Smith (Law Journal Seminars-Press, 1985–).
Laboratory Regulation Manual by H. Halper (Aspen Systems Corp., 1976–).
Lawyers' Guide to Medical Proof by M. Houts (Matthew Bender, 1966–).
Medical Directorship: Regulations and Guidelines (Natl. Law Pub. Corp., 1982–).
Medicare Home Health Agency Manual (U.S. Dept. of Health & Human Services, Health Care Financing Admin., 1980–).
Medicare Hospital Manual (U.S. Dept. of Health & Human Services, Health Care Financing Admin., 1981–).
Medicare-Medicaid Guide (CCH, 1969–).
Modern Health Care Forms by P. Selbst (Warren, Gorham & Lamont, 1976–).
Operating Standards in Health Care Facilities, M. Kander, ed. (Natl. Law Pub. Corp., 1984–).
Prospective DRG Payments, M. Kander, ed. (Natl. Law Pub. Corp., 1984–).
Prospective Payment: Laws, Regulations (Natl. Health Pub., 1984–).
Proving Medical Diagnosis and Prognosis by M. Houts (Matthew Bender, 1970–).
Reporter on Human Reproduction and the Law (1972).

TREATISES:
Accreditation Manual for Hospitals (Joint Commn. on Accred. of Hospitals, 1983).
Anesthesiology and the Law by J. Peters (Ann Arbor: Health Admin. Press, 1983).
Antitrust and the Health Care Provider by M. Thompson (Aspen Systems Corp., 1979).
Consent to Treatment by F. Rozovsky (Little, Brown, 1984).

Health and the Law: A Handbook for Health Professionals by T. Christoffel (Free Press, 1982).

Hospital Liability (Law Journal Seminars-Press, 1985).

Jury Instructions on Medical Issues, 3d ed. by G. Douthwaite (Michie, 1987).

Lawyers' Medical Cyclopedia, 3d ed. by C. Frankel (Michie, 1972).

Long Term Care and the Law (Natl. Health Pub., 1983).

Major Cases in Health Law, D. Wexler, ed. (Univ. Pubs. of America, 1984).

Mann's Medical Handbook for Litigation by A. Mann (Michie, 1985).

Medical Legal Issues for Radiologists (American College of Radiology; Precept Press, 1987).

Medical Risk Management: Preventive Legal Strategies for Health Care Providers by E. Richards (Aspen Systems Corp., 1983).

Medicare and Medicaid Claims and Procedures, 2d ed. by H. McCormick (West, 1986).

Sociobiology and the Law by J. Beckstrom (Univ. of Illinois Press, 1985).

Sourcebook on Asbestos Diseases: Medical, Legal, and Engineering Aspects by G. Peters (Gale; Law Pub., 1986).

Where to Write for Vital Records: Births, Deaths, Marriages, and Divorces (U.S. Dept of Health and Human Services, Public Health Service, Nat'l Center for Health Statistics, 1987).

ENCYCLOPEDIAS:

AMERICAN JURISPRUDENCE 2D (Am Jur 2d)

Check the following topics in the *General Index* volumes for Am Jur 2d:

Autopsy	Mental Capacity
Chiropractors	Nurses
Contagious or Communicable Diseases	Optometry and Optometrists
Coroners	Physical or Mental Examination
Dentists	
Diagnosis	Physician-Patient Privileges
Health	
Hospitals and Asylums	Physicians and Surgeons
Incompetent or Insane Persons	Social Security and Medicare
Malpractice	Veterinarians
Medical Care	

CORPUS JURIS SECUNDUM (CJS)

Check the following topics in the *General Index* volumes for CJS:

Autopsy	Medical Reports
Chiropractors	Mentally Deficient
Convalescent and Nursing Homes	Nurses
	Occupational Diseases
Coroners	Optometrists and Optometry
Dead Bodies	
Dentists	Osteopaths
Diagnosis	Physical Examination
Disease	Physicians and Surgeons
Druggists	Psychiatrists
Drugs and Narcotics	Quarantine
Health and Environment	Sanitariums
Hospitals	Social Security and Public Welfare
Illness	
Malpractice	Veterinarians
Medical Care and Treatment	

DIGESTS:

CASE SEARCH IN WEST DIGESTS BY KEY TOPIC
In the *Descriptive Word Index* of the West digests, look for key topics and numbers under the following subject headings:

Abortion	Medical Care and
Autopsy	Malpractice
Chiropractors	Medical Reports
Convalescent and Nursing	Mentally Deficient
Homes	Nurses
Coroners	Occupational Diseases
Dead Bodies	Optometrists and
Dentists	Optometry
Diagnosis	Osteopaths
Disease	Physical Examination
Druggists	Physicians and Surgeons
Drugs and Narcotics	Phychiatrists
Health and Environment	Quarantine
Hospitals	Sanitariums
Illness	Social Security and Public
Insurance	Welfare
Licenses	States
Malpractice	Veterinarians

ALR:

ANNOTATIONS
Check the index volumes for ALR, ALR2d, ALR3d, ALR4th, and ALR Fed for annotations under the following subject headings:

Acupuncture	Health
Allergy	Heart
Anesthetist	Hill-Burton Act
Autopsy	Hospital
Biopsy	Impotency
Birth	Informed Consent
Black Lung Disease	Insurance
Bleeding	Malpractice
Blood Test	Medical Treatment
Brain	Mental Illness
Bruises	Nurses
Burns	Opticians
Cancer	Osteopaths
Chiropractor	Patients
Coroners	Permanent Disability
Dentists	Physicians
Diagnosis	Pregnancy
Diseases	Prior Injury
Druggist	Sterility
Eyesight	Suicide
Fractures	Therapy

PERIODICALS:

CURRENT LAW INDEX (CLI) & LEGAL RESOURCE INDEX (LRI)
In the CLI and LRI, look for references to periodical literature under the following subject headings:

Abnormalities	Asthma
Alcoholism	Bioengineering
Arteries	Bioethics

Blood

Brain Death

Cancer

Communicable Disease

Community Health

Conception

Confidential

   Communication

Consent

Dead Bodies

Dialysis

Disability

Donation of Organs

Embryology

Environmental Health

Euthanasia

Fertilization in Vitro

Genetic Engineering

Health

Herpes

Hospitals

Kidneys

Malpractice

Medicaid

Medical Care

Medical Ethics

Midwives

Occupational Diseases

Opticians

Optometrists

Physicianss

Physicians' Assistants

Psychology

Psychotherapy

Public Health

Right to Die

Sports Medicine

Surgeons

Terminal Care

Tort Liability of Hospitals

Transplantation

Venereal Diseases

Vocational Rehabilitation

Wrongful Life

INDEX TO LEGAL PERIODICALS (ILP)

In the ILP, look for references to legal periodical literature under the following subject headings:

Autopsy

Behavior Modification

Civil Rights

Coroners

Dead Bodies

Dentists

Eugenics

Euthanasia

Fraud

Genetic Engineering

Genocide

Health

Hospitals

Industrial Diseases

Medicaid

Medical Examiners

Medical Jurisprudence

Medicare

Negligence

Nurses

Occupational Safety and

   Health

Pharmacists

Physicians

Psychiatry

Psychology

Right to Die

Sterilization

Workers' Compensation

HEARING: See Administrative Law, Legislative History, Trial & Appellate Practice

HEARING IMPAIRED: See Handicapped & the Law

HEARSAY: See Trial & Appellate Practice

HEART: See Health & Medicine

HEIRS: See Estate Planning, Family Law, Real Estate

HELSINKI: See Human Rights

HERBICIDES: See Environmental Law

HEREDITAMENT: See Estate Planning, Real Estate

HERPES: See Health & Medicine

HIGHER EDUCATION: See Church & State, Education Law

HIGH SEAS: See International Law, Maritime Law, Sea
HIGHWAYS: See State & Local Government, Torts
HIJACKING: See Terrorism
HILL–BURTON: See Health & Medicine
HIRING: See Employee Benefits, Law Office Management

HISTORIC PRESERVATION

SEE ALSO: Government Contracts, Legal History, Real Estate, State & Local Government

**RESEARCH GUIDES &
BIBLIOGRAPHIES:**
"Annotated Bibliography of Law-Related Journal Citations on Historic Preservation"
by T. French, 9 *Northern Kentucky Law Review* 45 (1982).
Historic Preservation Law: An Annotated Bibliography by E. Kettler & B. Reams
(Preservation Press, 1976).

**TREATISES &
LOOSELEAFS:**
Directory of Preservation Lawyers (Wash. D.C.: Natl. Trusts for Historic Preservation).
Federal Historic Preservation Case Law by the Advisory Council on Historic
Preservation (GPO, 1985).
Historic Preservation Law and Tax Planning . . . (ALI–ABA Comm. on Cont. Prof. Ed.,
1985).
Information: A Preservation Sourcebook (Wash. D.C.: Natl. Trusts for Historic
Preservation, 1979–).
Preservation Law Reporter (Wash. D.C.: Natl. Trusts for Historic Preservation, 1982–).
Reusing Old Buildings: Preservation Law and the Development Process (Wash. D.C.:
Conservation Foundation; Natl. Trusts for Historic Preservation, 1984).
Saving Southern Buildings: The Law and the Profits (VA: Mary Washington College
Center for Historic Preservation, 1983).
State Enabling Legislation for Local Preservation Commissions by P. Thurber (Wash.
D.C.: Natl. Trusts for Historic Preservation, 1984).

HISTORY: See Legal History, Legislative History, Statistics
HIT AND RUN: See Criminal Law
HOLDING COMPANY: See Banking Law, Corporate Law, Securities Law
HOME: See Real Estate
HOME CARE: See Family Law, Health & Medicine
HOME OWNERS ASSOCIATION: See Real Estate
HOMEOWNERS POLICY: See Insurance
HOME RULE: See State & Local Government
HOMESTEAD: See Bankruptcy, Estate Planning, Real Estate
HOMICIDE: See Criminal Law

HOMOSEXUALITY

SEE ALSO: AIDS, Civil Rights, Constitutional Law, Criminal Law, Employment Discrimination,
Family Law, Human Rights

**RESEARCH GUIDE &
BIBLIOGRAPHY:**
Lesbian Mothers and Their Children: An Annotated Bibliography, 2d ed. by D.
Hitchens & A. Thomas (San Francisco: Lesbian Rights Project, 1983).

**JOURNALS, NEWSLETTERS
& OTHER PERIODICALS:**   *AALS Section on Gay and Lesbian Legal Issues Newsletter* (Association of American
          Law Schools, 1985–).
          Lesbian/Gay Law Notes (NY: Bar Assn. for Human Rights of Greater New York, 1984–).
          Sexual Law Reporter (Gaunt, 1975–).

DIRECTORY: *National Attorneys' Directory for Lesbian & Gay Rights,* 3d ed. (Boston: Gay &
          Lesbian Advocates & Defenders, 1984).

**TREATISES &
LOOSELEAFS:**   *Anti-Gay Legislation* by R. Richter (NY: Lambda Legal Defense & Education Fund,
          1982).
          Homosexuality and the Law, D. Knutson, ed. (Haworth Press, 1980).
          A Legal Guide for Gay and Lesbian Couples by H. Curry & D. Clifford (Nolo Press,
          1985).
          Legalizing Homosexual Conduct by C. Rice (VA: Center for Judicial Studies, 1984).
          Lesbian Mother Litigation Manual by D. Hitchens (San Francisco: Lesbian Rights
          Project, 1982).
          Sexual Orientation and the Law, R. Achtenberg, ed. (Clark Boardman, 1985–).

ENCYCLOPEDIAS: AMERICAN JURISPRUDENCE 2D (Am Jur 2d)
          Check the following topics in the *General Index* volumes for Am Jur 2d:

Civil Rights	Homosexuality
Constitutional Law	Sex and Sexual Matters
Discrimination	Sexual Relations and
Equal Protection of	Offenses
the Law	

          CORPUS JURIS SECUNDUM (CJS)
          Check the following topics in the *General Index* volumes for CJS:

Civil Rights	Sex
Constitutional Law	Sex Offenses
Discrimination	Sexual Relations
Homosexuality	Sodomy
Right of Privacy	

DIGESTS: CASE SEARCH IN WEST DIGESTS BY KEY TOPIC
          In the *Descriptive Word Index* of the West digests, look for key topics and numbers
          under the following subject headings:

Civil Rights	Right of Privacy
Constitutional Law	Sex
Discrimination	Sex Offenses
Health	Sexual Relations
Homosexuality	Sodomy

ALR: ANNOTATIONS
          Check the index volumes for ALR, ALR2d, ALR3d, ALR4th, and ALR Fed for annotations
          under the following subject headings:

Discrimination	Sodomy
Equal Protection of the	Homosexuality
Law	Privacy

PERIODICALS: CURRENT LAW INDEX (CLI) & LEGAL RESOURCE INDEX (LRI)
In the CLI and LRI, look for references to periodical literature under the following subject headings:

Civil Rights	Discrimination
Constitutional Law	Homosexuals
Crimes Without Victims	Lesbians
Criminal Law	Sex Offenders
Deviant Behavior	Sodomy

INDEX TO LEGAL PERIODICALS (ILP)
In the ILP, look for references to legal periodical literature under the following subject headings:

Behavior Modification	Discrimination
Civil Rights	Freedom of Association
Civil Service	Homosexuality
Constitutional Law	Sex Crime
Criminal Law	Transsexualism

HONDURAS

SEE ALSO: International Law, Latin America, United Nations

**RESEARCH GUIDES &
BIBLIOGRAPHIES:**   *A Guide to the Official Publications of Honduras* (Library of Congress, 1947).
Honduras Bibliography and Research Guide by C. Danby & R. Swedberg
    (Cambridge, MA: Central America Information Office, 1984).

**TREATISES &
LOOSELEAFS:**   *Capital Formation and Investment Incentives Around the World* (Honduras) by
    W. Diamond & D. Diamond (Matthew Bender, 1984–).
Digest of Commercial Laws of the World (Honduras) (Natl. Assn. of Credit
    Management; Oceana, 1977–).
Honduras: A Crisis on the Border (NY: Lawyers Committee for Intl. Human Rights,
    1985).
Information Guide: Doing Business in Honduras (Price Waterhouse).
Latin America . . . A Tax Tour (Honduras) (Arthur Anderson & Co., 1985).
A Statement of the Laws of Honduras in Matters Affecting Business (Organization of
    American States, 1981).
Tax Laws of the World—Honduras (FL: Foreign Tax Law Assn.).

ARTICLES: "Honduras" (Human Rights in the World), *International Commission of Jurists Review*
    6 (1982).
"Latin American Tax Update: Honduras" by M. Marti, 12 *Lawyer of the Americas* 654
    (1980).

HONG KONG

SEE ALSO: Asia, International Law, United Nations

**RESEARCH GUIDE &
BIBLIOGRAPHY:**   *Legal Literature in Hong Kong* by P. Wesley-Smith (Univ. of Hong Kong, 1979).

TREATIES: "People's Republic of China-United Kingdom: Agreement on the Future of Hong Kong," 23 *International Legal Materials* 1366 (1984).

JOURNALS & OTHER PERIODICALS: *Hong Kong Current Law* (Hong Kong: Sweet & Maxwell, 1985–).
Hong Kong Law Journal (Gaunt, 1971–).

TREATISES & LOOSELEAFS: *Asia and the Pacific: A Tax Tour* (Hong Kong) Arthur Anderson & Co., 1986).
Capital Formation and Investment Incentives Around the World (Hong Kong) by W. Diamond & D. Diamond (Matthew Bender, 1984–).
Commercial, Business, and Trade Laws: Hong Kong (Oceana, 1982–).
Hong Kong Current Law (London: Sweet & Maxwell, 1985–).
Hong Kong Revenue Law by P. Willoughby (Matthew Bender, 1981–).
Hong Kong Taxation: Law and Practice by D. Flux (Hong Kong: Chinese Univ. Press, 1984).
Industrial Relations and Law in Hong Kong by J. England & J. Rear (Oxford Univ. Press, 1981).
Information Guide: Doing Business in Hong Kong (Price Waterhouse).
The Law of Intellectual and Industrial Property in Hong Kong by M. Pendleton (Butterworths, 1984).
Taxes and Investment in Asia and the Pacific (Hong Kong) (Amsterdam: Intl. Bureau of Fiscal Documentation, 1983–).
Tax Havens Encyclopedia (Hong Kong) by B. Spitz (Butterworths, 1975–).
Tax Laws of the World—Hong Kong (FL: Foreign Tax Law Assn.).

ARTICLES: "Hong Kong's Future: Can the People's Republic of China Invalidate the Treaty of Nanking as an Unequal Treaty?" by K. Greenberg, 7 *Fordham International Law Journal* 534 (1984).
"Hong Kong Under the Chinese Revolution" by W. Clarke, 14 *Hong Kong Law Journal* 71 (1984).
"A Requiem for Chinese Customary Law in Hong Kong" by D. Lewis, 32 *International & Comparative Law Quarterly* 347 (1983).
"Self-Determination in Hong Kong" by E. Amberg, 22 *San Diego Law Review* 839 (1985).
"The Transition from British to Chinese Rule in Hong Kong" by R. Mushkat, 14 *Denver Journal of International Law & Policy* 171 (1986).
"Understanding the Hong Kong Tax System" by A. Au-Yeung, 8 *The International Tax Journal* 337 (1981–82).

HORSE: See Agriculture, Animals, Art & Entertainment, Sports Law
HOSPITAL: See Health & Medicine, Mental Health, State & Local Government
HOSTAGES: See Terrorism
HOURS: See Employee Benefits, Labor Law
HOUSE OF REPRESENTATIVES: See Legislative History
HOUSING: See Civil Rights, Real Estate, State & Local Government, Zoning & Land Planning

HUMAN EXPERIMENTATION, GENETICS & BIOETHICS

SEE ALSO: Criminal Law, Death, Health & Medicine, Jurisprudence, Mental Health, Torts

RESEARCH GUIDES & BIBLIOGRAPHIES: *Bibliography of Bioethics* (Free Press, 1975–).

Bibliography of Bioethics, L. Waters, ed. (Georgetown Institute of Ethics, 1985).
"Bibliography on Human Experimentation" by M. Voges, 73 *Law Library Journal* 986 (1980).

JOURNALS: *Journal of Bioethics* (Human Sciences Press, 1983–).

LOOSELEAFS & TREATISES:

Bioethics Reporter by J. Childress (Univ. Pubs. of America, 1983–).
BioLaw: A Legal and Ethical Reporter (Univ. Pubs. of America).
Biotechnology and the Law by I. Cooper (Clark Boardman, 1982–).
Encyclopedia of Bioethics, R. Reich, ed. (Free Press, 1978).
Genetics and Man's Future: Legal, Social and Moral Implications of Genetic Engineering by M. Santos (Thomas, 1981).
Genetics and the Law II, A. Milunsky, ed. (Plenum Press, 1980).
Genetics, Ethics, and the Law by G. Smith (Associated Faculty Press, 1981).
The Human Body and the Law: Legal and Ethical Considerations in Human Experimentation, 2d ed. by C. Levy (Oceana, 1983).
Human Experimentation by B. Reams (Oceana, 1985–).
Reflections on Medicine, Biotechnology and the Law by Z. Cowen (Univ. of Nebraska Press, 1986)

HUMAN REPRODUCTION: See Family Law, Health & Medicine, Women & the Law

HUMAN RIGHTS

SEE ALSO: Africa, Asia, Caribbean, Civil Rights, Constitutional Law, Indians, International Law, Jurisprudence, Latin America; see also entries under individual countries

RESEARCH GUIDES & BIBLIOGRAPHIES:

A Bibliography of Selected Human Rights Bibliographies . . . by E. Stanek (Monticello, IL: Vance Bibliographies, 1987).
Human Rights: A Topical Bibliography by Columbia Univ. Center for the Study of Human Rights (Westview, 1983).
"Human Rights Law: A Research Guide to the Literature" by D. Vincent-Davies, 14 *New York University Journal of International Law and Policy* 209, 487 (1981–82).
"Human Rights Research in Periodicals" by H. Hood, 13 *Vanderbilt Journal of Transnational Law* 519 (1980).

JOURNALS, NEWSLETTERS & OTHER PERIODICALS:

Checklist of Human Rights Documents (Austin: Univ. of Texas Tarlton Law Library, 1976–).
Columbia Human Rights Law Review (1967–).
Human Rights (ABA, 1970–).
Human Rights Law Journal (N. P. Engel, 1980–).
Human Rights Quarterly (Johns Hopkins Univ. Press, 1979–).
Human Rights: Research and Education Bulletin (Univ. of Ottawa, Human Rights Centre, 1984–).
Human Rights Review (Oxford Univ. Press, 1976–).
The International League for Human Rights (NY, 1981/83–).
LAWASIA Human Rights Newsletter (Sydney: LAWASIA Human Rights Comm., 1986–).
South African Journal of Human Rights (Ravan Press, 1985–).
Yearbook on Human Rights (UN Publications, 1946–).

DIRECTORY:	*Human Rights Organizations and Periodicals Directory,* 5th ed. by D. Christiano (Meiklejohn Civil Liberties Institute, 1983).
LOOSELEAFS:	*Human Rights: The Inter-American System,* T. Buergenthal, ed. (Oceana, 1982–). *Human Rights: The International Petition System* by M. Tardu (Oceana, 1979–). *International Human Rights Instruments* by R. Lillich (Hein, 1982–). *International Human Rights: Law and Practice* (ABA, Prof. Education Pub., 1978–). *The Regulation of Statelessness under International and National Law* by P. Mutharika (Oceana, 1977–). *Universal Human Rights* (Stanfordville, NY: Earl M. Coleman, 1979–).
TREATISES:	*Basic Documents on Human Rights,* 2d ed., I. Brownlie, ed. (Oxford Univ. Press, 1981). *Essays on Human Rights in the Helsinki Process,* A. Bloed, ed. (Martinus Nijhoff, 1985). *European Human Rights Convention in Domestic Law* by A. Drzemczewski (Oxford Univ. Press, 1983). *Human Rights and Human Diversity: An Essay in the Philosophy of Human Rights* by A. Milne (Albany: State Univ. of N.Y. Press, 1986). *Human Rights in Third World Perspective* by T. Franck (Oceana, 1982). *Human Rights: Status of International Instruments* (UN Publications, 1987). *International Human Rights in a Nutshell* by T. Buergenthal (West, 1988). *The International Law of Human Rights* by P. Sieghart (Oxford Univ. Press, 1984). *The Lawful Rights of Mankind: An Introduction to the International Legal Code of Human Rights* by P. Sieghart (Oxford Univ. Press, 1985). *Prevention of Genocide* by L. Kuper (Yale Univ. Press, 1985).

HUMAN RIGHTS AMENDMENT: See Abortion

HUNGARY

SEE ALSO:	Communism, Soviet Union, Europe, International Law, United Nations
RESEARCH GUIDE & BIBLIOGRAPHY:	"Hungarian Legal Institutions and Their Publications: A Legal Bibliography with Translations and Annotations" by S. Csaky, 75 *Law Library Journal* 490 (1982).
CONSTITUTION:	*The Constitutions of the Communist World* (Hungary), W. Simons, ed. (Sijthoff & Noordhoff, 1980).
TREATIES & OTHER AGREEMENTS:	*Aviation Laws and Treaties of . . . the German Democratic Republic, Hungary, the Democratic People's Republic of Korea, Laos, Poland, the USSR, Yugoslavia and the Republic of Vietnam* (6 vols.) by J. Kneifel (Munich: J. Kneifel, 1985). Bulgaria . . . German Democratic Republic . . . Hungary . . . Mongolia . . . Agreement on the Establishment of the International Investment Bank and Statutes of the Bank, 23 *International Legal Materials* 641 (1984).
JOURNALS & OTHER PERIODICALS:	*Hungarian Law Review* (Budapest: Hungarian Lawyers' Assn.).
TREATISES & LOOSELEAFS:	*Administrative Secrecy in Developed Countries* (Hungary) by D. Rpwat (Columbia Univ. Press, 1979).

Digest of Commercial Laws of the World (Hungary) (Natl. Assn. of Credit
Management; Oceana, 1966–).
Digest of Commercial Laws of the World (Hungary) (Natl. Assn. of Credit
Management; Oceana, 1977–).
Doing Business with Eastern Europe (NY: Business Intl. Corp., 1975–).
Employment and Wage Policies in Poland, Czechoslovakia, and Hungary Since 1950
by J. Adam (London: Macmillan, 1984).
Legal Aspects of Joint Ventures in Eastern Europe (Hungary). D. Campbell, ed.
(Deventer, 1981).
The Legal Effects of a Revolution by W. Slyom-Fekete (Library of Congress, 1982).
Questions of International Law: Hungarian Perspectives, H. Bokor-Szego (S. Simon,
transl.) (Budapest: Akademiai Kiado, 1988).
Taxation in European Socialist Countries (vol. 5, Hungary) (Amsterdam: Intl. Bureau
of Fiscal Documentation).
Travel Abroad and Emigration Under New Rules Adopted by Hungary (Library of
Congress, 1979).

ARTICLES:

"Hungary: Legal Education" by K. Bard, 5 *Comparative Law Yearbook* 83 (1981).
"Hungary: Toward a Strengthening of Marriage" by M. Soltesz, 26 *Journal of Family
Law* 113 (1987–88).
"The Law on Economic Competition and Restraints of Trade in Hungary" by I. Voros,
24 *Ind. Prop.* 354 (1985).
"Legal Aspects of Doing Business with and in Hungary" by L. Schmidt, 15 *Vanderbilt
Journal of Transnational Law* 253 (1982).
"Legal Framework of the Economic and Foreign Trade System of Hungary and other
CMEA Countries" by I. Szasz, 10 *International Business Lawyer* 99 (1982).
"New Business Opportunity for Foreign Investors" by M. Mijoule, *Tax Management
International Journal* 10 (Feb., 1979).
"The Organization of Forensic Medicine and the Function of the Medicolegal Expert
in Hungary" by I. Fazekas, 2 *Case Western Reserve Journal of International Law*
19 (1970).
"The Role and Functions of Legal Professions in Hungary" by L. Nvai, 11
International Journal of the Sociology of the Law 219 (1983).
"Trademark Infringement Law and Practice in Hungary" by A. Vida, 75 *Trademark
Reporter* 86 (1985).
"Transport Law in Hungary" by J. Maly, 10 *International Business Lawyer* 18 (1982).

HUNGER: See Food, Poverty Law, Social Security
HUSBAND & WIFE: See Estate Planning, Family Law, Women & the Law
HYDROELECTRIC POWER: See Energy, Natural Resources, Oil & Gas, Water Law
HYPNOSIS: See Forensic Science

ICC: See Transportation

ICELAND

SEE ALSO: International Law, Scandinavian Law, United Nations

**TREATIES &
OTHER AGREEMENTS:** "Iceland-Norway: Agreement on the Continental Shelf …," 21 *International Legal Materials* 1222 (1982).

**TREATISES &
LOOSELEAFS:** *Digest of Commercial Laws of the World* (Iceland) (Natl. Assn. of Credit Management; Oceana, 1977–).
Labor Law and Practice in Iceland by F. Groemping (Bureau of Labor Statistics Report; Govt. Printing Office, 1970).
Laws of Early Iceland: by A. Dennis (Canada: Univ. of Manitoba Press, 1980).

ARTICLES: "Avoiding Legal Judgment: The Submission of Disputes to Arbitration in Medieval Iceland" by I. Miller, 28 *American Journal of Legal History* 95 (1984).
"Changing Characteristics of Homicide in Iceland" by G. Gudjonsson, 26 *Medicine, Science, and the Law* 299 (1986) (see also vol. 22, p. 91).
"Islandic Law" by L. Orfield, 56 *Dickinson Law Review* 42 (1951).
"The Nature of Shoplifting in Iceland" by G. Gudjonsson, 19 *Forensic Science International* 209 (1982).
"Prohibition of Beer in Iceland" by H. Gunnlaugsson, 20 *Law & Society Review* 335 (1986).

IDAHO

SEE ALSO: Circuit Courts (Ninth Circuit), Community Property

**STATUTES & OTHER
LEGISLATIVE MATERIALS:** *Idaho Code* (Bobbs-Merrill).
Session Laws, Idaho (Secretary of State; Caxton).
CCH Advance Session Laws Reporter. Idaho.
Idaho Legislative Report (JAG Corp.).

COURT OPINIONS: *Idaho Reports* (1866–).
Pacific Reporter (1881–).

COURT RULES: *Idaho Court Rules* (Michie, 1980).

JURY INSTRUCTIONS: *Idaho Jury Instructions* (Idaho State Bar, 1982–).

**COURT
ADMINISTRATION:** *Judicial Reports* (Supreme Court).

**OPINIONS OF THE
ATTORNEY GENERAL:** *Attorney General Opinions* (Attorney General).

**JOURNALS & OTHER
PERIODICALS:** *The Advocate Newsletter* (Idaho State Bar).

SURVEY OF STATE LAW: "Survey of Developments in Idaho Law" in *Idaho Law Review*. See, for example, vol. 14, p. 235; vol. 20, p. 365.

**TREATISES, LOOSELEAFS &
OTHER MONOGRAPHS:** *Community Property Law of Idaho* (Idaho Law Foundation, 1982).
Idaho Estate Planning Deskbook by E. Ahrens (Idaho Law Foundation, 1983).

Idaho Family Law Handbook, P. Buser, ed. (Idaho Law Foundation, 1981).
Idaho Pre-trial Civil Procedure by C. Lewis (Idaho Law Foundation, 1977).
Idaho Probate System Book (Idaho Law Foundation, 1977).
Permit Requirements for Development of Energy... for the State of Idaho (Office of the Governor, 1981).
State Tax Reporter (Idaho) (CCH).

DIGESTS & CITATOR: *Idaho Digest* (West).
Pacific Digest (West).
Idaho Advance Annotation Service (Michie).
Shepard's Idaho Citations.

IDENTIFICATION: See Criminal Law, Forensic Science
ILLEGITIMATE CHILDREN: See Estate Planning, Family Law, Juvenile Law

ILLINOIS

SEE ALSO: Circuit Courts (Seventh Circuit)

RESEARCH GUIDES & BIBLIOGRAPHIES: *Illinois Legal Research Sourcebook* by R. Jacobs et al. (Ill. Inst. Cont. Legal Ed., 1977).
Legal Research and Writing: A Guide for Illinois & Federal Law by M. Merzon (Ill. Bar, 1985).
Reseach in Illinois Law by B. Davies (Oceana, 1954).

STATUTES & OTHER LEGISLATIVE MATERIALS: *Illinois Advance Session Laws* (CCH).
Illionis Legislative Service (West).
Illinois Revised Statutes.
Laws of Illinois.
Smith-Hurd Illinois Annotated Statutes.

STATE ADMINISTRATIVE REGULATIONS: *Illinois Administrative Code.*
Illinois Register.

COURT OPINIONS: *Illinois Appellate Court Reports* (1977–).
Illinois Court of Claims Reports (1889–).
Illinois Courts Bulletin (Ill. Bar, 1955–).
Illinois Reports (1849–)
North Eastern Reporter (1885–).

COURT RULES: *Illinois Code of Civil Procedure and Court Rules* (West).
Illinois Court Rule Book, 3d ed. (Law Bulletin Pub. Co.)
Illinois Rules and Practice Handbook, 2d ed. (Pantagraph Printing Co., 1982–).

JURY INSTRUCTIONS: *Illinois Jury Instructions* (Burdette Smith, 1951).
Illinois Pattern Jury Instructions—Civil, 2d ed. (West, 1986).
Illinois Pattern Jury Instructions—Criminal, 2d ed. (West, 1987).

ETHICS & PROFESSIONAL RESPONSIBILITY: *Legal Advertising: The Illinois Experiment* (ABA, 1984).

Opinions on Professional Ethics (Ill. Bar, 1980).
Professional Liability (Ill. Bar, 1982).

**OPINIONS OF THE
ATTORNEY GENERAL:** *Attorney General Opinion Service* (Fidlar and Chambers).

**JOURNALS & OTHER
PERIODICALS:** *Chicago Bar Record* (1910–).
Chicago Daily Law Bulletin.
Illinois Bar Journal (1912–).
Illinois Family Law Report (1978–).
Illinois Jury Verdict Reporter (1963–).

SURVEY OF STATE LAW: "Supreme Court of Illinois Review" in *University of Illinois Law Forum.* See, for example, vol. 1976, p. 116; vol. 1980, p. 425.

**TREATISES, LOOSELEAFS
& OTHER MONOGRAPHS:** *Callaghan's Illinois Legal Forms With Tax Notes* (Callaghan, 1982).
CCH State Tax Reporter, Illinois.
Chicago Lawyers: The Social Structure of the Bar by J. Heinz & E. Laumann (American Bar Foundation, 1983).
Cleary and Graham's Handbook of Illinois Evidence, 4th ed. by M. Graham, (Little, Brown, 1984–).
Estate Planning and Administration in Illinois, 2d ed. by R. Hunter (Lawyers Co-op., 1981).
Illinois Civil Trial Evidence (Ill. Bar, 1983–).
Illinois Criminal Practice (Ill. Bar, 1980–).
Illinois Estate Administration (Ill. Bar, 1981–).
Illinois Lawyer's Manual, 3d ed. by B. Becker (Callaghan, 1975–).
Illinois Natural Resources Law by R. Beck (Butterworths, 1985).
Illinois Product Liability Practice (Ill. Bar, 1980).
Illinois Tort Law by M. Polelle (Butterworths, 1986).
Illinois Uniform Commerical Code Forms by W. Davenport (West, 1967).
Kenoe on Land Trusts (Ill. Bar, 1981–).

**DIGESTS, ENCYCLOPEDIA
& CITATOR:** *Illinois Digest* (Callaghan).
Illinois Digest, 2d.
Illinois Law and Practice (West).
Illinois Law Finder (West).
Shepard's Illinois Citations.

ILL, MENTALLY: See Mental Health
ILLNESS: See Death, Health & Medicine
ILO: See Czechoslovakia

IMMIGRATION LAW

SEE ALSO: Civil Rights, Constitutional Law, Criminal Law, Human Rights, International Law, Labor Law, United Nations

**RESEARCH GUIDES &
BIBLIOGRAPHIES:**
"Immigration Law" in *Specialized Legal Research,* L.Chanin, ed. (Little, Brown, 1987).
"Immigration Law and Practice" by E. Schander, 5 *International Journal of Law
Libraries* 228 (1977).
"Introduction to Immigration Law Materials and Where to Find Them" by
M. Churgin, 3 *Legal References Services Quarterly* 73 (1983).
"Research Guide to Immigration, Aliens, and the Law" by S. Pagel, 77 *Law Library
Journal* 466 (1984–85).

LEGISLATIVE HISTORY:
Immigration and Nationality Acts. Legislative Histories and Related Documents,
O. Trelles & J. Bailey, eds. (Hein, 1979).
Legislative History of the Immigration and Naturalization Act of 1981 (Major Briefs
Congressional Research Service).

**ADMINISTRATIVE
DECISIONS &
COURT OPINIONS:**
Administrative Decisions under Immigration and Nationality Laws (Dept. of Justice,
Board of Immigration Appeals).
Federal Immigration Law Reporter (CCH, 1982–).
Hein's Interim Decision Service.
Immigration-Labor Certification Reporter (Matthew Bender, 1981–85).
Immigration Law and Procedure Reporter (Matthew Bender, 1985–).
Interim Decisions (Dept. of Justice, Board of Immigration Appeals).
United States Immigration Reports (Wash. D.C.: Stetson Butler, 1984–).

**PUBLICATIONS OF THE
IMMIGRATION AND
NATURALIZATION
SERVICE:**
Annual Report of the Immigration and Naturalization Service (INS).
Basic Guide to Naturalization, Form M–230 (INS).
Deportation Officer Handbook (INS).
Documentary Requirements for Aliens in the United States, Form M–97 (INS).
Examination Handbook (INS, 1982–).
Guide to Immigration Benefits, Form M–210 (INS).
Immigration Detention Officer Handbook (1987).
Law of Arrest, Search and Seizure for Immigration Officers (INS).
Naturalization Procedures for Clerks of Court, Form M–77 (INS).
Operations, Instructions, Regulations, and Interpretations (INS, 1979–).
Statistical Yearbook of the Immigration and Naturalization Service (INS).
Student and School Regulations, Form M–242 (INS).

**JOURNALS, NEWSLETTERS,
& OTHER PERIODICALS:**
Georgetown Immigration Law Journal (1985–).
Immigration and Nationality Law Review (Hein, 1976–).
Immigration Journal (NY: Assn. of Immigration and Nationality Lawyers, 1979–).
Immigration Law Report (Clark Boardman, 1981–).
Immigration Newsletter (Natl. Lawyers Guild, Natl. Immigration Project, 1971–).
In Defense of the Alien (NY: Center for Migration Studies, 1978–).
INS Reporter (Immigration and Naturalization Service, 1976–).
International Journal of Refugee Law (Oxford University Press, 1989–).
International Migration Review (NY: Center for Migration Studies, 1966–).
Interpreter Releases (Amer. Council for Nationalities Service).
Refugee Reports (Wash. D.C.: Amer. Council for Nationalities Service, 1980–).

San Diego Law Review (see first issue since vol. 13, 1975).
Transnational Immigration Law Reporter (Palo Alto Intl. Common Law Exchange Society, 1979–).

INSTITUTES, SYMPOSIA:
Advanced Immigration Workshop (Practicing Law Institute).
Annual Immigration and Naturalization Institute (Practicing Law Institute).
Annual Immigration and Naturalization Symposium (Los Angeles County Bar Assn.).
Immigration and Nationality Law: Symposium of the American Immigration Lawyers Association (Law & Business, Inc.).

LOOSELEAFS:
The Alien under American Law by P. Mutharika (Oceana, 1980–).
Employers' Immigration Compliance Guide by R. Klasko (Matthew Bender, 1987–).
Immigration Law and Business by A. Fragomen et al. (Clark Boardman, 1983–).
Immigration Law and Crimes by the Natl. Immigration Project of the Natl. Lawyers Guild (Clark Boardman, 1984–).
Immigration Law and Defense by the Natl. Immigration Project of the Natl. Lawyers Guild (Clark Boardman, 1979–).
Immigration Law and Procedure by C. Gordon & H. Rosenfield (Matthew Bender, 1966–).
Immigration Law and Procedure: Desk Edition by C. & E. Gordon (Matthew Bender, 1980–).
Immigration Law Service (Lawyers Co-op., 1985–).

TREATISES:
Getting into America: The United States Visa and Immigration Handbook by H. Deutsch (Random House, 1984).
Handbook for Employers (CCH, 1987).
Handling Immigration Cases by B. Hing (Wiley, 1985).
History of the Immigration and Naturalization Service by S. Masanz (Congressional Research Service; GPO, 1980).
Immigration Compliance in Employment and Business by P. Zulkie (Callaghan, 1987).
Immigration Law and Practice, 3d ed. (ALI–ABA Comm. on Cont. Prof. Ed., 1979).
Immigration Law and Procedure in a Nutshell by D. Weissbrodt (West, 1984).
Immigration Procedures Handbook by A. Fragomen et al. (Clark Boardman, 1987).
Immigration: Process and Policy by T. Aleinikoff, (West, 1985).
Litigating the Asylum Case by I. Kurzban (Natl. Lawyers Guild, 1981).
Outline on Appellate Practice Before the Board of Immigration Appeals (NY: Lawyers Comm. for Intl. Human Rights, 1983).
Review of the U.S. Refugee Resettlement Programs and Policies by C. Moore (Congressional Research Service; GPO, 1980).
Steel on Immigration Law by R. Steel (Lawyers Co-op., 1985).
Taxation of Foreign Nationals by the United States (NY: Deloitte, Haskins & Sells, 1984).
United States Immigration for Businesses, Investors, and Workers by A. Gellman et al. (Hein, 1981).
U.S. Immigration Law and Policy (Congressional Research Service; GPO, 1979).

CITATORS & DIGESTS:
Danilov's U.S. Immigration Law Citator by D. Danilov (Butterworths, 1981–).
Patel's Citations of Administrative Decisions under Immigration and Nationality Laws by P. Patel (NY: Legal Research Bureau, 1982–).
Patel's Digest of Administrative Decisions under Immigration and Nationality Laws by P. Patel (Clark Boardman, 1982–).

Patel's Immigration Law Digest: Digest of Opinions in Immigration and Naturalization Cases by P. Patel (Lawyers Co-op., 1985–).
Shepard's Immigration and Naturalization Citations.

ENCYCLOPEDIAS:
AMERICAN JURISPRUDENCE 2D (Am Jur 2d)
Check the following topics in the *General Index* volumes for Am Jur 2d:

Administrative Law	Constitutional Law
Aliens and Citizens	Due Process
Civil Rights	

CORPUS JURIS SECUNDUM (CJS)
Check the following topics in the *General Index* volumes for CJS:

Administrative Bodies	Immigration
Alien	Nationality
Civil Rights	Naturalization
Constitutional Law	Passports and Visas
Discrimination	

DIGESTS:
CASE SEARCH IN WEST DIGESTS BY KEY TOPIC
In the *Descriptive Word Index* of the West digests, look for key topics and numbers under the following subject headings:

Administrative Law	Immigration
Aliens	Nationality
Civil Rights	Naturalization
Constitutional Law	Passports
Discrimination	

ALR:
ANNOTATIONS
Check the index volumes for ALR, ALR2d, ALR3d, ALR4th, and ALR Fed for annotations under the following subject headings:

Administrative Law	Immigration and
Aliens	Nationality Act
Deportation	Naturalization
Due Process of Law	

PERIODICALS:
CURRENT LAW INDEX (CLI) & LEGAL RESOURCE INDEX (LRI)
In the CLI and LRI, look for references to periodical literature under the following subject headings:

Administrative Law	Emigration and
Admission of	Immigration
Nonimmigrant	Identification Cards
Alien Labor	Naturalization
Aliens	Refugees
Citizenship	Taxation of Aliens
Deportation	United States Immigration
	and Naturalization Service

INDEX TO LEGAL PERIODICALS (ILP)
In the ILP, look for references to legal periodical literature under the following subject headings:

Administrative Law	Citizens
Alien Property	Civil Rights
Aliens	Constitutional Law
Asylum	Deportation

Discrimination	Fraud
Emigration and	International Law
Immigration	Naturalization
Foreign Agents in the	Refugees
United States	

IMMUNITY: See Family Law, International Law, State & Local Government, Torts

IMMUNOLOGY: See AIDS, Forensic Science, Health & Medicine

IMPAIRMENT OF CONTRACTS: See Constitutional Law, Contracts

IMPEACHMENT: See Constitutional Law, Trial & Appellate Practice

IMPLEADER: See Trial & Appellate Practice

IMPLIED CONSENT: See Contracts, Equity, Torts

IMPLIED CONTRACTS: See Contracts, Equity

IMPLIED POWERS: See Constitutional Law

IMPLIED WARRANTY: See Contracts, Torts, Uniform Commercial Code

IMPORT: See Customs, International Law, Maritime Law

IMPOSSIBILITY: See Contracts, Equity

IMPOTENCY: See Family Law, Health & Medicine

IMPRISONMENT: See Corrections, Criminal Law, Torts

IMPROVEMENTS: See Real Estate

IMPUTED NEGLIGENCE: See Torts

INCAPACITY: See Contracts, Family Law, Mental Health

INCEST: See Criminal Law, Family Law

INCOME TAXATION: See Employee Benefits, Estate Planning, State & Local Government, Taxation

INCOMPATIBILITY: See Family Law

INCOMPETENT: See Family Law, Mental Health, Trial & Appellate Practice

INCONTESTABLE: See Insurance

INCORPORATION: See Corporate Law, Nonprofit Corporations, State & Local Government

INCORPOREAL HEREDITAMENT: See Estate Planning

INDECENCY: See Media Law

INDECENT ASSAULT: See Criminal Law

INDEMNITY: See Architecture, Contracts, Government Contracts, Insurance, Torts, Trial & Appellate Practice

INDEPENDENCE: See International Law

INDEPENDENT COLLEGES: See Education Law

INDEPENDENT CONTRACTOR: See Agency, Architecture, Business Law, Contracts, Torts

INDEPENDENT PARALEGAL: See Paralegal

INDEPENDENT SCHOOL DISTRICTS: See Education Law, State & Local Government

INDETERMINATE SENTENCE: See Criminal Law

INDIA

SEE ALSO: Asia, International Law, Islam, United Nations

RESEARCH GUIDE & BIBLIOGRAPHY: *Indian Legal Materials: A Bibliographic Guide* by H. Jain (Oceana, 1970).

CASES: *All India Criminal Law Reporter* (Chandigarh: Jagjit Singh Chawla, 1983–).
Index to Case Law by J. Arora (Chandigarh: Punjab Law Agency, 1985–).

**JOURNALS & OTHER
PERIODICALS:**

Commerical Law Gazette (Delhi: Commercial Law Gazette, 1978–).

Delhi Law Review (1972–).

Index to Indian Legal Periodicals (New Delhi: Indian Law Institute, 1963 –).

Indian Journal of International Law (New Delhi: The Indian Society of Intl. Law, 1960–).

Indian Year Book of International Law (Madras, India: Indian Society Group of Intl. Affairs, 1952–).

International Law Reporter (New Delhi: Intl. Law Publishers, Corp., 1970–).

Journal of the Bar Council of India (1981–).

Journal of the Indian Law Institute (1961–).

**TREATISES &
LOOSELEAFS:**

Asia and the Pacific: A Tax Tour (India) (Arthur Anderson & Co., 1986).

Business Law in India by S. Sengupta (Oxford Univ. Press, 1979).

Capital Formation and Investment Incentives Around the World (India) by W. Diamond & D. Diamond (Matthew Bender, 1984–).

Company Failures in India by S. Vijaya (Delhi: New Heights Publishers & Distributors, 1976).

Digest of Commercial Laws of the World (India) (Natl. Assn. of Credit Management; Oceana, 1977–).

India: A Country Study (GPO, 1986).

Indian Legal System by The Indian Law Institute (Oceana, 1978).

Industrial Licensing by L. Kamar (New Delhi: Indu Pubs., 1983).

Information Guide: Doing Business in India (Price Waterhouse).

Introduction to the Constitution of India, 9th ed. by D. Das Basu (Prentice-Hall of India, 1982).

The Judicial and Legislative Systems in India by K. Nehra (Library of Congress, 1981).

The Law of Torts by R. Iyer (Bombay: N.M. Tripathi, 1975).

Mulla on the Law of Insolvency in India by D. Mulla (Bombay: N.M. Tripathi, 1977).

Patent Law, 2d ed. by P. Narayanan (Calcutta: Eastern Law House, 1985).

Readings in the Constitutional History of India, 1757–1947, S. V. Desika Char., ed. (Delhi: Oxford, 1983).

The Republic of India: The Development of its Laws and Constitution by A. Gledhill (Greenwood Press, 1951).

The Sino-Indian Border Dispute: A Legal Study by C. Lu (Greenwood Press, 1986).

Taxes and Investment in Asia and the Pacific (India) (Amersterdam: Intl. Bureau of Fiscal Documentation, 1983–).

Tax Laws of the World—India (FL: Foreign Tax Law Assn.).

ARTICLES:

"India: Legal Education" by P. Anklesaria, 5 *Comparative Law Yearbook* 103 (1981).

"India's Compulsory Sterilization Laws" by D. Castetter, 8 *California Western International Law Journal* 342 (1978).

"Taxation Aspects of Foreign Investments in India" by U. Singh, 11 *Georgia Journal of International & Comparative Law* 133 (1981)

INDIANA

SEE ALSO:

Circuit Courts (Seventh Circuit)

**RESEARCH GUIDES &
BIBLIOGRAPHIES:**

Checklist of Indiana State Documents (Ind. State Library, 1973–).

An Introduction to Indiana State Publications for the Law Librarian by L. Fariss & K. Buckley (Amer. Assn. of Law Libraries, 1982).

1978 Model Bibliography of Indiana Legal Materials by S. Taylor & K. Welker (Ind. State Library).

STATUTES & OTHER
LEGISLATIVE MATERIALS: *Indiana Code.*

Burns Indiana Statutes Annotated Code Edition (Bobbs-Merrill).

Annotated Indiana Code (West).

Acts, Indiana.

West's Indiana Legislative Service.

CCH Advance Session Laws Reports. Indiana

Daily Legislative Service (Ind. State Chamber of Commerce, 1946–).

STATE ADMINISTRATIVE
REGULATIONS: *Indiana Administrative Code* (Indiana Leg. Council, 1984).

Indiana Register (Legislative Services Agency, 1978–).

COURT OPINIONS: *Indiana Reports* (1848–1981).

North Eastern Reporter (1885–).

COURT RULES: *Indiana Rules of Court* (West).

Indiana Rules of Procedure Annotated by W. Harvey (West, 1987).

JURY INSTRUCTIONS: *Indiana Pattern Jury Instructions: Civil* (Michie, 1968).

Indiana Pattern Jury Instructions: Criminal (Michie, 1980).

OPINIONS OF THE
ATTORNEY GENERAL: *Annual Reports and Official Opinions of Attorney General* (Off. of Atty. Gen., 1882–).

JOURNALS & OTHER
PERIODICALS: *Indianapolis Commercial.*

Res Gestae (Ind. State Bar, 1956–).

DIRECTORY: *Indiana Legal Directory* (Legal Directories Pub., 1935–).

TREATISES, LOOSELEAFS
& OTHER MONOGRAPHS: *Administrative Law* (Ind., Cont. Legal Ed., 1983).

Bankruptcy (Ind. Cont. Legal Ed., 1981).

CCH State Tax Reporter. Indiana.

Estate Planning and Administration in Indiana (Ind. State Bar, 1979).

Ewbanks Indiana Criminal Law, 3d ed. by F. Symmes (Bobbs-Merrill, 1956).

Henty's Probate Law and Practice, 7th ed. by J. Grimes (Bobbs-Merrill, 1978).

Indiana Appellate Procedure by B. Bagni (West, 1979).

Indiana Corporate Practice Manual by L. Richie (Michie, 1983).

Indiana Evidence by R. Miller (West, 1984).

Indiana Forms of Pleading and Practice by C. Thompson (Matthew Bender, 1972–).

Indiana Legal Business Forms by C. Peeples (West, 1967).

Indiana Police Officer's Legal Manual (Allen Smith, 1983).

Indiana Procedural Forms by W. Harvey et al. (West, 1973).

Indiana Trial Evidence Manual by J. Tanford (Michie, 1982).

Indiana Uniform Commercial Code Forms by D. Johnson (West, 1986).

The Law of Evidence in Indiana by M. Seidman (Michie, 1977).

Midwest Transactions Guide (Indiana) (Matthew Bender, 1980).

Thompson's Indiana Forms, 3d ed. by H. Grube (Bobbs-Merrill, 1961–).
Work's Indiana Practice, 5th ed. by A. Bobbitt (Anderson, 1973).

DIGESTS, ENCYCLOPEDIA
& CITATOR: *Indiana Digest* (West, 1953–).
Indiana Law Encyclopedia (West, 1957–).
Shepard's Indiana Citations.

INDIANS (NATIVE AMERICANS)

SEE ALSO: Administrative Law, Alaska, Canada, Civil Rights, Constitutional Law, Legal History, Natural Resources, Oil & Gas, Oklahoma, Real Estate, State & Local Government, Water, Zoning & Land Planning

RESEARCH GUIDES &
BIBLIOGRAPHIES: "American Indian Law: Research and Source" by N. Carter, 4 *Legal Reference Services Quarterly* 5 (1984–1985).
American Indian Legal Materials: A Union List by L. Gasaway (Stanfordville, NY: Earl Coleman Enterprises, 1980).
"American Indian Tribal Codes" by S. Lupton, 1 *Legal Reference Services Quarterly* 40 (1981).
"Basic Bibliography for Native American Law" by Dees, 69 *Law Library Journal* 78 (1976).
A Bibliographic Guide to the History of Indian-White Relations in the United States by F. Prucha (Univ. of Chicago Press, 1977).
Guide to Records in the National Archives of the United States Relating to American Indians (GPO, 1981).
Indian-White Relations in the United States: A Bibliography of Works Published 1975–1980 by F. Prucha (Univ. of Nebraska Press, 1982).
National Indian Law Catalog: An Index to Indian Legal Materials and Resources (Boulder: Native American Rights Fund, 1973–).
Native Law Bibliography by L. Fritz (Univ. of Saskatchewan, Native Law Center, 1984).
"Sources of American Indian Law" by R. Strickland, 67 *Law Library Journal* 496 (1974).

CODES, TREATIES, EXECUTIVE
ORDERS, REGULATIONS &
DECISIONS: *American Indian Treaty Series,* 9 vols. (Institute for the Development of Indian Law, 1973).
Annual Report (Indian Claims Commission).
Cases Decided (Indian Claims Commission).
A Chronological List of Treaties and Agreements Made by Indian Tribes with the United States (Institute for the Development of Indian Law, 1973).
Code of Federal Regulations, title 25.
Decisions, Alaska Native Claims Appeals Board (U.S. Dept. of Interior, 1975–82).
Decisions, Indian Claims Commission (1948–78) (Clearwater Pub. Co.) (Microform).
Decisions, Interior Board of Indian Appeals (U.S. Dept. of Interior, 1970–).
Decisions, Interior Board of Land Appeals (U.S. Dept. of Interior, 1970–).
Executive Orders Relating to Indian Reservations, 1855–1922 (GPO, 1912, 1922) (reprint by Scholarly Resources, 1975).

Index to the Decisions of the Indian Claims Commission, N. Ross, ed. (Clearwater Pub. Co., 1973).
Indian Tribal Codes: A Microfiche Collection of Indian Tribal Law Codes, R. Johnson, comp. (Univ. of Wash. Law Library, 1981).
Kappler's Indian Affairs: Laws and Treaties (U.S. Dept. of Interior; GPO, 1979).
Navajo Tribal Code (Equity Pub. Co.).
Opinions of the Solicitor of the Department of the Interior Relating to Indian Affairs, 1917–1974 (GPO, 1979).
United States Code, title 25.
U.S. Indian Claims Commission Decisions, 1948–1978 (Law Library Microform Consortium).

JOURNALS, NEWSLETTERS & OTHER PERIODICALS:
American Indian Journal (Institute for the Development of Indian Law, 1975–).
American Indian Law Newsletter (Univ. of New Mexico, American Indian Law Center, 1968–).
American Indian Law Review (Univ. of Okla. Sch. of Law, 1973–).

TREATISES & LOOSELEAFS:
The American Indian and the United States: A Documentary History, W. Washburn, comp. (Random House, 1973).
American Indian Law in a Nutshell, 2d ed. by W. Canby (West, 1988).
American Indian Tribal Courts: The Costs of Separate Justice by S. Brakel (American Bar Foundation, 1978).
The Bureau of Indian Affairs: Public Policy Toward Indian Citizens by T. Tayler (Westview, 1984).
Felix S. Cohen's Handbook of Federal Indian Law, R. Strickland, ed. (Michie, 1982).
Indian Law Reporter (Oakland: Amerian Indian Lawyer Training Program, 1974–).
Indians of the Americas: Human Rights and Self-Determination by Ortiz (Praeger, 1984).
Protecting Indian Natural Resources by A. Sanders (Boulder: Native American Rights Fund, 1982).

PERIODICALS:
CURRENT LAW INDEX (CLI) & LEGAL RESOURCE INDEX (LRI)
In the CLI and LRI, look for references to periodical literature under the following subject headings:

Apache Indians	Mescalero Indians
Eskimos	Navaho Indians
Indians of North America	

INDICTMENT: See Criminal Law
INDIGENT: See Poverty Law
INDIVIDUAL RETIREMENT ACCOUNT: See Banking Law, Employee Benefits

INDONESIA

SEE ALSO: Asia, International Law, United Nations

RESEARCH GUIDES & BIBLIOGRAPHIES:
Bibliography of Material on Indonesian Law in the English Language, 3d ed. by J. Ball (Sydney: Univ. of Sydney Faculty of Law, 1981).
"Current Legal Research in Indonesia" by T. Radhie, 7 *International Journal of Law Libraries* 211 (1979).

TREATISES & LOOSELEAFS:

Adat Law in Modern Indonesia by M. Hooker (Oxford Univ. Press, 1978).

Asia and the Pacific: A Tax Tour (Indonesia) (Arthur Anderson & Co., 1986).

Capital Formation and Investment Incentives Around the World (Indonesia) by W. Diamond & D. Diamond (Matthew Bender, 1984–).

Digest of Commercial Laws of the World (Indonesia) (Natl. Assn. of Credit Management; Oceana, 1977–).

Fiscal Policy and Tax Structure in Australasia (Indonesia) (Amsterdam: Intl. Bureau of Fiscal Docmentation).

A Guide to Doing Business in the ASEAN Region: Brunei/Indonesia/Malaysia/ Philippines/Singapore/Thailand (U.S. Dept. of Commerce, Intl. Trade Admin., Office of Pacific Basin, 1985).

Indonesia and the Rule of Law, J. Thoolen, ed. (London: Printer Press, 1987).

Information Guide: Doing Business in Indonesia (Price Waterhouse).

An Introduction to Javanese Law by M. Hoadley (Univ. of Arizona Press, 1981).

Investment Laws of the World (Indonesia) (Oceana, 1981–).

Taxes and Investment in Asia and the Pacific (Indonesia) (Amsterdam: Intl. Bureau of Fiscal Documentation, 1983–).

Tax Laws of the World—Indonesia (FL: Foreign Tax Law Assn.).

ARTICLES:

"Company Insolvency in Singapore, Thailand and Indonesia" by R. Singam, *International Business Lawyer* 451 (Nov., 1985).

"Foreign Banking in Indonesia" by R. Hornick, 6 *Northwestern Journal of International Law and Business* 760 (1984).

"Formation of Contract ... Indonesia ..." by O. Lee, 17 *International Lawyer* 257 (1983).

"Issues under Indonesia's New Tax Laws" by R. Hammer, 7 *East Asian Executive Reports* 18 (1985).

"Joint Development of Resources in Indonesia" by A. Granucci, 4 *Journal of Energy & Natural Resources Law* 116 (1986).

"Taxation for Foreigners in Indonesia" by R. Hornick, 1 *International Tax & Business Lawyer* 83 (1983).

INDUSTRIAL BOARDS: See State & Local Government

INDUSTRIAL DISEASES: See Health & Medicine, Occupational Safety

INDUSTRIAL RELATIONS: See Employment Discrimination, Labor Law

INDUSTRIAL TOXINS: See Environmental Law, Occupational Safety, Torts

INDUSTRY: See Business Law, Corporate Law, Labor Law, State & Local Government

INEQUALITY: See Civil Rights, Constitutional Law, Jurisprudence

INFANTICIDE: See Abortion, Criminal Law

INFLATION: See Economics

INFORMATION: See Freedom of Information, Statistics

INFORMATION RETRIEVAL & STORAGE: See Computers, Law Office Management

INFORMED CONSENT: See Health & Medicine, Mental Health, Nursing, Torts

INFORMER: See Criminal Law

INHERITANCE: See Estate Planning, Real Estate, Taxation

INITIATIVE: See Election, State & Local Government

INJUNCTION: See Labor Law, Trial & Appellate Practice

INJURY: See Occupational Safety, Sports Law, Torts, Worker's Compensation

INK: See Forensic Science

IN LOCO PARENTIS: See Family Law, Juvenile Law

INNKEEPER: See Business Law, Torts

INNOCENCE: See Criminal Law
IN PARI MATERIA: See Statutes
IN PERSONAM: See Trial & Appellate Practice
IN REM: See Trial & Appellate Practice
INSANITY: See Age, Criminal Law, Forensic Science, Health & Medicine, Mental Health
INSECTICIDES: See Environmental Law
INSIDER TRADING: See Securities Law, Switzerland
INSOLVENCY: See Banking Law, Bankruptcy
INSPECTION: See Occupational Safety
INSTALLMENT CONTRACTS: See Consumer Law, Contracts, Uniform Commercial Code
INSTITUTIONALIZATION: See Age, Corrections, Health & Medicine, Juvenile Law,
   Mental Health
INSTRUCTIONS TO JURY: See Trial & Appellate Practice
INSUBORDINATION: See Employment Discrimination, Military Law

INSURANCE

SEE ALSO:
Accounting, Age, AIDS, Air & Aviation, Business Law, Consumer Law, Contracts, Corporate Law, Economics, Employee Benefits, Estate Planning, Health & Medicine, Labor Law, Maritime Law, Military Law, Occupational Safety, Real Estate, Torts, Unemployment Compensation, Workers' Compensation

RESEARCH GUIDES & BIBLIOGRAPHIES:
National Index of Insurance Laws, 9th ed. (CA: Natl. Ins. Law Service, 1983–).
National Index of Insurance Regulations, 6th ed. (CA: Natl. Ins. Law Service, 1983–).

JOURNALS, NEWSLETTERS & OTHER PERIODICALS:
Defense Law Journal (Michie).
Federation of Insurance & Corporate Counsel Quarterly (Federation, 1950–).
The Forum (ABA Section of Insurance, Negligence & Compensation Law, 1965–).
Insurance Counsel Journal (Intl. Assn. of Ins. Counsel, 1934–).
Insurance Law Journal (CCH, 1939–).
Insurance Review (NY: Insurance Information Institute, 1984–).
Journal of Insurance Regulation (FL: Natl. Assn. of Insurance Commissioners, 1983–).
Journal of the American Society of CLU (1984–).
National Insurance Law Review (NY: Insurance Information Institute, 1984–).
The Tort and Insurance Law Journal (ABA Tort & Ins. Prac. Sec., 1986–).

DIRECTORIES:
Best's Directory of Recommended Insurance Attorneys, 55th ed. (NJ: A.M. Best Co., 1984).
The Insurance Bar, 58th ed. (Directory) (Bar List Publishing Co., 1983–84).

LOOSELEAFS:
Automobile Law Reports (CCH, 1966–).
Automobile Liability Insurance by I. Schermer (Clark Boardman, 1979–).
Bad Faith Actions: Liability and Damages by S. Ashley (Callaghan, 1984–).
Benefits Review Board Service. (CCH).
Federal Income Taxation of Life Insurance Companies by R. Antes et al. (Matthew Bender, 1984–).
Federal Taxation of Insurance Companies by K. Tucker & D. Van Mieghem (Prentice-Hall, 1983–).
Handling Property and Casualty Claims, R. Cushman & C. Stamm, eds. (Wiley).
Insurance Bad Faith Litigation by W. Shernoff et al. (Matthew Bender, 1984–).

Insurance Guide (Prentice-Hall, 1961–).

Insurance Industry Litigation Reporter (Andrews Pub.).

Insurance Law Reports: Fire and Casualty (CCH, 1929–).

Insurance Law Reports: Life, Health, & Accident (CCH, 1929–).

Insurance: Letter and Revenue Rulings by M. Walsh (Natl. Law Pub., 1981–).

Insurance Pleadings & Briefs (San Francisco: Litigation Research Group).

The Law of Liability Insurance by R. Long (Matthew Bender, 1966–).

Loss Prevention and Control (BNA, 1979–).

National Insurance Advertising Regulation Service, R. Strand, ed. (MN: NIARS Corp., 1972–).

No-Fault and Uninsured Motorist Automobile Insurance (Matthew Bender, 1984–).

Official N.A.I.C. Model Insurance Laws, Regulations and Guidelines by the Natl. Assn. of Insurance Commissioners (MN: NIARS Corp., 1975–).

Responsibilities of Insurance Agents and Brokers by B. Hartnett (Matthew Bender, 1974–).

TREATISES:

Annotations to the Homeowners' Policy (ABA Tort and Insurance Practice Section, 1980).

Arson for Profit: The Insurer's Defense (ABA Natl. Institutes, 1981).

Automobile Insurance and No-Fault Law by M. Woodroof et al. (Lawyers Co-op., 1974).

Basic Protection for the Traffic Victim: A Blueprint for Reforming Automobile Insurance by R. Keeton & J. O'Connell (Little, Brown, 1966).

The Business Insurance Handbook, G. Castle et al., eds. (Dow Jones-Irwin, 1981).

Casualty Investigation Checklists, 3d ed. by P. Magarick (Clark Boardman, 1985).

Conference on Life Insurance Company Products (ALI–ABA, 1984).

Couch on Insurance Law by Anderson (Lawyers Co-op., 1959).

Dictionary of Insurance, 6th ed. by L. Davids (Rowman & Allanheld, 1984).

Directors' and Officers' Liability, Insurance and Self Insurance (Practicing Law Institute, 1986).

Excess Liability, 3d ed. by P. Magarick (Clark Boardman, 1988).

Federal Disability Law and Practice by F. Bloch (Wiley, 1984).

Handbook on the Law of Insurance, 3d ed. by W. Vance (Lawyers Co-op., 1951).

Handling Fidelity and Surety Claims, R. Cushman & C. Stamm, eds. (Wiley, 1984).

Insurance Claims and Disputes by A. Windt (Shepard's 1982).

Insurance Excess, and Reinsurance Coverage Disputes 1986 (Practicing Law Institute, 1986).

Insurance Law by R. Keeton & A. Widiss (West, 1988).

Insurance Law and Practice by J. Appleman (West, 1941–1966).

Insurance Law in a Nutshell by J. Dobbyn (West, 1981).

Insurance Rate Litigation by J. Mintell Kluwer, 1983).

Introduction to Commercial Insurance (Practicing Law Institute, 1986).

Law and the Life Insurance Contract by J. Greider (IL: Irwin, 1984).

Litigation and Prevention of Insurer Bad Faith by D. Wall (Shepard's, 1985).

The Practical Lawyer's Insurance Manual (ALI–ABA, 1975).

Professional Liability Insurance Coverage Problems: Attorneys, Accountants and Insurance Brokers (Practicing Law Institute, 1984).

Property and Liability Insurance, 3d ed. by S. Huebner et al. (Prentice-Hall, 1982).

Property Insurance Annotations (ABA Tort and Insurance Practice Section, 1977).

Punitive Damages in Bad Faith Cases, 3d ed. by J. McCarthy (Lawpress).

Studies in Modern Choice-of-Law: Torts, Insurance, Land Titles by M. Hancock (Hein, 1984).

Successful Handling of Casualty Claims by P. Magarick (Clark Boardman, 1974).

Uninsured and Uninsured Motorist Insurance, 2d ed. by A. Widiss (Anderson, 1985).

CITATORS: *Becker's Insurance Index/Citator,* 3d ed. by O. Becker (St. Louis: Index/Citator System, 1986).

ENCYCLOPEDIAS: AMERICAN JURISPRUDENCE 2D (Am Jur 2d)
Check the following topics in the *General Index* volumes for Am Jur 2d:

Actuaries	Insurance
Adjusters	Insurance Agents and
Annuities	Brokers
Assignments	Life Expectancy
Automobile Insurance	Life Insurance
Fidelity Bonds and	Marine Insurance
Insurance	Servicemen's and Veterans'
Fire Insurance	Insurance
Indemnity	

CORPUS JURIS SECUNDUM (CJS)
Check the following topics in the *General Index* volumes for CJS:

Accident and Health	Liability Insurance
Insurance	Life Expectancy
Annuities	Life Insurance
Assignments	Marine Insurance
Death	Monthly Tables
Disability Insurance	Motor Vehicle Insurance
Federal Deposit Insurance	Mutual Insurance
Act	Companies
Fire Insurance	National Service Life
Group Insurance	Insurance
Guaranty or Fidelity	No-Fault Insurance
Insurance	Title Insurance
Indemnity	Underwritings
Insurance	Uninsured Motorists
Insurance Adjusters	War Risk Insurance

DIGESTS: CASE SEARCH IN WEST DIGESTS BY KEY TOPIC
In the *Descriptive Word Index* of the West digests, look for key topics and numbers under the following subject headings:

Accident and Health	Insurance
Insurance	Insurance Adjusters
Annuities	Liability Insurance
Assignments	Life Expectancy
Automobiles	Life Insurance
Bonds	Marine Insurance
Brokers	Mortality Tables
Death	Motor Vehicle Insurance
Disability Insurance	Mutual Insurance
Federal Deposit	Companies
Insurance Act	No-Fault Insurance
Fire Insurance	Title Insurance
Group Insurance	Underwriting
Guaranty Insurance	Uninsured Motorists
Indemnity	War Risk Insurance

ALR: ANNOTATIONS
Check the index volumes for ALR, ALR2d, ALR3d, ALR4th, and ALR Fed for annotations
under the following subject headings:

Additional Insurance	Incontestable Clause
Adjusters	Indemnity
Automobile Insurance	Insurance
Binder	Insurance Agent
Brokers	Liability Insurance
Coinsurance	Life Insurance
Comprehensive	Marine Insurance
Insurance	No-Fault Insurance
Federal Employees'	Principal and Surety
Compensation Act	Public Liability Insurance
Fire Insurance	Risk of Loss
Health and Accident	Subrogation
Insurance	Theft Insurance
Homeowners' Insurance	Title Insurance

PERIODICALS: CURRENT LAW INDEX (CLI) & LEGAL RESOURCE INDEX (LRI)
In the CLI and LRI, look for references to periodical literature under the following
subject headings:

Accident Insurance	Insurance
Annuities	Life Insurance Trusts
Bad Faith	Risk (Insurance)
Indemnity Against Liability	

INDEX TO LEGAL PERIODICALS (ILP)
In the ILP, look for references to legal periodical literature under the following subject
headings:

Accident Insurance	Liability Insurance
Agency	Life Insurance
Annuities	Marine Insurance
Automobile Insurance	Motor Vehicles
Bonds	Old Age Insurance
Contracts	Subrogation
Disability Insurance	Title Insurance
Fire Insurance	Unemployment Insurance
Flood Insurance	War Risk Insurance
Health Insurance	Workers' Compensation

INSURRECTION: See Criminal Law, War
INTANGIBLE PROPERTY: See Intellectual Property, Personal Property, Estate
    Planning
INTEGRATED BAR: See Professional Responsibility
INTEGRATION: See Civil Rights, Constitutional Law

INTELLECTUAL PROPERTY

(Copyright, Patent, Trademark, Trade Secret)

SEE ALSO: Advertising, Antitrust Law, Art & Entertainment, Business Law, Computers,
International Law, Personal Property, Torts; see also entries under individual countries

**JOURNALS, NEWSLETTERS
& OTHER PERIODICALS
—GENERAL:**

AILPA Quarterly Journal (American Intellectual Property Law Assn., 1984–).

Bulletin of Law, Science & Technology (ABA).

Developments (John Marshall Law Sch.., Center for Intellectual Property Law, 1984–).

European Intellectual Property Review (Oxford: ESC Pub., 1978–).

IDEA: The Journal of Law and Technology (Franklin Pierce Law Center, 1957–).

Intellectual Property Journal (Canada: Carswell, 1985–).

Intellectual Property Law Review (Clark Boardman, 1969–).

Jurimetrics: Journal of Law, Science and Technology (ABA).

Patent and Trade Mark Review.

Patent, Trademark & Copyright Journal (BNA, 1970–).

A Practical Approach to Patents, Trademarks and Copyrights: An International Journal (NY: Harwood Academic Pub., 1979–).

PTC Newsletter (ABA Section of Patent, Trademark, and Copyright Law, 1981–).

**TREATISES & LOOSELEAFS
—GENERAL:**

BNA's Law Reprints, Patent, Trademark and Copyright Series (BNA, 1977–).

Digest of Commercial Laws of the World: Patents and Trademarks, L. Nelson, ed. (Natl. Assn. of Credit Management; Oceana, 1975–).

Federal Taxation of Intellectual Property Transfers by J. Olson (Law Journal Seminars-Press, 1986–).

Forms and Agreements on Intellectual Property and International Licensing, 3d ed. by L. Melville (Clark Boardman, 1979–).

Intellectual Property and Antitrust Law by W. Holmes (Clark Boardman, 1983–).

Intellectual Property in a Nutshell by A. Miller (West, 1983).

Intellectual Property Management: Law/Business/Strategy by P. Sperber (Clark Boardman, 1974–).

An Intellectual Property Primer by E. Kinter (Clark Boardman, 1982).

Jury Instructions in Intellectual Property Cases by D. Burton (Denver: Big Foot Press, 1980–).

Litigating Copyright, Trademark, and Unfair Competition Cases (Practicing Law Institute, 1986).

Manual of Classification by the U.S. Patent & Trademark Office (GPO, 1979–).

Media Law Reporter (BNA).

Modern Intellectual Property by M. Epstein (Law & Business, Inc., 1984–).

Patent and Trademark Forms by A. Jacobs (Clark Boardman, 1977–).

Patents, Trademarks, Copyrights and Trade Secrets by P. Saidman (MD: Inst. for Cont. Prof. Ed. for Lawyers, 1980–).

Rules of Practice in Patent and Trademark Cases (Rules Service Co., 1978–).

CITATORS—GENERAL:

United States Patents and Trademarks Citations (Shepard's).

**APPELLATE BRIEFS
—GENERAL:**

Patent, Trademark & Copyright Series (Congressional Information Service, 1984–).

**RESEARCH GUIDES &
BIBLIOGRAPHIES
—COPYRIGHT LAW:**

"Bibliography," 31 *Journal of the Copyright Society* 643 (1984).

"Copyright Law" by J. Beard in *Specialized Legal Research,* L. Chanin, ed. (Little, Brown, 1987).

"Selected Bibliography of Copyright Materials with Annotations" by J. Lomino & S. Kuklin, 4 *Legal Reference Services Quarterly* 39 (1984).

LEGISLATIVE HISTORIES
—COPYRIGHT LAW: *Kamenstein Legislative History Project . . . Copyright Act of 1976,* A. Latman & J. Lightstone, eds. (Rothman, 1985).
Omnibus Copyright Revision Legislative History, G. Grossman, comp. (Hein, 1976).

TREATISES—COPYRIGHT
LAW: *Copyright Laws and Treaties of the World* (UNESCO; BNA, 1957–).
Design Laws and Treaties of the World, A. Bogsch, ed. (BNA, 1960–).

JOURNALS, NEWSLETTERS
& OTHER PERIODICALS
—COPYRIGHT LAW: *ASCAP Copyright Law Symposium* (American Society of Composers, Authors and Publishers, 1939–).
Copyright (World Intellectual Property Organization—WIPO, 1965–).
The Copyright Law Journal, N. Boorstyn, ed. (San Francisco: 1984–).
ICIC Information Bulletin (Paris: UNESCO, Intl. Copyright Info. Centre, 1973–).
International Review of Industrial Property and Copyright Law (Munich: Max Planck Institute, 1969–).
Journal of the Copyright Society of the U.S.A. (NYU Law Center, 1981–).

TREATISES & LOOSELEAFS
—COPYRIGHT LAW: *An Author's Guide to Copyright Law* by W. Patton (D.C. Heath, 1980).
Copyright Law: A Practitioner's Guide, 2d ed. by H. Henn (Practicing Law Institute, 1988).
Copyright Law Reporter (CCH, 1978–).
Copyright Protection in the Americas (Organization of American States; Oceana, 1979–).
Howell's Copyright Law Revised and the 1976 Act, 5th ed. by A. Latman (BNA, 1979).
Musician's Guide to Copyright by G. Erickson (Scribner's, 1983).
Nimmer on Copyright by M. Nimmer (Matthew Bender, 1963–).
Software Protection by G. Davis (Van Nostrand Reinhold, 1985).
A Treatise on the Fair Use Privilege by W. Patry (BNA, 1985).
The Visual Artist's Guide to the New Copyright Law by T. Crawford (Graphic Arts Guild, 1978). ·

TREATIES—PATENT LAW: *Patent Cooperation Treaty and Regulations* (Rules Service Co., 1981–).

JOURNALS, NEWSLETTERS
& OTHER PERIODICALS
—PATENT LAW: *APLA Quarterly Journal* (American Patent Law Assn., 1972–).
Journal of the Patent Office Society.
Patent Law Annual (Dallas: Southwestern Legal Foundation, 1963–).

DIRECTORIES
—PATENT LAW: *Directory of Intellectual Property Lawyers and Patent Agents* (Clark Boardman, 1988).
Directory of Patent Attorneys and Agents (Pergamon Press, 1980).

TREATISES &
LOOSELEAFS
—PATENT LAW: *Biotechnology and the Law* by I. Cooper (Clark Boardman, 1982–).
Court Review of Patent Office Decisions (Matthew Bender, 1973–).
Drafting Patent License Agreements, 2d ed. by H. Mayers (BNA, 1984).
Encyclopedia of United Kingdom and European Patent Law, by T. Blancoland et al. (Maxwell & Sweet, 1977–).
European Patents Handbook by Chartered Institute of Patent Agents (Matthew

Bender, 1978–).

International Patent Litigation, M. Meller, ed. (BNA, 1983–).

Manual of Patent Examining Procedure, 4th ed. by the U.S. Dept. of Commerce Patent & Trademark Office (GPO, 1979–).

Patent Law and Practice Series (Matthew Bender).

Patent Law Fundamentals, 2d ed. by P. Rosenberg (Clark Boardman, 1980–).

Patent Law Perspectives, 2d ed. by J. Cambrell (Matthew Bender, 1982–).

Patent Licensing Transactions by H. Einhorn (Matthew Bender, 1968–).

Patent Litigation by R. Whitem (Matthew Bender, 1971–).

Patent Office Rules and Practice by L. Horwitz (Matthew Bender, 1959–).

Patents by D. Chisum (Matthew Bender, 1978–).

Patents Throughout the World, 2d ed., A. Green, ed. (Clark Boardman, 1978–).

The United States Patent Quarterly, 2d Series (BNA, 1987–).

What the General Practitioner Should Know about Patent Law and Practice, 4th ed. by A. Seidel (ALI–ABA Comm. on Cont. Prof. Ed.; Gaunt, 1984).

World Patent Law by J. Sinnott (Matthew Bender).

World Patent Law and Practice by J. Baxter & J. Sinnott (Matthew Bender).

**TREATISES & LOOSELEAFS
—TRADEMARK LAW:**

Callmann's Unfair Competition, Trademarks and Monopolies, 3d ed. by R. Callmann (Callaghan, 1967–).

Current Developments in Trademark Law (Practicing Law Institute, 1986).

Protection of Corporate Names: A Country-by-Country Survey by the U.S. Trademark Assn. (Clark Boardman, 1982–).

State Trademark Statutes (Law-Arts, 1967–).

Trademark Law and Practice by A. Seidel (Matthew Bender, 1963–).

Trademark Law and Procedure, 2d ed. by E. Vandenburgh (Michie, 1968).

Trademark Law Handbook by K. Germain (Clark Boardman, 1984).

Trademark Manual of Examining Procedure by U.S. Dept. of Commerce Patent Office (GPO, 1974–).

Trademark Protection and Practice by J. Gilson (Matthew Bender, 1974–).

Trademark Reporter (U.S. Trademark Assn., 1911–).

Trademark Rules of Practice by U.S. Dept. of Commerce Patent and Trademark Office (GPO, 1976–).

Trademarks Throughout the World, 3d ed. by A. Greene (Clark Boardman, 1979–).

U.S. Trademark Law (U.S. Trademark Assn., 1984–).

World Trademark Law and Practice by E. Horwitz (Matthew Bender, 1982).

**TREATISES & LOOSELEAFS
—TRADE SECRET:**

Protecting Trade Secrets (Practicing Law Institute).

Trade Secrets by R. Milgrim (Matthew Bender, 1957–).

Trade Secrets and Know-How Throughout the World by A. Wise (Clark Boardman, 1977–).

Trade Secrets Law Handbook by M. Jager (Clark Boardman, 1984).

What the General Practitioner Should Know about Trade Secrets and Employment Agreements, 2d ed. by A. Seidel (ALI–ABA Comm. on Cont. Prof. Ed., 1984).

ENCYCLOPEDIAS:

AMERICAN JURISPRUDENCE 2D (Am Jur 2d)

Check the following topics in the *General Index* volumes for Am Jur 2d:

Administrative Law	Patents
Copyright and Literary Property	Trademarks and Tradenames
Monopolies, Restraint of Trade and Unfair Trade Practices	

CORPUS JURIS SECUNDUM (CJS)
Check the following topics in the *General Index* volumes for CJS:

Administrative Law	Marks, Brands and Labels
Copyright and Literary	Monopolies
Property	Patents
Damages	Trade Marks, Trade Names,
Inventions	and Unfair Competition

DIGESTS:

CASE SEARCH IN WEST DIGESTS BY KEY TOPIC
In the *Descriptive Word Index* of the West digests, look for key topics and numbers under the following subject headings:

Administrative Law	Inventions
Contracts	Marks, Brands and Labels
Copyright and Intellectual	Monopolies
Property	Patents
Damages	Torts
Equity	Trade-Marks, Trade-Names,
Forgery	and Unfair Competition
Fraud	Trade Regulation
Injunction	

ALR:

ANNOTATIONS
Check the index volumes for ALR, ALR2d, ALR3d, ALR4th, and ALR Fed for annotations under the following subject headings:

Administrative Law	Literary and Artistic
Damages	Property
Diagram or Chart	Patents
Fraud	Trademarks, Trade Names,
Lanham Trade-Mark Act	Unfair Trade Practices

PERIODICALS:

CURRENT LAW INDEX (CLI) & LEGAL RESOURCE INDEX (LRI)
In the CLI and LRI, look for references to periodical literature under the following subject headings:

Administrative Law	Inventions
Brand Name Products	Patent Laws
Copyrights	Patents
Design Protection	Trade-Marks
Fair Use	United States Customs and
Industrial Property	Patent Appeals
Intangible Property	United States Patent and
Intellectual Property	Trademark Office

INDEX TO LEGAL PERIODICALS (ILP)
In the ILP, look for references to legal periodical literature under the following subject headings:

Administrative Law	Intellectual Property
Assignments	Patents
Authors and Publishers	Technology
Communications	Trademarks and Trade
Copyright	Names
Fraud	Trade Secrets
Industrial Property	

INTELLIGENCE TESTS: See Education Law, Handicapped & the Law, Mental Health
INTENT, INTENTIONAL: See Contracts, Criminal Law, Torts
INTER–AMERICAN: See Latin America
INTEREST: See Banking Law, Consumer Law, Uniform Commercial Code
INTERIOR DEPARTMENT: See Natural Resources, Oil & Gas, Water Law
INTERLOCUTORY APPEAL: See Trial & Appellate Practice
INTERNAL REVENUE SERVICE: See Business Law, Corporate Law, Estate Planning,
    Family Law, Taxation

INTERNATIONAL LAW

SEE ALSO:

Africa, Asia, Caribbean, Communism, Customs, Europe, European Economic
Community, Human Rights, Islam, Latin America, Middle East, Terrorism, United
Nations, War; see also entries under individual countries

RESEARCH GUIDES &
BIBLIOGRAPHIES:

A Bibliography of Foreign and Comparative Law: Books and Articles in English,
    C. Szladits, comp. (Oceana, 1955–).
Bibliography of Multinational Corporations and Foreign Direct Investment by
    E. Browndorf & S. Riemer (Oceana, 1978–).
Catalogue of International Law and Relations (Harvard Univ. Law School Library,
    1967).
Directory of Periodicals Published by International Organizations, 3d ed. (Brussels:
    Union of Intl. Assns., 1969).
Documents of International Organizations: A Bibliographic Handbook, T. Dimitrov,
    ed. (American Library Assn., 1973).
"Foreign Law in English" by C. Szladits, 28 *American Journal of Comparative Law*
    152 (1980).
A Guide to Bibliographic Tools for Research in Foreign Affairs, 2d ed., H. Conover,
    comp. (Library of Congress, 1958).
"Guide to International Legal Research," 20 *George Washington Journal of*
    International Law and Economics 1 (1986).
Index to Foreign Legal Periodicals (Univ. of London, 1960–).
"International and Foreign Law Sources in English for the Businessman and the
    Business Lawyer" by Szladits in *Digest of Commercial Laws of the World,* XV   ,
    G. Kohlik, ed. (1977–).
"International Business Transactions: A Guide to Research Sources" by I. Kavass, 76
    Law Library Journal 503 (1983).
International Commercial Arbitration Reference and Finding Tools (Oceana, 1988–).
International Sources: A Guide to Information Sources by A. Atherton (Gale Research
    Co., 1976).
Major Publications of the Department of State, An Annotated Bibliography (U.S.
    Dept. of State, 1971).
"Research Sources in International and Commercial Law," 9 *North Carolina Journal*
    of International Law and Commercial Regulation 319 (1984).
"Research Tips in International Law" by J. Williams, 15 *The Journal of International*
    Law and Economics 1 (1981).
Social Science Literature: A Bibliography for International Law by W. Gould &
    M. Barkun (Princeton Univ. Press, 1972).

LEGISLATION
—UNITED STATES:

United States Legislation on Foreign Relations and International Commerce Current
    Index by I. Kavass (Hein, 1986).

TREATIES
—UNITED STATES:

International Legal Materials (American Society for Intl. Law., 1961–).
Treaties and Other International Act Series (U.S. Dept. of State, 1946–).
Treaties and Other International Agreements of the United States of America,
   1776–1949, C. Bevins (Govt. Printing Office, 1968–1976).
Treaties in Force: A List of Treaties and Other International Agreements of the United
   States (Govt. Printing Office, 1929–).
United States Treaties and Other International Agreements (U.S. Dept. of State, 1950–).
United States Treaties and Other International Agreements Cumulative Index,
   1776–1949, I. Kavass & M. Michael, comps. (Hein, 1975).
Unperfected Treaties of the United States of America, C. Wiktor (Oceana, 1976–).
U.S.T. Cumulative Index 1950–1970, I Kavass & A. Sprudzs (Hein, 1973).
U.S.T. Cumulative Index 1971–1975, I. Kavass & A. Sprudzs (Hein, 1977).

TREATIES
—INTERNATIONAL:

Catalogue of Treaties 1814–1918 (Oceana, 1964).
A Collection of Neutrality Laws, Regulations and Treaties of Various Countries,
   F. Deak & P. Jessup (Greenwood Press, 1974).
Commercial Treaty Index, 2d ed. (ABA Sec. of Intl. Law, 1974–).
Consolidated Treaty Series, C. Perry, ed. (Oceana, 1969).
Cumulative List and Index to Treaties and International Agreements Registered or
   Filed and Recorded with the Secretariat of the United States, V. & R. Vambery
   (Oceana, 1977).
Glossary of International Treaties by Renoux and Yates (Amsterdam: Elsevier Pub.
   Co., 1970).
Index to Multilateral Treaties . . . Through 1963, V. Mostecky (Harvard Law School
   Library Pub., 1965; Oceana, 1966–68).
International Tax Treaties of All Nations, W. & D. Diamond (Oceana, 1975–) (Series
   B, 1978–).
Laws and Treaties of the World on the Protection of Performers, Producers of
   Phonograms and Broadcasting Organizations (BNA, 1970–).
League of Nations, Treaty Series: Treaties and International Engagements Registered
   with the Secretariat of the League (1920–1946).
Manual of Collections of Treaties and of Collections Relating to Treaties, D. Myers, ed.
   (NY: Burt Franklin, 1966).
Multilateral Treaties, Conventions, Protocols and Agreements of the United Nations
   and the Specialized Agencies (Geneva: World Peace through Law Center, 1967).
Office of Legal Affairs, List of Treaty Collections (United Nations, 1966).
Treaty Profiles, P. Rohn, comp. (Clio Press, 1976).
United Nations Treaty Series: Treaties and International Agreements Registered or
   Filed and Recorded with the Secretariat of the United Nations (1946).
World Treaty Index, 2d ed., P. Rohn, comp. (Clio Press, 1983).

CONSTITUTIONS:

A Compilation of the Political Constitutions of the Independent Nations of the World
   by A. Rodriguez (Govt. Printing Office, 1907).
Constitutions of Dependencies and Special Sovereignties, A. & E. Blaustein (Oceana,
   1975–).
Constitutions of Nations by A. Peaslee, 4th ed. by D. Xydis (Martinus Nijhoff, 1974).
Constitutions of Modern States by L. Wolf-Phillips (Praeger, 1968).
Constitutions of the Countries of the World, A. Blaustein & G. Flanz (Oceana, 1971–).
Independence Documents of the World by A. Blaustein et al. (Oceana, 1976).

RESTATEMENT:

Restatement of the Law (Third); Foreign Relations Law of the United States (American
   Law Institute, 1987).

CASES:

American International Law Cases, F. Deak, F. Ruddy, eds. (Oceana, 1793–1978).
British International Law Cases, C. Perry, ed. (Oceana, 1964–1967).
Common Market Law Reports (European Law Centre Ltd., 1951–).
European Human Rights Reports (London: European Law Centre Ltd., 1979–).
International Arbitrations by J. Moore (1898) (microfilm by Oceana).
International Law Reports, H. Lauterpacht (Butterworths, 1919–).
Reports of Judgments, Advisory Opinions and Orders (Netherlands: Intl. Court of
     Justice, 1947–).
World Court Reports by M. Hudson (Carnegie Endowment; reprint by Oceana,
     1922–1944).

**JOURNALS & OTHER
PERIODICALS:**

American Journal of Comparative Law (U.C. Berkeley, 1952–).
The American Journal of International Law (Wash. D.C., 1907–).
American Society of International Law Newsletter (1970–).
ASILS International Law Journal (Wash. D.C.: Assn. of Student Intl. Law Societies,
     1977–).
Boston College International and Comparative Law Journal (Boston College School
     of Law, 1977–).
Brooklyn Journal of International Law (Brooklyn Law School, 1975–).
California Western International Law Journal (Cal. Western School of Law, 1969–).
Case Western Reserve Journal of International Law (Case Western Reserve Univ.,
     1968–).
Columbia Journal of Transnational Law (Columbia Univ. School of Law, 1961–).
Connecticut Journal of International Law (1986–).
Cornell International Law Journal (Cornell Law School, 1968–).
Current Legal Problems (London: 1948–).
Denver Journal of International Law and Policy (Univ. of Denver College of Law,
     1971–).
Eastern Journal of International Law (India: Eastern Centre of International Studies,
     1969–).
Emory Journal of International Dispute Resolution (1986–).
Fordham International Law Forum (Fordham Univ. School of Law, 1977–).
Foreign Affairs (NY: Council on Foreign Relations, 1922–).
Foreign Tax Law Biweekly Bulletin (FL: Foreign Tax Law Assn., 1950–).
Georgia Journal of International and Comparative Law (Univ. of Ga. School of Law,
     1970–).
Harvard International Law Journal (Harv. Law School, 1967–).
Hastings International and Comparative Law Review (Hastings College of Law, 1977–).
Houston Journal of International Law (Univ. of Houston College of Law, 1978–).
Indian Journal of International Law (New Delhi: The Indian Society of International
     Law, 1960–).
International Affairs (London: Royal Institute of International Affairs, 1922–).
International Affairs (Moscow: All Union Znaniye Society, 1954–).
International and Comparative Law Quarterly (London: British Institute of Intl. and
     Comp. Law, 1952–).
International Bar Association Ombudsman Committee Newsletter (PA: Intl. Bar Assn.,
     1974–).
International Business and Trade Law Reporter (Wash. D.C.: 1985–).
International Business Lawyer (Netherlands: Intl. Bar Assn., 1973–).
International Center for Law and Development Newsletter (NY: 1980–).
International Commission of Jurists Review (Geneva: Intl. Comm. of Jurists, 1969–).
International Conciliation (NY: Carnegie Endowment for Intl. Peace, 1907–).
International Institute for the Unification of Private Law News Bulletin (Rome, 1973–).

International Journal of Comparative and Applied Criminal Justice (Wichita State Univ., 1977–).

International Law Association Newsletter (Intl. Law Assn., American Branch, B 1974–).

International Law News (ABA Sect. of Intl. Law, 1972–).

International Law Perspective (Wash. D.C., 1974–).

The International Lawyer (ABA Sect. of Intl. Law, 1966–).

International Legal Education Newsletter (Wash. D.C.: Assn. of American Law Schools, 1973–).

International Organization (Univ. of Wisc. Press, 1947–).

The International Tax Journal (Panel Publishers, 1974–).

International Tax News (Deloitte, Haskins & Sells, 1985–).

International Trade Law Journal (Univ. of Maryland School of Law, 1975–).

Journal of Conflict Resolution (Sage Publications, 1957–).

Journal of International Affairs (Columbia Univ. School of Intl. Affairs, 1947–).

Journal of International Arbitration (Geneva: 1984–).

Journal of International Law and Economics (George Wash. Univ. Natl. Law Center, 1971–).

Journal of World Trade Law (England, 1967–).

Law & Policy in International Business (Georgetown Univ. Law Center, 1969–).

Lawyer of the Americas (Univ. of Miami School of Law, 1969–).

Loyola of Los Angeles International and Comparative Law Annual (Loyola Univ. of LA School of Law, 1978–).

New York University Journal of International Law (NYU School of Law, 1968–).

North Carolina Journal of International Law and Commercial Regulation (Univ. of N.C. School of Law, 1976–).

Northwestern Journal of International Law and Business (NW Univ. School of Law, 1979–).

Proceedings of the American Society of International Law (Wash. D.C.: 1908–).

Public International Law (Berlin: Springer-Verlag, 1975–).

Stanford Journal of International Law (Stanford Univ. School of Law, 1966–).

Suffolk Transnational Law Journal (Suffolk Univ. Law School, 1977–).

Syracuse Journal of International Law and Commerce (Syracuse Univ. College of Law, 1972–).

Temple International and Comparative Law Journal (1985–).

Texas International Law Journal (Univ. of Texas School of Law, 1965–).

Vanderbilt Journal of Transnational Law (Vanderbilt Univ. School of Law, 1967–).

Virginia Journal of International Law (Univ. of Va. School of Law, 1960–).

World Affairs (Wash. D.C.: American Peace Society, 1837–).

World Politics (Princeton Univ. Press, 1948–).

Yale Studies in World Public Order (Yale Univ., 1974–).

DIRECTORIES:

Allen's International Directory of English Speaking Attorneys (NY: Natl. Legal Directory Publishing, 1986).

Directory of International Agencies by J. Angell (vol. 5 of American Encyclopedia of Intl. Information) (Simon & Schuster, 1970).

International Institutions and International Organizations, G. Speekaert, comp. (Brussels: Union of Intl. Assns., 1956).

YEARBOOKS & ANNUALS:

Australian Book of International Law (Butterworths, 1965–).

British Year Book of International Law (Oxford Univ. Press, 1920–).

Canadian Yearbook of International Law (Univ. of British Columbia Press, 1963–).

Indian Year Book of International Law (Madras, India: Indian Society Group of

International Affairs, 1952–).

International Court of Justice Yearbook (The Hague, 1946–).

Italian Yearbook of International Law (Oceana, 1975–).

Japanese Annual of Law & Politics (Tokyo: Science Council of Japan, 1952–).

Netherlands Yearbook of International Law (Sijthoff & Noordhoff, 1970–).

Philippines Yearbook of International Law (Quezon City: Phil. Society of Intl. Law, 1974–).

Polish Yearbook of International Law (Wroclaw, Poland: Publishing House of the Polish Academy of Sciences, 1966–).

Soviet Yearbook of International Law (Moscow: Nauka, 1958–).

Yearbook of International Organizations (Brussels: Union of Intl. Assn., 1949–).

Yearbook of World Affairs (London Institute of World Affairs, 1947–).

ENCYCLOPEDIAS (see also Am. Jur. 2d and Corpus Juris Secundum below):

Encyclopedia of American Foreign Policy, A. DeConte, ed. (Ch. Scribner's Sons, 1978).

Encyclopedia of Public International Law (Amsterdam, NY: Max Planck Institute of Public Comparative Law; North-Holland, 1981–).

International Encyclopedia of Comparative Law by J. Mohr (Sijthoff & Noordhoff).

International Encyclopedia of Comparative Law, K. Zweigert, ed. (Intl. Assn. of Legal Science).

TREATISES & LOOSELEAFS:

Antidumping and Countervailing Duty Laws by J. Pattison (Clark Boardman, 1984).

Antitrust and American Business Abroad, 2d ed. by J. Atwood & K. Brewster (Shepard's, 1981).

Applicable Law in International Arbitration by J. Lew (Oceana, 1978).

Arbitration and the Licensing Process, R. Goldscheider & M. de Haas, eds. (Clark Boardman, 1981–).

Capital Formation and Investment Incentives around the World by W. & D. Diamond (Matthew Bender, 1981–).

Commercial, Business and Trade Laws of the World, K. Simmonds, ed. (Oceana, 1981–).

Commercial Laws of the World (FL: Foreign Tax Law Assn., 1947–).

Customary International Law and Treatises by M. Villiger (Nijhoff, 1985).

Customs Law and Administration, 3d ed. by R. Sturm (Oceana, 1982–).

Customs Regulations of the United States (U.S. Customs Service, 1981–).

Digest of Commercial Laws of the World, L. Nelson, ed. (Natl. Assn. of Credit Management; Oceana, 1968–).

Digest of Commercial Laws of the World: Patents and Trademarks, L. Nelson, ed. (Natl. Assn. of Credit Management; Oceana, 1975–).

Digest of Legal Activities of International Organizations and other Institutions, 4th ed. (Oceana, 1980–).

Export Shipping Manual (BNA, 1947–).

The Export Trading Company Act of 1982 by W. Hancock (Ohio: Business Laws, Inc., 1983–).

Federal Regulation of International Business by S. Malawer (Wash. D.C.: Natl. Chamber Foundation, 1980–).

Financing Foreign Operations (NY: Business Intl. Corp., 1957–).

Foreign Business Practices: Materials on Practical Aspects of Exporting, International Licensing, and Investing (U.S. Dept. of Commerce).

Foreign Tax and Trade Briefs by W. Diamond (Matthew Bender, 1951–).

Foreign Tax Law Association Country Income Tax Services (FL: Foreign Tax Law Assn.).

GAAP Practice Manual by A. Afterman (Warren, Gorham & Lamont, 1985–).

Guide to Antidumping and Countervailing Duties and Other Unfair Import Laws (OH: Business Laws, Inc., 1983–).

Guide to International Commerce Law by P. Vishny (Shepard's, 1981–).

Guide to Legislation on Restrictive Business Practices (Paris: The Organization for Economic Cooperation and Development, 1960–).

History of the Tariff Schedules of the United States Annotated (U.S. Intl. Trade Commn., 1981–).

Income Taxation of Foreign-Related Transactions by R. Rhoades & M. Langer (Matthew Bender, 1971–).

International Arbitration, 2d ed., C. Schmitthof, ed. (Oceana, 1976).

International Boycotts by W. Hancock (OH: Business Laws, Inc., 1978–).

International Business & Law Series (Clark Boardman, 1981–).

International Business Planning: Law and Taxation by W. Streng & J. Salacuse (Matthew Bender, 1982–).

International Commercial Arbitration by K. Simmonds & C. Schmitthoff (Oceana, 1979–).

International Corporate Taxation by P. Postlewaite (Shepard's, 1980).

International Estate Planning by W. Newton (Shepard's, 1981–).

International Exporting Agreements by S. Ezer (Matthew Bender, 1985–).

International Handbook on Commercial Arbitration by P. Sanders (Gaunt, 1984–).

International Individual Taxation by P. Postlewaite & M. Collins (Shepard's, 1982).

International Law and Organization by J. Robinson (Sijthoff, 1967).

The International Relations Dictionary, 2d ed. by J. Plano & R. Olton (Western Mich. Univ., New Issues Press, 1979).

International Tax and Business Service (NY: Deloitte, Haskins and Sells, 1976–).

International Trade Practice by H. Kaye et al. (Shepard's, 1981–).

International Trade Reporter (BNA, 1984–).

International Trade Reports: Export Shipping Manual (1980–).

International Withholding Tax Treaty Guide by W. Diamond (Matthew Bender, 1973–).

Investing, Licensing & Trading Conditions Abroad (NY: Business Intl. Corp., 1955–).

Investment Laws of the World: The Developing Nations (Oceana, 1973–).

Investment Regulation Around the World, R. Hammer et al., eds. (Wiley, 1983).

Joint Venturing Abroad: A Case Study, D. Goldsweig (ABA, Section of Intl. Law and Practice, 1985).

Law and Judicial Systems of Nations, 3d ed. C. Rhyne (Wash. D.C.: The World Peace Through Law Center, 1978–).

The Law and Practice of International Finance by P. Wood (Clark Boardman, 1981–).

The Law of International Business Transactions by V. Nanda (Clark Boardman, 1981–).

Law and Practice under the GATT by K. Simmonds & B. Hill (Oceana, 1988–).

A Lawyer's Guide to International Business Transactions, 2d ed., W. Surrey & D. Wallace eds. (ALI–ABA Comm. on Cont. Prof. Ed., 1977, 1979).

Licensing in Foreign and Domestic Operations, 3d ed. by L. Eckstrom (Clark Boardman, 1972–).

Litigation of International Disputes in U.S. Courts by V. Nanda (Clark Boardman, 1986–).

Manual of International Law, 6th ed. by G. Schwarzenberger & E. Brown (NY: Professional Books, Ltd., 1976).

The Modern Law of Treaties by T. Elias (Oceana, 1971).

Modern Legal Systems Cyclopedia by K. Redden (Hein, 1983–).
Multinational Corporations Law, K. Simmonds, ed., (Oceana, 1979–).
Parry and Grant Encyclopedic Dictionary of International Law, C. Parry, J. Grant et
    al., eds. (Oceana, 1985).
Pinner's World Unfair Competition Law, H. Dawid, ed. (BNA, 1978–).
Principles of Public International Law by I. Brownlie (Clarendon Press, 1979).
The Process of International Arbitration by K. Carlston (Greenwood Press, 1972).
Private Investors Abroad: Problems and Solutions in International Business by
    J. Cohen & J. Horsley (Matthew Bender, 1983).
The Regulation of Statelessness Under International Law: Text and Documents by
    P. Murtharika (Oceana, 1977–).
Tariff Schedules of the United States Annotated (U.S. Intl. Trade Commn., 1981–).
Taxation of International Executives by Deloitte, Haskins & Sells (Kluwer, 1985).
Tax Free Zones of the World by D. & W. Diamond (Matthew Bender, 1977–).
Tax Havens Encyclopedia, B. Spitz (Butterworths, 1975–).
Tax Havens of the World by W. & D. Diamond (Matthew Bender, 1974–).
Tax Laws of the World (FL: Foreign Tax Law Assn., 1947–).
Trade Secrets and Know-How Throughout the World by A. Wise (Clark Boardman,
    1974–).
Transnational Contracts, Applicable Law and Settlement of Disputes by G. Delaume
    (Oceana, 1980–).
Transnational Economic and Monetary Law by L. Lazar (Oceana, 1978–).
Transport Laws of the World, D. Hill & M. Evans, eds. (Oceana, 1977–).
United States Court of International Trade—Rules (NY: Invictus Pub. Co., 1980–).
The United States Department of State Fact Book of the Countries of the World (NY:
    Crown, 1970).
United States International Trade Reports by E. Newman & E. Wypyski (Oceana,
    1981–).
U.S. Court of International Trade Rules and Annotation Service (MD: Rules Service
    Co., 1984–).
U.S. Customs and International Trade Guide by P. Feller (Matthew Bender, 1979–).
U.S. Export Weekly (BNA, 1974–).
U.S. Import Weekly (BNA, 1979–).
U.S. International Trade Laws, A Stowell, ed. (BNA, 1986).
U.S. Taxation of International Operations (Prentice-Hall, 1973–).
World Law of Competition, J. von Kalinowski, ed. (Matthew Bender, 1978–).
World Litigation & Practice, R. Myrick, ed. (Matthew Bender, 1986–).
World Shipping Laws, D. Jackson, ed. (Oceana, 1979–).

DIGESTS:

Digest of International Law, G. Hackworth, comp. (Govt. Printing Office, 1940–
    1944; reprint by Garland Pub., 1973; microfilm by Oceana).
Digest of International Law by M. Whiteman (Govt. Printing Office, 1963–1973).
Digest of United States Practice in International Law (U.S. Dept. of State, 1973–).

ENCYCLOPEDIAS:

AMERICAN JURISPRUDENCE 2d (Am Jur 2d)
Check the following topics in the *General Index* volumes for Am Jur 2d:

Ambassadors and Other	International Law
Diplomatic Officers	Military and Civil Defense
Customs Duties and	Passports
Import Regulations	Treaties
Foreign Corporations	War
Foreign State or Country	

CORPUS JURIS SECUNDUM (CJS)
Check the following topics in the *General Index* volumes for CJS:

Ambassadors and Consuls	International Law
Customs Duties	Passports and Visas
Exports and Imports	Treaties
Foreign Corporations	United States
Foreign Law	War and National Defense

DIGESTS:

CASE SEARCH IN WEST DIGESTS BY KEY TOPIC
In the *Descriptive Word Index* of the West digests, look for key topics and numbers under the following subject headings:

Aliens	International Law
Ambassadors and Consuls	Passports and Visas
Customs Duties	Treaties
Exports and Imports	United States
Foreign Corporations	War and National Security
Foreign Law	

ALR:

ANNOTATIONS
Check the index volumes for ALR, ALR2d, ALR3d, ALR4th, and ALR Fed for annotations under the following subject headings:

Extraterritoriality	International Law
Foreign State or Country	

PERIODICALS:

CURRENT LAW INDEX (CLI) & LEGAL RESOURCE INDEX (LRI)
In the CLI and LRI, look for references to periodical literature under the following subject headings:

Act of State	Extraterritoriality
Arbitration, International	Foreign Trade
Asylum, Right of	Immunities of Foreign
Civil Procedure	States
(International)	Import Controls
Civil Rights (International)	International. . .
Commercial Treaties	Intvestments, Foreign
Diplomatic and	Jurisdiction (International)
Consular Service	Neutrality
Diplomatic Protection	Nontariff Trade Barriers
Domestic International	Treaties
Sales Corporations	UNESCO Nations
European Community	United States
Export Sales	War
Extradition	

INDEX TO LEGAL PERIODICALS (ILP)
In the ILP, look for references to legal periodical literature under the following subject headings:

Aggression	Colonies
Alien Property	Comity
Ambassadors	Commerce
Antitrust/Foreign	Comparative Law
Asylum	Concessions,
Blockade	International Law
Citizens	Confiscation

Developing Countries	Government Immunity
Diplomacy	High Seas
Diplomatic . . .	Human Rights
Disarmament	International. . .
Embargo	Jurisdiction (International)
Enemy Aliens	Mandates
Executive Agreements	Neutrality
Expatriation	Passports
Exports and Imports	Patents/Foreign
Expropriation and	Peace
Nationalization	Prisoners of War
Extraterritoriality	Refugees
Fishing (International	Self-Determination
Law)	Sovereignty
Foreign Agents	Tax Treaties
Foreign Exchange	Treaties
Foreign Relations	War

INTERNATIONAL MONETARY FUND (IMF): See Africa, International Law, Peru, Uruguay

INTERPLEADER: See Trial & Appellate Practice

INTERPRETATION: See Legal Research, Statutes

INTERROGATORIES: See Trial & Appellate Practice

INTERSPOUSAL TORT IMMUNITY: See Family Law, Torts

INTERSTATE COMMERCE: See Constitutional Law

INTERSTATE COMMERCE COMMISSION: See Transportation

INTERSTATE COMPACTS: See State & Local Government

INTERVENING CAUSE: See Torts

INTERVENTION: See Trial & Appellate Practice

INTOXICATION: See Alcohol, Criminal Law, Health & Medicine, Mental Health

INVASION OF PRIVACY: See Constitutional Law, Torts

INVENTION: See Intellectual Property

INVENTORY: See Business Law, Personal Property, Uniform Commercial Code

INVESTIGATION: See Criminal Law, Death, Forensic Science

INVESTMENTS: See Banking Law, Business Law, Employee Benefits, International Law, Oil & Gas, Real Estate, Securities Law, Taxation

INVESTOR: See Franchise Law, Securities Law

INVITEE: See Torts

IN VITRO: See Family Law, Health & Medicine

INVOLUNTARY SERVITUDE: See Civil Rights, Constitutional Law

IOWA

SEE ALSO: Circuit Courts (Eighth Circuit)

STATUTES & OTHER LEGISLATIVE MATERIALS: *Code of Iowa.*
Iowa Code Annotated (West).
Acts and Joint Resolutions of the State of Iowa.
Iowa Legislative Service (West).
CCH Advance Session Laws Reports. Iowa.
Iowa Legislative News Service Bulletin (Des Moines, 1980–).

STATE ADMINISTRATIVE REGULATIONS:	*Iowa Administrative Bulletin.* *Iowa Administrative Code.*
CASES & OPINIONS:	*Iowa Reports* (1855–1968). *North Western Reporter* (1878–).
COURT RULES:	*Iowa Court Rules* (Iowa Gen. Services, Printing Div.). *Iowa Rules of Court* (West).
JURY INSTRUCTIONS:	*Iowa Uniform Jury Instructions: Civil* (Iowa Bar, 1978–). *Iowa Uniform Jury Instructions: Criminal* (Iowa Bar).
ETHICS & PROFESSIONAL RESPONSIBILITY:	*Formal Opinions of the Committee on Professional Ethics and Conduct of the Iowa State Bar.*
OPINIONS OF THE ATTORNEY GENERAL:	*Attorney General Opinions* (Iowa Gen. Services, Printing Div.).
JOURNALS & OTHER PERIODICALS:	*Daily Business Report* (Des Moines). *Daily Register* (Sioux City). *Iowa State Bar Newsletter* (1940–).
TREATISES, LOOSELEAFS & OTHER MONOGRAPHS:	*CCH State Tax Reporter. Iowa.* *Employment in Iowa* by M. Sautter (St. Paul: Mason Pub. Co., 1984–). *Iowa Bankruptcy* (Butterworths). *Iowa Business Organizations,* 2d ed. by E. Hayes (West, 1985). *Iowa Civil Procedure Forms* by M. Smith (West, 1984). *Iowa Criminal Law and Procedure,* 2d ed. by J. Yeager & R. Carlson (West, 1979). *Iowa Legal Forms* (St. Paul: Mason Pub. Co.). *Iowa Litigation Manual* (St. Paul: Mason Pub. Co., 1982–). *Iowa Matrimonial Law* by D. Braw (Butterworths, 1986). *Iowa Methods of Practice,* 2d ed. by M. Volz et al. (West, 1976). *Iowa Practice* by A. Vestal (Callaghan, 1983). *Iowa Probate,* 2d ed. by D. McCarthy (Callaghan, 1964). *Iowa Real Estate Mortgage Foreclosure* by J. Sullivan (Harrison, 1983). *Iowa Workers' Compensation Law and Practice* by J. Lawyer (Harrison, 1984). *Real Estate Practice Manual* (Iowa Bar, 1982–).
DIGESTS & CITATOR:	*Iowa Digest* (Callaghan). *Iowa Digest* (West). *North Western Digest* (West). *Shepard's Iowa Citations.*

IRA: See Banking Law, Employee Benefits

IRAN

SEE ALSO:	International Law, Islam, Middle East, United Nations
CONSTITUTION:	*Constitutions of Eastern Countries* (Iran) by M. Ahmad (Karachi, Pakistan, 1951).

IRANIAN ASSETS/
CLAIM CASE:　　　　20 *International Legal Materials* 923 (1981).
22 *International Legal Materials* 1406 (1983).
23 *International Legal Materials* 1 (1984).

TREATISES &
LOOSELEAFS:　　　　*Commercial Laws of Iran* by S. Amin (Teheran: Vahid Pub., 1986).
Commercial Laws of the Middle East (Iran) by G. Vafai (Oceana, 1982–).
Current Aspects of Doing Business in the Middle East—Saudi Arabia, Egypt and Iran,
　　W. Wickersham & B. Fishburne, eds. (American Bar Assn., 1977).
Digest of Commercial Laws of the World (Iran) (Natl. Assn. of Credit Management;
　　Oceana, 1977–).
*Four Failures: A Report of the U.N. Special Rapporteurs on Human Rights in Chile,
　　Guatemala, Iran and Poland* (NY: Americas Watch, 1986).
"The Government of God:" Iran's Islamic Republic by C. Benard (Columbia Univ.
　　Press, 1984).
The Iran Crisis and International Law by R. Steele (John Bassett Society of Intl. Law,
　　1981).
The Iran Service (NY: Business Intl. Corp., 1978–).
The Iran-United States Claims Tribunal, 1981–1983, R. Lillich, ed. (Univ. of Virginia
　　Press, 1985).
Taxes and Investment in the Middle East (Intl. Bureau of Fiscal Documentation).
Tax Laws of the World—Iran (FL: Foreign Tax Law Assn.).

ARTICLES:　　　　"Iran: Family Law After the Islamic Revolution" by A. Bernardi, 25 *Journal of Family
　　Law* 151 (1986–87).
"The Iranian Asset Control Regulations and the International Monetary Fund" by N.
　　Simon 4 *Boston College International and Comparative Law Review* 203 (1981).
"The Iranian Hostage Agreement" by G. McLaughlin, 4 *Fordham International Law
　　Journal* 223 (1980–81).
"The Iranian Nationalization Cases" by W. Eskridge, 22 *Harvard International Law
　　Journal* 525 (1981).
"The Iran-U.S. Claims Tribunal" by S. Swanson, 18 *Case Western Reserve Journal of
　　International Law* 307 (1986).
"Jurisdiction: Service of Process on Iran," 21 *Harvard International Law Journal* 774
　　(1980).
"The Legal, Social and Political Position of Women in Iran" by H. Afshar, 13
　　International Journal of the Sociology of Law 47 (1985).
"Middle East Agency Law Survey" (Iran) by F. Taylor, 14 *International Lawyer* 337
　　(1980).

IRAQ

SEE ALSO:　　　　International Law, Islam, Middle East, United Nations

CONSTITUTIONS:　　　　*Constitutions of Eastern Countries* (Iraq) by M. Ahmad (Karachi, Pakistan, 1951).

TREATISES &
LOOSELEAFS:　　　　*Business Laws of Iraq* by N. Karam (London: Graham & Trotman, 1984–).
Commercial Laws of the Middle East by A. Keesee (Oceana, 1980–).
Digest of Commercial Laws of the World (Iraq) (Natl. Assn. of Credit Management;
　　Oceana, 1977–).

The Kurdish Question in Iraq by E. Ghareeb (Syracuse Univ. Press, 1981).
Property Law in the Arab World: Real Rights in Egypt, Iraq, Jordan, Lebanon, Libya, Saudi Arabia and the Gulf States by F. Ziadeh (London: Graham & Trotman, 1979).
The Shatt Al-Arab Dispute: A Legal Study, 3d ed. by K. al-Izzi (London: World Centre for Research and Pub., 1981).
Taxes and Investment in the Middle East (Intl. Bureau of Fiscal Documentation).
Tax Laws of the World—Iraq (FL: Foreign Tax Law Assn.).

ARTICLES:
"How Contracting Works in Iraq," 9 *Middle East Executive Reports* 8 (Aug., 1986).
"Middle East Agency Law Survey" (Iraq) by F. Taylor, 14 *International Lawyer* 338 (1980).
"Reform of the Legal System in Iraq" by T. Jamil, 8 *International Business Lawyer* 213 (1980).
"Sales Opportunities in Agriculture (Iraq)," 7 *Middle Eastern Executive Report* 14 (1984).

IRELAND (IRISH REPUBLIC)

SEE ALSO:
Europe, European Economic Community, International Law, Ireland (Northern), United Nations

RESEARCH GUIDES & BIBLIOGRAPHIES:
A Bibliography of Literature on British and Irish Labour Law by B. Hepple et al. (London: Mansell, 1975).
A Bibliography of Periodical Literature Relating to Irish Law, 2d ed. by P. O'Higgins (Belfast: SIS Publications, 1983).
"Gaelic Law in Early and Medieval Ireland: A Bibliography" by B. Pawloski, 79 *Law Library Journal* 305 (1987).
Smurfit Irish Law Center Bibliographic Guide, 5th ed. by J. Milles (St. Louis Univ., Sch. of Law, 1986).

TREATIES:
Treaty Series (Dublin: Dept. of Foreign Affairs, 1930–).

CONSTITUTION:
"Ireland" by J. Siger in *Constitutions of the Countries of the World* by A. Blaustein & G. Flanz (Oceana, 1983).

CASES:
Irish Law Reports Monthly (Dublin: Round Hall Press; Totowa, NJ: Irish Academic Press).

JOURNALS & OTHER PERIODICALS:
Dublin University Law Journal (1976–).
Gazette of the Incorporated Law Society of Ireland (1907–).
Irish Jurist (New Series) (1966–).
Irish Law Times and Solicitors' Journal (Dublin: Round Hall Press; Totowa, NJ: Irish Academic Press).
Journal of the Irish Society for European Law (1977–).
Journal of the Irish Society for Labour Law (1982–).

**TREATISES &
LOOSELEAFS:**
Admissibility of Illegally Obtained Evidence: Comparative Analysis of the Laws of England, Scotland, Ireland, Canada, Australia and New Zealand (Library of Congress, 1981).

Capital Acquisitions Tax, 3d ed. by N. Bale & J. Condon (Dublin: Institute of Taxation in Ireland, 1984).

Capital Formation and Investment Incentives Around the World (Ireland) by W. Diamond & D. Diamond (Matthew Bender, 1984–).

Company Law in the Republic of Ireland by R. Keane (Butterworths, 1985).

Competition Laws of United Kingdom and Republic of Ireland by W. Allan & G. Hogan (Matthew Bender, 1988–).

Constitutional Law and Constitutional Rights in Ireland (Dublin: Gill and Macmillan, 1984).

Constitutional Law of Ireland (Dublin: Round Hall Press; Totowa, NJ: Irish Academic Press, 1985).

Corporation Tax, 3d ed. by F. Brennan (Dublin: Institute of Taxation in Ireland, 1985).

Digest of Commercial Laws of the World (Ireland) (Natl. Assn. of Credit Management; Oceana, 1977–).

The Evolution of Irish Industrial Relations Law and Practice by B. O'Hara (Dublin: Folens, 1981).

Fundamental Rights in the Irish Law and Constitution, 2d ed. by J. Kelly (Oceana, 1968).

Information Guide: Doing Business in the Republic of Ireland (Price Waterhouse).

Introduction to Law in the Republic of Ireland by R. Grimes (Associated Book Publishers, 1981).

Irish Company Law, 1973–1983: A Guide and Handbook by B. Power (Dublin; NY: Gill and Macmillan, 1984).

Irish Law of Torts by B. McMahon (Abington: Professional Books, 1981).

The Private International Law of Matrimonial Causes in the British Isles and the Republic of Ireland by P. North (NY: North-Holland, 1977).

Taxation in Ireland (NY: Deloitte, Haskins & Sells, 1983).

Taxation of Intercompany Transactions in Selected Countries in Europe and USA (Kluwer, 1979).

Tax Laws of the World—Ireland (FL: Foreign Tax Law Assn.).

World Law of Competition (Ireland), J. von Kalinowski, ed. (Matthew Bender, 1979–).

ARTICLES:
"The European Community, the United States, and Ireland: An Intermesh of Statutory Provisions" by F. Murphy, 17 *Vanderbilt Journal of Transnational Law* 665 (1984).

"Foreign Investment in Ireland: A Symposium," 17 *Vanderbilt Journal of Transnational Law* 563 (1984).

"Ireland—1980 Sale of Goods Act" by M. Burke-Staunton, 9 *International Business Lawyer* 433 (1981).

"Ireland: Waiting for Divorce" by W. Duncan, 25 *Journal of Family Law* 155 (1986–87).

"Irish Tax Law and the Foreign Investor," 17 *Vanderbilt Journal of Transnational Law* 631 (1984).

"Planning Appeals in the Republic of Ireland" by C. Stevenson, 7 *Urban Law & Policy* 165 (1985).

"Trademark Infringement" by S. Bigger, 72 *Trademark Reporter* 312 (1982).

IRELAND (NORTHERN)

SEE ALSO: Europe, International Law, Ireland (Irish Republic), United Nations

**RESEARCH GUIDES &
BIBLIOGRAPHIES:** *A Bibliography of Periodical Literature Relating to Irish Law,* 2d ed. by P. O'Higgins
(Belfast: SIS Publications, 1983).
"Legal Information Services in Northern Ireland" by T. Burgess, *Computers and Law*
21 (Nov., 1982).
"A Legal System Responds to Political Violence: Northern Ireland, 1969–1984, A Select
Bibliography" by M. Sullivan, 5 *Legal Reference Services Quarterly* 91 (1985).

CONSTITUTION: "Northern Ireland" by L. Wolf-Phillips in *Constitutions of Dependencies and Special
Sovereignties* by A. Blaustein (Oceana, 1983).

**JOURNALS & OTHER
PERIODICALS:** *Northern Ireland Legal Quarterly* (Gaunt, 1936–).

TREATISES: *Information Guide: Doing Business in Northern Ireland* (Price Waterhouse).
The Legal Systems of Britain (Northern Ireland) (London: Her Majesty's Stationery
Office, 1976).
Sentencing Law and Practice in Northern Ireland by C. Boyle and M. Allen (Belfast:
SLS Publications, 1983).
Winding Up Companies in Northern Ireland: A Practitioner's Guide by J. Hunter
(Belfast: SIS Publications, 1984).

ARTICLES: "Human Rights in Northern Ireland" by D. Donahue, 3 *Boston College International
and Comparative Law Review* 377 (1980).
"Irish Terrorists and Extradition" by W. O'Brien, 18 *Texas International Law Journal*
249 (1983).
"Law Enforcement by Regulatory Agency: The Case of Employment Discrimination in
Northern Ireland" by C. McCrudden, 45 *Modern Law Review* 617 (1982).
"The Planning Appeals Commission of Northern Ireland" by B. Thompson, 11
International Journal of the Sociology of Law 401 (1983).
"Prisoner's Rights in Northern Ireland" by S. Livingstone, 37 *Northern Ireland Legal
Quarterly* 75 (1986).
"Public Security and Individual Freedom: The Dilemma of Northern Ireland" by
T. Foley, 8 *Yale Journal of World Public Order* 284 (1982).
"Quasi-Constitutional Developments in Northern Ireland" by G. Swan, 13 *California
Western International Law Journal* 378 (1983).

IRRIGATION: See Natural Resources, Water Law
IRS: See Taxation

ISLAM

SEE ALSO: Cameroon, Egypt, India, Iran, Iraq, International Law, Malaysia, Middle East, Pakistan,
Saudi Arabia, Senegal, Somalia, Sudan, Syria, Tanzania, Turkey, United Nations

**RESEARCH GUIDES &
BIBLIOGRAPHIES:** "Islamic Law Bibliography" by J. Makdisi, 78 *Law Library Journal* 103 (1986).
Islamic Law in the Contemporary World: Introduction, Glossary and Bibliography by

S. Amin (Glasgow: Royston; Teheran: Vahid Publications, 1985).

Law in the Muslim World: A Union List of Materials, J. Szentendry, ed. (Univ. of Houston Law Library, 1981).

JOURNALS & OTHER PERIODICALS: *Journal of Islamic and Comparative Law* (1967–).

TREATISES: *Commercial Law in the Gulf States: The Islamic Legal Tradition* (London: Graham & Trotman).

The Concept of State and Law in Islam by F. Hassan (Wash. D.C.: Univ. Press of America, 1981).

Introduction to Islamic Law by J. Schacht (Clarendon Press, 1982).

Introduction to Islamic Theology and Law by I. Goldziher (Princeton Univ. Press, 1980).

Islamic Banking by Z. Iqbal (Intl. Monetary Fund, 1987).

The Islamic Concept of Justice by M. Khadduri (Johns Hopkins Univ. Press, 1984).

The Islamic Criminal Justice System by C. Bassiouni (Oceana, 1982).

Islamic Law in South-East Asia by M. Hooker (Oxford Univ. Press, 1984).

Unlawful Gain and Legitimate Profit in Islamic Law by N. Saleh (Cambridge Univ. Press, 1986).

Women in Muslim Family Law by J. Esposito (Syracuse Univ. Press, 1982).

ARTICLES: "Islamic Law: Its Relation to Other Legal Systems" by G. Badr, 26 *American Journal of Comparative Law* 187 (1978).

"Legal Logic and Equity in Islamic Law" by J. Makdisi, 33 *American Journal of Comparative Law* 63 (1985).

"Muslim Divorce" by K. Hodkinson, *Journal of Social Welfare Law* 46 (Jan., 1984).

ISLE OF MAN

SEE ALSO: England, International Law, United Nations

RESEARCH GUIDE & BIBLIOGRAPHY: *A Bibliographic Guide to the Law of the United Kingdom, the Channel Islands and the Isle of Man,* 2d ed., A Chloros, ed. (Univ. of London, Inst. of Advanced Legal Studies, 1973).

CONSTITUTION: "Isle of Man" by N. Yell in *Constitutions of Dependencies and Special Sovereignties* by A. Blaustein (Oceana, 1981).

TREATISES: *Tax Havens Encyclopedia* (Isle of Man) by B. Spitz (Butterworths, 1975–).

ISRAEL & JEWISH LAW

SEE ALSO: International Law, Middle East, United Nations

RESEARCH GUIDES & BIBLIOGRAPHIES: "The Arab-Israel Conflict: A Legal Bibliography" by S. Silverburg, 72 *Law Library Journal* 12 (1979).

Bibliography of Israeli Law in European Languages by R. Sanilevici (Hebrew Univ. of Jerusalem, Fac. of Law, 1985).

"Bibliography of Jewish Law Articles in Selected Law Journals," 3 *Jewish Law Annual* 245 (1980).

"Guide to Israel Legal Bibliography: Primary Sources" by E. Snyder 70 *Law Library Journal* 14 (1977).

Jewish Women and Jewish Law: Bibliography by O. Hamelsdorf (NY: Biblio Press, 1980).

"Legal Implications of the Arab Economic Boycott of the State of Israel: A Research Guide" by R. Mersky & M. Richmond, 71 *Law Library Journal* 68 (1978).

TREATIES: *Treaty Series* (Jerusalem: Govt. Printer, 1949–).

STATUTES & RELATED LAWS: *Israel Criminal Procedural Law* (American Series of Foreign Penal Codes; Rothman, 1967).

Laws of the State of Israel: Authorized Translation (Jerusalem: Ministry of Justice, 1948–).

CASES: *Selected Judgments of the Supreme Court of Israel,* E. Gotein, ed. (Jerusalem: Ministry of Justice, 1962–).

JOURNALS & OTHER PERIODICALS: *Israel Law Review* (Hebrew Univ., 1966–).

Israel Yearbook on Human Rights (Tel Aviv Univ., 1971–).

The Jewish Law Annual (Leiden: Brill, 1978–).

National Jewish Law Review (Ann Arbor, MI: Natl. Jewish Law Students' Network, 1986–).

The Palestine Yearbook of International Law (Nicosia: Al-Shaybani Society of Intl. Law, 1984–).

Tel Aviv University Studies in Law (1975–).

Union List of Periodicals in Law Libraries in Israel by R. Bar-Niv (Jerusalem: Hebrew Univ., 1979).

DICTIONARIES: *Legal Dictionary: English-Hebrew* by M. Shely (Jerusalem: Dvir, 1980).

TREATISES & LOOSELEAFS: *Business Operations in Israel* by A. Rafael, Tax Management Foreign Income Portfolios, no. 250–4th (BNA, 1984).

Digest of Commercial Laws of the World (Israel, vol. 4) by the Natl. Assn. of Credit Management (Oceana, 1977–).

Divorce in Jewish Law and Life by I. Hunt (NY: Sepher-Hermon, 1983).

Inflation and Indexation: Argentina, Brazil, and Israel by J. Williamson (MIT Press, 1985).

The Islamic Criminal Justice System by M. Bassiouni (Oceana, 1982).

Israel and Palestine: Assault on the Law of Nations by J. Stone (Johns Hopkins Univ. Press, 1981).

Israel Nationality Law by M. Gouldman (Jerusalem: Hebrew Univ., 1970).

Israel, the West Bank and International Law by A. Gerson (NJ: Frank Cass & Co., 1978).

Jewish Jurisprudence: Its Sources and Modern Application by E. Quint & I. Hecht (NY: Harwood, 1980).

Jewish Law and Current Legal Problems (Jerusalem: Library of Jewish Law, 1984).

Jewish Law and Decision-Making: A Study Through Time by A. Schreiber (Temple Univ. Press, 1980).

Jewish Women in Jewish Law by Meiselman (NY: Ktav, 1978).

Labour Law in Israel by M. Goldberg (Tel Aviv: Sadan, 1982).

The Legal System of Israel by Z. Baker (Israel Univ. Press, 1968).

The Main Institutions of Jewish Law by I. Herzog (London: Soncino, 1965).

Military Government in the Territories Administered by Israel, 1967–1980: The Legal Aspects by M. Shamgar (Jerusalem: Hebrew Univ., 1982).

Occupier's Law: Israel and the West Bank by R. Shehadeh (Wash. D.C.: Institute for Palestine Studies, 1985).

The Parliamentary System of Israel by S. Sager (Syracuse Univ. Press, 1985).

Political Questions in the Courts: A Judicial Function in Democracies: Israel and the United States by Y. Zemach (Wayne State Univ. Press, 1976).

Religious Law in the Israel Legal System by I. Englard (Jerusalem: Hebrew Univ., 1975).

Tax Laws of the World—Israel (FL: Foreign Tax Law Assn.).

The Traditional Jewish Law of Sale by J. Karo, S. Passamaneck, transl. (Cincinnati: Hebrew Union College Press, 1983).

ARTICLES:
"Business Operations in Israel" by A. Rafael, *Tax Management Income Portfolios,* no. 250–3rd (1981).

"Israel: Legal Education" by C. Klein, 5 *Comparative Law Yearbook* 113 (1981).

"Jewish Law in the State of Israel" by D. Sinclair, 3 *Jewish Law Annual* 154 (1980).

"Registration of Designs in Israel" by Y. Tsur, 14 *International Review of Industrial Property and Copyright Law* 508 (1982).

"Requirements for the American Lawyer to Practice Law in Israel" by L. Roth, 15 *International Lawyer* 433 (1981).

ITALY

SEE ALSO:
Europe, European Economic Community, International Law, United Nations

RESEARCH GUIDES & BIBLIOGRAPHIES:
Guide to Foreign Legal Materials: Italian by A. Grisoli (Parker School of Foreign and Comparative Law; Oceana, 1964).

The Italian Legal System by G. Certoma (Butterworths, 1985).

"The Italian Parliament and Legislative Publications: A Concise Survey" by V. Pisano, 6 *International Journal of Law Libraries* 263 (1978).

STATUTES & RELATED LAWS:
Italian Penal Code (vol. 23), E. Wise, transl. (American Series of Foreign Penal Codes, 1978).

LAW REVIEWS & OTHER PERIODICALS:
Italian Yearbook of International Law (Oceana, 1975–).

Jus Gentium (Rome: Corso Vittorio Emanuele, 1950–) (periodical in Italian, English & French).

DICTIONARIES:
Dictionary of Italian Legal Terms and Relevant Definitions by J. Genco (1980).

Law and Commercial Dictionary in Five Languages by R. Epstein (English, German, Spanish, French, Italian) (West, 1985).

TREATISES &
LOOSELEAFS:

Business Operations in Italy by P. Alegi, Tax Management Foreign Income Portfolios, no. 84–4th (BNA, 1983).

Capital Formation and Investment Incentives Around the World by W. Diamond & D. Diamond (Matthew Bender, 1984–).

Civil Procedure in Italy by M. Cappelletti & J. Perillo (The Hague: Martinus Nijhoff, 1965).

Comparative Law by G. Gloss (Rothman, 1979).

Consumer Legislation in Italy by G. Ghidini (Van Nostrand Reinhold, 1980).

Digest of Commercial Laws of the World (Italy) by the Natl. Assn. of Credit Management (Oceana, 1977–).

Eurocommunism: The Italian Case by A. Ranney & G. Sarti (American Enterprise Inst., 1978).

Information Guide, Doing Business in Italy (Price Waterhouse).

Italian Company Law by P. Verrucoli (London: Oyez Publications, 1977).

The Italian Legal System: An Introduction by M. Cappellenti et al. (Stanford Univ. Press, 1967).

Italian Practice in International Law (Italian Society for Intl. Organization; Oceana).

Recognition and Enforcement of Foreign Judgments in Various Foreign Countries (Italy) by G. Roman (Library of Congress, 1984).

The Rule of Law in Italy (The Hague: the Intl. Commission of Jurists, 1958).

Tax Laws of the World—Italy (FL: Foreign Tax Law Assn.).

World Law of Competition (Italy), J. von Kalinowski, ed. (Matthew Bender, 1979–).

ARTICLES:

"Agency and Distributorship Laws in Italy" by D. Dobson, 20 *International Lawyer* 997 (1986).

"Banking Secrecy in Italy with Respect to the Tax Authorities after the 1982 Reform" by F. Bosello, 37 *Bul. Intl. Fisc. Doc.* 436 (1983).

"The Disintermediation of the Banking System in the 1980s," *Review of Economic Conditions in Italy* 191–319 (June, 1982).

"Italy" in *Business Law in Europe* by G. Ughi et al. (Kluwer, 1982).

"Italy's Law Firms Fight Tradition" by C. Blackhurst, 4 *International Financial Law Review* 5 (1985).

"The Legal Profession in Italy" by H. Sereni, 63 *Harvard Law Review* 1000 (1950).

"1981 Italian Deposit Requirement," 14 *Law and Policy in International Business* 927 (1982).

". . . Overview of the Italian Legal System" by Del Duca, 88 *Dickerson Law Review* 221 (1984).

"The Policy of Law and Order in Italy: The Voice of the Power and its Impact" by V. Ferrari, 9 *International Journal of the Sociology of Law* 38 (1981).

"Real Property Investment in Italy" by R. Danovi, 4 *Comparative Law Yearbook* 193 (1980).

IVORY COAST

SEE ALSO:

Africa, International Law, United Nations

TREATISES &
LOOSELEAFS:

African Tax Systems by R. Hammon & M. van den Abeelen (Ivory Coast) (Amsterdam: Intl. Bureau of Fiscal Documentation, 1980–).

Capital Formation and Investment Incentives Around the World (vol. 1, Ivory Coast) by W. Diamond & D. Diamond (Matthew Bender, 1984–).

The Civil Code of the Ivory Coast by A. Levasseur (Michie, 1976).

Information Guide, Doing Business in the Ivory Coast (Price Waterhouse).
An Introduction to Law in French-Speaking Africa by J. Salacuse (Michie, 1969).

ARTICLES: "Double Taxation Agreements" (Ivory Coast and Canada), *International Business Lawyer* 466 (1985).
"The Reform of Company Law" (Ivory Coast) by B. Dumonteil, 5 *The Company Lawyer* 47 (1984).
"Regulation of Business Activities of Petroleum Contractors in Cameroon, Congo, Gabon, and Ivory Coast" by M. Frilet, 30 *Oil and Gas Tax Quarterly* 485 (1982).

JAG: See Military Law
JAIL: See Corrections
JAILHOUSE LAWYERS: See Corrections, Paralegal

JAMAICA

SEE ALSO: Caribbean, International Law, Latin America, United Nations

CONSTITUTION: "Jamaica, 1971–1983" in *Constitutions of the Countries of the World* by A. Blaustein & G. Flanz (Oceana, 1983).

STATUTES & RELATED LAWS: *Jamaica Consolidated Index of Statutes and Subsidiary Legislation* by the Fac. of Law Library, Univ. of West Indies, Barbados (Gaunt, 1986).

JOURNALS & OTHER PERIODICALS: *Kingston Law Review* (1968–).
West Indian Law Journal (Kingston: Council of Legal Education, 1977–).

TREATISES & LOOSELEAFS: *Capital Formation and Investment Incentives Around the World* (Jamaica) by W. Diamond & D. Diamond (Matthew Bender, 1984–).
Caribbean Basin: A Tax Tour (Jamaica) Arthur Anderson & Co., 1985).
Commercial Laws of the World, Jamaica (1985–).
The Constitutional Law of Jamaica by L. Barnett (Oxford Univ. Press, 1977).
Democratic Socialism in Jamaica by H. Evelyne (Princeton Univ. Press, 1986).
Information Guide: Doing Business in Jamaica (Price Waterhouse).
Investment Laws of the World (Jamaica) (Oceana, 1981–).
The Taxation of Corporate Income in Jamaica by J. Wozny (Kingston: Board of Revenue, 1985).
Tax Laws of the World—Jamaica (FL: Foreign Tax Law Assn., 1983–).
West Indian Constitutions: Post Independence Reform (Jamaica) by F. Phillips (Oceana, 1985).

ARTICLES: "Bauxite for Butter: The U.S.-Jamaican Agreement and the Future of Barter in U.S. Trade Policy" by E. Lee, 16 *Law and Policy in International Business* 239 (1984).
"The Jamaican Admiralty Jurisdiction" by H. Hyman, 8 *West Indian Law Journal* 175 (1984).

"Jamaican Income Tax and the Foreign Employee" by C. Alexander *International Business Lawyer* 459 (Nov., 1984).

"Land versus Capital Value Taxation; by J. Follain, 34 *National Tax Journal* 451 (1986).

"Taxing the Corporate Person in Jamaica" by D. White, 5 *The Company Lawyer* 147 (1984).

JAPAN

SEE ALSO:	Asia, International Law, United Nations

RESEARCH GUIDES & BIBLIOGRAPHIES:

"Forms of Citation of Japanese Legal Materials," 42 *Washington Law Review* 589 (1966).

"Guide to Japanese Legal Literature" by N. Yamamoto, 7 *International Journal of Law Libraries* 175 (1979).

"A Guide to the Study of Japanese Law" by L. Beer & H. Tomatsu, 23 *American Journal of Comparative Law* 284 (1975).

"Index to Japanese Law," an annual index supplement to *Law in Japan* (see Journals below).

An Index to Japanese Law: A Bibliography of Western Language Materials, 1867–1973, R. Coleman & J. Haley, eds. (Univ. of Tokyo Press, 1975) (supplemented by *Law in Japan*—see below).

An Introduction to Japanese Government Publications by T. Kuroki (Oxford, 1981).

"Japanese Law: A Selective Bibliographical Guide" by T. Lee, 63 *Law Library Journal* 189 (1970).

Japanese National Government Publications in the Library of Congress: A Bibliography, T. Ohta, comp. (Lib. of Cong., 1981).

CONSTITUTION:

The Constitutional Case Law of Japan: Selected Supreme Court Decisions 1961–70 (Univ. of Wash. Press, 1978).

The Constitution of Japan, its First Fifty Years, 1947–67 by D. Henderson (Univ. of Wash. Press, 1969).

Japan's Commission on the Constitution: The Final Report, J. Maki transl. (Univ. of Wash. Press, 1981).

STATUTES & RELATED LAWS:

Japan Laws, Ordinances and Other Regulations Concerning Foreign Exchange and Foreign Trade (Tokyo: Chuo Shuppan Kikaku, 1985).

JOURNALS & OTHER PERIODICALS:

The Japan Annual of Law and Politics (Science Council of Japan, 1952–).

Japanese Annual of International Law (Intl. Law Assn. of Japan; Oceana, 1957–).

Japanese Legal Periodicals: A Checklist of Holdings by T. Nishioka (Library of Congress, 1982).

The Japan Law Letter (Tokyo: Eagle Enterprises, 1983–).

Japan Science Review, Law and Politics (Union of Japanese Societies of Law and Politics, 1950–).

Kobe University Law Review (Intl. Edition, 1961–).

Law in Japan (Tokyo: Japanese American Society for Legal Studies, 1967–). (Beginning with vol. 7, there is an annual index to Japanese law.)

**TREATISES &
LOOSELEAFS:**

Antimonopoly Legislation in Japan (Federal Legal Publications, 1969).

Antitrust in Japan by E. Hadley (Princeton Univ. Press, 1970).

Business Transactions with China, Japan, and South Korea, S. Parviz & H. Smit, eds. (Matthew Bender, 1983–).

Civil Procedure in Japan by T. Hattori & D. Henderson (Matthew Bender, 1983–).

Current Legal Aspects of Doing Business in Japan and East Asia (ABA, Intl. Law and Practice Sect., 1978).

Digest of Commercial Laws of the World (Japan) by the Natl. Assn. of Credit Management (Oceana, 1977–).

Doing Business in Japan by Z. Kitagawa (Matthew Bender, 1980–).

Environmental Law in Japan by J. Gresser et al. (MIT Press, 1981).

Guide to Japanese Taxes 1983–84 by Y. Gomi (Kluwer, 1984).

The Intellectual Property Law of Japan by T. Doi (Sijthoff & Noordhoff, 1980).

Introduction to Japanese Law by Y. Noda, A. Angelo, transl. (Univ. of Tokyo Press, 1976).

Japan Business: Obstacles and Opportunities, K. Ohmae, ed. (Wiley, 1983).

Japanese Business Law and the Legal System by E. Hahn (Quorum Books, 1984).

Japanese International Taxation by J. Huston et al. (Matthew Bender, 1983–).

Japanese Securities Regulation, M. Yazawa & B. Banoff (Little, Brown, 1983).

Labour Law and Industrial Relations in Japan, 2d ed. by T. Hanami (Kluwer, 1985).

Legal Aspects of Doing Business in Japan (Practicing Law Institute, annual).

Litigation in Japan (ABA Litigation Section, 1980).

Setting Up Enterprises in Japan by the Bank of Tokyo (Japan: Jetro, 1984).

The Sogo Shosha: Japan's Multinational Trading Companies by A. Young (Westview, 1979).

Tax Laws of the World—Japan (FL: Foreign Tax Law Assn.).

ARTICLES:

"Antitrust Sanctions and Remedies: A Comparative Study of German and Japanese Law" by J. Haley, 59 *Washington Law Review* 471 (1984).

"Briefing the American Negotiator in Japan" by R. Watts, 16 *International Lawyer* 597 (1982).

"Doing Business in Japan: The Importance of the Unwritten Law" by P. Lansing & M. Wechselbatt, 17 *International Lawyer* 647 (no. 4, Fall, 1983). (See also 7 Licensing L. & Bus. Rep. 159 (1984).

"Export Control and Export Cartel in Japan" by M. Matsushita, 20 *Harvard International Law Journal* 103 (1979).

"Foreign Investment in Japan: The Legal and Social Climate" by P. Reynolds, 18 *Texas International Law Journal* 175 (1983).

"Historical Development of the Japanese Bar" by R. Rabinowitz, 70 *Harvard Law Review* 61 (1956).

"Japanese Banking Law," by B. Semkow, 17 *Law and Policy in International Business* 81 (1985).

"The Japanese Judicial System: Thirty Years of Transition" by B. George, 12 *Loyola of Los Angeles Law Review* 807 (1979).

"The Japanese Law in English: Some Thoughts on Scope and Method" by D. Henderson, 16 *Vanderbilt Journal of Transnational Law* 601 (1983).

"Japan: The Rise of Children" by I. Shimazu, 25 *Journal of Family Law* 179 (1986–87).

"The Law of the Subtle Mind: The Traditional Japanese Conception of Law" by C. Kim & C. Lawson, 28 *International and Comparative Law Quarterly* 491 (1979).

"The Use and Non-Use of Contract Law in Japan" by W. Gray, 17 *Law in Japan* 98 (1984).

JAVANESE LAW: See Indonesia
JEHOVAH'S WITNESSES: See Church & State
JERSEY: See Channel Islands, New Jersey
JEWISH LAW: See Israel
JOB RIGHTS: See Employment Discrimination, Labor Law, Women & the Law
JOB SAFETY: See Occupational Safety, Torts, Workers' Compensation
JOINDER: See Trial & Appellate Practice
JOINT AND SEVERAL LIABILITY: See Trial & Appellate Practice
JOINT CUSTODY: See Family Law
JOINT STOCK COMPANY: See Corporate Law, Securities Law
JOINT TENANCY: See Estate Planning, Family Law, Real Estte
JOINT TORTFEASOR: See Torts
JOINT VENTURES: See Business Law, Contracts, International Law, Partnership Law, Torts
JONES ACT: See Maritime Law, Workers' Compensation

JORDAN

SEE ALSO: International Law, Islam, Middle East, United Nations

**TREATISES &
LOOSELEAFS:**
Commercial Laws of the Middle East by A. Keesee (Oceana, 1980–).
Investment Laws of the World (Jordan) (Oceana, 1981–).
Jordan: A Country Study, 3d ed., R. Nyrop, ed. (American Univ., Foreign Area Studies, 1979).
The Laws of Saudi Arabia, the UAE, Egypt, and Jordan: A Legal and Investment Guide for American Business (Wash. D.C.: American Arab Affairs Council, 1985).
Property Law in the Arab World: Real Rights in Egypt, Iraq, Jordan, Lebanon, Libya, Saudi Arabia and the Gulf States by F. Ziadeh (London: Graham & Trotman, 1979).
Taxes and Investment in the Middle East (Jordan) (Intl. Bureau of Fiscal Documentation).
Tax Laws of the World—Jordan (FL: Foreign Tax Law Assn.).

ARTICLES:
"Middle East Agency Law Survey" (Jordan) by F. Taylor, 14 *International Lawyer* 341 (1980).
"A Survey of Intellectual Property Laws in Egypt, Jordan, and Lebanon" by M. Rawls, 6 *Middle East Executive Reports* 20 (1983).

JOURNALISM: See Media
JUDGE ADVOCATE GENERAL: See Military Law
JUDGES: See Judicial Administration, Trial & Appellate Practice
JUDGES, NONLAWYER: See Paralegal
JUDGMENT: See Criminal Law, Torts, Trial & Appellate Practice
JUDGMENT CREDITOR: See Consumer Law, Trial & Appellate Practice
JUDGMENT NOTWITHSTANDING THE VERDICT: See Trial & Appellate Practice
JUDICATURE: See Professional Responsibility

JUDICIAL ADMINISTRATION

SEE ALSO: Administrative Law, Circuit Courts, Criminal Law, Jurisprudence, Juvenile Law, Law

Office Management, Legal History, Professional Responsibility, State & Local Government, Trial & Appellate Practice

RESEARCH GUIDES & BIBLIOGRAPHIES:
The Administration of Justice in the Courts: A Selected and Annotated Bibliography by F. Klein (Oceana, 1976).
Selected Literature on Judicial Conduct and Disability: An Annotated Bibliography by J. Van Schaick (American Judicature Society, 1983).

JOURNALS, NEWSLETTERS & OTHER PERIODICALS:
Appellate Court Administration Review (VA: Natl. Center for State Courts).
Court Management Journal (VA: National Center for State Courts).
Judges Journal (ABA, Judicial Admin. Div.).
Judicare (1917–).
Jurist (1941–).
The Justice System Journal (Denver: Institute for Court Management, 1974–).
State Court Journal (VA: Natl. Center for State Courts).

REPORTS:
Federal Judicial Workload Statistics (Administrative Office of the U.S. Courts).
National Symposium on Court Management Proceedings (VA: National Center for State Courts, 1982–).
Report of the Proceedings of the Judicial Conference of the United States (Administrative Conference of the United States).

DIRECTORIES:
Directory of State Courts, Judges, and Clerks (BNA, 1986).
Federal Judiciary Almanac (Wiley, 1984–).

TREATISES & LOOSELEAFS:
American Court Management by D. Saari (Quorum Books, 1982).
Encyclopedia of the American Judicial System (Scribner, 1987).
A Guide to Court Records Management by T. Dibble (VA: Natl. Center for State Courts, 1986).
The Improvement of the Administration of Justice, 6th ed. by F. Klein (ABA, 1981).
Judicial Conduct Reporter (American Judicature Society).
Justice on Appeal by P. Carrington (West, 1976).
Managing the State Courts by L. Berkson (West, 1977).
Personnel Administration in the Courts by H. Lawson (Westview, 1979).
The Role of Courts in American Society by the Council on the Role of the Courts (West, 1985).

ENCYCLOPEDIAS:
AMERICAN JURISPRUDENCE 2D (Am Jur 2d)
Check the following topics in the General Index volumes for Am Jur 2d:

Clerks of Court	Courts
Courthouse	Inferior Courts
Court Records	Judicial Councils and
Court Reporters	Conferences

CORPUS JURIS SECUNDUM (CJS)
Check the following topics in the *General Index* volumes for CJS:

Clerks of Court	Courts
Courthouses	Judges
Court Reporters	States

PERIODICALS:

CURRENT LAW INDEX (CLI) & LEGAL RESOURCE INDEX (LRI)
In the CLI and LRI, look for references to periodical literature under the following subject headings:

Appellate Courts   Courts
Court Administration   Judges
Court Calendars   Justice, Administration of
Court Congestion   State Courts

INDEX TO LEGAL PERIODICALS (ILP)
In the ILP, look for references to legal periodical literature under the following subject headings:

Administration of Justice   Courts
Court Congestion and   Judges
    Delay   Judicial Statistics
Court Reporting

JUDICIAL CONDUCT: See Judicial Administration, Professional Responsibility
JUDICIAL NOTICE: See Trial & Appellate Practice
JUDICIAL POWER: See Constitutional Law
JUDICIAL SALE: See Real Estate, Trial & Appellate Practice
JURISDICTION: See Conflict of Law, Trial & Appellate Practice

JURISPRUDENCE

SEE ALSO:

Constitutional Law, Criminal Law, Economics, Human Rights, International Law, Legal History, Legal Research, Professional Responsibility

RESEARCH GUIDE & BIBLIOGRAPHY:

A Bibliography of Jurisprudence, 3d ed. by R. Dias (Butterworths, 1979).

JOURNALS, NEWSLETTERS & OTHER PERIODICALS:

American Journal of Jurisprudence (formerly the Natural Law Journal) (Notre Dame Law School, 1969–).
International Journal of the Sociology of the Law (Academic Press).
Journal of Law and Politics (Univ. of VA School of Law, 1983–).
Law and Philosophy: An International Journal for Jurisprudence and Legal Philosophy (Boston: Reidel, 1982–).
Law and Society Review.
Ratio Juris: An International Journal of Jurisprudence and Philosophy of Law (England: Basel Blackwell, 1988–).
Research in Law and Sociology (Greenwich: JAI Press, 1978–).

TREATISES:

The Authoritative and the Authoritarian by J. Viking (Univ. of Chicago Press, 1986).
The Bramble Bush by K. Llewellyn (Oceana, 1960).
The Common Law by O.W. Holmes (Little, Brown, 1881).
The Common Law Tradition: Deciding Appeals by K. Llewellyn (1960).
The Concept of Law by H.L.A. Hart (Oxford Univ. Press, 1976).
Conflicts of Law and Morality by K. Greenwalt (Oxford Univ. Press, 1987).
Courts on Trial by J. Frank (1949).
The Critical Legal Studies Movement by M. Unger (Harvard Univ. Press).
Essays in Jurisprudence and Philosophy by H.L.A. Hart (Clarendon Press, 1984).

Introduction to the Philosophy of Law, 2d ed. by R. Pound (1954).
An Introduction to the Principles of Morals and Legislation, 2d ed. by Bentham (1823; Oxford Univ. Press, 1907).
Jurisprudence, by R. Pound (West, 1959).
Jurisprudence, 3d ed. by E. Bodenheimer (Harvard Univ. Press, 1974).
Jurisprudence: A Descriptive and Normative Analysis of Law by A. D'Amato (Kluwer; Gaunt, 1984).
Jurisprudence and Legal Essays by F. Pollock (Greenwood Press, 1961).
Jurisprudence, Realism in Theory and Practice by K. Llewellyn (Univ. of Chicago Press, 1962).
Law and the Modern Mind by J. Frank (1930).
The Legal Imagination: Studies in the Nature of Legal Thought and Expression by J. White (Little, Brown, 1973).
Legal Philosophy from Plato to Hegel by H. Cairns (Johns Hopkins Press, 1949; Greenwood Press, 1980).
Legal Thinking: Its Limits and Tensions by W. Read (Univ. of Pa. Press, 1986).
On Liberty by John Stuart Mill; E. Rapaport, ed. (Hackett Pub. Co., 1978).
Marx and Engles on Law by M. Cain (Academic Press, 1979).
Marxism and the Law, P. Beirne, ed. (Wiley, 1982).
A Matter of Principle by R. Dworkin (Harvard Univ. Press, 1985).
The Morality of Law by L. Fuller (Yale Univ. Press, 1969).
Natural Law and Human Dignity by E. Bloch (MIT Press, 1986).
Nature and Sources of the Law, 2d ed. by J. Gray (Beacon Press, 1963).
The Nature of the Common Law by M. Eisenberg (Harvard Univ. Press, 1988).
The Nature of the Judicial Process by B. Cardozo (Yale Univ. Press, 1921).
Paradoxes of Legal Science by B. Cardozo (Columbia Univ. Press, 1928).
Ronald Dworkin and Contemporary Jurisprudence by M. Cohen (Rowman & Allanheld, 1984).
Sociological Approaches to the Law by A. Podgorecki (St. Martins, 1981).
Tactics of Legal Reasoning by P. Schlag & D. Skover (Carolina Academic Press, 1986).
A Theory of Justice by Rawles (Harvard Univ. Press, 1971).

PERIODICALS:

CURRENT LAW INDEX (CLI) & LEGAL RESOURCE INDEX (LRI)
In the CLI and LRI, look for references to periodical literature under the following subject headings:

Common Law	Law and Ethics
Decision-Making	Medical Jurisprudence
Judges	Natural Law
Jurisprudence	Political Science
Justice, Administration of Law	Sociological Jurisprudence
	Sociology

INDEX TO LEGAL PERIODICALS (ILP)
In the ILP, look for references to legal periodical literature under the following subject headings:

Anthropology	Legal History
Common Law	Natural Law
Constitutional Law	Philosophy
Criminology	Political Science
Democracy	Roman Law
History	Rule of Law
Judge-Made Law	Science
Jurisprudence	Sociology

JURY: See Intellectual Property, Torts, Trial & Appellate Practice
JUSTICE: See Jurisprudence, Military Law
JUSTICE OF THE PEACE: See Trial & Appellate Practice
JUSTINIAN: See Legal History

JUVENILE LAW

SEE ALSO:

Abortion, Constitutional Law, Corrections, Criminal Law, Family Law, International Law, Labor Law, Mental Health; see also entries under individual states and countries.

**RESEARCH GUIDES &
BIBLIOGRAPHIES:**

Crime and Delinquency: A Bibliographic Guide to the Basic Microform Collection (Microfilming Corp. of America).
"Juvenile Justice: A Bibliographic Essay" by A. Kondak, 72 *Law Library Journal* 21 (1979).
Juvenile Rights Since 1967: An Annotated, Indexed Bibliography by H. von Pfeil (Rothman, 1974).
KINDEX: Am Index to Legal Periodical Literature Concerning Children (Natl. Center for Juvenile Justice, 1976–).

STANDARDS:

Standards for Juvenile Justice: A Summary and Analysis (Institute of Judicial Administration, ABA Joint Commission on Juvenile Justice Standards; Ballinger, 1977).
Standards Relating to Abuse and Neglect (Institute of Judicial Administration, ABA Joint Commission on Juvenile Justice Standards; Ballinger, 1977).

UNIFORM ACT:

Uniform Juvenile Court Act, 9A *Uniform Laws Annotated* 1 (West, 1986).

**JOURNALS, NEWSLETTERS
& OTHER PERIODICALS:**

Children's Legal Rights Journal (Wash. D.C.: Children's Legal Rights Information & Training Program).
Crime and Delinquency (Natl. Council on Crime and Delinquency, 1955–).
Crime and Delinquency Abstracts (1963–).
Journal of Juvenile Law (Univ. of La Verne College of Law, 1977–).
Juvenile & Family Courts Journal (Natl. Council of Juvenile and Family Court Judges, 1949–).
Juvenile & Family Law Digest (1967–).
Youth Law News (San Francisco: Natl. Center for Youth Law).

**TREATISES &
LOOSELEAFS:**

ABA Juvenile & Child Welfare Law Reporter (ABA Natl. Resource Center for Child Advocacy and Protection, 1986–).
The American Juvenile Justice System by G. Vito (Sage Pubs., 1985).
Children, Mental Health and the Law by D. Reppucci et al. (Sage Pubs., 1984).
Children's Competence and Consent by G. Melton (Plenum Press, 1983).
In the Interest of Children: Advocacy, Law Reform, and Public Policy by R. Mnookin (NY: Freeman & Co., 1985).
Juvenile Courts in a Nutshell, 3d ed. by S. Fox (West, 1984).
Juvenile Delinquency and Youth Crime: Task Force Report (The President's Commn. on Law Enforcement and Judicial Admin., 1967).
Juvenile Detention Facilities (American Correctional Assn., 1984).
Juvenile Offenders and the Juvenile Justice System by S. Rubin (Oceana, 1986).

Legal Directory of Children's Rights, T. Jacobs, ed. (Univ. Pub. of America, 1985).
Legal Rights of Children by R. Horowitz & H. Davidson (Shepard's, 1984).
Representing the Child Client (Matthew-Bender, 1987–).
Rights of Juveniles, 2d ed. by S. Davis (Clark Boardman, 1980–).
The Sexual Rights of Adolescents by H. Rodman et al. (Columbia Univ. Press, 1984).
Up Against the Law: Your Rights as a Minor by R. Olney (E.P. Dutton, 1985).

ENCYCLOPEDIAS:

AMERICAN JURISPRUDENCE 2D (Am Jur 2d)
Check the following topics in the *General Index* volumes for Am Jr 2d:

Constitutional Law	Juvenile Courts and Delinquent
Guardian and Ward	and Dependent Children
	Parent and Child

CORPUS JURIS SECUNDUM (CJS)
Check the following topics in the *General Index* volumes for Am Jr 2d:

Constitutional Law	Juvenile Courts
Guardian ad Litem	Juvenile Delinquents
Guardian and Ward	Parent and Child

DIGESTS:

CASE SEARCH IN WEST DIGESTS BY KEY TOPIC
In the *Descriptive Word Index* of the West digests, look for key topics and numbers under the following subject headings:

Constitutional Law	Juvenile Courts
Criminal Law	Juvenile Delinquents
Guardian ad Litem	Parent and Child
Guardian and Ward	Reformatories
Infants	

ALR:

ANNOTATIONS
Check the index volumes for ALR, ALR2d, ALR3d, ALR4th, and ALR Fed for annotations under the following subject headings:

Children	Guardian and Ward
Criminal Law	Juvenile Courts and
Detention	Delinquency
Due Process of Law	Rehabilitation
Expungement	Rehabilitation Institution

PERIODICALS:

CURRENT LAW INDEX (CLI) & LEGAL RESOURCE INDEX (LRI)
In the CLI and LRI, look for references to periodical literature under the following subject headings:

Delinquents	Juvenile Delinquents
Criminal Law	Juvenile Justice
Juvenile Corrections	Parent and Child
Juvenile Courts	

INDEX TO LEGAL PERIODICALS (ILP)
In the ILP, look for references to legal periodical literature under the following subject headings:

Administrative Agencies	Family Courts
Behavior Modification	Guardian and Ward
Civil Rights	Infants
Commitment	Juvenile Courts
Constitutional Law	Juvenile Delinquency
Criminal Law	

KAMPUCHEA: See Cambodia

KANSAS

SEE ALSO:	Circuit Courts (Tenth Circuit)

RESEARCH GUIDES & BIBLIOGRAPHIES:

A Guide to Kansas Legal Research by F. Snyder (Kansas Bar Assn., 1986).

Kansas State Documents for Law Libraries by M. Wisneski (American Assn. of Law Libraries, 1984).

STATUTES & OTHER PUBLICATIONS RELATING TO LEGISLATION:

Kansas Statutes Annotated.

Session Laws of Kansas.

CCH Advance Session Laws Reporter—Kansas.

Kansas Legislature: Summary of Legislation (Kansas Legislative Research Dept.).

REGULATIONS:

Kansas Administrative Regulations.

Kansas Register (Kansas Secretary of State, 1982–).

CASES & OPINIONS:

Kansas Reports (1862–).

Pacific Reporter (1883–).

Kansas Court of Appeals Reports (1895–1901) (1977–).

COURT RULES:

Kansas Court Rules and Procedure (West).

JURY INSTRUCTIONS:

Pattern Instructions for Kansas—Criminal, 2d ed. (Kansas Judicial Center, 1982).

Pattern Instructions for Kansas 2d (Civil) (Bancroft-Whitney, 1977–).

OPINIONS OF THE ATTORNEY GENERAL:

Attorney General Opinions (Office of the Attorney General).

Kansas Register (Kansas Secretary of State, 1982–).

JOURNALS & OTHER PERIODICALS:

Daily Record (Wichita)

Journal of Kansas Trial Lawyers Association (1977–).

Journal of the Kansas Bar Association (1932–).

Kansas Barletter (1951–).

Kansas Criminal Procedure Review (Univ. of Kansas School of Law Criminal Justice Clinic, 1984–).

Topeka Daily Legal News.

Wichita Journal.

DIRECTORIES:

Directory of the Kansas Bar (Kansas Bar Assn., 1982/83–).

TREATISES & LOOSELEAFS:

Kansas Administrative Law with Federal Refrences by D. Ryan (Kansas Bar Assn., 1982–).

Kansas Appellate Practice, J. Harman, ed. (Kansas Bar Assn., 1987–).

Kansas Attorney's Practice Manual by the Douglas County Legal Aid Society (Kansas

Bar Assn., 1978–).
Kansas Bankruptcy Handbook, 2d ed. (Kansas Bar Assn., 1982–).
Kansas Code of Civil Procedure 2d Annotated by S. Gard (Bancroft-Whitney, 1979–).
Kansas Corporation Law and Practice (Including Tax Aspects), 3d ed. by J. Logan et al. (Kansas Bar Assn., 1988).
Kansas Criminal Law Handbook by M. Barbara (Kansas Bar Assn., 1978–).
Kansas Family Law Handbook by L. Elrod (Kansas Bar Assn., 1983–).
Kansas Law of Sales Under the Uniform Commercial Code by P. Rasor (Kansas Bar Assn., 1981–).
Kansas Real Estate Practice and Procedure (Kansas Bar Assn., 1984–).
Kansas State and Local Tax Service (Prentice-Hall).
Kansas Statutes of Limitations and Time Standards Handbook, C. McNeil, ed. (Kansas Bar Assn., 1988).
Kansas Tax Reporter: State and Local Taxes (CCH).
Vernon's Kansas Forms Annotated: Code of Civil Procedure with Practice Commentaries by E. Hatcher (West, 1963).
Vernon's Kansas Forms Annotated: Uniform Commercial Code with Practice Commentaries by J. Howe & D. Dale (West, 1981).

DIGESTS & CITATOR: *Kansas Digest* (West).
Pacific Digest (West).
Shepard's Kansas Citations.

KENTUCKY

SEE ALSO: Circuit Courts (Sixth Circuit)

**BIBLIOGRAPHIES &
RESEARCH GUIDES:** *Guide to Kentucky Legal Research: A State Bibliography* by W. Gilmer (State Library, 1979).
Index to Kentucky Legal History by E. Lockwood (State Law Library, 1983).

**STATUTES & OTHER
LEGISLATIVE MATERIALS:** *Baldwin's Official Edition, Kentucky Revised Statutes Annotated.*
Kentucky Acts.
Kentucky Revised Statutes and Rules Service (Baldwin).
Kentucky Revised Statutes Annotated, Official Edition (Michie).

**STATE ADMINISTRATIVE
REGULATIONS:** *Kentucky Administrative Register.*
Kentucky Administrative Regulation Service.

CASES & OPINIONS: *Kentucky Reports* (1879–1951).
Kentucky Decisions (West).
South Western Reporter (1886–).

COURT RULES: *Kentucky Court Rules* (Rules Service Co., 1979–).
Kentucky Rules of Court Annotated (Michie).
Kentucky Rules of Court (West).
Kentucky Rules of Civil Procedure Annotated by W. Bertelsman (West, 1984).

JURY INSTRUCTIONS: *Kentucky Instructions to Juries*, 4th ed. by J. Palmore (Anderson, 1975, 1989).

ETHICS & PROFESSIONAL RESPONSIBILITY:	"Ethics Opinions of the Kentucky Bar Association" in vol. 9 of *Baldwin's Kentucky Revised Statutes.*
OPINIONS OF THE ATTORNEY GENERAL:	*Attorney General Opinions and Reports* (Banks-Baldwin, 1960–).
JOURNALS & OTHER PERIODICALS:	*Daily Record* (Louisville). *Kentucky Bench and Bar* (KY State Bar, 1936–).
SURVEY OF STATE LAW:	"Survey of Kentucky Opinions" in *Kentucky Law Journal.* See for example vol. 61, p. 512; vol. 68, p. 495.
TREATISES, LOOSELEAFS & OTHER MONOGRAPHS:	*Anderson's Kentucky Corporation Record Book* (Anderson, 1989). *Cadwell's Kentucky Form Book,* 4th ed. by M. Volz et al. (Anderson, 1989). *Kentucky Collections* by W. Mapother (Lawyers Co-op., 1981). *Kentucky Criminal Practice and Procedure* by T. Fitzgerald (West, 1978) *Kentucky Divorce* by R. Revell (Lawyers Co-op., 1982). *Kentucky Domestic Relations Law* by L. Graham & J. Keller (Banks-Baldwin, 1982–). *Kentucky Evidence Law Handbook,* 2d ed. by R. Lawson (Michie, 1984). *Kentucky Family Law,* 2d ed. by R. Petrilli (Anderson, 1988). *Kentucky Financial Institutions and Securities Law* (Banks-Baldwin, 1975–). *Kentucky Law of Evidence* by J. Richardson (Anderson, 1973–). *Kentucky Legal Forms* (Banks-Baldwin, 1963–). *Kentucky Methods of Practice* by J. Richardson (West, 1968). *Kentucky Mineral Law,* D. Short, ed. (Banks-Baldwin). *Kentucky Probate* by W. Schmitt (Lawyers Co-op., 1980–). *Kentucky Probate Methods* by R. Noe (Michie, 1976). *Kentucky Probate Practice and Procedure with Forms* by J. Merritt (West, 1984). *Kentucky Tort Law: Defamation and the Right of Privacy* by D. Elder (Michie, 1983). *Products Liability: The Law in Kentucky* by R. Eades (Harrison, 1981). *Trial Handbook for Kentucky Lawyers* by T. Osborne (Lawyers Co-op., 1984). *The Uniform Commercial Code of Kentucky* by D. Leibson (Michie, 1983).
DIGESTS, ENCYCLOPEDIAS & CITATOR:	*Kentucky Digest* (West). *Baldwin's Kentucky Practice.* *Kentucky Practice* (West). *Kentucky Jur* (Lawyers Co-op.). *Shepard's Kentucky Citations.*

KENYA

SEE ALSO:	Africa, International Law, United Nations
RESEARCH GUIDES & BIBLIOGRAPHIES:	"A Bibliography of the Customary Laws of Kenya" by R. Abel, 6 *East African Law Journal* 100 (1970). "Notes on Legal Literature in East Africa" (Kenya), 10 *Case Western Reserve Journal of International Law* 123 (1978).

CONSTITUTION:	"Kenya" in *Constitutions of the Countries of the World* by A. Blaustein & G. Flanz (Oceana, 1981).
JOURNALS & OTHER PERIODICALS:	*East African Law Journal* (Univ. of Nairobi, Kenya Institute of Administrations, 1965–).
TREATISES & LOOSELEAFS:	*Africa and Law* (Kenya), T. Hutchison, ed. (Univ. of Wisc. Press, 1968).
	African Tax Systems (Kenya) (Amsterdam: Intl. Bureau of Fiscal Documentation).
	Capital Formation and Investment Incentives Around the World (Kenya) by W. Diamond & D. Diamond (Matthew Bender, 1984–).
	Information Guide: Doing Business in Kenya (Price Waterhouse).
	Integration and Disintegration in East Aftica (Kenya) by C. Potholm & R. Fredland (Univ. Press of America, 1980).
	An Introduction to Taxation in Kenya by S. Butt (London: Cassel & Co., 1978).
	Investment Laws of the World (Kenya) (Oceana, 1981–).
	Kenya: Law of Criminal Procedure by C. Mwalimu (Library of Congress, 1983).
	The Kenyan Legal System: An Overview by C. Mwalimu (Library of Congress, 1988).
	The Legal System of Africa: Kenya by O. K'Ombudo (Michie).
	Multinational Corporations in the Political Economy of Kenya by S. Langdon (St. Martin's Press, 1981).
	The Status of Aliens in East Africa: Asians and Europeans in Tanzania, Uganda, and Kenya by D. Nanjira (Praeger, 1976).
	Tax Laws of the World—Kenya (FL: Foreign Tax Law Assn.).
ARTICLES:	"Detention without Trial in Kenya" by K. Conboy, 8 *Georgia Journal of International and Comparative Law* 441 (1978).
	"The Development and Reform of the Law in Kenya" by E. Cotrain, 27 *Journal of African Law* 42 (1983).
	"Development and the Legal Process in Kenya" by H. Okoth-Ogendo, 12 *International Journal of the Sociology of Law* 59 (1984).
	"Kenya's Petit-Bourgeois State, the Public, and the Rule/Misrule of Law" by S. Gutto, 10 *International Journal of the Sociology of Law* 341 (1982).
	"The Legal Status of the Child in Kenya's Political Economy" by H. Okoth-Ogendo, 13 *Columbia Human Rights Law Review* 495 (1981).
	"The Patent System. . .Kenya and Tanzania" by B. Seyoum, 16 *International Review of Industrial Property and Copyright Law* 704 (1985).

KEOGH: See Employee Benefits
KIDNAPPING: See Criminal Law
KILLING: See Criminal Law, Death, Torts
KINSHASA: See Congo

KIRIBATI

SEE ALSO:	England, International Law, United Nations
	Taxes and Investment in Asia and the Pacific (Kiribati) (Amsterdam: Intl. Bureau of Fiscal Documentation, 1983–).

KNOW–HOW: See Intellectual Property

KOREA (NORTH)

SEE ALSO: Asia, Communism, International Law, Korea (South), United Nations

CONSTITUTION: *The Constitution of the Democratic People's Republic of Korea* by S. Cho (Library of Congress, 1986).
The Constitutions of the Communist World (North Korea), W. Simons, ed. (Sijthoff & Noordhoof, 1980).

STATUTES, TREATIES & RELATED LAWS: "Democratic People's Republic of Korea: Joint Venture Law," 24 *International Legal Materials* 806 (1985).
Aviation Laws and Treaties of . . . the German Democratic Republic, Hungary, the Democratic People's Republic of Korea, Laos, Poland, the USSR, Yugoslavia and the Republic of Vietnam (6 vols.) by J. Kneifel (Munich: J. Kneifel, 1985).

TREATISES: *Human Rights in Korea* (NY: Asia Watch Committee, 1985).
Law and Literature of North Korea: A Guide by Sung Yoon Cho (Library of Congress, 1988).

ARTICLES: "Executive Decree Concerning the Joint Venture Act," 40 *Bulletin for International Fiscal Documentation* 15 (1986).
"The 50-Mile Military Boundary Zone of North Korea" by Choon-Ho Park, 72 *American Journal of International Law* 866 (1978).
"Recent Developments in the Constitutions of Asian Marxist-Socialist States" by C. Kim, 13 *Case Western Reserve Journal of International Law* 483, 491 (1981).

KOREA (SOUTH)

SEE ALSO: Asia, International Law, Korea (North)

RESEARCH GUIDE & BIBLIOGRAPHY: *Korean Law: An Annotated Bibliography of English-Language Monographs* by C. Baik (Library of Congress, 1980).

TREATIES: *Republic of Korea Treaty Series* (Seoul: Ministry of Foreign Affairs, 1948–).

STATUTES & RELATED LAWS: *Commercial, Business and Trade Laws: Republic of Korea* (Oceana, 1984–).
Current Laws of the Republic of Korea (Seoul: Statutes Compilation & Dissemination Foundation of Korea, 1983–).
Korea Customs, Laws and Regulations (Seoul: Korea Customs Research Institute, 1987).

JOURNALS, NEWSLETTERS & OTHER PERIODICALS: *Korea and World Affairs.*
Korean Journal of Comparative Law.
Korean Journal of International Law.

Korean Journal of International Studies.
Korean Law Journal.
Seoul Law Journal.

**TREATISES &
LOOSELEAFS:**

Asia and the Pacific: A Tax Tour (South Korea) (Arthur Anderson & Co., 1986).
Business Operations in Republic of Korea by R. Baskerville, Tax Management Foreign Income Portfolios, No. 461 (BNA, 1986).
Business Transactions with China, Japan, and South Korea, S. Parviz & H. Smit, eds. (Matthew Bender, 1983–).
Capital Formation and Investment Incentives Around the World (Korea) by W. Diamond & D. Diamond (Matthew Bender, 1984–).
Digest of Commercial Laws of the World (Korea) (Natl. Assn. of Credit Management; Oceana, 1977–).
Information Guide: Doing Business in Korea (Price Waterhouse)
The Intellectual Property Laws of Korea by K. Park (Seoul: Lee & Ko, 1986).
Introduction to the Law and Legal System of Korea, S. Song, ed. (Seoul: Kyung Mun Sa Pub. Co., 1983).
Investment Laws of the World: The Developing Nations (South Korea) (Oceana, 1972–).
Legal Norms in a Confucian State by W. Shaw (Berkeley: Univ. of Cal. Center for Korean Studies, 1981).
Securities Regulation in Korea by Y. Shin (Univ. of Wash. Press, 1983).
South Korea: A Country Study, 3d ed. by F. Bunge (Govt. Printing Office, 1982).
Taxation in Korea (Seoul: Peat Marwick, Mitchell & Co., 1984–).
Taxes and Investment in Asia and the Pacific (Korea) (Amsterdam: Intl. Bureau of Fiscal Documentation, 1983–).
Tax Laws of the World—Korea (FL: Foreign Tax Law Assn.).

ARTICLES:

"Evolving Industrial Property Law and Transfer of Technology in the Republic of Korea" by J. West, 18 *Texas International Law Journal* 127 (1983).
"Guide to Protecting Trademarks in Korea" by Y. Chang, 82 *Patent and Trademark Review* 412 (1984).
"Introduction to the Law and Legal System of Korea" by H. Knudsen, 13 *International Journal of Legal Information* 96 (1985).
"Legal Aspects of U.S.-Korea Trade" by T. Lee, 7 *University of Hawaii Law Review* (1985).
"Limitation of Shipowners' Liability under the Commercial Code of Korea" by B. Min & J. West, 16 *Journal of Maritime Law and Commerce* 21 (1985).
"Trademark Litigation Involving Foreign Business in the Republic of Korea" by R. Baskerville, 16 *International Lawyer* 521 (1982).

KURDISH QUESTION: See Iraq

KUWAIT

SEE ALSO:

International Law, Islam, Middle East, United Nations

ARBITRATION AWARD:

"Kuwait and the American Independent Oil Company (AMINOIL)," 21 *International Legal Materials* 976 (1982).

**TREATISES &
LOOSELEAFS:**

Banking Laws of Kuwait, N. Karam, transl. (London: Graham & Trotman, 1979).
Business Laws of Kuwait by N. Karam (London: Graham & Trotman, 1984–).

Capital Formation and Investment Incentives Around the World (Kuwait) by W. Diamond & D. Diamond (Matthew Bender, 1984–).

Commerical Laws of the Middle East by A. Keesee (Oceana, 1980–).

Digest of Commercial Laws of the World (Kuwait) (Natl. Assn. of Credit Management; Oceana, 1977–).

Information Guide: Doing Business in Kuwait (Price Waterhouse).

Kuwait and the Gulf: Small States and the International System by A. Hassan (Wash. D.C.: Center for Contemporary Arab Studies, 1984).

Taxes and Investment in the Middle East (Kuwait) (Intl. Bureau of Fiscal Documentation).

Tax Laws of the World—Kuwait (FL: Foreign Tax Law Assn.).

ARTICLES:
"The Arbitration between the Government of Kuwait and Aminoil" by A. Redfern, 55 *British Yearbook of International Law* 65 (1984) (see also 17 *Journal of World Trade Law* 177).

"Arbitration in Kuwait" by J. Chaudhri, 8 *Middle East Executive Reports* 14 (1985).

"Middle East Agency Law Survey" (Kuwait) by F. Taylor, 14 *International Lawyer* 343 (1980).

"State Contracts and Oil Expropriations: The Aminoil-Kuwait Arbitration" by F. Teson, *Virginia Journal of International Law* 323 (1984).

LABLES: See Intellectual Property
LABORATORY: See Health & Medicine

LABOR LAW & ARBITRATION

SEE ALSO:
Administrative Law, Argiculture, Air & Aviation, Antitrust Law, Architecture, Art & Entertainment, Business Law, Civil Service, Corporate Law, Employee Benefits, Employment Discrimination, Government Contracts, Maritime Law, Occupational Safety, State & Local Government, Unemployment Compensation, Workers' Compensation

RESEARCH GUIDES & BIBLIOGRAPHIES:
Bibliography: Labor Management Relations Act ... by S. Washington (Natl. Labor Relations Board Library, 1967).

Doing Research in Federal Labor Law by J. Jagelski (Library of Congress, 1978).

"Federal Labor Law and Its Sources" by S. Pagel, 5 *Legal References Services Quarterly* 5 (1985).

"Index to Selected Bibliography of Articles Relating to Labor Law" by L. Gardiner, 15 *Law Notes* 41 (1979).

"Labor and Employment Law" by M. Grogan & E. Holshouser in *Specialized Legal Research*, L. Chanin, ed. (Little, Brown, 1987).

Labor Management Relations in the Public Sector by J. Cayer & S. Dickerson (Garland, 1984).

STATUTES:
Compilation of Laws Relating to Mediation, Conciliation, and Arbitration Between Employers and Employees (Govt. Printing Office, 1982).

Fair Labor Standards Act, 29 U.S.C.A. §§ 201ff.
Federal Labor Laws, 6th ed. (West, 1984).
Labor-Management Relations Act of 1947, 29 U.S.C.A. §§ 144 ff.
Labor-Management Reporting and Disclosure Act of 1959, 29 U.S.C.A. §§ 153, 411 ff.
National Labor Relations Act, 29 U.S.C.A. §§ 151 ff.
Norris-LaGuardia Act, U.S.C.A. §§ 101 ff.

LEGISLATIVE HISTORIES: *The Economic Regulation of Business and Industry: A Legislative History of U.S. Regulatory Agencies,* B. Schwartz, ed. (NY: Chelsea House, 1973).
Federal Anti-Injunction Act of 1932 (Norris-LaGuardia Act), I. Sloan, ed., vol. 2 of *American Landmark Legislation,* 2d Series (Oceana, 1984).
The Labor-Management Relations Act of 1947 (Taft-Hartley Act), I. Sloan, ed., vol. 5 of *American Landmark Legislation,* 2d Series (Oceana, 1984).
The Labor Reform Law (Labor-Management Reporting and Disclosure Act of 1959) (Bureau of National Affairs, 1959).
Legislative History of the Labor Management Relations Act, 1947 (Govt. Printing Office, 1947; reprint, 1974).
Legislative History of the Labor-Management Reporting and Disclosure Act of 1959 (Govt. Printing Office, 1959; reprint Hein, 1977).
Legislative History of the Labor-Management Reporting and Disclosure Act of 1959, Titles I–VI (Govt. Printing Office 1964).
Legislative History of the National Labor Relations Act, 1935 (Govt. Printing Office, 1978).
"The Legislative History of the Taft-Hartley Act" by G. Reilly, 29 *George Washington University Law Review* 285 (1960).
National Labor Relations Act of 1935, I. Sloan, ed., vol. 3 of *American Landmark Legislation,* 2d Series (Oceana, 1984).

REGULATIONS: *Labor Law Reporter* (CCH, 1965–).
Labor Relations Reporter (Bureau of National Affairs, 1937–).
Rules and Regulations and Statements of Procedure of the National Labor Relations Board, Series 8 as Amended (Govt. Printing Office, 1982–).
29 Code of Federal Regulations

EXECUTIVE ORDERS: E.O. 11,411, 3 C.F.R. 179 (1964–65 Comp.).
E.O. 11,246, 3 C.F.R. 339 (1964–65 Comp.).
E.O. 11,478, 3 C.F.R. 803 (1966–70 Comp.).
E.O. 11,480, 3 C.F.R. 806 (1966–70 Comp.).
E.O. 11,491, 3 C.F.R. 861 (1966–70 Comp.).
E.O. 11,701, 3 C.F.R. 752 (1971–75 Comp.).
E.O. 11,758, 3 C.F.R. 841 (1971–75 Comp.).
E.O. 12,067, 3 C.F.R. 206 (1978).

ANNUAL REPORTS: *Annual Report* (Natl. Labor Relations Board, 1936–).
Annual Report of the National Mediation Board (Govt. Printing Office, 1935–).

ADMINISTRATIVE DECISIONS & COURT OPINIONS: *Administrative Law Judge Decisions Report* (Federal Labor Relations Authority, 1981–).
CCH NLRB Decisions (1960–).
Classification Outline with Topical Index for Decisions of the National Labor Relations Board and Related Court Decisions (Govt. Printing Office, 1982).
Classified Index of Decisions of Regional Directors of the National Labor Relations Board in Representation Proceedings (Govt. Printing Office, 1976–).

Classified Index of Dispositions of ULP Charges by the General Counsel of the National Labor Relations Board (Govt. Printing Office, 1975–).

Classified Index of National Labor Relations Board Decisions and Related Court Decisions (Govt. Printing Office, 1974–).

Court Decisions Relating to the National Labor Relations Act (Govt. Printing Office, 1944–).

Decisions and Orders of the National Labor Relations Board (Govt. Printing Office, 1936–).

Decsions of the Federal Labor Relations Authority (1981–).

Decisions of the United States Merit Systems Protection Board (1981–).

The Digest (United States Merit Systems Protection Board, 1980–).

Digest and Table of Cases for Decisions of the Federal Labor Relations Authority (1980–).

Digest of Decisons of the National Labor Relations Board (Govt. Printing Office, 1946–70).

Employment Practices Guide (CCH, 1972–).

Fair Employment Practice Cases, (BNA, 1969–).

Federal Labor Relations Reporter (Labor Relations Press, 1979–).

Federal Merit Systems Reporter (Labor Relations Press, 1981–).

Labor Arbitration Awards (CCH, 1961–).

Labor Arbitration Reports (BNA, 1946–).

Labor Cases (CCH, 1940–).

Labor Law Reports (CCH, 1934–).

Labor Relations Reference Manual (BNA, 1937–).

NLRB Advice Memorandum Reporter (Labor Relations Press, 1976–).

NLRB Election Report. Cases Closed (National Labor Relations Board, 1962–).

Public Employee Bargaining Reporter (CCH, 1971–).

Subject Matter Indexes to Decisions of the Federal Labor Relations Authority (1979–).

Wage and Hour Cases (BNA, 1942–).

Weekly Summary of NLRB Cases (National Labor Relations Board).

JOURNALS & OTHER PERIODICALS:

"Annual Survey of Labor Relations and Employment Discrimination Law" in *Boston College Law Review.*

Aribtration and the Law: AAA General Counsel's Annual Report (American Arbitration Assn., 1982–).

Arbitration Journal (American Arbitration Assn., 1937–).

Arbitration Times (American Arbitration Assn., 1982).

BNA Employee Relations Weekly (BNA, 1983–).

Comparative Labor Law (UCLA School of Law, 1976–).

Daily Labor Report (BNA, 1961–).

Employee Relations Law Journal (NY: Executive Enterprises, 1975–).

Government Employee Relations Report (BNA, 1963–).

Government Union Review (VA: Public Service Research Foundation, 1980–).

Hofstra Labor Law Forum (Hofstra Univ. School of Law, 1983–).

Industrial and Labor Relations Review (Cornell Univ., N.Y. State School of Industrial and Labor Relations, 1947–).

Industrial Law Journal (Industrial Law Society, 1972–).

Industrial Organization Review (1973–).

Industrial Relations: A Journal of Economy and Society (Univ. of Cal., Berkeley, Institute of Industrial Relations, 1961–).

Industrial Relations Law Journal (Univ. of Cal., Berkeley 1976–).

Institute on Labor Law (Southwestern Legal Foundation Labor Law Developments).

International Labour Documentation (Geneva: Intl. Labour Office, 1965–).
International Labour Office Bulletin of Labour Statistics (Geneva: Intl. Labour Office, 1965–).
International Labour Office Legislative Series (Geneva: Intl. Labour Office, 1919–).
International Labour Review (Geneva: Intl. Labour Office, 1921–).
Labor and Employment Law Newsletter (Matthew Bender, 1984–).
Labor Arbitration Information System (Labor Relations Press, 1970–).
Labor Arbitration in Government (American Arbitration Assn., 1971–).
Labor Law Developments: Proceedings of the Annual Institute on Labor Law (Matthew Bender, 1949–).
Labor Law Journal (CCH, 1949–).
The Labor Lawyer (ABA, 1985–).
Labor Relations Law Journal (NY: Executive Enterprises).
Labor Relations Yearbook, (BNA, 1965–).
Law and Employment Law (ABA, Section of Labor and Employment Law,1968–).
Lawyer's Arbitration Letter (American Arbitration Assn., 1960–).
Monthly Labor Review (BNA, 1915–).
Proceedings of the New York University … Annual National Conference on Labor (Matthew Bender, 1948–).
Retail/Services Labor Report (BNA, 1974–).
Summary of Arbitration Awards (American Arbitration Assn., 1959–).
Union Labor Report (BNA).
White Collar Report (1957–).
Yearbook: Commercial Arbitration (Kluwer, 1976–).

LOOSELEAFS:

American Labor Arbitration (Prentice-Hall).
BNA Policy and Practice Series for Employee Relations Executives (BNA, 1946–).
Business Organizations. Labor Law (vols. 18–18I) by T. Kheel (Matthew Bender, 1972–).
Casehandling Manual (NLRB, 1975–).
Collective Bargaining: Negotiations and Contracts (BNA, 1945–).
Employee and Union Member Guide to Labor Law by the Natl. Lawyers Guild (Clark Boardman, 1979–).
Employment and Training Reporter (BNA, 1969–).
Employment Coordinator (NY: Research Institute of America, 1984–).
Federal Labor Relations Reporter (Labor Relations Press, 1970–).
Federal Regulation of Employment Service (Lawyers Co-op., 1976–).
Human Resources Management (CCH, 1981–).
Industrial Relations Guide—Management and Unions: A Complete Manual (Prentice-Hall, 1970–).
Labor Arbitration and Dispute Settlements (BNA).
Labor Law Reporter (CCH, 1965–).
Labor Management Relations Act Manual by C. Cabot (Warren, Gorham & Lamont, 1978–).
Labor Relations Guide (Prentice-Hall, 1965–).
Labor Relations Reporter (BNA, 1937–).
LMRDA Interpretive Manual (Dept. of Labor, Office of Labor-Management and Welfare-Pension Reports, 1967–).
Modern Personnel Forms by D. Launer et al. (Warren, Gorham & Lamont, 1976–).
NLRB Advice Memorandum Reporter (Labor Relations Press, 1977).
NLRB Casehandling Manual (CCH, 1976–).
NLRB Representation Elections: Law, Practice and Procedure by J. Feerick et al. (Law & Business, Inc.,1980–).

Personnel Management: Communications (Prentice-Hall, 1959–).
Personnel Management: Policies and Practices (Prentice-Hall).
Public Employee Bargaining (CCH, 1977–).
Retail/Services Labor Report (BNA, 1949–).
Union Labor Report (BNA, 1947–).
White Collar Report (BNA, 1957–).

DIRECTORIES:
Directory of Labor Arbitrators (Labor Relations Press, 1982–).
Directory of U.S. Labor Organizations (BNA, 1982–).
Who's Who in Labor (Arno Press, 1976).

TREATISES:
Annual Institute on Employment Law (Practicing Law Institute).
Annual Labor and Employment Law Institute (Rothman).
Arbitration and Collective Bargaining by P. Prasow & E. Peters (McGraw-Hill, 1983).
The Arbitration Guide by R. Britton (Prentice-Hall, 1982).
Arbitration: Promise and Performance, J. Stern & B. Dennis, eds. (BNA).
Basic Patterns in Union Contracts, 10th ed. (BNA, 1983).
Collective Bargaining by G. Berendt (Michie, 1984).
Collective Bargaining Agreements. Private Sector (NC: Microfilming Corp. of America, 1981–).
Comparative Labour Law and Industrial Relations, 2d ed. by R. Blanpain (BNA, 1985).
Contract Administration: A Guide for Stewards and Local Officers by B. Repas (BNA, 1984).
The Deunionizing Handbook by F. Coleman (Federal Publications, 1983).
The Developing Labor Law, 2d ed. (BNA, 1983).
Employee Dismissal Law and Practice by H. Perritt (Wiley, 1984).
Employer's Guide to Strike Planning and Prevention by M. Hutcheson et al. (Practicing Law Institute, 1984).
Federal Legislation to End Strikes: A Documentary History (Govt. Printing Office, 1967).
The Future of Arbitration in America (American Arbitration Assn., 1976).
Grievance Guide, 6th ed. (BNA, 1982).
Guide for Hearing Officers in NLRB Representation Proceedings (Natl. Labor Relations Board, Office of the General Counsel, 1975).
How to Negotiate and Draft Labor Contracts (Practicing Law Institute, 1980).
How to Take a Case before the National Labor Relations Board, 4th ed. by K. MGuiness (BNA, 1976).
International Arbitration, 2d ed., C. Schmitthof, ed. (Oceana, 1976).
International Encyclopedia for Labour Law and Industrial Relations, R. Blanpain, ed. (Kluwer).
International Labour Law by N. Valticos (Kluwer, 1979).
Labor Agreement in Negotiation and Arbitration by A. Zack & R. Bloch (BNA, 1983).
Labor and Employment Law: Resource Material, 2d ed. (ALI–ABA Committee on Cont. Prof. Ed., 1984).
Labor Arbitration Development: A Handbook (BNA, 1983).
Labor Arbitration Law and Practice in a Nutshell by D. Nolan (West, 1979).
The Labor Injunction by F. Frankfurter & N. Greene (MacMillan, 1930).
Labor Law in a Nutshell, 2d ed. by D. Leslie (West, 1986).
Labor Relations and Employment for the Corporate Counsel and the General Practitioner (ABA–ALI Comm. on Cont. Prof. Ed., 1983).
Labor Relations and Social Problems (BNA) (monograph series).

Labor Relations in the Private Sector, 2d ed. by F. Bartosic (ALI–ABA Committee on Cont. Prof. Ed., 1986).

Labor Relations Law by B. Taylor (Prentice-Hall, 1983).

Litigation Manual Outline and Litigation Manual, 1956–1970 (Govt. Printing Office, 1972).

Manual; Division of Judges (Natl. Labor Relations Board, 1984).

Negotiating a Labor Contract by C. Loughran (BNA, 1984).

NLRB Elections: A Guide for Employers by J. Swann (BNA, 1980).

NLRB Practice by L. Modjeska (Lawyers Co-op., 1983).

NLRB Representation Elections: Law, Practice and Procedure by J. Feerick (Law & Business Inc., 1980).

Organizing and the Law, 3d ed. by S. Schlossberg & J. Scott (BNA, 1983).

Personal Rights in the Workplace (ABA, 1981).

Plant Closing Legislation, A. Aboud (Cornell Univ., N.Y. State School of Ind. & Labor Rel., 1984).

Pleadings Manual: Complaint Forms (Natl. Labor Relations Board, Office of the General Counsel) (Govt. Printing Office, 1979).

The Practical Lawyer's Manual on Labor Law (ALI–ABA Committee on Cont. Prof. Ed., 1983).

Practice and Procedure before the National Labor Relations Board, 3d ed. by T. Kammholz & S. Strauss (ALI–ABA Committee on Cont. Prof. Ed., 1980).

Practice and Procedure in Labor Arbitration by O. Fairweather (BNA, 1983).

Practice and Procedure in Labor Arbitration, 2d ed. by O. Fairweather (BNA, 1983).

Primer of Labor Relations, 23d ed. (BNA, 1986).

A Primer on American Labor Law (MIT Press, 1982).

The Process of Deunionization by A. DeMaria (NY: Executive Enterprise Pub., 1979).

Punitive Damages in Wrongful Discharge Cases by J. McCarthy (Lawpress, 1985).

Remedies in Arbitration by M. Hill & A. Sinicropi (BNA, 1981).

Representation Manual, rev. ed. (Natl. Mediation, Board, 1980).

Teacher Strikes and the Courts by D. Colton & E. Graber (Lexington Books, 1982).

Teamster Rank and File Legal Rights Handbook by E. Boal (Detroit: Teamster Rank and File Education and Legal Defense Foundation, 1984).

Unions, Workers, and the Law by B. Justuce (BNA, 1983).

Unjust Dismissal and At Will Employment (Practicing Law Institute, 1982).

Year Book of Labor Statistics (Gale Research Co.).

CITATORS:

Citator: Decisions of the Federal Labor Relations Authority (1980–).

Shepard's Federal Labor Law Citator (1975–).

ENCYCLOPEDIAS:

AMERICAN JURISPRUDENCE 2D (Am Jur 2d)
Check the following topics in the *General Index* volumes for Am Jur 2d:

Administrative Law	Labor and Labor Relations
Arbitration and Award	Removal or Discharge
Compensation	Unemployment Insurance
Contracts	Work, Labor and Services
Injunctions	

CORPUS JURIS SECUNDUM (CJS)
Check the following topics in the *General Index* volumes for CJS:

Administrative Bodies	Compensation and Salaries
Apprentices	Contracts
Arbitration	Fair Labor Standards Act
Child Labor	Injunctions

Labor and Employment   Seniority
Labor Disputes   Severance Pay
Labor Organizations   State Officers and
National Labor Relations   Employees
  Act   Unemployment
National Labor Relations   Compensation
  Board   Union Labels
National Mediation Board   Work and Labor
Norris-LaGuardia Act   Workmens' Compensation
Removal

DIGESTS:

CASE SEARCH IN WEST DIGESTS BY KEY TOPIC
In the *Descriptive Word Index* of the West digests, look for key topics and numbers under the following subject headings:

Administrative Law   National Mediation Board
Arbitration   Norris-LaGuardia Act
Child Labor   Removal
Compensation and Salaries   Schools
Contracts   Seniority
Elections   Severance Pay
Fair Labor Standards Act   State Officers and
Injunctions   Employees
Labor and Employment   Unemployment
Labor Disputes   Compensation
Labor Organizations   Union Labels
National Labor Relations   Work and Labor
  Act   Workmens' Compensation
National Labor Relations
  Board

ALR:

ANNOTATIONS
Check the index volumes for ALR, ALR2d, ALR3d, ALR4th, and ALR Fed for annotations under the following subject headings:

Administrative Law   Labor and Labor Unions
Agency Shops   Landrum-Griffin Act
Arbitration and Award   Lockout
Back Pay   Pensions
Child Labor   Pensions and Retirement
Civil Service   Funds
Commercial Arbitration   Picketing
Compensation   Right-to-Work Laws
Discharge   Seniority
Fair Labor Standards Act   Strikes

PERIODICALS:

CURRENT LAW INDEX (CLI) & LEGAL RESOURCE INDEX (LRI)
In the CLI and LRI, look for references to periodical literature under the following subject headings:

Absenteeism   Contracts for Work
Administrative Law   Dispute Resolution
Alien Labor   Employee
Arbitration   General Strike
Boycott   Grievance Procedures
Collective Bargaining   Industrial Relations

Injunctions	Seniority
Labor …	Strikes and Lockouts
Layoff Systems	Teachers' Unions
Maternity Leave	Tort Liability of Trade
Mediation and Concilation	Unions
Migrant Agricultural	Trade Unions
Laborers	Unemployed
Open and Closed Shop	Unfair Labor Practice
Part-Time Employment	Wages

INDEX TO LEGAL PERIODICALS (ILP)
In the ILP, look for references to legal periodical literature under the following subject headings:

Administrative Law	Labor Law
Agency	Labor Management
Arbitration	Loyalty and Loyalty Oaths
Boycotts	Migrant Labor
Child Labor	Occupational Safety and
Civil Service	Health
Collective Bargaining	Picketing
Employee Ownership	Profit Sharing
Employer and Employee	Safety Laws
Factories	Strikes and Lockouts
Holidays	Unfair Labor Practices
Industrial Arbitration	Unions
Injunctions	Wages
International Arbitration	Workers' Compensation

LATCHES: See Equity, Trial & Appellate Practice
LAKES: See Natural Resources, Water Law
LAND: See Natural Resources, Real Estate, Water Law, Zoning & Land Planning

LANDLORD—TENANT

SEE ALSO: Agriculture, Business Law, Consumer Law, Corporate Law, Franchise Law, Real Estate, Torts, Zoning & Land Planning; see also entries under individual states

RESTATEMENT: *Restatement of the Law, Second, Property* (Landlord and Tenant) (American Law Institute, 1977).

TREATISES & LOOSELEAFS:
American Law of Landlord and Tenant by R. Schoshinski (Lawyers Co-op., 1980).
Current Leasing Law and Techniques by P. Rohan (Matthew Bender, 1982–).
Displacement: How to Fight it by C. Hartmen (Berkeley: Natl. Housing Law Project, 1982).
Friedman on Leases, 2d ed. by M. Friedman (Practicing Law Institute, 1983).
Landlord and Tenant Breach and Remedies by N. Settle (Harrison, 1980)
Landlord and Tenant Law in a Nutshell, 2d ed. by D. Hill (West, 1986).
Landlord's—Owner's Liability by M. Levine (Denver: Prof. Pubs., 1981).
The Landlord-Tenant Relationship by J. Cotton (Prentice-Hall, 1979).
Modern Real Estate Leasing Forms by J. Kusnet (Warren, Gorham & Lamont, 1980–).

Shopping Center and Store Leases by E. Halper (Law Journal Seminars-Press, 1979–).
A Treatise on the American Law of Landlord and Tenant by J. Taylor (Hein, 1981).

LANDRUM–GRIFFIN ACT: See Labor Law
LANDSMEN: See Natural Resources, Oil & Gas
LAND USE: See Environmental Law, Real Estate, Zoning & Land Planning
LANGUAGE: See Legal Research, Quebec
LANHAM TRADE–MARK ACT: See Intellectual Property

LAOS

SEE ALSO: Asia, Communism, International Law, United Nations

Laos: A Country Study (GPO, 1985).
Laos: Keystone of Indochina by A. Dommen (Westview, 1985).
*Aviation Laws and Treaties of ... the German Democratic Republic, Hungary, the
Democratic People's Republic of Korea, Laos, Poland, the USSR, Yugoslavia and
the Republic of Vietnam* (6 vols.) by J. Kneifel (Munich: J. Kneifel, 1985).
"The Legal Terms of Soviet Development Credits to the Laotian People's Democratic
Republic" by G. Ginsburgs, 10 *Review of Socialist Law* 261 (1984).

LARCENY: See Criminal Law
LAST CLEAR CHANCE: See Torts
LATENT DEFECT: See Torts

LATIN AMERICA

SEE ALSO: Argentina, Bahamas, Barbados Belize, Bolivia, Brazil, British Virgin Islands,
Caribbean, Chile, Colombia, Costa Rica, Cuba, Dominican Republic, Ecuador, El
Salvador, Grenada, Guatemala, Guyana, Haiti, Honduras, International Law, Jamaica,
Mexico, Netherlands Antilles, Nicaragua, Panama, Paraguay, Peru, Trinidad and
Tobago, Uruguay, Venezuela, United Nations.

**RESEARCH GUIDES &
BIBLIOGRAPHIES:**
Basic Latin American Legal Materials 1970–1975, J. Aguilar & A. Gonzales, eds.
(Rothman, 1977).
"A Bibliography of Latin American Law: Primary and Secondary Sources in English"
by R. Navarro, 19 *Texas International Law Journal* 319 (1984).
Business Information Sources on Latin America and the Caribbean (Organization of
American States, 1982).
Human Rights in Latin America, 1964–1980: A Selective Bibliography (Library of
Congress, 1983).
Inter-American Legal Materials (ABA Sect. of Intl. Law & Practice, Fall, 1986).
Latin American Society and Legal Culture: A Bibliography by F. Snyder (Greenwood
Press, 1985).
"Legal Materials from Latin America and the Caribbean: Some Ideas for Acquisition"
by E. Schaffer, 12 *International Journal of Legal Information* 103 (1984).
*Multinational and International Investment in Latin America: A Selected and
Annotated Bibliography* by H. Molineu et al. (Ohio Univ. Center for Intl. Studies,
1978).

Nomenclature and Hierarchy: Basic Latin American Legal Sources by R. Medina &
    C. Medina-Quiroga (Library of Congress, GPO, 1979).
"A Selected Guide to Law Related Publications of Latin America and the Caribbean"
    by E. Schaffer, 6 *International Journal of Law Libraries* 75 (1978).

TREATIES & RELATED
AGREEMENTS:
    Instruments of Economic Integration in Latin America and in the Caribbean,
        F. Garcia-Amador, ed., Inter-American Institute of Intl. Legal Studies (Oceana,
        1976).
    Organization of American States Treaty Series (1957–).
    Pan American Union Treaty Series (Organization of American States, 1934–).
    Status of Inter-American Treaties and Conventions (Organization of American States).

CONSTITUTIONS:
    The Constitutions of Latin America by G. Fitzgerald (Chicago: H. Regnery Co., 1968).
    Constitutions of the American Republics (Organization of American States).
    The Constitutions of the Americas by R. Fitzgibbon (Univ. of Chicago Press, 1948).
    Constitutions of the Countries of the World, A. Blaustein & G. Flanz, eds. (Oceana,
        1971).

STATUTES & RELATED
LAWS:
    Index to Latin American Legislation (Library of Congress, Hispanic Law Division;
        G.K. Hall & Co., 1950–60, 1961–65, 1966–70).
    Statement of the Laws of the American Republics in Matters Affecting Business
        (Organization of American States).

JOURNALS & OTHER
PERIODICALS:
    Bank of London & South American Review (Lloyds Bank Intl. Ltd.).
    Comparative Juridical Review (FL: Pan American Institute of Comparative Law, 1964–).
    Lawyer of the Americas (Institute for Inter-American Legal Studies, Univ. of Miami
        School of Law, 1969–) (now called the University of Miami Inter-American Law
        Review).

TREATISES &
LOOSELEAFS:
    The Andean Legal Order: A New Community Law by F. Garcia-Amador (Oceana,
        1978).
    *The Civil Law Tradition: An Introduction to Legal Systems of Western Europe and
        Latin America,* 2d ed. by J. Merryman (Stanford Univ. Press, 1985).
    Copyright Protection in the Americas (Organization of American States; Oceana,
        1979).
    Corporate Taxation in Latin America, B. Zak, ed. (Amsterdam: Intl. Bureau of Fiscal
        Documentation, 1975–).
    *The Crisis of Social Security and Health Care: Latin American Experiences and
        Lessons* C. Mesa-Lago, ed. (Univ. of Pittsburgh, Center for Latin American Studies,
        1985).
    Current Legal Aspects of Doing Business in Latin America (ABA, Intl. Law and
        Practice Section, 1981).
    Digest of Commercial Laws of the World, (Natl. Assn. of Credit Management (Oceana,
        1977–).
    The Expropriation of Multinational Property in the Third World by A. Akinsanya
        (Praeger, 1980).
    Latin America and the Development of the Law of the Sea by A. Szekely (Oceana,
        1976–).
    Latin American Laws and Institutions, by Y. Nun & A. Golbert (Praeger, 1981).

Latin American Society and Legal Culture by F. Snyder (Greenwood Press, 1985).

Latin Migration North: The Problem for U.S. Foreign Policy by M. Teitelbaum (NY: Council on Foreign Relations, 1985).

Legal Aspects of Doing Business in Latin America (vol. 2, Intl. Business Series) (Kluwer; West, 1983–1984).

Legal Aspects of Doing Business in Latin America: Mexico, Brazil, Argentina, Chile, and the Andean Common Market (Practicing Law Institute, 1980).

Legal Imperialism: American Lawyers and Foreign Aid in Latin America by J. Gardner (Univ. of Wisc. Press, 1981).

Mining and Petroleum Legislation of Latin America and the Caribbean (Organization of American States; Oceana, 1978–).

Reference Manual on Doing Business in Latin America, D. Shea et al., eds. (Univ. of Wisc., Center for Latin America, 1979).

Taxation in Latin America (Amsterdam: Intl. Bureau of Fiscal Documentation).

Technology Transfer: Laws and Practice in Latin America, B. Carl. ed. (ABA Intl. Law and Practice Section, 1978, 1980).

ARTICLES:

"The Andean Common Market and the Importance of Effective Dispute Resolution Procedures" by T. O'Leary, 2 *International Tax & Business Lawyer* 101 (1984).

"Antitrust, Technology Transfers and Joint Ventures in Latin American Development" by R. Radway, 15 *Lawyer of the Americas* 47 (1983).

"The Foreign Investment Laws of Latin America: Present and Future" by S. Juncadella, 16 *International Lawyer* 463 (1982).

"Latin American Tax Update" by M. Marti, 12 *Lawyer of the Americas* 630 (1980).

"Survey of Changing Attitudes in Latin American Tax Policy" by M. Marti, 8 *International Tax Journal* 115 (1981).

"Technology Transfer Rules in Latin America: A Study in Comparative Law" by W. Barnes, 3 *Boston College International and Comparative Law Review* 1 (1979).

"Video and Satellite Transmission Piracy in Latin America" by R. Campagna, 20 *International Lawyer* 961 (1986).

LAW ENFORCEMENT: See Criminal Law, State & Local Government
LAW FIRM: See Law Office Management, Professional Responsibility
LAW LIBRARY: See Legal Research

LAW OFFICE MANAGEMENT

SEE ALSO: Accounting, Computers, Legal Education, Paralegals, Professional Responsibility

RESEARCH GUIDES & BIBLIOGRAPHIES:

"Applications of Computers in the Legal Profession: A Selected Bibliography" by E. Day, 3 *Legal Reference Services Quarterly* 75 (1983).

LOCATE: A Directory of Law Office Computer Software (ABA).

"Law Firm Branch Offices: A Selected Bibliography" by D. Davidson, 5 *Legal Reference Services Quarterly* 83 (1985).

Law Office Information Service: A Bibliography of Material on Law Office Economics (ABA & Inst. of Cont. Legal Ed., 1978–).

JOURNALS, NEWSLETTERS & OTHER PERIODICALS: *Computer Law* (Toronot, 1984–).

Computer Law Developments (Computer Law Reporter, 1984–).
Law Office Economics & Management (Callaghan).
Law Office Staff Manual by B. Rolston (ABA, 1987).
Lawyer Hiring & Training Report (Chicago: LawLetters, Inc.).
Legal Economics (ABA).
Legal Management (Assn. of Legal Administrators).
Legal Tech (Leader Pub., 1983–).
Marketing for Lawyers (Leader Pub., 1987–).
Of Counsel (Law & Business, Inc.).
Professional Office Design (Law Journal Seminars-Press).
The Profitable Lawyer (Law & Business, Inc.).
Software Law Journal (CA: Center for Computer Law, 1985–).

DIRECTORIES:

Directory of Corporate Counsel (Law & Business, Inc.).
Directory of the Legal Profession (Natl. Law Journal).
International Directory of Bar Associations (American Bar Foundation).
The Lawyer's Almanac (Law & Business, Inc., 1986).
Lawyers and Creditors Service Directory by T. Stetler (Warren, Gorham & Lamont).
Lawyer's Register by Specialties and Fields of Law, 9th ed. (Solon, OH: Lawyer's Register Pub. Co., 1987).
Martindale-Hubbell Law Directory.

LOOSELEAFS:

Accounting Systems for Law Offices by W. Burke (Matthew Bender, 1978–).
Computer Law: Drafting and Negotiating Forms and Agreements by R. Raysman & P. Brown (Law Journal Seminars-Press, 1984).
Computers and Litigation Support by S. Haynes (Law & Business, Inc., 1981–).
How to Manage Your Law Office by A. Altman & R. Weil (Matthew Bender, 1973–).
Law Office Automation and Technology by F. Arentowicz (Matthew Bender, 1980–).
Law Office Economics and Technology Manual by P. Hoffman (Callaghan, 1970–).
Manual for Managing the Law Office (Prentice-Hall, 1971–).

TREATISES:

The Art of Managing Your Support Staff (A.B.A., 1986).
The Business of Law: A Handbook on How to Manage Law Firms, E. Couric, ed. (Law & Business, Inc., 1984).
Compensation of Attorneys (Abbott, Langer & Associates).
Flying Sole: A Survival Guide for the Solo Lawyer, D. Killoughey, ed. (ABA, 1984).
Future Directions for Law Office Management, P. Ulrich, ed. (State Bar of Arizona, 1982).
How to Create a System for a Law Office, R. Ramo, ed. (ABA, 1975).
How to Go Directly into Solo Practice by G. Singer (Lawyers Co-op., 1976).
How to Market Legal Services by R. Denney (Van Nostrand Reinhold).
How to Start and Build a Law Practice, 2d ed. by J. Foonberg (ABA, 1984).
I'd Rather Do it Myself: How to Set Up Your Own Law Firm by S. Gillers (New York Law Pub. Co., 1977).
Law Firm Accounting by J. Quinn (Law Journal Seminars-Press, 1986).
Law Office Guide to Small Computers by F. Rhoads (Shepard's, 1984).
Law Office Staff Manual by B. Rolston (ABA, 1982).
Lawyering: A Realistic Approach to Legal Practice by J. Freund (Law Journal Seminars-Press, 1979).
Lawyers' Work by J. Hartje (Butterworths, 1984).
Litigation Support Systems by H. Kinney (Callaghan, 1980).
Management for In-House Counsel, J. Silvers et al. eds. (A.B.A., 1985)

Manual of In-House Training: A Guide for Law Firms and Legal Departments,
J. Henning, ed. (Chicago: LawLetters, Inc., 1982).
Partner Withdrawals and Breakups (ABA, 1986).
A Planning Workbook for Law Firm Management, 2d ed. by W. Cobb (A.B.A., 1985).
Practicing Law and Managing People by D. Heller & J. Hunt (Butterworths, 1988).
The Successful Law Firm by B. Hildebrandt (Law & Business, Inc., 1984).

PERIODICALS: CURRENT LAW INDEX (CLI) & LEGAL RESOURCE INDEX (LRI)
In the CLI and LRI, look for references to periodical literature under the following
subject headings:

Computer Programs	Law Offices
Electronic Data Processing	Legal Assistants
Filing Systems	Legal Composition
Information Retrieval	Legal Research
Information Storage	Litigation Support
Law Firms	Practice of Law

INDEX TO LEGAL PERIODICALS (ILP)
In the ILP, look for references to legal periodical literature under the following subject
headings:

Attorneys	Law Office Management
Automation	Legal Ethics
Computers	Paraprofessionals
Information Storage and Retrieval	

LAW OF THE SEA: See Antarctica, International Law, Sea
LAW TEACHERS: See Legal Education
LAWYER REFERRAL: See Professional Responsibility
LAWYERS: See Legal Education, Professional Responsibility, Trial & Appellate
Practice
LAY JUDGES: See Paralegal, Poland
LAYOFF: See Civil Service, Labor Law
LEAGUE OF NATIONS: See International Law, United Nations
LEARNING DISABILITY: See Education Law, Handicapped & the Law, Health &
Medicine, Mental Health
LEASE: See Business Law, Computers, Landlord-Tenant, Natural Resources, Oil &
Gas, Real Estate

LEBANON

SEE ALSO: International Law, Islam, Middle East, United Nations

**RESEARCH GUIDE &
BIBLIOGRAPHY:**   "Legal System of Lebanese: Summary and Bibliography' by W. Wickersham,
5 *International Lawyer* 300 (1971).

**TREATISES &
LOOSELEAFS:**   *Commercial Laws of the Middle East* by A. Keesee (Oceana, 1980–).
Digest of Commercial Laws of the World (Lebanon) (Natl. Assn. of Credit
Management; Oceana, 1977–).

Information Guide: Doing Business in Lebanon (Price Waterhouse).
The Lebanese Legal System by A. El-Gemayel (Wash. D.C.: Intl. Law Institute, 1984).
The Making of Modern Lebanon by H. Cobban (Westview, 1985).
Peacekeeping on Arab-Israeli Fronts: Lessons from the Sinai and Lebanon by
  N. Pelcovits (Westview, 1984).
*Property Law in the Arab World: Real Rights in Egypt, Iraq, Jordan, Lebanon, Libya,
  Saudi Arabia and the Gulf States* by F. Ziadeh (London: Graham & Trotman,
  1979).
Taxes and Investment in the Middle East (Intl. Bureau of Fiscal Documentation).
Tax Laws of the World—Lebanon (FL: Foreign Tax Law Assn.).

ARTICLES: "Internationalized Non-International Armed Conflicts: Case Studies of Afghanistan,
  Kampuchea, and Lebanon" by H. Gasser, 33 *American University Law Review*
  145 (1983).
"Middle East Agency Law Survey" (Lebanon) by F. Taylor, 14 *International Lawyer*
  346 (1980).
"Peacekeeping without the UN: The Multinational Force in Lebanon and International
  Law" by B. Zimber, 10 *Yale Journal of International Law* 222 (1984).
"A Survey of Intellectual Property Laws in Egypt, Jordan, and Lebanon" by M. Rawls,
  6 *Middle East Executive Reports* 20 (1983).

LEEWARD ISLANDS: See British Virgin Islands, Montserrat
LEGAL ADMINISTRATOR: See Law Office Management
LEGAL ADVERTISING: See Advertising, Professional Responsibility
LEGAL AID: See Poverty Law, Professional Responsibility
LEGAL ASSISTANTS: See Law Office Management, Paralegal
LEGAL ECONOMICS: See Economics, Law Office Management

LEGAL EDUCATION & BAR ADMISSION

SEE ALSO: Education Law, Jurisprudence, Law Office Management, Legal History, Legal
Research, Professional Responsibility

**RESEARCH GUIDE &
BIBLIOGRAPHY:** *Admission to the Bar: An Annotated Bibliography of Law Review Articles* by
  F. Houdek (Los Angeles County Law Library, 1976).

**JOURNALS, NEWSLETTERS
& OTHER PERIODICALS:** *The Bar Examiner* (Natl. Conference of Bar Examiners, 1931–).
Clinical Law Journal and Newsletter (Pepperdine Univ. Sch. of Law, 1977–).
International Legal Education Newsletter (Wash. D.C.: Assn. of American Law
  Schools, 1973–).
Journal of Law and Education (1972–).
Journal of Legal Education (1948–).
Law Library Journal (AALL, 1907–).
Legal Education Newsletter (ABA).
Student Lawyer (ABA, 1971–).
Syllabus (ABA).
BAR/BRI Digest.

TREATISES: *Annual Compilation of Bar Examination Questions and Answers* (Institute of Bar
  Review Study).

The Bar Examiner's Handbook, 2d ed., S. Duhl, ed. (Natl. Conference of Bar
Examiners, 1980).
Comprehensive Guide to Bar Admissions Requirements (ABA, 1986).
The Costs and Resources of Legal Education by P. Swords (1974).
Directory of Law Teachers (Association of American Law Schools; West).
An Evaluation of Multistate Bar Examinations (Natl. Conference of Bar Examiners,
1982).
The High Citadel: The Influence of Harvard Law School by J. Seligman (Houghton-
Mifflin, 1978).
Law School: Legal Education in America from the 1850s to the 1980s by R. Stevens
(Univ. of North Carolina Press, 1983).
The Law Schools of the World by H. Tseng (Hein, 1977).
Lawyers, Law Students and People by T. Shaffer (Shepard's, 1977).
Legal Education in the United States by A. Harno (Bancroft-Whitney, 1953).
New Directions in Legal Education by H. Packer & T. Ehrlich (McGraw-Hill, 1972).
Paper Chase by J. Osborne (Houghton-Mifflin, 1971).
Pass This Bar: A Readiness Guide for Bar Examination Preparation by L. Walder
(Wiley, 1982).
Present-Day Law Schools in the United States and Canada by A. Reed (Carnegie
Foundation, 1928).
The Regulation of Foreign Lawyers, 3d ed. by Cone (ABA, 1984).
*A Review of Legal Education in the United States; . . . Law Schools and Bar Admission
Requirements* (ABA, Section of Legal Education and Admissions to the Bar).
Rules for Admission to the Bar in the United States and Territories (West).
Training for the Public Profession of the Law by A. Reed (Carnegie Foundation,
1921).

PERIODICALS: CURRENT LAW INDEX (CLI) & LEGAL RESOURCE INDEX (LRI)
In the CLI and LRI, look for references to periodical literature under the following
subject headings:

Admission to the Bar	Bar Examinations
Attorney and Client	

INDEX TO LEGAL PERIODICALS (ILP)
In the ILP, look for references to legal periodical literature under the following subject
headings:

Admissior to the Bar	Legal Education
Bar Examinations	Legal Profession
Bar Examiners and	
Examinations	

LEGAL ETHICS: See Judicial Administration, Law Office Management, Paralegal,
Professional Responsibility

LEGAL HISTORY

SEE ALSO: Canon Law, Constitutional Law, International Law, Jurisprudence, Legislative History,
Professional Responsibility

**RESEARCH GUIDES &
BIBLIOGRAPHIES:** *Bibliography of Early American Law* by M. Cohen (Kraus, 1985).
Comprehensive Bibliography of American Constitutional and Legal History,

1896–1979 by K. Hall (Kraus, 1984).

American Law and Legal History: State and Territorial Documents, Catalogue 63 (Sharon, MA: Michael Ginsberg Books, Inc.).

"Law Books and Legal Publishing in America, 1760–1840" by J. Parrish, 72 *Law Library Journal* 355 (1979).

The Literature of American Legal History by J. Reid (Oceana, 1985).

JOURNALS, NEWSLETTERS & OTHER PERIODICALS:

American Journal of Legal History (Temple Univ. School of Law, 1957–).

The Colonial Lawyer (Marshall-Wythe School of Law, 1984–).

Journal of Legal History (London: Frank Cass & Co., 1980–).

Law and History (Cornell Law School & the American Society for Legal History, 1983–).

Supreme Court Historical Society Yearbook (1976–).

Western Legal History (Pasadena, CA: Ninth Judicial Circuit Historical Society, 1988–).

SYMPOSIUM ON LEGAL HISTORY (examples):

63 *Oregon Law Review* 558 (1984).

1984 *University of Illinois Law Review* 507.

TREATISES:

Ambivalent Legacy: A Legal History of the South, D. Bodenhamer & J. Ely, eds. (Univ. Press of Mississippi, 1984).

The American Law Institute Archive Publications (microfiche) (Hein, 1985).

American Law Publishing 1860–1900, B. Taylor & R. Munro, eds. (Glanville, 1984).

American Legal and Constitutional History, H. Hyman & S. Bruchey, eds. (Garland, 1986).

The Antifederalists, C. Kenyon, ed. (Northeastern Univ. Press, 1985; Bobbs-Merrill, 1966).

Blackstone's Commentaries by Tucker (Rothman reprint, 1969).

The Chief Sources of English Legal History by P. Winfield (Hein, 1983).

A Concise History of the Common Law, 5th ed. by T. Plucknett (Butterworths, 1956).

Crime and the Courts in England, 1660–1800 by J. Beattie (Princeton Univ. Press, 1986).

The Digest of Justinian by C. Morris (Cambridge Univ. Press, 1904, 1909).

Early English Legal History by T. Plucknett (Seer Books, 1980).

English Law and the Renaissance by F. Maitland (Cambridge Univ. Press, 1901; Rothman, 1985).

Essays in the History of Early American Law by D. Flaherty (Univ. of North Carolina Press, 1965).

The Formative Era of American Law by R. Pound (Little, Brown, 1950).

Fundamental Law in English Constitutional History by J. Gough (Rothman, 1985).

Governing the Hearth: Law and the Family in Nineteenth Century America by M. Grossberg (Univ. of North Carolina Press, 1985).

Historical Introduction to Roman Law, 2d ed. by H. Jolowicz (Cambridge Univ. Press, 1952).

A History of American Law, 2d ed by L. Friedman (Simon & Schuster, 1985).

History of English Law by W. Holdsworth (London: Sweet & Maxwell, 1937).

History of the American Bar by C. Warren (Little, Brown, 1911).

The Institutes of Gaius by F. de Zulueta (Clarendon Press, 1946–53).

Interpretations of Legal History by R. Pound (MacMillan, 1923; Gaunt, 1986).

An Introduction to English Legal History, 2d ed by J. Baker (Butterworths, 1979).

An Introduction to Roman Law by B. Nichols (Clarendon Press, 1976).

The Lawyer from Antiquity to Modern Times by R. Pound (West, 1953).

Legal and Administrative Texts of the Reign of Samsu-iluna by S. Feigin (Yale Univ. Press, 1979).

Legal Education in the United States by A. Harno (Greenwood Press, 1953).

Magna Carta: Text and Commentary, A. Howard, ed. (Univ. Press of Virginia, 1964).

Nineteenth Century Legal Treatises (microfiche, 10,000 titles) (Woodbridge, CT: Research Publications).

The Rise of the Barristers by W. Prest (Oxford Univ. Press, 1986).

Sources of English Legal History 1750–1950 by A. Manchester (England: Butterworths 1984).

The Supreme Court in United States History by C. Warren (Little, Brown, 1937).

The Transformation of American Law, 1780–1860 by M. Horwitz (Harvard Univ. Press, 1977).

INDEX TO LEGAL PERIODICALS (ILP)

In the ILP, look for references to legal periodical literature under the following subject headings:

Constitutional History   Legal History
History

LEGAL MALPRACTICE: See Professional Responsibility, Torts

LEGAL MEDICINE: See Death, Forensic Science, Health & Medicine, Torts

LEGAL PARAPROFESSIONALS: See Law Office Management, Paralegal

LEGAL PHILOSOPHY: See Jurisprudence

LEGAL PROFESSION: See Law Office Management, Professional Responsibility, Trial & Appellate Practice

LEGAL REASONING: See Jurisprudence

LEGAL RESEARCH & WRITING

SEE ALSO: International Law, Law Office Management, Legislative History, Professional Responsibility, Statutes; see also entries under individual states and countries

GENERAL
BIBLIOGRAPHIES: **A. Legal Research—**

A Bibliography of Bibliographies of Legal Materials by M. Howell (N.J. Appellate Printing Co., 1969).

Law Books and Serials in Print (R.R. Bowker, 1988).

Index to Legal Books (R.R. Bowker, 1988).

Index to Periodical Articles Related to Law (1958–).

Legal Bibliographies: General and International by J. Goedan (Transnational Pub., 1987).

Recommended Publications for Legal Research (Rothman, 1979–).

Searching the Law by E. Bander, F. Bae & F. Doyle (Transnational Pub., 1987).

Searching the Law: The States by F. Doyle (Transnational Pub. 1989).

Specialized Legal Research, L. Chanin, ed. (Little, Brown, 1987).

B. Legal Writing—

"Bibliography of Plain English for Lawyers" by G. Hathaway, 62 *Michigan Bar Journal* 989 (1983).

"Law and Language: A Selected Annotated Bibliography on Legal Writing" by T. Collins & D. Hattenhauer, 33 *Journal of Legal Education* 141 (1983).

"Research on Legal Writing: A Bibliography" by P. Kolin & R. Marquardt, 78 *Law Library Journal* 493 (1986).

JOURNALS, NEWSLETTERS & OTHER PERIODICALS:

Law Library Journal (AALL, 1908–).

Legal Bibliography Journal (Pasadena, CA: The Legal Institute, 1983–).

Legal Information Alert (Chicago: Alert Publications, Inc., 1981–).

Legal Information Management Index (Newton Highlands, MA: Legal Information Services).

Legal Reference Services Quarterly (Haworth Press, 1980–).

Legal Writing Journal (Pasadena, CA: The Legal Institute, 1981–).

INDEXES TO PERIODICALS:

CCH Federal Tax Articles (1954–).

Current Law Index (Information Access Co., 1980–).

Index to Federal Tax Articles (Warren, Gorham & Lamont).

Index to Foreign Legal Periodicals.

Index to Periodical Articles Related to Law (1958–).

Index to Periodical Literature (Wilson, 1886–).

Index to U.S. Government Periodicals (1970–).

Legal Reference Resource (Information Access Co.).

TREATISES:

A. Legal Research—

Attorney's Guide to Government Studies and Reports, B. Chase & S. Diamond, eds. (Matthew Bender, 1986).

Computer-Assisted Legal and Tax Research by T. Thomas (Prentice-Hall, 1986).

Effective Legal Research, 4th ed. by M. Price, H. Bitner & S. Bysiewicz (Little, Brown, 1979).

Fundamentals of Legal Research, 3d ed. by J. Jacobstein & R. Mersky (Foundation Press, 1985).

How to Find the Law, 9th ed. by M. Cohen, R. Berring & K. Olson (West, 1989).

The Law Library Reference Shelf: Annotated Subject Guide by E. Matthews (Hein, 1988).

Legal Problem Solving: Analysis, Research and Writing, 4th ed. by M. Rombauer (West, 1983).

Legal Research and Law Library Management by J. Marke & R. Stone (Law Journal Seminars-Press, 1986).

Legal Research in a Nutshell, 4th ed. by M. Cohen (West, 1985).

The Legal Research Manual, 2d ed. by C. & J. Wren (Madison, WI: Adams & Ambrose Pub., 1988).

Legal Research, Writing, and Analysis, 3d ed. by W. Statsky (West, 1986).

Practical Approaches to Legal Research (Haworth Press, 1988).

The Process of Legal Research, 2d ed. by C. Kunz et al. (Little, Brown, 1989).

B. Legal Writing—

Brief Writing and Oral Argument, 6th ed. by E. Re (Oceana, 1987).

Case Analysis and Fundamentals of Legal Writing, 3d ed. by W. Statsky & J. Wernet (West, 1989).

Clear and Effective Legal Writing by Charrow & M. Erhardt (Little, Brown, 1986).

Effective Legal Communications by I. Mehler (Philgor, 1975).

Effective Legal Writing, 3d ed. by G. Block (Foundation Press, 1986).

The Fundamentals of Legal Writing, 2d ed. by R. Dickerson (Little, Brown, 1986).

The Grammatical Lawyer by M. Freeman (ALI–ABA Comm. on Cont. Prof. Ed., 1979).

How to Write Plain English: A Book for Lawyers and Consumers by R. Flesch (Harper & Row, 1979).

Introduction to Advocacy, 3d ed. by the Harvard Board of Student Advisors (Foundation Press, 1981).
The Langugage of the Law by D. Melinkoff (Little, Brown, 1963).
Legal Writing: Getting it Right and Getting it Written by M. Ray & J. Ramsfield (West, 1987).
Legal Writing in a Nutshell by M. Rombauer (West, 1982).
Legal Writing: Sense and Nonsense by D. Melinkoff (Scribner, 1982).
Legal Writing: The Strategy of Persuasion, 2d ed. by N. Brand (St. Martin's Press, 1988).
Legal Writing Style, 2d ed. by H. Weihofen (West, 1980).
Plain English for Lawyers, 2d ed. by R. Wydick (Durham, NC: Carolina Academic Press, 1986).
A Practical Guide to Legal Writing and Legal Method by J. Dernbach & R. Singleton (Rothman, 1981).
When Lawyers Write by R. Weisberg (Little, Brown, 1987).
Writing Consumer Contracts in Plain English by C. Felsenfield & A. Siegal (West, 1981).
Writing from a Legal Perspective by G. Gopen (West, 1981).
Writing Persuasive Briefs by G. Peck (Little, Brown, 1984).
Written and Oral Advocacy by M. Fontham (Wiley, 1985).

CITATIONS:

Bieber's Current American Legal Citations, 2d ed. by D. Bieber (Hein, 1986).
Citing and Typing the Law by E. Good (Charlottesville, VA: Wordstore).
The Complete Guide to Citing Government Documents by D. Garner & D. Smith (Congressional Information Service, 1984)
How to Prepare a Legal Citation by E. Maier (Barron's 1986).
A Uniform System of Citation, 14th ed. (Harvard Law Review Assn., 1986).

PERIODICALS:

CURRENT LAW INDEX (CLI) & LEGAL RESOURCE INDEX (LRI)
In the CLI and LRI, look for references to periodical literature under the following subject headings:

Bill Drafting	Legal Composition
Briefs	Legal Documents
Citation	Legal Drafting
Forms (Law)	Legal Research
Legal Authorities	Libraries

INDEX TO LEGAL PERIODICALS (ILP)
In the ILP, look for references to legal periodical literature under the following subject headings:

Bibliography	Legal Education
Brief	Legal Drafting
Information Storage and	Legal Research
Retrieval	Legal Terminology
Language	Legislative Drafting

LEGAL SECRETARY: See Law Office Management, Paralegal
LEGAL SERVICES: See Poverty Law, Professional Responsibility
LEGAL WRITING: See Legal Research
LEGISLATION: See Legal Research, Legislative History, Statutes

LEGISLATIVE HISTORY

SEE ALSO: Legal Research, State & Local Government, Statutes

MAJOR COLLECTIONS &
INDEXES:

CIS Index to Publications of the United States Congress (Congressional Information Service, 1970–). (There are two parts to this service: an *Abstract* volume and an *Index* volume.)

CIS Legislative History Annual (Congressional Information Service). (Contains citations to bills, reports, debates, etc. for the year.)

CIS Legislative History Service: Annotated Directories (Congressional Information Service, 1982–). (Contains citations, summaries of reports, hearings, etc.)

CIS/Microfiche Library (Congressional Information Service, 1970–).

CIS U.S. Congressional Committee Hearings, 1833– (Congressional Information Service).

Congressional Index (CCH, 1938–). (Lists Senate and House bills and resolutions, names of sponsors, dates of introduction and reference to committee current status, etc.)

Congressional Information Service (1970–). Lists public laws with references to committee hearings, reports and related documents.)

Congressional Quarterly Almanac (Congressional Quarterly, Inc., 1948–). (Data on legislative histories of public laws, voting records, etc. Its weekly counterpart is the *CQ Weekly Report*.).

Congressional Record (Congress, 1873–).

Congressional Record Index. (The Index lists all bills by House and Senate number with page references in the Congressional Record where the bills are covered.)

Digest of Public General Bills and Resolutions. (Library of Congress, Congressional Research Service, 1971–). (Contains summaries of public laws, dates of committee reports, floor debates, enactment, etc.)

Journal of the House of Representatives of the United States (GPO, 1789–).

Journal of the Senate of the United States (GPO, 1789–).

Legislative Histories Microfiche Program (Information Handling Services).

Legislative History Files—General Accounting Office. (The GAO files cover most public laws since 1921.)

Monthly Catalog of United States Government Publications (GPO, 1895–). (The Index includes the publications of Congress.)

Sources of Compiled Legislative Histories: Bibliography of Government Documents, Periodical Articles and Books, 1st Congress–96th Congress, N. Johnson, comp. (American Association of Law Libraries; Rothman, 1988).

Union List of Legislative Histories, 47th Congress, 1881–92nd Congress, 1972, 4th ed. by the Wash. D.C. Law Librarian's Society (Rothman, 1979–). (The List states which libraries in the Wash. D.C. area contain collections of legislative histories.)

United States Code Congressional and Administrative News (West, 1939–). (USCCAN contains committee reports of major public legislation).

TREATISES:

A Bibliography of State Bibliographies, 1970–1982 by D. Parish (Libraries Unlimited, 1984).

Congress and Law-Making: Researching the Legislative Process by R. Goehlert (Clio Books, 1979).

Congressional Publications: A Guide to Legislation, Budgets, and Treaties by J. Zwirn (Libraries Unlimited, 1983).

Directory of Government Document Collections & Librarians, 4th ed., B. Kile &
A. Taylor, eds. (American Library Assn., CIS).

Guide to State Legislative Materials, M. Fisher, ed. (American Association of Law
Libraries; Rothman, 1979–).

Handbook of Legislative Research (Harvard Univ. Press, 1985).

How to Prepare a Legislative History by D. Siddall (Library of Congress, Congressional
Research Service, Report No. 78–48A, Feb. 28, 1978, revised May 10, 1978).

Introduction to United States Public Documents, 3d ed. by J. Morehead (Libraries
Unlimited, 1983).

Legislative History: Research for the Interpretation of Laws by G. Folsom (Rothman,
1979).

Legislative Reference Checklist: The Key to Legislative Histories from 1789–1903 by
E. Nabors (Rothman, 1982).

State Government Reference Publications: An Annotated Bibliography, 2d ed. by
D. Parish (Libraries Unlimited, 1981).

LEGISLATIVE POWERS: See Constitutional Law
LEGISLATIVE VETO: See Administrative Law, Constitutional Law
LEGISLATURE: See Constitutional Law, Legislative History, State & Local Government
LENDING: See Banking Law, Uniform Commercial Code
LESBIAN: See Homosexuality

LESOTHO

SEE ALSO: Africa, International Law, United Nations

**JOURNALS & OTHER
PERIODICALS:** *Lesotho Law Journal* (Natl. Univ. of Lesotho; Gaunt, 1985–).
  University of Botswana, Lesotho and Swaziland Law Journal.

**TREATISES &
LOOSELEAFS:** *African Tax Systems* (Lesotho) by R. Hammond & M. van den Abeelen (Amsterdam:
Intl. Bureau of Fiscal Documentation, 1980–).

Criminal Law and Procedure through Cases by M. Mofokeng (Lesotho: Morija Sesuto
Book Depot, 1985).

Investment Laws of the World (Lesotho) (Oceana, 1981–).

The Legal System of Lesotho by V. Palmer & S. Poulter (Michie, 1972).

Lesotho: Dilemmas of Dependence in Southern Africa by J. Bardill (Westview,
1985).

ARTICLES: "The Common Law in Lesotho" by S. Poulter, 13 *Journal of African Law* 127 (1969).

"Current Legal Developments" (Lesotho), 15 *Comparative and International Law
Journal of Southern Africa* 104 (1982).

"Human Rights in Africa . . . Lesotho . . ." by S. Neff, 33 *The International and
Comparative Law Quarterly* 331 (1984).

Legal Aspects of the Lesotho Constitutional Crisis" by M. & E. Stein, *6 East African
Law Journal* 210 (1970).

"Lesotho" by S. Poulter, 1969 *Annual Survey of African Law* 217 (London: Cass,
1973).

"Marriage, Divorce and Legitimacy in Lesotho" by S. Poulter, 21 *Journal of African
Law* 66 (1977).

"The Parliaments of Botswana, Lesotho and Swaziland" by W. Macartney, 50
  Parliamentarian 92 (1969).

LETTER RULINGS: See Estate Planning, Taxation
LETTERS OF CREDIT: See Banking Law, Uniform Commercial Code
LEVEES: See State & Local Government
LEVERAGED BUYOUT: See Corporate Law, Securities Law
LEWDNESS: See Criminal Law, Media Law
LIABILITY: See Professional Responsibility, Torts, Trial & Appellate Practice
LIABILITY INSURANCE: See Insurance
LIBEL: See Media Law, Torts

LIBERIA

SEE ALSO: Africa, International Law, United Nations

CONSTITUTION: *The Constitution of the Republic of Liberia* . . . by A. Dormu (NY: Exposition Press,
                         1970).
                         "Liberia" by M. Kitay in *Constitutions of the Countries of the World* by A. Blaustein &
                         G. Flanz (Oceana, 1982).

TREATISES &
LOOSELEAFS: *African Tax Systems* (Liberia) by R. Hammond & M. van den Abeelen (Amsterdam:
                         Intl. Bureau of Fiscal Documentation, 1980–).
                         Information Guide: Doing Business in Liberia (Price Waterhouse).
                         Investment Laws of the World The Developing Nations (Liberia) (Oceana, 1972–).
                         The Legal System of Liberia by M. Kitay & R. Culp (Michie, 1970).
                         Liberia: A Country Study, 3d ed., H. Nelson, ed. (Amer. Univ., Foreign Area Studies,
                         1985).
                         Tax Havens Encyclopedia (Liberia) by B. Spitz (Butterworths, 1975–).
                         Tax Laws of the World—Liberia (FL: Foreign Tax Law Assn.).
                         Tax Mission: The Tax System of Liberia by C. Shoup et al. (Columbia Univ. Press,
                         1970).
                         . . . *Violations of Human Rights in Liberia* . . . (NY: Fund for Free Expression, 1986).

ARTICLES: "Liberia (Civil Rights)," *International Commission of Jurists Review* 13 (1986).

LIBERTY: See Constitutional Law, Jurisprudence
LIBRARY: See Civil Rights, Corrections, Law Office Management, Legal Research

LIBYA

SEE ALSO: Africa, International Law, Islam, United Nations

TREATIES: "Libya-Morocco: Treaty Instituting the Arab-African Union of States," 23 *International
                         Legal Materials* 1022 (1984).

TREATISES &
LOOSELEAFS: *African Tax Systems* (Libya) by R. Hammond & M. van den Abeelen (Amsterdam:
                         Intl. Bureau of Fiscal Documentation, 1980–).

Commercial Laws of the Middle East (Libya) by A. Keesee (Oceana, 1980–).

Principles of Petroleum Legislation by A. Al-Qasem (Gaithersburg, MD: Graham & Trotman, 1985).

Property Law in the Arab World: Real Rights in Egypt, Iraq, Jordan, Lebanon, Libya, Saudi Arabia and the Gulf States by F. Ziadeh (London: Graham & Trotman, 1979).

Taxes and Investment in the Middle East (Libya) (Intl. Bureau of Fiscal Documentation).

Tax Laws of the World—Libya (FL: Foreign Tax Law Assn.).

ARTICLES: "International Arbitrations Between States and Foreign Private Parties: The Libyan Nationalization Cases" by R. Von Mehren, 75 *American Journal of International Law* 476 (1981).

"Law of the Sea: Delimitation of the Libya-Malta Continental Shelf" by L. Thomas, 27 *Harvard International Law Journal* 304 (1986).

"Libyan Legislation in Defense of Arabo-Islamic Sexual Mores" by A. Mayer, 28 *American Journal of Comparative Law* 287 (1980).

"Middle East Agency Law Survey" (Libya) by F. Taylor, 14 *International Lawyer* 348 (1980).

LICENSE: See Administrative Law, Dentistry, Health & Medicine, Natural Resources, Nursing

LICENSEE: See Torts

LICENSING: See Business Law, Europe, Intellectual Property, International Law, Partnership Law, Public Utilities, Securities Law, State & Local Government

LIECHTENSTEIN

SEE ALSO: Europe, International Law, United Nations

TREATISES & LOOSELEAFS: *Capital Formation and Investment Incentives Around the World* (Liechtenstein) by W. Diamond & D. Diamond (Matthew Bender, 1984–).

Tax Havens Encyclopedia (Liechtenstein) by B. Spitz (Butterworths, 1975–).

Tax Laws of the World—Liechtenstein (FL: Foreign Tax Law Assn.).

The Trust in Liechtenstein Law by K. Biedermann, H. Crossland, transl. (Oxford: Alvescot Press, 1984).

ARTICLES: "The Analysis of a Tax Haven: The Liechtenstein Anstalts" by G. Glos, 18 *International Lawyer* 929 (1984).

"Commentary on Liechtenstein Company Law" by H. Batliner, 14 *Case Western Reserve Journal of International Law* 613 (1984).

"Letter of the Law Hits Liechtenstein's Mailbox Firms." 102 *Wall Street Journal* 32(W), p. 10(C), col 4 (April 17, 1980).

"Recent Changes in the Law of Liechtenstein" by R. Wengle, 9 *Australian Tax Review* 235 (1980).

"United States Tax Treatment of Liechtenstein Anstalts" by H. Liebman, 19 *International Lawyer* 921 (1985).

LIE DETECTOR: See Criminal Law, Forensic Science, Trial & Appellate Practice

LIENS: See Bankruptcy, Business Law, Contracts, Equity, Estate Planning, Real Estate, Uniform Commercial Code

LIFE ESTATE: See Estate Planning, Real Estate
LIFE EXPECTANCY: See Insurance
LIFE IMPRISONMENT: See Corrections, Criminal Law
LIFE INSURANCE: See Employee Benefits, Estate Planning, Community Property,
    Insurance
LIMITATION OF LIABILITY: See Torts, Trial & Appellate Practice
LIMITED PARTNERSHIP: See Partnership Law, Real Estate, Taxation
LINEUP: See Criminal Law
LIQUIDATION: See Corporate Law
LIQUOR: See Alcohol, Criminal Law, Health & Medicine, Mental Health
LIS PENDENS: See Trial & Appellate Practice
LITERARY RIGHTS, LITERATURE: See Art & Entertainment, Intellectual Property,
    Media Law
LITIGATION: See Computers, Law Office Management, Paralegal, Torts, Trial &
    Appellate Practice
LITIGATION SUPPORT: See Computers, Law Office Management
LITURGY: See Canon Law, Church & State
LIVESTOCK: See Agriculture, Animals
LLOYD'S OF LONDON: See Maritime Law
LOANS: See Banking Law, Consumer Law, Uniform Commercial Code
LOBBYING: See Election
LOCAL GOVERNMENT: See State & Local Government
LOCKOUT: See Labor Law
LOCO PARENTIS: See Family Law, Juvenile Law
LOGS AND LOGGING: See Natural Resources, Water Law
LONG ARM STATUTE: See Maritime Law, Workers' Compensation, Trial & Appellate
    Practice
LONGSHOREMEN: See Maritime Law, Workers' Compensation
LOS ANGELES: See California
LOSS OF CONSORTIUM: See Family Law, Torts
LOST INSTRUMENTS: See Estate Planning, Real Estate, Trial & Appellate Practice
LOST PROPERTY: See Personal Property
LOTTERY: See Criminal Law

LOUISIANA

SEE ALSO: Circuit Courts (Fifth Circuit), Community Property

RESEARCH GUIDES &
BIBLIOGRAPHIES: *Bibliography of Basic Materials for a Louisiana Law Library* by D. Naylor (La. State
    Univ. Law Center Library, 1979).
    "Legislative History in Louisiana" by J. Jones, 37 *Louisiana Bar Journal* 253 (no. 4,
    1989).
    *Louisiana Legal Documents and Related Publications: A Selected Annotated
    Bibliography* by C. Corneil & M. Herbert (Assn. of American Law Libraries, 1984).
    "Louisiana Legal Publications: A Selected Bibliography" by C. Corneil, 43 *Louisiana
    Law Review* 835 (1983).
    Louisiana Legal Research by W. Chiang (Butterworths, 1985).

STATUTES & RELATED
LEGISLATIVE MATERIALS: *Civil Code of Louisiana and Ancillaries,* R. Slovenko, ed. (Claitor's, 1981).
    Acts of the Legislature—State of Louisiana (1804–).

Legislative Bulletin (Public Affairs Research Council of Louisiana).
West's Louisiana Session Law Service (1977–).
West's Louisiana Statutes Annotated—Revised Statutes (1951–).

STATE ADMINISTRATIVE CODE:
The Louisiana Administrative Code.
Louisiana Register (Dept. of the State Register, 1975–).

CASES & OPINIONS:
Louisiana Reports.
Southern Reporter (West, 1887–).

COURT RULES:
Louisiana Court Rules, 2d ed. (Claitor's, 1973–).
Rules of Supreme Court of Louisiana (West, 1973–).
Louisiana Rules of Court, State and Federal (West).

JURY INSTRUCTIONS:
Louisiana Jury Instructions: Civil and Criminal by J. Chency et al. (LSU Pub. Institute, 1980).

OPINIONS OF THE ATTORNEY GENERAL:
Opinions of the Attorney General of the State of Louisiana (Attorney General, 1853–).

JOURNALS & OTHER PERIODICALS:
Institute on Mineral Law (La. State Univ., 1953–).
Louisiana Law Review (1938–).
Louisiana State Bar Journal (La. Bar Assn., 1953–).
State-Times/Morning Advocate.

DIRECTORIES:
Arkansas, Louisiana and Mississippi Legal Directory (Los Angeles: Legal Directories Pub. Co., 1955–).
Biographies of Louisiana Judges, F. Cleveland, ed. (La. District Judges Assn., 1977).
Louisiana Legal Directory (Legal Directories Pub. Co., 1983).

TREATISES & LOOSELEAFS:
Community Property System by H. Daggett (LSU Press, 1945).
Eminent Domain in Louisiana by M. Dakin (Bobbs-Merrill, 1970).
Essays in the Civil Law of Obligations, J. Dainow, ed. (LSU Press, 1969).
A Formulary of Civil Procedure and Rules . . ., 3d ed. by H. McEnerny (Claitor's, 1956).
Guide to Louisiana Real Actions by J. Johnson (Claitor's, 1961).
Handook of Criminal Procedure and Forms by R. Slovenko (Claitor's, 1967).
Louisiana Appellate Practice Handbook (Lawyers Co-op., 1986).
Louisiana Civil Law Treatise Series (West).
Louisiana Law Primer by D. Tate (Claitor's, 1983).
Louisiana Legal Transactions by S. Litvinoff (Claitor's, 1969).
Louisiana Notarial Manual, 2d ed. by M. Woodward (A. Smith Co., 1962).
Louisiana Wills and Trusts (Baton Rouge: Update Seminars and Pubs.).
Precis in Conventional Obligations by A. Levasseur (Michie, 1980).
Proposed Louisiana Code of Evidence by the La. State Law Institute (West, 1986).
Trial Handbook for Louisiana Lawyers by E. Fallon (Lawyers Co-op., 1981).

DIGESTS & CITATOR:
Louisiana Digest (Bobbs-Merrill).
Louisiana Digest (West, 1936–).

Shepard's Louisiana Citations.
Southern Digest (West).

LOVERS: See Family Law, Homosexuality, Juvenile Law, Women & the Law
LOYALTY OATHS: See Civil Rights, Civil Service, Constitutional Law, Employment
    Discrimination, Labor Law

LUXEMBOURG

SEE ALSO: Europe, European Economic Community, International Law, United Nations

RESEARCH GUIDE &
BIBLIOGRAPHY: *Guide to Foreign Legal Materials, Belgium, Luxembourg, Netherlands* by P. Graulich,
         et al. (Oceana, 1968).

TREATISES &
LOOSELEAFS: *Business Operations in Luxembourg* by G. Kioes, Tax Management Foreign Income
         Portfolios, No. 164–4th (BNA, 1981).
     Capital Formation and Investment Incentives Around the World (Luxembourg) by
         W. Diamond & D. Diamond (Matthew Bender, 1984–).
     Digest of Commercial Laws of the World (Luxembourg) (Natl. Assn. of Credit
         Management; Oceana, 1977–).
     Information Guide: Doing Business in Luxembourg (Price Waterhouse).
     Tax Havens Encyclopedia (Luxembourg) by B. Spitz (Butterworths, 1975–).
     Tax Laws of the World—Luxembourg (FL: Foreign Tax Law Assn.).
     World Law of Competition (Luxembourg), J. von Kalinowski, ed. (Matthew Bender,
         1979–).

ARTICLES: "European Community Luxembourg Compromise" by K. Mason, 13 *Georgia Journal*
         of International and Comparative Law 135 (1983).
     "Freedom to Provide Services" by M. Weirich, 10 *European Law Review* 471 (1985).
     "Survey of Tax Developments, *Tax Management International Journal* 14 (June,
         1979).

MACAO

SEE ALSO: Asia, International Law, United Nations

TREATISES: *Information Guide: Doing business in Macao* (Price Waterhouse).
     Taxes and Investment in Asia and the Pacific (Macao) (Amsterdam: Intl. Bureau of
         Fiscal Documentation, 1983–).

ARTICLES: "Banking, Investment and Contracting Opportunities" (Macao), 5 *East Asian Exeuctive Reports* 11 (Dec. 15, 1983).
"The Nationality Law of . . . China and . . . Macao . . ." by T. Chen, 5 *New York Law School Journal of International & Comparative Law* 281, 323 (1984).
"New Banking Act" (Macao) by L. Niang, 3 *The Company Lawyer* 286 (1982) (see also vol. 6, p. 145).

MADAGASCAR

SEE ALSO: Africa, Communism, International Law, United Nations

Four African Constitutions: Two Models (Algeria, Ghana, Madagascar, and Nigeria) by S.K. Panter-Brick, *Government and Opposition,* vol. 14, pt. 3 (1979).
Indian Ocean: Five Island Countries (Madagascar) (GPO, 1982).

MAGAZINES: See Art & Entertainment, Media Law
MAGISTRATE: See Trial & Appellate Practice
MAGNA CHARTA: See England, Legal History

MAINE

SEE ALSO: Circuit Courts (First Circuit)

RESEARCH GUIDE & BIBLIOGRAPHY: *Maine Legal Research Guide* by W. Wells (Portland: Tower Pub. Co., 1989).

STATUTES & OTHER LEGISLATIVE MATERIALS: *Maine Revised Statutes Annotated.*
Laws of the State of Maine.
Acts, Resolves and Constitutional Resolutions of the State of Maine.
Maine Legislative Service (West).

CASES & OPINIONS: *Maine Reports* (1820–1965).
Maine Reporter (West).
Atlantic Reporter (1885–).

COURT RULES: *Maine Rules of Court* (West).

ETHICS & PROFESSIONAL RESPONSIBILITY: *Maine Advisory Opinions of the Grievance Commission Board of Overseers of the Bar* (Tower Pub. Co., 1983).

JOURNALS & OTHER PERIODICALS: *Maine Bar Bulletin* (1967–).

TREATISES, LOOSELEAFS & OTHER MONOGRAPHS: *Appellate Advocacy* (Maine Bar Assn., 1981).
Corporation Law (Maine Bar Assn., 1981).
Maine Administrative Procedure (Butterworths).

Maine Civil Practice, Rules of Civil Procedure by R. Field (West).
Maine Civil Remedies by A. Horton & P. McGehee (Portland: Tower Pub. Co. 1988).
Maine Criminal Practice by D. Cluchey (Tower Pub. Co., 1985–).
Maine Probate Manual by D. J. Mitchell (Tower Pub. Co., 1983).
Maine Workers Compensation Act: Practice and Procedure by C. Devoe (Tower Pub. Co., 1983).
Probate Law (Maine Bar Assn., 1982).
Products Liability (Maine Bar Assn., 1980).

DIGESTS & CITATOR: *Maine Digest* (West).
Atlantic Digest (West).
Shepard's Maine Citations.

MAINTENANCE: See Family Law, Women & the Law
MAJORITY: See Election, Family Law, Juvenile Law

MALAWI

SEE ALSO: Africa, International Law, United Nations

JOURNALS & OTHER PERIODICALS: *Society of Malawi Journal.*

TREATISES: *African Tax Systems* by R. Hammond & M. van den Abeelen (Malawi) (Amsterdam: Intl. Bureau of Fiscal Documentation, 1980–).
Information Guide: Doing Business in Malawi (Price Waterhouse).
Investment Laws of the World (Malawi) (Oceana, 1981–).
Law, Custom, and Social Order: The Colonial Experience in Malawi and Zambia by M. Chanock (NY: Cambridge Univ. Press, 1985).
The Legal System of Malawi by V. Davidson & C. Baker (Michie).
Malawi II: The Law of Land, Succession, Movable Property, Agreements and Civil Wrongs by J. Ibik (London: Sweet & Maxwell, 1971).
Tax Law of the World—Malawi (FL: Foreign Tax Law Assn.).

ARTICLES: "The Controversy on the Statutes of General Application of Malawi" by C. Nzunda, 25 *Journal of African Law* 115 (1981).
"Current Legal Developments" (Malawi), 15 *Comparative and International Law Journal of Southern Africa* 228 (1982).
"The Design and Implementation of Customary Land Reforms in Central Malawi" by C. Ng'ong'ola, 26 *Journal of African Law* 115 (1982).

MALAYSIA

SEE ALSO: Asia, International Law, Islam, United Nations

RESEARCH GUIDES & BIBLIOGRAPHIES: "Current Legal Research in Malaysia" by A Khalik, 7 *International Journal of Law Libraries* 221 (1979).
Malaysian Legal Source Materials in London, Oxford and Cambridge by S. Zakaria (Kuala Lumpur: Perpustaakan Univ. Malaya, 1985).

"Statement of Recommended Holdings of Malaysian Legal Materials" by S. Zakaria, 25 *Malaya Law Review* 238 (1983).

TREATIES: *A Collection of Treaties and Other Documents Affecting the States of Malaysia 1761–1963,* J. V. Allen et al., eds. (Oceana, 1981).

CONSTITUTION: *The Constitution of Malaysia,* F. Trinidade, ed. (Oxford Univ. Press, 1986).
The Constitution of Malaysia, 3d ed. by L. Sheridan & H. Groves (Singapore: Malayan Law Journal, 1979).
The Malaysian Constitution, T. Suffian et al., ed.s (Oxford Univ. Press, 1978).

STATUTES & CASES: *General Index of Acts, Enactments, Ordinances . . .,* S. Sivaswamy, comp. (Kuala Lumur: Malaysian Law Publishers, 1984).
Law Reports in the Law Library, University of Malaya: A Guide by S. Zakaria (Kuala Lumpur: Perpustaakan Univ. Malaya, 1983).

JOURNALS & OTHER PERIODICALS: *Journal of Malaysian and Comparative Law* (1974–).
Malaya Law Review (1959–).

TREATISES & LOOSELEAFS: *Asia and the Pacific: A Tax Tour* (Malaysia) (Arthur Anderson & Co., 1986).
Capital Formation and Investment Incentives Around the World (Malaysia) by W. Diamond & D. Diamond (Matthew Bender, 1984–).
Digest of Commercial Laws of the World (Malaysia) (Natl. Assn. of Credit Management; Oceana, 1977–).
Estate Duty, Executorship & Bankruptcy in Singapore & Malaysia by A. Singh (Singapore: Law Book Co., 1974).
A Guide to Doing Business in the ASEAN Region: Brunei/Indonesia/Malaysia/Philippines/Singapore/Thailand (U.S. Dept. of Commerce, Intl. Trade Admin., Office of Pacific Basin, 1985).
A Guide to the Employment Ordinance of Malaysia by S. Perumal (Petaling Jaya: Intl. Book Service, 1981).
Income Taxation and Foreign Investment in Developing Countries (Malaysia) by M. Dominic (Amsterdam: Intl. Bureau of Fiscal Documentation, 1980).
The Industrial Relations Law of Malaysia by M. Wu (Kuala Lumpur: Heinemann Educational Books, 1982).
Information Guide: Doing Business in Malaysia (Price Waterhouse).
The Insurance Law of Malaysia by U. Myint Soe (Singapore: Quins, 1979).
Investment Laws of the World (Malaysia) (Oceana, 1981–).
Law of Compulsory Purchase and Compensation: Singapore and Malaysia by N. Khublass (Butterworths, 1984).
The Law of Contract in Malaysia and Singapore by V. Sinnardurai (Oxford Univ. Press, 1980).
Legislation on Bankruptcy (Malaysian Law Pub., 1983).
Malaysia: A Country Study, 4th ed., F. Bunge, ed. (American Univ., Foreign Area Studies; GPO, 1985).
Malaysian Master Tax Guide, 3d ed. by B. Soin (Australia: CCH, 1985).
The Sale and Purchase of Real Property in Malaysia by V. Sinnadurai (Butterworths, 1984).
Taxes and Investment in Asia and the Pacific (Malaysia) (Amsterdam: Intl. Bureau of Fiscal Documentation, 1983–).
Tax Laws of the World—Malaya (FL: Foreign Tax Law Assn.).

ARTICLES: "The Constitutional Crisis of 1983" by H. Rawlings, 35 *International & Comparative Law Quarterly* 237 (1986).
"Malaysia: Responding to Religious and Cultural Pluralism" by J. Connors, 27 *Journal of Family Law* 195 (1988–89).
"The October Boycott: Its Causes, Consequences and Implications for Legal Practice in Malaysia" by A. Said, 9 *International Journal of the Sociology of Law* 383 (1981).
"Securities Regulation in Malaysia" by P. Pillai, 8 *Journal of Comparative Business and Capital Market Law* 39 (1986).

MALDIVES

SEE ALSO: Africa, International law, Islam, United Nations

Indian Ocean: Five Island Countries (Maldives) (GPO, 1982).

MALFEASANCE: See Torts

MALI

SEE ALSO: Africa, International Law, Islam, United Nations

"Mali" in *Constitutions of the Countries of the World* by A. Blaustein & G. Flanz (Oceana, 1983).
An Introduction to Law in French-Speaking Africa (Mali) by J. Salacuse (Michie, 1969).

MALICE: See Criminal Law, Torts
MALICIOUS MISCHIEF: See Criminal Law
MALICIOUS PROSECUTION: See Torts
MALPRACTICE: See Dentistry, Education Law, Health & Medicine, Mental Health, Nursing, Professional Responsibility, Torts

MALTA

SEE ALSO: International Law, United Nations

TREATISES: *Aspects of Maltese Law for Bankers* by P. Randon (Valletta: Institute of Bankers, 1983).
Information Guide: Doing Business in Malta (Price Waterhouse).
The Law on Commercial Partnerships in Malta by F. Cremona (Valletta: Malta Univ. Press, 1975).
Tax Laws of the World—Malta (FL: Foreign Tax Law Assn.).

ARTICLES: "Law of the Sea: Delimitation of the Libya-Malta Continental Shelf" by L. Thomas, 27 *Harvard International Law Journal* 304 (1986).
"Malta" (Human Rights), *International Commission of Jurists Review* 8 (Dec., 1984).
"Trade Preferences and Foreign Investment in Malta" by R. Pomfret, 16 *Journal of World Trade Law* 236 (1982).

MALVINAS: See Argentina, England, Falkland Islands
MANAGEMENT: See Business Law, Corporate Law, Law Office Management
MANDAMUS: See State & Local Government, Trial & Appellate Practice
MANDATE: See International Law, South Africa
MANGANESE MINES: See Natural Resources
MANSLAUGHTER: See Criminal Law
MANUFACTURING: See Business Law, Corporate Law, Torts
MARGIN TRANSACTIONS: See Securities Law
MARIANA ISLANDS: See Guam, Micronesia
MARINE INSURANCE: See Insurance, Maritime Law
MARINE POLLUTION: See Environmental Law
MARINE RESOURCES: See Natural Resources, Sea

MARITIME LAW

SEE ALSO: Administrative Law, Agency, Air & Aviation, Antitrust, Banking Law, Business Law, Commodities, Conflict of Law, Contracts, Customs, Government Contracts, Insurance, International Law, Labor Law, Sea, Torts, Transportation, Workers' Compensation

RESEARCH GUIDES &
BIBLIOGRAPHIES: "Admiralty and Maritime Law" by S. Wiant in *Specialized Legal Research,* L. Chanin, ed. (Little, Brown, 1987).
Marine Affairs Bibliography (Dalhousie University, 1980–).
"Maritime Law: An Annotated Bibliography of Essential Publications" by M. Newman, 15 *Journal of Maritime Law and Commerce* 585 (1984).
"Maritime Law: Research References" by E. Danoff, 1 *Legal Reference Services Quarterly* 27 (1981).

CASES & ADMINISTRATIVE
DECISIONS: *American Maritime Cases* (American Maritime Cases, Inc., 1923–).
American Maritime Cases Index-Digest.
Arbitration Award Service (Society of Maritime Arbitrators).
Benefits Review Board—Longshore Reporter (Matthew Bender, 1980–).
Decisions of the American Maritime Commission (1919–).
Decisions of the Maritime Subsidy Board (1961–).
Lloyd's Law Reports (Lloyd's of London Press, 1919–).
Lloyd's Law Reports Digest.
Maritime Advisor (Greenwich, CT: Maritime Advisory Services, Inc., 1981–).

JOURNALS, NEWSLETTERS
& OTHER PERIODICALS: *Fairplay International Shipping Weekly* (London: Fairplay Publications, 1883–).
Journal of Maritime Law and Commerce (Jefferson Law Book Co., 1969–).
Lloyd's Maritime and Commercial Law Quarterly (Lloyd's of London Press, 1974–).
Lloyd's Maritime Law Newsletter.
Maritime Lawyer (Tulane Maritime Law Society, 1975–).
Tulane Law Review (see "Admiralty Law Institute Symposium" in various issues of the review, e.g., vol. 33, p. 999).
Yearbook Maritime Law (Kluwer).

TREATISES &
LOOSELEAFS: *Admiralty in a Nutshell* by F. Maraist (West, 1983).
Admiralty Law of the Supreme Court, 3d ed. by H. Baer (Michie, 1978).

The American Law of Admiralty, 7th ed. by E. Benedict: M. Cohen & M. Norris, eds. (Matthew Bender, 1985–).

The American Law of Collision by J. Griffin (Baltimore: American Maritime Cases, Inc., 1949).

The American Law of Ocean Bills of Lading, 4th ed. by A. Knauth (Oceana, 1953).

Arnold's Law of Marine Insurance and Average, 16th ed., M. Mustill & J. Gilman, eds. in British Shipping Laws, vols. 9–10, (London: Stevens & Sons, 1981).

British Shipping Laws (London: Stevens & Sons, 1982–).

Carver's Carriage by Sea, 13th ed., R. Colinvaux, ed. in British Shipping Laws, vols. 2–3 (London: Stevens & Sons, 1982).

Chartering and Shipping Terms, 10th ed. by J. Bes (London: Baker & Howard, 1978).

Chorley and Giles' Shipping Law, 7th ed. by O. Giles (London: Pitman Press, 1980).

Damages Recoverable in Maritime Matters by R. Acomb (ABA Press, 1984).

Encyclopedia of Shipping Law Sources (Lloyd's of London Press, 1985).

Farwell's Rules of the Nautical Road, 6th ed., F. Bassett & R. Smith, eds. (Annapolis: Naval Institute Press, 1982).

Federal Maritime Commission Service (Arlington, VA: Hawkins Publishing Co., 1970–).

Glossary of Maritime Technical Terms (London: Lund Humphries, 1963).

How to Recover for Loss or Damage to Goods in Transit by S. Sorkin (Matthew Bender, 1976).

International Maritime Dictionary, 2d ed. by R. De Kerchove (Princeton, NJ: D. Van Nostrand Co., 1961).

International Maritime Law (Pacific Northwest Admiralty Law Institute, 1983).

Kennedy's Civil Salvage, 4th ed., K. McGuffie, ed. in British Shipping Laws, vol. 7 (London: Stevens & Sons, 1958).

The Law of Admiralty, 2d ed. by G. Gilmore (Foundation Press, 1975).

The Law of Collisions at Sea, 11th ed., K. McGuffie, ed. in British Shipping Laws, vol. 4 (London: Stevens & Sons, 1961).

The Law of General Average and the York-Antwerp Rules, 10th ed., J. Donaldson et al., eds. in British Shipping Laws, vol. 7 (London: Stevens & Sons, 1975).

The Law of Maritime Personal Injuries, 3d ed. by M. Norris (Lawyers Co-op., 1975).

The Law of Pilotage, 2d ed. by G. Geen & R. Douglas (Lloyd's of London Press, 1984).

The Law of Tugs and Towage by L. Kovats (London: Barry Rose, 1981).

The Law of Tug, Tow and Pilotage, 2d ed. by A. Parks (Centreville, MD: Cornell Maritime Press, 1982).

Lloyd's Register of Shipping (Lloyd's of London Press).

Marine Affairs—A World Handbook; a Reference Guide to Maritime Organizations, Conventions, and Disputes . . . by W. Degenhardt (Gale, 1985).

Marine Cargo Claims, 2d ed. by W. Tetley (Butterworths, 1978).

Marine Insurance, 3d ed. by E. Ivamy (Butterworths, 1979).

Marine Insurance and General Average in the United States: An Average Adjuster's Viewpoint, 2d ed. by L. Buglass (Centreville, MD: Cornell Maritime Press, 1981).

Marine Insurance Claims by L. Buglass (Centreville, MD: Cornell Maritime Press, 1972).

Marine Insurance Claims, 2d ed. by J. Goodacre (London: Witherby & Co., 1981).

Marine Insurance: Its Principles and Practice, 3d ed. by W. Winter (McGraw-Hill, 1952).

Marine P&I Policy Annotations (ABA Tort and Insurance Practice Section, 1982).

Marine Reinsuracne by R. Brown & P. Reed (London: Witherby & Co., 1981).

Maritime Law by C. Hill (Oceana, 1981).

Maritime Law and Practice (Fla. Cont. Legal Ed., 1980).

Maritime Law of Salvage by G. Brice (London: Stevens & Sons; USA: Carswell, 1983).

Maritime Law: The Need for a Comprehensive Maritime Code by G. Malia (NY: Associated Faculty Press, 1983).

Nautical Rules of the Road: International and Inland, 2d ed. by B. Farnsworth & L. Young (Centreville, MD: Cornell Maritime Press, 1983).

Navigational Rules: International-Inland (GPO, 1983).

Payne and Ivamy's Carriage of Goods by Sea, 11th ed. by E. Ivamy (Butterworths, 1979).

Preparing A Ship Collision Case for Trial by J. Meadows (Lawyers Co-op., 1970).

Scrutton on Charterparties and Bills of Lading, 18th ed., A. Mocatta et al., eds. (London: Sweet & Maxwell, 1974).

Seamen's Damages for Death and Injury by J. Hood & B. Hardy (Harrison, 1983).

Secured Financing for the Transportation Industry, R. DeKoven, ed. (Practicing Law Institute, 1980).

Shipping Regulation (Pike & Fischer, Inc., 1961–).

Templeton on Marine Insurance: Its Principles and Practice, 5th ed., R. Lambeth, ed. (Plymouth, England: MacDonald & Evans, 1981).

Time Charters, 2d ed. by M. Wilford et al. (Lloyd's of London Press, 1982).

World Shipping Laws: International Conventions, D. Jackson, ed. (Oceana, 1984).

ENCYCLOPEDIAS:

AMERICAN JURISPRUDENCE 2D (Am Jur 2d)
Check the following topics in the *General Index* volumes for Am Jur 2d:

Admiralty	Jones Act

CORPUS JURIS SECUNDUM (CJS)
Check the following topics in the *General Index* volumes for CJS:

Admiralty	Longshoremen and
Boats	Harbor Workers
Cargo	Maritime Contracts
Carriers	Maritime Law
Custodia Legis	Pilots
Customs	Ports and Harbors
Exports and Imports	Seamen
Ferries	Ships and Shipping
High Seas	Weights and Measure

DIGESTS:

CASE SEARCH IN WEST DIGESTS BY KEY TOPIC
In the *Descriptive Word Index* of the West digests, look for key topics and numbers under the following subject headings:

Administrative Law	Insurance
Admiralty	International Law
Boats	Longshoremen and
Cargo	Harbor Workers
Carriers	Maritime Liens
Commerce	Pilots
Customs	Ports and Harbors
Damages	Seamen
Exports and Imports	Ships and Shipping
Ferries	Torts
High Seas	Weights and Measures

ALR:

ANNOTATIONS
Check the index volumes for ALR, ALR2d, ALR3d, ALR4th, and ALR Fed for annotations under the following subject headings:

Admiralty	Longshoremen
Barges	Marine Insurance
Carriers	Maritime Liens
Customs Court	Navigable Waters
Death on High Seas	Seamen
Freight	Shipping and Shipments
Imports and Exports	Ships and Vessels
Jones Act	

PERIODICALS:

CURRENT LAW INDEX (CLI) & LEGAL RESOURCE INDEX (LRI)
In the CLI and LRI, look for references to periodical literature under the following subject headings

Abandonment (Maritime	Marine Accident
Law)	Marine Pollution
Admiralty	Maritime Liens
Collisions at Sea	Navigation
Contracts, Maritime	Ocean Bottoms
Economic Zones	Salvage
(Maritime Law)	Shipping
Freedom of the Seas	Shipwrecks
Freight and Freightage	United Nations Convention
Import Controls	on the Law of the Sea
Jurisdiction over Ships	Water-Rights
at Sea	

INDEX TO LEGAL PERIODICALS (ILP)
In the ILP, look for references to legal periodical literature under the following subject headings

Administrative Agencies	Demurrage
Admiralty Courts	Embargo
Agency	Exports and Imports
Antidumping Duties	Longshoremen and
Arbitration and Award	Stevedores
Bills of Lading	Maritime Law
Bonds	Maritime Liens
Bulk Transfers	Merchant Marine
Collisions at Sea	Seamen
Commerce	Shipping
Damage	Tariff and Customs Laws

MARKETABLE TITLE: See Real Estate
MARKETS: See Business Law, Commodities, Computers
MARKET VALUE: See Contracts, Real Estate
MARKS: See Intellectual Property
MARRIAGE: See Canon Law, Family Law, Women & the Law
MARRIED WOMENS ACTS: See Estate Planning, Family Law, Real Estate
MARTIAL LAW: See Military Law, Philippines, War
MARXISM: See Communism, Jurisprudence

MARYLAND

SEE ALSO:	Circuit Courts (Fourth Circuit)

**RESEARCH GUIDES &
BIBLIOGRAPHIES:**

Ghost Hunting: Finding Legislative Intent in Maryland, A Checklist of Sources by M. Miller (MD State Law Library, 1984).
An Introduction to Maryland State Publications for the Law Librarian by L. Davis (Amer. Assn. of Law Libraries, 1981).
Legal Information Resources: A Guide for Maryland Law Libraries by M. Miller (Law Library Assn. of Md., 1984).
Suggested Minimum Standards Law Collection Maryland Circuit Court Libraries: Collection Content (Md. State Bar, 1984).

STATUTES:

Annotated Code of Maryland.
Laws of Maryland.

**STATE ADMINISTRATIVE
REGULATIONS:**

Code of Maryland Regulations.
Maryland Register.

CASES & OPINIONS:

Maryland Reports (1951–).
Maryland Appellate Reports (1967–).
Atlantic Reporter (1885–).

COURT RULES:

Maryland Court Rules (Rules Service Co., 1966–).
Maryland District Rules (Rules Service Co., 1971–).
Maryland Rules Commentary by P. Neimeyer (Michie, 1984).
Maryland Rules of Procedure (Michie).

JURY INSTRUCTIONS:

Maryland Civil Pattern Jury Instructions, 2d ed (Md. Inst. for Cont. Prof. Ed. of Lawyers, 1984).
Maryland Pattern Jury Instructions: Civil (Lawyers Co-op., 1976).

**ETHICS & PROFESSIONAL
RESPONSIBILITY:**

Opinions on Ethics and Professional Responsibility (Md. State Bar).

**OPINIONS OF THE
ATTORNEY GENERAL:**

Annual Report and Official Opinions of the Attorney General of Maryland (1916–).
Attorney General's Digest (1979–).

**JOURNALS & OTHER
PERIODICALS:**

Maryland Bar Journal (Md. State Bar, 1968–).
The Maryland Researcher (Natl. Legal Research Group, 1970–).

**ANNUAL SURVEY OF
STATE LAW:**

"Survey of Developments in Maryland Law" in *Maryland Law Review.* See for example vol. 36, p. 351; vol. 45, p. 254.

DIRECTORIES:

Maryland Lawyers' Manual (Md. State Bar).

**TREATISES, LOOSELEAFS &
OTHER MONOGRAPHS:**

Introduction to Maryland Civil Litigation by C. Brown (Michie, 1982).

Maryland Appellate Practice Handbook, P. Sandler, ed. (Md. Inst. for Cont. Prof. Ed. for Lawyers, 1977–).
Maryland Civil Procedure Forms by G. Liebmann (West, 1984).
Maryland Corporate Forms: Practice by R. Shapiro (Md. Legal Pub., 1976–)
Maryland Criminal Law: Practice and Procedure by R. Gilbert (Michie, 1983).
Maryland District Court Practice by G. Liebmann (West, 1984).
Maryland Divorce and Separation Law by J. Alexander (Md. Inst. for Cont. Prof. Ed. for Lawyers, 1982).
Maryland Estate Planning, Will Drafting and Estate Administration Forms by A. Barr (Md. Legal Pub., 1982–).
Maryland Evidence by G. McLain (West, 1987).
Maryland Practice Forms by P. Junghans (Md. Inst. for Cont. Prof. Ed. for Lawyers, 1980–).
Maryland Real Estate Forms: Practice by R. Reno (Md. Legal Pub., 1983–).
Maryland Tort Damages (Md. Inst. for Cont. Prof. Ed. for Lawyers, 1979).
Practice Manual for the Maryland Lawyer (Md. State Bar, 1979–).

**DIGESTS, ENCYCLOPEDIAS
& CITATOR:**

Maryland Digest (West).
Atlantic Digest (West).
Maryland Law Encyclopedia (West).
Shepard's Maryland Citations.

MASSACHUSETTS

SEE ALSO:

Circuit Courts (First Circuit).

**RESEARCH GUIDES &
BIBLIOGRAPHIES:**

Annual State Bibliography by L. McAuliffe & S. Steinway (American Assn. of Law Libraries, 1985).
Handbook of Legal Research in Massachusetts, M. Botsford & R. Matz, eds. (Mass. Cont. Legal Ed., 1988).

**STATUTES & RELATED
LEGISLATIVE MATERIALS:**

Annotated Laws of Massachusetts (Lawyers Co-op).
General Laws of the Commonwealth of Massachusetts (Michie/Lawyers Co-op).
Massachusetts General Laws Annotated (West).
Guide to Massachusetts General and Special Acts (Legislative Reporting Service, 1976–).
Massachusetts Advance Legislative Service (Lawyers Co-op.).
City of Boston Code: Statutes, Ordinances, Regulations (Law Dept. 1975–).

**STATE ADMINISTRATIVE
CODE:**

Code of Massachusetts Regulations.
Massachusetts Register.

CASES & OPINIONS:

Massachusetts Reports (1867–).
Massachusetts Appeals Court Reports (1976–).
Northeast Reporter (1972–).

COURT RULES:

Current Court Rules for all Courts in Massachusetts, Including Forms and Periodic Updates (Mass. Lawyers Diary and Manual 1976–).

Massachusetts Rules of Court (West).

Massachusetts Rules Service (Mass. Lawyers Weekly, 1979–).

Rules of the Courts of the Commonwealth: Civil and Criminal (Mass. Cont. Legal Ed., 1981–).

ETHICS & PROFESSIONAL RESPONSIBILITY:

Ethical Opinions of the Massachusetts Bar Association.

JOURNALS & OTHER PERIODICALS:

Boston Bar Journal (1923–).

Massachusetts Update (West, 1987–).

Massachusetts Law Review (1915–).

Massachusetts Lawyers Weekly.

SURVEY OF STATE LAW:

Annual Survey of Massachusetts Law (Little, Brown, 1954–).

TREATISES & LOOSELEAFS:

Administrative Law (Mass. Cont. Legal Ed., 1982).

Criminal Practice in the District Courts (Mass. Cont. Legal Ed., 1981).

Estate Taxation by B. Rosales & A. Bove (Callaghan, 1980).

Handbook of Massachusetts Evidence, 5th ed. by P. Liacos (Little, Brown, 1981).

Inheritance, Estate and Gift Tax Reports (CCH, 1928–).

Juvenile Delinquency (Mass. Cont. Legal Ed., 1982).

Manual for District Court Clerk/Magistrates by R. Maloney (Lawyers Weekly Publications, 1980).

Massachusetts Corporations by D. Muir (Lawyers Co-op., 1981).

Massachusetts Criminal Law, 2d ed. by J. Nolan & B. Henry (West, 1988).

Massachusetts Domestic Relations by J. Harvey et al. (Lawyers Co-op, 1982–).

Massachusetts Legal Systems (Matthew Bender, 1979–).

Massachusetts Pleading and Practice—Forms and Commentary by E. Swartz (Matthew Bender, 1974–).

Massachusetts Practice Series (West).

Massachusetts Probate Manual by J. Warner & H. Reynolds (Mass. Cont. Legal Ed., 1981).

Massachusetts Researcher (VA: Research Group, 1970–).

Massachusetts Standardized Civil Practice Forms by P. Garrity (Little, Brown, 1986–).

Massachusetts Tax Reporter (CCH, 1938–).

State and Local Taxes (Prentice-Hall, 1967–).

Superior Court Civil Practice (Mass. Cont. Legal Ed., 1981).

DIGEST & CITATOR:

Massachusetts Digest (West).

Shepard's Massachusetts Citations.

MASS MEDIA: See Media Law

MASTER & SERVANT: See Agency, Business Law, Employee Benefits, Torts, Workers' Compensation

MATERNITY LEAVE: See Labor Law, Women & the Law

MATHEMATICAL STATISTICS: See Economics, Statistics

MATRIMONY: See Canon Law, Family Law

MAURITANIA

SEE ALSO: Africa, International Law, Islam, United Nations

CONSTITUTION: "Mauritania" by M. Tarantino in *Constitutions of the Countries of the World* by
  A. Blaustein & G. Flanz (Oceana, 1981).

**TREATISES &
LOOSELEAFS:**   *African Tax Systems* by R. Hammond & M. van den Abeelen (Mauritania)
  (Amsterdam: Intl. Bureau of Fiscal Documentation, 1980–).
  An Introduction to Law in French-Speaking Africa (Mauritania) by J. Salacuse
  (Michie, 1969).
  Investment Laws of the World (Mauritania) (Oceana, 1981–).

ARTICLES: "Mauritania" (Human rights), *International Commission of Jurists Review* 13 (Dec.,
  1984).

MAURITIUS

SEE ALSO: Africa, International Law, Islam, United Nations

CASES: "Cases" (Supreme Court of Mauritius), 26 *Journal of African Law* 117 (1982).

**JOURNALS & OTHER
PERIODICALS:**   *Mauritius Law Review* (1977–).

**TREATISES &
LOOSELEAFS:**   *Investment Laws of the World* (Mauritius) (Oceana, 1981–).
  Labour Laws of Mauritius by A. Angelo (Port Louis: Mauritius Law Publishers, 1983).
  Maruitius: The Law of Criminal Procedure by C. Kenyon (Library of Congress, 1983).
  Modern Mauritius: The Politics of Decolonization by A. Simmons (Indiana Univ.
  Press, 1982).
  Tax Laws of the World—Mauritius (FL: Foreign Tax Law Assn.).

ARTICLES: "Attorney Works to Build a Name for Mauritius" by T. Aarons, 99 *Los Angeles Daily
  Journal,* p. B1, col. 3 (Nov. 18, 1986).
  "Current Legal Developments" (Mauritius), 15 *Comparative and International Law
  Journal of Southern Africa* 230 (1982).
  "Diego Garcia: Competing Claims to a Strategic Isle" by T. Lynch, 16 *Case Western
  Reserve Journal of International Law* 101 (1984).

MAYHEM: See Criminal Law
MAYOR: See State & Local Government
MECHANICS' LIEN: See Architecture, Contracts

MEDIA LAW

SEE ALSO: Advertising, Agency, Art & Entertainment, Business Law, Constitutional Law, Freedom of Information, Intellectual Property, International Law, Labor Law, Public Utilities

RESEARCH GUIDES & BIBLIOGRAPHIES:

Doing Research in Federal Communications Law by J. Howard (Library of Congress Law Library, 1981).
"Video Technology and the Law: A Bibliography" by F. Houdek, 5 *Comm./Ent.* 341 (1982–83).

ADMINISTRATIVE PUBLICATIONS—FCC REPORTS & RULES:

Federal Communications Commission Reports.
Federal Communications Commission Rules and Regulations (Rules Service Co., 1963–).
Legal Guide to FCC Broadcast Rules, Regulations, and Policies (Natl. Assn. of Broadcasters, 1977–).
Radio Regulation, Second Series by J. Willis (Pike & Fischer, Inc., 1963–).
Reports, Decisions and Orders, Federal Communications Commission (GPO, 1934–).
Rules and Regulations, Federal Communications Commission (GPO).

JOURNALS, NEWSLETTERS & OTHER PERIODICALS:

Broadcasting and the Law (Miami: L&S Pub., 1971–).
Cable TV Franchising (Carmel, CA: Paul Kagan Associates, 1975–).
Cable TV Law and New Media Law & Finance (Leader Pub.; NY Law Pub., 1983–).
Cable TV Law Reporter (Carmel, CA: Paul Kagan Associates, 1984–).
Communications and the Law (NY: Earl Colemen Enterprises, 1979–).
Communications Daily (Wash. D.C.: Television Digest, Inc., 1981–).
Communications Lawyer (ABA Forum Comm. on Communication Law, 1983–).
Federal Communication Law Journal (UCLA Law Sch., 1937–).
International Media Law (London: Oyez Longman Pub., 1982–).
Journal of Broadcasting (Wash. D.C.: Broadcast Education Assn., 1956–).
Journal of Media Law and Practice (1980–).
Media Law Notes (Univ. of Wisc. Sch. of Journalism).
News Media and the Law (1977–).

SYMPOSIA & ANNUALS:

Communications Law (Practicing Law Institute).
Communications Law Symposium (UCLA).

LOOSELEAFS:

All About Cable by M. Hamburg (New York Law Pub. Co., 1981–).
Cable Television Law by C. Ferris (Matthew Bender, 1983–).
Encyclopedia of International Telecommunications Law (Butterworths, 1987–).
International Telecommunications Agreements by G. Wallenstein (Oceana, 1977–).
Libel and Privacy by F. Abrams (Law & Business, Inc.).
Media Law Reporter (BNA, 1977–).
Rights and Liabilities of Publishers, Broadcasters, and Reporters by S. Metcalf (Shepard's, 1982–).

TREATISES:

Broadcast Law and Regulation by J. Bittner (Prentice-Hall, 1982).
Cable Television: Handbook and Forms by I. Stein (Shepard's, 1985).
The Deregulation of International Telecomunications by R. Eward (Dedham, MA: Artech House, 1985).

The First Freedom Today: Issues Relating to Censorship and Intellectual Freedom by R. Downs & R. McCoy (American Library Assn., 1984).

Freedom of the High School Press by N. Kristof (Univ. Press of America, 1983).

Law of Mass Communications, 5th ed. by H. Nelson (Foundation Press, 1986).

Major Principles of Media Law by W. Overbeck (Holt, Rinehart, and Winston, 1982).

Mass Communications Law in a Nutshell by H. Zuckman (West, 1983).

Mass Media Law, 2d ed. by D. Pember (Dubuque: Brown, 1982).

Media Guide for Lawyers by E. Miller (Natl. Law Pub., 1982).

The Newspaperman and the Law by W. Steigleman (Greenwood Press, 1950).

Newspapers and the Antitrust Laws by S. Oppenheim (Michie, 1982).

Satellite and Cable: International Protection, 2d ed. by A. Mosteshar (London: Longman, 1986).

Telecommunications Regulation Today and Tomorrow by E. Noam (Law & Business, Inc., 1983).

ENCYCLOPEDIAS: AMERICAN JURISPRUDENCE 2D (Am Jur 2d)
Check the following topics in the *General Index* volumes for Am Jur 2d:

Administrative Law	Lewdness, Indecency,
Censorship	and Obscenity
Civil Rights	Libel and Slander
Constitutional Law	Newspapers, Periodicals
Freedom of Speech	and Press Associations
and Press	Telecommunications

CORPUS JURIS SECUNDUM (CJS)
Check the following topics in the *General Index* volumes for CJS:

Administrative Bodies	Lewdness or Obscenity
Censorship	Libel and Slander
Civil Rights	Magazines
Constitutional Law	Newspapers
First Amendment	Telecommunications
Freedom of Speech	
and Press	

DIGESTS: CASE SEARCH IN WEST DIGESTS BY KEY TOPIC
In the *Descriptive Word Index* of the West digests, look for key topics and numbers under the following subject headings:

Administrative Law	Lewdness or Obscenity
Blasphemy	Libel and Slander
Censorship	Licenses
Civil Rights	Magazines
Constitutional Law	Monopolies
First Amendment	Newspapers
Freedom of Speech	Obscenity
and Press	Telecommunications

ALR: ANNOTATIONS
Check the index volumes for ALR, ALR2d, ALR3d, ALR4th, and ALR Fed for annotations under the following subject headings:

Administrative Law	Commission
Blasphemy and Profanity	Freedom of Speech
Cable Television	and Press
Equal Time	Indecency, Lewdness
Federal Communications	and Obscenity

Libel and Slander	Privacy
News Media	Radio and Television
Newspapers	Telecommunications
New York Times Rule	

PERIODICALS:

CURRENT LAW INDEX (CLI) & LEGAL RESOURCE INDEX (LRI)
In the CLI and LRI, look for references to periodical literature under the following subject headings

Administrative Law	International
Broadcasters	Telecommunications
Broadcasting	Journalism
Cable Television	Mass Media
Censorship	Newspaper Publishing
Condemned Books	Obscenity
Electronic Publishing	Pornography
Equal Time Rule	Press
Erotic Literature	Prior Restraint
Expunged Books	Public Broadcasting
Fairness Doctrine	Radio
FM Broadcasting	Telecommunication
Freedom of Speech	United States Federal
Free Press and Fair Trial	Communications
Home Video	Commission

INDEX TO LEGAL PERIODICALS (ILP)
In the ILP, look for references to legal periodical literature under the following subject headings:

Administrative Law	Fraud
Authors and Publishers	Freedom of Speech
Censorship	Freedom of the Press
Civil rights	Newspapers
Communications	Obscenity
Constitutional Law	Radio and Television
Copyright	

MEDIATION

SEE ALSO:

Criminal Law, Family Law, Judicial Administration, Labor Law, Professional Responsibility, Trial & Appellate Practice

JOURNALS, NEWSLETTERS & OTHER PERIODICALS:

Mediation Quarterly: Journal of the Academy of Family Mediators (San Francisco: Jossey-Bass, 1983–).

Ohio State Journal of Dispute Resolution (1985–).

TREATISES & LOOSELEAFS:

Child Custody Mediation by F. Bienenfeld (Palo Alto: Science and Behavior Books, 1983).

Dispute Resolution Program Directory (ABA Special Committee on Alternative Dispute Resolution, 1983).

Divorce Mediation by K. & M. Schneider (Acropolis Books, 1984).

Family Mediation by J. Blades (Prentice-Hall, 1985).

Family Mediation Will Work for You by R. Coulson (American Arbitration Assn.).
Mediate Your Divorce by J. Blades (Prentice-Hall, 1985).
The Mediation Process by C. Moore (San Francisco: Jossey-Bass, 1986).
Negotiating Settlements: A Guide to Environmental Mediation (American Arbitration Assn.).
Professional Mediation of Civil Disputes (American Arbitration Assn.).
Project Early Settlement: An Alternative to the Courts (ABA).
The Psychology of a Mediator by J. Barrett (Wash. D.C.: Society of Professionals in Dispute Resolution, 1983).
Public Sector Mediation by R. Zack (BNA, 1985).
Techniques of Mediation, 2d ed. by W. Maggiolo (Oceana, 1985).
The Wayne County Mediation Program in the Eastern District of Michigan by K. Shuart (Wash. D.C.: Federal Judicial Center 1984).

ENCYCLOPEDIA:

AMERICAN JURISPRUDENCE 2D (Am Jur 2d)
Check the following topics in the *General Index* volumes for Am Jur 2d:

Arbitration and Award	Labor and Labor Relations
Divorce and Separation	Negotiations and Negotiators

PERIODICALS:

CURRENT LAW INDEX (CLI) & LEGAL RESOURCE INDEX (LRI)
In the CLI and LRI, look for references to periodical literature under the following subject headings:

Arbitration	Grievance Procedures
Dispute Resolution	Labor
Divorce Mediation	Mediation
Environmental Mediation	

INDEX TO LEGAL PERIODICALS (ILP)
In the ILP, look for references to legal periodical literature under the following subject headings:

Arbitration and Award	International Arbitration
Divorce and Separation	Mediation
Industrial Arbitration	

MEDICAID, MEDICARE: See Health & Medicine, Nursing, Social Security
MEDICAL EXAMINERS: See Health & Medicine
MEDICAL MALPRACTICE: See Dentistry, Mental Health, Torts
MEDICAL RECORDS: See Health & Medicine
MEDICAL RESEARCH: See Death
MEDICINE: See Food, Forensic Science, Health & Medicine, Mental Health, Occupational Safety, Sports Law
MELANESIAN: See Papua New Guinea
MENTAL ANGUISH: See Mental Health, Torts
MENTAL DISABILITY: See Criminal Law

MENTAL HEALTH

SEE ALSO:

Age, AIDS, Alcohol, Constitutional Law, Contracts, Corrections, Criminal Law, Education Law, Estate Planning, Family Law, Forensic Science, Handicapped & the Law, Health & Medicine, Human Experimentation, International Law, Juvenile Law, Labor Law, Poverty Law, Social Security, State & Local Government, Torts, Workers' Compensation

JOURNALS, NEWSLETTERS & OTHER PERIODICALS:

Behavioral Sciences and the Law.

Bulletin of the American Academy of Psychiatry and the Law (1973–).

International Journal of Law and Psychiatry (Pergamon Press, 1978–).

Journal of Psychiatry & Law (Federal Legal Pubs., 1973–).

Law and Psychology Review (Univ. of Alabama Sch. of Law, 1975–).

New England Journal on Criminal and Civil Confinement (New England School of Law).

TREATISES & LOOSELEAFS:

American Psychiatric Association Statement on the Insanity Defense (Amer. Psychiatric Assn., 1982).

Clinical Handbook of Psychiatry and the Law by T. Gutheil (McGraw-Hill, 1982).

Consent to Treatment: A Practical Guide by F. Rozovsky (Little, Brown, 1984).

Decision Making for Incompetent Persons: The Law and Morality of Who Shall Decide by S. Jordan (C. C. Thomas, 1985).

The Dismissal of Students with Mental Disorders: Legal Issues by G. Pavela (Ashville, NC: College Admin. Pubs., 1985).

Ethical and Legal Issues in Counseling and Psychotherapy, W. Van Hoose, ed. (San Francisco: Jossey-Bass, 1985).

Guidelines for Involuntary Civil Commitment (Natl. Center for State Courts, 1986).

The Law and Mental Health: Research and Policy, R. Lambert, ed. (Sage pubs., 1986).

Legal Guidebook in Mental Health by R. Jay (Free Press, 1982).

Legal Issues in the Private Practice of Psychiatry by J. Klein (American Psychiatric Press, 1984).

Major Cases in Mental Health Law, D. Wexler, ed. (Univ. Pubs. of America, 1984).

Medical Malpractice, Psychiatric Care by J. Smith (Shepard's, 1986).

Mental and Physical Disability Law Reporter (ABA, 1984–).

Mental Health and the Law by E. Beis (Aspen Systems Corp., 1984).

Mental Health Law Reporter (VA: Capitol Pubs, 1983–).

The Mentally Disabled and the Law, 3d ed. by S. Brakel et al. (Amer. Bar Foundation, 1985).

Mental Retardation: Its Social and Legal Context by S. Vitello (Prentice-Hall, 1985).

Proposed Criminal Justice Mental Health Standards (ABA Standing Committee on Assn. Standards for Criminal Justice, 1984).

Psychiatric Dictionary, 5th ed. by R. Campbell (NY: Oxford Univ. Press, 1981).

Psychiatric Justice by T. Szasz (Greenwood Press, 1965).

Psychiatry in Everyday Practice of Law, 2d ed. by M. Binder (Lawyers Co-op., 1982).

Psychoanalytic Psychiatry for Lawyers by D. Gesensway (ALI–ABA Comm. on Cont. Prof. Ed., 1982).

Psychology and Professional Practice: The Interface of Psychology and the Law, F. Fields, ed. (Quorum, 1982).

Psychology and the Law, J. Scheirer, ed. (Amer. Psychological Society, 1983).

The Transfer of Care: Psychiatric Deinstitutionalization and its Aftermath by P. Brown (London; Boston: Routledge & Kegan Paul, 1985).

ENCYCLOPEDIAS:

AMERICAN JURISPRUDENCE 2d (Am Jur 2D)

Check the following topics in the *General Index* volumes for Am Jur 2d:

Capacity or Incapacity	Mental Capacity or
Civil rights	Condition
Competency	Physical or Mental
Constitutional Law	Examination
Guardian and Ward	Physicians and Surgeons
Incompetent or Insane	
Persons	

CORPUS JURIS SECUNDUM (CJS)
Check the following topics in the *General Index* volumes for CJS:

Asylums and Institutional Care Facilities	Guardian and Ward
	Medical Care and
Capacity	Treatment
Civil Rights	Mentally Deficient and
Constitutional Law	Mentally Ill Person
Discharge	Physicians and Surgeons
Guardian ad Litem	Psychiatrists

DIGESTS:

CASE SEARCH IN WEST DIGESTS BY KEY TOPIC
In the *Descriptive Word Index* of the West digests, look for key topics and numbers under the following subject headings:

Administrative Law	Health and Environment
Asylums	Hospitals
Capacity	Medical Care and
Civil Rights	Treatment
Constitutional Law	Mental Health
Criminal Law	Mentally Deficient and
Discharge	Mentally Ill Person
Guardian ad Litem	Physicians and Surgeons
Guardian and Ward	Psychiatrists

ALR:

ANNOTATIONS
Check the index volumes for ALR, ALR2d, ALR3d, ALR4th, and ALR Fed for annotations under the following subject headings:

Capacity or Incapacity	Mental Anguish
Competency	Mental Illness
Conservator	M'Naghten Rule
Due Process of Law	Physicians and Surgeons
Incompetent or Insane Persons	Psychiatric Examination
	Psychiatrist
Medical Treatment or Care	Psychologist
	Rehabilitation Institution

PERIODICALS:

CURRENT LAW INDEX (CLI) & LEGAL RESOURCE INDEX (LRI)
In the CLI and LRI, look for references to periodical literature under the following subject headings:

Abnormality, Human	Institutional Care
Alcoholism	Intelligence Tests
Asylums	Mental Health Laws
Capacity and Disability	Mentally Handicapped
Conservatorship	Mentally Ill
Constitutional Law	Mental Retardation
Criminal Law	Facilities
Developmentally Disabled	Psychiatric Hospital Care
Deviant Behavior	Psychiatrists
Group Psychotherapy	Psychology
Guardian and Ward	Psychotherapist and Patient
Human Behavior	Psychotherapy
Insane	Psychotropic Drugs
Insanity	Suicide

INDEX TO LEGAL PERIODICALS (ILP)
In the ILP, look for references to legal periodical literature under the following subject headings

Administrative Law	Incompetents
Behavior Modification	Insanity
Civil Rights	Medical Jurisprudence
Commitment	Mental Health
Common Law	Physicians and Surgeons
Constitutional Law	Psychiatry
Criminal Responsibility	Psychology
Health	Sterilization
Hospitals	

MERCHANDISE: See Business Law, Personal Property, Uniform Commercial Code

MERCHANTABLE TITLE: See Real Estate

MERGER: See Antitrust Law, Business Law, Corporate Law, Employee Benefits, Securities law

MERIT SYSTEMS PROTECTION BOARD: See Civil Service, Labor Law

MESCALERO INDIANS: See Indians

METES & BOUNDS: See Real Estate

MEXICO

SEE ALSO: Caribbean, International Law, Latin America, United States

RESEARCH GUIDES & BIBLIOGRAPHIES:

A Revised Guide to the Law & Literature of Mexico by H. Clagett & D. Valderrama (Library of Congress, 1973).

"A Select Bibliography on Mexican Real Property Law" by E. Revilla, 12 *Arizona Law Review* 374 (1970).

"A Select Bibliography on Works in English and Spanish on Mexican Law" by J. Pags, 4 *California Western Law Review* 366 (1968).

Housing and Urban Development Planning in Mexico: A Bibliography (Dept. of Housing and Urban Development, Office of Intl. Affairs, 1980).

CONSTITUTION:

Constitutions of the Countries of the World, "Mexico 1972–1982," by A. Blaustein & G. Flanz (Oceana, 1982).

STATUTES & RELATED LAWS:

Mexican Civil Code by M. Gordon (Oceana, 1980).

Series of Statements of the Law of the OAS Member States in Matters Affecting Business—Mexico (Organization of American States, 1970).

TREATISES & LOOSELEAFS:

Business Operations in Mexico by N. del Castillo, Tax Management Foreign Income Portfolios, no. 136–4th (BNA, 1984).

Capital Formation and Investment Incentives Around the World (Mexico, vol. 1) by W. Diamond & D. Diamond (Matthew Bender, 1984).

Coming Home: A Handbook for Americans Incarcerated in Mexico by R. Fogelnest et al. (Philadelphia: Intl. Legal Defense Counsel, 1984).

Company Formation in Mexico, 2d ed. by A. Hoagland (London: Lloyd's Bank Intl., 1980).

Conflict of Laws: Mexico and the United States by S. Bayitch (FL: Univ. of Miami Press, 1968).

Doing Business in Mexico by T. Reiner et al. (Matthew Bender, 1980–).

Digest of Commercial Laws of the World (vol. 5) (Natl. Assn. of Credit Mangement; Oceana, 1977–).

Five Centuries of Law and Politics in Central Mexico, R. Spores & R. Hassig, eds. (Vanderbilt Univ., 1984).

Information Guide, Doing Business in Mexico (Price Waterhouse).

An Introduction to the History of Mexican Law by G. Margadant (Oceana, 1982).

An Introduction to the Mexican Legal System by J. Herget & J. Camil (Hein, 1978).

Judicial Review in Mexico by R. Baker (Austin: Univ. of Texas Press, 1971).

Land Reform in Mexico, 1910–1980 by S. Sanderson (Orlando: Academic Press, 1984).

Latin America. . . A Tax Tour (Mexico) (Arthur Anderson & Co., 1985).

Multinational Corporations Law: Mexico and Central America, M. Gordon, ed., (Oceana, 1980–).

Prospects for Adjustment in Argentina, Brazil, and Mexico, J. Williamson (Wash. D.C.: Institute for Intl. Economics, 1983).

Tax Laws of the World—Mexico (FL: Foreign Tax Law Assn.).

ARTICLES:

"Doing Business in Mexico: A Practical Legal Analysis" by R. Radway, 14 *International Lawyer* 361 (1980).

"Expropriation and Aftermath," 18 *Texas International Law Journal* 431 (1983).

"The Foreign Investment Transaction in Mexico" by F. Perry, 8 *Loyola of Los Angeles International and Comparative Law Journal* 67 (1985).

"International Banking: Nationalization of Mexican Banks and Foreign Exchange Control," 24 *Harvard International Law Journal* 212 (1983).

"Know-How Licensing in Mexico" by H. Rangel, 5 *Licensing Law & Business Rep.* 25 (1982). See also 81 Patent & Trademark Review 3 (1983).

"Legal Issues Arising from the Mexican Economic Crisis" by R. Morgan, 17 *Vanderbilt Journal of International Law* 367 (1984).

"The Mexican Debt Crisis in Perspective: Faulty Legal Structures and Aftershocks" by F. Vazquez Pando, 23 *Texas International Law Journal* 171 (1988).

"Mexican Law of Damages for Automobile Accidents" by B. Kozolchyk, 1 *Arizona Journal of International and Comparative Law* 189 (1982).

"Mexican Protectionist Policies and Their Implications for the Computer Industry" by M. Salehizadeh, 38 *Inter-American Economic Affairs* 85 (1984).

"Mexico: Law on the Control and Registration of the Transfer of Technology . . . of Patents and Trademarks," 80 *Patent & Trademark Review* 300 (Sept., 1982).

"The New Mexican Transfer of Technology Law" by W. Baird, 12 *Denver Journal of International Law & Policy* 107 (1982).

"1981 Mexican Transfer of Technology Law" by A. Hyde, 15 *Lawyer of the Americas* 37 (1983).

"Observations on the Nature of Joint Ventures in Mexico" by M. Gordon, 2 *Boston College International and Comparative Law Review* 337 (1979).

"Symposium on Doing Business in Mexico," 18 *The International Lawyer* 285 (1984).

"U.S. Trade and Investment in Mexico" by E. Murphy, 12 *Lawyer of the Americas* 573 (1980).

"The Vienna Convention on International Sales Contracts and Mexican Law" by J. Graf, 1 *Arizona Journal of International and Comparative Law* 122 (1982).

MICHIGAN

SEE ALSO:	Circuit Courts (Sixth Circuit)
RESEARCH GUIDES & BIBLIOGRAPHIES:	*Michigan Legal Documents: An Annotated Bibliography* by S. Yoak & M. Heinen (Amer. Assn. of Law Libraries, 1982). "Michigan Practice Materials: A Selective, Annotated Bibliography" by D. Johnson, 73 *Law Library Journal* 672 (1980).
STATUTES & OTHER LEGISLATIVE MATERIALS:	*Michigan Compiled Laws* (1979). *Michigan Compiled Laws Annotated* (West). *CCH Advance Session Law Reporter.* *Michigan Legislative Service* (West). *Michigan Statutes Annotated* (Callaghan).
STATE ADMINISTRATIVE CODE:	*Michigan Administrative Code* (1979). *Michigan Register.* *Gongwer's Administrative Rules Report* (Gongwer's News Service, 1961–).
CASES & OPINIONS:	*Michigan Reports* (Lawyers Co-op., 1949–). *Michigan Appeals Reports* (Lawyers Co-op., 1967–). *Michigan Reporter* (West, 1941–). *North Western Reporter* (West, 1879–).
COURT RULES:	*Court Rules Annotated* (West). *Court Rules of Michigan Service,* 2d ed. (Mich. Inst. of Cont. Legal Ed., 1985–). *Michigan Court Rules Practice: Forms* (West). *Michigan Rules of Court* (West).
JURY INSTRUCTIONS:	*Michigan Criminal Jury Instructions* (Mich. Inst. of Cont. Legal Ed., 1977–). *Michigan Standard Jury Instructions: Civil,* 2d ed. (Mich. Inst. of Cont. Legal Ed., 1981–).
OPINIONS OF THE ATTORNEY GENERAL:	*Attorney General Opinions.* *Index of Opinions* (Attorney General's Dept.).
JOURNALS & OTHER PERIODICALS:	*Detroit Letter* (1931–). *Michigan Bar Journal* (State Bar, 1921–).
ANNUAL SURVEY OF STATE LAW:	"Annual Survey of Michigan Law" in *Wayne Law Review.* See for example vol. 13, p. 1; vol. 30, p. 191.
TREATISES & LOOSELEAFS:	*CCH State Tax Reporter: Michigan.* *Comparative Negligence in Michigan* by T. Koernke (Inst. for Cont. Legal Ed., 1981–). *Michigan Administrative Law* (Inst. for Cont. Legal Ed., 1981–).

Michigan Administrative Law (Inst. for Cont. Legal Ed., 1978–).
Michigan Appellate Handbook by C. Gromek (Inst. for Cont. Legal Ed., 1985–).
Michigan Basic Practice Handbook, 2d ed. (Inst. for Cont. Legal Ed., 1985–).
Michigan Business Organizations: Corporations by C. Revelos (West, 1985).
Michigan Civil Procedure Manual with Forms, 2d ed. by J. Soave (West, 1985).
Michigan Courtroom Evidence by M. Wade (Inst. for Cont. Legal Ed., 1985–).
Michigan Divorce Manual by T. Oehmke (West, 1986).
Michigan Family Law, 2d ed., N. Robbins, ed. (Inst. for Cont. Legal Ed., 1983).
Michigan Marriage and Divorce, 3d ed. by A. Moore (West, 1980).
Michigan Real Estate Formbook By R. Jossman (Inst. for Cont. Legal Ed., 1985).
Michigan Uniform Commercial Code Forms by R. Steinheimer (West, 1969).
Probate Administratin in Michigan, 2d ed. by H. Draper (Inst. for Cont. Legal Ed., 1984–).

DIGESTS, ENCYCLOPEDIAS & CITATOR:

Michigan Appellate Digest (Secretary of State, 1978–).
Michigan Civil Jurisprudence (Callaghan).
Michigan Digest (Callaghan).
Michigan Digest (West).
Michigan Law and Practice (West).
North Western Digest (West).
Shepard's Michigan Digest.

MICROCOMPUTING: See Computers

MICRONESIA

SEE ALSO: Guam, International Law, United Nations

TREATISES: *Democracy in the Islands: The Micronesian Plebiscites of 1983* by A. Ranney (American Enterprise Institute, 1985).
Welcoming America's Newest Commonwealth: The Second Interim Report of the Northern Mariana Islands Commission of Federal Laws to the Congress of the United States (The Commission, 1985).

ARTICLES: "Compact of Free Association for Micronesia: Constitutional and International Law Issues" by H. Hills, 18 *International Lawyer* 583 (1984).
"The Constitution of the Federated States of Micronesia" by A. Burdick, 8 *Univesity of Hawaii Law Review* 419 (1983) (see also vol. 5, pp. 57, 361).
"The Constitution of the Northern Mariana Islands" by J. Branch, 9 *Denver Journal of International Law and Policy* 35 (1980).
"Micronesia and Free Association: Can Federalism Save Them?" by J. Metelski, 5 *California Western International Law Journal* 162 (1975).

MIDDLE EAST

SEE ALSO: United Nations, Bahrain, Egypt, International Law, Iran, Iraq, Israel, Jordan, Kuwait, Lebanon, Libya, Oman, Qatar, Saudi Arabia, Syria, United Arab Emirates, (Arab Republic), Yemen (People's Democratic Republic)

RESEARCH GUIDES & **BIBLIOGRAPHIES:**	"The Arab-Israel Conflict: A Legal Bibliography" by S. Silverburg, 72 *Law Library Journal* 12 (1979).

"The Law in the Near and Middle East: Basic Sources in English," 57 *Law Library Journal* 234 (1964).

United States/Middle East Diplomatic Relations, 1784–1978: An Annotated Bibliography by T. Bryson (Scarecrow Press, 1979).

JOURNALS & OTHER
PERIODICALS: *Middle East Executive Reports* (Wash. D.C.: Middle East Executive Reports, Inc., 1979–).

TREATISES &
LOOSELEAFS: *Commercial Arbitration in the Arab Middle East* (London: Graham & Trotman).

Commercial Laws of the Middle East by A. Keesee (Oceana, 1980–).

Commercial Laws of the World, Middle East States (FL: Foreign Tax Law Assn., 1985–).

Constitutions, Electoral Laws, Treaties of the States in the Near and Middle East by H. Davis (NY: AMS Press; Duke Univ. Press, 1953).

Current Aspects of Doing Business in the Middle East—Saudi Arabia, Egypt and Iran, W. Wickersham & B. Fishburne, eds. (American Bar Assn., 1977).

Doing Business in Saudi Arabia and the Gulf Arab States by N. Shilling (Dallas: Inter-Crescent, 1983–).

An Introduction to Contract Procedures in the Near East & North Africa by C. Loustaunau & J. Cohen (Intl. Trade Admin., 1980).

Law in the Middle East, M. Khadduri & H. Liebesny, eds. (Wash. D.C.: The Middle East Institute, 1955).

The Law of the Near and Middle East by H. Liebsny (State Univ. of N.Y. Press, 1975).

The Legal Status of the Arabian Gulf States by H. Albaharna (Oceana, 1968).

Middle East Legal Systems by S. Amin (Glasgow: Royston Ltd., 1985).

Negotiating for Peace in the Middle East by I. Fahmy (Johns Hopkins Univ. Press, 1983).

Oil and Gas Law by H. Williams & C. Meyers (Matthew Bender, 1959–).

Taxes and Investment in the Middle East (Intl. Bureau of Fiscal Documentation).

Tax Systems of Africa, Asia, and the Middle East by C. Platt (Gower, 1982).

ARTICLES: "Agency Law in the Arabian Peninsula and North Africa" by P. Homsy, 5 *Northwestern Journal of International Law and Business* 296 (1983).

"Tax Consequences of U.S. Investments in Select Middle Eastern Countries" by Ball & Walsh, 37 *New York University Institute of Federal Taxation* 8 (1979).

MIDWIFE: See Family Law, Health & Medicine, Nursing
MIGRANT WORKERS: See Agriculture, Labor Law

MILITARY LAW

SEE ALSO: Administrative Law, Air & Aviation, Criminal Law, Government Contracts, Human Rights, International Law, Legal History, Space, Terrorism, Torts, Transportation, Trial & Appellate Practice, War

RESEARCH GUIDE &
BIBLIOGRAPHY: "Military Law" in *Specialized Legal Research*, L. Chanin, ed. (Little, Brown, 1987).

STATUTES: *Military Justice Act of 1983*, 10 U.S.C. § 801ff.
Uniform Code of Military Justice, 10 U.S.C. § 801ff.

CASES, DECISIONS &
OPINIONS: *Boards of Review* (microfiche): (Law Library Consortium; Hein).
                         Military Justice Reporter (West, 1975–).
                         Military Law Reporter (Wash. D.C.: Public Law Education Institute, 1973–).

REGULATIONS & RELATED
GOVERNMENTAL
MATERIALS: *Manual for Courts-Martial of the United States* (Office of the President, 1984).
                         The Uniform System of Military Justice (Charlottesville: Judge Advocate General's
                             School, 1984).
                         32 C.F.R. 581 (Army).
                         32 C.F.R. 723 (Navy).
                         32 C.F.R. 865 (Air Force).

JOURNALS, NEWSLETTERS
& OTHER PERIODICALS: *The Advocate* (U.S. Army Legal Service Agency).
                         Air Force Law Review (Air Force J.A.G. School).
                         The Army Lawyer (1971–).
                         J.A.G. Journal (Navy, 1947–).
                         Military Law Review (Army J.A.G. School, 1958–).
                         Naval Law Review (Navy J.A.G., 1986–).
                         Reporter (Air Force, 1953–).

TREATISES &
LOOSELEAFS: *Conscripts and Volunteers* by R. Fullinwider (Rowman & Allanheld, 1983).
                         Fundamentals of Military Law (Army; GPO, 1976).
                         Military Criminal Justice, 2d ed. by D. Schlueter (Michie, 1987).
                         Military Discharge Upgrading and Introduction to Veterans Administration Law by
                             D. Addlestone et al. (Wash. D.C.: Veterans Education Project, 1982–).
                         Military Evidence, 2d ed. by J. Munster (Bobbs-Merrill, 1978).
                         Military Law, 3d ed. by E. Bryne (Annapolis: Naval Institute Press, 1981).
                         Military Law and Precedents, 2d ed. by W. Winthrop (GPO, 1920; Hein, 1979).
                         Military Law in a Nutshell by C. Shanor (West, 1980).
                         Military Law Under the Uniform Code of Military Justice by W. Aycock (Greenwood
                             Press, 1955).
                         Military Motions: A Handbook for Lawyers (ABA General Prac. Sect., 1986).
                         Military Personnel Law Manual (OGC; GAO, 1983).
                         Military Rules of Evidence Manual, 2d ed. by S. Saltzburg et al. (Michie, 1961).
                         Naval Officer's Guide, 9th ed. by W. Mack (MD: Naval Institute Press, 1983).

DIGESTS: *CMR Citations & Index* (GPO).
                         Military Justice Digest (GPO).
                         Shepard's Military Justice Citations.

ENCYCLOPEDIAS: AMERICAN JURISPRUDENCE 2D (Am Jur 2d)
                         Check the following topics in the *General Index* volumes for Am Jur 2d:

Administrative Law	Servicemen's and
Civil Rights	Veterans' Insurance
Military and Civil Defense	Veterans Administration
Navy	Veterans and Veterans'
Secretary of Air Force	Laws
Secretary of Army	War
Secretary of Navy	

CORPUS JURIS SECUNDUM (CJS)
Check the following topics in the *General Index* volumes for CJS:

Administrative Bodies	Military Reservation
Armed Services	Militia
Civil Rights	National Guard
Coast Guard	Veterans
Court-Martial	Veterans' Administration
Insubordination	War and National Defense

DIGESTS:

CASE SEARCH IN WEST DIGESTS BY KEY TOPIC
In the *Descriptive Word Index* of the West digests, look for key topics and numbers under the following subject headings:

Administrative Law	Military Justice
Armed Services	Militia
Civil Rights	National Guard
Coast Guard	Veterans
Court-Martial	War and National
Insubordination	Emergency
International Law	

ALR:

ANNOTATIONS
Check the index volumes for ALR, ALR2d, ALR3d, ALR4th, and ALR Fed for annotations under the following subject headings:

Administrative Law	Due Process of Law
Armed Forces	Servicemen
Court-Martial	Veterans' Administration
Dependents	

PERIODICALS:

CURRENT LAW INDEX (CLI) & LEGAL RESOURCE INDEX (LRI)
In the CLI and LRI, look for references to periodical literature under the following subject headings:

Air Warfare	Military Offense
Armed Services	National Security
Arms Control	Pensions (Military)
Astronautics (Military)	Soldiers
Deterrence (Military)	Space Weapons
Disarmament	United States Court of
Military Discharge	Military Appeals
Military Law	Veterans

INDEX TO LEGAL PERIODICALS (ILP)
In the ILP, look for references to legal periodical literature under the following subject headings:

Administrative Law	Judge Advocate-General
Armed Forces	Martial Law
Civil Rights	Military Law
Civil Service	Military Occupation
Conscientious Objectors	Military Pensions
Constitutional Law	Military Service
Courts-Martial	National Defense
International Military	Veterans
Tribunals	

MILITIA: See Military Law, War
MINERAL RESOURCES: See Energy, Natural Resources, Oil & Gas
MINE SAFETY: See Occupational Safety, Torts
MINES & MINERALS: See Environmental Law, Latin America, Natural Resources, Oil
    & Gas, Sea, Water Law
MINISTRY: See Canon Law, Church & State
MINNEAPOLIS GRAIN EXCHANGE: See Commodities

MINNESOTA

SEE ALSO: Circuit Courts (Eighth Circuit)

**RESEARCH GUIDES &
BIBLIOGRAPHIES:** *Minnesota Legal Research Guide* by A. Soderberg & B. Golden (Minn. State Law
    Library; Hein, 1985).
Legal Research: Beyond Tradition (Hamline Univ., Advanced Legal Ed., 1981).

**STATUTES & OTHER
LEGISLATIVE MATERIALS:** *Minnesota Statutes.*
Minnesota Statutes Annotated (West).
Laws of Minnesota.
Minnesota Session Law Service (West).

**STATE ADMINISTRATIVE
CODE:** *Minnesota Rules.*
Minnesota State Register.

CASES & OPINION: *Minnesota Reporter* (West).
Minnesota Reports (1851–1977).
North Western Reporter (1879–).

COURT RULES: *Appellate Rules Annotated,* 2d ed. by E. Magnunson (West, 1985).
Minnesota Rules of Civil Procedure Annotated, 2d ed. by D. Herr (West, 1985).
Minnesota Rules of Court (West).

JURY INSTRUCTIONS: *Minnesota Jury Instruction Guides: Civil,* 3d ed. (West, 1986).
Minnesota Jury Instruction Guides: Criminal, 2d ed. (West, 1985).

**OPINIONS OF THE
ATTORNEY GENERAL:** *Minnesota Legal Register* (1969–).

**JOURNALS & OTHER
PERIODICALS:** *Bench & Bar of Minnesota* (1944–).
Finance and Commerce (Minneapolis).
The Hennepin Lawyer.
Saint Paul Legal Ledger.

**TREATISES &
LOOSELEAFS:** *Fundamentals of Corporate Practice* . . . (Minn. Cont. Legal Ed., 1983).
Minnesota Collections by A. Zlimen (Lawyers Co-op., 1979–).
Minnesota Corporations Practice Manual (Butterworths, 1986).
Minnesota Criminal Practice and Procedure by H. McCarr (West, 1976).

> *Minnesota Dissolution* by W. Haugh (Lawyers Co-op., 1979–).
> *Minnesota Evidence* by P. Thompson (West, 1979).
> *Minnesota Family Law Practice Manual* (Butterworths, 1985).
> *Minnesota Judges' Criminal Benchbook* (Minn. Cont. Legal Ed., 1982).
> *Minnesota Juvenile Law and Practice* by J Sonsteng (West, 1985).
> *Minnesota Methods of Practice* by L. Arthur (West, 1975).
> *Minnesota Probate* by M. Helland (Lawyers Co-op., 1979–).
> *Minnesota Real Estate* by G. Shumaker (Lawyers Co-op., 1981–).
> *Minnesota Real Estate Law Practice Manual* (Butterworths, 1985).
> *Minnesota Tax Reporter* (CCH, 1982–).
> *State of Minnesota Directory of Licenses and Permits,* 5th ed. (St. Paul: The Minn. Small Business Assistance Office, 1988).
> *Workers' Compensation* (Minn. Inst. of Legal Ed., 1985).

DIGESTS & CITATOR: *Dunnell's Minnesota Digest* (Mason Pub.).
Minnesota Digest (West).
North Western Digest (West).
Shepard's Minnesota Citations.

MINORITIES: See Civil Rights
MINOR, MINORITY: See Contracts, Family Law, Juvenile Law
MIRANDA: See Criminal Law
MISCARRIAGE: See Abortion, Health & Medicine
MISCONDUCT: See Torts
MISDEMEANOR: See Criminal Law

MISSISSIPPI

SEE ALSO: Circuit Courts (Fifth Circuit)

RESEARCH GUIDE & BIBLIOGRAPHY: "A Selective Bibliography of Mississippi Practice Materials" by C. Bunnell, 8 *Southeastern Law Librarian* 3 (1983).

STATUTES & OTHER LEGISLATIVE MATERIALS: *Mississippi Code Annotated* (Secretary of State).
General Laws of Mississippi.
Daily Legislative Report (Miss. Economic Council).
Factual Reporting Service (1948–).
Legislative Action (Miss. Economic Council).

STATE ADMINISTRATIVE CODE: *Mississippi Register.*

CASES & OPINIONS: *Mississippi Reports* (1850–1966).
Southern Reporter (1866–).

COURT RULES: *Mississippi Rules of Court* (West).
Rules of the Supreme Court of Mississippi.

JURY INSTRUCTIONS: *Mississippi Model Jury Instructions: Civil and Criminal* (West, 1977).

ETHICS & PROFESSIONAL
RESPONSIBILITY: *Code of Professional Responsibility, Code of Judicial Conduct, Ethics Opinions* (Miss. State Bar).

OPINIONS OF THE
ATTORNEY GENERAL: *Attorney General Opinions* (Hein, 1968–).

JOURNALS & OTHER
PERIODICALS: *Mississippi Lawyer* (Miss. State Bar).

TREATISES &
LOOSELEAFS: *Arkansas, Louisiana and Mississippi Legal Directory* (Los Angeles: Legal Directories Pub. Co., 1955–).
Bad Faith Litigation in Mississippi by W. Denton (Masterfile Press, 1981).
Mississippi Supreme Court Practice by L. Munford (Jackson: On Point Press, 1988).
Products Liability: The Law in Mississippi by J. Wittenberg (Harrison, 1982).
Summary of Mississippi Law by L. Grant (Lawyers Co-op., 1969).

DIGESTS & CITATOR: *Mississippi Digest* (West).
Southern Digest (West).
Shepard's Mississippi Citations.

MISSOURI

SEE ALSO: Circuit Courts (Eighth Circuit)

RESEARCH GUIDES &
BIBLIOGRAPHIES: *A Law Librarian's Introduction to Missouri State Publications* by P. Aldrich et al. (American Assn. of Law Libraries, 1980).
Missouri State Government Publications (Mo. State Library, 1972–).

STATUTES & OTHER
LEGISLATIVE MATERIALS: *Missouri Revised Statutes.*
Vernon's Annotated Missouri Statutes (West).
Laws of Missouri.
Missouri Legislative Service.

STATE ADMINISTRATIVE
CODE: *Missouri Code of State Regulations* (1977–).
Missouri Register (1976–).

CASES & OPINIONS: *Missouri Reports* (1821–1956).
Missouri Appeal Reports (1876–1952).
South Western Reporter (1886–).

COURT RULES: *Missouri Civil Rules Practice* by C. Wheaton (West, 1976).
Missouri Rules of Court: State and Federal (West).
Vernon's Annotated Missouri Rules (West).

JURY INSTRUCTIONS: *Missouri Approved Charges: Criminal (MACH–CRI)* (Mo. Bar, 1979–).

Missouri Approved Instructions: Criminal (MAI–CR), 2d ed. (Mo. Bar, 1979).
Missouri Approved Jury Instructions: Civil (MAI), 3d ed. (West, 1981).

OPINIONS OF THE ATTORNEY GENERAL:

Digests of Official Opinions (Office of the Atty. Gen., 1933–).
Opinions (Office of the Atty. Gen., 1933–).

JOURNALS & OTHER PERIODICALS:

Journal of the Missouri Bar (1945–).
Kansas City Daily Record.
Missouri Bar Courts and CLE Bulletin (Mo. Bar, 1965–).
Springfield Daily Events.
St. Joseph Daily Courier.
St. Louis Countian.
St. Louis Daily Courier.

TREATISES & LOOSELEAFS:

Missouri Administrative Law (Mo. Bar, 1979–).
Missouri Administrative Practice and Procedure by A. Neely (West, 1987).
Missouri Appellate Practice and Extraordinary Remedies, 3d ed. (Mo. Bar, 1981).
Missouri Civil Procedure (Mo. Bar, 1983).
Missouri Civil Trial Practice, 2d ed. (Mo. Bar, 1988).
Missouri Corporation Law and Practice (Mo. Bar, 1988).
Missouri Creditors'—Debtors' Remedies, 4th ed. (Mo. Bar, 1985).
Missouri Criminal Practice, 2d ed. (Mo. Bar, 1983).
Missouri Criminal Practice and Procedure by W. Knox (West, 1985).
Missouri Estate Administration, 3d ed. (Mo. Bar, 1984–).
Missouri Evidence, 3d ed. (Mo. Bar, 1983).
Missouri Executions on Money Judgments by W. Henning (Harrison, 1984).
Missouri Family Law, 4th ed. (Mo. Bar, 1988).
Missouri Farm Law (Mo. Bar, 1983).
Missouri Insurance Practice, 3d ed. (Mo. Bar, 1986).
Missouri Jurisdiction, Venue and Limitations by C. Wheaton (West, 1965).
Missouri Local Government Law, 2d ed (Mo. Bar, 1986).
Missouri Methods of Practice by M. Volz (West, 1986).
Missouri Probate Code Manual by F. Hanna (West, 1986).
Missouri Probate Forms Manual by J. Borron (West, 1985).
Missouri Procedural Forms by C. Wheaton (West, 1986).
Missouri Products Liability by D. King (Harrison, 1983).
Missouri Real Estate Law by T. Hellmuth (West, 1985).
Missouri Real Estate Practice, 3d ed. (Mo. Bar, 1986).
Missouri Tort Law (Mo. Bar, 1978).
Missouri Uniform Commercial Code Forms by R. Duesenberg (West, 1966).
Possessory Estates, Future Interests and Conveyances in Missouri by W. Eckhardt (West, 1986).
Postmortem Taxes: Forms and Planning (Mo. Bar, 1982).

DIGESTS, INDEX & CITATOR:

Missouri Digest (West).
South Western Digest (West).
Missouri Law Finder (West, 1986).
Shepard's Missouri Citations.

MISTAKE: See Contracts, Equity, Torts
MISTRIAL: See Trial & Appellate Practice
MITIGATION: See Torts
M'NAGHTEN RULE: See Criminal Law, Mental Health
MOBILE HOME: See Nevada, Real Estate
MOBS: See Criminal Law
MONETARY LAW: See International Law
MONEY: See Banking Law, Economics

MONGOLIA

SEE ALSO: Asia, Communism, International Law, United Nations

**TREATIES & OTHER
AGREEMENTS:** Bulgaria . . . German Democratic Republic . . . Hungary . . . Mongolia . . . Agreement on the Establishment of the International Investment Bank and Statutes of the Bank, 23 *International Legal Materials* 641 (1984).

CONSTITUTION: "Mongolian People's Republic" in *Constitutions of the Countries of the World* by A. Blaustein & G. Flanz (Oceana, 1981).
The Constitutions of the Communist World (Mongolia), W. Simons, ed. (Sijthoff & Noordhoff, 1980).

TREATISES: *Mongolian English-Russian Dictionary of Legal Terms and Concepts*, W. Butler, ed. (Martinus Nijhoff).
The Mongolian Legal System by W. Butler (Martinus Nijhoff, 1982).
Commercial Business and Trade Laws: The Soviet Union and Mongolia by J. Hazard (Oceana, 1983).

ARTICLES: "Mongolia: Coming to Terms with Family Legislation" by W. Butler, 27 *Journal of Family Law* 211 (1988–89).
"Mongolian Foreign Trade: The Legal Framework" by W. Butler, 14 *Journal of World Trade* 329 (1980).

MONOPOLY: See Antitrust Law, Commodities, Corporate Law, Intellectual Property, Media Law, Public Utilities

MONTANA

SEE ALSO: Circuit Courts (Ninth Circuit)

**STATUTES & OTHER
LEGISLATIVE MATERIALS:** *Montana Code Annotated.*
Laws of Montana.
A Legislator's Handbook, 3d ed., P. Verdon, ed. (Mont. Legislative Council, 1984).

**STATE ADMINISTRATIVE
CODE:** *Administrative Rules of Montana.*
Montana Administrative Register.

CASES & OPINIONS: *Montana Reports* (1868–).
Pacific Reporter (1882–).

JURY INSTRUCTIONS: *Criminal Jury Instruction Guidelines* by J. McDonald (State Bar of Mont., 1984).
Montana Jury Instruction Guides (Mont. Judges Assn., 1966).

**JOURNALS & OTHER
PERIODICALS:** *The Montana Lawyer* (Mont. State Bar).

SURVEY OF STATE LAW: "Survey of Montana Law" in *Montana Law Review*. See for example vol. 38, p. 1; vol. 45, p. 1.

DIRECTORY: *Lawyer's Deskbook and Directory* (State Bar of Mont.).

**TREATISES &
LOOSELEAFS:** *General Practice Seminar* (State Bar of Mont. 1986).
Marriage & Divorce Handbook by J. McAllister (State Bar of Mont., 1984).
Montana Administrative Procedures Handbook by R. Tippy (State Bar of Mont., 1984).
Montana Lawyer's Rule Book (State Bar of Mont., 1977–).
Montana Probate Procedure by D. Niklas (State Bar of Mont., 1983–).
Workers' Compensation Manual by N. Grosfield (State Bar of Mont., 1985).

DIGESTS & CITATOR: *Montana Digest* (West).
Pacific Digest (West).
Shepard's Montana Citations.

MONTSERRAT

SEE ALSO: Caribbean, International Law, Latin America, United Nations

"British Dependent Territories—Montserrat" by N. Yell in *Constitutions of Dependencies and Special Sovereignties* by A. Blaustein (Oceana, 1982).
West Indian Constitutions: Post Independence Reform (Montserrat) by F. Phillips (Oceana, 1985).
"Tourist Divorces and the Abuse of a Small State's Legal System" by K. Patchett, 30 *American Journal of Comparative Law* 654 (1982).

MOOT QUESTION: See Trial & Appellate Practice
MORALITY: See Church & State, Jurisprudence

MOROCCO

SEE ALSO: Africa, International Law, Islam, United Nations

**TREATIES & OTHER
 AGREEMENTS:** "Libya-Morocco: Treaty Instituting the Arab-African Union of States," 23 *International Legal Materials* 1022 (1984).

CONSTITUTION: "Morocco" by I. Zartman in *Constitutions of the Countries of the World* by A. Blaustein & G. Flanz (Oceana, 1971).

STATUTES & RELATED LAWS: *Investment Codes of North Africa: Morocco,* E. de Brauw, transl. (Amsterdam: Intl. Bureau of Fiscal Documentation, 1979).

TREATISES & LOOSELEAFS:

African Tax Systems by R. Hammond & M. van den Abeelen (Morocco) (Amsterdam: Intl. Bureau of Fiscal Documentation, 1980–).

Capital Formation and Investment Incentives Around the World (Morocco) by W. Diamond & D. Diamond (Matthew Bender, 1984–).

Digest of Commercial Laws of the World (Morocco) (Natl.·Assn. of Credit Management; Oceana, 1977–).

Information Guide: Doing Business in Morocco (Price Waterhouse).

An Introduction to Law in French-Speaking Africa (Morocco) by J. Salacuse (Michie, 1975).

Investment Laws of the World (Morocco) (Oceana, 1981–).

ARTICLES:

"Equity Discretion in a Modern Islamic Legal System" by L. Rosen, 15 *Law & Society Review* 217 (1981).

"The First World Bank Arbitration (Holiday Inns v. Morocco)" by P. Lalive, 51 *British Yearbook of International Law* 123 (1980).

"New Maritime Investment Law" by S. Hughs, 8 *Middle East Executive Reports* 14 (May, 1985) (see also vol. 6, pp. 11, 15; vol. 7, p. 13; vol. 8, p. 8; and vol. 9, pp. 8, 15).

"Real Property Acquisition in Morocco" by A. West, 130 *Solicitor's Journal* 582 (1986).

MORTALITY TABLES: See Insurance, Statistics
MORTGAGES: See Banking Law, Bankruptcy, Personal Property, Real Estate
MOTHERS: See Family Law, Women & the Law
MOTION: See Trial & Appellate Practice
MOTION PICTURES: See Art & Entertainment, Cook Islands, Media Law
MOTIVE: See Criminal Law, Torts
MOTOR CARRIER: See Air & Aviation, Transportation
MOTORCYCLE: See Torts
MOTOR VEHICLE: See Consumer Law, Criminal Law, Insurance, Torts, Transportation

MOZAMBIQUE

SEE ALSO: Africa, Communism, International Law, Islam, United Nations

TREATISES:

A Difficult Road: The Transition to Socialism in Mozambique, J. Saul, ed. (NY: Monthly Review Press, 1985).

Mozambique: A Country Study, 3d ed. (GPO; Foreign Area Studies, American Univ., 1985).

Mozambique: From Colonialism to Revolution by A. Isaacman (Westview, 1983).

ARTICLES:

"Changing the Terms of the Debate: A Visit to a Popular Tribunal in Mozambique" by A. Sachs, 20 *Journal of African Law* 99 (1984).

"The Two Dimensions of Socialist Legality: Recent Experience in Mozambique" by A. Sachs, 13 *International Journal of the Sociology of Law* 133 (1985).

MULTI DISTRICT LITIGATION: See Trial & Appellate Practice
MULTI–FAMILY UNITS: See Family Law
MULTILATERAL TREATIES: See Intellectual Property, International Law
MULTINATIONAL COMPANIES: See Africa, Corporate Law, International Law, Kenya, Latin America, Yugoslavia
MULTINATIONAL ESTATE PLANNING: See Estate Planning
MULTIPLICITY OF ACTION: See Trial & Appellate Practice
MULTISTATE EXAMS: See Legal Education
MUNICIPAL BONDS: See State & Local Government, Securities Law
MUNICIPAL CORPORATIONS: See Administrative Law, Corporate Law, Education Law, Government Contracts, State & Local Government, Torts, Zoning & Land Planning
MUSEUMS: See Art & Entertainment
MUSIC: See Art & Entertainment, Intellectual Property
MUSLIM: See Islam, Middle East
MUTE: See Handicapped & the Law
MUTUAL FUNDS: See Securities Law
MUTUAL INSURANCE: See Insurance
MUTUALITY: See Contracts

NAMES: See Family Law, Intellectual Property

NAMIBIA

SEE ALSO: Africa, International Law, South Africa, United Nations

CONSTITUTION: "Namibia-Southwest Africa" by N. Rubin in *Constitutions of the Countries of the World* by A. Blaustein & G. Flanz (Oceana, 1982).

TREATISES: *Information Guide: Doing Business in South-West Africa/Namibia* (Price Waterhouse).
The International Mandate System for Namibia by I. Dore (Westview, 1985).

ARTICLES: "Admission to Membership in International Organizations: The Case of Namibia" by E. Osieke, 51 *British Yearbook of International Law* 189 (1980).
"Security Legislation in Namibia" by E. Landis, 11 *Yale Journal of International Law* 48 (1985).
"Self-Determination of Namibia and the United Nations" by I Dore, 27 *Harvard International Law Journal* 159 (1986).
"Settlement of the Namibian Dispute" by D. Jordan-Walker, 14 *Case Western Reserve Journal of International Law* 543 (1982).

NARCOTICS: See Criminal Law, Food, Health & Medicine, Mental Health
NATIONAL ARCHIVES: See Indians, Legal History
NATIONAL DEFENSE: See International Law, Military Law, War
NATIONAL ENVIRONMENTAL POLICY ACT: See Environmental Law
NATIONALITY: See Immigration Law

NATIONALIZATION: See France, International Law, Mexico, Venezuela
NATIONAL LABOR RELATIONS ACT: See Labor Law
NATIONAL MEDIATION BOARD: See Labor Law
NATIONALS: See Immigration Law
NATIONAL SECURITY: See Military Law
NATIONAL TRANSPORTATION SAFETY BOARD: See Transportation
NATIVE AMERICANS: See Indians
NATURAL GAS: See Energy, Oil & Gas
NATURALIZATION: See Constitutional Law, Immigration Law
NATURAL LAW: See Jurisprudence

NATURAL RESOURCES, MINES & MINING

SEE ALSO: Administrative Law, Agriculture, Animals, Energy, Environmental Law, Indians, International Law, Oil & Gas, Public Utilities, Sea, State & Local Government, Taxation, Water Law

**JOURNALS, NEWSLETTERS,
& OTHER PERIODICALS:** *Earth Law Journal* (Sijthoff, 1975–).
Eastern Mineral Law Foundation (Matthew Bender, 1980–).
Ecology Law Quarterly (Univ. of Cal. Berkeley, 1971–).
Journal of Energy & Natural Resources Law (United Kingdom).
Journal of Mineral Law and Policy (Univ. of Ky., College of Law, 1985–).
Mineral Law Newsletter (Rocky Mountain Mineral Law Foundation, 1984–).
Natural Resources and Environment (ABA Section of Natural Resources Law, 1985–)
    (old title: Natural Resources Lawyer).
Natural Resources Journal (Univ. of New Mex. Sch. of Law, 1961–).
Natural Resources Law Newsletter (ABA Section of Natural Resources Law).
Timber Tax Journal (1967–).
Virginia Journal of Natural Resources Law (1980–).

INSTITUTES: *Mineral Law Institute* (Louisiana State University, 1856–).
Rocky Mountain Mineral Law Institute Proceedings (1955–).

LOOSELEAFS: *The American Law of Mining* by Rocky Mountain Mineral Law Foundation (Matthew Bender, 1960–).
Coal Law and Regulation (Matthew Bender, 1983–).
Digest of Mining Claim Laws, 2d ed. by R. Pruitt (Rocky Mountain Mineral Law Foundation, 1982–).
Federal Land Use Law: Limitations, Procedures, Remedies by D. Mandelker (Clark Boardman, 1986–).
Gower Federal Service: Mining (Rocky Mountain Mineral Law Foundation, 1962–).
Income Taxation of Natural Resources by F. Burke (Prentice-Hall, 1975– ·).
The Public Land and Resources Law Digest (Rocky Mountain Mineral Law Foundation, 1963–).

TREATISES: *American Law of Mining,* 2d ed. by The Rocky Mountain Mineral Law Foundation (Matthew Bender, 1983).
Conflicts Over Resource Ownership by A. Church (Lexington Books, 1982).
Domestic Taxation of Hard Minerals, 2d ed. (ALI–ABA Comm. on Cont. Prof. Ed., 1983).
The Evolution of National Wildlife Law by M. Bean (Praeger, 1983).
Handbook of Accounting for Natural Resources by D. Crumbley (Shepard's, 1986).

Handbook of Mineral Law, 2d ed. by T. Maley (Boise: MMRC Pubs., 1979).
International Wildlife Law by S. Lyster (Grotius Pubs. Ltd., 1985).
Legal Aspects of Geology by R. Tank (Plenum Press, 1983).
Mineral Resources Permitting (Rocky Mountain Mineral Law Foundation, 1981).
Mineral Taxation (Rocky Mountain Mineral Law Foundation, 1977).
Mining Agreements (Rocky Mountain Mineral Law Foundation, 1979, 1981).
Mining Exploration Technology for Lawyers and Landmen (Rocky Mountain Mineral Law Foundation, 1980).
The Mining Law: A Study in Perpetual Motion by J. Leshy (Wash. D.C.: Resources for the Future, Inc., 1987).
Mining Law: From Location to Patent by T. Maley (Boise: Mineral Land Pub., 1985).
Mining Ventures in Developing Countries by C. Kirchner (Kluwer, 1979).
Natural Resources Administrative Law and Procedure (Rocky Mountain Mineral Law Foundation, 1981).
The Politics of Wilderness Preservation by C. Allin (Quorum Books, 1982).
Public Land and Mining Law, 3d ed. by L. Mall (Butterworths).
State and Local Taxation of Natural Resources in the Federal System (ABA).
Taxation of Mineral Resources by R. Conrad (Lexington Books, 1980).
Taxation of Mining Operations by P. Maxfield (Matthew Bender, 1981–).
Uranium Exploration and Development (Rocky Mountain Mineral Law Foundation, 1976).

ENCYCLOPEDIAS:

AMERICAN JURISPRUDENCE 2D (Am Jur 2d)
Check the following topics in the *General Index* volumes for Am Jur 2d:

Atomic Energy	Logs and Timber
Coal	Mines and Minerals
Electricity	Natural Resources
Environment and Conservation	Pipes and Pipelines
	Pollution
Fish and Game	Water
Gas and Oil	

CORPUS JURIS SECUNDUM (CJS)
Check the following topics in the *General Index* volumes for CJS:

Administrative Bodies	Mines and Minerals
Coal and Coal Mines	Natural Resources
Constitutional Law	Navigable Waters
Electricity	Oil and Gas
Federal Power Commission	Oil and Gas Leases
Fish and Game	Pipes and Pipelines
Fuel	Pollution
Gas	United States Secretary of the Interior
Gasoline	Waters
Health and Environment	Water Supply
Lakes and Ponds	Woods and Forests
Logs and Logging	

DIGESTS:

CASE SEARCH IN WEST DIGESTS BY KEY TOPIC
In the *Descriptive Word Index* of the West digests, look for key topics and numbers under the following subject headings:

Administrative Law	Coal and Coal Mines
Agriculture	Constitutional Law

Electricity
Federal Power
  Commission
Fish and Game
Fuel
Game
Gas
Gasoline
Health and Environment
Lakes and Ponds
Logs and Logging
Mines and Minerals

Natural Resources
Navigable Waters
Oil and Gas
Oil and Gas Leases
Pipes and Pipelines
Pollution
Public Lands
United States Secretary of
  the Interior
Waters
Water Supply
Woods and Forests

ALR:

ANNOTATIONS

Check the index volumes for ALR, ALR2d, ALR3d, ALR4th, and ALR Fed for annotations under the following subject headings:

Administrative Law
Air Pollution
Chemicals
Coal
Conservation
Environmental Law
Forests

Gas and Oil
Interior Department
Irrigation
Mines and Minerals
Public Land
Waste
Water Pollution

PERIODICALS:

CURRENT LAW INDEX (CLI) & LEGAL RESOURCE INDEX (LRI)

In the CLI and LRI, look for references to periodical literature under the following subject headings:

Administrative Law
Atomic Energy
Depletion Allowance
Energy Materials
Environmental Law
Forest Reserves
Gas
Gas, Natural
Hydroelectric Power
Manganese Mines
Mines and Mineral
  Resources
Mining Law
Mining Leases

Ocean Mining
Offshore Oil Industry
Oil and Gas Leases
Oil Well Drilling
Parks
Petroleum
Power Resources
Public Lands
Solar Energy
Strip Mining
Water Rights
Wildlife Conservation
Zoning

INDEX TO LEGAL PERIODICALS (ILP)

In the ILP, look for references to legal periodical literature under the following subject headings:

Administrative Law
Coastal Zone
Continental Shelf
Electricity
Environmental Law
Fish and Game
Forests
Marine Resources

Mines and Minerals
Natural Resources
Oil and Gas
Pollution
Solar Energy
Territorial Waters
Water

NAUTICAL ROAD: See Maritime Law
NAVAHO: See Indians
NAVIGABLE WATERS: See Natural Resources, Sea, Water Law
NAVIGATION: See Maritime Law
NAVY: See Government Contracts, Military Law
NEAR EAST: See Africa, Asia, Middle East

NEBRASKA

SEE ALSO: Circuit Courts (Eighth Circuit)

**RESEARCH GUIDE &
BIBLIOGRAPHY:** *Nebraska Legal Research and Reference Manual* by P. Hall (Mason Pub. Co., 1982).

STATUTES: *Revised Statutes of Nebraska.*
Laws of Nebraska.

**STATE ADMINISTRATIVE
CODE:** *Nebraska Administrative Rules & Regulations.*

CASES & OPINIONS: *Nebraska Reports* (1860–).
North Western Reporter (1879–).

COURT RULES: *Nebraska Rules of Court* (West).
Revised Rules of the Supreme Court of the State of Nebraska (Clerk of the Sup. Ct.).

JURY INSTRUCTIONS: *Nebraska Pattern Jury Instructions* (West, 1969).

**OPINIONS OF THE
ATTORNEY GENERAL:** *Attorney General Report.*

**JOURNALS & OTHER
PERIODICALS:** *Nebraska State Bar Newsletter* (1972–).
Daily Record (Omaha).

**TREATISES &
LOOSELEAFS:** *Agricultural Law* (Neb. Cont. Legal Ed., 1983).
The Courts of Nebraska (State Court Administrator, 1976–).
Nebraska Criminal Procedure (Neb. County Attorneys Assn., 1974–).
Nebraska Law on the Measure of Damages (Neb. Cont. Legal Ed., 1983).
Nebraska Legal Forms (Mason Pub. Co., 1981–).
Nebraska Limitations Manual by J. Forbess (Mason Pub. Co., 1981–).
Nebraska Practice Methods and Forms by W. Moore (West, 1969).
Nebraska Probate System III (Neb. Cont. Legal Ed., 1982).
Nebraska Property & Liability Insurance Law (Butterworths).
Nebraska Rules of Evidence (Neb. Cont. Legal Ed., 1980).
Nebraska Uniform Commercial Code Forms by W. Moore (West, 1965).
Nebraska Water Law and Administration by R. Narnsberger (Butterworths, 1984).
Real Estate Practice in the 80's (Neb. Cont. Legal Ed., 1982).
Trial Advocacy (Neb. Cont. Legal Ed., 1982).
Water Law (Neb. Cont. Legal Ed., 1981).

DIGESTS & CITATOR: *Nebraska Digest* (West).
North Western Digest (West).
Shepard's Nebraska Citations.

NECESSARIES, NECESSITIES: See Family Law
NEGLECT: See Family Law, Juvenile Law
NEGLIGENCE: See Architecture, Health & Medicine, Insurance, Professional
    Responsibility, Torts, Transportation
NEGOTIABLE INSTRUMENTS: See Banking Law, Uniform Commercial Code
NEGOTIATION: See Civil Service, Labor Law, Mediation, Sports Law, Trial &
    Appellate Practice
NEGROES: See Civil Rights

NEPAL

SEE ALSO: Asia, International Law, United Nations

Excise Taxation in Nepal by Hari Dhoj Pant (Kathmandu, Nepal: H. D. Pant, 1985).
Investment Laws of the World (Nepal) (Oceana, 1981–).
Nepal's Trade and Transit Agreements, 4th ed. (Kathmandu: Trade Promotion Centre,
    1983) (microfiche, Library of Congress).
Recent Laws of Nepal (Kathmandy, Nepal: Legal Research Associates, 1989–).
Taxes and Investment in Asia and the Pacific (Nepal) (Amsterdam: Intl. Bureau of
    Fiscal Documentation, 1983–).
Tax Laws of the World—Nepal (FL: Foreign Tax Law Assn.).

NETHERLANDS

SEE ALSO: Europe, International Law, United Nations

RESEARCH GUIDES &
BIBLIOGRAPHIES: *Guide to Foreign Legal Materials, Belgium, Luxembourg, Netherlands* by P. Graulich
    et al. (Oceana, 1968).
Netherlands: A Selected Bibliography of Reference Works by M. Krewson (Library of
    Congress, 1986).

TREATIES: "Netherlands-United States: Treaty on Mutual Legal Assistance" 21 *International Legal
    Materials* 48 (1982).

JOURNALS & OTHER
PERIODICALS: *Leiden Journal of International Law* (Leiden Univ. Faculty of Law, 1988–).
Netherlands International Law Review (Sijthoff & Noordhoff, 1953–).
Netherlands Review of International Law (Leiden, 1953–).
Netherlands Yearbook of International Law (Sijthoff & Noordhoff, 1970–).

TREATISES &
LOOSELEAFS: *Business Operations in Netherlands* by K. van Raad, Tax Management Foreign
    Income Portfolios, no. 150–4th (BNA, 1986).
Capital Formation and Investment Incentives Around the World (Netherlands) by
    W. Diamond & D. Diamond (Matthew Bender, 1984–).

Digest of Commercial Laws of the World (Netherlands) (Natl. Assn. of Credit Management; Oceana, 1977–).

Dutch Business Law, 2d ed. by S. Schuit et al. (Kluwer, 1983).

Information Guide: Doing Business in Netherlands (Price Waterhouse).

International Law of the Netherlands by H. Panhuys (Oceana, 1981).

Introduction to Dutch Law for Foreign Lawyers by D. Fokkema (Kluwer, 1978).

Recognition and Enforcement of Foreign Judgments in Various Foreign Countries (Netherlands) by G. Roman (Library of Congress, 1984).

Taxation in the Netherlands (NY: Deloitte, Haskins & Sells, 1979).

Taxation in the Netherlands by G. Spenke (Kluwer, 1985).

Taxation of Intercompany Transactions in Selected Countries in Europe and USA (Netherlands) (Kluwer, 1979).

Tax Laws of the World—Netherlands (FL: Foreign Tax Law Assn.).

World Law of Competition (Netherlands), J. von Kalinowski, ed. (Matthew Bender, 1979–).

ARTICLES:

"Corporate and Tax Law in the Netherlands" by F. Rosendaal, 15 *International Lawyer* 105 (1981).

"Leading Law Firms in the Netherlands" by C. Blackhurst, 4 *International Financial Law Review* 5 (1985).

"Merger Law of the Netherlands," 52 *Antitrust Law Journal* 1021 (1983).

"The Netherlands: How to Tackle New Social Problems" by M. Rood-de-Boer, 26 *Journal of Family Law* 141 (1987–88). See also 25 *Journal of Family Law* 187 (1986–87).

"The Netherlands: Riding the Carousel of Family Law" by M. Rood-de Boer, 27 *Journal of Family Law* 221 (1988–89).

"A New Arbitration Law for the Netherlands" by P. Sanders, 4 *Pace Law Review* 581 (1984).

"Recent Tax Planning Developments in the Netherlands" by K. de Vries, 14 *International Business Law*. 8 (1986).

"Tax Developments: the Netherlands and Netherlands Antilles" by J. Savelbergh, *International Business Lawyer* 11 (Jan., 1984).

NETHERLANDS ANTILLES

SEE ALSO:

Caribbean, International Law, Latin America, United Nations

TREATISES & LOOSELEAFS:

Business Operations in the Netherlands Antilles by R. Kramer, Tax Management Foreign Income Portfolios, no. 263 (BNA, 1987).

Capital Formation and Investment Incentives Around the World (Netherlands Antilles) by W. Diamond & D. Diamond (Matthew Bender, 1984–).

Caribbean Basin: A Tax Tour (Netherlands Antilles) (Arthur Anderson & Co., 1985).

Corporate Taxation in the Netherlands Antilles by F. Leo (Kluwer, 1978).

Information Guide: Doing Business in Netherlands Antilles (Price Waterhouse).

Tax and Investment Profile: Netherlands Antilles (Touche Ross International, 1983).

Tax Havens Encyclopedia (Netherlands Antilles) by B. Spitz (Butterworths, 1975–).

Tax Laws of the World—Netherlands Antilles (FL: Foreign Tax Law Assn.).

ARTICLES:

"Netherlands Antilles Bill" by C. Low, 97 *Los Angeles Daily Journal* 5, col. 1 (Feb. 9, 1984).

"The New U.S./Antilles Treaty" by D. Renfroe & A. Fogarasi, 82 *Taxes International* 3
(1986).
"Tax Developments: the Netherlands and Netherlands Antilles" by J. Savelbergh,
International Business Lawyer 11 (Jan., 1984).

NEUTRALITY: See International Law, War

NEVADA

SEE ALSO:	Circuit Courts (Ninth Circuit)
RESEARCH GUIDE & BIBLIOGRAPHY:	*Nevada State Documents Bibliography. Part I: Legal Publications and Related Materials* by K. Henderson (American Assn. of Law Libraries, 1984).
STATUTES & OTHER LEGISLATIVE MATERIALS:	*Legislative Manual of the Nevada Legislature* (Legislative Counsel Bureau). *Nevada Revised Statutes.* *Nevada Revised Statutes Annotated* (Michie). *Statutes of Nevada.* *Annotations to Revised Statutes* (Legislative Counsel Bureau). *Summary of Legislation* (Legislative Counsel Bureau, 1977–).
STATE ADMINISTRATIVE CODE:	*Nevada Administrative Code.*
CASES & OPINIONS:	*Nevada Reports* (1865–). *Pacific Reporter* (1882–). *The Nevada Supreme Court Bulletin* (Nev. Legal Research Services, 1984–).
COURT RULES:	*Nevada Civil Rules Handbook* (State Bar of Nev.).
JURY INSTRUCTIONS:	*Court's Instructions to the Jury* (Eighth Judicial District Court, 1985). *Nevada Pattern Civil Jury Instructions* (Nev. State Bar, 1966). *Nevada Pattern Jury Instructions* (Michie, 1986).
OPINIONS OF THE ATTORNEY GENERAL:	*Official Opinions of the Attorney General* (State Printing Office, 1875–).
JOURNALS & OTHER PERIODICALS:	*Inter Alia* (Nev. State Bar, 1973–).
TREATISES, LOOSELEAFS & OTHER MONOGRAPHS:	*The Function of Parole in the Criminal Justice System* (Legislative Counsel Bureau, 1984). *Gaming Control Law, The Nevada Model* by J. Goodwin (Publishing Horizons, 1985). *Handbook on Landlord/Tenant and Mobile Home Laws* (Las Vegas Justice Court, 1982). *Nevada Benchbook for Justice and Municipal Courts* (Admin. Office of the Courts, 1985). *The Nevada Constitution: Origin and Growth*, 5th ed. by E. Bushnell (Univ. of Nevada Press, 1980).

DIGESTS & CITATOR:	*Nevada Digest* (Legislative Counsel Bureau, 1966–).
	Pacific Digest (West).
	Shepard's Nevada Citations.

NEW BRUNSWICK: See Canada
NEW GUINEA: See Papua New Guinea

NEW HAMPSHIRE

SEE ALSO:	Circuit Courts (First Circuit)
RESEARCH GUIDE & **BIBLIOGRAPHY:**	*New Hampshire Secondary Materials for the Practice of Law* by T. Steele & C. Trainor (Franklin Pierce Law Center Library, 1980).
STATUTES:	*New Hampshire Revised Statutes Annotated.*
	Session Laws of the State of New Hampshire.
STATE ADMINISTRATIVE **CODE:**	*New Hampshire Code of Administrative Rules.*
	New Hampshire Rulemaking Register.
CASES & OPINIONS:	*New Hampshire Reports* (1816–).
	Atlantic Reporter (1886–).
COURT RULES:	*New Hampshire Court Rules Annotated* (Equity Pub. Corp., 1979–).
JOURNALS & OTHER **PERIODICALS:**	*New Hampshire Bar Journal* (1958–).
TREATISES & **LOOSELEAFS:**	*Administrative Law* (NH Bar CLI, 1983).
	Advanced Estate Planning (NH Bar CLI, 1980).
	Appellate Advocacy (NH Bar CLI, 1985).
	Fundamentals of Probate Administration (NH Bar CLI, 1983).
	Hazardous Waste: Regulation Compliance and Representation (NH Bar CLI, 1983).
	New Hampshire Practice and Procedure Handbook (NH Bar CLI, 1984).
	New Hampshire Practice: Civil Practice and Procedure by R. Wiebusch (Equity Pub. Corp.).
	New Hampshire Practice: Criminal Practice and Procedure by R. McNamara (Equity Pub. Corp.).
	New Hampshire Practice: Family Law by C. Douglas (Equity Pub. Corp.).
	New Hampshire Practice: Probate Law by W. Treat (Equity Pub. Corp.).
	Personal Injury Practice (NH Bar CLI, 1984).
	Representing the Small Business (NH Bar CLI, 1984).
	Tort Liability (NH Bar CLI, 1981).
DIGESTS & CITATOR:	*New Hampshire Digest* (West).
	Atlantic Digest (West).
	Shepard's New Hampshire Citations.

NEW JERSEY

SEE ALSO:	Circuit Courts (Third Circuit)

**RESEARCH GUIDES &
BIBLIOGRAPHIES:** *Checklist of Official New Jersey Publications* (Div. of the State Library, 1965–).
A Guide to New Jersey Legal Bibliography and Legal History by C. Allen (Rothman, 1984).
New Jersey Legal Research Handbook by P. Axel-Lute (NJ Inst. Cont. Legal Ed., 1984).
New Jersey State Publications: A Guide for Law Librarians by C. Senezak (Amer. Assn. of Law Libraries, 1984).

**STATUTES & OTHER
LEGISLATIVE MATERIALS:** *Laws of New Jersey.*
New Jersey Revised Statutes (1937).
New Jersey Statutes Annotated (West).
New Jersey Session Law Service (West).
New Jersey Advance Law Service (Office of Legis. Services).

**STATE ADMINISTRATIVE
CODE:** *New Jersey Administrative Code.*
New Jersey Register.

CASES & OPINIONS: *New Jersey Reports* (1948–).
New Jersey Superior Court Reports (1948–).
New Jersey Tax Court Reports (1981–).
Atlantic Reporter (1885–).

COURT RULES: *New Jersey Court Rules* (Gann Law Books).
New Jersey Court Rules Annotated, 3d ed. (West, 1971).
Rules Governing the Courts of . . . New Jersey (West).

JURY INSTRUCTIONS: *Model Jury Charges, Civil,* 2d ed. (NJ Inst. Cont. Legal Ed., 1978).
Model Jury Charges, Criminal, 2d ed. (NJ Inst. Cont. Legal Ed., 1983).

**ETHICS & PROFESSIONAL
RESPONSIBILITY:** *Opinions of the New Jersey Supreme Court Advisory Committee on Professional Ethics,*
2d ed. (NJ Inst. Cont. Legal Ed., 1982–).

**ADMINISTRATIVE
DECISIONS:** *New Jersey Administrative Reports* (1982–).

**OPINIONS OF THE
ATTORNEY GENERAL:** *Attorney General Opinions* (Dept. of Law, 1949–).

**JOURNALS & OTHER
PERIODICALS:** *Advocate* (NJ State Bar, 1976–).
New Jersey Law Journal (1878–).
New Jersey Lawyer (NJ State Bar, 1979–).

DIRECTORIES: *Lawyers Diary and Manual Including Bar Directory of New Jersey* (NJ Law Journal
Pub. Co.).

**TREATISES &
LOOSELEAFS:**

Alternative Adjudication: An Evaluation of the New Jersey Automobile Arbitration Program (Rand Corp., 1988).
CCH Tax Reporter: New Jersey.
Chancery Practice (NJ Inst. Cont. Legal Ed., 1983).
New Jersey Abstracts and Titles, 3d ed. by M. Lieberman (West, 1966).
New Jersey Close Corporations by R. Kessler (Callaghan, 1981–).
New Jersey Criminal Practice and Procedure, 2d ed. by L. Arnold (West, 1980).
New Jersey Family Law Practice, 4th ed. by G. Skoloff (NJ Inst. Cont. Legal Ed., 1984–).
New Jersey Law with Forms by Z. Seltzer (Matthew Bender, 1948–).
New Jersey Legal Business Forms by J. Lodge (West, 1965).
New Jersey Marriage, Divorce and Separation by P. Silverman (West, 1963).
New Jersey Practice Forms by M. Blacker (West, 1980).
New Jersey Wills and Administration, 3d ed. by A. Clapp (West, 1984).
Products Liability Law in New Jersey by W. Dreier (NJ Inst. Cont. Legal Ed., 1982–).
Trial Handbook for New Jersey Lawyers by J. Freeman (Lawyers Co-op., 1972).

**DIGESTS, ENCYCLOPEDIA
& CITATOR:**

Atlantic Digest (West).
New Jersey Digest (West).
New Jersey Practice (West).
Shepard's New Jersey Citations.

NEWLY DISCOVERED EVIDENCE: See Trial & Appellate Practice

NEW MEXICO

SEE ALSO:

Circuit Courts (Tenth Circuit)

**RESEARCH GUIDES &
BIBLIOGRAPHIES:**

Guide to New Mexico State Publications by P. Wagner (Amer. Assn. of Law Libraries, 1983).
Manual for Effective New Mexico Legal Research by A. Poldervaart (Univ. of NM Press, 1955).

**STATUTES & OTHER
LEGISLATIVE MATERIALS:**

New Mexico Statutes Annotated.
Laws of New Mexico.
Legislative Handbook (Legislative Council Service, 1975–).

**STATE ADMINISTRATIVE
CODE:**

List of Rules and Publications Filed.

CASES & OPINIONS:

New Mexico Reports (1890–).
Pacific Reporter (1883–).

COURT RULES:

New Mexico Local & Federal Rules Handbook (Butterworths, 1976–).

JURY INSTRUCTIONS:

New Mexico Uniform Jury Instructions. Civil (West, 1966).
Uniform Jury Instructions: Civil (Michie, 1980).

OPINIONS OF THE ATTORNEY GENERAL: *Reports and Opinions of the Attorney General of New Mexico* (Compilation Commn., 1912–).

JOURNALS & OTHER PERIODICALS: *New Mexico State Bar Bulletin* (1963–).

TREATISES & LOOSELEAFS:
New Mexico Appellate Practice Manual by M. Thompson (Butterworths, 1978–).
New Mexico Collections Manual by M. Matthews (Butterworths, 1980–).
New Mexico Divorce Manual by D. Kelsey (Butterworths, 1978–).
New Mexico Domestic Relations Manual: Divorce System by B. Shapiro (State Bar of NM, 1985).
New Mexico Estate Administration System by R. Ramo (State Bar of NM, 1980).
New Mexico Probate Manual by W. Henderson (Butterworths, 1978–).
Prosecutor's Manual for DWI Cases by W. McPherson (Institute of Public Law, 1984).
Real Estate Contracts in New Mexico by L. Buchmiller (Security Escrow Corp., 1985).
Search and Seizure Outlines of Federal and New Mexico Law, 2d ed. by M. Hermann (State of Bar of NM, 1983).
Treatise on New Mexico Rules of Evidence by J. Wentworth (Butterworths, 1983).

DIGESTS & CITATOR:
New Mexico Digest (West).
Pacific Digest (West).
New Mexico Advance Annotation and Rules Service (Michie).
Shepard's New Mexico Citations.

NEW SOUTH WALES: See Australia
NEWSPAPERS: See Media Law
NEW TRIAL: See Trial & Appellte Practice

NEW YORK

SEE ALSO: Circuit Courts (Second Circuit)

RESEARCH GUIDES & BIBLIOGRAPHIES:
A Checklist of Official Publications of the State of New York (NY State Library, 1947–).
New York Legal Documents: A Selective Annotated Bibliography by S. Dow & K. Spenser (Amer. Assn. of Law Libraries, 1985).
New York Legal Research Guide by E. Gibson (Hein, 1988).
New York Rules of Citation (St. John's Law Review, 1979).
Official Publications of the State of New York: A Bibliographic Guide to Their Use by D. Butch (NY State Library, 1980).

STATUTES & OTHER LEGISLATIVE MATERIALS:
Laws of New York (1777–).
McKinney's Consolidated Laws of New York Annotated (1939–).
McKinney's Session Laws of New York (West, 1951–).
New York Consolidated Laws Service (Lawyers Co-op., 1976–).
New York State Legislative Annual (NY State Legislative Service, 1946–).
Summary of Legislation (NYU Senate Research Service, 1977–).
The Administrative Code of the City of New York (CCH).

STATE ADMINISTRATIVE CODE:	*New York State Register* (1979–). *Official Compilation of Codes, Rules & Regulations of the State of New York* (1960–).
CASES & OPINIONS:	*New York Reports* (1847–). *Appellate Division Reports* (1896–). *New York Miscellaneous Reports* (1892–). *North Eastern Reporter* (1885–). *New York Supplement* (1888–).
COURT RULES:	*New York Rules of Court: McKinney's State and Federal* (West, 1965–). *Rules of the U.S. Courts in New York* (Clark Boardman, 1984–).
JURY INSTRUCTIONS:	*Charges to the Jury. . . in a Criminal Case in New York* by J. Dowsey (Callaghan, 1968–). *New York Pattern Jury Instructions: Civil,* 2d ed. (Lawyers Co-op., 1974). *Speiser's Negligence Jury Charges* (Central Book Co., 1961).
ETHICS & PROFESSIONAL RESPONSIBILITY:	*Code of Professional Responsibility* (NY State Bar Assn.). *Opinions of the Committees on Professional Ethics* (Assn. of the Bar of the City of NY; Oceana, 1980–).
OPINIONS OF THE ATTORNEY GENERAL:	*Opinions of the Attorney General* (1959–).
JOURNALS & OTHER PERIODICALS:	*New York County Lawyers Association Bar Bulletin* (1943–). *New York Law Journal* (1888–). *New York Legal Update* (West, 1987–). *New York Real Estate Law Reporter* (NY Law Pub. Co., 1986–). *New York State Bar Journal* (1928–). *Record* (Assn. of the Bar of the City of NY, 1947–).
SURVEY OF STATE LAW:	"Survey of New York Law" in *Syracuse Law Review.* See for example vol. 19, p. 207; vol. 34, p. 1. "Survey of New York Practice" in *St. John's Law Review.* See for example vol. 58, p. 633.
TREATISES & LOOSELEAFS:	*Administrative Law Practice in New York* (NY State Bar Assn., 1984). *Boardman's New York Family Law,* 2d ed. by E. Biskind (Clark Boardman, 1981–). *Guidebook to New York Taxes* (CCH). *McKinney's Forms* (West) (Business Corporation Law, Civil Practice Law and Rules, Criminal Procedure Law, Estates and Surrogates Practice, Matrimonial and Family Law, Not-for-Profit Corporation Law, Real Property, UCC). *New York Civil Practice* (Matthew Bender) (CPLR; Estates, Powers, Trusts; Family; Matrimonial; Surrogate Court Practice). *New York Collections* by J. Rubin (Lawyers Co-op., 1981–). *New York Corporate Handbook,* R. Merritt, ed. (NY State Bar Assn., 1983). *New York Criminal Practice* by M. Waxner (Matthew Bender, 1973–). *New York Estates, Wills, Trusts* (CCH, 1967–). *New York Forms: Legal and Business* (Lawyers Co-op., 1970).

New York Matrimonial Practice by W. DaSilva (Lawyers Co-op., 1980–).
New York Practice under the CPLR, 6th ed. by H. Wachtell (Practicing Law Institute, 1986).
New York Products Liability by M. Weinberger (Callaghan, 1982–).
New York Wills by L. Kass (Gould, 1979–).
Pre-Trial Criminal Practice (NY State Bar Assn., 1984).
White, New York Corporations, 13th ed. by I. Kantrowitz (Matthew Bender, 1963–).

**DIGESTS, ENCYCLOPEDIAS
& CITATORS:**
West's New York Digest (1962–).
New York Law Journal Digest-Annotator (1937–).
New York State Law Digest (NY State Bar Assn., 1965–).
Carmody-Wait 2d; Cyclopedia of New York Practice with Forms (Lawyers Co-op., 1969–).
Encyclopedia of New York Law (West).
New York Jurisprudence, 2d ed. (Lawyers Co-op., 1971–).
New York Law Finder (West, 1979–).
Shepard's New York Law Locator (1975).
Shepard's New York Citations.

RECORDS AND BRIEFS:
Union List of Cases and Points/Records and Briefs in New York State Law Libraries, 2d ed. by J. White (SUNYAB Law Library, 1982).

NEW YORK MERCANTILE EXCHANGE: See Commodities
NEW YORK STOCK EXCHANGE: See Securities Law
NEW YORK TIMES RULE: See Media Law, Torts

NEW ZEALAND

SEE ALSO:
Australia, International Law, United Nations

**RESEARCH GUIDES &
BIBLIOGRAPHIES:**
Current Australian and New Zealand Legal Literature Index (Sydney: Law Book Co., 1974–).
Legal Research Materials and Methods, 2d ed. by E. Glass (Melbourne: Ann Labore Law Books Co., 1979).

**TREATIES & OTHER
AGREEMENTS:**
"Australia-New Zealand: Closer Economic Relations-Trade Agreement," 22 *International Legal Materials* 945 (1983).
Treaty Series (Wellington: Dept. of External Affairs, 1943–).

**STATUTES & RELATED
LAWS:**
New Zealand Statutes.

CASES:
Abridgement of New Zealand Case Law (Butterworths).
Butterworths Current Law Digest (Butterworths, 1984–).
Current Law (New Zealand).

**JOURNALS & OTHER
PERIODICALS:**
Auckland University Law Review.
Australia and New Zealand Journal of Criminology.
Canterbery Law Review.

New Zealand Law Journal (1925–).
New Zealand Universities Law Journal (1963–).
Victoria University of Wellington Law Review.

TREATISES &
LOOSELEAFS:
Business Operations in New Zealand by P. Jenkin, Tax Mangement Foreign Income
    Portfolios, no. 172–2d (BNA, 1987).
Capital Formation and Investment Incentives Around the World (New Zealand) by
    W. Diamond & D. Diamond (Matthew Bender, 1984–).
Digest of Commercial Laws of the World (New Zealand) (Natl. Assn. of Credit
    Management; Oceana, 1977–).
Financial Institutions and Markets in the Southwest Pacific: A Study of Australia, Fiji,
    New Zealand, and Papua New Guinea, M. Skully, ed. (St. Martin's Press, 1985).
Guidebook to New Zealand Companies and Securities Law (CCH, 1985).
Information Guide: Doing Business in New Zealand (Price Waterhouse).
Insurance Law in Australia and New Zealand by P. Joske (Butterworths, 1975).
Introduction to Company Law in New Zealand by J. Northey (Butterworths, 1976).
Introduction to the New Zealand Legal System, 5th ed. by R. Mulholland
    (Butterworths, 1983).
New Zealand Master Tax Guide (CCH).
Spratt and McKenzie's Law of Insolvency by F. Spratt (Butterworths, 1972).
Tax Laws of the World—New Zealand (FL: Foreign Tax Law Assn.).

ARTICLES:
"Allocation of Income and Expenses Between Related Companies: New Zealand Tax
    Aspects" by P. Cook, 9 *International Tax Journal* 179 (1983).
"New Zealand: An Expanding Role for the Family Court" by W. Atkin, 26 *Journal of*
    Family Law 149 (1987–88). See also 25 *Journal of Family Law* 191 (1986–87).

ENCYCLOPEDIA:
Halsbury's Laws: New Zealand.

NICARAGUA

SEE ALSO:
International Law, Latin America, United Nations

RESEARCH GUIDE &
BIBLIOGRAPHY:
A Guide to the Official Publications of. . .Nicaragua (Library of Congress, 1947).

CONSTITUTION:
"A New Constitution for Nicaragua" by M. Stern, *The National Law Journal,* p. 13
    (Jan. 19, 1987).
"Nicaragua" by W. Eberle in *Constitutions of the Countries of the World* by A. Blaustein
    & G. Flanz (Oceana, 1982).

TREATISES &
LOOSELEAFS:
Digest of Commercial Laws of the World (Nicaragua) (Natl. Assn. of Credit
    Mangement; Oceana, 1977–).
Information Guide: Doing Business in Nicaragua (Price Waterhouse).
Latin America. . .A Tax Tour (Nicaragua) (Arthur Anderson & Co. 1985).
Nicaragua: A Country Study, 2d ed. by J. Rudolph (Wash. D.C.: Dept. of the Army,
    1982).
Nicaragua: Revolutionary Justice: A Report on Human Rights and the Judicial System
    (NY: Lawyers Committee for International Human Rights, 1985).

Statement of the Laws of Nicaragua in Matters Affecting Business, 4th ed.
(Organization of American States, 1978, 1981).
Tax Laws of the World—Nicaragua (FL: Foreign Tax Law Assn).

ARTICLES: "Evidence, the Court, and the Nicaragua Case" by K. Highet, 81 *American Journal of
International Law* 1 (1987).
"Latin American Tax Update: Nicaragua" by M. Marti, 12 *Lawyer of the Americas* 661
(1980).
"The Legitimacy of Economic Coercion: The Carter Foreign Aid Policy and
Nicaragua," 5 *Loyola of Los Angeles International and Comparative Law Journal*
101 (1982).
"Nicaragua and the Law of Self-Defense Revisited' by N. Rostow, 11 *Yale Journal of
Interntional Law* 437 (1986).
"Observations in Loco: Practice and Procedure of the Inter-American Commission on
Human Rights" (Nicaragua), 19 *Texas International Law Journal* 285, 314 (1984).

NIGER

SEE ALSO: Africa, International Law, Islam, United Nations

CONSTITUTION: "Niger" in *Constitutions of the Countries of the World* by A. Blaustein & G. Flanz
(Oceana, 1983).

**TREATISES &
LOOSELEAFS:**   *African Tax Systems* by R. Hammond & M. van den Abeelen (Niger) (Amsterdam:
Intl. Bureau of Fiscal Documentation, 1980–).
An Introduction to Law in French-Speaking Africa (Niger) by J. Salacuse (Michie,
1969).

ARTICLES: "Africa's Shared Water Resources: Legal and Institutional Aspects of the Nile, Niger
and Sengal River Systems" by G. Badr, 80 *American Journal of International
Law* 423 (1986).

NIGERIA

SEE ALSO: Africa, International Law, United Nations

**RESEARCH GUIDES &
BIBLIOGRAPHIES:**   *Bibliography on the Constitutions of Nigeria* by O. Jegede (Oceana, 1981).
Nigerian Legal Bibliography, 2d ed. by O. Jegede (Oceana, 1983).

TREATIES: *Nigeria's Treaties in Force* (Lagos: Federal Ministry of Justice, 1971–).

CONSTITUTIONS: "Nigeria" by T. Aguda in *Constitutions of the Countries of the World* by A. Blaustein &
G. Flanz (Oceana, 1982).
The Presidential Constitution of Nigeria by B. Nwabueze (St. Martin's Press, 1982).

**JOURNALS & OTHER
PERIODICALS:**   *Journal of Private and Property Law* (Univ. of Lagos, 1984–).
Nigerian Annual of International Law (1976–).

Nigerian Bar Journal.
Nigerian Journal of Contemporary Law (Univ. of Lagos).
Nigerian Law Journal (London: Sweet & Maxwell).

TREATISES &
LOOSELEAFS:

African Tax Systems by R. Hammond & M. van den Abeelen (Nigeria) (Amsterdam: Intl. Bureau of Fiscal Documentation, 1980–).
Capital Formation and Investment Incentives Around the World (Nigeria) by W. Diamond & D. Diamond (Matthew Bender, 1984–).
Digest of Commercial Laws of the World (Nigeria) (Natl. Assn. of Credit Management; Oceana, 1977–).
Federalism in Nigeria by S. Oyovbaire (St. Martin's Press, 1985).
Information Guide: Dong Business in Nigeria (Price Waterhouse).
Investment Laws of the World (Nigeria) (Oceana, 1981–).
The Legal System of Nigeria by M. Marasinghe (Michie).
Nigerian Business Law by G. Ezejiofor (London: Sweet & Maxwell, 1982).
Nigerian Family Law by A. Kasunmu & J. Salacuse (Butterworths, 1966).
Nigerian Law of Contract by I. Sagay (London: Sweet & Maxwell, 1985).
Nigerian Law of Torts by G. Kodilinye (London: Sweet & Maxwell, 1982).
Nigerian Legal System by A. Obilade (London: Sweet & Maxwell, 1979).
Tax Laws of the World—Nigeria (FL: Foreign Tax Law Asn.).

ARTICLES:

"The Claim Settlement Provisions of the Nigerian Insurance Act of 1976" by R. Ogunrinde, 19 *Journal of World Trade Law* 170 (1985).
"Foreign Direct Investment Climate in Nigeria" by S. Megwa, 21 *Columbia Journal of Transnational Law* 487 (1983).
"Nigeria: The Developing Family Law" by E. Nwogugu, 27 *Journal of Family Law* 243 (1988–89).
"Nigerian Foreign Policy. . ." by C. Okeke, 5 *Suffolk Transnational Law Journal* 201 (1981).
"Nigeria's Exclusive Economic Zone and Freedom of Navigation" by O. Okere, 13 *Ocean Development and International Law Journal* 535 (1984).
"Penal Policy. . .in Nigeria" by A. Rotimi, 47 *Federal Probation* 62 (Sept., 1983).
"Secured Leasing in Nigeria" by A. Keesee, 15 *The International Lawyer* 25 (1981).
"Transfer of Technology from the United States to Nigeria" by D. Hill, 6 *Texas Southern University Law Review* 380 (1981).

NINETEENTH CENTURY: See Legal History
NINTH CIRCUIT: See Circuit Courts
NO-ACTION LETTERS: See Securities Law
NO-FAULT: See Family Law, Insurance, Torts
NOISE: See Environmental Law
NOLLE PROSEQUI: See Criminal Law
NOLO CONTENDERE: See Criminal Law
NOMINAL DAMAGES: See Torts, Trial & Appellate Practice
NOMINATIONS: See Election

NONPROFIT CORPORATIONS & ASSOCIATIONS

SEE ALSO:

Accounting, Agency, Animals, Art, Business Law, Consumer Law, Corporate Law, Environmental Law, Estate Planning, Historic Preservation, Labor Law, Poverty Law, Taxation, Torts

**JOURNALS, NEWSLETTERS
& OTHER PERIODICALS:**
Charitable Gift-Planning News by L. Moerschbaecher & J. McCoy (Little, Brown, 1983–).

Conference on Charitable Foundations. New York University Proceedings. (Matthew Bender, 1953–).

**TREATISES &
LOOSELEAFS:**
Association Law Handbook by J. Jacobs (BNA, 1981).

Charitable Giving and Solicitation by S. Stern (Prentice-Hall, 1981–).

Charity Under Siege: Government Regulation of Fund-Raising by B. Hopkins (Wiley, 1980).

Exempt Organization Reports (CCH, 1971–).

Financial and Accounting Guide for Nonprofit Organizations, 3d ed. by M. Gross (Wiley, 1982).

Law of Associations, 2d ed. by G. Webster (Matthew Bender, 1975–).

The Law of Tax-Exempt Organizations, 5th ed. by B. Hopkins (Wiley, 1987).

Making the Non-Profit Organization Work: A Financial, Legal and Tax Guide for Administrators (Institute for Business Planning).

Nonprofit Enterprise Law and Taxation (Callaghan).

Nonprofit Organizations: Forms for Creation, Operation and Dissolution by M. Clifford et al. (Callaghan, 1987).

Nonprofit Organizations: Handbook for Administrators by B. Singer (Callaghan, 1987).

Nonprofit Organizations: Rights and Liabilities for Members, Directors and Officers by E. Hadden & B. French (Callaghan, 1987).

Parliamentary Law for Non-Profit Organizations by H. Oleck (ALI–ABA, 1978).

Planning Tax-Exempt Organizations by R. Desiderio & S. Taylor (Shepard's, 1983).

Representing Tax-Exempt Organizations (Georgetown University Law Center, CLE Div., 1983).

Representing the Nonprofit Organization by M. Phelan (Callaghan, 1987).

Survey of State Laws Regulating Charitable Solicitation (New Milford, CT: Philanthropy Monthly, 1976–).

Tax Economics of Charitable Giving, 8th ed. (Arthur Anderson & Co., 1981).

Tax Exempt-Charitable Organizations, 2d ed. by P. Treusch & N. Sugarman (ALI–ABA Comm. on Cont. Prof. Ed., 1983).

NONRESIDENT: See Trial & Appellate Practice
NORFOLK ISLAND: See Australia
NORMALIZATION: See China
NORRIS–LA GUARDIA: See Labor Law

NORTH CAROLINA

SEE ALSO:
Circuit Courts (Fourth Circuit)

**RESEARCH GUIDES &
BIBLIOGRAPHIES:**
Guide to North Carolina Legal Research by I. Kavass & B. Christensen (Hein, 1973).

North Carolina Code Research Guide (Lawyers Co-op., 1988).

**STATUTES & OTHER
LEGISLATIVE MATERIALS:**
General Statutes of North Carolina (Michie).

Session Laws of North Carolina.
Legislative Reporting Service (Univ. of NC at Chapel Hill; Inst. of Govt.).

STATE ADMINISTRATIVE
CODE:
North Carolina Administrative Code.
North Carolina Register.

CASES & OPINIONS:
North Carolina Reports (1868–).
North Carolina Court of Appeals Reports (1968–).
South Eastern Reporter (1887–).

COURT RULES:
North Carolina Rules Annotated (Michie, 1984).
North Carolina Rules of Court (West).

JURY INSTRUCTIONS:
North Carolina Pattern Jury Instructions: Civil (NC Bar, 1970–).
North Carolina Pattern Jury Instructions: Criminal (NC Bar, 1970–).
North Carolina Pattern Jury Instructions: Motor Vehicle Negligence (NC Bar, 1973–).

ETHICS & PROFESSIONAL
RESPONSIBILITY:
North Carolina State Bar Statutes, Rules and Regulations, Canons of Ethics and Opinions. . . (NC Bar, 1970–).

OPINIONS OF THE
ATTORNEY GENERAL:
Attorney General Reports.

JOURNALS & OTHER
PERIODICALS:
North Carolina State Bar Quarterly (1978–).
North Carolina State Bar Newsletter.

SURVEY OF STATE LAW:
"Survey of Developments in North Carolina Law. . ." in *North Carolina Law Review.*
See for example vol. 63, p. 1051.

TREATISES &
LOOSELEAFS:
The Administration of Decedent's Estates in North Carolina by J. Huggard (Michie, 1985).
Admissibility of Evidence in North Carolina by A. Fox (Harrison, 1988).
Brandis on North Carolina Evidence, 2d ed. by H. Brandis (Michie, 1982).
Business Entities: A North Carolina Law Practice System by D. Humphrey (Michie, 1983).
CCH North Carolina Tax Reporter (1982–).
Domestic Relations: A North Carolina Law Practice System by M. Johnson et al. (Michie, 1984–).
Douglas' Forms, 3d ed. by L. Long (Michie, 1983).
Guidebook to North Carolina Taxes (CCH, 1987).
North Carolina Criminal Trial Practice, 2d ed. by R. Price (Harrison, 1985).
North Carolina Estate Planning Practice Manual (Wake Forest Cont. Legal Ed., 1984).
North Carolina Family Law, 4th ed. by R. Lee (Michie, 1979).
North Carolina Methods of Practice by Melott (West).
North Carolina Real Estate Title Searches by L. Schiro (Harrison, 1982).
North Carolina Tort Practice Manual by D. Logan (Wake Forest Univ. School of Law, 1982).
North Carolina Uniform Commercial Code Forms by Smith & Clifford (West).
Suing in North Carolina Small Claims Court by D. Guth (Michie, 1983).

Thorp's North Carolina Trial Practice Forms, 2d ed. by W. Thorp (Harrison, 1984).
Webster's Real Estate Law in North Carolina, 3d ed. by P. Hetrick (Michie, 1988).

DIGESTS & CITATOR: *North Carolina Digest* (West).
North Carolina Index 2d.
Shepard's North Carolina Citations.

NORTH DAKOTA

SEE ALSO: Circuit Courts (Eighth Circuit)

STATUTES: *Laws of North Dakota.*
North Dakota Century Code (Allen Smith).

**STATE ADMINISTRATIVE
CODE:**   *North Dakota Administrative Code.*

CASES & OPINIONS: *North Dakota Reports* (1890–).
North Western Reporter (1890–).

COURT RULES: *Rules of Court: North Dakota Century Code Annotated* (Allen Smith).
North Dakota Rules of Court (West).

JURY INSTRUCTIONS: *North Dakota Jury Instructions* (State Bar of ND, 1966–).
North Dakota Pattern Jury Instructions, Criminal (State Bar Assn. of ND, 1985–).

**OPINIONS OF THE
ATTORNEY GENERAL:**   *Opinions of the Attorney General.*

**JOURNALS & OTHER
PERIODICALS:**   *The Gavel* (1976–).

**TREATISES &
LOOSELEAFS:**   *NDALS Handbook* (Mandan: North Dakota Association of Legal Secretaries).
Standards of Title (State Bar of ND, 1978–).

DIGESTS & CITATOR: *Dakota Digest* (West).
N.W. Reporter Digest (West).
Shepard's N.D. Digest.

NORTHERN MARIANA ISLAND: See Micronesia
NORTH KOREA: See Korea (North)
NORTH YEMEN: See Yemen Arab Republic

NORWAY

SEE ALSO: Europe, International Law, Scandinavian Law, United Nations

**RESEARCH GUIDES &
BIBLIOGRAPHIES:**   Developing Legal Information Services in Norway" by J. Bing, *Computers and Law*
11 (Aug., 1982) (see also 3 Computer Law Journal 515).

Norwegian Legal Publications in English, French and German by K. Haukaas (Oslo Universitetsforlaget, 1967) (see also 10 Scandinavian Studies in Law 239).

"Third Generation Text Retrieval Systems" (Norway) by J. Bing, 1 *Journal of Law and Information Science* 183 (1983).

STATUTES & RELATED LAWS:

Norwegian Laws. . .Selected for the Foreign Service (Norway: The Royal Ministry of Foreign Affairs, 1963).

Norwegian Penal Code, H. Schjoldager, transl. (Rothman, 1961).

TREATISES & LOOSELEAFS:

Administrative Justice in Norway, Royal Ministry of Justice, ed. (Columbia Univ. Press, 1980).

Administrative Secrecy in Developed Countries (Norway) by D. Rpwat (Columbia Univ. Press, 1979).

Capital Formation and Investment Incentives Around the World (Norway) by W. Diamond & D. Diamond (Matthew Bender, 1984–).

Danish and Norwegian Law: A General Survey (Copenhagen: Danish Committee on Comparative Law; G.E.C. Gad, 1963).

Digest of Commercial Laws of the World (Norway) (Natl. Assn. of Credit Management; Oceana, 1977–).

Information Guide: Doing Business in Norway (Price Waterhouse).

International Business Arbitration in Norway by H. Thomsen (Oslo: Norges Eksportrad, 1977).

Taxation of Intercompany Transactions in Selected Countries in Europe and USA (Norway) (Kluwer, 1979).

Tax Laws of the World—Norway (FL: Foreign Tax Law Assn.).

ARTICLES:

"Court Review of Administrative Discretion in Norway" by E. Boe, 27 *Scandinavian Studies in Law* 11 (1983).

"New Forms of Atypical Employment Relationships in Norway" by H. Jakhelln, 7 *Comparative Labor Law* 343 (1986).

"Norway (Debt Renegotiation)" by C. Kjelstrup, 8 *International Business Lawyer* 31 (1980) (see also vol. 8, pp. 29, 245).

"Norway: Reforming the Law of Divorce" by P. Lodrup, 25 *Journal of Family Law* 199 (1986–87).

"Norway's Law of the Sea Policy in the 1970s" by W. Ostrreng, 11 *Ocean Development and International Law Journal* 69 (1982).

"The Relation between the Judiciary and the Legislative and Executive Branches of the Government in Norway" by R. Ryssdal, 57 *North Dakota Law Review* 527 (1981).

"The Rights of the Child in Norway" by A. Bratholm, 13 *Columbia Human Rights Law Review* 537 (1982).

"Women's Right to Money in Norway" by T. Dahl, 12 *International Journal of the Sociology of Law* 137 (1984).

NOTARY PUBLIC

Anderson's Manual for Notaries Public, 5th ed. by W. Gilmer (Anderson Pub. Co., 1976).

NOTES: See Banking Law, Trial & Appellate Practice
NOT GUILTY: See Criminal Law
NOTICE: See Contracts, Real Estate, Torts, Trial & Appellate Practice
NOVA SCOTIA: See Canada
NUCLEAR ENERGY: See Energy, Environmental Law
NUCLEAR WEAPONS: See War
NUISANCE: See Environmental Law, Real Estate, Torts

NURSING & THE LAW

SEE ALSO: AIDS, Dentistry, Health & Medicine, Human Experimentation, Labor Law, Mental Health, Torts

**TREATISES &
LOOSELEAFS:**

Director of Nursing Manual by M. Kander (Natl. Law Pub. Corp., 1980–).
Dynamics of Law in Nursing and Health Care, 2d ed. by M. Hemelt (Reston Pub. Co., 1982).
Ethical Issues in Nursing, P. Chinn, ed. (Aspen Systems, 1986–).
Law and Liability: A Guide for Nurses by J. Fiesta (Wiley, 1983).
The Legal Dimensions of Nursing Practice by L. Rocereto (Springer, 1982).
Legal Status of Midwifery and Nurse Midwifery by H. Beaser (U.S. Dept. of HEW, Public Health Service, 1977).
Legislative Challenges for Nurses in the '80s (Natl. League for Nursing, 1985).
Medicare Skilled Nursing Facility Manual (U.S. Dept. of Health & Human Services, Health Care Financing Admin., 1980–).
Nurse's Legal Handbook (Springhouse Corp., 1985).
The Nurse's Liability for Malpractice, 3d ed. by E. Bernzeig (McGraw-Hill, 1981).
Nursing Administration and Law Manual, K. Henry, ed. (Aspen Systems, 1985–).
Nursing and Informed Consent by E. Hogue (Natl. Law Pub. Corp., 1985).
Nursing and Legal Liability by E. Hogue (Natl. Law Pub. Corp., 1985).
Nursing and the Law, 4th ed., by A. Rhodes (Aspen Systems Corp., 1984).
Nursing Case Law Reporter by E. Hogue (Natl. Law Pub. Corp., 1982–).
Nursing Practice and the Law, 2d ed. J. Lesnik (Greenwood Press, 1962).
Revocation of Professional Licenses by Government Agencies (Nurse) by W. Morris (Michie, 1984).

OAS: See Latin America (and South American countries)
OB/GYN: See Health & Medicine, Torts
OBJECTIONS: See Trial & Appellate Practice
OBSCENITY: See Constitutional Law, Media Law
OBSTRUCTING JUSTICE: See Criminal Law
OCCUPANTS: See Landlord-Tenant, Real Estate

OCCUPATIONAL SAFETY & HEALTH

SEE ALSO: Administrative Law, AIDS, Business Law, Employee Benefits, Environmental Law, Health & Medicine, Insurance, Labor Law, Nursing, Social Security, Workers' Compensation

**TREATISES &
LOOSELEAFS:**   *Employment Safety and Health Guide* (CCH, 1971–).

General Industry Standards and Interpretations (U.S. Dept. of Labor, Occupational Safety & Health Admin., 1981–).

Guidebook to Occupational Safety and Health (CCH, 1973–).

Job Safety and Health (BNA, 1977–).

Labor Management Relations Guide with OSHA (Prentice-Hall, 1943–).

Labor Relations Guide with OSHA (Prentice-Hall, 1943–). ⋅

Medical Screening of Workers by M. Rothstein (BNA, 1984).

Mine Safety & Health Reporter (BNA, 1979–).

Occupational Safety and Health Act by R. Hogan (Matthew Bender, 1977–).

Occupational Safety and Health Cases (BNA, 1972–).

Occupational Safety and Health Decisons (CCH, 1971–).

Occupational Safety and Health Law by S. Bokat & H. Thompson (BNA, 1988).

Occupational Safety and Health Law, 2d ed. by M. Rothstein (West, 1983).

Occupational Safety and Health Reporter (BNA, 1971–).

OSHA Compliance Guide (CCH, 1977–).

OSHA: History, Law, and Policy by B. Mintz (BNA, 1984).

OSHA Recordkeeping Forms (CCH, 1987).

A Practical Guide to the Occupational Safety and Health Act by W. Connolly (Law Journal Seminars-Press, 1982–).

CITATOR: *Federal Occupational Safety and Health Citations* (Shepard's).

ENCYCLOPEDIAS: AMERICAN JURISPRUDENCE 2d (Am Jur 2d)
Check the following topics in the *General Index* volumes for Am Jur 2d:

Occupational Disability	Occupational Safety and
Occupational Disease	Health Administration
	Workmen's Compensation

CORPUS JURIS SECUNDUM (CJS)
Check the following topics in the *General Index* volumes for CJS:

Labor	Workmen's Compensation
Occupational Diseases	

ALR: ANNOTATIONS
Check the index volumes for ALR, ALR2d, ALR3d, ALR4th, and ALR Fed for annotations under the following subject headings:

Occupational Disability	Occupational Safety
Occupational Disease	and Health Acts

PERIODICALS: CURRENT LAW INDEX (CLI) & LEGAL REOURCE INDEX (LRI)
In the CLI and LRI, look for references to periodical literature under the following subject headings:

Employers' Liability	Occupations, Dangerous
Factory Inspection	United States Occupational
Industrial Toxicology	Safety and Health
Medicine, Industrial	Administration
Occupational Diseases	Workers' Compensation
Occupational Health Services	

INDEX TO LEGAL PERIODICALS (ILP)

In the ILP, look for references to legal periodical literature under the following subject headings:

Industrial Diseases	United States Occupational
Occupational Safety	Safety and Health
and Health	Administration
	Workers' Compensation

OCCUPATION TAX: See Employee Benefits, Taxation

OCEAN: See Antarctica, International Law, Maritime Law, Natural Resources, Oil & Gas, Sea, Water Law

OFFER: See Contracts

OFFERING: See Securities Law

OFFICE OF FEDERAL CONTRACT COMPLIANCE: See Government Contracts

OFFSHORE OIL: See Oil & Gas

OHIO

SEE ALSO: Circuit Courts (Sixth Circuit)

RESEARCH GUIDES & BIBLIOGRAPHIES:
"A Bibliography of Ohio Statutory Materials and Court Decisons, 1787 to Date" by A. Martin, 4 *Legal Reference Services Quarterly* 51 (1984).

A Guide to Legislative History in Ohio by D. Gold (Ohio Legislative Service Commission, 1985).

Ohio Legal Resources: An Annotated Bibliography and Guide (Ohio Library Association, 1982).

STATUTES & OTHER LEGISLATIVE MATERIALS:
Ohio Revised Code Annotated (Anderson).

Ohio Revised Code Annotated (Baldwin).

State of Ohio: Legislative Acts Passed and Joint Resolutions Adopted.

Ohio Legislatuve Bulletin (Anderson).

Baldwin's Ohio Legislative Service.

ADMINISTRATIVE REGULATIONS & REPORTS:
Ohio Administrative Code (Banks-Baldwin).

Ohio Monthly Record (Banks-Baldwin).

Ohio Government Reports.

Ohio Departments Reports.

CASES & OPINIONS:
Ohio Appellate Reports (1913–).

Ohio Miscellaneous (1965–).

Ohio Bar Reports (1982–).

North Eastern Reporter (1885–).

Ohio Appellate Decisions Index for 1981–1985 (Banks-Baldwin).

Ohio State Reports (1852–).

COURT RULES:
Ohio Rules of Civil Procedure Annotated (West, 1970).

Ohio Rules of Court, State and Federal (West).

JURY INSTRUCTIONS: *Ohio Instructions to Juries* by L. Fess (Anderson, 1952–).
Ohio Jury Instructions (Anderson, 1968–).

OPINIONS OF THE
ATTORNEY GENERAL: *Attorney General Opinions* (Banks-Baldwin, 1964).

JOURNALS & OTHER
PERIODICALS: *Ohio Bar Journal* (1928–).
Ohio State Bar Association Report.
Cleveland Bar Journal (1927–).
Akron Legal News.
Court Index (Cincinnati).
Daily Court Reporter (Dayton).
Daily Reporter (Columbus).
Daily Legal News (Cleveland).
Daily Legal News (Youngstown).
Legal News (Toledo).

SURVEY OF STATE LAW: "Survey of Ohio Law" in *Ohio Northern University Law Review*. See for example vol. 1, p. 143; vol. 12, p. 33.

TREATISES &
LOOSELEAFS: *Anderson's Ohio Civil Practice* by McCormack (Anderson).
Comparative Negligence (Ohio Legal Center Institute, 1980).
Baldwin's Ohio Legal Forms (Banks-Baldwin, 1973–).
Baldwin's Ohio Tax Law and Rules (Banks-Baldwin, 1976–).
Baldwin's Ohio Tax Service by M. Gall (Banks-Baldwin, 1978).
Domestic Relations (Ohio Legal Center Institute, 1982).
Guidebook to Ohio Taxes (CCH, 1987).
Ohio Appellate Practice by A. Whiteside (Banks-Baldwin, 1972–).
Ohio Civil Procedure Forms by J. Lewis (West, 1973).
Ohio Commercial and Consumer Law by W. Tabac (West, 1981).
Ohio Corporation Law with Federal Tax Analysis by Z. Cavitch (Matthew Bender, 1961–).
Ohio Corporations by J. Beavers (Lawyers Co-op., 1980–).
Ohio Family Law by J. Milligan (West, 1975).
Ohio Forms: Legal and Business (Lawyers Co-op., 1970).
Ohio Probate by D. Carmack (Lawyers Co-op., 1979–).
Ohio Probate Practice, 6th ed. by C. Davies (Anderson, 1973–).
Ohio Real Estate by J. Graf (Lawyers Co-op., 1970).
Ohio Transaction Guide: Legal Forms by Z. Cavitch (Matthew Bender, 1975–).
Title to Real Estate (Ohio Legal Center Institute, 1979).
Trial Handbook for Ohio Lawyers by R. Markus (Lawyers Co-op., 1973).

DIGEST, ENCYCLOPEDIA
& CITATOR: *Ohio Digest* (West).
Ohio Jurisprudence, 3d (Lawyers Co-op.).
Shepard's Ohio Citations.

OIL & GAS

SEE ALSO: Agency, Antitrust Law, Business Law, Consumer Law, Corporate Law, Economics, Energy, Environmental Law, Franchise Law, Government Contracts, Insurance,

International Law, Kuwait, Labor Law, Maritime Law, Middle East, Natural Resources, Partnership Law, Real Estate, Saudi Arabia, Sea, Taxation, Zoning

RESEARCH GUIDES &
BIBLIOGRAPHIES: *A Bibliography of Oil and Gas Law* by D. Spencer (Scotland: Centre for Petroleum and Mineral Studies, 1978–).

"Compendium of Articles of Interest to the Oil and Gas Practitioner: 1972–1980," 58 *North Dakota Law Review* 689 (1982).

"Selective Bibliography on Legal Aspects of the Petroleum Industry in the IDB Regional Member Countries" by S. Rodriguez, 10 *International Journal of Legal Information* 158 (1982).

JOURNALS, NEWSLETTERS
& OTHER PERIODICALS: *Oil and Gas Tax Alert* (The Research Institute of America).

Oil and Gas Tax Quarterly (Matthew Bender, 1951–).

INSTITUTE: *Proceedings of the. . .Annual Institute on Oil and Gas Law and Taxation* Southwestern Legal Foundation (Matthew Bender).

LOOSELEAFS: *Federal Income Taxation of Oil and Gas Investments* by A. Bruen (Warren, Gorham & Lamont, 1980–).

Federal Taxation of Oil and Gas Transactions by L. Fiske (Matthew Bender, 1958–).

Gower Federal Service: Oil and Gas (Denver: Rocky Mountain Mineral Law Foundation, 1948–).

Institute on Oil and Gas Law and Taxation by the Southwestern Legal Foundation (Matthew Bender, 1949–).

Law of Federal Oil and Gas Leases by Rocky Mountain Mineral Law Foundation (Matthew Bender, 1964–).

Law of Oil and Gas Leases, 2d ed. by E. Brown (Matthew Bender, 1983–).

Manual of Oil and Gas Terms: Annotated, 3d ed. by H. Williams (Matthew Bender, 1984–).

Oil and Gas Accounting by the Southwestern Legal Foundation (Matthew Bender, 1965).

Oil and Gas Law by H. Williams (Matthew Bender, 1959–).

Oil and Gas Law International Conventions by H. Collins (Oceana).

Oil and Gas: Natural Resources (Prentice-Hall, 1964–).

Oil and Gas Reporter by the Southwestern Legal Foundation (Matthew Bender, 1952–).

Regulation of the Gas Industry by American Gas Assn. (Matthew Bender).

Summary of State Statutes and Regulations for Oil and Gas Production (Interstate Oil Compact Commission, 1979–).

TREATISES: *Contracts Used In Oil and Gas Operations,* L. Mosburg, ed. (Oklahoma City: Institutes for Energy Development, 1979).

Gas Contracts, L. Mosburg, ed. (Oklahoma City: Institutes for Energy Development, 1978).

The Law of Oil and Gas by W. Summers (Vernon Law Book Co., 1954).

The Law of Oil and Gas, 2d ed. by R. Hemingway (West, 1983).

Natural Gas Policy Information Service (Federal Programs Advisory Service).

Ocean Oil and Gas Drilling and the Law by P. Swan (Oceana, 1979).

Oil and Gas Drilling Programs: Preparing the Documentation by C. Wright (Clark Boardman, 1984).

Oil and Gas: Federal Income Taxation, 24th ed. (CCH, 1986).

Oil and Gas Law by H. Collins (Oceana).

Oil and Gas Law in a Nutshell, 2d ed. by J. Lowe (West, 1988).

Oil and Gas Title Examination by G. Morgenthaler (Practicing Law Institute, 1982).

Petroleum Marketing Practices Act Manual by D. Grissom (Austin, TX: Texas Oil Marketers Assn., 1981).

A Treatise on the Law of Oil and Gas by E. Kuntz (Anderson, 1962).

World Petroleum Arrangements (NY: Barrows).

ENCYCLOPEDIAS: AMERICAN JURISPRUDENCE 2D (Am Jur 2d)
Check the following topics in the *General Index* volumes for Am Jur 2d:

Butane Gas	Mines and Minerals
Coal	Natural Resources
Electricity, Gas and Steam	Pipes and Pipelines
Environment and	Pollution
Conservation	Public Utilities
Gas and Oil	

CORPUS JURIS SECUNDUM (CJS)
Check the following topics in the *General Index* volumes for CJS:

Electricity	Mines and Minerals
Federal Power	Natural Resources
Commission	Oil and Gas
Fuel	Oil and Gas Leases
Gas	Pipes and Pipelines
Gasoline	Pollution
Health and Environment	

DIGESTS: CASE SEARCH IN WEST DIGESTS BY KEY TOPIC
In the *Descriptive Word Index* of the West digests, look for key topics and numbers under the following subject headings:

Electricity	Mines and Minerals
Federal Power	Natural Resources
Commission	Oil and Gas
Fuel	Pipes and Pipelines
Gas	Pollution
Gasoline	Public Lands
Health and Environment	

ALR: ANNOTATIONS
Check the index volumes for ALR, ALR2d, ALR3d, ALR4th, and ALR Fed for annotations under the following subject headings:

Air Pollution	Gas and Oil
Chemicals	Mines and Minerals
Coal	Oil Pollution
Conservation	Public Land
Environmental Law	

PERIODICALS: CURRENT LAW INDEX (CLI) & LEGAL RESOURCE INDEX (LRI)
In the CLI and LRI, look for references to periodical literature under the following subject headings:

Atomic Energy	Gas
Depletion Allowance	Gas Companies
Energy Materials	Gas, Natural
Environmental Law	Hydroelectric Power

Mines and Mineral	Oil Pollution
Resources	Oil Spills
Mining Law	Oil Well Drilling
Mining Leases	Petroleum
Ocean Mining	Power Resources
Offshore Oil Industry	Public Lands
Oil and Gas Exploration	Strip Mining
Oil and Gas Leases	Zoning
Oil Industries	

INDEX TO LEGAL PERIODICALS (ILP)

In the ILP, look for references to legal periodical literature under the following subject headings:

Coastal Zone	Marine Resources
Continental Shelf	Mines and Minerals
Energy	Natural Resources
Environmental Law	Oil and Gas
Forests	Pollution

OKLAHOMA

SEE ALSO: Circuit Courts (Tenth Circuit), Indians, Oil & Gas

RESEARCH GUIDES & BIBLIOGRAPHIES:

Oklahoma Government Publications (Oklahoma Dept. of Libraries, 1980).

Oklahoma Legal and Law-Related Documents and Publications: A Selected Bibliography by C. Corcos (Amer. Assn. of Law Libraries, Govt. Documents SIS Program, 1983).

STATUTES:

Oklahoma Statutes (West).

Oklahoma Statutes Annotated (West).

Oklahoma Session Laws (West, 1936–).

Oklahoma Session Law Service.

Legislative Bills and Acts of the Current Legislative Session (Okla. Dept. of Libraries).

Oklahoma Legislative Reporter (Okla. Business Publishing Co., 1939–).

STATE ADMINISTRATIVE CODE:

Oklahoma Register (formerly the Oklahoma Gazette) (Okla. Dept. of Libraries, Legislative Reference Service, 1962–).

CASES & OPINIONS:

Oklahoma Decisions (West).

Oklahoma Reports (1890–1953).

Oklahoma Criminal Reports (1908–1953).

Oklahoma Tax Reporter (CCH, 1954–).

Pacific Reporter (West).

COURT RULES:

Oklahoma Court Rules and Procedure (West).

Handbook of the Workers' Compensation Court; State of Oklahoma; Rules of the Court and Title 85 Oklahoma Statutes.

Oklahoma District Court Judges Benchbook (vol. 1, criminal; vol. 2, civil) (1980–).

JURY INSTRUCTIONS:	*Oklahoma Uniform Jury Instructions (Civil)—OUJI—CIV* (Okla. Bar Assn., 1982).
	Oklahoma Uniform Jury Instructions (Criminal)—OUJI—CR (Center for Criminal Justice, 1981).
	Uniform Jury Instructions (Okla. Bar Assn., 1983).
OPINIONS OF THE ATTORNEY GENERAL:	*Opinions of the Attorney General* (Attorney General's Office, 1911–).
	Digest of Opinions of the Attorney General (Attorney General's Office).
JOURNALS & OTHER PERIODICALS	*Oklahoma Bar Journal* (1930–).
	Oklahoma City Law Review (1976–).
	Oklahoma Law Review (1948–).
	Travis' Oklahoma Law Summary (Travis Enterprises, 1981–).
	Tulsa Law Review (1964–).
TREATISES & LOOSELEAFS:	*Administration of Estates,* (Okla. Bar Assn., 1983).
	All Rise—Trial Procedure and Practice in State Court (Okla. Bar Assn., 1984).
	Anatomy of an Oil and Gas Venture (Okla. Bar Assn., 1984).
	Automobile and General Liability Coverages (Okla. Bar Assn., 1984).
	Basic Estate Planning (Okla. Bar Assn., 1983).
	Basic Workers' Compensation (Okla. Bar Assn., 1984).
	Child Custody Litigation in the 80's (Okla. Bar Assn., 1983).
	Consumer Credit (Okla. Bar Assn., 1984).
	Creditors' Rights in the Oil Patch (Okla. Bar Assn., 1983).
	May it Please the Court—Federal Practice and Procedure in the Western District (Okla. Bar Assn., 1984).
	Oklahoma Appellate Advocacy (Okla. Bar Assn., 1983).
	Oklahoma Discovery Code Manual by R. Davis (Okla. Cont. Legal Ed., 1982–).
	The Oklahoma Pleading Code Handbook with Committee Commentaries (Okla. Bar Assn., 1984).
	Oklahoma Probate Law and Practice, with Forms, 2d ed. by R. Huff (West, 1982–).
	An Outline of Oklahoma Government by J. Stewart (Central State University, 1982).
	Real Estate Transactions (Okla. Bar Assn., 1984).
	Status of Mineral Resource Information for the Chickasaw Nation Indian Lands, Oklahoma by S. Ashe & E. Peterson (BIA–102) (Bureau of Indian Affairs, 1983).
	Vernon's Oklahoma Forms with Practice Commentaries by R. Kleinschmidt (West, 1958–).
DIGESTS & CITATOR:	*Oklahoma Digest* (West).
	Pacific Digest (West).
	Shepard's Oklahoma Citations.

OLD AGE BENEFITS: See Age, Employee Benefits, Insurance, Poverty Law, Social Security

OLIGOPOLIES: See Corporate Law

OMAN

SEE ALSO:	International Law, Islam, Middle East, United Nations

**TREATISES &
LOOSELEAFS:**
    The Banking Law of Oman (Oceana, 1974).

Business Laws of Oman by M. Hall (London: Graham & Trotman, 1984–).

Commercial Business Laws of Oman, 3d ed. (Oman: Ministry of Commerce and Industry, 1977).

Commercial Laws of the Middle East by A. Keesee (Oceana, 1980–).

Commercial Laws of the World, Middle East States (Oman) (FL: Foreign Tax Law Assn., 1985–).

The General Principles of Saudi Arabian and Omani Company Laws by N. Saleh (London: Namara Pub., 1981).

Information Guide: Doing Business in Oman (Price Waterhouse).

The Maritime Law of Oman (Oceana, 1975).

Taxes and Investment in the Middle East (Intl. Bureau of Fiscal Documentation).

Tax Laws of the World—Oman (FL: Foreign Tax Law Assn.).

ARTICLES:
    "The Commercial Legal System of the Sultanate of Oman" by J. Hill, 17 *International Lawyer* 507 (1983).

"The Enforcement of an Arbitration Award in Oman" by S. Jarvin, *Journal of International Arbitration* 81 (1985) (see also International Business Lawyer, p. 471, Dec., 1985).

"Modern Business Law in the Sultanate of Oman" by L. Spoliansky, 13 *International Lawyer* 101 (1979).

"New Rules Announced for Settling Commercial Disputes" (Oman) by E. Kerrigan, 7 *Middle East Executive Reports* 9 (1984) (see also vol. 6, pp 9, 16, 17; vol. 7, pp. 10,11, 14, 18; vol. 8, pp. 9, 13, 20; vol. 9, p. 36).

OMBUDSMAN

SEE ALSO:
    Administrative Law, Civil Service, Finland, International Law, Labor Law, Mediation, State & Local Government, Zimbabwe

**TREATISES &
LOOSELEAFS:**
    International Ombudsman Institute: Bibliography (Edmonton, Alberta: Intl. Ombudsman Inst., 1981–).

International Handbook of the Ombudsman by G. Caiden (Greenwood Press, 1983).

Ombudsmen Around the World by K. Weeks (Univ. of Cal., Berkeley, Inst. of Govt. Studies, 1978).

Ombudsmen Compared by F. Stacey (Clarendon Press; Oxford Univ. Press, 1978).

ON-LINE SEARCHING: See Computers, Legal Research
ONTARIO: See Canada
OPEN SHOP: See Labor Law
OPINION TESTIMONY: See Trial & Appellate Practice
OPTICIAN: See Health & Medicine
OPTIONS: See Commodities, Contracts, Real Estate
OPTOMETRY: See Health & Medicine
ORAL ARGUMENT: See Legal Research, Trial & Appellate Practice
ORDINANCE: See Legal Research, State & Local Government
ORDINARY CARE: See Torts

OREGON

SEE ALSO: Circuit Courts (Ninth Circuit)

RESEARCH GUIDE &
BIBLIOGRAPHY: *Bibliography of Law Related Oregon Documents* by L. Buhlman, B. Studwell, C. Romaine & K. Faust (Assn. of American Law Libraries, 1984).

STATUTES & RELATED
LEGISLATIVE MATERIAL: *Oregon Laws and Resolutions.*
Oregon Revised Statutes.
Session Laws (Secretary of State).
Manual for Ordinance Drafting and Maintenance (Univ. of Oregon, Bureau of Govt. Research and Service, 1984).

STATE ADMINISTRATIVE
CODE: *Oregon Administrative Rules Compilation.*
Oregon Administrative Rules Bulletin.

CASES & OPINIONS: *Oregon Appeals Reporter Service* (Butterworths).
Oregon Cases (West, 1967–).
Oregon Decisions (West, 1969–).
Oregon Reports (1853–).
Oregon Reports, Court of Appeals (1969–).
Oregon Tax Reports (1962–).
Pacific Reporter (1883–).
Land Use Board Appeals (Butterworths, 1979–).
Land Conservation Decisions (Butterworths, 1974–).

COURT RULES: *Local Rules of the Circuit and District Courts: Oregon* (Butterworths, 1981–).
Oregon Rules of Court (West).

ETHICS & PROFESSIONAL
RESPONSIBILITY: *Professional Responsibility Manual* (Oregon Cont. Legal Ed., 1985–).

OPINIONS OF THE
ATTORNEY GENERAL: *Biennial Report and Opinions of the Attorney General* (1897–1968).
Opinions of the Attorney General (1968–).

JOURNALS & OTHER
PERIODICALS: *Oregon State Bar Bulletin* (1940–).

TREATISES &
LOOSELEAFS: *Advising Oregon Businesses* (Oregon Cont. Legal Ed., 1979).
Appeal and Review (Oregon Cont. Legal Ed., 1977).
Civil Litigation, 2d ed., R. Foster & J. Webb, eds. (Oregon Cont. Legal Ed., 1982).
Civil Pleading and Practice (Oregon Cont. Legal Ed., 1985).
Creditors Rights and Remedies (Oregon Cont. Legal Ed., 1978).
Criminal Law (Oregon Cont. Legal Ed., 1986).
Damages (Oregon Cont. Legal Ed., 1980).
Evidence (Oregon Cont. Legal Ed., 1973).
Family Law (Oregon Cont. Legal Ed., 1983).

Foreclosing Security Interests (Oregon Cont. Legal Ed., 1984).
Insurance (Oregon Cont. Legal Ed., 1979).
Juvenile Law (Oregon Cont. Legal Ed., 1984).
Land Use (Oregon Cont. Legal Ed., 1982).
Legislation Notebook (Oregon Cont. Legal Ed., 1983).
Local Government (Oregon Cont. Legal Ed., 1982).
Oregon Constitutional Law (Oregon Cont. Legal Ed., 1985).
Oregon Probate System Manual (Oregon Cont. Legal Ed., 1987).
Practical Corporate Law (Oregon Cont. Legal Ed., 1984).
Real Property (Oregon Cont. Legal Ed., 1975).
State Administrative Law (Oregon Cont. Legal Ed., 1985).
Torts (Oregon Cont. Legal Ed., 1981).
Uniform Civil and Criminal Jury Instructions (Oregon Cont. Legal Ed., 1984).
Workers' Compensation (Oregon Cont. Legal Ed., 1984).

DIGESTS & CITATOR: *Oregon Digest* (West).
Pacific Digest (West).
Shepard's Oregon Citations.

ORGANIZATION: See International Law, Nonprofit Corporations
ORGANIZATION OF AMERICAN STATES: See Latin America (and South American
   Countries)
ORGANIZING: See Labor Law
ORGANS: See Health & Medicine
ORPHAN: See Family Law, Juvenile Law
OSHA: See Occupational Safety
OSTEOPATH: See Health & Medicine, Torts
OTTAWA: See Canada
OVERTIME: See Employee Benefits, Labor Law
OWNERSHIP: See Real Este, Taxation

PACIFIC BASIN: See American Samoa, Asia, Australia, Cook Islands, Fiji, Guam, Japan,
   Kiribati, Macao, Malaysia, Micronesia, New Zealand, Papua New Guinea, Sea,
   Solomon Islands, Tahiti, Taiwan, Tonga, Vanuatu, Western Samoa
PAIN & SUFFERING: See Torts

PAKISTAN

SEE ALSO: Asia, Islam, International Law, Middle East, United Nations

CONSTITUTION: "The Islamic Republic of Pakistan" by L. Wolf-Phillips in *Constitutions of the
   Countries of the World* by A. Blaustein & G. Flanz (Oceana, 1982).

**JOURNALS & OTHER
PERIODICALS:** *Pakistan Development Review.*
The Pakistan Supreme Court Law Quarterly.

**TREATISES &
LOOSELEAFS:** *Annual Law Referencer* (Lahore: Ann. Law Ref., 1985–).

Asia and the Pacific: A Tax Tour (Pakistan) (Arthur Anderson & Co., 1986).

Capital Formation and Investment Incentives Around the World (Pakistan) by W. Diamond & D. Diamond (Matthew Bender, 1984–).

Digest of Commercial Laws of the World (Pakistan) (Natl. Assn. of Credit Mangement; Oceana, 1977–).

The Foreigners Law by Masud-ul-Hassan (Lahore, Khyber Law Pub., 1983).

Income Tax Law: With Practical Problems, 17th ed. by K. Saeed (Lahore: Pakistan Accountancy and Taxation Services Institute, 1983–84).

Information Guide: Doing Business in Pakistan (Price Waterhouse).

Interpersonal Conflict of Laws in India, Pakistan and Bangladesh by D. Pearl (London: Steven, 1981).

Investment Laws of the World (Pakistan) (Oceana, 1981–).

Labour Code of Pakistan (Karachi: Bureau of Labour Pubs.).

Pakistan: The Development of its Laws and Constitution by A. Gledhill (Greenwood Press, 1967).

Principles of Muhammaden Law: With Exhaustive Up-to-Date Caselaw of Bangladesh, Pakistan, and India (Dacca: Dacca Law Reports, 1984).

Taxes and Investment in Asia and the Pacific (Pakistan) (Amsterdam: Intl. Bureau of Fiscal Documentation, 1983–).

Tax Laws of the World—Pakistan (FL: Foreign Tax Law Assn.).

ARTICLES:

"Child Custody in Pakistan: The Role of Ijtihad" by M. Davis, *Boston College Third World Law Journal* 119 (1985).

"The Doctrine of State Necessity in Pakistan" by M. Stavsky, 16 *Cornell International Law Journal* 341 (1983).

"Foreign Investment Incentives in the Developing World: The Legislation of Greece, Eqypt, Pakistan, Thailand, and the Republic of China" by P. Dempsey, 11 *Case Western Reserve Journal of International Law* 575 (1979).

"Legal Aspects of Doing Business in Pakistan" by R. de Belder, 20 *International Lawyer* 535 (1986).

"Perspectives on Islamic Law Reform: The Case of Pakistan" by J. Esposito, 13 *New York University Journal of International Law* 217 (1980).

PALESTINE

SEE ALSO: International Law, Islam, Israel, United Nations

The Palestine Yearbook of International Law, Nicosia, Cyprus: Al-Shaybani Society of Intl. Law).

"The Palestinian Refugees: The Right to Return in International Law" by K. Radley, 72 *American Journal of International Law* 586 (1978).

PANAMA

SEE ALSO: International Law, Latin America, United Nations

**RESEARCH GUIDE &
BIBLIOGRAPHY:** *A Guide to the Official Publications of. . .Panama* (Library of Congress, 1947).

TREATIES: "Panama-United States: Treaty Concerning the Treatment and Protection of Investments," 21 *International Legal Materials* 1227 (1982).

CONSTITUTIONS: "Panama Canal Zone" in *Constitutions of the Countries of the World* by A. Blaustein & G. Flanz (Oceana, 1982).

STATUTES & RELATED LAWS: *Canal Zone Code* (Equity Pub. Co.).

TREATISES & LOOSELEAFS:

Asia and the Pacific: A Tax Tour (Panama) (Arthur Anderson & Co., 1986).

Business Operations in Panama by L. Smejda, Tax Management Foreign Income Portfolios, no 527 (BNA, 1986).

Capital Formation and Investment Incentives Around the World (Panama) by W. Diamond & D. Diamond (Matthew Bender, 1984–).

Digest of Commercial Laws of the World (Panama) (Natl. Assn. of Credit Management: Oceana, 1977–)

Information Guide: Doing Business in Panama (Price Waterhouse).

Panama: A Country Study, 3d ed. by R. Nyrop (Wash. D.C.: Dept. of the Army; GPO, 1981).

A Statement of the Laws of Panama in Matters Affecting Business, 3d ed. (Organization of American States, 1974).

Taxation in Panama (NY: Deloitte, Haskins & Sells, 1981).

Tax Havens Encyclopedia, (Panama) by B. Spitz (Butterworths, 1975–).

Tax Laws of the World—Panama (FL: Foreign Tax Law Assn.).

ARTICLES:

"The Common Law Zone in Panama" by C. Oliver, 24 *American Journal of Legal History* 280 (1980).

"Latin American Tax Update: Panama" by M. Marti, 12 *Lawyer of the Americas* 662 (1980).

"Panama Canal Treaty," 72 *American Journal of International Law* 225 (1978).

PAN AMERICAN UNION: See Latin America
PAPER: See Forensic Science, Natural Resources

PAPUA NEW GUINEA

SEE ALSO: Asia, Australia, International Law, United Nations

RESEARCH GUIDE & BIBLIOGRAPHY: *Traditional Law in Papua New Guinea: An Annotated and Selected Bibliography* by M. Potter (Australian Natl. Univ., 1973).

CONSTITUTION: "Papua New Guinea" by A. Toleris in *Constitutions of the Countries of the World* by A. Blaustein & G. Flanz (Oceana, 1981).

JOURNALS & OTHER PERIODICALS: *Malanesian Law Journal* (Univ. of Papua New Guinea Facilty of Law, 1970–).

TREATISES & LOOSELEAFS: *Asia and the Pacific: A Tax Tour* (Papua New Guinea) (Arthur Anderson & Co., 1986).

Financial Institutions and Markets in the Southwest Pacific: A Study of Australia, Fiji, New Zealand, and Papua New Guinea, M. Skully, ed. (St. Martin's Press, 1985).
Information Guide: Doing Business in Papua New Guinea (Price Waterhouse).
Investment Laws of the World (Papua New Guinea) (Oceana, 1981–).
Law and Order in the New Guinea Highlands by R. Gordon (Univ. of VT; Univ. Press of New England, 1985).
Law and Social Change in Papua New Guinea by D. Weisbrot (Butterworths, 1982).
Law and State in Papua New Guinea by P. Fitzpatrick (NY: Academic Press, 1980).
Taxes and Investment in Asia and the Pacific (Papua New Guinea) (Amsterdam: Intl. Bureau of Fiscal Documentation, 1983–).

ARTICLES:

"Criminal Law in Papua New Guinea" by B. Ottley, 31 *American Journal of Comparative Law* 251 (1983).
"Customary Land Law Reform in Papua New Guinea" by M. Trebilcock, 9 *Adelaide Law Review* 191 (1983).
"Foreign Direct Investment in Papua New Guinea" by T. Parry, 19 *Journal of World Trade Law* 411 (1985).
"Papua New Guinea: 'Lo Bilong Famili'" by C. Bradley and S. Tovey, 27 *Journal of Family Law* 261 (1988-89).
"The Reception of the Common Law and Equity in Papua New Guinea" by D. Srivastava, 34 *International & Comparative Law Quarterly* 850 (1985).
"A Review of the Legal Profession in Papua New Guinea" by S. Ross, 7 *International Journal of the Sociology of Law* 395 (1979).
"Stone Age and Twentieth Century Law in the Independent State of Papua New Guinea" by W. Stewart, 4 *Boston College Third World Law Journal* 48 (1983).

PARAGUAY

SEE ALSO:

International Law, Latin America, United Nations

RESEARCH GUIDES & BIBLIOGRAPHIES:

A Guide to the Law and Literature of Paraguay (Library of Congress, 1947).
A Guide to the Official Publications of. . .Paraguay (Library of Congress, 1947).

CONSTITUTION:

Constitutions of the Countries of the World (Paraguay) by A. Blaustein & G. Flanz (Oceana, 1982).

TREATISES & LOOSELEAFS:

Information Guide: Doing Business in Paraguay (Price Waterhouse).
Latin America. . .A Tax Tour (Paraguay) (Arthur Anderson & Co., 1985).
Paraguay: A Country Study, 2d ed. by G. Amado (Amer. Univ., Foreign Area Studies; GPO, 1984).
Series of Statements of the Law of the OAS Members States in Matters Affecting Business: Paraguay (Organization of American States, 1973, 1978, 1979).
Tax Laws of the World—Paraguay (FL: Foreign Tax Law Assn.).

ARTICLES:

"Foreign Investment in Paraguay" by M. Schley, 3 *Hastings International & Comparative Law Review* 177 (1979).
"Investment and Tax Provisions" by O. Mersan, *Tax Management International Journal* 5 (Nov., 1975).

"Latin American Tax Update: Paraguay" by M. Marti, 12 *Lawyer of the Americas* 664
    (1980).
"Paraguay Trademark Law No. 751," 81 *Patent and Trademark Review* 183, 222 (1985).

PARALEGAL

SEE ALSO:
Administrative Law, Employee Benefits, Law Office Management, Professional
Responsibility

RESEARCH GUIDES &
BIBLIOGRAPHIES:
"Bibliography" in *Introduction to Paralegalism,* 809, 3d ed. by W. Statsky (West, 1986).
"Selected Checklist of Materials on Paralegals/Legal Assistants," 33 *Record of the*
    Association of the Bar of the City of New York 91 (1978).

JOURNALS, NEWSLETTERS
& OTHER PERIODICALS:
Facts and Findings (Natl. Assn. of Legal Assistants).
Journal of Paralegal Education (American Assn. for Paralegal Education, 1984–).
Legal Professional.
Legal Assistant Update (American Bar Assn., Standing Committee on Legal Assistants).
Paralegal Reporter (Natl. Federation of Paralegal Assns.).

TREATISES:
Attorney's Guide to Practicing with Paralegals (State Bar of Texas, Legal Assistant
    Division, 1986).
Better Resumes for Attorneys and Paralegals by A. Lewis (Barron's, 1986).
California Paralegal's Guide, 2d ed. by Z. Mack (Parker, 1982).
Career Guide for Paralegals by H. Cornelius (Monarch Press, 1983).
CLA Study Guide (CLA: Certified Legal Assistant) by Florida Legal Assistants, Inc.
    (Butterworths, 1986).
Ethics for the Legal Assistant by D. Orlik (Scott, Foresman, 1986).
Fundamentals of Paralegalism, 2d ed. by T. Eimmerman (Little, Brown, 1987).
A Guide for Legal Assistancs, M. Gowan, ed. (Practicing Law Institute, 1986).
The Independent Paralegal's Handbook by R. Warner (Berkeley, CA: Nolo Press,
    1987).
Introduction to Paralegalism: Perspectives, Problems, and Skills, 3d ed. by W. Statsky
    (West, 1986).
Judging Credentials: Nonlawyer Judges and the Politics of Professionalism by
    D. Provine (Univ. of Chicago Press, 1986).
Law for the Legal Secretary and Paraprofessional (Illinois Institute for Continuing
    Legal Education, 1979–).
Legal Assistant Handbook by T. Brunner (BNA, 1982).
The Legal Assistant Managers and Legal Assistants National Survey of Compensation
    and Management Practices (N.Y.: Arthur Young, 1987/88).
Manual for the Lawyer's Assistant, 2d ed. (West, 1988).
Legal Assistants (Practicing Law Institute, 1984).
National Utilization and Compensation Survey Report (Natl. Assn. of Legal Assistants,
    1987).
Opportunities in Paralegal Careers by A. Fins (VGM Career Horizons, 1979).
Paralegal Careers by W. Fry (Enslow Pub., 1986).
Paralegal Discovery by D. Zalewski (Santa Ana, CA: James Pub., 1987).
Paralegal Employment: Facts and Strategies for the 1990s by W. Statsky (West, 1987).
The Paralegal's Guide to U.S. Government Jobs (Wash. D.C.: Federal Reports, Inc., 1986).

Paralegal Handbook by C. Nemeth (Prentice-Hall, 1986).
Paralegal Immigration Defense Manual (Los Angeles: Natl. Center for Immigrants Rights, 1982).
Paralegal Litigation Forms by M. Fawcett (Santa Ana, CA: James Pub., 1988).
Paralegal Practice and Procedure, 2d ed. by D. Larbalestrier (Prentice-Hall, 1986).
Paralegal's Litigation Handbook by C. Bruno (Inst. for Business Planning, 1980).
Paralegals: Progress and Prospects of a Satellite Occupation by Q. Johnstone (Greenwood Press, 1986).
Personal Injury Paralegal by B. Eldridge (Santa Ana, CA: James Pub., 1987).
Prisoner Litigation: The Paradox of the Jailhouse Lawyer by J. Thomas (Rowman & Littlefield, 1988).
The Regulation of Paralegals: Ethics, Professional Responsibility, and Other Forms of Control by W. Statsky (West, 1987).
Secretary to Paralegal by L. Prendergast (Inst. for Business Planning, 1984).
Working with Legal Assistants (ABA Section of Economics of Law Practice, 1980).

MISCELLANEOUS: *Paralegal Assistants,* Senate Committee of the Judiciary, Subcommittee on Representation of Citizen Interests (GPO, 1974).

PERIODICALS: CURRENT LAW INDEX (CLI) & LEGAL RESOURCE INDEX (LRI)
In the CLI and LRI, look for references to periodical literature under the following subject headings:

Attorney and Client	Legal Ethics
Law Offices	Unauthorized Practice of
Lawyers	Law
Legal Assistants	

INDEX TO LEGAL PERIODICALS (ILP)
In the ILP, look for references to legal periodical literature under the following subject headings:

Attorneys	Legal Profession
Economics	Paraprofessionals
Law Office Management	Unauthorized Practice of
Legal Ethics	Law

PARAPROFESSIONALS: See Law Office Management, Paralegal
PARDON: See Corrections, Criminal Law
PARENT & CHILD: See Estate Planning, Family Law, Juvenile Law, Women & the Law
PARKS: See Natural Resources, State & Local Government
PARLIAMENTARY LAW: See Nonprofit Corporations
PAROL CONTRACTS: See Contracts
PAROLE: See Corrections, Criminal Law
PAROL EVIDENCE: See Trial & Appellate Practice
PARTIES: See Trial & Appellate Practice
PARTITION: See Estate Planning, Real Estate

PARTNERSHIP LAW

SEE ALSO: Accounting, Agency, Business Law, Contracts, Corporate Law, Employment Discrimination, Franchise Law, Nonprofit Corporations, Oil & Gas, Real Estate, Securities Law, State & Local Government, Taxation, Torts

UNIFORM LAWS (Uniform Laws Annotated):

Revised Uniform Limited Partnership Act.
Uniform Limited Partnership Act.
Uniform Partnership Act.

JOURNALS, NEWSLETTERS & OTHER PERIODICALS:

Journal of Partnership Taxation (Warren, Gorham & Lamont).
The Partnership Record (Fairfield, CT: Southport Advisors, Inc., 1981–).

TREATISES & LOOSELEAFS:

Agency, Employment, and Partnership Law by M. Closen (Butterworths, 1984).
Agency-Partnership in a Nutshell by R. Steffen (West, 1977).
The Drafting of Partnership Agreements, 6th ed. by K. Pantzer (ALI–ABA Comm. on Cont. Prof. Ed., 1965).
Federal Taxation of Partnerships and Partners by M. McKee (Warren, Gorham & Lamont, 1977–).
A Hornbook on the Law of Agency, Partnership and Other Unincorporated Business Organizations by H. Reuschlein & W. Gregory (West, 1979).
How to Save Time and Taxes Preparing the Federal Partnership Return by E. Fiore (Matthew Bender, 1975–).
Law of Agency and Partnership by H. Gill (West, 1979).
Partnerships and Taxes by J. Sullivan (Panel Pub., 1977–).
Partnerships: UPA, ULPA, Securities, Taxation, and Bankruptcy, 6th ed. (ALI–ABA Comm. on Cont. Prof. Ed., 1985).
Partnership Taxation, 3d ed. by A. Willis (Shepard's, 1981–).
Partnership Taxation: An Advanced Tax Program (Practicing Law Institute, 1985).
Partnership Tax Digest (Warren, Gorham & Lamont, 1986).
Prepare Your Own Partnership Agreements by J. Cotton (Prentice-Hall, 1980).
R&D Partnerships: Structuring the Transaction by L. Petillon (Clark Boardman, 1984).
Rowley on Partnership, 2d ed. by S. Rowley (Bobbs-Merrill, 1960).
State Limited Partnership Laws (Prentice-Hall, 1987–).
State Tax Forms: Partnership and Fiduciary (Louisville: Tax Form Library).
Structured Partnership Agreements (Law & Business, Inc., 1985–).
Tax Sheltered Financing Through the R&D Limited Partnership by J. LaFleur (Wiley, 1983).

SHEPARD'S:

Partnership Law Citations (Shepard's).

ENCYCLOPEDIAS:

AMERICAN JURISPRUDENCE 2D (Am Jur 2d)
Check the following topics in the *General Index* volumes for Am Jur 2d:

Agency	Partnership
Limited Partnership	

CORPUS JURIS SECONDUM (CJS)
Check the following topics in the *General Index* volumes for CJS:

Agents and Agency	Partnership
Confidential and Fiduciary Relationship	

DIGESTS:

CASE SEARCH IN WEST DIGESTS BY KEY TOPIC
In the *Descriptive index volumes* of the West digests, look for key topics and numbers under the following subject headings:

Agents and Agency	Licenses
Contracts	Partnership
Corporations	

PERIODICALS: CURRENT LAW INDEX (CLI) & LEGAL RESOURCE INDEX (LRI)
In the CLI and LRI, look for references to periodical literature under the following subject headings:

Agency (Law)	Partnership
Limited Partnership	

INDEX TO LEGAL PERIODICALS (ILP)
In the ILP, look for references to legal periodical literature under the following subject headings:

Agency	Income Tax/Partnerships
Fraud	Partnerships

PART PERFORMANCE: See Contracts
PART-TIME WORK: See Labor Law
PARTY WALL: See Real Estate
PASSENGERS: See Torts
PASSPORT: See Immigrtion Law, International Law, Transportation
PASTORS: See Canon Law, Church & State
PATENT: See Intellectual Property, Natural Resources
PATERNITY: See Family Law, Juvenile Law, Women & the Law
PATHOLOGY: See Forensic Science
PATIENT: See AIDS, Health & Medicine, Mental Health
PAY, PAYMENT: See Contracts, Employee Benefits, Uniform Commercial Code,
     Women & the Law
PAYROLL TAX: See Taxation
PEACE: See International Law, United Nations, War
PENAL INSTITUTION: See Corrections, Criminal Law
PENALTY: See Criminal Law, Trial & Appellate Practice

PENNSYLVANIA

SEE ALSO: Circuit Courts (Third Circuit)

RESEARCH GUIDES &
BIBLIOGRAPHIES: *Checklist of Pennsylvania State Documents* (State Library of PA, 1962–).
An Introduction to Pennsylvania State Publications of the Law Librarian by
     J. Fishman (American Assn. of Law Libraries, 1985).
"Pennsylvania Practice Materials: A Selected Annotated Bibliography" by J. Fisham &
     M. Silverman, 78 *Law Library Journal* 74 (1986).

STATUTES & OTHER
LEGISLATIVE MATERIALS: *Laws of Pennsylvania.*
Pennsylvania Consolidated Statutes.
Pennsylvania Consolidated Statutes Annotated (Purdon).
Pennsylvania Legislative Service (Purdon).
Purdon's Pennsylvania Statutes Annotated.

ADMINISTRATIVE CODE: *Pennsylvania Bulletin.*
Pennsylvania Code.

CASES & OPINIONS: *Pennsylvania State Reports* (1845–).

	Pennsylvania Superior Court Reports (1970–). *Pennsylvania District and Courty Reports* (1921–). *Atlantic Reporter* (1885–).
COURT RULES:	*Pennsylvania Consolidated Rules* (Rules Service Co., 1972–). *Pennsylvania Rules of Court* (West).
JURY INSTRUCTIONS:	*Pennsylvania Suggested Standard Civil Jury Instructions* (PA Bar Institute, 1981–). *Pennsylvania Suggested Standard Criminal Jury Instructions* (PA Bar Institute, 1979–).
ETHICS & PROFESSIONAL RESPONSIBILITY:	*Summaries of Decisions* (PA Supreme Court, Disciplinary Board, 1972–).
OPINIONS OF THE ATTORNEY GENERAL:	*Attorney General Opinions* (Attorney General).
JOURNALS & OTHER PERIODICALS:	*Pennsylvania Bar Association Quarterly* (1929–). *Pennsylvania Law Journal-Reporter* (Packard Press). *Pennsylvania Lawyer* (PA Bar Assn., 1979–). *Legal Intelligencer* (Phil., 1842–). *Pittsburgh Legal Journal* (Smith Bros., 1853–). *The Shingle* (PA Bar Assn., 1938–).

SURVEY OF STATE LAW:	"Annual Survey of Legal Developments" in *Pennsylvania Bar Association Quarterly*.
	    See for example vol. 57, p. 113.
	"Pennsylvania Supreme Court Review" in *Temple Law Quarterly*. See for example vol.
	    47, p. 38; vol. 59, p. 545.

DIRECTORIES:	*Pennsylvania Bar Association Lawyers' Directory* (PA Bar Assn., 1982–). *Pennsylvania Legal Directory* (Dallas: Legal Directories Pub., 1936–).
TREATISES & LOOSELEAFS:	*Environmental Law Update* (PA Bar Institute, 1985). *Guidebook to Pennsylvania Taxes* (CCH, 1987). *Land Use Law & Litigation* (PA Bar Institute). *Mineral Resource Development Law* (PA Bar Institute). *Pennsylvania Business Corporations* by W. Sell (G. Bisel Co., 1969–). *Pennsylvania Civil Practice, Rules and Forms* by R. Anderson (West). *Pennsylvania Corporation* by J. Nasuti (BNA, 1982). *Pennsylvania Criminal Practice* by R. Wasserbly (Callaghan, 1981–). *Pennsylvania Evidence* by M. Greenberg (Michie, 1983). *Pennsylvania Family Law* by A. Momjian (Bisel Co., 1978–). *Pennsylvania Grand Jury Practice* by D. Savitt (Banks-Baldwin). *Pennsylvania Keystone: Lawyers Desk Library* by B. Laub (G. Bisel Co., 1964–). *Pennsylvania Probate and Estate Administration* by D. Cleaver (Harrison, 1983). *Pennsylvania Probate Law and Taxation of Transfers, Trusts and Estates* by F. Rothman & L. Levin (West, 1980). *Pennsylvania Transaction Guide* by J. Bongiovanni (Matthew Bender, 1974/75–). *Purdon's Pennsylvania Forms* by R. Anderson (West, 1956–). *Standard Pennsylvania Practice*, 2d ed. (Lawyers Co-op., 1982–). *Trial Handbook for Pennsylvania Lawyers* by J. Kleiner (Lawyers Co-op., 1980).

DIGESTS, ENCYCLOPEDIAS & CITATORS:	*Pennsylvania Digest*, 2d (West).
	Atlantic Digest (West).
	Pennsylvania Law Encyclopedia (West, 1957–).
	Pennsylvania Law Finder (West).
	Shepard's Pennsylvania Citations.
	Pennsylvania County Court Reports and District & County Reports: Parallel Citation Tables (Allegheny County Law Library, 1985–).

PENSION: See Employee Benefits, Labor Law, Military Law

PENSION TRUSTS: See Estate Planning

PEOPLES REPUBLIC: See Bulgaria, Cambodia, China, Communism, Congo, Korea (North), Laos, Mongolia, Mozambique, Poland, Yemen.

PEREMPTORY CHALLENGE: See Trial & Appellate Practice

PERFORMANCE: See Contracts

PERFORMING ARTS: See Art & Entertainment, Media Law, Sports Law

PERIODICALS: See Media Law

PERJURY: See Criminal Law, Trial & Appellate Practice

PERMANENT DISABILITY: See Health & Medicine, Workers' Compensation

PERMITS: See State & Local Government

PERPETUITIES: See Estate Planning, Real Estate

PERSONAL INJURY: See Maritime Law, Torts

PERSONAL JURISDICTION: See Trial & Appellate Practice

PERSONAL PROPERTY

SEE ALSO:	Agency, Agriculture, Art & Entertainment, Banking Law, Bankruptcy, Business Law, Community Property, Estate Planning, Family Law, Intellectual Property, Real Estate, Securities Law, Tax, Torts, Uniform Commercial Code
TREATISES & LOOSELEAFS:	*An Essay on the Law of Bailments* by W. Jones (Garland, 1978).
	Guidebook to Security Interests in Personal Property by E. Reilly (Clark Boardman, 1986–).
	Law of Personal Property by R. Brown (Callaghan, 1955).
	Unclaimed Property Law and Reporting Forms by D. Epstein (Matthew Bender, 1984–).

ENCYCLOPEDIAS: AMERICAN JURISPRUDENCE 2D (Am Jur 2d)

Check the following topics in the *General Index* volumes for Am Jur 2d:

Abandoned, Lost, and	Equity
Unclaimed Property	Escheat
Baggage	Gifts or Gratuities
Bailments	Personal Property
Conversion of Property	Possession
of Funds	Replevin

CORPUS JURIS SECUNDUM (CJS)

Check the following topics in the *General Index* volumes for CJS:

Abandonment	Conversion
Baggage	Custodian
Bailments	Delivery
Constructive Possession	Deposits

Equity
Escheat
Gifts
Goods, Wares and
   Merchandise
Perishable Goods or
   Property

Personal Property
Property Damage
Replevin
Storage
Trover and Conversion
Warehousemen and Safe
   Storage

DIGESTS:

CASE SEARCH IN WEST DIGESTS BY KEY TOPIC
In the *Descriptive Word Index* of the West digests, look for key topics and numbers under the following subject headings:

Abandoned and Lost
   Property
Automobiles
Baggage
Bailments
Chattel Mortgages
Constructive Possession
Consumer Protection
Conversion
Copyright and Intellectual
   Property
Custodian
Damages
Delivery

Deposits
Detinue
Equity
Escheat
Gifts
Goods
Insurance
Personal Property
Replevin
Storage
Trespass
Trovers and Conversion
Warehousemen

ALR:

ANNOTATIONS
Check the index volumes for ALR, ALR2d, ALR3d, ALR4th, and ALR Fed for annotations under the following subject headings:

Abandonment
Bailment
Chattel Mortgages
Conditional Gift

Equitable Conversion
Personal Property
Replevin
Trover and Conversion

PERIODICALS:

CURRENT LAW INDEX (CLI) & LEGAL RESOURCE INDEX (LRI)
In the CLI and LRI, look for references to periodical literature under the following subject headings:

Attachment and
   Garnishment
Auctions
Bailments
Fixtures
Gifts
Intangible Property

Intellectural Property
Personal Property
Possession
Property
Renunciation
Transfer

INDEX TO LEGAL PERIODICALS (ILP)
In the ILP, look for references to legal periodical literature under the following subject headings:

Assignments
Bailments
Chattel Mortgages
Common Law
Conditional Sales
Conversion

Damages
Escheat
Escrow
Excise Tax
Forfeiture
Fraud

Gifts	Property
Lost Goods	Replevin
Mortgages	Sales
Personal Property	Secured Transactions
Possession	

PERSONAL REPRESENTATIVE: See Estate Planning
PERSONNEL: See Civil Service, Employee Benefits, Labor Law

PERU

SEE ALSO: International Law, Latin America, United Nations

RESEARCH GUIDES & BIBLIOGRAPHIES:
Law and Legal Literature of Peru by D. Valderrama (Library of Congress, 1976).
A Guide to the Official Publications of. . .Peru (Library of Congress 1947).

STATUTES & RELATED LAWS:
"Draft Civil Code of Peru" by F. Parodi, 14 *Lawyer of the Americas* 593 (1983).
"Peru: Private International Law in New Civil Code of 1984," 24 *International Legal Materials* 997 (1985).

TREATISES & LOOSELEAFS:
The Andean Legal Order (Peru) by F. Garcia-Amador (Oceana, 1978).
Capital Formation and Investment Incentives Around the World (Peru) by W. Diamond & D. Diamond (Matthew Bender, 1984–).
Digest of Commercial Laws of the World (Peru) (Natl. Assn. of Credit Management; Oceana, 1977–).
Information Guide: Doing Business in Peru (Price Waterhouse).
Peru: A Country Study by R. Nyrup (Wash. D.C.: Dept. of the Army, 1981).
Peru and the International Monetary Fund by T. Scheetz (Univ. of Pittsburgh Press, 1986).
Series of Statements of the Law of the OAS Member States in Matters Affecting Business: Peru (Organization of American States, 1973).
Tax Laws of the World—Peru (FL: Foreign Tax Law Assn., 1985–).

ARTICLES:
"Court and Statute Law in Peru" by D. Furnish, 28 *American Journal of Comparative Law* 487 (1980).
"The Hierarchy of Peruvian Laws" by D. Furnish, 19 *American Journal of Comparative Law* 91 (1971).
"Latin American Tax Update: Peru" by M. Marti, 12 *Lawyer of the Americas* 666 (1980).
"Peru and ANCOM: A Study in the Integration of a Common Market" by S. Horton, 17 *Texas International Law Journal* 39 (1982).
"Peru's Recovery of Cultural Property" by F. Truslow, 5 *New York University Journal of International Law and Politics* 839 (1983).
"A Summary Analysis of Peruvian Taxation" by S. Rose, *Tax Management International Journal* 8 (March, 1979).

PESTICIDE: See Agriculture, Environmental Law
PETITION: See Trial & Appellate Practice
PETROLEUM: See Brazil, Cameroon, China, Congo, Gabon, Ivory Coast, Kuwait, Latin America, Libya, Oil & Gas, Sea, Sudan, Texas
PHARMACY: See Food, Health & Medicine, Torts

PHILIPPINES

SEE ALSO:	Asia, International Law, United Nations
RESEARCH GUIDES & BIBLIOGRAPHIES:	"Current Legal Research in the Philippines" by M. Feliciano, 7 *International Journal of Law Libraries* 229 (1979). "Law Libraries and Legal Documentation in the Philippines" by M. Feliciano, 4 *Intl. Journal of Law Libraries* 176 (1976).
TREATIES:	*Philippine Treaty Series* (Oceana; Univ. of Philippines Law Center; Manila: Dept. of Foreign Affairs, 1947–).
CONSTITUTION:	*Constitutions of the Countries of the World* (Philippines) by A. Blaustein & G. Flanz (Oceana, 1971–).
STATUTES & RELATED LAWS:	*Civil Code of the Philippines Annotated,* 11th ed. by E. Paras (Manila: Rex Book Store, 1984–). *Laws and Regulations.* *Official Gazette.* *Philippine Permanent and General Statutes* (Univ. of Philippines Law Center). *The Revised Penal Code,* 14th ed. (Manila: Central Book Supply, 1983). *Subject Index to Presidential Decrees and Other Presidential Issuances* (Univ. of Philippines Law Center).
CASES:	*Philippine Law Report* (Univ. of Philippines Law Center). *Philippine Reports* (Supreme Court Decisions). *Subject Index and Digest to Supreme Court Decisions* (Univ. of Philippines Law Center). *Supreme Court Reports Annotated.* *Velayo's Digest of Supreme Court Decisions and Court of Appeals Decisions* (Manila: Central Book Supply, Inc.).
JOURNALS & OTHER PERIODICALS:	*Journal of Philippine Statistics* (Manila: Natl. Econ. & Development Auth.). *Journal of the Integrated Bar of the Philippines.* *Philippine Law and Jurisprudence* (Manila: Current Events Digest, Inc., 1977–). *Philippine Law Journal* (Univ. of Philippines College of Law, 1914–). *Philippine Tax Journal.* *Philippine Yearbook of International Law* (Quezon City: Philippine Society of Intl. Law, 1974–).
TREATISES & LOOSELEAFS:	*The Administration, Adjudication and Enforcement of Labor Justice in the Philippines* by G. Quadra (Manila: Rex Book Store, 1979). *Asia and the Pacific: A Tax Tour* (Philippines) (Arthur Anderson & Co., 1986). *Banking Laws of the Philippines,* 14th ed. (Manila: Central Book Supply, 1984). *Basic Laws Governing the Financial System of the Philippines* (Manila: Central Bank of the Philippines, 1986). *Business Operations in Philippines* by R. Romulo, Tax Management Foreign Income Portfolios, no. 112–3d (BNA, 1983). *Capital Formation and Investment Incentives Around the World* (Philippines) by W. Diamond & D. Diamond (Matthew Bender, 1984).

Digest of Commercial Laws of the World, Natl. Assn. of Credit Management (Oceana, 1977–).

Doing Business in the Philippines (Price Waterhouse).

A Guide to Doing Business in the ASEAN Region: Brunei/Indonesia/Malaysia/ Philippines/Singapore/Thailand (U.S. Dept. of Commerce, Intl. Trade Admin., Office of Pacific Basin, 1985).

Investment Incentive Laws of ASEAN Countries by Z. Reyes (Philippines, 1978).

Investment Laws of the World: The Developing Nations (Philippines) (Oceana, 1973–).

The Labor Code of the Philippines (Quezon City: Philippine Law Gazette, 1982).

Marcos and Martial Law in the Philippines, D. Rosenberg, ed. (Cornell Univ. Press, 1979).

Phillipine Law on Private Corporations, 3d ed. By J. Salonga (Quezon City: Central Lawbook Pub. Co., 1968).

Philippines: A Country Study (GPO, 1984).

Taxation in the Philippines (NY: Deloitte, Haskins & Sells, 1981).

Tax Laws of the World—Philippines (FL: Foreign Tax Law Assn.).

ARTICLES: Freedom from Arbitrary Arrest and Detention in the Philippines" by C. Lopez, 4 *Boston College Third World Law Journal* 72 (1983).

"Laws Governing Foreign Investment in the Philippines," 14 *International Lawyer* 140 (1980).

"Philippine Law on Products Liability" by E. Cueva, 55 *Philippines Law Journal* 205 (1980).

"Sixty Years of Philippine Law" by P. Fernandez, 35 *Philippine Law Journal* 1389 (1960).

PHILOSOPHY: See Jurisprudence

PHOTOGRAPHIC EVIDENCE: See Trial & Appellate Practice

PHOTOGRAPHY: See Art & Entertainment

PHYSICAL DISABILITY: See Handicapped & the Law, Health & Medicine, Occupational Safety, Workers' Compensation

PHYSICAL EDUCATION: See Education Law, Handicapped & The Law, Sports Law

PHYSICAL EXAMINATION: See Health & Medicine, Sports Law, Trial & Appellate Practice

PHYSICIAN: See Death, Forensic Science, Handicapped & the Law, Health & Medicine, Mental Health, Torts

PHYSICIAN–PATIENT PRIVILEGE: See Health & Medicine, Trial & Appellate Practice

PHYSICIAN'S ASSISTANT: See Health & Medicine

PICKETING: See Labor Law

PILOTAGE: See Maritime Law

PIPES & PIPELINES: See Natural Resources, Oil & Gas, Water Law

PIRACY: See Criminal Law, Terrorism

PLAIN ENGLISH: See Legal Research, Statutes

PLANNED UNIT DEVELOPMENT (PUD): See Real Estate

PLANNING: See Zoning & Land Planning

PLEA BARGAINING: See Criminal Law

PLEADING: See Conflict of Law, Trial & Appellate Practice

POISON: See Food, Torts

POLAND

SEE ALSO: Communism, Europe, International Law, Soviet Union, United Nations

**RESEARCH GUIDES &
BIBLIOGRAPHIES:**
"Legal Education, Legal Research, and Law Reform in Poland" by A. Tay, 54 *Australian Law Journal* 142 (1980).
The Polish Crisis—Solidarity and Martial Law: A Bibliography by A. Lakos (Monticello, IL: Vance Bibliographies, 1987).

CONSTITUTION:
The Constitutions of the Communist World (Poland), W. Simons, ed. (Sijthoff & Noordhoff, 1980).

**STATUTES & RELATED
LAWS:**
Penal Code of the Polish People's Republic W. Kenney, transl. (Rothman, 1973).

**JOURNALS & OTHER
PERIODICALS:**
Poland Watch Digest (Wash. D.C.: Poland Watch Center, 1985–).
Polish Yearbook of International Law (Wroclaw, Poland: Publishing House of the Polish Academy of Sciences, 1966–).

**TREATISES &
LOOSELEAFS:**
Anglo-Polish Legal Essays, W. Butler, ed. (Transnational Pub., 1982).
Commercial, Business, and Trade Laws. Poland by J. Rajski (Oceana, 1985–).
Constitutions, Elections, and Legislatures of Poland, 1493–1977 by J. Jedruch (Wash. D.C.: Univ. Press of America, 1982).
Digest of Commercial Laws of the World (Poland) Natl. Assn. of Credit Management; Oceana, 1977–).
Doing Business with Eastern Europe (NY: Business Intl. Corp., 1975–).
Employment and Wage Policies in Poland, Czechoslovakia, and Hungary Since 1950 by J. Adam (London: Macmillan, 1984).
General Principles of Law of the Polish People's Republic by L. Kuronoski (Warsaw: Polish Scientific Pub., 1984).
Legal Aspects of Joint Ventures in Eastern Europe, D. Campbell, ed. (Kluwer, 1981).
Poland: A Country Study (GPO, 1984).
Poland: Three Years After (NY: Lawyers Committee for Intl. Human Rights, 1984).
Polish Law Through the Ages, W. Wagner, ed. (Stanford Univ., Hoover Institution, 1970).
Recognition and Enforcement of Foreign Judgments in Various Foreign Countries (Poland) by G. Roman (Library of Congress, 1984).
Taxation in the European Socialist Countries (vol. 5, Poland) (Amsterdam: Intl. Bureau of Fiscal Documentation).

ARTICLES:
"Dumping From 'Controlled Economy' Countries: The Polish Golf Car Case," 11 *Law & Policy in International Business* 777 (1979) (see also 128 University of PA Law Review).
"Lay Judges in the Polish Criminal Courts" by S. Pomorski, 7 *Case Western Journal of International Law* 198 (1975).
"Legal Protection of Software in Poland and Other Socialist Countries" by B. Czachorska, 2 *International Protection Ind. Property* 7 (1980).
"New Legislation on Foreign Private Firms in Poland," 10 *Review of Socialist Law* 119 (1984).
"Ownership and Investment in Poland" by C. Jadach, 18 *Cornell International Law Journal* 63 (1985).
"Poland: Cohabitation" by W. Stojanowska, 27 *Journal of Family Law* 275 (1988–89).
"Poland: The New Law on Personal Status" by W. Stojanowska, 26 *Journal of Family Law* 161 (1987–88). See also 25 *Journal of Family Law* 205 (1986–87).
"Poland's Trade Union Statute" by R. Wolff, 10 *Brooklyn Journal of International Law* 25 (1984).

"Polish Constitutional Development in the 1970's" by L. Garlicki, 3 *Comparative Law Yearbook* 247 (1979).

"Polish Foreign Investment Law 1988" by E. Prontek 23 *Journal of World Trade* 5 (Oct. 1989).

POLICE: See Civil Rights, Criminal Law, Forensic Science
POLICE POWER: See Constitutional Law, State & Local Government
POLITICAL ACTION COMMITTEE (PAC): See Constitutional Law, Election
POLITICAL PARTY: See Election
POLITICAL QUESTION: See Constitutional Law
POLITICAL RIGHTS: See Civil Rights, Constitutional Law
POLITICAL SCIENCE: See Jurisprudence
POLITICAL SUBDIVISION: See State & Local Government
POLITICAL TERRORISTS: See Terrorism
POLITICS: See Education Law, Election, Jurisprudence
POLL TAX: See Election, Taxation
POLLUTION: See Environmental Law, Natural Resources, Oil & Gas, Public Utilities, Water Law
POLYGRAPH: See AIDS, Employment Discrimination, Trial & Appellate Practice
POLYNESIA: See Tahiti
PONDS: See Natural Resources, Water Law
POOR: See Poverty Law
POPE: See Canon Law
POPULATION: See Abortion, Health & Medicine, Statistics
PORNOGRAPHY: See Constitutional Law, Media Law
PORT: See Maritime Law

PORTUGAL

SEE ALSO: Angola, Europe, European Economic Community, International Law, United Nations

CONSTITUTION: *Constitutions of the Countries of the World* (Portugal) by A. Blaustein & G. Flanz (Oceana, 1982).

TREATISES & LOOSELEAFS: *Capital Formation and Investment Incentives Around the World* (Portugal) by W. Diamond & D. Diamond (Matthew Bender, 1984–).

Digest of Commercial Laws of the World (Portugal) (Natl. Assn. of Credit Management; Oceana, 1977–).

Information Guide: Doing Business in Portugal (Price Waterhouse).

Tax Laws of the World—Portugal (FL: Foreign Tax Law Assn.).

ARTICLES: "European Economic Community: Entry of Spain and Portugal" by J. Abrams, 27 *Harvard International Law Journal* 250 (1986).

"Investment Legislation in Greece, Portugal, and Spain" by P. Artisien & P. Buckley, 17 *Journal of World Trade Law* 513 (1983).

"Portugal: From Empire to Nation-State" by J. Santos, 9 *Fletcher Forum* 125 (1985).

POSSESSION: See Personal Property, Real Estate
POST–CONVICTION REMEDIES: See Corrections, Criminal Law

POST MORTEM: See Death, Estate Planning, Forensic Science, Health & Medicine
POST OFFICE: See Civil Service

POVERTY LAW

SEE ALSO:

Abortion, Administrative Law, Age, Bankruptcy, Civil Rights, Constitutional Law, Consumer Law, Criminal Law, Education Law, Election, Employee Benefits, Employment Discrimination, Equity, Family Law, Handicapped & the Law, Health & Medicine, Insurance, Juvenile Law, Mental Health, Nonprofit Corporations, Occupational Safety, Professional Responsibility, Public Utilities, Social Security, State & Local Government, Taxation, Unemployment Compensation, Uniform Commercial Code, Women & the Law, Workers' Compensation

**JOURNALS, NEWSLETTERS
& OTHER PERIODICALS:**

Clearinghouse Review (Natl. Clearinghouse for Legal Services, 1967–).
Journal of Social Welfare Law (1978–).
N.L.A.D.A. Briefcase (Natl. Legal Aid and Defender Assn., 1942–).

**TREATISES &
LOOSELEAFS:**

Law of the Poor by A. LaFrance et al. (West, 1973).
Legal Representation of the Poor, 2d ed. by E. Jarmel (Matthew Bender, 1975).
*National Health Law Program Manual on State and Local Government
    Responsibilities to Provide Medical Care for Indigents* (Natl. Clearinghouse for
    Legal Services, 1985).
Welfare Law in a Nutshell by A. LaFrance et al. (West, 1979).
The Welfare State in America: Trends and Prospects, R. Lambert, ed. (Sage Pubs.,
    1985).

ENCYCLOPEDIAS:

AMERICAN JURISPRUDENCE 2D (Am Jur 2d)
Check the following topics in the *General Index* volumes for Am Jur 2d:
    Welfare and Welfare Laws

CORPUS JURIS SECUNDUM (CJS)
Check the following topics in the *General Index* volumes for CJS:

Forma Pauperis	Social Security and
Indigent Persons	Public Welfare
Old Age Assistance	

DIGESTS:

CASE SEARCH IN WEST DIGESTS BY KEY TOPIC
In the *Descriptive Word Index* of the West digests, look for key topics and numbers under the following subject headings:

Abortion	Old Age Assistance
Common Law	Social Security and
Consumer Protection	Public Welfare
Forma Pauperis	States
Indigent Persons	

ALR:

ANNOTATIONS
Check the index volumes for ALR, ALR2d, ALR3d, ALR4th, and ALR Fed for annotations under the following subject headings:

Administrative Law	Due Process of Law
Aged persons	Forma Pauperis
Discrimination	Poor and Poor Laws

PERIODICALS: CURRENT LAW INDEX (CLI) & LEGAL RESOURCE INDEX (LRI)
In the CLI and LRI, look for references to periodical literature under the following subject headings:

Aid to Families with Dependent Children	Poor
	Poverty
Discrimination	Public Defenders
Food Stamp Program	Public Housing
Income Maintenance Programs	Public Welfare
	Right to Counsel
Legal Aid	Supplemental Security
Legal Assistance to the Poor	Income Program
	Welfare Recipients

INDEX TO LEGAL PERIODICALS (ILP)
In the ILP, look for references to legal periodical literature under the following subject headings:

Administrative Agencies	Fraud
Civil Rights	Poverty Law
Common Law	Social Security
Constitutional Law	Social Welfare
Federal Aid	Subsidies

POWER: See Energy, Natural Resources, Public Utilities

POWER OF APPOINTMENT: See Estate Planning, Real Estate

POWER OF ATTORNEY: See Agency, Estate Planning, Real Estate

PRACTICE OF LAW: See Law Office Management, Legal Research, Trial & Appellate Practice

PRACTITIONER: See Transportation

PRECEDENTS: See Trial & Appellate Practice

PREEMPTION: See Constitutional Law

PREGNANCY: See Abortion, Family Law, Health & Medicine, Juvenile Law, Women & the Law

PRELIMINARY HEARING: See Criminal Law

PREMARITAL AGREEMENT: See Family Law, Women & the Law

PREMISES: See Landlord-Tenant, Real Estate, Torts

PRENATAL INJURY: See Torts

PREPAID LEGAL SERVICES: See Professional Responsibility

PREPAYMENT: See Estate Planning

PREPONDERANCE OF EVIDENCE: See Trial & Appellate Practice

PRESCRIPTION: See Real Estate

PRESERVATION: See Historic Preservation

PRESIDENT: See Administrative Law, Constitutional Law

PRESS: See Constitutional Law, Education Law, Grenada, Media Law

PRESUMPTION: See Trial & Appellate Practice

PRETERMTTED CHILDREN: See Estate Planning, Juvenile Law

PREVENTIVE LAW: See Employment Discrimination, Professional Responsibility

PRICE FIXING: See Antitrust Law

PRICES: See Business Law, Consumer Law, Contracts, Real Estate, Uniform Commercial Code

PRIMA FACIE: See Trial & Appellate Practice

PRINCIPAL & AGENT: See Agency, Architecture, Business Law, Partnership Law

PRINCIPAL IN CRIME: See Criminal Law

PRINCIPAL (SCHOOLS): See Education Law, Handicapped & the Law

PRIOR CONVICTIONS: See Criminal Law

PRIOR INJURY: See Torts, Workers' Compensation

PRIORITIES: See Bankruptcy, Real Estate, Uniform Commercial Code

PRIOR RESTRAINT: See Media Law

PRISON: See Corrections, Constitutional Law, Criminal Law

PRISONERS OF WAR: See International Law, War

PRIVACY: See Abortion, Civil Rights, Constitutional Law, Freedom of Information, Homosexuality, Media Law, Torts

PRIVATE OFFERING: See Securities Law

PRIVATE ROADS: See Real Estate, Zoning & Land Planning

PRIVATE SCHOOLS: See Church & State, Education Law

PRIVATE SECTOR: See Labor Law

PRIVILEGE: See Health & Medicine, Professional Responsibility, Torts, Trial & Appellate Practice

PRIVILEGES & IMMUNITIES: See Constitutional Law

PRIVITY: See Contracts

PROBABILITIES: See Insurance, Statistics, Torts

PROBABLE CAUSE: See Criminal Law

PROBATE: See Estate Planning, Real Estate

PROBATION: See Corrections, Criminal Law

PRO BONO: See Professional Responsibility

PROCEDURE: See Administrative Law, Circuit Courts, Trial & Appellate Practice

PROCESS: See Trial & Appellate Practice

PROCESS, ABUSE OF: See Torts

PROCUREMENT: See Government Contracts

PRODUCERS: See Business Law, Contracts, International Law, Torts

PRODUCTION OF DOCUMENTS: See Trial & Appellate Practice

PRODUCTS: See Business Law, Intellectual Property, Torts

PRODUCTS LIABILITY: See Architecture, Consumer Law, Food, Sports Law, Torts

PROFANITY: See Media Law

PROFESSIONAL ATHLETES: See Art & Entertainment, Sports Law

PROFESSIONAL NEGLIGENCE: See Health & Medicine, Professional Responsibility, Torts

PROFESSIONAL RESPONSIBILITY

SEE ALSO: Criminal Law, Judicial Administration, Law Office Management, Legal Education, Torts, Trial & Appellate Practice; see also entries under individual states

RESEARCH GUIDES & BIBLIOGRAPHIES:

Bibliography on Professional Responsibility (ABA, 1984).

Legal Ethics: An Annotated Bibliography and Resource Guide by F. Elliston (Rothman, 1984).

Research on the Legal Profession by O. Maru (American Bar Foundation, 1986).

CODES & CANONS:

Code of Professional Responsibility by State (Natl. Center for Professional Responsibility; ABA, 1980).

ABA Model Code of Professional Responsibility (1981).

ABA Model Rules of Professional Conduct (1983).

ABA Standards Relating to the Administration of Criminal Justice, 2d ed. (1979).

The American Lawyer's Code of Conduct (Roscoe Pound—American Trial Lawyers Foundation).

Annotated Code of Professional Responsibility (American Bar Foundation, 1979).

OPINIONS:

Opinions on Professional Ethics (ABA, 1967).

Formal and Informal Opinions (ABA, 1978–).

Informal Ethics Opinions (ABA, 1975).

Recent Ethics Opinions (ABA, 1974–).

Digest of Bar Association Ethics Opinions (American Bar Foundation, 1970).

1980 Supplement to the Digest of Bar Association Ethics Opinions (American Bar Foundation, 1982). (See also 1970 & 1975 Supplements).

"Attorneys' Ethics Opinions: A State-by-State Analysis" by A. Hunkeler, 2 *Legal Reference Services Quarterly* 70 (1982).

JOURNALS, NEWSLETTERS & OTHER PERIODICALS:

American Bar Association Journal.

Disciplinary Law & Procedure Advance Sheets (ABA).

The Georgetown Journal of Legal Ethics (Georgetown Univ. School of Law, 1988–).

Journal of the Legal Profession (Univ. of Alabama Sch. of Law, 1976–).

Judicature (American Judicature Society, 1917–).

Lawyers' Professional Liability Update (ABA).

Legal Referral Network (CCH, 1986–).

LRIS Newsletter (Lawyer Referral and Information Service) (ABA).

Notre Dame Journal of Law, Ethics and Public Policy (1984–).

Professional Negligence (Frank Cass, 1985–).

Research Journal (American Bar Foundation, 1976–).

Unauthorized Practice News (ABA, 1934–1980).

LOOSELEAFS:

ABA/BNA Lawyers' Manual on Professional Conduct (ABA/BNA, 1984–).

Disciplinary Law and Procedure Research System (ABA, 1975–).

Ethics in Government Reporter (Wash. Service Bureau, 1980).

Federal Ethics Handbook (Michie, 1981–).

The Law of Lawyering by G. Hazard (Law & Business, Inc. 1985–).

National Reporter on Legal Ethics and Professional Resonsibility, M. Jacobstein, R. Mersky, eds. (Univ. Pubs. of America, 1982–).

Professional Corporations Guide (Prentice-Hall, 1973–).

Professional Corporations Handbook (CCH, 1973–).

Reporter on the Legal Profession (Legal-Medical Studies, 1979–).

TREATISES:

Attorney Malpractice: Law and Procedure by D. Meiselman (Lawyers Co-op., 1980).

Attorney Malpractice: Prevention and Defense by D. Horan (Garland).

Compilation of Reference Materials on Prepaid Legal Services (ABA, 1975).

Conflict of Interest, E. Epstein, ed. (Natl. Law Pub., 1984).

Contingent Fees for Legal Services by B. MacKinnon (American Bar Foundation, 1964).

Data Manual for the Survey of the Legal Needs of the Public by B. Curran (American Bar Foundation, 1980).

Expanding Your Law Practice: The Ethical Risks by J. Haynsworth (ABA, 1984).

Group Legal Service Plans, W. Bolger, ed. (Natl. Resource Center for Consumers of Legal Services, 1981).

Handbook on Specialization (ABA, 1983).

Lawyers and Their Work by Q. Johnstone & D. Hopson (Bobbs-Merrill, 1967).

A Lawyer's Guide to Prepaid Legal Services by A. Schwartz (A.B.A., 1988).

Legal Advertising: The Illinois Experiment (ABA, 1984).

Legal Ethics by H. Drinker (Columbia Univ. Press, 1953).

Legal Ethics by L. Patterson (Matthew Bender, 1982).
Legal Fees and Representation Agreements by J. McRae (ABA, 1983).
Legal Malpractice, 3d ed. by R. Mallen & A. Widiss (West, 1988).
Modern Legal Ethics by C. Wolfram (West, 1986).
A Practical Guide to Preventing Legal Malpractice by D. Stern (Shepard's, 1983).
Prepaid Legal Services by R. Billings (Lawyers Co-op., 1981).
Professional Liability Insurance Coverage Problems: Attorneys, Accountants and Insurance Brokers (Practicing Law Institute, 1984).
Professional Responsibility in a Nutshell by R. Aronson (West, 1980).
Regulation of Advertising by Lawyers (ABA Commn. on Advertising, 1978).
The Resource: A Pro Bono Manual (ABA, 1983).
When a Lawyer Divorces by G. Skolok (ABA, 1986).

SHEPARD'S: *Professional and Judicial Conduct Citations* (1980–).

ENCYCLOPEDIAS: AMERICAN JURISPRUDENCE 2D (Am Jur 2d)
Check the following topics in the *General Index* volumes for Am Jur 2d:

Attorney-Client Privilege	Conflict of Interest
Attorneys	Contingent Fees
Attorneys Fees	

CORPUS JURIS SECUNDUM (CJS)
Check the following toics in the *General Index* volumes for CJS:

Advice	Fees
Argument and Conduct	Malpractice
of Counsel	Professions and
Conflict of Interest	Occupations
Ethics	

DIGESTS: CASE SEARCH IN WEST DIGESTS BY KEY TOPIC
In the *Descriptive Word Index* of the West digests, look for key topics and numbers under the following subject headings:

Attorney and Client	Conflict of Interest
Champerty and	Malpratice
Maintenance	Partnerships

ALR: ANNOTATIONS
Check the index volumes for ALR, ALR2d, ALR3d, ALR4th, and ALR Fed for annotations under the following subject headings:

Advice	Commingling of Funds
Appearances	Conflict of Interest
Argument of Counsel	Contingent Fee
Assistance of Counsel	Disciplinary Action
Attorneys	Ethics and Ethical Matters
Attorneys' Fees	Liability Insurance
Champerty and	Unauthorized Practice of
Maintenance	Law

PERIODICALS: CURRENT LAW INDEX (CLI) & LEGAL RESOURCE INDEX (LRI)
In the CLI and LRI, look for references to periodical literature under the following subject headings:

A.B.A.	Confidential
Adversary System	Communications
Attorney and Client	Conflict of Interest
Client's Funds	Ethics

Fees, Professional
Judicial Ethics
Judicial Process
Law and Ethics
Law Firms
Lawyers
Legal Assistance to the
    Poor
Legal Ethics
Malpractice

Partnership
Practice of Law
Prepaid Legal Services
Public Interest Law
Representation in
    Administrative Proceedings
Right to Counsel
Unauthorized Practice of
    Law

INDEX TO LEGAL PERIODICALS (ILP)
In the ILP, look for references to legal periodical literature under the following subject headings:

Admission to the Bar
Agency
Attorneys
Bar Associations
Bar Examiners and
    Examinations
Barristers
Champerty and
    Maintenance
Civil Rights
Common Law
Costs
Ethics
Fees
Fraud

Integrated Bar
Law Office Management
Legal Education
Legal Ethics
Legal Profession
Prepaid Legal Services
Professional Corporations
Professions
Public Interest
Public Legal Service
Referral Services
Right to Counsel
Solicitors
Unauthorized Practice of
    Law

PROFESSIONAL SPORTS: See Art & Entertainment, Sports Law
PROFIT: See Business Law, Taxation
PROFIT SHARING: See Employee Benefits, Labor Law
PROGNOSIS: See Health & Medicine, Mental Health
PROGRAMMING: See Computers
PROMISE: See Contracts, Equity
PROMISSORY ESTOPPEL: See Contracts
PROMOTERS: See Corporate Law, Securities Law
PROMOTION: See Employee Benefits
PROOF: See Trial & Appellate Practice
PROPERTY: See Community Property, Estate Planning, Family Law, Intellectual
    Property, Landlord-Tenant, Personal Property, Real Estate, Torts, Zoning & Land
    Planning
PROPERTY DAMAGE: See Torts
PROPERTY INSURANCE: See Insurance
PROPERTY SETTLEMENT: See Family Law
PROPERTY TAXES: See Real Estate, Taxation
PRO SE: See Trial & Appellate Practice
PROSECUTING ATTORNEY: See Criminal Law
PROSECUTION, MALICIOUS: See Torts
PROSTITUTION: See Criminal Law
PROTOCOLS: See International Law, United Nations

PROVOCATION: See Torts

PROXIMATE CAUSE: See Torts

PROXY: See Corporate Law, Securities Law

PSYCHIATRY: See Age, Forensic Science, Health & Medicine, Mental Health

PSYCHIC INJURY: See Mental Health, Torts

PSYCHOANALYSIS: See Mental Health

PSYCHOLOGY: See Education Law, Forensic Science, Health & Medicine, Mental Health

PSYCHOTHERAPY: See Health & Medicine, Mental Health

PSYCHOTROPIC DRUGS: See Mental Health

PUBLIC BROADCASTING: See Art & Entertainment, Media Law

PUBLIC CONTRACTS: See Architecture, Government Contracts, State & Local Government

PUBLIC CONVENIENCE OR NECESSITY: See Transportation

PUBLIC DEFENDER: See Criminal Law, Poverty Law

PUBLIC EMPLOYEE: See Civil Service, Labor Law

PUBLIC HEALTH: See AIDS, Health & Medicine, State & Local Government

PUBLIC HOUSING: See Poverty Law, Real Estate, Zoning & Land Planning

PUBLIC INTEREST LAW: See Professional Responsibility

PUBLIC INTERNATIONAL LAW: See International Law

PUBLICITY: See Advertising, Art & Entertainment, Media Law, Torts

PUBLIC LANDS: See Environmental Law, Natural Resources, Oil & Gas, Real Estate, State & Local Government, Water Law, Zoning & Land Planning

PUBLIC OFFERING: See Securities Law

PUBLIC OPINION POLLS: See Election Law

PUBLIC SCHOOLS: See Church & State, Education Law

PUBLIC SECTOR EMPLOYEES: See Civil Service, Labor Law

PUBLIC SERVICE COMMISSION: See Public Utilities

PUBLIC UTILITIES

SEE ALSO: Administrative Law, Air & Aviation, Antitrust Law, Business Law, Consumer Law, Corporate Law, Economics, Election, Energy, Environmental Law, Freedom of Information, Government Contracts, Insurance, Labor Law, Media Law, Natural Resources, Occupational Safety, Oil & Gas, State & Local Government, Transportation, Water Law, Zoning & Land Planning

JOURNALS, NEWSLETTERS
& OTHER PERIODICALS: *National Association of Regulatory Utility Commissioners Bulletin* (1926–).

Public Utilities Fortnightly (Arlington, VA: Public Utilities Reports).

Public Utilities Law Anthology (1974–).

Public Utilities Reports: Executive Information Service (Arlington, VA: Public Utilities Reports, 1934–).

Utility Section Newsletter (ABA Public Utility Law Section, 1960–).

LOOSELEAFS: *Accounting for Public Utilities* by R. Hahne (Matthew Bender, 1983–).

Federal Power Service (Matthew Bender, 1974–).

PUR Digest (Public Utilities Reports, 1953–).

Utilities Law Reports (CCH, 1928–).

Utility Holding Companies by D. Hawes (Clark Boardman, 1984–).

Utility Reporter: Fuels, Energy and Power (Schenectady, NY: Merton Allen Associates, 1984–).

TREATISES: *The Breakup of AT&T* (Law & Business, Inc., 1982).
Principles of Public Utility Regulation by A. Priest (Michie, 1969).
Regulation and Deregulation after the AT&T Divestiture (Practicing Law Institute, 1984).
The Regulation of Public Utilities: Theory and Practice, 2d ed. by C. Phillips (Arlington, VA: Public Utilities Reports, 1988).
Telecommunications 1986: Competition and Deregulation after the AT&T Divestiture (Practicing Law Institute, 1986).
Unnatural Monopolies: The Case for Deregulating Public Utilities, R. Poole, ed. (Lexington Books, 1985).
Utility Investors' Return and Accounting Adjustments in an Inflationary Economy (Natl. Assn. of Regulatory Utility Commissioners, 1980).

MISCELLANEOUS: *United States v. AT&T: Court Documents, 1974–1984* (microfilm) (University Publications of America).

ENCYCLOPEDIAS: AMERICAN JURISPRUDENCE 2D (Am Jur 2d)
Check the following topics in the *General Index* volumes for Am Jur 2d:

Administrative Law	Telecommunications
Public Utilities	

CORPUS JURIS SECUNDUM (CJS)
Check the following topics in the *General Index* volumes for CJS:

Administrative Bodies	Public Utilities
and Procedure	Rural Electric Cooperatives
Public Interest	Rural Telephone
Public Service	Telecommunications
Commissions	

DIGESTS: CASE SEARCH IN WEST DIGESTS BY KEY TOPIC
In the *Descriptive Word Index* of the West digests, look for key topics and numbers under the following subject headings:

Administrative Law	Public Interest
and Procedure	Public Service
Carriers	Commissions
Eminent Domain	Public Utilities
Licenses	Rural Telephones
Monopolies	Telecommunications

ALR: ANNOTATIONS
Check the index volumes for ALR, ALR2d, ALR3d, ALR4th, and ALR Fed for annotations under the following subject headings:

Administrative Law	Pollution
Aerials and Antennas	Public Utilities
Electricity and Electric	Telecommunications
Companies	

PERIODICALS: CURRENT LAW INDEX (CLI) & LEGAL RESOURCE INDEX (LRI)
In the CLI and LRI, look for references to periodical literature under the following subject headings:

Administrative Law	Energy Minerals
American Telephone	Energy Policy
and Telegraph Co.	Energy Utilities
Electric Power Plants	Gas
Electric Utilities	Hydroelectric Power

Nuclear Reactors   United States Federal
Power Resources   Regulatory Commission
Public Utilities   United States Nuclear
Telecommunications Regulatory Commission
Tetlphone

INDEX TO LEGAL PERIODICALS (ILP)
In the ILP, look for references to legal periodical literature under the following subject headings:

Administrative Agencies Public Utilities
Administrative Law   Telegraphs and
Bonds   Telephones
Electricity   Transportation
Energy Resources

PUBLIC WELFARE: See Handicapped & the Law, Health & Medicine, Poverty Law, Social Security, State & Local Government
PUBLIC WORKS: See Contracts, Government Contracts, State & Local Government
PUBLISHERS: See Art & Entertainment, Intellectual Property, Media Law

PUERTO RICO

SEE ALSO: Caribbean, International Law, United Nations

CONSTITUTION: *Constitutions of the United States: National and State* (Puerto Rico) (Oceana, 1982).

STATUTES: *Laws of Puerto Rico Annotated* (Equity Pub. Co.).
Puerto Rico Session Laws (Equity Pub. Co.).

STATE ADMINISTRATIVE CODE: *Puerto Rico Register* (Equity Pub. Co.).

JOURNALS & OTHER PERIODICALS: *Puerto Rican Journal of Human Rights* (1977–).

TREATISES, LOOSELEAFS & OTHER MONOGRAPHS: *Business Operations in Puerto Rico* by B. Woods, Tax Management Foreign Income Portfolios, no. 139–3d (BNA, 1979).
Capital Formation and Investment Incentives Around the World (Puerto Rico) by W. Diamond & D. Diamond (Matthew Bender, 1984–).
Caribbean Basin: A Tax Tour (Puerto Rico) (Arthur Anderson & Co., 1985).
Information Guide: Doing Business in Puerto Rico (Price Waterhouse).
The Supreme Court and Puerto Rico by J. Torruella (Univ. of Puerto Rico, 1985).
Tax and Trade Guide to Puerto Rico (Arthur Anderson & Co., 1978).
Taxation in Puerto Rico (NY: Deloitte, Haskins & Sells, 1982).
Tax Laws of the World—Puerto Rico (FL: Foreign Tax Law Assn.).

ARTICLES: "The Commonwealth of Puerto Rico," by A. Leibowitz, 11 *Georgia Journal of International and Comparative Law* 211 (1981).
"The Decolonization of Puerto Rico" by M. Rodrigueq-Orellana, 5 *Boston College Third World Law Journal* 45 (1984).

"Federal District Court in Puerto Rico" by D. Indiano, 13 *Case Western Reserve Journal of International Law* 231 (1983).

"Intercorporate Transfer Pricing and Puerto Rico, Revisited" by G. Schindler, 10 *International Tax Journal* 213 (1984).

"Puerto Rico: Improving Child Support Obligations" by P. Silva-Ruiz, 26 *Journal of Family Law* 169 (1987–88).

"Puerto Rico's Dealer's Act: Fourteen Years Later" by S. Antonetti, 83 *Commercial Law Journal* 453 (1978).

"U.S. and Puerto Rican Taxation of Section 936 Corporations," 9 *International Tax Journal* 234 (1983).

CITATOR: *Shepard's Puerto Rico Citations.*

PUNISHMENT: See Corrections, Criminal Law

PUNITIVE DAMAGES: See Employment Discrimination, Insurance, Labor Law, Torts, Trial & Appellate Practice

PURCHASE MONEY MORTGAGE: See Real Estate

PURCHASING: See Government Contracts

PUTATIVE MARRIAGE: See Family Law

QATAR

SEE ALSO: International Law, Islam, Middle East, United Nations

TREATISES & LOOSELEAFS:

Commercial Laws of the Middle East (Qatar) by A. Keesee (Oceana, 1980–).

Commercial Laws of the World, Middle East States (Qatar) (FL: Foreign Tax Law Assn., 1985–).

Information Guide: Doing Business in Qatar (Price Waterhouse).

Taxes and Investment in the Middle East (Qatar) (Intl. Bureau of Fiscal Documentation).

Tax Laws of the World—Qatar (FL: Foreign Tax Law Assn.).

ARTICLES:

"Modernizing the Rules" (Qatar) by K. Whittingham, 8 *Middle East Executive Reports* 20 (Sept., 1985) (see also vol. 6, pp. 14, 17; vol. 7, pp. 14, 18; vol. 8, p. 17; vol. 9, p. 8).

"Qatar: Trademarks and Commercial Indications," 81 *Patent and Trademark Review* 372 (Sept., 1983) (see also vol. 81, pp. 326, 336, 423).

QUALIFIED PLANS: See Employee Benefits

QUARANTINE: See Health & Medicine

QUASI–CONTRACT: See Contracts, Equity

QUASI–CORPORATION: See Corporate Law

QUASI IN REM: See Trial & Appellate Practice

QUEBEC

SEE ALSO: Canada, Civil Law, International Law

"The Quebec Legal System" by J. Goulet, 73 *Law Library Journal* 354 (1980).
"Language Politics: Doing Business in Quebec" by R. McCarney, 17 *The International Lawyer* 553 (1983).
"The Legality of an Independent Quebec" by M. Thibodeau, 3 *Boston College International and Comparative Law Review* 99 (1976).

QUESTION OF LAW: See Trial & Appellate Practice
QUIET ENJOYMENT: See Real Estate
QUIET TITLE: See Real Estate
QUITCLAIM DEED: See Real Estate
QUO WARRANTO: See Trial & Appellate Practice

RACE: See Africa, Civil Rights, Constitutional Law, Employment Discrimination
RACING: See Sports Law
RACKETEERING: See Criminal Law
RADIO: See Art & Entertainment, Media Law
RADIOLOGY: See Health
RAILWAY, RAILROADS: See Labor Law, Transportation
RAIN: See Water Law
RANCH: See Agriculture, Real Estate
R&D LIMITED PARTNERSHIP: See Partnership Law
RAPE: See Criminal Law, Women & the Law
RAS AL KHAIMAH: See United Arab Emirates
RATES: See Insurance, Transportation
RATIFICATION OF CONSTITUTION: See Constitutional Law

REAL ESTATE

SEE ALSO: Agency, Antitrust Law, Architecture, Banking Law, Bankruptcy, Business Law, Community Property, Contracts, Corporate Law, Economics, Energy, Environmental Law, Equity, Estate Planning, Family Law, Franchise Law, Historic Preservation, Insurance, International Law, Landlord-Tenant, Natural Resources, Nonprofit Corporations, Oil & Gas, Partnership Law, Personal Property, Public Utilities, Sea, State & Local Government, Taxation, Torts, Water Law, Zoning & Land Planning; see also entries under individual states and countries

RESTATEMENT: *Restatement of the Law of Property* (American Law Institute, 1977).

UNIFORM & MODEL LAWS
(in *Uniform Laws Annotated*):
Model Land Sales Practices Act
Model Real Estate Cooperative Act
Model Real Estate Time-Share Act
Uniform Condominium Act
Uniform Eminent Domain Code

Uniform Land Security Interest Act
Uniform Land Transactions Act

JOURNALS, NEWSLETTERS
& OTHER PERIODICALS: *Commercial Leasing Law and Strategy* (N.Y. Law Pub. Co.).
Community Association Law Reporter (Alexandria, VA: Community Assns. Inst. 1978–).
Conveyancer and Property Lawyer (1936–).
Journal of Real Estate Taxation (Warren, Gorham & Lamont, 1963–).
Lawyers Title Guaranty Funds News (ABA).
National Property Law Digests (1975–).
Real Estate Finance Law Journal (Boston: Federal Research Press).
Real Estate Law Journal (Warren, Gorham & Lamont, 1972–).
Real Estate Review (Warren, Gorham & Lamont, 1971–).
Real Estate Syndicator (New York Law Pub. Co., 1985–).
Real Estate Tax Analyst (Boston: Federal Research Press, 1985–).
Real Estate Tax Digest (Matthew Bender, 1983–).
Real Estate Tax Planning Newsletter (Miami: Taxplan, Inc., 1981–).
Real Property, Probate and Trust Journal (ABA, 1966–).
Title News (American Land Title Assn.).

LOOSELEAFS: *Condemnation. . .* by P. Rohan (Matthew Bender, 1965– ; 1968–).
Condominium Law. . . by P. Rohan (Matthew Bender, 1965–).
Cooperative Housing Law and Practice by P. Rohan (Matthew Bender, 1967–).
Environmental Regulation of Real Property by N. Robinson (New York Law Pub. Co., 1982–).
Federal Taxation of Foreign Investment in U.S. Real Estate (Wash. D.C.: Tax Management, 1986–).
Federal Taxes Affecting Real Estate, 5th ed. by I. Faggen (Matthew Bender, 1981–).
Home Owner Associations and Planned Unit Developments by P. Rohan (Matthew Bender, 1977–).
Housing and Development Reporter (BNA, 1977–).
The Law and Business of Time-Share Resorts by M. Henze (Clark Boardman, 1982–).
The Law of Distressed Real Estate by B. Dunaway (Clark Boardman, 1985–).
The Law of Real Estate Financing by M. Madison (Warren, Gorham & Lamont, 1981–).
The Law of Real Property by R. Powell & P. Rohan (Matthew Bender, 1949–).
Modern Condominium Forms by M. Reskin (Warren, Gorham & Lamont, 1971–).
Multi-Family Housing: Federal Programs for the Private Sector by J. Jones (New York Law Pub. Co., 1986–).
Nichols on Eminent Domain, 3d ed. by J. Sackman (Matthew Bender, 1956–).
Private Real Estate Syndications by M. Constas (New York Law Pub. Co., 1983–).
Property Taxes (Prentice-Hall, 1925–).
Real Estate Coordinator (Research Institute of America).
Real Estate Financing. . . by P. Rohan (Matthew Bender, 1973–).
Real Estate Guide (Prentice-Hall, 1946–).
Real Estate Investment Planning (Prentice-Hall, 1959–).
Real Estate Review Portfolios (Warren, Gorham & Lamont).
Real Estate Tax Appeals by P. Rohan (Matthew Bender, 1984–).
Real Estate Tax Planning Forms by M. Scott (Little, Brown, 1981–).
Secondary Mortgage Market Guide by C. Edson (Matthew Bender, 1985–).
Shopping Center and Store Leases by E. Halper (Law Journal Seminars-Press, 1979–).
State Legislative Compilations. . .Real Estate Finance Laws (Wash. D.C.: Mortgage Bankers Assn. of America, 1982–).
Urban Renewal Handbook (U.S. Dept. of Housing and Urban Development, 1977–).

TREATISES:

Alternative Mortgage Instruments by P. Barnett (Warren, Gorham & Lamont, 1984).

American Law of Real Property, A. Casner, ed. (Little, Brown, 1952).

The Appraisal of Real Estate, 8th ed. (American Institute of Real Estate Appraisers, 1983).

Appraising Real Property by B. Boyce (Lexington Books).

Clark on Surveying and Boundaries, 4th ed. by J. Grimes (Michie, 1976).

Clearing Land Titles, 2d ed. by P. Bayse (West, 1970).

Commercial Real Estate Leases by M. Senn (Wiley, 1985).

Condominiums and Home Owner Associations by W. Hyatt (Shepard's, 1985).

Contracts and Conveyances in Real Property, 4th ed. by M. Friedman (Practicing Law Institute, 1984).

Fair Housing: Discrimination in Real Estate. . . by J. Kushner (Shepard's, 1983).

Handbook on the Law of Future Interests, 2d ed. by L. Sims (West, 1956).

Handling the Land Use Case by F. Schnidman (Little, Brown, 1984).

A History of the Land Law, 2d ed. by A. Simpson (Oxford Univ. Press, 1986).

Hornbook on the Law of Property by R. Cunningham (West, 1984).

Introduction to the Law of Real Property by C. Moynihan (West, 1962).

Law of Real Estate Brokers by D. Burke (Little, Brown, 1982).

Law of Real Property, 3d ed. by H. Tiffany (Callaghan, 1971).

Law of Title Insurance by D. Burke (Little, Brown, 1986).

Mobile Homes. . . (Shepard's, 1975).

Pattern Discovery: Premises Liability, 2d ed. by D. Danner (Lawyers Co-op., 1986).

Real Estate Bankruptcies and Workouts (ABA, 1983).

Real Estate Finance Law by G. Osborne (West, 1979).

Real Estate Law Locator (R.R. Bowker, 1988).

Real Estate Limited Partnerships, 2d ed. by T. Lynn (Wiley, 1983).

Real Estate Syndication by S. Jarchow (Wiley, 1985).

Real Estate Transactions, 2d ed. by M. Levine (West, 1988).

Structuring Foreign Investment in U.S. Real Estate by W. Knight (Kluwer, 1981).

Yorkley's Law of Subdivisions, 2d ed. (Michie, 1981).

REALISM: See Jurisprudence

REAL PARTY IN INTEREST: See Trial & Appellate Practice

REAL PROPERTY: See Estate Planning, Environmental Law, Real Estate

REASONABLE: See Contracts, Torts

REASONABLE DOUBT: See Criminal Law

REASONING: See Jurisprudence

REBUTTAL: See Trial & Appellate Practice

RECALL: See Food

RECALL (ELECTIONS): See State & Local Government

RECEIVER: See Bankruptcy, Real Estate

RECEIVING STOLEN PROPERTY: See Criminal Law

RECIDIVISM: See Corrections, Criminal Law

RECKLESS DRIVING: See Criminal Law

RECONSTRUCTION: See Torts

RECORDING: See Art & Entertainment, Real Estate

RECORDS: See Estate Planning, Health & Medicine, Judicial Administration, Trial & Appellate Practice

RECOVERY: See Health & Medicine, Mental Health, Torts, Trial & Appellate Practice

RECREATION: See Art & Entertainment, Sports Law, Torts

REDEMPTION: See Corporate Law, Securities Law

REFERENDUM: See Election, State & Local Government

REFERRAL SERVICE: See Professional Responsibility
REFORMATION: See Contracts, Equity, Real Estate
REFORMATORIES: See Corrections, Criminal Law, Juvenile Law
REFUGEE: See Immigration Law, International Law
REGIONAL PLANNING: See State & Local Government, Zoning & Land Planning
REGISTER OF DEEDS: See Real Estate
REGISTRATION: See Securities Law
REGULATION: See Administrative Law, State & Local Government
REHABILITATION: See Juvenile Law, Handicapped & the Law, Mental Health
REINSURANCE: See Insurance Law
RELATIVES: See Estate Planning, Family Law
RELEASE: See Estate Planning, Real Estate, Torts, Trial & Appellate Practice
RELIANCE: See Contracts, Torts
RELIGION: See Canon Law, Church & State, Constitutional Law, Israel
REMAINDERS: See Estate Planning, Real Estate
REMARRIAGE: See Family Law
REMEDIES: See Contracts, Equity, Estate Planning, Trial & Appellate Practice
REMITTITUR: See Trial & Appellate Practice
REMOVAL: See Employment Discrimination, Labor Law
REMOVAL OF CASE: See Trial & Appellate Practice
RENDITION: See Criminal Law
RENT: See Landlord-Tenant, Real Estate
REORGANIZATION: See Bankruptcy, Corporate Law
REPAIRS: See Real Estate
REPLEVIN: See Personal Property
REPORTER: See Media Law, Legal Research
REPOSSESSION: See Consumer Law, Contracts, Personal Property, Uniform
    Commercial Code
REPRESENTATION PROCEEDINGS: See Labor Law
REPRODUCTION: See Abortion, Family Law, Health & Medicine
RESCISSION: See Contracts, Equity, Real Estate
RESERVATION: See Indians, Military Law
RESETTLEMENT: See Immigration Law, International Law, Zimbabwe
RES GESTAE: See Trial & Appellate Practice
RESIDENCE: See Community Property, Estate Planning, Family Law, Real Estate, Trial
    & Appellate Practice
RESIDENTIAL AREA: See Zoning & Land Planning
RESIDUARY ESTATE: See Estate Planning, Real Estate
RES IPSA LOQUITUR: See Torts
RESORTS: See Real Estate
RESPONDEAT SUPERIOR: See Agency, Torts
RESTAURANT: See Torts
RESTITUTION: See Contracts, Criminal law, Equity, Trial & Appellate Practice
RESTRAINT ON ALIENATION: See Estate Planning, Real Estate
RESTRAINT ON TRADE: See Antitrust Law, Intellectual Property
RESTRICTIVE COVENANT: See Real Estate
RETROACTIVE LAWS: See Constitutional Law, Statutes
RESULTING TRUST: See Equity
RETAIL SERVICES: See Business Law, Labor Law
RETARDATION: See Health & Medicine, Mental Health
RETIREMENT: See Age, Civil Service, Employee Benefits
REVERSIONS: See Estate Planning, Real Estate
REVIEW: See Administrative Law, Trial & Appellate Practice

REVOCABLE TRUSTS: See Estate Planning
REVOLUTION: See Algeria, Angola, Ethiopia, Guinea, Hungary, International Law,
    Nicaragua, Sudan, United Nations

RHODE ISLAND

SEE ALSO: Circuit Courts (First Circuit)

RESEARCH GUIDE: *Legal Research in Rhode Island* (Rhode Island Law Institute, 1989).

STATUTES: *Statutory Laws of Rhode Island.*
Public Laws of Rhode Island and Providence Plantations.
Acts and Resolves of Rhode Island and Providence Plantations.

**STATE ADMINISTRATIVE
CODE:** *Compilation of Rules of State Agencies.*
G.L.42-35 *General Laws of Rhode Island.*

CASES & OPINIONS: *Rhode Island Reports* (1828–1980).
Atlantic Reporter (1885–).

**JOURNALS & OTHER
PERIODICALS:** *Rhode Island Bar Journal* (1952–).

SURVEY OF STATE LAW: "Annual Survey of Rhode Island Laws" in *Suffolk University Law Review*. See for
    example vol. 16, p. 359.

**TREATISES &
LOOSELEAFS:** *Basics in Organizing a Rhode Island Business* (Rhode Island Law Institute, 1988).
Drafting Basic Wills and Trusts (Rhode Island Law Institute, 1988).
Handling Negligence Cases (Rhode Island Law Institute, 1988).
Rhode Island Appellate Practice by Weisberger (Butterworths, 1985).
Rhode Island Will and Trust Form Manual Service by D. Riedel & R. Adams (Bank of
    New England-Old Colony, 1989).

DIGEST & CITATOR: *Rhode Island Advance Annotation Service* (Michie).
Rhode Island Digest (West).
Shepard's Rhode Island Citations.

RHODESIA: See Zimbabwe
RIGHT OF PRIVACY: See Constitutional Law, Homosexuality, Media Law, Torts
RIGHT OF WAY: See Real Estate
RIGHT TO COUNSEL: See Constitutional Law, Criminal Law, Proverty Law,
    Professional Responsibility
RIGHT TO DIE: See Death, Health & Medicine, Mental Health
RIGHT TO LIFE: See Abortion, Women & the Law
RIGHT TO WORK: See Labor Law
RIOT: See Criminal Law
RISK OF LOSS: See Insurance
RIVERS: See Environmental Law, Natural Resources, Water Law
ROAD, PRIVATE: See Real Estate
ROBBERY: See Criminal Law

ROMANIA

SEE ALSO: International Law, United Nations

RESEARCH GUIDE & BIBLIOGRAPHY: *Legal Sources and Bibliography of Romania* by V. Stoicoiu (Praeger, 1964).

CONSTITUTION: *The Constitutions of the Communist World* (Romania), W. Simons, ed. (Sijthoff & Noordhoff, 1980).

STATUTES & RELATED LAWS: *The Penal Code of the Romanian Socialist Republic,* S. Kleckner, transl. (Rothman, 1976).

TREATISES & LOOSELEAFS: *Bleak Reality: Human Rights in Romania* (NY: U.S. Helsinki Watch Committee, 1985).
A Concise History of Romanian Law by P. Goseanu (Bucharest: Scientific and Encyclopedic Pub. House, 1981).
Foreign Investments and the Taxation of Foreign Enterprises and Persons in Romania by P. Buzescu (Library of Congress, 1986).
Investment Laws of the World (Romania) (Oceana, 1981–).
Recognition and Enforcement of Foreign Judgments in Varius Foreign Countries (Romania) by C. Roman (Library of Congress, 1984).
Taxation in European Socialists Countries (vol. 5, Romania) (Amsterdam: Intl. Bureau of Fiscal Documentation).

ARTICLES: "Development of Air Law. . .in Romania" by D. Popescu, 5 *Annals of Air and Space Law* 249 (1980).
"New Trends in the Development of Constitutional Law in Romania" by M. Cismarescu, 4 *Review of Socialist Law* 100 (1978).
"Romania and International Law at the United Nations" by R. Weiner, 32 *International & Comparative Law Quarterly* 1026 (1983).
"Socialist Concepts of Sovereignty: The Case for Romania" by A. Braun, 7 *Case Western Reserve Journal of International Law* 169 (1975).
"The Supreme Control Organs in Romania" by R. Szawlowski, 10 *Review of Socialist Law* 5 (1984).

ROMAN LAW: See Legal History
ROME: See Canon Law
RULE IN SHELLEY'S CASE: See Estate Planning, Real Estate
RULEMAKING: See Administrative Law, State & Local Government, Statutes
RULES: See Circuit Courts, Trial & Appellate Practice
RULE 10b: See Securities Law
RUSSIA: See Soviet Union

RWANDA

SEE ALSO: Africa, International Law, United Nations

TREATISES & LOOSELEAFS: *Area Handbook for Rwanda* by R. Nyrop (American Univ., Foreign Area Studies, 1969).

Guide to the Text of the Criminal Law and Criminal Procedure Codes of Burundi, Rwanda, and Zaire by A. Wekerle (Library of Congress, 1975).

An Introduction to Law in French-Speaking Africa (Rwanda) by J. Salacuse (Michie, 1969).

Investment Laws of the World (Rwanda) (Oceana, 1981–).

S

SABOTAGE: See Criminal Law, Terrorism
SAFETY: See Consumer Law, Food, Occupational Safety, Torts, Transportation, Workers' Compensation
SAHARA: See Africa
SALARY: See Civil Service, Employee Benefits, Labor Law, Paralegal
SALES: See Business Law, Contracts, Real Estate, Taxation, Uniform Commercial Code
SALESMEN: See Agency, Business Law
SALES TAX: See State & Local Government, Taxation
SALVAGE: See Maritime Law
SANITARIUMS: See Health & Medicine
SANITARY DISTRICTS: See State & Local Government
SASKATCHEWAN: See Canada
SATELLITES: See Media Law, Space
SATISFACTION OF JUDGMENT: See Trial & Appellate Practice

SAUDI ARABIA

SEE ALSO: International Law, Islam, Middle East, United Nations

STATUTES & RELATED LAWS: "Saudi Arabia: Regulations Concerning Arbitration," 22 *International Legal Materials* 1052 (1983).

TREATISES & LOOSELEAFS:

Business Laws of Saudi Arabia by N. Karam (London: Graham & Trotman, 1984–).

Capital Formation and Investment Incentives Around the World (Saudi Arabia) by W. Diamond & D. Diamond (Matthew Bender, 1984–).

Commercial Laws of the Middle East by A. Keesee (Saudi Arabia) (Oceana, 1980–).

Current Aspects of Doing Business in the Middle East—Saudi Arabia, Egypt and Iran, W. Wickersham & B. Fishburne, eds. (American Bar Assn., 1977).

Doing Business in Saudi Arabia and the Gulf Arab States by N. Shilling (Dallas: Inter-Crescent, 1983–).

Information Guide: Doing Business in Saudi Arabia (Price Waterhouse).

The Laws of Saudi Arabia, the UAE, Egypt, and Jordan: A Legal and Investment Guide for American Business (Wash. D.C.: American Arab Affairs Council, 1985).

The Legal Regime of Foreign Private Investment in the Sudan and Saudi Arabia by Fath el Rahman Abdalla El Sheikh (NY: Cambridge Univ. Press, 1984).

Property Law in the Arab World: Real Rights in Egypt, Iraq, Jordan, Lebanon, Libya, Saudi Arabia and the Gulf States by F. Ziadeh (London: Graham & Trotman, 1979).

Saudi Arabia: A Country Study, 4th ed., R. Nyrop, ed. (American Univ., Foreign Area Studies; GPO, 1984).

Saudi Business and Labor Law by A. Lerrick (Graham & Trotman, 1982).

Taxes and Investment in the Middle East (Saudi Arabia) (Intl. Bureau of Fiscal Documentation).

Tax Laws of the World—Saudi Arabia (FL: Foreign Tax Law Assn.).

ARTICLES: "Aspects of Saudi Arabian Law and Practice" by J. Brand, 9 *Boston College International and Comparative Law Review* 1, 46 (1986).
"Business and Tax Planning Considerations for Investment in Saudi Arabia" by M. Ahmad, 9 *International Tax Journal* 227 (1983).
"Establishing an Enterprise in Saudi Arabia" by M. Leavitt, 3 *Houston Journal of International Law* 299 (1981).
"Legal Aspects of Doing Business in Saudi Arabia" by P. Homsy, 16 *International Lawyer* 51 (1982).
"The New Saudi Commercial Agencies Regulation" by R. Cartwright, 16 *The International Lawyer* 443 (1982).
"A Practitioner's Introduction to Saudi Arabian Law," 16 *Vanderbilt Journal of Transnational Law* 113 (1983).
"Service Agents Regulation and Related Laws Affecting Foreign Companies in Saudi Arabia" by R. Cartwright, 17 *The International Lawyer* 203 (1983).

SCANDINAVIAN LAW

SEE ALSO: Denmark, Europe, Finland, Iceland, International Law, Norway, Sweden, United Nations

RESEARCH GUIDES & BIBLIOGRAPHIES: "Academic Law Libraries in Scandinavia" by S. Nevin, 78 *Law Library Journal* 697 (1986).
"Scandinavian Legal Bibliographies" by F. Henriksen, 6 *International Journal of Law Libraries* 91 (1978).
"Scandinavian Legal Bibliography" by S. Iuul et al. (Stockholm: Almquist & Wiskill, 1961).
A Selective Survey of English Language Studies on Scandinavian Law by R. Ginsburg (Rothman, 1970).

JOURNALS & OTHER PERIODICALS: *American Scandinavian Review.*
Scandinavian Studies in Law.

DICTIONARY: *Anglo-Scandinavian Law Dictionary* by R. Anderson (Columbia Univ. Press, 1977).

TREATISES & LOOSELEAFS: *The Growth of Scandinavian Law* by L. Orfield (Univ. of Pa. Press for Temple Univ. Press, 1953).
The Nordic Parliaments: A Comparative Analysis by D. Arter (St. Martin's Press, 1984).
Proceedings of the Regional Energy Law Seminar, Oslo, Norway (Univ. of Oslo, Scandinavian Institute of Maritime Law; Intl. Bar Assn. Section on Energy and Natural Resources Law, 1984).
The Quantum of Damages under the Scandinavian Sale of Goods Act by K. Rodhe (Stockholm: Almqvist & Wiksell, 1966).
Tax and Trade Guide: Scandinavia (Arthur Anderson & Co., 1979).

ARTICLES: "Computer-Assisted Crime in Scandinavia" by S. Schjolberg, 2 *Computer/Law Journal* 457 (1980).

"International Bankruptcy Law in Scandinavia" by M. Bogan, 34 *International and Comparative Law Quarterly* 49 (1985).

"Inter-Nordic Legislative Co-operation" by W. von Eyben, 6 *Scandinavian Studies in Law* 63 (1962).

"Transnational Data Flows and the Scandinavian Data Protection Legislation" by J. Bing, 24 *Scandinavian Studies in Law* 65 (1980).

SCHOLARSHIP: See Education Law, Taxation
SCHOOL INTEGRATION: See Constitutional Law, Education Law
SCHOOLS: See Church & State, Civil Rights, Education Law, State & Local Government
SCIENCE: See Forensic Science, Health & Medicine, Intellectual Property, Jurisprudence
SCIENTER: See Torts
SCIENTIFIC EVIDENCE: See Torts, Trial & Appellate Practice
SCOPE OF EMPLOYMENT: See Agency, Business Law, Torts, Workers' Compensation
S CORPORATION: See Corporate Law, Securities Law, Taxation

SCOTLAND

SEE ALSO:

England, International Law, United Nations

JOURNALS & OTHER PERIODICALS:

Journal of the Law Society of Scotland.
Juridical Review.

TREATISES & LOOSELEAFS:

Admissibility of Illegally Obtained Evidence: Comparative Analysis of the Laws of England, Scotland, Ireland, Canada, Australia and New Zealand (Library of Congress, 1981).

The Law of Contracts and Related Obligations in Scotland by D. Walker (Butterworths, 1980).

The Law of Delict in Scotland, 2d ed. by D. Walker (Edinburgh: W. Green & Sons, 1981).

The Law of Husband and Wife in Scotland, 2d ed. by E. Clive (Edinburgh: W. Green & Sons, 1982).

The Legal Systems of Britain (Scotland) (London: Her Majesty's Stationery Office, 1976).

Principles of Scottish Private Law by D. Walker (Oxford Univ. Press, 1983).

Professional Ethics and Practice for Scottish Solicitors by R. & J. Webster (Edinburgh: Law Society of Scotland, 1984).

Report on Bankruptcy and Related Aspects of Insolvency and Liquidation by the Scottish Law Commn. (Edinburgh: H.M.S.O., 1982).

"Scotland: The Reform Process Continues" by E. Sutherland, 26 *Journal of Family Law* 175 (1987–88). See also 25 *Journal of Family Law* 211 (1986–87).

Scots Mercantile Law by E. Marshall (Edinburgh: W. Green & Sons, 1983).

The Scottish Legal System, 5th ed. by D. Walker (Edinburgh: W. Green & Sons, 1981).

The Treaty of Union of Scotland and England, G. Pryde, ed. (Nelson, 1950; Greenwood Press, 1979).

ARTICLES:

"Receiving and Receivers in Scotland" by J. Mack, 11 *International Journal of the Sociology of Law* 241 (1983).

"Scotland: Legal Education" by W. Balekjian, 5 *Comparative Law Yearbook* 123 (1981).

SEA, LAW OF THE

SEE ALSO: Air & Aviation, Antarctica, Business Law, Commodities, Energy, Environmental Law, Insurance, International Law, Maritime Law, Military Law, Natural Resources, Oil & Gas, Public Utilities, Transportation, United Nations, Water Law

RESEARCH GUIDES &
BIBLIOGRAPHIES:
International Law of the Sea: A Bibliography by N. Papadakis (Martinus Nijhoff; Kluwer, 1980).
Law of the Sea: A Select Bibliography by the Office of the Special Representative of the General-Assembly for the Law of the Sea (UN Pubs., 1987).
Marine Affairs Bibliography (Halifax: Dalhousie Law School, 1980–).
The New Law of the Sea: A Bibliography by B. Kudej (Oceana, 1984).
Ocean Law: A Bibliography with Abstracts (Springfield: Natl. Technical Information Service, 1975–).
"Researching the Law of the Sea" by T. McDorman, 10 *International Journal of Legal Information* 147 (1983).
The World Oceans: A Selected Bibliography of Social and Natural Sciences by P. Huang (Halifax: Dalhousie Law School, 1985).

TREATIES, CONVENTIONS
& OTHER AGREEMENTS:
The Law of the Sea: Multilateral Treaties Relevant to the United Nations Convention on the Law of the Sea (UN Pubs., 1985).
The Law of the Sea: Status of the United Nations Convention on the Law of the Sea (Office of the Special Representative of the Secretary-General for the Law of the Sea, 1985).
Third United Nations Conference on the Law of the Sea: Documents (Oceana, 1982).
The UN Convention of the Law of the Sea, K. Simmonds, ed. (Oceana, 1983).
United Nations Convention on the Law of the Sea (UN Publications).

CASES & STATUTES:
Cases on Law of the Sea, K. Simmonds, ed. (Oceana, 1976–).
The Law of the Sea, National Legislation on the Exclusive Economic Zone, the Economic Zone and the Exclusive Fishery Zone (Office of the Special Representative of the Secretary-General for the Law of the Sea, 1986).

JOURNALS & OTHER
PERIODICALS:
New York Sea Grant Law and Policy Journal (NY Sea Grant Institute, 1976–).
Ocean Development and International Law: The Journal of Marine Affairs (Crane Russak, 1973–).
Ocean Management (1973–).
Ocean Yearbook (Univ. of Chicago Press).
Sijthoff Publications on Ocean Development (Sijthoff & Noordhoff, 1977–).

LOOSELEAFS:
The Eastern European States and the Development of the Law of the Sea by V. Sebek (Oceana, 1977–).
Latin America and the Development of the Law of the Sea by A. Szekely (Oceana, 1976–).
New Directions in the Law of the Sea by K. Simmonds (Oceana, 1983–).
North America and Asia Pacific and the Development of the Law of the Sea by M. Nordquist (Oceana, 1980–).
Ocean Development and International Law (NY: Crane, Russak & Co., 1973–).
The USSR, Eastern Europe and the Development of the Law of the Sea by W. Butler (Oceana, 1983–).

Western Europe and the Development of the Law of the Sea by F. Durante (Oceana, 1980–).

TREATISES:

Africa and the International Law of the Sea by N. Rembe (Sijthoff, 1980).
Arrest of Ships by C. Hill et al. (Lloyd's of London Press, 1985).
Canada and the New Law of the Sea by D. Johnston (Univ. of Toronto Press, 1985).
Deep Sea Mining and the Law of the Sea by A. Post (Martinus Nijhoff, 1983).
The Denuclearization of the Oceans (St. Martin's Press, 1986).
East Asia and the Law of the Sea by Choon-ho Park (Seoul Natl. Univ. Press, 1983).
International Regulation of Whaling, P. Birnie, ed. (Oceana, 1985).
Land-Locked States and the UNCLOS Regime by A. Sinjela (Oceana, 1983).
The Lawfulness of Deep Seabed Mining by T. Kronmiller (Oceana, 1980).
The Law of the Sea and International Shipping: Anglo-Soviet Post-UNCLOS Perspectives, W. Butler, ed. (Oceana, 1985).
The Law of the Sea in a Nutshell by L. John (West, 1984).
Marine Pollution and the Law of the Sea by J. Kindt (Hein, 1986).
Negotiating the Law of the Sea by J. Sebenius (Harvard Univ. Press, 1984).
Ocean Uses and Their Regulation by L. Cuyvers (Wiley, 1984).
The Public Order of the Oceans: A Contemporary International Law of the Sea by M. McDougal (New Haven Press, 1986).
The System for Settlement of Disputes under the United Nations Convention on the Law of the Sea by A. Adede (Martinus Nijhoff, 1986).

ENCYCLOPEDIAS:

AMERICAN JURISPRUDENCE 2D (Am Jur 2d)
Check the following topics in the *General Index* volumes for Am Jur 2d:

Continental Shelf	Oceans
Convention on Territorial	Ships and Shipping
Sea and Contiguous	Waters
Zone	

CORPUS JURIS SECUNDUM (CJS)
Check the following topics in the *General Index* volumes for CJS:

Oceans	Shipping
Seamen	Waters

DIGESTS:

CASE SEARCH IN WEST DIGESTS BY KEY TOPIC
In the *Descriptive Word Index* of the West digests, look for key topics and numbers under the following subject headings:

Oceans	Waters
Seamen	

ALR:

ANNOTATIONS
Check the index volumes for ALR, ALR2d, ALR3d, ALR4th, and ALR Fed for annotations under the following subject headings:

High Seas	Territorial Waters
Navigable Waters	Waters and Watercourses

PERIODICALS:

CURRENT LAW INDEX (CLI) & LEGAL RESOURCE INDEX (LRI)
In the CLI and LRI, look for references to periodical literature under the following subject headings:

Freedom of the Seas	Oceanographic Research
Marine Biology	Seamen
Marine Pollution	United Nations
Maritime Law	Conference/Convention
Ocean	on the Law of the Sea
Ocean Mining	

INDEX TO LEGAL PERIODICALS (ILP)
In the ILP, look for references to legal periodical literature under the following subject headings:

Merchant Marine	Territorial Waters
Seamen	Water and Watercourses

SEAMAN: See Maritime Law, Sea
SEARCH & SEIZURE: See Constitutional Law, Criminal Law, Customs, Immigration Law
SECONDARY EDUCATION: See Education Law
SECONDARY MORTGAGE: See Real Estate
SECOND CIRCUIT: See Circuit Courts
SECRETARIAT: See International Law, United Nations
SECRETARY: See Law Office Mangement, Paralegal
SECRETARY–GENERAL: See United Nations
SECRETARY OF THE AIR FORCE: See Military Law
SECRETARY OF THE ARMY: See Military Law
SECRETARY OF THE INTERIOR: See Natural Resources
SECRETARY OF THE NAVY: See Military Law
SECURED TRANSACTIONS: See Banking Law, Bankruptcy, Consumer Law,
     Contracts, Securities Law, Uniform Commercial Code
SECURITIES & EXCHANGE COMMISSION (SEC): See Accounting, Securities Law

SECURITIES LAW

SEE ALSO:
Accounting, Administrative Law, Agents, Agriculture, Antitrust Law, Banking Law, Business Law, Commodities, Corporate Law, Criminal Law, Franchise Law, International Law, Oil & Gas, Partnership Law, Personal Property, Public Utilities, State & Local Government, Taxation, Uniform Commercial Code

RESEARCH GUIDES & BIBLIOGRAPHIES:
"Bibliographic Overview of Securities Materials" by D. McFadden, 1 *Legal Reference Services Quarterly* 11 (1981).
Legal Bibliography on Federal Securities Regulation (SEC Library, 1963).
"Research in Securities Regulation: Access to the Sources of the Law" by M. Sargent & E. Greenberg, 75 *Law Library Journal* 98 (1982) (see also vol. 79, p. 255).
"Securities Regulation" by K. Todd in *Specialized Legal Research,* L. Chanin, ed. (Little, Brown, 1987).

STATUTES:
Investment Advisers Act of 1940.
Investment Company Act of 1940.
Public Utility Holding Company Act of 1935.
Securities Act of 1933.
Securities Exchange Act of 1934.
Trust Indenture Act of 1939.

LEGISLATIVE HISTORY:
Federal Securities Laws: Legislative History, 1933–1982 (BNA, 1983).
Legislative History of the Securities Act of 1933 and Securities Exchange Act of 1934 (Rothman, 1973).

ADMINISTRATIVE DECISIONS & REGULATIONS (govt. publications):
Decisions and Reports, Securities and Exchange Commission (1934–).

Index to Commission Decisions, Securities and Exchange Commission (1967–).
Code of Federal Regulations, title 17.

OTHER GOVERNMENT
MATERIALS:
Directory of Company Filing Annual Reports Under the Securities Exchange Act of 1934 (GPO).
List of Companies Registered Under the Investment Company Act of 1940 (SEC).
SEC Docket (GPO).
SEC News Digest (GPO).
SEC Monthly Statistical Review (GPO).

JOURNALS, NEWSLETTERS
& INSTITUTES:
Annual Institute on Securities Regulation (Practicing Law Institute).
Journal of Comparative Corporate Law and Securities Regulation (Amsterdam: North-Holland Pub., 1977–).
New York University Institute on Securities Law and Regulations (Matthew Bender, 1977–).
Review of Securities Regulation (Standard & Poors).
SEC Accounting Report (Warren, Gorham & Lamont).
Securities and Federal Corporate Law Report by H. Bloomenthal (Clark Boardman).
Securities Law Review (Clark Boardman, 1969–).
Securities Regulation Law Alert (Warren, Gorham & Lamont).
Securities Regulation Law Journal (Warren, Gorham & Lamont, 1973–).
Securities Regulation Series (Cong. Info. Service, 1984–).
Securities Week (McGraw-Hill).

LOOSELEAFS:
Accountants SEC Practice Manual by M. Poloway & D. Charles (CCH, 1976–).
Acquisitions and Mergers: Negotiated and Contested Transactions by S. Lorne (Clark Boardman).
American Stock Exchange Company Guide (Amer. Stock Exchange, 1983–).
American Stock Exchange Guide (CCH, 1960–).
Appeal Securities Act Handbook, 5th ed. (NY: Appeal Printing Co., 1981–).
Blue Sky Law Reports (CCH, 1928–).
Blue Sky Regulations by H. Sowards & N. Hirsch (Matthew Bender, 1977–).
Boston Stock Exchange Guide (CCH, 1970–).
Capital Adjustments (Prentice-Hall, 1940–).
Capital Changes Reporter (CCH, 1928–).
Corporate Regulation of Securities (vol. 2. of Corporate Planning) (Institute for Business Planning).
Executive Disclosure Guide—SEC Compliance (CCH, 1976–).
Exempted Transactions under the Securities Act of 1933 by W. Hicks (Clark Boardman, 1979–).
Federal Securities Act—Analysis, Procedures and Forms by H. Sowards (Matthew Bender, 1965–).
The Federal Securities Code and Corporate Disclosure by W. Painter (Michie, 1979–).
Federal Securities Exchange Act of 1934 by E. Gadsby (Matthew Bender, 1971–).
Federal Securities Law Reporter (CCH, 1933–).
Federal Securities Laws—Regulations—Forms (CCH, 1979–).
Going Private by A. Borden (Law Journal Seminars-Press, 1982–).
A Guide to Municipal Official Statements by J. Daley (Law & Business, Inc., 1980–).
International Capital Markets and Securities Regulation by H. Bloomenthal (Clark Boardman, 1982–).
Litigation and Practice Under Rule 10b-5, 2d ed. by A. Jacobs (Clark Boardman, 1981–).
Manual of Corporate Forms for Securities Practice by A. Jacobs (Clark Boardman, 1981–).

Municipal Securities Rulemaking Board Manual (CCH, 1977–).
Mutual Funds Guide (CCH, 1969–).
NASD Manual (CCH, 1967–).
New York Stock Exchange Guide (CCH, 1957–).
Opinion Letters in Securities Matters by A. Jacobs (Clark Boardman, 1980–).
Raising Capital: Private Placement Forms & Techniques by R. Frome & H. Max (Law & Business, Inc., 1981–).
SEC Accounting and Reporting Manual by W. Badecker & R. Harnek (Warren, Gorham and Lamont, 1983–).
SEC Accounting Rules (CCH, 1968–).
SEC Compliance—Financial Reporting and Forms by S. Weinstein et al. (Prentice-Hall, 1979–).
SEC Financial Reporting, Annual Reports to Shareholders, Form 10—K, Quarterly Financial Reporting, 2d ed. by D. Beresford et al. (Matthew Bender, 1983–).
SEC No-Action Letters Index and Summaries (Wash. Service Bureau, 1971–).
Securities and Federal Corporate Law by H. Bloomenthal (Clark Boardman, 1971–).
Securities Credit Transactions Handbook (Federal Reserve System, Board of Governors, 1981–).
Securities Fraud and Commodities Fraud by A. Bromberg & L. Lowenfels (Shepard's, 1967–).
Securities Law Series (Clark Boardman).
Securities: Liabilities and Remedies by M. Steinberg (Law Journal Seminars-Press, 1984–).
Securities: Public and Private Offerings by W. Prifti (Callaghan, 1983–).
Securities Regulation (Prentice-Hall, 1935–).
Securities Regulation & Law Report (BNA, 1969–).
Securities Regulation Forms by R. Shapiro et al. (Clark Boardman, 1975–).
Securities Regulation Guide (Prentice-Hall, 1935–).
Significant SEC Filings Reporter (Wash. Service Bureau, 1980–).
Takeovers and Freezeouts by M. Lipton & E. Steinberger (Law Journal Seminars-Press).
Taxation of Securities Transactions by M. Fried (Matthew Bender, 1971–).
The Transfer of Stock, 5th ed. by F. Christy (Lawyers Co-op., 1972–).
Venture Capital and Public Offering Negotiation, M. Halloran, ed. (Law & Business, Inc., 1983–).
Venture Capital and Small Business Financing by R. Haft (Clark Boardman, 1984–).

TREATISES:

Blue Sky Law by J. Long (Clark Boardman, 1985).
Blue Sky Practice for Public and Private Limited Offerings by P. Fass (Clark Boardman, 1986).
The Deregulation of the Banking and Securities Industries, L. Goldberg & L. White, eds. (D.C. Heath, 1979).
Federal Securities Code (American Law Institute, 1980).
Fundamentals of Securities Regulation by L. Loss (Little, Brown, 1983).
International Securities Regulation by R. Rosen (Oceana).
Key SEC No-Action Letters by R. Haft (Clark Boardman, 1984).
A Lawyer's Basic Guide to Secured Transactions by D. Baker (ALI–ABA Comm. on Cont. Prof. Ed., 1983).
New Dimensions in Securities Litigation (ALI–ABA Comm. on Cont. Prof. Ed., 1985).
The New Wrinkles in Corporate Financing Products (Law & Business, Inc., 1985).
Securities Enforcement Institute (Practicing Law Institute, 1986).
Securities Practice. . .Federal and State Enforcement by M. Steinberg & R. Ferrara (Callaghan, 1985).
Securities Regulation in a Nutshell, 2d ed. by D. Ratner (West, 1982).
Securities Regulation, Practitioner's Edition by T. Hazen (West).

ENCYCLOPEDIAS: AMERICAN JURISPRUDENCE 2D (Am Jur 2d)
Check the following topics in the *General Index* volumes for Am Jur 2d:

Administrative Law	Joint Stock Companies
Brokers	Margin Transactions
Corporations	Public Securities and
Fraud	Obligations
Fraudulent Conveyances	Secured Transactions
Investment Companies	Securities Regulation
and Advisors	Stock and Commodities
Investments	Exchanges
Investment Securities	

CORPUS JURIS SECUNDUM (CJS)
Check the following topics in the *General Index* volumes for CJS:

Administrative Bodies	Joint Stock Companies
Brokers	Secured Transactions
Contracts	Securities and Exchange
Corporations	Commission
Fraud	Stock and Stockholders
Investments	Stock Exchange

DIGESTS: CASE SEARCH IN WEST DIGESTS BY KEY TOPIC
In the *Descriptive Word Index* of the West digests, look for key topics and numbers under the following subject headings:

Administrative Law	Joint Stock Companies
Brokers	Licenses
Contracts	Secured Transactions
Corporations	Securities Regulation
Exchanges	Stock and Stockholders
Fraud	Stock Exchange
Investments	

ALR: ANNOTATIONS
Check the index volumes for ALR, ALR2d, ALR3d, ALR4th, and ALR Fed for annotations under the following subject headings:

Administrative Law	Investment Companies
Bonds (Securities)	and Advisors
Brokers	Investments
Corporate Stock and	Investments Securities
Stockholders	Securities
Fraud	Stockholders

PERIODICALS: CURRENT LAW INDEX (CLI) & LEGAL RESOURCE INDEX (LRI)
In the CLI and LRI, look for references to preriodical literature under the following subject headings:

Administrative Law	Securities
Disclosure of Information	Stock Companies
(Securities Law)	Stock Exchange
Going Public	Stockholders
Insider Trading	Stocks
Investments	Taxation of Bonds,
Money Market Funds	Securities, etc.
Preferred Stocks	Tender Offers
Redemption (Law)	United States Securities and
Restricted Stock Options	Exchange Commission

INDEX TO LEGAL PERIODICALS (ILP)
In the ILP, look for references to legal periodical literature under the following subject headings:

Administrative Law	Investment
Agency	Public Finance
Bonds	Securities
Capital Gains Tax	Stock Companies
Fraud	Stock Exchanges
Holding Companies	Stocks

SECURITY: See Banking Law, Bankruptcy, Real Estate
SECURITY INTERESTS: See Personal Property, Uniform Commercial Code
SEDITION: See Criminal Law
SEDUCTION: See Criminal Law, Family Law
SEGREGATION: See Civil Rights, Constitutional Law, Sports Law
SEIZIN: See Real Estate
SELF–DEFENSE: See Criminal Law, Torts, Women & the Law
SELF–DETERMINATION: See International Law
SELF–INCRIMINATION: See Constitutional Law, Criminal Law, Trial & Appellate
    Practice
SELF–INSURANCE: See Insurance, Workers' Compensation
SENATE: See Legislative History

SENEGAL

SEE ALSO: Africa, International Law, Islam, United Nations

**TREATIES & OTHER
AGREEMENTS:**   "Gambia-Senegal: Agreement and Protocols Concerning the Establishment of a
                    Senegambian Confederation," 22 *International Legal Materials* 260 (1983) (see
                    also vol. 21, p. 44).

CONSTITUTION: *Constitutions of the Countries of the World* (Senegal) by A. Blaustein & G. Flanz
                    (Oceana, 1983).

**TREATISES &
LOOSELEAFS:**   *African Tax Systems* by R. Hammond & M. van den Abeelen (Senegal) (Amsterdam:
                    Intl. Bureau of Fiscal Documentation, 1980–).
                    An Introduction to Law in French-Speaking Africa (Senegal) by J. Salacuse (Michie,
                    1969).

ARTICLES: "Africa's Shared Water Resources: Legal and Institutional Aspects of the Nile, Niger
                    and Senegal River Systems" by G. Badr, 80 *American Journal of International
                    Law* 423 (1986).
                    "Legal Paradigm and Legal Discourse" by E. Le Roy, 12 *International Journal of the
                    Sociology of Law* 1 (1984).
                    "Senegambian Confederation" by P. Coppa, 11 *New York Law School of International
                    & Comparative Law* 44 (1986).

SENIORITY: See Civil Service, Labor Law
SENTENCING: See Corrections, Criminal Law

SEPARATE PROPERTY: See Community Property, Family Law
SEPARATION: See Family Law
SEPARATION OF POWERS: See Constitutional Law
SEQUESTRATION: See Trial & Appellate Practice
SEROLOGY: See Forensic Science
SERVICEMEN: See Military Law
SERVICE OF PROCESS: See Trial & Appellate Practice
SERVICES: See Military Law
SERVITUDE: See Real Estate
SET-OFF: See Trial & Appellate Practice
SETTLEMENT: See Family Law, Mediation, Trial & Appellate Practice
SEVENTH CIRCUIT: See Circuit Courts
SEVERANCE PAY: See Employee Benefits, Labor Law
SEWAGE: See Environmental Law, Natural Resources
SEWER: See State & Local Government
SEX: See Abortion, Family Law, Homosexuality, Juvenile Law, Women & the Law
SEX CRIMES: See Criminal Law, Women & the Law
SEX DISCRIMINATION: See Civil Rights, Constitutional Law, Employment
    Discrimination, Women & the Law
SEXUAL HARASSMENT: See Women & the Law
SEXUAL ORIENTATION: See Homosexuality

SEYCHELLES

SEE ALSO: Africa, International Law, United Nations

CONSTITUTION: *Constitutions of the Countries of the World* (Seychelles) by A. Blaustein & G. Flanz
            (Oceana, 1983).

**TREATISES &
LOOSELEAFS:**   *Indian Ocean: Five Island Countries* (Seychelles) (GPO, 1982).
            Investment Laws of the World (Seychelles) (Oceana, 1981–).
            The Seychelles: Unquiet Islands by M. Franda (Westview, 1982).
            Tax Laws of the World—Seychelles (FL: Foreign Tax Law Assn.).

ARTICLES: "How Successful are Devolution Agreements: The Seychelles Experience" by I. Kawaley,
            35 *International & Comparative Law Quarterly* 717 (1986).

SHELLEY'S CASE: See Estate Planning, Real Estate
SHELTERS: See Poverty Law, Real Estate, Taxation
SHERIFF: See Criminal Law, State & Local Government
SHERIFF DEED: See Real Estate
SHIPPING: See International Law, Maritime Law, Sea, Transportation
SHOPPING CENTER: See Landlord-Tenant, Real Estate, Torts
SHOW CAUSE ORDER: See Trial & Appellate Practice
SICK LEAVE: See Employee Benefits
SICKNESS: See Death, Health & Medicine, Mental Health, Occupational Safety,
    Workers' Compensation
SIDEWALK: See State & Local Government, Torts
SIERRA CLUB: See Environmental Law
SIMULTANEOUS DEATH: See Estate Planning

SINGAPORE

SEE ALSO: Asia, International Law, United Nations

RESEARCH GUIDE &
BIBLIOGRAPHY: "Current Legal Research in Singapore" by K. Lian, 7 *International Journal of Law Libraries* 241 (1979).

CONSTITUTION: *Constitutions of the Countries of the World* (Singapore) by A. Blaustein & G. Flanz (Oceana, 1981).

DIRECTORY: *The Legal Profession Directory in Singapore,* C. Kian, ed. (Singapore: Carlton, 1984–).

TREATISES &
LOOSELEAFS: *Asia and the Pacific: A Tax Tour* (Singapore) (Arthur Anderson & Co., 1986).
Bankruptcy: The Law and Practice by C. Kian (Butterworths, 1984).
Business Operations in Singapore by B. Soin, Tax Managment Foreign Income Portfolios, no. 458 (BNA, 1987).
Capital Formation and Investment Incentives Around the World (Singapore) by W. Diamond & D. Diamond (Matthew Bender, 1984–).
Commercial Law of Singapore by W. Woon (Dover, NH: Woodhead-Faulkner, 1986).
Digest of Commercial Laws of the World (Singapore) (Natl. Assn. of Credit Management; Oceana, 1977–).
Financial Structure and International Banking in Singapore by R. Bryant (Brookings Institution, 1985).
A Guide to Doing Business in the ASEAN Region: Brunei/Indonesia/Malaysia/ Philippines/Singapore/Thailand (U.S. Dept. of Commerce, Intl. Trade Admin., Office of Pacific Basin, 1985).
Handbook of Singapore Tax Statutes by P. Hong & L. van Hien (Butterworths, 1983).
Information Guide: Doing Business in Singapore (Price Waterhouse).
Investment Laws of the World (Singapore) (Oceana, 1981–).
Land Law by W. Ricquier (Butterworths, 1985).
Law of Compulsory Purchase and Compensation: Singapore and Malaysia by N. Khublass (Butterworths, 1984).
The Law of Contract in Malaysia and Singapore by V. Sinnardurai (Oxford Univ. Press, 1980).
The Law of Copyright in Singapore by G. Wei (Singapore: Natl. Printers, 1989).
Singapore Master Tax Guide, 6th ed. by B. Soin (CCH, Australia, 1985).
Taxes and Investment in Asia and the Pacific (Singapore) (Amsterdam: Intl. Bureau of Fiscal Documentation, 1983–).
Tax Laws of the World—Singapore (FL: Foreign Tax Law Assn.).

ARTICLES: "A Favorable Climate for Foreign Investment in Singapore" by S. Zwart, 21 *International Lawyer* 357 (1987).
"The Intoxicated Offender under Singapore Law" by M. Cheang, 35 *International & Comparative Law Quarterly* 106 (1986).
"Legal Considerations for Structuring a Business" by C. Angus, 7 *East Asian Executive Reports* 24 (Oct. 15, 1985) (see also vol. 5, p. 23; vol. 7, p. 20; vol. 8, p. 18).
"Singapore: Some Recent Developments in Maritime and Admiralty Law" by G. Selvam, 1985 *Lloyd's Maritime and Commercial Law Quarterly* 209.
"Tax Planning for Investment in Singapore" by G. Clark, 9 *International Tax Journal* 339 (1983).

SINO–SOVIET RELATIONS: See China
SISTERS: See Estate Planning, Family Law
SIXTH CIRCUIT: See Circuit Courts
SLANDER: See Media Law, Torts
SLAVERY: See Africa, Civil Rights
SLUM CLEARANCE: See Zoning & Land Planning
SMALL BUSINESS: See Business Law
SMALL CLAIMS COURT: See Consumer Law, Trial & Appellate Practice
SMOKING: See Agriculture, Environmental Law, Torts
SMUGGLING: See Criminal Law, Customs
SOCCER: See Art & Entertainment, Sports Law
SOCIALISM: See Communism, Jurisprudence
SOCIAL SCIENCES: See International Law, Jurisprudence

SOCIAL SECURITY

SEE ALSO:

Administrative Law, Age, Civil Service, Employee Benefits, Estate Planning, Health & Medicine, Insurance, Labor Law, Nursing, Poverty Law, State & Local Government, Unemployment Compensation

STATUTES, REGULATIONS & RULINGS (govt. publications):

Social Security Act, 42 U.S.C. 401ff., 1301ff., 1381ff.
1 CFR 305.78–2; 20 CFR 401ff.; 42 CFR 400ff.
Cumulative Bulletin (Social Security Admin., 1960–).
Social Security Rulings on Federal Old Age, Survivors, Disability, Supplemental Security Income and Miners Benefits (Social Security Administration, 1960–).

JOURNALS, NEWSLETTERS & OTHER PERIODICALS:

Social Security News (West, 1986–).
Social Security Practice Advisory (Lawyers Co-op., 1987–).
West's Social Security News (West, 1985–).

LOOSELEAFS:

Medicare-Medicaid Guide (CCH, 1969–).
Social Security Disability Claims by R. Gilbert (Lawyers Co-op., 1983–).
Social Security Disability Claims Practice and Procedure by R. Francis (Callaghan, 1983–).
Social Security Practice Guide by the Natl. Organization of Social Security Claimant's Representatives (Matthew Bender, 1984–).
Unemployment Insurance Reporter: Federal Social Security and Medicare Taxes (Prentice-Hall, 1983–).
Unemployment Insurance Reports with Social Security (CCH, 1934–).
West's Social Security Reporting Service (West, 1983–).

TREATISES:

Attorney's Guide to Social Security Disability Claims by K. Laritz (Shepard's, 1986).
Federal Disability Law and Practice by F. Bloch (Wiley).
Medicare and Medicaid Claims and Procedures by H. McCormick (West, 1977).
Social Security Claims and Procedures, 3d ed. by H. McCormick (West).
Social Security Handbook, 8th ed. (Social Security Admin., 1984).
Social Security Law & Practice (Lawyers Co-op.).
Trial of a Social Security Disability Case by M. Schwartz (New Platz, NY: The Social Security Disability Foundation, 1983).

ENCYCLOPEDIAS: AMERICAN JURISPRUDENCE 2D (Am Jur 2d)
Check the following topics in the *General Index* volumes for Am Jur 2d:

Administrative Law	Unemployment Insurance
Social Security and Medicare	Welfare and Welfare Laws

CORPUS JURIS SECUNDUM (CJS)
Check the following topics in the *General Index* volumes for CJS:

Administrative Bodies	Unemployment
Social Security and Public Welfare	Compensation

DIGESTS: CASE SEARCH IN WEST DIGESTS BY KEY TOPIC
In the *Descriptive Word Index* of the West digests, look for key topics and numbers under the following subject headings:

Administrative Law	Workers' Compensation
Social Security and Public Welfare	

ALR: ANNOTATIONS
Check the index volumes for ALR, ALR2d, ALR3d, ALR4th, and ALR Fed for annotations under the following subject headings:

Administrative Law	Social Security
Disability	Unemployment Compensation

PERIODICALS: CURRENT LAW INDEX (CLI) & LEGAL RESOURCE INDEX (LRI)
In the CLI and LRI, look for references to periodical literature under the following subject headings:

Administrative Law	Social Security
Aid to Families with Dependent Children	Supplemental Security Income
Insurance, Unemployment	United States Social Security Administration
Medicaid	
Medicare	

INDEX TO LEGAL PERIODICALS (ILP)
In the ILP, look for references to legal periodical literature under the following subject headings:

Administrative Law	Old Age Insurance
Annuities	Poverty Law
Federal Aid	Social Security
Medicaid	Unemployment Insurance

SOCIAL WELFARE LAW: See Poverty Law, Social Security, State & Local Government
SOCIAL WORKERS: See Education Law, Health & Medicine, Mental Health
SOCIOBIOLOGY: See Health & Medicine
SOCIOLOGY: See Jurisprudence
SODOMY: See Criminal Law, Homosexuality
SOFTWARE: See Computers, Intellectual Property, Law Office Management
SOLAR ENERGY: See Energy, Natural Resources
SOLDIERS: See Military Law, War
SOLICITATION: See Criminal Law, Nonprofit Corporations

SOLICITORS: See England, Professional Responsibility
SOLID WASTE: See Environmental Law

SOLOMON ISLANDS

SEE ALSO: England, International Law, United Nations

Information Guide: Doing Business in Solomon Islands (Price Waterhouse).
Investment in Soloman Islands 2d ed. (Sydney: Peat, Marwick, Mitchell & Co.,1985).
Taxes and Investment in Asia and the Pacific (Solomon Islands) (Amsterdam: Intl.
      Bureau of Fiscal Documentation, 1983–).

SOMALIA

SEE ALSO: Africa, Communism, International Law, Islam, United Nations

**RESEARCH GUIDE &
BIBLIOGRAPHY:**   *Somalia: A Bibliographical Survey,* "Law," p. 360 by M. Salad (Greenwood Press, 1977).

CONSTITUTION: *Constitutions of the Countries of the World* (Somalia) by A. Blaustein & G. Flanz
      (Oceana, 1982).
      "The 1979 Somali Constitution" by G. Ajanti, 8 *Review of Socialist Law* 259 (1982).

**TREATISES &
LOOSELEAFS:**   *African Tax Systems* by R. Hammond & M. van den Abeelen (Somalia) (Amsterdam:
      Intl. Bureau of Fiscal Documentation, 1980–).
      Information Guide: Doing Business in Somalia (Price Waterhouse).
      Investment Laws of the World (Somalia) (Oceana, 1981–).
      The Legal System of the Somali Democratic Republic by Haji N.A. Noor Muhammad
      (Michie, 1972).
      Somalia: A Country Study, 3d ed., H. Nelson, ed. (American. Univ., Foreign Affairs
      Studies, 1982).

ARTICLES: "Colonial Origins of the Public Domain in Southern Somalia" by M. Guadagni, 22
      Journal of African Law 1 (1978).
      "Refugees in Somalia" by H. Nelson, 12 *Syracuse Journal of International Law and
      Commerce* 552 (1986).

SOUTH AFRICA

SEE ALSO: Africa, Human Rights, International Law, United Nations

**RESEARCH GUIDES &
BIBLIOGRAPHIES:**   *Apartheid: A Selective Bibliography on the Racial Policies of the Government of the
      Republic of South Africa 1970–1978* (UN Publications, Dag Hammerskjold
      Library, 1979).
      The Namibian Issue, 1920–1980: A. . .Bibliography by E. Schoeman (Boston: G.K.
      Hall, 1982).

TREATIES: *The Treaty Series* (Pretoria: Govt. Printer, 1949–).

CONSTITUTIONS: *Constitutions of Dependencies and Special Sovereignties* (Gazankulu, Kwazulu) by A. Blaustein (Oceana, 1983).
Constitutions of the Countries of the World (South Africa) by A. Blaustein & G. Flanz (Oceana, 1982).

JOURNALS & OTHER PERIODICALS:
Acta Juridica (Cape Town: Junta, 1958–).
Annual Survey of South African Law (Cape Town: Junta, 1947–).
The Comparative and International Law Journal of Southern Africa (Pretoria: 1968–).
Journal of South African Law (1976–).
South African Journal on Human Rights (1985–).
South African Law Journal (1884–).
South African Law Journal of Criminal Law and Criminology (Butterworths, 1977–).
South African Yearbook of International Law (Univ. of South Africa, 1975–).

TREATISES & LOOSELEAFS:
Bills of Exchange, Cheques and Promissory Notes in South Africa by F. Malan (Butterworths, 1984).
Capital Formation and Investment Incentives Around the World (South Africa) by W. Diamond & D. Diamond (Matthew Bender, 1984–).
Constitutional Reform and Apartheid by L. Boulle (St. Martin's Press, 1984).
Digest of Commercial Laws of the World (South Africa) (Natl. Assn. of Credit Management; Oceana, 1977–).
Human Rights in the Homelands (NY: Fund for Free Expression, 1984).
Information Guide: Doing Business in South Africa (Price Waterhouse).
The International Mandate System and Namibia by I. Dore (Westview, 1985).
Introduction to South African Law and Legal Theory by W. Hosten (Butterworths, 1977).
South Africa: A Country Study (GPO, 1984).
South Africa: Law of Criminal Procedure by C. Kenyon (Library of Congress, 1982).
The South African Law of Persons and Family Law, 2d ed. by P. Oliver (Butterworths, 1980).
Taxgram (Johannesburg: Junta, 1985–).
Tax Laws of the World—South Africa (FL: Foreign Tax Law Assn.).

ARTICLES:
"The Divestment of United States Companies in South Africa and Apartheid" by P. Lansing, 60 *Nebraska Law Review* 304 (1981).
"The Law and Policy of Divestment of South African Stock" by J. Chettle, 15 *Law & Policy in International Business* 445 (1983).
"The Pathology of a Legal System: Criminal Justice in South Africa" by S. Kentridge, 128 *University of Pennsylvania Law Review* 603 (1980).
"Public Interest Law in South Africa" by J. Pitts, 22 *Stanford Journal of International Law* 153 (1986).
"South Africa: Marriage, Property and Money" by J. Sinclair, 26 *Journal of Family Law* 187 (1987–88). See also 25 *Journal of Family Law* 225 (1986–87).

SOUTH AMERICA: See Caribbean, Latin America

SOUTH CAROLINA

SEE ALSO:	Circuit Courts (Fourth Circuit)
RESEARCH GUIDE & BIBLIOGRAPHY:	*South Carolina Legal Research Methods* by R. Mills & J. Schultz (Hein, 1976).
STATUTES:	*Code of Laws of South Carolina 1976 Annotated* (Lawyers Co-op). *Acts and Joint Resolutions, South Carolina.*
STATE ADMINISTRATIVE CODE:	*Code of Laws of South Carolina 1976 Annotated,* vols. 23–27 (Lawyers Co-op.). *South Carolina State Register.*
CASES & OPINIONS:	*South Carolina Reports* (1868–). *South Eastern Reporter* (1886–).
COURT RULES:	*Code of Laws of South Carolina 1976 Annotated,* vol. 22 (Lawyers Co-op.). *South Carolina Rules of Court* (West).
JURY INSTRUCTIONS:	*Jury Charges and Instructions: Guide for Magistrates* by H. Weingrow (SC Criminal Justice Academy, 1981).
OPINIONS OF THE ATTORNEY GENERAL:	*Attorney General Reports & Opinions* (Office of the Attorney General).
ANNUAL SURVEY OF STATE LAW:	"Annual Survey of South Carolina Law" in *South Carolina Law Review.* See for example vol. 7, p. 65; vol. 31, p. 1, vol. 40, p. 1.
TREATISES & LOOSELEAFS:	*Bankruptcy Procedure in the District of South Carolina* by G. Levy (SC Bar, 1982–). *CCH State Tax Reporter.* *Code Pleading,* 2d ed. by H. Lightsey (SC Bar, 1984). *Criminal Defense* by J. Thames (SC Bar, 1984). *Drafting Wills and Trust Agreements in South Carolina* by R. Wilkins (SC Bar, 1977). *South Carolina Administrative Law* by D. Shipley (SC Bar, 1983). *South Carolina Bench Book for Magistrates* (SC Bar, 1979–). *South Carolina Children's Code Handbook* (SC Bar, 1982–). *South Carolina Condominium Law Manual* by D. MacGregor (Butterworths, 1986). *South Carolina Consumer Law and Practice* (SC Bar, 1984–). *South Carolina Domestic Relations Manual* by R. Chastain (SC Bar, 1984–). *South Carolina Income Taxation,* 2d ed. by L. Boyle (SC Bar, 1984–). *South Carolina Law and Practice* by H. Haynsworth (SC Bar, 1984). *South Carolina Probate Practice Manual* by A. Moses (SC Bar, 1983).
DIGESTS & CITATOR:	*South Carolina Digest* (West). *South Eastern Digest* (West). *Shepard's South Carolina Citations.*

SOUTH DAKOTA

SEE ALSO:	Circuit Courts (Eighth Circuit)
RESEARCH GUIDE & BIBLIOGRAPHY:	*South Dakota Legal Research Guide* by D. Jorgensen (Hein, 1988).
STATUTES:	*South Dakota Codified Laws Annotated.* *Laws of South Dakota.*
STATE ADMINISTRATIVE CODE:	*Administrative Rules of South Dakota.* *South Dakota Register.*
CASES & OPINIONS:	*North Western Reporter* (1890–). *South Dakota Reports* (1890–1976).
COURT RULES:	*Rule of Procedure in the States' Circuit Courts* (title 15 of S.D. Codified Laws) (Allen Smith). *Supreme Court Rules* (title 16–3 of S.D. Codified Laws) (Allen Smith).
JURY INSTRUCTIONS:	*South Dakota Criminal Pattern Jury Instructions* (SD Bar, 1985). *South Dakota Pattern Jury Instructions, Civil* (SD Bar, 1968).
OPINIONS OF THE ATTORNEY GENERAL:	*Report of the Attorney General* (Office of the Attorney General).
JOURNALS & OTHER PERIODICALS:	*State Bar Newsletter* (1974–).
TREATISES:	*Customer's Guide to South Dakota Law* (SD Bar, 1986). *South Dakota Tribal Court Handbook* (SD Bar, 1987).
DIGESTS & CITATOR:	*South Dakota Digest* (West). *North Eastern Digest* (West). *Shepard's South Dakota Citations.*

SOUTHEAST ASIA: See Asia
SOUTH PACIFIC: See Asia, Australia, Fiji Islands, New Zealand
SOUTH–WEST AFRICA: See Namibia
SOVEREIGN IMMUNITY: See State & Local Government, Torts
SOVEREIGNTIES: See International Law

SOVIET UNION

SEE ALSO:	Communism, International Law, Mongolia, United Nations
RESEARCH GUIDES & BIBLIOGRAPHIES:	"Bibliographic Note: Soviet Union Materials", 13 *The Journal of International Law and Economics* 109 (1978). *Soviet Foreign Relations and World Communism: A Selected, Annotated Bibliography of 7,000 Books in Thirty Languages* by T. Hammond (Princeton Univ. Press, 1965).

"Soviet Laws Translated into the English Language: A Bibliographic List through December 31, 1984" by J. Brannon, 13 *International Journal of Legal Information* 50 (1985).

CONSTITUTIONS:

The Constitution of the USSR and the Union Republics by F. Feldbrugge (Sijthoff and Noordhoff, 1979).

The Constitutions of the Communist World (Soviet Union), W. Simons, ed. (Sijthoff & Noordhoff, 1980).

"The New Constitution" by R. Scarlet, 26 *Problems of Communism* 1 (1974).

STATUTES & RELATED LAWS:

Collected Legislation of the Union of Soviet Socialist Republics and the Constituent Union Republics, W. Butler, transl. and comp. (Oceana, 1978).

The Soviet Codes of Law, W. Simons, ed. (Kluwer, 1980).

JOURNALS & OTHER PERIODICALS:

International Affairs (Moscow: All Union Znaniye Society, 1954–).

Review of Socialist Law.

Soviet Law and Government (1962–).

Soviet Statutes and Decisions (1962–).

Soviet Yearbook of International Law (Moscow: Nauka, 1958–).

TREATISES & LOOSELEAFS:

Basic Documents of the Soviet Legal System by W. Butler (Oceana, 1984).

The Citizenship Law of the USSR by G. Ginsburgs (Martinus Nijhoff; Kluwer, 1983).

Comparative Law and the Legal System: Anglo-Soviet by W. Butler (Oceana, 1985).

Contract Law in the USSR and the United States by A. Farnsworth & V. Mozolin (Wash. D.C.: Intl. Law Institute, 1987).

Digest of Commercial Laws of the World (USSR) (Natl. Assn. of Credit Management; Oceana, 1977–).

Encyclopedia of Soviet Law, 2d ed., F. Feldbrugge, ed. (Oceana; Martinus Nijhoff; Kluwer, 1985).

The Law of Marital Property in Czechoslovakia and the Soviet Union by G. Glos (Library of Congress, 1981).

Lawyers in Soviet Work Life by L. Shelley (Rutgers Univ. Press, 1984).

Legal and Practical Aspects of Doing Business with the Soviet Union (Practicing Law Institute, 1988).

Moscow's City Government by E. Savas (Praeger, 1985).

Oil and Gas Law: The USSR by W. Butler (Oceana).

Recognition and Enforcement of Foreign Judgments in Various Foreign Countries (Russia) by G. Roman (Library of Congress, 1984).

Soviet Commercial and Maritime Arbitration, W. Butler, ed. (Oceana, 1980–).

Soviet Foreign Policy Since World War II, 2d ed. by J. Nogee (Pergamon Press, 1984).

The Soviet Government and the Jews, B. Pincus, ed. (Cambridge Univ. Press, 1984).

The Soviet Law in Theory and Practice by O. Ioffe & P. Maggs (Oceana, 1983).

The Soviet Law of Property by G. Armstrong (Kluwer, 1983).

The Soviet Legal System: The Law in the 1980's by J. Hazard et al. (Oceana, 1984).

The Soviet System of Justice by G. van den Berg (Kluwer, 1985).

Taxation in European Socialist Countries (USSR) (Amsterdam: Intl. Bureau of Fiscal Documentation).

Taxation in the Soviet Union by M. Newcity (Praeger, 1986).

USSR Contract Law (Helsinki: Union of Finnish Lawyers Pub. Co., 1982).

ARTICLES: "Civil Defamation Law in the Soviety Union" by F. Cate, 23 *Stanford Journal of International Law* 303 (1987).

"A Comparison of the Chinese and Soviet Codes of Criminal Law and Procedure" by H. Berman et al., 73 *Journal of Criminal Law and Criminology* 238 (1982).

"The Development of Inheritance Law in the Soviet Union and the People's Republic of China" by F. Foster-Simons, 33 *American Journal of Comparative Law* 33 (1985).

"An Examination of the Modern Soviet Law of Torts" by C. Osakwe, 54 *Tulane Law Review* 3 (1979).

"Letters of Credit in East-West Trade: Soviet Reception of Capitalist Custom" by G. Armstrong, 17 *Vanderbilt Journal of Transnational Law* 329 (1984).

"The Problem of Autonomy in Soviet International Contract Law" by G. Armstrong, 31 *American Journal of Comparative Law* 63 (1983).

"A Soviet Perspective on Foreign Sovereign Immunity" by C. Osakwe, 23 *Virginia Journal of International Law* 13 (1982).

"Transferring U.S. Technology to the Soviets: Some Practical Legal Problems," 16 *The International Lawyer* 737 (1982).

SPACE

SEE ALSO: Air & Aviation, International Law, Media Law, Torts, Transportation, United Nations

RESEARCH GUIDES & BIBLIOGRAPHIES: "Air and Space Law Research and Materials: A Bibliographic Essay" by K. Li, 5 *Annals of Air and Space Law* 720 (1980).

"Bibliography of the Law of Outer Space," 22 *Jurimetrics Journal of Law, Science and Technology* 195 (1982).

"Current Literature on Aerospace Law" by S. Wise 49 *Journal of Air Law and Commerce* 1063 (1984).

Outer Space: A Selective Bibliography (UN Dag Hammarskjold Library, 1982).

"Private Enterprise in Outer Space: A Selected Bibliography" by M. Kell, 2 *Houston Journal of International Law* 159 (1979).

"Private Sector Activities in Outer Space" by A. Dula, 19 *International Lawyer* 159 (1985).

World Wide Space Law Bibliography by K. Li (Montreal: De Daro Publishing, 1987).

TREATIES: *The United Nations Treaties on Outer Space* (E.84.I.10) (UN, 1984).

JOURNALS, NEWSLETTERS, & SYMPOSIA: *The Air and Space Lawyer* (ABA, Forum Comm. on Air & Space Law, 1984–).

Annals of Air and Space Law (McGill Univ., 1976–).

Journal of Air Law and Commerce (Southern Methodist Univ. Sch. of Law, 1939–).

Journal of Space Law (Univ. of Miss. Law Center, 1973–).

Proceedings of the. . .Colloquium on the Law of Outer Space (American Institute of Aeronautics and Astronautics).

Space in the 1980's and Beyond: . . .European Space Symposium (Univelt, Inc.).

Yearbook of Air and Space Law (McGill Univ., 1965–).

DICTIONARY: "Legal Terminology of the Upper Regions of the Atmosphere and for the Space Beyond the Atmosphere" by J. Hogan, 51 *American Journal of International Law* 362 (1957).

TREATISES &	
LOOSELEAFS:	*Aerospace Law: Telecommunications Satellites* by N. Matte (Butterworths, 1982).

Aerospace Law: Telecommunications Satellites by N. Matte (Butterworths, 1982).

American Enterprise: The Law, and the Commercial Use of Space (Wash. D.C.: Natl. Center for the Public Interest, 1986–).

American Space Law: International and Domestic by N. Goldman (Ames, IA: State Univ. Press, 1988).

Aspects of Space Law by E. von Bogaert (Kluwer, 1985).

Astrobusiness: A Guide to Commerce and the Law of Outer Space by Finch (Praeger, 1985).

International Space Law by G. Zhukov (Praeger, 1984).

The Legal Definition of Outer Space by A. Gorbiel (Lodz, 1979).

Manual on Space Law, Jasentuliyana, ed. (Oceana, 1979).

The Modern International Law of Outer Space by C. Christol (Pergamon Press, 1982).

Outer Space and Legal Liability by M. Forkosch (Martinus Nijhoff; Kluwer, 1982).

Outer Space: New Challenges to Law and Policy by J. Fawcett (Oxford Univ. Press, 1985).

Settlement of Space Law Disputes by K. Bockstiegel (Verlag; Rothman, 1980).

Space Activities and Emerging International Law, N. Matte, ed. (McGill, 1984).

Space Commerce: Free Enterprise on the High Frontier by N. Goldman (Ballinger, 1985).

Space Shuttle and the Law by S. Gorove (Miss. Univ. Law Center, 1980).

Space Stations and the Law (Congress, Office of Technology Assessment, 1986).

Space Stations, International Law and Policy by D. Smith (Westview, 1979).

United States Space Law: National and International Regulations by S. Garove (Oceana, 1982–).

Utilization of Outer Space and International Law by G. Reijnen (Elsevier, 1981).

ENCYCLOPEDIAS:

AMERICAN JURISPRUDENCE 2D (Am Jur 2d)
Check the following topic in the *General Index* volumes for Am Jur 2d:

        Space Law

CORPUS JURIS SECUNDUM (CJS)
Check the following topics in the *General Index* volumes for CJS:

Aeronautics and	Pilots
Aerospace	

DIGESTS:

CASE SEARCH IN WEST DIGESTS BY KEY TOPIC
In the *Descriptive Word Index* of the West digests, look for key topics and numbers under the following subject headings:

Aviation	Satellite
Carriers	Space

ALR:

ANNOTATIONS
Check the index volumes for ALR, ALR2d, ALR3d, ALR4th, and ALR Fed for annotations under the following subject headings:

Aviation	Civil Aeronautics Board

PERIODICALS:

CURRENT LAW INDEX (CLI) & LEGAL RESOURCE INDEX (LRI)
In the CLI and LRI, look for references to periodical literature under the following subject headings:

Aeronautics	Space Law
Airspace	Space Shuttles
Outer Space	

INDEX TO LEGAL PERIODICALS (ILP)
In the ILP, look for references to legal periodical literature under the following subject headings:

Air Law	Space Law
Airspace	Transportation

SPAIN

SEE ALSO: Europe, European Economic Community, International Law, United Nations

DICTIONARY: *Law and Commercial Dictionary in Five Languages* (English, German, Spanish, French, Italian) (West, 1985).

**TREATISES &
LOOSELEAFS:**

Business Operations in Spain by J. Russin, Tax Management Foreign Income Portfolios, no. 273–3d (BNA, 1984).

Capital Formation and Investment Incentives Around the World (Spain) by W. Diamond & D. Diamond (Matthew Bender, 1984–).

Digest of Commercial Laws of the World (Spain) (Natl. Assn. of Credit Management; Oceana, 1977–).

Guide to the Law and Literature of Spain by T. Palmer (Library of Congress, 1915).

Information Guide: Doing Business in Spain (Price Waterhouse).

Litigating in Spain: Considerations for Foreign Practitioners by B. Cremades & E. Cabiedes (Kluwer, 1989).

Spanish Business Law, B. Cremades, ed. (Kluwer, 1985).

Taxation of Non-Residents in Spain by E. Piedrabuena (Amsterdam: Intl. Bureau of Fiscal Documentation, 1985).

Tax Laws of the World—Spain (FL: Foreign Tax Law Assn.).

World Law of Competition (Spain), J. von Kalinowski, ed. (Matthew Bender, 1979–).

ARTICLES:

"Buying Time in Spain: The Spanish Law of Installment Sales" by J. Steadman, 15 *Georgia Journal of International and Comparative Law* 143 (1985).

"Creditor's Rights Under Spanish Law" by F. Anton, 33 *American Journal of Comparative Law* 259 (1985).

"Establishment of Foreign Banks in Spain" by F. Anton, 19 *International Lawyer* 567 (1985).

"An Introduction to Spain's Foreign Investment Law" by C. Hendel, 10 *Brooklyn Journal of International Law* 1 (1984).

"Investment Legislation in Greece, Portugal, and Spain" by P. Artisien & P. Buckley, 17 *Journal of World Trade Law* 513 (1983).

"Licensing Aspects of Trade Secrets and Know-How in Spain," 79 *Patent and Trademark Review* 99 (1981).

"Reciprocal Influences between the Laws of Spain and Louisiana" by V. Castan, 42 *Louisiana Law Review* 1473 (1982).

"Spain: Family Law in the Eighties" by G. Cantero, 27 *Journal of Family Law* 275 (1988–89).

"Spanish Administrative Courts and Procedure Before Them" by G. Glos, 9 *Memphis State University Law Review* 591 (1979).

"The Spanish Constitution of 1978" by J. Palou, 15 *Vanderbilt Journal of Transnational Law* 47 (1982).

"The Spanish Divorce Law of 1981" by G. Glos, 32 *International and Comparative Law Quarterly* 667 (1983).

SPECIAL ASSESSMENT: See Real Estate, State & Local Government, Taxation
SPECIAL DAMAGES: See Torts, Trial & Appellate Practice
SPECIALIST: See Law Office Management
SPECIALIZATION: See Professional Responsibility
SPECIAL NEEDS: See Education Law, Handicapped & the Law
SPECIAL VERDICT: See Trial & Appellate Practice
SPECIFIC PERFORMANCE: See Contracts, Equity
SPEECH: See Art & Entertainment, Civil Rights, Constitutional Law, Media Law
SPEEDY TRIAL: See Constitutional Law, Criminal Law, Trial & Appellate Practice
SPENDTHRIFT TRUST: See Estate Planning
SPILLS: See Environmental Law, Oil & Gas

SPORTS LAW

SEE ALSO: Agency, Antitrust Law, Art & Entertainment, Contracts, Labor Law, Media Law, Torts

RESEARCH GUIDES & BIBLIOGRAPHIES:
Covering all Bases: A Comprehensive Research Guide to Sports Law 2d ed. by G. Uberstine (Hein, 1988).
"Sports and the Law: A Comprehensive Bibliography of Law-Related Materials, Five Year Supplement 1979–1984" by F. Houdek, 6 *Comm/Ent Law Journal* 921 (Summer, 1984).

JOURNALS, NEWSLETTERS & OTHER PERIODICALS:
Comm/Ent Law Journal (A Journal of Communications and Entertainment Law) (Hastings College of Law).
The Entertainment & Sports Law Journal (Univ. of Miami School of Law; Darby Printing Co., 1984–).
The Entertainment and Sports Lawyer (ABA Forum Comm. on the Entertainment and Sports Industries).
Entertainment Law Journal (Loyola Law School of Los Angeles).
Journal of Copyright, Entertainment & Sports Law (Tennessee Bar Assn.).
Sports and the Courts: Physical Educational and Sports Law Quarterly by H. Appenzeller & R. Thomas (Winston-Salem, NC: Sports and the Courts, Inc.).
Sports Lawyers Association Newsletter (Chicago: Sports Lawyers Assn.).

TREATISES & LOOSELEAFS:
The Athlete and the Law by P. Sloan (Oceana, 1983).
The Business of Boxing & Its Secrets by G. Reed (Detroit: New National Publishing Co.).
Entertainment Law Reporter by L. Sobel (Santa Monica, CA).
Essentials of Amateur Sports Law by G. Wong (Dover, MA: Auburn House Pub. Co., 1988).
From the Gym to the Jury by H. Appenzeller (Michie, 1970).
Government and Sport: The Public Policy Issues by A. Johnson & J. Frey (Rothman & Littlefield).
International Sports Law by J. Nafziger (Transnational Pub., 1988).
Labor Relations in Professional Sports by R. Berry, W. Gould & P. Staudohar (Boston: Auburn House, 1985).
Law and Amateur Sports, R. Waicukauski, ed. (Indiana Univ. Press, 1982).
Law and Business of Sports Industries by R. Berry (Boston: Auburn House, 1986).
Law and Liability in Athletics, Physical Education, and Recreation by J. Baley & D. Matthews (Allyn & Bacon, 1984).

The Law of Professional and Amateur Sports, G. Uberstine, ed. (Clark Boardman, 1988–).

The Law of Sports by J. Weistart & C. Lowell (Michie, 1979).

The Legal Aspects of Athletics by A. Grieve (NJ: A.S. Barnes, 1969).

New Dimensions in Products Liability: Sports Injuries G. Holmes, ed. (Ann Arbor: Institute for Cont. Ed., 1980).

Owners versus Players: Baseball and Collective Bargaining by J. Dworkin (Boston: Auburn House, 1981).

Personal Management and Client Representation by M. Silfen (Totaltape Publishing).

Physical Education and the Law by H. Appenzeller (Michie, 1978).

Products Liability: Recreation and Sports Equipment by J. Wittenberg (Law Journal Seminars-Press, 1985–).

Professional Sports & The Law by L. Sobel (NY: Law-Arts Publishers, 1977).

Representing Professional Athletes and Teams (Practicing Law Institute, 1985).

The Right to Participate: The Law and Individuals with Handicapping Conditions in Physical Education and Sports by H. Appenzeller (Michie, 1983).

Sports and Recreational Injuries by J. Riffer (Shepard's, 1985).

Sports and Law, H. Appenzeller, ed. (Michie, 1985).

Sports and the Law in Canada by J. Barnes (Butterworths, 1983).

Sports Injury Litigation (Practicing Law Institute, 1979).

Sports Law by G. Schubert (West, 1986).

Sports Law Reporter, J. Garagiola, Jr., ed. (Phoenix, AZ).

Sports Officiating: A Legal Guide by A. Goldberger (NY: Leisure Press, 1984).

Tax Planning and Contract Negotiating Techniques for Creative Persons, Professional Athletes and Entertainers by G. Reed (Detroit: New National Publishing Co.).

Torts and Sports: Legal Liability in Professional and Amateur Athletics by R. Yasser (Greenwood Press; Quorum Books, 1985).

ENCYCLOPEDIAS: AMERICAN JURISPRUDENCE 2D (Am Jur 2d)
Check the following topics in the *General Index* volumes for Am Jur 2d:

Baseball	Sports
Boxing	

CORPUS JURIS SECUNDUM (CJS)
Check the following topics in the *General Index* volumes for CJS:

Athletic Fields and Stadiums	Boxing and Wrestling
	Football
Athletics	Hockey
Baseball	Professional Athletes

DIGESTS: CASE SEARCH IN WEST DIGESTS BY KEY TOPIC
In the *Descriptive Word Index* of the West digests, look for key topics and numbers under the following subject headings:

Athletics	Labor Relations
Contracts	Theaters and Shows

ALR: ANNOTATIONS
Check the index volumes for ALR, ALR2d, ALR3d, ALR4th, and ALR Fed for annotations under the following subject headings:

Baseball	Racing
Basketball	Sports
Contracts	Water Sports
Football	

PERIODICALS: CURRENT LAW INDEX (CLI) & LEGAL RESOURCE INDEX (LRI)
In the CLI and LRI, look for references to periodical literature under the following subject headings:

Antitrust Law, Sports	Soccer
Athletics	Sports
College Sports	Sports Agents
Professional Sports	Sports Medicine
Segregation in Sports	

INDEX TO LEGAL PERIODICALS (ILP)
In the ILP, look for references to legal periodical literature under the following subject headings:

Arbitration and Award	Sports

SQUATTER: See Landlord-Tenant, Real Estate

SRI LANKA

SEE ALSO: Asia, Communism, International Law, United Nations

RESEARCH GUIDE & BIBLIOGRAPHY: "A Bibliography of the Books and Periodicals in the Laws of Sri Lanka" by J. Marikar, 4 *Colombo Law Review* 130 (1978).

TREATIES & OTHER AGREEMENTS: "Sri Lanka-United Kingdom: Agreement on the Promotion and Protection of Investments," 19 *International Legal Materials* 886 (1980) (see also vol. 21, p. 399).

STATUTES: *A Guide to Current Statute Law,* 3d ed. by J. Paul (Colombo: J. Paul, 1983).
An Index to the Legislative Enactments of Sri Lanka (Colombo: Celon Chamber of Commerce, 1985).

JOURNALS & OTHER PERIODICALS: *Colombo Law Review* (1969–).
Mooter: Journal of the Moot Society (Colombo: Sri Lanka Law College, 1984–).

TREATISES & LOOSELEAFS: *Asia and the Pacific: A Tax Tour* (Sri Lanka) (Arthur Anderson & Co., 1986).
Constitutional Government in Sri Lanka by L. Cooray (Colombo: Lake House Investments, 1984).
The Contract of Employment by S. de Silva (Colombo: Employers' Federation of Celon, 1983).
Democracy in Peril by P. Hyndman (Sydney, 1985).
Fiscal Policy and Tax Structure in Australasia (Sri Lanka) (Amsterdam: Intl. Bureau of Fiscal Documentation, 1978).
The Ideology of Popular Justice in Sri Lanka: A Socio-Legal Inquiry by N. Tiruchelvam (New Delhi: Vikas Pub. House, 1984).
Income Taxation and Foreign Investment in Developing Countries (Sri Lanka) by M. Dominic (Amsterdam: Intl. Bureau of Fiscal Documentation, 1980).
Investment Laws of the World (Sri Lanka) (Oceana, 1981–).
Labor Standards in Sri Lanka (Colombo: Sri Lanka Foundation Institute, 1981).

The Proposed Foreign Investment Authority Law of Sri Lanka by S. Weeraranta (Colombo: Lake House Investments, Ltd., 1982).

Sri Lanka: A country Study (GPO, 1985).

Sri Lanka: Current Human Rights Concerns... (NY: Amnesty Intl., 1984).

Sri Lanka: Ethnic Fratricide and the Dismantling of Democracy by S. Tambiah (Univ. of Chicago Press, 1986).

Sri Lanka in Change and Crisis, J. Manor, ed. (St. Martin's Press, 1984).

Taxes and Investment in Asia and the Pacific (Sri Lanka) (Amsterdam: Intl. Bureau of Fiscal Documentation, 1983–).

Tax Laws of the World—Celon (Sri Lanka) (FL: Foreign Tax Law Assn.).

ARTICLES:

"The Administration of Justice in Sri Lanka" by L. Cooray, 6 *Hong Kong Law Journal* 67 (1976).

"The Ideology of Popular Justice in Sri Lanka," 35 *International & Comparative Law Quarterly* 491 (1986).

"A Perspective on Law and Legal Institutions" by M. Marasinghe, 7 *Review of Socialist Law* 305 (1981).

"Survey of Laws Controlling Ownership of Lands in Sri Lanka" by H. Tambiah, 2 *International Property Investment Journal* 217 (1984).

SSARJAH: See United Arab Emirates
STADIUM: See Sports Law
STAFF: See Labor Law, Law Office Management
STAMP TAX: See Taxation
STANDARD OF CARE: See Torts
STANDING: See Trial & Appellate Practice
STARE DECISIS: See Trial & Appellate Practice
STATE ACTION: See Constitutional Law

STATE & LOCAL GOVERNMENT

SEE ALSO:

Administrative Law, Alcohol, Animals, Architecture, Banking Law, Business Law, Civil Service, Corporate Law, Criminal Law, Election, Employee Benefits, Energy, Estate Planning, Family Law, Government Contracts, Health & Medicine, Historic Preservation, Insurance, Juvenile Law, Landlord-Tenant, Legal History, Mental Health, Natural Resources, Nonprofit Corporations, Oil & Gas, Public Utilities, Real Estate, Securities Law, Torts, Water Law, Workers' Compensation, Zoning & Land Planning

**RESEARCH GUIDES &
BIBLIOGRAPHIES:**

Guide to State Legislative and Administrative Materials, 4th ed. by M. Fisher (Rothman, 1988).

Index to Current Urban Documents (Greenwood Press).

National Legal Bibliography: Government Documents... (Part II), P. Ward & M. Goldblatt, eds. (Hein, 1984–).

Searching the Law: The States by F. Doyle (Transnational Publishers, 1989).

State Government Research Checklist (KY: Council of State Govts., 1959–).

State Government Reference Publications; An Annotated Bibliography by D. Parish (CO: Libraries Unlimited, 1974).

Subject Compilations of State Laws: Research Guide and Annotated Bibliography by L. Foster & C. Boast (Greenwood Press, 1981).

CONSTITUTIONS:	*Constitutions of the United States: National & State,* F. Grad, ed. (Oceana, 1976–). *State Constitutional Conventions* (microfiche) (Greenwood Press).
DIRECTORIES:	*The Book of the States* (KY: Council of State Govts.) (biennial) *National Directory of State Agencies* (Wash. D.C.: Info. Resources Press) (biennial).

**JOURNALS,
NEWSLETTERS &
OTHER PERIODICALS:**

Annual Conference on State and Local Government (J. Reuben Clark Law School, 1983–).

Current Municipal Problems (Callaghan).

Fordham Urban Affairs Law Journal (1972–).

Journal of State Taxation (1982–).

Municipal Attorney (Wash. D.C.: Natl. Institute of Municipal Law Officers).

Municipal Law Report Newsletter (Callaghan).

National Municipal Litigation Center of the National Municipal Legal Defense Fund: Newsletter (Wash. D.C.: Natl. Institute of Municipal Law Officers).

NIMLO'S Congressional News (Wash. D.C.: Natl. Institute of Municipal Law Officers, 1986–).

University of Detroit Journal of Urban Law (1931–).

Urban Law Annual (1968–).

Urban Law Review (Univ. of Texas Sch. of Law, 1975–).

The Urban Lawyer (ABA Urban, State, and Local Govt. Sect., 1969–).

Urban, State and Local Law Newsletter (ABA Urban, State, and Local Govt. Sect.).

Washington University Journal of Urban and Contemporary Law (1968–).

LOOSELEAFS:

All State Sales Tax Reports (CCH, 1940–).

All State Tax Guide (Prentice-Hall, 1960–).

Checklist of State Publications (CO: Info. Handling Services, 1977–).

Comparative State Income Tax Guide with Forms by W. Diamond (Oceana, 1977–).

Federal Grants and Cooperative Agreements by R. Cappalli (Callaghan, 1983–).

A Guide to Municipal Official Statements by J. Daley (Law & Business, Inc., 1980–).

Local Government Digest (Madison, WI: Local Govt. Services, Inc., 1983).

Local Government Law by C. Antieau (Matthew Bender, 1955–).

Local Government Law by C. Sands (Callaghan, 1981–).

Monthly Checklist of State Publications (Library of Congress, Exchange and Gift Div., 1910–).

Municipal Securities Rulemaking Board Manual (CCH, 1977–).

Revenue Sharing Handbook by D. Musselwhite (Wash. D.C.: Revenue Sharing Advisory Service, 1974–).

State and Local Taxes (Prentice-Hall, 1925–).

State-by-State Guide to State Laws on Taxation of Banking Institutions (ABA Taxation Sect., 1981–).

State Tax Action Coordinator (Research Institute of America).

State Tax Cases Reports (CCH, 1948–).

State Tax Forms (KY: The Tax Form Library).

State Tax Guide (CCH, 1937–).

State Tax Reports (CCH, 1917–).

TREATISES:

Cities by Contract: The Politics of Municipal Incorporation by G. Miller (MIT Univ. Press, 1981).

Fundamentals of Municipal Bond Law (Natl. Assn. of Bond Lawyers, 1984).

A Guide to the Microfilm Collection of Early State Records by Library of Congress and Univ. of N.C. (Library of Congress, 1950).

Handbook of Local Government Law by O. Reynolds (West, 1982).

Interstate Compacts and Agencies (KY: Council of State Govts., 1983).

Interstate Compacts: 1783–1977 (KY: Council of State Govts., 1977).

Labor Arbitration in State and Local Government by R. Lester (Princeton Univ., 1984).

Law of Municipal Corporations, 3d ed. by E. McQuillin (Callaghan, 1949–).

Local Government Law in a Nutshell, 2d ed. by D. McCarthy (West, 1983).

Municipal Bonds by L. Moak (Municipal Finance Officers Assn., 1982).

Municipal Legal Forms with Commentary by R. Moore (Callaghan).

Municipal Ordinances: Text and Forms, 2d ed. by T. Matthews (Callaghan).

Ordinance Law Annotations (Shepard's).

Preferred Accounting Practices for State Governments (KY: Council of State Govts., 1983).

State and Local Taxation and Finance in a Nutshell by D. Gelfand (West, 1985).

State Constitutional Law in a Nutshell by T. Marks (West, 1988).

State Constitutions in a Federal System, J. Kincaid, ed. (Sage Publications, 1988).

State Taxation (vol. I, Corporate Income and Franchise Taxes) by J. Hellerstein (Warren, Gorham & Lamont, 1983).

Tax Aspect of Municipal Finance (Practicing Law Institute, 1984).

ENCYCLOPEDIAS: AMERICAN JURISPRUDENCE 2D (Am Jur 2d)

Check the following topics in the *General Index* volumes for Am Jur 2d:

Charter	Municipal or State Tort
Civil Service	Liability
County	Parks
Drains and Sewers	Police Power
Fire Departments	Public Works
Governor	Sales and Use Taxes
Highways	Schools
Housing	Sheriff, Police
Legislature	Sovereign or Government
Licenses	Immunity
Local or Special Laws	Towns
Municipal Corporations	

CORPUS JURIS SECUNDUM (CJS)

Check the following topics in the *General Index* volumes for CJS:

Administrative Bodies	Industrial Boards
Boards and Commissions	Legislature
Charters	Levees and Flood Control
Civil Service	Licenses and Permits
Counties	Mayor
Dams	Municipal Corporations
Drains	Ordinances
Excise Taxes	Parks
Fire Departments	Police
Government Agencies	Political Subdivisions
Governor	Sanitary Districts
Highway	School
Home Rule	Sewers
Income Tax-State	Sidewalks
Independent School	Special or Local Laws
Districts	State

Streets	Traffic
Tax Boards	Villages
Town	

DIGESTS:　CASE SEARCH IN WEST DIGESTS BY KEY TOPIC
In the *Descriptive Word Index* of the West digests, look for key topics and numbers under the following subject headings:

Administrative Law	Municipal Corporations
Bridges	Public Contracts
Counties	Public Lands
Drains	Schools
Elections	States
Escheat	Towns
Health	Turnpikes
Highway	Water
Hospitals	Zoning
Mandamus	

ALR:　ANNOTATIONS
Check the index volumes for ALR, ALR2d, ALR3d, ALR4th, and ALR Fed for annotations under the following subject headings:

Administrative Law	Licenses and Permits
Boundaries	Municipal Corporations
Bridges	Parks
Cemeteries	Police
Counties	Public Lands
Fire Department	Schools
Government Immunity	Sewers
Highways	State-Taxes
Housing	

PERIODICALS:　CURRENT LAW INDEX (CLI) & LEGAL RESOURCE INDEX (LRI)
In the CLI and LRI, look for references to periodical literature under the following subject headings:

Agriculture and State	Public Works
Cities and Towns	Regional Planning
City Planning	State Bonds
Community Development	State Government
Education	State Taxation of
Industry and State	Corporate Income
Intergovernmental	Taxation
Tax Relations	Tort Liability of Municipal
Municipal Corporations	Corporations
Police	Traffic
Public Housing	Zoning

INDEX TO LEGAL PERIODICALS (ILP)
In the ILP, look for references to legal periodical literature under the following subject headings:

Administrative Agencies	Cemeteries
Beaches	City Planning
Bonds	Counties
Bridges	Crime Prevention
Budgets	Education

Excise Taxes	Municipal Corporations
Federal and State	Municipal Courts
Cooperation	Parking
Federalism	Parks
Fires	Police Power
Government Corporations	Recall
Government Immunity	Regional Planning
Governors	Rents and Rent Control
Highways	Safety Laws
Historic Preservation	Schools
Hospitals	Securities/State Regulation
Housing	States Rights
Initiative and Referendum	Traffic
Interstate Agreements	Unions/Public Sector
Land Use	Zoning
Licenses	

STATELESSNESS: See Human Rights, International Law
STATES' RIGHTS: See Constitutional Law, State & Local Government

STATISTICS

SEE ALSO: Economics, Trial & Appellate Practice

Federal Information Sources and Systems. Congressional Sourcebook Series (GAO, 1976–).

Historical Statistics of the United States Colonial Times to 1970 (Bureau of the Census, 1975).

Statistical Abstract of the United States (Bureau of the Census, 1878–).

Statistical Sources (Gale).

Statistics Concepts for Attorneys: A Reference Guide by W. Curtis (Greenwood Press, 1983).

Use of Statistics in Equal Employment Opportunity Litigation by W. Connolly (Law Journal Seminars-Press, 1979–).

Vital Statistics (Dept. of Health and Human Services, Natl. Center of Health Statistics, 1937–).

CURRENT LAW INDEX (CLI) & LEGAL RESOURCE INDEX (LRI)
In the CLI and LRI, look for references to periodical literature under the following subject headings:

Criminal Statistics	Regression Analysis
Gross National Product	Sampling (Statistics)
Judicial Statistics	Statistics
Probabilities	Vital Statistics

STATUTE OF FRAUDS: See Contracts
STATUTE OF USES: See Real Estate

STATUTES

SEE ALSO: Constitutional Law, Jurisprudence, Legal Research, Legislative History, State & Local Government

JOURNALS: *Journal of Legislation* (Notre Dame Law School, 1974–).
Harvard Journal on Legislation (1964–).
Seton Hall Legislative Journal (1975–).

TREATISES: *A Common Law for the Age of Statutes* by G. Calabresi (Harvard Univ. Press, 1982).
The Construction of Statutes by E. Crawford (MO: Thomas Law Book Co., 1940;
   Rothman, 1976).
Dealing with Statutes by J. Hurst (Columbia Univ. Press, 1982).
The Interpretation and Application of Statutes by R. Dickerson (Little, Brown, 1975).
Legislative Analysis and Drafting, 2d ed. by W. Statsky (West, 1984).
Legislative Law and Process in a Nutshell, 2d ed. by J. Davies (West, 1986).
Sutherland Statutory Construction, 4th ed. by C. Sands (Callaghan, 1973).

AMERICAN JURISPRUDENCE 2D (Am Jur 2d)
Check the following topics in the *General Index* volumes for Am Jur 2d:

Construction or	Judicial Legislation
Interpretation	Legislature
Ejusdem Generis	Organic Acts
Emergency Legislation	Statutes
In Pari Materia	

STEPCHILDREN: See Family Law, Juvenile Law
STERILITY: See Family Law, Health & Medicine, Women & the Law
STERILIZATION: See Abortion, Health & Medicine, Mental Health, Women & the Law
STEWARDS: See Labor Law
STIPULATION: See Trial & Appellate Practice

ST. LUCIA

SEE ALSO: Caribbean, Civil Law, England, International Law, Latin America, United Nations

"Equity in the Law of St. Lucia" by D. White, 1 *Comparative Law Yearbook* 153 (1978).
Essays on the Civil Codes of Quebec and St. Lucia, R. Landry, ed., (Univ. of Ottawa
   Press, 1984).
Saint Lucia Consolidated Index of Statutes and Subsidiary Legislation by the Faculty
   of Law Library, Univ. of West Indies Barbados (Gaunt, 1986).
"Some Problems of a Hybrid Legal System: A Case Study of St. Lucia" by D. White, 30
   International & Comparative Law Quarterly 862 (1981).
West Indian Constitutions: Post-Independence Reforms (St. Lucia) by F. Phillips
   (Oceana, 1985).

STOCK: See Commodities, Corporate Law, Securities Law
STOCKBROKERS: See Agency, Corporate Law, Securities Law
STORAGE: See Personal Property, Torts
STREET: See State & Local Government, Torts
STREETCAR: See Torts, Transportation
STRICT LIABILITY: See Torts
STRIKES: See Civil Service, Education Law, Labor Law
STRIP MINING: See Energy, Environmental Law, Natural Resources, Oil & Gas
STUDENTS: See Education Law, Handicapped & the Law, Mental Health

ST. VINCENT AND THE GRENADINES

SEE ALSO: Caribbean, England, International Law, Latin America, United Nations

Saint Vincent and the Grenadines Consolidated Index of Statutes and Subsidiary Legislation by the Faculty of Law Library, Univ. of West Indies, Barbados (Gaunt, 1986).
West Indian Constitutions: Post-Independence Reforms (Saint Vincent and the Grenadines) by F. Phillips (Oceana, 1985).

SUBCONTRACTOR: See Agency, Architecture, Business Law, Contracts, Government Contracts
SUBDIVISIONS: See Real Estate, State & Local Government, Zoning & Land Planning
SUBPOENA: See Criminal Law, Trial & Appellate Practice
SUBROGATION: See Contracts, Insurance
SUBSIDIARY: See Corporate Law
SUBSIDIES: See Poverty Law
SUCCESSION: See Estate Planning, Taxation

SUDAN

SEE ALSO: Africa, International Law, Islam, United Nations

STATUTES & RELATED LAWS: *The Laws of the Sudan* by C. Cumings (11 vols.) (London: Haycock Press).

TREATISES & LOOSELEAFS: *Africa and Law* (Sudan) (Univ. of Wisc. Press, 1968).
African Tax Systems by R. Hammond & M. van den Abeelen (Sudan) (Amsterdam: Intl. Bureau of Fiscal Documentation, 1980–).
The Common Law in the Sudan by Z. Mustafa (Clarendon Press, 1971).
Investment Laws of the World: The Developing Nations (Sudan) (Oceana, 1972).
The Law of Evidence in the Sudan by K. Vasdev (Butterworths, 1981).
The Law of Homicide in the Sudan by K. Vasdev (Butterworths, 1981).
The Legal Regime of Foreign Private Investment in the Sudan and Saudi Arabia by Fath el Rahman Abdalla El Sheikh (NY: Cambridge Univ. Press, 1984).
The Legal System of Sudan by Z. Mustafa (Michie, 1970).
Natural Resources Development and Protection under the Sudanese Petroleum Laws (Univ. of Utah College of Law, 1985).
Sudan: A Country Study, 3d ed., H. Nelson, ed. (American Univ., Foreign Affairs Studies, 1983).
The Sudan: Law of Criminal Procedure by C. Kenyon (Library of Congress, 1984).
Tax Laws of the World—Sudan (FL: Foreign Tax Law Assn.).

ARTICLES: "Circulars of the Shari's Courts in the Sudan" by C. Fluehr-Lobban, 27 *Journal of African Law* 79 (1983) (see also vol. 26, p. 133).
"The Islamic Legal Revolution: The Case of Sudan" by C. Gordon, 19 *International Lawyer* 793 (1985).
"Protection of Property Under Sudanese Law" by H. Tier, 5 *New York Law School Journal of International and Comparative Law* 17 (1983).
"Sudan: The Patents Regulations," 82 *Patent and Trademark Review* 181 (1984) (see also vol. 82, pp. 125, 175).

SUFFERING: See Health & Medicine, Mental Health, Torts
SUFFRAGE: See Election
SUGAR: See Agriculture, Commodities, Food
SUICIDE: See Death, Health & Medicine, Mental Health
SULTANATE: See Oman
SUMMARY JUDGMENT: See Trial & Appellate Practice
SUMMONS: See Trial & Appellate Practice
SUNDAY: See Church & State
SUPERFUND: See Environmental Law
SUPERSEDEAS BOND: See Trial & Appellate Practice
SUPERVISION: See Employee Benefits, Employment Discrimination, Labor Law, Law
    Office Management, Paralegal
SUPPLEMENTAL SECURITY INCOME: See Poverty Law, Social Security
SUPPORT: See Estate Planning, Family Law, Women & the Law
SUPREME COURT: See Constitutional Law, Legal History, Trial & Appellate Practice
SURETYSHIP: See Architecture, Contracts, Insurance
SURFACE MINING: See Environmental Law, Natural Resources
SURGEONS: See Death, Handicapped & the Law, Health & Medicine, Mental Health,
    Torts
SURROGATE COURT: See Estate Planning
SURROGATE MOTHERHOOD: See Family Law, Women & the Law
SURVEYING: See Real Estate
SURVIVORSHIP: See Estate Planning, Real Estate
SUSPENSION OF SENTENCE: See Crininal Law

SWAZILAND

SEE ALSO:	Africa, International Law, United Nations
TREATISES & LOOSELEAFS:	*African Tax Systems* by R. Hammond & M. van den Abeelen (Swaziland) (Amsterdam: Intl. Bureau of Fiscal Documentation, 1980–).
	Investment Laws of the World: The Developing Nations (Swaziland) (Oceana, 1972–).
	Tax Laws of the World—Swaziland (FL: Foreign Tax Law Assn.).
ARTICLES:	"Human Rights in Africa. . .Swaziland. . ." by S. Neff, 33 *The International and Comparative Law Quarterly* 331 (1984).
	"The Parliaments of Botswana, Lesotho and Swaziland" by W. Macartney, 50 *Parliamentarian* 92 (1969).
	"The Swaziland Contractual Regulation of Land Transactions" by P. Takirambudde, 14 *Comparative and International Law Journal of Southern Africa* 179 (1981).
	"The Swazi Law of Succession" by N. Rubin, 9 *Journal of African Law* 90 (1965).

SWEDEN

SEE ALSO:	Europe, International Law, Scandinavian Law, United Nations
RESEARCH GUIDE & BIBLIOGRAPHY:	"Swedish Legal Publications in English, French, and German" by L. Fryholm, 5 *Scandinavian Studies in Law* 155 (1961).
CONSTITUTION:	"New Swedish Constitution" by O. Nyman, 26 *Scandinavian Studies in Law* 171 (1982).

STATUTES & RELATED LAWS:

Penal Code of Sweden (Rothman, 1972).
The Swedish Code of Judicial Procedure (Rothman, 1979).

TREATISES & LOOSELEAFS:

Administrative Secrecy in Developed Countries (Sweden) by D. Rpwat (Columbia Univ. Press, 1979).
Arbitration in Sweden (Stockholm Chamber of Commerce, 1977).
Business Operations in Sweden by R. Dahlman, Tax Management Foreign Income Portfolios, no. 450 (BNA, 1987).
Capital Formation and Investment Incentives Around the World (Sweden) by W. Diamond & D. Diamond (Matthew Bender, 1984–).
Consumer Protection Experiments in Sweden by D. King (Rothman, 1974).
Digest of Commercial Laws of the World (Sweden) (Natl. Assn. of Credit Management; Oceana, 1977–).
The Hare and the Tortoise: Clean Air Policies in the United States and Sweden by L. Lundqvist (Univ. of Mich. Press, 1980).
Human Rights in Sweden: The Annual Report 1985 by J. Sundberg (Rothman, 1987).
Information Guide: Doing Business in Sweden (Price Waterhouse).
An Introduction to Swedish Law by S. Stromholm (Kluwer, 1981).
Law and Industrial Relations in Sweden by F. Schmidt (Rothman, 1977).
Tax Laws of the World—Sweden (FL: Foreign Tax Law Assn.).
World Law of Competiton (Sweden), J. von Kalinowski, ed. (Matthew Bender, 1979–).

ARTICLES:

"Antitrust Law and Economic Analysis: The Swedish Approach" by D. Gerber, 8 *Hastings International and Comparative Law Review* 1 (1984).
"International Trade and the New Swedish Provisions on Corruption" by M. Bogdan, 27 *American Journal of Comparative Law* 665 (1979).
"The 1987 Swedish Family Law Reform" by F. Nozari, 17 *International Journal of Legal Information*, 219 (1989).
"Regulating America, Regulating Sweden," 80 *Michigan Law Review* 614 (1982).
"Rules, Problems and Trends in Family Conflict of Laws—Especially in Sweden" by L. Paisson, 199 *Hague Academy of International Law* 313 (1986).
"Strategies for the Swedish Public Housing Sector" by L. Lundqvist, 6 *Urban Law & Policy* 215 (1984).
"Sweden: Legal Education" by M. Bogdan, 5 *Comparative Law Yearbook* 137 (1981).
"Sweden: More Rights for Children and Homosexuals" by A. Saldeen, 27 *Journal of Family Law* 295 (1988–89).
"Sweden: Reforms of Marriage, Inheritance and Cohabitation Proposed" by A. Saldeen, 26 *Journal of Family Law* 197 (1987–88). See also 25 *Journal of Family Law* 245 (1986– 87).

SWIMMING: See Sports Law, Torts

SWITZERLAND

SEE ALSO:

Europe, International Law, United Nations

RESEARCH GUIDE & BIBLIOGRAPHY:

Guide to Foreign Legal Materials: French, German, Swiss by C. Szladits (Oceana, 1959).

TREATIES & OTHER AGREEMENTS:

"Switzerland-United States: Memorandum of Understanding. . .Insider Trading," 22 *International Legal Materials* 1 (1983).

CONSTITUTION:

Constitutions of the Countries of the World (Switzerland) by A. Blaustein & G. Franz (Oceana, 1982).

STATUTES & RELATED LAWS:

The Swiss Civil Code: English Version, I. Williams, transl. (Zurich: ReMaK, 1925; Oxford Univ. Press, 1976).
The Swiss Federal Code of Obligations by S. Goren (Rothman, 1987).

JOURNALS & OTHER PERIODICALS:

Swiss Review of Internatinal Antitrust Law (1977–).

TREATISES & LOOSELEAFS:

Business Operations in Switzerland by S. Bianchi, Tax Management Foreign Income Portfolios, no. 82–6th (BNA, 1986).
Capital Formation and Investment Incentives Around the World (Switzerland) by W. Diamond & D. Diamond (Matthew Bender, 1984).
Digest of Commercial Laws of the World (Switzerland) (Natl. Assn. of Credit Management; Oceana, 1977–).
Information Guide: Doing Business in Switzerland (Price Waterhouse).
International Handbook on Comparative Business Law (Switzerland), D. Campbell, ed. (Kluwer, 1979).
Introduction to Swiss Law, F. Dessemontet, ed. (Kluwer, 1983).
Recognition and Enforcement of Foreign Judgments in Various Foreign Countries (Switzerland) by G. Roman (Library of Congress, 1984).
The Swiss Way of Welfare by R. Segalman (Praeger, 1986).
Taxation in Switzerland (NY: Deloitte, Haskins & Sells, 1979).
The Taxation of Corporations in Switzerland by A. Margairaz (Kluwer, 1983).
Taxation of Intercompany Transactions in Selected Countries in Europe and USA (Switzerland) (Kluwer, 1979).
Tax Havens Encyclopedia (Switzerland) by B. Spitz (Butterworths, 1975–).
Tax laws of the World—Switzerland (FL: Foreign Tax Law Assn.).
Transnational Contracts in the Swiss Draft Statute and in the General European Context (Library of Congress, 1981).
World Law of Competition (Switzerland), J. von Kalinowski, ed. (Matthew Bender, 1979–).

ARTICLES:

"Attachment of Swiss Bank Accounts" by M. Wirth, 36 *Business Lawyer* 1029 (1981).
"Banking Secrecy and Insider Trading," 23 *Virginia Journal of International Law* 605 (1983).
"The Effect of the U.S.-Swiss Agreement on Swiss Banking Secrecy and Insider Trading," 15 *Law and Policy in International Business* 565 (1983).
"Foreign Bank Operations in Switzerland" by P. Buzescu, 19 *The International Lawyer* 897 (1985).
"Legislative Developments in Swiss Banking" by E. Tavernier, 1 *International Financial Law Review* 29 (1987).
"The Limits of Swiss Banking Secrecy Under Domestic and International Law" by M. Aubert, 2 *International Tax and Business Lawyer* 273 (1984).
"Prevention of Child Abuse in Switzerland: Statutes and Court Decisions" by P. Buzescu, 13 *International Journal of Legal Information* 41 (June-Aug., 1985).

"Switzerland: Hard Cases" by J. Grossen, 26 *Journal of Family Law* 207 (1987–88). See also 25 *Journal of Family Law* 255 (1986–87).

SYDNEY: See Australia

SYNDICATION: See Agriculture, Business Law, Real Estate, Taxation

SYRIA

SEE ALSO: Islam, International Law, Middle East, United Nations

TREATISES &
LOOSELEAFS: *Commercial Laws of the Middle East* (Syria) by A. Keesee (Oceana, 1980–).
Digest of Commercial Laws of the World (Syria) (Natl. Assn. of Credit Management; Oceana, 1977–).
Property Law in the Arab World: Real Rights in Egypt, Iraq, Jordan, Lebanon, Libya, Saudi Arabia and the Gulf States by F. Ziadeh (London: Graham & Trotman, 1979).
Taxes and Investment in the Middle East (Syria) (Intl. Bureau of Fiscal Documentation).
Tax Laws of the World—Syria (FL: Foreign Tax Law Assn.).

ARTICLES: "The Legal System of Syria" by R. Khany, 1 *Comparative Law Yearbook* 137 (1978).
"Middle East Agency Law Survey" (Syria) by F. Taylor, 14 *International Lawyer* 352 (1980).
"Syria' (Human Rights), *International Commission of Jurists Review* 12 (June, 1980).

SYSTEMS: See Law Office Management

TAFT–HARTELY: See Labor Law

T

TAHITI

SEE ALSO: France, International Law, United Nations

Taxes and Investment in Asia and the Pacific (Tahiti, French Polynesia) (Amsterdam: Intl. Bureau of Fiscal Documentation, 1983–).
"The Tax System of Tahiti (French Polynesia)" by E. Jehle, 37 *Bulletin for International Fiscal Documentation* 358 (1983).

TAIWAN

SEE ALSO: Asia, China, International Law, United Nations

RESEARCH GUIDE &
BIBLIOGRAPHY: *The Republic of China on Taiwan: A Selectively Annotated Bibliography of English-Language Legal Materials* by C. Johnson (Library of Congress, 1988).

**TREATISES &
LOOSELEAFS:**

Asia and the Pacific: A Tax Tour (Taiwan) (Arthur Anderson & Co., 1986).

Business Operations in the Republic of China (Taiwan) by P. Hsu (BNA, Tax Management, 1988–).

Capital Formation and Investment Incentives Around the World (Taiwan) by W. Diamond & D. Diamond (Matthew Bender, 1984–).

Commercial, Business, and Trade Laws: Taiwan (Oceana, 1983–).

Information Guide: Doing Buisness in Taiwan (Price Waterhouse).

Investment Laws of the World (Taiwan) (Oceana, 1981–).

Martial Law in Taiwan (Wash. D.C.: Asia Resource Center; NY: Formosan Assn. for Human Rights, 1985).

Tax Laws of the World—Taiwan (FL: Foreign Tax Law Assn.).

ARTICLES:

"A Comparative Study of Foreign Investment Laws in Taiwan and China" by T. Wan, 11 *California Western International Law Journal* 236 (1981).

"Legal Aspects of Offshore Banking in Taiwan" by Y. Chen, 8 *Maryland Journal of International Law and Trade* 237, 266 (1984).

"The Legal Status of Taiwan in the Normalization of Sino-American Relations" by G. Hsiao, 14 *Rutgers Law Journal* 839 (1983).

"Patent Law," 82 *Patent and Trademark Review* 380, 434, 487, 523 (1984).

"Self-Determination for the People of Taiwan" by K. Christiansen, 14 *California Western International Law Journal* 471 (1984).

"The Status of U.S. Copyright Relations with Taiwan" by E. Yambrusic, 13 *International Journal of Legal Information* 1 (Feb.–April, 1985).

"A Study Tour of Taiwan's Legal System" by R. Ginsburg, 66 *American Bar Association Journal* 165 (1980).

"Taiwan Relations Act" by C. Gable, 12 *Vanderbuilt Journal of Translational Law* 511 (1979).

"The United States and Taiwan after Derecognition: Consequences and Legal Remedies" by A. Sheikh, 37 *Washington and Lee Law Review* 323 (1980).

"United States-China Relations: Has President Reagan's Communique Revised International Obligations towards Taiwan?" by J. Wolfinger, 14 *California Western International Law Journal* 326 (1984).

MISCELLANEOUS:

Taiwan Communique and Separation of Powers, Hearings before the Subcommittee on Separation of Powers of the Committee of the Judiciary, U.S. Senate, 97th Cong., Second Session (GPO, 1983).

TAKEOVER: See Corporate Law, Securities Law

TANZANIA

SEE ALSO:

Africa, International Law, Islam, United Nations

**RESEARCH GUIDE &
BIBLIOGRAPHY:**

"Notes on Legal Literature in East Africa" (Tanzania), 10 *Case Western Reserve Journal of International Law* 123 (1978).

CASES:

Law Reports of Tanzania (Univ. of Dar es Salaam, Faculty of Law, 1967–).

Tanzania High Court Digest.

JOURNALS & OTHER
PERIODICALS:
    Dar es Salaam University Law Journal (1966–).
    Tanzania Notes and Records.

TREATISES &
LOOSELEAFS:
    African Tax Systmes (Tanzania) by R. Hammond & M. van den Abeelen
        (Amsterdam: Intl. Bureau of Fiscal Documentation, 1980–).
    Custom and Law with Reference to the Tanganyika Legal System by R. Tenga (JSD
        thesis, Cornell) (Ann Arbor: Univ. Microfilms Intl., 1985).
    Customary Land Law of Tanzania by James & Fimbo (Rothmanb, 1973).
    Integration and Disintegration in East Africa (Tanzania) by C. Potholm & R. Fredland
        (Univ. Press of America, 1980).
    The Legal System of Tanzania by Y. Ghai (Michie, 1970).
    The Status of Aliens in East Africa: Asians and Europeans in Tanzania, Uganda, and
        Kenya by D. Nanjira (Praeger, 1976).
    Tax Laws of the World—Tanzania (FL: Foreign Tax Law Assn.).

ARTICLES:
    "The Exclusive Economic Zone Tanzania" by E. Mtango, 14 *Ocean Development and*
        International Law Journal 1 (1984).
    "The Patent System and Transfer of Technology in … Kenya and Tanzania" by
        Seyoum, 16 *International Review of Industrial Property and Copyright Law* 704
        (1985).
    "The Tanzanian Ombudsman" by P. Norton, 22 *International and Comparative Law*
        Quarterly 603 (1973). (See also 15 Journal of Modern African Studies 239).
    "Tanzania: The Law Reform Commission's Paper on Proposed Changes in Family
        Law" by B. Rwezaura, 26 *Journal of Family Law* 213 (1987–88). See also 25
        Journal of Family Law 261 (1986–87).

TARIFF: See Customs, International Law, Maritime Law, Taxation

TAXATION

SEE ALSO:
    Accounting, Agriculture, Art & Entertainment, Banking Law, Bankruptcy, Business
    Law, Commodities,Community Property, Corporate Law, Customs, Employee Benefits,
    Energy, Estate Planning, Family Law, Franchise Law, Insurance, Intellectual Property,
    International Law, Maritime Law, Natural Resources, Nonprofit Corporations, Oil &
    Gas, Partnership Law, Real Estate, Securities Law, State & Local Government; see also
    entries under individual states and countries.

RESEARCH GUIDES &
BIBLIOGRAPHIES:
    Computer-Assisted Legal and Tax Research: A Professional's Guide to Lexis, Westlaw,
        and PHINet by T. Thomas (Prentice-Hall, 1986).
    "Federal Income Taxation" by L. Chanin & P. McDermott in *Specialized Legal*
        Research, L. Chanin, ed. (Little, Brown, 1987).
    "Guide to Select Sources of Legislative History for Tax Legislation" by V. Maclay,
        6 *Legal Reference Services Quarterly* 107 (1986).
    Tax Law Locator (R.R. Bowker, 1988–).
    West's Federal Tax Research by W. Raabe (West, 1987).

LEGISLATIVE HISTORY:
    Cumulative Changes in the Internal Revenue Code of 1954 as Amended, 1954–
        (Prentice Hall).

Federal Tax Laws Correlated by W. Barton & C. Browning (Federal Tax Press, 1969).
*Internal Revenue Acts of the United States 1909–1950: Legislative Histories, Laws
    and Administrative Documents*, B. Reams, comp. (Hein, 1979).
Internal Revenue Service Cumulative Bulletin.
Legislative History of the Internal Revenue Code of 1954 by the Joint Committee on
    Internal Revenue Taxation, 90th Congress, 1st Session (GPO, 1967).
Tax Management-Primary Sources (BNA, 1970–).
U.S. Code Congressional and Administrative News (West).

DECISIONS:

American Federal Tax Reports (AFTR) (Prentice-Hall, 1884–1957).
American Federal Tax Reports 2d (AFRT2d) (Prentice-Hall, 1958–).
BTA Memorandum Decisions (Prentice-Hall, 1928–1942).
BTA Reports (Prentice-Hall, 1924–1942).
CCH Current Memo Decisions.
P–H Tax Court.
Standard Federal Tax Reports (U.S. Taxes Advance Sheet) (CCH).
Tax Court Memorandum Deicisons (CCH, 1942–).
Tax Court Reporter and Memorandum Decisions (Prentcie-Hall, 1924–).
Tax Court Reports (CCH, 1924–).
TC Memorandum Decisions (Prentice-Hall, 1928–).
U.S. Claims Court Reporter (West).
U.S. Court of Claims Reports (GPO, 1874–1982).
U.S. Tax Cases (CCH, 1913–).
U.S. Tax Court Reports (GPO, 1942–).

**JOURNALS, INSTITUTES,
NEWSLETTERS & OTHER
PERIODICALS:**

Federal Tax Articles (CCH, 1962–).
Institute on Federal Taxation (Matthew Bender).
Journal of Taxation (Warren, Gorham & Lamont, 1954–).
The Journal of Taxation and Investments (Warren, Gorham & Lamont, 1983–).
The Journal of Taxation Digest (Warren, Gorham & Lamont, 1981–).
Monthly Digest of Tax Articles (Albany: Newkirk Products, 1950–).
National Tax Journal (Natl. Tax Assn., 1948–).
New York University Annual Conference on Taxation of Investments (Matthew
    Bender, 1984–).
New York University Annual Institute on Federal Taxation (Matthew Bender, 1943–).
The Practical Tax Lawyer (ALI–ABA Comm. on Cont. Prof. Ed., 1986–).
Review of the Taxation of Individuals Warren, Gorham & Lamont 1977–).
Section of Taxation Newsletter (ABA).
Taxation for Lawyers (1972–).
Tax Conference (Marshall-Wythe School of Law, 1955–).
Taxes—The Tax Magazine (CCH, 1923–).
Tax Executive (1951–).
Tax Law Review (Warren, Gorham & Lamont).
Tax Lawyer (ABA, 1947–).
Tax Management Memorandum (Tax Management, Inc.).
Tax Notes (Tax Analysts).
Tax Planning and Research Indices for Periodicals (NY: ProDex, 1974–).
Tulane Tax Institute (Claitor's, 1952–).
University of Southern California School of Law Tax Institute (Matthew Bender).
Virginia Tax Review (1981–).

LOOSELEAFS:
Annotated Tax Forms (Prentice-Hall, 1969–).
Code and Regulations (CCH, 1946–).
Cumulative Changes, 1954 Code and Regulations (Prentice-Hall, 1954–).
Daily Tax Report (BNA).
Federal Excise Tax (Prentice-Hall, 1956–).
Federal Excise Tax Reports (Prentice-Hall, 1913–).
Federal Tax Compliance Planning (Prentice-Hall, 1982–).
Federal Tax Compliance Reporter (CCH, 1982–).
Federal Tax Coordinator, 2d (Research Inst. of America, 1955–).
Federal Taxes (Prentice-Hall, 1919–).
Federal Tax Forms (CCH, 1973–).
Federal Tax Guide (CCH, 1917–).
Federal Tax Guide (Prentice-Hall, 1931–).
How to Handle Tax Audits ... (Panel, 1967–).
Interest and Dividends: Withholding, Information Returns (CCH, 1982–).
Internal Revenue Code of 1954 as Amended (Prentice-Hall).
Internal Revenue Manual: Administration (CCH, 1977–).
Internal Revenue Manual: Audit (CCH, 1977–).
IRS Letter Rulings (CCH, 1977–).
IRS Positions (CCH, 1982–).
IRS Publications (CCH, 1977–).
Mertens Code Commentary by J. Dohney (Callaghan, 1981–).
Mertens Law of Federal Income Taxation by J. Mertens (Callaghan, 1954–).
Obtaining IRS Private Letter Rulings by Touche Ross & Co. (Oceana, 1983–).
Private Letter Rulings (Prentice-Hall, 1976–).
Publications of the IRS (Prentice-Hall, 1979–).
S Corporation (Tax Management, 1986–).
Standard Federal Tax Reports (CCH, 1913–).
Tax Action Coordinator (Research Inst. of America, 1970–).
Tax Court (Prentice-Hall, 1921–).
Tax Court Practice by M. Garbis (Warren, Gorham & Lamont, 1974–).
Tax Planning (Prentice-Hall, 1954–).
Tax Planning for Executive Compensation by H. Frutkin (Matthew Bender, 1983–).
Weekly Tax Report (BNA, 1982–).
West's Federal Tax Guide by W. Hoffman, (West, 1983–).

CITATORS:
Federal Tax Citator (Prentice-Hall, 1933–).
Federal Taxes Citator, 2nd Series (Prentice-Hall, 1978–).
Shepard's Administrative Citations.
Shepard's Code of Federal Regulations Citations.
Shepard's Federal Tax Citations.
Standard Federal Tax Reporter Citator (CCH).

DIGESTS:
Court of Claims Digest (1855–).
Cumulative Bulletin Index-Digest System.
Current Matters volume of Federal Taxes (Prentice-Hall).
Index-Digest volume of *Tax Court Reporter* (CCH).
Tax Court Digest (1924–1967).

ENCYCLOPEDIAS:
AMERICAN JURISPRUDENCE 2D (Am Jur 2d)
Check the following topics in the *General Index* volumes for Am Jur 2d:

Customs Duties	Federal Tax Enforcement
Deductions	Fuel Taxes

Gift Taxes	Sales and Use Taxes
Inheritance and Estate	Stamp Taxes
Taxes	Taxation
Profit or Income	Taxpayer's Actions

CORPUS JURIS SECUNDUM (CJS)
Check the following topics in the *General Index* volumes for CJS:

Ad Valorem Taxes	Income Tax
Assessment of Taxes	Occupation Tax
Customs Duties	Poll Taxes
Delinquent Taxes	Sales Tax
Excise Taxes	Tax …
Franchise Taxes	Taxation
Gasoline Taxes	Taxpayers Actions
Gross Receipts Tax	Use Taxes

DIGESTS:

CASE SEARCH IN WEST DIGESTS BY KEY TOPIC
In the *Descriptive Word Index* of the West digests, look for key topics and numbers under the following subject headings:

Customs Duties	Income Tax
Delinquent Taxes	Sales Tax
Excise Taxes	Taxation
Gross Receipts Tax	

ALR:

ANNOTATIONS
Check the index volumes for ALR, ALR2d, ALR3d, ALR4th, and ALR Fed for annotations under the following subject headings:

Administrative Law	Succession, Estate and
Business Expense	Gift Taxes
Capital Gain or Loss	Tax Court
Evasion of Taxes	Taxes
Fraud	Tax Sale
Income Taxes	

PERIODICALS:

CURRENT LAW INDEX (CLI) & LEGAL RESOURCE INDEX (LRI)
In the CLI and LRI, look for references to periodical literature under the following subject headings:

Allocation of Income	Recognition of Gain
Attribution of Ownership	or Loss
Business Tax	Sales Tax
Capital Gains Tax	State Taxation of
Capitalization	Corporate Income
Depletion Allowances	Tax Accounting
Foreign Tax Credit	Tax Administration and
Income Tax	Procedure
Intergovernmental Tax	Taxation
Relations	Tax Evasionl
Investment Tax Credit	United States Internal
Payroll Tax	Revenue Service
Real Property and	United States Tax Court
Taxation	Withholding Tax

INDEX TO LEGAL PERIODICALS (ILP)
In the ILP, look for references to legal periodical literature under the following subject headings:

Antidumping Duties	Stamp Duties
Capital Gains Tax	Tariff and Custom Laws
Double Taxation	Taxation
Excess Profits Tax	Taxation/Enforcement
Excise Tax	Tax Liens
Fraud	Tax Sales
Income Tax	Tax Shelters
Occupation Tax	Tax Treaties
Property Tax	Value Added Tax
Social Security Tax	

TAX EXEMPT: See Nonprofit Corporations, Taxation
TAX HAVEN: See International Law, Taxation
TAX LIEN: See Real Estate, Taxation
TAX SALE: See Real Estate, Taxation
TEACHER: See Education Law, Labor Law, Legal Education
TEAMS: See Sports Law, Torts
TEAMSTERS: See Labor Law
TECHNOLOGY: See Business Law, Computers, Intellectual Property, Law Office
    Management
TELECOMMUNICATIONS: See Media Law, Public Utilities
TELEPHONE: See Public Utilities
TELEVISION: See Art & Entertainment, Media Law
TENANCY: See Landlord-Tenant, Real Estate
TENANCY BY THE ENTIRETIES: See Estate Planning, Family Law
TENANCY IN COMMON: See Estate Planning, Landlord-Tenant
TENANTS: See Landlord-Tenant, Real Estate
TENDER: See Contracts, Real Estate, Securities Law

TENNESSEE

SEE ALSO: Circuit Courts (Sixth Circuit)

RESEARCH GUIDES &
BIBLIOGRAPHIES: "A Selected Bibliography of Tennessee Practice Materials" by D. Picquet, 8
                              Southeastern Law Librarian 6 (1982).
                          Tennessee Legal Research Handbook by L. Laska (Hein, 1977).

STATUTES: *Private Acts of the State of Tennessee.*
                          Public Acts of the State of Tennessee.
                          Tennessee Code Annotated.

STATE ADMINISTRATIVE
CODE: *Official Compilation Rules & Regulations of the State of Tennessee.*
                          Tennessee Administrative Register.

CASES & OPINIONS: *Tennessee Appeals* (1925–1971).
                          Tennessee Criminal Appeals Reports (1967–1971).

Tennessee Reports (1870–1971).
South Western Reporter (1886–).

COURT RULES:
Tennessee Court Rules Annotated (Michie).
Tennessee Rules of Civil Procedure Annotated (West, 1970).
Tennessee Rules of Court (West).

JURY INSTRUCTIONS:
Tennessee Pattern Jury Instructions: Criminal-Civil (West, 1988).

OPINIONS OF THE ATTORNEY GENERAL:
Attorney General Opinions.

JOURNALS & OTHER PERIODICALS:
Tennessee Attorneys Memo (M. Lee Smith Publishers).
Tennessee Bankruptcy Service (M. Lee Smith Publishers).
Tennessee Bar Journal (1965–).
Tennessee Business Litigation Service (M. Lee Smith Publishers).
Tennessee Judicial Newsletter (Public Law Institute).
Tennessee Litigation Reporter (Lewis Laska).
Tennessee Medico-Legal Reporter (Lewis Laska).
Tennessee Real Estate Law Letter (M. Lee Smith Publishers).

TREATISES & LOOSELEAFS:
The General Sessions Court by W. Hall (Michie, 1972).
Gibson's Suits in Chancery, 6th ed. by W. Inman (Michie, 1982).
Gore's Forms for Tennessee Annotated, 3d ed. by T. Gore (Michie, 1970).
Pritchard on the Law of Wills and Administration of Estates, 4th ed. by H. Phillips (Michie, 1983).
Products Liability: The Law in Tennessee by B. Finberg (Harrison, 1979).
Tennessee Adoption Authorities with Forms by B. Trimble (Michie, 1968).
Tennessee Civil Procedural Forms by W. Bigham (West, 1977).
Tennessee Corporations by R. Gilman (Lawyers Co-op., 1980–).
Tennessee Criminal Practice and Procedure by D. Raybin (West, 1984–85).
Tennessee Divorce Authorities by B. Trimble (Michie, 1966).
Tennessee Law of Evidence by D. Paine (Michie, 1974).
Tennessee Probate by A. Secor (Lawyers Co-op, 1980–).
Tennessee Uniform Commercial Code Forms by S. Ramp (West, 1987).
Trial Handbook for Tennessee Lawyers by R. Burch (Lawyers Co-op., 1980).

DIGESTS, ENCYCLOPEDIAS & CITATORS:
Michie's Digest of Tennessee Reports.
Shepard's Tennessee Citations.
Tennessee Advance Annotation Service (Michie).
Tennessee Digest (West).
Tennessee Jurisprudence (Michie, 1982).
West's Tennessee Digests 2d Law Finder (1987–).

TENTH CIRCUIT: See Circuit Courts
TERMINAL CARE: See Civil Service, Employment Discrimination, Labor Law
TERRITORIAL WATERS: See Sea, Water Law
TERRITORIES: See Legal History

TERRORISM

SEE ALSO: Air & Aviation, Criminal Law, International Law, Military Law, War

**RESEARCH GUIDES &
BIBLIOGRAPHIES:**
Global Terrorism: A Historical Bibliography, S. Ontiveros, ed. (ABC-Clio, 1986).
International Terrorism: A Bibliography by A. Lakos (Westview, 1986).
"International Terrorism: A Legal Bibliography of Selected Issues and Sources" by
    R. Lutz, S. Streiker & D. Johnson-Champ, 20 *International Lawyer* 1083 (1986).
International Terrorism: An Annotated Bibliography and Research Guide by
    A. Norton & M. Greenberg (Westview, 1979).

**TREATISES &
LOOSELEAFS:**
*Anti-Terrorism, Forensic Science, Psychology in Police Investigations: International
    Congress on Techniques for Criminal Identification* (Westview).
*International Terrorism: A Compilation of Major Laws, Treaties, Agreements, and
    Executive Documents* (G.P.O., 1987).
International Terrorism: Targets, Responses, and the Role of the Law (VA: John Basset
    More Society of Intl. Law, 1979).
Legal and Other Aspects of Terrorism (Practicing Law Institute, 1979).
Legal Aspects of International Terrorism, A. Evans, ed. (Lexington Books; D.C. Heath,
    1978).
Legal Responses to International Terrorism: U.S. Procedural Aspects, M. Bassiouni, ed.
    (Martinus Nijhoff, 1988).
Legislative Responses to Terrorism, Y. Alexander, ed. (Martinus Nijhoff, 1986).
Political Terrorism and Business, Y. Alexander, ed. (Praeger, 1979).
Punishing International Terrorists: The Legal Framework by J. Murphy (Totowa, NJ:
    Rowman & Allanheld, 1985).
Terrorism: Documents of International and Local Control by R. Friedlander (Oceana,
    1979).
Terrorism, the Media and the Law by A. Miller (Transnational Pub., 1982).
Transnational Terrorism: Conventions and Commentary, L. Lillich, ed. (Michie, 1982).

ENCYCLOPEDIA:
AMERICAN JURISPRUDENCE 2D (Am Jur 2d)
Check the following topics in the *General Index* volumes for Am Jur 2d:

Hijacking	Terror
Piracy	War

PERIODICALS:
CURRENT LAW INDEX (CLI) & LEGAL RESOURCE INDEX (LRI)
In the CLI and LRI, look for references to periodical literature under the following
subject headings:

Genocide	Sabotage
Hostages	Terrorism

INDEX TO LEGAL PERIODICALS (ILP)
In the ILP, look for references to legal periodical literature under the following subject
headings:

Piracy	Terrorism

TESTIMONIAL PRIVILEGE: See Trial & Appellate Practice
TESTING: See AIDS, Education Law, Employment Discrimination, Legal Education

TEXAS

SEE ALSO:	Circuit Courts (Fifth Circuit), Community Property, Oil & Gas

RESEARCH GUIDES & BIBLIOGRAPHIES:

"An Annotated Bibliography of Texas Practice Materials" by K. Gruben & L. Philipp, 74 *Law Library Journal* 87 (1981).

A Reference Guide to Texas Law and Legal History, 2d ed., K. Gruber & J. Hambleton, eds. (Butterworth, 1987).

Texas Legislative History & Administrative Agency Citation Guide (Texas Tech Univ. Press, 1986).

Texas State Documents for Law Librarians by M. Allison & K. Schlueter (American Assn. of Law Libraries, 1983).

STATUTES:

Texas Codes Annotated (Vernon).
General and Special Laws of the State of Texas.
Texas Session Law Service (Vernon).

STATE ADMINISTRATIVE CODE:

Texas Administrative Code (Secretary of State).
Texas Register (Secretary of State).

CASES & OPINIONS:

Texas Reports (1846–1962).
Texas Criminal Reports (1876–1963).
South Western Reporter (1886–).

COURT RULES:

Local Rules in the District Courts of Texas by S. Steves (Butterworths).
Texas Rules of Court: State and Federal (West).

JURY INSTRUCTIONS:

Texas Pattern Jury Charges (State Bar of Texas, 1969).

ETHICS & PROFESSIONAL RESPONSIBILITY:

Texas Lawyers' Professional Ethics (State Bar of Texas, 1979).

OPINIONS OF THE ATTORNEY GENERAL:

Attorney General Opinions (1939–).
Attorney General Digest of Opinions.

JOURNALS & OTHER PERIODICALS:

Texas Bar Journal (1938–).
Texas Legal Update (West, 1987–).

SURVEY OF STATE LAW:

"Annual Survey of Texas Law" in *Southwestern Law Review*. See for example vol. 39, p. 1.

DIRECTORY:

Texas Legal Directory (Dallas: Legal Directories Pub. Co.).

TREATISES & LOOSELEAFS:

Centennial History of the Texas Bar: 1882–1982 by the State Bar of Texas (Eakin Press, 1981).
Creditors' Rights in Texas (State Bar of Texas, 1981).
Criminal Evidence Trial Manual for Texas Lawyers by M. Larkin (Butterworths, 1986).

Family Law: Texas Practice and Procedure by B. Kazen (Matthew Bender, 1982–).
A Guide to Texas Environmental Regulatory Programs (Austin: Texas Energy and Natural Resources Advisory Council, 1982).
How to Live—and Die—with Texas Probate (Houston: Gulf Pub. Co., 1983).
Michie's Texas Tort Reporter (Michie).
Petroleum Marketing Practices Act Manual by D. Grissom (Austin, TX: Texas Oil Marketers Assn., 1981).
Texas Business Organizations by R. Hamilton (West, 1973).
Texas Civil Trial Handbook by H. Sprouse (State Bar of Texas, 1984–).
Texas Corporation Law by S. Pfeffer (D&S Pub., 1982–).
Texas Criminal Forms and Trial Manual by M. McCormick (West, 1985).
Texas Evidence, 3d ed. by R. Ray (West, 1980).
Texas Foreclosure: Law and Practice by W. Baggett (Shepard's, 1984).
Texas Forms: Legal and Business (Lawyers Co-op).
Texas Insurance Law Reporter by D. Irons (Butterworths, 1986).
Texas Litigation Guide by W. Dorsaneo (Matthew Bender, 1977–).
Texas Method of Practice by A. Mitchell et al. (West, 1970).
Texas Products Liability Law by W. Powers (Butterworths, 1986).
Texas Rules of Evidence Manual, 2d ed. by H. Wendorf & D. Schlueter (Michie, 1988).
Vernon's Texas Code Forms Annotated, 2d ed. by J. Krahmer (West, 1986).
West's Texas Forms by F. Elliott (West, 1977).

DIGESTS, ENCYCLOPEDIAS
& CITATORS:

Texas Digest (West).
Texas Jurisprudence III (Lawyers Co-op).
Texas Law Finder (West).
Texas Law Locator (Shepard's).
South Western Digest.
Shepard's Texas Citations.

THAILAND

SEE ALSO: Asia, International Law, United Nations

RESEARCH GUIDE &
BIBLIOGRAPHY: "Current Legal Research in Thailand" by K. Kamprasert, 7 *International Journal of Law Libraries* 261 (1979).

CONSTITUTION: *The Constitution of Thailand* by M. Shin (Library of Congress, 1981).

TREATISES &
LOOSELEAFS:

Asia and the Pacific: A Tax Tour (Thailand) (Arthur Anderson & Co., 1986).
Capital Formation and Investment Incentives Around the World (Thailand) by W. Diamond & D. Diamond (Matthew Bender, 1984–).
Code and Custom in a Thai Provincial Court by D. Engel (Univ. of Ariz. Press, 1978).
A Guide to Doing Business in the ASEAN Region: Brunei/Indonesia/Malaysia/ Philippines/Singapore/Thailand (U.S. Dept. of Commerce, Intl. Trade Admin., Office of Pacific Basin, 1985).
Investment Laws of the World (Thailand) (Oceana, 1981–).
Taxes and Investment in Asia and the Pacific (Thailand) (Amsterdam: Intl. Bureau of Fiscal Documentation, 1983–).
Tax Laws of the World—Thailand (FL: Foreign Tax Law Assn.).

Thailand: A Country Study, 5th ed., F. Bunge (Dept. of the Army, 1981).
Thailand Business Legal Handbook, 6th ed. (Intl. Legal Counselors Thailand Ltd.; Chase Manhattan Bank, Bangkok Branch, 1984).

ARTICLES:

"Company Insolvency in Singapore, Thailand and Indonesia" by R. Singam, *International Business Leader* 451 (Nov., 1985).
"Copyright Law: Protection in Thailand," 25 *Harvard International Law Journal* 205 (1984).
"Foreign Investment Incentives in the Developing World: The Legislation of Greece, Egypt, Pakistan, Thailand, and the Republic of China" by P. Dempsey, 11 *Case Western Reserve Journal of International Law* 575 (1979).
"The Legal System of Thailand" by R. Hicking, 2 *Hong Kong Law Journal* 8 (1972).
"The Legal System of Thailand" by S. Kraichitti, 7 *Washburn Law Journal* 239 (1968).
"Thailand's Fisheries: A Victim of 200 Mile Zones" by T. McDorman, 16 *Ocean Development and International Law* 183 (1986).
"Thailand: The Patent Act," 82 *Patent and Trademark Review* 328 (1984).

THEATER: See Art & Entertainment, Torts
THEFT INSURANCE: See Insurance
THEOLOGY: See Canon Law, Church & State
THERAPY: See Health & Medicine, Mental Health, Torts
THIRD CIRCUIT: See Circuit Courts
THIRD PARTY BENEFICIARY: See Contracts, Estate Planning
THIRD PARTY PRACTICE: See Trial & Appellate Practice
THIRD WORLD: See Africa, Asia, International Law, Latin America, United Nations
THREATS: See Criminal Law, Torts
TIMBER: See Natural Resources
TIME: See Contracts, Estate Planning, Real Estate, Trial & Appellate Practice
TIME SHARE: See Real Estate
TITLE: See Equity, Estate Planning, Real Estate
TITLE EXAMINATION: See Oil & Gas, Real Estate
TITLE INSURANCE: See Insurance, Real Estate
TITLE VII: See Civil Rights, Employment Discrimination
TOBACCO: See Agriculture, Environmental Law, Torts

TOGO

SEE ALSO:

Africa, International Law, United Nations

African Tax Systems by R. Hammond & M. van den Abeelen (Togo) Amsterdam: Intl. Bureau of Fiscal Documentation, 1980–).
An Introduction to Law in French-Speaking Africa (Togo) by J. Salacuse (Michie, 1969).

TONGA

SEE ALSO:

International Law, United Nations

CONSTITUTION:

Constitutions of the Countries of the World (Tonga) by A. Blaustein & G. Flanz (Oceana, 1982).

TREATISES & **LOOSELEAFS:**	*Taxes and Investment in Asia and the Pacific* (Tonga) (Amsterdam: Intl. Bureau of Fiscal Documentation, 1983–).
ARTICLES:	"Ocean Boundaries in the South Pacific" by S. Border, 4 *University of Hawaii Law* *Review* 1 (1982).

TORRENS SYSTEM: See Real Estate
TORTIOUS INTERFERENCE WITH CONTRACTS: See Contracts, Torts

TORTS

SEE ALSO:	Agency, Agriculture, Air & Aviation, Alcohol, Architecture, Art & Entertainment, Business Law, Civil Rights, Conflict of Law, Constitutional Law, Criminal Law, Death, Employment Discrimination, Environmental Law, Family Law, Health & Medicine, Insurance, Intellectual Property, International Law, Media Law, Occupational Safety, Professional Responsibility, Real Estate, Sports Law, Trial & Appellate Practice, Workers' Compensation; see also entries under individual states and countries
RESEARCH GUIDES & **BIBLIOGRAPHIES:**	"Products Liability Bibliography" by D. Vetri, 25 *The Trial Lawyers Guide* 1 (1981). "Products Liability: Bibliography" by M. Beaird, 73 *Law Library Journal* 968 (1980). *Tort Reform and Related Proposals: Annotated Bibliography,* B. Levin, ed. (ABA, 1979).
RESTATEMENT:	*Restatement of the Law, Second, Torts* (America Law Institute, 1965).
JOURNALS, NEWSLETTERS **& OTHER PERIODICALS:**	*American Trial Lawyers Association Law Journal.* *The Brief* (ABA Tort and Insurance Practice Section). *Defense Law Journal* (Allan Smith, 1957–). *For the Defense* (Defense Research Institute). *The Forum* (ABA Tort and Insurance Practice Section). *Hazardous Waste and Toxic Torts Law & Strategy* (Leader Pubs., 1985–). *Journal of Products Law* (Symposia Press, 1982–). *Journal of Products Liability* (Peron Press, 1977–). *Medical Malpractice Law & Strategy Newsletter* (Law Journal Seminars-Press). *Personal Injury Annual* (Matthew Bender, 1961–). *Personal Injury Deskbook* (Matthew Bender, 1983–). *Personal Injury Newsletter* (Matthew Bender, 1958–). *Product Liability Newsletter* (Law Journal Seminars-Press). *Professional Negligence* (Frank Cass, 1985–). *West's Personal Injury News.*
GOVERNMENT REPORT:	*Interagency Task Force on Product Liability, Final Report* (U.S. Dept. of Commerce, 1978).
LOOSELEAFS:	*Abdominal Injuries* by J. Kalisch (Matthew Bender, 1973–). *The American Law of Torts* by S. Speiser (Lawyers Co-op., 1983–). *Automobile Design Liability,* 2d ed. by R. Goodman (Lawyers Co-op., 1983–). *Avaition Accident Law* by L. Kreindler (Matthew Bender, 1963–). *Comparative Negligence Manual* by C. Heft (Callaghan, 1978–).

Consumer Product Safety Commission by M. Lemov (Shepard's, 1981–).
Consumer Product Safety Guide (CCH, 1972–).
Courtroom Medicine Series (Matthew Bender).
Courtroom Toxicology by M. Houts (Matthew Bender, 1981–).
Damages in Tort Actions by M. Minzer (Matthew Bender, 1982–).
Drug Product Liability by M. Dixon (Matthew Bender, 1974–).
Fire Litigation Sourcebook by A. Patton & J. Russel (Garland Law Pub.).
Handling Federal Torts Claims by L. Jayson (Matthew Bender, 1964–).
How to Recover for Loss or Damage to Goods in Transit by S. Sorkin (Matthew Bender, 1976–).
Law of Defamation by R. Smolla (Clark Boardman, 1986–).
Law of Toxic Torts by M. Dore (Clark Boardman, 1987–).
Litigation and Trial of Air Crash Cases by J. Kennelly (Callaghan, 1968–).
Medical Malpractice by D. Louisell (Matthew Bender, 1960–).
Pain and Suffering by L. Chapman (Matthew Bender, 1967–).
Personal Injury: Actions, Defenses, Damages by L. Frumer (Matthew Bender, 1957–).
Product Liability by J. Allee (Law Journal Seminars-Press, 1984–).
Product Liability by L. Frumer (Matthew Bender, 1960–).
Product Liability: A Manual of Practice in Selected Nations, H. Stucki et al., eds. (Oceana, 1981–).
Product Safety & Liability Reporter (BNA, 1973–).
Products Liability Reports (CCH, 1963–).
Professional Liability Reporter (Litigation Research Group).
Punitive Damages Law and Practice by J. Ghiardi & J. Kircher (Callaghan, 1981–).
Psychic Injuries by M. Lewis (Matthew Bender, 1975–).
The Rights of Publicity and Privacy by J. McCarthy (Clark Boardman, 1987–).
Scientific Automobile Accident Reconstruction by G. Lacy et al. (Matthew Bender, 1964–).
Tobacco Products Litigation Reporter.
Trial of Accident Cases, 3d ed. by L. Schwartz (Matthew Bender, 1958–).

TREATISES:

Aircrash Litigation Techniques by D. Cathcart (Michie, 1985).
American Law of Medical Malpractice by S. Pedalis (Lawyers Co-op., 1980).
American Law of Products Liability, 2d ed. by R. Hursch & H. Bailey (Lawyers Co-op., 1974).
Asbestos Litigation (Law & Business, Inc., 1982).
Automobile Law & Practice, 3d ed. by D. Blashfield (West, 1965).
Automobile Engineering and Litigation (Garland, 1984).
Aviation Tort Law by S. Speiser & C. Krause (Lawyers Co-op., 1978–80).
Basic Protection for the Traffic Victim: A Blueprint for Reforming Automobile Insurance by R. Keeton & J. O'Connell (Little, Brown, 1966).
The Blame Game by J. O'Connell & C. Kelly (Lexington Books, 1987).
Commercial Torts, 2d ed. by G. Alexander (Michie, 1988).
Comparative Fault: The Negligence Case, 2d ed. by H. Woods (Lawyers Co-op., 1987).
Comparative Negligence, 2d ed. by V. Schwartz (Michie, 1986).
Computing Economic Loss in Cases of Wrongful Death by E. King (Rand Corp., 1988).
Constitutional Torts. by K. Davis (K.C. Davis, 1984).
Damages and Recovery: Personal Injury and Death Actions by J. Stein (Lawyers Co-op., 1972).
Drugs in Litigation (Michie, 1988).
Economic Torts, 2d ed. by J. Heydon (London: Sweet & Maxwell, 1978).
Federal Consumer Product Safety Act by W. Kimble (West, 1975).
Handbook on the Law of Damages by C. McCormick (West, 1935).
Handling Accident Cases by A. Averbach (Lawyers Co-op., 1963–72).

Handling Birth Trauma Cases by S. Schwartz (Wiley, 1985).

Hazardous Products Litigation, 2d ed. by E. Schwartz (Lawyers Co-op., 1988).

How to Avoid Products Liability: A Management Guide by S. Klein (Institute for Business Planning, 1980).

How to Prove Damages in Personal Injury and Death Cases by D. Avnet (Prentice-Hall, 1978).

Informed Consent by P. Applebaum (Oxford Univ. Press, 1987).

Jury Instructions on Damages in Tort Actions by G. Douthwaite (Allen Smith, 1981).

The Law of Product Warranties by B. Clark & C. Smith (Warren, Gorham & Lamont, 1984).

The Law of Torts, 2d ed. by Harper & James (Little, Brown, 1986).

The Laws of Innkeepers, by J. Sherry (Cornell Univ. Press, 1981).

Libel and Privacy Litigation: Prevention and Defense by B. Sanford (Law & Business, Inc., 1985).

The Litigation Process of Tort Law by L. Green (Bobbs-Merrill, 1965).

Medical Malpractice, 2d ed. by D. Harney (Allen Smith, 1984).

Model Jury Instructions for Business Tort Litigation (ABA, 1980).

Modern Tort Law by J. Dooley; rev. by B. Lindhal (Callaghan, 1977).

OB/GYN Malpractice by S. Lewis (Wiley, 1986).

Personal Injury Practice by L. Charfoos & D. Christensen (Lawyers Co-op., 1986).

Personal Injury Practice Manual by A. Cone & V. Lawyer (Prentice-Hall).

The Preparation and Trial of Medical Malpractice Cases by R. Shandell (Law Journal Seminars-Press, 1981).

Preparing Products Liability Cases by T. Kiely (Wiley, 1986).

Products Liability by W. Kimble (West, 1979).

Professional Negligence, T. Roady & W. Anderson, eds. (Vanderbuilt Univ. Press, 1960).

Prosser and Keeton on Torts, 5th ed. by W. Keeton (West, 1984).

Punitive Damages by K. Redden (Michie, 1980).

Recovery for Wrongful Death, 2d ed. by S. Speiser (Lawyers Co-op., 1975).

Res Ipsa Loquitur by S. Speiser (Lawyers Co-op., 1972).

Toxic Torts: Litigation of Hazardous Substance Cases by G. Nothstein (Shepard's, 1984).

Wrongful Death Actions by R. Eades (Harrison, 1981).

Wrongful Imprisonment by R. Brandon (Hamden, CT: Archon Books, 1973).

CITATORS:

Federal Occupational Safety and Health Citations (Shepard's).

Products Liability Citations (Shepard's).

TOTTEN TRUST: See Estate Planning

TOXICOLOGY: See Forensic Science, Health & Medicine, Torts

TOXIC TORT: See Environmental Law, Torts

TOXINS: See Health & Medicine, Torts

TOW: See Maritime Law

TOWNS: See State & Local Government

TRACE ELEMENTS: See Forensic Science

TRADE: See Antitrust Law, Business Law, Corporate Law, Commodities, Customs, Family Law, International Law, Securities Law

TRADEMARK: See Antitrust Law, Customs, Intellectual Property

TRADE REGULATION: See Antitrust Law, Franchise Law

TRADE SECRET: See Business Law, Intellectual Property

TRADE UNION: See Labor Law

TRAFFIC: See Insurance, State & Local Government, Torts

TRAINING: See Education Law, Labor Law, Law Office Management

TRANSCRIPTS: See Trial & Appellate Practice
TRANSIT: See Maritime Law, Transportation
TRANSNATIONAL LAW: See International Law
TRANSPLANTATION: See Health & Medicine

TRANSPORTATION

SEE ALSO: Administrative Law, Agency, Air & Aviation, Antitrust Law, Business Law, Commodities, Contracts, Corporate Law, Customs, Economics, Energy, Environmental Law, Franchise Law, Government Contracts, Handicapped & the Law, Immigration Law, Insurance, International Law, Labor Law, Maritime Law, Military Law, Natural Resources, Occupational Safety, Oil & Gas, Personal Property, Public Utilities, Sea, Space, State & Local Government, Taxation, Torts, Uniform Commerical Code, War, Water Law

RESEARCH GUIDES & BIBLIOGRAPHIES:
Doing Research in Federal Transportation Law by C. Brookes & M. McGuirl (Library of Congress Law Div., 1981).
International Bibliography of Air Law, 1900–1971 by W. Heere (Oceana, 1972).
Research in Transportation Legal/Legislative and Economic Sources and Procedures by K. FLood (Gale).

CASES, DECISIONS, RULES (see also treatises & looseleafs below):
Decisions (National Transportation Safety Board, 1967–).
Interstate Commerce Commission Reports (1887–).
Interstate Commerce Commission Rules of Practice (MD: Rules Service Co., 1977–).
National Transportation Safety Board Regulations (MD: Rules Service Co., 1973–).
Reports (Civil Aeronautics Board, 1939–).
Reports (Federal Maritime Commission, 1960–).

JOURNALS, NEWSLETTERS & OTHER PERIODICALS:
Annual Transportation Law Institute (Univ. of Denver College of Law, and Law and Motor Carrier Lawyers Assn.).
ICC Practitioners Journal (Assn. of ICC Practitioners, 1933–).
Journal of Air Law and Commerce (Southern Methodist Univ. School of Law, 1975–).
Railway Age (NY: Simmons Boardman, 1856–).
Transit Law Review (American Public Transit Assn.).
Transportation Journal (American Society of Traffic and Transportation, 1961–).
Transportation Law Journal (Univ. of Denver Law School, 1961–).
Transportation Law Seminars (Assn. of Transportation Practitioners).
Transportation Practitioners Journal (Assn. of Transportation Practitioners, 1933–).

TREATISES & LOOSELEAFS:
Current Issues in International Ship Finance (Practicing Law Institute, 1984).
Encyclopedia of Shipping Law Sources (UK) by E. Ivamy (Lloyd's of London Press, 1985–).
Federal Carriers Reports (CCH, 1937–).
Fleet Safety Compliance Manual (Neenah, WI: J.J. Keller, 1978–).
Freight Claims Manual (Neenah, WI: J.J. Keller, 1979–).
Hazardous Material Transportation (BNA, 1977–).
How to Recover for Loss or Damage to Goods in Transit by S. Sorkin (Matthew Bender, 1976–).

Interstate Commerce Guide (Neenah, WI: J.J. Keller, 1982–).

Interstate Motor Carrier Forms Manual (Neenah, WI: J.J. Keller, 1976–).

Law and Economic Regulation in Transportation by Dempsey (Greenwood Press).

Legal Aspects of Travel Agency Operation, 2d ed. by J. Miller (Albany: Delmar Pub., 1987).

Miller's Law of Freight Loss and Damage Claims, 4th ed. by J. Miller (Dubuque, IA: W.C. Brown, 1974).

Motor Carrier: Freight Forwarder Service (Hawkins, Inc., 1937–).

Motor Carrier Rate Structures (Praeger, 1979).

National Transportation Safety Board Service (Arlington, VA: Hawkins, Inc., 1972–).

Pricing and Capacity in International Air Transport: A Legal Analysis by P. Haanappel (Kluwer, 1984).

Rail Carrier Service (Hawkins, Inc., 1927).

Rail Deregulation Act Monitor Wash. D.C.: Traffic Service Corp., 1980–).

Railroads and Regulation by G. Kolko (Greenwood Press, 1965).

Shipping Regulation by J. Willis (Pike & Fischer, 1961–).

State Motor Carrier Guide (CCH, 1940–).

State Regulations Manual for Private Truck Operations (Wash. D.C.: Private Truck Council of America, 1976–).

Transportation Facility Negligence (ABA).

Transportation Law, 4th ed. by J. Guandolor (Dubuque, IA: Wm. C. Brown, 1983).

Transportation Regulation, 8th ed. by M. Fair & J. Guandolo (Dubuque, IA: Wm C. Brown, 1979).

Transport Laws of the World, D. Hill & M. Evans, eds. (Oceana, 1977–).

Travel Abroad—Frontier Formalities: Passports and Visas, Customs ..., 27th ed. (Geneva: World Tourism Organization, 1979).

Travel Industry Problems (Practicing Law Institute, 1987).

Travel Law by T. Dickerson (New York Law Pub. Co., 1981–).

Trucking Regulation by T. Moore (American Enterprise Institute, 1976).

Truck Permit Guide (Neenah, WI: J.J. Keller, 1974–).

World Shipping Laws, D. Jackson, ed. (Oceana, 1979–).

ENCYCLOPEDIAS:

AMERICAN JURISPRUDENCE 2D (Am Jur 2d)
Check the following topincs in the *General Index* volumes for Am Jur 2d:

Administrative Law	Public Convenience or
Automobiles	Necessity
Aviation	Railroads
Boats	Ships and Shipping
Carriers	Streetcars
Customs	Transportation
Ferries	Trucks
Freight	Weights and Measures
Marine Insurance	

CORPUS JURIS SECUNDUM (CJS)
Check the following topics in the *General Index* volumes for CJS:

Administrative Bodies	Boats
Aeronautics and	Canals
Aerospace	Cargo
Aircraft	Carriers
Airports	Certificate of Public
Barges	Convenience
Bills of Lading	Customs

Ferries	Rates
Forwarding Agents	Ships
Freight	Transportation
Navigable Waters	Trucks
Ports and Harbors	Weights and Measures
Railroads	

DIGESTS:

CASE SEARCH IN WEST DIGESTS BY KEY TOPIC
In the *Descriptive Word Index* of the West digests, look for key topics and numbers under the following subject headings:

Administrative Law	Ferries
Admiralty	Shipping
Carriers	Transportation

ALR:

ANNOTATIONS
Check the index volumes for ALR, ALR2d, ALR3d, ALR4th, and ALR Fed for annotations under the following subject headings:

Aviation	Interstate Commerce Act
Buses	Railroads
Carriers	Shipping
Freight	Transportation

PERIODICALS:

CURRENT LAW INDEX (CLI) & LEGAL RESOURCE INDEX (LRI)
In the CLI and LRI, look for references to periodical literature under the following subject headings:

Administrative Law	Maritime Law
Aeronautics	Railroad
Airplanes	Shipping
Carriers	Transportation
Deregulation	United States Interstate
Freight	Commerce Commission

INDEX TO LEGAL PERIODICALS (ILP)
In the ILP, look for references to legal periodical literature under the following subject headings:

Administrative Law	Interstate Commerce
Bills of Lading	Motor Vehicles
Carriers	Railroads
Commerce	Rate Regulation
Exports	Shipping
Freight	Transportation

TRANSSEXUALISM: See Health & Medicine, Homosexuality
TRAUMA: See Health & Medicine, Mental Health, Torts
TRAVEL AGENTS: See Agency, Business Law, Transportation
TREATIES: See Constitutional Law, Indians, International Law, Taxation, United Nations
TREATMENT: See Death, Health & Medicine, Mental Health, Torts
TRESPASS: See Criminal Law, Real Estate, Torts

TRIAL & APPELLATE PRACTICE

SEE ALSO:

Administrative Law, Air & Aviation, Antitrust Law, Business Law, Circuit Courts, Constitutional Law, Criminal Law, Employment Discrimination, Environmental Law,

Family Law, Forensic Science, Freedom of Information, Judicial Administration, Jurisprudence, Labor Law, Law Office Management, Legal Research, Ombudsman, Professional Responsibility, Statistics, Torts, Women & the Law; see also entries under individual states and countries

**RESTATEMENTS
(American Law Institute):** *Restatement of the Law of Conflicts of Laws, Second* (1971).
Restatement of the Law of Judgments, Second (1982).
Restatement of the Law of Restitution (1937).

RULES: *Federal Circuit Court Rules Service* (Rules Service Co., 1982–).
Federal Local Court Rules, Pike & Fischer, ed. (Callaghan, 1964–).
Federal Rules Digest, 3d ed., Pike & Fischer, ed. (Callaghan).
Federal Rules of Civil Procedure by T. Coyne (Clark Boardman, 1982–).
Federal Rules of Evidence, 2d ed. by P. Rothstein (Clark Boardman, 1978–).
Federal Rules of Evidence Digest, Pike & Fischer, ed. (Callaghan, 1979).
Federal Rules of Evidence Service, Pike & Fischer, ed. (Callaghan, 1979).
Federal Rules Service, Pike & Fischer, ed. (Callaghan, 1958–).

**JOURNALS, NEWSLETTERS
& OTHER PERIODICALS:** *American Journal of Trial Advocacy* (Cumberland School of Law, 1977–).
Association of Trial Lawyers of America Law Journal.
Defense Law Journal (Michie).
Federal Rules of Evidence News (Callaghan, 1976–).
Inside Litigation (Law & Business, Inc.).
Litigation (ABA, 1975–).
Litigation News (ABA).
Negotiation Journal (Plenum Press, 1985–).
Trial Lawyer's Guide (Callaghan, 1953–).
Verdicts & Settlements (Litigation Research Group).

LOOSELEAFS: *Appeals* by M. Houts (Matthew Bender, 1981–).
Art of Advocacy (Matthew Bender, 1978–).
Bender's Federal Practice Forms by L. Frumer et al. (Matthew Bender, 1951–).
Bender's Federal Practice Manual, 2d ed. by I. Hall (Matthew Bender, 1952–).
Bender's Forms of Discovery (Matthew Bender, 1967–).
Bender's Forms of Pleading by O. Warren (Matthew Bender, 1946–).
BNA Civil Trial Manual (BNA, 1986–).
Civil Trial Manual II by R. McCullough et al. (ALI–ABA Comm. on Cont. Prof. Ed., 1981–).
Class Actions: The Law of 50 States by T. Dickerson (New York Law Pub. Co., 1988–).
Court Awarded Attorney Fees by M. Derfner (Matthew Bender, 1983–).
Deposition Strategy, Law and Forms (Matthew Bender, 1981–).
Economic Damages by M. Brookshire (Anderson, 1987)
Federal Lawyer's Manual by R. Needham (Callaghan, 1981–).
Federal Testimonial Privileges by M. Larkin (Clark Boardman, 1982–).
Goldstein Trial Technique, 2d ed. by F. Lane (Callaghan, 1969).
Jury Selection by W. Wagner (Matthew Bender, 1981–).
Jury Work, 2d ed. by Natl. Jury Project (Clark Boardman, 1983–).
Manual for Complex Litigation (Clark Boardman, 1982–).
Manual for Complex Litigation, 2d ed. (Matthew Bender, 1948–).
Modern Visual Evidence by G. Joseph (Law Journal Seminars-Press, 1984–).
Moore's Federal Practice, 2d ed. (Matthew Bender, 1951–).
Moore's Manual by J. Moore et al. (Matthew Bender, 1962–).
National Verdict Survey, M. Lurie et al., eds. (Jury Verdict Research, 1983–).

Practice Before Federal Magistrates by K. Sinclair (Matthew Bender, 1984–).
Scientific Evidence by P. Giannelli (Michie, 1986).
Settlement by H. Miller (Matthew Bender, 1983–).
Successful Litigation Techniques by J. Kelner (Matthew Bender, 1964–).
Weinstein's Evidence by J. Weinstein & M. Berger (Matthew Bender, 1975–).
Winning Attorney Fees from the Government by J. Bennett (Law Journal Seminars-Press, 1984–).

TREATISES:

Advocacy: The Art of Pleading a Case, 2d ed. by R. Givens (Shepard's, 1984).
American Jurisprudence Pleading and Practice Form (Lawyers Co-op., 1956).
American Jurisprudence Proof of Facts 3d (Lawyers Co-op., 1988).
Causes of Action (Shepard's).
Civil Practice and Litigation in Federal and State Courts, 2d ed. (ALI–ABA Comm. on Cont. Prof. Ed., 1984).
Cyclopedia of Federal Procedure, 3d ed. (Callaghan, 1965).
Cyclopedia of Trial Practice (Lawyers Co-op.).
Federal Jury Practice and Instructions, 3d ed. (West, 1977).
Federal Practice and Procedure by C. Wright et al. (West, 1969).
Federal Procedural Forms, L.Ed. (Lawyers Co-op., 1975).
Federal Procedure, L.Ed. (Lawyers Co-op., 1981).
Federal Trial Handbook, 2d ed. by R. Hunter (Lawyer's Co-op. 1984).
The Hearsay Handbook, 2d ed. by D. Binder (Shepard's, 1983).
Law of Federal Courts, 4th ed. by C. Wright (West, 1983).
Legal Negotiations and Settlement by G. Williams (West, 1983).
McCormick's Handbook of the Law of Evidence, 3d ed. by E. Cleary et al. (West, 1984).
Model Code of Evidence (American Law Institute, 1942).
Multidistrict Litigation by D. Herr (Little, Brown, 1986).
Pattern Deposition Checklists by D. Danner (Lawyers Co-op., 1973).
Pattern Interrogatories by D. Danner (Lawyers Co-op., 1970).
Photographic Evidence, 2d ed. by C. Scott (West, 1969).
Questioning Techniques and Tactics by J. Kestler (Shepard's, 1982).
Scientific Evidence by P. Giannelli (Michie, 1986).
Statistical Evidence in Litigation by D. Barnes (Little, Brown).
Supreme Court Practice, 6th ed. by R. Stern (BNA, 1986).
Testimonial Privileges, S. Stone, ed. (Shepard's, 1983).
A Treatise on the Anglo-American System of Evidence in Trials at Common Law, 3d ed. by J. Wigmore (Little, Brown, 1940).
West's Federal Forms.
West's Federal Practice Manual, 2d ed. by M. Volz (West).

SERIES:

Contemporary Litigation Series (Michie).
Federal Practice Series (Clark Boardman).
Litigation and Administrative Practice Series (Practicing Law Institute).
Trial and Appellate Library (ALI–ABA Comm. on Cont. Prof. Ed.).

TRIBAL LAW: See Customary Law, Indians
TRIBUNAL: See Military Law, Trial & Appellate Practice

TRINIDAD & TOBAGO

SEE ALSO:

Caribbean, International Law, Latin America, United Nations

CONSTITUTION:

Constitutions of the Countries of the World (Trinidad and Tobago) by A. Blaustein & C. Flanz (Oceana, 1982).

STATUTES & RELATED LAWS:	*Trinidad & Tobago Consolidated Index of Statutes and Subsidiary Legislation* by the Faculty of Law Library, Univ. of West Indies, Barbados (Gaunt, 1986).
JOURNALS & OTHER PERIODICALS:	*The Lawyer, Journal of the Trinidad and Tobago Bar Association* (1977–).
TREATISES & LOOSELEAFS:	*Caribbean Basin: A Tax Tour* (Trinidad and Tobago) (Arthur Anderson & Co., 1985). *The Evolution of Labour Relations Legislation in Trinidad and Tobago* by C. Okpaluba (St. Agustine, Univ. of West Indies, 1980). *Information Guide: Doing Business in Trinidad and Tobago* (Price Waterhouse). *Investment Laws of the World: The Developing Nations* (Trinidad and Tobago) (Oceana, 1972–). *Tax Laws of the World—Trinidad and Tobago* (FL: Foreign Tax Law Assn.). *Trinidad and Tobago: Democracy and Development in the Caribbean* by S. MacDonald (Praeger, 1986). *West Indian Constitutions: Post Independence Reform* (Trinidad and Tobago) by F. Phillips (Oceana, 1985).
ARTICLES:	"The Right of Appeal from Trinidad and Tobago's Industrial Court" by R. Castagne, 12 *Lawyer of the Americas* 343 (1980).

TROVER: See Personal Property, Torts
TRUCK: See Transportation, Torts
TRUST: See Equity, Estate Planning, Real Estate
TRUSTEE: See Bankruptcy, Employee Benefits
TRUST EXAMINERS: See Banking Law
TRUST TERRIROTY: See Micronesia
TRUTH IN LENDING: See Banking Law, Consumer Law
TSWANA: See Bophuthatswana
TUG: See Maritime Law
TUITION: See Education Law

TUNISIA

SEE ALSO:	Africa, International Law, Islam, United Nations
CONSTITUTION:	*Constitutions of the Countries of the World* (Tunisia) by A. Blaustein & G. Flanz (Oceana, 1982).
STATUTES & RELATED LAWS:	*Investment Codes of North Africa: Tunisa,* E. de Brauw, transl. (Amsterdam: Intl. Bureau of Fiscal Documentation, 1980).
TREATISES & LOOSELEAFS:	*African Tax Systems* (Tunisia) by R. Hammond & M. van den Abeelen (Amsterdam: Intl. Bureau of Fiscal Documentation, 1980–). *Capital Formation and Investment Incentives Around the World* (Tunisia) by W. Diamond & D. Diamond (Matthew Bender, 1984–). *Digest of Commercial Laws of the World* (Tunisia) (Natl. Assn. of Credit Management; Oceana, 1977–).

An Introduction to Law in French-Speaking Africa (Tunisia) by J. Salacuse (Michie, 1975).
Investment Laws of the World (Tunisia) (Oceana, 1981–).
Tax Laws of the World—Tunisia (FL: Foreign Tax Law Assn.).

ARTICLES: "Law of the Sea: Delimitation of the Tunisia-Libya Continental Shelf" by M. Sonenshine, 24 *Harvard International Law Journal* 225 (1983).
"The Tunisian Law of Personal Status" by J. Anderson, 7 *International and Comparative Law Quarterly* 262 (1958).

TURKEY

SEE ALSO: Asia, International Law, Islam, United Nations

CONSTITUTION: *Constitutions of Eastern Countries* (Turkey) by M. Ahmad (Karachi, Pakistan, 1951).
Constitutions of the Countries of the World (Turkey) by A. Blaustein & G. Flanz (Oceana, 1982).

STATUTES & RELATED LAWS: *Turkish Code of Criminal Procedure* (Rothman, 1962).
Turkish Criminal Code (Rothman, 1965).

TREATISES & LOOSELEAFS: *The Attalid Kingdom: A Constitutional History* by R. Allen (Oxford Univ. Press, 1983).
Capital Formation and Investment Incentives Around the World (Turkey) by W. Diamond & D. Diamond (Matthew Bender, 1984–).
A Crime of Silence: The Armenian Genocide by The Permanent People's Tribunal (London: Zed, 1985).
Digest of Commercial Laws of the World (Turkey) (Natl. Assn. of Credit Management; Oceana, 1977–).
Freedom and Fear: Human Rights in Turkey (NY: Helsinki Watch Committee, 1986).
Information Guide: Doing Business in Turkey (Price Waterhouse).
Introduction to Turkish Law, 3d ed., T. Ansay & D. Wallace, eds. (Oceana, 1987).
Investment Laws of the World (Turkey) (Oceana, 1981–).
Tax Laws of the World—Turkey (FL: Foreign Tax Law Assn.).
Turkey: Law on Legitimacy by B. Bayar (Library of Congress, 1983).

ARTICLES: "Dispute and Settlement in Rural Turkey," 45 *Modern Law Review* 230 (1982).
"Financial Crisis Management in Egypt and Turkey" by D. Radke, 17 *Journal of World Trade Law* 325 (1983).
"Turkey: Legal Education" by E. Orucu, 5 *Commercial Law Yearbook* 145 (1981).
"Turkey: Reconciling Traditional Society and Secular Demands" by E. Orucu, 26 *Journal of Family Law* 221 (1987–88).

TURKS & CAICOS ISLANDS

SEE ALSO: Caribbean, England, International Law, Latin America, United Nations

CONSTITUTION: *Constitutions of Dependencies and Special Sovereignties* (Turks & Caicos Islands) by A. Blaustein (Oceana, 1983).

**TREATISES &
LOOSELEAFS:**   *Tax Havens Encyclopedia* (Turks and Caicos Islands) by B. Spitz (Butterworths, 1975–).
West Indian Constitutions: Post Independence Reform (Turks and Caicos Islands) by F. Phillips (Oceana, 1985).

ARTICLES: "Incorporating Offshore in Turks and Caicos" by G. Moore, 9 *International Tax Journal* 125 (1982).

TURNPIKE: See Government Contracts, State & Local Government, Torts
TV: See Media Law

UAE: See United Arab Emirates
UCC: See Uniform Commerical Code

UGANDA

SEE ALSO: Africa, International Law, United Nations

**RESEARCH GUIDE &
BIBLIOGRAPHY:**   "Notes on Legal Literature in East Africa" (Uganda), 10 *Case Western Reserve Journal of International Law* 123 (1978).

CONSTITUTION: *Constitutions of the Countries of the World* (Uganda) by A. Blaustein & G. Flanz (Oceana, 1982).

CASES: *East Africa Law Reports.*
Uganda Law Reports.

**JOURNALS & OTHER
PERIODICALS:**   *Uganda Law Focus* (1972)–).

**TREATISES &
LOOSELEAFS:**   *African Tax Systems* (Uganda) by R. Hammond & M. van den Abeelen (Amsterdam: Intl. Bureau of Fiscal Documentation, 1980–).
Conflict Resolution in Uganda, K. Rupesinghe, ed. (Ohio Univ. Press, 1989).
Criminal Procedure in Uganda and Kenya, 2d ed. by Brown (London: Sweet & Maxwell, 1970).
Integration and Disintegration in East Africa (Uganda) by C. Potholm & R. Fredland (Univ. Press of America, 1980).
An Introduction to the Law of Uganda by Brown & Allen (London: Sweet & Maxwell, 1968).
Investment Laws of the World (Uganda) (Oceana, 1981–).
The Status of Aliens in East Africa: Asians and Europeans in Tanzania, Uganda, and Kenya by D. Nanjira (Praeger, 1976).
Uganda: A Modern History by J. Jorgensen (St. Martin's Press, 1981).
Uganda: The Development of its Laws and Constitution by H. Morris & J. Read (London: Sweet & Maxwell, 1966).

ARTICLES: "Autochthony: The Development of Law in Uganda" by F. Ssekandi, 5 *New York Law School Journal of International and Comparative Law* 1 (1983).

"Corporate Personality and the 'African' Company in Uganda" by P. Thomas, 1 *East Africa Law Review* (1968).

ULTRA VIRES: See Corporate Law

UMM ALL QUWAIN: See United Arab Emirates

UN: See United Nations

UNAUTHORIZED PRACTICE OF LAW: See Paralegal, Professional Responsibility

UNBORN CHILDREN: See Abortion, Estate Planning, Family Law, Juvenile Law

UNCLAIMED PROPERTY: See Personal Property

UNCLOS: See Sea

UNCONSCIONABLE: See Consumer Law, Contracts, Uniform Commercial Code

UNDERWRITING: See Insurance, Securities Law

UNDUE INFLUENCE: See Contracts, Equity, Estate Planning, Torts

UNEMPLOYMENT COMPENSATION

SEE ALSO: Administrative Law, Employment Benefits, Labor Law, Social Security, Workers' Compensation

TREATISES & LOOSELEAFS: *Comparison of State Unemployment Insurance Laws* by the U.S. Dept. of Labor (GPO, 1978–).

How to Collect Unemployment Benefits (Prentice-Hall, 1983).

Promoting Employment and Maintaining Incomes with Unemployment Insurance by B. Vavriechek (Congressional Budget Office, 1985).

Unemployment Compensation (Natl. Commn. on Unemployment Compensation, 1980).

Unemployment Insurance Reports with Social Security (CCH, 1934–).

UNESCO: See International Law, United Nations

UNFAIR COMPETITION: See Antitrust Law, Business Law, Intellectual Property, International Law

UNFAIR LABOR PRACTICE: See Labor Law

UNIFORM CODE OF MILITARY JUSTICE: See Military Law

UNIFORM COMMERCIAL CODE

SEE ALSO: Agency, Agriculture, Banking Law, Business Law, Commodities, Contracts, Corporate Law, Insurance, International Law, Personal Property, Securities Law, Torts

RESEARCH GUIDES & BIBLIOGRAPHIES: "Contemporary Commercial Law Literature in the United States" by P. Winship, 43 *Ohio State Law Journal* 643 (1982).

"The Uniform Commercial Code" by I. Kavass in *Specialized Legal Research,* L. Chanin, ed. (Little, Brown, 1987).

Uniform Commercial Code Bibliography by M. Ezer (ALI-ABA Comm. on Cont. Prof. Ed., 1972). (Supplement by A. Squillante, 1978).

JOURNALS, NEWSLETTERS
& OTHER PERIODICALS: *Annual Review of Banking Law* (Warren, Gorham & Lamont).
Bank Automation Newsletter (Warren, Gorham & Lamont).
Banker's Letter of the Law (Warren, Gorham & Lamont).
Banking Law Journal (Warren, Gorham & Lamont).
Banking Lawyer (ABA).
Commercial Law Journal (Commercial Law League of America, 1963–).
Secured Lending Alert (Warren, Gorham & Lamont, 1985–).
UCC Bulletin (Callaghan, 1984–).
Uniform Commercial Code Law Journal (Warren, Gorham & Lamont, 1968–).
Uniform Commercial Code Law Letter, T. Quinn, ed. (Warren, Gorham & Lamont, 1967–).

LOOSELEAFS: *Commercial Paper Under the Uniform Commercial Code* by F. Hart (Matthew Bender, 1972–).
Compendium of Commercial Finance Law (NY: Natl. Commercial Finance Conference).
Consumer and Commercial Credit-Installment Sales Service (Prentice-Hall, 1932–).
Forms and Procedures Under the Uniform Commercial Code by F. Hart (Matthew Bender, 1963–).
Modern UCC Litigation Forms by P. Bestos (Matthew Bender, 1969–).
Sales and Bulk Transfers Under the Uniform Commercial Code by R. Dusenberg (Matthew Bender, 1980–).
Secured Transactions Guide (CCH, 1969–).
Secured Transactions Under the Uniform Commercial Code by P. Coogan (Matthew Bender, 1963–).
Uniform Commercial Code Case Digest (Callaghan, 1976–).
Uniform Commercial Code Commentary and Law Digest, T. Quinn (Warren, Gorham & Lamont).
Uniform Commercial Code Reporter-Digest, F. Hart, ed. (Matthew Bender, 1965–).
Uniform Commercial Code Reporting Service (Callaghan, 1964–).
Uniform Commercial Code Series by D. Hawkland (Callaghan, 1982–).
Uniform Commercial Code Service (Callaghan, 1965–).

TREATISES: *Anderson's Uniform Commercial Code,* 3d ed. by R. Anderson (Lawyers Co-op., 1981).
Commercial Loan Documentation by W. Hillman (Practicing Law Institute, 1982).
Common Law and Equity under the Uniform Commercial Code by R. Hillman (Warren, Gorham & Lamont, 1985).
Consumer Credit Compliance Manual by J. Fonseca (Lawyers Co-op., 1975).
Handbook of Secured Transactions Under the Uniform Commercial Code, 2d ed. by R. Henson (West, 1979).
Handling Consumer Credit Cases, 2d ed. by J. Fonseca (Lawyers Co-op., 1980).
The Law of Bank Deposits, Collections and Credit Cards by B. Clark (Warren, Gorham & Lamont, 1981).
The Law of Electronic Fund Transfer Systems by N. Penney (Warren, Gorham & Lamont, 1980).
The Law of Letters of Credit by J. Dolan (Warren, Gorham & Lamont, 1984).
The Law of Modern Commercial Practices by A. Squillante (Lawyers Co-op., 1980).
The Law of Product Warranties by B. Clark (Warren, Gorham & Lamont, 1984).
The Law of Sales Under the Uniform Commercial Code by G. Wallach (Warren, Gorham & Lamont, 1981).
The Law of Secured Transactions Under the Uniform Commercial Code by B. Clark (Warren, Gorham & Lamont, 1988).
Transactional Guide to the Uniform Code, 2d ed. by R. Alderman (ALI–ABA Comm. on Cont. Prof. Ed., 1983).

Transfer of Stock, 6th ed., M. Rhodes, ed. (Lawyers Co-op., 1985).
The Uniform Commercial Code, 3d ed. by J. White & R. Summers (Practitioner's
   Edition, West, 1988).
Uniform Commercial Code in a Nutshell, 2d ed. by B. Stone (West, 1984).
Williston on Sales, 4th ed. by A. Squillante (Lawyers Co-op., 1973).

SHEPARD'S: *Shepard's Uniform Commercial Code Citations*

ENCYCLOPEDIAS: AMERICAN JURISPRUDENCE 2D (Am Jur 2d)
                        Check the following topics in the *General Index* volumes for Am Jur 2d:

Banks	Contracts
Bills and Notes	Credit
Bulk Sales	Debts
Business	Investment Companies
Commerce	Sales
Commercial Code	Secured Transactions
Consignment	Vendor and Purchaser
Corporations	

CORPUS JURIS SECUNDUM (CJS)
Check the following topics in the *General Index* volumes for CJS:

Bills and Notes	Goods
Bulk Sales	Income
Commerce	Law Merchant
Contracts	Principal and Surety
Corporations	Profits
Credit	

DIGESTS: CASE SEARCH IN WEST DIGESTS BY KEY TOPIC
                        In the *Descriptive Word Index* of the West digests, look for key topics and numbers
                        under the following subject headings:

Accounts	Corporations
Bills & Notes	Credit
Bulk Sales	Goods
Commerce	Vendor
Contracts	Wholesale

ALR: ANNOTATIONS
                        Check the index volumes for ALR, ALR2d, ALR3d, ALR4th, and ALR Fed for annotations
                        under the following subject headings:

Accounts	Merchandise
Commerce	Retailer
Franchises	Sales
Inventory	

PERIODICALS: CURRENT LAW INDEX (CLI) & LEGAL RESOURCE INDEX (LRI)
                        In the CLI and LRI, look for references to periodical literature under the following
                        subject headings:

Bills of Exchange	Commercial Law
Bulk Sales	Debtor and Creditor
Business	Deposits
Capital	Finance
Chattel Mortgage	Installment Sales
Checks	International Business

Interstate Commerce	Partnership
Joint Ventures	Sales
Liens	Security
Manufacturers	Vendors and Purchasers
Negotiable Instruments	

INDEX TO LEGAL PERIODICALS (ILP)

In the ILP, look for references to legal periodical literature under the following subject headings:

Banks and Banking	Franchising
Bills of Lading	Fraud
Bulk Transfer	International Trade
Business	Leases
Checks	Letters of Credit
Conditional Sales	Negotiable Instruments
Consumer Protection	Sales
Contracts	Vendor and Purchaser
Equipment Leasing	Warranty

UNIFORM LAWS: See Consumer Law, Estate Planning, Uniform Commercial Code

UNIFORM PARTNERSHIP ACT: See Partnership Law

UNIFORM RECIPROCAL ENFORCEMENT OF SUPPORT ACT: See Family Law, Women & the Law

UNILATERAL CONTRACT: See Contracts

UNINSURED MOTORIST: See Insurance

UNION: See Civil Service, Communism, Education Law, Labor Law, Poland, State & Local Government

UNION OF SOVIET SOCIALIST REPUBLICS: See Soviet Union

UNITED ARAB EMIRATES

SEE ALSO: International Law, Islam, Middle East, United Nations

CONSTITUTION: *Constitutions of the Countries of the World* (United Arab Emirates) by A. Blaustein & G. Flanz (Oceana, 1982).

TREATISES & LOOSELEAFS:
Business Law of UAE by N. Karam (London: Graham & Trotman, 1984–).

Commercial Laws of the Middle East (United Arab Emirates) by A. Keesee (Oceana, 1980–).

Commercial Laws of the World, Middle East States (United Arab Emirates) (FL: Foreign Tax Law Assn., 1985–).

Information Guide: Doing Business in United Arab Emirates (Price Waterhouse).

The Laws of Saudi Arabia, the UAE, Egypt, and Jordan: A Legal and Investment Guide for American Business (Wash. D.C.: American Arab Affairs Council, 1985).

Taxes and Investment in the Middle East (United Arab Emirates) (Intl. Bureau of Fiscal Documentation).

Tax Laws of the World-United Arab Emirates (FL Foreign Tax Law Assn.).

United Arab Emirates: Unity in Fragmentation by A. Khalifa (Westview, 1979).

ARTICLES: ". . . Business in the United Arab Emirates" by J. Beaven, 10 *Australian Business Law Review* 215 (1982).

"Commercial Agency Law" by J. Barlow, 7 *Middle East Executive Reports* 21 (Jan., 1984) (see also vol. 8, p. 21).

"Corporate Law" by N. Angell, 11 *International Business Lawyer* 42 (1983).

"Middle East Agency Law Survey" (UAR) by F. Taylor, 14 *International Lawyer* 355 (1980).

UNITED KINGDOM: See England, Ireland, Scotland, Wales

UNITED NATIONS

SEE ALSO:
Human Rights, International law, Maritime Law, Sea, War; see also entries under individual countries and continents

RESEARCH GUIDES & BIBLIOGRAPHIES:
"A Bibliography of Commentaries on the United Nations International Sales Convention" by P. Winship, 21 *International Lawyer* 585 (1987).

Bibliography of Publications on UNESCO (Paris: UNESCO Library, 1984).

The Complete Reference Guide to United Nations Sales Publications, 1946–1978 by M. Birchfield & J. Coolman (UNIFO, 1982).

Directory of United Nations Databases and Information Systems (UN Publications).

Guide to United Nations Organization, Documentation and Publishing by P. Hajnal (Oceana, 1978).

Publications of the United Nations System by H. Winton (Bowker, 1972).

UNDOC: Current Index (UN Publication, 1979–).

United Nations Bibliographic Information System (UNBIS).

United Nations Documents Index (UNDEX) (UN, 1969–).

"United Nations" in "Bibliographic Notes," 15 *The Journal of International Law and Economics* 33, 280 (1981).

TREATIES:
Cumulative List and Index to Treaties and International Agreements Registered or Filed and Recorded with the Secretariat of the United States by V. & R. Vambery (Oceana, 1977).

League of Nations, Treaty Series: Treaties and International Engagements Registered with the Secretariat of the League (1920–1946).

Multilateral Treaties, Conventions, Protocols and Agreements of the United Nations and the Specialized Agencies (Geneva: World Peace through Law Center, 1967).

Multilateral Treaties Deposited with the Secretary-General, Status as of 31 December, 1984 (1981–). (ST/LEG/ SER.E/3.)

Office of Legal Affairs, List of Treaty Collections (United Nations, 1966).

Statement of Treaties and International Agreements Registered or Filed and Recorded with the Secretariat of the United Nations (UN Office of Legal Affairs, 1947–).

Status of Multilateral Conventions in Respect of which the Secretary-General Acts as a Depository (UN Office of Legal Affairs, 1953– ; rev. ed., 1959–).

United Nations Treaty Series: Treaties and International Agreements Registered or Filed and Recorded with the Secretariat of the United Nations (1946).

CASES:
Report of Judgments, Advisory Opinions and Orders (Intl. Court of Justice).

JOURNALS, YEARBOOKS & OTHER PERIODICALS:
United Nations Commission on International Trade Law Yearbook (NY: 1970–).

United Nations International Law Commission Yearbook (UN Publications, 1949–).

United Nations Juridical Yearbook (UN Publications, 1965–).

United Nations Library Monthly Bibliography (Geneva, 1928–).
Yearbook of the United Nations (UN Dept. of Public Information, 1947–).

**TREATISES &
LOOSELEAFS:**

A Chronology and Fact Book of the United Nations, 1941–1979 by T. & E. Hovet
 (Oceana, 1979).
Encyclopedia of the United Nations and International Agreements by E. Osmanczyk
 (Philadelphia: Taylor & Francis, 1985).
*Everyman's United Nations, A Ready Reference to the Structure, Functions and Work
 of the United Nations and its Related Agencies* (UN Dept. of Pub. Info., 1945–).
Guide to UNESCO by P. Hajnal (Oceana, 1983).
*Manual on Licensing Procedures in the Member Countries of the United Nations
 Economic Commission for Europe* (Clark Boardman, 1984).
United Nations Law Reports, J. Carey, ed. (NY: Walker & Co.).

PERIODICALS:

CURRENT LAW INDEX (CLI) & LEGAL RESOURCE INDEX (LRI)
In the CLI and LRI, look for references to periodical literature under the following
subject headings:

Civil Rights (International Law)	International Law
	United Nations
International Court of Justice	World Health Organization

UNITED STATES ATTORNEYS: See Criminal Law
UNITED STATES COURT OF APPEALS: See Circuit Courts, Trial & Appellate Practice
UNITED STATES COURT OF CUSTOMS AND PATENT APPEALS: See Intellectual
 Property
UNITED STATES COURT OF INTERNATIONAL TRADE: See Customs
UNITED STATES COURT OF MILITARY JUSTICE: See Military Law
UNITED STATES DEPARTMENT OF COMMERCE: See Intellectual Property,
 International Law
UNITED STATES DEPARTMENT OF HOUSING & HUMAN DEVELOPMENT: See
 Poverty Law, Real Estate
UNITED STATES DEPARTMENT OF STATE: See International Law
UNITED STATES DEPARTMENT OF THE INTERIOR: See Natural Resources, Water Law
UNITED STATES FEDERAL COMMUNICATIONS COMMISSION: See Media Law
UNITED STATES IMMIGRATION AND NATURALIZATION SERVICE: See Immigration
 Law
UNITED STATES INTERNAL REVENUE SERVICE: See Taxation
UNITED STATES INTERSTATE COMMERCE COMMISSION: See Transportation
UNITED STATES MAGISTRATES: See Circuit Courts, Trial & Appellate Practice
UNITED STATES MERIT PROTECTION BOARD: See Civil Service
UNITED STATES OCCUPATIONAL SAFETY & HEALTH ADMINISTRATION: See
 Occupational Safety, Torts
UNITED STATES PATENT & TRADEMARK OFFICE: See Intellectual Property
UNITED STATES PENSION BENEFIT GUARANTEE CORPORATION: See Employee
 Benefits
UNITED STATES SOCIAL SECURITY ADMINISTRATION: See Social Security
UNITED STATES SUPREME COURT: See Constitutional Law, Trial & Appellate Practice
UNITED STATES TAX COURT: See Taxation
UNITED STATES TERRITORIES: See American Samoa, Guam, Virgin Islands

UNJUST DISMISSAL: See Civil Service, Employment Discrimination, Labor Law
UNJUST ENRICHMENT: See Contracts, Equity, Torts
UNMARRIED COUPLES: See Family Law, Juvenile Law, Women & the Law
UNPERFECTED TREATIES: See International Law, United Nations
UPGRADE: See Military Law
UPPER VOLTA: See Burkina Faso
URANIUM: See Natural Resources
URBAN PLANNING: See Real Estate, State & Local Government, Zoning & Land
    Planning
URESA: See Family Law

URUGUAY

SEE ALSO: International Law, Latin America, United Nations

RESEARCH GUIDES &
BIBLIOGRAPHIES: *A Guide to the Law and Literature of Uruguay* (Library of Congress, 1947).
                     A Guide to the Official Publications of Uruguay (Library of Congress, 1948).

CONSTITUTION: *Constitutions of the Countries of the World* (Uruguay) by A. Blaustein & G. Flanz
                     (Oceana, 1982).

TREATISES &
LOOSELEAFS: *Capital Formation and Investment Incentives Around the World* (Uruguay) by
                         W. Diamond & D. Diamond (Matthew Bender, 1984–).
                     Digest of Commercial Laws of the World (Uruguay) (Natl. Assn. of Credit Manage-
                         ment; Oceana, 1977–).
                     The Generals Give Back Uruguay (NY: Lawyers Committee for Intl. Human Rights,
                         1985).
                     Information Guide: Doing Business in Uruguay (Price Waterhouse).
                     Latin America . . . A Tax Tour (Uruguay) (Arthur Anderson & Co., 1985).
                     Legal Aspects in International Business (Uruguay) by C. Crosswell (Oceana, 1980).
                     A Statement of the Laws of Uruguay in Matters Affecting Business (Organization of
                         American States, 1971, 1978).
                     Taxation in Uruguay (NY: Deloitte, Haskins & Sells, 1983).
                     Tax Laws of the World—Uruguay (FL: Foreign Tax Law Assn.).

ARTICLES: "The International Monetary Fund: Its Code of Good Behavior and the Uruguayan
                         Stabilization Program of 1968," 10 *Virginia Journal of International Law* 359
                         (1970).
                     "Latin American Tax Update: Uruguay" by M. Marti, 12 *Lawyer of the Americas* 671
                         (1980).
                     "The Uruguayan-Argentinan Trade Co-Operation Agreement" by D. Ferrere, 18
                         Journal of World Trade Law 320 (1984).

USES, STATUTE OF: See Real Estate
USE TAX: See State & Local Government, Taxation
URINALYSIS: See AIDS, Employment Discrimination
USURY: See Banking Law, Consumer Law

UTAH

SEE ALSO:	Circuit Courts (Tenth Circuit)
STATUTES:	*Utah Code Annotated Laws of Utah*
STATE ADMINISTRATIVE CODE:	*Administrative Rules of the State of Utah* (Archives and Records Service). *State of Utah Bulletin* (Archives and Records Service). *Utah Administrative Rule Making Bulletin* (Archives and Records Service).
CASES & OPINIONS:	*Utah Reports* (1855–1974). *Pacific Reporter* (1881–).
COURT RULES:	*Utah Rules of Court* (Michie, 1984).
JURY INSTRUCTIONS:	*Jury Instruction Forms for Utah* (Utah State Bar Assn., 1957).
ETHICS & PROFESSIONAL RESPONSIBILITY:	*Deskbook* (Utah Bar Assn.).
OPINIONS OF THE ATTORNEY GENERAL:	*Attorney General Opinions* (Office of the Attorney General, 1896–).
JOURNALS & OTHER PERIODICALS:	*Utah Bar Journal.* *Utah Bar Newsletter.*
ANNUAL SURVEY OF STATE LAW:	"Recent Developments in Utah Law" in *Utah Law Review.* See for example vol. 1985, p. 131. "Utah Legislative Survey" in *Utah Law Review.* See for example vol. 1984, p. 115.
TREATISES & LOOSELEAFS:	*Statutory Time Limitations: Utah* (Butterworths-Wash., 1981–). *Utah Civil Procedure* by D. Thomas (Provo: Utah Civil Procedure, 1981). *Utah Probate Systems* (Utah Bar Assn., 1977). *Utah Rules of Civil Procedure* (Utah Bar Assn.).
DIGESTS & CITATOR:	*Utah Digest* (West). *Pacific Digest* (West). *Shepard's Utah Citations.*

UTILITY: See Energy, Public Utilities

VACATION OF JUDGMENT: See Trial & Appellate Practice
VAGRANCY: See Criminal Law
VALUE ADDED TAX: See Taxation
VALUE, VALUATION: See Business Law, Estate Planning, Real Estate, Taxation

VANUATU

SEE ALSO: International Law, United Nations

CONSTITUTION: *Constitutions of the Countries of the World* (Vanuatu) by A. Blaustein & G. Flanz (Oceana, 1982).

**TREATISES &
LOOSELEAFS:**   *Information Guide: Doing business in Vanuatu* (Price Waterhouse).
Investment Laws of the World (Vanuatu) (Oceana, 1981–).
Land Tenure in Vanuatu by H. Alatoa (Suva: Institute of Pacific Studies, Univ. of the South Pacific, 1984).

ARTICLES: "Land Regimes and Paradigms of Development: Reflections on Melanesian Constitutions" (Vanuatu) by Y. Ghai, 13 *International Journal of the Sociology of Law* 393 (1985).
"Registration of a Vessel under Vanuatu Law" by V. Hubbard, 13 *Journal of Maritime Law and Commerce* 235 (1982).

VARIANCE: See Zoning & Land Planning
VATICAN: See Canon Law
VENDOR & PURCHASER: See Business Law, Consumer Law, Contracts, Uniform Commercial Code

VENEZUELA

SEE ALSO: International Law, Latin America, United Nations

**RESEARCH GUIDES &
BIBLIOGRAPHIES:**   *A Guide to the Law and Literature of Venezuela* (Library of Congress, 1947).
A Guide to the Official Publications of ... Venezuela (Library of Congress, 1948).

CONSTITUTION: "Venezuela, 1972–1983" in *Constitutions of the Countries of the World* by A. Blaustein & G. Flanz (Oceana, 1983).

**TREATISES &
LOOSELEAFS:**   *The Andean Common Market Management Implications of Technology Legislation,* F. Robles, ed. (NY: Unipub, 1976).
The Andean Legal Order (Venezuela) by F. Garcia-Amador (Oceana, 1978).
Capital Formation and Investment Incentives Around the World (Venezuela) by W. Diamond & D. Diamond (Matthew Bender, 1984–).
Digest of Commercial Laws of the World (Venezuela), Natl. Assn. of Credit Management (Oceana, 1977–).
Information Guide, Doing Business in Venezuela (Price Waterhouse).
Latin America ... A Tax Tour (Venezuela) (Arthur Anderson & Co., 1985).
Latin American Democracies: Colombia, Costa Rica, Venezuela by J. Peeler (Univ. of North Carolina Press, 1985).
The Nationalization of Venezuelan Oil by J. Petras et al. (Praeger, 1977).
Series of Statements of the Law of the OAS Member States in Matters Affecting Business—Venezuela (Organization of American States, 1977).

Tax and Trade Guide to Venezuela, 3d ed. (Arthur Anderson & Co.).
Taxation in Venezuela (NY: Deloitte, Haskins & Sills, 1979).
Tax Laws of the World—Venezuela (FL: Foreign Tax Law Assn.).

ARTICLES:
"Constitutional and Administrative Rights of Private Enterprise in Venezuela and their Protection" by R. Campagna, 16 *International Lawyer* 541 (1982).
"Lawyers and Venezuelan Independence" (Venezuela), 7 *International Journal of the Sociology of Law* 377 (1979).
"Present and Future Venezuelan Technologies: Implementation and Implications for Technology Suppliers and Foreign Investors" by J. Pate, 9 *Lawyer of the Americas* 1 (1977) (see also vol. 12, p. 675; vol. 17, p. 195).
"Security Interests under the Laws of Venezuela: An Introductory Guide," 17 *International Lawyer* 625 (1983).
"Venezuela: Certain Legal Considerations for Doing Business" by R. Radway, 8 *Case Western Reserve Journal of International Law* 289 (1976).
"Venezuela Revisted: Foreign Investment, Technology, and Related Issues" by R. Radway & F. Hoet-Linares, 15 *Vanderbilt Journal of Transnational Law* 1 (1982).

VENTURE CAPITAL: See Business Law, Franchise Law, Securities Law
VENUE: See Trial & Appellate Practice
VERDICT: See Criminal Law, Trial & Appellate Practice

VERMONT

SEE ALSO:
Circuit Courts (Second Circuit)

**RESEARCH GUIDE &
BIBLIOGRAPHY:**
Checklist of Available Vermont State Publications (State Dept. of Libraries).

STATUTES:
Vermont Statutes Annotated.
Laws of Vermont

**STATE ADMINISTRATIVE
CODE:**
Vermont Administrative Procedures Compilation.
Vermont Administrative Procedures Bulletin.
Vermont Regulations Annotated (Fox Pub. Corp.).

CASES & OPINIONS:
Vermont Reports (1826–).
Atlantic Reporter (1885–).

COURT RULES:
Vermont Court Rules Annotated (Equity Pub. Corp., 1981–).

**ETHICS & PROFESSIONAL
RESPONSIBILITY:**
Advisory Ethics Opinions (Vermont Bar Assn.).

**JOURNALS & OTHER
PERIODICALS:**
Vermont Bar Journal and Law Digest.

**TREATISES &
LOOSELEAFS:**
Criminal Law (Vermont Bar Assn., 1985).
Domestic Relations (Vermont Bar Assn., 1985).
Estate Planning and Probate Practice (Vermont Bar Assn., 1985).

Residential Real Estate (Vermont Bar Assn., 1985).
Small Business (Vermont Bar Assn., 1985).

DIGESTS & CITATORS: *Vermont Digest* (West).
Pacific Digest (West).
Shepard's Vermont Citations.

VETERANS: See Military Law
VETERINARIAN: See Agriculture, Animals, Health & Medicine, Torts
VICARIOUS LIABILITY: See Torts, Trial & Appellate Practice
VICTIMS: See Criminal Law, Homosexuality, Torts
VIDEO: See Art & Entertainment, Media Law

VIETNAM

SEE ALSO: Asia, Communism, International Law, United Nations

**RESEARCH GUIDE &
BIBLIOGRAPHY:**   *Vietnamese Legal Materials, 1954–1975: Annotated Bibliography* by P. Nguyen
(Library of Congress, 1977).

**TREATIES & OTHER
AGREEMENTS:**   *Aviation Laws and Treaties of . . . the German Democratic Republic, Hungary, the
Democratic People's Republic of Korea, Laos, Poland, the USSR, Yugoslavia and
the Republic of Vietnam* (6 vols) by J. Kneifel (Munich: J. Kneifel, 1985).

CONSTITUTIONS: *The Constitutions of the Communist World* (Vietnam), W. Simons, ed. (Sijthoff &
Noordhoff, 1980).
Constitutions of the Countries of the World (Vietnam) by A. Blaustein & G. Flanz
(Oceana, 1982).

**TREATISES &
LOOSELEAFS:**   *History of Vietnamese Communism, 1925–1976* by D. Pike (Hoover Institution Press,
1978).
The Sino-Vietnamese Territorial Dispute by P. Chang (Praeger, 1986).

ARTICLES: "American Courts, International Law, and the War in Vietnam," 18 *Columbia Journal
of Law and Social Problems* 295 (1984).
"Foreign Investment Code of the Socialist Republic of Vietnam," 13 *The Inter-national
Lawyer* 329 (1979).
"Law and Socialist Agricultural Development in Vietnam" by A. Forde, 10 *Review of
Socialist Law* 315 (1984).
"Recent Developments in the Constitutions of Asian Marxist-Socialist States" by
C. Kim, 13 *Case Western Reserve Journal of International Law* 483, 495 (1981).
"Vietnam's Code of the Le Dynasty (1428–1788)" by Ta Van Tai, 30 *American Journal
of Comparative Law* 523 (1982).
"Vietnam's Legal Regulation of Foreign Trade and Investment" by J. Quigley, 6
International Trade Law Journal 24 (1980–81).

VILLAGES: See State & Local Government
VIOLENCE: See Criminal Law, Family Law, Torts

VIRGINIA

SEE ALSO:	Circuit Courts (Fourth Circuit)

RESEARCH GUIDES & BIBLIOGRAPHIES:

A Bibliography of Virginia Legal History before 1900 by W. Bryson (Univ. Press of VA, 1979).

Check-List of Virginia State Publications (VA State Library, 1927–).

A Law Librarian's Introduction to Virginia State Publications by M. Aycock, J. Lichtman & J. Stinson (Amer. Assn. of Law Libraries, 1981).

"A Selected Bibliography of Virginia Practice Materials" by E. Edmonds, 7 *Southeastern Law Librarian* 52 (1982).

STATUTES:

Acts of the General Assembly of the Commonweath of Virginia.

Advance Session Law Reports (CCH).

Code of Virginia Annotated.

STATE ADMINISTRATIVE CODE: *Virginia Register of Regulations.*

CASES & OPINIONS:

South Eastern Reporter (1887–).

Virginia Court of Appeals Reports (1985–).

Virginia Reports (1881–).

COURT RULES:

Bankruptcy Court: Local Rules of Practice (VA, Eastern District) (Michie, 1980–).

Virginia Rules Annotated (Michie, 1983).

JURY INSTRUCTIONS:

Instructions for Virginia and West Virginia, 2d ed. (Michie, 1962).

Virginia Jury Instructions by M. Doubles (West, 1964).

Virginia Model Jury Instructions: Civil (Michie, 1984–).

Virginia Model Jury Instructions: Criminal (Michie, 1985–).

ETHICS & PROFESSIONAL RESPONSIBILITY:

Annual Report of the Virginia State Bar (1938–).

Rules for the Integration of the Virginia State Bar ... Formal and Informal Opinions on Legal Ethics (VA State Bar, 1975–).

OPINIONS OF THE ATTORNEY GENERAL:

Opinions of the Attorney-General and Report to the Governor of Virginia (Attorney-General's Office, 1872–).

Civil Digest (Attorney-General's Office, 1973–).

JOURNALS & OTHER PERIODICALS:

Law Letter (VA Trial Lawyers Assn., 1962–).

Virginia Bar Association Journal (1975–).

Virginia Bar News (VA State Bar, 1853–).

The Virginia Researcher (Natl. Leg. Res. Group, 1970–).

TREATISES & LOOSELEAFS:

Administration of Estates by L. Bracey (Michie, 1984–).

The "Average" Personal Injury Case (VA Trial Lawyers Assn., 1980).

Estate Planning Fundamentals (VA Bar Assn., 1980).

A Handbook of Standard Procedures and Model Orders ... for Judges and Clerks (Supreme Court of VA, 1978).
The Law of Evidence in Virginia, 2d ed. by C. Friend (Michie, 1983).
Legal Education in Virginia, 1779–1979 by W. Bryson (Univ. of VA Press, 1982).
Product Liability (VA Trial Lawyers Assn., 1980).
Viginia Administrative Law and Practice, C. Midkiff, ed. (Joint Committee on Cont. Legal Ed., 1980–).
Virginia and West Virginia Products Liability (Harrison, 1983).
Virginia Forms (Michie, 1978–).
Virginia Law Practice Systems (Michie).
The Virginia Lawyer: A Basic Practice Handbook (VA Bar Assn.; Michie, 1979–).
Virginia Lawyers Deskbook (Michie, 1983).
Virginia Will and Trust Forms (VA Natl. Bank, 1979).

DIGESTS, ENCYCLOPEDIA
& CITATOR: *Virginia and West Virginia Digest* (West, 1861–).
South Eastern Digest (West, 1729–).
Jurisprudence of Virginia and West Virginia (Michie, 1948–).
Shepard's Virginia Citations.

VIRGIN ISLANDS (U.S.)

SEE ALSO: British Virgin Islands, Caribbean, International Law, Latin America, United Nations

CONSTITUTION: *Constitutions of the United States: National and State* (Virgin Islands) (Oceana, 1982).

STATUTES &
RELATED LAWS: *Virgin Islands Code Annotated* (Equity Pub. Co.).
Virgin Islands Register (Equity Pub. Co.).
Virgin Islands Rules and Regulations (Equity Pub. Co.).
Virgin Islands Session Laws (Equity Pub. Co.).

CASES: *Virgin Islands Reports* (Equity Pub. Co.).

ATTORNEY GENERAL: *Opinions of the Attorney General* (Equity Pub. Co.).

JOURNALS & OTHER
PERIODICALS: *Virginia Islands Bar Journal* (1967–).

TREATISES &
LOOSELEAFS: *Business Operations in U.S. Virgin Islands* by G. Danielson, Tax Management Foreign Income Portfolios, No. 336–2nd (BNA, 1978).
Caribbean Basin: A Tax Tour (U.S. Virgin Islands) (Arthur Anderson & Co., 1985).

ARTICLES: "Possessions Corporation System of Taxation in American Samoa, Guam, and the Virgin Islands," 9 *International Tax Journal* 343 (1983).
"U.S. Virgin Islands: The Ultimate Tax Shelter," 15 *Tax Management International Journal* 155 (1986).

VISA: See Immigration Law, International Law
VISITATION: See Family Law, Juvenile Law

VISUAL ARTIST: See Art & Entertainment, Intellectual Property
VITAL STATISTICS: See Family Law, Statistics
VITRO, IN: See Family Law, Health & Medicine
VIVISECTION: See Animals
VOCATIONAL REHABILITATION: See Handicapped & the Law, Health & Medicine
VOLUNTEERS: See Military Law
VOTING: See Election

WAGE: See Employee Benefits, Labor Law
WAIVER: See Contracts, Trial & Appellate Practice

WALES

SEE ALSO: England, International Law, United Nations

**JOURNALS & OTHER
PERIODICALS:**   *The Cambrian Law Review* (Aberystwyth: Univ. College of Wales Dept. of Law, 1970–).

**TREATISES &
LOOSELEAFS:**   *The Legal Profession in England and Wales* by R. Abel (NY: Basil Blackwell, 1980).
The Legal Systems of Britain (Wales) (London: Her Majesty's Stationery Office, 1976).
A Modern Legal History of England and Wales, 1750–1950 by A. Manchester
(Butterworths, 1981).
Precedence in England and Wales by G. Squibb (Oxford Univ. Press, 1981).
*System of Justice: An Introduction to the Criminal Justice System in England and
Wales* by M. Fitzgerald & J. Muncie (B. Blackwell, 1983).
Welsh Studies in Public Law, J. Andrews, ed. (Univ. of Wales Press, 1970).

ARTICLES: "England and Wales: Legal Education" by J. Peile, 5 *Comparative Law Yearbook* 29
(1981).

WANTON: See Torts

WAR

SEE ALSO: Human Rights, International Law, Military Law, United Nations

**TREATISES &
LOOSELEAFS:**   *To Chain the Dog of War: The War Power of Congress in History and Law* by
F. Wormuth (Southern Methodist Univ. Press, 1986).
The Code of International Armed Conflict by H. Levie (Oceana, 1985).
Defining International Aggression: The Search for World Peace by B. Ferencz
(Oceana, 1975).
Essays on the Modern Law of War by L. Green (Transnational Pub., 1985).
*"Government from Reflection and Choice": Constitutional Essays on War, Foreign
Relations, and Federalism* by C. Lofgrin (Oxford Univ. Press, 1986).
The Law of Armed Conflict by G. Schwarzenberger (London: Stevens, 1968).

The Law of Armed Conflicts by R. Bindschedler (Carnegie Endowment for Intl. Peace, 1971).

The Law of War, R. Miller, ed. (Heath, 1975).

The Laws of Armed Conflicts: A Collection of Conventions, Resolutions and Other Documents, 3d ed., D. Schindler, ed. (Martinus Nijhoff, 1988).

Military Laws of the United States from the Civil War to the War Powers Act of 1973 (Arno Press, 1979).

The New Humanitarian Law of Armed Conflict, A. Cassese, ed. (Oceana, 1979).

Nuclear Weapons and Law (Greenwood Press, 1985).

On the Law of War and Peace by H. Grotius (Carnegie, 1913).

The War Powers Resolution: Balance of War Powers in the Eighties by R. Clark (Wash. D.C.: Natl. Defense Univ. Press, 1985).

When Battle Rages: How Can Law Protect?, S. Levie, ed. (Oceana, 1971).

PERIODICALS:

CURRENT LAW INDEX (CLI) & LEGAL RESOURCE INDEX (LRI)
In the CLI and LRI, look for references to periodical literature under the following subject headings:

Arms Control	War
Atomic Warfare	War and Emergency
Martial Law	Powers

INDEX TO LEGAL PERIODICALS (ILP)
In the ILP, look for references to legal periodical literature under the following subject headings:

International Arbitration	War and Emergency
Neutrality	Powers
War	War Crimes

WARD: See Estate Planning, Family Law, Handicapped & the Law, Juvenile Law, Mental Health, State & Local Government

WAREHOUSE: See Business Law, Customs, Personal Property, Torts

WARRANTY: See Contracts, Real Estate, Torts, Uniform Commercial Code

WARSAW CONVENTION: See Air & Aviation, International Law, Transportation

WARSAW PACT: See Communism

WASHINGTON D.C.: See District of Columbia

WASHINGTON STATE

SEE ALSO:
Circuit Courts (Ninth Circuit), Community Property, District of Columbia

RESEARCH GUIDES & BIBLIOGRAPHIES:
CLE Publication Index (Wash. State Bar Assn., Cont. Legal Ed., 1975–).
Washington State Law-Related Publications: A Selective Bibliography with Commentary by S. Burson (American Assn. of Law Libraries, 1984).

STATUTES:
Revised Code of Washington.
Revised Code of Washington Annotated.
Laws of Washington.
Washington Legislative Service (West).

STATE ADMINISTRATIVE CODE:
Washington Administrative Code.
Washington State Register.

CASES & OPINIONS:	*Washington Reports* (1889–). *Washington Appellate Reports* (1969–). *Pacific Reporter* (1880–).
COURT RULES:	*Local Rules for the Superior Court* (Butterworths, 1981–). *Local Rules for the Superior Court for King County* (Seattle: Book Pub. Co., 1982–). *Rules of Court* (State Law Reports Office). *Washington Court Rules* (West, 1960–). *Washington Court Rules Annotated* (Lawyers Co-op., 1977). *Washington Rules of Court Annotated* (Law Book Pub.).
JURY INSTRUCTIONS:	*Washington Pattern Jury Instructions, Civil,* 2d ed. (West, 1980). *Washington Pattern Jury Instructions, Criminal* (West, 1977). *Washington Pattern Jury Instructions for Use in Comparative Negligence Cases* (Wash. State Bar, 1974).
OPINIONS OF THE ATTORNEY GENERAL:	*Annual Index* (1975–). *Attorney General Opinions* (1892–).
JOURNALS & OTHER PERIODICALS:	*Washington State Bar Journal.* *Judiciary* (Administrator for the Courts, 1980–).
SURVEY OF STATE LAW:	"Survey of Washington Law" in *Gonzaga Law Review.* See for example vol. 19 p. 403.
TREATISES & LOOSELEAFS:	*Corporation Handbook* (Secretary of State, 1979–). *The Law of Evidence in Washington* by R. Aronson (Butterworths Redmond, 1986). *Washington Business Law Deskbook* (Wash. State Bar Assn., 1981–). *Washington Civil Procedure Before Trial Deskbook* (Wash. State Bar Assn., 1981–). *Washington Civil Procedure Forms,* 2d ed. by M. Barbier (West, 1987). *Washington Commercial Law Deskbook* (Wash. State Bar Assn., 1982–). *Washington Community Property Deskbook* (Wash. State Bar Assn., 1977–). *Washington Criminal Practice and Procedure* by R. Ferguson (West, 1984). *Washington Evidence Law and Practice,* 3d ed. by K. Tegland (West, 1988). *Washington Methods of Practice with Forms,* 2d ed. by V. Towne (West, 1976). *Washington Real Property Deskbook* (Wash. State Bar Assn., 1979–). *Washington Rules Practice,* 3d ed. by L. Orland (West, 1978). *Washington Trial Practice,* 4th ed. by L. Orland (West, 1986). *Washington Uniform Commercial Code Forms* by W. Shattuck (West, 1967).
DIGESTS & CITATORS:	*Washington Digest,* 2d. *Pacific Digest.* *Shepard's Washington Citations.*

WASTE: See Environmental Law, Real Estate

WATER LAW

SEE ALSO:	Agriculture, Business Law, Consumer Law, Economics, Energy, Environmental Law,

International Law, Maritime Law, Oil & Gas, Public Utilities, Sea, Zoning and Land Planning

RESEARCH GUIDES &
BIBLIOGRAPHIES: *Bibliography of Water Law Publications, 1925–1985* by K. Garner (Southern Illinois University at Carbondale School of Law Library, 1986).
Water Law Bibliography (Jefferson Law Book, 1979).

JOURNALS, NEWSLETTERS
& OTHER PERIODICALS: *Land and Water Law Review* (Univ. of Wyoming, 1966–).
The Water Reporter (Wash. D.C.: Information News Service 1985–).

TREATISES &
LOOSELEAFS: *Environmental Law: Air and Water* by W. Rodgers (West, 1986).
Federal Policies in Water Resources Planning (NY: American Society of Civil Engineers, 1985).
Indian Reserved Water Rights (GPO, 1985).
Law of Water Rights and Resources by A. Tarlock (Clank Boardman, 1988–).
Legal and Administrative Systems for Water Allocation and Management, W. Walker, ed. (Virginia Polytechnic Institute and State Univ., Virginia Water Resources Center, 1984).
Water Law in a Nutshell by D. Getches (West, 1984).
Water Law in Historical Perspective by L. Teclaff (Hein, 1985).
Water Pollution and Water Quality by R. Beck (Allen Smith, 1984).
Water Pollution Control (BNA, 1979–).
Water Rights in the Western States, 3d ed. by S. Wiel (NY: Arno, 1979).
Water Rights: Scarce Resource Allocation, Bureaucracy, and the Environment, 2d ed. by T. Anderson (Ballinger, 1983).
Waters and Water Rights: A Treatise on the Law of Waters and Allied Problems, 3d ed. (Michie, 1988–).
Western Water Law in Transition (Univ. of Colorado School of Law, Natural Resources Law Center, 1985).

ENCYCLOPEDIAS: AMERICAN JURISPRUDENCE 2D (Am Jur 2d)
Check the following topics in the *General Index* volumes for Am Jur 2d:

Canals	Natural Resources
Dams	Pipes and Pipelines
Environment and	Pollution
Conservation	Waters
Fish and Game	Waterworks
Mines and Minerals	Wharves

CORPUS JURIS SECUNDUM (CJS)
Check the following topics in the *General Index* volumes for CJS:

Electricity	Oil and Gas
Fish and Game	Pipes and Pipelines
Gas	Pollution
Health and Environment	United States Secretary of
Lakes and Ponds	the Interior
Logs and Logging	Waters
Mines and Minerals	Water Supply
Natural Resources	Woods and Forests
Navigable Waters	

DIGESTS:

CASE SEARCH IN WEST DIGESTS BY KEY TOPIC
In the *Descriptive Word Index* of the West digests, look for key topics and numbers under the following subject headings:

Administrative Law	Oil and Gas
Agriculture	Pipes and Pipelines
Coal and Coal Mines	Pollution
Gas	Public Lands
Lakes and Ponds	United States Secretary
Logs and Logging	of the Interior
Mines and Minerals	Water District
Natural Resources	Waters
Navigable Waters	Woods and Forests

ALR:

ANNOTATIONS
Check the index volumes for ALR, ALR2d, ALR3d, ALR4th, and ALR Fed for annotations under the following subject headings:

Chemicals	Mines and Minerals
Conservation	Navigable Waters
Environmental Law	Pollution
Floods	Public Land
Interior Department	Water Pollution
Irrigation	Water Supply
Lakes	

PERIODICALS:

CURRENT LAW INDEX (CLI) & LEGAL RESOURCE INDEX (LRI)
In the CLI and LRI, look for references to periodical literature under the following subject headings:

Drinking Water	Parks
Energy Materials	Power Resources
Environmental Law	Public Lands
Hydroelectric Power	Rain and Rain Water
Irrigation Water	Rivers
Mines and Mineral	Water
Resources	Wells
Mining Law	Wildlife Conservation
Ocean Mining	Zoning
Offshore Oil Industry	

INDEX TO LEGAL PERIODICALS (ILP)
In the ILP, look for references to legal periodical literature under the following subject headings:

Coastal Zone	Mines and Minerals
Continental Shelf	Natural Resources
Electricity	Pollution
Environmental Law	Territorial Waters
Fish and Game	Water
Marine Resources	

WEAPONS: See Criminal Law, War
WEIGHT OF EVIDENCE: See Trial & Appellate Practice
WEIGHTS & MEASURES: See Maritime Law, Transportation
WELFARE: See Consumer Law, Handicapped & the Law, Health & Medicine, Juvenile Law, Poverty Law, Social Security, State & Local Government

WELLS, OIL: See Environmental Law, Oil & Gas
WEST BANK: See Islam, Israel, Middle East

WESTERN SAMOA

SEE ALSO: International Law, United Nations

CONSTITUTION: *Constitutions of the Countries of the World* (Western Samoa) by A. Blaustein & G. Flanz (Oceana, 1982).

JOURNALS: *Samoan Pacific Law Journal.*

TREATISES & LOOSELEAFS:
Fiscal Policy and Tax Structure in Australasia (Western Samoa) (Amsterdam: Intl. Bureau of Fiscal Documentation, 1978).
Information Guide: Doing Business in Western Samoa (Price Waterhouse).
Investment Laws of the World (Western Samoa) (Oceana, 1981–).
Taxes and Investment in Asia and the Pacific (Western Samoa) (Amsterdam: Intl. Bureau of Fiscal Documentation, 1983–).

ARTICLES:
"New Zealand Citizenship and Western Samoa" by F. Brookfield, 5 *Otago Law Review* 367 (1983).
"The Western Samoa Bill" (citizenship) by J. Mclay, *New Zealand Law Journal* 353 (Oct., 1982).

WEST INDIES: See Anguilla, Antigua, Bahamas, Barbados, Belize, Bermuda, British Virgin Islands, Caribbean, Cayman Islands, Dominica, Grenada, Guyana, Jamaica, Montserrat, Turks & Caicos Islands

WEST VIRGINIA

SEE ALSO: Circuit Courts (Fourth Circuit)

STATUTES: *West Virginia Code Annotated* (Michie).

STATE ADMINISTRATIVE CODE: *West Virginia Register.*

CASES & OPINIONS:
West Virginia Reports (1863–1973).
South Eastern Reporter (1886–).

COURT RULES: *West Virginia Rules Annotated* (Michie, 1984).

JURY INSTRUCTIONS: *Instructions for Virginia and West Virginia,* 2d ed. by E. Abbott (Michie, 1962).

ETHICS & PROFESSIONAL RESPONSIBILITY: *Opinions of the Committee on Legal Ethics of the West Virginia State Bar* (West VA State Bar).

JOURNALS & OTHER PERIODICALS: *West Virginia State Bar Journal* (1975–).

**TREATISES &
LOOSELEAFS:**

Administrative Law in West Virginia (Michie, 1982).

Burk's Pleading and Practice, 4th ed. by T. Boyd (Michie, 1952).

Handbook on Evidence for West Virginia Lawyers by F. Cleckley (Michie, 1978).

Handbook on West Virginia Criminal Procedure by F. Cleckley (Michie, 1985).

Harrison on Wills and Administration for Virginia and West Virginia, 3d ed. by G. Smith (Michie, 1984).

The Law of Coal, Oil and Gas in West Virginia and Virginia by R. Donley (Michie, 1951).

The Law of Domestic Relations in West Virginia by W. Morris (Michie, 1973).

West Virginia Practice Handbook, 2d ed. by D. Stern (Michie, 1977).

**DIGESTS, ENCYCLOPEDIA
& CITATOR:**

Virginia and West Virginia Digest (West, 1861–).

South Eastern Digest (West, 1729–).

Michie's Jurisprudence of Virginia and West Virginia (Michie, 1948–).

West Virginia Advance Annotation Service (Michie).

Shepard's West Virginia Citations.

WHALING: See Natural Resources, Sea
WHARVES: See Water Law
WHITE COLLAR: See Civil Service, Criminal Law, Labor Law
WIFE: See Estate Planning, Family Law, Women & the Law
WILDERNESS: See Environmental Law, Natural Resources
WILDLIFE: See Animals, Environmental Law, Natural Resources, Water Law
WILL: See Estate Planning
WILLFUL: See Criminal Law, Torts

WISCONSIN

SEE ALSO:

Circuit Courts (Seventh Circuit)

**RESEARCH GUIDES &
BIBLIOGRAPHIES:**

Legal Research in Wisconsin by R. Danner (Univ. of WI, Extension Law Dept., 1980).

Wisconsin Legal Research Guide, 2d ed. by W. Knudson (Univ. of WI, 1972).

STATUTES:

Laws of Wisconsin.

Wisconsin Legislative Service (West).

Wisconsin Statutes.

Wisconsin Statutes Annotated (West).

Wisconsin Statutes Looseleaf Up-Dating Service (Oconomowoc, WI: Midwest Legal Publisher).

**ADMINISTRATIVE
REGULATIONS &
DECISIONS:**

Administrative Law Digest.

Wisconsin Administrative Code.

Wisconsin Administrative Register.

CASES & OPINIONS:

North Western Reporter (1978–).

Wisconsin Reports (1853–).

COURT RULES:	*Wisconsin Rules of Court* (West).
JURY INSTRUCTIONS:	*Wisconsin Jury Instructions—Civil* (Cont. Legal Ed. for WI, 1981–).
	Wisconsin Jury Instructions—Criminal (Cont. Legal Ed. for WI, 1980–)
ETHICS & PROFESSIONAL RESPONSIBILITY:	*Ethics and Professional Responsibility* by K. Kaap (State Bar of WI, 1988–).
OPINIONS OF THE ATTORNEY GENERAL:	*Attorney General Opinions.*
JOURNALS & OTHER PERIODICALS:	*Milwaukee Lawyer* (1976–).
	Wisconsin Appellate Reporter (Law Reporter Co.).
	Wisconsin Bar Bulletin (1927–).
	Wisconsin Bar News Briefs (State Bar of WI, 1982–).
	Wisconsin Law Reporter (Law Reporter Co.).

TREATISES & LOOSELEAFS:

Annual Survey of Wisconsin Law (State Bar of WI).

Appellate Practice and Procedure in Wisconsin by D. Walther et al. (State Bar of WI, 1986–).

Guidebook to Wisconsin Taxes (CCH, 1987).

The Law of Damages in Wisconsin (State Bar of WI, 1988–).

The Lawyer's Basic Corporate Practice Manual (State Bar of WI, 1985–).

Marital Property Law in Wisconsin, 2d ed. (State Bar of WI, 1986–).

Real Estate Transactions Systems by J. Horwich (State Bar of WI, 1982–).

System Book for Family Law: A Forms and Procedures Handbook for Divorce by L. Loeb (State Bar of WI, 1988–).

Wisconsin Appellate Practice by R. Martineau (State Bar of WI, 1978–).

Wisconsin Avoiding Attorney Malpractice (Professional Education Systems, 1981).

Wisconsin Civil Practice Forms (Callaghan, 1970–).

Wisconsin Civil Procedure Forms by W. Harvey (West, 1976).

Wisconsin Collections by R. Kohn (Lawyers Co-op., 1980–).

Wisconsin Corporations by L. Postlewaite (Lawyers Co-op., 1980–).

Wisconsin Criminal Defense Manual by P. Devitt (State Bar of WI, 1981).

Wisconsin Divorce by K. Olson (Lawyers Co-op., 1979–).

Wisconsin Inheritance, Estate and Gift Tax Handbook by N. Schmidt (Cont. Legal Ed. for WI, 1982–).

Wisconsin Judicial Benchbook (State Bar of WI) (vol. 1, criminal; vol. 2, civil; vol. 3, family, probate, 1982).

Wisconsin Juvenile Court Practice by M. Melli (State Bar of WI, 1983).

Wisconsin Methods of Practice by G. Sherman (West, 1987).

Wisconsin Probate System Forms and Procedures Handbook by W. Mundt (State Bar of WI, 1981–).

Wisconsin Real Estate by M. Greenberg (Lawyers Co-op., 1982–).

Wisconsin Rules of Civil Procedure by W. Harvey (West, 1975).

The Wisconsin Rules of Evidence: A Courtroom Handbook by T. Barland & T. Bell (State Bar of WI, 1988–).

Wisconsin Taxes (Cont. Legal Ed. for WI, 1983).

DIGESTS & CITATOR:	*Wisconsin Digest* (West).
	Wisconsin Digest (Callaghan).

North Western Digest (West).
Shepard's Wisconsin Citations.

WITHHOLDING TAX: See Employee Benefits, Taxation
WITNESS: See Criminal Law, Trial & Appellate Practice

WOMAN & THE LAW

SEE ALSO: Abortion, Age, Civil Rights, Community Property, Constitutional Law, Employment Discrimination, Family Law, Health & Medicine, Homosexuality, Human Rights, International Law, Labor Law

RESEARCH GUIDES & BIBLIOGRAPHIES: "Annotated Bibliography on Sexual Harassment in Education" by P. Crocker, 7 *Women's Rights Law Reporter* 96 (1982).
Introduction to Library Research in Women's Studies by S. Searing (Westview, 1985).
Women's Annotated Legal Bibliography by the Benjamin Cardozo School of Law (Clark Boardman, 1984).
Women's Legal Rights in the United States: A Selective Bibliography by J. Ariel (Chicago: American Library Assn., 1985).

JOURNALS, NEWSLETTERS & OTHER PERIODICALS: *Berkeley Women's Law Journal* (Lincoln, NB: Joe Christensen, Inc., 1985–).
Harvard Women's Law Journal (1978–).
Wisconsin Women's Law Journal (Univ. of Wisc. Law School, 1985–).
Women and Law (Hofstra Univ. School of Law).
Women Lawyers Journal (Natl. Assn. of Women Lawyers, 1911–).
Women's Rights Law Reporter (Newark: Rutgers Law School, 1971–).

TREATISES & LOOSELEAFS: *Bargaining for Equality: A Guide to Legal and Collective Bargaining Solutions for Workplace Problems that Particularly Affect Women* (San Francisco: Women's Labor Project, 1981).
Battered Women Who Kill: Psychological Self-Defense as Legal Justification by C. Ewing (Lexington Books, 1879).
Comparable Worth, Pay Equity, and Public Policy, R. Kelly & J. Bayers, eds. (Greenwood Press, 1988).
The Criminal Justice System and Women by B. Price (Clark Boardman, 1982).
The Equal Pay Act: Implications for Comparable Worth by W. Fogel (Praeger, 1984).
Equal Pay for Comparable Worth by F. Hutner (Praeger, 1986).
Equal Pay for Equal Work: Federal Equity Pay Law of 1963 (BNA, 1963).
Everywoman's Legal Guide, B. Burnett, ed. (Doubleday, 1985).
Fathers to Daughters: The Legal Foundations of Female Emancipation by P. Rabkin (Greenwood Press, 1980).
Fundamentals of the Equal Pay Act of 1963 (Natl. Employment Law Project).
The Invisible Bar: The Woman Lawyer in America 1638 to the Present by K. Morello (Random House, 1986).
The Legal Rights of Women by L. Foster (1913; reprint by Rothman, 1986).
Legislative History of the Equal Pay Act of 1963 (Govt. Printing Office, 1963).
Legislative History of the Preganancy Discrimination Act of 1978 (Govt. Printing Office, 1979).

Sex-Based Discrimination: International Law and Organization by H. Taubenfeld (Oceana, 1978–).

Sex Discrimination and the Sexually Charged Work Environment (Natl. Employment Law Project).

Sex Discrimination in Employment by W. Pepper (Michie, 1981).

Sexual Harassment in Employment by S. Omilian (Callaghan, 1987).

U.S. Women's Legal Rights: International Covenants an Alternative to ERA? by M. Halberstam (Transnational Pub., 1987).

Why WE Lost the ERA by J. Mansbridge (Univ. of Chicago Press, 1986).

Women and the Law, C. Lefcourt, ed. (Clark Boardman, 1984–).

Women and the Law of Property in Early America by M. Salmon (Univ. of North Carolina Press, 1986).

Women Law Professors (American Bar Foundation, 1980).

Women, Sex, and the Law by R. Tong (Totowa, NJ: Rowman & Allanheld, 1984).

A Working Woman's Guide to Her Job Rights (GPO, 1985).

ENCYCLOPEDIAS:

AMERICAN JURISPRUDENCE 2d (Am Jur 2d)
Check the following topics in the *General Index* volumes for Am Jur 2d:

Civil Rights	Husband and Wife
Constitutional Law	Married Women's Acts
Discrimination	Rape
Equal Protection of Law	Separate Property

CORPUS JURIS SECUNDUM (CJS)
Check the following topics in the *General Index* volumes for CJS:

Civil Rights	Marriage
Common Law	Pregnancy
Constitutional Law	Rape
Discrimination	Sex Discrimination
Divorce	Support
Equity	Women
Husband and Wife	

DIGESTS:

CASE SEARCH IN WEST DIGESTS BY KEY TOPIC
In the *Descriptive Word Index* of the West digests, look for key topics and numbers under the following subject headings:

Abortion	Marriage
Civil Rights	Parent and Child
Common Law	Pregnancy
Constitutional Law	Rape
Discrimination	Sex Discrimination
Divorce	Social Security and Public
Equity	Welfare
Husband and Wife	Support
Joint Tenancy	Women
Labor Relations	

ALR:

ANNOTATIONS
Check the index volumes for ALR, ALR2d, ALR3d, ALR4th, and ALR Fed for annotations under the following subject headings:

Alimony	Change of Name
Antenuptial Contracts	Community Property
Bigamy	Dependents
Birth	Discrimination

Equal Protection of Law	Pregnancy
Equity	Rape
Husband abd Wufe	Sex Discrimination
Marriage	Support and Maintenance
Parent and Child	

PERIODICALS:

CURRENT LAW INDEX (CLI) & LEGAL RESOURCE INDEX (LRI)
In the CLI and LRI, look for references to periodical literature under the following subject headings:

Abortion	Husband and Wife
Abused Wives	Married Women
Alimony	Maternity Leave
Civil Rights	Mothers
Common Law	Parent and Child
Constitutional Law	Pregnancy
Custody	Rape
Desertion and and Non-Support	Separation
	Sex Crimes
Discrimination	Sex Discrimination
Divorce	Sexual Harassment
Domestic Relations	Wife Abuse
Equality	Women
Family	Women's Rights

INDEX TO LEGAL PERIODICALS (ILP)
In the ILP, look for references to legal periodical literature under the following subject headings:

Alimony and Maintenance	Equal Protection
Antenuptial Contract	Family Courts
Artifical Insemination	Guardian and Ward
Battered Women	Husband and Wife
Child Custody	Marriage
Civil Rights	Married Women
Common Law	Parent and Child
Community Property	Sex Crimes
Constitutional Law	Support and Dependents
Discrimination/Sex	Surrogate Motherhood
Divorce	Unmarried Couples
Dower and Curtesy	Women

WOODS: See Environmental Law, Natural Resources, Water Law

WORKER'S COMPENSATION

SEE ALSO:
Administrative Law, AIDS, Business Law, Employee Benefits, Handicapped & the Law, Health & Medicine, Insurance, Labor Law, Maritime Law, Occupational Safety, Unemployment Compensation; see also entries under individual states

JOURNALS & OTHER PERIODICALS:
Workmen's Compensation Law Journal (1918–1922; 1974–1980).
Workmen's Compensation Law Review (Hein).

TREATISES & LOOSELEAFS:
Benefits Review Board—Black Lung Reporter (Matthew Bender, 1980–).

Benefits Review Board—Longshore Reporter (Matthew Bender, 1980–).
Defending Workers' Compensation and Employers' Liability Cases, F. Bardenwerper,
    ed. (Milwaukee: Defense Research Institute, 1984).
Industrial Low Back Pain by S. Wiesel et al. (Michie).
The Law of Workmen's Compensation by A. Larson (Matthew Bender, 1952–).
Reference Guide to Workmen's Compensation Law by E. Blair (Thomas, 1968–).
The Self-Insurance Manual by C. Welch (NILS Pub. Co.).
Workers' Compensation Benefits: Adequacy, Equity, and Efficiency, J. Worrell, ed.
    (Ithaca, NY: ILP Press, 1985).
Workers' Compensation Law Reports (CCH, 1980–).
Workmen's Compensation, 3d ed. by Schneider (Thomas, 1939–).
Workmen's Compensation for Occupational Injuries and Death (desk edition) by
    A. Larson (Matthew Bender, 1972–).

ENCYCLOPEDIAS:

AMERICAN JURISPRUDENCE 2D (Am Jur 2d)
Check the following topics in the *General Index* volumes for Am Jur 2d:

Administrative Law	Longshoremen's and
Federal Employers	Harbor Workers'
Liability and	Compensation Act
Compensation Act	Scope of Employment or
Fellow Employee or	Authority
Servant	Workmens' Compensation
Jones Act	

CORPUS JURIS SECUNDUM (CJS)
Check the following topics in the *General Index* volumes for CJS:

Accident and Health	Fellow Servants
Insurance	Longshoremen and
Administrative Bodies	Harbor Workers
Federal Employers	Workmens' Compensation
Liability Act	

DIGESTS:

CASE SEARCH IN WEST DIGESTS BY KEY TOPIC
In the *Descriptive Word Index* of the West digests, look for key topics and numbers
under the following subject headings:

Administrative Law	Master and Servant
Common Law	Social Security
Labor Relations	Workers' Compensation

ALR:

ANNOTATIONS
Check the index volumes for ALR, ALR2d, ALR3d, ALR4th, and ALR Fed for annotations
under the following subject headings:

Administrative Law	Longshoremen
Disability	Master and Servant
Federal Employers'	Permanent Disability
Liability Act	Scope of Employment
Jones Act	Workers' Compensation

PERIODICALS:

CURRENT LAW INDEX (CLI) & LEGAL RESOURCE INDEX (LRI)
In the CLI and LRI, look for references to periodical literature under the following
subject headings:

Administrative Law	Labor Laws
Disability Evaluation	Master and Servant
Employers' Liability	Workmen's Compensation

INDEX TO LEGAL PERIODICALS (ILP)
In the ILP, look for refernces to legal periodical literature under the following subject headings:

Administrative Law	Insurance
Common Law	Labor Law
Disability Insurance	Workers' Compensation

WORKOUT: See Real Estate
WORKPLACE: See AIDS, Civil Service, Employment Discrimination, Labor Law,
    Women & the Law
WORLD: See International Law, United Nations
WRITING: See Art & Entertainment, Legal Research
WRONGFUL DEATH: See Death, Forensic Science, Torts
WRONGFUL DISCHARGE: See Civil Service, Employment Discrimination, Labor Law
WRONGFUL LIFE: See Family Law, Health & Medicine, Torts

WYOMING

SEE ALSO: Circuit Courts (Tenth Circuit)

RESEARCH GUIDE
& BIBLIOGRAPHY: *Wyoming State Legal Documents: An Annotated Bibliography* by N. Greene (Amer.
                        Assn. of Law Libraries, 1985).

STATUTES & OTHER
LEGISLATIVE MATERIALS: *Wyoming Statutes Annotated* (Michie).
                        Session Laws of Wyoming.
                        Wyoming Advanced Annotation Service (Michie, 1981–).
                        Legislative Summary Service (Wyo. Taxpayers Assn., 1965–).

ADMINISTRATIVE
REGULATIONS: *Index to Administrative Rules and Regulations of Wyoming State Agencies* (Secretary
                        of State, 1983–).

CASES & OPINIONS: *Wyoming Reports.*
                        Pacific Reporter (1883–).

COURT RULES: *Wyoming Court Rules Annotated* (Michie, 1979).
                        Civil and Criminal Rules of the United States District Court for the District of Wyoming
                            (District Court for the District of Wyo., 1980).
                        Rules of Practice of the United States Bankruptcy Court for the District of Wyoming
                            (Bankruptcy Court for the District of Wyo., 1982).

JURY INSTRUCTIONS: *Pattern Jury Instructions: Negligence* (Wyo. State Bar, 1963).
                        Wyoming Pattern Jury Instructions (Wyo. State Bar, 1981).
                        Wyoming Pattern Jury Instructions: Criminal (Wyo. State Bar, 1963).

OPINIONS OF THE
ATTORNEY GENERAL: *Opinions of the Attorney General of the State of Wyoming* (1940–).
                        Attorney General Opinion Index (Univ. of Wyo. Staff Attorney's Office, 1969–).

**JOURNALS & OTHER
PERIODICALS:**

The Coffeehouse: Wyoming Trial Lawyers Association Newsletter (1977–).
Corrections in Wyoming (Wyo. Attorney General).
Crime in Wyoming (Wyo. Attorney General, 1979–).
Wyoming Lawyer (Wyo. State Bar, 1976–).

DIRECTORIES:

Wyoming State Bar Directory (Wyo. State Bar).

**TREATISES &
LOOSELEAFS:**

Criminal Practice Manual by F. Chapman (Wyo. Public Defender Program, 1979).
Criminal Procedure in Wyoming Courts (Wyo. State Bar, Wyo. Trial Lawyers Assn.).
Handbook for Wyoming Mayors and City Councilmen by J. Miller (Univ. of Wyo.
    Institute of Business and Management Services, 1974–).
Madison on Wyoming Real Property Boundary Law by T. Madson (Gainesville, FL:
    LSS Pub. Co., 1984).
Real Estate Manual (Wyo. Real Estate Commn., 1984–).
Title Standards of the Wyoming State Bar (Wyo. State Bar, 1980).
Wyoming Juvenile Justice System: An Evaluation by the Columbia Research Center
    (Wyo. Attorney General, 1981).
The Wyoming Law of Real Mortgages by G. Rudolph (Wyo. Law Institute, 1969).
Wyoming Local Government Law by G. Rudolph (Wyo. State Bar, 1985).
Wyoming Manual of Legislative Procedures by H. Pownall (Wyo. State Legislature,
    1984).
Wyoming's Judicial System, 2d ed. by R. Duncan (Pioneer Printing Co., 1982).

DIGESTS & CITATOR:

Wyoming Digest (West).
Pacific Digest (West).
Shepard's Wyoming Citation.

YEAR-TO-YEAR TENANCY: See Estate Planning, Landlord-Tenant, Real Estate

YEMEN (North Yemen)

SEE ALSO:

International Law, Islam, Middle East, United Nations, Yemen (People's Democratic
Republic)

CONSTITUTION:

Constitutions of the Countries of the World (Yemen Arab Republic) by D. McClintock
    (Oceana, 1971).

**TREATISES &
LOOSELEAFS:**

Commercial Laws of the Middle East by A. Keesee (Oceana, 1980–).
*Law and Justice in Contemporary Yemen: People's Democratic Republic of Yemen and
    Yemen Arab Republic* by S. Amin (Glasgow: Royston, 1987).
Taxes and Investment in the Middle East (Intl. Bureau of Fiscal Documentation).
The Two Yemens by R. Bidwell (Westview, 1983).

Yemen Arab Republic: A Country Law Study by Y. Hakim for the Dept. of Navy, Off. of Judge Advocate General (Library of Congress, 1985).

Yemen: Political History, Social Structure and Legal System by I. Ghanem (London: Arthur Probsthain, 1981).

ARTICLES: "Choosing and Economic Future" (North Yemen) by D. Roy, 8 *Middle East Executive Reports* 8 (April, 1985).

"Yemen Arab Republic: Law No. 451 Pertaining to Trademarks and Commercial Names," 82 *Patent and Trademark Review* 208 (May, 1984).

YEMEN (SOUTHERN YEMEN)

SEE ALSO: Communism, International Law, Islam, Middle East, United Nations, Yemen Arab Republic

CONSTITUTION: *Constitutions of the Countries of the World: People's Democratic Republic of Yemen* by D. McClintock (Oceana, 1971).

**TREATISES
& LOOSELEAFS:**   *Commercial Laws of the Middle East* by A. Keesee (Oceana, 1980–).

South Yemen: A Marxist Republic in Arabia by R. Stookey (Westview, 1982).

Taxes and Investment in the Middle East (Intl. Bureau of Fiscal Documentation).

ARTICLES: "Legal Reform and Socialist Revolution in Democratic Yemen: Women and the Family" by M. Molyneux, 13 *International Journal of the Sociology of Law* 147 (1985).

YOUTH: See Contracts, Corrections, Family Law, Juvenile Law, Mental Health, Torts

YUGOSLAVIA

SEE ALSO: Communism, Europe, International Law, Soviet Union, United Nations

**RESEARCH GUIDE &
BIBLIOGRAPHY:**   *Legal Sources and Bibliography of Yugoslavia* by F. Gjupanovich (Praeger, 1964).

CONSTITUTION: *The Constitutions of the Communist World* (Yugoslavia), W. Simons, ed. (Sijthoff & Noordhoff, 1980).

**STATUTES & RELATED
LAWS:**   "Yugoslavia: Law on Investment of Resources of Foreign Persons" 24 *International Legal Materials* 315 (1985).

"Yugoslavia: Laws on Joint Ventures and the Transfer of Technology," 18 *International Legal Materials* 229 (1979).

**JOURNALS & OTHER
PERIODICALS:**   *Jugoslovenska Revija za Medjunarodno Pravo* (Belgrade: 1954–). (Articles in Serbo-Croatian, English, and French.)

TREATISES & LOOSELEAFS:	*Administrative Secrecy in Developed Countries* (Yugoslavia) by D. Rpwat (Columbia Univ. Press, 1979). *Digest of Commercial Laws of the World* (Yugoslavia) (Natl. Assn. of Credit Management; Oceana, 1977–). *Doing Business with Eastern Europe* (Yugoslavia) (NY: Business Intl. Corp., 1975–). *Investment Laws of the World* (Yugoslavia) (Oceana, 1981–). *Legal Aspects of Joint Ventures in Eastern Europe* (Yugoslavia), D. Campbell, ed. (Kluwer, 1981). *Taxation in European Socialist Countries* (Yugoslavia) (Amsterdam: Intl. Bureau of Fiscal Documentation). *Yugoslav Civil Law: History, Family, Property* by A. Chloros (Clarendon Press, 1970). *Yugoslavia: A Country Study*, 2d ed. by R. Nyrop (GOP, 1982). *Yugoslav Socialism* by H. Lydall (Oxford Univ. Press, 1984).

ARTICLES:

"The Concept of Social Property and the Rights of the Foreign Investor in Yugoslavia" by M. Coronna, 11 *Review of Socialist Law* 227 (1985).

"An Economic Analysis of Yugoslav Joint Ventures" by C. Coughlin, 17 *Journal of World Trade Law* 12 (1983) (see also vol. 18, p. 163).

"The Multinational in Yugoslavia" by L. Orbe, 19 *The International Lawyer* 623 (1985)

"The New Yugoslav Private International Law Act" by P. Sarevic, 38 *American Journal of Comparative Law* 283 (1985).

"The Right to Repatriation of Capital and Transfer of Profit for Foreign Investors in Yugoslav Joint-Ventures" by M. Coronna, 2 *Review of Socialist Law* 139 (1986).

"Yugoslavia: Adoption—Legislation and Practice" by N. Hlaca, 26 *Journal of Family Law* 247 (1987–88). See also 25 *Journal of Family Law* 279 (1986–87).

ZAIRE

SEE ALSO:

Africa, International Law, United Nations

**TREATISES &
LOOSELEAFS:**

African Tax Systems (Zaire) by R. Hammond & M. van den Abeelen (Amsterdam: Intl. Bureau of Fiscal Documentation, 1980–).

Guide to the Text of the Criminal Law and Criminal Procedure Codes of Burundi, Rwanda, and Zaire by A. Wekerle (Library of Congress, 1975).

Information Guide: Doing Business in Zaire (Price Waterhouse).

Investment Laws of the World (Zaire) (Oceana, 1981–).

The Rise and Decline of the Zairian State by C. Young & T. Turner (Univ. of Wisc. Press, 1985).,

Zaire: A Country Study, 3d ed., I. Kaplan, ed. (American Univ., Foreign Affairs Studies, 1979).

ZAMBIA

SEE ALSO: Africa, International Law, United Nations

JOURNALS & OTHER PERIODICALS:
University of Zambia Law Bulletin.
Zambia Law Journal.

TREATISES & LOOSELEAFS:
African Tax Systems (Zambia) by R. Hammond & M. van den Abeelen (Amsterdam: Intl. Bureau of Fiscal Documentation, 1980–).
Civil Liberties in Zambia by M. Ndulo (Oxford: African Law Reports, 1984).
Information Guide: Doing Business in Zambia (Price Waterhouse).
Investment Laws of the World: The Developing Nations (Zambia) (Oceana, 1972–).
Law, Custom, and Social Order: The Colonial Experience in Malawi and Zambia by M. Chanock (NY: Cambridge Univ. Press, 1985).
The Legal System of Zambia by J. Collingwood (Michie, 1970).
Tax Laws of the World—Zambia (FL: Foreign Tax Law Assn.).

ARTICLES:
"The Administration of the Judiciary in Zambia, 1889–1969" by D. Aihe, 67 *Nigerian Law Journal* 116 (1972).
"The Law of Succession in Zambia" by S. Coldham, 27 *Journal of African Law* 162 (1983).
"Patterns of Stock Theft Victimization and Formal Response Strategies among the Lla of Zambia," 9 *Victimiology* 137 (1984).
"The Requirement of Domestic Participation in New Mining Ventures in Zambia" by M. Ndulo, 7 *Georgia Journal of International and Comparative Law* 579 (1977).
"Zambia: Development or its Lack since Independence" by T. Mabula, 27 *Journal of Family Law* 329 (1988–89).

ZIMBABWE

SEE ALSO: Africa, International Law, United Nations

JOURNALS & OTHER PERIODICALS:
Zimbabwe Law Review (Harare: Univ. of Zimbabwe Dept. of Law, 1984–).

TREATISES & LOOSELEAFS:
Business Law in Zimbabwe, R. Christie (Cape Town: Junta, 1985).
Commercial, Business & Trade Laws: Zimbabwe, T. Aguda, ed. (Oceana, 1982).
Information Guide: Doing Business in Zimbabwe (Price Waterhouse).
Introduction to the Legal System of Zimbabwe by J. Redgment (Salisbury: Book Centre, 1981).
Tax Laws of the World—Zimbabwe (FL: Foreign Tax Law Assn.).
The United Nations, International Law, and the Rhodesian Independence Crisis by J. Nkala (Clarendon Press; Oxford Univ. Press, 1985).
Zimbabwe: A Country Study (GPO, 1983).
Zimbabwe Company Law by N. Chadwick (Univ. of Zimbabwe, Dept. of Law, Zimbabwe Law Journal, 1981).

ARTICLES:
"Customary Law in Zimbabwe" by W. Enwright, 49 *Saskatchewan Law Review* 37 (1984/85).

"The Evian Agreements on Algeria and the Lancaster Agreements on Zimbabwe: A Comparative Analysis" by O. Musamirapamwe, 12 *Georgia Journal of International & Comparative Law* 153 (1982).

"The Institution of Ombudsman in Africa with Special Reference to Zimbabwe" by J. Hatchard, 5 *Ombudsman Journal* 21 (1986).

"Minimum Wage Legislation in Developing Countries: Zimbabwe" by S. Fauber, 13 *Case Western Reserve Journal of International Law* 385 (1981).

"Rules of Recognition in the Primary Courts of Zimbabwe" by R. Seidman, 32 *International and Comparative Law Quarterly* 871 (1983) (see also vol. 30, p. 59).

"Zimbabwe: Away from the Customary Law" by A. Armstrong, 27 *Journal of Family Law* 339 (1988–89).

"Zimbabwe's Land Resettlement Program" by G. Sampliner, 5 *New York Law School of International & Comparative Law* 49 (1983).

ZONING & LAND PLANNING

SEE ALSO:
Administrative Law, Agriculture, Air & Aviation, Architecture, Business Law, Constitutional Law, Energy, Environmental Law, Handicapped & the Law, Historic Preservation, Natural Resources, Oil & Gas, Public Utilities, Real Estate, State & Local Government, Water Law; see also entries under individual states

RESEARCH GUIDES & BIBLIOGRAPHIES:
"Environmental Law and Land Use Planning" by F. Skillern in *Specialized Legal Research*, L. Chanin, ed. (Little, Brown, 1987).

National Planning in the United States: An Annotated Bibliography by D. Wilson (Westview, 1979).

JOURNALS, NEWSLETTERS & OTHER PERIODICALS:
American Land Forum Magazine (Bethesda, MD: American Land Forum, 1983–).

Institute on Planning, Zoning, and Eminent Domain Proceedings (Matthew Bender).

Land Use and Environment Law Review (Clark Boardman).

Land Use Law and Zoning Digest (Wash. D.C.: American Planning Assn.).

Zoning and Planning Law Report (Clark Boardman, 1977–).

Zoning Bulletin (Boston: Quinlan Pub. Co., 1952–).

Zoning Law Anthology (Gaylord, 1978–).

Zoning News (Wash. D.C.: American Planning Assn., 1984–).

TREATISES & LOOSELEAFS:
American Land Planning Law by N. Williams (Callaghan, 1974).

American Law of Zoning, 3d ed. by R. Anderson (Lawyers Co-op, 1986).

Decisions for Sale: Corruption in Local Land Use and Building Regulation by J. Gardiner (Praeger, 1978).

The Economics of Zoning Laws: A Property Rights Approach to American Land Use Controls by W. Fischel (Johns Hopkins Univ. Press, 1985).

Handling the Land Use Case by C. Schnidman (Little, Brown, 1984).

Handling Zoning and Land Use Litigation by C. Peterson (Michie, 1982).

How to Win the Zoning Game by S. Abrams (Michie, 1978).

Land Development Law Reporter by S. Bloch (Wash. D.C.: Land Development Institute 1979–).
Land Use and the States, 2d ed. by R. Healy (Johns Hopkins Univ. Press, 1979).
Land Use in a Nutshell, 2d ed. by R. Wright (West, 1985).
Land Use Law, 2d ed. by D. Madelker (Michie, 1988).
The Law of Zoning and Planning by A. Rathkopf (Clark Boardman, 1956–).
1985 Zoning and Planning Law Handbook, J. Gailey, ed. (Clark Boardman, 1985).
Performance Zoning (Wash. D.C.: American Planning Assn., 1980).
Strategy and Tactics in Municipal Zoning, 2d ed. by C. Crawford (Prentice-Hall, 1979).
Urban Land Use Planning, 3d ed. by F. Chapin (Urbana: Univ. of Ill. Press, 1979).
Urban Planning and Land Development Control Law, 2d ed. by D. Hagman (West, 1986).
Winning at Zoning by D. Hinds (McGraw-Hill, 1979).
Zoning and Land Use Controls by P. Rohan (Matthew Bender, 1977–).
Zoning and Planning Deskbook by D. Kmiec (Clark Boardman, 1986–).
Zoning Law and Practice, 3d ed. by E. Yokley (Michie, 1965).

ENCYCLOPEDIAS:

AMERICAN JURISPRUDENCE 2D (Am Jur 2d)
Check the following topics in the *General Index* volumes for Am Jur 2d:

Administrative Law	Zoning and Planning

CORPUS JURIS SECUNDUM (CJS)
Check the following topics in the *General Index* volumes for CJS:

Administrative Bodies	Zoning and Land
Subdivisions	Planning

DIGESTS:

CASE SEARCH IN WEST DIGESTS BY KEY TOPIC
In the *Descriptive Word Index* of the West digests, look for key topics and numbers under the following subject headings:

Administrative Law	Private Roads
Boundaries	Public Lands
Eminent Domain	Zoning and Planning

ALR:

ANNOTATIONS
Check the index volumes for ALR, ALR2d, ALR3d, ALR4th, and ALR Fed for annotations under the following subject headings:

Administrative Law	Land Use Planning and
Boards and Commissions	Control
Community Development	Parks
Discrimination	Residential Area or
Eminent Domain	Property
Housing and Slum	Variance
Clearance	Zoning
Land Development and
Developers

PERIODICALS:

CURRENT LAW INDEX (CLI) & LEGAL RESOURCE INDEX (LRI)
In the CLI and LRI, look for references to periodical literature under the following subject headings:

Administrative Law	Land Use
Building Laws	Public Housing
City Planning	Public Lands
Community Development	Regional Planning
Housing	Zoning

INDEX TO LEGAL PERIODICALS (ILP)

In the ILP, look for references to legal periodical literature under the following subject headings:

Administrative Law	Housing
Building Laws	Land Use
City Planning	Real Property
Common Law	Regional Planning
Historic Preservation	Zoning

STATE JUDICIAL SYSTEMS

Prepared by the Court Statistics and Information Management Project of the National Center for State Courts published in *State Court Caseload Statistics: Annual Report, 1986*. National Center for State Courts, 300 Newport Ave., Williamsburg, VA 23187–8798.

ALABAMA COURT STRUCTURE, 1987

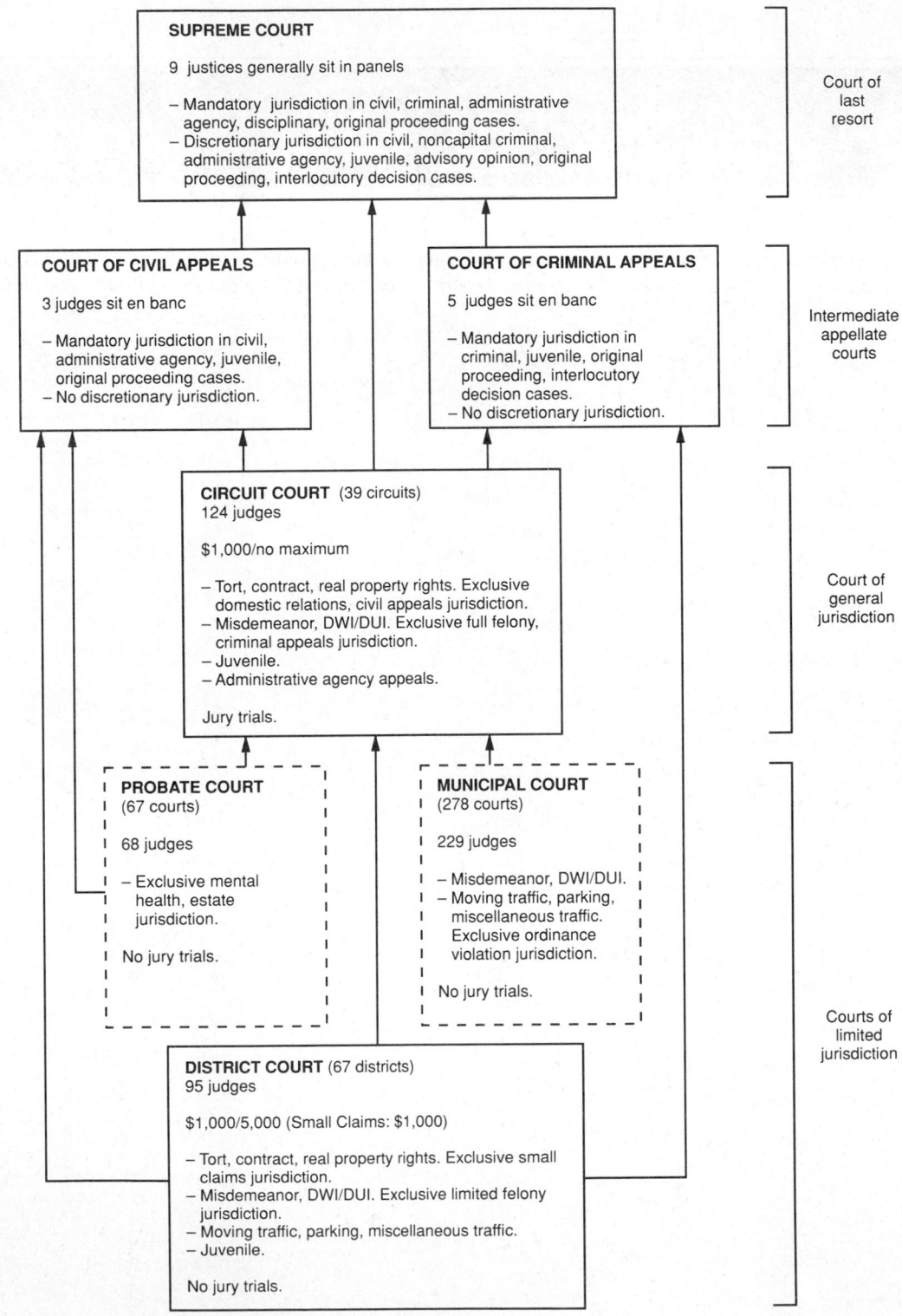

SUPREME COURT

9 justices generally sit in panels

– Mandatory jurisdiction in civil, criminal, administrative agency, disciplinary, original proceeding cases.
– Discretionary jurisdiction in civil, noncapital criminal, administrative agency, juvenile, advisory opinion, original proceeding, interlocutory decision cases.

Court of last resort

COURT OF CIVIL APPEALS

3 judges sit en banc

– Mandatory jurisdiction in civil, administrative agency, juvenile, original proceeding cases.
– No discretionary jurisdiction.

COURT OF CRIMINAL APPEALS

5 judges sit en banc

– Mandatory jurisdiction in criminal, juvenile, original proceeding, interlocutory decision cases.
– No discretionary jurisdiction.

Intermediate appellate courts

CIRCUIT COURT (39 circuits)
124 judges

$1,000/no maximum

– Tort, contract, real property rights. Exclusive domestic relations, civil appeals jurisdiction.
– Misdemeanor, DWI/DUI. Exclusive full felony, criminal appeals jurisdiction.
– Juvenile.
– Administrative agency appeals.

Jury trials.

Court of general jurisdiction

PROBATE COURT
(67 courts)

68 judges

– Exclusive mental health, estate jurisdiction.

No jury trials.

MUNICIPAL COURT
(278 courts)

229 judges

– Misdemeanor, DWI/DUI.
– Moving traffic, parking, miscellaneous traffic. Exclusive ordinance violation jurisdiction.

No jury trials.

DISTRICT COURT (67 districts)
95 judges

$1,000/5,000 (Small Claims: $1,000)

– Tort, contract, real property rights. Exclusive small claims jurisdiction.
– Misdemeanor, DWI/DUI. Exclusive limited felony jurisdiction.
– Moving traffic, parking, miscellaneous traffic.
– Juvenile.

No jury trials.

Courts of limited jurisdiction

ALASKA COURT STRUCTURE, 1987

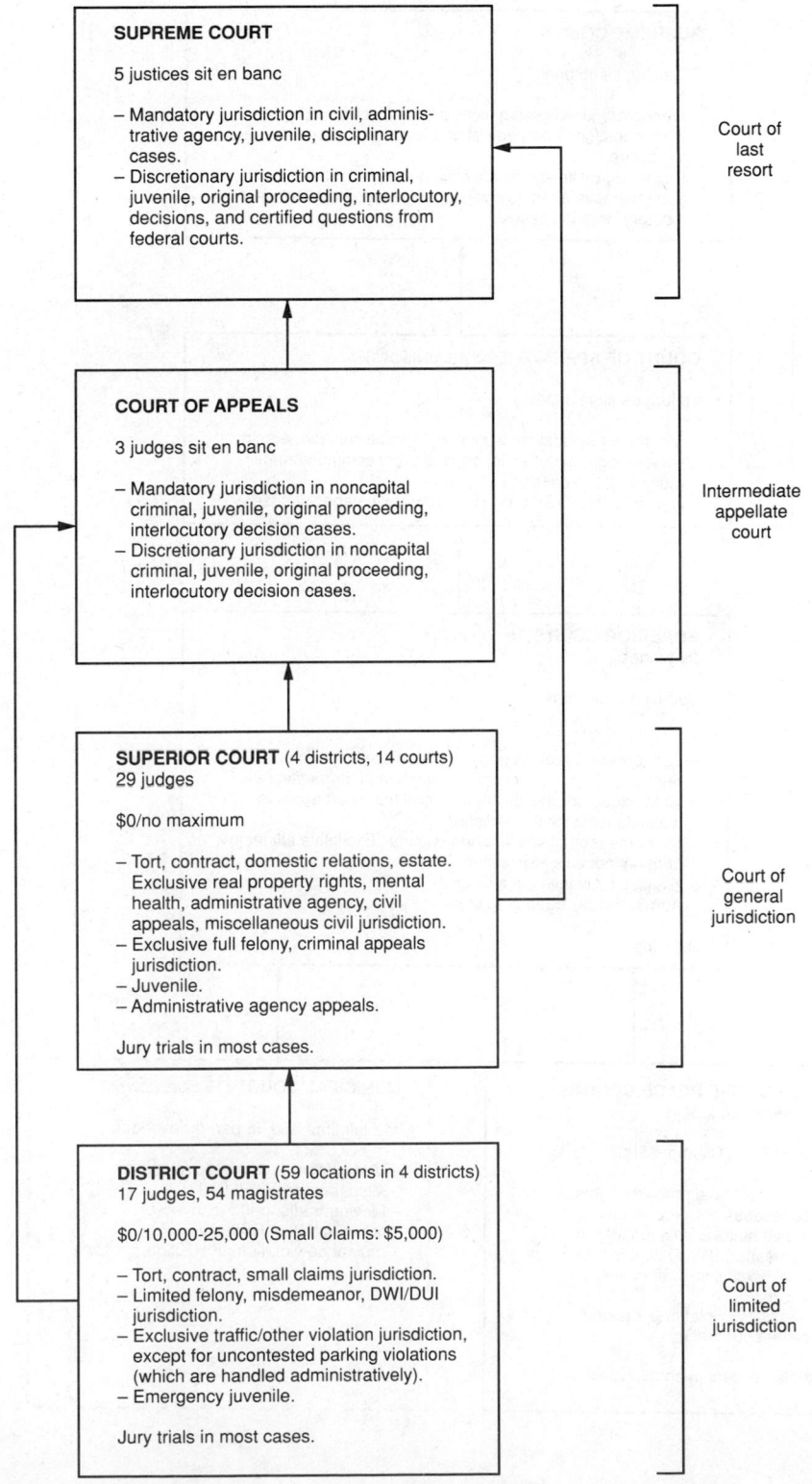

SUPREME COURT

5 justices sit en banc

– Mandatory jurisdiction in civil, administrative agency, juvenile, disciplinary cases.
– Discretionary jurisdiction in criminal, juvenile, original proceeding, interlocutory, decisions, and certified questions from federal courts.

Court of last resort

COURT OF APPEALS

3 judges sit en banc

– Mandatory jurisdiction in noncapital criminal, juvenile, original proceeding, interlocutory decision cases.
– Discretionary jurisdiction in noncapital criminal, juvenile, original proceeding, interlocutory decision cases.

Intermediate appellate court

SUPERIOR COURT (4 districts, 14 courts)
29 judges

$0/no maximum

– Tort, contract, domestic relations, estate. Exclusive real property rights, mental health, administrative agency, civil appeals, miscellaneous civil jurisdiction.
– Exclusive full felony, criminal appeals jurisdiction.
– Juvenile.
– Administrative agency appeals.

Jury trials in most cases.

Court of general jurisdiction

DISTRICT COURT (59 locations in 4 districts)
17 judges, 54 magistrates

$0/10,000-25,000 (Small Claims: $5,000)

– Tort, contract, small claims jurisdiction.
– Limited felony, misdemeanor, DWI/DUI jurisdiction.
– Exclusive traffic/other violation jurisdiction, except for uncontested parking violations (which are handled administratively).
– Emergency juvenile.

Jury trials in most cases.

Court of limited jurisdiction

ARIZONA COURT STRUCTURE, 1987

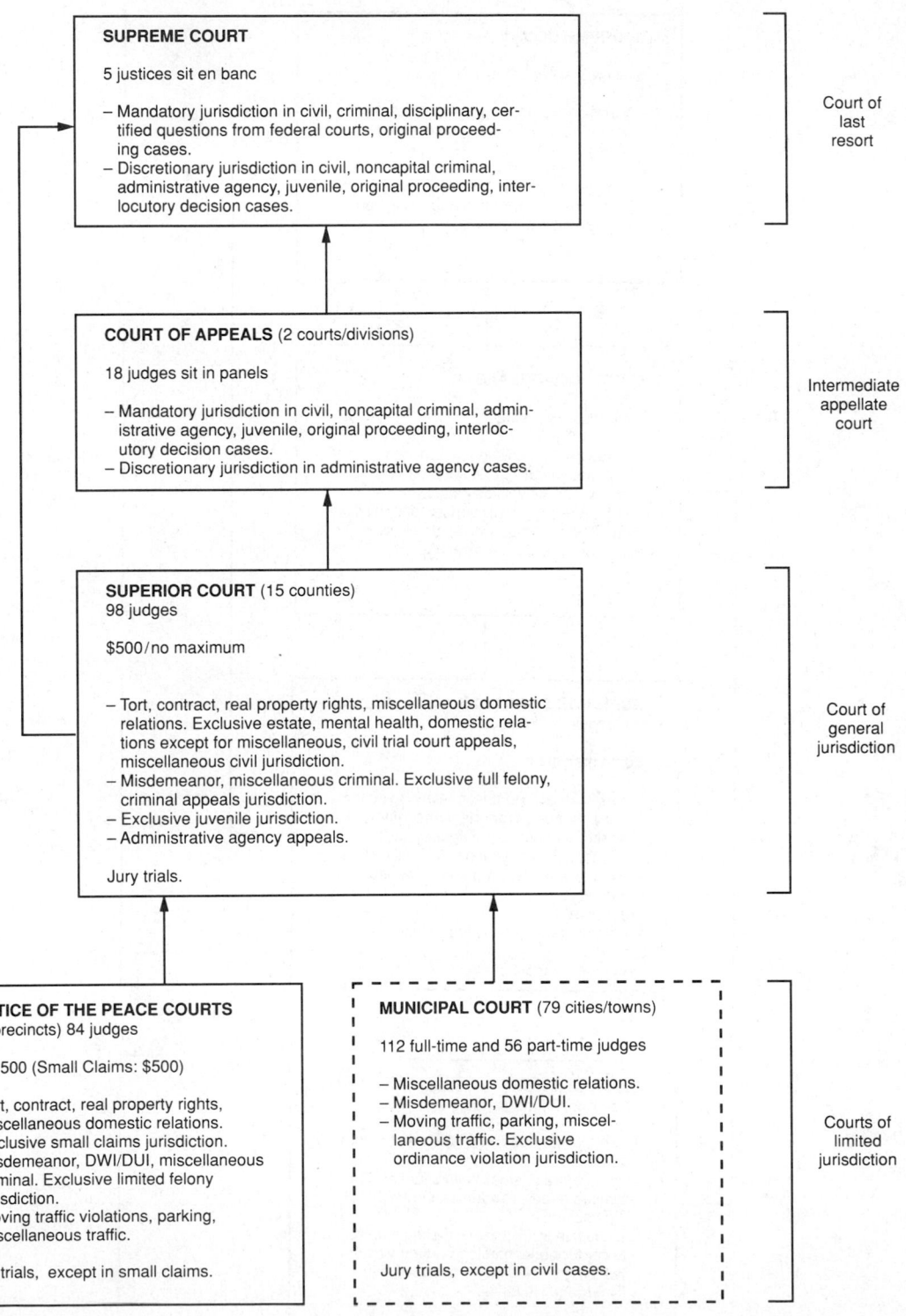

SUPREME COURT

5 justices sit en banc

– Mandatory jurisdiction in civil, criminal, disciplinary, certified questions from federal courts, original proceeding cases.
– Discretionary jurisdiction in civil, noncapital criminal, administrative agency, juvenile, original proceeding, interlocutory decision cases.

Court of
last
resort

COURT OF APPEALS (2 courts/divisions)

18 judges sit in panels

– Mandatory jurisdiction in civil, noncapital criminal, administrative agency, juvenile, original proceeding, interlocutory decision cases.
– Discretionary jurisdiction in administrative agency cases.

Intermediate
appellate
court

SUPERIOR COURT (15 counties)
98 judges

$500/no maximum

– Tort, contract, real property rights, miscellaneous domestic relations. Exclusive estate, mental health, domestic relations except for miscellaneous, civil trial court appeals, miscellaneous civil jurisdiction.
– Misdemeanor, miscellaneous criminal. Exclusive full felony, criminal appeals jurisdiction.
– Exclusive juvenile jurisdiction.
– Administrative agency appeals.

Jury trials.

Court of
general
jurisdiction

JUSTICE OF THE PEACE COURTS
(84 precincts) 84 judges

$0/2,500 (Small Claims: $500)

– Tort, contract, real property rights, miscellaneous domestic relations. Exclusive small claims jurisdiction.
– Misdemeanor, DWI/DUI, miscellaneous criminal. Exclusive limited felony jurisdiction.
– Moving traffic violations, parking, miscellaneous traffic.

Jury trials, except in small claims.

MUNICIPAL COURT (79 cities/towns)

112 full-time and 56 part-time judges

– Miscellaneous domestic relations.
– Misdemeanor, DWI/DUI.
– Moving traffic, parking, miscellaneous traffic. Exclusive ordinance violation jurisdiction.

Jury trials, except in civil cases.

Courts of
limited
jurisdiction

ARKANSAS COURT STRUCTURE, 1987

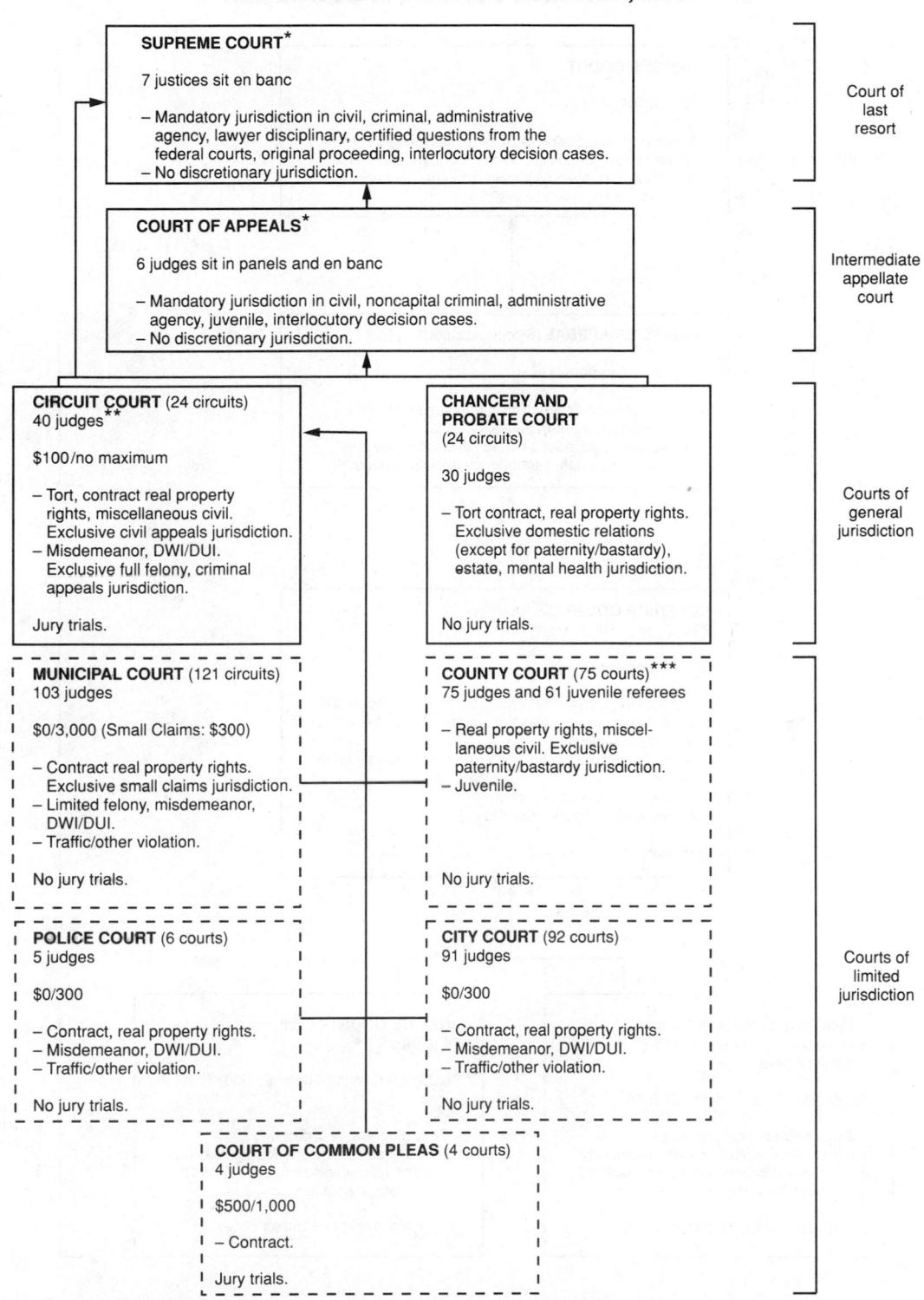

SUPREME COURT*

7 justices sit en banc

– Mandatory jurisdiction in civil, criminal, administrative
  agency, lawyer disciplinary, certified questions from the
  federal courts, original proceeding, interlocutory decision cases.
– No discretionary jurisdiction.

Court of
last
resort

COURT OF APPEALS*

6 judges sit in panels and en banc

– Mandatory jurisdiction in civil, noncapital criminal, administrative
  agency, juvenile, interlocutory decision cases.
– No discretionary jurisdiction.

Intermediate
appellate
court

CIRCUIT COURT (24 circuits)
40 judges**

$100/no maximum

– Tort, contract real property
  rights, miscellaneous civil.
  Exclusive civil appeals jurisdiction.
– Misdemeanor, DWI/DUI.
  Exclusive full felony, criminal
  appeals jurisdiction.

Jury trials.

**CHANCERY AND
PROBATE COURT**
(24 circuits)

30 judges

– Tort contract, real property rights.
  Exclusive domestic relations
  (except for paternity/bastardy),
  estate, mental health jurisdiction.

No jury trials.

Courts of
general
jurisdiction

MUNICIPAL COURT (121 circuits)
103 judges

$0/3,000 (Small Claims: $300)

– Contract real property rights.
  Exclusive small claims jurisdiction.
– Limited felony, misdemeanor,
  DWI/DUI.
– Traffic/other violation.

No jury trials.

COUNTY COURT (75 courts)***
75 judges and 61 juvenile referees

– Real property rights, miscellaneous civil. Exclusive
  paternity/bastardy jurisdiction.
– Juvenile.

No jury trials.

POLICE COURT (6 courts)
5 judges

$0/300

– Contract, real property rights.
– Misdemeanor, DWI/DUI.
– Traffic/other violation.

No jury trials.

CITY COURT (92 courts)
91 judges

$0/300

– Contract, real property rights.
– Misdemeanor, DWI/DUI.
– Traffic/other violation.

No jury trials.

Courts of
limited
jurisdiction

COURT OF COMMON PLEAS (4 courts)
4 judges

$500/1,000

– Contract.

Jury trials.

---

*   Each of the appellate courts is the court of last resort for specific casetypes. Only a very few
      cases are ever appealed to the Supreme Court from the Court of Appeals.
**   Eight judges also serve the Chancery and Probate Court.
***   Referred to as the Juvenile Court when handling juvenile matters.

CALIFORNIA COURT STRUCTURE, 1987

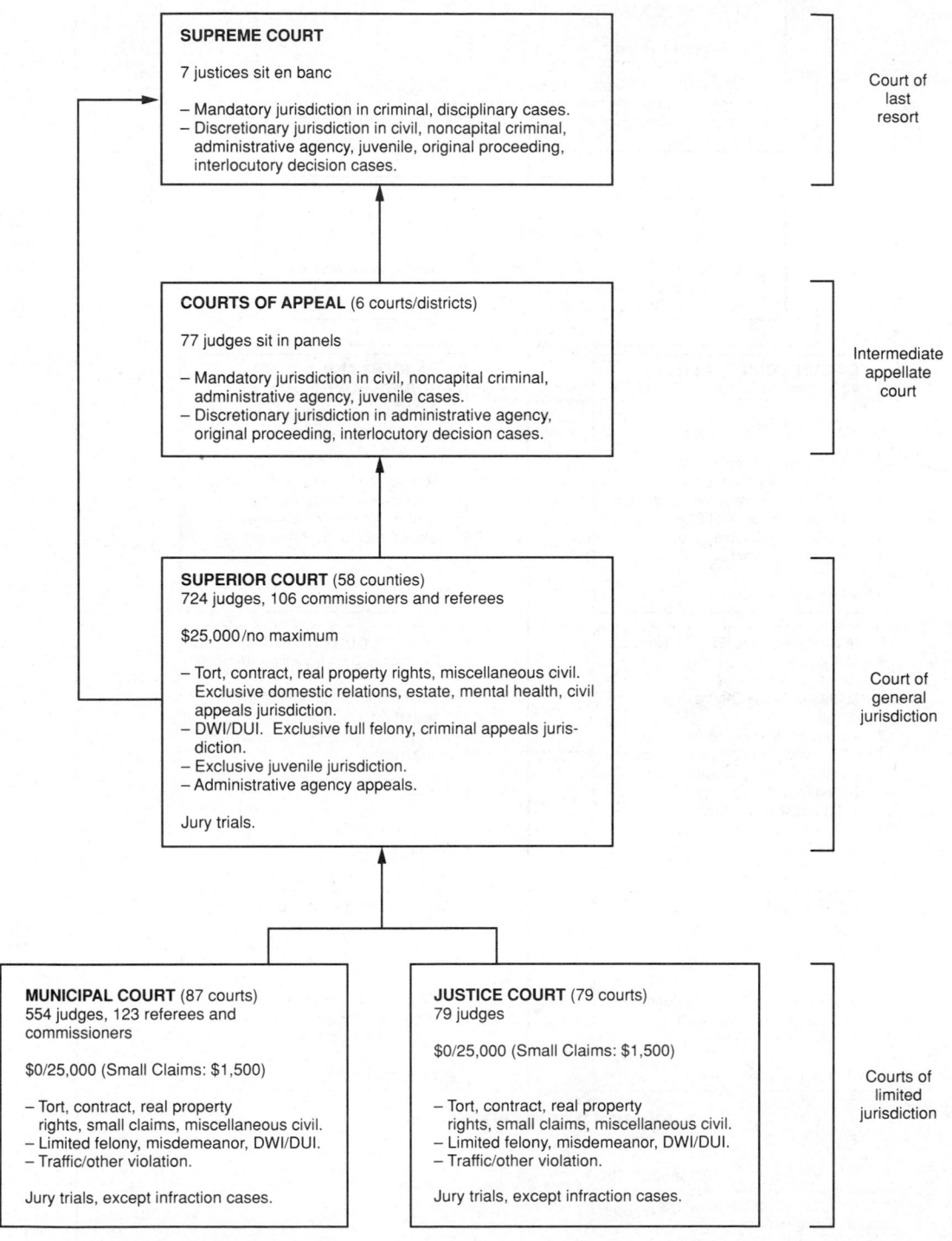

SUPREME COURT

7 justices sit en banc

– Mandatory jurisdiction in criminal, disciplinary cases.
– Discretionary jurisdiction in civil, noncapital criminal, administrative agency, juvenile, original proceeding, interlocutory decision cases.

Court of last resort

COURTS OF APPEAL (6 courts/districts)

77 judges sit in panels

– Mandatory jurisdiction in civil, noncapital criminal, administrative agency, juvenile cases.
– Discretionary jurisdiction in administrative agency, original proceeding, interlocutory decision cases.

Intermediate appellate court

SUPERIOR COURT (58 counties)
724 judges, 106 commissioners and referees

$25,000/no maximum

– Tort, contract, real property rights, miscellaneous civil. Exclusive domestic relations, estate, mental health, civil appeals jurisdiction.
– DWI/DUI. Exclusive full felony, criminal appeals juris-diction.
– Exclusive juvenile jurisdiction.
– Administrative agency appeals.

Jury trials.

Court of general jurisdiction

MUNICIPAL COURT (87 courts)
554 judges, 123 referees and commissioners

$0/25,000 (Small Claims: $1,500)

– Tort, contract, real property rights, small claims, miscellaneous civil.
– Limited felony, misdemeanor, DWI/DUI.
– Traffic/other violation.

Jury trials, except infraction cases.

JUSTICE COURT (79 courts)
79 judges

$0/25,000 (Small Claims: $1,500)

– Tort, contract, real property rights, small claims, miscellaneous civil.
– Limited felony, misdemeanor, DWI/DUI.
– Traffic/other violation.

Jury trials, except infraction cases.

Courts of limited jurisdiction

COLORADO COURT STRUCTURE, 1987

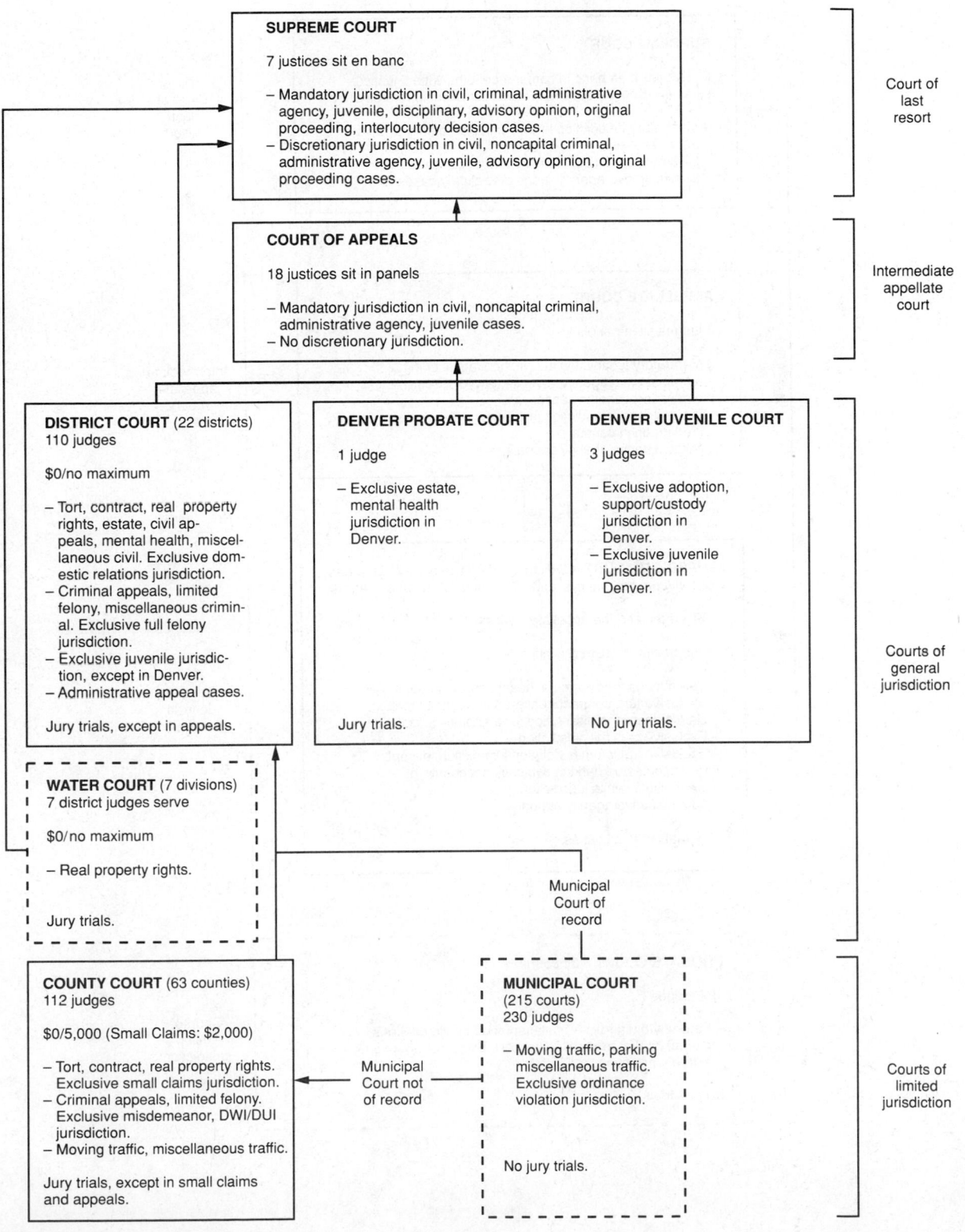

SUPREME COURT

7 justices sit en banc

– Mandatory jurisdiction in civil, criminal, administrative agency, juvenile, disciplinary, advisory opinion, original proceeding, interlocutory decision cases.
– Discretionary jurisdiction in civil, noncapital criminal, administrative agency, juvenile, advisory opinion, original proceeding cases.

Court of last resort

COURT OF APPEALS

18 justices sit in panels

– Mandatory jurisdiction in civil, noncapital criminal, administrative agency, juvenile cases.
– No discretionary jurisdiction.

Intermediate appellate court

DISTRICT COURT (22 districts)
110 judges

$0/no maximum

– Tort, contract, real property rights, estate, civil appeals, mental health, miscellaneous civil. Exclusive domestic relations jurisdiction.
– Criminal appeals, limited felony, miscellaneous criminal. Exclusive full felony jurisdiction.
– Exclusive juvenile jurisdiction, except in Denver.
– Administrative appeal cases.

Jury trials, except in appeals.

DENVER PROBATE COURT

1 judge

– Exclusive estate, mental health jurisdiction in Denver.

Jury trials.

DENVER JUVENILE COURT

3 judges

– Exclusive adoption, support/custody jurisdiction in Denver.
– Exclusive juvenile jurisdiction in Denver.

No jury trials.

Courts of general jurisdiction

WATER COURT (7 divisions)
7 district judges serve

$0/no maximum

– Real property rights.

Jury trials.

Municipal Court of record

COUNTY COURT (63 counties)
112 judges

$0/5,000 (Small Claims: $2,000)

– Tort, contract, real property rights. Exclusive small claims jurisdiction.
– Criminal appeals, limited felony. Exclusive misdemeanor, DWI/DUI jurisdiction.
– Moving traffic, miscellaneous traffic.

Jury trials, except in small claims and appeals.

Municipal Court not of record

MUNICIPAL COURT
(215 courts)
230 judges

– Moving traffic, parking miscellaneous traffic. Exclusive ordinance violation jurisdiction.

No jury trials.

Courts of limited jurisdiction

CONNECTICUT COURT STRUCTURE, 1987

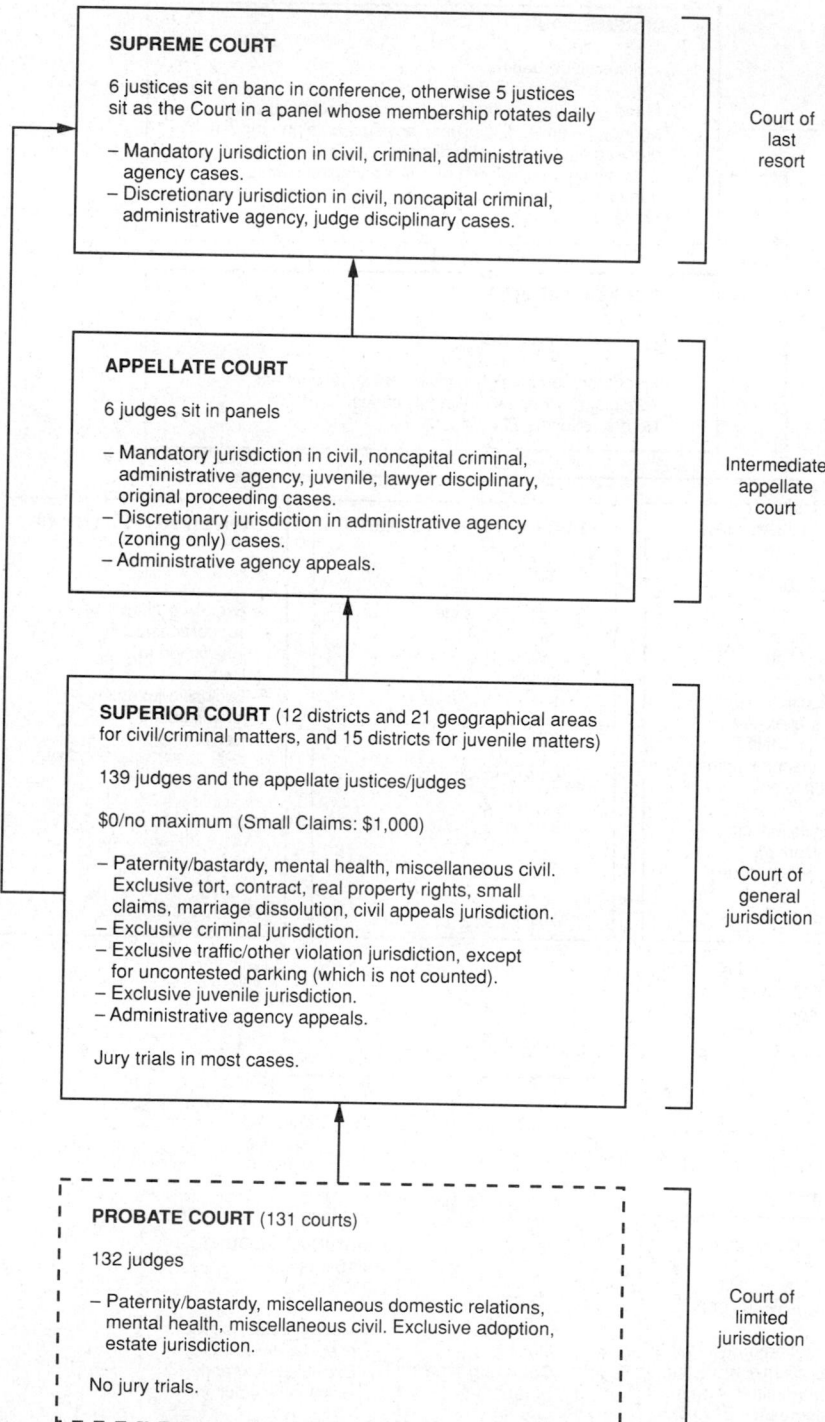

SUPREME COURT

6 justices sit en banc in conference, otherwise 5 justices
sit as the Court in a panel whose membership rotates daily

– Mandatory jurisdiction in civil, criminal, administrative
  agency cases.
– Discretionary jurisdiction in civil, noncapital criminal,
  administrative agency, judge disciplinary cases.

Court of
last
resort

APPELLATE COURT

6 judges sit in panels

– Mandatory jurisdiction in civil, noncapital criminal,
  administrative agency, juvenile, lawyer disciplinary,
  original proceeding cases.
– Discretionary jurisdiction in administrative agency
  (zoning only) cases.
– Administrative agency appeals.

Intermediate
appellate
court

SUPERIOR COURT (12 districts and 21 geographical areas
for civil/criminal matters, and 15 districts for juvenile matters)

139 judges and the appellate justices/judges

$0/no maximum (Small Claims: $1,000)

– Paternity/bastardy, mental health, miscellaneous civil.
  Exclusive tort, contract, real property rights, small
  claims, marriage dissolution, civil appeals jurisdiction.
– Exclusive criminal jurisdiction.
– Exclusive traffic/other violation jurisdiction, except
  for uncontested parking (which is not counted).
– Exclusive juvenile jurisdiction.
– Administrative agency appeals.

Jury trials in most cases.

Court of
general
jurisdiction

PROBATE COURT (131 courts)

132 judges

– Paternity/bastardy, miscellaneous domestic relations,
  mental health, miscellaneous civil. Exclusive adoption,
  estate jurisdiction.

No jury trials.

Court of
limited
jurisdiction

DELAWARE COURT STRUCTURE, 1987

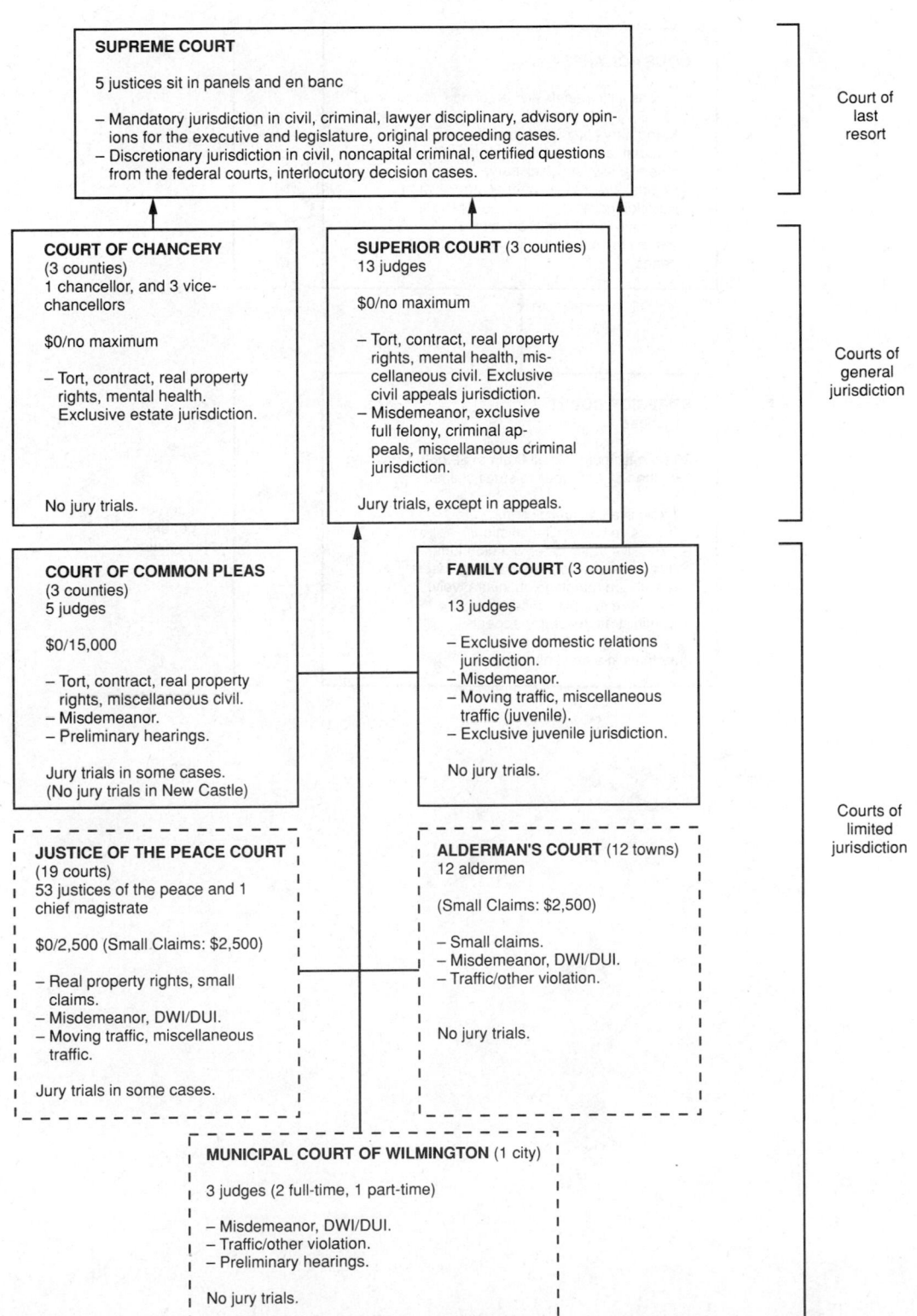

SUPREME COURT

5 justices sit in panels and en banc

– Mandatory jurisdiction in civil, criminal, lawyer disciplinary, advisory opinions for the executive and legislature, original proceeding cases.
– Discretionary jurisdiction in civil, noncapital criminal, certified questions from the federal courts, interlocutory decision cases.

Court of last resort

COURT OF CHANCERY
(3 counties)
1 chancellor, and 3 vice-chancellors

$0/no maximum

– Tort, contract, real property rights, mental health. Exclusive estate jurisdiction.

No jury trials.

SUPERIOR COURT (3 counties)
13 judges

$0/no maximum

– Tort, contract, real property rights, mental health, miscellaneous civil. Exclusive civil appeals jurisdiction.
– Misdemeanor, exclusive full felony, criminal appeals, miscellaneous criminal jurisdiction.

Jury trials, except in appeals.

Courts of general jurisdiction

COURT OF COMMON PLEAS
(3 counties)
5 judges

$0/15,000

– Tort, contract, real property rights, miscellaneous civil.
– Misdemeanor.
– Preliminary hearings.

Jury trials in some cases.
(No jury trials in New Castle)

FAMILY COURT (3 counties)

13 judges

– Exclusive domestic relations jurisdiction.
– Misdemeanor.
– Moving traffic, miscellaneous traffic (juvenile).
– Exclusive juvenile jurisdiction.

No jury trials.

JUSTICE OF THE PEACE COURT
(19 courts)
53 justices of the peace and 1 chief magistrate

$0/2,500 (Small Claims: $2,500)

– Real property rights, small claims.
– Misdemeanor, DWI/DUI.
– Moving traffic, miscellaneous traffic.

Jury trials in some cases.

ALDERMAN'S COURT (12 towns)
12 aldermen

(Small Claims: $2,500)

– Small claims.
– Misdemeanor, DWI/DUI.
– Traffic/other violation.

No jury trials.

Courts of limited jurisdiction

MUNICIPAL COURT OF WILMINGTON (1 city)

3 judges (2 full-time, 1 part-time)

– Misdemeanor, DWI/DUI.
– Traffic/other violation.
– Preliminary hearings.

No jury trials.

DISTRICT OF COLUMBIA COURT STRUCTURE, 1987

COURT OF APPEALS

9 judges sit in panels and en banc

– Mandatory jurisdiction in civil,
  criminal, administrative agency,
  juvenile, lawyer disciplinary,
  original proceeding, interlocutory
  decision cases.
– Discretionary jurisdiction in small claims,
  minor criminal, and original proceeding
  cases.

Court of
last
resort

SUPERIOR COURT
51 judges

$0/no maximum (Small Claims: $2,000) (anything
less than $2,000 goes to small claims)

– Exclusive civil jurisdiction.
– Exclusive criminal jurisdiction.
– Exclusive traffic/other violation juris-
  diction, except for most parking cases
  (which are handled administratively).
– Exclusive juvenile jurisdiction.
– Administrative agency appeals.

Jury trials in almost all cases.

Court of
general
jurisdiction

FLORIDA COURT STRUCTURE, 1987

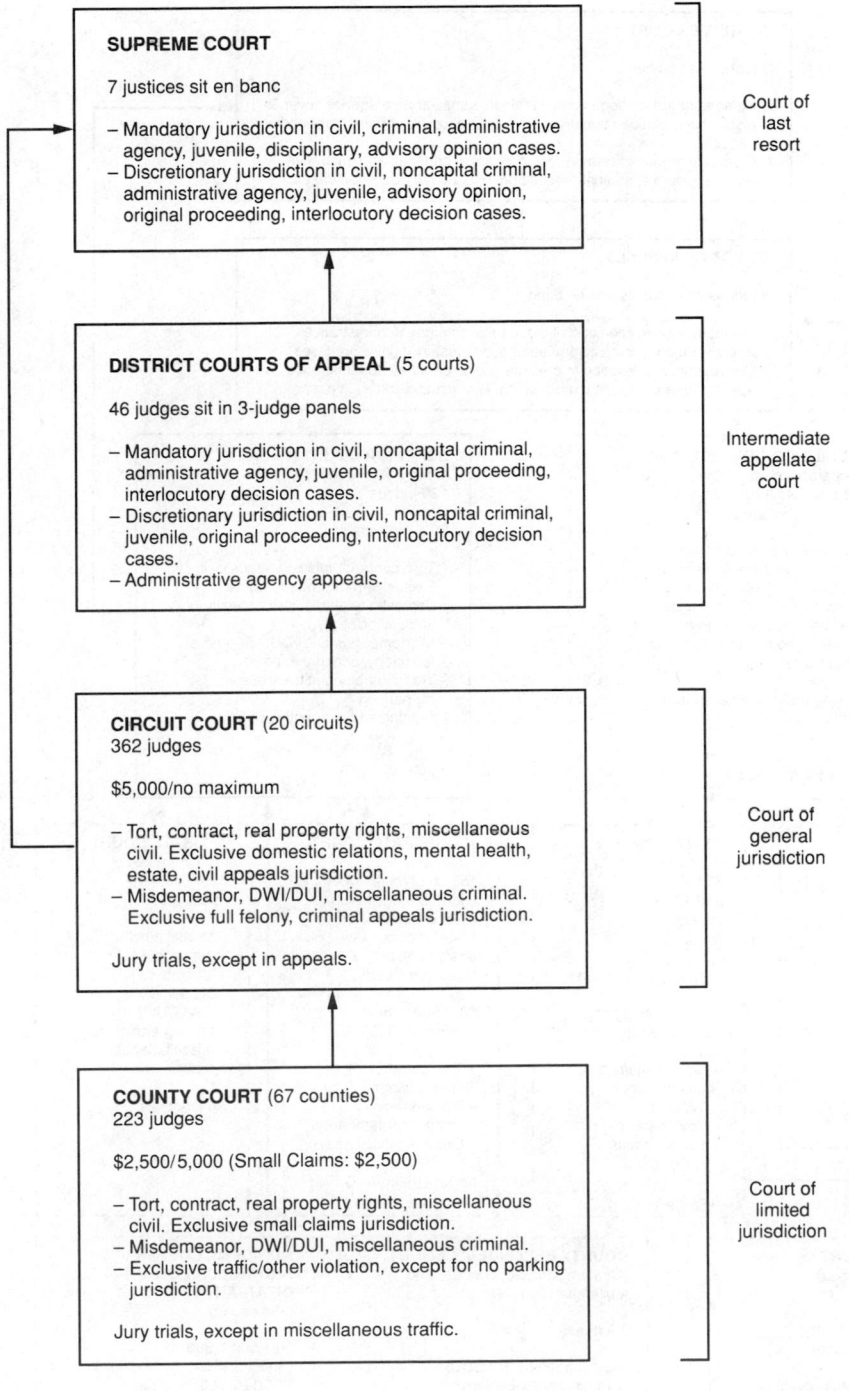

SUPREME COURT

7 justices sit en banc

– Mandatory jurisdiction in civil, criminal, administrative agency, juvenile, disciplinary, advisory opinion cases.
– Discretionary jurisdiction in civil, noncapital criminal, administrative agency, juvenile, advisory opinion, original proceeding, interlocutory decision cases.

Court of last resort

DISTRICT COURTS OF APPEAL (5 courts)

46 judges sit in 3-judge panels

– Mandatory jurisdiction in civil, noncapital criminal, administrative agency, juvenile, original proceeding, interlocutory decision cases.
– Discretionary jurisdiction in civil, noncapital criminal, juvenile, original proceeding, interlocutory decision cases.
– Administrative agency appeals.

Intermediate appellate court

CIRCUIT COURT (20 circuits)
362 judges

$5,000/no maximum

– Tort, contract, real property rights, miscellaneous civil. Exclusive domestic relations, mental health, estate, civil appeals jurisdiction.
– Misdemeanor, DWI/DUI, miscellaneous criminal. Exclusive full felony, criminal appeals jurisdiction.

Jury trials, except in appeals.

Court of general jurisdiction

COUNTY COURT (67 counties)
223 judges

$2,500/5,000 (Small Claims: $2,500)

– Tort, contract, real property rights, miscellaneous civil. Exclusive small claims jurisdiction.
– Misdemeanor, DWI/DUI, miscellaneous criminal.
– Exclusive traffic/other violation, except for no parking jurisdiction.

Jury trials, except in miscellaneous traffic.

Court of limited jurisdiction

GEORGIA COURT STRUCTURE, 1987

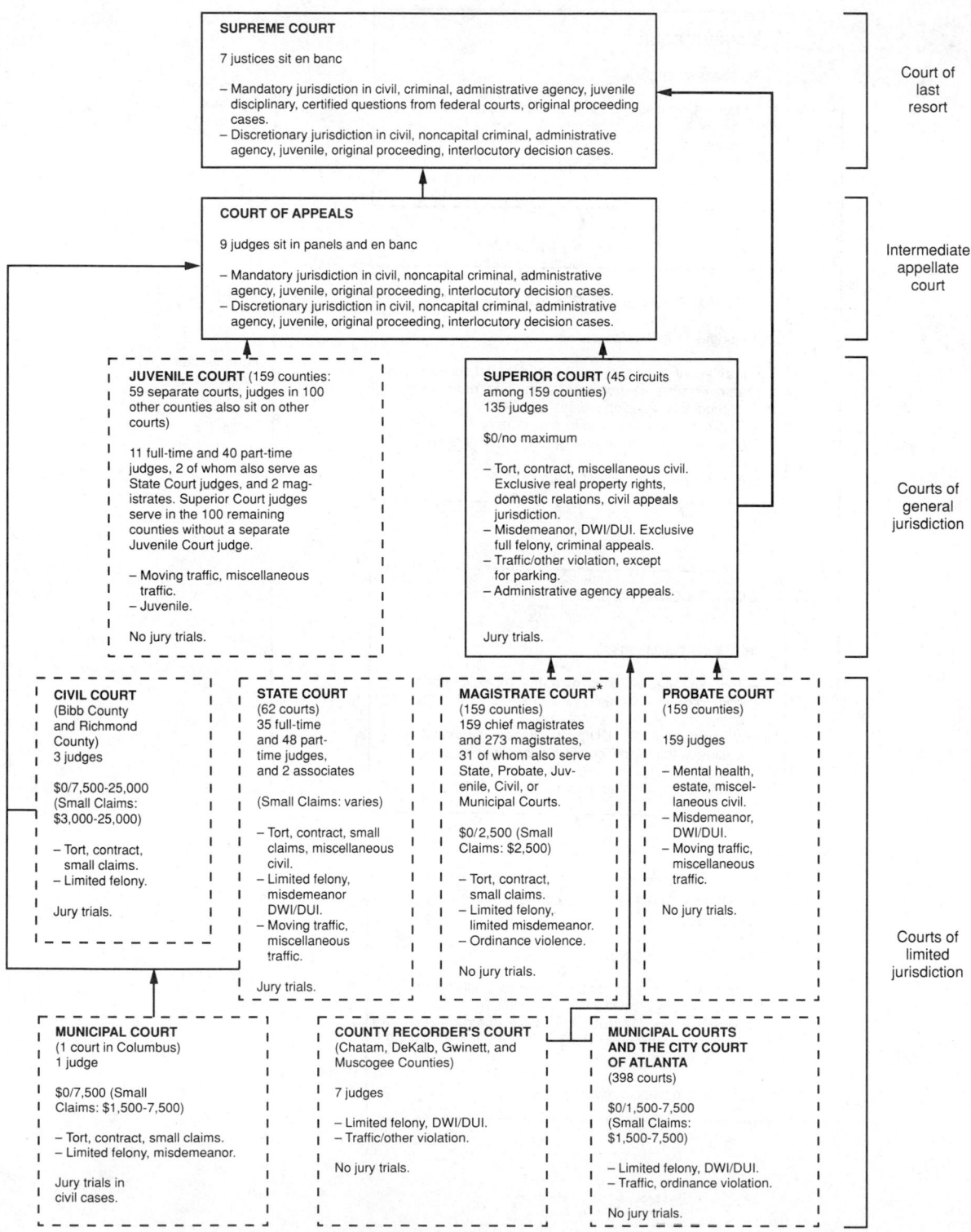

*In July of 1983 the Justice of the Peace Court and the Small Claims Court were merged into the Magistrate Court by Constitutional Article.

HAWAII COURT STRUCTURE, 1987

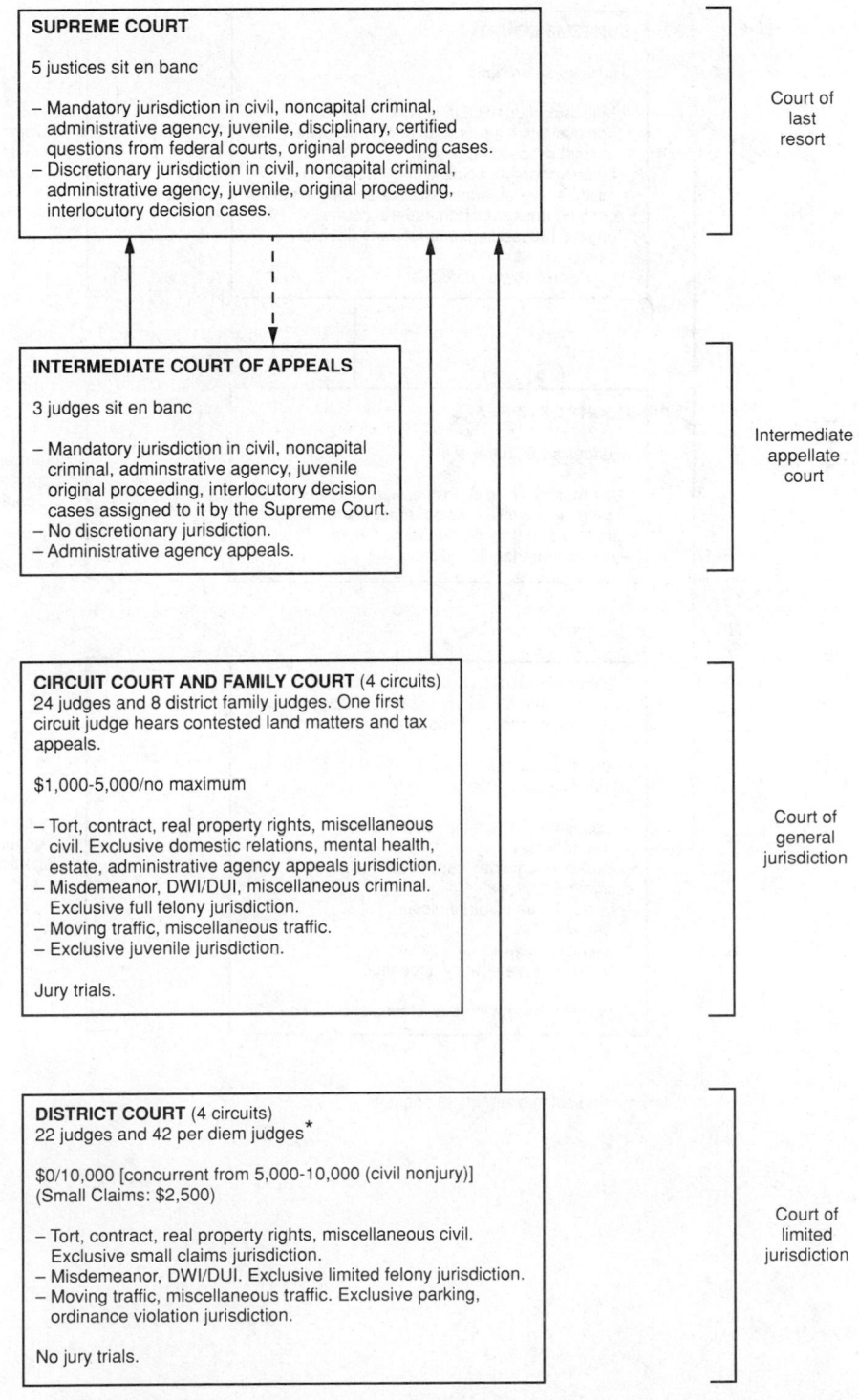

SUPREME COURT

5 justices sit en banc

– Mandatory jurisdiction in civil, noncapital criminal, administrative agency, juvenile, disciplinary, certified questions from federal courts, original proceeding cases.
– Discretionary jurisdiction in civil, noncapital criminal, administrative agency, juvenile, original proceeding, interlocutory decision cases.

Court of last resort

INTERMEDIATE COURT OF APPEALS

3 judges sit en banc

– Mandatory jurisdiction in civil, noncapital criminal, administrative agency, juvenile original proceeding, interlocutory decision cases assigned to it by the Supreme Court.
– No discretionary jurisdiction.
– Administrative agency appeals.

Intermediate appellate court

CIRCUIT COURT AND FAMILY COURT (4 circuits)
24 judges and 8 district family judges. One first circuit judge hears contested land matters and tax appeals.

$1,000-5,000/no maximum

– Tort, contract, real property rights, miscellaneous civil. Exclusive domestic relations, mental health, estate, administrative agency appeals jurisdiction.
– Misdemeanor, DWI/DUI, miscellaneous criminal. Exclusive full felony jurisdiction.
– Moving traffic, miscellaneous traffic.
– Exclusive juvenile jurisdiction.

Jury trials.

Court of general jurisdiction

DISTRICT COURT (4 circuits)
22 judges and 42 per diem judges[*]

$0/10,000 [concurrent from 5,000-10,000 (civil nonjury)]
(Small Claims: $2,500)

– Tort, contract, real property rights, miscellaneous civil. Exclusive small claims jurisdiction.
– Misdemeanor, DWI/DUI. Exclusive limited felony jurisdiction.
– Moving traffic, miscellaneous traffic. Exclusive parking, ordinance violation jurisdiction.

No jury trials.

Court of limited jurisdiction

– – –Indicates assignment of cases.
[*]Some per diem judges are assigned to serve as per diem District & Family Court judges in the First Circuit.

IDAHO COURT STRUCTURE, 1987

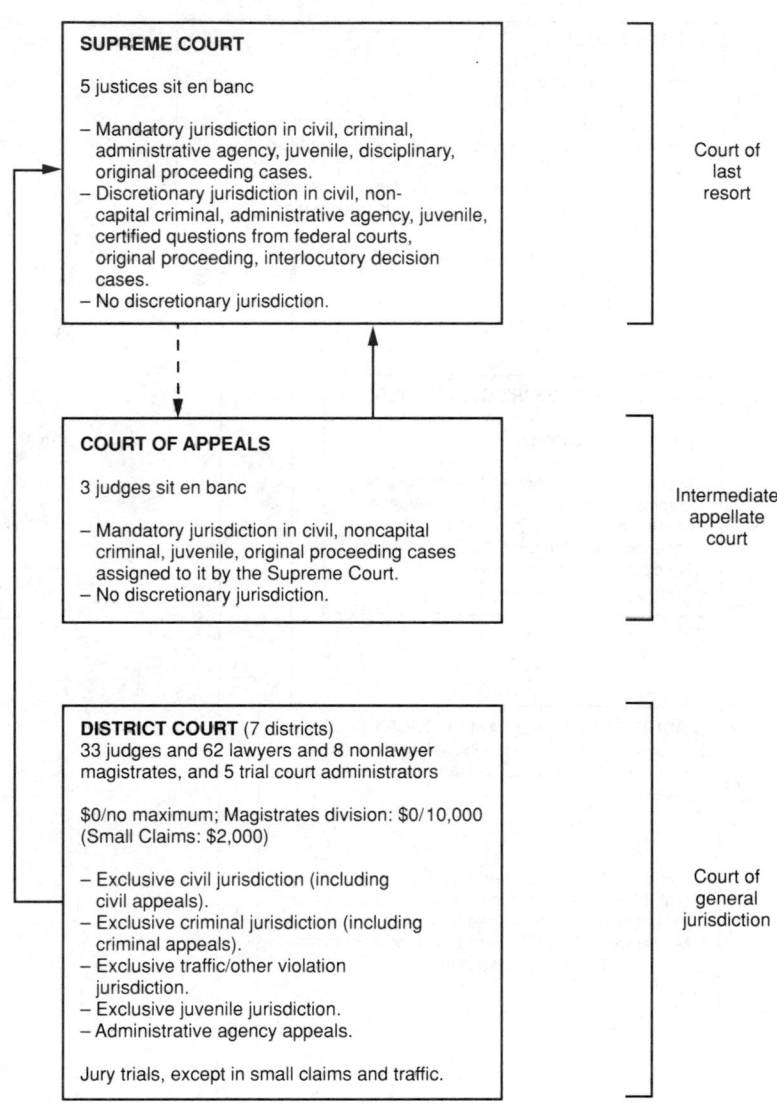

SUPREME COURT

5 justices sit en banc

– Mandatory jurisdiction in civil, criminal,
  administrative agency, juvenile, disciplinary,
  original proceeding cases.
– Discretionary jurisdiction in civil, noncapital criminal, administrative agency, juvenile,
  certified questions from federal courts,
  original proceeding, interlocutory decision
  cases.
– No discretionary jurisdiction.

Court of
last
resort

COURT OF APPEALS

3 judges sit en banc

– Mandatory jurisdiction in civil, noncapital
  criminal, juvenile, original proceeding cases
  assigned to it by the Supreme Court.
– No discretionary jurisdiction.

Intermediate
appellate
court

DISTRICT COURT (7 districts)
33 judges and 62 lawyers and 8 nonlawyer
magistrates, and 5 trial court administrators

$0/no maximum; Magistrates division: $0/10,000
(Small Claims: $2,000)

– Exclusive civil jurisdiction (including
  civil appeals).
– Exclusive criminal jurisdiction (including
  criminal appeals).
– Exclusive traffic/other violation
  jurisdiction.
– Exclusive juvenile jurisdiction.
– Administrative agency appeals.

Jury trials, except in small claims and traffic.

Court of
general
jurisdiction

– – – Indicates assignment of cases.

ILLINOIS COURT STRUCTURE, 1987

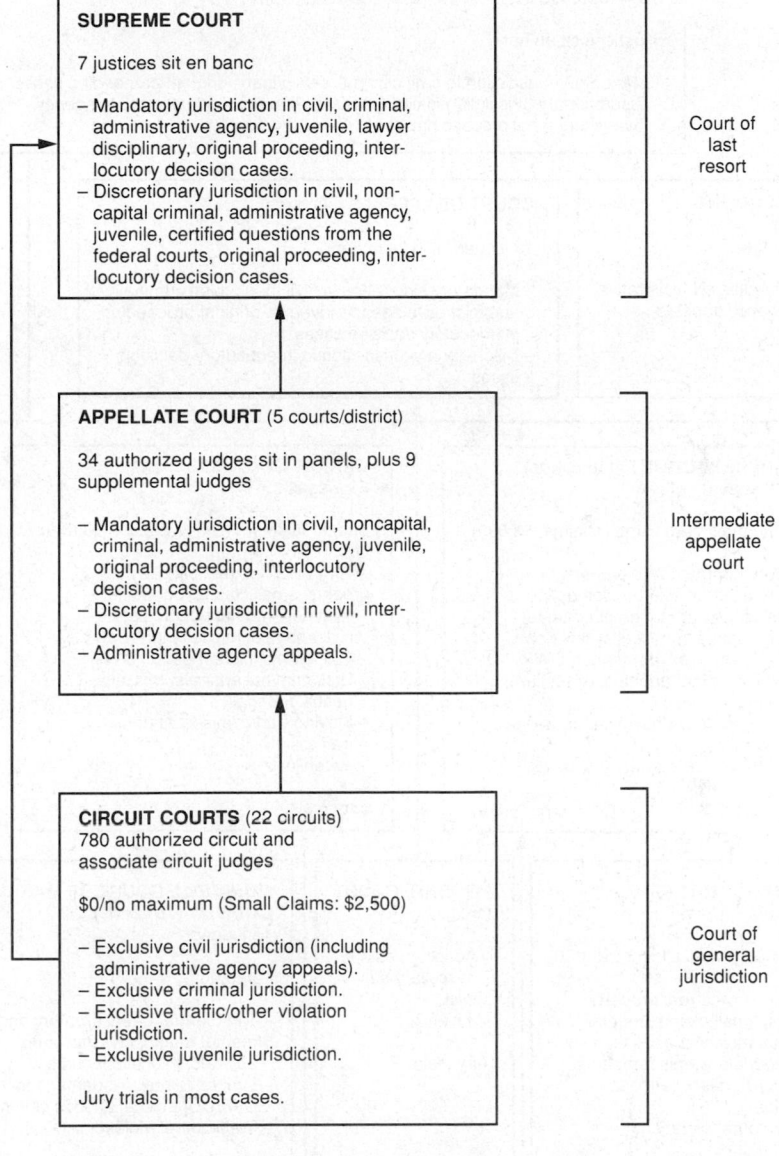

SUPREME COURT

7 justices sit en banc

– Mandatory jurisdiction in civil, criminal, administrative agency, juvenile, lawyer disciplinary, original proceeding, interlocutory decision cases.
– Discretionary jurisdiction in civil, non-capital criminal, administrative agency, juvenile, certified questions from the federal courts, original proceeding, interlocutory decision cases.

Court of
last
resort

APPELLATE COURT (5 courts/district)

34 authorized judges sit in panels, plus 9 supplemental judges

– Mandatory jurisdiction in civil, noncapital, criminal, administrative agency, juvenile, original proceeding, interlocutory decision cases.
– Discretionary jurisdiction in civil, interlocutory decision cases.
– Administrative agency appeals.

Intermediate
appellate
court

CIRCUIT COURTS (22 circuits)
780 authorized circuit and associate circuit judges

$0/no maximum (Small Claims: $2,500)

– Exclusive civil jurisdiction (including administrative agency appeals).
– Exclusive criminal jurisdiction.
– Exclusive traffic/other violation jurisdiction.
– Exclusive juvenile jurisdiction.

Jury trials in most cases.

Court of
general
jurisdiction

INDIANA COURT STRUCTURE, 1987

SUPREME COURT 5 justices sit en banc – Mandatory jurisdiction in civil, criminal, disciplinary, original proceeding cases. – Discretionary jurisdiction in civil, noncapital criminal, administrative agency, juvenile, original proceeding cases.	Court of last resort

TAX COURT[*] 1 judge – Handles administrative agency appeals.	**COURT OF APPEALS** (4 courts) 12 judges sit in four courts – Mandatory jurisdiction in civil, noncapital criminal, administrative agency, juvenile, original proceeding, interlocutory decision cases. – Discretionary jurisdiction in interlocutory decision cases.	Intermediate appellate court

SUPERIOR COURT (115 courts) 117 judges $0/no maximum (Small Claims: $3,000) – Tort, contract, real property rights, small claims, domestic relations, mental health, estate, civil appeals, miscellaneous civil. – Full felony, misdemeanor, DWI/DUI, criminal appeals, miscellaneous criminal. – Moving traffic, miscellaneous traffic. – Juvenile. – Administrative agency appeals. Jury trials.	**CIRCUIT COURT** (92 courts) 89 judges $0/no maximum (Small Claims: $3,000) – Tort, contract, real property rights, small claims, domestic relations, mental health, estate, civil appeals, miscellaneous civil. – Full felony, misdemeanor, DWI/DUI, criminal appeals, miscellaneous criminal. – Moving traffic, miscellaneous traffic. – Juvenile. Jury trials.	Courts of general jurisdiction

COUNTY COURT (57 courts) 54 judges $0/10,000 (Small Claims: $3,000) – Tort, contract, real property rights, small claims, mental health, miscellaneous civil. – Limited felony, misdemeanor, DWI/DUI, miscellaneous criminal. – Traffic/other violation. Jury trials.	**PROBATE COURT** (1 court) – Adoption, estate, miscellaneous civil. – Juvenile. Jury trials.	**MUNICIPAL COURT OF MARION COUNTY** (15 courts) 15 judges $0/20,000 – Tort, contract, real property rights, mental health, civil trial court appeals, miscellaneous civil. – Limited felony, misdemeanor, DWI/DUI, miscellaneous criminal. – Traffic/other violations. Jury trials.	Courts of limited jurisdiction
CITY COURT (52 courts) 52 judges $0/500-2,500 (most are $500 maximum) – Tort, contract. – Misdemeanor, DWI/DUI. – Traffic/other violation. Jury trials.	**TOWN COURT** (25 courts) – Misdemeanor, DWI/DUI. – Traffic/other violation. Jury trials.	**SMALL CLAIMS COURT OF MARION COUNTY** (8 courts) 8 judges $3,000 – Small claims. – Miscellaneous criminal. No jury trials.	

[*]The Tax Court was established in the beginning of 1986.

IOWA COURT STRUCTURE, 1987

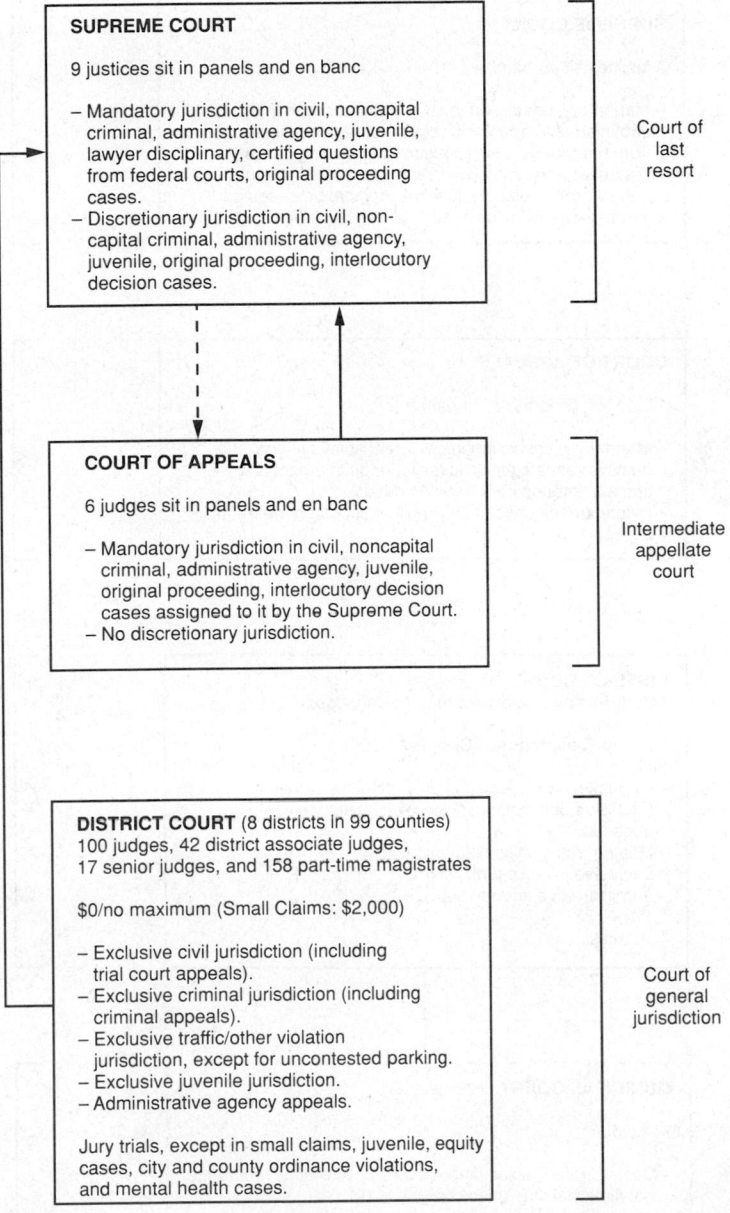

SUPREME COURT

9 justices sit in panels and en banc

– Mandatory jurisdiction in civil, noncapital criminal, administrative agency, juvenile, lawyer disciplinary, certified questions from federal courts, original proceeding cases.
– Discretionary jurisdiction in civil, non-capital criminal, administrative agency, juvenile, original proceeding, interlocutory decision cases.

Court of last resort

COURT OF APPEALS

6 judges sit in panels and en banc

– Mandatory jurisdiction in civil, noncapital criminal, administrative agency, juvenile, original proceeding, interlocutory decision cases assigned to it by the Supreme Court.
– No discretionary jurisdiction.

Intermediate appellate court

DISTRICT COURT (8 districts in 99 counties)
100 judges, 42 district associate judges,
17 senior judges, and 158 part-time magistrates

$0/no maximum (Small Claims: $2,000)

– Exclusive civil jurisdiction (including trial court appeals).
– Exclusive criminal jurisdiction (including criminal appeals).
– Exclusive traffic/other violation jurisdiction, except for uncontested parking.
– Exclusive juvenile jurisdiction.
– Administrative agency appeals.

Jury trials, except in small claims, juvenile, equity cases, city and county ordinance violations, and mental health cases.

Court of general jurisdiction

– – – Indicates assignment of cases.

KANSAS COURT STRUCTURE, 1987

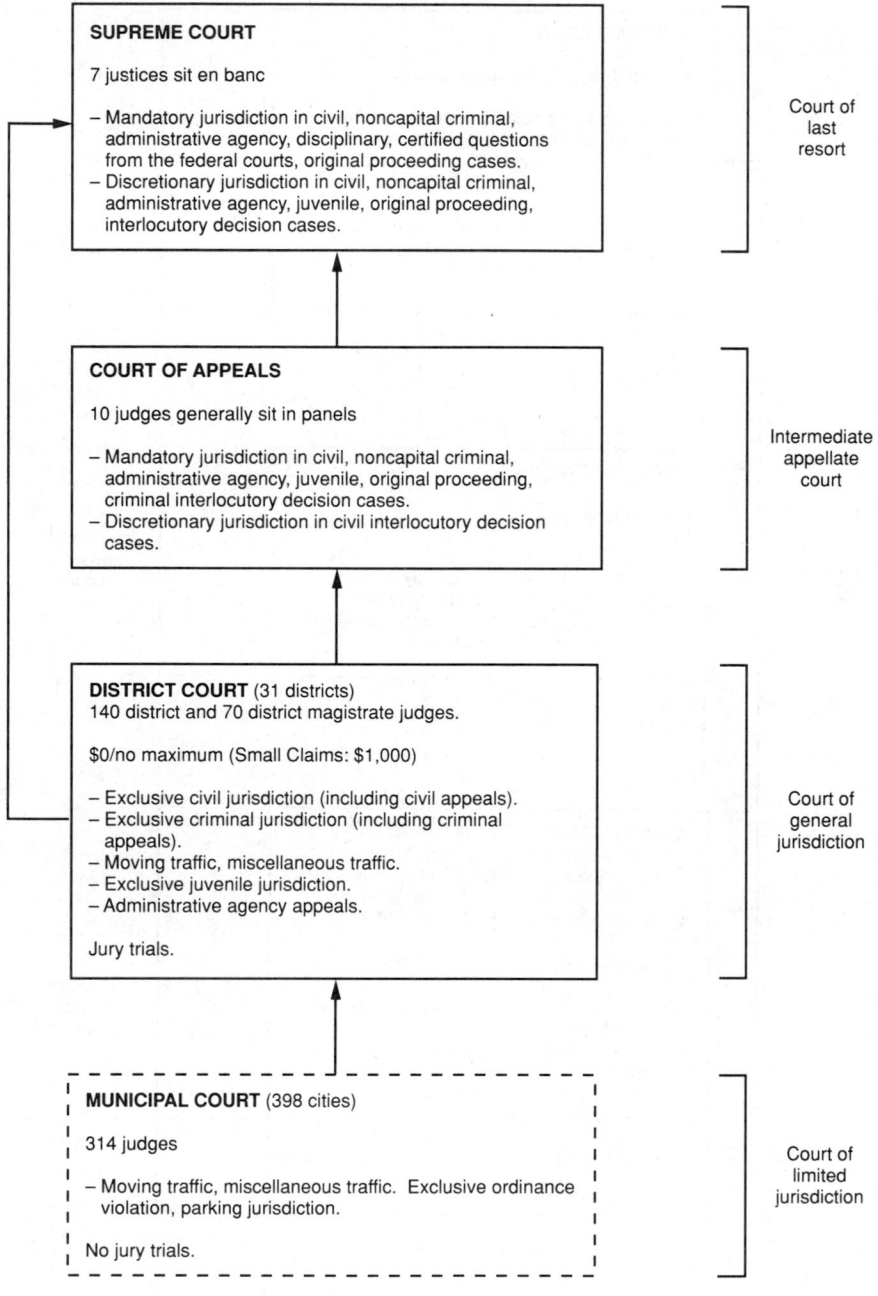

SUPREME COURT

7 justices sit en banc

– Mandatory jurisdiction in civil, noncapital criminal, administrative agency, disciplinary, certified questions from the federal courts, original proceeding cases.
– Discretionary jurisdiction in civil, noncapital criminal, administrative agency, juvenile, original proceeding, interlocutory decision cases.

Court of last resort

COURT OF APPEALS

10 judges generally sit in panels

– Mandatory jurisdiction in civil, noncapital criminal, administrative agency, juvenile, original proceeding, criminal interlocutory decision cases.
– Discretionary jurisdiction in civil interlocutory decision cases.

Intermediate appellate court

DISTRICT COURT (31 districts)
140 district and 70 district magistrate judges.

$0/no maximum (Small Claims: $1,000)

– Exclusive civil jurisdiction (including civil appeals).
– Exclusive criminal jurisdiction (including criminal appeals).
– Moving traffic, miscellaneous traffic.
– Exclusive juvenile jurisdiction.
– Administrative agency appeals.

Jury trials.

Court of general jurisdiction

MUNICIPAL COURT (398 cities)

314 judges

– Moving traffic, miscellaneous traffic. Exclusive ordinance violation, parking jurisdiction.

No jury trials.

Court of limited jurisdiction

KENTUCKY COURT STRUCTURE, 1987

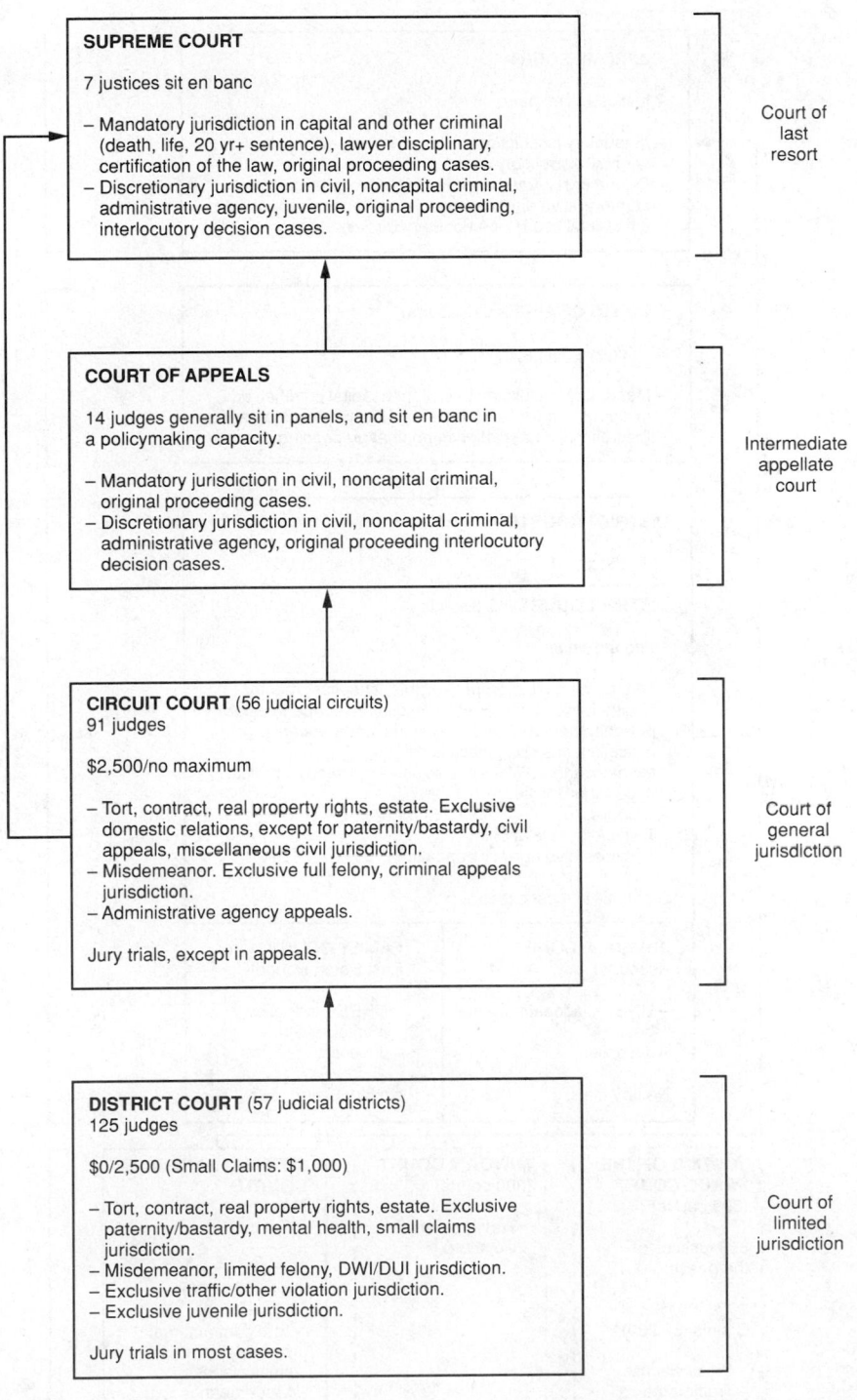

SUPREME COURT

7 justices sit en banc

– Mandatory jurisdiction in capital and other criminal (death, life, 20 yr+ sentence), lawyer disciplinary, certification of the law, original proceeding cases.
– Discretionary jurisdiction in civil, noncapital criminal, administrative agency, juvenile, original proceeding, interlocutory decision cases.

Court of last resort

COURT OF APPEALS

14 judges generally sit in panels, and sit en banc in a policymaking capacity.

– Mandatory jurisdiction in civil, noncapital criminal, original proceeding cases.
– Discretionary jurisdiction in civil, noncapital criminal, administrative agency, original proceeding interlocutory decision cases.

Intermediate appellate court

CIRCUIT COURT (56 judicial circuits)
91 judges

$2,500/no maximum

– Tort, contract, real property rights, estate. Exclusive domestic relations, except for paternity/bastardy, civil appeals, miscellaneous civil jurisdiction.
– Misdemeanor. Exclusive full felony, criminal appeals jurisdiction.
– Administrative agency appeals.

Jury trials, except in appeals.

Court of general jurisdiction

DISTRICT COURT (57 judicial districts)
125 judges

$0/2,500 (Small Claims: $1,000)

– Tort, contract, real property rights, estate. Exclusive paternity/bastardy, mental health, small claims jurisdiction.
– Misdemeanor, limited felony, DWI/DUI jurisdiction.
– Exclusive traffic/other violation jurisdiction.
– Exclusive juvenile jurisdiction.

Jury trials in most cases.

Court of limited jurisdiction

LOUISIANA COURT STRUCTURE, 1987

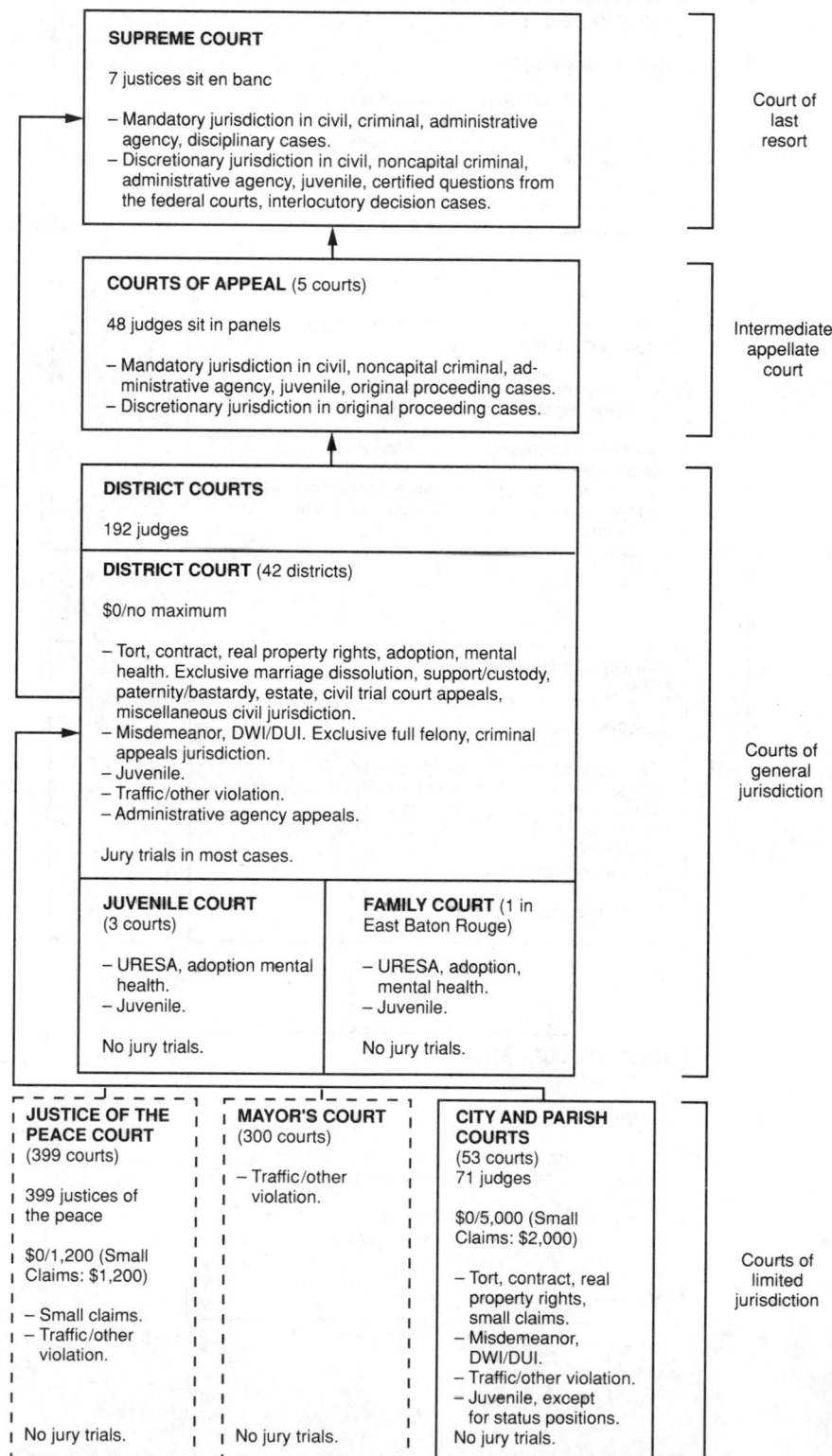

SUPREME COURT

7 justices sit en banc

– Mandatory jurisdiction in civil, criminal, administrative agency, disciplinary cases.
– Discretionary jurisdiction in civil, noncapital criminal, administrative agency, juvenile, certified questions from the federal courts, interlocutory decision cases.

Court of last resort

COURTS OF APPEAL (5 courts)

48 judges sit in panels

– Mandatory jurisdiction in civil, noncapital criminal, administrative agency, juvenile, original proceeding cases.
– Discretionary jurisdiction in original proceeding cases.

Intermediate appellate court

DISTRICT COURTS

192 judges

DISTRICT COURT (42 districts)

$0/no maximum

– Tort, contract, real property rights, adoption, mental health. Exclusive marriage dissolution, support/custody, paternity/bastardy, estate, civil trial court appeals, miscellaneous civil jurisdiction.
– Misdemeanor, DWI/DUI. Exclusive full felony, criminal appeals jurisdiction.
– Juvenile.
– Traffic/other violation.
– Administrative agency appeals.

Jury trials in most cases.

JUVENILE COURT (3 courts)

– URESA, adoption mental health.
– Juvenile.

No jury trials.

FAMILY COURT (1 in East Baton Rouge)

– URESA, adoption, mental health.
– Juvenile.

No jury trials.

Courts of general jurisdiction

JUSTICE OF THE PEACE COURT (399 courts)

399 justices of the peace

$0/1,200 (Small Claims: $1,200)

– Small claims.
– Traffic/other violation.

No jury trials.

MAYOR'S COURT (300 courts)

– Traffic/other violation.

No jury trials.

CITY AND PARISH COURTS (53 courts)
71 judges

$0/5,000 (Small Claims: $2,000)

– Tort, contract, real property rights, small claims.
– Misdemeanor, DWI/DUI.
– Traffic/other violation.
– Juvenile, except for status positions.

No jury trials.

Courts of limited jurisdiction

MAINE COURT STRUCTURE, 1987

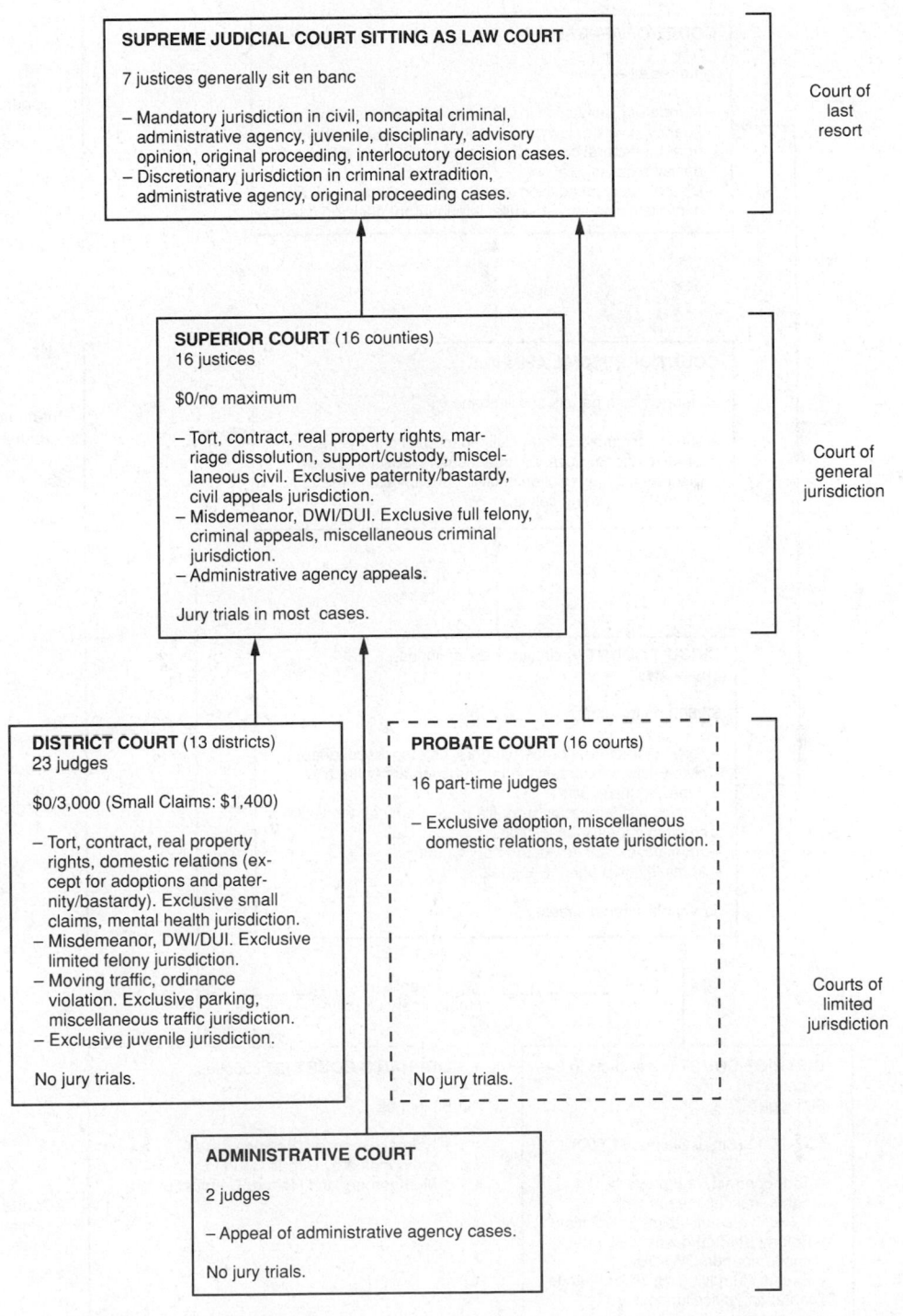

SUPREME JUDICIAL COURT SITTING AS LAW COURT

7 justices generally sit en banc

– Mandatory jurisdiction in civil, noncapital criminal, administrative agency, juvenile, disciplinary, advisory opinion, original proceeding, interlocutory decision cases.
– Discretionary jurisdiction in criminal extradition, administrative agency, original proceeding cases.

Court of last resort

SUPERIOR COURT (16 counties)
16 justices

$0/no maximum

– Tort, contract, real property rights, marriage dissolution, support/custody, miscellaneous civil. Exclusive paternity/bastardy, civil appeals jurisdiction.
– Misdemeanor, DWI/DUI. Exclusive full felony, criminal appeals, miscellaneous criminal jurisdiction.
– Administrative agency appeals.

Jury trials in most cases.

Court of general jurisdiction

DISTRICT COURT (13 districts)
23 judges

$0/3,000 (Small Claims: $1,400)

– Tort, contract, real property rights, domestic relations (except for adoptions and paternity/bastardy). Exclusive small claims, mental health jurisdiction.
– Misdemeanor, DWI/DUI. Exclusive limited felony jurisdiction.
– Moving traffic, ordinance violation. Exclusive parking, miscellaneous traffic jurisdiction.
– Exclusive juvenile jurisdiction.

No jury trials.

PROBATE COURT (16 courts)

16 part-time judges

– Exclusive adoption, miscellaneous domestic relations, estate jurisdiction.

No jury trials.

Courts of limited jurisdiction

ADMINISTRATIVE COURT

2 judges

– Appeal of administrative agency cases.

No jury trials.

MARYLAND COURT STRUCTURE, 1987

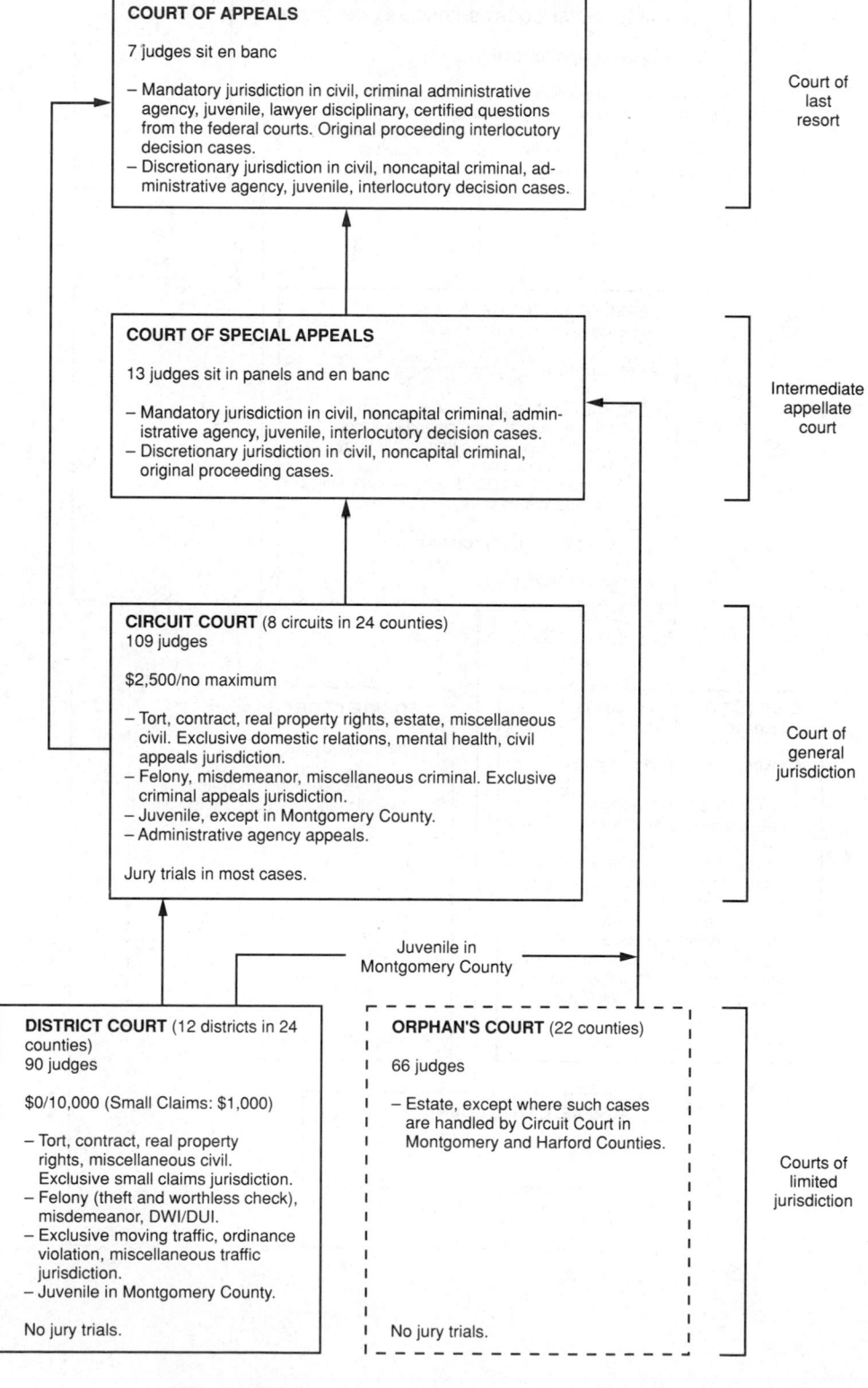

COURT OF APPEALS

7 judges sit en banc

– Mandatory jurisdiction in civil, criminal administrative agency, juvenile, lawyer disciplinary, certified questions from the federal courts. Original proceeding interlocutory decision cases.
– Discretionary jurisdiction in civil, noncapital criminal, administrative agency, juvenile, interlocutory decision cases.

Court of last resort

COURT OF SPECIAL APPEALS

13 judges sit in panels and en banc

– Mandatory jurisdiction in civil, noncapital criminal, administrative agency, juvenile, interlocutory decision cases.
– Discretionary jurisdiction in civil, noncapital criminal, original proceeding cases.

Intermediate appellate court

CIRCUIT COURT (8 circuits in 24 counties)
109 judges

$2,500/no maximum

– Tort, contract, real property rights, estate, miscellaneous civil. Exclusive domestic relations, mental health, civil appeals jurisdiction.
– Felony, misdemeanor, miscellaneous criminal. Exclusive criminal appeals jurisdiction.
– Juvenile, except in Montgomery County.
– Administrative agency appeals.

Jury trials in most cases.

Court of general jurisdiction

Juvenile in Montgomery County

DISTRICT COURT (12 districts in 24 counties)
90 judges

$0/10,000 (Small Claims: $1,000)

– Tort, contract, real property rights, miscellaneous civil. Exclusive small claims jurisdiction.
– Felony (theft and worthless check), misdemeanor, DWI/DUI.
– Exclusive moving traffic, ordinance violation, miscellaneous traffic jurisdiction.
– Juvenile in Montgomery County.

No jury trials.

ORPHAN'S COURT (22 counties)

66 judges

– Estate, except where such cases are handled by Circuit Court in Montgomery and Harford Counties.

No jury trials.

Courts of limited jurisdiction

MASSACHUSETTS COURT STRUCTURE, 1987

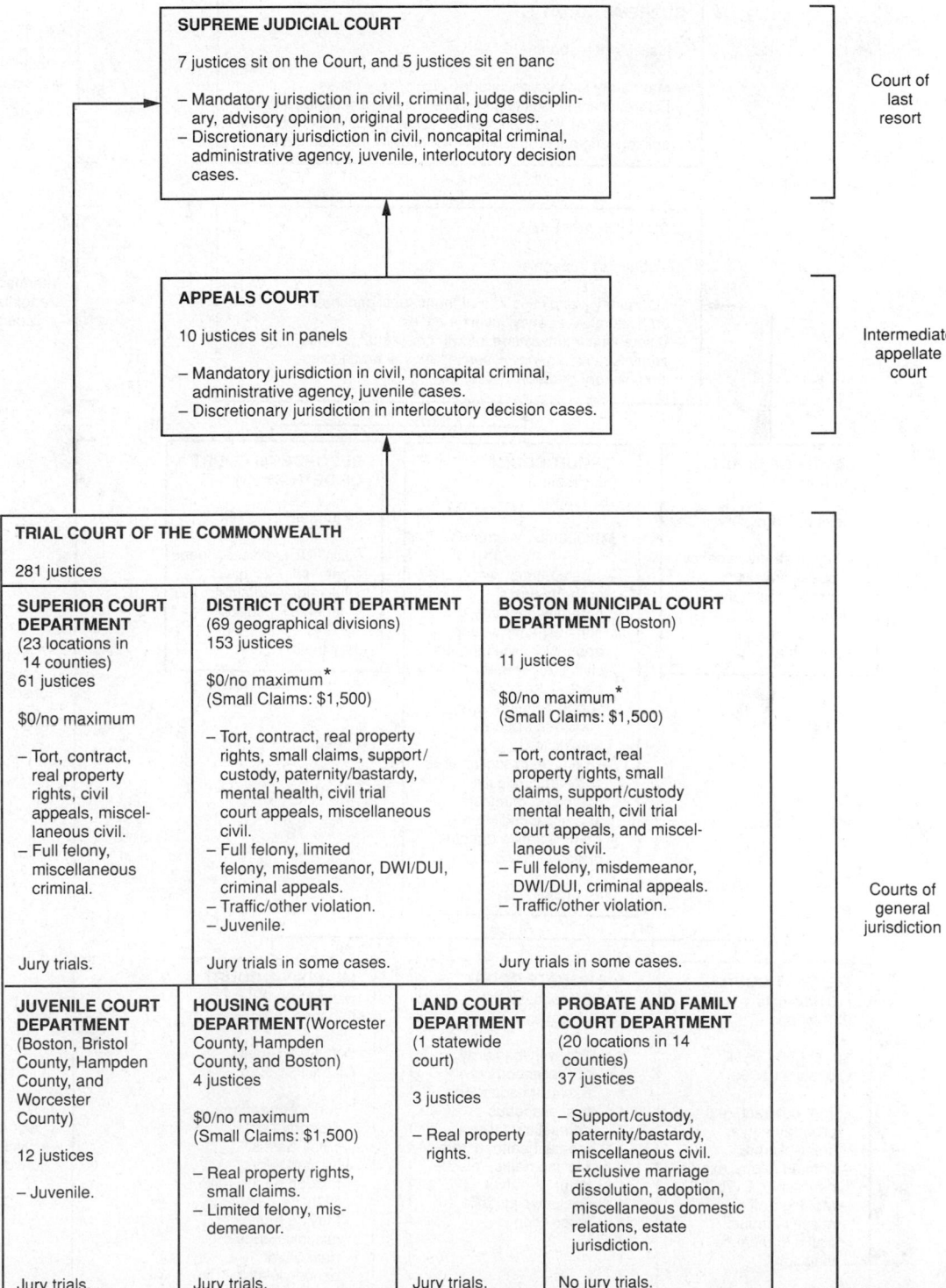

SUPREME JUDICIAL COURT

7 justices sit on the Court, and 5 justices sit en banc

– Mandatory jurisdiction in civil, criminal, judge disciplinary, advisory opinion, original proceeding cases.
– Discretionary jurisdiction in civil, noncapital criminal, administrative agency, juvenile, interlocutory decision cases.

Court of last resort

APPEALS COURT

10 justices sit in panels

– Mandatory jurisdiction in civil, noncapital criminal, administrative agency, juvenile cases.
– Discretionary jurisdiction in interlocutory decision cases.

Intermediate appellate court

TRIAL COURT OF THE COMMONWEALTH

281 justices

SUPERIOR COURT DEPARTMENT	**DISTRICT COURT DEPARTMENT**	**BOSTON MUNICIPAL COURT DEPARTMENT** (Boston)
(23 locations in 14 counties) 61 justices	(69 geographical divisions) 153 justices	11 justices
$0/no maximum	$0/no maximum* (Small Claims: $1,500)	$0/no maximum* (Small Claims: $1,500)
– Tort, contract, real property rights, civil appeals, miscellaneous civil. – Full felony, miscellaneous criminal.	– Tort, contract, real property rights, small claims, support/custody, paternity/bastardy, mental health, civil trial court appeals, miscellaneous civil. – Full felony, limited felony, misdemeanor, DWI/DUI, criminal appeals. – Traffic/other violation. – Juvenile.	– Tort, contract, real property rights, small claims, support/custody mental health, civil trial court appeals, and miscellaneous civil. – Full felony, misdemeanor, DWI/DUI, criminal appeals. – Traffic/other violation.
Jury trials.	Jury trials in some cases.	Jury trials in some cases.

JUVENILE COURT DEPARTMENT	**HOUSING COURT DEPARTMENT** (Worcester	**LAND COURT DEPARTMENT**	**PROBATE AND FAMILY COURT DEPARTMENT**
(Boston, Bristol County, Hampden County, and Worcester County)	County, Hampden County, and Boston) 4 justices	(1 statewide court) 3 justices	(20 locations in 14 counties) 37 justices
12 justices	$0/no maximum (Small Claims: $1,500)	– Real property rights.	– Support/custody, paternity/bastardy, miscellaneous civil. Exclusive marriage dissolution, adoption, miscellaneous domestic relations, estate jurisdiction.
– Juvenile.	– Real property rights, small claims. – Limited felony, misdemeanor.		
Jury trials.	Jury trials.	Jury trials.	No jury trials.

Courts of general jurisdiction

*Limited dollar jurisdiction in tort and contract cases is $25,000.

MICHIGAN COURT STRUCTURE, 1987

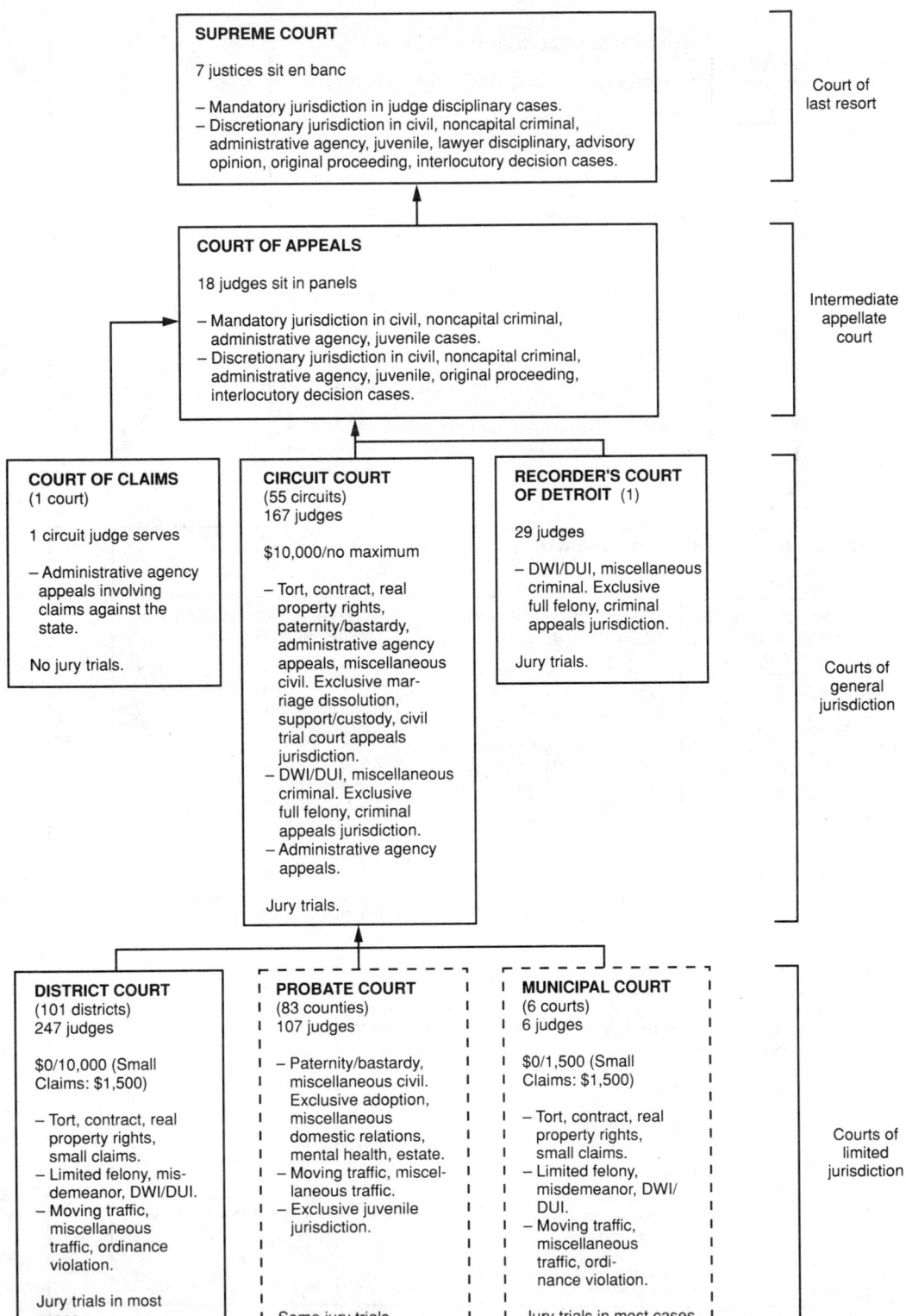

SUPREME COURT

7 justices sit en banc

– Mandatory jurisdiction in judge disciplinary cases.
– Discretionary jurisdiction in civil, noncapital criminal, administrative agency, juvenile, lawyer disciplinary, advisory opinion, original proceeding, interlocutory decision cases.

Court of last resort

COURT OF APPEALS

18 judges sit in panels

– Mandatory jurisdiction in civil, noncapital criminal, administrative agency, juvenile cases.
– Discretionary jurisdiction in civil, noncapital criminal, administrative agency, juvenile, original proceeding, interlocutory decision cases.

Intermediate appellate court

COURT OF CLAIMS
(1 court)

1 circuit judge serves

– Administrative agency appeals involving claims against the state.

No jury trials.

CIRCUIT COURT
(55 circuits)
167 judges

$10,000/no maximum

– Tort, contract, real property rights, paternity/bastardy, administrative agency appeals, miscellaneous civil. Exclusive marriage dissolution, support/custody, civil trial court appeals jurisdiction.
– DWI/DUI, miscellaneous criminal. Exclusive full felony, criminal appeals jurisdiction.
– Administrative agency appeals.

Jury trials.

RECORDER'S COURT OF DETROIT (1)

29 judges

– DWI/DUI, miscellaneous criminal. Exclusive full felony, criminal appeals jurisdiction.

Jury trials.

Courts of general jurisdiction

DISTRICT COURT
(101 districts)
247 judges

$0/10,000 (Small Claims: $1,500)

– Tort, contract, real property rights, small claims.
– Limited felony, misdemeanor, DWI/DUI.
– Moving traffic, miscellaneous traffic, ordinance violation.

Jury trials in most cases.

PROBATE COURT
(83 counties)
107 judges

– Paternity/bastardy, miscellaneous civil. Exclusive adoption, miscellaneous domestic relations, mental health, estate.
– Moving traffic, miscellaneous traffic.
– Exclusive juvenile jurisdiction.

Some jury trials.

MUNICIPAL COURT
(6 courts)
6 judges

$0/1,500 (Small Claims: $1,500)

– Tort, contract, real property rights, small claims.
– Limited felony, misdemeanor, DWI/DUI.
– Moving traffic, miscellaneous traffic, ordinance violation.

Jury trials in most cases.

Courts of limited jurisdiction

MINNESOTA COURT STRUCTURE, 1987

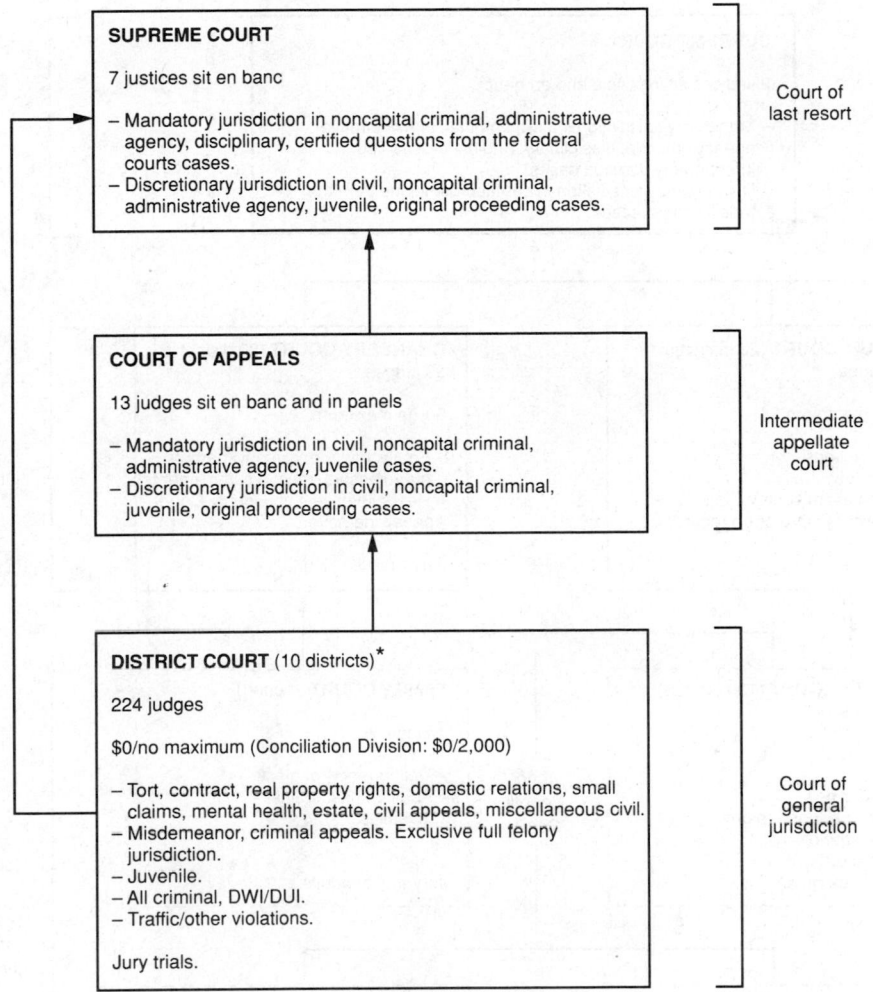

SUPREME COURT

7 justices sit en banc

– Mandatory jurisdiction in noncapital criminal, administrative agency, disciplinary, certified questions from the federal courts cases.
– Discretionary jurisdiction in civil, noncapital criminal, administrative agency, juvenile, original proceeding cases.

Court of last resort

COURT OF APPEALS

13 judges sit en banc and in panels

– Mandatory jurisdiction in civil, noncapital criminal, administrative agency, juvenile cases.
– Discretionary jurisdiction in civil, noncapital criminal, juvenile, original proceeding cases.

Intermediate appellate court

DISTRICT COURT (10 districts)*

224 judges

$0/no maximum (Conciliation Division: $0/2,000)

– Tort, contract, real property rights, domestic relations, small claims, mental health, estate, civil appeals, miscellaneous civil.
– Misdemeanor, criminal appeals. Exclusive full felony jurisdiction.
– Juvenile.
– All criminal, DWI/DUI.
– Traffic/other violations.

Jury trials.

Court of general jurisdiction

*The District Court was consolidated in September, 1987.

MISSISSIPPI COURT STRUCTURE, 1987

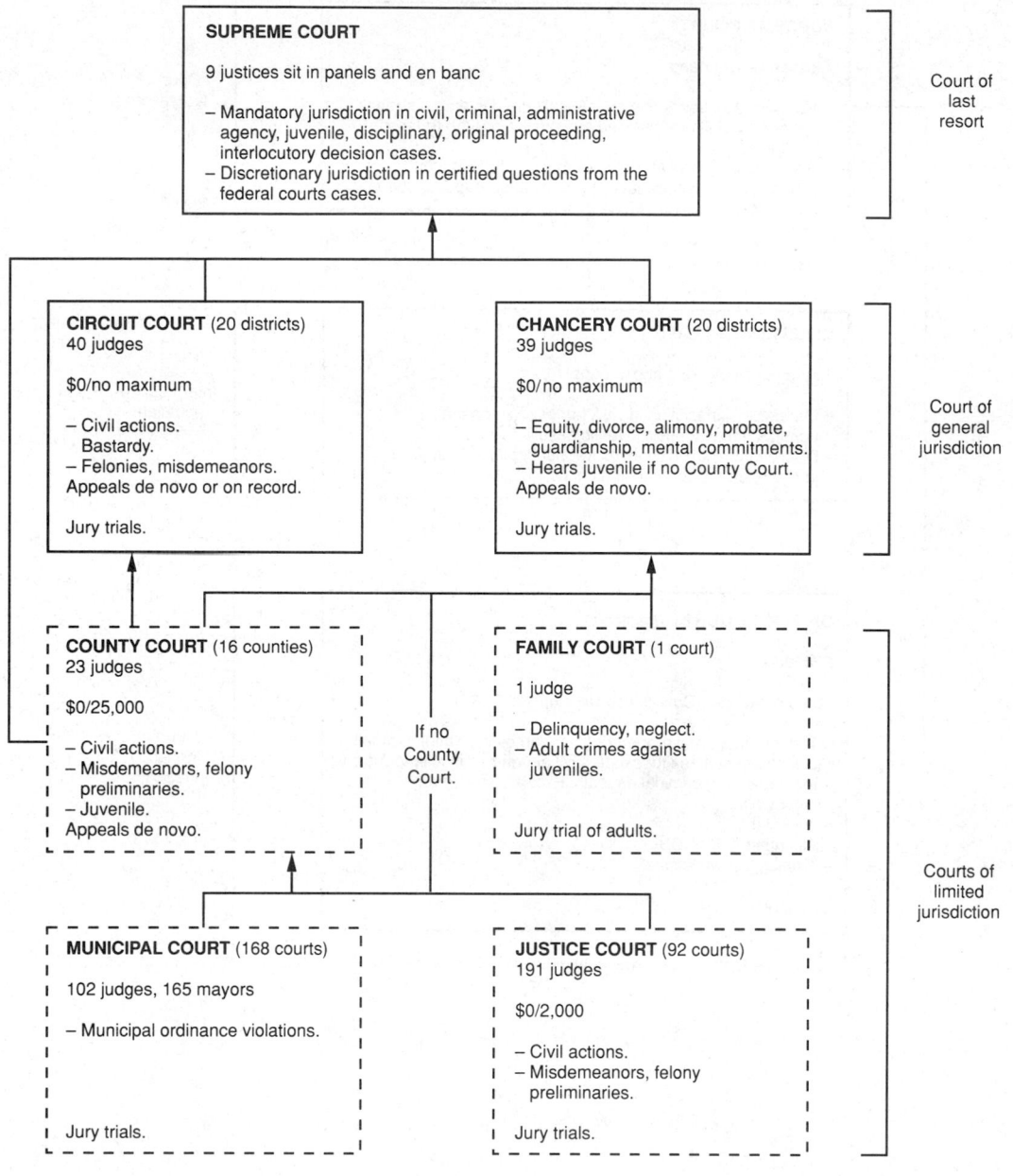

SUPREME COURT

9 justices sit in panels and en banc

– Mandatory jurisdiction in civil, criminal, administrative
  agency, juvenile, disciplinary, original proceeding,
  interlocutory decision cases.
– Discretionary jurisdiction in certified questions from the
  federal courts cases.

Court of
last
resort

CIRCUIT COURT (20 districts)
40 judges

$0/no maximum

– Civil actions.
  Bastardy.
– Felonies, misdemeanors.
Appeals de novo or on record.

Jury trials.

CHANCERY COURT (20 districts)
39 judges

$0/no maximum

– Equity, divorce, alimony, probate,
  guardianship, mental commitments.
– Hears juvenile if no County Court.
Appeals de novo.

Jury trials.

Court of
general
jurisdiction

COUNTY COURT (16 counties)
23 judges

$0/25,000

– Civil actions.
– Misdemeanors, felony
  preliminaries.
– Juvenile.
Appeals de novo.

If no
County
Court.

FAMILY COURT (1 court)

1 judge

– Delinquency, neglect.
– Adult crimes against
  juveniles.

Jury trial of adults.

MUNICIPAL COURT (168 courts)

102 judges, 165 mayors

– Municipal ordinance violations.

Jury trials.

JUSTICE COURT (92 courts)
191 judges

$0/2,000

– Civil actions.
– Misdemeanors, felony
  preliminaries.

Jury trials.

Courts of
limited
jurisdiction

MISSOURI COURT STRUCTURE, 1987

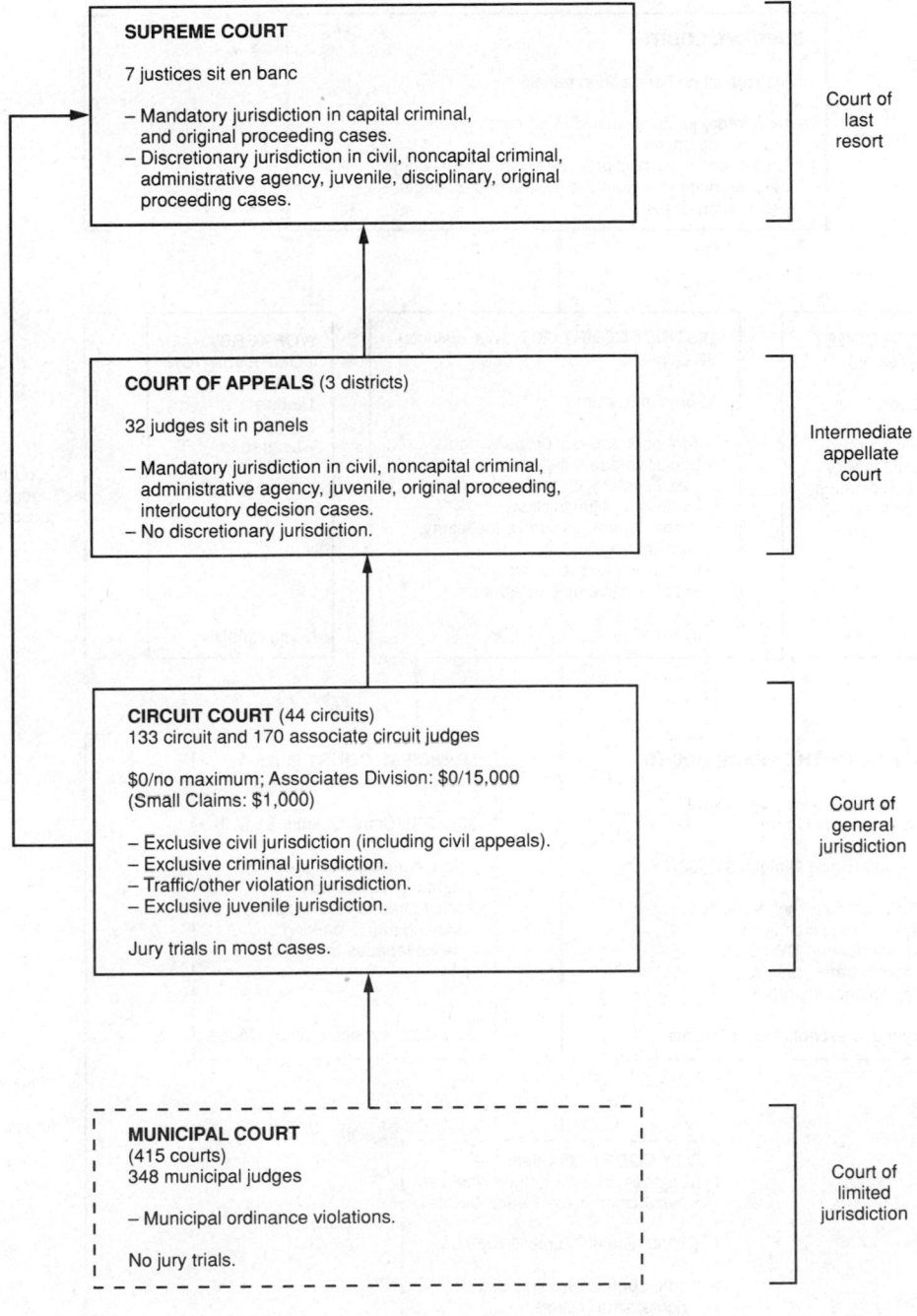

SUPREME COURT

7 justices sit en banc

– Mandatory jurisdiction in capital criminal, and original proceeding cases.
– Discretionary jurisdiction in civil, noncapital criminal, administrative agency, juvenile, disciplinary, original proceeding cases.

Court of last resort

COURT OF APPEALS (3 districts)

32 judges sit in panels

– Mandatory jurisdiction in civil, noncapital criminal, administrative agency, juvenile, original proceeding, interlocutory decision cases.
– No discretionary jurisdiction.

Intermediate appellate court

CIRCUIT COURT (44 circuits)
133 circuit and 170 associate circuit judges

$0/no maximum; Associates Division: $0/15,000
(Small Claims: $1,000)

– Exclusive civil jurisdiction (including civil appeals).
– Exclusive criminal jurisdiction.
– Traffic/other violation jurisdiction.
– Exclusive juvenile jurisdiction.

Jury trials in most cases.

Court of general jurisdiction

MUNICIPAL COURT
(415 courts)
348 municipal judges

– Municipal ordinance violations.

No jury trials.

Court of limited jurisdiction

MONTANA COURT STRUCTURE, 1987

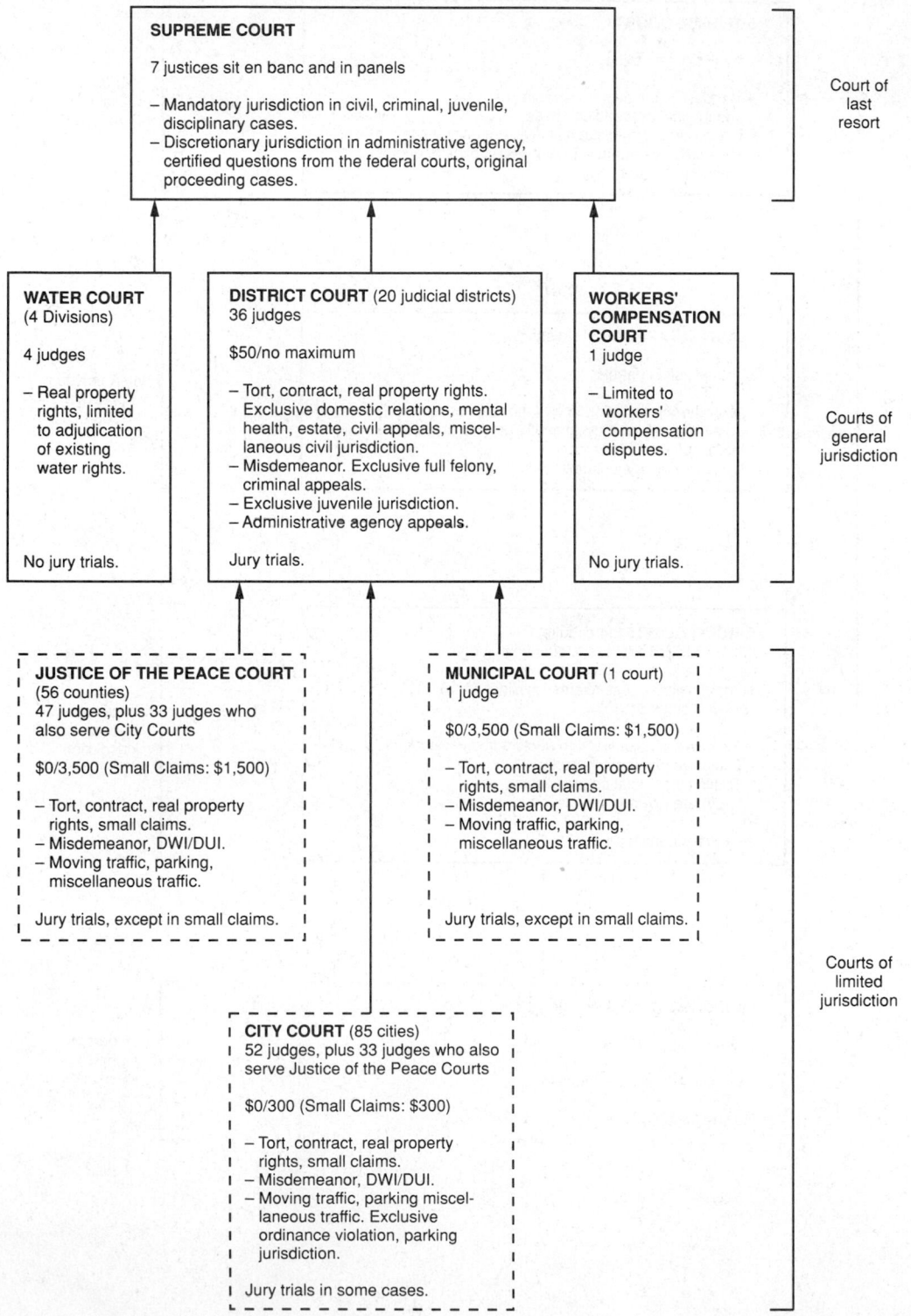

SUPREME COURT

7 justices sit en banc and in panels

– Mandatory jurisdiction in civil, criminal, juvenile, disciplinary cases.
– Discretionary jurisdiction in administrative agency, certified questions from the federal courts, original proceeding cases.

Court of last resort

WATER COURT
(4 Divisions)

4 judges

– Real property rights, limited to adjudication of existing water rights.

No jury trials.

DISTRICT COURT (20 judicial districts)
36 judges

$50/no maximum

– Tort, contract, real property rights. Exclusive domestic relations, mental health, estate, civil appeals, miscellaneous civil jurisdiction.
– Misdemeanor. Exclusive full felony, criminal appeals.
– Exclusive juvenile jurisdiction.
– Administrative agency appeals.

Jury trials.

WORKERS' COMPENSATION COURT
1 judge

– Limited to workers' compensation disputes.

No jury trials.

Courts of general jurisdiction

JUSTICE OF THE PEACE COURT
(56 counties)
47 judges, plus 33 judges who also serve City Courts

$0/3,500 (Small Claims: $1,500)

– Tort, contract, real property rights, small claims.
– Misdemeanor, DWI/DUI.
– Moving traffic, parking, miscellaneous traffic.

Jury trials, except in small claims.

MUNICIPAL COURT (1 court)
1 judge

$0/3,500 (Small Claims: $1,500)

– Tort, contract, real property rights, small claims.
– Misdemeanor, DWI/DUI.
– Moving traffic, parking, miscellaneous traffic.

Jury trials, except in small claims.

CITY COURT (85 cities)
52 judges, plus 33 judges who also serve Justice of the Peace Courts

$0/300 (Small Claims: $300)

– Tort, contract, real property rights, small claims.
– Misdemeanor, DWI/DUI.
– Moving traffic, parking miscellaneous traffic. Exclusive ordinance violation, parking jurisdiction.

Jury trials in some cases.

Courts of limited jurisdiction

NEBRASKA COURT STRUCTURE, 1987

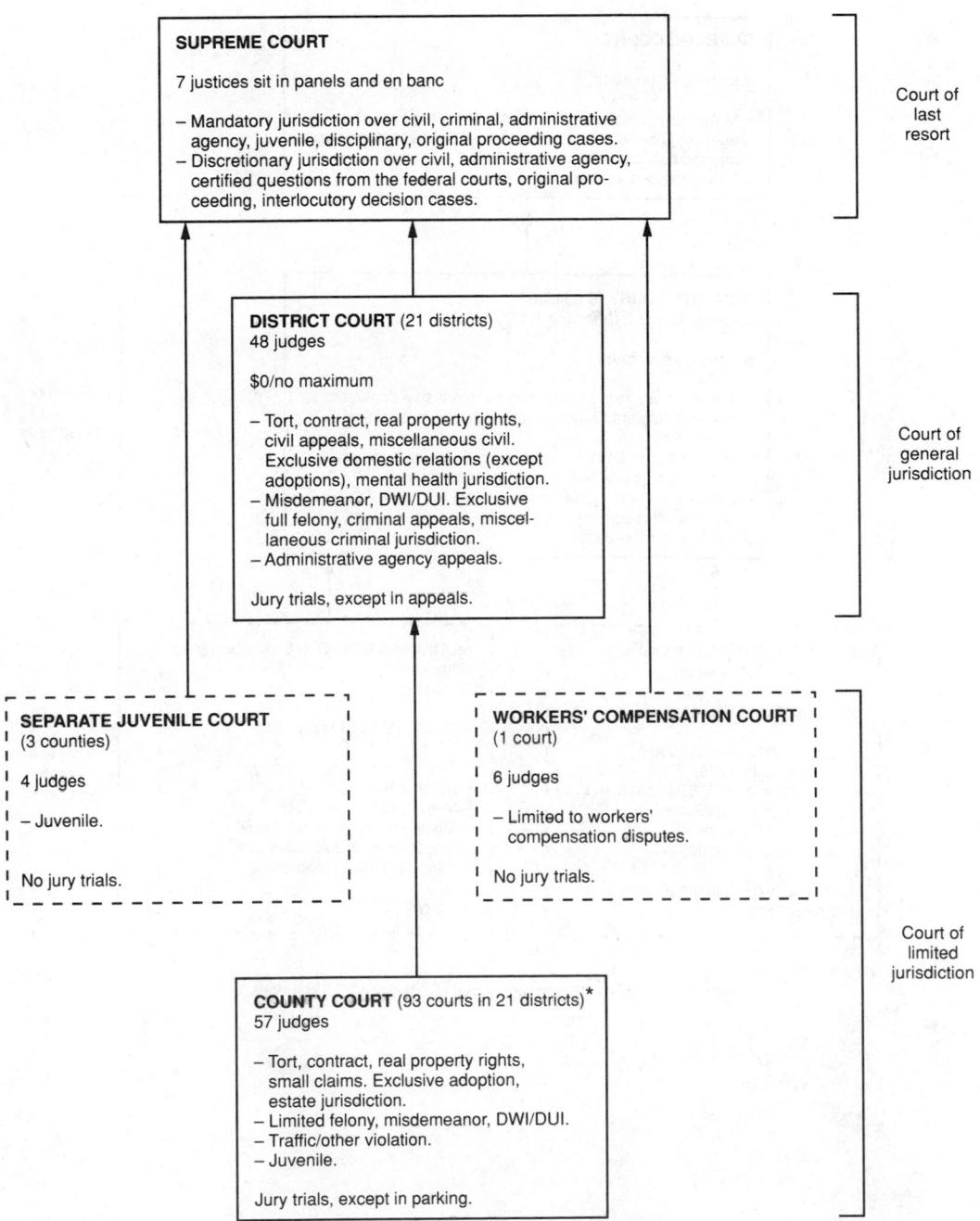

SUPREME COURT

7 justices sit in panels and en banc

– Mandatory jurisdiction over civil, criminal, administrative agency, juvenile, disciplinary, original proceeding cases.
– Discretionary jurisdiction over civil, administrative agency, certified questions from the federal courts, original proceeding, interlocutory decision cases.

Court of last resort

DISTRICT COURT (21 districts)
48 judges

$0/no maximum

– Tort, contract, real property rights, civil appeals, miscellaneous civil. Exclusive domestic relations (except adoptions), mental health jurisdiction.
– Misdemeanor, DWI/DUI. Exclusive full felony, criminal appeals, miscellaneous criminal jurisdiction.
– Administrative agency appeals.

Jury trials, except in appeals.

Court of general jurisdiction

SEPARATE JUVENILE COURT
(3 counties)

4 judges

– Juvenile.

No jury trials.

WORKERS' COMPENSATION COURT
(1 court)

6 judges

– Limited to workers' compensation disputes.

No jury trials.

Court of limited jurisdiction

COUNTY COURT (93 courts in 21 districts)*
57 judges

– Tort, contract, real property rights, small claims. Exclusive adoption, estate jurisdiction.
– Limited felony, misdemeanor, DWI/DUI.
– Traffic/other violation.
– Juvenile.

Jury trials, except in parking.

*In July 1985, the Municipal Courts were merged with the County Courts.

NEVADA COURT STRUCTURE, 1987

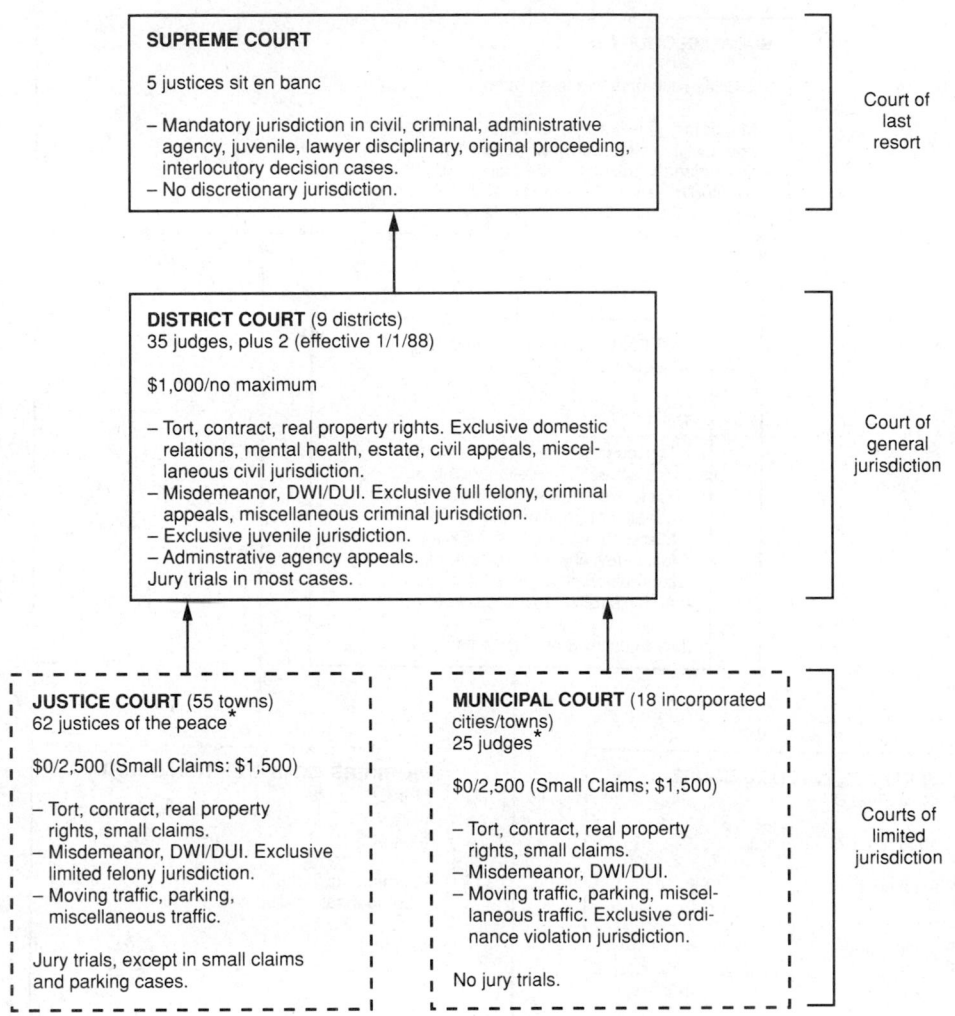

SUPREME COURT

5 justices sit en banc

– Mandatory jurisdiction in civil, criminal, administrative
   agency, juvenile, lawyer disciplinary, original proceeding,
   interlocutory decision cases.
– No discretionary jurisdiction.

Court of
last
resort

DISTRICT COURT (9 districts)
35 judges, plus 2 (effective 1/1/88)

$1,000/no maximum

– Tort, contract, real property rights. Exclusive domestic
   relations, mental health, estate, civil appeals, miscel-
   laneous civil jurisdiction.
– Misdemeanor, DWI/DUI. Exclusive full felony, criminal
   appeals, miscellaneous criminal jurisdiction.
– Exclusive juvenile jurisdiction.
– Adminstrative agency appeals.
Jury trials in most cases.

Court of
general
jurisdiction

JUSTICE COURT (55 towns)
62 justices of the peace[*]

$0/2,500 (Small Claims: $1,500)

– Tort, contract, real property
   rights, small claims.
– Misdemeanor, DWI/DUI. Exclusive
   limited felony jurisdiction.
– Moving traffic, parking,
   miscellaneous traffic.

Jury trials, except in small claims
and parking cases.

MUNICIPAL COURT (18 incorporated
cities/towns)
25 judges[*]

$0/2,500 (Small Claims; $1,500)

– Tort, contract, real property
   rights, small claims.
– Misdemeanor, DWI/DUI.
– Moving traffic, parking, miscellaneous traffic. Exclusive ordinance violation jurisdiction.

No jury trials.

Courts of
limited
jurisdiction

[*]Eight Justices of the Peace also serve as Municipal Court judges.

NEW HAMPSHIRE COURT STRUCTURE, 1987

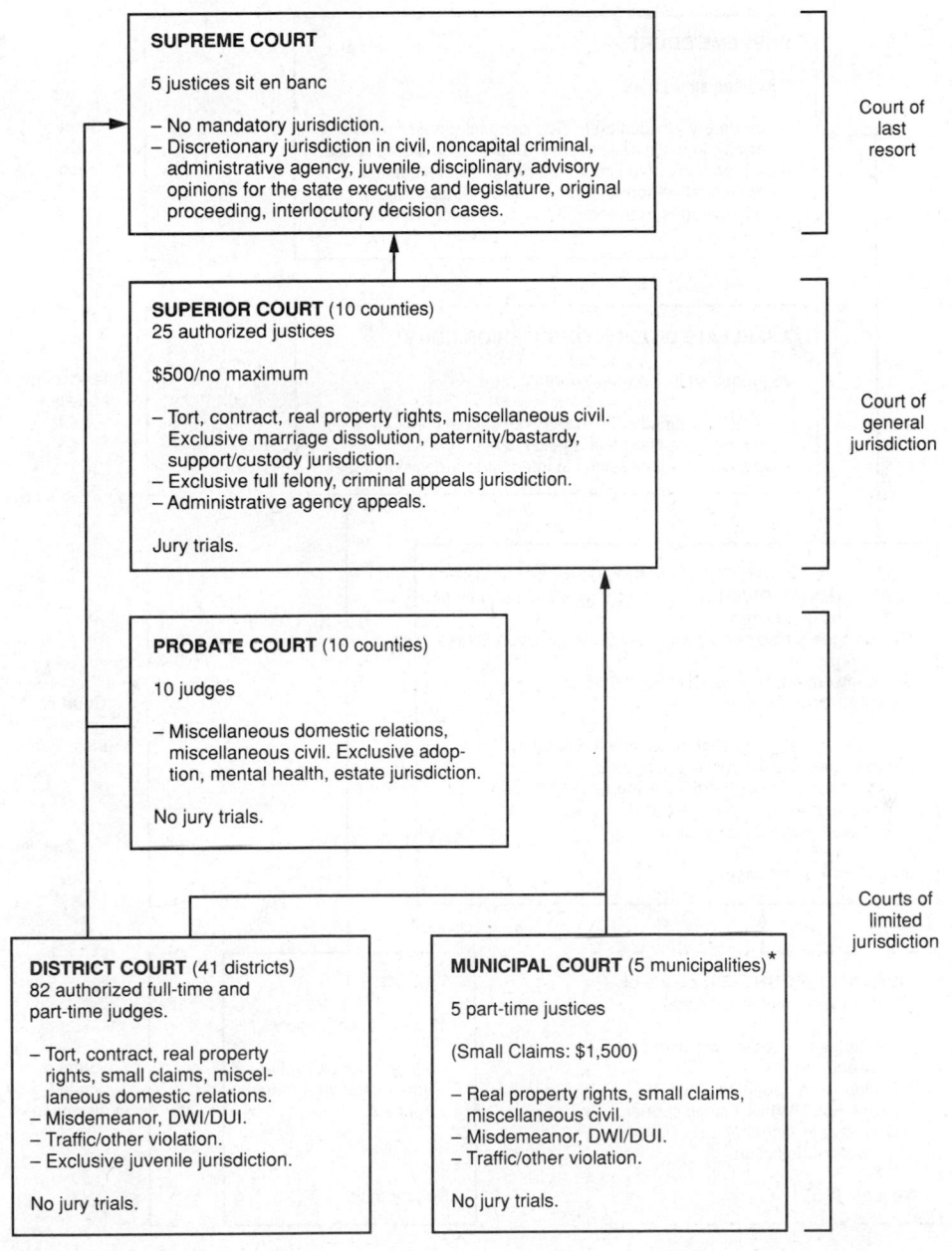

SUPREME COURT

5 justices sit en banc

– No mandatory jurisdiction.
– Discretionary jurisdiction in civil, noncapital criminal, administrative agency, juvenile, disciplinary, advisory opinions for the state executive and legislature, original proceeding, interlocutory decision cases.

Court of last resort

SUPERIOR COURT (10 counties)
25 authorized justices

$500/no maximum

– Tort, contract, real property rights, miscellaneous civil. Exclusive marriage dissolution, paternity/bastardy, support/custody jurisdiction.
– Exclusive full felony, criminal appeals jurisdiction.
– Administrative agency appeals.

Jury trials.

Court of general jurisdiction

PROBATE COURT (10 counties)

10 judges

– Miscellaneous domestic relations, miscellaneous civil. Exclusive adoption, mental health, estate jurisdiction.

No jury trials.

Courts of limited jurisdiction

DISTRICT COURT (41 districts)
82 authorized full-time and part-time judges.

– Tort, contract, real property rights, small claims, miscellaneous domestic relations.
– Misdemeanor, DWI/DUI.
– Traffic/other violation.
– Exclusive juvenile jurisdiction.

No jury trials.

MUNICIPAL COURT (5 municipalities)[*]

5 part-time justices

(Small Claims: $1,500)

– Real property rights, small claims, miscellaneous civil.
– Misdemeanor, DWI/DUI.
– Traffic/other violation.

No jury trials.

[*]The Municipal Court is being phased out (by statute) upon retirement and/or resignation of sitting justices.

NEW JERSEY COURT STRUCTURE, 1987

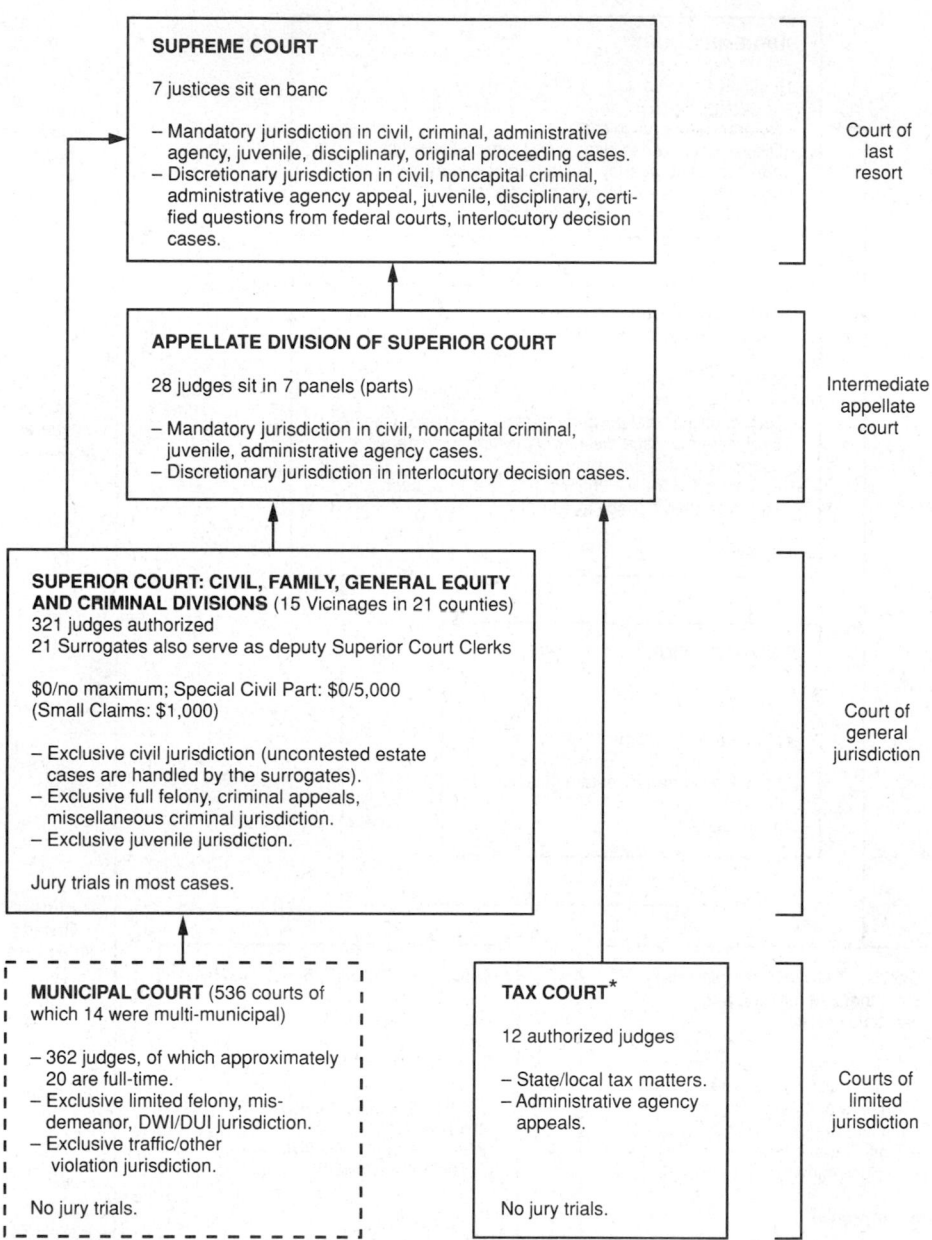

SUPREME COURT

7 justices sit en banc

– Mandatory jurisdiction in civil, criminal, administrative
  agency, juvenile, disciplinary, original proceeding cases.
– Discretionary jurisdiction in civil, noncapital criminal,
  administrative agency appeal, juvenile, disciplinary, certified questions from federal courts, interlocutory decision
  cases.

Court of
last
resort

APPELLATE DIVISION OF SUPERIOR COURT

28 judges sit in 7 panels (parts)

– Mandatory jurisdiction in civil, noncapital criminal,
  juvenile, administrative agency cases.
– Discretionary jurisdiction in interlocutory decision cases.

Intermediate
appellate
court

**SUPERIOR COURT: CIVIL, FAMILY, GENERAL EQUITY
AND CRIMINAL DIVISIONS** (15 Vicinages in 21 counties)
321 judges authorized
21 Surrogates also serve as deputy Superior Court Clerks

$0/no maximum; Special Civil Part: $0/5,000
(Small Claims: $1,000)

– Exclusive civil jurisdiction (uncontested estate
  cases are handled by the surrogates).
– Exclusive full felony, criminal appeals,
  miscellaneous criminal jurisdiction.
– Exclusive juvenile jurisdiction.

Jury trials in most cases.

Court of
general
jurisdiction

MUNICIPAL COURT (536 courts of
which 14 were multi-municipal)

– 362 judges, of which approximately
  20 are full-time.
– Exclusive limited felony, misdemeanor, DWI/DUI jurisdiction.
– Exclusive traffic/other
  violation jurisdiction.

No jury trials.

TAX COURT*

12 authorized judges

– State/local tax matters.
– Administrative agency
  appeals.

No jury trials.

Courts of
limited
jurisdiction

*Tax Court is considered a limited jurisdiction court because of its specialized subject matter.
Nevertheless, it receives appeals from administrative bodies and its cases are appealed to the
intermediate appellate court. Tax Court judges have the same general qualifications and terms
of service as Superior Court judges and can be cross assigned.

NEW MEXICO COURT STRUCTURE, 1987

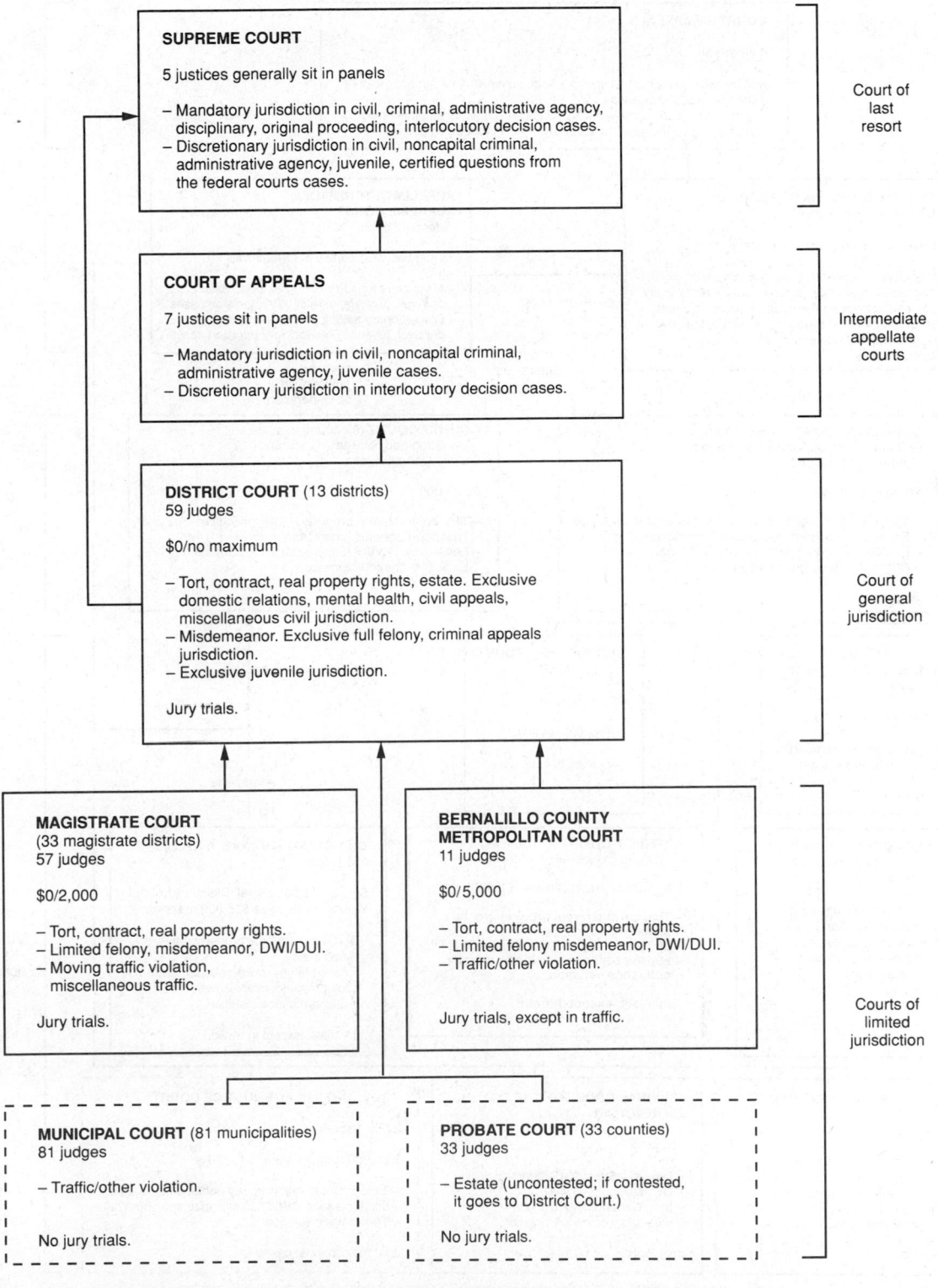

SUPREME COURT

5 justices generally sit in panels

– Mandatory jurisdiction in civil, criminal, administrative agency, disciplinary, original proceeding, interlocutory decision cases.
– Discretionary jurisdiction in civil, noncapital criminal, administrative agency, juvenile, certified questions from the federal courts cases.

Court of last resort

COURT OF APPEALS

7 justices sit in panels

– Mandatory jurisdiction in civil, noncapital criminal, administrative agency, juvenile cases.
– Discretionary jurisdiction in interlocutory decision cases.

Intermediate appellate courts

DISTRICT COURT (13 districts)
59 judges

$0/no maximum

– Tort, contract, real property rights, estate. Exclusive domestic relations, mental health, civil appeals, miscellaneous civil jurisdiction.
– Misdemeanor. Exclusive full felony, criminal appeals jurisdiction.
– Exclusive juvenile jurisdiction.

Jury trials.

Court of general jurisdiction

MAGISTRATE COURT
(33 magistrate districts)
57 judges

$0/2,000

– Tort, contract, real property rights.
– Limited felony, misdemeanor, DWI/DUI.
– Moving traffic violation, miscellaneous traffic.

Jury trials.

**BERNALILLO COUNTY
METROPOLITAN COURT**
11 judges

$0/5,000

– Tort, contract, real property rights.
– Limited felony misdemeanor, DWI/DUI.
– Traffic/other violation.

Jury trials, except in traffic.

MUNICIPAL COURT (81 municipalities)
81 judges

– Traffic/other violation.

No jury trials.

PROBATE COURT (33 counties)
33 judges

– Estate (uncontested; if contested, it goes to District Court.)

No jury trials.

Courts of limited jurisdiction

NEW YORK COURT STRUCTURE, 1987

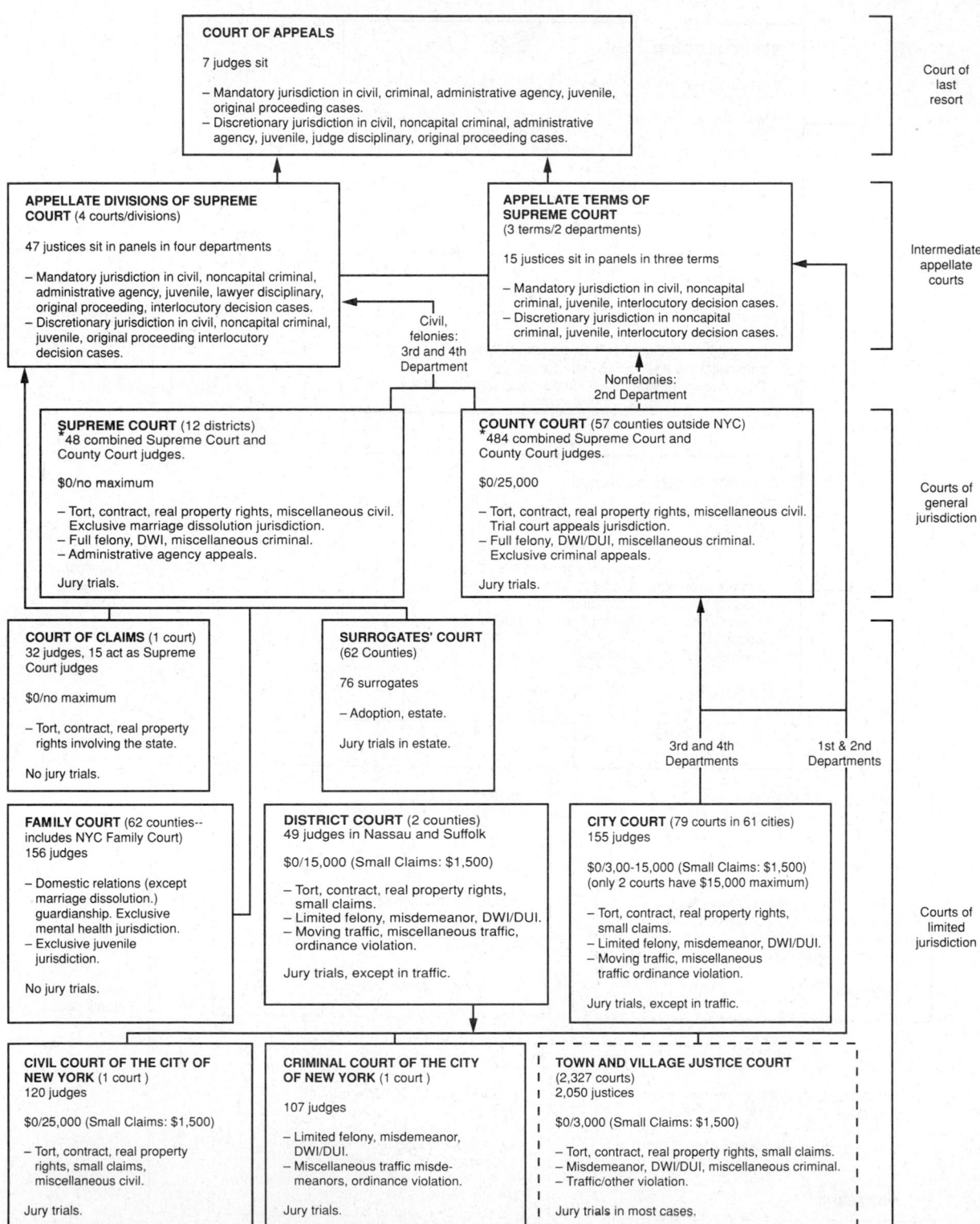

COURT OF APPEALS

7 judges sit

– Mandatory jurisdiction in civil, criminal, administrative agency, juvenile, original proceeding cases.
– Discretionary jurisdiction in civil, noncapital criminal, administrative agency, juvenile, judge disciplinary, original proceeding cases.

Court of last resort

APPELLATE DIVISIONS OF SUPREME COURT (4 courts/divisions)

47 justices sit in panels in four departments

– Mandatory jurisdiction in civil, noncapital criminal, administrative agency, juvenile, lawyer disciplinary, original proceeding, interlocutory decision cases.
– Discretionary jurisdiction in civil, noncapital criminal, juvenile, original proceeding interlocutory decision cases.

APPELLATE TERMS OF SUPREME COURT
(3 terms/2 departments)

15 justices sit in panels in three terms

– Mandatory jurisdiction in civil, noncapital criminal, juvenile, interlocutory decision cases.
– Discretionary jurisdiction in noncapital criminal, juvenile, interlocutory decision cases.

Intermediate appellate courts

Civil, felonies: 3rd and 4th Department

Nonfelonies: 2nd Department

SUPREME COURT (12 districts)
*48 combined Supreme Court and County Court judges.

$0/no maximum

– Tort, contract, real property rights, miscellaneous civil. Exclusive marriage dissolution jurisdiction.
– Full felony, DWI, miscellaneous criminal.
– Administrative agency appeals.

Jury trials.

COUNTY COURT (57 counties outside NYC)
*484 combined Supreme Court and County Court judges.

$0/25,000

– Tort, contract, real property rights, miscellaneous civil. Trial court appeals jurisdiction.
– Full felony, DWI/DUI, miscellaneous criminal. Exclusive criminal appeals.

Jury trials.

Courts of general jurisdiction

COURT OF CLAIMS (1 court)
32 judges, 15 act as Supreme Court judges

$0/no maximum

– Tort, contract, real property rights involving the state.

No jury trials.

SURROGATES' COURT
(62 Counties)

76 surrogates

– Adoption, estate.

Jury trials in estate.

3rd and 4th Departments

1st & 2nd Departments

FAMILY COURT (62 counties-- includes NYC Family Court)
156 judges

– Domestic relations (except marriage dissolution.) guardianship. Exclusive mental health jurisdiction.
– Exclusive juvenile jurisdiction.

No jury trials.

DISTRICT COURT (2 counties)
49 judges in Nassau and Suffolk

$0/15,000 (Small Claims: $1,500)

– Tort, contract, real property rights, small claims.
– Limited felony, misdemeanor, DWI/DUI.
– Moving traffic, miscellaneous traffic, ordinance violation.

Jury trials, except in traffic.

CITY COURT (79 courts in 61 cities)
155 judges

$0/3,00-15,000 (Small Claims: $1,500) (only 2 courts have $15,000 maximum)

– Tort, contract, real property rights, small claims.
– Limited felony, misdemeanor, DWI/DUI.
– Moving traffic, miscellaneous traffic ordinance violation.

Jury trials, except in traffic.

Courts of limited jurisdiction

CIVIL COURT OF THE CITY OF NEW YORK (1 court)
120 judges

$0/25,000 (Small Claims: $1,500)

– Tort, contract, real property rights, small claims, miscellaneous civil.

Jury trials.

CRIMINAL COURT OF THE CITY OF NEW YORK (1 court)

107 judges

– Limited felony, misdemeanor, DWI/DUI.
– Miscellaneous traffic misdemeanors, ordinance violation.

Jury trials.

TOWN AND VILLAGE JUSTICE COURT (2,327 courts)
2,050 justices

$0/3,000 (Small Claims: $1,500)

– Tort, contract, real property rights, small claims.
– Misdemeanor, DWI/DUI, miscellaneous criminal.
– Traffic/other violation.

Jury trials in most cases.

*Includes Acting Supreme Court Justices assigned administratively. Increase due to manner of reporting.

NORTH CAROLINA COURT STRUCTURE, 1987

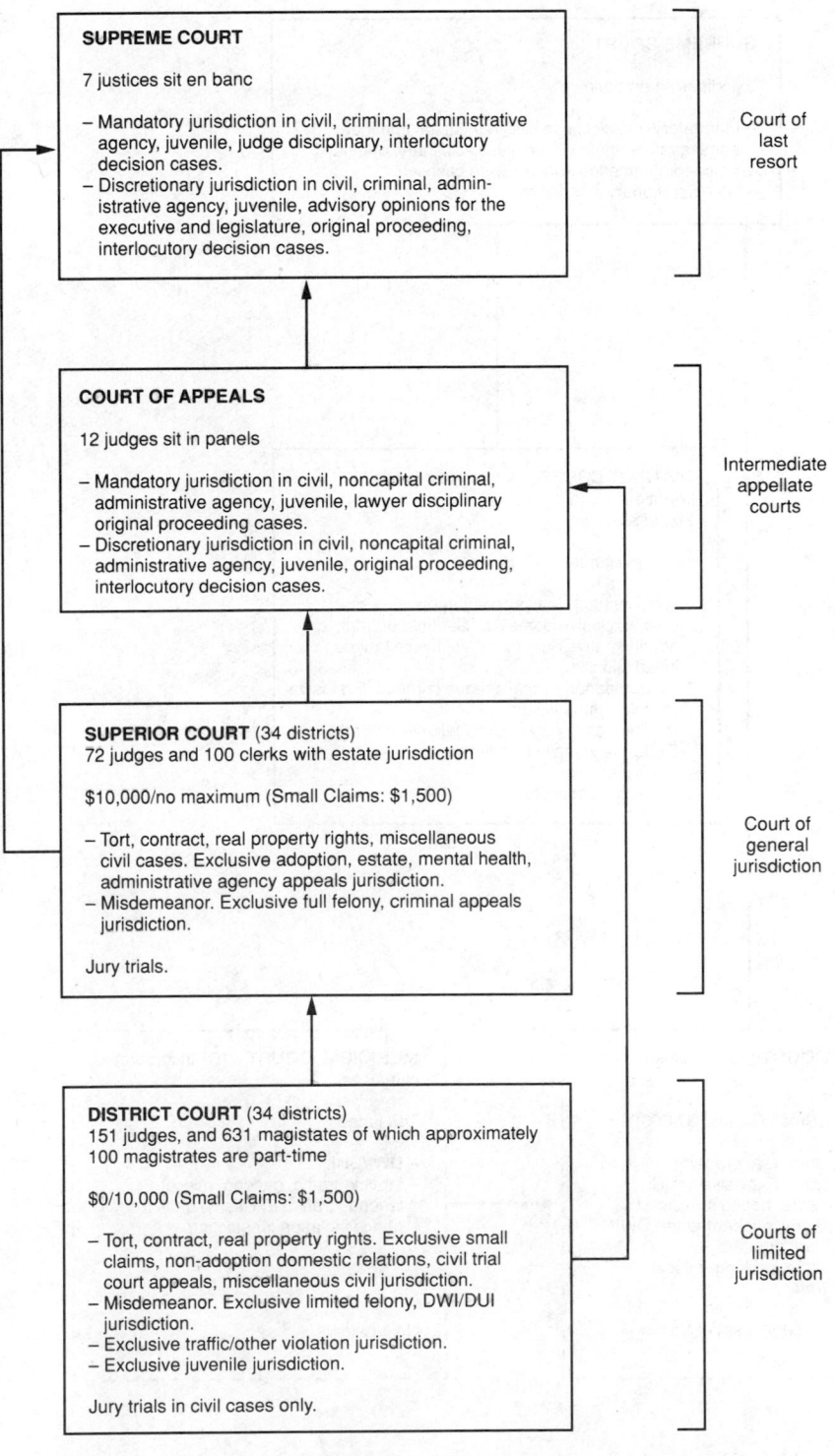

SUPREME COURT

7 justices sit en banc

- Mandatory jurisdiction in civil, criminal, administrative agency, juvenile, judge disciplinary, interlocutory decision cases.
- Discretionary jurisdiction in civil, criminal, administrative agency, juvenile, advisory opinions for the executive and legislature, original proceeding, interlocutory decision cases.

Court of last resort

COURT OF APPEALS

12 judges sit in panels

- Mandatory jurisdiction in civil, noncapital criminal, administrative agency, juvenile, lawyer disciplinary original proceeding cases.
- Discretionary jurisdiction in civil, noncapital criminal, administrative agency, juvenile, original proceeding, interlocutory decision cases.

Intermediate appellate courts

SUPERIOR COURT (34 districts)
72 judges and 100 clerks with estate jurisdiction

$10,000/no maximum (Small Claims: $1,500)

- Tort, contract, real property rights, miscellaneous civil cases. Exclusive adoption, estate, mental health, administrative agency appeals jurisdiction.
- Misdemeanor. Exclusive full felony, criminal appeals jurisdiction.

Jury trials.

Court of general jurisdiction

DISTRICT COURT (34 districts)
151 judges, and 631 magistates of which approximately 100 magistrates are part-time

$0/10,000 (Small Claims: $1,500)

- Tort, contract, real property rights. Exclusive small claims, non-adoption domestic relations, civil trial court appeals, miscellaneous civil jurisdiction.
- Misdemeanor. Exclusive limited felony, DWI/DUI jurisdiction.
- Exclusive traffic/other violation jurisdiction.
- Exclusive juvenile jurisdiction.

Jury trials in civil cases only.

Courts of limited jurisdiction

NORTH DAKOTA COURT STRUCTURE, 1987

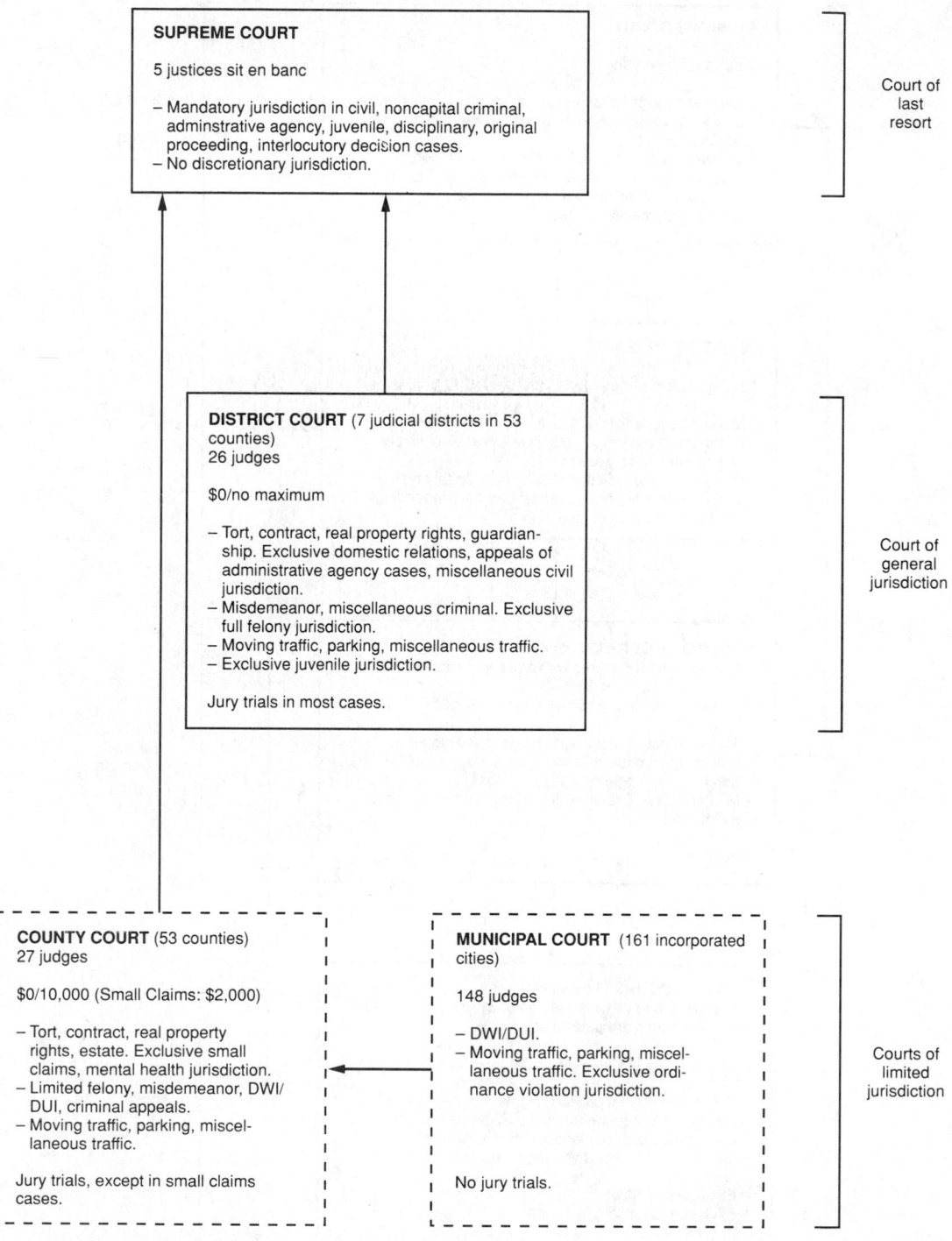

SUPREME COURT

5 justices sit en banc

– Mandatory jurisdiction in civil, noncapital criminal, adminstrative agency, juvenile, disciplinary, original proceeding, interlocutory decision cases.
– No discretionary jurisdiction.

Court of last resort

DISTRICT COURT (7 judicial districts in 53 counties)
26 judges

$0/no maximum

– Tort, contract, real property rights, guardianship. Exclusive domestic relations, appeals of administrative agency cases, miscellaneous civil jurisdiction.
– Misdemeanor, miscellaneous criminal. Exclusive full felony jurisdiction.
– Moving traffic, parking, miscellaneous traffic.
– Exclusive juvenile jurisdiction.

Jury trials in most cases.

Court of general jurisdiction

COUNTY COURT (53 counties)
27 judges

$0/10,000 (Small Claims: $2,000)

– Tort, contract, real property rights, estate. Exclusive small claims, mental health jurisdiction.
– Limited felony, misdemeanor, DWI/ DUI, criminal appeals.
– Moving traffic, parking, miscellaneous traffic.

Jury trials, except in small claims cases.

MUNICIPAL COURT (161 incorporated cities)

148 judges

– DWI/DUI.
– Moving traffic, parking, miscellaneous traffic. Exclusive ordinance violation jurisdiction.

No jury trials.

Courts of limited jurisdiction

OHIO COURT STRUCTURE, 1987

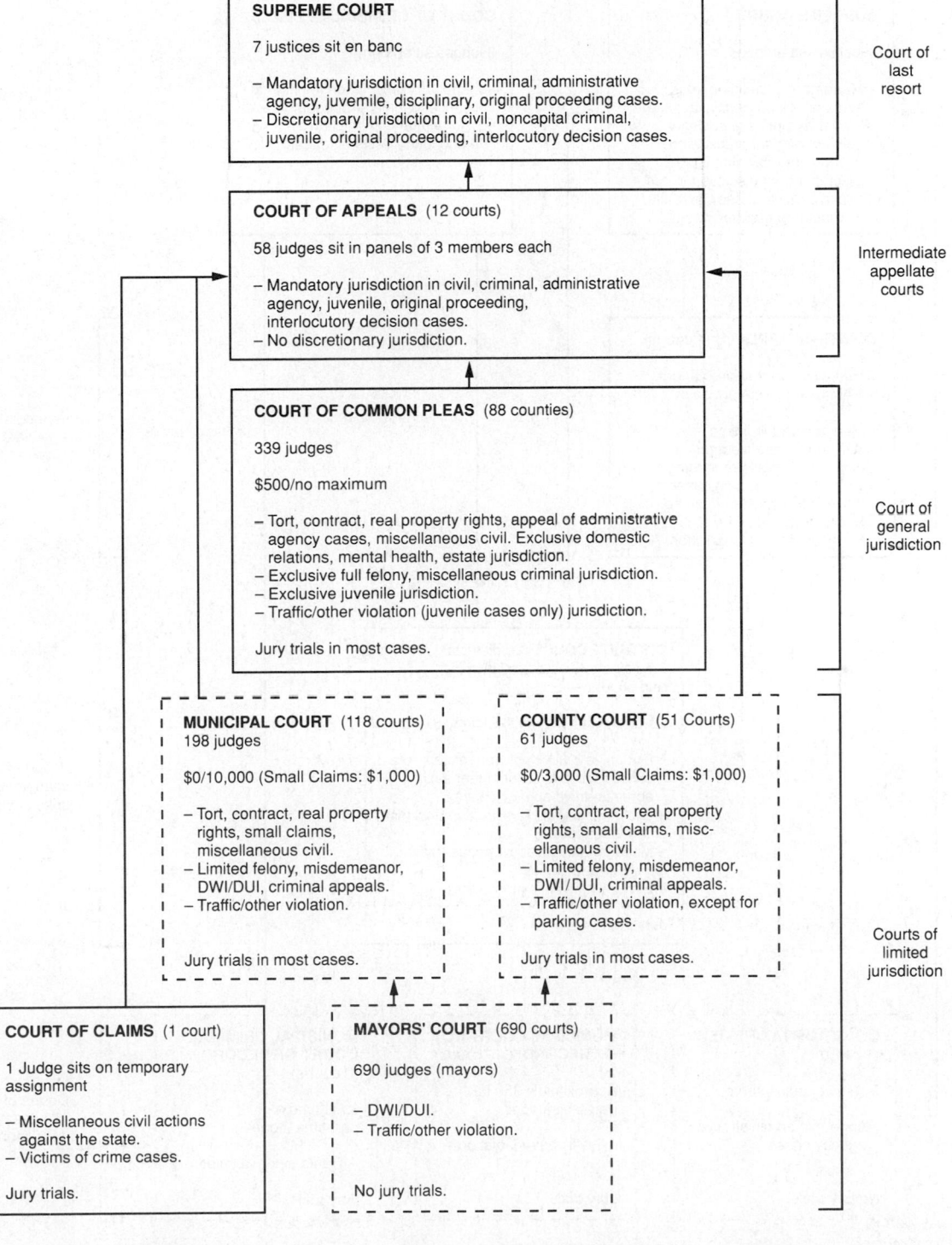

SUPREME COURT

7 justices sit en banc

– Mandatory jurisdiction in civil, criminal, administrative
  agency, juvenile, disciplinary, original proceeding cases.
– Discretionary jurisdiction in civil, noncapital criminal,
  juvenile, original proceeding, interlocutory decision cases.

Court of
last
resort

COURT OF APPEALS (12 courts)

58 judges sit in panels of 3 members each

– Mandatory jurisdiction in civil, criminal, administrative
  agency, juvenile, original proceeding,
  interlocutory decision cases.
– No discretionary jurisdiction.

Intermediate
appellate
courts

COURT OF COMMON PLEAS (88 counties)

339 judges

$500/no maximum

– Tort, contract, real property rights, appeal of administrative
  agency cases, miscellaneous civil. Exclusive domestic
  relations, mental health, estate jurisdiction.
– Exclusive full felony, miscellaneous criminal jurisdiction.
– Exclusive juvenile jurisdiction.
– Traffic/other violation (juvenile cases only) jurisdiction.

Jury trials in most cases.

Court of
general
jurisdiction

MUNICIPAL COURT (118 courts)
198 judges

$0/10,000 (Small Claims: $1,000)

– Tort, contract, real property
  rights, small claims,
  miscellaneous civil.
– Limited felony, misdemeanor,
  DWI/DUI, criminal appeals.
– Traffic/other violation.

Jury trials in most cases.

COUNTY COURT (51 Courts)
61 judges

$0/3,000 (Small Claims: $1,000)

– Tort, contract, real property
  rights, small claims, miscellaneous civil.
– Limited felony, misdemeanor,
  DWI/DUI, criminal appeals.
– Traffic/other violation, except for
  parking cases.

Jury trials in most cases.

Courts of
limited
jurisdiction

COURT OF CLAIMS (1 court)

1 Judge sits on temporary
assignment

– Miscellaneous civil actions
  against the state.
– Victims of crime cases.

Jury trials.

MAYORS' COURT (690 courts)

690 judges (mayors)

– DWI/DUI.
– Traffic/other violation.

No jury trials.

OKLAHOMA COURT STRUCTURE, 1987

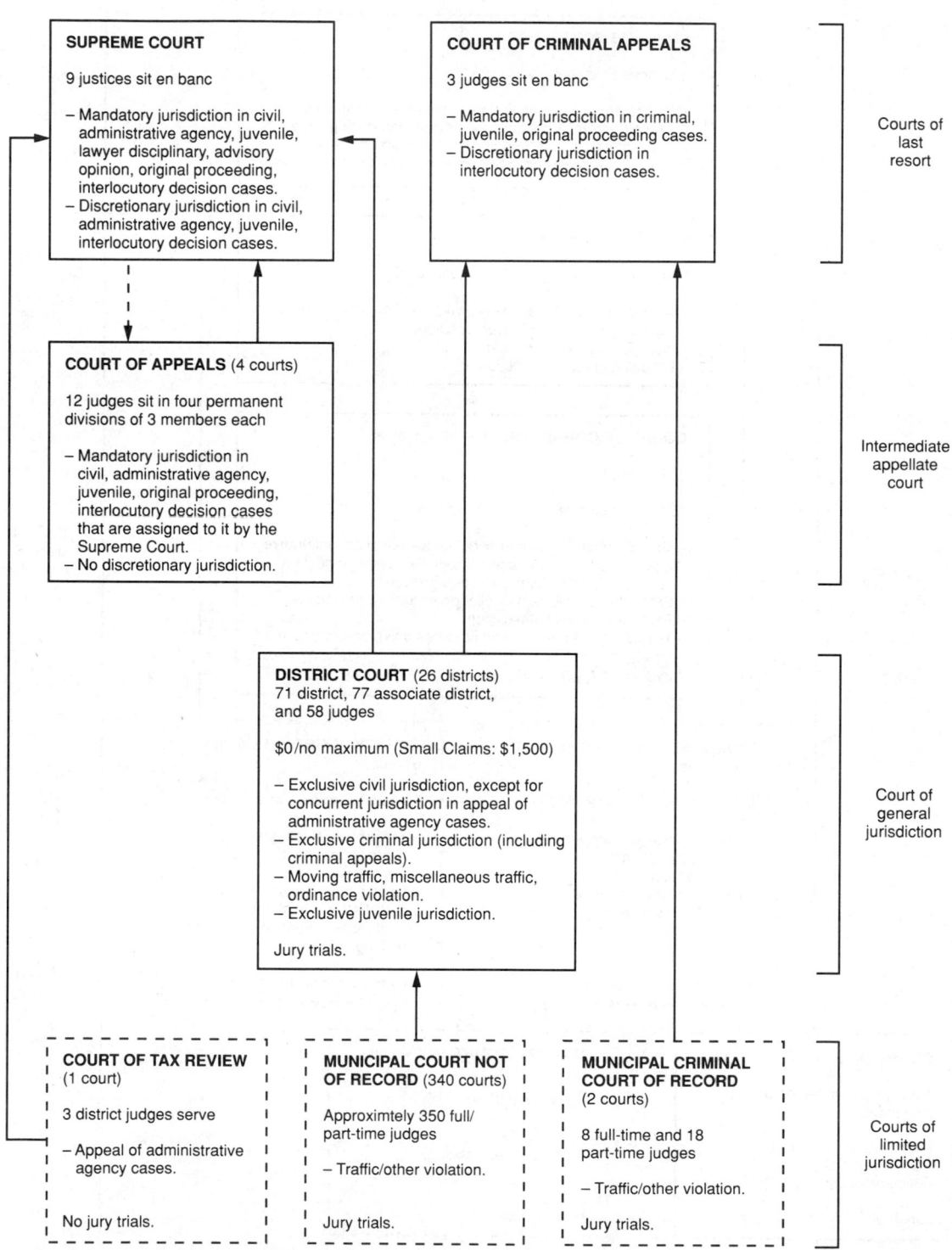

SUPREME COURT

9 justices sit en banc

– Mandatory jurisdiction in civil, administrative agency, juvenile, lawyer disciplinary, advisory opinion, original proceeding, interlocutory decision cases.
– Discretionary jurisdiction in civil, administrative agency, juvenile, interlocutory decision cases.

COURT OF CRIMINAL APPEALS

3 judges sit en banc

– Mandatory jurisdiction in criminal, juvenile, original proceeding cases.
– Discretionary jurisdiction in interlocutory decision cases.

Courts of last resort

COURT OF APPEALS (4 courts)

12 judges sit in four permanent divisions of 3 members each

– Mandatory jurisdiction in civil, administrative agency, juvenile, original proceeding, interlocutory decision cases that are assigned to it by the Supreme Court.
– No discretionary jurisdiction.

Intermediate appellate court

DISTRICT COURT (26 districts)
71 district, 77 associate district, and 58 judges

$0/no maximum (Small Claims: $1,500)

– Exclusive civil jurisdiction, except for concurrent jurisdiction in appeal of administrative agency cases.
– Exclusive criminal jurisdiction (including criminal appeals).
– Moving traffic, miscellaneous traffic, ordinance violation.
– Exclusive juvenile jurisdiction.

Jury trials.

Court of general jurisdiction

COURT OF TAX REVIEW
(1 court)

3 district judges serve

– Appeal of administrative agency cases.

No jury trials.

MUNICIPAL COURT NOT OF RECORD (340 courts)

Approximtely 350 full/part-time judges

– Traffic/other violation.

Jury trials.

MUNICIPAL CRIMINAL COURT OF RECORD
(2 courts)

8 full-time and 18 part-time judges

– Traffic/other violation.

Jury trials.

Courts of limited jurisdiction

– – – Indicates assignment of cases.
Oklahoma has a Workers' Compensation Court which hears complaints that are handled exclusively by administrative agencies in other states.

OREGON COURT STRUCTURE, 1987

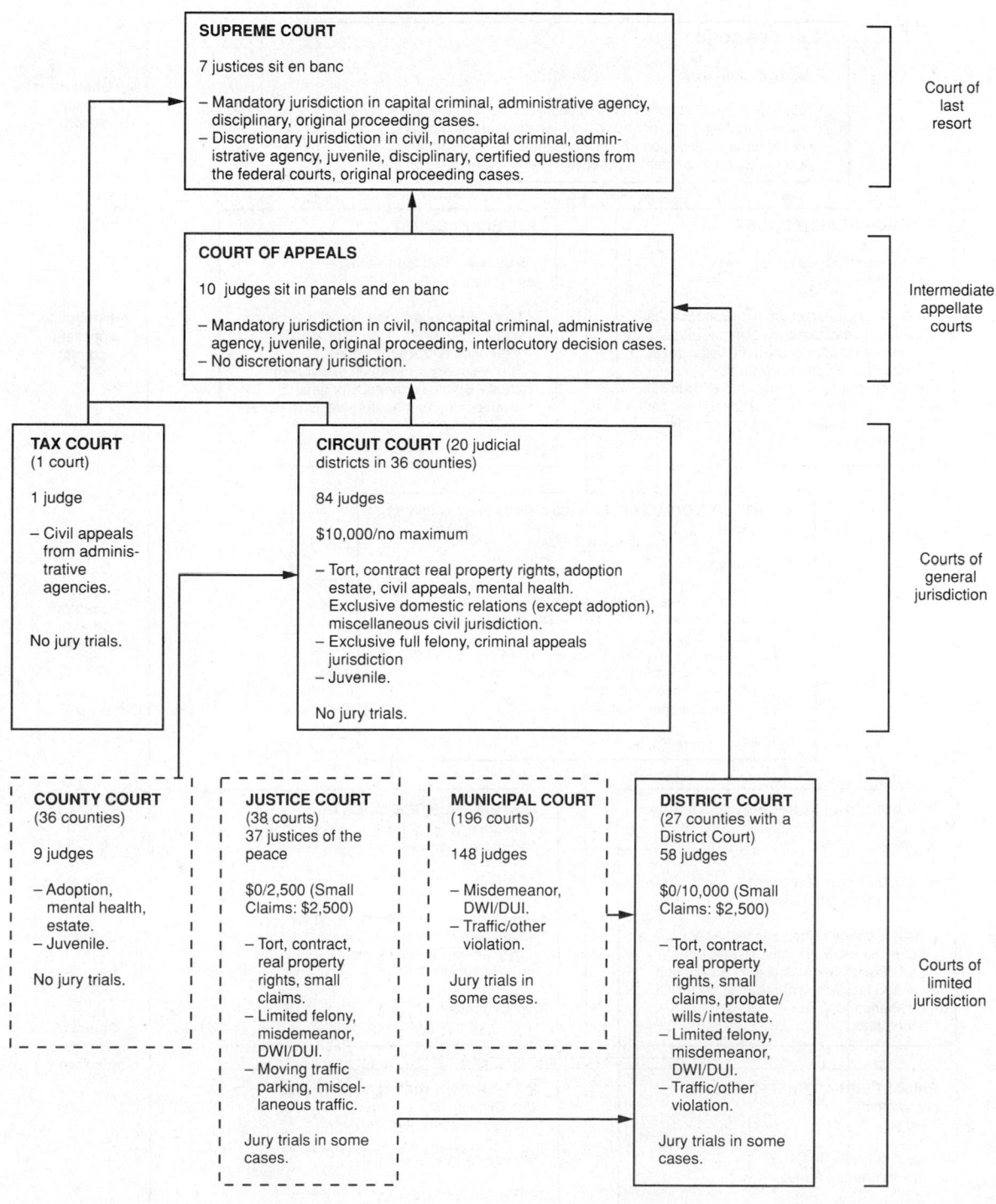

SUPREME COURT

7 justices sit en banc

- Mandatory jurisdiction in capital criminal, administrative agency, disciplinary, original proceeding cases.
- Discretionary jurisdiction in civil, noncapital criminal, administrative agency, juvenile, disciplinary, certified questions from the federal courts, original proceeding cases.

Court of last resort

COURT OF APPEALS

10 judges sit in panels and en banc

- Mandatory jurisdiction in civil, noncapital criminal, administrative agency, juvenile, original proceeding, interlocutory decision cases.
- No discretionary jurisdiction.

Intermediate appellate courts

TAX COURT
(1 court)

1 judge

- Civil appeals from administrative agencies.

No jury trials.

CIRCUIT COURT (20 judicial districts in 36 counties)

84 judges

$10,000/no maximum

- Tort, contract real property rights, adoption estate, civil appeals, mental health. Exclusive domestic relations (except adoption), miscellaneous civil jurisdiction.
- Exclusive full felony, criminal appeals jurisdiction
- Juvenile.

No jury trials.

Courts of general jurisdiction

COUNTY COURT
(36 counties)

9 judges

- Adoption, mental health, estate.
- Juvenile.

No jury trials.

JUSTICE COURT
(38 courts)
37 justices of the peace

$0/2,500 (Small Claims: $2,500)

- Tort, contract, real property rights, small claims.
- Limited felony, misdemeanor, DWI/DUI.
- Moving traffic parking, miscellaneous traffic.

Jury trials in some cases.

MUNICIPAL COURT
(196 courts)

148 judges

- Misdemeanor, DWI/DUI.
- Traffic/other violation.

Jury trials in some cases.

DISTRICT COURT
(27 counties with a District Court)
58 judges

$0/10,000 (Small Claims: $2,500)

- Tort, contract, real property rights, small claims, probate/wills/intestate.
- Limited felony, misdemeanor, DWI/DUI.
- Traffic/other violation.

Jury trials in some cases.

Courts of limited jurisdiction

PENNSYLVANIA COURT STRUCTURE, 1987

SUPREME COURT

7 justices sit en banc

– Mandatory jurisdiction in civil, criminal, administrative agency, juvenile disciplinary, original proceeding, interlocutory decision cases.
– Discretionary jurisdiction in civil, noncapital criminal, administrative agency, juvenile, original proceeding, interlocutory decision cases.

Court of last resort

COMMONWEALTH COURT

9 authorized judges sit in panels and en banc

– Mandatory jurisdiction in civil, noncapital criminal, administrative agency, original proceeding, interlocutory decision cases involving the Commonwealth.
– Discretionary jurisdiction in civil, administrative agency, original proceeding, interlocutory decision cases involving the Commonwealth.

SUPERIOR COURT

15 authorized judges sit in panels and en banc

– Mandatory jurisdiction in civil, noncapital criminal, juvenile, original proceeding, interlocutory decision cases.
– Discretionary jurisdiction in civil, noncapital criminal, juvenile, original proceeding, interlocutory decision cases.

Intermediate appellate courts

COURT OF COMMON PLEAS (60 districts in 67 counties)
330 judges

$0/no maximum

– Tort, contract, real property rights, miscellaneous civil, Exclusive domestic relations, estate, mental health, civil appeals jurisdiction.
– Misdemeanor, DWI/DUI. Exclusive full felony, criminal appeals, miscellaneous criminal jurisdiction.
– Exclusive juvenile jurisdiction.
– Administrative agency appeals.

Jury trials in most cases.

Court of general jurisdiction

PHILADELPHIA MUNICIPAL COURT
(1st District)
22 judges

$0/5,000 (only real property)
(Small Claims: $5,000)

– Real property rights, miscellaneous domestic relations, miscellaneous civil. Exclusive small claims jurisdiction.
– Limited felony, misdemeanor, DWI/DUI.
– Ordinance violation.
No jury trials.

DISTRICT JUSTICE COURT
(543 courts)
543 district justices

$0/4,000

– Tort, contract, real property rights.
– Limited felony/misdemeanor, misdemeanor, DWI/DUI.
– Traffic/other violation.

No jury trials.

PHILADELPHIA TRAFFIC COURT
(1st District)
7 judges

– Moving traffic, parking, miscellaneous traffic.

No jury trials.

PITTSBURGH CITY MAGISTRATES
(5th District)
6 magistrates

$0/no maximum

– Real property rights.
– Limited felony/misdemeanor, DWI/DUI, misdemeanor.
– Traffic/other violation.

No jury trials

Courts of limited jurisdiction

PUERTO RICO COURT STRUCTURE, 1987

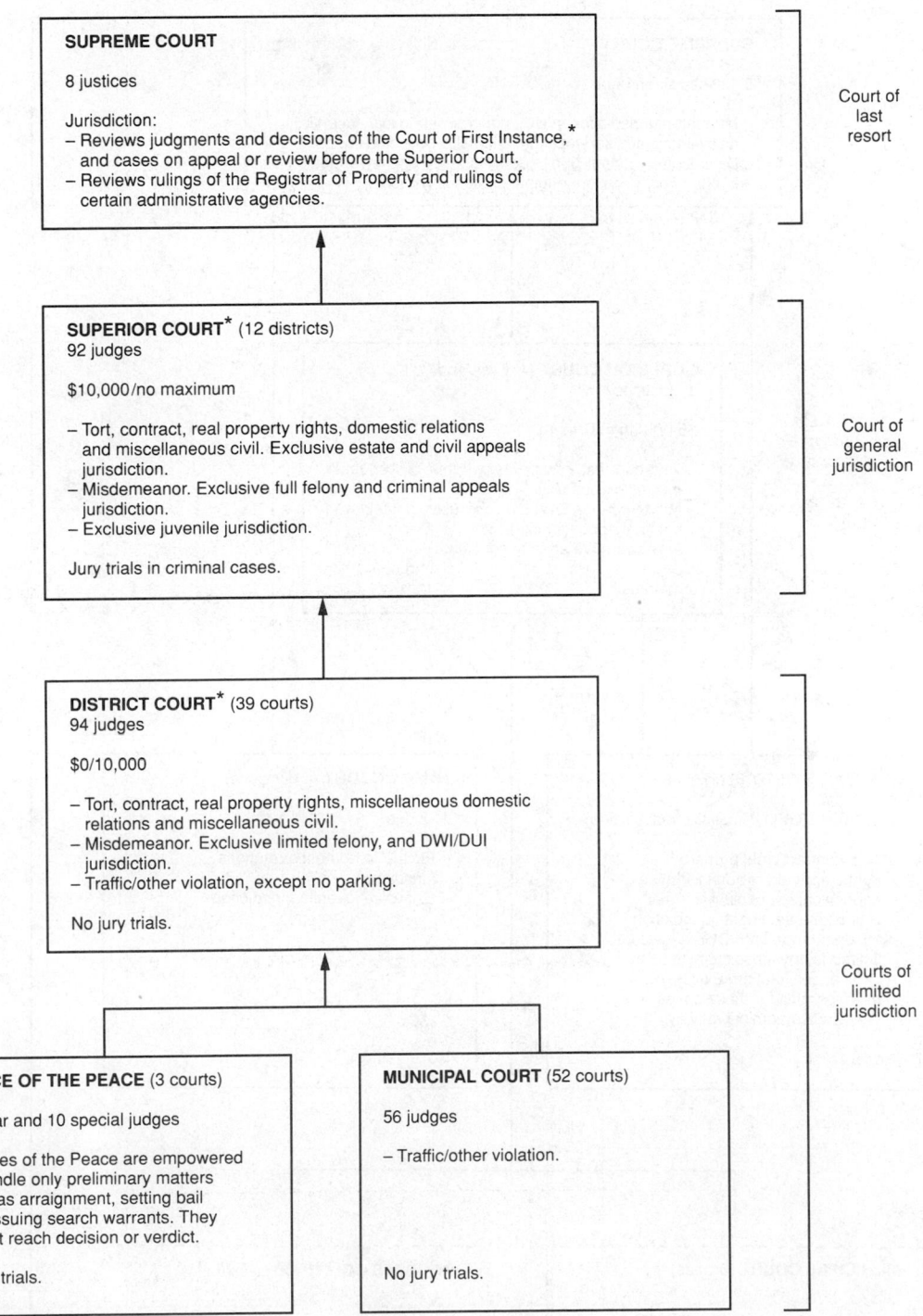

SUPREME COURT

8 justices

Jurisdiction:
– Reviews judgments and decisions of the Court of First Instance,[*] and cases on appeal or review before the Superior Court.
– Reviews rulings of the Registrar of Property and rulings of certain administrative agencies.

Court of last resort

SUPERIOR COURT[*] (12 districts)
92 judges

$10,000/no maximum

– Tort, contract, real property rights, domestic relations and miscellaneous civil. Exclusive estate and civil appeals jurisdiction.
– Misdemeanor. Exclusive full felony and criminal appeals jurisdiction.
– Exclusive juvenile jurisdiction.

Jury trials in criminal cases.

Court of general jurisdiction

DISTRICT COURT[*] (39 courts)
94 judges

$0/10,000

– Tort, contract, real property rights, miscellaneous domestic relations and miscellaneous civil.
– Misdemeanor. Exclusive limited felony, and DWI/DUI jurisdiction.
– Traffic/other violation, except no parking.

No jury trials.

Courts of limited jurisdiction

JUSTICE OF THE PEACE (3 courts)

3 regular and 10 special judges

– Justices of the Peace are empowered to handle only preliminary matters such as arraignment, setting bail and issuing search warrants. They do not reach decision or verdict.

No jury trials.

MUNICIPAL COURT (52 courts)

56 judges

– Traffic/other violation.

No jury trials.

[*]The Court of First Instance consists of two divisions: the Superior Court and the District Court.

RHODE ISLAND COURT STRUCTURE, 1987

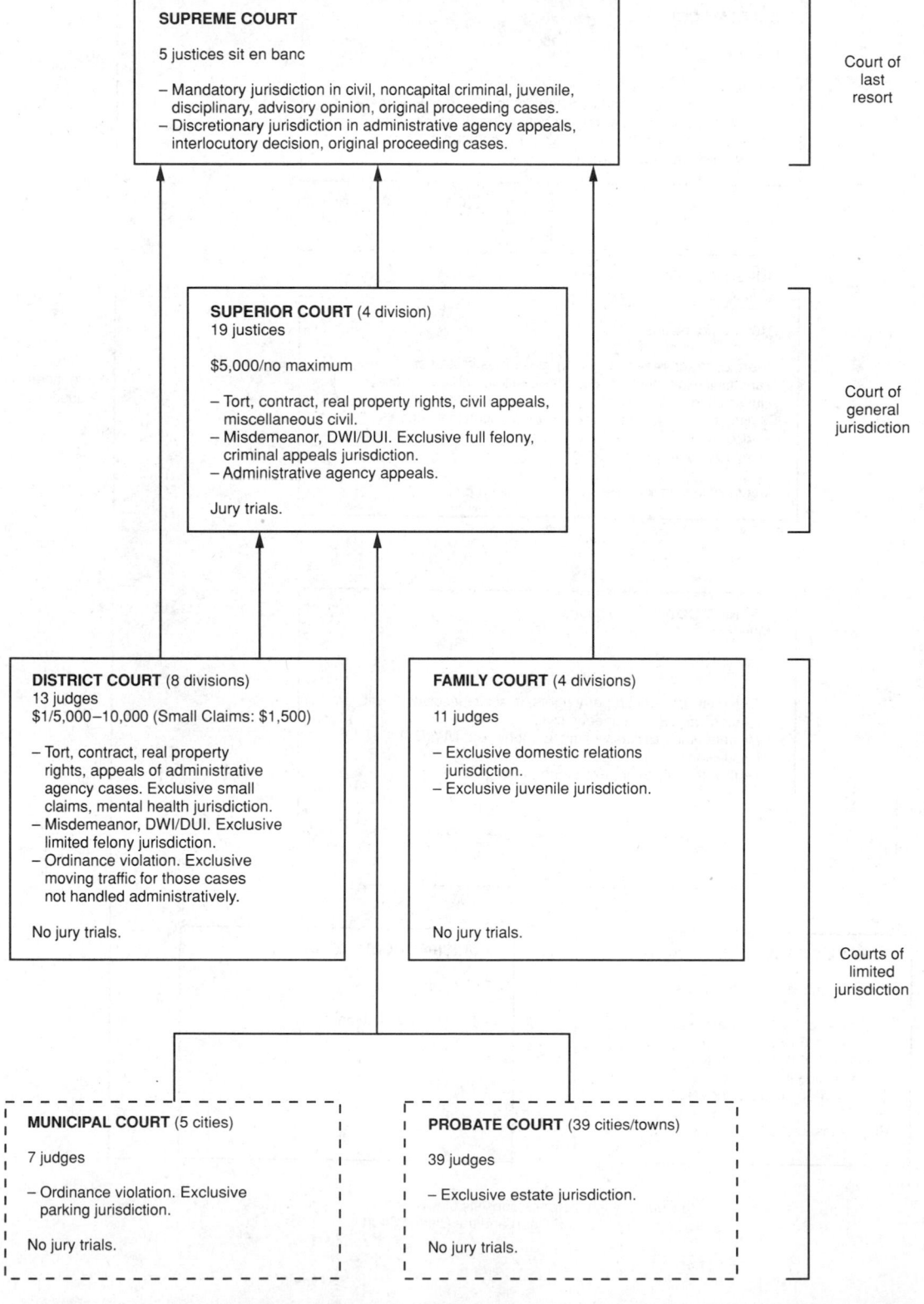

SUPREME COURT

5 justices sit en banc

– Mandatory jurisdiction in civil, noncapital criminal, juvenile,
  disciplinary, advisory opinion, original proceeding cases.
– Discretionary jurisdiction in administrative agency appeals,
  interlocutory decision, original proceeding cases.

Court of
last
resort

SUPERIOR COURT (4 division)
19 justices

$5,000/no maximum

– Tort, contract, real property rights, civil appeals,
  miscellaneous civil.
– Misdemeanor, DWI/DUI. Exclusive full felony,
  criminal appeals jurisdiction.
– Administrative agency appeals.

Jury trials.

Court of
general
jurisdiction

DISTRICT COURT (8 divisions)
13 judges
$1/5,000–10,000 (Small Claims: $1,500)

– Tort, contract, real property
  rights, appeals of administrative
  agency cases. Exclusive small
  claims, mental health jurisdiction.
– Misdemeanor, DWI/DUI. Exclusive
  limited felony jurisdiction.
– Ordinance violation. Exclusive
  moving traffic for those cases
  not handled administratively.

No jury trials.

FAMILY COURT (4 divisions)

11 judges

– Exclusive domestic relations
  jurisdiction.
– Exclusive juvenile jurisdiction.

No jury trials.

Courts of
limited
jurisdiction

MUNICIPAL COURT (5 cities)

7 judges

– Ordinance violation. Exclusive
  parking jurisdiction.

No jury trials.

PROBATE COURT (39 cities/towns)

39 judges

– Exclusive estate jurisdiction.

No jury trials.

SOUTH CAROLINA COURT STRUCTURE, 1987

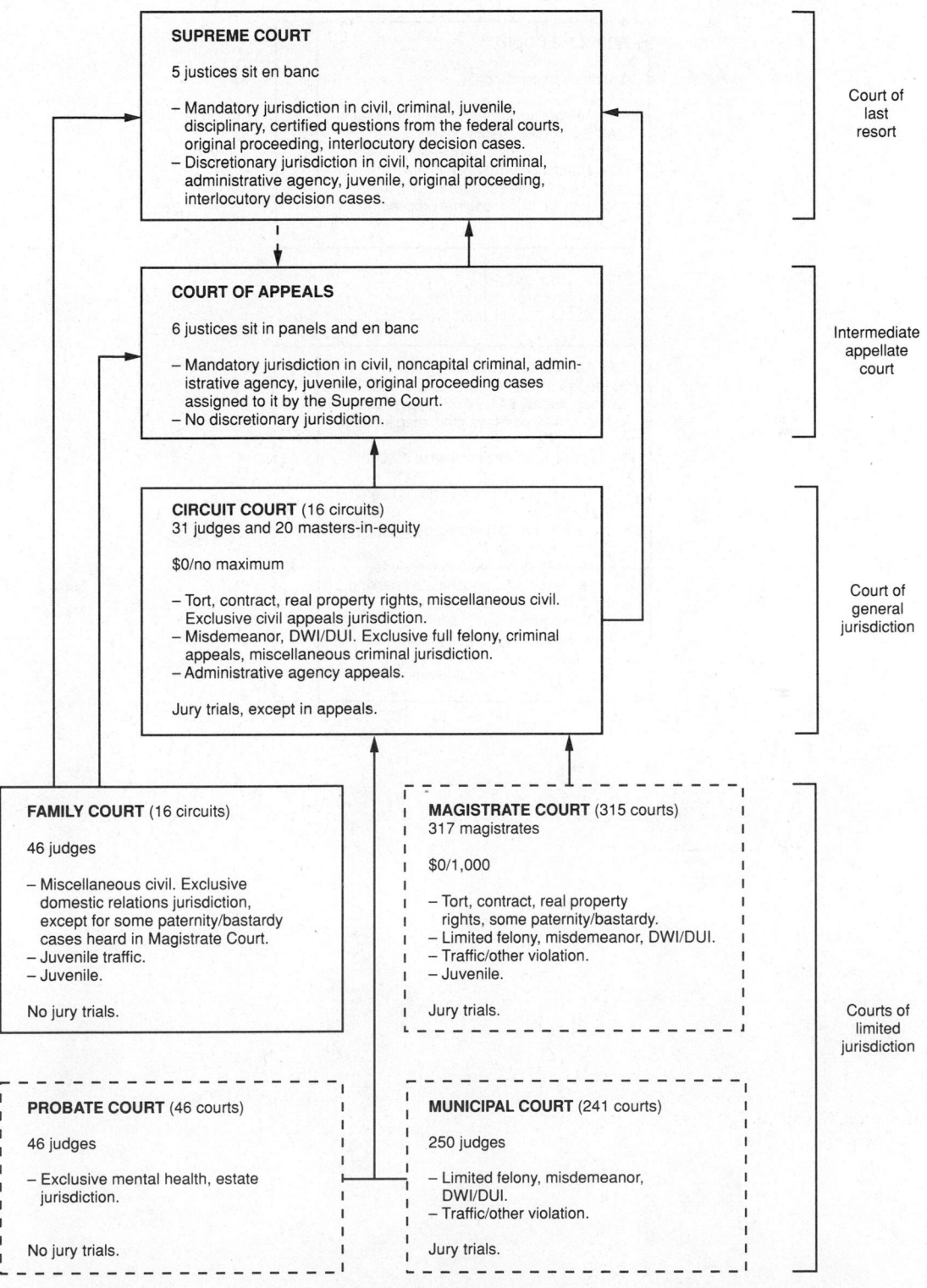

SUPREME COURT

5 justices sit en banc

– Mandatory jurisdiction in civil, criminal, juvenile, disciplinary, certified questions from the federal courts, original proceeding, interlocutory decision cases.
– Discretionary jurisdiction in civil, noncapital criminal, administrative agency, juvenile, original proceeding, interlocutory decision cases.

Court of last resort

COURT OF APPEALS

6 justices sit in panels and en banc

– Mandatory jurisdiction in civil, noncapital criminal, administrative agency, juvenile, original proceeding cases assigned to it by the Supreme Court.
– No discretionary jurisdiction.

Intermediate appellate court

CIRCUIT COURT (16 circuits)
31 judges and 20 masters-in-equity

$0/no maximum

– Tort, contract, real property rights, miscellaneous civil. Exclusive civil appeals jurisdiction.
– Misdemeanor, DWI/DUI. Exclusive full felony, criminal appeals, miscellaneous criminal jurisdiction.
– Administrative agency appeals.

Jury trials, except in appeals.

Court of general jurisdiction

FAMILY COURT (16 circuits)

46 judges

– Miscellaneous civil. Exclusive domestic relations jurisdiction, except for some paternity/bastardy cases heard in Magistrate Court.
– Juvenile traffic.
– Juvenile.

No jury trials.

MAGISTRATE COURT (315 courts)
317 magistrates

$0/1,000

– Tort, contract, real property rights, some paternity/bastardy.
– Limited felony, misdemeanor, DWI/DUI.
– Traffic/other violation.
– Juvenile.

Jury trials.

PROBATE COURT (46 courts)

46 judges

– Exclusive mental health, estate jurisdiction.

No jury trials.

MUNICIPAL COURT (241 courts)

250 judges

– Limited felony, misdemeanor, DWI/DUI.
– Traffic/other violation.

Jury trials.

Courts of limited jurisdiction

– – – Indicates assignment of cases.

SOUTH DAKOTA COURT STRUCTURE, 1987

SUPREME COURT

5 justices sit en banc

– Mandatory jurisdiction in civil, criminal,
administrative agency, juvenile,
disciplinary, original proceeding cases.
– Discretionary jurisdiction in advisory
opinions for the state executive, interlocutory decision, original proceeding
cases.

Court of
last
resort

CIRCUIT COURT (8 circuits)
35 judges, 18 law magistrates, 11 part-time
lay magistrates, 84 full-time clerk magistrates, and 49 part-time clerk magistrates.

$0/no maximum (Small Claims: $2,000)

– Exclusive civil jurisdiction (including
civil appeals).
– Exclusive criminal jurisdiction (including
criminal appeals).
– Exclusive traffic/other violation jurisdiction (except for uncontested parking
which is handled administratively).
– Exclusive juvenile jurisdiction.
– Administrative agency appeals.

Jury trials, except in small claims.

Court of
general
jurisdiction

TENNESSEE COURT STRUCTURE, 1987

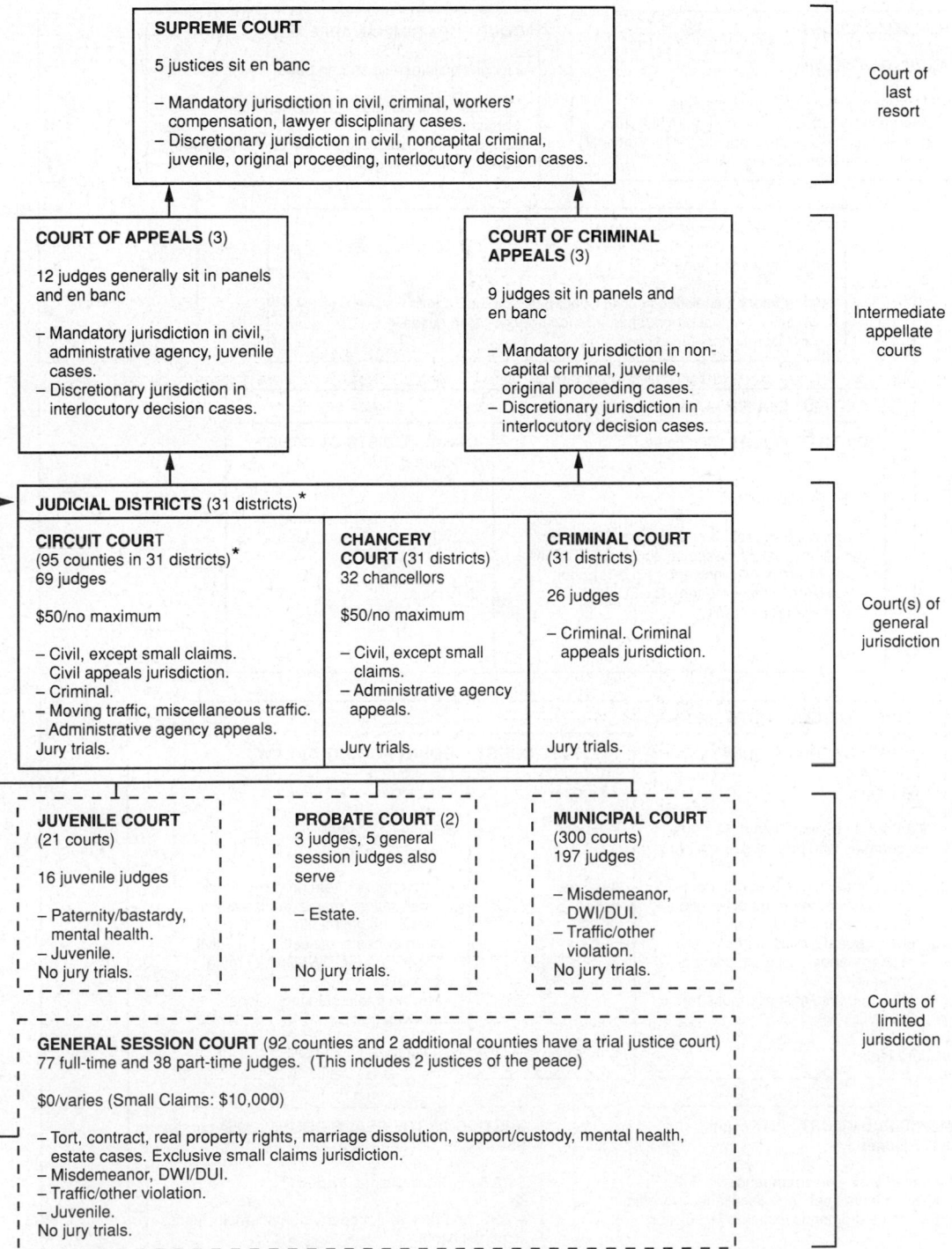

SUPREME COURT

5 justices sit en banc

– Mandatory jurisdiction in civil, criminal, workers'
compensation, lawyer disciplinary cases.
– Discretionary jurisdiction in civil, noncapital criminal,
juvenile, original proceeding, interlocutory decision cases.

Court of
last
resort

COURT OF APPEALS (3)

12 judges generally sit in panels
and en banc

– Mandatory jurisdiction in civil,
administrative agency, juvenile
cases.
– Discretionary jurisdiction in
interlocutory decision cases.

**COURT OF CRIMINAL
APPEALS** (3)

9 judges sit in panels and
en banc

– Mandatory jurisdiction in noncapital criminal, juvenile,
original proceeding cases.
– Discretionary jurisdiction in
interlocutory decision cases.

Intermediate
appellate
courts

JUDICIAL DISTRICTS (31 districts)*

CIRCUIT COURT
(95 counties in 31 districts)*
69 judges

$50/no maximum

– Civil, except small claims.
Civil appeals jurisdiction.
– Criminal.
– Moving traffic, miscellaneous traffic.
– Administrative agency appeals.
Jury trials.

**CHANCERY
COURT** (31 districts)
32 chancellors

$50/no maximum

– Civil, except small
claims.
– Administrative agency
appeals.

Jury trials.

CRIMINAL COURT
(31 districts)

26 judges

– Criminal. Criminal
appeals jurisdiction.

Jury trials.

Court(s) of
general
jurisdiction

JUVENILE COURT
(21 courts)

16 juvenile judges

– Paternity/bastardy,
mental health.
– Juvenile.
No jury trials.

PROBATE COURT (2)
3 judges, 5 general
session judges also
serve

– Estate.

No jury trials.

MUNICIPAL COURT
(300 courts)
197 judges

– Misdemeanor,
DWI/DUI.
– Traffic/other
violation.
No jury trials.

GENERAL SESSION COURT (92 counties and 2 additional counties have a trial justice court)
77 full-time and 38 part-time judges. (This includes 2 justices of the peace)

$0/varies (Small Claims: $10,000)

– Tort, contract, real property rights, marriage dissolution, support/custody, mental health,
estate cases. Exclusive small claims jurisdiction.
– Misdemeanor, DWI/DUI.
– Traffic/other violation.
– Juvenile.
No jury trials.

Courts of
limited
jurisdiction

*The State of Tennessee was divided into 31 judicial districts on September 1, 1984. There is a
Circuit in each district. Twenty seven districts have separate Chancery Courts, and thirteen districts
have separate Criminal Courts. The Circuit Court has jurisdiction over chancery and criminal matters
in the remaining circuits. There is one presiding judge for each district. As a result of the redistricting,
two Law and Equity Courts became Circuit Courts and the other two became Chancery Courts.

TEXAS COURT STRUCTURE, 1987

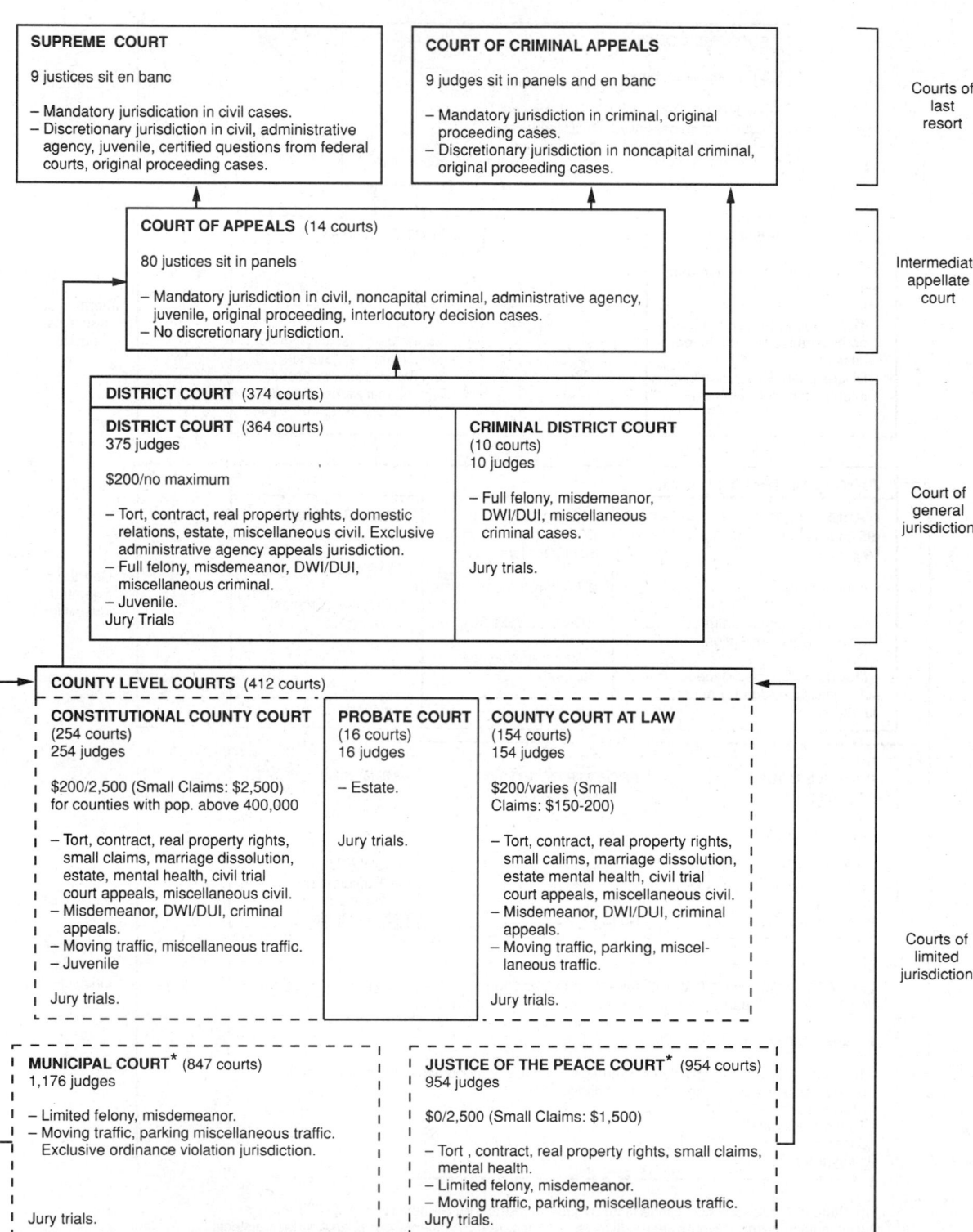

SUPREME COURT

9 justices sit en banc

– Mandatory jurisdication in civil cases.
– Discretionary jurisdiction in civil, administrative agency, juvenile, certified questions from federal courts, original proceeding cases.

COURT OF CRIMINAL APPEALS

9 judges sit in panels and en banc

– Mandatory jurisdiction in criminal, original proceeding cases.
– Discretionary jurisdiction in noncapital criminal, original proceeding cases.

Courts of last resort

COURT OF APPEALS (14 courts)

80 justices sit in panels

– Mandatory jurisdiction in civil, noncapital criminal, administrative agency, juvenile, original proceeding, interlocutory decision cases.
– No discretionary jurisdiction.

Intermediate appellate court

DISTRICT COURT (374 courts)

DISTRICT COURT (364 courts)
375 judges

$200/no maximum

– Tort, contract, real property rights, domestic relations, estate, miscellaneous civil. Exclusive administrative agency appeals jurisdiction.
– Full felony, misdemeanor, DWI/DUI, miscellaneous criminal.
– Juvenile.
Jury Trials

CRIMINAL DISTRICT COURT
(10 courts)
10 judges

– Full felony, misdemeanor, DWI/DUI, miscellaneous criminal cases.

Jury trials.

Court of general jurisdiction

COUNTY LEVEL COURTS (412 courts)

CONSTITUTIONAL COUNTY COURT
(254 courts)
254 judges

$200/2,500 (Small Claims: $2,500) for counties with pop. above 400,000

– Tort, contract, real property rights, small claims, marriage dissolution, estate, mental health, civil trial court appeals, miscellaneous civil.
– Misdemeanor, DWI/DUI, criminal appeals.
– Moving traffic, miscellaneous traffic.
– Juvenile

Jury trials.

PROBATE COURT
(16 courts)
16 judges

– Estate.

Jury trials.

COUNTY COURT AT LAW
(154 courts)
154 judges

$200/varies (Small Claims: $150-200)

– Tort, contract, real property rights, small calims, marriage dissolution, estate mental health, civil trial court appeals, miscellaneous civil.
– Misdemeanor, DWI/DUI, criminal appeals.
– Moving traffic, parking, miscellaneous traffic.

Jury trials.

Courts of limited jurisdiction

MUNICIPAL COURT * (847 courts)
1,176 judges

– Limited felony, misdemeanor.
– Moving traffic, parking miscellaneous traffic. Exclusive ordinance violation jurisdiction.

Jury trials.

JUSTICE OF THE PEACE COURT * (954 courts)
954 judges

$0/2,500 (Small Claims: $1,500)

– Tort , contract, real property rights, small claims, mental health.
– Limited felony, misdemeanor.
– Moving traffic, parking, miscellaneous traffic.
Jury trials.

*Some Municipal and Justice of the Peace Courts may appeal to the District Court.

UTAH COURT STRUCTURE, 1987

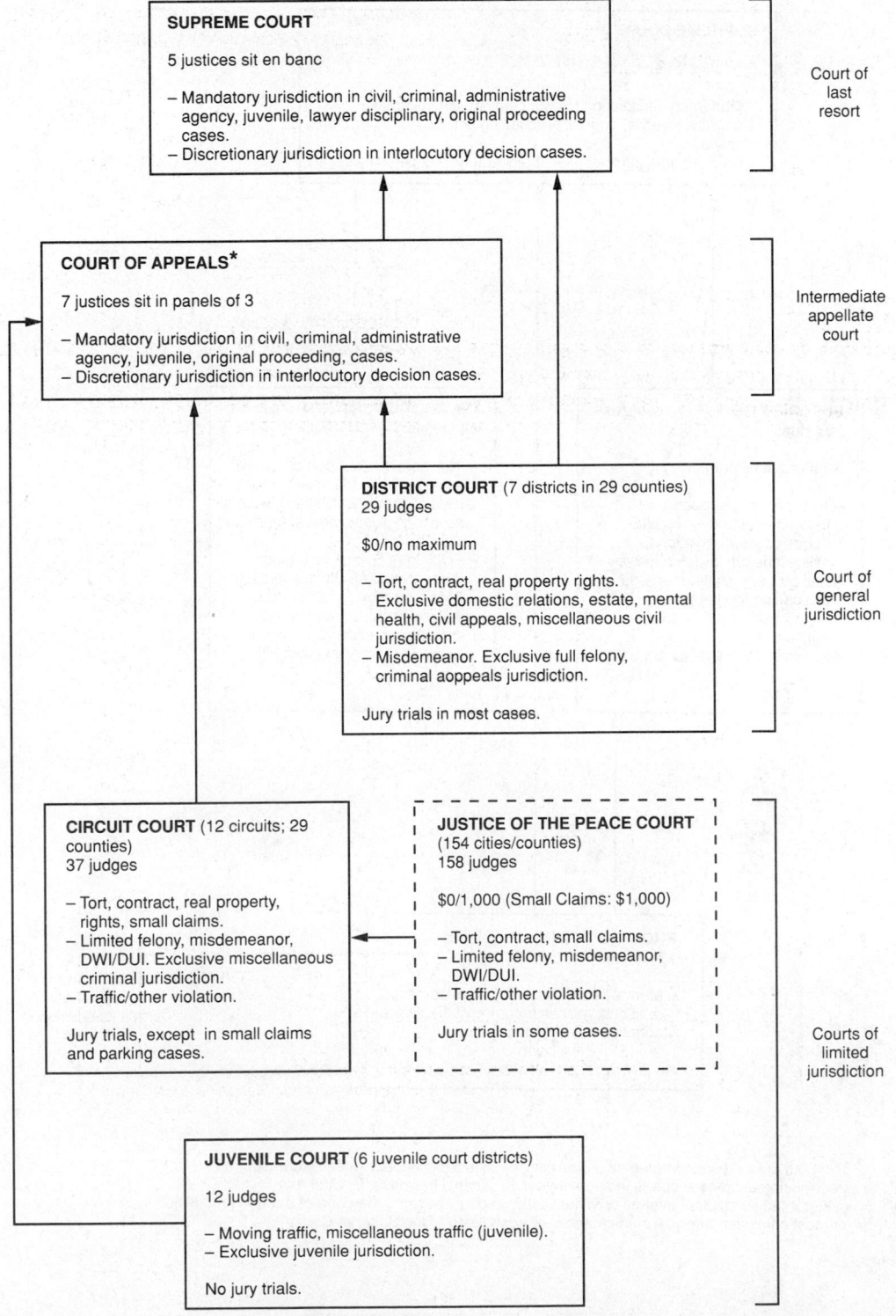

SUPREME COURT

5 justices sit en banc

- Mandatory jurisdiction in civil, criminal, administrative agency, juvenile, lawyer disciplinary, original proceeding cases.
- Discretionary jurisdiction in interlocutory decision cases.

Court of last resort

COURT OF APPEALS*

7 justices sit in panels of 3

- Mandatory jurisdiction in civil, criminal, administrative agency, juvenile, original proceeding, cases.
- Discretionary jurisdiction in interlocutory decision cases.

Intermediate appellate court

DISTRICT COURT (7 districts in 29 counties)
29 judges

$0/no maximum

- Tort, contract, real property rights. Exclusive domestic relations, estate, mental health, civil appeals, miscellaneous civil jurisdiction.
- Misdemeanor. Exclusive full felony, criminal aoppeals jurisdiction.

Jury trials in most cases.

Court of general jurisdiction

CIRCUIT COURT (12 circuits; 29 counties)
37 judges

- Tort, contract, real property, rights, small claims.
- Limited felony, misdemeanor, DWI/DUI. Exclusive miscellaneous criminal jurisdiction.
- Traffic/other violation.

Jury trials, except in small claims and parking cases.

JUSTICE OF THE PEACE COURT
(154 cities/counties)
158 judges

$0/1,000 (Small Claims: $1,000)

- Tort, contract, small claims.
- Limited felony, misdemeanor, DWI/DUI.
- Traffic/other violation.

Jury trials in some cases.

Courts of limited jurisdiction

JUVENILE COURT (6 juvenile court districts)

12 judges

- Moving traffic, miscellaneous traffic (juvenile).
- Exclusive juvenile jurisdiction.

No jury trials.

*The Court of Appeals became operational on Feb. 1, 1989.

VERMONT COURT STRUCTURE, 1987

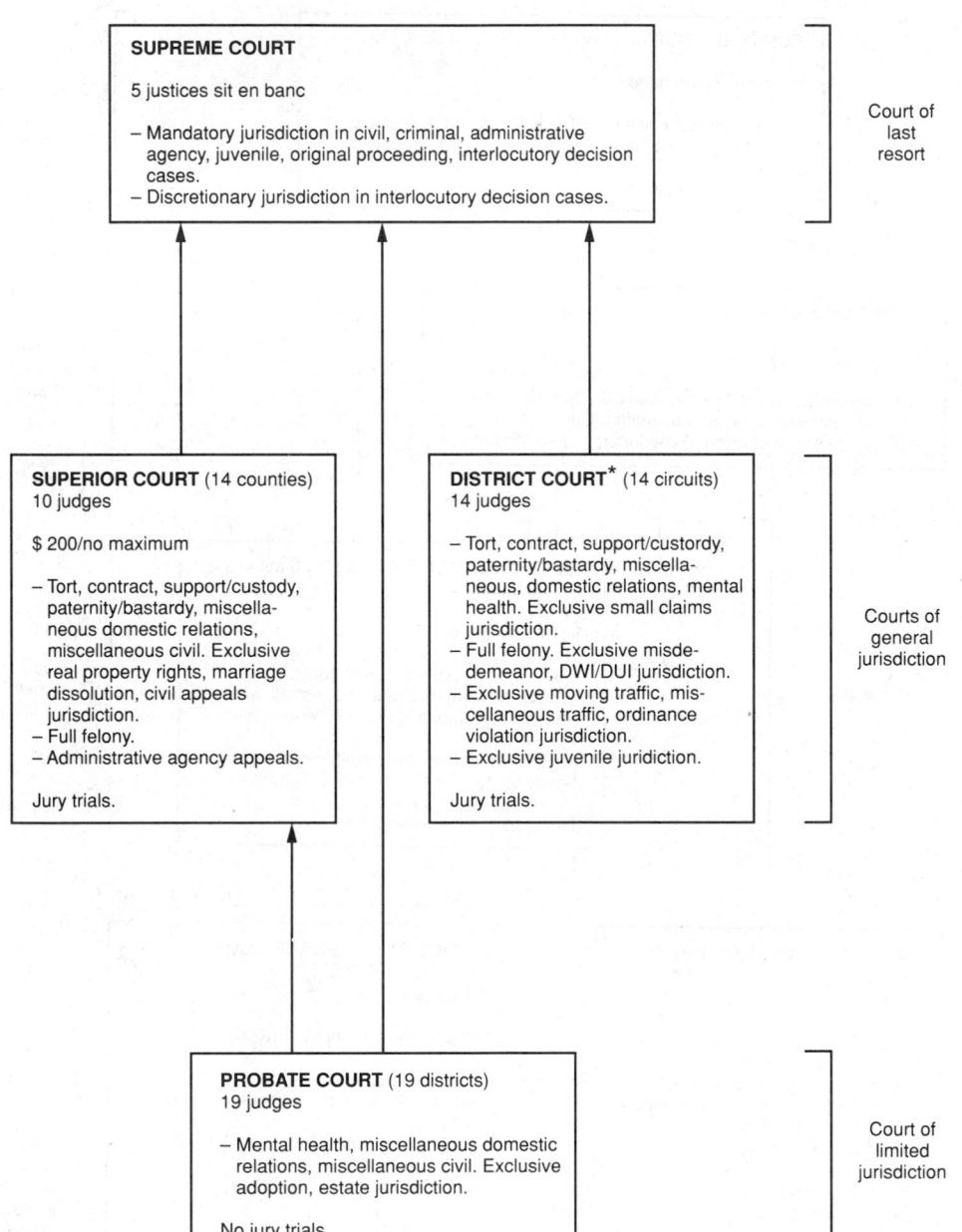

SUPREME COURT

5 justices sit en banc

– Mandatory jurisdiction in civil, criminal, administrative
  agency, juvenile, original proceeding, interlocutory decision
  cases.
– Discretionary jurisdiction in interlocutory decision cases.

Court of
last
resort

SUPERIOR COURT (14 counties)
10 judges

$ 200/no maximum

– Tort, contract, support/custody,
  paternity/bastardy, miscellaneous domestic relations,
  miscellaneous civil. Exclusive
  real property rights, marriage
  dissolution, civil appeals
  jurisdiction.
– Full felony.
– Administrative agency appeals.

Jury trials.

DISTRICT COURT[*] (14 circuits)
14 judges

– Tort, contract, support/custody,
  paternity/bastardy, miscellaneous, domestic relations, mental
  health. Exclusive small claims
  jurisdiction.
– Full felony. Exclusive misde-
  demeanor, DWI/DUI jurisdiction.
– Exclusive moving traffic, miscellaneous traffic, ordinance
  violation jurisdiction.
– Exclusive juvenile juridiction.

Jury trials.

Courts of
general
jurisdiction

PROBATE COURT (19 districts)
19 judges

– Mental health, miscellaneous domestic
  relations, miscellaneous civil. Exclusive
  adoption, estate jurisdiction.

No jury trials.

Court of
limited
jurisdiction

[*] The District Court was created as a court of limited jurisdiction, but since its creation, has
steadily increased its scope to include almost all criminal business. In 1983, the District Court
was granted jurisdiction over all criminal cases, and has become the court of general jurisdiction
for most criminal matters. A small number of appeals go to the Superior Court.

VIRGINIA COURT STRUCTURE, 1987

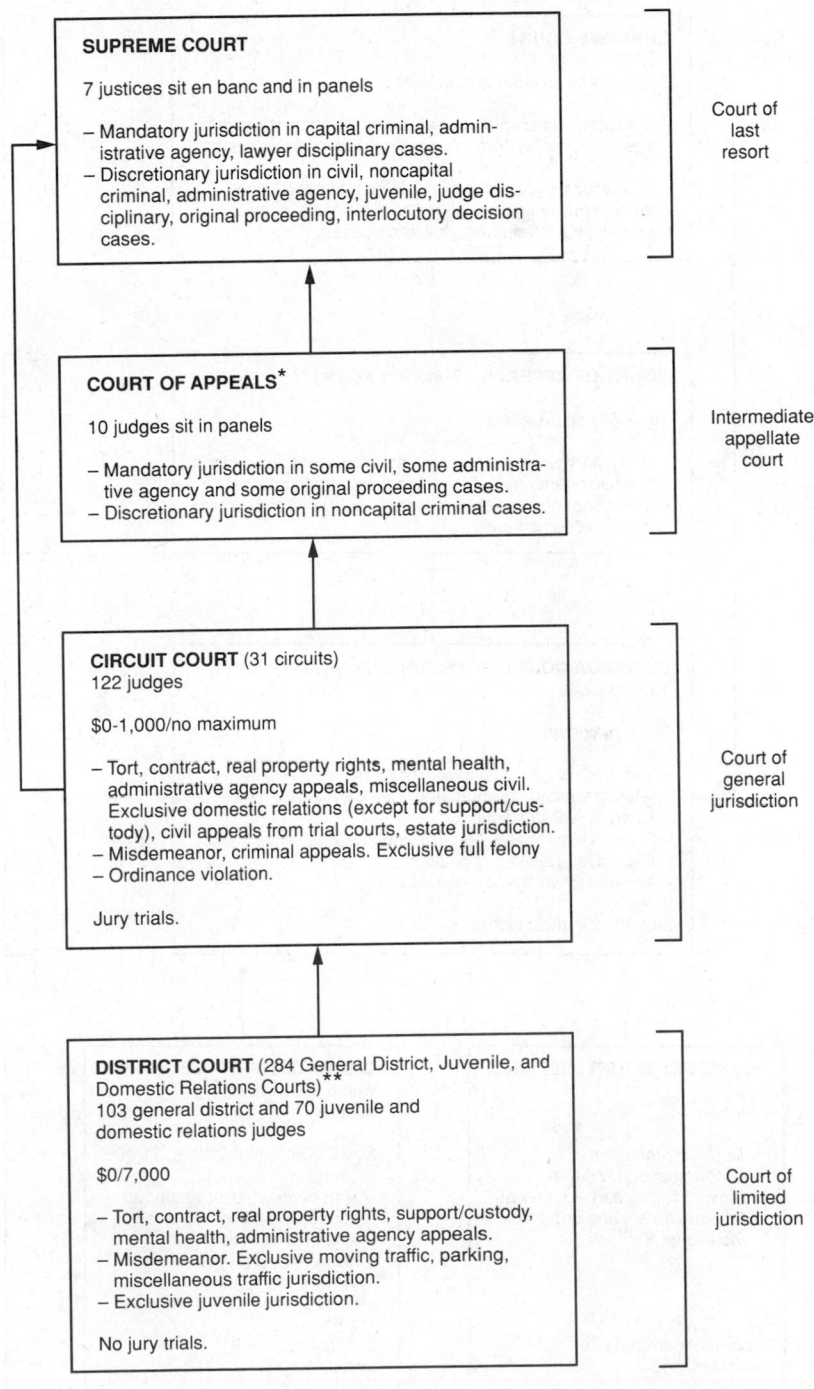

SUPREME COURT

7 justices sit en banc and in panels

— Mandatory jurisdiction in capital criminal, administrative agency, lawyer disciplinary cases.
— Discretionary jurisdiction in civil, noncapital criminal, administrative agency, juvenile, judge disciplinary, original proceeding, interlocutory decision cases.

Court of
last
resort

COURT OF APPEALS*

10 judges sit in panels

— Mandatory jurisdiction in some civil, some administrative agency and some original proceeding cases.
— Discretionary jurisdiction in noncapital criminal cases.

Intermediate
appellate
court

CIRCUIT COURT (31 circuits)
122 judges

$0-1,000/no maximum

— Tort, contract, real property rights, mental health, administrative agency appeals, miscellaneous civil. Exclusive domestic relations (except for support/custody), civil appeals from trial courts, estate jurisdiction.
— Misdemeanor, criminal appeals. Exclusive full felony
— Ordinance violation.

Jury trials.

Court of
general
jurisdiction

DISTRICT COURT (284 General District, Juvenile, and Domestic Relations Courts)**
103 general district and 70 juvenile and domestic relations judges

$0/7,000

— Tort, contract, real property rights, support/custody, mental health, administrative agency appeals.
— Misdemeanor. Exclusive moving traffic, parking, miscellaneous traffic jurisdiction.
— Exclusive juvenile jurisdiction.

No jury trials.

Court of
limited
jurisdiction

* The Virginia Court of Appeals, an intermediate appellate court, became effective January 1, 1985.
**The District Court is referred to as the Juvenile and Domestic Relations Court when hearing juvenile and domestic relations cases, and as the General District Court for the balance of the cases.

WASHINGTON COURT STRUCTURE, 1987

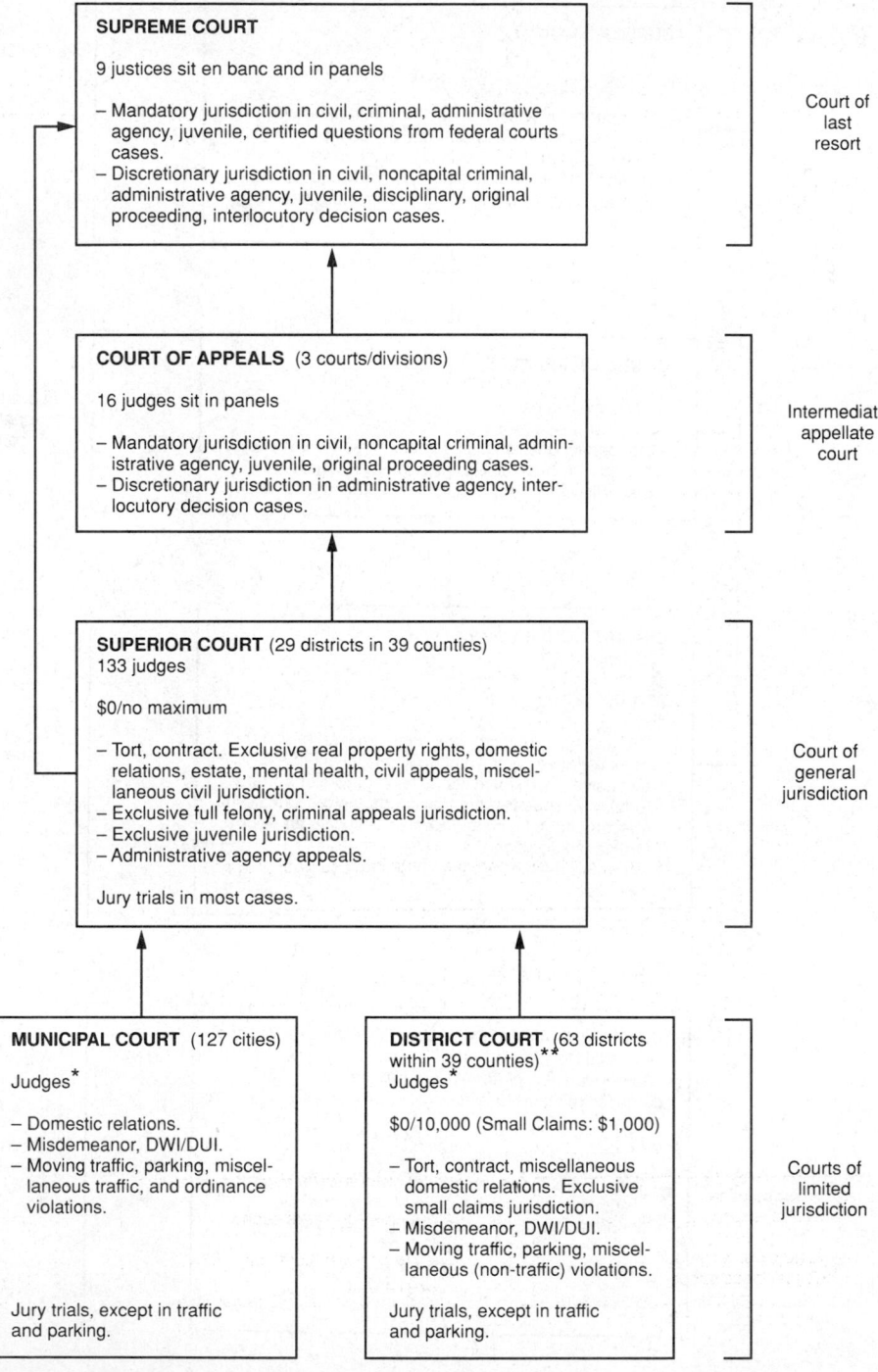

SUPREME COURT

9 justices sit en banc and in panels

– Mandatory jurisdiction in civil, criminal, administrative
agency, juvenile, certified questions from federal courts
cases.
– Discretionary jurisdiction in civil, noncapital criminal,
administrative agency, juvenile, disciplinary, original
proceeding, interlocutory decision cases.

Court of
last
resort

COURT OF APPEALS (3 courts/divisions)

16 judges sit in panels

– Mandatory jurisdiction in civil, noncapital criminal, administrative agency, juvenile, original proceeding cases.
– Discretionary jurisdiction in administrative agency, interlocutory decision cases.

Intermediate
appellate
court

SUPERIOR COURT (29 districts in 39 counties)
133 judges

$0/no maximum

– Tort, contract. Exclusive real property rights, domestic
relations, estate, mental health, civil appeals, miscel-
laneous civil jurisdiction.
– Exclusive full felony, criminal appeals jurisdiction.
– Exclusive juvenile jurisdiction.
– Administrative agency appeals.

Jury trials in most cases.

Court of
general
jurisdiction

MUNICIPAL COURT (127 cities)

Judges[*]

– Domestic relations.
– Misdemeanor, DWI/DUI.
– Moving traffic, parking, miscellaneous traffic, and ordinance
violations.

Jury trials, except in traffic
and parking.

DISTRICT COURT (63 districts
within 39 counties)[**]
Judges[*]

$0/10,000 (Small Claims: $1,000)

– Tort, contract, miscellaneous
domestic relations. Exclusive
small claims jurisdiction.
– Misdemeanor, DWI/DUI.
– Moving traffic, parking, miscellaneous (non-traffic) violations.

Jury trials, except in traffic
and parking.

Courts of
limited
jurisdiction

[*] There are 194 judges assigned to the Municipal Court and District Court:
169 are attorneys, 25 are non-attorneys; 79 are full-time, 82 are part-time.
[**] District Court provides services to municipalities that do not have a Municipal Court.

WEST VIRGINIA COURT STRUCTURE, 1987

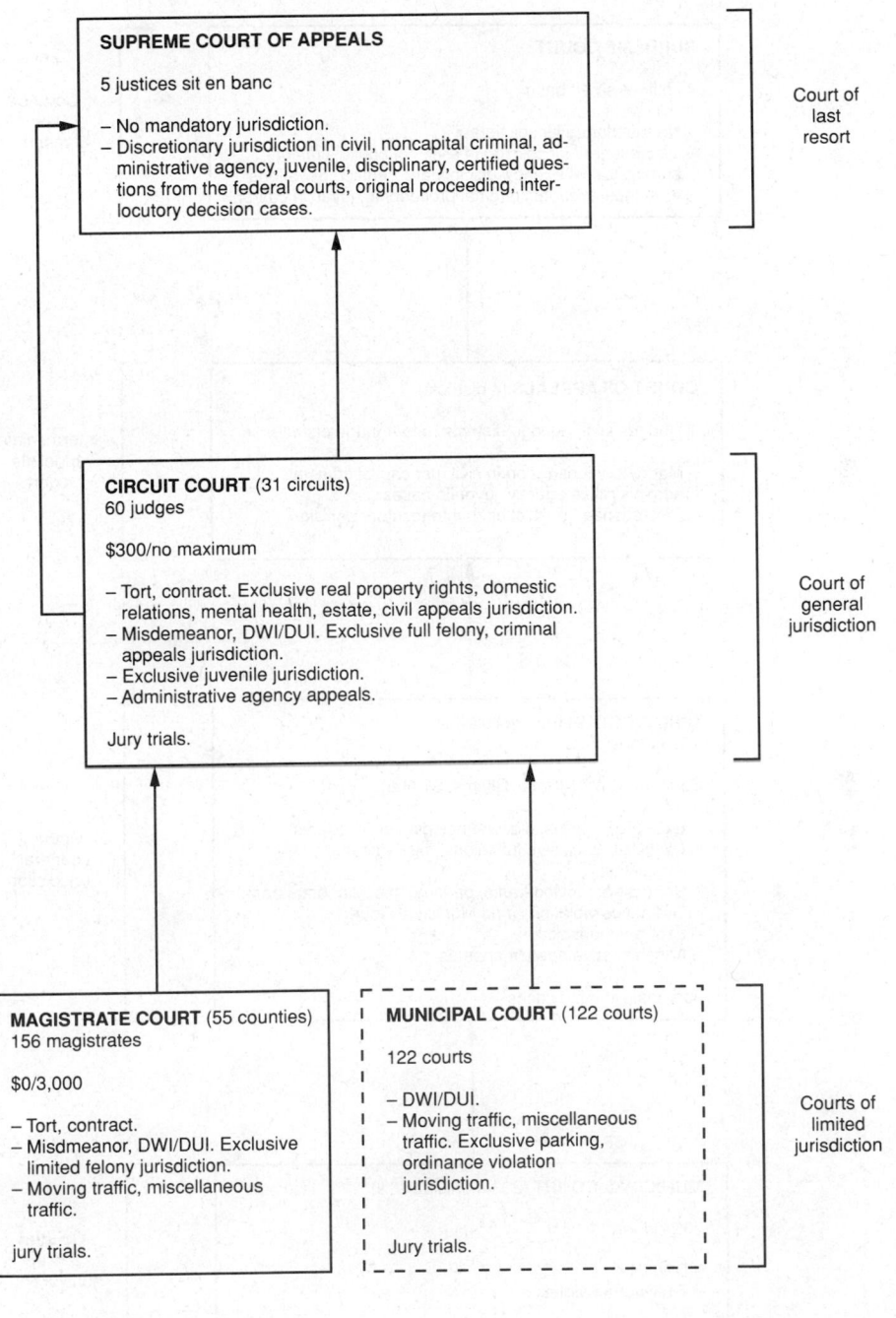

SUPREME COURT OF APPEALS

5 justices sit en banc

– No mandatory jurisdiction.
– Discretionary jurisdiction in civil, noncapital criminal, administrative agency, juvenile, disciplinary, certified questions from the federal courts, original proceeding, interlocutory decision cases.

Court of
last
resort

CIRCUIT COURT (31 circuits)
60 judges

$300/no maximum

– Tort, contract. Exclusive real property rights, domestic relations, mental health, estate, civil appeals jurisdiction.
– Misdemeanor, DWI/DUI. Exclusive full felony, criminal appeals jurisdiction.
– Exclusive juvenile jurisdiction.
– Administrative agency appeals.

Jury trials.

Court of
general
jurisdiction

MAGISTRATE COURT (55 counties)
156 magistrates

$0/3,000

– Tort, contract.
– Misdmeanor, DWI/DUI. Exclusive limited felony jurisdiction.
– Moving traffic, miscellaneous traffic.

jury trials.

MUNICIPAL COURT (122 courts)

122 courts

– DWI/DUI.
– Moving traffic, miscellaneous traffic. Exclusive parking, ordinance violation jurisdiction.

Jury trials.

Courts of
limited
jurisdiction

WISCONSIN COURT STRUCTURE, 1987

SUPREME COURT

7 justices sit en banc

– No mandatory jurisdiction.
– Discretionary jurisdiction in civil, noncapital criminal, administrative agency, disciplinary, certified questions from federal courts, original proceeding, juvenile cases.

Court of last resort

COURT OF APPEALS (4 districts)

13 judges sit in 3-judge districts (one 4-judge district)

– Mandatory jurisdiction in civil, noncapital criminal, administrative agency, juvenile cases.
– Discretionary jurisdiction in interlocutory decision cases.

Intermediate appellate court

CIRCUIT COURT (69 circuits)
197 judges

$0/no maximum (Small Claims: $1,000)

– Exclusive civil jurisdiction (including civil appeals).
– DWI/DUI. Exclusive full felony, misdemeanor jurisdiction.
– Contested: moving traffic, parking, miscellaneous traffic. Ordinance violations if no Municipal Court.
– Exclusive jurisdiction.
– Administrative agency appeals.

Jury trials in most cases.

Court of general jurisdiction

MUNICIPAL COURT (203 municipalities)

205 judges

– DWI/DUI.
– Traffic/other violation.

No jury trials.

Court of limited jurisdiction

WYOMING COURT STRUCTURE, 1987

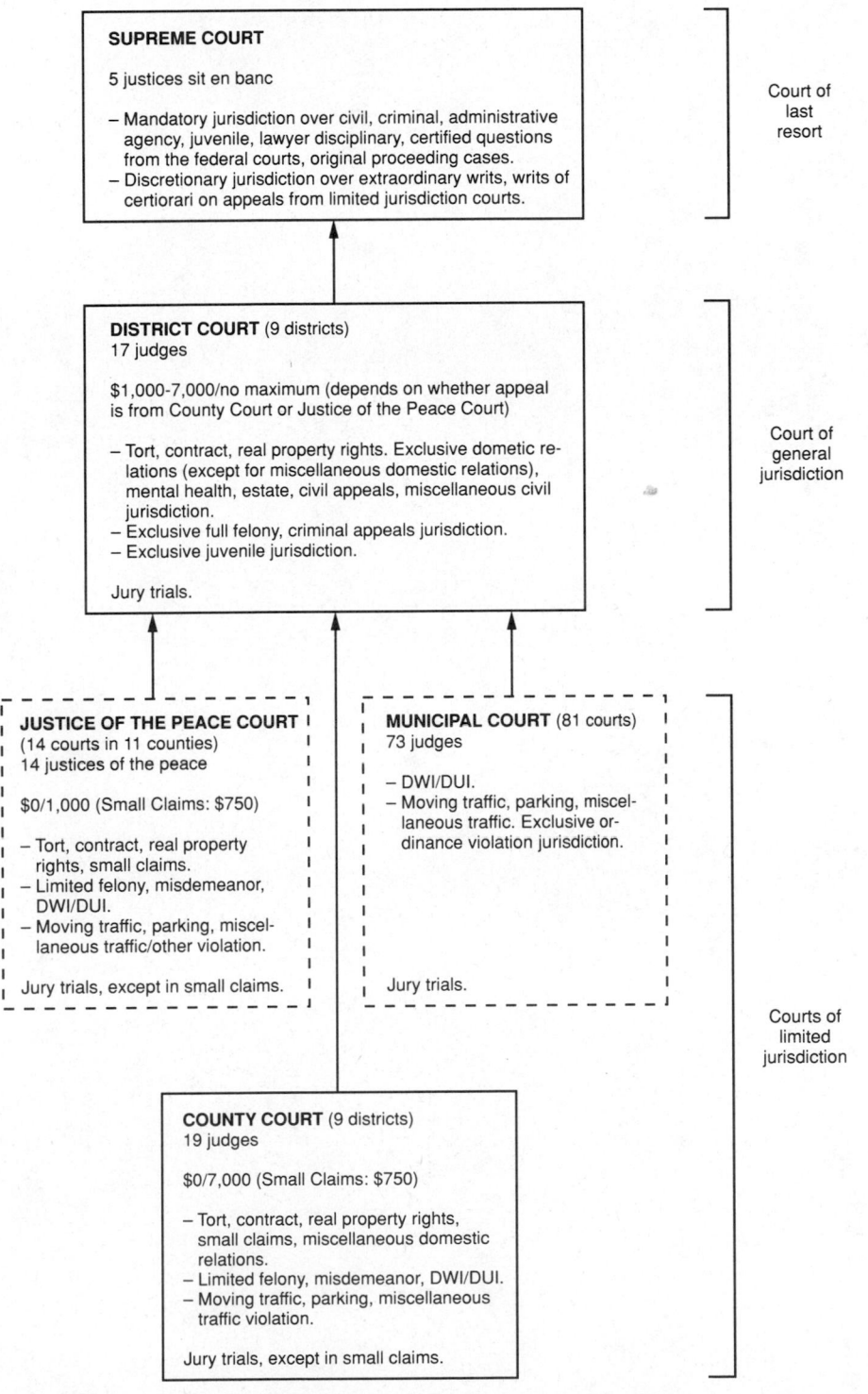

SUPREME COURT

5 justices sit en banc

– Mandatory jurisdiction over civil, criminal, administrative
  agency, juvenile, lawyer disciplinary, certified questions
  from the federal courts, original proceeding cases.
– Discretionary jurisdiction over extraordinary writs, writs of
  certiorari on appeals from limited jurisdiction courts.

Court of
last
resort

DISTRICT COURT (9 districts)
17 judges

$1,000-7,000/no maximum (depends on whether appeal
is from County Court or Justice of the Peace Court)

– Tort, contract, real property rights. Exclusive dometic relations (except for miscellaneous domestic relations),
  mental health, estate, civil appeals, miscellaneous civil
  jurisdiction.
– Exclusive full felony, criminal appeals jurisdiction.
– Exclusive juvenile jurisdiction.

Jury trials.

Court of
general
jurisdiction

JUSTICE OF THE PEACE COURT
(14 courts in 11 counties)
14 justices of the peace

$0/1,000 (Small Claims: $750)

– Tort, contract, real property
  rights, small claims.
– Limited felony, misdemeanor,
  DWI/DUI.
– Moving traffic, parking, miscel-
  laneous traffic/other violation.

Jury trials, except in small claims.

MUNICIPAL COURT (81 courts)
73 judges

– DWI/DUI.
– Moving traffic, parking, miscellaneous traffic. Exclusive ordinance violation jurisdiction.

Jury trials.

Courts of
limited
jurisdiction

COUNTY COURT (9 districts)
19 judges

$0/7,000 (Small Claims: $750)

– Tort, contract, real property rights,
  small claims, miscellaneous domestic
  relations.
– Limited felony, misdemeanor, DWI/DUI.
– Moving traffic, parking, miscellaneous
  traffic violation.

Jury trials, except in small claims.

Selected Federal Statutes

The following list contains the codified citation of selected Acts of Congress that are alphabetically listed by Popular Name. When Congress passes a statute, portions of it may go into several different titles of the United States Code and in potentially hundreds of different sections of these titles. We have *not* included all of these sections in the following list. Rather, you will find the first section number and the last section number for every title that contains portions of the Act. For a list of *every* section number, consult the Popular Name Table within the United States Code Annotated. The word "see" (when not providing a cross-reference) indicates that the Act has been repealed in whole or in part, but that certain provisions of the Act have been restated in the title and section following the word "see."

AAA Farm Relief and Inflation Act: 7 U.S.C.A. 601, 620; 12 U.S.C.A. 347, 1019; See 31 U.S.C.A. 5301, 5304.

Abacá Production Act of 1950: 50 U.S.C.A. 541, 546.

Abandoned Infants Assistance Act of 1988: 42 U.S.C.A. 670 note.

Abandoned Military Reservations Acts: 43 U.S.C.A. 1073.

Abandoned Shipwreck Act of 1987: 43 U.S.C.A. 2101, 2106.

Able Seamen Act: 46 U.S.C.A. 672-2.

Academic Research Facilities Modernization Act of 1988: 42 U.S.C.A. 1862a, 1862d.

Accident Reports Acts (Railroads): 45 U.S.C.A. 32, 43.

Accounting and Auditing Act of 1950: See 31 U.S.C.A. 713, 3524.

Accounting Simplification Acts (Meter Readings): See 31 U.S.C.A. 1308.

Acid Precipitation Act of 1980: 42 U.S.C.A. 8901, 8912.

Acid Transportation Act (Carriage by Sea): See 18 U.S.C.A. 2278.

Ackia Battleground National Monument Act: 16 U.S.C.A. 450r, 450t.

Act for the Prevention and Punishment of Crimes Against Internationally Protected Persons: 18 U.S.C.A. 11, 1201.

Act for the Prevention and Punishment of the Crime of Hostage-Taking: 18 U.S.C.A. 1203.

Act to Authorize the United States to Participate in Chapter II of the Patent Cooperation Treaty: 35 U.S.C.A. 351, 376.

Act to Prevent Pollution from Ships: 16 U.S.C.A. 742c; 33 U.S.C.A. 1001, 1912; see 46 U.S.C.A. 3301, 3702.

Adjustment Act (Irrigation Projects): 43 U.S.C.A. 423, 423g.

Adjustment Act (Railroad Land Grants): 43 U.S.C.A. 894, 899.

Administrative Assistants Acts (Executive Departments): 3 U.S.C.A. 106.

Administrative Conference Act: 5 U.S.C.A. 575, 576; see 5 U.S.C.A. 571, 576.

Administrative Expenses Act of 1946: See 5

U.S.C.A. 302, 7903; 19 U.S.C.A. 1645; 22 U.S.C.A. 287o, 287q; see 28 U.S.C.A. 1823; see 31 U.S.C.A. 1343, 3324; 41 U.S.C.A. 5, 5a; 44 U.S.C.A. 321.

Administrative Orders Review Act: See 28 U.S.C.A. 41, 2352.

Administrative Procedure Act: 5 U.S.C.A. 551, 7521.

Admiralty Act: 46 U.S.C.A. 743, 752.

Admiralty Bond Act: See 28 U.S.C.A. 2464.

Admiralty Interlocutory Decrees Appeals Act: 28 U.S.C.A. 1292, 2107.

Admiralty Jurisdiction Act (Extension): 46 U.S.C.A. 740.

Admiralty Rules Enabling Act: 28 U.S.C.A. 2073.

Adoption Assistance and Child Welfare Act of 1980: 26 U.S.C.A. 50B; 42 U.S.C.A. 602, 1397d.

Adult Education Act: 20 U.S.C.A. 1201,1213.

Adult Education Amendments of 1988: 20 U.S.C.A. 1201, 1213d.

Adult Indian Vocational Training Act: 25 U.S.C.A. 309, 309a.

Adulterated Seeds Act: See 7 U.S.C.A. 1581, 1596.

Advance Pay and Allotment Act of 1961: See 5 U.S.C.A. 5521, 5527.

Advertising Act (Public Purchases): 41 U.S.C.A. 5.

Advisory Commission on Intergovernmental Relations Act of 1959: 42 U.S.C.A. 4271, 4279.

Advisory Committee on Intergovernmental Relations Act of 1959: 42 U.S.C.A. 4271, 4279.

African Development Bank Act: 12 U.S.C.A. 24; 22 U.S.C.A. 290d, 290i-9.

African Development Foundation Act: 22 U.S.C.A. 290h, 290h-9.

African Development Fund Act: 22 U.S.C.A. 290g, 290g-14.

African Elephant Conservation Act: 16 U.S.C.A. 1538, 4245.

African Famine Relief and Recovery Act of 1985: 22 U.S.C.A. 2292q.

Age Discrimination Act of 1975: 42 U.S.C.A. 6101, 6107.

Age Discrimination in Employment Act of 1967: 29 U.S.C.A. 621, 634.

Age Discrimination in Employment Act Amendments of 1978: 5 U.S.C.A. 8335, 8339; 29 U.S.C.A. 623, 634.

Age Discrimination in Employment Amendments of 1986: 29 U.S.C.A. 623, 631.

Agricultural Act of 1948: 7 U.S.C.A. 602, 1385; 15 U.S.C.A. 713a-8 note; 16 U.S.C.A. 590h.

Agricultural Act of 1949: 7 U.S.C.A. 397; 1471e; 12 U.S.C.A. 1134c, 1134j; 15 U.S.C.A. 713a-4; see 26 U.S.C.A. 3121, 7701; 42 U.S.C.A. 410.

Agricultural Act of 1954: 7 U.S.C.A. 397, 1769.

Agricultural Act of 1956: 7 U.S.C.A. 1301, 1860; 16 U.S.C.A. 568e, 568g.

Agricultural Act of 1958: 7 U.S.C.A. 1313, 1784.

Agricultural Act of 1961: 5 U.S.C.A. 577; 7 U.S.C.A. 602, 1990; 16 U.S.C.A. 590p.

Agricultural Act of 1964: 7 U.S.C.A. 1301, 1445a.

Agricultural Act of 1970: 7 U.S.C.A. 428b, 2654; 16 U.S.C.A. 590p, 1510; 42 U.S.C.A. 3122.

Agricultural Act of 1980: 7 U.S.C.A. 4004.

Agricultural Adjustment Act: 7 U.S.C.A. 601, 624; 19 U.S.C.A. 2112 note.

Agricultural Adjustment Act of 1937: 7 U.S.C.A. 601, 674.

Agricultural Adjustment Act of 1938: 7 U.S.C.A. 608c, 1519; 16 U.S.C.A. 590h, 590p.

Agricultural Adjustment Act of 1980: 7 U.S.C.A. 1308, 1445b.

Agricultural Aid and Trade Missions Act: 7 U.S.C.A. 1726, 1736bb-6.

Agricultural and Mechanical Colleges Acts: 7 U.S.C.A. 301, 329.

Agricultural Competitiveness and Trade Act of 1988: 7 U.S.C.A. 608c, 5235; 16 U.S.C.A. 2112; 21 U.S.C.A. 620, 1403.

Agricultural Credit Act of 1978: 7 U.S.C.A. 1309, 2908; 16 U.S.C.A. 2201, 2205.

Agricultural Credit Act of 1987: 7 U.S.C.A. 1927, 5106; 12 U.S.C.A. 393, 5103; 16 U.S.C.A. 3835; 31 U.S.C.A. 9105.

Agricultural Credit Corporations Act: 12 U.S.C.A. 1401, 1404.

Agricultural Credit Technical Corrections Act of 1988: 7 U.S.C.A. 1988, 5103; 12 U.S.C.A. 2001, 2279aa-12; 31 U.S.C.A. 9105.

Agricultural Credits Act of 1923: 12 U.S.C.A. 10, 1322.

Agricultural Enabling Amendments Act of 1961: 7 U.S.C.A. 602, 1913; 16 U.S.C.A. 590p.

Agricultural Entry Acts: 30 U.S.C.A. 121, 124.

Agricultural Experiment Stations Acts: 7 U.S.C.A. 361a, 361i.

Agricultural Extension Work Acts: 7 U.S.C.A. 341, 349.

Agricultural Fair Practices Act of 1967: 7 U.S.C.A. 2301, 2306.

Agricultural Foreign Investment Disclosure Act of 1978: 7 U.S.C.A. 3501, 3508.

Agricultural Marketing Act: 12 U.S.C.A. 1141, 1141j.

Agricultural Marketing Act of 1946: 7 U.S.C.A. 1621, 1627.

Agricultural Marketing Agreement Act of 1937: 7 U.S.C.A. 601; 674.

Agricultural Programs Adjustment Act of 1984: 7 U.S.C.A. 1431, 1994.

Agricultural Reconciliation Act of 1987: 7 U.S.C.A. 608c, 2371; 15 U.S.C.A. 713a-11; 42 U.S.C.A. 7545 note.

Agricultural Research Act: 7 U.S.C.A. 329; see 7 U.S.C.A. 341, 348; see, also, 7 U.S.C.A. 341, 348.

Agricultural Subterminal Facilities Act of 1980: 7 U.S.C.A. 1932, 3703.

Agricultural Trade Act of 1978: 5 U.S.C.A. 5314; 7 U.S.C.A. 612c-3, 2211a; 19 U.S.C.A. 2431 note.

Agricultural Trade and Export Policy Commission Act: 7 U.S.C.A. 1691 note.

Agricultural Trade Development and Assistance Act of 1954: 7 U.S.C.A. 1427, 1736g.

Agricultural Trade Suspension Adjustment Act of 1980: 7 U.S.C.A. 1444c, 4005; 15 U.S.C.A. 714c note.

Agriculture and Consumer Protection Act of 1973: 7 U.S.C.A. 428b, 2654; 13 U.S.C.A. 142 note; 16 U.S.C.A. 1501, 1510; 45 U.S.C.A. 71 note.

Agriculture and Food Act of 1981: 5 U.S.C.A. 5315; 7 U.S.C.A. 79, 4319; 15 U.S.C.A. 714b, 16 U.S.C.A. 582a, 3473; 21 U.S.C.A. 620; 30 U.S.C.A. 1236; 40 U.S.C.A. 483; 42 U.S.C.A. 6651, 8852.

Agriculture and Related Agencies Appropriation Act, 1978: 7 U.S.C.A. 411b, 2254; 15 U.S.C.A. 713a-10; 16 U.S.C.A. 590e-1, 590e-2; 21 U.S.C.A. 129.

Agriculture-Environmental and Consumer Protection Appropriation Act, 1975: 7 U.S.C.A. 411b, 2254; 15 U.S.C.A. 713a-10; 16 U.S.C.A. 590e-1, 590e-2; 21 U.S.C.A. 129.

Agriculture Regulatory Act: 7 U.S.C.A. 450c, 450g.

Agriculture, Rural Development, and Related Agencies Appropriations Act, 1987: 7 U.S.C.A. 411b, 2254; 15 U.S.C.A. 638 note; 16 U.S.C.A. 590e-1, 3831; 20 U.S.C.A. 191 note; 21 U.S.C.A. 129; 42 U.S.C.A. 1776a, 1776b.

Aid to American Republics Act: 22 U.S.C.A. 521, 527.

Aider and Abettor Act: 18 U.S.C.A. 2.

AIDS Amendments of 1988: 42 U.S.C.A. 242c, 300aaa-13.

Air Brakes Act (Railroads): 45 U.S.C.A. 9.

Air Carrier Access Act of 1986: 49 U.S.C.A. 1374.

Air Carrier Economic Regulation Act: 49 U.S.C.A. 481, 496.

Air Commerce Act of 1926: 15 U.S.C.A. 1505 note; 49 U.S.C.A. 171, 184.

Air Engineering Development Center Act of 1949: 50 U.S.C.A. 521, 524.

Air Force Academy Act: 10 U.S.C.A. 9331 note; see 10 U.S.C.A. 541, 9331.

Air Force Headquarters Act: See 10 U.S.C.A. 3961, 3991.

Air Mail Acts: See 39 U.S.C.A. 5401.

Air Pollution Control Act: 42 U.S.C.A. 1857, 1857g.

Air Quality Act of 1967: 42 U.S.C.A. 1857, 1857*l*.

Air Safety Board Act: 49 U.S.C.A. 581, 582.

Air Transportation Security Act of 1974: 49 U.S.C.A. 1301, 1516.

Aircraft Development Act: 50 U.S.C.A. 95.

Aircraft Parts Secrecy Act: See 10 U.S.C.A. 2301, 2305.

Aircraft Prize Act: See 10 U.S.C.A. 7651.

Aircraft Registration Act: 49 U.S.C.A. 521, 524.

Aircraft Sabotage Act: 18 U.S.C.A. 31, 32; 49 U.S.C.A. 1301, 1472.

Airline Deregulation Act of 1978: 49 U.S.C.A. 334, 1729.

Airport and Airway Development Act of 1970: 49 U.S.C.A. 1701, 1741; see 49 U.S.C.A. 322, 1741.

Airport and Airway Development Act Amendments of 1976: 49 U.S.C.A. 1356a; see 49 U.S.C.A. 332, 1742.

Airport and Airway Improvement Act of 1982: 49 U.S.C.A. 1349, 2225; 49 App. U.S.C.A. 2101, 2227; 50 App. U.S.C.A. 1622.

Airport and Airway Revenue Act of 1970: 4 U.S.C.A. 104 note; 23 U.S.C.A. 120 note; 26 U.S.C.A. 39, 7605; 49 U.S.C.A. 1742.

Airport and Airway Revenue Act of 1987: 26 U.S.C.A. 4041, 9502.

Airport and Airway Safety and Capacity Expansion Act of 1987: 23 U.S.C.A. 401 notes; 26 U.S.C.A. 4041, 9502; 49 U.S.C.A. 334; 49 App. U.S.C.A. 1301, 2227.

Airport Development Acceleration Act of 1973: 49 U.S.C.A. 1513, 1717.

Airports Acts: 16 U.S.C.A. 7a, 7e; 49 U.S.C.A. 211, 1108.

Alaska Agricultural Experiment Stations Acts: See 7 U.S.C.A. 341, 361a.

Alaska Communications Disposal Act: 40 U.S.C.A. 771, 792.

Alaska Federal-Civilian Energy Efficiency Swap Act of 1980: 40 U.S.C.A. 795, 795d.

Alaska Fur Farming Act: 43 U.S.C.A. 687c, 687c-1.

Alaska Hydroelectric Power Development Act: 42 U.S.C.A. 1962d-14a.

Alaska Livestock Grazing Act: 43 U.S.C.A. 316, 316*o*.

Alaska Mental Health Enabling Act: 42 U.S.C.A. 273, 274.

Alaska National Interest Lands Conservation Act: 10 U.S.C.A. 3148; 16 U.S.C.A. 410hh, 3233; 43 U.S.C.A. 1602, 1784.

Alaska Native Claims Settlement Act: 26 U.S.C.A. 1620; 30 U.S.C.A. 1702; 43 U.S.C.A. 1601, 1629e.

Alaska Native Claims Settlement Act Amendments of 1987: 15 U.S.C.A. 78m; 30 U.S.C.A. 1702; 43 U.S.C.A. 1602, 1636.

Alaska Natural Gas Transportation Act of 1976: 15 U.S.C.A. 719, 719*o*; 43 U.S.C.A. 1651 note.

Alaska Omnibus Act: 1 U.S.C.A. 1 note; 7 U.S.C.A. 101, 1837; 10 U.S.C.A. 101, 2662; 12 U.S.C.A. 144, 1748e; 14 U.S.C.A. 634; 15 U.S.C.A. 77b, 80b-2; 16 U.S.C.A. 590h, 777k; 18 U.S.C.A. 1385, 5024; See Popular Name Table for other titles.

Alaska Railroad Acts: 16 U.S.C.A. 353a.

Alaska Railroad Transfer Act of 1982: 5 U.S.C.A. 305, 7327; 16 U.S.C.A. 353a, 410hh-1; 30 U.S.C.A. 208a; 42 U.S.C.A. 251; 43 U.S.C.A. 975, 975g; 45 U.S.C.A. 231, 1214; 48 U.S.C.A. 301a; 49 U.S.C.A. 1655, 10749.

Alaska Statehood Bill: 48 U.S.C.A. note prec. 21.

Alcohol Abuse, Drug Abuse, and Mental Health Amendments of 1984: 21 U.S.C.A. 802, 1165; 42 U.S.C.A. 218, 300x-9.

Alcohol and Drug Abuse Amendments of 1983: 21 U.S.C.A. 1117, 1194; 42 U.S.C.A. 218, 4856.

Alcohol and Drug Abuse Amendments of 1986: 21 U.S.C.A. 331, 350a; 42 U.S.C.A. 218, 300y-2.

Alcohol and Drug Abuse Education Act: 21 U.S.C.A. 1001, 1007.

Alcohol and Drug Abuse Education Act Amendments of 1974: 21 U.S.C.A. 1001, 1007.

Alcohol and Drug Abuse Education Amendments of 1978: 20 U.S.C.A. 1070e-1; 21 U.S.C.A. 1001, 1007; 38 U.S.C.A. 246.

Alcohol Plants Transfer Act: 7 U.S.C.A. 439, 439e.

Alcoholic and Narcotic Addict Rehabilitation Amendments of 1968: 42 U.S.C.A. 2688e, 2697a.

Alcoholic Beverage Labeling Act of 1988: 27 U.S.C.A. 213, 219a.

Alcoholic Rehabilitation Act of 1968: 42 U.S.C.A. 2688e; 2688j.

Aldrich Act (Currency): 12 U.S.C.A. 90, 178.

Aldrich-Vreeland Act (National Currency Associations): 12 U.S.C.A. 104.

Aleutian and Pribilof Islands Restitution Act: 50 App. U.S.C.A. 1989c, 1989c-8.

Alien Registration Act, 1940: See 8 U.S.C.A. 1101, 1351; 18 U.S.C.A. 2385, 2387.

Aliens' Real Estate Ownership Acts (Territories): 48 U.S.C.A. 1501, 1508.

All Writs Act: See 28 U.S.C.A. 1651.

Allied Health Professions Personnel Training Act of 1966: 12 U.S.C.A. 1717; 42 U.S.C.A. 293e, 298c-8.

Alternative Mortgage Transaction Parity Act of 1982: 12 U.S.C.A. 3801, 3805.

Alternative Motor Fuels Act of 1988: 15 U.S.C.A. 2001, 2013; 42 U.S.C.A. 6374, 6374d.

Alzheimer's Disease and Related Dementias Services Research Act of 1986: 42 U.S.C.A. 11201, 11294.

Amateur Sports Act of 1978: 36 U.S.C.A. 371, 396.

Amendments of 1973 to Federal Law Relating to Explosives: 18 U.S.C.A. 845, 921.

American Aid to Poland Act of 1988: 7 U.S.C.A. 1431.

American Fire Act: 46 U.S.C.A. 182.

American Fisheries Promotion Act: 15 U.S.C.A. 713c-3, 1511b; 16 U.S.C.A. 917, 1855; 22 U.S.C.A. 1972, 1980; 33 U.S.C.A. 1321; 43 U.S.C.A. 1843; 46 U.S.C.A. 1271, 1275.

American Folklife Preservation Act: 20 U.S.C.A. 2101, 2107.

American Heart Month Act: 36 U.S.C.A. 169b.

American Indian, Alaska Native, and Native Hawaiian Culture and Art Development Act: 20 U.S.C.A. 4401, 4451.

American Indian Religious Freedom Act: 42 U.S.C.A. 1996.

American Legion Acts: 36 U.S.C.A. 41, 51.

American-Mexican Boundary Treaty Act of 1972: 19 U.S.C.A. 1322; 22 U.S.C.A. 277d-34, 277d-42.

American-Mexican Chamical Convention Act of 1964: 22 U.S.C.A. 277d-17, 277d-25.

American-Mexican Treaty Act of 1950: 22 U.S.C.A. 277d-1, 277d-9.

American National Red Cross Acts: See, also, 18 U.S.C.A. 1, 917; 36 U.S.C.A. 1, 9.

American National Red Cross Headquarters Act: 36 U.S.C.A. 13.

American Samoa Labor Standards Amendments of 1956: 29 U.S.C.A. 206, 216.

American Society of International Law Incorporation Act: 36 U.S.C.A. 341, 352.

American Television and Radio Archives Act: 2 U.S.C.A. 170.

American War Mothers Incorporation Act: 36 U.S.C.A. 91, 104.

Amtrak Improvement Act of 1974: 5 U.S.C.A. 5313; 26 U.S.C.A. 250; 45 U.S.C.A. 544, 644; See 49 U.S.C.A. 102, 1653.

Amtrak Reauthorization Act of 1985: 45 U.S.C.A. 502, 1111; 49 U.S.C.A. 1654.

Amtrak Reorganization Act of 1979: 45 U.S.C.A. 501, 650; 49 App. U.S.C.A. 1653.

Amvets Incorporation Act: 36 U.S.C.A. 67, 67s.

Anadromous Fish Conservation Act: 16 U.S.C.A. 757a, 757g.

Anarchist Exclusion Acts: See 8 U.S.C.A. 1182.

Anchorage Grounds Act: 33 U.S.C.A. 472.

Animal Cancer Research Act: 7 U.S.C.A. 3901, 3904.

Animal Drug Amendments of 1968: 21 U.S.C.A. 321, 392.

Animal Industry Act: 7 U.S.C.A. 391; 21 U.S.C.A. 112, 130.

Animal Virus, Serum, Toxin, Antitoxin Act: 21 U.S.C.A. 151, 158.

Animal Welfare Act: 7 U.S.C.A. 2131, 2157; 39 U.S.C.A. 3001.

Annual and Sick Leave Act of 1951: See 5 U.S.C.A. 5508, 6311.

Antarctic Conservative Act of 1978: 16 U.S.C.A. 2401, 2412; 22 U.S.C.A. 1971.

Antarctic Marine Living Resources Convention Act of 1984: 16 U.S.C.A. 2431, 2444.

Anthracite Mine Water Control Act: 30 U.S.C.A. 571, 576.

Anthropological Research Act: 20 U.S.C.A. 69, 70.

Anti-Assignment Act: See 31 U.S.C.A. 3727.

Anti-Deficiency Act: See 31 U.S.C.A. 1341, 1519.

Anti-Drug Abuse Act of 1988: 5 U.S.C.A. 4501, 5315; 8 U.S.C.A. 1101, 1254; 10 U.S.C.A. 9441 note; 12 U.S.C.A. 635, 3420; 14 U.S.C.A. 2, 637; 15 U.S.C.A. 1245, 2057a; 16 U.S.C.A. 559c, 559g; 18 U.S.C.A. 13, 6003; 18 App. U.S.C.A. 9, 14. See Popular Name Table for other titles.

Anti-Drug Abuse Amendments Act of 1988: 5 U.S.C.A. 5315 note, 5541 note; 12 U.S.C.A. 1730d, 3420; 15 U.S.C.A. 1245; 16 U.S.C.A. 559, 559g. See Popular Name Table for other titles.

Anti-Dumping Act, 1921: 19 U.S.C.A. 160, 171.

Anti-Heroin Act: 21 U.S.C.A. 173.

Anti-Hijacking Act of 1974: 49 U.S.C.A. 1301, 1515.

Anti-Immunity Act (Trusts and Interstate Commerce): 49 U.S.C.A. 48.

Anti-Injunction Law: 29 U.S.C.A. 101, 115.

Anti-Kickback Acts: 40 U.S.C.A. 276b, 276c; 41 U.S.C.A. 51, 54.

Anti-Lobbying Act: See 18 U.S.C.A. 1913.

Anti-Merger Act: 15 U.S.C.A. 18, 21.

Anti-Moiety Act (Informers): 19 U.S.C.A. 494, 537.

Anti-Pass Acts: See 49 U.S.C.A. 10102, 11916.

Anti-Peonage Act: See, also, 18 U.S.C.A. 1581; 42 U.S.C.A. 1994.

Antiquities Act of 1906: 16 U.S.C.A. 431, 433.

Anti-Racketeering Act: 15 U.S.C.A. 17 note; see 18 U.S.C.A. 1951; 29 U.S.C.A. 52, 101.

Anti-Rebate Act (Railroads): See 49 U.S.C.A. 11703, 11916.

Anti-Reviver Act (Repeals): 1 U.S.C.A. 108.

Anti-Secrecy Act (Departmental Information): See 5 U.S.C.A. 301.

Anti-Smuggling Act: See 14 U.S.C.A. 638; 19 U.S.C.A. 170, 1711; 46 U.S.C.A. 60, 325.

Anti-Strikebreaking Act: See 18 U.S.C.A. 1231.

Anti-Subversive Activities Act: See 18 U.S.C.A. 2386.

Anti-Terrorism Act of 1987: 22 U.S.C.A. 5201, 5203.

Antitrust Acts: 15 U.S.C.A. 1, 27; see 18 U.S.C.A. 402, 3691; 29 U.S.C.A. 52, 53.

Antitrust Civil Process Act: 15 U.S.C.A. 1311, 1314; 18 U.S.C.A. 1505.

Antitrust Procedural Improvements Act of 1980: 15 U.S.C.A. 15, 1314; 18 U.S.C.A. 1905; 28 U.S.C.A. 1927.

Antitrust Procedures and Penalties Act: 15 U.S.C.A. 1, 29; 47 U.S.C.A. 401; see 49 U.S.C.A. 11703.

Appalachian Regional Development Act of 1965: 40 U.S.C.A. 461; 40 App. U.S.C.A. 1, 405.

Appalachian Regional Development Act Amendments of 1967: 5 U.S.C.A. 5334; 40 U.S.C.A. 461; 40 App. U.S.C.A. 102, 403; 42 U.S.C.A. 3183, 3204.

Apportionment Acts: 2 U.S.C.A. 2a, 5; see 13 U.S.C.A. 2, 214; 42 U.S.C.A. 244a.

Arbitration: 9 U.S.C.A. 1, 208.

Archaeological Resources Protection Act of 1979: 16 U.S.C.A. 470aa, 470mm.

Architectural Barriers Act of 1968: 42 U.S.C.A. 4151, 4157.

Arctic Research and Policy Act of 1984: 15 U.S.C.A. 4101, 4111.

Area Redevelopment Act: 15 U.S.C.A. 696; 40 U.S.C.A. 461; 42 U.S.C.A. 1464, 2525.

Arid Land Act: 43 U.S.C.A. 662.

Arizona-Idaho Conservation Act of 1988: 16 U.S.C.A. 460xx, 460zz-11; 25 U.S.C.A. 640d-11, 640d-31; 40 U.S.C.A. 188a, 188c-1.

Arizona Wilderness Act of 1984: 16 U.S.C.A. 1274.

Armed Career Criminal Act of 1984: 18 App. U.S.C.A. 1201, 1202.

Armed Forces: 10 U.S.C.A. 1, 9842.

Armed Forces Damages Settlement Act: See 10 U.S.C.A. 2734, 2735.

Armed Forces Enlisted Personnel Bonus Revision Act of 1974: 37 U.S.C.A. 308, 308a.

Armed Forces Leave Act of 1946: See 37 U.S.C.A. 501.

Armed Services Procurement Act of 1947: See 10 U.S.C.A. 2202, 2383.

Armistice Day Act: See 5 U.S.C.A. 6103.

Arms Control and Disarmament Act: 22 U.S.C.A. 2551, 2593.

Arms Export Control Act: 22 U.S.C.A. 2344, 2796c.

Army Air Base Act: See 10 U.S.C.A. 9773, 9774.

Army Experimental Test Act: 50 U.S.C.A. 89.

Army-Foreign Service Act: See 10 U.S.C.A. 3544, 8544.

Army Medical Department Act: See 10 U.S.C.A. 3298, 8302.

Army Nurse and Medical Specialist Act of 1957: 10 U.S.C.A. 3069, 3991.

Army Organization Act of 1950: 10 U.S.C.A. 101, 4532; see 10 U.S.C.A. 3067, 3210.

Army Promotion Act: See 10 U.S.C.A. 3294, 8991.

Arrest Facilitation Act: See 18 U.S.C.A. 752, 3187.

Arthritis, Diabetes, and Digestive Disease Amendments of 1976: 42 U.S.C.A. 289c-2, 289c-8.

Arts and Artifacts Indemnity Act: 20 U.S.C.A. 971, 977.

Arts and Humanities Act of 1980: 20 U.S.C.A. 952, 3473.

Arts, Humanities, and Cultural Affairs Act of 1976: 20 U.S.C.A. 954, 1867.

Arts, Humanities, and Museums Amendments of 1985: 2 U.S.C.A. 177; 20 U.S.C.A. 951, 974.

Arts in Education Act of 1978: 20 U.S.C.A. 2961, 2963.

Asbestos Hazard Emergency Response Act of 1986: 15 U.S.C.A. 2614, 2654; 20 U.S.C.A. 4014, 4022.

Asbestos School Hazard Abatement Act of 1984: 20 U.S.C.A. 4011, 4021.

Asbestos School Hazard Detection and Control Act of 1980: 20 U.S.C.A. 1411, 3611.

Ash Pan Act (Railroads): 45 U.S.C.A. 17, 21.

Ashurst-Sumners Act: See 4 U.S.C.A. 111.

Asia Foundation Act, The: 22 U.S.C.A. 4401, 4403.

Asian Development Bank Act: 22 U.S.C.A. 285, 285x.

Asset Forfeiture Amendments Act of 1988: 19 U.S.C.A. 1954; 21 U.S.C.A. 801, 1509; 28 U.S.C.A. 524; 49 App. U.S.C.A. 782.

Assignment of Claims Act of 1940: 15 U.S.C.A. 203; see 31 U.S.C.A. 3727; 41 U.S.C.A. 15.

Assimilative Crimes Statute: See 18 U.S.C.A. 13.

Atlantic Salmon Convention Act of 1982: 16 U.S.C.A. 3601, 3608.

Atlantic Striped Bass Conservation Act: 16 U.S.C.A. 757g.

Atlantic Tunas Convention Act of 1975: 16 U.S.C.A. 971, 971h.

Atomic Energy Act of 1954: 42 U.S.C.A. 2011, 2286i.

Atomic Energy Community Act of 1955: 12 U.S.C.A. 1715n; 20 U.S.C.A. 243; 42 U.S.C.A. 2301, 2394.

Atomic Energy Damages Act: 42 U.S.C.A. 2012, 2239.

Atomic Weapons and Special Nuclear Materials Rewards Act: 40 U.S.C.A. 47a, 47e.

Atomic Weapons Rewards Act of 1955: 50 U.S.C.A. 47a, 47f.

Augustus F. Hawkins-Robert T. Stafford Elementary and Secondary School Improvement Amendments of 1988: 5 U.S.C.A. 5315; 20 U.S.C.A. 236, 4909; 25 U.S.C.A. 13d-2, 2651; 42 U.S.C.A. 9833, 11421; 47 U.S.C.A. 223.

Automatic Coupler Act (Interstate Commerce): 45 U.S.C.A. 1, 7.

Automobile Dealers' Day in Court Act: 15 U.S.C.A. 1221, 1225.

Automobile Fuel Efficiency Act of 1980: 15 U.S.C.A. 1901, 2012.

Automobile Information Disclosure Act: 15 U.S.C.A. 1231, 1233.

Automobile Tax Act: See 26 U.S.C.A. 4061, 6416 (c).

Automobile Products Trade Act of 1965: 19 U.S.C.A. 1202, 2033.

Automotive Propulsion Research and Development Act of 1978: 15 U.S.C.A. 2701, 2710; 42 U.S.C.A. 2451.

Aviation Career Incentive Act of 1974: 37 U.S.C.A. 301, 301a.

Aviation Day Act: 36 U.S.C.A. 151.

Aviation Drug-Trafficking Control Act: 49 U.S.C.A. 1401, 1903.

Aviation Pilots Act: See 10 U.S.C.A. 6915; 14 U.S.C.A. 758a, 759a.

Aviation Safety and Noise Abatement Act of 1979: 49 U.S.C.A. 2101, 2104; 49 App. U.S.C.A. 1359, 2125.

Aviation Safety Research Act of 1988: 49 U.S.C.A. 106; 49 App. U.S.C.A. 1353, 2205.

Baby Doe Amendment: 42 U.S.C.A. 5102, 5103.

Bail Reform Act of 1984: 18 U.S.C.A. 3041, 4282, 18 U.S.C.A. Rules 5, 15, 40, 46, 54; 28 U.S.C.A. 636; 28 U.S.C.A. 9.

Bailey Merchant Marine Act: 46 U.S.C.A. 1242a.

Balanced Budget and Emergency Deficit Control Act of 1985: 2 U.S.C.A. 602, 922; 31 U.S.C.A. 1104, 1109; 42 U.S.C.A. 911.

Balanced Budget and Emergency Deficit Control Reaffirmation Act of 1987: 2 U.S.C.A. 622, 922;

31 U.S.C.A. 1105; 42 U.S.C.A. 1320b-8 note, 1395ww notes.

Bald Eagle Protection Act: 16 U.S.C.A. 668, 668d.

Baldwin Amendment: See 23 U.S.C.A. 402(a).

Ballistic Knife Prohibition Act of 1986: 15 U.S.C.A. 1245; 18 U.S.C.A. 1716.

Bangladesh Disaster Assistance Act of 1988: 7 U.S.C.A. 1727.

Bank Bribery Amendments Act of 1985: 18 U.S.C.A. 215.

Bank Conservation Act: 12 U.S.C.A. 201, 211.

Bank Export Services Act: 12 U.S.C.A. 372, 1843.

Bank Holding Company Act of 1956: 12 U.S.C.A. 1841, 1978; 26 U.S.C.A. 1101, 1103.

Bank Holding Company Act Amendments of 1970: 12 U.S.C.A. 1841, 1978; see 31 U.S.C.A. 5111, 5112.

Bank Holding Company Tax Act of 1976: 26 U.S.C.A. 311, 6601.

Bank Merger Acts: 12 U.S.C.A. 1828.

Bank Official Loan Act: 12 U.S.C.A. 375a.

Bank Protection Act of 1968: 12 U.S.C.A. 1729, 1884.

Bank Robbery Act: See 18 U.S.C.A. 2113, 3231.

Bank Secrecy Act: 12 U.S.C.A. 1730d; 1959; see 18 U.S.C.A. 6002; see 31 U.S.C.A. 321, 5322.

Bank Service Corporation Act: 12 U.S.C.A. 1861, 1867.

Bankhead-Jones Act: 7 U.S.C.A. 343c, 1624.

Bankhead-Jones Farm Tenant Act: 7 U.S.C.A. 1010, 1013a.

Banking Act of 1933: 12 U.S.C.A. 64a, 378; 12 U.S.C.A. distributed throughout chapters 2, 3, and 6.

Banking Act of 1935: See 11 U.S.C.A. 345; 12 U.S.C.A. 51b-1, 371; 12 U.S.C.A. generally dispersed throughout chapters 1–6, 13; 15 U.S.C.A. 19, 19a.

Banking Affiliates Act of 1982: 12 U.S.C.A. 371c, 1972.

Banking and Related Programs Authorization Adjustment Act: 12 U.S.C.A. 461, 635e; see 31 U.S.C.A. 5132.

Bankrupt Railroad Service Preservation and Employment Protection Act of 1982: 45 U.S.C.A. 797c, 1017.

Bankruptcy: 11 U.S.C.A. 101, 151326; 11 U.S.C.A. Rules 2002, 3001; 11 U.S.C.A. Form No. 1.

Bankruptcy Acts: 11 U.S.C.A. 101, 151326.

Bankruptcy Amendments and Federal Judgeship Act of 1984: 5 U.S.C.A. 8331, 8714c; 11 U.S.C.A. 101, 151302; 11 U.S.C.A. Rules 2002, 3001; 11 U.S.C.A. Form No. 1; 28 U.S.C.A. 44, 2256; 28 U.S.C.A. Rule 1101.

Bankruptcy Judges, United States Trustees, and Family Farmer Bankruptcy Act of 1986: 11 U.S.C.A. 101, 15326; 11 App. U.S.C.A. Form No. 1; 28 U.S.C.A. 49, 2075.

Bankruptcy Reform Act of 1978: 11 U.S.C.A. 101, 151326; 11 App. U.S.C.A. 408.

Bankruptcy Rules: 11 App. U.S.C.A. Rule 2002.

Bankruptcy Tax Act of 1980: 26 U.S.C.A. 108, 7508.

Barbour Fight Film Act: 15 U.S.C.A. 1001.

Barrow Gas Field Transfer Act of 1984: 42 U.S.C.A. 6502, 6504.

Bartlett Act (Twelve Mile Fishery Jurisdiction): 16 U.S.C.A. 1091, 1094.

Bayh-Dole Act: 35 U.S.C.A. 200, 212.

Beef Promotion and Research Act of 1985: 7 U.S.C.A. 2901, 2918.

Beef Research and Information Act: 7 U.S.C.A. 2901, 2918.

Bennett Amendment (Civil Rights): 42 U.S.C.A. 2000e-2(h).

Berne Convention Implementation Act of 1988: 17 U.S.C.A. 101, 801.

Beverage Tax Acts: 19 U.S.C.A. 460.

Big Brothers—Big Sisters of America: 36 U.S.C.A. 881, 1101.

Bilingual Education Act: 20 U.S.C.A. 880b, 3341.

Bill of Lading Act (Interstate and Foreign Commerce): 49 U.S.C.A. 81, 124.

Biomass Energy and Alcohol Fuels Act of 1980: 7 U.S.C.A. 341, 3154; 15 U.S.C.A. 753, 3391a; 16 U.S.C.A. 590h, 1642; 42 U.S.C.A. 8801, 8871.

Biomedical Research and Research Training Amendments of 1978: 42 U.S.C.A. 241, 4585.

Biomedical Research Extension Act of 1977: 42 U.S.C.A. 280b, 289*l*-1.

Black Bass Act: 16 U.S.C.A. 851, 856.

Black Lung Benefits Act of 1972: 30 U.S.C.A. 901, 951.

Black Lung Benefits Reform Act of 1977: 26 U.S.C.A. 4121 note; 29 U.S.C.A. 675 note; 30 U.S.C.A. 901, 945.

Black Lung Benefits Revenue Act of 1977: 26 U.S.C.A. 192, 7454; 30 U.S.C.A. 934, 934a.

Black Lung Benefits Revenue Act of 1981: 26 U.S.C.A. 501, 9602; 30 U.S.C.A. 902, 934a.

Bland Change of Masters Act: 46 U.S.C.A. 276.

Bland Merchant Marine Act: 46 U.S.C.A. 822, 1274.

Block Signal, Resolution (Railroads): 45 U.S.C.A. 35.

Blood Transfusion Act: 24 U.S.C.A. 30.

Blue Star Mothers of America Act: 36 U.S.C.A. 941, 958.

Board for International Broadcasting Act of 1973: 22 U.S.C.A. 2871, 2883.

Board for International Broadcasting Authoriza-

tion Act, Fiscal Years 1982 and 1983: 22 U.S.C.A. 2872, 2880.

Board for International Broadcasting Authorization Act, Fiscal Years 1984 and 1985: 22 U.S.C.A. 2877, 2882.

Boggs Act: 21 U.S.C.A. 174.

Boiler Inspection Acts (Railroads): 45 U.S.C.A. 22, 34.

Bomb Threats Act: 18 U.S.C.A. 844(e).

Bond Act (Public Officers): 6 U.S.C.A. 1, 3.

Bond Purchase Clause (Sundry Civil Appropriation Act): See 31 U.S.C.A. 3110.

Bonneville Project Act: 16 U.S.C.A. 832, 832*l*.

Borah Act: See 18 U.S.C.A. 155.

Boulder Canyon Project Act: 43 U.S.C.A. 617, 617t.

Boulder Canyon Project Adjustment Act: 43 U.S.C.A. 618, 618*o*.

Boulder City Act of 1958: 12 U.S.C.A. 1715n; 43 U.S.C.A. 617u note.

Boykin Merchant Marine Act: 46 U.S.C.A. 1159.

Bretton Woods Agreements Act: 22 U.S.C.A. 286, 286gg; see 31 U.S.C.A. 5302.

Bretton Woods Agreements Act Amendments of 1978: See 31 U.S.C.A. 1103.

Bridge Act: 33 U.S.C.A. 491, 498.

Brooks Architect-Engineers Act: 40 U.S.C.A. 541, 544.

Brush Disposal Act: 16 U.S.C.A. 490.

Bryson Act: 15 U.S.C.A. 1071; 35 U.S.C.A. 1, 293.

Buck Act: See 4 U.S.C.A. 105, 110.

Budget and Accounting Act, 1921: See 31 U.S.C.A. 501, 3702.

Budget and Accounting Procedures Act of 1950: 16 U.S.C.A. 452; 24 U.S.C.A. 278; see 31 U.S.C.A. 701, 9504.

Bureau of Land Management Drug Enforcement Supplemental Authority Act: 16 U.S.C.A. 559g; 18 U.S.C.A. 1855, 1864; 21 U.S.C.A. 841, 886; 43 U.S.C.A. 2 note.

Bureau of Marine Inspection and Navigation Act: See 46 U.S.C.A. 373, 6301.

Bureau of Mines Act: 30 U.S.C.A. 1, 7.

Bureau of Standards Act: 15 U.S.C.A. 203, 278h.

Burke Act (Indians): 25 U.S.C.A. 349.

Burnt Timber Act: 16 U.S.C.A. 614, 615.

Burton-Hill Hospital Survey and Construction Act: See Hospital Survey and Construction Act.

Bus Regulatory Reform Act of 1982: 15 U.S.C.A. 77c; 26 U.S.C.A. 250; 39 U.S.C.A. 5201; 49 U.S.C.A. 10101, 11911.

Business Opportunity Development Reform Act of 1988: 15 U.S.C.A. 631, 645; 40 U.S.C.A. 541.

Business Records Act: 28 U.S.C.A. 1732, 1733.

Butter Standard Act: 21 U.S.C.A. 6.

Buy American Act: 41 U.S.C.A. 10a, 10c.

Buy American Act of 1988: 19 U.S.C.A. 2511, 2515; 41 U.S.C.A. 10a, 10d.

Buy Indian Act: 25 U.S.C.A. 47.

Byrnes Act (Transporting Strikebreakers): See 18 U.S.C.A. 1231.

Cable Communications Policy Act of 1984: 15 U.S.C.A. 21; 18 U.S.C.A. 2511; 46 U.S.C.A. 484, 487; 47 U.S.C.A. 35, 611; 50 U.S.C.A. 1805.

Calder Act (Daylight Saving): 15 U.S.C.A. 261, 263.

California Wilderness Act of 1984: 16 U.S.C.A. 543, 1274.

Campaign Communications Reform Act: 47 U.S.C.A. 312, 805.

Canada-United States Interparliamentary Group Act: 25 U.S.C.A. 276d, 276g.

Canal Act of 1890: 43 U.S.C.A. 945.

Canal Zone Code: 18 U.S.C.A. 14, 4210; 22 U.S.C.A. 1934; 24 U.S.C.A. 196; 28 U.S.C.A. 414, 1406; 50 U.S.C.A. 191a, 858.

Cape Cod National Seashore Act: 16 U.S.C.A. 459b, 459b-8.

Capper-Ketcham Act: 7 U.S.C.A. 343a, 343b.

Car Service Act: See 49 U.S.C.A. 10102, 11128.

Career Compensation Act of 1949: 14 U.S.C.A. 309; see 37 U.S.C.A. 201; 42 U.S.C.A. 209, 216.

Career Criminals Amendment Act of 1986: 18 U.S.C.A. 924.

Career Education Incentive Act: 20 U.S.C.A. 1865, 2614; 21 U.S.C.A. 1001, 1007.

Career Incentive Act of 1955: See 10 U.S.C.A. 6912; see 37 U.S.C.A. 201.

Carey Act (Irrigation): 43 U.S.C.A. 641.

Cargo Preference Laws: 46 U.S.C.A. 1241, 1241-1.

Caribbean Basin Economic Recovery Act: 19 U.S.C.A. 1202, 2706; 26 U.S.C.A. 274, 7652; 33 U.S.C.A. 1311 note.

Carl D. Perkins Vocational Education Act: 20 U.S.C.A. 2301, 2471.

Carlin Act (Larceny from Interstate Carriers): See 18 U.S.C.A. 659, 2117.

Carlisle Act (Internal Revenue): 19 U.S.C.A. 468, 469.

Carmack Amendment to Hepburn Act (Interstate Commerce): See 49 U.S.C.A. 10103, 11707.

Carriage of Goods by Sea Act: 46 U.S.C.A. 1300, 1315.

Cash Discount Act: 12 U.S.C.A. 29; 15 U.S.C.A. 1602, 1666f; 42 U.S.C.A. 205, 212.

Cattle Contagious Diseases Acts: See 18 U.S.C.A. 111; 21 U.S.C.A. 102, 153.

Celler-Hennings Act of 1958: 18 U.S.C.A. 4208, 4209; 28 U.S.C.A. 334.

Census: 13 U.S.C.A. 1, 307.

Center for Cultural and Technical Interchange Between East and West Act of 1960: 22 U.S.C.A. 2054, 2057.

Central Idaho Wilderness Act of 1980: 16 U.S.C.A. 1274.

Central Intelligence Agency Act of 1949: 50 U.S.C.A. 403a, 403q.

Central Intelligence Agency Information Act: 5 U.S.C.A. 552a; 50 U.S.C.A. 431, 432.

Central Intelligence Agency Spouses' Retirement Equity Act of 1982: 50 U.S.C.A. 403n.

Central, Western, and South Pacific Fisheries Development Act: 16 U.S.C.A. 758e, 758e-5.

Challenge Grant Amendments of 1983: 20 U.S.C.A. 1065a, 1069c.

Chandler Act, Bankruptcy Revision: 11 U.S.C.A. generally.

Change in Bank Control Act of 1978: 12 U.S.C.A. 1817.

Change in Savings and Loan Control Act of 1978: 12 U.S.C.A. 1730.

Charitable Assistance and Food Bank Act of 1987: 7 U.S.C.A. 2014.

Charity Games Advertising Clarification Act of 1988: 18 U.S.C.A. 1304, 1307; 39 U.S.C.A. 3005.

Cherokee Leasing Act: 25 U.S.C.A. 415, 450i; 26 U.S.C.A. 3121; 42 U.S.C.A. 410.

Chesapeake and Ohio Canal Development Act: 16 U.S.C.A. 410y, 410y-6.

Chesapeake Bay Research Coordination Act of 1980: 16 U.S.C.A. 3001, 3007.

Child Abuse Amendments of 1984: 42 U.S.C.A. 5101, 10412.

Child Abuse Prevention, Adoption, and Family Services Act of 1988: 42 U.S.C.A. 5101, 10413.

Child Abuse Prevention and Treatment Act: 42 U.S.C.A. 5101, 10412.

Child Abuse Prevention and Treatment and Adoption Reform Act of 1978: 42 U.S.C.A. 5101, 5115.

Child Abuse Victims' Rights Act of 1986: 18 U.S.C.A. 2251, 2256.

Child Development Associate Scholarship Assistance Act of 1985: 42 U.S.C.A. 10901, 10905.

Child Nutrition Act of 1966: 42 U.S.C.A. 1771, 1789.

Child Nutrition Amendments of 1986: 7 U.S.C.A. 1431e note; 42 U.S.C.A. 1752, 1789.

Child Protection Act of 1966: 15 U.S.C.A. 1261, 1273.

Child Protection Act of 1984: 18 U.S.C.A. 2251, 2516; 28 U.S.C.A. 522 note.

Child Protection and Obscenity Enforcement Act of 1988: 18 U.S.C.A. 1460, 2516; 19 U.S.C.A. 1305; 47 U.S.C.A. 223.

Child Protection and Toy Safety Act of 1969: 15 U.S.C.A. 1261, 1274.

Child Sexual Abuse and Pornography Act of 1986: 18 U.S.C.A. 2251, 2424.

Child Support Enforcement Amendments of 1984: 26 U.S.C.A. 6103, 7213; 42 U.S.C.A. 602, 1396a.

Children's Justice Act: 42 U.S.C.A. 290dd-3, 10603a.

Children's Justice and Assistance Act of 1986: 42 U.S.C.A. 290dd-3, 10603a.

China Trade Acts: 15 U.S.C.A. 141, 162.

Choctaw-Chickasaw Supplemental Agreement: 16 U.S.C.A. 151.

Chrysler Corporation Loan Guarantee Act of 1979: 15 U.S.C.A. 1861, 2512.

Circuit Court of Appeals Act: See 28 U.S.C.A. 43, 2107.

Citron Flood Compact Act: 33 U.S.C.A. 567a.

Civil Aeronautics Act of 1938: See 49 U.S.C.A. 646, 1542.

Civil Aeronautics Board Sunset Act of 1984: 5 U.S.C.A. 5314, 5315; 7 U.S.C.A. 1622, 2145; 10 U.S.C.A. 4746, 9746; 15 U.S.C.A. 18, 1692*l*; 16 U.S.C.A. 18b; 26 U.S.C.A. 47, 7701; 31 U.S.C.A. 3726; 39 U.S.C.A. 3401, 5402; 44 U.S.C.A. 3502; 49 U.S.C.A. 329, 1557.

Civil Aeronautics and Space Administration Authorization Act, 1971: 42 U.S.C.A. 2462.

Civil Functions Appropriation Acts: 24 U.S.C.A. 290; 33 U.S.C.A. 574, 701b-10; 41 U.S.C.A. 6b; 42 U.S.C.A. 6b.

Civil Liberties Act of 1988: 50 App U.S.C.A. 1989b, 1989b-8.

Civil Obedience Act of 1968: 18 U.S.C.A. 231, 233.

Civil Relief Act (Soldiers and Sailors): See Soldiers' and Sailors' Civil Relief Act of 1940.

Civil Rights Act of 1957: See 5 U.S.C.A. 5319(19); 28 U.S.C.A. 1343, 1861; 42 U.S.C.A. 1971, 1995.

Civil Rights Act of 1960: 18 U.S.C.A. 837, 1509; 20 U.S.C.A. 241, 640; 42 U.S.C.A. 1971, 1975d.

Civil Rights Act of 1964: 28 U.S.C.A. 1447; 42 U.S.C.A. 1971, 2000h-6.

Civil Rights Act of 1968: 18 U.S.C.A. 231, 2102; 25 U.S.C.A. 1301, 1341; 28 U.S.C.A. 1360 note; 42 U.S.C.A. 1973j, 3631.

Civil Rights Acts: See 42 U.S.C.A. 1971, 1981 et seq.

Civil Rights Attorney's Fees Awards Act of 1976: 42 U.S.C.A. 1988.

Civil Rights Commission Act of 1978: 42 U.S.C.A. 1975b, 1975e.

Civil Rights Commission Authorization Act of 1979: 42 U.S.C.A. 1975c, 1975e.

Civil Rights of Institutionalized Persons Act: 42 U.S.C.A. 1997, 1997j.

Civil Rights Restoration Act of 1987: 20 U.S.C.A. 1687, 1688; 29 U.S.C.A. 706, 794; 42 U.S.C.A. 2000d-4a, 6107.

Civil Service Act: See 5 U.S.C.A. 1101, 7352; see 18 U.S.C.A. 1, 1917; 40 U.S.C.A. 42.

Civil Service Examination in State of Domicile Act: See 5 U.S.C.A. 3305, 3306.

Civil Service Miscellaneous Amendments Act of 1983: 5 U.S.C.A. 1304, 7122.

Civil Service Reform Act of 1978: 5 U.S.C.A. 552, 8913; 10 U.S.C.A. 4540, 9540; 15 U.S.C.A. 1715; 28 U.S.C.A. 2342; 38 U.S.C.A. 2014 note; 39 U.S.C.A. 410, 1002; 42 U.S.C.A. 246, 4766.

Civil Service Retirement Acts: See 5 U.S.C.A. 1308, 8348.

Civil Service Retirement Spouse Equity Act of 1984: 5 U.S.C.A. 3135, 8913; 10 U.S.C.A. 1602; 31 U.S.C.A. 731.

Civilian Nautical School Act: 46 U.S.C.A. 1332, 1333.

Clarke-McNary Act (Reforestation): 16 U.S.C.A. 471, 570.

Classification Act of 1949: See 5 U.S.C.A. 305, 7154; 12 U.S.C.A. 1138f.

Classification Act Amendments of 1962: See 5 U.S.C.A. 5108, 5337; 7 U.S.C.A. 1857; 10 U.S.C.A. 3535 note; 16 U.S.C.A. 742b; 42 U.S.C.A. 2521.

Classified Information Procedures Act: 18 App. U.S.C.A. 14.

Clayton Act (Anti-Trust Act): 15 U.S.C.A. 12, 27; see 18 U.S.C.A. 402, 3691; 29 U.S.C.A. 52, 53.

Clayton Antitrust Act: 15 U.S.C.A. 26a, 27.

Clean Air Act: 42 U.S.C.A. 1857c-10, 7642.

Clean Air Act Amendments of 1977: 15 U.S.C.A. 792 note; 42 U.S.C.A. 4362, 7626.

Clean Air Amendments of 1970: 42 U.S.C.A. 1857a, 1858a; 49 App. U.S.C.A. 1421, 1430; 50 App. U.S.C.A. 456.

Clean Water Act of 1977: 33 U.S.C.A. 1251, 1376.

Clean Water Restoration Act of 1966: 33 U.S.C.A. 431, 466n.

Clinical Laboratories Improvement Act of 1967: 42 U.S.C.A. 263a.

Clinical Laboratory Improvement Amendments of 1988: 42 U.S.C.A. 263a.

Coast and Geodetic Survey Commissioned Officers' Act of 1948: 33 U.S.C.A. 852a, 864d.

Coast Guard: 14 U.S.C.A. 1, 894.

Coast Guard Authorization Act of 1982: 14 U.S.C.A. 52, 475; 33 U.S.C.A. 401, 2073; 37 U.S.C.A. 306; 46 U.S.C.A. 9, 1484.

Coast Guard Authorization Act of 1988: 10 U.S.C.A. 1054; 14 U.S.C.A. 2, 665; 16 U.S.C.A. 777, 777*l*; 26 U.S.C.A. 9503, 9504; 31 U.S.C.A. 1105 note; 33 U.S.C.A. 59x, 2027; 42 U.S.C.A. 3374; 46 U.S.C.A. 8301, 13110.

Coast Guard Personnel Act: See 14 U.S.C.A. 47, 48.

Coast Guard Retirement Act: See 14 U.S.C.A. 355, 633.

Coastal Barrier Resources Act: 16 U.S.C.A. 3501, 3510; 42 U.S.C.A. 4028.

Coastal Zone Management Act Amendments of 1976: 5 U.S.C.A. 5316; 15 U.S.C.A. 1511a; 16 U.S.C.A. 1451, 1464.

Coastwise Load Line Act, 1935: 46 U.S.C.A. 88, 88i.

Cochran-Hull Act: See 18 U.S.C.A. 876, 3239.

Cochran-Patterson Acts: See 18 U.S.C.A. 10, 1201.

Coinage Act of 1965: 18 U.S.C.A. 337, 485; see 31 U.S.C.A. 321, 5133.

Coinage Act (Silver Dollar): See 31 U.S.C.A. 5116.

Collateral Security Act: 12 U.S.C.A. 347b, 445.

College Housing Amendments of 1955: 12 U.S.C.A. 1749.

Color Additive Amendments of 1960: 21 U.S.C.A. 321, 376.

Color of Title Act: 43 U.S.C.A. 1068, 1068a.

Colorado River Basin Project Act: 43 U.S.C.A. 616aa-1, 1556.

Colorado River Basin Salinity Control Act: 43 U.S.C.A. 620d, 1599.

Colorado River Floodway Protection Act: 42 U.S.C.A. 4029; 43 U.S.C.A. 1600, 1600*l*.

Columbia Basin Project Act: 16 U.S.C.A. 835, 835c-5.

Combined Hydrocarbon Leasing Act of 1981: 30 U.S.C.A. 181, 352.

Commerce Under-Secretary Act: 15 U.S.C.A. 1502, 1503.

Commercial Fisheries Research and Development Act of 1964: 16 U.S.C.A. 742c, 779f.

Commercial Fishing Industry Vessel Anti-Reflagging Act of 1987: 16 U.S.C.A. 1802; 46 U.S.C.A. 251, 12108; 46 App. U.S.C.A. 883.

Commercial Fishing Industry Vessel Safety Act of 1988: 46 U.S.C.A. 2101, 10603; 46 App. U.S.C.A. 531, 534.

Commercial Motor Vehicle Safety Act of 1986: 49 U.S.C.A. 521, 2716.

Commercial Print Copyright Act: See 17 U.S.C.A. 5, 25.

Commercial Space Launch Act: 49 U.S.C.A. 2601, 2623; 49 App. U.S.C.A. 2623.

Commercial Space Launch Act Amendments of 1988: 49 App. U.S.C.A. 2603, 2615.

Commodity Clause of Railroad Rate Act: See 49 U.S.C.A. 10746.

Commodity Credit Corporation Act: 15 U.S.C.A. 713a-1, 713a-11.

Commodity Credit Corporation Charter Act: 15 U.S.C.A. 714, 714o.

Commodity Distribution Reform Act and WIC Amendments of 1987: 7 U.S.C.A. 1431e; 42 U.S.C.A. 1755, 1786.

Commodity Exchange Act: 7 U.S.C.A. 2, 87b; 7 U.S.C.A. generally dispersed throughout chapter 1.

Commodity Futures Trading Commission Act of 1974: 5 U.S.C.A. 5108, 5316; 7 U.S.C.A. 2, 22.

Commodore Bill: See 10 U.S.C.A. 5501, 5787; 14 U.S.C.A. 351, 438; 42 U.S.C.A. 212.

Communicable Disease Control Amendments of 1970: 42 U.S.C.A. 247b.

Communicable Disease Control Amendments Act of 1972: 42 U.S.C.A. 247b, 300.

Communications Act of 1934: 15 U.S.C.A. 21; 17 U.S.C.A. 223; 18 U.S.C.A. 1343; 46 U.S.C.A. 484, 487; 47 U.S.C.A. 35, 613.

Communications Act Amendments, 1952: 18 U.S.C.A. prec. 1341, 1343; 47 U.S.C.A. 153, 410.

Communications Amendments Act of 1982: 18 U.S.C.A. 1118; 47 U.S.C.A. 153, 605.

Communications Satellite Act of 1962: 47 U.S.C.A. 701, 757.

Communist Control Act of 1954: 50 U.S.C.A. 782, 844.

Community and Migrant Health Centers Amendments of 1988: 42 U.S.C.A. 254b, 254c.

Community Economic Development Act of 1981: 42 U.S.C.A. 9801, 9822.

Community Emergency Drought Relief Act of 1977: 42 U.S.C.A. 3121, 5184.

Community Health Services and Facilities Act of 1961: 42 U.S.C.A. 246, 292g.

Community Mental Health Centers Act: 42 U.S.C.A. 2681, 2697b.

Community Mental Health Centers Extension Act 1978: 42 U.S.C.A. 246, 4588.

Community Reinvestment Act of 1977: 12 U.S.C.A. 2901, 2905.

Community Schools Act: 20 U.S.C.A. 1864.

Community Schools and Comprehensive Community Education Act of 1978: 20 U.S.C.A. 3281, 3295.

Community Services Act of 1974: 42 U.S.C.A. 2706, 2995b.

Community Services Block Grant Act: 42 U.S.C.A. 9901, 9912.

Community Services Extension Amendments of 1965: 42 U.S.C.A. 24, 247b.

Compact of Free Association Act of 1985: 16 U.S.C.A. 460ff-3, 460ff-5; 48 U.S.C.A. 1681 note.

Competition in Contracting Act of 1984: 10 U.S.C.A. 2301, 2356, 31 U.S.C.A. 3551, 3556; 40 U.S.C.A. 759; 41 U.S.C.A. 252, 419.

Competitive Equality Amendments of 1987: 12 U.S.C.A. 24, 1846.

Competitive Equality Banking Act of 1987: 2 U.S.C.A. 905; 12 U.S.C.A. 24, 4010; 15 U.S.C.A. 45, 57a; 31 U.S.C.A. 3328, 9105.

Competitiveness Policy Council Act: 15 U.S.C.A. 4801, 4809.

Comprehensive Alcohol Abuse and Alcoholism Prevention, Treatment and Rehabilitation Act of 1970: 42 U.S.C.A. 218, 4594.

Comprehensive Alcohol Abuse, Drug Abuse, and Mental Health Amendments Act of 1988: 21 U.S.C.A. 801 note; 40 U.S.C.A. 484; 42 U.S.C.A. 242a, 300y-2.

Comprehensive Anti-Apartheid Act of 1986: 12 U.S.C.A. 635; 22 U.S.C.A. 2151c, 5116.

Comprehensive Child Development Act: 20 U.S.C.A. 9881, 9887.

Comprehensive Child Development Centers Act of 1988: 42 U.S.C.A. 9833, 9887.

Comprehensive Crime Control Act of 1984: 5 U.S.C.A. 5314, 5315; 8 U.S.C.A. 1182, 1252; 15 U.S.C.A. 1116, 1118; 16 U.S.C.A. 460-3, 460n-8; 18 U.S.C.A. 7, 5042; 19 U.S.C.A. 1589, 1644; 21 U.S.C.A. 802, 1204; 23 U.S.C.A. 114; 26 U.S.C.A. 5871, 7607; 28 U.S.C.A. 504, 2901; 29 U.S.C.A. 186, 1695; 41 U.S.C.A. 35 note; 42 U.S.C.A. 186, 10604; 49 U.S.C.A. 1472, 11507; 50 App. U.S.C.A. 460.

Comprehensive Drug Abuse Prevention Act of 1978: 21 U.S.C.A. 881.

Comprehensive Drug Abuse Prevention and Control Act of 1970: 18 U.S.C.A. 1114, 4251; 19 U.S.C.A. 2079, 2080; 21 U.S.C.A. 198a, 967; 26 U.S.C.A. 4901, 7655; 31 U.S.C.A. 529e, 529f; 40 U.S.C.A. 304m; 42 U.S.C.A. 201, 3509; 46 U.S.C.A. 239a; see 46 U.S.C.A. 7302; 49 U.S.C.A. 787.

Comprehensive Employment and Training Act: 18 U.S.C.A. 665; 29 U.S.C.A. 801, 999; 42 U.S.C.A. 2571 note.

Comprehensive Environmental Response, Compensation, and Liability Act of 1980: 10 U.S.C.A. 2701, 2810; 26 U.S.C.A. 26, 9508; 29 U.S.C.A. 655 note; 33 U.S.C.A. 1364, 1416; 42 U.S.C.A. 6901, 11050; 49 U.S.C.A. 11901.

Comprehensive Forfeiture Act of 1984: 18 U.S.C.A. 1961, 1963; 19 U.S.C.A. 1589, 1644; 21 U.S.C.A. 824, 967; 26 U.S.C.A. 7607; 28 U.S.C.A. 524.

Comprehensive Health Manpower Training Act of 1971: 42 U.S.C.A. 201, 295h-9.

Comprehensive Health Planning and Public Health Services Amendments of 1966: 42 U.S.C.A. 242g, 246.

Comprehensive Older Americans Act Amendments of 1978: 42 U.S.C.A. 3001, 6107.

Comprehensive Smoking Education Act: 15 U.S.C.A. 1331, 1341.

Comprehensive Smokeless Tobacco Health Education Act of 1986: 15 U.S.C.A. 4401, 4408; 21 U.S.C.A. 342.

Comptroller General Annuity Adjustment Act of 1978: See 31 U.S.C.A. 772, 777.

Computer Fraud and Abuse Act of 1986: 18 U.S.C.A. 1030.

Computer Security Act of 1987: 15 U.S.C.A. 272, 278h; 40 U.S.C.A. 759.

Comstock Act: See 18 U.S.C.A. 1461.

Condemnation Act (Lands for Public Uses): 40 U.S.C.A. 257.

Condominium and Cooperative Abuse Relief Act of 1980: 15 U.S.C.A. 3601, 3616.

Congregate Housing Services Act of 1978: 42 U.S.C.A. 1437e, 8010.

Congressional Award Act: 2 U.S.C.A. 801, 808.

Congressional Budget Act of 1974: 1 U.S.C.A. 105; 2 U.S.C.A. 109a-1, 661; see 31 U.S.C.A. 702, 1552.

Congressional Budget and Impoundment Control Act of 1974: 1 U.S.C.A. 105; 2 U.S.C.A. 190a-3, 688; see 31 U.S.C.A. 702, 1552.

Congressional Committees Witness Immunity Act: 18 U.S.C.A. 3486.

Congressional Merit Scholarship in Mathematics, Science, and Engineering Education: 20 U.S.C.A. 3931, 3933.

Congressional Operations Appropriation Act, 1978: 2 U.S.C.A. 31a-1, 287d; 40 U.S.C.A. 166a, 851; 44 U.S.C.A. 103 note.

Congressional Reports Elimination Act of 1986: 5 U.S.C.A. 3104, 7701; 12 U.S.C.A. 1701z-4, 1701z-5; 15 U.S.C.A. 713a-10; 16 U.S.C.A. 758e-2, 1821; 18 U.S.C.A. 2101; 19 U.S.C.A. 81p; 20 U.S.C.A. 1017, 1453; 26 U.S.C.A. 6103; 33 U.S.C.A. 1106; 40 U.S.C.A. 484; 42 U.S.C.A. 1883, 9210; 49 U.S.C.A. 1307; 50 App. U.S.C.A. 1746.

Conrail Privatization Act: 45 U.S.C.A. 726, 1346; 49 U.S.C.A. 10362, 10713.

Conservation Service Reform Act of 1986: 42 U.S.C.A. 8201, 8284.

Consolidated Farm and Rural Development Act: 17 U.S.C.A. 1013a, 2006.

Consolidated Federal Funds Report Act of 1982: 31 U.S.C.A. 6102 note.

Consolidated Federal Funds Report Amendments of 1985: 31 U.S.C.A. 6101, 6207.

Consolidated Omnibus Budget Reconciliation Act of 1985: 5 U.S.C.A. 5504, 8906; 7 U.S.C.A. 511d, 1445-3; 10 U.S.C.A. 1095. See Popular Name Table for other titles.

Consolidated Omnibus Reconciliation Act of 1985: 19 U.S.C.A. 58c; 42 U.S.C.A. 603 note.

Consolidated Refugee Education Assistance Act: 8 U.S.C.A. 1522 note; 20 U.S.C.A. 239a, 1211b.

Conspiracy Act (Offenses Against U.S.): 18 U.S.C.A. 371.

Constitution Heritage Act of 1988: 16 U.S.C.A. 407aa, 407ee.

Consular Reorganization Acts: 22 U.S.C.A. 9, 107.

Consumer Checking Account Equity Act of 1980: 12 U.S.C.A. 371a, 1832.

Consumer Credit Protection Act: 15 U.S.C.A. 1601, 1693r; 18 U.S.C.A. 891, 896.

Consumer Education Act of 1978: 20 U.S.C.A. 2981, 2986.

Consumer Goods Pricing Act of 1975: 15 U.S.C.A. 1, 45.

Consumer Home Mortgage Assistance Act of 1974: 12 U.S.C.A. 371, 1788.

Consumer Leasing Act of 1976: 15 U.S.C.A. 1601, 1667e.

Consumer Product Safety Act: 5 U.S.C.A. 5314, 5315; 15 U.S.C.A. 2051, 2083.

Consumer Product Safety Amendments of 1981: 7 U.S.C.A. 135; 12 U.S.C.A. 24; 15 U.S.C.A. 1193, 2083; 21 U.S.C.A. 343, 362.

Consumer-Patient Radiation Heal and Safety Act of 1981: 42 U.S.C.A. 10001, 10008.

Continental Scientific Drilling and Exploration Act: 43 U.S.C.A. 31 note.

Continuing Drug Enterprises Act of 1986: 21 U.S.C.A. 848.

Contraband Seizure Act: 49 U.S.C.A. 781, 789.

Contract Disputes Act of 1978: 5 U.S.C.A. 5108; 28

Defense Industrial Reserve Act: 50 U.S.C.A. 451, 462.

Defense Officer Personnel Management Act: 10 U.S.C.A. 101, 9837; 14 U.S.C.A. 286a, 438; 32 U.S.C.A. 303, 716; 33 U.S.C.A. 857a; 37 U.S.C.A. 101, 1011; 42 U.S.C.A. 213a; 50 U.S.C.A. 1651; 50 App. U.S.C.A. 326, 460.

Defense Procurement Improvement Act of 1985: 10 U.S.C.A. 1621, 2415; 18 U.S.C.A. 287 notes; 31 U.S.C.A. 3729 note; 40 U.S.C.A. 759; 41 U.S.C.A. 253, 418a; 50 App. U.S.C.A. 2168.

Defense Procurement Reform Act of 1984: 10 U.S.C.A. 139a, 2416.

Defense Production Act of 1950: 50 App. U.S.C.A. 2061, 2170.

Defense Technical Correction Act of 1987: 5 U.S.C.A. 5314, 5315; 10 U.S.C.A. 101, 8723; 15 U.S.C.A. 632, 644; 20 U.S.C.A. 4703; 37 U.S.C.A. 101, 1014; 41 U.S.C.A. 416.

Defense Workers Housing Act: 42 U.S.C.A. 1523.

Deficiency Appropriation Act, 1934: 2 U.S.C.A. 33.

Deficit Reduction Act of 1984: 26 U.S.C.A. 1, 6695; 38 U.S.C.A. 1816 note; 40 U.S.C.A. 759 note; 42 U.S.C.A. 1395f, 1396b.

Delaware Water Gap National Recreation Area Act: 16 U.S.C.A. 460o, 460o-7.

Demonstration Cities and Metropolitan Development Act of 1966: 12 U.S.C.A. 24, 1749aaa-5; 15 U.S.C.A. 77ddd, 637; 16 U.S.C.A. 470b-1; 40 U.S.C.A. 461; 42 U.S.C.A. 1416, 3374.

Department of Agriculture Act: 21 U.S.C.A. 119.

Department of Agriculture and Farm Credit Administration Appropriation Act, 1961: 7 U.S.C.A. 411b, 2254; 12 U.S.C.A. 1020a-3; 15 U.S.C.A. 713a-10; 16 U.S.C.A. 590e-1, 590e-2; 21 U.S.C.A. 129.

Department of Agriculture and Related Agencies Appropriation Act, 1962: 7 U.S.C.A. 411b, 2254; 12 U.S.C.A. 1020a-3; 15 U.S.C.A. 713a-10; 16 U.S.C.A. 590e-1, 590e-2; 21 U.S.C.A. 129.

Department of Agriculture Appropriation Act, 1954: 7 U.S.C.A. 367, 2254; 12 U.S.C.A. 1020a-2, 1131a-1; 15 U.S.C.A. 713a-10; 16 U.S.C.A. 571a, 590g-1; 21 U.S.C.A. 129.

Department of Agriculture Organic Act of 1944: 7 U.S.C.A. 57a, 1605; 12 U.S.C.A. 832, 2258; 16 U.S.C.A. 500, 590q-1; 21 U.S.C.A. 114a.

Department of Agriculture Organic Act of 1956: 7 U.S.C.A. 428a, 2233; 16 U.S.C.A. 579b, 590n; 21 U.S.C.A. 114a, 114c.

Department of Commerce and Labor Act: 15 U.S.C.A. 1501, 1519; 16 U.S.C.A. 631; 29 U.S.C.A. 557; 40 U.S.C.A. 483.

Department of Commerce and Related Agencies Appropriation Act, 1956: 15 U.S.C.A. 329; see 23 U.S.C.A. 314; 33 U.S.C.A. 851, 872; 41 U.S.C.A. 6b; 46 U.S.C.A. 1241b, 1242-1; 50 App. U.S.C.A. 1738b.

Department of Commerce Appropriation Act, 1954: 15 U.S.C.A. 329; 33 U.S.C.A. 851, 872; 46 U.S.C.A. 1242-1; 50 App. U.S.C.A. 1738b.

Department of Defense Appropriations Act, 1989: 10 U.S.C.A. 2324; 31 U.S.C.A. 3554; 41 U.S.C.A. 405b; 50 App. U.S.C.A. 2410a note.

Department of Defense Reorganization Act 1958: 10 U.S.C.A. 141, 8074; 50 U.S.C.A. 401.

Department of Defense Supplemental Authorization Act, 1981: 10 U.S.C.A. 701 note; 37 U.S.C.A. 301c.

Department of Education Appropriation Act, 1985: 12 U.S.C.A. 1749a; 20 U.S.C.A. 238.

Department of Education Organization Act: 3 U.S.C.A. 19; 5 U.S.C.A. 101, 5316; 5 App. U.S.C.A. 2, 11; 20 U.S.C.A. 928, 3510; 21 U.S.C.A. 1004; 29 U.S.C.A. 761b, 952.

Department of Energy Act of 1978—Civilian Applications: 15 U.S.C.A. 2506, 2710; 22 U.S.C.A. 3224a; 30 U.S.C.A. 1121, 1145; 42 U.S.C.A. 2391, 7151a.

Department of Energy National Security and Military Applications of Nuclear Energy Authorization Act of 1988: 15 U.S.C.A. 4621, 4631; 42 U.S.C.A. 7256a, 7261a.

Department of Energy Organization Act: 3 U.S.C.A. 19; 5 U.S.C.A. 101, 5316; 7 U.S.C.A. 916; 12 U.S.C.A. 1701z-8; 15 U.S.C.A. 766, 2002; 42 U.S.C.A. 2036, 7352.

Department of Health, Education, and Welfare Appropriation Act, 1960: 20 U.S.C.A. 612; 42 U.S.C.A. 227a, 3508.

Department of Housing and Urban Development Act: 3 U.S.C.A. 19; see 5 U.S.C.A. 101, 5316; 12 U.S.C.A. 1723; 42 U.S.C.A. 1451, 3537.

Department of Housing and Urban Development—Independent Agencies Appropriation Act, 1976: 12 U.S.C.A. 1428a; 36 U.S.C.A. 121b, 122a.

Department of Housing and Urban Development; Space, Science, Veterans, and Certain Other Independent Agencies Appropriation Act, 1975: 12 U.S.C.A. 1428a; 36 U.S.C.A. 121b; 122a.

Department of Interior Airports Act: 16 U.S.C.A. 7a, 7e; 49 U.S.C.A. 1102, 1108.

Department of Justice and Related Agencies Appropriation Act, 1984: 11 App. U.S.C.A. 408; 23 U.S.C.A. 114 note; 28 U.S.C.A. 533 note; 42 U.S.C.A. 252a.

Department of Justice Appropriations Act, 1989: 8 U.S.C.A. 1101, 1455; 23 U.S.C.A. 114 note; 28 U.S.C.A. 533 note; 42 U.S.C.A. 250a.

Department of Justice Appropriation Authorization Act, Fiscal Year 1980: 5 U.S.C.A. 5315, 5924; 8 U.S.C.A. 1151 note, 1551 note; 21 U.S.C.A. 802, 904; 28 U.S.C.A. 509 note, 533 note; 42 U.S.C.A. 250a.

Department of Justice Assets Forfeiture Fund Amendments Act of 1986: 18 U.S.C.A. 1963; 19 U.S.C.A. 1613a, 1613b; 21 U.S.C.A. 853; 28 U.S.C.A. 524.

Department of Labor Acts: 29 U.S.C.A. **1, 562.**

Department of Labor Appropriations Act, 1989: 30 U.S.C.A. 962.

Department of Labor Executive Level Conforming Amendments of 1986: 5 U.S.C.A. 5313, 5316; 29 U.S.C.A. 552, 1721; 38 U.S.C.A. 222, 2010.

Department of State and Related Agencies Appropriation Act, 1984: 22 U.S.C.A. 269a.

Department of State Appropriations Act, 1989: 22 U.S.C.A. 287e, 287e-1.

Department of State Authorization Act, Fiscal Years 1984 and 1985: 5 U.S.C.A. 5314, 5944; 8 U.S.C.A. 1522; 22 U.S.C.A. 269f, 4154; 50 U.S.C.A. 1546a.

Department of the Interior and Related Agencies Appropriations Act, 1989: 2 U.S.C.A. 178, 178*l*; 5 U.S.C.A. 1511 note; 16 U.S.C.A. 20b note, 1604 note; 18 U.S.C.A. 208 note; 20 U.S.C.A. 4420. For other titles see Popular Name Table.

Department of Transportation Act: 3 U.S.C.A. 19; 5 U.S.C.A. 101, 5317; 10 U.S.C.A. 801; 15 U.S.C.A. 1404; 18 U.S.C.A. 1020; 23 U.S.C.A. 401 note; 29 U.S.C.A. 213; 33 U.S.C.A. 981, 1102; 40 App. U.S.C.A. 201, 206; 42 U.S.C.A. 1376; 49 U.S.C.A. 1652, 1659; 49 App. U.S.C.A. 1655; see 49 U.S.C.A. 101, 10925; 50 U.S.C.A. 123.

Department of Transportation and Related Agencies Appropriations Act, 1989: 5 U.S.C.A. 5532, 8344; 10 U.S.C.A. 2304 note; 14 U.S.C.A. 92 note; 20 U.S.C.A. 241 note; 23 U.S.C.A. 129; 33 U.S.C.A. 594, 1517a; 40 U.S.C.A. 817 note; 45 U.S.C.A. 581; 49 U.S.C.A. 301 note, 10344 note; 49 App. U.S.C.A. 1551, 1553.

Department of Veterans Affairs Act: 3 U.S.C.A. 19; 5 U.S.C.A. 101, 5316; 5 App. U.S.C.A. 2, 11; 38 U.S.C.A. 210, 1000.

Departments of Commerce, Justice, and State, the Judiciary, and Related Agencies Appropriations Act, 1989: 8 U.S.C.A. 1101, 1455; 19 U.S.C.A. 2171 note; 22 U.S.C.A. 287e, 287e-1; 23 U.S.C.A. 114 note; 28 U.S.C.A. 332, 603; 33 U.S.C.A. 851; 42 U.S.C.A. 250a; 47 U.S.C.A. 303 note.

Departments of Labor, and Health, Education and Welfare, and Related Agencies Appropriation Act, 1956: 29 U.S.C.A. 34 note; 42 U.S.C.A. 210, 3508; 45 U.S.C.A. 355a.

Departments of Labor and Health, Education, and Welfare Appropriations Act, 1979: 2 U.S.C.A. 88b-1 note; 30 U.S.C.A. 962; 42 U.S.C.A. 421 note.

Departments of Labor, Health and Human Services, and Education, and Related Agencies Appropriations Act, 1989: 20 U.S.C.A. 1070a note; 24 U.S.C.A. 168b, 170a; 30 U.S.C.A. 962; 42 U.S.C.A. 210 notes, 1383 note.

Departments of State, Justice, and Commerce, the Judiciary, and Related Agencies Appropriation Act, 1980: 22 U.S.C.A. 269a, 1928b; 28 U.S.C.A. 604 note; 33 U.S.C.A. 851; 42 U.S.C.A. 250a.

Dependents Assistance Act of 1950: 50 App. U.S.C.A. 2201, 2216.

Deposit Insurance Extension Act: See 12 U.S.C.A. 1811, 1831.

Deposit Insurance Flexibility Act: 12 U.S.C.A. 1431, 1843.

Depository Institution Management Interlocks Act: 12 U.S.C.A. 1464, 3208.

Depository Institutions Deregulation Act of 1980: 12 U.S.C.A. 3501, 3508.

Depository Institutions Deregulation and Monetary Control Act of 1980: 12 U.S.C.A. 4a, 3524; 15 U.S.C.A. 57a, 1691f.

Depository Library Act of 1962: See 44 U.S.C.A. 1119, 1914.

Deputy Chief of Staff Act: See 10 U.S.C.A. 3031.

Desert Land Acts: 43 U.S.C.A. 321, 323.

Destruction of Records Act (Interstate Commerce): See 49 U.S.C.A. 11144, 11910.

Destruction of War Material Act: 50 U.S.C.A. 101, 103.

Development Disabilities Assistance and Bill of Rights Act: 21 U.S.C.A. 360aa note; 42 U.S.C.A. 6000, 6083.

Developmental Disabilities Services and Facilities Construction Act: 42 U.S.C.A. 266, 6081.

Developmentally Disabled Assistance and Bill of Rights Act: 42 U.S.C.A. 295, 6081.

Dingley Act (Shipping): 46 U.S.C.A. 47, 703.

Diplomatic Relations Act: 22 U.S.C.A. 254a, 254e; 28 U.S.C.A. 1251, 1364.

Diplomatic Security Act: 3 U.S.C.A. 208; 5 U.S.C.A. 5315; 5 App. U.S.C.A. 2, 11; 22 U.S.C.A. 300, 4862.

Disabled American Veterans Acts: 36 U.S.C.A. 90a, 90k.

Disabled Veterans' and Servicemen's Automobile Assistance Act of 1970: 38 U.S.C.A. 1901, 1903.

Disaster Assistance Act of 1988: 7 U.S.C.A. 1314e, 2267; 12 U.S.C.A. 2252 note; 16 U.S.C.A. 3834; 29 U.S.C.A. 1672 note; 43 U.S.C.A. 502 note.

Disaster Loan Act: 12 U.S.C.A. 1703; 15 U.S.C.A. 605k.

Disaster Relief and Emergency Assistance Amendments of 1988: 7 U.S.C.A. 1421, 2014; 12 U.S.C.A. 1706c, 1715*l*; 15 U.S.C.A. 636; 16 U.S.C.A. 1536, 3505. For other titles, see Popular Names Table.

Disbursing Officers' Relief Act: See 31 U.S.C.A. 3527.

Disease Control Amendments of 1976: 42 U.S.C.A. 243, 4843.

Dispute Resolution Act: 28 App. U.S.C.A. 1, 10.

Distilled Spirits Tax Revision Act of 1979: 26 U.S.C.A. 5001, 5691.

Distribution System Loan Act: 43 U.S.C.A. 421a, 421h.

District of Columbia Appropriations Act, 1987: 20 U.S.C.A. 4206.

District of Columbia Criminal Justice Act: 18 U.S.C.A. 3006A.

District of Columbia Jury System Act: 28 U.S.C.A. 1869.

District of Columbia Public Postsecondary Education Reorganization Act: 7 U.S.C.A. 361a.

District of Columbia Self-Government and Governmental Reorganization Act: 2 U.S.C.A. 167h note; 5 U.S.C.A. 8101 note; 29 U.S.C.A. 49b, 50; see 31 U.S.C.A. 715, 6701; 40 U.S.C.A. 71a, 71g.

Dockery Act (Accounting): 22 U.S.C.A. 1191; 25 U.S.C.A. 96, 97; see 31 U.S.C.A. 331, 3702; 41 U.S.C.A. 20, 21; 42 U.S.C.A. 112; 43 U.S.C.A. 14.

Doctors Draft Act: 50 App. U.S.C.A. 454, 454b.

Domestic and Foreign Investment Improved Disclosure Act of 1977: 15 U.S.C.A. 78m, 78*o*.

Domestic Housing and International Recovery and Financial Stability Act: 12 U.S.C.A. 635, 3912; 19 U.S.C.A. 1671a, 1671g; 22 U.S.C.A. 262d, 290g-12; 40 U.S.C.A. 484b; 42 U.S.C.A. 1437a, 8107; 50 App. U.S.C.A. 2166.

Domestic Minerals Program Extension Act of 1953: 50 U.S.C.A. 2181 note.

Domestic Relations Tax Reform Act of 1984: 26 U.S.C.A. 2, 7701.

Domestic Volunteer Service Act of 1973: 5 U.S.C.A. 8332; 42 U.S.C.A. 3067, 5085.

Doughton Unemployment Compensation Act: 42 U.S.C.A. 501.

Drug Abuse Control Amendments of 1965: 18 U.S.C.A. 1114; 21 U.S.C.A. 321, 372.

Drug Abuse Education Act of 1970: 21 U.S.C.A. 1001, 1007.

Drug Abuse Office and Treatment Act of 1972: 5 U.S.C.A. 5313, 5316; 21 U.S.C.A. 1101, 1191; 42 U.S.C.A. 218, 2688t.

Drug Abuse Prevention, Treatment, and Rehabilitation Act: 5 U.S.C.A. 5313, 5316; 21 U.S.C.A. 1101, 1194; 42 U.S.C.A. 218, 2688t.

Drug Amendments of 1962: 21 U.S.C.A. 321, 381.

Drug and Alcohol Dependent Offenders Treatment Act of 1986: 18 U.S.C.A. 3672, 4255; 19 U.S.C.A. 1608, 1616a; 21 U.S.C.A. 802, 881.

Drug Export Amendments Act of 1986: 21 U.S.C.A. 382; 42 U.S.C.A. 241, 262.

Drug Listing Act of 1972: 21 U.S.C.A. 331, 360.

Drug Possession Penalty Act of 1986: 21 U.S.C.A. 844.

Drug Price Competition and Patent Term Restoration Act of 1984: 15 U.S.C.A. 68b, 70b; 21 U.S.C.A. 355, 360cc; 28 U.S.C.A. 2201; 35 U.S.C.A. 156, 282.

Drug-Free Public Housing Act of 1988: 42 U.S.C.A. 1121, 1125.

Drug-Free Schools and Communities Act of 1986: 20 U.S.C.A. 241cc, 4664; 25 U.S.C.A. 2001, 2009.

Drug-Free Workplace Act of 1988: 41 U.S.C.A. 701, 707.

Drunk Driving Prevention Act of 1988: 23 U.S.C.A. 403, 410.

Dual Compensation Act: 2 U.S.C.A. 162; see 5 U.S.C.A. 3326, 8701; 13 U.S.C.A. 23; 15 U.S.C.A. 327; 20 U.S.C.A. 907; 22 U.S.C.A. 277d-3, 2584. For other titles, see Popular Name Table.

Duck Stamp Act: 16 U.S.C.A. 718b.

Dwight D. Eisenhower Mathematics and Science Education Act: 20 U.S.C.A. 2981, 2993.

Earthquake Hazards Reduction Act of 1977: 42 U.S.C.A. 7701, 7706.

Eastern Pacific Tuna Licensing Act of 1984: 16 U.S.C.A. 972, 972h.

Economic Cooperation Act of 1948: 7 U.S.C.A. 612c note; 22 U.S.C.A. 272b, 1513.

Economic Dislocation and Worker Adjustment Assistance Act: 29 U.S.C.A. 565, 1752.

Economic Opportunity Act of 1964: 42 U.S.C.A. 2701, 2996*l*.

Economic Opportunity Amendments of 1966: 20 U.S.C.A. 425, 1077; 42 U.S.C.A. 2581, 3161.

Economic Recovery Tax Act of 1981: 26 U.S.C.A. 1, 7701; 42 U.S.C.A. 409, 430; 45 U.S.C.A. 231n; 46 U.S.C.A. 46, 857.

Economic Stabilization Act Amendments of 1971: 5 U.S.C.A. 5305 note; 12 U.S.C.A. 1904 notes; 15 U.S.C.A. 1026.

Economy Acts: 15 U.S.C.A. 276; 30 U.S.C.A. 7; see 31 U.S.C.A. 1535, 3728; 36 U.S.C.A. 13; 40 U.S.C.A. 278a, 303b; 41 U.S.C.A. 10a, 10c.

Edge Act (Federal Reserve Banks): 12 U.S.C.A. 611, 631.

Edmunds-Tucker Act (Polygamy): 48 U.S.C.A. 1480a.

Education Amendments of 1972: 7 U.S.C.A. 326a, 1626; 12 U.S.C.A. 24, 1757; 16 U.S.C.A. 582a-3, 582a-7; 20 U.S.C.A. 1, 1688; 29 U.S.C.A. 203, 213; 42 U.S.C.A. 2000c, 2756a.

Education and Training for a Competitive America Act of 1988: 20 U.S.C.A. 1018, 5124; 22 U.S.C.A. 4604; 29 U.S.C.A. 565, 1752; 42 U.S.C.A. 1862a, 1862b.

Education Consolidation and Improvement Act of 1981: 20 U.S.C.A. 2844, 3876.

Education for All Handicapped Children Act of 1975: 20 U.S.C.A. 1232, 1453.

Education for Economic Security Act: 20 U.S.C.A. 3901, 4086.

Education of Blind Acts: 20 U.S.C.A. 101, 105.

Education of the Deaf Act of 1986: 20 U.S.C.A. 681, 4362.

Education of the Handicapped Act: 20 U.S.C.A. 871, 1485.

Education Professions Development Act: 20 U.S.C.A. 1091, 1119c-4.

Educational Agencies Financial Aid Act: 20 U.S.C.A. 236, 647.

Educational Broadcasting Facilities and Tele-communications Demonstration Act of 1976: 47 U.S.C.A. 390, 399.

Educational Partnerships Act of 1988: 20 U.S.C.A. 5031, 5039.

Egg Products Inspection Act: 15 U.S.C.A. 633, 636; 21 U.S.C.A. 1031, 1056.

Egg Research and Consumer Information Act: 7 U.S.C.A. 2701, 2718.

Egg Research and Consumer Information Act Amendments of 1980: 7 U.S.C.A. 2707, 2714.

Electoral Count Act: See 3 U.S.C.A. 5, 18.

Electric and Hybrid Vehicle Research, Development, and Demonstration Act of 1976: 15 U.S.C.A. 2501, 2514; 42 U.S.C.A. 2451, 2473.

Electric Consumers Protection Act of 1986: 16 U.S.C.A. 797, 825h.

Electric Utility Companies Act: 16 U.S.C.A. 824, 825r.

Electronic Communications Privacy Act of 1986: 18 U.S.C.A. 1367, 3126.

Electronic Fund Transfer Act: 15 U.S.C.A. 1693, 1693r.

Elementary and Secondary Education Act of 1965: 20 U.S.C.A. 236, 3389.

Elementary and Secondary Education Amendments of 1967: 15 U.S.C.A. 1381 note; 20 U.S.C.A. 237, 1233g; 42 U.S.C.A. 2000d-5, 2494.

Elkins Act (Interstate Commerce): 49 U.S.C.A. 41, 43; see 49 U.S.C.A. 11703, 11916.

Ellender Sugar Act: See Sugar Act of 1937.

Emergency Agricultural Credit Act of 1984: 7 U.S.C.A. 1921 note.

Emergency Agricultural Credit Adjustment Act of 1978: 5 U.S.C.A. 8340; 7 U.S.C.A. note prec. 1961.

Emergency Appropriation Acts: 2 U.S.C.A. 36, 67; 7 U.S.C.A. 604, 605; 16 U.S.C.A. 587a; 40 U.S.C.A. 22a.

Emergency Banking Relief Act: 12 U.S.C.A. 51a, 445; 50 App. U.S.C.A. 5, 5a.

Emergency Cargo-Ship Construction Act: 46 U.S.C.A. 1119a, 1214.

Emergency Community Facilities Act of 1970: 42 U.S.C.A. 3102, 3108.

Emergency Compensation and Special Unemployment Assistance Extension Act of 1975: 26 U.S.C.A. 44, 3302.

Emergency Copyright Act of 1941: See 17 U.S.C.A. 9.

Emergency Daylight Saving Time Energy Conservation Act of 1973: 15 U.S.C.A. 260a note.

Emergency Detention Act of 1950: 18 U.S.C.A. 4001; 50 U.S.C.A. 811, 826.

Emergency Employment Act of 1971: 42 U.S.C.A. 4871, 4883.

Emergency Energy Conservation Act of 1979: 42 U.S.C.A. 6261, 8541.

Emergency Extension Act of 1985: 19 U.S.C.A. 2271 note; 26 U.S.C.A. 5701 note; 42 U.S.C.A. 1395ww notes; 45 U.S.C.A. 360.

Emergency Farm Mortgage Act of 1933: 12 U.S.C.A. 347, 1019; see 31 U.S.C.A. 5301; 43 U.S.C.A. 403, 404.

Emergency Food Stamp Vendor Accountability Act of 1976: 7 U.S.C.A. 2012, 2016.

Emergency Health Personnel Act of 1970: 42 U.S.C.A. 233, 254b.

Emergency Health Personnel Act Amendments of 1972: 42 U.S.C.A. 234, 294a.

Emergency Highway Energy Conservation Act: 23 U.S.C.A. 101 note; 49 U.S.C.A. 1421.

Emergency Home Finance Act of 1970: 12 U.S.C.A. 82, 1749; 42 U.S.C.A. 3906, 3941.

Emergency Home Purchase Assistance Act of 1974: 12 U.S.C.A. 347b, 1723e.

Emergency Homeowners Relief Act: 12 U.S.C.A. 2701, 2712.

Emergency Housing Act of 1975: 12 U.S.C.A. 1723e, 2712; 42 U.S.C.A. 1452b, 4106.

Emergency Immigrant Education Act of 1984: 20 U.S.C.A. 3121, 4108.

Emergency Insured Student Loan Act of 1969: 20 U.S.C.A. 421, 1078a; 42 U.S.C.A. 2751.

Emergency Interim Consumer Product Safety Standard Act of 1978: 15 U.S.C.A. 2068, 2082.

Emergency Job Programs Extension Act of 1976: 26 U.S.C.A. 3304 note; 29 U.S.C.A. 815, 984; 38 U.S.C.A. 2002 note.

Emergency Jobs and Unemployment Assistance Act of 1974: 18 U.S.C.A. 665; 26 U.S.C.A. 3304 note; 29 U.S.C.A. 818, 992; 38 U.S.C.A. 2002 note; 42 U.S.C.A. 3222, 3246g.

Emergency Livestock Credit Act of 1974: 7 U.S.C.A. note prec. 1961.

Emergency Livestock Feed Assistance Act of 1988: 7 U.S.C.A. 1471, 1471j.

Emergency Loan Guarantee Act: 15 U.S.C.A. 1841, 1852.

Emergency Low Income Housing Preservation Act of 1987: 12 U.S.C.A. 1715z-6, 1715z-15; 42 U.S.C.A. 1437f, 1487.

Emergency Medical Services Amendments of 1976: 42 U.S.C.A. 295f-6, 4577.

Emergency Medical Services Systems Act of 1973: 33 U.S.C.A. 763c; 42 U.S.C.A. 211a, 300d-9.

Emergency Petroleum Allocation Act of 1973: 15 U.S.C.A. 751, 760h.

Emergency Planning and Community Right-To-Know Act of 1986: 42 U.S.C.A. 11001, 11050.

Emergency Rail Services Act of 1970: 45 U.S.C.A. 661, 669; see 49 U.S.C.A. 10301, 11914.

Emergency Railroad Transportation Act, 1933: 45 U.S.C.A. 662, 669.

Emergency Relief and Construction Act of 1932: 12 U.S.C.A. 343, 1148a; 15 U.S.C.A. generally dispersed throughout chapter 14; 40 U.S.C.A. 258a note.

Emergency Relief Appropriation Acts: 7 U.S.C.A. 612c note; 15 U.S.C.A. 609i; 16 U.S.C.A. 584g-1, 831*l*; 29 U.S.C.A. 205, 206.

Emergency School Aid Act: 20 U.S.C.A. 1601, 3207.

Emergency Ship Repair Act of 1954: 50 App. U.S.C.A. 2391, 2394.

Emergency Technical Provisions Act: 20 U.S.C.A. 1615; 42 U.S.C.A. 2756.

Emergency Unemployment Compensation Act of 1971: 26 U.S.C.A. 3304 note; 42 U.S.C.A. 1103.

Emergency Unemployment Compensation Extension Act of 1977: 2 U.S.C.A. 359, 360; 26 U.S.C.A. 3302, 3309.

Emergency Wetlands Resources Act of 1986: 16 U.S.C.A. 460*l*-8, 4104.

Employee Polygraph Protection Act of 1988: 29 U.S.C.A. 2001, 2009.

Employee Retirement Income Security Act of 1974: 5 U.S.C.A. 5108, 5109; 18 U.S.C.A. 664, 1954; 26 U.S.C.A. 37, 7802; 29 U.S.C.A. 441, 1461; see 31 U.S.C.A. 9101; 42 U.S.C.A. 1320b-1.

Employers' Liability Acts (Railroads): 45 U.S.C.A. 51, 60.

Employment Act of 1946: 15 U.S.C.A. 1021, 1024.

Employment Opportunities for Disabled Americans Act: 42 U.S.C.A. 1382, 1396s.

Employment Opportunities for Handicapped Individuals Act: 29 U.S.C.A. 795, 795i.

Employment Security Act of 1960: 26 U.S.C.A. 3301, 3309; 29 U.S.C.A. 49d; 42 U.S.C.A. 501, 1400c.

Endangered American Wilderness Act of 1978: 16 U.S.C.A. 1132 note.

Endangered Species Act of 1973: 7 U.S.C.A. 136; 16 U.S.C.A. 460*l*-9, 3375.

Endangered Species Conservation Act of 1969: 16 U.S.C.A. 668aa, 668cc-6.

Energy and Water Development Appropriation Act, 1980: 40 U.S.C.A. 174b-1 note; 43 U.S.C.A. 377a.

Energy Conservation and Production Act: 12 U.S.C.A. 1701z-8; 15 U.S.C.A. 757, 790h; 42 U.S.C.A. 5818, 6892.

Energy Conservation in Existing Buildings Act of 1976: 12 U.S.C.A. 1701z-8; 42 U.S.C.A. 6323, 6892.

Energy Conservation Standards for New Buildings Act of 1976: 42 U.S.C.A. 6831, 6840.

Energy Emergency Preparedness Act of 1982: 42 U.S.C.A. 6239, 6385.

Energy Organization Act of 1974: 42 U.S.C.A. 5818.

Energy Policy and Conservation Act: 12 U.S.C.A. 1904 note; 15 U.S.C.A. 753, 2012; 42 U.S.C.A. 2, 6422; 50 App. U.S.C.A. 2071.

Energy Reorganization Act of 1974: 5 U.S.C.A. 5313, 5316; 42 U.S.C.A. 5801, 5891.

Energy Security Act: 7 U.S.C.A. 341, 3154; 10 U.S.C.A. 7430; 12 U.S.C.A. 1451, 3620; 15 U.S.C.A. 753, 3391a; 16 U.S.C.A. 590h, 2708; 30 U.S.C.A. 1141, 1542; 42 U.S.C.A. 6240, 8912; 50 App. U.S.C.A. 2062, 2166.

Energy Supply and Environmental Coordination Act of 1974: 15 U.S.C.A. 791, 798; 42 U.S.C.A. 1857b-1, 1957*l*.

Energy Tax Act of 1978: 23 U.S.C.A. 120 note; 26 U.S.C.A. 39, 6504.

Engle Act (National Defense Withdrawals): 10 U.S.C.A. 2671; 40 U.S.C.A. 472; 43 U.S.C.A. 155, 158.

Enlarged Homestead Acts: 43 U.S.C.A. 218, 302.

Environmental Education Act: 20 U.S.C.A. 1531, 1536.

Environmental Education Act of 1978: 20 U.S.C.A. 3011, 3018.

Environmental Financing Act of 1972: 33 U.S.C.A. 1281 note.

Environmental Programs Assistance Act of 1984: 42 U.S.C.A. 4368a.

Environmental Quality Improvement Act of 1970: 42 U.S.C.A. 4371, 4375.

Environmental Research, Development, and Demonstration Authorization Act of 1978: 42 U.S.C.A. 300j-3a, 4367.

Equal Access Act, The: 20 U.S.C.A. 4071, 4074.

Equal Access to Justice Act: 5 U.S.C.A. 504; 15 U.S.C.A. 634b; 28 U.S.C.A. 2412; 42 U.S.C.A. 1988.

Equal Credit Opportunity Act: 15 U.S.C.A. 1691, 1691f.

Equal Educational Opportunities Act of 1974: 20 U.S.C.A. 1228, 1758.

Equal Employment Opportunity Act of 1972: 5 U.S.C.A. 5108, 2000e-17.

Equal Export Opportunity Act: 50 App. U.S.C.A. 2401, 2413.

Equal Pay Act of 1963: 29 U.S.C.A. 206.

Equal Time Act: See Communications Acts.

ERISA: See Employee Retirement Income Security Act of 1974.

Esch Act (Hours of Service on Railroads): 45 U.S.C.A. 61, 64.

Esch Car Service Act: See 49 U.S.C.A. 11121.

Espionage Act: See 18 U.S.C.A. 11, 3241; 22 U.S.C.A. 213, 408; 50 U.S.C.A. 191, 194.

Espionage and Sabotage Act of 1954: 18 U.S.C.A. 794, 2156.

Ethics in Government Act of 1978: 2 U.S.C.A. 288, 1018a; 5 U.S.C.A. 5314, 5316; 5 App. U.S.C.A. 201, 408; 18 U.S.C.A. 207; 28 U.S.C.A. 49, 1364; 28 App. U.S.C.A. 301, 308; 39 U.S.C.A. 3210, 3219.

EURATOM Cooperation Act of 1958: 42 U.S.C.A. 2291, 2296.

Everglades National Park Acts: 16 U.S.C.A. 410, 410r-4.

Excellence in Education Act: 20 U.S.C.A. 4031, 4037.

Excellence in Minority Health Education and Care Act: 42 U.S.C.A. 295g-8a.

Exchange Rates and International Economic Policy Coordination Act of 1988: 12 U.S.C.A. 225a; 22 U.S.C.A. 5301, 5306.

Excise, Estate, and Gift Tax Adjustment Act of 1970: 15 U.S.C.A. 1232a; 26 U.S.C.A. 56, 6905; 31 U.S.C.A. 322.

Excise-Tax Rate Extension Act of 1964: 26 U.S.C.A. 165, 6412.

Excise Tax Reduction Act of 1965: 13 U.S.C.A. 120 note; 26 U.S.C.A. 39, 7652.

Executive Exchange Program Voluntary Services Act of 1986: 5 U.S.C.A. 4103 note.

Executive Office Appropriations Act, 1989: 26 U.S.C.A. 7443 note; 33 U.S.C.A. 776; 40 U.S.C.A. 490a-1, 490d.

Executive Salary Cost-of-Living Adjustment Act: 2 U.S.C.A. 31, 356; 3 U.S.C.A. 104; 5 U.S.C.A. 5305, 5318; 28 U.S.C.A. 5, 792; see 31 U.S.C.A. 703, 731; 40 U.S.C.A. 162a, 166b; 44 U.S.C.A. 303.

Expatriation Act of 1954: 8 U.S.C.A. 1481.

Expedited Funds Availability Act: 12 U.S.C.A. 248a, 4010.

Expediting Act: 15 U.S.C.A. 28, 29; see 49 U.S.C.A. 11703.

Expediting Acts (Trusts and Interstate Commerce): 15 U.S.C.A. 28, 29; see 49 U.S.C.A. 11703, 11916.

Explosives Act: 50 U.S.C.A. 121, 144.

Explosives Transportation Acts: See 18 U.S.C.A. 831, 835.

Export Administration Act of 1969: 50 App. U.S.C.A. 2401, 2413.

Export Administration Act of 1979: 7 U.S.C.A. 1732; 22 U.S.C.A. 2778, 3108; 26 U.S.C.A. 993; 42 U.S.C.A. 6212, 6274; 50 App. U.S.C.A. 2401, 2420.

Export Apple and Pear Act: 7 U.S.C.A. 581, 590.

Export Control Act of 1949: 50 App. U.S.C.A. 2021, 2032.

Export Enhancement Act of 1988: 5 U.S.C.A. 5314, 5315; 7 U.S.C.A. 1431, 1708; 12 U.S.C.A. 635q, 635s; 15 U.S.C.A. 4003, 4726; 19 U.S.C.A. 1864; 22 U.S.C.A. 2151f, 3310a; 50 App. U.S.C.A. 5, 2419.

Export Expansion Finance Act of 1971: 12 U.S.C.A. 635, 635f.

Export Grape and Plum Act: 7 U.S.C.A. 591, 599.

Export-Import Bank Act of 1945: 12 U.S.C.A. 635, 635i-4.

Export-Import Bank Act Amendments of 1978: 12 U.S.C.A. 635, 635g; 42 U.S.C.A. 2153e-1.

Export-Import Bank Act Amendments of 1986: 12 U.S.C.A. 635, 635i; 22 U.S.C.A. 262h.

Export-Import Bank and Reconstruction Finance Corporation Appropriation Act, 1950: 15 U.S.C.A. 603b, 603c.

Export-Import Bank and Tied Aid Credit Amendments of 1988: 12 U.S.C.A. 635, 635i-3.

Export-Import Bank Extension Act: 15 U.S.C.A. 713, 173c.

Export Trade Act: 15 U.S.C.A. 61, 66.

Export Trading Company Act of 1982: 15 U.S.C.A. 4001, 4003.

Export Trading Company Act Amendments of 1988: 12 U.S.C.A. 1843.

Ex-Servicemen's Unemployment Compensation Act of 1958: See 5 U.S.C.A. 8501, 8525.

Extra Long Staple Cotton Act of 1983: 7 U.S.C.A. 1308, 1444.

Fact Finders' Act: 21 U.S.C.A. 129; see 28 U.S.C.A. 571; 43 U.S.C.A. 371, 526.

Fair Credit and Charge Card Disclosure Act of 1988: 15 U.S.C.A. 1610, 1646.

Fair Credit Billing Act: 15 U.S.C.A. 1601, 1666j.

Fair Credit Reporting Act: 15 U.S.C.A. 1681, 1681t.

Fair Debt Collection Practices Act: 15 U.S.C.A. 1692, 1692o.

Fair Housing Act of 1968: 42 U.S.C.A. 3601, 3619.

Fair Housing Amendments Act of 1988: 28 U.S.C.A. 2341, 2342; 42 U.S.C.A. 3602, 3631.

Fair Labor Standards Act of 1938: 29 U.S.C.A. 201, 260.

Fair Packaging and Labeling Act: 15 U.S.C.A. 1451, 1461.

Fair Share Refugee Act: 8 U.S.C.A. 1182, 1255.

Fair Trade Act: 15 U.S.C.A. 1.

Fair Trade in Auto Parts Act of 1988: 15 U.S.C.A. 4701, 4704.

False Branding or Marking Act: 21 U.S.C.A. 16, 17.

False Claims Act: See 31 U.S.C.A. 3629, 3731.

False Identification Crime Control Act of 1982: 18 U.S.C.A. 1028, 1738; 39 U.S.C.A. 3001.

Family Educational Rights and Privacy Act of 1974: 20 U.S.C.A. 1232g.

Family Planning and Population Research Act of 1975: 42 U.S.C.A. 300, 300a-8.

Family Planning Services and Population Research Act of 1970: 33 U.S.C.A. 763c; 42 U.S.C.A. 211a, 3505c.

Family Practice of Medicine Act: 42 U.S.C.A. 295, 295e.

Family Support Act of 1988: 5 U.S.C.A. 5315, 26 U.S.C.A. 51, 6109; 42 U.S.C.A. 405, 1397e.

Family Violence Prevention and Services Act: 42 U.S.C.A. 10401, 10413.

Farm Credit Act of 1971: 5 U.S.C.A. 5314, 5315; 7 U.S.C.A. 1983, 5106; 12 U.S.C.A. 393, 2297aa-12; 16 U.S.C.A. 3835; 31 U.S.C.A. 9105.

Farm Disaster Assistance Act of 1987: 7 U.S.C.A. 1441-1, 1446; 16 U.S.C.A. 3835 note; 31 U.S.C.A. 701n.

Farm Interest Act: 12 U.S.C.A. 771, 1016.

Farm Labor Contractor Registration Act of 1963: 7 U.S.C.A. 2041, 2055.

Farm labor Supply Appropriation Act, 1944: 50 App. U.S.C.A. 1351, 1355.

Farm Mortgage Foreclosure Act: 12 U.S.C.A. 1016.

Farm Research Act: 7 U.S.C.A. 427, 427g.

Farmers' Home Administration Act of 1946: 7 U.S.C.A. 1032a; 12 U.S.C.A. 371.

Farmer-to-Consumer Direct Marketing Act of 1976: 7 U.S.C.A. 3001, 3006; 42 U.S.C.A. 5145 note.

Farmington Wild and Scenic River Study Act: 16 U.S.C.A. 1276.

Farmland Protection Policy Act: 7 U.S.C.A. 4201, 4209.

Fascell Fellowship Act: 22 U.S.C.A. 4901, 4904.

Father's Day Act: 36 U.S.C.A. 142a.

Federal Advisory Committee Act: 5 App. U.S.C.A. 7, 10.

Federal-Aid Highway Act of 1987: 18 U.S.C.A. 1761; 23 U.S.C.A. 101, 409; 33 U.S.C.A. 494, 535d; 49 U.S.C.A. 303, 2716.

Federal Airport Act: 49 U.S.C.A. 1101, 1120.

Federal Alcohol Administration Act: 27 U.S.C.A. 201, 220.

Federal Anti-Injunction Act: 29 U.S.C.A. 101, 115.

Federal Anti-Tampering Act: 18 U.S.C.A. 1365; 35 U.S.C.A. 155A.

Federal Assistance and Related Programs Appropriation Act of 1985: 12 U.S.C.A. 24; 22 U.S.C.A. 254p, 2761.

Federal Aviation Act of 1958: 5 U.S.C.A. 5314 note; 14 U.S.C.A. 81, 90; 15 U.S.C.A. 45; 16 U.S.C.A. 7a; see 31 U.S.C.A. 1535; 40 U.S.C.A. 474; 48 U.S.C.A. 485, 485d; 49 U.S.C.A. 212, 1551; see 49 U.S.C.A. 106, 1432; 49 App. U.S.C.A. 1301, 1553; 50 U.S.C.A. 123; 50 App. U.S.C.A. 1622, 1622c.

Federal Aviation Administration Drug Enforcement Assistance Act of 1988: 49 U.S.C.A. 334; 49 App. U.S.C.A. 1303, 1472.

Federal Banking Agency Audit Act: 18 U.S.C.A. 1906; See 31 U.S.C.A. 714, 719.

Federal Boat Safety Act of 1971: 16 U.S.C.A. 1606a; 46 U.S.C.A. 526u, 1489.

Federal Boating Act of 1958: 46 U.S.C.A. 526*l*, 527h.

Federal Capital Investment Program Information Act of 1984: 31 U.S.C.A. 1105.

Federal Caustic Poison Act: 15 U.S.C.A. 401, 411; 50 App. U.S.C.A. 2255, 2281.

Federal Cave Resources Protection Act of 1988: 16 U.S.C.A. 4301, 4309.

Federal Child Support Enforcement Act: 42 U.S.C.A. 651, 662.

Federal Cigarette Labeling and Advertising Act: 15 U.S.C.A. 1331, 1340.

Federal Civil Defense Act of 1950: 50 App. U.S.C.A. 2251, 2302.

Federal Civilian Employee and Contractor Travel Expenses Act of 1985: 2 U.S.C.A. 476; 5 U.S.C.A. 5701, 5734; 22 U.S.C.A. 2396; 26 U.S.C.A. 4941; 28 U.S.C.A. 456; 31 U.S.C.A. 326; 41 U.S.C.A. 420; 42 U.S.C.A. 2477.

Federal Claims Collection Act of 1966: See 31 U.S.C.A. 3701, 3718.

Federal Coal Leasing Amendments Act of 1975: 30 U.S.C.A. 184, 352.

Federal Coal Mine Health and Safety Act of 1969: 15 U.S.C.A. 633, 636; 30 U.S.C.A. 801, 960.

Federal Coal Mine Safety Act: 30 U.S.C.A. 451, 932a.

Federal Coal Mine Safety Act Amendments of 1965: 30 U.S.C.A. 471, 482.

Federal Columbia River Transmission System Act: 16 U.S.C.A. 838, 838k.

Federal Communications Commission Authorization Act of 1983: 47 U.S.C.A. 154, 503.

Federal Contested Election Act: 2 U.S.C.A. 381, 396.

Federal Corrupt Practices Acts: 2 U.S.C.A. 241; see 18 U.S.C.A. 602.

Federal Courts Improvement Act of 1982: 2 U.S.C.A. 356; 5 U.S.C.A. 7703, 8912; 7 U.S.C.A. 2461; 10 U.S.C.A. 2273; 15 U.S.C.A. 714b, 2210; 16 U.S.C.A. 831s; 18 U.S.C.A. 204, 6001; 19 U.S.C.A. 1337, 2395. For more titles, see Popular Name Table.

Federal Courts Study Act: 5 U.S.C.A. 5108; 28 U.S.C.A. 331 note.

Federal Credit Union Act: 12 U.S.C.A. 1751, 1795k.

Federal Credit Union Insurance Act: 12 U.S.C.A. 1790a.

Federal Crop Insurance Act of 1980: 7 U.S.C.A. 1441, 1518.

Federal Crop Insurance Commission Act of 1988: 7 U.S.C.A. 1508 note.

Federal Deposit Insurance Act: 12 U.S.C.A. 264, 1831d.

Federal Deposit Insurance Corporation Act: 12 U.S.C.A. 462a–1, 1831.

Federal District Court Organization Act of 1984: 28 U.S.C.A. 85, 126.

Federal Drivers Act: 28 U.S.C.A. 2679(b), 2679(e).

Federal Election Campaign Act of 1971: 2 U.S.C.A. 431, 490c; 18 U.S.C.A. 591, 611; 47 U.S.C.A. 312, 805.

Federal Election Campaign Act Amendments of 1979: 2 U.S.C.A. 431, 441i; 5 U.S.C.A. 3132; 18 U.S.C.A. 602, 607; 22 U.S.C.A. 901a; 26 U.S.C.A. 9008; 42 U.S.C.A. 5043.

Federal Employee Substance Abuse Education and Treatment Act of 1986: 5 U.S.C.A. 7361, 7904; 21 U.S.C.A. 801 notes; 42 U.S.C.A. 290dd–1, 290ee–1.

Federal Employees Benefits Improvement Act of 1986: 5 U.S.C.A. 1103, 8909; 24 U.S.C.A. 35.

Federal Employees' Compensation Act: See 1 U.S.C.A. 1; see 5 U.S.C.A. 5342, 8150; see 18 U.S.C.A. 1, 1922.

Federal Employees Flexible and Compressed Work Schedules Act of 1982: 5 U.S.C.A. 3401, 6133.

Federal Employees' Group Life Insurance Act of 1954: See 5 U.S.C.A. 1308, 8716.

Federal Employees' Group Life Insurance Act of 1980: 5 U.S.C.A. 8701, 8714c.

Federal Employees Health Benefits Act of 1959: See 5 U.S.C.A. 1104, 8913.

Federal Employees Leave Sharing Act of 1988: 5 U.S.C.A. 5724, 8112.

Federal Employees Liability Reform and Tort Compensation Act of 1988: 16 U.S.C.A. 831c–2; 28 U.S.C.A. 2671, 2679.

Federal Employees Part-Time Career Employment Act of 1978: 5 U.S.C.A. 3391, 8913.

Federal Employees Pay Act of 1945: 2 U.S.C.A. 60e–2, 60e–4; see 5 U.S.C.A. 305, 6101; see 28 U.S.C.A. 604; 39 U.S.C.A. 3573.

Federal Employees' Retirement System Act of 1986: 5 U.S.C.A. 2105, 8905; 10 U.S.C.A. 1605; 22 U.S.C.A. 4041, 4071k; 26 U.S.C.A. 3121, 6103; 39 U.S.C.A. 1005; 42 U.S.C.A. 410; 50 U.S.C.A. 402 note, 403 notes.

Federal Employees Salary Act of 1966: See 5 U.S.C.A. 5332, 5545; 16 U.S.C.A. 590h note; 22 U.S.C.A. 867, 870; 28 U.S.C.A. 548 note; 38 U.S.C.A. 4107.

Federal Employees Salary Increase Act of 1960: 2

U.S.C.A. 60e–9; see 5 U.S.C.A. 5332, 8913; 16 U.S.C.A. 590h note; 22 U.S.C.A. 867, 870; 28 U.S.C.A. 753; 38 U.S.C.A. 4103, 4108.

Federal Employees Uniform Allowance Act: See 5 U.S.C.A. 5901, 8331.

Federal Employees Vacation Act: See 5 U.S.C.A. ch. 63.

Federal Employment Pay Act of 1946: 2 U.S.C.A. 60e–2, 60e–4; see 5 U.S.C.A. 5342, 8331; see 28 U.S.C.A. 604.

Federal Employment Service Act: 29 U.S.C.A. 49, 49*l*.

Federal Energy Administration Act of 1974: 15 U.S.C.A. 761, 790h.

Federal Energy Administration Authorization Act of 1977: 15 U.S.C.A. 766, 796; 42 U.S.C.A. 6246, 6881.

Federal Energy Management Improvement Act of 1988: 15 U.S.C.A. 5001; 42 U.S.C.A. 6361, 8261.

Federal Environmental Pesticide Control Act of 1972: 7 U.S.C.A. 136, 136y; 15 U.S.C.A. 1261, 1471; 21 U.S.C.A. 321, 346a.

Federal Escape Act: See 18 U.S.C.A. 751, 1791.

Federal Executive Pay Act of 1956: 3 U.S.C.A. 105; see 5 U.S.C.A. 1102, 8348; 21 U.S.C.A. 113a; 22 U.S.C.A. 387n, 1787; 42 U.S.C.A. 210, 3504; 50 U.S.C.A. 158.

Federal Executive Salary Act of 1964: 3 U.S.C.A. 104, 105; see 5 U.S.C.A. 5311, 5364; 8 U.S.C.A. 1104; 10 U.S.C.A. 137, 8013. See Popular Name Table for more titles.

Federal Explosives Act: 50 U.S.C.A. 121, 144.

Federal Farm Board Act: 12 U.S.C.A. 1141, 1141j.

Federal Farm Loan Acts: 12 U.S.C.A. 636c, 1134*l*.

Federal Farm Mortgage Corporation Act: 12 U.S.C.A. 347, 1138b.

Federal Financial Institutions Examination Council Act of 1978: 12 U.S.C.A. 3301, 3308; See 31 U.S.C.A. 714.

Federal Financing Bank Act of 1973: 12 U.S.C.A. 24, 2294.

Federal Fire Prevention and Control Act of 1974: 15 U.S.C.A. 278f, 2223; 42 U.S.C.A. 290a.

Federal Firearms Act: See 18 U.S.C.A. 921 et seq.

Federal Flood Insurance Act of 1956: 42 U.S.C.A. 2401, 2421.

Federal Food, Drug, and Cosmetic Act: 21 U.S.C.A. 301, 393.

Federal Grant and Cooperative Agreement Act of 1977: See 31 U.S.C.A. 6301, 6308.

Federal Hazardous Substances Act: 15 U.S.C.A. 1261, 1277.

Federal Highway Acts: See 4 U.S.C.A. 104; 16 U.S.C.A. 8–1, 460c; see 23 U.S.C.A. 101, 311; 25 U.S.C.A. 318b.

Federal Highway Act of 1960: See 23 U.S.C.A. 104, 305.

Federal Home Loan Bank Act: 12 U.S.C.A. 1421, 1449.

Federal Home Loan Mortgage Corporation Act: 12 U.S.C.A. 1451, 1459.

Federal Information Centers Act: 40 U.S.C.A. 760.

Federal Insecticide, Fungicide, and Rodenticide Act: 7 U.S.C.A. 135, 136y.

Federal Insurance Contributions Act (1939): See 26 U.S.C.A. 3101, 3125.

Federal Insurance Contributions Act (1954): 26 U.S.C.A. 3101, 3125.

Federal Interpleader Act: See 28 U.S.C.A. 1335, 2361.

Federal Judicial Salary Act of 1964: 10 U.S.C.A. 867; 26 U.S.C.A. 7443; 38 U.S.C.A. 5, 792.

Federal Juvenile Delinquency Act: 18 U.S.C.A. 5031, 5042; see 18 U.S.C.A. 5031, 5037.

Federal Laboratory Animal Welfare Act: 7 U.S.C.A. 2131, 2154.

Federal Land Exchange Facilitation Act of 1988: 16 U.S.C.A. 505a, 1723.

Federal Land Policy and Management Act of 1976: 7 U.S.C.A. 1010, 1012a; 16 U.S.C.A. 5, 1340; 30 U.S.C.A. 50, 191; 40 U.S.C.A. 319, 319c; 43 U.S.C.A. 315b, 1782.

Federal Lands Cleanup Act of 1985: 36 U.S.C.A. 169i, 169i–1.

Federal Legislative Salary Act of 1964: 2 U.S.C.A. 31, 273a; see 31 U.S.C.A. 703, 731; 40 U.S.C.A. 162a, 166b–1; see 44 U.S.C.A. 303.

Federal Magistrates Act: 18 U.S.C.A. 202, 3771; 28 U.S.C.A. 604, 639.

Federal Magistrate Act of 1979: 18 U.S.C.A. 3401; 28 U.S.C.A. 604, 1915.

Federal Managers' Financial Integrity Act of 1982: See 31 U.S.C.A. 1105, 3512.

Federal Marshals Act: See 18 U.S.C.A. 3053; see 28 U.S.C.A. 567.

Federal Mass Transportation Act of 1987: 23 U.S.C.A. 101 notes; 49 U.S.C.A. 1602, 10922.

Federal Meat Inspection Act: 19 U.S.C.A. 1306; 21 U.S.C.A. 601, 691.

Federal Metal and Nonmetallic Mine Safety Act: 30 U.S.C.A. 721, 740.

Federal Mine Safety and Health Act of 1977: 5 U.S.C.A. 5314, 4315; 29 U.S.C.A. 557a; 30 U.S.C.A. 801, 961; see 31 U.S.C.A. 1105; 43 U.S.C.A. 1456.

Federal National Mortgage Association Act: 12 U.S.C.A. 1721.

Federal National Mortgage Association Charter Act: 12 U.S.C.A. 1454, 1723h.

Federal Nonnuclear Energy Research and De-velopment Act of 1974: 42 U.S.C.A. 5901, 5920.

Federal Noxious Weed Act of 1974: 7 U.S.C.A. 2801, 2813; 19 U.S.C.A. 2112 note.

Federal Oil and Gas Royalty Management Act of 1982: 30 U.S.C.A. 188, 1757.

Federal Onshore Oil Gas Leasing Reform Act of 1987: 16 U.S.C.A. 3148; 30 U.S.C.A. 187a, 226-3.

Federal Pay Comparability Act of 1970: 2 U.S.C.A. 60a note; 5 U.S.C.A. 5108, 5947; 39 U.S.C.A. 410.

Federal Pesticide Act of 1978: 7 U.S.C.A. 136, 136y.

Federal Photovoltaic Utilization Act: 42 U.S.C.A. 8271, 8278.

Federal Physicians Comparability Allowance Act of 1978: 5 U.S.C.A. 5948.

Federal Plant Pest Act: 7 U.S.C.A. 147a, 150jj; 19 U.S.C.A. 2112 note.

Federal Possession and Control Act (Railroads in War): See 10 U.S.C.A. 4742, 9742.

Federal Power Act: 16 U.S.C.A. 791, 825r.

Federal Program Information Act: See 31 U.S.C.A. 6101, 6105.

Federal Property and Administrative Services Act: 40 U.S.C.A. 541.

Federal Property and Administrative Services Act of 1949: 40 U.S.C.A. 471, 760; 41 U.S.C.A. 5, 260; 44 U.S.C.A. chs. 21, 25, 27, 29, 31; see 44 U.S.C.A. 2101, 3107; 50 App. U.S.C.A. 1622, 1641.

Federal Property Management Improvement Act of 1988: 40 U.S.C.A. 481, 493.

Federal Public Transportation Act of 1978: 15 U.S.C.A. 1418; 49 App. U.S.C.A. 1601, 1618.

Federal Question Jurisdictional Amendments Act of 1980: 15 U.S.C.A. 2072; 28 U.S.C.A. 1331.

Federal Railroad Safety Act of 1970: 45 U.S.C.A. 39, 445.

Federal Railroad Safety Authorization Act of 1980: 43 U.S.C.A. 975; 45 U.S.C.A. 6, 444; 49 U.S.C.A. 26.

Federal Records Act of 1950: See 44 U.S.C.A. chs. 21, 25, 27, 29, 31.

Federal Records Management Amendments of 1976: 44 U.S.C.A. 2103, 3302.

Federal Register Act: See 44 U.S.C.A. 1501, 1511.

Federal Regulation of Lobbying Act: 2 U.S.C.A. 261, 270.

Federal Reports Act of 1942: See 44 U.S.C.A. 3501, 3511.

Federal Reserve Act: 12 U.S.C.A. 82, 1972; generally dispersed throughout U.S.C.A. title 12; 50 App. U.S.C.A. prec. 634.

Federal Reserve Note Security Act: 12 U.S.C.A. 412.

Federal Reserve Reform Act of 1977: 12 U.S.C.A. 208, 302.

Federal Revenue Sharing Act (National Forest Revenues for National Forest Road and Trail Expenditures): 16 U.S.C.A. 501.

Federal Revenue Sharing Act (National Forest Revenues for Public School and Road Expenditures): 16 U.S.C.A. 500.

Federal Rules of Appellate Procedure: 28 U.S.C.A. Rules 4, 9.

Federal Rules of Civil Procedure: 28 U.S.C.A. Rules 17, 35, 71A.

Federal Rules of Civil Procedure Amendments Act of 1982: 18 U.S.C.A. 951; 28 U.S.C.A. 2071 note; 28 App. U.S.C.A. Rule 4; 28 App. U.S.C.A. Form 18-A.

Federal Rules of Criminal Procedure: 18 U.S.C.A. Rules 5, 6, 11, 12.2, 12.3, 29, 32, 32.1, 35, 38, 40, 46, 54.

Federal Rules of Evidence: 28 App. U.S.C.A.

Federal Salary Act of 1967: 2 U.S.C.A. 60e–14, 361; 3 U.S.C.A. 102 note; 5 U.S.C.A. 3110, 8339; 16 U.S.C.A. 590h note; 22 U.S.C.A. 867, 870; 28 U.S.C.A. 603, 792; see 31 U.S.C.A. 703, 731; 38 U.S.C.A. 4107; 40 U.S.C.A. 162a, 166b–3.

Federal Salary and Fringe Benefits Act of 1966: 2 U.S.C.A. 293b, 16 U.S.C.A. 590h note; 22 U.S.C.A. 867, 870; 28 U.S.C.A. 548 note, 753 note; 38 U.S.C.A. 4107.

Federal Salary Reform Act of 1962: 2 U.S.C.A. 60e–10; see 5 U.S.C.A. 3104, 8331; 7 U.S.C.A. 1857; 10 U.S.C.A. 1581. See Popular Name Table for other titles.

Federal Savings and Loan Insurance Corporation Recapitalization Act of 1987: 12 U.S.C.A. 1430, 1730; 31 U.S.C.A. 9101.

Federal Security Agency Appropriation Act: 16 U.S.C.A. 584h–1, 584n–1; 21 U.S.C.A. 46a; 24 U.S.C.A. 169; 29 U.S.C.A. 31; 41 U.S.C.A. 6a note; 42 U.S.C.A. 209c; 1301a.

Federal Seed Act: 7 U.S.C.A. 1551, 1611; 19 U.S.C.A. 2112 note.

Federal Ship Financing Act of 1972: 46 U.S.C.A. 1271, 1279b.

Federal Ship Mortgage Insurance Act: 46 U.S.C.A. 1274.

Federal Sick Leave Act: See 5 U.S.C.A. 6302; see 5 U.S.C.A. ch. 63.

Federal-State Communications Joint Board Act: 47 U.S.C.A. 410.

Federal-State Extended Unemployment Compensation Act of 1970: 26 U.S.C.A. 3304.

Federal-State Tax Collection Act of 1972: 26 U.S.C.A. 6361, 7463.

Federal Supplemental Compensation Amend-

ments of 1983: 26 U.S.C.A. 3306; 42 U.S.C.A. 1323, 1397b.

Federal Tax Lien Act of 1966: 26 U.S.C.A. 545, 7810; 28 U.S.C.A. 1346, 2410; 40 U.S.C.A. 270a.

Federal Technology Transfer Act of 1986: 15 U.S.C.A. 3701, 3714; 35 U.S.C.A. 210.

Federal Timber Contract Payment Modification Act: 16 U.S.C.A. 539f, 619.

Federal Tort Claims Act: 28 U.S.C.A. 1291, 2680.

Federal Trade Commission Act: 7 U.S.C.A. 610; 15 U.S.C.A. 41, 58.

Federal Trade Commission Improvements Act of 1980: 15 U.S.C.A. 45, 58.

Federal Triangle Development Act: 40 U.S.C.A. 1101, 1109.

Federal Unemployment Tax Act (1954): 26 U.S.C.A. 3301, 3310; see 26 U.S.C.A. 3311.

Federal Urban Land-Use Act: 40 U.S.C.A. 531, 535.

Federal Voting Assistance Act of 1955: 42 U.S.C.A. 1973cc, 1973cc–26; 50 U.S.C.A. 301 note, 355 note.

Federal Water Pollution Control Act: 33 U.S.C.A. 1152, 1387.

Federal Water Pollution Control Act Amendments of 1972: 12 U.S.C.A. 24; 15 U.S.C.A. 633, 636; see 31 U.S.C.A. 1305; 33 U.S.C.A. 1251, 1376.

Federal Water Power Act: 16 U.S.C.A. 791, 825r; 16 U.S.C.A. ch. 12 note.

Federal Water Project Recreation Act: 16 U.S.C.A. 460*l*–5, 662.

Federal Youth Corrections Act: 18 U.S.C.A. 5005, 5026.

Feed Grain Act of 1963: 7 U.S.C.A. 1339a, 1444b; 16 U.S.C.A. 590p.

Fencing Act (Public Lands): 43 U.S.C.A. 1061, 1066.

Fess-Kenyon Act (Vocational Rehabilitation): 29 U.S.C.A. 31, 44.

Fifth Circuit Court of Appeals Reorganization Act of 1980: 28 U.S.C.A. 41, 48.

Filled Milk Act: 21 U.S.C.A. 61, 63.

Financial Institutions Emergency Acquisitions Amendments of 1987: 2 U.S.C.A. 905, 906; 12 U.S.C.A. 1439–1, 1849.

Financial Institutions Regulatory and Interest Rate Control Act of 1978: 5 U.S.C.A. 5108, 5316; 12 U.S.C.A. 27, 3422; 15 U.S.C.A. 1693, 1693r; 28 U.S.C.A. 709, 1114; see 31 U.S.C.A. 714, 9101; 42 U.S.C.A. 2153e–1.

Financial Institutions Supervisory Act of 1966: 12 U.S.C.A. 1464, 1821.

Financial Regulation Simplification Act of 1980: 12 U.S.C.A. 3521, 3524.

Financial Reports Act of 1988: 22 U.S.C.A. 5351, 5354.

Fine Arts Commission Act: 40 U.S.C.A. 104, 106.

Fire Research and Safety Act of 1968: 15 U.S.C.A. 278f, 278g.

Firearms Owners' Protection Act: 18 U.S.C.A. 921, 929; 18 App. U.S.C.A. 1201, 1203; 26 U.S.C.A. 5845.

First Decontrol Act of 1947: 50 App. U.S.C.A. 645.

First Deficiency Appropriation Act, 1926: 2 U.S.C.A. 64a, 196.

First Liberty Bond Act: See 31 U.S.C.A. 3110, 3129.

First Supplemental Surplus Appropriation Rescission Act, 1946: 42 U.S.C.A. 1543.

First War Powers Act of 1941: 12 U.S.C.A. 95a; 50 App. U.S.C.A. 5, 37.

Fiscal Year Adjustment Act: 2 U.S.C.A. 139; 5 U.S.C.A. 8147; 7 U.S.C.A. 324, 950; 10 U.S.C.A. 279, 6386; 12 U.S.C.A. 1783. See Popular Name Table for other titles.

Fiscal Year Transition Act: 5 U.S.C.A. 5532 note, 8147 note; 7 U.S.C.A. 343 note, 2652 note; 8 U.S.C.A. 1151 note. See Popular Name Table for more titles.

Fish and Game Sanctuary Act: 16 U.S.C.A. 694, 694b.

Fish and Seafood Promotion Act of 1986: 15 U.S.C.A. 713c–3; 16 U.S.C.A. 4001, 4017.

Fish and Wildlife Act of 1956: 15 U.S.C.A. 713c–3; 16 U.S.C.A. 742a, 742j–2.

Fish and Wildlife Conservation Act of 1980: 16 U.S.C.A. 2901, 2912.

Fish and Wildlife Coordination Act: 16 U.S.C.A. 661, 666c.

Fish and Wildlife Improvement Act of 1978: 16 U.S.C.A. 460k–3, 753a; 18 U.S.C.A. 1114, 3112.

Fish Restoration and Management Projects Act: 16 U.S.C.A. 777, 777*l*.

Fisheries Amendments of 1982: 16 U.S.C.A. 779b, 3608; 46 U.S.C.A. 688, 883.

Fishermen's Protective Act of 1967: 22 U.S.C.A. 1971, 1980.

Fishery Conservation Zone Transition Act: 16 U.S.C.A. 1826.

Flag and Seal, Seat of Government, and the States: 4 U.S.C.A. 1, 146.

Flammable Fabrics Act: 15 U.S.C.A. 1191, 1204.

Flexible Tariff Act: 19 U.S.C.A. 1336.

Flood Control Act of 1917: 33 U.S.C.A. 701, 703.

Flood Control Act of 1970: 5 U.S.C.A. 5315; 10 U.S.C.A. 3013; 16 U.S.C.A. 460d; 33 U.S.C.A. 426e, 709a; 42 U.S.C.A. 1962–2, 1962d–5b; 43 U.S.C.A. 1511a.

Flood Disaster Protection Act of 1973: 12 U.S.C.A. 24, 1709–1; 42 U.S.C.A. 4001, 4128.

Floral Research and Consumer Information Act: 7 U.S.C.A. 4301, 4319.

Florida Canal-Pipe Line Act: 15 U.S.C.A. note prec. 715.

Florida Indian Land Claims Settlement Act of 1982: 25 U.S.C.A. 1741, 1749.

Florida Wilderness Act of 1983: 16 U.S.C.A. 1132 note.

Follow Through Act: 42 U.S.C.A. 9861, 9868.

Food Additives Amendment of 1958: 21 U.S.C.A. 321, 348, 42 U.S.C.A. 210.

Food and Agriculture Act of 1977: 7 U.S.C.A. 75, 6651; 15 U.S.C.A. 714b; 16 U.S.C.A. 590h, 1505; 42 U.S.C.A. 1382e note.

Food and Drug Administration Act of 1988: 5 U.S.C.A. 5315, 5316; 21 U.S.C.A. 393.

Food for Peace Act of 1966: 7 U.S.C.A. 1427, 1736d.

Food for Progress Act of 1985: 7 U.S.C.A. 1736o.

Food Security Act of 1985: 7 U.S.C.A. 76, 5007; 12 U.S.C.A. 2129; 15 U.S.C.A. 713a-4, 714b; 16 U.S.C.A. 580q, 3845; 21 U.S.C.A. 151, 881a; 29 U.S.C.A. 49b; 42 U.S.C.A. 503; 46 U.S.C.A. 1241d, 1241p.

Food Security Improvements Act of 1986: 5 U.S.C.A. 5312; 7 U.S.C.A. 259, 1736v; 15 U.S.C.A. 714b.

Food Security Wheat Reserve Act of 1980: 7 U.S.C.A. 1736f–1.

Food Stamp Act of 1964: 7 U.S.C.A. 2011, 2027; 42 U.S.C.A. 1382e note.

Food Stamp and Commodity Distribution Amendments of 1981: 7 U.S.C.A. 2012, 2270.

Foot-and-Mouth Disease Act (Mexico): 21 U.S.C.A. 114b; 114d–1.

Foraker Act (Puerto Rico): See Puerto Rico Civil Code.

Fordney-McCumber Act (Tariff): 19 U.S.C.A. 5, 1333; 46 U.S.C.A. 11, 333.

Foreign Agents Registration Act of 1938: 22 U.S.C.A. 611, 621.

Foreign Aid and Related Agencies Appropriation Act, 1964: 2 U.S.C.A. 46a, 46c; 22 U.S.C.A. 2151 note, 2370 note.

Foreign Assistance Act of 1974: 22 U.S.C.A. 278, 2776.

Foreign Assistance and Related Programs Appropriations Act, 1987: 22 U.S.C.A. 262h, 2414a.

Foreign Corrupt Practices Act of 1977: 15 U.S.C.A. 78m, 78ff.

Foreign Disaster Assistance Act of 1974: 22 U.S.C.A. 2262, 2399–la.

Foreign Earned Income Act of 1978: 26 U.S.C.A. 43, 6091.

Foreign Gifts and Decorations Act of 1966: 22 U.S.C.A. 804, 2626.

Foreign Intelligence Surveillance Act of 1978: 18 U.S.C.A. 2511, 2519; 50 U.S.C.A. 1801, 1811.

Foreign Investment in Real Property Tax Act of 1980: 26 U.S.C.A. 861, 6652.

Foreign Investment Study Act of 1974: 15 U.S.C.A. 78b note.

Foreign Investors Tax Act of 1966: 26 U.S.C.A. 1, 7701.

Foreign Language Assistance Act of 1988: 20 U.S.C.A. 3001, 5015.

Foreign Military Sales Act: 22 U.S.C.A. 2314, 2794.

Foreign Missions Act: 22 U.S.C.A. 254a, 4314.

Foreign Operations, Export Financing, and Related Programs Appropriations Act, 1989: 3 U.S.C.A. 101 note; 7 U.S.C.A. 3602 note; 8 U.S.C.A. 1101 note, 1182 note; 22 U.S.C.A. 262h, 4802.

Foreign Relations Authorization Act, Fiscal Years 1988 and 1989: 1 U.S.C.A. 112b note; 5 U.S.C.A. 5313, 8332; 8 U.S.C.A. 1182; 15 U.S.C.A. 2901 note; 18 U.S.C.A. 3181 note; 19 U.S.C.A. 2492, 2605; 22 U.S.C.A. 288f–3, 5203; 28 U.S.C.A. 1364.

Foreign Securities Act: See 18 U.S.C.A. 955.

Foreign Service Act: 22 U.S.C.A. 2654, 2664.

Foreign Service Act of 1946: 22 U.S.C.A. 801, 1160; see 26 U.S.C.A. 115, 943.

Foreign Service Act of 1980: 5 U.S.C.A. 3323, 8501; 7 U.S.C.A. 1765a, 1766c; 10 U.S.C.A. 2002; 20 U.S.C.A. 906; 22 U.S.C.A. 99, 4173; 26 U.S.C.A. 104, 2055; see 31 U.S.C.A. 325; 37 U.S.C.A. 405a; 38 U.S.C.A. 235; 42 U.S.C.A. 5055.

Foreign Service Annuity Adjustment Act of 1965: 22 U.S.C.A. 1076, 1121.

Foreign Service Appointment Act: 22 U.S.C.A. 293, 297; see 22 U.S.C.A. 906, 907.

Foreign Service Buildings Act, 1926: 22 U.S.C.A. 292, 302.

Foreign Service Pension System Act of 1986: 22 U.S.C.A. 4041, 4071k.

Foreign Service Retirement Amendments of 1976: 22 U.S.C.A. 915, 1229.

Foreign Service Salary Reform Act of 1962: 22 U.S.C.A. 867, 1017.

Foreign Shipping Practices Act of 1988: 46 U.S.C.A. 3302 note; 46 App. U.S.C.A. 1122b, 1710a.

Foreign Sovereign Immunities Act of 1976: 28 U.S.C.A. 1330, 1611.

Foreign Trade Antitrust Improvements Act of 1982: 15 U.S.C.A. 6a, 45.

Foreign Trade Zones Act: 19 U.S.C.A. 81a, 810.

Forest and Rangeland Renewable Resources Research Act of 1978: 16 U.S.C.A. 1641, 1647.

Forest Ecosystems and Atmospheric Pollution Research of 1988: 16 U.S.C.A. 1642.

Forest Exchange Act: 16 U.S.C.A. 485, 486.
Forest Pest Control Act: 16 U.S.C.A. 594–1, 594–5.
Forest Products Act: 16 U.S.C.A. 581, 581i.
Forest Reserve Acts (General): 16 U.S.C.A. 471, 610; 24 U.S.C.A. 58; 25 U.S.C.A. 426, 495; 30 U.S.C.A. 35, 48; see 31 U.S.C.A. 303, 5111; 43 U.S.C.A. 161, 1181; see 44 U.S.C.A. 732, 1324.
Forest Reserve Homestead Act: 16 U.S.C.A. 506, 509.
Forest Transfer Act: 16 U.S.C.A. 472, 615b.
Forest Wildfire Emergency Pay Equity Act of 1988: 5 U.S.C.A. 5547.
Form Disaster Assistance Act of 1987: 7 U.S.C.A. 1441–1, 1446, 16 U.S.C.A. 3835 note; 33 U.S.C.A. 701n.
Former Prisoner of War Benefits Act of 1981: 38 U.S.C.A. 101, 612.
Foundation for the Advancement of Military Medicine Act of 1983: 10 U.S.C.A. 178, 2113.
Fourth Liberty Bond Act: See 31 U.S.C.A. 3102, 3122.
Free Homestead Act: 43 U.S.C.A. 179.
Free Trade Zone Act: 19 U.S.C.A. 81a, 81u.
Freedom of Information Act: 5 U.S.C.A. 552.
Fugitive Felon Act: See 18 U.S.C.A. 1073.
Full Employment and Balanced Growth Act of 1978: 2 U.S.C.A. 632, 636; 12 U.S.C.A. 225a; 15 U.S.C.A. 1021, 3152.
Fund for the Improvement and Reform of Schools and Teaching Act: 20 U.S.C.A. 4801, 4843.
Fur Products Labeling Act: 15 U.S.C.A. 69, 69j.
Fur Seal Act of 1966: 16 U.S.C.A. 1151, 1187.
Futures Trading Act of 1978: 7 U.S.C.A. 2, 23; 18 U.S.C.A. 6001.
Futures Trading Act of 1986: 7 U.S.C.A. 2a, 2271a; 16 U.S.C.A. 590h, 3831; 21 U.S.C.A. 606, 676.

Gambling Devices Act of 1962: 15 U.S.C.A. 1171, 1178.
Gambling Devices Transportation Act: 15 U.S.C.A. 1171, 1177.
Game and Wild Life Act: 16 U.S.C.A. 141b, 718e; see 18 U.S.C.A. 42, 3112.
Garn-St. Germain Depository Institutions Act of 1982: 11 U.S.C.A. 109; 12 U.S.C.A. 22, 3805; 15 U.S.C.A. 1602, 1603; 20 U.S.C.A. 1099; 42 U.S.C.A. 8103, 8105.,

Garrison Diversion Unit Reformulation Act of 1986: 43 U.S.C.A. 390a.
Gas Guzzler Tax: 26 U.S.C.A. 4064.
Gasohol Competition Act of 1980: 15 U.S.C.A. 26a, 27.
Gearhart Armistice Day Act: See 15 U.S.C.A. 6103.
General Accounting Act of 1974: 7 U.S.C.A. 1513; 12 U.S.C.A. 1701y, 1827; 20 U.S.C.A. 1082; see 31 U.S.C.A. 702, 9106; 38 U.S.C.A. 4207; 40 U.S.C.A. 756; 44 U.S.C.A. 309; 49 U.S.C.A. 1537.
General Accounting Office Act of 1980: See 31 U.S.C.A. 702, 3524; 42 U.S.C.A. 3523, 7138.
General Accounting Office Personnel Act of 1980: 5 U.S.C.A. 2108, 7328; see 31 U.S.C.A. 711, 755; 42 U.S.C.A. 2000e–16.
General Appropriation Act, 1951: 2 U.S.C.A. 52, 65a; 3 U.S.C.A. 201 note; 7 U.S.C.A. 367, 435. See Popular Name Table for more titles.
General Bridge Act of 1946: 33 U.S.C.A. 59x, 533.
General Education Provisions Act: 20 U.S.C.A. 240, 1234i.
General Government Matters Appropriation Act, 1960: See 31 U.S.C.A. 1108, 1551; 36 U.S.C.A. 121b, 122a; 40 U.S.C.A. 33a.
General Leasing Act: 43 U.S.C.A. 98a.
General Provisions: 1 U.S.C.A. 1, 213.
Generalized System of Preferences Renewal Act of 1984: 19 U.S.C.A. 2461, 2466.
Generic Animal Drug and Patent Term Restoration Act: 21 U.S.C.A. 321, 360b; 28 U.S.C.A. 2201; 35 U.S.C.A. 156, 271.
Genocide Convention Implementation Act of 1987 (the Proxmire Act): 18 U.S.C.A. 1091, 1093.
George Bill: 12 U.S.C.A. 1801, 1804.
George Washington Commemorative Coin Act: See 31 U.S.C.A. 5112.
Georgia Wilderness Act of 1986: 16 U.S.C.A. 1132.
Geothermal Energy Act of 1980: 16 U.S.C.A. 796, 824j; 30 U.S.C.A. 1141, 1542.
Geothermal Energy Research, Development, and Demonstration Act of 1974: 30 U.S.C.A. 1101, 1164.
Geothermal Steam Act of 1970: 30 U.S.C.A. 1001, 1025.
G.I. Bill Improvement Act of 1977: 38 U.S.C.A. 101, 2014.
G.I. Bill of Rights: See Servicemen's Readjustment Act of 1944.
Gifted and Talented Children's Education Act of 1978: 20 U.S.C.A. 3311, 3318.
Glacier National Park Act: 16 U.S.C.A. 163, 177.
Glass Bank Official Loan Act: 12 U.S.C.A. 375a.
Glass Federal Reserve Note Act: 12 U.S.C.A. 412.

Glass-Steagall Act, 1932: 12 U.S.C.A. 347a, 412.

Glen Canyon National Recreation Area Act: 16 U.S.C.A. 460dd, 460dd–9.

Gold Bullion Coin Act of 1985: 31 U.S.C.A. 5112, 5132.

Gold Clause Act: See 31 U.S.C.A. 5118.

Gold Hoarding Act: 12 U.S.C.A. 248.

Gold Labeling Act of 1976: 15 U.S.C.A. 295.

Gold Repeal Joint Resolution: See 31 U.S.C.A. 5118.

Gold Reserve Act of 1934: 12 U.S.C.A. 411, 467; see 31 U.S.C.A. 325, 5304.

Golden Gate National Recreation Area Act: 16 U.S.C.A. 460bb, 460bb–5.

Golden Nematode Act: 7 U.S.C.A. 150, 150g.

Goldwater Nichols Department of Defense Reorganization Act of 1986: 10 U.S.C.A. 101, 8074; 22 U.S.C.A. 2795, 2795b; 37 U.S.C.A. 204, 406; 50 U.S.C.A. 402, 833.

Government-Aided Railroad and Telegraph Act: 47 U.S.C.A. 9, 15.

Government Corporation Control Act: See 31 U.S.C.A. 1105, 9109.

Government Corporations Appropriation Act, 1948: 16 U.S.C.A. 831h–2; see 31 U.S.C.A. 9104; 40 U.S.C.A. 33a, 129; 42 U.S.C.A. 1431.

Government Employees Incentive Awards Act: See 5 U.S.C.A. 1308, 4506.

Government Employees Salary Reform Act of 1964: 2 U.S.C.A. 31, 273a; 3 U.S.C.A. 104, 105; see 5 U.S.C.A. 5108, 8331; 8 U.S.C.A. 1104. See Popular Name Table for more titles.

Government Employees Training Act: See 5 U.S.C.A. 1308, 4118.

Government in the Sunshine Act: 5 U.S.C.A. 551, 557; 5 App. U.S.C.A. 10; 39 U.S.C.A. 410.

Government Losses in Shipment Act: See 31 U.S.C.A. 321, 3331; 40 U.S.C.A. 721, 729.

Government Organization and Employees: 5 U.S.C.A. 101, 9341; 41 U.S.C.A. 420.

Government Printing Office Inspector General Act of 1988: 44 U.S.C.A. 3901, 3903.

Government Securities Act of 1986: 15 U.S.C.A. 78c, 80b–3; 31 U.S.C.A. 3121, 9110.

Government Surplus Airports and Equipment Act: 50 App. U.S.C.A. 1622, 1622c.

Graduate Public Health Training Amendments of 1964: 42 U.S.C.A. 242d, 242g.

Grain Futures Act: 7 U.S.C.A. 1, 17.

Grain Quality Improvement Act of 1986: 7 U.S.C.A. 74, 87b.

Gramm-Rudman-Hollings Act: See Balanced Budget and Emergency Deficit Control Act of 1985.

Grand Canyon National Park Enlargement Act: 16 U.S.C.A. 227, 228j.

Great Lakes Coastal Barrier Act of 1988: 16 U.S.C.A. 3501, 3503.

Great Lakes Fishery Act of 1956: 16 U.S.C.A. 931, 939c.

Great Lakes Pilotage Act of 1960: See 46 U.S.C.A. 2101, 9308.

Great Lakes Planning Assistance Act of 1988: 16 U.S.C.A. 3501, 3503; 33 U.S.C.A. 426p.

Griffin-Landrum Act: See Labor-Management Reporting and Disclosure Act of 1959.

Guam Development Fund Act of 1968: 48 U.S.C.A. 1428, 1428e.

Guam Elective Governor Act: 10 U.S.C.A. 335; 48 U.S.C.A. 1421a, 1423i.

Guard and Reserve Forces Facilities Authorization Act, 1976: 10 U.S.C.A. 2233a.

Guatemala Relief and Rehabilitation Act of 1976: 22 U.S.C.A. 2292g.

Guayule Rubber Act: 7 U.S.C.A. 171, 173.

Gun Control Act of 1968: 18 U.S.C.A. 921, 928; 18 App. U.S.C.A.; 26 U.S.C.A. 5801, 7273.

Gwynne Act (Portal to Portal): 29 U.S.C.A. 216, 262.

Haleakala National Park Act: 16 U.S.C.A. 396b.

Hall-Mark Act: 15 U.S.C.A. 291, 293.

Halogeton Glomeratus Control Act: 7 U.S.C.A. 1651, 1656.

Handicapped Children's Early Education Assistance Act: 20 U.S.C.A. 621, 624.

Handicapped Children's Protection Act of 1986: 20 U.S.C.A. 1415.

Handicapped Programs Technical Amendments Act of 1988: 20 U.S.C.A. 1401, 1482; 29 U.S.C.A. 702, 796i; 36 U.S.C.A. 155.

Harbor Development and Navigation Improvement Act of 1986: 33 U.S.C.A. 2231, 2241.

Harbor Maintenance Revenue Act of 1986: 26 U.S.C.A. 4042, 9506; 33 U.S.C.A. 984, 1804.

Hart-Scott-Rodino Antitrust Improvements Act of 1976: 15 U.S.C.A. 12, 1314; 18 U.S.C.A. 1505; 28 U.S.C.A. 1407.

Harter Act (Carriage of Goods by Sea): 46 U.S.C.A. 190, 195.

Hastings Amendment: 18 U.S.C.A. 1156.

Hatch Act (Agricultural Experiment Stations): 7 U.S.C.A. 361a, 379.

Hatch Political Activity Act: See 1 U.S.C.A. 1; see 5 U.S.C.A. 1302, 7327; see 18 U.S.C.A. 594, 1918.

Hatch-Sumners Act (Additional Judgeships): See 28 U.S.C.A. 44, 132.

Hawaii Omnibus Act: 7 U.S.C.A. 1837; 10 U.S.C.A. 101, 4744; 12 U.S.C.A. 1422, 1748; 15 U.S.C.A. 77b, 80b–2. See Popular Name Table for more titles.

Hawaii Statehood Bill: 48 U.S.C.A. note prec. 491.

Hawes-Cooper Act: See 49 U.S.C.A. 11507.

Hawley-Smoot Tariff Act: See Tariff Act of 1930.

Hayden-Cartwright Act: See 23 U.S.C.A. 101, 118; 25 U.S.C.A. 318b.

Hazardous and Solid Waste Amendments of 1984: 42 U.S.C.A. 6901, 6991i.

Hazardous Liquid Pipeline Safety Act of 1979: 49 U.S.C.A. 1811, 2014; 49 App. U.S.C.A. 2002, 2015.

Hazardous Materials Transportation Act: 46 U.S.C.A. 170; see 46 U.S.C.A. 2106; 49 U.S.C.A. 1471, 1813; see 49 U.S.C.A. 103, 106.

Hazardous Materials Transportation Control Act of 1970: 49 U.S.C.A. 1761, 1762.

Hazardous Substance Response Revenue Act of 1980: 26 U.S.C.A. 4611, 4682; 42 U.S.C.A. 9641.

Head Start Act: 42 U.S.C.A. 9831, 9852.

Headstart, Economic Opportunity, and Community Partnership Act of 1974: 42 U.S.C.A. 2706, 5103.

Headstart-Follow Through Act: 42 U.S.C.A. 2921, 2930f.

Health Amendments Act of 1956: 20 U.S.C.A. 15aa, 15jj; 42 U.S.C.A. 242a, 291s.

Health Care Quality Improvement Act of 1986: 42 U.S.C.A. 11101, 11152.

Health Care Services in the Home Act of 1987: 42 U.S.C.A. 280c, 280c–5.

Health Education Act of 1978: 20 U.S.C.A. 3021, 3024.

Health Insurance for the Aged Act: 26 U.S.C.A. 72, 6051; 42 U.S.C.A. 303, 1396d; 45 U.S.C.A. 228e, 228s–2.

Health Maintenance Organization Act of 1973: 12 U.S.C.A. 1721; 42 U.S.C.A. 280c, 2001.

Health Manpower Act of 1968: 42 U.S.C.A. 242d, 298c–1.

Health Omnibus Programs Extension of 1988: 5 U.S.C.A. 5315, 5316; 21 U.S.C.A. 393; 42 U.S.C.A. 210, 11283.

Health Planning and Health Services Research and Statistics Extension Act of 1977: 42 U.S.C.A. 201, 1396b.

Health Planning and Resources Development Amendments of 1979: 21 U.S.C.A. 1176; 42 U.S.C.A. 201, 4573.

Health Professions Educational Assistance Act of 1976: 8 U.S.C.A. 1101, 1182; 42 U.S.C.A. 201, 300s–3.

Health Professions Reauthorization Act of 1988: 42 U.S.C.A. 254a, 295j.

Health Professions Training Assistance Act of 1985: 42 U.S.C.A. 254*l*, 300aa–14; 50 App. U.S.C.A. 462 note.

Health Programs Extension Act of 1980: 8 U.S.C.A. 1182; 42 U.S.C.A. 286e, 300n–1.

Health Promotion and Disease Prevention Amendments of 1984: 21 U.S.C.A. 360bb, 360ee; 42 U.S.C.A. 242b, 300u–9.

Health Research and Health Services Amendments of 1976: 21 U.S.C.A. 321, 378; 42 U.S.C.A. 213, 6064.

Health Research Extension Act of 1985: 42 U.S.C.A. 217a, 300c–12.

Health Research Facilities Act of 1956: 33 U.S.C.A. 763c note; 42 U.S.C.A. 201, 292i; 46 U.S.C.A. 654 note.

Health Services Amendments of 1985: 15 U.S.C.A. 1333; 42 U.S.C.A. 207, 300aa–4.

Health Services and Centers Amendments of 1978: 42 U.S.C.A. 218, 1396b.

Health Services Extension Act of 1977: 8 U.S.C.A. 1101, 1182; 21 U.S.C.A. 1112, 1176; 25 U.S.C.A. 1614; 42 U.S.C.A. 210, 4577.

Health Services Research and Evaluation and Health Statistics Act of 1974: 42 U.S.C.A. 235, 253b.

Health Services Research, Health Statistics, and Health Care Technology Act of 1978: 42 U.S.C.A. 210, 7617.

Health Services Research, Health Statistics, and Medical Libraries Act of 1974: 42 U.S.C.A. 235, 280b–11.

Health Training Improvement Act of 1970: 42 U.S.C.A. 295f–1, 295h–9.

Hearing Aid Compatibility Act of 1988: 47 U.S.C.A. 610.

Heart Disease, Cancer, and Stroke Amendments of 1965: 33 U.S.C.A. 763c; 42 U.S.C.A. 221a, 299i.

Helium Act: 50 U.S.C.A. 167, 167n.

Helium Gas Act: 50 U.S.C.A. 161, 166.

Hepburn Act (Interstate Commerce): See 49 U.S.C.A. 10102, 11916.

Hickenlooper Amendment: 22 U.S.C.A. 2370(e)(2).

High Plains States Groundwater Demonstration Program Act of 1983: 43 U.S.C.A. 390g, 390g–8.

High Speed Ground Transportation Act: 49 U.S.C.A. 1643.

Higher Education Act of 1965: 20 U.S.C.A. 403, 1221d; 42 U.S.C.A. 56a, 2761.

Higher Education Facilities Act of 1963: 20 U.S.C.A. 701, 758.

High-Speed Ground Transportation Act: 49 U.S.C.A. 1631, 1642; see 49 U.S.C.A. 329, 1642.

Highway Beautification Act of 1965: 23 U.S.C.A. 131, 319.

Highway Improvement Act of 1982: 23 U.S.C.A. 101, 307.

Highway Safety Act of 1987: 23 U.S.C.A. 402, 408; 49 U.S.C.A. 2314.

Highways: 23 U.S.C.A. 101, 512.

Hill-Burton Act: See Hospital Survey and Construction Act.

Hiss Act (Pensions): See 5 U.S.C.A. 2101, 8322; see 18 U.S.C.A. 3282.

Historic Sites, Buildings and Antiquities Act: 16 U.S.C.A. 461, 467.

Hobbs Bridge Act: 33 U.S.C.A. 511, 523.

Holiday Pay Act: See 5 U.S.C.A. 6103, 6104.

Home Energy Assistance Act of 1980: 7 U.S.C.A. 2014; 42 U.S.C.A. 8601, 8612.

Home Equity Loan Consumer Protection Act of 1988: 15 U.S.C.A. 1632, 1665b.

Home Mortgage Disclosure Act of 1975: 12 U.S.C.A. 1703, 2811; 42 U.S.C.A. 1452, 5302.

Home Mortgage Relief Act: 12 U.S.C.A. generally dispersed throughout chs. 11-13.

Home Owners' Loan Act: 12 U.S.C.A. 1461.

Home Owners' Loan Act of 1933: 12 U.S.C.A. 347, 1468.

Home Port Act: 46 U.S.C.A. 18.

Homeless Eligibility Clarification Act: 7 U.S.C.A. 2012, 2019; 29 U.S.C.A. 1531, 1603; 38 U.S.C.A. 3003, 3020; 42 U.S.C.A. 1383, 1396a.

Homeownership Opportunity Act of 1979: 12 U.S.C.A. 1715z–10.

Homestead Acts: 43 U.S.C.A. 161, 277.

Homesteaders' Relief Act: 43 U.S.C.A. 237b.

Honey Research Promotion, and Consumer Information: 7 U.S.C.A. 4601, 4612.

Honeybee Act: 7 U.S.C.A. 281, 282.

Hoopa-Yurok Settlement Act: 16 U.S.C.A. 460ss–3; 25 U.S.C.A. 1300i, 1300i–11.

Hoover Power Plant Act of 1984: 16 U.S.C.A. 839b note; 42 U.S.C.A. 7275, 7276; 43 U.S.C.A. 617a, 1543.

Horse Protection Act of 1970: 15 U.S.C.A. 1821, 1831.

Hospital and Medical Facilities Amendments of 1964: 42 U.S.C.A. 247c, 291o.

Hospital and Medical Facilities Construction and Modernization Assistance Amendments of 1968: 42 U.S.C.A. 291a, 291b.

Hospital Survey and Construction Act: 24 U.S.C.A. 219; 33 U.S.C.A. 763c; 42 U.S.C.A. 2, 191o; 46 U.S.C.A. 654; 48 U.S.C.A. 1011; 49 U.S.C.A. 177, 181.

Hot-Oil Act: 15 U.S.C.A. 715, 715*l*.

Hours of Service Acts (Public Works): 45 U.S.C.A. 61, 64a.

Hours of Service Acts (Railroads): 45 U.S.C.A. 61, 66.

House Employees Position Classification Act: 2 U.S.C.A. 88c, 303.

Household Goods Transportation Act of 1980: 26 U.S.C.A. 250; 28 U.S.C.A. 2342; 39 U.S.C.A. 5201; 49 U.S.C.A. 10102, 11917.

Housing Act of 1948: 12 U.S.C.A. 1437, 1747*l*; see 31 U.S.C.A. 9101; see 38 U.S.C.A. 1801, 1803; 42 U.S.C.A. 1403, 1432.

Housing Act of 1949: 7 U.S.C.A. 1981a; 12 U.S.C.A. 24, 2811; 42 U.S.C.A. 1401, 5302.

Housing Act of 1950: 7 U.S.C.A. 1001, 1017; 12 U.S.C.A. 371, 1749c; 15 U.S.C.A. 604; see 38 U.S.C.A. 1801, 1823; 42 U.S.C.A. 1412, 1590.

Housing Act of 1954: 12 U.S.C.A. 24, 1750jj; 18 U.S.C.A. 709; 20 U.S.C.A. 272; see 38 U.S.C.A. 1810; 40 U.S.C.A. 459, 462; 42 U.S.C.A. 1407, 1592a.

Housing Act of 1964: 12 U.S.C.A. 24, 2811; 15 U.S.C.A. 636, 637; 20 U.S.C.A. 801, 811; 38 U.S.C.A. 1820, 1823; 40 U.S.C.A. 461, 462; 42 U.S.C.A. 1402, 5302.

Housing and Community Development Act of 1974: 5 U.S.C.A. 5315, 5316; 12 U.S.C.A. 24, 5312; 20 U.S.C.A. 801, 807; see 31 U.S.C.A. 1305; 40 U.S.C.A. 460, 461; 42 U.S.C.A. 1437, 5426; 49 U.S.C.A. 1602, 1602a.

Housing and Rent Act of 1947: 50 App. U.S.C.A. 1884, 1898.

Housing and Rent Act of 1953: 50 App. U.S.C.A. 1884, 1898.

Housing and Urban Development Act of 1970: 12 U.S.C.A. 371, 1817; 15 U.S.C.A. 692, 1705; 16 U.S.C.A. 617; 18 U.S.C.A. 1014; 20 U.S.C.A. 803; 40 U.S.C.A. 461, 484b; 42 U.S.C.A. 1401, 4532.

Housing and Urban-Rural Recovery Act of 1983: 12 U.S.C.A. 1701g–5b, 3804; 40 U.S.C.A. 484b; 42 U.S.C.A. 1437a, 8107.

Housing Authorization Act of 1976: 5 U.S.C.A. 5315; 12 U.S.C.A. 1464, 2710; 40 U.S.C.A. 461; 42 U.S.C.A. 1437a, 5316.

Hovering Vessels: 19 U.S.C.A. 1401, 1709; 46 U.S.C.A. 91.

Howard University Endowment Act: 20 U.S.C.A. 123, 130aa–5.

Human Services Reauthorization Act: 20 U.S.C.A. 1070d–31, 4206; 42 U.S.C.A. 2991b, 9910a.

Humane Methods of Slaughter Act of 1978: 7 U.S.C.A. 1902, 1904; 21 U.S.C.A. 603, 620.

Hump Law: 10 U.S.C.A. 6387.

Humphrey-Durham Drug Prescriptions Act: 21 U.S.C.A. 333, 353.

Humphrey-Thye-Blatnik-Andersen Act: 16 U.S.C.A. 577d–1, 577h.

Hunger Prevention Act of 1988: 7 U.S.C.A. 2012, 2026; 15 U.S.C.A. 713a–14; 42 U.S.C.A. 1761, 1786.

I Am An American Day Act: 36 U.S.C.A. 152, 391.

Illinois and Michigan Canal National Heritage Corridor Act of 1984: 16 U.S.C.A. 450jj–3, 450jj–9.

Immigration Acts: 46 U.S.C.A. 151, 162.

Immigration and Nationality Act: 8 U.S.C.A. 1101, 1524; 18 U.S.C.A. 1114, 1546, 19 U.S.C.A. 2112 note; 22 U.S.C.A. 618, 1446; see 49 U.S.C.A. 177, 10721; 50 App. U.S.C.A. 1952, 1961.

Immigration and Nationality Act of 1952: 8 U.S.C.A. 1356.

Immigration Marriage Fraud Amendments of 1986: 8 U.S.C.A. 1154, 1325.

Immigration Reform and Control Act of 1986: 7 U.S.C.A. 2025; 8 U.S.C.A. 1101, 1365; 18 U.S.C.A. 1546; 20 U.S.C.A. 1091, 1096; 29 U.S.C.A. 1802, 1851; 42 U.S.C.A. 303, 1437r.

Immunity Act of 1954: 18 U.S.C.A. 3486.

Immunity Acts (Trusts and Interstate Commerce): 15 U.S.C.A. 32, 33; 49 U.S.C.A. 47, 48; see 49 U.S.C.A. 47, 11913.

Immunity of Witnesses Act: 18 U.S.C.A. 6001, 6005.

Impact Aid Reauthorization Act of 1988: 20 U.S.C.A. 236, 647.

Import Milk Act: 21 U.S.C.A. 141, 149.

Imported Vehicle Safety Compliance Act of 1988: 15 U.S.C.A. 1397.

Impoundment Control Act of 1974: 2 U.S.C.A. 681, 688; see 31 U.S.C.A. 1512.

Income Tax Acts: See Internal Revenue Code of 1954.

Independent Agencies Appropriation Act, 1989: 40 U.S.C.A. 490c; 50 U.S.C.A. 98-h note.

Independent Counsel Reauthorization Act of 1987: 5 App. U.S.C.A. 203, 205; 18 U.S.C.A. 202; 28 U.S.C.A. 49, 599.

Independent Offices Act, 1928: 46 App. U.S.C.A. 810a.

Independent Offices Appropriation Act, 1967: 12 U.S.C.A. 1701g–5; 38 U.S.C.A. 1823 note; 40 U.S.C.A. 313–2 note; 42 U.S.C.A. 1431; 49 U.S.C.A. 10344 note.

Independent Offices and Department of Housing and Urban Development Appropriation Act, 1971: 12 U.S.C.A. 1701g–5; 40 U.S.C.A. 313–2 note; 42 U.S.C.A. 1431.

Independent Safety Board Act of 1974: 49 U.S.C.A. 1653, 1907; 49 App. U.S.C.A. 1903, 1907.

Indian Affairs Administration Act: 25 U.S.C.A. 1a.

Indian Alcohol and Substance Abuse Prevention and Treatment Act of 1986: 25 U.S.C.A. 1302, 2478.

Indian Arts and Crafts Act: 25 U.S.C.A. 305, 305e.

Indian Child Welfare Act of 1978: 25 U.S.C.A. 1901, 1963.

Indian Civil Rights Act of 1968: 25 U.S.C.A. 1301, 1341.

Indian Claims Commission Act: 25 U.S.C.A. 70, 70v–3.

Indian Claims Limitation Act of 1982: 28 U.S.C.A. 2415.

Indian Crimes Act of 1976: 18 U.S.C.A. 113, 3242.

Indian Education Act: 20 U.S.C.A. 240, 3385b.

Indian Education Act of 1988: 25 U.S.C.A. 2601, 2651.

Indian Education Assistance Act: 25 U.S.C.A. 455, 458e.

Indian Elementary and Secondary School Assistance Act: 20 U.S.C.A. 241aa, 241ff.

Indian Financing Act of 1974: 25 U.S.C.A. 1451, 1544.

Indian Gaming Regulatory Act: 18 U.S.C.A. 1166, 1168; 25 U.S.C.A. 2701. 2721.

Indian General Allotment Act: 25 U.S.C.A. 331, 381.

Indian Health Care Improvement Act: 25 U.S.C.A. 1601, 1680j; 42 U.S.C.A. 234, 1396j.

Indian Housing Act of 1988: 42 U.S.C.A. 1437, 1437ee.

Indian Land Consolidation Act: 25 U.S.C.A. 483a, 2211.

Indian Long-Term Leasing Act: 25 U.S.C.A. 415, 415d.

Indian Major Crimes Act: 18 U.S.C.A. 1153.

Indian Mineral Development Act of 1982: 25 U.S.C.A. 2101, 2108.

Indian Omnibus Law: 25 U.S.C.A. 404.

Indian Peaks Wilderness Area, the Arapaho National Recreation Area and the Oregon Islands Wilderness Area Act: 16 U.S.C.A. 460jj, 460jj–7.

Indian Reorganization Act: 25 U.S.C.A. 461 et seq.

Indian Self-Determination Act: 5 U.S.C.A. 3371, 3372; 25 U.S.C.A. 450f, 450n; 42 U.S.C.A. 2004b, 4762; 50 App. U.S.C.A. 456.

Indian Self-Determination and Education Assistance Act: 5 U.S.C.A. 3371; 25 U.S.C.A. 13a, 458e; 42 U.S.C.A. 2004b, 4762; 50 App. U.S.C.A. 456.

Indian Tribal Governmental Tax Status Act of 1982: 26 U.S.C.A. 41, 7871.

Indian Tribal Judgment Funds Use or Distribution Act: 25 U.S.C.A. 1401.

Indochina Refugee Children Assistance Act of 1976: 20 U.S.C.A. 1211b.

Industrial Loans Act: 15 U.S.C.A. 601, 617.

Industrial Productivity and Labor Costs Act: 29 U.S.C.A. 2b.

Infant Formula Act of 1980: 21 U.S.C.A. 321, 873.

Inflation Act: 12 U.S.C.A. 462b; see 31 U.S.C.A. 5301, 5304.

Informer's Act: See 31 U.S.C.A. 3730.

Injury Prevention Act of 1986: 42 U.S.C.A. 280b, 280b–3.

Inland Navigational Rules Act of 1980: 33 U.S.C.A. 151, 2073.

Inland Rules: 33 U.S.C.A. 154, 331.

Inland Waterways Revenue Act of 1978: 26 U.S.C.A. 4042, 4293; 33 U.S.C.A. 1801, 1804.

Insanity Defense Reform Act of 1984: 18 U.S.C.A. 20 note.

Insect Control Act: 7 U.S.C.A. 148.

Insecticide Act: 7 U.S.C.A. 121, 134.

Insider Trading and Securities Fraud Enforcement Act of 1988: 15 U.S.C.A. 78c, 80b–4a.

Insider Trading Sanctions Act of 1984: 15 U.S.C.A. 78c, 78ff.

Inspector General Act of 1978: 5 U.S.C.A. 5315, 5316; 5 App. U.S.C.A. 1, 12; 42 U.S.C.A. 3522.

Installment Sales Revision Act of 1980: 26 U.S.C.A. 311, 1255.

Institute of Inter-American Affairs Act: 22 U.S.C.A. 281, 281*l*.

Insular Areas Drug Abuse Amendments of 1988: 42 U.S.C.A. 10603; 48 U.S.C.A. 1494, 1494c.

Insurance Act of 1951: See 38 U.S.C.A. 701, 784.

Insurance Regulation Act: 15 U.S.C.A. 1101 et seq.

Intelligence Authorization Act, Fiscal Year 1989: 5 U.S.C.A. 9101 note; 10 U.S.C.A. 136, 1607; 50 U.S.C.A. 403q, 405.

Inter-American Coffee Agreement Act: 19 U.S.C.A. 1355, 1356.

Inter-American Development Bank Act: 12 U.S.C.A. 24; 22 U.S.C.A. 283, 283z–3.

Inter-American Foundation Act: 22 U.S.C.A. 290f.

Inter-American Investment Corporation Act: 22 U.S.C.A. 276c–2, 283ii.

Inter-American Statistical Institute Act: 22 U.S.C.A. 269d.

Intercoastal Shipping Act: 46 U.S.C.A. 843, 848.

Interest and Dividend Tax Compliance Act of 1983: 26 U.S.C.A. 31, 7701.

Interest Equalization Tax Act: 26 U.S.C.A. 263, 7241.

Intergovernmental Anti-recession Assistance Act of 1977: 42 U.S.C.A. 6722, 6736.

Intergovernmental Cooperation Act of 1968: See 31 U.S.C.A. 6501, 6508; 40 U.S.C.A. 531, 535.

Intergovernmental Personnel Act of 1970: 5 U.S.C.A. 1304, 3376; 42 U.S.C.A. 4701, 4772.

Interior Department Appropriation Act, 1938: 24 U.S.C.A. 169.

Interior Department Appropriation Act, 1955: 43 U.S.C.A. 50, 775; 48 U.S.C.A. 1401f, 1436.

Interjurisdictional Fisheries Act of 1986: 16 U.S.C.A. 742c, 4007.

Internal Revenue Code of 1954: 26 U.S.C.A. 1, 9602.

Internal Revenue Code of 1986: 26 U.S.C.A. 1, 9508.

Internal Security Act of 1950: 50 U.S.C.A. 831, 835.

International Air Transportation Competition Act of 1979: 49 U.S.C.A. 1159b, 1517; see 49 U.S.C.A. 334.

International Air Transportation Fair Competitive Practices Act of 1974: 22 U.S.C.A. 2122; 49 U.S.C.A. 1159a, 1517; 49 App. U.S.C.A. 1159b.

International Atomic Energy Agency Participation Act of 1957: 22 U.S.C.A. 2021, 2026; 42 U.S.C.A. 2074.

International Aviation Facilities Act: 49 U.S.C.A. 1151, 1160.

International Banking Act of 1978: 12 U.S.C.A. 72, 3108.

International Bridge Act of 1972: 33 U.S.C.A. 535, 535i.

International Broadcasting Act of 1973: 22 U.S.C.A. 2871, 2873.

International Carriage of Perishable Foodstuffs Act: 5 U.S.C.A. 5315, 5316; 5 App. U.S.C.A. 1953 Reorg. Plan No. 2; 7 U.S.C.A. 2212c, 4406.

International Child Abduction Remedies Act: 42 U.S.C.A. 663, 1610.

International Claims Settlement Act of 1949: 22 U.S.C.A. 1621, 1645o.

International Coffee Agreement Act of 1980: 19 U.S.C.A. 1356k, 1356n.

International Communication Agency Authorization Act, Fiscal Years 1980 and 1981: 5 U.S.C.A. 1304; 22 U.S.C.A. 1461, 2458a; 40 U.S.C.A. 474.

International Cultural Exchange and Trade Fair Participation Act of 1956: 22 U.S.C.A. 1991, 2001.

International Debt Management Act of 1988: 12 U.S.C.A. 3912; 22 U.S.C.A. 5321, 5333.

International Development and Food Assistance Act of 1977: 5 U.S.C.A. 5315; 7 U.S.C.A. 1702, 1736b; 22 U.S.C.A. 2151,2429b.

International Development Association Act: 22 U.S.C.A. 284, 284q.

International Development Cooperation Act of 1979: 5 U.S.C.A. 5314, 5924; 7 U.S.C.A. 1703, 1736g; 22 U.S.C.A. 2151–1, 3513.

International Economic Policy Act of 1972: 22 U.S.C.A. 2841, 2849.

International Education Act of 1966: 20 U.S.C.A. 511, 1177; 22 U.S.C.A. 2452, 2455.

International Emergency Economic Powers Act: 50 U.S.C.A. 1701, 1706.

International Environment Protection Act of 1983: 22 U.S.C.A. 2151q, 2452.

International Finance Corporation Act: 22 U.S.C.A. 282, 282j.

International Financial Institutions Act: 22 U.S.C.A. 262c, 290g–10.

International Health Research Act of 1960: 22 U.S.C.A. 2101, 2104; 42 U.S.C.A. 242f.

International Investment and Trade in Services Survey Act: 22 U.S.C.A. 3101, 3108.

International Lending Supervision Act of 1983: 12 U.S.C.A. 3901, 3912.

International Maritime and Port Security Act: 33 U.S.C.A. 1226; 46 U.S.C.A. 1801, 1809.

International Maritime Satellite Telecommunications Act: 47 U.S.C.A. 751, 757.

International Narcotics Control Act of 1988: 8 U.S.C.A. 1103 note; 12 U.S.C.A. 635; 18 U.S.C.A. 3181 note; 19 U.S.C.A. 2492; 21 U.S.C.A. 1502 note; 22 U.S.C.A. 2222, 2714; 31 U.S.C.A. 5311 note; 41 U.S.C.A. 701 note; 46 App. U.S.C.A. 1902 note.

International Navigational Rules Act of 1977: 33 U.S.C.A. 1051, 1608.

International Organizations Immunities Act: 22 U.S.C.A. 288, 288f–3; 42 U.S.C.A. 409.

International Regulations for Preventing Collisions at Sea: 33 U.S.C.A. 1051, 1094.

International Rules (Collisons at Sea): 33 U.S.C.A. 301.

International Safe Container Act: 46 U.S.C.A. 1501, 1508.

International Security and Development Assistance Authorizations Act of 1983: 22 U.S.C.A. 2151 note.

International Security and Development Cooperation Act of 1985: 7 U.S.C.A. 1431, 1736b; 10 U.S.C.A. 7307; 15 U.S.C.A. 4011 note; 16 U.S.C.A. 469j; 22 U.S.C.A. 290f, 2795; 49 U.S.C.A. 1356, 1515a.

International Security Assistance Act of 1977: 22 U.S.C.A. 2261, 2778.

International Security Assistance Act of 1978: 22 U.S.C.A. 1754, 2776; 50 App. U.S.C.A. 2403.

International Security Assistance and Arms Export Control Act of 1976: 22 U.S.C.A. 2183, 2794.

International Trade and Investment Act: 19 U.S.C.A. 2112, 3104.

International Travel Act of 1961: 22 U.S.C.A. 2121, 2128.

International Understanding Act: 20 U.S.C.A. 3063, 3065.

International Voyage Load Line Act of 1973: 46 U.S.C.A. 86, 86i.

International Waterways Act: 22 U.S.C.A. 267b; 33 U.S.C.A. 1, 631.

International Wheat Agreement Act of 1949: 7 U.S.C.A. 1641, 1642.

Interparliamentary Union Acts: 22 U.S.C.A. 276, 276c.

Interpleader Act: See 28 U.S.C.A. 1335, 2361.

Interstate Agreement on Detainers Act: 18 App. U.S.C.A. 9.

Interstate Commerce Act: 15 U.S.C.A. 77c; 49 U.S.C.A. 26, 1240; 49 App. U.S.C.A. 26.

Interstate Commerce Commission Dangerous Article Act: See Dangerous Cargo Act.

Interstate Horseracing Act of 1978: 15 U.S.C.A. 3001, 3007.

Interstate Land Sales Full Disclosure Act: 15 U.S.C.A. 1701, 1720.

Intervention on the High Seas Act: 33 U.S.C.A. 1471, 1487.

Invention Secrecy Act of 1951: See 35 U.S.C.A. 181, 188.

Investment Advisers Act of 1940: 15 U.S.C.A. 80a–9, 80b–21.

Investment Company Act of 1940: 15 U.S.C.A. 80a–1, 80a–64.

Investment Company Amendments Act of 1970: 15 U.S.C.A. 77b, 80b–6a.

Irrigation Acts: 16 U.S.C.A. 471, 613; 25 U.S.C.A. 426; 43 U.S.C.A. 161, 1197.

Isolated Tract Act: 43 U.S.C.A. 1171.

Jackson-Vanik Amendment: 19 U.S.C.A. 2192, 2439.

Jacob K. Javits Gifted and Talented Students Education Act of 1988: 20 U.S.C.A. 3061, 3068.

Japan-United States Friendship Act: 22 U.S.C.A. 2901, 2906.

Japanese Technical Literature Act of 1986: 15 U.S.C.A. 3704.

Japanese-American Evacuation Claims Act of 1948: 50 App. U.S.C.A. 1981, 1987.

Jefferson National Expansion Memorial Act: 16 U.S.C.A. 450jj, 450jj–2.

Jencks Act: 18 U.S.C.A. 3500.

Jewelers' Liability Act (Gold and Silver Articles): 15 U.S.C.A. 294, 300.

Job Training Partnership Act: 18 U.S.C.A. 665; 29 U.S.C.A. 49, 1791j; 42 U.S.C.A. 602, 633.

Jobs for Employable Dependent Individuals Act: 29 U.S.C.A. 49, 1791j; 42 U.S.C.A. 602.

John F. Kennedy Center Act: 20 U.S.C.A. 76h, 76q.

John C. Stennis Center for Public Service Training and Development Act: 2 U.S.C.A. 72a, 1110; 40 U.S.C.A. 216c; 44 U.S.C.A. 309.

Johnson Act (Immigration): See 8 U.S.C.A. 1181, 1322.

Johnson Act (Injunctions Affecting Utility Rates): 28 U.S.C.A. 1331, 1354.

Johnson Act (Maritime Workers' Compensation): See 18 U.S.C.A. 3231; 28 U.S.C.A. 1251, 1356.

Johnson Amendment: 15 U.S.C.A. 77bb, 77mm.

Johnson Debt Default Act: See 18 U.S.C.A. 955; 31 U.S.C.A. 804b.

Johnson-O'Malley Act: 25 U.S.C.A. 452, 457.

Joint Funding Simplification Act of 1974: See 31 U.S.C.A. 7101, 7112.

Jones Act (Puerto Rico): 2 U.S.C.A. 46; 48 U.S.C.A. 731, 893.

Jones-Connally Farm-Relief Act: 7 U.S.C.A. 608, 612a.

Jones-Costigan Sugar Act: 7 U.S.C.A. 608, 620.

Jones-Miller Act (Narcotics Import and Export): 21 U.S.C.A. 171, 185.

Jones-White Act: 46 U.S.C.A. 866, 891x.

Judgeship Act (Additional Judges): 28 U.S.C.A. 44, 134; 48 U.S.C.A. 1392a.

Judicial Code: See 28 U.S.C.A. 5, 2640; see 28 U.S.C.A. chs. 1–13.

Judicial Councils Reform and Judicial Conduct and Disability Act of 1980: 28 U.S.C.A. 331, 604.

Judicial Housekeeping Act of 1986: 28 U.S.C.A. 90, 121.

Judicial Improvements Act of 1985: 2 U.S.C.A. 288d; 5 U.S.C.A. 8706, 8714c; 28 U.S.C.A. 376, 2342.

Judicial Improvements and Access to Justice Act: 5 U.S.C.A. 5108, 5584; 9 U.S.C.A. 15; 16 U.S.C.A. 460n–8; 17 U.S.C.A. 912; 18 U.S.C.A. 3402, 3772; 28 U.S.C.A. 89, 2520; 42 U.S.C.A. 10702, 10713.

Judicial Survivors' Annuities Reform Act: 28 U.S.C.A. 376.

Judiciary and Judicial Procedure: 19 U.S.C.A. 2112 note; 28 U.S.C.A. 1, 2901; 28 U.S.C.A. Rule 1101.

Judiciary Appropriations Act, 1989: 28 U.S.C.A. 332, 603.

Judiciary Office Building Development Act: 40 U.S.C.A. 816, 1208.

Jury Selection and Service Act of 1968: 28 U.S.C.A. 1821, 1871.

Jury System Improvements Act of 1978: 28 U.S.C.A. 1363, 1875.

Justice System Improvement Act of 1979: 5 U.S.C.A. 5314, 5315; 18 U.S.C.A. 1761; 41 U.S.C.A. 35; 42 U.S.C.A. 3701, 3797.

Juvenile Delinquency and Youth Offenses Control Act of 1961: 42 U.S.C.A. 2541, 2548.

Juvenile Delinquency Prevention and Control Act of 1968: 42 U.S.C.A. 3801, 3890.

Juvenile Drug Trafficking Act of 1986: 21 U.S.C.A. 841, 845b.

Juvenile Justice Amendments of 1977: 5 U.S.C.A. 5316; 18 U.S.C.A. 4351, 5038; 42 U.S.C.A. 3723, 5751.

Juvenile Justice and Delinquency Prevention Act of 1974: 5 U.S.C.A. 5108; 18 U.S.C.A. 4351, 5042; 42 U.S.C.A. 3701, 5776.

Juvenile Justice, Runaway Youth, and Missing Children's Act Amendments of 1984: 42 U.S.C.A. 5601, 5777.

Kellogg Act (Cable Companies): 47 U.S.C.A. 34, 39.
Kern-McGillicuddy Act (Federal Employees' Workmen's Compensation): See 5 U.S.C.A. 8101 et seq.
Kidnapping Act: See 18 U.S.C.A. 10, 1202.
Kilday Bill: 10 U.S.C.A. 1401, 8991; 14 U.S.C.A. 423; 33 U.S.C.A. 853o.
Kinkaid Act (Homestead Entries in Nebraska): 43 U.S.C.A. 224.
Klamath Indian Tribe Restoration Act: 25 U.S.C.A. 566, 566h.
Klamath River Basin Fishery Resources Restoration Act: 16 U.S.C.A. 460ss–2, 460ss–5.
Klamath Termination Act: 25 U.S.C.A. 564, 564w–1.
Klamath Welfare Act: 25 U.S.C.A. 544, 545.
Knutson-Vandenberg Act: 16 U.S.C.A. 576, 576b.
Kramer Patent Act: See 35 U.S.C.A. 101, 282.
Ku Klux Act: See 2 U.S.C.A. 9; see 10 U.S.C.A. 333; 18 U.S.C.A. 371, 2384; 28 U.S.C.A. 1343, 1861; 28 App. U.S.C.A. Rule 40; 42 U.S.C.A. 1983, 1986.

Labor Disputes Act: See Norris-La Guardia Act (Labor Disputes).
Labor-Federal Security Appropriation Acts: 21 U.S.C.A. 46a, 372a; 24 U.S.C.A. 169; 29 U.S.C.A. 31, 49c–5; 41 U.S.C.A. 6a note; 42 U.S.C.A. 209c, 1918.
Labor Management Cooperation Act of 1978: 29 U.S.C.A. 173, 186.
Labor-Management Relations Act, 1947: See 18 U.S.C.A. 610; 29 U.S.C.A. 141, 504.
Labor-Management Reporting and Disclosure Act of 1959: 29 U.S.C.A. 153, 1111.
Labor Relations Act: See National Labor Relations Act.
Laboratory Animal Act of 1966: 7 U.S.C.A. 2131, 2154.
Lac Vieux Desert Band of Lake Superior Chippewa Indians Act: 25 U.S.C.A. 1300h, 1300h–8.

Lacey Act (Game): 16 U.S.C.A. 667e, 701; 18 U.S.C.A. 43, 44.
La Follette Hours of Labor Act (Railroads): 45 U.S.C.A. 61, 64.
Lake Ontario Protection Act of 1976: 33 U.S.C.A. 426l.
Land Acquisition Policy Act of 1960: 33 U.S.C.A. 596, 597.
Land and Water Conservation Fund Act of 1965: 16 U.S.C.A. 460d, 4601–11; 23 U.S.C.A. 120 note.
Land Remote-Sensing Commercialization Act of 1984: 15 U.S.C.A. 4201, 4292.
Land Remote-Sensing Commercialization Act Amendments of 1987: 15 U.S.C.A. 4212, 4273.
Landrum-Griffin Act: See Labor-Management Reporting and Disclosure Act of 1959.
Lanham Act (Public War Housing): 42 U.S.C.A. 1506, 1590.
Lanham Patent Act: See 35 U.S.C.A. 134, 146.
Latin American Development Act: 22 U.S.C.A. 1943.
Law-Related Education Act of 1978: 20 U.S.C.A. 3001, 3003.
Lea Act (Radio-Coercive Practices): 47 U.S.C.A. 506.
Lead-Based Paint Poisoning Prevention Act: 42 U.S.C.A. 4801, 4846.
Lead Contamination Control Act of 1988: 42 U.S.C.A. 247b–1, 300j–26.
Lead-Zinc Small Producers Stabilization Act of Oct. 3, 1961: 30 U.S.C.A. 681, 689.
Leadership in Educational Administration Development Act of 1984: 20 U.S.C.A. 4201, 4206.
Leasehold Management Bankruptcy Amendments Act of 1983: 11 U.S.C.A. 362, 541.
Leavitt Act (Indians): 25 U.S.C.A. 386a.
Lee Metcalf Wilderness and Management Act of 1983: 16 U.S.C.A. 460ll–3.
Legal Services Corporation Act: 42 U.S.C.A. 2996, 2996l.
Legislative Appropriation Act, 1954: 2 U.S.C.A. 31c, 122; 40 U.S.C.A. 164a, 166a; see 44 U.S.C.A. 309, 1117.
Legislative Branch Appropriations Act, 1989: 2 U.S.C.A. 58, 1110; 40 U.S.C.A. 166a, 216c; 44 U.S.C.A. 309.
Legislative-Judiciary Appropriation Act, 1955: 2 U.S.C.A. 38a, 125; 28 U.S.C.A. 604 note; 40 U.S.C.A. 164a, 166a.
Legislative Reorganization Act of 1970: 2 U.S.C.A. 28, 8332; 5 U.S.C.A. 2107, 8332; 8 U.S.C.A. 1106 note; see 31 U.S.C.A. 702, 1113; 40 U.S.C.A. 166b–1a, 851.

Lemon Law: See Magnuson-Moss Warranty—Federal Trade Commission Improvement Act.

Lend-Lease Act: 22 U.S.C.A. 411, 419.

Liability Risk Retention Act of 1986: 15 U.S.C.A. 3901, 3903.

Liberty Coin Act: 31 U.S.C.A. 5112, 5132.

Liberty Loan Acts: See 12 U.S.C.A. 84, 221; see 31 U.S.C.A. 331, 3129; 50 App. U.S.C.A. 5.

Library of Congress Police Act: 2 U.S.C.A. 167, 167j.

Library of Congress Trust Fund Board Act: 2 U.S.C.A. 154, 163.

Library Services and Construction Act: 20 U.S.C.A. 351, 375.

Lieu Lands Acts (Indian Reservations): 16 U.S.C.A. 152; 25 U.S.C.A. 52a, 292; 43 U.S.C.A. 149.

Lieutenant General Act: See 10 U.S.C.A. 3036, 3212.

Life Insurance Company Income Tax Act of 1959: 26 U.S.C.A. 34, 6501.

Life Insurance Company Tax Act for 1955: 26 U.S.C.A. 316, 4371.

Lighthouse Service Retirement Act: 33 U.S.C.A. 763, 765.

Limited Liability Acts (Shipping): 46 U.S.C.A. 189, 196.

Liquor Enforcement Act of 1936: See 18 U.S.C.A. 1263, 1265.

Liquor Law Repeal and Enforcement Act: 27 U.S.C.A. 122.

Liquor Tax Administration Act: See 18 U.S.C.A. 1114, 2231; 19 U.S.C.A. 1201, 1313; 27 U.S.C.A. 205; 48 U.S.C.A. 1402.

Little Cigar Act of 1973: 15 U.S.C.A. 1332, 1335.

Livable Cities Act of 1978: 42 U.S.C.A. 8141, 8146.

Livestock Transportation Act: 45 U.S.C.A. 71, 74.

Lloyd-La Follette Act: See 5 U.S.C.A. 5595, 7501.

Load Line Act: 46 U.S.C.A. 85, 85g.

Local Government Antitrust Act of 1984: 15 U.S.C.A. 34, 36.

Local Government Fiscal Assistance Amendments of 1983: 31 U.S.C.A. 6701, 6723.

Local Public Works Capital Development and Investment Act of 1976: 42 U.S.C.A. 6701, 6710.

Local Rail Service Assistance Act of 1978: 49 U.S.C.A. 1654.

Lodge Act (Consular Reorganization): 19 U.S.C.A. 338, 341; 22 U.S.C.A. 1180, 1203; see 46 U.S.C.A. 10308, 11104.

Logan Act (Foreign Relations): See 18 U.S.C.A. 953.

Longshore and Harbor Workers' Compensation Act: 33 U.S.C.A. 901, 950.

Lower Mississippi Delta Development Act: 7 U.S.C.A. 1981a note; 16 U.S.C.A. 590e–1, 590e–2; 42 U.S.C.A. 3121 note.

Lower Saint Croix River Act of 1972: 16 U.S.C.A. 1274.

Low-Income Home Energy Assistance Act of 1981: 7 U.S.C.A. 2014; 42 U.S.C.A. 8601, 8629.

Low-Level Radioactive Waste Policy Act: 42 U.S.C.A. 2021b, 2021j.

Lower Colorado River Basin Project Act: 43 U.S.C.A. 1543.

Luce Patent Act: See 35 U.S.C.A. 12, 151.

McCarran Act: See Immigration and Nationality Act.

McCarran Amendment (Department of Justice Appropriation Act, 1953): 43 U.S.C.A. 666.

McCarran-Ferguson Act: 15 U.S.C.A. 1011, 1015.

McCumber Act (Transportation): 10 U.S.C.A. 2631; see 10 U.S.C.A. 2631.

McDuffie-Tydings Acts: 2 U.S.C.A. 31; see 15 U.S.C.A. 2102.

McFadden Act (Branch Banks): 12 U.S.C.A. 24, 593.

McGuire Bill: 15 U.S.C.A. 45.

McIntire-Stennis Act of 1962: 16 U.S.C.A. 582a, 582a–7.

Magistrates' Retirement Parity Act of 1987: 5 U.S.C.A. 8331, 8339.

Magnetic Fusion Energy Engineering Act of 1980: 42 U.S.C.A. 9301, 9312.

Magnuson Fishery Conservation and Management Act: 16 U.S.C.A. 971, 1882; 22 U.S.C.A. 1972, 1973.

Magnuson-Moss Warranty—Federal Trade Commission Improvement Act: 15 U.S.C.A. 45, 2312.

Mahaffie Act: See 49 U.S.C.A. 10321, 11367.

Mail Fraud Act: See 18 U.S.C.A. 1341, 1342.

Mail Order Consumer Protection Amendments of 1983: 39 U.S.C.A. 3005, 3013.

Mail Order Drug Paraphernalia Control Act: 21 U.S.C.A. 857.

Maine Indian Claims Settlement Act: 25 U.S.C.A. 1721, 1735.

Major Fraud Act of 1988: 10 U.S.C.A. 2324; 18 U.S.C.A. 293, 1031; 28 U.S.C.A. 522 note; 31 U.S.C.A. 3730; 41 U.S.C.A. 256.

Malcolm Baldrige National Quality Improvement Act of 1987: 15 U.S.C.A. 3708, 3714.

Management Interlocks Revision Act of 1988: 12 U.S.C.A. 3201, 3205.

Mandamus Act: 28 U.S.C.A. 1361.

Mann Acts: See White-Slave Laws.

Mann-Elkins Act: See 49 U.S.C.A. 501, 11914.

Man-Power Act: 43 U.S.C.A. 183.

Manpower Act of 1965: 42 U.S.C.A. 2571, 2620.

Manpower Development and Training Act of 1962: 42 U.S.C.A. 2571, 2628.

Marine Mammal Protection Act of 1972: 16 U.S.C.A. 1361, 1407.

Marine Plastic Pollution Research and Control Act of 1987: 33 U.S.C.A. 1901, 1912.

Marine Protection, Research, and Sanctuaries Act of 1972: 16 U.S.C.A. 1431, 1445; 33 U.S.C.A. 1401, 1445.

Marine Resources and Engineering Development Act of 1966: 33 U.S.C.A. 1101, 1131.

Marine Sanctuaries Amendments of 1984: 5 App. U.S.C.A. Reorg. Plan No. 4 of 1970; 10 U.S.C.A. 1174; 15 U.S.C.A. 1511 note; 16 U.S.C.A. 742c, 1439. See Popular Name Table for other titles.

Marine Science, Technology, and Policy Development Act of 1987: 33 U.S.C.A. 1121, 1131.

Maritime Academy Act of 1958: 46 U.S.C.A. 1381, 1388.

Maritime Act of 1981: 46 U.S.C.A. 18, 1382; see 46 U.S.C.A. 382b, 1132; 46 App. U.S.C.A. 1606. See Popular Name Table for other titles.

Maritime Appropriation Authorization Act for Fiscal Year 1978: 5 U.S.C.A. 5315; 15 U.S.C.A. 1507b; 46 U.S.C.A. 1119, 1385.

Maritime Drug Law Enforcement Act: 21 U.S.C.A. 955a, 955d; 46 App. U.S.C.A. 1903.

Maritime Education and Training Act of 1980: 46 U.S.C.A. 1119, 1295f; see 46 U.S.C.A. 1259g.

Maritime Labor Agreements Act of 1980: 46 U.S.C.A. 801, 842.

Maritime Safety Act of 1984: 46 U.S.C.A. 2301, 6103; 46 App. U.S.C.A. 183.

Martin Luther King, Jr., Federal Holiday Commission Extension Act: 36 U.S.C.A. 169j.

Mashantucket Pequot Indian Claims Settlement Act: 25 U.S.C.A. 1751, 1760.

Massachusetts Bay Protection Act of 1988: 33 U.S.C.A. 1330.

Materials Act of 1947: 30 U.S.C.A. 601, 604.

Maternal and Child Health and Mental Retardation Planning Amendments of 1963: 42 U.S.C.A. 701, 1394.

Maternal and Child Health Services Block Grant Act: 42 U.S.C.A. 236, 1396a.

Mayfield Act: See 49 U.S.C.A. 10103, 11707.

Meat Import Act of 1979: 19 U.S.C.A. 1202, 2253.

Medals of Honor Act (Railroads and Motor Vehicles): 49 U.S.C.A. 1201, 1203.

Medical Care Recovery Act: 42 U.S.C.A. 2651, 2653.

Medical Device Amendments of 1976: 15 U.S.C.A. 55; 21 U.S.C.A. 321, 381.

Medical Facilities Construction and Modernization Amendments of 1970: 12 U.S.C.A. 1717; 21 U.S.C.A. 186, 187; 42 U.S.C.A. 229b, 300a-7.

Medical Facilities Survey and Construction Act of 1954: 42 U.S.C.A. 291, 291v.

Medical Library Assistance Act of 1965: 42 U.S.C.A. 277, 280b-11.

Medical Malpractice Immunity Act: 10 U.S.C.A. 1089; 32 U.S.C.A. 334; 42 U.S.C.A. 2458a, 2459.

Medical Waste Tracking Act of 1988: 18 U.S.C.A. 3063; 42 U.S.C.A. 6903, 6992k.

Medicare Act: See Health Insurance for the Aged Act.

Medicare-Medicaid Anti-Fraud and Abuse Amendments: 42 U.S.C.A. 254e, 3524.

Medicare and Medicaid Amendments of 1981: 26 U.S.C.A. 162; 42 U.S.C.A. 301, 1396n.

Medicare and Medicaid Budget Reconciliation Amendments of 1985: 29 U.S.C.A. 623, 1144; 42 U.S.C.A. 401, 1396s.

Medicare and Medicaid Patient and Program Protection Act of 1987: 21 U.S.C.A. 824; 42 U.S.C.A. 704, 1397d.

Medicare Catastrophic Coverage Act of 1988: 1 U.S.C.A. 106 note; 5 U.S.C.A. 8902 note; 26 U.S.C.A. 59B, 650F; 42 U.S.C.A. 254o, 1397d.

Mellon Art Gallery Act: 20 U.S.C.A. 71, 75.

Menominee Restoration Act: 25 U.S.C.A. 903, 903f.

Mental Health Amendments of 1967: 42 U.S.C.A. 225a, 2691.

Mental Health Study Act of 1955: 42 U.S.C.A. 242b.

Mental Health Systems Act: 42 U.S.C.A. 210, 9523.

Mental Retardation Amendments of 1967: 20 U.S.C.A. 617; 42 U.S.C.A. 2661, 2698b.

Mental Retardation Facilities and Community Mental Health Centers Construction Act Amendments of 1965: 20 U.S.C.A. 615, 618; 42 U.S.C.A. 2672, 3514.

Merchant Marine Acts: 46 U.S.C.A. 801, 842.

Merchant Marine Act, 1920: 46 U.S.C.A. 13, 984; see 46 U.S.C.A. 3304, 10504; 46 App. U.S.C.A. 13, 984.

Merchant Marine Act, 1928: 46 U.S.C.A. 866, 1295f; see 46 U.S.C.A. 1295g.

Merchant Marine Act, 1936: 46 U.S.C.A. 871, 1295*l*; 46 App. U.S.C.A. 1113, 1271; 46 U.S.C.A. generally dispersed throughout title 46.

Merchant Marine Act of 1970: 5 U.S.C.A. 5315; 5 App. U.S.C.A.; 15 U.S.C.A. 1507a; 33 U.S.C.A. 985,

988; 40 U.S.C.A. 270f; 46 U.S.C.A. 1101, 1294.

Merchant Marine Emergency Act: 40 U.S.C.A. 326 note.

Merchant Ship Sales Act of 1946: 46 U.S.C.A. 864b, 1274; 50 App. U.S.C.A. 1735, 1746.

Mesa Verde National Park Acts: 16 U.S.C.A. 111, 118; see 16 U.S.C.A. 6; see, also, 18 U.S.C.A. 13, 3141; 18 App. U.S.C.A. Rules 4, 5(c), 9; 28 U.S.C.A. 85, 634; 28 App. U.S.C.A. Rule 4.

Methane Transportation Research, Development, and Demonstration Act of 1980: 15 U.S.C.A. 3801, 3810.

Metric Conversion Act of 1975: 15 U.S.C.A. 205a, 205k.

Metric Education Act of 1978: 20 U.S.C.A. 2951, 2954.

Metropolitan Washington Airports Act of 1986: 49 U.S.C.A. 2451, 2461.

Mexican Agricultural Workers Importation Act: 7 U.S.C.A. 1461, 1468.

Mexican Border Act: 7 U.S.C.A. 149.

Mexico-United States Interparliamentary Group Act: 22 U.S.C.A. 276h, 276k.

Micronesian Claims Act of 1971: 50 App. U.S.C.A. 2018, 2020b.

Middle East Peace and Stability Act: 22 U.S.C.A. 1961, 1965.

Middle Income Student Assistance Act: 20 U.S.C.A. 1070a, 1088f.

Migrant and Community Health Centers Amendments of 1978: 42 U.S.C.A. 218, 1396b.

Migrant and Seasonal Agricultural Worker Protection Act: 29 U.S.C.A. 1801, 1872.

Migrant Health Act: 42 U.S.C.A. 247d, 254b.

Migration and Refugee Assistance Act of 1962: 8 U.S.C.A. 1104; 22 U.S.C.A. 2601, 2606.

Migratory Bird Conservation Act: 16 U.S.C.A. 715, 715r.

Migratory Bird Treaty Act: 16 U.S.C.A. 668aa, 711.

Military Appropriation Acts: 10 U.S.C.A. 2776 note; 22 U.S.C.A. 412 note; 37 U.S.C.A. 406 note, 412 note; 50 App. U.S.C.A. 1191.

Military Construction Act of 1961: 10 U.S.C.A. 2674; 12 U.S.C.A. 1748b; 42 U.S.C.A. 1594j.

Military Construction Authorization Act, 1989: 10 U.S.C.A. 2391, 2828.

Military Construction Codification Act: 7 U.S.C.A. 1704b, 1704c; 10 U.S.C.A. 138, 9774; 30 U.S.C.A. 1002a; 42 U.S.C.A. 1592d, 5042; 48 U.S.C.A. 1409b; 50 U.S.C.A. 491; 50 App. U.S.C.A. 2287.

Military Family Act of 1985: 5 U.S.C.A. 5911; 10 U.S.C.A. 113 note, 133 note; 37 U.S.C.A. 403, 1011.

Military Functions Appropriation Act, 1949: See 10

U.S.C.A. 1081; 37 U.S.C.A. 406 note, 412 note; 50 U.S.C.A. 406.

Military Health Care Amendments: 10 U.S.C.A. 533, 8855; 37 U.S.C.A. 302; 50 App. U.S.C.A. 460.

Military Justice Act of 1983: 10 U.S.C.A. 801, 1553; 28 U.S.C.A. 1259, 2101.

Military Medical Benefits Amendments of 1966: 10 U.S.C.A. 1071, 1087.

Military Pay and Allowances Benefits Act of 1980: 10 U.S.C.A. 520, 9355; 37 U.S.C.A. 101, 403.

Military Personnel and Civilian Employees' Claims Act of 1964: 10 U.S.C.A. 2732 note, 2735 note; 14 U.S.C.A. 490 note; see 31 U.S.C.A. 3701, 3721.

Military Personnel and Compensation Amendments of 1980: 10 U.S.C.A. 1201, 8962; 37 U.S.C.A. 203, 1006.

Military Retirement Reform Act of 1986: 5 U.S.C.A. 5313, 5314; 10 U.S.C.A. 101, 8992; 14 U.S.C.A. 46, 424; 33 U.S.C.A. 853o; 42 U.S.C.A. 211, 212.

Military Selective Service Act: 10 U.S.C.A. 673a; 37 U.S.C.A. 302, 303; 50 App. U.S.C.A. 451, 2216.

Miller Act: 40 U.S.C.A. 270a, 270d.

Miller-Tydings Fair Trade Act: See Fair Trade Act.

Mills Act (Customs Reorganization): 19 U.S.C.A. 4, 52.

Milwaukee Railroad Restructuring Act: 42 U.S.C.A. 231f, 922; 45 U.S.C.A. 902, 916.

Mineral Land Free Timber Act: 16 U.S.C.A. 604, 606.

Mineral Lands Leasing Act of 1920: 30 U.S.C.A. 22, 352.

Mineral Leasing Act for Acquired Lands: 30 U.S.C.A. 351, 359.

Mineral Leasing Act Revision of 1960: 30 U.S.C.A. 181, 241.

Minimum Wage and Hour Act: See Fair Labor Standards Act of 1938.

Mining and Mineral Resources Research Institute Act of 1984: 30 U.S.C.A. 1221, 1230.

Mineral and Minerals Policy Act of 1970: 30 U.S.C.A. 21a.

Mining Claims Rights Restoration Act of 1955: 30 U.S.C.A. 621.

Minnesota Valley National Wildlife Refuge Act: 16 U.S.C.A. 668kk, 668ss.

Miscellaneous International Affairs Authorizations Act of 1988: 22 U.S.C.A. 2191, 2200a.

Miscellaneous Purposes Act of 1920 (Surplus Water): 43 U.S.C.A. 521.

Miscellaneous Revenue Act of 1982: 5 U.S.C.A. 8509, 8521; 19 U.S.C.A. 2291 note; 26 U.S.C.A. 48, 7463; 46 U.S.C.A. 601.

Missing Children Act: 28 U.S.C.A. 534.

Missing Children's Assistance Act: 42 U.S.C.A. 5771, 5778.

Missing Persons Act: See 5 U.S.C.A. 5561, 5568; see 37 U.S.C.A. 551, 558.

Mississippi River Flood Control Act: 33 U.S.C.A. 702a, 704.

Mitchell Act (Columbia River Basin Fishery Development): 16 U.S.C.A. 755, 757.

Mni Wiconi Project Act of 1988: 43 U.S.C.A. 615aaa, 615 *llll*–6.

Model Secondary School for the Deaf Act: 20 U.S.C.A. 693, 693b; 31 U.S.C.A. 3102.

Monetary Act: See 31 U.S.C.A. 5301, 5302.

Monetary Control Act of 1980: 12 U.S.C.A. 248, 1425a.

Money and Finance: 31 U.S.C.A. 1, 9702.

Money Laundering Control Act of 1986: 12 U.S.C.A. 1464, 3413; 18 U.S.C.A. 981, 2516; 31 U.S.C.A. 5312, 5324.

Money Laundering Prosecution Improvements Act of 1988: 12 U.S.C.A. 1730d, 3420; 18 U.S.C.A. 1956, 1957; 31 U.S.C.A. 5312, 5326.

Monroe Doctrine Act: 22 U.S.C.A. 504.

Montgomery GI Bill Act of 1984: 10 U.S.C.A. 708, 2138; 38 U.S.C.A. 1401, 1795.

Morrill Acts (Agricultural Colleges): 7 U.S.C.A. 301, 328.

Morris Act (Chippewa Indians of Minnesota): 25 U.S.C.A. 197.

Morrison Act (Tariff): 12 U.S.C.A. 541, 545.

Mortgage Purchase Amendments of 1981: 12 U.S.C.A. 1454, 1717.

Mortgage Subsidy Bond Tax Act of 1980: 26 U.S.C.A. 103, 103A.

Mother's Day Act: 36 U.S.C.A. 141, 142.

Motorboat Act of 1940: 46 U.S.C.A. 526b, 526t; see 46 U.S.C.A. 2101, 4106.

Motor Carrier Act of 1980: 18 U.S.C.A. 1114; 49 U.S.C.A. 10101, 11902a.

Motor Carrier Safety Act of 1984: 28 U.S.C.A. 2342; 49 U.S.C.A. 507, 11914; 49 App. 2505, 2521.

Motor Vehicle Air Pollution Control Act: 42 U.S.C.A. 1857f–1, 1857f–8.

Motor Vehicle and Schoolbus Safety Amendments of 1974: 15 U.S.C.A. 1391, 1964.

Motor Vehicle Information and Cost Savings Act: 15 U.S.C.A. 1901, 2034.

Motor Vehicle Theft Law Enforcement Act of 1984: 15 U.S.C.A. 2021, 2034; 18 U.S.C.A. 511, 2320; 19 U.S.C.A. 1627.

Mrs. Murphy (Civil Rights Act) Exemption: 42 U.S.C.A. 3603(b)(2).

Multiemployer Pension Plan Amendments Act of 1980: 5 U.S.C.A. 8521; 26 U.S.C.A. 194, 6511; 29 U.S.C.A. 1001a, 1461.

Multifamily Mortgage Foreclosure Act of 1981: 12 U.S.C.A. 3701, 3717.

Multilateral Development Banks Procedurement Act of 1988: 22 U.S.C.A. 262q.

Multilateral Export Control Enhancement Amendments Act: 19 U.S.C.A. 1864; 50 App. U.S.C.A. 2404, 2413.

Multinational Force and Observers Participation Resolution: 22 U.S.C.A. 3421, 3427.

Multinational Force in Lebanon Resolution: 50 U.S.C.A. 1541.

Multiple Mineral Development Act: 30 U.S.C.A. 521, 530.

Multiple Use Law: 30 U.S.C.A. 521, 530.

Multiple-Use Sustained-Yield Act of 1960: 16 U.S.C.A. 528, 531.

Municipal Wastewater Treatment Construction Grant Amendments of 1981: 33 U.S.C.A. 1281, 1314.

Museum Services Act: 20 U.S.C.A. 958, 968.

Mustering-Out Payment Act of 1944: See 38 U.S.C.A. 101, 2104.

Mutual Defense Assistance Control Act of 1951: 22 U.S.C.A. 1613a, 1613d.

Mutual Educational and Cultural Exchange Act of 1961: 8 U.S.C.A. 1101, 1258; 22 U.S.C.A. 1221, 2460; 26 U.S.C.A. 117, 3402; 42 U.S.C.A. 410; 50 App. U.S.C.A. 1641.

Mutual Educational Exchange Act of 1961: 22 U.S.C.A. 2460.

Mutual Security Act of 1951: 7 U.S.C.A. 612c; 22 U.S.C.A. 272b, 1434.

Mutual Security Appropriation Acts: 22 U.S.C.A. 1811 note, 1819 note; 42 U.S.C.A. 1975c.

Myers Patent Act: See 35 U.S.C.A. 132, 135.

Narcotic Addict Rehabilitation Act of 1966: 18 U.S.C.A. 4251, 4255; 28 U.S.C.A. 2901, 2906; 42 U.S.C.A. 3411, 3442.

Narcotic Addict Treatment Act of 1974: 21 U.S.C.A. 802, 827.

Narcotic Control Act of 1956: 8 U.S.C.A. 1182, 1251; 18 U.S.C.A. 1401, 1407; 21 U.S.C.A. 174, 198; 26 U.S.C.A. 4744, 7608.

Narcotic Drugs Import and Export Acts: 21 U.S.C.A. 171, 200a.

Narcotics Acts: See 6 U.S.C.A. 15; see 31 U.S.C.A. 9303; 48 U.S.C.A. 845.

Narcotics Control Trade Act: 19 U.S.C.A. 2462, 2702.

Narcotics Manufacturing Act of 1960: 21 U.S.C.A. 182, 517; 26 U.S.C.A. 4702, 4731.

Narcotics Penalties and Enforcement Act of 1986: 18 U.S.C.A. 3553, 3583; 18 App. U.S.C.A. Rule 35; 21 U.S.C.A. 802, 960; 28 U.S.C.A. 994.

NASA Authorization Act, 1970: 42 U.S.C.A. 2462.

National Advisory Committee on Oceans and Atmosphere Act of 1977: 33 U.S.C.A. 857–13, 857–18.

National Advisory Committee on Semiconductor Research and Development Act of 1988: 15 U.S.C.A. 4632.

National Aeronautics and Space Act of 1958: 10 U.S.C.A. 2302, 2303; 18 U.S.C.A. 799, 1114; 42 U.S.C.A. 2451, 2484; 50 U.S.C.A. 511, 515.

National Aeronautics and Space Administration Authorization Act, Fiscal Year 1989: 15 U.S.C.A. 1534; 31 U.S.C.A. 1105 note; 42 U.S.C.A. 2451, 8906; 49 App. U.S.C.A. 2623.

National Agricultural Policy Commission Act of 1985: 7 U.S.C.A. 178c, 5007.

National Agricultural Research Extension, and Teaching Policy Act of 1977: 7 U.S.C.A. 341, 3323.

National Agricultural, Research, Extension, and Teaching Policy Act Amendments of 1981: 5 U.S.C.A. 5315; 7 U.S.C.A. 321, 3336; 16 U.S.C.A. 582a, 582a–5; 40 U.S.C.A. 483; 42 U.S.C.A. 6651, 8852.

National Air Museum Amendments Act of 1965: 20 U.S.C.A. 77, 77d.

National Appliance Energy Conservation Act of 1987: 42 U.S.C.A. 6291, 6309.

National Apprenticeship Act: 29 U.S.C.A. 50, 50b.

National Aquaculture Act of 1980: 16 U.S.C.A. 2801, 2810.

National Archives and Records Administration Act of 1984: 1 U.S.C.A. 106a, 201; 3 U.S.C.A. 6, 13; 4 U.S.C.A. 141, 145; 5 U.S.C.A. 552a, 5314; 25 U.S.C.A. 199a; 44 U.S.C.A. 710, 3513.

National Archives Trust Fund Board Act: See 44 U.S.C.A. 2301, 2308.

National Arthritis Act of 1974: 42 U.S.C.A. 289a, 289c–6.

National Arts and Cultural Development Act of 1964: 20 U.S.C.A. 781, 790.

National Assessment of Educational Progress Improvement Act: 20 U.S.C.A. 1221e, 1221e–1.

National Aviation Day Act: 36 U.S.C.A. 151.

National Bank Acts: 12 U.S.C.A. 24, 165.

National Bank Tax Act: 12 U.S.C.A. 548.

National Bureau of Standards: 15 U.S.C.A. 278a, 278h.

National Cancer Act of 1971: 42 U.S.C.A. 218, 2862*l*.

National Cancer Institute Act: 42 U.S.C.A. 281.

National Capital Planning Act of 1952: 20 U.S.C.A. 76 note; 40 U.S.C.A. 71, 128.

National Capital Transportation Act of 1969: 12 U.S.C.A. 24; 40 U.S.C.A. 684.

National Cattle Theft Act: See 18 U.S.C.A. 10, 3237.

National Cemeteries Act of 1973: 5 U.S.C.A. 5316; 24 U.S.C.A. 271, 275, 38 U.S.C.A. 218, 3505.

National Center for the Study of Afro-American History and Culture Act: 20 U.S.C.A. 3701, 3703.

National Childhood Vaccine Injury Act of 1986: 42 U.S.C.A. 218, 300cc–15.

National Climate Program Act: 15 U.S.C.A. 2901, 2908; see 31 U.S.C.A. 1105.

National Coal Imports Reporting Act of 1985: 15 U.S.C.A. 2903, 2905; 42 U.S.C.A. 7277.

National Commission on Libraries and Information Science Act: 20 U.S.C.A. 1501, 1506.

National Commission on Supplies and Shortages Act of 1974: 50 App. U.S.C.A. 2169.

National Consumer Cooperative Bank Act: 5 U.S.C.A. 5315; 12 U.S.C.A. 3001, 3051; see 31 U.S.C.A. 9101, 9108.

National Consumer Health Information and Health Promotion Act of 1976: 42 U.S.C.A. 300u, 300u–5.

National Cooley's Anemia Control Act: 42 U.S.C.A. 300b, 300c–4.

National Cooperative Research Act of 1984: 15 U.S.C.A. 4301, 4305.

National Credit Union Central Liquidity Facility Act: 12 U.S.C.A. 1757, 1795i; 18 U.S.C.A. 709; see 31 U.S.C.A. 9101.

National Critical Materials Act of 1984: 30 U.S.C.A. 1801, 1810.

National Currency Association Acts: 12 U.S.C.A. 104; 12 U.S.C.A. generally dispersed throughout Title 12.

National Deafness and Other Communication Disorders Act of 1988: 42 U.S.C.A. 281, 285m–6.

National Defense Act: See 10 U.S.C.A. 771, 8612; see 32 U.S.C.A. 109, 708.

National Defense Education Act of 1958: 20 U.S.C.A. 15aaa, 602; 42 U.S.C.A. 1876, 1879.

National Defense Emergency Appropriation Act: 42 U.S.C.A. 1523 note.

National Defense Facilities Act of 1950: 10 U.S.C.A.

2233 note; see 10 U.S.C.A. 2231, 2238.

National Defense Stockpile Amendments of 1987: 50 U.S.C.A. 98a, 98h–5.

National Dental Research Act: 42 U.S.C.A. 201, 291k.

National Diabetes Mellitus Research and Education Act: 42 U.S.C.A. 247b, 289c–3.

National Drug Interdiction Improvement Act of 1986: 10 U.S.C.A. 374, 911; 14 U.S.C.A. 89 note; 19 U.S.C.A. 507, 2081; 21 U.S.C.A. 959; 23 U.S.C.A. 403 note; 31 U.S.C.A. 5316; 46 U.S.C.A. 1901, 1904; 47 U.S.C.A. 312a; 49 U.S.C.A. 1401, 1509.

National Emergencies Act: 8 U.S.C.A. 1481; 10 U.S.C.A. 2667; 16 U.S.C.A. 831d; 50 U.S.C.A. 1601, 1651.

National Emission Standards Act: 42 U.S.C.A. 1857f–1, 1857f–7.

National Employment Service Act: 29 U.S.C.A. 49, 557.

National Endowment for Democracy Act: 22 U.S.C.A. 4411, 4415.

National Energy Conservation Policy Act: 12 U.S.C.A. 1451, 1735f–4; 15 U.S.C.A. 2006, 2008; 23 U.S.C.A. 217 note; 42 U.S.C.A. 300k–2, 8287c.

National Energy Extension Service Act: 42 U.S.C.A. 5813, 7011.

National Environmental Policy Act of 1969: 42 U.S.C.A. 4321, 4347.

National Film Preservation Act of 1988: 2 U.S.C.A. 178a, 178*l*.

National Firearms Act: 26 U.S.C.A. 5801, 5872.

National Fish and Wildlife Foundation Establishment Act: 16 U.S.C.A. 3701, 3709.

National Fishing Enhancement Act of 1984: 16 U.S.C.A. 1220, 1220d; 33 U.S.C.A. 2102, 2106.

National Flag Week Act: 36 U.S.C.A. 157a.

National Flood Insurance Act of 1968: 12 U.S.C.A. 1703, 2811; 42 U.S.C.A. 1401, 5302.

National Forest Management Act of 1976: 16 U.S.C.A. 472a, 1614.

National Forest Ski Area Permit Act of 1986: 16 U.S.C.A. 497b.

National Forest System Drug Control Act of 1986: 16 U.S.C.A. 559b, 559g.

National Forests Act of 1972: 16 U.S.C.A. 558d.

National Foundation on the Arts and the Humanities Act of 1965: 20 U.S.C.A. 784, 974.

National Gallery of Art Act: 20 U.S.C.A. 71, 75.

National Geography Studies Centers Act: 20 U.S.C.A. 3156a, 3157.

National Gold and Silver Stamping Act of 1906: 15 U.S.C.A. 294, 300.

National Guard: 32 U.S.C.A. 1, 716.

National Guard Act of 1933: See 10 U.S.C.A. 101, 9621; 32 U.S.C.A. 101, 705; 37 U.S.C.A. 231.

National Guard Officers' Act: See 10 U.S.C.A. 3015; see 32 U.S.C.A. 304, 709.

National Guard Technicians Act of 1968: 5 U.S.C.A. 2105, 8339; 10 U.S.C.A. 3848, 8851; 32 U.S.C.A. 709, 715; 42 U.S.C.A. 418.

National Health Planning and Resources Development Act of 1974: 42 U.S.C.A. 300e–4, 300t.

National Health Survey Act: 42 U.S.C.A. 241, 242c.

National Heart Act: 42 U.S.C.A. 201, 287d.

National Heart, Blood Vessel, Lung and Blood Act of 1972: 42 U.S.C.A. 218, 289*l*–2.

National Historic Preservation Act: 16 U.S.C.A. 469c–2, 470w–6.

National Defense Authorization Act, Fiscal Year 1989: 5 U.S.C.A. 5314, 8140; 10 U.S.C.A. 101, 9511; 15 U.S.C.A. 632; 22 U.S.C.A. 2592a, 2796d; 32 U.S.C.A. 101, 712; 37 U.S.C.A. 101, 1013; 38 U.S.C.A. 101; 42 U.S.C.A. 248d, 2286i; 44 U.S.C.A. 502 note; 50 U.S.C.A. 98b, 1521.

National Historical Publications and Records Commission Amendments of 1988: 44 U.S.C.A. 2501, 2504.

National Housing Act: See 10 U.S.C.A. 4387; 12 U.S.C.A. 24, 3631; 15 U.S.C.A. 609k; 41 U.S.C.A. 22; 50 App. U.S.C.A. 1830, 1909.

National Housing Census Act: See 13 U.S.C.A. 142.

National Industrial Reserve Act of 1948: 50 U.S.C.A. 451, 455.

National Institute of Standards and Technology Act: 15 U.S.C.A. 203, 282.

National Institute on Deafness & Other Communication Disorders & Health Research Extension Act of 1988: 42 U.S.C.A. 241, 11283.

National Insurance Development Act of 1975: 12 U.S.C.A. 1749bbb.

National Labor Relations Act: 29 U.S.C.A. 151, 169.

National Library of Medicine Act: 42 U.S.C.A. 275, 281.

National Manufactured Housing Construction and Safety Standards Act of 1974: 42 U.S.C.A. 5401, 5426.

National Mass Transportation Assistance Act of 1974: 42 U.S.C.A. 3303; 49 U.S.C.A. 1601b, 1611.

National Materials and Minerals Policy, Research and Development Act of 1980: 30 U.S.C.A. 1601, 1605.

National Materials Policy Act of 1970: 42 U.S.C.A. 3251 note.

National Mental Health Act: 42 U.S.C.A. 201, 246.

National Mobile Home Construction and Safety Standards Act of 1974: 42 U.S.C.A. 5419, 5425.

National Monument Act (Preservation of Antiquities): 16 U.S.C.A. 431, 433.

National Motor Vehicle Theft Act: See 18 U.S.C.A. 10, 2313.

National Museum Act of 1966: 20 U.S.C.A. 65a.

National Narcotics Act of 1984: 21 U.S.C.A. 1111, 1204.

National Narcotics Leadership Act of 1988: 5 U.S.C.A. 5312, 5315; 21 U.S.C.A. 1105, 1508; 31 U.S.C.A. 1105; 50 U.S.C.A. 402.

National Ocean Pollution Planning Act of 1978: 33 U.S.C.A. 1701, 1709.

National Oceanic and Atmospheric Administration Marine Fisheries Program Authorization Act: 46 U.S.C.A. 801.

National Organ Transplant Act: 42 U.S.C.A. 273, 274e.

National Park Foundation Act: 16 U.S.C.A. 19e, 19n.

National Park Service Organic Act: 16 U.S.C.A. 1, 43.

National Park System Concessions Policy Act: 16 U.S.C.A. 20, 20g.

National Park System Visitor Facilities Fund Act: 16 U.S.C.A. 19aa, 19gg.

National Parks and Recreation Act of 1978: 16 U.S.C.A. 1a–5, 2514.

National Portrait Gallery Act: 20 U.S.C.A. 752, 75g.

National Productivity and Quality of Working Life Act of 1975: 15 U.S.C.A. 2401, 2471.

National Research Act: 42 U.S.C.A. 218, 300a–7.

National Research Service Award Act of 1974: 42 U.S.C.A. 218, 300a–7.

National School Lunch Act: 42 U.S.C.A. 1751, 1874.

National Science and Technology Policy, Organization, and Priorities Act of 1976: 5 App. U.S.C.A.; 7 U.S.C.A. 6651; 42 U.S.C.A. 1863; 6671; 50 App. U.S.C.A. 2271 note.

National Science, Engineering, and Mathematics Authorization Act of 1986: 20 U.S.C.A. 351a, 4059; 29 U.S.C.A. 1503, 1753; 42 U.S.C.A. 1862, 1886.

National Science Foundation Act of 1950: 42 U.S.C.A. 1861, 1875.

National Science Foundation Authorization Act of 1988: 20 U.S.C.A. 3011, 3012; 42 U.S.C.A. 1862a, 1885c.

National Science Foundation Authorization and Science and Engineering Equal Opportunities Act: 42 U.S.C.A. 1885, 1885d.

National Science Foundation Authorization and Science and Technology Equal Opportunities Act: 42 U.S.C.A. 1863, 1885d.

National Science Foundation University Infrastructure Act of 1988: 42 U.S.C.A. 1862a, 1862b.

National Sea Grant College Program Act: 33 U.S.C.A. 1121, 1131.

National Security Act of 1947: See 5 U.S.C.A. 101, 5315(16); see 10 U.S.C.A. 101(5), 8062; 50 U.S.C.A. 401, 432.

National Service Life Insurance Act of 1940: See 38 U.S.C.A. 701, 788.

National Sickle Cell Anemia Control Act: 33 U.S.C.A. 763c note; 42 U.S.C.A. 300b, 300b–5.

National Sickle Cell Anemia, Cooley's Anemia, Tay-Sachs, and Genetic Diseases Act: 42 U.S.C.A. 300b, 300c–22.

National Space Grant College and Fellowship Act: 16 U.S.C.A. 1244, 1249; 42 U.S.C.A. 2486, 2486*l*.

National Stolen Property Act: See 18 U.S.C.A. 10, 3237.

National Superconductivity and Competitiveness Act of 1988: 15 U.S.C.A. 5201, 5209.

National Swine Flu Immunization Program of 1976: 42 U.S.C.A. 247b.

National Technical Information Act of 1988: 15 U.S.C.A. 3704b, 3710.

National Technical Institute for the Deaf Act: 20 U.S.C.A. 681, 685.

National Tourism Policy Act: 5 U.S.C.A. 5314; 22 U.S.C.A. 2121, 2128.

National Traffic and Motor Vehicle Safety Act of 1966: 15 U.S.C.A. 1391, 1431; 23 U.S.C.A. 313 note.

National Trails System Act: 16 U.S.C.A. 1241, 1251.

National Transportation Policy: 15 U.S.C.A. 605; 49 U.S.C.A. throughout title generally.

National Urban Policy and New Community Development Act of 1970: 42 U.S.C.A. 4502, 4518.

National Venereal Disease Prevention and Control Act: 42 U.S.C.A. 247c note.

National Visitor Center Facilities Act of 1968: 40 U.S.C.A. 801, 831.

National Vocational Student Loan Insurance Act of 1965: 20 U.S.C.A. 981, 1086.

National War Agencies Appropriation Acts: 41 U.S.C.A. 6a note.

National Weather Modification Policy Act of 1976: 15 U.S.C.A. 330e.

National Wildlife Refuge System Administration Act of 1966: 16 U.S.C.A. 668dd, 668ee.

National Wool Act of 1954: 7 U.S.C.A. 1781, 1787.

Nationality Act of 1940: See 8 U.S.C.A. 1101.

Native American Programs Act of 1974: 42 U.S.C.A. 2991, 2992d.

Native Hawaiian Health Care Act of 1988: 25 U.S.C.A. 1621d; 42 U.S.C.A. 11701, 11710.

Natural Gas Act: 15 U.S.C.A. 717, 717w.

Natural Gas Pipeline Safety Act of 1968: 49 U.S.C.A. 1671, 2003; 49 App. U.S.C.A. 1672, 1687.

Natural Gas Policy Act of 1978: 15 U.S.C.A. 3301, 3432; 42 U.S.C.A. 7255.

Nautical Education Act: See 14 U.S.C.A. 148.

Navajo Community College Act: 25 U.S.C.A. 640a, 640c–2.

Navajo-Hopi Land Settlement Act of 1974: 25 U.S.C.A. 640d, 640d-30.

Navajo-Hopi Rehabilitation Act: 25 U.S.C.A. 631, 640.

Navajo and Hopi Indian Relocation Amendments Act of 1980: 25 U.S.C.A. 640d–7, 640d–28.

Naval Air Base Act: See 10 U.S.C.A. 7212.

Naval Aircraft Public Works Act: See 10 U.S.C.A. 6022.

Naval Appropriation Acts: 22 U.S.C.A. 412 note; 24 U.S.C.A. 16a; 42 U.S.C.A. 70; 50 App. U.S.C.A. 1152.

Naval Auxiliary Vessel Acts: See 10 U.S.C.A. 7296.

Naval Aviation Cadet Act of 1942: See 10 U.S.C.A. 6911, 6915; 14 U.S.C.A. 758a, 759a.

Naval Aviation Personnel Act of 1940: See 10 U.S.C.A. 5942, 6914.

Naval Aviation Reserve Act: See 10 U.S.C.A. 6148.

Naval Expansion Acts: See 10 U.S.C.A. 6022, 7344.

Naval Line-Officer Act: See 10 U.S.C.A. 5404, 6021.

Naval Parity Act: See 10 U.S.C.A. 2382, 7343; 40 U.S.C.A. 474.

Naval Petroleum Reserves Production Act of 1976: 10 U.S.C.A. 7420, 7438; 42 U.S.C.A. 6244, 6507.

Naval Reserve Act of 1938: See 10 U.S.C.A. 261, 6521; 37 U.S.C.A. 231.

Naval R.O.T.C. Act: See 10 U.S.C.A. 6901, 6902.

Naval Service Appropriations Act, 1922: 48 U.S.C.A. 1393.

Naval Special Duty Act: See 10 U.S.C.A. 5231, 5501.

Naval Staff Corps Act: See 10 U.S.C.A. 5571.

Naval Stores Act: 7 U.S.C.A. 91, 99.

Navigation Acts: 19 U.S.C.A. 289; 33 U.S.C.A. 152, 687; 46 U.S.C.A. 49, 124; see 46 U.S.C.A. 2101, 8101.

Navy and Marine Corps Officer Augmentation Act of 1955: See 10 U.S.C.A. 3212, 9353.

Navy-Marine Advancement Act: See 10 U.S.C.A. 6150, 6483.

Navy-Marine Corps Enlisted Strength Act: See 10 U.S.C.A. 5401.

Navy Public Works Act: See 10 U.S.C.A. 7213; 40 U.S.C.A. 276a–7.

Nebraska Wilderness Act of 1985: 16 U.S.C.A. 460rr, 460rr–2.

Negotiated Shipbuilding Contracting Act of 1976: 46 U.S.C.A. 1152.

Neighborhood Reinvestment Corporation Act: 42 U.S.C.A. 8101, 8107.

Neighborhood Self-Help Development Act of 1978: 42 U.S.C.A. 8121, 8124.

Nelson Act (Bankruptcy Act of 1898): 11 U.S.C.A. generally dispersed throughout title 11.

Nelson Amendment (Agricultural Colleges): 7 U.S.C.A. 322, 2245; 15 U.S.C.A. 320; 16 U.S.C.A. 471, 499; 21 U.S.C.A. 71, 91; 43 U.S.C.A. 203, 957.

Nelson Bill: 2 U.S.C.A. 25 note; 5 U.S.C.A. 2106; 10 U.S.C.A. 4342, 9342; 18 U.S.C.A. 201, 595; 42 U.S.C.A. 1973i.

Nematocide, Plant Regulator, Defoliant, and Desiccant Amendment of 1959: 7 U.S.C.A. 135.

New Worth Certificate Act: 12 U.S.C.A. 1464, 1823.

Neutrality Acts: See 18 U.S.C.A. 960; 22 U.S.C.A. 441, 457.

Neutrality Proclamations: 50 App. U.S.C.A. note prec. 1.

Nevada-Florida Land Exchange Authorization Act of 1988: 16 U.S.C.A. 670g note.

New Communities Act of 1968: 42 U.S.C.A. 3901, 3914.

New GI Bill Continuation Act: 10 U.S.C.A. 2132; 38 U.S.C.A. 1401, 1412.

New Hampshire Wilderness Act of 1984: 16 U.S.C.A. 1276.

New York City Loan Guarantee Act of 1978: 12 U.S.C.A. 2285a; 26 U.S.C.A. 103.

Newlands Act (Irrigation): 43 U.S.C.A. 372, 1457.

Newspaper Preservation Act: 15 U.S.C.A. 1801, 1804.

Newton Amendment to the Carmack Amendment: See 49 U.S.C.A. 10103, 11707.

Niagara Power Project Act: 16 U.S.C.A. 836, 836a.

1984 Act to Combat International Terrorism: 5 U.S.C.A. 5928 note; 18 U.S.C.A. 3071, 3077; 22 U.S.C.A. 2669, 2708.

No Net Cost Tobacco Program Act of 1982: 7 U.S.C.A. 1301, 1445–2; 16 U.S.C.A. 590h note.

Noise Control Act of 1972: 42 U.S.C.A. 4901, 4918; 49 App. U.S.C.A. 1431.

Noise Pollution and Abatement Act of 1970: 42 U.S.C.A. 1858, 1858a.

Noise Reduction Reimbursement Act of 1989: 49 App. U.S.C.A. 2212.

Nonappropriated Fund Instrumentalities Employees' Retirement Credit Act of 1986: 5 U.S.C.A. 2105, 8332.

Nonprofit Institutions Act: 15 U.S.C.A. 13c.

Norris-La Guardia Act (Labor Disputes): 29 U.S.C.A. 101, 115.

North Atlantic Treaty Organization Mutual Support Act of 1979: 10 U.S.C.A. 2321, 2331.

North Pacific Fisheries Act of 1954: 16 U.S.C.A. 1021, 1035.

Northeast Rail Service Act of 1981: 45 U.S.C.A. 159a, 1116.

Northern Pacific Halibut Act of 1982: 16 U.S.C.A. 772. 773k.

Northwest Atlantic Fisheries Act of 1950: 16 U.S.C.A. 981, 991.

Notaries Public Expense Act of 1955: See 5 U.S.C.A. 5945.

Nuclear Career Incentive Act of 1975: 37 U.S.C.A. 312, 312c.

Nuclear Non-Proliferation Act of 1978: 22 U.S.C.A. 3201, 3282; 42 U.S.C.A. 2074, 2160a.

Nuclear Safety Research, Development and Demonstration Act of 1980: 42 U.S.C.A. 9701, 9708.

Nuclear Waste Policy Act of 1982: 42 U.S.C.A. 10101, 10270.

Nurse Education Amendments of 1985: 15 U.S.C.A. 1332, 1341; 26 U.S.C.A. 6103; 42 U.S.C.A. 296, 298b-5.

Nurse Training Act of 1964: 33 U.S.C.A. 763c note; 42 U.S.C.A. 291c, 298b.

Nursery Stock Quarantine Act: 7 U.S.C.A. 151, 167; 46 U.S.C.A. 103, 106.

Nursing Shortage Reduction and Education Extension Act of 1988: 42 U.S.C.A. 210, 298b-6.

Occupational Safety and Health Act of 1970: 5 U.S.C.A. 5108, 7902; 15 U.S.C.A. 633, 636; 18 U.S.C.A. 1114; 29 U.S.C.A. 553, 678; 42 U.S.C.A. 3142-1; 49 App. U.S.C.A. 1421.

Ocean Dumping Ban Act of 1988: 33 U.S.C.A. 1268, 1415.

Ocean Shipping Act of 1978: 46 U.S.C.A. 801, 817.

Ocean Thermal Energy Conversion Act of 1980: 42 U.S.C.A. 9101, 9168; 46 U.S.C.A. 1271, 1279c.

OCS Paperwork and Reporting Act: 43 U.S.C.A. 1343, 1865.

Odometer Disclosure Act: 15 U.S.C.A. 1981.

Office of Federal Procurement Policy Act: 5 U.S.C.A. 5315; 40 U.S.C.A. 474, 487; 41 U.S.C.A. 401, 424.

Officer Grade Limitation Act of 1954: See 10 U.S.C.A. 686, 8202.

Officer Personnel Act of 1947: See 10 U.S.C.A. 5701 note.

Officers Competency Certificates Act: 46 U.S.C.A. 224a.

Offshore Shrimp Fisheries Act of 1973: 16 U.S.C.A. 1085, 1100b-10.

Oil and Gas Prospecting Act: 30 U.S.C.A. 185, 236a.

Oil Pipe Line Act: 43 U.S.C.A. 962, 965.

Oil Pollution Act of 1924: 33 U.S.C.A. 431, 437.

Oil Pollution Act, 1961: 33 U.S.C.A. 1001, 1015.

Oklahoma Welfare Act: 25 U.S.C.A. 501, 1461.

Old Age Assistance Claims Settlement Act: 25 U.S.C.A. 2301, 2307.

Old-Age, Survivors, and Disability Insurance Amendments of 1965: 26 U.S.C.A. 451, 6674; 42 U.S.C.A. 401, 1306; 45 U.S.C.A. 228a, 228e.

Old Series Currency Adjustment Act: 12 U.S.C.A. 415, 416; see 31 U.S.C.A. 5119.

Older American Community Service Employment Act: 42 U.S.C.A. 3056, 3067.

Older Americans Act of 1965: 42 U.S.C.A. 3001, 3058d.

Older Americans Comprehensive Services Amendments of 1973: 20 U.S.C.A. 315b, 1505; 42 U.S.C.A. 3001, 3067.

Older Americans Personal Health Education and Training Act: 42 U.S.C.A. 3058, 3058d.

Oleomargarine Acts: 21 U.S.C.A. 25.

Olympic Commemorative Coin Act: 31 U.S.C.A. 5112 note.

Omnibus Adjustment Act of May 25, 1926: 43 U.S.C.A. 423e.

Omnibus Budget Reconciliation Act of 1981: 5 U.S.C.A. 3393, 8521; 7 U.S.C.A. 15b, 2028; 8 U.S.C.A. 1522 note, 1524 note; 10 U.S.C.A. 1401a note, 1448 note; 11 U.S.C.A. 523; 12 U.S.C.A. 24, 3717; 15 U.S.C.A. 632, 2083. See Popular Name Table for other titles.

Omnibus Claims Act: See 28 U.S.C.A. 121, 2501.

Omnibus Crime Control Act of 1970: 5 U.S.C.A. 5108, 5316; 18 U.S.C.A. 351, 3731; 42 U.S.C.A. 3711, 3795.

Omnibus Crime Control and Safe Streets Act of 1968: 5 U.S.C.A. 5108, 7313; 18 U.S.C.A. 921, 3731; 18 App. U.S.C.A. 1201, 1203; 28 U.S.C.A. 522 note, 532 note; 40 U.S.C.A. 484; 41 U.S.C.A. 35; 42 U.S.C.A. 3334, 3797; 47 U.S.C.A. 605.

Omnibus Diplomatic Security and Antiterrorism Act of 1986: 3 U.S.C.A. 208; 5 U.S.C.A. 5315, 6325; 5 App. U.S.C.A. 2, 11; 10 U.S.C.A. 1051, 2185; 18 U.S.C.A. 793, 3671; 22 U.S.C.A. 300, 4904; 33

U.S.C.A. 1226; 37 U.S.C.A. 559, 1013; 42 U.S.C.A. 2160b, 2169; 46 U.S.C.A. 1801, 1809; 50 App. U.S.C.A. 2405.

Omnibus Education Reconciliation Act of 1981: 8 U.S.C.A. 1522 note; 20 U.S.C.A. 239a, 3851; 21 U.S.C.A. 1002 note; 22 U.S.C.A. 287 note; 25 U.S.C.A. 13 note; 42 U.S.C.A. 2000c–2 note, 2751 note.

Omnibus Flood Control Act: 33 U.S.C.A. 558b–1, 707.

Omnibus Judgeship Act: 28 U.S.C.A. 44, 134; see 28 U.S.C.A. 132.

Omnibus Oregon Wild and Scenic Rivers Act of 1988: 16 U.S.C.A. 1274, 1276.

Omnibus Reconciliation Act of 1980: 5 U.S.C.A. 5551, 8714; 26 U.S.C.A. 103, 7213; 39 U.S.C.A. 2401; 42 U.S.C.A. 402, 1788; 45 U.S.C.A. 231.

Omnibus Small Business Capital Formation Act of 1980: 15 U.S.C.A. 80c, 775.

Omnibus Taxpayer Bill of Rights: 5 U.S.C.A. 504; 26 U.S.C.A. 6159 7811.

Omnibus Territories Act of 1977: 26 U.S.C.A. 7651 note; 43 U.S.C.A. 1457 note; 48 U.S.C.A. 1421i, 1681b.

Omnibus Trade and Competitiveness Act of 1988: 7 U.S.C.A. 511r, 5235; 15 U.S.C.A. 78m, 4913; 16 U.S.C.A. 2112, 3912; 19 U.S.C.A. 58b, 3111; 20 U.S.C.A. 1018, 5124. See Popular Name Table for other titles.

Onion Futures Act: 7 U.S.C.A. 13–1.

Opium Acts: 21 U.S.C.A. 171, 193.

Opium Poppy Control Act of 1942: 21 U.S.C.A. 188, 188n.

Oregon Wilderness Act of 1984: 16 U.S.C.A. 460oo.

Organ Transplant Amendments Act of 1988: 42 U.S.C.A. 273, 300y–27.

Organic Act of Guam: See 8 U.S.C.A. 1407, 1422; 48 U.S.C.A. 1421, 1424b.

Organic Act of Puerto Rico: 2 U.S.C.A. 46; 48 U.S.C.A. ch. 4.

Organic Act of the Virgin Islands of the United States: 48 U.S.C.A. 1405, 1406m.

Organized Crime Control Act of 1970: 7 U.S.C.A. 15, 2115; 12 U.S.C.A. 1820; 15 U.S.C.A. 49, 1714; 16 U.S.C.A. 825f; 18 U.S.C.A. 835, 6005. See Popular Name Table for other titles.

Organotin Antifouling Paint Control Act of 1988: 33 U.S.C.A. 2401, 2410.

Original Packages Act (Intoxicating Liquors): 27 U.S.C.A. 121.

Orphan Drug Act: 15 U.S.C.A. 1274, 2080; 21 U.S.C.A. 360aa, 904; 26 U.S.C.A. 44H, 6096; 35 U.S.C.A. 155; 42 U.S.C.A. 209, 4587.

Osage Tribe of Indians Technical Corrections Act of 1984: 25 U.S.C.A. 883.

Outer Continental Shelf Lands Act: See 10 U.S.C.A. 7421, 7438; 43 U.S.C.A. 1331, 1356.

Outer Continental Shelf Operations Indemnification Clarification Act of 1988: 16 U.S.C.A. 668dd note; 43 U.S.C.A. 1815.

Overseas Citizens Voting Rights Act of 1975: 42 U.S.C.A. 1973dd, 1973dd–6.

Overseas Differentials and Allowances Act: See 5 U.S.C.A. 5509, 6310; 22 U.S.C.A. 287e, 2669; 26 U.S.C.A. 912; 50 U.S.C.A. 403a, 403e.

Overseas Private Investment Corporation Amendments Act of 1974: 22 U.S.C.A. 2191, 2200a.

Over-the-Counter Market Act: 15 U.S.C.A. 78cc, 78q.

Overton-Whittington Flood Control Act: See Flood Control Act of 1936.

Ozark National Scenic Riverways Act: 16 U.S.C.A. 460m, 460m–7.

Pacific Northwest Electric Power Planning and Conservation Act: 16 U.S.C.A. 837, 839h.

Pacific Salmon Treaty Act of 1985: 16 U.S.C.A. 776, 3644.

Packers and Stockyards Act: 7 U.S.C.A. 181, 229.

Packwood-Magnuson Amendment: 16 U.S.C.A. 971(4), 1882; 22 U.S.C.A. 1972, 1973(a).

Paiute Indian Tribe of Utah Restoration Act: 25 U.S.C.A. 761, 768.

Panama Canal Act of 1979: 5 U.S.C.A. 305, 8901; 8 U.S.C.A. 1101, 1182; 22 U.S.C.A. 2778, 3871; 29 U.S.C.A. 213; 39 U.S.C.A. 403, 3682; 50 U.S.C.A. 191, 196.

Panama Canal Acts: 15 U.S.C.A. 31; 46 U.S.C.A. 11; see 49 U.S.C.A. 10503, 11914.

Panama Canal Commission Authorization Act, Fiscal Year 1987: 22 U.S.C.A. 3751; 46 U.S.C.A. 1295b.

Panama Canal Revolving Fund Act: 5 U.S.C.A. 8348; 22 U.S.C.A. 3683, 3793.

Pan-American Naval Academy Act: 20 U.S.C.A. 221.

Pandering Law: 39 U.S.C.A. 3008.

Paperwork Reduction Act of 1980: 5 U.S.C.A. 5315; 20 U.S.C.A. 1221–3; 30 U.S.C.A. 1211; 42 U.S.C.A. 292h; 44 U.S.C.A. 2904, 3520.

Postal Service Appropriation Act, 1987: 18 U.S.C.A. 2254; 39 U.S.C.A. 2003.

Postsecondary Student Assistance Amendments of 1981: 20 U.S.C.A. 1075, 1232.

Potato Research and Promotion Act: 7 U.S.C.A. 2611, 2627.

Poultry Producers Financial Protection Act of 1987: 7 U.S.C.A. 182, 228b–4.

Poultry Products Inspection Act: 21 U.S.C.A. 451, 470.

Poultry Racket Act: 7 U.S.C.A. 192, 224.

Power or Train Brakes Safety Appliance Act of 1958: 45 U.S.C.A. 9.

Powerplant and Industrial Fuel Use Act of 1978: 15 U.S.C.A. 796; 42 U.S.C.A. 6211, 8484; 45 U.S.C.A. 821, 825; see 49 U.S.C.A. 10382.

Practical Nurse Training Extension Act of 1961: 20 U.S.C.A. 15aa, 15jj.

Pre-emption Acts: 43 U.S.C.A. 251.

Preferred Surety Bond Guarantee Program Act of 1988: 15 U.S.C.A. 694b, 694c.

Pregnancy Discrimination Act: 42 U.S.C.A. 2000e(k).

Prescription Drug Marketing Act of 1987: 21 U.S.C.A. 331, 381.

Presidential Election Campaign Fund Act: 26 U.S.C.A. 9001, 9013.

Presidential Inaugural Ceremonies Act: 36 U.S.C.A. 721, 730.

Presidential Libraries Act: 44 U.S.C.A. 2101, 2108.

Presidential Primary Matching Payment Account Act: 26 U.S.C.A. 9031, 9042.

Presidential Protection Assistance Act of 1976: 18 U.S.C.A. 3056 note.

Presidential Recordings and Materials Preservation Act: 44 U.S.C.A. 3315, 3324.

Presidential Records Act of 1978: 44 U.S.C.A. 2107, 2207.

Presidential Science Technology Advisory Organization Act of 1976: 42 U.S.C.A. 6611, 6618.

Presidential Succession Act: 3 U.S.C.A. 17; see 3 U.S.C.A. 1, 19.

Presidential Transitions Effectiveness Act: 3 U.S.C.A. 102 notes; 5 U.S.C.A. 3345, 5723.

President's Emergency Food Assistance Act of 1984: 7 U.S.C.A. 1723, 1728b.

President's Media Commission on Alcohol and Drug Abuse Prevention Act: 21 U.S.C.A. 1301, 1308.

Pretrial Services Act of 1982: 18 U.S.C.A. 3152, 3155; 28 U.S.C.A. 604.

Preventive Health Amendments of 1984: 42 U.S.C.A. 247b, 300w–10.

Price Adjustment Act of 1938: 7 U.S.C.A. 1302.

Price Discrimination Act: See Robinson-Patman Price Discrimination Act.

Primary Dealers Act of 1988: 22 U.S.C.A. 5341, 5342.

Primary Health Care Act of 1978: 42 U.S.C.A. 254a, 294t.

Printing Act: See 44 U.S.C.A. 906.

Printing and Binding Acts: 1 U.S.C.A. 30; 15 U.S.C.A. 187; 43 U.S.C.A. 1457; 44 U.S.C.A. generally dispersed throughout title 44.

Priorities and Allocations Act: 41 U.S.C.A. 40; 42 U.S.C.A. 1501, 1505.

Prison Escape Act: See 18 U.S.C.A. 751.

Prison Testing Act of 1988: 42 U.S.C.A. 300ee–6.

Privacy Act of 1974: 5 U.S.C.A. 552a.

Privacy Protection Act of 1980: 42 U.S.C.A. 2000aa, 2000aa–12.

Privacy Protection for Rape Victims Act of 1978: 28 App. U.S.C.A. 1103 note; 28 App. U.S.C.A. Fed. Rules of Evidence, Rule 412.

Private Ownership of Special Nuclear Materials Act: 42 U.S.C.A. 2012, 2234.

Probation Act: See 18 U.S.C.A. 3651, 3656.

Process Patent Amendments Act of 1988: 35 U.S.C.A. 154, 295.

Processed Products Inspection Improvement Act of 1986: 21 U.S.C.A. 606, 676.

Produce Agency Act: 7 U.S.C.A. 491, 497.

Producing Facilities Disposal Act of 1953: 50 App. U.S.C.A. 1941y.

Product Liability Risk Retention Act of 1981: 15 U.S.C.A. 3901, 3906.

Program Fraud Civil Remedies Act of 1986: 5 U.S.C.A. 504; 31 U.S.C.A. 3801, 3812.

Prohibition Reorganization Act of 1930: 19 U.S.C.A. 1001, 2072.

Prompt Payment Act: See 31 U.S.C.A. 3901, 3906.

Propaganda Agency Act: 22 U.S.C.A. 611, 621.

Protection and Advocacy for Mentally Ill Individuals Act of 1986: 42 U.S.C.A. 247a, 10851.

Protection Island National Wildlife Refuge Act: 16 U.S.C.A. 668dd note.

Protection of Children Against Sexual Exploitation Act of 1977: 18 U.S.C.A. 2251, 2423.

Protection of Foreign Officials and Official Guests of the United States Act: 18 U.S.C.A. 112, 1201.

Protection of Public Property Act: 40 U.S.C.A. 318, 318d.

Psychotropic Substances Act of 1978: 21 U.S.C.A. 352, 965; 42 U.S.C.A. 242a.

Public Broadcasting Act of 1967: 47 U.S.C.A. 390, 399.

Public Buildings Act of 1949: 40 U.S.C.A. 37a, 356a.

Public Buildings Cooperative Use Act of 1976: 40 U.S.C.A. 490, 612a.

Public Buildings Purchase Contract Act of 1954: 40 U.S.C.A. 356, 357.

Public Contracts Act: 29 U.S.C.A. 557; 41 U.S.C.A. 35, 45.

Public Debt Act: See 31 U.S.C.A. 3101.

Public Debt and Tax Rate Extension Act of 1960: 26 U.S.C.A. 11, 6412.

Public Documents Act: 44 U.S.C.A. 3315, 3324.

Public Health and Marine-Hospital Service Act: 46 U.S.C.A. 654.

Public Health Cigarette Smoking Act of 1969: 15 U.S.C.A. 1331, 1340.

Public Health Service Act: 21 U.S.C.A. 360aa note; 33 U.S.C.A. 763c, 857a; 42 U.S.C.A. 201, 3733; 46 U.S.C.A. 654, 48 U.S.C.A. 508, 49 App. U.S.C.A. 177, 181.

Public Health Service Commissioned Corps Personnel Act of 1960: 42 U.S.C.A. 201, 415.

Public Housing Anti-Crime Amendments of 1980: 12 U.S.C.A. 1701z–6 note.

Public Housing Drug Elimination Act of 1988: 42 U.S.C.A. 11901, 11908.

Public Housing Security Demonstration Act of 1978: 12 U.S.C.A. 1701z–6 note.

Public Land Administration Act: 43 U.S.C.A. 1361, 1383.

Public Lands and National Parks Act of 1983: 16 U.S.C.A. 433e, 460x; 40 U.S.C.A. 872, 885.

Public Lands Sales Acts: 43 U.S.C.A. 1171, 1435.

Public Printing and Documents: 44 U.S.C.A. 101, 3903.

Public Rangelands Improvement Act of 1978: 16 U.S.C.A. 1332, 1333; 43 U.S.C.A. 1739, 1908.

Public Safety Officers' Benefits Act of 1976: 42 U.S.C.A. 3768, 3796c.

Public Salary Tax Act of 1939: See 4 U.S.C.A. 111.

Public Telecommunications Act of 1988: 47 U.S.C.A. 391, 605.

Public Utilities Review Act: See 28 U.S.C.A. 1342.

Public Utility Holding Company Act: 15 U.S.C.A. 79, 79z–6.

Public Utilities Regulatory Policies Act of 1978: 15 U.S.C.A. 717f, 3211; 16 U.S.C.A. 796, 2708; 30 U.S.C.A. 1311, 1316; 42 U.S.C.A. 6802, 6808; 43 U.S.C.A. 2001, 2012.

Public Vessels Act: 46 U.S.C.A. 781, 790.

Public Welfare Amendments of 1962: 42 U.S.C.A. 301, 1385.

Public Works Acceleration Act: 40 U.S.C.A. 462; 42 U.S.C.A. 1492, 2643.

Public Works and Atomic Energy Commission Appropriation Act, 1968: 43 U.S.C.A. 377a.

Public Works and Economic Development Act of 1965: 42 U.S.C.A. 3121, 3266.

Public Works Appropriation Act, 1967: 43 U.S.C.A. 377a.

Public Works Employment Act of 1976: 33 U.S.C.A. 1287 note; 42 U.S.C.A. 6701, 6736.

Public Works for Water and Power Development and Atomic Energy Commission Appropriation Act, 1975: 43 U.S.C.A. 377a.

Public Works for Water and Power Development and Energy Research Appropriation Act, 1978: 43 U.S.C.A. 377a.

Public Works for Water, Pollution Control, and Power Development and Atomic Energy Commission Appropriation Act, 1970: 43 U.S.C.A. 377a.

Publicity in Taking Evidence Act (Anti-Trust): 15 U.S.C.A. 30.

Puerto Rican Federal Relations Act: 48 U.S.C.A. 731, 893.

Puerto Rico Civil Code: 48 U.S.C.A. 733, 866.

Purnell Act (Corn Borer Eradication): 7 U.S.C.A. 146.

Puyallup Tribe of Indians Settlement Act of 1989: 25 U.S.C.A. 1773.

Quiet Communities Act of 1978: 42 U.S.C.A. 4905, 6984; 49 App. U.S.C.A. 1431.

Racketeer Influenced and Corrupt Organizations Act (RICO): 18 U.S.C.A. 1961, 1968.

Radiation Control for Health and Safety Act of 1968: 42 U.S.C.A. 263b, 263n.

Radiation-Exposed Veterans Compensation Act of 1988: 38 U.S.C.A. 312.

Radio Broadcasting to Cuba Act: 22 U.S.C.A. 1465, 1465g.

Radon Gas and Indoor Air Quality Research Act of 1986: 42 U.S.C.A. 7401 note.

Rail Amendments of 1976: 15 U.S.C.A. 80a–3 note; 20 U.S.C.A. 960; 45 U.S.C.A. 702, 854; see 49 U.S.C.A. 10327, 11503.

Rail Passenger Service Act: 26 U.S.C.A. 250; 45 U.S.C.A. 501, 658.

Rail Safety and Service Improvement Act of 1982: 5 U.S.C.A. 305, 7327; 16 U.S.C.A. 353a, 410hh–1; 30 U.S.C.A. 208a; 33 U.S.C.A. 59t; 42 U.S.C.A. 251; 43 U.S.C.A. 975, 975g; 45 U.S.C.A. 13, 1214; 48 U.S.C.A. 301a; 49 U.S.C.A. 10713, 10910; 49 App. U.S.C.A. 1654, 2005.

Rail Safety Improvement Act of 1988: 23 U.S.C.A. 401 note; 45 U.S.C.A. 1, 854; 49 App. U.S.C.A. 26.

Rail Transportation Improvement Act: 15 U.S.C.A. 80a–3 note; 20 U.S.C.A. 960; 45 U.S.C.A. 543, 854; see 49 U.S.C.A. 10327, 11729; 49 App. U.S.C.A. 1653.

Railroad Control Acts: See 49 U.S.C.A. 10301, 11914.

Railroad Land Grant Forfeiture Act: 43 U.S.C.A. 904, 907.

Railroad Reorganization Acts: 11 U.S.C.A. 1161, 1174.

Railroad Retirement Act of 1974: 45 U.S.C.A. 231, 354.

Railroad Retirement Board Appropriation Acts: 26 U.S.C.A. 3201, 3233.

Railroad Retirement Revenue Act of 1983: 26 U.S.C.A. 72, 6601; 42 U.S.C.A. 430; 45 U.S.C.A. 231n note.

Railroad Retirement Solvency Act of 1983: 26 U.S.C.A. 72, 6601; 42 U.S.C.A. 430; 45 U.S.C.A. 231, 358.

Railroad Retirement Tax Act: 26 U.S.C.A. 3201, 3233; 45 U.S.C.A. 228a, 351.

Railroad Revitalization and Regulatory Reform Act of 1976: 15 U.S.C.A. 77c, 80a–3; see 31 U.S.C.A. 1108, 9101; 45 U.S.C.A. 543, 916; 49 U.S.C.A. 1613, 1653a; see 49 U.S.C.A. 306, 11914; 49 App. U.S.C.A. 1613, 10504.

Railroad Right of Way Acts: 25 U.S.C.A. 312, 318; 43 U.S.C.A. 934, 939.

Railroad Unemployment Insurance Act: See 26 U.S.C.A. 3231, 7701; 42 U.S.C.A. 503, 1107; 45 U.S.C.A. 228a, 368.

Railroad Unemployment Insurance and Retirement Improvement Act of 1988: 26 U.S.C.A. 3321, 6601; 45 U.S.C.A. 231, 369.

Railway Labor Act: See 15 U.S.C.A. 21, 45; 18 U.S.C.A. 373; 28 U.S.C.A. 1291, 1294; 45 U.S.C.A. 151, 188.

Raker Act (Reclamation and Irrigation): 12 U.S.C.A. 773; 43 U.S.C.A. 511, 513.

Ramspeck Act: See 5 U.S.C.A. 2102, 3304.

Randolph-Sheppard Vending Stand Act: 20 U.S.C.A. 107, 107f.

Real Estate Settlement Procedures Act of 1974: 12 U.S.C.A. 1730f, 2617.

Reapportionment Act of 1929: 2 U.S.C.A. 2a.

Reciprocal Tariff Act: 19 U.S.C.A. 1351, 1354.

Reclamation Acts (Irrigation of Arid Lands): 43 U.S.C.A. 372, 1457.

Reclamation Project Act of 1939: 43 U.S.C.A. 357a, 485k.

Reclamation Reform Act of 1982: 25 U.S.C.A. 383; 43 U.S.C.A. 373a, 485h.

Reclamation Safety of Dams Act of 1978: 43 U.S.C.A. 506, 1511.

Reconstruction Finance Corporation Act: 15 U.S.C.A. 603, 609.

Reconstruction Finance Corporation Disaster Loan Act: 12 U.S.C.A. 1703; 15 U.S.C.A. 605k.

Reconstruction Finance Corporation Exports Resolution: 15 U.S.C.A. 616a.

Reconstruction Finance Corporation Liquidation Act: 15 U.S.C.A. 603; 40 U.S.C.A. 459; 50 U.S.C.A. 98 note, 544 note; 50 App. U.S.C.A. 1929 note, 2261 note.

Record Carrier Competition Act of 1981: 45 U.S.C.A. 1017; 47 U.S.C.A. 222.

Record Rental Amendment of 1984: 17 U.S.C.A. 101, 115.

Recreation and Public Purposes Act: 43 U.S.C.A. 869, 869–4.

Recreation and Public Purposes Amendment Act of 1988: 43 U.S.C.A. 869, 869–2.

Recreational Boating Fund Act of 1980: 23 U.S.C.A. 120 notes; 26 U.S.C.A. 4041 note; 46 U.S.C.A. 1451 note; see 46 U.S.C.A. 13106, 13107.

Recreational Boating Safety and Facilities Improvement Act of 1980: 46 U.S.C.A. 1451, 1452; see 46 U.S.C.A. 13101, 13108.

Reed-Bulwinkle Act: See 49 U.S.C.A. 10706.

Reed-Jenkins Act: See 8 U.S.C.A. 1103, 1353.

Refuge Recreation Act: 16 U.S.C.A. 460k, 460k–4.

Refuge Revenue Sharing Act: 16 U.S.C.A. 715s.

Refugee Act of 1980: 8 U.S.C.A. 1101, 1525; 22 U.S.C.A. 2601.

Refugee Assistance Extension Act of 1986: 8 U.S.C.A. 1522, 1524.

Refuse Act of 1899: 33 U.S.C.A. 407.

Regional Action Planning Commission Improvement Act of 1975: 42 U.S.C.A. 3181, 3196.

Regional Development Act of 1975: 40 App. U.S.C.A. 2, 405; 42 U.S.C.A. 3181, 3196.

Regional Rail Reorganization Act of 1973: See 31 U.S.C.A. 9101; 45 U.S.C.A. 701, 797m; See 49 U.S.C.A. 10361, 10710.

Regulatory Fairness Act: 16 U.S.C.A. 824e.

Regulatory Flexibility Act: 5 U.S.C.A. 601, 612.

Rehabilitation Act of 1973: 29 U.S.C.A. 701, 796i.

Rehabilitation and Betterment Act of 1949: 43 U.S.C.A. 504.

Rehabilitation, Comprehensive Services and Developmental Disabilities Amendments of 1978: 29 U.S.C.A. 701, 796i; 38 U.S.C.A. 1904; 42 U.S.C.A. 6000, 6862.

Reindeer Industry Act of 1937: 25 U.S.C.A. 500z.

Renegotiation Act: 50 App. U.S.C.A. 1191.

Renewable Energy Industry Development Act of 1983: 42 U.S.C.A. 6276.

Renewable Energy Resources Act of 1980: 16 U.S.C.A. 2705, 2708; 42 U.S.C.A. 7371, 8276.

Reorganization Act of 1939: See 3 U.S.C.A. 106; see 31 U.S.C.A. 701, 1101.

Reorganization Act of 1949: See 5 U.S.C.A. 901, 913.

Reorganization Act of 1977: 5 U.S.C.A. 901, 912.

Research Facilities Act: 7 U.S.C.A. 390, 390j.

Research on Aging Act of 1974: 42 U.S.C.A. 289k–2, 289k–5.

Reserve Forces Act of 1955: See 10 U.S.C.A. 268, 1162; 50 App. U.S.C.A. 454, 456.

Reserve Forces Bill of Rights and Vitalization Act: 10 U.S.C.A. 136, 8850; 32 U.S.C.A. 502; 37 U.S.C.A. 404.

Reserve Forces Facilities Act of 1958: 10 U.S.C.A. 2233, 2233a.

Reserve Forces Facilities Authorization Act, 1974: 10 U.S.C.A. 2674, 9774; 42 U.S.C.A. 1594k, 3374.

Reserve Officers' Training Corps Vitalization Act of 1964: 10 U.S.C.A. 1475, 9348; 37 U.S.C.A. 205, 422.

Resource Conservation and Recovery Act of 1976: 42 U.S.C.A. 6901, 6986.

Resource Recovery Act of 1970: 42 U.S.C.A. 3251, 3259.

Retired Federal Employees Health Benefits Act: See 5 U.S.C.A. 8901, 8913.

Retiree Benefits Bankruptcy Protection Act of 1988: 11 U.S.C.A. 1101, 1129.

Retirement and Survivors' Annuities for Bankruptcy Judges and Magistrates Act of 1988: 5 U.S.C.A. 8334, 8440a; 28 U.S.C.A. 155, 636.

Retirement Equity Act of 1984: 26 U.S.C.A. 72, 6652; 29 U.S.C.A. 1025, 1144.

Retirement-Straight Line Adjustment Act of 1958: 26 U.S.C.A. 1016 note.

Revenue Acts: 2 U.S.C.A. 271, 277; 7 U.S.C.A. 610, 659; 15 U.S.C.A. 71, 80a–3; 19 U.S.C.A. 460, 1617; see 31 U.S.C.A. 301, 9303; 40 U.S.C.A. 301, 308; 42 U.S.C.A. 401; 48 U.S.C.A. 845; 50 App. U.S.C.A. 527, 1192.

Revenue Act of 1987: 26 U.S.C.A. 11, 9508.

Revenue Adjustment Act of 1980: 26 U.S.C.A. 103, 6655; 42 U.S.C.A. 409.

Revenue and Expenditure Control Act of 1968: 26 U.S.C.A. 51, 7701; 42 U.S.C.A. 603, 1396b.

Revised Organic Act of the Virgin Islands: 21 U.S.C.A. 104, 111; see 26 U.S.C.A. 7652; 48 U.S.C.A. 1405c, 1644.

R.F.C. Extension Act: 15 U.S.C.A. 609.

Rhode Island Indian Claims Settlement Act: 25 U.S.C.A. 1701, 1716.

Rice Production Act of 1975: 7 U.S.C.A. 428c, 1441.

Right of Way Act of 1891: 16 U.S.C.A. 471, 613; 25 U.S.C.A. 495; 30 U.S.C.A. 35, 52; 43 U.S.C.A. 161, 1181.

Right to Financial Privacy Act of 1978: 12 U.S.C.A. 3401, 3422.

Right to Work Law: 29 U.S.C.A. 164.

Rio Grande Pollution Correction Act of 1987: 22 U.S.C.A. 277g, 277g–3.

Risk Retention Amendments of 1986: 15 U.S.C.A. 3901, 3906; 42 U.S.C.A. 9671, 9675.

River and Harbor Act of 1970: 33 U.S.C.A. 426g, 1293a.

River Basin Monetary Authorization Act of 1971: 42 U.S.C.A. 1962d–5b.

R.M.S. Titanic Maritime Memorial Act of 1986: 16 U.S.C.A. 450rr, 450rr–6.

Roads Employment Act: See 23 U.S.C.A. 126.

Robert T. Stafford Disaster Relief and Emergency Assistance Act: 42 U.S.C.A. 5121, 5202.

Roberts Act: 40 U.S.C.A. 701, 703.

Robinson-Patman Anti-Discrimination Act: 15 U.S.C.A. 13, 21a.

Rock Island Railroad Transition and Employee Assistance Act: 45 U.S.C.A. 231f, 1018.

Rocky Mountain National Park Act: 16 U.S.C.A. 191, 195.

Roosevelt Campobello International Park Act: 16 U.S.C.A. 1101, 1113.

Rubber Act of 1948: 50 App. U.S.C.A. 1921, 1941t.

Rubber Producing Facilities Disposal Act of 1953: 50 App. U.S.C.A. 1941w, 1941x.

Rules of Decisions Act: 28 U.S.C.A. 1652.

Rumanian Declaration of War: 50 App. U.S.C.A. note prec. 1.

Runaway and Homeless Youth Act: 42 U.S.C.A. 5701, 5751.

Runaway Youth Act: 42 U.S.C.A. 5701, 5751.

Rural Crisis Recovery Program Act of 1987: 7 U.S.C.A. 2662.

Rural Development Act of 1972: 5 U.S.C.A. 5315; 7 U.S.C.A. 1006, 2670; 16 U.S.C.A. 590g, 1005; 42 U.S.C.A. 3122.

Rural Development, Agriculture, Related Agencies Appropriations Act, 1989: 7 U.S.C.A. 1981a note; 16 U.S.C.A. 590e–1, 590e–2; 42 U.S.C.A. 3121 note.

Rural Development Policy Act of 1980: 5 U.S.C.A. 5314; 7 U.S.C.A. 1926, 2667; 42 U.S.C.A. 3122.

Rural Electrification Act of 1936: 7 U.S.C.A. 901, 950b.

Rural Electrification Administration Technical Amendments Act of 1976: 7 U.S.C.A. 931, 935.

Rural Health Clinics Act of 1983: 42 U.S.C.A. 254g.

Rural Housing Amendments of 1983: 42 U.S.C.A. 1471, 1490o.

Rural Industrial Assistance Act of 1986: 7 U.S.C.A. 1932.

Rural Rehabilitation Corporation Trust Liquidation Act: 7 U.S.C.A. 1001 note; 40 U.S.C.A. 440, 444.

Saccharin Study and Labeling Act: 21 U.S.C.A. 321, 343a; 42 U.S.C.A. 218 notes, 298*l*–1 note.

Safe Drinking Water Act: 21 U.S.C.A. 349; 42 U.S.C.A. 201, 300j–25.

Safety Appliance Acts (Interstate Commerce): 15 U.S.C.A. 77c; 45 U.S.C.A. 1, 43; 49 U.S.C.A. 26, 27; 49 U.S.C.A. generally dispersed throughout Title 49; 49 App. U.S.C.A. 26.

Sailing School Vessels Act of 1982: 46 U.S.C.A. 390, 672; see 46 U.S.C.A. 8101.

Saint Elizabeths Hospital and District of Columbia Mental Health Services Act: 24 U.S.C.A. 161, 324; 42 U.S.C.A. 300aa–3.

Saint Lawrence Seaway Act: See 31 U.S.C.A. 9101; 33 U.S.C.A. 981, 990.

Saline Act (Public Lands): 30 U.S.C.A. 162.

Saline Water Conversion Act: 42 U.S.C.A. 1951, 1958.

Salmon and Steelhead Conservation and Enhancement Act of 1980: 16 U.S.C.A. 3301, 3345.

Salt River Pima-Maricopa Indian Community Water Rights Settlement Act of 1988: 43 U.S.C.A. 1522 note.

Saltonstall-Kennedy Act: 15 U.S.C.A. 713c–3.

Salvage Act: 46 U.S.C.A. 727, 731.

San Antonio Missions National Historical Park: 16 U.S.C.A. 410ee.

San Francisco Maritime National Historical Park Act of 1988: 16 U.S.C.A. 410nn, 460bb–3.

San Juan Basin Wilderness Protection Act of 1984: 16 U.S.C.A. 1132 note; 25 U.S.C.A. 640d–10.

Satellite Home Viewer Act of 1988: 17 U.S.C.A. 111, 804; 47 U.S.C.A. 605, 613.

Save Your Vision Week Act: 36 U.S.C.A. 169a.

Savings and Loan Holding Company Amendments of 1967: 12 U.S.C.A. 1730a.

Savings Bond Act: 6 U.S.C.A. 15; see 12 U.S.C.A. 221; see 31 U.S.C.A. 3101, 9303.

School Dropout Demonstration Assistance Act of 1988: 20 U.S.C.A. 3241, 5057.

School Facilities Construction Act: 20 U.S.C.A. 241–1, 646.

School Lunch and Child Nutrition Amendments of 1986: 42 U.S.C.A. 1431e, 1929a.

Science and Technology Equal Opportunities Act: 42 U.S.C.A. 1885, 1885d.

Sea Food Inspection Act: 21 U.S.C.A. 372a.

Sea Grant Program Improvement Act of 1976: 5 U.S.C.A. 5314, 5315; 5 App. U.S.C.A. 1970 Reorg. Plan No. 4; 15 U.S.C.A. 1511 note; 33 U.S.C.A. 1121, 1131.

Seamen Discharge Act: See 46 U.S.C.A. 8701, 10503.

Seamen's Act: 22 U.S.C.A. 258; 33 U.S.C.A. 365, 366; 46 U.S.C.A. 688; see 46 U.S.C.A. 2102, 11507.

Seamen's Service Act: 10 U.S.C.A. 2604; 46 U.S.C.A. 1151, 1223.

Search Warrant Act: See 18 U.S.C.A. 11, 3109.

Second Decontrol Act of 1947: 50 App. U.S.C.A. 645.

Second Defense Aid Supplemental Appropriation Act, 1942: 22 U.S.C.A. 412 note.

Second Deficiency Appropriation Act, 1946: 40 U.S.C.A. 164a.

Second Independent Offices Appropriation Act of 1954: See 38 U.S.C.A. 5011.

Second Liberty Bond Act: See 12 U.S.C.A. 221; see 31 U.S.C.A. 331, 3129.

Second Morrill Act: 7 U.S.C.A. 326a.

Second Revenue Act of 1940: See 26 U.S.C.A. 11, 7423; see 38 U.S.C.A. 701, 721; 45 U.S.C.A. 228c–1; 46 U.S.C.A. 1155a.

Second Supplemental Appropriations Act, 1984: 5 U.S.C.A. 5532, 8344. See Popular Name Table for other titles.

Second Urgent Deficiency Appropriation Act, 1957: 15 U.S.C.A. 633 note.

Second War Powers Act, 1942: 12 U.S.C.A. 355; 50 App. U.S.C.A. 643, 1152.

Secondary Mortgage Market Enhancement Act of 1984: 12 U.S.C.A. 24, 1757; 15 U.S.C.A. 77r–1, 78k.

Secondary Schools Basic Skills Demonstration Assistance Act of 1988: 20 U.S.C.A. 3261, 5066.

Secrecy of Military Information Act: See 22 U.S.C.A. 1934.

Securities Act of 1933: 15 U.S.C.A. 77a, 77aa.

Securities Exchange Act of 1934: 15 U.S.C.A. 77b, 80b–3.

Securities Investor Protection Act of 1970: 15 U.S.C.A. 78o, 78lll.

"Seeing-Eye" Dogs on Railroads Act: See 49 U.S.C.A. 10723.

Selective Service Act of 1948: 50 App. U.S.C.A. 451, 471.

Selective Service Extension Act of 1950: 50 App. U.S.C.A. 460, 471.

Self-Employed Individuals Tax Retirement Act of 1962: 26 U.S.C.A. 37, 7207.

Self-Employment Contributions Act of 1954: 26 U.S.C.A. 1401, 1403.

Semiconductor Chip Protection Act of 1984: 17 U.S.C.A. 901, 914.

Seminole Indian Land Claims Settlement Act of 1987: 25 U.S.C.A. 1772, 1772g.

Senior Citizens Housing Act of 1962: 12 U.S.C.A. 84, 1701r; 42 U.S.C.A. 1471, 1485.

Sentencing Act of 1987: 18 U.S.C.A. 3006A, 4106; 28 U.S.C.A. 994; 29 U.S.C.A. 504, 1111.

Sentencing Guidelines Act of 1986: 28 U.S.C.A. 994.

Sentencing Reform Act of 1983: 28 U.S.C.A. 524, 1921.

Sentencing Reform Amendments Act of 1985: 18 U.S.C.A. 3551 notes; 28 U.S.C.A. 994.

Service Contract Act of 1965: 41 U.S.C.A. 351, 358.

Service Flag and Button: 36 U.S.C.A. 179, 182.

Servicemen's and Veterans' Survivor Benefits Act: See 10 U.S.C.A. 1441, 6148; 14 U.S.C.A. prec. 461; 26 U.S.C.A. 121, 6051; 33 U.S.C.A. 857; see 38 U.S.C.A. 101, 3502; 42 U.S.C.A. 213, 417; 45 U.S.C.A. 228a, 228c–1.

Servicemen's Readjustment Act of 1944: 12 U.S.C.A. 672, 1020d; see 38 U.S.C.A. 1801.

Sexual Abuse Act of 1986: 18 U.S.C.A. 113, 3185; 42 U.S.C.A. 300w–3, 9511; 49 U.S.C.A. 1472.

Shareholder Communications Act of 1985: 15 U.S.C.A. 78n.

Shenandoah National Park Acts: 16 U.S.C.A. 403, 459s; see 18 U.S.C.A. 3041, 3141; 18 App. U.S.C.A.

Rules 4, 5(c), 9; 28 U.S.C.A. 127, 634; 28 App. U.S.C.A. Rule 4.

Sherman Anti-Trust Act (Trusts): 15 U.S.C.A. 1, 7.

Ship Load Line Act: 46 U.S.C.A. 88a.

Ship Mortgage Act of 1920: 46 U.S.C.A. 911, 984.

Shipping: 46 U.S.C.A. 71, 31343; 46 App. U.S.C.A. 531, 534.

Shipping Acts: See, also, Merchant Marine Acts; 22 U.S.C.A. 1186, 33 U.S.C.A. 320, 364; 46 U.S.C.A. 8, 826; see 46 U.S.C.A. 2101, 11110.

Shipping Act, 1916: 46 U.S.C.A. 801, 842; 46 App. U.S.C.A. 808, 840.

Shipping Act, 1984: 46 U.S.C.A. 801, 1720.

Shipping Commissioners Acts: 46 U.S.C.A. 544; see 46 U.S.C.A. 11110.

Shipstead-Nolan Act: 16 U.S.C.A. 577, 577b.

Shoreline Erosion Control Demonstration Act of 1974: 42 U.S.C.A. 1962d–5 note.

Shore Line Erosion Protection Act (Public Property): 33 U.S.C.A. 426g.

Shore Protection Act of 1988: 33 U.S.C.A. 2601, 2609.

Sikes Act: 16 U.S.C.A. 670a, 670o.

Siletz Indian Tribe Restoration Act: 25 U.S.C.A. 711, 711f.

Silver Purchase Acts: 12 U.S.C.A. 122, 145.

Single Audit Act of 1984: 31 U.S.C.A. 7501, 7507.

Single-Employer Pension Plan Amendments Act of 1986: 26 U.S.C.A. 402, 501; 29 U.S.C.A. 1001b, 1370.

Sixth Supplemental National Defense Appropriation Act, 1942: 7 U.S.C.A. 174; 22 U.S.C.A. 412 note; see 31 U.S.C.A. 3325, 3528; 42 U.S.C.A. 1602; 50 App. U.S.C.A. 1191.

Small Business Act: 12 U.S.C.A. 371; 15 U.S.C.A. 631, 649–1.

Small Business Act Amendments of 1961: 15 U.S.C.A. 631, 639; 50 App. U.S.C.A. 2158.

Small Business Act Amendments of 1967: 15 U.S.C.A. 633, 692; 42 U.S.C.A. 2902.

Small Business Administration Reauthorization and Amendment Act of 1988: 15 U.S.C.A. 631, 697b.

Small Business and Federal Procurement Competition Enhancement Act of 1984: 10 U.S.C.A. 2302, 2320; 15 U.S.C.A. 637, 644; 41 U.S.C.A. 253, 419.

Small Business Budget Reconciliation and Loan Consolidation/Improvement Act of 1981: 15 U.S.C.A. 632; 696.

Small Business Competitiveness Demonstration Program Act of 1988: 15 U.S.C.A. 632; 40 U.S.C.A. 541.

Small Business Computer Security and Education Act of 1984: 15 U.S.C.A. 632, 637.

Small Business Development Center Act of 1980: 15 U.S.C.A. 636, 648.

Small Business Economic Policy Act of 1980: 15 U.S.C.A. 631a, 631b.

Small Business Employee Ownership Act of 1980: 15 U.S.C.A. 632, 636.

Small Business Energy Loan Act: 15 U.S.C.A. 633, 639.

Small Business Export Expansion Act of 1980: 15 U.S.C.A. 696.

Small Business Innovation Development Act of 1982: 15 U.S.C.A. 638.

Small Business International Trade and Competitiveness Act: 15 U.S.C.A. 631, 649.

Small Business Investment Act of 1958: 12 U.S.C.A. 352a note; 15 U.S.C.A. 77c, 697c; 18 U.S.C.A. 217, 1014.

Small Business Investment Incentive Act of 1980: 15 U.S.C.A. 77b, 775.

Small Business Issuers' Simplification Act of 1980: 15 U.S.C.A. 77b, 77d.

Small Business Protection Act of 1967: 15 U.S.C.A. 634 note.

Small Business Secondary Market Improvements Act of 1984: 15 U.S.C.A. 633, 639.

Small Business Tax Revision Act of 1958: 26 U.S.C.A. 165, 6601.

Small Reclamation Projects Act of 1956: 43 U.S.C.A. 422a, 422k–1.

Small Tract Act of 1938: 43 U.S.C.A. 682a.

Small Tract Act of 1983: 16 U.S.C.A. 484a, 521i.

Smith Act (Reclamation and Irrigation): 43 U.S.C.A. 621, 630.

Smith Act of 1940: See 10 U.S.C.A. 2385.

Snyder Act (Indian Affairs Bureau): 25 U.S.C.A. 13.

Social Security Act: 42 U.S.C.A. 1, 8821. See Popular Name Table for other titles.

Social Security Disability Amendments of 1980: 26 U.S.C.A. 6103, 7213; 42 U.S.C.A. 401, 1397b; 45 U.S.C.A. 231f.

Social Security Disability Benefits Reform Act of 1984: 26 U.S.C.A. 6103; 42 U.S.C.A. 405, 1383b.

Social Services Block Grant Act: 42 U.S.C.A. 303, 1397f.

Sockeye Salmon or Pink Salmon Fishing Act of 1947: 16 U.S.C.A. 776, 3642.

Sodbuster Law: 7 U.S.C.A. 4207, 4209; 16 U.S.C.A. 590g, 3812.

Soft Drink Interbrand Competition Act: 15 U.S.C.A. 3501, 3503.

Soil and Water Resources Conservation Act of 1977: 16 U.S.C.A. 2001, 2009.

Soil Bank Act: 7 U.S.C.A. 1801, 1837.

Soil Conservation and Domestic Allotment Act: 7 U.S.C.A. 608–1, 1391; 16 U.S.C.A. 590a, 590q.

Solar Energy and Energy Conservation Act of 1980: 12 U.S.C.A. 1451, 3620; 42 U.S.C.A. 6347, 8286b.

Solar Energy and Energy Conservation Bank Act: 12 U.S.C.A. 1451, 3620.

Solar Energy Research Development and Demonstration Act of 1974: 42 U.S.C.A. 5551, 5566.

Solar Heating and Cooling Demonstration Act of 1974: 42 U.S.C.A. 2473, 5517.

Solar Photovoltaic Energy Research, Development, and Demonstration Act of 1978: 42 U.S.C.A. 5581, 5594.

Soldiers' and Sailors' Civil Relief Act of 1940: 50 App. U.S.C.A. 501, 591.

Solid Waste Disposal Act: 42 U.S.C.A. 3251, 6992k.

South Pacific Tuna Act of 1988: 16 U.S.C.A. 973, 973r.

Southern Nevada Project Act: 43 U.S.C.A. 616ggg, 616mmm.

Soviet-Eastern European Research and Training Act of 1983: 22 U.S.C.A. 4501, 4509.

"SPARS" Act: See 14 U.S.C.A. 751, 826.

Special Central American Assistance Act of 1979: 22 U.S.C.A. 2346e.

Special Drawing Rights Act: 12 U.S.C.A. 412, 467; 22 U.S.C.A. 286n, 286r.

Special Foreign Assistance Act of 1986: 22 U.S.C.A. 290f, 3929.

Special Health Revenue Sharing Act of 1975: 42 U.S.C.A. 246.

Special International Security Assistance Act of 1979: 22 U.S.C.A. 2349, 3408.

Special Laws Prohibition Act (Territories): 48 U.S.C.A. 1471, 1479.

Special Projects Act: 20 U.S.C.A. 1851, 1853.

Specie Payment Resumption Act: See 31 U.S.C.A. 5115, 5122.

Speedy Trial Act of 1974: 18 U.S.C.A. 3152, 3174; 28 U.S.C.A. 604.

Spence Act (Savings and Loan Holding Companies): 12 U.S.C.A. 1730a.

Spending Reduction Act of 1984: 5 U.S.C.A. 5315.

Sponge Act: 16 U.S.C.A. 781, 785.

Springer Act: 48 U.S.C.A. 1471, 1479.

Spruce Knob-Seneca Rocks National Recreation Area Act: 16 U.S.C.A. 460p, 460p–5.

Stabilization Act of 1942: 15 U.S.C.A. 713a–8.

Staggers Rail Act of 1980: 11 U.S.C.A. 1170, 1172; 45 U.S.C.A. 231f, 1018; 49 U.S.C.A. 10101, 11913a; 49 App. U.S.C.A. 1654a.

Standard Barrel Act (Apple Barrels): 15 U.S.C.A. 231, 233; 21 U.S.C.A. 20, 23.

Standard Barrel Act (Fruits, Vegetables, etc.): 15 U.S.C.A. 234, 236.

Standard Barrel Act (Lime Barrels): 15 U.S.C.A. 237, 242

Standard Baskets Act: 15 U.S.C.A. 251, 256.

Standard Reference Data Act: 15 U.S.C.A. 290, 290f.

Standard Time Acts: 15 U.S.C.A. 261, 265.

Star Schools Program Assistance Act: 20 U.S.C.A. 4081, 4086.

State and Local Fiscal Assistance Act of 1972: 26 U.S.C.A. 6017A, 6687; see 31 U.S.C.A. 321, 6724.

State and Local Government Cost Estimate Act of 1981: 2 U.S.C.A. 653.

State and Local Law Enforcement Assistance Act of 1986: 42 U.S.C.A. 3741, 3797.

State Appropriation Act of 1937: 22 U.S.C.A. 2661.

State Comprehensive Mental Health Services Plan Act of 1986: 42 U.S.C.A. 290aa–3, 300x–13.

State Department Basic Authorities Act of 1956: 22 U.S.C.A. 254a, 4343.

State Department/USIA Authorization Act, Fiscal Year 1975: 5 U.S.C.A. 5924; 22 U.S.C.A. 901a, 2676.

State Forest Aid Act: 16 U.S.C.A. 567a, 567c.

State Justice Institute Act of 1984: 28 U.S.C.A. 620; 42 U.S.C.A. 10701, 10713.

State Selection Acts (Public Lands): 15 U.S.C.A. 203; 20 U.S.C.A. 83; 43 U.S.C.A. 276, 863.

State Taxation of Depositories Act: 12 U.S.C.A. 548 note.

State Technical Services Act of 1965: 15 U.S.C.A. 1351, 1368.

Statutes of Limitations Act: See 18 U.S.C.A. 3287.

Steagall Commodity Credit Act: 15 U.S.C.A. 713a–1, 713a–8.

Steagall National Housing Act of 1939: 12 U.S.C.A. 1703, 1716.

Steagall R. F. C. Relief Obligations Act: 15 U.S.C.A. 603, 611b.

Steamboat Inspection Act: See 28 U.S.C.A. 411; 33 U.S.C.A. 152, 157; 46 U.S.C.A. 2, 416.

Steel and Aluminum Energy Conservation and Technology Competitiveness Act of 1988: 15 U.S.C.A. 5101, 5110.

Steel Industry Compliance Extension Act of 1981: 42 U.S.C.A. 7410, 7413.

Sterling Act (Employers' Liability): 45 U.S.C.A. 51, 71.

Stevenson-Wydler Technology Innovation Act of 1980: 15 U.S.C.A. 3701, 3714.

Stewart B. McKinney Homeless Assistance Act: 7 U.S.C.A. 2012, 2025; 20 U.S.C.A. 1205, 1207a; 29 U.S.C.A. 1503, 1551; 40 U.S.C.A. 484; 42 U.S.C.A. 254e, 11472.

Stock Reservoir Act: 43 U.S.C.A. 952, 955.

Stone Act: 30 U.S.C.A. 161.

Strategic and Critical Materials Stock Piling Revision Act of 1979: 7 U.S.C.A. 1743, 1745; 15 U.S.C.A. 714b; 50 U.S.C.A. 98, 98h–4; 50 App. U.S.C.A. 2093.

Strategic Petroleum Reserve Amendments Act of 1981: 42 U.S.C.A. 6231, 6247.

Strategic War Materials Act: 50 U.S.C.A. 98, 98h.

Streambank Erosion Control Evaluation and Demonstration Act of 1974: 42 U.S.C.A. 1962d–5 note.

Strikebreaker Act: See 18 U.S.C.A. 1231.

Student Financial Assistance Amendments of 1985: 20 U.S.C.A. 1072, 1094.

Student Loan Consolidation and Technical Amendments Act of 1983: 20 U.S.C.A. 1077, 1098.

Subchapter S Revision Act of 1982: 26 U.S.C.A. 31, 6661; 29 U.S.C.A. 1108.

Subcontractors' Gratuities and Kick-Backs Act (Public Contracts): 41 U.S.C.A. 51, 54.

Submarine Cable Act: 47 U.S.C.A. 21, 33.

Submerged Lands Act: See 10 U.S.C.A. 7421, 7438; 43 U.S.C.A. 1301, 1315.

Subversive Activities Control Act of 1950: 8 U.S.C.A. 156; see 8 U.S.C.A. 1102, 1451; 18 U.S.C.A. 793, 1507; 22 U.S.C.A. 611, 618; 50 U.S.C.A. 591, 826; see, also, 50 U.S.C.A. 851, 852.

Subversive Activities Control Board Tenure Act: 50 U.S.C.A. 791.

Sudden Infant Death Syndrome Act of 1974: 42 U.S.C.A. 289d, 300c–11.

Sugar Act of 1948: 7 U.S.C.A. 1100, 1161; 26 U.S.C.A. 4501, 6412.

Sugar Control Act: 7 U.S.C.A. 608, 620.

Suits in Admiralty Act: 46 U.S.C.A. 741, 752.

Sumners-Amherst Act: See 18 U.S.C.A. 1761.

Sumners Courts Act: See 18 U.S.C.A. 3141, 3771.

Sumners-McCarran Act: See 28 U.S.C.A. 294, 371.

Superfund Revenue Act of 1986: 26 U.S.C.A. 26, 9632; 42 U.S.C.A. 9601, 9653.

Supplemental Appropriations and Rescission Act, 1981: 2 U.S.C.A. 58b, 126b; 5 U.S.C.A. 5318 note; 10 U.S.C.A. 2304 note; 20 U.S.C.A. 1070a note; 33 U.S.C.A. 1517a; 40 U.S.C.A. 756a; 42 U.S.C.A. 5915 note.

Supplemental Housing Authorization Act of 1977: 12 U.S.C.A. 1706e, 1749bbb–8; 42 U.S.C.A. 1437c, 1451.

Surety Bonds: 6 U.S.C.A. 1, 15.

Surface Freight Forwarder Deregulation Act of 1986: 26 U.S.C.A. 250; 39 U.S.C.A. 5201; 49 U.S.C.A. 10102, 11910.

Surface Mining Control and Reclamation Act of 1977: 18 U.S.C.A. 1114; 30 U.S.C.A. 1201, 1328.

Surface Transportation and Uniform Relocation Assistance Act of 1987: 16 U.S.C.A. 460*l*–11; 18 U.S.C.A. 1761; 23 U.S.C.A. 101, 409. See Popular Name Table for other titles.

Surface Transportation Assistance Act of 1978: 15 U.S.C.A. 1418; 16 U.S.C.A. 460*l*–11; 23 U.S.C.A. 101, 407. See Popular Name Table for other titles.

Surface Transportation Assistance Act of 1982: 15 U.S.C.A. 713c–3; 16 U.S.C.A. 460*l*–11, 1606a; 23 U.S.C.A. 103, 402. See Popular Name Table for other titles.

Surplus Agricultural Commodities Disposal Act of 1982: 7 U.S.C.A. 1433b.

Surplus Commodities Corporation Act: 15 U.S.C.A. 713c.

Surplus Fund-Certified Claims Act of 1949: See 31 U.S.C.A. 1502.

Surplus Property Act of 1944: 50 App. U.S.C.A. 1622, 1641.

Survivor Benefit Plan Amendments of 1985: 10 U.S.C.A. 1447, 1455.

Susan B. Anthony Dollar Coin Act of 1978: See 31 U.S.C.A. 5112.

Swamp Land Act: See 43 U.S.C.A. 982, 984.

Swampbuster Provision: 16 U.S.C.A. 3821, 3823.

Swine Health Protection Act: 7 U.S.C.A. 3801, 3813.

Synthetic Fuels Corporation Act of 1985: 42 U.S.C.A. note prec. 8791.

Synthetic Liquid Fuels Act: 30 U.S.C.A. 321.

Taft-Hartley Act: See Labor Management Relations Act, 1947.

Taiwan Relations Act: 22 U.S.C.A. 3301, 3316.

Talmadge-Aiken Act: 7 U.S.C.A. 450.

Tandem Truck Safety Act of 1984: 49 U.S.C.A. 2311, 2316.

Tank Vessel Act: 19 U.S.C.A. 1202; see 46 U.S.C.A. 3301, 3702.

Tariff Acts: 12 U.S.C.A. 541, 545; 15 U.S.C.A. 8, 11; 19 U.S.C.A. 5, 1333; 46 U.S.C.A. 11, 333.

Tariff Act of 1930: 6 U.S.C.A. 1; 19 U.S.C.A. 6, 2395; 22 U.S.C.A. 401; see 31 U.S.C.A. 5151; 46 U.S.C.A. 28, 333.

Tariff Classification Act of 1962: 7 U.S.C.A. 1856; 19 U.S.C.A. prec. 1202, 1312; 21 U.S.C.A. 41; 26 U.S.C.A. 4501, 6418; 40 U.S.C.A. 470; 42 U.S.C.A. 2201.

Tariff Commission of 1882: 19 U.S.C.A. 1202.

Tariff Schedules Technical Amendments Act of 1965: 19 U.S.C.A. note prec. 1202.

Tax Adjustment Act of 1966: 19 U.S.C.A. 1202; 26 U.S.C.A. 276, 7701; 42 U.S.C.A. 428.

Tax Equity and Fiscal Responsibility Act of 1982: 26 U.S.C.A. 5, 9502; 28 U.S.C.A. 1346, 2412; 29 U.S.C.A. 623; see 31 U.S.C.A. 3102, 6709; 42 U.S.C.A. 410, 1397b; 45 U.S.C.A. 231f; 47 U.S.C.A. 331; 49 App. U.S.C.A. 1349, 2225; 50 App. U.S.C.A. 1622.

Tax Rate Extension Act of 1963: 26 U.S.C.A. 11, 6412.

Tax Reduction Act of 1975: 26 U.S.C.A. 3, 6428; 42 U.S.C.A. 402 note.

Tax Reduction and Simplification Act of 1977: 5 U.S.C.A. 5520; 15 U.S.C.A. 1673, 1675; 26 U.S.C.A. 1, 6654; 42 U.S.C.A. 652, 6736.

Tax Reform Act of 1969: 26 U.S.C.A. 1, 7701; 42 U.S.C.A. 402, 428.

Tax Reform Act of 1976: 26 U.S.C.A. 1, 6698.

Tax Reform Act of 1984: 26 U.S.C.A. 1, 6695.

Tax Reform Act of 1986: 5 U.S.C.A. 504, 8440; 15 U.S.C.A. 638 note; 16 U.S.C.A. 429b, 460*l*–11; 19 U.S.C.A. 58c, 2703; 20 U.S.C.A. 1113 note; 25 U.S.C.A. 71, 500g; 26 U.S.C.A. 1, 9510; 28 U.S.C.A. 1581, 1961; 29 U.S.C.A. 1002, 1461; 31 U.S.C.A. 3102; 42 U.S.C.A. 300bb–2, 1397f; 45 U.S.C.A. 231, 369; 46 U.S.C.A. 1177; 46 App. U.S.C.A. 1177; 48 U.S.C.A. 1424c note, 1681 note; 49 U.S.C.A. 1741.

Tax Treatment Extension Act of 1977: 26 U.S.C.A. 167.

Tax Treatment of Partnership Items Act of 1982: 26 U.S.C.A. 702, 7485; 28 U.S.C.A. 1346, 1508.

Taylor Grazing Act: 43 U.S.C.A. 315, 1171.

Tea Importation Act: 21 U.S.C.A. 41, 50.

Technical Amendments Act of 1958: 26 U.S.C.A. 35, 7514.

Technical and Miscellaneous Revenue Act of 1988: 5 U.S.C.A. 504, 8440; 15 U.S.C.A. 638 note; 16 U.S.C.A. 429b, 429b–1; 19 U.S.C.A. 58c, 2703; 20 U.S.C.A. 1113 note; 25 U.S.C.A. 71; 26 U.S.C.A. 1, 9510; 29 U.S.C.A. 1167; 31 U.S.C.A. 3102; 42 U.S.C.A. 300bb–8, 1396r–6; 45 U.S.C.A. 231, 369;

46 App. U.S.C.A. 1177; 48 U.S.C.A. 1424c note, 1681 note.

Technology Assessment Act of 1972: 2 U.S.C.A. 471, 481; 42 U.S.C.A. 1862.

Technology Competitiveness Act: 5 U.S.C.A. 5315; 15 U.S.C.A. 205a, 4632; 30 U.S.C.A. 1803 note.

Technology-Related Assistance for Individuals with Disabilities Act of 1988: 29 U.S.C.A. 2201, 2271.

Telecommunications Accessibility Enhancement Act of 1988: 40 U.S.C.A. 762, 762d.

Telecommunications for the Disabled Act of 1982: 47 U.S.C.A. 610, 734.

Telecommunications Trade Act of 1988: 19 U.S.C.A. 3101, 3111.

Temporary Child Care for Handicapped Children and Crisis Nurseries Act of 1986: 42 U.S.C.A. 5117, 5117d.

Temporary Emergency Wildfire Suppression Act: 42 U.S.C.A. 1856p, 5117d.

Temporary Extended Railroad Unemployment Insurance Benefits Act of 1961: 45 U.S.C.A. 401, 404.

Temporary Extended Unemployment Compensation Act of 1961: 26 U.S.C.A. 3301, 3302; 42 U.S.C.A. 1105, 1400v.

Temporary Unemployment Compensation Act of 1958: 42 U.S.C.A. 1400, 1400k.

Tennessee Valley Authority Act of 1933: 16 U.S.C.A. 831, 831dd.

Tennessee Valley Authority Bond Limitation Act: 16 U.S.C.A. 831n–4.

Tennessee Valley Authority Bridge Act: 16 U.S.C.A. 831c–1.

Territorial Enabling Act of 1950: 48 U.S.C.A. 910, 1408e.

Territorial Practice Act: 48 U.S.C.A. 1464.

Texas Wilderness Act of 1984: 16 U.S.C.A. 1132 note.

Textile Fiber Products Identification Act: 15 U.S.C.A. 70, 70k.

Thanksgiving Day Act: See 5 U.S.C.A. 6103.

The Judiciary Appropriation Act, 1988: 2 U.S.C.A. 356; 28 U.S.C.A. 153, 634; 31 U.S.C.A. 1344.

The President: 3 U.S.C.A. 1, 303.

Thomas Amendment: 12 U.S.C.A. 462b; see 31 U.S.C.A. 5301, 5304.

Threatening Communication Act: See 18 U.S.C.A. 875, 3239.

Thrift Industry Recovery Act: 12 U.S.C.A. 1442a, 1730i; 31 U.S.C.A. 9105.

Thrift Institutions Restructuring Act: 12 U.S.C.A. 1425a, 3505.

Thrift Savings Fund Investment Act of 1987: 5 U.S.C.A. 8438.

Timber and Stone Act: 43 U.S.C.A. 311, 313.

Title I of the Elementary and Secondary Education Act of 1965: 20 U.S.C.A. 241b, 886; 42 U.S.C.A. 2000d–5.

Title to Movable Property Act: 43 U.S.C.A. 499a.

Tobacco Adjustment Act of 1983: 7 U.S.C.A. 511r, 1445–2.

Tobacco Control Act: 7 U.S.C.A. 515, 515k.

Tobacco Inspection Act: 7 U.S.C.A. 511, 511q.

Tonnage Measurement Simplification Act: 46 U.S.C.A. 4, 496.

Toxic Substances Control Act: 15 U.S.C.A. 2601, 2671.

Toy Safety Act of 1984: 15 U.S.C.A. 1274.

Trade Act of 1974: 5 U.S.C.A. 5312, 5316; 19 U.S.C.A. 160, 2702; 26 U.S.C.A. 3302; see 31 U.S.C.A. 1513, 1514.

Trade Adjustment Assistance Reform and Extension Act of 1986: 19 U.S.C.A. 58b, 2346.

Trade Agreements Act of 1979: 5 U.S.C.A. 5315; 13 U.S.C.A. 301; 19 U.S.C.A. 993, 2582; 26 U.S.C.A. 5001, 5691; 28 U.S.C.A. 1582, 2637.

Trade Agreements Extension Act of 1958: 19 U.S.C.A. 1333, 1360; see 19 U.S.C.A. 1801 et seq.

Trade and Development Enhancement Act of 1983: 12 U.S.C.A. 635q, 635t.

Trade and Tariff Act of 1984: 18 U.S.C.A. 925; 19 U.S.C.A. 58b, 2806; 22 U.S.C.A. 3103, 3104; 26 U.S.C.A. 162, 7607; 28 U.S.C.A. 2631, 2647.

Trade Expansion Act of 1962: 19 U.S.C.A. prec. 1202, 1991; 26 U.S.C.A. 172, 6511.

Trade Fair Act of 1959: 19 U.S.C.A. 1751, 1756.

Trademark Act of 1946: 15 U.S.C.A. 1051, 1128; see, also, 28 U.S.C.A. 1254.

Trademark Clarification Act of 1984: 2 U.S.C.A. 437g, 687; 5 U.S.C.A. 552; 7 U.S.C.A. 8, 1601; 10 U.S.C.A. 2304 note; 12 U.S.C.A. 1464. See Popular Name Table for more titles.

Trademark Counterfeiting Act of 1984: 15 U.S.C.A. 1116, 1118; 18 U.S.C.A. 2320.

Trademark Law Revision Act of 1988: 15 U.S.C.A. 1051, 1128.

Trading With the Enemy Act: 3 U.S.C.A. 46; 5 U.S.C.A. 636; 12 U.S.C.A. 95a; 50 U.S.C.A. 176; 40 U.S.C.A. 485; 50 U.S.C.A. 176; 50 App. U.S.C.A. 1, 619.

Training Technology Transfer Act of 1988: 20 U.S.C.A. 5091, 5097.

Tramroad Act: 43 U.S.C.A. 956.

Trans-Alaska Pipeline Authorization Act: 43 U.S.C.A. 1651, 1655.

Transportation: 49 U.S.C.A. 101, 11917.

Transportation Acts: 40 U.S.C.A. 316; see 49 U.S.C.A. 10102, 11914.

Transportation Act, 1920: 40 U.S.C.A. 316.

Transportation Act, 1940: See 31 U.S.C.A. 3726; see 49 U.S.C.A. 10101, 11914.

Transportation of Foreign Mail by Aircraft Act: 49 U.S.C.A. 485a, 485b.

Transportation Payment Act of 1972: see 31 U.S.C.A. 3726.

Transportation Safety Act of 1974: 45 U.S.C.A. 39, 441; see 46 U.S.C.A. 2106; see 49 U.S.C.A. 103, 1907.

Travel Act: 18 U.S.C.A. 1952.

Travel Expense Act of 1949: See 5 U.S.C.A. 102, 5708.

Treasury and Post Office Departments Appropriation Act, 1954: 12 U.S.C.A. 362; 20 U.S.C.A. 241 note.

Treasury Department Appropriations Act, 1988: 19 U.S.C.A. 1613b.

Treasury, Postal Service and General Government Appropriations Act, 1989: 3 U.S.C.A. 102 note; 5 U.S.C.A. 5724; 22 U.S.C.A. 211a note; 26 U.S.C.A. 7443 note; 31 U.S.C.A. 1343 note, 5114 note; 33 U.S.C.A. 776; 39 U.S.C.A. 403 note; 40 U.S.C.A. 490c, 490a–1; 50 U.S.C.A. 98h note.

Tribally Controlled Community College Assistance Act of 1978: 25 U.S.C.A. 640c, 1836.

Tribally Controlled Community College Assistance Amendments of 1986: 25 U.S.C.A. 640c–1, 1836.

Tribally Controlled Schools Act of 1988: 25 U.S.C.A. 2501, 2511.

Truck and Bus Safety and Regulatory Reform Act of 1988: 49 U.S.C.A. 3102, 11707; 49 App. U.S.C.A. 2505, 2521.

Truman-Hobbs Act: 33 U.S.C.A. 511, 524.

Trust Fund Code of 1981: 26 U.S.C.A. 9500, 9501.

Trust Indenture Act of 1939: 15 U.S.C.A. 77aaa, 77yyy.

Truth in Lending Act: 15 U.S.C.A. 1601, 1677; 18 U.S.C.A. 891 note.

Truth in Lending Simplification and Reform Act: 15 U.S.C.A. 57a, 1694.

Truth in Mileage Act of 1986: 15 U.S.C.A. 1982, 1990c.

Truth in Negotiations Act: 10 U.S.C.A. 2304(a), 2311.

Tucker Act (Admiralty-Limitations): 46 U.S.C.A. 745.

Tucker Act (Claims): See 28 U.S.C.A. 507, 2512.

Tuna Conventions Act of 1950: 16 U.S.C.A. 951, 961.

Tunnel Site Act: 30 U.S.C.A. 27.

Twentieth Amendment Adjustment Act: 2 U.S.C.A. 1, 7; see 3 U.S.C.A. 7, 101; 48 U.S.C.A. 891.

Tydings-McDuffie Acts: 2 U.S.C.A. 31.

Uintah and Ouray Reservation Termination Act of 1954: 25 U.S.C.A. 677, 677p.

Underwood Tariff Act: See 18 U.S.C.A. 1905; 19 U.S.C.A. 124, 131; 46 U.S.C.A. 146.

Undetectable Firearms Act of 1988: 18 U.S.C.A. 922, 925; 49 App. U.S.C.A. 1356 note.

Unemployment Compensation Amendments of 1976: 5 U.S.C.A. 8501, 8522; 26 U.S.C.A. 3301, 6157; 29 U.S.C.A. 49b, 49d; 42 U.S.C.A. 603a, 1382e.

Unfair Competition Act: 15 U.S.C.A. 71, 77; see 18 U.S.C.A. 1905; 19 U.S.C.A. 1333, 1335.

Uniform Code of Military Justice: 10 U.S.C.A. 801, 1553; see 10 U.S.C.A. 801, 940; 28 U.S.C.A. 1259, 2101; 50 U.S.C.A. 552.

Uniform Cotton Classing Fees Act of 1987: 7 U.S.C.A. 473a.

Uniform Federal Crime Reporting Act of 1988: 28 U.S.C.A. 534 note.

Uniform Regulatory Jurisdiction Act of 1988: 15 U.S.C.A. 717f.

Uniform Relocation Act Amendments of 1987: 42 U.S.C.A. 4601, 4655.

Uniform Relocation Assistance and Real Property Acquisition Policies Act of 1970: 42 U.S.C.A. 1415, 4655; 49 App. U.S.C.A. 1606.

Uniform Retirement Date Act: See 5 U.S.C.A. 5532.

Uniform Time Act of 1966: 15 U.S.C.A. 260, 267.

Uniformed and Overseas Citizens Absentee Voting Act: 18 U.S.C.A. 608, 609; 39 U.S.C.A. 2401, 3684; 42 U.S.C.A. 1973c, 1973ff–6; 50 U.S.C.A. 301, 355 notes.

Uniformed Services Contingency Option Act of 1953: See 10 U.S.C.A. 1431, 1444.

Uniformed Services Former Spouses' Protection Act: 10 U.S.C.A. 1072, 1450.

Uniformed Services Health Professions Revitalization Act of 1972: 10 U.S.C.A. 2112, 2127.

Uniformed Services Health Provisions Special Pay Act of 1980: 37 U.S.C.A. 302, 313.

Uniformed Services Pay Act of 1981: 10 U.S.C.A. 2107, 9342; 37 U.S.C.A. 203, 1006; 50 App. U.S.C.A. 460.

Unitary Wind Tunnel Plan Act of 1949: 50 U.S.C.A. 511, 515.

United Nations Environment Program Participation Act of 1973: 22 U.S.C.A. 287 note.

United Nations Participation Act of 1945: 22 U.S.C.A. 287, 287e–1.

United States Arbitration Act: See 9 U.S.C.A. 1, 208.

United States Commission on Civil Rights Act of 1983: 42 U.S.C.A. 1975, 1975f.

United States Commissioners Act: See 5 U.S.C.A. 3341; see 18 U.S.C.A. 203, 3569; 20 U.S.C.A. 3; 22 U.S.C.A. 257; see 28 U.S.C.A. 502, 1929; see 31 U.S.C.A. 1302, 3302; 46 U.S.C.A. 603, 604.

United States Cotton Futures Acts: 7 U.S.C.A. 71, 2209; 16 U.S.C.A. 490, 683; see 31 U.S.C.A. 1343.

United States Cotton Standards Act: 7 U.S.C.A. 51, 65.

United States Fishing Fleet Improvement Act: 46 U.S.C.A. 1401, 1413.

United States Futures Act: 7 U.S.C.A. 15b.

United States Grain Standards Act: 7 U.S.C.A. 71, 2209; 16 U.S.C.A. 490, 683; see 31 U.S.C.A. 1343.

United States Grain Standards Act of 1976: 5 U.S.C.A. 5316; 7 U.S.C.A. 74, 87h; 18 U.S.C.A. 1114.

United States Housing Act of 1937: 42 U.S.C.A. 1401, 1585.

United States-India Fund for Cultural, Educational, and Scientific Cooperation Act: 22 U.S.C.A. 290j, 290j–1.

United States Information Agency Authorization Act, Fiscal Years 1984 and 1985: 22 U.S.C.A. 287e–1, 2460.

United States Information and Educational Exchange Act of 1948: 22 U.S.C.A. 272b, 1479.

United States Institute of Peace Act: 22 U.S.C.A. 4601, 4611.

United States Insular Areas Drug Abuse Act of 1986: 48 U.S.C.A. 1494, 1494c.

United States-Israel Free Trade Area Implementation Act of 1985: 19 U.S.C.A. 2112, 2518.

United States-Japan Fishery Agreement Approval Act of 1987: 16 U.S.C.A. 1801 note, 1823 note; 33 U.S.C.A. 1121, 1912; 42 U.S.C.A. 6981 notes.

United States Participation Act of 1945: 22 U.S.C.A. 287, 287e.

United States Public Vessel Medical Waste Anti-Dumping Act of 1988: 33 U.S.C.A. 2501, 2504.

United States Railway Association Amendments Act of 1978: 43 U.S.C.A. 975; 45 U.S.C.A. 701, 825.

United States Synthetic Fuels Corporation Act of 1980: 42 U.S.C.A. 8702, 8795.

United States Warehouse Act: 7 U.S.C.A. 71, 2209; 16 U.S.C.A. 490, 683; see 31 U.S.C.A. 1343.

Universal Military Training and Service Act: See 10 U.S.C.A. 3292; 50 App. U.S.C.A. 451, 471.

Unjust Conviction Law: See 28 U.S.C.A. 1495, 2513.

Unlisted Securities Trading Act: 15 U.S.C.A. 78*l*, 78hh–1.

Upper Colorado Act: 43 U.S.C.A. 620, 620*o*.

Upper Mississippi River Management Act of 1986: 33 U.S.C.A. 652.

Upper Mississippi River Wild Life and Fish Refuge Act: 16 U.S.C.A. 721, 731.

Uranium Mill Tailings Radiation Control Act of 1978: 42 U.S.C.A. 2014, 7942.

Uranium Mill Tailings Remedial Action Amendments Act of 1988: 42 U.S.C.A. 7916, 7922.

Urban Growth and New Community Development Act of 1970: 12 U.S.C.A. 371, 1464; 40 U.S.C.A. 461; 42 U.S.C.A. 1453, 4532.

Urban Mass Transportation Act of 1964: 49 U.S.C.A. 1601, 1621; 49 App. U.S.C.A. 1604, 1608.

Urban Park and Recreation Recovery Act of 1978: 16 U.S.C.A. 2501, 2514.

Urban Property Protection and Reinsurance Act of 1968: 5 U.S.C.A. 5315; 12 U.S.C.A. 1701s, 1749bbb–21; 15 U.S.C.A. 2636; 42 U.S.C.A. 1462, 3533a.

Urgent Deficiencies Appropriation Acts: 2 U.S.C.A. 72a–2; 15 U.S.C.A. 713a–10; 42 U.S.C.A. 1523 note.

Used Oil Recycling Act of 1980: 42 U.S.C.A. 6901a, 6948.

Utah Wilderness Act of 1984: 16 U.S.C.A. 1132 note.

Vaccination Assistance Act of 1962: 42 U.S.C.A. 247b.

Vaccine Compensation Amendments of 1987: 42 U.S.C.A. 300aa–11, 300aa–34.

Valley Forge National Historical Park Act: 16 U.S.C.A. 410aa, 410aa–3.

Valuation Act (Interstate Commerce): See 49 U.S.C.A. 10301, 11901.

Van Zandt Patent Act: See 35 U.S.C.A. 133, 267.

Vermont Wilderness Act of 1984: 16 U.S.C.A. 460nn, 460nn–3.

Vessel Bridge-to-Bridge Radiotelephone Act: 33 U.S.C.A. 1201, 1208.

Vessel Documentation Act: 46 U.S.C.A. 4, 496.

Veterans' Administration and Department of Defense Health Resources Sharing and Emer-gency Operations Act: 38 U.S.C.A. 1786, 5011A.

Veterans' Administration Health-Care Amendments of 1985: 38 U.S.C.A. 210, 5035.

Veterans' Administration Health-Care Programs Improvement and Extension Act of 1982: 38 U.S.C.A. 601, 5054.

Veterans' Administration Medical School Assistance and Health Manpower Training Act of 1972: 38 U.S.C.A. 4121, 5096.

Veterans' Administration Physician and Dentist Pay Comparability Act of 1975: 5 U.S.C.A. 5314, 5315; 38 U.S.C.A. 4104, 4118.

Veterans' and Survivors' Pension Improvement Act of 1978: 328 U.S.C.A. 101, 3203.

Veterans' Benefits: 36 U.S.C.A. 125b; 38 U.S.C.A. 101, 5228.

Veterans' Benefits Act of 1957: 10 U.S.C.A. 1218, 6160; 26 U.S.C.A. 121; 38 U.S.C.A. generally dispersed throughout title 38; see 38 U.S.C.A. 102, 5207.

Veterans' Benefits and Programs Improvement Act of 1988: 10 U.S.C.A. 2131, 2135; 16 U.S.C.A. 3198; 29 U.S.C.A. 1721 note; 38 U.S.C.A. 105, 3103A.

Veterans' Benefits and Services Act of 1988: 36 U.S.C.A. 138c; 38 U.S.C.A. 101, 5035; 42 U.S.C.A. 402 note.

Veterans' Day: See Armistice Day Act.

Veterans' Dioxin and Radiation Exposure Compensation Standards Act: 38 U.S.C.A. 354.

Veterans' Disability Compensation and Housing Benefits Amendments of 1980: 36 U.S.C.A. 121; 38 U.S.C.A. 230, 4109.

Veterans' Disability Compensation and Survivors' Benefits Act of 1978: 24 U.S.C.A. 295a note; 36 U.S.C.A. 121; 38 U.S.C.A. 314, 3101.

Veterans' Education and Employment Assistance Act of 1976: 5 U.S.C.A. 2108; see 31 U.S.C.A. 1321; 38 U.S.C.A. 1502, 1763.

Veterans' Judicial Review Act: 5 U.S.C.A. 5315; 38 U.S.C.A. 211, 4092.

Veterans' Preference Act of 1944: See 5 U.S.C.A. 1302, 7701.

Veterinary Medical Education Act of 1966: 42 U.S.C.A. 293, 294b.

Victim and Witness Protection Act of 1982: 18 U.S.C.A. 1503, 3580; 18 App. U.S.C.A. Rule 32.

Victims of Crime Act of 1984: 18 U.S.C.A. 3013, 4215; 42 U.S.C.A. 10601, 10605.

Victims of Terrorism Compensation Act: 5 U.S.C.A. 5569, 6325; 10 U.S.C.A. 1051, 2185; 37 U.S.C.A. 559, 1013.

Victory Liberty Loan Acts: See 12 U.S.C.A. 221; see 31 U.S.C.A. 3103, 3129.

Video Privacy Protection Act of 1988: 18 U.S.C.A. 2710, 2711.

Vietnam Era Veterans' Readjustment Assistance Act of 1974: 38 U.S.C.A. 219, 2026; 50 App. U.S.C.A. 459.

Vinson-Trammell Parity Act: See 10 U.S.C.A. 2382, 7343; 40 U.S.C.A. 474.

Virgin Islands Acquisition Act: 48 U.S.C.A. 1391, 1396.

Virgin Islands Corporation Act: See 31 U.S.C.A. 9101; 48 U.S.C.A. 1407, 1407i.

Virgin Islands Elective Governor Act: 10 U.S.C.A. 336; 48 U.S.C.A. 1541,1641.

Virgin Islands Nonimmigrant Alien Adjustment Act of 1981: 8 U.S.C.A. 1255 note.

Virgin Islands Organic Act Amendments of 1959: 48 U.S.C.A. 1572, 1617.

Virginia Wilderness Act of 1984: 16 U.S.C.A. 1132 notes.

Virus-Serum-Toxin Act: 21 U.S.C.A. 151, 157.

Vocational Education Act of 1917: 20 U.S.C.A. 11, 28.

Vocational Education Act of 1963: 20 U.S.C.A. 1241, 2461; see 20 U.S.C.A. 1241.

Vocational Rehabilitation Acts: 29 U.S.C.A. 31, 42b.

Volstead Act (Drainage under State Laws): 43 U.S.C.A. 1021, 1027.

Voluntary Home Mortgage Credit Act: 12 U.S.C.A. 1750a, 1750jj.

Voluntary Service Acts: See 31 U.S.C.A. 1341, 1519; 44 U.S.C.A. 219a.

Volunteers in the National Forests Act of 1972: 16 U.S.C.A. 558a, 558d.

Volunteers in the Parks Act of 1969: 16 U.S.C.A. 18g, 18j.

Voorhis Anti-Propaganda Act: See 18 U.S.C.A. 2386.

Voting Accessibility for the Elderly and Handicapped Act: 42 U.S.C.A. 1973ee, 1973ee–6.

Voting Rights Act of 1965: 42 U.S.C.A. 1971, 1973bb–4.

Voting Rights Act Amendments of 1970: 42 U.S.C.A. 1973b, 1973bb–4.

Voting Rights Act Amendments of 1982: 42 U.S.C.A. 1971, 1973aa–6.

Vreeland-Aldrich Act (National Currency Associations): 12 U.S.C.A. 104.

Wadsworth-Kahn Act: See 40 U.S.C.A. 483, 484.

Wages-Hours Act Amendment: 29 U.S.C.A. 207, 213.

Wagner Foreign Credits Act: 12 U.S.C.A. 95a; 50 App. U.S.C.A. 5.

Wagner-O'Day Act: 41 U.S.C.A. 46, 48c.

Wagner-Peyser Act: 29 U.S.C.A. 49, 557.

Wagner-Peyser National Employment System Act: 29 U.S.C.A. 49, 557.

Walsh Act: See 28 U.S.C.A. 1783, 1784.

Walsh Act (Additional Federal Judges): See 28 U.S.C.A. 44, 456.

Walsh-Healey Act: 29 U.S.C.A. 557; 41 U.S.C.A. 35, 45.

Wampanoag Tribal Council of Gay Head, Inc., Indian Claims Settlement Act of 1987: 25 U.S.C.A. 1771, 1771i.

War Claims Act of 1948: 42 U.S.C.A. 1702; 50 App. U.S.C.A. 39, 2017p.

War Declaration Against Germany: 50 App. U.S.C.A. note prec. 1.

War Declaration Against Italy: 50 App. U.S.C.A. note prec. 1.

War Declaration Against Japan: 50 App. U.S.C.A. note prec. 1.

War Department Civil Appropriation Acts: 24 U.S.C.A. 46b, 290; 33 U.S.C.A. 701b–5, 701h; 41 U.S.C.A. 6b.

War Finance Corporation Acts: 12 U.S.C.A. 82.

War Hazards Compensation Act: 42 U.S.C.A. 1651, 1717.

War Manpower Commission Appropriation Acts: 29 U.S.C.A. 50, 50b.

War Orphans Education Assistance Act of 1956: See 18 U.S.C.A. 1001, 1621; 38 U.S.C.A. 111, 1768.

War Pay and Allowances Act of 1942: 50 App. U.S.C.A. 1001, 1016.

War Powers Resolution: 50 U.S.C.A. 1541, 1548.

War Risk Insurance Acts: 46 U.S.C.A. 1281, 1294.

Warren Act (Reclamation): 43 U.S.C.A. 523, 525.

Warsaw Convention (International Air Transportation): 49 U.S.C.A. 1502 note.

Washington Park Wilderness Act of 1988: 16 U.S.C.A. 90b, 1274(a)(60).

Washington State Wilderness Act of 1984: 16 U.S.C.A. 460pp.

Water Bank Act: 16 U.S.C.A. 1301, 1311.

Water Facilities Act: 16 U.S.C.A. 590r, 590x–4.

Water Pollution Control Act: 33 U.S.C.A. 1256; see 33 U.S.C.A. 1151.

Water Quality Act of 1965: See 33 U.S.C.A. 1151.

Water Quality Act of 1987: 33 U.S.C.A. 1251, 1414a; 42 U.S.C.A. 1962d–20 note.

Water Quality Improvement Act of 1970: 33 U.S.C.A. 1152, 1175.

Water Research and Development Act of 1978: 42 U.S.C.A. 1959, 7883.

Water Resources Development Act of 1986: 10 U.S.C.A. 3036; 16 U.S.C.A. 460*ll*, 1002; 26 U.S.C.A. 4042, 9506; 33 U.S.C.A. 59, 4260; 40 U.S.C.A. 403b, 483d; 42 U.S.C.A. 1962d–5a, 1962d–20; 43 U.S.C.A. 390, 390b; 46 U.S.C.A. 1121–1.

Water Resources Planning Act: 42 U.S.C.A. 1962, 1962d–3.

Water Resources Research Act of 1984: 42 U.S.C.A. 1959, 10309.

Water Supply Act of 1958: 43 U.S.C.A. 390b.

Watermelon Research and Promotion Act: 7 U.S.C.A. 4901, 4916.

Watershed Protection and Food Prevention Act: 16 U.S.C.A. 1001, 1008; 33 U.S.C.A. 701b.

Weather Modification Reporting Act of 1972: 15 U.S.C.A. 330, 330e.

Webb Exporter Combination Act: 15 U.S.C.A. 63, 65.

Webb-Kenyon Act: 27 U.S.C.A. 122.

Weeks Law: 16 U.S.C.A. 480, 563.

Welfare and Pension Plans Disclosure Act: 29 U.S.C.A. 301, 309.

West Point Act: 16 U.S.C.A. 590y, 590z–3.

West Point Cadet Act: See 10 U.S.C.A. 4342, 9342.

West Virginia National Interest River Conservation Act of 1987: 16 U.S.C.A. 460m–15, 1274.

Wetlands Loan Act: 16 U.S.C.A. 715K–3, 715K–5.

Wetlands Loan Extension Act of 1976: 16 U.S.C.A. 668dd, 718d.

Whale Conservation and Protection Study Act: 16 U.S.C.A. 917, 917d.

Whaling Convention Act of 1949: 16 U.S.C.A. 916, 916*l*.

Whaling Treaty Act: 16 U.S.C.A. 901, 915.

Wheat and Wheat Foods Research and Nutrition Education Act: 7 U.S.C.A. 3401, 3417.

Wheeler-Case Act: 16 U.S.C.A. 590y, 590z–3.

Wheeler-Howard Act: 25 U.S.C.A. 461, 479.

Wheeler-Lea Act: 15 U.S.C.A. 41, 58.

Wheeler-Lea Transportation Act: See Transportation Act, 1940.

Wherry Act (Housing Near Military Establishments): 12 U.S.C.A. 1702, 1748g.

Whistleblower Protection Act of 1989: 5 U.S.C.A. 1201, 7703; 22 U.S.C.A. 4139.

White Act (Collisions on Great Lakes): 33 U.S.C.A. 241, 301; 46 U.S.C.A. 381.

White Cane Safety Day Act: 36 U.S.C.A. 169d.

White House Police Act: See 3 U.S.C.A. 203.

White Pine Blister Rust Protection Act: 16 U.S.C.A. 594a.

White-Slave Laws: See 18 U.S.C.A. 2421, 2424.

Wholesome Meat Act: 19 U.S.C.A. 1306; 21 U.S.C.A. 601, 691.

Wholesome Poultry Products Act: 21 U.S.C.A. 451, 470.

Wilcox Air Base Act: See 10 U.S.C.A. 9774.

Wild and Scenic Rivers Act: 16 U.S.C.A. 1271, 1287.

Wild Free-Roaming Horses and Burros Act: 16 U.S.C.A. 1331, 1340.

Wild Horse Annie Act: 18 U.S.C.A. 47.

Wild Life Restoration Act: 16 U.S.C.A. 669, 669i.

Wilderness Act: 16 U.S.C.A. 1131, 1136.

Wildfire Suppression Assistance Act: 42 U.S.C.A. 1856p.

Wilson Act (Original Packages): 27 U.S.C.A. 121.

Wilson Act (Tariff): 15 U.S.C.A. 8, 11.

WIN Demonstration Program Extension Act of 1988: 42 U.S.C.A. 645.

Wind Energy Systems Act of 1980: 42 U.S.C.A. 9201, 9213.

Winding Stair Mountain National Recreation and Wilderness Area Act: 16 U.S.C.A. 460vv, 460vv–19.

Wine Equity and Export Expansion Act of 1984: 19 U.S.C.A. 2801, 2806.

Wisconsin Wilderness Act of 1984: 16 U.S.C.A. 1132 note.

Witness Security Reform Act of 1984: 18 U.S.C.A. 3521 note.

Wolf Trap Farm Park Act: 16 U.S.C.A. 284, 284b.

Women's Business Ownership Act of 1988: 13 U.S.C.A. 131 note; 15 U.S.C.A. 631, 1691b; 41 U.S.C.A. 417a.

Women's Educational Equity Act: 20 U.S.C.A. 3041, 3047.

Wood Residue Utilization Act of 1980: 16 U.S.C.A. 1681, 1687.

Wool Products Labeling Act of 1939: 15 U.S.C.A. 68, 68j.

Work Hours and Safety Act of 1962: 28 U.S.C.A. 1499; 40 U.S.C.A. 327, 333.

Worker Adjustment and Retraining Notification Act: 29 U.S.C.A. 2101, 2109.

Workmen's Compensation Acts: See 5 U.S.C.A. 8101.

Wright Brothers Day Act: 36 U.S.C.A. 169.

Wunderlich Act: 41 U.S.C.A. 321, 322.

Wyoming Land Act: 43 U.S.C.A. 82, 224.

Yellowstone National Park Protection Act: 16 U.S.C.A. 24, 31.

Young Adult Act: 18 U.S.C.A. 4209.

Young Adult Offender Act: 18 U.S.C.A. 4216.

Youth Conservation Corps Act of 1972: 16 U.S.C.A. 1701, 1706.

Youth Employment and Demonstration Projects Act of 1977: 29 U.S.C.A. 802, 993i.

Ysleta del Sur Pueblo and Alabama and Coushatta Indian Tribes of Texas Restoration Act: 25 U.S.C.A. 731, 1300g–7.

Zuni-Cibola National Historical Park Establishment Act of 1988: 16 U.S.C.A. 410pp, 460uu–12.

QUICK CITE: CASES

Selected U.S. Supreme Court Cases

Abate v. Mundt, 403 U.S. 182, 91 S.Ct. 1904, 29 L.Ed.2d 399 (1971).

Abood v. Detroit Board of Education, 431 U.S. 209, 97 S.Ct. 1782, 52 L.Ed.2d 261 (1977).

Abrams v. United States, 250 U.S. 616, 40 S.Ct. 17, 63 L.Ed. 1173 (1919).

Adamson v. California, 332 U.S. 46, 67 S.Ct. 1672, 91 L.Ed. 1903 (1947).

Addington v. Texas, 441 U.S. 418, 99 S.Ct. 1804, 60 L.Ed.2d 323 (1979).

Adkins v. Children's Hospital, 261 U.S. 525, 43 S.Ct. 394, 67 L.Ed. 785 (1923).

Afroyim v. Rusk, 387 U.S. 253, 87 S.Ct. 1660, 18 L.Ed.2d 757 (1967).

Aquilar v. Felton, 473 U.S. 402, 105 S.Ct. 3232, 87 L.Ed.2d 290 (1985).

Akron v. Akron Center for Reproductive Health, Inc., 462 U.S. 416, 103 S.Ct. 2481, 76 L.Ed.2d 687 (1983).

Alabama v. King & Boozer, 314 U.S. 1, 62 S.Ct. 43, 86 L.Ed. 3 (1941).

Albertini, United States v., 472 U.S. 675, 105 S.Ct. 2897, 86 L.Ed.2d 536 (1985).

Allen v. Wright, 468 U.S. 737, 104 S.Ct. 3315, 82 L.Ed.2d 556 (1984).

Allgeyer v. Louisiana, 165 U.S. 578, 17 S.Ct. 427, 41 L.Ed. 832 (1897).

Allied Structural Steel Co. v. Spannaus, 438 U.S. 234, 98 S.Ct. 2716, 57 L.Ed.2d 727 (1978).

Ambach v. Norwick, 441 U.S. 68, 99 S.Ct. 1589, 60 L.Ed.2d 49 (1979).

American Communications Assn'n v. Douds, 339 U.S. 382, 70 S.Ct. 674, 94 L.Ed. 925 (1950).

American Insurance Co. v. Canter, 26 U.S. (1 Pet.) 511, 7 L.Ed. 242 (1828).

American Party of Texas v. White, 415 U.S. 767, 94 S.Ct. 1296, 39 L.Ed.2d 744 (1974).

Anderson v. Celebrezze, 460 U.S. 780, 103 S.Ct. 1564, 75 L.Ed.2d 547 (1983).

Anderson v. Liberty Lobby, Inc., 477 U.S. 242, 106 S.Ct. 2505, 91 L.Ed.2d 202 (1986).

Arcara v. Cloud Books, Inc., 478 U.S. 697, 106 S.Ct. 3172, 92 L.Ed.2d 568 (1986).

Arizona Governing Committee for Tax Deferred Annuity and Deferred Compensation Plans v. Norris, 463 U.S. 1073, 103 S.Ct. 3492, 77 L.Ed.2d 1236 (1983).

Arkansas Electric Cooperative Corp. v. Arkansas Public Service Comm'n, 461 U.S. 375, 103 S.Ct. 1905, 76 L.Ed.2d 1 (1983).

Arlington Heights v. Metropolitan Housing Development Corp., 429 U.S. 252, 97 S.Ct. 555, 50 L.Ed.2d 450 (1977).

Arnett v. Kennedy, 416 U.S. 134, 94 S.Ct. 1633, 40 L.Ed.2d 15 (1974).

ASARCO Inc. v. Idaho State Tax Comm'n, 458 U.S. 307, 102 S.Ct. 3103, 73 L.Ed.2d 787 (1982).

Ash, United States v., 413 U.S. 300, 93 S.Ct. 2568, 37 L.Ed.2d 619 (1973).

Assn. of Data Processing Service Organizations, Inc. v. Camp, 397 U.S. 150, 90 S.Ct. 827, 25 L.Ed.2d 184 (1970).

Atascadero State Hospital v. Scanlon, 473 U.S. 234, 105 S.Ct. 3142, 87 L.Ed.2d 171 (1985).

Augenblick, United States v., 393 U.S. 348, 89 S.Ct. 528, 21 L.Ed.2d 537 (1969).

Austin v. New Hampshire, 420 U.S. 656, 95 S.Ct. 1191, 43 L.Ed.2d 530 (1975).

Avery v. Midland County, 390 U.S. 474, 88 S.Ct. 1114, 20 L.Ed.2d 45 (1968).

Baker v. Carr, 369 U.S. 186, 82 S.Ct. 691, 7 L.Ed.2d 663 (1962).

Bakke, Regents of the University of California v., 438 U.S. 265, 98 S.Ct. 2733, 57 L.Ed.2d 750 (1978).

Baldwin v. Fish & Game Comm'n of Montana, 436 U.S. 371, 98 S.Ct. 1852, 56 L.Ed.2d 354 (1978).

Baldwin v. G.A.F. Seelig, Inc., 294 U.S. 511, 55 S.Ct. 497, 79 L.Ed. 1032 (1935).

Ball v. James, 451 U.S. 355, 101 S.Ct., 1811, 68 L.Ed.2d 150 (1981).

Ballard, United States v., 322 U.S. 78, 64 S.Ct. 882, 88 L.Ed. 1148 (1944).

Bank of Augusta v. Earle, 38 U.S. (13 Pet.) 519, 10 L.Ed. 274 (1839).

Bantam Books, Inc. v. Sullivan, 372 U.S. 58, 83 S.Ct. 631, 9 L.Ed.2d 584 (1963).

Barber v. Page, 390 U.S. 719, 88 S.Ct. 1318, 20 L.Ed.2d 255 (1968).

Barenblatt v. United States, 360 U.S. 109, 79 S.Ct. 1081, 3 L.Ed.2d 1115 (1959).

Barron v. Mayor and City Council of Baltimore, 32 U.S. (7 Pet.) 243, 8 L.Ed. 672 (1833).

Barrows v. Jackson, 346 U.S. 249, 73 S.Ct. 1031, 97 L.Ed. 1586 (1953).

Barry v. Barchi, 443 U.S. 55, 99 S.Ct. 2642, 61 L.Ed.2d 365 (1979).

Barsky v. Board of Regents, 347 U.S. 442, 74 S.Ct. 650, 98 L.Ed. 829 (1954).

Beauharnais v. Illinois, 343 U.S. 250, 72 S.Ct. 725, 96 L.Ed. 919 (1952).

Belle Terre, Village of v. Boraas, 416 U.S. 1, 94 S.Ct. 1536, 39 L.Ed.2d 797 (1974).

Belmont, United States v., 301 U.S. 324, 57 S.Ct. 758, 81 L.Ed. 1134 (1937).

Belton, New York v., 453 U.S. 454, 101 S.Ct. 2860, 69 L.Ed.2d 768 (1981).

Bender v. Williamsport Area School District, 475 U.S. 534, 106 S.Ct. 1326, 89 L.Ed.2d 501 (1986).

Bibb v. Navajo Freight Lines, Inc., 359 U.S. 520, 79 S.Ct. 962, 3 L.Ed.2d 1003 (1959).

Bivens v. Six Unknown Named Agents, 403 U.S. 388, 91 S.Ct. 1999, 29 L.Ed.2d 619 (1971).

Blair v. Commissioner of Internal Revenue, 300 U.S. 5, 57 S.Ct. 330, 81 L.Ed. 465 (1937).

Blum v. Yaretsky, 457 U.S. 991, 102 S.Ct. 2777, 73 L.Ed.2d 534 (1982).

Board of Directors of Rotary International v. Rotary Club of Duarte, 481 U.S. 537, 107 S.Ct. 1940, 95 L.Ed.2d 474 (1987).

Board of Regents of State Colleges v. Roth, 408 U.S. 564, 92 S.Ct. 2701, 33 L.Ed.2d 548 (1972).

Bob-Lo Excursion Co. v. Michigan, 333 U.S. 28, 68 S.Ct. 358, 92 L.Ed. 455 (1948).

Boddie v. Connecticut, 401 U.S. 371, 91 S.Ct. 780, 28 L.Ed.2d 113 (1971).

Bolger v. Youngs Drug Products Corp., 463 U.S. 60, 103 S.Ct. 2875, 77 L.Ed.2d 469 (1983).

Bolling V. Sharpe, 347 U.S. 497, 74 S.Ct. 693, 98 L.Ed. 884 (1954).

Bose Corp. v. Consumers Union of the United States, Inc., 466 U.S. 485, 104 S.Ct. 1949, 80 L.Ed.2d 502 (1984).

Bowen v. Roy, 476 U.S. 693, 106 S.Ct. 2147, 90 L.Ed.2d 735 (1986).

Bowers v. Hardwick, 478 U.S. 186, 106 S.Ct. 2841, 92 L.Ed.2d 140 (1986).

Bowsher v. Synar, 478 U.S. 714, 106 S.Ct. 3181, 92 L.Ed.2d 583 (1986).

Bradfield v. Roberts, 175 U.S. 291, 20 S.Ct. 121, 44 L.Ed. 168 (1899).

Brandenburg v. Ohio, 395 U.S. 444, 89 S.Ct. 1827, 23 L.Ed.2d 430 (1969).

Branti v. Finkel, 445 U.S. 507, 100 S.Ct. 1287, 63 L.Ed.2d 574 (1980).

Branzburg v. Hayes, 408 U.S. 665, 92 S.Ct. 2646, 33 L.Ed.2d 626 (1972).

Braunfeld v. Brown, 366 U.S. 599, 81 S.Ct. 1144, 6 L.Ed.2d 563 (1961).

Brinkerhoff-Faris Trust & Savings Co. v. Hill, 281 U.S. 673, 50 S.Ct. 451, 74 L.Ed. 1107 (1930).

Broadrick v. Oklahoma, 413 U.S. 601, 93 S.Ct. 2908, 37 L.Ed.2d 830 (1973).

Brotherhood of Locomotive Firemen and Enginemen v. Chicago, R.I. & P.R. Co., 393 U.S. 129, 89 S.Ct. 323, 21 L.Ed.2d 289 (1968).

Brotherhood of Railroad Trainmen v. Virginia ex rel. Virginia State Bar, 377 U.S. 1, 84 S.Ct. 1113, 12 L.Ed.2 89 (1964).

Brown v. Board of Education of Topeka, 347 U.S. 483, 74 S.Ct. 686, 98 L.Ed. 873 (1954).

Brown v. Board of Education of Topeka, 349 U.S. 294, 75 S.Ct. 753, 99 L.Ed. 1083 (1955).

Brown v. Illinois, 422 U.S. 590, 95 S.Ct. 2254, 45 L.Ed.2d 416 (1975).

Brown v. Socialist Workers '74 Campaign Committee, 459 U.S. 87, 103 S.Ct. 416, 74 L.Ed.2d 250 (1982).

Brown v. Thomson, 462 U.S. 835, 103 S.Ct. 2690, 77 L.Ed.2d 214 (1983).

Brown, United States v., 381 U.S. 437, 85 S.Ct. 1707, 14 L.Ed.2d 484 (1965).

Buchanan v. Warley, 245 U.S. 60, 38 S.Ct. 16, 62 L.Ed. 149 (1917).

Buck v. Bell, 274 U.S. 200, 47 S.Ct. 584, 71 L.Ed. 1000 (1927).

Buck v. California, 343 U.S. 99, 72 S.Ct. 502, 96 L.Ed. 775 (1952).

Buckley v. Valeo, 424 U.S. 1, 96 S.Ct. 612, 46 L.Ed.2d 659 (1976).

Bullock v. Carter, 405 U.S. 134, 92 S.Ct. 849, 31 L.Ed.2d 92 (1972).

Bunting v. Oregon, 243 U.S. 426, 37 S.Ct. 435, 61 L.Ed. 830 (1917).

City of Burbank v. Lockheed Air Terminal, Inc., 411 U.S. 624, 93 S.Ct. 1854, 36 L.Ed.2d 547 (1973).

Burgess v. Salmon, 97 U.S. (7 Otto) 381, 24 L.Ed. 1104 (1878).

Burton v. Wilmington Parking Authority, 365 U.S. 715, 81 S.Ct. 856, 6 L.Ed.2d 45 (1961).

Butz v. Economou, 438 U.S. 478, 98 S.Ct. 2894, 57 L.Ed.2d 895 (1978).

Cabell v. Chavez-Salido, 454 U.S. 432, 102 S.Ct. 735, 70 L.Ed.2d 677 (1982).

Calder v. Bull, 3 U.S. (3 Dall.) 386, 1 L.Ed. 648 (1798).

Califano v. Boles, 443 U.S. 282, 99 S.Ct. 2767, 61 L.Ed.2d 541 (1979).

Califano v. Goldfarb, 430 U.S. 199, 97 S.Ct. 1021, 51 L.Ed.2d 270 (1977).

Califano v. Westcott, 443 U.S. 76, 99 S.Ct. 2655, 61 L.Ed.2d 382 (1979).

California v. Green, 399 U.S. 149, 90 S.Ct. 1930, 26 L.Ed.2d 489 (1970).

California v. Zook, 336 U.S. 725, 69 S.Ct. 841, 93 L.Ed. 1005 (1949).

California Bankers Ass'n v. Schultz, 416 U.S. 21, 94 S.Ct. 1494, 39 L.Ed.2d 812 (1974).

California Federal Savings & Loan Ass'n v. Guerra, 479 U.S. 272, 107 S.Ct. 683, 93 L.Ed.2d 613 (1987).

California Medical Ass'n v. Federal Election Comm'n, 453 U.S. 182, 101 S.Ct. 2712, 69 L.Ed.2d 567 (1981).

Campbell v. Hussey, 368 U.S. 297, 82 S.Ct. 327, 7 L.Ed.2d 299 (1961).

Cantwell v. Connecticut, 310 U.S. 296, 60 S.Ct. 900, 84 L.Ed. 1213 (1940).

Capital Cities Cable, Inc. v. Crisp, 467 U.S. 691, 104 S.Ct. 2694, 81 L.Ed.2d 580 (1984).

Carey v. Brown, 447 U.S. 455, 100 S.Ct. 2286, 65 L.Ed.2d 263 (1980).

Carey v. Piphus, 435 U.S. 247, 98 S.Ct. 1042, 55 L.Ed.2d 252 (1978).

Carey v. Population Services International, 431 U.S. 678, 97 S.Ct. 2010, 52 L.Ed.2d 675 (1977).

Carolene Products Co., United States v., 304 U.S. 144, 58 S.Ct. 778, 82 L.Ed. 1234 (1938).

Carrington v. Rash, 380 U.S. 89, 85 S.Ct. 775, 13 L.Ed.2d 675 (1965).

Carter v. Carter Coal Co., 298 U.S. 238, 56 S.Ct. 855, 80 L.Ed. 1160 (1936).

Castle v. Hayes Freight Lines, 348 U.S. 61, 75 S.Ct. 191, 99 L.Ed. 68 (1954).

Central Greyhound Lines v. Mealey, 334 U.S. 653, 68 S.Ct. 1260, 92, L.Ed. 1633 (1948).

Central Hudson Gas & Electric Corp. v. Public Service Comm'n, 447 U.S. 557, 100 S.Ct. 2343, 65 L.Ed.2d 341 (1980).

Chandler v. Florida, 449 U.S. 560, 101, S.Ct. 802, 66 L.Ed.2d 740 (1981).

Chaplinsky v. New Hampshire, 315 U.S. 568, 62 S.Ct. 766, 86 L.Ed. 1031 (1942).

Cherokee Nation v. Georgia, 30 U.S. (5 Pet.) 1, 8 L.Ed. 25 (1831).

Chiarella v. United States, 445 U.S. 222, 100 S.Ct. 1108, 63 L.Ed.2d 348 (1980).

Chicago & Southern Air Lines, Inc. v. Waterman Steamship Corp., 333 U.S. 103, 68 S.Ct. 431, 92 L.Ed. 568 (1948).

Chicago Teachers Union, Local No. 1, AFT, AFL–CIO v. Hudson, 475 U.S. 292, 106 S.Ct. 1066, 89 L.Ed.2d 232 (1986).

Chimel v. California, 395 U.S. 752, 89 S.Ct. 2034, 23 L.Ed.2d 685 (1969).

Chisholm v. Georgia, 2 U.S. (2 Dall.) 419, 1 L.Ed. 440 (1793).

Cipriano v. City of Houma, 395 UY.S. 701, 89 S.Ct. 1897, 23 L.Ed.2d 647 (1969).

Cities Services Gas Co. v. Peerless Oil and Gas Co., 340 U.S. 179, 71 S.Ct. 215, 95 L.Ed. 190 (1950).

Citizens Against Rent Control/Coalition for Fair Housing v. City of Berkeley, 454 U.S. 290, 102 S.Ct. 434, 70 L.Ed.2d 492 (1981).

City of Los Angeles v. Lyons, 461 U.S. 95, 103 S.Ct. 1660, 75 L.Ed.2d 675 (1983).

Civil Rights Cases, In re, 109 U.S. 3, 3 S.Ct. 18, 27 L.Ed. 835 (1883).

Clark v. Community For Creative Non-Violence, 468 U.S. 288, 104 S.Ct. 3065, 82 L.Ed.2d 221 (1984).

Cleburne, Texas v. Cleburne Living Center, 473 U.S. 432, 105 S.Ct. 3249, 87 L.Ed.2d 313 (1985).

Clements v. Fashing, 457 U.S. 957, 102 S.Ct. 2836, 73 L.Ed.2d 508 (1982).

Cleveland Board of Education v. LaFleur, 414 U.S. 632, 94 S.Ct. 791, 39 L.Ed.2d 52 (1974).

Cleveland Board of Education v. Loudermill, 470 U.S. 532, 105 S.Ct. 1487, 84 L.Ed.2d 494 (1985).

Coates v. Cincinnati, 402 U.S. 611, 91 S.Ct. 1686, 29 L.Ed.2d 214 (1971).

Codd v. Velger, 429 U.S. 624, 97 S.Ct. 882, 51 L.Ed.2d 92 (1977).

Cohen v. California, 403 U.S. 15, 91 S.Ct. 1780, 29 L.Ed.2d 284 (1971).

Coker v. Georgia, 433 U.S. 584, 97 S.Ct. 2861, 53 L.Ed.2d 982 (1977).

Coleman v. Miller, 307 U.S. 433, 59 S.Ct. 972, 83 L.Ed. 1385 (1939).

Colgate v. Harvey, 296 U.S. 404, 56 S.Ct. 252, 80 L.Ed. 299 (1935).

Colorado Anti-Discrimination Comm'n v. Continental Air Lines, Inc., 372 U.S. 714, 83 S.Ct. 1022, 10 L.Ed.2d 84 (1963).

Colorado Springs Amusements, Ltd. v. Rizzo, 428 U.S. 913, 96 S.Ct. 3228, 49 L.Ed.2d 1222 (1976).

Columbus Board of Education v. Penick, 443 U.S. 449, 99 S.Ct. 2941, 61 L.Ed.2d 666 (1979).

Columbia Broadcasting System v. Democratic National Committee, 412 U.S. 94, 93 S.Ct. 2080, 36 L.Ed.2d 772 (1973).

Commissioner of Internal Revenue v. Tufts, 461 U.S. 300, 103 S.Ct. 1826, 75 L.Ed.2d 863 (1983).

Committee for Public Education v. Nyquist, 413 U.S. 756, 93 S.Ct. 2955, 37 L.Ed.2d 948 (1973).

Committee for Public Education and Religious Liberty v. Regan, 444 U.S. 646, 100 S.Ct. 840, 63 L.Ed.2d 94 (1980).

Commodity Futures Trading Comm'n v. Schor, 478 U.S. 833, 106 S.Ct. 3245, 92 L.Ed.2d 675 (1986).

Commonwealth Edison Co. v. Montana, 453 U.S. 609, 101 S.Ct. 2946, 69 L.Ed.2d 884 (1981).

Communist Party of Indiana v. Whitcomb, 414 U.S.

441, 94 S.Ct. 656, 38 L.Ed.2d 635 (1974).

Complete Auto Transit, Inc. v. Brady, 430 U.S. 274, 97 S.Ct. 1076, 51 L.Ed.2d 326 (1977).

Connecticut Board of Pardons v. Dumschat, 452 U.S. 458, 101 S.Ct. 2460, 69 L.Ed.2d 158 (1981).

Connick v. Myers, 461 U.S. 138, 103 S.Ct. 1684, 75 L.Ed.2d 708 (1983).

Consolidated Edison Co. v. Public Service Comm'n, 447 U.S. 530, 100 S.Ct. 2326, 65 L.Ed.2d 319 (1980).

Container Corporation of America v. Franchise Tax Board, 463 U.S. 159, 103 S.Ct. 2933, 77 L.Ed.2d 545 (1983).

Cooley v. Board of Wardens of the Port of Philadelphia, 53 U.S. (12 How.) 299, 132 L.Ed. 996 (1851).

Cooper v. Aaron, 358 U.S. 1, 78 S.Ct. 1401, 3 L.Ed.2d 5 (1958).

Coppage v. Kansas, 236 U.S. 1, 35 S.Ct. 240, 59 L.Ed. 441 (1915).

Cornelius v. NAACP Legal Defense and Educational Fund, Inc., 473 U.S. 788, 105 S.Ct. 3439, 87 L.Ed.2d 567 (1985).

Corn Products Refining Co. v. Commissioner of Internal Revenue, 350 U.S. 46, 76 S.Ct. 20, 100 L.Ed. 29 (1955).

Corporation of the Presiding Bishop of Church of Jesus Christ of Latter-Day Saints v. Amos, 483 U.S. 327, 107 S.Ct. 2862, 97 L.Ed.2d 273 (1987).

Cory v. White, 457 U.S. 85, 102 S.Ct. 2325, 72 L.Ed.2d 694 (1982).

Cousins v. Wigoda, 419 U.S. 477, 95 S.Ct. 541, 42 L.Ed.2d 595 (1975).

Cox v. Louisiana, 379 U.S. 536, 85 S.Ct. 453, 13 L.Ed.2d 471 (1965).

Cox Broadcasting Corp. v. Cohn, 420 U.S. 469, 95 S.Ct. 1029, 43 L.Ed.2d 328 (1975).

Coyle v. Smith, 221 U.S. 559, 31 S.Ct. 688, 55 L.Ed. 853 (1911).

Craig v. Boren, 429 U.S. 190, 97 S.Ct. 451, 50 L.Ed.2d 397 (1976).

Crane v. Commissioner of Internal Revenue, 331 U.S. 1, 67 S.Ct. 1047, 91 L.Ed. 1301 (1947).

Crawford v. Borad of Education of the City of Los Angeles, 458 U.S. 527, 102 S.Ct. 3211, 73 L.Ed.2d 948 (1982),

Crews, United States v., 445 U.S. 463, 100 S.Ct. 1244, 63 L.Ed.2d 537 (1980).

Crowell v. Benson, 285 U.S. 22, 52 S.Ct. 285, 76 L.Ed. 598 (1932).

Cummings v. Missouri, 71 U.S. (4 Wall.) 277, 18 L.Ed. 356 (1866).

Curtiss-Wright Export Corp., United States v., 299 U.S. 304, 57 S.Ct. 216, 81 L.Ed. 255 (1936).

Cuyler v. Adams, 449 U.S. 433, 101 S.Ct. 703, 66 L.Ed.2d 641 (1981).

Dames & Moore v. Regan, 453 U.S. 654, 101 S.Ct. 2972, 69 L.Ed.2d 918 (1981).

Dandridge v. Williams, 397 U.S. 471, 90 S.Ct. 1153, 25 L.Ed.2d 491 (1970).

Daniels v. Williams, 474 U.S. 327, 106 S.Ct. 662, 88 L.Ed.2d 662 (1986).

Darby, United States v., 312 U.S. 100, 61 S.Ct. 451, 86 L.Ed. 609 (1941).

Dartmouth College v. Woodward, 17 U.S. (4 Wheat) 518, 4 L.Ed. 629 (1819).

Davidson v. Cannon, 474 U.S. 344, 106 S.Ct. 668, 88 L.Ed.2d 677 (1986).

Davis v. Alaska, 415 U.S. 308, 94 S.Ct. 1105, 39 L.Ed.2d 347 (1974).

Davis v. Bandemer, 478 U.S. 109, 106 S.Ct. 2797, 92 L.Ed.2d 85 (1986).

Davis v. United States (I), 160 U.S. 469, 16 S.Ct. 353, 40 L.Ed. 499 (1895).

Davis v. United States (II), 165 U.S. 373, 17 S.Ct. 360, 41 L.Ed. 750 (1897).

Dayton Board of Education v. Brinkman, 433 U.S. 406, 97 S.Ct. 2766, 53 L.Ed.2d 851 (1977).

Dayton Board of Education v. Brinkman (Brinkman II), 443 U.S. 526, 99 S.Ct. 2971, 61 L.Ed.2d 720 (1979).

DeFunis v. Odegaard, 416 U.S. 312, 94 S.Ct. 1704, 40 L.Ed.2d 164 (1974).

Democratic Party of the United States v. Wisconsin ex rel. La Follette, 450 U.S. 107, 101 S.Ct. 1010, 67 L.Ed.2d 82 (1981).

Dennis v. United States, 341 U.S. 494, 71 S.Ct. 857, 95 L.Ed. 1137 (1951).

Deposit Guaranty National Bank v. Roper, 445 U.S. 326, 100 S.Ct. 1166, 63 L.Ed.2d 427 (1980).

Dobbert v. Florida, 432 U.S. 282, 97 S.Ct. 2290, 53 L.Ed.2d 344 (1977).

Doe v. Bolton, 410 U.S. 179, 93 S.Ct. 739, 35 L.Ed.2d 201 (1973).

Doe v. McMillan, 412 U.S. 306, 93 S.Ct. 2018, 36 L.Ed.2d 912 (1973).

Doremus v. Board of Education, 342 U.S. 429, 72 S.Ct. 394, 96 L.Ed. 475 (1952).

Dothard v. Rawlinson, 433 U.S. 321, 97 S.Ct. 2720, 53 L.Ed.2d 786 (1977).

Douglas v. California, 372 U.S. 353, 83 S.Ct. 814, 9 L.Ed.2d 811 (1963).

Dred Scott v. Sandford, 60 U.S. (19 How.) 393, 15 L.Ed. 691 (1857).

Drope v. Missouri, 420 U.S. 162, 95 S.Ct. 896, 43 L.Ed.2d 103 (1975).

Dunn v. Blumstein, 405 U.S. 330, 92 S.Ct. 995, 31 L.Ed.2d 274 (1972).

Dun & Bradstreet, Inc. v. Greenmoss Builders, Inc., 472 U.S. 749, 105 S.Ct. 2939, 86 L.Ed.2d 593 (1985).

Dutton v. Evans, 400 U.S. 74, 91 S.Ct. 210, 27 L.Ed.2d 213 (1970).

City of Eastlake v. Forest City Enterprises, Inc., 426 U.S. 668, 96 S.Ct. 2358, 49 L.Ed.2d 132 (1976).

Edelman v. Jordon, 415 U.S. 651, 94 S.Ct. 1347, 39 L.Ed.2d 662 (1974).

Edgar v. MITE Corp., 457 U.S. 624, 102 S.Ct. 2629, 73 L.Ed.2d 269 (1982).

Edwards v. Aguillard, 482 U.S. 578, 107 S.Ct. 2573, 96 L.Ed.2d 510 (1987).

Edwards v. California, 314 U.S. 160, 62 S.Ct. 164, 86 L.Ed. 119 (1941).

Edwards v. South Carolina, 372 U.S. 229, 83 S.Ct. 680, 9 L.Ed.2d 697 (1963).

EEOC v. Wyoming, 460 U.S. 226, 103 S.Ct. 1054, 75 L.Ed.2d 18 (1983).

Eisenstadt v. Baird, 405 U.S. 438, 92 S.Ct. 1029, 31 L.Ed.2d 349 (1972).

Ellis v. Brotherhood of Railway, Airline & S.S. Clerks, 466 U.S. 435, 104 S.Ct. 1883, 80 L.Ed.2d 428 (1984).

Empresa Siderurgica, S.A. v. Merced County, 337 U.S. 154, 69 S.Ct. 995, 93 L.Ed. 1276 (1949).

Energy Reserves Group, Inc. v. Kansas Power and Light Co., 459 U.S. 400, 103 S.Ct. 697, 74 L.Ed.2d 569 (1983).

Engel v. Vitale, 370 U.S. 421, 82 S.Ct. 1261, 8 L.Ed.2d 601 (1962).

Epperson v. Arkansas, 393 U.S. 97, 89 S.Ct. 266, 21 L.Ed.2d 228 (1968).

Ernst & Ernst v. Hochfelder, 425 U.S. 185, 96 S.Ct. 1375, 47 L.Ed.2d 668 (1976).

Erznoznik v. Jacksonville, 422 U.S. 205, 95 S.Ct. 2268, 45 L.Ed.2d 125 (1975).

Escobedo v. Illinois, 378 U.S. 478, 84 S.Ct. 1758, 12 L.Ed.2d 977 (1964).

Estate of Thornton v. Caldor, Inc., 472 U.S. 703, 105 S.Ct. 2914, 86 L.Ed.2d 557 (1985).

Estelle v. Gamble, 429 U.S 97, 97 S.Ct. 285, 50 L.Ed.2d 251 (1976).

Estelle v. Williams, 425 U.S. 501, 96 S.Ct. 1691, 48 L.Ed.2d 126 (1976).

Village of Euclid v. Ambler Realty Co., 272 U.S. 365, 47 S.Ct. 114, 71 L.Ed. 303 (1926).

Evansville-Vanderburgh Airport Authority District v. Delta Airlines, 405 U.S. 707, 92 S.Ct. 1349, 31 L.Ed.2d 620 (1972).

Everson v. Board of Education, 330 U.S. 1, 67 S.Ct. 504, 91 L.Ed. 711 (1947).

Ex Parte Virginia, 100 U.S. (10 Otto) 339, 25 L.Ed. 676 (1879).

Exxon Corp. v. Eagerton, 462 U.S. 176, 103 S.Ct. 2296, 76 L.Ed.2d 497 (1983).

Exxon Corp. v. Governor of Maryland, 437 U.S. 117, 98 S.Ct. 2207, 57 L.Ed.2d 91 (1978).

Exxon Corp. v. Wisconsin Department of Revenue, 447 U.S. 207, 100 S.Ct. 2109, 65 L.Ed.2d 66 (1980).

Farmer v. United Brotherhood of Carpenters and Joiners of America, Local 25, 430 U.S. 290, 97 S.Ct. 1056, 51 L.Ed.2d 338 (1977).

Fay v. Noia, 372 U.S. 391, 83 S.Ct. 822, 9 L.Ed.2d 837 (1963).

Federal Communications Comm'n v. League of Women Voters, 468 U.S. 364, 104 S.Ct. 3106, 82 L.Ed.2d 278 (1984).

Federal Communications Comm'n v. Pacifica Foundation, 438 U.S. 726, 98 S.Ct. 3026, 57 L.Ed.2d 1073 (1978).

Federal Election Comm'n v. National Conservative Political Action Committee, 470 U.S. 480, 105 S.Ct. 1459, 84 L.Ed.2d 455 (1985).

Federal Election Comm'n v. Massachusetts Citizens for Life, Inc., 479 U.S. 238, 107 S.Ct. 616, 93 L.Ed.2d 539 (1986).

Federal Election Comm'n v. National Right to Work Committee, 459, U.S. 197, 103 S.Ct. 552, 74 L.Ed.2d 364 (1982).

Feiner v. New York, 340 U.S. 315, 71 S.Ct. 303, 95 L.Ed. 295 (1951).

Ferguson v. Skrupa, 372 U.S. 726, 83 S.Ct. 1028, 10 L.Ed.2d 93 (1963).

First Nat'l Bank of Boston v. Bellotti, 435 U.S. 765, 98 S.Ct. 1407, 55 L.Ed.2d 707 (1978).

Fisher v. City of Berkeley, 475 U.S. 260, 106 S.Ct. 1045, 89 L.Ed.2d 206 (1986).

Fitzpatrick v. Bitzer, 427 U.S. 445, 96 S.Ct. 2666, 49 L.Ed.2d 614 (1976).

Flagg Brothers, Inc. v. Brooks, 436 U.S. 149, 98 S.Ct. 1729, 56 L.Ed.2d 185 (1978).

Flast v. Cohen, 392 U.S. 83, 88 S.Ct. 1942, 20 L.Ed.2d 947 (1968).

Flint v. Stone Tracy Co., 220 U.S. 107, 31 S.Ct. 342, 55 L.Ed. 389 (1911).

Florida Lime and Avocado Growers, Inc. v. Paul, 373 U.S. 132, 83 S.Ct. 1210, 10 L.Ed.2d 248 (1963).

Foley v. Connelie, 435 U.S. 291, 98 S.Ct. 1067, 55 L.Ed.2d 287 (1978).

Fong Yue Ting v. United States, 149 U.S. 698, 13 S.Ct. 1016, 37 L.Ed. 905 (1893).

Foremost-McKesson, Inc. v. Provident Securities Co., 423 U.S. 232, 96 S.Ct. 508, 46 L.Ed.2d 464 (1976).

Foster-Fountain Packing Co. v. Haydel, 278 U.S. 1, 49 S.Ct. 1, 73 L.Ed. 147 (1928).

Franks v. Bowman Transportation Co., 424 U.S. 747, 96 S.Ct. 1251, 47 L.Ed.2d 444 (1976).

Frontiero v. Richardson, 411 U.S. 677, 93 S.Ct. 1764, 36 L.Ed.2d 583 (1973).

Fuentes v. Shevin, 407 U.S. 67, 92 S.Ct. 1983, 32 L.Ed.2d 556 (1972).

Fullilove v. Klutznick, 448 U.S. 448, 100 S.Ct. 2758, 65 L.Ed.2d 902 (1980).

F.W. Woolworth Co. v. Taxation and Revenue Department of New Mexico, 458 U.S. 354, 102 S.Ct. 3128, 73 L.Ed.2d 819 (1982).

Gaffney v. Cummings, 412 U.S. 735, 93 S.Ct. 2321, 37 L.Ed.2d 298 (1973).

Gagnon v. Scarpelli, 411 U.S. 778, 93 S.Ct. 1756, 36 L.Ed.2d 656 (1973).

Gannett Co. v. DePasquale, 443 U.S. 368, 99 S.Ct. 2898, 61 L.Ed.2d 608 (1979).

Garcia v. San Antonio Metropolitan Transit Authority, 469 U.S. 528, 105 S.Ct. 1005, 83 L.Ed.2d 1016 (1985).

Garrison v. Louisiana, 379 U.S. 64, 85 S.Ct. 209, 13 L.Ed.2d 125 (1964).

Geduldig v. Aiello, 417 U.S. 484, 94 S.Ct. 2485, 41 L.Ed.2d 256 (1974).

Geer v. Connecticut, 161 U.S. 519, 16 S.Ct. 600, 40 L.Ed. 793 (1896).

General Electric Co. v. Gilbert, 429 U.S. 125, 97 S.Ct. 401, 50 L.Ed.2d 343 (1976).

General Motors Corp. v. District of Columbia, 380 U.S. 553, 85 S.Ct. 1156, 14 L.Ed.2d 68 (1965).

General Motors Corp. v. Washington, 377 U.S. 436, 84 S.Ct. 1564, 12 L.Ed.2d 430 (1964).

Gertz v. Robert Welch, Inc., 418 U.S. 323, 94 S.Ct. 2997, 41 L.Ed.2d 789 (1974).

Gibbons v. Ogden, 22 U.S. (9 Wheat.) 1, 6 L.Ed. 23 (1824).

Gibson v. Berryhill, 411 U.S. 564, 93 S.Ct. 1689, 36 L.Ed.2d 488 (1973).

Gideon v. Wainwright, 372 U.S. 335, 83 S.Ct. 792, 9 L.Ed.2d 799 (1963).

Gillette v. United States, 401 U.S. 437, 91 S.Ct. 828, 28 L.Ed.2d 168 (1971).

Gilligan v., Morgan, 413 U.S. 1, 93 S.Ct. 2440, 37 L.Ed.2d 407 (1973).

Gitlow v. New York, 268 U.S. 652, 45 S.Ct. 625, 69 L.Ed. 1138 (1925).

Glidden Co. v. Zdanok, 370 U.S. 530, 82 S.Ct. 1459, 8 L.Ed.2d 671 (1962).

Globe Newspaper Co. v. Superior Court of Norfolk County, 457 U.S. 596, 102 S.Ct. 2613, 73 L.Ed.2d 248 (1982).

Goesaert v. Cleary, 335 U.S. 464, 69 S.Ct. 198, 93 L.Ed. 163 (1948).

Goldberg v. Kelly, 397 U.S. 254, 90 S.Ct. 1011, 25 L.Ed.2d 287 (1970).

Golden State Transit Corp. v. City of Los Angeles, 475 U.S. 608, 106 S.Ct. 1395, 89 L.Ed.2d 616 (1986).

Goldman v. Weinberger, 475 U.S. 503, 106 S.Ct. 1310, 89 L.Ed.2d 478 (1986).

Goldstein v. California, 412 U.S. 546, 93 S.Ct. 2303, 37 L.Ed.2d 163 (1973).

Goldwater v. Carter, 444 U.S. 996, 100 S.Ct. 533, 62 L.Ed.2d 428 (1979).

Gomillion v. Lightfoot, 364 U.S. 339, 81 S.Ct. 125, 5 L.Ed.2d 110 (1960).

Goss v. Board of Education, 373 U.S. 683, 83 S.Ct. 1405, 10 L.Ed.2d 632 (1963).

Goss v. Lopez, 419 U.S. 565, 95 S.Ct. 729, 42 L.Ed.2d 725 (1975).

Grace, United States v., 461 U.S. 171, 103 S.Ct. 1702, 75 L.Ed.2d 736 (1983).

Graham v. Richardson, 403 U.S. 365, 91 S.Ct. 1848, 29 L.Ed.2d 534 (1971).

Grand Rapids School District v. Ball, 473 U.S. 373, 105 S.Ct. 3216, 87 L.Ed.2d 267 (1985).

Gray v. Sanders, 372 U.S. 368, 83 S.Ct. 801, 9 L.Ed.2d 821 (1963).

Green, California v., 399 U.S. 149, 90 S.Ct. 1930, 26 L.Ed.2d 489 (1970).

Green v. County School Board, 391 U.S. 430, 88 S.Ct. 1689, 20 L.Ed.2d 716 (1968).

Greene v. Lindsey, 456 U.S. 444, 102 S.Ct. 1874, 72 L.Ed.2d 249 (1982).

Greenholtz v. Inmates of the Nebraska Penal and Correctional Complex, 442 U.S. 1, 99 S.Ct. 2100, 60 L.Ed.2d 668 (1979).

Griffin v. Breckenridge, 403 U.S. 88, 91 S.Ct. 1790, 29 L.Ed.2d 338 (1971).

Griffin v. County School Board of Prince Edward County, 377 U.S. 218, 84 S.Ct. 1226, 12 L.Ed.2d 256 (1964).

Griffin v. Illinois, 351 U.S. 12, 76 S.Ct. 585, 100 L.Ed. 891 (1956).

Griffiths, In re, 413 U.S. 717, 93 S.Ct. 2851, 37 L.Ed.2d 910 (1973).

Griswald v. Connecticut, 381 U.S. 479, 85 S.Ct. 1678, 14 L.Ed.2d 510 (1965).

Guest, United States v., 383 U.S. 745, 86 S.Ct. 1170, 16 L.Ed.2d 239 (1966).

Hadley v. Junior College District, 397 U.S. 50, 90 S.Ct. 791, 25 L.Ed.2d 45 (1970).

Hague v. CIO, 307 U.S. 496, 59 S.Ct. 954, 83 L.Ed. 1423 (1939).

Haig v. Agee, 453 U.S. 280, 101 S.Ct. 2766, 69 L.Ed.2d 640 (1981).

Hale v. Bimco Trading, 306 U.S. 375, 59 S.Ct. 526, 83 L.Ed. 771 (1939).

Hall v. De Cuir, 95 U.S. (5 Otto) 485, 24 L.Ed. 547 (1877).

Hampton v. Mow Sun Wong, 426 U.S. 88, 96 S.Ct. 1895, 48 L.Ed.2d 495 (1976).

Hans v. Louisiana, 134 U.S. 1, 10 S.Ct. 504, 33 L.Ed. 842 (1890).

Harisiades v. Shaughnessy, 342 U.S. 580, 72 S.Ct. 512, 96 L.Ed. 586 (1952).

Harper v. Virginia State Board of Elections, 383 U.S. 663, 86 S.Ct. 1079, 16 L.Ed.2d 169 (1966).

Harris v. McRae, 448 U.S. 297, 100 S.Ct. 2671, 65 L.Ed.2d 784 (1980).

Hayburn's Case, 2 U.S. (2 Dall.) 409, 1 L.Ed. 436 (1792).

Head v. New Mexico Board of Examiners, 374 U.S. 424, 83 S.Ct. 1759, 10 L.Ed.2d 983 (1963).

Heart of Atlanta Motel v. United States, 379 U.S. 241, 85 S.Ct. 348, 13 L.Ed.2d 258 (1964).

Heffron v. International Society for Krishna Consciousness, Inc., 452 U.S. 640, 101 S.Ct. 2559, 69 L.Ed.2d 298 (1981).

Heim v. McCall, 239 U.S. 175, 36 S.Ct. 78, 60 L.Ed. 206 (1915).

Helvering v. Clifford, 309 U.S. 331, 60 S.Ct. 554, 84 L.Ed. 788 (1940).

Helvering v. Gerhardt, 304 U.S. 405, 58 S.Ct. 969, 82 L.Ed. 1427 (1938).

Henneford v. Silas Mason Co., 300 U.S. 577, 57 S.Ct. 524, 81 L.Ed. 814 (1937).

Henry v. Mississippi, 379 U.S. 443, 85 S.Ct. 564, 13 L.Ed.2d 408 (1965).

Herbert v. Lando, 441 U.S. 153, 99 S.Ct. 1635, 60 L.Ed.2d 115 (1979).

Hess v. Indiana, 414 U.S. 105, 94 S.Ct. 326, 38 L.Ed.2d 303 (1973).

Hewitt v. Helms, 459 U.S. 460, 103 S.Ct. 864, 74 L.Ed.2d 675 (1983).

Hicklin v. Orbeck, 437 U.S. 518, 98 S.Ct. 2482, 57 L.Ed.2d 397 (1978).

Hills v. Gautreaux, 425 U.S. 284, 96 S.Ct. 1538, 47 L.Ed.2d 792 (1976).

Hines v. Davidowitz, 312 U.S. 52, 61 S.Ct. 399, 85 L.Ed. 581 (1941).

Hisquierdo v. Hisquierdo, 439 U.S. 572, 99 S.Ct. 802, 59 L.Ed.2d 1 (1979).

Hobbie v. Unemployment Appeals Comm'n of Florida, 480 U.S. 136, 107 S.Ct. 1046, 94 L.Ed.2d 190 (1987).

Hodel v. Virginia Surface Mining and Reclamation Ass'n, Inc., 452 U.S. 264, 101 S.Ct. 2352, 69 L.Ed.2d 1 (1981).

Hodges v. United States, 203 U.S. 1, 27 S.Ct. 6, 51 L.Ed. 65 (1906).

Holden v. Hardy, 169 U.S. 366, 18 S.Ct. 383, 42 L.Ed. 780 (1898).

Holt Civic Club v. Tuscaloosa, 439 U.S. 60, 99 S.Ct. 383, 58 L.Ed.2d 292 (1978).

Hood & Sons, H.P. v. Du Mond, 336 U.S. 525, 69 S.Ct. 657, 93 L.Ed.865 (1949).

Hooper v. Bernalillo County Assessor, 472 U.S. 612, 105 S.Ct. 2862, 86 L.Ed.2d 487 (1985).

Houchins v. KQED, Inc., 438 U.S. 1, 98 S.Ct. 2588, 57 L.Ed.2d 553 (1978).

Hoyt v. Florida, 368 U.S. 57, 82 S.Ct. 159, 7 L.Ed.2d 118 (1961).

Hudgens v. National Labor Relations Board, 424 U.S. 507, 96 S.Ct. l029, 47 L.Ed.2d 196 (1976).

Hudson v. Palmer, 468 U.S. 517, 104 S.Ct. 3194, 82 L.Ed.2d 393 (1984).

Hughes v. Alexandria Scrap Corp., 426 U.S. 794, 96 S.Ct. 2488, 49 L.Ed.2d 220 (1976).

Hughes v. Oklahoma, 441 U.S. 322, 99 S.Ct. 1727, 60 L.Ed.2d 250 (1979).

Hunt v. Washington State Apple Advertising Comm'n, 432 U.S. 333, 97 S.Ct. 2434, 53 L.Ed.2d 383 (1977).

Hunter v. Erickson, 393 U.S. 385, 89 S.Ct. 557, 21 L.Ed.2d 616 (1969).

Hunter v. Underwood, 471 U.S. 222, 105 S.Ct. 1916, 85 L.Ed.2d 222 (1985).

Huron Cement Co. v. Detroit, 362 U.S. 440, 80 S.Ct. 813, 4 L.Ed.2d 852 (1960).

Hurtado v. California, 110 U.S. 516, 4 S.Ct. 111, 28 L.Ed. 232 (1884).

Hutchinson v. Proxmire, 443 U.S. 111, 99 S.Ct. 2675, 61 L.Ed.2d 411 (1979).

Hutto v. Finney, 437 U.S. 678, 98 S.Ct. 2565, 57 L.Ed.2d 522 (1978).

Illinois v. Allen, 397 U.S. 337, 90 S.Ct. 1057, 25 L.Ed.2d 353 (1970).

Illinois v. Gates, 462 U.S. 213, 103 S.Ct. 2317, 76 L.Ed.2d 527 (1983).

Illinois ex rel. McCollum v. Board of Education, 333 U.S. 203, 68 S.Ct. 461, 92 L.Ed. 649 (1948).

Illinois State Board of Elections v. Socialist Workers Party, 440 U.S. 173, 99 S.Ct. 983, 59 L.Ed.2d 230 (1979).

Immigration and Naturalization Service v. Chadha, 462 U.S. 919, 103 S.Ct. 2764, 77 L.Ed.2d 317 (1983).

Ingraham v. Wright, 430 U.S. 651, 97 S.Ct. 1401, 51 L.Ed.2d 711 (1977).

Innis, Rhode Island v., 446 U.S. 291, 100 S.Ct. 1682, 64 L.Ed.2d 297 (1980).

Insurance Corporation of Ireland v. Compagnie des Bauxites de Guinee, 456 U.S. 694, 102 S.Ct. 2099, 72 L.Ed.2d 492 (1982).

International Harvester Co. v. Department of Treasury, 322 U.S. 340, 64 S.Ct. 1019, 88 L.Ed. 1313 (1944).

Jackson v. Metropolitan Edison Co., 419 U.S. 345, 95 S.Ct. 449, 42 L.Ed.2d 477 (1974).

Jago v. Van Curen, 454 U.S. 14, 102 S.Ct. 31, 70 L.Ed.2d 13 (1981).

James v. Dravo Contracting Co., 302 U.S. 134, 58 S.Ct. 208, 82 L.Ed. 155 (1937).

James v. Valtierra, 402 U.S. 137, 91 S.Ct. 1331, 28 L.Ed.2d 678 (1971).

Japan Line, Ltd. v. County of Los Angeles, 441 U.S. 434, 99 S.Ct. 1813, 60 L.Ed.2d 336 (1979).

Jefferson v. Hackney, 406 U.S. 535, 92 S.Ct. 1724, 32 L.Ed.2d 285 (1972).

Jenness v. Fortson, 403 U.S. 431, 91 S.Ct. 1970, 29 L.Ed.2d 554 (1971).

Johnson v. Transportation Agency, Santa Clara County, 480 U.S. 616, 107 S.Ct. 1442, 94 L.Ed.2d 615 (1987).

Johnson, United States v., 319 U.S. 302, 63 S.Ct. 1075, 87 L.Ed. 1413 (1943).

Joint Anti-Fascist Refugee Committee v. McGrath, 341 U.S. 123, 71 S.Ct. 624, 95 L.Ed. 817 (1951).

Jones v. Alfred H. Mayer Co., 392 U.S. 409, 88 S.Ct. 2186, 20 L.Ed.2d 1189 (1968).,

Jones v. Rath Packing Co., 430 U.S. 519, 97 S.Ct. 1305, 51 L.Ed.2d 604 (1977).

Jones v. Wolf, 443 U.S. 595, 99 S.Ct. 3020, 61 L.Ed.2d 775 (1979).

Kahn v. Shevin, 416 U.S. 351, 94 S.Ct. 1734, 40 L.Ed.2d 189 (1974).

Kaiser Aetna v. United States, 444 U.S. 164, 100 S.Ct. 383, 62 L.Ed.2d 332 (1979).

Karcher v. Daggett, 462 U.S. 725, 103 S.Ct. 2653, 77 L.Ed.2d 133 (1983).

Kassel v. Consolidated Freightways Corp. of Delaware, 450 U.S. 662, 101 S.Ct. 1309, 67 L.Ed.2d 580 (1981).

Katz v. United States, 389 U.S. 347, 88 S.Ct. 507, 19 L.Ed.2d 576 (1967).

Katzenbach v. Morgan, 384 U.S. 641, 86 S.Ct. 1717, 16 L.Ed.2d 828 (1966).

Kedroff v. St. Nicholas Cathedral, 344 U.S. 94, 73 S.Ct. 143, 97 L.Ed. 120 (1952).

Kelley v. Johnson, 425 U.S. 238, 96 S.Ct. 1440, 47 L.Ed.2d 708 (1976).

Kendall v. United States, 37 U.S. (12 Pet.) 524, 9 L.Ed. 1181 (1838).

Kent v. Dulles, 357 U.S. 116, 78 S.Ct. 1113, 2 L.Ed.2d 1204 (1958).

Kern County Land Co. v. Occidental Petroleum Corp., 411 U.S. 582, 93 S.Ct. 1736, 36 L.Ed.2d 503 (1973).

Kern-Limerick, Inc. v. Scurlock, 347 U.S. 110, 74 S.Ct. 403, 98 L.Ed. 546 (1954).

Keyes v. School District No. 1, 413 U.S. 189, 93 S.Ct. 2686, 37 L.Ed.2d 548 (1973).

Kilbourn v. Thompson, 103 U.S. (13 Otto) 168, 26 LEd. 377 (1881).

Kirby v. Illinois, 406 U.S. 682, 92 S.Ct. 1877, 32 L.Ed.2d 411 (1972).

Kirchberg v. Feenstra, 450 U.S. 455, 101 S.Ct. 1195, 67 L.Ed.2d 428 (1981).

Kirkpatrick v. Preisler, 394 U.S. 526, 89 S.Ct. 1225, 22 L.Ed.2d 519 (1969).

Klein, United States v., 80 U.S. (13 Wall.) 128, 20 L.Ed. 519 (1871).

Kleppe v. New Mexico, 426 U.S. 529, 96 S.Ct. 2285, 49 L.Ed.2d 34 (1976).

Korematsu v. United States, 323 U.S. 214, 65 S.Ct. 193, 89 L.Ed. 194 (1944).

Kotch v. Board of River Port Pilot Commissioners, 330 U.S. 552, 67 S.Ct. 910, 91 L.Ed. 1093 (1947).

Kramer v. Union Free School District No. 15, 395
U.S. 621, 89 S.Ct. 1886, 23 L.Ed.2d 583 (1969).

Kras, United States v., 409 U.S. 434, 93 S.Ct. 631, 34
L.Ed.2d 626 (1973).

Kusper v. Pontikes, 414 U.S. 51, 94 S.Ct. 303, 38
L.Ed.2d 260 (1973).

Labine v. Vincent, 401 U.S. 532, 91 S.Ct. 1017, 28
L.Ed.2d 288 (1971).

Laird v. Tatum, 408 U.S. 1, 92 S.Ct. 2318, 33 L.Ed.2d
154 (1972).

Lalli v. Lalli, 439 U.S. 259, 99 S.Ct. 518, 58 L.Ed.2d 503
(1978).

Landmark Communications, Inc. v. Virginia, 435
U.S. 829, 98 S.Ct. 1535, 56 L.Ed.2d 1 (1978).

Larkin v. Grendel's Den, Inc., 459 U.S. 116, 103 S.Ct.
505, 74 L.Ed.2d 297 (1982).

Larson v. Valente, 456 U.S. 228, 102 S.Ct. 1673, 72
L.Ed.2d 33 (1982).

Lassiter v. Dept. of Social Services, 452 U.S. 18, 101
S.Ct. 2153, 68 L.Ed.2d 640 (1981).

Lassiter v. Northhampton Board of Elections, 360
U.S. 45, 79 S.Ct. 985, 3 L.Ed.2d 1072 (1959).

Lawrence v. State Tax Comm'n, 286 U.S. 276, 52
S.Ct. 556, 76 L.Ed. 1102 (1932).

***Law Students Civil Rights Research Council v.
Wadmond,*** 401 U.S. 154, 91 S.Ct. 720, 27 L.Ed.2d
749 (1971).

Lee, United States v., 455 U.S. 252, 102 S.Ct. 1051, 71
L.Ed.2d 127 (1982).

Leis v. Flynt, 439 U.S. 438, 99 S.Ct. 698, 58 L.Ed.2d 717
(1979).

Leisy v. Hardin, 135 U.S. 100, 10 S.Ct. 681, 34 L.Ed.
128 (1890).

Lemke v. Farmers' Grain Co., 258 U.S. 50, 42 S.Ct.
244, 66 L.Ed. 458 (1922).

Lemon v. Kurtzman, 403 U.S. 602, 91 S.Ct. 2105, 29
L.Ed.2d 745 (1971).

Leslie Miller, Inc. v. Arkansas, 352 U.S. 187, 77 S.Ct.
257, 1 L.Ed.2d 231 (1956).

Levin v. Mississippi River Fuel Corp., 386 U.S. 162,

87 S.Ct. 927, 17 L.Ed.2d 834 (1967).

Levy v. Louisiana, 391 U.S. 68, 88 S.Ct. 1509, 20
L.Ed.2d 436 (1968).

Lewis v. BT Investment Managers, Inc., 447 U.S. 27,
100 S.Ct. 2009, 64 L.Ed.2d 702 (1980).

Lewis v. United States, 146 U.S. 370, 13 S.Ct. 136, 36
L.Ed. 1011 (1892).

Lindsey v. Normet, 405 U.S. 56, 92 S.Ct. 862, 31
L.Ed.2d 36 (1972).

Linn v. United Plant Guard Workers, Local 114,
383 U.S. 53, 86 S.Ct. 657, 15 L.Ed.2d 582 (1966).

Little v. Streater, 452 U.S. 1, 101 S.Ct. 2202, 68
L.Ed.2d 627 (1981).

Lloyd Corp. v. Tanner, 407 U.S. 551, 92 S.Ct. 2219, 33
L.Ed.2d 131 (1972).

***Local 28 of the Sheet Metal Workers' Inter-
national Ass'n v. Equal Employment Opportunity Commission,*** 478 U.S. 421, 106 S.Ct. 3019,
92 L.Ed.2d 344 (1986).

***Local No. 93, International Association of Fire-
fighters v. Cleveland,*** 478 U.S. 501, 106 S.Ct.
3063, 92 L.Ed.2d 405 (1986).

Lochner v. New York, 198 U.S. 45, 25 S.Ct. 539, 49
L.Ed. 937 (1905).

Loretto v. Teleprompter Manhattan CATV Corp.,
458 U.S. 419, 102 S.Ct. 3164, 73 L.Ed.2d 868
(1982).

Los Angeles, City of v. Lyons, 461 U.S. 95, 103 S.Ct.
1660, 75 L.Ed.2d 675 (1983).

Los Angeles, County of v. Davis, 440 U.S. 625, 99
S.Ct. 1379, 59 L.Ed.2d 642 (1979).

Louisiana Public Service Comm'n v. FCC, 476 U.S.
355, 106 S.Ct. 1890, 90 L.Ed.2d 369 (1986).

Lovett, United States v., 328 U.S. 303, 66 S.Ct. 1073,
90 L.Ed. 1252 (1946).

Loving v. Virginia, 388 U.S. 1, 87 S.Ct. 1817, 18
L.Ed.2d 1010 (1967).

Lubin v. Panish, 415 U.S. 709, 94 S.Ct. 1315, 39
L.Ed.2d 702 (1974).

Lucas v. Earl, 281 U.S. 111, 50 S.Ct. 241, 74 L.Ed. 731
(1930).

***Lucas v. Forty-Fourth Colorado General Assem-
bly,*** 377 U.S. 713, 84 S.Ct. 1459, 12 L.Ed.2d 632
(1964).

Luther v. Borden, 48 U.S. (7 How.) 1, 12 L.Ed. 581
(1849).

Lynch v. Donnelly, 465 U.S. 668, 104 S.Ct. 1355, 79
L.Ed.2d 604 (1984).

Lyng v. Castillo, 477 U.S. 635, 106 S.Ct. 2727, 91
L.Ed.2d 527 (1986).

Madden v. Kentucky, 309 U.S. 83, 60 S.Ct. 406, 84 L.Ed. 590 (1940).

Mahan v. Howell, 410 U.S. 315, 93 S.Ct. 979, 35 L.Ed.2d 320 (1973).

Maher v. Roe, 432 U.S. 464, 97 S.Ct. 2376, 53 L.Ed.2d 484 (1977).

Maine v. Taylor, 477 U.S. 131, 106 S.Ct. 2440, 91 L.Ed.2d 110 (1986).

Mancusi v. Stubbs, 408 U.S. 204, 92 S.Ct. 2308, 33 L.Ed.2d 293 (1972).

Manual Enterprises, Inc. v. Day, 370 U.S. 478, 82 S.Ct. 1432, 8 L.Ed.2d 639 (1962).

Mapp v. Ohio, 367 U.S. 643, 81 S.Ct. 1684, 6 L.Ed.2d 1081 (1961).

Marbury v. Madison, 5 U.S. (1 Cranch.) 137, 2 L.Ed. 60 (1803).

Marchioro v. Chaney, 442 U.S. 191, 99 S.Ct. 2243, 60 L.Ed.2d 816 (1979).

Marsh v. Alabama, 326 U.S. 501, 66 S.Ct. 276, 90 L.Ed. 265 (1946).

Marsh v. Chambers, 463 U.S. 783, 103 S.Ct. 3330, 77 L.Ed.2d 1019 (1983).

Marshall v. Jerrico, Inc., 446 U.S. 238, 100 S.Ct. 1610, 64 L.Ed.2d 182 (1980).

Martin v. Hunter's Lessee, 14 U.S. (1 Wheat.) 304, 4 L.Ed. 97 (1816).

Martinez v. Bynum, 461 U.S. 321, 103 S.Ct. 1838, 75 L.Ed.2d 879 (1983).

Martinez v. California, 444 U.S. 277, 100 S.Ct. 553, 62 L.Ed.2d 481 (1980).

Maryland v. Louisiana, 451 U.S. 725, 101 S.Ct. 2114, 68 L.Ed.2d 576 (1981).

Maryland v. Wirtz, 392 U.S. 183, 88 S.Ct. 2017, 20 L.Ed.2d 1020 (1968).

Maryland Committee for Fair Representation v. Tawes, 377 U.S. 656, 84 S.Ct. 1429, 12 L.Ed.2d 595 (1964).

Massachusetts Board of Retirement v. Murgia, 427 U.S. 307, 96 S.Ct. 2562, 49 L.Ed.2d 520 (1976).

Massiah v. United States, 377 U.S. 201, 84 S.Ct. 1199, 12 L.Ed.2d 246 (1964).

Mathews v. Diaz, 426 U.S. 67, 96 S.Ct. 1883, 48 L.Ed.2d 478 (1976).

Mathews v. Eldridge, 424 U.S. 319, 96 S.Ct. 893, 47 L.Ed.2d 18 (1976).

McCardle, Ex Parte, 74 U.S. (7 Wall.) 506, 19 L.Ed. 264 (1868).

McCready v. Virginia, 94 U.S. (4 Otto) 391, 24 L.Ed. 248 (1877).

McCulloch v. Maryland, 17 U.S. (4 Wheat.) 316, 4 L.Ed. 579 (1819).

McDaniel v. Paty, 435 U.S. 618, 98 S.Ct. 1322, 55 L.Ed.2d 593 (1978).

McGoldrick v. Berwind-White Coal Mining Co., 309 U.S. 33, 60 S.Ct. 388, 84 L.Ed. 565 (1940).

McGowan v. Maryland, 366 U.S. 420, 81 S.Ct. 1101, 6 L.Ed.2d 393 (1961).

McLeod v. J.E. Dilworth Co., 322 U.S. 327, 64 S.Ct. 1023, 88 L.Ed. 1304 (1944).

Meachum v. Fano, 427 U.S. 215, 96 S.Ct. 2532, 49 L.Ed.2d 451 (1976).

Meese v. Keene, 481 U.S. 465, 107 S.Ct. 1862, 95 L.Ed.2d 415 (1987).

Memorial Hospital v. Maricopa County, 415 U.S. 250, 94 S.Ct. 1076, 39 L.Ed.2d 306 (1974).

Memphis v. Greene, 451 U.S. 100, 101 S.Ct. 1584, 67 L.Ed.2d 769 (1981).

Memphis Light, Gas and Water Division v. Craft, 436 U.S. 1, 98 S.Ct. 1554, 56 L.Ed.2d 30 (1978).

Mendoza, United States v., 464 U.S. 154, 104 S.Ct. 568, 78 L.Ed.2d 379 (1984).

Mennonite Board of Missions v. Adams, 462 U.S. 791, 103 S.Ct. 2706, 77 L.Ed.2d 180 (1983).

Meyer v. Nebraska, 262 U.S. 390, 43 S.Ct. 625, 67 L.Ed. 1042 (1923).

Miami Herald Publishing Co. v. Tornillo, 418 U.S. 241, 94 S.Ct. 2831, 41 L.Ed.2d 730 (1974).

Michelin Tire Corp. v. Wages, 423 U.S. 276, 96 S.Ct. 535, 46 L.Ed.2d 495 (1976).

Michigan v. Long, 463 U.S. 1032, 103 S.Ct. 3469, 77 L.Ed.2d 1201 (1983).

Michigan v. Summers, 452 U.S. 692, 101 S.Ct. 2587, 69 L.Ed.2d 340 (1981).

Middendorf v. Henry, 425 U.S. 25, 96 S.Ct. 1281, 47 L.Ed.2d 556 (1976).

Milk Control Board v. Eisenberg Farm Products, 306 U.S. 346, 59 S.Ct. 528, 83 L.Ed. 752 (1939).

Miller v. California, 413 U.S. 15, 93 S.Ct. 2607, 37 L.Ed.2d 419 (1973)

Miller v. Schoene, 276 U.S. 272, 48 S.Ct. 246, 72 L.Ed. 568 (1928).

Miller Bros., Co. v. Maryland, 347 U.S. 340, 74 S.Ct. 535, 98 L.Ed. 744 (1954).

Milliken v. Bradley, 418 U.S. 717, 94 S.Ct. 3112, 41 L.Ed.2d 1069 (1974).

Milliken v. Bradley (Milliken II), 433 U.S. 267, 97 S.Ct. 2749, 53 L.Ed.2d 745 (1977).

Mills v. Electric Auto-Lite Co., 396 U.S. 375, 90 S.Ct. 616, 24 L.Ed.2d 593 (1970).

Mills v. Habluetzel, 456 U.S. 91, 102 S.Ct. 1549, 71 L.Ed.2d 770 (1982).

Minneapolis Star and Tribune Co. v. Minnesota Commissioner of Revenue, 460 U.S. 575, 103 S.Ct. 1365, 75 L.Ed.2d 295 (1983).

Minnesota v. Blasius, 290 U.S. 1, 54 S.Ct. 34, 78 L.Ed. 131 (1933).

Minnesota v. Clover Leaf Creamery Co., 449 U.S. 456, 101 S.Ct. 715, 66 L.Ed.2d 659 (1981).

Miranda v. Arizona, 384 U.S. 436, 86 S.Ct. 1602, 16 L.Ed.2d 694 (1966).

Mississippi v. Johnson, 71 U.S. (4 Wall.) 475, 18 L.Ed. 437 (1866).

Mississippi University for Women v. Hogan, 458 U.S. 718, 102 S.Ct. 3331, 73 L.Ed.2d 1090 (1982).

Missouri v. Holland, 252 U.S. 416, 40 S.Ct. 382, 64 L.Ed. 641 (1920).

Mitchell v. W. T. Grant Co., 416 U.S. 600, 94 S.Ct. 1895, 40 L.Ed.2d 406 (1974).

Mobile v. Bolden, 446 U.S. 55, 100 S.Ct. 1490, 64 L.Ed.2d 47 (1980).

Monitor Patriot Co. v. Roy, 401 U.S. 265, 91 S.Ct. 621, 28 L.Ed.2d 35 (1971).

Moore v. City of East Cleveland, 431 U.S. 494, 97 S.Ct. 1932, 52 L.Ed.2d 531 (1977).

Moore v. Ogilvie, 394 U.S. 814, 89 S.Ct. 1493, 23 L.Ed.2d 1 (1969).

Moorman Manufacturing Co. v. Bair, 437 U.S. 267, 98 S.Ct. 2340, 57 L.Ed.2d 197 (1978).

Moose Lodge No. 107 v. Irvis, 407 U.S. 163, 92 S.Ct. 1965, 32 L.Ed.2d 627 (1972).

Mora v. McNamara, 389 U.S. 934, 88 S.Ct. 282, 19 L.Ed.2d 287 (1967).

Morehead v. New York ex rel Tipaldo, 298 U.S. 587, 56 S.Ct. 918, 80 L.Ed. 1347 (1936).

Morey v. Doud, 354 U.S. 457, 77 S.Ct. 1344, 1 L.Ed.2d 1485 (1957).

Mueller v. Allen, 463 U.S. 388, 103 S.Ct. 3062, 77 L.Ed.2d 721 (1983).

Muller v. Oregon, 208 U.S. 412, 28 S.Ct. 324, 52 L.Ed. 551 (1908).

Munro v. Socialist Workers Party, 479 U.S. 189, 107 S.Ct. 533, 93 L.Ed.2d 499 (1986).

Murdock v., City of Memphis, 87 U.S. (20 Wall.) 590, 22 L.Ed. 429 (1875).

Murdock v. Pennsylvania, 319 U.S. 105, 63 S.Ct. 870, 87 L.Ed. 1292 (1943).

Murray's Lessee v. Hoboken Land and Improvement Co., 59 U.S. (18 How.) 272, 15 L.Ed. 372 (1855).

Muskrat v. United States, 219 U.S. 346, 31 S.Ct. 250, 55 L.Ed. 246 (1911).

Myers v. United States, 272 U.S. 52, 47 S.Ct. 21, 71 L.Ed. 160 (1926).

NAACP v. Alabama ex rel. Patterson, 357 U.S. 449, 78 S.Ct. 1163, 2 L.Ed.2d 1488 (1958).

NAACP v. Button, 371 U.S. 415, 83 S.Ct. 328, 9 L.Ed.2d 405 (1963).

Naim v. Naim, 350 U.S. 891, 76 S.Ct. 151, 100 L.Ed. 784 (1955)

Namet v. United States, 373 U.S. 179, 83 S.Ct. 1151, 10 L.Ed.2d 278 (1963).

Nash v. Florida Industrial Comm'n, 389 U.S. 235, 88 S.Ct. 362, 19 L.Ed.2d 438 (1967).

Nashville Gas Co. v. Satty, 434 U.S. 136, 98 S.Ct. 347, 54 L.Ed.2d 356 (1977).

National Bellas Hess, Inc. v. Department of Revenue, 386 U.S. 753, 87 S.Ct. 1389, 18 L.Ed.2d 505 (1967).

National League of Cities v. Usery, 426 U.S. 833, 96 S.Ct. 2465, 49 L.Ed.2d 245 (1976).

Near v. Minnesota, 283 U.S. 697, 51 S.Ct. 625, 75 L.Ed. 1357 (1931).

Nebraska Press Ass'n v. Stuart, 427 U.S. 539, 96 S.Ct. 2791, 49 L.Ed.2d 683 (1976).

New Jersey Welfare Rights Organization v. Cahill, 411 U.S. 619, 93 S.Ct. 1700, 36 L.Ed.2d 543 (1973).

New Mexico v. Mescalero Apache Tribe, 462 U.S. 324, 103 S.Ct. 2378, 76 L.Ed.2d 611 (1983).

New Mexico, United States v., 455 U.S. 720, 102 S.Ct. 1373, 71 L.Ed.2d 580 (1982).

New Orleans, City of v. Dukes, 427 U.S. 297, 96 S.Ct. 2513, 49 L.Ed.2d 511 (1976).

New York v. Belton, 453 U.S. 454, 101 S.Ct. 2860, 69 L.Ed.2d 768 (1981).

New York v. Ferber, 458 U.S. 747, 102 S.Ct. 3348, 73 L.Ed.2d 1113 (1982).

New York v. Miln, 36 U.S. (11 Pet.) 102, 9 L.Ed. 648 (1837).

New York v. United States, 326 U.S. 572, 66 S.Ct. 310, 90 L.Ed. 326 (1946).

New York State Department of Social Services v. Dublino, 413 U.S. 405, 93 S.Ct. 2507, 37 L.Ed.2d 688 (1973).

New York Times Co. v. Sullivan, 376 U.S. 254, 84 S.Ct. 710, 11 L.Ed.2d 686 (1964).

New York Times Co. v. United States, 403 U.S. 713, 91 S.Ct. 2140, 29 L.Ed.2d 822 (1971).

Nippert v. City of Richmond, 327 U.S. 416, 66 S.Ct. 586, 90 L.Ed. 760 (1946).

Nixon v. Administrator of General Services, 433 U.S. 425, 97 S.Ct. 2777, 53 L.Ed.2d 867 (1977).

Nixon v. Herndon, 273 U.S. 536, 47 S.Ct. 446, 71 L.Ed. 759 (1927).

Nixon, United States v., 418 U.S. 683, 94 S.Ct. 3090, 41 L.Ed.2d 1039 (1974).

NLRB v. Jones & Laughlin Steel Corp., 301 U.S. 1, 57 S.Ct. 615, 81 L.Ed. 893 (1937).

Nollan v. California Coastal Commission, 483 U.S. 825, 107 S.Ct. 3141, 97 L.Ed.2d 677 (1987).

Northeast Bancorp, Inc. v. Board of Governors of the Federal Reserve System, 472 U.S. 159, 105 S.Ct. 2545, 86 L.Ed.2d 112 (1985).

Northern Pipeline Construction Co. v. Marathon Pipe Line Co., 458 U.S. 50, 102 S.Ct. 2858, 73 L.Ed.2d 598 (1982).

North Georgia Finishing, Inc. v. Di-Chem, 419 U.S. 601, 95 S.Ct. 719, 42 L.Ed.2d 751 (1975).

Northwest Airlines v. Minnesota, 322 U.S. 292, 64 S.Ct. 950, 88 L.Ed. 1283 (1944).

Northwestern States Portland Cement Co. v. Minnesota, 358 U.S. 450, 79 S.Ct. 357, 3 L.Ed.2d 421 (1959).

Norwood v. Harrison, 413 U.S. 455, 93 S.Ct. 2804, 37 L.Ed.2d 723 (1973).

Nyquist v. Mauclet, 432 U.S. 1, 97 S.Ct. 2120, 53 L.Ed.2d 63 (1977).

O'Bannon v. Town Court Nursing Center, 447 U.S. 773, 100 S.Ct. 2467, 65 L.Ed.2d 506 (1980).

O'Brien, United States v., 391 U.S. 367, 88 S.Ct. 1673, 20 L.Ed.2d 672 (1968).

O'Conner v. Donaldson, 422 U.S. 563, 95 S.Ct. 2486, 45 L.Ed.2d 396 (1975).

Ogden v. Saunders, 25 U.S. (12 Wheat.) 213, 6 L.Ed. 606 (1827).

Ohio v. Roberts, 448 U.S. 56, 100 S.Ct. 2531, 65 L.Ed.2d 597 (1980).

Ohralik v. Ohio State Bar, 436 U.S. 447, 98 S.Ct. 1912, 56 L.Ed.2d 444 (1978).

Old Colony Trust Co. v. Commissioner of Internal Revenue, 279 U.S. 716, 49 S.Ct. 499, 73 L.Ed. 918 (1929).

Oliver, In re, 333 U.S. 257, 68 S.Ct. 499, 92 L.Ed. 682 (1948).

Olmstead v. United States, 277 U.S. 438, 48 S.Ct. 564, 72 L.Ed. 944 (1928).

O'Lone v. Estate of Shabazz, 482 U.S. 342, 107 S.Ct. 2400, 96 L.Ed.2d 282 (1987).

Oregon v. Hass, 420 U.S. 714, 95 S.Ct. 1215, 43 L.Ed.2d 570 (1975).

Orito, United States v., 413 U.S. 139, 93 S.Ct. 2674, 37 L.Ed.2d 513 (1973).

Orr v. Orr, 440 U.S. 268, 99 S.Ct. 1102, 59 L.Ed.2d 306 (1979).

O'Shea v. Littleton, 414 U.S. 488, 94 S.Ct. 669, 38 L.Ed.2d 674 (1974).

Oyama v. California, 332 U.S. 633, 68 S.Ct. 269, 92 L.Ed. 249 (1948).

Pacific Gas and Electric Co. v. Public Utilities Comm'n, 475 U.S. 1, 106 S.Ct 903, 89 L.Ed.2d 1 (1986).

Pacific Gas and Electric Co. v. State Energy Resources Conservation and Development Comm'n, 461 U.S. 190, 103 S.Ct. 1713, 75 L.Ed.2d 752 (1983).

Pacific States Telephone and Telegraph Co. v. Oregon, 223 U.S. 118, 32 S.Ct. 224, 56 L.Ed. 377 (1912).

Palko v. Connecticut, 302 U.S. 319, 58 S.Ct. 149, 82 L.Ed. 288 (1937).

Palmer v. Thompson, 403 U.S. 217, 91 S.Ct. 1940, 29 L.Ed.2d 438 (1971).

Palmore v. Sidoti, 466 U.S. 429, 104 S.Ct. 1879, 80 L.Ed.2d 421 (1984).

Panama Refining Co. v. Ryan, 293 U.S. 388, 55 S.Ct. 241, 79 L.Ed. 446 (1935).

Parden v. Terminal Railway Co., 377 U.S. 184, 84 S.Ct. 1207, 12 L.Ed.2d 233 (1964).

Parham v. Hughes, 441 U.S. 347, 99 S.Ct. 1742, 60 L.Ed.2d 269 (1979).

Paris Adult Theater I v. Slaton, 413 U.S. 49, 93 S.Ct. 2628, 37 L.Ed.2d 446 (1973).

Parker v. Brown, 317 U.S. 341, 63 S.Ct. 307, 87 L.Ed. 315 (1943).

Parratt v. Taylor, 451 U.S. 527, 101 S.Ct. 1908, 68 L.Ed.2d 420 (1981).

Pasadena Board of Education v. Spangler, 427 U.S. 424, 96 S.Ct. 2697, 49 L.Ed.2d 599 (1976).

Paul v. Davis, 424 U.S. 693, 96 S.Ct. 1155, 47 L.Ed.2d 405 (1976).

Paul v. United States, 371 U.S. 245, 83 S.Ct. 426, 9 L.Ed.2d 292 (1963).

Paul v. Virginia, 75 U.S. (8 Wall.) 168, 19 L.Ed. 357 (1869).

Penn Central Transportation Co. v. City of New York, 438 U.S. 104, 98 S.Ct. 2646, 57 L.Ed.2d 631 (1978).

Pennhurst State School and Hospital v. Halderman, 465 U.S. 89, 104 S.Ct. 900, 79 L.Ed.2d 67 (1984).

Pennsylvania v. Board of Directors of City Trusts of Philadelphia, 353 U.S. 230, 77 S.Ct. 806, 1 L.Ed.2d 792 (1957).

Pennsylvania v. Nelson, 350 U.S. 497, 76 S.Ct. 477, 100 L.Ed. 640 (1956).

Pennsylvania Coal Co. v. Mahon, 260 U.S. 393, 43 S.Ct. 158, 67 L.Ed. 322 (1922).

Pension Benefit Guaranty Corp. v. R.A. Gray & Co., 467 U.S. 717, 104 S.Ct. 2709, 81 L.Ed.2d 601 (1984).

Pentagon Papers Case, 403 U.S. 713, 91 S.Ct. 2140, 29 L.Ed.2d 822 (1971).

Perez v. United States, 402 U.S. 146, 91 S.Ct. 1357, 28 L.Ed.2d 686 (1971).

Perry v. Sindermann, 408 U.S. 593, 92 S.Ct. 2694, 33 L.Ed.2d 570 (1972).

Personnel Administrator of Massachusetts v. Feeney, 442 U.S. 256, 99 S.Ct. 2282, 60 L.Ed.2d 870 (1979).

Phoenix v. Kolodziejski, 399 U.S. 204, 90 S.Ct. 1990, 26 L.Ed.2d 523 (1970).

Pickering v. Board of Education, 391 U.S. 563, 88 S.Ct. 1731, 20 L.Ed.2d 811 (1968).

Pickett v. Brown, 462 U.S. 1, 103 S.Ct. 2199, 76 L.Ed.2d 372 (1983).

Pierce v. Society of Sisters, 268 U.S. 510, 45 S.Ct. 571, 69 L.Ed. 1070 (1925).

Pike v. Bruce Church, Inc., 397 U.S. 137, 90 S.Ct. 844, 25 L.Ed.2d 174 (1970).

Pinkus v. United States, 436 U.S. 293, 98 S.Ct. 1808, 56 L.Ed.2d 293 (1978).

Piper v. Chris-Craft Industries, Inc., 430 U.S. 1, 97 S.Ct. 926, 51 L.Ed.2d 124 (1977).

Pittsburg Press Co. v. Pittsburg Comm'n on Human Relations, 413 U.S. 376, 93 S.Ct. 2553, 37 L.Ed.2d 669 (1973).

Planned Parenthood of Central Missouri v. Danforth, 428 U.S. 52, 96 S.Ct. 2831, 49 L.Ed.2d 788 (1976).

Plessy v. Ferguson, 163 U.S. 537, 16 S.Ct. 1138, 41 L.Ed. 256 (1896).

Plyler v. Doe, 457 U.S. 202, 102 S.Ct. 2382, 72 L.Ed.2d 786 (1982).

Poe v. Ullman, 367 U.S. 497, 81 S.Ct. 1752, 6 L.Ed.2d 989 (1961).

Pointer v. Texas, 380 U.S. 400, 85 S.Ct. 1065, 13 L.Ed.2d 923 (1965).

Police Dept. of City of Chicago v. Mosley, 408 U.S. 92, 92 S.Ct. 2286, 33 L.Ed.2d 212 (1972).

Polk County v. Dodson, 454 U.S. 312, 102 S.Ct. 445, 70 L.Ed.2d 509 (1981).

Pollock v. Farmer's Loan and Trust Co., 157 U.S. 429, 15 S.Ct. 673, 39 L.Ed. 759 (1895).

Pollock v. Farmer's Loan and Trust Co., 158 U.S. 601, 15 S.Ct. 912, 39 L.Ed. 1108 (1895).

Posadas de Puerto Rico Associates v. Tourism Co. of Puerto Rico, 478 U.S. 328, 106 S.Ct. 2968, 92 L.Ed.2d 266 (1986).

Poulos v. New Hampshire, 345 U.S. 395, 73 S.Ct. 760, 97 L.Ed. 1105 (1953).

Powell v. McCormack, 395 U.S. 486, 89 S.Ct. 1944, 23 L.Ed.2d 491 (1969).

Powell v. Texas, 392 U.S. 514, 88 S.Ct. 2145, 20 L.Ed.2d 1254 (1968).

Presbyterian Church v. Mary Elizabeth Blue Hull Memorial Presbyterian Church, 393 U.S. 440, 89 S.Ct. 601, 21 L.Ed.2d 658 (1969).

Prince v. Massachusetts, 321 U.S. 158, 64 S.Ct. 438, 88 L.Ed. 645 (1944).

Prize Cases, The, 67 U.S. (2 Black) 635, 17 L.Ed. 459 (1863).

Prudential Insurance Co. v. Benjamin, 328 U.S. 408, 66 S.Ct. 1142, 90 L.Ed. 1342 (1946).

PruneYard Shopping Center v. Robins, 447 U.S. 74, 100 S.Ct. 2035, 64 L.Ed.2d 741 (1980).

Railroad Comm'n v. Pullman Co., 312 U.S. 496, 61 S.Ct. 643, 85 L.Ed. 971 (1941).

Railway Express Agency, Inc. v. New York, 336 U.S. 106, 69 S.Ct. 463, 93 L.Ed. 533 (1949).

Ray v. Atlantic Richfield Co., 435 U.S. 151, 98 S.Ct. 988, 55 L.Ed.2d 179 (1978).

Raymond Motor Transportation, Inc. v. Rice, 434 U.S. 429, 98 S.Ct. 787, 54 L.Ed.2d 664 (1978).

Reed v. Reed, 404 U.S. 71, 92 S.Ct. 251, 30 L.Ed.2d 225 (1971).

Reeves, Inc. v. Stake, 447 U.S. 429, 100 S.Ct. 2271, 65 L.Ed.2d 244 (1980).

Regan v. Taxation With Representation of Washington, 461 U.S. 540, 103 S.Ct. 1997, 76 L.Ed.2d 129 (1983).

Regents of the University of California v. Bakke, 438 U.S. 265, 98 S.Ct. 2733, 57 L.Ed.2d 750 (1978).

Regional Rail Reorganization Act Cases, 419 U.S. 102, 95 S.Ct. 335, 42 L.Ed.2d 320 (1974).

Reid v. Covert, 354 U.S. 1, 77 S.Ct. 1222, 1 L.Ed.2d 1148 (1957).

Reitman v. Mulkey, 387 U.S. 369, 87 S.Ct. 1627, 18 L.Ed.2d 830 (1967).

Rendell-Baker v. Kohn, 457 U.S. 830, 102 S.Ct. 2764, 73 L.Ed.2d 418 (1982).

Renton, City of v. Playtime Theatres, Inc., 475 U.S. 41, 106 S.Ct. 925, 89 L.Ed.2d 29 (1986).

Reynolds v. Sims, 377 U.S. 533, 84 S.Ct. 1362, 12 L.Ed.2d 506 (1964).

Reynolds v. United States, 98 U.S. (8 Otto) 145, 25 L.Ed. 244 (1879).

Richardson v. Ramirez, 418 U.S. 24, 94 S.Ct. 2655, 51 L.Ed.2d 551 (1974).

Richmond Newspapers, Inc. v. Virginia, 448 U.S. 555, 100 S.Ct. 2814, 65 L.Ed.2d 973 (1980).

Rinaldi v. Yeager, 384 U.S. 305, 86 S.Ct. 1497, 16 L.Ed.2d 577 (1966).

Rhode Island v. Innis, 446 U.S. 291, 100 S.Ct. 1682, 64 L.Ed.2d 297 (1980).

Richardson, United States v., 418 U.S. 166, 94 S.Ct. 2940, 41 L.Ed.2d 678 (1974).

Richmond Newspapers, Inc. v. Virginia, 448 U.S. 555, 100 S.Ct. 2814, 65 L.Ed.2d 973 (1980).

Rizzo v. Goode, 423 U.S. 362, 96 S.Ct. 598, 46 L.Ed.2d 561 (1976).

Robins v. Shelby County Taxing District, 120 U.S. 489, 7 S.Ct. 592, 30 L.Ed. 694 (1887).

Robel, United States v., 389 U.S. 258, 88 S.Ct. 419, 19 L.Ed.2d 508 (1967).

Roberts, Ohio v., 448 U.S. 56, 100 S.Ct. 2531, 65 L.Ed.2d 597 (1980).

Roberts v. United States Jaycees, 468 U.S. 609, 104 S.Ct. 3244, 82 L.Ed.2d 462 (1984).

Robinson, United States v., 414 U.S. 218, 94 S.Ct. 467, 38 L.Ed.2d 427 (1973).

Rochin v. California, 342 U.S. 165, 72 S.Ct. 205, 96 L.Ed. 183 (1952).

Rodriguez v. Popular Democratic Party, 457 U.S. 1, 102 S.Ct. 2194, 72 L.Ed.2d 628 (1982).

Roe v. Wade, 410 U.S. 113, 93 S.Ct. 705, 35 L.Ed.2d 147 (1973).

Roemer v. Board of Public Works, 426 U.S. 736, 96 S.Ct. 2337, 49 L.Ed.2d 179 (1976).

Rogers v. Bellei, 401 U.S. 815, 91 S.Ct. 1060, 28 L.Ed.2d 499 (1971).

Rome, City of v. United States, 446 U.S. 156, 100 S.Ct. 1548, 64 L.Ed.2d 119 (1980).

Rosario v. Rockefeller, 410 U,.S. 752, 93 S.Ct. 1245, 36 L.Ed.2d 1 (1973).

Rosenbloom v. Metromedia, Inc., 403 U.S. 29, 91 S.Ct. 1811, 29 L.Ed.2d 296 (1971).

Ross v. Moffitt, 417 U.S. 600, 94 S.Ct. 2437, 41 L.Ed.2d 341 (1974).

Rostker v. Goldberg, 453 U.S. 57, 101 S.Ct. 2646, 69 L.Ed.2d 478 (1981).

Rotary International v. Rotary Club of Duarte, 481 U.S. 537, 107 S.Ct. 1940, 95 L.Ed.2d 474 (1987).

Roth v. United States, 354 U.S. 476, 77 S.Ct. 1304, 1 L.Ed.2d 1498 (1957).

Ruckelshaus v. Monsanto Co., 467 U.S. 986, 104 S.Ct. 2862, 81 L.Ed.2d 815 (1984).

Runyon v. McCrary, 427 U.S. 160, 96 S.Ct. 2586, 49 L.Ed.2d 415 (1976).

Sailors v. Board of Education, 387 U.S. 105, 87 S.Ct. 1549, 18 L.Ed.2d 650 (1967).

Salyer Land Co. v. Tulare Water District, 410 U.S. 719, 93 S.Ct. 1224, 35 L.Ed.2d 659 (1973).

San Antonio Independent School District v. Rodriguez, 411 U.S. 1, 93 S.Ct. 1278, 36 L.Ed.2d 16 (1973).

San Diego Building Trades Council v. Garmon, 353 U.S. 26, 77 S.Ct. 607, 1 L.Ed.2d 618 (1957).

Scales v. United States, 367 U.S. 203, 81 S.Ct. 1469, 6 L.Ed.2d 782 (*1961).

Schad v. Borough of Mount Ephraim, 452 U.S. 61, 101 S.Ct. 2176, 68 L.Ed.2d 671 (1981).

Schaumburg, Village of v. Citizens for a Better Environment, 444 U.S. 620, 100 S.Ct. 826, 63 L.Ed.2d 73 (1980).

Schenck v. United States, 249 U.S. 47, 39 S.Ct. 247, 63 L.Ed. 470 (1919).

Schlesinger v. Ballard, 419 U.S. 498, 95 S.Ct. 572, 42 L.Ed.2d 610 (1975).

Schlesinger v. Reservists Committee to Stop the War, 418 U.S. 208, 94 S.Ct. 2925, 41 L.Ed.2d 706 (1974).

Schmerber v. California, 384 U.S. 757, 86 S.Ct. 1826, 16 L.Ed.2d 908 (1966).

Schneider v. State of N.J., 308 U.S. 147, 60 S.Ct. 146, 84 L.Ed. 155 (1939).

Schware v. Board of Bar Examiners, 353 U.S. 232, 77 S.Ct. 752, 1 L.Ed.2d 796 (1957).

Schweiker v. McClure, 456 U.S. 188, 102 S.Ct. 1665, 72 L.Ed.2d 1 (1982).

Screws v. United States, 325 U.S. 91, 65 S.Ct. 1031, 89 L.Ed. 1495 (1945).

Sears, Roebuck & Co. v. Stiffel Co., 376 U.S. 225, 84 S.Ct. 784, 11 L.Ed.2d 661 (1964).

Seattle Times Co. v. Rhinehart, 467 U.S. 20, 104 S.Ct. 2199, 81 L.Ed.2d 17 (1984).

Secretary of Public Welfare of Pennsylvania v. Institutionalized Juveniles, 442 U.S. 640, 99 S.Ct. 2523, 61 L.Ed.2d 142 (1979).

Secretary of State of Maryland v. Joseph H. Munson Co., 467 U.S. 947, 104 S.Ct. 2839, 81 L.Ed.2d 786 (1984).

Selective Service System v. Minnesota Public Interest Research Group, 468 U.S. 841, 104 S.Ct. 3348, 82 L.Ed.2d 632 (1984).

Serbian Eastern Orthodox Diocese v. Milivojevich, 426 U.S. 696, 96 S.Ct. 2372, 49 L.Ed.2d 151 (1976).

Shapiro v. Thompson, 394 U.S. 618, 89 S.Ct. 1322, 22 L.Ed.2d 600 (1969).

Shelley v. Kraemer, 334 U.S. 1, 68 S.Ct. 836, 92 L.Ed. 1161 (1948).

Shelton v. Tucker, 364 U.S. 479, 81 S.Ct. 247, 5 L.Ed.2d 231 (1960).

Sherbert v. Verner, 374 U.S. 398, 83 S.Ct. 1790, 10 L.Ed.2d 965 (1963).

Shuttlesworth v. City of Birmingham, 394 U.S. 147, 89 S.Ct. 935, 22 L.Ed.2d 162 (1969).

Silkwood v. Kerr-McGee Corp., 464 U.S. 238, 104 S.Ct. 615, 78 L.Ed.2d 443 (1984).

Simon v. Eastern Kentucky Welfare Rights Organization, 426 U.S. 26, 96 S.Ct. 1917, 48 L.Ed.2d 450 (1976).

Sinclair v. United States, 279 U.S. 263, 49 S.Ct. 268, 73 L.Ed. 692 (1929).

Singleton v. Wulff, 428 U.S. 106, 96 S.Ct. 2868, 49 L.Ed.2d 826 (1976).

Skinner v. Oklahoma, 316 U.S. 535, 62 S.Ct. 1110, 86 L.Ed. 1655 (1942).

Slaughter-House Cases, The, 83 U.S. (16 Wall.) 36, 21 L.Ed. 394 (1873).

Smith v. Allwright, 321 U.S. 649, 64 S.Ct. 757, 88 L.Ed. 987 (1944).

Smith v. Cahoon, 283 U.S. 553, 51 S.Ct. 482, 75 L.Ed. 1264 (1931)

Smith v. Illinois, 390 U.S. 129, 88 S.Ct. 748, 19 L.Ed.2d 956 (1968).

Smith v. Maryland, 442 U.S. 735, 99 S.Ct. 2577, 61 L.Ed.2d 220 (1979).

Snepp v. United States, 444 U.S. 507, 100 S.Ct. 763, 62 L.Ed.2d 704 (1980).

Sniadach v. Family Finance Corp., 395 U.S. 337, 89 S.Ct. 1820, 23 L.Ed.2d 349 (1969).

Socialist Labor Party v. Gilligan, 406 U.S. 583, 92 S.Ct. 1716, 32 L.Ed.2d 317 (1972).

Sonzinsky v. United States, 300 U.S. 506, 57 S.Ct. 554, 81 L.Ed. 772 (1937).

Sosna v. Iowa, 419 U.S. 393, 95 S.Ct. 553, 42 L.Ed.2d 532 (1975).

South Carolina State Highway Dept. v. Barnwell Brothers, 303 U.S. 177, 58 S.Ct. 510, 82 L.Ed. 734 (1938).

South Carolina v. Katzenbach, 383 U.S. 301, 86 S.Ct. 803, 15 L.Ed.2d 769 (1966).

South-Central Timber Development, Inc. v. Wunnicke, 467 U.S. 82, 104 S.Ct. 2237, 81 L.Ed.2d 71 (1984).

Southeastern Promotions, Ltd. v. Conrad, 420 U.S. 546, 95 S.Ct. 1239, 43 L.Ed.2d 448 (1975).

Southern Pacific Co. v. Arizona ex rel Sullivan, 325 U.S. 761, 65 S.Ct. 1515, 89 L.Ed. 1915 (1945).

Southern Pacific Terminal Co. v. Interstate Commerce Comm'n, 219 U.S. 498, 31 S.Ct. 279, 55 L.Ed. 310 (1911).

Southland Corp. v. Keating, 465 U.S. 1, 104 S.Ct. 852, 79 L.Ed.2d 1 (1984).

Spence v. Washington, State of, 418 U.S. 405, 94 S.Ct. 2727, 41 L.Ed.2d 842 (1974).

Spinelli v. United States, 393 U.S. 410, 89 S.Ct. 584, 21 L.Ed.2d 637 (1969).

Sporhase v. Nebraska, 458 U.S. 941, 102 S.Ct. 3456, 73 L.Ed.2d 1245 (1982).

Stack v. Boyle, 342 U.S. 1, 72 S.Ct. 1, 96 L.Ed. 3 (1951).

Stanley v. Georgia, 394 U.S. 557, 89 S.Ct. 1243, 22 L.Ed.2d 542 (1969).

Stanley v. Illinois, 405 U.S. 645, 92 S.Ct. 1208, 31 L.Ed.2d 551 (1972).

Stanton v. Stanton, 421 U.S. 7, 95 S.Ct. 1373, 43 L.Ed.2d 688 (1975).

Steel Seizure Case, The, 343 U.S. 579, 72 S.Ct. 863, 96 L.Ed. 1153 (1952).

Stone v. Graham, 449 U.S. 39, 101 S.Ct. 192, 66 L.Ed.2d 199 (1980).

Storer v. Brown, 415 U.S. 724, 94 S.Ct. 1274, 39 L.Ed.2d 714 (1974).

Stovall v. Denno, 388 U.S. 293, 87 S.Ct. 1967, 18 L.Ed.2d 1199 (1967).

Strauder v. West Virginia, 100 U.S. (10 Otto) 303, 25 L.Ed. 664 (1879).

Stromberg v. California, 283 U.S. 359, 51 S.Ct. 532, 75 L.Ed. 1117 (1931).

Sturges v. Crowinshield, 17 U.S. (4 Wheat.) 122, 4 L.Ed. 529 (1819).

Sugarman v. Dougall, 413 U.S. 634, 93 S.Ct. 2842, 37 L.Ed.2d 853 (1973).

Sullivan v. Little Hunting Park, Inc., 396 U.S. 229, 90 S.Ct. 400, 24 L.Ed.2d 386 (1969).

Swann v. Charlotte-Mecklenburg Board of Education, 402 U.S. 1, 91 S.Ct. 1267, 28 L.Ed.2d 554 (1971).

Swift v. Tyson, 41 U.S. (16 Pet.) 1, 10 L.Ed. 865 (1842).

Takahashi v. Fish and Game Comm'n, 334 U.S. 410, 68 S.Ct. 1138, 92 L.Ed., 1478 (1948).

Talley v. California, 362 U.S. 60, 80 S.Ct. 536, 4 L.Ed.2d 559 (1960).

Tashjian v. Republican Party of Connecticut, 479 U.S. 208, 107 S.Ct. 544, 93 L.Ed.2d 514 (1986).

Tate v. Short, 401 U.S. 395, 91 S.Ct. 668, 28 L.Ed.2d 130 (1971).

Taylor v. United States, 414 U.S. 17, 94 S.Ct. 194, 38 L.Ed.2d 174 (1973).

Terminiello v. Chicago, 337 U.S. 1, 69 S.Ct. 894, 93 L.Ed. 1131 (1949).

Terrace v. Thompson, 263 U.S. 197, 44 S.Ct. 15, 68 L.Ed. 255 (1923).

Terry v. Adams, 345 U.S. 461, 73 S.Ct. 809, 97 L.Ed. 1152 (1953).

Terry v. Ohio, 392 U.S. 1, 88 S.Ct. 1868, 20 L.Ed.2d 889 (1968).

Thomas v. Review Board, 450 U.S. 707, 101 S.Ct. 1425, 67 L.Ed.2d 624 (1981).

Thomas v. Union Carbide Agricultural Products Co., 473 U.S. 568, 105 S.Ct. 3325, 87 L.Ed.2d 409 (1985).

Thornburg v. Gingles, 478 U.S. 30, 106 S.Ct. 2752, 92 L.Ed.2d 25 (1986).

Thornhill v. Alabama, 310 U.S. 88, 60 S.Ct. 736, 84 L.Ed. 1093 (1940).

Thornton, Estate of v. Caldor, Inc., 472 U.S. 703, 105 S.Ct. 2914, 86 L.Ed.2d 557 (1985).

Time, Inc. v. Hill, 385 U.S. 374, 87 S.Ct. 534, 17 L.Ed.2d 456 (1967).

Tinker v. Des Moines Independent Community School District, 393 U.S. 503, 89 S.Ct. 733, 21 L.Ed.2d 731 (1969).

Toll v. Moreno, 458 U.S. 1, 102 S.Ct. 2977, 73 L.Ed.2d 563 (1982).

Toomer v. Witsell, 334 U.S. 385, 68 S.Ct. 1156, 92 L.Ed. 1460 (1948).

Torcaso v. Watkins, 367 U.S. 488, 81 S.Ct. 1680, 6 L.Ed.2d 982 (1961).

Trafficante v. Metropolitan Life Insurance Co., 409 U.S. 205, 93 S.Ct. 364, 34 L.Ed.2d 415 (1972).

Trimble v. Gordon, 430 U.S. 762, 97 S.Ct. 1459, 52 L.Ed.2d 31 (1977).

Truax v. Raich, 239 U.S. 33, 36 S.Ct. 7, 60 L.Ed. 131 (1915).

Tufts, Commissioner of Internal Revenue v., 461 U.S. 300, 103 S.Ct. 1826, 75 L.Ed.2d 863 (1983).

Turner v. Fouche, 396 U.S. 346, 90 S.Ct. 532, 24 L.Ed.2d 567 (1970).

Twining v. New Jersey, 211 U.S. 78, 29 S.Ct. 14, 53 L.Ed. 97 (1908).

United Air Lines, Inc. v. Mahin, 410 U.S. 623, 93 S.Ct. 1186, 35 L.Ed.2d 545 (1973).

United Building and Construction Trades Council v. City of Camden, 465 U.S. 208, 104 S.Ct. 1020, 79 L.Ed.2d 249 (1984).

United Mine Workers v. Illinois State Bar Ass'n, 389 U.S. 217, 88 S.Ct. 353, 19 L.Ed.2d 426 (1967).

United Public Workers v. Mitchell, 330 U.S. 75, 67 S.Ct. 556, 91 L.Ed. 754 (1947).

United States v. (see entry under name of opposing party).

United States Dept. of Agriculture v. Moreno, 413 U.S. 528, 93 S.Ct. 2821, 37 L.Ed.2d 782 (1973).

United States Dept. of Agriculture v. Murry, 413 U.S. 508, 93 S.Ct. 2832, 37 L.Ed.2d 767 (1973).

United States Parole Comm'n v. Geraghty, 445 U.S. 388, 100 S.Ct. 1202, 63 L.Ed.2d 479 (1980).

United States Postal Service v. Council of Greenburgh Civic Associations, 453 U.S. 114, 101 S.Ct. 2676, 69 L.Ed.2d 517 (1981).

United States Railroad Retirement Board v. Fritz, 449 U.S. 166, 101 S.Ct. 453, 66 L.Ed.2d 368 (1980).

United States Trust Co. of New York v. New Jersey, 431 U.S. 1, 97 S.Ct. 1505, 52 L.Ed.2d 92 (1977).

United Steelworkers of America v. Weber, 443 U.S. 193, 99 S.Ct. 2721, 61 L.Ed.2d 480 (1979).

United Transportation Union v. Long Island Railroad Co., 455 U.S. 678, 102 S.Ct. 1349, 71 L.Ed.2d 547 (1982).

United Transportation Union v. State Bar of Michigan, 401 U.S. 576, 91 S.Ct. 1076, 28 L.Ed.2d 339 (1971).

Usery v. Turner Elkhorn Mining Co., 428 U.S. 1, 96 S.Ct. 2882, 49 L.Ed.2d 752 (1976).

Uphaus v. Wyman, 360 U.S. 72, 79 S.Ct. 1040, 3 L.Ed.2d 1090 (1959).

Valentine v. Chrestensen, 316 U.S. 52, 62 S.Ct. 920, 86 L.Ed. 1262 (1942).

Valley Forge Christian College v. Americans United For Separation of Church and State, Inc., 454 U.S. 464, 102 S.Ct. 752, 70 L.Ed.2d 700 (1982).

Vance v. Bradley, 440 U.S. 93, 99 S.Ct. 939, 59 L.Ed.2d 171 (1979).

Vance v. Universal Amusement Co., 445 U.S. 308, 100 S.Ct. 1156, 63 L.Ed.2d 413 (1980).

Veazie Bank v. Fenno, 75 U.S. (8 Wall.) 533, 19 L.Ed. 482 (1869).

Village of Belle Terre v. Boraas, 416 U.S. 1, 94 S.Ct. 1536, 39 L.Ed.2d 797 (1974).

Village of Euclid v. Ambler Realty Co., 272 U.S. 365, 47 S.Ct. 114, 71 L.Ed. 303 (1926).

Village of Hoffman Estates v. Flipside, 455 U.S. 489, 102 S.Ct. 1186, 71 L.Ed.2d 362 (1982).

Village of Schaumburg v. Citizens for a Better Environment, 444 U.S. 620, 100 S.Ct. 826, 63 L.Ed.2d 73 (1980)

Virginia, Ex parte, 100 U.S. (10 Otto) 339, 25 L.Ed. 676 (1879).

Virginia State Board of Pharmacy v. Virginia Citizens Council, Inc., 425 U.S. 748, 96 S.Ct. 1817, 48 L.Ed.2d 346 (1976).

Vitek v. Jones, 445 U.S. 480, 100 S.Ct. 1254, 63 L.Ed.2d 552 (1980).

Vlandis v. Kline, 412 U.S. 441, 93 S.Ct. 2230, 37 L.Ed.2d 63 (1973).

Wade, United States v., 388 U.S. 218, 87 S.Ct. 1926, 18 L.Ed.2d 1149 (1967).

Walker v. City of Birmingham, 388 U.S. 307, 87 S.Ct. 1824, 18 L.Ed.2d 1210 (1967).

Wallace v. Jaffree, 472 U.S. 38, 105 S.Ct. 2479, 86 L.Ed.2d 29 (1985).

Walters v. Nat'l Ass'n of Radiation Survivors, 473 U.S. 305, ,105 S.Ct. 3180, 87 L.Ed.2d 220 (1985).

Walz v. Tax Comm'n, 397 U.S. 664, 90 S.Ct. 1409, 25 L.Ed.2d 697 (1970).

Wardair Canada, Inc. v. Florida Dept. of Revenue, 477 U.S. 1, 106 S.Ct. 2369, 91 L.Ed.2d 1 (1986).

Warth v. Seldin, 422 U.S. 490, 95 S.Ct. 2197, 45 L.Ed.2d 343 (1975).

Washington v. Davis, 426 U.S. 229, 96 S.Ct. 2040, 48 L.Ed.2d 597 (1976).

Washington v. Seattle School District No. 1, 458 U.S. 457, 102 S.Ct. 3187, 73 L.Ed.2d 896 (1982).

Watson v. Jones, 80 U.S. (13 Wall.) 679, 20 L.Ed. 666 (1872).

Webb's Fabulous Pharmacies v. Beckwith, 449 U.S. 155, 101 S.Ct. 446, 66 L.Ed.2d 358 (1980).

Weber v. Aetna Casualty & Surety Co, 406 U.S. 164, 92 S.Ct. 1400, 31 L.Ed.2d 768 (1972).

Webster v. Reproductive Health Services, __ U.S. __, 109 S.Ct. 3040, 106 L.Ed.2d 410 (1989).

Weinberger v. Salfi, 422 U.S. 749, 95 S.Ct. 2457, 45 L.Ed. 2d 522 (1975).

Weinberger v. Wiesenfeld, 420 U.S. 636, 95 S.Ct. 1225, 43 L.Ed.2d 514 (1975).

Wengler v. Druggists Mutual Insurance Co., 446 U.S. 142, 100 S.Ct. 1540, 64 L.Ed.2d 107 (1980).

Wesberry S. Sanders, 376 U.S. 1, 84 S.Ct. 526, 11 L.Ed.2d 481 (1964).

West Coast Hotel Co. v. Parrish, 300 U.S. 379, 57 S.Ct. 478, 81 L.Ed. 703 (1937).

West Point Wholesale Grocery Co. v. City of Opelika, 354 U.S. 390, 77 S.Ct. 1096, 1 L.Ed.2d 1420 (1957).

West Virginia State Board of Education v. Barnette, 319 U.S. 624, 63 S.Ct. 1178, 87 L.Ed. 1628 (1943).

Western and Southern Life Insurance Co. v. State Board of Equalization of California, 451 U.S. 648, 101 S.Ct. 2070, 68 L.Ed.2d 514 (1981).

Western Live Stock v. Bureau of Revenue, 303 U.S. 250, 58 S.Ct. 546, 82 L.Ed. 823 (1938).

Westinghouse Electric Corp. v. Tully, 466 U.S. 388, 104 S.Ct. 1856, 80 L.Ed.2d 388 (1984).

Whalen v. Roe, 429 U.S. 589, 97 S.Ct. 869, 51 L.Ed.2d 64 (1977).

Whitcomb v. Chavis, 403 U.S. 124, 91 St.Ct. 1858, 29 L.Ed.2d 363 (1971).

White v. Weiser, 412 U.S. 783, 93 S.Ct. 2348, 37 L.Ed.2d 335 (1973).

White v. Regester, 412 U.S. 755, 93 S.Ct. 2332, 37 L.Ed.2d 314 (1973).

Whitney v. California, 274 U.S. 357, 47 S.Ct. 641, 71 L.Ed. 1095 (1927).

Wickard v. Filburn, 317 U.S. 111, 63 S.Ct. 82, 87 L.Ed. 122 (1942).

Widmar v. Vincent, 454 U.S. 263, 102 S.Ct. 269, 70 L.Ed.2d 440 (1981).

Wiener v. United States, 357 U.S. 349, 78 S.Ct. 1275, 2 L.Ed.2d 1377 (1958).

Williams v. Illinois, 399 U.S. 235, 90 S.Ct. 2018, 26 L.Ed.2d 586 (1970).

Williams v. Rhodes, 393 U.S. 23, 89 S.Ct. 5, 21 L.Ed.2d 24 (1968).

Williamson v. Lee Optical of Okl., 348 U.S. 483, 75 S.Ct. 461, 99 L.Ed. 563 (1955).

Wisconsin v. Constantineau, 400 U.S. 433, 91 S.Ct. 507, 27 L.Ed.2d 515 (1971).

Wisconsin v. Yoder, 406 U.S. 205, 92 S.Ct. 1526, 32 L.Ed.2d 15 (1972).

Witters v. Washington Dept. of Services for the Blind, 474 U.S. 481, 106 S.Ct. 748, 88 L.Ed.2d 846 (1986).

Wolf v. Colorado, 338 U.S. 25, 69 S.Ct. 1359, 93 L.Ed. 1782 (1949).

Wolff v. McDonnell, 418 U.S. 539, 94 S.Ct. 2963, 41 L.Ed.2d 935 (1974).

Wolman v. Walter, 433 U.S. 229, 97 S.Ct. 2593, 53 L.Ed.2d 714 (1977).

Wong Sun v. United States, 371 U.S. 471, 83 S.Ct. 407, 9 L.Ed.2d 441 (1963).

Wooley v. Maynard, 430 U.S. 705, 97 S.Ct. 1428, 51 L.Ed.2d 752 (1977).

Woolworth Co., F.W. v. Taxation and Revenue Dept. of New Mexico, 458 U.S. 354, 102 S.Ct. 3128, 73 L.Ed.2d 819 (1982).

Worcester v. State of Georgia, 31 U.S. (6 Pet.) 515, 8 L.Ed. 483 (1832).

Wright v. City Council of Emporia, 407 U.S. 451, 92 S.Ct. 2196, 33 L.Ed.2d 51 (1972).

Wright v. United States, 302 U.S. 583, 58 S.Ct. 395, 82 L.Ed. 439 (1938).

Wygant v. Jackson Board of Education, 476 U.S. 267, 106 S.Ct. 1842, 90 L.Ed.2d 260 (1986).

Xerox Corp. v. Harris County, Texas, 459 U.S. 145, 103 S.Ct. 523, 74 L.Ed.2d 323 (1982).

Yates v. United States, 354 U.S. 298, 77 S.Ct. 1064, 1 L.Ed.2d 1356 (1957).

Yick Wo v. Hopkins, 118 U.S. 356, 6 S.Ct. 1064, 30 L.Ed. 220 (1886).

Young v. American Mini Theatres, Inc., 427 U.S. 50, 96 S.Ct. 2440, 49 L.Ed.2d 310 (1976).

Youngberg v. Romeo, 457 U.S. 307, 102 S.Ct. 2452, 73 L.Ed.2d 28 (1982).

Younger v. Harris, 401 U.S. 37, 91 S.Ct. 746, 27 L.Ed.2d 669 (1971).

Youngstown Sheet & Tube Co. v. Sawyer, 343 U.S. 579, 72 S.Ct. 863, 96 L.Ed. 1153 (1952).

Zablocki v. Redhail, 434 U.S. 374, 98 S.Ct. 673, 54 L.Ed.2d 618 (1978).

Zobel v. Williams, 457 U.S. 55, 102 S.Ct. 2309, 72 L.Ed.2d 672 (1982).

Zoracb v. Cla'uson, 343 U.S. 306, 72 S.Ct. 679, 96 L.Ed. 954 (1952).

Zurcber v. Stanford Daily, 436 U.S. 547, 98 S.Ct. 1970, 56 L.Ed.2d 525 (1978).

UNITED STATES SUPREME COURT JUSTICES

PRESIDENT Party Dates of his Administration	JUSTICE Political Party Years of Service	Born/Died Law School Residence Prior Experience
GEORGE WASHINGTON Fed. 1789–1797	* JOHN JAY Fed. 1789–1795	1745–1829 N.Y. Cont. Cong. (5); N.Y. prov. cong. (1); State judge (2); Minister to Spain (1); U.S. Sec'y of Foreign Affairs (5)
	JOHN RUTLEDGE Fed. 1789–1791	1739–1800 S.C. Confirmed but never sat with the Court. Col. legis. (15); Col. Atty. Gen. (1); Cont. Cong. (3); State legis. (9); Gov. (3); Const. Conv., 1787; State judge (1)
	WILLIAM CUSHING Fed. 1789–1810	1732–1810 Mass. Local judge (1); State judge (17)
	JAMES WILSON Fed 1789–1798	1724–1798 Pa. Cont. Cong. (4); Const. Conv., 1787
	JOHN BLAIR Fed. 1789–1796	1732–1800 Va. House of Burgesses (4); Clerk, Va. council (5); State privy council (1); Const. Conv., 1787; State judge (11)
	JAMES IREDELL Fed. 1790–1799	1750–1799 N.C. Customs collector (3); State judge (1); State Atty. Gen. (1); State council (1)

PRESIDENT Party Dates of his Administration	JUSTICE Political Party Years of Service	Born/Died Law School Residence Prior Experience
WASHINGTON *(Cont)*	THOMAS JOHNSON Fed. 1791–1793	1732–1819 Md. Cont. Cong. (2)
	WILLIAM PATERSON Fed. 1793–1806	1745–1806 N.J. State legis. (2); State Atty. Gen. (7); Const. Conv., 1787; Senate (1); Gov. (3)
	* JOHN RUTLEDGE Fed. 1795	1739–1800 S.C. (See entry above) Unconfirmed recess appointment since 1791; State judge (4)
	SAMUEL CHASE Fed. 1796–1811	1741–1811 Md. Col. & state legis. (20); Cont. Cong. (6); Local judge (1); State judge (5)
	* OLIVER ELLSWORTH Fed. 1796–1800	1745–1807 Conn. State legis. (1); State's atty. (1); Cont. Cong. (6); Gov's council (4); State judge (5); Const. Conv., 1787; Senate (7)
JOHN ADAMS Fed. 1797–1801	BUSHROD WASHINGTON Fed. 1798–1829	1762–1829 Pa. State legis. (1)
	ALFRED MOORE Fed. 1799–1804	1755–1810 N.C. State legis. (2); State Atty. Gen. (9); State judge (1)
	* JOHN MARSHALL Fed. 1801–1835	1755–1835 Va. House of Burgesses (7); Gov's council (13); City recorder (2); House (1); Mem., special comm'n to France, XYZ Affair (1); Sec'y of State (1)
THOMAS JEFFERSON Dem.-Rep. 1801–1809	WILLIAM JOHNSON Dem.-Rep. 1804–1834	1771–1834 S.C. State legis. (4); State judge (6)
	HENRY BROCKHOLST LIVINGSTON Dem.-Rep. 1806–1823	1757–1823 N.Y. State judge (5)

PRESIDENT Party Dates of his Administration	JUSTICE Political Party Years of Service	Born/Died Law School Residence Prior Experience
JEFFERSON *(Cont)*	THOMAS TODD Dem.-Rep. 1807–1826	1765–1826 Ky. Court clerk (14); State judge (6)
JAMES MADISON Dem.-Rep. 1809–1817	GABRIEL DUVALL Dem.-Rep. 1811–1835	1752–1844 Md. Gov's council (2); State legis. (7); House (1-1/2) State judge (6); Comptr., U.S. Treasury (9)
	JOSEPH STORY Dem.-Rep. 1811–1845	1779–1845 Mass. State legis. (4); House (1)
JAMES MONROE Dem.-Rep. 1817–1825	SMITH THOMPSON Dem.-Rep. 1823–1843	1768–1843 N.Y. State legis. (1); State judge (16); Sec'y of the Navy (4)
JOHN QUINCY ADAMS Dem.-Rep. 1825–1829	ROBERT TRIMBLE Dem.-Rep. 1826–1828	1777–1828 Ky. State legis. (1); State judge (2); U.S. atty. (4); Fed. judge (9)
ANDREW JACKSON Dem. 1829–1837	JOHN McLEAN Dem., later Rep. 1829–1861	1785–1861 Ohio House (3-1/2); State judge (6); Fed. agency (1); Post. Gen. (4)
	HENRY BALDWIN Dem. 1830-1844	1780–1844 Pa. House (5)
	JAMES M. WAYNE Dem. 1835–1867	1790–1867 Ga. State legis. (1); Mayor (1); State judge (5); House (6)
	* ROGER B. TANEY Dem. 1836–1864	1777–1864 Md. State legis. (5); State Atty. Gen. (4); U.S. Atty Gen. (4); Acting Sec'y of War (1); Sec'y of the Treasury (1)
	PHILIP P. BARBOUR Dem. 1836–1841	1783–1841 Va. State legis. (2); House (14); Fed. judge (6)
MARTIN VAN BUREN Dem. 1837–1841	JOHN CATRON Dem. 1837–1865	1778–1865 Tenn. State judge (10)

PRESIDENT Party Dates of his Administration	JUSTICE Political Party Years of Service	Born/Died Law School Residence Prior Experience
VAN BUREN (Cont)	JOHN McKINLEY Dem. 1837–1852	1780–1852 Ky. State legis. (1); Senate (5); House (2)
	PETER V. DANIEL Dem. 1841–1860	1784–1860 Va. State legis. (1); State privy council (23); Lt. Gov. (1); Fed. judge (4)
JOHN TYLER Whig 1841–1845	SAMUEL NELSON Dem. 1845–1872	1792–1873 N.Y. State judge (22)
JAMES KNOX POLK Dem. 1845–1849	LEVI WOODBURY Dem. 1845–1851	1789–1851 N.H. State judge (6); Gov. (1); State legis. (1); Senate (10); Sec'y of the Navy (3); Sec'y of the Treasury (7)
	ROBERT C. GRIER Dem. 1846–1870	1794–1870 Pa. Local judge (13)
MILLARD FILLMORE Whig 1850–1853	BENJAMIN R. CURTIS Whig 1851–1857	1809–1874 Mass. State legis. (1)
FRANKLIN PIERCE Dem. 1853–1857	JOHN A. CAMPBELL Dem. 1853–1861	1811–1889 Ala. State legis. (2)
JAMES BUCHANAN Dem. 1857–1861	NATHAN CLIFFORD Dem. 1858–1881	1803–1881 Maine State legis. (4); State Atty. Gen. (4); House (4); U.S. Atty. Gen. (2)
ABRAHAM LINCOLN Rep. 1861–1865	NOAH H. SWAYNE Rep. 1862–1881	1804–1884 Ohio Pros. atty. (1); State legis. (1); U.S. atty. (9)
	SAMUEL F. MILLER Rep. 1862–1890	1816–1890 Iowa Private practice
	DAVID DAVIS Rep., later Dem. 1862–1877	1815–1886 Ill. State legis. (1); State judge (14)

PRESIDENT Party Dates of his Administration	JUSTICE Political Party Years of Service	Born/Died Law School Residence Prior Experience
LINCOLN *(Cont)*	STEPHEN J. FIELD Dem. 1863–1897	1816–1899 Calif. State legis. (1); State judge (6)
	* SALMON P. CHASE Rep. 1864–1873	1808–1873 Ohio Senate (7); Gov. (4); Sec'y of the Treasury (3)
ULYSSES S. GRANT Rep. 1869–1877	WILLIAM STRONG Rep. 1870–1880	1808–1895 Pa. House (4); State judge (11)
	JOSEPH P. BRADLEY Rep. 1870–1892	1803–1892 N.J. Private practice
	WARD HUNT Rep. 1872–1882	1810–1886 N.Y. State legis. (1); Mayor (1); State judge (8)
	* MORRISON R. WAITE Rep. 1874–1888	1816–1888 Ohio State legis. (1)
RUTHERFORD B. HAYES Rep. 1877–1881	JOHN MARSHALL HARLAN Rep. 1877–1911	1833–1911 Ky. Local judge (1); State Atty. Gen. (4); Repub. cand. for Gov., 1871, 1875
	WILLIAM B. WOODS Rep. 1880–1887	1824–1887 Ga. Private practice
JAMES A. GARFIELD Rep. 1881	STANLEY MATTHEWS Rep. 1881–1889	1824–1889 Ohio Asst. pros. atty. (1); Local judge (4); State legis. (3); U.S. atty. (3); Senate (2)
CHESTER ALAN ARTHUR Rep. 1881–1885	HORACE GRAY Rep. 1881–1902	1828–1902 Mass. Court reporter (7); State judge (18)
	SAMUEL BLATCHFORD Rep. 1882–1893	1820–1893 N.Y. Resident minister to the Vatican (1); Fed. judge (15)

PRESIDENT Party Dates of his Administration	JUSTICE Political Party Years of Service	Born/Died Law School Residence Prior Experience
GROVER CLEVELAND Dem. 1885–1889	LUCIUS Q. C. LAMAR Dem. 1888–1893	1825–1893 Miss. Coll. prof. (2); State legis. (1); House (8); Law prof. (1); Senate (8); Sec'y of the Interior (3)
	* MELVILLE W. FULLER Dem. 1888–1910	1833–1910 Ill. City atty. & councilman (1); State legis. (2)
BENJAMIN HARRISON Rep. 1889–1893	DAVID J. BREWER Rep. 1889–1910	1837–1910 Kan. U.S. commissioner (1); Local judge (1); County atty. (1); State judge (18); Fed. judge (5)
	HENRY B. BROWN Rep. 1890–1906	1836–1913 Mich. Dep. U.S. marshal (2); Asst. U.S. atty. (5); Local judge (1/2); Fed. judge (15)
	GEORGE SHIRAS Rep. 1892–1903	1832–1924 Yale Pa. Private practice
	HOWELL E. JACKSON Dem. 1893–1895	1832–1895 Tenn.. State judge (4); State legis. (1); Senate (5); Fed. judge (7)
GROVER CLEVELAND Dem. 1893–1897	EDWARD D. WHITE Dem. 1894–1910	1845–1921 LA. State legis. (1); Stage judge (1); Senate (3) Promoted to Chief Justice, 1910
	RUFUS W. PECKHAM Dem. 1895–1909	1838–1909 N.Y. Dist. atty. (1); City atty. (1); State judge (12)
WILLIAM McKINLEY Rep. 1897–1901	JOSEPH McKENNA Rep. 1898–1925	1843–1926 Calif. Dist. atty. (2); State legis. (1); House (7); Fed. judge (5); U.S. Atty. Gen. (1)
THEODORE ROOSEVELT Rep. 1901–1908	OLIVER WENDELL HOLMES, Jr. Rep. 1902–1932	1841–1935 Harvard Mass. Law prof. (2); State judge (20)

PRESIDENT Party Dates of his Administration	JUSTICE Political Party Years of Service	Born/Died Law School Residence Prior Experience
ROOSEVELT (Cont)	WILLIAM R. DAY Rep. 1903–1922	1849–1923 Ohio Local judge (4); Asst. Sec'y of State (1); Sec'y of State (1/2); Fed judge (4)
	WILLIAM H. MOODY Rep. 1906–1910	1853–1917 Mass. City atty. (2); Dist. atty. (5); House (7); Sec'y of the Navy (2); U.S. Atty. Gen. (1-1/2)
WILLIAM HOWARD TAFT Rep. 1909–1913	HORACE H. LURTON Dem. 1909–1914	1844–1914 Cumberland Tenn. State judge (10); Law prof. & dean (12); Fed. judge (17)
	CHARLES EVANS HUGHES Rep. 1910–1916	1862–1948 Columbia N.Y. Spec. counsel to legis. invest. comms. (2); Law prof. (4); Gov. (2) Later appointed Chief Justice
	* EDWARD D. WHITE Dem. 1910–1921	1845–1921 La. Promoted from Associate Justice
	WILLIS VAN DEVANTER Rep. 1910–1937	1859–1941 Cincinnati Wyo. City atty. (1); Terr. legis. (1); State judge (1); Chmn., Rep. state comm. (1); Chmn., Rep. nat. comm. (1); Asst. U.S. Atty. Gen. (6); Fed. judge (7)
	JOSEPH R. LAMAR Dem. 1910–1916	1857–1916 Ga. State legis. (3); State judge (4)
	MAHLON PITNEY Rep. 1912–1922	1858–1924 N.J. House (4); State legis. (2); State judge (14)
WOODROW WILSON Dem. 1913–1921	JAMES C. McREYNOLDS Dem. 1914–1941	1862–1946 Virginia Tenn. Asst. U.S. Atty. Gen. (4); U.S. Atty. Gen (1)
	LOUIS D. BRANDEIS Rep. 1916–1939	1856–1941 Harvard Mass. Private practice and public interest law in antitrust, labor, and consumer matters. Counsel for fed. and state govts. in rate regulation, minimum wage, and maximum hours cases.

PRESIDENT Party Dates of his Administration	JUSTICE Political Party Years of Service	Born/Died Law School Residence Prior Experience
WILSON *(Cont)*	JOHN H. CLARKE Dem. 1916–1922	1857–1945 Ohio Railroad counsel (13); Fed. judge (2)
WARREN G. HARDING Rep. 1921–1923	* WILLIAM HOWARD TAFT Rep. 1921–1930	1857–1930 Cincinnati Ohio Asst. pros. atty. (3); County atty. (2); Local judge (3); U.S. Sol. Gen. (2); Fed. judge (8); Law prof. & dean (4); Gov. of Philippines (4); Sec'y of War (3-1/2); President (4); Law prof. (8)
	GEORGE SUTHERLAND Rep. 1922–1938	1862–1942 Utah State legis. (1); House (2); Senate (12)
	PIERCE BUTLER Dem. 1922–1939	1866–1939 Minn. Private practice
	EDWARD T. SANFORD Rep. 1923–1930	1865–1930 Harvard Tenn. Asst. U.S. Atty. Gen. (1); Fed. judge (15)
CALVIN COOLIDGE Rep. 1923–1929	HARLAN F. STONE Rep. 1925–1941	1872–1946 Columbia N.Y. Law prof. & dean (24); U.S. Atty. Gen. (1) Promoted to Chief Justice, 1941
HERBERT HOOVER Rep. 1929–1933	* CHARLES EVANS HUGHES Rep. 1930–1941	1862–1948 Columbia N.Y. (See entry above) Since 1916: Repub. pres. candid., 1916; Sec'y of State (4); Perm. Court of Arbitration (4); World Court (2)
	OWEN J. ROBERTS Rep. 1930–1945	1875–1955 Pennsylvania Pa. Dist. atty. (3); Law prof. (20)
	BENJAMIN N. CARDOZO Dem. 1932–1938	1870–1938 N.Y. State judge (18)
FRANKLIN D. ROOSEVELT Dem. 1933–1945	HUGO L. BLACK Dem. 1937–1971	1886–1971 Alabama Ala. Local judge (1-1/2); Pros. atty. (2); Senate (10)

PRESIDENT Party Dates of his Administration	JUSTICE Political Party Years of Service	Born/Died Law School Residence Prior Experience
ROOSEVELT *(Cont)*	STANLEY F. REED Dem. 1938–1957	1884–1980 Ky. State legis. (4); Counsel, fed. agencies (6); Sol. Gen. (3)
	FELIX FRANKFURTER Ind. 1939–1962	1882–1965 Harvard Mass. Asst. U.S. atty. (4); Fed. agencies (3); Law prof. (25)
	WILLIAM O. DOUGLAS Dem. 1939–1975	1898–1980 Columbia Wash. Law prof. (9); SEC, chmn. and commn'r (3)
	FRANK MURPHY Dem. 1940–1949	1893–1949 Michigan Mich. Asst. U.S. atty. (1); Local judge (7); Mayor (3); Gov. (3); U.S. Atty. Gen. (1)
	JAMES F. BYRNES Dem. 1941–1942	1879–1972 S.C. Senate (12)
	* HARLAN F. STONE Rep. 1941–1946	1872–1946 Columbia N.Y. Promoted from Associate Justice
	ROBERT H. JACKSON Dem. 1941–1954	1892–1954 N.Y. Counsel, IRS (2); Asst. U.S. Atty. Gen. (2); Sol. Gen. (1); U.S. Atty. Gen. (1-1/2)
	WILEY B. RUTLEDGE Dem. 1943–1949	1894–1949 Colorado Iowa Law prof. & dean (15); Fed. judge (4)
HARRY S. TRUMAN Dem. 1945–1953	HAROLD H. BURTON Rep. 1945–1958	1888–1964 Harvard Ohio State legis. (1); City atty. (3); Mayor (5); Senate (4)
	* FRED M. VINSON Dem. 1946–1953	1890–1953 Centre College, Ky. Ky. City atty. (1); Pros. atty. (3); House (14); Fed. judge (5); Fed. agencies (2); Sec'y of the Treasury (1)
	TOM C. CLARK Dem. 1949–1967	1899–1977 Texas Tex. Dist. atty. (6); U.S. Justice Dept. (8); U.S. Atty. Gen. (4)

PRESIDENT Party Dates of his Administration	JUSTICE Political Party Years of Service	Born/Died Law School Residence Prior Experience
TRUMAN *(Cont)*	SHERMAN MINTON Dem. 1949–1956	1890–1965 Indiana Ind. Senate (6); Fed. judge (8)
DWIGHT D. EISENHOWER Rep. 1953–1961	* EARL WARREN Rep. 1953–1969	1891–1974 California Calif. Dep. city atty. (1); Dep. dist. atty. (5); Dist. atty. (14); State Atty. Gen. (4); Gov. (10); Repub. vice-pres. cand., 1948
	JOHN MARSHALL HARLAN Rep. 1955–1971	1899–1971 New York Law School N.Y. Asst. U.S. atty. (2); Spec. asst. state Atty. Gen. (4); Chief counsel, state crime comm'n (2); Fed. judge (1)
	WILLIAM J. BRENNAN, Jr. Dem. 1956–1990	1906– Harvard N.J. State judge (7)
	CHARLES E. WHITTAKER Rep. 1957–1962	1901–1973 Univ. of Kansas City Mo. Fed. judge (3)
	POTTER STEWART Rep. 1958–1981	1915–1985 Yale Ohio City council (3); Fed. judge (4)
JOHN F. KENNEDY Dem. 1961–1963	BYRON R. WHITE Dem. 1962–	1917– Yale Colo. Dep. U.S. Atty. Gen. (1)
	ARTHUR J. GOLDBERG Dem. 1962–1965	1908–1990 Northwestern Ill. Counsel to AFL-CIO (13); Sec'y of Labor (1)
LYNDON B. JOHNSON Dem. 1963–1969	ABE FORTAS Dem. 1965–1969	1910–1982 Yale Tenn. Law prof. (4); Fed. agencies (4); Under sec'y of the Interior (4)
	THURGOOD MARSHALL Dem. 1967–	1908–1990 Howard N.Y. Counsel, NAACP (25); Sol. Gen. (2); Fed. judge (4)
RICHARD M. NIXON Rep. 1969–1974	* WARREN E. BURGER Rep. 1969–1986	1907– St. Paul College of Law Minn. Asst. U.S. Atty. Gen. (3); Fed. judge (13)

PRESIDENT Party Dates of his Administration	JUSTICE Political Party Years of Service	Born/Died Law School Residence Prior Experience
NIXON *(Cont)*	HARRY A. BLACKMUN Rep. 1970–	1908– Harvard Minn. Counsel, Mayo Clinic (9); Fed. judge (11)
	LEWIS F. POWELL, Jr. Dem. 1972–1987	1907– Washington & Lee Va. Private practice
	WILLIAM H. REHNQUIST Rep. 1972–	1924– Stanford Ariz. Asst. U.S. Atty. Gen. (2)
GERALD R. FORD Rep. 1974–1977	JOHN PAUL STEVENS Rep. 1975–	1920– Northwestern Ill. Fed. judge (5)
RONALD REAGAN Rep. 1981–	SANDRA DAY O'CONNOR Rep. 1981–	1930– Stanford Ariz. Asst. state Atty. Gen. (4); State legis. (5); State judge (7)
	* WILLIAM H. REHNQUIST Rep. 1986–	1924– Stanford Ariz. Promoted from Associate Justice
	ANTONIN SCALIA Rep. 1986–	1936– Harvard D.C. Asst. U.S. Atty. Gen. (3); Law prof. (9)
	ANTHONY M. KENNEDY Rep. 1988–	1936– Harvard Calif. Fed. judge (13); Law prof. (23)

* Chief Justice

Source: Constitutional Interpretation, Chase and Ducat, published by West Publishing Co.

HARRY A. BLACKMUN, Associate Justice of the Supreme Court of the United States; born November 12, 1908, Nashville, IL; A.B. (summa cum laude), Harvard College, 1929; LL.B., Harvard Law School, 1932; admitted to the Minnesota Bar September 1932; law clerk to the Honorable John B. Sanborn, judge of the U.S. Court of Appeals for the Eighth Circuit, August 1, 1932 through December 31, 1933; in practice, as associate, junior partner and general partner, Dorsey, Colman, Barker, Scott & Barber and predecessor firms, Minneapolis, MN, January 1, 1934 through September 30, 1950; occasional member of the faculties of St. Paul College of Law (now William Mitchell College of Law) and University of Minnesota Law School; resident counsel, Mayo Clinic and Mayo Association (now Mayo Foundation), and member of the Section of Administration, Mayo Clinic, Rochester, MN, October 1, 1950 through November 3, 1959; Republican; nominated by President Eisenhower as judge of the U.S. Court of Appeals for the Eighth Circuit, August 18, 1959; nominated Associate Justice by President Nixon, April 14, 1970; confirmed by the Senate, May 12, 1970.

WILLIAM J. BRENNAN, JR., of Rumson, N.J. Associate Justice of the Supreme Court of the United States; born April 25, 1906, in Newark, N.J.; B.S. (with honors) Wharton School of Business, University of Pennsylvania 1928; LL.B., Harvard 1931; joined firm Pitney, Hardin & Skinner, Newark, N.J., as associate in 1931; member from 1937–42 and again 1945–49, firm name Pitney, Hardin, Ward & Brennan; major, later colonel, United States Army, specializing in manpower and personnel work, 1942–45, awarded Legion of Merit; appointed by Governor Driscoll, New Jersey Superior Court, 1949, served as assignment judge, Hudson County, to 1951; appointed to Appellate Division of that court 1951; appointed by Governor Driscoll, associate justice of New Jersey Supreme Court, 1952; appointed as an Associate Justice of the Supreme Court of the United States by President Eisenhower, a recess appointment on October 15, 1956; took the oath and his seat on October 16, 1956; was nominated by President Eisenhower on January 14, 1957; the nomination was confirmed by the Senate on March 19, 1957; was given a new commission on March 21, 1957, and again took the oath on March 22, 1957.

ANTHONY M. KENNEDY, Associate Justice of the Supreme Court of the United States; born, July 23, 1936, Sacramento, CA; Stanford University, 1954–57; London School of Economics, 1957–58; Stanford University, B.A., 1958; Harvard Law School, LL.B., 1961; admitted to the California bar, 1962; admitted to the United States Tax Court bar, 1971; associate, Thelen, Marrin, John & Bridges, San Francisco, 1961–63; sole practitioner, Sacramento, 1963–67; partner, Evans, Jackson & Kennedy, Sacramento, 1967–75; professor of constitutional law, McGeorge School of Law, University of the Pacific, 1965–88; California Army National Guard, 1961; member, the Judicial Conference of the United States Advisory Panel on Financial Disclosure Reports and Judicial Activities, subsequently renamed the Advisory Committee on Codes of Conduct, 1979–87; member, the Committee on Pacific Territories, 1979–88, named chairman, 1982; member, Board of the Federal Judicial Center, 1987–88; nominated by President Ford to the United States Court of Appeals for the Ninth Circuit; took oath of office May 30, 1975; nominated by President Reagan as Associate Justice; took oath of office, February 18, 1988.

THURGOOD MARSHALL, Associate Justice of the Supreme Court of the United States; born in Baltimore, MD, July 2, 1908; attended public schools in Baltimore; graduated with honors from Lincoln University in 1930, and in 1933 graduated, at the head of his class, from Howard University Law School in Washington; entered private law practice in Baltimore, and in 1934 became counsel for the Baltimore branch, National Association for the Advancement of Colored People; in 1936, joined the organization's national legal staff, and in 1938 appointed chief legal officer, serving from 1940 until appointed to the Federal bench as director-counsel of the NAACP legal defense and educational fund; nominated by President Kennedy for appointment to the Second Circuit Court of Appeals on September 23, 1961, given recess appointment in October 1961, confirmed by the Senate on September 11, 1962; nominated by President Johnson for appointment as Solicitor General of the United States on July 13, 1965, taking oath of office August 24, 1965; nominated by President Johnson as Associate Justice of the Supreme Court of the United States on June 13, 1967, confirmed by the Senate on August 30, 1967.

SANDRA DAY O'CONNOR, Associate Justice of the Supreme Court of the United States; born March 26, 1930, at El Paso, TX; B.A. (magna cum laude), Stanford University, 1950; LL.B., Stanford Law School, 1952; Order of the Coif,

Board of Editors, Stanford Law Review; deputy county attorney, San Mateo County, CA, 1952–53; civilian attorney for Quartermaster Market Center, Frankfurt, Germany, 1954–57; private practice of law in Maryvale, AZ, 1958–60; assistant attorney general, Arizona, 1965–69; Arizona State senate from 1969–75; senate majority leader in 1972 and 1975; chairman of the State, County, and Municipal Affairs Committee in 1972 and 1973; also served on the Legislative Council, on the Probate Code Commission, and on the Arizona Advisory Council on Intergovernmental Relations; elected judge of the Maricopa County Superior Court, Phoenix, AZ, 1975–79; appointed o the Arizona Court of Appeals by Gov. Bruce Babbitt and served from 1979–81; nominated by President Reagan as Associate Justice of the U.S. Supreme Court on July 7, 1981; took the oath of office on September 25, 1981.

WILLIAM HUBBS REHNQUIST, Chief Justice of the United States; born October 1, 1924, in Milwaukee, WI; member of Emmanuel Lutheran Church, Bethesda, MD; served in the U.S. Army Air Corps in this country and overseas from 1943 to 1946; discharged with the rank of sergeant; Stanford University, B.A., M.A., 1948; Harvard University, M.A., 1950; Stanford University, LL.B., 1952, ranking first in Class; Order of the Coif; member of the Board of Editors of the Stanford Law Review; February 1952–June 1953, law clerk for Justice Robert H. Jackson, Supreme Court of the United States; private practice of law, Phoenix, AZ, 1953–69; engaged in a general practice of law with primary emphasis on civil litigation; appointed Assistant Attorney General, Office of Legal Counsel, by President Nixon in January 1969; nominated Associate Justice of the Supreme Court of the United States by President Nixon on October 21, 1971, confirmed December 10, 1971, sworn in on January 7, 1972; nominated by President Reagan as Chief Justice of the United States on June 17, 1986; sworn in on September 26, 1986.

ANTONIN SCALIA, Associate Justice of the Supreme Court of the United States, born Trenton, NJ, March 11, 1936; A.B., Georgetown University and University of Fribourg (Switzerland), 1957; LL.B., Harvard Law School, 1960; note editor, Harvard Law Review; Sheldon fellow, Harvard University, 1960–61; admitted to practice in Ohio (1962), Virginia (1970); in private practice with Jones, Day, Cockley, and Reavis (Cleveland, OH), 1961–67; professor of law, University of Virginia Law School; general counsel, Office of Telecommunications Policy, Executive Office of the President, 1971–72; chairman, Administrative Conference of the United States, 1972–74; Assistant Attorney General, Office of Legal Counsel, U.S. Department of Justice, 1974–77; scholar in residence, American Enterprise Institute, 1977; visiting professor of law, Georgetown University, 1977; professor of law, University of Chicago, 1977–82; visiting professor of law, Stanford University, 1980–81; editor, Regulation Magazine, 1979–82; chairman, ABA Section of Administrative Law, 1981–82; chairman, ABA Conference of Section Chairmen, 1982–83; appointed by President Reagan as Circuit Judge of the U.S. Court of Appeals for the District of Columbia Circuit, taking office August 17, 1982; appointed by President Reagan as Associate Justice of the U.S. Supreme Court, taking office September 26, 1986.

JOHN PAUL STEVENS, Associate Justice of the Supreme Court of the United States, born in Chicago, IL, April 20, 1920; A.B., University of Chicago, 1941; J.D., Northwestern University, 1947; admitted to Illinois Bar 1949, practiced law in Chicago; law clerk to U.S. Supreme Court Justice Wiley Rutledge, 1947–48; served in the U.S. Navy, 1942–45; associate counsel, Subcommittee on the Study of Monopoly Power, Judiciary Committee of the U.S. House of Representatives, 1951–52; member of the Attorney General's National Committee to Study Antitrust Laws, 1953–55; appointed U.S. Circuit Judge for the Seventh Circuit, October 14, 1970; nominated to the Supreme Court December 1, 1975, by President Ford; took the oath of office on December 10, 1975.

BYRON RAYMOND WHITE, Associate Justice of the Supreme Court of the United States; born in Fort Collins, CO, June 8, 1917; B.A., University of Colorado, 1938; Rhodes scholar, Oxford, England, 1939; LL.B., Yale Law School, 1946; law clerk to Chief Justice of the Supreme Court of the United States, 1946–47; associate, Lewis, Grant, Newton, Davis & Henry, 1947–50, partner, 1950–60; Deputy Attorney General of the United States, January 1961–April 1962; nominated Associate Justice of the Supreme Court of the United States by President Kennedy on April 3, 1962; took the oath of office on April 16, 1962.

1865

From left to right: David Davis, Noah H. Swayne, Robert C. Grier, James M. Wayne, Salmon P. Chase, Samuel Nelson, Nathan Clifford, Samuel F. Miller, Stephen J. Field.

1904

First row, *from the left:* Henry Brown, John Marshall Harlan, Melville W. Fuller, David J. Brewer, Edward D. White. Second row, *from the left:* Oliver Wendell Holmes Jr., Rufus W. Peckham, Joseph McKenna, William R. Day.

1936

First row, *from the left:* Louis D. Brandeis, Willis Van Devanter, Charles Evans Hughes, James C. McReynolds, and George Sutherland. Second row, *from the left:* Owen J. Roberts, Pierce Butler, Harlan Fiske Stone, and Benjamin N. Cardozo.

Seated, *from the left:* Felix Fankfurter, Hugo Black, Earl Warren, Stanley Reed, William O. Douglas. Standing, *from the left:* John Harlan, Harold Burton, Tom C. Clark, William J. Brennan, Jr.

First row, *left to right:* Thurgood Marshall, William J. Brennan, Jr., Warren E. Burger, Byron R. White, Harry A. Blackmun. Second row, *left to right:* John Paul Stevens, Lewis F. Powell, William H. Rehnquist, and Sandra Day O'Connor.

First row, *from left to right:* Thurgood Marshall, William J. Brennan, Jr., William H. Rehnquist, Byron R. White, Harry A. Blackmun. Second row, *from left to right:* Antonin Scalia, John Paul Stevens, Sandra Day O'Connor, Anthony M. Kennedy.

JUSTICES OF THE UNITED STATES SUPREME COURT

The following table is designed to aid the user in identifying the composition of the Court at any given time in the Court's history. Each listing is headed by the chief justice, whose name is italicized. Associate justices are then placed below the chief justice in order of seniority, with the most senior associate justice immediately following the chief justice.

1789
Jay
J. Rutledge
Cushing
Wilson
Blair

1790–91
Jay
J. Rutledge
Cushing
Wilson
Blair
Iredell

1792
Jay
Cushing
Wilson
Blair
Iredell
T. Johnson

1793–94
Jay
Cushing
Wilson
Blair
Iredell
Paterson

1795
*J. Rutledge*ª
Cushing
Wilson
Blair
Iredell
Paterson

1796–97
Ellsworth
Cushing
Wilson
Iredell
Paterson
S. Chase

1798–99
Ellsworth
Cushing
Iredell
Paterson
S. Chase
Washington

1800
Ellsworth
Cushing
Paterson
S. Chase
Washington
Moore

1801–03
J. Marshall
Cushing
Patterson
S. Chase
Washington
Moore

1804–05
J. Marshall
Cushing
Paterson
S. Chase
Washington
W. Johnson

1806
J. Marshall
Cushing
S. Chase
Washington
W. Johnson
Livingston

1807–10
J. Marshall
Cushing
S. Chase
Washington
W. Johnson
Livingston
Todd

1811–22
J. Marshall
Washington
W. Johnson
Livingston
Todd
Duvall
Story

1823–25
J. Marshall
Washington
W. Johnson
Todd
Duvall
Story
Thompson

1826–28
J. Marshall
Washington
W. Johnson
Duvall

1826–28 (CONT)
Story
Thompson
Trimble

1829
J. Marshall
Washington
W. Johnson
Duvall
Story
Thompson
McLean

1830–34
J. Marshall
W. Johnson
Duvall
Story
Thompson
McLean
Baldwin

1835
J. Marshall
Duvall
Story
Thompson
McLean
Baldwin
Wayne

1836
Taney
Story
Thompson
McLean
Baldwin
Wayne
Barbour

1837–40
Taney
Story
Thompson
McLean
Baldwin
Wayne
Barbour
Catron
McKinley

1841–43
Taney
Story
Thompson
McLean
Baldwin
Wayne
Catron
McKinley
Daniel

1844
Taney
Story
McLean
Baldwin
Wayne
Catron
McKinley
Daniel

1845
Taney
McLean
Wayne
Catron
McKinley
Daniel
Nelson
Woodbury

1846–50
Taney
McLean
Wayne
Catron
McKinley
Daniel
Nelson
Woodbury
Grier

1851–52
Taney
McLean
Wayne
Catron
McKinley
Daniel
Nelson
Grier
Curtis

1853–57
Taney
McLean
Wayne
Catron
Daniel
Nelson
Grier
Curtis
Campbell

1858–60
Taney
McLean
Wayne
Catron
Daniel
Nelson
Grier
Campbell
Clifford

1861
Taney
McLean
Wayne
Catron
Nelson
Grier
Campbell
Clifford

1862
Taney
Wayne
Catron
Nelson
Grier
Clifford
Swayne
Miller
Davis

1863
Taney
Wayne
Catron
Nelson
Grier
Clifford
Swayne
Miller
Davis
Field

1864–65
S. P. Chase
Wayne
Catron[b]
Nelson
Grier
Clifford
Swayne
Miller
Davis
Field

1866
S. P. Chase
Wayne[b]
Nelson
Grier
Clifford
Swayne
Miller
Davis
Field

1867–69
S. P. Chase
Nelson
Grier
Clifford
Swayne
Miller
Davis
Field

1870–71
S. P. Chase
Nelson
Clifford
Swayne
Miller
Davis
Field
Strong
Bradley

1872–73
S. P. Chase
Clifford
Swayne
Miller
Davis
Field
Strong
Bradley
Hunt

1874–76
Waite
Clifford
Swayne
Miller
Davis
Field
Strong
Bradley
Hunt

1877–79
Waite
Clifford
Swayne
Miller
Field
Strong
Bradley
Hunt
Harlan (Ky.)

1880
Waite
Clifford
Swayne
Miller
Field
Bradley
Hunt
Harlan (Ky.)
Woods

1881
Waite
Miller
Field
Bradley
Hunt
Harlan (Ky.)
Woods
Matthews
Gray

1882–87	**1893**	**1903–05**	**1914–15**
Waite	*Fuller*	*Fuller*	*E.White*
Miller	Field	Harlan (Ky.)	McKenna
Field	Harlan (Ky.)	Brewer	Holmes
Bradley	Gray	Brown	Day
Harlan (Ky.)	Blatchford	E. White	Hughes
Woods	Brewer	Peckham	Van Devanter
Matthews	Brown	McKenna	J. Lamar
Gray	Shiras	Holmes	Pitney
Blatchford	H. Jackson	Day	McReynolds

1888	**1894**	**1906–08**	**1916–20**
Fuller	*Fuller*	*Fuller*	*E. White*
Miller	Field	Harlan (Ky.)	McKenna
Field	Harlan (Ky.)	Brewer	Holmes
Bradley	Gray	E. White	Day
Harlan (Ky.)	Brewer	Peckham	Van Devanter
Matthews	Brown	McKenna	Pitney
Gray	Shiras	Holmes	McReynolds
Blatchford	H. Jackson	Day	Brandeis
L. Lamar	E. White	Moody	Clarke

1889	**1895–97**	**1909**	**1921**
Fuller	*Fuller*	*Fuller*	*Taft*
Miller	Field	Harlan (Ky.)	McKenna
Field	Harlan (Ky.)	Brewer	Holmes
Bradley	Gray	E. White	Day
Harlan (Ky.)	Brewer	McKenna	Van Devanter
Gray	Brown	Holmes	Pitney
Blatchford	Shiras	Day	McReynolds
L. Lamar	E. White	Moody	Brandeis
Brewer	Peckham	Lurton	Clarke

1890–91	**1898–1901**	**1910–11**	**1922**
Fuller	*Fuller*	*E. White*	*Taft*
Field	Harlan (Ky.)	Harlan (Ky.)	McKenna
Bradley	Gray	McKenna	Holmes
Harlan (Ky.)	Brewer	Holmes	Van Devanter
Gray	Brown	Day	Pitney
Blatchford	Shiras	Lurton	McReynolds
L. Lamar	E. White	Hughes	Brandeis
Brewer	Peckham	Van Devanter	Sutherland
Brown	McKenna	J. Lamar	Butler

1892	**1902**	**1912–13**	**1923–24**
Fuller	*Fuller*	*E. White*	*Taft*
Field	Harlan (Ky.)	McKenna	McKenna
Harlan (Ky.)	Brewer	Holmes	Holmes
Gray	Brown	Day	Van Devanter
Blatchford	Shiras	Lurton	McReynolds
L. Lamar	E. White	Hughes	Brandeis
Brewer	Peckham	Van Devanter	Sutherland
Brown	McKenna	J. Lamar	Butler
Shiras	Holmes	**Pitney**	**Sanford**

1925–29	**1939**	**1946–48**	**1957**
Taft	*Hughes*	*Vinson*	*Warren*
Holmes	McReynolds	Black	Black
Van Devanter	Butler	Reed	Frankfurter
McReynolds	Stone	Frankfurter	Douglas
Brandeis	Roberts	Douglas	Burton
Sutherland	Black	Murphy	Clark
Butler	Reed	R. Jackson	Harlan (N.Y.)
Sanford	Frankfurter	W. Rutledge	Brennan
Stone	Douglas	Burton	Whittaker
1930–31	**1940**	**1949–52**	**1958–61**
Hughes	*Hughes*	*Vinson*	*Warren*
Holmes	McReynolds	Black	Black
Van Devanter	Stone	Reed	Frankfurter
McReynolds	Roberts	Frankfurter	Douglas
Brandeis	Black	Douglas	Clark
Sutherland	Reed	R. Jackson	Harlan (N.Y.)
Butler	Frankfurter	Burton	Brennan
Stone	Douglas	Clark	Whittaker
Roberts	Murphy	Minton	Stewart
1932–36	**1941–42**	**1953–54**	**1962–65**
Hughes	*Stone*	*Warren*	*Warren*
Van Devanter	Roberts	Black	Black
McReynolds	Black	Reed	Douglas
Brandeis	Reed	Frankfurter	Clark
Sutherland	Frankfurter	Douglas	Harlan (N.Y.)
Butler	Douglas	R. Jackson	Brennan
Stone	Murphy	Burton	Stewart
Roberts	Byrnes	Clark	B. White
Cardozo	R. Jackson	Minton	Goldberg
1937	**1943–44**	**1955**	**1965–67**
Hughes	*Stone*	*Warren*	*Warren*
McReynolds	Roberts	Black	Black
Brandeis	Black	Reed	Douglas
Sutherland	Reed	Frankfurter	Clark
Butler	Frankfurter	Douglas	Harlan (N.Y.)
Stone	Douglas	Burton	Brennan
Roberts	Murphy	Clark	Stewart
Cardozo	R. Jackson	Minton	B. White
Black	W. Rutledge	Harlan (N.Y.)	Fortas
1938	**1945**	**1956**	**1967–69**
Hughes	*Stone*	*Warren*	*Warren*
McReynolds	Black	Black	Black
Brandeis	Reed	Reed	Douglas
Butler	Frankfurter	Frankfurter	Harlan (N.Y.)
Stone	Douglas	Douglas	Brennan
Roberts	Murphy	Burton	Stewart
Cardozo	R. Jackson	Clark	B. White
Black	W. Rutledge	Harlan (N.Y.)	Fortas
Reed	Burton	**Brennan**	T. Marshall

1969
Burger
Black
Douglas
Harlan (N.Y.)
Brennan
Stewart
B. White
Fortas
T. Marshall

1969–70
Burger
Black
Douglas
Harlan (N.Y.)
Brennan
Stewart
B. White
T. Marshall

1970
Burger
Black
Douglas
Harlan (N.Y.)
Brennan
Stewart
B. White
T. Marshall
Blackmun

1971
Burger
Douglas
Brennan
Stewart
B. White
T. Marshall
Blackmun

1972–75
Burger
Douglas
Brennan
Stewart
B. White
T. Marshall
Blackmun
Powell
Rehnquist

1975–81
Burger
Brennan
Stewart
B. White
T. Marshall
Blackmun
Powell
Rehnquist
J. Stevens

1981–86
Burger
Brennan
B. White
T. Marshall
Blackmun
Powell
Rehnquist
J. Stevens
O'Connor

1986–87
Rehnquist
Brennan
B. White
T. Marshall
Blackmun
Powell
J. Stevens
O'Connor
Scalia

1987—
Rehnquist
Brennan
B. White
T. Marshall
Blackmun
J. Stevens
O'Connor
Scalia
Kennedy

[a] Rutledge was a recess appointment whose confirmation was rejected by the Senate after the 1795 Term.
[b] Upon the death of Catron in 1865 and Wayne in 1867 their positions were abolished according to a congressional act of 1866. The Court's membership was reduced to eight until a new position was created by Congress in 1869.

Source: Constitutional Interpretation, Chase and Ducat, published by West Publishing Co.

BIOGRAPHY OF LITIGATION: DOCUMENTS, STRATEGIES, AND SKILLS

NADER v. ALLEGHENY AIRLINES

TABLE OF CONTENTS

INTRODUCTION

Litigation can be a creative and exhilarating experience. It can also be complex, technical, and daunting. The material in this section is designed to take the reader, step by step, through a case in federal litigation. In doing so, we will use various documents developed for the case in order to follow it from the onset of the cause of action to the decision in the Supreme Court. The textual discussion accompanying each document will focus on the nature of the document, its relation to the Federal Rules of Civil Procedure, the strategic options that were open to the attorneys, and an analysis of the choices they made. We hope that this will assist you in understanding the litigation process and the preparation of litigation documents. It should be kept in mind that this section is *not* designed to be a text in substantive law. Rather, it is designed to aid in the development of litigation skills such as drafting, analysis, strategizing, and argumentation.

While we recognize that case handling differs from jurisdiction to jurisdiction and that cases themselves differ within any particular jurisdiction, we believe that there are enough commonalities to make the approach we have adopted useful. With that in mind, we have chosen a case that has a recognizable fact situation, a wide variety of documents and procedural devices, and a number of opportunities for strategic decision making. The case is *Nader v Allegheny Airlines*, a suit involving a confirmed, ticketed airline passenger who was involuntarily denied boarding ("bumped") from an overbooked commercial flight.

On April 28, 1972, Ralph Nader was not permitted to board Allegheny flight 864 from Washington, D.C. to Hartford, Connecticut for which he had a confirmed reservation. Nader had booked the flight in advance. He was scheduled to appear that day at a rally in Hartford on behalf of the Connecticut Citizen Action Group (CCAG), a co-plaintiff in the case. When Nader could not secure timely alternate transportation to Hartford, the purpose of the rally was frustrated and CCAG was thereby injured. The suit sought compensatory and punitive damages for both plaintiffs.

We chose to use this case for several reasons. First, it involves an issue that is directly or indirectly familiar to most people today, being bumped from an overbooked airplane.

Second, it involves a public figure who is widely identified with consumerism (adding a touch of irony to the fact situation). Third, and most importantly, the case involves a broad panoply of documents as it moves from the district court to the court of appeals and to the Supreme Court.

The documents we have used are arranged chronologically in the order that they were filed in the case. We have edited some of them so that the focus would be primarily on the most important issues in the dispute. For those who wish to read the entire opinions in the court of appeals or the Supreme Court, the citations are 512 F.2d 527 for the court of appeals and 426 U.S. 290 for the Supreme Court.

Finally, we would like to offer a word of thanks to the litigation group at Public Citizen, the public interest law firm that helped represent Mr. Nader at the Supreme Court. Alan Morrison and David Vladek made their files available to us for extended periods of time. David Vladek also spent considerable amounts of his limited time answering questions and generally assisting us to understand and develop the case. We appreciate their efforts.

DOCUMENT #1: COMPLAINT

The first pleading in a case is the *complaint*. It is used to allege the basis of the court's jurisdiction, to set out the factual elements of the plaintiff's claim, and to request the desired relief. An examination of the Complaint in *Nader v Allegheny* will provide clear illustrations of these functions.

Like all pleadings, the complaint begins by identifying various participants in the lawsuit. At the top of the first page, the court in which the suit is pending is set out. Then comes the "caption" in which Ralph Nader and Connecticut Citizen Action Group (CCAG) are identified as plaintiffs, and Allegheny Airlines is named as defendant. Immediately to the right of the caption is the Civil Action Number. This is the number, assigned by the clerk when the suit is filed, that will identify the case on all documents submitted to the court and on all court records. The number in this case, 1346-72, indicates that this is case 1346 of 1972. Finally, the document itself is identified. In this instance, we have *COMPLAINT FOR COMPENSATORY AND PUNITIVE DAMAGES*. From this heading, we know the plaintiffs are bringing this action to recover for injuries actually suffered (the compensatory damages) and for an amount that will punish the defendant for its particularly wrongful act (the punitive damages).

Next comes the plaintiffs' statement of the facts supporting their claim. Federal Rule of Civil Procedure (FRCP) 8 says that a claim for relief "shall contain (1) a short and plain statement of the. . .court's jurisdiction. . ., (2) a short and plain statement of the claim showing that the pleader is entitled to relief, and (3) a demand for judgment for the relief the pleader seeks."

The court's jurisdiction is alleged in paragraph 1 of the complaint in which the plaintiffs state that the case arises under various laws of the United States (federal laws) regulating commerce. Therefore, the court has jurisdiction under title 28, section 1337 of the United States Code (USC) which gives district courts jurisdiction of cases arising under any Act of Congress regulating Interstate Commerce. This is the court's "federal question" jurisdiction. Plaintiffs also assert jurisdiction under 28 USC 1332 which then gave district courts jurisdiction over actions when there is a diversity of citizenship between the various parties to the suit and where the amount in controversy exceeds $10,000. (Today, the amount is $50,000.)

Paragraphs 6–30 describe in some detail the facts, according to plaintiffs, and the basis for their claim for relief. The paragraphs indicate the method by which Allegheny sought passengers and took reservations. The airline knew people relied on its representations concerning travel reservations. It knew that Nader obtained and confirmed a reservation. Yet despite this confirmed reservation, he was not permitted to board the flight on which he had reserved a space. Because he could not board his flight and because he was unable, despite his efforts to do so, to obtain other accommodations, he missed a public meeting sponsored by the CCAG which defeated the purpose of the meeting.

Paragraphs 31–36 lay out the specific charge against Allegheny. In this case, the charge is that Allegheny knew it could not assure Nader, or any confirmed passenger, that they would actually be seated on an Allegheny flight due to Allegheny's regular practice of over-selling space on its planes. Allegheny did not inform Nader of this practice nor of the risk that the practice presented to him prior to refusing him a seat. This knowing disregard for the well-being of passengers amounts, according to plaintiffs, to a willful, wanton breach of Allegheny's obligations to passengers.

The claim is presented in the nature of a *tort* rather than as a *breach of contract.* One reason for this may have been that as a matter of general policy, punitive damages are not available in breach-of-contract actions. Injured plaintiffs are left to compensatory damages to make them whole. In this case, compensatory damages were either very small or unascertainable. Therefore, a claim sounding in fraud provided a better vehicle for greater relief through punitive damages.

Finally, there is a "WHEREFORE" clause at the end of the complaint in which the plaintiffs demand their relief. In this case, Nader seeks only ten dollars compensatory damages but $50,000 punitive damages, together with interest and costs. The relatively small number for compensatory damages is due to the fact that, in monetary terms, Nader suffered very little actual injury. CCAG, on the other hand, sought $100,000 compensatory damages because it felt it was actually injured by Nader's inability to attend the meeting. CCAG also sought $100,000 punitive damages plus interest and costs. Each plaintiff also asked for "such other or further relief as the Court may deem proper." This catchall phrase is standard in civil complaints. It asks the court to use its flexibility to fashion appropriate relief.

There are a number of concerns that the drafter of a complaint needs to keep in mind. Some of those listed here will appear self-evident. Unfortunately, they are not. Others are somewhat more subtle, posing difficulties that cannot be overcome by mechanical rules.

We should caution the reader here that neither this discussion, nor similar discussions on other documents, are intended to be exhaustive. They will merely point out some common problems to watch for and, where possible, methods to solve them. Also, different jurisdictions have different rules, sometimes *very* different rules, for drafting documents. It is, therefore, extremely important to check the rules of the jurisdiction in question when preparing any litigation document.

First, the drafter must make certain that all the defendants are properly designated. This is particularly important when a defendant is an organization or when the defendant is being sued in a representative, rather than a personal, capacity. The failure to designate a defendant properly can lead to embarrassment and inconvenience (due to the necessity of re-filing) or to the more serious problem of losing an improperly designated defendant due to the running of the statute of limitations before the error can be corrected.

Second, the drafter must allege the jurisdiction of the court. Where this depends on statute, the statute should be specifically identified.

Third, the body of the complaint containing the allegations about the wrong done to the plaintiff, must be clearly and concisely set out in separately numbered paragraphs. FRCP 8(a) requires "a short and plain statement of the claim. . . ." This generally means that each paragraph should contain only one main thought. A series of paragraphs should be used to develop a cause of action. (It should be noted, however, that "no technical forms of pleading. . .are required." FRCP 8 (e)). The allegations generally should be *factual* and not conclusory and, when taken together, must make out each element of the cause of action the plaintiff is pursuing. If plaintiff is pursuing several different causes of action, these may be separately laid out in different "counts" of the complaint (e.g., Count I, Breach of Warranty; Count II, Strict Liability in Tort). The various counts may rely on the same facts which need not be repeated or repled. Existing paragraphs of general allegations or ones from a particular count may be incorporated by reference (to their paragraph numbers) in any other part of the complaint).

After all the factual allegations have been made, plaintiff should set out its "demand for judgment for the relief" sought. This may be done with specificity or in a more general sense. For instance, plaintiff may demand damages in a specific amount or in the amount the court deems appropriate. If relief other than damages is sought (e.g., injunctive or declaratory relief) the prayer should be more specific. Plaintiff may also seek interest, costs, attorneys fees and "such other or further relief as the Court may deem proper."

Finally, the complaint must be signed by an attorney (if the plaintiff is represented) or by the plaintiff (if not represented) together with the signer's address. The complaint need not be verified unless otherwise specifically required.

DRAFTING A COMPLAINT

- Properly identify each party to the action.
- Set out with specificity all the bases of the court's jurisdiction.
- Allege facts sufficient to make out each element of your cause(s) of action.
- Where specifics are not known, more general allegations, or those on information and belief, may be made, pending discovery (provided some legitimate basis exists for the allegations).
- Sign, or have the plaintiff sign, the complaint.

UNITED STATES DISTRICT COURT
FOR THE DISTRICT OF COLUMBIA

Ralph Nader
and
Connecticut Citizen Action Group,

Plaintiffs,

v

Allegheny Airlines, Inc.,

Defendant.

Civil Action No. 1346-72

COMPLAINT FOR COMPENSATORY AND PUNITIVE DAMAGES

Plaintiffs allege as follows:

1. This action arises under the laws of the United States regulating interstate and foreign air commerce, U.S.C. Title 49, Sections 1301 et. seq., and particularly U.S.C. Title 49, Section 1374. This Court has jurisdiction under U.S.C. Title 28, Section 1337 and

U.S.C. Title 28, Section 1332. The amount in controversy exceeds the sum of $10,000, exclusive of interest and costs.

2. Plaintiff Ralph Nader is a citizen of the United States and resides in the District of Columbia.

3. Plaintiff Connecticut Citizen Action Group (hereinafter referred to as CCAG) is a non-profit corporation, organized and existing under the laws of the District of Columbia and having its principal place of business at 57 Farmington Avenue, Hartford, Connecticut. Plaintiff CCAG is a public interest advocate for environmental, consumer and human rights issues arising throughout the State of Connecticut, which has been supported and sponsored by Plaintiff Nader since its inception.

4. Defendant Allegheny Airlines, Inc., is a corporation, having its principal place of business at National Airport, Washington, D.C., and at all times relevant herein transacted business and maintained offices in the District of Columbia, at 16th and K Streets, N.W., at Washington National Airport, and at other locations within the said District.

5. Defendant is an air carrier engaged in interstate commerce pursuant to a certificate of public convenience and necessity issued by the Civil Aeronautics Board and is regulated by the laws of the United States relating to such interstate commerce and by the rules, orders and regulations promulgated by the Board in accordance with the Federal Aviation Act of 1958.

6. Prior to April 28, 1972, Defendant advertised, publicized and published tariffs stating that it transported passengers on a reservation basis by jet aircraft on scheduled flights between Washington, D.C. and Hartford, Connecticut.

7. Defendant knew or should have known that passengers and others alike rely heavily upon such representations and upon the confirmed reservations and tickets which are sold by Defendant for transportation on particular flights.

8. Several days prior to April 28, 1972, Plaintiff Nader's representative contacted Defendant and requested a reservation for Plaintiff Nader for one seat on Allegheny flight 864 from Washington National Airport to Hartford, Connecticut, on the morning of Friday, April 28, 1972.

9. Defendant's agent represented to Plaintiff Nader's representative that Defendant had made a reservation which would assure him passage from Washington on Allegheny flight 864 scheduled to depart on April 28, 1972, provided he purchased his ticket at least 30 minutes prior to flight time.

10. Plaintiff Nader's representative communicated to Plaintiff CCAG the fact that Plaintiff Nader had a reservation on flight 864 on April 28, 1972 and would be arriving at Bradley Field in Hartford, Connecticut on that flight.

11. Early on the morning of April 28, 1972 Defendant's agent, Ober Steamship and Tour Agency, issued a ticket to Plaintiff Nader for Allegheny flight 864 to depart Washington National Airport at 10:15 a.m. on April 28, 1972.

12. At the time the ticket was issued, Defendant's agent marked the symbol "OK" in the status column of the ticket thereby confirming the previously made reservation in writing.

13. The Defendant intended by its representations aforesaid to induce the Plaintiffs to rely upon its said representations so that Plaintiff Nader's travel arrangements would not be made with any other competitor of Defendant.

14. When Plaintiff Nader arrived at the gate at National Airport where flight 864 was boarding on April 28, 1972, several people, some of whom had tickets and had not yet been boarded, were also present at the gate.

15. Plaintiff Nader presented his ticket to Defendant's gate agent and was then informed by this agent that the flight had been oversold and that all seats had been taken.

16. At this point Plaintiff Nader explained to Defendant's agents at the gate that he was due to speak to a fund-raising rally organized by and for Plaintiff CCAG, which was to occur at noon that day, and that if he didn't appear on schedule, the rally would be ruined.

17. The purpose of the rally was to organize citizen opposition to utilities rate increases, raise funds for CCAG's public interest work and to give interested citizens the opportunity to hear Plaintiff Nader speak on consumer issues. Plaintiff Nader was to be introduced at the rally by the Mayor of Hartford, Connecticut. The rally and Plaintiff Nader's appearance were heavily advertised both on the radio and by leaflet distribution for several days prior to April 28, 1972. Plaintiff CCAG anticipated a crowd well in excess of 2,000 persons and planned to raise substantial funds through the sale of bumper stickers and other similar items.

18. In making such plans and arrangements, Plaintiff CCAG relied on the expectation that Plaintiff Nader would be accommodated on flight 864 for which he had a confirmed reservation.

19. After being informed that the flight had been oversold and he would not be accommodated, Plaintiff Nader then asked Defendant's agent, in view of his urgent circumstances, to ascertain whether standby passengers had been improperly boarded in lieu of persons holding confirmed reservations, and to recheck whether Plaintiff Nader could be accommodated.

20. Defendant's agent refused to board Plaintiff on flight 864.

21. Other persons holding confirmed reservations were also denied boarding on flight 864.

22. Defendant's refusal to accommodate Plaintiff Nader on flight 864 was in breach of its contract with Plaintiff Nader.

23. Defendant's refusal to accommodate Plaintiff Nader was in violation of its published tariff.

24. Plaintiff Nader then requested Defendant's agents to explain his situation to the passengers already boarded on flight 864 and ask if any such passenger would volunteer to take a later flight in order to allow Plaintiff Nader to get to Hartford in time for the rally.

25. Defendant's agents refused Plaintiff Nader's request described in paragraph 24.

26. No other certificated airline service was available at that time to transport Plaintiff Nader to Hartford in time for the rally.

27. Defendant's flight 864 departed Washington National Airport approximately on schedule at about 10:15 a.m. on April 28, 1972, and said flight arrived at Hartford approximately on schedule that morning.

28. Defendant in fact sold more seats for flight 864 on April 28, 1972 from Washington to Hartford than were available on the aircraft.

29. Plaintiff Nader was forced to take the next available flight to Boston, Massachusetts in order to arrive in time for an engagement that afternoon in Storrs, Connecticut, thereby incurring additional charges for airfare in the amount of $3.00, plus other costs and expenses for Plaintiffs.

30. As a direct and proximate result of Defendant's conduct, the Director of Plaintiff CCAG had to and in fact did appear before an expectant crowd of hundreds of persons and inform the audience that Plaintiff Nader had missed his flight and would not appear. Consequently, the purpose of the meeting was frustrated, the large anticipated turn-out failed to materialize, no funds were raised, the publicity work of a large number of CCAG supporters and volunteers went for naught, and the reputation, esteem, and fund-raising ability of Plaintiff CCAG was seriously damaged and impaired.

31. Defendant knew that it could not assure passage to Plaintiff Nader on flight 864 on April 28, 1972 or other flights on Defendant's system because such flights had been and were being consistently over-reserved and oversold.

32. Defendant knew that ticket holders with confirmed reservations were regularly being denied space on such oversold flights and that any prospective passenger on any such flight might be denied accommodation on such flight despite holding a confirmed reservation.

33. Defendant failed to inform Plaintiff Nader, at any time prior to his arrival at Washington National Airport to take flight 864, of the possibility that his confirmed reservation might not be or would not be honored because of Defendant's practice of overbooking such flights.

34. Defer.dant arbitrarily and capriciously denied Plaintiff Nader passage and at the same time afforded passage on said flight to one or more persons holding tickets issued subsequent to this ticket or to persons otherwise not entitled to occupy the space reserved and confirmed for Plaintiff Nader by Defendant's agent, thereby subjecting Plaintiff Nader to unjust discrimination, or undue or unreasonable prejudice or disadvantage.

35. Defendant regularly overbooks, on a confirmed reservation basis, various of its flights including flight 864 with the result that said flights are frequently oversold, and regularly subjects ticket holders with confirmed reservations on said flights to unjust discrimination or undue or unreasonable prejudice or disadvantage by arbitrarily and capriciously refusing passage to ticket holders with confirmed reservations without regard to their contractual rights, and by arbitrarily and capriciously allowing passage to other persons not entitled to the space which Defendant had previously contractually reserved.

36. Defendant's actions as aforesaid were knowing, and were undertaken in such conscious and deliberate disregard of the interests of its prospective passengers and others that such actions were willful, wanton and accomplished in willful disregard of the provisions of Defendant's own tariffs and the Federal Aviation Act of 1958 (49 U.S.C. 1301 et. seq.).

WHEREFORE, Plaintiffs demand judgment against the Defendant as follows:

1. Plaintiff Nader demands compensatory damages in the amount of $10.00 and punitive damages in the amount of $50,000.00 together with interest, costs of this suit, and such other or further relief as the Court may deem proper.

2. Plaintiff CCAG demands compensatory damages in the sum of $100,000.00 and punitive damages in the sum of $100,000.00 together with interest, costs of this suit, and such other or further relief as the Court may deem proper.

PLAINTIFFS DEMAND TRIAL BY JURY AS TO ALL ISSUES.

Don Crockett
1001 Connecticut Avenue, N.W.
Suite 800
Washington, D.C. 20036
Telephone: (202) 628-7234

Reuben B. Robertson, III
1156 – 19th Street, N.W.
Washington, D.C. 20036
Telephone: (202) 833-3400

ATTORNEYS FOR PLAINTIFFS

DOCUMENT #2: ANSWER

The next document is the *answer,* which is the responsive pleading to the complaint. It may also add new material to the legal or factual dispute. For example, in *Nader v Allegheny,* the defendant has chosen not only to respond to the allegations in the complaint, but also to raise various legal questions about the validity of the complaint and the jurisdiction of the court to entertain it.

An answer is very different from a complaint in many ways, although there are some similarities. For the most part, the complaint dictates what is included in the answer. In this sense, the answer is truly "responsive." FRCP 8(b) requires a party to state, "in short and plain terms," his or her defenses to the averments made by the adverse party. In doing so, the answering party may admit, deny, or state that he or she is without knowledge or information to respond. The latter statement has the effect of a denial so far as issues of fact are concerned. The answering party will generally be barred from contesting facts not denied. If an averment that requires a response is not denied, it is deemed to be admitted. Therefore, the answering party must carefully read the averments contained in the document being answered (such as the complaint) and deny each paragraph *or part of a paragraph* that the answering party does not wish to admit.

If the answering party must admit an averment but wishes to explain it, he or she may do so through "affirmative defenses" FRCP 8(c). For example, if a complaint alleges that the defendant borrowed $100 from the plaintiff, the defendant may admit this fact without conceding the debt. The defendant may respond by saying that the obligation had been repaid or that the defendant was a minor when the debt was contracted. These claims are more like those in a complaint because they are, essentially, new matters being pled. Thus, the answering party develops a theory of law concerning his or her defense, and pleads facts supporting that theory.

As in a complaint, the statements in the answer should be short, to the point, and in numbered paragraphs. Enough must be said to permit the answering party to introduce at trial evidence of the facts alleged. Whether a more complete statement should be given is often a matter of strategy. Given the extensive nature of discovery, it is likely that even a skeletal statement of a defense will eventually be fleshed out before trial.

Finally, counterclaims may (and sometimes must) be raised in an answer. A counterclaim is a claim that the answering party has against the party whose pleading is being answered. In this sense, a counterclaim is much like a complaint and is treated this way by the rules.

Turning to the answer in *Nader v Allegheny,* note the designation of the court and the caption which must appear on all documents in this litigation. The defendant then proceeds with the substance of its answer. It begins by separately listing its defenses. The first two defenses argue that even if the facts alleged by plaintiffs are fully believed by the court, the complaint does not state a legally recognizable claim against Allegheny for either compensatory or punitive relief. The Third Defense argues that the nature of the claim against Allegheny, if cognizable at all, *must* be heard first at the Civil Aeronautics Board, the administrative agency charged with regulating air transportation. Defendant is saying that the law assigns primary jurisdiction over this type of complaint to the Board and that the court cannot act until the Board acts. Finally, in its Fourth Defense, Allegheny alleges that, even if the court can generally hear this suit, plaintiffs cannot maintain it because they have not complied with a regulatory requirement concerning timely written notice of the events giving rise to the claim.

Defendant then turns to the specific allegations of the complaint. In the Fifth Defense, it addresses with specificity plaintiffs' factual claims. Paragraph 1 admits the allegations contained in various numbered paragraphs of plaintiffs' complaint. These allegations are now deemed proved and will not be contested at trial. Paragraph 2 admits the allegations of plaintiffs' paragraph 4 except to the extent that the paragraph places National Airport in

Washington, D.C. While this will not be a major issue in the case, defendant is contesting the location of the airport. In paragraph 3, defendant is denying the factual allegations in specific paragraphs of the complaint. Since these facts are in dispute, plaintiffs will have to introduce evidence to support them. The defendant, of course, will introduce evidence to disprove them. The trier of fact will then have to sort through the evidence to resolve the differences on these factual issues. In paragraph 4, defendant is saying it does not have sufficient knowledge to answer specified paragraphs of the complaint. Plaintiffs will have to introduce evidence to substantiate its claims in these paragraphs.

In paragraph 7, defendant responds to plaintiffs' allegation that boarding of the flight was still in progress by saying that boarding had been completed by the time Nader had arrived. The implication here is that Nader was partly at fault for arriving at the boarding gate later than he should have. Defendant also attempts to minimize the overbooking problem by responding to plaintiffs' claim that "several people, some of whom had tickets" had not been boarded by indicating that only two such people other than Nader were at the gate. Paragraph 8 seeks to show that Allegheny did offer Nader alternate transportation which would have resulted in only minor disruption of plaintiffs' plans. Thus, part of any damage suffered by plaintiffs was caused by Nader's refusal of alternate transportation. Similarly, paragraph 9 alleges that Nader was aware of the possibility of being "bumped" and that the possibilities increase if one arrives at the boarding gate after boarding is complete. Again, the effort is clearly to cast at least some of the blame for the situation on Nader. While this tactic might influence the outcome of the case on the merits, it was most probably intended to influence the decision on punitive damages, the area of Allegheny's largest exposure.

As a result of the complaint and answer, all parties and the court are at least preliminarily aware of the issues in dispute and the theories to be used by the parties in pressing their claims or defenses.

DRAFTING AN ANSWER:

* Read the complaint carefully; examine all of the factual allegationsand their legal implications.
* Deny any allegations about which there is any doubt; the failure to deny is deemed an admission.
* Explain in affirmative defenses all aspects of allegations which, while true, are out of context, incomplete, or otherwise inaccurate.
* Consider whether your client has claims against the plaintiff and, if so, whether they must be pled in a counterclaim.
* Even if a counterclaim is not mandatory, determine whether it is strategically sound to include it anyway.

UNITED STATES DISTRICT COURT
FOR THE DISTRICT OF COLUMBIA

Ralph Nader and the Connecticut
Citizen Action Group,

Plaintiffs,

v

Allegheny Airlines, Inc.,

Defendant.

Civil Action No. 1346-72

ANSWER

First Defense

The Complaint fails to state a claim upon which relief can be granted against the Defendant Allegheny Airlines, Inc.

Second Defense

The Complaint fails to state a claim upon which punitive damages can be granted against Defendant Allegheny Airlines, Inc.

Third Defense

This action does not appropriately belong within the jurisdiction of this Court in that it challenges the legality and propriety of Defendant Allegheny's reservation and denied boarding practices, which considerations are by law assigned to the Civil Aeronautics Board and not to the courts.

Fourth Defense

This action is barred for the failure of the Plaintiffs to comply with Rule 40(B), Tariff C.A.B. 142, Local and Joint Passenger Rules Tariff No. PR-6 in that they failed to present to Defendant Allegheny a written notice of claim within 45 days of the alleged occurrence of the events giving rise to this claim.

Fifth Defense

1. Defendant Allegheny admits the allegations of paragraphs 5, 6, 8, 11, 12, 15, 20, 21 24, 25, 27, and 28 of the Complaint.

2. Defendant Allegheny admits the allegations of paragraph 4 of the Complaint except that National Airport is in Washington, D.C., which Defendant denies.

3. Defendant Allegheny denies the allegations of paragraphs 7, 9, 13, 18, 22, 23, 29, 30, 31, 32, 34, and 36 of the Complaint.

4. Defendant Allegheny is without knowledge or information sufficient to form a belief as to the truth of the averments in paragraphs 2, 3, 10, and 17 of the Complaint.

HOGAN & HARTSON
815 CONNECTICUT AVENUE
WASHINGTON, D.C. 20006

5. Defendant Allegheny admits the allegations of paragraph 16 of the Complaint except that it is denied that Plaintiff Nader told the Defendant's agent that the rally would be ruined if he failed to appear.

6. Defendant Allegheny admits the allegations of paragraph 19 of the Complaint and avers that Defendant's agent did take the actions requested by Plaintiff Nader as described in said paragraph 19 of the Complaint.

7. In answer to paragraph 14 of the Complaint, Defendant Allegheny states that at the time Plaintiff Nader arrived at the gate from which Flight 864 was departing the boarding of Flight 864 had been completed. Two people were at the gate at that time with tickets, but they had not been boarded.

8. In answer to paragraph 26 of the Complaint, Defendant Allegheny alleges that Plaintiff Nader was offered transportation on Allegheny Commuter Flight 145 from Washington to Philadelphia connecting with Allegheny Flight 906 to Hartford, Connecticut, scheduled to arrive in Hartford at 12:10 p.m., 55 minutes after the arrival of Plaintiff Nader's ticketed flight.

9. In answer to paragraph 33 of the Complaint, Defendant states that Plaintiff Nader was already aware of the possibility that a confirmed reservation would not be honored because of the reservation practices of airlines, and Defendant avers that Plaintiff Nader was aware that the possibility of such denied boarding increases when the passenger arrives at the boarding gate after the conclusion of the boarding of the airplane and at the time that the flight was scheduled to take off, as Plaintiff Nader did in this instance.

10. In answer to paragraph 35 of the Complaint, Defendant Allegheny states that Defendant, in an effort to minimize the effect of the no-show passenger problem upon Defendant and the public, accepts a limited number of reservations in excess of flight capacity based upon statistical studies of the percentage of likely cancellations and no-shows on each flight. The remainder of paragraph 35 is denied.

11. The allegations of injuries and damages in the Complaint are denied, as are all other allegations of the Complaint not specifically answered above.

By _____
Frank F. Roberson

By _____
William A. Bradford, Jr.

By _____
Robert S. Bennett

815 Connecticut Avenue, N.W.
Washington, D.C. 20006
298-5500

Attorneys for Defendant

HOGAN & HARTSON
815 CONNECTICUT AVENUE
WASHINGTON, D.C. 20006

CERTIFICATE OF SERVICE

I hereby certify that a true copy of the foregoing Answer was mailed, postage prepaid, this 20th day of October, 1972, to Don W. Crockett, Esquire, Suite 880, 1700 Pennsylvania Avenue, N.W., Washington, D.C. 20006, and Reuben B. Robertson, III, Esquire, 1156–19th Street, N.W., Washington, D.C. 20036, Attorneys for Plaintiffs.

_____

William A. Bradford, Jr.

DOCUMENT #3: INTERROGATORIES

Once the answer has been filed, the factual dispute between the parties is brought into greater focus. Nevertheless, there are many details of the broader dispute that remain unknown, uncertain, or confused. The FRCP provide for various methods by which each side may learn facts known to opponents. These methods are called, in the aggregate, *discovery*. The purpose of discovery is to narrow the factual disputes between the parties and to provide the parties with important information so that the trial can move more quickly and efficiently.

Among the methods of discovery permitted by the FRCP are interrogatories, depositions, and notices to produce. Here we will focus on interrogatories and the responses to them. Later we will examine depositions and notices to produce as well as motions compelling or limiting discovery.

Rule 33 of the FRCP provides for interrogatories to parties. The Rule permits *any* party to serve on any other *party* "written interrogatories to be answered by the party served." They must be answered in writing and under oath. If there is an objection to an interrogatory, the reasons for the objection must be stated. If the party seeking discovery is dissatisfied with the answers submitted, believes any objections to questions are unfounded, or has not been given any responses at all, that party may seek an order of the court compelling the other party to respond or to respond more fully. Similarly, if the party to whom discovery is directed believes that the discovery sought is overly burdensome or harassing, it may seek a protective order in which the court limits the scope of the discovery or makes other provisions to protect the party to whom the discovery is directed.

In the *Nader* case, Plaintiffs served Allegheny with a *First Set of Interrogatories*—our Document #3. After the standard opening, the document states to whom it is directed, the authority under which it has been served, and the terms by which defendant must answer including the due date for answers to be submitted to plaintiffs' attorney. The document then goes on to ask the questions plaintiffs want to have answered. It should be noted that several questions are conditioned upon receiving a particular answer to a previous question. For instance, interrogatory 1 asks whether Allegheny has an established policy concerning the retention or destruction of business records and documents. Interrogatory 2 is to be answered only if the answer to the previous question is "yes." Note that an interrogatory may have several parts. For example, in interrogatory 7, a variety of information is sought through parts (a) to (e) for each document or record that Allegheny may have destroyed.

Beginning with interrogatory 8, plaintiffs ask questions designed to show Allegheny's practice concerning overbooking in general and flight 864 (the flight from which Nader was bumped) in particular. Interrogatory 8 specifically seeks information as to whether and how often (during a specific period) flight 864 had been oversold causing confirmed passengers to be bumped. If there have been such occurrences, interrogatory 9 seeks more detailed information about the circumstances. The purpose of these interrogatories, through number 16, is to show that Allegheny had a practice of overbooking which resulted in confirmed passengers being denied boarding, and that some of these passengers had complained to Allegheny or to the governmental regulatory agency. Thus, Allegheny could be shown to be on notice of the problem which it failed to correct.

Interrogatories 16–23 are intended to seek answers that show an affirmative policy of overbooking and that this policy was not disclosed to customers or prospective customers. Again, the goal is to box Allegheny into a corner where its culpability is apparent. Many of the remaining interrogatories seek information about employees and other passengers bumped from the flight. The information concerning these people is sought so that plaintiffs might contact them to obtain more information or to seek their participation as witnesses.

Finally, the document is signed by plaintiffs' attorney who also signs a *Certificate of Service* indicating that a copy of the document, the original of which is filed with the court, has been mailed on a particular date to the attorney for the defendant.

PREPARING INTERROGATORIES

- Know what kind of information you are seeking.
- Ask questions designed to elicit that information.
- Ask very focused questions when you know the information you are seeking and want to try to commit your opponent to a certain position.
- Ask questions requiring a narrative answer or a descriptive answer when you are seeking general or new information.
- Keep in mind that you may be able to serve additional sets of interrogatories in the future seeking more information.

UNITED STATES DISTRICT COURT
FOR THE DISTRICT OF COLUMBIA

Ralph Nader and the Connecticut
Citizen Action Group,

                                    Plaintiffs,

        v   } Civil Action No. 1346-72

Allegheny Airlines, Inc.,

                                    Defendant.

**PLAINTIFFS' FIRST SET OF
INTERROGATORIES TO DEFEN-
DANT ALLEGHENY AIRLINES**

TO: Allegheny Airlines, Inc.
Washington National Airport
Washington, D.C. 20001
Attention: Mr. Edwin I. Colodny

Pursuant to Rule 33 of the Federal Rules of Civil Procedure, the plaintiffs herein require that the defendant, through its officers having actual knowledge of the matters referred to herein, answer the following interrogatories fully, in writing and under oath and serve a copy of said answers upon plaintiffs' counsel on or before September 7, 1972.

1. Does Allegheny Airlines, Inc. (hereinafter referred to as "Allegheny" have an established policy for the retention and destruction of business records and documents?

2. If the answer to Interrogatory No. 1 is yes, is any part of that policy set forth in writing?

* * *

6. State whether any records or documents of any kind, including records stored on computer tape, microfilm or microfische, which in any way relate to or refer to Allegheny flight 864 on April 28, 1972 have been destroyed?

7. If the answer to Interrogatory No. 6 is yes, list the following:

(a) Each document or record destroyed.

(b) The contents of each such document or record.

(c) The date of the destruction.

(d) The name of the person authorizing or supervising such destruction.

(e) The reason for the said destruction.

8. During the period January 1, 1969 through June 30, 1972, has Allegheny flight 864 or any predecessor flight with a different number departing for Hartford at approximately the same time, been oversold thereby causing any confirmed ticketed passenger to be denied boarding?

9. If the answer to Interrogatory No. 8 is yes, state the date of each such occurrence, the number of seats available on each such flight, the number of tickets sold for each such flight and the number of such confirmed ticketed passengers denied boarding on each such flight.

10. With respect to all Allegheny flights between Washington D.C. and Hartford Connecticut during the period January 1, 1969 through June 30, 1972, list the flight number, date, and the number of passengers denied boarding on each and every flight where any confirmed ticketed passenger was denied boarding.

11. State the total number of Allegheny flights on which one or more confirmed ticketed passengers have been denied boarding for each of the following periods:

(a) 1969.

(b) 1970.

(c) 1971.

(d) First six months of 1972.

12. List the ten Allegheny markets which had the highest incidence of denied boarding in calandar year 1971 and for each such market list the following:

    (a) Total number of flights performed.

    (b) Total number of passengers carried.

    (c) Total seats available.

    (d) Average Load factor.

    (e) Total number of confirmed ticketed passengers denied boarding.

13. For each of the years 1969, 1970, 1971 and the first half of 1972, separately state the following with respect to Allegheny's denial of boarding on a system-wide basis to confirmed ticketed passengers by year or portion of each year:

    (a) Total number of ticket holders denied boarding.

    (b) Number of such ticket holders accommodated on later flights within a two hour period from the original departure time.

    (c) Number of ticket holders accepting denied boarding compensation.

    (d) Number of ticket holders not receiving either denied boarding compensation or a flight within two hours.

    (e) Number of persons filing suit as a result of being denied boarding.

    (f) Total amount paid out in denied boarding compensation by Allegheny.

14. List the name and address of each person who wrote a letter of complaint to Allegheny with respect to being denied boarding on Allegheny during the period January 1, 1969 through June 30, 1972. Copies of such letters may be attached in response to this Interrogatory.

15. List the name, address and date of complaint of every person (of which Allegheny is aware) that complained to the Civil Aeronautics Board with respect to denied boarding on Allegheny during the period January 1, 1969 through June 30, 1972.

16. Is Allegheny's reservation or ticketing system designed, programmed or operated to permit acceptance of more reservations than the number of seats in fact available on any particular flight or flights under any circumstances?

17. Is Allegheny's reservation or ticketing system designed or operated or programmed to permit the issuance of more tickets for confirmed reserved space than the number of seats in fact available on any particular flight or flights under any circumstances?

18. Does Allegheny as a matter of corporate policy or practice purposefully oversell certain flights on the statistical assumption that a certain percentage of ticketed passengers will not show up for any such flight?

19. If the answer to Interrogatory No. 18 is yes:

    (a) Is the fact of the possibility of such oversales and resultant denied boarding stated in Allegheny's tariff?

    (b) Is the fact of the possibility of such oversales communicated to all customers at the time they purchase their tickets?

20. If the answer to Interrogatory No. 18 is yes, does Allegheny have any plan or intention to eliminate the policy of oversales?

21. Does Allegheny have written rules or criteria for determining which passengers holding confirmed tickets shall be denied boarding on an oversold flight?

22. If the Answer to Interrogatory No. 21 is yes, set forth:

    (a) The effective date of such rules or criteria.

    (b) The text of such rules or criteria.

    (c) All instructions given to employees and agents with respect to such rules or criteria.

23. If the Answer to Interrogatory No. 21 is yes, are such rules or criteria set forth in Allegheny's current tariff and, if so, state the date on which such rules or criteria were first set forth in the tariff and list the sections of the tariff in which such rules or criteria are set forth.

24. State the name, position or title, business address and home address of each of the following described employees, officers or agents of Allegheny:

(a) The agents on duty at the ticket counter at Washington National Airport at the time Allegheny flight 864 was boarding on April 28, 1972.

(b) The agents on duty at the gate at Washington National Airport at which Allegheny flight 864 was boarded on April 28, 1972.

(c) The agents who refused to allow Mr. Nader to board the aircraft.

(d) The supervisor, if any, to whom the first report of Mr. Nader's denied boarding was made.

(e) The employee directly in charge of computer programming for Allegheny.

(f) The employee or employees or agents who actually write the computer programs which set the parameters for booking reservations and issuing tickets for Allegheny flights.

25. With respect to Allegheny flight 864 on April 28, 1972 from Washington to Hartford, state the following:

(a) The name, address and telephone number of each person holding a reservation on said flight as of April 27, 1972. (A computer printout containing all of the above information and attached to the answers will suffice.)

(b) The name, address, and telephone number of each additional person obtaining or holding a reservation up until 10:00 A.M. on April 28, 1972. (A computer printout containing all of the above information will suffice.)

(c) The name, address and telephone number of each person holding a ticket for said flight. (A copy of the passenger manifest together with a supplemental computer printout containing all of the above information will suffice.)

(d) The name, address and telephone number of each person accommodated on such flight.

(e) The date, the time of ticketing, and the class of ticket for each person listed in response to subparagraphs (c) and (d) above.

(f) The name, address and telephone number of each person denied boarding on said flight.

(g) The time at which flight 864 departed from the gate at Washington National Airport.

(h) The time at which flight 864 arrived at the gate at Bradley field.

* * *

29. State the written instructions given by Allegheny to its ticket agents and travel agents for making reservations, confirming reservations and ticketing passengers onto Allegheny flights.

30. Does Allegheny intend to rely upon any part of its Airline tariff in defense of this action?

31. If the answer to Interrogatory No. 30 is yes, specifically list each such section, sentence or rule upon which Allegheny intends to rely.

32. State the cause or causes of the oversale of Allegheny flight 864 on April 28, 1972 as reported by any and all of Allegheny's agents or employees.

Submitted this 8th Day of August 1972.

———————————————————

Don W. Crockett
Attorney for Plaintiffs

CERTIFICATE OF SERVICE

I hereby certify that a copy of the foregoing Interrogatories was mailed, postage prepaid, this 8th day of August, 1972 to David Armstrong, attorney for Allegheny Airlines, Washington National Airport, Washington, D.C. 20001.

———————————————————

DOCUMENT #4: ANSWERS TO INTERROGATORIES

Within thirty days of being served with a set of interrogatories, the recipient must answer under oath or object (and give the reasons for the objection) to each interrogatory. (FRCP 33.) The answers must be signed by the person answering the interrogatories; the objections must be signed by the attorney objecting. The answers are contained in a document that may be entitled *Answers to Plaintiff's Interrogatories* or *Answers and Objections to Plaintiff's Interrogatories*. The heading of the document is the same as the others we have seen thus far. The body of the document will number and repeat each interrogatory just as it appeared in the interrogatories served on the answering party. Following the restating of a particular interrogatory, the responding party will give its answer, or state that the question is objected to and give the reason for the objection.

In the *Nader* case, Allegheny responded to Plaintiffs' interrogatories both by answering (e.g., see A.1) and by objecting (e.g., see A.5.a). Note that defendant objects to interrogatories 11 through 15. (See A.11–15.) These were questions designed by plaintiffs to obtain information about the existence and magnitude of the bumping problem. Allegheny's objection is based on the fact that the problem is industry-wide. Such a problem should be dealt with by the experts at the administrative agency with regulatory authority to resolve it, and not by courts and juries in ad hoc civil trials based on a single incident of bumping.

In interrogatory 19.(b) plaintiffs asked whether the possibility of oversales and bumping, which defendant had previously acknowledged as occasionally occurring, was communicated to customers when they bought their tickets. Allegheny's answer is that the question is irrelevant, but, in any event, plaintiff Nader, himself, was aware of the possibility of being bumped. In fact, he had been bumped from an American Airlines flight earlier that same month. Defendant here wants to avoid giving information to plaintiffs, but also wants to point out Nader's own responsibility in not protecting himself from a known risk.

Many of Allegheny's answers are quite short and offer as little information as the questions will allow. Many questions are objected to and the objections begin to lay out Allegheny's theory of defense. The objections are designed to limit the information given to plaintiffs, or to force them to take further steps to obtain the information they want.

PREPARING ANSWERS TO INTERROGATORIES

- Evaluate what is being asked for and why.
- Answer questions the law or good sense demands be answered, but limit the responses to the questions asked.
- Object to questions when appropriate for legal or strategic reasons.
- Be prepared to support objections with appropriate theories of law.

UNITED STATES DISTRICT COURT
FOR THE DISTRICT OF COLUMBIA

Ralph Nader and the Connecticut
Citizen Action Group,

Plaintiffs,

v

Allegheny Airlines, Inc.,

Defendant.

Civil Action No. 1346-72

ANSWERS AND OBJECTIONS TO
PLAINTIFFS' FIRST SET OF
INTERROGATORIES

Q.1. Does Allegheny Airlines, Inc. (hereinafter referred to as "Allegheny") have an established policy for the retention and destruction of business records and documents?

A.1. Yes, though not company-wide and not written.

Q.2. If the answer to Interrogatory No. 1 is yes, is any part of that policy set forth in writing?

A.2. No.

Q.3. If the answer to Interrogatory No. 2 is yes, set forth or attach a copy of all such portions of such policy which have been set forth in writing.

A.3. Inapplicable.

Q.4. Specifically, state the time periods for which the following documents are retained by Allegheny:

    (a) General business correspondence.

    (b) Letters of complaint from customers.

    (c) Flight coupons.

    (d) Passenger manifests.

    (e) Passenger reservation information, lists or printouts.

    (f) Documentation with respect to cases of denied boarding.

A.4.   (a) Period of retaining general business correspondence varies with department.

    (b) Customer Relations Department retains customer complaint letters in active files for one year.

    (c) One year (if issued by Allegheny).

    (d) Three months.

    (e) Three months.

    (f) Three months.

Q.5. State the name title or position of the person or persons having custody of each category of documents or records listed in Interrogatory No. 4 and the location of each such group or category of documents.

A.5.   (a) Objection—Too broad for Answer.

    (b) Director, Customer Relations, Washington, D.C.

            Customer Services, Pittsburgh, Pennsylvania.

    (c) Director, Revenue Accounting, Washington, D.C.

  (d) (e) Director, Passenger Accommodation System, Washington, D.C.

    (f) Director, Reservations, Pittsburgh, Pennsylvania.

Q.6. State whether any records or documents of any kind, including records stored on computer tape, microfilm or microfische, which in any way relate to or refer to Allegheny flight 864 on April 28, 1972 have been destroyed?

A.6. No relevant records relative to Flight 864, April 28, 1972, have been destroyed.

Q.7. If the answer to Interrogatory No. 6 is yes, list the following:

    (a) Each document or record destroyed.

    (b) The contents of each such document or record.

    (c) The date of the destruction.

    (d) The name of the person authorizing or supervising such destruction.

    (e) The reason for the said destruction.

A.7. Inapplicable.

Q.8. During the period January 1, 1969 through June 30, 1972, has Allegheny flight 864 or any predecessor flight with a different number departing for Hartford at approximately the same time, been oversold thereby causing any confirmed ticketed passenger to be denied boarding?

A.8. Defendant has no oversale records prior to January 1, 1971. The flight was oversold only 3 times during the year and a half period from 1/1/71 through 6/30/72.

Q.9. If the answer to Interrogatory No. 8 is yes, state the date of each such occurrence, the number of seats available on each such flight, the number of tickets sold for each such flight and the number of such confirmed ticketed passengers denied boarding on each such flight.

A.9. Tickets may be issued by Allegheny offices, other carriers and travel agencies and may be issued on an open or wait basis. Therefore defendant cannot accurately state how many tickets were sold for a particular flight; however, it does know when a confirmed reservation passenger is denied boarding. As to flight 864:

  November 28, 1971, capacity 100, 1 denied boarding;

  April 24, 1972, capacity 100, 3 denied boarding;

  April 28, 1972, capacity 100, 3 denied boarding.

Q.10. With respect to all Allegheny flights between Washington, D.C. and Hartford Connecticut during the period January 1, 1969 through June 30, 1972, list the flight number, date and the number of passengers denied boarding on each and every flight where any confirmed ticketed passenger was denied boarding.

A.10. Information as to Flight 864 is in 9, *supra*. Information as to other flights is objected to as irrelevant as experience varies among flights.

Q.11. State the total number of Allegheny flights on which one or more confirmed ticketed passengers have been denied boarding for each of the following periods:

  (a) 1969. (b) 1970. (c) 1971. (d) First six months of 1972.

Q.12. List the ten Allegheny markets which had the highest incidence of denied boarding in calendar year 1971 and for each such market list the following:

  (a) Total number of flights performed.

  (b) Total number of passengers carried.

  (c) Total seats available.

  (d) Average load factor.

  (e) Total number of confirmed ticketed passengers denied boarding.

Q.13. For each of the years 1969, 1970, 1971 and the first half of 1972, separately state the following with respect to Allegheny's denial of boarding on a system-wide basis to confirmed ticketed passengers by year or portion of each year:

  (a) Total number of ticket holders denied boarding.

  (b) Number of such ticket holders accommodated on later flights within a two hour period from the original departure time.

  (c) Number of ticket holders accepting denied boarding compensation.

  (d) Number of ticket holders not receiving either denied boarding compensation or a flight within two hours.

  (e) Number of persons filing suit as a result of being denied boarding.

  (f) Total amount paid out in denied boarding compensation by Allegheny.

Q.14. List the name and address of each person who wrote a letter of complaint to Allegheny with respect to being denied boarding on Allegheny during the period January 1, 1969 through June 30, 1972. Copies of such letters may be attached in response to this Interrogatory.

Q.15. List the name, address and date of complaint of every person (of which Allegheny is aware) that complained to the Civil Aeronautics Board with respect to denied boarding on Allegheny during the period January 1, 1969 though June 30, 1972.

A.11–15. See answers and objection to 9 and 10 *supra*. The problem of no-shows and denied boarding is an industry-wide problem and the appropriate forum for dealing with it are the expert personnel of the Civil Aeronautics Board, not a court in civil litigation arising out of a single instance of denied boarding concerning which plaintiff Nader declined the tendered denied boarding compensation required under CAB regulations.

Q.16. Is Allegheny's reservation or ticketing system designed, programmed or operated to permit acceptance of more reservations than the number of seats in fact available on any particular flight or flights under any circumstances?

Q.17. Is Allegheny's reservation or ticketing system designed or operated or programmed to permit the issuance of more tickets for confirmed reserved space than the number of seats in fact available on any particular flight or flights under any circumstances?

A.16–17. Yes, acceptance of reservations and issuance of tickets are based upon continuing statistical analysis of traffic according to traffic, flight, and date.

Q.18. Does Allegheny as a matter of corporate policy or practice purposefully oversell certain flights on the statistical assumption that a certain percentage of ticketed passengers will not show up for any such flight?

A.18. To minimize the effect of the no-show problem upon defendant and the public defendant accepts a limited number of reservations in excess of actual capacity based upon statistical studies.

Q.19. If the answer to Interrogatory No. 18 is yes:

(a) Is the fact of the possibility of such oversales and resultant denied boarding stated in Allegheny's tariff?

(b) Is the fact of the possibility of such oversales communicated to all customers at the time they purchase their tickets?

A.19. (a) This is implicit in the tariff provisions providing for the CAB required denied boarding compensation payment.

(b) Irrelevant. In any event, plaintiff Nader in April, 1972, was well aware of the possibility of denied boarding on an airline inasmuch as he had been denied boarding on American Airline's 3:25 P.M. flight from Washington, D.C. to Boston, Massachusetts on April 23, 1972.

Q.20. If the answer to Interrogatory No. 18 is yes, does Allegheny have any plan or intention to eliminate the policy of oversales?

A.20. Allegheny intends to abide by Civil Aeronautics Board regulations on the industry-wide problems resulting from no-shows.

Q.21. Does Allegheny have written rules or criteria for determining which passengers holding confirmed tickets shall be denied boarding on an oversold flight?

A.21. Yes.

Q.22. If the Answer to Interrogatory No. 21 is yes, set forth:

(a) The effective date of such rules or criteria.

(b) The text of such rules or criteria.

(c) All instructions given to employees and agents with respect to such rules or criteria.

A.22. The currently effective revision of defendant's boarding priority rules and handling procedures are contained in its Passenger Service Manual, the pertinent pages of which are attached as Exhibit 1.

*   *   *

Allegheny Airlines
By: _____
David Armstrong

Answers sworn to and subscribed before me, this ___10th___ day of October, 1972.

_____
Notary Public

My Commission expires ___2/26/73___ .

Objections made by Hogan & Hartson, attorneys for Allegheny Airlines.

HOGAN & HARTSON

By: _____

Frank F. Roberson
815 Connecticut Avenue, N.W.
Washington, D.C. 20006
298-5500
Attorneys for Defendant Allegheny Airlines

CERTIFICATE OF SERVICE

I hereby certify that a copy of the foregoing Answers and Objections to Plaintiffs' First Set of Interrogatories was mailed, postage prepaid, this 20th day Of October, 1972, to Don W. Crockett, Esq., Suite 880, 1700 Pennsylvania Avenue, N.W., Washington, D.C. 20006, and to Reuben B. Robertson, III, Esq., 1156–19th Street, N.W., Washington, D.C. 20036, Attorneys for Plaintiffs.

HOGAN & HARTSON

By: _____

Frank F. Roberson

DOCUMENT #5: REQUEST FOR PRODUCTION OF DOCUMENTS

Another form of discovery is a request, which may be made by *any* party to any other *party*, to produce for inspection (including copying or testing, as appropriate) any document or tangible thing in its "possession, custody or control" (FRCP 34(a)). As with interrogatories, the scope of discovery for requests to produce is very broad. Therefore, most pertinent documents or objects may be discovered.

Generally, requests include an introductory paragraph in which the requesting party tells the other party when and where the items to be produced should be made available. FRCP 34(b) requires that the request state "a reasonable time, place and manner" of inspection. Also included in most introductions is a series of definitions to be used by the responding party in producing the items requested. For example, plaintiffs in *Nader* defined the terms "records" and "government agency."

The actual requests must be drafted with "reasonable particularity" so as to allow the responding party the opportunity to identify the item requested and to produce it, or to object to its production. When the requesting party knows of a particular document, the request for its production should be made with specific language. If, however, the requesting party believes there is a class of documents pertaining to certain aspects of the case, a more general request may be warranted so as not to give the responding party a legitimate opportunity to omit potentially useful documents. On the other hand, the request cannot be made so broadly that the responding party cannot determine what is being requested. Such a request can be objected to as vague or overbroad. A solution may be for the requesting party to identify categories of documents (e.g., correspondence or government reports), situations (e.g., flight 864 or the merger with XYZ, Inc.) or time frames (e.g., March, 1983 through August, 1986) and make requests within these somewhat descriptive limitations.

The plaintiffs in *Nader v Allegheny* made a request to Allegheny in which they sought production of various records, including several that they had also asked about in their interrogatories. For example, plaintiffs requested that Allegheny produce flight coupons and the passenger manifest for flight 864 on April 28, 1972. They had previously, in their interrogatories, asked Allegheny to list the name and address of each passenger on that flight. Plaintiffs may be using the requests for production to check the defendant's answers to the interrogatories to be sure that they are correct or, perhaps, to try to find discrepancies. They can also try to use the requests to obtain physical proof of the facts in question, or to gain new information or leads from the documents requested.

PREPARING REQUEST FOR PRODUCTION OF DOCUMENTS

- The request should be made to obtain evidence supporting known facts or to obtain new information,
- The request should identify with the appropriate degree of specificity, given the particular purpose of the request, whatever is being requested.

UNITED STATES DISTRICT COURT

FOR THE DISTRICT OF COLUMBIA

Ralph Nader and the Connecticut
Citizen Action Group,

Plaintiffs,

v

} Civil Action No. 1346-72

Allegheny Airlines, Inc.,

Defendant.

REQUEST FOR PRODUCTION OF DOCUMENTS

Pursuant to Rule 34 of the Federal Rules of Civil Procedure, the plaintiffs request that the defendant produce at its offices in the District of Columbia (or any other place agreed upon by counsel) on or before the 21st day of September, 1972, the following described records for inspection and copying by plaintiffs' counsel.

For the purposes of this request, the term "records" includes but is not limited to any records, documents, letters, correspondence, memoranda, studies, reports, interoffice memoranda, minutes of management or Directors meetings, books and accounts, notes, charts, tables, lists, logs, computer printouts, reports submitted to any government agency, information stored on computer tape or microfilm and any and all documentation connected with reserving space, ticketing passengers and boarding passengers on Allegheny flights. The term "government agency" includes but is not limited to the Civil Aeronautics Board, the U.S. Department of Transportation, the Federal Aviation Administration, and any officials, employees or agents thereof.

CATEGORIES OF RECORDS REQUESTED

1. The flight coupons for all passengers boarded on Allegheny flight 864 on April 28, 1972.

2. The passenger manifest for Allegheny flight 864 on April 28, 1972.

3. All records which in any way relate to or refer to the denial of boarding to any confirmed ticketed passenger on Allegheny flight 864 on April 28, 1972.

4. All records transmitted by Allegheny to any government agency or received by Allegheny from any government agency during the period January 1, 1967 to date which discuss, concern or relate or refer to the subjects of over-reserving flights, oversales, denial of boarding to confirmed ticketed passengers, or the consequences thereof.

5. All records transmitted between Allegheny and the Air Transport Association of America (ATA) or any other association or group of airlines during the period January 1, 1967 to date which discuss, concern or relate or refer to the subjects of over-reserving flights, oversales, denial of boarding to confirmed ticketed passengers or the consequences thereof.

6. All records comprising, containing, or referring to instructions, documents or information given to ticket agents or employees of Allegheny concerning or setting forth the procedures to be followed in making reservations, confirming or re-confirming reservations, issuing tickets, handling cases of denied boarding and treatment of denied boarding passengers. This request includes Allegheny's ticketing manual and other company manuals.

7. All records now in Allegheny's possession or control which discuss, refer to or relate to over-reserving flights, oversales, denial of boarding to confirmed ticketed passengers or the consequences, or problems connected therewith for the period January 1, 1967 to date.

8. All records containing flight histories and/or statistics of the occurrence of denied boarding on any flight or flights for the period January 1, 1967 to date.

Submitted this 21st day of August, 1972.

_____

Don W. Crockett

_____

Reuben B. Robertson, III
Attorneys for Plaintiffs

CERTIFICATE OF SERVICE

I hereby certify that I mailed a copy of the foregoing Request, postage prepaid, to Robert S. Bennett, Hogan and Hartson, 815 Connecticut Avenue, N.W., Washington, D.C., 20006, attorneys for defendant, this 21st day of August, 1972.

_____

Don W. Crockett

DOCUMENT #6: RESPONSE TO REQUEST TO PRODUCE

The party on whom a Request to Produce has been served generally has thirty days to respond. The response must state that inspection will be permitted as requested, or that the production of particular items is objected to, in which case, the reasons for the objection must be stated. Allegheny agreed to produce most of what plaintiffs sought but it did object to some of the requests. In request No. 5, plaintiffs sought all records transmitted from "January 1, 1967 to date" between Allegheny and the Air Transport Association of America, a trade association, pertaining to overbooking flights and bumping ticketed passengers. Allegheny objected on the ground that much of what was requested was irrelevant to this case which deals only with plaintiff Nader's being bumped on a particular day. Allegheny also pointed out that the comments of the Association were already on public record and, thus, available to plaintiffs.

Interestingly, in response to Request No. 4 which sought the same information concerning records between Allegheny and "any governmental agency" such as the Civil Aeronautics Board (CAB), Allegheny did not object. Its response, however, was somewhat circumspect and surely not as broad as the request.

In Request No. 7, plaintiffs sought *all* records in Allegheny's control concerning overbooking and bumping. Allegheny objected on the ground that the information was largely irrelevant, and also that the search would be burdensome and oppressive and would take "hundreds of man hours." This objection serves to remind us that while the discovery provisions of the Federal Rules are generous and offer great latitude, there are limits of reasonableness which courts will examine and occasionally assert in denying some aspect of discovery.

UNITED STATES DISTRICT COURT
FOR THE DISTRICT OF COLUMBIA

Ralph Nader and the Connecticut
Citizen Action Group,

Plaintiffs,

v

} Civil Action No. 1346-72

Allegheny Airlines, Inc.,

Defendant.

RESPONSE OF DEFENDANT ALLEGHENY AIRLINES, INC., TO PLAINTIFFS' REQUEST FOR PRODUCTION OF DOCUMENTS

The Defendant Allegheny Airlines, Inc., pursuant to Rule 34, F.R.Civ.P., hereby responds to the Plaintiffs' Request for Production of Documents.

Request No. 1. The flight coupons for all passengers boarded on Allegheny flight 864 on April 28, 1972.

Response No. 1. These documents will be produced.

Request No. 2. The passenger manifest for Allegheny flight 864 on April 28, 1972.

Response No. 2. These documents will be produced.

Request No. 3. All records which in any way relate to or refer to the denial of boarding to any confirmed ticketed passenger on Allegheny flight 864 on April 28, 1972.

Response No. 3. These documents will be produced.

Request No. 4. All records transmitted by Allegheny to any government agency or received by Allegheny from any government agency during the period January 1, 1967 to date which discuss, concern or relate or refer to the subjects of over-reserving flights, oversales, denial of boarding to confirmed ticketed passengers, or the consequences thereof.

Response No. 4. The portions of Defendant Allegheny's ticketing manual relating to oversales and denied boarding and Allegheny's quarterly Report of Unaccommodated Passengers to the Civil Aeronautics Board from December 1967 to date will be produced.

Request No. 5. All records transmitted between Allegheny and the Air Transport Association of America (ATA) or any other association or group of airlines during the period January 1, 1967 to date which discuss, concern or relate or refer to the subjects of over-reserving flights, oversales, denial of boarding to confirmed ticketed passengers or the consequences thereof.

Response No. 5. Defendant Allegheny objects to this request on the ground that it calls for documents not relevant to this lawsuit involving only the denied boarding of Plaintiff Nader on Flight 864 on April 28, 1972 and on the additional ground that the comments of the Air Transport Association of America on oversales and denied boarding is a matter of public record on file in C.A.B. Docket 16-563.

Request No. 6. All records comprising, containing, or referring to instructions, documents or information given to ticket agents or employees of Allegheny concerning or setting forth the procedures to be followed in making reservations, confirming or re-confirming reservations, issuing tickets, handling cases of denied boarding and treatment of denied boarding passengers. This request includes Allegheny's ticketing manual and other company manuals.

Response No. 6. Portions of Defendant Allegheny's manuals relevant to this action will be made available for inspection and copying.

Request No. 7. All records now in Allegheny's possession or control which discuss, refer to or relate to over-reserving flights, oversales, denial of boarding to confirmed ticketed passengers or the consequences, or problems connected therewith for the period January 1, 1967 to date.

Response No. 7. Defendant Allegheny objects to this request on the ground that the material requested is irrelevant to this action involving only the denied boarding of Plaintiff Nader on Flight 864 on April 28, 1972 and on the additional ground that the request is burdensome and oppressive in that a search of Defendant's files from 1967 to date for the requested information would take hundreds of man hours.

Request No. 8. All records containing flight histories and/or statistics of the occurrence of denied boarding on any flight or flights for the period January 1, 1967 to date.

Response No. 8. Please see the response to request number 4. To the extent that request number 8 calls for material not produced in response to request number 4 it is objected to on the same grounds as is request number 7.

Respectfully submitted,

HOGAN & HARTSON

By _____
Frank F. Roberson

By _____
William A. Bradford, Jr.

DOCUMENT #7: MOTION TO COMPEL DISCOVERY

DOCUMENT #8: MEMORANDUM OF POINTS AND AUTHORITIES IN SUPPORT OF MOTION TO COMPEL DISCOVERY

What happens when a person to whom discovery is directed fails to respond, or responds incompletely or frivolously? Alternatively, he or she may raise objections to particular components of a discovery request. At this point, the court is asked to intervene. This is what happened in the *Nader* case. Plaintiffs sought assistance from the court in obtaining responses from Allegheny. The approach they took, after a good deal of discussion and negotiation between the attorneys, was to move the court for an order compelling Allegheny to answer the interrogatories it did not answer and to produce the documents it did not produce.

Motions are devices by which a party asks the court for an order on some matter before it. Generally, motions are prepared in writing and served on the other parties who then have an opportunity to respond. Exceptions exist, e.g., motions made in open court during a hearing are often made orally. Written motions must follow the rules pertaining to caption and form that apply to pleadings. The motion must also state the grounds for the motion together with the relief sought (FRCP 7 (b)). A motion is often accompanied by a *Memorandum* of *Points and Authorities* which lays out the legal and/or factual arguments supporting the request made in the motion. Supporting cases, if available, are cited.

Motions to Compel Discovery are covered by FRCP 37. A court can impose sanctions on a person for failing to obey the court's order compelling compliance with discovery requests. The most serious sanctions are holding the person in contempt, prohibiting the recalcitrant person from introducing evidence on designated issues, or ruling that certain evidentiary positions will be considered established in favor of the moving party. It should be pointed out that while sanctions are permitted under the federal rules, as a practical matter, they are not often applied. What generally happens is that a party who is not satisfied with a response, moves for an order compelling the response. The responding party will usually make an argument on the inappropriateness of the request. Before the court acts, the parties will often settle the matter between themselves. Even when there is a court order compelling discovery, it usually will not include a sanction (although it might include an admonition from the court). If a responding party still does not comply, the moving party may seek sanctions anew. On a second noncompliance, a court may be ready to impose a sanction. Even here, however, the sanction may be conditioned on a further noncompliance. The typical sanction, when one is imposed, is that the responding party must pay the moving party's legal fees and costs for the preparation and argument of the motions to compel and to impose sanctions.

When seeking the court's assistance in compelling discovery, it is useful to give the court a description of the dispute. While not required by the rules, plaintiffs in the *Nader* case laid out in their Motion to Compel (Document #7) the interrogatory and the request to produce which they served on defendant, together with defendant's unsatisfactory response or objection. Plaintiffs also stated their own position as to each interrogatory and request to produce. This procedure, whether it is in the motion or in the accompanying Memorandum of Points and Authorities, is extremely useful to the court in understanding the particular problems presented. The citation of legal authority, of course, gives the court a basis on which to make its ruling.

In *Nader*, plaintiffs moved for an order to compel and for the imposition of a sanction (expenses, including attorneys fees, for the preparation of the motion). Plaintiffs basically argue that defendant's objections to certain interrogatories and requests for production are unjustified and dilatory, and that some of its responses are evasive or incomplete.

Keep in mind that one of the goals of the plaintiffs is to go beyond Nader's ticket on flight 864. Their discovery strategy is to elicit information showing a pattern of tortious behavior. This is relevant to the punitive damage claim.

UNITED STATES DISTRICT COURT
FOR THE DISTRICT OF COLUMBIA

Ralph Nader and the Connecticut
Citizen Action Group,

Plaintiffs,

v

Civil Action No. 1346-72

Allegheny Airlines, Inc.,

Defendant.

MOTION TO COMPEL ANSWERS TO INTERROGATORIES AND THE PRODUCTION OF DOCUMENTS

Pursuant to Rule 37 of the Federal Rules of Civil Procedure, the plaintiffs herein move this court to order the defendant, Allegheny Airlines, Inc., to answer Interrogatories and produce documents on the grounds shown below.

The defendant has filed its answers and objections to plaintiffs' First Set of Interrogatories and has filed its response to plaintiffs' Request for Documents. While a substantial portion of the requested discovery has been accomplished, defendant has unjustifiably and without excuse refused to answer or objected to the following.

I
INTERROGATORIES

Q.10. With respect to all Allegheny flights between Washington, D.C. and Hartford Connecticut during the period January 1, 1969 through June 30, 1972, list the flight number, date and the number of passengers denied boarding on each and every flight where any confirmed ticketed passenger was denied boarding.

A.10. Information as to Flight 864 is in 9, *supra.* Information as to other flights is objected to as irrelevant as experience varies among flights.

The foregoing Interrogatory is clearly relevant to plaintiffs' primary allegation that Allegheny willfully, wantonly and systematically causes large numbers of innocent passengers to be denied boarding. The Washington-Hartford-Washington market is a logical test sample in view of the fact that the instant tort was committed in that market. This market is relatively small and Allegheny will not be burdened by providing this information.

*   *   *

Q.19. (a) Is the fact of the possibility of such oversales and resultant denied boarding stated in Allegheny's tariff?

(b) Is the fact of the possibility of such oversales communicated to all customers at the time they purchase their tickets?

A.19. (a) This is implicit in the tariff provision providing for the CAB required denied boarding compensation payment.

(b) Irrelevant. In any event, plaintiff Nader in April 1972, was well aware of the possibility of denied boarding on an airline inasmuch as he had been denied boarding on American Airline's 3:25 P.M. flight from Washington, D.C. to Boston, Massachusetts on April 23, 1972.

The foregoing gratuitous remarks are irrelevant. The failure of Allegheny to communicate the possibility of oversales to its customers is a primary element of plaintiff's cause of action. Defendant must be required to answer this crucial interrogatory.

Q.20. If the answer to Interrogatory No. 18 is yes, does Allegheny have any plan or intention to eliminate the policy of oversales?

A.20. Allegheny intends to abide by Civil Aeronautics Board regulations on the industry-wide problems resulting from no-shows.

Once again the answer is evasive and unresponsive. Allegheny's future intentions with respect to its admitted practice of lying to the public is certainly relevant with respect to the issue of awarding punitive damages and the amount. These intentions have nothing whatsoever to do with any regulations of the Civil Aeronautics Board. Defendant should be compelled to answer Interrogatory 20 in a forthright manner.

* * *

II
PRODUCTION OF DOCUMENTS

Request No. 5. All records transmitted between Allegheny and the Air Transport Association of America (ATA) or any other association or group of airlines during the period January 1, 1967 to date which discuss, concern or relate or refer to the subjects of over-reserving flights, oversales, denial of boarding to confirmed ticketed passengers or the consequences thereof.

Response to No. 5. Defendant Allegheny objects to this request on the ground that it calls for documents not relevant to this lawsuit involving only the denied boarding of Plaintiff Nader on Flight 864 on April 28, 1972 and on the additional ground that the comments of the Air Transport Association of America on oversales and denied boarding is a matter of public record on file in C.A.B. Docket 16-563.

Allegheny's objection begs the question. As Allegheny well knows, the test is not whether the documents are relevant but whether or not they "may lead to relevant evidence". In any event, the correspondence between Allegheny and the ATA is clearly relevant to the degree of willfulness and wantonness of Allegheny's actions in overselling flights. If, as Allegheny asserts in its answer to Interrogatory No. 11, the problem is industry-wide, then correspondence on this subject with the industry association is clearly relevant. ATA's comments on file in CAB Docket 16-563 may be excluded from this request. Plaintiffs are entitled to all other records on this subject in Allegheny's possession and control.

Request No. 7. All records now in Allegheny's possession or control which discuss, refer to or relate to over-reserving flights, oversales, denial of boarding to confirmed ticketed passengers or the consequences, or problems connected therewith for the period January 1, 1967 to date.

Response No. 7. Defendant Allegheny objects to this request on the ground that the material requested is irrelevant to this action involving only the denied boarding of Plaintiff Nader on Flight 864 on April 28, 1972 and on the additional ground that the request is burdensome and oppressive in that a search of Defendant's files from 1967 to date for the requested information would take hundreds of man hours.

Allegheny's objection is clearly evasive. Certainly, intra-company correspondence regarding oversales and related problems is relevant to this case. Certainly complaints from other customers, Allegheny's replies thereto and minutes of company meetings where oversale policies were discussed are relevant. The fact that some person will have to go through this material to select it out, is not a legitimate excuse for failing to respond. Examples of such intra-company correspondence are attached as Exhibits A and B.

*   *   *

WHEREFORE, Plaintiffs respectfully request this court to require the defendant to fully and completely answer Interrogatories 10, 11, 12, 13, 14, 15, 19, 20, and 28(i) and to produce for inspection each and every document encompassed by Documentary Requests 5, 7 and 8. Plaintiffs further request that the court require Allegheny to pay the plaintiffs expenses incurred in prosecuting this motion including reasonable attorneys fees.

Respectfully submitted,

Don W. Crockett
1700 Pennsylvania Ave. N.W.
Washington, D.C. 20006
872-0331

Reuben B. Robertson, III
1156 19th St., N.W.
Washington, D.C. 20036
833-3400
Attorneys for Plaintiffs

UNITED STATES DISTRICT COURT
FOR THE DISTRICT OF COLUMBIA

Ralph Nader and the Connecticut
Citizen Action Group,

Plaintiffs,

v

Allegheny Airlines, Inc.,

Defendant.

} Civil Action No. 1346-72

MEMORANDUM OF POINTS AND AUTHORITIES IN SUPPORT OF PLAINTIFFS' MOTION TO COMPEL ANSWERS TO INTERROGATORIES AND THE PRODUCTION OF DOCUMENTS.

This action seeks compensatory and punitive damages from Allegheny Airlines arising from Allegheny's refusal to honor a confirmed ticket held by Mr. Nader on April 28, 1972.

Plaintiffs have alleged that Allegheny purposefully and systematically oversells certain flights, including the flight on April 28, 1972, knowing full well that a certain percentage of its passengers are going to be denied boarding and thereby sustain serious damages.

In its answer to Interrogatory Number 17 herein, Allegheny has admitted that its reservation and ticketing system is programmed to permit the issuance of more tickets for confirmed reserved space than the number of seats in fact available. Allegheny has refused to state whether it informs its customers of this fact and refuses to give further particulars with respect to the nature and extent of this fraudulent practice. It attempts to restrict plaintiffs' discovery to the documents and events surrounding Mr. Nader's flight on April 28, 1972. The issues herein are much broader than defendant would lead the court to believe.

Thus far, we know that when Allegheny's computer shows that all available seats have been sold to confirmed and ticketed customers, the airline will continue to sell a certain amount of non-existent space on the statistical assumption that some of the previously ticketed passengers will "no-show".

Rather than informing the later customers that the flight is full and of then conditioning their tickets on the fulfillment of Allegheny's no-show forecasts, the airline represents that it has space and sells a confirmed ticket to the passenger for the flight. When the no-shows don't materialize, the person who purchased the first seat on the flight is as likely to be bumped as the person who bought the last non-existent seat on the day of the flight. This is all we *know* at this point.

The interrogatories and document requests which Allegheny has refused to answer seek further information as to Allegheny's practices in overselling flights. This information is required to determine whether or not and to what extent punitive damages may be assessed. The appropriateness of punitive damages in denied boarding cases was first established in *Wills v. Trans World Airways*, 200 F. Supp. 360 (S.D. Calif. 1961). As stated by Judge Mathes in awarding $5,000 in punitive damages to an oversold passenger:

> . . . the purpose of the award is twofold, to complement the criminal
> and injunctive provisions of the Act, and to afford the courts the
> means to make effective vindication of the rights of the individual
> airline passenger which have been willfully or wantonly violated. 200
> F. Supp at 368.

Since all of the contested interrogatory answers and document requests may obviously lead to evidence bearing on the willful and wanton nature of defendant's dishonest oversales policies, Defendant is required to produce this discovery.

Respectfully submitted,

_____

Don W. Crockett

_____

Reuben B. Robertson, III
Attorneys for Plaintiffs

DOCUMENT #9: DEFENDANT'S MEMORANDUM OF POINTS AND AUTHORITIES IN OPPOSITION TO PLAINTIFFS' MOTION TO COMPEL DISCOVERY

DOCUMENT #10: REPLY TO DEFENDANT'S MEMORANDUM OF POINTS AND AUTHORITIES

Defendant opposed plaintiffs' Motion to Compel and submitted a *Memorandum of Points and Authorities* (Document #9) arguing that opposition. Plaintiffs believed a response to defendant's opposition was desirable so they submitted a Reply to defendant's opposition (Document #10). A moment should be taken here to examine what the parties attempted to do with their memos. Note how defendant attempts to limit the scope of the case and the type of damages available, while plaintiffs seek to retain the right to punitive damages by attempting to characterize the matter as just a common law case.

Defendant appears to have had several related purposes in its memo. First, it tries to characterize Nader as a crusading reformer rather than as an injured party. His crusade, defendant argues, is to change a policy that exists throughout the air transport industry, but he attempts to do so by bringing suit against one carrier only, Allegheny. To support this contention, Allegheny argues that other passengers bumped from the flight were offered, and accepted, alternate transportation which subjected them to only minor disruption in their travel schedules. Since only Nader refused this accommodation, Allegheny argues that Nader is intent on litigating the industry-wide policy rather than his own injury. This characterization is then used in arguing that Nader is not entitled to punitive damages due to his own wrongful or, at least, inequitable position.

The second purpose of the defendant's memo is to persuade the court that the big issue, the industry-wide problem of "no-shows," should be dealt with by the administrative agency set up to regulate and control air transport, the Civil Aeronautics Board (CAB). This argument by Allegheny will recur several times throughout this litigation, and ultimately will be presented to the Supreme Court. Allegheny asserts that the award of large punitive damages against individual carriers would throw the industry into regulatory chaos. Therefore, Allegheny argues, the court should limit its decision to the actual damages of one complaining individual, Nader. It should not usurp the authority statutorily entrusted to the experts at the CAB by considering the broader issues presented by Nader's claim for punitive damages.

Finally, Allegheny argues that it has already provided plaintiffs all the information reasonably relevant to the limited issue that Allegheny believes is before the court. Therefore, the court should deny plaintiffs' motion to compel because the information sought is irrelevant and is not likely to lead to evidence that is relevant to any issue properly before the court.

Plaintiffs' *Reply to Defendant's Memorandum of Points and Authorities* (Document #10) is short and rather direct. First, they state that the purpose of the lawsuit is not to examine industry-wide problems nor to establish policies that properly should be made by the CAB. Instead, they argue, the suit is an attempt to recover "substantial actual damages sustained by plaintiffs" and punitive damages for defendant's "callous disregard of *these plaintiffs*" (emphasis in original).

Plaintiffs go on to characterize the suit as a standard common law action for fraud or breach of contract. They cite a case specifically permitting punitive damages in such a suit without overstepping the boundary between the administrative agency and the court. They then liken the information sought through their motion to compel to the information sought in the cited case in which the court allowed punitive damages. Thus, they argue, the questions are relevant and their answers should be compelled.

UNITED STATES DISTRICT COURT
FOR THE DISTRICT OF COLUMBIA

Ralph Nader and the Connecticut
Citizen Action Group,

Plaintiffs,

v

Allegheny Airlines, Inc.,

Defendant.

Civil Action No. 1346-72

DEFENDANT'S MEMORANDUM OF POINTS AND AUTHORITIES IN OPPOSITION TO PLAINTIFFS' MOTION TO COMPEL DISCOVERY

Background

The individual plaintiff asks $10 in compensatory damages and $50,000 punitive damages and the Connecticut Citizen Action Group $100,000 compensatory and $100,000 punitive because Mr. Nader was unable to board defendant's Flight 864 to Hartford, Connecticut on April 28, 1972, where he was scheduled to address a CCAG fund raising rally. Mr. Nader was the last of three persons holding confirmed reservations who could not be accommodated. The other two took proffered alternate transportation which arrived in Hartford some 55 minutes after Flight 864. Mr. Nader declined the alternate transportation.

The real purpose of the litigation is an effort by Mr. Nader and one of his groups to force Allegheny Airlines to abandon its efforts to ameliorate the no-show problem which has plagued the airline carriers over the years. Our Court of Appeals has aptly referred to this industry-wide situation as "the perennial no-show problem of the airlines". *Delta Air Lines, et al.* v. *Civil Aeronautics Board*, 455 F.2d 1340, 1341 (D.C. Cir. Dec. 1, 1971). Plaintiffs' attorney, in rejecting for Mr. Nader the denied boarding compensation which Allegheny had tendered, as required by CAB regulations, unabashedly revealed the purpose of this threatened litigation by writing defendant on June 19, 1972, (Exhibit B to Crockett affidavit, filed herein August 24, 1972):

> "Recent CAB statistics reveal that the airline industry is apparently unwilling to take steps necessary to eliminate the oversales of their flights, a problem that has plagued consumers for many years and which remains a matter of serious public concern.

> "If you are interested in discussing settlement of this matter before the complaint is filed, please let me know before June 23, 1972. We anticipate that *any such settlement would include an assurance on Allegheny's part that it would take immediate steps to eliminate overbooking and oversales*". (Emphasis supplied)

Yet it is the experts of the Civil Aeronautics Board to whom Congress has entrusted the control of the public interest in having efficient and reasonable air carrier service, regulations and practices. No more chaotic situation can be imagined than to have juries, through imposition of large punitive damage awards, force one domestic airline carrier to abandon reasonable efforts to minimize its no-show problem, while competing airlines could continue their practices to that end. As Judge Richey recently ruled in an Interstate Commerce Act case, a court does not have power to afford a judicial remedy inconsistent with Congressional policy, which "should not be frustrated or circumvented by the courts". See *Baltimore & Ohio R.R.* v. *Alabama Great Southern R.R.*, U.S. Dist. Ct. D.C. Civil No. 906-72 (October 3, 1972).

As the Complaint filed herein alleges, in paragraph 5:

> "Defendant is an air carrier engaged in interstate commerce pursuant to a certificate of public convenience and necessity issued by the Civil Aeronautics Board and is regulated by the laws of the United States relating to such interstate commerce and by the rules, orders and regulations promulgated by the Board in accordance with the Federal Aviation Act of 1958."

As appears from defendant's answer to plaintiffs' Interrogatory 18:

> "To minimize the effect of the no-show problem upon defendant and the public defendant accepts a limited number of reservations in excess of actual capacity based upon statistical studies."

As appears from defendant's answers to Interrogatories 21 and 22 its rules and criteria for determining which passengers holding confirmed tickets shall be denied boarding on an oversold flight are contained in its Passenger Service Manual (Exhibit 1 to the Interrogatory Answers, filed herein 28 October 1972).

A mere oversale is not actionable; only an *unreasonable* policy would create such a civil right in an individual. Thus the court said, in *Archibald* v. *Pan American*, 460 F.2d 14, 16 (9th Cir. 1972):

> "Some overselling is an economic necessity for an airline in view of inevitable cancellations and no-shows. However, when a flight is thus oversold, the airline must fill the plane in a reasonable and just manner. *Slough* and *Wills* indicate that bumping which is outwardly discriminatory or preferential may be legitimated by proof that the airline adhered to its established policy and that the policy is reasonable.

Plaintiffs in this case have already been voluntarily supplied by defendant through answers to interrogatories and response to requests for documents with all the material reasonably necessary and relevant on whether plaintiff's inability to obtain a seat on Flight 864 if "outwardly discriminatory or preferential" was in fact "legitimated" by adherence to defendant's established and reasonable policy. What plaintiffs' Motion to Compel seeks to do is to convert this civil action into a wide-ranging investigation by non-experts of defendant's reasonable efforts to ameliorate its no-show problem. Such a broad inquiry is a function of the Civil Aeronautics Board, charged with maintaining the national interest, not that of a court and jury in a judicial proceeding.

To compel defendant to provide more than it has already voluntarily supplied would be unduly onerous and oppressive. Having answered most of plaintiffs interrogatories (which with sub-questions number 86) and supplied most of the documents in response to the eight sweeping categories requested, defendant has supplied all material properly pertinent to this case. The Court should not allow its process to be converted to a Civil Aeronautics Board type of administrative investigation. To order more than has been supplied already would be to go beyond the intent and scope of relevant discovery as expressed in Federal Rule of Civil Procedure 26(b)(1).

Respectfully submitted,

HOGAN & HARTSON

By: _____

Frank F. Roberson

By: _____

William A. Bradford, Jr.
815 Connecticut Avenue
Washington, D.C. 20008
298-5500
Attorneys for Defendant
Allegheny Airlines, Inc.

CERTIFICATE OF SERVICE

A copy of the foregoing Defendant's Memorandum In Opposition to Plaintiffs' Motion to Compel and of a proposed Order thereon were mailed this ___15th___ day of December, 1972, to Don W. Crockett, Esq., 1700 Pennsylvania Avenue, N.W., Washington, D.C. 20006 and to Reuben B. Robertson, III, Esq., 1156–19th Street, N.W., Washington, D.C. 20036, Attorneys for Plaintiffs.

HOGAN & HARTSON

By: _____

Frank F. Roberson

UNITED STATES DISTRICT COURT
FOR THE DISTRICT OF COLUMBIA

Ralph Nader and the Connecticut
Citizen Action Group,
_____

                        Plaintiffs,

      v   } Civil Action No. 1346-72

Allegheny Airlines, Inc.,
_____

                        Defendant.

REPLY TO DEFENDANT'S MEMORANDUM
OF POINTS AND AUTHORITIES

Allegheny Airlines has answered plaintiffs' Motion to Compel Discovery with a memorandum of points and authorities that requires a brief reply.

It appears that defendant's only defense to the discovery motion is the specious argument that the courts should not allow a plaintiff to have discovery with respect to an airline's fraudulent consumer practices for fear of invading the territory occupied by the Civil Aeronautics Board.

First, the purpose of this action is not to investigate any "reasonable efforts" Allegheny claims to have made to "ameliorate its no-show problem". This action has been filed to recover substantial actual damages sustained by the plaintiffs and punitive damages for Allegheny's callous disregard of *these plaintiffs* due to its admitted policy of *selling* and *confirming non-existent seats to an unsuspecting public.* This is outright fraudulent misrepresentation. Needless to say, fraud is never "reasonable" and no public policy can or could sanction its use to increase the profits of a public utility.

Second, a long line of Federal cases beginning with *Wills v. Trans World Airways, Inc.,* 200 F. Supp. 161 (S.D. Calif. 1956) have established the power of the courts to award both actual and punitive damages in denied boarding cases without interfering with the legitimate functions of the CAB. In the *Wills* case the court awarded $5,000.00 in punitive damages after finding that the airline purposefully followed a corporate practice of over-selling its flights. The information requested of Allegheny in this suit is exactly the same type of information used by the court in *Wills* to determine punitive damages.

Third, Allegheny makes the unbelieveable assertion that "a mere oversale is not actionable". We do not know how defendant defines an oversale. However, we do know in this case that defendant breached its contract of carriage with plaintiffs, that it made fraudulent misrepresentations to plaintiffs and that it committed an intentional tort upon plaintiffs. The foregoing causes of action have been pled herein and they are in addition and pendant to the Federal cause of action for unjust discrimination. Plaintiffs are entitled to all pertinent discovery with respect to each of its four causes of action.

Respectfully submitted,

Don W. Crockett
1700 Pennsylvania Ave. N.W.
Washington, D.C. 20006
872-0331
Attorney for Plaintiffs

CERTIFICATE OF SERVICE

I hereby certify that a copy of the foregoing Reply was mailed postage prepaid to Frank F. Roberson, Hogan & Hartson, 815 Connecticut Ave. N.W., Washington, D.C. 20006, this 27th day of December, 1972.

DOCUMENT #11:
RECOMMENDATION OF PRETRIAL EXAMINER

DOCUMENT #12: COURT ORDER

After receiving the Motion to Compel from plaintiffs and the memoranda of the parties, the Court appointed a Trial Examiner to read the memos, hear arguments on the Motion to Compel and recommend a decision to the court on the points raised. A Trial Examiner is like a Special Master, that is, someone appointed by the court to take testimony or to evaluate evidence, and then recommend a decision. In this case, the Examiner made a recommendation to the court (Document #11). Each side then had an opportunity to argue to the court why the recommendation should or should not be followed. Each party submitted Objections to the Recommendation of the Pretrial Examiner. The Objections are not included here since they are similar to the arguments in each party's Points and Authorities on the Motion to Compel. The court adopted the recommendation of the Examiner in full (Document #12) and Allegheny filed Supplemental Responses to the interrogatories it was ordered to answer.

UNITED STATES DISTRICT COURT
FOR THE DISTRICT OF COLUMBIA

Ralph Nader, et al.,

Plaintiffs,

v

Civil Action No. 1346-72

Allegheny Airlines, Inc.,

Defendant.

RECOMMENDATION OF PRETRIAL EXAMINER

In this action plaintiffs seek to recover punitive and compensatory damages from the defendant because the plaintiff Nader had a ticket for a specific flight from Washington, D.C. to Hartford, Connecticut, and when he presented himself for the flight, he was advised that the flight had been oversold and all seats had been taken, as a result of which he was not allowed on the flight and was unable to keep an engagement in Hartford, Connecticut.

Motions to Compel Answers to Interrogatories and the Production of Documents are presented by which the plaintiffs seek, in part, to obtain information about company-wide operations and certain documents which are matters of public record.

Upon consideration of said motions, the plaintiffs' claims, the entire file, the memoranda of the parties and oral arguments, it is . . . therefore this 18th day of January, 1973

RECOMMENDED that in respect of interrogatories that the defendant answer or further answer, on or before February 17, 1973, the following interrogatories restricted to all flights between Washington, D.C. and Hartford, Connecticut and Hartford, Connecticut and Washington, D.C. during the period January 1, 1969 through June 30, 1972:

Nos. 10, 11, 14, 15 19, 20, and 28, and it is

FURTHER RECOMMENDED that the plaintiffs' motion otherwise be denied in respect of interrogatories, and it is

FURTHER RECOMMENDED in respect of plaintiffs' Motion for Production of Documents that plaintiffs' request No. 5 be denied; that plaintiffs' request No. 7 be allowed restricted to the period between January 1, 1969 and June 30, 1972; that plaintiffs' request No. 8 be allowed restricted to the aforesaid dates and flights restricted to those between Washington, D.C. and Hartford, Connecticut and Hartford, Connecticut and Washington, D.C. and it is

FURTHER RECOMMENDED that with respect to the documents, where a recommendation is made herein for production, that said documents be produced for inspection, and copying by counsel for the plaintiffs if he is so disposed and at his expense, at a time and place mutually convenient to counsel for the parties and in any event, on or before February 17, 1973.

Copies mailed to counsel on January 18, 1973.

_____

PRETRIAL EXAMINER

NOTE: Under Local Civil Rule 9(i)(1) the above Recommendation becomes the order of the Court unless objections thereto are filed within five days in conformity with Rule 9(i)(2).

UNITED STATES DISTRICT COURT
FOR THE DISTRICT OF COLUMBIA

Ralph Nader, et al.,
_____
                                    Plaintiffs,

v   Civil Action No. 1346-72

Allegheny Airlines, Inc.,
_____
                                    Defendant.

ORDER

Upon consideration of the plaintiff Nader's Objections to the Recommendation of the Pretrial Examiner, and the defendant Allegheny's separate Objections to the

Recommendation of the Pre-trial Examiner, it is, by the Court this __16th__ day of February, 1973,

ORDERED, that the recommendation of the Pretrial Examiner entered on January 18, 1973 will be and the same is hereby affirmed, and that the parties shall comply with the provisions contained therein.

Charles R. Richey
United States District Judge

DOCUMENT #13: NOTICE TO TAKE ORAL DEPOSITION

DOCUMENT #14: DEPOSITION OF RALPH NADER

DOCUMENT #15: CERTIFICATE OF NOTARY PUBLIC

Depositions are another form of discovery which generally involve the taking of oral testimony of an adverse witness prior to trial. FRCP 30 provides that after "the commencement of the action, any party may take the testimony of any person, including a party, . . ." The attendance of a witness to be deposed may be obtained by subpoena. The party seeking to depose a witness must give reasonable notice to every other *party* to the action. The notice must state the time and place of the deposition, and the name and address of each person to be deposed. If the name is not known, a general description that identifies the person(s) will suffice (e.g., the person in the XYZ company who took minutes at the September 26, 1988 meeting of the Board of Directors).

Each party may attend the deposition and question the witness, or object to questions asked by another party. The witness is placed under oath by an officer (eg., a notary public) before whom the deposition is conducted. The witness's testimony is recorded stenographically or electronically. A party may object to a question asked. Generally the evidence objected to is received subject to the objection which is preserved for a decision by the judge. Occasionally, however, an attorney will instruct his or her client not to answer a particular question. If the attorneys cannot resolve the matter between them, a Motion to Compel the answer is the appropriate procedure for relief.

In the *Nader* case, several depositions were noticed. A Motion for a *Protective Order* was made against the taking of a deposition. A Protective Order is a device permitted under

FRCP 26(c) whereby a party or a witness from whom discovery is sought may seek protection from the court against the request for discovery. The reasons for the protection may be "annoyance, embarrassment, oppression, or undue burden or expense". The rule gives a wide range of discretion to the court in fashioning an order. For instance, the court may prohibit the discovery altogether or limit its scope; it may permit discovery but only upon specified terms or by a specified method; or it may limit the people who may be present at a deposition or the use to be made of the material discovered.

Here, we focus on the *Notice to Take Oral Deposition* (Document #13) and the *Deposition* of Ralph Nader (Document #14). Later will will look at the Motion for a Protective Order (Document #16) which was denied, and portions of the subsequent deposition of Leslie O. Barnes, the President of Allegheny Airlines (Document #20).

The Notice to Take Oral Deposition is very short and direct. As always, the caption is set out first and is followed by the body of the document. The notice states who is taking the deposition and whose deposition is to be taken. The date, time, and place of the deposition are stated along with the name of the officer before whom it is to be taken. The notice is then signed by the attorney seeking the deposition and served on all parties and on the witness.

For strategic reasons, it is useful to consider carefully the timing and site of the deposition. Generally, it is wise to conduct it in your own office. If you believe the deposition will be a long one, an early start may be advisable rather than having to break and schedule a continuation on another day.

PREPARING A NOTICE TO TAKE ORAL DEPOSITION

- Identify clearly, by name or description, the witness to be deposed.
- Include the date and time of the deposition after considering its expected length.
- Include the location of the deposition after considering strategy and convenience factors.
- Serve the witness and all parties.

The deposition of Ralph Nader was taken by defendant's attorney at his office before a notary public. As you will see in Document #14, the transcript of the deposition begins by identifying the witness. The date, time, and address of the deposition is also stated as is the name and title of the officer before whom it is to be taken. The appearances of counsel are then noted together with a brief index of the transcript. The witness is called and sworn, and the examination begins. It should be noted that all parties have the right to question the witness and to object to questions asked by any other party. It is rare, however, for any significant questioning to be done by parties other than the one who sought the deposition. On the other hand, objections are routine, and are preserved for disposition by the judge even if the question objected to is answered.

The examination of Ralph Nader begins by counsel asking him to identify himself. It then goes into the background of the events in question. Counsel for Allegheny asks about CCAG and its purposes, and about the purpose of Nader's trip. While focusing on the cancelled speaking engagement, counsel sought information about what was to be discussed, and who else was to be on the program. He asked about whether admission was to be charged and whether items were to be sold to people attending the speech. He also asked about the effect of Nader's nonappearance.

The apparent goal of these questions was to establish that the rally had a variety of purposes involving several well known speakers. Therefore, Nader's nonappearance did not defeat the entire event. Moreover, since admission was not charged and there were no items sold to the public, any financial loss was entirely speculative and, thus, not compensable.

There was also a good deal of questioning as to whether Nader was partially at fault for his being bumped. Defendant's theory appears to be, in part, that Nader knew that airlines sometimes overbook flights. This is common knowledge among experienced travelers such as Nader. In any event, it was specifically known to Nader who had been bumped from another flight less than a week before the Allegheny experience, and once before, within six months of the Allegheny bumping. Despite this knowledge, defendant argues, Nader arrived at the gate at the time of the scheduled departure of the flight. Since he had a scheduled speaking engagement, defendant suggests that Nader not only should have been at the airport earlier to be sure of making his flight, but also that he should have booked an earlier flight, perhaps one leaving the night before the engagement.

Defendant asks why Nader refused alternative transportation, and how CCAG's reputation and fund-raising abilities were injured by his not attending the rally. These questions, too, were designed to show Mr. Nader's culpability in not arriving at the rally, and that any harm to him or to CCAG is purely speculative. This theory would limit or, perhaps, negate compensatory damages and would go a long way towards denying punitives as well.

Throughout this deposition it is interesting to note the interplay among the defendant's attorney, plaintiffs' attorneys, and Nader. There is an obvious jockeying for position by Mr. Nader and a cautiousness in answering. The questioner, Mr. Roberson, almost had to drag answers from him. Examine the excerpt of the deposition not only for its content but for its tone and manner. Note that despite objections to several questions, Nader answers them anyway. Only rarely does an attorney for a witness instruct that witness not to answer a question to which the attorney objected. The objections are preserved for decision by the judge. If an objection is sustained, the question and answer may be stricken from the record.

DEPOSING A WITNESS

- Know what information you hope to get from the witness.
- Know how that information will fit into your theory of the case.
- In representing a witness at a deposition you must decide:
  - when to object but let the witness answer;
  - when to instruct the witness not to answer;
  - when to intervene to change the tone or direction of the deposition.

UNITED STATES DISTRICT COURT
FOR THE DISTRICT OF COLUMBIA

Ralph Nader and the Connecticut
Citizen Action Group,

Plaintiffs,

v

Allegheny Airlines, Inc.,

Defendant.

} Civil Action No. 1346-72

NOTICE TO TAKE ORAL DEPOSITION

Please take notice that defendant Allegheny Airlines, Inc., will take the oral deposition of Ralph Nader, Washington, D.C., pursuant to the Federal Rules of Civil Procedure, at 10:00 A.M., Monday, November 13, 1972, in the offices of Hogan &

Hartson, 600 Chanin Building, 815 Connecticut Avenue, Washington, D.C., before George M. Poe, Notary Public, or some other person authorized to administer an oath.

HOGAN & HARTSON

By: _____
Frank F. Roberson

_____
William A. Bradford, Jr.
815 Connecticut Avenue
Washington, D.C. 20006
298-5500
Attorneys for Defendant Allegheny Airlines, Inc.

CERTIFICATE OF SERVICE

I hereby certify that a copy of the foregoing Notice To Take Oral Deposition was mailed, postage prepaid, this 12th day of October, 1972, to Don W. Crockett, Esq., 1700 Pennsylvania Avenue, N.W., Washington, D.C., 20006 and to Reuben B. Robertson, III, Esq., 1156–19th Street, N.W., Washington, D.C. 20036, Attorneys for Plaintiffs.

HOGAN & HARTSON

By: _____
Frank F. Roberson

UNITED STATES DISTRICT COURT
FOR THE DISTRICT OF COLUMBIA

Ralph Nader and the Connecticut
Citizen Action Group, _____

                                    Plaintiffs,

    v   } Civil Action No. 1346-72

Allegheny Airlines, Inc., _____

                                    Defendant.

DEPOSITION OF
RALPH NADER,

a plaintiff, was called for examination by counsel for the defendant, pursuant to notice, copy of which is attached to the court copy of this deposition, at the offices of Hogan & Hartson, 600 Chanin Building, 815 Connecticut Avenue, Washington, D.C., by Frank F. Roberson, Esquire, before George M. Poe, Jr., a Notary Public in and for the District of Columbia, beginning at 10:00 o'clock a.m., when were present on behalf of the respective parties:

For the Plaintiffs:

> DON W. CROCKETT, ESQUIRE and
> REUBEN B. ROBERTSON, III, ESQUIRE

For the Defendant:

> HOGAN & HARTSON
> By: FRANK F. ROBERSON, ESQUIRE

— — —

INDEX

WITNESS	EXAMINATION BY COUNSEL FOR THE DEFENDANT	PLAINTIFFS
RALPH NADER	3	

EXHIBITS

NADER DEPOSITION EXHIBIT NOS.	FOR IDENTIFICATION
1. Plan of airport layout	39
2. Plan of airport layout	39

WHEREUPON,

RALPH NADER,

a plaintiff, was called for examination by counsel for the defendant and, after being first duly sworn by the Notary Public, was examined and testified as follows:

EXAMINATION BY COUNSEL FOR THE DEFENDANT

BY MR. ROBERSON:

Q. Will you state your full name, Mr. Nader?

A. Ralph Nader.

Q. And what is your residence address?

A. 1719–19th Street, N.W.

Q. And what is your business address?

A. 2000–P Street, N.W.

Q. What is your occupation, sir?

A. Lawyer.

Q. Are you admitted to practice in the District of Columbia?

A. No.

Q. Where are you admitted to practice?

A. Connecticut and Massachusetts.

Q. Have you ever been in private practice?

A. Yes.

Q. Where was that?

A. Connecticut.

Q. Do you have a law firm here in the District of Columbia?

A. No, as conventionally defined.

Q. You say you have an office address, what is the nature of that office?

A. That is where lawyers and scientists and other researchers are engaged in studying problems relating to the public interest.

Q. Back in April of this year, April 28, 1972, you had a speaking engagement up in Hartford, Connecticut, did you not?

A. That's right.

Q. What was the nature of the speaking engagement?

A. It was an address relating to the fund raising program of the Connecticut Citizen Action Group, Hartford, Connecticut.

Q. Can you tell me what the Connecticut Citizen Action Group is?

A. That is a group of citizens that is engaged in researching issues dealing with consumer and environmental and other public issues.

* * *

Q. Do you know whether anybody else was scheduled to talk at the meeting other than you and the Mayor?

A. Just Mr. Moffett who sort of was to be like the master of ceremonies.

Q. Mr. Moffett did make some sort of talk, did he?

A. Yes.

Q. Was it planned to solicit contributions to this group at this meeting?

A. Generally I believe he had that in mind but I doubt whether he passed the hat around, but the general purpose of the meeting was informative and fund raising.

Q. How did you think he intended to raise money if he wasn't going to pass the hat around so to speak?

MR. CROCKETT: I object to the question because what Mr. Nader thinks has no bearing on the facts in this case.

BY MR. ROBERSON:

Q. It was alleged in this lawsuit it was to be a fund raising method and I want to know how they expect to raise it? Can you help us any along these lines?

A. No, the specifics you would have to ask Mr. Moffett.

Q. For instance, do you know whether they were going to sell any objects to the group?

A. I don't know.

Q. Like bumper stickers for instance?

A. I don't know.

Q. Do you know whether any effort was made to raise funds at the meeting?

A. I don't know.

Q. You can tell me this even by hearsay. Have you heard one way or the other whether they tried to raise any money?

974 ☐ *West's Legal Desk Reference*

A. All I heard was basically that the purpose of the meeting collapsed and the wrinkles on the nature of its collapse you will have to ask Mr. Moffett.

Q. You don't know whether they even tried to raise any money, is that right?

A. I would assume.

Q. I don't want you to assume

A. I don't know for a fact what they did.

Q. And he hasn't told you one way or the other?

A. He told me it was a collapse.

Q. Did he tell you that he tried to raise some money?

A. He didn't specify.

Q. Do you know how long the meeting lasted?

A. No.

*   *   *

Q. Do you fly frequently, Mr. Nader?

A. Yes.

Q. Do you make several trips every week by air?

A. There is no average, it's sporadic.

Q. Well, there must be an average?

A. There is no specific, you know, routine.

Q. Would you fly in the course of a year, would you make as many as fifty round trips by plane?

A. Yes.

Q. That would be just one a week?

A. Yes.

Q. Would you fly a good deal more than that in an average year?

A. There is no average year as I stated, it depends, but at least fifty round trips.

Q. Are these primarily for speaking engagements, your travel?

A. To some extent, but certainly not exclusively.

Q. I didn't say exclusively, I said primarily.

A. To some extent.

Q. Primarily means mostly, do you agree with that?

A. No. I have never totaled it up but there are other reasons to travel besides speaking engagements.

Q. Of course, but this is the reason for which you generally travel more often than not, is that right?

A. I couldn't say.

Q. How far in advance do you ordinarily schedule your speaking arrangements time wise?

A. Several weeks at least for the most part.

Q. Can you recall where you were on the day before Friday the 28th of April 1972?

A. No.

Q. You don't know whether you were in Washington or elsewhere?

A. I believe I was in Washington but I would have to refresh my recollection. Correction. I was in Washington that evening, whether I was in Washington that whole day I would have to refresh my recollection.

Q. You are speaking about Thursday evening?

A. Yes.

Q. Was there a particular reason why you could not go up to Connecticut on Thursday instead of Friday?

A. Yes.

Q. What was the reason?

A. Work.

Q. What, just office work you are speaking of?

A. Yes.

Q. Is it your custom to schedule events so close that you arrive on the day of your speaking engagements?

A. That is my custom, to schedule them efficiently and if that involves relying on airline schedules then it is so scheduled.

Q. But you fly enough to know that you can't always rely on airline schedules, don't you?

MR. CROCKETT: I object to that as being a leading question.

MR. ROBERSON: I have a right to lead the witness. Go ahead and answer it.

THE WITNESS: I like to rely on the airlines representations of leaving on time and according to schedule. They certainly spend enough money trying to convince us of that.

BY MR. ROBERSON:

Q. That wasn't the question, whether you like to rely on them or not. I said, you know you can't rely on them one hundred per cent, can you?

MR. ROBERTSON: I object to that because you haven't laid a basis for that question.

BY MR. ROBERSON:

Q. Then you do know it's a fact that you can't rely on them one hundred per cent, don't you?

A. Nothing can be relied on one hundred per cent in this world.

Q. Specifically, you know that from time to time a particular flight will be over booked and you won't be able to get on the plane. You know that, don't you?

MR. CROCKETT: I object to that again because there has been no foundation laid.

MR. ROBERSON: Go ahead and answer it.

THE WITNESS: What does my counsel instruct?

MR. ROBERTSON: Go ahead and answer it.

THE WITNESS: Rephrase the question.

MR. ROBERTSON: Yes, please rephrase the question.

*　　*　　*

BY MR. ROBERSON:

Q. What is the ambiguity?

A. You often make reservations and the airlines will tell you that there is no more room, and in that sense your question might cover that area. What are you specifically directing your question to?

Q. You know from time to time although you have a confirmed reservation that more people show up than customarily show up and you can't get on the plane. You know that, don't you?

A. With what frequency?

Q. I said from time to time this happens.

A. I would not agree with the characterization of from time to time.

Q. Well it happened to you within the week of April the 24th, 1972, hadn't it?

A. Yes, but that still doesn't qualify it for that.

Q. Tell me about the previous things that have happened to you that we can—

MR. CROCKETT: I object to this entire line of questioning because I fail to see any relevance whatsoever.

MR. ROBERSON: You have your objection on the record now go ahead and answer it.

MR. CROCKETT: I don't know whether I am going to let it go because it seems to me we are reaching a point—

MR. ROBERSON: We will terminate the deposition and get a ruling from the Judge if you are going to stop him on that sort of thing because we are just wasting our time here. I am going to have an answer to this because it's relevant.

MR. CROCKETT: Let's go off the record.

(Brief discussion off the record.)

*   *   *

BY MR. ROBERSON:

Q. You knew what denied boarding compensation was at the time of your Friday April 28, 1972 incident at Allegheny Airlines didn't you? You knew about denied boarding compensation, didn't you?

A. I knew about the card that the airlines proffer.

Q. Didn't the Allegheny passenger representative that talked to you give you such a card?

A. I don't recollect to what extent he characterized it because I refused to accept any such card.

Q. You said you already had one from American Airlines in fact, isn't that right?

MR. ROBERTSON: He didn't say that.

THE WITNESS: No, I didn't say that.

*   *   *

Q. On Friday morning the 28th of April did you go to your office?

A. No.

*   *   *

Q. How did you get to the airport on that morning?

A. Taxi.

Q. Was it from your home that you went to the airport?

A. From downtown Washington, yes.

Q. You are saying it was not your home?

A. There was another stop made.

Q. Where did you go first? Tell me about this: After you got up that morning what did you do. You had breakfast at home?

A. That's not a relevant question.

Q. You tell me what you did that is relevant.

A. A call was made to the office to obtain the ticket for which a reservation had been made, and the ticket was prepared and then conveyed to me and then I went to the airport.

Q. The ticket was sent out to your home, or did you stop somewhere and pick it up?

A. No, it was delivered to me.

* * *

Q. What time did you leave the city to go to the airport?

A. About twenty of ten.

Q. That flight, and by the way we are talking about Allegheny flight number 864, what time was it scheduled to depart?

A. I believe 10:15.

Q. That would be indicated on your ticket, wouldn't it?

A. Yes.

Q. On a weekday morning between nine and ten what do you estimate the travel time would be from where you started in downtown Washington to the Washington National Airport?

A. About twenty minutes.

Q. How long did it take you on this occasion?

A. Oh, about twenty five minutes.

Q. Were you traveling alone, Mr. Nader?

A. Yes.

Q. Did you have any luggage with you?

A. Just a small hand bag.

Q. An attache type of thing?

A. Yes.

Q. Where did the taxi let you off when it got over to the Washington National Airport?

A. In front of the Allegheny sign at the National Airport, main terminal.

* * *

Q. Did you stop at the Allegheny ticket counter when you got in?

A. Just in order to see the board and find out where the gate was.

Q. You did not intend to check any baggage?

A. No, there was no baggage to check.

Q. What did you see when you looked at the board?

A. The gate number.

Q. Did it indicate whether it was boarding on time or late?

A. I just ascertained what was the gate number.

Q. What time was it then?

A. About five after ten, or four after ten, something like that.

Q. Were you concerned that you might miss the flight?

A. No.

Q. You thought that you had plenty of time?

A. Oh, yes.

Q. Did you walk from the Allegheny ticket counter to the gate?

A. I always walk fast.

Q. You walked this time, didn't you?

A. Yes.

Q. You weren't running?

A. No, I was walking fast.

Q. Did you say anything to any of the people at the Allegheny ticket counter on the main floor there when you ascertained the gate number?

A. I don't believe so.

* * *

Q. What was the gate number?

* * *

A. It was down near the end of the corridor.,

Q. It was the last gate in fact on the corridor, wasn't it?

A. Yes, probably.

Q. And it's a considerable distance from the airline ticket counter to that gate, isn't it?

A. About three minutes.

Q. It's a matter of three or four hundred yards, isn't it?

A. I don't know, but I have done it before in three minutes.

* * *

CERTIFICATE OF NOTARY PUBLIC

I, George M. Poe, Jr., the officer before whom the foregoing deposition was taken, do hereby certify that the witness whose testimony appears in the foregoing deposition was duly sworn by me; that the testimony of said witness was taken by me stenographically and thereafter reduced to typewriting under my direction; that said deposition is a true record of the testimony given by said witness; that I am neither counsel for, related to, nor employed by any of the parties to the action in which this deposition was taken; and, further, that I am not a relative or employee of any attorney or counsel employed by the parties hereto, nor financially or otherwise interested in the outcome of the action.

_____
Notary Public in and for the District of Columbia

My Commission Expires:
December 14, 1973

— — —

DOCUMENT #16: MOTION FOR A PROTECTIVE ORDER

DOCUMENT #17:
MEMORANDUM OF POINTS AND AUTHORITIES IN SUPPORT OF MOTION FOR PROTECTIVE ORDER

DOCUMENT #18:
OPPOSITION TO MOTION FOR A PROTECTIVE ORDER

DOCUMENT #19: COURT ORDER

DOCUMENT #20:
DEPOSITION OF PRESIDENT OF ALLEGHENY AIRLINES

Plaintiffs wanted to take the deposition of Leslie O. Barnes, the President of Allegheny Airlines. Defendant objected, and sought a Protective Order (Document #16) from the court vacating the Notice of Deposition to Mr. Barnes and prohibiting the deposition. It asserted that Mr. Barnes had "no information or knowledge relevant to the instant action," and that taking the deposition would be "burdensome," "oppressive," and would constitute "harassment."

Defendant submitted a Memorandum of Points and Authorities in support of its Motion for a Protective Order (Document #17). In it, after briefly reiterating the basic sequence of events, defendant again characterizes the dispute as limited to whether Allegheny wrongfully injured Nader or CCAG due to Nader's being bumped from his confirmed flight. If this characterization is accepted by the court, it is argued (and, no doubt, would be conceded by plaintiffs) that the President of Allegheny has no firsthand knowledge of the facts in this case. If a witness has no knowledge of the facts and thus, arguably, can give no competent testimony, calling that witness for a deposition *is* burdensome and oppressive. Defendant alludes to Mr. Barnes' heavy daily responsibilities, the interruption of which would burden both him and Allegheny, and cites cases protecting witnesses such as Mr. Barnes from being deposed. Allegheny goes on to state that the facts concerning the incident in question have already been laid out in discovery. Therefore, Mr. Barnes could serve no useful purpose at a deposition.

As noted in our discussion of defendant's Opposition to plaintiffs' Motion to Compel (Document #9), defendant's characterization of the case is very different from that of plaintiffs. Defendant describes this situation as an isolated incident, while plaintiffs portray it as the result of a deliberate and unnecessary policy that defrauds the public as a whole. Based on this portrayal, plaintiffs seek punitive damages. They want the testimony of Mr. Barnes in order to lay the foundation for this damage claim. They wish to know more about the policy, its origin and the alternatives to it. On this basis, the court entered an Order (Document #19) denying defendant's motion for a protective order and allowed Mr. Barnes to be deposed. We are reproducing limited excerpts from the deposition (Document #20) merely to suggest its flavor.

The introductory material in this deposition is similar to that in the Nader deposition seen earlier (Document #14). Similarly, the interaction between Mr. Barnes and plaintiffs' counsel displays much of the same jockeying that was evident in the Nader deposition. It is interesting to note, however, that this deposition was taken after a Motion for a Protective Order was denied. Thus, there seems to be a bit more tension in the discussion.

Plaintiffs' goal is to establish that Allegheny had an unstated and economically unnecessary policy of overbooking flights. They hope to show that travellers rely on airline schedules and on confirmed reservations, and that the policy of overbooking and the resultant bumping of passengers unreasonably and fraudulently defeats that reliance. This is particularly harmful when the airlines, through their advertising, attempt to foster and increase that reliance by emphasizing their record of timely arrivals and general reliability. The questions put to Mr. Barnes are designed to elicit information about that policy and its essential contradiction with the image developed and promulgated by the industry, including Allegheny. This knowing deception is the basis for the punitive damage claim.

PREPARING A MOTION FOR A PROTECTIVE ORDER

In the motion, state:
- the authority for the motion;
- the relief sought;
- the basis for that relief.

UNITED STATES DISTRICT COURT
FOR THE DISTRICT OF COLUMBIA

Ralph Nader, et al.,

               Plaintiffs,

    v

Allegheny Airlines, Inc.,

               Defendant.

Civil Action No. 1346-72

MOTION OF DEFENDANT ALLEGHENY AIRLINES, INC.
FOR PROTECTIVE ORDER

The defendant Allegheny Airlines, Inc., pursuant to Federal Rule of Civil Procedure 26(c), hereby moves for a Protective Order that the noted deposition of Leslie O. Barnes, President of defendant Allegheny, not be had and that the Notice to Take Oral Deposition of Mr. Barnes be vacated and set aside on the grounds that Mr. Barnes has no information or knowledge relevant to the instant action and on the further grounds that the deposition of Mr. Barnes would be burdensome and oppressive to the defendant and would constitute harassment of the defendant, all of which is more fully set forth in the Memorandum of Points and Authorities in Support of defendant's Motion for Protective Order filed herewith and by reference made a part hereof.

Respectfully submitted,

HOGAN & HARTSON

By: _____
Frank F. Roberson

William A. Bradford, Jr.
815 Connecticut Avenue, N.W.
Washington, D.C. 20006
298-5500
Attorneys for Defendant Allegheny Airlines, Inc.

UNITED STATES DISTRICT COURT
FOR THE DISTRICT OF COLUMBIA

Ralph Nader, et al.,

Plaintiffs,

v

Allegheny Airlines, Inc.,

Defendant.

} Civil Action No. 1346-72

MEMORANDUM OF POINTS AND AUTHORITIES
IN SUPPORT OF DEFENDANT'S MOTION FOR
A PROTECTIVE ORDER

Statement of the Case

This action was brought by Mr. Ralph Nader and the Connecticut Citizen Action Group ("CCAG") on July 7, 1972. A non-jury trial date of September 7 was set in open court on May 10, 1973, and that trial date was changed to September 4 by written notice to the parties served by the Court on July 31, 1973.

*   *   *

The plaintiffs have filed, and the defendant has responded to 32 interrogatories with subparts and 8 Requests for Production of Documents and subparts. The defendant has taken the deposition of Mr. Nader and Mr. Moffett, a principal of CCAG, and the plaintiffs have taken the deposition of Mr. John McDonald, an Allegheny passenger service representative who dealt directly with Mr. Nader at the time of the denied boarding incident and who has personal knowledge of what transpired at that time.

On August 3, 1973 the plaintiffs served by mail on the defendant a Notice to Take Oral Deposition of Mr. Leslie O. Barnes, the President of Allegheny Airlines, on August 13, 1973. Subsequently counsel for the parties agreed that Mr. Barnes' deposition, if the Motion for Protective Order is not granted, will be held at 10:30 a.m. on August 20, 1973.

ARGUMENT

The defendant, pursuant to Federal Rule of Civil Procedure 26(c), moves for a Protective Order that the deposition of Mr. Barnes not be held and that the Notice to Take Oral Deposition be vacated and set aside on the grounds that the President of Allegheny Airlines has no relevant knowledge of the incident that is the subject of this lawsuit and that the Notice to Take Oral Deposition of President Barnes constitutes harassment of the defendant and is otherwise burdensome and oppressive.

The gravamen of plaintiffs' claim is that Mr. Nader had a confirmed reservation ticket for Allegheny's flight to Hartford, Connecticut, but that when he appeared at the airport a minute or two before the plane began its take-off taxi he was informed that the flight had been oversold, that there was no seat for him, and that he would be able to take Allegheny's alternative transportation to Hartford. The plaintiff CCAG claims that it was damaged by Mr. Nader's failure to appear at its meeting. . . .

President Barnes has absolutely no personal knowledge of the denied boarding incident that is the basis of this lawsuit, nor of CCAG's alleged injuries, and thus his deposition cannot be for the purpose of gaining any knowledge relevant to the lawsuit, but is simply unjustified harassment of the defendant.

The law is clear that a judge, pursuant to Federal Rule 26(c), can set aside a deposition notice if the proposed deponent can have no knowledge relevant to the action. Thus, in a personal injury action against an airline a judge in the Southern District of New York vacated the plaintiffs' notice to take the deposition of the president of Northwest Orient Airlines where "It [was] apparent that the defendant's president has no firsthand knowledge of the facts and circumstances concerning the accident out of which this action arose." *Spencer v. Northwest Orient Airlines, Inc.*, 201 F. Supp. 504, 507-08 (S.D.N.Y. 1962).

*   *   *

UNITED STATES DISTRICT COURT
FOR THE DISTRICT OF COLUMBIA

Ralph Nader and the Connecticut
Citizen Action Group,

Plaintiffs,

v

Civil Action No. 1346-72

Allegheny Airlines, Inc.,

Defendant.

PLAINTIFFS' OPPOSITION TO DEFENDANT'S MOTION FOR PROTECTIVE ORDER

The defendant Allegheny Airlines has now moved for a protective order which would prohibit plaintiffs from taking the company's deposition through its president, Mr. Leslie O. Barnes, now scheduled for August 20, 1973. For the reasons set forth herein, plaintiffs submit that no good cause to cut off normal discovery rights has been shown and respectfully urge that this Court deny the instant motion.

The plaintiffs' right to discover relevant information from the defendant company, based on the Federal Rules of Civil Procedure, is clear. Rule 26 provides for discovery of any unprivileged matter that is relevant to the subject matter of the action, and it is well established that the pre-trial discovery rules must be accorded liberal treatment. Protective orders to bar the taking of a deposition are quite rare and must be supported by a strong showing of good cause. 4 Moore's Federal Practice § 26.69 (2d Ed. 1972).

*   *   *

This litigation involves several disputed issues concerning the defendant's corporate policies and practices. For example, the plaintiffs have alleged—and Allegheny has denied—that the company's deliberate overbooking of its flights is done with willful and wanton disregard of its passengers' rights, a test for punitive damages articulated in the leading case of *Wills* v. *Trans World Airlines*, 200 F. Supp. 360 (S.D. Cal. 1961).

*   *   *

The defendant bases its request to prohibit the deposition of Mr. Barnes upon two arguments. First it is contended that he has no knowledge or information relevant to the *incident* in which Mr. Nader was refused accommodation on Allegheny's flight or to the consequences visited upon the plaintiffs. This argument, however, misconceives the scope of discovery contemplated under the Federal Rules, since plaintiffs are entitled to examine on any matter relevant to the subject matter of the litigation. Obviously this must include the issues of company policy and potential defenses described in the preceding paragraph, important matters of which the chief executive of the company must be presumed to have some knowledge. *Chemical Specialties Co.* v. *Ciba Pharmaceutical Products, Inc.*, 10 F.R.D. 500, 502 (D.N.J. 1950).

*   *   *

UNITED STATES DISTRICT COURT
FOR THE DISTRICT OF COLUMBIA

Ralph Nader and the Connecticut
Citizen Action Group,

                              Plaintiffs,

    v   Civil Action No. 1346-72

Allegheny Airlines, Inc.,

                              Defendant.

ORDER

Upon consideration of the Motion of Defendant Allegheny Airlines, Inc. for a Protective Order to prevent the deposition of Leslie O. Barnes, President of Allegheny Airlines, Inc., and the plaintiffs' opposition thereto, it is this 16th day of August, 1973.

ORDERED that the defendant's motion for a protective order be and is hereby denied; and it is

FURTHER ORDERED that Leslie O. Barnes appear Monday, August 20, 1973 at 10:30 A.M. at the requested location and give testimony upon oral deposition in accordance with Rule 26 of the Federal Rules of Civil Procedure.

CHARLES R. RICHEY
UNITED STATES DISTRICT JUDGE

UNITED STATES DISTRICT COURT

FOR THE DISTRICT OF COLUMBIA

Ralph Nader and the Connecticut
Citizen Action Group,

                                          Plaintiffs,

    v   } Civil Action No. 1346-72

Allegheny Airlines, Inc.,

                                          Defendant.

Washington, D.C.
Monday, August 20, 1973

**DEPOSITION OF
LESLIE O. BARNES**

Deposition of LESLIE O. BARNES, taken on behalf of the plaintiffs in the above-entitled action, at 1156 Nineteenth Street, N.W. (Second Floor), Washington, D.C., pursuant to notice, beginning at 10:30 o'clock a.m., before Doris F. Hoover, a notary public in and for the District of Columbia, when were present on behalf of the respective parties:

For the Plaintiffs:
    REUBEN B. ROBERTSON, III, ESQ.
    1156 Nineteenth Street, N.W.
    Washington, D.C. 20036
For the Defendant:
    FRANK F. ROBERSON, ESQ.
    HOGAN & HARTSON
    815 Connecticut Avenue
    Washington, D.C. 20006

PROCEEDINGS

WHEREUPON,

LESLIE O. BARNES,

was called for examination by counsel for plaintiffs, and having been first duly sworn by the notary public, was examined and testified as follows:

EXAMINATION BY COUNSEL FOR PLAINTIFFS

BY MR. ROBERTSON:

Q. For the record, would you state your name and your residence and address.

A. Leslie Barnes, 4625 Holly Road, Rockville.

Q. And your phone?

A. It's unlisted.

Q. Could you give it to us for the record?

A. No. Why?

Q. Would you give it to me off the record so I may be able to find you if I need you?

A. You know where my office is, and that's where.

MR. ROBERSON: Without calling any unlisted phone.

BY MR. ROBERTSON:

Q. What is your business address?

A. It's Washington National Airport, Hanger Club.

*   *   *

Q. How do people find out about Allegheny's services and about the reservations that are available for its flights?

A. Through advertising, through the numbers that are given and through the calls that they make.

Q. Excuse me. Through the numbers that are given?

A. The number to call. Either in—every advertisement gives a number or go through your travel agency.

Q. So the company does want them to know about them?

A. Of course.

Q. In your advertising, do you try to convey an image of reliability and dependability?

A. Certainly.

Q. Do Allegheny's tariffs set forth the reservation services?

A. The tariffs?

Q. Yes.

A. Well, I don't know where it all is, where it's all set forth. But, certainly, the passengers through advertising, through publications of various kinds, do know what the number is to call, whether it's through the tariffs, or the schedules, or the telephone bill.

Q. Do you know what the tariffs might say about—

A. No, I do not.

Q. —who's entitled to a seat on a particular flight?

A. No.

Q. Well, is a person, would you say that a person is justified, would be justified in actually relying on having confirmed reservation for a particular Allegheny flight when he's making business or personal plans?

A. Yes, and I think our record in that area is identical, or is in cadence with the rest of the news. But I think that the person making reservation would have normal expectancy of completing that flight as planned.

*   *   *

Q. What is overbooking?

A. What do you mean "What is overbooking"? I just told you.

Q. Well, you were setting up a balance or attempts between finding the number of correct balance between no-shows and the number of passengers you carry.

A. Right.

Q. And then you said to the extent that you come out to a zero excess that you overbook. I don't think I understand you.

A. No. I said the extent that you come out with zero overbooking to zero oversales and zero empty seats. That's the optimum.

Q. That's the optimum.

I'm just asking you what is overbooking for the record.

A. I have to go right back what do you mean, 'cause I just got through telling you.

Q. Well, would you say the correct definition of "overbooking" would be the reservation or expectance of reservation for more seats on the flight than you have?

A. We have a factor of two per cent.

MR. ROBERSON: Wait just a minute. Listen to the question until he finishes it, rather than anticipate, because you never know what he'll tell at the end of the questions if you do that.

*   *   *

BY MR. ROBERTSON:

Q. What is planned capacity?

A. One hundred seats is to go out with one hundred passengers.

Q. That's all that it is? Doesn't the term imply a system as used by Allegheny, or an approach used by Allegheny?

A. It could, I don't know.

Q. You're not familiar with the term?

A. No.

Q. Is it true that Allegheny under—that Allegheny intentionally overbooks certain of its flights?

A. I don't know. I mean I don't know of an instance in this. I would assume that in the fulfillment of that policy there would be some overbooking.

Q. On what flights does this apply?

A. I don't know.

Q. Are there any flights on which overbooking is prohibited?

A. I don't know.

Q. Well, how does the planned capacity system work?

A. I don't know.

Q. Who's in charge?

A. The—Mr. Jenkins is responsible for that.

Q. You know who sets up the authorized number of oversales on a particular flight?

A. No, I do not.

Q. You know whether it's set by a particular flight or by market?

A. I don't know.

*   *   *

Q. You're not aware that Allegheny's record on oversales is substantially above the industry average?

A. No. In fact, I have the opposite impression that it is not. It's about at industry average.

Q. So when the system gets out of balance, you do get some reports about this, is that right?

A. I would hear about it, I think.

Q. And have you received any of such reports?

A. No.

Q. None that you can remember?

A. I have not received any.

Q. What happens when the authorized number for a particular flight is reached and that number of reservations come in?

A. You mean on a given flight?

Q. Yeah.

A. This flight is dispatched.

Q. I'm referring to when the reservations are received in advance of flight up to the top number that they will accept.

A. I don't know.

Q. You know what closing flight is for reservations?

A. No, I would have to guess at that. I don't know.

Q. What is confirming a flight?

A. I don't know.

Q. Do you know where a flight is overbooked in advance Allegheny might have people call up some of the persons holding reservations to check and see whether they're actually going?

A. I would think that a good administration would do that, yes.

Q. Do you know whether Allegheny does that?

A. I don't know. No, I don't.

Q. When was planned capacity, as it's now operated by Allegheny, first put into effect?

A. I don't know.

* * *

Q. Do you know what the other reasons are for denied boarding? We've talked about some of the equipment change problems and—

A. There are other reasons than just this one, but I'm not the one who can give you that, because I don't have the facts and I'm not familiar with all the operation of reservations in this area. So I have to sit here and tell you I haven't thought about it, and that's exactly the answer you're going to get.

Q. Well, if you don't know, just tell me. There's no problem.

* * *

Q. Why are Allegheny's agents instructed to tell a passenger, who's been bumped because of an oversale, everything but the planned capacity is the reason?

A. You have information that indicates they are.

Q. I'd like to show you a copy of the *Allegheny Passenger Service Manual,* 6-100, at Page 4, and if you'd just like to read that over.

* * *

Q. Mr. Barnes, would you tell me what the Allegheny agent is supposed to do when an oversale occurs, based on the Allegheny manual here.

A. I would simply suggest you put this in the deposition, 'cause all I would be doing is reading from it.

Q. Well, I'd like you to tell me in your own words what that means (indicating).

A. I'm not going to tell you in my own words. All I'm going to do is tell you this. Do you want me to read it?

* * *

DOCUMENT #21: MOTION FOR SUMMARY JUDGMENT

DOCUMENT #22:
MEMORANDUM OF POINTS AND AUTHORITIES
IN SUPPORT OF MOTION FOR SUMMARY JUDGMENT

DOCUMENT #23:
DEFENDANT'S STATEMENT OF UNDISPUTED MATERIAL FACTS

Summary judgment is a method by which a lawsuit may be decided on the merits before the trial actually begins. It is available when there are no issues of material fact in dispute between the parties. All that is left be be decided is what law applies to the agreed upon facts and how it applies. These are questions for the court to decide without the need for a fact-finder. FRCP 56 sets out the method by which a party may move the court for an order granting summary judgment in its favor. A "defending party" may move, at any time, for such an order (Document #21). Allegheny Airlines did so after the complaint was served but before it had filed an answer. Allegheny alleged that there was "no genuine issue as to any material fact" in the suit and that it was entitled, as a matter of law, to judgment. As always, the party submitting a motion must support it with a Memorandum of Points and Authorities which sets out its arguments on the law (cases, statutes, regulations, etc.) and the policy supporting its position (Document #22).

In its memorandum, Allegheny presents two theories to convince the court to rule in its favor. Neither theory goes directly to the substance of the dispute raised by plaintiffs, the bumping of Ralph Nader from his confirmed flight, but involve instead a procedural issue and a legal relationship. In particular, Allegheny alleges, first, that each plaintiff failed to comply in a timely manner with a notice requirement which it claims was a prerequisite to a suit. Second, Allegheny argues that CCAG had no legally recognized relationship with it so that CCAG had not stated a claim upon which relief can be granted. (Technically, this is the basis for a motion to dismiss for failure to state a claim upon which relief can be granted pursuant to FRCP 12(b) and not a motion for summary judgment).

Allegheny begins by briefly stating the relevant facts in the case. Some are the same facts plaintiffs alleged in their complaint which Allegheny does not dispute. For instance, Allegheny concedes that Nader was bumped from a confirmed flight, that CCAG was to have a rally at which Nader was to be a featured speaker, and that Nader did not make the rally. Allegheny, however, also alleges new facts. On the day Nader was bumped, Allegheny alleges that it had on file with the CAB a tariff which, in essence, required that a person with a claim against Allegheny must notify Allegheny, in writing, of that claim within forty-five days of the occurrence or else be barred from suing. Allegheny then points out that the first written notice from Nader was delivered to Allegheny more than forty-five days from the date of the incident and that therefore he may not maintain the present suit. (It is also claimed that CCAG never notified Allegheny and, thus, it too is barred.)

Allegheny's second argument, which goes only to the claims made by CCAG, is that there was no contract between it and CCAG nor was there any other legally cognizable relationship between them that could lead to a recovery in this case. Allegheny's position is that it did not know of CCAG's existence until *after* Nader was denied boarding on the flight. Therefore, Allegheny could not have intended to injure CCAG by bumping Nader.

Accompanying Allegheny's motion and memorandum is a Table of Cases and a Statement of Undisputed Material Facts (Document #23). The latter is critical since if any material facts are in dispute, a motion for summary judgment cannot lie. Next, there is an affidavit from an attorney for Allegheny who states under oath that the tariff alluded to in the motion was on file with the CAB and that a search was conducted of Allegheny's records which turned up no notice by either plaintiff within the time permitted by the tariff. Finally, there is attached to the motion a certified copy of the tariff provision itself. (Neither the affidavit nor the copy of the tariff are included below.)

With the submission of these documents, defendant has shown facts it believed are incontestable, identified a body of law concerning the incident in question, and developed an argument tying the law to the facts so as to require judgment in its favor.

Moving for summary judgment is a strategic as well as a legal maneuver. In deciding whether to do so, you should consider the following:

- are there any material facts in dispute;
- do the undisputed facts favor your party;
- how clear is the law on the issue;
- does the law favor your party;
- would presenting testimonial and other evidence strengthen your case?

PREPARING SUMMARY JUDGMENT DOCUMENTS

- State all the facts necessary to make out your case.
- Provide clear support through evidence or affidavit for each fact not conceded by your opponent which you allege.
- Cite all relevant law supporting your position.
- Provide the judge with a clear and concise argument, citing appropriate authorities that support your position.
- Consider the likely response of your opponent and be able to meet it either in your memorandum, in oral argument, or in a supplemental memorandum.

UNITED STATES DISTRICT COURT
FOR THE DISTRICT OF COLUMBIA

Ralph Nader and the Connecticut
Citizen Action Group,

                              Plaintiffs,

      v   } Civil Action No. 1346-72

Allegheny Airlines, Inc.,

                              Defendant.

DEFENDANT'S MOTION FOR SUMMARY JUDGMENT

Comes now defendant Allegheny Airlines, Inc., and, pursuant to Federal Rule of Civil Procedure 56(b), moves the court for summary judgment in its favor upon the claims asserted against it herein by plaintiffs Ralph Nader and Connecticut Citizen Action Group upon the ground that there is no genuine issue as to any material fact and that it is entitled to judgment as a matter of law, as more fully set forth in the pleadings and Exhibits A and B, attached hereto.

HOGAN & HARTSON

By: _____
Frank S. Roberson

_____
Robert S. Bennett

_____
William A. Bradford, Jr.
Attorneys for Defendant
Allegheny Airlines, Inc.
815 Connecticut Avenue
Washington, D.C. 20006
298-5500

CERTIFICATE OF SERVICE

Copies of the foregoing Motion for Summary Judgment, attached Exhibits, Statement of Material Facts, Supporting Memorandum and proposed Order were mailed, this 16th day of August, 1972, to Don W. Crockett, Esq., Suite 880, 1700 Pennsylvania Avenue, N.W., Washington, D.C. 20006, and to Reuben B. Robertson, III, Esquire, 1156–19th Street, N.W., Washington, D.C. 20036, Attorneys for Plaintiffs.

HOGAN & HARTSON

By: _____
Frank F. Roberson

UNITED STATES DISTRICT COURT
FOR THE DISTRICT OF COLUMBIA

Ralph Nader and the Connecticut
Citizen Action Group,

                         Plaintiffs,

     v

Allegheny Airlines, Inc.,

                       Defendant.

}

Civil Action No. 1346-72

DEFENDANT'S MEMORANDUM OF POINTS AND AUTHORITIES IN SUPPORT OF MOTION FOR SUMMARY JUDGMENT

Defendant, pursuant to U.S. District Court for the District of Columbia Rule 9(b) presents herein its memorandum of points and authorities in support of its Motion for Summary Judgment. The Table of Cases with asterisks placed alongside those chiefly relied on is attached at the end of this memorandum.

I. Facts

*   *   *

II. Law

1. The claims of both plaintiff Nader and plaintiff Connecticut Citizen Action Group are barred for failure to comply with the 45 day written notice provision of defendant's Tariff C.A.B. 142, Rule 42(B).

Tariffs of air carriers are filed pursuant to the provisions of the Federal Aviation Act which provides in pertinent part, 49 U.S.C.A. §1373:

> "(a) Every air carrier . . . shall file with the Board, and print, and keep open to public inspection, tariffs showing all rates, fares, and charges for air transportation between points served by it. . . and showing to the extent required by regulations of the Board, all classifications, rules, regulations, practices, and services in connection with such air transportation. Tariffs shall be filed, posted, and published in such form and manner, and shall contain such information, as the Board shall by regulation prescribe; and the Board is empowered to reject any tariff so filed which is not consistent with this section and such regulations."

Limitations of liability in air carrier tariffs are valid and binding even on passengers who lack actual notice of the limitations.

*   *   *

2. Plaintiff Connecticut Citizen Action Group has not stated a claim upon which relief can be granted against defendant Allegheny Airlines, Inc.

The complaint (par. 22) alleges a breach of defendant's contract with plaintiff Nader. There was no contract between the defendant carrier and plaintiff CCAG and none is alleged. No other legally recognizable theory of recovery by CCAG is enunciated in the complaint.

Not until *after* denial of boarding to plaintiff Nader was his speaking engagement at plaintiff CCAG's even revealed to the defendant carrier (Complaint, par. 16). Thus, at most, CCAG was "a mere incidental beneficiary" of the contract to transport Nader to Hartford on defendant's flight 864. A mere incidental beneficiary has no right to claim under a contract between two other parties even though it might have derived a benefit from performance of the contract. *Schwartz* v. *Brown*, 64 A.2d 298, 299 (D.C. Mun. App. 1949).

*   *   *

Respectfully submitted,

HOGAN & HARTSON

By: _____
Frank F. Roberson

_____
Robert S. Bennett

_____
William A. Bradford, Jr.
815 Connecticut Avenue
Washington, D.C. 20006
Attorneys for Defendant Allegheny Airlines, Inc.

TABLE OF CASES

*Cases chiefly relied upon are marked by asterisks.

UNITED STATES DISTRICT COURT
FOR THE DISTRICT OF COLUMBIA

Ralph Nader and the Connecticut
Citizen Action Group,

Plaintiffs,

v

Allegheny Airlines, Inc.,

Defendant.

Civil Action No. 1346-72

DEFENDANT'S STATEMENT OF UNDISPUTED MATERIAL FACTS

Defendant Allegheny Airlines, Inc., pursuant to U.S. District Court for the District of Columbia Rule 9(h) states the following material facts as to which it contends there is no genuine issue.

1. Defendant is an air carrier engaged in interstate commerce pursuant to a certificate of public convenience and necessity issued by the Civil Aeronautics Board and is regulated by the laws of the United States relating to such interstate commerce and by the rules, orders and regulations promulgated by the Board in accordance with the Federal Aviation Act of 1958. (Complaint, par. 5).

2. The complaint filed herein seeks damages arising from denial by defendant on April 28, 1972, notwithstanding plaintiff Nader's confirmed reservation, of a seat for him on its flight 864 from Washington, D.C., to Hartford, Connecticut, where he was scheduled to speak at a fund-raising rally organized by and for plaintiff Connecticut Citizen Action Group. (Complaint).

3. On April 28, 1972, defendant had on file with the Civil Aeronautics Board, Washington, D.C., Tariff C.A.B. 142, Local and Joint Passenger Rules Tariff No. PR-6, Rule 40(B) providing as follows:

> "*No action shall be maintained for* any loss of, or any damage to, or *any delay in the delivery of, any property or baggage, or on any other claim* (excepting only personal injury or death), *arising out of or in connection with transportation of, or failure to transport any passenger* or property or baggage *unless notice of the claim is presented in writing to an office of the carrier* participating in this Rule 40(B) alleged to be responsible therefor *within 45 days after the alleged occurrence of the events giving rise to the claim*, and unless the action is commenced within 2 years after such alleged occurrence, but failure to give the above notice shall not be a bar if the claimant establishes to the satisfaction of the carrier that he was unable to give such notice." (Emphasis added). (Exhibits A, par. 2., and B).

4. The first notice of the plaintiffs' claims presented in writing to an office of defendant was not delivered until June 19, 1972. (Exhibit A, par. 4).

5. No effort has been made by plaintiffs to establish to the satisfaction of defendant that either plaintiff was unable to give written notice of claim within 45 days of April 28, 1972. (Exhibit A, par. 5).

HOGAN & HARTSON

By: _____
Frank F. Roberson

_____
Robert S. Bennett

_____
William A. Bradford, Jr.
Attorneys for Defendant Allegheny Airlines, Inc.
815 Connecticut Avenue
Washington, D.C. 20006

DOCUMENT #24:
MEMORANDUM OF POINTS AND AUTHORITIES
IN OPPOSITION TO MOTION FOR SUMMARY JUDGMENT

DOCUMENT #25: COURT ORDER

Plaintiffs filed a responsive memorandum opposing defendant's Motion for Summary Judgment (Document #24). In it they agree with some of the facts stated by defendant but raise questions concerning others. Both sides apparently agree about the events leading up to Ralph Nader's being bumped from flight 864. Plaintiffs, however, take issue with defendant's legal position, including its reliance on the terms of the tariff it filed with the CAB (which purport to bar plaintiffs' suit) and to its argument relating to the lack of privity between CCAG and Allegheny. Other objections are factual in nature which, if permitted to be interposed, would defeat a Motion for Summary Judgment and would require findings of fact at a trial.

Plaintiffs argue the invalidity of the requirement in Allegheny's tariff that one with a claim must file a written notificaton with Allegheny within forty-five days of the incident.

The authority to file tariffs is restricted to issues relating to fares and service. Limitations of liability in these tariffs are not binding. Therefore, the filing was not valid as to the limitation, and since neither Nader nor CCAG *actually* knew about the forty-five day rule, it does not bar them from suit.

Plaintiffs go on to distinguish cases cited by defendant on baggage claims where the claimants did not declare the extra value of their belongings nor pay the higher fees necessary to have those belongings fully covered by insurance. In such cases, plaintiffs concede that the tariff limiting airline liability was proper because the tariff was directly related to fares (the extra cost of covering valuable belongings). The *Nader* case is different in that the tariff filed had nothing to do with fares and thus was not controlling here.

Next, plaintiffs argue that even if the tariff was valid, defendant waived its applicability in this case. Shortly after bumping Mr. Nader, defendant tendered him a check which included a statement that his signature on the check would operate as a release of all claims against Allegheny. The offer of payment indicated that it would remain open for sixty days, not the forty-five days stated in the tariff. In addition, plaintiffs argue that defendant had actual knowledge of the incident and, according to its own operations manual, should have received written notice of it from its employees. Therefore, defendant is estopped from raising the forty-five day rule in an attempt to bar plaintiffs' suit.

Plaintiff also responds to defendant's argument that CCAG is barred from suing due to its lack of privity with Allegheny. Contrary to defendant's reading of its claim, CCAG is not suing on a contract theory but on a theory of statutory discrimination, fraudulent misrepresentation, and prima facie tort. In none of these theories is privity required. All that is necessary is that defendant committed the wrongful act and that the injurious consequences were within the range of reasonable foreseeability. Since CCAG's injuries were clearly foreseeable here, its claim is enforceable.

Plaintiffs include a Table of Citations to authorities they rely on, an affidavit verifying some attached correspondence, a copy of defendant's settlement check, and excerpts from one of defendant's manuals which discusses staff procedures in bumping cases. It is also interesting to note that throughout their responsive memo, plaintiffs do not dispute the underlying facts but only the way Allegheny has characterized them. On this state of the facts, it is even conceivable that *plaintiffs* might have cross-moved for summary judgment on the liability issue while leaving the damages issue to be tried.

Defendant responded to plaintiffs' memo with a Supplementary Memorandum in support of their motion. Plaintiffs then filed a Response to Defendant's Supplementary Memorandum (not included here). Each new document seeks to add new facts or case law, and to characterize the other party's arguments as fallacious, dilatory, or inapplicable. After reading these documents, but without oral argument on the point, the Judge, without opinion, denied the motion for summary judgment (Document #25).

UNITED STATES DISTRICT COURT
FOR THE DISTRICT OF COLUMBIA

Ralph Nader and the Connecticut
Citizen Action Group,

Plaintiffs,

v

Civil Action No. 1346-72

Allegheny Airlines, Inc.,

Defendant.

MEMORANDUM OF POINTS AND AUTHORITIES IN OPPOSITION TO MOTION FOR SUMMARY JUDGMENT

STATEMENT OF THE FACTS

*　　*　　*

ARGUMENT

I. Defendant Cannot Rely on Its Purported 45-Day Notification Rule to Bar This Action

Defendant has moved for summary judgment on the ground that the plaintiffs herein failed to adhere to an Allegheny tariff provision which purports to require the filing of written notice of all claims (excepting personal injury and death) with the carrier within 45 days of the occurrence giving rise to the claim.

Assertion of this "45-day notification rule" as a bar to this action is frivolous and outrageous. Defendants have made no showing whatever that its 45-day notification requirement is legally authorized or required, or that any notice of its existence has been given to the public or to the plaintiffs herein. It lies in hiding as a trap for the unwary. Such rules have uniformly been held to be ineffective by numerous state and federal courts. The Civil Aeronautics Board has held similar provisions to be unreasonable and against public policy. Nevertheless, defendant Allegheny has had the temerity to raise it as a defense in this action.

A. Allegheny's "45-day Notification Rule" is Without Statutory Authority and is Therefore a Nullity.

Section 403 of the Federal Aviation Act of 1958, (49 U.S.C. 1373), requires all air carriers to file tariffs stating their fares, rates and charges. This statute is not permissive. It allows carriers to file related "rules" only "to the extent required or permitted by the regulations of the Board."

No regulation of the CAB requires or allows air carriers to file private statutes of limitation or "notification rules". To the contrary, the Board has consistently found that tariff rules which attempt to limit the carriers' common law liability are against public policy.

*　　*　　*

B. Allegheny Has Waived Its "45-day Rule" And Is Estopped To Assert It.

Even if Allegheny could establish the validity of its "rule," it would be of no value to it in this case. As shown by plaintiffs' supporting affidavit herein, on April 28, 1972 Allegheny tendered plaintiff Nader a draft in the amount of $32.41 for denied boarding compensation. The draft was good for sixty days and contained an endorsement which would have required plaintiff to waive all rights against the carrier as a condition of accepting the proffered payment. (Crockett Affidavit, Exhibit A)

This tender constituted an irrevocable offer of settlement for a period of sixty days. Had Mr. Nader signed the endorsement and presented the draft on or before June 27, 1972, he would have waived his rights and settled the claim. Instead, on June 19, 1972, a week before the expiration of the 60-day period, Mr. Nader returned the draft to Allegheny and offered to discuss other settlement terms on or before June 23, 1972, (Crockett Affidavit, Exhibit B) and further discussions were in fact held (Exhibit C).

Allegheny now for the first time claims that plaintiff had no rights after June 12, 1972 by virtue of its hitherto unannounced "45-day rule." This defense is a disingenuous attempt to renege upon a written settlement offer which it made to plaintiff Nader and upon which plaintiffs' counsel relied in conducting their negotiations with Allegheny.

By holding its settlement offer open for more than 45 days, Allegheny effectively waived its "45 day rule." As to the effective waiver of tariff provisions, see *Bernard* v. *U.S. Aircoach*, 117 F.Supp. 134 (S.D. Calif. 1953). In any event, after making a settlement offer which plaintiffs responded to within the period stated, Allegheny is clearly estopped to raise this spurious and unconscionable defense.

There are several other reasons why the defendant cannot successfully assert its purported limitation rule as a bar to this action. First, the carrier obviously had actual notice of the denial of boarding to Mr. Nader. Second, written notices and reports of the incident presumably were prepared and presented by defendant's own agents to an office of the carrier within the 45-day period. (See Affidavit of Don W. Crockett filed herewith, paragraph 5.)

*   *   *

II. Defendant Allegheny Airlines Is Liable to Plaintiff CCAG for Its Intentional Torts

Defendant also urges, as a subsidiary ground for summary judgment as to plaintiff Connecticut Citizen Action Group, that CCAG was an incidental beneficiary of the contract between Nader and Allegheny, with no right of recovery on its own. This contention is fallacious, since plaintiff CCAG does not rest its claim for relief in this action on the theory that it is a third party beneficiary as apparently assumed by defendant. To the contrary, the complaint is clearly predicated upon at least three other legally cognizable bases for relief: (1) The statutory cause of action for unreasonable discrimination. *Archibald* v. *Pan American World Airways*, 12 CCH Avi. 17,399 (9th Cir., No. 71-1535, decided May 12, 1972); *Wills* v. *Trans World Airlines, Inc.*, 200 F. Supp. 360 (S.D. Calif. 1961); *Fitzgerald* v. *Pan American World Airways*, 229 F. 2d 499 (2nd Cir. 1956); (2) the tort of fraudulent misrepresentation, *Isen* v. *Calvert Corp.*, 379 F.2d 126 (D.C. Cir. 1967); and (3) the "prima facie" or intentional tort, *Advance Music Corp.* v. *American Tobacco Co.*, 296 N.Y. 79, 70 N.E.2d 401 (1946).

As the facts alleged in the complaint show, plaintiff CCAG's damage was due directly to defendant's action of inducing Mr. Nader to believe and rely on the fact that he had a confirmed reservation and then refusing to allow him to travel to Hartford at the last minute. But for defendant's tortious conduct, Mr. Nader would have appeared on schedule and the damages would all have been avoided.

As stated in Prosser on Torts, 4th Ed. at page 244:

> Once it has been established that the defendant's conduct has in fact been one of the causes of the plaintiff's injury, there remains the question of whether the defendant should be legally responsible for what he caused.

One well established approach used in determining legal responsibilities of tortfeasors in negligence cases is expressed in the case of *Palsgraf* v. *Long Island R. Co.*, 248 N.Y. 339, 162 N.E. 99 (1928). Under the doctrine of the Palsgraf case, plaintiffs need only show that they were within the "scope of the risk" which the defendant took.

The instant case is not merely a negligence action but arises from an intentional tort. Nevertheless, even under the more stringent negligence rule, CCAG's damage was certainly within the scope of the risk of Allegheny's deliberate oversales program.

Allegheny is an experienced airline. It has dealt with millions of passengers and thousands of denied boarding instances. It must know that speakers of all kinds rely on the airlines to get them to their audiences—on time. It must know that the failure of a speaker to arrive on time will cause great inconvenience and disappointment to those who are left waiting. Accordingly, plaintiff CCAG is within the scope of the risk to which defendant Allegheny must be held responsible.

However, in this case Allegheny did not even have to make the slightest speculation. It was told, while it still had the opportunity to cease its tortious conduct, that CCAG would invariably be damaged unless the carrier performed its duty. Allegheny, at that time, willfully and wantonly refused to transport plaintiff Nader, thereby assuring and intending plaintiff CCAG's ultimate damage.

As stated by Justice Holmes in *Aikens* v. *Wisconsin*, 195 U.S. 194, 204 (1904):

> It has been considered that, prima facie, the intentional infliction of temporal damage is a cause of action, which, as a matter of substantive law, whatever may be the form of pleading, requires justification if the defendant is to escape.

Plaintiff CCAG has stated a legally sufficient cause of action and upon proof of its allegations is entitled to redress against Allegheny Airlines.

For the foregoing reasons defendant's motion for summary judgment must be denied.

Respectfully submitted,

Don W. Crockett
1700 Pennsylvania Avenue, N.W.
Suite 880
Washington, D.C. 20006
(202) 872 0331

Reuben B. Robertson, III
1156 19th Street, N.W.
Washington, D.C. 20036
(202) 833 3400
Attorneys for Plaintiffs

CERTIFICATE OF SERVICE

The foregoing Memorandum of Points and Authorities in opposition to Motion for Summary Judgment, and the accompanying Affidavit, attached exhibits and draft Order, together with the Memorandum of Points and Authorities in Opposition to Defendant's Motion to Delay Answering Interrogatories and accompanying draft Order have been served by mail upon Frank F. Robertson, Robert S. Bennett and William A. Bradford, Jr., Hogan & Hartson, 815 Connecticut Avenue, N.W., Washington, D.C. 20006, attorneys for defendant Allegheny Airlines, Inc., this 24th day of August, 1972.

Don W. Crockett

TABLE OF CITATIONS

*Cases chiefly relied upon are marked by asterisks.

UNITED STATES DISTRICT COURT
FOR THE DISTRICT OF COLUMBIA

Ralph Nader and the Connecticut
Citizen Action Group,

                           Plaintiffs,

    v   } Civil Action No. 1346-72

Allegheny Airlines, Inc.,

                      Defendant.

ORDER

Upon consideration of the motion of defendant Allegheny Airlines for summary judgment, the memoranda of points and authorities on file herein and the argument of counsel, it is by the Court this ___29___ day of ___September___ 1972

ORDERED, that the defendant's motion for summary judgment is denied.

UNITED STATES DISTRICT JUDGE

DOCUMENT #26: PLAINTIFFS' TRIAL BRIEF

DOCUMENT #27: DEFENDANT'S TRIAL BRIEF

After discovery has been completed and pretrial motions disposed of, the parties are ready for trial. In large or complex cases, a great deal of time has probably passed from the date the case was first assigned to a judge. During this time, many issues were raised, discussed and often argued before that judge who has a workload of many other cases. One may thus assume that the judge is not completely informed on the status and history of any particular case. Many lawyers therefore find it useful to submit a "Trial Brief." This document serves several purposes. Most obviously, it brings the judge up to date on the status of the case and highlights the issues in dispute between the parties. The Trial Brief also gives the attorneys a chance to argue various points they expect to arise in the course of the trial. Therefore, the Trial Brief is also an advocacy instrument.

In *Nader* v *Allegheny* both sides submitted Trial Briefs (Documents #26 and 27). Two things to note about these Briefs are that they are somewhat different in form and style and also that they are not really responsive to one another. Rather, each side sets out its position instead of directly attacking the position of the other side.

Plaintiffs' Brief begins with an Introductory Statement in which they continually repeat and reinforce their theory of the case that Allegheny, through its conscious but unpublished policy of overbooking, defrauded plaintiffs who were unaware of the overbooking on this flight. Nader complied fully with all check-in requirements but was nevertheless bumped from the flight. No adequate alternative transportation was available and therefore Nader missed the fund-raising rally at which he was scheduled to speak; the rally as thereby "effectively ruined."

Following the Introductory Statement, the Brief contains a section headed "Issues to be Tried." Here, plaintiffs attempt to narrow and focus the issues as they see them. Note how the first four issues relate to plaintiffs' specific causes of action:

1. illegal discrimination in violation of federal statutes and regulations;
2. fraudulent misrepresentation;
3. prima facie tort; and
4. breach of contract.

The remaining issues go to the amount and type of damages to which plaintiffs are entitled.

Plaintiffs then set out the facts they expect to prove and the witnesses and evidence they will introduce to establish those facts. Interestingly, several of their witnesses are (or were) Allegheny employees. A history of CCAG is provided, including its financial status and goals, and its activities in preparation for the rally such as the arrangements involved in getting Nader as a speaker. Other facts are laid out: the date and time of Nader's confirmed reservation, the fact that the reserved flight would get him to Hartford on time, and the fact that there were other flights before flight 864 which Nader could have taken. The latter fact goes to Nader's reliance argument. Had he known earlier of the overbooking, he might have taken another flight to get him to the rally on time.

The Brief then develops facts concerning Allegheny's policies, plaintiffs' reliance on them, Nader's actions, and Allegheny's knowing acts and omissions. Among the acts described is the alleged discriminatory boarding by Allegheny of persons whose reservations were confirmed after Nader's or whose reservation status was lower than his. Plaintiffs' injuries are then described including a history of public injury caused by Allegheny's policy of overbooking. Plaintiffs' argument is that the history of injury should have led Allegheny to change its policy, or at least to inform the public that it exists. The failure to do either in the face of large numbers of bumped passengers should permit the court to award punitive damages.

Other factual and legal arguments are made in the Trial Brief, although they are not the kind of full-blown arguments that might be found in an Appellate Brief. They are merely capsulizations of arguments with appropriate citations. It must be remembered that the Trial Brief is submitted *before* the trial begins and before evidence is taken. It is forward looking, suggesting what will be shown, rather than retrospective.

Plaintiffs also attach several appendices to their Brief which, among other things, attempt to make graphic what they argued in the Brief. For example, they attach an appendix that lists the date and time of Nader's confirmed reservation as well as the date and time of each reservation made after Nader's, for passengers who *were* boarded on the flight. Similarly, they list by month the number of confirmed Allegheny ticket holders who had been bumped from all Allegheny flights for the previous several years and those bumped between Hartford and the District of Columbia during an eighteen month period surrounding the incident involved in this case. Finally, plaintiffs attach a list of their witnesses and a list of their exhibits so that the defendant and the court can see the source of their evidence.

Defendant's Trial Brief is different in form but is intended to accomplish much the same purpose as plaintiffs'. Defendant's Brief begins with a statement of the "Issues" as it wishes the court to view them. Some of defendant's issues are merely the reverse of plaintiffs', but others are quite different. For example, defendant raises a procedural objection which, if sustained, will bar plaintiffs from prosecuting their claims. This is the same argument that defendant made (and which was unsuccessful) in its Motion for Summary Judgment. Allegheny can raise it again here because the standards for evaluating the argument are different at trial from what they are in a summary judgment situation.

Similarly, defendant in paragraph (3) raises the issue of whether the court is barred from addressing parts of this suit because jurisdiction rests first with the CAB, the administrative agency that regulates the airlines. In paragraph (4), defendant questions whether CCAG, which had no direct relationship with Allegheny, has any basis for a claim at all. Defendant then answers each of the questions raised in its "Issues" section, giving a short statement or argument supporting its positions.

Defendant lists the "Facts and Elements" it will prove to defeat plaintiffs' claims, and gives the sources for the evidence it will introduce. Defendant has numbered each fact (and its source) in such a way as to correspond to the numbered issues it listed in the previous sections. This, of course, allows the reader to relate the evidence and argument directly to the issue to which it applies. Defendant then provides a short legal argument (with citations) relating to each aspect of the defense. These arguments are also numbered to correspond with the prior sections of the brief.

PREPARING A TRIAL BRIEF

While there is no particular form for a trial brief, there are several things to keep in mind.

- Be organized, clear, and concise in the brief.
- Give an overview of the case to the judge.
- Characterize the facts as favorably to your side as is reasonable.
- To the extent your strategy does not require otherwise, place the facts in the context of your theory of the case.
- Remember that this is an advocacy document; build an argument.
- Remember, too, that it is not an appellate brief; keep it short.

UNITED STATES DISTRICT COURT
FOR THE DISTRICT OF COLUMBIA

Ralph Nader and the Connecticut
Citizen Action Group,

Plaintiffs,

v

Allegheny Airlines, Inc.,

Defendant.

Civil Action No. 1346-72

PLAINTIFFS' TRIAL BRIEF

Introductory Statement

On April 28, 1972 Ralph Nader arrived at Washington National Airport to take Allegheny's flight 864 to Hartford, Connecticut, where he was scheduled to appear at a "rate-payers rally" organized by the Connecticut Citizen Action Group. The purpose of this rally was to raise funds and public support in the Hartford Community for the group's consumer rights activities, and particularly its efforts to oppose pending electric utility rate increases. Mr. Nader's reservation on the flight had been made and confirmed by Allegheny several days in advance, and in reliance on that reservation elaborate plans had been made for the rally. These included arrangements for the Hartford community leaders, including the Mayor, to appear and introduce Mr. Nader, obtaining permission to use the privately-owned Constitution Plaza in downtown Hartford, organizing numerous volunteer workers, and extensive advance publicity.

Unknown to the plaintiffs, it was—and is—Allegheny's practice to intentionally sell more reservations for its flights than the number of seats actually available, and Allegheny had in fact oversold flight 864 on April 28. As a result, when Mr. Nader arrived at the departure gate, having purchased his ticket in advance and in full compliance with all check-in requirements, he was told that the plane was oversold and he would not be accommodated. At least two other persons were also denied boarding although they too held confirmed reservations for the flight.

Mr. Nader explained to Allegheny's gate agent that he was scheduled to appear and speak at the fund-raising rally for CCAG and it was very important that he get there by noon that day. In light of these facts, he requested the agent to double-check whether any stand-by passengers or others had been improperly boarded ahead of those holding confirmed reservations. When he was informed there were none, Mr. Nader requested the agent to explain the urgent situation to the passengers already boarded on the flight, in case anyone might volunteer to take a later flight so that the rally would not be ruined. This request was refused, and the plane departed without Mr. Nader or the other bumped passengers.

Flight 864 arrived in Hartford on schedule, at approximately 11:15 a.m. But for having been denied boarding, Mr. Nader would have arrived in ample time for his promised appearance, and the rally could have proceeded as planned. Instead, because of Allegheny's action he was unable to appear at all, and the rally was effectively ruined.

This litigation seeks to recover compensatory damages for the losses suffered by Mr. Nader and CCAG, as well as punitive damages based upon the willful and wanton nature of Allegheny's treatment of its passengers and others acting in reliance on its reservations.

Issues to be Tried

1. Did Allegheny discriminate against plaintiff Nader in dishonoring his confirmed reservation and denying him boarding on its flight 864 on April 28, 1972, by accommodating other persons on the flight who had no confirmed reservations or who had a lower boarding priority?

2. Did Allegheny knowingly misrepresent to plaintiffs that Mr. Nader had a confirmed reservation on flight 864 by failing to state the true nature of such reservation and the likelihood that some passengers would not be accommodated, and did the plaintiffs justifiably rely thereon to their detriment?

3. Did Allegheny commit a prima facie tort against plaintiffs by refusing to allow Mr. Nader to board the aircraft and, knowing of the likely harm its action would cause, refusing even to seek a possible volunteer on flight 864 who would be willing to take a later flight, thereby causing and assuring the failure of the rally in Hartford?

4. Did Allegheny breach its contract with plaintiff Nader?

5. What compensatory damages should be award to plaintiffs?

6. What punitive damages should be awarded, if any?

Facts to be Presented

1. The Connecticut Citizen Action Group was organized in April, 1971 with the assistance and advice of Ralph Nader. Its purpose was to serve throughout the state of Connecticut as a full-time citizen-supported public interest group to deal with consumer, environmental and human rights issues. Initial fund-raising efforts produced approximately $50,000 in 1971 and the group's substantive efforts commenced in August, 1971. During the ensuing period through March, 1972 the group built up a reputation as an active and responsible public interest spokesman on various consumer, environmental, safety, transportation and government issues.

> —Testimony of Anthony J. (Toby) Moffett, Jr., director of Connecticut
> —Citizen Action Group.
> —Plaintiffs Exhibits 20, 22.

2. During the spring of 1972, CCAG initiated its second major fund-raising program, setting a goal of $150,000 to be raised from public solicitations and canvassing. A key element in its campaign was the active support of Mr. Nader who is a native of Connecticut and widely known there, and he agreed to make a number of appearances in the state to urge public support for and participation in the group's activities, including a speech at the University of Connecticut in Storrs on the afternoon of Friday, April 28. During the preceding weeks, CCAG became actively involved in a controversy over proposed public utility rate increases, and a unique opportunity was presented for a major "rate-payers" rally at which the group could attract major interest and support for its efforts, both in the form of monetary contributions and word-of-mouth publicity, as well as obtaining volunteers for canvassing and other projects.

> —Moffett testimony

*　　　*　　　*

8. CCAG was informed that Mr. Nader had a reservation on flight 864 on Friday, April 28 sometime early in that week, and Toby Moffett was specifically advised by Allegheny, upon his telephone inquiry, that Mr. Nader in fact did hold a confirmed reservation for the flight. CCAG relied heavily upon these representations in making its plans for the rally. It was unaware and was never advised of the overbooking policy or the risks associated therewith.

> —Moffett testimony

*　　　*　　　*

10. The reliance of plaintiffs Nader and CCAG upon Allegheny's representation that Mr. Nader had a confirmed reservation was entirely justified, since Allegheny conducts corporate advertising and promotional programs in the communities it serves, including Washington and Hartford, to create a public image for the company of integrity and reliability and to make known its flight schedules and reservations service. Allegheny is well aware that prospective passengers as well as others in the communities it serves in fact do take actions and make plans for business and personal matters in reliance on confirmed reservations on its flights, and Allegheny in fact intends that such persons feel they can rely upon its reservations.

> —Testimony of Leslie O. Barnes.
>
> —Plaintiffs' Exhibit 14.

*　　　*　　　*

15. Allegheny knew in advance that flight 864 was overbooked, since its computer reservation system showed that substantially more passengers were holding confirmed reservations than the capacity of the plane (100), and since the flight had been intentionally overbooked under the "planned capacity" scheme. As of one hour prior to the flight's scheduled departure, 107 passengers were holding confirmed reservations, and this information was available to Allegheny's gate agents through the computer system.

—Plaintiffs' Exhibit 4.
—Testimony of Leslie O. Barnes.
—Testimony of John H. McDonald, Allegheny passenger service represen-
—tative on duty at gate for flight 864.

* * *

17. Instead of applying the procedures and criteria set forth in the company manual, Allegheny's agents in fact boarded passengers on flight 864 on a completely haphazard basis. One passenger was denied boarding only after he was first put on the aircraft and then removed by the agent. One of the passengers who was denied boarding presented himself at the boarding gate at least 45 minutes before the flight. Allegheny's agents did not use the available reservations lists or check-in tools to ascertain whether persons presenting themselves for boarding actually held valid confirmed reservations for the flight or otherwise ascertain their boarding priorities.

—Testimony of John H. McDonald, Allegheny passenger service representative.
—Testimony of Sheila Hartney, Allegheny gate agent.

* * *

Legal Points

1. The Statutory Cause of Action for Unjust Discrimination

An implied cause of action for unjust discrimination by an airline, arising under the Federal Aviation Act, 49 U.S.C. 1347(b), has been uniformly recognized in the federal courts since the Second Circuit's decision in *Fitzgerald* v. *Pan American World Airways*, 229 F.2d 499 (2nd Cir. 1956). This cause of action has been most frequently employed in denied boarding cases arising because of oversales. *Wills* v. *Trans World Airlines, Inc.*, 200 F. Supp. 360 (S.D. Cal. 1961); *Mortimer* v. *Delta Air Lines*, 302 F. Supp. 276 (N.D. Ill. 1969); *Archibald* v. *Pan American World Airways*, 460 F.2d 14 (9th Cir. 1972); *Kaplan* v. *Lufthansa German Airlines*, 12 CCH Avi. L. Rep. 17, 933, E.D. Penna., No. 68-2611, decided April 9, 1973.

In the *Wills* case, the plaintiff held a confirmed second class reservation but was denied boarding on an oversold flight in order to accommodate excess first class passengers whose reservations had been made later than his. The court held that plaintiff "was entitled to priority in flight accommodations over all other passengers who had made later reservations than he and yet were permitted to board the flight," and that the airline had violated that right. The court awarded compensatory and punitive damages, noting that "what is here condemned is any unwarranted interference with a passenger's right to accommodations aboard a particular flight, on the basis of a prior and reconfirmed reservation, which results in his exclusion from the space to which he is entitled." 200 F. Supp. 365.

* * *

2. Fraudulent Misrepresentation

The plaintiffs also submit that the facts of this case satisfy all of the elements of the action for deceit or fraudulent misrepresentation. The essential elements of a fraud case are (1) a false representation, (2) in reference to a material fact, (3) made with knowledge of its falsity, (4) and with intent to deceive, (5) with action taken in reliance upon the representation. *Sankin* v. *5410 Connecticut Ave. Corp.*, 281 F. Supp. 524 (D.D.C. 1968), affirmed *sub. nom.*, *Benn* v. *Sankin*, 410 F.2d 1060 (D.C. Cir. 1969), cert. denied, 396 U.S. 1041. The Court of Appeals has stated that, to recover damages for deceit, the misrepresentation must be of a material fact which is relied upon, the reliance must be reasonable, and damages must be shown. *Isen* v. *Calvert Corp.*, 379 F.2d 126 (D.C. Cir. 1967). See also 37 Am. Jur. 2d, Fraud and Deceit, §12, setting forth the elements of this cause of action.

Third persons such as those in the position of CCAG are entitled to recover for their injuries suffered as a result of the misrepresentation. It is noted in 37 Am. Jur. 2d, Fraud and Deceit, §298 that "the right to recover for fraud or deceit is not restricted to the parties to a transaction, but extends to third persons injured thereby, at least where such third persons are intended to rely and act upon false representations and they do so rely and act thereon, to their damage." See also, *Id.*, §§189 et seq., 244 et seq.; Prosser, Misrepresentations and Third Persons," 19 Vanderbilt L. Rev. 231.

3. The Intentional or Prima Facie Tort

*   *   *

4. Breach of Contract

*   *   *

Respectively submitted,

_____

Reuben B. Robertson, III
Attorney for Plaintiffs

August 30, 1973

UNITED STATES DISTRICT COURT
FOR THE DISTRICT OF COLUMBIA

Ralph Nader, et al.,
_____

Plaintiffs,

v

Allegheny Airlines, Inc.,
_____

Defendant.

}

Civil Action No. 1346-72

TRIAL BRIEF OF DEFENDANT
ALLEGHENY AIRLINES, INC.

I. *Issues*

(1) Whether plaintiff Nader and plaintiff Connecticut Citizen Action Group are barred from maintaining an action on a claim "arising out of . . .failure to transport any passenger" by reason of the Tariff Civil Aeronautics Board 142, Local and Joint Passenger Rules Tariff No. PR-6, Rule 40(B) requirement that

> ". . .notice of the claim is presented in writing to an office of the
> carrier. . .within 45 days after the alleged occurrence of the events
> giving rise to the claim. . . ."

(2) Whether failure to provide plaintiff Nader with a seat on Allegheny Airlines' Flight 864 results in liability as an "unreasonable preference" or "unjust discrimination" where the airline adhered to its established policy of boarding the first hundred confirmed passenger arrivals at its boarding gate. [49 U.S.C.A. §1374(b)].

(3) Whether an air carrier's practices of accepting a limited number of reservations in excess of flight capacity based upon statistical studies of the percentage of likely cancellations and no-shows and, in case of an oversell, of treating the last passenger to arrive at the gate as the oversale, must be accepted by the Court as reasonable unless and until declared otherwise by the Civil Aeronautics Board. If not, whether the practices are, in fact, unreasonable.

(4) Whether plaintiff Connecticut Citizen Action Group, having no contractual relationship with the defendant carrier, has any cause of action against it for failure to accommodate plaintiff Nader on Allegheny Flight 864.

(5) Whether either plaintiff sustained compensatory damage and, if so, the amount thereof.

(6) Whether the reservation and boarding practices adopted by the defendant carrier and applied to plaintiff Nader are wanton or malicious so as to warrant imposition of punitive damages.

II. *Each Element of Defense*

(1) The CAB Tariff Notice of Claim In Writing Requirement.

   That neither plaintiff attempted to comply with the 45 day notice in writing claim is undisputed.

(2) The Federal Aviation Act prohibition on "unreasonable" preference.

   It is not an "unreasonable" preference to give priority in boarding, in case of an oversale on a particular flight, to confirmed passengers who are on hand at the gate when the flight is loaded. [Federal Aviation Act of 1958, §404(b), 49 U.S.C.A. §1374(b)].

(3) C.A.B. primary jurisdiction over Air Carrier Practices.

49 U.S.C.A. §1482(g) provides with respect to complaints to and investigations by the Civil Aeronautics Board that:

> "whenever any air carrier shall file with the Board a tariff stating a new . . . rate, fare, or charge. . . or *any regulation affecting* such rate, fare, or charge, or the *value of the service thereunder*, the Board is empowered. . .to enter upon a hearing concerning *the lawfulness of such. . .regulation.*" (emphasis added).

Part 250.3 of the Civil Aeronautics Board Regulations requires that:

> "*every carrier shall establish priority rules* and criteria *for determining which passengers* holding confirmed reserved space *shall be denied boarding on an oversold flight. Every carrier shall file with the Board two copies of such rules and criteria, including that portion of its company manual instructing employees on the order of boarding priorities* in case of an oversold flight. Such rules and regulations shall not make, give or cause any undue or unreasonable preference or advantage to any particular person, or subject any particular person to any unjust discrimination or any undue or unreasonable prejudice or disadvantage in any respect whatsoever." (emphasis added)

Defendant Allegheny's Passenger Service Manual (6-100 Page 1, March 10, 1971), on file with the C.A.B. defines "OVERSALES":

> "an oversale is a passenger who holds a confirmed ticket for a flight, and who checks in for the flight (this means appearing at our local ticket lift point before scheduled departure time), but who cannot be accommodated on that flight because of insufficient seats or seats being blocked."

and, at Page 3, paragraph 5:

> "If the oversale is not known until the flight is being boarded, (this applies particularly where gate check-in is used) *the last passenger to arrive at the gate is the oversale and is not permitted to board.* Selection is automatic. Do not delay the flight seeking a passenger who would be least inconvenienced." (emphasis added).

Plaintiff Nader was the 103rd passenger to arrive at the ticket lift position for Flight 864, which could accommodate but 100 passengers. Defendant was not guilty of an "unjust discrimination" in applying to him its established and C.A.B. filed priority rule. The C.A.B., not the Court, would have primary jurisdiction to hear and deal with any claim that the carrier's rule was unreasonable. (This is likewise true of the 45 day written notice Tariff, dealt with *supra*).

(4) Connecticut Citizen Action Group states no claim entitling it to relief against Allegheny Airlines.

Defendant Allegheny Airlines knew of no speech arrangement between plaintiff Nader and plaintiff CCAG until *after* Nader had been denied boarding. Accordingly, defendant could not have committed an intentional tort with respect to an organization it had never even heard of, much less had any legally recognized relationship with. At most, CCAG was a mere "incidental beneficiary" of a contract of carriage between the airline and prospective passenger, Nader. As such, CCAG would not be entitled to any damages for breach of the contract of carriage. Moreover, the other defenses, including lack of the 45 day written notice tariff, asserted with respect to plaintiff Nader's claim are *a fortiori* applicable to plaintiff CCAG's claims.

(5) Plaintiff Nader sustained no substantial compensatory damage and plaintiff CCAG sustained no damages at all without resort to speculation.

*   *   *

(6) The case is not one where punitive damages could be imposed.

*   *   *

III. *Facts And Elements Which Will Be Proved To Defeat The Claims Of Plaintiffs.*

(1) The CAB Tariff Notice of Claim in Writing

Defendant will prove the tariff through a certified copy of 11th Revised page 16 to C.A.B. No. 142 issued by Airline Tariff Publishers, Inc. Agent, which page was in effect April 28, 1972.

Defendant will prove that the first notice of claim presented in writing to an office of Allegheny Airlines was a letter from plaintiffs' attorney, Don W. Crockett, Esquire, hand-delivered to the office of Mr. Edwin I. Colodny, Executive Vice President, June 19, 1972.

(2) (3) Defendant did not unlawfully discriminate against plaintiff Nader by reason of denying him boarding.

Through John McDonald, 8 South Ingram Street, Alexandria, Virginia, defendant will prove:

That McDonald was on duty as Passenger Service Representative at Allegheny's ticket lift position when Flight 864 was boarded on April 28, 1972; the flight was scheduled to depart at 10:15 a.m.; passengers were allowed to start boarding at 10:05 a.m.; by 10:10 a.m. the full flight capacity of 100 passengers were on board the aircraft, between 10:10 and 10:12 a.m., two additional passengers, a Mr. Koskinen and a Mr. Poulson, had arrived at the ticket lift position and were denied boarding. McDonald started to process the forms required to be filled out when a passenger is denied boarding. When he was about half through the second of the denied boarding reports, Mr. Nader arrived at the ticket lift position, the time then being about 10:15-1/2 a.m.

*   *   *

(4) Plaintiff Connecticut Citizen Action Group has no claim upon which relief can be granted against Defendant Allegheny Airlines.

CCAG had no contractual relationship with Allegheny Airlines. It was, at most, an incidental beneficiary of the contract between plaintiff Nader and Allegheny. Nader did not mention his speech to defendant when buying the ticket, but only after he had been denied boarding as the 103rd passenger showing up for the 100 passenger capacity flight.

Denial of boarding having already occurred when defendant first learned of the speech engagement, defendant could have had no malice toward CCAG and committed no intentional tort with respect to it.

(5) Neither plaintiff can prove compensatory damages.

*   *   *

(6) Punitive damages are not recoverable.

*   *   *

IV. *Trial Memorandum of Law.*

(1) The CAB Tariff requiring 45 day written notice of claim is valid and enforceable.

*   *   *

(2) (3) A carrier which applies priority rules that have not been declared unreasonable by the C.A.B. is not liable in an "unjust discrimination" claim under 49 U.S.C.A. §1374(b).

A passenger holding a confirmed reservation who is denied boarding makes out a *prima facie* case of discrimination, but this does not per se give rise to a §1374(b) action. As the court said in *Archibald* v. *Pan American World Airways, Inc.*, 460 F.2d 14, 16 (9th Cir. 1972):

> "Some overselling is an economic necessity for an airline in view of inevitable cancellations and no-shows. However, when a flight is thus oversold, the airline must fill the plane in a reasonable and just manner. *Stough* and *Wills* indicate that bumping which is outwardly discriminatory or preferential may be legitimized by proof that the airline adhered to its established policy and that the policy is reasonable."

*   *   *

(4) Plaintiff Connecticut Citizen Action Group has no legally cognizable claim against defendant.

*   *   *

V. *Conclusion*

Defendant Allegheny Airlines believes that the evidence will show that it did not receive written notice of plaintiffs claims within 45 days of the denied boarding incident. The evidence will show that the Civil Aeronautics Board has never declared Allegheny's tariffs, oversale practices and regulations to be unreasonable, that plaintiff Nader was treated as the priority rules required that he be treated, that he unreasonably failed to mitigate or wipe out his claimed compensatory damage and that the case is certainly not one for punitive damages when Allegheny has acted only as C.A.B. permits. The claim of plaintiff CCAG is unknown in the law. Even if it were not, plaintiff will be unable to prove any damage, at least for which it would have a claim against Allegheny Airlines, to which CCAG is a stranger.

Respectfully submitted,

HOGAN & HARTSON

BY: _____
Frank F. Roberson

William A. Bradford, Jr.
815 Connecticut Avenue, N.W.
Washington, D.C. 20006
298-5500
Attorneys for Defendant Allegheny Airlines, Inc.

DOCUMENT #28: TRIAL TRANSCRIPT

The testimony at the trial presented no surprises to either side. There was little real dispute about the facts. Instead, the dispute was about the meaning and effect of those facts. Each side produced testimony and other evidence supporting its positions. Much of it was admitted by stipulation, that is, an agreement in advance by both attorneys that certain evidence could be admitted and that neither would object. As to evidence actually taken, Ralph Nader testified about booking his ticket, his arrival for the flight, and the consequences of his being bumped. John McDonald, Allegheny's passenger service representative on the day of Nader's bumping, testified as to his version of what happened. Little substantive difference existed between McDonald's account and Nader's account of these facts.

There was extensive cross examination of Mr. McDonald concerning discrepancies between his testimony and information gained through discovery from company records, as well as discrepancies between his testimony on direct examination and his deposition. The goal was to discredit McDonald's testimony, but the exchange did not really effect the substance of the case. There was also cross examination as to Allegheny's procedures concerning boarding and oversales. Plaintiffs attempted to show that defendant's own procedures were not followed. Had they been, it is implied, Mr. Nader either would have been on the flight or would have had time to make satisfactory alternative arrangements.

Perhaps the most interesting aspect of the trial transcript is the interplay and informality between the attorneys and the judge. Since this was not a jury trial, the court gave the lawyers a great deal of leeway. Much of the evidentiary formality, for example, was dispensed with. We have included some of this interaction in order to give a flavor of the courtroom in a nonjury trial. Note in particular how the judge deals with objections and with the introduction of evidence. Note also how much of the evidence is not discussed at trial but is submitted for the judge to read on his own. This would not occur in a jury trial.

UNITED STATES DISTRICT COURT
FOR THE DISTRICT OF COLUMBIA

Ralph Nader, et al.,

Plaintiffs,

v

Allegheny Airlines, Inc.,

Defendant.

Civil Action No. 1346-72

Washington, D.C.
September 4, 1973

The above-entitled matter came on for trial before the Honorable CHARLES R. RICHEY, United States District Judge, at ten o'clock a.m.

APPEARANCES

FOR THE PLAINTIFFS:

REUBEN B. ROBERTSON, Esq.

FOR THE DEFENDANT:

FRANK ROBERSON, Esq., and
WILLIAM A. BRADFORD, JR., Esq.

— — —

TOM DOURIAN, OFFICIAL REPORTER
6808 U.S. Court House
Washington, D.C. 20001

TRANSCRIPT OF PROCEEDINGS

THE CLERK: Civil Action 1346-72, Ralph Nader and others versus Allegheny Airlines.

MR. ROBERTSON: Good morning, Your Honor. I am Reuben Robertson, counsel for Mr. Nader and the Connecticut Citizen Action Group, which is another plaintiff in this action. It is a non-profit corporation which is engaged in citizens' work and consumer activities in Connecticut.

What we have this morning, Your Honor, is a consumer fraud case.

THE COURT: Well, unless you insist on making an opening statement, I have reviewed the pleadings and the briefs that you have filed, and I do not believe we need opening statements.

We can go right into the trial, if that is all right with you.

MR. ROBERTSON: That is very fine with me.

THE COURT: I have no objection to your making opening statements on the part of either side, but I just want to tell you that I have examined the trial briefs of each side, the list of exhibits, and the pleadings.

So I think I am pretty familiar with what happened here.

I might inquire as to this:

Is there any disagreement with respect to the exhibits that you propose to offer in evidence?

MR. ROBERTSON: There is some disagreement with respect to a few of the exhibits that I intend to offer. There is no disagreement—

THE COURT: That you intend to offer?

MR. ROBERTSON: Yes, Your Honor. There is no disagreement with the defendant's exhibits.

THE COURT: All right. All defendant's exhibits may be admitted?

MR. ROBERTSON: So far as I am concerned, that is fine.

THE COURT: Well, I assume Mr. Roberson does not want to do that until you rest, is that correct, Mr. Roberson?

MR. ROBERSON: That is right, Your Honor.

THE COURT: All right.

Now, what ones does Mr. Roberson object to with respect to your proposed exhibits?

MR. ROBERSON: I filed with the court, Your Honor, a statement of those.

THE COURT: Oh, you did?

MR. ROBERSON: As well as my reason for each one, Your Honor.

THE COURT: Now, just a minute.

MR. ROBERSON: Incidentally, Your Honor, I would like a rule on witnesses before anybody testifies.

THE COURT: All right. I think that is in order, gentlemen.

THE CLERK: All persons who expect to testify in this case will please stand and follow the Marshal to the witness room until called.

MR. ROBERSON: Not Mr. Nader. He is the plaintiff.

THE COURT: You can sit at counsel table, Mr. Nader, if you wish. There is no reason you cannot.

MR. NADER: Thank you, Your Honor.

THE COURT: Just a minute, now.

All right. In other words, as I understand it, Mr. Roberson, on behalf of the defendant, would admit and offer no objection to 1, 3, 4, 5, 6, 7, 8, 9, 10, 11 and 12?

MR. ROBERSON: That is correct, sir.

THE COURT: All right. Let us go back to 2. You had better argue that, because I am not sure I understand it.

MR. ROBERSON: The objection, Your Honor, you want argued?

THE COURT: Yes, I think you had better, Mr. Roberson. I am not sure I understand your position. You say it is irrelevant.

MR. ROBERSON: I say it is irrelevant whether we tendered the amount. The draft that we tendered him is irrelevant because he did not accept it.

You are required under CAB tariffs filed with the CAB to tender in case of oversale in a scheduled amount that is fixed by the CAB.

We did that by mailing this draft to him. He did not accept it.

To the contrary, he sent it back through his counsel as an enclosure to the letter of June 19th, which I will introduce into evidence.

So I don't really see why we should encumber the record with a copy of the draft, which was never accepted.

THE COURT: Well, I will receive it for what it is worth. Now, let us go to 13.

I am inclined to think that Mr. Roberson's objection there makes sense, Mr. Robertson.

MR. ROBERTSON: Your Honor, the authenticity of these reports is not questioned.

THE COURT: I realize that, but that is not the test.

MR. ROBERTSON: No, of course not. These are relevant, Your Honor, to show two things:

First is the fact that Allegheny well knew, by virtue of its own records, that its flights were regularly overbooked. These statistics show, or the statistics that are drawn from these figures and reports show, that almost 16,000 people were bumped during the period shortly—in the three years prior to the incident that we are talking about here.

THE COURT: That may be so. How does that affect this case?

MR. ROBERTSON: Because one of the allegations that is denied by the defendant is that Allegheny was well aware that its flights were frequently overbooked and that people were frequently being denied boarding on these flights.

I mean what we have here is somewhere between 12 and 15 people a day that Allegheny is bumping off the flights for which they have confirmed reservations.

Secondly, it goes to the issue of punitive damages, and it is very clearly set forth in the Wills case, Your Honor, which is really the leading case in this field, that the statistical evidence of systematic overbooking is directly relevant to the issue of punitive damages.

THE COURT: All right. Let me hear from Mr. Roberson.

MR. ROBERSON: Your Honor, we are firmly satisfied that this is not the place to go into whether or not a certain amount of overbooking is an economic necessity for airlines or not.

We think that all that is material in this case is whether or not Mr. Nader was overbooked on this occasion, and, if he was, then was it improper for us to have overbooked as much as we did on the flight from Washington to Hartford.

Experience with overbooking, Your Honor, differs according to the particular flight involved, the time of day, the season of the year, and your history as to what happened on some flight from Washington to Memphis has not a thing to do with, or any proper relevancy to, this Washington to Hartford flight.

The evidence will show that, despite his talking about 10 or 20, or whatever he says is overbookings each day, on this particular flight, Flight 864 from Washington to Hartford, which leaves at 10:15 in the morning, it has only been overbooked twice in 16 months until this incident.

This was the third time in 16 months, and I think that is all that is relevant in this case, and we should not be going out and this court trying to decide whether or not on your overall system that is too much, or you are overbooked too much.

The issue in this case is whether or not we overbooked too much, or whether this is just one of the few occasions, on this particular flight where more no-shows—where fewer no-shows failed to keep their reservations than our statistical studies indicate was probable.

We think the history—

THE COURT: Well, let me ask you this:

Certainly, this does not go to any issue in the case. I say that by way of indicating that it is not an underlying or basic issue in the case. It may go to the issues of damages. But it certainly does not go to the issue in this case.

MR. ROBERSON: I can't even see how it would go to damages if the evidence is undisputed—and I do not see how they can dispute it—that on this particular flight, the one that is at issue in this case, it had only been overbooked twice in the previous 16 months.

So what difference does it make whether there is excessive overbooking or the computer is not working right on other flights?

The computer is evidently doing a very good job on this flight, and that is all we are involved in, in this lawsuit, Your Honor.

THE COURT: Do you have evidence to show that there had been no overbooking on this flight in the last 16 months?

MR. ROBERSON: I did not say "no". I said there had been two instances of it, only two instances on two dates since the first of January, 1970, through April 27, 1972. There had only been two instances.

THE COURT: All right.

MR. ROBERTSON: Well, Your Honor, I think that what will come out in the course of the testimony—

THE COURT: Let me say this, Mr. Roberson:

As you obviously know, the court is sitting without a jury, and I believe the court can give it the appropriate weight. It may have no bearing on any issue in this case, and I am not ruling, by letting it in, that it does at this point. I am going to receive it for what it is worth at this time.

MR. ROBERTSON: Thank you, Your Honor.

*   *   *

THE COURT: All right. Are you ready to proceed with your first witness?

MR. ROBERTSON: Yes.

Mr. Ralph Nader.

Whereupon,

RALPH NADER

was called as a witness, and, having been first duly sworn, was examined and testified as follows:

* * *

THE COURT: Now, gentlemen, I note the hour is 12:10. What can we accomplish before our luncheon recess? We are nearing our luncheon recess, but, of course, as I told you I believe on Friday, whenever it was that you were here last, I must finish this trial today.

I kept my staff here until 12:00 midnight taking testimony Friday night in order to accommodate you and your trial here today, and it is no easy task to ask a court reporter like Mr. Dourian, and one as strong as he is, to transcribe notes from 9:30 a.m. until 12:00 midnight, which he did, to say nothing of the Marshal and Miss Moore.

So I do want to finish at the end of the day.

MR. ROBERTSON: Your Honor, in an effort to accommodate the court—and I think you are absolutely right—as you know, we have two witnesses who are out of town and out of the country.

THE COURT: Right.

MR. ROBERTSON: In one case.

THE COURT: Was there a subpoena served?

MR. ROBERTSON: Well, I am not exactly certain, Your Honor. We did attempt to serve a subpoena on Mr. Barnes at his home. Mr. Barnes was out of the country, and the subpoena was left at his home in the care of a responsible person, together with the requisite witness fee.

We are informed that Mr. Barnes has been out of the country virtually—well, for several days or weeks, and we have not served him personally, although we have served him at home.

We have asked counsel to help make him available, and I gather he is not available.

THE COURT: Well, I think that is a matter we are going to have to argue today. That was one question I left up in the air, did I not?

MR. ROBERTSON: Well, I had understood that, if we subpoenaed him—

THE COURT: I do not know who Mr. Barnes is. Is he the president of Allegheny Airlines?

MR. ROBERTSON: Yes, he is.

THE COURT: And you had not issued your subpoena on Friday of last week?

MR. ROBERTSON: Well, it was Thursday that we were discussing it.

THE COURT: You had not issued it as of that time?

MR. ROBERTSON: We had understood that he had been out of town all of that week, as well.

THE COURT: Well, all right. But up to that time you had not issued it?

MR. ROBERTSON: That is right.

THE COURT: Knowing a week prior to that, that this trial was to take place today, correct?

MR. ROBERTSON: Yes, we did know it was to take place today. Of course, we had the pending question of rescheduling, because of Mr. Moffett's absence, which we were attempting to work out with the opposing counsel. So we had anticipated we would be able to work out the problems.

THE COURT: Well, there was one other witness that we dealt with and talked about.

MR. ROBERTSON: Now, that is Mr. Moffett, Your Honor, who today is delivering a keynote address in San Francisco.

THE COURT: And that is another plaintiffs' witness?

MR. ROBERTSON: Yes, and other than that—

THE COURT: I think I said I would excuse you from having to call him today.

MR. ROBERTSON: I understood your ruling to be—I hope I am correct—that because we are not sitting with a jury, and you were going to make the decision in the case, that we could bring Mr. Moffett on, and the other witness, if he were also unavailable, at a time to be scheduled by the court.

THE COURT: That may have been your impression, but it was the court's understanding that Mr. Moffett, having been previously notified and served and within your control and also out of the jurisdiction, I would allow that testimony to be taken later.

On the question of whether or not the president of Allegheny Airlines—and I assume that is the one you are talking about—would be treated in the same fashion, since he had not been served with a notice or subpoena prior to last Thursday, I reserved decision on that question, and I think the record will support that.

Is that not correct gentlemen?

MR. ROBERSON: Yes, sir, that is correct.

MR. ROBERTSON: As I recall Your Honor's ruling—

THE COURT: Well, you can argue that after lunch.

Now, what other evidence can we get in now that will be helpful to the court?

MR. ROBERTSON: Well, we have tried to limit the case that we are going to put on in front of Your Honor. Most of our case was documentary. We had to prove Mr. Nader's damages and the fact of the occurrence.

We are not going to put on any other direct case, Your Honor.

THE COURT: This is your direct case except for—

MR. ROBERTSON: Except for Mr. Barnes and Mr. Moffett and the documentary evidence.

THE COURT: I see. I see.

Mr. ROBERTSON: Yes, Your Honor.

THE COURT: Then you would rest except for those two gentlemen?

MR. ROBERTSON: That is right, so far as the direct case is concerned. We may have a rebuttal witness, Your Honor.

THE COURT: All right. Let me hear from Mr. Roberson.

MR. ROBERSON: Your Honor, if that is all his case, I think I am entitled to a judgment. First, let us take the Connecticut Citizen Action Group.

THE COURT: May I just ask you a question, Mr. Roberson?

MR. ROBERSON: Yes, sir.

THE COURT: How can you be entitled to a judgment at this stage of the case, when neither you nor I, nor the plaintiffs, know with precision what either of these gentlemen will say?

You know better than I do, because I assume you have deposed them.

MR. ROBERSON: I have deposed Mr. Moffett, and it is perfectly clear on the record that he is the director of the Connecticut Citizen Action Group, and I think as a matter of law—and it is clear on the record—that they did not buy any ticket from Allegheny Airlines.

I think as a matter of law if anybody has a right of action, it is Mr. Nader. It is not some other group that would like him to have been up there.

THE COURT: Well, Mr. Nader—

MR. ROBERSON: I think that in all the years of common carriers, ships, railroads, and airplanes, there is not one single instance where a third party has been able to recover from the carrier because of failure to transport a passenger.

If that were the law, certainly with the millions and millions of people that have been carried there would have been some recovery.

So I, therefore, say that Mr. Moffett's expectation and his testimony is immaterial in this case.

Since it is clear from the record that there was no ticket sold by Allegheny to the Connecticut Citizen Action Group—Mr. Nader bought his own ticket—that, therefore, I am entitled to a judgment with respect to Connecticut Citizen Action Group.

If Your Honor grants that, then I will go to Mr. Nader.

THE COURT: Well, I am not going to be precipitous. I want to hear all the evidence, and there was some discussion last Thursday about using Mr. Moffett's testimony that he gave on oral deposition, was there not?

MR. ROBERSON: He gave his deposition.

THE COURT: Can you not use that?

MR. ROBERTSON: No, Your Honor.

MR. ROBERSON: Counsel said that the reason he did not use it was because he did not go into Connecticut Citizen Action Group relying on the—

THE COURT: All right. Well, we do not have to go into that now.

MR. ROBERSON: But I think if you assume that that is true, I am still entitled to a judgment.

THE COURT: Why do you not work out whatever you wish and whatever you deem appropriate by way of a stipulation, if you can. If you cannot do so, you tell me after the luncheon break. And I, then, will rule with respect to Mr. Roberson's motion for a directed verdict at this stage of the case, if Mr. Moffett's testimony by way of oral deposition is admitted with the addendum of a couple of stipulations, or a stipulation.

MR. ROBERTSON: I do not think—

THE COURT: Do you think that might be possible, Mr. Robertson?

MR. ROBERTSON: I think it is very unlikely, Your Honor, since there are so many areas that were not inquired into on the deposition.

THE COURT: Well, Mr. Roberson may consent to a stipulation with respect to that, and you have not tried that, have you?

MR. ROBERTSON: I have tried to obtain stipulations, but I am certainly glad to try again, Your Honor.

THE COURT: Well, all right.

MR. ROBERTSON: And I would be glad to have some stipulations on that.

THE COURT: Whatever you intend to elicit from the stand, were he called to testify.

MR. ROBERTSON: Yes, Your Honor.

THE COURT: And then, Mr. Roberson, here is what I would suggest that you do, something along these lines:

Mr. Moffett, if called to testify on direct examination, would say the following in addition to that which is already of record in this case in his deposition which was taken on such and such a date.

MR. ROBERSON: Your Honor, we will see what we can do about that. I don't know how sweeping he will want Mr. Moffett's testimony to be, but my position is that it does not make any difference what he says.

THE COURT: Then you ought to be very generous in your willingness to stipulate.

MR. ROBERSON: I may be. I may be, sir. And I would also like to bring to Your Honor's attention that Mr. Nader's case, himself, I think that they have not made out a prima facie case.

THE COURT: Well, I will deal with that.

MR. ROBERSON: And I want the motion to go to both, in other words.

THE COURT: All right. Well, let us get the testimony elements straightened out first. We will resume at 1:45, and I hope that you gentlemen can work something out.

(Whereupon, at 12:15 o'clock p.m., the court adjourned, to reconvene at 1:45 o'clock p.m., of the same day.)

DOCUMENT #29:
PLAINTIFFS' PROPOSED FINDINGS OF FACT AND CONCLUSIONS OF LAW

DOCUMENT #30:
DEFENDANT'S PROPOSED FINDINGS OF FACT AND CONCLUSIONS OF LAW

In a trial without a jury, as in *Nader* v *Allegheny*, the judge makes the findings of fact. FRCP 52 requires that judges specify what facts they have found and what legal conclusions they have reached. In order to assist the judge in this task, parties are asked to submit Proposed Findings of Fact and Conclusions of Law for the judge to consider. In doing so, each party will highlight evidence that supports its version of the facts. Many of the proposed findings will overlap. Others will be contradictory, while still others will concern facts offered only by one side. Both sides agree, as plaintiffs state in their proposed finding 3, that Nader arrived at the gate, presented his ticket, and was denied boarding. Plaintiffs, however, also propose that the judge find that Nader complied with all "applicable requirements" for boarding. Defendant, on the other hand, does not accept that position, and suggests that Nader arrived too late for boarding and, in any event, was not entitled to board due to Allegheny's oversale regulations.

Plaintiffs propose several findings that support their theories of the case. Their proposed findings 10 and 11 state Allegheny's practice of inducing the public, through advertising and other means, to rely on its reservation system without disclosing its policy of overbooking. Proposals 12 and 13 conclude that plaintiffs had no knowledge of Allegheny's overbooking policy and relied on the confirmed reservation held by Nader. Proposal 16 points out that Allegheny, by offering to pay Nader for being bumped, was aware of the incident and his claim. Plaintiffs also propose to find that even if the forty-five day rule was not waived, it was complied with due to the notice of the incident Allegheny actually received from its own employees (proposal 17).

As might be expected, defendant's proposed findings highlight different facts and seek to sustain different theories of the case. For example, proposed finding 6 says that in advertising CCAG's rally, no mention was made of its intention to raise funds. This conclusion, if adopted, would significantly reduce Allegheny's exposure to a damage award. In proposal 12, defendant indicates that Nader was late, or at best, had left little margin for error in his arrival time at the gate. This focus on Nader's culpability would counter plaintiffs' contract, discrimination, and prima facie tort theories, and would also help to negate plaintiffs' claim for punitive damages.

Each side also proposed conclusions of law in terms of applicable statutory or common law. Defendant's conclusions follow directly from the arguments it has made throughout the case. Plaintiffs' conclusions address each theory they have developed and each relevant response by defendant.

PREPARING PROPOSED FINDINGS OF FACT AND CONCLUSIONS OF LAW

- Be sure to include facts to cover each element of each of your causes of action.
- Be sure there is support in the record for each fact proposed.
- Be sure to account for the proposals of your adversary.
- Use the facts to draw your conclusions.
- Draw conclusions as to each claim or cause of action you are asserting.
- Draw conclusions to negate the expected proposals of your adversary.

UNITED STATES DISTRICT COURT
FOR THE DISTRICT OF COLUMBIA

Ralph Nader, et al.,

Plaintiffs,

v

Allegheny Airlines, Inc.,

Defendant.

Civil Action No. 1346-72

PLAINTIFFS' PROPOSED FINDINGS OF FACT AND CONCLUSIONS OF LAW

In accordance with the Court's request that the parties submit preliminary proposed findings of fact and conclusions of law by Monday, September 10, recognizing that further evidence is to be introduced at that time and that the trial transcript will not be available until after that date, the plaintiffs hereby submit the following tentative proposed findings and conclusions:

Findings of Fact

1. The plaintiff Ralph Nader made a confirmed reservation for Allegheny Airlines flight 864 from Washington National Airport to Bradley Field, Hartford, Connecticut on April 28, 1972, and Allegheny advised the plaintiff Connecticut Citizen Action Group that Mr. Nader had such a reservation.

2. In advance of the flight Mr. Nader purchased a valid ticket through an authorized agent of Allegheny showing his confirmed reservation, which entitled him to passage on flight 864 from Washington to Hartford.

3. Upon arrival at the Allegheny departure gate and presentation of his ticket, in compliance with all applicable requirements, Mr. Nader was denied boarding on flight 864 because it had been oversold by Allegheny.

4. Allegheny permitted other persons to be boarded on the flight who had later reservations than Mr. Nader or no reservations at all.

5. Allegheny knew in advance that flight 864 had been overbooked, yet its agents did not follow the company's established procedures for the selection of passengers to be denied boarding in such cases.

*   *   *

7. Allegheny's practice is to systematically overbook its flights by accepting more confirmed reservations and selling more tickets for a flight than the number of seats actually available on the aircraft.

8. Allegheny is aware that its overbooking practice inevitably results in denials of boarding to some persons on flights for which they hold confirmed reservations, and that its dishonoring of reservations in such cases is likely to cause severe distress, disruption of personal and business plans made in reliance on the reservations, and financial losses for the victimized passengers as well as other persons.

*   *   *

10. Through advertising and other means Allegheny holds out and represents to the public that it offers reliable reservations which, if available and confirmed, will assure any prospective passenger of a seat on the flight designated.

11. Allegheny does not in its advertising, tariffs or by any other means make known to the public or to its prospective passengers its intentional practice of overbooking flights or the fact that this practice creates a substantial risk that confirmed reservations will be dishonored. Instead, the company and its agents attempt to conceal the practice from the public and even from persons who have been denied boarding as a result of the intentional overbooking.

12. Prior to April 28 neither plaintiff was in fact aware of Allegheny's intentional overbooking of its flights or of the fact that flight 864 in particular was intentionally overbooked.

*   *   *

Conclusions of Law

1. The Court has jurisdiction over the subject matter of this action pursuant to 28 U.S.C., sections 1332 and 1337.

2. In dishonoring his confirmed reservation for its oversold flight, while accommodating persons who had made later reservations or none at all, Allegheny *prima facie* subjected Mr. Nader to unjust discrimination or undue or unreasonable prejudice or disadvantage in contravention of the Federal Aviation Act of 1958, 49 U.S.C. section 1374(b).

* * *

4. Allegheny knowingly misrepresented to plaintiffs that Mr. Nader had a confirmed reservation which would assure him of a seat on flight 864 by failing to disclose the true nature of its reservations and the risk that he would not be accommodated because of its intentional overbooking of flights, and the plaintiffs justifiably relied upon Allegheny's representation to their detriment.

* * *

6. Allegheny's denial of boarding to Mr. Nader was a breach of its contract with him.

7. This action is not barred by any tariff rule concerning written notice of claims to the company within a certain period, since any such rule otherwise applicable to this action was waived by Allegheny or complied with. In any event, Allegheny cannot avoid liability for its intentional torts by an unreasonable exculpatory rule which is not set forth on the ticket, express notice of which is not otherwise given to passengers, and which has not been approved for filing by the Civil Aeronautics Board or other competent authority.

8. This action is not barred by the primary jurisdiction of the Civil Aeronautics Board, or any action or regulation thereof.

9. Plaintiffs are entitled to compensatory damages for the injuries suffered by them as a result of Allegheny's conduct in the amount of $10 for Mr. Nader and $100,000 for Connecticut Citizen Action Group, plus interest. Mr. Nader is also entitled to recover $35 for the unused portion of his ticket which Allegheny did not honor on its Washington to Hartford flight.

10. Because of the willful and wanton nature of Allegheny's misconduct, the plaintiffs are entitled to punitive damages of $50,000 to Mr. Nader and $100,000 to Connecticut Citizen Action Group, plus interest.

11. In addition the plaintiffs are entitled to recover the costs of this litigation, including reasonable attorneys fees as an additional measure of punitive damages.

Respectfully submitted,

Reuben B. Robertson, III
1156—19th Street, N.W.
Washington, DC 20036
202/833-3400

September 10, 1973   Attorney for Plaintiffs

UNITED STATES DISTRICT COURT
FOR THE DISTRICT OF COLUMBIA

Ralph Nader and the Connecticut
Citizen Action Group,

Plaintiffs,

v

Civil Action No. 1346-72

Allegheny Airlines, Inc.,

Defendant.

DEFENDANT ALLEGHENY AIRLINES, INC.'S FINAL PROPOSED FINDINGS OF FACT AND CONCLUSIONS OF LAW

This case came on to be heard before the court without a jury, and the Court, having considered the evidence introduced at the trial, the stipulations entered into by the parties and the arguments of counsel in the trial briefs, hereby makes the following findings of fact and conclusions of law.

Findings of Fact

*   *   *

5. At 3:20 p.m. Tuesday, April 25, 1972, Nader's representative made a confirmed reservation for Allegheny Flight 864, scheduled to depart Washington National Airport at 10:15 a.m., April 28, 1972 and to arrive at Hartford's Bradley International Airport at 11:15 a.m.

6. CCAG volunteers began on Wednesday, April 26th to distribute flyers for a 12:15 p.m., April 28, 1972, "rate payers" rally to protest proposed electric utility rates (Exhibit G) and on April 28, 1972, the "rate payers" rally at 12:15 today (Exhibit F). Neither flyer mentioned CCAG's undisclosed intention to try at the rally to raise funds for CCAG.

7. Mr. Nader's ticket was picked up from a travel agent in downtown Washington, D.C., on the morning of April 28, 1972. At 9:40 a.m., plaintiff Nader took a taxi in downtown Washington, arrived at the north entrance to the main terminal at about 10:05 [Tr. 53–54.] He ascertained at the Allegheny ticket counter on the main floor that Flight 864 was to leave from gate 17, which is located some 1037 feet from the ticket counter and on a lower level. [Tr. 55–56.]

8. Allegheny employees had started checking in Flight 864 confirmed reservation passengers at the gate 17 ticket lift position at about 9:30 a.m. [Tr. 172.] The flight began boarding at 10:05 a.m. [Tr. 172.] By 10:10 a.m. the aircraft's full flight capacity of 100 seats was filled with passengers holding "OK" status tickets, meaning they held confirmed reservations for the flight. [Tr. 173, 215.] Under Allegheny's practice, tickets bearing an "OK" are honored as establishing a confirmed reservation status and such status could also be otherwise established in the absence of an OK ticket such as by consulting the Passenger Name List. [Tr. 207, 215.]

9. Allegheny Airlines, Inc., makes and periodically reviews and revises statistical studies of its records of each of its flights to determine the number of passengers who actually showed up for a flight for which a confirmed reservation has been made. [Tr. 217–18, stipulated testimony of John S. Jenkins.] The company's policy is, based on the statistical information thus obtained from the history of the particular flight, to attempt to off-set the probable no-shows and late cancellations by booking a limited number of reservations in excess of the number of seats on the aircraft. [Tr. 217–18, stipulated testimony of John S. Jenkins.] Such reservations practices, the CAB has found, "on balance, worked reasonably well in the public interest." [Exhibit D, page 3.]

10. An "oversale" is a passenger who holds a confirmed ticket for a flight, and who checks in for the flight (appears at the ticket lift position *before* scheduled departure time), but who cannot be accommodated on that flight because of insufficient seats or seats being blocked. [Exhibit D, page 1.] If the oversale is not known until the flight is being boarded, (this applies particularly where gate check-in is used) the last passenger to arrive at the gate is the oversale and is not permitted to board. Selection is automatic and the flight is not to be delayed by seeking a passenger who would be least inconvenienced. [Exhibit C, page 3; Tr. 181–82.] Because of the desire for flexibility for each carrier to draft its individual "priority rules," the CAB deems them inappropriate as tariff material but requires that the carrier file copies of their priority rules with the Board. [Exhibit D, page 13; Tr. 117–18.] CAB requires that such rules and criteria shall not make, give or cause any undue or unreasonable preference or advantage to any particular person or subject any particular person to any unjust discrimination or any undue or unreasonable prejudice or disadvantage in any respect whatsoever. [Exhibit E, page 20.] As to the reasonableness of such priority rules the CAB has primary jurisdiction and a Court must accept them as such, although the Court may determine whether the carrier has in a particular case violated its own rules. [Tr. 118–19.]

*   *   *

12. For Flight 864 on April 28, 1972, however, three additional passengers appeared at the ticket lift position for check in after 100 passengers with OK status had already been boarded. The first two were a Mr. Koskinen, an aide to a United States Senator from Connecticut, and a Mr. Pulzun. [Tr. 173–74.] The Allegheny Passenger Service Representative, John McDonald, denied them boarding with the statement that the plane was already full [Tr. 174.] He then started to fill out the denied boarding reports which are required whenever such an incident occurs. When he was about one-half through the second of these reports he heard running footsteps in the corridor, looked up and saw Mr. Nader running toward him. [Tr. 175.] It was then about 10:15 a.m., which was the scheduled departure time although the plane had not yet left. [Tr. 175.] Final weight and tear sheets had already been taken out to the plane. [Tr. 177.] Nader was told by McDonald that he was sorry but the plane was full. [Tr. 19, 177.] McDonald had already checked the ticket coupons and knew that 100 confirmed reservation passengers were aboard. [Tr. 176, 215.]

*   *   *

19. The CCAG rate payers rally went forward. Mr. Moffett, its head, spoke for five minutes and announced that Mr. Nader had not been able to take his intended flight, the Mayor spoke 10 or 15 minutes and City Councilman Carbone spoke for 10. About 1000 people were present when Moffett first spoke. About one-third left when he announced Nader wasn't going to be able to appear and about 200 to 300 people were still present after the politicians spoke. [Moffett dep. 30.] Because of Mr. Nader's non-appearance CCAG decided not to seek to raise funds from those entering and leaving the rally. [Moffett dep. 31.]

20. Even had Mr. Nader appeared and spoken, it is impossible to determine, without speculation, the amount of funds CCAG would have been able to raise. Carrying out its intention of selling buttons and bumper stickers at the public entrances to Constitution Plaza would have been unlawful on April 28, 1972. An ordinance contained in Hartford Code, Article II, Sec. 25–25, provides in pertinent part that:

> "No person. . . .shall set or offer for sale any goods, wares or merchandise other than newspapers, upon any sidewalk of the city within the area bounded as follows except on days observed as holidays. . . ."

* * *

Conclusions of Law

1. Because of the 52 day delay in giving notice of claim *in writing* to the carrier within 45 days of April 28, 1972, no action can be maintained arising out of or in connection with failure to transport any passenger.

> [*Herman v. Northwest Airlines*, 222 F.2d 326 (2d Cir. 1955) (Time limitations in tariffs for legal actions, other than personal injury or death actions, are binding and enforceable). A tariff provision binding on the passenger is likewise binding on CCAG as someone claiming through the passenger. *Tishman & Lish, Inc. v. Delta Air Lines*, 413 F.2d 1401 (2d Cir. 1969). A tariff requirement of "written notice" of claim is not met by proof of oral notice. *Scheinman v. Eastern Airlines*, 138 N.Y. Supp.2d 992 (Civ. Ct. N.Y. County, 1971).]

2. The Civil Aeronautics Board, charged by Congress with the duty of regulating the airlines in the public interest, has not prohibited the practice of the airlines to overbook reservations to a limited extent in an effort to ameliorate the industry-wide problem of no-shows and cancellations but has made a conscious policy choice to require the carriers to offer oversold passengers deferred boarding compensation in an amount specified by the CAB and to file with the CAB copies of their priority rules for selecting which passengers on an oversold flight will be boarded.

> [CAB Economics Regulations, Enactment of Part 250, adopted August 3, 1967; Exhibit E.]

3. While a passenger holding a confirmed reservation who is denied boarding makes out a *prima facie* case of discrimination, this does not *per se* give rise to an "unjust" discrimination claim under 49 U.S.C.A. §1347(b). Bumping, outwardly discriminatory or preferential, may be legitimized by proof that the airline adhered to its established policy and that the policy is reasonable.

> [*Archibald v. Pan American World Airways, Inc.*, 460 F.2d 14, 16 (9th Cir. 1972).]

4. The doctrine of primary jurisdiction requires that inquiry into reasonableness of CAB permitted tariffs and priority rules required by CAB be addressed to that expert body and not as an original matter be brought to the Court.

> [*Alco-Gravure v. American Airlines*, 173 F. Supp. 752, 755 (D. Md. 1959); see *Ambassador, Inc. v. United States*, 325 U.S. 317, 324 (1945).]

* * *

9. Plaintiff CCAG has not established, without resort to speculation, its compensatory damages, if it were entitled to any damages.

10. The evidence has not established any right to punitive damages with respect to either plaintiff.

11. Defendant Allegheny Airlines, Inc., should have judgment in its favor plus costs.

Respectfully submitted,

HOGAN & HARTSON

By _____
Frank F. Roberson

_____
William A. Bradford, Jr.
815 Connecticut Avenue, N.W.
Washington, D.C. 20006
298-5500
Attorneys for Defendant

DOCUMENT #31:
FINDINGS OF FACT AND CONCLUSIONS OF LAW

DOCUMENT #32: COURT ORDER

After the trial, plaintiffs submitted a Post-Trial Brief. While such a Brief is not required by the rules, many lawyers find it useful in nonjury cases (in lieu of a closing statement to the jury) to restate their position for the judge while citing particular items of supporting evidence.

The Court eventually made its Findings of Fact and Conclusions of Law (Document #31), and entered an Order (Document #32) giving judgment to plaintiffs. In all nonjury cases, FRCP 52 requires the judge to "find the facts specifically and state separately its conclusions of law thereon," and then to enter judgment.

The judge, after reviewing the record, substantially accepted plaintiffs' version of the facts. In finding 6 the judge finds that CCAG relied on Nader's confirmed reservation in its continuing efforts to organize and promote its rally. In finding 7 the judge describes what happened when Nader arrived at the airport and at the boarding gate. Interestingly, he makes no finding as to the time Nader arrived at the gate, an issue defendant raised in its attempt to cast at least some blame on Nader. The judge also found that:

—Allegheny's conduct caused Nader $10 actual damage (finding 9);

—Upon learning that Nader would not be able to attend, the crowd at CCAG's rally dwindled from 1000 persons to 200. This caused CCAG to lose contributions it expected to raise at the rally and to suffer "extreme and very real embarrassment, loss of professional esteem and prestige" and to incur $50 actual expense (10);

—Allegheny had a practice of systematic overbooking which was substantial (11,12);

—Allegheny was aware that many of its confirmed passengers were bumped and that this caused "distress and financial loss" to those who relied on confirmed reservations (13);

—Allegheny held itself out, through advertising and other means as having reliable reservations policies and never disclosed to the public (in fact the court finds it concealed from the public) its policy of overbooking (14,15);

—Neither of the plaintiffs, prior to Nader's being bumped, was aware of Allegheny's overbooking policy (16); and

—Allegheny, by tendering Nader an offer of settlement to which he might respond within sixty days, together with its employees submitting to it reports about Nader's bumping, either waived the forty-five day notice rule, or the rule was complied with (19,20).

The judge also reached conclusions of law. He ruled that Nader had made out a *prima facie* case of discrimination under the Federal Aviation Act and that defendant had not sustained its burden under that statute to show that the discrimination was reasonable (conclusion 2). Similarly, the Court found that Allegheny had knowingly misrepresented a material fact—that Nader's confirmed reservation guaranteed him a seat on the plane—and that Nader relied on this representation (3). These findings make out a case of common law fraud. CCAG was also entitled to recover under the fraud theory. The Court accepted plaintiffs' position that CCAG's cause of action sounded in tort, not contract. This eliminated the need for privity which Allegheny had argued was required (4). The Court concluded, however, that CCAG had not proved the loss of contributions or injury to its reputation and prestige with sufficient certainty to support an award of compensatory damages with regard to these items; these damages were too speculative (6). The Court also concluded that punitive damages were available to both plaintiffs and that Allegheny's forty-day notice rule was not a bar to the suit. The Court then entered an order giving judgment against Allegheny. Nader received $10 compensatory damages and $25,000 punitive damages, and CCAG received $51 compensatory damages and $25,000 punitive damages.

UNITED STATES DISTRICT COURT
FOR THE DISTRICT OF COLUMBIA

Ralph Nader and the Connecticut
Citizen Action Group,

Plaintiffs,

v

Allegheny Airlines, Inc.,

Defendant.

Civil Action No. 1346-72

APPEARANCES: REUBEN B. ROBERTSON, III, ESQ.
Attorney for the Plaintiffs

FRANK F. ROBERSON, ESQ.
Attorney for the Defendant

FINDINGS OF FACT AND CONCLUSIONS OF LAW

This case came on to be heard before the Court, sitting without a jury, and the Court, having considered the evidence introduced at the trial, the stipulations entered into by the parties, and upon consideration thereof including the arguments of counsel as well as the trial briefs, hereby makes the following Finds of Fact and Conclusions of Law.

Findings of Fact

1. Plaintiff Ralph Nader is a citizen of the United States and resides in the District of Columbia.

2. Plaintiff Connecticut Citizens Action Group (hereinafter CCAG), is a non-profit corporation, organized and existing under the laws of the District of Columbia and has its principal place of business in Hartford, Connecticut. It is a public interest advocate for environmental and consumer issues arising in the State of Connecticut.

3. Defendant, Allegheny Airlines, Inc., is a corporation having a principal place of business at the Washington National Airport near Alexandria, Virginia. It is an air carrier and holds a certificate of public convenience and necessity issued by the Civil Aeronautics Board and is regulated by the laws of the United States relating to such carriers and by the rules, regulations and orders promulgated by the CAB in accordance with the Federal Aviation Act of 1958.

*   *   *

21. The Defendant Allegheny airlines is a common carrier which is licensed or authorized to do business by the Civil Aeronautics Board, as hereinbefore stated, and is the holder of a certificate of public convenience and necessity. As such it has a public duty and an especially large and high fiduciary obligation to make its policies known to all of its customers with regard to its intentional over-booking. The fact that it conceals such practices in its advertising and otherwise, and, by virtue of its failure and refusal to take reasonable steps to avoid harm to the Plaintiffs herein is tantamount to willful and wanton misconduct which gives rise to and provides a proper basis for each of the Plaintiffs' claims for damages.

Conclusions of Law

1. This Court has jurisdiction over the subject matter (28 U.S.C. 1331, 1332, 1337), *Fitzgerald* v. *Pan American World Airways*, 229 F.2d 499, 502 (2nd Cir., 1956); moreover, the amount in controversy, exclusive of interest and costs, exceeds $10,000.00. The Court also has pendant jurisdiction over any non-federal claims, *United Mine Workers* v. *Gibbs*, 383 U.S. 715 (1966).

2. The Plaintiff, Mr. Nader, is entitled to both compensatory and punitive damages under the antidiscrimination provisions of the Federal Aviation Act of 1958, Section 404(b), 49 U.S.C. §1374(b). Mr. Nader has established a *prima facie* case of unreasonable discrimination. . . .

*   *   *

Conclusion

By virtue of the foregoing, an order will be entered of even date herewith awarding the Plaintiff Nader $10.00 in compensatory damages and $25,000 as punitive damages of and from the Defendant. The Plaintiff CCAG is awarded $51.00 in nominal damages and $25,000 in punitive damages, of and from the Defendant.

CHARLES R. RICHEY
UNITED STATES DISTRICT JUDGE

DATED: October 18th, 1973

UNITED STATES DISTRICT COURT
FOR THE DISTRICT OF COLUMBIA

Ralph Nader and the Connecticut
Citizen Action Group,

Plaintiffs,

v

Allegheny Airlines, Inc.,

Defendant.

} Civil Action No. 1346-72

ORDER

This cause came on for trial before the Court sitting without a jury on September 4, 1973, and the Court having heard the testimony and having examined the proofs offered by the respective parties, and having filed herein of even date its Findings of Fact and Conclusions of Law, and having directed that judgment be entered in accordance therewith,

Now, therefore, by reason of said law and findings, it is this 18th day of October, 1973,

ORDERED that Judgment be entered against the Defendant and that the Defendant pay to Plaintiff Nader $10 in compensatory damages and $25,000 in punitive damages, and pay to Plaintiff Connecticut Citizens Action Group $51 in nominal damages and $25,000 in punitive damages; and it is

FURTHER ORDERED, that the Plaintiffs shall have judgment against the Defendant for their costs.

CHARLES R. RICHEY
UNITED STATES DISTRICT JUDGE

DOCUMENT #33: NOTICE OF APPEAL

Allegheny, pursuant to Federal Rules of Appellate Procedure (FRAP) 3, filed a *Notice of Appeal* (Document #33) with the clerk of the District Court. As per the rule, Allegheny's notice specifies that the defendant is appealing to the Court of Appeals for the District of Columbia from the judgment of the District Court in favor of Nader and CCAG and against Allegheny. FRAP 4 requires the filing of a Notice of Appeal within thirty days of the entry of the judgment or order appealed from. The filing of the notice is, however, only the first step in any appeal. An appeal must be "perfected" by the appellant (the party appealing) compiling and transmitting the record to the appellate court. Then there is the filing of the appellate briefs, and finally, the oral argument.

UNITED STATES DISTRICT COURT
FOR THE DISTRICT OF COLUMBIA

Ralph Nader, et al.,

Plaintiffs,

v

Allegheny Airlines, Inc.,

Defendant.

Civil Action No. 1346-72

NOTICE OF APPEAL

Notice is hereby given this 16th day of November, 1973, that defendant Allegheny Airlines, Inc. hereby appeals to the United States Court of Appeals for the District of Columbia from the judgment of this Court entered on the 18th day of October, 1973 in favor of plaintiffs Ralph Nader and Connecticut Citizen Action Group against said defendant Allegheny Airlines, Inc.

Hogan & Hartson

By: Frank F. Roberson
Attorney for defendant Allegheny Airlines, Inc.
815 Connecticut Avenue, N.W.
Washington, D.C. 20006
298-5500

Please mail copy to:
Reuben B. Robertson, III, Esq.
1156—19th Street, N.W.
Washington, D.C. 20036,
Attorney for plaintiffs
Ralph Nader and Connecticut
Citizen Action Group

Don Crockett
1700 Pennsylvania Ave., N.W.,
Washington, D.C. 20006

DOCUMENT #34: APPELLATE BRIEF OF APPELLANT

At the beginning of Allegheny's *appellate brief*, there is a Table of Contents and a Table of Authorities. The asterisks in the Table of Authorities indicate the items chiefly relied on in the brief.

In its Statement of Issues presented for review, Allegheny raises four questions:

—whether plaintiffs proved their discrimination claim;

—whether plaintiffs proved their fraud claim;

—whether the doctrine of primary jurisdiction bars the court from awarding punitive damages; and

—whether the action is barred by plaintiffs' failure to comply with Allegheney's 45 day notice rule.

In its Statement of the Facts (not included here) within the Statement of the Case, Allegheny begins to argue its points. The facts included in this statement were carefully selected and organized to paint the most favorable picture of Allegheny's position. The Court is made aware of the "industry-wide" problem of "no-shows," that is, passengers with confirmed reservations who do not show up for boarding (causing fully booked planes to depart with empty seats), as well as the industry's solution to the problem, overbooking. Allegheny admits that this practice occasionally results in a confirmed passenger being denied boarding, but this is kept to a very small percentage of ticket holders due to its careful statistical monitoring of the problem. In fact, it had occurred only twice on flight 864 in the eighteen months prior to Nader's being bumped. Allegheny goes on to point out that the CAB, in addressing this very problem, did not ban the overbooking practice but, rather, provided for financial compensation for any passenger bumped from a flight. In addition, the CAB allowed each airline to establish procedures to determine who shall have priority in boarding. Its only requirement was that there be no discrimination in applying these procedures.

The Statement of the Facts is argumentative in nature. The selection of the facts to highlight and their presentation are forms of advocacy that should not be ignored. They create a context for the judge(s) and start a chain of thinking about the case that the party presenting the facts hopes will carry over into its discussion of the law.

In the Argument section of its brief, Allegheny repeats positions it took in its Trial Brief (Document #27). In referring to plaintiffs' discrimination claim, Allegheny, using prior case law for support, identifies the elements needed to make out a cause of action:

1. The plaintiff must have a ticket entitling him or her to board the plane;

2. The plaintiff must appear on time and be denied boarding; and

3. The denial must be discriminatory, that is, contrary to the reasonable priority rules of the carrier.

Allegheny then argues that neither plaintiff nor CCAG has met all of these tests. CCAG was never a ticket holder nor was it denied boarding. As to Nader, Allegheny argues that it did not violate its prior rules which must be accepted by the court as *prima facie* reasonable. Moreover, even if the rules were violated, the violation did not cause Nader's bumping. Plaintiffs argued that two passengers with lower boarding priority than Nader were boarded. The record, however, shows that there were two bumped passengers with similar ticketing as Nader who arrived prior to Nader and, thus, would have been entitled to those seats. Therefore, even if there was discrimination against Nader, it was not the cause of his being denied boarding.

With reference to plaintiffs' fraudulent misrepresentation claim, Allegheny again lays out the elements of the cause of action and attempts to show how plaintiffs have failed to prove them. In particular, Allegheny argues that there was no evidence that it ever represented to the public or to plaintiffs that holding a ticket was a guarantee that the ticket-holder would have a seat on the flight. Even if there was such evidence, plaintiffs would have to prove that they believed such statements and the record shows that Nader was bumped from a flight on another airline only days before the flight in question and from still another flight within six months before that. Therefore, he must have known that holding a ticket does not guarantee passage on a particular flight.

Allegheny then goes on to address the issue of primary jurisdiction. It is important to realize that Allegheny is not attempting to remove from the court the power to award Nader compensation for his injuries. Rather, Allegheny wants to prevent the Court, through its power to award punitive damages, from making airline industry policy. Questions about such policy should be presented, in the first instance, to the CAB. Questions about the reasonableness of Allegheny's boarding priority rules, and of its nondisclosure, through advertising, of its overbooking policy are matters of industry-wide concern and should be addressed by the Civil Aeronautics Board. Allegheny also argues that the entire action is barred due to plaintiffs' noncompliance with Allegheny's forty-five day notice rule.

Note the development of the Argument. Allegheny's attorneys first establish the elements of the claim they are contesting. After listing each element, they give evidentiary support in the record for why the element was not proved, or why it is not actionable if it was proved. Allegheny creates a logical sequence in its Argument, and makes very efficient use of the cases and other authorities cited.

PREPARING AN APPELLLANT'S BRIEF

- Clearly state the issues raised.
- Select facts and organize their presentation with an eye to the arguments you will make.
- Provide legal support in each argument.
- Be effective but efficient in your use of authorities.
- Give due consideration to the implications of policy and social justice.
- Break down legal issues into understandable elements.
- Develop your arguments logically and concisely.

BRIEF FOR APPELLANT

IN THE

United States Court of Appeals

FOR THE DISTRICT OF COLUMBIA CIRCUIT

No. 73-2243

RALPH NADER, ET AL., *Appellees*

v.

ALLEGHENY AIRLINES, INC., Appellant

**Appeal from the United States District Court for the
District of Columbia**

FRANK F. ROBERSON
WILLIAM A. BRADFORD, JR.
815 Connecticut Avenue
Washington, D.C. 20006
298-5500
Attorneys for Appellant

Of Counsel:

HOGAN & HARTSON
815 Connecticut Avenue
Washington, D.C. 20006

PRESS OF BYRON S. ADAMS PRINTING, INC., WASHINGTON, D. C.

TABLE OF CONTENTS

TABLE OF AUTHORITIES

*Cases and authorities chiefly relied upon are marked by asterisks.

I. STATEMENT OF ISSUES PRESENTED FOR REVIEW

1. Whether Nader and CCAG Proved Claims Against Allegheny Under the Antidiscrimination Provisions of the Federal Aviation Act?

2. Whether Nader and CCAG Proved Claims Against Allegheny for Fraudulent Misrepresentation?

3. Whether the Doctrine of Primary Jurisdiction Bars the Awarding of Punitive Damages, the Findings that Allegheny's Overbooking Policy and Lack of Publicity with Respect Thereto Were Unreasonable, and the Finding of Liability for Fraudulent Misrepresentation?

4. Whether this Action is Barred for Failure of Nader and CCAG to Comply with the Written Notice of Claim Provisions of Allegheny's Tariff?

This case has not previously been before this Court under the same or similar title.

II. REFERENCES TO PARTIES AND RULINGS

The order and opinion below presenting the issues for review are the Order and Findings of Fact and Conclusions of Law of United States District Judge Richey dated October 18, 1973 in Civil Action No. 1346-72 (App. 147; 137–146).

III. STATEMENT OF THE CASE

A. Nature of the Case

*   *   *

B. Course of Proceedings and Disposition by the Court Below

*   *   *

C. Statement of the Facts

*   *   *

IV. ARGUMENT

A. Nader and CCAG Did Not Prove a Claim Under the Antidiscrimination Provisions of the Federal Aviation Act

Federal and state courts, since the case of *Wills* v. *Trans World Airlines, Inc.*, 200 F. Supp. 360 (S.D. Calif. 1961), have recognized that a civil action for damages will be available *under certain circumstances* to oversold passengers. The *Wills* court constructed the action for damages from Section 404(b) of the Federal Aviation Act of 1958, 49 U.S.C. § 1374(b) (1970), upon which Nader and CCAG also rely:

> No air carrier . . . shall make, give, or cause any undue or unreasonable preference or advantage to any particular person . . . in air transportation in any respect whatsoever or subject any particular person . . . to any unjust discrimination or any undue or unreasonable prejudice or disadvantage in any respect whatsoever. [49 U.S.C. § 1374(b) (1970).]

The plaintiff-passenger in *Wills* had been denied boarding on an overbooked flight by the defendant airline, while at least seven other passengers who had made reservations after Wills were allowed to fly, such *preference* to the seven passengers *being in contravention of that defendant airline's own priority rules*. The court found as follows:

> In a word, defendant took plaintiff's tourist seat and arbitrarily and capriciously gave it to a first-class passenger who, even under the airline's established procedure in event of oversales, was not entitled to it. [*Wills* v. *Trans World Airlines, Inc.*, supra at 365.]

The court awarded Mr. Wills $1.54 compensatory damages and $5,000 punitive damages after finding that the airline acted "wantonly" under the circumstances. *Id.* at 368.

Thus, the elements for an action for denied boarding as set forth in *Wills* were:

1. The plaintiff must have a ticket entitling him to passage on the flight in question.

2. The plaintiff must make a timely appearance for the flight and be denied boarding.

3. The denied boarding of the plaintiff must be discriminatory, that is, it must be contrary to the reasonable priority rules of the air carrier. [*E.g. Mortimer* v. *Delta Air Lines,* 302 F. Supp. 276 (N.D. Ill. 1969); *Stough* v. *North Central Airlines, Inc.,* 55 Ill. App. 2d 338, 204 N.E.2d 792 (App. Ct. Ill. 1965).]

* * *

Neither CCAG nor Nader established the elements necessary for denied boarding damages, and the district court's award of damages to them is a reversible error. The judgment against Allegheny on behalf of CCAG does not appear to be grounded on a violation of 49 U.S.C. § 1374(b) but rather on fraudulent misrepresentation. *See* App. 144. To the extent, however, that Allegheny's liability in damages to CCAG is based on the antidiscrimination provisions of the Federal Aviation Act such a finding of liability is error. The first element of the antidiscrimination cause of action—that the plaintiff hold a ticket for carriage—was not met by CCAG, and *no recorded case has ever extended the antidiscriminatory cause of action to non-ticketholders.*

Nor did the evidence establish that Nader was entitled to damages under the antidiscrimination provisions of the Federal Aviation Act. First, Nader did not establish that Allegheny violated its own priority rules, and the Court made no finding of fact that Allegheny did so. Second, Allegheny's priority rules were *prima facie* reasonable. And, third, Nader did not establish that Allegheny's violations of its own priority rules, if any occurred, caused Nader's denied boarding.

* * *

Thirdly, and most importantly, Nader failed to prove a necessary element in an antidiscrimination cause of action—that he was discriminated against. Or, put another way, Nader did not prove that any discriminatory actions by Allegheny, if any occurred, proximately caused his denied boarding. Thus, assuming *arguendo* that the boarding of passengers Biscomb and Rucienski was discriminatory, Nader would have to show that the discriminatory action was the proximate cause of his denied boarding. But he cannot make this indispensable proof because even if no alleged discrimination had taken place, and the two passengers had not been boarded, *Nader still would have been denied boarding* because two other oversold passengers presented their tickets for check-in before he did (App. 77–78). Thus, no discrimination on the part of Allegheny caused Nader's denied boarding since he would have been denied boarding regardless of the discriminatory acts of which he accuses Allegheny.

* * *

B. Nader and CCAG Did Not Prove that They Had Been Damaged by Fraudulent Misrepresentations Made by Allegheny

The district court found that Allegheny was liable to both Nader and CCAG for the tort of fraudulent misrepresentation in that Allegheny intentionally misrepresented a material fact—that Nader "had a *guaranteed* reservation for a seat"—upon which Nader and CCAG reasonably relied to their injury (App. 144). Such a finding is barred in this case by the doctrine of primary jurisdiction, as will be discussed below. In addition, however, to the primary jurisdiction bar, both Nader and CCAG failed to prove the elements necessary to sustain an action for fraudulent misrepresentation.

The elements of the tort of fraudulent misrepresentation in the District of Columbia, where Allegheny's headquarters are, where Nader resides, where Nader purchased his ticket, from where Nader informed CCAG of his flight to Hartford, and under whose laws CCAG is incorporated, have been set forth as follows:

> The general rules of law governing such cases are clear. Generally actionable fraud is the concealment of a fact which should have been disclosed, or is the representation of the existence of a material fact which did not exist. That representation must be positively made knowing it to be false, or recklessly and positively made without knowledge of its truth. The party to whom the representation is made must not only be warranted in accepting it, but he must actually accept it, and, relying on its truth, act as contemplated by the party making it. [*Rosenberg* v. *Howle*, 56 A.2d 709, 710 (Mun. Ct. App. D.C. 1948).]

*   *   *

The most glaring omission from the appellees' proof at trial was the misrepresentation itself. *There was no evidence that Allegheny ever represented to the public, much less to the appellees, that holding a ticket for a flight was an absolute assurance that the ticket-holder would be flown*, or as the district court put it, that Nader "had a *guaranteed* reservation for a seat" (App. 144). No advertisements or any other public statements of Allegheny were introduced into evidence. Without evidence of the misrepresentation, the district court had no basis for finding Allegheny liable for making any misrepresentation.

*   *   *

Even if the record contained a statement by Allegheny to the effect that every ticket-holder was absolutely guaranteed a seat, Nader failed to adduce any credible evidence that he believed such a statement to be true, a prerequisite to Allegheny's liability. On the contrary, the evidence showed that five days before the incident in question Nader had been denied boarding by American Airlines and had received the standard CAB form explaining his denied boarding rights, and that he was so familiar with the form that he told the Allegheny representative that he did not need one of theirs (App. 33–35, 80). The evidence further showed that within the prior six months Nader had similarly been denied boarding on an overbooked Eastern Airlines flight (App. 24–25). Mr. Nader had no reasonable basis for believing that Allegheny's reservations practices with respect to overbooking would be any different than those of its two competitors with which he had so recently experienced being an oversale. In view of this undisputed evidence, it was error for the district court to find that the much-traveled Nader was unaware of the risk of oversales or that Allegheny overbooked flights.

The finding of liability to CCAG for fraudulent misrepresentation is likewise unsupportable. None of the parties to this action, nor apparently the district court, have discovered any case against a common carrier in which a third party unknown to the carrier has recovered for the failure of the carrier to make a timely delivery of a passenger. Such individuals are merely incidental beneficiaries of the contract of carriage between the passenger and common carrier and, as such, are not entitled to damages for breach of a contract to which they are not parties. Notwithstanding this lack of law, the district court has tortured the tort of fraudulent misrepresentation to find Allegheny liable to CCAG.

The lack of evidence of the misrepresentation itself is as fatal to CCAG's case as it is to Nader's. Moreover, CCAG has failed to show any misrepresentation made by Allegheny with the intent to influence CCAG to act in reliance on it to its injury, a necessary element of the tort of fraudulent misrepresentation. At the time Nader purchased his ticket, and, indeed at the time he was denied boarding, Allegheny had never heard of CCAG nor of Nader's plans to speak at its rally. Allegheny cannot be said to have reasonably contemplated that CCAG would act to arrange a rally in reliance on any statements Allegheny might have made about airline reservations.

The very case relied on by the district court to support its finding of liability to CCAG, *Rusch Factors, Inc.* v. *Levin*, 284 F. Supp. 85 (D.R.I. 1968), supports Allegheny's contention that the reliance of CCAG, by way of planning a rally, on any misrepresentation that Allegheny might have made was not reasonably foreseeable by Allegheny and thus cannot support a finding of liability. In *Rusch*, the plaintiff-lender, before it would lend money to a potential corporate borrower, requested certified financial statements, and those statements were provided by the defendant accountants. Thus, the accountants, who the court found to have made fraudulent misrepresentations, knew the persons to whom it made the misrepresentations and knew that those persons would rely on the misrepresentations. . . .

*   *   *

C. The Doctrine of Primary Jurisdiction Bars the Awarding of Punitive Damages, the Findings that Allegheny's Overbooking Policy and Lack of Publicity with Respect Thereto Were Unreasonable, and the Finding of Liability for Fraudulent Misrepresentation

The district court, after it found that Allegheny engaged in the practice of discrimination and fraudulent misrepresentation by overbooking flights, awarded exorbitant punitive damages in the total amount of $50,000 to the plaintiffs below ". . . to deter others from such conduct" (Total compensatory damages were but $61) (App. 145). By so doing, the district court usurped the function of the Civil Aeronautics Board, which is charged by Congress with the "regulation of air transportation . . . [to promote] . . . adequate, economical, and efficient service by air carriers at reasonable charges, without unjust discriminations, undue preferences or advantages, or unfair or destructive competitive practices". 49 U.S.C. § 1302 (1970).

*   *   *

Similarly, in the instant case, the determination of whether the no-show problem should be remedied by higher fares to all passengers to compensate for the revenues lost to no-shows, by a no-show penalty, by permitting airlines to overbook, or by other methods, was intended by Congress to be left to the CAB not to the courts (App. 152–205).

While it is true, as the *Price* court mentioned, that courts may award damages to individual passengers who had been denied boarding discriminatorily, the doctrine of primary jurisdiction bars courts from using punitive damages as a vehicle to stop the industry-wide practice of overbooking, *as is the district court's stated intent herein*. The very case that recognized a "bumping" cause of action, *Wills* v. *Trans World Airlines*, 200 F. Supp. 360 (S.D. Cal., 1961), held that judicial action to restrain future oversales was beyond the competence of the court as long as the avenues of administrative redress provided by the CAB were available. *Id.* at 365–66. And apparently in *Wills* the principle of primary jurisdiction was not urged by counsel for the carrier with respect to awarding punitive damages, as it was, most emphatically, in the instant case.

*   *   *

D. This Action Is Barred as a Matter of Law by Allegheny's Tariff

*   *   *

V. CONCLUSION

Because Nader and CCAG did not prove the elements necessary for recovery under the antidiscrimination provisions of the Federal Aviation Act or under a theory of misrepresentation and because neither complied with the 45 day written notice of claim tariff provisions, neither was entitled to recover compensatory damages. Because under the doctrine of primary jurisdiction it was for the CAB, not the court, to decide what the public policy should be with respect to airline overbooking and notice reservation practices, the imposition of punitive damages was precluded. Therefore, the appellant Allegheny Airlines Inc. prays that this Court reverse the judgment of the district court and order that judgment be entered for Allegheny Airlines, Inc.

Respectfully submitted,

Frank F. Roberson
William A. Bradford, Jr.
815 Connecticut Avenue
Washington, D.C. 20006
298-5500
Attorneys for Appellant

Of Counsel:
Hogan & Hartson
815 Connecticut Avenue
Washington, D.C. 20006

APPENDIX FOR APPELLANT

INDEX TO APPENDIX

* * *

DOCUMENT #35: APPELLATE BRIEF OF APPELLEES

Plaintiffs filed an *appellate brief* (Document #35) which responded to Allegheny's arguments and affirmatively made its own points in support of the decision of the Court below. As appellees (against whom an appeal is brought), plaintiffs cite many more authorities than Allegheny but both briefs chiefly rely on only a few.

In its Counter Statement of the Issues, plaintiffs attempt to narrow the Court's focus. Instead of discussing the issues on their merits, plaintiffs are asking whether the lower Court's findings were "clearly erroneous." They argue that this is the proper standard for reviewing the findings of the Court below. If the appellate court adopts this standard of review, it must accept the trial court's findings (even if it does not agree with them) unless they are found to be "clearly erroneous." This standard gives the appellate court a very narrow scope of review and limited ability to overturn the trial judge's findings.

In their statement of the facts and in their arguments, plaintiffs point to evidence in the record that supports the trial judge's views. They also attempt to shape the way in which the Court of Appeals views the facts. For example, Allegheny argued that any discrimination in not boarding Nader was not actionable because Allegheny merely followed its rules as to boarding priorities. In fact, the rules applied by Allegheny were to be used only when oversales could not be determined before boarding. Plaintiffs argue that those rules do not apply because the oversale could have been known by Allegheny prior to boarding. Judge Richey made no specific finding on this point, but if plaintiffs' position were to be accepted, different rules would have been invoked under which Nader *would* have been boarded. Given Judge Richey's ultimate decision in the case, plaintiffs hope that the appellate judges will infer that Allegheny should have known about the problem prior to boarding. In fact, they point to testimony of the Allegheny employee at the gate when Nader was bumped to establish that there were ways he could have known of the situation in advance, but that he did not utilize those methods.

United States Court of Appeals

FOR THE DISTRICT OF COLUMBIA CIRCUIT

No. 73-2243

RALPH NADER AND THE CONNECTICUT
CITIZEN ACTION GROUP,
Plaintiffs-Appellees,

v.

ALLEGHENY AIRLINES, INC.,
DEFENDANT-APPELLANT.

Appeal from the United States District Court for the District of Columbia

BRIEF FOR APPELLEES

REUBEN B. ROBERTSON III
ALAN B. MORRISON

Suite700
2000 P Street, N.W.
Washington, D.C. 20036
(202) 785-3704

Attorneys for Plaintiffs-Appellees

TABLE OF CONTENTS

TABLE OF AUTHORITIES

              *   *   *

*Authorities principally relied upon.

              *   *   *

BRIEF FOR APPELLEES

    This litigation arose because of the purposeful concealment by the defendant,
Allegheny Airlines, of its deliberate company policy to sell more tickets on its flights than

there are seats on the planes, and the inevitable adverse consequences flowing from this practice. The result of Allegheny's intentional overbooking is to leave thousands of its passengers each year literally stranded at the gate, their travel plans shattered without warning. Allegheny has thus victimized, on the average, over 4000 unsuspecting passengers a year by dishonoring confirmed reservations, knowing full well that this would result in serious inconvenience, disruption of personal and business plans, and economic losses, not only for the passengers but for others as well.

*   *   *

COUNTER-STATEMENT OF THE ISSUES

1. Was it "clearly erroneous" for the trial court to find that the plaintiffs had established a prima facie case of unreasonable discrimination, and that Allegheny had failed to meet its burden of showing that it had followed its own procedures in denying boarding to Mr. Nader?

2. Was it "clearly erroneous" for the trial court fo find that Allegheny intentionally misrepresented a material fact, and that the plaintiffs justifiably relied thereupon to their detriment?

3. Does the doctrine of primary jurisdiction preclude liability against Allegheny for the common law tort of fraudulent misrepresentation or the award of punitive damages for such conduct or for unjust discrimination in violation of section 404(b) of the Federal Aviation Act?

4. Did the trial court err in holding that Allegheny's exculpatory tariff rule concerning notice of claims does not bar this suit?

This case has not previously been before this Court.

COUNTER-STATEMENT OF THE CASE

The Facts

*   *   *

What appeared at first blush to have caused such inconvenience and embarrassment to the plaintiffs—bureaucratic inefficiency—turned out not to be the source of their problems at all. For what neither Mr. Nader nor CCAG had known was that Allegheny had intentionally "overbooked" flight 864—sold more confirmed reservation tickets than the 100 seats actually available on the aircraft—hoping that someone would cancel or fail to show up for the flight (App. 24, 108, 137, 141). Nor were they aware that Allegheny systematically overbooks its flights in order to enhance its profits (App. 25, 108, 123–124, 140–141). They could not have known this either, because not only does Allegheny not disclose this practice to the public, but it affirmatively conceals it. For example, when the Company responds to complaints from victims of oversales, it is invariably with an assurance that the incident was isolated and accidental, rather than the inevitable consequence of Alleghenys intentional practices:

> The oversale at Hartford was indeed unplanned, and I wish to assure you that Allegheny does not purposely oversell any flight. (Pl. Exh. 14, letter dated Sept. 16, 1969).

> . . . I agree that the oversale of this flight or any other flight is not the kind of service our valued customers deserve. Please be advised that each and every oversale is investigated with corrective action instituted in an effort to prevent recurrence. (Pl. Exh. 14, letter dated March 18, 1970).

Oversales are few when compared to the number of departures . . . .
However, through human or computer error if we are not properly advised,
our total number of commitments do occasionally exceed our total number
of seats available. (*Id.*).

. . . I deeply regret the fact that you were denied a seat on one of our
March 9 flights to Washington . . . . In today's computerized environment,
this should not have happened and we are probably more interested in the
cause than even you are. (Pl. Exh. 14, letter dated May 1, 1970).

. . . in August of 1970, Allegheny introduced a computerized name and
flight reservation system and this has reduced the number of oversale incidents considerably. (Pl. Exh. 14, letter dated Jan. 11, 1971).

And when a passenger is bumped because of overbooking, Allegheny's company
manual instructs its gate agents to say it was "caused by an unintentional error made in
confirming reservations for the flight," or by "equipment substitution" or "weight
restriction"—anything but the true reason (App. 220). . . .

*   *   *

Proceedings Below

*   *   *

ARGUMENT

In its appeal, Allegheny has fired a shotgun blast of miscellaneous arguments, joined
in some of them by its trade association, the Air Transportation Association, which has
filed a brief as *amicus curiae*. Most of these are aimed at Judge Richey's findings on
factual issues, which are, of course, subject to reversal only if "clearly erroneous." See
Rule 52(a), Federal Rules of Civil Procedure. Allegheny also insists now that because of
the doctrine of "primary jurisdiction" several of the issues in the case should not have
been before the court, but, as we shall show, these arguments are without merit and
moreover, since they were not properly presented below, are untimely at this stage.

I. The Trial Court's Finding That Allegheny Unreasonably Discriminated Against the Plaintiff Nader Was Not "Clearly Erroneous."

*   *   *

Rule 52(a) of the Federal Rules of Civil Procedure, which Allegheny conveniently
omits from its brief, states that "Findings of fact shall not be set aside unless clearly erroneous, and due regard shall be given for the opportunity of the trial court to judge the
credibility of the witnesses." Analysis of the record in this case shows that there is substantial evidentiary support for each of Judge Richey's findings and factual inferences.
His order must therefore be affirmed. . . .

*   *   *

There is convincing evidence that Allegheny did not adhere to its procedures in
boarding flight 864. Allegheny's own reservations department concluded in internal
reports that "boarding discrepancies" had been at fault in the denial of boarding to Mr.
Nader on the oversold flight (App. 210, 211), a conclusion that could not be reconciled
with the company's insistence that the flight was properly boarded. Thus, among the
persons who were accommodated on the flight, one was a standby with no reservation,
one had a cancelled reservation, and no reservation record of any kind existed for two

(App. 210, 211; Pl. Exh. 8, 11). On this basis, the trial court quite properly concluded that Mr. Nader's right to boarding, based upon his confirmed, ticketed reservation, had been violated, and that he had been subjected to "unjust discrimination" within the meaning of section 404(b).

*   *   *

II. The Finding That Allegheny Had Engaged in Fraudulent Misrepresentation Which Caused Injury To Plaintiffs Was Not "Clearly Erroneous."

Allegheny also takes issue with Judge Richey's holding that Allegheny was liable to both plaintiffs for the tort of fraudulent misrepresentation. The District Court held (App. 144) that in such cases recovery may be had upon showing that (a) the defendant knowingly misrepresented or concealed a fact; (b) the fact was material to the parties' conduct; (c) reliance on the defendant's representation was reasonable; and (d) the plaintiff actually relied thereupon to his detriment. *Isen* v. *Calvert Corp.*, 126 U.S. App. D.C. 349, 379 F.2d 126 (1967). While privity of contract is not required in a case of deliberate misrepresentation, third parties must also demonstrate that they are within a class of persons whose reliance upon the misrepresentation is contemplated by the defendant. *Ultramares Corp.* v. *Touche*, 255 N.Y. 170, 174 N.E. 441 (1931); *Rusch Factors, Inc.* v. *Levin*, 284 F. Supp. 85 (D. R.I. 1968); 37 Am. Jur. 2d, Fraud and Deceit § 298; Prosser, "Misrepresentation and Third Parties," 19 Vand. L. Rev. 231, 246, 250 (1966). Allegheny does not take issue with the rule of law applied below; rather, it claims error in the court's findings of facts, asserting that there was no evidence of Allegheny's misrepresentation, of actual reliance thereupon by the plaintiffs, or of the foreseeability that persons such as CCAG would be injured by its misrepresentation. The record is clear, however, that on each of these findings there is more than adequate evidence to support the trial court's judgment.

First, as to the element of misrepresentation, it is undisputed that Allegheny expressly advised Mr. Nader that he had a confirmed reservation for flight 864. It is likewise undisputed that this flight, unknown to Mr. Nader and CCAG, had been intentionally overbooked by the airline, and that it is Allegheny's practice to overbook regularly, without any warning to potential victims. Clearly, Allegheny intends by confirming a reservation to convey the understanding that a seat is available for that passenger on that flight. It is Allegheny's purpose to induce reliance by the passenger on the confirmed reservation as a reasonable assurance that, except for some mechanical or weather emergency, his travel plans will be fulfilled on that flight, and this purpose is reinforced by Allegheny's advertising and promotion campaigns stressing the reliability and integrity of its reservations and other services (App. 117–119, 141) Allegheny's president Leslie Barnes testified that a confirmed reservation gives "within the normal latitudes" of weather and mechanical problems a "reasonable assurance of fulfilling one's plan, whether it be business or pleasure." (App. 117). . . .

*   *   *

Second, Allegheny raises the issue of reliance. It was established that Mr. Nader and CCAG believed that his reservation on flight 864 would assure him of a seat on that flight which would put him in Hartford in ample time for his speaking engagement (App. 24, 108). The plaintiffs clearly relied on this confirmed reservation in making their plans, and in foregoing the opportunity to arrange for an earlier flight or another means of transportation (App. 24, 31, 32, 108). It is undisputed that by the time plaintiffs learned that Mr. Nader's reservation had been dishonored because the flight was overbooked, it was too late to make such alternate arrangements.

As to the reasonableness of this reliance, Allegheny suggests that, because Mr. Nader had been bumped before by other airlines (Eastern and American) and had received from them the printed statements required by the CAB regulations, he could not possibly have believed that his reservation on Allegheny assured him of a seat (Al. Br. 20). But these earlier incidents did not dismantle Mr. Nader's reasonable expectation that his Allegheny reservation could be relied upon. . . . .

III. The Doctrine of Primary Jurisdiction is Inapplicable to this Case

On appeal, Allegheny vigorously urges that the District Court's rulings transgressed the "primary jurisdiction" of the Civil Aeronautics Board and for that reason must be reversed. Primary jurisdiction is a doctrine designed for "cases raising issues of fact not within the conventional experience of judges or cases requiring the exercise of administrative discretion." *Far East Conference* v. *United States*, 342 U.S. 570, 574 (1952). It is a policy of suspension and deferral, rather than prohibition, which "applies where a claim is originally cognizable in the courts, and comes into play whenever enforcement of the claim requires the resolution of issues which, under a regulatory scheme, have been placed within the special competence of an administrative body; in such a case the judicial process is suspended pending referral of such issues to the administrative body for its views." . . .

As to this much, at least, it appears that the parties essentially agree. Where they part company is when Allegheny contends that, even though the issues in this litigation have nothing to do with tariff construction or antitrust immunity, the primary jurisdiction doctrine is at all relevant here, let alone that it requires the reversal of the District Court's judgment and substantially bars liability here. Allegheny seems to believe that the creation of the CAB by Congress erected an impermeable shield protecting airlines from responsibility for their deliberate torts, a proposition finding no support in law or logic.

*   *   *

IV. Allegheny's Exculpatory Tariff Rule Is No Bar to this Action

*   *   *

CONCLUSION

For the foregoing reasons, it is apparent that Allegheny's appeal is without merit and the District Court's judgment should be affirmed.

Respectfully submitted,

Reuben B. Robertson III
Alan B. Morrison
Attorneys for Plaintiffs-Appellees
Suite 700
2000 P Street NW
Washington, D.C. 20036
(202) 785-3704

March 4, 1974

DOCUMENT 36: AMICUS CURIAE BRIEF

Allegheny filed a *Reply Brief* (not included here) in response to plaintiffs' submission. A Reply Brief is not designed to raise new material but, rather, to respond to the arguments made by the appellee.

In addition to the briefs of the parties, the Civil Aeronautics Board and the Air Transport Association of America filed *Amicus Curiae Briefs* supporting the position of Allegheny in this suit. An Amicus Curiae (or Friend of the Court) must obtain the consent of all parties or obtain court permission to file a brief. In this case, Amicus came in by motion. As might be expected, the Amicus brief for the CAB argued that the issues before the trial court should have been presented first to the Board (Document #36). The Air Transport Association of America, a trade association of airlines, took the position in its Amicus brief (not included here) that overbooking was a permissible and reasonable response to the industry-wide problem of no-shows. Since many airline members of the Association practiced the same policy, an award of punitive damages in this case would have a negative and widespread effect on the industry, one that the Association desired to avoid. Plaintiffs, as was their right, filed reply briefs to each of the amicus briefs submitted to the Court.

**BRIEF FOR CIVIL AERONAUTICS BOARD
AS AMICUS CURIAE**

IN THE

United States Court of Appeals

FOR THE DISTRICT OF COLUMBIA CIRCUIT

No. 73-2243

RALPH NADER AND THE CONNECTICUT
CITIZEN ACTION GROUP,
Plaintiffs-Appellees,

v.

ALLEGHENY AIRLINES, INC
Defendant-Appellant..

**On Appeal from the United States
District Court for the District of Columbia**

O.D. OZMENT
Deputy General Counsel

GLEN M. BENDIXSEN
Associate General Counsel
Litigation and Research

BARBARA THORSON
Attorney

WARREN L. SHARFMENN
Special Counsel
Civil Aeronautics Board
Washington, D.C. 20428

THOMAS E. KAUPER
Assistant Attorney General
Department of Justice
Washington, D.C. 20530

RICHARD LITTELL
General Counsel
Civil Aeronautics Board
Washington, D.C. 20428

INDEX

*   *   *

DOCUMENT #37: OPINION OF THE COURT OF APPEALS

The Court of Appeals, in a partially split decision, reversed and remanded *Nader* v *Allegheny* to the District Court. The Court attempted to sort out a muddled set of findings by the Court below. The Court of Appeals examined the issues of whether plaintiffs were discriminated against in violation of statute, whether they were the victims of common law misrepresentation, and whether, assuming any liability was found against Allegheny, punitive damages were available. On the first issue, the Court of Appeals held that the findings of the lower court were not clear enough to determine the precise basis upon which it ruled for plaintiffs. On the second issue, the Court of Appeals turned the question of Allegheny's "nonrepresentation" to the public of its overbooking practices into a question of the primary jurisdiction of the CAB. On the issue of punitive damages, the Court of Appeals held that there must be a showing of malice or a conscious disregard for the rights of others in order for punitive damages to be available. There was no such showing concerning the discrimination claim, and the trial judge failed to consider whether Allegheny had a good faith defense concerning its nondisclosure to the public of its overbooking policy. We will briefly discuss the Court's rationale on each of these issues.

The Court held that overbooking does not, *per se*, give rise to a discrimination claim under the statute. Nevertheless, the failure of an airline to follow its own priority rules in cases of overbooking may be actionable. In this case, however, the Court of Appeals held that the findings of the trial judge did not make clear whether he found that Allegheny did not follow its rules or whether he found those rules to be unreasonable. An examination of the record by the appellate judges indicated there was conflicting evidence on this issue which must be resolved, in the first instance, by the trial judge. If it was his intention to find that Allegheny violated its rules, Nader may have proved his discrimination claim. If, however, the judge intended to find that Allegheny's rules were unreasonable, he would be violating the principle of *primary jurisdiction* which requires that the administrative agency charged with regulating a field be given the first opportunity to pass on policy questions such as this. Since the findings and the record did not allow the Court of Appeals to determine the trial judge's meaning, the judgment for plaintiffs on this claim was vacated and the issue remanded for further findings and clarification by the trial court.

The misrepresentation issue was interpreted by the Court of Appeals to be one of "non-representation." There was no evidence that Allegheny made actual false statements to plaintiffs or, through its advertising, to plaintiffs, or to the public at large. The Court of Appeals went on to hold that the nondisclosure to the public of Allegheny's overbooking policy could be categorized under the Aviation Act as an "unfair or deceptive" practice which would be, under the doctrine of primary jurisdiction, for the CAB to determine. The Court then asked whether the CAB's jurisdiction over this issue precluded the courts from entertaining a common law tort action for the same nondisclosure. Its answer was that Congress expected some alteration of the common law by allowing the CAB to regulate so comprehensively. Therefore, if the CAB found that the nondisclosure was not "deceptive" under the Act, a tort action for misrepresentation by virtue of the nondisclosure would have to fail as a matter of law.

The Court then examined whether the CAB had ever addressed this question and found that there was a proceeding pending at the CAB in which the question had been raised. The Court therefore vacated the District Court's judgment in favor of Nader on the misrepresentation issue, and remanded the case to the District Court with instructions to stay the matter until the CAB's proceeding was completed.

On CCAG's misrepresentation claim, the Court ruled that, although privity of contract is not required to assert a misrepresentation claim, some relationship must exist between the parties. CCAG had no direct relationship and its indirect relationship was too remote to allow it to recover from Allegheny, even if misrepresentation were to be established.

Concerning punitive damages, the court decided to examine the discrimination and misrepresentation claims separately. It found no evidence in the record that there was malice toward Nader in bumping him from the flight. It was not even contended that this was the case. Therefore, the Court reversed outright the lower Court finding that punitive damages were available on the discrimination claim. On the misrepresentation claim, the court held that the trial judge had not inquired into whether Allegheny had a good faith belief that its procedures were lawful (due to their acceptance by the CAB or, at least, its acquiescence in them). Since malice is a prerequisite for an award of punitive damages, the failure to inquire was fatal and the issue was remanded for further examination.

Judge Fahy concurred in the Court's decision except in relation to the misrepresentation issue. On that point he dissented and offered an opinion which the Supreme Court eventually adopted in substantial part. Judge Fahy argued that the issue of misrepresentation was one for the *Court*, not an administrative agency, to decide.

Ralph NADER et al.

v.

**ALLEGHENY AIRLINES,
INC., Appellant**

512 F.2d 527 (D.C. Cir. 1975)

No. 73-2243

United States Court of Appeals,

District of Columbia Circuit

Argued Dec. 10, 1974.

Decided May 2, 1975.

Rehearing and Rehearing En Banc
Denied June 23, 1975.

Appeal from the United States District Court for the District of Columbia (D.C. Civil Action 1346-72).

Frank F. Roberson, Washington, D.C., with whom William A. Bradford, Jr., Washington, D.C., was on the brief, for appellant.

Reuben B. Robertson, Washington, D.C., with whom Alan B. Morrison, Washington, D.C., was on the brief, for appellees.

James E. Landry and Donald C. Comlish, Washington, D.C., filed a brief on behalf of certain members of the Air Transport Association of America as amici curiae urging reversal.

Richard Littell, Gen. Counsel, C.A.B., O. D. Ozment, Deputy Gen. Counsel, Glen M. Bendixsen, Associate Gen. Counsel, Litigation and Research, Barbara Thorson, Atty., C.A.B., and Warren L. Sharfman, Sp. Counsel, C.A.B., filed a brief on behalf of Civil Aeronautics Board as amicus curiae urging reversal.

Before FAHY, Senior Circuit Judge, and McGOWAN and TAMM, Circuit Judges.

Opinion for the Court filed by Circuit Judge TAMM.

Opinion filed by Senior Circuit Judge FAHY, concurring in part and dissenting in part.

TAMM, Circuit Judge:

Plaintiffs-appellees Ralph Nader and the Connecticut Citizen Action Group (CCAG) brought this suit in district court against defendant-appellant Allegheny Airlines, Inc. (Allegheny) after Allegheny dishonored Nader's reservation for one of its flights. Appellees alleged that as a consequence of Allegheny's actions, Nader was unable to appear at a fund-raising rally in behalf of CCAG, thereby causing the loss of $100,000 in contributions. Appellees claimed that the incident gave rise to a private damage remedy for unjust discrimination under section 404(b) of the Federal Aviation Act of 1958, 49 U.S.C. § 1374(b) (1970) and that Allegheny's failure to disclose the risk of being denied a seat constituted fraudulent misrepresentation. They sought compensatory damages for lost contributions, and for various out-of-pocket expenses, and punitive damages of $150,000. After a non-jury trial, the district judge entered judgments for Nader on the section 404(b) claim and for both appellees on the claim of fraudulent misrepresentation. He assessed compensatory damages at $10 for Nader and $51 for CCAG and also awarded $25,000 punitive damages to each appellee. Nader v. Allegheny Airlines, Inc., 365 F.Supp. 128 (D.D.C. 1973). Allegheny appeals the decision of the district court both with respect to liability and damages. The Air Transport Association of America, on behalf of certain of its members, and the Civil Aeronautics Board (the Board) have submitted briefs as amicus curiae.

Parts I and II of this opinion discuss the facts that led to the suit and the pertinent regulatory background. In part III, we first conclude that the trial judge's holding that Nader can recover under section 404(b) of the Act must be reversed and remanded because his findings of fact appear tainted by erroneous legal conclusions. We next hold that the finding that Allegheny committed fraudulent misrepresentation must be reversed and the case stayed until the Board determines whether the airlines' reservation practices are deceptive. Lastly, we conclude even assuming *arguendo* that Allegheny committed fraudulent misrepresentation, CCAG is not within the class that can recover. In part IV, we hold that punitive damages may not be awarded for a section 404(b) violation based on the record in this case. We also hold that while punitive damages ultimately may be assessed against Allegheny for fraudulent misrepresentation, the trial judge must consider whether Allegheny was relying upon the belief that its actions carried the approval of the Board, and therefore was acting in good faith.

I. FACTS

*   *   *

III. LIABILITY

*   *   *

B. Common Law Misrepresentation

Both Nader and CCAG recovered on the second cause of action, the common law tort of fraudulent misrepresentation. Applying the accepted definition of the tort, the trial judge found that: Allegheny "knowingly and intentionally misrepresented a material fact, namely that Mr. Nader had a guaranteed reservation for a seat;" Nader and CCAG relied to their detriment on the misrepresentation; their reliance was reasonable; and CCAG could recover because it was foreseeable that members of the public would rely on Allegheny's misrepresentations. Nader v. Allegheny Airlines, Inc., *supra*, 365 F.Supp. at 132.

Although the trial judge found that Alle-gheny, "through advertising and other means," affirmatively misrepresented to Nader that he had a guaranteed reservation for a seat, *id.* at 131, there is absolutely no probative evidence in the record to support a specific finding of an affirmative misrepresentation. In fact, the only record evidence on this issue is the testimony of Nader and of Allegheny's President, Leslie Barnes. Nader testified that since Allegheny advertises its reliability, publishes its schedule of flights, and accepts reservations, it was his understanding that a reservation would not be accepted unless a seat could be provided. He was unable to show any specific instances of affirmative misrepresentations. Barnes testified that Allegheny attempts to portray an image of reliability in its advertising, that Allegheny advertises that reservations may be made by contacting the airline or a travel agent, and that a passenger who makes a reservation has, "within normal latitudes," a reasonable expectation of receiving a seat. Thus, we reverse the finding that Allegheny affirmatively represented to Nader that he had a guaranteed reservation for a seat because it is clearly erroneous and without evidentiary support.

In reality, the gravamen of appellees' complaint is *nonrepresentation* rather than misrepresentation. The issue that the court must decide is, assuming *arguendo* that the public shares the perception, created either by the aura of Allegheny's advertising or more generally, by shared societal notions about the meaning of a confirmed reservation, that a confirmed reservation guarantees a seat, whether Allegheny had a duty to disclose the possibility that its policy of deliberate overbooking could alter these expectations. To resolve this question, we address the contention, pressed by Allegheny and the Civil Aeronautics Board, that the existence of the Board's power under section 411 of the Federal Aviation Act, 49 U.S.C. § 1381 (1970), to investigate and determine whether an air carrier "has been or is engaged in unfair or deceptive practices or unfair methods of competition" precludes a common law tort action for fraudulent misrepresentation. In effect, appellant and amicus curiae argue that the Board's regulatory power over reservation practices, which are inter-

twined with the level and structure of air fares, gives it exclusive jurisdiction over these practices and eliminates common law remedies. Nader's response is that Congress did not intend to pre-empt all private tort actions involving airline practices when it passed the Federal Aviation Act. Thus framed, the issue becomes the effect, if any, the passage of the Federal Aviation Act had on the remedies available for the common law misrepresentational torts of air carriers.

It seems clear that the deceptive practices that the Board has power to proscribe under the Act would include all of the carrier misrepresentations actionable under the common law. However, we simply cannot accept the proposition that the existence of the Board's power under section 411 eliminates all private remedies for common law torts arising from those types of misrepresentations or other forms of unfair or deceptive practices. The Supreme Court has noted in American Airlines, Inc. v. North American Airlines, Inc., 351 U.S. 79, 85, 76 S.Ct. 600, 100 L.Ed. 953 (1956) that section 411 of the Federal Aviation Act was modeled after section five of the Federal Trade Commission Act, and this court indicated in Holloway v. Bristol-Myers Corp., 158 U.S. App.D.C. 207, 485 F.2d 986, 989 (1973), that the remedies of section five were additional to rather than in derogation of the common law remedies for fraud and deceit. Moreover, while the arsenal of remedies available to the Civil Aeronautics Board is significant, it does not include the power to award damages to injured parties. Finally, to hold that the Act pre-empts the common law remedies would ignore section 1106 of the Act, 49 U.S.C. § 1506 (1970), which states: "Nothing contained in this chapter shall in any way abridge or alter the remedies now existing at common law or by statute, but the provisions of this chapter are in addition to such remedies."

However, despite the similarities be-tween section 5 of the Federal Trade Commission Act and 411 of the Federal Aviation Act, the differences between the two would itself suggest that the common law misrepresentational torts did not remain unaffected by the Act. The Supreme Court recognized as much in American Airlines, Inc. v. North American Airlines, Inc., *supra*, 351 U.S. at 83–84, 76 S.Ct. at 604:

> Section 5 is concerned with purely private business enterprises which cover the full spectrum of economic activity. On the other hand, the air carriers here conduct their business under a regulated system of limited competition. The business so conducted is of especial and essential concern to the public, as is true of all common carriers. . . .

Finally, Congress has committed the regulation of this industry to an administrative agency of special competence that deals only with the problems of the industry.

This conclusion, that the common law remedies for fraud and deceit cannot remain totally unaffected by the Act, is buttressed by the fact that the practices at issue have a significant rate making effect. Besides the Board's power to control deceptive practices, section 102 of the Act, 49 U.S.C. § 1302 (1970), charges the Board with the responsibility for promoting a number of goals that Congress specifically found to be in the public interest. In carrying out its functions, the Board is to encourage the "development of an air-transportation system properly adapted to the present and *future* needs of . . . foreign and domestic commerce . . . ," and is to promote "adequate, economical, and efficient service . . . by air carriers at reasonable charges. . . ." (emphasis supplied). Further, section 1002(e), 49 U.S.C. § 1482(e) (1970) requires the Board, in its rate making capacity to balance "[t]he need in the public interest of adequate and efficient transportation service . . . at the lowest cost consistent with the furnishing of such service . . . " with "[t]he need of each air carrier for revenue sufficient . . . to provide adequate and efficient . . . service." Having charged the Board with these important responsibilities, Congress must have necessarily given the Board the power to carry out its functions. We think that this power must be read broadly to include the approval in the public interest of some practices that might be considered common law misrepresentations. The effect of such approval, or a holding that they do not represent deceptive practices, would be to establish that the practices, as a matter of law, do not constitute common law misrepresentations. . . .

We believe that the factors outlined above indicate that Congress, by enacting the Federal Aviation Act, expected some alteration of the common law so that the Board could effectively regulate the airline industry in the public interest. Thus, if the Board properly finds that a practice is not deceptive, a common law action for misrepresentation must fail as a matter of law. Given this interpretation, when the allegedly tortious practice is one that has been directly regulated by the Board, or while not directly regulated is so obviously tied to a regulated practice or rate that a change in one would require a change in the other, the Board must determine, in the first instance, whether the practice

falls within the ambit of the deceptive practices provision of section 411.

This result is but another application of the principles of primary jurisdiction, a doctrine whose purpose is the coordination of the workings of agency and court., *See* 3 K. Davis, Administrative Law Treatise, § 19.01 (1958). Primary jurisdiction recognizes that even though a claim may be cognizable in the courts, technical questions often call for the judgment of an agency presumably expert in the field under judicial consideration. Perhaps more importantly, where Congress has entrusted the regulation of an industry to a single regulatory body, uniformity of policy and practice can only be achieved by submitting relevant issues to the affected agency for consideration. *See generally* Far East Conference v. United States, 342 U.S. 570, 72 S.Ct. 492, 96 L.Ed. 576 (1952); Price v. Trans World Airlines, Inc., 481 F.2d 844 (9th Cir. 1973); Lichten v. Eastern Airlines, Inc., 189 F.2d 939 (2d Cir. 1951); Adler v. Chicago & Southern Air Lines, Inc., 41 F.Supp. 366 (E.D.Mo. 1941).

It is beyond peradventure that the requisites for submission to the Board are met in this case. As demonstrated in part II, the Board has been quite active in this area and has recognized the relationship of the carriers' reservations policies to the structure and level of air fares. Moreover, the discussion of deliberate overbooking in part II illustrates that the determination whether overbooking is or is not a deceptive practice involves technical and policy judgments that should properly be submitted to the Board in the first instance. Finally, since the problems are as wide as the industry itself, a single, industry-wide resolution is appropriate. Thus, in the absence of an existing Board decision disposing of this question, the issue of whether the air carriers' overbooking policies, including their policy of nondisclosure, may be characterized as a tortious misrepresentation must first be submitted to the Board to ascertain whether the conduct violates section 411.

*   *   *

There is one final question in this area requiring resolution—assuming Allegheny's liability for misrepresentation, whether appellees may recover for their reliance. The trial judge's award of damages to CCAG raises one of the most troublesome problems in this area of tort law: when may a third party recover his pecuniary losses for reliance on a misrepresentation that was not made to him. In this case, the trial judge employed the following reasoning to conclude that CCAG as well as Nader could recover for Allegheny's misrepresentation:

CCAG is eligible and entitled to recover herein for damages it has incurred due to the Defendant's intentional misrepresentation even though they were not direct parties to the transacton in issue because: (1) The misrepresentation was knowingly and intentionally made; privity of contract is not required here; (2) CCAG was within the class of foreseeable plaintiffs (the class is determined by the Defendant's legal duty to the public at large both under its license and by its better position to prevent injury to the public by full disclosure of its practices affecting the public); (3) CCAG made a reasonable reliance on the misrepresentation and was thereby damaged. . . .

Nader v. Allegheny Airlines, Inc., *supra*, 365 F.Supp. at 132–33 (citations omitted).

Of course, questions involving the scope of liability for fraudulent misrepresentation are questions of "local" rather than federal law. Thus, we must look to the common law of the District of Columbia since, under all of the various choice of law principles, the law of this jurisdiction would be applied. *See generally* Dovell v. Arundel Supply Corp., 124 U.S. App.D.C. 89, 361 F.2d 543 (1966); Emmert v. United States, 300 F.Supp. 45 (D.D.C. 1969). Apparently, the question of third party recovery for fraudulent misrepresentation is virtually one of the first impression, as the parties have not referred us to any District of Columbia decisions that have confronted this issue, and our research has uncovered only one such case. In that case, New York Title & Mortgage Co. v. Hutton, 63 App.D.F.C. 266, 17 F.2d 989, cert. denied, 293 U.S. 605, 55 S.Ct. 122, 79, L.Ed. 696 (1934), the court applied the then prevalent rule to determine that a title company which lauded the facilities of another title company by letter in order to obtain title business could not be held liable for fraudulent misrepresentation where the letter was used by the other title company to aid in the sale of its stock. We therefore turn to the legal principles that have guided other courts and commentators. . . .

*   *   *

Although the trial judge apparently did not explicitly consider Nader's position, it is manifest that Nader was not in privity with Allegheny at the time of the misrepresentation, nor was he identified as a person to whom the misrepresentation was directed. However, he was within an identifiable class of third persons—potential passengers—that Allegheny intended to influence. Although the class of persons is large, liability is justified by the notion that, in

general, loss caused by intentional wrongdoing should be placed on the wrongdoer rather than on the innocent party. *See* Rusch Factors, Inc. v. Levin, 284 F.Supp. 85, 90 (D.R.I. 1968).

CCAG, however, is a party more remote from the transaction than Nader. It was not identified to Allegheny until this law suit was instituted. Allegheny had no special reason to know of CCAG's reliance or even of its existence. In fact, CCAG is really a member of a vast indeterminate class that may be equated with the public itself. The trial judge seems to have recognized this, as he stated: "It was foreseeable that the Defendant's intentional misrepresentation would be relayed to other *members of the public* and that they would rely upon the Defendant's representation . . . ." Nader v. Allegheny Airlines, Inc., *supra*, 365 F.Supp. at 132 (emphasis supplied). However, as discussed above, foreseeability is not the test to be used in determining the class of third persons who may recover; otherwise, liability in a case such as this could become indeterminate. To hold that CCAG is within the class of persons who may recover would mean that virtually any plaintiff, no matter how far removed from the transaction or incident, can recover the full amount of his damages. We are unwilling to extend liability that far and consequently hold that CCAG cannot recover as Allegheny's duty did not extend to it.

*   *   *

V. CONCLUSION

For the reasons stated in part III of this opinion:

(1) the judgement entered in favor of Nader based on Allegheny's alleged violation of section 404(b) is reversed, and the district court is instructed to make new findings of fact and conclusions of law in accordance with this opinion. In addition, the district court may take appropriate action to resolve conflicts in the evidence;

(2) the judgment in favor of CCAG based on fraudulent misrepresentation is reversed ,and the district court is instructed to enter a judgment in favor of Allegheny on this issue; and

(3) the judgment entered in favor of Nader based on fraudulent misrepresentation is reversed, and the district court is instructed to stay further action on this issue in accordance with this opinion.

For the reasons stated in part IV of this opinion:

(1) the punitive damage award to Nader and CCAG is reversed. Punitive damage shall be awarded only on the terms set forth in this opinion.

So ordered.

FAHY, Senior Circuit Judge (concurring in part, dissenting in part):

I concur in the conclusion reached in the opinion of Judge Tamm for the court that the question whether appellee Nader was entitled to recover under section 404(b) of the Federal Aviation Act must be remanded for further consideration. I also concur in the conclusion of the court, assuming *arguendo* that Alle-gheny committed fraudulent misrepresentation, that appellee Connecticut Citizen Action Group (CCAG) is not within the class which can recover on that ground. Furthermore, I concur that punitive damages may not be awarded on the present record for a section 404(b) violation.

My dissent is due to the court's disposition of the claim of Mr. Nader based on allegedly fraudulent misrepresentation by Allegheny. The court holds that the finding of the District Court in that regard must be reversed and the case stayed until the Board determines whether the reservation practices of the airlines are deceptive. In my opinion the finding by the District Court of fraudulent misrepresentation is ripe for review now by this court without reference to the Board, under section 411, of the reservation practices of the airlines. . . .

DOCUMENT #38:
PETITION FOR A WRIT OF CERTIORARI

Opinions of the U.S. Courts of Appeals may be brought to the Supreme Court for review in one of several ways. Among them are *appeal, certification,* or *writ of certiorari.* Review by appeal is a matter of right in certain cases (which are set out in title 28 of the United States Code, section 1254). Review by certification or certiorari is discretionary with the Supreme Court. Section 1254 states that a writ of certiorari may be granted "upon the petition of any party to any civil or criminal case." The Supreme Court has elaborated on this statutory mandate in the Supreme Court Rules (SCR). SCR 10 indicates that review on certiorari is *not* a matter of right and that such writs will be granted only when there are "special and important" reasons for doing so.

A *Petition for Writ of Certiorari* must contain, in the order required by SCR 14, the following:

- A concise statement of the question(s) presented for review (only questions so presented or fairly included in the questions presented will be considered by the Court).
- A list of all parties to the proceeding to be reviewed (unless all parties are contained in the caption).
- A table of contents and table of authorities.
- A reference to the official and unofficial reports of opinions (judicial or administrative) delivered below.

- A concise statement of the jurisdiction of the Court including:
  —the date of the judgment or decree to be reviewed and the time of its entry;
  —the date of any order concerning a rehearing or an extension of time to petition; and
  —the statutory provision conferring jurisdiction on the Court.
- A citation and verbatim statement of the constitutional, statutory, regulatory, treaty, or ordinance provision involved in the case.
- A concise statement of the case including the basis for federal jurisdiction.
- A "direct and concise" argument of the reasons relied on for the granting of the writ.
- An appendix including orders and decrees from the court whose decision is sought to be reviewed.

All arguments in support of the petition must be contained in it and no separate brief will be allowed. Forty copies of the petition must be filed. The petition cannot exceed thirty pages excluding certain basic material and the appendix. Forty copies of any *brief in opposition* to the petition must be filed within thirty days after receipt of the petition. It, too, is limited to thirty pages. Finally, a *reply brief* addressed to arguments first raised in the opposition brief may be filed at any time after receipt of the brief in opposition and must be limited to ten pages. If the Court grants the petition, it will set the case down for briefing and oral argument.

Plaintiffs, in their *Petition for a Writ of Certiorari* (Document #38), had to make several choices about which arguments they would present to the Supreme Court. They had to choose the arguments that had the best chance of being reviewed by the Court, and that had the best chance of prevailing once reviewed.

Plaintiffs chose to pursue only one of the issues decided against them by the court of appeals. They argued in their petition that the question of whether nondisclosure of the overbooking policy was actionable as a common law tort was for the courts to decide, not the CAB. Note how the *Question Presented* is drafted narrowly as an issue of the construction of a federal statute. Also note how the *Statutes Involved* are limited to two sections of the Federal Aviation Act which plaintiffs argue were misconstrued by the Court of Appeals. The broad possibilities for relief outlined in the original complaint and argued through the Court of Appeals have been narrowed. The focus is now on these two statutory sections.

Plaintiffs are no longer arguing about discrimination or failure to follow priority rules. They are, instead, asking the Court to decide whether the Court of Appeals has properly construed two federal statutes so as to limit the ability of courts to examine common law issues which are also within the purview of an administrative agency, even though the agency charged with regulating the particular field of conduct has not yet passed on the point in question. This is the issue they wish the Court to examine. In their petition, they must show the Court that there are "special and important" reasons for the Court to address this issue. Nader presents the reasons in two parts. First, he argues that the decision below "disrupts the traditional allocation of functions between the courts and [in this case] the Civil Aeronautics Board." Second, the retroactive immunization from liability for common law fraud, which the decision of the Court of Appeals would permit the CAB to do, is "unprecedented and contrary to the statutory limitation" of the CAB.

Nader's discussion of the first reason focuses on the fact that the CAB was designed to vindicate the *public* interest and not individual rights, which is the province of the courts. The Court of Appeals decision negates this distinction in letting the Board decide whether the carrier may be liable on a private tort claim by determining whether the airline practice in question was "unfair or deceptive." Moreover, the decision of the Court of Appeals requires the Board to make a determination on an issue which it had previously decided not to resolve. This directive by the court is a usurpation of a power reserved to the CAB and is an issue which the Court should examine.

The second reason put forward by the plaintiffs is the retroactivity of the immunization from tort liability implicit in the opinion of the Court of Appeals. While the Board arguably may have the power to declare certain practices *not* unfair or deceptive and, thus, remove them thereafter from the realm of tortious conduct, Nader asserts that there has never been a ruling that allows an agency to do so *after* the conduct has occurred. Furthermore, a holding allowing plaintiffs to proceed with their tort claim would not infringe on the regulatory power of the agency which would remain able to legitimize certain conduct prospectively. Since the Board has not yet legitimized Allegheny's conduct, the ruling by the District Court in favor of plaintiffs' tort claim in no way conflicts with any ruling of the CAB. Moreover, the Federal Aviation Act specifically indicates that its provisions do not abridge common law remedies but are in addition to them. Thus, the ruling by the Court of Appeals departs from the norm of judicial proceedings on an issue which should be decided by the Supreme Court.

PREPARING A PETITION FOR A WRIT OF CERTIORARI

- Follow the format and meet the deadlines of the Supreme Court Rules.
- Choose which issues to pursue very carefully based upon your assessment of the chances for ultimate success, and on the importance of the issues to the Court.
- Distinguish between your issue(s) on the merits and your "special and important" reasons for having the Court decide it.
- Be brief and to the point.

IN THE

SUPREME COURT OF THE UNITED STATES

OCTOBER TERM, 1975

RALPH, NADER,

Petitioner,

V.

ALLEGHENY AIRLINES, INC.,

PETITION FOR A WRIT OF CERTIORARI TO THE UNITED STATES COURT OF APPEALS FOR THE DISTRICT OF COLUMBIA CIRCUIT

REUBEN B. ROBERTSON III
ALAN B. MORRISON
Suite 700
2000 P Street NW
Washington, D.C. 20036
(202) 785-3704
Attorneys for Petitioner

Ralph Nader, the plaintiff and appellee in the proceedings below, petitions for a writ of certiorari to review the judgment of the United States Court of Appeals for the District of Columbia Circuit in this case.

INDEX

CITATIONS

Cases:

Statutes:

Civil Aeronautics Board Orders, Regulations and Reports:

OPINIONS BELOW

The opinion of the court of appeals (Appendix A, *infra*) is reported at 512 F.2d 527.
The decision of the district court (Appendix B, *infra*) is reported at 365 F. Supp. 128.

JURISDICTION

The judgment of the court of appeals was entered on May 2, 1975. A timely petition for rehearing, with suggestion for rehearing en banc, was denied by order of the court of appeals entered on June 23, 1975. (Appendix C, *infra.*). The jurisdiction of this Court is invoked under 28 U.S.C. § 1254(1). See *Morse* v. *United States*, 270 U.S. 151 (1926); *Department of Banking* v. *Pink*, 317 U.S. 264, 266 (1942); *United States* v. Healy, 376 U.S. 75, 78 (1964).

QUESTION PRESENTED

Whether, notwithstanding a statutory provision preserving common law remedies, the Federal Aviation Act requires that the Civil Aeronautics Board be given the opportunity retroactively to approve fraudulent misrepresentations by an airline that would otherwise constitute actionable torts under state common law, with the effect of extinguishing any private right of action arising form such misrepresentations.

STATUTES INVOLVED

Sections 411 and 1106 of the Federal Aviation Act of 1958, as amended, 49 U.S.C. §§ 1381, 150-6, provide:

> Section 411. The [Civil Aeronautics] Board may, upon its own initiative or upon complaint by any air carrier, foreign air carrier, or ticket agent, if it considers that such action by it would be in the interest of the public, investigate and determine whether any air carrier, foreign air carrier, or ticket agent has been or is engaged in unfair or deceptive practices or unfair methods of competition in air transportation or the sale thereof. If the Board shall find, after notice and hearing, that such air carrier, foreign air carrier, or ticket agent is engaged in such unfair or deceptive practices or unfair methods of competition,it shall order such air carrier, foreign air carrier, or ticket agent to cease and desist from such practices or methods of competition.
>
> Section 1106. Nothing contained in this Act shall in any way abridge or alter the remedies now existing at common law or by statute, but the provisions of this Act are in addition to such remedies.

STATEMENT

A. The Facts

*   *   *

B. Proceedings Below

*   *   *

REASONS FOR GRANTING THE WRIT

1. The decision below disrupts the traditional allocation of functions between the courts and the Civil Aeronautics Board, both in the adjudication of private disputes under state law and in the invocation of statutory powers to regulate air transportation, contrary to the Federal Aviation Act and to decisions of this Court.

Since this Court's decision in *American Airlines* v. *North American Airlines*, 351 U.S. 79 (1956), it has been clear that the powers of the Civil Aeronautics Board under Section 411 of the Federal Aviation Act are to be exercised only as a means of vindicating the public interest, and not to adjudicate the rights and liabilities of parties in private disputes. As Judge Fahy correctly noted in his dissent, Section 411 "looks only to the future cessation of practices determined by the Board to be unfair or deceptive," having nothing whatever to do with remedies "for past tortious conduct of a carrier injurious to an individual." (App. A, *infra*, p. A51.) The courts of law, rather than the regulatory agencies charged with the protection of the overall public interest, are available for the resolution of private legal rights against air carriers.

The court of appeals has sharply departed from that rule. Its holding that damages may not be awarded against a regulated airline for its past tortious acts, without first referring the matter to CAB for a ruling as to whether the conduct is deemed unfair or deceptive under Section 411, will deeply affect the historic relationships between federal agencies and courts throughout the nation—not only the federal courts, but state and local courts as well. The decision effectively withdraws from judicial bodies at every level their traditional role in adjudicating private tort claims under both the common law and specific statutes, and reassigns an important part of that job to a federal administrative agency. Yet the circuit court never mentioned and apparently did not even consider the effect its decision would have on these important functional divisions of responsibilities as between the state and federal courts and the federal regulatory agencies.

Moreover the court of appeals has seriously misconstrued the Board's role under Section 411 as illuminated by this Court's *North American Airlines* decision. The existence of unfair or deceptive practices in the airline industry does not automatically trigger investigations, cease and desist proceedings, or other adjudications before the Board; only when the Board—*not* the court of appeals—makes a specific determination that, in the language of Section 411, it is "in the interest of the public", is the Board authorized to exercise those powers. The decision below simply ignores that it is the agency's duty to decide whether and when these powers should be invoked, in effect forcing from the Board an adjudication of whether certain carrier practices should be condemned or approved on an industry-wide basis.

The CAB has long recognized that intentional overbooking may be inherently deceptive and misleading to passengers. It has studiously refrained, however, from finding that the public interest requires it to attempt the detailed regulation and control of overbooking or other airline reservations practices under Section 411. Instead, it has sought to deal with the problem through rulemaking by focusing on the treatment of passengers when oversales occur and by requiring prompt, effective and adequate monetary compensation, in the expectation that this would stimulate the carriers to improve their own reservations systems. That this may not have proved to be a very successful way of dealing with the problem still does not justify the court of appeals in intruding into an issue of regulatory strategy—when to use Section 411—by forcing the Board to determine the merits of a particular private dispute.

2. The decision that the Board may retroactively immunize common law frauds from civil liability is unprecedented and contrary to the statutory limitations on that agency's powers.

In *Hughes Tool Co.* v. *Trans World Airlines*, 409 U.S. 363 (1973), the Court held that a private antitrust suit for damages could not proceed where the CAB had asserted jurisdiction over and actually approved the transactions involved. The court of appeals in this litigation has gone far beyond the holding in *Hughes Tool*, however, in asserting that the Board not only has the power to approve airline conduct and thus insulate it from civil liability, but that it may do so *retroactively*—after the injury has already occurred. The court of appeals recognized that its holding on this point involved a fundamental "alteration of the common law," (App. A, *infra*, p. A31) yet it was unable to cite any helpful precedent. The doctrine of retroactive agency immunization of torts is indeed unknown to the common law; moreover it seriously misconstrues the CAB's powers and conflicts directly with the preservation of remedies that is explicitly provided for in Section 1106 of the Aviation Act.

Certainly this is not a situation in which the award of damages in a civil action would inherently conflict with the agency's exercise of its jurisdiction and powers. As Judge Fahy correctly pointed out in his dissent, whatever the courts might decide as to particular claims of fraudulent misrepresentation for past conduct, the Board remains free to exercise its statutory authority in accordance with the policies of the Aviation Act. (App. A, *infra*, p. A53.) It is not a situation such as was found in *Ricci* v. *Chicago Mercantile Exchange*, 409 U.S. 289 (1973), where there was a possible clash between two major federal regimes—in that case the Sherman Act and the Commodity Exchange Act—and where resolution of an essential issue of fact within the agency's special competence might materially aid the court in resolving that clash. Here, as Judge Fahy stated, the issue is simply whether the plaintiff was the victim of a common law tort, a matter well within the competence of courts to decide.

Finally, it is clear that this is not a case like *Hughes Tool* in which the agency has already acted so as to preempt any private damage claims. The Board has quite plainly taken no action to sanction any airlines' conduct or grant immunity for it from civil liability. Instead its consistent approach has been to *avoid* assertion of its regulatory powers over the airlines' reservations practices, leaving that field open to what it hoped would be informed and enlightened management discretion. At the same time, the Board has repeatedly made clear its intention to preserve the common law remedies of persons who are denied boarding, as an alternative to the optional liquidated damages remedy provided in its Part 250 regulations. Thus the choice by Mr. Nader to pursue his common law damage claim for fraudulent misrepresentation by Allegheny, and the ruling in his favor by the trial court, were in no way in conflict with CAB policy or regulations but indeed were entirely consonant with them.

The question presented on this petition is whether the court of appeals was correct in reversing the trial court's judgment that a common law tort had occurred, and remanding solely to allow the regulatory agency an opportunity to extinguish petitioner's right of action retroactively. Even assuming, as the court of appeals did, that the Board could ever approve common law misrepresentations, the notion that it could do so to immunize an airline's past misconduct is plainly wrong. Certainly nothing in *Hughes Tool* or any other decision of this Court lends support to that holding. It is, moreover, squarely in conflict with Section 1106 of the Aviation Act, which specifically preserves common law remedies so long as they are not fundamentally repugnant to the duties of the CAB.

CONCLUSION

A central purpose of the Aviation Act is the elimination of deceptive practices in the airline industry. Yet the circuit court's decision turns the Act on its head by erecting an enormous new barrier to common law recovery for those very practices. The court's holding that the CAB's regulatory jurisdiction may be invoked to extinguish retroactively a common law right of action is wholly unprecedented, and in plain conflict with the statutory preservation of common law remedies, as well as the CAB's own regulatory pronouncements. This sweeping decision, which embraces principles of law that were never briefed or argued, not only disrupts traditional relationships between state and federal courts and agencies and interferes with common law remedies, but it imposes additional, potentially enormous burdens on the agency (or agencies) which will be affected by it. And neither Allegheny nor the CAB—the agency on which this mandatory funnelling of every federal and state case arguably within its sphere of authority would be imposed—ever suggested or endorsed the result reached by the court of appeals. All of these factors, we submit, demonstrate the need for review of the case by this Court.

Respectfully submitted,

REUBEN B. ROBERTSON III
ALAN B. MORRISON
Suite 700
2000 P Street, NW
Washington, D.C. 20036
(202) 785-3704
Attorneys for Petitioner

September 22, 1975

DOCUMENT #39:
OPPOSITION TO PETITION FOR WRIT OF CERTIORARI

Allegheny, of course, opposed plaintiff's petition for certiorari. In its Opposition to the Petition (Document #39), Allegheny attempted to change the focus of the case by characterizing the questions presented as administrative law issues of "finality" and primary jurisdiction. First, since the Court of Appeals remanded the case for further fact finding by the District Court and the CAB, it would be premature for the Supreme Court to review the matter until a final order is entered. Second, the concept of primary jurisdiction requires that the CAB have the opportunity to rule on whether Allegheny's allegedly tortious conduct was permissible under its regulatory scheme. The latter argument is supported in Allegheny's Statement of the Facts where it points out that the CAB, in examining the problem of overbooking, has chosen not to prohibit it, and expressly rejected a proposed rule that would have required airlines to inform passengers that they could be bumped from overbooked flights.

In its first argument, Allegheny outlines the nature of the factual findings still to be made. The District Court was asked by the Court of Appeals to determine:

—whether Allegheny's operations manual established priority boarding rules;

—if so, what these rules were and whether they had been properly interpreted in this case; and

—whether the testimony of Allegheny's ticket agent was credible in light of conflicting documentary evidence.

Allegheny then discusses the necessity of allowing an agency, charged with regulating an industry, the first opportunity to rule on any issue within its regulatory domain. The CAB has a statutory mandate to prohibit unfair or deceptive practices in air transportation. The question of whether Allegheny's policy of nondisclosure to the public of its overbooking practices is actionable should therefore go to the CAB first. The Court of Appeals apparently recognized this requirement when it stayed the remanded District Court proceeding until the CAB had completed its then current study of the issue. The result of that study, together with the new fact finding required of the district court, would complete the record and could moot the case. For both of these reasons, the lack of finality and the possibility of mootness, Allegheny argues that the Court should not grant plaintiff's petition and should not review the decision of the Court of Appeals.

Allegheny further argues that the Court should not grant the petition because plaintiff failed to show "special and important" reasons to review the case. The decision of the Court of Appeals did not depart from the norm of judicial proceedings. In fact, it was "consistent with well established principles of primary jurisdiction." Allegheny also points out that it is well established that agencies, acting within their delegated authority, may change the common law through their rulings. While it is clear that agencies may do so prospectively, the question was raised by plaintiff as to whether they may do so retroactively. Allegheny answers that they can and cites various cases in support of its argument. Allegheny also suggests that the validity of nondisclosure of overbooking was established in a CAB proceeding *before* the action challenged in plaintiffs' suit. Therefore, the ruling has no retroactive effect. Thus there are no special reasons for the Court to review this issue.

IN THE

Supreme Court of the United States

OCTOBER TERM, 1975

No. 75-455

RALPH NADER,
Petitioner,

v.

ALLEGHENY AIRLINES, INC.,
Respondent.

On Petition for a Writ of Certiorari to the United States Court of Appeals for the District of Columbia Circuit

---

BRIEF FOR RESPONDENT IN OPPOSITION

FRANK F. ROBERSON
WILLIAM A. BRADFORD, JR.

815 Connecticut Avenue, N.W.
Washington, D.C. 20006
(202) 331-4500

Of Counsel: *Attorneys for Respondent*

HOGAN & HARTSON
815 Connecticut Avenue, N.W.
Washington, D.C. 20006
October 24, 1975

WILSON · EPES PRINTING CO., · **RE 7-6002** · WASHINGTON, D. C. 20001

INDEX

CITATIONS

Questions Presented

Whether the judgment of the court of appeals is final so as to permit review by this Court.

Whether the court of appeals has deviated from well established principles of the doctrine of primary jurisdiction by deferring petitioner's tort claim until the agency statutorily charged with regulating the allegedly tortious activities has spoken on the permissibility of the activities.

STATUTES INVOLVED

* * *

STATEMENT

A. The Facts

* * *

B. The Proceedings Below

* * *

ARGUMENT

I. The Judgment of the Court of Appeals Sought to be Reviewed is not Final, and There is no Compelling Reason for Premature Review

As the preceding Statement demonstrates, the judgment of the court of appeals sought to be reviewed by the Petition is not final. The court of appeals' opinion calls for further proceedings that may entail the taking of additional evidence, both at the district court and at the CAB, before Nader's rights are finally determined. According to the standards for review applied by this Court, the court of appeals' interim judgment should not be reviewed and the Petition for a Writ of Certiorari should be denied.

An examination of the directions of the court of appeals on remand reveals the various proceedings yet to occur in this litigation. The outcomes of those proceedings might moot the issue that the Court is asked to review and render advisory any decision the Court might reach if it grants this Petition. The examination will also reveal that there are conflicting factual contentions that remain to be resolved, not only by the district court, but also by the CAB whose expertise the court of appeals has ordered should be brought to bear on the deceptiveness, *vel non*, of Allegheny's overbooking practices, the issue at the heart of the present dispute.

The district court was directed by the court of appeals to resolve three factual issues, by reopening the trial record, if necessary, on Nader's claim under the antidiscrimination provision of the Federal Aviation Act. The district court was asked to resolve: whether Allegheny's own operations manual properly established denied boarding priority rules, as it is required to do by CAB regulations; what those rules were and whether they were properly interpreted by Allegheny's agent; and whether the agent's testimony was credible in light of certain documentary evidence. (App. A24.) While it might be contended that these factual issues do not bear directly on Nader's misrepresentation claim, they do go to the heart of Nader's claimed injury—his denied boarding. Resolution of the issues might also affect Allegheny's defense to the imposition of punitive damages on the misrepresentation claim that the district court was directed to consider, *i.e.*, whether Allegheny reasonably believed that its overbooking practices had been approved by the CAB. (App. A48–49.) Moreover, the issues are certainly ones that an appellate court would want resolved before rendering a judgment on review.

A second reason for the unreviewability of the court of appeals' judgment is the nature of the stay imposed by the court on the proceedings below. The court of appeals, in an "application of the principles of primary jurisdiction" (App. A32), directed the district court to defer further proceedings on Nader's misrepresentation claim until the CAB had spoken on the issue of whether Allegheny's failure affirmatively to disclose its overbooking practices was deceptive or unfair. (App. A50.) After noting that the CAB in 1967 had ruled that airlines *need not disclose* the overbooked condition of their flights to prospective passengers (App. A10), the court found that the CAB was again considering the fairness and reasonableness of airlines' overbooking practices, that an administrative law judge had initially found the overbooking practices not to be deceptive, and that this decision was on review by the full CAB. (App. A33–A37.) It has been pointed out *supra* at p. 6 that the CAB is now in the process of insuring that the issue raised in this litigation will be specifically considered in the Board's proceedings.

In asking the district court to await the CAB's decision on the deceptiveness *vel non* of Allegheny's overbooking practices before continuing its own proceedings, the court of appeals was honoring the primary jurisdiction doctrine, which holds that "a court should not act upon subject matter that is peculiarly within the agency's specialized field without taking into account what the agency has to offer, for otherwise parties who are subject to the agency's continuous regulation may become the victims of uncoordinated and conflicting requirements." 3 K. Davis, Administrative Law Treatise, § 19.01 at 5 (1958). By granting the instant Petition, which seeks a ruling on the relationship between the courts and the CAB on the matter of airlines' overbooking practices, *before* the CAB has definitively spoken on those practices and *before* the district court has considered the CAB's expertise, the Court would be ignoring the doctrine of primary jurisdiction and would, perforce, be violating the doctrine of finality of judgments, which will be discussed more fully below.

A third reason for the unreviewability of the court of appeals' judgment is that the outcomes of further proceedings before the CAB and the district court contemplated by the court of appeals' decision may moot the issue for which review is sought by the Petition and, consequently, render advisory any opinion that the Court might reach if it granted the Petition. . . .

In the instant case, not only has the court of appeals directed further litigation on unresolved factual issues, from which further appeals would lie, but the administrative proceedings to which the district court was directed to show deference have yet to be completed. When the administrative proceedings are complete they may moot entirely the issue that the Court is being asked to review. Furthermore, the Petition mentions no extraordinary reasons for disregarding the doctrine of finality and granting premature review. Accordingly, the Petition for Writ of Certiorari should be denied as seeking review of a judgment that is not final.

II. The Decision Below was Correct and Did Not Deviate From Well Established Principles of Primary Jurisdiction.

Far from being without precedent as the petitioner intimates (Petition at 18–19), the ruling of the court of appeals that Allegheny's policies may be immune from private damage actions if found by the CAB to be necessary to its regulatory scheme is consistent with well established principles of primary jurisdiction.

Petitioner argues that there is no precedent for the court of appeals' holding that Allegheny's overbooking practices may not as a matter of law constitute fraudulent misrepresentation if found by the CAB not to be deceptive or unfair pursuant to § 411 of the Federal Aviation Act. However, Petitioner does not, because he cannot, contend that the CAB is without power prospectively to immunize airlines from private actions that are inconsistent with the regulatory scheme. Notwithstanding § 1106 of the Federal Aviation Act (text of Petition, p. 3) preserving common law remedies, a contention that the CAB may not prospectively immunize is untenable in view of *Texas & Pac. Ry. Co.* v. *Abilene Cotton Oil Co.*, 204 U.S. 426 (1907), and its progeny, and *Hughes Tool Co.* v. *Trans World Airlines, Inc.*, 409 U.S. 363 (1973).

*   *   *

The question, then, is whether the law has permitted regulatory agencies to do retroactively what they indisputably can do prospectively. The answer to that question must be yes in order to avoid the anomaly described by this Court when it held, in *Pan American World Airways, Inc.* v. *United States*, 371 U.S. 296 (1963), that the CAB could *retroactively immunize* activity within its § 411 jurisdiction—the same section that is invoked in the instant case—from the antitrust laws. In dismissing a suit against regulated airlines and others charging that their activities prior to the 1938 adoption of the Civil Aeronautics Act violated the antitrust laws, this Court held that the CAB, and not the courts, should retroactively approve or condemn the challenged practices:

> It would be strange, indeed, if a division of territories or an allocation of routes which met the requirement of the "public interest" as defined in § 2 were held to be antitrust violations. It would also be odd to conclude that an affiliation between a common carrier and an air carrier that passed muster under § 408 should run afoul of the antitrust laws. [*Id.* at 309.]

Manifestly, it wold likewise be "strange" and "odd" if overbooking practices found by the CAB to be within its regulatory scheme, lawful, and in the public interest were held to subject the airlines to damages in common law actions.

If a regulatory agency has the power within its implementing statute to approve certain practices of the industry it regulates, as the CAB without question does with respect to airlines' overbooking practices (App. A5–A14), this Court has held that the courts must defer to such agency approval and resultant immunity even if the alleged injury caused by the challenged practices occurred *before* the practices had been submitted to the agency for approval. *Far East Conf.* v. *United States*, 342 U.S. 570 (1952); *U.S. Nav. Co., Inc.* v. *Cunard S.S. Co., Inc.*, 284 U.S. 474, 486–87 (1932). Such deferral must *a fortiori* occur if the challenged practices, as has arguably occurred in the instant case, have been referred to the agency for consideration, but the agency has not yet ruled. *Laveson* v. *Trans World Airlines*, 471 F.2d 76, 81 (3d Cir. 1972).

Turning finally to petitioner's argument (Petition at 14–18) that deferral to the CAB is improper because his claim is a "private dispute" seeking damages, that issue, too, has well-reasoned precedent supporting the court of appeals' decision. In *Laveson* v. *Trans World Airlines, supra*, a "private dispute" between a passenger and an airline, the plaintiffs argued as does petitioner here that because their suit was solely for antitrust law treble damages, which the CAB has no power to award, the deferral to the agency for its possible immunization of the challenged activities was improper. The court rejected that argument, quoting from the rationale of *S.S.W., Inc.* v. *Air Transport Association of America*, 191 F.2d 658 (D.C. Cir. 1951), *cert. denied*, 343 U.S. 955 (1952):

> The fact remains that, regardless of the particular remedy sought, the subject matter of this action falls within the regulatory jurisdiction of the CAB. If courts fail to apply the primary jurisdiction doctrine in suits for damages, "we might [still] have the [spectacle] of courts throughout the country enjoining practices as violations of the antitrust laws even though the agency specifically authorized to deal with them has determined *or may decide*, subject to judicial review, that such practices serve the interests of the national air transportation policy. [*Laveson* v. *Trans World Airlines, supra*, at 83 (emphasis added).]

The same "private action" argument against deferral to the CAB was rejected in *Price* v. *Trans World Airlines, Inc.*, 481 F.2d 844, 848 (9th Cir. 1973).

CONCLUSION

The Petition should be denied because it seeks review of a judgment that is not final and that contemplates further proceedings, both before the CAB and the district court, which may moot the issue raised by the Petition. Moreover, the judgment of the court of appeals is correct and follows well established principles of the doctrine of primary jurisdiction. Finally, petitioner has failed to show any conflict between the circuits or other factors that would warrant review of the decision below. Accordingly, this Court should deny the Petition for Certiorari.

Respectfully submitted,

Frank F. Roberson
William A. Bradford, Jr.
815 Connecticut Avenue,. N.W.
Washington, D.C. 20006
(202) 331-4500

Of Counsel:

Attorneys for Respondent

HOGAN & HARTSON
815 Connecticut Avenue, N.W.
Washington, D.C. 20006

October 24, 1975

DOCUMENT #40:
PETITIONER'S SUPREME COURT BRIEF

Nader was granted a writ of certiorari on November 11, 1975. Pursuant to SCR 25, he had forty-five days from the order granting the writ to file with the Clerk forty copies of Petitioner's Supreme Court Brief (Document #40) on the merits. SCR 33 provides general details as to the form of documents which are to be filed with the Court, while SCR 24 deals specifically with the form of briefs on the merits.

The brief must contain the following items (in this order):
—the question(s) presented for review;
—a list of all parties to the proceeding in the court whose judgment is to be reviewed;
—a table of contents and of authorities;
—citations to opinions or judgments of the courts below;
—a concise statement of the basis of jurisdiction;
—a verbatim statement of the constitutional, statutory, regulatory, treaty, or ordinance
provisions (with citations) that are involved in the case;
—a concise statement of the case;

—a summary of the arguments;
—the arguments; and
—the conclusion.

Briefs are generally limited to fifty pages (SCR 33) and must be "compact, logically arranged with proper headings, concise and free from burdensome, irrelevant, immaterial, and scandalous matter." (SCR 24.6)

Nader's brief on the merits (Document #40) is limited in scope to the question raised in his petition for the writ of certiorari (Document #38). He asks whether, notwithstanding a provision in the Federal Aviation Act which preserves common law remedies, the CAB was empowered by that Act to approve, retroactively, fraudulent misrepresentations by an airline that would otherwise be actionable as torts, with the effect of extinguishing any private right of action to redress them. Again, it should be noted how this very narrow and focused question differs from the broad issues to be derived from the allegations of the complaint and even from the questions presented for review to the Court of Appeals.

It should also be noted that CCAG, a plaintiff in the District Court and an appellee in the Court of Appeals, is *not* a party in the Supreme Court. This is primarily due to a strategic decision made by plaintiffs that the CCAG claims either were not strong enough to be successful or would otherwise dilute the critical argument of the bumped passenger.

Nader lays out in his brief the required preliminary material together with his Statement, including the facts and descriptions of the decisions of the District Court and Court of Appeals. He characterizes the Court of Appeals decision concerning misrepresentation as "imposing a solution that had not been suggested in any brief or at oral argument by any party or amicus, including the Board." (Br. pg. 17) The solution of the Court of Appeals was to remand the case to the District Court and to stay proceedings there until the CAB decided whether the failure to disclose to the public Allegheny's overbooking policies was a deceptive or unfair practice under the Act. If not, according to the Court of Appeals, the practice would be protected and would be insulated from common law tort liability. This was, according to Nader, despite the plain language of the very Act in question which called for its remedies to be *in addition to*, and not in substitution for, common law remedies. Moreover, it was clear that the CAB had never expressly approved overbooking and nondisclosure and, therefore, not only did the Court of Appeals misread the statute but also it provided for the *retroactive* insulation of tortious conduct.

Nader then provides a Summary of Argument. This is a very important part of the brief, serving several practical purposes. First, it capsulizes the arguments and states them, without the citation of any supporting authorities, in their most concise form. This gives the Court a clear indication of the direction to be taken and helps the reader in following the more complex positions contained in the argument itself. Second, it allows a judge who has not read, or who has not recently read, the brief to quickly determine the party's position on the issues. In this case, there is only one argument being made, and Nader summarizes it by stating that the Court of Appeals:

—"misapprehended the manner in which the CAB has chosen to deal with airline oversales" by equating conscious nonintervention with approval;
—misreads the intent of the Act to preserve common law remedies;
—misreads the Act, which was intended to prevent deceptions, into a basis for approving misrepresentations; and
—disrupts the balance between the traditional roles of courts and administrative agencies.

Nader's Argument is divided into the same four subparts as indicated in the Summary. The first argument, that the CAB has never sanctioned deliberate nondisclosure of overbooking and has consistently acted to preserve all common law remedies, is largely an historical and chronological statement of various proceedings in the CAB. The remedy imposed by the Court of Appeals, which included a requirement of agency action on the issue, was an unwarranted invasion of the agency's discretionary authority.

In Nader's second argument, he restates Allegheny's position that the mere existence of statutory authority to determine deceptive and unfair practices pre-empts the courts from adjudicating claims of common law misrepresentation involving companies subject to CAB jurisdiction. This argument was not accepted by the Court of Appeals. Nader believes that this refusal comports with the history of the Federal Aviation Act and with its terms (which preserve common law remedies). The CAB's authority under the Act was to apply only to issues of broad public concern and not to every potentially unfair or deceptive activity. Allegheny's interpretation of the statute would involve the CAB in every case of alleged deception, no matter how trivial.

Nevertheless, the decision of the Court of Appeals would have the effect of inserting the CAB into all claims of misrepresentation. The majority of the Court of Appeals held that a claim of misrepresentation against an airline must first be litigated at the CAB to determine whether the practice is unfair or deceptive. If it is found not to be, the claimant would be foreclosed from pursuing a remedy through the courts. While the majority realized that its decision involved "a fundamental alteration of the common law," it indicated that some-times the purpose of a federal statute involves such an alteration. This case, with a uniform air transport system in issue, was such a situation. Nader agreed with the general principle that a federal statute might modify the common law, but took issue with the position that this was such a case.

Nader's third argument involves the question of whether the CAB has the power, retroactively, to affect private relations. The CAB has been authorized to inquire whether particular practices are within the public interest and, if not, to order a carrier to cease and desist from their use. Nothing in the Act authorizes the CAB to approve fraudulent misrepre-sentations which are otherwise actionable at common law. The question of overbooking, which may properly be an issue before the CAB, is distinct from deception about that policy, which is an issue for the courts. What is even worse in this case is that the Court of Appeals purports to give the CAB the authority to insulate such tortious conduct *after* it has occurred. There is nothing in the Act, argues Nader, authorizing such a broad sweep of administrative power.

His final argument is that any doubts as to statutory interpretation should be resolved against the decision of the Court of Appeals because that decision disrupts the long standing allocation of functions between the courts and the CAB. The CAB has historically dealt with issues of public interest and not with the resolution of private claims. The courts, on the other hand, have been charged with protecting individual rights, not the public interest. The decision of the Court of Appeals casts upon the agency the power to affect private rights by retroactively insulating actions which would otherwise be tortious and withdraws from the courts the ability to redress the wrong. The decision also thrusts the courts into the policy making arena previously reserved to the agencies by allowing the courts to order an agency to decide a policy issue it previously had declined to resolve.

IN THE

Supreme Court of the United States

OCTOBER TERM, 1975

_____

No. 75-455

_____

RALPH NADER,
Petitioner,

v.

ALLEGHENY AIRLINES, INC.,
Respondent.

_____

ON A WRIT OF CERTIORARI
TO THE UNITED STATES COURT OF APPEALS
FOR THE DISTRICT OF COLUMBIA CIRCUIT

_____

BRIEF FOR PETITIONER

REUBEN B. ROBERTSON, III
ALAN B. MORRISON
LINDA F. DONALDSON

Suite 700
2000 P Street, N.W.
Washington, D.C. 20036
(202) 785-3704

Attorneys for Petitioner

ABS DUPLICATORS, INC.–1732 Eye Street, N.W.–Washington, D.C.–296-5537

INDEX

TABLE OF AUTHORITIES

Cases:

Statutes:

CAB Orders, Notices and Regulations:

OPINIONS BELOW

The opinion of the court of appeals is reported at 512 F.2d 527 and is set forth as Appendix A to the petition for a writ of certiorari. (Pet. App. A 1–60.)* The decision of the district court is reported at 365 F.Supp. 128 and is set forth as Appendix B to the petition. (Pet. App. B 1–11.)

JURISDICTION

The judgment of the court of appeals was entered on May 2, 1975. A timely petition for rehearing, with suggestion for rehearing en banc, was denied by the court of appeals on June 23, 1975. (Pet. App. C 1–2.) The petition for a writ of certiorari was filed on September 22, 1975, and was granted on November 11, 1975, with Mr. Justice Douglas taking no part in the consideration or decision of the matter. The jurisdiction of this Court is conferred by 28 U.S.C. § 1254(1).

QUESTION PRESENTED

Whether, notwithstanding a statutory provision preserving common law remedies, the Federal Aviation Act requires that the Civil Aeronautics Board be given the opportunity retroactively to approve fraudulent misrepresentations by an airline that would otherwise constitute actionable torts under state common law, with the effect of extinguishing any private right of action arising from such practices.

STATUTES INVOLVED

*   *   *

STATEMENT

A. The Facts

*   *   *

B. The Decision of the District Court

*   *   *

C. The Decision of the Court of Appeals

*   *   *

SUMMARY OF ARGUMENT

The decision below is premised on several fundamental misconceptions. First, it misapprehends the manner in which the CAB has chosen to deal with airline oversales by viewing a policy of deliberate non-intervention as positive approval of all practices adopted by the airlines. Second, it reads into the interstices of the Federal Aviation Act an intent to abrogate a common law claim of misrepresentation, despite the fact that the tort claim is perfectly consistent with the Act and is preserved by a savings clause. Third, it misreads section 411 of the Act, which was designed to prevent deception, and thereby converts it into a basis for approving fraudulent misrepresentations. And, finally, it disrupts the traditional functional balance between federal regulatory agencies and common law courts.

The CAB has on a number of occasions reviewed the problem of airline oversales but, contrary to the opinion of the circuit court, has never sanctioned deliberate, concealed overbooking. The Board has consistently adhered to the view that close, direct federal supervision of carrier reservations systems would entail more drawbacks than potential benefits. It has thus avoided exercising the full extent of its powers under section 411 to ban all overbooking, instead seeking through its regulations to provide some degree of compensation for passengers injured by oversales, and to provide a variety of incentives for the airlines to bring about improvements in their own systems. In taking such actions the CAB has consistently cautioned the carriers against deceiving the public in connection with their reservation practices, and has consistently sought to preserve the rights of persons injured as a result of dishonored confirmed reservations to pursue their remedies under the common law, as an alternative to the acceptance of denied boarding compensation as liquidated damages.

The circuit court also erred in assuming that national uniformity is so essential in matters involving airline reservations practices that the common law remedies for deliberate nondisclosure of overbooking must be overridden or altered, notwithstanding the express savings provision of section 1106 of the Aviation Act. In fact, the CAB itself has consistently rejected the notion that uniform practices are required in the area of reservations, and has permitted carriers great latitude in determining what kind of reservation systems to offer the public. Certainly any such interest as may exist in having uniform air carrier reservations systems does not meet the test of absolute repugnancy for abridgment or alteration of common law remedies, as established by this Court.

Even more fundamentally, the appellate court concluded that the CAB has power to approve fraudulent misrepresentations, and thus insulate them from tort liability, and that the CAB could do so on a retroactive basis. However, there is nothing in the language, purpose or history of the Aviation Act to support that conclusion, and indeed all of the evidence points to the conclusion that a statute basically intended to assure the public an effective air transportation system cannot be the basis for denying a passenger his day in court.

Finally, the decision of the court of appeals will result in administrative chaos, since every tortious misrepresentation case brought in a state or federal court will have to be funneled through the CAB for a preliminary determination. This will surely impose an unnecessary and inappropriate burden on the CAB, requiring it to proceed in countless cases of a routine nature. The decision thus constitutes a fundamental reallocation of responsibility between the CAB (and presumably other federal agencies) on the one hand and the state and federal courts on the other. Whatever the wisdom of such a reallocation might be, it is a change that can be dictated only by Congress and not by the courts.

ARGUMENT

I. THE CIVIL AERONAUTICS BOARD HAS NEVER SANCTIONED DELIBERATE NONDISCLOSURE OF OVERBOOKING BY RESPONDENT, AND IT HAS CONSISTENTLY ACTED TO PRESERVE ALL COMMON LAW REMEDIES OF OVERSOLD PASSENGERS.

*   *   *

II. THERE IS NOTHING EITHER EXPLICIT OR INHERENT IN THE AVIATION ACT THAT IS INCOMPATIBLE WITH ALLOWING PASSENGERS TO PURSUE THEIR COMMON LAW REMEDIES FOR DELIBERATE NONDISCLOSURE OF OVERBOOKING

In the court of appeals, respondent argued that the existence of section 411 was sufficient to oust the courts of jurisdiction to adjudicate claims for common law misrepresentation involving companies subject to CAB regulation. Thus, according to respondent, since the CAB had the power to ban overbooking as "unfair or deceptive" under section 411 of the Aviation Act, and even though it had not done so, petitioner's common law remedies for fraudulent misrepresentation were abrogated, and he was left without a remedy other than the denied boarding compensation which he had declined. The court of appeals rejected that broad claim of immunity, relying on the history and purpose of section 411 and the savings provisions of section 1106, which it found would have to be ignored in order to sustain respondent's position. (Pet. App. A 28–29.)

In so holding, the court of appeals was plainly correct. Initially it should be noted that nothing in section 411—or any other provision of the Aviation Act for that matter—suggests that the powers granted to the CAB were intended to modify in any way traditional controls over deceptive practices under state common law or statute. See *American Airlines* v. *North American Airlines*, 351 U.S. 79, 83 (1956); *cf., Polansky* v. *Trans World Airlines, Inc.*, 523 F.2d 332, 337 (3d Cir. 1975); *Holiday Magic, Inc.* v. *Warren*, 357 F. Supp. 20, 28 (D.Wis. 1973), *vacated on other grounds*, 497 F.2d 607 (7th Cir. 1974).

Section 411 was modeled on section 5 of the Federal Trade Commission Act, 15 U.S.C. § 45, as amended by the Wheeler-Lea Amendments of 1938. See *American Airlines* v. *North American Airlines*, 351 U.S. 79, 82 (1956); Hearings on Regulation of Transportation of Passengers and Property By Aircraft, Before A Subcommittee of the Committee on Interstate Commerce, U.S. Senate, 75th Cong., 1st Sess. 514 (1937) (Statement of E.S. Gorell, Prsident of Air Transport Association of America). Since section 5 was intended to provide new and additional administrative remedies, not to assign to one small agency in Washington the exclusive role of determining for all purposes what is and what is not deceptive, *Federal Trade Commission* v. *Klesner*, 280 U.S. 19 (1929), section 411 must be construed in that light as well. This is particularly appropriate in view of section 1106 which provides that "Nothing contained in this Act shall in any way abridge or alter the remedies now existing at common law or by statute, but the provisions of this Act are in addition to such remedies." 49 U.S.C. § 1506. To rule that section 411 automatically pre-empts all common law remedies involving unfair or deceptive practices would be to override section 1106, and this the court of appeals correctly refused to do.

That refusal was appropriate for another reason as well. This Court has construed section 411 to apply only to those practices which the CAB decides are of broad public interest and not to every activity which might arguably be unfair or deceptive. *American Airlines* v. *North American Airlines, supra.* To interpret section 411 in the manner suggested by respondent would require the CAB to concern itself with all manner of trivial issues in order to assure that section 411's prohibition extended to any conduct arguably within its ambit. Such a position would run counter to the broad public interest purpose of section 411.

Nonetheless, the majority of the court of appeals ruled that a damage claimant may not maintain a common law action against an airline for intentional, tortious misrepresentations, without first litigating before the CAB to determine whether the conduct is deemed "unfair or deceptive" under section 411. Thus, at least where a CAB-regulated company is concerned, the common-law standards of liability for fraud and deceit developed over the course of hundreds of years have been modified by the addition of a new, threshold test derived from federal legislation—namely, whether there has been a violation of section 411. If no such violation is found, it was held, the common law action would necessarily fail and the remedies otherwise available would be extinguished. (Pet. App. A31.)

The court below seems to have correctly recognized that its holding involves a fundamental "alteration of the common law." (*Id.*) Indeed on its face it presents a square conflict with the savings provisions of section 1106, but the court held that section 1106 could not be read literally and must be examined in light of the remainder of the Aviation Act to determine whether the particular common law action survives, relying on *Texas & Pacific Ry. Co.* v. *Abiline Cotton Oil Co.*, 204 U.S. 426 (1907). (Pet. App. A31.) Petitioner does not dispute the general proposition that in some specific instances the overriding purpose and operation of a federal regulatory statute will be so inconsistent with the continuing vitality of a common law remedy that the remedy cannot survive, notwithstanding a provision such as section 1106; his position is simply that the facts of this case do not place it within the narrow group of cases to which that proposition applies.

The fundamental flaw in the approach of the majority below is that it focuses on the refusal of this Court in *Texas & Pacific Ry. Co., supra,* to apply a savings clause similar to section 1106, but fails to examine the special circumstances and reasons that led to that result. In that case a shipper sued for overcharges, claiming that the railroad had exacted an unreasonable rate in violation of the common law. The rate in question, however, was filed as required by the Interstate Commerce Act; the carrier was required to charge it and no other rate until it had been disapproved by the ICC or a new tariff had been accepted. Therefore, if a court were to hold the rate unreasonable, the carrier would be violating the federal law if he gave the shipper the court-awarded refund. Since this Court found that one of the primary purposes of the Interstate Commerce Act was to eliminate discrimination among shippers, and that to allow the common law remedy to survive would result in that very discrimination, albeit in a different form, this Court ruled that the retention of the common law action based on unreasonable rates would be "absolutely inconsistent" with the Interstate Commerce Act, so that the savings provision could not apply. "In other words, the act cannot be held to destroy itself." 204 U.S. at 446. Or as the Court said in an earlier portion of that opinion:

> a statute will not be construed as taking away a common-law right
> existing at the date of its enactment unless that result is imperatively
> required; that is to say, unless it is found that the pre-existing right is
> so repugnant to the statute that the survival of such right would in

effect deprive the subsequent statute of its efficacy; in other words
render its provision nugatory. (*Id.* at 437.)

Judged by that standard, it is apparent that the majority below was in error in its
holding that petitioner's common law rights were necessarily altered by the Aviation Act.
While it cannot be doubted that the effects of no-shows and overbooking may show up
in a carrier's profit or loss column, that is true of virtually every aspect of its operations.
That, therefore, cannot be the touchstone for overruling section 1106 as the majority
below suggested. (Pet. App. A30.) Similarly, deliberate and undisclosed overbooking is
not a practice which is integral to respondent's rates and fares, since it is not set forth in
any tariff and has never been required by the CAB to be filed under section 403(a). A
practice which respondent has concealed from the public obviously stands on a very different footing from a publicly filed tariff insofar as section 1106 in concerned.

Nor is this an area where uniformity is essential, so that retention of common law
rights would be inherently repugnant to the Aviation Act. The best evidence of the
absence of need for uniformity is the action, or more properly non-action, by the CAB
each time it has considered the possibility of issuing uniform standards for all carriers
concerning their reservation practices. First, there is no requirement that carriers provide
reservations for their flights (JA 117), and non-reservation services have been highly successful in some major markets (*e.g.*, the Eastern Air-Shuttle). Similarly, while most carriers now provide for confirmation of reservations by telephone, the CAB has repeatedly
made clear that they are not obliged to do so, with the matter left entirely to the carrier's
own judgment. See PS-52, 38 F.R. 14823, 14824 (1973); PS-58, 39 F.R. 38095, 38096
(1974).

Most importantly with regard to the overbooking question, the CAB has on
numerous occasions considered proposals that would have taken the discretion from the
airlines and established across-the-board standards that all the carriers would have to
meet. Yet each time the Board has opted in favor of stimulating airline management to
innovate and improve their reservation systems, rather than imposing a uniform,
inflexible federal regime in this area. Plainly, this *laissez faire* attitude on the part of the
CAB is wholly inconsistent with any claimed need for uniformity, and surely falls well
below the standard of outright repugnancy established in the *Texas & Pacific* case as the
test for overriding a specific savings clause such as section 1106.

Indeed this has been clearly demonstrated by an innovative approach conceived by
Eastern Air Lines, which was approved in *Delta Air Lines, Inc.* v. *CAB*, 455 F.2d 1340
(D.C. Cir. 1971) (affirming CAB Order 71-6-120). Eastern's proposal provided for a system
of limited overbooking in which passengers subject to a denial of boarding would be
advised at the outset of their status, a status with both advantages (*e.g.*, the possibility of
being compensated if there is no space available) and disadvantages (*e.g.*, the possibility
of not being accommodated on the flight). A major benefit of this system, as the court of
appeals noted in *Delta*, is that the passenger is fully apprised of all the facts, and it is
entirely his own decision whether the arrangement offered is acceptable. While this
concept was originally approved for only a nine-month trial period, it is still in effect
almost five years later on Eastern and has since been added by several other carriers. At
a minimum the CAB's continuation of its permission to operate a different kind of reservations system demonstrates that uniformity is hardly essential in this area.

Finally, whatever may be said of the need for standardized reservations practices
regarding overbooking, there is no purpose of the Federal Aviation Act of which we are
aware that is fostered by the refusal of Allegheny and other carriers to disclose their
practices to the public, let alone by their willful concealment in the face of direct
inquiries about them. Unless it can be shown that Congress required the CAB to give
paramount consideration to uniformity in all aspects of airline operations, it is difficult to
imagine how a system which deludes more than 100,000 passengers annually into

believing they have confirmed reservations, and then leaves them stranded at the gate, can be said to be so important to the aviation system in this country that it eliminates the common law remedies of those who are injured by it. Concealment and misrepresentation are plainly not essential ingredients in an airline reservation system, and there is utterly no public interest in insulating those who use such practices from damage actions under the common law. Accordingly, the majority below was in error in holding that section 411, either alone or in conjunction with other portions of the Aviation Act, requires a uniform policy, imposed by the CAB, for all reservation practices including concealed overbooking.

III. THE CIVIL AERONAUTICS BOARD HAS NO POWER TO INSULATE DELIBERATE NONDISCLOSURE OF OVERBOOKING BY AIRLINES FROM LIABILITY UNDER THE COMMON LAW, AND CERTAINLY COULD NOT DO SO RETROACTIVELY AS THE COURT OF APPEALS HELD.

In dictating that the trial court must refer petitioner's common law misrepresentation claim to the CAB for a determination of whether Allegheny's conduct was deceptive under section 411, the court of appeals has seriously misconceived that agency's functions and powers. This is not a case where petitioner bases his claim for damages on a violation of section 411, in which case the court would first have to decide whether any such cause of action existed and then whether the tests of section 411 had been met. This case has not been referred to the CAB by the court of appeals in order to establish petitioner's right to recovery, but rather to provide an opportunity for the agency to insulate the carrier from liability for its practices.

The appellate court's conclusion that the CAB could perform such a function arose from its belief that the Aviation Act "must be read broadly to include the approval in the public interest of some practices that might be considered common law misrepresentations." (Pet. App. A 30.) This, we believe, was a crucial misreading of that statute. Section 411 provides authority to the CAB *only* to investigate the practices of its regulatees and, when they are found to be unfair and deceptive, to issue cease and desist orders, and even this authority can be exercised *only* when the public interest so requires. Nothing in that section even purports to empower the agency to approve fraudulent misrepresentations that are otherwise actionable at common law. And to infer such authority from section 411 would turn its fundamental purpose—the protection of consumers from potentially deceptive acts or practices—on its head.

Nor is there any other provision of the Act that authorizes the Board to approve intentional deceptions by an air carrier. To be sure, the agency has a legitimate concern in seeing that the companies it regulates make a reasonable return on their investment, but its general interest in their profits and financial welfare can hardly be translated into a license for deceit. Concededly, some kind of tortious misrepresentations might be of financial benefit to an airline, and such benefits might somehow be passed through to the public in lowered fares. Yet that would still be no basis to infer a sweeping power in the CAB to insulate such conduct from accountability at law to those injured by the deception—nor, it might be noted, has the agency ever claimed to have such a power. As Mr. Justice Cardozo wrote in *Federal Trade Commission* v. *Algoma Lumber Co.*, 291 U.S. 67, 78–79 (1934):

> But saving to the consumer, though it be made out, does not obliterate the prejudice. Fair competition is not attained by balancing a gain in money against a misrepresentation of the thing supplied. The courts must set their faces against a conception of business standards so corrupting in its tendency . . . . The careless and the unscrupulous must rise to the standards of the scrupulous and diligent. The Commission was not organized to drag the standards down.

That is not to say, however, that the CAB could never approve overbooking, for petitioner does not contend that overbooking is *per se* deceptive at all times and under all conditions. Indeed, when one carrier demonstrated that its proposed overbooking system would not be deceptive because all participants would be fully informed, its tariff regulations were quite properly approved and allowed to go into effect. *Delta Air Lines, Inc.* v. *CAB*, 455 F.2d 1340 (D.C. Cir. 1971). What is at issue here, however, is not just Allegheny's overbooking, but its deliberate concealment of that material fact in confirming petitioner's reservation. That conduct is simply beyond the CAB's power to approve. *Cf. Aloha Airlines, Inc.* v. *Hawaiian Airlines, Inc.*, 489 F.2d 203, 211–212 (9th Cir. 1973), *cert. denied*, 417 U.S. 913 (1974).

Even assuming for the sake of argument that the court of appeals was right in inferring authority for the CAB to approve fraudulent conduct and shield it from future liability, the concept that it could do so *retroactively*—issuing ad hoc determinations after injuries have already occurred to extinguish any cause of action—cannot be supported. Even where the agency has been given express power to insulate particular conduct from liability under the antitrust laws, this is not done on a retroactive basis. In *Hughes Tool Co.* v. *Trans World Airlines*, 409 U.S. 363 (1973), for example, this Court held that a private antitrust suit for damages could not proceed where the CAB had actually taken jurisdiction over and approved the transactions and relationships which were at the heart of the controversy. If the agency had declined to approve the transactions or to exercise its regulatory jurisdiction, it is inconceivable that this Court would have felt it appropriate to send the case back to see whether the Board might want to give retroactive approval. Whatever immunizing powers the Board may have in these areas is inherently prospective, not retroactive in nature. See *Pan American World Airways* v. *United States*, 371 U.S. 296, 305 (1963); *Aloha Airlines, Inc.* v. *Hawaiian Airlines, Inc., supra*.

The CAB's powers are broad, but not limitless. The fact that the court of appeals might think that the agency should have the power to approve affirmative misrepresentations "in the public interest" in the manner contemplated by its decision is irrelevant, for the Board's powers are necessarily limited to those assigned it by Congress. *Civil Aeronautics Board* v. *Delta Air Lines*, 367 U.S. 316, 322 (1961). And those powers do not include those inferred by the majority below.

IV. ALL DOUBTS ON THE QUESTIONS OF STATUTORY INTERPRETATION SHOULD BE RESOLVED AGAINST THE DECISION BELOW, BECAUSE IT DISRUPTS THE ALLOCATION OF FUNCTIONS BETWEEN THE COURTS AND THE CIVIL AERONAUTICS BOARD.

*　　　*　　　*

CONCLUSION

For the foregoing reasons, the decision of the court of appeals requiring referral of petitioner's common law claim to the Civil Aeronautics Board should be reversed.

Respectfully submitted,

REUBEN B. ROBERTSON III
ALAN B. MORRISON
LINDA F. DONALDSON
Suite 700
2000 P Street, N.W.
Washington, D.C. 20036
(202) 785-3704
Attorneys for Petitioner

January 9, 1976

DOCUMENT #41:
RESPONDENT'S SUPREME COURT BRIEF

Forty copies of a Brief in Opposition (Document #41) must be filed with the Clerk within thirty days of receipt of the petitioner's brief. Rule 25 indicates that the brief of a respondent must conform to the requirements of a brief for petitioner except for certain items, such as the question presented and the list of the parties below. Even the statement of the case, may be omitted unless respondent is dissatisfied with those items in petitioner's brief. Most of these items *are* included in a respondent's brief because they are, in fact, tools of advocacy. Allegheny, for instance, omitted only a list of the parties below, citations to opinions of the lower courts, and citations to the grounds for the jurisdiction of the Supreme Court.

In phrasing its "Question Presented," Allegheny continues to present the case as a question of an agency's right to examine issues peculiarly within its regulatory ambit before, and sometimes to the exclusion of, the courts. Thus, Allegheny asks whether it was wrong for the Court of Appeals to decide that the issue of Allegheny's nondisclosure of over-booking practices must be ruled upon by the CAB under its authority to determine whether particular practices are unfair or deceptive. If not unfair or deceptive under the Act, it is Allegheny's position (concurred in by a majority of the court of appeals) that the courts would be foreclosed from granting relief for misrepresentation based upon that practice.

Allegheny's factual statement includes an historical analysis, which is somewhat different from Nader's, of the CAB's involvement with the problem of overbooking. Here the CAB is shown to have expressed at least an acquiescence in the practice of overbooking as distinct from the problem of oversales. According to Allegheny, overbooking is an economic necessity whereby airlines accept more reservations than they can accommodate on a particular flight. This is because a statistically discernible number of those passengers will, for one reason or another, fail to show up for the flight. The *overbooking* policy allows some passengers to fail to appear for boarding yet permits the plane to depart substantially full. An *oversale* occurs when more people show up for boarding than there are seats to accommodate them. This, according to Allegheny, is a very rare occurrence and is the result of statistical aberration rather than deliberate planning by an airline.

After showing the CAB's acceptance of *overbooking*, Allegheny goes on to discuss the opinions of the courts below. Here, too, Allegheny takes an aggressive stance. "Nader's intent in asserting his claim against Allegheny was not to be made whole for any tortious injury . . . but rather to force Allegheny to cease its practice of overbooking flights." Allegheny goes on to discuss the rulings in the Court of Appeals against Nader and CCAG before stating that those rulings are not before the Supreme Court. It also discusses the remaining proceedings mandated by the Court of Appeals which, once completed, could render the question before the Supreme Court moot. Thus, even before Allegheny's formal argument has begun, it has attempted to shape the Court's view of the case.

In its Summary of Argument, Allegheny points out that Nader has, in fact, presented to the Court a very narrow issue, whether this case presents one of the "specific instances" which Nader concedes would warrant the "subordination of a common law claim to regulation by the CAB." It divides its response into three points, the first of which is to explain the difference between *overbooking* and *oversales* which Allegheny claims Nader has confused. The second is that this is precisely the type of case to be decided by the agency, which has the expertise to balance the competing issues. The third point goes to the relationship between the doctrine of primary jurisdiction and judicial determinations contrary to agency views.

The ability of the courts to examine and rule on the issue of deceptive practices would confront the airline industry with countless different decisions by a myriad of courts. This would throw the reservation and tariff schemes of the airlines into chaos with significant harm likely to be inflicted on some carriers. The need for a uniform policy in this area is so strong that it would override Nader's asserted "private grievance" exception to the doctrine of primary jurisdiction. (Recall that Nader argued that agencies deal with issues of public interest while courts deal with rectifying private grievances. Therefore, the agency may not pre-empt a court from examining and remedying fraudulent behavior by an airline against one of its passengers.)

When the doctrine of primary jurisdiction applies, it is converted into an exclusive jurisdiction of the agency. This is because certain regulatory schemes must be protected from the dissipating influence of large numbers of judges and juries around the country. This would remove from a trial court any right to examine the reasonableness of those practices committed to CAB regulation. It would also allow the agency to sanitize, within its sphere of regulation, otherwise unlawful or tortious conduct.

This brings Allegheny to the issue of retroactivity. Allegheny responds to Nader's argument on this point by arguing that since the CAB has repeatedly allowed overbooking to stand, any ruling now that it is not deceptive would merely be enunciating already existing law. But even if such a ruling were to be viewed as retroactive, Nader does not point to any prohibition against retroactivity. To the contrary, Allegheny argues that the courts have permitted retroactive application of agency rulings when appropriate to a regulatory scheme as is the situation here. Allegheny then asks the Supreme Court to affirm the decision of the Court of Appeals.

Note how much of Allegheny's argument is draped around policy considerations. These are related to the doctrine of primary jurisdiction which is, itself, a cornerstone of efficient public administration.

IN THE

Supreme Court of the United States

OCTOBER TERM, 1975

No. 75-455

RALPH NADER, *Petitioner,*

V.

ALLEGHENY AIRLINES, INC., *Respondent.*

On Writ of Certiorari to the United States Court of Appeals for the District of Columbia Circuit

BRIEF FOR RESPONDENT

E. BARRETT PRETTYMAN, JR.
FRANK F. ROBERSON
WILLIAM A. BRADFORD, JR.

815 Connecticut Avenue, N.W.
Washington, D.C. 20006
(202) 331-4500

Attorneys for Respondent

Of Counsel:

HOGAN & HARTSON
815 Connecticut Avenue N.W.
Washington, D.C. 20006

PRESS OF BYRON S. ADAMS PRINTING, INC., WASHINGTON, D. C.

INDEX

TABLE OF AUTHORITIES

CASES:

*   *   *

CAB ORDERS, NOTICES, REPORTS AND REGULATIONS:

*   *   *

OTHER AUTHORITIES:

*   *   *

STATUTES:

*   *   *

QUESTION PRESENTED

Whether the Court of Appeals deviated from well established principles of the doctrine of primary jurisdiction by conditioning petitioner's tort claim on a finding by the agency statutorily charged with regulating the allegedly tortious activities that those activities are not sanctioned by the regulatory scheme.

STATUTES INVOLVED

*   *   *

STATEMENT OF THE CASE

A. The Facts

*   *   *

B. The Decisions Below

Nader's intent in asserting his claim against Allegheny was not to be made whole for any tortious injury that might have occurred to him, but rather to force Allegheny to cease its practice of overbooking flights. . . .

*   *   *

On review by the United States Court of Appeals for the District of Columbia Circuit, in which Allegheny was supported by amicus briefs of the CAB and the Air Transport Association of America, that court reversed the District Court and remanded the case for further proceedings.

With respect to the District Court's judgment for Nader on the antidiscrimination claim, the Court of Appeals held that the lower court made errors of law and clearly erroneous findings of fact, and it remanded that portion of the case with directions to make new findings of fact and conclusions of law and to reopen the record if necessary. Pet. App. A14–A24, A49–A50. Because the Court of Appeals found no record evidence of malice or wanton conduct on behalf of Allegheny, and because it found that it was improper to use punitive damages to deter other members of a regulated industry from conduct within the ambit of regulation, the court held that no punitive damages could be awarded as a matter of law on Nader's misrepresentation claim. *Id.* at A49–A50. Review is not sought here by Nader of these portions of the Court of Appeals' judgment.

The Court of Appeals further held that co-plaintiff CCAG could not recover from Allegheny on its claim of misrepresentation because it was not within the class of persons whom Allegheny had reason to expect might act in reliance on its statements, and the court reversed the judgment for CCAG. Pet. App. A40. That portion of the Court of Appeals' decision is likewise not before the Court.

*   *   *

C. The Remaining Proceedings

*   *   *

SUMMARY OF ARGUMENT

The extremely narrow issue presented by petitioner is whether the particular facts of this case present one of the "specific instances" conceded by him to warrant the subordination of a common law claim to regulation by the CAB. In Part I, we demonstrate that petitioner has confused "oversales," which neither Allegheny nor any other airline engages in intentionally, with "overbooking," which the airlines do engage in and which the CAB has said works to the public's benefit. Overbooking is designed to prevent flights from departing with empty seats because of people who make reservations but then fail to appear for those flights. This overbooking is carefully and statistically monitored for each flight so as to *prevent* oversales. The CAB not only has found overbooking advantageous to both carriers and prospective passengers but has designed an elaborate scheme of rules and criteria for dealing with it and with the rare oversale that may result from it. Thus, carriers must report oversales, provide boarding compensation for "bumped" passengers, establish priorities for those denied boarding, etc. Even more significantly, the CAB has considered and *rejected* a proposal that passengers be informed in advance of their flights that they could become oversales, pointing out, among other things, the terrible anxiety and confusion on behalf of passengers that would result. Thus, the CAB has investigated and regulated—and continues to do so in a current investigation—the very conduct for which petition seeks damages in the courts.

In Part II, respondent shows that this is precisely the kind of case where the issue (the deceptiveness and validity of respondent's overbooking practices) should be decided *vel non* by the agency which regulates those practices. The CAB has the expertise to balance all the competing interests in this difficult field. This is particularly important where rates are affected, as the CAB has noted is true in this case. The necessity for uniformity is demonstrated by the kind of situation which would result if some airlines were forced by court rulings or jury awards to disclose overbookings while others were silent on the subject.

In Part III, we demonstrate that the doctrine of exclusive primary jurisdiction is properly applied here where the courts would merely be deferring the question of respondent's overbooking practices to the CAB for sanction or disapproval. If the CAB sanctions such practices, it would violate every concept of the primary jurisdiction doctrine, and would completely disrupt this regulated industry, to allow passengers to recover substantial awards in court based on the very practices that have been sanctioned by the regulatory agency. The two-fold answer to petitioner's argument that the CAB cannot retroactively declare practices legal and valid is that (a) the CAB, when it rules here in the exercise of its primary jurisdiction, will merely be declaring what its policy has been all along, and (b) even if this turns out not to be the case, the doctrine of primary jurisdiction fully allows an agency to declare practices legal and valid retroactively, and they have frequently done so with court approval.

ARGUMENT

I. THE CAB, AFTER SCRUTINIZING AIRLINE OVERBOOKING, HAS PERMITTED THAT PRACTICE AND HAS FOUND THAT DISCLOSURE OF THE PRACTICE IS NOT IN THE PUBLIC INTEREST.

* * *

II. THE DOCTRINE OF PRIMARY JURISDICTION COMPELS REFERENCE TO THE CAB OF THE DECEPTIVENESS VEL NON AND LEGITIMACY OF ALLEGHENY'S OVERBOOKING PRACTICES.

The Court of Appeals ruled that Nader's fraudulent misrepresentation claim should be deferred until the CAB had spoken on whether Allegheny's overbooking practices were deceptive or nevertheless legitimate within § 411 of the Act. If the CAB finds that those practices were not deceptive, then the practices cannot as a matter of law constitute common law misrepresentations. Pet. App. A30. This result was "but another application of the principles of primary jurisdiction, a doctrine whose purpose is the coordination of the workings of agency and court." Pet. App. A32.

The court's application of the doctrine of primary jurisdiction was proper. The doctrine has been fashioned so that those regulated by government agencies will not be subject to conflicting and contradictory directions from court and agency. . . .

A subsidiary rationale of the doctrine is that the expertise of regulatory agencies should be made available to each court, "thereby aid[ing] the court by laying a foundation for a more intelligent disposition of the question * * *." *Weidberg* v. *American Airlines, Inc.*, 336 F. Supp. 407, 409 (N.D. Ill. 1972). *Accord, Ricci* v. *Chicago Mercantile Exchange*, 409 U.S. 289, 305–306 (1973). This rationale was also recognized by the Court of Appeals. Pet. App. A32.

Thus, considering the rationale of the doctrine, it is not necessary that the regulatory agency have actually engaged in regulation of the practice or matter referred to it by the court, as long as the matter referred is within the agency's power to regulate—"within the sphere of regulation of the administrative agency" (*Adler* v. *Chicago & Southern Air Lines, Inc.*, 41 F. Supp. 366, 367 (E.D. Mo. 1941))— and involves the agency's specialized field. Here, as Part I of the Argument has shown, the CAB has been continually active in the area of overbooking and oversales, but such activity need not be a prerequisite to the invocation of primary jurisdiction.

* * *

With this understanding of the doctrine of primary jurisdiction, the correctness of the invocation of the doctrine by the Court of Appeals in the instant case cannot be questioned. Applying the uniformity rationale first, it is obvious that uniformity of the regulation of airlines' overbooking disclosure practices must obtain. The consequences to the airline industry would be disastrous if some airlines, through court rulings and punitive damages awards, were forced to disclose the overbooked conditions of flights and the resultant risk of oversales, while their competitors remained silent. . . .

*　　*　　*

Petitioner's statement that airline overbooking practices are not "an area where uniformity is essential" (Brief for Pet. at 42) is absurd. The Court of Appeals found that the overbooking disclosure problem was "as wide as the industry itself [and] a single, industry-wide resolution is appropriate." Pet. App. A32. By adopting the regulatory scheme it has in this area, the CAB has implicitly recognized that uniformity is essential. . . .

In its amicus brief filed with the Court of Appeals the CAB urged the doctrine of primary jurisdiction because the practice challenged by petitioner's tort suit should be the subject of uniform regulation by the Board:

> [The District Court] departed from the salutary principle that carriers' practices should be regulated on a uniform basis and that the agency charged with their regulation should specify in the first instance what those practices should be. [Brief for Civil Aeronautics Board as Amicus Curiae at 15–16; footnote omitted.]

Similarly, the need for agency expertise in the area of airline overbooking and its disclosure is manifest. . . .

*　　*　　*

Finally, petitioner suggests that the adjudication of private disputes under state law is not a matter within the primary jurisdiction of the CAB, and that the statutory powers of the agency "are to be exercised only as a means of vindicating the public interest * * *." . . .

The considerations of uniformity and consistency in the regulatory scheme, and of agency expertise, underlying the doctrine of primary jurisdiction point clearly to the non-existence of any asserted "private grievance" exception to the doctrine. It matters not that the courts are equipped by experience and tradition to adjudicate private common law claims if those claims raise issues whose resolution may affect the uniformity of regulation or may be aided by an agency determination. . . .

*　　*　　*

III. IF THE CAB SANCTIONS ALLEGHENY'S OVERBOOKING PRACTICES, SUCH PRACTICES CANNOT CONSTITUTE A COMMON LAW TORT.

Petitioner argues that the facts of this case do not warrant the extinguishing of his common law tort claim, although he concedes that the law permits such an extinguishing in certain circumstances. Brief for Pet. at 40. He argues further that even assuming his common law tort could be taken away by the action of an agency, "the concept that it could do so *retroactively* * * * cannot be supported." *Id.* at 48. His contention rests primarily on the common law rights savings clause of the Act, 49 U.S.C. § 1506.

The doctrine of primary jurisdiction, which has been properly applied in this case, contemplates the subordination of common law claims when those claims are repugnant to the regulatory scheme. This is what Nader concedes. . . .

*　　*　　*

In light of the cases on exclusive primary jurisdiction, we respectfully submit that the task of this Court is to determine merely whether the Court of Appeals erred in its finding that a continued tort of fraudulent misrepresentation in this case would be inconsistent with the regulatory scheme which treats nondisclosure of overbooking not to be deceptive. The Court of Appeals' decision in this regard was manifestly correct. It has already been shown that to permit oversold passengers, at their whim, to sue and collect punitive damage awards from overbooking airlines would be completely disruptive of the regulatory scheme that contemplates overbooking as an economic necessity and that has found nondisclosure of overbooking to be in the public interest. There is no practical distinction between the fluctuating standard of duty with respect to overbooking disclosure that would be placed on airlines by the varying judgments of judges and juries throughout the country and the varying standards of court-determined reasonableness of rates found to be impermissible by this Court in the *Abilene Cotton Oil Co.* case.

Petitioner's contention that an airline's "deliberate concealment of * * * [a] material fact * * * is simply beyond the CAB's power to approve" (Brief for Pet. at 47–48) is wrong. It is wrong, first, as conflicting with petitioner's own concession that certain common law remedies must give way to regulatory schemes. It is also wrong in light of the operation of the doctrine of primary jurisdiction as hereinabove described. The courts have frequently held that a regulatory statute may contemplate conduct which would be unlawful but for the regulatory legislation. . . .

Nader's argument throughout his Brief that the common law savings clause of the Act somehow operates to alter the doctrine of primary jurisdiction is in error. The common law savings clause, which is often found in regulatory schemes, is not an exception to the doctrine of primary jurisdiction. This has been clear since *Texas & Pacific Ry.* v. *Abilene Cotton Oil Co., supra*, which held that a common law savings clause virtually identical to the one invoked by Nader was no bar to the exercise of the doctrine of primary jurisdiction. This Court held that the clause would not preserve a common law right "the continued exercise of which would be absolutely inconsistent with the provisions of the act. In other words, the act cannot be held to destroy itself." 204 U.S. at 446. *Accord, Pennsylvania R.R.* v. *Puritan Coal Co.*, 237 U.S. 121, 129–130 (1915); *Danna* v. *Air France*, 334 F. Supp. 52, 57 (S.D.N.Y. 1971), *aff'd, supra*, 463 F.2d 407 (construing § 1106 of the Federal Aviation Act). Congress, by including the common law savings clause in the Federal Aviation Act that authorized the entire regulatory scheme, clearly did not intend it to operate to permit private plaintiffs to recover damage awards for activities by air carriers—here, the nondisclosure of overbooking—that were found to be necessary and in the public interest by the regulatory agency.

Furthermore, it should be remembered that the Court of Appeals' decision does not leave oversold passengers without a common law remedy against the airlines. The Court of Appeals reinvigorated the traditional common law claim of an oversold passenger, which is a court-made cause of action founded on the antidiscrimination provision of the Act. Pet. App. A16–18. After applying the elements of the "bumping" cause of action to Nader, the Court of Appeals found that Nader had not fully proved the elements of that claim in the trial court, and that portion of the case was remanded. The traditional "bumping" cause of action, pursuant to § 404(b) of the Act that has been characterized as "more generous" than the common law (*Mason* v. *Pan American World Airways, Inc.*, 13 Av. L. Rep. 17,114, 17,117 (D.D.C. 1974) (Gesell, J.)), is not inconsistent with the regulatory scheme because it allows recovery only against airlines that deviate from their own boarding priority rules (which are required to be filed with the Board by 14 C.F.R. § 250.3) in determining which passengers are oversold. In other words, a passenger has no cause of action under § 404(b) if he becomes an oversale as a result of properly applied boarding priority rules on file with the CAB. But if airlines deviate from CAB-filed practices and an oversale results, the airlines may be liable for compensatory and punitive damages. Nothing in the Court of Appeals' decision changes this law.

Lastly, Nader contends that even though the doctrine of primary jurisdiction might extinguish some common law claims that are inconsistent with regulatory schemes, the doctrine cannot operate retroactively. Nader cites no authority for his anti-retroactivity argument other than instances in which the doctrine has operated prospectively rather than retroactively. Brief for Pet. at 48. The two-fold answer to Nader's argument on retroactivity is that a CAB ruling that Allegheny's overbooking practices are not deceptive will not be a retroactive ruling and that, even if the ruling could be construed to be retroactive, the doctrine of primary jurisdiction permits such retroactive rulings.

The CAB has been wrestling with the overbooking problem for years, as we have shown. We think it is clear that it has both approved overbooking and determined that passenger-by-passenger disclosure would be highly prejudicial to the public. If the CAB agrees in its forthcoming proceedings, it will not be declaring these policies for the first time—and thus validating *future* overbooking and nondisclosure—but rather it will be reasserting that which it has said for many years. It will, in effect, be making clear that Allegheny's practices have been valid in the past and that the common law remedy has to that extent been displaced.

Even if, however, an eventual Board ruling could be construed as retroactive, there is nothing in the doctrine of primary jurisdiction that prohibits such retroactive rulings, and they have occurred frequently. Considering the rationale of the doctrine of primary jurisdiction, this must be so. The factors of uniformity of regulation and agency expertise come as much into play when the agency has not yet ruled as when it has already ruled. In looking at the question in the manner posed by Nader, what difference is there between a person prevented from recovering on a claim because, as Nader argues here, the reference to the agency will result in a ruling sanctioning the allegedly tortious practices, and a person prevented from recovering on a claim because the agency has already made such a ruling? In both cases a common law claim has given way to a regulatory scheme, as Nader concedes can occur. Why the operation of the doctrine of primary jurisdiction can operate "prospectively" but not "retroactively" Nader has not even attempted to explain or find authority to support.

The courts have made no distinction between retroactivity and prospectivity in their application of the doctrine of primary jurisdiction. A complicated question of whether car-mileage allowance from railroads should be paid over to the lessor of the cars or to the lessee, when the filed tariff contained no provisions answering the question, was held to lie within the primary jurisdiction of the ICC in *General American Tank Car Corp.* v. *El Dorado Terminal Co., supra.* Any doubt that the Court there recognized the agency's primary jurisdiction to determine the reasonableness of a past practice was effectively removed by this Court's subsequent decision upon appeal of the ICC's determination in the same matter. In *El Dorado Oil Works* v. *United States,* 328 U.S. 12, 17 (1946), this Court noted that by its previous decision it had "accepted [the] contention that determination of the validity of the challenged past practices was for the Commission."

> The question before us when this case was first here did not relate to future but to past allowances. Relying on past decisions, we held that the "reasonableness and legality" of the past dealings here involved were matters which Congress had entrusted to the Commission. [*Id.* at 19.]

Similarly, in *Far East Conf.* v. *United States, supra,* 342 U.S. 570, the question was the lawfulness under the antitrust laws of a system of dual freight rates which had not themselves been filed with the Federal Maritime Commission ("FMC"). This Court showed no hesitation in holding that resort must first be made to the FMC which had primary jurisdiction of the issue of the rates' lawfulness under the Shipping Act, although its determination could effectively be retroactive. *See also United States Nav. Co.* v. *Cunard S.S. Co., supra,* 284 U.S. at 486–487. Mr. Justice Brennan later interpreted these two cases as invoking the doctrine "when 'there is a possibility that a *subsequent* administrative decision would approve the questioned activities * * *.' " *Pan American World Airways, Inc.* v. *United States*, 371 U.S. 296, 332 (1963) (Brennan, J., dissenting) (emphasis added), quoting Schwartz, "Legal Restriction of Competition in the Regulated Industries: An Abdication of Judicial Responsibility," 67 Harv. L. Rev. 436, 464 (1954). The primary jurisdiction doctrine was also applied by this Court retroactively in *Port of Boston Marine Terminal Ass'n* v. *Rederiaktiebolaget Transatlantic*, discussed *supra*. Accord, *S.S.W., Inc.* v. *Air Transport Ass'n of America, supra*.

CONCLUSION

For each of these reasons, we respectfully submit that the judgment of the Court of Appeals should be affirmed.

Respectfully submitted,

E. BARRETT PRETTYMAN, JR.
FRANK F. ROBERSON
WILLIAM A. BRADFORD, JR.
815 Connecticut Avenue, N.W.
Washington, D.C. 20006
Attorneys for Respondent

Of Counsel:

HOGAN & HARTSON
815 Connecticut Avenue, N.W.
Washington, D.C. 20006

DOCUMENT #42: OPINION OF THE SUPREME COURT

The Supreme Court had before it the entire record, the briefs of the parties, including a reply brief from Nader, Amicus briefs from the CAB and the Air Transport Association of America, and had heard oral argument from the parties. The decision of the Court, written by Justice Powell, was unanimous in reversing the Court of Appeals.

Powell first points out that the Federal Aviation Act contains a clause which preserves common law remedies and makes the remedies under the Act cumulative. The Court of Appeals held that the common law savings clause did not apply in this case. Justice Powell, on the other hand, distinguished the present case as one in which there was no irreconcilable conflict between the statutory scheme and the common law issues involved. There was no call in this case for the courts to substitute their judgment on the reasonableness of any carrier practice for that of the agency. The CAB had not required that the airlines overbook or that they not disclose their policies. No violation of any CAB regulatory provision would result from permitting the common law remedy sought here.

Powell goes on to indicate that the Act conferred no power on the CAB to immunize common law misrepresentation. The language of section 411 authorizes the Board to investigate, when the public interest demands, unfair and deceptive practices and to issue cease and desist orders when such practices are found. Other sections of the Act specifically permit the CAB to immunize certain actions from the operation of the antitrust laws. Section 411 has no similar provision. In addition, the CAB has no authority under the Act to redress private wrongs, but may only issue cease and desist orders. Private parties may not even institute CAB proceedings under the provisions of section 411. Therefore, the common law remedies must be maintained or private redress would be lost altogether.

On the issue of "primary jurisdiction," Powell agrees that its purpose is to promote and maintain proper relationships between the agencies and the courts. In this case, however, there is no issue of technical complexity beyond the reach of the courts or of policy considerations that the agency would best be able to resolve. Instead, there is a traditional issue of tort liability which affects CAB regulation only tangentially, if at all.

Under these circumstances, the Court reverses the decision of the Court of Appeals on the issue of whether Nader's misrepresentation claim must be referred to the CAB before it can be passed upon by the District Court. The case was thus remanded for "further proceedings consistent with [the Court's] opinion."

Ralph NADER, Petitioner,

v.

ALLEGHENY AIRLINES, INC.

No. 75-455

Argued March 24, 1976.

Decided June 7, 1976.

426 U. S. 290, 96 S.Ct. 1978, 48 L.Ed.2d 643

Reuben B. Robertson, III, Washington, D.C., for petitioner.

E. Barrett Prettyman, Jr., Washington, D.C., for respondent.

Mr. Justice POWELL delivered the opinion of the Court.

In this case we address the question whether a common-law tort action based on alleged fraudulent misrepresentation by an air carrier subject to regulation by the Civil Aeronautics Board (Board) must be stayed pending reference to the Board for determination whether the practice is "deceptive" within the meaning of § 411 of the Federal Aviation Act of 1958, 72 Stat. 769, 49 U.S.C. § 1381. We hold that under the

circumstances of this case a stay pending reference is inappropriate.

I

The facts are not contested. Petitioner agreed to make several appearances in Connecticut on April 28, 1972, in support of the fundraising efforts of the Connecticut Citizen Action Group (CCAG), a nonprofit public interest organization. His two principal appearances were to be at a noon rally in Hartford and a later address at the Storrs campus of the University of Connecticut. On April 25, petitioner reserved a seat on respondent's flight 864 for April 28. The flight was scheduled to leave Washington, D.C., at 10:15 a.m. and to arrive in Hartford at 11:15 a.m. Petitioner's ticket was purchased from a travel agency on the morning of the flight. It indicated, by the standard "OK" notation, that the reservation was confirmed.

Petitioner arrived at the boarding and check-in area approximately five minutes before the scheduled departure time. He was informed that all seats on the flight were occupied and that he, like several other passengers who had arrived shortly before him, could not be accommodated. Explaining that he had to arrive in Hartford in time for the noon rally, petitioner asked respondent's agent to determine whether any standby passengers had been allowed to board by mistake or whether anyone already on board would voluntarily give up his or her seat. Both requests were refused. In accordance with respondent's practice, petitioner was offered alternative transportation by air taxi to Philadelphia, where connections could be made with an Allegheny flight scheduled to arrive in Hartford at 12:15 p.m. Fearing that the Philadelphia connection, which allowed only 10 minutes between planes, was too close, petitioner rejected this offer and elected to fly to Boston, where he was met by a CCAG staff member who drove him to Storrs.

Both parties agree that petitioner's reservation was not honored because respondent had accepted more reservations for flight 864 than it could in fact accommodate. One hour prior to the flight, 107 reservations had been confirmed for the 100 seats actually available. Such overbooking is a common industry practice, designed to ensure that each flight leaves with as few empty seats as possible despite the large number of "no-shows"— reservation-holding passengers who do not appear at flight time. By the use of statistical studies of no-show patterns on specific flights, the airlines attempt to predict the appropriate number of reservations necessary to fill each flight. In this way, they attempt to ensure the most efficient use of aircraft while preserving a flexible booking system that permits passengers to cancel and change reservations without notice or penalty. At times the practice of overbooking results in oversales, which occur when more reservation-holding passengers than can be accommodated actually appear to board the flight. When this occurs, some passengers must be denied boarding ("bumped"). The chance that any particular passenger will be bumped is so negligible that few prospective passengers aware of the possibility would give it a second thought. In April 1972, the month in which petitioner's reservation was dishonored, 6.7 confirmed passengers per 10,000 enplanements were denied boarding on domestic flights. For all domestic airlines, oversales resulted in bumping an average of 5.4 passengers per 10,000 enplanements in 1972, and 4.6 per 10,000 enplanements in 1973. In domestic operations respondent oversold 6.3 seats per 10,000 enplanements in 1972 and 4.5 seats per 10,000 enplanements in 1973. Thus, based on the 1972 experience of all domestic airlines, there was only slightly more than one chance in 2,000 that any particular passenger would be bumped

on a given flight. Nevertheless, the total number of confirmed ticket holders denied seats is quite substantial, numbering over 82,000 passengers in 1972 and about 76,000 in 1973.

Board regulations require each airline to establish priority rules for boarding passengers and to offer "denied boarding compensation" to bumped passengers. These "liquidated damages" are equal to the value of the passenger's ticket with a $25 minimum and a $200 maximum. 14 C.F.R. § 250.5 (1975). Passengers are free to reject the compensation offered in favor of a common-law suit for damages suffered as a result of the bumping. Petitioner refused the tender of denied boarding compensation ($32.41 in his case) and, with CCAG, filed this suit for compensatory and punitive damages. His suit did not seek compensation for the bumping *per se* but asserted two other bases of liability: a common-law action based on fraudulent misrepresentation arising from respondent's alleged failure to inform petitioner in advance of its deliberate overbooking practices, and a statutory action under § 404(b) of the Act, 49 U.S.C. § 1374(b), arising from respondent's alleged failure to afford petitioner the boarding priority specified in its rules filed with the Board under 14 CFR § 250.3 (1975).

The District Court entered a judgment for petitioner on both claims, awarding him a total of $10 in compensatory damages and $25,000 in punitive damages. Judgment also was entered for CCAG on its misrepresentation claim, with an award of $51 in compensatory damages and $25,000 in punitive damages.

The Court of Appeals for the District of Columbia Circuit reversed. 167 U.S.App. D.C. 350, 512 F.2d 527 (1975). A number of its rulings were not presented to this Court in the petition for certiorari. The award of damages to CCAG was reversed on the ground that the organization was too "remote from the transaction" to fall "within the class of persons who may recover." *Id.*, at 372, 512 F.2d, at 549. The merits of petitioner's statutory claim were remanded for further findings. The award of punitive damages to petitioner on the statutory claim was reversed on the ground that respondent's conduct contained no "elements of intentional wrongdoing or conscious disregard for" petitioner's rights. *Id.*, at 373, 512 F.2d, at 550. The question of punitive damages for the common-law claim was remanded for further findings on respondent's good faith. In particular, the trial court was to consider "whether Allegheny reasonably believed that its policies were completely lawful and in fact carried the approval of the Board." *Id.*, at 374,

512 F.2d, at 551. None of these rulings was presented to this Court in the petition for certiorari.

The only issue before us concerns the Court of Appeals' disposition on the merits of petitioner's claim of fraudulent misrepresentation. Although the court rejected respondent's argument that the existence of the Board's cease-and-desist power under § 411 of the Act eliminates all private remedies for common-law torts arising from unfair or deceptive practices by regulated carriers, it held ˈˈat a determination by the Board that a practice is not deceptive within the meaning of § 411 would, as a matter of law, preclude a common-law tort action seeking damages for injuries caused by that practice. Therefore, the court held that the Board must be allowed to determine in the first instance whether the challenged practice (in this case, the alleged failure to disclose the practice of overbooking) falls within the ambit of § 411. The court took judicial notice that a rulemaking proceeding concerning possible changes in reservation practices in response to the 1973–1974 fuel crisis was already underway and that a challenge to the carriers' overbooking practices had been raised by an intervenor in that proceeding. The District Court was instructed to stay further action on petitioner's misrepresentation claim pending the outcome of the rulemaking proceeding. The Court of Appeals characterized its holding as "but another application of the principles of primary jurisdiction, a doctrine whose purpose is the coordination of the workings of agency and court." 167 U.S. App. D.C., at 367, 512 F.2d, at 544.

II

The question before us, then, is whether the Board must be given an opportunity to determine whether respondent's alleged failure to disclose its practice of deliberate overbooking is a deceptive practice under § 411 before petitioner's common-law action is allowed to proceed. The decision of the Court of Appeals requires the District Court to stay the action brought by petitioner in order to give the Board an opportunity to resolve the question. If the Board were to find that there had been no violation of § 411, respondent would be immunized from common-law liability.

A

Section 1106 of the Act, 49 U.S.C. § 1506, provides that "[n]othing contained in this chapter shall in any way abridge or alter the remedies now existing at common law or by statute, but the provisions of this

chapter are in addition to such remedies." The Court of Appeals found that "although the saving clause of section 1106 purports to speak in absolute terms it cannot be read so literally." 167 U.S.App. D.C., at 367, 512 F.2d, at 544. In reaching this conclusion, it relied on *Texas & Pacific R. Co.* v. *Abilene Cotton Oil Co.*, 204 U.S. 426, 27 S.Ct. 350, 51 L.Ed. 553 (1907). In that case, the Court, despite the existence of a saving clause virtually identical to § 1106, refused to permit a state-court common-law action challenging a published carrier rate as "unjust and unreasonable." The Court conceded that a common-law right, even absent a saving clause, is not to be abrogated "unless it be found that the preexisting right is so repugnant to the statute that the survival of such right would in effect deprive the subsequent statute of its efficacy; in other words, render its provisions nugatory." 204 U.S., at 437, 27 S.Ct., at 354, 51 L.Ed., at 557. But the Court found that the continuance of private damages actions attacking the reasonableness of rates subject to the regulation of the Interstate Commerce Commission would destroy the purpose of the Interstate Commerce Act, which was to eliminate discrimination by requiring uniform rates. The saving clause, the Court found, "cannot in reason be construed as continuing in shippers a common law right, the continued existence of which would be absolutely inconsistent with the provisions of the act. In other words, the act cannot be held to destroy itself." *Id.*, at 446, 27 S.Ct., at 358, 51 L.Ed., at 561.

In this case, unlike *Abilene*, we are not faced with an irreconcilable conflict between the statutory scheme and the persistence of common-law remedies. In *Abilene* the carrier, if subject to both agency and court sanctions, would be put in an untenable position when the agency and a court disagreed on the reasonableness of a rate. The carrier could not abide by the rate filed with the Commission, as required by statute, and also comply with a court's determination that the rate was excessive. The conflict between the court's common-law authority and the agency's ratemaking power was direct and unambiguous. The court in the present case, in contrast, is not called upon to substitute its judgment for the agency's on the reasonableness of a rate—or, indeed, on the reasonableness of any carrier practice. There is no Board requirement that air carriers engage in overbooking or that they fail to disclose that they do so. And any impact on rates that may result from the imposition of tort liability or from practices adopted by a carrier to avoid such liability would be merely incidental. Under the circumstances, the common-law action and the statute are not "absolutely inconsistent" and may coexist, as contemplated by § 1106.

B

Section 411 of the Act allows the Board, where "it considers that such action . . would be in the interest of the public," "upon its own initiative or upon complaint by any air carrier, foreign air carrier, or ticket agent," to "investigate and determine whether any air carrier . . . has been or is engaged in unfair or deceptive practices or unfair methods of competition . . . ." Practices determined to be in violation of this section "shall" be the subject of a cease-and-desist order. The Court of Appeals concluded—and respondent does not challenge the conclusion here—that this section does not totally preclude petitioner's common-law tort action. But the Court of Appeals also held, relying on the nature of the airline industry as "a regulated system of limited competition," *American Airlines, Inc.* v. *North American Airlines, Inc.*, 351 U.S. 79, 84, 76 S.Ct. 600, 604, 100 L.Ed. 953, 961 (1956), and the Board's duty to promote "adequate, economical, and efficient service," § 102(c) of the Act, 49 U.S.C. § 1302(c), "at the lowest cost consistent with the furnishing of such service," § 1002(e)(2) of the Act, 49 U.S.C. § 1482(e)(2), that the Board has the power in a § 411 proceeding to approve practices that might otherwise be considered deceptive and thus to immunize carriers from common-law liability. 167 U.S.App.D.C., at 366, 512 F.2d, at 543.

We cannot agree. No power to immunize can be derived from the language of § 411. And where Congress has sought to confer such power it has done so expressly, as in § 414 of the Act, 49 U.S.C. § 1384, which relieves those affected by certain designated orders (not including orders issued under § 411) "from the operations of the 'antitrust laws.'" When faced with an exemptive provision similar to § 414 in *United States Navigation Co.* v. *Cunard S.S. Co.*, 284 U.S. 474, 52 S.Ct. 247, 76 L.Ed. 408 (1932), this Court dismissed an antitrust action because initial consideration by the agency had not been sought. The Court pointed out that the Act in question was "restrictive in its operation upon some of the activities of common carriers . . ., and permissive in respect of others." *Id.*, at 485, 52 S.Ct., at 250, 76 L.Ed., at 414. See also *Far East Conference* v. *United States*, 342 U.S. 570, 72 S.Ct. 492, 96 L.Ed. 576 (1952). Section 411, in contrast, is purely restrictive. It contemplates the elimination of "unfair or deceptive practices" that impair the public interest. Its role has been described in *American*

Airlines, Inc. v. *North American Airlines, Inc., supra*, 351 U.S., at 85, 76 S.Ct., at 605, 100 L.Ed., at 962:

> "'Unfair or deceptive practices or unfair methods of competition,' as used in § 411, are broader concepts than the common-law idea of unfair competition. . . . The section is concerned not with punishment of wrongdoing or protection of injured competitors, but rather with protection of the public interest."

As such, § 411 provides an injunctive remedy for vindication of the public interest to supplement the compensatory common-law remedies for private parties preserved by § 1106.

Thus, a violation of § 411, contrary to the Court of Appeals' conclusion, is not coextensive with a breach of duty under the common law. We note that the Board's jurisdiction to initiate an investigation under § 411 is expressly premised on a finding that the "public interest" is involved. The Board "may not employ its powers to vindicate private rights." 351 U.S., at 83, 76 S.Ct., at 604, 100 L.Ed., at 961. Indeed, individual consumers are not even entitled to initiate proceedings under § 411, a circumstance that indicates that Congress did not intend to require private litigants to obtain a § 411 determination before they could proceed with the common-law remedies preserved by § 1106. Cf. *Rosado* v. *Wyman*, 397 U.S. 397, 406, 90 S.Ct. 1207, 1214, 25 L.Ed.2d 442, 452 (1970).

Section 411 is both broader and narrower than the remedies available at common law. A cease-and-desist order may issue under § 411 merely on the Board's conclusion, after an investigation determined to be in the public interest, that a carrier is engaged in an "unfair or deceptive practice." No findings that the practice was intentionally deceptive or fraudulent or that it in fact has caused injury to an individual are necessary. *American Airlines, Inc.* v. *North American Airlines, Inc., supra*, 351 U.S. at 86, 76 S.Ct., at 605, 100 L.Ed., at 962. On the other hand, a Board decision that a cease-and-desist order is inappropriate does not represent approval of the practice under investigation. It may merely represent the Board's conclusion that the serious prohibitory sanction of a cease-and-desist order is inappropriate, that a more flexible approach is necessary. A wrong may be of the sort that calls for compensation to an injured individual without requiring the extreme remedy of a cease-and-desist order. Indeed, the Board, in dealing with the problem of overbooking by air carriers, has declined to issue cease-and-desist orders, despite the determination by an examiner in one case that a § 411 violation had occurred. Instead, the Board has elected to establish boarding priorities and to ensure that passengers will be compensated for being bumped either by a liquidated sum under Board regulations or by resort to a suit for compensatory damages at common law.

In sum, § 411 confers upon the Board a new and powerful weapon against unfair and deceptive practices that injure the public. But it does not represent the only, or best, response to all challenged carrier actions that result in private wrongs.

C

The doctrine of primary jurisdiction "is concerned with promoting proper relationships between the courts and administrative agencies charged with particular regulatory duties." *United States v. Western Pacific R. Co.*, 352 U.S. 59, 63, 77 S.Ct. 161, 165, 1 L.Ed.2d 126, 132 (1956). Even when common-law rights and remedies survive and the agency in question lacks the power to confer immunity from common-law liability, it may be appropriate to refer specific issues to an agency for initial determination where that procedure would secure "[u]niformity and consistency in the regulation of business entrusted to a particular agency" or where

"the limited functions of review by the judiciary [would be] more rationally exercised, by preliminary resort for ascertaining and interpreting the circumstances underlying legal issues to agencies that are better equipped than courts by specialization, by insight gained through experience, and by more flexible procedure. *Far East Conference v. United States*, 342 U.S., at 574–575, 72 S.Ct., at 494, 96 L.Ed., at 582.

See Also *United States v. Western Pacific R. Co.*, *supra*, 352 U.S., at 64, 77 S.Ct., at 165, 1 L.Ed.2d, at 132.

The doctrine has been applied, for example, when an action otherwise within the jurisdiction of the court raises a question of the validity of a rate or practice included in a tariff filed with an agency, *e.g.*, *Danna v. Air France*, 463 F.2d 407 (C.A.2 1972); *Southwestern Sugar & Molasses Co. v. River Terminals Corp.*, 360 U.S. 411, 417–418, 79 S.Ct. 1210, 1214–1215, 3 L.Ed.2d 1334, 1340–1341 (1959), particularly when the issue involves technical questions of fact uniquely within the expertise and experience of an agency—such as matters turning on an assessment of industry conditions, *e.g.*, *United States v. Western Pacific R.Co.*, *supra*, 352 U.S., at 66–67, 77 S.Ct., at 166, 1 L.Ed.2d, at 133–134. In this case, however, considerations of uniformity in regulation and of

technical expertise do not call for prior reference to the Board.

Petitioner seeks damages for respondent's failure to disclose its overbooking practices. He makes no challenge to any provision in the tariff, and indeed there is no tariff provision or Board regulation applicable to disclosure practices. Petitioner also makes no challenge, comparable to those made in *Southwestern Sugar & Molasses Co. v. River Terminals Corp.*, *supra*, and *Lichten v. Eastern Airlines, Inc.*, 189 F.2d 939 (C.A.2 1951), to limitations on common-law damages imposed through exculpatory clauses included in a tariff.

Referral of the misrepresentation issue to the Board cannot be justified by the interest in informing the court's ultimate decision with "the expert and specialized knowledge," *United States v. Western Pacific R. Co.*, *supra*, at 64, 77 S.Ct., at 165, 1 L.Ed.2d, at 132, of the Board. The action brought by petitioner does not turn on a determination of the reasonableness of a challenged practice—a determination that could be facilitated by an informed evaluation of the economics or technology of the regulated industry. The standards to be applied in an action for fraudulent misrepresentation are within the conventional competence of the courts, and the judgment of a technically expert body is not likely to be helpful in the application of these standards to the facts of this case.

We are particularly aware that, even where the wrong sought to be redressed is not misrepresentation but bumping itself, which has been the subject of Board consideration and for which compensation is provided in carrier tariffs, the Board has contemplated that there may be individual adjudications by courts in common-law suits brought at the option of the passenger. The present regulations dealing with the problems of overbooking and oversales were promulgated by the Board in 1967. They provide for denied boarding compensation to bumped passengers and require each carrier to establish priority rules for seating passengers and to file reports of passengers who could not be accommodated. The order instituting these regulations contemplates that the bumped passenger will have a choice between accepting denied boarding compensation as "liquidated damages for all damages incurred . . . as a result of the carrier's failure to provide the passenger with confirmed reserved space," or pursuing his or her common-law remedies. The Board specifically provided for a 30-day period before the specified compensation need be accepted so that the passenger will not be forced to make a decision before "the consequences of denied boarding have occurred and are known." After evaluating the consequences, passengers may choose as an alternate "to pursue their remedy under the common law."

III

We conclude that petitioner's tort action should not be stayed pending reference to the Board and accordingly the decision of the Court of Appeals on this issue is reversed. The Court of Appeals did not address the question whether petitioner had introduced sufficient evidence to sustain his claim. We remand the case for consideration of that question and for further proceedings consistent with this opinion.

It is so ordered.

EPILOGUE

The case was remanded, through the Court of Appeals, to the District Court. The Court of Appeals issued an amended judgment in which it reversed the judgment of the District Court on all issues except the issue of fraudulent misrepresentation as to which the Court of Appeals vacated the judgment of the District Court. The Court of Appeals then remanded the entire matter to the District Court for further proceedings consistent with the judgments of the Supreme Court and of the Court of Appeals. The District Court, after a new trial in accordance with the instructions of both higher courts, rendered a new judgment awarding a total of $10 compensatory damages and $15,000 punitive damages in favor of Nader on his discrimination and his fraudulent misrepresentation claims. Judgment was entered against CCAG on its misrepresentation claim which was its only remaining cause of action.

Allegheny appealed to the Court of Appeals on the issue of fraudulent misrepresentation and on the issue of punitive damages. Allegheny did not challenge the judgment for Nader on the issue of its violating its own priority boarding rules. The Court of Appeals again overturned the District Court's award of punitive damages to Nader and also its finding that Allegheny's failure to disclose its overbooking practices was misrepresentation. Nader, therefore, came away from nearly eight years of litigation with a judgment against Allegheny, but an award of only $10.

One might ask whether the result was worth all that time and expense. Allegheny gained a judgment which makes it unlikely that a passenger bumped (under typical circumstances) will be able to recover punitive damages from an airline. This, in turn, makes it very unlikely that such a passenger would sue an airline at all. This is a significant victory for Allegheny and the airline industry. On the other hand, Nader was able to show that he was bumped in violation of Allegheny's priority boarding rules. This may make airlines more conscious of their rules and more likely to follow them. Whether this will inure to the benefit of the typical air traveler is uncertain, particularly in light of the limited recovery likely to be obtained against the airlines.

On a much broader level, the judgment for Nader in the Supreme Court helped to clarify the relationship between courts and agencies and left the courts with more power than Allegheny, the airline industry, or the CAB had desired. This meant that individual actions might proceed against airlines for common law violations without the intervening presence of the CAB.

Finally, CCAG appears not to have gained anything at all. The Court of Appeals held that it was, in this case, too remote a party to fall within any theory of tort compensation. It should be remembered here that Nader had not informed Allegheny of the purpose of his trip until *after* he was bumped from the flight. Had Allegheny known in advance of CCAG's activities in reliance on the reservation, would a court have permitted its recovery? Alas, that question must await another litigation biography.

THE CONSTITUTION OF THE UNITED STATES

We the People of the United States, in Order to form a more perfect Union, establish Justice, insure domestic Tranquility, provide for the common defence, promote the general Welfare, and secure the Blessings of Liberty to ourselves and our Posterity, do ordain and establish this Constitution for the United States of America.

Article I

Section 1. All legislative Powers herein granted shall be vested in a Congress of the United States, which shall consist of a Senate and House of Representatives.

Section 2. The House of Representatives shall be composed of Members chosen every second Year by the People of the several States, and the Electors in each State shall have the Qualifications requisite for Electors of the most numerous Branch of the State Legislature.

No Person shall be a Representative who shall not have attained to the Age of twenty five Years, and been seven Years a Citizen of the United States, and who shall not, when elected, be an Inhabitant of that State in which he shall be chosen.

Representatives and direct Taxes shall be apportioned among the several States which may be included within this Union, according to their respective Numbers, which shall be determined by adding to the whole Number of free Persons, including those bound to Service for a Term of Years, and excluding Indians not taxed, three fifths of all other Persons. The actual Enumeration shall be made within three Years after the first Meeting of the Congress of the United States, and within every subsequent Term of ten Years, in such Manner as they shall by Law direct. The Number of Representatives shall not exceed one for every thirty Thousand, but each State shall have at Least one Representative; and until such enumeration shall be made, the State of New Hampshire shall be entitled to chuse three, Massachusetts eight, Rhode Island and Providence Plantations one, Connecticut five, New York six, New Jersey four, Pennsylvania eight, Delaware one, Maryland six, Virginia ten, North Carolina five, South Carolina five, and Georgia three.

When vacancies happen in the Representation from any State, the Executive Authority thereof shall issue Writs of Election to fill such Vacancies.

The House of Representatives shall chuse their Speaker and other Officers; and shall have the sole Power of Impeachment.

Section 3. The Senate of the United States shall be composed of two Senators from each State, chosen by the Legislature thereof, for six Years; and each Senator shall have one Vote.

Immediately after they shall be assembled in Consequence of the first Election, they shall be divided as equally as may be into three Classes. The Seats of the Senators of the first Class shall be vacated at the Expiration of the second Year, of the second Class at the Expiration of the fourth Year, and of the third Class at the Expiration of the sixth Year, so that one third may be chosen every second Year; and if Vacancies happen by Resignation, or otherwise, during the Recess of the Legislature of any State, the Executive thereof may make temporary Appointments until the next Meeting of the Legislature, which shall then fill such Vacancies.

No Person shall be a Senator who shall not have attained to the Age of thirty Years, and been nine Years a Citizen of the United States, and who shall not, when elected, be an Inhabitant of that State for which he shall be chosen.

The Vice President of the United States shall be President of the Senate, but shall have no Vote, unless they be equally divided.

The Senate shall chuse their other Officers, and also a President pro tempore, in the Absence of the Vice President, or when he shall exercise the Office of President of the United States.

The Senate shall have the sole Power to try all Impeachments. When sitting for that Purpose, they shall be on Oath or Affirmation. When the President of the United States is tried, the Chief Justice shall preside: And no Person shall be convicted without the concurrence of two thirds of the Members present. Judgment in Cases of Impeachment shall not extend further than to removal from Office, and disqualification to hold and enjoy any Office of honor, Trust, or Profit under the United States: but the Party convicted shall nevertheless be liable and subject to Indictment, Trial, Judgment, and Punishment, according to law.

Section 4. The Times, Places and Manner of holding Elections for Senators and Representatives, shall be prescribed in each State by the Legislature thereof; but the Congress may at any time by Law make or alter such Regulations, except as to the Places of chusing Senators.

The Congress shall assemble at least once in every Year, and such Meeting shall be on the first Monday in December, unless they shall by Law appoint a different Day.

Section 5. Each House shall be the Judge of the Elections, Returns, and Qualifications of its own Members, and a Majority of each shall constitute a Quorum to do business; but a smaller Number may adjourn from day to day, and may be authorized to compel the Attendance of absent Members, in such Manner, and under such Penalties as each House may provide.

Each House may determine the Rules of its Proceedings, punish its Members for disorderly Behaviour, and, with the Concurrence of two thirds, expel a Member.

Each House shall keep a Journal of its Proceedings, and from time to time publish the same, excepting such Parts as may in their Judgment require Secrecy; and the Yeas and Nays of the Members of either House on any question shall, at the Desire of one fifth of those Present, be entered on the Journal.

Neither House, during the Session of Congress, shall, without the Consent of the other, adjourn for more than three days, nor to any other place than that in which the two Houses shall be sitting.

Section 6. The Senators and Representatives shall receive a Compensation for their Services, to be ascertained by Law, and paid out of the Treasury of the United States. They shall in all Cases, except Treason, Felony and Breach of the Peace, be privileged from Arrest during their Attendance at the Session of their respective Houses, and in going to and returning from the same; and for any Speech or Debate in either House, they shall not be questioned in any other Place.

No Senator or Representative shall, during the Time for which he was elected, be appointed to any civil Office under the Authority of the United States, which shall have been created, or the Emoluments whereof shall have been encreased during such time; and no Person holding any Office under the United States, shall be a Member of either House during his Continuance in Office.

Section 7. All Bills for raising Revenue shall originate in the House of Representatives; but the Senate may propose or concur with Amendments as on other Bills.

Every Bill which shall have passed the House of Representatives and the Senate, shall, before it become a Law, be presented to the President of the United States; If he approve he shall sign it, but if not he shall return it, with his Objections to that House in which it shall have originated, who shall enter the Objections at large on their Journal, and proceed to reconsider it. If after such Reconsideration two thirds of that House shall agree to pass the Bill, it shall be sent, together with the Objections, to the other House, by which it shall likewise be reconsidered, and if approved by two thirds of that House, it shall become a Law. But in all such Cases the Votes of both Houses shall be determined by yeas and Nays, and the Names of the Persons voting for and against the Bill shall be entered on the Journal of each House respectively. If any Bill shall not be returned by the President within ten Days (Sundays excepted) after it shall have been presented to him, the Same shall be a Law, in like Manner as if he had signed it, unless the Congress by their Adjournment prevent its Return in which Case it shall not be a Law.

Every Order, Resolution, or Vote, to which the Concurrence of the Senate and House of Representatives may be necessary (except on a question of Adjournment) shall be presented to the President of the United States; and before the Same shall take Effect, shall be approved by him, or being disapproved by him, shall be repassed by two thirds of the Senate and House of Representatives, according to the Rules and Limitations prescribed in the Case of a Bill.

Section 8. The Congress shall have Power To lay and collect Taxes, Duties, Imposts and Excises, to pay the Debts and provide for the common Defence and general Welfare of the United States; but all duties, Imposts and Excises shall be uniform throughout the United States;

To borrow Money on the Credit of the United States;

To regulate Commerce with foreign Nations, and among the several States, and with the Indian Tribes;

To establish an uniform Rule of Naturalization, and uniform Laws on the subject of Bankruptcies throughout the United States;

To coin Money, regulate the Value thereof, and of foreign Coin, and fix the Standard of Weights and Measures;

To provide for the Punishment of counterfeiting the Securities and current Coin of the United States;

To establish Post Offices and post Roads;

To promote the Progress of Science and useful Arts, by securing for limited Times to Authors and Inventors exclusive Right to their respective Writings and Discoveries;

To constitute Tribunals inferior to the supreme Court;

To define and punish Piracies and Felonies committed on the high Seas, and Offences against the Law of Nations;

To declare War, grant Letters of Marque and Reprisal, and make rules concerning Captures on Land and Water;

To raise and support Armies, but no Appropriation of Money to that Use shall be for a longer Term than two Years;

To provide and maintain a Navy;

To make Rules for the Government and Regulation of the land and naval Forces;

To provide for calling forth the Militia to execute the Laws of the Union, suppress Insurrections and repel Invasions;

To provide for organizing, arming, and disciplining, the Militia, and for governing such Part of them as may be employed in the Service of the United States, reserving to the States respectively, the Appointment of the Officers, and the Authority of training the Militia according to the discipline prescribed by Congress;

To exercise exclusive Legislation in all Cases whatsoever, over such District (not exceeding ten Miles square) as may, by Cession of particular States, and the Acceptance of Congress, become the Seat of the Government of the United States, and to exercise like Authority over all Places purchased by the Consent of the Legislature of the State in which the Same shall be, for the Erection of Forts, Magazines, Arsenals, dock-Yards, and other needful Buildings;—And

To make all Laws which shall be necessary and proper for carrying into Execution the foregoing Powers, and all other Powers vested by this Constitution in the Government of the United States, or in any Department or Officer thereof.

Section 9. The Migration or Importation of such Persons as any of the States now existing shall think proper to admit, shall not be prohibited by the Congress prior to the Year one thousand eight hundred and eight, but a Tax or duty may be imposed on such Importation, not exceeding ten dollars for each Person.

The Privilege of the Writ of Habeas Corpus shall not be suspended, unless when in Cases of Rebellion or Invasion the public Safety may require it.

No Bill of Attainder or ex post facto Law shall be passed.

No Capitation, or other direct, Tax shall be laid, unless in Proportion to the Census or Enumeration herein before directed to be taken.

No Tax or Duty shall be laid on Articles exported from any State.

No Preference shall be given by any Regulation of Commerce or Revenue to the Ports of one State over those of another: nor shall Vessels bound to, or from, one State, be obliged to enter, clear, or pay Duties in another.

No money shall be drawn from the Treasury, but in Consequence of Appropriations made by Law; and a regular Statement and Account of the Receipts and Expenditures of all public Money shall be published from time to time.

No Title of Nobility shall be granted by the United States: And no Person holding any Office of Profit or Trust under them, shall, without the Consent of the Congress, accept of any present, Emolument, Office, or Title, of any kind whatever, from any King, Prince, or foreign State.

Section 10. No State shall enter into any Treaty, Alliance, or Confederation; grant Letters of Marque and Reprisal; coin Money; emit Bills of Credit; make any Thing but gold and silver Coin a Tender in Payment of Debts; pass any Bill of Attainder, ex post facto Law, or Law impairing the Obligation of Contracts, or grant any Title of Nobility.

No State shall, without the Consent of the Congress, lay any Imposts or Duties on Imports or Exports, except what may be absolutely necessary for executing it's inspection Laws: and the net Produce of all Duties and Imposts, laid by any State on Imports or Exports, shall be for the Use of the Treasury of the United States; and all such Laws shall be subject to the Revision and Controul of the Congress.

No State shall, without the Consent of Congress, lay any Duty of Tonnage, keep Troops, or Ships of War in time of Peace, enter into any Agreement or Compact with another State, or with a foreign Power, or engage in War, unless actually invaded, or in such imminent Danger as will not admit of delay.

Article II

Section 1. The executive Power shall be vested in a President of the United States of America. He shall hold his Office during the Term of four Years, and, together with the Vice President, chosen for the same Term, be elected, as follows

Each State shall appoint, in such Manner as the Legislature thereof may direct, a Number of Electors, equal to the whole Number of Senators and Representatives to which the State may be entitled in the Congress; but no Senator or Representative, or Person holding an Office of Trust or Profit under the United States, shall be appointed an Elector.

The Electors shall meet in their respective States, and vote by Ballot for two Persons, of whom one at least shall not be an Inhabitant of the same State with themselves. And they shall make a List of all the Persons voted for, and of the Number of Votes for each; which List they shall sign and certify, and transmit sealed to the Seat of the Government of the United States, directed to the President of the Senate. The President of the Senate shall, in the Presence of the Senate and House of Representatives, open all the Certificates, and the Votes shall then be counted. The Person having the greatest Number of Votes shall be the President, if such Number be a Majority of the whole Number of Electors appointed; and if there be more than one who have such Majority, and have an equal Number of Votes, then the House of Representatives shall immediately chuse by Ballot one of them for President; and if no Person have a Majority, then from the five highest on the List the said House shall in like Manner chuse the President. But in chusing the President, the Votes shall be taken by States, the Representation from each State having one Vote; A quorum for this Purpose shall consist of a Member or Members from two thirds of the States, and a Majority of all the States shall be necessary to a Choice. In every Case, after the Choice of the President, the Person having the greater Number of Votes of the Electors shall be the Vice President. But if there should remain two or more who have equal Votes, the Senate shall chuse from them by Ballot the Vice President.

The Congress may determine the Time of chusing the Electors, and the Day on which they shall give their Votes; which Day shall be the same throughout the United States.

No Person except a natural born Citizen, or a Citizen of the United States, at the time of the Adoption of this Constitution, shall be eligible to the Office of President; neither shall any Person be eligible to that Office who shall not have attained to the Age of thirty five Years, and been fourteen Years a Resident within the United States.

In Case of the Removal of the President from Office, or of his Death, Resignation, or Inability to discharge the Powers and Duties of the said Office, the Same shall devolve on the Vice President, and the Congress may by Law provide for the Case of Removal, Death, Resignation or Inability, both of the President and Vice President, declaring what Officer shall then act as President, and such Officer shall act accordingly, until the Disability be removed, or a President shall be elected.

The President shall, at stated Times, receive for his Services, a Compensation, which shall neither be increased nor diminished during the Period for which he shall have been elected, and he shall not receive within that Period any other Emolument from the United States, or any of them.

Before he enter on the Execution of his Office, he shall take the following Oath or Affirmation:—"I do solemnly swear (or affirm) that I will faithfully execute the Office of President of the United States, and will to the best of my Ability, preserve, protect and defend the Constitution of the United States."

Section 2. The President shall be Commander in Chief of the Army and Navy of the United States, and of the Militia of the several States, when called into the actual Service of the United States; he may require the Opinion, in writing, of the principal Officer in each of the executive Departments, upon any Subject relating to the Duties of their respective Offices, and he shall have Power to grant Reprieves and Pardons for Offences against the United States, except in Cases of Impeachment.

He shall have Power, by and with the Advice and Consent of the Senate to make Treaties, provided two thirds of the Senators present concur; and he shall nominate, and by and with the Advice and Consent of the Senate, shall appoint Ambassadors, other public Ministers and Consuls, Judges of the supreme Court, and all other Officers of the United

States, whose Appointments are not herein otherwise provided for, and which shall be established by Law; but the Congress may by Law vest the Appointment of such inferior Officers, as they think proper, in the President alone, in the Courts of Law, or in the Heads of Departments.

The President shall have Power to fill up all Vacancies that may happen during the Recess of the Senate, by granting Commissions which shall expire at the End of their next Session.

Section 3. He shall from time to time give to the Congress Information of the State of the Union, and recommend to their Consideration such Measures as he shall judge necessary and expedient; he may, on extraordinary Occasions, convene both Houses, or either of them, and in Case of Disagreement between them, with Respect to the Time of Adjournment, he may adjourn them to such Time as he shall think proper; he shall receive Ambassadors and other public Ministers; he shall take Care that the Laws be faithfully executed, and shall Commission all the Officers of the United States.

Section 4. The President, Vice President and all civil Officers of the United States, shall be removed from Office on Impeachment for, and Conviction of, Treason, Bribery, or other high Crimes and Misdemeanors.

Article III

Section 1. The judicial Power of the United States, shall be vested in one supreme Court, and in such inferior Courts as the Congress may from time to time ordain and establish. The Judges, both of the supreme and inferior Courts, shall hold their Offices during good Behaviour, and shall, at stated Times, receive for their Services, a Compensation, which shall not be diminished during their Continuance in Office.

Section 2. The judicial Power shall extend to all Cases, in Law and Equity, arising under this Constitution, the Laws of the United States, and Treaties made, or which shall be made, under their Authority;—to all Cases affecting Ambassadors, other public Ministers and Consuls;—to all Cases of admiralty and maritime Jurisdiction;—to Controversies to which the United States shall be a Party;—to Controversies between two or more States;—between a State and Citizens of another State;—between Citizens of different States;—between Citizens of the same State claiming Lands under Grants of different States, and between a State, or the Citizens thereof, and foreign States, Citizens or Subjects.

In all Cases affecting Ambassadors, other public Ministers and Consuls, and those in which a State shall be Party, the supreme Court shall have original Jurisdiction. In all the other Cases before mentioned, the supreme Court shall have appellate Jurisdiction, both as to Law and Fact, with such Exceptions, and under such Regulations as the Congress shall make.

The Trial of all Crimes, except in Cases of Impeachment, shall be by Jury; and such Trial shall be held in the State where the said Crimes shall have been committed; but when not committed within any State, the Trial shall be at such Place or Places as the Congress may by Law have directed.

Section 3. Treason against the United States, shall consist only in levying War against them, or, in adhering to their Enemies, giving them Aid and Comfort. No Person shall be convicted of Treason unless on the Testimony of two Witnesses to the same overt Act, or on Confession in open Court.

The Congress shall have Power to declare the Punishment of Treason, but no Attainder of Treason shall work Corruption of Blood, or Forfeiture except during the Life of the Person attainted.

Article IV

Section 1. Full Faith and Credit shall be given in each State to the public Acts, Records, and judicial Proceedings of every other State. And the Congress may by general Laws prescribe the Manner in which such Acts, Records and Proceedings shall be proved, and the Effect thereof.

Section 2. The Citizens of each State shall be entitled to all Privileges and Immunities of Citizens in the several States.

A Person charged in any State with Treason, Felony, or other Crime, who shall flee from Justice, and be found in another State, shall on Demand of the executive Authority of the State from which he fled, be delivered up, to be removed to the State having Jurisdiction of the Crime.

No Person held to Service or Labour in one State, under the Laws thereof, escaping into another, shall, in Consequence of any Law or Regulation therein, be discharged from such Service or Labour, but shall be delivered up on Claim of the Party to whom such Service or Labour may be due.

Section 3. New States may be admitted by the Congress into this Union; but no new State shall be formed or erected within the Jurisdiction of any other State; nor any State be formed by the Junction of two or more States, or Parts of States, without the Consent of the Legislatures of the States concerned as well as of the Congress.

The Congress shall have Power to dispose of and make all needful Rules and Regulations respecting the Territory or other Property belonging to the United States; and nothing in this Constitution shall be so construed as to Prejudice any Claims of the United States, or of any particular State.

Section 4. The United States shall guarantee to every State in this Union a Republican Form of Government, and shall protect each of them against Invasion; and on Application of the Legislature, or of the Executive (when the Legislature cannot be convened) against domestic Violence.

Article V

The Congress, whenever two thirds of both Houses shall deem it necessary, shall propose Amendments to this Constitution, or, on the Application of the Legislatures of two thirds of the several States, shall call a Convention for proposing Amendments, which, in either Case, shall be valid to all Intents and Purposes, as Part of this Constitution, when ratified by the Legislatures of three fourths of the several States, or by Conventions in three fourths thereof, as the one or the other Mode of Ratification may be proposed by the Congress; Provided that no Amendment which may be made prior to the Year One thousand eight hundred and eight shall in any Manner affect the first and fourth Clauses in the Ninth Section of the first Article; and that no State, without its Consent, shall be deprived of its equal Suffrage in the Senate.

Article VI

All Debts contracted and Engagements entered into, before the Adoption of this Constitution shall be as valid against the United States under this Constitution, as under the Confederation.

This Constitution, and the Laws of the United States which shall be made in Pursuance thereof; and all Treaties made, or which shall be made, under the Authority of the United States, shall be the supreme Law of the Land; and the Judges in every State shall be bound thereby, any Thing in the Constitution or Laws of any State to the Contrary notwithstanding.

The Senators and Representatives before mentioned, and the Members of the several State Legislatures, and all executive and judicial Officers, both of the United States and of the several States, shall be bound by Oath or Affirmation, to support this Constitution; but no religious Test shall ever be required as a Qualification to any Office or public Trust under the United States.

Article VII

The Ratification of the Conventions of nine States shall be sufficient for the Establishment of this Constitution between the States so ratifying the Same.

done in Convention by the Unanimous Consent of the States present the Seventeenth Day of September in the Year of our Lord one thousand seven hundred and Eighty seven and of the Independence of the United States of America the Twelfth *In witness whereof We have hereunto subscribed our Names,*

G°Washington—Presid^t
and deputy from Virginia

New Hampshire	John Langdon Nicholas Gilman
Massachusetts	Nathaniel Gorham Rufus King
Connecticut	W^m. Saml. Johnson Roger Sherman
New York	Alexander Hamilton
New Jersey	Wil: Livingston David Brearley. W^m. Paterson. Jona: Dayton
Pennsylvania	B Franklin Thomas Mifflin Robt Morris Geo. Clymer Thos FitzSimons Jared Ingersoll James Wilson Gouv Morris
Delaware	Geo: Read Cunning Bedford jun John Dickinson Richard Bassett Jaco: Broom
Maryland	James McHenry Dan of St Tho.^sJenifer Danl Carroll
Virginia	John Blair— James Madison Jr.

North Carolina
{
Wm Blount
Richd Dobbs Spaight
Hu Williamson

South Carolina
{
J. Rutledge
Charles Cotesworth Pinckney
Charles Pinckney
Pierce Butler.

Georgia
{
William Few
Abr Baldwin

Amendments

(The first 10 Amendments were ratified December 15, 1791, and form what is known as the Bill of Rights)

Amendment 1

Congress shall make no law respecting an establishment of religion, or prohibiting the free exercise thereof; or abridging the freedom of speech, or of the press; or the right of the people peaceably to assemble, and to petition the Government for a redress of grievances.

Amendment 2

A well regulated Militia, being necessary to the security of a free State, the right of the people to keep and bear Arms, shall not be infringed.

Amendment 3

No Soldier shall, in time of peace be quartered in any house, without the consent of the Owner, nor in time of war, but in a manner to be prescribed by law.

Amendment 4

The right of the people to be secure in their persons, houses, papers, and effects, against unreasonable searches and seizures, shall not be violated, and no Warrants shall issue, but upon probable cause, supported by Oath or affirmation, and particularly describing the place to be searched, and the persons or things to be seized.

Amendment 5

No person shall be held to answer for a capital, or otherwise infamous crime, unless on a presentment or indictment of a Grand Jury, except in cases arising in the land or naval forces, or in the Militia, when in actual service in time of War or public danger; nor shall any person be subject for the same offence to be twice put in jeopardy of life or limb; nor shall be compelled in any criminal case to be a witness against himself, nor be deprived of life, liberty, or property, without due process of law; nor shall private property be taken for public use, without just compensation.

Amendment 6

In all criminal prosecutions, the accused shall enjoy the right to a speedy and public trial, by an impartial jury of the State and district wherein the crime shall have been committed, which district shall have been previously ascertained by law, and to be informed of the nature and cause of the accusation; to be confronted with the witnesses against him; to have compulsory process for obtaining witnesses in his favor, and to have the Assistance of Counsel for his defence.

Amendment 7

In Suits at common law, where the value in controversy shall exceed twenty dollars, the right of trial by jury shall be preserved, and no fact tried by a jury, shall be otherwise re-examined in any Court of the United States, than according to the rules of the common law.

Amendment 8

Excessive bail shall not be required, nor excessive fines imposed, nor cruel and unusual punishments inflicted.

Amendment 9

The enumeration in the Constitution, of certain rights, shall not be construed to deny or disparage others retained by the people.

Amendment 10

The powers not delegated to the United States by the Constitution, nor prohibited by it to the States, are reserved to the States respectively, or to the people.

Amendment 11

(Ratified February 7, 1795)

The Judicial power of the United States shall not be construed to extend to any suit in law or equity, commenced or prosecuted against one of the United States by Citizens of another State, or by Citizens or Subjects of any Foreign State.

Amendment 12

(Ratified July 27, 1804)

The Electors shall meet in their respective states, and vote by ballot for President and Vice-President, one of whom, at least, shall not be an inhabitant of the same state with themselves; they shall name in their ballots the person voted for as President, and in distinct ballots the person voted for as Vice-President, and they shall make distinct lists of all persons voted for as President, and of all persons voted for as Vice-President, and of the number of votes for each, which lists they shall sign and certify, and transmit sealed to the seat of the government of the United States, directed to the President of the Senate;—The President of the Senate shall, in the presence of the Senate and House of Representatives, open all the certificates and the votes shall then be counted;—The person having the greatest number of votes for President, shall be the President, if such number be a majority of the whole number of Electors appointed; and if no person have such majority, then from the persons having the highest numbers not exceeding three on the list of those voted for as President, the House of Representatives shall choose immediately, by ballot, the President. But in choosing the President, the votes shall be taken by states, the representation from each state having one vote; a quorum for this purpose shall consist of a member or members from two-thirds of the states, and a majority of all the states shall be necessary to a choice. And if the House of Representatives shall not choose a President whenever the right of choice shall devolve upon them, before the fourth day of March next following, then the Vice-President shall act as President, as in the case of the death or other constitutional disability of the President.—The person having the greatest number of votes as Vice-President, shall be the Vice-President, if such number be a majority of the whole number of Electors appointed, and if no person have a majority, then from the two highest numbers on the list, the Senate shall choose the Vice-President; a quorum for the purpose shall consist of two-thirds of the whole number of Senators, and a majority of the whole number shall be necessary to a choice. But no person constitutionally ineligible to the office of President shall be eligible to that of Vice-President of the United States.

Amendment 13

(Ratified December 6, 1865)

Section 1. Neither slavery nor involuntary servitude, except as a punishment for crime whereof the party shall have been duly convicted, shall exist within the United States, or any place subject to their jurisdiction.

Section 2. Congress shall have power to enforce this article by appropriate legislation.

Amendment 14

(Ratified July 9, 1868)

Section 1. All persons born or naturalized in the United States, and subject to the jurisdiction thereof, are citizens of the United States and of the State wherein they reside. No State shall make or enforce any law which shall abridge the privileges or immunities of citizens of the United States; nor shall any State deprive any person of life, liberty, or property, without due process of law; nor deny to any person within its jurisdiction the equal protection of the laws.

Section 2. Representatives shall be apportioned among the several States according to their respective numbers, counting the whole number of persons in each State, excluding Indians not taxed. But when the right to vote at any election for the choice of electors for President and Vice President of the United States, Representatives in Congress, the Executive and Judicial officers of a State, or the members of the Legislature thereof, is denied to any of the male inhabitants of such State, being twenty-one years of age, and citizens of the United States, or in any way abridged, except for participation in rebellion, or other crime, the basis of representation therein shall be reduced in the proportion which the number of such male citizens shall bear to the whole number of male citizens twenty-one years of age in such State.

Section 3. No person shall be a Senator or Representative in Congress, or elector of President and Vice President, or hold any office, civil or military, under the United States, or under any State, who having previously taken an oath, as a member of Congress, or as an officer of the United States, or as a member of any State legislature, or as an executive or judicial officer of any State, to support the Constitution of the United States, shall have engaged in insurrection or rebellion against the same, or given aid or comfort to the enemies thereof. But Congress may by a vote of two-thirds of each House, remove such disability.

Section 4. The validity of the public debt of the United States, authorized by law, including debts incurred for payment of pensions and bounties for services in suppressing insurrection or rebellion, shall not be questioned. But neither the United States nor any State shall assume or pay any debt or obligation incurred in aid of insurrection or rebellion against the United States, or any claim for the loss or emancipation of any slave; but all such debts, obligations and claims shall be held illegal and void.

Section 5. The Congress shall have power to enforce, by appropriate legislation, the provisions of this article.

Amendment 15

(Ratified February 3, 1870)

Section 1. The right of citizens of the United States to vote shall not be denied or abridged by the United States or by any State on account of race, color, or previous condition of servitude.

Section 2. The Congress shall have power to enforce this article by appropriate legislation.

Amendment 16

(Ratified February 3, 1913)

The Congress shall have power to lay and collect taxes on incomes, from whatever source derived, without apportionment among the several States, and without regard to any census or enumeration.

Amendment 17

(Ratified April 8, 1913)

The Senate of the United States shall be composed of two Senators from each State, elected by the people thereof, for six years; and each Senator shall have one vote. The electors in each State shall have the qualifications requisite for electors of the most numerous branch of the State legislatures.

When vacancies happen in the representation of any State in the Senate, the executive authority of such State shall issue writs of election to fill such vacancies: *Provided,* That the legislature of any State may empower the executive thereof to make temporary appointments until the people fill the vacancies by election as the legislature may direct.

This amendment shall not be so construed as to affect the election or term of any Senator chosen before it becomes valid as part of the Constitution.

Amendment 18

(Ratified January 16, 1919. Repealed December 5, 1933 by Amendment 21)

Section 1. After one year from the ratification of this article the manufacture, sale, or transportation of intoxicating liquors within, the importation thereof into, or the exportation thereof from the United States and all territory subject to the jurisdiction thereof for beverage purposes is hereby prohibited.

Section 2. The Congress and the several States shall have concurrent power to enforce this article by appropriate legislation.

Section 3. This article shall be inoperative unless it shall have been ratified as an amendment to the Constitution by the legislatures of the several States, as provided in the Constitution, within seven years from the date of the submission hereof to the States by the Congress.

Amendment 19

(Ratified August 18, 1920)

The right of citizens of the United States to vote shall not be denied or abridged by the United States or by any State on account of sex.

Congress shall have power to enforce this article by appropriate legislation.

Amendment 20

(Ratified January 23, 1933)

Section 1. The terms of the President and Vice President shall end at noon on the 20th day of January, and the terms of Senators and Representatives at noon on the 3d day of January, of the years in which such terms would have ended if this article had not been ratified; and the terms of their successors shall then begin.

Section 2. The Congress shall assemble at least once in every year, and such meeting shall begin at noon on the 3d day of January, unless they shall by law appoint a different day.

Section 3. If, at the time fixed for the beginning of the term of the President, the President elect shall have died, the Vice President elect shall become President. If a President shall not have been chosen before the time fixed for the beginning of his term, or if the President elect shall have failed to qualify, then the Vice President elect shall act as President until a President shall have qualified; and the Congress may by law provide for the case wherein neither a President elect nor a Vice President elect shall have qualified, declaring who shall then act as President, or the manner in which one who is to act shall be selected, and such person shall act accordingly until a President or Vice President shall have qualified.

Section 4. The Congress may by law provide for the case of the death of any of the persons from whom the House of Representatives may choose a President whenever the right of choice shall have devolved upon them, and for the case of the death of any of the persons from whom the Senate may choose a Vice President whenever the right of choice shall have devolved upon them.

Section 5. Sections 1 and 2 shall take effect on the 15th day of October following the ratification of this article.

Section 6. This article shall be inoperative unless it shall have been ratified as an amendment to the Constitution by the legislatures of three-fourths of the several States within seven years from the date of its submission.

Amendment 21

(Ratified December 5, 1933)

Section 1. The eighteenth article of amendment to the Constitution of the United States is hereby repealed.

Section 2. The transportation or importation into any State, Territory, or possession of the United States for delivery or use therein of intoxicating liquors, in violation of the laws thereof, is hereby prohibited.

Section 3. This article shall be inoperative unless it shall have been ratified as an amendment to the Constitution by conventions in the several States, as provided in the Constitution, within seven years from the date of the submission hereof to the States by the Congress.

Amendment 22

(Ratified February 27, 1951)

Section 1. No person shall be elected to the office of the President more than twice, and no person who has held the office of President, or acted as President, for more than two years of a term to which some other person was elected President shall be elected to the office of the President more than once. But this Article shall not apply to any person holding the office of the President when this Article was proposed by the Congress, and shall not prevent any person who may be holding the office of President, or acting as President, during the term within which this Article becomes operative from holding the office of President or acting as President during the remainder of such term.

Section 2. This article shall be inoperative unless it shall have been ratified as an amendment to the Constitution by the legislatures of three-fourths of the several States within seven years from the date of its submission to the States by the Congress.

Amendment 23

(Ratified March 29, 1961)

Section 1. The District constituting the seat of Government of the United States shall appoint in such manner as the Congress may direct:

A number of electors of President and Vice President equal to the whole number of Senators and Representatives in Congress to which the District would be entitled if it were a State, but in no event more than the least populous State; they shall be in addition to those appointed by the States, but they shall be considered, for the purposes of the election of President and Vice President, to be electors appointed by a State; and they shall meet in the District and perform such duties as provided by the twelfth article of amendment.

Section 2. The Congress shall have power to enforce this article by appropriate legislation.

Amendment 24

(Ratified January 23, 1964)

Section 1. The right of citizens of the United States to vote in any primary or other election for President or Vice President, for electors for President or Vice President, or for Senator or Representative in Congress, shall not be denied or abridged by the United States, or any State by reason of failure to pay any poll tax or other tax.

Section 2. The Congress shall have power to enforce this article by appropriate legislation.

Amendment 25

(Ratified February 10, 1967)

Section 1. In case of the removal of the President from office or of his death or resignation, the Vice President shall become President.

Section 2. Whenever there is a vacancy in the office of the Vice President, the President shall nominate a Vice President who shall take office upon confirmation by a majority vote of both Houses of Congress.

Section 3. Whenever the President transmits to the President pro tempore of the Senate and the Speaker of the House of Representatives his written declaration that he is unable to discharge the powers and duties of his office, and until he transmits to them a written declaration to the contrary, such powers and duties shall be discharged by the Vice President as Acting President.

Section 4. Whenever the Vice President and a majority of either the principal officers of the executive departments or of such other body as Congress may by law provide, transmit to the President pro tempore of the Senate and the Speaker of the House of Representatives their written declaration that the President is unable to discharge the powers and duties of his office, the Vice President shall immediately assume the powers and duties of the office as Acting President.

Thereafter, when the President transmits to the President pro tempore of the Senate and the Speaker of the House of Representatives his written declaration that no inability exists, he shall resume the powers and duties of his office unless the Vice President and a majority of either the principal officers of the executive department or of such other body as Congress may by law provide, transmit within four days to the President pro tempore of the Senate and the Speaker of the House of Representatives their written declaration that the President is unable to discharge the powers and duties of his office. Thereupon Congress shall decide the issue, assembling within forty-eight hours for that purpose if not in session. If the Congress, within twenty-one days after receipt of the latter written declaration, or, if Congress is not in session, within twenty-one days after Congress is required to assemble, determines by two-thirds vote of both Houses that the President is unable to discharge the powers and duties of his office, the Vice President shall continue to discharge the same as Acting President; otherwise, the President shall resume the powers and duties of his office.

Amendment 26

(Ratified July 1, 1971)

Section 1. The right of citizens of the United States, who are eighteen years of age or older, to vote shall not be denied or abridged by the United States or by any State on account of age.

Section 2. The Congress shall have power to enforce this article by appropriate legislation.

PROPOSED AMENDMENTS TO THE CONSTITUTION
NOT RATIFIED BY THE STATES

During the course of our history, in addition to the 26 amendments that have been ratified by the required three-fourths of the States, other amendments have been submitted to the States but have not been ratified by them.

Beginning with the proposed Eighteenth Amendment, Congress has customarily included a provision requiring ratification within seven years from the time of the submission to the States. The Supreme Court in *Coleman* v. *Miller*, 307 U.S. 433 (1939), declared that the question of the reasonableness of the time within which a sufficient number of States must act is a political question to be determined by the Congress.

In 1789, twelve proposed articles of amendment were submitted to the States. Of these, Article III-XII were ratified and became the first ten amendments to the Constitution, popularly known as the Bill of Rights. Proposed Articles I and II were not ratified. The following is the text of those articles:

ARTICLE I. After the first enumeration required by the first article of the Constitution, there shall be one Representaive for every thirty thousand, until the number shall amount to one hundred, after which the proportion shall be so regulated by Congress, that there shall be not less than one hundred Representatives, nor less than one Representative for every forty thousand persons, until the number of Representatives shall amount to two hundred; after which the proportion shall be so regulated by Congress, that there shall not be less than two hundred Representatives, nor more than one Representative for every fifty thousand persons.

ARTICLE II. No law varying the compensation for the services of the Senators and Representatives shall take effect, until an election of Representatives shall have intervened.

Thereafter, in the 2d session of the Eleventh Congress, the Congress proposed the following article of amendment to the Constitution relating to acceptance by citizens of the United States of titles of nobility from any foreign government.

The proposed amendment, which was not ratified by three-fourths of the States, is as follows:

Resolved by the Senate and House of Representatives of the United States of America in Congress assembled (two thirds of both houses concurring), That the following section be submitted to the legislatures of the several states, which, when ratified by the legislatures of three fourths of the states, shall be valid and binding, as a part of the constitution of the Untied States.

If any citizen of the United States shall accept, claim, receive or retain any title of nobility or honour, or shall, without the consent of Congress, accept and retain any present, pension, office or emolument of any kind whatever, from any emperor, king, prince or foreign power, such person shall cease to be a citizen of the United States, and shall be incapable of holding any office of trust or profit under them, or either of them.

The following amendment to the Constitution relating to slavery was proposed by the 2d session of the Thirty-sixth Congress on March 2, 1861, when it passed the Senate, having previously passed the House on February 28, 1861. It is interesting to note in this connection that this is the only proposed amendment to the Constitution ever signed by the President. The President's signature is considered unnecessary because of the constitutional provision that on the concurrence of two-thirds of both Houses of Congress the proposal shall be submitted to the States for ratification.

Resolved by the Senate and House of Representatives of the United States of America in Congress assembled, That the following article be proposed to the Legislatures of the several States as an amendment to the Constitution of the United States, which, when ratified by three-fourths of said Legislatures, shall be valid, to all intents and purposes, as part of the said Constitution, viz:

ARTICLE THIRTEEN

No amendment shall be made to the Constitution which will authorize or give to Congress the power to abolish or interfere, within any State, with the domestic institutions thereof, including that of persons held to labor or service by the laws of said State.

A child labor amendment was proposed by the 1st session of the Sixty-eighth Congress on June 2, 1926, when it passed the Senate, having previously passed the House on April 26, 1926. The proposed amendment, which has been ratified by 28 States to date, is as follows:

JOINT RESOLUTION PROPOSING AN AMENDMENT TO THE
CONSTITUTION OF THE UNITED STATES

Resolved by the Senate and House of Representatives of the United States of America in Congress assembled (two-thirds of each House concurring therein), That the following article is proposed as an amendment to the Constitution of the United States, which, when ratified by the legislatures of three-fourths of the several States, shall be valid to all intents and purposes as a part of the Constitution:

ARTICLE—.

SECTION 1. The Congress shall have power to limit, regulate, and prohibit the labor of persons under eighteen years of age.

SECTION 2. The power of the several States is unimpaired by this article except that the operation of State laws shall be suspended to the extent necessary to give effect to legislation enacted by the Congress.

An amendment relative to equal rights for men and women was proposed by the 2d session of the Ninety-second Congress on March 22, 1972, when it passed the Senate, having previously passed the House on October 12, 1971. The seven-year deadline for ratification of the proposed amendment was extended to June 30, 1982, by the 2d session of the Ninety-fifth Congress. The proposed amendment, which was not ratified by three-fourths of the States by June 30, 1982; is as follows:

JOINT RESOLUTION PROPOSING AN AMENDMENT TO THE
CONSTITUTION OF THE UNITED STATES RELATIVE TO
EQUAL RIGHTS FOR MEN AND WOMEN

Resolved by the Senate and House of Representatives of the United States of America in Congress assembled (two-thirds of each House concurring therein), That the following article is proposed as an amendment to the Constitution of the United States, which shall be valid to all intents and purposes as a part of the Constitution when ratified by the legislatures of three-fourths of the several States within seven years from the date of its submission by the Congress:

ARTICLE—

SECTION 1. Equality of rights under the law shall not be denied or abridged by the United States or by any State on account of sex.

SEC. 2. The Congress shall have the power to enforce, by appropriate legislation, the provisions of this article.

SEC. 3. This amendment shall take effect two years after the date of ratification.

An amendment relative to voting rights for the District of Columbia was proposed by the 2d session of the Ninety-fifth Congress on August 22, 1978, when it passed the House on March 2, 1978. The proposed amendment, which was not ratified by three-fourths of the States within the specified seven-year period, is as follows:

JOINT RESOLUTION PROPOSING AN AMENDMENT TO THE
CONSTITUTION TO PROVIDE FOR REPRESENTATION
OF THE DISTRICT OF COLUMBIA IN THE CONGRESS.

Resolved by the Senate and House of Representatives of the United States of America in Congress assembled (two-thirds of each House concurring therein), That the following article is proposed as an amendment to the Constitution of the United Sates, which shall be valid to all intents and purposes as part of the Constitution when ratified by the legislatures of three-fourths of the several States within seven years from the date of its submission by the Congress:

ARTICLE—

SECTION 1. For purposes of representation in the Congress, election of the President and Vice President, and article V of this Constitution, the District constituting the seat of government of the United States shall be treated as though it were a State.

SEC. 2. The exercise of the rights and powers conferred under this article shall be by the people of the District constituting the seat of government, and as shall be provided by the Congress.

SEC. 3. The twenty-third article of amendment to the Constitution of the United States is hereby repealed.

SEC. 4. This article shall be inoperative, unless it shall have been ratified as an amendment to the Constitution by the legislatures of three-fourths of the several States within seven years from the date of its submission.

Dates Related To The Ratification Of The Constitution

September 20, 1787:   Congress receives the proposed Constitution.

September 26–27, 1787:   Congress resolves to submit the Constitution to special state ratifying conventions. Article VII of the document stipulates that it will become effective when ratified by nine states.

October 27, 1787:   The first Federalist paper appears in New York City newspapers, one of 85 to argue in favor of the adoption of the new frame of government. Written by Alexander Hamilton, James Madison and John Jay, the essays attempt to counter the arguments of Antifederalists, who fear a strong centralized national government.

December 7, 1787:   Delaware ratifies the Constitution, the first state to do so, by unanimous vote.

December 12, 1787:   Pennsylvania ratifies the Constitution in the face of considerable opposition. The vote in convention is 46 to 23.

December 18, 1787:   New Jersey ratifies unanimously.

January 2, 1788:   Georgia ratifies unanimously.

January 9, 1788:   Connecticut ratifies by a vote of 128 to 40.

February 6, 1788:   The Massachusetts convention ratifies by a close vote of 187 to 168, after vigorous debate. Many Antifederalists, including Sam Adams, change sides after Federalists propose nine amendments, including one which would reserve to the states all powers not "expressly delegated" to the national government by the Constitution.

March 24, 1788:   Rhode Island, which had refused to send delegates to the Constitutional Convention, declines to call a state convention and holds a popular referendum instead. Federalists do not participate, and the voters reject the Constitution, 2,708 to 237.

April 28, 1788:   Maryland ratifies by a vote of 63 to 11.

March 23, 1788:   South Carolina ratifies by a vote of 149 to 73.

June 21, 1788:   New Hampshire becomes the ninth state to ratify, by a vote of 57 to 47. The convention proposes twelve amendments.

June 25, 1788:   Despite strong opposition led by Patrick Henry, Virginia ratifies the Constitution by 89 to 79. James Madison leads the fight in favor. The convention recommends a bill of rights, composed of twenty articles, in addition to twenty further changes.

July 2, 1788:   The President of Congress, Cyrus Griffin of Virginia, announces that the Constitution has been ratified by the requisite nine states. A committee is appointed to prepare for the change in government.

July 26, 1788:   New York ratifies by vote of 30 to 27 after Alexander Hamilton delays action, hoping that news of ratification from New Hampshire and Virginia would influence Antifederalist sentiment.

August 2, 1788:   North Carolina declines to ratify until the addition to the Constitution of a bill of rights.

October 10, 1788:   The congress of the Confederation transacts its last official business.

Source: The Guide to American Law, published by West Publishing Co., 1983.

CHARTS, TABLES, MAPS

METRIC SYSTEM AND ENGLISH CONVERSION

The gram, that is the primary unit of weights, is the weight of one cubic centimeter of pure distilled water at a temperature of 39.2° F., the kilogram is the weight of 1 liter of water; the ton is the weight of 1 cubic meter of water. The gram is used in weighing gold, jewels, and small quantities of things. The kilogram, commonly called kilo for brevity, is used by grocers; the ton is used for weighing heavy articles.

Measures of Pressure

1 Pound per square inch =
- 144 pounds per square foot
- 0.068 atmosphere
- 2.042 inches of mercury at 62° F.
- 27.7 inches of water at 62° F.
- 2.31 feet of water at 62° F.

1 Atmosphere =
- 30 inches of mercury at 62° F.
- 14.7 pounds per square inch
- 2116.3 pounds per square foot
- 33.95 feet of water at 62° F.

1 Foot of water at 62° F. =
- 62.355 pounds per square foot
- 0.433 pounds per square inch

1 Inch of mercury at 62° F. =
- 1.132 foot of water
- 13.58 inches of water
- 0.491 pound per square inch

Metric and English Conversion Table

Measures of Length

1 millimeter	=	0.03937 inch
1 centimeter	=	0.3937 inch
1 meter	=	39.37 inches
		3.2808 feet
		1.0936 yards
1 kilometer	=	0.6214 miles
1 inch	=	25.4 millimeters
		2.54 centimeters
1 foot	=	304.8 millimeters
		0.3048 meter
1 yard	=	0.9144 meter
1 mile	=	1.609 kilometer

Square Measure—Measures of Surface

1 square millimeter	=	0.00155 square inch
1 square centimeter	=	0.155 square inch
1 square meter	=	10.764 square feet
		1.196 square yard
1 are	=	0.0247 acre
		1076.4 square feet
1 hectare	=	2.471 acres
		107,640 square feet
1 square kilometer	=	0.3861 square mile
		247.1 acres
1 square inch	=	6.452 square centimeters
		645.2 square millimeters
1 square foot	=	0.0929 square meter
		9.290 square centimeters
1 square yard	=	0.836 square meter
1 acre	=	0.4047 hectare
		40.47 ares
1 square mile	=	2.5899 square kilometers

Cubic Measure—Measures of Volume and Capacity

1 cubic centimeter	=	0.061 cubic inch
1 cubic decimeter	=	61.023 cubic inches
		0.0353 cubic foot

Metric Prefixes

Micro, a millionth	=	$1/1{,}000{,}000$
Milli, a thousandth	=	$1/1000$
Centi, a hundredth	=	$1/100$
Deci, a tenth	=	$1/10$
Deca, ten	=	10
Hecto, one hundred	=	100

* *Patternmaker 3 & 2*, Trauman, U.S. Navy (Naval Publications & Forms Center, Navy Education and Training Program, 1985).

Kilo, one thousand	=	1000
Myria, ten thousand	=	10,000
Mega, one million	=	1,000,000

Principal Units of Metric System

The meter for lengths
The square meter for surfaces
The cubic meter for large volumes
The liter for small volumes
The gram for weights

Measures of Length

10 millimeters (mm.)	= 1 centimeter (cm.)
10 centimeters	= 1 decimeter (dm.)
10 decimeters	= 1 meter (m)
10 meters	= 1 decameter (Dm.)
10 decameters	= 1 hectometer (Hm.)
10 hectometers	= 1 kilometer (Km.)
10 kilometers	= 1 myriameter

A meter is used in ordinary measurements; the centimeter or millimeter in calculating very small distances; and the kilometer for long distances.

Square Measure—Measures of Surface

100 square millimeters (mm.²)	= 1 square centimeter (cm.²)
100 square centimeters	= 1 square decimeter (dm.²)
100 square decimeters	= 1 square meter (m.²)
100 centiares, or square meters	= 1 are (a.)
100 ares	= 1 hectare (ha.)

The square meter is used for ordinary surfaces; the are, a square, each of whose sides is 10 meters, is the unit of land measure.

Cubic Measure—Measures of Volume

1000 cubic millimeters (mm.³)	= 1 cubic centimeter (cm.³ or cc.)
1000 cubic centimeters	= 1 cubic decimeter (dm.³)
1000 cubic decimeters	= 1 cubic meter (m.³)

The term stere is used to designate the cubic meter in measuring wood and timber. A tenth of a stere is a decistere, and ten steres are a decastere.

Liquid and Dry Measures—Measures of Capacity

10 milliliters (ml.)	= 1 centiliter (cl.)
10 centiliters	= 1 deciliter (dl.)
10 deciliters	= 1 liter (l.)
10 liters	= 1 decaliter (Dl.)
10 decaliters	= 1 hectoliter (Hl.)
10 hectoliters	= 1 kiloliter (Kl.)

The liter, which is a cube each of whose edges is $1/10$ of a meter in length, is the principal unit of measures of capacity. The hectoliter is the unit that is used in measuring large quantities of grain, fruits, roots, and liquids.

Measures of Weight

10 milligrams (mg.)	= 1 centigram (cg.)
10 centigrams	= 1 decigram (dg.)
10 decigrams	= 1 gram (g.)
10 grams	= 1 decagram (Dg.)
10 decagrams	= 1 hectogram (Hg.)
10 hectograms	= 1 kilogram (Kg.)
1000 kilograms	= 1 (metric) ton (T.)

Useful Factors, English Measures

Inches	×	0.08333	=	feet
"	×	0.02778	=	yards
"	×	0.00001578	=	miles
Square inches	×	0.00695	=	square feet
"	×	0.0007716	=	square yards
Cubic inches	×	0.00058	=	cubic feet
"	×	0.0000214	=	cubic yards
"	×	0.004329	=	U.S. gallons
Feet	×	0.3334	=	yards
"	×	0.00019	=	miles
Square feet	×	144.0	=	square inches
"	×	0.1112	=	square yards
Cubic feet	×	1,728	=	cubic inches
"	×	0.03704	=	cubic yards
"	×	7.48	=	U.S. gallons
Yards	×	36	=	inches
"	×	3	=	feet
"	×	0.0005681	=	miles

Square yards	×	1,296	= square inches
"	×	9	= square feet
Cubic Yards.........	×	46,656	= cubic inches
"	×	27	= cubic feet
Miles.........	×	63,360	= inches
"	×	5,280	= feet
Miles.........	×	1,760	= yards
Avoirdupois ounces	×	0.0625	= pounds
" "	×	0.00003125	= tons
" pounds..	×	16	= ounces
" "	×	.001	= hundredweight
" "	×	.0005	= tons
" "	×	27.681	= cubic inches of water at 39.2°F.
" tons.....	×	32,000	= ounces
" "	×	2,000	= pounds
Watts.........	×	0.00134	= horse power
Horse power	×	746	= watts

Weight of round iron per foot = square of diameter in quarter inches ÷ 6.
Weight of flat iron per foot = width × thickness × 10/3.

Cubic centimeters ÷ 29.57	= fluid ounce U.S. Pharmacopoeia
Cubic meters × 35.315	= cubic feet
Cubic meters × 1.038	= cubic yards
Cubic meters × 264.2	= gallons, United States
Liters × 61.022	= cubic inches
Liters × 33.84	= fluid ounces
Liters × 0.2642	= gallons, United States
Liters ÷ 3.78	= gallons, United States
Liters ÷ 28.316	= cubic feet
Hectoliters × 3.531	= cubic feet
Hectoliters × 2.84	= bushels, United States
Hectoliters × 0.131	= cubic yards
Hectoliters × 26.42	= gallons, United States
Grams × 15.432	= grains
Grams (water) ÷ 29.57	= fluid ounces
Grams ÷ 28.35	= ounces, avoirdupois
Kilograms × 2.2046	= pounds
Kilograms × 35.3	= ounces, avoirdupois
Kilograms ÷ 1102.3	= tons, 2000 pounds

Useful Factors, Metric Measures

Millimeters × 0.03937	= inches
Millimeters ÷ 25.4	= inches
Centimeters × 0.3937	= inches
Centimeters ÷ 2.54	= inches
Meters × 39.37	= inches
Meters × 3.281	= feet
Meters × 1.094	= yards
Kilometers × 0.621	= miles
Kilometers ÷ 1.6093	= miles
Kilometers × 3280.7	= feet
Square millimeters × 0.0155	= square inches
Square millimeters ÷ 645.1	= square inches
Square centimeters × 0.155	= square inches
Square centimeters ÷ 6.451	= square inches
Square meters × 10.764	= square feet
Square kilometers × 247.1	= acres
Hectares × 2.471	= acres
Cubic centimeters ÷ 16.385	= cubic inches
Cubic centimeters ÷ 3.69	= fluid drachms, U.S. Pharmacopoeia

INCHES AND EQUIVALENTS IN MILLIMETERS

Inches	MM	Inches	MM	Inches	MM
1/64	.397	45/64	17.859	26	660.4
1/32	.794	23/32	18.256	27	685.8
3/64	1.191	47/64	18.653	28	711.2
1/16	1.588	3/4	19.050	29	637.6
5/64	1.984	49/65	19.447	30	762.0
3/32	2.381	25/32	19.844	31	787.4
7/64	2.778	51/64	20.241	32	812.8
1/8	3.175	13/16	20.638	33	838.2
9/64	3.572	53/64	21.034	34	863.6
5/32	3.969	27/32	21.431	35	889.0
11/64	4.366	55/64	21.828	36	914.4
3/16	4.763	7/8	22.225	37	939.8
13/64	5.159	57/64	22.622	38	965.2
7/32	5.556	29/32	23.019	39	990.6
15/64	5.953	59/64	23.416	40	1016.0
1/4	6.350	15/16	23.813	41	1041.4
17/64	6.747	61/64	24.209	42	1066.8
9/32	7.144	31/32	24.606	43	1092.2
19/64	7.540	63/64	25.003	44	1117.6
5/16	7.938	1	25.400	45	1143.0
21/64	8.334	2	50.8	46	1168.4
11/32	8.731	3	76.2	47	1193.8
23/64	9.128	4	101.6	48	1219.2
3/8	9.525	5	127.0	49	1244.6
25/64	9.922	6	152.4	50	1270.0
13/32	10.319	7	177.8	51	1295.4
27.64	10.716	8	203.2	52	1320.8
7/16	11.113	9	228.6	53	1346.2
29/64	11.509	10	254.0	54	1371.6
15/32	11.906	11	279.4	55	1397.0
31/64	12.303	12	304.8	56	1422.4
1/2	12.700	13	330.2	57	1447.8
33/64	13.097	14	355.6	58	1473.2
17/32	13.494	15	381.0	59	1498.6
35/64	13.891	16	406.4	60	1524.0
9/16	14.288	17	431.8	61	1549.4
37/64	14.684	18	457.2	62	1574.8
19/32	15.081	19	482.6	63	1600.2
39/64	15.478	20	508.0	64	1625.6
5/8	15.875	21	533.4	65	1651.0
41/64	16.272	22	558.8	66	1676.4
21/32	16.669	23	584.2	67	1701.8
43/64	17.066	24	609.6	68	1727.2
11/16	17.463	25	635.0	69	1752.6

MATHEMATICS SYMBOLS

Symbol	Name or Meaning	Symbol	Name or Meaning
+	Addition or positive value	$\sqrt{}$	Square root symbol
−	Subtraction or negative value	$\sqrt[n]{}$	Radical symbol. Letter n represents a number indicating which root is to be taken.
±	Positive or negative value		
·	Multiplication dot (Centered; not to be mistaken for decimal point.)	i or j	Imaginary unit; operator j for electronics; represents $\sqrt{-1}$.
×	Multiplication symbol	∞	Infinity symbol
( )	Parentheses ⎫	…	Ellipses. Used in series of numbers in which successive numbers are predictable by their conformance to a pattern; meaning is approximated by "etc."
[ ]	Brackets ⎬ Grouping symbols		
{ }	Braces ⎭		
%	Percent	$\log_a N$	Logarithm of N to the base a.
÷	Division symbol	$\log N$	Logarithm of N to the base 10. (understood)
:	Ratio symbol		
::	Proportion symbol	$\ln N$	Natural or Napierian logarithm of N. Base of the natural or Napierian logarithm system.
=	Equality symbol		
≠	"Not equal" symbol		
<	Less than	[X]	Absolute value of X.
≦	Less than or equal to	π	Pi. The ratio of the circumference of any circle to its diameter. Approximate numerical value is 22/7.
>	Greater than		
≧	Greater than or equal to		
∝	"Varies directly as" or "is proportional to" (Not to be mistaken for Greek alpha (α).)	∠ or ∡	Angle

TABLE OF DECIMAL EQUIVALENTS OF FRACTIONS OF AN INCH

1/64	0.0156	17/64	0.2656	33/64	0.5156	49/64	0.7656
1/32	.0313	9/32	.2813	17/32	.5313	25/32	.7813
3/64	.0469	19/64	.2969	35/64	.5469	51/64	.7969
1/16	.0625	5/16	.3125	9/16	.5625	13/16	.8125
5/64	.0781	21/64	.3281	37/64	.5781	53/64	.8281
3/32	.0938	11/32	.3438	19/32	.5938	27/32	.8438
7/64	.1094	23/64	.3594	39/64	.6094	55/64	.8594
1/8	.125	3/8	.375	5/8	.625	7/8	.875
9/64	.1406	25/64	.3906	41/64	.6406	57/64	.8906
5/32	.1563	13/32	.4063	21/32	.6563	29/32	.9063
11/64	.1719	27/64	.4219	43/64	.6719	59/64	.9219
3/16	.1875	7/16	.4375	11/16	.6875	15/16	.9375
13/64	.2031	29/64	.4531	45/64	.7031	61/64	.9531
7/32	.2188	15/32	.4688	23/32	.7188	31/32	.9688
15/64	.2344	31/64	.4844	47/64	.7344	63/64	.9844
1/4	.25	1/2	.5	3/4	.75	1	1.0

WEIGHTS AND MEASURES

Distance

12 inches	=	1 foot (ft)
3 feet	=	1 yard (yd)
5½ yards	=	1 rod (rd)
16½ feet	=	1 rod
1,760 yards	=	1 statute mile (mi)
5,280 feet	=	1 statute mile

Additional measures of length occasionally used

1000 mils = 1 inch; 3 inches = 1 palm; 4 inches = 1 hand;
9 inches = 1 span; 2½ feet = 1 military space;
5½ yards or 16½ feet = 1 rod; 2 yards = 1 fathom;
a cable length = 120 fathoms = 720 feet;
1 inch = 0.0001157 cable length = 0.013889 fathom = 0.111111 span

Old Land or Surveyors' Measure*

7.92 inches = 1 link (l.)
100 links, or 66 feet, or 4 rods = 1 chain (ch.)
10 chains or 220 yards = 1 furlong
8 furlongs or 80 chains = 1 mile (mi)

* Sometimes called Gunter's Chain.

Nautical Measure

6080.26 feet or 1.15156 statute miles = 1 nautical mile or knot†
3 nautical miles = 1 league
60 nautical miles, or 69.169 statute miles = 1 degree at the equator
360 degrees = circumference of the earth at the equator
†The value varies according to different measures of the earth's diameter

Square Measures—Measures of Surface

144 square inches (sq. in.)	=	1 square foot (sq. ft.)
9 square feet	=	1 square yard (sq. yd.)
30¼ square yards or 272¼ square feet	=	1 square rod (sq. rd.)
160 square rods or 43,560 square feet	=	1 acre (A.)
640 acres	=	1 square mile (sq. mi.)

Surveyors' Measure

16 square rods	=	1 square chain (sq. ch.)
10 square chains	=	1 acre (A.)
640 acres	=	1 square mile (Sq. mi.)
1 square mile	=	1 section (sec.)
36 sections	=	1 township (tp.)

Solid or Cubic Measure—Measures of Volume

1728 cubic inches (cu. in.)	=	1 cubic foot (cu. ft.)
27 cubic feet	=	1 cubic yard (cu. yd.)

The following measures are also used for wood and masonry.

1 cord of wood	=	a pile, 4 × 4 × 8 feet = 128 cubic feet
1 perch of masonry	=	16½ × 1½ × 1 foot = 24¾ cubic feet

Shipping Measure

Register Ton—For register tonnage or for measuring entire internal capacity of a ship or vessel:

100 cubic feet = 1 register ton

Shipping Ton—For the measurement of cargo.
40 cubic feet = 1 United States shipping ton = 32.143 U.S. bushels
42 cubic feet = 1 British shipping ton = 32.719 imperial bushels.

Carpenter's Rule—To find the weight a vessel will carry multiply the length of keel by the breadth at main beam by the depth of the hold in feet and divide by 95 (the cubic feet allowed for a ton). The result will be the tonnage.

Old Liquid Measure

31½ gallons	= 1 barrel (bbl.)
42 gallons	= 1 tierce
2 barrels or 63 gallons	= 1 hogshead (hhd.)
84 gallons or 2 tierces	= 1 puncheon
2 hogsheads or 4 barrels or 126 gallons	= 1 pipe or butt
2 pipes or 3 puncheons	= 1 tun

Apothecaries' Fluid Measure

60 minims = 1 fluid drachm; 8 drachms = 1 fluid ounce

1 U.S. fluid ounce = 8 drachms = 1.805 cubic inch = $\frac{1}{128}$ U.S. gallon. The fluid ounce in Great Britain is 1.732 cubic inches.

Measures of Weight

Avoirdupois or Commercial Weight

16 drachms or 437.5 grains	= 1 ounce (oz.)
16 ounces or 7000 grains	= 1 pound (lb.)
2000 pounds	= 1 net or short ton
2240 pounds	= 1 gross or long ton
2204.6 pounds	= 1 metric ton

Measures of weight occasionally used in collecting duties on foreign goods at U.S. custom houses and in freighting coal are:

1 hundredweight = 4 quarters = 112 pounds (1 gross or long ton = 20 hundredweight); 1 quarter = 28 pounds; 1 stone = 14 pounds; 1 quintal = 100 pounds.

Troy Weight*

24 grains	= 1 pennyweight (pwt.)
20 pennyweights	= 1 ounce
12 ounces or 5760 grains	= 1 pound (lb.)

A carat of the jewelers, for precious stones = 3.2 grains in the United States. The International carat = 3.168 grains or 200 milligrams. In avoirdupois, apothecaries' and troy weights, the grain is the same, 1 pound troy = 0.82286 pound avoirdupois.

*Used for weighing gold, silver, jewels, etc.

Dry Measure

2 cups	= 1 pint (pt)
2 pints	= 1 quart (qt)
4 quarts	= 1 gallon (gal)
8 quarts	= 1 peck (pk)
4 pecks	= 1 bushel (bu)

Counting Units

12 units	= 1 dozen (doz)
12 dozen	= 1 gross
144 units	= 1 gross
24 sheets	= 1 quire
480 sheets	= 1 ream

Equivalents

1 cubic foot of water weighs 62.5 pounds (approx) = 1,000 ounces
1 gallon of water weighs 8⅓ pounds (approx)
1 cubic foot = 7.48 gallons
1 inch = 2.54 centimeters
1 foot = 30.4801 centimeters
1 meter = 39.37 inches
1 liter = 1.05668 quarts (liquid) = 0.90808 quart (dry)
1 nautical mile = 6,080 feet (approx)
1 fathom = 6 feet
1 shot of chain = 15 fathoms

Liquid Measure

3 teaspoons (tsp)	= 1 tablespoon (tbsp)
16 tablespoons	= 1 cup
2 cups	= 1 pint (pt.)
16 fluid ounces (oz)	= 1 pint
4 gills (gi.)	= 1 pint (pt.)
2 pints	= 1 quart (qt.)
4 quarts	= 1 gallon (gal.) { U.S. 231 cubic inches / British 277.274 cubic inches

1 cubic foot = 7.48 U.S. gallons

Apothecaries' Weight†

20 grains (gr.)	=	1 scruple
3 scruples	=	1 drachm
8 drachms	=	1 ounce
12 ounces	=	1 pound troy

†This table is used in compounding medicines and prescriptions.

Measures of Time

one millionth of a second	=	1 microsecond (μsec.)
one thousandth of a second	=	1 millisecond (msec.)
1/3600 hour	=	1 second (sec.)
60 seconds	=	1 minute (min.)
60 minutes	=	1 hour (hr.)
24 hours	=	1 day (da.)
7 days	=	1 week (wk.)
365 days	=	1 solar year (yr.)
366 days	=	1 leap-year (every four years)
100 years	=	1 century

By the Gregorian calendar every year in which the number is divisible by 4 is a leap year except that the centesimal years (each 100 years: 1800, 1900, 2000, etc.) are leap-years only when the number of the year is divisible by 400.

Water Conversion Factors

U.S. gallons	×	8.33	= pounds
U.S. gallons	×	0.13368	= cubic feet

U.S. gallons	×	231	=	cubic inches
U.S. gallons	×	0.83	=	English gallons
U.S. gallons	×	3.78	=	liters
English gallons (Imperial)	×	10	=	pounds
English gallons (Imperial)	×	0.16	=	cubic feet
English gallons (Imperial)	×	277.274	=	cubic inches
English gallons (Imperial)	×	1.2	=	U.S. gallons
English gallons (Imperial)	×	4.537	=	liters
Cubic inches of water (39.1°)	×	0.036024	=	pounds
Cubic inches of water (39.1°)	×	0.004329	=	U.S. gallons
Cubic inches of water (39.1°)	×	0.003607	=	English gallons
Cubic inches of water (39.1°)	×	0.576384	=	ounces
Cubic feet (of water) (39.1°)	×	62.425	=	pounds
Cubic feet (of water) (39.1°)	×	7.48	=	U.S. gallons
Cubic feet (of water) (39.1°)	×	6.232	=	English gallons
Cubic feet (of water) (39.1°)	×	0.028	=	tons
Pounds of water	×	27.72	=	cubic inches
Pounds of water	×	0.01602	=	cubic feet
Pounds of water	×	0.12	=	U.S. gallons
Pounds of water	×	0.10	=	English gallons

Miscellaneous Tables

Numbers

12 units	=	1 dozen
12 dozen	=	1 gross
12 gross	=	1 great gross
20 units	=	1 score

Circular and Angular Measures

60 seconds (″)	=	1 minute (′)
60 minutes	=	1 degree (°)
90 degrees	=	1 quadrant
360 degrees	=	1 circumference

ROMAN NUMERAL

I	1
II	2
III	3
IV	4
V	5
VI	6
VII	7
VIII	8
IX	9
X	10
XI	11
XII	12
XIII	13
XIV	14
XV	15
XVI	16
XVII	17
XVIII	18
XIX	19
XX	20
XXI	21
XXIX	29
XXX	30
XL	40
XLVIII	48
IL	49
L	50
LX	60
XC	90
XCVIII	98
IC	99
C	100
CI	101
CC	200
D	500
DC	600
CM	900
M	1000
MDCLXVI	1666
MCMLXXX	1980

MATHEMATICAL NOTATION

Mathematical Power	Name
10^{18} or 1,000,000,000,000,000,000	one quintillion
10^{15} or 1,000,000,000,000,000	one quadrillion
10^{12} or 1,000,000,000,000	one trillion
10^{9} or 1,000,000,000	one billion
10^{6} or 1,000,000	one million
10^{3} or 1,000	one thousand
10^{2} or 100	one hundred
10^{1} or 10	ten
10^{0} or 1	one
10^{-1} or 0.1	one tenth
10^{-2} or 0.01	one hundredth
10^{-3} or 0.001	one thousandth
10^{-6} or 0.000 001	one millionth
10^{-9} or 0.000 000 001	one billionth
10^{-12} or 0.000 000 000 001	one trillionth
10^{-15} or 0.000 000 000 000 001	one quadrillionth
10^{-18} or 0.000 000 000 000 000 001	one quintillionth

INTERNATIONAL ATOMIC WEIGHTS

Element	Symbol	Atomic number	Atomic weight	Element	Symbol	Atomic number	Atomic weight
Actinium	Ac	89	(227)	Mercury	Hg	80	200.59
Aluminum	Al	13	26.9815	Molybdenum	Mo	42	95.94
Americium	Am	95	(243)	Neodymium	Nd	60	144.24
Antimony	Sb	51	121.75	Neon	Ne	10	20.183
Argon	Ar	18	39.948	Neptunium	Np	93	(237)
Arsenic	As	33	74.9216	Nickel	Ni	28	58.70
Astatine	At	85	(210)	Niobium	Nb	41	92.906
Barium	Ba	56	137.34	Nitrogen	N	7	14.0067
Berkelium	Bk	97	(247)	Nobelium	No	102	(254)
Beryllium	Be	4	9.0122	Osmium	Os	76	190.2
Bismuth	Bi	83	208.980	Oxygen	O	8	15.9994
Boron	B	5	10.811	Palladium	Pd	46	106.4
Bromine	Br	35	79.909	Phosphorus	P	15	30.9738
Cadmium	Cd	48	112.40	Platinum	Pt	78	195.09
Calcium	Ca	20	40.08	Plutonium	Pu	94	(244)
Californium	Cf	98	(249)	Polonium	Po	84	(210)
Carbon	C	6	12.01115	Potassium	K	19	39.102
Cerium	Ce	58	140.12	Praesodymium	Pr	59	140.907
Cesium	Cs	55	132.905	Promethium	Pm	61	(145)
Chlorine	Cl	17	35.453	Protactinium	Pa	91	(231)
Chromium	Cr	24	51.996	Radium	Ra	88	(226)
Cobalt	Co	27	58.9332	Radon	Rn	86	(222)
Copper	Cu	29	63.54	Rhenium	Re	75	186.2
Curium	Cm	96	(245)	Rhodium	Rh	45	102.905
Dysprosium	Dy	66	162.50	Rubidium	Rb	37	85.47
Einsteinium	Es	99	(254)	Ruthenium	Ru	44	101.07
Erbium	Er	68	167.26	Samarium	Sm	62	150.35
Europium	Eu	63	151.96	Scandium	Sc	21	44.956
Fermium	Fm	100	(252)	Selenium	Se	34	78.96
Fluorine	F	9	18.9984	Silicon	Si	14	28.086
Francium	Fr	87	(223)	Silver	Ag	47	107.870
Gadolinium	Gd	64	157.25	Sodium	Na	11	22.9898
Gallium	Ga	31	69.72	Strontium	Sr	38	87.62
Germanium	Ge	32	72.59	Sulfur	S	16	32.064
Gold	Au	79	196.967	Tantalum	Ta	73	180.948
Hafnium	Hf	72	178.49	Technetium	Tc	43	(99)
Helium	He	2	4.0026	Tellurium	Te	52	127.60
Holmium	Ho	67	164.930	Terbium	Tb	65	158.924
Hydrogen	H	1	1.00797	Thallium	Tl	81	204.37
Indium	In	49	114.82	Thorium	Th	90	232.038
Iodine	I	53	126.9044	Thulium	Tm	69	168.934
Iridium	Ir	77	192.2	Tin	Sn	50	118.69
Iron	Fe	26	55.847	Titanium	Ti	22	47.90
Krypton	Kr	36	83.80	Tungsten	W	74	183.85
Lanthanum	La	57	138.91	Uranium	U	92	238.03
Lawrencium	Lw	103	(257)	Vanadium	V	23	50.942
Lead	Pb	82	207.19	Xenon	Xe	54	131.30
Lithium	Li	3	6.942	Ytterbium	Yb	70	173.04
Lutetium	Lu	71	174.97	Yttrium	Y	39	88.905
Magnesium	Mg	12	24.312	Zinc	Zn	30	65.37
Manganese	Mn	25	54.9380	Zirconium	Zr	40	91.22
Mendelevium	Mv	101	(256)				

Numbers in parentheses indicate mass number of most stable known isotope.

STATES OF THE UNION—HISTORICAL DATA

State or other jurisdiction	Capital	Source of state lands	Date organized as Territory	Date admitted to Union	Chronological order of admission to Union
ALABAMA	Montgomery	Mississippi Territory, 1798[a]	March 3, 1817	Dec. 14, 1819	22
ALASKA	Juneau	Purchased from Russia, 1867	Aug. 24, 1912	Jan. 3, 1959	49
ARIZONA	Phoenix	Ceded by Mexico, 1848[b]	Feb. 24, 1863	Feb. 14, 1912	48
ARKANSAS	Little Rock	Louisiana Purchase, 1803	March 2, 1819	June 15, 1836	25
CALIFORNIA	Sacramento	Ceded by Mexico, 1848	[c]	Sept. 9, 1850	31
COLORADO	Denver	Louisiana Purchase, 1803[d]	Feb. 28, 1861	Aug. 1, 1876	38
CONNECTICUT	Hartford	Fundamental Orders, Jan. 14, 1638; Royal charter, April 23, 1662[e]	—	Jan, 9, 1788[f]	5
DELAWARE	Dover	Swedish charter, 1638; English charter, 1683[e]	—	Dec. 7, 1787[f]	1
FLORIDA	Tallahassee	Ceded by Spain, 1819	March 30, 1822	March 3, 1845[f]	27
GEORGIA	Atlanta	Charter, 1732, from George II to Trustees for Establishing the Colony of Georgia[e]	–	Jan. 2, 1788[f]	4
HAWAII	Honolulu	Annexed, 1898	June 14, 1900	Aug. 21, 1959	50
IDAHO	Boise	Treaty with Britain, 1846	March 4, 1863	July 3, 1890	43
ILLINOIS	Springfield	Northwest Territory, 1787	Feb. 3, 1809	Dec. 3, 1818	21
INDIANA	Indianapolis	Northwest Territory, 1787	May 7, 1800	Dec. 11, 1816	19
IOWA	Des Moines	Louisiana Purchase, 1803	June 12, 1838	Dec. 28, 1846	29
KANSAS	Topeka	Louisiana Purchase, 1803[d]	May 30, 1854	Jan. 29, 1861	34
KENTUCKY	Frankfort	Part of Virginia until admitted as State	[c]	June 1, 1792	15
LOUISIANA	Baton Rouge	Louisiana Purchase, 1803[g]	March 26, 1804	April 30, 1812	18
MAINE	Augusta	Part of Massachusetts until admitted as State	[c]	March 15, 1820	23
MARYLAND	Annapolis	Charter, 1632, from Charles I to Calvert[e]	—	April 28, 1788[f]	7
MASSACHUSETTS	Boston	Charter to Massachusetts Bay Company, 1629[e]	—	Feb. 6, 1788[f]	6
MICHIGAN	Lansing	Northwest Territory, 1787	Jan. 11, 1805	Jan. 26, 1837	26
MINNESOTA	St. Paul	Northwest Territory, 1787[h]	March 3, 1849	May 11, 1858	32
MISSISSIPPI	Jackson	Mississippi Territory[i]	April 7, 1798	Dec. 10, 1817	20
MISSOURI	Jefferson City	Louisiana Purchase, 1803	June 4, 1812	Aug. 10, 1821	24
MONTANA	Helena	Louisiana Purchase, 1803[j]	May 26, 1864	Nov. 8, 1889	41
NEBRASKA	Lincoln	Louisiana Purchase, 1803	May 30, 1854	March 1, 1867	37

State or other jurisdiction	Capital	Source of state lands	Date organized as Territory	Date admitted to Union	Chronological order of admission to Union
NEVADA	Carson City	Ceded by Mexico, 1848	March 2, 1861	Oct. 31, 1864	36
NEW HAMPSHIRE	Concord	Grants from Council for New England, 1622 and 1629. Made Royal province, 1679[e]	—	June 21, 1788[f]	9
NEW JERSEY	Trenton	Dutch settlement, 1618; English charter, 1664[e]	—	Dec. 18, 1787[f]	3
NEW MEXICO	Santa Fe	Ceded by Mexico, 1848[b]	Sept. 9, 1850	Jan. 6, 1912	47
NEW YORK	Albany	Dutch settlement, 1623; English control, 1664[e]	—	July 26, 1788[f]	11
NORTH CAROLINA	Raleigh	Charter, 1663, from Charles II[e]	—	Nov. 21, 1789[f]	12
NORTH DAKOTA	Bismarck	Louisiana Purchase, 1803[k]	March 2, 1861	Nov. 2, 1889	39
OHIO	Columbus	Northwest Territory, 1787	May 7, 1800	March 1, 1803	17
OKLAHOMA	Oklahoma City	Louisiana Purchase, 1803	May 2, 1890	Nov. 16, 1907	46
OREGON	Salem	Settlement and treaty with Britain, 1846	Aug. 14, 1848	Feb. 14, 1859	33
PENNSYLVANIA	Harrisburg	Grant from Charles II to William Penn, 1681[e]	—	Dec. 12, 1787[f]	2
RHODE ISLAND	Providence	Charter, 1663, from Charles II[e]	—	May 29, 1790[f]	13
SOUTH CAROLINA	Columbia	charter, 1663, from Charles II[e]	—	May 23, 1788[f]	8
SOUTH DAKOTA	Pierre	Louisiana Purchase, 1803	March 2, 1861	Nov. 2, 1889	40
TENNESSEE	Nashville	Part of North Carolina until land ceded to U.S. in 1789	June 8, 1790[l]	June 1, 1796	16
TEXAS	Austin	Republic of Texas, 1845	[c]	Dec. 29, 1945	28
UTAH	Salt Lake City	Ceded by Mexico, 1848	Sept. 9, 1850	Jan. 4, 1896	45
VERMONT	Montpelier	From lands of New Hampshire and New York	[c]	March 4, 1791	14
VIRGINIA	Richmond	Charter, 1609 from James I to London Company[e]	—	June 25, 1788[f]	10
WASHINGTON	Olympia	Oregon Territory, 1848	March 2, 1853	Nov. 11, 1889	42
WEST VIRGINIA	Charleston	Part of Virginia until admitted as State	[c]	June 20, 1863	35
WISCONSIN	Madison	Northwest Territory, 1787	April 20, 1836	May 29, 1848	30
WYOMING	Cheyenne	Louisiana Purchase, 1803[dj]	July 25, 1868	July 10, 1890	44
D.C.	—	Maryland[m]			—
AMERICAN SAMOA	Pago Pago	—	Became a Territory, 1900		—
FEDERATED STATES OF MICRONESIA	Kalonia	—	May 10, 1979		—
GUAM	Agana	Ceded by Spain 1898	Aug. 1, 1950		—
MARSHALL ISLANDS	Majuro	—	May 1, 1979		—

State or other jurisdiction	Capital	Source of state lands	Date organized as Territory	Date admitted to Union	Chronological order of admission to Union
PUERTO RICO	San Juan	Ceded by Spain, 1898	—	July 25, 1952[n]	—
NO. MARIANA IS.	Saipan	—	March 24, 1976	—	—
REPUBLIC OF BELAU	Korok	—	Jan. 1, 1981	—	—
VIRGIN ISLANDS	Charlotte Amalie	Purchased from Denmark, March 31, 1917			—

a. By the Treaty of Paris, 1783, England gave up claim to the thirteen original Colonies, and to all land within an area extending along the present Canadian border to the Lake of the Woods, down the Mississippi River to the 31st parallel, east to the Chattahoochie, down that river to the mouth of the Flint, east to the source of the St. Mary's, down that river to the ocean. The major part of Alabama was acquired by the Treaty of Paris, and the lower portion from Spain in 1813.

b. Portion of land obtained by Gadsden Purchase, 1853.

c. No territorial status before admission to Union.

d. Portion of land ceded by Mexico, 1848.

e. One of the original thirteen Colonies.

f. Date of ratification of U.S. Constitution.

g. West Feliciana District (Baton Rouge) acquired from Spain, 1810, added to Louisiana, 1812.

h. Portion of land obtained by Louisiana Purchase, 1803.

i. See footnote (a). The lower portion of Mississippi was also acquired from Spain in 1813.

j. Portion of land obtained from Oregon Territory, 1848.

k. The northern portion and the Red River Valley were acquired by treaty with Great Britain in 1818.

l. Date Southwest Territory (identical boundary as Tennessee) was created.

m. Area was originally 100 square miles, taken from Virginia and Maryland. Virginia's portion south of the Potomac was given back to that State in 1846. Site chosen in 1790, city incorporated 1802.

n. On this date Puerto Rico became a self-governing Commonwealth by compact approved by the United States Congress and the voters of Puerto Rico as provided in U.S. Public Law-600 of 1950.

Source: The Book of the States 1884-85 is published biennially by The Council of State Governments, Lexington, KY.

Estimated average monthly number of wage and salary workers covered by workers' compensation, 1981 and 1984

(Numbers in thousands)

State	1981	1984
Total	78,316	81,909
Alabama	955	990
Alaska	139	172
Arizona	830	950
Arkansas	595	625
California	9,400	9,940
Colorado	1,020	1,100
Connecticut	1,240	1,310
Delaware	185	200
District of Columbia	371	382
Florida	2,950	3,330
Georgia	1,690	1,900
Hawaii	384	389
Idaho	265	270
Illinois	3,860	3,910
Indiana	1,610	1,660
Iowa	945	940
Kansas	795	805
Kentucky	910	925
Louisiana	1,120	1,100
Maine	400	420
Maryland	1,340	1,430
Massachusetts	2,070	2,280
Michigan	2,900	2,900
Minnesota	1,520	1,580
Mississippi	605	610
Missouri	1,635	1,700
Montana	230	235
Nebraska	555	565
Nevada	355	370
New Hampshire	350	390
New Jersey	2,730	2,970
New Mexico	375	400
New York	6,110	6,360
North Carolina	2,020	2,230
North Dakota	208	212
Ohio	3,860	3,840
Oklahoma	875	865
Oregon	895	890
Pennsylvania	4,190	4,140
Rhode Island	310	320
South Carolina	930	990
South Dakota	175	184
Tennessee	1,210	1,260
Texas	3,710	4,160
Utah	475	515
Vermont	197	209
Virginia	1,880	2,050
Washington	1,470	1,470
West Virginia	540	510
Wisconsin	1,830	1,860
Wyoming	163	148
Federal Employees	2,939	2,948

Source: 51 Social Security Bulletin 20, No. 7 (July, 1988)

Minimum and Maximum Benefits for Temporary Total Disability Under Workers' Compensation Laws July 1, 1986

State	Maximum percentage of wages	Payments per week		Percentage of State average weekly wage	Maximum duration of benefit[1]
		Minimum	Maximum		
Alabama	$66^2/_3$	$88 or worker's average weekly wage, if less.[2]	$319.00	100	...
Alaska	80% of spendable earnings.	$110 or worker's spendable weekly wage, if less.	$1,114.00	200	...
Arizona	$66^2/_3$	...	$203.86	...	...
Arkansas	$66^2/_3$	$20	$175.00	(5)	450 weeks
California	$66^2/_3$	$112.00	$224.00	...	...
Colorado	$66^2/_3$	...	$351.68	80	...
Connecticut	$66^2/_3$	$79.40 or 80% of worker's average weekly wage, if less.[2]	$397.00	100	Duration of disability
Delaware	$66^2/_3$	$81.41 or actual wage, if less.[2]	$244.22	$66^2/_3$	...
District of Columbia	The lesser of $66^2/_3$ or 80% of spendable earnings.	$107.80	$431.70	100	...
Florida	$66^2/_3$	$20 or actual wage, if less.	$315.00	100	350 weeks
Georgia	$66^2/_3$	$25 or average wage, if less.	$175.00	...	...
Hawaii	$66^2/_3$	$74.75 or worker's average wage if less, but not lower than $38.[2]	$299.00	100	...
Idaho	60–90	$134.55	$269.10 to $373.75	90	After 52 weeks, maximum weekly benefit is 60% of State average weekly wage.
Illinois	$66^2/_3$	$100.90 to $124.30 or worker's average wage if less.[1]	$525.45	$133^1/_3$	...
Indiana	$66^2/_3$	$50 or worker's average wage, if less.	$190.00	...	500 weeks or $95.00
Iowa	80% of worker's spendable earnings.	$107.30 or actual wage, if less.[2]	$613.00	200	...
Kansas	$66^2/_3$	$25	$247.00	75	$75,000

State	Maximum percentage of wages	Payments per week		Percentage of State average weekly wage	Maximum duration of benefit[1]
		Minimum	Maximum		
Kentucky	66⅔	[2]$63.31	$316.54	100	...
Louisiana	66⅔	$68 or actual wage if less.[2]	$254.00	75	...
Maine	66⅔	$25	$447.92	([5])	...
Maryland	66⅔	$50 or actual wage, if less.	$344.00	100	...
Massachusetts	66⅔	$40 or worker's average wage, if less, but not less than $20 if normal working hours amount to 15 or more.	[3]$360.50	100	250 multiplied by state average weekly wage.
Michigan	80% of spendable worker's earnings.	...	$375.00	90	...
Minnesota	66⅔	$171 or actual wage, if less, but not less than $68.40[2]	$342.00	100	...
Mississippi	66⅔	$25	$140.00	...	450 weeks or $63,000
Missouri	66⅔	$40	$243.78	70	400 weeks
Montana	66⅔	...	$299.00	100	...
Nebraska	66⅔	$49 or actual wage, if less.	$225.00	...	...
Nevada	66⅔	...	$341.95	100	...
New Hampshire	66⅔	$131 or actual wage, if less.[2]	$492.00	150	...
New Jersey	70	$76[2]	$284.00	75	400 weeks
New Mexico	66⅔	$36 or actual wage.	$308.38	100	600 weeks
New York	66⅔	$30 or actual wage, if less.	$300.00	...	...
North Carolina	66⅔	$30	$294.00	100	...
North Dakota	66⅔	$178 or actual wage, if less.[2]	[3]$296.00	100	...
Ohio	72% for first 12 weeks; thereafter 66⅔	$121.67 or actual wage, if less.[2]	$365.00	100	...
Oklahoma	66⅔	$30 or actual wage, if less.	$217.00	([5])	300 weeks
Oregon	66⅔	$50 or 90% of actual wage, if less.	$344.77	100	...
Pennsylvania	66⅔	[2]$115.67	$347.00	100	Duration of disability
Puerto Rico	66⅔	$10	$45.00	...	312 weeks
Rhode Island	66⅔	...	[3]$307.00	100	Duration of disability
South Carolina	66⅔	$75 or actual wage, if less	$294.95	100	500 weeks
South Dakota	66⅔	$131 or worker's average wage, if less.	$262.00	100	...
Tennessee	66⅔	$25	$189.00	...	$75,600
Texas	66⅔	[2]$37	$217.00	([6])	401 weeks
Utah	66⅔	$45	[3]$329.00	100	312 weeks

State	Maximum percentage of wages	Payments per week		Percentage of State average weekly wage	Maximum duration of benefit[1]
		Minimum	Maximum		
Vermont	66⅔	$155 or worker's average wage, if less.[2]	$465.00	150	...
Virgin Islands	66⅔	$60 or actual wages, if less.	$187.00	66⅔	...
Virginia	66⅔	$81.50 or actual wage, if less.[2]	$326.00	100	500 weeks
Washington	'60–75	$42.69 to $81.23[1]	$269.70	75% of State's monthly wage.	...
West Virginia	70	[2]$114.35	$343.06	100	208 weeks
Wisconsin	66⅔	$20	$329.00	100	...
Wyoming	66⅔	$43.39	$353.00	100	...
United States:					
Federal employees	'66⅔–75	$141.46 or actual wage.	$979.90	(7)	...
Longshore	66⅔	$148.81 or worker's wage, if less.[2]	$595.24	200% of national average weekly wage.	...

[1] Benefits payable for duration of disability without any dollar limit unless stated otherwise.

[2] Adjusted automatically as States average weekly wage increases (with respect to the Longshore program as national average weekly wage rises).

[3] Plus dependents' allowance. Arizona, $10 monthly for one or more percent of basic benefit or 75 percent of worker's wage. Massachusetts, $6 per dependent if weekly benefits are below $150 and 100 percent of wage. North Dakota, $5 per dependent child not to exceed workers' net wage. Rhode Island, $9 per dependent, not to exceed 80 percent of workers' wage. Utah, $5 for dependent spouse and per child up to 4, not to exceed State average wage. Vermont, $10 per dependent under age 21.

[4] According to number of dependents (and in Washington, marital status). Idaho, 7 percent ($20.23) of State average weekly wage for each dependent child up to 5.

[5] Under current law, the maximum weekly benefit will be set as percentage of the State average weekly wage at a specified future date.

[6] Maximum increased by $7 for each $10 increase in average weekly wage for manufacturing at a specified future date.

[7] Based on 75 percent of the pay of specific grade level in the Federal civil service.

Selected Benefit Provisions Under State Unemployment Insurance Laws, September 6, 1986

State	Weekly benefit amount for total unemployment			Duration of benefits (weeks)[3]	
	Computation (fraction of high-quarter wages unless otherwise indicated)[1]	Minimum[2]	Maximum[2]	Minimum[4]	Maximum
Alabama	1/24	$22	$120	11+	26
Alaska	3.8-0.95% of annual wages, plus dependents' allowance	38-62	188-260	[5]16	[5]26
Arizona	1/25	40	135	12+	26
Arkansas	1/52 of wage in two highest quarters, up to 66⅔% of State average weekly wage	44	196	10	26
California	1/24—1/33	30	166	[5]12+	[5]26
Colorado	55% of 1/22 of wage in two highest quarters up to 55% of State average weekly wage	25	213	8+-13	[5]26
Connecticut	1/26 up to 60% of State average weekly wage plus dependents' allowance	15-22	192-242	[5]26	[5]26
Delaware	1/78 of wage in three highest quarters, up to 66⅔% of State average weekly wage	20	205	18	26
District of Columbia	1/23 plus dependents' allowance	26	[5]50	17	26
Florida	1/2 of claimant's average weekly wage	10	175	10	26
Georgia	1/50 of wage in two highest quarters	27	145	4	26
Hawaii	1/25 up to 66⅔% of State average weekly wage	5	188	[5]26	[5]26
Idaho	1/26 up to 60% of State average weekly wage	45	173	10	26
Illinois	48% of claimant's average weekly wage up to 48% of State average weekly wage plus dependent's allowance	50	161-209	26	26
Indiana	4.3% plus dependents' allowance	40	96-161	9+	26
Iowa	1/19—1/23 up to 53% of State average weekly wage plus dependents' allowance	23-28	162-199	11+	26
Kansas	4.25% up to 60% of State average weekly wage	49	197	10	26
Kentucky	1.185% of base period wages up to 55% of State average weekly wage	22	140	15	26
Louisiana	1/20—1/25 of average wage in highest two quarters up to 66⅔% of State average weekly wage[5]	10	205	12	26
Maine	1/22 up to 52% of State average weekly wage plus dependents' allowance	25-37	152-228	7+-22	26
Maryland	1/24 plus dependents' allowance	25-29	[5]195	26	26
Massachusetts	1/52 of wage in two highest quarters up to 57.5% of State average weekly wage plus dependents' allowance	14-21	207-310	9+-30	30
Michigan	70% of claimant's weekly wage up to 53% of State average weekly wage (from January 1, 1987) after tax earnings plus dependents' allowance	54	197	15	26

State	Weekly benefit amount for total unemployment			Duration of benefits (weeks)[3]	
	Computation (fraction of high-quarter wages unless otherwise indicated)[1]	Minimum[2]	Maximum[2]	Minimum[4]	Maximum
Minnesota	[6]	$58	$239	11	26
Mississippi	$1/26$	30	130	13+	26
Missouri	4.5%	14	125	10	26
Montana	44% of claimant's average weekly wage up to 60% of State average weekly wage	44	171	8	26
Nebraska	$1/17$–$1/24$	12	126	17	26
Nevada	$1/25$ up to 50% of State average weekly wage	16	171	12+	26
New Hampshire	1.8–1.2% of annual wages	36	150	26	26
New Jersey	60% of claimant's average weekly wage up to $56\frac{2}{3}$% of State average weekly wage plus dependents' allowance	20	[1]214	15	26
New Mexico	$1/26$ up to 50% of State average weekly wage	30	154	19+	26
New York	67–50% of claimant's average weekly wage	40	180	26	26
North Carolina	$1/52$ of wage in two highest quarters, up to $66\frac{2}{3}$% of State average weekly wage	16	175	13–26	26
North Dakota	$1/52$ of wage in two highest quarters, up to 67% of State average weekly wage	60	197	12	26
Ohio	$1/2$ claimant's average weekly wage plus dependents' allowance[5]	10	147–233	20	26
Oklahoma	$1/25$ up to 50–60% of State average weekly wage	16	197	20+	[5]26
Oregon	1.25% of base period wage up to 64% of State average weekly wage	50	261	6	26
Pennsylvania	$1/23$–$1/25$ up to $66\frac{2}{3}$% of State average weekly wage, plus dependents' allowance	35–40	232–240	16	26
Puerto Rico	$1/11$–$1/26$ up to 50% of State average weekly wage	7	95	16	[5]20
Rhode Island	55% of claimant's average weekly wage up to 60% of State average weekly wage, plus dependent's allowance	36–41	191–236	[5]20	[5]20
South Carolina	$1/26$ up to $66\frac{2}{3}$% of State average weekly wage	21	125	12	26
South Dakota	$1/26$ up to 62% of State average weekly wage[4]	28	129	14	26
Tennessee	$1/25$–$1/31$ of average wage in two highest quarters	30	125	18+	26
Texas	$1/25$[9]	32	203	12	26
Utah	$1/26$ up to 60% of State average weekly wage	13	197	13+	26
Vermont	$1/2$ of claimant's average weekly wage up to 60% of State average weekly wage	18	154	10	26
Virginia	$1/50$ of wage in two highest quarters	58	167	26	26
Virgin Islands	$1/26$ up to 50% of State average weekly wage	30	140	12	26
Washington	$1/25$ of average of wage in two highest quarters up to 55% of State average weekly wage	53	197	14+	26
				16+–30	30

State	Weekly benefit amount for total unemployment			Duration of benefits (weeks)[3]	
	Computation (fraction of high-quarter wages unless otherwise indicated)[1]	Minimum[2]	Maximum[2]	Minimum[4]	Maximum
West Virginia............	1.0% of annual wage up to 70% of State average weekly wage[5]	24	225	26	26
Wisconsin...............	50% of claimant's average weekly wage up to 66⅔% of State average week wage[5]	37	196	1–14+	26
Wyoming...............	1/25 up to 55% of State average weekly wage	36	198	12–26	26

[1]When States use a weighted high-quarter, annual wage, or average weekly wage formula, approximate fractions or percentages are figured at midpoint of lowest and highest normal wage brackets. When dependents' allowances are provided, the fraction applies to the basic benefit amount. In some States, variable amounts above maximum basic benefits are limited to claimants with specified number of dependents and earnings in excess of amounts applicable to maximum basic benefit. In the District of Columbia, Maryland, and New Jersey the maximum is the same with or without dependents' allowances.

[2]When two amounts are given, the higher includes dependents' allowances.

[3]Benefits extended under exclusively State funded program when unemployment in State reaches specified levels: Alaska, California, by 50 percent; Connecticut, Hawaii, by 13 weeks. In Puerto Rico, benefits extended by 32 weeks in certain industries, occupations, or establishments when special unemployment situations exist. In all States, benefits may be extended during periods of high unemployment by 50 percent for up to 13 weeks under Federal-State extended unemployment compensation program.

[4]For claimants with minimum qualifying wages and minimum weekly benefit amount. In States noted, range of duration applies to claimants with minimum qualifying wages in base period; longer duration applies with maximum possible concentration of wages in the high quarter, and therefore the highest weekly benefit amount possible for such base period earnings.

[5]The minimum and maximum weekly benefit amounts are frozen indefinitely in Louisiana and Wisconsin. The maximum weekly benefit is frozen until July 1988 in West Virginia, and indefinitely in South Dakota.

[6]Sixty percent of first $85, 40 percent of next $85, 50 percent of balance of claimant's average weekly wage, up to 66⅔% of State fund.

[7]Maximum weekly benefit amount may be frozen or be a variable percent of State average weekly wage depending on condition of State fund.

[8]Duration can be as low as 10 weeks for individuals with only one employer in a base period.

[9]Maximum amount adjusted annually by $7 for each $10 increase in average weekly wage of manufacturing production workers.

Source: *Comparison of Unemployment Insurance Laws*, Department of Labor, Washington, D.C., September 6, 1986.

Consumer Price Index for All Urban Consumers, 1940–87[1]

[1982–84 = 100]

Year and Month	All Items	Food and beverages	Housing	Apparel and upkeep	Transportation	Medical care	Entertainment	Other goods and services	Personal care	All services	All items less medical care
Annual Average:											
1940	14.0	...	...	21.8	14.2	10.4	...	...	...	12.6	...
1945	18.0	...	...	31.3	15.9	11.9	...	...	...	13.9	...
1950	24.1	...	...	40.3	22.7	15.1	...	...	26.2	17.0	...
1955	26.8	...	...	42.9	25.8	18.2	...	...	29.9	20.5	...
1960	29.6	...	...	45.7	29.8	22.3	...	...	34.6	24.0	30.2
1965	31.5	...	...	47.7	31.9	25.2	...	...	36.6	26.6	32.0
1970	38.8	40.1	36.4	59.2	37.5	34.0	47.5	41.0	43.5	35.1	39.2
1975	53.8	60.2	50.6	72.5	50.1	47.5	62.0	53.9	57.9	48.0	54.3
1980	82.4	86.8	81.1	90.9	83.1	74.9	83.6	75.2	81.9	77.9	82.8
1985	107.6	105.6	107.7	105.0	106.5	113.5	107.9	114.5	108.3	109.9	107.2
1986	109.6	109.1	110.9	105.9	102.3	122.0	111.6	121.4	111.9	115.4	108.8
1987	113.6	113.5	114.2	110.6	105.4	130.1	115.3	128.5	115.1	120.2	112.6
1987											
March	112.1	112.5	112.8	109.7	103.3	128.1	113.9	126.3	113.9	118.5	111.1
April	112.7	112.8	113.2	111.5	104.2	128.7	114.5	126.6	114.2	118.9	111.7
May	113.1	113.3	113.6	111.1	104.7	129.2	114.8	126.9	114.9	119.3	112.1
June	113.5	113.8	114.3	109.3	105.4	129.9	114.9	127.2	114.9	120.1	112.5
July	113.8	113.7	114.7	107.3	106.0	130.7	115.4	128.0	115.3	120.5	112.7
August	114.4	113.8	115.4	109.4	106.5	131.2	115.6	128.5	115.6	121.2	113.3
September	115.0	114.2	115.6	113.3	106.6	131.7	116.1	131.1	116.0	121.7	113.9
October	115.3	114.3	115.5	115.4	107.1	132.3	116.9	131.6	116.2	121.9	114.2
November	115.4	114.3	115.5	115.4	107.8	132.8	117.3	131.8	116.3	122.0	114.4
December	115.4	114.8	115.6	112.7	107.6	133.1	117.4	132.1	116.5	122.2	114.3

[1] Beginning January 1988, Consumer Price Index rebased from 1967 = 100 to 1982–84 = 100.

Source: Bureau of Labor Statistics.

Civilian population and labor force, 1940–87

[Numbers in thousands]

Period	Resident population, total1	Civilian population			Civilian labor force aged 16 or older2			Unemployment as percent of civilian labor force	
		Total	Under age 18	Aged 65 or older	Total	Employed	Unemployed	Unadjusted	Seasonally Adjusted
1940	132,457	132,129	...	...	55,640	47,520	8,120	14.6	...
1945	133,434	128,112	...	...	53,860	52,820	1,040	1.9	...
1950	151,868	150,790	...	...	62,208	58,920	3,288	5.3	...
1955	165,069	162,967	...	...	65,023	62,171	2,852	4.4	...
1960	179,979	178,140	64,463	16,675	69,628	65,778	3,852	5.5	...
1961	182,992	181,143	65,750	17,089	70,459	65,746	4,714	6.7	...
1962	185,771	183,677	67,087	17,457	70,614	66,702	3,911	5.5	...
1963	188,483	186,493	68,383	17,778	71,833	67,762	4,070	5.7	...
1964	191,141	189,141	69,644	18,127	73,091	69,305	3,786	5.2	...
1965	193,526	191,605	69,688	18,451	74,455	71,088	3,366	4.5	...
1966	195,576	193,420	69,857	18,755	75,770	72,895	2,875	3.8	...
1967	197,457	195,264	69,903	19,071	77,347	74,372	2,975	3.8	...
1968	199,399	197,113	69,865	19,365	78,737	75,920	2,817	3.6	...
1969	201,385	199,145	69,728	19,680	80,734	77,902	2,832	3.5	...
1970	203,984	201,895	66,222	20,107	82,771	78,678	4,093	4.9	...
1971	206,827	204,866	66,173	20,561	84,382	79,367	5,016	5.9	...
1972	209,824	207,511	66,075	21,020	87,034	82,153	4,882	5.6	...
1973	211,357	209,600	65,597	21,525	89,429	85,064	4,365	4.9	...
1974	213,342	211,636	64,877	22,061	91,949	86,794	5,156	5.6	...
1975	215,465	213,788	63,980	22,696	93,775	85,846	7,929	8.5	...
1976	217,563	215,894	63,102	23,278	96,158	88,752	7,406	7.7	...
1977	219,760	218,106	62,150	23,892	99,009	92,017	6,991	7.1	...
1978	222,095	220,467	61,427	24,502	102,251	96,048	6,202	6.1	...
1979	224,567	222,969	60,661	25,134	104,962	98,824	6,137	5.8	...
1980	227,236	225,632	60,087	25,708	106,940	99,303	7,637	7.1	...
1981	229,518	227,870	59,551	26,253	108,670	100,397	8,273	7.6	...
1982	231,786	230,117	62,810	26,826	110,238	99,541	10,696	9.7	...
1983	233,981	232,286	62,575	27,384	111,501	100,817	10,684	9.6	...
1984	236,108	234,395	63,756	27,959	113,544	105,005	8,539	7.5	...
1985	238,291	236,569	63,014	28,530	115,490	107,171	8,320	7.8	...
1986	240,750	239,077	63,266	29,172	117,841	109,600	8,241	7.0	...
1987	243,249	241,519	...	...	119,952	112,727	7,224	6.3	...

[1]Includes Alaska and Hawaii for all years. Annual data are estimated as of July 1. Data not adjusted for Census undercounts and of age misreporting. Comparability of estimates for data in the 1970's in tables published earlier affected by recomputations based on data from the 1980 census of the population. Source for data is Bureau of the Census, **Current Population Reports** (Population Estimates and Projections, Series P-25).

[2]Annual data are averages of monthly figures. Beginning 1960, includes Alaska and Hawaii. Data for 1950 and 1955 adjusted to reflect definitions adopted January 1957; two groups (those on temporary layoff and those waiting to start new wage and salary jobs within 30 days) formerly classified as employed—with a job, not at work—were assigned to other classifications, chiefly to the unemployed. Beginning 1962, comparability with previous years affected somewhat by the introduction of material from the 1960 census (level of labor force and employment lowered by about 150,000). Before January 1967, series show aged 14 or older. Source for data is the Bureau of Labor Statistics, **Employment and Earnings**.

[3]Rate computed from data in Department of Commerce, **Survey of Current Business**.

Custody Laws

State	A — States with statutory custody guidelines	B — States that consider the children's wishes	C — States with joint custody laws
Alabama	x	x	
Alaska	x	x	
Arizona	x	x	x
Arkansas			
California	x	x	x
Colorado	x	x	x
Connecticut		x	x
Delaware	x	x	x
Florida	x	x	x
Georgia		x	
Hawaii	x	x	x
Idaho	x	x	x
Illinois	x	x	x
Indiana	x	x	x
Iowa	x	x	x
Kansas	x	x	x
Kentucky	x	x	x
Louisiana	x	x	x
Maine	x	x	x
Maryland			x¹
Massachusetts			x
Michigan	x	x	x
Minnesota	x	x	x
Mississippi	x		x
Missouri	x	x	x
Montana	x	x	x
Nebraska	x	x	x
Nevada	x	x	x
New Hampshire		x	x
New Jersey		x	x¹
New Mexico	x	x	x
New York			
North Carolina			x
North Dakota	x	x	
Ohio		x	x
Oklahoma		x	x
Oregon	x		x
Pennsylvania		x	x
Rhode Island			
South Carolina			
South Dakota		x	
Tennessee		x	x
Texas		x	x
Utah		x	
Vermont	x		
Virginia	x	x	x
Washington	x	x	
West Virginia		x	
Wisconsin	x	x	x
Wyoming		x	
Washington, D.C.	x	x	
Puerto Rico		x	
Virgin Islands			

¹Case law only.

Source: *Reprinted from Family Law Quarterly, Volume XIX, Number 4, Winter 1987, copyright 1986 American Bar Association*

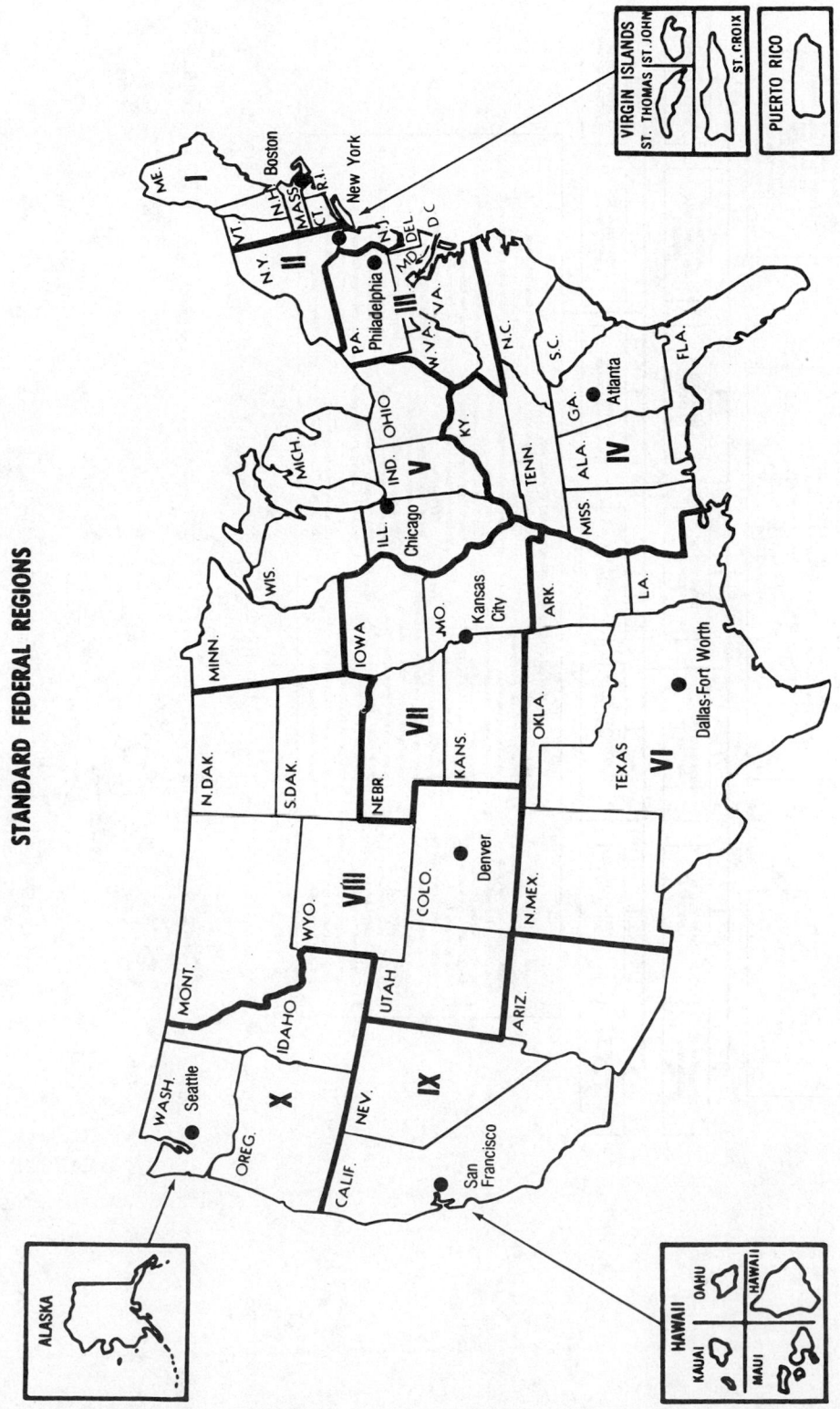

STANDARD FEDERAL REGIONS

THE GOVERNMENT OF THE UNITED STATES

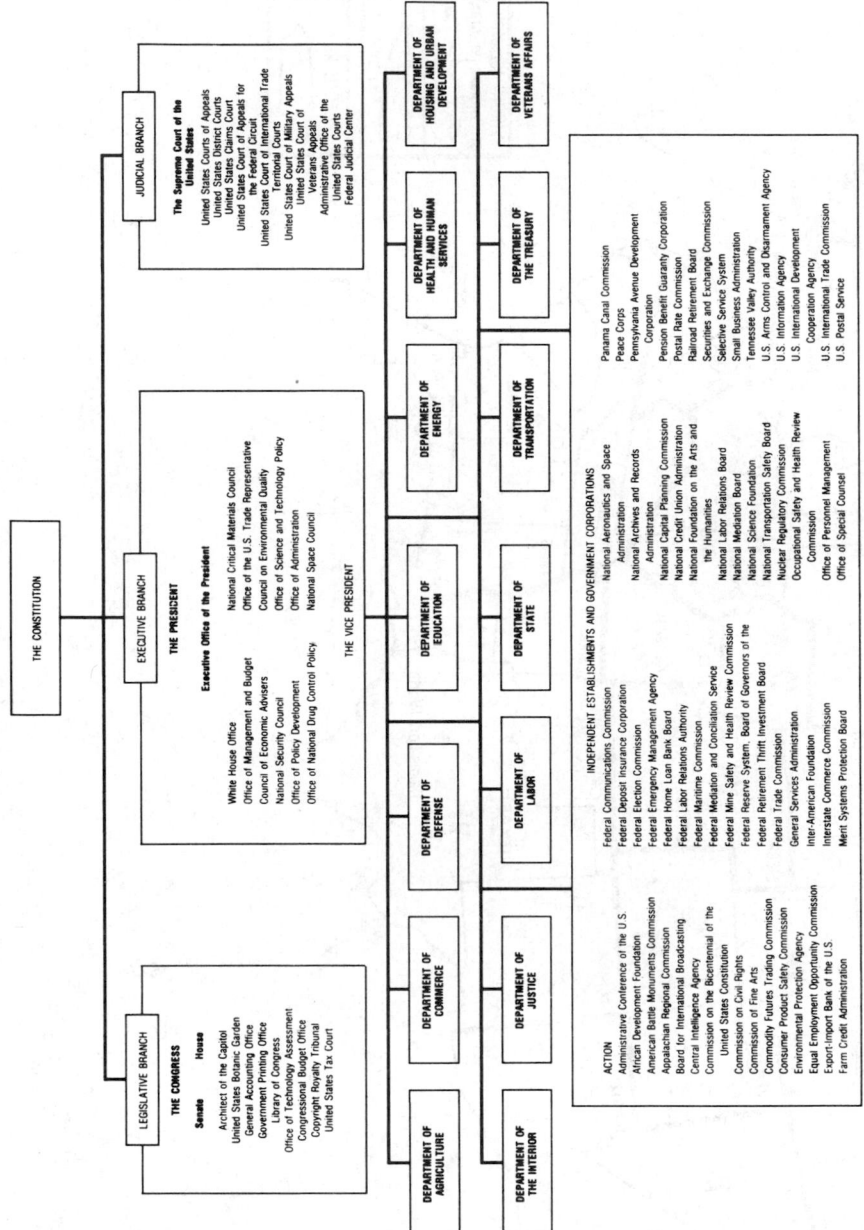

THE CONSTITUTION

LEGISLATIVE BRANCH

THE CONGRESS

Senate   House

Architect of the Capitol
United States Botanic Garden
General Accounting Office
Government Printing Office
Library of Congress
Office of Technology Assessment
Congressional Budget Office
Copyright Royalty Tribunal
United States Tax Court

EXECUTIVE BRANCH

THE PRESIDENT

Executive Office of the President

White House Office
Office of Management and Budget
Council of Economic Advisers
National Security Council
Office of Policy Development
Office of National Drug Control Policy

National Critical Materials Council
Office of the U.S. Trade Representative
Council on Environmental Quality
Office of Science and Technology Policy
Office of Administration
National Space Council

THE VICE PRESIDENT

JUDICIAL BRANCH

The Supreme Court of the United States

United States Courts of Appeals
United States District Courts
United States Claims Court
United States Court of Appeals for the Federal Circuit
Territorial Courts
United States Court of Military Appeals
United States Court of Veterans Appeals
Administrative Office of the United States Courts
Federal Judicial Center

DEPARTMENT OF AGRICULTURE

DEPARTMENT OF COMMERCE

DEPARTMENT OF DEFENSE

DEPARTMENT OF EDUCATION

DEPARTMENT OF ENERGY

DEPARTMENT OF HEALTH AND HUMAN SERVICES

DEPARTMENT OF HOUSING AND URBAN DEVELOPMENT

DEPARTMENT OF THE INTERIOR

DEPARTMENT OF JUSTICE

DEPARTMENT OF LABOR

DEPARTMENT OF STATE

DEPARTMENT OF TRANSPORTATION

DEPARTMENT OF THE TREASURY

DEPARTMENT OF VETERANS AFFAIRS

INDEPENDENT ESTABLISHMENTS AND GOVERNMENT CORPORATIONS

ACTION
Administrative Conference of the U.S.
African Development Foundation
American Battle Monuments Commission
Appalachian Regional Commission
Board for International Broadcasting
Central Intelligence Agency
Commission on the Bicentennial of the United States Constitution
Commission on Civil Rights
Commission of Fine Arts
Commodity Futures Trading Commission
Consumer Product Safety Commission
Environmental Protection Agency
Equal Employment Opportunity Commission
Export-Import Bank of the U.S.
Farm Credit Administration

Federal Communications Commission
Federal Deposit Insurance Corporation
Federal Election Commission
Federal Emergency Management Agency
Federal Home Loan Bank Board
Federal Labor Relations Authority
Federal Maritime Commission
Federal Mediation and Conciliation Service
Federal Mine Safety and Health Review Commission
Federal Reserve System, Board of Governors of the
Federal Retirement Thrift Investment Board
Federal Trade Commission
General Services Administration
Inter-American Foundation
Interstate Commerce Commission
Merit Systems Protection Board

National Aeronautics and Space Administration
National Archives and Records Administration
National Capital Planning Commission
National Credit Union Administration
National Foundation on the Arts and the Humanities
National Labor Relations Board
National Mediation Board
National Science Foundation
National Transportation Safety Board
Nuclear Regulatory Commission
Occupational Safety and Health Review Commission
Office of Personnel Management
Office of Special Counsel

Panama Canal Commission
Peace Corps
Pennsylvania Avenue Development Corporation
Pension Benefit Guaranty Corporation
Postal Rate Commission
Railroad Retirement Board
Securities and Exchange Commission
Selective Service System
Small Business Administration
Tennessee Valley Authority
U.S. Arms Control and Disarmament Agency
U.S. Information Agency
U.S. International Development Cooperation Agency
U.S. International Trade Commission
U.S. Postal Service

LIBRARY OF CONGRESS

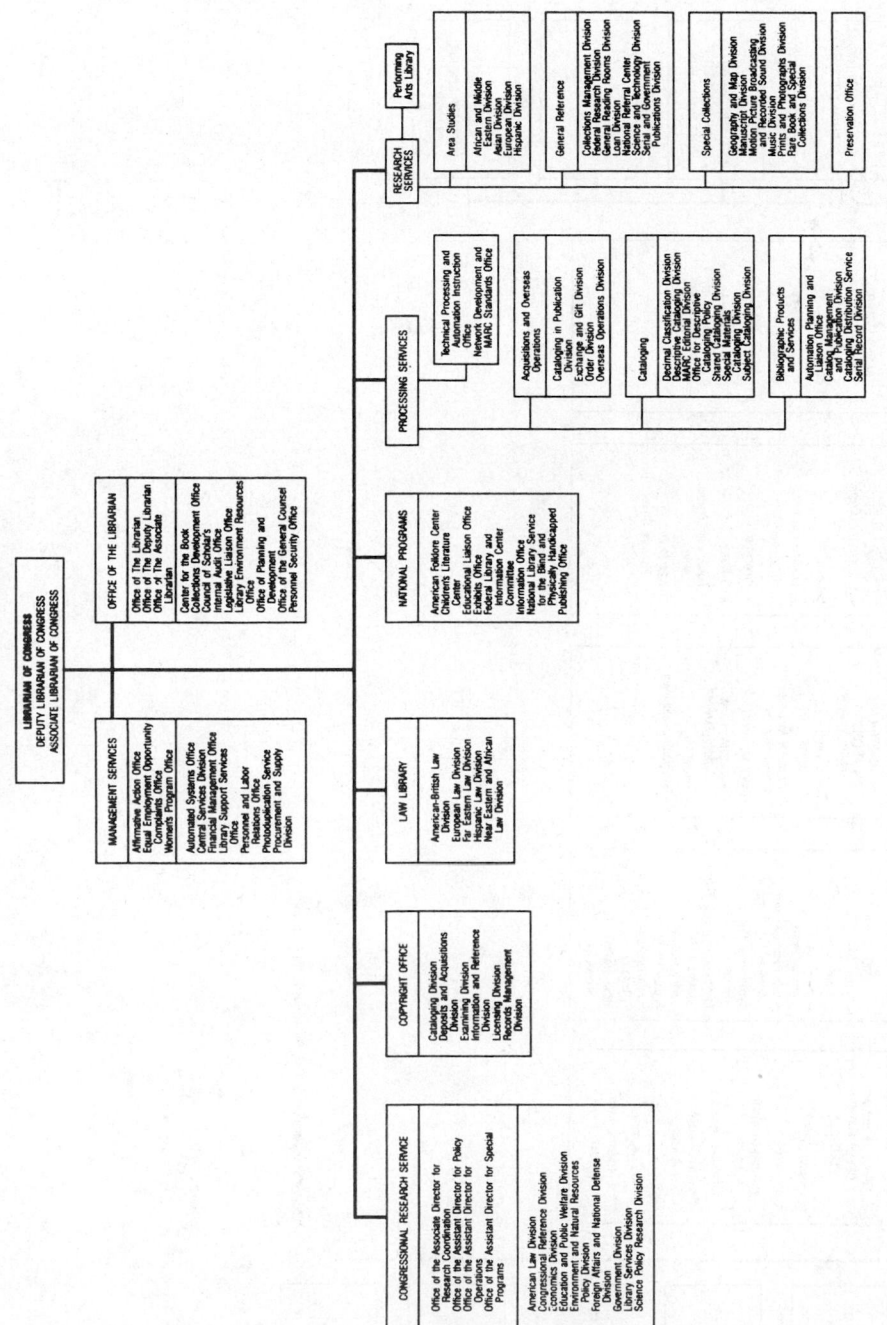

DEPARTMENT OF HEALTH AND HUMAN SERVICES

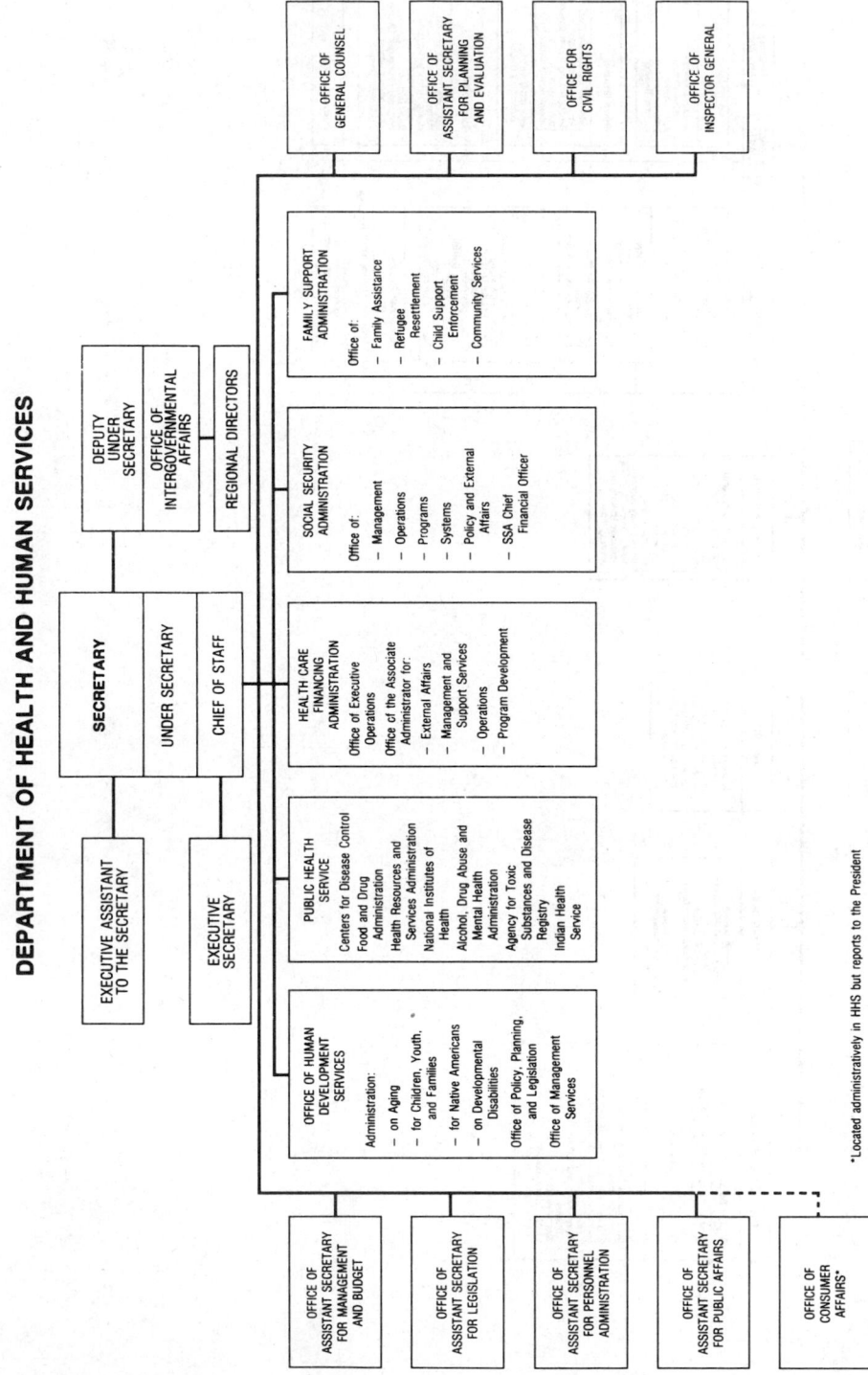

*Located administratively in HHS but reports to the President

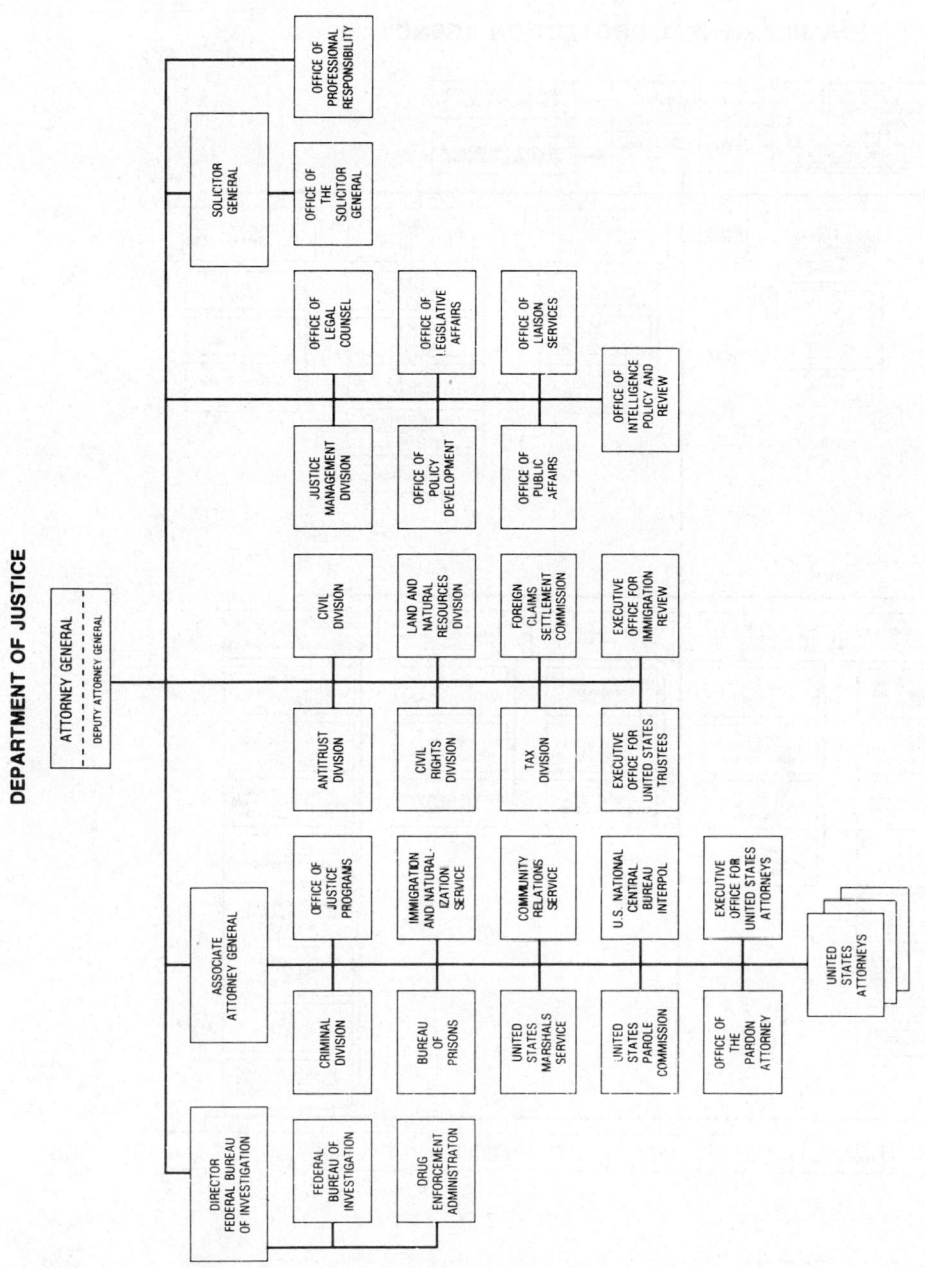

DEPARTMENT OF JUSTICE

ENVIRONMENTAL PROTECTION AGENCY

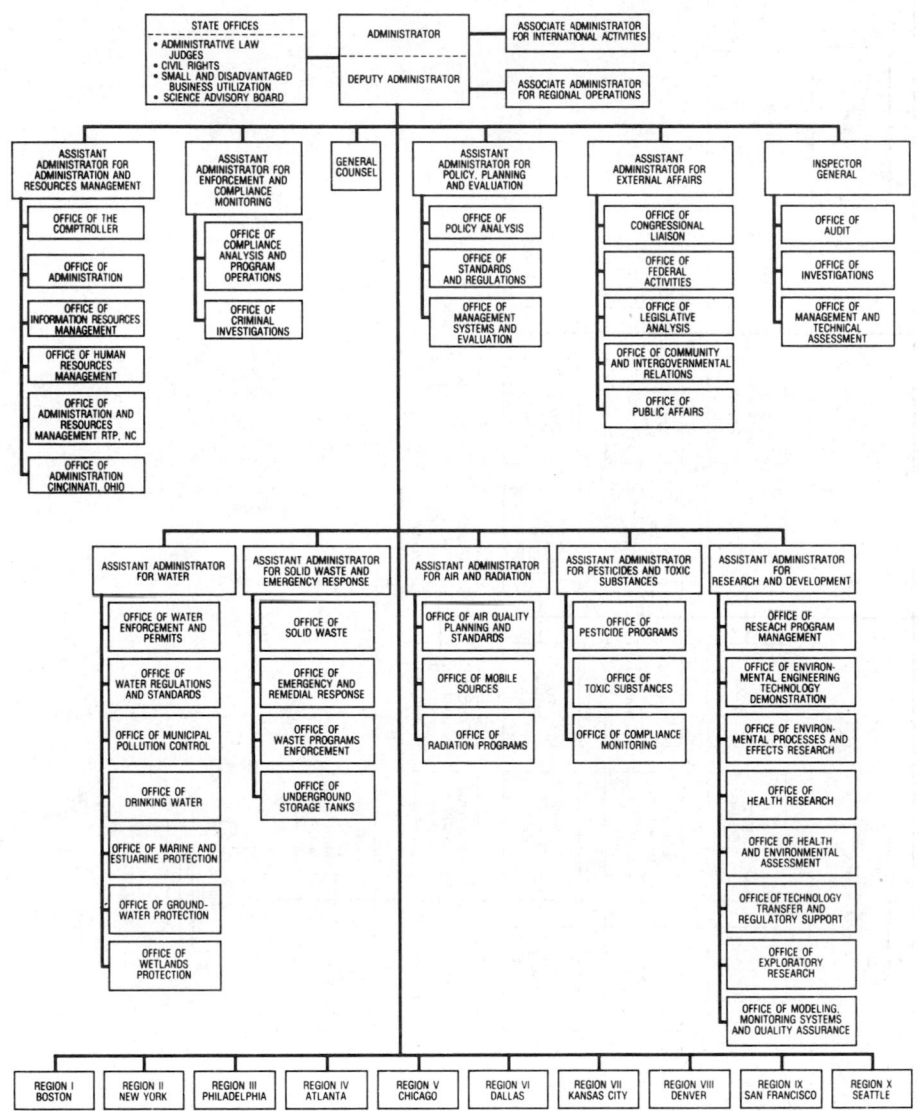

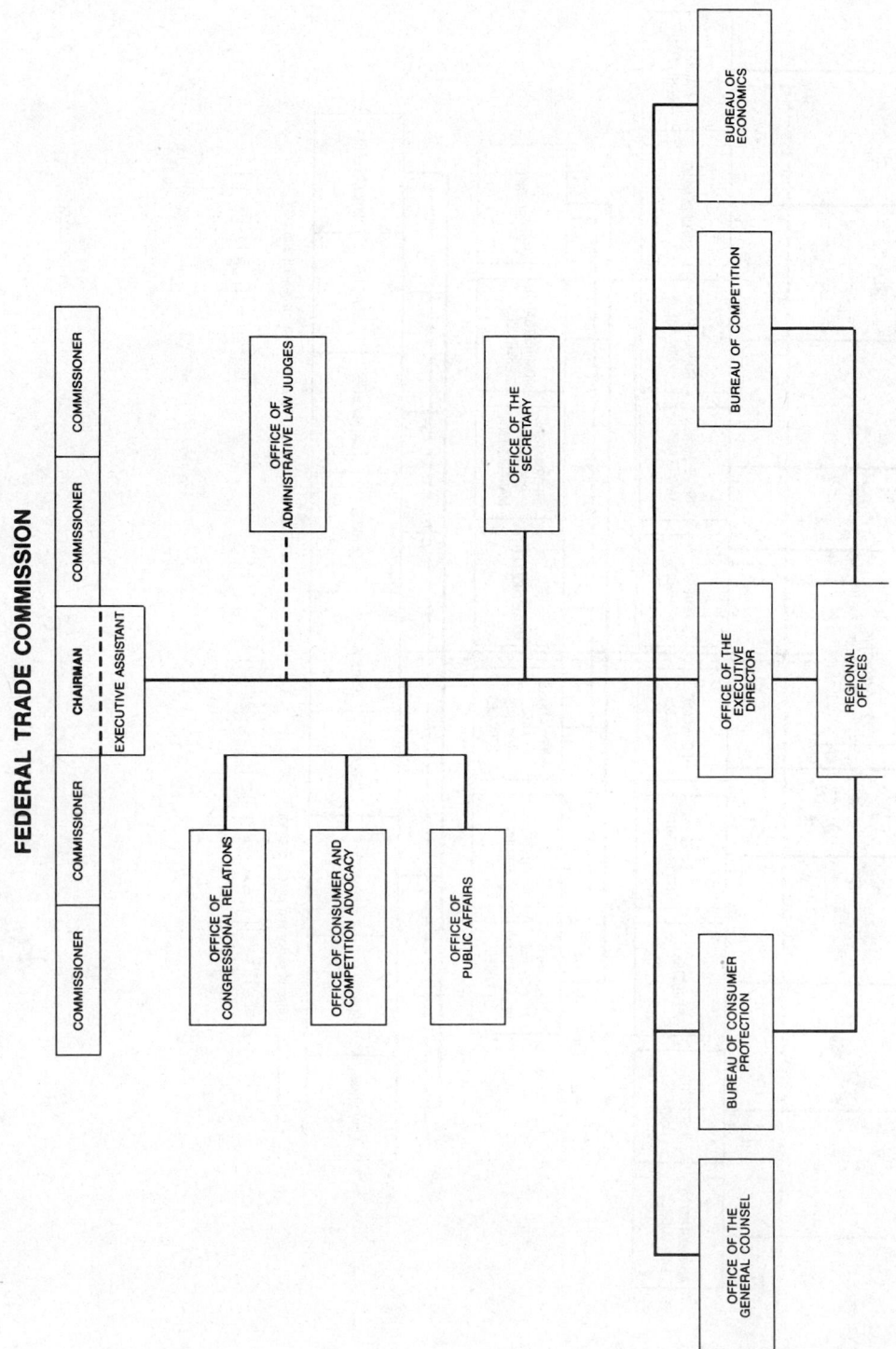

FEDERAL TRADE COMMISSION

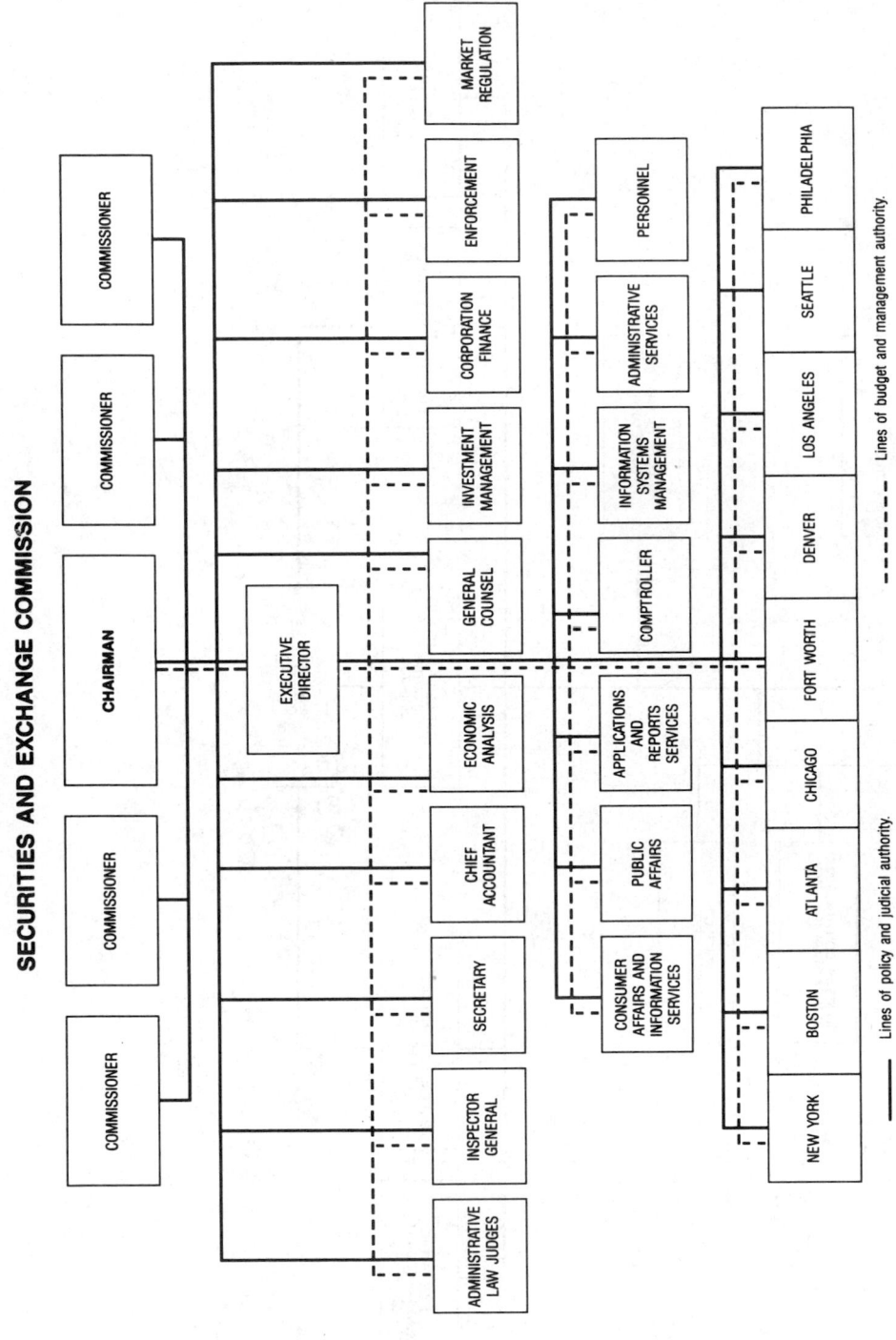

SECURITIES AND EXCHANGE COMMISSION

Lines of budget and management authority. ----

Lines of policy and judicial authority. ——

Highway Mileage

	Wash., D.C.	Toronto, Canada	Seattle, WA	San Fran., CA	Phoenix, Arizona	Phila., PA	New York, NY	New Orleans, LA	Mpls./St. Paul, MN	Los Angeles, CA	Las Vegas, NV	Indianapolis, IN	Houston, TX	Detroit, MI	Denver, CO	Dallas, TX	Columbus, OH	Chicago, IL	Boston, MA	Atlanta, GA
Atlanta, GA	605	925	2623	2499	1793	741	844	483	1073	2187	1971	495	789	704	1407	759	533	674	1037	
Baltimore, MD	41	446	2681	2796	2261	96	196	1114	1075	2637	2399	563	1417	500	1623	1356	391	666	389	645
Bismarck, ND	1502	1305	1193	1607	1463	1569	1632	1584	427	1615	1335	1012	1386	1093	672	1150	1136	831	1796	1495
Boise, ID	2343	2196	501	658	952	2411	2478	2073	1407	848	668	1802	1779	1942	811	1584	1968	1685	2639	2174
Boston, MA	432	539	2982	3099	2609	296	207	1512	1371	2814	2734	910	1816	699	1961	1748	735	958		1037
Buffalo, NY	352	100	2533	2653	2174	351	372	1217	927	2554	2286	480	1452	253	1508	1343	323	519	444	857
Chicago, IL	671	492	2013	2142	1713	738	804	920	411	2080	1780	181	1083	269	1001	917	308		958	674
Cincinnati, OH	481	485	2300	2362	1804	569	647	788	692	2180	1941	106	1029	259	1166	920	108	287	840	440
Cleveland, OH	345	287	2348	2468	1992	413	475	1030	740	2367	2099	296	1274	171	1321	1160	139	335	628	672
Charleston, SC	899	1215	2910	2786	2090	664	764	810	1359	2254	2273	731	1081	851	1726	1095	660	914	972	289
Columbus, OH	387	418	2321	2423	1869	462	542	897	718	2252	2021	171	1152	192	1229	1028		308	735	533
Dallas, TX	1316	1369	2080	1757	1015	1452	1557	498	950	1399	1229	867	244	1148	781		1028	917	1748	759
Denver, CO	1628	1479	1329	1240	817	1702	1782	1276	843	1110	788	1062	1024	1251		779	1229	1001	1961	1407
Des Moines, IA	969	810	1754	1827	1427	1057	1130	1003	253	1752	1449	467	924	586	671	689	624	330	1291	892
Detroit, MI	509	226	2290	2431	1971	581	642	1051	677	2336	2041	281	1278		1261	1148	192	269	699	704
Hartford, CT	335	552	2918	3056	2543	204	111	1428	1299	2901	2671	816	1713	723	1879	1662	644	889	105	947
Houston, TX	1378	1491	2291	1923	1153	1522	1616	357	1184	1546	1428	994		1278	1024	244	1152	1083	1816	789
Indianapolis, IN	564	504	2200	2273	1704	635	716	805	590	2083	1848		994	281	1062	867	171	181	910	495
Jackson, MS	991	1140	2488	2180	1429	1117	1219	180	1051	1817	1632	652	419	917	1193	407	766	744	1409	392
Jacksonville, FL	728	1160	2950	2491	1993	863	963	556	1380	2394	2219	802	892	1008	1710	997	815	984	1161	306
Kansas City, MO	1047	969	1848	1851	1219	1126	1207	826	454	1604	1374	490	728	751	606	494	657	500	1396	801
Knoxville, TN	490	744	2554	2531	1833	617	718	597	938	2217	1979	346	897	515	1334	839	346	528	912	193
Las Vegas, NV	2417	2255	1154	565	286	2481	2567	1724	1610	283		1848	1428	2041	788	1229	2021	1780	2734	1971
Little Rock, AR	1001	1064	2251	1999	1325	1149	1251	426	823	1701	1470	562	433	846	954	322	720	646	1437	511
Los Angeles, CA	2653	2537	1154	379	389	2726	2799	1899	1943		283	2083	1546	2336	1110	1399	2252	2080	2814	2187
Louisville, KY	583	586	2313	2352	1737	668	749	687	699	2117	1890	111	930	361	1124	823	210	292	944	382
Memphis, TN	870	939	2326	2147	1456	1008	1111	394	839	1820	1598	438	566	715	1049	460	578	539	1299	312
Mexico, D.F.	2357	2469	2854	2295	1550	2488	2588	1337	2074	1917	1834	1965	979	2243	1746	1138	2115	2045	2783	1768

	Wash., D.C.	Toronto, Canada	Seattle, WA	San Fran., CA	Phoenix, Arizona	Phila., PA	New York, NY	New Orleans, LA	Mpls./St. Paul, MN	Los Angeles, CA	Las Vegas, NV	Indianapolis, IN	Houston, TX	Detroit, MI	Denver, CO	Dallas, TX	Columbus, OH	Chicago, IL	Boston, MA	Atlanta, GA
Miami, FL	1087	1510	3297	3082	2321	1214	1316	858	1734	2701	2547	1156	1197	1359	2050	1311	1168	1334	1513	658
Milwaukee, WI	761	579	1991	2193	1792	831	899	1014	333	2116	1812	269	1153	355	1034	1027	397	87	1054	753
Mpls./St. Paul, MN	1081	900	1640	1962	1644	1148	1212	1232		1943	1610	590	1184	677	843	950	781	411	1371	1073
Mobile, AL	948	1239	2665	2372	1590	1077	1178	144	1177	1989	1821	718	479	696	1361	591	817	854	1373	336
Nashville, TN	622	754	2380	2333	1676	765	898	519	829	2014	1812	280	771	530	1162	664	378	448	1090	243
New Orleans, LA	1088	1271	2643	2267	1510	1215	1317		1232	1899	1724	805	357	1051	1276	498	897	920	1512	483
New York, NY	234	469	2832	2948	2422	102		1317	1212	2799	2562	716	1616	642	1782	1557	542	804	207	844
Okla. City, OK	1293	1241	1910	1657	947	1368	1448	668	796	1349	1125	735	449	1013	609	206	906	787	1641	839
Omaha, NE	1118	942	1640	1685	1292	1185	1253	1009	359	1597	1315	589	867	718	539	646	752	461	1414	988
Orlando, FL	869	1307	3057	2835	2080	1002	1102	638	1507	2469	2303	932	972	1138	1819	1082	954	1113	1298	439
Phila., PA	135	453	2753	2863	2333		102	1215	1148	2726	2481	635	1522	581	1702	1452	462	738	298	741
Phoenix, AZ	2258	2183	1439	765		2333	2422	1510	1644	389	286	1704	1153	1971	817	1015	1869	1713	2609	1793
Pittsburgh, PA	221	316	2465	2578	2051	288	368	1070	857	2426	2188	353	1313	287	1411	1204	182	452	561	687
Portland, ME	531	561	3055	3174	2699	395	308	1609	1447	3074	2804	1001	1906	775	2028	1850	837	1042	106	1139
Portland, OR	2783	2566	172	639	1268	2842	2901	2545	1699	976	985	2241	2238	2369	1261	2032	2399	2108	3046	2601
Providence, RI	396	604	2965	3084	2571	263	173	1474	1357	2946	2708	873	1771	787	1931	1715	704	952	46	1004
Rapid City, SD	1567	1386	1134	1414	1186	1634	1698	1507	565	1363	1081	1071	1288	1162	394	1050	1204	896	1859	1487
Reno, NV	2578	2393	735	230	747	2638	2716	2181	1754	472	448	2031	1876	2183	1026	1683	2208	1936	2870	2378
Richmond, VA	111	592	2766	2867	2261	244	344	994	1158	2636	2412	615	1303	588	1673	1271	449	753	540	515
St. Louis, MO	795	739	2090	2093	1481	873	952	686	552	1852	1626	237	789	515	860	640	410	290	1146	546
Salt Lake City, UT	2053	1870	852	761	659	2127	2189	1746	1212	722	434	1509	1445	1655	508	1252	1691	1416	2346	1879
San Diego, CA	2607	2538	1256	504	355	2682	2762	1827	1938	125	331	2049	1482	2308	1108	1331	2220	2064	2955	2126
San Francisco, CA	2802	2625	833		769	2863	2948	2267	1962	379	565	2273	1923	2431	1240	1757	2423	2142	3099	2499
Seattle, WA	2687	2496		833	1439	2753	2832	2643	1640	1154	1154	2200	2291	2290	1329	2080	2321	2013	2982	2623
Spokane, WA	2406	2218	278	882	1335	2473	2537	2343	1330	1205	1050	1916	2102	2001	1089	1864	2043	1735	2698	2340
Tampa, FL	930	1336	3082	2837	2080	1064	1161	640	1533	2471	2298	972	974	1177	1821	1082	989	1157	1362	458
Tulsa, OK	1189	1135	1962	1760	1077	1264	1344	647	695	1452	1228	631	478	909	681	257	802	683	1537	772
Vancouver, B.C.	2830	2639	143	976	1582	2896	2975	2786	1783	1297	1297	2343	2434	2433	1472	2223	2464	2156	3125	2766
Washington, D.C.		456	2687	2802	2258	135	234	1088	1081	2653	2417	564	1378	509	1628	1316	387	671	432	605
Wichita, KS	1239	1165	1825	1695	1032	1314	1394	823	647	1392	1176	681	618	940	510	375	852	703	1587	903
Yellowstone N. Pk.	2142	1903	766	1133	1148	2104	2160	1892	1015	1210	932	1542	1727	1628	715	1492	1667	1364	2325	1968

Air Distances between Some Major Cities in the World
(in Statute Miles)

	Athens	Baghdad	Beijing	Berlin	Bombay	Buenos Aires	Cairo	Calcutta	Caracas	Chicago	Copenhagen
Athens		1198	4705	1123	3211	7275	693	3925	6693	5445	1331
Baghdad	1198		3905	2038	2018	8118	788	2768	8070	6428	2188
Beijing	4705	3905		4565	2965	11968	4678	2024	8950	6592	4496
Berlin	1123	2038	4565		3908	7370	1798	4372	5247	4406	222
Bombay	3211	2018	2965	3908		9270	2698	1039	10383	8050	3870
Buenos Aires	7275	8118	11968	7370	9270		7328	10250	3168	5601	7519
Cairo	693	788	4678	1798	2698	7328		3535	6335	6125	1988
Calcutta	3925	2768	2024	4372	1039	10250	3535		9605	7979	4385
Caracas	6693	8070	8950	5247	10383	3168	6335	9605		2499	6078
Chicago	5445	6428	6592	4406	8050	5601	6125	7979	2499		4262
Copenhagen	1331	2188	4496	222	3870	7519	1988	4385	6078	4262	
Hong Kong	5309	4258	1230	5495	2675	11471	5045	1535	10169	7785	5385
Honolulu	8276	8448	5068	7308	8012	7565	8835	7035	6012	4248	6998
Istanbul	440	1008	4396	1075	2990	7568	762	3650	6048	5470	1236
Lisbon	1789	2988	6003	1399	4976	5990	2367	5637	4041	3999	1512
London	1501	2568	5054	575	4458	6915	2170	4952	4660	3948	606
Los Angeles	6889	7568	6250	5780	8696	6115	7470	8145	3632	1742	5606
Mexico City	6964	8068	7735	6035	9720	4635	7685	9488	2232	1675	5835
Montreal	4720	5754	6495	3724	7508	5618	5418	7569	2449	749	3586
Moscow	1402	1594	3597	995	3130	8378	1804	3447	6173	4988	965
New York	4921	5974	6823	3959	7796	5301	5594	7919	2132	713	3848
Paris	1305	2384	5101	542	4360	6878	1994	4890	4735	4133	642
Rio de Janeiro	6035	7015	10765	6145	8255	1215	6145	9375	2810	5295	6330
Rome	648	1824	5047	735	3843	6929	1321	4496	5198	4808	955
San Francisco	6791	7447	5905	5657	8393	6475	7449	7809	3903	1857	5475
Santiago	7890	8820	12072	7782	9978	734	7946	10560	3050	5310	7890
Shanghai	5293	4386	646	5213	3133	12199	5186	2113	9501	7053	5163
Singapore	5625	4444	2775	6165	2430	9868	5145	1790	11401	9368	6190
Sydney	9565	8364	5590	9996	6315	7330	8955	5680	9513	9270	10009
Tokyo	5905	5180	1307	5535	4190	11389	5949	3185	8799	6304	5409
Vienna	785	1758	4660	328	3718	7368	1470	4259	6190	4695	555
Warsaw	995	1747	7501	320	4969	7662	1630	4048	5517	4667	414
Washington	5125	6140	6920	4167	7988	5216	5800	8088	2059	591	4053

	Hong Kong	Honolulu	Istanbul	Lisbon	London	Los Angeles	Mexico City	Montreal	Moscow	New York	Paris
Athens	5309	8276	440	1789	1501	6889	6964	4720	1402	4921	1305
Baghdad	4258	8448	1008	2988	2568	7568	8068	5754	1594	5974	2384
Beijing	1230	5068	4396	6003	5054	6250	7735	6495	3597	6823	5101
Berlin	5495	7308	1075	1399	575	5780	6035	3724	995	3959	542
Bombay	2675	8012	2990	4976	4458	8696	9720	7508	3130	7796	4360
Buenos Aires	11471	7565	7568	5990	6915	6115	4635	5618	8378	5301	6878
Cairo	5045	8835	762	2367	2170	7470	7685	5418	1804	5594	1994
Calcutta	1535	7035	3650	5637	4952	8145	9488	7569	3447	7919	4890
Caracas	10169	6012	6048	4041	4660	3632	2232	2449	6173	2132	4735
Chicago	7785	4248	5470	3999	3948	1742	1675	749	4988	713	4133
Copenhagen	5385	6998	1236	1512	606	5606	5835	3586	965	3848	642
Hong Kong		5535	4975	6850	5982	7236	8777	7696	4440	8049	5955
Honolulu	5535		8108	7770	7222	2551	3779	4909	7035	4949	7435
Istanbul	4975	8108		1998	1552	6848	7106	4299	1085	5013	1398
Lisbon	6850	7770	1998		972	5629	5382	3241	2420	3353	890
London	5982	7222	1552	972		5441	5536	3249	1550	3459	215
Los Angeles	7236	2551	6848	5629	5441		1540	2469	6065	2449	5598
Mexico City	8777	3779	7106	5382	5536	1540		2312	6688	2085	5702
Montreal	7696	4909	4299	3241	3249	2469	2312		4388	330	3419
Moscow	4440	7035	1085	2420	1550	6065	6688	4388		4659	1540
New York	8049	4949	5013	3353	3459	2449	2085	330	4659		3622
Paris	5955	7435	1398	890	215	5598	5702	3419	1540	3622	
Rio de Janeiro	10995	8190	6395	4795	5775	6300	4770	5095	7180	4820	5705
Rome	5768	8020	852	1161	885	6325	6353	4090	1473	4273	682
San Francisco	6895	2391	6699	5669	5357	347	1887	2539	5869	2571	5441
Santiago	11430	6860	8182	6390	7252	5572	4194	5502	8780	5122	7240
Shanghai	776	4933	4989	6676	5709	6476	8039	7069	4236	7356	5753
Singapore	1650	6715	5375	7385	6745	8770	10305	9200	5240	9630	6670
Sydney	4585	5073	9355	11335	10550	7465	8050	9899	9003	9932	10545
Tokyo	1795	3849	5555	6930	5935	5470	7034	6455	4650	6735	6033
Vienna	5429	7626	785	1405	772	6105	6306	4005	1044	4224	642
Warsaw	5144	7355	863	1715	899	5922	6365	4009	715	4344	849
Washington	8148	4829	5216	3565	3655	2300	1878	437	4883	205	3828

	Rio de Janeiro	Rome	San Francisco	Santiago	Shanghai	Singapore	Sydney	Tokyo	Vienna	Warsaw	Washington
Athens	6035	648	6791	7890	5293	5625	9565	5905	785	995	5125
Baghdad	7015	1824	7447	8820	4386	4444	8364	5180	1758	1747	6140
Beijing	10765	5047	5905	12072	646	2775	5590	1307	4660	7501	6920
Berlin	6145	735	5657	7782	5213	6165	9996	5535	328	320	4167
Bombay	8255	3843	8393	9978	3133	2430	6315	4190	3718	4969	7988
Buenos Aires	1215	6929	6475	734	12199	9868	7330	11389	7368	7662	5216
Cairo	6145	1321	7449	7946	5186	5145	8955	5949	1470	1630	5800
Calcutta	9375	4496	7809	10560	2113	1790	5680	3185	4259	4048	8088
Caracas	2810	5198	3903	3050	9501	11401	9513	8799	6190	5517	2059
Chicago	5295	4808	1857	5310	7053	9368	9270	6304	4695	4667	591
Copenhagen	6330	955	5475	7890	5163	6190	10009	5409	555	414	4053
Hong Kong	10995	5768	6895	11430	776	1650	4585	1795	5429	5144	8148
Honolulu	8190	8020	2391	6860	4933	6715	5073	3849	7626	7355	4829
Istanbul	6395	852	6699	8182	4989	5375	9355	5555	785	863	5216
Lisbon	4795	1161	5669	6390	6676	7385	11335	6930	1405	1715	3565
London	5775	885	5357	7252	5709	6745	10550	5935	772	899	3655
Los Angeles	6300	6325	347	5572	6476	8770	7465	5470	6105	5922	2300
Mexico City	4770	6353	1887	4194	8039	10305	8050	7034	6306	6365	1878
Montreal	5095	4090	2539	5502	7069	9200	9899	6455	4005	4009	437
Moscow	7180	1473	5869	8780	4236	5240	9003	4650	1044	715	4883
New York	4820	4273	2571	5122	7356	9630	9932	6735	4224	4344	205
Paris	5705	682	5441	7240	5753	6670	10545	6033	642	849	3828
Rio de Janeiro		5685	6617	1812	11346	9775	8396	11535	6136	6467	4797
Rome	5685		6239	7362	5679	6230	10137	6125	465	817	4435
San Francisco	6617	6239		5930	6133	8480	7415	5130	5990	5841	2442
Santiago	1812	7362	5930		11715	10190	7058	10709	7810	9333	3987
Shanghai	11346	5679	6133	11715		2375	4905	1093	5299	4951	7442
Singapore	9775	6230	8480	10190	2375		3918	3304	6035	7764	9834
Sydney	8396	10137	7415	7058	4905	3918		4859	9970	9696	9667
Tokyo	11535	6125	5130	10709	1093	3304	4859		5681	5249	6769
Vienna	6136	465	5990	7810	5299	6035	9970	5681		342	4429
Warsaw	6467	817	5841	9333	4951	7764	9696	5249	342		4457
Washington	4797	4435	2442	3987	7442	9834	9667	6769	4429	4457	

Countries and Capitals

Countries and Capitals	Population (in 1000s)	Rank	Square Miles	National Day	Language Spoken (o) Official (n) National
Afghanistan, Kabul	14177	44	251750	Aug 19	Dari Persian (o), Pushtu
Albania, Tirana	2846	110	11100	Nov 29	Albanian
Algeria, Algiers	20695	37	919950	Jul 5	Arabic (o), French
Andorra, Andorra la Vella	38	185	180		Catalan (o), French, Spanish
Angola, Luanda	7567	73	481350	Nov 11	Bantu, Portugese (o)
Antigua & Barbuda, St. Johns	79	176	171	Nov 1	English
Argentina, Buenos Aires	29627	29	1072065	Jul 9	Spanish
Australia, Canberra	15265	48	2967910	Jan 26	English
Austria, Vienna	7574	69	32375	Oct 26	German
Bahamas, Nassau	223	154	4404	Jul 10	English
Bahrain, Manama	393	143	258	Aug 14	Arabic (o), English
Bangladesh, Dacca	96539	8	55125	Mar 26	Bengali (o), English
Barbados, Bridgetown	280	151	166	Nov 30	English
Belgium, Brussels	9865	57	11780	Jul 21	Dutch, French
Belize, Belmopan	154	160	8865	Sep 20	English (o), Spanish
Benin, Porto Novo	3792	100	43490	Noiv 30	French and Local Dialects
Bhutan, Thimphu	1386	125	17900	Dec 17	Dzongkha (o), Nepali
Bolivia, La Paz (adm) Sucre (jud)	5883	85	424150	Aug 6	Spanish, Quechua
Botswana, Gaborone	1001	132	223000	Sep 30	English (o), Setswana (n)
Brazil, Brasilia	131305	6	3286470	Sep 7	Portuguese
Bulgaria, Sofia	8944	62	42823	Sep 9	Bulgarian
Burma, Rangoon	37061	25	261500	Jan 4	Burmese
Burundi, Bujumbura	4561	93	10750	Jul 1	Kirundi (o), French
Cambodia, Phnom Penh	5996	78	69950	Apr 17	Khmer (o), French
Cameroon, Yaounde	9251	65	182000	May 20	English (o), French (o), Bantu Dialects
Canada, Ottawa	24882	31	3851809	Jul 1	English, French
Cape Verde, Praia	297	147	1557	Sep 12	Portuguese, Local Dialects
Central Africa, Bangui	2512	114	240320	Dec 1	French (o), Sango
Chad, N'djamena	4990	92	495750	Apr 13	French (o), Arabic, Others
Chile, Santiago	11486	54	292100	Sep 18	Spanish
China, Peking	1059802	1	3691520	Sep 21	Mandarin Chinese (o), and Others
China (Taiwan), Taipei	18810	38	13590		Mandarin Chinese and Others
Colombia, Bogotá	27663	30	455300	Jul 20	Spanish
Comoros, Moroni	442	144	692		French
Congo, Brazzaville	1694	121	132046	Aug 15	French (o), Dialects
Costa Rica, San Jose	2624	116	19650	Sep 15	Spanish
Cuba, Havana	9858	59	44215	Jan 1	Spanish
Cyprus, Nicosia	653	135	3572	Oct 1	Greek, Turkish, English
Czechoslovakia, Prague	15420	43	49370	May 9	Czech, Slovak
Denmark, Copenhagen	5115	87	16615	Apr 16	Danish
Greenland (Kalaallit Nunaat), Gothaab (Nuuk)	52	183	840000	May 1	Danish
Djibouti, Dijbouti	276	142	9000	Jun 27	Somali, Arabic, French, Afar
Dominica, Roseau	74	175	300	Nov 3	English, French, Patois
Dominican Republic, Santo Domingo	6248	81	18700	Feb 27	Spanish

Countries and Capitals	Population (in 1000s)	Rank	Square Miles	National Day	Language Spoken (o) Official (n) National
Ecuador, Quito	8811	67	113425	Aug 10	Spanish, Quechua
Egypt, Cairo	45851	20	385200	Jul 23	Arabic
El Salvador, San Salvador	4685	91	8260	Sep 15	Spanish
Equatorial Guinea, Malabo	268	152	10831	Mar 5	Spanish (o), Fang
Ethiopia, Addis Ababa	31305	26	465000	Sep 12	Amharic (o), Tigri, Galla
Fiji, Suva	672	136	7056	Oct 10	English (o), Hindi, Fajian
Finland, Helsinki	4850	90	130119	Dec 6	Finnish, Swedish
France, Paris	54604	15	212950	Jul 14	French
Gabon, Libreville	921	134	103347	Aug 17	French (o), Bantu Dialects
Gambia, Banjul	638	137	4016	Feb 18	English (o), Mandinba, Wolof
German Dem. Republic (East Germany), East Berlin	16724	41	41825	Oct 7	German
Federal Rep. of Germany (West Germany), Bonn	61543	12	96011	May 23	German
Ghana, Accra	13367	53	92100	Mar 6	English, Native Dialects
Greece, Athens	9898	60		Mar 25	Greek
Grenada, St. George's	111	170	133	Feb 7	English
Guatemala, Gautemala City	7714	71	42042	Sep 15	Spanish
Guinea, Conakry	5430	84	94925	Oct 2	French (o), Tribal Language
Guinea-Bissau, Bissau	827	133	13948	Sep 12	Portuguese (o)
Guyana, Georgetown	833	131	83000	May 26	English (o), Hindi, Negro Patois
Haiti, Port Au Prince	5690	79	10714	Jan 1	French (o), Creole
Honduras, Tegucigalpa	4276	96	43277	Sep 15	Spanish, Indian Dialects
Hungary, Budapest	10691	55	35919	Apr 4	Hungarian (Magyar)
Iceland, Reykjavik	236	155	39702	Jun 17	Icelandic
India, New Delhi	730572	2	1269420	Jan 26	Hini (o), 15 other languages including English
Indonesia, Jakarta	160932	5	735268	Aug 17	Bahasa Indonesia (o), Dutch, Javanese and over 60 dialects
Iran, Teheran	42490	22	636363	Apr 1	Farsi, Turk, Kurdish, Azerbaijani
Iraq, Baghdad	14509	52	170000	Jul 14	Arabic (o), Kurdish
Ireland, Dublin	3534	101	27000	Mar 17	English, Irish
Israel, Jerusalem	3960	95	8000	Apr 1	Hebrew, English, Arabic
Italy, Rome	58345	13	116300	Jun 2	Italian
Ivory Coast, Abidjan	8890	68	124500	Dec 7	French, Local Dialects
Jamaica, Kingston	2335	115	4300	Aug 1	English, Creole
Japan, Tokyo	119205	7	145000	Apr 29	Japanese
Jordan, Amman	3420	103	37300	May 25	Arabic
Kenya, Nairobi	18580	42	224500	Dec 12	Swahili (o), English, Local Dialects
Kiribati, Tarawa	60	182	265	Jul 12	English (o), Gilbertese
North Korea, Pyongyang	19185	35	47000	May 1	Korean
South Korea, Seoul	41366	21	38000	Aug 15	Korean
Kuwait, Kuwait	1652	124	7500	Feb. 25	Arabic, English
Laos, Vientiane	3647	98	91500	Dec 2	Lao (o), English, French
Lebanon, Beirut	2598	107	4000	Nov 22	Arabic (o), French
Lesotho, Maseru	1438	123	11700	Oct 4	Sotho (o), English
Liberia, Monrovia	2091	119	40000	Jul 26	English (o), Tribal Dialects
Libya, Tripoli	3498	108	6795000	Sep 1	Arabic
Liechtenstein, Vaduz	26	189	62		German
Luxembourg, Luxembourg	366	145	1000	Jun 23	French (o), German, Letzeburgesch

Countries and Capitals	Population (in 1000s)	Rank	Square Miles	National Day	Language Spoken (o) Official (n) National
Madagascar, Antananarivo	9389	64	227000	Jun 26	French (o), Malagasy
Malawi, Lilongwe	6612	77	45750	Jul 6	English (o), Chichewa
Malaysia, Kuala Lampur	14995	50	128000	Aug 31	Malay (o), English, Chinese
Maldives, Male	168	161	115	Jul 26	Bivehi
Mali, Bamako	7393	74	465000	Sep 22	French (o), Tribal Dialects
Malta, Valetta	363	146	123	Mar 31	English (o), Maltese (o)
Mauritania, Nouakchott	1591	122	410000	Nov 28	French (o), Arabic
Mauritius, Port Louis	1002	128	785	Mar 12	English (o), French, Hindi, Creole
Mexico, Mexico City	75702	11	761500	Sep 16	Spanish
Monaco, Monacoville	28	188	0.75		French (o), Monegasque
Mongolia, UlaanBaatar	1809	120	604200	Jul 11	Mongolian (o), Russian, Chinese
Morocco, Rabat	22889	34	172000	Mar 3	Arabic (o), Spanish, French
Mozambique, Maputo	13047	56	308500	Jun 25	Portuguese (o), Bantu
Nauru, Yaren	8	196	8	Jan 31	English, Nauruan
Nepal, Kathmandu	16169	45	55000	Dec 28	Napali (o), Others
Netherlands, Amsterdam	14374	49	16000	Apr 30	Dutch
New Zealand, Wellington	3142	106	104000	Feb 6	English (o), Maori
Nicaragua, Managua	2812	112	57140	Sep 15	Spanish
Niger, Niamey	6083	83	449400	Dec 18	French (o), Arabic, Others
Nigeria, Lagos	85219	10	372670	Oct 1	French (o)
Norway, Oslo	4131	94	125000	May 17	Norwegian
Oman, Muscat	978	130	85500	Nov 18	Arabic
Pakistan, Islamabad	94780	9	323000	Mar 23	English (o), Urdu
Panama, Panama City	2058	117	28570	Nov 3	Spanish
Papua/New Guinea, Port Moresby	3259	105	183000	Sep 16	English & Others
Paraguay	3526	104	157000	May 14	Spanish (o), Guarant
Peru, Lima	19161	40	482250	Jul 28	Spanish
Philippines, Quezon City	53162	17	114850	Jun 12	Pilipino (n), Spanish, English
Poland, Warsaw	36556	24	120300	Jul 22	Polish
Portugal, Lisbon	10008	58	34300	Jun 10	Portuguese
Qatar, Doha	254	158	4000	Sep 3	Arabic
Rumania, Bucharest	22649	33	91700	Aug 23	Romanian, Hungarian, German
Rwanda, Kigali	5644	88	10160	Jul 1	French, Kinyarwand
St. Lucia, Castries	134	166	238	Dec 31	English, Patois
St. Vincent & The Grenadines, Kingstown	100	169	150	Oct 27	English
San Marino, San Marino	22	190	23		Italian
Sao Tome & Principe, Sao Tome	88	174	369	Jul 12	Portuguese
Saudi Arabia, Rivadh	10443	61	900000	Sep 23	Arabic
Sengegal, Dakar	6335	82	76100	Apr 4	French (o), Other Tribal Dialects
Sychelles, Victoria	65	178	156	Jun 5	English (o), French (o), Creole
Sierra Leone, Freetown	3705	102	27900	Apr 19	English (o), Creole Temne
Singapore, Singapore	2501	113	234	Aug 9	English, Chinese, Mandarin, Malay, Others
Solomon Islands, Honiara on Guadalcanal	267	156	16000	Jul 7	English, Dialects
Somalia, Mogadishu	6248	97	250000	Oct 21	Somali
South Africa, Cape Town (Leg) Pretoria (Admin)	30938	28	471400	May 31	English, Afrikaans, Bantu

Countries and Capitals	Population (in 1000s)	Rank	Square Miles	National Day	Language Spoken (o) Official (n) National
Spain, Madrid	37234	23	184599	Oct 12	Spanish, Catalan, Galician, Basque
Sri Lanka, Colombo	15647	46	25300	Feb 4	Sinhala (o), English, Tamil
Sudan, Khartoum	20539	36	967500	Jan 1	English, Arabic, Dialects
Surinami, Paramaribo	363	141	55150	Nov 25	Dutch, Surinamese
Swaziland, Mbabane	632	138	6700	Sep 6	Siswati (o), English
Sweden, Stockholm	8331	66	158500	Apr 30	Swedish
Switzerland, Bern	6463	75	15940		German, French, Italian
Syria, Damascus	9739	63	71500	Apr 17	Arabic
Tanzania, Dar-es-Salaam	20524	39	362500	Apr 26	English, Arabic, Bantu, Swahili
Thailand, Bangkok	50731	18	198300	Dec 5	Thai, Chinese, English
Togo, Lome	2823	111	20750	Apr 27	French (o), Many Dialects
Tonga, Naku'Alofa	104	172	270	Jun 4	English, Tongan
Trinidad & Tobago, Port of Spain	1211	126	1980	Aug 31	English (o), Spanish, French
Tunisia, Tunis	7020	76	48300	Jun 1	Arabic, French
Turkey, Ankara	49155	19	296200	Oct 29	Turkish
Tuvalu, Funa Futi	8	197	10		Samoan-Gilberese
Uganda, Kampala	13819	51	93980	Oct 9	English (o), Swahili, Others
Union of Soviet Socialist Republics, Moscow	272308	3	8570500	Nov 7	Russian, Ukranian
United Arab Emirates, Abu Dhabi	1374	129	31000	Dec 2	Arabic
United Kingdom of Great Britain and Northern Ireland, London	56006	14	94210		English, Welsh, Gaelic
United States of America, Washington, D.C.	234193	4	3615211	Jul 4	English
Upper Volta, Ouagadougou	6569	72	106000	Dec 11	French, African Languages
Uruguay, Montevideo	2916	109	72100	Jul 18	Spanish
Venezuela, Caracas	17993	47	352150	Jul 5	Spanish (o)
Vietnam, Hanoi	57036	16	129600	Sep 2	Vietnamese (o), Chinese, French
West Samoa, Apia	160	159	1133	Jul 1	English, Samoan
North Yemen, Sanaa	5744	86	75300	Oct 14	Arabic
South Yemen	2086	118	111000	Nov 30	Arabic
Yugoslavia, Belgrade	22826	32	98700	Nov 29	Serbo-Croatian, Slovene, Macedonian (all o)
Zaire, Kinshasa	31250	27	905000	Jun 30	French, Bantu Dialects
Zambia, Lusaka	6346	80	290300	Oct 24	English, Local Dialects
Zimbabwe	8376	70	150500	Apr 18	English (o), Sindebele, Shona

Presidents, Vice Presidents of the United States

Order	President	Vice President	Service
1.	George Washington	John Adams	1789–1797
2.	John Adams	Thomas Jefferson	1797–1801
3.	Thomas Jefferson	Aaron Burr	1801–1805
	Thomas Jefferson	George Clinton	1805–1809
4.	James Madison	George Clinton[1]	1809–1813
	James Madison	Elbridge Gerry[2]	1813–1817
5.	James Monroe	Daniel D. Tompkins	1817–1825
6.	John Quincy Adams	John C. Calhoun	1825–1829
7.	Andrew Jackson	John C. Calhoun[3]	1829–1833
	Andrew Jackson	Martin Van Buren	1833–1837
8.	Martin Van Buren	Richard M. Johnson	1837–1841
9.	William Henry Harrison[1]	John Tyler	1841
10.	John Tyler		1841–1845
11.	James K. Polk	George M. Dallas	1845–1849
12.	Zachary Taylor[5]	Millard Fillmore	1849–1850
13.	Millard Fillmore		1850–1853
14.	Franklin Pierce	William R. King[6]	1853–1857
15.	James Buchanan	John C. Breckinridge	1857–1861
16.	Abraham Lincoln	Hannibal Hamlin	1861–1865
	Abraham Lincoln[7]	Andrew Johnson	1865
17.	Andrew Johnson		1865–1869
18.	Ulysses S. Grant	Schuyler Colfax	1869–1873
	Ulysses S. Grant	Henry Wilson[8]	1873–1877
19.	Rutherford B. Hayes	William A. Wheeler	1877–1881
20.	James A. Garfield[9]	Chester A. Arthur	1881
21.	Chester A. Arthur		1881–1885
22.	Grover Cleveland	Thomas A. Hendricks[10]	1885–1889
23.	Benjamin Harrison	Levi P. Morton	1889–1893
24.	Grover Cleveland	Adlai E. Stevenson	1893–1897
25.	William McKinley	Garret A. Hobart[11]	1897–1901
	William McKinley[12]	Theodore Roosevelt	1901
26.	Theodore Roosevelt		1901–1905
	Theodore Roosevelt	Charles W. Fairbanks	1905–1909
27.	William H. Taft	James S. Sherman[13]	1909–1913
28.	Woodrow Wilson	Thomas R. Marshall	1913–1921
29.	Warren G. Harding[14]	Calvin Coolidge	1921–1923
30.	Calvin Coolidge		1923–1925
	Calvin Coolidge	Charles G. Dawes	1925–1929

Order	President	Vice President	Service
31.	Herbert C. Hoover	Charles Curtis	1929–1933
32.	Franklin D. Roosevelt	John N. Garner	1933–1941
	Franklin D. Roosevelt	Henry A. Wallace	1941–1945
	Franklin D. Roosevelt[15]	Harry S. Truman	1945
33.	Harry S. Truman		1945–1949
	Harry S. Truman	Alben W. Barkley	1949–1953
34.	Dwight D. Eisenhower	Richard M. Nixon	1953–1961
35.	John F. Kennedy[16]	Lyndon B. Johnson	1961–1963
36.	Lyndon B. Johnson		1963–1965
	Lyndon B. Johnson	Hubert H. Humphrey	1965–1969
37.	Richard M. Nixon	Spiro T. Agnew[17]	1969–1973
	Richard M. Nixon[19]	Gerald R. Ford[18]	1973–1974
38.	Gerald R. Ford[20]	Nelson A. Rockefeller[21]	1974–1977
39.	Jimmy Carter	Walter F. Mondale	1977–1981
40.	Ronald W. Reagan	George H.W. Bush	1981–1989
41.	George H. W. Bush	James D. Quayle	1989–

[1]Died in office, April 20, 1812.
[2]Died in office, November 23, 1814.
[3]Resigned December 28, 1832 to become U.S. Senator.
[4]Died in office, April 4, 1841.
[5]Died in office, July 9, 1850.
[6]Died in office, April 18, 1853.
[7]Died in office, April 15, 1865.
[8]Died in office, November 22, 1875.
[9]Died in office, September 19, 1881.
[10]Died in office, November 25, 1885.
[11]Died in office, November 21, 1899.
[12]Died in office, September 14, 1901.

[13]Died in office, October 30, 1912.
[14]Died in office, August 2. 1923.
[15]Died in office, April 12, 1945.
[16]Died in office, November 22, 1963.
[17]Resigned October 12, 1973.
[18]Appointed and confirmed as Vice President under the 25th Amendment.
[19]Resigned August 9, 1974.
[20]Succeeded to the Presidency on resignation of the President, August 9, 1974.
[21]Appointed and confirmed as Vice President under the 25th Amendment.

UNITED STATES COURTS OF APPEALS AND UNITED STATES DISTRICT COURTS

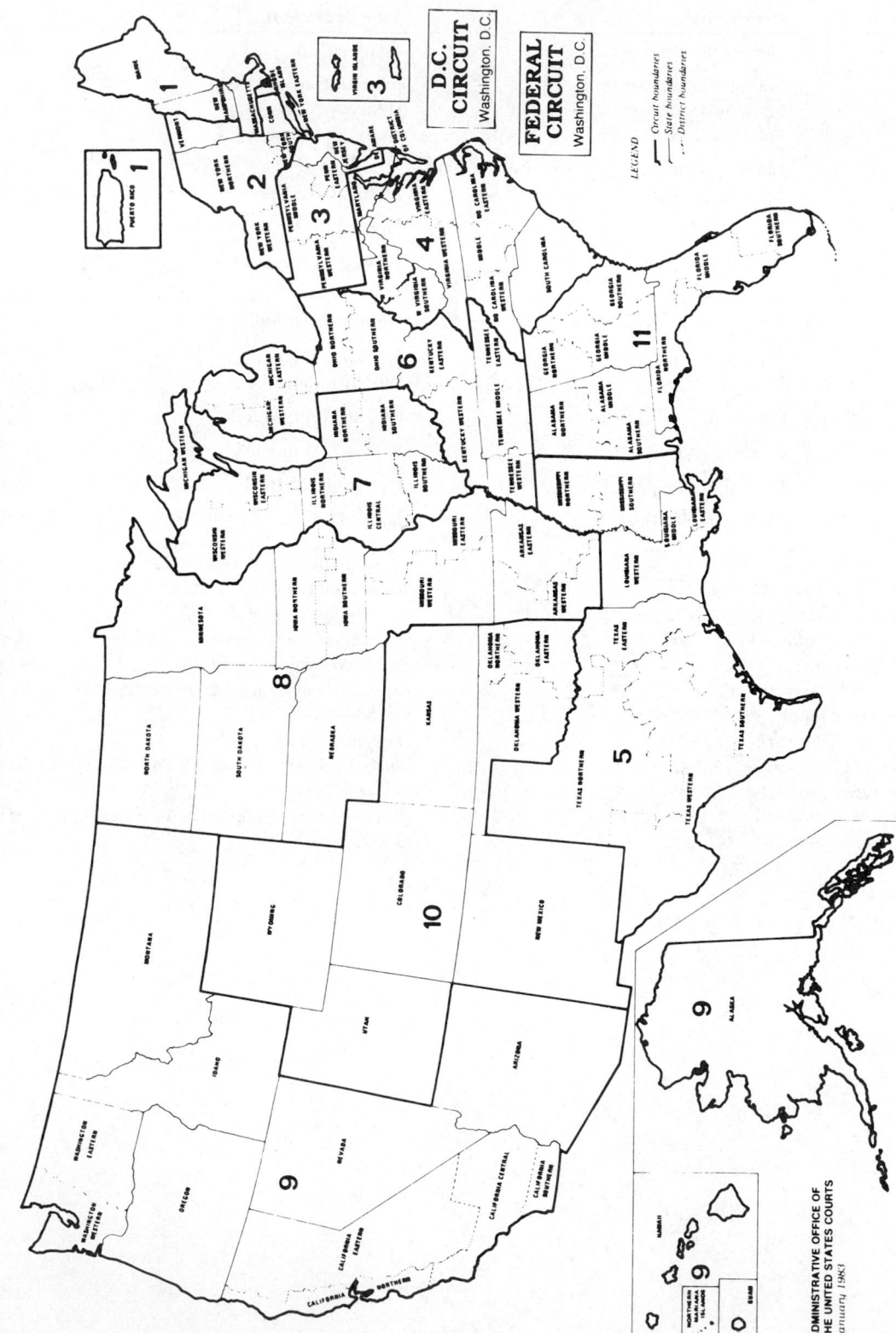

ADMINISTRATIVE OFFICE OF
THE UNITED STATES COURTS
January 1983

NATIONAL REPORTER SYSTEM
REGIONAL/FEDERAL

Regional Reporters	Coverage Beginning	Coverage
Atlantic Reporter	1885	Connecticut, Delaware, Maine, Maryland, New Hampshire, New Jersey, Pennsylvania, Rhode Island, Vermont, and District of Columbia Municipal Court of Appeals
North Eastern Reporter	1885	Illinois, Indiana, Massachusetts, New York and Ohio
North Western Reporter	1879	Iowa, Michigan, Minnesota, Nebraska, North Dakota, South Dakota and Wisconsin
Pacific Reporter	1883	Alaska, Arizona, California, Colorado, Hawaii, Idaho, Kansas, Montana, Nevada, New Mexico, Oklahoma, Oregon, Utah, Washington and Wyoming
South Eastern Reporter	1887	Georgia, North Carolina, South Carolina, Virginia and West Virginia
South Western Reporter	1886	Arkansas, Kentucky, Missouri, Tennessee and Texas
Southern Reporter	1887	Alabama, Florida, Louisiana and Mississippi

Federal Reporters

Federal Reporter	1880	United States Circuit Court from 1880 to 1912; Commerce Court of the United States from 1911 to 1913; District Courts of the United States from 1880 to 1932; U.S. Court of Claims from 1929 to 1932 and from 1960 to 1982; the U.S. Court of Appeals from its organization in 1891; the U.S. Court of Customs and Patent Appeals from 1929 to 1982; and the U.S. Emergency Court of Appeals from 1943.
Federal Supplement	1932	United States Court of Claims from 1932 to 1960; United States District Courts since 1932; United States Customs Court from 1956 to 1981; United States Court of International Trade since 1981.
Federal Rules Decisions	1939	United States District Courts involving the Federal Rules of Civil Procedure since 1939 and the Federal Rules of Criminal Procedure since 1946.
Supreme Court Reporter	1882	U.S. Supreme Court beginning with the October term of 1882.
Bankruptcy Reporter	1980	Bankruptcy decisions of U.S. Bankruptcy Courts, U.S. District Courts, U.S. Courts of Appeals and the U.S. Supreme Court.
Military Justice Reporter	1978	United States Court of Military Appeals and Courts of Military Review for the Army, Navy, Air Force and Coast Guard.
Claims Court Reporter	1982	Decisions of the U.S. Claims Court and of the U.S. Court of Appeals for the Federal Circuit and Supreme Court of the United States in review of decisions of the Claims Court.

NATIONAL REPORTER SYSTEM MAP

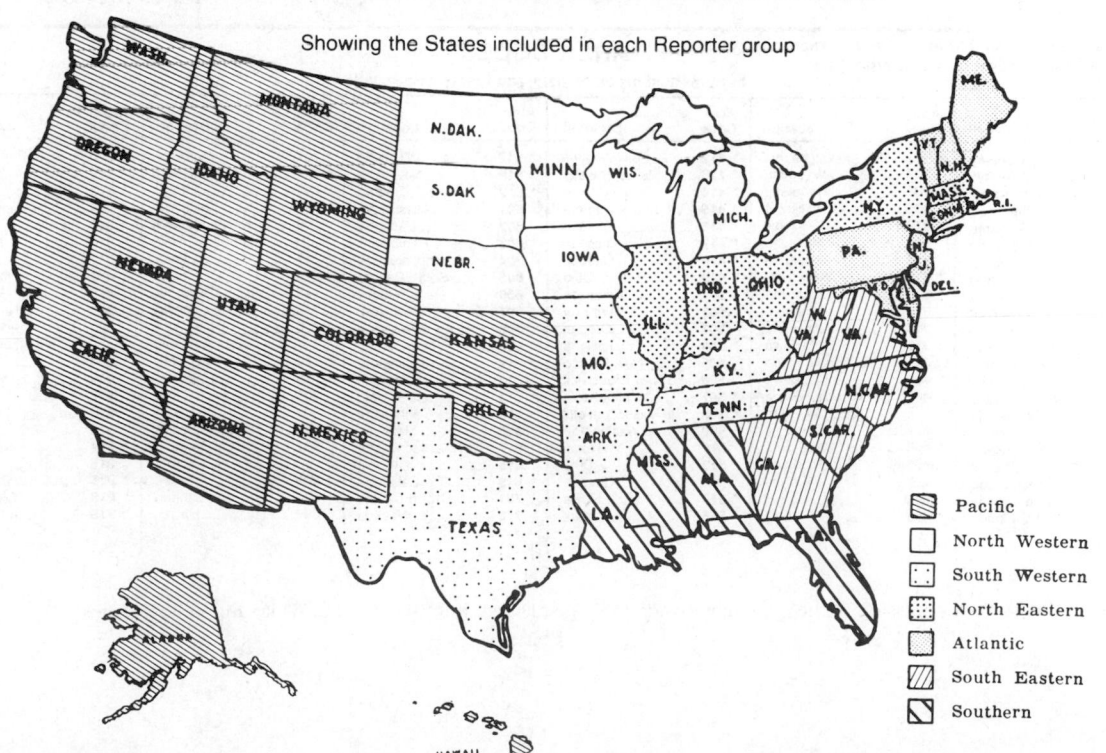

Showing the States included in each Reporter group

Pacific
North Western
South Western
North Eastern
Atlantic
South Eastern
Southern

U. S. TIME ZONES/TELEPHONE AREA CODES

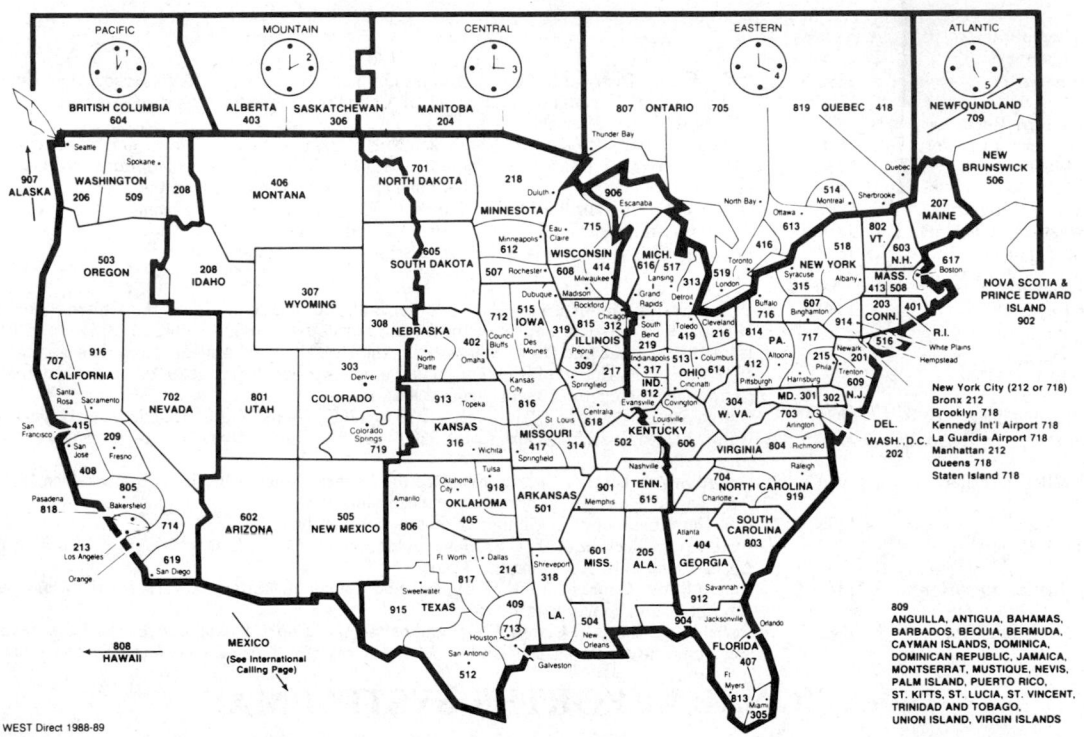

ʻ U S WEST Direct 1988-89

States or provinces that are served by more than one area code are shown by an asterisk (*).

AREA CODES
In numerical order, to help you identify your calls.

Area Code	Location	Area Code	Location	Area Code	Location	Area Code	Location	Area Code	Location	Area Code	Location
* 201	New Jersey	306	Saskatchewan	* 412	Pennsylvania	* 517	Michigan	* 703	Virginia	809	Puerto Rico
202	Dist. of Columbia	307	Wyoming	* 413	Massachusetts	* 518	New York	* 704	North Carolina	* 812	Indiana
203	Connecticut	* 308	Nebraska	* 414	Wisconsin	* 519	Ontario	* 705	Ontario	* 813	Florida
204	Manitoba	* 309	Illinois	* 415	California	601	Mississippi	* 707	California	* 814	Pennsylvania
205	Alabama	* 312	Illinois	* 416	Ontario	602	Arizona	709	Newfoundland	* 815	Illinois
* 206	Washington	* 313	Michigan	* 417	Missouri	603	New Hampshire		and Labrador	* 816	Missouri
207	Maine	314	Missouri	* 418	Quebec	604	Br. Columbia	* 712	Iowa	* 817	Texas
208	Idaho	315	New York	* 419	Ohio	605	South Dakota	* 713	Texas	* 818	California
* 209	California	* 316	Kansas	501	Arkansas	* 606	Kentucky	* 714	California	* 819	Quebec
* 212	New York	317	Indiana	* 502	Kentucky	* 607	New York	* 715	Wisconsin	* 901	Tennessee
* 213	California	* 318	Louisiana	503	Oregon	* 608	Wisconsin	* 716	New York	902	P. E. I. and
* 214	Texas	* 319	Iowa	* 504	Louisiana	* 609	New Jersey	* 717	Pennsylvania		Nova Scotia
215	Pennsylvania	401	Rhode Island	505	New Mexico	* 612	Minnesota	* 718	New York	* 904	Florida
* 216	Ohio	* 402	Nebraska	506	New Brunswick	* 613	Ontario	* 719	Colorado	* 906	Michigan
* 217	Illinois	403	Alberta, Yukon	* 507	Minnesota	* 614	Ohio	801	Utah	907	Alaska
* 218	Minnesota		and N.W. Terr.	* 508	Massachusetts	* 615	Tennessee	802	Vermont	* 912	Georgia
* 219	Indiana	* 404	Georgia	* 509	Washington	* 616	Michigan	803	South Carolina	* 913	Kansas
301	Maryland	405	Oklahoma	* 512	Texas	* 617	Massachusetts	* 804	Virginia	* 914	New York
302	Delaware	406	Montana	* 513	Ohio	* 618	Illinois	* 805	California	* 915	Texas
* 303	Colorado	* 407	Florida	* 514	Quebec	* 619	California	* 806	Texas	* 916	California
304	West Virginia	* 408	California	* 515	Iowa	701	North Dakota	* 807	Ontario	* 918	Oklahoma
* 305	Florida	* 409	Texas	* 516	New York	702	Nevada	808	Hawaii	* 919	North Carolina

Reprinted with the permission of the copyright owner, U.S. West Direct, publishers of the White and Yellow Pages.

TELEPHONE CODE DIRECTORY: DOMESTIC

Alabama
  All Points, 205
Alaska
  All Points, 907
Arizona
  All Points, 602
Arkansas
  All Points, 501

California
  Alameda, 415
  Alamo, 415
  Albany, 415
  Alhambra, 818
  Alisal, 408
  Alpine (Alpine Co.),
    916
  Alpine (San Diego
    Co.), 619

Altadena, 818
Alta Loma, 714
Alturas, 916
Anaheim, 714
Anderson, 916
Angels Camp, 209
Antioch, 415
Apple Valley, 619
Aptos, 408
Arcadia, 818
Arcata, 707
Armona, 209
Arroyo Grande, 805
Artesia, 213
Arvin, 805
Atascadero, 805
Atherton, 415
Atwater, 209
Auburn, 916
Avon, 415
Azua, 818
Bakersfield, 805
Baldwin Park, 818
Banning, 714
Barstow, 619
Beaumont, 714
Bell, 213
Bellflower, 213
Belmont, 415
Belvedere (Marin
  Co.), 415
Benicia, 707
Berkeley, 415
Beverly Hills, 213
Big Bear Lake, 714

Bishop, 619
Bloomington, 714
Blythe, 619
Boulder Creek, 408
Brawley, 619
Brea, 714
Brentwood, 213
Brisbane, 415
Broderick, 916
Bryte, 916
Buena Park, 714
Burbank (Los Angeles
  Co.), 818
Burbank (Santa Clara
  Co.), 408
Burlingame, 415
Calexico, 619
Calipatria, 619
Calistoga, 707
Calwa, 209
Camarillo, 805
Campbell, 408
Capistrano Beach,
  714
Carlsbad, 619
Carmel, 408
Carmichael, 916
Carpinteria, 805
Castro Valley, 415
Castroville, 408
Cathedral City, 619
Centerville (Alameda
  Co.), 415
Centerville (Fresno
  Co.), 209

Central Valley, 916
Ceres, 209
Chester, 916
Chico, 916
Chino, 714
Chowchilla, 209
Chula Vista, 619
Claremont, 714
Cloverdale, 707
Clovis, 209
Coachella, 619
Coalinga, 209
Colton, 714
Colusa, 916
Compton, 213
Concord, 415
Corcoran, 209
Corning, 916
Corona, 714
Coronado, 619
Corte Madera, 415
Costa Mesa, 714
Cotati, 707
Covina, 818
Crescent City, 707
Cucamonga, 714
Culver City, 213
Cutler, 209
Cypress, 714
Daly City, 415
Danville, 415
Davis, 916
Delano, 805
Del Mar, 619
Dinuba, 209

Dixon, 916
Dos Palos, 209
Downey, 213
Duarte, 818
Dunsmuir, 916
Earlimart, 805
Edwards Air Force
  Base, 805
El Cajon, 619
El Centro, 619
El Cerrito, 415
Elk Grove, 916
El Monte, 818
El Rio, 805
El Segundo, 213
Elsinore, 714
El Sobrante, 415
Emeryville, 415
Empire, 209
Encinitas, 619
Escalon, 209
Escondido, 619
Eureka, 707
Exeter, 209
Fairfax, 415
Fairfield, 707
Fair Oaks
  (Sacramento Co.),
  916
Fair Oaks (San Luis
  Obsipo Co.), 805
Fallbrook, 619
Felton, 408
Fillmore, 805
Firebaugh, 209
Folsom, 916
Fontana, 714
Fort Bragg, 707
Fortuna, 707
Fowler, 209
Fremont, 415
Fresno, 209
Fullerton, 714
Galt, 209
Gardena, 213
Garden Grove, 714
Gilroy, 408
Glendale, 818
Glendora, 818
Goleta, 805
Gonzales, 408
Grass Valley, 916
Greenbrae, 415

Greenfield (Kern Co.),
  805
Greenfield (Monterey
  Co.), 408
Grover City, 805
Gustine, 209
Half Moon Bay, 415
Hanford, 209
Hawthorne, 213
Hayward, 415
Healdsburg, 707
Hemet, 714
Hermosa Beach, 213
Hesperia, 619
Highland, 714
Hollister, 408
Holtville, 619
Hughson, 209
Huntington Beach,
  714
Huntington Park, 213
Imperial Beach, 619
Indio, 619
Inglewood, 213
Irwindale, 818
Ivanhoe, 209
Jackson, 209
Kentfield, 415
Kerman, 209
Keyes, 209
King City, 408
Kingsburg, 209
La Canada, 818
La Crescenta, 818
Lafayette, 415
Laguna Beach, 714
La Habra, 213
La Jolla, 619
Lakeport, 707
Lakeside, 619
Lakewood, 213
La Mesa, 619
La Mirada, 714
Lamont, 805
Lancaster, 805
La Puente, 213
Larkspur, 415
La Verne, 714
Lawndale, 213
Lemon Grove, 619
Lemoore, 209
Lincoln, 916
Lindsay, 209

Live Oak (San Benito
  Co.), 408
Live Oak (Sutter Co.),
  916
Livermore, 415
Livingston, 209
Lodi, 209
Loma Linda, 714
Lomita, 213
Lompoc, 805
Long Beach, 213
Los Angeles, 213
Los Banos, 209
Los Gatos, 408
Los Nietos, 213
Lynwood, 213
Madera, 209
Manhattan Beach, 213
Marina, 408
Marin City, 415
Martinez, 415
Marysville, 916
Mather Air Force
  Base, 916
Maywood, 213
McClellan Air Force
  Base, 916
Mendota, 209
Menlo Park, 415
Merced, 209
Millbrae, 415
Mill Valley, 415
Milpitas, 408
Modesto, 209
Moffett Field (Naval
  Air Station), 415
Mojave, 805
Monrovia, 818
Montclair, 714
Montebello, 213
Montecito, 805
Monterey, 408
Monterey Park, 213
Moorpark, 805
Morgan Hill, 408
Morro Bay, 805
Mountain View, 415
Mount Shasta, 916
Napa, 707
National City, 619
Needles, 619
Nevada City, 916
Newark, 415

Newhall, 805
Newman, 209
Newport Beach, 714
Norco, 714
North Highlands, 916
North Sacramento, 916
Norwalk, 213
Novato, 415
Oakdale, 209
Oakland, 415
Oak View, 805
Oceanside, 714
Oildale, 619
Ojai, 805
Ontario, 714
Orange, 714
Orange Cove, 209
Orinda, 415
Orland, 916
Oroville, 916
Oxnard, 805
Pacifica, 415
Pacific Beach, 619
Pacific Grove, 408
Palmdale, 805
Palm Springs, 619
Palo Alto, 415
Paradise, 916
Paramount, 213
Parlier, 209
Pasadena, 818
Paso Robles, 805
Patterson, 209
Perris, 714
Petaluma, 707
Pico Rivera, 213
Piedmont, 415
Pinedale, 209
Pismo Beach, 805
Pittsburg, 415
Placentia, 714
Placerville, 916
Planada, 209
Pleasant Hill, 415
Pleasanton, 415
Pomona, 714
Port Chicago, 415
Porterville, 209
Port Hueneme, 805
Portola, 916
Poway, 619
Presidio of Monterey,
  408

Presidio of San
   Francisco, 415
Quartz Hill, 805
Ramona, 619
Rancho Santa Fe, 619
Red Bluff, 916
Redding, 916
Redlands, 714
Redondo Beach, 213
Redwood City, 415
Reedley, 209
Rialto, 714
Richmond, 415
Ridgecrest, 619
Rio Dell, 707
Rio Linda, 916
Rio Vista, 707
Ripon, 209
Riverbank, 209
Riverside, 714
Rosamond, 805
Rosemead, 818
Roseville, 916
Ross, 415
Sacramento, 916
St. Helena, 707
Salinas, 408
San Anselmo, 415
San Bernardino, 714
San Bruno, 415
San Clemente, 714
San Diego, 619
San Dimas, 714
San Fernando, 818
San Francisco, 415
San Gabriel, 818
Sanger, 209
San Jacinto, 714
San Jose, 408
San Juan Capistrano,
   714
San Leandro, 415
San Lorenzo, 415
San Luis Obispo, 805
San Marcos, 619
San Marino, 818
San Mateo, 415
San Pablo, 415
San Rafael, 415
Santa Ana, 714
Santa Barbara, 805
Santa Clara, 408
Santa Cruz, 408

Sante Fe Springs, 213
Santa Maria, 805
Santa Monica, 213
Santa Paula, 805
Santa Rosa, 707
Santa Susana, 805
Santee, 619
Saratoga, 408
Saticoy, 805
Sausalito, 415
Seal Beach, 213
Seaside, 408
Sebastopol, 707
Selma, 209
Shafter, 805
Sierra Madre, 818
Sierra Ordnance
   Depot, 916
Signal Hill, 213
Simi Valley, 805
Solana Beach, 619
Soledad, 408
Sonoma, 707
Sonora, 209
South Gate, 213
South Pasadena, 818
South San Francisco,
   415
Spring Valley, 714
Stanton, 714
Stockton, 209
Suisun, 707
Sunnymead, 714
Sunnyvale, 408
Susanville, 916
Taft, 805
Tehachapi, 805
Temple City, 818
Thousand Oaks, 805
Tiburon, 415
Torrance, 213
Tracy, 209
Travis Air Force Base,
   707
Treasure Island, 415
Tulare, 209
Turlock, 209
Tustin, 714
Twentynine Palms,
   619
Ukiah, 707
U.S. Naval
   Hdqrs.—Twelfth

Naval Dist., 415
Upland, 714
Vacaville, 707
Vallejo, 707
Vandenberg Air Force
   Base, 805
Ventura, 805
Victorville, 619
Visalia, 209
Vista, 619
Walnut Creek, 415
Wasco, 805
Waterford, 209
Watsonville, 408
Weaverville, 916
Weed, 916
West Covina, 818
Westminster, 714
West Sacramento, 916
Whittier, 213
Willits, 707
Willows, 916
Winters, 916
Woodlake, 209
Woodland, 916
Yreka, 916
Yuba City, 916
Yucaipa, 714

Colorado
Aberdeen, 303
Aguilar, 719
Air Force Academy,
   719
Akron, 303
Alliston, 303
Anton, 303
Aspen, 303
Ault, 303
Avon, 303
Bailey, 303
Bayfield, 303
Bennett, 303
Boulder, 303
Breckenridge, 303
Brighton, 303
Bristol, 719
Broomfield, 303
Buena Vista, 719
Burlington, 719
Byers, 303
Capitol Hill, 303
Carbondale, 303
Central City, 303

Colorado City, 719
Colorado Springs, 719
Colorado Springs
   East, 719
Columbine, 303
Copper Mountain, 303
Craig, 303
Crestone, 719
De Beque, 303
Del Norte, 719
Denver, 303
Dillon, 303
Durango, 303
Eads, 719
Eaton, 303
Eckert, 303
Edwards, 303
Elizabeth, 303
El Paso, 719
Englewood, 303
Erie, 303
Evergreen, 303
Flagler, 719
Fleming, 303
Ft. Collins, 303
Ft. Morgan, 303
Fraser, 303
Frederick, 303
Frisco, 303
Gardener, 719
Gateway, 303
Georgetown, 303
Gilcrest, 303
Glenwood Springs,
   303
Grand Junction, 303
Grand Lake, 303
Grover, 303
Gunnison, 303
Hartman, 719
Hayden, 303
Hillrose, 303
Hot Sulphur Springs,
   303
Howard, 719
Hudson, 303
Idaho Springs, 303
Johnstown, 303
Kirk, 303
Kremmling, 303
La Junta, 719
Lake George, 719
La Salle, 303

Lafayette, 303
Lake City, 303
Lakewood, 303
Limon, 719
Littleton, 303
Longmont, 303
Louisville, 303
Lyons, 303
Mancos, 303
McCoy, 303
Mead, 303
Mesa, 303
Mesa Verde National
 Park, 303
Montbello, 303
Monte Vista, 719
Montrose, 303
Morrison, 303
Nederland, 303
New Castle, 303
Norwood, 303
Nunn, 303
Ordway, 719
Otis, 303
Pagosa Springs, 303
Palisade, 303
Palmer Lake, 719
Parker, 303
Parkview, 303
Penrose, 719
Plesant View, 303
Pueblo, 719
Pueblo West, 719
Rico, 303
Ridgway, 303
Roggen, 303
Rye, 719
Salida, 719
San Luis, 719
Sheridan Lake, 719
Silt, 303
Snowmass, 303
Somerset, 303
Springfield, 719
Stoneham, 303
Strasburg, 303
Stratton, 719
Sullivan, 303
Sunset, 719
Telluride, 303
Trinidad, 719
Vail, 303
Vineland, 719

Walden, 303
Walsh, 719
Ward, 303
Wellington, 303
Westminster, 303
Weston, 719
Wiggins, 303
Wiley, 719
Windsor, 303
Woodland Park, 719
Woodrow, 303
Wray, 303
Yampa, 303
Yuma, 303
Connecticut
All Points, 203

Delaware
All Points, 302
District of Columbia
Washington, D.C., 202

Florida
Alachua, 904
Apalachicola, 904
Apopka, 407
Arcadia, 813
Atlantic Beach, 904
Auburndale, 813
Avon Park, 813
Bartow, 813
Belleair, 813
Belle Glade, 407
Blountstown, 904
Boca Raton, 407

Bonifay, 904
Boynton Beach, 407
Bradenton, 813
Brooksville, 904
Bunnell, 904
Cape Canaveral, 407
Cape Kennedy, 407
Casselberry, 407
Century, 904
Chattahoochee, 904
Chipley, 904
Clearwater, 813
Clermont, 904
Clewiston, 813
Cocoa, 407
Coral Gables, 305
Crescent City, 904
Crestview, 904
Dade City, 904
Dania, 305
Daytona Beach, 904
Deerfield Beach, 305
De Funiak Springs,
 904
De Land, 904
Delray Beach, 407
Dunedin, 813
Edgewater, 904
Eglin Air Force Base,
 904
Ellenton, 813
Ellyson Field, 904
Englewood, 813
Eustis, 904
Fernandina Beach,
 904
Fort Lauderdale, 305
Fort Meade, 813
Fort Myers, 813
Fort Myers Beach, 813
Fort Ogden, 813
Fort Pierce, 407
Fort Walton Beach,
 904
Fort White, 904
Frostproof, 813
Fruitville, 813
Gainesville, 904
Gibsonton, 813
Green Cove Springs,
 904
Groveland, 904
Gulf Port, 813

Haines City, 813
Hallandale, 305
Havana, 904
Hialeah, 305
High Springs, 904
Holly Hill, 904
Hollywood, 305
Homestead, 305
Immokalee, 813
Indian Rocks Beach,
 813
Inverness, 904
Jacksonsville, 904
Jacksonville Beach,
 904
Jasper, 904
Kendall, 305
Kennedy Space
 Center, 407
Key Biscayne, 305
Key Largo, 305
Key West, 305
Kissimmee, 407
Lake Alfred, 813
Lake City, 904
Lakeland, 813
Lake Park, 407
Lake Wales, 813
Lake Worth, 407
Lantana, 407
Largo, 813
Leesburg, 904
Lehigh Acres, 813
Live Oak, 904
Long Beach (Bay
 Co.), 904
Long Beach (Sarasota
 Co.), 813
Lynn Haven, 904
Macclenny, 904
MacDill Air Force
 Base, 813
Madeira Beach, 813
Madison, 904
Maitland, 407
Marathon, 305
Marianna, 904
Marietta, 904
Mayport U.S. Naval
 Air Sta., 904
Melbourne, 407
Miami, 305
Miami Beach, 305

Miami Shores, 305
Miami Springs, 305
Milton, 904
Monticello, 904
Mount Dora, 904
Mulberry, 813
Naples, 813
Neptune Beach, 904
New Port Richey, 813
New Smyrna Beach, 904
Niceville, 904
North Miami Beach, 305
Oakland, 407
Ocala, 904
Ocoee, 407
Ojus, 305
Okeechobee, 813
Opa Locka, 305
Orange Park, 904
Orlando, 407
Ormond Beach, 904
Oviedo, 407
Pahokee, 407
Palatka, 904
Palm Beach, 407
Palmetto, 813
Panama City, 904
Panama City Naval Sta., 904
Patrick Air Force Base, 407
Pensacola, 904
Pensacola Naval Air Sta., 904
Perry, 904
Pinellas Park, 813
Plant City, 813
Pompano Beach, 305
Port Orange, 904
Port St. Joe, 904
Punta Gorda, 813
Quincy, 904
Riviera Beach, 407
Rockledge, 305
Ruskin, 813
Safety Harbor, 813
St. Augustine, 904
St. Petersburg, 813
Samoset, 813
Sanford, 407
Sarasota, 813

Sebring, 813
South Bay, 407
South Miami, 305
Springfield, 904
Starke, 904
Tallahassee, 904
Tampa, 813
Tarpon Springs, 813
Tavares, 904
Temple Terrace, 813
Tice, 813
Titusville, 407
Treasure Island, 813
Tyndall Air Force Base, 904
Tyndall Field, 904
Umatilla, 904
Valparaiso, 904
Venice, 813
Vero Beach, 407
Warrington, 904
Watertown, 904
Wauchula, 813
West Palm Beach, 407
White City (Gulf Co.), 904
White City (St. Lucie Co.), 305
Wildwood, 904
Winter Garden, 407
Winter Haven, 813
Winter Park, 407
Zephyrhills, 813

Georgia
Albany, 912
Americus, 912
Athens, 404
Atlanta, 404
Augusta 404
Bainbridge, 912
Barnesville, 404
Blakely, 912
Brunswick, 912

Cairo, 912
Camilla, 912
Carrollton, 404
Cartersville, 404
Cedartown, 404
Centerville (De Kalb Co.), 404
Centerville (Houston Co.), 912
Centerville (Wilkes Co.), 404
Chamblee, 404
Cochran, 912
College Park, 404
Columbus, 404
Cordele, 912
Covington, 404
Dalton, 404
Dawson, 912
Decatur, 404
Douglas, 912
Dublin, 912
Eastman, 912
East Point, 404
Elberton, 404
Fitzgerald, 912
Forest Park, 404
Fort Valley, 912
Gainesville, 404
Glynco Naval Air Station, 912
Griffin, 404
Hapeville, 404
Hartwell, 404
Huynter Field, 912
Jesup, 912
La Fayette, 404
La Grange, 404
Mableton, 404
Macon, 912
Marietta, 404
Milledgeville, 912
Monroe, 404
Moultrie, 912
Newnan, 404
Pelham, 912
Perry, 912
Quitman, 912
Robins Air Force Base, 912
Rome, 404
Rossville, 404
Sandersville, 912

Sandy Springs, 404
Savannah, 912
Scottdale, 404
Smyrna, 404
Statesboro, 912
Summerville, 404
Swainsboro, 912
Thomaston, 404
Thomasville, 912
Tifton, 912
Toccoa, 404
U.S. Army—Hdqrs. of Service Commands —Third Army, 404
Valdosta, 912
Valdosta Air Force Base, 912
Vidalia, 912
Warner Robins, 912
Waycross, 912
West Point, 404
Winder, 404

Hawaii
All Points, 808

Idaho
All Points, 208
Illinois
Abingdon, 309
Albion, 618
Aledo, 309
Alsip, 312
Altamont, 618
Alton, 618

Amboy, 815
Anna, 618
Antioch, 708
Arcola, 217
Arlington Heights, 708
Arthur, 217
Auburn, 217
Aurora, 708
Barrington, 708
Bartonville, 309
Beardstown, 217
Belleville, 618
Belvidere, 815
Benld, 217
Benton, 618
Bethalto, 618
Bismarck, 217
Bloomington, 309
Blue Island, 708
Bourbonnais, 815
Bradley, 815
Braidwood, 815
Breese, 618
Bridgeport, 618
Broadview, 708
Brookfield, 708
Brooklyn (St. Clair Co.), 618
Brooklyn (Schuyler Co.), 309
Bushnell, 309
Calumet Park, 708
Canton, 309
Carbondale, 618
Carlinville, 217
Carlyle, 618
Carmi, 618
Carrollton, 217
Carterville, 618
Carthage, 217
Carthage Junction, 309
Casey, 217
Central City (Grundy Co.), 815
Central City (Marion Co.), 618
Centralia, 618
Champaign-Urbana, 217
Chanute Air Force Base, 217
Charleston, 217

Chester, 618
Chicago, 312
Chillicothe, 309
Christopher, 618
Cicero, 708
Clinton, 217
Coal City, 815
Collinsville, 618
Columbia, 618
Country Club Hills, 312
Creve Coeur, 309
Crystal Lake, 815
Danville, 217
Decatur, 217
De Kalb, 815
Des Plaines, 708
Dixon, 815
Dupo, 618
Du Quoin, 618
Dwight, 815
East Alton, 618
East Moline, 309
East Peoria, 309
East St. Louis, 618
Edwardsville, 618
Effingham, 217
Eldorado, 618
Elgin, 708
Elk Grove, 708
Eureka, 309
Evanston, 708
Fairbury, 815
Fairfield, 618
Fairview (Fulton Co.), 309
Fairview (St. Clair Co.), 618
Farmington, 309
Flora, 618
Freeport, 815
Fulton, 815
Galena, 815
Galesburg, 309
Galva, 309
Geneseo, 309
Geneva, 708
Genoa, 815
Georgetown, 217
Germantown (Clinton Co.), 618
Germantown Hills, 309

Gibson City, 217
Gillespie, 217
Glen Ellyn, 312
Glenview, 708
Godfrey, 618
Granite City, 618
Greenville, 618
Harmony (Jefferson Co.), 618
Harmony (McHenry Co.), 815
Harrisburg, 618
Harvard, 815
Harvey, 708
Havana, 309
Herrin, 618
Highland, 618
Highland Park, 708
Hillsboro, 217
Indian Point (Menard Co.), 217
Irwin (Kankakee Co.), 815
Jacksonville, 217
Jerseyville, 618
Johnston City, 618
Joliet, 815
Kankakee, 815
Kingston (DeKalb Co.), 815
Kingston (Kingston Mines) (Peoria Co.), 309
Knoxville, 309
La Grange, 708
Lancaster (Stephenson Co.), 815
Lancaster (Wabash Co.), 618
La Salle, 815
Lawrenceville, 618
Lebanon, 618
Lewistown, 309
Libertyville, 708
Lidice, 815
Lily Lake (McHenry Co.), 815
Lincoln, 217
Litchfield, 217
Lockport, 815
Long Lake (Madison Co.), 618
Loves Park, 815

Lyons (Vermilion Co.), 217
Macomb, 309
Madison, 618
Manteno, 815
Marengo, 815
Marion, 618
Markham (Morgan Co.), 217
Marseilles, 815
Mascoutah, 618
Matton, 217
Maywood, 708
McHenry, 815
McLensaboro, 618
Metropolis, 618
Milan, 309
Millersburg (Bond Co.), 618
Millersburg (Mercer Co.), 309
Moline, 309
Momence, 815
Monmouth, 309
Monticello, 217
Morris, 815
Morrison, 815
Mount Carmel, 618
Mount Morris, 815
Mount Vernon, 618
Murphysboro, 618
Nashville, 618
Newton, 618
Nokomis, 217
Normal, 309
Northbrook, 708
Oak Lawn, 708
Oak Park, 708
O'Fallon, 618
Oglesby, 815
Oregon, 815
Ottawa, 815
Pana, 217
Park Forest, 708
Park Ridge, 708
Paxton, 217
Pekin, 309
Peoria, 309
Peoria Heights, 309
Peru, 815
Petersburg, 217
Pittsfield, 217
Polo, 815

Pontiac, 815
Quincy, 217
Rantoul, 217
Robinson, 618
Rochelle, 815
Rock Falls, 815
Rockford, 815
Rock Island, 309
Roodhouse, 217
Rushville, 217
Salem, 618
Sandwich, 815
Savanna, 815
Scott Air Force Base, 618
Skokie, 708
South Beloit, 815
Sparta, 618
Spaulding (Sangamon Co.), 217
Springfield, 217
Spring Valley, 815
Staunton, 618
Sterling, 815
Summit, 708
Sunnyland, 309
Swansea, 618
Sycamore, 815
Taylorville, 217
Thomas (Bureau Co.), 309
Thomas (Vermilion Co.), 217
Tilton, 217
Tuscola, 217
Urbana, 217
Vandalia, 618
Villa Grove, 217
Virden, 217
Washington, 309
Waterloo, 618
Watseka, 815
Waukegan, 708
West Chicago, 708
West Frankfort, 618
Westville, 217
Wheaton, 708
White Hall, 217
Wilmette, 708
Wilmington, 815
Winnetka, 708
Winthrop Harbor, 312
Wonder Lake, 815

Wood River, 618
Woodstock, 815

Indiana
Albany, 317
Alexandria, 317
Anderson, 317
Angola, 219
Ardmore, 219
Attica, 317
Auburn, 219
Austin, 812
Batesville, 812
Bedford, 812
Beech Grove, 317
Bloomfield, 812
Bloomington, 812
Bluffton, 219
Boonville, 812
Brazil, 812
Brownsburg, 317
Bunker Hill Air Force Base, 317
Cedar Lake, 219
Charlestown, 812
Chestertown, 219
Clarksville (Clark Co.), 812
Clarksville (Hamilton Co.), 317
Clinton, 317
Columbia City, 219
Columbus, 812
Connersville, 317
Crane Naval Ordnance Depot, 812
Crawfordsville, 317
Crown Point, 219
Decatur, 219
East Chicago, 219
East Gary, 219
Edinburg, 812
Elkhart, 219
Elwood, 317
Evansville, 812
Fairmount, 317
Fort Wayne, 219
Frankfort, 317
Franklin, 317
Garrett, 219
Gary, 219
Gas City, 317
Goshen, 219

Greencastle, 317
Greenfield, 317
Greensburg, 812
Greenwood, 317
Griffith, 219
Hammond, 219
Hartford City, 317
Highland, 219
Hobart, 219
Huntington, 219
Indianapolis, 317
Jasonville, 812
Jeffersonville, 812
Jonesboro, 317
Kendallville, 219
Knox, 219
Kokomo, 317
La Porte, 219
Lawrence, 317
Lebanon, 317
Lewisville (Henry Co.), 317
Lewisville (Morgan Co.), 317
Ligonier, 219
Linton, 812
Logansport, 219
Madison, 812
Marion, 317
Martinsville, 317
Michigan City, 219
Michigantown, 317
Milford, 219
Monticello, 219
Mooresville, 317
Mount Vernon, 812
Muncie, 317
Munster, 219
New Albany, 812
New Castle, 317
Noblesville, 317
Notre Dame, 219
Oakland City, 812
Peru, 317
Plainfield, 317
Plymouth, 219
Portland, 317
Princeton, 812
Rensselaer, 219
Richmond, 317
Rochester, 219
Rushville, 317
Salem, 812

Scottsburg, 812
Sellersburg, 812
Seymour, 812
Shelbyville, 317
South Bend, 219
Sullivan, 812
Tell City, 812
Terre Haute, 812
Tipton, 317
Valparaiso, 219
Wabash, 219
Washington, 812
Whiting, 219
Wolf Lake (Lake Co.), 219
Wolf Lake (Noble Co.), 219

Iowa
Albia, 515
Algona, 515
Ames, 515
Anamosa, 319
Ankeny, 515
Atlantic, 712
Belle Plaine, 319
Boone, 515
Burlington, 319
Carroll, 712
Cedar Falls, 319
Cedar Rapids, 319
Centerville, 515
Chariton, 515
Charles City, 515
Cherokee, 712
Clarinda, 712
Clear Lake, 515
Clinton, 319
Council Bluffs, 712
Cresco, 319
Creston, 515
Davenport, 319
Decorah, 319
Denison, 712
Des Moines, 515
Dubuque, 319
Eagle Grove, 515
Emmetsburg, 712
Estherville, 712
Fairfield, 515
Fort Dodge, 515
Fort Madison, 319
Glenwood, 712
Grinnell, 515

Hampton, 515
Harlan, 712
Humboldt, 515
Independence, 319
Indianola, 515
Iowa City, 319
Iowa Falls, 515
Jefferson, 515
Keokuk, 319
Knoxville, 515
Le Mars, 712
Manchester, 319
Maquoketa, 319
Marion, 319
Marshalltown, 515
Mason City, 515
Mount Pleasant, 319
Muscatine, 319
Nevada, 515
Newton, 515
Oelwein, 319
Oskaloosa, 515
Ottumwa, 515
Pella, 515
Perry, 515
Sac City, 712
Sheldon, 712
Shenandoah, 712
Sioux City, 712
Spencer, 712
Storm Lake, 712
Tama, 515
Washington, 319
Waterloo, 319
Waverly, 319
Webster City, 515
West Des Moines, 515

Kansas
Abilene, 913
Arkansas City, 316
Atchison, 913

Augusta, 316
Baxter Springs, 316
Beloit, 913
Chanute, 316
Clay Center, 913
Coffeyville, 316
Derby, 316
Dodge City, 316
El Dorado, 316
Emporia, 316
Fairway, 913
Forbes Air Force
    Base, 913
Fort Scott, 316
Garden City, 316
Great Bend, 316
Hays, 913
Haysville, 316
Herington, 913
Hiawatha, 913
Hutchinson, 316
Independence, 316
Iola, 316
Junction City, 913
Kansas City, 913
Kingman, 316
Larned, 316
Lawrence, 913
Leavenworth, 913
Liberal, 316
Lyons, 316
Marysville, 913
McPherson, 316
Merriam, 913
Mission, 913
Naval Air Sta.
    (Gardner), 913
Naval Air Sta.
    (Hutchinson), 316
Newton, 316
Norton, 913
Olathe, 913
Oswatomie, 913
Ottawa, 913
Overland Park, 913
Paola, 913
Parsons, 316
Phillipsburg, 913
Pittsburg, 316
Prarie Village, 913
Pratt, 316
Russell, 913

Salina, 913
Schilling Air Force
    Base, 913
Scott City, 316
Shawnee, 913
Topeka, 913
Ulysses, 316
Valley Falls, 913
Victoria, 913
Wellington, 316
Wichita, 316
Winfield, 316

Kentucky
Ashland, 606
Bardstown, 502
Bowling Green, 502
Buechel, 502
Campbellsville, 502
Catlettsburg, 606
Central City, 502
Clarksville Army Air
    Base, 502
Corbin, 606
Corinth (Grant Co.),
    606
Corinth (Logan Co.),
    502
Covington, 606
Cumberland, 606
Cynthiana, 606
Danville, 606
Dawson Springs, 502
Dayton, 606
Elizabethtown, 502
Fairview (Bleming
    Co.), 606
Fairview (Todd Co.),
    502
Florence, 606
Fort Thomas, 606
Frankfort, 502
Franklin, 502
Garrett (Floyd Co.),
    606
Garrett (Meade Co.),
    502
Georgetown, 502
Glasgow, 502
Harrodsburg, 606
Hayward (Carter Co.),
    66
Haywood (Barren

Co.), 502
Hazard, 606
Henderson, 502
Hopkinsville, 502
Jeffersontown, 502
Lebanon, 502
Lewisburg (Logan
    Co.), 502
Lewisburg (Mason
    Co.), 606
Lexington, 606
London, 606
Louisville, 502
Ludlow, 606
Madisonville, 502
Mayfield, 502
Maysville, 606
Middlesboro, 606
Morehead, 606
Mount Sterling, 606
Murray, 502
Newport, 606
Nicholasville, 606
Okolona, 502
Owensboro, 502
Paducah, 502
Paris, 606
Pikeville, 606
Princeton, 502
Richmond, 606
Roundhill (Edmonson
    Co.), 502
Roundhill (Madison
    Co.), 606
Russellville, 502
St. Helens (Jefferson
    Co.), 502
St. Helens (Lee Co.),
    606
St. Matthews, 502
Shelbyville, 502
Shiveley, 502
Somerset, 606
Valley Station, 502
Versailles, 606
Winchester, 606
Worthington
    (Greenup Co.),
    606
Worthington
    (Jefferson Co.),
    502

Louisiana

Abbeville, 318
Alexandria, 318
Arabi, 504
Bastrop, 318
Baton Rouge, 504
Bogalusa, 504
Bossier City, 318
Bunkie, 318
Chalmette, 504
Covington, 504
Crowley, 318
Denham Springs, 504
De Ridder, 318
Donaldsonville, 504
Eunice, 318
Franklin, 318
Greenwood (Caddo
   Par.), 318
Greenwood (St. Mary
   Par.), 504
Gretna, 504
Hammond, 504
Harahan, 504
Harvey, 504
Houma, 504
Jeanerette, 318
Jennings, 318
Kaplan, 318
Kenner, 504
Lafayette, 318
Lake Charles, 318
Leesville (Vernon
   Par.), 318
Leesville (Lafourche
   Par.), 504
Mansfield, 318
Marrero, 504
Metairie, 504
Minden, 318
Monroe, 318
Morgan City, 504
Natchitoches, 318
New Iberia, 318
New Orleans, 504

Oakdale, 318
Opelousas, 318
Plaquemine, 504
Rayne, 318
Ruston, 318
St. Martinville, 318
Scotlandville, 504
Shreveport, 318
Slidell, 504
Springhill
   (Washington Par.),
   504
Springhill (Webster
   Par.), 318
Sulphur, 318
Thibodaux, 504
Ville Platte, 318
West Monroe, 318
Westwego, 504
Winnfield, 318
Winnsboro, 318

Maine
All Points, 207
Maryland
All Points, 301
Massachusetts
Abington, 617
Adams, 413
Amesbury, 508
Amherst, 413
Andover, 508
Arlington, 617
Ashland, 508
Athol, 508
Attleboro, 508
Avon, 508
Ayer, 508
Bedford, 617
Belmont, 617
Beverly, 508
Boston, 617
Braintree, 617

Bridgewater, 508
Brighton, 617
Brookline, 617
Burlington, 617
Cambridge, 617
Canton, 508
Centerville, 617
Chelmsford, 508
Chelsea, 617
Chicopee, 413
Clinton, 508
Cochituate, 617
Concord, 508
Danvers, 508
Dedham, 617
Dracut, 508
Easthampton, 413
East Longmeadow,
   413
Everett, 617
Fairhaven, 508
Fall River, 508
Feeding Hills, 413
Fitchburg, 508
Framingham, 508
Franklin, 508
Gardner, 508
Gloucester, 508
Greenfield, 413
Hingham, 617
Holyoke, 413
Hopedale, 508
Hudson, 508
Hyannis, 508
Ipswich, 508
Lawrence, 508
Leominster, 508
Lexington, 617
Longmeadow, 413
Lowell, 508
Ludlow, 413
Lynn, 617
Lynnfield, 617
Lynnfield Center, 617
Malden, 617
Manchester, 508
Mansfield, 508
Marblehead, 617
Marlboro, 508
Maynard, 508
Medford, 617
Melrose, 617

Methuen, 508
Middleborough, 508
Milford, 508
Millbury, 508
Mill River (Berkshire
   Co.), 413
Mill River (Franklin
   Co.), 413
Milton, 617
Natick, 508
Naval Reserve Air
   Sta., 617
Needham, 617
New Bedford, 508
Newburyport, 508
Newton, 617
North Abington, 617
North Dartmouth, 508
Norwood, 617
Orange, 508
Palmer, 413
Peabody, 508
Pittsfield, 413
Plainville, 508
Plymouth, 508
Quincy, 617
Randolph, 617
Reading, 617
Revere, 617
Riverside (Franklin
   Co.), 413
Riverside (Middlesex
   Co.), 617
Salem, 508
Saugus, 617
Scituate, 617
Sharon, 617
Shrewsbury, 508
Somerset, 508
Somerville, 617
Southbridge, 508
South Hadley (Falls),
   413
Springfield, 413
Stoneham, 617
Stoughton, 617
Swampscott, 617
Taunton, 508
Turners Falls, 413
Walpole, 508
Waltham, 617
Ware, 413

Watertown, 617
Wellesley, 617
Westborough, 508
Westfield, 413
Weston, 617
Westover Air Force
    Base, 413
West Springfield, 413
Westwood, 617
Weymouth, 617
Whitinsville, 508
Whitman, 617
Williamstown, 413
Williamsville
    (Berkshire Co.),
    413
Williamsville
    (Worcester Co.),
    617
Winchendon, 508
Winchester, 617
Winthrop, 617
Woburn, 617
Woods Hole, 508
Worcester, 508
Michigan
Adrian, 517
Albion, 517
Algonac, 313
Allegan, 616
Allen Park, 313
Alma, 517
Alpena, 517
Ann Arbor, 313
Auburn Heights, 313
Augusta, 616
Bad Axe, 517
Bangor, 616
Battle Creek, 616
Bay City, 517
Bay View (Emmet
    Co.), 616
Bay View (Kalamazoo
    Co.), 616
Belding, 616
Benton Harbor, 616
Berkley, 313
Big Rapids, 616
Birmingham, 313
Blissfield, 517
Bloomfield Hills, 313
Boyne City, 616
Bridgeport, 517

Brighton, 313
Bronson, 517
Buchanan, 616
Cadillac, 616
Carlisle (Eaton Co.),
    517
Carlisle (Kent Co.),
    616
Carrollton, 517
Cedarville, 906
Center Line, 313
Charlevoix, 616
Charlotte, 517
Cheboygan, 616
Chesaning, 517
Clare, 517
Clawson, 313
Coldwater, 517
Comstock, 616
Covert, 616
Crawford, 517
Croswell, 313
Custer Air Force Sta.,
    616
Cutlerville, 616
Dearborn, 313
Detroit, 313
Dowagiac, 616
Drayton Plains, 313
East Detroit, 313
East Grand Rapids,
    616
East Lansing, 517
Eaton Rapids, 517
Ecorse, 313
Escanaba, 906
Essexville, 517
Farmington, 313
Fenton, 313
Ferndale, 313
Flat Rock, 313
Flint, 313
Fort Custer, 616
Frankfort, 616
Freeland, 517
Fremont, 616
Garden City, 313
Gaylord, 517
Gladstone, 906
Grand Haven, 616
Grand Ledge, 517
Grand Rapids, 616
Grandville, 616

Greenville, 616
Grosse Ile, 313
Grosse Ile (Naval Air
    Sta.), 313
Grosse Pointe, 313
Gwinn, 906
Hamtramck, 313
Hancock, 906
Harper Woods, 313
Hart, 616
Hastings, 616
Hazel Park, 313
Helena (Antrim Co.),
    616
Helena (Huron Co.),
    517
Highland, 313
Highland Park, 313
Hillsdale, 517
Holland, 616
Holt, 517
Howell, 517
Huntington Woods,
    313
Inkster, 313
Ionia, 616
Iron Mountain, 906
Ironwood, 906
Ishpeming, 906
Jackson, 517
Jenison, 616
Kalamazoo, 616
Kalkaska, 616
Kincheloe Air Force
    Base, 906
Lakeview, 517
Lakewood (Monroe
    Co.), 313
Lakewood (Muskegon
    Co.), 616
Lansing, 517
Lapeer, 313
Lathrup Village, 313
Lincoln Park, 313
Litchfield, 517
Livonia, 313
Long Lake (Alpena
    Co.), 517
Long Lake (Iosco
    Co.), 517
Ludington, 616
Madison Heights, 313
Manistee, 616

Manistique, 906
Marcellus, 616
Marine City, 313
Marlette, 517
Marquette, 906
Marshall, 616
Marysville, 313
Mason, 517
Melvindale, 313
Menominee, 906
Michigan Center, 517
Midland, 517
Milan, 313
Milford, 313
Monroe, 313
Montague, 616
Morenci, 517
Mount Clemens, 313
Mount Pleasant, 517
Munising, 906
Muskegon, 616
Muskegon Heights,
    616
Negaunee, 906
Niles, 616
Novi, 313
Oak Park, 313
Okemos, 517
Otsego, 616
Owosso, 517
Petoskey, 616
Pleasant Lake
    (Jackson Co.), 517
Pleasant Lake
    (Washtenaw Co.),
    313
Plymouth, 313
Pontiac, 313
Portage (Kalamazoo
    Co.), 616
Portage (Manistee
    Co.), 616
Portage Coast Guard
    Sta. No. 300, 906
Port Huron, 313
Rawsonville, 313
River Rouge, 313
Riverview, 313
Rochester, 313
Rogers City, 517
Romeo, 313
Romulus, 313
Roseville, 313

Round Lake (Jackson
Co.), 517
Round Lake (Lenawee
Co.), 517
Round Lake (Oakland
Co.), 313
Round Lake
(Shiawassee Co.),
517
Royal Oak, 313
Saginaw, 517
St. Clair, 313
St. Clair Shores, 313
St. Johns, 517
St. Joseph, 616
Saline, 313
Sand Lake (Kent Co.),
616
Sand Lake (Lenawee
Co.), 313
Sault Ste. Marie, 906
Sawyer Air Force
Base, 906
Selfridge Air Force
Base, 313
Silver Lake
(Dickinson Co.),
906
Silver Lake (Kent
Co.), 616
Southfield, 313
South Haven, 616
Sturgis, 616
Taylor, 313
Tecumseh, 517
Tekonsha, 517
Three Rivers, 616
Traverse City, 616
Trenton, 313
Troy, 313
Twin Lake (Muskegon
Co.), 616
Twin Lakes, 906
Union City, 517
U.S. War Department
Detroit Ordnance
Plant Center Line,
313
Utica, 313
Vandercook Lake, 517
Warren, 313
Watson (Allegan Co.),
616

Watson (Marquette
Co.), 906
Wayne, 313
White Lake
(Muskegon Co.),
616
White Lake (Oakland
Co.), 313
Willow Run, 313
Wixom, 313
Wolf Lake (Jackson
Co.), 517
Wolf Lake (Muskegon
Co.), 616
Wurtsmith Air Force
Base, 517
Wyandotte, 313
Wyoming, 616
Ypsilanti, 313
Zeeland, 616

Minnesota
Albert Lea, 507
Alexandria, 612
Anoka, 612
Austin, 507
Belle Plaine, 612
Bemidji, 218
Bloomington, 612
Blue Earth, 507
Brainerd, 218
Breckenridge, 218
Brooklyn Center, 612
Camp Ripley, 612
Carlton, 218
Chisholm, 218
Cloquet, 218
Cohasset, 218
Columbia Heights,
612
Coon Rapids, 612
Crookston, 218
Crystal, 612
Detroit Lakes, 218
Duluth, 218
East Grand Forks, 218
Edina, 612
Elk River, 612
Ely, 218
Eveleth, 218
Excelsior, 612
Fairmont, 507
Faribault, 507
Fergus Falls, 218

Fort Snelling, 612
Franklin (Renville
Co.), 507
Franklin (St. Louis
Co.), 218
Fridley, 612
Glencoe, 612
Golden Valley, 612
Grand Rapids, 218
Granite Falls, 612
Hastings, 612
Hibbing, 218
Hopkins, 612
International Falls,
218
Isanti, 612
La Crescent, 50]7
Lake City, 612
Lakeville, 612
Le Sueur, 612
Litchfield, 612
Little Falls, 612
Luverne, 507
Mankato, 507
Marshall, 507
Minneapolis, 612
Minnetonka, 612
Moorhead, 218
Mora, 612
Mound, 612
Mountain Iron, 218
New Brighton, 612
New Ulm, 507
Northfield, 507
North St. Paul, 612
Orono, 612
Osseo, 612
Owatonna, 507
Pipestone, 507
Red Wing, 612
Redwood Falls, 507
Richfield, 612
Robbinsdale, 612
Rochester, 507
St. Cloud, 612
St. James, 507
St. Louis Park, 612
St. Paul, 612
St. Paul Park, 612
St. Peter, 507
Sartell, 612
Sauk Rapids, 612
Shakopee, 612

Silver Bay, 218
South St. Paul, 612
Spring Grove, 507
Stillwater, 612
Taconite, 218
Taconite Harbor, 218
Taylors Falls, 612
Thief River Falls, 218
Two Harbors, 218
Virginia, 218
Wadena, 218
Waseca, 507
West St. Paul, 612
White Bear Lake, 612
Williams, 218
Willmar, 612
Windom, 507
Worthington, 507
Wyoming, 612

Mississippi
All Points, 601

Missouri
Affton, 314
Aurora, 417
Ballwin, 314
Belton, 816
Berkeley, 314
Boonville, 816
Boss, 314
Brentwood, 314
Bridgeton, 314
Brookfield, 816
Brunswick, 816
Butler, 816
California, 314
Cameron, 816
Cape Girardeau, 314
Carrollton, 816
Carsonville, 314
Carthage, 417
Caruthersville, 314
Charleston, 314
Chillicothe, 816
Claycomo, 816
Clayton, 314
Clinton, 816
Columbia, 314
Creve Coeur, 314
Crystal City, 314
Denton (Johnson
Co.), 816
Denton (Pemiscot
Co.), 314

Desloge, 314
De Soto 314
Dexter, 314
El Dorado Springs, 417
Ellington, 314
Excelsior Springs, 816
Farber, 314
Farmington, 314
Fenton, 314
Ferguson, 314
Festus, 314
Florissant, 314
Fort Leonard Wood, 314
Fredericktown, 314
Fulton, 314
Gladstone, 816
Glendale, 314
Grandview, 816
Hannibal, 314
Helena, 816
Higginsville, 816
Hollister, 417
Independence, 816
Ironton, 314
Jackson, 314
Jefferson City, 314
Jennings, 314
Joplin, 417
Kansas City, 816
Kennett, 314
Kirksville, 816
Kirkwood, 314
Knob Noster, 816
La Due (Henry Co.), 816
Ladue (St. Louis Co.), 314
Lake Ozark, 314
Lebanon, 417
Lees Summit, 816
Lemay, 314
Lexington, 816
Liberty, 816
Linden (Christian Co.), 417
Linden (Clay Co.), 816
Louisiana, 314
Macon, 816
Malden, 314
Maplewood, 314

Marshall, 816
Maryville, 816
Mexico, 314
Miller, 417
Moberly, 816
Monett, 417
Mount Vernon, 417
Neosho, 417
Nevada, 417
Noel, 417
Normandy, 314
North Kansas City, 816
Overland, 314
Pacific, 314
Palmyra, 314
Perryville, 314
Pine Lawn, 314
Poplar Bluff, 314
Potosi, 314
Raytown, 816
Reeds Spring, 417
Richards-Gebaur Air Force Base, 816
Richmond, 816
Richmond Heights, 314
Rock Hill, 314
Rolla, 314
St. Ann, 314
St. Charles, 314
Ste. Genevieve, 314
St. Joseph, 816
St. Louis, 314
Salem, 314
Sarcoxie, 417
Scott City, 314
Sedalia, 816
Sedalia Air Force Base, 816
Shelbina, 314
Sikeston, 314
Springdale, 816
Springfield, 417
Sullivan, 314
Trenton, 816
University City, 314
Vandalia, 314
Warrensburg, 816
Washington, 314
Waynesville, 314
Webb City, 417
Webster Goves, 314

Wellston, 314
Wellsville, 314
Wentzville, 314
West Plains, 417
Whiteman Air Force Base, 816
Windsor, 816
Wright City, 314

Montana
All Points, 406

Nebraska
Auburn, 402
Beatrice, 402
Bellevue, 402
Broken Bow, 308
Chadron, 308
Fremont, 402
Grand Island, 308
Hastings, 402
Holdrege, 308
Kearney, 308
Lexington, 308
Lincoln, 402
Minatare, 308
Nebraska City, 402
Norfolk, 402
North Bend, 402
North Platte, 308
Offutt Air Force Base, 402
Ogallala, 308
Omaha, 402
Oshkosh, 308
Plattsmouth, 402
Schuyler, 402
Scottsbluff, 308
Sidney, 308
Valley, 402

Nevada
All Points, 702

New Hampshire
All Points, 603

New Jersey

Absecon, 609
Allentown, 609
Ancora, 609
Asbury Park, 201
Atlantic City, 609
Audubon, 609
Avalon, 609
Avenel, 201
Barrington, 609
Bayonne, 201
Belford, 201
Belleville, 201
Bellmawr (Camden Co.), 609
Belmar (Monmouth Co.), 201
Belvidere, 201
Bergenfield, 201
Berkeley Heights, 201
Bernardsville, 201
Beverly, 609
Birmingham, 609
Blackwood, 609
Bloomfield, 201
Bloomfield-Glen Ridge-Montclair, 201
Bloomingdale, 201
Bogota, 201
Boonton, 201
Bordentown, 609
Bound Brook, 201
Bradley Beach, 201
Bridgeton, 609
Brugantine, 609
Burlington, 609
Butler, 201
Caldwell, 201
Camden, 609
Cardiff, 609
Carlstadt, 201
Carneys Point, 609
Carteret, 201
Carteret Sub Post-Raritan Arsenal U.S. Army, 201
Cedar Grove (Essex Co.), 201
Cedar Grove (Mercer Co.), 609
Cedar Knolls, 201
Chatham, 201
Chester, 201

Cinnaminson, 609
Clark, 201
Clayton, 609
Clementon, 609
Cliffside, 201
Cliffside Park, 201
Clifton, 201
Closter, 201
Collingswood, 609
Colonia, 201
Cranbury, 609
Cranford, 201
Cresskill, 201
Deal, 201
Delair, 609
Delanco, 609
Demarest, 201
Denville, 201
Deptford, 609
Dover, 201
Dumont, 201
Dunellen, 201
Earle U.S. Naval
    Ammunition
    Depot., 201
East Brunswick, 201
East Orange, 201
East Paterson, 201
East Rutherford, 201
Eatontown, 201
Edgewater, 201
Edison, 201
Egg Harbor, 609
Elizabeth, 201
Emerson, 201
Englewood, 201
Englewood Cliffs, 201
Fair Haven, 201
Fair Lawn, 201
Fairview (Bergen
    Co.), 201
Fairview (Camden
    Co.), 609
Fairview (Gloucester
    Co.), 609
Fairview (Monmouth
    Co.), 201
Fanwood, 201
Fieldsboro, 609
Finderne, 201
Flemington, 201
Florence, 609
Florham Park, 201

Fords, 201
Forked River, 609
Fort Dix, 609
Fort Lee, 201
Fort Monmouth, 201
Franklin, 201
Freehold, 201
Frenchtown, 201
Garfield, 201
Garwood, 201
Gibbsboro, 609
Gibbstown, 609
Glassboro, 609
Glendora, 609
Glen Ridge, 201
Glen Rock, 201
Gloucester, 609
Guttenberg, 201
Hackensack, 201
Hackettstown, 201
Haddonfield, 609
Haddon Heights, 609
Haddon Township,
    609
Haledon, 201
Hamburg, 201
Hamilton Square, 609
Hammonton, 609
Hanover, 201
Harrison, 201
Hasbrouck Heights,
    201
Haskell, 201
Hawthorne, 201
Hazlet, 201
High Bridge, 201
Highland Park
    (Camden Co.), 609
Hightstown, 609
Hillsdale, 201
Hillside, 201
Hoboken, 201
Hohokus, 201
Holmdel, 201
Hopewell
    (Cumberland Co.),
    609
Hopewell (Mercer
    Co.), 609
Irvington, 201
Iselin, 201
Jersey City, 201
Keansburg, 201

Kearny, 201
Keasbey, 201
Kenilworth, 201
Keyport, 201
Kinnelon, 201
Lake Hiawatha, 201
Lakehurst, 201
Lakehurst U.S. Naval
    Air Station, 201
Lakewood, 201
Lambertville, 609
Lawrenceville, 609
Lebanon, 201
Leonia, 201
Lincoln Park, 201
Linden, 201
Lindenwold, 609
Little Falls, 201
Little Ferry, 201
Little Silver, 201
Livingston, 201
Lodi, 201
Long Branch, 201
Lumberton, 609
Lyndhurst, 201
Madison, 201
Magnolia, 609
Mahwah, 201
Manahawkin, 609
Manasquan, 201
Manasquan Radio
    Compass Station
    U.S. Navy, 201
Manville, 201
Maple Shade, 609
Maplewood, 201
Margate City, 609
Matawan, 201
Mays Landing, 609
Maywood, 201
McGuire Air Force
    Base, 609
Mendham, 201
Menlo Park, 201
Mercerville, 609
Merchantville, 609
Metuchen, 201
Middlesex, 201
Middletown, 201
Midland Park, 201
Milford, 201
Milburn, 201
Milltown (Middlesex

Co.), 201
Milltown (Morris Co.),
    201
Millville, 609
Monmouth Junction,
    201
Montclair, 201
Montvale, 201
Montville, 201
Moonachie, 201
Moorestown, 609
Morris Plains, 201
Morristown, 201
Mountain Lake
    (Warren Co.), 201
Mountain Lakes
    (Morris Co.), 201
Mountainside, 201
Mount Ephraim, 609
Mount Holly, 609
Mount Laurel, 609
Murray Hill, 201
Neptune, 201
Neptune City, 201
Netcong, 201
Newark, 201
New Brunswick, 201
New Market, 201
New Milford, 201
New Providence, 201
New Shrewsbury, 201
Newton, 201
Nixon, 201
North Arlington, 201
North Bergen, 201
North Brunswick, 201
North Caldwell, 201
Northfield, 609
North Haledon, 201
North Plainfield, 201
Northvale, 201
Norwood, 201
Nutley, 201
Oakhurst, 201
Oakland, 201
Oaklyn, 609
Oak Tree, 201
Ocean City, 609
Ocean Gate, 201
Oceanport, 201
Old Bridge, 201
Oradell, 201
Orange, 201

Oxford, 201
Packanack Lake, 201
Palisade, 201
Palisades Park, 201
Palmyra, 609
Paramus, 201
Park Ridge, 201
Parlin, 201
Parsippany, 201
Passaic, 201
Paterson, 201
Paulsboro, 609
Pennsauken, 609
Penns Grove, 609
Pennsville, 609
Perth Amboy, 201
Phillipsburg, 201
Picatinny U.S. Army
    Arsenal, 201
Pitman, 609
Plainfield, 201
Pleasantville, 609
Point Pleasant, 201
Pompton Lakes, 201
Pompton Plains, 201
Port Monmouth, 201
Princeton, 609
Rahway, 201
Ramsey, 201
Raritan, 201
Red Bank, 201
Richfield, 201
Ridgefield Park, 201
Ridgewood, 201
Ringwood, 201
River Edge, 201
Riverside, 609
River Vale, 201
Rochelle Park, 201
Rockaway, 201
Roselle, 201
Roselle Park, 201
Rumson, 201
Runnemede, 609
Rutherford, 201
Saddle Brook, 201
Salem, 609
Sayreville, 201
Scotch Plains, 201
Secaucus, 201
Somerdale, 609
Somerset, 201
Somers Point, 609

Somerville, 201
South Amboy, 201
South Brunswick, 201
South Hackensack,
    201
South Orange, 201
South Plainfield, 201
South River, 201
Spotswood, 201
Springfield, 201
Stirling, 201
Stratford, 609
Succasunna, 201
Summit, 201
Teaneck, 201
Tenafly, 201
Teterboro, 201
Toms River, 201
Totowa, 201
Trenton, 609
Tuckerton, 609
Union, 201
Union Beach, 201
Union City, 201
Upper Montclair, 201
Ventnor, 609
Verona, 201
Vincentown, 609
Vineland, 609
Waldwick, 201
Wallington, 201
Wanaque, 201
Washington, 201
Washington
    Township, 201
Wayne, 201
Weehawken, 201
West Caldwell, 201
West Creek, 609
Westfield, 201
West Long Branch,
    201
Westmont, 609
West New York, 201
West Orange, 201
West Paterson, 201
Westville, 609
Westwood, 201
Wharton, 201
Whippany, 201
Wilburtha, 609
Wildwood, 609
Williamstown, 609

Willingboro, 609
Woodbine, 609
Woodbridge, 201
Woodbury, 609
Woodcliff Lake, 201
Wood-Ridge, 201
Wrightstown, 609
Wyckoff, 201

New Mexico
All Points, 505

New York
Akron, 716
Albany, 518
Albion, 716
Alden, 716
Allegany, 716
Amityville, 516
Amsterdam, 518
Aqueduct (Queens
    Co.), 718
Aqueduct
    (Schenectady Co.),
    518
Arcade, 716
Ardsley, 914
Arlington, 914
Armonk Village, 914
Atlantic Beach, 516
Attica, 716
Auburn, 315
Au Sable Forks, 518
Babylon, 516
Bainbridge, 607
Baldwin, 516
Baldwinsville, 315
Ballston Spa, 518
Batavia, 716
Bath, 607
Bayport, 516
Bay Shore, 516
Bayside, 718
Beacon, 914
Bethpage, 516
Binghamton, 607
Bohemia, 516
Brentwood, 516
Brewster, 914
Briarcliff Manor, 914
Bridgewater, 315
Brockport, 716
Bronx, 212
Bronxville, 914
Brooklyn, 718

Buchanan, 914
Buffalo, 716
Buffalo U.S. Naval
    Radio Station, 716
Burke, 518
Cairo, 518
Caledonia, 716
Calverton, 516
Camillus, 315
Canandaigua, 315
Canton, 315
Carle Place, 516
Caroline (Center)
    (Depot), 607
Carthage, 315
Castleton, 518
Catskill, 518
Cedarhurst, 516
Centereach, 516
Centerport (Cayuga
    Co.), 315
Centerport (Suffolk
    Co.), 516
Central Islip, 516
Champlain, 518
Charleston (Charleston
    Four Corners)
    (Montgomery Co.),
    518
Charleston (Richmond
    Co.), 718
Chateaugay, 518
Chautauqua, 716
Cheektowaga, 716
Clifton (Monroe Co.),
    716
Clifton (Richmond
    Co.), 718
Cohoes, 518
Cold Brook
    (Herkimer Co.),
    315
Cold Spring, 914
Cold Spring Harbor,
    516
Cold Springs (Steuben
    Co.), 607
Colonie, 518
Commack, 516
Cooperstown, 607
Copiague, 516
Corning, 607
Cornwall, 914

Cortland, 607
Croton-on-Hudson, 914
Crystal Lake (Cattaraugus Co.), 716
Crystal Lake (Lewis Co.), 315
Crystal Lake (Schoharie Co.), 518
Dannemora, 518
Dansville, 716
Deer Park, 516
Deferiet, 315
Delmar, 518
Depauville, 315
Depew, 716
Dewitt, 315
Dobbs Ferry, 914
Dunkirk, 817
East Aurora, 716
East Islip, 516
East Northport, 516
East Patchogue, 516
East Rochester, 716
East Rockaway, 516
East Syracuse, 315
Ellenville, 914
Elmira, 607
Elmsford, 914
Endicott, 607
Endwell, 607
Fairmount, 315
Fairport, 716
Farmingdale, 516
Fayetteville, 315
Fredona, 716
Freeport, 516
Fulton, 315
Garden City, 516
Geneva, 315
Glen Cove, 516
Glen Head, 516
Glens Falls, 518
Glenwood (Erie Co.), 716
Glenwood (Nassau Co.), 516
Glenwood (Tompkins Co.), 607
Glenwood Landing, 516

Goshen, 914
Gouverneur, 315
Grand Island, 716
Great Neck, 516
Green Island, 518
Greenlawn, 516
Greenport (Columbia Co.), 518
Greenport (Suffolk Co.), 516
Greenvale (Station), 516
Greenville (Greene Co.), 518
Greenville (Orange Co.), 914
Greenwich, 518
Griffis Air Force Base, 315
Hamburg, 716
Harrison, 914
Hartsdale, 914
Hastings-on-Hudson, 914
Hauppauge, 516
Haverstraw, 914
Hawthorne, 914
Hempstead, 516
Herkimer, 315
Hicksville, 516
Hoosick Falls, 518
Hornell, 607
Horseheads, 607
Hudson, 518
Hudson Falls, 518
Huguenot (Orange Co.), 914
Huguenot (Richmond Co.), 718
Huntington, 516
Ilion, 315
Inwood, 516
Irondequoit, 716
Islip, 516
Ithaca, 607
Jamestown, 716
Jericho (Clinton Co.), 518
Jericho (Nassau Co.), 516
Johnson, 914
Johnson City, 607
Kenmore, 716

Kings Park, 516
Kings Point, 516
Kingston, 914
La Grange (Dutchess Co.), 914
Lagrange (Wyoming Co.), 716
Lakewood, 716
Lancaster, 716
Larchmont, 914
Latham, 518
Lawrence, 516
Lawrenceville (Greene Co.), 518
Lawrenceville (St. Lawrence Co.), 315
Levittown, 516
Liberty, 914
Lindenhurst, 516
Litchfield (Oneida Co.), 315
Litchfield (Tioga Co.), 607
Little Falls, 315
Liverpool, 315
Lockport, 716
Long Beach, 516
Long Lake (Hamilton Co.), 518
Long Lake (Oneida Co.), 315
Loudonville, 518
Lynbrook, 516
Lyons, 315
Malone, 518
Mamaroneck, 914
Manhasset, 516
Manhattan, 212
Massapequa, 516
Massena, 315
Mastic, 516
Meadow Brook (Nassau Co.), 516
Meadow Brook (Orange Co.), 914
Media, 716
Melville, 516
Meredith, 607
Middletown, 914
Millwood, 914
Mineola, 516
Mitchell Air Force Base, 516

Mohawk, 315
Montezuma, 315
Monticello, 914
Mount Kisco, 914
Mount Vernon, 914
Mount Vision, 607
Newark, 315
Newburgh, 914
New City, 914
Newfane, 716
New Hyde Park, 516
New Paltz, 914
Newport, 315
New Rochelle, 914
New York City, 212
Niagara Falls, 716
North Pelham, 914
Northport, 516
North Syracuse, 315
North Tarrytown, 914
North Tonawanda, 716
Norwich, 607
Nyack, 914
Oceanside, 516
Ogdensburg, 315
Olean, 716
Oneida, 315
Oneonta, 607
Orangeburg, 914
Ossining, 914
Oswego, 315
Owego, 607
Oyster Bay, 516
Painted Post, 607
Palmyra, 315
Patchogue, 516
Pawling, 914
Pearl River, 914
Peekskill, 914
Penn Yan, 315
Pinelawn, 516
Plainfield, 516
Plattsburgh, 518
Pleasant Plains (Richmond Co.), 718
Pleasant Plains (Dutchess Co.), 914
Pleasant Valley (Steuben Co.), 607
Pleasantville, 914

Port Chester, 914
Port Jefferson, 516
Port Jervis, 914
Port Washington, 516
Postdam, 315
Poughkeepsie, 914
Queens, 718
Rensselaer, 518
Ripley, 716
Riverhead, 516
Rochester, 716
Rockville Centre, 516
Rome, 315
Ronkonkoma, 516
Roslyn, 516
Rotterdam, 518
Rouses Point, 518
Rye, 914
Sackets Harbor, 315
Sag Harbor, 516
St. James, 516
Salamanca, 716
Salem, 518
Saranac Lake, 518
Saratoga Springs, 518
Saugerties, 914
Sayville, 516
Scarsdale, 914
Schenectady, 518
Schoharie, 518
Schuylerville, 518
Sciota, 518
Scotia, 518
Scottsville, 716
Scranton, 716
Sea Cliff, 516
Seaford, 516
Selden, 516
Selkirk (Albany Co.), 518
Selkirk (Oswego Co.), 315
Seneca Falls, 315
Sherburne, 607
Sherrill, 315
Shirley (Suffolk Co.), 516
Shirly (Erie Co.), 716
Sidney, 607
Silver Creek, 716
Silver Lake (Clinton Co.), 518

Silver Lake (Dutchess Co.), 914
Silver Lake (Richmond Co.), 718
Silver Lake (Wyoming Co.), 716
Sloan, 716
Smithtown, 516
Solvay, 315
Southampton, 516
South Corning, 607
South Floral Park, 516
South Hempstead, 516
South Nyack, 914
Spencerport, 716
Spring Valley, 914
Springville, 716
Stony Brook, 516
Stony Point (Rockland Co.), 914
Stottville, 518
Suffern, 914
Syosset, 516
Syracuse, 315
Tarrytown, 914
Tonawanda, 716
Troy, 518
Tuckahoe, 914
Tupper Lake, 518
Upton, 516
Utica, 315
Valhalla, 914
Valley Stream, 516
Vestal, 607
Walden, 914
Wantagh, 516
Wappingers Falls, 914
Warsaw, 716
Waterloo, 315
Watertown, 315
Watervliet, 518
Waverly, 607
Webster, 716
Wellsville, 716
Westbury (Cayuga Co.), 315
Westbury (Nassau Co.), 516
West Nyack, 914
Whitehall, 518
White Plains, 914

Whitesboro, 315
Whitney Point, 607
Williamsville, 716
Williston Park, 516
Wilson, 716
Yonkers, 914
Yorktown, 914
Yorktown Heights, 914
Youngstown, 716

North Carolina
Ahoskie, 919
Albemarle, 704
Arden, 704
Asheboro, 919
Asheville, 704
Belmont, 704
Boone, 704
Brevard, 704
Burlington, 919
Canton, 704
Cary, 919
Chapel Hill, 919
Charlotte, 704
Cherryville, 704
Clinton, 919
Concord, 704
Conover, 704
Davidson, 704
Dunn, 919
Durham, 919
Edenton, 919
Elkin, 919
Farmville, 919
Fayetteville, 919
Forest City, 704
Fuquay-Varina, 919
Gastonia, 704
Gibsonville, 919
Goldsboro, 919
Graham, 919
Greensboro, 919
Greenville, 919
Hamlet, 919
Henderson, 919
Hendersonville, 704
Hickory, 704
High Point, 919
Jacksonville, 919
Kannapolis, 704
Kernersville, 919
Kings Mountain, 704

Kinston, 919
Laurinburg, 919
Leaksville-Spray, 919
Lenoir, 704
Lexington, 704
Lincolnton, 704
Lowell, 704
Lumberton, 919
Maiden, 704
Marion, 704
Monroe, 704
Mooresville, 704
Morehead City, 919
Morganton, 704
Mount Airy, 919
Mount Holly, 704
Mount Olive, 919
Murphy, 704
New Bern, 919
Newland, 704
Newton, 704
Old Fort, 704
Oxford, 919
Pilot Mountain, 919
Plymouth, 919
Raleigh, 919
Roanoke Rapids, 919
Rockingham, 919
Rocky Mount, 919
Salisbury, 704
Sanford, 919
Seymour Johnson Air Force Base, 919
Shelby, 704
Siler City, 919
Smithfield, 919
Southern Pines, 919
Spindale, 704
Spray, 919
Spruce Pine, 704
Statesville, 704
Swannanoa, 704
Tarboro, 919
Taylorsville, 704
Thomasville, 919
Valdese, 704
Wake Forest, 919
Washington, 919
Waynesville, 704
Whiteville, 919
Wilkesboro, 919
Williamston, 919

Wilmington, 919
Wilson, 919
Winston-Salem, 919
Yanceyville, 919
North Dakota
All Points, 701

Ohio
Ada, 419
Akron, 216
Alliance, 216
Amherst, 216
Ashland, 419
Ashtabula, 216
Athens, 614
Aurora, 216
Austin, 614
Barberton, 216
Barnesville, 614
Bay Village, 216
Bedford, 216
Bellaire, 614
Bellefontaine, 513
Bellevue, 419
Belpre, 614
Berea, 216
Bethany, 513
Bexley, 614
Blue Ash, 513
Bluffton, 419
Boardman, 216
Bowling Green, 419
Brecksville, 216
Bridgeport, 614
Broadview Heights, 216
Brook Park, 216
Brunswick, 216
Bryan, 419
Bucyrus, 419
Cadiz, 614
Cambridge, 614
Camden, 513

Campbell, 216
Canton, 216
Carrollton, 216
Celina, 419
Centerville (Belmont Co.), 614
Centerville (Gallia Co.), 614
Centerville (Montgomery Co.), 513
Chagrin Falls, 216
Chardon, 216
Chesterland, 216
Chillicothe, 614
Cincinnati, 513
Circleville, 614
Cleveland, 216
Cleveland Heights, 216
Clinton County Air Force Base, 513
Clyde, 419
Columbiana, 216
Columbus, 614
Conneaut, 216
Coshocton, 614
Crestline, 419
Cuyahoga Falls, 216
Dayton, 513
Deer Park, 513
Defiance, 419
Delaware, 614
Delphos, 419
Dennison, 614
Dover, 216
Duffy, 614
Eastlake, 216
East Liverpool, 216
East Richland, 614
Eaton, 513
Elmwood Place, 513
Elyria, 216
Euclid, 216
Fairborn, 513
Fairfield, 513
Fairpoint, 614
Fairport, 216
Fairview Park, 216
Findlay, 419
Fostoria, 419
Franklin, 513

Fremont, 419
Galion, 419
Gallipolis, 614
Garfield Heights, 216
Geneva, 216
Germantown, 513
Girard, 216
Golf Manor, 513
Grandview Heights, 614
Greenfield, 513
Greenhills, 513
Greenville, 513
Hamilton, 513
Harrisburg (Franklin Co.), 614
Harrisburg (Stark Co.), 216
Harrison, 513
Heath, 614
Hilliard, 614
Hillsboro, 513
Hubbard, 216
Hudson, 216
Huron, 419
Independence (Cuyahoga Co.), 216
Indian Hill, 513
Ironton, 614
Jackson, 614
Kent, 216
Kenton, 419
Kettering, 513
Lakewood, 216
Lancaster, 614
Lebanon (Monroe Co.), 614
Lima, 419
Lincoln Heights, 513
Lisbon (Clark Co.), 513
Lisbon (Columbiana Co.), 216
Lockbourne, 614
Lockbourne Air Force Base, 614
Lockland, 513
Logan, 614
London, 614
Lorain, 216
Louisville, 216

Loveland, 513
Lyndhurst, 216
Macedonia, 216
Madeira, 513
Manchester (Adams Co.), 513
Manchester (Summit Co.), 216
Mansfield, 419
Maple Heights, 216
Mariemont, 513
Marietta, 614
Marion, 614
Martins Ferry, 614
Marysville, 513
Mason, 513
Massillon, 216
Masury, 216
Maumee, 419
Mayfield Heights, 216
Medina, 216
Mentor, 216
Miamisburg, 513
Middleburgh Heights, 216
Middletown, 513
Milan, 419
Minerva, 216
Mingo Junction, 614
Mogadore, 216
Montpelier, 419
Moran, 216
Mount Gilead, 419
Mount Healthy, 513
Mount Vernon, 614
Napoleon, 419
Nelsonville, 614
New Albany (Franklin Co.), 614
New Albany (Mahoning Co.), 216
Newark, 614
New Boston, 614
Newburgh Heights, 216
New Carlisle, 513
Newcomerstown, 614
New Lexington, 614
New Philadelphia, 216
Newton Falls, 216

Niles, 216
North Canton, 216
North College Hill,
   513
North Olmsted, 216
North Ridgeville, 216
North Robinson, 419
Norwalk, 419
Norwood, 513
Oakwood
   (Montgomery Co.),
   513
Oakwood (Paulding
   Co.), 419
Oberlin, 216
Oregon, 419
Orrville, 216
Ottawa Hills, 419
Oxford, 513
Painesville, 216
Parma (Heights), 216
Perrysburg, 419
Piqua, 513
Portage Leaks, 216
Port Clinton, 419
Portsmouth, 614
Ravenna, 216
Reading, 513
Reynoldsburg, 614
Richmond Heights,
   216
Rittman, 216
Rocky Ridge, 419
Rossford, 419
St. Bernard, 513
St. Clairsville, 614
St. Marys, 419
Salem, 216
Sandusky, 419
Sebring, 216
Seven Hills, 216
Shadyside, 614
Shaker Heights, 216
Sharonville, 513
Sheffield Lake, 216
Shelby, 419
Shiloh, 419
Sidney, 513
Silverton, 513
Solon, 216
South Euclid, 216
South Point, 614
Springfield, 513

Steubenville, 614
Stow, 216
Strongsville, 216
Struthers, 216
Sylvania, 419
Tallmadge, 216
Tiffin, 419
Tipp City, 513
Toledo, 419
Toronto, 614
Trotwood, 513
Troy, 513
Twinburg, 216
Uhrichsville, 614
University Heights,
   216
Upper Arlington, 614
Upper Sandusky, 419
Urbana, 513
Urbancrest, 614
Vandalia, 513
Van Wert, 419
Vermilion, 216
Wadsworth, 216
Wapakoneta, 419
Warren, 216
Washington Court
   House, 614
Wauseon, 419
Waverly, 614
Wellington, 216
Wellston, 614
Wellsville, 216
West Carrollton, 513
Westerville, 614
West Lafayette, 614
Westlake, 216
Whitehall, 614
Wickliffe, 216
Willard, 419
Willoughby, 216
Willowick, 216
Wilmington, 513
Windham, 216
Wintersville, 614
Wooster, 216
Worthington, 614
Wright-Patterson Air
   Force Base, 513
Wyoming, 513
Xenia, 513
Yellow Springs-
   Clifton, 513

Youngstown, 216
Zanesville, 614

Oklahoma
Ada, 405
Altus, 405
Anadarko, 405
Ardmore, 405
Bartlesville, 918
Bethany, 405
Broken Arrow, 918
Chicasha, 405
Claremore, 918
Clinton, 405
Cushing, 918
Duncan, 405
Durant, 405
Edmond, 405
Elk City, 405
El Reno, 405
Enid, 405
Frederick, 405
Guthrie, 405
Guymon, 405
Henryetta, 918
Hobart, 405
Lawton, 405
Maysville, 405
McAlester, 918
Miami, 918
Midwest City, 405
Muskogee, 918
Mustang, 405
Norman, 405
Oklahoma City, 405
Okmulgee, 918
Pauls Valley, 405
Perry, 405
Ponca City, 405
Pryor, 918
Sallisaw, 918
Sand Springs, 918
Sapulpa, 918
Shawnee, 405
Stillwater, 405
Tahlequah, 918
Tecumseh, 405
Tinker Air Force
   Base, 405
Tulsa, 918
Vinita, 918
Wewoka, 405
Woodward, 405
Wynnewood, 405

Yukon, 405
Oregon
All Points, 503

Pennsylvania
Abington, 215
Aldan (Delaware
   Co.), 215
Alden (Luzerne Co.),
   717
Aliquippa, 412
Allentown (Allegheny
   Co.), 412
Allentown (Lehigh
   Co.), 215
Allentown-Bethlehem
   Airport, 215
Allison Park, 412
Altoona, 814
Ambler, 215
Ambridge, 412
Annville, 717
Archbald, 717
Ardmore, 215
Arnold, 412
Ashland (Clearfield
   Co.), 814
Ashland (Schuylkill
   Co.), 717
Ashley, 717
Aspinwall, 412
Athens, 717
Avalon, 412
Avondale (Chester
   Co.), 215
Avondale (Delaware
   Co.), 215
Bala-Cynwyd, 215
Bangor, 215
Bear Lake (Luzerne
   Co.), 717
Bear Lake (Warren
   Co.), 814
Beaver, 412

Fullerton, 215
Georgetown (Adams
  Co.), 717
Georgetown (Beaver
  Co.), 412
Georgetown
  (Lancaster Co.),
  717
Georgetown (Luzerne
  Co.), 717
Gettysburg, 717
Glasgow (Beaver
  Co.), 412
Glasgow (Cambria
  Co.), 814
Glassport, 412
Glenolden, 215
Glenshaw, 412
Glenside, 215
Goshen (Clearfield
  Co.), 814
Goshen (Lancaster
  Co.), 717
Green Ridge
  (Delaware Co.),
  215
Green Ridge
  (Northumberland
  Co.), 717
Greensburg, 412
Greentree (Allegheny
  Co.), 412
Green Tree (Chester
  Co.), 215
Green Tree (Lancaster
  Co.), 717
Greenville, 412
Grove City, 412
Hamilton (Jefferson
  Co.), 814
Hamilton
  (Northumberland
  Co.), 717
Hanover (Luzerne
  Co.), 717
Harrisburg, 717
Haverford, 215
Hazleton, 717
Hellertown, 215
Hershey, 717
Hickory, 412
Highland Park
  (Cumberland Co.),

717
Highland Park
  (Delaware Co.),
  215
Hillside (Luzerne
  Co.), 717
Hillside
  (Westmoreland
  Co.), 412
Hollidaysburg, 814
Homestead, 412
Honesdale, 717
Independence
  (Beaver Co.), 412
Independence
  (Snyder Co.), 717
Independence
  (Washington Co.),
  412
Indiana, 412
Isabella (Chester Co.),
  215
Isabella (Fayette Co.),
  412
Island Park
  (Northampton
  Co.), 215
Island Park
  (Northumberland
  Co.), 717
Jacksonville (Centre
  Co.), 814
Jacksonville
  (Cumberland Co.),
  717
Jacksonville (Indiana
  Co.), 412
Jacksonville (Lebanon
  Co.), 717
Jacksonville (Lehigh
  Co.), 215
Jamestown (Carbon
  Co.), 215
Jamestown (Mercer
  Co.), 412
Jeannette, 412
Jefferson (Schuylkill
  Co.), 717
Jefferson (York Co.),
  717
Jenkintown, 215
Jersey Shore, 717
Jessup, 717

Jim Thorpe, 717
Juniata (Blair Co.),
  814
Juniata (Fayette Co.),
  412
Kingston, 717
Kittanning, 412
Klinesville (Berks
  Co.), 215
Klinesville (Lancaster
  Co.), 717
Knoxville (Allegheny
  Co.), 412
Knoville (Tioga Co.),
  814
Kutztown (Berks
  Co.), 215
Kutztown (Lebanon
  Co.), 717
Lancaster, 717
Lansdale, 215
Lansdowne, 215
Lansford, 717
Lebanon, 717
Lehighton, 215
Levittown, 215
Lewisburg, 717
Lewistown (Mifflin
  Co.), 717
Lewistown (Schuylkill
  Co.), 717
Lewisville (Chester
  Co.), 215
Lewisville (Potter
  Co.), 814
Liberty (Allegheny
  Co.), 412
Liberty (Tioga Co.),
  717
Lititz, 717
Lock Haven, 717
Locust Valley (Lehigh
  Co.), 215
Locust Valley
  (Schuylkill Co.),
  717
Logan (Columbia
  Co.), 717
Logan (Philadelphia
  Co.), 215
Lumber City
  (Clearfield Co.),
  814

Lumber City (Mifflin
  Co.), 717
Mahanoy City, 717
Manchester (Erie Co.),
  814
Manchester (York
  Co.), 717
McKees Rocks, 412
Mechanicsburg, 717
Mechanicsville, 215
Merion Station, 215
Middletown (Blair
  Co.), 814
Middletown (Dauphin
  Co.), 717
Middletown (Luzerne
  Co.), 717
Midland, 412
Midway (Adams Co.),
  717
Midway (Washington
  Co.), 412
Millcreek (Erie Co.),
  814
Mill Creek
  (Huntingdon Co.),
  814
Millerstown (Blair
  Co.), 814
Millerstown (Perry
  Co.), 717
Mill Grove (Columbia
  Co.), 717
Millgrove (Erie Co.),
  814
Milltown (Allegheny
  Co.), 412
Milltown (Bradford
  Co.), 717
Millvale, 412
Milton, 717
Minersville, 717
Monaca, 412
Monessen, 412
Monongahela, 412
Monroeville, 412
Morrisville (Bucks
  Co.), 215
Morrisville (Greene
  Co.), 412
Mount Airy (Lancaster
  Co.), 717
Mount Airy

(Philadelphia Co.),
215
Mount Carmel, 717
Mount Lebanon, 412
Mount Oliver, 412
Mount Pleasant
(Adams Co.), 717
Mount Pleasant
(Berks Co.), 215
Mount Pleasant
(Franklin Co.), 717
Mount Pleasant
(Juniata Co.), 717
Mount Pleasant
(Lebanon Co.), 717
Mount Pleasant
(Mifflin Co.), 717
Mount Pleasant
(Westmoreland
Co.), 412
Mount Pleasant (York
Co.), 717
Nanticoke, 717
Narberth, 215
Natrona Heights, 412
Nazareth, 215
New Brighton, 412
Newburg
(Cumberland Co.),
717
Newburg
(Huntingdon Co.),
814
New Castle, 412
New Kensington, 412
New Town (Bucks
Co.), 215
Newtown (Lancaster
Co.), 717
Norristown, 215
Norwood (Delaware
Co.), 215
Norwood (Lancaster
Co.), 717
Oakdale (Allegheny
Co.), 412
Oakdale (Luzerne
Co.), 717
Oakmont (Allegheny
Co.), 412
Oakmont (Delaware
Co.), 215
Old Forge, 717

Orangeville
(Columbia Co.),
717
Orangeville (Mercer
Co.), 412
Overbrook
(Allegheny Co.),
412
Overbrook
(Philadelphia Co.),
215
Palmyra, 717
Paoli, 215
Penfield (Clearfield
Co.), 814
Penfield (Delaware
Co.), 215
Penn Hill, 717
Philadelphia, 215
Phoenixville, 215
Pittsburgh, 412
Pittston, 717
Pleasant Hill
(Lebanon Co.), 717
Pleasant Hills
(Allegheny Co.),
412
Pleasant Valley
(Bucks Co.), 215
Pleasant Valley
(Fayette Co.), 412
Pleasant Valley
(Lycoming Co.),
717
Pleasant Valley
(Schuylkill Co.),
717
Pleasant Valley
(Westmoreland
Co.), 412
Pleasantville (Bedford
Co.), 814
Pleasantville (Berks
Co.), 215
Pleasantville
(Venango Co.), 814
Plymouth, 717
Port Vue, 412
Pottstown, 215
Pottsville, 717
Presque Isle Coast
Guard Sta. No.
236, 814

Prospect Park, 215
Punxsutawney, 814
Quakertown, 215
Rankin, 412
Reading, 215
Red Lion, 717
Richmond
(Northampton
Co.), 215
Richmond (York Co.),
717
Ridgway, 814
Ridley Park, 215
Rochester, 412
Rosedale (Allegheny
Co.), 412
Rosedale (Chester
Co.), 215
Roslyn, 215
St. Clair, 717
St. Lawrence (Berks
Co.), 215
St. Lawrence
(Cambria Co.), 814
Salisbury (Lancaster
Co.), 717
Salisbury (Somerset
Co.), 814
Sandy Run (Bedford
Co.), 814
Sandy Run (Luzerne
Co.), 717
Sayre, 717
Scottdale, 412
Scranton, 717
Sewickley, 412
Sharon, 412
Sharon Hill, 215
Sharpsburg (Blair
Co.), 814
Sharpsville, 412
Sheridan (Allegheny
Co.), 412
Sheridan (Lebanon
Co.), 215
Sheridan (Schuylkill
Co.), 717
Shippensburg, 717
Smithfield (Fayette
Co.), 412
Smithfield
(Huntingdon Co.),
814

Smithton
(Westmoreland
Co.), 412
Smithtown (Bucks
Co.), 215
Souderton, 215
South Williamsport,
717
Springdale, 412
Springfield (Bradford
Co.), 717
Springfield
(Cumberland Co.),
717
Springfield (Delaware
Co.), 215
Standing Stone
(Bradford Co.), 717
Standing Stone
(Huntingdon Co.),
814
State College, 814
State Line (Bedford
Co.), 814
State Line (Franklin
Co.), 717
Stroudsburg, 717
Summerhill (Cambria
Co.), 814
Summer Hill
(Columbia Co.),
717
Sunbury, 717
Swarthmore, 215
Swissvale, 412
Swoyersville, 717
Tamaqua, 717
Tarentum, 412
Taylor, 717
Trevose, 215
Turtle Creek, 412
Tyrone, 814
Uniontown (Fayette
Co.), 412
Uniontown (Indiana
Co.), 814
Uniontown
(Northumberland
Co.), 717
Unionville (Centre
Co.), 814
Unionville (Chester
Co.), 215

Upper Darby, 215
Villanova, 215
Warren, 814
Washington, 412
Wayne, 215
West Chester, 215
West Hazleton, 717
Westmont, 814
West View, 412
White Hall (Adams
    Co.), 717
Whitehall (Allegheny
    Co.), 412
Whitehall (Mifflin
    Co.), 717
White Hall (Montour
    Co.), 717
White Oak, 717
Wildwood (Allegheny
    Co.), 412
Wildwood (Bradford
    Co.), 717
Wilkes-Barre, 717
Wilkes-Barre,
    Wyoming Valley
    Airport, 717
Wilkinsburg, 412
Williamsport 717
Willow Grove
    (Bedford Co.), 814
Wilow Grove
    (Columbia Co.),
    717
Willow Grove
    (Montgomery Co.),
    215
Wilson, 412
Woodland (Clearfield
    Co.), 814
Woodland (Mifflin
    Co.), 717
Woodlyn, 215
Wrightsville (Warren
    Co.), 814
Wrightsville (York
    Co.), 717
Wyncote, 215
Wyndmoor, 215
Wynnewood, 215
Yeadon, 215
Puerto Rico
All Points, 809

Rhode Island
All Points, 401

South Carolina
All Points, 803
South Dakota
All Points, 605

Tennessee
Alcoa, 615
Athens, 615
Bristol, 615
Brownfield, 901
Chattanooga, 615
Clarksville, 615
Cleveland, 615
Columbia, 615
Cookeville, 615
Covington, 901
Donelson, 615
Dyersburg, 901
Elizabethton, 615
Fayetteville, 615
Franklin, 615
Gallatin, 615
Greeneville, 615

Harriman, 615
Humboldt, 901
Jackson, 901
Johnson City, 615
Kingsport, 615
Knoxville, 615
La Follette, 615
Lawrenceburg, 615
Lebanon, 615
Lenoir City, 615
Lewisburg, 615
Madison, 615
Maryville, 615
Memphis, 901
Midland, 615
Millington, 901
Morristown, 615
Murfreesboro, 615
Nashville, 615
Newport, 615
Oak Ridge, 615
Oakville, 901
Paris, 901
Pulaski, 615
Rockwood, 615
Savannah, 901
Shelbyville, 615
Springfield, 615
Union City, 901
Texas
Abilene, 915
Alamo, 512
Alice, 512
Amarillo, 806
Andrews, 915
Aransas Pass, 512
Arlington, 817
Aten, 915
Austin, 512
Bay City, 409
Baytown, 713
Beaumont, 409
Beeville, 512
Bellevue, 817
Big Spring, 915
Bonham, 214
Borger, 806
Brady, 915
Breckenridge, 817
Brownfield, 806
Brownsville, 512
Brownwood, 915

Bryan, 409
Burkburnett, 817
Cameron, 817
Canyon, 806
Carrizo Springs, 512
Carthage, 215
Childress, 817
Cleburne, 817
Coleman, 915
College Station, 409
Colorado City, 915
Commerce, 214
Corpus Christi, 512
Corsicana, 214
Crystal City, 512
Cuero, 512
Dallas, 214
Del Rio, 512
Denison, 214
Denton, 817
Eagle Pass, 512
Edinburg, 512
Edna, 512
El Paso, 915
Ennis, 214
Falfurrias, 512
Farmers Branch, 214
Fort Stockton, 915
Fort Worth, 817
Freeport, 409
Gainesville, 817
Galveston, 409
Garfield, 512
Georgetown, 512
Gladewater, 214
Gonzales, 512
Graham, 817
Grand Prairie, 214
Greenville, 214
Greggton, 214
Harlingen, 512
Henderson, 214
Hereford, 806
Hillsboro, 817
Hitchcock, 409
Houston, 713
Irving, 214
Jacksonville, 214
Kermit, 915
Kerrville, 512
Kilgore, 214
Killeen, 817

Kingsbury, 512
Lampasas, 512
Lancaster, 214
Laredo, 512
Levelland, 806
Littlefield, 806
Lockhart, 512
Longview, 214
Lubbock, 806
Marlin, 817
Marshall, 214
Mathis, 512
McAllen, 512
McKinney, 214
Mercedes, 512
Mesquite, 214
Mexia, 817
Midland, 915
Mineral Wells, 817
Mission, 512
Monahans, 915
New Braunfels, 512
North Richland Hills, 817
Orange, 409
Palestine, 214
Pampa, 806
Paris, 214
Pasadena, 713
Pecos, 915
Pharr, 512
Plainview, 806
Port Lavaca, 512
Raymondville, 512
Richardson, 214
San Angelo, 915
San Antonio, 512
San Benito, 512
San Marcos, 512
Seguin, 512
Seminole, 915
Sherman, 214
Sinton, 512
Slaton, 806
Snyder, 915
Stamford, 915
Stephenville, 817
Sulphur Springs, 214
Sweetwater, 915
Temple, 817
Terrell, 214
Texarkana, 214

Tyler, 214
Uvalde, 512
Vernon, 817
Victoria, 512
Waco, 817
Waxahachie, 214
Weatherford, 817
Weslaco, 512
White Settlement, 817
Wichita Falls, 817
Yoakum, 512

Utah
All Points, 801

Vermont
All Points, 802
Virginia
Alexandria, 703
Annandale, 703
Arlington, 703
Bedford, 703
Belleview, 703
Blacksburg, 703
Bluefield, 703
Bon Air, 804
Bristol, 703
Buena Vista, 703
Charlottesville, 804
Chesapeake, 804
Chester, 804
Christianburg, 703
Clifton Forge, 703

Collinsville, 703
Colonial Heights, 804
Covington, 703
Culpepper, 703
Dale, 703
Danville, 804
Emporia, 804
Fairfax, 703
Falls Church, 703
Fort Belvoir, 703
Fort Lee, 804
Franklin, 804
Fredericksburg, 703
Front Royal, 703
Galax, 703
Hampton, 804
Harrisonburg, 703
Highland Springs, 804
Hopewell, 804
Jefferson, 804
Lexington, 703
Lynchburg, 804
Manassas, 703
Marion, 703
Martinsville, 703
McLean, 703
Mechanicsville, 804
Newport News, 804
Norfolk, 804
Petersburg, 804
Poquoson, 804
Portsmouth, 804
Pulaski, 703
Quantico Station, 703
Radford, 703
Reston, 703
Richmond, 804
Roanoke, 703
Rose Hill, 703
Salem, 703
South Boston, 804
Springfield, 703
Staunton, 703
Sterling Park, 703
Suffolk, 804
Vienna, 703
Vinton, 703
Virginia Beach, 804
Waynesboro, 703
Williamsburg, 804
Winchester, 703
Wytheville, 703

Washington
Aberdeen, 206
Alderwood Manor, 206
Anacortes, 206
Arlington, 206
Auburn, 206
Bellevue, 206
Bellingham, 206
Benton City, 509
Black Diamond, 206
Blaine, 206
Bothell, 206
Bremerton, 206
Bryn Mawr, 206
Buckley, 206
Burlington, 206
Camas, 206
Cashmere, 509
Castle Rock, 206
Centralia, 206
Chehalis, 206
Cheney, 509
Chewelah, 509
Clarkston, 509
Cle Elum, 509
Colfax, 509
College Place, 509
Colville, 509
Cosmopolis, 206
Coulee Dam, 509
Darrington, 206
Davenport, 509
Dayton, 509
Deer Park, 509
Des Moines, 206
Dishman, 509
Edmonds, 206
Ellensburg, 509
Elma, 206
Enumclaw, 206
Ephrata, 509
Everett, 206
Ferndale, 206
Gig Harbor, 206

Goldendale, 509
Grand Coulee, 509
Grandview, 509
Granger, 509
Hoquiam, 206
Houghton, 206
Issaquah, 206
Kalama, 206
Kelso, 206
Kenmore, 206
Kennewick, 509
Kennydale, 206
Kent, 206
Kirkland, 206
Lacey, 206
Lake Stevens, 206
Lakewood, 206
Leavenworth, 509
Longview, 206
Lowell, 206
Marysville, 206
Medical Lake, 509
Mercer Island, 206
Midway, 206
Millwood, 509
Monroe, 206
Montesano, 206
Morton, 206
Moses Lake, 509
Mountlake Terrace,
    206
Mount Vernon, 206
Mukilteo, 206
Newport, 509
Oak Harbor, 206
Odessa, 509
Okanogan, 509
Olympia, 206
Omak, 509
Opportunity, 509
Oroville, 509
Orting, 206
Othello, 509
Parkland, 206

Pasco, 509
Pinehurst, 206
Pomeroy, 509
Port Angeles, 206
Port Orchard, 206
Poulsbo, 206
Prosser, 509
Pullman, 509
Puyallup, 206
Quincy, 509
Raymond, 206
Redmond, 206
Renton, 206
Republic, 509
Richland, 509
Richmond Beach, 206
Ritzville, 509
Roslyn, 509
Seattle, 206
Sedro Woolley, 206
Selah, 509
Sequim, 206
Shelton, 206
Silverdale, 206
Snohomish, 206
Snoqualmie, 206
Soap Lake, 509
South Bend, 206
Spanaway, 206
Spokane, 509
Stanwood, 206
Steilacoom, 206
Sumner, 206
Sunnyside, 509
Tacoma, 206
Tillicum, 206
Toppenish, 509
Trentwood, 509
Tulalip, 206
Tumwater, 206
Union Gap, 509
Vancouver, 206
Waitsburg, 509
Walla Walla, 509

Wapato, 509
Washougal, 206
Wenatchee, 509
West Richland, 509
White Salmon, 509
Wilbur, 509
Woodland, 206
Yakima, 509
Zillah, 509
West Virginia
All Points, 304
Wisconsin
Antigo, 715
Appleton, 414
Baraboo, 608
Beaver Dam, 414
Beloit, 608
Brookfield, 414
Brown Deer, 414
Burlington, 414
Cedarburg, 414
Chippewa Falls, 715
Cudahy, 414
De Pere, 414
Eau Claire, 715
Fond Du Lac, 414
Fort Atkinson, 414
Fox Point, 414
Franklin, 414
Green Bay, 414
Greendale, 414
Greenfield, 414
Hales Corners, 414
Hartford, 414
Janesville, 608
Kaukauna, 414
Kenosha, 414
La Crosse, 608
Little Chute, 414
Madison, 608
Manitowoc, 414
Menasha, 414
Menomonee Falls,
    414

Menomonie, 715
Mequon, 414
Merrill, 715
Milwaukee, 414
Mondovi, 715
Monroe, 608
Muskego, 414
New Lisbon, 608
Oak Creek, 414
Oconomowoc, 414
Oshkosh, 414
Platteville, 608
Plymouth, 414
Port Washington, 414
Racine, 414
Rhinelander, 715
Rice Lake, 715
Ripon, 414
St. Francis, 414
Shorewood, 414
South Milwaukee, 414
Sparta, 608
Stevens Point, 715
Stoughton, 608
Sturgeon Bay, 414
Superior, 715
Tomah, 608
Two Rivers, 414
Watertown, 414
Waucousta, 414
Waupaca, 715
Wausau, 715
Wauwatosa, 414
West Allis, 414
West Bend, 414
West Milwaukee, 414
Whitefish Bay, 414
Whitewater, 414
Wisconsin Rapids,
    715
Wyoming
All Points, 307

TELEPHONE CODE DIRECTORY: INTERNATIONAL

(Calling information: 1-800-874-4000)

Dial 011 + Country Code + City Code + Local Number (for direct dialing)

For example, to make a call to London, you would dial:

Dial 01 + Country Code + City Code + Local Number (for operator-assisted calls)

*City Codes (an asterisk means city codes are not required)

Algeria, 213*
American Samoa, 684*
Andorra, 33
  All Points 628
Argentina, 54
  Buenos Aires, 1
  Cordoba, 51
  La Plata, 21
  Rosario, 41
Aruba, 297
  All Points, 8
Ascension Island, 247*
Australia, 61
  Adelaide, 8
  Brisbane, 7
  Melbourne, 3

Sydney, 2
Austria, 43
  Graz, 316
  Linz Donau, 732
  Vienna 1 or 222

B

Bahrain, 973*
Bangladesh, 880
  Barisal, 431
  Chittagong, 31
  Dhaka, 2
  Khulna, 41
Belgium, 32
  Antwerp, 3
  Brussels, 2

Ghent, 91
  Liege, 41
Belize, 501
  Belize City, 2
  Corozal Town, 4
  Punta Gorda, 7
Benin, 229*
Bolivia, 591
  Cochabamba, 42
  La Paz, 2
  Santa Cruz, 33
Botswana, 267
  Francistown, 21
  Gaborone, 31
  Jwaneng, 33
  Kanye, 34
  Lobatse, 33
Brazil, 55
  Belo Horizonte, 31
  Rio de Janeiro, 21
  Sao Paulo, 11
Brunei, 673
  Bandar Seri Begawan, 2

Kuala Belait, 3
  Tutong, 4
Bulgaria, 359
  Plovdiv, 32
  Rousse (Ruse), 82
  Sofia, 2
  Varna, 52

Cameroon, 237*
Canada
  See end of list
Cape Verde Islands, 238*
Caribbean/Atlantic
  See end of list
Chile, 56

Japan, 81
  Kyoto, 75
  Osaka, 6
  Sapporo, 11
  Tokyo, 3
  Yokohama, 45
Jordan, 962
  Amman, 6
  Irbid, 2
  Jerash, 4
  Karak, 3
  Ma'an, 3

Kenya, Rep. of, 254
  Kisumu, 35
  Mombasa, 11
  Nairobi, 2
  Nakuru, 37
Korea, Rep. of, 82
  Inchon, 32
  Pusan, 51
  Seoul, 2
  Taegu, 53
Kuwait, 965*

Lesotho, 266*
Liberia, 231*
Libya, 218
  Benghazi, 61
  Misuratha, 51
  Tripoli, 21

Zawai, 23
Liechtenstein, 41
  All Points, 75
Luxembourg, 352*

Macao, 853*
Malawi, 265
  Domasi, 531
  Makwasa, 474
  Zomba, 50
Malaysia, 60
  Ipoh, 5
  Johor Bahru, 7
  Kajang, 3
  Kuala Lumpur, 3
Malta, 356*
Marshall Islands, 692
  Ebeye, 871
  Majuro, 9
Mexico
  See end of list
Micronesia, Fed. States
  of, 691
  Kosrae, 370
  Ponape, 320
  Truk, 330
  Yap, 350
Monaco, 33
  All Points, 93
Morocco, 212
  Agadir, 8
  Beni-Mellal, 48
  Casablanca*
  El Jadida, 34

Namibia, 264
  Grootfontein, 673

Keetmanshoop, 631
  Mariental, 661
Nepal, 977*
Netherlands, 31
  Amsterdam, 20
  Rotterdam, 10
  The Hague, 70
Netherlands Antilles, 599
  Bonaire, 7
  Curacao, 9
  St. Eustatius, 3
  St. Maarten, 5
New Caledonia, 687*
New Zealand, 64
  Auckland, 9
  Christchurch, 3
  Dunedin, 24
  Hamilton, 71
Nicaragua, 505
  Chinandega, 341
  Diriamba, 42
  Leon, 311
  Managua, 2
Niger Republic, 227*
Nigeria, 234
  Lagos, 1
Norway, 47
  Bergen, 5
  Oslo, 2
  Stavanger, 4
  Trondheim, 7

Oman, 968*

Pakistan, 92
  Islamabad, 51

Karachi, 21
Lahore, 42
Panama, 507*
Papua New Guinea, 675*
Paraguay, 595
  Asuncion, 21
  Concepcion, 31
Peru, 51
  Arequipa, 54
  Callao, 14
  Lima, 14
  Trujillo, 44
Philippines, 63
  Cebu, 32
  Davao, 82
  Iloilo City, 33
  Manila, 2
Poland, 48
  Crakow, 12
  Gdansk, 58
  Warsaw, 22
Portugal, 351
  Coimbra, 39
  Lisbon, 1
  Porto, 2
  Setubal, 65

Qatar, 974*
Romania, 40
  Bucharest, 0
  Cluj-Napoca, 51
  Constanta, 16

Saipan, 670
  Rota Island, 532
  Susupe City, 234

Tinian Island, 433
San Marino, 39
  All Points, 549
Saudi Arabia, 966
  Hofuf, 3
  Jeddah, 2
  Makkah (Mecca), 2
  Riyadh, 1
Senegal Rep., 221*
Singapore, 65*
South Africa, 27
  Cape Town, 21
  Durban, 31
  Johannesburg, 11
Spain, 34
  Barcelona, 3
  Madrid, 1
  Seville, 54
  Valencia, 6
Sri Lanka, 94
  Colombo Central, 1
  Kandy, 8
  Kotte, 1
St. Pierre and Miquelon, 508*
Suriname, 597*
Swaziland, 268*
Sweden, 46
  Goteborg, 31
  Malmo, 40
  Stockholm, 8
  Vasteras, 21
Switzerland, 41
  Basel, 61
  Berne, 31
  Geneva, 22
  Zurich, 1

Taiwan, Rep. of China, 886
  Kaohsiung, 7
  Tainan, 6
  Taipei, 2

Tanzania, 255
  Dar Es Salaam, 51
  Dodoma, 61
  Mwanza, 68
  Tanga, 53
Thailand, 66
  Bangkok, 2
  Burirum, 44
  Chanthaburi, 39
Togo, Rep. of, 228*
Tunisia, 216
  Bizerte, 2
  Kairouan, 7
  Msel Bourguiba, 2
  Tunis, 1
Turkey, 90
  Adana, 711
  Ankara, 4
  Istanbul, 1
  Izmir, 51

Uganda, 256
  Entebbe, 42
  Jinja, 43
  Kampala, 41
  Kyambogo, 41
United Arab Emirates, 971
  Abu Dhabi, 2
  Ajman, 6
  Al Ain, 3
  Dubai, 4
  Sharjah, 6
United Kingdom, 44
  Belfast, 232
  Birmingham, 21
  Glasgow, 41
  London, 1
Uruguay, 598
  Canelones, 332
  Mercedes, 532
  Montevideo, 2

Vatican City, 39
  All Points, 6
Venezuela, 58
  Barquisimeto, 51
  Caracas, 2
  Maracaibo, 61
  Valencia, 41
Yemen Arab Repubic, 967
  Amran, 2
  Sanaa, 2
  Taiz, 4
  Yarim, 4
  Zabid, 3

Yugoslavia, 38
  Belgrade, 11
  Sarajevo, 71
  Zagreb, 41

Zaire, Rep. of, 243
  Kinshasa, 12
  Lubumbashi, 222
Zambia, 260
  Chingola, 2
  Kitwe, 2
  Luanshya, 2
  Lusaka, 1
  Ndola, 2
Zimbabwe, 263

  Bulawayo, 9
  Harare, 4
  Mutare, 20

Canada
  Dial 1 + Area Code + Local Number

Caribbean/Atlantic
  Dial 1 + 809 + Local Number
  Anguilla, British Virgin Islands, Antigua, Barbados, Dominica, Montserrat, Nevis, St. Kitts, St. Lucia, St. Vincent and the Grenadines (including Bequia, Mustique, Palm Island, Union Island), Trinidad, and Tobago (Dem. Rep. of), Bahamas, Bermuda, Cayman Islands, Dominican Republic, Grenada (including Carriacou), Jamaica, Turks and Caicos Islands

Mexico
  Dial 011 + 52 + City Code + Local Number
  Acapulco, GO, 748
  Cancun, QR, 988
  Celaya, GU, 461
  Cordoba, VE, 271
  Culiacan, SI, 671
  Guadalajara, JA, 36
  Hermosillo, SO, 621
  Jalapa, VE, 281
  Leon, GU, 471
  Mérida, YU, 99
  Mexico City, ME, 5
  Monterrey, NL, 83
  Tampico, TS, 121
  Tijuana, BC, 66
  Toluca, ME, 721
  Torreon, CO, 17
  Veracruz, VE, 29

USEFUL ADDRESSES

(Words in brackets are used to keep groupings of addresses together. They are not part of the proper name of an organization.)

Academy for State & Local Government
444 N. Capitol St., NW, Rm. 349
Wash. D.C. 20001
202-638-1445

Academy of Family Mediators
P.O. Box 10501
Eugene, OR 97440
503-345-1205

AETNA Life & Casualty
151 Farmington Ave.
Hartford, CT 06156
203-273-7694
800-243-0185

AIDS Hotline
800-342-AIDS

[Alabama] Information & Referral (State Government)
205-261-2500

[Alabama] Information Center (Federal Government)
205-322-8591 (Birmingham)
205-438-1421 (Mobile)

[Alabama] Aeronautics, Department of
627 Highway Bldg.
Montgomery, AL 36130
205-242-4480

[Alabama] Aging, Commission on
136 Catoma St.
Montgomery, AL 36130
205-261-5743
800-243-5463

[Alabama] Agricultural Chemistry & Plant Industry Division
P.O. box 3336
Montgomery, AL 36193
205-242-2656

[Alabama] Agriculture & Industries, Department of
1445 Federal Dr.
P.O. Box 3336
Montgomery, AL 36193
205-261-2650

[Alabama] Alcoholic Beverage Control Board
2715 Gunter Park Dr., West
P.O. Box 1151
Montgomery, AL 36109
205-271-3840

[Alabama] Archives & History, Department of
624 Washington Ave.
Montgomery, AL 26130
205-242-4361

Alabama Arts & Humanities, State Council on the
1 Dexter Ave.
Montgomery, AL 36130
205-261-4076

Alabama Association of Legal Assistants
P.O. Box 2069
Montgomery, AL 36197

[Alabama] Attorney General, Office of
11 S. Union St.
Montgomery, AL 36130
205-261-7305

[Alabama] Auditor, Office of the
11 Union St.
Montgomery, AL 36130
105-261-7010

[Alabama] Banks, Superintendent of
166 Commerce St., 3rd Fl.
Montgomery, AL 36130
205-261-3452

Alabama Bar Association
P.O. Box 671
Montgomery AL 36101
205-269-1515

[Alabama] Bar Examiners, Board of
P.O. Box 671
Montgomery, AL 36101
205-269-1515

[Alabama] Bar Institute for Continuing Legal Education
P.O. Box 870384
Tuscaloosa, AL 35487
205-348-6230

[Alabama] Better Business Bureau
1214 S. 20th St.
Birmingham, AL 35205
205-558-2222
205-533-1640 (Huntsville)
205-433-5494 (Mobile)
205-262-5606 (Montgomery)

[Alabama] Birmingham Bar Association
109 N. 20th St., 2nd Fl.
Birmingham, AL 35203
205-251-8006

[Alabama] Budget Office, State
237 State House
Montgomery, AL 36130
295-242-3117

[Alabama] Building Commission
800 S. McDonald St.
Montgomery, AL 36104
205-242-4082

[Alabama] Child Support Enforcement Division
64 N. Union St.
Montgomery, AL 36130
205-261-2734

[Alabama] Conservation & Natural Resources, Department of
64 N. Union St., Rm. 702
Montgomery, AL 36130
205-261-3486

[Alabama] Consumer Protection Division
Office of Attorney General

11 S. Union St.
Montgomery, AL 36130
205-261-7334
800-392-5658

[Alabama] Corporations Division
501 Dexter Ave., Rm. 524
Montgomery, AL 36130
205-261-5324

[Alabama] Corrections, Department of
101 S. Union St.
Montgomery, AL 36130
205-834-1227

[Alabama] Court Administration, State
817 S. Court St.
Montgomery, AL 36130
205-834-7990

[Alabama] Criminal Justice Information Center
858 S. Court St.
Montgomery, AL 36130
205-832-4930

[Alabama] Cumberland School of Law
Cordell Hull Law Library
800 Lakeshore Dr.
Birmingham, AL 35229
205-870-2714

[Alabama] Dallas County
P.O. Box 997
Selma, AL 36702
205-875-4401

[Alabama] Data System Management
64 N. Union St., Suite 250
Montgomery, AL 36130
205-242-3100

Alabama Development Office
135 S. Union St.
Montgomery, AL 36130
205-263-0048

[Alabama] Education, Department of
501 Dexter Ave.
Montgomery, AL 36130
205-261-5156

[Alabama] Elections Division
11 S. Union St.
Montgomery, AL 36130
205-261-7210

[Alabama] Emergency Management, Department of
520 S. Court St.
Montgomery, AL 36130
205-834-1375

[Alabama] Energy Division
3465 Norman Bridge Rd.
Montgomery, AL 36105
205-284-8952

[Alabama] Environmental Management, Department of
1751 Congressman Dickinson Dr.
Montgomery, AL 36130
205-271-7861

[Alabama] Equal Opportunity Employment Office
649 Monroe St.
Montgomery, AL 36130
205-242-5393

[Alabama] Ethics Commission
817 S. Court St., Suite 2B
Montgomery, AL 36104
205-261-2997

[Alabama] Family & Children's Services, Division of
64 N. Union St., Rm. 503
Montgomery, AL 36130
205-261-3409

[Alabama] Finance, Department of
Alabama State House Bldg., Rm. 207
Montgomery, AL 36130
205-261-7160

[Alabama] Fire Marshall
135 S. Union St., Suite 140
Montgomery, AL 36130
205-269-3575

[Alabama] Forestry Commission
513 Madison Ave.
Montgomery, AL 36130
205-240-9304

[Alabama] Game & Fish, Division of
64 N. Union St.
Montgomery, AL 36130
205-261-3465

[Alabama] Geological Survey
P.O. Drawer O
University, AL 35846
205-349-2852

[Alabama] Governor, Office of
11 S. Union St.
Montgomery, AL 36130
205-261-7100

[Alabama] Higher Education,
Commission on
1 Court Sq., Suite 221
Montgomery, AL 36197
205-269-2700

[Alabama] Highway Department
1409 Coliseum Blvd
Montgomery, AL 36130
205-261-6311

Alabama Historical Commission
725 Monroe St.
Montgomery, AL 36130
205-261-3184

[Alabama] House of
Representatives
State Capitol
Montgomery, AL 36130
205-261-7600
205-261-7667 (Judiciary)

[Alabama] Human Resources,
Department of
64 N. Union St.
Montgomery, AL 36130
205-261-3190

[Alabama] Industrial Relations,
Department of
649 Monroe St.
Montgomery, AL 36130
205-261-5386

[Alabama] Insurance
Commissioner
135 S. Union St., #181
Montgomery, AL 36130
205-269-3550

[Alabama] Jefferson County
716 N. 21st St.
Birmingham, AL 35263
205-325-5300

[Alabama] Jefferson County Law
Library
900 Jefferson County Courthouse

Birmingham, AL 35263
205-325-5628

[Alabama] Labor, Department of
64 N. Union St., Rm. 651
Montgomery, AL 36130
205-261-3460

[Alabama] Law Enforcement
Planning Agency
3465 Norman Bridge Rd.
Montgomery, AL 36105
205-261-3891

[Alabama] Law
Enforcement–Traffic Safety
P.O. Box 2939
Montgomery, AL 36105
205-261-3897

Alabama Law Institute
P.O. Box 1425
University, AL 35486
205-348-7411

[Alabama] Law Library, State
445 Dexter Ave., Judicial Bldg.
Montgomery, Al 36130
205-261-4347

Alabama, Legal Service
Corporation of
207 Montgomery St., 900 Bell Bldg.
Montgomery, AL 36104
205-832-4570

[Alabama] Legislative Reference
Service
11 S. Union St., Rm. 613
Montgomery AL 36130
205-261-7560
205-261-7560 (Code Revision)

[Alabama] Lieutenant Governor,
Office of
11 S. Union St.
Montgomery, AL 36130
205-261-7900

[Alabama] Macon County
101 E. Northside St.
Tuskegee, AL 36083
205-727-5120

[Alabama] Marine Police
Division
64 N. Union St.
Montgomery, AL 36130
205-242-3673

[Alabama] Mental Health &
Mental Retardation,
Department of
Bureau of Mental Illness &
Substance Abuse
P.O. Box 3710
Montgomery, AL 36193
205-271-9253

[Alabama] Mobile Association of
Legal Assistants
P.O. Box 81382
Mobile, AL 36689

[Alabama] Mobile County
101 Government St.
Mobile, AL 36602
205-690-8615

[Alabama} Mobile County Public
Law Library
Mobile County Court House
Mobile, AL 366602
205-690-8436

{Alabama] Motor Vehicle
Division
Department of Revenue
2721 Gunter Park Dr. W
Montgomery, AL 36109
205-244-6700

[Alabama] Pardons & Paroles,
Board of
750 Washington Ave., Suite 312
Montgomery, AL 36130
205-261-5533

[Alabama] Personnel
Department, State
64 N. Union St., Rm. 402
Montgomery, AL 36130
205-261-3389

[Alabama] Planning & Federal
Programs Office
3465 Norman Bridge Rd.
Montgomery, AL 36105
205-284-8707

[Alabama] Public Health,
Department of
434 Monroe St.
Montgomery, AL 36130
205-261-5052

[Alabama] Public Safety,
Department of
500 Dexter Ave.

Montgomery, AL 36130
205-261-4393

**[Alabama] Public Service
Commission**
P.O. Box 991
Montgomery, AL 36101
205-261-5207
800-392-8050

**[Alabama] Purchases & Stores,
Division of**
11 S. Union St., Rm. 200
Montgomery, AL 36130
205-261-7250

**[Alabama] Real Estate
Commission**
750 Washington Ave.
Montgomery, AL 36130
205-261-5544

**[Alabama] Rehabilitation &
Crippled Children Service**
P.O. Box 11586
Montgomery, AL 36111
205-281-8780

[Alabama] Retirement Systems
135 S. Union St.
Montgomery, AL 36130
205-832-4140

**[Alabama] Revenue,
Department of**
64 N. Union St.
Montgomery, AL 36130
205-261-3362

**[Alabama] Safety & Inspection,
Division of**
P.O. Box 10444
Birmingham, AL 35202
205-251-1181

[Alabama] Secretary of State
11 S. Union St., Rm. 208
Montgomery, AL 36130
205-261-7200

Alabama Securities Commission
166 Commerce St., 2d Fl.
Montgomery, AL 36130
205-261-2984

[Alabama] Senate
State Capitol
Montgomery, AL 36130

205-261-7800
205-261-7871 (Judiciary)

[Alabama] Supreme Court
445 Dexter Ave.
Montgomery, AL 36104
205-261-4609
205-834-7990 (Clerk)
205-261-4347 (Law Library)

[Alabama] Treasury Department
11 S. Union St., Rm. 204
Montgomery, AL 36130
205-261-7500

**[Alabama] Unemployment
Compensation Division**
649 Monroe St.
Montgomery, AL 36130
205-261-5467

**[Alabama] United States
Bankruptcy Court**
Northern Alabama
500 S. 22nd St.
Birmingham, AL 35233
205-731-1615

**[Alabama] United States
Bankruptcy Court**
Middle Alabama
P.O. Box 1248
Montgomery, AL 36192
205-832-7250

**[Alabama] United States
Bankruptcy Court**
Southern Alabama
P.O. Box 2865
Mobile, AL 36652
205-690-2391

**[Alabama] United States Courts
Library**
113 St. Joseph St.
Mobile, AL 36602
205-694-4297

**[Alabama] United States District
Court**
Southern District
P.O. Box 2625
Mobile, AL 36652
205-690-2371

**[Alabama] United States District
Court**
Northern District

104 Federal Courthouse
1729 5th Ave. North
Birmingham, AL 35203
205-731-1025

**[Alabama] United States District
Court**
Middle District
P.O. Box 711
Montgomery, AL 36101
205-832-7308

**[Alabama] United States
Government Bookstore**
2021 3rd Ave., N.
Birmingham, AL 35203
205-731-1056

Alabama, University of
School of Law
Law Library
Tuscaloosa, AL 35487
205-348-1113

**[Alabama] Veterans Affairs,
Department of**
P.O. Box 1509
Montgomery, AL 36192
205-261-5077

**[Alabama] Victims of Crime
Compensation**
P.O. Box 1548
Montgomery, AL 36102
205-242-4007

[Alabama] Vital Statistics
434 Monroe St., Rm. 215
Montgomery, AL 36130
205-261-5033

Alabama Washington Office
444 N. Capitol St., Suite 343
Wash. D.C. 20001
202-624-5820

**[Alabama] Weights & Measures
Division**
P.O. Box 3336
Montgomery, AL 36193
205-261-2613

Alabama Women's Commission
Box 204, Route 2
Troy, AL 36081

**[Alabama] Workmen's
Compensation Division**

649 Monroe St.
Montgomery, AL 36130
205-261-2868

**[Alabama] Youth Services,
Department of**
P.O. Box 66, AL 36057
205-272-9100

**[Alaska] Information & Referral
(State Government)**
907-465-2111

**[Alaska] Information Center
(Federal Government)**
Anchorage 907-271-2898

**[Alaska] Administration,
Department of**
P.O. Box C
Juneau, AK 99811
907-465-2200

[Alaska] Agriculture, Division of
P.O. Box 949
Palmer, AK 99645
907-745-7200

**[Alaska] Air Quality
Management Section**
P.O. Box O
Juneau, AK 99811
907-465-2666
907-465-2653 (Water Quality)

**[Alaska] Alcoholic Beverage
Control Board**
550 W. 7th, Suite 350
Anchorage, AK 99501
907-277-8638

**[Alaska] Alcoholism & Drug
Abuse, Office of**
P.O. Box H-OSF
Juneau, AK 99811
907-586-6201

[Alaska] Anchorage Law Library
303 K. St.
Anchorage, AK 99501
907-265-0580

**[Alaska] Anchorage,
Municipality of**
P.O. Box 196650
Anchorage, AK 99519
907-343-4311

**[Alaska] Archives & Records
Management**
P.O. Box C-0207
Juneau, AK 99801
907-465-2275

**[Alaska] Association of Legal
Assistants**
P.O. Box 101956
Anchorage, AK 99510

**[Alaska] Attorney General,
Office of**
P.O. Box K
Juneau, AK 99811
907-465-3600

**[Alaska] Audit & Management
Division**
P.O. Box AM
Juneau, AK 99811
907-465-3568

**[Alaska] Banking, Corporations
& Securities, Division of**
P.O. Box D
Juneau, AK 99811
907-465-2521

[Alaska] Bar Association
P.O. Box 100279
Anchorage, AK 99510
907-272-7469

[Alaska] Better Business Bureau
3380 C. St., Suite 100
Anchorage, AK 99503
907-562-0704

[Alaska] Business Development
P.O. Box D
Juneau, AK 99811
907-465-2017

**[Alaska] Child Support
Enforcement Division**
550 W. 7th, 4th Fl.
Anchorage, AK 99501
907-276-3441

**[Alaska] Code Revision
Commission**
P.O. Box Y
Juneau, AK 99811
907-465-2450

**[Alaska] Commerce & Economic
Development, Department of**
P.O. Box D

Juneau, AK 99811
907-465-2500

**[Alaska] Community & Regional
Affairs, Department of**
P.O. Box B
Juneau, AK 99811
907-465-4700

**[Alaska] Consumer Protection
Section**
Attorney General
1031 W. 4th Ave., Suite 110
Juneau, AK 99501
907-276-3550
907-279-0428 (Anchorage)
907-456-8588 (Fairbanks)

[Alaska] Corporation Section
Commerce & Economic
Development
P.O. Box D
Juneau, AK 99811
907-465-2530

**[Alaska] Corrections,
Department of**
P.O. Box T
Juneau, AK 99811
907-465-3376
907-561-4426 (Anchorage)

Alaska Council on the Arts
619 Warehouse, #220
Anchorage, AK 99501
907-279-1588

Alaska Court Libraries
303 K. St.
Anchorage, AK 99507
907-264-0585

[Alaska] Court of Appeals
303 K. St.
Anchorage, AK 99501
907-264-0751

**[Alaska] Data Network Services,
Division of**
P.O. Box C, MS 0206
Juneau, AK 98811
907-465-2220

**[Alaska] Education,
Department of**
P.O. Box F
Juneau, AK 99811
907-465-2800

[Alaska] Elections, Division of
P.O. Box AF
Juneau, AK 99811
907-465-4611

[Alaska] Emergency Services,
Division of
3501 E. Bogard Rd.
Wasilla, AK 99687
907-376-3061

[Alaska] Employment Security,
Division of
P.O. Box 2-7000
Juneau, AK 99802
907-465-2712

[Alaska] Environmental
Conservation, Department of
P.O. Box O
Juneau, AK 99811
907-465-2600

[Alaska] Equal Employment
Division
P.O. Box AE
Juneau, AK 99811
907-465-3570

[Alaska] Fairbanks Association
of Legal Assistants
P.O. Box 73503
Fairbanks, AK 99707

[Alaska] Family & Youth
Services, Division of
P.O. Box H-05
Juneau, AK 99811
907-465-3170

[Alaska] Finance, Division of
P.O. Box H-02
Juneau, AK 99811
907-465-3082

[Alaska] Fire Prevention,
Division of
P.O. Box 6313
Anchorage, AK 99502
907-269-5604

[Alaska] Fish & Game,
Department of
P.O. Box 3-2000
Juneau, AK 99802
907-465-4100

[Alaska] Forestry, Division of
P.O. Box 107005

Anchorage, AK 99510
907-762-2501

[Alaska] Geological &
Geophysical Surveys,
Division of
3700 Airport Way
Fairbanks, AK 99709
907-451-2760

[Alaska] Governor, Office of
P.O. Box A
Juneau, AK 99811
907-465-3500

[Alaska] Health & Social
Services, Department of
P.O. Box H-06
Juneau, AK 99811
907-465-3030

[Alaska] House of
Representatives
P.O. Box V
Juneau, AK 99811
907-465-4648
907-465-3755

Alaska Housing Market Council
P.O. Box 240048
Anchorage, AK 99524
907-563-3325

[Alaska] Human Rights
Commission
800 A. St., Suite 202
Anchorage, AK 99501
907-276-7474

[Alaska] Industrial Development
& Export Authority
1577 C. St., Suite 304
Anchorage, AK 99501
907-274-1651

[Alaska] Insurance, Division of
P.O. Box D
Juneau, AK 99811
907-465-2515

[Alaska] International Trade,
Office of
3601 C. St., Suite 798
Anchorage, AK 99503
907-561-5585

[Alaska] Investments,
Division of
P.O. Box DI

Juneau, AK 99811
907-465-2510

[Alaska] Judicial Conduct,
Commission on
303 K. St., Rm. 241
Anchorage, AK 99501
907-264-0528

Alaska Judicial Council
303 K. St.
Anchorage, AK 99501
907-264-0618

[Alaska] Juneau Borough
155 S. Seward St.
Juneau, AK 99801
907-586-3300

[Alaska] Juneau Legal Assistants
Association
P.O. Box 22336
Juneau, AK 99802

[Alaska] Labor, Department of
P.O. Box 21149
Juneau, AK 99802
907-465-2700

[Alaska] Labor Relations,
Division of
P.O. Box C
Juneau, AK 99811
907-465-4044

[Alaska] Labor Standards &
Safety, Division of
P.O. Box 20630
Juneau, AK 99811
901-465-4870

[Alaska] Land & Water
Management, Division of
P.O. Box 107005
Anchorage, AK 99510
907-762-2692

[Alaska] Land Recorder's Office
3601 C. St., Suite 1134
Anchorage, AK 99503
907-762-2438

[Alaska] Law, Department of
P.O. Box K
Juneau, AK 99811
907-465-3600

[Alaska] Legislative Affairs
Agency
P.O. Box Y

Juneau, AK 99811
907-465-3867

**[Alaska] Legislative Audit,
Division of**
P.O. Box W
Juneau, AK 99811
907-465-3830

**[Alaska] Libraries & Museums,
Division of**
P.O. Box G
Juneau, AK 99811
907-465-2910

**[Alaska] Lieutenant Governor,
Office of**
P.O. Box AA
Juneau, AK 99811
907-465-3520

**[Alaska] Management & Budget,
Office of**
P.O. Box AM
Juneau, AK 99811
907-465-3586

**[Alaska] Marine Highway
System**
P.O. Box R
Juneau, AK 99811
907-465-3950

**[Alaska] Measurement
Standards, Division of**
P.O. Box 111686
Anchorage, AK 99511
907-345-7750

**[Alaska] Mental Health &
Developmental Disabilities,
Division of**
P.O. Box H–04
Juneau, AK 99811
907-465-3370

[Alaska] Mental Health Board
416 6th St., Rm. 124
Juneau, AK 99811
907-465-3071

**[Alaska] Military & Veterans
Affairs, Department of**
3601 C. St., Suite 620
Anchorage, AK 99503
907-249-1253

[Alaska] Mining, Division of
P.O. Box 107016

Anchorage, AK 99510
907-762-2165

**[Alaska] Motor Vehicles,
Division of**
5700 E. Tudor Rd.
Anchorage, AK 99507
907-269-5551

**[Alaska] Municipal & Regional
Assistance, Division of**
949 E. 36th, Rm. 400
Anchorage, AK 99508
907-561-8586

**[Alaska] Natural Resources,
Department of**
400 Willoughby Ave.
Juneau, AK 99801
907-465-2400

[Alaska] North Star Borough
P.O. Box 1267
Fairbanks, AK 99707
907-452-4761

**[Alaska] Occupational Licensing,
Division of**
P.O. Box D
Juneau, AK 99811
907-465-2534

**[Alaska] Occupational Safety &
Health Division**
P.O. Box 1149
Juneau, AK 99802
907-465-4855

**[Alaska] Oil & Gas Conservation
Commission**
3001 Porcupine Dr.
Anchorage, AK 99501
907-279-1433

[Alaska] Oil & Gas, Division of
P.O. Box 10734
Anchorage, AK 99510
907-762-2547

**[Alaska] Older Alaskans
Commission**
P.O. Box C
Juneau, AK 99811
907-465-3250

**[Alaska] Ombudsman, Office of
the**
P.O. Box WO, MS 3000
Juneau, AK 99811

907-465-4970
907-277-8848 (Anchorage)

**[Alaska] Parks & Outdoor
Recreation, Division of**
P.O. Box 107001
Anchorage, AK 99510
907-762-2600

[Alaska] Parole, Board of
P.O Box T
Juneau, AK 99811
907-465-3384

**[Alaska] Personnel & Payroll,
Office of**
P.O. Box H
Juneau, AK 99811
907-465-3024

[Alaska] Personnel, Division of
P.O. Box C
Juneau, AK 99811
907-465-4430

[Alaska] Policy, Division of
P.O. Box AB
Juneau, AK 99811
907-465-3573

**[Alaska] Postsecondary
Education Commission**
P.O. Box FP
Juneau, AK 99811
907-465-2854

[Alaska] Power Authority
P.O. Box AM
Juneau, AK 99811
907-465-3575

**[Alaska] Professional Teaching
Practices Commission**
4100 Spenard Rd.
Anchorage, AK 99503
907-243-4344

**[Alaska] Public Advocacy, Office
of**
900 W. 5th, Suite 525
Anchorage, AK 99501
907-274-1684

**[Alaska] Public Assistance,
Division of**
P.O. Box H-07
Juneau, AK 99811
907-465-3347

[Alaska] Public Defender, Office of the State
900 W. 5th, Suite 200
Anchorage, AK 99501
907-279-7541

[Alaska] Public Health, Division of
350 Main St.
Juneau, AK 99811
907-465-3030

Alaska Public Offices Commission
2221 E. Northen Lights, Rm.. 128
Anchorage, AK 99508
907-276-4176

[Alaska] Public Safety, Department of
P.O. Box N
Juneau, AK 99811
907-465-4322

[Alaska] Public Utilities Commission
420 L. St., Suite 100
Anchorage, AK 99501
907-276-6222

Alaska Railroad Corporation
P.O. Box 107500
Anchorage, AK 99510
907-265-2403

[Alaska] Real Estate Commission
3601 C. St.
Anchorage, AK 99503
907-563-2169

[Alaska] Retirement & Benefits, Division of
P.O. Box CR
Juneau, AK 99811
907-465-4460

[Alaska] Revenue, Department of
P.O. Box S
Juneau, AK 99811
907-465-2300

[Alaska] Rural Development Division
949 E. 36th, Rm. 403
Anchorage, AK 99508
907-561-0900

Alaska Seafood Marketing Institute
111 W. 8th St.
Juneau, AK 99801
907-586-2902

[Alaska] Senate
P.O. Box V
Juneau, AK 99811
907-465-4648
907-465-3755 (Judiciary)

[Alaska] Service & Supply, Division of
P.O. Box C
Juneau, AK 99811
907-465-2250

Alaska State Building Authority
P.O. Box 100080
Anchorage, AK 99510
907-562-2813

[Alaska] State/Federal Relations
444 N. Capitol St., NW, Suite 305
Wash. D.C. 20001
202-624-5858

Alaska State Troopers
5700 E. Tudor Rd.
Anchorage, AK 99507
907-269-5641

[Alaska] Superior Court
First District
415 Main St.
Ketchikan, AK 99901
907-225-3141

[Alaska] Superior Court
Second District
P.O. Box 100
Nome, AK 99762
907-443-5216

[Alaska] Superior Court
Third District
303 K. St.
Anchorage, AK 99501
907-264-0430

[Alaska] Superior Court
Fourth District
604 Narnette, Rm. 430
Fairbanks, AK 99701
907-456-9319

[Alaska] Supreme Court
303 K. St.
Anchorage, AK 99501
907-264-0618
907-264-0607 (Clerk)

[Alaska] Tourism, Division of
P.O. Box E
Juneau, AK 99811
907-465-2010

[Alaska] Transportation & Public Facilities, Department of
P.O. Box Z
Juneau, AK 99811
907-465-3900

[Alaska] United States Bankruptcy Court
605 W. 4th Ave., Suite 138
Anchorage, AK 99501
907-271-2655

[Alaska] United States District Court
Box 4, 701 C. St.
Anchorage, AK 99513
907-271-5568

[Alaska] United States District Court Library
222 W. 7th Ave.
Anchorage, AK 99513
907-271-5564

[Alaska] Vital Records, Bureau of
P.O. Box H
Juneau, AK 99811
907-465-3391

[Alaska] Vocational Rehabilitation, Division of
Box F, M.S. 0581
Juneau, AK 99811
907-465-2814

[Alaska] Weights & Measures, Office of
P.O. Box 111686
Anchorage, AK 99511
907-345-7750

Alaska Women's Commission
3601 C. St., Suite 742
Anchorage, AK 99503
907-561-4227

[Alaska] Workers' Compensation, Division of
P.O. Box 1149
Juneau, AK 99802
907-465-2790

Alcoholic Beverage Legislative Council
5101 River Rd., Suite 108
Bethesda, MD 20816
301-656-1494

ALI–ABA Committee on Continuing Professional Education
4025 Chestnut St.
Philadelphia, PA 19104
215-243-1650

Alliance for American Insurers
1501 Woodfield Rd., Suite 400 West
Schaumburg, IL 60173
312-330-8500

Alliance for Justice
600 New Jersey Ave, NW
Wash. D.C. 20001
202-662-9548

Allied Van Lines
P.O. Box 4403
Chicago, IL 60680
312-717-3000

Allstate Insurance Co.
Allstate Plaza – F3
Northbrook, IL 60062
312-281-6718

Altman & Weil Inc.
P.O. Box 472
Ardmore, PA 19003
215-649-4646

American Academy of Forensic Psychology
100 Church Lane, Suite 2B
Baltimore, MD 21208
301-486-6963

American Academy of Forensic Sciences
218 E. Cache La Poudre
Colorado Springs, CO 80903
719-636-1100

American Academy of Hospital Attorneys
American Hospital Association

840 N. Lake Shore Dr.
Chicago, IL 60611
312-280-6600

American Academy of Matrimonial Lawyers
20 N. Michigan Ave., Suite 540
Chicago. IL 60602
312-263-6477

American Academy of Medical–Legal Analysis
522 Rossmore Dr.
Las Vegas, NV 89110
702-385-6886

American Academy of Psychiatry & the Law
1211 Cathedral St.
Baltimore, MD 21201
301-539-0379

American Agricultural Law Association
University of Arkansas
Waterman Hall
Fayetteville, AR 72701
501-575-3706

American Apparel Manufacturers Association
2500 Wilson Blvd., Suite 301
Arlington, VA 22201
703-524-1864

American Arbitration Association
140 W. 51st St.
New York, NY 10020
212-484-4100
202-296-8510 (Wash. D.C.)

American Association for Paralegal Education
P.O. Box 40244
Overland Park, KS 66204
913-381-4458

American Association for Protecting Children
9725 E. Hampden Ave.
Denver, CO 80231
303-695-0811

American Association of Law Libraries
52 W. Jackson Blvd., Suite 940

Chicago, IL 60604
312-939-4764

American Association of Marriage & Family Therapists
1717 K. St., NW
Wash. D.C. 22036
202-429-1825

American Association of Port Authorities
1010 Duke St.
Alexandria, VA 22314
703-684-5700

American Association of Public Welfare Attorneys
810 1st St., NE, Suite 500
Wash. D.C. 20002
202-682-0100

American Association of School Administrators
1801 N. Moore St.
Arlington, VA 22209
703-528-0700

American Association of Small Cities
P.O. Box 128, Route 2
De Leon, TX 76444
817-893-5818

American Bankers Association
1120 Connecticut Ave. NW
Wash. D.C. 20036
202-663-5000
202-663-5221 (Law Library)

American Bankruptcy Institute
107 2nd St., NE
Wash, D.C. 20002
202-543-1234

American Bar Association
750 N. Lake Shore Dr.
Chicago, IL 60611
312-988-5000
800-621-6159
312-988-6500 (American Bar Foundation)
800-435-7342 (ABA/NET)
312-988-5618 (Committee on Legal Assistants)
202-331-2200 (Wash. D.C.)
317-274-8071 (Indianapolis)

**American Blind Lawyers
Association**
1010 Vermont Ave., NW, Suite 1100
Wash. D.C. 20005
202-393-3666
800-424-8666

**American Board of Professional
Liability Attorneys**
175 E. Shore Rd.
Great Neck, NY 11023
516-487-1990

**American Board of Trial
Advocates**
16633 Ventura Blvd., Suite 1015
Encino, CA 91436
818-501-3250

American Bus Association
1015 15th St., NW
Wash. C.C. 20005
202-842-1645

American Collectors Association
4040 West 70th St.
Minneapolis, MN 55435
612-926-6547

**American College of Healthcare
Executives**
840 N. Lake Shore Dr.
Chicago, IL 60611
312-943-0544

**American College of Probate
Counsel**
2716 Ocean Park Blvd., Suite 1080
Santa Monica, CA 90405
213-450-2033

**American College of Trial
Lawyers**
10886 Wilshire Blvd.
Los Angeles, CA 90024
213-879-0143

**American Corporate Counsel
Association**
1225 Connecticut Ave., Suite 302
Wash. D.C. 20036
202-296-4522

**American Correctional
Association**
4321 Hartwick Rd., Suite L208
College Park, MD 20740
800-888-8784

**American Council of Life
Insurance**
1101 Pennsylvania Ave., NW
Wash. D.C. 20004
202-624-2000
202-624-2472 (Information
  Resource Center)

American Express Co.
World Financial Center
New York, NY 10285
212-640-5619
800-528-4800

American Federation of Police
1000 Connecticut Ave., NW, Suite 9
Wash. D.C. 20036
202-293-9088

American Gas Association
1515 Wilson Blvd.
Arlington, VA 22209
703-841-8583

**American Health Care
Association**
1201 L. St. NW
Wash. D.C. 20005
202-842-4444

**American Hotel & Motel
Association**
1201 New York Ave., NW, Suite 600
Wash. D.C. 20005
202-289-3100

American Humane Association
9725 E. Hampden Ave.
Denver, CO 80231
303-695-0811

**American Immigration Lawyers
Association**
1000 16th St., NW, Suite 604
Wash. D.C. 20036
202-331-0046

American Institute of Architects
1735 New York Ave., NW
Wash. D.C. 20006
202-626-7300

**American Institute of Certified
Planners**
1776 Massachusetts Ave., NW
Wash. D.C. 20036
202-872-0611

**American Institute of Certified
Public Accountants**
1211 Avenue of the Americas
New York, NY 10036
212-575-6209

**American Intellectual Property
Law Association**
2001 Jefferson Davis Hwy, Suite 203
Arlington, VA 22202
703-521-1680

American Jail Association
162 W. Washington St.
Hagerstown, MD 21740
301-790-3930

American Judges Association
300 Newport Ave.
Williamsburg, VA 23187
804-253-2000

American Judicature Society
25 E. Washington St., Suite 1600
Chicago, IL 60602
312-558-6900

American Land Title Association
1828 L. St., NW, Suite 705
Wash. D.C. 20036
202-296-3671

American Law Institute
4025 Chestnut St.
Philadelphia, PA 19104
215-243-1600

American Law Network
4025 Chestnut St.
Philadelphia, PA 19104
215-243-1600

American Library Association
50 E. Huron St.
Chicago, IL 60611
312-944-6780

**American National Standards
Institute**
1430 Broadway
New York, NY 10018
212-354-3300

**American Newspaper
Publishers Association**
P.O. Box 17022
Dulles International Airport
Wash. D.C. 20041
703-648-1038

American Planning Association
1776 Massachusetts Ave., NW
Wash. D.C. 20036
202-872-0611

American Polygraph Association
Box 8037
Chattanooga, TN 37411
615-892-3992

American Prepaid Legal Services Institute
750 N. Lake Shore Dr.
Chicago, IL 60611
312-988-5751

American Probation & Parole Association
P.O. Box 11910
Lexington, KY 40578
606-252-2291

American Prosecutors Research Institute
1033 N. Fairfax St., Suite 200
Alexandria, Va 22314
703-549-4253

American Public Health Association
1015 15th St., NW
Wash. D.C. 20005
202-789-5600

American Public Power Association
2301 M. St., NW
Wash. D.C. 20037
202-775-8300

American Public Welfare Association
810 1st St., NE
Wash. D.C. 20002
202-682-0100

[American Samoa] Chamber of Commerce
P.O. Box 2446
Pago Pago, AS 96799
684-633-5583

[American Samoa] Consumer Protection Bureau
P.O. Box 7
Pago Pago, AS 96799
684-633-4163

[American Samoa] Department of Legal Affairs
Attorney General
P.O. Box 7
Pago Pago, AS 96799
684-633-4163

[American Samoa] Department of Public Safety
P.O. Box 1086
Pago Pago, AS 96799
684-633-1115

American Samoa, Development Bank of
Pago Pago, AS 96799
684-633-4031

[American Samoa] High Court & District Court
P.O. Box 309
Pago Pago, AS 96799
684-633-4131

[American Samoa] Office of the Governor
Pago Pago, AS 96799
684-633-4116

Americans for Effective Law Enforcement
5519 N. Cumberland Ave.
Chicago, IL 60656
312-763-2800

American Society for Information Science
1424 16th St., NW, Suite 404
Wash. D.C. 20036
202-462-1000

American Society for Public Administration
1120 G. St., NW, Suite 500
Wash. D.C. 20005
202-393-7878

American Society of Appraisers
P.O. Box 17265
Wash. D.C. 20041
703-478-2228

American Society of Composers, Authors & Publishers
1 Lincoln Plaza
New York, NY 10023
212-595-3050

American Society of International Law
2223 Massachusetts Ave., NW
Wash. D.C. 20008
202-265-4313

American Society of Law & Medicine
765 Commonwealth Ave.
Boston, MA 02215
617-262-4990

American Society of Notaries
918 16th St., NW
Wash. D.C. 20006
202-955-6162

American Society of Questioned Document Examiners
1432 Esperson Bldg.
Houston, TX 77002
713-227-4451

American Society of Travel Agents
P.O. Box 23992
Wash. D.C. 20026
703-739-2782

American Textile Manufacturers Institute
1801 K. St. NW, Suite 900
Wash. D.C. 20006
202-862-0552

Amoco Oil Co.
200 E. Randolph
Chicago, IL 60601
312-856-4074

AMTRAK
60 Massachusetts Ave., NE
Wash. D.C. 20002
202-906-2121
800-USA-RAIL

Anderson Publishing Co.
2035 Reading Rd.
Cincinnati, OH 45202
513-421-4142
800-543-0883

Andrews Publications
5123 W. Chester Pike
Edgemont, PA 19028
215-343-2565
800-345-1101

Apple Computer, Inc.
20525 Mariani Ave.
Cupertino, CA 95014
408-974-2244
800-538-9585

**[Arizona] Information &
Referral (State Government)**
602-542-4900

**[Arizona] Information Center
(Federal Government)**
602-261-3313

[Arizona] Accountancy Board
3110 N. 19th Ave., Suite 140
Phoenix, AZ 85015
602-255-3648

**[Arizona] Administration,
Department of**
1700 W. Washington
Phoenix, AZ 85007
602-542-1500

[Arizona] Aeronautics Division
1801 W. Jefferson, Rm. 426M
Phoenix, AZ 85007
602-255-7691

[Arizona] Affirmative Action
1700 W. Washington, Rm. 104
Phoenix, AZ 85007
602-542-3711

**[Arizona] Aging & Adult
Administration**
1400 W. Washington, No. 950a
Phoenix, AZ 85077
602-255-4446

**[Arizona] Agricultural
Employment Relations Board**
1937 W. Jefferson, Bldg. E
Phoenix, AZ 85009
602-542-5989

**[Arizona] Agriculture &
Horticulture, Commission of**
1688 W. Adams, Rm. 421
Phoenix, AZ 85007
602-542-4373

[Arizona] Air Quality Management
2005 N. Central, Suite 603
Phoenix, AZ 85004
602-257-2277

[Arizona] Arts, Commission on the
417 W. Roosevelt
Phoenix, AZ 85003
602-255-5882

**[Arizona] Attorney General,
Office of**
1275 W. Washington
Phoenix, AZ 85007
602-542-4266

[Arizona] Auditor General
2700 N. Central Ave., Suite 700
Phoenix, AZ 85004
602-255-4385

[Arizona] Banks, Superintendent of
3225 N. Central Ave., Suite 815
Phoenix, AZ 85012
602-255-4421

Arizona, Bar of
363 N. 1st Ave.
Phoenix, AZ 85003
602-252-4804

**[Arizona] Behavioral Health,
Division of**
411 N. 24th St.
Phoenix, AZ 85008
602-220-6506

[Arizona] Better Business Bureau
4428 N. 12th St.
Phoenix, AZ 85014
602-264-1721
602-622-7651 (Tucson)

[Arizona] Blind, Industries for the
3013 W. Lincoln
Phoenix, AZ 85009
602-269-5131

[Arizona] Boating Administrator
2222 W. Greenway Rd.
Phoenix, AZ 85023
602-942-3000

Arizona Boxing Commission
1645 W. Jefferson, Rm. 212
Phoenix, AZ 85007
602-542-1417

[Arizona] Budget Office, Executive
1700 W. Washington, Rm. 210
Phoenix, AZ 85007
602-542-4886

**[Arizona] Building & Fire Safety,
Department of**
701 E. Jefferson, Suite 200
Phoenix, AZ 85034
602-255-4072

**[Arizona] Child Support
Enforcement Administration**
2222 W. Encanto
P.O. Box 6123—State Code 776A
Phoenix, AZ 85005
602-252-0236

[Arizona] Coconino County
100 E. Birth
Flagstaff, AZ 86001
602-779-6806

**[Arizona] Commerce,
Department of**
1700 W. Washington
State Capitol, West Wing, 4th Fl.
Phoenix, AZ 85007
602-542-5371

**[Arizona] Community Services
Administration**
1601 W. Jefferson
Phoenix, AZ 85007
602-542-3726

**[Arizona] Compensation Fund,
State**
3031 N. 2nd St.
Phoenix, AZ 85012
602-631-2050
602-631-2156 (Legal Division)

[Arizona] Consumer Affairs
3030 N. 3rd St., Suite 111
Phoenix, AZ 85012
602-255-4783

[Arizona] Contractors, Registrar of
800 W. Washington, 6th Fl.
Phoenix, AZ 85007
602-255-4082

**[Arizona] Corporation
Commission**
Incorporating Division
1200 W. Washington St.
Phoenix, AZ 85007
602-542-3521

**[Arizona] Corrections,
Department of**
1601 W. Jefferson

Phoenix, AZ 85007
602-542-5536

**[Arizona] Court of
Appeals—Division One**
1700 W. Washington, Rm. 101
Phoenix, AZ 85007
602-542-4828 (Chief Judge)
602-542-4821 (Clerk)

**Arizona Court of
Appeals—Division Two**
416 W. Congress
Tucson, AZ 85701
602-884-1346 (Vice Chief Judge)
602-628-1999 (Clerk)

**[Arizona] Courts, Administrative
Office of the**
1314 N. 3rd St., Suite 200
Phoenix, AZ 85004
602-253-5700

**Arizona Criminal Justice
Commission**
1700 N. 7th Ave., Suite 250
Phoenix, AZ 85007
602-255-1928

**[Arizona] Data Management
Division**
1616 W. Adams St.
Phoenix, AZ 85007
602-542-5791

**[Arizona] Disease Control Services
Division**
1740 W. Adams St., Rm. 408
Phoenix, AZ 85007
602-255-1181

**[Arizona] Economic Security,
Department of Unemployment
Insurance**
1717 W. Jefferson
Phoenix, AZ 85007
602-542-5678

**[Arizona] Education,
Department of**
1535 W. Jefferson
Phoenix, AZ 85007
602-542-5393

**[Arizona] Emergency & Military
Affairs, Department of**
5636 E. McDowell Rd.

Phoenix, AZ 85008
602-267-2710

[Arizona] Energy Commission
1700 W. Washington St.
Phoenix, AZ 85007
602-542-3632

**[Arizona] Environmental Quality,
Department of**
2005 N. Central Ave.
Phoenix, AZ 85004
602-257-2300

**[Arizona] Environment,
Commission on the**
1645 W. Jefferson, Rm. 416
Phoenix, AZ 85007
602-542-2102

**[Arizona] Family Support,
Division of**
P.O. Box 6123
Phoenix, AZ 85007
602-255-3596

[Arizona] Finance, Division of
1700 W. Washington St., Rm. 210
Phoenix, AZ 85007
602-542-4886

[Arizona] Financial Fraud Division
Office of the Attorney General
1275 W. Washington St.
Phoenix, AZ 85007
602-542-3702
800-352-8431
602-779-6518 (Flagstaff)
602-628-5501 (Tucson)

[Arizona] Fire Marshal
701 E. Jefferson, Suite 200
Phoenix, AZ 85034
602-255-4072

**[Arizona] Game & Fish,
Department of**
2222 W. Greenway Rd.
Phoenix, AZ 85023
602-942-3000

[Arizona] General Services Division
Department of Administration
1805 W. Madison
Phoenix, AZ 85007
602-542-1593

[Arizona] Glendale Public Library
Law Section
5959 W. Brown St.
Glendale, AZ 85302
602-931-5662

[Arizona] Governor, Office of the
1700 W. Washington, 9th Fl.
State Capitol, West Wing
Phoenix, AZ 85007
602-542-4331

**[Arizona] Health Services,
Department of**
1740 W. Adams
Phoenix, AZ 85007
602-542-1000

**[Arizona] Hearing Impaired,
Council for the**
1300 W. Washington, 2nd Fl.
Phoenix, AZ 85007
602-542-3323

[Arizona] Highway Patrol
2102 W. Encanto
P.O. Box 6638
Phoenix, AZ 85005
602-223-2354

[Arizona] Highways, Division of
206 S. 17th Ave.
Phoenix, AZ 85007
602-255-7437

Arizona Historical Society
949 E. 2nd St.
Tucson, AZ 85719
602-628-5774

Arizona House of Representatives
State Capitol
Phoenix, AZ 85007
602-542-4221
602-542-5503 (Judiciary)

**Arizona Indian Affairs,
Commission of**
1645 W. Jefferson, Rm. 130
Phoenix, AZ 85007
602-542-3123

[Arizona] Industrial Commission
800 W. Washington
Phoenix, AZ 85007
602-542-4411

[Arizona] Insurance Department
3030 N. 3rd St., Suite 1100
Phoenix, AZ 85012
602-255-5400

[Arizona] Labor Department
800 W. Washington St., Rm. 102
Phoenix, AZ 85007
602-542-4515

[Arizona] Land Department
1616 W. Adams, Rm. 329
Phoenix, AZ 85007
602-542-4621

[Arizona] Law Enforcement Merit System Council
2102 W. Encanto Blvd., Suite 250
Phoenix, AZ 85009
602-223-2286

[Arizona] LawTemps
7234 E. Shoeman Ln.
Scottsdale, AZ 85251
602-947-8094

[Arizona] Legal Assistants, Southeast Valley Association of
10463 E. University Dr.
Apache Junction, AZ 85220

[Arizona] Legislative Council
Legislative Services Wing, Suite 100
1700 W. Washington
Phoenix, AZ 85007
602-542-4236

[Arizona] Library, State
1700 W. Washington, 3rd Fl.
Phoenix, AZ 85007
602-542-3701
602-542-4035 (Archives & Public Records)

[Arizona] Liquor Licenses & Control, Department of
800 W. Washington, 5th Fl.
Phoenix, AZ 85007
602-542-5141

[Arizona] Lottery, State
4740 E. University Dr.
Phoenix, AZ 85034
602-255-1438

[Arizona] Maricopa County
111 S. 3rd Ave.

Phoenix, AZ 85003
602-262-3011

[Arizona] Maricopa County Bar Association
333 W. Roosevelt
Phoenix, AZ 85003
602-257-4200

[Arizona] Maricopa County Law Library
101 W. Jefferson St., 2nd Fl.
Phoenix, AZ 85003
602-262-3461

[Arizona] Medical Examiners, Board of
2001 W. Camelback Rd., Suite 300
Phoenix, AZ 85015
602-255-3751

[Arizona] Mines & Mineral Resources, Department of
Mineral Bldg.
Phoenix, AZ 85007
602-255-3791

[Arizona] Motor Vehicle Division
1801 W. Jefferson St.
Phoenix, AZ 85007
602-255-7427

[Arizona] Natural Resources Division
1616 W. Adams Ave.
Phoenix, AZ 85007
602-542-4625

[Arizona] Occupational Safety & Health, Division of
800 W. Washington St., Rm. 202
Phoenix, AZ 85007
602-542-5795

[Arizona] Oil & Gas Conservation Commission
3110 N. 19th Ave., Rm. 190
Phoenix, AZ 85015
602-255-5161

Arizona Paralegal Association
P.O. Box 392
Phoenix, AZ 85001

[Arizona] Paralegal Association, Northern Arizona
Box 15005
Flagstaff, AZ 86011

[Arizona] Paralegals, Association of Professional
P.O. Box 2511
Phoenix, AZ 85002

[Arizona] Pardons & Paroles, Board of
1645 W. Jefferson, Rm. 326
Phoenix, AZ 85007
602-542-5656

[Arizona] Parks, State
800 W. Washington, Suite 415
Phoenix, AZ 85007
602-542-4174

[Arizona] Personnel Division
1831 W. Jefferson St.
Phoenix, AZ 85007
602-542-5482

[Arizona] Phoenix City Hall
251 W. Washington St.
Phoenix, AZ 85003
602-262-6011

[Arizona] Phoenix, Legal Assistants of Metropolitan
P.O. Box 13005
Phoenix, AZ 85002

[Arizona] Phoenix Public Library
12 E. McDowell Rd.
Phoenix, AZ 85004
602-262-4766

[Arizona] Physicians Assistants, Joint Board on the Regulation of
2001 W. Camelback Rd., Suite 300
Phoenix, AZ 85015
602-255-3751

[Arizona] Pima County Law Library
110 W. Congress St., Rm. 256
Tucson, AZ 85716
602-740-8456

[Arizona] Planning & Policy Development, Division of
1700 W. Washington St.
Phoenix, Az 85007
602-542-4331

[Arizona] Postsecondary Education, Commission for
3030 N. Central, Suite 1407
Phoenix, AZ 85012
602-255-3109

[Arizona] Postsecondary Education, State Board for Private
1624 W. Adams, Rm. 102
Phoenix, AZ 85007
602-542-5709

[Arizona] Power Authority
1810 W. Adams
Phoenix, AZ 85007
602-542-4263

Arizona Public Employees Association/AFSCME
420 N. 15th Ave.
Phoenix, AZ 85007

[Arizona] Public Safety, Department of
2102 W. Encanto
P.O. Box 6638
Phoenix, AZ 85005
602-223-2000
602-223-2365 (Criminal Investigations)

[Arizona] Racing, Department of
800 W. Washington, 5th Fl.
Phoenix, AZ 85007
602-542-5151

[Arizona] Radiation Regulatory Agency
4814 S. 40th St.
Phoenix, AZ 85040
602-255-4845

[Arizona] Real Estate Department
202 E. Earll Dr., Suite 400
Phoenix, AZ 85012
602-255-4345

Arizona Regents, Board of
3030 N. Central, Suite 1400
Phoenix, AZ 85012
602-255-4082

[Arizona] Rehabilitation Services Administration
1300 W. Washington St.
Phoenix, AZ 85007
602-542-3332

[Arizona] Reporters, Northern Arizona
317 N. Humphreys
P.O. Box 22142

Flagstaff, AZ 86002
602-774-0422

[Arizona] Residential Utility Consumer Office
34 W. Monroe, Suite 512
Phoenix, AZ 85003
602-255-1431

[Arizona] Revenue, Department of
1600 W. Monroe
Phoenix, AZ 85007
602-542-3381

[Arizona] Secretary of State
State Capitol, West Wing
1700 W. Washington, 7th Fl.
Phoenix, AZ 85007
602-542-4285

[Arizona] Securities Division
1200 W. Washington St.
Phoenix, AZ 85007
602-542-4242

Arizona Senate
State Capitol
Phoenix, AZ 85007
602-542-3559
602-542-3171 (Judiciary)

Arizona State University
College of Law Library
Tempe, AZ 85287
602-965-6141

[Arizona] Supreme Court
State Capitol, West Wing
1700 W. Washington, RM 201
Phoenix, AZ 85007
602-542-4531 (Chief Judge)
602-542-4536 (Clerk)

[Arizona] Supreme Court
Committee on Examinations
Committee on Character & Fitness
363 N. 1st Ave.
Phoenix, AZ 85003
602-252-4804

[Arizona] Tax Appeal, Board of
1645 W. Jefferson
Phoenix, AZ 85007
602-542-5462

[Arizona] Technical Registration, Board of
5060 N. 19th Ave., Suite 306

Phoenix, AZ 85015
602-255-4053

[Arizona] Tourism, Office of
1100 W. Washington
Phoenix, AZ 85007
602-542-8687

[Arizona] Transportation, Department of
206 S. 17th Ave., Rm. 100A
Phoenix, AZ 85007
602-255-7011

[Arizona] Treasurer, Office of
State Capitol, West Wing
1700 W. Washington, 1st Fl.
Phoenix, AZ 85007
602-542-5815

[Arizona] Tucson Association of Legal Assistants
P.O. Box 257
Tucson, AZ 85702

[Arizona] Tucson City Hall
255 W. Alameda St.
Tucson, AZ 85701
602-791-4911

[Arizona] Unemployment Insurance Administration
1717 W. Jefferson
Phoenix, AZ 85007
602-542-5678

[Arizona] Uniform State Laws, Commission on
6900 E. Camelback, Suite 1040
Scottsdale, AZ 85251
602-949-8998

Arizona, United States Arbitration & Mediation of
7226 N. 16th St.
Phoenix, AZ 85008
602-870-4400

[Arizona] United States Bankruptcy Court
230 N. 1st Ave.
Phoenix, AZ 85025
602-261-6965

[Arizona] United States Courts Library
55 E. Broadway
Tucson, AZ 85701
602-629-6117

[Arizona] United States Courts Library
230 N. 1st Ave., Rm. 6434
Phoenix, AZ 85025
602-261-3879

[Arizona] United States District Court
230 N. 1st Ave., Rm. 1400
Phoenix, AZ 85025
602-261-3341

Arizona, University of
College of Law
Law Library
Tucson, AZ 85721
602-621-1413

[Arizona] Utilities Division
1200 W. Washington St.
Phoenix, AZ 85007
602-542-4251

[Arizona] Veteran's Service Commission
3225 N. Central, Suite 910
Phoenix, AZ 85012
602-255-4713

[Arizona] Vital Records, Office of
P.O. Box 3887
Phoenix, AZ 85037
602-542-1084

[Arizona] Water Resources, Department of
15 S. 15th Ave.
Phoenix, AZ 85004
602-542-1540

[Arizona] Weights & Measures Division
1951 W. North Lane
Phoenix, AZ 85021
602-255-5211

[Arkansas] Information & Referral (State Government)
501-371-3000

[Arkansas] Information Center (Federal Government)
501-378-6177

[Arkansas] Adult Probation Commission
323 Center St., Suite 1210
Little Rock, AR 72201
501-371-5222

[Arkansas] Aeronautics Department
Old Terminal, Adams Field
Little Rock, AR 72202
501-376-6781

[Arkansas] Aging & Adult Services, Office of
P.O. Box 1437
Little Rock, AR 72203
501-682-2441

[Arkansas] Alcohol & Drug Abuse, Office on
Donaghey Plaza North
P.O. Box 1437
Little Rock, AR 72203
501-682-6653

[Arkansas] Assessment Coordination Division
1614 W. 3rd St.
Little Rock, AR 72201
501-371-1261

Arkansas at Little Rock, University of
Pulaski County Law Library
400 W. Markham
Little Rock, AR 72201
501-371-0167

[Arkansas] Attorney General, Office of
4th & Center Streets, Suite 200
Little Rock, AR 72201
501-682-2007

[Arkansas] Auditor of State
230 State Capitol Bldg.
Little Rock, AR 72201
501-682-6030

[Arkansas] Bank Commissioner
323 Center St., Suite 500
Little Rock, AR 72201
501-371-1117

Arkansas Bar Association
400 W. Markham
Little Rock, AR 72201
501-375-4605
501-375-3957 (CLE)

[Arkansas] Better Business Bureau
1415 S. University Ave.

Little Rock, AR 72204
501-664-7274

[Arkansas] Boating Law Administrator
2 Natural Resources Dr.
Little Rock, AR 72205
501-223-6300

[Arkansas] Building Service, State
1515 Tower Bldg.
Little Rock, AR 72201
501-682-1833

[Arkansas] Children & Family Services, Division of
Donaghey Plaza South
P.O. Box 1437
Little Rock, AR 72203
501-682-8772

[Arkansas] Children & Victims Advocate
323 Center St., No. 200
Little Rock, AR 72201
501-682-2341

[Arkansas] Child Support Enforcement, Division of
P.O. Box 3358
Little Rock, AR 72203
501-682-8398

[Arkansas] Claims Commission
State Capitol Bldg.
Little Rock, AR 72201
501-682-1619

[Arkansas] Code Revision Commission
1400 W. Capitol Ave.
Little Rock, AR 72201
501-371-2128

[Arkansas] Computer Services, Department of
1 Capitol Mall, Rm. 3D-410
Little Rock, AR 72201
501-682-2701

[Arkansas] Consumer Protection Division
4th & Center Streets
Little Rock, AR 72201
501-682-2007
800-482-8982

[Arkansas] Contractor's Licensing Board
621 E. Capitol
Little Rock, AR 72202
501-372-4661

[Arkansas] Corrections, Department of
P.O. Box 8707
Pine Bluff, AR 71611
501-247-1800

[Arkansas] Court Administration
Justice Bldg.
Little Rock, AR 72201
501-371-2295

[Arkansas] Court of Appeals
Justice Bldg., 2nd Fl.
Little Rock, AR 72201
501-682-7460

[Arkansas] Courts, Administrative Office of the
Justice Bldg.
Little Rock, AR 72201
501-376-6655

[Arkansas] Crime Information Center
One Capitol Mall
Little Rock, AR 72201
501-682-2222

[Arkansas] Crime Laboratory, State
Three Natural Resources Dr.
Little Rock, AR 72215
501-227-5747

[Arkansas] Development Finance Authority
100 Main St.
P.O. Box 8023
Little Rock, AR 72203
501-682-5900

[Arkansas] Economic & Medical Services
Donaghey Plaza South
P.O. Box 1437
Little Rock, AR 72203
501-682-8375

[Arkansas] Educational Television Commission
350 S. Donaghey

Conway, AR 72032
501-682-2386

[Arkansas] Education, Department of
1220 W. 3rd St.
Little Rock, AR 72201
501-371-1441

[Arkansas] Education, Department of Higher
1220 W. 3rd St.
Little Rock, AR 72201
501-371-1441

[Arkansas] Emergency Services, Office of
P.O. Box 758, Hwy 286 Spur
Conway, AR 72032
501-329-5601

[Arkansas] Employment Security Division
Unemployment Insurance
2 Capitol Mall
Little Rock, AR 72201
501-682-2121

[Arkansas] Energy Office
One State Capitol Mall
Little Rock, AR 72201
501-371-1370

[Arkansas] Finance & Administration, Department of
1509 W. 7th St., Rm. 401
Little Rock, AR 72201
501-682-2242
501-682-2242 (Equal Employment)
501-682-5372 (Budget)

[Arkansas] Fire Marshall
3 Natural Resources Dr.
Little Rock, AR 72205
501-224-3103

[Arkansas] Food & Dairy Section
4815 W. Markham St.
Little Rock, AR 72205
501-661-2581

[Arkansas] Forestry Commission
3821 W. Roosevelt Rd.
Little Rock, AR 72204
501-664-2531

[Arkansas] Game & Fish Commission
Two Natural Resources Dr.
Little Rock, AR 72205
501-223-6300

[Arkansas] Governor, Office of
State Capitol, Rm. 250
Little Rock, AR 72201
501-682-2345

[Arkansas] Health, Department of
4815 W. Markham St.
Little Rock, AR 72205
501-661-2500

[Arkansas] Heritage Publishing Co.
P.O. Box 9067
North Little Rock, AR 72119
501-835-9111

Arkansas Highway & Transportation
P.O. Box 2261
Little Rock, AR 72203
501-569-2000

Arkansas Historic Preservation Program
225 E. Markham
Little Rock, AR 72201
501-371-2763

[Arkansas] History Commission
1 Capitol Mall
Little Rock, AR 72201
501-682-6900

[Arkansas] House of Representatives
State Capitol
Little Rock, AR 72201
501-375-7771

[Arkansas] Human Services, Department of
Donaghey Plaza South
P.O. Box 1467
Little Rock, AR 72203
501-682-1001

[Arkansas] Industrial Development Commission
One State Capitol Mall, Rm. 4C300
Little Rock, AR 72201
501-682-1121

[Arkansas] Insurance Commissioner
400 University Tower Bldg.
Little Rock, AR 72204
501-371-1325

[Arkansas] Judicial Department
Justice Bldg.
Little Rock, AR 72201
501-371-2295

[Arkansas] Labor, Department of
10421 W. Markham
Little Rock, AR 72205
501-682-4500

[Arkansas] Land Commissioner, State
109 State Capitol Bldg.
Little Rock, AR 72201
501-371-1222

[Arkansas] Law Enforcement Standards & Training
P.O. Box 3106
East Camden, AR 71701
501-574-1810

[Arkansas] Law Examiners, Board of
P.O. Box 5581
One Financial Centre, Suite 450
650 S. Shackleford Rd.
Little Rock, AR 72211
501-225-1071

Arkansas Law Letter, Inc.
P.O. Box 1304
Little Rock, AR 72203
501-375-3058

Arkansas Legal Services, Central
209 W. Capitol, Suite 36
Little Rock, AR 72201
501-376-3423

[Arkansas] Legislative Audit
State Capitol Bldg., Rm. 172
Little Rock, AR 72201
501-371-1931

[Arkansas] Legislative Council
State Capitol Bldg., Rm. 315
Little Rock, AR 72201
501-682-1937

Arkansas Legislative Digest, Inc.
1401 W. 6th St.
Little Rock, AR 72201
501-376-2843

[Arkansas] Library, State
One Capitol Mall, 5th Fl.
Little Rock, AR 72201
501-682-1527

[Arkansas] Lieutenant Governor, Office of
270 State Capitol Bldg.
Little Rock, AR 72201
501-682-2144

[Arkansas] Mental Health Services
4313 W. Markham
Little Rock, AR 72205
501-686-9000

Arkansas Military Department
Camp Robinson
North Little Rock, AR 72118
501-771-5100

[Arkansas] Mine Inspection Division
616 Garrison Ave., Rm. 209
Fort Smith, AR 72901
501-783-2103

[Arkansas] Oil & Gas Commission
P.O. Box 1472, 2215 W. Hillsboro
El Dorado, AR 71730
501-862-4965

[Arkansas] Pardons & Paroles, Division of
P.O. Box 8707
Pine Bluff, AR 71611
501-247-1800

[Arkansas] Parks & Tourism, Department of
One Capitol Mall
Little Rock, AR 72201
501-682-777

[Arkansas] Planning Division
One State Capitol Mall, Rm. 4B-210
Little Rock, AR 72201
501-682-5193

[Arkansas] Pollution Control & Ecology, Department of
8001 National Dr.
Little Rock, AR 72209
501-562-7444

Arkansas Prosecuting Attorneys' Association
Justice Bldg.
Little Rock, AR 72201
501-682-3671

[Arkansas] Prosecutor Coordinator, Office Of
Tower Bldg., Suite 750
4th & Center Streets
Little Rock, AR 72201
501-682-3671

[Arkansas] Public Service Commission
1000 Center St.
Little Rock, AR 72202
501-682-1453
800-482-1164

Arkansas Pulaski County
405 W. Markham St.
Little Rock, AR 72201
501-372-8305

[Arkansas] Purchasing, Office of State
1509 W. 7th St.
Little Rock, AR 72201
501-371-2336

[Arkansas] Real Estate Commission
One Riverfront Pl., Suite 660
North Little Rock, AR 72114
501-371-1247

[Arkansas] Rehabilitation Services Division
P.O. Box 3781
Little Rock, AR 72203
501-682-6697

[Arkansas] Revenues, Division of
7th & Wolfe Streets
Little Rock, AR 72203
501-682-7000

[Arkansas] Safety Division
10421 W. Markham St.
Little Rock, AR 72205
501-569-2235

[Arkansas] Secretary of State
265 State Capitol Bldg.
Little Rock, AR 72201
501-682-1020

**Arkansas Securities
Commissioner**
Heritage West Bldg.
201 E. Markham St., 3rd Fl.
Little Rock, AR 72201
501-371-1011
501-371-1010 (Corporate Records)

[Arkansas] Senate
State Capitol
Little Rock, AR 72201
501-682-6107

**[Arkansas] Services for the
Blind, Division of**
P.O. Box 3237
Little Rock, AR 72203
501-371-2587

**[Arkansas] Soil & Water
Conservation Commission**
One Capitol Mall, Suite 2D
Little Rock, AR 72201
501-682-1611

[Arkansas] Solid Waste Division
8001 National Dr.
Little Rock, AR 72209
501-562-7444

[Arkansas] Standards, Bureau of
4608 W. 61st St.
Little Rock, AR 72209
501-371-1759

**Arkansas State Employees
Association**
P.O. Box 1588
Little Rock, AR 72203
501-378-0187

[Arkansas] State Police
P.O. Box 5901
Three Natural Resources Dr.
Little Rock, AR 72215
501-224-4111

[Arkansas] Supreme Court
Justice Bldg.
Little Rock, AR 72202
501-682-6849
501-682-6841 (Clerk)
501-682-2147 (Law Library)

**[Arkansas] Transportation &
Safety**
Justice Bldg., Suite 100
Little Rock, AR 72201
501-682-1341

[Arkansas] Treasurer of State
State Capitol Bldg., Rm. 220
Little Rock, AR 72201
501-682-5888

**Arkansas Trial Lawyers
Association**
1700 First Commercial Bldg.
Little Rock, AR 72201
501-372-5847

**[Arkansas] Unemployment
Insurance**
Two State Capitol Mall
Little Rock, AR 72201
501-682-1160

**[Arkansas] United States
Bankruptcy Court**
P.O. Box 2381
Little Rock, AR 72203
501-378-6357

**[Arkansas] United States Courts
Branch Library**
600 W. Capitol, Rm. 224
Little Rock, AR 72201
501-387-5039

**[Arkansas] United States District
Court**
Eastern District
P.O. Box 869
Little Rock, AR 72203
501-378-5353

**[Arkansas] United States District
Court**
Western District
P.O. Box 1523
Fort Smith, AR 72902
501-783-6833

Arkansas, University of
School of Law
Law Library
Waterman Hall
Fayetteville, AR 72701
501-575-5604

**[Arkansas] Veterans Services
Division**
P.O. Box 1280
North Little Rock, AR 72115
501-370-3820

**[Arkansas] Vital Records,
Division of**
4815 W. Markham St.
Little Rock, AR 72205
501-661-2134

**[Arkansas] Water Resources
Division**
One State Capitol Mall, Suite 2D
Little Rock, AR 72201
501-682-1611

**[Arkansas] Workers'
Compensation Commission**
Justice Bldg., 2nd Fl.
Little Rock, AR 72201
501-682-3930

Armour Food Co.
1 Central Park Plaza
Omaha, NE 68102
502-449-7272

Arthur Andersen & Co.
633 W. 5th St.
Los Angeles, CA 90071
213-614-6500

Asian Development Bank
2330 Roxas Blvd.
Metro Manila, Philippines

Aspen Systems Corp.
1600 Research Blvd.
Rockville, MD 20850
301-251-5000

**Associated Public-Safety
Communications Officers,
Inc.**
P.O. Box 669
New Smyrna Beach, FL 32070
904-427-3461

**Association for Library &
Information Science
Education**
5623 Palm Aire Dr.
Sarasota, FL 34243
813-355-1795

**Association of American Law
Schools**
1 DuPont Circle, NW
Wash. D.C. 20036
202-296-8851

**Association of College &
Research Libraries**
50 E. Huron St.
Chicago, IL 60611
312-944-6780

**Association of Continuing Legal
Education Administrators**
2001 6th Ave.
Seattle, WA 98121
206-448-0433

**Association of Defense Trial
Attorneys**
600 Jefferson Bank Bldg.
Peoria, IL 61602
309-676-0400

**Association of Family &
Conciliation Courts**
329 W. Wilson
Madison, WI 53703
608-251-4001

**Association of Federal
Investigators**
1612 K. St., NW, Suite 506
Wash. D.C. 20006
202-466-7288

**Association of Government
Accountants**
601 Wythe St., Suite 204
Alexandria, VA 22314
703-684-6931

**Association of Legal
Administrators**
175 E. Hawthorn Parkway,
Suite 325
Vernon Hills, IL 60061
708-816-1212

**Association of Life Insurance
Counsel**
201 Park Ave. South
New York, NY 10003
212-679-1110

**Association of Research
Libraries**
1527 New Hampshire Ave., NW
Wash. D.C. 20036
202-232-2466

**Association of Transportation
Practitioners**
1211 Connecticut Ave., NW,
Suite 310
Wash. D.C. 20036
202-466-2080

**Association of Trial Lawyers of
America**
1050 31st St., NW
Wash. D.C. 20007
202-965-3500
800-424-2727

AT&T
295 North Maple Ave.
Basking Ridge, NJ 07920
201-221-7105
201-221-4359 (Law Library)

Atlantic Richfield Co.
1005 W. 7th St.
Los Angeles, CA 90051
800-322-ARCO

Atlas Van Lines
1212 St. George Rd.
Evansville, IN 47703
800-457-3705

Attorneys Group, The
292 Madison Ave., 7th Fl.
New York, NY 10017
212-949-5900

Attorneys Software Inc.
4800 Lincoln Blvd., Suite 470
Marina Del Ray, CA 90292
213-551-0766
800-443-5763

**Automotive Consumer Action
Program**
8400 Westpark Dr.
McLean, VA 22102
703-821-7144

**Auxiliary of the Decalogue
Society of Lawyers**
179 W. Washington St., Suite 350
Chicago, IL 60602
312-263-6493

Avis Rent-A-car System
900 Old Country Rd.
Garden City, NY 11530
516-222-4200

BBB Auto Line
Council of Better Business Bureaus
4200 Wilson Blvd., Suite 800
Arlington, VA 22203
703-276-0100

Bancroft-Whitney
3250 Van Ness Ave.
San Francisco, CA 94112
415-848-4000
716-546-5530 (Rochester)

Banking Law Institute
22 W. 21st St.
New York, NY 10010
212-645-7880

Bank of America, NT & SA
555 California St.
San Francisco, CA 94104
415-622-3590

Bank of New York Co.
48 Wall St.
New York, NY 10286
212-495-2066

**Banks-Baldwin Law Publishing
Co.**
P.O. Box 1974
Cleveland, OH 44106
216-721-7373

**Barrister Information Systems
Corp.**
45 Oak St.
Buffalo, NY 14203

716-845-5010
213-380-0342 (Los Angeles)

Bell Atlantic Corp.
1310 N. Court House Road
Arlington, VA 22201
703-974-5553

Better Hearing Institute
P.O. Box 1840
Wash. D.C. 20013
703-642-0580
800-EAR-WELL

**Black Entertainment & Sports
Lawyers Association**
111 Broadway
New York, NY 10006
212-587-0300

Blacks in Government
1424 K. St., NW, Suite 604
Wash. D.C. 20005
202-638-7767

**Blue Cross & Blue Shield
Association**
655 15th St. NW, Suite 350
Wash. D.C. 20005
202-626-4780

**Boat Owners Association of the
United States**
880 South Pickett St.
Alexandria, VA 22304
703-823-9550

Borden, Inc.
180 E. Broad St.
Columbus, OH 43215
614-225-4411

**Bowker Legal Reference
Publishing**
245 W. 17th St.
New York, NY 10011
212-337-6934
800-521-8110

Bristol-Myers Products
685 Rt. 202/206 North
Somerville, NJ 08876
800-468-7746

Budget Rent-A-Car Corp.
3350 Boyington Dr.
Carrollton, TX 75006
800-621-2844

**Building Officials & Code
Administrators International**
4051 W. Flossmoor Rd.
Country Club Hills, IL 60477
312-799-2300

Bureau of National Affairs
1231 25th St., NW
Wash. D.C. 20037
202-452-5742
800-372-1033

Burlington Industries
3330 W. Friendly Ave.
Greensboro, NC 27420
919-379-3376

Butterworth Legal Publishers
90 Stiles Rd.
Salem, NH 03079
800-548-4001
617-438-8464

**Cable Television Information
Center**
1500 N. Beauregard St., Suite 205
Alexandria, VA 22311
703-845-1700

**[California] Information &
Referral (State Government)**
916-322-9900

**[California] Information Center
(Federal Government)**
Los Angeles 213-894-3800
San Diego 619-557-6030
San Francisco 415-556-6600
Santa Ana 415-836-2386

**[California] Aeronautics,
Division of**
P.O. Box 942874
Sacramento, CA 94274
916-322-9941

**[California] Aging,
Department of**
1600 K. St.
Sacramento, CA 95814
916-322-5290

[California] Air Resources Board
1102 Q. St.
Sacramento, CA 95814
916-445-4383

[California] Alameda County
1225 Fallon St.
Oakland, CA 94612
415-272-6790

**[California] Alameda County Bar
Association**
405 145h St., Suite 208
Oakland, CA 94612
415-893-7160

**[California] Alameda County
Law Library**
1225 Fallon St., Rm. 200
Oakland, CA 94612
415-272-6481
415-670-5230 (Haywood)

**[California] Alcohol & Drug
Programs, Department of**
111 Capital Mall
Sacramento, CA 95814
916-445-0834

**California Alliance of Paralegal
Associations**
P.O. Box 2234
San Francisco, CA 94126

**[California] American Law
Books**
11477 Silvergate Dr.
Dublin, CA 94568
800-635-5648

**[California] American Paralegal
Association**
P.O. Box 35233
Los Angeles, CA 90035

[California] Archives, State
1020 O. St., Rm. 130
Sacramento, CA 95814
916-445-4293

[California] Arts Council
1901 Broadway, Suite A

Sacramento, CA 95818
916-322-8911

[California] Assembly
State Capitol
Sacramento, CA 95814
916-445-3614
916-445-1611 (Judiciary)

**California Association of
Freelance Paralegals**
P.O. Box 3267
Berkeley, CA 94703

**California Association of
Independent Paralegals**
466 Santa Clara Ave., Suite 220
Oakland, CA 94610
415-452-4602

**[California] Auditor General,
Office of the**
660 J. St., Suite 300
Sacramento, CA 95814
916-445-0255

**[California] Banks,
Superintendent of**
111 Pine St., Suite 1100
San Francisco, CA 94111
415-557-3535
800-622-0620
213-736-2479 (Los Angeles)
916-322-5966 (Sacramento)

**[California] Bar, Continuing
Education of the**
2300 Shattuck Ave.
Berkeley, CA 94704
415-642-8000
800-858-4545

**[California] Bar Examiners,
Committee of**
(attorney applicants)
P.O. Box 7908
San Francisco, CA 94120
415-561-8303

**[California] Bar Examiners,
Committee of**
(first time applicants & repeaters)
333 S. Beaudry, 10th Fl.
Los Angeles, CA 90017
213-580-5500

California, Bar of
555 Franklin St.

San Francisco, CA 94102
415-561-8200

**[California] Barclays Law
Publishers**
P.O. Box 3066
South San Francisco, CA 94083
800-888-3600

**[California] Better Business
Bureau**
400 S. St.
Sacramento, CA 95814
916-443-6843
805-322-2074 (Bakersfield)
213-383-0992 (Los Angeles)
619-234-0966 (San Diego)
415-775-9999 (San Francisco)

**[California] Beverly Hills Bar
Association**
300 S. Beverly Dr., #201
Beverly Hills, CA 90212
213-553-6644

**[California] Boating &
Waterways, Department of**
1629 S. St.
Sacramento, CA 95814
916-445-2615

**[California] Central Coast Legal
Assistants**
P.O. Box 93
San Luis Obispo, CA 93406

**[California] Channel Cities Legal
Assistant Association**
P.O. Box 2695
Santa Barbara, CA 93120

**[California] Child Support
Program Management
Branch**
744 P. St., MS 9-011
Sacramento, CA 95814
916-322-8495

**[California] Codes & Standards,
Division of**
6007 Folson Blvd., Suite A
Sacramento, CA 95819
916-445-9471

**[California] Commerce,
Department of**
1121 L. St., Suite 600
Sacramento, CA 95814
916-332-3241

**[California] Conservation,
Department of**
1416 9th St.
Sacramento, CA 95814
916-322-1080

**[California] Consumer Affairs,
Department of**
1020 N. St.
Sacramento, CA 95814
916-445-0660
800-952-5225
800-952-5210 (Automotive repairs)
213-974-1452 (Los Angeles)
619-531-4070 (San Diego)
415-552-7400 (San Francisco)

**[California] Contra Costa
County Law Library**
1020 Ward St., 1st Fl.
Martinez, CA 94553
415-646-2783

[California] Controller, State
P.O. Box 942850
300 Capitol Mall, 18th Fl.
Sacramento, Ca 94250
916-445-2636

**[California] Corporations,
Department of**
1107 9th St., Rm. 800
Sacramento, CA 95814
916-324-9011

**[California] Corrections,
Department of**
630 K. St.
Sacramento, CA 94283
916-445–7688

California Court of Appeals
First Appellate District
350 McAllister St.
San Francisco, CA 94102
415-557-9580
415-557-0859 (Law Library)

California Court of Appeals
Second Appellate District
3580 Wilshire Blvd.
Los Angeles, CA 90010
213-736-2391
213-736-7887

California Court of Appeals
Second Appellate District,
Division Six

1280 S. Victoria, Rm. 201
Ventura, CA 93003
805-654-4502

California Court of Appeals
Third Appellate District
119 Liberty & Courts Bldg.
Sacramento, CA 95814
916-445-4677

California Court of Appeals
Fourth Appellate District,
Division One
1350 Front St., Rm. 6010
San Diego, CA 92101
619-237-6558
618-237-6023

California Court of Appeals
Fourth Appellate District,
Division Two
303 W. 3rd St.
San Bernardino, CA 92401
714-383-4442
714-383-4088 (Law Library)

California Court of Appeals
Fourth Appellate District,
Division Three
P.O. Box 1378
Santa Ana, CA 92701
714-558-6777

California Court of Appeals
Fifth Appellate District
2550 Mariposa St.
Fresno, CA 93721
209-445-5491
209-445-5686

California Court of Appeals
Sixth Appellate District
333 W. Santa Clara St., Suite 1060
San Jose, CA 95113
408-277-1004
4098-277-9788

[California] Courts,
Administrative Office of the
350 McAllister St., Rm. 3154
San Francisco, CA 94102
415-557-1581

[California] Criminal Justice
Planning, Office of
1130 K. St., Suite 300
Sacramento, CA 95814
916-324-9100

[California] East Bay Association
of Legal Assistants
P.O. Box 424
Oakland, CA 94604

[California] Economic
Opportunity, Department of
1600 9th St.
Sacramento, CA 95814
916-322-2940

[California] Education
Commission, Postsecondary
1020 12th St., 3rd Fl.
Sacramento, CA 95814
916-445-1000

[California] Education,
Department of
721 Capitol Mall, Rm. 524
Sacramento, CA 95814
916-445-2700

[California] Election Division
1230 J. St., Rm. 232
Sacramento, CA 95814
916-445-0820

[California] Employment
Development, Department of
800 Capitol Mall
Sacramento, CA 95814
916-445-8008

[California] Energy Commission
1516 9th St.,
Sacramento, CA 95814
916-324-3331

[California] Environmental
Affairs Agency
1102 Q. St.
Sacramento, CA 95814
916-322-4203

[California] Equalization, State
Board of (Taxation &
Revenue)
1020 N. St.
Sacramento, CA 95814
916-445-3956
926-445-7356 (Law Library)

[California] Fair Employment &
Housing, Department of
2016 T. St., Suite 210
Sacramento, CA 95814
916-323-5256

[California] Fair Political
Practices Commission
428 J. St., Suite 800
Sacramento, CA 95814
916-322-5901

[California] Finance,
Department of
State Capitol, Rm. 1145
Sacramento, CA 95814
916-445-4141

[California] Fire Marshall
7171 Bowling Dr., Suite 600
Sacramento, CA 95823
916-427-4161

[California] Fish & Game,
Department of
1416 9th St.
Sacramento, CA 95814
916-445-3535

[California] Food & Agriculture,
Department of
1220 N. St.
Sacramento, CA 94271
916-445-7128

[California] Fresno County Law
Library
1100 Van Ness Ave., Rm. 600
Fresno, CA 93721
209-237-2227

[California] General Services,
Department of
915 Capitol Mall, Suite 590
Sacramento, CA 95814
916-445-3441

[California] Glendale University
College of Law Library
220 N. Glendale Ave.
Glendale, CA 91206
818-247-0770

[California] Golden Gate
University
School of Law Library
536 Mission St.
San Francisco, CA 94105
415-442-7260

[California] Governor, Office of
the
State Capitol, 1st Fl.
Sacramento, CA 95814
916-445-2841

[California] Health Data & Statistics Branch
410 N. St.
Sacramento, CA 95814
916-445-1719

[California] Health Services, Department of
714 P. St., Rm. 1253
Sacramento, CA 95814
916-445-1248

California Highway Patrol
P.O. Box 942898
Sacramento, CA 94298
916-445-1564

[California] Housing & Community Development, Department of
1800 3rd St.
Sacramento, CA 95814
916-322-1560
916-322-9648 (Law Library)

[California] Industrial Relations, Department of
525 Golden Gate Ave.
San Francisco, CA 94102
415-557-3356

[California] Information Technology, Office of
915 L. St.
Sacramento, CA 95814
916-445-1932

[California] Inland Counties Paralegal Association
P.O. Box 192
Riverside, CA 92502

[California] Insurance, Commissioner of
100 Van Ness Ave.
San Francisco, CA 94102
415-557-3245
800-233-9045
213-736-2551 (Los Angeles)

[California] John F. Kennedy University
Law Library
547 Ygnacio Valley Rd.
Walnut Creek, CA 94596
415-930-6434

[California] Justice, Department of
Office of the Attorney General
1515 K. St.
Sacramento, CA 95814
916-324-5437
916-324-5314

[California] Kern County
1415 Truxtun Ave.
Bakersfield, CA 93301
805-861-2111

[California] Kern County Law Library
1415 Truxtun Ave.
Bakersfield, CA 93301
805-861-2379

[California] Kern County Paralegal Association
P.O. Box 2673
Bakersfield, CA 93303

[California] Legislative Council, Office of
State Capitol, Rm. 3021
Sacramento, CA 95814
916-445-3057

[California] Legislative Intent Service
712 Main St.
Woodland, CA 95695
916-666-1917

[California] Library, State
P.O. Box 942837
Sacramento, CA 94237
916-445-4027
916-445-8833 (Law Library)

[California] Lieutenant Governor, Office of
State Capitol, Rm. 1114
Sacramento, Ca 95814
916-445-8994

[California] Long Beach City Hall
333 W. Ocean Blvd.
Long Beach, CA 90802
213-590-6101

[California] Los Angeles City Attorney
Law Library
City Hall East, Rm. 1700
Los Angeles, CA 90012
213-485-5400

[California] Los Angeles Copyright Society
3000 W. Alameda Ave.
Burbank, CA 91523
818-840-3508

[California] Los Angeles County
111 N. Hill St.
Los Angeles, CA 90012
213-974-1234

[California] Los Angeles County Bar Association
617 S. Olive St.
Los Angeles, CA 90014
213-627-2727

[California] Los Angeles County Counsel Law Library
500 W. Temple St., Rm. 610
Los Angeles, CA 90012
213-974-1982

[California] Los Angeles County Law Library
301 W. 1st St.
Los Angeles, CA 90012
213-629-3531

[California] Los Angeles County Municipal Courts & Research Unit Library
110 N. Grand, Rm. 536
Los Angeles, CA 90012
213-974-6181

[California] Los Angeles County Superior Court Law Library
111 N. Hill St., Rm. 623
Los Angeles, CA 90012
213-974-4867

[California] Los Angeles, Lawyers Club of
P.O. Box 58525
Los Angeles, CA 90058
213-624-2525

[California] Los Angeles, Legal Aid Foundation of
1550 W. 8th St.
Los Angeles, CA 90017
213-252-3824

[California] Los Angeles Mayor's Office
200 N. Spring St.
Los Angeles, CA 90012
213-485-3311

[California] Los Angeles Paralegal Association
P.O. Box 241928
Los Angeles, CA 90024
213-284-2118

[California] Los Angeles Times
Times Mirror Sq.
Los Angeles, CA 90053
213-237-5000

[California] Lottery, State
600 N. 10th St.
Sacramento, CA 95814
916-323-0400

[California] Loyola Marymount University
Law Library
1440 W. 9th St.
Los Angeles, CA 90015
213-736-1117

[California] Marin Association of Legal Assistants
P.O. Box 13051
San Rafael, CA 94913

[California] Marin County Law Library
Hall of Justice, Civic Center, Rm. C-33
San Rafael, CA 94903
415-499-6355

[California] Measurement Standards, Division of
8500 Fruitridge Rd.
Sacramento, CA 95826
916-366-5119

[California] Mental Health, Department of
1600 9th St., Rm. 151
Sacramento, CA 95814
916-323-8173

[California] Mines & Geology, Division of
1416 9th St.
Sacramento, CA 95814
916-445-1825

[California] Motor Vehicles, Department of
2415 1st Ave.
Sacramento, CA 95818
916-732-0250

[California] National Association of Independent Paralegals
585 5th St. West, Suite 111
Sonoma, CA 95476

[California] National University
Law Library
8380 Miramar Rd.
San Diego, CA 92126
619-492-5180

[California] Nolo Press
950 Parker St.
Berkeley, CA 94710
415-548-5902

[California] North County Legal Assistants
911 Hacienda Dr., Suite A
Vista, CA 92083

[California] Oakland City Hall
1 City Hall Plaza
Oakland, CA 94612
415-444-2489

[California] Occupational Safety & Health
525 Golden Gate Ave.
San Francisco, CA 94102
415-557-1946

[California] Occupational Safety & Health Standards Board
1006 4th St., 3rd Fl.
Sacramento, CA 95814
916-322-3640

[California] Orange County
700 Civic Center Dr. W.
Santa Ana, CA 92701
714-834-2200

[California] Orange County Bar Association
601 Civic Center Dr. West
Santa Ana, CA 92701
714-541-6222

[California] Orange County Law Library
515 N. Flower St.
Santa Ana, CA 92703
714-834-3397

[California] Orange County Paralegal Association
P.O. Box 8512
Newport Beach, CA 92658

California Paralegal Associations, Alliance of
P.O. Box 2234
San Francisco, CA 94126

[California] Parker & Sons Publications
P.O. Box 60001
Los Angeles, CA 90060
213-727-1088
800-452-9873

[California] Parks & Recreation, Department of
P.O. Box 942896
Sacramento, CA 94296
916-445-6477

[California] Parole & Community Services Division
501 J. St.
Sacramento, CA 95814
916-445-6200

[California] Pepperdine University
Law Library
Malibu, CA 90265
213-456-4647

[California] Personnel Board, State
801 Capitol Mall
Sacramento, CA 94244
916-322-2530

[California] Planning & Research, Office of
1400 10th St., Rm. 156
Sacramento, CA 95814
916-322-8515

[California] Police, State
815 S. St.
Sacramento, CA 95814
916-445-1150

[California] Prison Terms, Board of
545 Downtown Plaza, Suite 200
Sacramento, CA 95814
916-445-4071

[California] Procurement, Office of
P.O. Box 942804
Sacramento, CA 95204
916-445-6942

[California] Public Defender, Office of State
1390 Market St., Suite 425
San Francisco, CA 94102
415-557-1600
213-620-5402 (Los Angeles)
916-322-7520 (Sacramento)

[California] Public Employees Retirement System
400 P. St.
Sacramento, CA 95814
916-326-3232

[California] Public Utilities Commission
505 Van Ness Ave., Rm. 5207
San Francisco, CA 94102
415-557-2444

[California] Real Estate, Department of
P.O. Box 187000
Sacramento, CA 95818
916-739-3600

[California] Redwood Empire Association of Legal Assistants
1275 4th St., #226
Santa Rosa, CA 95404

[California] Rehabilitation, Department of
830 K. St. Mall
Sacramento, CA 95814
916-445-3971

[California] Resources Agency
1416 9th St., Rm. 1311
Sacramento, CA 95814
916-445-6371

[California] Riverside County Law Library
3535 10th St., Suite 100
Riverside, CA 92501
714-787-2460

[California] Rutter Group, The
15760 Ventura Blvd., Suite 630
Encino, CA 91436
818-990-3260
800-367-2053

[California] Sacramento Association of Legal Assistants

P.O. Box 453
Sacramento, CA 95812

[California] Sacramento County
720 9th St.
Sacramento, Ca 95814
916-440-5522

[California] Sacramento County Law Library
720 9th St., Rm. 16
Sacramento, CA 95814
916-440-6011

[California] San Bernardino County Law Library
401 N. Arrowhead
San Bernardino, CA 92415
714-885-3020

[California] San Diego Association of Legal Assistants
P.O. Box 87449
San Diego, CA 92138

[California] San Diego City Administration
202 C. St.
San Diego, CA 92101
619-236-5555

[California] San Diego City Attorney
Law Library
202 C. St. MS/3A
San Diego, CA 92101
619-236-6220

[California] San Diego County Bar Association
1434 5th Ave.
San Diego, CA 92101
619-231-0781

[California] San Diego County Law Library
1105 Front St.
San Diego, CA 92101
619-531-3900

[California] San Francisco Association of Legal Assistants
P.O. Box 26668
San Francisco, CA 94126
415-982-2586

[California] San Francisco, Bar Association of
685 Market St., # 700
San Francisco, CA 94105
415-764-1600

[California] San Francisco Board of Supervisors
City Hall, Rm. 235
San Francisco, CA 94102
415-554-5184

[California] San Francisco, City & County Libraries of
P.O. Box 11108
San Francisco, CA 94101
415-821-7762

California San Francisco City Hall
400 Van Ness Ave.
San Francisco, CA 94102
415-554-4000

[California] San Francisco County
400 Van Ness Ave., Rm. 317
San Francisco, CA 94102
415-554-4114

[California] San Francisco Law Library
400 Van Ness Ave., Rm. 436
San Francisco, CA 94102
415-554-6821
415-554-6821 (Market St.)

[California] San Francisco, Lawyers' Club of
685 Market St., #750
San Francisco, CA 94105
415-433-2514

[California] San Joaquin Association of Legal Assistants
P.O. Box 1306
Fresno, CA 93715

[California] San Joaquin College of Law
Law Library
3385 E. Shields
Fresno, CA 93726
209-225-4959

[California] San Luis Obispo County Law Library

County Government Center, Rm. 125
San Luis Obispo, CA 93408
805-549-5855

[California] San Mateo County Law Library
710 Hamilton St.
Redwood City, CA 94063
415-363-4000

[California] San Mateo, Paralegal Association of
250 Wheeler Ave.
Redwood City, CA 94061

[California] Santa Barbara County Law Library
County Court House
1100 Anacapa St.
Santa Barbara, CA 93101
805-568-2296

[California] Santa Clara County
70 W. Heddding St.
San Jose, CA 95110
408-299-2424

[California] Santa Clara County Bar Association
2001 Gateway Pl., #220 West
San Jose, CA 95110
408-288-8840

[California] Santa Clara County Law Library
360 N. 1st St.
San Jose, CA 95113
408-299-3567

[California] Santa Clara County, Paralegal Association of
P.O. Box 26736
San Jose, CA 95159

[California] Santa Clara University
Heafey Law Library
Santa Clara, CA 95053
408-554-5318

[California] Santa Cruz County Law Library
701 Ocean St.
Santa Cruz, CA 95060
408-425-2211

[California] Secretary of State
1230 J. St.
Sacramento, CA 95814
916-445-6371
916-324-1485 (Corporate Filings)

[California] Senate
State Capitol
Sacramento, CA 95814
916-445-4202
916-445-5957 (Judiciary)

[California] Sequoia Paralegal Association
P.O. Box 93278
Visalia, CA 93278

[California] Social Services, Department of
744 P. St.
Sacramento, CA 95814
916-445-4500

[California] Sonoma County Law Library
600 Administration Dr., Rm. 213J
Santa Rosa, CA 95403
707-527-2668

[California] Southwestern University
School of Law Library
675 S. Westmoreland Ave.
Los Angeles, CA 90005
213-738-6723

[California] Stanford University
Law Library
Stanford, CA 94305
415-723-2478

[California] Stanislaus County Law Library
1100 I St., Rm. 223
Modesto, CA 95354
209-525-6967

California State Office
444 N. Capitol St., NW, Suite 305
Wash. D.C. 20001
202-347-6894

[California] Supreme Court
350 McAllister St.
San Francisco, CA 94102
415-557-0587
415-557-1388 (Clerk)
415-557-1922 (Law Library)

916-445-7525 (Sacramento)
213-736-2902 (Los Angeles)

[California] Tourism, Office of
1121 L. St., Suite 600
Sacramento, CA 95814
916-322-1396

[California] Transportation, Department of
1120 N. St.
Sacramento, CA 95814
916-445-2201

[California] Treasurer
915 Capitol Mall, Rm. 110
Sacramento, CA 95814
916-445-6562

[California] Tulare County Law Library
County Civic Center, Rm. 1
Visalia, CA 93291
209-733-6395

[California] Unemployment Appeals Board
P.O. Box 944275
Sacramento, CA 95814
916-445-8351

[California] Unemployment Insurance Division
800 Capitol Mall
Sacramento, CA 95814
916-445-9212

[California] Uniform Commercial Code Division
1230 J. St.
Sacramento, CA 95814
916-445-6371

[California] United States Bankruptcy Court
Central District
312 N. Spring St.
Los Angeles, CA 90012
213-894-4696
213-894-3636 (Law Library)

[California] United States Bankruptcy Court
Eastern District
8308 U.S. Courthouse
650 Capitol Mall
Sacramento, CA 95814
916-551-2662

[California] United States Bankruptcy Court
Northern District
P.O. Box 36053
450 Golden Gate Ave.
San Francisco, CA 94102
415-556-2250

[California] United States Bankruptcy Court
Southern District
940 Front St.
San Diego, CA 92189
619-557-5620
619-557-5066 (Law Library)

[California] United States Court of Appeals for the Ninth Circuit
P.O. Box 547
San Francisco, CA 94101
415-556-7340
415-556-4690 (Law Library)
818-405-7018 (Law Library, Pasadena)
818-405-7906 (Bankruptcy Appellate Panel)

[California] United States District Court
Central District
312 N. Spring St.
Los Angeles, CA 90012
213-894-3535
213-894-3636 (Law Library)

[California] United States District Court
Eastern District
650 Capitol Mall
2546 U.S. Courthouse
Sacramento, CA 95814
916-551-2615

[California] United States District Court
Northern District
P.O. Box 36060
450 Golden Gate Ave.
San Francisco, CA 94102
415-556-3031

[California] United States District Court
Southern District
940 Front St.
San Diego, CA 92189
619-557-5600
619-557-5066 (Law Library)

[California] United States District Court Library
1130 O. St., Rm. 5023
Fresno, CA 93721
209-487-5836

[California] United States District Court Library
Box 36060-450
Golden Gate Ave.
San Francisco, CA 94102
415-556-7979

[California] United States Government Printing Office
450 Golden Gate Ave., Rm. 1023
San Francisco, CA 94102
415-556-0643

[California] United States Government Printing Office
ARCO Plaza, C-Level
505 S. Flower St.
Los Angeles, CA 90071
213-894-5841

[California] University of California (Berkeley)
Law Library
Berkeley, CA 94720
415-642-4044

[California] University of California (Davis)
Law Library
Davis, CA 95616
916-752-3327

[California] University of California (Hastings)
Law Library
200 McAllister St.
San Francisco, CA 94102
415-621-4859

[California] University of California (Los Angeles)
Law Library
Los Angeles, CA 90024
213-825-7826

[California] University of LaVerne
College of Law Library

1950 3rd St.,
LaVerne, CA 91750
714-593-7184

[California] University of San Diego
Law Library
Alcala Park
San Diego, CA 92110
619-260-4542

[California] University of San Francisco
School of Law Library
San Francisco, CA 94117
415-666-6679

[California] University of Southern California
Law Library
University Park
Los Angeles, CA 90089
213-743-6314

[California] University of the Pacific
McGeorge School of Law Library
3282 5th Ave.
Sacramento, CA 95817
916-739-7131

[California] University of West Los Angeles
Law Library
12201 Washington Pl.
Los Angeles, CA 90066
213-313-2117

[California] Ventura County Association of Legal Assistants
P.O. Box 24229
Ventura, CA 93002

[California] Ventura County Law Library
800 S. Victoria Ave.
Ventura, CA 93009
805-654-2695

[California] Veterans Affairs, Department of
1227 O. St.
Sacramento, CA 94295
916-323-3287

[California] Waste Management Board

1020 9th St., Suite 300
Sacramento, CA 95814
916-322-3330

**[California] Water Resources
Control Board**
P.O. Box 100
Sacramento, CA 95801
916-322-4142

**California Western School of
Law Library**
350 Cedar St.
San Diego, CA 92101
619-239-0391

**[California] Western State
University College of Law**
Law Library
1111 N. State College Blvd.
Fullerton, CA 92631
714-738-1000

**[California] Western State
University College of Law**
Law Library
2121 San Diego Ave.
San Diego, CA 92110
619-297-9700

[California] Whittier College
Law Library
5353 W. 3rd St.
Los Angeles, CA 90020
213-938-3460

**California Water Resources,
Department of**
P.O. Box 942386
Sacramento, CA 95236
916-445-9248

**[California] Women,
Commission on the Status of**
1303 J. St., Rm. 400
Sacramento, CA 95814
916-445-3173

**[California] Yolo County Law
Library**
625 Court St., Rm. B-07
Woodland, CA 95695
916-666-8918

**[California] Youth &
Correctional Agency**
1027 10th St., Suite 300

Sacramento, CA 95814
916-323-6001

**[California] Youth Authority,
Department of the**
4241 Williamsbourgh Dr.
Sacramento, Ca 95823
916-427-4822

**[California] Youthful Offender
Parole Board**
4241 Williamsbourgh Dr.
Sacramento, CA 95823
916-427-4873

Callaghan & Co.
155 Pfingsten Rd.
Deerfield, IL 60015
312-948-7000
800-323-1336

Campbell Soup Co.
Campbell Pl.
Camden, NJ 08101
609-342-3714

Canada Law Book
240 Edward St.
Aurora, Ontario
Canada L4G 3S9
416-773-6300
800-263-2037

**Canadian Association of Law
Libraries**
York University School of Law
4700 Keele St.
North York, Ontario M3J 2R5
  Canada
416-667-2100

**Canadian Association of Legal
Assistants**
Box 30, Toronto-Dominion Centre
Toronto, ON Canada M5K 1C1

**[Canal Zone] United States
District Court**
Box 2006
Balboa Heights
U.S.A. Postal Zone #8
Phone Canal Zone 52-7675

Cancer Hotline
800-4-CANCER

Carnation Co.
5045 Wilshire Blvd.

Los Angeles, CA 90036
213-932-6000

Carpet & Rug Institute
1155 Connecticut Ave., NW,
  Suite 500
Wash. D.C. 20036
202-429-6629

Carswell Co., Ltd.
2330 Midland Ave.
Ontario, Canada M1S 1P7
416-291-8421

CBS Broadcast Group
524 W. 57th St.
New York, NY 10019
212-975-3166

**Cemetery Consumer Service
Council**
P.O. Box 3574
Wash. D.C. 20007
703-379-6426

Center for Auto Safety
2001 S. St., NW
Wash. D.C. 20009
202-328-7700

**Center for Computer-Assisted
Legal Instruction**
University of Minnesota School of
  Law
229 19th Ave., South
Minneapolis, MN 55455
612-373-5352

Center for Computer/Law
P.O. Box 3280
Manhattan Beach, CA 90266
213-470-6361

Center for Dispute Settlement
1666 Connecticut Ave., NW,
  Suite 501
Wash. D.C. 20009
202-265-9572

Center for Judicial Studies
Box 93, Route 2
Cumberland, VA 23040
804-492-1776

Center for Law and Education
14 Appian Way
Cambridge, MA 02138
617-495-4666

Center for Law & Social Policy
1616 P. St., NW, Suite 350
Wash. D.C. 20036
202-328-5140

**Center for Law in the Public
Interest**
11835 W. Olympic Blvd.,
Suite 1155
Los Angeles, CA 90064
213-470-3000

**Center for Litigation Risk
Analysis**
3000 Sand Hill Road
Menlo Park, CA 94025
415-854-1104

**Center for Local Prosecution of
Drug Offenses**
1033 N. Fairfax St., Suite 200
Alexandria, VA 22314
703-549-9222

Center for Local Tax Research
121 E. 30th St.
New York, NY 10016
212-889-8020

**Center for Professional
Responsibility**
American Bar Association
750 N. Lake Shore Dr.
Chicago, IL 60611
312-988-5000

Center for Seafarers' Rights
50 Broadway
New York, NY 10004
212-269-2710

**Center for Study of Responsive
Law**
P.O. Box 19367
Wash. D.C. 20036
202-387-8030

**Center on Social Welfare Policy
& Law**
95 Madison Ave.
New York, NY 10016
212-679-3709

Chemical Bank
277 Park Ave.
New York, NY 10172
212-310-5800

Chevron U.S.A., Inc.
P.O. Box H
Concord, CA 94524
415-827-6412
800-CHEVRON

Chicago Title
111 W. Washington St.
Chicago, IL 60602
312-630-2207

Christic Institute
1324 N. Capitol St., NW
Wash. D.C. 20002
202-797-8106

Chrysler Motors Corp.
P.O. Box 1718
Detroit, MI 48288
800-992-1997

**CIGNA Property & Casualty
Companies**
1600 Arch St.
Philadelphia, PA 19103
215-523-2729

Citicorp/Citibank
399 Park Ave.
New York, NY 10043
212-559-0043

**Citizens' Commission on Civil
Rights**
1424 M. St., NW
Wash. D.C. 20026
202-822-7708

**Citizens' Committee for the
Right to Keep and Bear Arms**
600 Pennsylvania Ave., SE
Wash. D.C. 20003
202-543-3363

Citizens Legal Protective League
5466 Lake Ave.
Sanford, FL 32771
407-322-7011

Clark Boardman Co.
35 Hudson St.
New York, NY 10014
212-929-7500
800-221-9428

Coca-Cola Co.
Drawer 1734

Atlanta, GA 30301
800-438-2653

Colgate-Palmolive Co.
300 Park Ave.
New York, NY 10022
800-221-4607

Colonial Penn Group, Inc.
1818 Market, 23rd Fl.
Philadelphia, PA 19181
215-988-8000

**[Colorado] Information &
Referral (State Government)**
303-866-5000

**[Colorado] Information Center
(Federal Government)**
Colorado Springs 719-471-9491
Denver 303-844-6575
Pueblo 303-544-9523

**Colorado Accounts & Control
Division**
1525 Sherman St., 7th Fl.
Denver, CO 80203
303-866-3281

**[Colorado] Administration,
Department of**
1525 Sherman St., 7th Fl.
Denver, CO 80203
303-866-3221

**[Colorado] Aging & Adult
Services Division**
1575 Sherman St., 10th Fl.
Denver, CO 80203
303-294-5912

**[Colorado] Agriculture,
Department of**
1525 Sherman St., 14th Fl.
Denver, CO 80203
303-866-2811

**[Colorado] Air Quality
Commission**
4210 E. 11th Ave.
Denver, CO 80220
303-331-8500

**[Colorado] Alcohol & Drug
Abuse Division**
4210 E. 11th Ave.
Denver, CO 80220
303-331-8201

[Colorado] Archives & Public Records Division
1313 Sherman St., Rm. 1-B20
Denver, CO 80203
303-866-2055

[Colorado] Arts & Humanities, Council on the
770 Pennsylvania St.
Denver, CO 80203
303-866-2617

[Colorado] Attorney General, Office of
1525 Sherman St., 3rd Fl.
Denver, CO 80203
303-866-3611

[Colorado] Auditor, Office of State
200 E. 14th Ave.
Denver, CO 80203
303-866-2051

[Colorado] Bank Commissioner
303 W. Colfax Ave., Suite 650
Denver, CO 80204
303-620-4358

Colorado Bar Association
1900 Grant St., #950
Denver, CO 80203
303-860-1112
800-322-6737
303-860-0608 (CLE)

[Colorado] Better Business Bureau
1780 S. Bellaire, Suite 700
Denver, CO 80222
303-758-2100
719-636-1155 (Colorado Springs)
719-484-1348 (Ft. Collins)
303-542-6464 (Pueblo)

[Colorado] Boating Administrator
13787 South Hwy 85
Littleton, CO 80125
303-791-1954

[Colorado] Boulder County
P.O. Box 471
Boulder, CO 80306
303-441-3131

[Colorado] Buildings Division, State
1525 Sherman St.
Denver, CO 80203
303-620-4451

[Colorado] Child Support Enforcement, Division of
1575 Sherman St., Rm. 504
Denver, CO 80203
303-866-5994

[Colorado] Child Welfare Services, Division of
1575 Sherman St., 2nd Fl.
Denver, CO 80203
303-866-5957

[Colorado] Citizens Advocate Office
State Capitol, Rm. 121
Denver, CO 80203
303-866-2885

[Colorado] Civil Rights Division
1525 Sherman St., Rm. 600
Denver, CO 80203
303-866-2621

[Colorado] Colorado Springs, City Attorney's Office
Law Library
30 S. Nevada Ave., Suite 501
Colorado Springs, CO 80903
719-578-6670

[Colorado] Commerce & Development, Division of
1625 Broadway, Suite 1710
Denver, CO 80202
303-892-3840

[Colorado] Commercial Recordings Division
1560 Broadway, Rm. 200
Denver, CO 80202
303-894-2251

[Colorado] Computer Center, General Government
690 Kipling St.
Lakewood, CO 80215
303-239-4313

[Colorado] Consumer Protection Unit
1525 Sherman St., 3rd Fl.
Denver, CO 80203
303-866-5167
303-441-3700 (Boulder)

[Colorado] Corrections, Department of
2862 S. Circle Dr., Suite 400
Colorado Springs, CO 80906
719-579-9580

[Colorado] Court Administrator, Office of the State
1301 Pennsylvania Ave., Rm. 300
Denver, CO 80203
303-866-1111

[Colorado] Court of Appeals
2 E. 14th Ave.
Denver, CO 80203
303-861-1111

[Colorado] Criminal Justice, Division of
700 Kipling St., Suite 3000
Denver, CO 80215
303-239-4442

[Colorado] Data Legal Publishing
P.O. Box 620205
Littleton, CO 80162
303-972-4165

[Colorado] Denver Bar Association
1900 Grant St., Suite 950
Denver, CO 80203
303-860-1112

[Colorado] Denver City Hall
14th & Bannock
Denver, CO 80202
303-575-5555

[Colorado] Denver County
City-County Bldg., Rm. 350
Denver, CO 80202
303-575-2721

[Colorado] Disaster Emergency Services, Division of
Camp George W
Golden, CO 80401
303-273-1624

[Colorado] Education, Commission on Higher
1300 Broadway, 2nd Fl.
Denver, CO 80203
303-866-2723

[Colorado] Education, Department of
201 E. Colfax Ave.

Denver, CO 80203
303-866-6806
303-866-3694 (State Library)

[Colorado] Elections, Division of
1560 Broadway, Suite 200
Denver, CO 80202
303-866-2041

[Colorado] El Paso County
20 E. Vermijo St.
Colorado Springs, CO 80903
719-630-2800

**[Colorado] El Paso County Law
Library**
20 E. Jermijo
104 Judicial Bldg.
Colorado Springs, CO 80903
719-630-2880

**[Colorado] Energy
Conservation, Office of**
112 E. 14th Ave.
Denver, CO 80203
303-894-2144

**[Colorado] Fire Safety,
Director of**
700 Kipling St.
Lakewood, CO 80215
303-239-4463

[Colorado] Forest Service, State
Colorado State University
Ft. Collins, CO 80523
303-491-6303

[Colorado] Governor, Office of
136 State Capitol Bldg.
Denver, CO 80203
303-866-2471

**[Colorado] Hazardous Materials
& Waste Management
Division**
4210 E. 11th Ave.
Denver, CO 80220
303-331-4830

**[Colorado] Health & Statistics
Division**
4210 E. 11th Ave.
Denver, CO 80220
303-331-4902

**[Colorado] Health,
Department of**
4210 E. 11th Ave.

Denver, CO 80220
303-331-4600

**[Colorado] Highways, State
Department of**
4201 E. Arkansas Ave.
Denver, CO 80222
303-757-9011

**[Colorado] House of
Representatives**
State Capitol
Denver, CO 80203
303-866-2904
303-866-2938 (Judiciary)

**[Colorado] Institutions,
Department of**
3520 W. Oxford
Denver, CO 80236
303-762-4410

**[Colorado] Insurance,
Commissioner of**
303 W. Colfax Ave., Suite 500
Denver, CO 80204
303-620-4647

[Colorado] Judicial Department
2 E. 14th Ave.
Denver, CO 80203
303-866-1111

**[Colorado] Juvenile Parole
Board**
4255 S. Knox Court
Denver, CO 80236
303-762-4696

**[Colorado] Labor &
Employment, Department of**
600 Grant St, 9th Fl.
Denver, CO 80203
303-873-3800

[Colorado] Law, Department of
1525 Sherman St., 3rd Fl.
Denver, CO 80203
303-866-5005

**[Colorado] Law Examiners,
Board of**
600 17th St., Suite 520, South
Denver, CO 80202
303-893-8096

Colorado Lawyers for the Arts
P.O. Box 300428

Denver, CO 80203
303-892-7122

**[Colorado] Legal Research
Clearing House, Inc.**
140 19th Ave., Suite 100
Denver, CO 80203
303-839-8104

[Colorado] Legislative Council
200 E. Colfax Ave.
Denver, CO 80203
303-866-3521

**[Colorado] Lieutenant Governor,
Office of**
130 State Capitol Bldg.
Denver, CO 80203
303-866-2088

**[Colorado] Local Affairs,
Department of**
1313 Sherman St.
Denver, CO 80203
303-866-2205

Colorado Lottery
P.O. Box 7
Pueblo, CO 81002
303-546-2400

**[Colorado] Measurement
Standards Section**
3125 Wyandot St.
Denver, CO 80211
303-866-2845

**[Colorado] Mental Health,
Division of**
3520 W. Oxford Ave.
Denver, CO 80236
303-762-4073

[Colorado] Mines, Division of
1313 Sherman St., Rm. 215
Denver, CO 80203
303-866-3401

**[Colorado] Motor Vehicle
Division**
140 W. 6th Ave., Rm. 100
Denver, CO 80204
303-620-4100

**[Colorado] National Indian Law
Library**
1522 Broadway
Boulder, CO 80302
303-447-8760

[Colorado] Natural Resources, Department of
1313 Sherman St., Rm. 718
Denver, CO 80203
303-866-3311

[Colorado] Oil & Gas Conservation Commission
1580 Logan St., Suite 380
Denver, CO 80203
303-894-2100

[Colorado] Parole, State Board of
1580 Lincoln St., Suite 920
Denver, CO 80203
303-894-2465

[Colorado] Personnel, Department of
1313 Sherman St.
Denver, CO 80203
303-866-2321

[Colorado] Pitkin County Law Library
Courthouse
506 E. Main St.
Aspen, CO 81611

[Colorado] Planning & Budgeting, Office of State
111 State Capitol Bldg.
Denver, CO 80203
303-866-3386

[Colorado] Public Defender, State
110 16th St., Suite 800
Denver, CO 80202
303-620-4888

[Colorado] Public Utilities Commission
1580 Logan St.
Denver, CO 80203
303-894-2001
800-888-0170

[Colorado] Purchasing, Division of
303 W. Colfax St.
Denver, CO 80204
303-620-4441

[Colorado] Radiation Control Division
4210 E. 11th Ave.
Denver, CO 80220
303-331-8480

[Colorado] Real Estate Commission
1776 Logan St., 4th Fl.
Denver, CO 80203
303-894-2166

[Colorado] Regulatory Agencies, Department of
1525 Sherman St., Rm. 110
Denver, CO 80203
303-866-3304

[Colorado] Residential Inspection Engineer
Department of Local Affairs
1313 Sherman St.
Denver, CO 80203
303-866-2033

[Colorado] Revenue, Department of
1375 Sherman St.
Denver, CO 80261
303-534-1208

[Colorado] Revisor of Statutes, Office of
State Capitol Bldg., Rm. 079
Denver, CO 80203
303-866-2045

[Colorado] Rocky Mountain Legal Assistants Association
P.O. Box 304
Denver, CO 80201
303-369-1606

[Colorado] Secretary of State
1560 Broadway, Suite 200
Denver, CO 80202
303-894-2200

[Colorado] Securities Commissioner
1560 Broadway, Suite 1450
Denver, CO 80202
303-894-2320

[Colorado] Senate
State Capitol
Denver, CO 80203
303-866-4866
303-866-5500 (Judiciary)

[Colorado] Social Services & Rehabilitation Services, Department of
1575 Sherman St., 4th Fl.

Denver, CO 80203
303-866-2866

[Colorado] State Patrol
700 Kipling St., Suite 3000
Denver, CO 80215
303-239-4403

[Colorado] Supreme Court
2 E. 14th Ave.
Denver, CO 80203
303-861-1111
303-861-1111 x171 (Law Library)

Colorado Tourism Board
1625 Broadway, Suite 1700
Denver, CO 80202
303-592-5510

[Colorado] Treasury, Department of
200 E. Colfax Ave., Rm. 140
Denver, CO 80203
303-866-2442

[Colorado] Unemployment Insurance Division
600 Grant St., 8th Fl.
Denver, CO 80203
303-837-3805

Colorado Uniform Commercial Code Administrator
1525 Sherman St., 3d Fl.
Denver, CO 80203
303-866-5181

[Colorado] United States Bankruptcy Court
400 Columbine Bldg.
1845 Sherman St.
Denver, CO 80203
303-844-4045

[Colorado] United States Court of Appeals for the Tenth Circuit
U.S. Courthouse, C-404
1929 Stout St.
Denver, CO 80294
303-844-3157
303-844-3591 (Law Library)

[Colorado] United States District Court
U.S. Courthouse, C-145
1929 Stout St.
Denver, CO 80294
303-844-3433

[Colorado] United States Government Printing Office
720 N. Main St.
Pueblo, CO 81003
719-544-3142

[Colorado] United States Government Printing Office
1961 Stout St., Rm. 117
Denver, CO 80294
303-844-3964

Colorado, University of
School of Law Library
Boulder, CO 80309
303-492-1233

[Colorado] University of Denver
College of Law Library
1900 Olive St.
Denver, CO 80220
303-871-6188

[Colorado] Water Quality Control Division
4210 E. 11th Ave.
Denver, CO 80220
303-331-4530

[Colorado] Water Resources, Division of
1313 Sherman St., Rm. 818
Denver, CO 80203
303-866-3581

[Colorado] Worker's Compensation
Division of Labor
1313 Sherman St., Rm. 314
Denver, CO 80203
303-866-2782

Commerce Clearing House
4025 W. Peterson Ave.
Chicago, IL 60646
312-583-8500
800-248-3248

Commercial Law League of America
222 W. Adams St., Suite 599
Chicago, IL 60606
312-236-4942

Commission for International Due Process of Law
105 W. Adams St.
Chicago, IL 60603
312-782-1946

Community Dispute Services
140 W. 51st St.
New York, NY 10020
212-484-4000

Compaq Computer Corp.
20555 State Hwy 249
Houston, TX 77070
713-370-0412

Conference on Critical Legal Studies
State University of New York—Buffalo
School of Law
Buffalo, NY 14260
716-636-3035

Congressional Information Service (CIS)
4520 East-West Hwy
Bethesda, MD 20814
301-654-1550

[Connecticut] Information & Referral (State Government)
203-566-2750
800-842-2220

[Connecticut] Information Center (Federal Government)
203-527-2617 (Hartford)
203-624-4720 (New Haven)

[Connecticut] Agriculture Department
165 Capitol Ave.
Hartford, CT 06106
203-566-4667

[Connecticut] Administrative Services, Department of
165 Capitol Ave.
Hartford, CT 06106
203-566-7528

[Connecticut] Adult Probation, Office of
643 Maple Ave.
Hartford, CT 06114
203-566-8350

[Connecticut] Aeronautics, Bureau of
24 Wolcott Hill Rd.
Wethersfield, CT 06109
203-566-4417

[Connecticut] Aging, Department on
175 Main St.
Hartford, CT 06106
203-566-3238
800-443-9946

[Connecticut] Air Compliance Unit
165 Capitol Ave., Rm. 144
Hartford, CT 06106
203-566-4030

[Connecticut] Alcohol & Drug Abuse Commission
999 Asylum Ave.
Hartford, CT 06105
203-566-4145

[Connecticut] Archivist, State
231 Capitol Ave.
Hartford, CT 06106
203-566-3690

[Connecticut] Arts, Commission on the
227 Lawrence St.
Hartford, CT 06106
203-566-4770

Connecticut Association of Paralegals
P.O. Box 862
New Haven, CT 06504

Connecticut Association of Paralegals—Fairfield County
P.O. Box 134
Bridgeport, CT 06601

[Connecticut] Attorney General, Office of
55 Elm St.
Hartford, CT 06114
203-566-2026
203-566-3603 (Law Library)

Connecticut Banking Commissioner
44 Capitol Ave.
Hartford, CT 06106
203-566-4560
800-842-2220

Connecticut Bar Association
101 Corporate Pl.
Rocky Hill, CT 06067
203-721-0025

[Connecticut] Bar Examining Committee
P.O. Box 6430
Station A
Hartford, CT 06106
203-566-3770

[Connecticut] Better Business Bureau
2345 Black Rock Turnpike
Fairfield, CT 06430
203-374-6161
203-529-3575 (Rocky Hill)
203-269-2700 (Wallingford)

[Connecticut] Boating Administrator
333 Ferry Rd.
Old Lyme, CT 06371
203-434-9840

[Connecticut] Budget & Finance Division
80 Washington St.
Hartford, CT 06106
203-566-5086

[Connecticut] Building Inspector, State
Department of Public Safety
294 Colony St.
Meriden, CT 06450
203-238-0611

[Connecticut] Central Connecticut Association of Legal Assistants
P.O. Box 3954
Hartford, CT 06103

[Connecticut] Children & Youth Services, Department of
170 Sigourney St.
Hartford, CT 06106
203-566-3536

[Connecticut] Child Support Enforcement, Bureau of
1049 Asylum Ave.
Hartford, CT 06105
203-566-3053

[Connecticut] Comptroller, Office of State
55 Elm St.
Hartford, CT 06106
203-566-5565

[Connecticut] Consumer Protection, Department of
165 Capitol Ave.
Hartford,CT 06106
203-566-4999
800-842-2649

[Connecticut] Correction, Department of
340 Capitol Ave.
Hartford, CT 06106
203-566-4457

[Connecticut] Court Administrator, Office of Chief
231 Capitol Ave.
Hartford, CT 06106
203-566-4461

[Connecticut] Criminal Injury Compensation
1155 Silas Deane Hwy
Wethersfield, CT 06109
203-529-3089

[Connecticut] Economic Development, Department of
210 Washington St.
Hartford, CT 06106
203-566-3787

[Connecticut] Education, Department of
165 Capitol Ave.
Hartford, CT 06106
203-566-5061

[Connecticut] Education, Department of Higher
61 Woodland St.
Hartford, CT 06105
203-566-3913

[Connecticut] Elections Division
30 Trinity St.
Hartford, CT 06106
203-566-3106

[Connecticut] Emergency Management, Office of
360 Broad St.
Hartford, CT 06105
203-566-3180

[Connecticut] Employment Security Division
200 Folly Brook Blvd.
Wethersfield, CT 06109
203-566-4280

[Connecticut] Energy Division
80 Washington St.
Hartford, CT 06106
203-566-2800

[Connecticut] Environmental Protection, Department of
165 Capitol Ave.
Hartford, CT 06106
203-566-2110

[Connecticut] Ethics Commission, State
97 Elm St.
Hartford, CT 06106
203-566-4472

[Connecticut] Fairfield Judicial District
1061 Main St.
Hartford, CT 06604
203-579-6527

[Connecticut] Fire Marshall, Bureau of State
294 Colony St.
Meriden, CT 06450
203-238-6623

[Connecticut] Governor, Office of
210 Capitol Ave.
Hartford, CT 06106
203-566-4840

[Connecticut] Hartford Judicial District
95 Washington St.
Hartford, CT 06106
203-566-3170

[Connecticut] Health Services, Department of
150 Washington St.
Hartford, CT 06106
203-566-2038

[Connecticut] Highways, Bureau of
24 Wolcott Hill Rd.
Wethersfield, CT 06109
203-566-3854

[Connecticut] Housing, Department of
1179 Main St.
Hartford, CT 06103
203-566-8208

[Connecticut] House of Representatives
State Capitol
Hartford, CT 06114
203-566-4544
203-240-0530 (Judiciary)

[Connecticut] Human Resources, Department of
1049 Asylum Ave.
Hartford, CT 06105
203-566-4329

[Connecticut] Human Rights & Opportunities, Commission on
90 Washington St.
Hartford, CT 06106
203-566-4895

[Connecticut] Income Maintenance, Department of
110 Batholomew Ave.
Hartford, CT 06106
203-566-2008
800-842-1508

[Connecticut] Information Systems & Data Processing
340 Capitol Ave., 1st Fl.
Hartford, CT 06106
203-566-7093

[Connecticut] Insurance Commissioner
165 Capitol Ave., Rm. 425
Hartford, CT 06106
203-297-3800

[Connecticut] Justice Planning Division
80 Washington St.
Hartford, CT 06106
203-566-3020

[Connecticut] Juvenile Matters, Superior Court
28 Grand St.
Hartford, CT 06106
203-566-7971

[Connecticut] Labor, Department of
200 Folly Brook Blvd.
Wethersfield, CT 06109
203-566-4384

[Connecticut] Law Revision Commission
State Capitol, Rm. 509A
Hartford, CT 06106
203-240-0220

Connecticut, Legal Assistants of Southeastern
P.O. Box 409
New London, CT 06320

[Connecticut] Legislative Commissioners' Office
Legislative Office Bldg., Rm. 5500
Hartford, CT 06106
203-240-8410

[Connecticut] Legislative Library
Legislative Office Bldg., Rm. 5400
Hartford, CT 06106
203-240-8888

[Connecticut] Library, State
231 Capitol Ave.
Hartford, CT 06106
203-566-4301
203-566-7850 (Law Library)

[Connecticut] Licensing & Administration Division
165 Capitol Ave.
Hartford, CT 06106
203-566-7177

[Connecticut] Lieutenant Governor, Office of
210 Capitol Ave.
Hartford, CT 06106
203-566-2614

[Connecticut] Litchfield Judicial District
West St.
Litchfield, CT 06759
203-567-0885

[Connecticut] Lottery, State
P.O. Box 11424
Newington, CT 06111
203-566-2912

[Connecticut] Mental Health, Department of
90 Washington St.
Hartford, CT 06106
203-566-3650

[Connecticut] Mental Retardation, Department of
90 Pitkin St.
East Hartford, CT 06108
203-528-7141

[Connecticut] Middlesex Judicial District
265 DeKoven Dr.
Middletown, CT 06457
203-344-2966

[Connecticut] Motor Vehicles, Department of
60 State St.
Wethersfield, CT 06109
203-566-2240

[Connecticut] Natural Resources Center
165 Capitol Ave.
Hartford, CT 06106
203-566-3540

[Connecticut] New Haven, Association of Paralegals
P.O. Box 862
New Haven, CT 06504

[Connecticut] New Haven Judicial District
235 Church St.
New Haven, CT 06510
203-789-7883

[Connecticut] Occupational Safety & Health, Division of
200 Folly Brook Blvd.
Wethersfield, CT 06109
203-566-4550

[Connecticut] Parole, Division of
340 Capitol Ave.
Hartford, CT 06106
203-566-5203

[Connecticut] Personnel Division
165 Capitol Ave.
Hartford, CT 06106
203-566-3081

[Connecticut] Public Defender, Office of Chief
1 Hartford Sq. West
Hartford, CT 06106
205-566-5328

[Connecticut] Public Utility Control, Department of
1 Central Park Plaza
New Britain, CT 06051
203-827-1553
800-382-4586

[Connecticut] Public Works, Bureau of
165 Capitol Ave.
Hartford, CT 06106
203-566-3360

[Connecticut] Real Estate Commission
165 Capitol Ave.
Hartford, CT 06106
203-566-5131

[Connecticut] Rehabilitation Services
600 Asylum Ave.
Hartford, CT 06105
203-566-7153

[Connecticut] Revenue Services, Department of
92 Farmingham Ave.
Hartford, CT 06105
203-566-8520

[Connecticut] Secretary of State
State Capitol Bldg.
Hartford, CT 06106
203-566-2739
203-566-2446 (Corporations, UCC)

[Connecticut] Securities/Business Investments Division
44 Capitol Ave.
Hartford, CT 06106
203-566-4560

[Connecticut] Senate
State Capitol
Hartford, CT 06114
203-566-4544
203-240-0530 (Judiciary)

[Connecticut] Solid Waste Management Bureau
122 Washington St.
Hartford, CT 06106
203-566-3672

Connecticut State Law Library—Bridgeport
1061 Main St.

Bridgeport, CT 06604
203-579-6237

Connecticut State Law Library—Danbury
146 White St., Court House
Danbury, CT 06810
203-685-5885

Connecticut State Law Library—Hartford
95 Washington St.
Hartford, CT 06106
203-566-3900

Connecticut State Law Library—Litchfield
West St., Court House
Litchfield, CT 06759
203-567-0598

Connecticut State Law Library—Middletown
DeKoven Dr., Court House
Middletown, CT 06457
203-344-2955

Connecticut State Law Library—New Haven
235 Church St.
New Haven, CT 06510
203-789-7889

Connecticut State Law Library—New London
70 Huntington St.
New London, CT 06320
203-442-7561

Connecticut State Law Library—Norwich
1 Courthouse Sq.
Norwich, CT 06360
203-887-2398

Connecticut State Law Library—Putnam
155 Church St.
Putnam, CT 06260
203-928-3716

Connecticut State Law Library—Rockville
Brooklyn St., Court House
Rockville, CT 06066
203-872-3824

Connecticut State Law Library—Stamford

123 Hoyt St.
Stamford, CT 06905
203-359-1114

Connecticut State Law Library—Waterbury
300 Grand St.
Waterbury, CT 06722
203-754-2644

Connecticut State Law Library—Williamantic
108 Valley St.
Willimantic, CT 06226

[Connecticut] State Police, Division of
100 Washington St.
Hartford, CT 06106
203-566-3200

[Connecticut] Supreme Court
231 Capitol Ave.
Hartford, CT 06106
203-566-8160

[Connecticut] Tolland Judicial District
69 Brooklyn St.
Rockville, CT 06066
203-875-6294

[Connecticut] Tourism Division
210 Washington St.
Hartford, CT 06106
203-566-2496

[Connecticut] Transportation, Department of
24 Wolcott Hill Rd.
Wethersfield, CT 06109
203-566-3477

[Connecticut] Treasurer, Office of
20 Trinity St.
Hartford, CT 06106
203-566-5050

[Connecticut] Unemployment Compensation Division
2000 Folly Brook Blvd.
Wethersfield, CT 06109
203-566-4288

[Connecticut] Uniform Commercial Code Division
30 Trinity St.
Hartford, CT 06106
203-660-8888

[Connecticut] United States Bankruptcy Court
450 Main St.
Hartford, CT 06103
203-240-3675

[Connecticut] United States District Court
141 Church St.
New Haven, CT 06510
203-773-2140

Connecticut, University of
School of Law Library
120 Sherman St.
Hartford, CT 06105
203-241-4636

[Connecticut] University of Bridgeport
School of Law Library
Washington Bldg.
Bridgeport, CT 06601
203-576-4056

[Connecticut] Vital Records
Division of Health Statistics
150 Washington St.
Hartford, CT 06106
203-566-1124

Connecticut Washington Office
444 N. Capitol St., Suite 317
Wash. D.C. 20001
202-347-4535

[Connecticut] Water Resources Unit
165 Capitol Ave.
Hartford, CT 06106
203-566-7220

[Connecticut] Weights & Measures Division
165 Capitol Ave.
Hartford, CT 06106
203-566-5230

[Connecticut] Windham Judicial District
155 Church St.
Putnam, CT 06260
203-928-7749

[Connecticut] Women, Commission on the Status of
90 Washington St.

Hartford, CT 06106
203-566-5702

[Connecticut] Worker's Compensation Commission
1890 Dixwell Ave.
Hamden, CT 06514
203-789-7783
800-223-9675

[Connecticut] Yale University
School of Law Library
127 Wall St.
New Haven, CT 06520
203-432-1608

Control Data Corp.
8100 34th Ave. South
Minneapolis, MN 55425
612-853-3400
800-232-1985

Continental Banks, N.A.
231 LaSalle St.
Chicago, IL 60697
312-828-5795

Copyright Clearance Center
21 Congress St.
Salem, MA 01970
508-744-3350

Copyright Society of the USA
New York University School of Law
40 Washington Sq. S.
New York, NY 10012
212-998-6194

Correctional Industries Information Clearinghouse
8025 Laurel Lakes Court
Laurel, MD 20207
301-206-5100

Council of Better Business Bureaus, Inc.
4200 Wilson Blvd.
Arlington, VA 22203
703-276-0100

Council for Court Excellence
1025 Vermont Ave., NW, Suite 510
Wash. D.C. 20005
202-783-7736

Council of National Library & Information Associations
461 W. Lancaster Ave.

Haverford, PA 19041
215-649-5251

Council of State Governments
P.O. Box 11910
Lexington, KY 40578
606-252-2291
212-693-0400 (New York)
708-810-0210 (Illinois)
404-266-1271 (Georgia)
415-974-6422 (California)
202-624-5460 (Wash. D.C.)

Council on Legal Education Opportunity
1800 M. St., NW, Suite 290
Wash. D.C. 20036
202-785-4840

Council on Ocean Law
1717 Massachusetts Ave., NW, Suite 302
Wash. D.C. 20036
202-462-3737

Council on Religion & Law
512 Edgewood Pl.
Ithaca, NY 14850
607-273-5928

CT Corp
2 Peachtree St., NW
Atlanta, GA 30383
800-241-5824

Decalogue Society of Lawyers
179 W. Washington St., Suite 350
Chicago, IL 60602
312-263-6493

[Delaware] Information & Referral (State Government)
302-736-4000
800-222-3383

[Delaware] Administrative Services, Department of
Townsend Bldg.

Lockerman & Federal Streets
Dover, DE 19903
302-736-3611

**[Delaware] Aeronautics
Administration**
Department of Transportation
Dover, DE 19901
302-736-3264

[Delaware] Aging, Division of
1901 N. DuPont Hwy.
New Castle, DE 19720
302-421-6791
800-223-9074

**[Delaware] Agriculture,
Department of**
2320 DuPont Hwy
Dover, DE 19901
302-736-4811

**[Delaware] Alcohol Beverage
Control**
820 N. Carvel St.
Wilmington, DE 19801
302-571-3200

**[Delaware] Alcoholism, Drug
Abuse & Mental Health,
Division of**
1901 N. DuPont Hwy
New Castle, DE 19720
302-421-6107

**[Delaware] Archives & Records
Management Bureau**
Hall of Records
Dover, DE 19901
302-736-5318

[Delaware] Arts Council, State
820 N. French St.
Dover, DE 19901
302-571-3540

**[Delaware] Attorney General,
Office of**
820 N. French St., 8th Fl.
Wilmington, DE 19801
302-571-3838

**[Delaware] Auditor of Accounts,
Office of**
P.O. Box 1401
Dover, DE 19903
302-736-4241

**[Delaware] Bank Commissioner,
State**
555 E. Lockerman St., Suite 210
Dover, DE 19901
302-736-4235

Delaware Bar Association
706 Market St. Mall
Wilmington, DE 19801
302-658-5278

**[Delaware] Bar Examiners,
Board of**
P.O. Box 8965
Wilmington, DE 19899
302-888-6800

**Delaware Better Business
Bureau**
P.O. Box 5361
Wilmington, DE 19808
302-966-9200
302-422-6300 (Kent)
302-856-6969 (Sussex)

**[Delaware] Boating Law
Administrator**
P.O. Box 1401
Dover, DE 19903
302-736-3440

**[Delaware] Budget Office, Office
of the**
P.O. Box 1401
Dover, DE 19903
302-736-4204

**[Delaware] Business &
Occupational Regulation
Division**
P.O. Box 1401
Dover, DE 19903
302-736-4522

**[Delaware] Child Protective
Services, Division of**
330 E. 30th St.
Wilmington, DE 19802
302-571-6410

**[Delaware] Child Support
Enforcement, Division of**
P.O. Box 904
New Castle, DE 19720
302-421-8300

[Delaware] Code Revisor
P.O. Box 951

Wilmington, DE 19899
302-658-6771

**[Delaware] Commerce
Department**
800 N. French St., 9th Fl.
Wilmington, DE 19801
302-571-4169

**[Delaware] Community Affairs,
Department of**
P.O. Box 1401
Dover, DE 19903
302-736-4456

**[Delaware] Community
Corrections, Division of**
38 Todd's Lane
Wilmington, DE 19802
302-571-3039

[Delaware] Comptroller General
P.O. Box 1401
Dover, DE 19903
302-736-4131

**[Delaware] Consumer Affairs,
Division of**
820 N. French St., 4th Fl.
Wilmington, DE 19801
302-571-3250
302-571-3849 (Office of Attorney
General)

**[Delaware] Correction,
Department of**
80 Monrovia Ave.
Smyrna, DE 19977
302-736-5601

**[Delaware] Courts,
Administrative Office of the**
820 N. French St.
Wilmington, DE 19801
302-571-2480

**[Delaware] Criminal Justice
Council**
820 N. French St.
Wilmington, DE 19801
302-571-3420

[Delaware] Development Office
99 Kings Hwy
Dove, DE 19901
302-736-4271
800-441-8846

[Delaware] EEO/AA Program
State Personnel Office
Townsend Bldg.
Dover, DE 19901
302-571-3950

[Delaware] Election Commissioner, State
P.O. Box 1401
Dover, DE 19901
302-736-4277

[Delaware] Employment & Training, Division of
P.O. Box 9499
Newark, DE 19714
302-368-6810

[Delaware] Finance, Department of
540 S. DuPont Hwy
Dover, DE 19901
302-736-4393

[Delaware] Fish & Wildlife, Division of
P.O. Box 1401
Dover, DE 19903
302-736-5295

[Delaware] Governor, Office of the
Legislative Hall
Dover, DE 19901
302-736-4101

[Delaware] Highways, Division of
Route 113
Dover, DE 19903
302-736-4301

[Delaware] House of Representatives
Legislative Hall
Dover, DE 19901
302-736-4351
302-736-4161 (Judiciary)

[Delaware] Housing Authority, State
P.O. Box 1401
Dover, DE 19903
302-736-4263

[Delaware] Human Relations, Division of
820 N. French St.

Wilmington, DE 19801
302-571-3716

[Delaware] Industrial Affairs, Division of
820 N. French St.
Wilmington, DE 19801
302-571-2877
302-571-3594 (Industrial Accident Board)

[Delaware] Information Systems, Office of
801 Silver Lake Blvd.
Dover, DE 19901
302-736-9628

[Delaware] Insurance Commissioner
841 Silver Lake Blvd.
Dover, DE 19901
302-736-4251
800-282-8611

[Delaware] Justice, Department of
820 N. French St., 8th Fl.
Wilmington, DE 19801
302-571-3838

[Delaware] Kent County
141 Federal St.
Dover, DE 19901
302-736-2040

[Delaware] Labor, Department of
820 N. French St., 6th Fl.
Wilmington, DE 19801
302-571-2710

Delaware Legislative Council
P.O. Box 1401
Dover, DE 19901
302-736-4414

[Delaware] Libraries, Division of
43 S. DuPont Hwy
Dover, DE 19901
302-736-4748
800-282-8696

[Delaware] Lieutenant Governor, Office of the
Legislative Hall
Dover, DE 19901
302-736-4151

[Delaware] Lottery, State
Blue Hen Mall, Suite 202
Dover, DE 19901
302-736-5291

[Delaware] Mental Retardation, Division of
802 Silverlake Rd.
Dover, DE 19901
302-736-4386

[Delaware] Motor Vehicles, Division of
P.O. Box 698
Dover, DE 19903
302-736-4421

[Delaware] Natural Resources & Environmental Control, Department of
89 Kings Hwy
Dover, DE 19901
302-736-4403

[Delaware] New Castle County
800 French St.
Wilmington, DE 19801
302-571-4011

[Delaware] New Castle County Law Library
Public Bldg.
Wilmington, DE 19801
302-571-2437

[Delaware] Occupational Safety & Health
820 N. French St.
Wilmington, DE 19801
302-571-3908

Delaware Paralegal Association
P.O. Box 1362
Wilmington, DE 19899

[Delaware] Parole, Board of
820 N. French St.
Wilmington, DE 19801
302-571-3452

[Delaware] Pensions, Office of
540 S. DuPont Hwy
Dover, DE 19901
302-736-4208

[Delaware] Personnel Office, State
Loockerman & Federal Streets

Dover, DE 19901
302-736-4195

**[Delaware] Planning &
Operations, Division of**
Governor Bacon Health Center
Delaware City, DE 19706
302-834-4531

**[Delaware] Police, Division of
State**
P.O. Box 430
Dover, DE 19903
302-736-5911

**[Delaware] Public Defender,
Office of**
820 N. French St.
Wilmington, DE 19801
302-571-3230

**[Delaware] Public Health,
Division of**
802 Silverlake Blvd.
Dover, DE 19901
302-736-4701

**[Delaware] Public Instruction,
Department of**
P.O. Box 1402
Dover, DE 19903
302-736-4601

**[Delaware] Public Service
Commission**
1560 S. DuPont Hwy
Dover, DE 19903
302-736-4247
800-282-8574

**[Delaware] Public Utilities
Control, Division of**
P.O. Box 457
Dover, DE 19903
302-736-4247

**[Delaware] Purchasing,
Division of**
P.O. Box 299
Delaware City, DE 19706
302-834-7081

**[Delaware] Real Estate
Commission**
P.O. Box 1401
Dover, DE 19903
302-736-4522

[Delaware] Revenue, Division of
820 N. French St.
Wilmington, DE 19801
302-736-5251

**[Delaware] Securities
Commissioner**
820 N. French St., 8th Fl.
Wilmington, DE 19801
302-571-2515

[Delaware] Senate
Legislative Hall
Dover, DE 19901
302-736-4129
302-736-4163 (Judiciary)

**[Delaware] Soil & Water
Conservation, Division of**
P.O. Box 1401
Dover, DE 19903
302-736-4411

**[Delaware] Solid Waste
Management**
89 Kings Hwy
Dover, DE 19901
302-736-4781

**[Delaware] Standards &
Inspection, Division of**
Department of Agriculture
2320 S. DuPont Hwy
Dover, DE 19901
302-736-4811

[Delaware] State, Department of
Townsend Bldg.
Dover, DE 19901
302-736-4111
302-736-3073 (Corporate Records)

[Delaware] Supreme Court
820 N. French St.
Wilmington, DE 19801
302-571-2427
302-736-4155 (Clerk)

[Delaware] Sussex County
P.O. Box 609
Georgetown, DE 19947
302-856-5601

**[Delaware] Sussex County Law
Library**
Courthouse, Box 390
Georgetown, DE 19947
302-856-5483

Delaware Tourism Office
P.O. Box 1401
Dover, DE 19903
302-736-4271

**[Delaware] Transportation,
Department of**
P.O. Box 778
Dover, DE 19903
302-736-4303

**[Delaware] Treasurer, Office of
State**
Route 13 Thomas Collins Bldg.
Dover, DE 19901
302-736-3382

**[Delaware] Unemployment
Insurance Division**
Route 273 & Chapman Rd.
Newark, DE 19711
302-368-6730

**[Delaware] United States
Bankruptcy Court**
844 King St.
Lockbox 38
Wilmington, DE 19801
302-573-6174

**[Delaware] United States District
Court**
844 King St.
Lockbox 18
Wilmington, DE 19801
302-573-6170
302-573-6178 (Law Library)

**[Delaware] Veterans Affairs,
Commission of**
P.O. Box 1401
Dover, DE 19903
302-736-2792

**[Delaware] Violent Crime
Compensation Board**
1500 E. Newport Pike, Suite 10
Wilmington, DE 19802
302-995-8383

**[Delaware] Visually Impaired,
Division for the**
305 W. 8th St.
Wilmington, DE 19801
302-571-3570

[Delaware] Vital Statistics, Office of
P.O. Box 637
Dover, DE 19903
302-736-4721

[Delaware] Vocational Rehabilitation, Division of
321 E. 11th St.
Wilmington, DE 19801
302-571-2851

Delaware Washington Office
444 N. Capitol St., Suite 378
Wash. D.C. 20001
202-624-7724

[Delaware] Water Resources, Division of
P.O. Box 1401
Dover, DE 19903
302-736-4860

[Delaware] Weights & Measures, Office of
2320 S. DuPont Hwy
Dover, DE 19903
302-736-4811

[Delaware] Widener University
School of Law Library
P.O. Box 7475
401 Concord Pike
Wilmington, DE 19803
302-478-5280

[Delaware] Women, Commission for
820 N. French St.
Wilmington, DE 19801
302-571-2660

[Delaware] Youth Rehabilitation Services, Division of
Centre & Faulkland Roads
Wilmington, DE 19805
302-995-8334

Del Monte Corp.
P.O. Box 3575
San Francisco, CA 94119
415-442-4804
800-543-3090

Digital Equipment Corp.
40 Old Bolton Rd.
Stow, MA 01777

508-493-7161
800-332-4636

Diners Club International
183 Inverness Dr. West
Englewood, CO 80112
303-790-2433
800-525-9135

Direct Marketing Association
6 E. 43rd St.
New York, NY 10017
212-689-4977

Direct Selling Association
1776 K. St., NW, Suite 600
Wash. D.C. 20006
202-293-5760

[District of Columbia] Information & Referral (City Government)
202-727-1000

[District of Columbia] Aging, Office on
1424 K. St., NW, 2nd Fl.
Wash. D.C. 20005
202-724-5623

[District of Columbia] American Civil Liberties Union
1400 20th St., NW, Rm. 119
Wash. D.C. 20036
202-457-0800

[District of Columbia] American University
Washington College of Law Library
4400 Massachusetts Ave., NW
Wash. D.C. 20016
202-885-2626

District of Columbia Archives
Office of Public Records
  Management
515 D. St., NW, Rm. 307
Wash. D.C. 20001
202-727-2052

[District of Columbia] Banking & Financial Institutions, Superintendent of
1250 I. St., NW, Suite 1000
Wash. D.C. 20005
202-727-1563

District of Columbia Bar
1707 L. St., NW, 6th Fl.
Wash. D.C. 20036
202-331-3883

District of Columbia, Bar Association of the
1819 H. St., NW, 12th Fl.
Wash. D.C. 20006
202-223-1480

[District of Columbia] Bar Association, Washington
P.O. Box 605
Wash. D.C. 20044
202-887-1990

[District of Columbia] Better Business Bureau
1012 14th St., NW
Wash. D.C. 20005
202-393-8000

[District of Columbia] Budget, Office of the
1350 Pennsylvania Ave., NW,
  Rm. 427
Wash. D.C. 20004
202-727-6343

[District of Columbia] Catholic University of America
Columbus School of Law Library
620 Michigan Ave., NE
Wash. D.C. 20064
202-635-5155

District of Columbia Circuit, United States Court of Appeals
3rd & Constitution Ave., NW
Wash. D.C. 20001
202-535-3308
202-535-3400 (Law Library)

[District of Columbia] City Administrator
1350 Pennsylvania Ave., NW,
  Rm. 507
Wash. D.C. 20004
202-727-6053

[District of Columbia] Codification Counsel
1350 Pennsylvania Ave., NW
Wash. D.C. 20004
202-724-8093

[District of Columbia] Consumer & Regulatory Affairs, Department of
614 H. St., NW
Wash. D.C. 20001
202-727-7000

[District of Columbia] Corporation Counsel
1350 Pennsylvania Ave., NW
Wash. D.C. 20004
202-727-6248

[District of Columbia] Corporations Division
614 H. St., NW, Rm. 407
Wash. D.C. 20001
202-727-7278

[District of Columbia] Corrections, Department of
1923 Vermont Ave., NW
Wash. D.C. 20001
202-673-7316

[District of Columbia] Council of Lawyers, Washington
1200 New Hampshire Ave., NW, Suite 700
Wash. D.C. 20036
202-659-5964

District of Columbia, Council of the
1350 Pennsylvania Ave., NW
Wash. D.C. 20004
202-724-8000
202-724-8062 (Judiciary)

District of Columbia Court of Appeals
500 Indiana Ave., NW
Wash. D.C. 20001
202-879-2700
202-879-2725 (Clerk)
202-879-2767 (Law Library)
202-879-2710 (Committee on Admissions)

District of Columbia Courts
Administrative Office
500 Indiana Ave., NW
Wash. D.C. 20001
202-879-1700

[District of Columbia] Elections & Ethics, Board of
1350 Pennsylvania Ave., NW
Wash. D.C. 20004
202-727-2525

[District of Columbia] Family Services Administration
1st & I. St., SW
Wash. D.C. 20024
202-727-5947

District of Columbia] Finance & Revenue, Department of
300 Indiana Ave., NW
Wash. D.C. 20001
202-727-6020

[District of Columbia] Georgetown University
Law Library
111 G. St., NW
Wash. D.C. 20001
202-662-9131

[District of Columbia] George Washington University
Jacob Burns Law Library
716 20th St., NW
Wash. D.C. 20052
202-994-7336

[District of Columbia] Housing & Community Development, Department of
1133 N. Capitol St., NE, Suite 217
Wash. D.C. 20002
202-535-1500

[District of Columbia] Howard University
School of Law Library
2935 Van Ness St., NW
Wash. D.C. 20008
202-686-6684

[District of Columbia] Human Rights, Office of
2000 14th St., NW, 3rd Fl.
Wash. D.C. 20009
202-939-8780

[District of Columbia] Human Services, Department of
801 N. Capitol St., NE
Wash. D.C. 20002
202-727-0310

[District of Columbia] Information Resources Management
613 G. St., NW, Rm. 803
Wash. D.C. 20001
202-727-2277

[District of Columbia] Inspector General, Office of
415 12th St., NW
Wash. D.C. 20004
202-727-2540

[District of Columbia] Insurance, Superintendent of
614 G. St., NW, Suite 516
Wash. D.C. 20001
202-727-7424

[District of Columbia] Intergovernmental Relations, Office of
1350 Pennsylvania Ave., NW
Wash. D.C. 20004
202-727-6265

District of Columbia Lottery Board
2101 Marin Luther King, Jr. Ave., SE
Wash. D.C. 20020
202-433-8011

[District of Columbia] Mayor, Office of the
1350 Pennsylvania Ave., NW
Wash. D.C. 20004
202-727-6319

[District of Columbia] Metropolitan Police Department
300 Indiana Ave., NW, Rm. 5080
Wash. D.C. 20001
202-727-4218

[District of Columbia] Motor Vehicle Services
301 C. St., NW
Wash. D.C. 20001
202-727-7360

[District of Columbia] Occupational & Health Office
950 Upshur St., NW
Wash. D.C. 20011
202-576-6339

[District of Columbia] Occupational & Professional Licensing Administration
614 H. St., NW, Rm. 93
Wash. D.C. 20001
202-727-7480

[District of Columbia] Paralegal Association, National Capital Area
P.O. Box 65152
Wash. D.C. 20035
202-659-0243

[District of Columbia] Parole, Board of
1111 E. St., NW, Rm. 600
Wash. D.C. 20004
202-727-2264

[District of Columbia] Paternity & Child Support Enforcement
425 I. St., Suite 3013
Wash. D.C. 20001
202-724-5610

[District of Columbia] Personnel, Office of
613 G. St., NW
Wash. D.C. 20001
202-727-6406

[District of Columbia] Public Defender Service
451 Indiana Ave., NW
Wash. D.C. 20001
202-628-1200

[District of Columbia] Public Health Commission
1875 Connecticut Ave., NW
Wash. D.C. 20009
202-673-7700

[District of Columbia] Public Service Commission
450 5th St., NW
Wash. D.C. 20001
202-626-5110

District of Columbia Rehabilitation Services
605 G. St., NW, Rm. 1111
Wash. D.C. 20001
202-727-3227

[District of Columbia] Securities, Director of
450 5th St., NW, Suite 820
Wash. D.C. 20001
202-626-5105

District of Columbia, Superior Court of the
500 Indiana Ave., NW
Wash. D.C. 20001
202-879-1600
202-879-1435 (Law Library)

[District of Columbia] Treasurer, Office of the
300 Indiana Ave., NW, Rm. 1132
Wash. D.C. 20001
202-727-6055

[District of Columbia] Unemployment Compensation Office
500 C. St., NW, Rm. 515
Wash. D.C. 20001
202-639-1163

[District of Columbia] United States Attorney
Law Library
555 4th St., NW
Wash. D.C. 20001
202-272-9112

[District of Columbia] United States Bankruptcy Court
3rd & Constitution Ave., NW
Wash. D.C. 20001
202-535-3042

District of Columbia, United States District Court
3rd & Constitution Ave., NW
Wash. D.C. 20001
202-535-3594

[District of Columbia] United States Government Printing Office
1510 H. St., NW
Wash. D.C. 20005
202-653-5075
202-275-2091 (701 N. Capitol)

[District of Columbia] Vital Records Branch
425 I. St., NW
Wash. D.C. 20001
202-727-5319

[District of Columbia] Washington Document Service, Inc.
450 5th St., NW, Suite 1110
Wash. D.C. 20001
800-247-8774

[District of Columbia] Washington Service Bureau
655 15th St., NW
Wash. D.C. 20005
202-833-9200
800-828-5354

[District of Columbia] Weights & Measures
1110 U. St., SE
Wash. D.C. 20020
202-767-7923

[District of Columbia] Worker's Compensation Office
1200 Upshur St., NW, 3rd Fl.
Wash. D.C. 20011
202-576-6265

Eastern Mineral Law Foundation
P.O. Box 6130
Morgantown, WV 26506
304-293-2470

Eastman Kodak Co.
343 State St.
Rochester, NY 14650
800-242-2424

Edison Electric Institute
1111 19th St., NW
Wash. D.C. 20036
202-778-6560

E.I. duPont de Nemours & Co.
1007 Market St.
Wilmington, DE 19898
800-441-7515

**Electronic Industries
    Association**
Consumer Electronics Group
2001 I. St., NW
Wash. D.C. 20006
202-457-4977

Eli Lilly & Co.
Lilly Corporate Center
Indianapolis, IN 46285
317-276-2339

Emery Worldwide
Old Danbury Rd.
Wilton, CT 06897
203-762-8601

Environmental Law Institute
1616 P. St., NW, Suite 200
Wash. D.C. 20036
202-328-5150
202-387-3500 (Defense Fund)

Equal Rights Advocates
1370 Mission St.
San Francisco, CA 94103
415-621-0505

Equitable Life Assurance Society
787 7th Ave.
New York, NY 10019
212-554-1234

Exxon Co. U.S.A.
P.O. Box 2180
Houston, TX 77252
713-656-3151

Federal Bar Association
1815 H. St., Suite 408
Wash. D.C. 20006
202-638-0252
202-638-1956 (Law Library)

**Federal Communications Bar
    Association**
P.O. Box 34434
Bethesda, MD 20817
301-299-7299

**Federal Criminal Investigators
    Association**
P.O. Box 1256
Detroit, MI 48231
512-229-5610

Federal Energy Bar Association
1900 M. St., NW, Suite 620
Wash. D.C. 20036
202-223-5625

Federal Express Corp.
P.O. Box 727
Memphis, TN 38194
901-395-3846
800-238-5355

Federal Government
See United States and entries under
    individual states.

**Federal Information Center
    (Federal Government)**
See entries under individual states.

**Federalist Society for Law &
    Public Policy Studies**
1625 I. St., NW
Wash. D.C. 20006
202-822-8138

**Federal Law Enforcement
    Officers Association**
106 Cedarhurst Ave.
Selden, NY 11784
516-698-0179

Federal Managers Association
1000 16th St., Suite 701
Wash. D.C. 20036
202-778-1500

**Federal National Mortgage
    Association**
3900 Wisconsin Ave., NW
Wash. D.C. 20016
202-752-7000
202-752-7175 (Law Library)

Federal Publications, Inc.
120 20th St. NW
Wash. D.C. 20036
202-337-7000

**Federation of Insurance &
    Corporate Counsel**
15 Ridge Rd.
Marblehead, MA 01945
617-639-0698

**Federation of Tax
    Administrators**
444 N. Capitol St.
Wash. D.C. 20001
202-624-5890

Fidelity Bank, N.A.
100 Constitution Dr.
Upper Darby, PA 19082
215-734-5090

First National Supermarkets, Inc.
17000 Rockside Rd.
Cleveland, OH 44137
216-587-7100

First Nationwide Bank
700 Market St.
San Francisco, CA 94102
800-237-0756

First Union Bank
P.O. Box 2870
Jacksonville, FL 32231
904-361-2265
800-433-4195

**[Florida] Information & Referral
    (State Government)**
904-488-1234

**[Florida] Information Center
    (Federal Government)**
Ft. Lauderdale 305-522-8531
Jacksonville 904-354-4756
Miami 305-536-4155
Orlando 407-422-1800
St. Petersburg 813-893-3495
Tampa 813-229-7911
West Palm Beach 407-833-7566

[Florida] Aging & Adult Services
1321 Winewood Blvd., Rm. 323
Tallahassee, FL 32399
904-488-2650

**[Florida] Agriculture &
    Consumer Services,
    Department of**
407 S. Calhoun St.
Tallahassee, FL 32399
904-488-3022
800-342-3581
305-377-5619 (Miami)

**[Florida] Air Resources
    Management, Bureau of**
2600 Blair Stone Rd.

Tallahassee, FL 32399
904-488-1344

[Florida] Athletic Commission
725 S. Bronough St.
Tallahassee, FL 32399
904-488-8448

**[Florida] Attorney General,
Office of**
Capitol Bldg.
Tallahassee, FL 32399
904-487-1963

**[Florida] Auditor General, Office
of the**
P.O. Box 1735
Tallahassee, FL 32302
904-488-5534

**[Florida] Banking & Finance,
Department of**
State Capitol
Tallahassee, FL 32399
904-488-0520
800-848-3792

Florida Bar
650 Apalachee Parkway
Tallahassee, FL 32399
904-222-5286
904-561-5600
800-342-8060
800-874-0005 (Out-of-state)
904-561-5843 (CLE)

**[Florida] Bar Examiners,
Board of**
P.O. Box 2254
Orlando, FL 32802
407-843-7300
1300 E. Park Ave.
Tallahassee, FL 32399
904-487-1294

[Florida] Better Business Bureau
16291 NW 57th Ave.
Miami, FL 33014
305-625-1302
813-875-6200
800-432-7159 (Auto Complaints)

**[Florida] Brevard County Bar
Association**
231 N. Courtenay Parkway
Merritt Island, FL 32953
407-453-5285

**[Florida] Brevard County Law
Library**
50 S. Nieman Ave.
Melbourne, FL 32901
407-727-9720
407-269-8197 (Titusville)

[Florida] Broward County
201 SE 6th St.
Fort Lauderdale, FL 33301
305-357-6586

**[Florida] Broward County Bar
Association**
1051 SE 3rd Ave.
Ft. Lauderdale, FL 33316
305-764-8040

**[Florida] Broward County Law
Library**
444 County Court House
Ft. Lauderdale, FL 33301
305-357-6226

**[Florida] Broward County
Paralegal Association**
P.O. Box 1900
Ft. Lauderdale, FL 33302

**[Florida] Building Construction,
Division of**
200 E. Gains St., Rm. 512
Tallahassee, FL 32399
904-488-2774

**[Florida] Child Support
Enforcement, Office of**
1317 Winewood Blvd., Bldg. 3
Tallahassee, FL 32399
904-488-9900
800-622-5437

**[Florida] Clearwater Bar
Association**
P.O. Box 1609
Clearwater, FL 33517
813-461-4869

**[Florida] Collier County Bar
Association**
3301 E. Tamiami
Naples, FL 33962
813-775-8566

**[Florida] Commerce,
Department of**
107 W. Gains St.
Collins Bldg., Suite 510-C

Tallahassee, FL 32399
904-488-3104

**[Florida] Community Affairs,
Department of**
2740 Centerview Dr.
Tallahassee, FL 32399
904-488-8466

[Florida] Comptroller, State
Department of Banking & Finance
The Capitol
Tallahassee, FL 32399
904-488-0286
800-848-3792

**[Florida] Consumer Services,
Division of**
508 Mayo Bldg.
Tallahassee, FL 32399
904-488-2226

[Florida] Corporate Records
409 E. Gaines St.
Tallahassee, FL 32301
904-487-6900

**[Florida] Corrections,
Department of**
1311 Winewood Blvd.
Tallahassee, FL 32399
904-488-5021

**[Florida] Court of Appeal, First
District**
300 Martin Luther King, Jr. Blvd.
Tallahassee, FL 32399
904-488-6151

**[Florida] Court of Appeal,
Second District**
1005 E. Memorial Blvd.
Lakeland, FL 33802
813-686-8171
813-272-3430 (Tampa)

**[Florida] Court of Appeal, Third
District**
2001 SW 117 Ave., P.O. Box 650307
Miami, FL 33265
305-221-1200

**[Florida] Court of Appeal,
Fourth District**
1525 Palm Beach Lakes Blvd., P.O.
Box A
West Palm Beach, FL 33402
407-686-1903

[Florida] Court of Appeal, Fifth District
300 S. Beach St.
Daytona Beach, FL 32014
904-253-7909

[Florida] Courts Administrator, Office of State
Supreme Court Bldg.
Tallahassee, FL 32399
904-488-8621

[Florida] Crimes Compensation
2728 Centerview, Suite 122
Tallahassee, FL 32399
904-488-0848
800-342-1741

[Florida] Cultural Affairs, Division of
State Capitol
Tallahassee, FL 32399
904-487-2980

[Florida] Dade County
111 NW 1st St., Suite 220
Miami, FL 33128
305-375-5124

[Florida] Dade County Bar Association
111 NW 1st Ave., No. 214
Miami, FL 33128
305-371-2220

[Florida] Dade County Law Library
73 W. Flagler St., Rm. 2101
Miami, FL 33130
305-375-5422
305-538-0313 (Miami Beach)

[Florida] Duval County
330 E. Bay St.
Jacksonville, FL 32202
904-630-2028

[Florida] Duval County Law Library
220 County Courthouse, Rm. 220
Jacksonville, FL 32202
904-630-2560

[Florida] Economic Development, Division of
107 W. Gains St.
Tallahassee, FL 32399
904-488-6300

[Florida] Education, Department of
State Capitol Plaza Level 08
Tallahassee, FL 32399
904-487-1785

[Florida] Emergency Management, Division of
2740 Centerview Dr.
Tallahassee, FL 32399
904-487-4918

[Florida] Energy Office
214 S. Bronough St.
Tallahassee, FL 32301
904-488-6764

[Florida] Environmental Regulation, Department of
2600 Blair Stone Rd.
Tallahassee, FL 32399
904-488-4805

[Florida] Escambia-Santa Rosa Bar Association
32 W. Government St.
Pensacola, FL 32501
904-434-6009

[Florida] Ethics, Commission on
P.O. Box 6
Tallahassee, FL 32302
904-488-7864

[Florida] General Services, Department of
Larson Bldg., Rm. 133
Tallahassee, FL 32399
904-488-2786

[Florida] Governor, Office of
Capitol Bldg.
Tallahassee, FL 32399
904-488-4441

[Florida] Health & Rehabilitative Services, Department of
1317 Winewood Blvd Bldg 1, Suite 115
Tallahassee, FL 32399
904-488-4115

[Florida] Hearings, Division of
2009 Apalachee Parkway
Tallahassee, FL 32399
904-488-9675

[Florida] Hillsborough County
419 Pierce St.

Tampa, FL 33602
813-272-5000

[Florida] Hillsborough County Bar Association
315 E. Madison, Suite 1010, P.O. Box 26
Tampa, FL 33601
813-226-6431

[Florida] Hillsborough County Law Library
County Court House, Rm. 230
419 Pierce St.
Tampa, FL 33602
813-272-5818

[Florida] Historical Resources, Division of
R.A. Gray Bldg.
Tallahassee, FL 32399
904-488-1480

[Florida] House of Representatives
State Capitol
Tallahassee, FL 32399
904-488-1152
800-342-1827
904-488-2873 (Judiciary)

[Florida] Human Relations Commission
325 John Knox Rd., Suite 240
Tallahassee, FL 32399
904-488-7082
800-342-8170

[Florida] Immigration Judge, Office of the
7880 Biscayne Blvd., 8th Fl.
Miami, FL 33138
305-536-5008

[Florida] Insurance Commissioner
State Capitol, Plaza Level 11
Tallahassee, FL 32399
904-488-3440
800-342-2762

Florida Jacksonville Bar Association
802 Barnett Bank Bldg.
Jacksonville, FL 32202
904-354-2144

[Florida] Jacksonville City Hall
220 E. Bay St.
Jacksonville, FL 32202
904-630-1919

[Florida] Jacksonville Legal Assistants
P.O. Box 52264
Jacksonville, FL 32201

Florida Judicial Qualifications Commission
The Historic Capitol, Rm. 102
Tallahassee, FL 32301
904-488-1581

[Florida] Justice Administrative Commission
124 W. Jefferson St.
Tallahassee, FL 32302
904-488-2415

[Florida] Labor Employment & Training, Division of
1320 Executive Center Dr.
Tallahassee, FL 32399
904-488-7228

[Florida] Law Enforcement, Department of
208 W. Carolina St.
Tallahassee, FL 32301
904-488-8771

[Florida] Lee County Bar Association
P.O. Box 1387
Ft. Myers, FL 33902
813-334-0047

[Florida] Legal Affairs, Department of
The Capitol
Tallahassee, FL 32399
904-487-1963

Florida Legal Assistants
P.O. Box 503
Bradenton, FL 34206

[Florida] Leon County
301 S. Monroe St.
Tallahassee, FL 32301
904-488-4710

[Florida] Leon County Law Library
301 S. Monroe St.

Tallahassee, FL 32301
904-488-1357

[Florida] Library & Information Services, Division of
500 Bronough St.
Tallahassee, FL 32399
904-487-2651

[Florida] Licensing, Division of
City Central Bldg.
Tallahassee, FL 32301
904-488-5381

[Florida] Lieutenant Governor, Office of
State Capitol Plaza Level 5
Tallahassee, FL 32399
904-488-4711

Florida Marine Patrol
3900 Commonwealth Blvd.
Tallahassee, FL 32399
904-487-3671

[Florida] Miami City Hall
3500 Pan American Dr.
Miami, FL 33133
305-579-6065

[Florida] Miami, Legal Services of Greater
225 NE 34th St., Suite 300
Miami, FL 33137
305-576-0080

[Florida] Natural Resources, Department of
3900 Commonwealth Blvd.
Tallahassee, FL 32399
904-488-1554

[Florida] North Central Florida Association of Legal Assistants
4224 SW 70th Terrace, #B
Gainesville, FL 32608

[Florida] Nova University Law Library
3100 SW 9th Ave.
Ft. Lauderdale, FL 33315
305-760-5700

[Florida] Orange County Bar Association
880 N. Orange Ave., Suite 100
Orlando, FL 32801
407-422-4551

[Florida] Orange County Law Library
101 E. Central Blvd.
Orlando, FL 32801
407-425-4694

[Florida] Orlando Legal Assistants
P.O. Box 1107
Orlando, FL 32802

[Florida] Palm Beach County
301 N. Olive
West Palm Beach, FL 33401
407-820-2754

[Florida] Palm Beach County Bar Association
105 S. Narcissus Ave.
West Palm Beach, FL 33401
407-659-1537

[Florida] Palm Beach County Law Library
300 N. Dixie Hwy, Rm. 339
West Palm Beach, FL 33401
407-355-2928

[Florida] Parole & Probation Commission
1309 Winewood Blvd.
Tallahassee, FL 32399
904-488-1653

[Florida] Pensacola Legal Assistants
P.O. Box 1333
Pensacola, FL 32581

[Florida] Pinellas County Law Library
545 1st Ave., North, Rm. 500
St. Petersburg, FL 33701
813-892-7875
813-462-3411 (Clearwater)

[Florida] Planning & Budgeting, Office of
Carlton Bldg., Rm. 415
Tallahassee, FL 32399
904-488-5393

Florida Power & Light Co.
P.O. Box 029110
Miami, FL 33102
305-552-3552
800-432-6563

[Florida] Professional Regulation, Department of
130 N. Monroe St.
Tallahassee, FL 32399
904-487-2252
800-342-7940

[Florida] Public Counsel
111 W. Madison St.
801 Pepper Bldg.
Tallahassee, FL 32302
904-488-9330

[Florida] Public Employees Relations Commission
2586 Seagate Dr., Suite 100
Tallahassee, FL 32399
904-488-8641

[Florida] Public Safety Planning Management, Bureau of
2740 Centerview Dr.
Tallahassee, FL 32399
904-488-0090

[Florida] Public Service Commission
101 E. Gains St.
Tallahassee, FL 32399
904-488-7001
800-342-3552

[Florida] Public Transportation, Office of
Burns Bldg.
Tallahassee, FL 32399
904-488-5704

[Florida] Purchasing, Division of
200 E. Gains St.
Tallahassee, FL 32399
904-488-1194

[Florida] Real Estate, Division of
400 W. Robinson St.
Orlando, FL 32801
407-423-6053

[Florida] Retirement, Division of
2639 N. Monroe St.
Tallahassee, FL 32303
904-488-5541

[Florida] Revenue, Department of
Carlton Bldg., Rm. 104
Tallahassee, FL 32399

904-488-5050
800-872-9909

[Florida] Sarasota County Bar Association
P.O. Box 507
Sarasota, FL 34230
813-366-6703

[Florida] Securities, Division of
The Capitol
Tallahassee, FL 32301
904-488-9805

[Florida] Seminole County Bar Association
608 E. Altamonte Ave., Suite 203
Altamonte Springs, FL 32701
407-834-0530

[Florida] Senate
State Capitol
Tallahassee, FL 32301
904-487-5270
800-342-1827
904-487-5094 (Judiciary, Civil)
904-487-5068 (Judiciary, Criminal)

[Florida] South Palm Beach County Bar Association
2281 Whistling Pine Lane
Boca Raton, FL 33428
407-479-2648

[Florida] State, Department of
The Capitol
Tallahassee, FL 32399
904-488-3680

Florida State University
College of Law Library
Tallahassee, FL 32306
904-644-4578

[Florida] Statutory Revision Division
Joint Legislative Management Committee
The Capitol, Rm. 726
Tallahassee, FL 32399
904-488-8404

[Florida] Stetson University Law Library
1401 61st St. South
St. Petersburg, FL 33707
813-345-1300

[Florida] St. Petersburg Bar Association
P.O. Box 7538
St. Petersburg,FL 33734
813-823-7474

[Florida] St. Petersburg City Hall
175 5th St. N.
St. Petersburg, FL 33701
813-893-7171

[Florida] St. Thomas University Law Library
16400 NW 32nd Ave.
Miami, FL 33054
305-623-2330

[Florida] Supreme Court
500 S. Duvall St.
Tallahassee, FL 32399
904-488-0125
904-488-1531 (Law Library)

[Florida] Tallahassee Bar Association
307 E. 7th Ave.
Tallahassee, FL 32303
904-222-3292

[Florida] Tampa City Hall
306 E. Jackson St.
Tampa, FL 33602
813-223-8211

[Florida] Transportation, Department of
605 Suwannee Burns Bldg.
Tallahassee, FL 32399
904-488-6721

Florida Trial Lawyers, Academy of
218 S. Monroe St.
Tallahassee, FL 32301
904-224-9403

[Florida] Unemployment Appeals Commission
1321 Executive Center Drive East, Suite 221
Tallahassee, FL 32399
904-487-2685

[Florida] Unemployment Compensation Bureau
201 Caldwell Bldg.
Tallahassee, FL 32399
904-488-6093
800-342-9909 (Fraud)

[Florida] United States Attorney's Office Library
155 S. Miami Ave., Suite 700
Miami, FL 33130
305-536-5461

[Florida] United States Bankruptcy Court
Middle Florida
4921 Memorial Hwy, Suite 205
Tampa, FL 33634
813-228-2139

[Florida] United States Bankruptcy Court
Northern Florida
227 N. Bronough St.
Tallahassee, FL 32301
904-681-7500

[Florida] United States Bankruptcy Court
Southern Florida
51 SW 1st Ave.
Miami, FL 33130
305-536-5216

[Florida] United States District Court
Middle District
P.O. Box 53558
Jacksonville, FL 32201
904-791-2854

[Florida] United States District Court
Northern District
110 E. Park Ave.
Tallahassee, FL 32301
904-681-7165

[Florida] United States District Court
Southern District
301 N. Miami Ave.
Miami, FL 33128
305-536-4131

[Florida] United States Government Printing Office
400 W. Bay St., Rm. 158
Jacksonville, FL 32202
904-791-3801

Florida, University of
College of Law
Legal Information Center

Gainesville, FL 36211
904-392-0417

[Florida] University of Miami
Law Library
P.O. Box 248087
Coral Gables, FL 33124
305-284-2349

[Florida] Vital Statistics, Office of
1217 Pearl St.
Jacksonville, FL 32202
904-359-6971

[Florida] Vocational Rehabilitation, Division of
1709 A. Mahan Dr.
Tallahassee, FL 32399
904-488-6210

[Florida] Volusia County Bar Association
P.O. Drawer 15050
Daytona Beach, FL 32015
904-255-3434

[Florida] Volusia County Law Library
125 E. Orange Ave., Rm. 208
Daytona Beach, FL 32014
904-257-6041

Florida Washington Office
444 N. Capitol St., Suite 287
Wash. D.C. 20001
202-624-5885

[Florida] Weights & Measures, Bureau of
3125 Conner Blvd.
Tallahassee, FL 32399
904-488-9140

[Florida] Women Lawyers, Association for
P.O. Box 10617
Tallahassee, FL 32302
904-561-6344

[Florida] Worker's Compensation, Division of
301 Forest Bldg.
Tallahassee, FL 32399
904-488-2514
800-342-5860 (Benefits)
800-342-1741 (Claims)

Food & Drug Law Institute
1000 Vermont Ave., 12 Fl.

Wash. D.C. 20005
202-371-1420

Forbes, Inc.
60 5th Ave.
New York, NY 10011
212-620-2248

Ford Consumer Appeals Board
P.O. Box 1805
Dearborn, MI 48126
313-337-6950
800-241-8450
800-255-1433

Forensic Sciences Foundation
218 E. Cache La Poudre
Colorado Springs, CO 80903
719-636-1100

Fred B. Rothman & Co.
See Rothman

Fund for Modern Courts
36 W. 44th St., Rm. 310
New York, NY 10036
212-575-1577

Funeral Service Consumer Arbitration Program
11121 W. Oklahoma Ave.
Milwaukee, WI 53227
414-541-2500

Gannett Co., Inc.
P.O. Box 7858
Wash. D.C. 20044
703-284-6048

General Electric
3135 Easton Turnpike
Fairfield, CT 06431
203-373-2211
800-626-2000

General Foods Corp.
250 North St.
White Plains, NY 10625
800-431-1003

General Mills, Inc.
P.O. Box 1113
Minneapolis, MN 55440
612-540-4295
800-328-6787

**General Motors Acceptance
Corp.**
3044 W. Grand Blvd.
Detroit, MI 48202
313-556-0510

**[Georgia] Information &
Referral (State Government)**
404-656-2000
404-656-7000

**[Georgia] Information Center
(Federal Government)**
Atlanta 404-331-6891

**[Georgia] Administrative
Services, Department of**
Piedmont Ave., SE, Suite 1520-D
Atlanta, GA 20334
404-656-5514

[Georgia] Aging, Office of
878 Peachtree St., NE, Suite 632
Atlanta, GA 30309
404-894-5333

**[Georgia] Agriculture,
Department of**
19 Martin Luther King, Jr. Dr., SW
Agriculture Bldg., Rm. 204
Atlanta, GA 30334
404-656-3600
800-282-5852

**[Georgia] Air Quality
Control Section**
205 Butler St. SE
East Tower, Rm. 1162
Atlanta, GA 30334
404-656-6900

**[Georgia] Archives & History,
Department of**
330 Capitol Ave. SE
Atlanta, GA 30334
404-656-2358

[Georgia] Arts, Council for the
2082 E. Exchange Pl., Suite 100
Tucker, GA 30084
404-493-5780

**[Georgia] Atlanta Bar
Association**
100 Peachtree St., NW
Atlanta, GA 30303
404-521-0781

[Georgia] Atlanta City Hall
68 Mitchell ST. SW
Atlanta, GA 30335
404-658-6000

**[Georgia] Atlanta Regional
Commission**
100 Edgewood Ave., No. 1801
Atlanta, GA 30303
404-656-7700

**[Georgia] Attorney General,
Office of**
132 State Judicial Bldg.
Atlanta, GA 30334
404-656-4586

**[Georgia] Audits, State
Depart-ment of**
270 Washington St., SW, Rm. 214
Atlanta, GA 30334
404-656-2174

**[Georgia] Banking & Finance,
Commissioner of**
2990 Brandywine Rd., Suite 200
Atlanta, GA 30341
404-986-1633

**[Georgia] Bar Admissions,
Office of**
47 Trinity Ave.
Atlanta, GA 30334
404-656-3490

Georgia, Bar of
800 The Hurt Bldg.
Atlanta, GA 30303
404-527-8700

**[Georgia] Bar Examiners,
Board of**
P.O. Box 38466
Atlanta, GA 30334
404-656-3490

**[Georgia] Better Business
Bureau**
100 Edgewood Ave., Suite 1012
Atlanta, GA 30303
404-688-4910
404-722-2574 (Augusta)

**Georgia, Board of Regents of the
University Sytem of**
244 Washington St., SW
Atlanta, GA 30334
404-656-2200

Georgia Building Authority
1 Martin Luther King, Jr., Dr., SW
Atlanta, GA 30334
404-656-3250

**[Georgia] Business Services &
Regulation**
2 Martin Luther King, Jr. Dr. SE
Atlanta, GA 30334
404-656-2190

**[Georgia] Carl Vinson Institute
of Government**
University of Georgia
Terrell Hall
Athens, GA 30602
404-542-2736

[Georgia] Chatham County
133 Montgomery St.
Savannah, GA 31401
912-944-4641

**[Georgia] Child Support
Recovery, Office of**
878 Peachtree St., NE, Rm. 529
Atlanta, GA 30309
404-894-4119

**[Georgia] Community Affairs,
State Department of**
400 Marietta St., NW, Suite 800
Atlanta, GA 30303
404-656-3836

**[Georgia] Consumer Affairs,
Governor's Office of**
2 Martin Luther King, Jr. Dr., SE
Atlanta, GA 30334
404-656-3790
800-282-5808

**[Georgia] Continuing Legal
Education, Center for**
University Plaza, Box 642
Atlanta, GA 30303
404-651-2040

**[Georgia] Corrections,
Department of**
2 Martin Luther King, Jr., Dr., SE
Atlanta, GA 30334
404-656-6002

[Georgia] Court of Appeals
433 Judicial Bldg.
Atlanta, GA 30334
404-656-3450

[Georgia] Courts, Administrative Office of the
244 Washington St., SW, Suite 550
Atlanta, GA 30334
404-656-5171

[Georgia] Criminal Justice Coordinating Council
205 Butler St., SE
Balcony Level East Tower, Suite 470
Atlanta, GA 30334
404-656-1721

[Georgia] Defense, Department of
P.O. Box 17965
Atlanta, GA 30316
404-624-6000

[Georgia] DeKalb County
556 N. McDonough St.
Decatur, GA 30030
404-371-2000

Georgia Diagnostic & Classification Center
P.O. Box 3877
Jackson, GA 30233
404-775-3161

[Georgia] Drugs & Narcotics Agency
166 Pryor St., SW, Rm. 503
Atlanta, GA 30303
404-656-5100

[Georgia] Education, State Department of
205 Butler St., Suite 2066
Atlanta, GA 30334
404-656-2534

[Georgia] Emory University
School of Law Library
Gambrell Hall
Atlanta, GA 30322
404-727-6824

[Georgia] Employees' Retirement System
Two Northside 75
Beta Bldg., Suite 300
Atlanta, GA 30381
404-352-6400

[Georgia] Energy Resources, Office of
270 Washington St. SW, Suite 615
Atlanta, GA 30334
404-656-5176

[Georgia] Environmental Protection Division
205 Butler St., Suite 1252
Atlanta, GA 30334
404-656-3500

[Georgia] Ethics Commission, State
3080 East Exchange Pl., Suite 235
Tucker, GA 30084
404-493-5795

[Georgia] Examining Boards Division
166 Pryor St. SE
Atlanta, GA 30303
404-656-3900

[Georgia] Fair Employment Practices, Office of
156 Trinity Ave., Suite 206
Atlanta, GA 30303
404-656-1736

[Georgia] Forestry Commission, State
200 Piedmont Ave., SE
800 West Tower
Atlanta, GA 30334
404-656-3204

[Georgia] Fulton County
165 Central Ave. SW, Rm. 208
Atlanta, GA 30303
404-572-2457

[Georgia] Fulton County Law Library
136 Pryor St., SW
Atlanta, GA 30303
404-730-4544

[Georgia] Governor, Office of the
State Capitol, Rms. 201-203
Atlanta, GA 30334
404-656-1776

[Georgia] Gwinnett County Law Library
75 Langley Dr.
Lawrenceville, GA 30245
404-822-8577

[Georgia] Highway Safety, Office of
100 Peachtree St., Suite 2000
Atlanta, Ga 30303
404-656-6996

[Georgia] House of Representatives
State Capitol
Atlanta, GA 30334
404-656-5082

[Georgia] Human Resources, Department of
47 Trinity Ave., SW, Room 520–H
Atlanta, GA 30334
404-656-5542

[Georgia] Industry & Trade, Department of
230 Peachtree St., NW, 7th Fl.
Atlanta, GA 30303
404-656-3589

[Georgia] Insurance Commissioner
2 Martin Luther King, Jr. Dr., SE
Atlanta, GA 30334
404-656-2056

[Georgia] Investigation, Bureau of
3121 Pantherville Rd.
Decatur, GA 30034
404-244-2501

Georgia, Judicial Council of
244 Washington St.
Atlanta, GA 30334
404-656-5171

[Georgia] Juvenile Court Judges, Council of
244 Washington St., Suite 550
Atlanta, GA 30334
404-656-6411

[Georgia] Labor, Department of
148 International Blvd.
Atlanta, GA 30303
404-656-3011

[Georgia] Law, Department of
Judicial Bldg., Rm. 132
40 Capitol Square
Atlanta, GA 30334
404-656-3300

Georgia Legal Assistants, Association of
P.O.Box 1802
Atlanta, GA 30301

Georgia Legal Services
161 Spring St., 5th Fl.
Atlanta, GA 30303
404-656-6021

[Georgia] Legislative Counsel
Legislative Services Committee
State Capitol, Rm. 316
Atlanta, GA 30334
404-656-5000

[Georgia] Library, State
40 Mitchell St.
Atlanta, GA 30334
404-656-3468

[Georgia] Lieutenant Governor, Office of the
State Capitol, Rm. 240
Atlanta, GA 30334
404-656-5030

[Georgia] Medical Assistance, Department of
2 Martin Luther King, Jr., Dr., SE
Atlanta, GA 30334
404-656-4479

[Georgia] Mercer University
School of Law Library
Macon, GA 31207
912-744-2612

Georgia Merit System of Personnel Administration
200 Piedmont Ave., SE, 5th Fl.
Atlanta, GA 30334
404-656-2705

[Georgia] Natural Resources, Department of
205 Butler St., SE, Suite 1252
Atlanta, GA 30334
404-656-3530

Georgia-Pacific Corp.
133 Peachtree St., NE
Atlanta, GA 30303
404-521-4708
800-447-2882

[Georgia] Pardons & Paroles, State Board of
2 Martin Luther King, Jr., Dr., SE

East Tower, 5th Fl.
Atlanta, GA 30334
404-656-5651

[Georgia] Planning & Budget, Office of
Trinity-Washington Bldg., 6th Fl.
270 Washington St., SW
Atlanta, GA 30334
404-656-3820

Georgia Professional Standards Commission
Koger Executive Center
2945 Flowers Road South, No. 107
Atlanta, GA 30341
404-656-2535

[Georgia] Properties Commission, State
1 Martin Luther King, Jr., Dr., SW
Atlanta, GA 30334
404-656-5602

Georgia, Prosecuting Attorneys Council of
5500 Highlands Parkway, SE, Suite 1700
Smyrna, GA 30082
404-438-2550

[Georgia] Public Health, Division of
878 Peachtree St., Suite 201
Atlanta GA 30309
404-894-7505

[Georgia] Public Safety, Department of
959 E. Confederate Ave., SE
P.O. Box 1456
Atlanta, GA 30371
404-656-6063

[Georgia] Public Service Commission, Office of the
244 Washington St., SW
Atlanta, GA 30334
404-656-4556
800-282-3813

Georgia Public Telecommunications Commission
1540 Stewart Ave., SW
Atlanta, GA 30310
404-656-5943

[Georgia] Purchasing & Surplus Property, Division of
200 Piedmont Ave., Suite 1302
Atlanta, GA 30334
404-656-3240

[Georgia] Real Estate Commission
40 Pryor St. SW
Atlanta, GA 30303
404-656-3916

[Georgia] Rehabilitation Services, Division of
878 Peachtree St. NE, Rm. 706
Atlanta, GA 30390
404-894-6670

Georgia Residential Finance Authority
60 Executive Parkway South
Atlanta, GA 30329
404-320-4840

[Georgia] Revenue, State Department of
270 Washington St., SW, Rm. 410
Atlanta, GA 30334
404-656-4015

[Georgia] Secretary of State, Office of the
State Capitol, Rm. 214
Atlanta, GA 30334
404-656-2881
404-656-2817 (Corporations)

[Georgia] Senate
State Capitol
Atlanta, GA 30334
404-656-0028

[Georgia] Soil & Water Conservation Commission
624 S. Milledge Ave., Suite 203
Smith-Boley-Brown Bldg.
P.O. Box 8024
Athens, GA 30603
404-542-3065

[Georgia] State Patrol
959 E. Confederate Ave. SE
Atlanta, GA 30371
404-624-7400

Georgia State University
College of Law Library
University Plaza

Atlanta, GA 30303
404-651-2479

Georgia Subsequent Injury Trust Fund
Two Northside
75 Beta Bldg., Suite 124
Atlanta, GA 30318
404-894-5674

[Georgia] Superior Court Judges Council of
50 Hurt Plaza, SE, Suite 411
Atlanta, GA 30303
404-656-4964

Georgia, Superior Courts Sentence Review Panel of
18 Capitol Square, Suite 108
Atlanta, GA 30334
404-656-5154

[Georgia] Supreme Court, Office of the
506 Judicial Bldg. & Annex, 5th Fl.
Atlanta, GA 30334
404-656-3476 (Chief Justice)
404-656-3470 (Clerk)
404-656-3490 (Bar Admissions)

[Georgia] Technical & Adult Education, Department of
One CNN Center
South Tower, Suite 660
Atlanta, GA 30303
404-656-5845

[Georgia] Transportation, Department of
2 Capitol Sq. SW
Atlanta, GA 30334
404-656-5267

[Georgia] Treasurer
200 Piedmont Ave. SE
Atlanta, GA 30334
404-656-2168

[Georgia] Unemployment Insurance Division
254 Washington St., SW
Atlanta, GA 30334
404-656-3050

[Georgia] United States Bankruptcy Court
Middle Georgia
P.O. Box 1957

Macon, GA 31202
912-752-3497

[Georgia] United States Bankruptcy Court
Northern Georgia
75 Spring St., SW, Rm. 1340
Atlanta, GA 30303
404-331-6490
404-331-3744 (Law Library)

[Georgia] United States Bankruptcy Court
Southern Georgia
P.O. Box 8347
Savannah, GA 31412
912-944-4100

[Georgia] United States Court of Appeals for the Eleventh Circuit
56 Forsyth St., NW
Atlanta, GA 30303
404-331-6187
404-331-2510 (Law Library)

[Georgia] United States District Court
Middle District
P.O. Box 128
Macon, GA 31202
912-752-3497

[Georgia] United States District Court
Northern District
75 Spring St., SW, Rm. 2211
Atlanta, GA 30335
404-331-6496

[Georgia] United States District Court
Southern District
P.O. Box 8286
Savannah, GA 31412
912-944-4281

[Georgia] United States Government Printing Office
275 Peachtree St., NE, Rm. 100
P.O. Box 56445
Atlanta, GA 30343
404-331-6947

Georgia, University of
School of Law Library
Athens, GA 30601
404-542-1922

[Georgia] Veterans Service, State Department of
Loyd Veterans Memorial Bldg.,
Suite E. 970
Atlanta, GA 30334
404-656-2300

[Georgia] Vital Records Service
47 Trinity Ave. SW
Atlanta, GA 30334
404-656-4900

[Georgia] Water Protection Branch
205 Butler St., SE
Atlanta, GA 30334
404-656-3605

[Georgia] Weights & Measures, Division of
Agriculture Bldg.
Atlanta, GA 30334
404-656-3605

[Georgia] Workers' Compensation, State Board of
1000 S. Omni International
Atlanta, GA 30335
404-656-2034

[Georgia] Youth Services, Division of
878 Peachtree St., NE
Atlanta, GA 30309
404-894-5922

Gerber Products Co.
445 State St.
Fremont, MI 49412
616-928-2000

Gillette Co.
Prudential Tower Bldy., 24th Fl.
Boston, MA 02199
617-421-7000

GM Service Parts Operations
6060 W. Bristol Rd.
Flint, MI 48456
313-635-5412

Gould Publications
199 State St.
Binghamton, NY 13901
607-724-3000

Governmental Accounting Standards Board
401 Merritt 7

P.O. Box 5116
Norwalk, CT 06856
203-847-0700

Great Lakes Commission
400 S. 4th St.
Ann Arbor, MI 48103
313-665-9135

Greenwood Press, Inc.
88 Post Road, Box 5007
Westport, CT 06881
203-226-3571

GTE Corp.
1 Stamford Forum
Stamford, CT 06904
203-965-2000

**[Guam] Administration,
Department of**
P.O. Box 884
Agana, GU 96910
671-472-8481

[Guam] Aging, Office of
Department of Human Services
P.O. Box 2816
Agana, Gu 96910
671-734-2942

[Guam] Banking Commissioner
855 W. Marine Dr.
Agana, Gu 96910
671-477-1040

[Guam] Bar Examiners, Board of
110 W. O'Brian Dr.
Agana, GU 96910
671-472-8961

**[Guam] Child Support
Enforcement Office**
194 Hernan Cortez Ave., Suite 309
Agana, GU 96910
671-477-2036

**[Guam] Corrections,
Department of**
P.O. Box 3236
Agana, GU 96910
671-734-2458
671-734-2476 (Parole Board)

[Guam] Governer, Office of the
Agana, GU 96910
671-472-8931

[Guam] Insurance Commissioner
P.O. Box 2796

Agana, GU 96910
671-477-1040

[Guam] Law, Department of
Attorney General, Office of
P.O. Box 2950
Agana, GU 96910
671-472-6841

[Guam] Legislature
P.O. Box CB–1
Agana, GU 96910
671-472-3444 (Judiciary)
671-472-6841 (Compiler of Law)

**[Guam] Revenue & Taxation,
Department of**
P.O. Box 2796
Agana, GU 96910

Guam, Superior Court of
110 W. O'Brian Dr.
Agana, GU 96910
671-472-9861

Guam Territorial Law Library
141 San Ramon Rd.
Agana, GU 96910
671-477-7623

**[Guam] United States District
Court**
238 O'Hara St.
Agana, GU 96910
671-472-7411

**HALT–An Organization of
Americans for Legal Reform**
1319 F. St., NW, Suite 300
Wash. D.C. 20004
202-347-9600

Handgun Control
1400 K. St., NW
Wash. D.C. 20005
202-898-0792

Harrison Co.
3110 Crossing Park

Norcross, GA 30071
404-447-9150
800-241-3561

**[Hawaii] Information & Referral
(State Government)**
808-548-2211

**[Hawaii] Information Center
(Federal Government)**
Honolulu 808-541-1365

**[Hawaii] Accounting & General
Services Department**
1151 Punchbowl St.
Honolulu, HI 96813
808-548-3050

**[Hawaii] Affirmative Action,
Office of**
State Capitol, Rm. 443
Honolulu, HI 96813
808-548-3432

**[Hawaii] Aging, Executive
Office on**
335 Merchant St., Rm. 241
Honolulu, HI 96813
808-548-2593

**[Hawaii] Agriculture,
Department of**
1428 S. King St.
Honolulu, HI 96814
808-548-7101

Hawaiian Home Lands
335 Merchant St.
Honolulu, HI 96813
808-548-6450

[Hawaii] Archives, State
Iolani Palace Grounds
Honolulu, HI 96813
808-548-2355

**[Hawaii] Attorney General,
Office of**
Hawaii State Capitol Bldg., Rm. 405
Honolulu, HI 96813
808-548-4740

Hawaii Bar Association
1001 Bishop St., Suite 950
Honolulu, HI 96813
808-537-1868

[Hawaii] Bar Examiners, Board of
P.O. Box 2560

Honolulu, HI 96804
808-548-7430

[Hawaii] Better Business Bureau
1600 Kapiolani Blvd., Suite 704
Honolulu, HI 96814
808-942-2355

**[Hawaii] Budget & Finance,
Department of**
P.O. Box 150
Honolulu, HI 96810
808-548-2325

**[Hawaii] Business & Economic
Development, Department of**
250 S. King St.
Honolulu, HI 96813
808-548-6914

**[Hawaii] Business Registration
Division**
P.O. Box 40
Honolulu, HI 96810
808-548-6521

**[Hawaii] Child Support
Enforcement Agency**
P.O. Box 1860
Honolulu, HI 96805
808-548-5779

**[Hawaii] Children & Youth,
Office of**
P.O. Box 3044
Honolulu, HI 96802
808-548-7582

**[Hawaii] Commerce & Consumer
Affairs, Department of**
1010 Richards St.
Honolulu,HI 96813
808-548-7505

**[Hawaii] Consumer Advocacy,
Division of**
1010 Richards St., 2nd Fl.
Honolulu, HI 96813
808-548-6590

**[Hawaii] Consumer Protection
Office**
P.O. Box 3767
Honolulu, HI 96812
808-548-2560

**Hawaii Corporation &
Securities Administrator**
1010 Richards St.

Honolulu, HI 96810
808-548-6421

**[Hawaii] Corrections,
Department of**
677 Ala Moana Blvd., Suite 700
Honolulu, HI 96813
808-548-3608

Hawaii County
25 Aupuni St.
Hilo, HI 96720
808-961-8255

**[Hawaii] Culture & Art,
Foundation on**
335 Merchant St., RM. 202
Honolulu, HI 96813
808-548-4145

**[Hawaii] Criminal Injuries
Compensation Commission**
1149 Bethel St., Rm. 412
Honolulu, HI 96813
808-548-4680

[Hawaii] Defense, Department of
3949 Diamond Head Rd.
Honolulu, HI 96816
808-734-2195

**[Hawaii] Disability
Compensation Division**
830 Punchbowl St.
Honolulu, HI 96813
808-548-5414

**[Hawaii] Education,
Department of**
1390 Miller St.
Honolulu, HI 96813
808-548-6405

**[Hawaii] Employees' Retirement
System**
888 Mililani St.
Honolulu, HI 96813
808-548-7593

[Hawaii] Employment Service
P.O. Box 3680
Honolulu, HI 96811
808-548-6468

[Hawaii] Energy Division
335 Merchant St., Rm. 110
Honolulu, HI 96813
808-548-4080

**[Hawaii] Environmental
Protection & Health Services**
P.O. Box 3378
Honolulu, HI 96801
808-548-6455

**[Hawaii] Environmental Quality
Control, Office of**
465 S. King St. Rm. 104
Honolulu, HI 96813
808-548-6915

**[Hawaii] Ethics Commission,
State**
P.O. Box 616
Honolulu, HI 96809
808-548-6401

[Hawaii] Family & Adult Services
P.O. Box 339
Honolulu, HI 96809
808-548-5908

**[Hawaii] Financial Institutions,
Commissioner of**
P.O. Box 2054
Honolulu, HI 96805
808-548-5855

**[Hawaii] Forestry & Wildlife,
Division of**
1151 Punchbowl St.
Honolulu, HI 96813
808-548-8850

[Hawaii] Governor, Office of
State Capitol Bldg., 5th Fl.
Honolulu, HI 96813
808-548-5420

**[Hawaii] Handicapped,
Commission on the**
335 Merchant St.
Honolulu, HI 96813
808-548-7606

[Hawaii] Health, Department of
1250 Punchbowl St.
Honolulu, HI 96813
808-548-6505

[Hawaii] Highways Division
869 Punchbowl St.
Honolulu, HI 96813
808-548-5710

[Hawaii] Honolulu City Hall
530 King St.

Honolulu, HI 96813
808-523-4385

[Hawaii] Honolulu County
City Hall
Honolulu, HI 96817
808-523-4141

**[Hawaii] House of
Representatives**
State Capitol
Honolulu, HI 96813
808-548-7843
808-548-2267 (Judiciary)

**[Hawaii] Human Services,
Department of**
1390 Miller St.
Honolulu, HI 86813
808-548-6260

**[Hawaii] Insurance
Commissioner**
P.O. Box 3614
Honolulu, HI 96811
808-548-5450

**[Hawaii] Judiciary
Department, State**
P.O. Box 2560
Honolulu, HI 96804
808-548-4605

**[Hawaii] Labor & Industrial
Relations, Department of**
830 Punchbowl St., Rm. 321
Honolulu, HI 96813
808-548-3150

**[Hawaii] Land & Natural
Resources Department**
1151 Punchbowl St., Rm. 131
Honolulu, HI 96813
808-548-6550

**[Hawaii] Law Enforcement
Planning Agency, State**
426 Queen St.
Honolulu, HI 96813
808-548-3800

**Hawaii Legal Assistants,
Association of**
P.O. Box 674
Honolulu, HI 96809

[Hawaii] Legislative Auditor
465 S. King St.

Honolulu, HI 96813
808-548-2450

**[Hawaii] Lieutenant Governor,
Office of**
415 S. Beretenia St.
Honolulu, HI 96813
808-548-2544

**[Hawaii] Measurements
Standards**
725 Llalo St.
Honolulu, HI 96813
808-548-7152

**[Hawaii] Occupational Safety &
Health, Division of**
830 Punchbowl St., Rm. 423
Honolulu, HI 96813
808-548-4155

**[Hawaii] Ombudsman,
Office of the**
465 S. King St.
Honolulu, HI 96813
808-548-7811

[Hawaii] Paroling Authority
250 S. King St.
Honolulu, HI 86813
808-548-2530

**[Hawaii] Personnel Services,
Department of**
830 Punchbowl St.
Honolulu, HI 96813
808-548-7405

**[Hawaii] Professional &
Vocational Licensing Division**
1010 Richards St.
Honolulu, HI 96813
808-548-6520

**[Hawaii] Public Defender,
Office of**
1130 N. Nimitz Hwy
Honolulu, HI 96817
808-548-6273

**[Hawaii] Public Utilities
Commission**
465 S. King St., Rm. 103
Honolulu, HI 96813
808-548-3990

**[Hawaii] Public Works,
Division of**
1151 Punchbowl St.

Honolulu, HI 96813
808-548-4560

**[Hawaii] Purchasing &
Supply Division**
P.O. Box 119
Honolulu, HI 96810
808-5548-4057

[Hawaii] Real Estate Commission
1010 Richard St.
Honolulu, HI 96813
808-548-7464

[Hawaii] Regents, Board of
University of Hawaii
Bachman Hall, Rm. 209
Honolulu, HI 96822
808-548-8213

**[Hawaii] Research &
Statistics Office**
1250 Punchbowl St.
Honolulu, HI 96813
808-548-6454

**[Hawaii] Resource
Coordination Division**
426 Queen St., Rm. 201
Honolulu, HI 96813
808-548-3800

[Hawaii] Secretary of State
415 S. Beretania St.
Honolulu, HI 96813
808-548-2544

[Hawaii] Senate
State Capitol
Honolulu, HI 96813
808-548--4675
808-548-7825 (Judiciary)

[Hawaii] Sheriff's Department
111 Alakea St.
Honolulu, HI 96813
808-548-4220

**[Hawaii] Statutes Office,
Revisor of**
Legislative Reference Bureau
State Capitol, Rm. 004
Honolulu, HI 96813
808-548-6237

[Hawaii] Supreme Court
417 S. King St.
Honolulu, HI 96813

808-548-7431
808-548-7432 (Law Library)

[Hawaii] Taxation Department
830 Punchbowl St.
Honolulu, HI 96813
808-548-7650

[Hawaii] Tourism Office
P.O. Box 2359
Honolulu, HI 96804
808-548-3958

**[Hawaii] Transportation,
Department of**
869 Punchbowl St.
Honolulu, HI 96813
808-548-3205

**[Hawaii] Unemployment
Insurance Division**
830 Punchbowl St., Rm. 325
Honolulu, HI 96813
808-548-6951

**[Hawaii] United States
Bankruptcy Court**
P.O. Box 50121
Honolulu, HI 96850
808-541-1791

**[Hawaii] United States
District Court**
P.O. Box 50129
Honolulu, HI 96850
808-541-1300
808-541-1797 (Law Library)

Hawaii, University of
School of Law Library
2525 Dole St.
Honolulu, HI 96822
808-948-7583

**[Hawaii] Vocational
Rehabilitation & Services for
the Blind, Division of**
P.O. Box 339
Honolulu, HI 96809
808-548-4769

**[Hawaii] Women, Commission
on the Status of**
335 Merchant St.
Honolulu, HI 96813
808-548-4199

Hearing Industries Association
1255 23rd St., NW
Wash. D.C. 20037
202-833-1411

Hein & Co., William S.
1285 Main St.
Buffalo, NY 14209
716-882-2600
800-828-7571

Heintz U.S.A.
P.O. Box 57
Pittsburgh, PA 15230
412-237-5740

Hershey Foods Corps
P.O. Box 815
Hershey, PA 17033
800-468-1714

Hertz Corp.
225 Brae Blvd.
Parkridge, NJ 07656
201-307-2000
800-654-3131

Hildebrandt Inc.
50 Division St.
Somerville, NJ 08876
201-725-1600

**Hispanic National Bar
Association**
1 Farragut Sq. South, Suite 901
1634 I. St., NW
Wash. D.C. 20006
202-628-7147

**Home Owners Warranty
Corporation**
HOW Operation Center
P.O. Box 152087
Irving, TX 75015
800-433-7657

Honeywell, Inc.
1885 Douglas Dr.
Golden Valley, MN 55422
800-328-8194

H.W. Wilson Co.
See Wilson

IBM Corp.
Old Orchard Rd.

Armonk, NY 10504
914-765-5546

**[Idaho] Information & Referral
(State Government)**
208-334-2411

[Idaho] Ada County
650 Main St.
Boise, ID 83702
208-383-4417

**[Idaho] Administration,
Department of**
650 W. State
Boise, ID 83720
208-334-3380

[Idaho] Aging, Office on
Statehouse, Rm. 108
Boise, ID 83720
208-334-3833

**[Idaho] Agriculture,
Department of**
P.O. Box 790
Boise, ID 83701
208-334-3240

[Idaho] Air Quality, Bureau of
450 W. State
Boise, ID 83720
208-334-5860

**[Idaho] Alcohol Beverage
Control Division**
6023 Clinton St.
Boise, ID 83704
208-334-2572

[Idaho] Archives & Records
610 N. Julia Davis Dr.
Boise, ID 83702
208-334-3356

**[Idaho] Attorney General,
Office of**
Statehouse, Rm. 210
Boise, ID 83720
208-334-2400

[Idaho] Auditor, Office of State
700 W. State
Boise, ID 83720
208-334-3100

Idaho Bar Association
204 W. State
Boise, ID 83702
208-342-8958

Idaho Bar Association
Bar Admissions
P.O. Box 895
Boise, ID 83701
208-342-8958

[Idaho] Better Business Bureau
409 W. Jefferson
Boise, ID 83702
208-342-4649

**Idaho Bureau of Child Support
Enforcement**
450 W. State St., 7th Fl.
Boise, ID 83720
208-334-5710

[Idaho] Code Commission
101 S. Capitol Blvd., Suite 1500
Boise, ID 83702
208-345-7832

**[Idaho] Commerce,
Department of**
Hall of Mirrors, 2nd Fl.
Boise, ID 83720
208-334-2470

**[Idaho] Consumer
Protection Unit**
State Capitol Bldg., Rm. 117
Boise, ID 83720
208-334-2424

[Idaho] Corporation Division
Secretary of State
Statehouse, Rm. 203
Boise, ID 83720
208-334-2966

**[Idaho] Corrections,
Department of**
1075 Park Blvd.
Boise, ID 83720
208-334-2318

[Idaho] Court of Appeals
537 W. Bannock St.
Boise, ID 83720
208-334-5166

**[Idaho] Courts, Administrative
Office of the**
451 W. State St.
Boise, ID 83720
208-334-2246

**[Idaho] Criminal Identification,
Bureau of**
6083 Clinton

Boise, ID 83704
208-334-2537

**[Idaho] Dairy Products
Commission**
1365 N. Orchard, Suite 203
Boise, ID 83706
208-334-4316

**[Idaho] Disaster Services,
Bureau of**
650 W. State St.
Boise, ID 83720
208-334-3460

**[Idaho] Economic Opportunity
Office, State**
450 W. State St.
Boise, ID 83720
208-334-5731

**[Idaho] Education,
Department of**
650 W. State St.
Boise, Id 83720
208-334-3301

**[Idaho] Education, Office of the
State Board of**
Len. B. Jordan Bldg., Rm. 307
Boise, ID 83720
208-334-2270

**[Idaho] Employment,
Department of**
317 Main
Boise, ID 83735
208-334-6100

**[Idaho] Environmental Quality,
Division of**
450 W. State
Boise, ID 83720
208-334-5839

[Idaho] Examiners, Board of
700 W. State
Boise, ID 83720
208-334-3100

**[Idaho] Family & Children's
Services, Division of**
450 W. State
Boise, ID 83720
208-334-5700

[Idaho] Finance, Department of
700 W. State St., 2nd Fl.
Boise, ID 83720
208-334-3319

**[Idaho] Fish & Game,
Department of**
600 S. Walnut
Boise, ID 83707
208-334-3700

[Idaho] Governor, Office of
State Capitol, West Wing, 2nd Fl.
Boise, ID 83720
208-334-2200

**[Idaho] Hazardous Materials,
Bureau of**
450 W. State
Boise, ID 83720
208-334-5879

**[Idaho] Health & Welfare,
Department of**
450 W. State
Boise, ID 83720
208-334-5500

**[Idaho] Health Statistics,
Center for**
450 W. State, 1st Fl.
Boise, ID 83720
208-334-5976

[Idaho] Highways, Division of
8150 Chinten Blvd.
Boise, ID 83714
208-334-8300

**[Idaho] House of
Representatives**
State Capitol Bldg.
Boise, ID 83720
208-334-2360

**Idaho Human Rights
Commission**
450 W. State St.
Boise, ID 83720
208-334-2873

[Idaho] Industrial Commission
317 Main
Boise, ID 83720
208-334-6000

[Idaho] Insurance, Department of
500 S. 10th St.
Boise, ID 83720
208-334-2250

[Idaho] Insurance Fund, State
Worker's Compensation
317 Main St.

Boise, ID 83720
208-334-2370

**[Idaho] Labor & Industrial
Services, Department of**
277 N. 6th
Boise, ID 83720
208-334-3950

[Idaho] Lands, Department of
State Capitol Bldg., Rm. 121
Boise, ID 83720
208-334-3280

**[Idaho] Law Enforcement,
Department of**
3310 W. State
P.O. Box 55
Boise, ID 83707
208-334-2521

[Idaho] Law Library, State
451 W. State St.
Boise, ID 83720
208-334-3316

**Idaho Legal Assistants,
Association of**
P.O. Box 1254
Boise, ID 83701

[Idaho] Legislative Council
State Capitol
Boise, ID 83720
208-334-2475

**[Idaho] Lieutenant Governor,
Office of**
Statehouse, Rm. 225
Boise, ID 83720
208-334-2200

[Idaho] Liquor Dispensary, State
7185 Bethel
P.O. Box 59
Boise, ID 83707
208-334-3265

[Idaho] Medicine, Board of
500 S. 10th St., Suite 103
Boise, ID 83720
208-334-2822

[Idaho] Mental Health, Bureau of
450 W. State
Boise, ID 83720
208-334-5531

[Idaho] Military, Division of the
Adjutant General's Office

Boise, ID 83707
208-389-5011

[Idaho] Motor Vehicle Bureau
P.O. Box 7129
Boise, ID 83707
208-334-8606

**[Idaho] Occupational Licenses,
Bureau of**
2417 Bank Dr., Rm. 312
Boise, ID 83705
208-334-3233

**[Idaho] Pardons & Parole,
Commission for**
1075 Park Blvd.
Boise, ID 83720
208-334-2318

**[Idaho] Parks & Recreation,
Department of**
2177 Warm Springs Ave.
Boise, ID 83720
208-334-2154

[Idaho] Personnel Commission
700 W. State
Boise, ID 83720
208-334-2263

[Idaho] Potato Commission
303 N. 5th
P.O. Box 1068
Boise, ID 83701
208-334-2350

**Idaho Prosecuting Attorneys
Association, Inc.**
900 W. Washington St.
Boise, ID 83702
208-345-3460

**[Idaho] Public Instruction,
Superintendent of**
650 W. State, Rm. 200
Boise, ID 83720
208-334-3300

**[Idaho] Public Utilities
Commission**
State House
Boise, ID 83720
208-334-3427

[Idaho] Public Works, Division of
502 N. 4th St.
Boise, ID 83720
208-334-3453

[Idaho] Real Estate Commission
633 N.4th
Boise, ID 83720
208-334-3285

**[Idaho] Revenue & Taxation,
Department of**
700 W. State
Boise, ID 83702
208-334-7500

**[Idaho] Secretary of State,
Office of**
Statehouse, Rm. 203
Boise, ID 83720
208-334-2300

[Idaho] Securities Bureau
700 W. State St.
Boise, ID 83720
208-334-3684

Idaho Senate
State Capitol Bldg., Rm. 351
Boise, ID 83720
208-334-2085
208-334-3016 (Judiciary & Rules)

**[Idaho] Soil Conservation
Commission**
801 Capitol Blvd.
Boise, ID 83720
208-334-2148

Idaho State Police Division
3311 W. State
Boise, ID 83703
208-334-3850

[Idaho] Supreme Court
451 W. State
Boise, ID 83720
208-334-2210
208-334-3317 (Law Library)

**[Idaho] Transportation,
Department of**
3311 W. State
Boise, ID 83703
208-334-8000

[Idaho] Treasurer, Office of State
State Capitol Bldg., Rms. 101–107
Boise, ID 83720
208-334-3200

**[Idaho] Unemployment
Insurance Division**
317 Main

Boise, ID 83735
208-334-6466

**[Idaho] Uniform Commercial
Code Division**
Statehouse, West Wing, Basement
Boise, ID 83720
208-334-3191

**[Idaho] United States
Bankruptcy Court**
550 W. Fort St.
Boise, ID 83724
208-334-1361

**[Idaho] United States
District Court**
P.O. Box 039
550 W. Fort St.
Boise, ID 83724
208-334-1361

[Idaho] University of
College of Law Library
Moscow, ID 83843
208-885-6521

**[Idaho] Veterans Services,
Division of**
320 Collins Rd.
P.O. Box 7765
Boise, ID 83707
208-334-5000

**[Idaho] Vital Statistics Standards
& Local Health Services,
Bureau of**
450 W. State St.
Boise, ID 83720
208-334-5976

**[Idaho] Vocational
Rehabilitation, Division of**
650 West State, Rm. 150
Boise, ID 83720
208-334-3390

**[Idaho] Water Resources,
Department of**
1301 N. Orchard
Statehouse Mail
Boise, ID 83720
208-334-7900

**[Idaho] Weights & Measures,
Bureau of**
2216 Kellogg Lane
Boise, ID 83712
208-334-2345

**[Idaho] Women's Programs,
Commission on**
250 N. 5th St.
Pocatello, ID 83205
208-234-0020

**[Illinois] Information & Referral
(State Government)**
217-782-2000

**[Illinois] Information Center
(Federal Government)**
Chicago 312-353-4242

[Illinois] Aging, Department on
421 E. Capitol Ave.
Springfield, IL 62701
217-785-2870
800-252-8966

Illinois Agricultural Association
1701 Towanda Ave.
P.O. Box 2901
Bloomington, IL 61701
309-557-2542

**[Illinois] Agriculture
Department**
P.O. Box 19281
Springfield, IL 62794
217-782-2172

**[Illinois] Air Pollution,
Division of**
1340 N. 9th St.
Springfield, IL 62706
217-782-7326

**[Illinois] Alcoholism &
Substance Abuse,
Department of**
100 W. Randolph St.
Chicago, IL 60601
312-917-3840

**[Illinois] Appellate Court,
First District**
Richard J. Daley Center, Rm. 3060
Chicago, IL 60602
312-793-5484

**[Illinois] Appellate Court,
Second District**
Appellate Court Bldg.
Elgin, IL 60120
312-695-3750

**[Illinois] Appellate Court,
Third District**
111 E. Jefferson St.

Ottawa, IL 61350
815-434-5050

**Illinois Appellate Court,
Fourth District**
INB Center, Suite 560
Springfield, IL 62701
217-782-4154

**[Illinois] Appellate Court,
Fifth District**
Appellate Court Bldg.
Mt. Vernon, IL 62864
618-242-3120

**[Illinois] Appellate Defender's
Office, State**
300 E. Monroe St., Suite 100
Springfield, IL 62701
217-782-7203

[Illinois] Archives, State
Archives Bldg.
Springfield, IL 62756
271-782-4682

[Illinois] Arts Council
100 W. Randolph St., Suite 10-500
Chicago, IL 60601
312-917-6750

**[Illinois] Attorney General,
Office of**
500 S. 2nd St.
Springfield, IL 62701
217-782-1090

**[Illinois] Auditor General, Office
of the**
509 S. 6th St.
Springfield, IL 62701
217-782-6046

**[Illinois] Banks & Trust
Companies, Commissioner of**
117 S. 5th St., Rm. 100
Springfield, IL 62701
217-785-2837
800-634-5452

Illinois Bar Association
424 S. 2nd St.
Springfield, IL 62701
217-525-1760
800-252-8908
217-787-2080 (CLE)
312-726-8775 (Chicago)

**[Illinois] Bar Examiners,
Board of**
340 INB Center
Springfield, IL 62701
217-522-5917

Illinois Bell
225 W. Randolph St.
Chicago, IL 60606
312-727-3386
800-872-8002

[Illinois] Better Business Bureau
211 W. Wacker Dr.
Chicago, IL 60606
312-444-1188
309-673-5194 (Peoria)

[Illinois] Budget, Bureau of the
State Capitol, Rm. 108
Springfield, IL 62706
217-782-4520

**[Illinois] Capital
Development Board**
401 S. Spring St.
Springfield, IL 62706
217-782-8725

**[Illinois] Central Illinois
Paralegal Association**
P.O. Box 153
Normal, IL 61761

**[Illinois] Chicago Bar
Association**
29 S. LaSalle St., Suite 1040
Chicago, IL 60603
312-782-7348

**[Illinois] Chicago Council
of Lawyers**
220 S. State St., Rm. 800
Chicago, IL 60604
312-427-0710

[Illinois] Chicago-Kent
College of Law Library
77 S. Wacker Dr.
Chicago, IL 60606
312-567-5014

**[Illinois] Chicago Law
Department**
Corporation Counsel Library
121 N. LaSalle
Chicago, IL 60602
312-744-5124

**[Illinois] Chicago
Mayor's Office**
121 N. LaSalle St., Rm. 507
Chicago, IL 60602
312-744-5000

**[Illinois] Children & Family
Services, Department of**
406 E. Monroe St.
Springfield, IL 62701
217-785-2509

**[Illinois] Child Support
Enforcement, Division of**
201 S. Grand Ave., East
Springfield, IL 62794
217-782-1366

**[Illinois] Circuit Court of
Cook County**
2650 S. California Ave.
Chicago, IL 60608
312-890-3333

**[Illinois] Citizens Assistance &
Consumer Affairs, Office of**
201 W. Monroe St.
Springfield, IL 62706
217-782-0244
800-642-3112
312-917-3580 (Chicago)

**[Illinois] Commerce &
Community Affairs,
Department of**
620 E. Adams St.
Springfield, IL 62701
217-782-7500

[Illinois] Commerce Commission
527 E. Capitol Ave.
P.O. Box 19280
Springfield, IL 62794
217-782-7295

[Illinois] Comptroller, State
State Capitol, Rm. 201
Springfield, IL 62706
217-782-6000

**[Illinois] Conservation,
Department of**
542 S. 2nd St., Rm. 425
Springfield, IL 62701
217-782-6302

**[Illinois] Consumer Protection
Division**
500 S. 2nd St.

Springfield, IL 62706
217-782-9011
312-917-3580 (Chicago)

[Illinois] Cook County
118 N. Clark
Chicago, IL 60602
312-443-6398

**[Illinois] Cook County
Department of Corrections**
2700 S. California Ave.
Chicago, IL 60608
312-890-7100

**[Illinois] Cook County
Law Library**
2900 Richard J. Daley Center
Chicago, IL 60602
312-443-5423

**[Illinois] Corrections,
Department of**
1301 Concordia Court
Springfield, IL 62794
217-522-2666

**[Illinois] Courts, Administrative
Office of the**
Supreme Court Bldg.
Springfield, IL 62706
217-782-7770

**[Illinois] Criminal Justice
Authority**
120 S. Riverside Plaza
Chicago, IL 60606
312-793-8550

**[Illinois] De Paul University Law
Library**
25 E. Jackson Blvd.
Chicago, IL 60604
312-341-8121

**[Illinois] DuPage County
Law Library**
201 S. Reber St.
Wheaton, IL 60187
312-682-7337

**[Illinois] Education,
State Board of**
100 N. 1st St.
Springfield, IL 62777
217-782-2221

[Illinois] Elections, Board of
P.O. Box 4187

Springfield, IL 62708
217-782-4141

**[Illinois] Emergency Services &
Disaster Agency**
110 E. Adams St.
Springfield, IL 62706
217-782-7860

**[Illinois] Employment Security,
Department of**
401 S. State St.
Chicago, IL 60605
312-973-5700

**[Illinois] Energy & Natural
Resources, Department of**
235 W. Adams St., 3rd Fl.
Springfield, IL 62704
217-785-2800

**[Illinois] Environmental
Protection Agency**
2200 Churchill Rd.
Springfield, IL 62702
217-782-3397

[Illinois] Ethics, Board of
100 W. Randolph St.
Springfield, IL 60601
217-917-4100

[Illinois] Governor, Office of
207 State House
Springfield, IL 62706
217-782-6830

**[Illinois] Higher Education,
Board of**
4 W. Old State Capitol Plaza
Springfield, IL 62701
217-782-2551

[Illinois] Highways, Division of
2300 S. Dirksen Pkwy.
Springfield, IL 62764
217-782-2151

**[Illinois] Historic Preservation
Agency**
Old State Capitol
Springfield, IL 62701
217-782-4836

**[Illinois] House of
Representatives**
State Capitol
Springfield, IL 62706

217-782-8223
217-782-8398 (Judiciary I)
217-782-0425 (Judiciary II)

**[Illinois] Human Rights,
Department of**
100 W. Randolph St.
Chicago, IL 60601
312-793-6245

**Illinois, Independent
Contractors Association of**
6400 Woodward Ave.
Downers Grove, IL 60516

[Illinois] Industrial Commission
100 W. Randolph St.
Chicago, IL 60601
312-917-6500
312-917-6555 (Workers'
Compensation)

**[Illinois] Insurance,
Department of**
320 W. Washington St., 4th Fl.
Springfield, IL 62767
217-782-4515

**[Illinois] John Marshall Law
School Library**
315 S. Plymouth Court
Chicago, IL 60604
312-987-1413

[Illinois] Labor, Department of
1 W. Old State Capitol Plaza
Springfield, IL 62701
217-782-6206
217-782-9386 (Occupational Safety)

**[Illinois] Lake County Law
Library**
18 N. County St.
Waukegan, IL 60085
312-360-6654

**Illinois Legislative Information
System**
705 Stratton Bldg.
Springfield, IL 62706
217-782-3944

**[Illinois] Legislative Reference
Bureau**
State House, Rm. 112
Springfield, IL 62706
217-782-6625

[Illinois] Library, State
Centennial Bldg., Rm. 275
Springfield, IL 62756
217-782-2994

**[Illinois] Lieutenant Governor,
Office of**
214 State House
Springfield, IL 62706
217-782-7884

**[Illinois] Liquor Control
Commission**
100 W. Randolph St.
Chicago, IL 60601
312-917-2206

[Illinois] Lottery, State
676 N. St. Clair, Suite 2040
Chicago, IL 60611
312-793-1681

**[Illinois] Loyola University
of Chicago**
School of Law Library
1 E. Pearson St.
Chicago, IL 60606
312-670-2950

**[Illinois] Management Services,
Department of Central**
401 S. Spring St., Rm. 614
Springfield, IL 62706
217-782-2141

**[Illinois] McHenry County
Law Library**
2200 Seminary St.
Woodstock, IL 60098
815-338-2040

**[Illinois] Mental Health &
Developmental Disabilities,
Department of**
401 S. Spring St.
Springfield, IL 62706
217-782-7179

**[Illinois] Mines & Minerals,
Department of**
400 S. Spring St., Suite 704
Springfield, IL 62706
217-782-6791

**[Illinois] Municipal Reference
Library**
City Hall, Rm. 1004
Chicago, IL 60602
312-744-4992

[Illinois] Northern Illinois University
College of Law Library
De Kalb, IL 60115
815-753-0505

[Illinois] Northwestern University
School of Law Library
357 E. Chicago Ave.
Chicago, IL 60611
312-908-8451

[Illinois] Nuclear Safety, Department of
1035 Outer Park Dr.
Springfield, IL 62704
217-785-9000

[Illinois] Oil & Gas, Division of
400 S. Spring St., Stratton Bldg.
Springfield, IL 62706
217-782-7756

Illinois Paralegal Association
P.O. Box 857
Chicago, IL 60690

[Illinois] Peoria County
324 Main St.
Peoria, IL 61602
309-672-6059

[Illinois] Peoria County Law Library
Court House, Rm. 209
Peoria, IL 61602
309-672-6084

[Illinois] Planning, Office of
107 Stratton Bldg.
Springfield, IL 62706
217-782-2654

[Illinois] Prisoner Review Board
319 E. Madison St.
Springfield, IL 62701
217-782-7273

[Illinois] Procurement Services Division
401 S. Spring St.
Springfield, IL 62706
217-782-4705

[Illinois] Professional Regulation, Department of
320 W. Washington St.

Springfield, IL 62786
217-785-0800

[Illinois] Public Health, Department of
535 W. Jefferson St.
Springfield, IL 62761
217-782-4977

[Illinois] Public Utility Division
527 E. Capitol Ave., 3rd Fl.
Springfield, IL 62701
217-782-7892

[Illinois] Real Estate Commissioner
320 W. Washington St.
Springfield, IL 62786
217-785-0800

[Illinois] Rehabilitation Services, Department of
623 E. Adams St.
Springfield, IL 62705
217-785-0218

[Illinois] Revenue, Department of
101 W. Jefferson St.
Springfield, IL 62702
217-785-2602

[Illinois] Sagamon County
800 E. Monroe
Springfield, IL 62701
217-753-6600

[Illinois] Secretary of State
213 State House
Springfield, IL 62756
217-782-2201

[Illinois] Securities Department
188 W. Randolph St., #426
Chicago, IL 60601
312-793-3384

[Illinois] Senate
State Capitol
Springfield, IL 62706
217-782-4517
217-782-8503 (Judiciary)

[Illinois] Southern Illinois University
School of Law Library
Lesar Law Bldg.

Carbondale, IL 62901
618-536-7711

[Illinois] State Police, Department of
103 Armory Bldg.
Springfield, IL 62706
217-782-2841

[Illinois] Statesville Correctional Center Library
P.O. Box 112
Joliet, IL 60424
815-727-3607

[Illinois] Supreme Court
Supreme Court Bldg.
Springfield, IL 62706
217-782-2035
217-782-7864 (Clerk)
217-782-2424 (Law Library)

[Illinois] Transportation, Department of
2300 S. Dirksen Parkway
Springfield, IL 62764
217-782-5597

[Illinois] Treasurer
State Capitol, Rm. 219
Springfield, IL 62706
217-782-2211

[Illinois] Unemployment Insurance, Division of
401 S. State St.
Chicago, IL 60605
312-793-4240

[Illinois] United States Bankruptcy Court
Central Illinois
P.O. Box 2438
Springfield, IL 62705
217-492-4550

[Illinois] United States Bankruptcy Court
Northern Illinois
219 S. Dearborn St.
Chicago, IL 60604
312-435-5587

[Illinois] United States Bankruptcy Court
Southern Illinois
750 Missouri Ave.

P.O. Box 309
East St. Louis, IL 62202
618-482-9365

[Illinois] United States Court of Appeals for the Seventh Circuit
219 S. Dearborn St.
Chicago, IL 60604
312-435-5850
312-435-5661 (Law Library)

[Illinois] United States District Court
Central District
P.O. Box 315
Springfield, IL 62705
217-492-4020

[Illinois] United States District Court
Northern District
219 S. Dearborn St.
Chicago, IL 60604
312-435-5670

[Illinois] United States District Court
Southern Illinois
750 Missouri Ave.
P.O. Box 249
East St. Louis, IL 62202
618-482-9371

[Illinois] United States Government Printing Office
219 S. Dearborn St., Rm. 1365
Chicago, IL 60604
312-353-5133

[Illinois] University of Chicago
D'Angelo Law Library
1121 E. 60th St.
Chicago, IL 60637
312-702-9615

[Illinois] University of Illinois
Law Library
504 E. Pennsylvania Ave.
Champaign, IL 61820
217-333-2914

[Illinois] Vehicle Services Department
Centennial Bldg., Rm. 312
Springfield, IL 62756
217-785-3000

[Illinois] Veterans' Affairs, Department of
P.O. Box 19432
Springfield, IL 62794
217-782-6641

[Illinois] Vital Records, Division of
605 W. Jefferson St.
Springfield, IL 62702
217-782-6553

[Illinois] Water Resources, Division of
2300 S. Dirksen Pkwy.
Springfield, IL 62764
217-782-2152

[Illinois] Weights & Measures Program
801 E. Sangamon Ave.
Springfield, IL 62794
217-782-3817

[Illinois] Will County Law Library
14 W. Jefferson St, 4th Fl.
Joliet, IL 60431
815-727-8536

[Illinois] Women's Affairs
100 W. Randolph St.
Chicago, IL 60601
312-917-6709

Immigration Reform Law Institute
1666 Connecticut Ave., NW,
Suite 402
Wash. D.C. 20009
202-462-1969

Incorporated Society of Irish/American Lawyers
15140 Farmington Rd.
Livonia, MI 48154
313-522-5900

Independent Association of Questioned Document Examiners
403 W. Washington
Red Oak, IA 51566
712-623-9130

Independent Truckers & Drivers Association
1109 Plover Dr.
Baltimore, MD 21227
301-242-0507

[Indiana] Information & Referral (State Government)
317-232-3140

[Indiana] Information Center (Federal Government)
Gary 219-883-4100
Indianapolis 317-226-7373

[Indiana] Accounts, Board of
100 N. Senate Ave.
Indianapolis, IN 46204
317-232-2524

[Indiana] Administration, Department of
100 N. Senate Ave., Rm. 507
Indianapolis, IN 46204
317-232-3114

[Indiana] Agriculture Division
1 N. Capitol
Indianapolis, IN 46204
317-232-8770

[Indiana] Air Management, Office of
105 S. Meridian St., Rm. 201
Indianapolis, IN 46225
317-232-8222

[Indiana] Alcoholic Beverage Commission
251 N. Illinois
Indianapolis, IN 46204
317-232-2448

[Indiana] Archives Division
140 N. Senate Ave.
State Office Bldg., Rm. 501
Indianapolis, IN 46204
317-232-3661

[Indiana] Arts Commission
47 S. Pennsylvania Ave.
Indianapolis, IN 46204
317-232-1286

[Indiana] Attorney General, Office of
219 State House
Indianapolis, IN 46204
317-232-6201

Indiana Bar Association
230 E. Ohio St., 6th Fl.
Indianapolis, IN 46204
317-639-5465

Indiana Bell
220 N. Meridian St.
Indianapolis, IN 46204
317-265-5628
800-562-2612

[Indiana] Better Business Bureau
22 E. Washington St.
Indianapolis, IN 46204
317-637-0197
219-980-1511 (Gary)

[Indiana] Budget Agency
100 N. Senate Ave., Rm. 212
Indianapolis, IN 46204
317-232-5610

**[Indiana] Business Expansion,
Office of**
One N. Capitol St.
Indianapolis, IN 46204
317-232-0160

**[Indiana] Child Support
Division**
141 S. Meridian St., 4th Fl.
Indianapolis, IN 46225
317-232-4885

**[Indiana] Civil Defense,
Department of**
100 N. Senate Ave., Rm. 90B
Indianapolis, IN 46204
317-232-3830

**[Indiana] Civil Rights
Commission**
32 E. Washington St.
Indianapolis, IN 46204
317-232-2613

**[Indiana] Code Revision,
Office of**
Legislative Services Agency
State House, Rm. 302
Indianapolis, IN 46204
317-232-9572

**[Indiana] Commerce,
Department of**
1 N. Capitol St., Suite 700
Indianapolis, IN 46204
317-232-8801

**[Indiana] Consumer Protection
Division**
219 State House

Indianapolis, IN 46204
317-232-6330
800-382-5516

[Indiana] Corporation Division
State House, Rm. 201
Indianapolis, IN 46204
317-232-6587

**[Indiana] Correction,
Department of**
804 State Office Bldg.
Indianapolis, IN 46204
317-232-5766

**[Indiana] Court Administration,
State**
State House, Rm. 323
Indianapolis, IN 46204
317-232-2542

**[Indiana] Crime Compensation
Division, Violent**
100 N. State Ave.
Indianapolis, IN 46204
317-232-7103

**[Indiana] Criminal Justice
Institute**
101 W. Ohio St.
Indianapolis, IN 46204
317-232-1233

**[Indiana] Education,
Department of**
200 W. Washington St.
229 State House
Indianapolis, IN 46204
317-232-6610

[Indiana] Election Board, State
850 N. Meridian St.
Indianapolis, IN 46204
317-232-3939

**[Indiana] Employment &
Training Services,
Department of**
100 N. Senate Ave.
Indianapolis, IN 46204
317-232-7670

**[Indiana] Employment Security
Division**
10 N. Senate Ave., Rm. 300
Indianapolis, IN 46204
317-232-0195

**[Indiana] Energy Policy,
Division of**
1 N. Capitol St.
Indianapolis, IN 46204
317-232-8940

**[Indiana] Environmental
Management, Department of**
105 S. Meridian
Indianapolis, IN 46225
317-232-3120

**[Indiana] Ethics Commission,
State**
One N. Capitol
Indianapolis, IN 46204
317-232-3850

**[Indiana] Financial Institutions,
Department of**
State Office Bldg., Rm. 1024
Indianapolis, IN 46204
317-232-3955
800-382-4880

[Indiana] Governor, Office of
206 State House
Indianapolis, IN 46204
317-232-4567

[Indiana] Health, State Board of
1330 W. Michigan St.
Indianapolis, IN 46202
317-633-8400

**[Indiana] Health Statistics,
Public**
1330 W. Michigan St., Rm. 236
Indianapolis, IN 46202
317-633-8512

**[Indiana] Higher Education,
Commission for**
101 W. Ohio St., Rm. 550
Indianapolis, IN 46204
317-232-1900

**[Indiana] Highways,
Department of**
100 N. Senate Ave.
Indianapolis, IN 46204
317-232-5526

**[Indiana] House of
Representatives**
State House
Indianapolis, IN 46204

317-232-9856
317-232-3140 (Judiciary)

[Indiana] Human Services, Department of
P.O. Box 7083
Indianapolis, IN 46207
317-232-7000
317-232-6500 (Vocational Rehabilitation)

[Indiana] Indianapolis Bar Association
1 Indiana Sq.
Indianapolis, IN 46204
317-632-8240

[Indiana] Indianapolis City Hall
200 E. Washington St.
Indianapolis, IN 46204
317-236-3200

[Indiana] Industrial Hygiene & Radiological Health, Division of
1330 W. Michigan St.
Indianapolis, IN 46202
317-633-0147

[Indiana] Insurance, Commissioner of
311 W. Washington St., Suite 300
Indianapolis, IN 46204
317-232-2385
800-622-4461

[Indiana] Labor, Department of
100 N. Senate Ave., Rm. 1013
Indianapolis, IN 46204
317-232-2663

[Indiana] Lake County Central Law Library
3400 Broadway
Gary, IL 46408
219-980-6797

[Indiana] Law Examiners, State Board of
101 W. Ohio St., Suite 450
Indianapolis, IN 46204
317-232-2552

Indiana Library, State
140 N. Senate Ave.
Indianapolis, IN 46204
317-232-3692

[Indiana] Licensing Agency, Professional
100 N. Senate Ave.
Indianapolis, IN 46204
317-232-2980

[Indiana] Lieutenant Governor, Office of
333 State House
Indianapolis, IN 46204
317-232-4545

[Indiana] Marion County
201 E. Washington St., Rm. W-122
Indianapolis, IN 46204
317-236-3200

[Indiana] Marion County Law Library
602 City County Bldg.
Indianapolis, IN 46204
317-236-5499

[Indiana] Mental Health, Department of
117 E. Washington St.
Indianapolis, IN 46204
317-232-7844

[Indiana] Mines & Mine Safety, Bureau of
6 NE 21st St.
Washington, IN 47501
812-254-1040

[Indiana] Motor Vehicle Bureau
100 N. Senate Ave.
Indianapolis, IN 46204
317-232-2800

[Indiana] Natural Resources, Department of
State Office Bldg., Rm. 608
Indianapolis, IN 46204
317-232-4020

[Indiana] Notre Dame Law School
Kresge Library
Notre Dame, IN 46556
219-239-7024

[Indiana] Oil & Gas, Division of
100 N. Senate Ave., Rm. 911B
Indianapolis, IN 46204
317-232-4055

Indiana Paralegal Association, Inc.
P.O. Box 44518, Federal Station
Indianapolis, IN 46204

[Indiana] Parole Board
803 State Office Bldg.
Indianapolis, IN 46204
317-232-5737

[Indiana] Parole Services Section
100 N. Senate Ave., Suite 804
Indianapolis, IN 46204
317-232-5726

[Indiana] Personnel Department
100 N. Senate Ave.
Indianapolis, IN 46204
317-232-3056

[Indiana] Probation Administration
1800 N. Meridian St., Suite 404
Indianapolis, IN 46202
317-232-1313

[Indiana] Procurement Division
100 N. Senate Ave.
Indianapolis, IN 46204
317-232-3032

[Indiana] Public Defender, Office of
309 W. Washington St., 5th Fl.
Indianapolis, IN 46204
317-232-2475

[Indiana] Public Records, Commission on
State Office Bldg., Rm. 501
Indianapolis, IN 46204
317-232-3373

[Indiana] Public Welfare, Department of
100 N. Senate Ave.
Indianapolis, IN 46204
317-232-4705

[Indiana] Public Works, Division of
100 N. Senate Ave., Rm. 510
Indianapolis, IN 46204
317-232-3000

[Indiana] Revenue, Department of
100 N. Senate Ave.

Indianapolis, IN 46204
317-232-2101

[Indiana] Secretary of State
201 State House
Indianapolis, IN 46203
317-232-6531

[Indiana] Securities Division
1 N. Capitol St., Suite 560
Indianapolis, IN 46204
317-232-6690

[Indiana] Senate
State House
Indianapolis, IN 46204
317-232-9856
317-232-3140 (Judiciary)

**[Indiana] Service Commission,
Public**
913 State Office Bldg.
Indianapolis, IN 46204
317-232-2700

**[Indiana] Solid & Hazardous
Waste Management, Office of**
105 S. Meridian St.
Indianapolis, IN 46225
317-232-4454

[Indiana] State Police
100 N. Senate Ave., Rm. 101
Indianapolis, IN 46204
317-232-8241

[Indiana] Supreme Court
217 State House
Indianapolis, IN 46204
317-232-1930
317-232-2540 (Administration)
317-232-2557 (Law Library)

**[Indiana] Transportation,
Department of**
143 W. Market St., Suite 300
Indianapolis, IN 46204
317-232-1470

[Indiana] Treasurer
242 State House
Indianapolis, IN 46204
317-232-6386

**[Indiana] Unemployment
Insurance**
10 N. Senate Ave., Rm. 209

Indianapolis, IN 46204
317-232-8087

**[Indiana] United States
Bankruptcy Court**
Northern Indiana
204 S. Main St., Rm. 224
South Bend, IN 46601
219-236-8247

**[Indiana] United States
Bankruptcy Court**
Southern Indiana
46 E. Ohio St., Rm. 123
Indianapolis, IN 46204
317-226-6710

**[Indiana] United States
District Court**
Northern District
204 S. Main St., Rm. 102
South Bend, IN 46602
219-236-8260
219-236-8767 (Law Library)

**[Indiana] United States
District Court**
Southern District
46 E. Ohio St., Rm. 105
Indianapolis, IN 46204
317-226-6770
317-269-2092 (Law Library)

**Indiana University School of
Law Library**
735 W. New York St.
Indianapolis, IN 46202
317-274-8825
812-855-9666 (Bloomington)

**[Indiana] Utility Regulatory
Commission**
913 State Office Bldg.
100 N. Senate Ave.
Indianapolis, IN 46204
317-232-2701

[Indiana] Valparaiso University
School of Law Library
Valparaiso, IN 46383
219-465-7838

**[Indiana] Vanderburgh County
Law Library**
207 City-County Courts Bldg.
Evansville, IL 47708
812-426-5175

**[Indiana] Veterans' Affairs,
Department of**
100 N. Senate Ave.
Indianapolis, IN 46204
317-232-3910

[Indiana] Water, Division of
2475 Directors Row
Indianapolis, IN 46241
317-232-4161

**[Indiana] Water Management,
Office of**
105 S. Meridian St.
Indianapolis, IN 46225
317-232-8670

[Indiana] Weights & Measures
1330 W. Michigan St.
Indianapolis, IN 46206
317-633-0350

**[Indiana] Worker's
Compensation Board**
601 State Office Bldg.
Indianapolis, IN 46204
317-232-3808

**Information Industry
Association**
555 New Jersey Ave., NW, Suite 800
Wash. D.C. 20001
202-639-8262

Institute for Court Management
1331 17th St., Suite 402
Denver, CO 80202
303-293-3063

**Institute for Government
Forums**
1710 Rhode Island Ave., Suite 600
Wash. D.C. 20036
202-466-8204

**Institute for International Legal
Information**
P.O. Box 158927
Nashville, TN 37215

**Institute for Mediation &
Conflict Resolution**
99 Hudson St.
New York, NY 10013
212-966-3660

Institute of Advanced Law Study
3419 Thom Blvd.

Las Vegas, NV 89106
702-873-4542

Institute of Continuing Legal Education
1020 Green St.
Ann Arbor, MI 48109
313-764-0533

Institute of Internal Auditors, Inc.
249 Maitland Ave.
Altamonte Springs, FL 32701
407-830-7600

Institute of Judicial Information
1 Washington Sq. Village
New York, NY 10012
212-998-6280

Institute of Legal Executives
Kempston Manor
Kempston, Bedford England

Institute of Public Administration
55 W. 44th St.
New York, NY 10036
212-730-5480

Insurance Information Institute
110 William St.
New York, NY 10038
212-669-9200

Inter-American Bar Association
1889 F. St., NW, Suite LL-2
Wash. D.C. 20006
202-789-2747
202-293-1455 (Foundation)

Inter-American Defense Fund
2600 16th St., NW
Wash. D.C. 20441
202-939-6660

Inter-American Development Bank
1300 New York Ave., NW
Wash. D.C. 20577
202-623-1000
202-623-2164 (Law Library)

International Academy of Trial Lawyers
210 S. 1st St., Suite 206
San Jose, CA 95113
408-275-6767

International Association for Financial Planning
2 Concourse Parkway, Suite 800
Atlanta, GA 30328
404-395-1605

International Association of Arson Investigators
5428 Del Maria Way
Louisville, KY 40291
502-491-7482

International Association of Auto Theft Investigators
255 S. Vernon
Dearborn, MI 48124
313-561-8583

International Association of Chiefs of Police
13 Firstfield Rd.
Gaithersburg, MD 20878
301-948-0922

International Association of Credit Card Investigators
1620 Grant Ave.
Novato, CA 94945
415-897-8800

International Association of Defense Counsel
20 N. Wacker Dr., Suite 3100
Chicago, IL 60606
312-368-1494

International Association of Fire Chiefs
1329 18th St., NW
Wash. D.C. 20036
202-833-3420

International Association of Law Libraries
University of Chicago Law Library
1121 E. 60th St.
Chicago, IL 60637
312-702-9599

International Bank for Reconstruction & Development
1818 H. St., NW
Wash. D.C. 20433
202-477-1234
202-477-2128 (Law Library)

International Bar Association
2 Harewood Pl.
Hanover Sq.
London W1R 9HB England
01-629-1206

International Bureau of Fiscal Documentation
P.O. Box 20237
NL-1000 HE Amsterdam
The Netherlands

International Center for Law in Development
777 United Nations Plaza
New York, NY 10017
212-687-0036

International Centre for Settlement of Investment Disputes
1818 H. St., NW
Wash. D.C. 20433
202-477-1234

International City Management Association
1120 G. St., NW
Wash. D.C. 20005
202-626-4600

International Civil Service Commission
2 United Nations Plaza, Rm. 1060
New York, NY 10017
212-963-8466

International Common Law Exchange Society
P.O. Box 51
Palo Alto, CA 94302
415-962-8073

International Federation of Library Associations & Institutions
Postbus 95312
NL-2509 Ch The Hague
Netherlands
70 140884

International Federation of Women Lawyers
186 5th Ave.
New York, NY 10010
212-206-1666

**International Finance
  Corporation**
1818 H. St., NW
Wash. D.C. 20433
202-477-1234

**International Footprint
  Association**
1095 Market St., Rm. 206
San Francisco, CA 94103
415-431-3324

**International Institute of
  Municipal Clerks**
160 N. Altadena Dr.
Pasadena, CA 91107
818-795-6153

International Law Institute
888 16th St.
Wash. D.C. 20006
202-463-7979

**International Legal Defense
  Counsel**
111 S. 15th St., 24th Fl.
Philadelphia, PA 19102
215-977-9982

International Monetary Fund
700 19th St., NW
Wash. D.C. 20431
202-623-7000
202-623-7054

**International Narcotic
  Enforcement Officers
  Association**
112 State St., Suite 1200
Albany, NY 12207
518-463-6232

**International Patent &
  Trademark Association**
33 W. Monroe
Chicago, IL 60603
312-641-1500

**International Society of
  Barristers**
3586 E. Huron River Rd.
Ann Arbor, MI 48104
313-577-3933

International Tax Institute
200 Park Ave.
New York, NY 10166
212-880-4408

**International Trade
  Commission Trial Lawyers
  Association**
815 Connecticut Ave., NW
Wash. D.C. 20006
202-659-5070

**[Iowa] Information & Referral
  (State Government)**
515-281-5011

**[Iowa] Information Center
  (Federal Government)**
800-532-1556

**[Iowa] Agriculture & Land
  Stewardship, Department of**
E. 9th & Grand Ave.
Des Moines, IA 50319
515-281-8852

**[Iowa] Air Quality & Solid Waste
  Protection Bureau**
900 E. Grand Ave.
Des Moines, IA 50319
515-281-5322

**[Iowa] Appellate Defender
  Department of Inspections &
  Appeals**
Lucas State Office Bldg.
Des Moines, IA 50319
515-281-8828

**[Iowa] Attorney General,
  Office of**
1300 E. Walnut St.
Des Moines, IA 50319
515-281-5164

**[Iowa] Banking,
  Superintendent of**
200 E. Grand, Suite 300
Des Moines, IA 50309
515-281-4014

Iowa Bar Association
1101 Fleming Bldg.
Des Moines, IA 50309
515-243-3179

[Iowa] Bar Examiners, Board of
Supreme Court of Iowa
State Capitol Bldg.
Des Moines, IA 50319
515-281-5911

[Iowa] Better Business Bureau
615 Insurance Exchange Bldg.

Des Moines, IA 50309
515-243-8137
319-366-5401 (Cedar Rapids)

**[Iowa] Campaign Finance
  Disclosure Commission**
507 10th St.
Des Moines, IA 50319
515-281-4411

**[Iowa] Citizens
  Aide/Ombudsman**
215 E. 7th St.
Des Moines, IA 50319
515-281-3592
800-358-5510

[Iowa] Civil Rights Commission
211 E. Maple St., 2nd Fl.
Des Moines, IA 50319
515-281-4121

[Iowa] Collections, Bureau of
Child Support Enforcement
Hoover Bldg., 5th Fl.
Des Moines, IA 50319
515-281-5580

**[Iowa] Commerce,
  Department of**
1918 SE Hulsizer, 5th Fl.
Des Moines, IA 50021
515-281-7400

**[Iowa] Consumer Protection
  Division**
1300 E. Walnut St.
Des Moines, IA 50319
515-281-5926

**[Iowa] Corrections,
  Department of**
523 E. 12th St.
Capitol Annex
Des Moines, IA 50319
515-281-4811

[Iowa] Court Administrator
Statehouse
Des Moines, IA 50319
515-281-5241

Iowa, Court of Appeals of
Statehouse
Des Moines, IA 50319
515-281-5221

[Iowa] Crime Victim Assistance
Attorney General's Office

Des Moines, IA 50319
515-281-5044

**[Iowa] Disaster Services,
Office of**
1300 E. Walnut St.
Des Moines, IA 50319
515-281-3231

[Iowa] Drake University
School of Law Library
Des Moines, IA 50311
515-271-2141

[Iowa] Dubuque County
720 Central
Dubuque, Ia 52001
319-589-4418

**[Iowa] Economic Development,
Department of**
200 E. Grand Ave.
Des Moines, IA 50319
515-281-7636

[Iowa] Education, Department of
Grimes State Office Bldg.
Des Moines, IA 50319
515-281-5294

**[Iowa] Elder Affairs,
Department of**
914 Grand Ave.
Des Moines, IA 50319
515-281-5187

**[Iowa] Employment Appeal
Board**
Lucas State Office Bldg., 2nd Fl.
Des Moines, IA 50319
515-281-4159

**[Iowa] Employment Services,
Department of**
1000 E. Grand Ave., Suite 236
Des Moines, IA 50319
515-281-5187
800-532-3213

[Iowa] Energy Division
900 E. Grand Ave.
Des Moines, IA 50319
515-281-8681

**[Iowa] Environmental
Protection Division**
900 E. Grand Ave.
Des Moines, IA 50319
515-281-6284

Iowa Finance Authority
200 E. Grand St.
Des Moines, IA 50319
515-281-4058

**[Iowa] General Services
Department**
1300 E. Walnut St., A Level
Des Moines, IA 50319
515-281-3196

[Iowa] Governor, Office of
Capitol Bldg.
Des Moines, IA 50319
515-281-5211

[Iowa] Highways Division
800 Lincoln Way
Ames, IA 50010
515-239-1124

[Iowa] House of Representatives
State Capitol Bldg.
Des Moines, IA 50319
515-281-3221
512-281-6996 (Judiciary & Law
Enforcement)

Iowa Humanities Board
University of Iowa
Oakdale Hall
Iowa City, IA 52242
319-335-4153

**[Iowa] Human Services,
Department of**
Hoover Bldg.
Des Moines, IA 50319
515-281-5452

**[Iowa] Industrial Services,
Division of**
100 E. Grand Ave.
Des Moines, IA 50319
515-281-5934

**[Iowa] Insurance,
Commissioner of**
Lucas State Office Bldg., 6th Fl.
Des Moines, IA 50319
515-281-5705

[Iowa] Job Insurance, Bureau of
1000 E. Grand Ave.
Des Moines, IA 50319
515-281-5526

[Iowa] Johnson County
417 S. Clinton St.

Iowa City, IA 52240
319-356-6060

[Iowa] Judicial Department
10th St. & Grand Ave.
Des Moines, IA 50319
515-281-5241

[Iowa] Labor Division
1000 Grand Ave.
Des Moines, IA 50319
515-281-3606

[Iowa] Law Library, State
State Capitol Bldg.
Des Moines, IA 50319
515-281-5124

**[Iowa] Legislative Service
Bureau**
State Capitol
Des Moines, IA 50319
515-281-3566

**[Iowa] Library/Archives,
Bureau of**
600 E. Locust St.
Des Moines, IA 50319
515-281-3007

**[Iowa] Licensing & Regulation,
Professional**
1918 SE Hulsizer Ave
Des Moines, IA 50021
515-281-4126

**[Iowa] Lieutenant Governor,
Office of**
Capitol Bldg.
Des Moines, IA 50319
515-281-3421

[Iowa] Linn County
P.O. Box 1468
Cedar Rapids, IA 52406
319-398-3411

Iowa Lottery
2015 Grand Ave.
Des Moines, IA 50312
515-281-7900

**[Iowa] Management,
Department of**
1000 E. Grand Ave.
State Capitol Bldg., Rm. 12
Des Moines, IA 50319
515-281-3322

[Iowa] Motor Vehicle Division
5268 NW 2nd Ave.
Des Moines, IA 50313
515-281-3697

**[Iowa] Natural Resources,
Department of**
900 E. Grand Ave.
Des Moines, IA 50319
515-281-5385

**[Iowa] Occupational Safety &
Health Administration**
1000 E. Grand
Des Moines, IA 50319
515-281-3606

[Iowa] Paralegals of Iowa, Ltd.
P.O. Box 1943
Cedar Rapids, IA 52406

[Iowa] Parole, Board of
523 E. 12th St.
Capitol Annex
Des Moines, IA 50319
515-281-4820

[Iowa] Patrol, State
E. 9th & Grand Ave.
Des Moines, IA 50319
515-281-5824

[Iowa] Personnel, Department of
E. 14th St. & Grand Ave.
Des Moines, IA 50319
515-281-3351

[Iowa] Polk County
500 Mulberry
Des Moines, IA 50309
515-286-3772

**[Iowa] Public Health,
Department of**
E. 12th & Walnut Sts.
Des Moines, IA 50319
515-281-5605

**[Iowa] Purchasing & Material
Management Division**
Hoover Bldg., Level A
Des Moines, IA 50319
515-281-5981

**[Iowa] Real Estate Examining
Board**
1918 SE Hulsizer Ave.
Des Moines, IA 50021
515-281-3183

[Iowa] Regents, State Board of
E. 12th & Walnut Sts.
Des Moines, IA 50319
515-281-3934

**[Iowa] Revenue & Finance,
Department of**
1300 E. Walnut St.
Des Moines, IA 50319
515-281-3204

[Iowa] Secretary of State
National Capitol Bldg.
Des Moines, IA 50319
515-281-5864

**[Iowa] Securities,
Superintendent of**
Lucas State Office Bldg.
Des Moines, IA 50319
515-281-4441

[Iowa] Senate
State Capitol Bldg.
Des Moines, IA 50319
515-281-3371
512-281-7347 (Judiciary)

[Iowa] Supreme Court
State Capitol Bldg.
Des Moines, IA 50319
515-281-5911

**[Iowa] Transportation,
Department of**
800 Lincoln Way
Ames, IA 50010
515-239-1111

[Iowa] Treasurer
State Capitol Bldg.
Des Moines, IA 50319
515-281-5366

**[Iowa] Uniform Commercial
Code Division**
300 E. Walnut St.
Des Moines, IA 50319
515-281-6560

**[Iowa] United States Bankruptcy
Court**
Northern Iowa
P.O. Box 74890
Cedar Rapids, IA 52407
319-399-2473

**[Iowa] United States Bankruptcy
Court**
Southern Iowa

1st & Walnut Streets, Rm. 318
Des Moines, IA 50309
515-284-6230

**[Iowa] United States District
Court**
Northern District
101 1st St. SE
Cedar Rapids, IA 52401
319-399-2566

**[Iowa] United States District
Court**
Southern District
1st & Walnut Streets, Rm. 200
Des Moines, IA 50309
515-284-6248
515-284-6228 (Law Library)

Iowa, University of
Law Library
Boyd Law Bldg.
Iowa City, IA 52242
319-335-9002

[Iowa] Utilities Board, State
State Office Bldg.
Des Moines, IA 50319
515-281-5979

[Iowa] Vital Records & Statistics
Lucas Bldg, 4th Fl.
Des Moines, IA 50319
515-281-5871

**[Iowa] Vocational Rehabilitation
Services, Division of**
510 E. 12th St.
Des Moines, IA 50319
515-281-4311

**[Iowa] Weights & Measures
Division**
Henry Wallace Bldg.
Des Moines, IA 50319
515-281-5716

**[Iowa] Women, Commission on
the Status of**
E. 12th & Walnut Sts.
Des Moines, IA 50319
515-281-4461

**[Iowa] Woodbury County Bar
Association**
County Court House, 6th Fl.
Sioux City, IA 51101
712-279-6609

[Iowa] Woodbury County Law Library
County Court House, 6th Fl.
Sioux City, IA 51101
712-279-6609

Japanese American Society for Legal Studies
University of Washington School of Law
Seattle, WA 98105
206-545-1897

John Hancock Financial Services
P.O. Box 111
Boston, MA 02117
617-572-6272

Johnson & Johnson Consumer Products
199 Grandview Rd.
Skillman, NJ 08558
800-526-2433

Judge Advocates Association
1815 H. St., NW, Suite 420
Wash. D.C. 20006
202-628-0979

Juris, Inc.
151 Athens Way
Nashville, TN 37228
615-242-2870

Jurisoft
763 Massachusetts Ave.
Cambridge, MA 02139
617-864-6151
800-262-5656

Jury Verdict Research, Inc.
30700 Bainbridge Rd.
Solon, OH 44139
216-248-7960
800-321-6910

[Kansas] Information & Referral (State Government)
913-296-0111

[Kansas] Information Center (Federal Government)
800-432-2934

[Kansas] Administration, Department of
9th & Jackson Sts., Rm. 263E
Topeka, KS 66612
913-296-3011

[Kansas] Aging, Department on
915 SW Harrison St.
Topeka, KS 66612
913-296-4986
800-432-3535

[Kansas] Agriculture, Board of
109 SW 9th St.
Topeka, KS 66612
913-296-3558

[Kansas] Air Quality & Radiation Control, Bureau of
Forbes Field Bldg. 740
Topeka, KS 66620
913-296-1540

[Kansas] Archives & Records
120 W. 10th St.
Topeka, KS 66612
913-296-3251

Kansas Association of Legal Assistants
700 Fourth Financial Center
Wichita, KS 67202

[Kansas] Attorney Admissions
Kansas Judicial Center
301 W. 10th St.
Topeka, KS 66612
913-296-3229

[Kansas] Attorney General, Office of
301 W. 10th St., 2nd Fl.

Topeka, KS 66612
913-296-2215

[Kansas] Bank Commissioner, State
700 Jackson, Suite 300
Topeka, KS 66603
913-296-2266

Kansas Bar Association
1200 Harrison St.
P.O. Box 1037
Topeka, KS 66601
913-234-5696

[Kansas] Better Business Bureau
501 Jefferson, Suite 24
Topeka, KS 66607
913-232-0455
316-263-3146 (Wichita)

[Kansas] Child Support Enforcement Program
300 SW Oakley St., P.O. Box 497
Topeka, KS 66603
913-296-3237

[Kansas] Civil Rights, Commission on
900 SW Jackson St.
Topeka, KS 66612
913-296-3206

[Kansas] Commerce, Department of
400 SW 8th
Topeka, KS 66603
913-296-3480

[Kansas] Consumer Protection Division
Kansas Judicial Center
Topeka, KS 66612
913-296-3751
800-432-2310

[Kansas] Corporation Commission
Docking State Office Bldg.
Topeka, KS 66612
913-296-3324
800-662-0027

[Kansas] Corrections, Department of
900 SW Jackson St., 4th Fl.
Topeka, KS 66612
913-296-3317

[Kansas] Crime Victims Reparations Boards
117 W. 10th St.
Topeka, KS 66612
913-926-2359

[Kansas] Development Division
400 W. 8th St., Suite 500
Topeka, KS 66603
913-296-3483

[Kansas] Economic Development, Department of
400 W. 8th St., Suite 500
Topeka, KS 66603
913-296-3483

[Kansas] Education, Department of
120 E. 10th St.
Topeka, KS 66612
913-296-3201

[Kansas] Emergency Preparedness, Division of
2800 Topeka Ave.
Topeka, KS 66601
913-233-9253

[Kansas] Employment, Division of
401 Topeka Blvd.
Topeka, KS 66603
913-296-5076

[Kansas] Environment, Division of
Forbes Field Bldg. 740
Topeka, KS 66620
913-296-1535

[Kansas] Equal Employment Opportunity
Landon St. Office Bldg., Rm. 951
Topeka, KS 66612
913-296-4288

[Kansas] Governor, Office of
State Capitol, 2nd Fl.
Topeka, KS 66612
913-296-3232
913-296-4030 (Constituent Services)

[Kansas] Highway Patrol
122 SW 7th St.
Topeka, KS 66603
913-296-6800

[Kansas] House of Representatives
State Capitol
Topeka, KS 66612
913-296-7500
913-296-7679 (Judiciary)

[Kansas] Income Maintenance
Docking Bldg., 6th Fl.
Topeka, KS 66612
913-296-2111

[Kansas] Indigent Defense Services
900 SW Jackson St., Rm. 506
Topeka, KS 66612
913-296-4505

[Kansas] Industrial Safety & Health Section
512 W. 6th St.
Topeka, KS 66603
913-296-4386

[Kansas] Insurance, Commissioner of
420 SW 9th St.
Topeka, KS 66612
913-296-7801
800-432-2484

[Kansas] Judicial Branch
Judicial Administrator
310 W. 10th St.
Topeka, KS 66612
913-296-4873

[Kansas] Labor-Management Relations & Employment Standards, Division of
1430 SW Topeka Blvd.
Topeka, KS 66612
913-296-7475

Kansas Legal Assistants Society
P.O. Box 1300
Topeka, KS 66117

[Kansas] Library, State
State House
Topeka, KS 66612
913-296-3296

[Kansas] Lieutenant Governor, Office of
State Capitol, Rm. 222-S
Topeka, KS 66612
913-296-2213

Kansas Lottery
128 N. Kansas Ave.
Topeka, KS 66603
913-296-5700

[Kansas] Parole Board
900 SW Jackson St., 4th Fl.
Topeka, KS 66612
913-296-3469

[Kansas] Personnel Services, Division of
900 SW Jackson St.
Topeka, KS 66612
913-296-4278

[Kansas] Public Disclosure Commission
109 W. 9th St.
Topeka, KS 66612
913-296-4219

[Kansas] Purchasing, Division of
900 SW Jackson St., Rm. 102N
Topeka, KS 66612
913-296-2376

[Kansas] Real Estate Commission
900 SW Jackson St.
Topeka, KS 66612
913-296-3411

[Kansas] Regents, Board of
400 SW 8th St.
Topeka, KS 66603
913-296-3421

[Kansas] Research & Energy Analysis Division
915 Harrison St.
Topeka, KS 66612
913-296-5460

[Kansas] Revenue, Department of
State Office Bldg., 2nd Fl.
Topeka, KS 66612
913-296-3041

[Kansas] Secretary of State
State Capitol, 2nd Fl.
Topeka, KS 66612
913-296-2236

[Kansas] Securities Commissioner
900 SW Jackson St., Suite 552

Topeka, KS 66612
913-296-3307

[Kansas] Sedgwick County
455 N. Main
Wichita, KS 67202
316-268-4331

[Kansas] Sedgwick County Law Library
301 N. Main St., Suite 700
Wichita, KS 67202

[Kansas] Senate
State Capitol
Topeka, KS 66612
913-296-7300
913-296-7364 (Judiciary)

[Kansas] Shawnee County
200 E. 7th
Topeka, KS 66603
913-291-4040

[Kansas] Social & Rehabilitative Services, Department of
Docking Bldg., 6th Fl.
Topeka, KS 66612
913-296-3959

[Kansas] Statutes, Revisor of
State House, Rm. 322-S
Topeka, KS 66612
913-296-2321

[Kansas] Supreme Court
301 W. 10th St.
Topeka, KS 66612
913-296-3229
913-296-3257 (Law Library)

[Kansas] Transportation, Department of
Docking State Office Bldg., 7th Fl.
Topeka, KS 66612
913-296-3461

[Kansas] Treasury Department, State
900 SW Jackson St.
Topeka, KS 66612
913-296-3171

[Kansas] Unemployment Insurance Program
401 Topeka Ave.
Topeka, KS 66603
913-296-1796

[Kansas] United States Bankruptcy Court
401 N. Market St., No. 167
Wichita, KS 67202
316-269-6486

[Kansas] United States District Court
401 N. Market St., No. 204
Wichita, KS 67202
316-269-6491

Kansas, University of
School of Law Library
Green Hall
Lawrence, KS 66045
913-864-3025

[Kansas] Utilities Division
Docking State Office Bldg., 4th
Topeka, KS 66612
913-296-4191

[Kansas] Vital Statistics, Office of
900 SW Jackson
Topeka, KS 66612
913-296-1400

[Kansas] Washburn University of Topeka
School of Law Library
1700 College
Topeka, KS 66621
913-295-6688

[Kansas] Waste Management, Bureau of
Forbes Field Bldg. 729
Topeka, KS 66620
913-296-1593

[Kansas] Water Office
109 SW 9th St., Suite 200
Topeka, KS 66612
913-296-3185

[Kansas] Weights & Measures Division
2016 SW 37th St.
Topeka, KS 66611
913-267-4641

[Kansas] Wildlife & Parks, Department of
900 SW Jackson St., Rm. 502
Topeka, KS 66612
913-296-2281

[Kansas] Workers Compensation, Division of
Landon St. Office Bldg., Rm. 651
Topeka, KS 66612
913-296-3441

Kellogg Co.
P.O. Box CAMB
Battle Creek, MI 49016
616-916-2277

Kemper Group
Corporate Relations F-3
Long Grove, IL 60049
800-833-0355

[Kentucky] Information & Referral (State Government)
502-564-2500

[Kentucky] Information Center (Federal Government)
Louisville 502-582-6261

[Kentucky] Adjutant General
Department of Military Affairs
Boone National Guard Center
Frankfort, KY 40601
502-564-8558

[Kentucky] Aging Services, Division for
275 E. Main St., 6th Fl.
Frankfort, KY 40621
502-564-6930
800-372-2991

[Kentucky] Agriculture, Department of
Capitol Plaza Tower, 7th Fl.
Frankfort, KY 40601
502-564-4696

[Kentucky] Air Pollution Control, Division of
18 Reilly Rd.
Frankfort, KY 40601
502-564-2150

[Kentucky] Arts, Department of the
Berry Hill Mansion
Frankfort, KY 40601
502-564-8076

[Kentucky] Attorney General, Office of
Capitol Bldg., Rm. 116

Frankfort, KY 40601
502-564-7600

Kentucky Bar Association
West Main at Kentucky River
Frankfort, KY 40601
502-564-3795

**[Kentucky] Bar Examiners,
Board of**
1220 Haarrodsburg Rd., Suite 403
Lexington, KY 40504
606-253-2733

**[Kentucky] Better Business
Bureau**
154 Patchen Dr., Suite 90
Lexington, KY 40502
606-268-4128

[Kentucky] Budget Director, State
Capitol Annex, Rm. 201
Frankfort, KY 40601
502-564-2611

**[Kentucky] Child Support
Enforcement, Division of**
275 E. Main St., 6th Fl. East
Frankfort, KY 40621
502-564-2285
800-248-1163

[Kentucky] Commerce Cabinet
Capital Plaza Tower, 24th Fl.
Frankfort, KY 40601
502-564-7670

**[Kentucky] Consumer
Protection, Division of**
209 St. Clair St.
Frankfort, KY 40601
502-564-2200
800-432-9257

**[Kentucky] Corporation
Division**
State Office Bldg., Rm. 150
Frankfort, KY 40601
502-564-3490

[Kentucky] Corrections Cabinet
State Office Bldg., 5th Fl.
Frankfort, KY 40601
502-564-4726

**[Kentucky] Courts,
Administrative Office of the**
403 Wapping St.

Frankfort, KY 40601
502-564-2350

[Kentucky] CPAs, Society of
310 W. Liberty St., Suite 604
Louisville, KY 40202
502-589-9239

**[Kentucky] Crime Victims
Compensation Board**
115 Myrtle Ave
Frankfort, KY 40601
502-564-2290

**[Kentucky] Disaster &
Emergency Services,
Division of**
Boone National Guard Center
Frankfort, KY 40601
502-564-8682

**[Kentucky] Economic
Development, Cabinet for**
Capitol Plaza Tower, 24th Fl.
Frankfort, KY 40601
502-564-7670

**[Kentucky] Education &
Humanities Cabinet**
State Office Bldg., 5th Fl.
Frankfort, KY 40601
502-564-4726

**[Kentucky] Education,
Department of**
Capital Plaza Tower, 1st Fl.
Frankfort, KY 40601
502-564-4770

[Kentucky] Elections, Board of
State Office Bldg., Rm. 71
Frankfort, KY 40601
502-564-7100

**[Kentucky] Employment
Services, Department for**
275 E. Main St.
Frankfort, KY 40601
502-564-5331

[Kentucky] Energy Cabinet
Iron Works Pike
P.O. Box 11888
Lexington, KY 40578
606-252-5535

**[Kentucky] Engineering,
Division of**
State Capitol Annex, Rm. 229

Frankfort, KY 40601
502-564-2980

**[Kentucky] Environmental
Protection, Department of**
18 Reilly Rd.
Frankfort, KY 40601
502-564-2150

**[Kentucky] Ethics of the General
Assembly, Board of**
P.O. Box 456
Frankfort, KY 40602
502-564-3296

[Kentucky] Fayette County
162 E. Main St.
Lexington, KY 40507
606-253-3344

**[Kentucky] Fayette County Bar
Association**
701 Beechmont Rd.
Lexington, KY 40502
606-266-9897

**[Kentucky] Finance &
Administration Cabinet**
301 Capitol Annex
Frankfort, KY 40601
502-564-4240

**[Kentucky] Financial
Institutions, Department of**
911 Leawood Dr.
Frankfort, KY 40601
502-564-3390

[Kentucky] Franklin County
P.O. Box 338
Frankfort, KY 40602
502-875-8702

[Kentucky] Governor, Office of
State Capitol Bldg., Rm. 100
Frankfort, KY 40601
502-564-2611

**[Kentucky] Health Services,
Department for**
275 E. Main St.
Frankfort, KY 40601
502-564-3970

**[Kentucky] Higher Education,
Council on**
U.S. Hwy 127 South
Frankfort, KY 40601
502-564-3553

[Kentucky] Highways, Department of
Clinton & High Sts.
Frankfort, KY 40622
502-564-4890

[Kentucky] House of Representatives
State Capitol
Frankfort, KY 40601
502-564-8100
502-564-8167 (Judiciary)

Kentucky Housing Corporation
1231 Louisville Rd.
Frankfort, KY 40601
502-564-7630

[Kentucky] Human Resources, Cabinet for
275 E. Main St.
Frankfort, KY 40601
502-564-7130

[Kentucky] Human Rights Commission
Capital Plaza Tower
Frankfort, KY 40601
502-564-3550

[Kentucky] Insurance Commissioner
229 W. Main St.
P.O. Box 517
Frankfort, KY 40602
502-564-3630

[Kentucky] Jefferson County Public Law Library
514 W. Liberty, Suite 240
Louisville, KY 40202
502-625-5943

[Kentucky] Justice Cabinet
Commonwealth Credit Union Bldg.
Frankfort, KY 40601
502-564-7554

[Kentucky] Labor Cabinet
U.S. Hwy 127 South
Frankfort, KY 40601
502-564-3070

[Kentucky] Law Library, State
State Capitol, Rm. 200
Frankfort, KY 40601
502-564-4848

[Kentucky] Lexington Paralegal Association
P.O. Box 574
Lexington, KY 40507

[Kentucky] Libraries & Archives, Department for
300 Coffee Tree Rd.
Frankfort, KY 40601
502-875-7000

[Kentucky] Lieutenant Governor, Office of
Capitol Bldg., Rm. 142
Frankfort, KY 40601
502-564-7562

[Kentucky] Louisville Association of Paralegals
P.O. Box 962
Louisville, KY 40201

[Kentucky] Louisville Bar Association
717 W. Main St., #200
Louisville, KY 40202
502-583-5314

[Kentucky] Medicaid Services, Department of
275 E. Main St.
Frankfort, KY 40601
502-564-4321

[Kentucky] Mines & Minerals, Department of
120 Graham Ave.
Lexington, KY 40506
606-257-8818

[Kentucky] Natural Resources & Environmental Protection
Capital Plaza Tower, 5th Fl.
Frankfort, KY 40601
502-564-3350

[Kentucky] Northern Kentucky Bar Association
522 Nunn Hall
Highland Heights, KY 41076
606-781-1300

[Kentucky] Occupational & Professional Licensing, Division of
Berry Hill Annex
Frankfort, KY 40602
502-564-3296

[Kentucky] Occupational Safety & Health Compliance
The 127 Bldg.
Frankfort, KY 40601
502-564-7360

[Kentucky] Oil & Gas Division
120 Graham Ave.
Lexington, KY 40506
606-257-3812

[Kentucky] Parole Board
State Office Bldg., 5th Fl.
Frankfort, KY 40601
502-564-3620

[Kentucky] Personnel, Department of
Capitol Annex Bldg., Rm. 373
Frankfort, KY 40601
502-564-4460

[Kentucky] Policy & Management, Office for
Capitol Annex Bldg., Rm. 201
Frankfort, KY 40601
502-564-7300

[Kentucky] Probation & Parole Division
Holmes & High Sts., Rm. 514
Frankfort, KY 40601
502-564-4221

[Kentucky] Public Advocacy, Office for
State Office Bldg. Annex
Frankfort, KY 40601
502-564-5213
502-564-8006 (Law Library)

[Kentucky] Public Defender, Department of
1264 Louisville Rd.
Frankfort, KY 40601
502-564-8006

[Kentucky] Public Protection & Regulation Cabinet
Capital City Airport
Louisville Road
Frankfort, KY 40601
502-564-7760

[Kentucky] Public Service Commission
730 Schenkel Ln.
Frankfort, KY 40602
502-564-3940

[Kentucky] Purchases, Division of
State Capitol Annex, Rm. 348
Frankfort, KY 40601
502-564-4510

[Kentucky] Real Estate Commission
222 S. 1 St., Suite 300
Lexington, KY 40202
502-588-4462

[Kentucky] Retirement Systems
151 Elkhorn Ct.
Frankfort, KY 40601
502-564-4646

[Kentucky] Revenue Cabinet
Capitol Annex, 4th Fl.
Frankfort, KY 40601 ·
502-564-3226

[Kentucky] Salmon P. Chase
College of Law Library
Highland Heights, KY 41076
606-572-5394

[Kentucky] Secretary of State
Capitol Bldg., Rm. 150
Frankfort, KY 40601
502-564-3490

[Kentucky] Securities, Division of
911 Leawood Dr.
Frankfort, KY 40601
502-564-2180

[Kentucky] Senate
State Capitol
Frankfort, KY 40601
502-564-8100
502-564-8167 (Judiciary)

[Kentucky] State Police, Department of
919 Versailles Rd.
Frankfort, KY 40601
502-695-6300

[Kentucky] Statutes, Revisor of
Legislative Research Committee
State Capitol
Frankfort, KY 40601
502-564-8100

Kentucky, Supreme Court of
Capitol Bldg., Rm. 231
Frankfort, KY 40601

502-564-6753
502-564-4720 (Clerk)
606-233-0664 (Lexington)

[Kentucky] Transportation Cabinet
State Office Bldg., 10th Fl.
Frankfort, KY 40601
502-564-4890

[Kentucky] Treasury Department
Capitol Annex Bldg.
Frankfort, KY 40601
502-564-4722

[Kentucky] Trial Lawyers, Academy of
12700 Shelbyville Rd.
Middletown, KY 40243
502-244-1320

[Kentucky] Unemployment Insurance, Division of
275 E. Main St.
Frankfort, KY 40601
502-564-2900

[Kentucky] United States Bankruptcy Court
Eastern Kentucky
P.O. Box 1050
Lexington, KY 40588
606-233-2608

[Kentucky] United States Bankruptcy Court
Western Kentucky
601 W. Broadway, No. 414
Louisville, KY 40202
502-582-5145

[Kentucky] United States District Court
Eastern District
P.O. Box 741
Lexington, KY 40586
606-233-2503

[Kentucky] United States District Court
Western District
601 W. Broadway, No. 230
Louisville, KY 40202
502-582-5156

Kentucky, University of
School of Law Library

Lexington, KY 40506
606-257-8346

[Kentucky] University of Louisville Law Library
Belknap Campus
Louisville, KY 40292
502-588-6392

[Kentucky] Vehicle Registration, Department of
State Office Bldg., Rm. 1001
Frankfort, KY 40622
502-564-7000

[Kentucky] Veterans Affairs, Center for
600 Federal Pl.
Louisville, KY 40202
502-588-4447

[Kentucky] Vital Statistics, Division of
275 E. Main St.
Frankfort, KY 40601
502-564-4212

[Kentucky] Vocational Rehabilitation, Office of
Capital Plaza Tower, 9th Fl.
Frankfort, KY 40601
502-564-4566

[Kentucky] Waste Management, Division of
18 Reilly Rd.
Frankfort, KY 40601
502-564-6716

[Kentucky] Water, Division of
18 Reilly Rd.
Frankfort, KY 40601
502-564-3410

[Kentucky] Weights & Measures, Division of
106 W. 2nd St.
Frankfort, KY 40601
502-564-4870

[Kentucky] Women, Commission on
614A Shelby
Frankfort, KY 40601
502-564-6643

[Kentucky] Worker's Claims, Department of
1270 Louisville Pl.

Perimeter Park W., Bldg. C.
Frankfort, KY 40601
502-564-3070

**Kluwer Law & Taxation
  Publishers**
101 Philip Dr.
Norwell, MA 02061
617-871-6600

K Mart Corp.
3100 W. Big Beaver Rd.
Troy, MI 48084
800-63K-MART

Kraft, Inc.
Kraftcourt
Glenview, IL 60025
800-323-0768

**Labor-Management
  Relations Service**
1620 Eye St., NW, 4th Fl.
Wash. D.C. 20006
202-293-7330

Law & Society Association
University of Massachusetts
Amherst, MA 01003
413-545-4617

Law Firm Management, Inc.
4–6 SW 96 Ct.
Miami, FL 33174
305-472-4531

Law Journal Seminars-Press
111 8th Ave.
New York, NY 10011
212-741-8300
800-888-8300

**Law Library Microform
  Consortium**
P.O. Box 11033
Honolulu, HI 96828
808-949-4280

Law of the Sea Institute
2515 Dole St., Rm. 208
Honolulu, HI 96822
808-948-6750

Lawpress Corporation
P.O. Box 5024
Westport, CT 06881
800-622-1181

**Law School Admission
  Council/Services**
P.O. Box 40
New Town, PA 18940
215-968-1111

LAWTRAC Development Corp.
57 E. 11th St.
New York, NY 10003
212-979-8920

**Lawyers Committee for Civil
  Rights Under Law**
1400 I. St., NW, Suite 400
Wash. D.C. 20005
202-371-1212

**Lawyers Committee for
  Human Rights**
330 7th Ave., 10th Fl.
New York, NY 10001
212-921-2160

**Lawyers Co-Operative
  Publishing**
Aquesduct Bldg.
Rochester, NY 14694
716-546-5530
800-448-3400

Lawyers Liability Review
10655 NE 4th St., Suite 604
Bellevue, WA 98004
206-462-7714
800-444-7714

Leader Publications
111 8th Ave., Suite 900
New York, NY 10011
212-741-8300

**Leadership Conference on
  Civil Rights**
2027 Massachusetts Ave., NW
Wash. D.C. 20036
202-667-1780

League of Women Voters
1730 M. St., NW

Wash. D.C. 20036
202-429-1965

**Legal Assistant Management
  Association**
P.O. Box 40129
Overland Park, KS 66204
913-381-4458

Legal Assistant Today
See Legal Professional

**Legal Education Society of
  Alberta**
2005 IPL Tower
10201 Jasper Ave.
Edmonton, AL Canada T5J 3N7

Legal Malpractice Institute
103 Washington St.
Morristown, NJ 07960
800-289-2090

Legal Professional
6060 N. Central Expressway,
  Suite 670
Dallas, TX 75206
214-369-6868
800-225-8347

Lever Brothers Corp.
390 Park Ave.
New York, NY 10022
800-451-6679

LEXIS
See Mead Data Central

Libel Defense Resource Center
404 Park Ave., S, 16th Fl.
New York, NY 10016
212-889-2306

Liberty Mutual Insurance Group
175 Berkeley St.
Boston, MA 02117
617-357-9500
800-225-2390

Licensing Executives Society
71 East Ave., Suite S
Norwalk, CT 06851
203-852-7168

Little Brown & Co.
34 Beacon St.
Boston, MA 02108
617-227-0730

[Louisiana] Information & Referral (State Government)
504-342-6600

[Louisiana] Information Center (Federal Government)
New Orleans 504-589-6696

[Louisiana] Administration, Division of
P.O. Box 94095
Baton Rouge, LA 70804
504-342-7000

[Louisiana] Agriculture & Forestry, Department of
P.O. Box 94305, State Capitol
Baton Rouge, LA 70804
504-922-1234

[Louisiana] Air Quality Division
P.O. Box 44096
Baton Rouge, LA 70804
504-342-1206

[Louisiana] Archives, Records Management & History, Division of
3851 Essen Lane
Baton Rouge, LA 70809
504-992-1213

[Louisiana] Attorney General, Office of
State Capitol Bldg., 22nd Fl.
Baton Rouge, LA 70804
504-342-7013

[Louisiana] Auditor, Office of the Legislative
P.O. Box 94397
Baton Rouge, LA 70804
504-342-7237

[Louisiana] Bar Admissions, Committee on
601 St. Charles Ave.
New Orleans, LA 70130
504-566-1600

Louisiana Bar Association
210 O'Keefe Ave., #600
New Orleans, LA 70112
504-566-1600

[Louisiana] Baton Rouge City Hall
222 Saint Louis St.

Baton Rouge, LA 70802
504-389-3000

[Louisiana] Baton Rouge Paralegal Association
P.O. Box 306
Baton Rouge, LA 70821

[Louisiana] Better Business Bureau
2055 Wooddale Blvd.
Baton Rouge, LA 70806
504-926-3010
504-581-6222 (New Orleans)

[Louisiana] Budget Office
State Capitol Annex
Baton Rouge, LA 70804
504-342-7071

[Louisiana] Civil Service Commission, State
P.O. Box 94111
Baton Rouge, LA 70804
504-925-1877

[Louisiana] Consumer Protection Section
P.O. Box 94005
State Capitol Bldg.
Baton Rouge, LA 70804
504-342-7013
504-568-5472 (New Orleans)

[Louisiana] Court of Appeal, First Circuit
222 St. Louis St., Rm. 902
Baton Rouge, LA 70801
504-342-6920

[Louisiana] Court of Appeal, Second Circuit
1430 Fannin St., 6th Fl.
Shreveport, LA 71101
318-227-3700

[Louisiana] Court of Appeal, Third Circuit
Courthouse
Lake Charles, LA 70601
318-433-9403

[Louisiana] Court of Appeal, Fourth Circuit
421 Loyola Ave.
210 Civil Courts Bldg.
New Orleans, LA 70112
504-568-4700

[Louisiana] Court of Appeal, Fifth Circuit
Courthouse Bldg., 4th Fl.
Gretna, LA 70053
504-361-7399

[Louisiana] Crime Victims Reparations Board
2121 Wooddale Blvd.
Baton Rouge, LA 70806
504-925-4437

[Louisiana] Culture, Recreation & Tourism, Department of
P.O. Box 94361
Baton Rouge, LA 70804
504-342-8115

[Louisiana] East Baton Rouge Parish
222 Saint Louis St.
Baton Rouge, LA 70802
504-389-3100

[Louisiana] Economic Development, Department of
P.O. Box 94185
Baton Rouge, LA 70804
504-342-5359

[Louisiana] Education, Department of
P.O. Box 94064
Baton Rouge, LA 70804
504-342-3602

[Louisiana] Elder Affairs, Governor's Office of
P.O. Box 80374
Baton Rouge, LA 70898
504-925-1700

[Louisiana] Elections & Registration, Department of
P.O. Box 14179
Baton Rouge, LA 70898
504-925-7885

Louisiana Elections Integrity Commission
P.O. Box 44321
Baton Rouge, LA 70804
504-342-5958

[Louisiana] Emergency Preparedness, Office of
625 N. 4th St.

Baton Rouge, LA 70802
504-342-5470

**[Louisiana] Employment
Security, Office of**
1001 N. 23rd St.
Baton Rouge, LA 70802
504-342-3013

[Louisiana] Energy Division
625 N. 4th St.
Baton Rouge, LA 70802
504-342-1399

**[Louisiana] Environmental
Quality, Department of**
P.O. Box 44066
Baton Rouge, LA 70804
504-342-9103

**[Louisiana] Financial Institutions,
Commissioner of**
P.O. Box 94095
Baton Rouge, LA 70804
504-925-4660

[Louisiana] Governor, Office of
State Capitol Bldg.
Baton Rouge, LA 70804
504-342-7015

**[Louisiana] Health & Hospitals,
Department of**
P.O. Box 3776
Baton Rouge, LA 70821
504-342-6711

[Louisiana] Highways, Office of
P.O. Box 94245
Baton Rouge, LA 70804
504-379-1208

**[Louisiana] House of
Representatives**
State Capitol
Baton Rouge, LA 70804
504-342-7259

**[Louisiana] Insurance,
Commissioner of**
P.O. Box 94214
Baton Rouge, LA 70804
504-342-5328

**[Louisiana] Judicial
Administrator**
Supreme Court Bldg., Rm. 109
New Orleans, LA 70112
504-568-5747

**[Louisiana] Justice,
Department of**
P.O. Box 94005
Baton Rouge, LA 70804
504-342-7103

[Louisiana] Labor, Department of
P.O. Box 94094
Baton Rouge, LA 70804
504-342-3111
504-925-4221 (Workers
Compensation)

**[Louisiana] Lafayette Paralegal
Association**
P.O. Box 2775
Lafayette, LA 70502

**[Louisiana] Law Enforcement &
Administration of Criminal
Justice, Commission on**
2121 Wooddale Blvd.
Baton Rouge, LA 70806
504-925-4418

Louisiana, Law Library of
301 Loyola Ave.
New Orleans, LA 70112
504-568-5705

**Louisiana, Legal Assistants of
Northeast**
P.O. Drawer 8032
Monroe, LA 71211

**[Louisiana] Licensing &
Certification, Division of**
P.O. Box 3767
Baton Rouge, LA 70821
504-342-6448

**[Louisiana] Lieutenant
Governor, Office of**
State Capitol Bldg.
Baton Rouge, LA 70804
504-342-7009

**[Louisiana] Loyola University
Law School Library**
7214 St. Charles Ave.
New Orleans, LA 70118
504-861-5539

**[Louisiana] Mineral Resources,
Office of**
625 N. 4th St.
Baton Rouge, LA 70802
504-342-4615

**[Louisiana] Natural Resources,
Department of**
P.O. Box 44396
Baton Rouge, LA 70804
504-342-4500

**[Louisiana] New Orleans
City Hall**
1300 Perdido St.
New Orleans, LA 70112
504-586-4311

**[Louisiana] New Orleans Legal
Assistance Corporation**
144 Elk Pl., Suite 100
New Orleans, LA 70112
504-529-1000

**[Louisiana] New Orleans
Paralegal Association**
P.O. Box 30604
New Orleans, LA 70190

**[Louisiana] Northshore
Paralegal Association**
P.O. Box 1916
Hammond, LA 70404

**[Louisiana] Northwest Louisiana
Paralegal Association**
P.O. Box 1913
Shreveport, LA 71166

**[Louisiana] Nuclear Energy
Division**
2845 Jamestown Ave.
Baton Rouge, LA 70808
504-925-4518

**[Louisiana] Occupational Safety
& Health Survey**
1001 N. 23rd St.
Baton Rouge, LA 70802
504-342-3126

[Louisiana] Orleans Parish
1300 Perdido St.
New Orleans, LA 70112
504-586-4322

[Louisiana] Pardon Board, State
P.O. Box 94304
Baton Rouge, LA 70804
504-342-5421

[Louisiana] Parole, Board of
P.O. Box 94304, Capitol Station
Baton Rouge, LA 70804
504-342-6622

[Louisiana] Probation & Parole, Division of
P.O. Box 94304, Capitol Station
Baton Rouge, LA 70804
504-342-6609

[Louisiana] Public Safety & Corrections, Department of
P.O. Box 94304, Capital Station
Baton Rouge, LA 70804
504-342-6740

[Louisiana] Public Service Commission
1 American Pl., Suite 1630
Baton Rouge, LA 70825
504-342-4404
800-228-9368

[Louisiana] Public Works, Office of
1201 Capitol Access Rd., Rm. 211
Baton Rouge, LA 70802
504-379-1220

[Louisiana] Real Estate Commission
P.O. Box 14785
Baton Rouge, LA 70898
504-925-4771

[Louisiana] Regents, Board of
150 Riverside Mall
Baton Rouge, LA 70801
504-342-4253

[Louisiana] Rehabilitation Services, Division of
P.O. Box 94371
Baton Rouge, LA 70804
504-342-2285

[Louisiana] Revenue & Taxation, Department of
P.O. Box 201
Baton Rouge, LA 70821
504-925-7537

[Louisiana] Securities Commission
315 Loyola Ave.
New Orleans, LA 70112
504-568-5515

[Louisiana] Senate
State Capitol
Baton Rouge, LA 70804
504-342-2040

[Louisiana] Social Services, Department of
P.O. Box 3776
Baton Rouge, LA 70821
504-342-0286

[Louisiana] Solid & Hazardous Waste Management, Office of
625 N. 4th St.
Baton Rouge, LA 70802
504-342-8925

[Louisiana] Southern University Law Library
P.O. Box 9294
Baton Rouge, LA 70813
504-771-2315

Louisiana Southwest Association of Paralegals
P.O. Box 1143
Lake Charles, LA 70602

[Louisiana] State, Department of
P.O. Box 94125
Baton Rouge, LA 70804
504-922-1000

Louisiana State Paralegal Association
Rt 1, Box 1507
Breaux Bridge, LA 70517

[Louisiana] State Police, Office of
P.O. Box 66614
Baton Rouge, LA 70896
504-925-6117

Louisiana State University Law Library
Paul M. Hebert Law Center
Baton Rouge, LA 70803
504-388-8802

[Louisiana] Support Enforcement Services
P.O. Box 94065
Baton Rouge, LA 70804
504-342-4780

Louisiana, Supreme Court of
301 Loyola Ave.
New Orleans, LA 70112
504-568-5707

[Louisiana] Tax Appeals, Board of
1111 S. Foster Dr., Suite A

Baton Rouge, LA 70806
504-922-0172

Louisiana Tax Commission
P.O. Box 66788
Baton Rouge, LA 70806
504-925-7830

[Louisiana] Transportation & Development, Department of
P.O. Box 94245
Baton Rouge, LA 70804
504-379-1100

[Louisiana] Treasury, Department of
P.O. Box 44154
Baton Rouge, LA 70804
504-343-0010

[Louisiana] Trial Lawyers Association
442 Europe St.
P.O. Drawer 4289
Baton Rouge, LA 70821
504-383-5554

[Louisiana] Tulane University Law Library
6801 Freret St.
New Orleans, LA 70118
504-865-5951

[Louisiana] Unemployment Insurance Services
1002 N. 23rd St.
Baton Rouge, LA 70802
504-342-3017

[Louisiana] United States Bankruptcy Court
Eastern Louisiana
500 Camp St., C104
New Orleans, LA 70130
504-589-6506

[Louisiana] United States Bankruptcy Court
Middle Louisiana
412 N. 4th St.
Baton Rouge, LA 70802
504-389-0211

[Louisiana] United States Bankruptcy Court
Western Louisiana
500 Fannin St., Rm. 4A18

Shreveport, LA 71101
318-226-5267

**[Louisiana] United States Court of
 Appeals for the Fifth Circuit**
600 Camp Street
New Orleans, LA 70130
504-589-6514
504-589-6510 (Law Library)

**[Louisiana] United States District
 Court**
Eastern District
500 Camp St., C-151
New Orleans, LA 70130
504-589-2946

**[Louisiana] United States District
 Court**
Middle District
P.O. Box 2630
Baton Rouge, LA 70821
504-389-0321

**[Louisiana] United States District
 Court**
Western District
500 Fannin St., Rm. 106
Shreveport, LA 71101
318-226-5273

**[Louisiana] Veterans' Affairs,
 Department of**
P.O. Box 94095
Baton Rouge, LA 70804
504-342-5863

**[Louisiana] Vital Records
 Section**
Office of Health Services
P.O. Box 60630
New Orleans, LA 70160
504-568-5175

**[Louisiana] Water Resources,
 Office of**
625 N. 4th St.
Baton Rouge, LA 70802
504-342-6363

[Louisiana] Weights & Measures
P.O. Box 3098
Baton Rouge, LA 70821
504-925-3780

**[Louisiana] Wildlife & Fisheries,
 Department of**
P.O. Box 98000

Baton Rouge, LA 70898
504-765-2803

**[Louisiana] Women's Services,
 Office of**
P.O. Box 94095
Baton Rouge, LA 70804
504-342-2715

**[Louisiana] Worker's
 Compensation Commission
 Administration, Office of**
101 N. 23rd St.
Baton Rouge, LA 70804
504-342-7558

Magazine Publishers of America
575 Lexington Ave.
New York, NY 10022
212-752-0055

**[Maine] Information & Referral
 (State Government)**
207-289-1110

**[Maine] Administration,
 Department of**
State Office Bldg., Rm. 424
Augusta, ME 04333
207-289-4505

**[Maine] Agriculture,
 Department of**
State House, Station #28
Augusta, ME 04333
207-289-3871

**[Maine] Air Quality Control,
 Bureau of**
Hospital St.
Augusta, ME 04333
207-289-2437

[Maine] Archives, State
Capitol-State House 84
Augusta, ME 04333
207-289-5790

Maine Association of Paralegals
P.O. Box 7554 DTS
Portland, ME 04112

**[Maine] Attorney General,
 Office of**
State House, Station #6
Augusta, ME 04333
207-289-3661

[Maine] Audit, Department of
State Office Bldg., Rm. 700
Augusta, ME 04333
207-289-2201

**[Maine] Banking,
 Superintendent of**
State House, State #36
Augusta, ME 04333
207-582-8713

Maine Bar Association
124 State St.
P.O. Box 788
Augusta, ME 04330
207-662-7523

[Maine] Bar Examiners, Board of
P.O. Box 30
Augusta, ME 04330
207-623-2464

[Maine] Better Business Bureau
812 Stevens Ave.
Portland, ME 04103
207-878-2715

[Maine] Cleves Law Library
142 Federal St.
Portland, ME 04101
207-773-9712

**[Maine] Conservation,
 Department of**
State House, Station #22
Augusta, ME 04333
207-289-4900

**[Maine] Consumer Credit
 Protection, Bureau of**
State House, Station #35
Augusta, ME 04333
207-582-8718
207-797-8978 (Portland)

**[Maine] Corrections,
 Department of**
State House, Station #111, Rm. 400

Augusta, ME 04333
207-289-2711

**[Maine] Courts, Administrative
Office of the**
70 Center St.
Portland, ME 04112
207-879-4792
207-879-4704 (Law Library)

[Maine] Cumberland County
142 Federal St.
Portland, ME 04101
207-871-8380

**[Maine] Data Research & Vital
Statistics, Office of**
51 Capitol St.
State House, Station #11
Augusta, ME 04333
207-289-3181

**[Maine] Economic &
Community Development,
Department of**
193 State St.
State House, Station #59
Augusta, ME 04333
207-289-2656

**[Maine] Educational & Cultural
Services, Department of**
State House, Station #119
Augusta, ME 04333
207-289-2183

Maine's Elderly, Bureau of
Statehouse, Station #11
Augusta, ME 04333
207-289-2561

**[Maine] Emergency
Management Agency**
State Office Bldg. Station #72
Augusta, ME 04333
207-289-4080

**[Maine] Employment Security,
Bureau of**
State House Station #54
Augusta, ME 04333
207-289-2411

**[Maine] Energy Resources,
Office of**
State Office Bldg., 5th Fl.
Augusta, ME 04333
207-289-3811

**[Maine] Environmental
Protection, Department of**
State House, Station #17
Augusta, ME 04333
207-289-2811

[Maine] Finance, Department of
State Office Bldg., Rm. 317
Augusta, ME 04333
207-289-3446

[Maine] Governor, Office of
State House, Station #1
Augusta, ME 04333
207-289-3531

[Maine] Health, Bureau of
151 Capitol St.
Augusta, ME 04333
207-289-3201

**[Maine] House of
Representatives**
State House, Station #2
Augusta, ME 04330
207-289-2900
800-423-2900
207-289-1327 (Judiciary)

[Maine] Housing Authority, State
P.O. Box 2669
Augusta, ME 04330
207-623-2981

**[Maine] Human Rights
Commission**
State House, Station #51
Augusta, ME 04333
207-289-2326

**[Maine] Human Services,
Department of**
State House, Station #11
Augusta, ME 04333
207-289-5060

**[Maine] Insurance,
Superintendent of**
State House, Station #34
Augusta, ME 04333
207-582-8707

[Maine] Kennebec County
95 State St.
Augusta, ME 04330
207-662-0971

[Maine] Labor, Department of
State House, Station #54
Augusta, ME 04333
207-289-3788

**[Maine] Law & Legislative
Reference Library, State**
State House Station #43
Augusta, ME 04330
207-289-1600

[Maine] Law Library, State
State House, Station #43
Augusta, ME 04333
207-289-1600

**[Maine] Legislative Information
Office**
Legislative Council
State House, Station #115
Augusta, ME 04333
207-289-1692

**[Maine] Licensing &
Enforcement, Division of**
Professional & Financial Regulation
State House, Station #35
Augusta, ME 04333
207-289-3671

[Maine] Lottery, Bureau of the
State House, Station #30
Augusta, ME 04333
207-289-6700

[Maine] Motor Vehicle Division
State House, Station #29
Augusta, ME 04333
207-289-2761

Maine Parole Board
State House, Station #111
Augusta, ME 04333
207-289-2711

**[Maine] Penobscot County
Law Library**
97 Hammond St.
Bangor, ME 04401
207-947-0751

[Maine] Planning Office
184 State St.
State House, Station #38
Augusta, ME 04333
207-289-3261

[Maine] Probation & Parole, Division of
State House, Station #111, Rm. 400
Augusta, ME 04333
207-289-2711

[Maine] Public Improvements, Bureau of
State Office Bldg. Station #77
Augusta, ME 04333
207-289-3881

[Maine] Public Utilities Commission
242 State St.
State House, Station #18
Augusta, ME 04333
207-289-3831
800-452-4699

[Maine] Real Estate Commission
State House, Station #35, Rm. 35
Augusta, ME 04333
207-289-3735

[Maine] Regulations, Division of
State House Station #28
Augusta, ME 04333
207-289-3841

[Maine] Rehabilitation Services, Bureau of
32 Winthrop St.
Augusta, ME 04333
207-289-2266
800-332-1003

[Maine] Revisor of Statutes, Office of
Legislative Council
State House, Station #7
Augusta, ME 04333
207-289-1650

[Maine] Safety, Division of
Hall Owell Annex, Rm. 100
Augusta, ME 04333
207-289-2591

[Maine] Secretary of State
State House, Station #29
Augusta, ME 04333
207-289-1090

[Maine] Securities Division
Bureau of Banking
State House, Station #36
Augusta, ME 04333
207-582-8760

[Maine] Senate
State House, Station #2
Augusta, ME 04330
207-289-1540
800-423-6900
207-289-1327 (Judiciary)

[Maine] State Police, Bureau of
36 Hospital St.
Augusta, ME 04333
207-289-2950

[Maine] Support Enforcement & Location Unit
State House, Station #11
Augusta, ME 04333
207-289-2886

[Maine] Supreme Court
142 Federal St.
Portland, ME 04101
207-879-4765

[Maine] Taxation, Bureau of
Capitol St. Station
Augusta, ME 04330
207-289-2076

[Maine] Transportation, Department of
State House, Station #16
Augusta, ME 04333
207-289-2551

[Maine] Treasury Department
State Office Bldg., Rm. 318
Augusta, ME 04333
207-289-2771

[Maine] Unemployment Compensation Division
20 Union St.
Augusta, ME 04330
207-289-2316

[Maine] Uniform Commercial Code Bureau
State House, Station #101
Augusta, ME 04333
207-289-4177

[Maine] United States Bankruptcy Court
P.O. Box 48 DTS
76 Pearl St.
Portland, ME 04112
207-780-3482

[Maine] United States District Court
P.O. Box 7505 DTS
Portland, ME 04112
207-780-3357

Maine, University of
Garbrecht Law Library
246 Deering Ave.
Portland, ME 04102
207-780-4350

[Maine] Water & Gas Division
242 State St.
State House, Station #18
Augusta, ME 04333
207-289-3831

[Maine] Women, Commission for
State House, Station #93
Augusta, ME 04333
207-289-3417

[Maine] Worker's Compensation Commission
AMHI Grounds Station #27
Augusta, ME 04333
207-289-3751

Major Appliance Consumer Action Panel
20 N. Wacker Dr.
Chicago, IL 60606
312-984-5858
800-621-0477

Manufacturers Hanover Trust Co.
270 Park Ave.
New York, NY 10017
212-286-7370

Manville Corp.
P.O. Box 5108
Denver, CO 80217
800-654-3130

Maritime Law Association of the United States
1 Battery Park Plaza
New York, NY 10004
212-422-7585

Marriott Corp.
1 Marriott Dr.
Wash. D.C. 20058
301-294-3601

**[Maryland] Information &
Referral (State Government)**
301-974-2000

**[Maryland] Information Center
(Federal Government)**
Baltimore 301-962-4980

[Maryland] Aging, Office on
301 W. Preston St., 10th Fl.
Baltimore, MD 21201
301-225-1100
800-423-3425

**[Maryland] Agriculture,
Department of**
50 Harry S. Truman Parkway
Annapolis, MD 21401
301-841-5880

**[Maryland] Air Management
Administration**
2500 Broening Hwy
Baltimore, MD 21224
301-631-3255

**[Maryland] Anne Arundel
County**
44 Calvert
Annapolis, MD 21401
301-280-1821

**[Maryland] Anne Arundel
County Circuit Court Library**
Court House—Church Circle
Annapolis, MD 21401
301-280-1387

[Maryland] Archives, State
350 Rowe Blvd.
Annapolis, MD 21401
301-974-3915

**[Maryland] Attorney General,
Office of**
7 Calvert St., 2nd Fl.
Baltimore, MD 21202
301-576-6300
301-576-6400 (Law Library)

**[Maryland] Baltimore
Association of
Legal Assistants**
P.O. Box 13244
Baltimore, MD 21203

**[Maryland] Baltimore City, Bar
Association of**
111 N. Calvert St.

Baltimore, MD 21202
301-539-5936
301-727-0280 (Law Library)

[Maryland] Baltimore City Hall
100 N. Holiday St.
Baltimore, MD 21202
301-396-3100

[Maryland] Baltimore County
400 Washington Ave.
Towson, MD 21204
301-887-3196

**[Maryland] Baltimore County
Circuit Court Law Library**
401 Bosley Ave.
Towson, MD 21204
301-887-3086

[Maryland] Bank Commissioner
34 Market Pl.
Baltimore, MD 21202
301-333-6262
800-492-7521

Maryland Bar Association
520 W. Fayette St.
Baltimore, MD 21122
301-685-7878

**[Maryland] Bar Examiners,
Board of**
580 Taylor Ave., Suite 403
Annapolis, MD 21401
301-974-2140

**[Maryland] Bay Area Paralegal
Association**
P.O. Box 2313
Annapolis, MD 21404

**[Maryland] Better Business
Bureau**
2100 Huntingdon Ave.
Baltimore, MD 21211
301-347-3990

**[Maryland] Children & Youth,
Office for**
301 W. Preston St.
Baltimore, MD 21201
301-225-4160

**[Maryland] Child Support
Enforcement Administration**
311 West Saratoga St.
Baltimore, MD 21201
301-333-3979

**[Maryland] Circuit Court Library
for Prince George's County**
14735 Main St., Rm. 118
Upper Marlboro, MD 20772
301-952-3438

**[Maryland] Comptroller of the
Treasury**
P.O. Box 466
Annapolis, MD 21404
301-974-3801

**[Maryland] Consumer
Protection Division**
7 N. Calvert St.
Baltimore, MD 21202
301-528-8662
800-492-2114

[Maryland] Court Administrator
361 Rowe Blvd.
Annapolis, MD 21401
301-974-2141

[Maryland] Court of Appeals
361 Rowe St.
Annapolis, MD 21401
301-974-3341

**[Maryland] Court of
Special Appeals**
Annapolis, MD 21401
301-974-3646

**[Maryland] Criminal Justice
Coordinating Council**
6776 Reisterstown Rd., Suite 301
Baltimore, MD 21215
301-764-4336

**[Maryland] Economic &
Employment Development,
Department of**
217 E. Redwood St.
Baltimore, MD 21202
301-333-6904

**[Maryland] Education,
Department of**
200 W. Baltimore St.
Baltimore, MD 21201
301-333-2648

**[Maryland] Election Laws,
Administrative Board of**
P.O. Box 231
Annapolis, MD 21404
301-974-3711

**Maryland Environmental
Service**
2020 Industrial Dr.
Annapolis, MD 21401
301-261-8596

**[Maryland] Ethics
Commission, State**
301 W. Preston St.
Baltimore, MD 21201
301-225-1030

[Maryland] Governor, Office of
State House
Annapolis, MD 21401
301-974-3901

**[Maryland] Health & Mental
Hygiene, Department of**
201 W. Preston St.
Baltimore, MD 21201
301-225-6500

**[Maryland] Higher Education,
State Board for**
16 Francis St.
Annapolis, MD 21401
301-974-2971

**[Maryland] Highway
Administration**
707 N. Calvert St.
Baltimore, MD 21202
301-333-1111

[Maryland] House of Delegates
State House
Annapolis, MD 21401
301-585-3000
800-492-7122
301-841-3488 (Judiciary)

**[Maryland] Housing &
Community Development,
Department of**
Office of Management Services
45 Calvert St.
Annapolis, MD 21401
301-974-2700

**Maryland Human Relations,
Commission on**
20 E. Franklin St.
Baltimore, MD 21202
301-333-1715

**[Maryland] Income Tax
Division**
60 Calvert St.
Annapolis, MD 21401
301-974-3441

**[Maryland] Insurance
Commissioner**
501 St. Paul Pl., 7th Fl. South
Baltimore, MD 21202
301-333-2520
800-492-7521

**[Maryland] Juvenile
Services Agency**
321 Fallsway
Baltimore, MD 21202
301-333-6751

**[Maryland] Labor & Industry,
Division of**
501 St. Paul Pl., 3rd Fl.
Baltimore, MD 21202
301-333-4195

[Maryland] Law Library, State
361 Rowe Blvd.
Annapolis, MD 21401
301-974-3395

[Maryland] Legal Aid Bureau, Inc.
714 E. Pratt St.
Baltimore, MD 21202
301-539-5340

**[Maryland] Licensing &
Regulation, Department of**
501 St. Paul Pl.
Baltimore, MD 21202
301-333-6200

**[Maryland] Lieutenant
Governor, Office of**
State House
Annapolis, MD 21404
301-974-2804

[Maryland] Lottery, State
6776 Reisterstown Rd.
Baltimore, MD 21215
301-764-5700

[Maryland] Mines, Bureau of
69 Hill St.
Frostburg, MD 21532
301-689-4136

[Maryland] Montgomery County
101 Monroe St., 2nd Fl.
Rockville, MD 20850
301-217-2500

**[Maryland] Montgomery County
Circuit Court Law Library**
Judicial Center, 50 Courthouse Sq.
Rockville, MD 20850
301-217-7165

**[Maryland] Motor Vehicle
Administration**
6601 Ritchie Hwy, NE
Glen Burnie, MD 21062
301-768-7274

**[Maryland] Natural Resources,
Department of**
580 Taylor Ave.
Annapolis, MD 21401
301-974-3041

**[Maryland] Occupational Safety
& Health Program**
501 St. Paul Pl.
Baltimore, MD 21202
301-333-4182

**[Maryland] Parole & Probation,
Division of**
6776 Reisterstown Rd., Suite 305
Baltimore, MD 21215
301-764-4274

[Maryland] Parole Commission
6776 Reisterstown Rd., Suite 307
Baltimore, MD 21215
301-764-4231

**[Maryland] Personnel,
Department of**
301 W. Preston St.
Baltimore, MD 21201
301-225-4715

**[Maryland] Planning
Department**
301 W. Preston St., Rm. 1101
Annapolis, MD 21404
301-225-4500

**[Maryland] Power Plant
Research Program**
580 Taylor Ave.
Annapolis, MD 21401
301-974-2261

[Maryland] Prosecutor, Office of the State
One Investment Pl., Rm. 100
Towson, MD 21204
301-321-4067

[Maryland] Public Defender Program
201 St. Paul Pl.
Baltimore, MD 21202
301-333-4826

[Maryland] Public Safety & Correctional Services, Department of
6776 Reisterstown Rd., Suite 310
Baltimore, MD 21215
301-764-4003.

[Maryland] Public Service Commission
231 E. Baltimore St.
Baltimore, MD 21202
301-333-6000
800-492-0474

[Maryland] Public Works, Board of
State Treasury Bldg., Rm. 309
Annapolis, MD 21404
301-994-3443

[Maryland] Purchasing Bureau
301 W. Preston St., Rm. M2
Baltimore, MD 21201
301-225-4620

[Maryland] Real Estate Commission
501 Saint Paul Pl.
Baltimore, MD 21201
301-333-6230

[Maryland] Retirement Agency, State
301 W. Preston St.
Baltimore, MD 21201
301-225-4030

[Maryland] Secretary of State
State House, Rm. H-105
Annapolis, MD 21401
301-841-3908

[Maryland] Securities Commissioner
7 N. Calvert St.

Baltimore, MD 21202
301-576-6360

[Maryland] Senate
State House
Annapolis, MD 21401
301-585-3000
800-492-7122
301-841-4623 (Judiciary)

Maryland Social Services Administration
311 W. Saratoga St.
Baltimore, MD 21201
301-333-0103

[Maryland] State Police
State Police Headquarters
Pikesville, MD 21208
301-486-3101

[Maryland] Statutory Revision, Division of
Department of Legislative
Reference
90 State Circle
Annapolis, MD 21401
301-841-3771

[Maryland] St. Mary's College of Maryland
Law Library
P.O. Box 366
St. Mary's, MD 20686
301-862-0265

[Maryland] Transportation, Department of
BWI Airport
Baltimore, MD 21201
301-859-7397

[Maryland] Treasurer
60 Calvert St.
Annapolis, MD 21401
301-974-3533

[Maryland] Unemployment Insurance Division
1100 N. Eutaw St., Rm. 404
Baltimore, MD 21201
301-333-5435

[Maryland] United States Bankruptcy Court
101 W. Lombard St.
Baltimore, MD 21201
301-962-2688

[Maryland] United States District Court
101 W. Lombard St.
Baltimore, DD 21201
301-962-2600

[Maryland] United States Government Printing Office
8660 Cherry Lane
Laurel, MD 20707
301-953-7974
301-792-0262

[Maryland] University of Baltimore Law Library
1415 Maryland Ave.
Baltimore, MD 21201
301-625-3400

[Maryland] University of Maryland Law Library
20 N. Paca St.
Baltimore, MD 21201
301-328-7270

[Maryland] Vital Records, Division of
201 W. Preston St.
Baltimore, MD 21203
301-225-5950

[Maryland] Vocational Rehabilitation, Division of
200 W. Baltimore St.
Baltimore, MD 21201
301-333-2294

[Maryland] Water Resources Administration
580 Taylor Ave.
Annapolis, MD 21401
301-974-3846

[Maryland] Weights & Measures
50 Harry S. Truman Hwy
Annapolis, MD 21401
301-841-5790

[Maryland] Women, Commission for
311 W. Saratoga St.
Baltimore, MD 21201
301-333-0054

[Maryland] Worker's Compensation Commission
6 N. Liberty St.
Baltimore, MD 21201
301-333-4775

**[Massachusetts] Information &
Referral (State Government)**
617-727-7030
800-392-6090

**[Massachusetts] Information
Center (Federal Government)**
Boston 617-565-8121

**[Massachusetts] Administration
& Finance, Office for**
State House, Rm. 373
Boston, MA 02133
617-727-2040

**[Massachusetts] Air Quality
Control, Division of**
1 Winter St., 8th Fl.
Boston, MA 02108
617-292-5593

**[Massachusetts] Beverages
Control Commission**
100 Cambridge St.
Boston, MA 02202
617-727-3040

**[Massachusetts] Archives
Division**
220 Morrissey Blvd.
Boston, MA 02125
617-727-2816

**[Massachusetts] Arts &
Humanities, Council on the**
80 Boylston St., 10th Fl.
Boston, MA 02116
617-727-3668

**[Massachusetts] Attorney
General, Department of**
1 Ashburton Pl.
Boston, MA 02108
617-727-2200

**[Massachusetts] Banks,
Commissioner of**
100 Cambridge St.
Boston, MA 02202
617-727-3120

Massachusetts Bar Association
20 West St.
Boston, MA 022111
617-542-3602
413-584-4438 (Northhampton)

**[Massachusetts] Bar Examiners,
Board of**
77 Franklin St.
Boston, MA 02110
617-482-0409

**[Massachusetts] Barnstable Law
Library**
First District Courthouse
Barnstable, MA 02630
508-362-8539

**[Massachusetts] Berkshire Law
Library**
76 East St.
Pittsfield, MA 01201
413-442-5059

**[Massachusetts] Better Business
Bureau**
8 Winter St.
Boston, MA 02108
617-482-9151
413-734-3114 (Springfield)

**[Massachusetts] Blind,
Commission for the**
88 Kingston St.
Boston, MA 02111
617-727-5550
800-392-6450

**[Massachusetts] Boston Bar
Association**
16 Beacon St.
Boston, MA 02108
617-742-0615

[Massachusetts] Boston City Hall
1 City Hall Plaza
Boston, MA 02201
617-725-4000

**[Massachusetts] Boston College
School of Law Library**
885 Centre St.
Newton Centre, MA 02159
617-552-8612

**[Massachusetts] Boston
University Law Library**
765 Commonwealth Ave.
Boston, MA 02215
617-353-3151

**[Massachusetts] Bristol Law
Library**
9 Court St.

Taunton, MA 02780
617-824-7632

**[Massachusetts] Brockton Law
Library**
72 Belmont St., Trial Court
Brockton, MA 02401
508-586-7110

**[Massachusetts] Business
Development, Office of**
100 Cambridge St.
Boston, MA 02202
617-727-3206

**[Massachusetts] Children,
Office for**
10 West St.
Boston, MA 02111
617-727-8900

**[Massachusetts] Child Support
Enforcement Division**
215 1st St.
Cambridge, MA 02124
617-621-4200

**[Massachusetts] Civil Defense
Agency**
400 Worcester Rd.
Framingham, MA 01701
508-820-2000

**[Massachusetts] Communities &
Development, Office of**
100 Cambridge St.
Boston, MA 02202
617-727-7765

**[Massachusetts] Comptroller,
Office of the**
1 Ashburton Pl., Rm. 909
Boston, MA 02108
617-727-5000

**[Massachusetts] Consumer
Affairs & Business
Regulation, Office of**
1 Ashburton Pl., Rm. 1411
Boston, MA 02108
617-727-7755

**[Massachusetts] Consumer
Protection Division**
131 Tremont St.
Boston, MA 02111
617-727-8400

[Massachusetts] Corporations Division
1 Ashburton Pl., Rm. 1710
Boston, MA 02108
617-727-2853

[Massachusetts] Corrections, Department of
100 Cambridge St.
Boston, MA 02202
617-727-3300

[Massachusetts] Criminal Justice, Committee on
100 Cambridge St.
Boston, MA 02202
617-727-6300

[Massachusetts] Discrimination, Commission Against
1 Ashburton Pl., Rm. 601
Boston, MA 02108
617-727-3990

[Massachusetts] Economic Affairs, Office of
1 Ashburton Pl., Rm. 2101
Boston, MA 02108
617-727-8380

[Massachusetts] Education, Department of
1385 Hancock St.
Quincy, MA 02169
617-770-7300

[Massachusetts] Elder Affairs, Office of
38 Chauncy St.
Boston, MA 02111
617-727-7750
800-882-2003

[Massachusetts] Employment Training, Department of
19 Staniford St.
Boston, MA 02114
617-727-6600

[Massachusetts] Energy Resources, Executive Office of
100 Cambridge St., Rm. 1500
Boston, MA 02202
617-727-4732

[Massachusetts] Environmental Affairs, Executive Office of
100 Cambridge St., 20th Fl.
Boston, MA 02202
617-727-9800

[Massachusetts] Ethics Commission, State
1 Ashburton Pl., Rm. 619
Boston, MA 02108
617-727-0060

[Massachusetts] Fall River Law Library
441 N. Main St.
Fall River, MA 02720
617-676-8971

[Massachusetts] Fitchburg Law Library
84 Elm St.
Fitchburg, MA 01420
617-345-6726

[Massachusetts] Food & Agriculture, Department of
100 Cambridge St.
Boston, MA 02202
617-727-3000

[Massachusetts] Franklin Law Library
725 Main St.
Greenfield, MA 01301
413-772-6580

[Massachusetts] Governor, Office of
State House Executive Office
Boston, MA 02115
617-727-3600

[Massachusetts] Hampden Law Library
50 State St., Box 559
Springfield, MA 01101
413-781-8100

[Massachusetts] Harvard Law School Library
Langdell Hall
Boston, MA 02138
617-495-3174

[Massachusetts] Higher Education, Board of Regents of
1 Ashburton Pl., Rm. 1401

Boston, MA 02108
617-727-8872

[Massachusetts] House of Representatives
State House
Boston, MA 02133
617-727-2000
617-727-2121 (Judiciary)
617-722-2360 (Counsel)

[Massachusetts] Human Services, Office of
1 Ashburton Pl., Rm. 109
Boston, MA 02108
617-727-7600

[Massachusetts] Industrial Accident Board
600 Washington St., 7th Fl.
Boston, MA 02111
617-727-4900

[Massachusetts] Insurance, Commissioner of
280 Friend St.
Boston, MA 02114
617-727-7189

[Massachusetts] Labor & Industries, Department of
100 Cambridge St., 11th Fl.
Boston, MA 02202
617-727-3454

[Massachusetts] Legislative Research Bureau
30 Winter St., Suite 1100
Boston, MA 02133
617-722-2345

[Massachusetts] Library, State
State House, Rm. 341
Boston, MA 02133
617-727-2592

[Massachusetts] Lieutenant Governor, Office of
State House, Rm. 259
Boston, MA 02133
617-727-7200

[Massachusetts] Lottery Commission
15 Rockdale St.
Braintree, MA 02184
617-849-5555

[Massachusetts] Lowell Law Library
360 Gorham St.
Lowell, MA 01852
617-452-9301

[Massachusetts] Mental Health, Department of
160 N. Washington St.
Boston, MA 02114
617-727-5600

[Massachusetts] Middlesex Law Library
40 Thorndike St.
East Cambridge, MA 02141
617-494-4148

[Massachusetts] Mutual Life Insurance Co.
1295 State St.
Springfield, MA 01111
413-788-8411

[Massachusetts] Neighborhoods & Economic Opportunity, Division of
100 Cambridge St., Rm. 1103
Boston, MA 02202
617-727-3246

[Massachusetts] New England School of Law Library
154 Stuart St.
Boston, MA 02116
617-451-0010

[Massachusetts] Norfolk Law Library
650 High St.
Dedham, MA 02026
617-329-1856

[Massachusetts] Northeastern University Law Library
400 Huntington Ave.
Boston, MA 02115
617-437-3332

Massachusetts Paralegal Association
P.O. Box 423
Boston, MA 02102
617-642-8338

Massachusetts Paralegal Association, Central
P.O Box 444
Worcester, MA 01614

[Massachusetts] Parole Board
27-43 Wormwood St., Ft. Point Pl.
Boston, MA 02210
617-727-3271

[Massachusetts] Personnel Administration, Department of
1 Ashburton Pl.
Boston, MA 02108
617-727-3555

[Massachusetts] Plymouth Law Library
S. Russel St.
Plymouth, MA 02360
617-747-4796

[Massachusetts] Probation Office of the Commissioner
1 Ashburton Pl., Rm. 405
Boston, MA 02108
617-727-5300

[Massachusetts] Public Counsel Services, Committee for
80 Boylston St., Suite 600
Boston, MA 02116
617-482-6212

[Massachusetts] Public Health, Department of
150 Tremont St.
Boston, MA 02111
617-727-0201

[Massachusetts] Public Safety, Department of
1010 Commonwealth Ave.
Boston, MA 02215
617-566-4500

[Massachusetts] Public Utilities, Department of
100 Cambridge St., 12th Fl.
Boston, MA 02202
617-727-3500

[Massachusetts] Public Works, Department of
10 Park Plaza
Bosotn, MA 02116
617-973-7800

[Massachusetts] Registration, Division of
100 Cambridge St., Suite 1520

Boston, MA 02202
617-727-3084
617-727-7376 (Real Estate Brokers)

[Massachusetts] Registry of Motor Vehicles
100 Nashua St.
Boston, MA 02114
617-727-3700

[Massachusetts] Registry of Vital Records & Statistics
150 Tremont St.
Boston, MA 02111
617-727-0036

[Massachusetts] Retirement, State Board of
1 Ashburton Pl., Rm. 1219
Boston, MA 02108
617-367-7770

[Massachusetts] Revenue, Department of
100 Cambridge St.
Boston, MA 02202
617-727-4201

[Massachusetts] Secretary of State
1 Ashburton Pl., Rm. 425
Boston, MA 02133
617-727-7030

[Massachusetts] Securities Division
1 Ashburton Pl., Rm. 1719
Boston, MA 02108
617-727-3548

[Massachusetts] Senate
State House
Boston, MA 02133
617-727-1276
617-727-2121 (Judiciary)
617-722-1470 (Counsel)

Massachusetts Social Law Library
1200 Court House
Boston, MA 02108
617-523-0018

[Massachusetts] Social Services, Department of
150 Causeway St.
Boston, MA 02114
617-727-0900

[Massachusetts] Standards, Division of
1 Ashburton Pl.
Boston, MA 02108
617-727-3480

[Massachusetts] Suffolk County
County Courthouse
Government Center
Boston, MA 02114
617-725-8000

[Massachusetts] Suffolk University
Law Library
41 Temple St.
Boston, MA 02114
617-573-8176

[Massachusetts] Supreme Court
1412 Pemberton Sq.
Boston, MA 02108
617-725-8055
617-725-8083 (Public Information)

[Massachusetts] Transportation Department
10 Park Plaza
Boston, MA 02116
617-973-7031

[Massachusetts] Treasurer, State
State House, Rm. 227
Boston, MA 02133
617-367-6900

[Massachusetts] Unemployment Insurance Program
19 Staniford St.
Boston, MA 02114
617-727-6638

[Massachusetts] United States Bankruptcy Court
10 Causeway St.
1101 Thomas O'Neill Federal Bldg.
Boston, MA 02222
617-565-6050

[Massachusetts] United States Court of Appeals for the First Circuit
1606 John W. McCormack Post Office & Courthouse Bldg.
Boston, MA 02109
617-223-9057
617-223-9044 (Law Library)

[Massachusetts] United States District Court
1525 John W. McCormack Post Office & Courthouse Bldg.
Boston, MA 02109
617-223-9152

[Massachusetts] United States Government Printing Office
10 Causeway St., Rm. 179
Boston, MA 02222
617-565-6680

[Massachusetts] Veterans' Services, Office of
100 Cambridge St.
Boston, MA 02202
617-727-3570

[Massachusetts] Waste Disposal, Bureau of Solid
1 Winter St., 4th Fl.
Boston, MA 02108
617-292-5961

[Massachusetts] Water Resources, Division of
100 Cambridge St., Rm. 1304
Boston, MA 02202
617-727-3267

[Massachusetts] Western New England School of Law Library
1215 Wilbraham Rd.
Springfield, MA 01119
413-782-1454

[Massachusetts] Women's Issues, Office on
State House, Rm. 109A
Boston, MA 02133
617-727-7853

[Massachusetts] Worcester County Law Library Association
Court House
Worcester, MA 01608
617-756-2441

[Massachusetts] Youth, Department of
27-43 Wormwood St., Suite 400
Boston, MA 02210
617-727-7575

Matthew Bender
11 Penn Plaza
New York, NY 10001
800-223-1940

McDonald's Corp.
McDonald's Plaza
Oak Brook, IL 60521
312-575-6198

McGraw-Hill
Princeton Rd.
Highstown, NJ 08520
800-426-4729

Mead Data Central
P.O. Box 933
Dayton, OH 45401
800-227-4908

Medical Library Association
6 N. Michigan Ave., Suite 300
Chicago, IL 60602
312-419-9094

Meiklejohn Civil Liberties Institute
Box 673
Berkeley, CA 94701
415-848-0599

Mellon Bank Corp.
1 Mellon Center
Pittsburgh, PA 15258
412-234-4003

Merrill Lynch, Pierce, Fenner & Smith, Inc.
165 Broadway
New York, NY 10080
212-637-1212

Metropolitan Life & Affiliated Companies
1 Madison Ave.,
New York, NY 10010
212-578-2544

Mexican-American Legal Defense & Education Fund
1430 K. St. NW
Wash. D.C. 20005
202-628-4074

Michie Company
P.O. Box 7587
Charlottesville, VA 22906
804-972-7600
800-446-3410

[Michigan] Information & Referral (State Government)
517-373-1837

[Michigan] Information Center (Federal Government)
Detroit 313-226-7016
Grand Rapids 616-732-2739

[Michigan] Adams–Pratt Law Library Division
Oakland County Library
1200 N. Telegraph Rd.
Pontiac, MI 48053
313-858-1445

[Michigan] Aging, Office of Services to the
P.O. Box 30026
Lansing, MI 48909
517-373-8230

[Michigan] Agriculture, Department of
P.O. Box 30017
Lansing, MI 48909
517-373-1104

[Michigan] Air Quality Division
Mason Building, Fourth Floor
530 W. Allegan
Lansing, MI 48933
517-373-7023

[Michigan] Archives & Historic Preservation Division
717 W. Allegan
Lansing, MI 48918
517-373-0510

[Michigan] Attorney Discipline Board
1 Kennedy Sq., Suite 1910
Detroit, MI 48226
313-963-5553

[Michigan] Attorney General, Office of
525 W. Ottawa
Lansing, MI 48913
517-373-1110

Michigan Attorney Grievance Commission
243 W. Congress St.
Detroit, MI 48226
313-961-6585

[Michigan] Auditor General
333 S. Capitol Ave., Suite A
Lansing, MI 48913
517-373-3773

Michigan, Bar Association of
306 Townsend St.
Lansing, MI 48933
517-372-9030

[Michigan] Bar Examiners, Board of
200 Washington Sq. North
P.O. Box 30104
Lansing, MI 48909
517-334-6992

Michigan Bell Telephone Co.
1365 Cass Ave.
Detroit, MI 48226
313-223-7224
800-482-3141

[Michigan] Better Business Bureau
150 Michigan Ave.
Detroit, MI 48226
313-962-7566

[Michigan] Child Support, Office of
300 S. Capitol Ave., Suite 621
Lansing, MI 48909
517-373-7570

[Michigan] Civil Rights
303 W. Kalamazoo, 4th Fl.
Lansing, MI 48913
417-334-6079

[Michigan] Civil Service Commission
320 S. Walnut
Lansing, MI 48909
517-373-3020

[Michigan] Commerce, Department of
525 W. Ottawa, 4th Fl.
Lansing, MI 48909
517-373-1820

[Michigan] Consumer Protection Division
670 Law Bldg.
Lansing, MI 48913
517-373-1140
800-292-4204 (Automotive)

[Michigan] Consumers Council
404 Hollister Bldg.
P.O. Box 30036
Lansing, MI 48909
517-373-0947

[Michigan] Corporation/ Securities Bureau
6546 Mercantile Way
P.O. Box 30222
Lansing, MI 48909
517-334-6206

[Michigan] Corrections, Department of
Grand View Plaza Bldg.
P.O. Box 30003
Lansing, MI 48909
517-373-0720

[Michigan] Court Administrative Office, State
611 W. Ottawa, 1st Fl.
P.O. Box 30048
Lansing, MI 48909
517-373-0130

Michigan Court of Claims
333 S. Capitol Ave., Suite C
Lansing, MI 48933
517-482-0650

[Michigan] Crime Victims Compensation Board
P.O. Box 30026
Lansing, MI 48909
517-373-7373

[Michigan] Criminal Justice, Office of
P.O. Box 30026
Lansing, MI 48909
517-373-6665

[Michigan] Detroit Bar Association
2380 Penobscot Bldg.
Detroit, MI 48226
313-961-6120
313-961-3507 (Law Library)

[Michigan] Detroit City Clerk's Office
2 Woodward Ave.
Detroit, MI 48220
313-575-5555

[Michigan] Detroit Law Department Library
1010 City-County Bldg.
Detroit, MI 48226
313-224-4550

[Michigan] Education, Department of
P.O. Box 30008
Lansing, MI 48909
517-373-3324
517-335-4933 (Postsecondary Education)

[Michigan] Employment Security Commission
7310 Woodwood Ave.
Detroit, MI 48202
313-373-3400

[Michigan] Environmental & Occupational Health, Bureau of
3423 N. Logan
Lansing, MI 48906
517-335-9218

Michigan Financial Institutions Bureau
P.O. Box 30224
Lansing, MI 48909
517-373-3460

[Michigan] Food Division
Department of Agriculture
P.O. Box 30017
Lansing, MI 48909
517-373-1060

[Michigan] Governor, Office of
State Capitol Bldg., 2nd Fl.
P.O. Box 30013
Lansing, MI 48909
417-272-3400

[Michigan] Grand Rapids Bar Association
200 Monroe, NW, Suite 400
Grand Rapids, MI 49503
616-454-5000
616-454-7681

[Michigan] Health Statistics, Center for
P.O. Box 30195
Lansing, MI 48909
517-335-8655

[Michigan] History, Bureau of
717 W. Allegan
Lansing, MI 48918
517-335-2717

[Michigan] House of Representatives
Capitol Building
Lansing, MI 48909
517-373-0135
517-373-0153 (Judiciary)

Michigan Insurance Bureau
P.O. Box 30220
Lansing, MI 48909
517-373-9273

[Michigan] Kent County
300 Monroe NW
Grand Rapids, MI 49503
616-774-3548

[Michigan] Labor, Department of
P.O. Box 30015
Lansing, MI 48909
517-322-1287

[Michigan] Law Examiners, State Board of
200 Washington Sq. North, Suite 20
P.O. Box 30104
Lansing, MI 48909
517-334-6992

[Michigan] Law Library, State
P.O. Box 30012
Lansing, MI 48909
517-373-3915

Michigan, Legal Assistants Association of
P.O. Box 12316
Birmingham, MI 48012

[Michigan] Legal Education, Institute of Continuing
1020 Green St.
Ann Arbor, MI 48109
313-764-0533

[Michigan] Legislative Service Bureau
P.O. Box 30036
Lansing, MI 48909
517-373-0175
517-373-0472 (Law Library)

[Michigan] Licensing & Regulation, Department of
P.O. Box 30018
Lansing, MI 48909
517-373-1870

[Michigan] Lieutenant Governor, Office of
State Capitol Bldg., Rm. 128
P.O. Box 30013
Lansing, MI 48909
517-373-6800

[Michigan] Liquor Control Commission
P.O. Box 30005
Lansing, MI 48909
517-322-1345

[Michigan] Management & Budget, Department of
320 S. Walnut
Lansing, MI 48909
517-373-1004

[Michigan] Mental Health, Department of
320 S. Walnut
Lansing, MI 48913
517-373-3740

[Michigan] Military Affairs, Department of
2500 S. Washington Ave.
Lansing, MI 48913
517-473-5500

[Michigan] Natural Resources, Department of
Mason Bldg., 7th Fl.
P.O. Box 30028
Lansing, MI 48909
517-373-1220

[Michigan] Oakland County Bar Association
1200 N. Telegraph Rd., Suite 532
Pontiac, MI 48053
313-338-2100

[Michigan] Occupational Health Standards Commission
P.O. Box 30035
Lansing, MI 48909
517-335-8250

[Michigan] Oil & Gas Section
P.O. Box 30028

Lansing, MI 48909
517-334-6951

[Michigan] Parole Board
Grandview Plaza, 2nd Fl.
P.O. Box 30003
Lansing, MI 48909
517-373-0270

[Michigan] Public Health, Department of
P.O. Box 30035
Lansing, MI 48909
517-335-8000

[Michigan] Public Service Commission
P.O. Box 30221
Lansing, MI 48909
517-334-6445
800-292-9555

[Michigan] Purchasing, Office of
P.O. Box 30026
Lansing, MI 48909
517-373-0300

[Michigan] Rehabilitation, Bureau of
P.O. Box 30010
Lansing, MI 48909
517-373-3390
800-373-7831

[Michigan] Revenue, Bureau of
Treasury Bldg., 1st Fl.
Lansing, MI 48922
517-373-3196

[Michigan] Senate
Capitol Building
Lansing, MI 48909
517-373-2400
517-373-2417 (Judiciary)

[Michigan] Social Services, Department of
300 S. Capitol Ave.
P.O. Box 30037
Lansing, MI 48909
517-373-2000

[Michigan] State Department
Treasury Bldg., 1st Fl.
430 W. Allegan
Lansing, MI 48918
517-373-2510

[Michigan] State Police, Department of
714 S. Harrison Rd.
East Lansing, MI 48823
517-332-2521

[Michigan] Supreme Court
525 W. Ottawa
P.O. Box 30052
Lansing, MI 48909
517-373-0120

[Michigan] Transportation, Department of
P.O. Box 30050
Lansing, MI 48933
517-373-2090

[Michigan] Treasury, Department of
430 W. Allegan
Lansing, MI 48922
517-373-3200

[Michigan] Unemployment Insurance, Bureau of
7310 Woodward Ave., Rm. 506
Detroit, MI 48202
313-876-5465

[Michigan] United States Bankruptcy Court
Eastern Michigan
231 W. Lafayette Blvd.
Detroit, MI 48226
313-226-7064

[Michigan] United States Bankruptcy Court
Western Michigan
P.O. Box 49501
Grand Rapids, MI 49501
616-456-2231

[Michigan] United States District Court
Eastern District
231 W. Lafayette Blvd., Rm. 133
Detroit, MI 48226
313-226-7200
313-226-7825 (Law Library)

[Michigan] United States District Court
Western District
110 Michigan St., NW
Grand Rapids, MI 49503
616-456-2381

[Michigan] United States Government Printing Office
477 Michigan Ave., Suite 160
Detroit, MI 48226
313-226-7816

[Michigan] Water Quality Division, Surface
P.O. Box 30028
Lansing, MI 48909
517-373-1949

[Michigan] Tax Tribunal
P.O. Box 30232
Lansing, MI 48909
517-334-6521

[Michigan] Wayne County
600 Randolph St.
Detroit, MI 48226
313-224-0286

[Michigan] Women's Commission
P.O. Box 30026
Lansing, MI 48909
517-373-2884

[Michigan] Worker's Disability Compensation, Bureau of
309 N. Washington Sq.
Box 30016
Lansing, MI 48909
517-373-3490

[Michigan] Youth Parole & Review Board
300 S. Capitol Ave.
Lansing, MI 48909
517-373-0957

Migrant Legal Action Program
2001 S. St., NW
Wash. D.C. 20009
202-462-7744

Military Law Task Force
1168 Union
San Diego, CA 92101
619-233-1701

[Minnesota] Information & Referral (State Government)
612-296-6013

[Minnesota] Information Center (Federal Government)
Minneapolis 612-370-3333

**[Minnesota] Administration,
Department of**
50 Sherburne Ave.
St. Paul, MN 55155
612-296-6013

**[Minnesota] Administrative
Hearings Office**
310 4th Ave. South
Minneapolis, MN 55415
612-241-7600

**[Minnesota] Adult Release,
Office of**
450 N. Syndicate, Suite 300
St. Paul, MN 55104
612-642-0270
612-642-0274 (Juvenile Release)

[Minnesota] Aging, Board on
444 Lafayette Rd.
St. Paul, MN 55155
612-296-2544
800-652-9747

**[Minnesota] Agriculture,
Department of**
90 W. Plato Blvd.
St. Paul, MN 55107
612-297-2200

**[Minnesota] Air Quality,
Division of**
520 Lafayette Rd.
St. Paul, MN 55155
612-296-7331

**[Minnesota] Anoka County Law
Library**
325 E. Main St.
Anoka, MN 55303
612-422-7487

[Minnesota] Archives, State
1500 Mississippi St.
St. Paul, MN 55101
612-296-6980

**Minnesota Association of Legal
Assistants**
P.O. Box 15165
Minneapolis, MN 55415

**[Minnesota] Attorney General,
Office of**
State Capitol Bldg., Rm. 102
St. Paul, MN 55155

612-296-6196
612-296-8152 (Law Library)

[Minnesota] Auditor, State
525 Park St., Suite 400
St. Paul, MN 55103
612-296-2551

Minnesota Bar Association
430 Marquette Ave., Suite 403
Minneapolis, MN 55401
612-333-1183
800-292-4152
612-339-1128 (CLE)

**[Minnesota] Bar Examiners,
Board of**
200 S. Robert St.
St. Paul, MN 55107
612-297-1800

**[Minnesota] Better Business
Bureau**
1745 University Ave.
St. Paul, MN 55104
612-646-7700

**[Minnesota] Building
Construction Division**
50 Sherburne Ave., Rm. 610
St. Paul, MN 55155
612-296-4645

**[Minnesota] Child Support
Enforcement, Office of**
444 Lafayette Rd., 4th Fl.
St. Paul, MN 55155
612-296-2499

**[Minnesota] Commerce,
Department of**
500 Metro Square., 5th Fl.
St. Paul, MN 55101
612-296-2135

**[Minnesota] Consumer Services,
Office of**
117 University Ave.
St. Paul, MN 55155
612-296-2331

**[Minnesota] Corrections,
Department of**
450 N. Syndicate, Suite 300
St. Paul, MN 55104
612-642-0200

**[Minnesota] Court
Administration, State**
230 State Capitol
St. Paul, MN 55155
612-296-2474

[Minnesota] Court of Appeals
1300 Landmark Towers
St. Paul, MN 55102
612-296-2581

**[Minnesota] Criminal Justice,
Department of**
550 Cedar St.
St. Paul, MN 55101
612-297-2436

**Minnesota District Judges
Association**
73 Spruce St.
Mahtomedi, MN 55115
612-426-1746

**[Minnesota] Economic
Opportunity Office**
150 E. Kellogg Blvd.
St. Paul, MN 55101
612-296-4657

**[Minnesota] Education,
Department of**
550 Cedar St.
St. Paul, MN 55101
612-296-6104

**[Minnesota] Emergency
Services, Division of**
Aurora Ave. & Oark St. B5 State
Capitol
St. Paul, MN 55155
612-296-2233

[Minnesota] Employee Relations
520 Lafayette Rd.
St. Paul, MN 55155
612-296-2616

**[Minnesota] Environmental
Quality Board**
658 Cedar St., 3rd Fl.
St. Paul, MN 55155
612-296-2603

**[Minnesota] Ethical Practices
Board**
625 N. Robert St.
St. Paul, MN 55101
612-296-5148

[Minnesota] Finance, Department of
50 Sherburne Ave.
St. Paul, MN 55155
612-296-5900

[Minnesota] Governor, Office of
130 State Capitol Bldg.
St. Paul, MN 55155
612-296-3391

[Minnesota] Health Department
717 Delaware St. SE
Minneapolis, MN 55440
612-623-5000

[Minnesota] Hennepin County
300 S. 6th St.
Minneapolis, MN 55487
612-348-7574

[Minnesota] Hennepin County Bar Association
430 Marquette Ave., No. 402
Minneapolis, MN 55401
612-340-0022

[Minnesota] Hennepin County Law Library
2451 Government Center
Minneapolis, MN 55487
612-348-3022

[Minnesota] House of Representatives
State Office Bldg.
St. Paul, MN 55155
612-296-2146
612-296-4277 (Juciciary)

Minnesota Housing Finance Agency
400 Sibley St., Suite 300
St. Paul, MN 55101
612-296-7608

[Minnesota] Human Services, Department of
444 Lafayette Rd.
St. Paul, MN 55155
612-296-6117

[Minnesota] Insurance, Commissioner of
500 Metro Square Bldg.
St. Paul, MN 55101
612-296-6848
800-652-9747

[Minnesota] Jobs & Training, Department of
390 N. Robert St.
St. Paul, MN 55101
612-296-5359

[Minnesota] Judicial Standards, State Board on
200 S. Robert St.
St. Paul, MN 55107
612-296-3999

[Minnesota] Labor & Industry, Department of
444 Lafayette Rd.
St. Paul, MN 55101
612-296-6105

[Minnesota] Law Examiners, State Board of
200 S. Robert St., Suite 310
St. Paul, MN 55107
612-297-1800

[Minnesota] Law Library, State
117 University Ave.
St. Paul, MN 55155
612-296-2084

[Minnesota] Lawyers Joint Law Library
3930 IDS Tower
Minneapolis, MN 55402
612-338-4320

[Minnesota] Legislative Auditor, Office of the
20 W. 12th St.
St. Paul, MN 55155
612-296-4708

[Minnesota] Lieutenant Governor, Office of
State Capitol Bldg., Rm. 121
St. Paul, MN 55155
612-296-2374

[Minnesota] Materials Management Division
50 Sherburne Ave., Rm. 112
St. Paul, MN 55155
612-296-6152

[Minnesota] Mediation Services, Bureau of
1380 Energy Lane, Suite 2
St. Paul, MN 55108
612-649-5421

[Minnesota] Medical Examiners, State Board of
2700 University Ave. West, Rm. 106
St. Paul, MN 55114
612-642-0538

[Minnesota] Minerals, Division of
500 Lafayette Rd.
St. Paul, MN 55155
612-296-4807

[Minnesota] Minneapolis City Hall
350 S. 5th St.
Minneapolis, MN 55415
612-348-3000

[Minnesota] Natural Resources, Department of
500 Lafayette Rd.
St. Paul, MN 55155
612-296-6157

[Minnesota] Occupational Safety & Health Division
444 Lafayette Rd.
St. Paul, MN 55101
612-296-2116

[Minnesota] Olmsted County
515 2nd St. SW
Rochester, MN 55902
507-285-8145

[Minnesota] Ombudsman for Corrections
333 Sibley, Rm. 895
St. Paul, MN 55101
612-296-4500

[Minnesota] Ombudsman for Mental Health & Mental Retardation
Metro Square Bldg., Rm. 103
St. Paul, MN 55101
612-296-3848
800-652-9747

[Minnesota] Planning Agency
658 Cedar St.
St. Paul, MN 55155
612-296-3985

Minnesota Pollution Control Agency
520 Lafayette Rd.
St. Paul, MN 55155
612-296-6300

[Minnesota] Probation, Parole & Supervised Release Offices
Box 1493
St. Cloud, MN 56302
612-255-3940

[Minnesota] Professional Employees, Association of
411 Main, Rm. 400
St. Paul, MN 55102
612-227-6457
800-652-9721

[Minnesota] Professional Responsibility, State Board of
520 Lafayette Rd., 1st Fl.
St. Paul, MN 55155
612-296-3952

[Minnesota] Public Defender
University of Minnesota
95 Law Center
Minneapolis, MN 55487
612-625-5008

[Minnesota] Public Safety
Transportation Bldg.
John Ireland Blvd.
St. Paul, MN 55155
612-296-6642

[Minnesota] Public Service, Department of
150 E. Kellogg Blvd.
St. Paul, MN 55101
612-296-7107

[Minnesota] Public Utilities Commission
150 E. Kellogg Blvd., Rm. 780
St. Paul, MN 55101
'612-296-7124
800-852-8747

Minnesota Racing Commission
11000 W. 78th St., Suite 201
Eden Prairie, MN 55344
612-341-7555

[Minnesota] Ramsey County
County Courthouse, Rm. 286
St. Paul, MN 55102
612-298-5980

[Minnesota] Ramsey County Law Library
1815 Court House

St. Paul, MN 55102
612-298-5208

[Minnesota] Red River Valley Legal Assistants
Box 1077
Moorehead, MN 56560

[Minnesota] Rehabilitation Services, Division of
390 N. Robert St., 5th Fl.
St. Paul, MN 55101
612-296-1822

[Minnesota] Revenue, Department of
658 Cedar St.
St. Paul, MN 55145
612-296-6185

[Minnesota] Saint Louis County
100 N. 5th Ave. W.
Duluth, MN 55802
218-726-2380

[Minnesota] Saint Louis County Law Library
100 N. 5th Ave., #515
Duluth, MN 55802
218-726-2611

[Minnesota] Saint Paul City Hall
15 Kellogg Blvd. W.
St. Paul, MN 55102
612-298-4012

[Minnesota] Secretary of State
180 State Office Bldg.
St. Paul, MN 55155
612-296-3266

[Minnesota] Securities Registration Unit
7th & Robert Sts.
St. Paul, MN 55101
612-296-4520

[Minnesota] Senate
Capitol Bldg.
Aurora Ave.
St. Paul, MN 55155
612-296-0504
612-296-4191 (Judiciary)

[Minnesota] Sentencing Guidelines Commission
100 Constitution Ave., Rm. 51

St. Paul, MN 55155
612-296-0144

[Minnesota] Solid & Hazardous Waste, Division of
520 Lafayette Rd.
St. Paul, MN 55155
612-296-7282

[Minnesota] State Patrol Division
Transportation Bldg., Rm. 107
St. Paul, MN 55155
612-296-3080

[Minnesota] Statutes, Revisor of
700 State Office Bldg.
St. Paul, MN 55155
612-296-0949

[Minnesota] Supreme Court
230 State Capitol Bldg.
St. Paul, MN 55155
612-296-2581

Minnesota Tax Court
520 Lafayette Rd.
St. Paul, MN 55155
612-296-2806

[Minnesota] Treasurer's Office
50 Sherburne Ave., Rm. 303
St. Paul, MN 55155
612-296-2122

[Minnesota] Trade & Economic Development, Department of
150 E. Kellogg Blvd.
St. Paul, MN 55101
612-297-1291

[Minnesota] Transportation, Department of
Transportation Bldg.
John Ireland Blvd.
St. Paul, MN 55155
612-296-3000

[Minnesota] United States Bankruptcy Court
330 2nd Ave. South
Minneapolis, MN 55401
612-348-1855

[Minnesota] United States District Court
316 N. Robert
St. Paul, MN 55101

612-290-3212
612-290-3177 (Law Library)

[Minnesota] Veterans Affairs, Department of
20 W. 12th St.
St. Paul, MN 55155
612-296-5262

[Minnesota] Vital Records & Statistics
717 Delaware St. SE
P.O. Box 9441
St. Paul, MN 55440
612-623-5121

[Minnesota] Water & Soil Resources, Board of
90 W. Plato Blvd.
St. Paul, 55107
612-296-3767

[Minnesota] Water, Division of
500 Lafayette Rd.
St. Paul, MN 55155
612-296-4810

[Minnesota] Weights & Measures, Division of
2277 Hwy 36
St. Paul, MN 55113
612-341-7200

[Minnesota] Women, Commission on the Economic Status of
100 Constitution Ave.
State Office Bldg., Rm. 85
St. Paul, MN 55155
612-296-8590

[Minnesota] Worker's Compensation Court of Appeals
345 St. Peter St., Rm. 775
St. Paul, MN 55102
612-296-6526

[Minnesota] Worker's Compensation Division
443 Lafayette Rd.
St. Paul, MN 55101
612-296-6490

[Mississippi] Information & Referral (State Government)
601-359-1000
601-354-7011

[Mississippi] Aging & Adult Services, Division of
421 W. Pascagoula St.
Jackson, MS 39201
601-949-2070
800-949-2070

[Mississippi] Aging, Council on
301 W. Pearl St.
Jackson, MS 39203
601-949-2013

[Mississippi] Agriculture & Commerce, Department of
1604 Sillers Bldg.
Jackson, MS 39201
601-359-3639

[Mississippi] Alcoholic Beverage Control
P.O. Box 540
Jackson, MS 39110
601-877-3711

[Mississippi] Archives & History, Department of
100 S. State St.
Jackson, MS 39201
601-359-1424

Mississippi Association of Legal Assistants
P.O. Box 966
Jackson, MS 39205

Mississippi Association of Legal Secretaries
4622 Lewis St.
Gulfport, MS 39501

[Mississippi] Attorney General, Office of
450 High St.
Jackson, MS 39201
601-359-3680

[Mississippi] Audit, Department of
P.O. Box 956
Jackson, MS 39205
601-359-3561

[Mississippi] Banking & Consumer Finance, Department of
P.O. Box 23729
Jackson, MS 39225
601-359-1031
800-826-2499

[Mississippi] Bar Admissions, Board of
P.O. Box 1449
Jackson, MS 39215
601-359-1268

Mississippi Bar Association
643 N. State St.
Jackson, MS 39202
601-948-4471

[Mississippi] Better Business Bureau
P.O. Box 390
Jackson, MS 39205
601-948-8222
601-327-8594 (Columbus)

[Mississippi] Child Support Division
P.O. Box 352
515 E. Amite St.
Jackson, MS 39205
601-354-0341

[Mississippi] Consumer Protection Division
P.O. Box 220
Jackson, MS 39205
601-354-6018

[Mississippi] Corporations Division
401 Mississippi St.
Jackson, MS 39205
601-359-1350

[Mississippi] Corrections, Department of
723 N. President St.
Jackson, MS 39202
601-354-6454

[Mississippi] Crime Lab
P.O. Box 5008
Jackson, MS 39216
601-987-1600

[Mississippi] Criminal Justice Planning
301 W. Pearl St.
Jackson, MS 39203
601-949-2225

[Mississippi] Economic Development, Department of
1201 Walter Sillers Bldg.

Jackson, MS 39201
601-359-3449

**[Mississippi] Education,
Department of**
Walter Sillers Bldg., Rm. 501
Jackson, MS 39201
601-359-3513

**[Mississippi] Emergency
Operations Center**
1410 Riverside Dr.
Jackson, MS 39202
601-352-9100

**[Mississippi] Employment
Security Commission**
1520 W. Capitol St.
Jackson, MS 39203
601-354-8711

**[Mississippi] Energy &
Transportation,
Department of**
510 George St.
Dickson Bldg.
Jackson, MS 39202
601-961-4733

**[Mississippi] Equal Employment
Opportunity Commission**
1520 W. Capitol
Jackson, MS 39203
601-961-7421

[Mississippi] Ethics Commission
P.O. Box 22746
Jackson, MS 39205
601-359-1285

**[Mississippi] Fiscal Management
Board**
550 High St., Rm. 906
Jackson, MS 39201
601-359-3402

[Mississippi] Governor's Office
P.O. Box 139
Jackson, MS 39205
601-359-3150

**[Mississippi] Harrison County
Law Library**
1801 23rd Ave.
Gulfport, MS 39501
601-865-4068

**[Mississippi] Health,
Department of**
2423 N. State St.
Jackson, MS 39216
601-960-7634

**[Mississippi] Higher Learning,
Institutions of**
3825 Ridgewood Rd.
Jackson, MS 39211
601-982-6611

**[Mississippi] Highway
Department**
P.O. Box 1850
Jackson, MS 39215
601-359-1209

**[Mississippi] Highway Safety
Patrol**
1900 E. Woodrow Wilson Dr.
Jackson, MS 39216
601-987-1212

[Mississippi] Hinds County
P.O. Box 686
Jackson, MS 39205
601-968-6501

**[Mississippi] House of
Representatives**
New Capitol
Jackson, MS 39205
601-359-3770
601-359-3388 (Judiciary)

**[Mississippi] Housing Finance
Corporation**
510 George St.
Jackson, MS 39201
601-961-4514

**[Mississippi] Insurance,
Commissioner of**
1804 Walter Sillers Bldg.
Jackson, MS 39201
601-359-3569

**Mississippi Judicial
Performance, Commission on**
P.O. Box 22527
Jackson, MS 39225
601-359-1273

[Mississippi] Law Library, State
450 High St., Rm. 219
Jackson, MS 39215
601-359-3672

**[Mississippi] Lieutenant
Governor's Office**
P.O. Box 1018
Jackson, MS 39215
601-359-3200

**[Mississippi] Medical Licensure,
Board of**
2688-D Insurance Center Dr.
Jackson, MS 39216
601-354-6645

**[Mississippi] Mental Health,
Department of**
239 N. Lamar St.
Jackson, MS 39201
601-359-1288

**[Mississippi] Mining &
Reclamation Division**
2525 Northwest St.
Jackson, MS 39216
601-354-6228

**[Mississippi] Motor Vehicle
Commission**
P.O. Box 1212
Jackson, MS 39205
601-354-7572

[Mississippi] Narcotics Bureau
P.O. Box 6462
Jackson, MS 39212
601-359-1570

**[Mississippi] Natural Resources,
Department of**
2380 Hwy 80 W. & Ellis Ave.
Jackson, MS 39204
601-961-5000

**[Mississippi] Occupational
Safety & Health Branch**
305 W. Lorenz Blvd.
Jackson, MS 39213
601-987-3981

[Mississippi] Oil & Gas Board
Walter Sillers Bldg., Rm. 1400
P.O. Box 1332
Jackson, MS 39215
601-359-3736

**Mississippi, Paralegal
Association of**
P.O. Box 22887
Jackson, MS 39205

[Mississippi] Parole Board
723 N. President St.
Jackson, MS 39202
601-354-6200

[Mississippi] Personnel Board, State
301 N. Lamar St.
Jackson, MS 39201
601-359-1406

[Mississippi] Planning & Policy, Department of
637 N. President St.
Ilk Sanford Bldg., 1st Fl.
Jackson, MS 39202
601-354-7017

[Mississippi] Pollution Control, Bureau of
2380 Hwy 80 W
Jackson, MS 39204
601-961-5171

[Mississippi] Public Health Statistics, Office of
2423 N. State St., Rm. 110
Jackson, MS 39216
601-960-7960

[Mississippi] Public Safety, Department of
P.O. Box 958
Jackson, MS 39205
601-982-1212

[Mississippi] Public Service Commission
P.O. Box 1174
Jackson, MS 39215
601-961-5400

Mississippi Public Welfare, Department of
P.O. Box 352
Jackson, MS 39205
601-354-0341

[Mississippi] Purchasing, Bureau of
550 High St.
Jackson, MS 39201
601-359-3409

[Mississippi] Real Estate Commission
1920 Dunbarton St.

Jackson, MS 39216
601-987-3969

Mississippi Revisor of Statutes
P.O. Box 220
Jackson, MS 39215
601-359-3860

[Mississippi] Secretary of State
401 Mississippi St.
Jackson, MS 39201
601-359-1350

[Mississippi] Security Division
401 Mississippi St.
Jackson, MS 39205
601-359-1350

[Mississippi] Senate
New Capitol
Jackson, MS 39205
601-359-3770
601-359-3237 (Judiciary)

[Mississippi] Solid Waste Management, Division of
2380 Hwy 80 W.
Jackson, MS 39204
601-961-5062

Mississippi Supreme Court
P.O. Box 117
Carroll Gartin Bldg.
Jackson, MS 39205
601-359-3694

[Mississippi] Tax Commission
102 Woolfolk Bldg.
Jackson, MS 39205
601-359-1098

[Mississippi] Treasurer, State
404 Sillers Bldg.
P.O. Box 138
Jackson, MS 39201
601-359-3531

[Mississippi] Unemployment Insurance Division
1520 W. Capitol St.
Jackson, MS 39203
601-961-7700

[Mississippi] United States Bankruptcy Court
Northern Mississippi
P.O. Box 867
Aberdeen, MS 39730
601-369-2596

[Mississippi] United States Bankruptcy Court
Southern Mississippi
P.O. Drawer 2448
Jackson, MS 39225
601-965-5301

[Mississippi] United States District Court
Northern District
P.O. Box 727
Oxford, MS 38655
601-234-1971

[Mississippi] United States District Court
Southern District
245 E. Capitol St., Suite 416
Jackson, MS 39201
601-960-4439

[Mississippi] Veterans Affairs Board
4607 Lindberg Dr.
Jackson, MS 39209
601-354-7205

[Mississippi] Vital Records, Division of
P.O. Box 1700
Jackson, MS 39215
601-960-6606

[Mississippi] Vocational Rehabilitation for the Blind
P.O. Box 4872
Jackson, MS 39296
601-354-6411

[Mississippi] Weights & Measures Division
500 Greymont Ave.
Jackson, MS 39205
601-354-7077

[Mississippi] Workers Compensation Commission
1428 Lakeland Dr.
Jackson, MS 39216
601-987-4200

[Mississippi] Youth Services, Department of
301 N. Lamar St., Suite 410
Jackson, MS 39201
601-359-1066

**[Missouri] Information &
Referral (State Government)**
314-751-2000

**[Missouri] Information Center
(Federal Government)**
St. Louis 314-539-2106
Elsewhere in state 800-393-7711

**[Missouri] Administration,
Office of**
P.O. Box 809
Jefferson City, MO 65102
314-751-3311

[Missouri] Aging, Division of
P.O. Box 1337
Jefferson City, MO 65102
314-751-3082
800-392-0210

**[Missouri] Agriculture,
Department of**
P.O. Box 630
Jefferson City, MO 65102
314-751-4211

**[Missouri] Air Pollution Control
Program**
205 Jefferson St.
Jefferson City, MO 65101
314-751-4817

**[Missouri] Attorney General,
Office of**
Supreme Court Bldg., 1st Fl.
Jefferson City, MO 65101
314-751-3321

**[Missouri] Auditor, Office of the
State**
P.O. Box 869
Jefferson City, MO 65102
314-751-4824

Missouri Bar Association
326 Monroe
Jefferson City, MO 65102
314-635-4128

**[Missouri] Bar Examiners,
Board of**
P.O. Box 150
Jefferson City, MO 65102
314-751-4144

**[Missouri] Better Business
Bureau**
5100 Oakland, Suite 200

St. Louis, MO 63110
314-531-3300
816-421-7800 (Kansas City)

**[Missouri] Budget & Planning,
Division of**
State Capitol, Rm. 124
Jefferson City, MO 65101
314-751-2345

**[Missouri] Child Support
Enforcement, Division of**
P.O. Box 1527
Jefferson City, MO 65102
314-751-4301

[Missouri] Cole County
301 E. High St.
Jefferson City, MO 65101
314-634-9110

**[Missouri] Community
Sanitation, Bureau of**
P.O. Box 570
Jefferson City, MO 65102
314-751-6090

**[Missouri] Consumer Protection
Division**
P.O. Box 899
Jefferson City, MO 65102
314-751-2389

[Missouri] Corporation Division
P.O. Box 778
Jefferson City, MO 65102
314-751-4194

**[Missouri] Corrections & Human
Resources, Department of**
2729 Plaza Dr.
Jefferson City, MO 65109
314-751-2389

**[Missouri] Court Administrator,
Office of State**
1105 Rear Southwest Blvd.
Jefferson City, MO 65109
314-751-4377

**[Missouri] Court of
Appeals—Eastern District**
Wainwright State Office Bldg.
111 N. 7th St.
St. Louis, MO 63101
314-444-6967
314-444-6964 (Law Library)

**[Missouri] Court of
Appeals—Southern District**
300 Hammons Parkway
Springfield, MO 65806
417-837-6820
417-837-6813 (Law Library)

**[Missouri] Court of
Appeals—Western District**
1300 Oak
Kansas City, MO 64106
816-474-5511

**[Missouri] Design &
Construction, Division of**
301 W. High St.
Jefferson City, MO 65101
314-751-3339

**[Missouri] Economic
Development,
Department of**
P.O. Box 1157
Jefferson City, MO 65102
314-751-4962
800-392-8222

[Missouri] Elections, Division of
P.O. Box 778
Jefferson City, MO 65102
314-751-2301

**[Missouri] Elementary &
Secondary Education,
Department of**
205 Jefferson St.
Jefferson City, MO 65101
314-751-3503

**[Missouri] Emergency
Management Agency, State**
1717 Industrial Dr.
Jefferson City, MO 65109
314-751-9571

**[Missouri] Employees'
Retirement System, State**
P.O. Box 209
Jefferson City, MO 65102
314-751-2342

**[Missouri] Employment
Security, Division of**
421 E. Dunklin St.
Jefferson City, MO 65104
314-751-3215

[Missouri] Energy, Division of
205 Jefferson St.

Jefferson City, MO 65101
314-751-4000

[Missouri] Environmental Protection Agency
1103 Southwest Blvd.
Jefferson City, MO 65109
314-636-5223

[Missouri] Environmental Quality, Division of
205 Jefferson St.
Jefferson City, MO 65101
314-751-4810

[Missouri] Family Services, Division of
P.O. Box 88
Jefferson City, MO 65103
314-751-4247

[Missouri] Finance, Commissioner of
P.O. Box 716
Jefferson City, MO 65102
314-751-3242

[Missouri] Governor, Office of
216 Capitol Bldg.
Jefferson City, MO 65101
314-751-3222

[Missouri] Health, Department of
1730 E. Elm St.
Jefferson City, MO 65101
314-751-6001

[Missouri] Higher Education, Department of
101 Adams St.
Jefferson City, MO 65101
314-751-2361

[Missouri] Highway & Transportation Department
Capitol Ave. & Jefferson Sts.
Jefferson City, MO 65101
314-751-4622

[Missouri] Highway Patrol
P.O. Box 568
Jefferson City, MO 65102
314-751-3313

[Missouri] Housing Development Commission
3770 Broadway
Kansas City, MO 64111
816-756-3790

[Missouri] House of Representatives
State Capitol
Jefferson City, MO 65101
314-751-4043
314-751-4473 (Judiciary)

[Missouri] Human Rights, Commission on
Truman Bldg., Box 1129
Jefferson City, MO 65102
314-751-3325

[Missouri] Insurance, Division of
301 W. High St., Rm. 600
P.O. Box 690
Jefferson City, MO 65102
314-751-2451

[Missouri] Jackson County
415 E. 12th St.
Kansas City, MO 64106
816-881-3333

[Missouri] Jackson County Law Library
818 Grand-Walnut Level
Kansas City, MO 64106
816-221-2221

[Missouri] Kansas City Association of Legal Assistants
P.O. Box 13223
Kansas City, MO 64199

[Missouri] Kansas City Hall
414 E. 12th St.
Kansas City, MO 64106
816-274-2000

[Missouri] Kansas City Metropolitan Bar Association
818 Grand Ave.
Kansas City, MO 64106
816-474-4322

[Missouri] Labor & Industrial Relations, Department of
421 E. Dunklin St.
Jefferson City, MO 65101
314-751-4091

[Missouri] Lawyer's Library
12761 Halls Ferry Rd.
Florissant, MO 63033
314-837-5649

[Missouri] Lieutenant Governor, Office of
316 State Capitol Bldg.
Jefferson City, MO 65101
314-751-3000

[Missouri] Lottery Commission, State
P.O. Box 1603
Jefferson City, MO 65102
314-751-4050

[Missouri] Mental Health, Department of
P.O. Box 687
Jefferson City, MO 65102
314-751-3070

[Missouri] Motor Vehicles & Drivers Licensing, Division of
P.O. Box 629
Jefferson City, MO 65102
314-751-4429

[Missouri] Natural Resources, Department of
205 Jefferson St.
Jefferson City, MO 65101
314-751-4422

[Missouri] Personnel, Division of
P.O. Box 388
Jefferson City, MO 65102
314-751-4162

[Missouri] Probation & Parole, Board of
Box 267, 117 Commerce Plaza Dr.
Jefferson City, MO 65102
314-751-2389

[Missouri] Professional Registration, Division of
3523 N. Ten Mile Dr.
Jefferson City, MO 65109
314-751-2334

[Missouri] Public Defender Commission
Plaza Towers, Suite 811
Springfield, MO 65804
417-887-9800

[Missouri] Public Defender, State Office
209B E. Green Meadows Rd.

Columbia, MO 65203
314-442-1101

**[Missouri] Public Safety,
Department of**
301 W. High St.
Jefferson City, MO 65101
314-751-4905

**[Missouri] Public Service
Commission**
P.O. Box 360
Jefferson City, MO 65102
314-751-3234
800-392-4211

**[Missouri] Purchasing,
Division of**
301 W. High St., Rm. 580
Jefferson City, MO 65101
314-751-2387

**[Missouri] Real Estate
Commission**
3523 N. Ten Mile Dr.
Jefferson City, MO 65109
314-751-2334

**[Missouri] Records Management
& Archives**
1001 Industrial Dr.
Jefferson City, MO 65101
314-751-4702

**[Missouri] Revenue,
Department of**
301 W. High St.
Jefferson City, MO 65101
314-751-4450

**[Missouri] Safety & Health
Consultation Service**
P.O. Box 449
Jefferson City, MO 65102
314-751-3403

[Missouri] Secretary of State
301 W. High St.
Jefferson City, MO 65101
314-751-3318

**[Missouri] Securities
Commissioner**
Truman State Office Bldg.
Jefferson City, MO 65102
314-751-4136

[Missouri] Senate
State Capitol

Jefferson City, MO 65101
314-751-3824
314-751-4106 (Judiciary)

**[Missouri] Social Services,
Department of**
P.O. Box 1527
Jefferson City, MO 65102
314-751-4815

**[Missouri] Soil & Water
Conservation Program**
205 Jefferson St.
Jefferson City, MO 65101
314-751-4932

**[Missouri] Southwest Missouri
Paralegal Association**
517 E. Seminole
Springfield, MO 65807

**[Missouri] St. Louis Association
of Legal Assistants**
P.O. Box 9690
St. Louis, MO 63122

**[Missouri] St. Louis, Bar
Association of Metropolitan**
One Mercantile Center, Suite 3600
St. Louis, MO 63101
314-421-4134

[Missouri] St. Louis City Hall
1200 Market St.
St. Louis, MO 63103
314-622-4000

**[Missouri] St. Louis County Law
Library**
7900 Forsythe
Clayton, MO 63105
314-889-2512

**[Missouri] St. Louis, Law Library
Association of**
1300 Civil Courts Bldg.
St. Louis, MO 63101
314-622-4386

[Missouri] Statutes, Revisor of
State Capitol, Rm. 117A
Jefferson City, MO 65101
314-751-2393

[Missouri] Supreme Court
P.O. Box 150
Jefferson City, MO 65102
314-751-4144
314-751-2636 (Law Library)

**[Missouri] Trade Offense
Division**
Supreme Court Bldg.
Jefferson City, MO 65101
314-751-5333

[Missouri] Treasurer, State
State Capitol, Rm. 229
Jefferson City, MO 65101
314-751-4123

**[Missouri] Unemployment
Insurance Operations**
421 E. Dunklin St.
Jefferson City, MO 65104
314-751-3643

**[Missouri] United States
Bankruptcy Court**
Eastern Missouri
1114 Market St.
St. Louis, MO 63101
314-539-2222

**[Missouri] United States
Bankruptcy Court**
Western Missouri
811 Grand Ave.
Kansas City, MO 64106
816-426-2811

**[Missouri] United States Court of
Appeals for the Eighth Circuit**
1114 Market St.
St. Louis, MO 63101
314-539-3609
314-539-2930 (Law Library)
402-221-4768 (Law Library, Omaha)
701-232-1326 (Law Library, Fargo)

**[Missouri] United States District
Court**
Eastern District
1114 Market St.
St. Louis, MO 63101
314-539-6056

**[Missouri] United States District
Court**
Western District
811 Grand Ave., Rm. 201
Kansas City, MO 64106
816-426-2811
816-426-2937 (Law Library)

**[Missouri] United States
Government Printing Office**
5600 E. Bannister Rd.

120 Bannister Mall
Kansas City, MO 64137
816-765-2256

**[Missouri] Vital Records,
Bureau of**
P.O. Box 570
Jefferson City, MO 65102
314-751-6400

**[Missouri] Vocational
Rehabilitation, Division of**
2401 E. McCarty
Jefferson City, MO 65101
314-751-3251

**[Missouri] Waste Management
Program**
205 Jefferson St.
Jefferson City, MO 65101
314-751-4533

**[Missouri] Weights & Measures
Division**
P.O. Box 630
Jefferson City, MO 65102
314-751-4278

**[Missouri] Women's Economic
Development & Training,
Council on**
P.O. Box 1684
Jefferson City, MO 65102
314-751-0810

**[Missouri] Worker's
Compensation, Division of**
722 Jefferson St., Box 58
Jefferson City, MO 65102
314-751-4231

**[Missouri] Youth Services,
Division of**
P.O. Box 447
Jefferson City, MO 65102
314-751-3324

Mobile Oil Corp.
3225 Gallows Rd.
Fairfax, VA 22037
703-849-3986

**[Montana] Information &
Referral (State Government)**
406-444-2511

[Montana] Aging Services Bureau
P.O. Box 8005

Helena, MT 59604
406-444-5900
800-332-2272

**[Montana] Agriculture,
Department of**
Agriculture-Livestock Bldg.
  Capitol Station
Helena, MT 59620
406-444-3144

[Montana] Air Quality Bureau
Cogswell Bldg.
Helena, MT 59620
406-444-3454

**[Montana] Architecture &
Engineering Division**
1520 E. 6th Ave.
Helena, MT 59601
406-444-3104

**[Montana] Archives & Library
Division**
225 N. Roberts St.
Helena, MT 59620
406-444-2694

**[Montana] Attorney General,
Office of**
215 N. Sanders St.
Helena, MT 59201
406-444-2026

**[Montana] Auditor & Securities
Commissioner, State**
126 N. Sanders St., Rm. 270
Helena, MT 59604
406-444-2040

Montana Bar Association
46 N. Last Chance Gulch, Suite 2A
P.O. Box 577
Helena, MT 59264
406-442-7660

**[Montana] Bar Examiners,
Board of**
215 N. Sanders
Helena, MT 59620
406-444-2621

**[Montana] Budget & Program
Planning, Office of**
State Capitol Bldg., Rm. 237
Helena, MT 59620
406-444-3616

**[Montana] Business Regulation
Division**
1424 9th Ave.
Helena, MT 59601
406-444-3737

**[Montana] Child Support
Enforcement Division**
P.O. Box 5955
Helena, MT 59604
406-444-4614

**[Montana] Citizen's Advocate,
Office of**
Capitol Bldg., Rm. 213
Helena, MT 59620
406-444-3468

**[Montana] Commerce,
Department of**
1424 9th Ave.
Helena, MT 59601
406-444-3797

**[Montana] Community
Corrections Bureau**
1539 11th Ave.
Helena, MT 59601
406-444-4912

[Montana] Consumer Affairs Unit
1424 9th Ave.
Helena, MT 59620
406-444-4312

[Montana] Corporation Bureau
State Capitol, Rm. 225
Helena, MT 59620
406-444-3665

**[Montana] Court
Administrator's Office**
Supreme Court
Justice Bldg., Rm. 315
Helena, MT 59620
406-444-2621

**[Montana] Crime Control
Division**
303 N. Roberts St., 4th Fl.
Helena, MT 59601
406-444-3604

**[Montana] Disaster &
Emergency Services Division**
1100 N. Main St.
Helena, MT 59601
406-444-6911

[Montana] Economic Assistance Division
P.O. Box 4210
Helena, MT 59604
406-444-4540

[Montana] Energy Division
1520 E. 6th Ave.
Helena, MT 59601
406-444-6754

[Montana] Environmental Sciences Division
Cogswell Bldg., Capitol Station
Helena, MT 59620
406-444-3948

[Montana] Family Services, Department of
Box 8005
Helena, MT 59604
406-444-5901

[Montana] Financial Institutions, Commissioner of
1520 E. 6th Ave., Rm. 50
Helena, MT 59620
406-444-2091

[Montana] Governor, Office of
State Capitol Bldg.
Helena, MT 59620
406-444-3111

[Montana] Health & Environmental Sciences, Department of
Cogswell Bldg., Rm C108
Helena, MT 59620
406-444-2544

[Montana] Highway Patrol
303 N. Roberts
Helena, MT 59601
406-444-3780

[Montana] Highways, Department of
2701 Prospect Ave.
Helena, MT 59601
406-444-6201

[Montana] House of Representatives
State Capitol
Helena, MT 59620
406-444-4800
406-444-4828 (Judiciary)

[Montana] Housing, Board of
2001 11th Ave.
Helena, MT 59620
406-444-3040

[Montana] Human Rights Division
P.O. Box 1728
Helena, MT 59624
406-444-2884

[Montana] Institutions, Department of
1539 11th Ave.
Helena, MT 59620
406-444-3930

[Montana] Insurance Commissioner of
126 N. Sanders, Rm. 270
Helena, MT 59604
406-444-2040
800-332-6148

[Montana] Investigation & Enforcement
Sam Mitchell Bldg., Rm. 465
Helena, MT 59620
406-444-2846

[Montana] Justice, Department of
215 N. Sanders St.
Helena, MT 59620
406-444-2026

[Montana] Labor & Industry, Department of
1327 Lockey Labor & Industry Bldg.
Helena, MT 59624
406-444-3555

Montana, Law Library of, State
215 N. Sanders
Helena, MT 59620
406-444-3660

[Montana] Legislative Council
State Capitol, Rm. 138
Helena, MT 59620
406-444-3064

[Montana] Lieutenant Governor, Office of
Capitol Station
Helena, MT 59620
406-444-3111

[Montana] Mines & Geology, Bureau of
W. Park St.
Butte, MT 59701
406-496-4180

[Montana] Missoula County
100 W. Broadway
Missoula, MT 59802
406-721-5700

[Montana] Motor Vehicle Division
303 N. Roberts St.
Helena, MT 59620
406-444-4536

[Montana] Natural Resources & Conservation, Department of
1520 E. 6th Ave.
Helena, MT 59620
406-444-6699

[Montana] Occupational Health Bureau
Cogswell Bldg., Rm. A113
Helena, MT 59620
406-444-3671

[Montana] Oil & Gas Conservation Division
1520 E. 6th Ave.
Helena, MT 59601
406-444-6675

Montana Paralegal Association, Inc.
P.O. Box 693
Billings, MT 59103

[Montana] Pardons, Board of
300 Maryland Ave.
Deer Lodge, MT 58722
406-846-1404

[Montana] Personnel, State
205 Roberts St.
Helena, MT 59620
406-444-3871

[Montana] Political Practices, Commissioner of
1208 8th Ave.
Helena, MT 59620
406-444-2942

Montana Promotion Division
1424 9th Ave.
Helena, MT 59620

406-444-2654
800-548-3390

[Montana] Public Instruction, Office of
Capitol Bldg., Rm. 106
Helena, MT 59620
406-444-3654

[Montana] Public Service Commission
2701 Prospect Ave.
Helena, MT 59620
406-444-6199

[Montana] Purchasing Division
205 Robert St., Rm. 165
Helena, MT 59620
406-444-2575

[Montana] Realty Regulation, Board of
1424 9th Ave.
Helena, MT 59601
406-444-2961

[Montana] Revenue, Department of
Sam W. Mitchell Bldg., Rm. 455
Helena, MT 59620
406-444-2460

[Montana] Secretary of State
State Capitol Bldg.
Helena, MT 59620
406-444-2034

[Montana] Senate
State Capitol
Helena, MT 59620
406-444-4800
406-444-4886 (Judiciary)

[Montana] Social & Rehabilitation Services, Department of
P.O. Box 4210
Helena, MT 59604
406-444-2590

[Montana] Solid & Hazardous Waste Bureau
Cogswell Bldg., Rm. B-201
Helena, MT 59620
406-444-2821

[Montana] Supreme Court
215 N. Sanders St., Rm. 323
Helena, MT 59620

406-444-3858
406-444-3660 (Library)

[Montana] Transportation Division
2701 Prospect Ave.
Helena, MT 59601
406-444-6190

[Montana] Treasurer
205 Robert St., Rm. 155
Helena, MT 59620
406-444-2032

[Montana] Unemployment Insurance Division
1327 Lockey St.
Helena, MT 59624
406-444-2723

[Montana] United States Bankruptcy Court
215 1st Ave., North
Great Falls, MT 59401
406-761-3811

[Montana] United States District Court
316 N. 26th St., No. 5405
Billings, MT 59101
406-657-6366

[Montana] Vital Records & Statistics Bureau
Cogswell Bldg. C118
Helena, MT 59620
406-444-2614

[Montana] Water Resources Division
1520 E. 6th Ave.
Helena, MT 59601
406-444-6601

[Montana] Weights & Measures, Bureau of
1424 9th Ave.
Helena, MT 59620
406-444-3164

[Montana] Women & Employment, Council on
Capitol Bldg.
Helena, MT 59620
406-444-3946

[Montana] Workers' Compensation, Division of
5 S. Last Chance Gulch

Helena, MT 59601
406-444-6518

[Montana] Yellowstone County
P.O. Box 35001
Billings, MT 59107
406-256-2785

Montgomery Ward
Montgomery Ward Plaza
Chicago, IL 60671
312-467-2628

Monument Builders of America
1612 Central St.
Evanston, IL 60201
312-869-2031

Mortgage Bankers Association of America
1125 15th St., NW, 7th Fl.
Wash. D.C. 20005
202-861-1929

Multistate Tax Commission
444 N. Capitol St., NW, Suite 409
Wash. D.C. 20001
202-624-8699

Music Library Association
P.O. Box 487
Canton, MA 02021
617-828-8450

Mutual Life Insurance Company of New York
500 Frank W. Burr Blvd.
Teaneck, NJ 07666
201-907-6669

Mutual of Omaha Insurance Co.
Mutual of Omaha Plaza
Omaha, NE 68175
402-342-7600

NAACP Legal Defense & Educational Fund, Inc.
1275 K. St., NW, Suite 301

Wash. D.C. 20005
202-682-1300

Nabisco Brands, Inc.
100 DeForest Ave.
East Hanover, NJ 07936
800-932-7800

National Abortion Rights Action League
1101 14th St., NW
Wash. D.C. 20005
202-371-0779

National Academy of Code Administration
803 County Administration Bldg.
138 E. Court St.
Cincinnati, OH 45202
513-632-8643

National Academy of Conciliators
7315 Wisconsin Ave., Suite 1255
Bethesda, MD 20814
301-907-7000

National Academy of Elder Law Attorneys
1730 E. River Rd., Suite 107
Tucson, AZ 85718

National Advertising Division
Council of Better Business Bureaus
845 3rd Ave.
New York, NY 10022
212-754-1320

National American Indian Court Judges Association
1000 Connecticut Ave., NW
Wash. D.C. 20036
202-296-0685

National Association for Independent Paralegals
585 5th St. West, Suite 111
Sonoma, CA 95476
707-935-3595

National Association for Law Placement
440 1st St., NW, Suite 302
Wash. D.C. 20001
202-783-5157

National Association for Public Interest Law
215 Pennsylvania Ave., SE

Wash. D.C. 20003
202-546-4918

National Association for State Information Systems
350 Elaine Dr., Suite 203
Lexington, KY 40504
606-254-7017

National Association for the Advancement of Colored People
1025 Vermont Ave. NW
Wash. D.C. 20005
202-638-2269
(see also NAACP)

National Association of American School Employees & Retirees Legal Defense Counsel
13902 Robson St.
Detroit, MI 48227
313-837-0627

National Association of Attorneys General
444 N. Capitol St., NW, Suite 403
Wash. D.C. 20001
202-628-0435

National Association of Bankruptcy Trustees
3008 Milkwood Ave.
Columbia, SC 29205
803-252-5646

National Association of Bar Executives
750 N. Lake Shore Dr.
Chicago, IL 60611
312-988-5346

National Association of Black Women Attorneys
506 5th St., NW
Wash. D.C. 20001
202-966-9693

National Association of Bond Attorneys
P.O. Box 397
Hinsdale, IL 60522
312-920-0160

National Association of Business & Professional Women's Clubs, Inc.
2012 Massachusetts Ave., NW

Wash. D.C. 20036
202-293-1100

National Association of Chiefs of Police
1110 N. Glebe Rd.
Arlington, VA 22201
703-293-9088

National Association of Civil Service Employees
7185 Navajo Rd., Suite C
San Diego, CA 92119
619-464-1014

National Association of College & University Attorneys
1 Dupont Circle, Suite 620
Wash. D.C. 20036
202-833-8390

National Association of Counsel for Children
1205 Oneida St.
Denver, CO 80220
303-321-3963

National Association of Counties
440 1st St., NW
Wash. D.C. 20001
202-393-6226

National Association of County Civil Attorneys
440 1st St., NW
Wash. D.C. 20001
202-393-6226

National Association of Crime Victim Compensation Boards
1900 L St. NW, Suite 500
Wash. D.C. 20016
202-293-5420

National Association of Criminal Defense Lawyers
1110 Vermont Ave., Suite 1150
Wash. D.C. 20005
202-872-8688

National Association of Criminal Justice Planners
1511 K St. NW
Wash. D.C. 20005
202-347-0501

National Association of Document Examiners
20 Nassau St.

Princeton, NJ 08542
609-924-8193

**National Association of Enrolled
Agents**
6000 Executive Blvd., Suite 205
Rockville, MD 20852
301-984-6232
800-424-4339

**National Association of Enrolled
Federal Tax Accountants**
6108 N. Harding Ave.
Chicago, IL 60659
312-463-5577

**National Association of
Evangelicals**
1023 15th St. NW
Wash. D.C. 20005
202-789-1011

**National Association of Home
Builders**
15th & M. Streets, NW
Wash. D.C. 20005
202-822-0409
800-568-5242

**National Association of Housing
& Redevelopment Officials**
1320 18th St., NW
Wash. D.C. 20036
202-429-2960

**National Association of
Insurance Commissioners**
120 W. 12th St., Suite 1100
Kansas City, MO 64105
816-842-3600

**National Association of Law
Firm Marketing
Administrators**
60 Revere Dr., Suite 500
Northbrook, IL 60062
312-480-9641

**National Association of Law
Placement**
1666 Connecticut Ave., NW,
Suite 450
Wash. D.C. 20009
202-667-1666

**National Association of Legal
Assistants**
1601 S. Main St., Suite 300

Tulsa, OK 74119
918-587-6828

**National Association of Legal
Search Consultants**
1025 Thomas Jefferson St., NW,
Suite 400
Wash. D.C. 20007
202-944-3719

**National Association of Legal
Secretaries**
2250 E. 73rd St., Suite 550
Tulsa, OK 74136
918-493-3540

**National Association of
Personnel Consultants**
3133 Mt. Vernon Ave.
Alexandria, VA 22303
703-684-0180

**National Association of
Professional Process Servers**
306 H. St. NE
Wash. D.C. 20002
202-547-5710

**National Association of Railroad
Trial Counsel**
88 Alma Real Dr., Suite 103A
Pacific Palisades, CA 90272
213-459-7659

**National Association of Real
Estate License Law Officials**
P.O. Box 129
Centerville, UT 84014
801-298-5572

**National Association of Retired
Federal Employees**
1533 New Hampshire Ave., NW
Wash. D.C. 20036
202-234-0832

**National Association of
Secretaries of State**
Council of State Governments
P.O. Box 11910
Lexington, KY 40578
606-252-2291

**National Association of
Securities Dealers, Inc.**
33 Whitehall St., 10th Fl.
New York, NY 10004
212-858-4000

**National Association of State
Auditors, Comptrollers, &
Treasurers**
2401 Regency Rd.
Lexington, KY 40503
606-276-1147

**National Association of State
Boards of Accountancy**
545 5th Ave.
New York, NY 10017
212-490-3868

**National Association of State
Utility Consumer Advocates**
1101 14th St., NW, Suite 808
Wash. D.C. 20005
202-727-3908

**National Association of Tax
Consultants**
454 N. 13th St.
San Jose, CA 95112
408-298-1458

**National Association of Tax
Practitioners**
1015 W. Wisconsin Ave.
Kaukauna, WI 54130
414-766-9491

**National Association of
Technical & Trade Schools**
2251 Wisconsin Ave., NW
Wash. D.C. 20007
202-333-1021

**National Association of Towns
& Townships**
1522 K. St., Suite 730
Wash. D.C. 20005
202-737-5200

**National Association of Women
Judges**
300 Newport Ave.
Williamsburg, VA 23185
804-253-2000

**National Association of Women
Lawyers**
750 N. Lake Shore Dr.
Chicago, IL 60611
312-988-6186

National Bar Association
1225 11th St. NW
Wash. D.C. 20001
202-842-3900

**National Black Police
Association**
1100 17th St., NW, Suite 1000
Wash. D.C. 20036
202-457-0564

**National Board of Trial
Advocacy**
Suffolk University Law School
Beacon Hill, MA 02114
Boston, MA 02114
617-573-8700

National Car Rental System, Inc.
7700 France Ave., South
Minneapolis, MN 55435
800-627-7777

**National Center for Automated
Information Retrieval**
145 E. 74th St., Suite 1C
New York, NY 10021
212-249-0760

**National Center for Legal
Administration**
1401 19th St.
Denver, CO 80202
800-848-0550

**National Center for Mediation
Education**
2083 West St., Suite 3C
Annapolis, MD 21401
301-261-8445

**National Center for Missing and
Exploited Children**
2101 Wilson Blvd., Suite 550
Arlington, VA 22201
800-843-5678

**National Center for
Preservation Law**
1233 20th St., NW, Suite 501
Wash. D.C. 20036
202-828-9611

**National Center for Preventive
Law**
1900 Olive St.
Denver, CO 80220

National Center for State Courts
300 Newport Ave.
Williamsburg, VA 23185
804-253-2000

**National Center for the
Prosecution of Child Abuse**
1033 N. Fairfax St., Suite 200
Alexandria, VA 22314
703-549-9222

National Center for Youth Law
114 Sansone St., Suite 900
San Francisco, CA 94104
415-543-3307

**National Center on Institutions
& Alternatives**
635 Slaters Lane
Alexandria, VA 22314
703-684-0373

**National Center on Women &
Family Law, Inc.**
799 Broadway, Rm. 402
New York, NY 10003
212-674-8200

**National Child Support
Enforcement Association**
444 N. Capitol St., NW, Suite 613
Wash. D.C. 20001
202-624-8180

**National Clearinghouse for
Legal Services**
407 S. Dearborn, Suite 400
Chicago, IL 60605
312-939-3830

**National Clearinghouse on
Licensure, Enforcement &
Regulation**
P.O. Box 11910
Lexington, KY 40578
606-252-2291

National Clients Council
2617 Martha St.
Philadelphia, PA 19125
215-686-2913

**National Coalition Against
Domestic Violence**
P.O. Box 15127
Wash. D.C. 20003
202-293-8860

**National Coalition Against
Surrogacy**
1133 17th St. NW
Wash. D.C. 20036
202-466-2823

**National Coalition to Ban
Handguns**
100 Maryland Ave., NE
Wash. D.C. 20002
202-544-7190

**National College of District
Attorneys**
University of Houston Law Center
Houston, TX 77204
713-747-6232

**National Committee Against
Repressive Legislation**
265 Massachusetts Ave. NE
Wash. D.C. 20002
202-543-7659

**National Committee for
Adoption**
1930 17th St.. NW
Wash. D.C. 20009
202-328-1200

**National Committee for a
Human Life Amendment**
1430 K St. NW
Wash. D.C. 20005
202-393-0703

**National Committee for
Employer Support of the
Guard & Reserve**
1111 20th St., NW, Suite 414
Wash. D.C. 20036
202-653-0852
800-336-4590

**National Committee for
Prevention of Child Abuse**
2001 O. St., NW
Wash. D.C. 20036
202-965-1900

**National Committee on
Uniform Traffic Laws &
Ordinances**
405 Church St.
Evanston, IL 60204
312-491-5280

**National Conference of Bar
Examiners**
333 N. Michigan, Suite 1025
Chicago, IL 60601
312-641-0963

National Conference of Bar Presidents
750 N. Lake Shore Dr.
Chicago, IL 60611
312-988-5346

National Conference of Black Lawyers
126 W. 119th St.
New York, NY 10026
212-864-4000

National Conference of Catholic Bishops
Committee for Pro-Life Activities
1312 Massachusetts Ave. NW
Wash. D.C. 20005
202-659-6673

National Conference of Commissioners on Uniform State Laws
676 N. St. Clair, Suite 1700
Chicago, IL 60611
312-915-0195

National Conference of State Legislatures
1050 17th St., Suite 2100
Denver, CO 80265
303-623-7800
202-624-5400

National Conference of State Liquor Administrators
P.O. Box 12971
Austin, TX 78711
512-458-2500

National Conference of States on Building Codes & Standards, Inc.
481 Carlisle Dr.
Herndon, VA 22070
703-437-0100

National Conference of Women's Bar Associations
113 W. Franklin St.
Baltimore, MD 21201
504-835-6705

National Consumer Law Center
11 Beacon St.
Boston, MA 02108
617-523-8010

National Council of Churches
110 Maryland Ave. NE
Wash. D. C. 20002
202-544-2350

National Council of Juvenile & Family Court Judges
P.O. Box 8970
Reno, NV 89507
701-784-6012

National Council on Crime & Delinquency
77 Maiden Ln, 4th Fl.
San Francisco, CA 94108
415-956-5651

National Crime Prevention Council
733 15th St. NW
Wash. D.C. 20005
202-393-7141

National Criminal Defense College
1021 Georgia Ave.
Macon, GA 31207
912-746-4151

National Criminal Justice Association
444 N. Capitol St. NW
Wash. D.C. 20001
202-347-4900

National District Attorneys Association
1033 N. Fairfax St., Suite 200
Alexandria, VA 22314
703-549-9222

National Dropout Prevention Center
P.O. Box 1864
Clemson, SC 29631
803-656-2599

National Employment Law Institute
444 Magnolia Ave.
Larkspur, CA 94939
415-924-3844

National Environmental Health Association
720 S. Colorado Blvd., Suite 970
Denver, CO 80222
303-861-9090

National Federation of Paralegal Associations
104 Wilmot Rd., Suite 201
Deerfield, IL 60015
708-940-8800

National Food Processors Association
1401 New York Ave., NW
Wash. D.C. 20005
202-639-5939

National Forensic Center
17 Temple Terrace
Lawrenceville, NJ 08648
609-883-0550

National Foundation for Unemployment Compensation & Workers Compensation
600 Maryland Ave., SW
Wash. D.C. 20024
202-484-3346

National Futures Association
200 W. Madison St.
Chicago, IL 60606
312-781-1410
800-621-3570

National Gay Rights Advocates
540 Castro St.
San Francisco, CA 94114
415-863-3624

National Governors' Association
444 N. Capitol St., NW
Wash. D.C. 20001
202-624-5300

National Health Law Association
1620 I. St., NW, Suite 900
Wash. D.C. 20006
202-833-1100

National Home Study Council
1601 18th St., NW
Wash. D.C. 20009
202-234-5100

National Housing Law Project
1950 Addison St.
Berkeley, CA 94704
415-548-9400

National Immigration Project
National Lawyers Guild

14 Beacon St., Suite 506
Boston, MA 02108
617-227-9727

**National Indian Paralegal
Association**
7524 Major Ave.
Brooklyn Park, MN 55443

**National Institute for Citizen
Education in the Law**
25 E. St., Suite 400
Wash. D.C. 20001
202-662-9620

**National Institute for Dispute
Resolution**
1901 L. St., Suite 600
Wash. D.C. 20036
202-466-4764

**National Institute for Trial
Advocacy**
Notre Dame Law School
Notre Dame, IN 46556
219-239-7770
800-225-6482

National Institute of Justice
633 Indiana Ave. NW
Wash. D.C. 20531
202-724-2942

**National Institute of Municipal
Law Officers**
1000 Connecticut Ave., NW
Wash. D.C. 20036
202-466-5424

**National Institute on Economic
Crime**
1785 Massachusetts Ave. NW
Wash. D.C. 20036
202-232-6012

National Judges Association
P.O. Box 85
Beulah, MI 49617
616-882-4389

National Judicial College
University of Nevada-Reno
Reno, NV 89557
702-784-6747

National Jury Project
1540 San Pablo Ave.

Oakland, CA 94612
415-832-2583

**National Juvenile Court Services
Association**
University of Nevada
P.O. Box 8970
Reno, NV 89507
702-784-4859

**National Law Enforcement
Council**
1140 Connecticut Ave. NW
Wash. D.C. 20036
202-223-6850

National Law Institute
330 2nd Ave. S.
Minneapolis, MN 55401
612-338-1977
800-328-4444

National Lawyers Club
1815 H. St., NW
Wash. D.C. 20006
202-638-3200

National League of Cities
1301 Pennsylvania Ave., NW
Wash. D.C. 20004
202-626-3000

**National Legal Aid & Defender
Association**
1625 K. St., Suite 800
Wash. D.C. 20006
202-452-0620

**National Legal Center for the
Medically Dependent &
Disabled**
P.O. Box 441069
Indianapolis, IN 46244
317-632-6245

**National Legal Center for the
Public Interest**
1000 16th St., NW Suite 301
Wash. D.C. 20036
202-296-1683

National Legal Foundation
P.O. Box 64845
Virginia Beach, VA 23464
804-424-4242

National Legal Research Group
P.O. Box 7187

Charlottesville, VA 22906
800-446-1870

National Notary Association
8236 Remmet Ave.
Canoga Park, CA 91304
818-713-4000
800-876-6827

**National Office for Social
Responsibility**
222 S. Washington St.
Alexandria, VA 22314
703-549-5305

National Organization for Men
381 Park Ave. South
New York, NY 10016
212-766-4030

**National Organization for the
Reform of Marijuana Laws**
2001 S St. NW
Wash. D.C. 20009
202-483-5500

**National Organization for
Victim Assistance**
717 D. St., NW
Wash. D.C. 20004
202-393-6682

**National Organization for
Women (NOW)**
1401 New York Ave., NW
Wash. D.C. 20005
202-347-2279

**National Organization of Social
Security Claimants
Representatives**
19 E. Central Ave., 2d Fl.
Pearl River, NY 10965
914-735-8812
800-431-2804

**National Organization on Legal
Problems of Education**
3601 W. 29th St., Suite 223
Topeka, KS 66614
913-273-3550

National Paralegal Association
P.O. Box 629
Doylestown, PA 18901
215-348-5575

National Police Officers Association of America
1316 Gardiner Ln., Suite 204
Louisville, KY 40213
502-451-7550

National Pro-Family Coalition
721 2nd St. NE
Wash. D.C. 20002
202-546-3003

National PTA
700 N. Rush St.
Chicago, IL 60611
312-787-0977

National Public Employer Labor Relations Association
1444 Eye St. NW
Wash. D.C. 20005
202-842-3505

National Resource Center for Consumers of Legal Services
1444 Eye St. NW
Wash. D.C. 20005
202-842-3503

National Resource Center on Child Abuse & Neglect
9725 E. Hampden Ave.
Denver, CO 80231
303-695-0811
800-227-5242

National Rifle Association
1600 Rhode Island Ave., NW
Wash. D.C. 20036
202-828-6000

National Right to Life Committee
419 7th St., NW
Wash. D.C. 20004
202-626-8800

National Right to Work Legal Defense Foundation
8001 Braddock Rd., Suite 600
Springfield, VA 22160
703-321-8510
800-336-3600

National Runaway Switchboard
800-621-4000

National Safety Council Library
444 N. Michigan Ave.

Chicago, IL 60611
312-527-4800

National School Boards Association
1680 Duke St.
Alexandria, VA 22314
703-838-6722

National Senior Citizens Law Center
2025 M. St., NW
Wash. D.C. 20036
202-887-5280

National Sheriffs' Association
1450 Duke St.
Alexandria, VA 22314
703-836-7827

National Shorthand Reporters Association
118 Park St., SE
Vienna, VA 22180
703-281-4677

National Tax Association—Tax Institute of America
5310 E. Main St.
Columbus, OH 43213
614-864-1221

National Tax Equality Association
1615 M. St., NW
Wash. D.C. 20036
202-466-8310

National Tire Dealers & Retreaders Association
1250 I. St., NW
Wash. D.C. 20005
202-789-2300
800-876-8372

National Turkey Federation
11319 Sunset Hills Road
Reston, VA 22090
703-435-7206

National United Law Enforcement Officers Association
256 E. McLemore Ave.
Memphis, TN 38106
901-774-1118

National Veterans Legal Services Project
2001 S. St., NW
Wash. D.C. 20009
202-265-8305

National Victims Resource Center
Box 6000-AHG
Rockville, MD 20850
301-251-5525

National Women & the Law Association
99 Hudson St., 12 Fl.
New York, NY 10013
212-219-2850

National Women's Health Network
1325 G St. NW
Wash. D.C. 20005
202-347-1140

National Women's Political Caucus
1275 K. St. NW
Wash. D.C. 20005
202-898-1100

National Women's Law Center
1616 P. St., NW
Wash. D.C. 20036
202-328-5160

Nationwide Insurance Companies
One Nationwide Plaza
Columbus, OH 43216
614-249-6985

Native American Rights Fund
1712 N. St., NW
Wash. D.C. 20036
202-785-4166

Natural Rights Center
156 Drakes Ln.
Summertown, TN 38483
615-964-2334

NBC
30 Rockefeller Plaza
New York, NY 10112
212-664-4444

[Nebraska] Information & Referral (State Government)
402-471-2311

[Nebraska] Information Center (Federal Government)
Omaha 402-221-3353
Elsewhere in state 800-642-8383

[Nebraska] Administrative Services, Department of
P.O. Box 94664
Lincoln, NE 68509
402-471-2331

[Nebraska] Affirmative Action Office
P.O. Box 94905
Lincoln, NE 68509
402-471-3678

Nebraska Aging, Department on
P.O. Box 95044
Lincoln, NE 68509
402-471-2306

[Nebraska] Agriculture, Department of
301 Centennial Mall South
Lincoln, NE 68508
402-471-2341

[Nebraska] Air Quality Division
301 Centennial Mall South, 4th Fl.
Lincoln, NE 68508
402-471-2189

[Nebraska] Archives/Library, Division of
1500 R. St.
Lincoln, NE 68508
402-471-4750

Nebraska Association of Legal Assistants
P.O. Box 81434
Lincoln, NE 68501

[Nebraska] Attorney General, Office of
2115 State Capitol Bldg.
Lincoln, NE 68509
402-471-2682

[Nebraska] Auditor of Public Accounts
P.O. Box 94786
Lincoln, NE 68509
402-471-2111

[Nebraska] Banking & Finance, Director of
301 Centennial Mall South

Lincoln, NE 68509
402-471-2171

Nebraska Bar Association
635 S. 14th St.
Lincoln, NE 68508
402-475-7091

[Nebraska] Beef Industry Development Board
East Hwy 30, Box 2408
Kearney, NE 68848
308-236-7551

[Nebraska] Better Business Bureau
719 N. 48th St.
Lincoln, NE 68504
402-467-5261

[Nebraska] Building Division, State
1445 K. St.
Lincoln, NE 68508
402-471-3191

[Nebraska] Child Support Enforcement Office
P.O. Box 95026
Lincoln, NE 68509
402-471-9125

[Nebraska] Civil Defense Agency
1300 Military Rd
Lincoln, NE 68508
402-471-3241

[Nebraska] Consumer Fraud Division
605 S. 14th
Lincoln, NE 68508
402-471-4723

[Nebraska] Consumer Protection Division
2115 State Capitol
P.O. Box 98920
Lincoln, NE 68509
402-471-4723

[Nebraska] Correctional Services, Department of
P.O. Box 94661
Lincoln, NE 68509
402-471-2654

Nebraska Court Administrator, State
State Capitol Bldg.

Lincoln, NE 68509
402-471-3730

[Nebraska] Douglas County
1819 Farnam St.
Omaha, NE 68183
402-444-7000

[Nebraska] Douglas County Law Library
17th & Farnam St.
Omaha, NE 68183
402-444-7174

[Nebraska] Economic Development, Department of
301 Centennial Mall South
Lincoln, NE 68508
402-471-3111

[Nebraska] Educational Telecommunications Commission
P.O. Box 83111
Lincoln, NE 68501
402-472-3611

[Nebraska] Education, Department of
P.O. Box 94987
Lincoln, NE 68509
402-471-2295

[Nebraska] Energy Office
P.O. Box 95085
Lincoln, NE 68509
402-471-2867

[Nebraska] Environmental Control, Department of
P.O. Box 98922
Lincoln, NE 68509
402-471-2186

[Nebraska] Equal Opportunity Commission
P.O. Box 94934
Lincoln, NE 68509
402-471-2024

[Nebraska] Games & Parks Commission
P.O. Box 30370
Lincoln, NE 68503
402-471-0641

[Nebraska] Governor, Office of
State Capitol Bldg., 2nd Fl.

Lincoln, NE 68509
402-471-2244

**[Nebraska] Health, State
Department of**
P.O. Box 95007
Lincoln, NE 68509
402-471-2133

**Nebraska Historical Society,
State**
P.O. Box 82554
Lincoln, NE 68501
402-471-4783

Nebraska Indian Commission
P.O. Box 94981
Lincoln, NE 68509
402-471-3475

**[Nebraska] Insurance,
Director of**
941 O. St., Suite 400
Lincoln, NE 68508
402-471-2201

[Nebraska] Labor, Department of
P.O. Box 94600
Lincoln, NE 68509
402-475-8451

[Nebraska] Lancaster, County
555 S. 10th St.
Lincoln, NE 68508
402-471-7481

**[Nebraska] Law Enforcement &
Criminal Justice,
Commission on**
301 Centennial Mall South, 3rd Fl.
Lincoln, NE 68508
402-471-2194

[Nebraska] Legislative Council
State Capitol, Rm. 2018
Lincoln, NE 68509
402-471-2271

[Nebraska] Legislature
State Capitol
Lincoln, NE 68509
402-471-2271
402-471-2327 (Judiciary)

[Nebraska] Library, State
P.O. Box 94926
Lincoln, NE 68509
402-471-3189

**[Nebraska] Lieutenant Governor,
Office of**
2315 State Capitol Bldg.
Lincoln, NE 68509
402-471-2256

**[Nebraska] Lincoln Correctional
Center**
3210 W. Van Dorn St.
Lincoln, NE 68522
402-471-2861

**[Nebraska] Liquor Control
Commission**
P.O. Box 95046
Lincoln, NE 68509
402-471-2571

**[Nebraska] Mexican-American
Commission**
P.O. Box 94965
Lincoln, NE 68509
402-471-2791

**[Nebraska] Motor Vehicles,
Department of**
P.O. Box 94789
Lincoln, NE 68509
402-471-2281

**[Nebraska] Natural Resources
Commission**
P.O. Box 94876
Lincoln, NE 68509
402-471-2081

**[Nebraska] Oil & Gas
Conservation Commission**
1135 Jackson St.
Sidney, NE 69162
308-254-4595

[Nebraska] Omaha City Hall
1819 Farnam St.
Omaha, NE 68183
402-444-7000

**[Nebraska] Ombudsman (Public
Counsel)**
P.O. Box 94712
Lincoln, NE 68509
402-471-2035

[Nebraska] Pardons, Board of
P.O. Box 94754
Lincoln, NE 68509
402-471-2156

**[Nebraska] Parole
Administration**
P.O. Box 94661
Lincoln, NE 68509
402-471-2654

[Nebraska] Parole, Board of
P.O. Box 94754
Lincoln, NE 68509
402-471-2156

**[Nebraska] Personnel,
Department of**
P.O. Box 94905
Lincoln, NE 68509
402-471-2075

**[Nebraska] Policy Research &
Energy Office**
P.O. Box 94601
Lincoln, NE 68509
402-471-2414

**[Nebraska] Probation System,
State**
P.O. Box 94652
Lincoln, NE 68509
402-471-2141

**[Nebraska] Public Employees
Retirement Systems**
P.O. Box 94816
Lincoln, NE 68509
402-471-2053

**[Nebraska] Public Institutions,
Department of**
P.O. Box 94728
Lincoln, NE 68509
402-471-2851

**[Nebraska] Public Service
Commission**
P.O. Box 94927
Lincoln, NE 68509
402-471-3101

[Nebraska] Purchasing Division
301 Centennial Mall South, 1st Fl.
Lincoln, NE 68508
402-471-2401

**Nebraska Racing Commission,
State**
P.O. Box 94927
Lincoln, NE 68509
402-471-2577

[Nebraska] Real Estate Commission
P.O. Box 94667
Lincoln, NE 68509
402-471-2004

[Nebraska] Rehabilitation Services, Division of
301 Centennial Mall South, 6th Fl.
Lincoln, NE 68509
402-471-2961

[Nebraska] Revenue, Department of
P.O. Box 94818
Lincoln, NE 68509
402-471-5607

[Nebraska] Revisor of Statutes
State Capitol, Rm. 358
Lincoln, NE 68509
402-471-2225

[Nebraska] Roads, Department of
P.O. Box 94759
Lincoln, NE 68509
402-471-4567

[Nebraska] Safety, Division of
301 Centennial Mall South
Lincoln, NE 68508
402-471-2239

Nebraska Secretary of State
P.O. Box 94608
Lincoln, NE 68509
402-471-2554

[Nebraska] Securities, Bureau of
301 Centennial Mall South
Lincoln, NE 68508
402-471-3445

[Nebraska] Social Services, Department of
P.O. Box 95026
Lincoln, NE 68509
402-471-3121

Nebraska State Patrol
14th & Burnham Sts.
Lincoln, NE 68509
402-471-4545

Nebraska State Penitentiary
14th & Pioneer Blvd.
Lincoln, NE 68502
402-471-3161

[Nebraska] Supreme Court
Supreme Court Bldg., Rm. 2413
Lincoln, NE 68509
402-471-3731

[Nebraska] Surveyor, State
555 N. Cotner Blvd.
Lincoln, NE 68505
402-471-2566

[Nebraska] Treasurer
State Capitol Bldg.
Lincoln, NE 68509
402-471-2455

[Nebraska] Unemployment Insurance Division
P.O. Box 94600
Lincoln, NE 68509
402-475-8451

[Nebraska] Uniform Commercial Code Division
P.O. Box 95104
Lincoln, NE 68509
402-471-4080

[Nebraska] United States Bankruptcy Court
P.O. Box 428
Omaha, NE 68101
402-221-4687

[Nebraska] United States District Court
P.O. Box 129, DTS
Omaha, NE 68101
402-221-4761

[Nebraska] Veterans' Affairs, Department of
P.O. Box 95083
Lincoln, NE 68509
402-471-2458

[Nebraska] Vital Statistics, Bureau of
301 Centennial Mall South
P.O. Box 95007
Lincoln, NE 68508
402-471-2871

[Nebraska] Water Resources, Department of
P.O. Box 94676
Lincoln, NE 68509
402-471-2363

[Nebraska] Weights & Measures, Division of
301 Centennial Mall South, 4th Fl.
Lincoln, NE 68509
402-471-4292

Nebraska Wheat Board
P.O. Box 94912
Lincoln, NE 68509
402-471-2358

[Nebraska] Women's Commission
P.O. Box 94985
Lincoln, NE 68509
402-471-2039

[Nebraska] Worker's Compensation Court
P.O. Box 98908
Lincoln, NE 68509
402-471-2568

Nestle Foods Corp.
100 Manhattanville Rd.
Purchase, NY 10577
800-NESTLES

[Nevada] Information & Referral (State Government)
702-885-5000

[Nevada] Administration, Department of
209 E. Musser St.
Carson City, NV 89710
702-885-4065

[Nevada] Aging Services, Division for
505 E. King St.
Carson City, NV 89710
702-885-4210

[Nevada] Agriculture, Department of
P.O. Box 11100
Reno, NV 89510
702-789-0180

[Nevada] Assembly
State Capitol
Carson City, NV 89710
702-885-4848
702-885-3657 (Judiciary)

[Nevada] Attorney General, Office of
198 S. Carson St.

Carson City, NV 89710
702-885-4170

Nevada, Bar Association of
(and Bar Admissions)
295 Holcomb Ave., Suite 2
Reno, NV 89502
702-329-4100
702-329-4443 (CLE)

[Nevada] Better Business Bureau
1022 E. Sahara Ave.
Las Vegas, NV 89104
702-735-6900

**[Nevada] Child Support
Enforcement Program**
2527 N. Carson St.
Carson City, NV 89710
702-885-4744

[Nevada] Clark County
200 S. 3rd St.
Las Vegas, NV 89155
702-455-4011

**[Nevada] Clark County Bar
Association**
P.O. Box 657
Las Vegas, NV 89125
702-387-6011

**[Nevada] Clark County Law
Library**
304 E. Carson
Las Vegas, NV 89101
702-455-4696

**[Nevada] Commerce,
Department of**
210 S. Fall St., Rm. 321
Carson City, NV 89710
702-885-4250

**[Nevada] Conservation &
Natural Resources,
Department of**
201 S. Fall St.
Carson City, NV 89710
702-885-4360

**[Nevada] Consumer Affairs,
Commissioner of**
State Mail Room Complex
Las Vegas, NV 89158
702-486-4150

**[Nevada] Courts, Administrative
Office of the**
400 W. King St., Suite 406
Carson City, NV 89710
702-885-5076

**[Nevada] Data Processing,
Department of**
Blasdel Bldg., Rm. 304
Carson City, NV 89710
702-687-4090

**[Nevada] Economic
Development, Commission on**
600 E. William St., Suite 203
Carson City, NV 89710
702-885-4325

**[Nevada] Education,
Department of**
400 W. King St.
Carson City, NV 89710
702-885-3104

**[Nevada] Emergency
Management, Division of**
2525 S. Carson St.
Carson City, NV 89710
702-885-4240

**[Nevada] Employment Security,
Department of**
500 E. 3rd St.
Carson City, NV 89713
702-885-4635

**[Nevada] Environmental
Protection, Division of**
201 S. Fall St., Rm. 221
Carson City, NV 89710
702-885-4670

**[Nevada] Financial Institutions,
Commissioner of**
406 E. 2nd St.
Carson City, NV 89710
702-885-4260

**[Nevada] Gaming Control Board,
State**
1150 E. William St.
Carson City, NV 89710
702-687-6500

**[Nevada] General Services,
Department of**
Kinkead Bldg., Rm. 400

Carson City, NV 89710
702-885-4094

[Nevada] Governor, Office of
Capitol Bldg. Executive Office
Carson City, NV 89710
702-885-5670

[Nevada] Health Division
505 E. King St.
Carson City, NV 89710
702-885-4740

[Nevada] Highway Patrol
555 Wright Way
Carson City, NV 89711
702-885-5300

**[Nevada] Human Resources,
Department of**
505 E. King St., Rm. 600
Carson City, NV 89710
702-885-4400

**[Nevada] Incline Village Bar
Association**
P.O. Box 7100
Incline Village, NV 89450
702-831-0326

**Nevada Indian Rural Legal
Services**
600 E. William St., Suite 301
Carson City, NV 89710
702-885-5100

**[Nevada] Industrial Insurance
System, State**
515 E. Musser St.
Carson City, NV 89714
702-885-5284

**[Nevada] Industrial Relations,
Department of**
1390 S. Curry St.
Carson City, NV 89710
702-687-3032

**[Nevada] Institute of Advanced
Law Study**
3419 Thom Blvd.
Las Vegas, NV 89106
702-873-4542

**[Nevada] Insurance,
Commissioner of**
201 S. Fall St.
Carson City, NV 89710

702-885-4270
800-992-0900

[Nevada] Judicial Discipline, Commission on
106 E. Adams St., P.O. Box 48
Carson City, NV 89702
702-885-4017

[Nevada] Labor Commission
505 E. King St., Rm. 602
Carson City, NV 89710
702-885-4850

[Nevada] Las Vegas City Hall
400 Stewart Ave.
Las Vegas, NV 89101
702-386-6011

[Nevada] Las Vegas Municipal Court Library
400 E. Stewart Ave.
Las Vegas, NV 89101
702-799-6139

[Nevada] Legislative Counsel Bureau
Legislative Bldg., Capitol Complex
Carson City, NV 89710
702-687-6800

Nevada Library & Archives, State
401 Carson St.
Carson City, NV 89710
702-887-2615

[Nevada] Lieutenant Governor, Office of
Capitol Complex
Carson City, NV 89710
702-885-3037

[Nevada] Military, Department of
2525 S. Carson St.
Carson City, NV 89710
702-885-4240

[Nevada] Minerals, Department of
400 W. King St., Suite 106
Carson City, NV 89710
702-885-5050

[Nevada] Motor Vehicles & Public Safety, Department of
555 Wright Way
Carson City, NV 89711
702-885-5375

[Nevada] Nuclear Projects, Agency for
Capitol Complex
Carson City, NV 89710
702-885-3744

[Nevada] Occupational Safety & Health, Division of
1370 S. Curry St.
Carson City, NV 89710
702-885-5240

[Nevada] Parole & Pardons Board
5500 E. Snyder, Bldg. #6
Carson City, NV 89710
702-885-5049

[Nevada] Personnel, Department of
209 E. Musser St., Rm. 200
Carson City, NV 89710
702-885-4050

[Nevada] Prisons, Department of
P.O. Box 7011
Carson City, NV 89702
702-887-3216

[Nevada] Probation & Parole, Department of
1000 E. William, Suite 210
Carson City, NV 89710
702-885-5040

Nevada Public Defender, State
308 N. Curry St., Room 200
Carson City, NV 89710
702-885-4880

[Nevada] Public Employees Retirement System
693 W. Nye Lane
Carson City, NV 89703
702-885-4208

[Nevada] Public Service Commission
727 Fairview Dr.
Carson City, NV 89710
702-687-6000

Nevada Public Works Board
505 E. King St., Rm. 301
Carson City, NV 89710
702-885-4870

[Nevada] Purchasing Division
505 E. King St., Rm. 400

Carson City, NV 89710
702-885-4094

[Nevada] Real Estate Division
201 S. Fall St.
Carson City, NV 89710
702-885-4280

[Nevada] Rural Housing Authority
2100 California St.
Carson City, NV 89710
702-885-5747

[Nevada] Secretary of State
Capitol Complex
Carson City, NV 89710
702-885-5203

[Nevada] Securities Division
2501 E. Sahara Ave., Suite 201
Las Vegas, NV 89158
702-486-4400

[Nevada] Senate
State Capitol
Carson City, NV 89710
702-885-4848
702-885-3645 (Judiciary)

Nevada Supreme Court
100 N. Carson St.
Carson City, NV 89710
702-885-5180
800-992-0900
702-885-5140 (Law Library)

[Nevada] Taxation, Department of
1340 S. Curry St.
Carson City, NV 89710
702-885-4892

[Nevada] Transportation, Department of
1263 S. Stewart St.
Carson City, NV 89712
702-885-5585

[Nevada] Treasurer
Capitol Complex
Carson City, NV 89710
702-885-5200

[Nevada] Unemployment Insurance Division
500 E. 3rd St.
Carson City, NV 89713
702-885-4615

[Nevada] United States Bankruptcy Court
300 Las Vegas Blvd. South
Las Vegas, NV 89101
702-385-6257

[Nevada] United States District Court
300 Las Vegas Blvd. South
Las Vegas, NV 89101
702-388-6351

[Nevada] Vital Statistics Section
505 E. King St., Rm. 102
Carson City, NV 89710
702-885-4480

[Nevada] Washoe County
P.O. Box 11130
Reno, NV 89502
702-785-5454

[Nevada] Washoe County Bar Association
P.O. Box 1548
Reno, NV 89505
702-323-7631

[Nevada] Washoe County Law Library
P.O. Box 11130
Reno, NV 89520
702-328-3250

[Nevada] Water Resources, Division of
201 S. Fall St., Suite 211
Carson City, NV 89710
702-885-4380

[Nevada] Weights & Measures
P.O. Box 11100
Reno, NV 89510
702-789-0166

[Nevada] Youth Parole Bureau
869 N. Eastern Ave.
Las Vegas, NV 89158
702-486-5661

[Nevada] Youth Services Division
505 E. King St., Rm. 606
Carson City, NV 89710
702-885-5982

[New Hampshire] Information & Referral (State Government)
603-271-1110
603-271-2239

[New Hampshire] Administrative Services, Department of
25 Capitol St., Rm. 120
Concord, NH 03301
603-271-3201

[New Hampshire] Agriculture, Department of
10 Ferry St., CB 2042
Concord, NH 03302
603-271-3551

[New Hampshire] Arts, Council on the
40 N. Main St.
Concord, NH 03301
603-271-2789

[New Hampshire] Attorney General, Office of
25 Capitol St.
Concord, NH 03301
603-271-3655

[New Hampshire] Audit Division
P.O. Box 457
Concord, NH 03302
603-271-3400

[New Hampshire] Bank Commissioner
45 S. Main St.
Concord, NH 03301
603-271-3561

New Hampshire Bar Association
18 Centre Street
Concord, NH 03301
603-224-6942

[New Hampshire] Better Business Bureau
410 S. Main St.
Concord, NH 03301
603-224-1991
800-852-3757

[New Hampshire] Children & Youth Services, Division for
H & HS Bldg. 6, Hazen Dr.
Concord, NH 03301
603-271-4319

[New Hampshire] Child Support Enforcement Services, Office of
Hazen Dr.

Concord, NH 03301
603-271-4426

[New Hampshire] Consumer Protection & Antitrust Bureau
State House Annex
Concord, NH 03301
603-271-3641

[New Hampshire] Corporations Division
Secretary of State
State House, Rm. 204
Concord, NH 03301
603-271-3244

[New Hampshire] Corrections, Department of
P.O. Box 769
Concord, NH 03302
603-224-3500

[New Hampshire] Courts, Administrative Office of the
Supreme Court Bldg.
Concord, NH 03301
603-271-2647

[New Hampshire] Education, Department of
101 Pleasant St.
Concord, NH 03301
603-271-3144

[New Hampshire] Elderly & Adult Services, Division of
6 Hazen Dr.
Concord, NH 03301
603-271-4680
800-351-1888

New Hampshire Emergency Management
107 Pleasant St.
Concord, NH 03301
603-271-2231

[New Hampshire] Employment Security, Department of
32 S. Main St.
Concord, NH 03301
603-271-3311

[New Hampshire] Energy Office
$2\frac{1}{2}$ Beacon St., 2nd Fl.
Concord, NH 03301
603-271-2711

[New Hampshire] Environmental Services, Department of
6 Hazen Dr.
Concord, NH 03301
603-271-3503

[New Hampshire] Field Services Division
105 Pleasant St.
Concord, NH 03301
603-271-5600

[New Hampshire] Fish & Game, Department of
6 Hazen Dr.
Concord, NH 03301
603-271-3512

[New Hampshire] Governor, Office of
208 State House
Concord, NH 03301
603-271-2121

[New Hampshire] Highway Safety Agency
117 Manchester St.
Concord, NH 03301
603-271-2131

[New Hampshire] Hillsborough County Law Library
300 Chestnut St.
Manchester, NH 03103
603-627-5629

[New Hampshire] House of Representatives
State House
Concord, NH 03301
603-271-3315
603-271-3184 (Judiciary)

[New Hampshire] Housing Finance Authority
P.O. Box 5087
Manchester, NH 03108
603-472-8623

[New Hampshire] Human Rights Commission
163 Loudon Rd.
Concord, NH 03301
603-271-2767

[New Hampshire] Inspection Division
19 Pillsbury St.

Concord, NH 03301
603-271-3179

[New Hampshire] Insurance Commissioner
169 Manchester St.
Concord, NH 03301
603-271-2261
800-852-3416

[New Hampshire] Juvenile Parole Board
1056 N. River Rd.
Manchester, NH 03104
603-625-5471

[New Hampshire] Labor, Department of
19 Pillsbury St.
Concord, NH 03301
603-271-3176

[New Hampshire] Law Library, State
Supreme Court Bldg, Noble Dr.
Concord, NH 03301
603-271-3777

[New Hampshire] Legislative Services, Office of
State House, Rm. 109
Concord, NH 03301
603-271-3435

[New Hampshire] Liquor Commission
P.O. Box 503
Concord, NH 03302
603-271-3132

[New Hampshire] Merrimack County
111 N. Main St.
Concord, NH 03301
603-223-0331

[New Hampshire] Parole, Board of
New Hampshire State Prison
P.O. Box 14
Concord, NH 03302
603-271-2569

[New Hampshire] Personnel, Division of
25 Capitol St.
Concord, NH 03301
603-271-3261

[New Hampshire] Planning, Office of State
$2\frac{1}{2}$ Beacon St.
Concord, NH 03301
603-271-2155

[New Hampshire] Postsecondary Education Commission
$2\frac{1}{2}$ Beacon St.
Concord, NH 03301
603-271-2555

[New Hampshire] Public Health Services, Division of
6 Hazen Dr.
Concord, NH 03301
603-271-4501

[New Hampshire] Public Utilities Commission
8 Old Suncook Rd.
Concord, NH 03301
603-271-2431
800-852-3793

[New Hampshire] Public Works, Bureau of
P.O. Box 483
Concord, NH 03301
603-271-3516

[New Hampshire] Real Estate Commission
107 Pleasant St.
Concord, NH 03301
603-271-2701

[New Hampshire] Records Management & Archives, Division of
71 S. Fruit St.
Concord, NH 03301
603-271-2236

[New Hampshire] Resources & Economic Development Department
P.O. Box 856
Concord, NH 03301
603-271-2411

[New Hampshire] Revenue Administration, Department of
61 S. Spring St.
Concord, NH 03301
603-271-2191

[New Hampshire] Safety, Department of
State Police Division
Hayes Bldg.
Concord, NH 03301
603-271-2575

[New Hampshire] Secretary of State
State House, Rm. 204
Concord, NH 03301
603-271-3242

[New Hampshire] Securities Regulation, Office of
157 Manchester St.
Concord, NH 03301
603-271-1463

[New Hampshire] Senate
State House
Concord, NH 03301
603-271-3315
603-271-3096 (Judiciary)

New Hampshire Solid Waste Bureau
6 Hazen Dr.
Concord, NH 03301
603-271-2925

[New Hampshire] Supreme Court
Supreme Court Bldg.
Noble Dr.
Concord, NH 03301
603-271-2646
603-271-2646 (Bar Admissions)

New Hampshire Sweepstakes Commission
P.O. Box 1217
Concord, NH 03301
603-271-3391

[New Hampshire] Transportation, Department of
P.O. Box 483
Concord, NH 03301
603-271-3734

[New Hampshire] Treasury Department
25 Capitol St.
Concord, NH 03301
603-271-2621

[New Hampshire] Unemployment Insurance Bureau
32 S. Main St.
Concord, NH 03301
603-224-3311

[New Hampshire] United States Bankruptcy Court
275 Chestnut St.
722 Norris Cotton Federal Bldg.
Manchester, NH 03103
603-666-7532

[New Hampshire] United States District Court
P.O. Box 1498
Concord, NH 03301
603-225-1423

[New Hampshire] Vital Records & Health Statistics, Bureau of
6 Hazen Dr.
Concord, NH 03301
603-271-4654

[New Hampshire] Vocational Rehabilitation, Division of
78 Regional Dr.
Concord, NH 03301
603-271-3800

[New Hampshire] Water Resources, Division of
P.O. Box 2008
Concord, NH 03301
603-271-3406

[New Hampshire] Weights & Measures, Bureau of
Caller Box 2042
Concord, NH 03302
603-271-3700

[New Jersey] Information & Referral (State Government)
609-292-2121
800-792-8600

[New Jersey] Information Center (Federal Government)
Newark 201-645-3600
Trenton 609-396-4400

[New Jersey] Aging, Division on
101 S. Broad St., CN 807
Trenton, NJ 08625

609-292-4833
800-792-8820

[New Jersey] Agriculture, Department of
CN 330, John Fitch Plaza
Trenton, NJ 08625
609-292-3976

[New Jersey] Appellate Division of Superior Court
CN 006, Richard J. Hughes Justice Complex
Trenton, NJ 08625
609-292-4693

[New Jersey] Archives & Records Management, Division of
CN 307, 2300 Stuyvesant Ave.
Trenton, NJ 08625
609-530-3203

[New Jersey] Arts, Council on the
CN 306, 4 N. Broad St.
Trenton, NJ 08625
609-292-6130

[New Jersey] Attorney General, Office of
CN 080, Hughes Justice Complex
Trenton, NJ 08625
609-292-4925
609-292-4958 (Law Library)

[New Jersey] Banking, Commissioner of
CN 040, 200 W. State St.
Trenton, NJ 08625
609-292-3420
800-421-0069

New Jersey Bar Association
1 Constitution Sq.
New Brunswick, NJ 08901
201-249-5000

[New Jersey] Bar Examiners, Board of
CN 973
Trenton, NJ 08625
609-984-7783

[New Jersey] Better Business Bureau
34 Park Pl.
Newark, NJ 07102
201-642-INFO

**[New Jersey] Building &
Construction Division**
3131 Princeton Pike
Lawrenceville, NJ 08648
609-530-8820

**[New Jersey] Child Support &
Paternity Programs,
Office of**
CN 716, Department of Human
Services
Trenton, NJ 08625
609-588-2401

**[New Jersey] Commerce, Energy
& Economic Development,
Department of**
CN 820, 20 W. State St.
Trenton, NJ 08625
609-292-2444

**[New Jersey] Community
Affairs, Department of**
CN 800, 101 S. Broad St.
Trenton, NJ 08625
609-292-6420

**[New Jersey] Consumer Affairs,
Division of**
1100 Raymond Blvd., Rm. 504
Newark, NJ 07102
201-648-4010

**[New Jersey] Corrections,
Department of**
CN 863, Whittlesey
Trenton, NJ 08625
609-292-4036

**[New Jersey] Courts,
Administrative Office of the**
CN 037, Judicial Complex
Trenton, NJ 08625
609-292-1589
609-292-8386 (Law Library)

**[New Jersey] Education,
Department of**
CN 542, 20 W. State St.
Trenton, NJ 08625
609-292-4310

**[New Jersey] Environmental
Protection, Department of**
CN 402, 401 E. State St.
Trenton, NJ 08625
609-292-2885

[New Jersey] Essex County
469 King Blvd.
Newark, NJ 07102
201-621-4916

**[New Jersey] Essex County Bar
Association**
Gateway One, 16th Fl.
Newark, NJ 07102
201-622-6207

**[New Jersey] Financial
Management, Office of**
1 W. State St., 3rd Fl.
Trenton, NJ 08625
609-292-9200

[New Jersey] General Assembly
State House Annex
Trenton, NJ 08625
609-292-4840
800-792-8630
609-292-5526 (Judiciary)

[New Jersey] Governor, Office of
CN 001, 125 W. State St.
Trenton, NJ 08625
609-292-6000

**[New Jersey] Health,
Department of**
CN 360, John Fitch Plaza
Trenton, NJ 08625
609-292-7837

**[New Jersey] Higher Education,
Department of**
20 W. State St.
Trenton, NJ 08625
609-292-4310

**[New Jersey] Hudson County
Law Library**
595 Newark Ave.
Jersey City, NJ 07306
201-795-6629

**[New Jersey] Human Services,
Department of**
CN 700, 222 S. Warren St.
Trenton, NJ 08625
609-292-3717

**[New Jersey] Insurance,
Department of**
CN 325, 20 W. State St.
Trenton, NJ 08625
609-292-5363

**[New Jersey] Investigation, State
Commission of**
CN 045, 28 W. State St.
Trenton, NJ 08625
609-292-6767

**[New Jersey] Labor,
Department of**
CN 110, John Fitch Plaza
Trenton, NJ 08625
609-292-2323

**[New Jersey] Law & Public
Safety, Department of**
CN 081, Justice Complex
Trenton, NJ 08625
609-292-8740

**[New Jersey] Law Enforcement
Planning Agency, State**
CN 083, 200 Woolverton St.
Trenton, NJ 08625
609-984-2090

[New Jersey] Law Library, State
CN 520, 185 W. State St.
Trenton, NJ 08625
609-292-6230

**New Jersey, Legal Assistants
Association of**
P.O. Box 142
Caldwell, NJ 07006

**[New Jersey] Medical
Examiners, Board of**
28 W. State St., Rm. 914
Trenton, NJ 08625
609-292-4843

[New Jersey] Mercer County
P.O. Box 8068
Trenton, NJ 08650
609-989-6517

**[New Jersey] Military &
Veterans' Affairs,
Department of**
CN 340, Eggert Crossing Rd.
Trenton, NJ 08625
609-530-6892

**[New Jersey] Morris County Law
Library**
Court House
Morristown, NJ 07960
201-285-6371

[New Jersey] Motor Vehicles, Division of
25 S. Montgomery St.
Trenton, NJ 08666
609-292-4750

[New Jersey] Paralegal Association of Central Jersey
93 Princeton Court
Mercerville, NJ 08619

[New Jersey] Parole, Bureau of
CN 864, Whittlesey Rd.
Trenton, NJ 08628
609-292-4256
609-292-4257 (Parole Board)

[New Jersey] Patterson Free Public Library
250 Broadway
Paterson, NJ 07501
201-881-1060

[New Jersey] Pensions, Division of
20 W. Front St.
Trenton, NJ 08625
609-292-3463

[New Jersey] Personnel, Department of
CN 317, Front & Montgomery Streets
Trenton, NJ 08625
609-292-4144

[New Jersey] Policy & Planning, Office of
CN 001, 125 W. State St.
Trenton, NJ 08625
609-292-6000

[New Jersey] Prison System, State
3rd & Federal Streets
Trenton, NJ 08625
609-292-9700

[New Jersey] Public Advocate, Department of
25 Market St.
Trenton, NJ 08625
609-292-7087

[New Jersey] Public Affairs Research Institute of
212 Carnegie Center
Princeton, NJ 08540
609-452-0220

[New Jersey] Public Information, Office of
CN 068, Office of Legislative Services
State House Annex
Trenton, NJ 08625
609-292-4840
800-792-8630

[New Jersey] Public Utilities, Board of
2 Gateway Center
Newark, NJ 07102
201-648-2027
800-824-0241

[New Jersey] Real Estate Commission
20 W. State St.
Trenton, NJ 08625
609-292-7053

[New Jersey] Revisor of Statutes
Office of Legislative Services
State House Annex
Trenton, NJ 08625
609-292-5430

[New Jersey] Securities, Bureau of
2 Gateway Center, 8th Fl.
Newark, NJ 07102
201-648-2040

[New Jersey] Senate
State House Annex
Trenton, NJ 08625
609-292-4840
800-792-8630
609-292-5526 (Judiciary)

[New Jersey] Somerset County Law Library
New Courthouse
Somerville, NJ 08876
201-231-7000

[New Jersey] South Jersey Paralegal Association
P.O. Box 355
Haddonfield, NJ 08033

[New Jersey] State, Department of
CN 300, State House
Trenton, NJ 08625
609-984-1900
609-530-6400 (Corporations)

[New Jersey] State Police, Division of
P.O. Box 7068
West Trenton, NJ 08628
609-882-2000

[New Jersey] Superior Court
CN 971, Richard J. Hughes Justice Complex
Trenton, NJ 08625
609-292-4987

[New Jersey] Supreme Court
CN 970, 25 Market St.
Trenton, NJ 08611
609-292-4837

[New Jersey] Taxation, Division of
CN 269, 50 Barrack St.
Trenton, NJ 08646
609-292-5185

[New Jersey] Transportation, Department of
CN 600, 1035 Parkway Ave.
Trenton, NJ 08625
609-530-3535

[New Jersey] Treasury, Department of
CN 002, State House
Trenton, NJ 08625
609-292-5031

[New Jersey] Unemployment & Disability Insurance, Division of
Labor & Industry Bldg., Rm. 601
Trenton, NJ 08625
609-292-2460

[New Jersey] United States Bankruptcy Court
970 Broad St.
Newark, NJ 07102
201-645-2630

[New Jersey] United States District Court
P.O. Box 419
Newark, NJ 07102
201-645-3730

[New Jersey] Vital Statistics & Registration, Bureau of
CN 360, Health Niagara Falls Bldg., Rm. 504
Trenton, NJ 08625
609-292-4087

[New Jersey] Vocational Rehabilitation Services, Division of
Labor & Industry Bldg., Rm. 1005
Trenton, NJ 08625
609-292-5987

[New Jersey] Weights & Measures, State Office of
1261 Routes 1 & 9 South
Avenel, NJ 07001
201-815-4840

[New Jersey] Workplace Standards Division
CN 386, John Fitch Plaza
Trenton, NJ 08625
609-292-7036

[New Jersey] Worker's Compensation, Division of
Labor & Industry Bldg.
Trenton, NJ 08625
609-292-5275

[New Mexico] Information & Referral (State Government)
505-827-4011

[New Mexico] Information Center (Federal Government)
Albuquerque 505-766-3091

[New Mexico] Adult Parole Board
604 W. San Mateo St.
Santa Fe, NM 87503
505-827-3560
505-827-3592 (Juvenile Parole Board)

[New Mexico] Aging, State Agency on
224 E. Palace Ave., 4th Fl.
Santa Fe, NM 87501
505-827-7640
800-432-2080

[New Mexico] Agriculture, Department of
Gregg & Espina Streets
Las Cruces, NM 88003
505-646-3007

[New Mexico] Air Quality Bureau
1190 St. Francis Dr., Rm. S2100
Santa Fe, NM 87501
505-827-0042

[New Mexico] Attorney General, Office of
Bataan Memorial Bldg., Rm. 260
Santa Fe, NM 87501
505-827-6000

[New Mexico] Auditor, State
PERA Bldg., Rm. 302
Santa Fe, NM 87503
505-827-4740

New Mexico, Bar Association of
1117 Stamford, NE
Albuquerque, NM 87130
505-842-6132
800-876-6227

[New Mexico] Bar Examiners, Board of
P.O. Box 848
Santa Fe, NM 85704
505-827-4860

[New Mexico] Bernalillo County
5th & Marquitto
Albuquerque, NM 87102
505-768-4090

[New Mexico] Better Business Bureau
1210 Luisa St., Suite 5
Santa Fe, NM 87502
505-988-3648
800-445-1461 (Albuquerque)

[New Mexico] Child Support Enforcement Division
P.O. Box 25109—Channel 2 Bldg.
2009 S. Pacheco
Santa Fe, NM 87505
505-827-7200

[New Mexico] Civil Emergency Preparedness Division
4499 Cerrillos Rd.
Santa Fe, NM 87501
505-827-9236

[New Mexico] Consumer Protection & Economic Crimes
Bataan Memorial Bldg.
Santa Fe, NM 87503
505-827-6060
800-432-2070

[New Mexico] Corporations Commission
P.O. Drawer 1269

Santa Fe, NM 87504
505-827-4508

[New Mexico] Corrections Department
1422 Paseo de Peralta
Santa Fe, NM 87503
505-827-8709
505-827-8848 (Library Services)

[New Mexico] Court of Appeals
237 Don Gasper Ave.
Santa Fe, NM 87503
505-827-4925

[New Mexico] Courts, Adminsitrative Office of the
State Supreme Court Bldg., Rm. 25
Santa Fe, NM 87503
505-827-4800

[New Mexico] Disciplinary Counsel, Chief
400 Gold SW, Suite 712
Albuquerque, NM 87102
505-842-5781

[New Mexico] Economic Development & Tourism Department
1100 St. Francis Dr.
Santa Fe, NM 87503
505-827-0274

[New Mexico] Education, Department of
300 Don Gaspar Ave.
Santa Fe, NM 87501
505-827-6635

[New Mexico] Elections, Bureau of
State Capitol, Rm. 400
Santa Fe, NM 87503
505-827-3621

[New Mexico] Employment Security Department
401 Broadway NE
Albuquerque, NM 87102
505-841-8437

[New Mexico] Energy Minerals & Natural Resources Department
525 Camino de los Marquez
Santa Fe, NM 87503
505-827-5950

[New Mexico] Environmental Improvement Division
1190 St. Francis Dr.
Santa Fe, NM 87503
505-827-2850

[New Mexico] Finance & Administration Department
Capitol Bldg., Rm. 425
Santa Fe, NM 87503
505-827-3060

[New Mexico] Financial Institutions Division
Bataan Memorial Bldg., Rm. 307
Santa Fe, NM 87503
505-827-7740

[New Mexico] Game & Fish, Department of
408 Galisteo St.
Santa Fe, NM 87503
505-827-7899

[New Mexico] Governor, Office of
State Capitol Bldg.
Santa Fe, NM 87501
505-827-3000

[New Mexico] Health Services Division
1190 St. Francis Dr.
Santa Fe, NM 87503
505-827-0020

[New Mexico] Higher Education, Commission on
1068 Cerrillos Rd.
Santa Fe, NM 87501
505-827-8300

[New Mexico] Highway & Transportation Department
1120 Cerrillos Rd.
Santa Fe, NM 87504
505-827-5110

[New Mexico] House of Representatives
State Capitol
Santa Fe, NM 87503
505-984-9300

[New Mexico] Human Rights Division
1596 Pacheco St.
Santa Fe, NM 87502
505-827-6838

[New Mexico] Human Services Department
P.O. Box 2348
Santa Fe, NM 87504
505-827-4065

[New Mexico] Institute of Public Law
1117 Stanford NE
Albuquerque, NM 87131
505-277-5006

[New Mexico] Insurance, Superintendent of
PERA Bldg., P.O. Drawer 1269
Santa Fe, NM 87504
505-827-4500

[New Mexico] Judicial Standards Commission
2539 Wyoming NE, Suite A
Albuquerque, NM 87112
505-841-6382

[New Mexico] Juvenile Facilities & Programs Division
1422 Paseo de Peralta
Santa Fe, NM 87503
505-827-8845

[New Mexico] Labor & Industrial Commission
1596 Pacheco St., Aspen Plaza
Santa Fe, NM 87507
505-827-6835

[New Mexico] Labor, Department of
P.O. Box 1928
Albuquerque, NM 87203
505-841-8408

New Mexico, Legal Assistants of
P.O. Box 1113
Albuquerque, NM 87103
505-848-9104

[New Mexico] Legislative Council Service
State Capitol, Rm. 334
Santa Fe, NM 87503
505-984-9600

[New Mexico] Lieutenant Governor, Office of
421 State Capitol Bldg.
Santa Fe, NM 87503
505-827-3050

[New Mexico] Mining & Minerals Division
525 Camino de los Marquez
Santa Fe, NM 87501
505-827-5970

[New Mexico] Motor Vehicles, Department of
P.O. Box 1028
Santa Fe, NM 87504
505-827-2294

[New Mexico] Natural Resources Department
408 Galisteo St., Vilagra Bldg.
Santa Fe, NM 87503
505-827-7835

[New Mexico] Occupational Health & Safety
P.O. Box 968
Santa Fe, NM 87504
505-827-2888

[New Mexico] Oil Conservation Division
310 Old Santa Fe Trail, Rm. 206
Santa Fe, NM 87503
505-827-5800

[New Mexico] Personnel Office, State
810 W. San Mateo
Santa Fe, NM 87503
505-827-8120

[New Mexico] Probation & Parole Division
1422 Paseo de Peralta
Santa Fe, NM 87503
505-827-8694

[New Mexico] Property Control Division
1100 St. Francis Dr.
Santa Fe, NM 87503
505-827-2141

New Mexico Public Defender
142 Lincoln Ave., Suite 500
Santa Fe, NM 87501
505-827-3900

[New Mexico] Public Service Commission
P.O. Box 2205
Santa Fe, NM 87504
505-827-6940

[New Mexico] Purchasing Division
1100 St. Francis Dr., Rm. 2016
Santa Fe, NM 87503
505-827-0472

[New Mexico] Real Estate Commission
4125 Carlisle NE
Albuquerque, NM 87107
505-841-6524

[New Mexico] Records Center & Archives, State
404 Montezuma Ave.
Santa Fe, NM 87503
505-827-8860

[New Mexico] Regulation & Licensing Department
Bataan Memorial Bldg., Rm. 133
Santa Fe, NM 87503
505-827-6318

[New Mexico] Santa Fe County
102 Grant Ave.
Santa Fe, NM 87501
505-984-5080

[New Mexico] Secretary of State
Capitol Bldg., Rm. 400
Santa Fe, NM 87503
505-827-3600

[New Mexico] Securities Division
Bataan Memorial Bldg., Rm. 165
Santa Fe, NM 87503
505-827-7750

[New Mexico] Senate
State Capitol
Santa Fe, NM 87503
505-984-9300

[New Mexico] State Police
4491 Cerrillos Rd.
Santa Fe, NM 87501
505-827-9000

[New Mexico] Supreme Court
237 Don Gasper Ave.
Santa Fe, NM 87503
505-827-4860
505-827-4850 (Law Library)

[New Mexico] Taxation & Revenue Department
1100 St. Francis Dr.

Santa Fe, NM 87509
505-827-0700

[New Mexico] Treasury Department
224 E. Palace Ave.
Santa Fe, NM 87501
505-827-6400

New Mexico Trial Lawyers' Association Foundation
P.O. Box 301
Albuquerque, NM 87103
505-243-6003

[New Mexico] Unemployment Insurance Bureau
401 Broadway NE
Albuquerque, NM 87103
505-841-8431

[New Mexico] United States Bankruptcy Court
P.O. Box 546
Albuquerque, NM 87103
505-766-2051

[New Mexico] United States District Court
P.O. Box 689
Albuquerque, NM 87103
505-766-2851

[New Mexico] Vital Statistics Bureau
P.O. Box 968
Santa Fe, NM 87504
505-827-2338

[New Mexico] Vocational Rehabilitation, Division of
604 W. San Mateo
Santa Fe, NM 87503
505-827-3500

[New Mexico] Women, Commission on the Status of
5006 Cooper NE
Albuquerque, NM 87108
505-841-4662
800-432-9168

[New Mexico] Worker's Compensation Administration
P.O. Box 27190
Albuquerque, NM 87203
505-841-8790

Newsweek, Inc.
444 Madison Ave.
New York, NY 10022
212-350-4000

[New York] Information & Referral (State Government)
518-474-8390 2121

[New York] Information Center (Federal Government)
Albany 518-463-4421
Buffalo 716-846-4010
New York 212-264-4464
Rochester 716-546-5075
Syracuse 315-476-8545

[New York] Aging, Office for the
Empire State Plaza, Agency Bldg. 2
Albany, NY 12223
518-474-5731
800-342-9871

[New York] Agriculture & Markets, Department of
Capitol Plaza, 1 Winners Circle
Albany, NY 12235
518-457-4188

[New York] Air Resources, Division of
50 Wolf Rd., Rm. 128
Albany, NY 12233
518-475-7320

[New York] Appellate Division, First Department
27 Madison Ave.
New York, NY 10010
212-340-0400

[New York] Appellate Division, Second Department
45 Monroe Pl.
Brooklyn, NY 11201
518-875-1300

[New York] Appellate Division, Third Department
P.O. Box 7288
Capitol Station
Albany, NY 12224
518-474-3609

[New York] Appellate Division, Fourth Department
501 Hall of Justice
Civic Center Plaza

Rochester, NY 14614
716-232-6220
716-428-5480 (Law Library)

[New York] Archives & Records Administration, State
10A46 Cultural Education Center
Albany, NY 12230
518-474-1195

[New York] Arts, Council on the
915 Broadway
New York, NY 10010
212-614-2900

[New York] Assembly
State Capitol
Albany, NY 12224
518-455-4100
518-455-5965 (Judiciary)

[New York] Banks, Superintendent of
2 Rector St.
New York, NY 10006
212-618-6642
800-522-3330
800-823-1838

New York Bar Association
1 Elk St.
Albany, NY 12207
518-463-3200

[New York] Bar Examiners, Board of
7 Executive Centre Dr.
Albany, NY 12203
518-452-8700

[New York] Berkshire Association for Paralegals & Legal Secretaries
P.O. Box 433
New Lebanon, NY 12125

[New York] Better Business Bureau
257 Park Ave., South
New York, NY 10010
212-533-6200
716-856-7180 (Buffalo)
315-479-6635 (Syracuse)

[New York] Bronx County
851 Grand Concourse
Bronx, NY 10451
212-590-3644

[New York] Child Support Enforcement, Office of
P.O. Box 14, 1 Commerce Plaza
Albany, NY 12260
518-474-9081

New York City, Association of the Bar of
42 W. 44th St.
New York, NY 10036
212-382-6600
212-382-6741 (Law Library)

New York City Department of Corrections
60 Hudson St.
New York, NY 10013
212-266-1000

New York City Department of Juvenile Justice
365 Broadway
New York, NY 10013
212-925-7779

New York City Department of Probation
115 Leonard St.
New York, NY 10013
212-374-3775

New York City, Mayor's Office
61 Chambers St.
New York, NY 10007
212-566-5700

[New York] Civil Service Department
1 Harriman State Office Bldg.
Albany, NY 12239
518-457-3701

[New York] Comptroller, Office of the State
Washington Ave. & S. Swan St.
Albany, NY 12236
518-474-4044

[New York] Consumer Protection Board
99 Washington Ave.
Albany, NY 12210
518-474-8583

[New York] Correction Commission of
Tower Bldg., Empire State Plaza

Albany, NY 12223
518-474-1416

[New York] Correctional Services, Department of
State Office Campus Bldg. 2
Albany, NY 12226
518-457-8134

New York County
60 Centre St.
New York, NY 10007
212-374-8328

New York County Lawyers Association
14 Vesey St.
New York, NY 10007
212-267-6646
212-267-6646 (Law Library)

[New York] Court Administration
270 Broadway
New York, NY 10007
212-587-2004

New York Court of Appeals
Court of Appeals Hall
20 Eagle St.
Albany, NY 12207
518-455-7700

[New York] Design & Construction
Empire State Plaza, Rm. 3508
Corning Tower
Albany, NY 12242
518-474-0335

[New York] Disaster Preparedness Commission
330 Old Niskayuna Rd., Rm. 414
Latham, NY 12110
518-786-4501

[New York] Economic Development, Department of
1 Commerce Plaza
Albany, NY 12245
518-474-4100

[New York] Economic Opportunity, Division of
162 Washington Ave.
Albany, NY 12231
518-474-5700

[New York] Elections, Board of
P.O. Box 4
Albany, NY 12260
518-474-8100

**[New York] Elementary &
Secondary Education,
Office of**
Education Bldg. Annex, Rm. 875
Albany, NY 12234
518-474-4688

[New York] Energy Office
Agency Bldg. 2
Albany, NY 12223
518-486-4376

**[New York] Environmental
Conservation, Department of**
50 Wolf Rd.
Albany, NY 12233
518-457-3446

[New York] Erie County
25 Delaware Ave.
Buffalo, NY 14202
716-846-8785

**[New York] Ethics Commission,
State**
11 N. Pearl St.
Albany, NY 12207
518-432-8207

**[New York] Facilities
Development Corporation**
44 Holland Ave., 5th Fl.
Albany, NY 12208
518-473-4362

[New York] Governor, Office of
State Capitol Bldg.
Albany, NY 12202
518-474-8390

**[New York] Health,
Department of**
Tower Bldg., Rm. 1408
Albany, NY 12237
518-457-2011

**[New York] Health Statistics,
Bureau of**
Corning Tower, Rm. 308
Albany, NY 12237
518-474-8260

**[New York] Higher &
Professional Education,
Office of**
Empire State Plaza
Albany, NY 12230
518-474-5851

**[New York] Human Rights,
Division of**
55 W. 125th St.
New York, NY 10027
212-870-8790

**[New York] Insurance,
Superintendent of**
160 W. Broadway
New York, NY 10013
212-602-0429
800-342-3736

**[New York] Investor Protection
& Securities, Division of**
120 Broadway, 23rd Fl.
New York, NY 10271
212-341-2222

[New York] Kings County
360 Adam St.
Brooklyn, NY 11201
718-643-5771

[New York] Labor, Department of
State Office Campus Bldg. 12
Albany, NY 12240
518-457-2741

[New York] Law, Department of
Attorney General
State Capitol
Albany, NY 12224
518-474-7330
518-474-3840 (Law Library)

[New York] Legal Aid Society
15 Park Row
New York, NY 10038
212-577-3333

**[New York] Legal Assistants of
Broome County**
P.O. Box 2039
Binghamton, NY 13902

**[New York] Legal Professionals
of Duchess County**
51 Maloney Rd.
Wappingers Falls, NY 12590

**[New York] Legislative Library,
State**
State Capitol, Rm. 337
Albany, NY 12224
518-455-4000

New York Legislative Service, Inc.
299 Broadway
New York, NY 10007
212-962-2826

**[New York] Lieutenant
Governor, Office of**
State Capitol Bldg., Rm. 326
Albany, NY 12224
518-474-4623

**New York Life Insurance
Company**
51 Madison Ave.
New York, NY 10010
212-576-5081

**[New York] Liquor Authority,
State**
250 Broadway
New York, NY 10007
212-587-4191

**[New York] Long Island
Paralegal Association**
P.O. Box 361
Oyster Bay, NY 11771

**[New York] Manhattan Paralegal
Association, Inc.**
200 Park Ave, Suite 303 East
New York, NY 10166
212-986-2304

**[New York] Mineral Resources,
Division of**
50 Wolf Rd., Rm 202
Albany, NY 12233
518-457-9337

[New York] Monroe County
39 W. Main St.
Rochester, NY 14614
716-428-5151

**[New York] Motor Vehicles
Department**
Swan Street Bldg.
Albany, NY 12228
518-474-0841

[New York] Onondaga County
407 Courthouse
Syracuse, NY 13208
315-425-2070

[New York] Paralegal Association of Central New York
P.O. Box 860
Syracuse, NY 13201

[New York] Paralegal Association of Rochester
P.O. Box 40567
Rochester, NY 14604

[New York] Parole, Board of
97 Central Ave.
Albany, NY 12206
518-473-5424

[New York] Parole, Division of
97 Central Ave.
Albany, NY 12206
518-473-9400

[New York] Probation & Correctional Alternatives, Division of
60 S. Pearl St.
Albany, NY 12207
518-474-1210

[New York] Probation Commission
60 S. Pearl St.
Albany, NY 12207
518-474-1210

[New York] Professional Licensing Services, Division of
Cultural Education Center
Albany, NY 12230
518-474-3830

[New York] Public Interest Research Group
Tax Reform Project
9 Murray St.
New York, NY 10007
212-349-6460

[New York] Public Service Commission
Empire State Plaza Bldg. 3
Albany, NY 12223
518-474-7080
800-342-3377

[New York] Purchasing, Division of
Empire State Plaza
Corning Tower, 38th Fl.
Albany, NY 12242
518-474-3695

[New York] Safety & Health, Division of
State Office Campus Bldg.
Albany, NY 12240
518-457-3518

[New York] Secretary of State
162 Washington Ave.
Albany, NY 12231
518-474-4750

[New York] Senate
State Capitol
Albany, NY 12224
518-455-2800
518-455-2831 (Judiciary)

[New York] Social Services, Department of
40 N. Pearl St.
Albany, NY 12243
518-474-9475

[New York] Solid & Hazardous Waste, Division of
50 Wolf Rd.
Albany, NY 12233
518-457-6603

New York Southern Tier Association of Paralegals
P.O. Box 2555
Binghamton, NY 13902

[New York] State, Department of
162 Washington Ave.
Albany, NY 12231
518-474-4750

[New York] State Police
Public Security Bldg.
Albany, NY 12226
518-457-6721

[New York] Supreme Court Library—Bronx
851 Grand Concourse
Bronx, NY 10451
212-590-3679

[New York] Supreme Court Library—Brooklyn
360 Adams St., Rm. 349
Brooklyn, NY 11201
718-643-8080

[New York] Supreme Court Library—Buffalo
92 Franklin St., 4th Fl.
Buffalo, NY 14202
716-852-0712

[New York] Supreme Court Library—Elmira
203–205 Lake St.
Elmira, NY 14901
607-737-2983

[New York] Supreme Court Library—Kingston
U.P.O. Box 3535
Kingston, NY 12401
914-339-5680

[New York] Supreme Court Library—Manhattan
100 Centre St.
New York, NY 10013
212-374-6267
212-374-8385 (Civil Branch)

[New York] Supreme Court Library—Nassau County
100 Supreme Court Dr.
Mineola, NY 11501
516-535-3883

[New York] Supreme Court Library—Norwich
5 Maple St.
Norwich, NY 13815
607-334-9463

[New York] Supreme Court Library—Saratoga Springs
474 Broadway
Saratoga Springs, NY 12866
518-584-4862

[New York] Supreme Court Library—Staten Island
Richmond County Courthouse
Staten Island, NY 10301
718-390-5291

[New York] Supreme Court Library—Syracuse
500 Court House

Syracuse, NY 13202
315-425-2063

**[New York] Supreme Court
Library—Troy**
Courthouse, 2nd St. Annex
Troy, NY 12180
518-274-0590

**[New York] Supreme Court
Library—Utica**
Oneida County Court House
Elizabeth St.
Utica, NY 13501
315-798-5703

**[New York] Supreme Court
Library—Watertown**
Court House
Watertown, NY 13601
315-785-3064

**[New York] Taxation & Finance,
Department of**
Campus Tax & Finance Bldg. 9
Albany, NY 12227
518-457-2244

New York Times Co.
229 W. 43rd St.
New York, NY 10036
212-556-7171

**[New York] Transportation,
Department of**
State Office Campus, Bldg. 5
Albany, NY 12232
518-457-4422

**[New York] Treasury, Division
of the**
Alfred E. Smith Office Bldg., 5th Fl.
Albany, NY 12225
518-474-4250

**[New York] Trial Lawyers
Association, State**
132 Nassau St.
New York, NY 10038
212-349-5890

**[New York] Unemployment
Insurance Division**
State Office Campus Bldg. 12,
  Rm. 554
Albany, NY 12240
518-457-2878

**[New York] United States
Bankruptcy Court**
Eastern New York
75 Clinton St.
Brooklyn, NY 11201
718-330-2188

**[New York] United States
Bankruptcy Court**
Western New York
68 Court St.
312 U.S. Courthouse
Buffalo, NY 14202
716-846-4130

**[New York] United States
Bankruptcy Court**
Northern New York
P.O. Box 398
Albany, NY 12201
518-472-4226

**[New York] United States
Bankruptcy Court**
Southern New York
1 Bowling Green, 6th Fl.
New York, NY 10004
212-791-2247

**[New York] United States Court
of Appeals for the Second
Circuit**
Foley Sq.
New York, NY 10007
212-791-0103
212-791-1052 (Law Library)

**[New York] United States
District Court**
Eastern District
225 Cadman Plaza East
Brooklyn, NY 11201
718-330-2105

**[New York] United States
District Court**
Western District
68 Court St.
304 U.S. Courthouse
Buffalo, NY 14202
716-846-4211

**[New York] United States
District Court**
Northern District
Box 1037

Albany, NY 12201
518-562-5651

**[New York] United States
District Court**
Southern District
Foley Sq.
New York, NY 10007
212-791-0108

**[New York] United States
Government Printing Office**
26 Federal Plaza, Rm. 110
New York, NY 10278
212-264-3825

**[New York] Vital Records,
Bureau of**
Empire State Plaza, Tower Bldg.
Albany, NY 12237
518-474-3075

**[New York] Vocational
Rehabilitation, Office of**
1 Commerce Plaza, Rm. 1907
Albany, NY 12234
518-474-2714
800-222-JOBS

[New York] Water, Division of
50 Wolf Rd., Rm. 306
Albany, NY 12233
518-457-1627

**[New York] Weights & Measures,
Bureau of**
1220 Washington Ave.
Albany, NY 12235
518-457-3452

**[New York] Western New York
Paralegal Association**
P.O. Box 207
Niagara Square Station
Buffalo, NY 14202

**[New York] Worker's
Compensation Board**
180 Livingston St.
Brooklyn, NY 11248
718-802-6700

NILS Publishing Co.
21625 Prairie St.
Chatsworth, CA 91311
818-988-8830
800-423-5910

**[North Carolina] Information &
Referral (State Government)**
919-733-1110

**[North Carolina] Information
Center (Federal Government)**
Charlotte 704-376-3600

**[North Carolina]
Administration,
Department of**
116 W. Jones St.
Raleigh, NC 27603
919-733-7232

**[North Carolina] Administrative
Hearings, Office of**
424 N. Blount St.
Raleigh, NC 27601
919-733-2691

**[North Carolina] Adult Probation
& Parole, Division of**
401 Glenwood Ave.
Raleigh, NC 27603
919-733-7333

**[North Carolina] Aging,
Division of**
1985 Umstead Dr.
Raleigh, NC 27603
919-733-3983
800-662-7030

**[North Carolina] Agriculture,
Department of**
1 W. Edenton St.
Raleigh, NC 27601
919-733-7125

**[North Carolina] Air Quality
Section**
512 N. Salisbury St.
Raleigh, NC 27604
919-733-3340

**[North Carolina] Archives &
History, Division of**
109 E. Jones St.
Raleigh, NC 27611
919-733-7305

**North Carolina Association of
Professional Legal Assistants**
P.O. Box 31951
Raleigh, NC 27622

**[North Carolina] Attorney
General, Office of**
2 E. Morgan St.
Raleigh, NC 27601
919-733-3377

**[North Carolina] Auditor,
Department of the State**
300 N. Salisbury St.
Raleigh, NC 27611
919-733-3217

**[North Carolina] Banks,
Commissioner of**
P.O. Box 29512
Raleigh, NC 27626
919-733-3016

North Carolina Bar Association
1312 Annapolis Dr.
Raleigh, NC 27608
919-828-0561
919-828-4620 (State Bar Association)

**[North Carolina] Bar Examiners,
Board of**
208 Fayetteville St. Mall
P.O. Box 2946
Raleigh, NC 27602
919-828-4886

**[North Carolina] Benefit Claims
Administration**
700 Wade Ave.
Raleigh, NC 27605
919-733-7883

**[North Carolina] Better Business
Bureau**
3120 Poplarwood Dr., Suite 101
Raleigh, NC 27604
919-872-9240
800-532-0477 (Charlotte)

**[North Carolina] Budget
Management, Office of State**
115 W. Jones St., Rm. 5111
Raleigh, NC 27603
919-733-7061

**[North Carolina] Building
Division, State**
300 N. Salisbury St., Rm. 403
Raleigh, NC 27603
919-733-7962

**[North Carolina] Charlotte Law
Library**
730 E. Trade St.
Charlotte, NC 28202
704-334-4912

**[North Carolina] Child Support
Enforcement Section**
437 N. Harrington St.
Raleigh, NC 27603
919-733-4120

**[North Carolina] Commerce,
Department of**
430 N. Salisbury St., Rm. 6122
Raleigh, NC 27611
919-733-4962

**[North Carolina] Consumer
Protection**
Department of Justice Bldg.
P.O. Box 629
Raleigh, NC 27602
919-733-7741

**[North Carolina] Consumer
Standards Division**
P.O. Box 27647
Raleigh, NC 27611
919-733-3313

**[North Carolina] Corrections,
Department of**
840 W. Morgan St.
Raleigh, NC 27603
919-733-4926

**[North Carolina] Courts,
Administrative Office of the**
Fayetteville & Morgan Streets
Raleigh, NC 27602
919-733-7107

**[North Carolina] Cumberland
County Paralegal Association**
P.O. Box 1358
Fayetteville, NC 28302

**[North Carolina] Economic
Opportunity, Division of**
2413–19 Crabtree Blvd.
Raleigh, NC 27611
919-733-2633

**[North Carolina] Elections, State
Board of**
P.O. Box 1166

Raleigh, NC 27602
919-733-7173

**[North Carolina] Emergency
Management, Division of**
116 W. Jones St.
Raleigh, NC 27603
919-733-3867

**[North Carolina] Employment
Security Commission**
700 Wade Ave.
Raleigh, NC 27605
919-733-7546

**[North Carolina] Energy
Division**
430 N. Salisbury St.
Raleigh, NC 27603
919-733-2230

**[North Carolina] Environmental
Management, Division of**
512 N. Salisbury St.
Raleigh, NC 27604
919-733-7015

**[North Carolina] Governor,
Office of**
State Capitol
Raleigh, NC 27603
919-733-4240

**[North Carolina] Health
Services, Division of**
225 N. McDowell St.
Raleigh, NC 27603
919-733-3446

**[North Carolina] Highway Patrol
Division, State**
P.O. Box 27687
Raleigh, NC 27611
919-733-7952

**[North Carolina] Highways,
Division of**
1 S. Wilmington St.
Raleigh, NC 27601
919-733-7384

**[North Carolina] House of
Representatives**
State Capitol
Raleigh, NC 27611
919-733-7761
919-733-1110 (Judiciary)

**[North Carolina] Housing
Finance Agency**
P.O. Box 28066
Raleigh, NC 27611
919-781-6115

**[North Carolina] Human
Resources, Department of**
705 Palmer Dr.
Raleigh, NC 27603
919-733-4534

**[North Carolina] Insurance,
Commissioner of**
Dobbs Bldg., P.O. Box 26387
Raleigh, NC 27611
919-733-7343

**[North Carolina] Interstate
Compact on Juveniles**
325 N. Salisbury St.
Raleigh, NC 27611
919-733-4622

**[North Carolina] Labor,
Department of**
4 W. Edenton St.
Raleigh, NC 27601
919-733-7166

**[North Carolina] Legislative
Services Office**
Legislative Office Bldg., Rm. 100
Raleigh, NC 27611
919-733-6660
919-733-7779 (Bill Status)

**[North Carolina] Lieutenant
Governor, Office of**
Legislative Office Bldg., Rm. 301
Raleigh, NC 27611
919-733-7350

**[North Carolina] Mecklenburg
County**
P.O. Box 31787
Charlotte, NC 28231
704-342-6233

**[North Carolina] Metrolina
Paralegal Association**
P.O. Box 36260
Charlotte, NC 28236

**[North Carolina] Motor Vehicles,
Division of**
1100 New Bern Ave.

Raleigh, NC 27697
919-733-2403

**[North Carolina] Natural
Resources & Community
Development, Department of**
512 N. Salisbury St.
Raleigh, NC 27604
919-733-4984

**[North Carolina] Occupational
Safety & Health, Division of**
214 W. Jones St.
Raleigh, NC 27603
919-733-4880

**North Carolina Paralegal
Association**
P.O. Box 31507
Raleigh, NC 27622

**[North Carolina] Parole
Commission**
831 W. Morgan St.
Raleigh, NC 27603
919-733-3414

**[North Carolina] Personnel,
Office of State**
116 W. Jones St.
Raleigh, NC 27603
919-733-7108

**[North Carolina] Policy &
Planning, Division of**
116 W. Jones St.
Raleigh, NC 27603
919-733-4131

**[North Carolina] Prisons,
Division of**
831 W. Morgan St.
Raleigh, NC 27603
919-733-3226

**[North Carolina] Public
Education, Department of**
116 W. Edenton St.
Raleigh, NC 27603
919-733-3813

**[North Carolina] Purchase &
Contract, Division of**
116 W. Jones St.
Raleigh, NC 27603
919-733-3581

[North Carolina] Real Estate Commission
1313 Navaho Dr.
Raleigh, NC 27609
919-733-9580

[North Carolina] Revenue, Department of
Revenue Bldg., Rm. 210
Raleigh, NC 27640
919-733-7211

[North Carolina] Secretary of State
300 N. Salisbury St.
Raleigh, NC 27603
919-733-3433

[North Carolina] Securities Division
300 N. Salisbury St., Rm. 404
Raleigh, NC 27611
919-733-3924

[North Carolina] Senate
State Capitol
Raleigh, NC 27611
919-733-7761
919-733-5874 (Judiciary I)
919-733-5651 (Judiciary II & III)

North Carolina Solid & Hazardous Waste Management Branch
401 Oberlain Rd.
Raleigh, NC 27605
919-733-2178

North Carolina State Bar Association
208 Fayetteville St. Mall
Raleigh, NC 27611
919-828-4620

[North Carolina] Supreme Court
P.O. Box 2170
Raleigh, NC 27602
919-733-3723
919-733-3425 (Law Library)

[North Carolina] Transportation, Department of
1 S. Wilmington St.
Raleigh, NC 27611
919-733-2520

[North Carolina] Treasurer, State
325 N. Salisbury St.
Raleigh, NC 27611
919-733-3951

[North Carolina] Triad Paralegal Association
Drawer U
Greensboro, NC 27402

[North Carolina] Triangle Association of Professional Legal Assistants
2924 Tutman Court
Raleigh, NC 27614

[North Carolina] United States Bankruptcy Court
Eastern North Carolina
Box 2807
Wilson, NC 27894
919-273-0248

[North Carolina] United States Bankruptcy Court
Middle North Carolina
P.O. Box 26100
Greensboro, NC 27420
919-333-5647

[North Carolina] United States Bankruptcy Court
Western North Carolina
401 W. Trade St.
Charlotte, NC 28202
704-371-6103

[North Carolina] United States District Court
Eastern District
Box 25670
Raleigh, NC 27611
919-856-4370

[North Carolina] United States District Court
Middle District
P.O. Box V-1
Greensboro, NC 27420
919-333-5347

[North Carolina] United States District Court
Western District
100 Otis St.
Asheville, NC 28801
704-259-0648

[North Carolina] University of North Carolina
910 Raleigh Rd.
Chapel Hill, NC 27514
919-962-6981

[North Carolina] Utilities Commission
P.O. Box 29510
Raleigh, NC 27626
919-733-4249

[North Carolina] Vital Records Branch
225 N. McDowell St.
Raleigh, NC 27603
919-733-3000

[North Carolina] Vocational Rehabilitation, Division of
P.O. Box 26053
Raleigh, NC 27611
919-733-3364

[North Carolina] Wade County
336 Fayetteville Mall
Raleigh, NC 27602
919-755-6160

[North Carolina] Water Resources Division
512 N. Salisbury St.
Raleigh, NC 27604
919-733-4064

[North Carolina] Women, Council on the Status of
526 N. Wilmington St.
Raleigh, NC 27604
919-733-2455

[North Carolina] Youth Services, Division of
705 Palmer Dr.
Raleigh, NC 27603
919-733-3011

[North Dakota] Information & Referral (State Government)
701-224-2000

[North Dakota] Adjutant General
Fraine Barracks
Bismarck, ND 58502
701-224-5102

[North Dakota] Aging Services
600 E. Blvd.
Bismarck, ND 58505

701-224-2310
800-472-2622

[North Dakota] Agriculture, Department of
600 E. Blvd., 6th Fl.
Bismarck, ND 58505
701-224-2231

[North Dakota] Archivist, State
North Dakota Heritage Center
Bismarck, ND 58505
701-224-2668

[North Dakota] Arts, Council on the
Black Bldg., Suite 606
Fargo, ND 58102
701-237-8962

[North Dakota] Attorney General, Office of
600 E. Blvd.
Bismarck, ND 58505
701-224-3404
800-472-2600

[North Dakota] Banking & Financial Institutions, Commissioner of
600 E. Blvd. Ave., 13th Fl.
Bismarck, ND 58505
701-224-2256

North Dakota, Bar Association of
515½ E. Broadway, Suite 101
Bismarck, ND 58501
701-255-1404
800-472-2685

[North Dakota] Bar Examiners, Board of
600 E. Boulevard Ave.
Bismarck, ND 58505
701-224-2221

[North Dakota] Burleigh County
514 E. Thayer Ave.
Bismarck, ND 58501
701-222-6702

[North Dakota] Child Support Enforcement Agency
State Capitol
Bismarck, ND 58505
701-224-3582

[North Dakota] Code Revisor
Legislative Council

State Capitol
Bismarck, ND 58505
701-224-2916

[North Dakota] Consumer Fraud & Antitrust Bldg.
State Capitol Bldg.
Bismarck, ND 58505
701-224-3404

[North Dakota] Court Administrator, Office of State
Supreme Court, 2nd Fl.
State Capitol Bldg.
Bismarck, ND 58505
701-224-4216

[North Dakota] Economic Development Commission
Liberty Memorial Bldg.
Bismarck, ND 58505
701-224-2810

[North Dakota] Game & Fish Department
100 N. Bismarck Expressway
Bismarck, ND 58501
701-221-6300

[North Dakota] Governor, Office of
State Capitol Bldg.
Bismarck, ND 58505
701-224-2200

[North Dakota] Health, Department of
State Capitol Bldg.
Bismarck, ND 58505
701-224-2372

[North Dakota] Higher Education, Board of
State Capitol Bldg., 10th Fl.
Bismarck, ND 58505
701-224-2960

[North Dakota] Highway Department
600 E. Boulevard Ave.
Bismarck, ND 58505
701-224-2581

[North Dakota] Highway Patrol
State Capitol Bldg.
Bismarck, ND 58505
701-224-2455

[North Dakota] House of Representatives
Capitol Bldg.
Bismarck, ND 58505
701-224-3508

[North Dakota] Institutions, Director of
State Capitol Bldg., 10th Fl.
Bismarck, ND 58505
701-224-2471

[North Dakota] Insurance, Commissioner of
600 E. Blvd. Ave., 5th Fl.
Bismarck, ND 58505
701-224-2440
800-247-0560

[North Dakota] Job Insurance Department
1000 E. Divide Ave.
Bismarck, ND 58501
701-224-2832

[North Dakota] Labor, Department of
State Capitol Bldg., 5th Fl.
Bismarck, ND 58505
701-224-2660

[North Dakota] Land Department
State Capitol, 6th Fl.
Bismarck, ND 58505
701-224-2800

[North Dakota] Lieutenant Governor, Office of
State Capitol Bldg., 1st Fl.
Bismarck, ND 58505
701-224-2200

[North Dakota] Management & Budget, Office of
State Capitol Bldg.
Bismarck, ND 58505
701-224-2680

[North Dakota] Motor Vehicle Department
Capitol Grounds
Bismarck, ND 58505
701-224-2725

[North Dakota] Natural Resources Division
Liberty Memorial Bldg.

Bismarck, ND 58505
701-224-4187

[North Dakota] Occupational Safety & Health Program
1200 Missouri Ave.
Bismarck, ND 58504
701-224-2348

[North Dakota] Oil & Gas Division
900 E. Boulevard Ave.
Bismarck, ND 58505
701-224-2969

[North Dakota] Pardon Board, State
P.O. Box 5521
Bismarck, ND 58502
701-221-6190

[North Dakota] Parole & Probation Department
P.O. Box 5521
Bismarck, ND 58502
701-221-6190

[North Dakota] Parole Board
P.O. Box 5521
Bismarck, ND 58502
701-221-6190

[North Dakota] Public Instruction, Department of
State Capitol Bldg.
Bismarck, ND 58505
701-224-2260

[North Dakota] Public Service Commission
State Capitol Bldg.
Bismarck, ND 58505
701-224-2400
800-932-2400

[North Dakota] Real Estate Commission
314 E. Thayer Ave.
Bismarck, ND 58501
701-224-2749

[North Dakota] Red River Valley Legal Assistants
P.O. Box 547
Mayville, ND 58257

[North Dakota] Secretary of State
State Capitol Bldg., 1st Fl.

Bismarck, ND 58505
701-224-2900

[North Dakota] Securities Commissioner
State Capitol Bldg.
Bismarck, ND 58505
701-224-2910

[North Dakota] Senate
Capitol Bldg.
Bismarck, ND 58505
701-224-3508

[North Dakota] Supreme Court
State Capitol Bldg.
Bismarck, ND 58505
701-224-2221
701-224-2227 (Law Library)

[North Dakota] Tax Department
State Capitol Bldg.
Bismarck, ND 58505
701-224-2770

[North Dakota] Treasurer
State Capitol Bldg., 3rd Fl.
Bismarck, ND 58505
701-224-2643

[North Dakota] United States Bankruptcy Court
P.O. Box 1110
Fargo, ND 58107
701-239-5120

[North Dakota] United States District Court
P.O. Box 1193
Bismarck, ND 58102
701-250-4295

[North Dakota] Vital Records, Division of
State Capitol Bldg.
Bismarck, ND 58505
701-224-2360

[North Dakota] Vocational Rehabilitation, Office of
600 E. Blvd.
Bismarck, ND 58505
701-224-2907

[North Dakota] Waste Management, Division of
1200 Missouri Ave.
Bismarck, ND 58504
701-224-2366

[North Dakota] Water Commission
900 E. Boulevard Ave.
Bismarck, ND 58505
701-224-2750

[North Dakota] Weights & Measures, Division of
State Capitol
Bismarck, ND 58505
701-224-2400

[North Dakota] Western Dakota Association of Legal Assistants
P.O. Box 2056
Bismarck, ND 58502

[North Dakota] Workmen's Compensation Bureau
4007 N. State St.
Bismarck, ND 58501
701-224-2700

Northwestern Mutual Life Insurance Co.
720 E. Wisconsin Ave.
Milwaukee, WI 53202
414-271-1444

NOW Legal Defense & Legal Education Fund
1333 H. St., NW, 11th Fl.
Wash. D.C. 20005
202-682-0940

OCLC Online Computer Library Center, Inc.
6565 Frantz Rd.
Dublin, OH 43017
614-764-6000
800-848-5878

[Ohio] Information & Referral (State Government)
614-466-2000

[Ohio] Information Center (Federal Government)
Akron 216-375-5638
Cincinnati 513-684-2801
Cleveland 216-522-4040
Columbus 614-221-1014
Dayton 513-223-7377
Toledo 419-241-3223

[Ohio] Administrative Services, Department of
40 E. Broad St.
Columbus, OH 43266
614-446-2000

Ohio Aging, Department of
50 W. Broad St., 9th Fl.
Columbus, OH 43266
614-446-5500

[Ohio] Agriculture, Department of
65 S. Front St.
Columbus, OH 43266
614-466-2732

[Ohio] Akron Law Library Association
209 S. High St.
Akron, OH 44308
216-379-2804

[Ohio] Archivist, State
1985 Velma Ave.
Columbus, OH 43211
614-297-2500

[Ohio] Arts Council
727 E. Main St.
Columbus, OH 43205
614-466-2613

[Ohio] Ashland County Law Library Association
Court House, 2nd St.
Ashland, OH 44805
419-289-0000

[Ohio] Ashtabula County Law Library Association
County Courthouse
Jefferson, OH 44047
216-576-9553

[Ohio] Attorney General, Office of
30 E. Broad St., 17th Fl.
Columbus, OH 43266
614-466-4320

[Ohio] Auditor of State
P.O. Box 1140
Columbus, OH 43266
614-446-4514

[Ohio] Banks, Superintendent of
77 S. High St.
Columbus, OH 43266
614-466-2932

Ohio Bar Association
33 W. 11th Ave.
Columbus, OH 43201
614-421-2121

[Ohio] Bar Examiners, Board of
30 E. Broad St.
Columbus, OH 43215
614-466-1541

Ohio Bell Telephone Co.
45 Erie View
Cleveland, OH 44114
216-822-2124

[Ohio] Better Business Bureau
527 S. High St.
Columbus, OH 43215
614-221-6336
513-421-3015 (Cincinnati)
800-521-8357 (Dayton)

[Ohio] Budget & Management, Office of
30 E. Broad St., 34th Fl.
Columbus, OH 43266
614-466-3034

Ohio Building Authority
40 E. Broad St., 40th Fl.
Columbus, OH 43266
614-446-5959

[Ohio] Butler County Law Library Association
141 Court St.
Hamilton, OH 45011
513-887-3456

[Ohio] Child Support, Bureau of
30 E. Broad St., 27th Fl.
Columbus, OH 43266
614-466-3233

[Ohio] Cincinnati Bar Association
35 E. 7th St., 8th Fl.
Cincinnati, OH 45202
513-381-8213

[Ohio] Cincinnati City Hall
801 Plum St.
Cincinnati, OH 45202
513-352-3000

[Ohio] Cincinnati Law Library Association
601 Hamilton County Courthouse
Cincinnati, OH 45202
513-632-8371

[Ohio] Cincinnati Paralegal Association
P.O. Box 1515
Cincinnati, OH 45201

Ohio Civil Rights Commission
220 Parsons Ave.
Columbus, OH 43266
614-446-2785

[Ohio] Clermont County Law Library
Courthouse, Main St.
Batavia, OH 45103
513-732-7109

[Ohio] Cleveland Association of Paralegals, Inc.
P.O. Box 14247
Cleveland, OH 44114

[Ohio] Cleveland Bar Association
118 St. Clair Ave., 2nd Fl.
Cleveland, OH 44114
216-696-33525

[Ohio] Cleveland City Hall
601 Lakeside Ave. E.
Cleveland, OH 44114
216-664-2000

[Ohio] Cleveland Law Library Association
404 Cuyahoga County Court House
1 Lakeside Ave.
Cleveland, OH 44113
216-861-5070

[Ohio] Code Revision
Legislative Services Commission
Vern Riffe Center
Columbus, OH 43215
614-466-7854
614-466-4489 (Bill Status Clerk)

[Ohio] Columbus Bar Association
40 S. 3rd St., 6th Fl.
Columbus, OH 43215
614-221-4112

[Ohio] Columbus City Hall
90 W. Broad St.
Columbus, OH 43215
614-222-8100

[Ohio] Columbus Law Library Association
369 S. High St., 10th Fl.
Columbus, OH 43215
614-221-4181

[Ohio] Commerce, Department of
77 S. High St.
Columbus, OH 43266
614-466-3636

[Ohio] Consumers' Counsel, Office of
77 S. High St., 15th Fl.
Columbus, OH 43266
614-446-9605
800-282-9448

Defiance County Law Library
500 Court St.
Defiance, OH 43512
419-782-4181

Ohio, Court of Claims of
65 E. State St., Suite 1100
Columbus, OH 43266
614-446-7190

[Ohio] Cuyahoga County
1219 Ontario St.
Cleveland, OH 44113
216-443-7950

[Ohio] Cuyahoga County Bar Association
850 Euclid Ave., # 715
Cleveland, OH 44114
216-621-5112

[Ohio] Dayton Law Library Association
41 N. Perry St.
Dayton, OH 45422
513-225-4496

[Ohio] Dayton Paralegal Association, Greater
P.O. Box 515

Mid City Station
Dayton, OH 45402

[Ohio] Delaware County Law Library Association
91 N. Sandusky St.
Delaware, OH 43015
614-363-4632

[Ohio] Development, Department of
30 E. Broad St.
Columbus, OH 43266
614-466-2480

[Ohio] Education, Board of
65 S. Front St., Rm. 808
Columbus, OH 43266
614-466-5327

[Ohio] Education, Department of
65 S. Front St.
Columbus, OH 43266
614-466-3641

[Ohio] Emergency Management Agency
2825 W. Dublin-Granville Rd.
Columbus, OH 43235
614-889-7150

[Ohio] Employment Services, Bureau of
P.O. Box 1618
Columbus, OH 43266
614-466-4636

[Ohio] Environmental Protection Agency
1800 Water Mark Dr.
Columbus, OH 43266
614-644-3020

Ohio Ethics Commission
8 E. Long St.
Columbus, OH 43266
614-446-7090

[Ohio] Franklin County
410 S. High St.
Columbus, OH 43215
614-462-3322

[Ohio] Governor, Office of
State House
Columbus, OH 43215
614-466-3555

[Ohio] Governor's Office of Advocacy for People with Disabilities
8 E. Long St.
Columbus, OH 43266
614-446-9956
800-228-5405

[Ohio] Hamilton County
1000 Main St.
Cincinnati, OH 45202
513-632-6500

[Ohio] Handcock County Law Library Association
300 S. Main St.
Findlay, OH 45840
419-424-7077

[Ohio] Health, Department of
P.O. Box 118
Columbus, OH 43266
614-466-3543

[Ohio] Highway Patrol
660 E. Main St.
Columbus, OH 43205
614-466-2990

[Ohio] Highway Safety, Department of
240 Parsons Ave.
Columbus, OH 43266
614-466-2550

[Ohio] House of Representatives
State Capitol
Columbus, OH 43215
614-446-8842
800-282-0253
614-446-2591 (Judiciary)

Ohio Human Services, Department of
30 E. Broad St.
Columbus, OH 43266
614-466-7987

Ohio, Industrial Commission of
246 N. High St.
Columbus, OH 43266
614-446-6136

[Ohio] Industrial Relations, Department of
2323 W. 5th Ave.
Columbus, OH 43266
614-644-2223

[Ohio] Insurance, Director of
2100 Stella Ct.
Columbus, OH 43266
614-644-2651
800-282-4658

[Ohio] Law Library Association
of Geauga County
Geauga County Courthouse
Chardon, OH 44024
216-285-2222

[Ohio] Legal Assistants of
Central Ohio
P.O. Box 15182
Columbus, OH 43215

Ohio Legal Rights Service
8 E. Long St.
Columbus, OH 43266
614-446-7264

[Ohio] Licensing, Division of
77 S. High St., 23rd Fl.
Columbus, OH 43266
614-466-4130

[Ohio] Lieutenant Governor,
Office of
State House
Columbus, OH 43215
614-466-3396

[Ohio] Liquor Control,
Department of
2323 W. 5th Ave.
Columbus, OH 43266
614-644-2360

[Ohio] Lorain County Law
Library Association
Lorain County Courthouse
Elyria, OH 44035
216-329-5567

Ohio Lottery Commission
615 W. Superior Ave.
Cleveland, OH 44113
216-622-3344

[Ohio] Lucus County
1 Government Center, Suite 800
Toledo, OH 43604
419-245-4000

[Ohio] Mahoning Law Library
Association
120 Market St.

Youngstown, OH 44503
216-740-2295

[Ohio] Medical Board, State
77 S. High St., 17th Fl.
Columbus, OH 43266
614-446-3934

[Ohio] Medina County Law
Library Association
93 Public Sq.
Medina, OH 44256
216-723-3641
216-725-9744

[Ohio] Mental Health,
Department of
30 E. Broad, Rm. 1180
Columbus, OH 43266
614-466-2596

[Ohio] Montgomery County
451 W. 3rd St.
Dayton, OH 45422
513-225-4000

[Ohio] Natural Resources,
Department of
Fountain Square
Columbus, OH 43224
614-265-6994

[Ohio] Oil & Gas, Division of
Fountain Sq. Bldg. A-1
Columbus, OH 43224
614-265-6893

[Ohio] Parole & Community
Services, Division of
1050 Freeway Dr. N.
Columbus, OH 43229
614-431-2776

[Ohio] Portage County Law
Library
203 W. Main St.
Ravenna, OH 44266
216-297-3661

[Ohio] Public Defender
E. Long St., 11th Fl.
Columbus, OH 43266
614-466-5394

[Ohio] Public Utilities
Commission
180 E. Broad St.

Columbus, OH 43266
614-466-3016
800-282-0198

[Ohio] Real Estate, Division of
77 S. High St., 20th Fl.
Columbus, OH 43266
614-466-4100

[Ohio] Regents, Board of
30 E. Broad St., Suite 3600
Columbus, OH 43266
614-466-6000

[Ohio] Rehabilitation &
Correction, Department of
1050 Freeway Dr. N.
Columbus, OH 43229
614-431-2762
614-438-1210

[Ohio] Safety & Hygiene,
Division of
246 N. High St., 4th Fl.
Columbus, OH 43215
614-466-1276

[Ohio] Secretary of State
30 E. Broad St., 14th Fl.
Columbus, OH 43266
614-466-2655

[Ohio] Securities,
Commissioner of
2 Nationwide Plaza
Columbus, OH 43215
614-644-7381

[Ohio] Senate
State Capitol
Columbus, OH 43215
614-446-4884
800-282-0253
614-466-8909 (Judiciary)

[Ohio] Seneca County Law
Library
Courthouse, 4th Fl.
Tiffin, OH 44883
419-447-2636

[Ohio] Solid & Hazardous Waste
Management, Division of
1018 Watermark Dr.
Columbus, OH 43216
614-466-7220

Ohio Stark County Law Library Association
Court House, 4th Fl.
Canton, OH 44702
216-456-2330

[Ohio] Supreme Court
30 E. Broad St.
Columbus, OH 43266
614-466-3456
614-466-2044 (Law Library)

[Ohio] Surface Mines, Division of
2242 S. Hamilton Rd.
Columbus, OH 43232
614-866-0578

[Ohio] Tax Appeals, Board of
30 E. Broad St.
Columbus, OH 43266
614-446-6700

[Ohio] Taxation Department
30 E. Broad St., 22nd Fl.
Columbus, OH 43266
614-466-2166

[Ohio] Toledo Association of Legal Assistants
P.O. Box 1322
Toledo, OH 43603

[Ohio] Toledo City Hall
1 Government Center
Toledo, OH 43604
419-245-1000

[Ohio] Toledo Law Association Library
Lucas County Courthouse
Toledo, OH 43624
419-245-4747

[Ohio] Transportation, Department of
25 S. Front St.
Columbus, OH 43215
614-466-7170

[Ohio] Treasurer
30 E. Broad St.
Columbus, OH 43266
614-466-2160

[Ohio] Trumbull County Law Library Association
High St.

Warren, OH 44481
216-841-0525

[Ohio] Unemployment Insurance Division
P.O. Box 1618
Columbus, OH 43266
614-466-9755
614-466-3628 (Board of Review)

[Ohio] Uniform Commercial Code Office
30 E. Broad St.
Columbus, OH 43266
614-466-3623

[Ohio] United States Bankruptcy Court
Northern Ohio
201 Superior Ave., NE, No. 427
Cleveland, OH 44114
216-942-7555

[Ohio] United States Bankruptcy Court
Southern Ohio
85 Marconi Blvd., No. 124
Columbus, OH 43215
614-469-2087

[Ohio] United States Court of Appeals for the Sixth Circuit
5th & Walnut Streets
Cincinnati, OH 45202
513-684-2953
513-684-2678 (Law Library)

[Ohio] United States District Court
Northern District
201 Superior Ave., NE, No. 102
Cleveland, OH 44114
216-522-5359
216-522-2253 (Law Library)

[Ohio] United States District Court
Southern District
85 Marconi Blvd., No. 328
Columbus, OH 43215
614-469-6945
614-469-2019 (Law Library)

[Ohio] United States Government Printing Office
200 N. High St., Rm. 207

Columbus, OH 43215
614-469-6956

[Ohio] United States Government Printing Office
1240 E. 9th St., Rm. 1653
Cleveland, OH 44199
216-522-4922

[Ohio] Vital Statistics, Division of
65 S. Front St.
Columbus, OH 43266
614-466-2533

[Ohio] Water Development Authority
50 W. Broad St.
Columbus, OH 43215
614-265-5822

[Ohio] Weights & Measures, Division of
8995 E. Main St.
Reynoldsburg, OH 43068
614-866-6361

[Ohio] Women's Information Center
State House, Rm. 19
Columbus, OH 43266
614-446-5580
800-282-3040

[Ohio] Wood County Law Library
Courthouse Sq.
Bowling Green, OH 43402
419-353-3921

[Ohio] Worker's Compensation
246 N. High St.
Columbus, OH 43266
614-466-1000
800-282-9536

[Ohio] Youth Services, Department of
51 N. High St.
Columbus, OH 43266
614-466-8783

[Oklahoma] Information & Referral (State Government)
405-521-1601

[Oklahoma] Information Center (Federal Government)
Oklahoma City 405-231-4868
Tulsa 918-584-4193

[Oklahoma] Aging, Special Unit on
P.O. Box 25352
Oklahoma City, OK 73125
405-521-2281

[Oklahoma] Agriculture, Department of
2800 N. Lincoln Blvd.
Oklahoma City, OK 73105
405-521-3864

[Oklahoma] Appellate Public Defender
1660 Cross Center Dr.
Norman, OK 73019
405-325-3128

[Oklahoma] Attorney General, Office of
State Capitol Bldg., Rm. 112
Oklahoma City, OK 73105
405-521-3921
405-521-3921 (Consumer Affairs)

[Oklahoma] Auditor & Inspector, State
State Capitol, Rm. 100
Oklahoma City, OK 73105
405-521-3495

[Oklahoma] Bank Commissioner
4100 N. Lincoln Blvd.
Oklahoma City, OK 73105
405-521-2783

Oklahoma Bar Association
1901 N. Lincoln
Oklahoma City, OK 73105
405-524-2365
800-522-8065

[Oklahoma] Bar Examiners, Board of
P.O. Box 53036
Oklahoma City, OK 73152
405-524-2365

[Oklahoma] Better Business Bureau
17 S. Dewey
Oklahoma City, OK 73102
405-239-6081

[Oklahoma] Central Oklahoma Association of Legal Assistants
P.O. Box 2146
Oklahoma City, OK 73101

[Oklahoma] Central Purchasing Division
State Capitol Bldg., Rm. B-4
Oklahoma City, OK 73105
405-521-2115

[Oklahoma] Child Support Enforcement Division
P.O. Box 25352
Oklahoma City, OK 73125
405-424-5871

[Oklahoma] Civil Defense, Department of
2401 N. Lincoln Blvd.
Oklahoma City, OK 73105
405-521-2481

[Oklahoma] Commerce, Department of
6601 N. Broadway Extension
Oklahoma City, OK 73116
405-843-9770

[Oklahoma] Conservation Commission
2800 N. Lincoln Blvd., Suite 160
Oklahoma City, OK 73105
405-521-2384

[Oklahoma] Consumer Credit, Department of
4545 Lincoln Bldg., Suite 104
Oklahoma City, OK 73105
405-521-3653

[Oklahoma] Corporation Commission
Jim Thorpe Office Bldg.
Oklahoma City, OK 73125
405-521-2264
800-522-8154

[Oklahoma] Corrections, Department of
3400 Martin Luther King Ave.
Oklahoma City, OK 73136
405-425-2500

Oklahoma County Bar Association
500 W. Main, # 100
Oklahoma City, OK 73102
405-236-8421

Oklahoma County Law Library
County Courthouse, Rm. 247
Oklahoma City, OK 73102
405-278-1353

[Oklahoma] Court of Appeals
440 S. Houston, Rm. 601
Tulsa, OK 74127
918-581-2711

[Oklahoma] Court of Criminal Appeals
State Capitol Bldg., Rm. 230
Oklahoma City, OK 73105
405-521-2156

[Oklahoma] Courts, Administrative Office of the
1915 N. Stiles, Suite 305
Oklahoma City, OK 73105
405-521-2450

[Oklahoma] Education, Department of
2500 N. Lincoln Blvd.
Oklahoma City, OK 73105
405-521-3301

[Oklahoma] Election Board
P.O. Box 53156
Oklahoma City, OK 73152
405-521-2391

[Oklahoma] Employment Security Commission
2401 N. Lincoln Blvd.
Oklahoma City, OK 73105
405-557-7200

[Oklahoma] Finance Office, State
State Capitol Bldg., Rm. 122
Oklahoma City, OK 73105
405-521-2141

[Oklahoma] Governor, Office of
State Capitol Bldg., Rm. 212
Oklahoma City, OK 73105
405-521-2342

**[Oklahoma] Health,
Department of**
1000 NE 10th St.
Oklahoma City, OK 73152
405-271-4200

**[Oklahoma] Higher Education,
State Regents for**
2500 N. Lincoln Blvd.
Oklahoma City, OK 73105
405-521-2444

[Oklahoma] Highway Patrol
3600 N. King Ave.
Oklahoma City, OK 73111
405-425-2424

**[Oklahoma] House of
Representatives**
State Capitol
Oklahoma City, OK 73105
405-521-2711

**[Oklahoma] Human Rights
Commission**
2101 N. Lincoln Blvd.
Oklahoma City, OK 73105
405-521-2360

**[Oklahoma] Human Services,
Department of**
Sequoyah Memorial Bldg., Box
25352
Oklahoma City, OK 73125
405-521-3646

**[Oklahoma] Insurance
Commissioner**
P.O. Box 53408
Oklahoma City, OK 73152
405-521-2828
800-522-0071

**[Oklahoma] Labor,
Department of**
1315 Broadway Pl.
Oklahoma City, OK 73103
405-235-0530

**[Oklahoma] Libraries,
Department of**
200 NE 18th St.
Oklahoma City, OK 73105
504-521-2502

**[Oklahoma] Lieutenant
Governor, Office of**
State Capitol Bldg., Suite 211
Oklahoma City, OK 73105
405-521-2161

**[Oklahoma] Mental Health,
Department of**
P.O. Box 53277
Oklahoma City, OK 73152
405-271-7474

**[Oklahoma] Merit Protection
Commission**
310 NE 28th St.
Oklahoma City, OK 73105
405-525-9144

**[Oklahoma] Mines,
Department of**
4040 N. Lincoln Blvd., Suite 107
Oklahoma City, OK 73105
405-521-3859

**[Oklahoma] Motor Vehicle
Commission**
4400 Will Rogers Parkway
Oklahoma City, OK 73108
405-521-2375

**[Oklahoma] Oil & Gas
Conservation Division**
2101 N. Lincoln Blvd., 2nd Fl.
Oklahoma City, OK 73105
405-521-2302

[Oklahoma] Oklahoma County
321 Park Ave.
Oklahoma City, OK 73102
405-236-2727

Oklahoma Paralegal Association
P.O. Box 18476
Oklahoma City, OK 73154

**[Oklahoma] Pardon & Parole
Board**
4040 N. Lincoln Blvd., Suite 219
Oklahoma City, OK 73105
405-427-8601

[Oklahoma] Personnel, Office of
2101 N. Lincoln Blvd.
Oklahoma City, OK 73105
405-521-2177

**[Oklahoma] Pollution Control,
Department of**
P.O. Box 53504
Oklahoma City, OK 73152
405-271-4677

**[Oklahoma] Programs &
Services, Division of**
3400 Marin Luther King Ave.
Oklahoma City, OK 73111
405-425-2500

[Oklahoma] Public Affairs Office
State Capitol Bldg., Rm. 104
Oklahoma City, OK 73105
405-521-2121

**[Oklahoma] Public Utilities
Division**
2101 N. Lincoln Blvd., 5th Fl.
Oklahoma City, OK 73105
405-521-3908

**[Oklahoma] Real Estate
Commission**
4040 N. Lincoln Blvd., Suite 100
Oklahoma City, OK 73105
405-521-3387

**[Oklahoma] Rehabilitation
Services, Division of**
P.O. Box 25352
Oklahoma City, OK 73125
405-424-4311

**[Oklahoma] Safety Standards
Division**
1315 Broadway Pl.
Oklahoma City, OK 73103
405-235-5568

[Oklahoma] Secretary of State
State Capitol Bldg., Rm. 101
Oklahoma City, OK 73105
405-521-3911

**[Oklahoma] Securities
Commission**
2401 N. Lincoln Blvd., 4th Fl.
Oklahoma City, OK 73152
405-521-2451

[Oklahoma] Senate
State Capitol
Oklahoma City, OK 73105
405-524-0126

[Oklahoma] Supreme Court
State Capitol Bldg., Rm. 1
Oklahoma City, OK 73105
405-521-2163

Oklahoma Tax Commission
2501 N. Lincoln Blvd.
Oklahoma City, OK 73194
405-521-3115

**[Oklahoma] Transportation,
Department of**
200 NE 21st St.
Oklahoma City, OK 73105
405-521-2701

[Oklahoma] Treasurer
State Capitol Bldg., Rm. 217
Oklahoma City, OK 73105
405-521-3191

**[Oklahoma] Tulsa Association of
Legal Assistants**
P.O. Box 1484
Tulsa, OK 74101

[Oklahoma] Tulsa City Hall
200 Civil Center
Tulsa, OK 74103
918-592-7777

[Oklahoma] Tulsa County
500 S. Denver
Tulsa, OK 74103
918-584-0471

**[Oklahoma] Tulsa County Bar
Association**
1446 S. Boston
Tulsa, OK 74119
918-584-5243

**[Oklahoma] Tulsa County Law
Library**
500 S. Denver
Tulsa, OK 74103
918-584-0471

**[Oklahoma] Unemployment
Insurance Division**
2401 N. Lincoln Blvd.
Oklahoma City, OK 73105
405-557-7219

**[Oklahoma] United States
Bankruptcy Court**
Eastern Oklahoma
P.O. Box 1347

Okmulgee, OK 74447
918-758-0126

**[Oklahoma] United States
Bankruptcy Court**
Northern Oklahoma
333 W. 4th St., Rm. 4-540
Tulsa, OK 74103
918-581-7181

**[Oklahoma] United States
Bankruptcy Court**
Western Oklahoma
201 Dean A. McGee Ave.
Oklahoma City, OK 73102
405-231-5143

**[Oklahoma] United States
District Court**
Eastern District
P.O. Box 607
Muskogee, OK 74401
918-687-2471

**[Oklahoma] United States
District Court**
Northern District
333 W. 4th St., Rm. 411
Tulsa, OK 74103
918-581-7796

**[Oklahoma] United States
District Court**
Western District
200 NW 4th St.
Oklahoma City, OK 73102
405-231-4792

**[Oklahoma] Vital Records
Section**
Northeast 10th St. & Stonewall
P.O. Box 53551
Oklahoma City, OK 73152
405-271-4040

**[Oklahoma] Waste Management
Service**
1000 NE 10th St.
Oklahoma City, OK 73152
405-271-5338

**[Oklahoma] Water Resources
Board**
1000 NE 10th St., 12th Fl.
Oklahoma City, OK 73152
405-271-2555

**[Oklahoma] Women,
Commission on the Status of**
440 S. Houston St.
Tulsa, OK 74127
918-581-2801

**[Oklahoma] Workers
Compensation Court**
1915 N. Stiles
Oklahoma City, OK 73105
405-557-7600

**[Oregon] Information &
Referral (State Government)**
503-378-3131

**[Oregon] Information Center
(Federal Government)**
Portland 503-326-2222

**[Oregon] Accident Prevention
Division**
Labor & Industries Bldg., Rm. 21
Salem, OR 97310
503-378-3272

**[Oregon] Agriculture,
Department of**
635 Capitol St. NE
Salem, OR 97310
503-378-3773

[Oregon] Air Quality Division
811 SW 6th St.
Portland, OR 97204
503-229-5397

[Oregon] Archives Division
1005 Broadway NE
Salem, OR 97310
503-378-4242

**[Oregon] Attorney General,
Office of**
1162 Court St. NE
Salem, OR 97310
503-378-6002

Oregon Bar Association
5200 SW Meadows Rd.
P.O. Box 1689
Lake Oswego, OR 97035
503-620-0222

**[Oregon] Bar Examiners,
Board of**
5200 SW Meadows Rd.
P.O. Box 1689

Lake Oswego, OR 97035
530-620-0222 x410

[Oregon] Better Business Bureau
601 SW Alder St., Suite 615
Portland, OR 97205
503-226-3981

[Oregon] Budget & Management Division
155 Cottage St. NE
Salem, OR 97310
503-378-3104

[Oregon] Building Codes Agency
1535 Edgewater NW
Salem, OR 97310
503-378-3176

[Oregon] Children's Services Division
198 Commercial SE
Salem, OR 97310
503-378-4374

[Oregon] Consumer Affairs Division
100 Justice Bldg.
Salem, OR 97310
503-229-5725

[Oregon] Corporation Division
158 12th St. NE
Salem, OR 97310
503-378-4166

[Oregon] Corrections, Department of
2575 Center St. NE
Salem, OR 97310
503-378-2467

[Oregon] Court Administrator, Office of the State
Supreme Court Bldg.
Salem, OR 97310
503-378-6046

[Oregon] Court of Appeals
Justice Bldg., 3rd Fl.
Salem, OR 97310
503-378-6381

[Oregon] Douglas County Law Library
Justice Bldg.
Roseburg, OR 97470
503-440-4341

[Oregon] Economic Development Department
595 Cottage St. NE
Salem, OR 97310
503-373-1200

[Oregon] Education, Department of
700 Pringle Parkway SE
Salem, OR 97310
503-378-3573

[Oregon] Emergency Management Division
43 State Capitol Bldg.
Salem, OR 97310
503-378-4124

[Oregon] Employment Relations Board
528 Cottage St. NE
Salem, OR 97310
503-378-3807

[Oregon] Energy, Department of
625 Marion St. NE
Salem, OR 97310
503-378-4040

[Oregon] Environmental Quality, Department of
811 SW 6th Ave.
Portland, OR 97204
503-229-5696

[Oregon] Ethics Commission, Government
700 Pringle Parkway SE
Salem, OR 97310
503-378-3147

[Oregon] Executive Department
155 Cottage St. NE
Salem, OR 97310
503-378-3147

[Oregon] Finance & Corporate Securities, Division of
Labor & Industries Bldg., Rm. 21
Salem, OR 97310
503-378-4140

[Oregon] Financial Fraud Section
Department of Justice
Justice Bldg.
Salem, OR 97310
503-378-4320

[Oregon] Financial Institutions & Corporate Securities
21 Labor & Industries Bldg.
Salem, OR 97310
503-378-4140

[Oregon] Fish & Wildlife, Department of
506 SW Mill St.
Portland, OR 97201
503-229-5403

[Oregon] Forestry Department
2600 State St.
Salem, OR 97310
503-378-2560

[Oregon] General Services, Department of
1225 Ferry St. SE
Salem, OR 97310
503-378-4691

[Oregon] Geology & Mineral Industries, Department of
910 State Office Bldg.
Portland, OR 97201
503-229-5580

[Oregon] Governor, Office of
254 State Capitol
Salem, OR 97310
503-378-3111

[Oregon] Hazardous & Solid Waste Division
811 SW 6th Ave.
Portland, OR 97204
503-229-5913

[Oregon] Health Division
1400 SW 5th Ave.
Portland, OR 97201
503-229-5806

[Oregon] Health Statistics, Center for
1400 SW 5th Ave.
Portland, OR 97201
503-229-5895

[Oregon] Higher Education, State System of
P.O. Box 3175
Eugene, OR 97403
503-686-5794

[Oregon] Highway Division
Transportation Bldg.
Salem, OR 97310
503-378-6516

[Oregon] House of Representatives
State Capitol
Salem, OR 97310
503-378-8551
503-378-5962 (Judiciary)

Oregon Housing Agency
110 Labor & Industries Bldg.
Salem, OR 97310
503-373-1614

[Oregon] Human Resources, Department of
318 Public Service Bldg.
Salem, OR 97310
503-378-3033

[Oregon] Insurance Commissioner
21 Labor & Industries Bldg.
Salem, OR 97310
503-378-4271

[Oregon] Justice, Department of
P.O. Box 2134
Lake Oswego, OR 97035
503-244-3156

[Oregon] Labor & Industries, Bureau of
1400 SW 5th Ave.
Portland, OR 97201
503-229-5737

[Oregon] Land Conservation & Development, Department of
1175 Court St. NE
Salem, OR 97310
503-373-0050

[Oregon] Lane County Law Library
125 E. 8th St.
Eugene, OR 97401
503-687-4337

Oregon Legal Assistants Association
P.O. Box 8523
Portland, OR 97207

Oregon Liquor Control Commission
9079 SE McLoughlin Blvd.
Portland, OR 97222
503-653-3054

[Oregon] Lottery, State
2767 22nd St. SE
Salem, OR 97302
503-378-3545

[Oregon] Measurement Standards
635 Capitol St., NE
Salem, OR 97310
503-378-3792

[Oregon] Medical Examiners, Board of
1500 SW 1st Ave., Suite 620
Portland, OR 97201
503-229-5770

[Oregon] Mental Health Division
2575 Bittern St. NE
Salem, OR 97310
503-378-2430

[Oregon] Multnomah Bar Association
711 SW Adler, Suite 311
Portland, OR 97205
503-222-3275

[Oregon] Multnomah County
1021 SW 4th St., Rm. 605
Portland, OR 97204
503-248-3277

[Oregon] Multnomah Law Library
1021 SW 4th Ave.
Portland, OR 97204
503-248-3394

[Oregon] Natural Resources Department
State Capitol Bldg., Rm. 160
Salem, OR 97310
503-378-3548

[Oregon] Parole, Board of
2575 Center St. NE
Salem, OR 97310
503-378-2334

[Oregon] Police, State Department of
107 Public Service Bldg.

Salem, OR 97310
503-378-3720

[Oregon] Portland City Hall
1220 SW 5th Ave.
Portland, OR 97204
503-226-3161

[Oregon] Public Defender, Office of the
1655 State St.
Salem, OR 97310
503-378-3349

[Oregon] Public Utility Commission
300 Labor & Industries Bldg.
Salem, OR 97310
503-378-6611
800-522-2404

[Oregon] Purchasing Division
1225 Ferry St. SE
Salem, OR 97310
503-378-4643

[Oregon] Real Estate Agency
158 12th St. NE
Salem, OR 97310
503-378-4170

[Oregon] Recovery Services Section
Child Support Enforcement
P.O. Box 14506
Salem, OR 97309
503-378-5439

[Oregon] Revenue, Department of
955 Center St. NE
Salem, OR 97310
503-378-3363

[Oregon] Secretary of State
136 State Capitol Bldg.
Salem, OR 97310
503-378-4139

[Oregon] Senate
State Capitol
Salem, OR 97310
503-378-8551
503-378-5781 (Judiciary)

[Oregon] Senior Services Division
313 Public Service Bldg.
Salem, OR 97310

503-378-4728
800-232-3020

[Oregon] Supreme Court
Supreme Court Bldg.
Salem, OR 97310
503-378-5912
503-378-6030 (Law Library)

[Oregon] Tax Court
520 Justice Bldg.
Salem, OR 97310
503-378-5251

[Oregon] Transportation, Department of
135 Transportation Bldg.
Salem, OR 97310
503-378-6570

[Oregon] Treasury, State
158 State Capitol Bldg.
Salem, OR 97310
503-378-4329

[Oregon] Uniform State Laws, Commission on
520 SW Yamhill St., Suite 800
Salem, OR 97310
503-378-2000

[Oregon] United States Bankruptcy Court
1001 SW 5th Ave.
Portland, OR 97204
503-221-2231

[Oregon] United States District Court
620 SW Main St.
Portland, OR 97205
503-221-2202

[Oregon] United States Government Printing Office
1305 SW 1st Ave.
Portland, OR 97201
503-221-6217

[Oregon] Vital Statistics Section
Oregon State Health Division
P.O. Box 116
Portland, OR 97207
503-229-6123
503-229-5895 (Vital Records)

[Oregon] Vocational Rehabilitation, Division of
2045 Silverton Rd., NE

Salem, OR 97310
503-378-3850

[Oregon] Washington County Law Library
230 NE 2nd Ave.
Hillsboro, OR 97124
503-648-8880

[Oregon] Water Resources Department
3850 Portland Rd. NE
Salem, OR 97310
503-378-3739

[Oregon] Willamette Valley Legal Assistants
P.O. Box 1835
Eugene, OR 97440

[Oregon] Women, Commission for
695 Summer NE
Salem, OR 97310
503-378-2780

[Oregon] Workers' Compensation Board
480 Church St. SE
Salem, OR 97310
503-378-3308

[Oregon] Workers' Compensation Division
Labor & Industries Bldg., Rm. 21
Salem, OR 97310
503-378-3304

Organization of American States
17th St. & Constitution Ave., NW
Wash. D.C. 20006
202-458-3000

Pacific Bell
140 Montgomery St.
San Francisco, CA 94105
415-811-6222

Pacific Legal Foundation
2700 Gateway Oaks Dr., Suite 200
Sacramento, CA 95833
916-641-8888

Paine Webber, Inc.
1200 Harbor Blvd.
Weehawken, NJ 07087
201-902-3000

Panel Publishers, Inc.
14 Plaza Rd.
Greenvale, NY 11548
516-484-0006

Patent Resources Group, Inc.
2000 Pennsylvania Ave. NW
Wash. D.C. 20006
202-223-1175

[Pennsylvania] Information & Referral (State Government)
717-787-2121

[Pennsylvania] Information Center (Federal Government)
Philadelphia 215-597-7042
Pittsburgh 412-644-3456

[Pennsylvania] Administration, Office of
207 Finance Bldg.
Harrisburg, PA 17120
717-787-9945

[Pennsylvania] Aging, Department of
231 State St.
Harrisburg, PA 17101
717-787-1549

[Pennsylvania] Agriculture, Department of
2301 N. Cameron St.
Harrisburg, PA 17110
717-787-4737

[Pennsylvania] Air Quality Control, Bureau of
101 S. 2nd St.
Executive House, Rm. 116
Harrisburg, PA 17120
717-787-9702

[Pennsylvania] Allegheny County
436 Grant St.
Pittsburgh, PA 15219
412-355-5300

[Pennsylvania] Allegheny County Bar Association
420 Grant Bldg.
Pittsburgh, PA 15219
412-261-6161

[Pennsylvania] Allegheny County Law Library
921 City-County Bldg.
Pittsburgh, PA 15219
412-355-5353

[Pennsylvania] Archives & History, Bureau of
P.O. Box 1026
3rd & Forster St.
Harrisburg, PA 17108
717-787-3051

[Pennsylvania] Attorney General, Office of
4th & Walnut St.
Strawberry Sq., 16th Fl.
Harrisburg, PA 17120
717-787-3391
717-787-3176 (Law Library)

Pennsylvania Auditor General, Office of the
229 Finance Bldg.
Harrisburg, PA 17120
717-787-2543

[Pennsylvania] Banking, Secretary of
333 Market St., 16th Fl.
Harrisburg, PA 17101
717-787-6991
800-PA-BANKS

Pennsylvania Bar Association
100 South St.
P.O. Box 186
Harrisburg, PA 17108
717-238-6715

[Pennsylvania] Bar Examiners, Board of
674 Public Ledger Bldg.
Independence Sq.
Philadelphia, PA 19106
215-627-3246

Pennsylvania Bar Institute, CLE
104 South St.
Harrisburg, PA 17108
717-233-5774
800-932-4637

[Pennsylvania] Beaver County Law Library
Court House
Beaver, PA 15009
412-728-5700

[Pennsylvania] Berks County Law Library
Court House
Reading, PA 19601
215-378-8189

[Pennsylvania] Better Business Bureau
511 N. Broad St.
Philadelphia, PA 19123
215-574-3600
412-456-2700 (Pittsburgh)

[Pennsylvania] Bucks County Law Library
Courthouse
Doylestown, PA 18901
215-348-6023

[Pennsylvania] Butler County Law Library
Court House
Butler, PA 16001
412-284-5206

[Pennsylvania] Central Pennsylvania Paralegal Association
P.O. Box 11814
Harrisburg, PA 17108

[Pennsylvania] Chester County Law Library
15 W. Gay St.
West Chester, PA 19380
215-344-6166

[Pennsylvania] Child Support Enforcement, Bureau of
P.O. Box 8018
Harrisburg, PA 17105
717-787-3672

[Pennsylvania] Commerce, Department of
433 Forum Bldg.
Harrisburg, PA 17120
717-787-3003

[Pennsylvania] Consumer Protection, Bureau of
Strawberry Sq., 14th Fl.

Harrisburg, PA 17120
717-787-9707

[Pennsylvania] Corporations Bureau
Commonwealth Ave. & North St.
Harrisburg, PA 17120
717-787-1997

[Pennsylvania] Corrections, Department of
Box 598, 2520 Lisbourn Rd.
Camp Hill, PA 17011
717-975-4860

[Pennsylvania] Courts, Administrative Office of the
1515 Market St.
Philadelphia, PA 19102
215-560-6337

[Pennsylvania] Dauphin County
P.O. Box 1295
Harrisburg, PA 17108
717-255-2741

[Pennsylvania] Dauphin County Law Library
Front & Market Sts, Court House
Harrisburg, PA 17101
717-255-2797

[Pennsylvania] Delinquent Youth, Office of State Facilities for
P.O. Box 2675, Health & Welfare Bldg., Annex
Harrisburg, PA 17105
717-787-8834

[Pennsylvania] Education, Department of
333 Market St.
Harrisburg, PA 17126
717-783-6788

[Pennsylvania] Emergency Management Agency
Commonwealth Ave. & Forster St.
Harrisburg, PA 17105
717-783-8150

[Pennsylvania] Environmental Resources, Department of
3rd & Locust St.
Harrisburg, PA 17120
717-787-2814

[Pennsylvania] Erie County Law Library
Court House
Erie, PA 16501
814-451-6319

[Pennsylvania] Ethics Commission, State
P.O. Box 11470
Harrisburg, PA 17108
717-787-1610

[Pennsylvania] General Services, Department of
North Office Bldg.
Harrisburg, PA 17120
717-787-5295

[Pennsylvania] Governor, Office of
225 Main Capitol Bldg.
Harrisburg, PA 17120
717-787-2500

[Pennsylvania] Governor's Energy Council
116 Pine St., 2nd Fl.
Harrisburg, PA 17101
717-783-9981

[Pennsylvania] Health Data Center, State
Commonwealth Ave. & Forster St.
Harrisburg, PA 17120
717-787-3810

[Pennsylvania] Health, Department of
Commonwealth Ave. & Forster St.
Harrisburg, PA 17110
717-787-6436

[Pennsylvania] Highway Administration, Office of
Commonwealth Ave. & Forster St., Rm. 1220
Harrisburg, PA 17120
717-787-6875

[Pennsylvania] House of Representatives
State Capitol
Harrisburg, PA 17120
717-787-2372
717-787-3525 (Judiciary)

[Pennsylvania] Housing Finance Agency
P.O. Box 8029

Harrisburg, PA 17105
717-780-3911

[Pennsylvania] Human Relations Commission
101 S. 2nd St.
Harrisburg, PA 17101
717-787-5173

[Pennsylvania] Insurance Commissioner
Strawberry Sq., 13th Fl.
Harrisburg, PA 17120
717-787-5173

[Pennsylvania] Jenkins Memorial Law Library
841 Chestnut St., Suite 1220
Philadelphia, PA 19107
215-592-5690

[Pennsylvania] Juvenile Court Judges' Commission
Box 1234, Federal Square Station
Harrisburg, PA 17108
717-787-6910

[Pennsylvania] Labor & Industry, Department of
7th & Forster St., Rm. 1700
Harrisburg, PA 17120
717-787-3907

[Pennsylvania] Lackawanna Bar Association Law Library
Court House, 2nd Fl.
Scranton, PA 18503
717-963-6712

[Pennsylvania] Lancaster County Law Library
50 N. Duke St.
Lancaster, PA 17603
717-299-8090

[Pennsylvania] Law Library of Pennsylvania, State
Forum Bldg.,Box 1601
Harrisburg, PA 17105
717-787-3273

[Pennsylvania] Lawrence County Law Library
Government Center
New Castle, PA 16101
412-658-2541

[Pennsylvania] Legislative Reference Bureau
Main Capitol Bldg., Rm. 641
Harrisburg, PA 17120
717-787-2142

[Pennsylvania] Lehigh County Law Library
5th & Hamilton St.
Allentown, PA 18105
215-820-3308

[Pennsylvania] Lieutenant Governor, Office of
Main Capitol Bldg., Rm. 200
Harrisburg, PA 17120
717-787-3300

[Pennsylvania] Liquor Control Board
3rd & Forster St.
Harrisburg, PA 17124
717-787-2696

[Pennsylvania] Mining & Reclamation, Bureau of
2nd & Chestnut St.
Harrisburg, PA 17120
717-787-5103

[Pennsylvania] Montgomery County Law Library
Court House
Norristown, PA 19404
215-278-3806

[Pennsylvania] Motor Vehicles, Bureau of
Commonwealth Ave. & Forster St.
Harrisburg, PA 17122
717-787-2304

[Pennsylvania] Northampton County Law Library
7th & Washington St.
Easton, PA 18042
215-253-4111

[Pennsylvania] Oil & Gas Management, Bureau of
3rd & Reilly St.
Harrisburg, PA 17120
717-783-9645

Pennsylvania, Paralegal Association of Northwestern
P.O. Box 1504
Erie, PA 16507

[Pennsylvania] Pardons, Board of
333 Market St.
Harrisburg, PA 17126
717-787-2596

[Pennsylvania] Personnel,
Bureau of
Commonwealth Ave. & North St.
Harrisburg, PA 17120
717-787-5545

[Pennsylvania] Philadelphia
Association of Paralegals
1411 Walnut St., Suite 200
Philadelphia, PA 19102
215-564-0525

[Pennsylvania] Philadelphia Bar
Association
One Reading Bldg.
Philadelphia, PA 19107
215-238-6300

[Pennsylvania] Philadelphia
City Hall
City Hall, Rm. 616
Philadelphia, PA 19107
215-686-5665

[Pennsylvania] Philadelphia
Common Pleas & Municipal
Court Law Library
City Hall, Rm. 600
Philadelphia, PA 19107
215-686-3799

[Pennsylvania] Philadelphia
County
City Hall
Philadelphia, PA 19107
215-686-1776

[Pennsylvania] Philadelphia
Prisons
8201 State Rd.
Philadelphia, PA 19136
215-335-8201

[Pennsylvania] Pittsburgh City
Hall
414 Grant St.
Pittsburgh, PA 15219
412-255-2100

[Pennsylvania] Pittsburgh
Paralegal Association
P.O. Box 1053
Pittsburgh, PA 15230

[Pennsylvania] Probation &
Parole, Board of
3101 N. Front St., P.O. Box 1661
Harrisburg, PA 17105
717-787-5100

[Pennsylvania] Public Utility
Commission
P.O. Box 3265
Harrisburg, PA 17120
717-787-1740
800-782-1110

[Pennsylvania] Public Works,
Office of
18th & Herr St.
Harrisburg, PA 17125
717-787-7095

[Pennsylvania] Purchases,
Bureau of
Commonwealth Ave. & North St.
Harrisburg, PA 17125
717-787-4718

[Pennsylvania] Radiation
Protection, Bureau of
200 N. 3rd St.
Harrisburg, PA 17120
717-787-2480

[Pennsylvania] Real Estate,
Bureau of
Commonwealth Ave. & North St.,
Rm. 503
Harrisburg, PA 17125
717-787-4394

[Pennsylvania] Revenue,
Department of
4th & Walnut St.
Strawberry Sq., 11th Fl.
Harrisburg, PA 17128
717-787-3680

[Pennsylvania] Secretary of the
Commonwealth
North Office Bldg., Rm. 302
Harrisburg, PA 17120
717-787-7630

[Pennsylvania] Securities
Commission
1010 N. 7th St., 2nd Fl.
Harrisburg, PA 17102
717-787-8061

[Pennsylvania] Senate
State Capitol
Harrisburg, PA 17120
717-787-5920
717-787-6599 (Judiciary)

[Pennsylvania] Soil & Water
Conservation, Bureau of
1 Ararat Blvd., Rm. 214
Harrisburg, PA 17110
717-787-5267

[Pennsylvania] Solid Waste
Management, Bureau of
200 N. 3rd St.
Harrisburg, PA 17120
717-787-9870

[Pennsylvania] State Police
1800 Elmerton Ave.
Harrisburg, PA 17110
717-783-5561

[Pennsylvania] Supreme Court
City Hall, Rm. 468
Philadelphia, PA 19107
215-560-6370

[Pennsylvania] Transportation,
Department of
Transportation & Safety Bldg.
Harrisburg, PA 17120
717-787-3154

[Pennsylvania] Treasury
Department
Commonwealth Ave. & North St.
Harrisburg, PA 17105
717-787-2465

[Pennsylvania] Unemployment,
Bureau of
7th & Forster Streets
Harrisburg, PA 17121
717-787-3547

[Pennsylvania] United States
Bankruptcy Court
Eastern Pennsylvania
601 Market St.
Philadelphia, PA 19106
215-597-7704

[Pennsylvania] United States
Bankruptcy Court
Middle Pennsylvania
197 S. Main St.

Wilkes-Barre, PA 18701
717-826-6450

[Pennsylvania] United States Bankruptcy Court
Western Pennsylvania
1000 Liberty Ave.
Pittsburgh, PA 15222
412-644-2700

[Pennsylvania] United States Court of Appeals for the Third Circuit
601 Market St.
Philadelphia, PA 19106
215-597-2995
215-597-2009 (Law Library)
201-645-3034 (Law Library, Newark)

[Pennsylvania] United States District Court
Eastern District
601 Market St.
Philadelphia, PA 19106
215-597-7704

[Pennsylvania] United States District Court
Middle District
P.O. Box 1148
Scranton, PA 18501
717-347-5623

[Pennsylvania] United States District Court
Western District
P.O. Box 1805
Pittsburgh, PA 15230
412-644-3528

[Pennsylvania] United States Government Printing Office
1000 Liberty Ave., Rm. 118
Pittsburgh, PA 15222
412-644-2721

[Pennsylvania] United States Government Printing Office
100 N. 17th St.
Philadelphia, PA 19103
215-597-0677

[Pennsylvania] Vital Statistics, Division of
101 S. Mercer St.
New Castle, PA 16103
412-656-3100

[Pennsylvania] Vocational Rehabilitation, Office of
7th & Forster Streets
Harrisburg, PA 17120
717-787-5244

[Pennsylvania] Weights & Measures, Bureau of
2301 N. Cameron St.
Harrisburg, PA 17110
717-787-6772

[Pennsylvania] Westmoreland County Law Library
202 Courthouse Sq.
Greenburg, PA 15601
412-834-2191

[Pennsylvania] Workers' Compensation
3607 Derry St., 4th Fl.
Harrisburg, PA 17111
717-787-5421

Pepsi-Cola Co.
Route 100
Somers, NY 10589
914-767-6000

Pfizer Inc.
235 E. 42nd St.
New York, NY 10017
212-573-2323

Philip Morris, Inc.
120 Park Ave.
New York, NY 10017
212-880-3489

Phillips Petroleum Co.
16 Phillips Bldg.
Bartlesville, OK 74004
918-661-1215

Photo Marketing Association
3000 Picture Pl.
Jackson, MI 42901
517-788-8100

Pillsbury Co.
P.O. Box 550
Minneapolis, MN 55440
800-328-4466

Police Executive Research Forum
2300 M St. NW
Wash. D.C. 20037
202-466-7820

Police Foundation
1001 22nd St. NW
Wash. D.C. 20037
202-833-1460

Police Management Association
1001 22nd St., Suite 200
Wash. D.C. 20037
202-833-1460

Practicing Law Institute
810 7th Ave.
New York, NY 10017
212-765-5700

Prentice-Hall Law & Business
910 Sylvan Ave.
Englewood Cliffs, NJ 07632
201-894-6000
800-223-0231

Prison Fellowship Ministries
P.O. Box 17500
Wash. D.C. 20041
202-478-0100

Private Satellite Network
215 Lexington Ave.
New York, NY 10016
212-696-9476

Proctor & Gamble Co.
P.O. Box 599
Cincinnati, OH 45201
513-983-2200

Professional Legal Assistants, Inc.
120 Penmarc Dr., Suite 118
P.O. Box 31951
Raleigh, NC 27622
919-821-7762

Provident Mutual Insurance
1600 Market St.
Philadelphia, PA 19101
215-636-5000

Prudential Bache Securities, Inc.
One Seaport Plaza
New York, NY 10292
212-214-1000

Prudential Insurance Co. of America
Prudential Plaza
Newark, NJ 07101
201-802-6000

Prudential Property & Casualty Co.
P.O. Box 300
Lindwood, NJ 08221
609-653-3000

Public Citizen Litigation Group
2000 P. St., NW, Rm. 700
Wash. D.C. 20036
202-785-3704

Public Law Education Institute
1601 Connecticut Ave., NW, Suite 450
Wash. D.C. 20036
202-232-1400

Public Risk Management Association
1120 G. St., Suite 400
Wash. D.C. 20005
202-626-4650

Public Securities Association
40 Broad St., 12th Fl.
New York, NY 10004
202-809-7000

Public Welfare Foundation
2600 Virginia Ave. NW
Wash. D.C. 20037
202-965-1800

Puerto Rican Bar Association
888 Grand Concourse, Suite 1-0
Bronx, NY 10451
212-292-8201

Puerto Rican Legal Defense & Education Fund
99 Hudson St., 24th Fl.
New York, NY 10013
212-219-3360

Puerto Rico Association of Legal Assistants
GPO Box 4225
San Juan, PR 00936

[Puerto Rico] Banking, Commissioner of
G.P.O. Box 70324
San Juan, PR 00936
809-721-7064

Puerto Rico Bar Association
Ponce de Leon 808

San Juan, PR 00908
809-721-3358

[Puerto Rico] Bar Examiners, Board of
Supreme Court of Puerto Rico
P.O. Box 2392
San Juan, PR 00903

[Puerto Rico] Better Business Bureau
GPO Box 70212
San Juan, PR 00936
809-756-5400

[Puerto Rico] Child Support Enforcement Program
Call Box 3349
San Juan, PR 00904
809-722-4731

[Puerto Rico] Consumer Affairs, Department of
P.O. Box 41059
Santurce, PR 00940
809-722-7555

[Puerto Rico] Correction, Administration of
Call Box 71308
San Juan, PR 00936
809-766-4700

[Puerto Rico] Demographic Registry & Vital Statistics, Division of
Department of Health
San Juan, PR 00908
809-728-4300

[Puerto Rico] Elder Affairs, Office of
Call Box 50063
San Juan, PR 00902
809-721-0753

[Puerto Rico] Financial Institutions, Commissioner of
GPO Call Box 70324
San Juan, PR 00936
809-751-7064

[Puerto Rico] General Archives
Ponce de Leon #500
Puerta de Tierra

San Juan, PR 00905
809-722-0331

[Puerto Rico] Insurance, Commissioner of
P.O. Box 8330
Santurce, PR 00910
809-722-8686

Puerto Rico Interstate Compact Office
Probation & Parole
Call Box 71308
San Juan, PR 00936
809-753-0870

[Puerto Rico] Juvenile Courts
P.O. Box 887, Hato Rey Station
San Juan, PR 00919
809-763-6377

[Puerto Rico] Parole, Board of
P.O. Box 40945
Minillas Station
San Juan, PR 00940
809-759-7127

[Puerto Rico] Public Service Commission
Call Box 870
Hato Rey, PR 00919
809-751-5050

[Puerto Rico] Securities Office
GPO Call Box 70324
San Juan, PR 00936
809-751-5606

[Puerto Rico] United States Bankruptcy Court
Federal Bldg. & U.S. Courthouse, Ch. 105D
Hato Rey, PR 00918
809-766-5123

[Puerto Rico] United States District Court
P.O. Box 3671
San Juan, PR 00904
809-729-6701

[Puerto Rico] Vocational Rehabilitation Program
P.O. Box 1118, Bldg. 10
Hato Rey, PR 00919
809-725-1792

Quaker Oats Co.
P.O. Box 9003
Chicago, IL 60604
312-222-7843

Ralston Purina Co.
Checkerboard Sq.
St. Louis, MO 63164
800-345-5678

Rand Corporation
2100 M St. NW
Wash. D.C. 20037
202-296-5000

Reliance Insurance Co.
4 Penn Center Plaza
Philadelphia, PA 19103
215-864-4445

Religious Coalition for Abortion Rights
100 Maryland Ave. NE
Wash. D.C. 20002
202-543-7032

Research Institute of America
90 5th Ave.
New York, NY 10011
212-337-4100
800-431-9025

Reserve Officers Association of the United States
1 Constitution Ave., NE
Wash. D.C. 20002
202-479-2200

[Rhode Island] Information & Referral (State Government)
401-277-2000

[Rhode Island] Information Center (Federal Government)
Providence 401-331-5565

[Rhode Island] Administration, Department of
82 Smith St.
Providence, RI 02904
401-457-4100

[Rhode Island] Agriculture & Marketing Division
22 Hayes St.
Providence, RI 02908
401-277-2781

[Rhode Island] Archives, State
State House, Rm. 43
Providence, RI 02903
410-277-2353

[Rhode Island] Arts, Council on the
95 Cedar St., Suite 10
Providence, RI 02903
401-277-3880

[Rhode Island] Atomic Energy Commission
S. Ferry Rd.
Narragansett, RI 02882
401-789-9391

[Rhode Island] Attorney General, Department of
72 Pine St.
Providence, RI 02903
401-274-4400

[Rhode Island] Banking & Securities, Superintendent of
233 Richmond St., Suite 231
Providence, RI 02903
401-277-2405

Rhode Island Bar Association
91 Friendship St.
Providence, RI 02903
401-421-5740

[Rhode Island] Bar Examiners, Board of
Supreme Court

250 Benefit St.
Providence, RI 02903
401-277-3272

[Rhode Island] Benefits, Division of
24 Mason St.
Providence, RI 02903
401-277-3649

[Rhode Island] Better Business Bureau
P.O. Box 1300
Warwick, RI 02887
401-785-1212

[Rhode Island] Business Regulation, Department of
233 Richmond St.
Providence, RI 02903
401-277-2246

[Rhode Island] Children & Their Families, Department for
610 Mt. Pleasant Ave.
Providence, RI 02908
401-457-4750

[Rhode Island] Consumer Protection Division
72 Pine St.
Providence, RI 02903
401-277-2104
800-852-7776

[Rhode Island] Consumer's Council
365 Broadway
Providence, RI 02909
401-277-2764

[Rhode Island] Correction, Department of
75 Howard Ave.
Cranston, RI 02920
401-464-2611

[Rhode Island] Court Administrator, Office of the State
250 Benefit St.
Providence, RI 02903
401-277-3263

[Rhode Island] Economic Development, Department of
7 Jackson Walkway

Providence, RI 02903
401-277-2601

**[Rhode Island] Education,
Department of**
22 Hayes St.
Providence, RI 02908
401-277-2031

**[Rhode Island] Elderly Affairs,
Department of**
160 Pine St.
Providence, RI 02903
401-277-2880
800-322-2880

**[Rhode Island] Emergency
Management Agency**
82 Smith St.
State House, Rm. 27
Providence, RI 02903
401-421-7333

**[Rhode Island] Employment
Security, Department of**
24 Mason St.
Providence, RI 02903
401-277-3648

**[Rhode Island] Environmental
Management, Department of**
83 Park St.
Providence, RI 02908
401-277-3434

**Rhode Island Ethics
Commission**
43 Jefferson Blvd.
Warwick, RI 02888
401-277-3790

**[Rhode Island] Family Support,
Bureau of**
77 Dorance St.
Providence, RI 02903
401-277-2409

**[Rhode Island] Governor,
Office of**
111 State House
Providence, RI 02903
401-277-2080

**[Rhode Island] Governor's
Office of Energy Assistance**
275 Westminster Mall
Providence, RI 02903
401-277-6920

**[Rhode Island] Health,
Department of**
75 Davis St.
Providence, RI 02908
401-277-2233

**[Rhode Island] Higher
Education, Office of**
199 Promenade St., Rm. 217
Providence, RI 02908
401-277-2685

**[Rhode Island] House of
Representatives**
State House
Providence, RI 02903
401-277-2466
401-277-2258 (Judiciary)

**[Rhode Island] Human Rights,
Commission for**
10 Abbott Park Pl.
Providence, RI 02903
401-277-2661

**[Rhode Island] Human Services,
Department of**
600 New London Ave.
Cranston, RI 02920
401-464-2121

**[Rhode Island] Insurance
Commissioner**
233 Richmond St.
Providence, RI 02903
401-277-2246

[Rhode Island] Kent County
222 Quaker Ln.
West Warwick, RI 02893
401-822-1311

**[Rhode Island] Labor,
Department of**
220 Elmwood Ave.
Providence, RI 02907
401-457-1800

[Rhode Island] Law Library, State
250 Benefit St.
Providence, RI 02903
401-277-3275

**[Rhode Island] Law Revision
Office**
State House
Providence, RI 02903
401-277-3614

**[Rhode Island] Legislative
Council**
State House, Rm. 17
Providence, RI 02903
401-277-2653

**[Rhode Island] Lieutenant
Governor, Office of**
State House, Rm. 317
Providence, RI 02903
401-277-2371

**[Rhode Island] Maximum
Security Facility at Cranston**
P.O. Box 8273
Cranston, RI 02920
401-464-2054

[Rhode Island] Newport County
Washington Sq.
Newport, RI 02840
401-846-5556

**[Rhode Island] Occupational
Safety, Division of**
220 Elmwood Ave.
Providence, RI 02907
401-457-1829

**Rhode Island Paralegal
Association**
P.O. Box 1003
Providence, RI 02901

[Rhode Island] Parole Board
250 Benefit St.
Providence, RI 02903
401-277-3262

**[Rhode Island] Personnel
Administration, Office of**
289 Promenade St.
Providence, RI 02908
401-277-2160

**[Rhode Island] Planning,
Division of**
165 Melrose St.
Providence, RI 02907
401-277-2656

**[Rhode Island] Probation &
Parole, Division of**
1 Dorrance Plaza
Providence, RI 02903
401-277-3496

[Rhode Island] Professional Regulation, Division of
75 Davis St.
Providence, RI 02908
401-277-2827

[Rhode Island] Providence County
250 Benefit St.
Providence, RI 02903
401-277-3220

[Rhode Island] Public Defender, Department of
250 Benefit St.
Providence, RI 02903
401-277-3492

[Rhode Island] Public Utilities Commission
100 Orange St.
Providence, RI 02903
401-277-3500
800-341-1000

[Rhode Island] Purchases, Division of
301 Promenade St.
Providence, RI 02908
401-277-2321

[Rhode Island] Secretary of State
State House, Rm. 217
Providence, RI 02903
401-277-2357

[Rhode Island] Securities Division
233 Richmond St., Suite 232
Providence, RI 02903
401-277-3048

[Rhode Island] Senate
State House
Providence, RI 02903
401-277-2370
401-277-6896 (Judiciary)

[Rhode Island] Solid Waste Management Program
291 Promenade St.
Providence, RI 02908
401-277-2797

[Rhode Island] State Police
P.O. Box 185
North Scituate, RI 02857
401-647-3311

[Rhode Island] Supreme Court
250 Benefit St.
Providence, RI 02903
401-277-3272

[Rhode Island] Taxation, Division of
289 Promenade St.
Providence, RI 02908
401-277-3050

[Rhode Island] Transportation, Department of
State Office Bldg., Rm. 210
Providence, RI 02903
401-277-2481

[Rhode Island] Treasury Department
198 Dyer St.
Providence, RI 02903
401-277-2287

[Rhode Island] United States Bankruptcy Court
380 Westminster Mall
Providence, RI 02903
401-528-4477

[Rhode Island] United States District Court
119 Federal Bldg.
Providence, RI 02903
401-528-5100

[Rhode Island] Utilities Commission
100 Orange St.
Providence, RI 02903
401-277-2443

[Rhode Island] Vital Statistics, Division of
75 Davis St., Rm. 101
Providence, RI 02908
401-277-2811

[Rhode Island] Vocational Rehabilitation Services
40 Fountain St.
Providence, RI 02903
401-421-7005

[Rhode Island] Washington County
4800 Tower Hill Rd.
Wakefield, RI 02879
401-783-5441

[Rhode Island] Water Resources Board
265 Melrose St.
Providence, RI 02907
401-277-2217

[Rhode Island] Women, Advisory Commission on
220 Elmwood Ave.
Providence, RI 02907
401-457-1802

[Rhode Island] Workers' Compensation, Department of
610 Manton Ave.
Providence, RI 02909
401-277-0700

Rocky Mountain Mineral Law Foundation
7039 E. 18th Ave.
Denver, CO 80220
303-321-8100

Roscoe Pound Foundation
1050 31st St., NW
Wash. D.C. 20007
202-965-3500

Rothman & Co., Fred B.
10368 W. Centennial Rd.
Littleton, CO 80127
800-457-1986

Safeway Stores, Inc.
Oakland, CA 94660
415-891-3267

[Saipan] Commonwealth Trial Court
P.O. Box 307CK
Saipan, CM 96950
670-234-6401

SCRIBES
P.O. Box 7206

Wake Forest University School of
Law
Winston-Salem, NC 27109
919-761-5440

Shepard's/McGraw-Hill Inc.
420 N. Cascade Ave.
Colorado Springs, CO 80901
719-475-7230
800-525-2474

Sierra Club Legal Defense Fund
2044 Fillmore St.
San Francisco, CA 94115
415-567-6100

Soap & Detergent Association
475 Park Ave. S.
New York, NY 10016
212-725-1262

Society of Financial Examiners
5 W. Hargett St.
Raleigh, NC 27601
919-821-1435

Society of Forensic Toxicologists
1013 Three Mile Dr.
Grosse Pointe Park, MI 48230
313-884-4718

Society of Maritime Arbitrators
26 Broadway
New York, NY 10004
212-483-0616

**Society of Professional Benefit
Administrators**
2033 M St. NW, Suite 605
Wash, D.C. 20036
202-223-6413

**Society of Professionals in
Dispute Resolution**
1730 Rhode Island Ave., NW,
Suite 909
Wash. D.C. 20036
202-833-2188

Society of Real Estate Appraisers
225 N. Michigan Ave.
Chicago, IL 60601
312-819-2400
800-331-7732

Songwriters Guild of America
276 5th Ave.
New York, NY 10001
212-686-6820

**[South Carolina] Information &
Referral (State Government)**
803-734-1000

**[South Carolina] Aging,
Commission on**
400 Arbor Lake Dr.
Columbia, SC 29223
803-735-0210

**[South Carolina] Agriculture,
Department of**
1200 Senate St.
Columbia, SC 29201
803-734-2210
803-737-2080 (Weights & Measures)

**[South Carolina] Air Quality
Control, Bureau of**
2600 Bull St.
Columbia, SC 29201
803-734-4750

**[South Carolina] Appellate
Defense, Office of**
1122 Lady St., Suite 301
Columbia,SC 29201
803-734-1330

**[South Carolina] Archives &
History, Department of**
1430 Senate St., P.O. Box 11669
Columbia, SC 29211
803-734-8577

**[South Carolina] Attorney
General's Office**
P.O. Box 11549
Columbia, SC 29211
803-734-3970
803-734-3769 (Law Library)

**[South Carolina] Banking,
Commissioner of**
State Board of Financial Institutions
1026 Sumter St., Rm. 217
Columbia, SC 29201
803-734-1050

South Carolina Bar Association
950 Taylor St.
Columbia, SC 29201
803-799-6653

**[South Carolina] Bar Examiners,
Board of**
P.O. Box 11330

Columbia, SC 29211
803-734-1080

**[South Carolina] Better Business
Bureau**
1830 Bull St.
Columbia, SC 29201
803-254-2525

**[South Carolina] Child Support
Enforcement Division**
P.O. Box 1520
Columbia, SC 29202
803-737-9939

**[South Carolina] Code
Commissioner**
Legislative Council
P.O. Box 11417
Columbia, SC 29211
803-734-2145

**[South Carolina] Columbia Legal
Assistant Association**
P.O. Box 11634
Columbia, SC 29211

**[South Carolina] Comptroller
General**
Wade Hampton Office Bldg.,
Rm. 305
Columbia, SC 29201
803-734-2121

**[South Carolina] Consumer
Affairs, Department of**
P.O. Box 5757
Columbia, SC 29250
803-734-9452
800-922-1594

**[South Carolina] Corporations
Division**
P.O. Box 11350
Columbia, SC 29211
803-734-2158

**[South Carolina] Corrections,
Department of**
4444 Broad River Rd., P.O. Box
21787
Columbia, SC 29221
803-737-8555

**South Carolina Court
Administration**
P.O. Box 50447

Columbia, SC 29250
803-734-1800

[South Carolina] Court of Appeals
1224 Sumter St.
Columbia, SC 29211
803-734-1890

[South Carolina] Development Board, State
P.O. Box 927
Columbia, SC 29202
803-737-0400

[South Carolina] Economic Development Division
1201 Main St.
Columbia, SC 29201
803-734-1400

[South Carolina] Economic Opportunity, Division of
1205 Pendleton St.
Columbia, SC 29201
803-734-0662

[South Carolina] Education, Department of
1429 Senate St.
Columbia, SC 29201
803-734-8500

[South Carolina] Election Commission, State
P.O. Box 5987
Columbia, SC 29250
803-734-9060

[South Carolina] Emergency Preparedness Division
1429 Senate St.
Columbia, SC 29201
803-734-8020

[South Carolina] Employment Security Commission
1550 Gadsen St.
Columbia, SC 29202
803-737-2400

[South Carolina] Energy Research & Development Center
302 Seneca Rd.
Clemson, SC 29634
803-656-2267

[South Carolina] Environmental Quality Control, Department of
2600 Bull St.
Columbia, SC 29201
803-734-5360

[South Carolina] Governor, Office of
State House
Columbia, SC 29201
803-734-9818

[South Carolina] Grand Jury, State
P.O. Box 11508
Columbia, SC 29211
803-734-2350

[South Carolina] Greenville Association of Legal Assistants
P.O. Box 10207
Greenville, SC 29603

[South Carolina] Health & Environmental Control
2600 Bull St.
Columbia, SC 29201
803-734-5000

[South Carolina] Health & Human Services Finance Commission
P.O. Box 8206
Columbia, SC 29202
803-253-6100

[South Carolina] Higher Education, Commission on
1333 Main St., Suite 650
Columbia, SC 29201
803-253-6260

[South Carolina] Highways & Transportation, Department of
955 Park St.
Columbia, SC 29201
803-737-1302

[South Carolina] House of Representatives
State House, P.O. Box 11867
Columbia, SC 29211
803-734-2923

800-922-1539
803-734-3120 (Judiciary)

[South Carolina] Housing Authority, State
1710 Gervais St.
Columbia, SC 29201
803-734-8831

South Carolina Human Affairs Commission
P.O. Drawer 11009
Columbia, SC 29211
803-737-6570

[South Carolina] Insurance Commission
1612 Marion St., P.O. Box 100105
Columbia, SC 29202
803-737-6117

South Carolina Labor Department
3600 Forest Dr., P.O. Box 11329
Columbia, SC 29211
803-734-9600

[South Carolina] Land Resources Conservation Commission
2221 Devine St., Suite 222
Columbia, SC 29205
803-734-9100

[South Carolina] Law Enforcement Division, State
P.O. Box 21398
Columbia, SC 29221
803-734-9000

[South Carolina] Legislative Information Systems
1105 Pendleton St.
Columbia, SC 29201
803-734-2923
800-922-1539
800-922-2221

[South Carolina] Lieutenant Governor, Office of
State House
Columbia, SC 29201
803-734-2080

[South Carolina] Medical Examiners, State Board of
P.O. Box 12245
Columbia, SC 29201
803-734-8901

[South Carolina] Mental Health, Department of
P.O. Box 485
Columbia, SC 29202
803-734-7766

[South Carolina] Mining & Reclamation, Division of
2221 Devine St.
Columbia, SC 29205
803-734-9100

[South Carolina] Occupational Safety & Health
3600 Forest Dr.
Columbia, SC 29204
803-734-9643

[South Carolina] Probation, Parole & Pardon Services, Department of
P.O. Box 50666
Columbia, SC 29201
803-734-9244

[South Carolina] Public Safety Program, Division of
1205 Pendleton St.
Columbia, SC 29201
803-734-0425

[South Carolina] Public Service Commission
P.O. Drawer 11649
Columbia, SC 29211
803-737-5100
800-922-1531

[South Carolina] Radiological Health, Bureau of
2600 Bull St.
Columbia, SC 29201
803-734-4634

[South Carolina] Real Estate Commission
1201 Main St., Suite 201
Columbia, SC 29201
803-734-9480

[South Carolina] Retirement System
P.O. Box 11960
Columbia, SC 29211
803-734-1660

[South Carolina] Richland County
P.O. Box 1781
Columbia, SC 29202
803-748-4684

[South Carolina] Secretary of State
P.O. Box 11350
Columbia, SC 29211
803-734-2170

[South Carolina] Securities Division
1205 Pendleton St., # 501
Columbia, SC 29201
803-734-1087

[South Carolina] Senate
State House, P.O. Box 142
Columbia, SC 29202
803-734-2923
803-734-2735 (Judiciary)

[South Carolina] Social Services, Department of
P.O. Box 1520
Columbia, SC 29202
803-734-6179

[South Carolina] Solid & Hazardous Waste Management, Bureau of
2600 Bull St.
Columbia, SC 29201
803-734-5200

[South Carolina] Supreme Court
1231 Gervais St.
Columbia, SC 29211
803-734-1080

[South Carolina] Tax Commission
301 Gervais St.
Columbia, SC 29201
803-737-9820

[South Carolina] Treasurer's Office, State
P.O. Box 11778
Columbia, SC 29211
803-734-2101

[South Carolina] Unemployment Insurance Program
1550 Gadsen St., Rm. 411

Columbia, SC 29202
803-737-2787

[South Carolina] Uniform Commercial Code Division
P.O. Box 11350
Columbia, SC 29201
803-734-2175

[South Carolina] United States Bankruptcy Court
P.O. Box 1448
Columbia, SC 29202
803-765-5211

[South Carolina] United States District Court
P.O. Box 867
Columbia, SC 29202
803-765-5816

[South Carolina] Veterans' Affairs, Department of
1205 Pendleton St., Rm. 227
Columbia, SC 29201
803-734-0200

[South Carolina] Victim's Compensation Fund
P.O. Box 210009
Columbia, SC 29221
803-734-9450
800-521-6576

[South Carolina] Vital Records & Public Health Statistics, Office of
2600 Bull St.
Columbia, SC 29201
803-734-4830

[South Carolina] Vocational Rehabilitation Department
P.O. Box 15
West Columbia, SC 29171
803-734-4300

[South Carolina] Water Resources Commission
1201 Main St., Suite 1100
Columbia, SC 29201
803-734-0800

[South Carolina] Women, Commission on
2221 Devine St., Suite 408

Columbia, SC 29205
803-734-9144

[South Carolina] Worker's Compensation Commission
1612 Marion St., P.O. Box 1715
Columbia, SC 29202
803-737-5700
800-521-6576

[South Carolina] Youth Services, Department of
NBSC Center, 1122 Lady St.,
Suite 500
Columbia, SC 29201
803-734-1440

[South Dakota] Information & Referral (State Government)
605-773-3011

[South Dakota] Administration, Bureau of
500 E. Capitol Ave.
Pierre, SD 57501
605-773-3688

[South Dakota] Adult Services & Aging, Office of
700 Governors Dr.
Pierre, SD 57501
605-773-3656

[South Dakota] Agriculture, Department of
445 E. Capitol Ave.
Anderson Bldg.
Pierre, SD 57501
605-773-3375

[South Dakota] Alternative Energy, Division of
217½ W. Missouri Ave.
Pierre, SD 57501
605-773-3603

[South Dakota] Archivist, State
800 Governor's Dr.
Pierre, SD 57501
605-773-3616

[South Dakota] Attorney General, Office of
500 E. Capitol Ave.
Pierre, SD 57501
605-773-3215

[South Dakota] Banking & Finance, Director of
State Capitol Bldg.
Pierre, SD 57501
605-773-2236

South Dakota Bar Association
222 E. Capitol
Pierre, SD 57501
605-224-7554

[South Dakota] Bar Examiners, Board of
P.O. Box 1037
Pierre, SD 57501
605-773-4898

[South Dakota] Charities & Corrections, Board of
523 E. Capitol Ave., Suite 405
Pierre, SD 57501
605-773-3478

[South Dakota] Child Protection Services
700 Governors Dr.
Pierre, SD 57501
605-773-3227

[South Dakota] Child Support Enforcement, Office of
700 Governors Dr.
Pierre, SD 57501
605-773-3641

[South Dakota] Code Counsel
500 E. Capitol
Pierre, SD 57501
605-773-3251

[South Dakota] Commerce & Regulation, Department of
910 E. Sioux Ave.
Pierre, SD 57501
605-773-3178

South Dakota Consumer Affairs Division
State Capitol Bldg.
Pierre, SD 57501
605-773-4400

[South Dakota] Corporations Division
500 E. Capitol Ave.

Pierre, SD 57501
605-773-4845

[South Dakota] Court Services Department
Supreme Court, State Capitol Bldg.
Pierre, SD 57501
605-773-4871

[South Dakota] Education, Division of
700 Governors Dr.
Pierre, SD 57501
605-773-3243

[South Dakota] Emergency & Disaster Services, Division of
500 E. Capitol Ave.
Pierre, SD 57501
605-773-3231

[South Dakota] Finance & Management Bureau
State Capitol Bldg., 2nd Fl.
Pierre, SD 57501
605-773-3411

[South Dakota] Game, Fish & Parks, Department of
445 E. Capitol St.
Pierre, SD 57501
605-773-3718

[South Dakota] Governor, Office of
500 E. Capitol Ave.
Pierre, SD 57501
605-773-3212

[South Dakota] Health, Department of
523 E. Capitol Ave.
Pierre, SD 57501
605-773-3361

[South Dakota] Health Policy & Statistics, Center for
Vital Records
523 E. Capitol
Pierre, SD 57501
605-773-3355

[South Dakota] Highway Patrol
300 N. Nicollet Ave.
Pierre, SD 57501
605-773-4094

[South Dakota] House of Representatives
State Capitol
Pierre, SD 57501
605-734-2060
605-773-4498 (Public Information)
605-773-3011 (Judiciary)

[South Dakota] Housing Development Authority
P.O. Box 1237
Pierre, SD 57501
605-773-3181

[South Dakota] Hughes County
104 E. Capitol Ave.
Pierre, SD 57501
605-773-3713

[South Dakota] Human Rights, Division of
500 E. Capitol
Pierre, SD 57501
605-773-4493

[South Dakota] Insurance, Director of
910 E. Sioux Ave.
Pierre, SD 57501
605-773-3563

[South Dakota] Labor & Management
700 Governors Dr.
Pierre, SD 57501
605-773-3681

[South Dakota] Legislative Audit, Department of
435 S. Chapelle St.
Pierre, SD 57501
605-773-3595

[South Dakota] Legislative Research Council
500 E. Capitol
Pierre, SD 57501
605-773-3251

[South Dakota] Lieutenant Governor, Office of
500 E. Capitol Ave.
Pierre, SD 57501
605-773-3661

[South Dakota] Minerals & Mining, Office of
523 E. Capitol Ave.
Pierre, SD 57501
605-773-4201

[South Dakota] Motor Vehicles, Division of
118 W. Capitol Ave.
Pierre, SD 57501
605-773-3541

[South Dakota] Pardons & Paroles, Board of
Box 911
Sioux Falls, SD 57117
605-339-6780

[South Dakota] Personnel, Bureau of
500 E. Capitol
Pierre, SD 57501
605-773-3148

[South Dakota] Professional & Occupational Licensing, Division of
910 E. Sioux Ave.
Pierre, SD 57501
605-773-3178

[South Dakota] Public Utilities Commission
500 E. Capitol Ave.
Pierre, SD 57501
605-773-3201

[South Dakota] Purchasing & Printing
523 E. Capitol Ave.
Pierre, SD 57501
605-773-3405

[South Dakota] Real Estate Commission
212 E. Capitol Ave.
Pierre, SD 57501
605-773-3600

[South Dakota] Regents, State Board of
700 Governors Dr.
Pierre, SD 57501
605-773-3455

[South Dakota] Rehabilitation Services, Division of
700 E. Illinois St.
Pierre, SD 57501
605-773-3195

[South Dakota] Revenue, Department of
700 Governors Dr.
Pierre, SD 57501
605-773-5131

[South Dakota] Secretary of State
500 E. Capitol Ave., 2nd Fl.
Pierre, SD 57501
605-773-3537

[South Dakota] Securities, Division of
910 E. Sioux Ave.
Pierre, SD 57501
605-773-4823

[South Dakota] Senate
State Capitol
Pierre, SD 57501
605-734-2060
605-773-4498 (Public Information)
605-773-3011 (Judiciary)

[South Dakota] Social Services, Department of
700 Governors Dr.
Pierre, SD 57501
605-773-3165

[South Dakota] Supreme Court
500 E. Capitol
Pierre, SD 57501
605-773-3511
605-773-4898 (Law Library)

[South Dakota] Transportation, Department of
700 Broadway Ave. E.
Pierre, SD 57501
605-773-3265

[South Dakota] Treasurer, Office of
500 E. Capitol Ave., 2nd Fl. Annex
Pierre, SD 57501
605-773-3378

[South Dakota] Unemployment Insurance Division
420 S. Roosevelt St.
Aberdeen, SD 57401
605-622-2452

South Dakota, Unified Judicial System of
State Court Administrator's Office
500 E. Capitol Ave.
Pierre, SD 57501
605-773-3474

[South Dakota] United States Bankruptcy Court
P.O. Box 5060
Sioux Falls, SD 57117
605-330-4541

[South Dakota] United States District Court
400 S. Phillips Ave.
Sioux Falls, SD 57102
605-338-5566

[South Dakota] Water & Natural Resources, Department of
523 E. Capitol Ave.
Pierre, SD 57501
605-773-3151

Southern Building Code Congress, International
900 Montclair Rd.
Birmingham, AL 35213
205-591-1853

Southwestern Legal Foundation
P.O. Box 830707
Richardson, TX 75083
214-690-2377

Special Libraries Association
1700 18th St., NW
Wash. D.C. 20009
202-234-4700

Sports Lawyers Association
P.O. Box 5684
Lakeland, FL 33807
813-646-5091

State Justice Institute
120 S. Fairfax St.
Alexandria, VA 22314
703-684-6100

Tax Executives Institute
1001 Pennsylvania Ave., NW
Wash. D.C. 20004
202-638-5601

Tax Foundation
470 L'Enfant Plaza SW
Wash. D.C. 20024
202-863-5454

[Tennessee] Information & Referral (State Government)
615-741-3011

[Tennessee] Information Center (Federal Government)
Chattanooga 615-265-8231
Memphis 901-521-3285
Nashville 615-242-5056

[Tennessee] Aging, Commission on
706 Church St., Suite 201
Nashville, TN 37219
615-741-2056

[Tennessee] Agriculture, Department of
P.O. Box 40627
Nashville, TN 37204
615-360-0100

[Tennessee] Air Pollution Control Division
701 Broadway
Nashville, TN 37203
615-741-3931

[Tennessee] Alcoholic Beverage Commission
226 Capitol Blvd.
Nashville, TN 37219
615-741-1602

[Tennessee] Antitrust & Consumer Protection Division
450 James Robertson Pkwy.
Nashville, TN 37219
615-741-2672

[Tennessee] Attorney General, Office of
450 James Robertson Pkwy.
Nashville, TN 37219
615-741-3491

Tennessee Bar Association
3622 W. End Ave.
Nashville, TN 37205
615-383-7421

[Tennessee] Bar Examiners, Board of
401 Church St.
Nashville, TN 37219
615-741-3234

[Tennessee] Better Business Bureau
1 Commerce St.
Nashville, TN 37239
615-254-5872
901-272-9641 (Memphis)

[Tennessee] Child Support Services
400 Deaderick St., 12th Fl.
Nashville, TN 37219
615-741-1820

Tennessee Code Committee
G-10 War Memorial Bldg.
Nashville, TN 37219
615-741-3056

[Tennessee] Conservation, Department of
701 Broadway
Nashville, TN 37203
615-742-6749

[Tennessee] Consumer Affairs, Division of
500 James Robertson Pkwy.
Nashville, TN 37219
615-714-4737

[Tennessee] Corrections, Department of
320 6th Ave. North
Nashville, TN 37219
615-741-2071

[Tennessee] East Tennessee Paralegal Association
450 Maclellan Bldg.
Chattanooga, TN 37402

**[Tennessee] Economic &
Community Commission,
Department of**
320 6th Ave. North, 8th Fl.
Nashville, TN 37219
615-741-1888

**[Tennessee] Education,
Department of**
436 6th Ave. North
Nashville, TN 37219
615-741-2731

**[Tennessee] Emergency
Management Agency**
3041 Sidco Dr.
Nashville, TN 37204
615-252-3311

**[Tennessee] Employment
Security, Department of**
500 James Robertson Pkwy., 12 Fl.
Nashville, TN 37219
615-741-2131

**[Tennessee] Environment,
Bureau of**
159th Ave. North
Terra Bldg., 1st Fl.
Nashville, TN 37219
615-741-3657

**[Tennessee] Finance & Admin-
istration, Department of**
Andrew Jackson State Office Bldg.
Nashville, TN 37219
615-741-3478

**[Tennessee] Financial Institu-
tions, Commissioner of**
John Sevier Bldg., 4th Fl.
Nashville, TN 37219
615-741-2236

**[Tennessee] General Services,
Department of**
503 5th Ave. North
Nashville, TN 37219
615-741-2081

[Tennessee] Governor, Office of
State Capitol Bldg.
Nashville,TN 37204
615-741-2001

**[Tennessee] Health &
Environment, Department of**
436 6th Ave. North, Rm. 347
Nashville, TN 37219
615-741-3111

**[Tennessee] Higher Education
Commission**
Parkway Towers, Suite 1900
Nashville, TN 37219
615-741-3605

**[Tennessee] House of
Representatives**
State Capitol
Nashville, TN 37219
615-741-3511
615-741-1351 (Judiciary)

**[Tennessee] Housing
Development Agency**
700 Land Mark Center
Nashville, TN 37219
615-741-2473

**Tennessee Human Rights
Commission**
226 Capitol Blvd.
Nashville, TN 37219
615-741-5825

**[Tennessee] Human Services,
Department of**
400 Deaderick St.
Nashville, TN 37219
615-741-5124

**[Tennessee] Insurance,
Commissioner of**
500 James Robertson Pkwy.
Nashville, TN 37219
615-741-2241
800-342-4029

[Tennessee] Knox County
P.O. Box 1566
Knoxville, TN 37901
615-521-2385

**[Tennessee] Labor,
Department of**
501 Union Bldg.
Nashville, TN 37219
615-741-2582

[Tennessee] Law Library, State
Supreme Court Bldg.
Nashville, TN 37219
615-741-2016

**[Tennessee] Legislative
Administration**
G-11 War Memorial Bldg.
Nashville, TN 37219
615-741-3569

**[Tennessee] Legislative Services,
Office of**
State Capitol, Rm. G-3
Nashville, TN 37219
615-741-3511

**[Tennessee] Library & Archives,
State**
403 7th Ave. North
Nashville,TN 37219
615-741-2764

**[Tennessee] Lieutenant
Governor, Office of**
Legislative Plaza, Suite 1
Nashville, TN 37219
615-741-2368

**[Tennessee] Memphis Bar
Association Law Library**
140 Adams Ave., Rm. 315
Memphis, TN 38103
901-527-7041

[Tennessee] Memphis City Hall
125 N. Main St.
Memphis, TN 38103
901-576-6500

**[Tennessee] Memphis Paralegal
Association**
P.O. Box 3646
Memphis, TN 38173

**[Tennessee] Mental Health &
Mental Retardation,
Department of**
706 Church St.
Nashville, TN 37219
615-741-3107

**[Tennessee] Middle Tennessee
Paralegal Association**
P.O. Box 198006
Nashville, TN 37219

[Tennessee] Mid-South Association of Legal Assistants
P.O. Box 3646
Memphis, TN 38173

[Tennessee] Mines, Division of
Queener Rd.
Caryville, TN 37714
615-562-4914

[Tennessee] Motor Vehicle Division
500 Deaderick St.
Nashville, TN 37242
615-741-3381

[Tennessee] Nashville City Hall
110 Public Sq.
Nashville, TN 37201
615-259-5620

[Tennessee] Occupational Safety & Health, Division of
501 Union Blvd., 3rd Fl.
Nashville, TN 37219
615-741-2793

[Tennessee] Paroles, Board of
404 James Robertson Parkway
Nashville, TN 37219
615-741-1673

[Tennessee] Personnel, Department of
505 Deaderick St.
Nashville, TN 37219
615-741-2958

[Tennessee] Planning Office
500 Charlotte Ave.
Nashville, TN 37219
615-741-1676

[Tennessee] Probation, Division of
320 6th Ave. North
Nashville, TN 37219
615-741-3141

[Tennessee] Public Service Commission
460 James Robertson Pkwy.
Nashville, TN 37219
615-741-2904
800-342-8359

[Tennessee] Public Works Division
910 8th Ave. North
Nashville, TN 37208
615-741-1886

[Tennessee] Purchasing, Division of
503 5th Ave. North, Rm. C2-211
Nashville, TN 37219
615-741-1035

[Tennessee] Real Estate Commission
500 James Robertson Pkwy.,
Suite 180
Nashville, TN 37219
615-741-2273

[Tennessee] Regulatory Boards
500 James Robertson Pkwy.
Nashville,TN 37219
615-741-3449

[Tennessee] Rehabilitation Services, Commissioner of
400 Deaderick St.
Nashville, TN 37248
615-741-2019

[Tennessee] Retirement, Division of
500 Deaderick St.
Andrew Jackson Bldg., 13th Fl.
Nashville, TN 37219
615-741-7063

[Tennessee] Revenue, Department of
Andrew Jackson Bldg., Suite 1200
Nashville, TN 37219
615-741-2461

[Tennessee] Safety, Department of
1226 Andrew Jackson State Office
Bldg.
Nashville, TN 37219
615-251-5166

[Tennessee] Secretary of State
State Capitol Bldg., 1st Fl.
Nashville, TN 37219
615-741-2816

[Tennessee] Securities Division
500 James Robertson Pkwy., 6th Fl.

Nashville, TN 37219
615-741-2947

[Tennessee] Senate
State Capitol
Nashville, TN 37219
615-741-3511
615-741-7821 (Judiciary)

[Tennessee] Shelby County
160 N. Mid-America Mall
Memphis, TN 38103
901-576-4244

[Tennessee] Solid Waste Management, Division of
701 Broadway
Nashville, TN 37203
615-741-3424

[Tennessee] Standards Administration
Weights & Measures
P.O. Box 40627
Nashville, TN 37204
615-360-0109

[Tennessee] State Police
1150 Foster Ave.
Nashville, TN 37210
615-741-2102

[Tennessee] Supreme Court
401 7th Ave., North
Supreme Court Bldg., Rm. 100
Nashville, TN 37219
615-741-2681

[Tennessee] Transportation, Department of
James K. Polk Bldg., Suite 700
Nashville, TN 37219
615-741-2848

[Tennessee] Treasury, Comptroller of the
State Capitol
Nashville, TN 37219
615-741-2501

[Tennessee] Treasury, Department of the
State Capitol Bldg., 1st Fl.
Nashville, TN 37219
615-741-2956

[Tennessee] United States Bankruptcy Court
Eastern Tennessee
P.O. Box 1189
Chattanooga, TN 37401
615-742-5163

[Tennessee] United States Bankruptcy Court
Middle Tennessee
701 Broadway, No. 207
Nashville, TN 37203
615-736-5590

[Tennessee] United States Bankruptcy Court
Western Tennessee
969 Madison Ave.
Memphis, TN 38104
901-534-3202

[Tennessee] United States District Court
Eastern District
P.O. Box 2348
Knoxville, TN 37901
615-673-4227

[Tennessee] United States District Court
Middle District
801 Broadway
Nashville, TN 37203
615-736-5728

[Tennessee] United States District Court
Western District
167 N. Main St.
Memphis, TN 38103
901-521-3317

Tennessee Vital Records
Cordell Hull Bldg.
Nashville, TN 37219
615-741-1763
800-423-1901

[Tennessee] Water Management, Division of
150 9th Ave. North, 1st Fl.
Nashville, TN 37203
615-741-6610

[Tennessee] Worker's Compensation Division
501 Union St.

Nashville, TN 37219
615-741-2395

Texaco Refining & Marketing
P.O. Box 2000
Bellaire, TX 77402
713-432-2255

[Texas] Information & Referral (State Government)
512-463-4630

[Texas] Information Center (Federal Government)
Austin 513-472-5494
Dallas 214-767-8585
Ft. Worth 817-334-3624
Houston 713-653-3025
San Antonio 512-224-4471

Texas Adult Probation Commission
P.O. Box 12427, Capitol Station
Austin, TX 78711
512-834-8188

[Texas] Aging, Department on
P.O. Box 12786
Austin, TX 78711
512-444-2727
800-252-9240

[Texas] Agriculture, Department of
P.O. Box 12847
Austin, TX 78711
512-463-7446

[Texas] Alamo Area Professional Legal Assistants
P.O. Box 524
San Antonio, TX 78292

[Texas] Alcohol & Drug Abuse, Commission on
1705 Guadalupe
Austin, TX 78701
512-463-5510

Texas Alcoholic Beverage Commission
P.O. Box 13127
Austin, TX 78711
512-458-2500

[Texas] Archives, State
P.O. Box 12927
Austin, TX 78711
512-463-5480

[Texas] Attorney General's Department
Supreme Court Bldg.
P.O. Box 12548
Austin, TX 78711
512-463-2100

[Texas] Auditor's Office, State
409 John H. Reagan State Office Bldg.
P.O. Box 12067
Austin, TX 78711
512-463-5776

[Texas] Austin City Hall
124 W. 8th St.
Austin, TX 78701
512-499-2000

[Texas] Banking Commissioner
2601 N. Lamar
Austin, TX 78705
512-479-1200

Texas Bar Association
1414 Colorado
P.O. Box 12487
Austin, TX 78701
512-475-1463

[Texas] Bar Examiners, Board of
P.O. Box 13486
Austin, TX 78711
512-463-1621

[Texas] Better Business Bureau
1005 American Plaza
Austin, TX 78701
512-476-1616
214-220-2000 (Dallas)
713-868-9500 (Houston)

[Texas] Brazoria County Law Library
315-A Courthouse
Angleton, TX 77515
409-849-5711

[Texas] Capital Area Paralegal Association
P.O. Box 200343
Austin, TX 78720

[Texas] Child Support Enforcement Division
P.O. Box 12548
Austin, TX 78711
512-463-2181

[Texas] Coastal Authority
1200 Smith St., Suite 2260
Houston, TX 77002
713-658-9020

**[Texas] Collin County Law
Library**
210 S. McDonald Courthouse
McKinney, TX 75069
214-548-4255

**[Texas] Commerce,
Department of**
816 Congress, 12th Fl.
P.O. Box 12728
Austin, TX 78711
512-472-5059

[Texas] Common Law Library
306 W. Wall St., Suite 320
Midland, TX 79701
915-683-5492

**[Texas] Community Affairs,
Department of**
8317 Cross Park Dr.
Austin, TX 78711
512-834-6000

**[Texas] Comptroller of Public
Accounts**
Lyndon B. Johnson State Office
Bldg.
Austin, TX 78774
512-463-4000

**[Texas] Consumer Credit
Commissioner**
2601 N. Lamar
Austin, TX 78705
512-479-1280

**[Texas] Consumer Protection
Division**
P.O. Box 12548
Austin, TX 78711
512-463-2070
214-630-6300 (Dallas)

**[Texas] Corrections,
Department of**
P.O. Box 99
Huntsville, TX 77342
409-295-6371

[Texas] Counties, Association of
P.O. Box 2131

Austin, TX 78768
512-478-8753

**[Texas] Court Administration,
State Office of**
P.O. Box 12066
Austin, TX 78711
512-463-1625

[Texas] Court of Appeals
First District
1307 San Jacinto, 10th Fl.
Houston, TX 77002
713-655-2700

[Texas] Court of Appeals
Second District
100 W. Weatherford
Fort Worth, TX 76196
817-334-1900

[Texas] Court of Appeals
Third District
14th & Colorado
P.O. Box 12547
Austin, TX 78711
512-463-1733

[Texas] Court of Appeals
Fourth District
500 Bexar County Courthouse
San Antonio, TX 78205
512-220-2635

[Texas] Court of Appeals
Fifth District
Dallas County Government Center,
2d Fl.
Dallas, TX 75202
214-653-7382

[Texas] Court of Appeals
Sixth District
100 N. State Line Ave.
Texarkana, TX 75501
214-798-3046

[Texas] Court of Appeals
Seventh District
P.O. Box 9540
Amarillo, TX 79105
806-379-2470

[Texas] Court of Appeals
Eighth District
500 City-County Bldg.
El Paso, TX 79901
915-546-2240

[Texas] Court of Appeals
Ninth District
1001 Pearl, Suite 330
Beaumont, TX 77701
409-835-8402

[Texas] Court of Appeals
Tenth District
P.O. Box 1606
Waco, TX 76703
817-757-5200

[Texas] Court of Appeals
Eleventh District
100 W. Main St.
P.O. Box 271
Eastland, TX 76448
817-629-2638

[Texas] Court of Appeals
Twelfth District
306 Smith County Courthouse
Tyler, TX 75702
214-593-8471

[Texas] Court of Appeals
Thirteenth District
Nueces County Courthouse, 10th Fl.
Corpus Christi, TX 78401
512-888-0416

[Texas] Court of Appeals
Fourteenth District
1307 San Jacinto, 11th Fl.
Houston, TX 77002
713-655-2800

**[Texas] Court of Criminal
Appeals**
Supreme Court Bldg.
P.O. Box 12308
Austin, TX 78711
512-463-1551

**[Texas] Court Reporters
Certification Board**
510 S. Congress Ave., Suite 312
Austin, TX 78711
512-463-1630

**[Texas] Criminal Justice
Coordinating Council**
Sam Houston State Office Bldg.
P.O. Box 13332
Austin, TX 78711
512-463-1810

[Texas] Dallas Association of Legal Assistants
P.O. Box 2938
Dallas, TX 75221

[Texas] Dallas Bar Association
2101 Ross Ave.
Dallas, TX 75201
214-969-7066

[Texas] Dallas City Hall
1500 Marilla St.
Dallas, TX 75201
214-670-3011

[Texas] Dallas County
500 Main St.
Dallas, TX 75202
214-653-7131

[Texas] Dallas County Law Library
600 Commerce St., 2nd Fl.
Dallas, TX 75202
214-653-7481

[Texas] Depository Board, State
P.O. Box 12608
Austin, TX 78711
512-463-6000

Texas Education Agency
1701 N. Congress Ave.
Austin, TX 78701
512-463-9734

[Texas] Education, State Board of
1701 N. Congress Ave.
Austin, TX 78701
512-463-9007

[Texas] El Paso Association of Legal Assistants
P.O. Box 983
El Paso, TX 79946

[Texas] El Paso City Hall
2 Civic Center Plaza
El Paso, TX 79901
915-541-4000

[Texas] El Paso County Law Library
500 San Antonio St.
El Paso, TX 79901
915-546-2245

[Texas] Emergency Management, Division of
5805 N. Lamar Blvd.

P.O. Box 4087
Austin, TX 78773
512-465-2138

Texas Employment Commission
Congress Ave. & 15th St.
Austin, TX 78778
512-463-2222

[Texas] Energy Research & Policy Analysis
201 E. 14th St.
Austin, TX 78711
512-463-2198

[Texas] Environmental Protection Division
1124 S. 1H-35, 2nd Fl.
Austin, TX 78704
512-463-2012

[Texas] Facilities Construction & Space Management Division
1711 San Jacinto Blvd.
Austin, TX 78701
512-463-3214

[Texas] Finance Commission, State
2601 N. Lamar
Austin, TX 78705
512-479-1200

[Texas] Fort Worth City Hall
1000 Throckmorton St.
Fort Worth, TX 76102
817-870-6000

[Texas] Fort Worth Paralegal Association
P.O. Box 17021
Fort Worth, TX 76102

[Texas] General Land Office
837 Stephen F. Austin State Office Bldg.
Austin, TX 78701
512-463-5001

[Texas] Governor's Office
State Capitol, Rm. 200
Austin, TX 78701
512-463-2000

[Texas] Harris County Law Library
1019 Congress, 17th Fl.
Houston, TX 77002
713-221-5183

Texas Health, Department of
1100 W. 49th St.
Austin, TX 78756
512-458-7111

[Texas] Higher Education Coordinating Board
200 E. Riverside Dr.
Austin, TX 78704
512-462-6400

[Texas] Highways & Public Transportation, State Department of
11th & Brazos Streets
Austin, TX 78701
512-463-8585

[Texas] House of Representatives
State Capitol, Rm. 241
P.O. Box 2910
Austin, TX 78769
512-463-1252
512-463-0720 (Judiciary)

[Texas] Houston Bar Association
707 Travis St., Suite 1300
Houston, TX 77002
713-222-1441

[Texas] Houston City Hall
901 Bagby St.
Houston, TX 77002
713-247-1000

[Texas] Houston Legal Assistants Association
P.O. Box 52241
Houston, TX 77052

[Texas] Human Rights, State Commission on
8100 Cameron Rd., #525
P.O. Box 13493
Austin, TX 78711
512-837-8534

[Texas] Human Services, Department of
701 W. 51st St.
P.O. Box 2960
Austin, TX 78769
512-450-3011

Texas Indian Commission
4800 N. Lamar, #201
P.O. Box 12030

Austin, TX 78711
512-458-1203

[Texas] Industrial Accident Board
200 E. Riverside Dr.
Austin, TX 78704
512-448-7960

[Texas] Insurance, Commissioner of
1110 San Jacinto Blvd.
Austin, TX 78701
512-463-6501
800-252-3438

[Texas] Judicial Conduct, Commission on
400 W. 14th St.
P.O. Box 12265
Austin, TX 78711
512-463-5533

Texas Judicial Council
P.O. Box 12066
Austin, TX 78711
512-463-1625

[Texas] Juvenile Probation Commission
P.O. Box 13547
Austin, TX 78711
512-443-2001

[Texas] Labor & Standards, Department of
Ernest O. Thompson State Office Bldg.
P.O. Box 12157
Austin, TX 78711
512-463-5520

Texas Law Book Co.
427 N. Milam
Seguin, TX 78155
1-800-55-BOOKS

[Texas] Law Examiners, State Board of
P.O. Box 13486
Austin, TX 78711
512-463-1621

[Texas] Law Library, State
Supreme Court Bldg., B107
P.O. Box 12367
Austin, TX 78711
512-463-1722

Texas Legal Assistant Division
State Bar of Texas
P.O. Box 12487
Austin, TX 78711

[Texas] Legal Assistants Association/Permian Basin
P.O. Box 1540
Midland, TX 79702

[Texas] Legal Specialization, Board of
P.O. Box 12487
Austin, TX 78711
512-463-1454

[Texas] Legislative Reference Library
P.O. Box 12488
Austin, TX 78711
512-463-1252

Texas Legislative Service
303 W. 12th
Austin, TX 78767
512-476-7596

[Texas] Lieutenant Governor's Office
State Capitol, Rm. 219
P.O. Box 12068
Austin, TX 78711
412-463-0005

[Texas] Medical Examiners, State Board of
1101 Camino La Costa, #201
P.O. Box 13562
Austin, TX 78711
512-452-1078

Texas Motor Vehicle Commission
815 Brazos
P.O. Box 2293
Austin, TX 78768
512-476-3587

[Texas] Northeast Texas Association of Legal Assistants
P.O. Box 1869
Longview, TX 75606

[Texas] Nueces County Association of Legal Assistants
P.O. Box 3474
Corpus Christi, TX 78404

[Texas] Occupational Safety Division
1100 W. 49th St.
Austin, TX 78756
512-458-7287

[Texas] Oil & Gas Division
1701 N. Congress Ave.
Austin, TX 78701
512-463-6893

Texas Panhandle Association of Legal Assistants
P.O. Box 9158
Amarillo, TX 79105

[Texas] Pardons & Paroles, Board of
P.O. Box 13401
Austin, TX 78711
512-459-2700

Texas Parks & Wildlife Commission
4200 Smith School Rd.
Austin, TX 78744
512-389-4800

[Texas] Pension Review Board, State
18th & Brazos
P.O. Box 13498
Austin, TX 78711
512-463-1736

[Texas] Petroleum & Minerals Development Division
1700 N. Congress Ave.
Austin, TX 78701
512-463-5022

Texas Planning Council for Developmental Disabilities
118 E. Riverside
Austin, TX 78704
512-445-8867

[Texas] Planning Office
201 E. 14th St.
Austin, TX 78701
512-463-1778

[Texas] Property Tax Board, State
P.O. Box 15900
Austin, TX 78761
512-834-4901

[Texas] Prosecuting Attorney, State
Supreme Court Bldg.

P.O. Box 12405
Austin, TX 78711
512-463-1660

Texas Public Employees Association
512 E. 11th
Austin, TX 787111
512-476-2691

Texas Public Finance Authority
P.O. Box 12906
Austin, TX 78711
512-463-5544

[Texas] Public Safety, Department of
5805 N. Lamar Blvd.
Ausitn, TX 78773
512-465-2000

[Texas] Public Utility Commission
7800 Shoal Creek Blvd., Suite 400N
Austin, TX 78757
512-458-0100

[Texas] Purchasing & General Services Commission, State
P.O. Box 13047
Austin, TX 78711
512-463-3446

Texas, Railroad Commission of
P.O. Box 12967
Austin, TX 78711
512-463-7288

Texas, Real Estate Commission of
P.O. Box 12188
Austin, TX 78711
512-459-6544

Texas Rehabilitation Commission
4900 N. Lamar
Austin, TX 78751
512-445-8100

[Texas] San Antonio City Hall
Military Plaza
San Antonio, TX 78205
512-299-7011

[Texas] Savings & Loan Department of
2601 N. Lamar, Suite 201

Austin, TX 78705
512-479-1250

[Texas] Secretary of State
Capitol Bldg., Rm. 127
Austin, TX 78711
512-463-5701

[Texas] Securities Commissioner
P.O. Box 13167
Ausitn, TX 78711
512-474-2233

[Texas] Senate
State Capitol
Austin, TX 78711
512-463-1252
512-463-0122 (Jurisprudence)

[Texas] Soil & Water Conservation Board, State
P.O. Box 658
Temple, TX 76503
817-773-2250

[Texas] Solid Waste Management, Division of
1100 W. 49th. St.
Austin, TX 78756
512-458-7271

[Texas] Southeast Texas Association of Legal Assistants
P.O. Box 813
Beaumont, TX 77704

[Texas] State-Federal Relations, Office of
600 Maryland Ave., SW, Suite 255
Wash. D.C. 20024
202-488-3927

[Texas] Sunset Advisory Commission
P.O. Box 13066
Austin, TX 78711
512-463-1300

Texas, Supreme Court of
P.O. Box 12248
Austin, TX 78711
512-463-1312

[Texas] Tarrant County
100 W. Weatherford
Fort Worth, TX 76196
817-334-1195

[Texas] Tarrant County Law Library
420 County Courthouse
Ft. Worth TX 76196
817-334-1481

[Texas] Travis County
1000 Guadalupe St.
Austin, TX 78701
512-473-9188

[Texas] Travis County Law Library
P.O. Box 1748
Austin, TX 78701
512-473-9519

[Texas] Treasury Department, State
P.O. Box 12608
Austin, TX 78711
512-463-6000

Texas Turnpike Authority
P.O. Box 190369
Dallas, TX 75219
214-522-6200

[Texas] Tyler Area Association of Legal Assistants
P.O. Box 1178
Tyler, TX 75711

[Texas] Unemployment Insurance
101 E. 15th St.
Austin, TX 78778
512-463-2611

[Texas] United States Bankruptcy Court
Eastern Texas
211 W. Ferguson St., 4th Fl.
Tyler, TX 75712
214-592-1212

[Texas] United States Bankruptcy Court
Northern Texas
1100 Commerce St.
Dallas, TX 75242
214-767-0814

[Texas] United States Bankruptcy Court
Southern Texas
P.O. Box 61010

Houston, TX 77208
713-221-9505

[Texas] United States Bankruptcy Court
Western Texas
655 E. Durango Blvd.
San Antonio, TX 78206
512-229-6550

[Texas] United States District Court
Eastern District
211 W. Ferguson St., No. 309
Tyler, TX 75702
214-592-8195

[Texas] United States District Court
Northern District
1100 Commerce St., Rm. 14A20
Dallas, TX 75242
214-767-0787

[Texas] United States District Court
Southern District
P.O. Box 61010
Houston, TX 77208
713-221-9505

[Texas] United States District Court
Western District
655 E. Durango Blvd.
San Antonio, TX 78206
512-229-6550

[Texas] United States Government Printing Office
801 Travis St., Suite 120
Houston, TX 77002
713-653-3100

[Texas] United States Government Printing Office
1100 Commerce St., Rm. 1C46
Dallas, TX 75242
214-767-0076

Texas Veterans Commission
10th & Colorado
P.O. Box 12277
Austin, TX 78711
512-463-5538

[Texas] Vital Statistics, Bureau of
1100 W. 49th St.

Austin, TX 78756
512-458-7380

Texas Water Commission
1700 N. Congress
P.O. Box 13087
Austin, TX 78711
512-463-7898

Texas Water Development Board
1700 N. Congress
P.O. Box 13231
Austin, TX 78711
512-463-7847

[Texas] Weights & Measures Section
P.O. Box 12847
Austin, TX 78711
512-463-7602
800-835-5832

[Texas] Women, Governor's Commission for
P.O. Box 12428
Austin, TX 78711
512-463-1782

Texas Youth Commission
8900 Shoal Creek Blvd.
P.O. Box 9999
Austin, TX 78766
512-452-8111

Time, Inc.
1271 6th Ave.
New York, NY 10020
212-522-1212

Toy Manufacturers of America
2000 5th Ave., Rm. 740
New York, NY 10010
212-675-1141

Transportation Lawyers Association
3310 Harrison
Topeka, KS 66611
913-266-7014

Travelers Companies
One Tower Sq.
Hartford, CT 06183
203-277-6565
800-243-0191

Trial Lawyers for Public Justice
1625 Massachusetts Ave., NW,
  Suite 100

Wash. D.C. 20036
202-797-8600

Uniform Commerical Code Institute
P.O. Box 812
Carlisle, PA 17013
717-249-6831

Unisys Corp.
P.O. Box 5000
Bluebell, PA 19424
215-542-4011

United Nations
New York, NY 10017
212-963-1234

United Parcel Service of America, Inc.
51 Weaver St.
Greenwich, CT 06836
203-862-6000

[United States] ACTION
1100 Vermont Ave., NW
Wash. D.C. 20525
202-634-9380

[United States] Administration, Office of
Old Executive Office Bldg.
Wash. D.C. 20500
202-456-7050

United States, Administrative Conference of the
2120 L. St., NW
Wash. D.C. 20037
202-254-7020

[United States] African Development Foundation
1625 Massachusetts Ave., NW
Wash. D.C. 20036
202-673-3916

[United States] Agricultural Library, National
Beltsville, MD 20705
301-344-4248

[United States] Agricultural Stabilization & Conservation Service
Department of Agriculture
P.O. Box 2415
Wash. D.C. 20013
202-447-5237

[United States] Agriculture, Department of
14th St. & Independence Ave. SW
Wash. D.C. 20250
202-447-2791
202-447-7751 (Law Library)
202-447-3351 (General Counsel)

[United States] AIDS Hotline
800-342-AIDS

[United States] Air Force, Department of the
The Pentagon
Wash. D.C. 20330
202-545-6700
202-697-0941 (General Counsel)

[United States] Alcohol, Drug Abuse, & Mental Health Administration
5600 Fishers Lane
Rockville, MD 20857
301-443-4797

[United States] Alcohol, Tobacco & Firearms, Bureau of
1200 Pennsylvania Ave., NW
Wash. D.C. 20226
202-566-7777
800-424-9555

[United States] American Battle Monuments Commission
20 Massachusetts Ave., NW
Wash. D.C. 20314
202-272-0533

[United States] Appalachian Regional Commission
1666 Connecticut Ave., NW
Wash. D.C. 20235
202-673-7893

[United States] Architect of the Capitol
U.S. Capitol Bldg.
Wash. D.C. 20515
202-225-1200

[United States] Architectural & Transportation Barriers Compliance Board
1111 18th St., NW
Wash. D.C. 20036
202-653-7834

[United States] Archives & Records Administration, National
7th St. & Pennsylvania Ave., NW
Wash. D.C. 20408
202-523-3218
202-523-5240 (Law Library)

[United States] Armed Services Board of Contract Appeals
5109 Leesburg Pike, Skyline Six
Falls Church, VA 22041
201-756-8501

United States Arms Control & Disarmament Agency
320 21st St., NW
Wash. D.C. 20451
202-647-4000
202-647-3582 (General Counsel)

[United States] Army, Department of the
The Pentagon
Wash. D.C. 20310
202-545-6700
202-695-0441
202-697-9235 (General Counsel)

[United States] Arts, National Endowment for the
1100 Pennsylvania Ave., NW
Wash. D.C. 20506
202-682-5400
202-682-5418 (General Counsel)

United States Bankruptcy Courts
See entries under individual states.

[United States] Bilingual Education, National Clearinghouse on
Department of Education
8737 Colesville Rd., Suite 900

Silver Spring, MD 20910
301-588-6898
800-647-0123

United States Botanic Garden
245 1st St., SW
Wash. D.C. 20024
202-225-8333

[United States] Capital Planning Commission, National
1325 G. St., NW
Wash. D.C. 20576
202-724-0174

[United States] Census, Bureau of the
Department of Commerce
Wash. D.C. 20233
301-763-4040

[United States] Centers for Disease Control
1600 Clifton Road NE
Atlanta, GA 30333
404-329-3311

[United States] Central Intelligence Agency
Wash. D.C. 20505
703-482-1100
703-482-2422 (Law Library)

[United States] Child Abuse & Neglect, National Center on
Department of Health & Human Services
P.O. Box 1182
Wash. D.C. 20013
202-245-0586

[United States] Child Support Enforcement, Office of
370 L`Enfant Promenade SW
Wash. D.C. 20447
202-252-5349

[United States] Civil Rights, Commission on
1121 Vermont Ave., NW
Wash. D.C. 20425
202-376-8177
800-552-6843

United States Claims Court
717 Madison Pl., NW
Wash. D.C. 20005
202-633-7257

United States Coast Guard
Department of Transportation
2100 2nd St., SW
Wash. D.C. 20593
202-426-1587
800-368-5647

[United States] Commerce, Department of
14th St. between Constitution Ave. & E. St., NW
Wash. D.C. 20230
202-377-2000
202-377-4901 (Public Affairs)
202-377-5517 (Law Library)
202-377-4772 (General Counsel)

[United States] Commodity Credit Corporation
Department of Agriculture
P.O. Box 2415
Wash. D.C. 20013
202-447-5237

[United States] Commodity Futures Trading Commission
2033 K. St., NW
Wash. D.C. 20581
202-254-6387
202-254-5901 (Law Library)
202-254-9880 (General Counsel)

[United States] Comptroller of the Currency, Office of the
490 L'Enfant Plaza East, SW
Wash. D.C. 20219
202-447-1810
202-447-1843 (Law Library)

[United States] Congressional Budget Office
Second & D. Streets, SW
Wash. D.C. 20515
202-226-2621
202-226-2600 (Information)

[United States] Consumer Advisor, Office of the
Department of Agriculture
Wash. D.C. 20250
202-382-9681

[United States] Consumer Information Center
Pueblo, CO 81009
719-948-3334

[United States] Consumer Product Safety Commission
5401 Westbard Ave.
Bethesda, MD 20207
301-492-6580
301-492-6980 (General Counsel)

[United States] Contract Appeals Board
Department of Transportation
400 7th St., SW
Wash. D.C. 20590
202-366-4305

[United States] Contracts Compliance Programs, Office of Federal
Department of Labor
200 Constitution Ave., NW, Rm. C-3325
Wash. D.C. 20210
202-523-9474

[United States] Copyright Royalty Tribunal
1111 20th St., NW
Wash. D.C. 20036
202-653-5175

[United States] Copyrights, Register of
James Madison Memorial Bldg., Rm. LM-401
101 Independence Ave., SE
Wash. D.C. 20540
202-707-9100

United States Court of Appeals
See entries under California, Colorado, District of Columbia, Georgia, Illinois, Louisiana, Massachusetts, Missouri, New York, Ohio, Pennsylvania, and Virginia,

United States Court of Appeals for the Federal Circuit
717 Madison Pl., NW
Wash. D.C. 20439
202-633-6550
202-633-5871 (Law Library)

United States Court of International Trade
One Federal Plaza
New York, NY 10007

212-264-2814
212-264-2816 (Law Library)

United States Court of Military Appeals
450 E. St., NW
Wash. D.C. 20442
202-272-1448
202-272-1466 (Law Library)

United States Courts, Administrative Office of the
Wash. D.C. 20544
202-633-6236
202-633-6127 (General Counsel)

[United States] Credit Union Administraton, National
1776 G. St., NW
Wash. D.C. 20456
202-682-9600

[United States] Criminal Police Organization, International
United States National Central Bureau
Department of Justice
Wash. D.C. 20530
202-272-8383

[United States] Critical Materials Council, National
18th & C. Streets, NW
Wash. DC. 20240
202-343-1847

United States Customs Service
1301 Constitution Ave., NW
Wash. D.C. 20229
202-566-8195
800-USA-FAKE
800-BE-ALERT
202-566-5642 (Law Library)

[United States] Debt, Bureau of the Public
Department of the Treasury
999 E. St., NW
Wash. D.C. 20239
202-376-4300

[United States] Defense Advanced Research Projects Agency
1400 Wilson Blvd.
Arlington, VA 22209
202-694-5469

[United States] Defense Communications Agency
8th St. & S. Courthouse Road
Arlington, VA 22204
202-692-9012

[United States] Defense Computer Institute, Department of
Washington Navy Yard, Bldg. 175
Wash. D.C. 20374
202-433-2013

[United States] Defense Contract Audit Agency
Bldg. 4, Cameron Station
Alexandria, VA 22304
202-274-6785

[United States] Defense, Department of
The Pentagon
Wash. D.C. 20301
202-545-6700
202-697-5737 (Public Affairs)
202-695-2957 (Law Library)
202-695-3341 (General Counsel)

[United States] Defense Intelligence Agency
The Pentagon
Wash. D.C. 20340
202-697-8844

[United States] Defense Investigative Service
1900 Half St., SW
Wash. D.C. 20324
202-475-0966

[United States] Defense Legal Services Agency
The Pentagon
Wash. D.C. 20301
202-695-3341

[United States] Defense Logistics Agency
Cameron Station
Alexandria, VA 22304
202-274-6000

[United States] Defense Mapping Agency
8613 Lee Hwy
Fairfax, VA 22031
703-756-9368

[United States] Defense Nuclear Agency
Wash. D.C. 20305
202-325-7095

[United States] Defense Security Assistance Agency
The Pentagon
Wash. D.C. 20301
202-695-3291

[United States] Disabilities, President's Committee on Employment of People with
1111 20th St., NW
Wash. D.C. 20036
202-653-5050

United States District Courts
See entries under individual states.

[United States] Drug Control Policy, Office of National
Executive Office of the President
Wash. D.C. 20500
202-673-2520

[United States] Drug Enforcement Administration
1600-700 Army Navy Dr.
Arlington, VA 22202
202-307-1000

[United States] Economic Advisers, Council of
Old Executive Office Bldg.
Wash. D.C. 20500
202-395-5084

[United States] Economic Analysis, Bureau of
Department of Commerce
Wash. D.C. 20230
202-523-0777

[United States] Economic Development Administration
Department of Commerce
Wash. D.C. 20230
202-377-5113

[United States] Education, Department of
400 Maryland Ave., SW
Wash. D.C. 20202
202-245-3192
202-732-2600 (General Counsel)

[United States] Energy, Department of
1000 Independence Ave., SW
Wash. D.C. 20585
202-586-5000
202-252-4848 (Law Library)
202-586-5281 (General Counsel)

[United States] Engraving & Printing, Bureau of
Department of the Treasury
14th & C. Streets, SW
Wash. D.C. 20228
202-447-0193

[United States] Environmental Protection Agency
401 M. St., SW
Wash. D.C. 20460
202-382-2090
202-382-5919 (Law Library)
202-475-8064 (General Counsel)

[United States] Environmental Quality, Council on
722 Jackson Pl., NW
Wash. D.C. 20503
202-395-5750

[United States] Equal Employment Opportunity Commission
1801 L. St., NW
Wash. D.C. 20507
202-634-6036
800-USA-EEOC
202-634-4603 (Law Library)
202-663-4702 (General Counsel)

[United States] Export Administration, Bureau of
Department of Commerce
    14th St. & Constitution Ave., NW
Wash. D.C. 20230
202-377-2721

United States, Export-Import Bank of the
811 Vermont Ave., NW
Wash. D.C. 20571
202-566-8990

[United States] Family Support Administration
Department of Health & Human Services

370 L'Enfant Promenade,
Independence Ave., SW
Wash. D.C. 20447
202-252-4500

**[United States] Farm Credit
Administration**
1501 Farm Credit Dr.
McLean, VA 22102
703-883-4000

**[United States] Farmers Home
Administration**
Department of Agriculture
Wash. D.C. 20250
202-447-4323

**[United States] Federal Aviation
Administration**
Department of Transportation
800 Independence Ave., SW
Wash. D.C. 20591
202-366-4000
800-FAA-SURE
202-267-3174 (Law Library)

**[United States] Federal Bureau of
Investigation**
9th St. & Pennsylvania Ave., NW
Wash. D.C. 20535
202-324-3000

**[United States] Federal
Communications
Commission**
1919 M. St., NW
Wash. D.C. 20554
202-632-7000
202-632-7020 (General Counsel)

**[United States] Federal Crop
Insurance Corporation**
Department of Agriculture
Wash. D.C. 20250
202-447-6795

**[United States] Federal Deposit
Insurance Corporation**
550 17th St., NW
Wash. D.C. 20429
202-393-8400
800-424-5488
202-898-3620 (Law Library)

**[United States] Federal Election
Commission**
999 E. St., NW

Wash. D.C. 20463
202-376-3120
800-424-9530

**[United States] Federal
Emergency Management
Agency**
500 C. St., SW
Wash. D.C. 20472
202-646-4600

**[United States] Federal Grain
Inspection Service**
Department of Agriculture
Wash. D.C. 20250
202-475-3367

**[United States] Federal Highway
Administration**
Department of Transportation
400 7th St., SW
Wash. D.C. 20590
202-366-0660

**[United States] Federal Home
Loan Bank Board**
See [United States] Thrift
Supervision

**[United States] Federal Judicial
Center**
1520 H. St., NW
Wash. D.C. 20005
202-633-6011

**[United States] Federal Labor
Relations Authority**
500 C. St., SW
Wash. D.C. 20424
202-382-0711
202-382-0742 (General Counsel)

**[United States] Federal Register,
Office of the**
National Archives & Records
Administration
Wash. D.C. 20408
202-523-5230

**[United States] Federal Reserve
System, Board of Governors
of the**
20th St. & Constitution Ave., NW
Wash. D.C. 20551
202-452-3000
202-452-3293 (General Counsel)
202-452-3284 (Law Library)

**[United States] Federal Trade
Commission**
Pennsylvania Ave. at 6th St., NW
Wash. D.C. 20580
202-326-2222
202-326-2395 (Law Library)
202-326-2480 (General Counsel)

**United States Fidelity &
Guarantee Co.**
100 Light St.
Baltimore, MD 21202
301-547-3000

**[United States] Financial
Management Service**
Department of the Treasury
401 14th St. SW
Wash. D.C. 20227
202-287-0669

**[United States] Fine Arts,
Commission on**
708 Jackson Pl., NW
Wash. D.C. 20006
202-566-1066

**[United States] Fish & Wildlife
Service**
Department of the Interior
Wash. D.C. 20240
202-343-5634

**[United States] Food & Drug
Administration**
Department of Health & Human
Services
5600 Fishers Lane
Rockville, MD 20857
301-443-1544

**United States, Foreign Claims
Settlement of the**
1111 20th St., NW
Wash. D.C. 20579
202-653-5883
202-653-5883 (General Counsel)

[United States] Forest Service
Department of Agriculture
P.O. Box 96090
Wash. D.C. 20090
202-447-3760

**[United States] Gallaudet
University**
800 Florida Ave., NE

Wash. D.C. 20002
202-651-5000

**[United States] General
Accounting Office**
441 G. St., NW
Wash. D.C. 20548
202-275-5067
202-275-2585 (Law Library)
202-275-5205 (General Counsel)
202-275-2812 (Public Information)

**[United States] General Services
Administration**
18th & F. Streets, NW
Wash. D.C. 20405
202-472-1082

United States Geological Survey
Department of the Interior
119 National Center
Reston, VA 22092
703-648-4460

**[United States] Government
Printing Office**
North Capitol & H. Streets, NW
Wash. D.C. 20401
202-275-2051
202-275-3204 (Public Affairs)

**[United States] Graduate School,
Department of Agriculture**
14th & Independence Ave. SW
Wash. D.C. 20250
202-447-4419

**[United States] Handicapped,
Clearinghouse on the**
Department of Education
Mail Stop 2319
Wash. D.C. 20202
202-732-1241

**[United States] Health & Human
Services, Department of**
200 Independence Ave., SW
Wash. D.C. 20201
202-245-6296
202-475-0257 (Information Center)
202-245-7741 (General Counsel)

**[United States] Health Care
Financing Administration**
Department of Health & Human
Services
200 Independent Ave., SW

Wash. D.C. 20201
202-245-6113

**[United States] Health
Information Center, National**
Department of Health & Human
Services
P.O. Box 1133
Wash. D.C. 20013
301-565-4167

**[United States] Health, National
Institutes of**
Department of Health & Human
Services
9000 Rockville Pike
Bethesda, MD 20892
301-496-4000

**[United States] Health Resources
& Services Administration**
Department of Health & Human
Services
5600 Fishers Lane
Rockville, MD 20857
301-443-2086

**[United States] Health Services,
Public**
Department of Health & Human
Services
5600 Fishers Lane
Rockville, MD 20857
301-443-2404

**[United States] Hearings &
Appeals, Office of**
Department of the Interior
4015 Wilson Blvd.
Arlington, VA 22203
703-345-3810

**[United States] Highway Traffic
Safety Administration,
National**
Department of Transportation
400 7th St., SW
Wash. D.C. 20590
202-366-9550
800-424-9393

**United States House of
Representatives**
The Capitol
Wash. D.C. 20515
202-224-3121

**[United States] Housing & Equal
Opportunity, Office of Fair**
Department of Housing & Urban
Development
Rm. 5100
Wash. D.C. 20410
202-755-7252
800-424-8590

**[United States] Housing & Urban
Development, Department of**
451 7th St. SW
Wash. D.C. 20410
202-755-5111
202-755-6420 (Information)
202-755-0009 (General Counsel)

**[United States] Human
Development Services,
Office of**
Department of Health & Human
Services
200 Independence Ave. SW
Wash. D.C. 20201
202-245-7246

**[United States] Humanities,
National Endowment for the**
1100 Pennsylvania Ave., NW
Wash. D.C. 20506
202-786-0438
202-786-0322 (General Counsel)

**[United States] Immigration &
Naturalization Service**
425 I. St., NW
Wash. D.C. 20536
202-633-4316
703-235-4055
202-633-1270 (General Counsel)

**[United States] Immigration
Judge, Office of the Chief**
5201 Leesburg Pike, Suite 1501
Falls Church, VA 22041
703-756-6247

**[United States] Immigration
Review, Executive Office for**
Department of Justice
Falls Church, VA 22401
202-756-6171

**[United States] Indian Affairs,
Bureau of**
Department of the Interior

Wash. D.C. 20240
202-343-4576
202-343-4072

[United States] Indian Health Services
Department of Health & Human Services
5600 Fishers Land
Rockville, MD 20857
301-443-1083

United States Information Agency
301 4th St., NW
Wash. D.C. 20547
202-485-7700
202-485-7979 (General Counsel)

[United States] Inter-American Foundation
1515 Wilson Blvd.
Rosslyn, VA 22209
703-841-3800
703-841-3812 (General Counsel)

[United States] Interior, Department of the
1800 C. St., NW
Wash. D.C. 20240
202-343-3171
202-343-4571 (Law Library)
202-343-6115 (Solicitor)
202-343-4423 (General Counsel)

[United States] Internal Revenue Service
Department of the Treasury
111 Constitution Ave., NW
Wash. D.C. 20224
202-566-5000
202-566-6364 (General Counsel)

[United States] International Broadcasting, Board for
1201 Connecticut Ave., NW
Wash. D.C. 20036
202-254-8040

[United States] International Development, Agency for
320 21st St., NW
Wash. D.C. 20523
202-647-1850
202-647-8548 (General Counsel)

United States International Trade Commission
500 E. St., SW
Wash. D.C. 20436
202-252-1000
202-252-1287 (Law Library)
202-252-1061 (General Counsel)

[United States] Interstate Commerce Commission
12th St. & Constitution Ave., NW
Wash. D.C. 20423
202-275-7119
202-275-7312 (General Counsel)

[United States] Judge Advocate General
Department of the Navy
200 Stovall St.
Alexandria, VA 22332
202-694-7420

[United States] Judge Advocate General's School Library
United States Army
Charlottesville, VA 22903
804-972-6306

[United States] Judicial Panel on Multidistrict Litigation
1120 Vermont Ave., NW, Suite 1002
Wash. D.C. 20005
202-653-6090

[United States] Justice, Department of
Constitution Ave. & 10th St., NW
Wash. D.C. 20530
202-633-2000
202-633-2133 (Law Library)
202-633-2201 (Solicitor General)
202-633-2292 (Antitrust)
202-633-4224 (Civil Rights)
202-633-2601 (Criminal Division)
202-633-1100 (Drug Enforcement)
202-633-2701 (Land & Natural Resources)

United States Justice Foundation
2091 E. Valley Parkway
Escondido, CA 92027
619-741-8086

[United States] Justice Programs, Office of
Department of Justice

633 Indiana Ave., NW
Wash. D.C. 20531
202-724-7782

[United States] Juvenile Justice & Delinquency Prevention, Coordinating Council on
633 Indiana Ave., NW
Wash. D.C. 20531
202-724-7655

[United States] Labor, Department of
200 Constitution Ave., NW
Wash. D.C. 20210
202-523-8165
202-523-6992 (Law Library)
202-523-7675 (General Counsel)

[United States] Labor-Management Standards, Office of
Department of Labor
Wash. D.C. 20210
202-523-7343

[United States] Labor Statistics, Bureau of
Department of Labor
200 Constitution Ave., NW
Wash. D.C. 20210
202-523-1327

[United States] Land Management, Bureau of
Department of the Interior
Wash. D.C. 20240
202-343-9435

[United States] Law Enforcement Training Center, Federal
Department of the Treasury
Glynco, GA 31524
912-267-2100

United States League of Savings Institutions
1709 New York Ave., NW
Wash. D.C. 20006
202-637-8900

[United States] Legal Services Corporation
400 Virginia Ave., SW
Wash. D.C. 20024
202-863-1820

[United States] Library of Congress
101 Independence Ave., SE
Wash. D.C. 20540
202-707-5000
202-707-5065 (Law Library)
202-707-5081 (British Div.)
202-707-5088 (European Div.)
202-707-5085 (Far Eastern Div.)
202-707-5073 (Near East & African Div.)
202-707-8999 (CRS)

[United States] Management & Budget, Office of
Executive Office Bldg.
Wash. D.C. 20503
202-395-3080

United States Marine Corps
Department of the Navy
Wash. D.C. 20380
202-694-2500

[United States] Marine Fisheries Service, National
1335 East-West Hwy
Silver Spring, MD 20910
301-427-2355

[United States] Maritime Administration
Department of Transportation
400 7th St., SW
Wash. D.C. 20590
202-366-5807
202-523-5740 (General Counsel)

[United States] Maritime Commission, Federal
1100 L. St., NW
Wash. D.C. 20573
202-523-5773

United States Marshals Service
600 Army Navy Dr.
Arlington, VA 22202
202-307-9000

[United States] Mayors, Conference of
1620 I. St., NW
Wash. D.C. 20006
202-293-7330

[United States] Mediation & Conciliation Service, Federal
2100 K. St., NW

Wash. D.C. 20427
202-653-5290
202-653-5305 (General Counsel)

[United States] Mediation Board, National
1425 K. St., NW
Wash. D.C. 20572
202-523-5920

[United States] Merit Systems Protection Board
1120 Vermont Ave., NW
Wash. D.C. 20419
202-653-7124
202-653-7168 (General Counsel)

[United States] Metric Programs, Office of
Department of Commerce
Rm. H4082
Wash. D.C. 20230
202-377-0944

United States Military Academy
West Point, NY 10996
914-938-4261

[United States] Mine Safety & Health Administration
Department of Labor
Ballston Towers #3
Arlington, VA 22203
703-235-1452

[United States] Mine Safety & Health Review Commission, Federal
1730 K. St., NW
Wash. D.C. 20006
202-653-5625

[United States] Mines, Bureau of
Department of the Interior
2401 E. St., NW
Wash. D.C. 20241
202-634-1004

[United States] Minority Business Development Agency
Department of Commerce
Wash. D.C. 20230
202-377-1936

United States Mint
Department of the Treasury
633 3rd St., NW

Wash. D.C. 20220
202-376-0560
301-436-7400

[United States] Museum Services, Institute of
1100 Pennsylvania Ave., NW, Rm. 510
Wash. D.C. 20506
202-786-0536

[United States] National Aeronautics & Space Administration
600 Independence Ave., SW
Wash. D.C. 20546
202-453-1000
202-453-2450 (General Counsel)

[United States] National Labor Relations Board
1717 Pennsylvania Ave., NW
Wash. D.C. 20570
202-655-4000
202-254-9055 (Law Library)
202-254-9150 (General Counsel)

United States Naval Academy
Annapolis, MD 21402
800-638-9156
301-267-4361

[United States] Naval Legal Service Command
Department of the Navy
200 Stovall St., Hoffman Bldg. 2
Alexandria, VA 22332
202-325-9850

[United States] Navy, Department of the
The Pentagon
Wash. D.C. 20350
202-545-6700
202-694-1994 (General Counsel)

[United States] Navy Judge Advocate General
200 Stovall St.
Alexandria, VA 22332
202-325-9565

[United States] Nuclear Regulatory Commission
Wash. D.C. 20555
301-492-7000
301-492-1743 (General Counsel)

[United States] Occupational Safety & Health Administration
Department of Labor
200 Constitution Ave., NW
Wash. D.C. 20210
202-523-8017

[United States] Occupational Safety & Health Review Commission
1825 K. ST., NW
Wash. D.C. 20006
202-634-7943

[United States] Oceanic & Atmospheric Administration, National
Department of Commerce
Wash. D.C. 20230
202-377-2985

[United States] Overseas Citizen Services
Department of State
Wash. D.C. 20520
202-647-3666
202-647-5225

[United States] Panama Canal Commission
2000 L. St., NW, Rm. 550
Wash. D.C. 20036
202-634-6441

[United States] Park Service, National
Department of the Interior
P.O. Box 37127
Wash. D.C. 20013
202-343-7394

United States Parole Commission
5550 Friendship Blvd.
Chevy Chase, MD 20815
301-492-5990

[United States] Passport Services
Department of State
1425 K. St., NW
Wash. D.C. 20524
202-647-0518

[United States] Patent & Trademark Office
Department of Commerce

Wash. D.C. 20231
202-377-4190
202-557-4035 (General Counsel)

[United States] Patent & Trademark Office (Operations)
2021 Jefferson Davis Hwy
Arlington, VA 20231
703-557-3341

[United States] Peace Corps
1990 K. St., NW
Wash. D.C. 20526
202-254-6886
202-254-3114 (General Counsel)

[United States] Peace, Institute of
1550 M. St., NW
Wash. D.C. 20005
202-457-1700

[United States] Pennsylvania Avenue Development Corporation
1331 Pennsylvania Ave., NW, Suite 1220
Wash. D.C. 20004
202-724-9091

[United States] Pension Benefit Guaranty Corporation
2020 K. St., NW
Wash. D.C. 20006
202-778-8800

[United States] Pension & Welfare Benefits Administration
Department of Labor
Office of Program Services
Wash. D.C. 20210
202-523-8921

[United States] Personnel Management, Office of
1900 E. St., NW
Wash. D.C. 20415
202-632-1212

[United States] Physical Fitness & Sports, President's Council on
Department of Health & Human Services
450 5th St., NW
Wash. D.C. 20001
202-272-3430

[United States] Policy Development, Office of
1600 Pennsylvania Ave., NW
Wash. D.C. 20500
202-456-1414

[United States] Postal Rate Commission
1333 H. St., NW
Wash. D.C. 20268
202-789-6800
202-789-6820 (General Counsel)

United States Postal Service
475 L'Enfant Plaza, SW
Wash. D.C. 20260
202-268-2000
202-268-4267 (Postal Inspector)
202-268-2284 (Consumer Advocate)
202-268-2904 (Law Library)
202-268-2950 (General Counsel)

United States, President of the
1600 Pennsylvania Ave., NW
Wash. D.C. 20500
202-456-1414

[United States] Prisons, Bureau of
Department of Justice
320 1st St., NW
Wash. D.C. 20534
202-724-3198

[United States] Railroad Adjustment Board, National
175 W. Jackson Blvd., Rm. A931
Chicago, IL 60604
312-886-7300

[United States] Railroad Administration, Federal
Department of Transportation
400 7th St., SW
Wash. D.C. 20590
202-366-4000

[United States] Railroad Passenger Corporation (AMTRAK), National
60 Massachusetts Ave., NE
Wash. D.C. 20002
202-906-3000

[United States] Railroad Retirement Board
844 Rush St.
Chicago, IL 60611

312-751-4776
202-653-9540 (Wash. D.C.)

**[United States] Reclamation,
Bureau of**
Department of the Interior
Wash. D.C. 20240
202-343-4662

**[United States] Research &
Special Programs
Administration**
Department of Transportation
400 7th St., SW
Wash. D.C. 20590
202-366-4347

**[United States] Resolution Trust
Corporation**
550 17th St., NW
Wash. D.C. 20429
202-789-6313

**[United States] Resolution Trust
Corporation Oversight Board**
1825 Connecticut Ave., NW
Wash. D.C. 20232
202-387-7667

**[United States] Retirement Thrift
Investment Board, Federal**
805 15th St., NW
Wash. D.C. 20005
202-523-4511

**[United States] Rural
Electrification Administration**
Department of Agriculture
Wash. D.C. 20250
202-382-1255

**[United States] Saint Lawrence
Seaway Development
Corporation**
Department of Transportation
400 7th St., SW
Wash. D.C. 20590
202-366-0091
315-764-3200 (Massena, NY)

**United States Savings Bond
Division**
Department of the Treasury
1111 20th St., NW
Wash. D.C. 20226
202-634-5350
800-US-BONDS

**[United States] Science &
Technology Policy, Office of**
Old Executive Office Bldg.
Wash. D.C. 20506
202-395-7347

**[United States] Science
Foundation, National**
1800 G. St., NW
Wash. D.C. 20550
202-357-5000
202-357-9435 (General Counsel)

United States Secret Service
Department of the Treasury
1800 G. St., NW
Wash. D.C. 20223
202-535-5708

**[United States] Securities &
Exchange Commission**
450 5th St., NW
Wash. D.C. 20549
202-272-3100
202-272-7450 (Investor Complaints)
202-272-5624 (Filings)
202-272-3171 (General Counsel)

**[United States] Security
Agency/Central Security
Service, National**
Fort George Meade, MD 20755
301-688-6311

**[United States] Security Council,
National**
Old Executive Office Bldg.
Wash. D.C. 20506
202-395-4974

**[United States] Selective Service
System**
National Headquarters
Wash. D.C. 20435
202-724-0820
202-724-1167 (General Counsel)

United States Senate
The Capitol
Wash. D.C. 20510
202-224-3121

**United States Sentencing
Commission**
1331 Pennsylvania Ave., NW
Wash. D.C. 20004
202-662-8800
202-626-8500 (Law Library)

**[United States] Small Business
Administration**
1441 L. St., NW
Wash. D.C. 20416
202-653-6554
800-368-5855
202-653-6659 (General Counsel)

**[United States] Smithsonian
Institution**
1000 Jefferson Dr., SW
Wash. D.C. 20560
202-357-1300
202-357-2583 (General Counsel)

**[United States] Social Security
Administration**
Department of Health & Human
Services
6401 Security Blvd.
Baltimore, MD 21235
301-965-1234
301-965-7700 (Public Inquiries)
800-2345-SSI
301-965-6107 (Law Library)

**[United States] Special Counsel,
Office of the**
1120 Vermont Ave., NW
Wash. D.C. 20005
202-653-7188
800-872-9855

**[United States] Standards &
Technology, National
Institute of**
Department of Commerce
Gaithersburg, MD 20899
301-975-2000
301-975-4004 (Weights & Measures)

**[United States] State,
Department of**
2201 C. St., NW
Wash. D.C. 20520
202-647-4000
202-647-6575 (Public Affairs)
202-647-9598 (Legal Adviser)

**[United States] State Justice
Institute**
120 S. Fairfax St.
Alexandria, VA 22314
703-684-6100

**[United States] Student Financial
Aid Program, Federal**
Department of Education

P.O. Box 84
Wash. D.C. 20044
800-333-INFO
800-MIS-USED

**United States, Supreme Court
of the**
United States Supreme Court Bldg.
One 1st St., NE
Wash. D.C. 20543
202-479-3000
202-479-3011 (Clerk)
202-479-3177 (Law Library)

**[United States] Surface Mining
Reclamation & Enforcement,
Office of**
Department of the Interior
Wash. D.C. 20240
202-343-4719

United States Tax Court
400 2nd St., NW
Wash. D.C. 20217
202-376-2754
202-376-2707 (Law Library)

**[United States] Technical
Information Service, National**
Department of Commerce
5285 Port Royal Rd.
Springfield, VA 22161
703-487-4650

**[United States] Technology
Assessment, Office of**
600 Pennsylvania Ave. SE
Wash. D.C. 20510
202-224-8713
202-224-9241 (Public Affairs)

**[United States] Technology
Assistance Service, National
Appropriate**
Department of Energy
P.O. Box 2525
Butte, MT 59702
800-428-1718

**[United States]
Telecommunications &
Information Administration,
National**
Department of Commerce
Wash. D.C. 20230
202-377-1832

**United States Telephone
Association**
900 19th St. NW, Suite 800
Wash. D.C. 20006
202-835-3100

**United States Temporary
Emergency Court of Appeals**
3rd & Constitution Ave., NW
Wash. D.C. 20001
202-535-3390

**[United States] Tennessee Valley
Authority**
400 W. Summit Hill Dr.
Knoxville, TN 37902
615-632-2101
202-479-4412 (Wash. D.C.)

**[United States] Thrift
Supervision, Office of**
Department of the Treasury
1700 G. St., NW
Wash. D.C. 20552
202-906-6000

**[United States] Title I Insurance
Division**
Department of Housing & Urban
Development
Rm. 9158
Wash. D.C. 20410
202-755-6680

**[United States] Toxic Substances
& Disease Registry, Agency for**
Department of Health & Human
Services
1600 Clifton Road, NE
Atlanta, GA 30333
404-42-4111

**[United States] Trade
Administration, International**
Department of Commerce
Wash. D.C. 20230
202-377-3808

**United States Trademark
Association**
6 E. 45th St.
New York, NY 10017
212-986-5880

**United States Trade
Representatives, Office of the**
600 17th St., NW

Wash. D.C. 20506
202-395-3230

**[United States] Transportation,
Department of**
400 7th St., SW
Wash. D.C. 20590
202-366-4000
202-366-4702 (General Counsel)

**[United States] Transportation
Safety Board, National**
800 Independence Ave., SW
Wash. D.C. 20594
202-382-6600
202-382-6540 (General Counsel)

**United States Travel & Tourism
Administration**
Department of Commerce
Wash. D.C. 20230
202-377-3811

**[United States] Treasury,
Department of the**
1500 Pennsylvania Ave. NW
Wash. D.C. 20220
202-566-2000
202-566-2777 (Law Library)
202-566-2093 (General Counsel)

**[United States] United Nations,
Mission to the**
799 United Nations Plaza
New York, NY 10017

**[United States] Urban Mass
Transportation
Administration**
Department of Transportation
400 7th St., SW
Wash. D.C. 20590
202-366-4043
202-366-9157 (Transit Research)

**[United States] Veterans Affairs,
Department of**
810 Vermont Ave., NW
Wash. D.C. 20420
202-233-2300
202-233-6442 (Law Library)

**[United States] Vice President,
Office of the**
Old Executive Office Bldg.
Wash. D.C. 20501
202-456-2326

[United States] Visa Services
Department of State
Wash. D. C. 20520
202-647-0510

**[United States] Wage & Hour
Division**
Department of Labor
200 Constitution Ave., NW,
Rm. S-3502
Wash. D. C. 20210
202-523-8305

**[United States] Weather Service,
National**
Department of Commerce
Wash. D.C. 20901
301-427-7258

[United States] White House
1600 Pennsylvania Ave., NW
Wash. D.C. 20500
202-456-1414
202-395-3397

[United States] Women's Bureau
The Work & Family Clearinghouse
Department of Labor
Division of Information &
Publications
Wash. D.C. 20210
202-523-6652

United Van Lines, Inc.
1 United Dr.
Fenton, MO 63026
800-325-3870

Upjohn Co.
7000 Portage Rd.
Kalamazoo, MI 49001
616-323-6004

Urban Institute Press
4720 Boston Way
Lanham, MD 20706
301-459-3366

Urban Land Institute
1090 Vermont Ave., NW
Wash. D.C. 20005
202-289-8500

U.S. Sprint
8001 Stemmons Freeway
Dallas, TX 75247
214-688-5707
800-877-4646

U.S. Tour Operators Association
211 E. 51st St., Suite 12-B
New York, NY 10022
212-944-5727

**[Utah] Information & Referral
(State Government)**
801-538-3000

**[Utah] Information Center
(Federal Government)**
Salt Lake City 801-524-5353

**[Utah] Administrative Services,
Department of**
State Office Bldg.
Salt Lake City, UT 84114
801-538-3010

**[Utah] Aging & Adult Services,
Division of**
P.O. Box 45500
Salt Lake City, UT 84145
801-538-3910

**[Utah] Agriculture,
Department of**
350 N. Rosewood Rd.
Salt Lake City, UT 84116
801-538-7100

[Utah] Air Quality, Bureau of
288 N. 1460 West, 2nd Fl.
Salt Lake City, UT 84116
801-538-6108

**Utah Archives & Records
Service, State**
Archives Bldg.
Salt Lake City, UT 84114
801-538-3012

**[Utah] Attorney General,
Office of**
State Capitol Bldg., Rm. 236
Salt Lake City, UT 84114
801-538-1015

**[Utah] Auditor, Office of the
State**
State Capitol, Rm. 211
Salt Lake City, UT 84114
801-538-1361

Utah Bar Association
645 S. 200 East
Salt Lake City, UT 84111
801-531-9077

[Utah] Better Business Bureau
1588 S. Main St.
Salt Lake City, UT 84115
801-487-4656

**[Utah] Business Regulation,
Department of**
160 E. 300 South, 2nd Fl.
Salt Lake City, UT 84111
801-530-6700

**[Utah] Community & Economic
Development, Department of**
6290 State Office Bldg.
Salt Lake City, UT 84114
801-538-3368

**[Utah] Consumer Protection
Division**
160 E. 3rd South, P.O. Box 45802
Salt Lake City, UT 84145
801-530-6601

**[Utah] Corrections,
Department of**
6100 S. 300 East
Salt Lake City, UT 84107
801-264-2150

**[Utah] Courts, Administrative
Office of the**
230 S. 500 East, Suite 300
Salt Lake City, UT 84102
801-533-6371

**[Utah] Crime Prevention,
Council for**
4501 S. 2700 West, 1st Fl.
Salt Lake City, UT 84119
801-965-4587

[Utah] Education, Office of
250 E. 500 South
Salt Lake City, UT 84111
801-538-7500

**[Utah] Emergency Management,
Division of Comprehensive**
1543 E. Sunnyside Ave.
Salt Lake City, UT 84105
801-533-5271

**[Utah] Employment Security,
Department of**
174 Social Hall Ave.
Salt Lake City, UT 84111
801-533-2400

Utah Energy Office
355 W. North Temple, Suite 450
Salt Lake City, UT 84180
801-538-5428

[Utah] Finance, Division of
State Office Bldg., Rm. 2110
Salt Lake City, UT 84114
801-538-3020

[Utah] Financial Institutions,
Commissioner of
P.O. Box 89
Salt Lake City, UT 84110
801-530-6502

[Utah] Governor, Office of
210 State Capitol Bldg.
Salt Lake City, UT 84114
801-538-1000

[Utah] Health, Department of
288 N. 1460 West
Salt Lake City, UT 84116
801-538-6101

[Utah] Higher Education,
System of
355 W. North Temple St., Suite 550
Salt Lake City, UT 84180
801-538-5247

[Utah] Highway Patrol Division
4501 S. 2700 West
Salt Lake City, UT 84119
801-965-4518

[Utah] House of Representatives
State Capitol
Salt Lake City, UT 84114
801-538-1029
801-538-4000 (Judiciary)

[Utah] Human Resource
Management, Department of
State Office Bldg., Rm. 2229
Salt Lake City, UT 84114
801-538-3025

[Utah] Insurance,
Commissioner of
P.O. Box 45803
Salt Lake City, UT 84145
801-530-6400

[Utah] Labor/Anti-
Discrimination Division
160 E. 300 South, 3rd Fl.

Salt Lake City, UT 84111
801-530-6922

[Utah] Law Library, State
125 State Capitol Bldg.
Salt Lake City, UT 84114
801-538-1045

Utah, Legal Assistants
Association of
P.O. Box 11019
Salt Lake City, UT 84111

[Utah] Legislative Research,
Office of
State Capitol, Rm. 436
Salt Lake City, UT 84114
801-538-1032

[Utah] Lieutenant Governor,
Office of
203 State Capitol Bldg.
Salt Lake City, UT 84114
801-538-1040

[Utah] Motor Vehicle Division
1095 Motor Ave.
Salt Lake City, UT 84116
801-538-8321

[Utah] Natural Resources
Department
1636 W. North Temple St., Suite 316
Salt Lake City, UT 84114
801-538-7200

[Utah] Oil, Gas & Mining,
Division of
355 W. North Temple, Suite 350
Salt Lake City, UT 84180
801-538-5340

[Utah] Pardons, Board of
6100 S. 300 East
Murray, UT 84107
801-261-2825

[Utah] Planning & Budget,
Office of
State Capitol Bldg., Rm. 116
Salt Lake City, UT 84114
801-538-1540

[Utah] Public Service
Commission
P.O. Box 45585
Salt Lake City, UT 84145
801-530-6716

[Utah] Real Estate Division
160 E. 300 South
Salt Lake City, UT 84111
801-530-6747

[Utah] Recovery Services,
Office of
120 N. 200 West
P.O. Box 45011
Salt Lake City, UT 84145
801-538-4400

[Utah] Rehabilitation Services,
Division of
250 E. 5th South
Salt Lake City, UT 84111
801-538-7530

[Utah] Salt Lake County
240 E. 4th South
Salt Lake City, UT 84111
801-535-7541

[Utah] Salt Lake County Law
Library
240 E. 400 South, Rm. 219
Salt Lake City, UT 84111
801-535-5818

[Utah] Secretary of State
State Capitol Bldg.
Salt Lake City, UT 84114
801-530-6700

[Utah] Securities Division
160 E. 300 South
Salt Lake City, UT 84145
801-530-6600

[Utah] Senate
State Capitol
Salt Lake City, UT 84114
801-538-1035
801-535-4000 (Judiciary)

[Utah] Social Services,
Department of
120 North 200 West
Salt Lake City, UT 84145
801-538-4171

[Utah] Solid & Hazardous Waste
Management, Bureau of
288 N. 1460 West
Salt Lake City, UT 84116
801-538-6170

[Utah] Supreme Court
332 State Capitol Bldg.

Salt Lake City, UT 84114
801-538-1044

[Utah] Tax Commission
160 E. 300 South
Salt Lake City, UT 84111
801-538-6088

**[Utah] Telecommunications
Office**
State Office Bldg., Rm. 1226
Salt Lake City, UT 84114
801-538-3330

**[Utah] Transportation,
Department of**
4501 S. 2700 West
Salt Lake City, UT 84119
801-965-4113

[Utah] Treasurer, State
State Capitol, Rm. 215
Salt Lake City, UT 84114
801-538-1042

**[Utah] Unemployment
Insurance Division**
P.O. Box 11249
Salt Lake City, UT 84147
801-533-2201

**[Utah] United States Bankruptcy
Court**
350 S. Main St., No. 361
Salt Lake City, UT 84101
801-524-5157

**[Utah] United States District
Court**
350 S. Main St., No. 204
Salt Lake City, UT 84101
801-524-5160

[Utah] Vital Records, Bureau of
288 N. 1460 West
Salt Lake City, UT 84116
801-538-6105

**[Utah] Weights & Measures,
Division of**
350 N. Redwood Rd.
Salt Lake City, UT 84116
801-538-7159

[Utah] Workers' Compensation
160 E. 300 South
Salt Lake City, UT 84111
801-530-6800

**[Utah] Youth Corrections,
Division of**
120 N. 200 West, 4th Fl.
Salt Lake City, UT 84103
801-538-4330

Veralex
One Graves St.
Rochester, NY 14692
716-546-7111
800-448-3400

**[Vermont] Information &
Referral (State Government)**
802-828-1110

**[Vermont] Administration,
Agency of**
109 State St.
Montpelier, VT 05602
802-828-3322

**[Vermont] Agriculture,
Department of**
116 State St.
Montpelier, VT 05602
802-828-2430

**[Vermont] Air Pollution Control
Division**
103 S. Main St. Bldg. 3-S
Waterbury, VT 05676
802-244-8731

**[Vermont] Alcohol & Drug
Abuse, Office of**
103 S. Main St.
Waterburg, VT 05676
802-241-2170

[Vermont] Archivist, State
26 Terrace St.
Montpelier, VT 05602
802-828-2369

**[Vermont] Attorney General,
Office of**
109 State St.

Montpelier, VT 05602
802-828-3171

[Vermont] Auditor of Accounts
132 State St.
Montpelier, VT 05602
802-828-2281

**[Vermont] Banking & Insurance,
Commissioner of**
State Office Bldg.
Montpelier, VT 05602
802-828-3301

[Vermont] Bar Admissions
Judiciary—Court Administration
c/o Pavilion Office Bldg. P.O.
Montpelier, VT 05602
802-828-3281

Vermont Bar Association
P.O. Box 100
Montpelier, VT 05602
802-223-2020
800-642-3153

**[Vermont] Child Support
Division**
103 S. Main St.
Waterbury, VT 05676
802-241-2910

**[Vermont] Conservation &
Renewable Energy Unit**
120 State St.
Montpelier, VT 05602
802-828-2393

[Vermont] Consumer Division
109 State St.
Montpelier, VT 05602
802-828-3171

**[Vermont] Corrections,
Department of**
103 S. Main St.
Waterbury, VT 05676
802-241-2263

**[Vermont] Court Administrator,
Office of the**
111 State St.
Pavilion Office Bldg.
Montpelier, VT 05602
802-828-3276

[Vermont] Defender General
141 Main St.

Montpelier, VT 05602
802-828-3168

**[Vermont] Development &
Community Affairs**
109 State St.
Montpelier, VT 05602
802-828-3168

**[Vermont] Economic
Development Department**
109 State St.
Montpelier, VT 05602
802-828-3221

**[Vermont] Economic
Opportunity Office**
103 S. Main St.
Waterbury, VT 05676
802-241-2450

**[Vermont] Education,
Department of**
120 State St.
Montpelier, VT 05602
802-828-3135

**[Vermont] Emergency
Management**
103 S. Main St.
Waterbury, VT 05676
802-244-8721

**[Vermont] Employment &
Training, Department of**
P.O. Box 488
Montpelier, VT 05602
802-229-0311

[Vermont] Environmental Board
58 E. State St.
Montpelier, VT 05602
802-828-3309

**[Vermont] Environmental
Conservation, Department of**
103 S. Main St.
Waterburg, VT 05676
802-244-8755

**[Vermont] Finance &
Management, Department of**
109 State St.
Montpelier, VT 05602
802-828-2309

[Vermont] Governor, Office of
109 State St., 4th Fl.

Montpelier, VT 05602
802-828-3333

[Vermont] Health, Department of
60 Main St.
Burlington, VT 05402
802-863-7280

**[Vermont] Higher Education
Council**
Main St.
Hyde Park, VT 05655
802-888-7771

**[Vermont] House of
Representatives**
State House
Montpelier, VT 05602
802-828-2228
802-828-1110 (Judiciary)

**[Vermont] Historic Preservation,
Division for**
58 E. State St.
Montpelier, VT 05602
802-828-3226

**[Vermont] Housing &
Community Affairs**
109 State St.
Montpelier, VT 05602
802-828-3217

**[Vermont] Human Services,
Agency for**
103 S. Main St.
Waterbury, VT 05676
802-241-2220

**[Vermont] Insurance,
Commissioner of**
State Office Bldg.
Montpelier, VT 05602
802-828-3301

**[Vermont] Judicial Conduct
Board**
111 State St.
Montpelier, VT 05602
802-828-3281

**[Vermont] Labor & Industry,
Department of**
State Office Bldg.
Montpelier, VT 05602
802-828-2286

[Vermont] Legislative Council
115 State St.

Montpelier, VT 05602
802-828-2231

**Vermont Libraries,
Department of**
Law Library
State Office Bldg.
Montpelier, VT 05602
802-828-3268

**[Vermont] Licensing &
Registration, Department of**
26 Terrace St.
Montpelier, VT 05602
802-828-2363

**[Vermont] Lieutenant Governor,
Office of**
State House
Montpelier, VT 05602
802-828-2226

**[Vermont] Liquor Control,
Department of**
120 State St.
Montpelier, VT 05602
802-828-2345

**[Vermont] Mental Health,
Department of**
103 S. Main St.
Waterbury, VT 05676
802-241-2214

**[Vermont] Motor Vehicles,
Department of**
120 State St.
Montpelier, VT 05602
802-828-2011

**[Vermont] Municipal Retirement
Board of Trustees**
133 State St.
Montpelier, VT 05602
802-828-2305

**[Vermont] Natural Resources,
Agency for**
103 S. Main St.
Waterbury, VT 05676
802-244-7347
802-244-5164 (Conservation
Council)

**[Vermont] Occupational &
Radiological Health Division**
10 Baldwin St.
Montpelier, VT 05602
802-828-2886

[Vermont] Oil & Gas Resources Board
109 State St.
Montpelier, VT 05602
802-828-3326

[Vermont] Parole, Board of
103 S. Main St.
Waterbury, VT 05676
802-241-2295

[Vermont] Policy Research and Coordination
109 State ST.
Montpelier, VT 05602
802-828-3326

[Vermont] Probation & Parole, Division of
103 S. Main St.
Waterbury, VT 05676
802-241-2295

[Vermont] Public Protection Division
109 State St.
Montpelier, VT 05602
802-828-3171

[Vermont] Public Safety, Department of
103 S. Main St.
Waterbury, VT 05676
802-244-8718

[Vermont] Public Service, Department of
120 State St..
Montpelier, VT 05602
802-828-2811
802-828-2358 (Public Service Board)
800-622-4496

[Vermont] Racing Commission
State Office Building
Montpelier, VT 05602
802-828-3429

[Vermont] Real Estate Commission
Pavilion Office Bldg.
Montpelier, VT 05602
802-828-3228

[Vermont] Rehabilitation & Aging, Department of
103 S. Main St.

Waterbury, VT 05676
802-241-2400

[Vermont] Secretary of State
26 Terrace St.
Montpelier, VT 05602
802-828-2363
800-642-5155

[Vermont] Securities Division
120 State St.
Montpelier, VT 05602
802-828-2379

[Vermont] Senate
State House
Montpelier, VT 05602
802-828-2228
802-828-1110 (Judiciary)

[Vermont] Social Welfare Department
103 S. Main St.
Waterbury, VT 05676
802-241-2800

[Vermont] State Police
103 S. Main St.
Waterbury, VT 05676
802-244-7345

[Vermont] State's Attorneys, Department of
12 Baldwin St.
Montpelier, VT 05602
802-828-2891

[Vermont] Statutory Revision Committee
Supreme Court Bldg.
Montpelier, VT 05602
802-828-3276

Vermont, Supreme Court of
111 State St.
Montpelier, VT 05602
802-828-3276

[Vermont] Taxes, Department of
109 State St.
Montpelier, VT 05602
802-828-2501

[Vermont] Transportation, Agency of
133 State St.
Montpelier, VT 05602
802-828-2657

[Vermont] Treasurer, State
133 State St.
Montpelier, VT 05602
802-828-2301

[Vermont] Unemployment Compensation Division
5 Green Mountain Dr.
Montpelier, VT 05602
802-229-0311

[Vermont] United States Bankruptcy Court
P.O. Box 6648
Rutland, VT 05701
802-773-0219

[Vermont] United States District Court
P.O. Box 945
Burlington, VT 05402
802-951-6301

[Vermont] Vital Records Section
60 Main St., Box 70
Burlington, VT 05402
802-863-7275

[Vermont] Washington County
P.O. Box 426
Montpelier, VT 05602
802-223-2091

[Vermont] Waste Management Division
103 S. Main St., W. Bldg.
Waterbury, VT 05676
802-244-8702

[Vermont] Water Resources & Environmental Engineering, Department of
103 S. Main St.
Waterbury, VT 05676
802-244-8755

[Vermont] Weights & Measures, Division of
116 State St.
Montpelier, VT 05602
802-828-2436

[Vermont] Women, Commission on
126 State St.
Montpelier, VT 05602
802-828-2851

[Virginia] Information & Referral (State Government)
804-786-0000
800-422-2319

[Virginia] Information Center (Federal Government)
Norfolk 804-441-3101
Richmond 804-643-4920
Roanoke 703-982-8591

[Virginia] Administration, Secretary of
202 N. 9th St., Rm. 633
Richmond, VA 23219
804-786-1201

[Virginia] Aging, Department for the
700 E. Franklin St., 10th Fl.
Richmond, VA 23219
804-225-2271
800-552-4464

[Virginia] Agriculture & Consumer Services, Department of
1100 Bank St.
Richmond, VA 23219
804-225-3501
800-552-9963

[Virginia] Albemarle County
401 McIntire Rd.
Charlottesville, VA 22901
804-296-5841

[Virginia] Alexandria Law Library
520 King St., Rm. L34
Alexandria, VA 22314
703-838-4077

[Virginia] Archives Branch
Virginia State Library
11th & Capitol Sq.
Richmond, VA 23219
804-786-2306

[Virginia] Arlington County
1400 N. Courthouse Rd.
Arlington, VA 22201
703-358-3000

[Virginia] Attorney General, Office of
101 N. 8th St.

Supreme Court Bldg.
Richmond, VA 23219
804-786-2071

[Virginia] Auditor of Public Accounts
P.O. Box 1295
Richmond, VA 23210
804-225-3350

Virginia Bar Association
701 E. Franklin St., Suite 1515
Richmond, VA 23219
804-664-0041
804-786-2061 (Virginia State Bar)

[Virginia] Bar Examiners, Board of
9th & Main Streets, Suite 303
Richmond, VA 23219
804-786-7490

[Virginia] Better Business Bureau
701 E. Franklin St., Suite 712
Richmond, VA 23219
804-648-0016

[Virginia] Child Welfare Services, Bureau of
8007 Discovery Dr.
Richmond, VA 23229
804-662-9695

[Virginia] Civil Rights, Office of
1503 Santa Rosa Rd.
Richmond, VA 23288
804-662-9971

[Virginia] Conservation & Historic Resources, Department of
203 Governor St., Suite 302
Richmond, VA 23219
804-786-2121

[Virginia] Consumer Affairs, Office of
1100 Bank St., Rm. 101
Richmond, VA 23219
804-786-2042
800-552-9963

[Virginia] Corporation Commission, State
P.O. Box 1197
Richmond, VA 23209
804-786-3608
800-552-7945

[Virginia] Corrections, Department of
6900 Atmore Dr.
Richmond, VA 23261
804-674-3000

[Virginia] Criminal Justice Services, Department of
805 E. Broad St.
Richmond, VA 23219
804-786-4000

[Virginia] Economic Development, Department of
1000 Washington Bldg.
Richmond, VA 23075
804-786-3791

[Virginia] Education, Department of
101 N. 14th St.
Richmond, VA 23219
804-225-2023

[Virginia] Elections, Board of
9th & Grace Streets
Richmond, VA 23219
804-786-6551

[Virginia] Emergency Services, Department of
310 Turner Rd.
Richmond, VA 23225
804-674-2449

[Virginia] Employment Commission
703 E. Main St.
Richmond, VA 23219
804-786-3001

[Virginia] Energy Division
2201 W. Broad St.
Richmond, VA 23220
804-367-1310

[Virginia] Engineering & Buildings, Division of
805 E. Broad St.
Richmond, VA 23219
804-786-3263

[Virginia] Environment, Council on the
N. 9th St. Bldg., Rm. 903
Richmond, VA 23219
804-786-4500

[Virginia] Fairfax Law Library
4110 Chain Bridge Rd.
Fairfax, VA 22030
703-246-2170

[Virginia] Financial Institutions, Commissioner of
P.O. Box 2-AE
Richmond, VA 23205
804-786-3657
800-552-7945

[Virginia] Governor, Office of
State Capitol Bldg.
Richmond, VA 23219
804-786-2211

[Virginia] Health, Department of
109 Governor St.
Richmond, VA 23219
804-786-3561

[Virginia] Henrico County
P.O. Box 27032
Richmond, VA 23273
804-747-4435

[Virginia] Higher Education, Council of
101 N. 14th St.
Richmond, VA 23219
804-225-2600

[Virginia] House of Delegates
State Capitol
Richmond, VA 23219
804-786-3591
804-786-6530 (Legislative Information)
804-786-7202 (Courts of Justice Committee)

[Virginia] Housing & Community Development, Department of
205 N. 4th St.
Richmond, VA 23219
804-786-1575

Virginia, Industrial Commission of
1000 DMV Dr.
Richmond, VA 23220
804-367-8600

[Virginia] Insurance, Commissioner of
P.O. Box 1157

Richmond, VA 23209
804-786-3741
800-552-7945

[Virginia] Labor & Industry, Department of
4th St. Office Bldg., Suite 205
Richmond, VA 23219
804-786-2376

[Virginia] Law, Department of
101 N. 8th St.
Richmond, VA 23219
804-786-2071

[Virginia] Law Library, Public
800 E. Marshall St., Rm. 302
Richmond, VA 23219
804-780-6500

[Virginia] Law Library, State
100 N. 9th St., 2nd Fl.
Richmond, VA 23219
804-786-2075

[Virginia] Legal Assistants, American Academy of
1022 Park Ave., NE
Norton, VA 24273

[Virginia] Lieutenant Governor, Office of
101 N. 8th St.
Richmond, VA 23219
804-786-2078

[Virginia] Mental Health, Mental Retardation & Substance Abuse Services, Department of
P.O. Box 1797
Richmond, VA 23005
804-786-4868

[Virginia] Mines, Division of
219 Wood Ave.
Big Stone Gap, VA 24219
703-523-0335

[Virginia] Motor Vehicles, Department of
2300 W. Broad St.
Richmond, VA 23220
804-367-6600

[Virginia] Norfolk Law Library
999 Waterside Dr.
Norfolk, VA 23510
804-622-2910

[Virginia] Occupational Health & Safety, Division of
205 N. 4th St.
Richmond, VA 23219
804-786-5873

[Virginia] Parole Board
6900 Atmore Dr.
Richmond, VA 23261
804-674-3081

[Virginia] Peninsula Legal Assistants, Inc.
P.O. Box 1003
Newport News, VA 23601

[Virginia] Personnel & Training, Department of
101 N. 14th St.
Richmond, VA 23219
804-255-2131

[Virginia] Planning & Budget, Department of
9th & Grace St.
Richmond, VA 23219
804-786-5375

[Virginia] Pollution Control Board
P.O. Box 10089
Richmond, VA 23240
804-786-3248

[Virginia] Prince William County Law Library
9311 Lee Ave.
Manassas, VA 22110
703-335-6262

[Virginia] Public Defender Commission
701 E. Franklin St.
Richmond, VA 23219
804-225-3297

[Virginia] Real Estate Board
3600 W. Broad St.
Richmond, VA 23230
804-367-8526

[Virginia] Regulations, Registrar of
Virginia Code Committee
P.O. Box 3-AG
Richmond, VA 23208
804-786-3591

[Virginia] Rehabilitative Services, Department of
P.O. Box 11045
Richmond, VA 23230
804-367-0316

[Virginia] Richmond Association of Legal Assistants
P.O. Box K-121
Richmond, VA 23288

[Virginia] Roanoke Law Library
315 Church Ave., SW
Roanoke, VA 24016
703-981-2268

[Virginia] Roanoke Valley Paralegal Association
P.O. Box 1018
Roanoke, VA 24005

[Virginia] Secretary of the Commonwealth
200–202 N. 9th, Rm. 114
Richmond, VA 23219
804-786-2441

[Virginia] Securities & Retail Franchising, Division of
P.O. Box 1197
Richmond, VA 23209
804-786-7751

[Virginia] Senate
State Capitol
Richmond, VA 23219
804-786-3591
804-786-6882 (Courts of Justice Committee)

[Virginia] Social Services, Department of
8007 Discovery Dr.
Richmond, VA 23229
804-662-9236

[Virginia] Solid & Hazardous Waste Management, Division of
101 N. 14th St.
Richmond, VA 23219
804-225-2667

Virginia State Bar
801 E. Main St., Suite 100
Richmond, VA 23219
804-786-2061

804-644-0041 (Virginia Bar Association)

[Virginia] State Police, Department of
7700 Midlothin Turnpike
Richmond, VA 23235
804-674-2000

[Virginia] Support Enforcement Program, Division of
8007 Discovery Dr.
Richmond, VA 23288
804-662-9297

[Virginia] Supreme Court
100 N. 9th St.
Richmond, VA 23219
804-786-2251

[Virginia] Taxation, Department of
2220 W. Broad St.
Richmond, VA 23220
804-367-8005

[Virginia] Transportation, Department of
1401 E. Broad St.
Richmond, VA 23219
804-786-2801

[Virginia] Treasury, Department of
101 N. 14th St.
Richmond, VA 23219
804-225-2142

[Virginia] Unemployment Insurance Division
P.O. Box 1358
Richmond, VA 23211
804-786-3004

[Virginia] United States Bankruptcy Court
Eastern Virginia
P.O. Box 676
Richmond, VA 23206
804-771-2878

[Virginia] United States Bankruptcy Court
Western Virginia
P.O. Box 2390
Roanoke, VA 24010
703-982-6391

[Virginia] United States Court of Appeals for the Fourth Circuit
10th & Main Streets
Richmond, VA 23219
804-771-2213
804-771-2219 (Law Library)

[Virginia] United States District Court
Eastern District
P.O. Box 21449
200 S. Washington St.
Alexandria, VA 22302
703-557-5127

[Virginia] United States District Court
Western District
P.O. Box 1234
Roanoke, VA 24006
703-982-6224

[Virginia] Vital Records, Division of
P.O. Box 1000
Richmond, VA 23208
804-786-6228

[Virginia] Water Control Board, State
2111 N. Hamilton St.
Richmond, VA 23230
804-367-0056

[Virginia] Weights & Measures Bureau
P.O. Box 1163
Richmond, VA 23209
804-786-2476

[Virginia] Women, Council on the Status of
8007 Discovery Dr.
Richmond, VA 23229
804-662-9200

[Virgin Islands] Bar Association
P.O. Box 990
St. Thomas, VI 00801
809-776-3470
809-778-7497 (St. Croix)

[Virgin Islands] Bar Examiners, Board of
P.O. Box 720
St. Thomas, VI 00801
809-774-5480

[Virgin Islands] Economic Development & Agriculture, Department of
81 AB Kronprindsens Gade
St. Thomas, VI 00801
809-774-8784

[Virgin Islands] Governor, Office of
Government House
21–222 Kongens Gade
St. Thomas, VI 00802
809-774-0001
809-773-1404 (St. Croix)

[Virgin Islands] Human Services, Department of
Barbel Plaza South
St. Thomas, VI 00802
809-774-0930

[Virgin Islands] Insurance, Commissioner of
Kangens Garde #18
St. Thomas, VI 00802
809-774-2991

[Virgin Islands] Justice, Department of
46 Norre Gade
St. Thomas, VI 00801
809-774-5666

[Virgin Islands] Law Revision Commission
Corporate Pl., Royal Dane Mall
St. Thomas, VI 00802
809-776-9825
809-774-0739 (Legislative Counsel)

[Virgin Islands] Legislature
P.O. Box 477
St. Thomas, VI 00801
809-774-0880

Virgin Islands Paralegals
P.O. Box 10197
St. Thomas, VI 00801

[Virgin Islands] Parole, Board of
P.O. Box 2931
Christiansted
St. Croix, VI 00820
809-773-1507

[Virgin Islands] Public Services Commission
P.O. Box 40

St. Thomas, VI 00804
809-776-1291

[Virgin Islands] Support & Paternity Division
46 Norre Gade
St. Thomas, VI 00801
809-776-0372

Virgin Islands Territorial Court
Barbel Plaza
P.O. Box 70
St. Thomas, VI 00801
809-774-6680

[Virgin Islands] United States Customs Service
Federal Bldg.
P.O. Box 510
St. Thomas, VI 00801
809-774-2501
809-773-1490 (St. Croix)

[Virgin Islands] United States District Attorney
Federal Office Bldg.
St. Thomas, VI 00802
809-774-5757

[Virgin Islands] United States District Court
P.O. Box 720
Charlotte Amalie, St. Thomas 00801
809-774-0640
809-773-1130 (St. Croix)

[Virgin Islands] United States Immigration & Naturalization Service
Federal Office Bldg.
St. Thomas, VI 00802
809-774-1390
809-778-6559 (St. Croix)

[Virgin Islands] United States Internal Revenue Service
Federal Office Bldg.
St. Thomas, VI 00802
809-774-7870
809-778-6080 (St. Croix)

[Virgin Islands] Vital Statistics, Registrar of
Charles Harwood Memorial Hospital
St. Croix, VI 00820

Volunteer Lawyers for the Arts
1285 Avenue of the Americas
New York, NY 10019
212-977-9270

Voters for Choice
2000 P. St. NW
Wash. D.C. 20036
202-822-6640

Wang Laboratories
1 Industrial Ave.
Lowell, MA 01851
508-967-6061

Warren, Gorham & Lamont, Inc.
1 Penn Plaza
New York, NY 10019
212-971-5000
800-950-1216

[Washington] Information & Referral (State Government)
206-753-5000

[Washington] Information Center (Federal Government)
Seattle 206-442-0570
Tacoma 206-383-7970

[Washington] Actuary, Office of the State
Lakeridge Way S.W., Suite C 919
Olympia, WA 98504

[Washington] Administrative Hearings, Office of
4224 6th Ave., S.E., M/S PY-15
Lacey, WA 98504
206-459-6353

[Washington] Aging & Adult Services Administration
M/S OB-44A
Olympia, WA 98504
206-753-2502
800-422-3263

[Washington] Agriculture, Department of
406 General Administration Bldg.
Olympia, WA 98504
206-753-5063

[Washington] Air Programs Division
4224 6th Ave. SE, M/S PV-11
Lacey, WA 98503
206-459-6256

[Washington] Archives & Records Management
P.O. Box 9000
Olympia, WA 98504
206-753-5485

[Washington] Asian American Affairs, Commission on
110 Prefontaine Pl. South, Suite 202
Seattle, WA 98104
206-464-5820

[Washington] Attorney General, Office of
Highway-Licenses Bldg., M/S PB-71
Olympia, WA 98504
206-753-6200 (Olympia)
206-464-7744 (Seattle)
509-456-6373 (Spokane)

[Washington] Auditor, Office of State
Legislative Bldg.
Olympia, WA 98504
206-753-5277

[Washington] Banking, Supervisor of
General Administration Bldg.
Olympia, WA 98504
206-753-6520

[Washington] Bar Association
500 Westin Bldg.
2001 6th Ave.
Seattle, WA 98121
206-448-0441
206-448-0433 (CLE)
206-448-0563 (Bar Admissions)

[Washington] Better Business Bureau
2220 6th Ave., Suite 828
Seattle, WA 98121
206-448-8888

[Washington] Children & Family Services Administration
Office Bldg. #2, M/S OB-41
Olympia, WA 98504
206-586-8654

[Washington] Code Reviser
Legislative Bldg.
Olympia, WA 98504
206-753-6804

[Washington] Community Development, Department of
9th & Columbia Bldg.
Olympia, WA 98504
206-753-2200

[Washington] Consumer & Business Fair Practices Division
N. 122 Capitol Way
Olympia, WA 98501
206-753-6210
800-551-4636

[Washington] Convention & Trade Center, State
720 Olive Way, 15th Fl., Suite 1515
Seattle, WA 98101
206-464-5305

[Washington] Corrections, Department of
P.O. Box 9699
Capital Center Bldg., M/S FN-61
Olympia, WA 98504
206-753-1573

[Washington] Counties, State Association of
206 10th Ave., S.E.
Olympia, WA 98501
206-753-1886

[Washington] Court of Appeals
Division I
1 Union Square
600 University St.
Seattle, WA 98101
206-464-7750

[Washington] Court of Appeals
Division II
945 Market St., Suite 600
Tacoma, WA 98402
206-593-2970

[Washington] Court of Appeals
Division III
N. 500 Cedar, P.O. Box 2159
Spokane, WA 99210
509-456-3082 (clerk)

[Washington] Courts, Office of the Administrator for the
1206 S. Quince St., M/S EZ-11
Olympia, WA 98504
206-753-3365

Washington Dairy Products Commission
1107 N.E. 45th St., Suite 205
Seattle, WA 98105
206-545-6763

Washington Defender Association
810 3rd Ave., Central Bldg., 8th Fl.
Seattle, WA 98104
206-623-4321

[Washington] Deferred Compensation, Committee for
2600 Martin Way, Suite D
Olympia, WA 98504
206-586-4980

[Washington] Disability Issues & Employment, Governor's Committee on
212 Maple Park
Olympia, WA 98504
206-753-1547

[Washington] Ecology, Department of
M/S PV-11
Lacey, WA 98504
206-459-6168

[Washington] Economic Development Board
18000 Pacific Hwy S., #408
Seattle, WA 98188
206-764-4090

[Washington] Education, Department of
Legion Way & Washington St.
Olympia, WA 98504
206-586-6904

[Washington] Emergency Management, Division of
4220 E. Martin Way, M/S PT-11

Olympia, WA 98504
206-753-5255

[Washington] Employment Security Department
212 Maple Park
Olympia, WA 98504
206-753-5116

[Washington] Energy Facility Site Evaluation Council
4224 6th Ave. S.E., Bldg. #1
Lacey, WA 98504
206-459-6490

[Washington] Energy Office, State
809 Legion Way S.E.
Olympia, WA 98504
206-586-5000

[Washington] Family Independence Program, State
924 E. 7th
Olympia, WA 98504
206-586-4280

[Washington] Financial Management, Office of
300 Insurance Bldg.
Olympia, WA 98504
206-753-5459

[Washington] Fisheries, Department of
115 General Administration Bldg.
Olympia, WA 98504
206-753-6600

[Washington] Forest Practices Appeals Board
4224 6th Ave., S.E., Bldg. #2
Lacey, WA 98504
206-459-6327

[Washington] Gambling Commission
1110 S. Jefferson
Olympia, WA 98504
206-753-0861

[Washington] General Administration, Department of
218 General Administration Bldg., M/S AX-22
Olympia, WA 98504
206-753-5439

[Washington] Governor, Office of the
Legislative Bldg.
Olympia, WA 98504
206-753-6780

[Washington] Health Care Authority, State
1400 Evergreen Park Dr., S.W.
Olympia, WA 98504
206-753-3096

[Washington] Health Care Facilities Authority
504 E. 14th, Suite 130
Olympia, WA 98504
206-753-6185

[Washington] Higher Education Coordinating Board
908 E. 5th Ave.
Olympia, WA 98504
206-753-2210

Washington Hispanic Affairs, State Commission on
1515 S. Cherry
Olympia, WA 98504
206-753-3159

[Washington] Hospital Commission, State
206 Evergreen Plaza
711 S. Capitol Way
Olympia, WA 98504
206-753-1990

[Washington] House of Representatives
Legislative Bldg.
Olympia, WA 98504
206-786-7550
206-786-7886 (Judiciary)

[Washington] Housing Finance Commission
710 2nd Ave., Suite 1090
Seattle, WA 98104
206-464-7139

[Washington] Human Rights Commission
402 Evergreen Plaza Bldg.
711 S. Capitol Way
Olympia, WA 98504
206-753-6770

[Washington] Hydraulics Appeals Board
4224 6th Ave. S.E., Bldg. #2
Lacey, WA 98504
206-459-6327

[Washington] Indeterminate Sentence Review Board
700 Capitol Center Bldg., M/S FN-71
Olympia, WA 98504
206-753-6797

[Washington] Indian Affairs, Governor's Office of
605 11th Ave. So., Suite 112
Olympia, WA 98504
206-753-2411

[Washington] Industrial Insurance Appeals, Board of
410 W. 5th Ave.
Olympia, WA 98504
206-753-6823

[Washington] Industrial Safety & Health Division
P.O. Box 207
Olympia, WA 98504
206-753-6500

[Washington] Insurance Commissioner
Insurance Bldg., M/S AQ-21
Olympia, WA 98504
206-753-7301
800-562-6900

[Washington] Investment Board, State
421 S. Capitol Way
Olympia, WA 98504
206-753-6810

[Washington] Judicial Conduct, Commission on
12th & Jefferson Bldg., Suite 9
Olympia, WA 98504
206-753-4585

[Washington] Judicial Council
Temple of Justice
Olympia, WA 98504
206-753-5078

[Washington] Juvenile Rehabilitation, Division of
M/S OB-32

Olympia, WA 98504
206-753-7402

[Washington] King County
King County Courthouse
Seattle, WA 98104
206-296-0100

**[Washington] King County Law
Library**
621 County Courthouse
Seattle, WA 98104
206-296-0940

**[Washington] King County
Superior Court**
Arbitration Office
W. 855 King County Courthouse
Seattle, WA 98104
206-296-9365

**[Washington] Labor &
Industries, Department of**
General Administration Bldg., M/S
HC-101
Olympia, WA 98504
206-753-6341

[Washington] Law Library, State
Temple of Justice, M/S AV-02
Olympia, WA 98504
206-357-2136

**[Washington] Law Reports,
Commission on State**
Temple of Justice
Olympia, WA 98504
206-753-3013

**Washington Legal Assistants
Association**
P.O. Box 2114
Seattle, WA 98111

Washington Legal Foundation
1705 N. St., NW
Wash. D.C. 20036
202-857-0240

**[Washington] Legislative Service
Center**
Legislative Bldg.
Olympia, WA 98504
206-786-7725

[Washington] Library, State
State Library Bldg.

Olympia, WA 98504
206-753-5590

**[Washington] Licensing,
Department of**
Highway-Licenses Bldg., M/S PB-01
Olympia, WA 98504
206-753-6918

**[Washington] Lieutenant
Governor, Office of the**
Legislative Bldg., 3rd Fl.
Olympia, WA 98504
206-786-7700

**[Washington] Liquor Control
Board**
1025 E. Union
Olympia, WA 98504
206-753-6262

**[Washington] Lottery
Commission, State**
814 4th Ave.
Olympia, WA 98504
206-753-1412

**[Washington] Military
Department**
Headquarters
Camp Murray
Tacoma, WA 98430
206-581-1950

**[Washington] Minority &
Women's Business
Enterprises, Office of**
406 S. Water
Olympia, WA 98504
206-753-9693

**[Washington] Municipal
Research Council**
4719 Brooklyn Ave., N.E.
Seattle, WA 98105
206-543-9050

**[Washington] Natural Resources,
Department of**
201 John A. Cherberg Bldg.
Olympia, WA 98504
206-753-5327

**[Washington] Northwest Power
Planning Council**
809 Legion Way, S.E.

Olympia, WA 98504
206-586-8071

**[Washington] Parks & Recreation
Commission, State**
7150 Cleanwater Lane
Olympia, WA 98504
206-753-5755

**[Washington] Personnel Appeals
Board**
2828 Capitol Blvd.
Olympia, WA 98504
206-586-1481

**[Washington] Personnel,
Department of**
521 Capitol Way So.
P.O. Box 1789
Olympia, WA 98504
206-753-5368

[Washington] Pierce County
930 Tacoma Ave. South
Tacoma, WA 98402
206-591-7272

**[Washington] Pierce County Law
Library**
930 Tacoma Ave. South
Tacoma, WA 98402
206-591-7494

**[Washington] Pollution Control
Hearings Board**
4224 6th Ave. S.E., Bldg. #2
Lacey, WA 98504
206-459-6327

[Washington] Productivity Board
Legislative Bldg.
Olympia, WA 98504
206-753-3174

**[Washington] Prosecuting
Attorneys, Association of**
206 10th Ave. SE
Olympia, WA 98501
206-753-2175

**[Washington] Public Deposit
Protection Commission**
Office of the State Treasurer
General Administration Bldg.
Olympia, WA 98504
206-753-7477

[Washington] Public Disclosure Commission
403 Evergreen Plaza
Olympia, WA 98504
206-753-1111

[Washington] Public Employment Relations Commission
603 Evergreen Plaza
Olympia, WA 98504
206-753-3444

[Washington] Public Instruction, Superintendent of
Old Capitol Bldg.
Olympia, WA 98504
206-753-6738

[Washington] Puget Sound Water Quality Authority
217 Pine St., Suite 1100
Seattle, WA 98101
206-464-7320

[Washington] Real Estate Commission
P.O. Box 9012
Olympia,WA 98504
206-753-6974

[Washington] Revenue, Department of
General Administration Bldg,
M/S AX-02
Olympia, WA 98504
206-753-5540

[Washington] Road Administration Board
206 10th S.E.
Olympia, WA 98504
206-753-5989

[Washington] Seattle, City of
600 4th Ave.
Seattle, WA 98104
206-386-1234

[Washington] Seattle-King County Bar Association
320 Central Bldg.
Seattle, WA 98104
206-624-9365

[Washington] Secretary of State, Office of the
Legislative Bldg.

Olympia, WA 98504
206-753-7121

[Washington] Securities Division
P.O. Box 648
Olympia, WA 98504
206-753-6928

[Washington] Senate
Legislative Bldg.
Olympia, WA 98504
206-786-7550
206-786-7692 (Law & Justice
Committee)

[Washington] Sentencing Guidelines Commission
3400 Capitol Blvd.
Olympia, WA 98504
206-753-3084

[Washington] Shorelines Hearing Board
4224 6th Ave., S.E., Bldg. #2
Lacey, WA 98504
206-459-6327

[Washington] Snohomish County Law Library
Courthouse
Everett, WA 98201
206-259-5326

[Washington] Social Services, Department of
12th & Franklin
Olympia, WA 98504
206-753-7039

[Washington] Solid & Hazardous Waste Program
4224 6th Ave. S.E. Bldg. 4, M/S
PV-11
Olympia, WA 98504
206-459-6316

[Washington] Spokane, City of
808 West Spokane Falls Blvd.
Spokane, WA 99201
509-456-3232

[Washington] Spokane County
W. 1116 Broadway
Spokane, WA 99201
509-456-2211

[Washington] Spokane County Law Library
1020 Paulsen Bldg.

Spokane, WA 99201
509-456-3680

[Washington] Support Enforcement, Office of
P.O. Box 9162. M/S HJ-31
Olympia, WA 98504
206-586-6111

[Washington] Supreme Court
Highways/Licenses Bldg., 6th Fl.
12th & Washington, M/S AV-11
Olympia, WA 98504
206-753-5080

[Washington] Tax Appeals, Board of
910 E. 5th Ave.
Olympia, WA 98504
206-753-5449

Washington Trade & Economic Development, Department of
101 General Administration Bldg.
Olympia, WA 98504
206-753-5630

Washington Traffic Safety Commission
1000 S. Cherry St.
Olympia, WA 98504
206-753-6197

Washington Transportation, Department of
Transportation Bldg, M/S KF-01
Olympia, WA 98504
206-753-6005

[Washington] Transportation Improvement Board
Transportation Bldg.
Olympia, WA 98504
206-753-7199

[Washington] Treasurer, State
Legislative Bldg.
Olympia, WA 98504
206-753-7130

[Washington] Unemployment Compensation Division
212 Maple Park
Olympia, WA 98504
206-753-5120

[Washington] United States Bankruptcy Court
Eastern Washington

P.O. Box 2164
Spokane, WA 99210
509-456-3830

[Washington] United States Bankruptcy Court
Western Washington
1200 6th Ave.
Seattle, WA 98101
206-442-2751

[Washington] United States District Court
Eastern District
P.O. Box 1493
Spokane, WA 99210
509-456-3728

[Washington] United States District Court
Western District
1010 5th Ave.
Seattle, WA 98104
206-442-5598

[Washington] United States Government Printing Office
915 2nd Ave., Rm. 194
Seattle, WA 98174
206-442-4270

[Washington] Utilities & Transportation Commission
1300 S. Evergreen Park Dr., South
Olympia, WA 98504
206-753-6423
800-652-6150

[Washington] Veterans Affairs, Department of
505 E. Union Republic Bldg., 3rd Fl.
P.O. Box 9770
Olympia, WA 98504
206-753-5586

[Washington] Vital Records
P.O. Box 9709, M/S ET-11
Olympia, WA 98504
206-753-5396
800-551-0562
800-331–0680

[Washington] Vocational Rehabilitation, Division of
M/S OB 21-C
Olympia, WA 98504
206-753-0293

[Washington] Water Resources Division
Baran Hall, 3rd Fl., M/S PV-11
Olympia, WA 98504
206-459-6056

[Washington] Weights & Measures
General Administration Bldg., Rm. 406
Olympia, WA 98504
206-753-5042

[Washington] Wildlife, Department of
600 N. Capitol Way
Olympia, WA 98504
206-753-5700

[Washington] Worker's Benefits
11th Ave. & Columbia St.
Olympia, WA 98504
206-753-6376

Western Center on Law & Poverty
3535 W. 6th St.
Los Angeles, CA 90020
213-487-7211

Western Union Corp.
1 Lake St.
Upper Saddle River, NJ 07458
201-818-5000

West Publishing Co.
50 W. Kellogg Blvd.
St. Paul, MN 55164
612-288-2500
800-328-9352
800-328-0109 (WESTLAW)

[West Virginia] Information & Referral (State Government)
304-348-3456

[West Virginia] Administration, Department of
State Capitol Complex, Bldg. 1, Rm. E-119
Charleston, WV 25305
304-340-2300

[West Virginia] Aging, Commission on
1710 Kanawha Blvd. E.
Charleston, WV 25317

304-348-3317
800-642-3671

[West Virginia] Agriculture, Department of
Guthrie Agricultural Center
Charleston, WV 25305
304-348-3350

[West Virginia] Air Pollution Control Commission
1558 Washington St. E.
Charleston, WV 25311
304-348-2275

[West Virginia] Alcohol Beverage Control Commission
310 57th St. SE
Charleston, WV 25305
304-348-2481

[West Virginia] Archives & History Division
Cultural Center, Capitol Complex
Charleston, WV 25305
304-348-0162

[West Virginia] Arts & Humanities Division
Cultural Center, 2nd Fl.
Charleston, WV 25305
304-348-0240

[West Virginia] Attorney General, Office of
State Capitol Complex, Rm. E-26
Charleston, WV 25305
304-348-2021

[West Virginia] Auditor, Office of
State Capitol, Rm. W-100
Charleston, WV 25305
304-348-2251

[West Virginia] Banking, Commissioner of
State Capitol Complex, Rm. 311
Charleston, WV 25305
304-348-2294
800-642-9056

West Virginia Bar Association
100 Capitol St.
Charleston, WV 25301
304-342-1474
304-346-8414 (WV State Bar)

[West Virginia] Child Advocate Office
1900 Washington St. East
Charleston, WV 25305
304-348-3780

[West Virginia] Civil Service System
Building 6, Rm. B-456
Charleston, WV 25305
304-348-3950

[West Virginia] Commerce, Labor & Environmental Resources, Department of
State Capitol Complex, Bldg. 1
Charleston, WV 25305
304-348-1600

[West Virginia] Community & Industrial Development Division
State Capitol Complex Bldg. 1, Rm. M-146
Charleston, WV 25305
304-348-0400

[West Virginia] Consumer Protection Division
812 Quarrier St., 6th Fl
Charleston, WV 25301
304-348-8986
800-368-8808

[West Virginia] Corrections, Department of
112 California Ave., Bldg. 4
Charleston, WV 25305
304-348-2037

[West Virginia] Court of Claims
Bldg. 1, Rm. 4
Charleston, WV 25305
304-348-03470

[West Virginia] Courts, Administrative Director of the
State Capitol Bldg., Rm. E-402
Charleston, WV 25305
304-348-0145

[West Virginia] Crime Victims Compensation Fund
Bldg. 1, Rm. 6
Charleston, WV 25305
304-348-3471

[West Virginia] Economic Opportunity, Office of
1204 Kanawha Blvd. E.
Charleston, WV 25301
304-348-8860

[West Virginia] Education & the Arts, Department of
950 Kanawha Blvd., East
Charleston, WV 25301
304-348-2101

[West Virginia] Emergency Services, Office of
State Capitol Bldg., Rm. EB-80
Charleston, WV 25305
304-348-5380

[West Virginia] Employment Security, Department of
112 California Ave.
Charleston, WV 25305
304-348-2630

[West Virginia] Environmental Health Services, Office of
1800 Washington St. E.
Charleston, WV 25312
304-348-2981

[West Virginia] Farm Management Commission
703 N. Main St.
New Martinsville, WV 26155
304-455-1922

[West Virginia] Finance & Administration, Department of
State Capitol Bldg., Rm. E-119
Charleston, WV 25305
304-348-2300
304-348-2344 (Budget)

[West Virginia] Fuel & Energy, Department of
1204 Kanawha Blvd. E.
Charleston, WV 25301
304-348-8860

[West Virginia] Governor, Office of
Capitol Bldg.
Charleston, WV 25305
304-340-1600
800-227-4865

[West Virginia] Health & Human Resources, Department of
State Capitol Complex, Bldg. 6, Rm. B-617
Charleston, WV 25305
304-348-2400

[West Virginia] Highways, Department of
1900 Washington St. E.
Charleston, WV 25305
304-348-3505

[West Virginia] House of Delegates
Bldg. 1, Rm. 212
State Capitol
Charleston, WV 25305
304-340-3200
304-340-3252 (Judiciary)

[West Virginia] Human Rights Commission
1036 Quarrier St.
Charleston, WV 25301
304-348-2616

[West Virginia] Human Services, Department of
State Capitol
Charleston, WV 25305
304-348-2400

[West Virginia] Insurance Commissioner
2019 Washington St. East
Charleston, WV 25305
304-348-3394
800-642-9004

[West Virginia] Kanawha County
P.O. Box 3226
Charleston, WV 25332
304-357-0101

[West Virginia] Labor, Department of
1800 Washington St. E., Rm. 319
Charleston, WV 25305
304-348-7890

[West Virginia] Law Examiners, Board of
Bldg. 1, Rm. E-400
State Capitol Complex
Charleston, WV 25305
304-348-7815

West Virginia Law Library
Capitol Bldg., Rm. E-404
Charleston, WV 25305
304-348-2607

West Virginia, Legal Assistants of
P.O. Box 553
Charleston, WV 25322

[West Virginia] Legislative Auditor's Office
Bldg. 1, Rm. WW-202
Charleston, WV 25305
304-348-2151

[West Virginia] Legislative Services
State Capitol, Rm. E-132
Charleston, WV 25305
304-348-2040

[West Virginia] Medicine, Board of
100 Dee. Dr., Suite 104
Charleston, WV 25311
304-348-2921

[West Virginia] Motor Vehicles, Department of
Bldg. 3, Rm. 113
Charleston, WV 25317
304-348-2723
800-642-9066

[West Virginia] Natural Resources, Department of
State Capitol Bldg. 3
Charleston, WV 25305
304-348-2754

[West Virginia] Ohio County
City County Bldg.
Wheeling, WV 26003
304-234-3656

[West Virginia] Oil & Gas Conservation Commission
322 70th St. SE
Charleston, WV 25304
304-348-3092

[West Virginia] Planning Unit
State Capitol Complex Bldg. 6,
Rm. 553
Charleston, WV 25301
304-348-4010

[West Virginia] Probation & Parole, Board of
112 California Ave., Rm. 304
Charleston, WV 25305
304-348-6366

[West Virginia] Public Legal Services Council
Bldg. 3, Rm. 330
Charleston, WV 25305
304-348-3905

[West Virginia] Public Safety, Department of
State Capitol Complex, Box 2930
Charleston, WV 25305
304-348-2930

[West Virginia] Public Service Commission
P.O. Box 812
Charleston, WV 25323
304-340-0300
800-344-5113

[West Virginia] Real Estate Commission
1033 Quarrier St., Suite 400
Charleston, WV 25301
304-348-3555

[West Virginia] Regents, Board of
950 Kanawha Blvd. E.
Charleston, WV 25301
304-348-2101

[West Virginia] Rehabilitation, Division of
State Board of Rehabilitation
State Capitol
Charleston, WV 25305
304-766-4600

[West Virginia] Secretary of State
State Capitol Bldg., Rm. W-157
Charleston, WV 25305
304-345-4000

[West Virginia] Securities Division
State Capitol Bldg.
Charleston, WV 25305
304-348-2257

[West Virginia] Senate
Bldg. 1, Rm. W-131
State Capitol
Charleston, WV 25305
304-357-7800

West Virginia State Bar
E-400 State Capitol
Charleston, WV 25305
304-346-8414
304-342-1474 (WV Bar Association)

[West Virginia] Supreme Court of Appeals
State Capitol Bldg., Rm. 317-E
Charleston, WV 25305
304-348-2601

[West Virginia] Tax & Revenue, Department of
State Office Bldg., Bldg. 1, Rm.
W-300
Charleston, WV 25305
304-348-2500

[West Virginia] Treasury, Office of the
State Capitol Complex, Rm. E141
Charleston, WV 25305
304-348-4000

[West Virginia] Trial Lawyers Association
P.O. Box 3968
Charleston, WV 25339
304-344-0692

[West Virginia] Unemployment Compensation Division
112 California Ave., 6th Fl.
Charleston, WV 25305
304-348-2624

[West Virginia] United States Bankruptcy Court
Northern West Virginia
P.O. Box 70
Wheeling, WV 26003
304-233-1655

[West Virginia] United States Bankruptcy Court
Southern West Virginia
500 Quarrier St.
Charleston, WV 25301
304-347-5114

[West Virginia] United States District Court
Northern District
P.O. Box 1518
Eakins, WV 26241
304-636-1445

[West Virginia] United States District Court
Southern District
P.O.Box 2546
Charleston, WV 25329
304-342-5154

[West Virginia] Veterans Affairs, Department of
605 Atlas Bldg.
Charleston, WV 25301
304-348-3661

[West Virginia] Vital Statistics, Division of
1800 Washington St. E., 5th Fl.
Charleston, WV 25305
304-348-2931

[West Virginia] Waste Management, Division of
1260 Greenbrier St.
Charleston, WV 25311
304-348-5935

[West Virginia] Water Resources Board
1201 Greenbrier St.
Charleston, WV 25311
304-348-2107

[West Virginia] Weights & Measures, Division of
1800 Washington St., East
Charleston, WV 25305
304-348-7890

[West Virginia] Worker's Compensation Fund
601 Morris St.
Charleston, WV 25301
304-348-2580

Wildlife Conservation Fund of America
50 W. Broad St., Suite 1025
Columbus, OH 43215
614-221-2684

Wildlife Society, The
5410 Grosvenor Ln.
Bethesda, MD 20814
301-897-9770

Wiley Law Publications
721 N. Tejon St.
Colorado Springs, CO 80903
719-578-0600

William S. Hein & Co.
See Hein

Wilson Co., H.W.
950 University St.
Bronx, NY 10452
800-622-4002

[Wisconsin] Information & Referral (State Government)
608-266-2211

[Wisconsin] Information Center (Federal Government)
Milwaukee 414-271-2273

[Wisconsin] Administration, Department of
P.O. Box 7864
Madison, WI 53707
608-266-1741

[Wisconsin] Adult Probation & Parole Services
P.O. Box 7925
Madison, WI 53707
608-266-3834

[Wisconsin] Aging, Bureau on
P.O. Box 7851
Madison, WI 53707
608-266-2536

[Wisconsin] Agriculture Trade & Consumer Protection, Department of
801 W. Badger Rd.
Madison, WI 53713
608-266-7100

[Wisconsin] Air Management, Bureau of
101 S. Webster St.
Madison, WI 53702
608-266-0603

[Wisconsin] Archivist, State
816 State St.
Madison, WI 53716
608-262-7304

[Wisconsin] Assembly
State Capitol
Madison, WI 53702
608-266-0341
608-266-9960 (Legislative Hotline)
608-266-8590 (Judiciary)

[Wisconsin] Attorney General, Office of
P.O. Box 7857
Madison, WI 53707
608-266-1221

[Wisconsin] Attorneys Professional Competence, Board of
119 Martin Luther King, Jr. Blvd., Rm. 405
Madison, WI 53703
608-266-9760

[Wisconsin] Attorneys Professional Responsibility, Board of
110 E. Main St., Suite 410
Madison, WI 53703
608-267-7274

[Wisconsin] Banking, Commissioner of
131 W. Wilson, 8th Fl.
Madison, WI 53703
608-266-1621

Wisconsin Bar Association
402 W. Wilson
Madison, WI 53707
608-257-3838
800-362-8096
608-257-9569 (Bar Foundation)

Wisconsin Bell
722 N. Broadway
Milwaukee, WI 53202
414-678-0681
800-237-8576

[Wisconsin] Better Business Bureau
740 N. Plankinton Ave.
Milwaukee, WI 53202
414-273-1600

[Wisconsin] Budget & Planning, Division of
101 S. Webster St.
Madison, WI 53702
608-266-1353

[Wisconsin] Child Support, Bureau of
1 W. Wilson St., Rm. 382
P.O. Box 7935
Madison, WI 53707
608-266-1175

[Wisconsin] Community Corrections, Bureau of
1 W. Wilson St., Rm. 951
Madison, WI 53702
608-266-3834

[Wisconsin] Consumer Protection & Citizen Advocacy
P.O. Box 7856
Madison,WI 53702
608-266-1852
800-362-8189

Wisconsin Correctional Center System
5140 County Hwy M
Oregon, WI 53575
608-835-5711

[Wisconsin] Corrections, Division of
1 W. Wilson St., P.O. Box 7925
Madison, WI 53707
608-266-2471

Wisconsin Court of Appeals, District I
901 N. 9th St., Suite 609
Milwaukee, WI 53233
414-227-4684

Wisconsin Court of Appeals, District II
2727 N. Grandview Blvd., Suite 300
Waukesha, WI 53188
414-521-5232

Wisconsin Court of Appeals, District III
740 3rd St.
Wausau, WI 54401
715-845-6404

Wisconsin Court of Appeals, District IV
119 Martin Luther King, Jr. Blvd,
7th Fl.
Madison, WI 53703
608-266-9360

[Wisconsin] Dane County
210 Martin Luther King Ave.
Madison, WI 53709
608-266-4121

[Wisconsin] Development, Department of
123 W. Washington Ave.
Madison, WI 53702
608-266-1916

[Wisconsin] Election Board, State
2912 S. Delaware Ave.
Bay View, WI 53207
414-481-6237

[Wisconsin] Energy & Intergovernmental Relations, Division of
101 S. Webster St.
Madison, WI 53702
608-266-8234

[Wisconsin] Ethics Board
125 S. Webster St.
Madison, WI 53702
608-266-8123

[Wisconsin] Facilities Management, Division of
101 S. Webster St.
Madison, WI 53702
608-266-1031

[Wisconsin] Finance & Program Management, Division of State
101 S. Webster St.
Madison, WI 53707
608-266-3628

[Wisconsin] Governor, Office of
115 E. State Capitol Bldg.
Madison, WI 53703
608-266-1212

[Wisconsin] Health & Social Services, Department of
1 W. Wilson St., P.O. Box 7850
Madison, WI 53707
608-266-3681

[Wisconsin] Health Statistics, Bureau of
P.O. Box 309
Madison, WI 53701
608-266-1371

[Wisconsin] Housing & Economic Development Authority
1 S. Pickney

Madison, WI 53703
608-266-2767

[Wisconsin] Industry, Labor & Human Relations, Department of
201 E. Washington Ave.
Madison, WI 53702
608-266-7552

[Wisconsin] Insurance, Commissioner of
P.O. Box 7873
Madison, WI 53702
608-266-3582
800-236-8517

[Wisconsin] Juvenile Offender Review Board
1 W. Wilson St., P.O. Box 7850
Madison, WI 53707
608-266-6463

[Wisconsin] Law Library, State
P.O. Box 7881
Madison, WI 53707
608-266-1424

[Wisconsin] Legislative Audit Bureau
131 W. Wilson St.
Madison, WI 53703
608-266-2818

[Wisconsin] Legislative Reference Bureau
State Capitol, Rm. 201
Madison, WI 53702
608-266-7098

[Wisconsin] Licensing & Real Estate, Bureau of Direct
P.O. Box 8935
Madison,WI 53708
608-266-5514

[Wisconsin] Lieutenant Governor, Office of
State Capitol Bldg., Rm. 22E
Madison, WI 53702
608-266-3516

[Wisconsin] Midwest Legal Publisher
806 Lincoln Ct.
Oconomowoc, WI 53066
414-567-2521

[Wisconsin] Milwaukee Bar Association
605 E. Wisconsin Ave.
Milwaukee, WI 53202
414-274-6760

[Wisconsin] Milwaukee City Hall
200 E. Wells St.
Milwaukee, WI 53202
414-278-3200

[Wisconsin] Milwaukee County Law Library
901 N. 9th St.
Milwaukee, WI 53233
414-278-4900

[Wisconsin] Mine Reclamation Section
101 S. Webster St.
Madison, WI 53702
608-266-2050

[Wisconsin] Motor Vehicles, Division of
4802 Sheboygan Ave.
Madison, WI 53702
608-266-2233

[Wisconsin] Natural Resources, Department of
101 S. Webster St.
Madison, WI 53702
608-266-2121

Wisconsin, Paralegal Association of
P.O. Box 92882
Milwaukee, WI 53202
414-272-7168

[Wisconsin] Parole Board
1 W. Wilson St., P.O. Box 7850
Madison, WI 53707
608-266-2957

[Wisconsin] Public Defender, State
131 W. Wilson St., Rm. 100
Madison, WI 53703
608-266-0087

[Wisconsin] Public Instruction, Department of
101 S. Webster St.
Madison, WI 53707
608-266-1771

[Wisconsin] Public Representation, Center for
520 University Ave.

Madison, WI 53703
608-251-4008

[Wisconsin] Public Service Commission
4802 Sheboygan Ave., P.O. Box 7854
Madison, WI 53707
608-266-2001

[Wisconsin] Regulation & Licensing, Department of
1400 E. Washington Ave.
Madison, WI 53703
608-266-8609

[Wisconsin] Revenue, Department of
101 S. Webster St.
Madison, WI 53708
608-266-6466

[Wisconsin] Revisor of Statutes
30 W. Mifflin St., Rm. 702
Madison, WI 53703
608-266-2011

Wisconsin Safety & Buildings Division
201 E. Washington Ave.
Madison, WI 53702
608-266-1816

[Wisconsin] Secretary of State
30 W. Mifflin, 10th Fl.
Madison, WI 53703
608-266-5594

[Wisconsin] Securities Commissioner
111 W. Wilson St.
Madison, WI 53701
608-266-3431

[Wisconsin] Senate
State Capitol
Madison, WI 53702
608-266-0341
608-266-9960 (Legislative Hotline)
608-266-5400 (Judiciary)

[Wisconsin] Solid Waste Management, Bureau of
101 S. Webster St.
Madison, WI 53702
608-266-1327

[Wisconsin] State Patrol, Division of
4802 Sheboygan Ave.

Madison, WI 53702
608-266-3212

[Wisconsin] Supreme Court
P.O. Box 1688
Madison, WI 53701
608-266-1880

[Wisconsin] Transportation, Department of
4802 Sheboygan Ave., Rm. 120-B
Madison, WI 53702
608-266-1113

[Wisconsin] Treasury, State
125 S. Webster St.
Madison, WI 53707
608-266-1714

[Wisconsin] Unemployment Compensation Division
201 E. Washington Ave.
Madison, WI 53702
608-266-2284

[Wisconsin] United States Bankruptcy Court
Eastern Wisconsin
517 E. Wisconsin Ave., Rm. 216
Milwaukee, WI 53202
414-291-3293

[Wisconsin] United States Bankruptcy Court
Western Wisconsin
P.O. Box 548
Madison, WI 53701
608-264-5178

[Wisconsin] United States District Court
Eastern District
517 E. Wisconsin Ave., Rm. 362
Milwaukee, WI 53202
414-291-3372
414-291-1698 (Law Library)

[Wisconsin] United States District Court
Western District
P.O. Box 432
Madison, WI 53701
608-264-5156
698-264-5448 (Law Library)

[Wisconsin] United States Government Printing Office
517 E. Wisconsin Ave., Rm. 190

Milwaukee, WI 53202
414-297-1304

**[Wisconsin] Vocational
Rehabilitation, Division of**
1 W. Wilson, 8th Fl.
Madison, WI 53707
608-266-5466

**[Wisconsin] Water Regulation &
Zoning, Bureau of**
101 S. Webster St.
Madison, WI 53702
608-266-8030

**[Wisconsin] Weights &
Measures, Bureau of**
P.O. Box 8911
Madison, WI 53708
608-266-9836
800-362-3020

**[Wisconsin] Women's Issues &
Employment**
State House, Rm. 115E
Madison, WI 53702
608-266-1212

**[Wisconsin] Worker's
Compensation Division**
201 E. Washington Ave.
Madison, WI 53702
608-266-1340

**Women Executives in State
Government**
1730 Rhode Island Ave., NW
Wash. D.C. 20036
202-293-7006

Women's Equity Action League
1250 I. St., NW, Suite 305
Wash. D.C. 20005
202-898-1588

Women's Legal Defense Fund
2000 P. St., NW
Wash. D.C. 20036
202-887-0364

Word Perfect Corp.
1555 N. Technology Way
Orem, UT 84057
801-225-5000
800-541-5096

**World Association of Document
Examiners**
111 N. Canal St.

Chicago, IL 60606
312-930-9446

World Association of Judges
1000 Connecticut Ave., NW, Suite
800
Wash. D.C. 20036
202-466-5428

World Association of Lawyers
1000 Connecticut Ave., NW,
Suite 800
Wash. D.C. 20036
202-466-5428

World Bank
See International Bank for
Reconstruction & Development

World Peace Through Law Center
1000 Connecticut Ave. NW
Wash. D.C. 20036
202-466-5428

**[Wyoming] Information &
Referral (State Government)**
301-777-7220

**[Wyoming] Administration &
Fiscal Control**
2001 Capitol Ave.
Cheyenne, WY 82002
307-777-7201

**[Wyoming] Aging,
Commission on**
Hathaway Bldg.
Cheyenne, WY 82002
307-777-7986
800-442-2766

**[Wyoming] Agriculture,
Department of**
2219 Carey Ave.
Cheyenne, WY 82002
307-777-7321

[Wyoming] Air Quality Division
122 W. 25th St., 4th Fl.
Cheyenne, WY 82002
307-777-7391

[Wyoming] Archives, State
Museums & Historical Department
Barrett Bldg.
Cheyenne, WY 82002
307-777-7013

**[Wyoming] Attorney General,
Office of**
200 W. 24th St., Rm. 123

Cheyenne, WY 82002
307-777-7841

[Wyoming] Auditor's Office, State
200 W. 24th St.
Cheyenne, WY 82002
307-777-7831

**[Wyoming] Banking Examiner,
State**
Herschell Bldg.
Cheyenne, WY 82002
307-777-6600

Wyoming Bar Association
500 Redell Ave.
Cheyenne, WY 82001
307-632-9061

**[Wyoming] Better Business
Bureau**
Lincoln Park & Teton Counties
208-523-9754
800-873-3222

**[Wyoming] Charities & Reform,
Board of**
Herschler Bldg.
Cheyenne, WY 82002
307-777-7405

**[Wyoming] Child Support
Enforcement Services**
Hathaway Bldg.
Cheyenne, WY 82002
307-777-7892

**[Wyoming] Consumer Affairs
Division**
100 W. 24th St.
Cheyenne, WY 82002
307-777-6286

**[Wyoming] Economic
Development & Stabilization
Board**
122 W. 25th St., 3rd Fl.
Cheyenne, WY 82002
307-777-7284
800-262-3425

**[Wyoming] Education,
Department of**
2300 Capitol Ave.
Cheyenne, WY 82002
307-777-7673

**[Wyoming] Emergency
Management Agency**
5500 Bishop Blvd.

Cheyenne, WY 82009
307-777-7566

**[Wyoming] Employment
Security Commission**
100 W. Midwest St.
Casper, WY 82606
307-235-3200

**[Wyoming] Environmental
Quality, Department of**
122 W. 25th St., 4th Fl.
Cheyenne, WY 82002
307-777-7938

[Wyoming] Governor, Office of
State Capitol Bldg.
Cheyenne, WY 82002
307-777-7434

**[Wyoming] Health & Social
Services, Department of**
117 Hathaway Bldg.
Cheyenne, WY 82002
307-777-7656

[Wyoming] Highway Patrol
5300 Bishop Blvd.
Cheyenne, WY 82002
307-777-7301

**[Wyoming] House of
Representatives**
State Capitol
Cheyenne, WY 82002
307-777-7330
307-777-7220 (Judiciary)

**[Wyoming] Insurance
Commissioner**
122 W. 25th St.
Cheyenne, WY 82002
307-777-7401

**[Wyoming] Labor & Statistics
Department**
122 W. 25th St.
Cheyenne, WY 82002
307-777-7261

**[Wyoming] Labor Standards &
Fair Employment**
122 W. 25th St.
Cheyenne, WY 82002
307-777-7261

[Wyoming] Laramie County
19th & Cary

Cheyenne, WY 82001
307-638-4296

**[Wyoming] Law Examiners,
State Board of**
P.O. Box 109
Cheyenne, WY 82003
307-632-9061

[Wyoming] Law Library, State
Supreme Court Bldg.
Cheyenne, WY 82002
307-777-7509

**[Wyoming] Legislative Service
Office**
State Capitol, Rm. 213
Cheyenne, WY 82002
307-777-7881

[Wyoming] Liquor Commission
1520 E. 5th St.
Cheyenne, WY 82002
307-777-7231

[Wyoming] Mines, Board of
P.O. Box 1094
Rock Springs, WY 82902
307-362-5222

**[Wyoming] Occupational Health
& Safety Commission**
604 E. 25th St.
Cheyenne, WY 82002
307-777-7786

**[Wyoming] Oil & Gas
Commission**
777 W. 1st St.
Casper, WY 82601
307-234-7147

[Wyoming] Parole, Board of
1700 Pacific St.
Cheyenne, WY 82002
301-777-7208

[Wyoming] Personnel Division
2001 Capitol Ave.
Cheyenne, WY 82002
307-777-6713

**[Wyoming] Probation & Parole,
Department of**
1700 Pacific St.
Cheyenne, WY 82002
301-777-7208

**[Wyoming] Public Defender,
State**
1712 Carey, 2nd Fl.
Cheyenne, WY 82002
307-777-7137

**[Wyoming] Public Lands,
Department of**
122 W. 25th St.
Cheyenne, WY 82002
307-777-7331

**[Wyoming] Public Service
Commission**
700 W. 21st St.
Cheyenne, WY 82002
307-777-7427

**[Wyoming] Purchasing &
Property Control, Division of**
2001 Capitol Ave., Rm. 301
Cheyenne, WY 82002
307-777-7253

**[Wyoming] Real Estate
Commission**
122 W. 25th St., Rm. 4301
Cheyenne, WY 82002
307-777-7141

**[Wyoming] Revenue & Taxation,
Department of**
122 W. 25th St., 1st Fl.
Cheyenne, WY 82002
307-777-7961

[Wyoming] Secretary of State
200 W. 24th St.
Cheyenne, WY 82002
307-777-7378

**[Wyoming] Securities
Commissioner**
State Office Bldg.
Cheyenne, WY 82002
307-777-7370

[Wyoming] Senate
State Capitol
Cheyenne, WY 82002
307-777-7733
307-777-7220 (Judiciary)

**[Wyoming] Solid Waste
Management Program**
122 W. 25th St.
Cheyenne, WY 82002
307-777-7752

[Wyoming] Supreme Court
2301 Capitol Ave.
Cheyenne, WY 82002
307-777-7560

[Wyoming] Treasurer, State
200 W. 24th St.
Cheyenne, WY 82002
307-777-7408

**[Wyoming] Unemployment
Insurance Division**
100 W. Midwest St.
Casper, WY 82601
307-235-3200

**[Wyoming] United States
Bankruptcy Court**
P.O. Box 1107
Cheyenne, WY 82003
307-772-2191

**[Wyoming] United States
District Court**
P.O. Box 727

Cheyenne, WY 82001
307-772-2145

**[Wyoming] Vital Records
Services**
Hathaway Bldg.
Cheyenne, WY 82002
307-777-7591

**[Wyoming] Vocational
Rehabilitation, Division of**
347 Hathaway Bldg.
Cheyenne, WY 82002
307-777-7385

**[Wyoming] Water Development
Commission**
Herschler Bldg., 3rd Fl.
Cheyenne, WY 82002
307-777-7626

**[Wyoming] Women,
Commission for**
122 W. 25th St.
Cheyenne, WY 82002
307-777-7349

**[Wyoming] Worker's
Compensation**
122 W. 25th St., 2nd Fl.
Cheyenne, WY 82002
307-777-7441

Xerox Corp.
100 Clinton Ave. South
Rochester, NY 14644
716-423-5480
800-334-6200

LEGAL, MEDICAL AND COMPUTER ABBREVIATIONS

A, a Atlantic Reporter, First Series; Abbott; affirmed on appeal; Louisiana Annuals; annual; asked price; bond rating (Standard & Poor); Selective Service classification (e.g., 1-A); answer; acquiescence; amended; agricultural; anterior; act; association; anonymous; absolute; approved; adult; age; acre; ampere; acceleration; amateur; admiral; academy; academician; about; are; anode; ante; anno; annum; angstrom unit; mass number; atomic weight; arctic; Ahmad; Arabic; Anglican; American; Australian; Austria; Alabama; Arkansas; Alberta; accumulator; amplitude; the number 10 (in the hexadecimal number system); absorbency; artery; anus; allergy.

A/- United Nations General Assembly.

A2d Atlantic Reporter, Second Series.

A1 first class, superior in quality.

A1C airman, first class.

A$_2$ second aortic sound.

A$ Australian dollar.

Aa bond rating (Moody).

AA, aa Administration on Aging; Ars Aequi (Holland); able and available; affirmative action; affected areas; automobile accident; administrative assistant; assistant administrator; approving authority; arrival approved; arrival angle; aviation annex; always afloat; Aluminum Association; bond rating (Standard & Poor); American Assembly; American anthropologist; antiaircraft; associate in arts; Alcoholics Anonymous; achievement age; approximate absolute; of each; ana; author's alterations; atomic absorption; arithmetic average; anterior aorta; antibody activity.

aA azure A.

AAA, aaa American Arbitration Association; Agricultural Adjustment Act; Agricultural Adjustment Administration; Association of Attenders and Alumni of the Hague Academy of International Law; Automobile Association of America; Amateur Athletic Association; Ambulance Association of America; American Academy of Advertising; American Accounting Association; Army Audit Agency; Association of Average Adjusters of the United States; Appraisers Association of America; Bond rating (Moody); approved as amended; accumulated adjustment account; antiaircraft artillery; abdominal aortic aneurysm; acute anxiety attack.

Aaa bond rating (Moody).

AAAA Antique Appraisal Association of America; Associated Actors and Artists of America.

AAAC American Association for the Advancement of Criminology.

AAA-CPA American Association of Attorney-Certified Public Accountants.

aaad aromatic amino acid decarboxylase.

AAAE, aaae American Association of Airport Executives; amino acid activating enzymes.

AA Ag Associate in Arts in Agriculture.

AAAL American Academy of Arts and Letters.

AAAS American Association for the Advancement of Science.

AAB Army Air Base.

AABB American Association of Blood Banks.

aabd aid to the aged, blind, or disabled.

AABM, aabm Australian Association of British Manufacturers; airborne antiballistic missiles.

AABP American Association of Book Publishers.

aabs automobile accident, broadside.

AABT Association for Advancement of Behavior Therapy.

aaby as amended by.

AAC, aac Aeronautical Advisory Council; in the year before Christ (anno ante Christum); air approach control; Alaskan Air Command; American Association of Criminology; Army Air Corps; Association of American Colleges; Anglo-American Code; antiaircraft command; antibiotic associated colitis.

AACB Aviation and Astronautics Coordinating Board.

AACC Airport Association Coordinating Council; American Association of Credit Counselors; Army Aviation Control Center.

AACCP American Association of Colleges of Chiropody-Podiatry.

AACD American Association for Counseling and Development.

AACE American Association for Cancer Education.

aacft army aircraft.

AACHP American Association for Comprehensive Health Planning.

AACJC American Association of Community and Junior Colleges.

AACM American Academy of Comprehensive Medicine.

aacn the year before the birth of Christ (anno ante Christum natum).

AACOM American Association of Colleges of Osteopathic Medicine.

A&A Corp Angell & Ames on Corporations.

AACP American Association of Correctional Psychologists; American Academy of Child Psychiatry; American Association of Colleges of Pharmacy; Advanced Airborne Command Post.

AACPM American Association of Colleges of Podiatric Medicine.

AACR Anglo American Cataloging Rules.

AACS Airways and Air Communications Service.

AACSL American Association for the Comparative Study of Law.

AACU American Association of Clinical Urologists.

AAD, aad American Academy of Dermatology; Arms and Ammunition Division; Association of American Dentists; admission and disposition; aircraft assignment directive.

AADE American Association of Dental Examiners.

AADGP American Academy of Dental Group Practice.

AADLA Art and Antique Dealers League of America.

AADM American Academy of Dental Medicine.

aado accepted alternative designation of.

AADR Association Academy of Dental Radiology.

AADS American Association of Dental Schools.

aadt annual average daily traffic.

A Ae Are Aequi (Netherlands).

AAE, aae Aeronautical and Astronautical Engineering; American Association of Endodontists; Accounting and Auditing Enforcement (IRS); apparent activation energy; active assertive exercise; acute allergic encephalitis.

AAEC Australian Atomic Energy Commission.

AAEE American Academy of Environmental Engineers.

AAF, aaf American Advertising Federation; American Architectural Foundation; ascorbic acid factor; Army airfield.

AAFB Andrews Air Force Base.

AAFC Air Accounting and Finance Center.

AAFCM American Association of Family Counselors and Mediators.

AAFCPB Army Air Force Clemency and Parole Board.

aafg amino acid formula with glutamate.

AAFI Associated Accounting Firms International.

AAFOIC Army Air Force Officer in Charge.

AAFP American Academy of Family Physicians.

AAfPE American Association for Paralegal Education.

AAFRC American Association of Fund Raising Counsel.

AAFS American Academy of Forensic Sciences; Association for the Advancement of Family Stability.

AAFSW Association of American Foreign Service Women.

aafu augmented assault fire units.

AAFWB Army and Air Force Wage Board.

AAG, aag Assistant Adjutant General; Association of American Geographers; autoantigen.

aagcm awaiting action general court-martial.

aagm antiaircraft guided missile.

AAGUS American Association of Genito Urinary Surgeons.

aah adrenal androgenic hyperfunction.

AAHA American Association of Handwriting Analysts; American Academy of Health Administration; American Association of Homes for the Aging; American Animal Hospital Association.

AAHD American Association of Hospital Dentists.

AAHE American Association for Higher Education.

AAI, aai American Association of Immunologists; air-to-air identification (intercept); acute alveolar injury.

AAIA Association on American Indian Affairs.

AAIB Aircraft Accident Investigation Board.

AAICJ American Association for the International Commission of Jurists.

AAID American Academy of Implant Dentistry.

AAIE American Association of Industrial Engineers.

AAII Association for the Advancement of Invention and Innovation.

aain acute allergic intestinal nephritis.

AAIS American Association of Insurance Services.

AAIT American Association of Inhalation Therapists.

AAJE American Academy of Judicial Education.

aal anterior axillary line; acoustical absorption loss; anterior axillary line.

AALA American Automotive Leasing Association; Alaska Association of Legal Assistants; Arrowhead Association of Legal Assistants.

AALC Afro-Asian Lawyers Conference.

AALD Australian Army Legal Department.

AALL American Association of Law Libraries; Arkansas Association of Legal Assistants.

AALPP American Association for Legal and Political Philosophy.

AALR Anglo American Law Review.

AALS Association of American Law Schools; Alabama Association of Legal Assistants.

AALS Proc Association of American Law Schools Proceedings.

AAM, aam American Association of Museums; American Academy of Microbiology; air-to-air missile.

AAMA American Association of Medical Assistants.

AAMC American Association of Medico-Legal Consultants; American Association of Marriage Counselors; American Association of Medical Clinics; Association of American Medical Colleges.

aame acetylarginine methyl ester.

AAML American Academy of Matrimonial Lawyers.

AAMP American Association of Meat Processors.

AAMRL American Association of Medical Record Librarians.

AAN, aan American Academy of Nutrition; American Academy of Neurology; alpha-amino nitrogen.

A and C or **A&C, a&c** New York State Department of Audit and Control; addenda and corrigenda.

A and C Cir or **A&C Cir** Accounts and Collection Unit Circulars.

A and E or **A&E** Adolphus & Ellis' Queen's Bench Reports (NS: New Series) (England); admiralty and ecclesiastical.

A and EAC or **A&EAC** or **A&E Ann Cases** or **A&E Anno** or **A&E Cas** American and English Annotated Cases.

A and ECC or **A&ECC** or **A&E Corp Cases** American and English Corporation Cases (NS: New Series).

A and E Enc L & Pr American and English Encyclopedia of Law and Practice.

A and E Ency or **A&E Ency** or **A&E Ency Law** American and English Encyclopedia of Law.

A and E (NS) or **A&E (NS)** Adolphus & Ellis' New Series (England).

A and E Pat Cases or **A&E Pat Cases** American and English Patent Cases.

A and E P&P or **A&E P&Pr** American and English Pleading and Practice.

A and E R Cas or **A&E R Cases** or **A&E RR Cas** American and English Railroad Cases (NS: New Series).

A and H or **A&H** Arnold and Hodges' English Queen's Bench Reports (England).

a and m agricultural and mechanical; ancient and modern.

a and p or **a&p** anterior and posterior; auscultation and percussion.

a and r or **a&r** artists and repertory.

a and w or **a&w** alive and well.

AANP American Association of Neuropathologists.

AAO, aao American Academy of Optometry; American Academy of Osteopathy; awake alert oriented; amino acid oxidase.

AAOA Ambulance Association of America.

aaoc antacid of choice.

AAOG American Association of Obstetricians and Gynecologists.

AAP, aap Association of American Publishers; American Academy of Pediatrics; American Academy of Psychotherapists; Association of American Publishers; affirmative action plan; advise if able to proceed.

AAPA American Association of Physicians' Assistants.

AAPCA American Association of Pesticide Control Officials.

AAPL American Academy of Psychiatry and the Law; American Association of Petroleum Landsmen.

AAPP Arizona Association of Professional Paralegals.

AAPS Arizona Articulation Proficiency Scale.

AAPSO Afro-Asian People's Solidarity Organization.

aar administrative adjustment request; against all risks.

aare automobile accident, rear end.

aarf acute alveolar respiratory failure.

AARP American Association of Retired Persons.

AAS, aas Associate in Applied Science; acute abdominal series; aortic arch syndrome.

AASCU American Association of State Colleges and Universities.

aash adrenal androgen stimulating hormone.

AASM Associated African States and Madagascar.

AASR Ancient Accepted Scottish Rite.

aat auditory apperception test; acute abdominal tympany.

AAU, aau Amateur Athletic Union; acute anterior uveitis.

AAUN American Association for the United Nations.

AAUP American Association of University Professors.

AAUW American Association of University Women.

aav adeno associated virus.

aaw anterior aortic wall.

AB, Ab, ab Abstracts of Treasury Decisions; Assembly Bill; Anonymous Reports at end of Benloe (England); Armory Board (District of Columbia); Nederlandse Jurisprudentie (Holland); aid to the blind; abortion; abnormal; antibody; acid base; about; abridgment;

abstracts; airborne; air base; airman basic; active bilaterally; Alberta; Bachelor of Arts (artium baccalaureus); ace bandage; abbot; abdominal; antigen binding.

ABA, aba American Bar Association; American Bankers Association; American Booksellers Association; Amateur Boxing Association; American Basketball Association; abscissic acid; antibacterial activity.

ABA Antitrust LJ American Bar Association Antitrust Law Journal.

ABABJ American Bar Association Banking Journal.

ABA Comp L Bull American Bar Association Comparative Law Bulletin.

ABACPD American Bar Association Center for Professional Discipline.

ABA Intl & Comp L Sec American Bar Association International and Comparative Law Section.

ABAJ American Bar Association Journal.

ABA Model Bus Corp Act Ann American Bar Association Model Business Corporation Act Annotated (2d: Second Series).

Aband Prop Abandoned Property (one of the New York Codes).

ABA Rep American Bar Association Reports or Reporter.

ABA Sec Lab Rel L American Bar Association Section of Labor Relations Law.

ABA Sect Ins N&CL American Bar Association Section of Insurance, Negligence & Compensation Law.

Abb Abbott's Circuit and District Court Reports (United States); abbey.

Abb Ad or **Abb Adm** or **Abb Ad R** Abbott's Admiralty Reports

(United States).

Abb Ap Dec or **App Ct App** Abbott's Court of Appeals Decisions (New York).

Abb App Dec Abbott's Appeals Decisions (New York).

Abb CC Abbott's Circuit Court Reports (United States).

Abb Ct App or **Abb Ct of App Dec** or **Abb Ap Dec** or **Abb App Dec** Abbott's Court of Appeals Decisions (New York).

Abb Dec Abbott's Decisions or Abbott's Court of Appeals Decisions (New York).

Abb Dict or **Abb Law Dict** Abbott's Law Dictionary.

Abb Dig Abbott's New York Digest.

Abb Law Dict Abbott's Law Dictionary.

Abb NC or **Abb N Cas** Abbott's New Cases (New York).

Abb NS Abbott's Practice Reports, New Series.

Abb NY App Abbott's Court of Appeals Decisions (New York).

Abb NY Dig Abbott's New York Digest.

Abbott See Abb entries above.

Abbott's Adm or **Abbott's Ad Rep** Abbott's Admiralty Reports (United States).

Abbott's NC Abbott's New Cases (New York).

Abbott's Prac Rep Abbott's Practice Reports (New York).

Abb PR or **Abb Pr** or **Abb Pract Cas** or **Abb Pr Rep** Abbott's New York Practice Reports; Abbott's Practice Reports (New York); Abbott's Practice Cases (New York); Abbott's Practice (New York).

Abb Prac Abbott's Practice (New York) (see also Abb PR).

Abb PR (NS) Abbott's Practice Reports (New York) New Series.

aabr or **abbrev** abbreviated; abbreviation.

ABBREV PLAC Placitorum Abbreviatis, Record Commissioner (England).

Abb RPS Abbott's Real Property Statutes

Abb Sh Abbott on Shipping.

Abb US Abbott's Circuit Court Reports, United States; Abbott's Circuit and District Courts, United States.

Abb USCC Abbott's Circuit and District Court Reports, United States.

ABC, abc American Bar Center; Australian Bankruptcy Cases; Alcoholic Beverages Commission; American Broadcasting Company; American Business Conference; Australian Broadcasting Company; Audit Bureau of Circulations; American Bowling Congress; a better chance; advanced booking charter; atomic, biological and chemical; absolute bone count; apnea, bradycardia cyanosis; acalculous biliary colic.

ABCC Association of British Chambers of Commerce.

abcd accelerated business collection and delivery.

ABCm alum, blood, clay method.

ABC Newsl International Association of Accident Boards and Commissions Newsletter.

ABCNY Association of the Bar of the City of New York.

abd abdomen; abdominal; abduction; all but the dissertation; average body dose.

abd hyst abdominal hysterectomy.

Abdy R Pr Abdy's Roman Civil Procedure.

ABE, abe American Bar Endowment; acute bacterial endocarditis.

A'Beck Judg Vict or **A'Beck Res Judg** A'Beckett's Reserved Judgments, Victoria.

A'Beck RJNSW A'Beckett's Reserved Judgments, New South Wales.

aber aberration.

ABF, abf American Bar Foundation; airborne freight.

ABFP American Board of Family Practice.

ABF Research J or **ABF Res J** or **ABFRJ** American Bar Foundation Research Journal.

ABF Res Newsl American Bar Foundation Research Newsletter.

abg arterial blood gases.

abi atherothrombotic brain infarction.

ab initio from the beginning.

AB in Th Bachelor of Arts in Theology.

ABL, abl Automated Biological Laboratory; Amateur Bicycling League; ablative; antigen binding lymphocytes.

ABLA American Blind Lawyers Association; American Business Law Association; Amateur Bicycle League of America.

ABLE Adult Basic Learning Exam.

ABM, abm antiballistic missiles; abductor muscle; autologous bone marrow.

ABMC American Battle Monuments Commission.

Ab N, abn Abstracts, Treasury Decisions (NS: New Series); airborne; abnormal.

ABO, abo blood groups; abortion.

Abogada Intl Abogada International.

abor abortion.

abp arterial blood pressures; archbishop; actin binding protein.

abpc antibody producing cell.

ABR, abr American Bankruptcy Reports; Army Board of Review; abridged; abridgement; abrasion; absolute bed rest.

Abr Ca Eq or **Abr Cas Eq** Abridgement of Cases in Equity

Abr Cas Abridged Cases.

AB Rep American Bankruptcy Reports.

AB Rev American Bankruptcy Review.

ABRNS American Bankruptcy Reports, New Series.

ABS, Abs, abs Ohio Law Abstract; Abstracts, Treasury Decisions; Abstracts, Decisions of the Board of United States General Appraisers; American Bible Society; American Bureau of Shipping; able-bodied seaman; abstain; abstract; absent; absolute; absolutely; acrylonitrile-butadiene-styrene; acute brain syndrome; at bedside; anti B serum.

absc abscissa.

Abs Crim Pen Abstracts on Criminology and Penology.

Abs (NS) Abstracts, Treasury Decisions, New Series.

absol absolutely.

abs re the defendant being absent (absente reo).

abst, abstr abstract; abstracted.

abstn abstain.

ABT, abt American Ballet Theatre; about; arteria basilaris thrombus.

ABTA American Board of Trial Advocates.

A Bus L Rev Australian Business Law Review.

abv above; arthropod borne virus.

abw actual body weight.

aby antibody; abortion; acid bismuth yeast.

AC, Ac, ac Advance California Reports; Appeal Cases (Canada); Appeal Cases, Third Series (England); Court of Appeal in Chancery (England); Assemblee Consultative of Conseil de l'Europe; actinium; appellate court; air corps; air craftsman; army corps; aviation cadet; alternating current; area code; author's changes; author's correction;

account; acute; money of account; alicyclic; adult contemporary; acre; in the year of Christ (anno Christi); before Christ (ante Christum); before a meal (ante cibum); athletic club; anticomplementary; American Can; Air Canada; automobile club; ATM use charge; acid; altocumulus; Access Index 1975+; abdominal compression; ascending colon; alcoholic cirrhosis; aortocoronary; anodal closure; aortic closure.

A/C account; account current; alternating current; absolute ceiling; air conditioning; anterior chamber.

A&C, a&c New York State Department of Audit and Control; addenda and corrigenda.

ACA, aca Advance California Appellate Reports; Australian Corporate Affairs Reporter (Commerce Clearing House); American Correctional Association; Administrator of Civil Aeronautics; American Casting Association; American Canoe Association; American Camping Association; ammonia, copper, arsenic; acute cerebellar ataxia; anterior cerebral artery.

ACAA Agricultural Conservation and Adjustment Administration.

ACABQ Advisory Committee on Administrative and Budgetary Questions.

acac activated charcoal artificial cell.

acad academy; academic.

Acad L Rev Academy Law Review (India).

Acad Pol Sci Proc Academy of Political Science Proceedings.

AC and U Association of Colleges and Universities.

ACAST United Nations Advisory Committee on Application of Science and Technology to Development.

ACB, abc Association of the Customs Bar; antibody coated bacteria.

acbg aorta coronary bypass graft.

ACC, acc Allahabad Criminal Cases (India); Agricultural Credit Corporation; United Nations Administrative Committee on Coordination; Air Coordinating Committee; Atlantic Coast Conference; accident; automatic color control; acceptance; accepted; account; accountant; accusative; accompanied; accompaniment; according; accord; accordant; accumulator; alveolar cell carcinoma; acute care center; adenoid cystic carcinoma.

A&C Cir Accounts and Collection Unit Circulars.

acce acceptance.

accel accelerando.

accid accidental.

accom accommodation.

accomp accompaniment.

Accountancy L Rep (CCH) Accountancy Law Reports (Commerce Clearing House).

accpt acceptance; accepted; accompaniment.

accrd accrued.

accred accredited.

acct account; accountant; accounting; accountancy.

acctg accounting.

acctng accounting.

accts pay accounts payable.

accts rec accounts receivable.

ACCTU All-Union Central Council of Trade Unions.

accum accumulated.

ACCUS, accus Automobile Competition Committee for the United States; accusative.

Accy Accountancy Board.

acd adjourn in contemplation of dismissal; automatic call distributor; absolute cardiac dullness; acid citrate dextrose;

anterior chest diameter; adult celiac disease.

ACDA Arms Control and Disarmament Agency.

ac/dc alternating current, direct current; bisexual.

ACDD Advisory Committee on Drug Dependence.

ACD solution acid-citrate-dextrose solution.

ACE, ace American Council on Education; Active Corps of Executives; automatic computing engine; acentric fragment; adrenal cortical extract; alcohol chloroform ether.

A Ce adriamycin cyclophosphamide.

a cells alpha cells.

acf acute care facility; accessory clinical finding.

acf/min actual cubic feet per minute.

acfn additional cost of false negatives.

acfp additional cost of false positives.

acft aircraft.

acg, AcG aortocoronary graft; accelerator globulin (factor V).

ach arm, chest, height; adrenal cortical hormone; active chronic hepatitis; acetylcholine.

AChE acetylcholinesterase.

aci average cost of illness; acute coronary infarction.

acia asynchronous communications interface adapter.

acid phos acid phosphate.

ACJA-LAE American Criminal Justice Association - Lambda Alpha Epsilon.

ACJS Academy of Criminal Justice Sciences.

ack acknowledge; acknowledge character (computer communications); acknowledgement.

ackgt acknowledgement.

ACL, acl Australian Current Law; adjective check list; alternate concentration list; access control list; anterior cruciate ligament.

ACLC Australian Company Law Cases.

ACLD Australian Current Law Digest.

ACLEA Association of Continuing Legal Education Administrators.

ACLJ American Civil Law Journal.

ACLR Australian Company Law Reports.

ACL Rev Australian Current Law Review.

ACLS, acls American Council of Learned Societies; advanced cardiac life support.

ACLU American Civil Liberties Union.

ACLUF American Civil Liberties Union Foundation.

ACLU Leg Action Bull American Civil Liberties Union Legislative Action Bulletin.

ACM, acm Air Force Cases, Court Martial Reports; Association for Computer Machinery; Asbestos Containing Material; army court martial; Arab Common Market; albumin, calcium, magnesium; anticardiac myosin.

acme automated classification of medical entities.

ACMR Army Court of Military Review.

ACMS Automated Career Management System.

acn before the birth of Christ (ante Christum natum); acute conditioned necrosis.

ACNM American College of Nurse-Midwives.

aco alert, cooperative, and oriented; acute coronary occlusion.

acoa adult children of alcoholics.

ACOG American College of Obstetricians and Gynecologists.

ACP American College of Physicians; Agricultural Conservation Program;

African, Caribbean, and Pacific States; All Union Communist Party; aspirin, caffeine, phenacetin; acyl carrier protein.

ACPC American College of Probate Counsel.

ac ph acid phosphate.

ACPO Association of Chief Police Officers.

ACPS Advisory Council on the Penal System.

acpt acceptance.

acq acquitted; acquittal; acquiescence by IRS Commissioner in Tax Court decision or Board of Tax Appeals decision.

acq in result acquiescence in result; acquitted in result.

acqu acquisition.

ACR, acr American Criminal Reports; anticonstipation regimen; absolute catabolic rate.

A Crim R Australian Criminal Reports.

acrs accelerated cost recovery system.

ACS, acs American College of Surgeons; American Chemical Society; American Cancer Society; aircraft control system; autograph card signed; automated collection system; antireticular cytotoxic serum; acute cervical strain or sprain; anticytotoxic serum; acute confusional state.

ACSW Academy of Certified Social Workers.

Act, ACT, act a public law; Acton Prize Cases, Privy Council (England); Australian Capital Territory; American College Test(ing); Association of Classroom Teachers; active; active motion; action; actuary; actual; actor; atropine coma therapy; anticoagulation therapy; activating clotting time.

Acta or **Acta Cancelariae** Acta

Cancelariae Chancery Reports (England).

Acta Crim Acta Criminologica.

Acta Jur Acta Juridica.

acts acute cervical traumatic syndrome.

Acts Ass Acts of the General Assembly, Church of Scotland.

Act Can Acta Cancellaria (England).

Act Cur Ad Sc Acta Curiae Admiralatus Scotiae.

actg acting; actuating.

Actg Legal Adv Acting Legal Advisor.

acth adrenocorticotropic hormone.

ACTION A federal agency that runs the Peace Corps, VISTA, etc.

ACTL American College of Trial Lawyers.

ACTLRC Australian Capital Territory Law Reform Commission.

Acton Acton Prize Cases, Privy Council (12 English Reprint) (England).

Act PC Acts of Privy Council (Dasent) (England) (NS: New Series).

Act Pr C Acton's Reports, Prize Cases (England).

ACTR Australian Capitol Territory Reports.

Act Reg Acta Regia.

Acts & Ords Interregnum Acts and Ordinances of the Interregnum.

act und activity undetermined.

ACU, acu American Conservative Union; American Cycling Union; Association of Colleges and Universities; automatic calling unit; acute care unit.

ACUS Administration Conference of the United States.

ACV, acv Australian and New Zealand Conveyancing Report; Alberto-Culver; actual cash value; air-cushion vehicle.

acvd acute cardiovascular disease.

acw alternating continuous wave; aircraftwoman.

ACY American Cyanamid.

ACYF Administration for Children, Youth and Families.

AD, Ad, ad Appellate Division Reports (New York Supreme Court); Appellate Division Reports (South African Supreme Court); American Decisions (United States); Annual Digest and Reports of Public International Law Cases; Agriculture Decisions; Australian Digest; Adams' Ecclesiastical Reports (England); addendum; additur; before the day (ante diem); in the year of our Lord (anno domini); administration; administrator; assembly district; average deviation; adult; active duty; after date; advantage; associate director; assistant director; adapted; advertisement; Alzheimer's disease; air-dried; ATM deposit; addict; after discharge; acute dermatomyositis; adjuvant disease; alcohol dehydrogenase; adrenalin.

AD 2d Appellate Division Reports, Second Series (New York Supreme Court).

A/D, a/d analog to digital; after date.

ADA, ada American Dental Association; American Dairy Association; Americans for Democratic Action; American Dietetic Association; American Diabetes Association; Automobile Dealers Association; assistant district attorney; a modular programming language; average daily attendance; approved dietary allowance; anterior descending artery.

ADAMHA Alcohol, Drug Abuse and Mental Health Administration.

Adams Adams' Reports (Maine); Adams' Reports (New Hampshire); Adams County Legal Journal (Pennsylvania).

Adams Eq Adams' Equity.

Adams LJ Adams County Legal Journal (Pennsylvania).

adapt adaptation.

ADB Asian Development Bank; African Development Bank; Air Defense Board.

ADC, adc Appeal Cases, District of Columbia Reports; aid to dependent children; Assistant Division Commander; Air Defense Command; American Distilling Company; Asian Development Center; analog to digital converter; aide-de-camp; axiodistocervical; anodal duration contraction.

AdC adrenal cortex.

adccp advanced data communication control protocol.

ADCON administrative control.

Ad Con Addison's Contracts.

Ad Ct Dig Administrative Court Digest.

ADD, add Addison's Reports (Pennsylvania); Addams Ecclesiastical Reports (England); Abstracts of Declassified Documents; Administration on Development Disabilities; American Dialect Dictionary; addendum; additur; addiction; additional; adduction; let be added; average daily dose; adenosine deaminase.

Addams Addams Ecclesiastical Reports (England).

Add Eccl Rep or **Add ER** Addams Ecclesiastical Reports (England).

Addis See Addison.

Addison Pennsylvania State Reports.

addl or **addnl** additional.

addn addition.

Add Pa Addison's County Court Reports (Pennsylvania).

Add Penn See Addison.

add poll adductor pollicis.

Add Rep Addison's Reports (Pennsylvania).

ADDS American Digestive Disease Society.

addt additive.

ADE, ade Air Defense Emergency; adenine; acute disseminated encephalitis.

Ad&E or **Ad & El** Adolphus and Ellis' King's Bench Reports (England) (NS: New Series).

ADEA Age Discrimination in Employment Act.

addee addressee.

Adel L Rev Adelaide Law Review.

adeq adequate.

ADF, adf African Development Fund; Air Defense Force; American Duty Free; Assured Destruction Force; automatic document feed; automatic direction finder.

ad feb fever being present (adstante febre).

ad fin at the end; near the end; to the end (ad finem).

adg average daily gain; axiodistogingival.

adh adhesions; antidiuretic hormone.

adi allowable daily intake; acceptable daily intake; altitude direction indicator; analog devices; antral diverticulum of the ileum.

ADIL Annual Digest of International Law; air defense identification line.

ad inf to infinity (ad infinitum).

ad init at the beginning (ad initium).

ad int in the meantime; to meanwhile (ad interim).

ADIS automatic data interchange system; a data interchange system.

ADIZ air defense identification zone.

adj adjudged; adjudication; adjourned; adjoining; adjutant; adjusted; adjunct; adjective.

Adj AG Adjudications of the Attorney General.

Adj Gen Adjutant General.

ADJGEN Ohio Adjutant General.

Adjt adjutant.

adk adenosine kinase.

Ad L, adl Administrative Law; acceptable defect level; anti-defamation league; authorized data list; activities of daily living.

Ad L2d Administrative Law, Second Series (Pike and Fischer).

Ad L Bull Administrative Law Bulletin.

ad lib as desired; at pleasure; freely (ad libitum).

Ad L News Administrative Law News.

ad loc to or at the place (ad locum).

ADLR Automated Direct Labor Reporting.

Ad L Rep (P&F) Administrative Law Reporter (Pike & Fischer).

Ad L Rev Administrative Law Review.

ADM, Adm, adm Admiralty Court; admiral; admiralty; admitted; admission; adminis-tration; administrative; air defense missile; adrenal medulla; administrative medicine; ambulatory.

Adm & Ecc Law Reports, Admiralty and Ecclesiastical (England).

adm Dr admitting doctor.

ADMI American Dairy Milk Institute.

admin administration; adminis-trative.

Admin Conf Administrative Conference of the United States.

Admin Dec Administrative Decisions.

Admin L Rev Administrative Law Review.

administr administrator.

admino administrative orders.

Admin Trib Administrative Tribunal of the League of Nations.

admir admiralty.

admis admissions.

admix or **admrx** or **adm'x** administratrix.

adml admiral.

Adm L Rev Administrative Law Review.

adm ph admitting physician.

adm'r administrator.

admr administrator; average daily metabolic rate.

admrx administratrix.

adms administrator.

Adm Sci Q Administrative Science Quarterly.

ADMSER Ohio Administrative Services.

admstr administrator.

admty admiralty.

admx administratrix.

adn aortic depressor nerve.

ad naus ad nauseam.

ADO administration duty officer; air defense operations; axiodisto-occlusal.

Adol & El Adolphus & Ellis' Queens Bench Reports (England) (NS: New Series).

ADP, adp Academy of Denture Prosthetics; actual deferral percentage; automated (auto-matic) data processing; alpha delta phi or pi; adenosine diphosphate; adductor pollicis; advanced pancreatitis.

adpe automatic data processing equipment.

adps automatic data processing system.

ADPSO Association of Data Process Service Organizations.

ADR, adr Massachusetts Appellate Division Reports; alternative dispute resolution; American Depositary Receipts; Applied Data Research; asset depreci-ation range; address; adverse drug reaction; accepted dental remedy.

ADRB Army Disability Review Board; Army Discharge Review Board.

ad s or **ads** or **ADS** at the suit of (ad sectam); Air Defense System, American Denture Society; autograph document signed; alternate delivery system; antibody deficiency syndrome.

ad sat to saturation (ad satu-randum).

adt accelerated development test; approved departure time; average daily traffic; adenosine triphosphate.

ADTC American District Telegraph Co.

ADTS Automated Data Telecommunications Service.

adu acute duodenal ulcer.

ad us according to custom (ad usum).

ad us exter for external use (ad usum externum).

adv advocate; advisory; adver-tising; advance; advice; against (adversus); adverb; arc drop voltage; adenovirus.

ADVA Administrator's Decisions, Veterans' Administration.

ad val according to value (ad valorem).

advg advertising.

advpmt advance payment.

advo advocate.

Adv O or **Adv Op** Advance Opinion.

Advocate The Advocate (Army); The Advocate (University of Toronto).

Advocates Q Advocates Quarterly.

advr advisor.

Adv Rep Advanced Reports.

Advry advisory.

Adv Sh Advance Sheet.

advt advertisement.

advtg advertising.

ADW assault with a deadly weapon; Air Defense Warning.

ADX Adnexa.

AE, ae accrued expenditure; added entry; account exec-utive; Atomic Energy; Agricultural Engineer; All England; Arab Emirates (United); associate in edu-cation; adult education; above elbow; analysis and evaluation; acrodermatitis enteropathica; of age (aetatis); aged; adult erythrocyte; anti epileptic.

A&E, a&e Adolphus and Ellis; active and equal; admiralty and ecclesiastical; aircraft and engines.

A-E architect-engineer.

A/E absorptivity/emissivity; Registration Board of Architects and Professional Engineers.

AEA, aea Association of Enrolled Agents; Atomic Energy Agency; Atomic Energy Act; Actors Equity Association; Adult Education Association; American Economic Association; alcohol, ether, acetone.

A&EAC or **A&E Ann Cases** or **A&E Cas** American and English Annotated Cases.

aeb acute erythroblastopenia.

AEC, aec Atomic Energy Commission Reports; American Engineering Council; average electrode current; at earliest convenience.

AECB Arms Export Control Board; Atomic Energy Control Board.

A&ECC or **A&E Corp Cases** American and English Corporation Cases (NS: New Series).

A Ed, aed Associate in Education; anti epileptic drug.

aeda ammunition, explosives, and other dangerous articles.

AEDS Atomic Energy (also Atmospheric Electric) Detection System

AeE Aeronautical Engineer.

A&E Adolphus & Ellis' Queen's Bench Reports (England) (NS: New Series).

A&E Enc L&Pr American and English Encyclopedia of Law and Practice.

A&E Ency American and English Encyclopedia of Law.

AEF, aef American (or Allied) Expeditionary Force; American Euthanasia Foundation; amyloid enhancing factor.

aeg air encephalogram.

AEI, aei American Enterprise Institute for Public Policy Research; air express international; atrial emptying index.

AELE European Free Trade Association; Americans for Effective Law Enforcement.

AELJ Atomic Energy Law Journal

AELR All England Law Reports.

aem accelerated evaluation method; avian encephalomyelitis.

AEO Appeals Examining Office.

AEP, aep American Electrical Power; accrued expenditure paid; acute edematous pancreatitis.

A&E P&P American and English Pleading and Practice.

A&E Pat Cases American and English Patent Cases.

aeq equal (aequalis); age equivalent.

AER, aer All England Law Reports; American Economic Review; aeronautics; acute external rhabdomyolysis; average evoked response.

A&E R Cases or **A&E RRC** American and English Railroad Cases (NS: New Series).

aero aeronautics.

aert acceptable environmental range test.

AES, aes American Epilepsy Society; American Electrochemical Society; American Eugenics Society; atomic emission spectroscopy; acetone extracted serum.

AESC American Engineering Standards Committee.

aesp applied extrasensory perception.

AET, aet Aetna Life & Casualty; of age (aetatis); actual (or approximate) exposure time;

absorption equivalent thickness.

AEU, aeu American Ethical Union; accrued expenditure unpaid.

AF, Af, af Air Force; Air France; Anglo-French; Africa; Afghanistan; Admiral of the Fleet; advance freight; next year (anno futuro); audio frequency; abnormal frequency; accumulation factor; air fuel; at, to the end (ad finem); affix; acre foot; auricular fibrillation; attenuation factor; angiogenesis factor; antibody forming; atrial flutter.

AFA, afa American Forensic Association; Air Force Academy; American Finance Association; alcohol formalin acetic acid.

AFB, afb American Farm Bureau; Air Force Base; aorto femoral bypass; acid-fast bacillus.

AFBR Air Force Board of Review.

afc average fixed cost; automatic flight control, automatic frequency control; antibody forming cell.

AFCM Air Force Court Martial.

AFCMR Air Force Court of Military Review.

AfDB African Development Bank.

AFDC Aid to Families with Dependent Children.

AFDEA American Funeral Directors and Embalmers Association.

AFDRB Air Force Discharge Review Board.

Afeb a febrile.

aff affirmed; affirming; affirmative; affairs.

aff act affirmative action.

aff'd affirmed.

aff'd mem affirmed without opinion.

aff'g affirming.

affil or **affl** affiliate.

affr affray.

aff reh affirmed on rehearing.

afft affidavit.

Afg, Afgh Afghanistan.

AFHG Air Force Headquarters Command.

AFI, afi Armed Forces Institute, Association of Federal Investigators; amaurotic familial idiocy.

AFIA American Foreign Insurance Association.

AFIDA Agricultural Foreign Investment Disclosure Act.

AFIPS American Federation of Information Processing Societies.

AFIS American Forces Information Service.

AFJAG Air Force Judge Advocate General.

AF JAG L Rev Air Force JAG (Judge Advocate General) Law Review.

AFL, afl American Federation of Labor; American Football League; artificial limb; anti fatty liver.

AFLA American Foreign Law Association.

AFL-CIO American Federation of Labor and Congress of Industrial Organizations.

AFLD American Foundation for Learning Disabilities.

AFLR or **AFL Rev** Air Force Law Review.

Af L Stud African Law Studies; African Language Studies.

a flutter atrial flutter.

AFM, afm Air Force Manual; American Federation of Musicians; application functions module; aflatoxin M.

AFMA American Feed Manufacturers Association.

AFO, afo Admiralty Fleet Order; ankle foot orthosis.

AF of L American Federation of Labor.

AFP, afp American Federation of Police; authority for purchase; alpha-fetoprotein; affiliated physician.

AFPC Air Force Policy (or Personnel) Council.

AFPDAB Air Force Physical Disability Appeals Board.

afpp acute fibrinopurulent pneumonia.

AFR, Afr, afr Armed Forces Radio; Air Force Reserve; Africa; applicable federal rates; available for release; acceptable failure rate; antifibrinolysin reaction.

AFRC Air Force Records Center.

AF Rep Alaska Federal Reports.

AF Res Air Force Reserves.

afri acute febrile respiratory illness.

Afrik Afrikaans.

Afr L Dig African Law Digest.

Afr L R African Law Reports.

Afr L R Mal Ser African Law Reports, Malawi Series.

Afr L R Sierre L Ser African Law Reports, Sierre Leone Series.

Afr L Stud African Law Studies; African Language Studies.

AFRKB American Federation of Retail Kosher Butchers.

AFROTC Air Force Reserve Officers' Training Corps.

AFRRI Armed Forces Radiobiology Research Institute.

afrt air freight.

AFS, afs Air Force Standard; American Finance System; automatic firing sequencer; acquired Fanconi syndrome; antifibroblast serum.

AFSA American Federation of School Administrators; American Foreign Service Association.

AFSC Armed Forces Staff College.

afsd aforesaid

AFT, aft American Federation of Teachers; Air Freight Terminal; afternoon; after; automatic fine tuning; agglutination flocculation test.

AFTR, aftr American Federal Tax Reports (2d: Second Series); atrophy, fasciculation, tremor, rigidity.

AFTRA American Federation of Television and Radio Artists.

AG, Ag, ag Attorney General; Opinions of the Attorney General; Adjutant General; Department of Agriculture; corporation (Germany); agriculture; August; accountant general; auditor general; agent general; agency; armed guard; against gravity; silver (argentum); antigravity; axiogingival; antiglobulin; antigen.

A/G albumin/globulin ratio in blood; air-to-ground.

AGA, aga American Gas Association; American Genetic Association; Association of Government Accountants; Amateur Gymnastics Association; appropriate for gestational age; accelerated growth area; as good as.

agb any good brand.

AGBCA Department of Agriculture Board of Contract Appeals.

agc automatic gain control; advanced graduate certificate; absolute granulocyte count.

agcy agency.

agd agreed; agar gel diffusion.

AGDA American Gasoline Dealers Association; American Gun Dealers Association.

AG Dec, Ag Dec Attorney General Decisions; Agricultural Decisions.

age angle of greatest extension; automatic ground equipment; acute gastroenteritis.

agf angle of greatest flexion; adrenal growth factor.

agg aggravated; agglutination; aggregate; agammaglobulinemia.

aggl, agglut agglutination.

AGI, agi American Geological Institute; adjusted gross income.

AGIS Attorney General's Information Service.

agl above ground level; acute granulocytic leukemia.

AGO Attorney General Opinions;

Adjutant General's Office; Angola.

agr agree; agreement; agriculture.

agri agriculture; agricultural.

Agri Dec Agriculture Decisions.

Agr LJ Agricultural Law Journal.

agrm agreement.

agron agronomy.

AGS, ags American Gynecological Society; air ground system; adrenogenital syndrome.

agt agreement; agent; against; abnormal glucose tolerance; acute generalized tuberculosis.

agtr agitator.

agtt abnormal glucose tolerance test.

agw actual gross weight; allowable gross weight.

agy agency.

ah ampere-hour; in the year of the hegira; abdominal hysterectomy; arterial hypertension; artificial heart; alcoholic hepatitis.

A&H Arnold and Hodges' Queen's Bench Reports (England).

AHA, aha American Hospital Association; American Historical Association; American Heart Association; antiheart antibody; acute hemolytic anemia.

AHC, ahc American Horse Council; acute hemorrhagic cystitis.

ahd acute heart disease.

AHERA Asbestos Hazard Emergency Response Act.

AHF, ahf American Health Foundation; American Heritage Foundation; antihemophilic factor; acute heart failure.

ahg anti-human globulin; anti hemophilic globulin.

AHgb normal adult hemoglobin.

AHL, ahl American Hockey League; average hearing level.

ahm anterior hyaloid membrane.

AHP, ahp Affordable Housing Program; American Home

Products; air at high pressure; air horsepower; acute hemorrhagic pancreatitis.

AHQ Arkansas Historical Quarterly; Army Headquarters.

AHR, ahr American Historical Review; Academy of Human Rights; active high resolution; antihyaluronidase reaction.

AHS American Hospital Society; American Humane Society.

AHST Alaska/Hawaii standard time.

ahv at this word (ad hanc vocem); avian herpes virus.

AI, ai Amnesty International; accidently incurred; accidental injury; accountants' index; artificial intelligence; in the meantime (ad interim); Air India; aircraft interception; aptitude index; active ingredient; artificial insemination; atherogenic index; aortic insufficiency; autoimmune.

AIA, aia Association of Insurance Attorneys; American Institute of Architects; Aircraft Industries Association; aspirin induced asthma; anti immunoglobulin antibodies.

AI Arb Associate of the Institute of Arbitrators.

AIB, aib American Institute of Banking; Accidents Investigation Branch; avian infectious bronchitis.

AIC American Institute of Criminology.

AIChE American Institute of Chemical Engineers.

AICLE Alabama Institute for Continuing Legal Education.

AICPA American Institute of Certified Public Accountants.

AID, a/i/d, aid Agency for International Development; accident/injury/damages; artificial insemination by donor; autoimmune disease; acute infectious disease.

AIDA Automobile Information Disclosure Act.

AIDP Advanced Institutional Development Program; International Association of Penal Law.

AIDS acquired immune deficiency syndrome; automated identification division system.

aie acute infectious encephalitis.

AIEE American Institute of Electrical Engineers.

AIFB American Institute of Financial Brokers.

AIG, aig American International Group; anti immunoglobulin.

AIH artificial insemination homologous; artificial insemination by husband.

aii allowable installment indebtedness.

Aik Aikens' Reports (Vermont); assistance in kind.

AILC American Indian Law Center; American International Law Cases.

AIM, aim Abridged Index Medicus; Accuracy in Media; American Indian Movement; American Institute of Management; air intercept missile; assessment of interactive mode.

AINL Association of Immigration and Nationality Lawyers.

aio applicable installment obligations; amyloid of immunoglobulin origin.

AIP, aip American Independent Party; American Institute of Planners; air intake panel; acute intermittent porphyria; average intravascular pressure.

AIPLU American Institute for Property and Liability Underwriters.

AIPPI International Association for the Protection of Industrial Property.

AIR, air All India Reporter; after initial release; average impairment rating.

Air L, Air LR, Air L Rev Air Law Review.

AIR (C) All India Reporter (Supreme Court).

Air U Rev Air University Review.

AIS, ais International Sociological Association; advance in schedule; automated information systems; anti insulin serum.

AISJ International Association of Legal Science.

AIT, ait Ameritech; acute intensive treatment.

AITR Australian and New Zealand Income Tax Reports.

AIUSA Amnesty International, USA.

AJ, aj Associate Justice, American Jurist; American Jurisprudence; ankle jerk.

aje adjusting journal entry.

AJHQ American Jewish Historical Quarterly.

AJIL American Journal of International Law.

AJR or **A Jur Rep** Australian Jurist Reports.

AJS American Judicature Society; American Journal of Sociology.

AK, ak Alaska; assault to kill; above knee; artificial kidney; acetate kinase.

aka also known as; above knee amputation; antikeratin antibody.

AK Marsh A.K. Marshall's Reports (Kentucky).

Akron L Rev Akron Law Review.

akp alkaline phosphatase.

AL, al Alabama; American Legion; American League; Albania; aluminum; alias; annual leave; assembly language; automatic transfer loan; allowance list; alley; all lengths; annoyance level; adaptation level; avian leukosis; acinar lumina; left ear (auris laeva); allergy; acute leukemia. See also Aleyn.

ALA, Ala, ala Alabama Supreme Court; Alabama Reports (NS: New Series); American Library Association; Alliance

for Labor Action; Automobile Legal Association; Association of Legal Administrators; aminolevulinic acid; anterior lip of the acetabulum; alanine.

ALAA Association of Legal Aid Attorneys of the City of New York; American Labor Arbitration Awards.

Ala Acts Acts of Alabama.

Ala Admin Code Alabama Administrative Code.

Ala App Alabama Appellate Court Reports.

ALAB NRC Atomic Safety and Licensing Appeal Board.

Ala Bar Bull Alabama Bar Bulletin.

Ala Code Code of Alabama.

Ala Cr App or **Ala Crim App** Alabama Court of Criminal Appeals.

Ala Ct App Alabama Court of Appeals.

Ala Law Alabama Lawyer.

Ala LJ Alabama Law Journal

Ala L Rev Alabama Law Review.

Ala Rep Alabama Reports (NS: New Series).

Ala Sel Cas Alabama Select Cases.

Alaska Alaska Reports.

Alaska B Brief Alaska Bar Brief.

Alaska BJ Alaska Bar Journal.

Alaska Ct App Alaska Court of Appeals.

Alaska Fed Alaska Federal Reports.

Alaska LJ Alaska Law Journal.

Alaska Sess Laws Alaska Session Laws.

Alaska Stat Alaska Statutes.

Ala St B Found Bull Alabama State Bar Foundation Bulletin.

ALB, Alb, alb Alberta; Automobile Labor Board; albumin.

Alba Alberta.

Albany Law J Albany Law Journal.

Albany L Rev Albany Law Review.

Alb LQ Alberta Law Quarterly.

Alb LR Alberta Law Reports.

Alb L Rev Alberta Law Review; Albany Law Review.

ALC, alc American Labor Cases (Prentice Hall); alcohol; assembly language coding; axiolinguocervical; absolute lymphocyte count.

ACLM Air Launched Cruise Missile.

Alc & N or **Alc & Nap** or **Al & N** Alcock & Napier's King's Bench Reports (Ireland).

Alco Bev Cont Alcoholic Beverage Control.

Alcock See Alc & N.

Alcoh alcoholic.

Alcr alcohol rub.

Alc Reg Cas or **Alc R Cas** Alcock's Registry Cases (Ireland).

ALD, Ald Alden's Condensed Reports; alderman; at a later date; Actualite Legislative Dalloz; anterior latissimus dorsi; aldolase; approximate lethal dose.

Alden See Ald.

ALEC American Legislative Exchange Council.

Alexander Alexander's Reports (Mississippi).

Aleyn Aleyn's Kings Bench Reports (England).

alf acute liver failure.

ALG, Alg, alg Algeria; algebra; allergy; antilymphocyte globulin; axiolinguogingival.

Alg Med Holland, Statutes and Decrees (Algemene Mededelingen).

ALGOL ALGOrithmic Language.

alh anterior lobe hormone.

ALI American Law Institute.

ALI-ABA American Law Institute - American Bar Association Committee on Continuing Professional Education (Course MJ: Course Materials Journal).

ALI Proc American Law Institute Proceedings.

Alison Pr Alison's Practice (Scotland).

ALJ, alj Administrative Law Judge; Albany Law Journal.

ALJR Australian Law Journal Reports.

Alk, alk Alaska Reports; alkaline.

alk phos alkaline phosphatase.

alky alkalinity.

All, all Allen's Reports (Massachusetts); acute lymphoblastic leukemia; allergy; air life line.

alld allowed.

alleg allegiance.

Allen or **Allen Rep** Allen's Reports (Massachusetts); Allen's Reports (Washington Territory); Allen's Reports (New Brunswick); Allen Telegraph Cases.

Allen NB Allen's Reports, New Brunswick.

All ER or **All Eng** All England Law Reports.

Allin Allinson's Reports (Pennsylvania).

All India Crim Dec All India Criminal Decisions.

All India Rptr or **All Ind Rep** All India Reporter (NS: New Series).

Allinson Allinson Reports, Pennsylvania Superior District Courts.

All Nig L R All Nigeria Law Reports.

All NLR All Nigeria Law Reports.

All Pak Leg Dec All Pakistan Legal Decisions.

All St Sales Tax Rep All State Sales Tax Reporter.

ALM, alm American Law Magazine; air launched missile; alarm; acral lentiginous melanoma.

ALMA Association of Labor Mediation Agencies; Adoptees Liberty Movement Association.

Al & N Alcock & Napier's King's Bench Reports (Ireland).

aln accounting line number; anterior lateral nerve; anterior lymph node.

ALO American Liaison Office;

average lymphocyte output.

alos average length of stay.

alot allotment.

ALP American Labor Party; assembly language program; anterior lobe of pituitary; acute lupus pericarditis.

ALPAI International Air Line Pilots Association.

ALR American Law Reports; Argus Law Reports; Alberta Law Reports; Alden Law Reports; Adelaide Law Review.

ALR2d American Law Reports, Second Series.

ALR3d American Law Reports, Third Series.

ALR4th American Law Reports, Fourth Series.

ALRA Associated Legislative Rabbinate of America.

ALR Fed American Law Reports, Federal.

AL Rec American Law Record.

AL Reg American Law Register (NS: New Series) (OS: Old Series).

AL Rep American Law Reporter.

ALRI American Law Research Institute.

als alias; autograph signed letter; anticipated life span; antilymphocyte serum; acute lumbar strain; amyotrophic lateral sclerosis.

ALSA American Law Student Association.

ALST Alaska Standard Time.

ALT, alt Australian Law Times; administrative lead time; alteration; alter; alternate; alternator; altitude; avian laryngotracheitis.

ALTA, Alta American Land Title Association; Alberta Law Reports.

Alta Gaz Alberta Gazette.

Alta L Alberta Law.

Alta LQ Alberta Law Quarterly.

Alta L Rev or **Alta LR** Alberta Law Review.

Alta Rev Stat Revised Statutes of Alberta.

Alta Stat Statutes of Alberta.

alter alteration; alternative.

alt hor every two hours (alternis horis).

altm altimeter.

altn alternate; alteration.

altr alteration.

alts acute lumbar trauma syndrome.

alu arithmetic and logic unit.

alum alumnus; aluminum.

alv alveolar; avian leukosis virus.

alw allowance.

aly alloy; alley.

AM, Am, a/m, am Master of Arts; American; Aeromexico; ampere per meter; administrative manual; amendment; arms material; before noon (ante meridiem); in the year of the world (anno mundi); ammeter; acoustic-magnetic; amplitude modulation; ammunition; air marshal; air mail; awaiting maintenance; assumed mean; adult male; axiomesial; ampicillin; amacrine cell.

a&m agricultural and mechanical.

AMA, ama American Medical Association; American Management Association; American Maritime Association; American Municipal Association; Automobile Manufacturers Association; American Ministerial Association; American Motel Association; American Motorcycle Association; as many as; against medical advice; anti myosin antibody.

Am & E Corp Cas American and English Corporation Cases (NS: New Series).

Am & ER Cas American and English Railroad Cases (NS: New Series).

Am & Eng Ann Cas American and English Annotated Cases.

Am & Eng Eq D American and English Decisions in Equity.

Am & Eng Pat Cas American and English Patent Cases.

Am Acad Matri Law J American Academy of Matrimonial Lawyers Journal.

Am Acad Pol & Soc Sci American Academy of Political and Social Science.

Am A Psych L Bull American Academy of Psychiatry and the Law Bulletin.

amagl amalgamated.

AM&O Armstrong, Macartney & Ogle's Nisi Prius Reports (Ireland).

Amb, amb Ambler's Chancery Reports (England); ambassador; ambulatory; ambient; American Brands; ambulance.

Am Bank Rev American Bankruptcy Review.

Am Bankr LJ American Bankruptcy Law Journal.

Am Bank Rep American Bankruptcy Reports (NS: New Series).

Am Bankr LJ American Bankruptcy Law Journal.

Am Bankr Reg American Bankruptcy Register (United States).

Am Bankr Rep American Bankruptcy Reports (NS: New Series).

Am Bankr Rev or **Am Bank Rev** American Bankruptcy Review.

Am Bar AJ American Bar Association Journal.

Am B Found Res J American Bar Foundation Research Journal.

Ambl Ambler, Chancery Reports (England).

Am B News American Bar News.

Ambo amboceptor.

AMBOP American Board of Oral Pathology.

Am BR American Bankruptcy Reports (NS: New Series).

Ambt, ambt Ambtenarengerecht (Holland civil service court); ambulatory.

Am Bus Law or **Am Bus LJ** American Business Law Journal.

AMC, amc American Maritime Cases; Association of Management Consultants; American Mining Congress; American Motors Corporation; average monthly consumption; air mail center; arm muscle circumference; acetyl methyl carbinol.

AMCC American Mexican Claims Commission.

amcom AMEX communications.

Am Corp Cas American Corporation Cases.

Am Cr American Criminal Reports.

Am Crim Law American Criminal Law Review.

Am Crim LQ American Criminal Law Quarterly.

Am Crim L Rev or **Am Crim Law** American Criminal Law Review.

Am Crim Rep American Criminal Reports.

am cur amicus curiae.

amd advanced micro devices; amend; anti morphine dose.

Am Dec or **Am D** American Decisions.

amdg to the greater glory of God (ad majorem dei gloriam).

Am Dig American Digest.

amdt amendment.

AME, ame African Methodist Episcopal; amphotericin methyl ester.

Am & E Corp Cas American and English Corporation Cases (NS: New Series).

Am Ec Rev or **Am Econ Rev** American Economic Review.

Am Ed American Edition.

Am Elect Cas American Electrical Cases.

amemb American embassy.

amend amendment.

-Amend United Nations amendment or addendum to the main document.

Am & Eng Ann Cas American and English Annotated Cases.

Am & Eng Eq D American and English Decisions in Equity.

Am & Eng Pat Cas American and English Patent Cases.

Amer Amerman's Reports (Pennsylvania); American.

Am & ER Cas American and English Railroad Cases (NS: New Series).

Amer Fed Tax Rep American Federal Tax Reports (Prentice Hall) (2d: Second Series).

Amer J Comp L American Journal of Comparative Law.

Amer Law Reg American Law Register.

Amer Petrol Inst Stand American Petroleum Institute Standard.

Amer St Papers For Rels American State Papers, Legislative and Executive Documents of the Congress of the United States, Class I, Foreign Relations.

Ames Ames (Minnesota); Ames (Rhode Island).

Ames K&B Ames, Knowles & Bradley (Rhode Island).

Ameslan American sign language.

AMEX American Stock Exchange; American Express Co.

amf air mail field; anti muscle factor.

Am Fed American Federationist.

Am Fed Tax R or **Amer Fed Tax Rep** American Federal Tax Reports (Prentice Hall) (2d: Second Series).

AMFIE Association of Mutual Fire Insurance Engineers.

Am For L Assn Newsl American Foreign Law Association Newsletter.

AMG, amg American military government; allied military government; among; anti macrophage globulin.

Am Gas J American Gas Journal.

AMGP Association of Medical Group Psychoanalysts.

AMHA Association of Mental Health Administrators.

Am Hist R or **Am Hist Rev** American Historical Review.

AMI, ami American Maritime Institute; American Medical International; American Meat Institute; axiomesio incisal; acute myocardial infarction.

Amicus Amicus (South Bend, Ind.); Amicus (Thousand Oaks, CA).

Am Ind J American Indian Journal.

Am Ind L Newsl American Indian Law Newsletter.

Am Ind L Rev or **Am Ind LR** American Indian Law Review.

AMINOIL American Independent Oil Co.

Am Insolv Rep or **Am Ins Rep** American Insolvency Reports.

Am Inst Bank Bul American Institute of Banking Bulletin.

Am J American Jurisprudence (2d: Second Edition).

Am J Comp L American Journal of Comparative Law.

Am J Crim L American Journal of Criminal Law.

Am J For Psych American Journal of Forensic Psychiatry.

AMJI Arkansas Model Jury Instructions.

Am J Int L American Journal of International Law.

Am J Juris American Journal of Jurisprudence.

Am JL & Med or **Am J of Law & Med** American Journal of Law and Medicine.

Am J Legal Hist American Journal of Legal History.

Am J Leg Forms Ann American Jurisprudence Legal Forms Annotated.

Am JL Rev American Journal Law Review.

Am J Pl & Pr Forms Ann American Jurisprudence Pleading and Practice Forms Annotated.

Am J Police Sci American Journal of Police Science.

Am J Proof of Facts American Jurisprudence Proof of Facts.

Am J Tax Poly American Journal of Tax Policy.

Am J Trial Advoc American Journal of Trial Advocacy.

Am J Trials American Jurisprudence Trials.

Am Jr American Jurisprudence; American Jurist.

Am Jud Soc American Judicature Society.

Am Jur American Jurisprudence (2d: Second Edition); American Jurist.

Am Jur Legal Forms American Jurisprudence Legal Forms (2d: Second Edition).

Am Jur Pl & Pr Forms American Jurisprudence Pleading and Practice Forms.

Am Jur Proof of Facts American Jurisprudence Proof of Facts.

Am Jur Trials American Jurisprudence Trials.

aml acute myeloblastic leukemia; anterior mitral leaflet.

Am Lab Arb Awards American Labor Arbitration Awards.

Am Lab Arb Cas American Labor Arbitration Cases.

Am Lab Cas American Labor Cases.

Am Lab Leg Rev American Labor Legislation Review.

Am Law American Lawyer.

Am Law Inst American Law Institute.

Am Law J American Law Journal (Pennsylvania) (NS: New Series).

Am Law Mag American Law Magazine.

Am Law Rec American Law Record.

Am Law Reg American Law Register.

Am L Ins American Law Institute.

Am LJ American Law Journal (Pennsylvania) (NS: New Series).

Am L Mag or **Am L Mag** American Law Magazine.

Am L Rec American Law Record (Ohio).

Am L Reg American Law Register

(NS: New Series) (OS: Old Series).

Am L Rev American Law Review.

Am L School Rev or **Am LS Rev** American Law School Review.

Am LT Bankr or **Am LT Bankr Rep** American Law Times Bankruptcy Reports.

amm ammonia; agnogenic myeloid metaplasia.

Am Mar Cas American Maritime Cases.

amn alloxazine mononucleotide; anterior median nucleus.

amnd amendment.

Am Neg Cas American Negligence Cases.

Am Neg Dig American Negligence Digest.

Am Negl Cas American Negligence Cases.

Am Negl Rep or **Am Neg Rep** American Negligence Reports.

amnio amniocentesis.

Am Notary American Notary.

AMO, amo American Motors Corporation; air mass zero; axiomesio occlusal; amorphous.

A Moo A. Moore's Reports (England).

AM&O Armstrong, Macartney & Ogle's Nisi Prius Reports (Ireland).

amp ampere; amplifier; amputation; ampul; average mean pressure; adenosine monophosphate; amputation; ampicillin.

AMPAS Academy of Motion Picture Arts and Sciences.

Am Pat LA Bull or **Am Pat L Ass Bull** American Patent Law Association Bulletin.

Am Pet Inst Proc American Petroleum Institute Proceedings.

amph or **amphib** amphibious.

amp hr ampere hour.

Am Pol Sci Rev American Political Science Review.

Am Pr Rep American Practice Reports (D.C.).

Am Prob or **Am Prob Rep**
American Probate Reports
(NS: New Series).

amps amperes; abnormal
mucopolysacchariduria.

Am R, amr American Reports;
alternating motion rate;
activity metabolic rate.

Am R&C Rep American Railroad
and Corporation Reports.

Am Rail Cas or **Am R Ca**
American Railway Cases
(Smith & Bates).

Am Rep American Reports.

AMREX American Real Estate
Exchange.

Am R Rep American Railway
Reports.

Am Ry Rep American Railway
Reports.

AMS, ams Agricultural Marketing
Service; American
Mathematical Society; aggravated in military service; anti-
macrophage serum.

Am Samoa American Samoa
Reports (2d: Second Series).

Am Samoa Admin Code
American Samoa
Administrative Code.

Am Samoa Code Ann American
Samoa Code Annotated.

amsl above mean sea level.

Am Soc Intl L Proc or **Am Soc
Int Law Proc** American
Society of International Law
Proceedings.

Am Soc Rev American
Sociological Review.

Am St Papers American State
Papers.

Am St R or **Am St Rep** or **Am SR**
American State Reports.

Am St RD American Street
Railway Decisions.

Am St Rep American State
Reports.

AMT, amt American Medical
Technologists; amount;
available machine time; alternative minimum tax; active
maintenance time; acute
miliary tuberculosis.

Am Tax Q American Taxpayer's
Quarterly.

Am Trial Law Assn J American
Trial Lawyers Association
Journal.

Am Trial Law LJ American Trial
Lawyers Law Journal.

Am Tr M Cas American
Trademark Cases (Cox).

amu atomic mass unit; average
monthly usage.

Am U Int L Rev American
University Intramural Law
Review.

Am UL Rev American University
Law Review.

amv avian myeloblastosis virus.

AMVETS American Veterans of
World War II, Korea, and
Vietnam.

An, an Anonymous Reports at
end of Benloe (England);
arrival notice; anonymous;
animate; annex; year (annus);
above named; army-navy;
alphanumeric; atmosphere
normal; atomic number; acid
number; anterior; aneurysm;
anorexia nervosa.

ANA, ana American Newspaper
Association; American Nurses
Association; Administration for
Native Americans; antinuclear
antibodies; anesthesia.

anad anorexia nervosa and associated disorders.

ANAF Army Navy Air Force.

anag anagram; acute narrow
angle glaucoma.

anal analysis; analogous.

Anales Jur Anales de
Jurisprudencia (Mexico).

anat anatomy; anatomic.

An B Anonymous Reports at end
of Benloe (England).

ANC, anc Abbott's New Cases
(New York); American
Negligence Cases; Advisory
Neighborhood Commission;
African National Council;
ancient; antigen neutralizing
capacity.

anch anchorage.

And, and Anderson's Common
Pleas Reports (England);
Andrew's King's Bench
Reports (England); Andorra;
alphanumeric display; algo-
neurodystrophy.

Anderson Anderson's Common
Pleas Reports (England).

Andr Andrew's King's Bench
Reports (England).

anes anesthesiology.

anf antinuclear factor; agriculture,
nutrition, and forestry.

Ang, ang Angell's Reports (Rhode
Island); Angola; Anglican;
angular; angle; angiogram.

Ang & Dur Angell & Durfee's
Reports (Rhode Island).

Angl Anglican.

Anglo-Am L Rev or **Ang & AL Rev**
Anglo-American Law Review.

anh anhydrous.

anhy or **anhyd** anhydrous.

ani animal; automatic number
identification; acute nerve irritation.

Animal Rights L Rep Animal
Rights Law Reporter.

aniso anisocytosis.

ank ankle.

anl animal; analog; annual;
anneal; acute nonlymphocytic
leukemia.

Ann, ann Annaly's Harwicke
King's Bench Reports
(England); annotation; annotated; annals; annuity; annual;
years (anni); annex.

Annals Annals of the American
Academy of Political and
Social Science.

Annals Air & Space Annals of Air
and Space Law.

Annaly Annaly's Harwicke King's
Bench Reports (England).

Ann Cas American Annotated
Cases; New York Annotated
Cases.

Ann Code Annotated Code.

Ann Dig Annual Digest of Public
International Law Cases.

Ann Hum Gen Annals of Human
Genetics.

Ann Indus Prop L Annual of Industrial Property Law.

Ann L Reg US or **Ann Law Reg** Annual Law Register.

Ann Leg Forms Mag Annotated Legal Forms Magazine.

anno, annot annotated.

annova analysis of variance.

Ann Rev Intl Aff Annual Review of International Affairs.

Ann R Gen Annual Review of Genetics.

Ann Rev Bank L Annual Review of Banking Law.

Ann Surv Afr L Annual Survey of African Law.

Ann Surv Am L Annual Survey of American Law.

Ann Surv Banking L Annual Survey of Banking Law.

Ann Surv Colo L Annual Survey of Colorado Law.

Ann Surv Commonw L Annual Survey of Commonwealth Law.

Ann Surv Ind L Annual Survey of Indian Law.

Ann Surv Mass L Annual Survey of Massachusetts Law.

Ann Surv S Afr L Annual Survey of South African Law.

Ann Tax Cas Annotated Tax Cases.

ano another.

anon anonymous.

anp acute necrotizing pancreatitis.

ANPA American Newspapers Publishers Association.

ANR American Negligence Reports.

ANRC American National Red Cross.

ANS, Ans, ans American Nuclear Society; American national standard; automatic navigation system; answer; anterior nasal spine; autonomic nervous system.

ANSCII American National Standard Code for Information Interchange.

ANSI American National Standards Institute.

Anst Ansthruther's Exchequer Reports (England).

Ant, ant Antarctica; Netherlands Antilles; anticipated; antonym; antiquity; anterior; antenna; acoustic noise test.

ante before.

anth anthology.

Anth NP Anthon's Nisi Prius Reports (New York).

anthro anthropology.

antiq antiquarian.

Antitrust Bull Antitrust Bulletin.

Antitrust L & Econ Rev Antitrust Law and Economics Review.

Antitrust LJ Antitrust Law Journal.

Antitrust L Sym Antitrust Law Symposium.

ant sup sp anterior superior spine.

antu alpha naphthylthiourea.

anx anxiety; annex.

ANZUK Australia, New Zealand, United Kingdom.

ANZUS Australia, New Zealand, United States.

AO, ao, a/o Angola; authorized order; area office; area of operation; among others; and others; account of; accounts office; administrative office; administrative order; atomic orbital; avoidance of others; alert and oriented; anterior oblique; abdominal aorta.

AOA, aoa Administration on Aging; American Optometric Association; American Osteopathic Association; at or above; average orifice area.

aoaa aminooxoacetic acid.

aob alcohol on breadth; angle of beam; approved operation budget; at or below; accessory olfactory bulb.

AOC, aoc Architect of the Capitol; average operating cost; auditor overcharge claims; abridged ocular chart.

AOC Newsl Administrative Office of the Courts Newsletter.

aod administrative officer on duty;

angle of descent; arterial occlusive disease; auriculo osteodysplasia.

aodm adult onset diabetes mellitus.

AOHA American Osteopathic Hospital Association.

aoi area of interest.

aol absent over leave; acro osteolysis.

aoo anodal opening odor.

aop acetoxypregnenolone.

AOPA Aircraft Owners and Pilots Association.

aoq average outgoing quality.

aor angle of reflection; area of responsibility; auditory oculogyric reflex.

AORN Association of Operating Room Nurses.

aos add or subtract; anodal opening sound.

aot average operation time; anti ovotransferrin.

AOTA American Occupational Therapy Association.

AOUSC Administrative Office of United States Courts.

aov aortic valve.

aow admitted on ward.

AP, A&P, Ap, a&p, a/p, ap Associated Press; Alliance for Progress; Great Atlantic and Pacific Tea Co.; April; agency procedure; air pollution; airport; all purpose; asking price; account paid; accounts payable; as purchased; authority to pay; authority to purchase; additional premium; advanced pay; assumed position; auscultation and percussion; author's proof; above proof; access permit; automatic pilot; airplane; according to (apud); attached processor; alkaline phosphatase; acid phosphatase; anterior and posterior; anterior pituitary; anal pore; aortic pressure; alum precipitated; aspiration pneumonia; angina pectoris.

APA, apa Administrative Procedure Act; American Psychiatric Association; Amalgamated Printers Association; American Polygraph Association; Airline Passengers Association; American Pilots Association; American Philosophical Association; amino penicillanic acid.

APAI Association of Paroling Authorities, International.

APAP, apap Association of Physician Assistant Programs; acetyl para amino phenol.

APB, apb Accounting Principles Board; all points bulletin; abductor pollicis brevis.

Ap Bre Breese's Illinois Reports Appendix.

APC, apc All Peoples Congress; aspirin, phenacetin, caffeine; armored personnel carrier; all purpose capsule; antiphlogistic corticoid.

apch approach.

APCO Air Pollution Control Office.

apd acute polycystic disease; afferent pupillary defect.

APDAB Army Physical Disability Appeal Board.

ape available power efficiency; anterior pituitary extract; acute polio encephalitis.

APF, apf American Psychological Foundation; animal protein factor; acidulated phosphofluoride.

apg acid precipitable globulin.

APGA American Public Gas Association.

ASH, aph Association of Private Hospitals; access permit holder; anterior pituitary hormone; alcohol positive history.

APHA American Public Health Association.

API, api American Petroleum Institute; American Press Institute; Amalgamated Publishers, Inc.; Animal Protection Institute; air position indicator; alkaline protease inhibitor.

APJI Alabama Pattern Jury Instructions.

apl a programming language; assembly programming language; authorized price list; applied physics lab; approved parts list; abductor pollicis longus; anterior pituitary like.

APLA American Patent Law Association.

APLAQJ APLA Quarterly Journal.

APLS American Psychology Law Society.

apm anterior papillary muscle.

apn artificial pneumothorax; acute pyelonephritis.

apo assault on police officer; adductor pollicis obliquus.

App, app Appleton's Reports (Maine); Ohio Appellate Reports; appellate; appeal; apprentice; appendix, apparatus; applied; apparent; appearance; approximately; appraised; appointed; air pollution potential; anti platelet plasma.

APPA American Probation and Parole Association.

App Bd OCS Decisions of the Appeal Board, Office of Contract Settlement.

App Cas Appeal Cases (District of Columbia); Law Reports Appeal Cases (England) (2d: Second Series).

App Court Ad Rev Appellate Court Administration Review.

appd approved.

App DC United States Court of Appeals for the District of Columbia; Appeal Cases (District of Columbia).

App Dept Appellate Department.

App Div Appellate Division Reports (New York) (2d: Second Series).

appl applicable; appliance.

appln application.

appmt appointment.

appn appropriation.

App NZ Appeal Reports (New Zealand) (2d: Second Series).

appr approved; apprentice; apprehend; approximately.

App Rep Ont Ontario Appeal Reports.

Appleton Appleton's Reports (Maine)

appt appointment.

appv approved.

appx appendix.

appy appendectomy.

APR, Apr, apr Atlantic Provinces Reports; April; apprentice; annual progress report; annual percentage rate; anterior primary rami; abdominal perineal resection.

APRA American Petroleum Refiners Association.

APRRB Airman Performance Report Review Board.

APRS American Performing Rights Society; Association of Public Radio Stations.

aprx approximately.

APS, aps American Pediatric Society; automatic pilot system; assimilations per second; adenosine phosphosulfate.

APSA American Political Science Association.

APSR American Political Science Review.

apt appointment; aptitude; apartment; automatically programmed tools; alum precipitated toxoid.

APTA, apta American Physical Therapy Association; aneurysm of persistent trigeminal artery.

aptd aid to the permanently and totally disabled.

apvd approved.

APW American Prisoner of War.

APWU American Postal Workers Union.

apx appendix.

aq water (aqua); accomplishment

quotient; alcohol quotient; air quality; any quantity.

AQA Air Quality Act.

aq bull boiling water (aqua bulliens).

AQCR Air Quality Control Region.

aq dest distilled water (aqua destillata).

aq ferv boiling water (aqua fervens).

AR, Ar, ar, a/r Alberta Reports; Atlantic Reports; American Reports; Administrative Ruling; Army Regulation; Arkansas; Argentina; Arabic; argon; antiracketeering; approved for release; all risks; as required; accounts receivable; at the rate of; acknowledgement of receipt; annual report; annual return; average revenue; acceptance review; artists and repertory; automatic rifle; area; arrival; applied research; active resistance; alcohol related; aortic regurgitation; admitting room; artificial respiration.

ARA, ara Artists Rights Association; American Railway Association; Agricultural Research Administration; aortic root angiogram.

ARAMCO Arabian American Oil Company.

ARB, arb Administratiefrechtelijke Beslissingen (Holland); arbitrary; arbitrageur; any reliable brand.

Arb Ct Arbitration Court (New Zealand).

Arb J Arbitration Journal (NS: New Series) (OS: Old Series).

Arb L Dig Arbitration Law: A Digest of Court Decisions.

Arb Schools Arbitration in the Schools.

Arb Trib Arbitration Tribunal.

arbtrn arbitration.

ARC, arc American Ruling Cases; American Railway Cases; Appalachian Regional Commission; Atlantic Richfield

Company; American Red Cross; Annual Review Committee; AIDS related condition; antigen reactive cell.

ARCA American Retail Coal Association; Automobile Racing Club of America.

arccot arccotangent.

Arch, arch Archbishop; architect; archive; archaic; archipelago.

Archer Archer's Reports (Florida).

Archer & H Archer & Hogue's Reports (Florida).

Arch PL Cas Archbold's Poor Law Cases (England).

archt architect.

ARCO Atlantic Richfield Company.

ard application for review decisions; acute respiratory disease; AIDS related disease; atopic respiratory disease.

A Rep American Reports; Atlantic Reports.

ARES Association of Real Estate Syndicators.

arf acute respiratory failure; acute renal failure.

Arg, arg Argentina; arguendo; argentum.

Argus LR Argus Law Reports (Australia).

ARI, ari Aluminum Research Institute; Agricultural Research Institute; anxiety reaction, intense; acute respiratory infection.

ARIT American Registered Inhalation Therapist.

Ariz Arizona.

Ariz App Arizona Appeals Reports.

Ariz BJ Arizona Bar Journal.

Ariz Ct App Arizona Court of Appeals.

Ariz L Rev or **Ariz Law R** Arizona Law Review.

Ariz St LJ Arizona State Law Journal.

Ark Arkansas.

Ark Acts General Acts of Arkansas.

Ark Just Arkley's Justiciary Cases (Scotland).

Ark LJ Arkansas Law Journal.

Ark L Rev or **Ark Law R** Arkansas Law Review.

Ark Law The Arkansas Lawyer.

Ark Law Q Arkansas Lawyer Quarterly.

Ark Reg Arkansas Register.

Ark Stat Ann Arkansas Statutes Annotated.

arl anti-riot laws; applied research lab; average remaining lifetime.

ARM, Arm, arm Appeals & Review Memorandum Committee (I.R. Bulletin); all risk management; Armenia; armature; armament; adjustable rate mortgage; artificial rupture of membrane; allergy relief medicine.

ARMA Association of Records Managers and Administrators.

Armour Manitoba Queen's Bench Reports, Temp. Wood, by Armour.

Arms Con Elec Armstrong's Contested Elections (New York).

Army Law Army Lawyer.

Arn or **Arnold** Arnold's Common Pleas Reports (England).

ArNG Army National Guard.

Arn & H or **Arn & Hod** Arnold & Hodges' Queen's Bench Reports (England).

aro after receipt of order.

arom aromatic; artificial rupture of membranes.

arp at risk period.

ARPANET Advanced Research Projects Agency Network.

arpt airport.

arq automatic request for repeat.

ARR, arr American Railway Reports; arrive; arrangement; arrester; arrested.

ARRT American Registered Respiratory Therapist; American Registry of Radiologic Technologists.

ARS, ars Arizona Revised Statutes; advanced record system; arsenal; anti rabies serum.

ART, art Accredited Record Technician; alert reaction time; article; artist; artificial; artery; arthritis; autologous reactive T cell.

Art & L Art and the Law.

artc air route traffic control.

artf artificial.

arth arthritic.

artl awaiting results of trial.

aru audio response unit.

ARWA American Right-of-Way Association.

AS, As, as, a/s American Samoa; Act of Sederunt (Scotland); Associate in Science; Anglo Saxon; arsenic; account sales; apprentice seaman; as stated; at sight; after sight; automatic transfer-shares; arts and sciences; air speed; area surveillance; along side; astigmatism; arsenic; applied science; artificial sweetener; aerospace standards; left ear (auris sinistra); aortic stenosis; arteriosclerosis.

ASA, asa American Standards Association; American Statistical Association; American Society of Appraisers; American Society of Anesthesiologists; Army Security Agency; as soon as; anti static additive; acetylsalicylic acid; aspirin sensitive asthma.

ASA Code American Standards Association Code for Information Exchange.

ASA Newsl Association for the Study of Abortion Newsletter.

asap as soon as possible.

ASB, asb Acoustical Standards Board; Air Safety Board; analytical support branch; asbestos; asymptomatic bacteriuria.

ASBCA Armed Services Board of Contract Appeals.

ASC, asc American Safety Council; American Society of Criminology; altered state of consciousness; asthma symptom checklist; arteriosclerosis.

ASCAP Copyright L Symp Copyright Law Symposium of the American Society of Composers, Authors, and Publishers.

ASCE American Society of Civil Engineers.

ASCI American Society of Construction Inspectors.

ASCII American Standard Code for Information Interchange.

ASCP American Society of Clinical Pathologists.

ASCS Agricultural Stabilization and Conservation Service.

ASCU, ascu Association of State Colleges and Universities; automatic scanning control unit.

ascvd arteriosclerotic cardiovascular disease.

ASD, asd Association of Steel Distributors; atrial septal defect; arthritis syphilitic deformans.

ASDSO Association of State Dam Safety Officials.

ASE American Stock Exchange; American Society of Engineers.

ASEAN Association of South East Asian Nations.

ASET Associate in Engineering Technology.

ASF, asf Automotive Safety Foundation; amperes per square foot; assignable square feet; African swine fever.

ASFO American Society of Forensic Odontology.

ASFPM Association of State Floodplan Managers.

asg, asgmt assignment.

Ash, ASH, ash Ashmead's Reports (Pennsylvania); Action on Smoking and Health; Ashland Oil; antistreptococcal hyaluronidase.

ASHA American Society of Hospital Attorneys.

ashd arteriosclerotic heart disease.

Ashm Ashmead's Reports (Pennsylvania).

ASI, asi American Safety Institute; amended shipping instruction; addiction severity index.

Asian Comp L Rev Asian Comparative Law Review.

ASIL American Society of International Law.

ASILS Association of Student International Law Societies.

ASILS Intl LJ ASILS International Law Journal.

ASIS, asis American Society for Informtaion Science; anterior superior iliac spine.

ASL, Asl, asl American Soccer League; American sign language; average service life; above sea level; antistreptolysin.

ASLH American Society for Legal History.

ASLIB Association of Special Libraries and Information Bureaus.

ASLL American Savings and Loan League.

ASLM American Society of Law and Medicine.

A/SLMR Decisions and Reports on Rulings of the Assistant Secretary of Labor for Labor Management Relations pursuant to Executive Order 11491, as amended.

ASLRA Association of State Labor Relations Agencies.

ASM, asm American Samoa; air to surface missile; airway smooth muscle.

ASMA Association of State Mediation Agencies.

ASME American Society of Mechanical Engineers.

asmi anteroseptal myocardial infarction.

ASN, asn American Society of Notaries; army service number; arteriosclerotic nephritis.

ASNE American Society of Newspaper Editors.

asot antistreptolysin-o titer.

Asp, ASP, asp Aspinall's Maritime Cases (England); American State Papers; American selling price; attached support processor; aspartic acid; area systolic pressure.

ASPA American Society of Personnel Administration.

ASPAC Asian and Pacific Council.

ASPCA American Society for the Prevention of Cruelty to Animals.

Asp or **Asp Cas** or **Asp MC** Aspinall's Maritime Cases (England).

Aspin Aspinall's Maritime Cases (England).

ASPL American Society for Pharmacy Law.

ASPLP American Society for Political and Legal Philosophy.

ASPM American Society of Paramedics.

Asp MC Aspinall's Maritime Cases (England).

aspr armed services procurement regulation.

ASQ Administrative Science Quarterly.

ASQDE American Society of Questioned Document Examiners.

ASR, asr American State Reports; American Sociological Review; airport surveillance radar; automatic send/receive; atrial septal resection.

ASR- Accounting Series (IRS Release Designations).

ass association; acute spinal stenosis.

assd assigned.

ASSE American Society of Safety Engineers.

assmt assessment.

assn association.

Assn Trial Law Am Newsl Association of Trial Lawyers of America Newsletter.

ASSR, assr Autonomous Soviet Socialist Republic; adult situation stress reaction.

asst assistant.

Assyr Assyrian.

AST, ast Atlantic Standard Time; all systems test; at same time; anterior spinothalamic tract.

ASTM American Society for Testing Materials.

ASU, asu Arab Socialist Union; administrative service unit.

Asv, asv American standard version; avian sarcoma virus; anodic stripping voltametry.

asvd arteria sclerotic vascular disease.

asw air to surface weapon.

asym asymmetric.

asx asymptomatic.

AT, At, at, a/t Alcohol Tax Unit (Internal Revenue Bulletin); Alcohol and Tobacco Tax Ruling; Atlantic Standard Time; American Tobacco Co.; atmosphere; attorney; American terms; air temperature; ampere turn; additional term; amount tendered; access time; action taken; achievement test; assay ton; automatic transmission; achilles tendon; adjunctive therapy; anterior tibial.

AT/- United Nations Administrative Tribunal.

ATA, ata American Taxpayer Association; American Title Association; American Teachers Association; atmospheric temperature absolute; alimentary toxic aleukia.

ATAA Air Transport Association of America.

ATB Air Transportation Board.

ATC, atc Annotated Tax Cases; Australian Tax Cases (Commerce Clearing House); air traffic control; average total cost; around the clock; activated thymus cell.

atch attachment.

ATD, atd Australia Tax Decisions; actual time of departure; anti thyroid drug; alzheimer type dementia.

atdm asynchronous time division multiplexing.

ate automatic test equipment.

Ateneo LJ Ateneo Law Journal.

ATF, atf Alcohol, Tobacco, and Firearms, Bureau of; actual time of fall; ascitic tumor fluid.

ATFB Alcohol, Tobacco, and Firearms Bureau, Quarterly Bulletin.

ATFCB Alcohol, Tobacco, and Firearms Cumulative Bulletin.

ATF Qtrly Bull Quarterly Bulletin, Alcohol, Tobacco and Firearms Bureau, Quarterly Bulletin.

ATF Rul Alcohol, Tobacco, and Firearms Bureau Rulings.

atg antithyroglobulin.

ATGC Attorney Grievance Commission of Maryland.

ATGSB Admissions Test for Graduate Study in Business.

Atk Atkyn's Chancery Reports (England).

Atl, ATL, atl Atlantic Reporter (2d: Second Series); antitrust law; American Tariff League; anterior tricuspid leaflet

ATLA American Trial Lawyers Association; adult T cell leukemia antigen.

ATLAJ American Trial Lawyers Association Journal.

Atl Com Q Atlantic Community Quarterly.

Atl PR Atlantic Province Reports (Canada).

atm atmosphere; automated teller machine; acute transverse myelitis.

atn acute tubular necrosis.

atog allowable takeoff gross weight.

Atom Energy LJ Atomic Energy Law Journal.

atp authority to proceed; admissions testing program; adenosine triphosphate; attending physician.

ATR, atr Australian Tax Review; air traffic regulations; atrophy; achilles tendon reflex.

atr fib atrial fibrillation.

ATRR Antitrust and Trade Regulation Reporter.

ATR Rul Ruling of Alcohol, Tobacco, and Firearms Bureau (Treasury Department).

ats administrative terminal system; automatic test scoring; action tracking system; anti-tetanic serum; arteriosclerosis.

ATSDR Agency for Toxic Substances and Disease Registry.

ATST Atlantic Standard Time.

AT&T, att American Telephone and Telegraph Co.; attorney; attempt.

ATTD Alcohol and Tobacco Tax Division.

attr average time to repair.

atty attorney.

Atty Gen Attorney General.

Atty Gen LJ Attorney General Law Journal.

Atty Gen Op Attorney General Opinions.

Atty Gen Rep United States Attorney General's Reports.

ATU Alcohol Tax Unit.

Atw or **Atwater** Atwater Reports (Minnesota).

at wt atomic weight.

atv all terrain vehicle; avian tumor virus.

AU, Au, au Austria; American University; gold; according to custom (ad usum); antitoxin unit; angstrom unit; accounting unit; astronomical unit; both ears (aures utrae).

Auckland UL Rev or **Auck UL Rev** Auckland University Law Review.

aud audit; auditor; audible.

Aug, aug August; augment.

aul average useful life.

aup actual unit price.

AUS, Aus Army of the United States; Austria; Australia.

Aust Bus L Rev Australian Business Law Review.

Aust Jur Australian Jurist.

Aust Law Australian Lawyer.

Aust LJ Australian Law Journal.

Aust LT Australian Law Times.

Aust & NZJ Crim or **Aust NZ JC** Australian and New Zealand Journal of Criminology.

Austl Acts P Acts of the Australian Parliament.

Austl AD Australian Annual Digest.

Austl Argus LR Australian Argus Law Reports.

Austl Bankr Cas Australian Bankruptcy Cases.

Austl Bus L Rev Australian Business Law Review.

Austl C Acts Commonwealth Acts (Australia).

Austl Cap Terr Laws Laws of the Australian Capital Territory.

Austl Cap Terr Ord Ordinances of the Australian Capital Territory.

Austl Com J Australian Commercial Journal

Austl Convey & Sol J Australian Conveyancer and Solicitors Journal.

Austl Current L Rev Australian Current Law Review.

Austl D Australian Digest (2d: Second Edition).

Austl J For Sci Australian Journal of Forensic Sciences.

Austl JL Socy Australian Journal of Law and Society.

Austl Jr Australian Jurist.

Austl Law Australian Lawyer.

Austl LJ Australian Law Journal.

Austl LJ Rep Australian Law Journal Reports.

Austl LMD Australia Legal Monthly Digest.

Austl L Times Australian Law Times.

Austl Tax Australian Tax Decisions.

Austl Tax Rev Australian Tax Review.

Austl TS Australia Treaty Series.

Austl YB Intl L Australian Yearbook of International Law.

Austr CLR Commonwealth Law Reports, Australia.

Aust Y Int L Australian Yearbook of International Law.

auth authority; authorized; author; authentic.

Auto Cas Automobile Cases (2d: Second Series).

Auto L. Rep Automobile Law Reporter (Commerce Clearing House).

aux auxiliary.

av according to the value (ad valorem); average; avoirdupois; avulsion; audio visual; avenue; acid value; actual value; average value; aortic valve; atrioventricular; arteria venous.

AVA, ava American Vocational Association; aortic valve atresia.

avc automatic volume control; aberrant ventricular conduction.

Av Cas Aviation Cases.

avcd atrioventricular conduction defect.

avd aortic valve disease.

ave avenue; average.

avg average.

avh acute viral hepatitis.

Av L Rep Aviation Law Reporter (CCH).

AVS, avs Anti Vivisection Society; aneurysm of ventricular septum.

aw, a&w, a/w actual weight; atomic weight; articles of war; above water; automatic weapon; alive and well; able to work; above waist; anterior wall.

AWACS Airborne Warning And Control System.

AWC Army War College.

awd award.

AWE, awe Alliance of Women for Equality; average weekly earnings.

awg American wire gauge.

awi anterior wall infarction.

awik assault with intent to kill.

awl absent with leave; average work load.

awm awaiting maintenance.

AWMD Air and Waste Management Division.

awmi anterior wall myocardial infarction.

awo airway obstruction.

awol absent without leave.

aws area working standards.

ax axiom; axillary.

AYC American Youth Congress.

AZ, az Arizona; azimuth; active zone; Ascheim-Zondek test for pregnancy.

AZF Ascheim-Zondek test modified by Freidman.

AZLR Arizona Law Review.

B, b Weekly Law Bulletin (Ohio); Barbour's Reports (New York); Belgium; British; British thermal unit; bond; bid; battery; buoyancy; byte; Bible; birth; billion; before; brotherhood; behavior; broken; bulletin; base; bar; ballistic; back; the number 11 (in the hexadecimal number system); bacillus.

BA, Ba; ba Bank of America; Book of Awards, barium; burglar alarm; blood alcohol; bureau of accounts; budget authority; bachelor of arts; base activity; blind approach; boolean algebra; breathing apparatus; bromoacetyl; butyl acrylate; benzanthracene; buccoaxial; bronchial asthma.

B&A or **B&Ald** Barnewall & Alderson's King's Bench Reports (England).

BAA Bureau of African Affairs; Brewers Association of America.

BAB Budget Advisory Board.

BAC, bac International Union of Bricklayers and Allied Craftsmen; blood alcohol concentration; bachelor; below all clouds; barometric altitude control; binary analog conversion; buccoaxiocervical.

Bac Abr Bacon's Abridgment (England).

Bac Dec Bacon's Decisions (England).

BACP Business Advisory Committee on Procurement.

bact bacteria; bacterium; bacteriological; best available control technology.

B&Ad Barnewall & Adolphus' King's Bench Reports (England).

bad biological aerosol detection.

BAE, BaE, bae Bureau of Africa and Europe; Bachelor of Agricultural Engineering; Bachelor of Architectural Engineering; Bachelor of Aeronautical Engineering; barium enema.

b&e breaking and entering.

BA Ed Bachelor of Arts in Education.

BAF, baf British Air Force; budget, accounting, and finance.

BAFT Bankers Association for Foreign Trade.

BAg; bag Bachelor of Agriculture; baggage; buccoaxiogingival.

Bag & Har Bagley & Harman's Reports (California).

Bagl Bagley's Reports (California).

Bai or **Bail** or **Bailey** Bailey's Law Reports (South Carolina).

Bai Eq or **Bail Eq** Bailey's Equity Reports (South Carolina).

Bail Ct Cas Lowndes & Maxwell's Bail Court Cases (England).

Baild Baildon's Select Cases in Chancery (England).

Bail Eq Bailey's Equity Reports (South Carolina).

BAL, bal British Anti Lewisite; blood alcohol level; basic assembly language; balance;

base authorization list; ballistics.

BALA Baltimore Association of Legal Assistants.

Bal Ann Codes Ballinger's Annotated Cases and Statutes (Washington).

Bald Baldwin's Reports.

Bald CC Baldwin's Circuit Court Reports.

Balf Pr Balfour's Practice (Scotland).

Ball & B Ball and Beatty's Chancery Reports (Ireland).

bal pa balance of payments.

Bal Payt Rep Balance of Payments Reports (Commerce Clearing House).

BALSA Black American Law Students Association.

Balt CR Baltimore City Reports.

Balt LT Baltimore Law Transcript.

bam basic access method.

bamn by any means necessary.

BAN British approved name.

Ban & A Banning and Arden's Patent Cases.

B&A or **B&Ald** Barnewall & Alderson's King's Bench Reports (England).

B&Ad Barnewall & Adolphus' King's Bench Reports (England).

B&Arn Barron & Arnold's Election Cases (England).

B&Aust Barron & Austin's Election Cases (England).

B&B Ball & Beatty's Chancery Reports (Ireland); Broderip & Bingham's Common Pleas (England).

B&Bar Bench & Bar.

B&C Barnewall & Cresswell's King's Bench Reports (England).

B&CR Reports of Bankruptcy & Companies Winding Up Cases (England).

B&D Benloe & Dalison's Common Pleas Reports (England).

B&F Broderip & Freemantle's Ecclesiastical (England).

B&G Brownlow &

Goldesborough's Reports (England).

B&H Blatchford & Howland's Reports (England).

B&H Cr Cas or **B&H Crim Cas** Bennett & Heard's Criminal Cases (England).

b&j bone and joint.

B&L Browning & Lushington's Reports (England).

B&M Brown & MacNamara's Reports (England).

B&Macn Brown & Macnamara's Railway Cases (England).

B&P Bosanquet & Puller's Common Pleas (England) (NR: New Reports).

B&S Best & Smith's Queen's Bench Reports (England).

Ban & A Banning and Arden's Patent Cases.

Bank & Ins R Bankruptcy and Insolvency Reports (England).

Bank Cas Banking Cases.

Bank Ct Rep Bankrupt Court Reports.

Bank LJ or **Banking LJ** Banking Law Journal.

bankr bankruptcy.

Bankr B Bull Bankruptcy Bar Bulletin.

Bankr L Rep Bankruptcy Law Reports (Commerce Clearing House).

Bankr Reg National Bankruptcy Register (New York).

Banks Banks Reports (Kansas).

Bann Bannister's Common Pleas Reports (England).

Bann & A or **Bann & Ard** Banning and Arden's Patent Cases.

bans back, arm, neck, scalp.

bao basal acid output.

Bap, bap Baptist; basic adaptive process; benzyl amino phenol.

BAR, Bar, bar Board of Appeals and Review; Barbour's Reports (New York); Browning automatic rifle; barometer; barrel; budget adjustment request.

Bar & Ad Barnewall & Adolphus' King's Bench Reports (England).

Bar & Al Barnewall & Alderson's King's Bench Reports (England).

Bar & Arn Barron & Arnold's Election Cases (England).

Bar & Aust Barron & Austin's Election Cases (England).

Barb Barbour's Supreme Court Reports (New York); Barber Reports (Arkansas).

Barb Ch Barbour's Chancery Reports (New York).

Bar Bull Bar Bulletin.

Bar & Cr Barnewall & Cresswell's King's Bench Reports (England).

Bar Exam Bar Examiner.

Barn Barnardiston's King's Bench Reports (England).

Barn & Ad or **Barn & A** Barnewall & Adolphus' King's Bench Reports (England).

Barn & Al or **Barn & A** Barnewall & Alderson's King's Bench Reports (England).

Barn & C or **Barn & Cr** or **Barn & Cress** Barnewall & Cresswell's King's Bench Reports (England).

Barn Ch Barnardiston's Chancery Reports (England).

Barnes Barnes' Practice Cases (England).

Barn KB Barnardiston's King's Bench Reports (England).

Barnes Notes Barnes' Notes (England).

Barnet Barnet's Reports Common Pleas (England).

Barnf & St Barnfield and Stiness Reports (Rhode Island).

Barr, barr Barr's Reports (Pennsylvania); barrister; barratry.

Barr Ch Pr Barroll's Chancery Practice (Maryland).

Barr Mss Barradall's Manuscript Reports (Virginia).

bars budget analysis reporting system.

Bart Elec Cas Bartlett's Election Cases.

BAS, bas Bachelor of Applied Science; basic; basic allowance for subsistence; benzyl antiserotonin; boric acid solution.

BASIC Beginner's All-purpose Symbolic Instruction Code; Banking and Securities Industry Committee.

bast bastardy.

BAT, bat Bureau of Apprenticeship and Testing; battery; best available technology; basic air temperature; brown adipose tissue; behavioral avoidance test.

Bates Ch Bates' Chancery Reports (Delaware).

BATM Bureau of Air Traffic Management.

batn battalion.

batt battery; battalion; battle.

Batty Batty's King's Bench Reports (Ireland).

baw bare aluminum wire.

Bax or **Baxt** Baxter's Reports (Tennessee).

Bay Bay's Reports (Missouri) (South Carolina).

Baylor Law Baylor Law Review.

Baylor L Rev Baylor Law Review.

BB, bb Ball & Beatty's Chancery Reports (Ireland); Broderip & Bingham's Common Pleas Reports (England); B'nai B'rith; blue book; bank burglary; bail bond; bearer bond; bank book, blood book; best of breed; ball bearing; breast biopsy; breakthrough bleeding.

BBA, bba Bachelor of Business Administration; born before arrival.

B Bar or **B&Bar** Bench & Bar.

BBB, bbb Better Business Bureau; bed, breakfast, and bath; blood brain barrier; bundle branch block; blood buffer base.

BBC, bbc British Broadcasting Corporation; bromo benzyl cyanide.

bbd baby born dead.

bbf bronchial blood flow.
BBI B'nai B'rith International.
bbl barrels.
BBM Bachelor of Business Management.
bbt basal body temperature.
B Bull Bar Bulletin.
b bx breast biopsy.
BC, bc Barnewall & Cresswell's King's Bench Reports (England); British Columbia Reports; Bankruptcy Cases; Bail Court; Bureau of the Census; Bureau of Customs; Black Code; Blue Cross; Before Christ; bail court; borough council; broadcasting; bad check, bogus check; banking and currency; battery commander; board of control; body count; binary code; buccal cartilage; birth control.
b/c because.
BCA, bca Board of Contract Appeals; breast cancer antigen.
B Can L Bachelor of Canon Law.
BC/BS Blue Cross, Blue Shield.
BCC, bcc Bail Court Cases (England); body centered cubic; basal cell carcinoma.
bcd bad conduct discharge; behind completion date; binary coded decimal.
BCE, bce Bachelor of Civil Engineering; basal cell epithelioma.
BC Envt Aff L Rev Boston College Environmental Affairs Law Review.
BCF, bcf Bureau of Commercial Fisheries; billion cubic feet; breast cyst fluid.
BCG bacillus Calmette Guérin.
bch basal cell hyperplasia.
B Ch Barbour's Chancery Reports (New York).
BCI Bituminous Coal Institute.
BC Ind & Com LR Boston College Industrial and Commercial Law Review.
BC Intl & Comp LJ Boston

College International and Comparative Law Journal.
BCL Business Corporation Law; Bachelor of Civil Law; Bachelor of Canon Law; Bachelor of Commercial Law.
BCL Notes British Columbia Law Notes.
BCLR British Columbia Law Reports.
BC L Rev Boston College Law Review.
bcls basic cardiac life support.
bcm become; birth control medication; body cell mass.
bcn beacon; bilateral cortical necrosis.
bco binary coded octal.
BCOA Bituminous Coal Operators Association.
bcp budget change proposal; byte control protocol; birth control pill.
BCR, bcr Bail Court Reports; British Columbia Reports; budget change request.
B&CR Reports of Bankruptcy & Companies Winding Up Cases (England).
BC Rev Stat Revised Statutes of British Columbia.
BCS, bcs Bachelor of Chemical Science; British Computer Society; basic contract specification; backup control system; battered child syndrome.
BCSE Board of Civil Service Examiners.
BC Stat British Columbia Statutes.
BC Gaz British Columbia Gazette.
bct basic combat training; best conventional technology.
bcv basal cell vigilance.
bcw biological and chemical warfare.
BD, bd Benloe & Dalison's Common Pleas Reports (England); board; bond; boundary; back dividends; bill discounted; base deficit; bank draft; basic documents; barrels per day; baud; boulevard; bomb disposal; twice a day

(bis die); behavioral differential; bile duct.
BDAC Bureau of Drug Abuse Control.
bdam basic direct access method.
bdb bis diazotized benzidine.
bdc burn dressing change; binary decimal counter; bottom dead center.
bdd binary digital data.
bde bile duct examination; brigade.
BDFJ Biographical Dictionary of the Federal Judiciary.
bd ft board foot.
bdg binding.
BDGC Bad Conduct Discharge, General Court Martial.
BDI, bdi Burundi; both dates inclusive.
bdl below detectable limits.
BD&O Blackham, Dundas & Osborne's Nisi Prius Reports (Ireland).
bdos basic disk operating system.
bdp bilateral diaphragm paralysis.
BDPA Bureau of Data Processing and Accounts; Birth Defect Prevention Act.
bdr border; boundary.
bdry boundary.
bds boards; biological detection system.
BDSI Bad Conduct Discharge, Summary Court Martial Sentence, Immediate.
bdsld bid solicited.
bdy boundary; body.
BE, Be, be Belgium; Bank of England; Board of Education; Bureau of Economics; Bachelor of Education; Bachelor of Engineering; beryllium; bill of exchange; bill of entry; bank error; biennial; barium enema; below elbow.
b&e breaking and entering.
BEA Bureau of European Affairs; Bureau of Economic Analysis.
beam brain electrical activity map.
Beasl Beasley's Reports (New Jersey).

beat breaking and entering and auto theft.

Beav Beavan's Rolls Court (England).

Beav R&C Cas Beavan's Railway and Canal Cases (England).

Beav & W Ry Cas Beavan and Walford's Railway and Canal Cases (England).

Beaw Lex Mer Beawes' Lex Mercatoria (England).

BEC, bec Bureau of Employee Compensation; bioelectrochemistry.

Bedell Bedell's Reports (New York).

Bee or **Bee Adm** Bee's Admiralty District Court Reports.

Bee CCR Bee's Crown Cases Reserved (England).

bef before.

beg beginning.

BEH Bureau of Education for the Handicapped.

Bel, bel Bellewe's King's Bench Reports (England); Belgium; below; basic equipment list.

Bel Cas t H VIII or **Bell Cas t H VIII** Bellewe's Cases King's Bench temp. Henry VIII (England).

Belg Belgium.

Bell Bellewe's King's Bench Reports (England); Bell's Crown Cases, Reserved (England).

Bell App Cas Bell's Appeal Cases, House of Lords (Scotland).

Bell CC Bell's Crown Cases, Reserved (England).

Bell Cas Bell's Cases (Scotland).

Bell Cas t H VIII Bellewe's Cases King's Bench temp. Henry VIII (England).

Bell Cas t R II Bellewe's Cases King's Bench temp. Richard II (England).

Bell Comm Bell's Commentaries (England).

Bell Cr Cas or **Bell Cr C** Bell's Crown Cases Reserved (England).

Bell HL Bell's Appeal Cases House of Lords (Scotland).

Bell PC Bell's Parliament Cases (Scotland).

Bell Sc Cas or **Bell Ses Cas** Bell's Scotch Court of Sessions Cases.

Bellewe Bellewe's Cases King's Bench temp. Richard II (England).

BelSSR Byelorussian Soviet Socialist Republic.

Belt Bro Brown's Chancery Cases by Belt (England).

Ben Benedict's District Court Reports; Benloe's King's Bench Reports (England); Benin.

Bendl or **Benl** Bendloe's or Benloe's Common Pleas (England).

Bened Benedict's District Court Reports.

BENELUX Belgium, Netherlands, Luxembourg.

Ben & Dal or **Benl & D** Benloe and Dalison's Common Pleas Reports (England).

Ben & H LC Bennett and Heard's Leading Criminal Cases (England).

Benl Benloe's Common Pleas Reports (England); Benloe's King's Bench Reports (England).

Benl & D or **Benl & Dal** Benloe and Dalison's Common Pleas Reports (England).

Benl KB Benloe's King's Bench Reports (England).

Benl Old Benloe's Old English Common Pleas (England).

Ben Monroe Ben Monroe's Reports (Kentucky).

Benn Bennett's Reports (California, Dakota, Missouri).

Bent Bentley's Chancery (Ireland).

BEOG Basic Educational Opportunity Grant.

BEP, bep Bureau of Engraving and Printing; best efficiency point.

BER, Ber, ber Bureau of Economic Regulation; Berton's Reports (New Brunswick); budget execution review; blood ethanol response.

Berry Berry's Reports (Missouri).

besd basic enlisted service date.

BESE Bureau of Elementary and Secondary Education.

Best & Sm Best and Smith's Queen's Bench Reports (England).

bet between.

BEU Black Education Union.

bev beverage; billion electron volts.

BEWT Bureau of East West Trade.

B Exam Bar Examiner.

BF, bf Bank of France; brief; bona fide; board foot; brought forward; bold face; beat frequency; black female; breast fed.

B&F Broderip & Freemantle's Ecclesiastical Cases (England).

bfc benign febrile convulsion.

BFCU Bureau of Federal Credit Unions.

bfe blood flow energy.

BFOQ Bona Fide Occupational Qualification.

bfp bona fide purchaser; biologic false positive.

bfpv bona fide purchaser for value.

bfr blood flow rate.

BFS Bureau of Family Services; Bureau of Flight Standards.

bft bladder flap tube.

bfv bovine feces virus.

bfy budget fiscal year.

BG, bg Bender-Gestalt test; Bulgaria; British Guiana; bonded goods; board of governors; background; blood glucose.

B&G Brownlow & Goldesborough's Reports (England).

BGAg blood group antigen.

bgc blood group class.

BGD Bangladesh.

BGFRS Board of Governors of the Federal Reserve System.

bgg bovine gamma globulin.

bght bought.

BGR Bulgaria.

bgt bought.

BGU British Guiana.

BH, Bh, bh British Honduras; Bahrain; brinell hardness; board of health; bill of health.

B&H Blatchford & Howland's Reports (England).

B&H Cr Cas or **B&H Crim Cas** Bennett & Heard's Criminal Cases (England).

bha butylated hydroxyanisole.

BHb, bHb bovine hemoglobin.

bhc barbers, hairdressers, cosmetologists; benzene hexachloride.

BHCA Bank Holding Company Act.

BHE Bureau of Higher Education.

BHI, bhi Bureau of Health Insurance; biosynthetic human insulin.

bhp bishop; brake horsepower; benign hypertrophic prostatitis.

BHR, bhr Bahrain; basal heart rate.

BHS Bureau of Health Services; Bahamas.

bht butylated hydroxytoluene.

bhu basic health unit.

bhv bovine herpes virus.

BI, Bi, bi Burundi; bismuth; background investigation; bureau of investigation; biceps; body injury; bone injury; bisexual.

B&I Bankruptcy and Insolvency Cases (England).

BIA, bia Board of Immigration Appeals; Bureau of Indian Affairs; Bachelor of Industrial Arts; Boating Industry Association; bioimmunoassay.

Bib, bib Bible; drink (bibe); brought in by.

Bibb Bibb's Reports (Kentucky).

bibl bibliography.

BIBO Bureau of International Business Operations.

BIC, bic Bank Investment Contract; Bureau of International Commerce; biceps.

BICIL British Institute of Comparative and International Law.

Bick or **Bick & Haw** Bicknell and Hawley's Reports (Nevada).

bid two times a day (bis in die); brought in dead.

BIF Bank Insurance Fund.

big best in group.

Big Ov Cas Bigelow's Overruled Cases.

bih benign intracranial hypertension.

bil billion; brother in law; bilateral.

BILA Bureau of International Labor Affairs.

bilat bilateral.

BILC British International Law Cases.

bili bilirubin.

bildg bill of lading.

Bill of Rights J Bill of Rights Journal.

bim bimonthly; BIT image memory.

bin twice a night (bis in noctus).

Bing Bingham's Common Pleas Reports (England).

Binn Binney's Reports (Pennsylvania).

B Int L Bachelor of International Law.

bio biography; biology.

biol biology.

bior business input - output return.

bios basic input output system.

BIP, bip Bureau of International Programs; brief infertile period; bacterial intravenous protein.

BIPAC Business Industry Political Action Committee.

BIS, Bis, bis Bank for International Settlements; Bissell's Circuit Court Reports; brain information service.

bisam basic indexed sequential access method.

bisync binary synchronous communication.

bit binary digit.

Bitt Rep in Ch Bittleson's Queen's Bench Reports (England).

Bitt W&P Bittleson, Wise and Parnell's Practice Cases (England).

bitum bituminous.

biw biweekly; battle injury or wound.

BJ, bj Bachelor of Journalism; biceps jerk.

b&j bone and joint.

BJA Bureau of Justice Assistance.

BJS Bureau of Justice Statistics.

B Jur Bachelor of Jurisprudence.

Bk, bk Black's Supreme Court Reports; berkelium; bank; black; book; block; brook; below knee.

bka below knee amputation.

bkcy bankruptcy.

bkf breakfast.

bkg bookkeeping; banking.

bkgd background.

bkpg bookkeeping.

bkpt bankrupt.

bks barracks.

bkt bracket.

bktcy bankruptcy.

bky bankruptcy.

Bl, BL, bl Blackstone's Commentaries; Henry Blackstone's Common Pleas Reports (England); Bligh's House of Lord's Reports (England) (NS: New Series); Bureau of Litigation; Bachelor of Laws; Barrister at Law; bill of lading; building and loan; bank larceny; building line; bale; block; baseline; breadth and length; buccolingual.

B&L Browning & Lushington's Reports (England).

BLA, Bla Bills of Lading Act; Blackstone.

Bla Ch Bland's Chancery Reports (Maryland).

Black Black's Supreme Court Reports; Blackford's Reports (Indiana); Henry Blackstone's Common Pleas Reports (England); William

Blackstone's King's Bench Reports (England).

Black Cond Rep or **Blackw Cond** Blackwell's Condensed Reports (Illinois).

Black D&O Blackham, Dundas and Osborne's Nisi Prius Reports (Ireland).

Blackf Blackford's Reports (Indiana).

Black H Henry Blackstone's Common Pleas Reports (England).

Black Jus Blackerby's Justices' Cases (England).

Black LJ Black Law Journal.

Blackst R William Blackstone's King's Bench Reports (England).

Bla H Henry Blackstone's Common Pleas Reports (England).

Bl & H Blake and Hedges' Reports (Montana); Blatchford and Howland's District Court Reports.

Blair Co LR Blair County Law Reports (Pennsylvania).

Blake Blake's Reports (Montana).

Blake & H Blake and Hedges' Reports (Montana).

Bland Bland's Chancery Reports (Maryland).

Blatch & H Blatchford and Howland's District Court Reports.

Blatchf Blatchford's Circuit Court Reports.

Blatch Pr Cas Blatchford's Prize Cases.

Bla W William Blackstone's King's Bench Reports (England).

blc blood culture.

Bl Comm Blackstone's Commentaries.

bld below limit of detection; building; blood; beryllium lung disease.

bldg building.

bldr bleeder; builder.

BLE, ble Brotherhood of Locomotive Engineers; both lower extremities.

Bleck Bleckley's Reports (Georgia).

BLFE Brotherhood of Locomotive Firemen and Enginemen.

Bl H Henry Blackstone's Common Pleas Reports (England).

Bli or **Bligh** Bligh's House of Lord's Reports (England) (NS: New Series).

Bliss Bliss' Delaware County Reports (Pennsylvania).

blk block; blank; bulk.

BLL, bll Bachelor of Laws; below lower limit.

BLM, blm Bureau of Land Management; black lipid membrane.

BLMR Bureau of Labor Management Reports.

bln bronchial lymph nodes.

Bl NS Bligh's House of Lord's Reports (England) (NS: New Series).

Bloom Bloomfield's Manumission Cases (New Jersey).

blp blood pressure.

Bl Pr Cas Blatchford's Prize Cases.

blr boiler; breech loading rifle.

BLS, bls Bureau of Labor Standards; Bureau of Labor Statistics; blood and lymphatic system; blood sugar.

blsd bovine lumpy skin disease.

blst ballast.

blt built; blood type; but less than.

BLTDA Burley Leaf Tobacco Dealers Association.

Blue Sky L Rep Blue Sky Law Reporter (Commerce Clearing House).

Bluett Bluett's Isle of Man Cases.

blv blood volume.

blvd boulevard.

Bl W William Blackstone's King's Bench Reports (England).

blzd blizzard.

BM, bm Bermuda; Bureau of the Mint; Bureau of Mines; Bureau of Medicine; bill of material; branch memorandum; bench mark; burgomaster; beam;

bimonthly; board measure; black male; before marriage; basilar membrane; basal metabolism; bone marrow; bowel movement.

B&M Browne & MacNamara's Reports (England).

BMA, bma British Medical Association; Boat Manufacturers Association; Bicycle Manufacturers Association; butyl methacrylate; bone marrow arrest.

B&Macn Brown & Macnamara's Railway Cases (England).

BMC, bmc Bureau of Motor Carriers; binary magnetic core; bone marrow cell.

BMCS Bureau of Motor Carrier Safety.

BMDDP Bureau of Medical Devices and Diagnostic Products.

bme biomedical electronics.

bmep break mean effective pressure.

bmews ballistic missile early warning system.

bmfl bidders master file listing.

bmg benign monoclonal gammopathy.

BMI, bmi Book Manufacturers Institute; body mass index.

B Mon Ben Monroe's Reports (Kentucky).

bmp bricklayers, masons and plasterers; best management practice; bone morphogenic protein.

bmr basal metabolic rate.

BMS Bureau of Medical Services.

bmt basic military training; bone marrow transplant.

BMU Bermuda.

bmw bare molybdenum wire.

BN, bn Brunei; Bureau of Narcotics; Bachelor of Nursing; bank note; binary number; battalion; been; but not; boron nitride; bladder neck.

BNA, bna Bureau of National Affairs; basle nomina anatomica.

BNA Sec Reg Bureau of National Affairs Securities Regulation and Law Report.

bnb blood nerve barrier.

BNC Busbee's Reports (North Carolina); Bingham's New Cases (England).

BNCA Bureau of National Capital Airports.

bncw bare nickel chrome wire.

bnd bound.

BNDD Bureau of Narcotics and Dangerous Drugs.

bndry boundary.

bne but not exceeding.

BNF, bnf Backus normal form; Backus naur form; boron nitride fiber.

BNG Bureau of Natural Gas.

bno bowels not opened; but not over; bladder neck obstruction.

BN&R Botswana Notes and Records.

bns binary number system; benign nephrosclerosis.

bnth beneath.

BO, bo Bolivia; broker's order; branch office; buyer option; back order; base order; bad order; black-out; born; box office; bowels open.

boa born on arrival.

BOASI Bureau of Old Age and Survivors Insurance.

BOB, bob Bureau of the Budget; beginning of business; best of breed.

BOCA Building Officials and Code Administrators.

BOD, bod Board of Directors, buy off date; bid opening date; biological oxygen demand.

BOE or **B of E** Board of Education; Bureau of Enforcement.

bof beginning of file; barium oxide ferrite; basic oxygen furnace.

BOFSA Bureau of Oceans, Fisheries and Scientific Affairs.

BOH or **B of H** Board of Health.

BOIA Bureau of Indian Affairs.

BOL, bol Bolivar; be on the lookout; beginning of life; bolus.

BOLO be on the lookout.

BOM, bom Bureau of Mines; by other means; business office must; bill of materials; beginning of month; bilateral otitis media.

Bond Bond's Circuit Court Reports.

Book of Judg Book of Judgments (England).

Boor Booraem's Reports (California).

BOP, bop United Nations Bureau of Operations and Programming; beginning of period; balance of payments; bit oriented protocol.

BOPA Balance of Payments Act.

bopd barrels of oil per day.

BOR, bor Bureau of Reclamation; Bureau of Review; Bureau of Operating Rights; borough; bowels open regularly.

Bos Bosworth's Superior Court Reports (New York).

Bos & P or **Bos & Pul** Bosanquet and Puller's Common Pleas Reports (NR: New Reports) (England).

Bos Pol Rep Boston Police Reports.

Bost LR Boston Law Reporter.

Bost BJ Boston Bar Journal.

Boston ULR Boston University Law Review.

Bosw Bosworth's Superior Court Reports (New York).

BOT, bot Board of Transport; Board of Trade; balance of trade; beginning of tape; botany; bottle; bought.

Bott Poor Law Cas or **Bott's Set Cas** Bott's Poor Laws Settlement Cases (England).

Bould Bouldin's Reports (Alabama).

Bouv Bouvier Law Dictionary.

Bov Pat Cas Bovill's Patent Cases.

bow bill of work; bag of waters.

Boyce Boyce's Reports (Delaware).

BP, bp Bureau of Prisons; Board of Parole; Bachelor of Pharmacy; bishop; breach of promise; public good (bonum publicum); breach of peace; balance of payments; border patrol; bypass; birth place; bills payable; bonus point; bill of parcels; bid/proposal; base pay; baptized; blue print; before present; boiling point; barometric pressure; back pressure; blood pressure; benzopyrene.

B&P Bosanquet & Puller's Common Pleas Reports (England) (NR: New Reports).

BPA, bpa Bureau of Public Assistance; basic pressure altitude; bronchopulmonary aspergillosis.

bpac budget program activity code.

bpam basic partitioned access method.

bpb bank post bill.

bpc base point configuration; bile phospholipid concentration.

BPD, bpd Bureau of Public Debt; barrels per day; biparietal diameter.

BPDP Brotherhood of Painters, Decorators, and Paperhangers.

BPE Bureau of Postsecondary Education.

bpf bronchopleural fistula.

bpg blood pressure gauge.

bph barrels per hour; benign prostatic hypertrophy.

BPI, bpi Board of Patent Interferences; Bituminous Pipe Institute; buying power index; bytes per inch; bits per inch; blood pressure increase.

BPL, bpl Bachelor of Patent Law; birthplace; benign proliferative lesion.

bpm beats per minute.

bpn brachial plexus neuropathy.

BPNR Bosanquet & Puller's Common Pleas, New Reports (England).

bpo bile phospholipid output.

BPOE Benevolent and Protective Order of Elks.

BPP, bpp Black Panther Party; border patrol police; breast parenchymal pattern.

bpr bypass ratio blood; blood pressure recorder; blood per rectum.

BPS, bps Bureau of Product Safety; basic programming support; bits per second; beats per second.

bpt best practicable technology.

bpv bioprosthetic valve.

BPW Board of Public Works, business and professional women.

bq base quota.

BQA Bureau of Quality Assurance.

BR, Br, br Board of Review (Army); Bankruptcy Reports; Brazil; British; British Railways; Bureau of Reclamation; bromine; break; bills receivable; bill of rights; bank robbery; bank rate; brief; builder's risk; building and repair; bridge; brigade; brother; basic research; birth rate; branch; bronchitis.

Bra Bracton's De Legibus et Consuetudinibus Angliae (England); Brazil.

Br Abr or **Brook Abr** Brook's Abridgment (England).

Bracton or **Bract** Bracton's De Legibus et Consuetudinibus Angliae (England).

Brad, **BRAD** Bradford's Reports (Iowa); Bradwell's Reports (Illinois); Bradford's Surrogate Court Reports (New York); Bureau of Research and Development.

Bradb Bradbury's Pleading and Practice Reports (New York).

Bradf Bradford's Surrogate Court Reports (New York); Bradford's Reports (Iowa).

Bradl Bradley's Reports (Rhode Island).

Bradw Bradwell's Appellate Reports (Illinois).

Brame Brame's Reports (Mississippi).

Branch Branch's Reports (Florida).

Brant Brantly's Reports (Maryland).

BRB, brb Barbados; bright red blood.

Br & B Broderip & Bingham's Common Pleas Reports (England).

brby bribery.

BRC British Ruling Cases; Brotherhood of Railway Carmen; Budget Review Committee.

Br CC or **Brit Cr Cas** British Crown Cases.

Br & Col Pr British and Colonial Prize Cases.

brd board; bladder retraining drills.

Breese Breese's Reports (Illinois).

Brev Brevard's Reports (South Carolina).

Brew Brewer's Reports (Maryland); Brewster's Reports (Pennsylvania).

brf brief.

Br & F Ecc Broderick & Freemantle's Ecclesiastical Cases (England).

brg bridge.

Br & G or **Br & Gold** Browndow & Goldesborough's Common Pleas Reports (England).

Br & L Browning & Lushington's Admiralty Reports (England).

BRI Brain Research Institute; Building Research Institute; Behavior Research Institute.

Bridg J J. Bridgman's Common Pleas Reports (England)

Bridg O Orlando Bridgman's Common Pleas Reports (England)

Brief Case Legal Aid Brief Case.

brig brigade.

Bright Brightly's Nisi Prius Reports (Pennsylvania).

Brightly El Brightly's Leading Election Cases (Pennsylvania).

Brisb Brisbin's Reports (Minnesota).

Brit British.

Brit J Crim British Journal of Criminology.

Brit Cr Cas or **Br CC** British Crown Cases.

Brit J Admin L British Journal of Administrative Law.

Brit Ship L British Shipping Law.

Brit Tax Rev British Tax Review.

Brit Y Int L British Yearbook of International Law.

BR JC Board of Review and Judicial Council (Army).

Br J Crim British Journal of Criminology.

brl barrel.

Br & L Browning & Lushington's Admiralty Reports (England).

brm barometer.

BRN, brn Brunei; brown.

Br NC or **Br N Cas** Brook's New Cases King's Bench (England).

Bro, bro See Brown; see Brooke; brother; bronze.

Bro A&R Brown's District Court Reports, Admiralty and Revenue.

Bro Adm Brown's Admiralty Reports.

Bro Ch Brown's Chancery Reports (England).

Brock Brockenbrough's Marshall's Decisions, United States Circuit Court.

Brock Cas Brockenbrough's Cases (Virginia).

Brock & H Cas Brockenbrough and Holmes' Cases (Virginia).

Brod & Bing Broderip & Bingham's Common Pleas Reports (England).

Brod & F Ecc Cas Broderick & Freemantle's Ecclesiastical Cases (England).

Brodix Am & E Pat Cas Brodix' American and English Patent Cases.

Bro Ecc Brown's Ecclesiastical Reports (England).

Bro & F or **Bro & Fr** Broderick & Freemantle's Ecclesiastical Cases (England).

Bro & G Brownlow &

Goldesborough's Common
Pleas Reports (England).

Bro & H Brown and
Hemingway's Reports
(Mississippi).

Bro Just Brown's Justiciary Cases
(Scotland).

Bro & H Brown and
Hemingway's Reports
(Mississippi).

Bro & L Browning and
Lushington's Admiralty Cases
(England).

Bro NP Brown's Nisi Prius
Reports (Michigan).

Brook Abr or **Br Abr** Brook's
Abridgment (England).

Brooke Brooke's New Cases,
King's Bench (England).

Brooklyn Bar Brooklyn Barrister.

Brooklyn J Intl L Brooklyn
Journal of International Law.

Brooklyn L Rev Brooklyn Law
Review.

Brook NC or **Br NC** Brook's New
Cases King's Bench (England).

Brooks Brooks' Reports
(Michigan).

Bro Pa Browne's Reports
(Pennsylvania).

Bro PC Brown's Parliamentary
Cases (England).

Brown Brown's Reports
(Massachusetts); Brown's
Reports (Michigan); Brown's
Reports (Nebraska); Brown's
Reports (Mississippi); Brown's
Chancery Reports (England).

Brown Adm Brown's Admiralty
Reports.

Brown A&R Brown's District
Court Reports, Admiralty and
Revenue.

Brown & Gold Brownlow &
Goldesborough's Common
Pleas Reports (England).

Brown & H Brown and
Hemingway's Reports
(Mississippi).

Brown & L Browning and
Lushington's Admiralty Cases
(England).

Brown & MacN Brown and

Macnamara's Railway Cases
(England).

Brown & R or **Br & R** Brown and
Rader's Reports (Missouri).

Brown Ch Brown's Chancery
Cases (England).

Brown Dict Brown Law
Dictionary.

Browne Browne's Common Pleas
Reports (Pennsylvania);
Browne's Reports
(Massachusetts); Browne's
Civil Procedure Reports (New
York).

Browne & G Browne and Gray's
Reports (Massachusetts).

Browne Bank Cas Browne's
National Bank Cases.

Brown Eccl Brown's
Ecclesiastical Reports
(England).

Brownl & G Brownlow &
Goldesborough's Common
Pleas Reports (England).

Brown NP Brown's Nisi Prius
Reports (Michigan).

Brown Parl Cas Brown's House
of Lords Cases (England).

Brown PC Brown's Parliamentary
Cases (England).

Br & R or **Brown & R** Brown and
Rader's Reports (England).

brp bathroom privileges.

BRS Brotherhood of Railroad
Signalmen; Bureau of Railway
Safety.

BRSC Brotherhood of Railway and
Steamship Clerks.

BRT, brt Brotherhood of Railroad
Trainmen; brought.

Bruce Bruce's Court of Session
Reports (Scotland).

Brunn Coll Cas Brunner's
Collected Cases.

BS, bs Bureau of Standards;
Bahamas; Bachelor of Science;
British Standard; Blue Shield;
bill of sale; bill of store;
balance sheet; behind
schedule; border surveillance;
basic sediment; "bull shit;"
backspace; breadth sounds;
bowel sounds; blood sugar.

B&S Best & Smith's Queen's
Bench Reports (England).

BSA, bsa Boy Scouts of America;
Bachelor of Science in
Agriculture; body surface area;
bowel sounds active; bovine
serum albumin.

bsam basic sequential access
method.

bsb body surface burned.

bsc basic; binary symmetric
channel; binary synchronous
communications; bedside care.

B Sc L Bachelor in the Science of
Law.

bse breast self examination.

bsh bushel.

BSI, bsi British Standards Institute;
bound serum iron.

BSL, bsl Bachelor of Science in
Law; blue sky laws; blood
sugar level.

BSLE Bachelor of Science in Law
Enforcement.

BSLS Bachelor of Science in
Library Science.

bsmt basement.

bsn bowel sounds normal.

bso benzene soluble organics;
bile salt output; bilateral
salpingo oophorectomy.

bsp body segment parameter.

BSR, bsr Board of Standards
Review; blood sedimentation
rate.

bsso bilateral sagittal split
osteotomy.

BST, bst British Standard Time;
bill of sight; blood serological
test.

BSU Black Students Union.

BSUI Benefit Service Series,
Unemployment Insurance.

bsv boolean simple variable.

BSW Boot and Shoe Workers
Union.

BSWM Bureau of Solid Waste
Management.

Bt, BT, bt Benedict's United States
District Reports; Bhutan;
Board of Trade; balance of
trade; bill tomorrow; basic
training; bought; berth terms;

boat; biceps tendon; brain tumor; bacillus thuringiensis.

BTA, bta Board of Tax Appeals, better than average.

btam basic telecommunications access method.

btb break through bleeding.

bte bulk tape eraser.

btg beating.

btl below the line; bottle; bilateral tubal ligation.

btm benign tertian malaria.

BTN, btn Brussels Tariff Nomenclature; Bhutan, battalion; between.

btp batch transfer program; biliary tract pain.

BTR British Tax Review.

btry battery.

BTS Board of Thoracic Surgery.

BTU, btu British Thermal Unit; basic transmission unit.

BTUH British thermal unit per hour.

btw back to work.

btx benzene, toluene, xylene.

bty battery.

BU, bu Bulgaria; Burma; Bodansky Unit; bulletin; bushel; back up; bureau; burn unit.

bua blood uric acid.

BuB Bureau of the Budget.

Buch Buchanan's Reports (New Jersey).

Buck Buck's Reports (Montana).

Buck Bank Buck's Bankruptcy Cases (England).

Buck Cooke Bucknill's Cooke's Cases of Practice, Common Pleas Reports (England).

Buck Dec Buckner's Decisions in Freeman's Chancery Reports (Mississippi).

bud budget; benefits and use division.

BUdR bromodeoxyuridine.

bue both upper extremities.

BUF Black United Front.

Buffalo L Rev Buffalo Law Review.

Buff L Rev Buffalo Law Review.

Buff Sup Ct Buffalo Superior

Court Reports (New York).

bug buccal ganglion.

BUJ Bachelor of Both Laws (Canon and Civil) (Baccalaureus Utriusque Juris).

Bulg Bulgaria.

Bull Bulletin; Weekly Law Bulletin.

Bull Am Acad Psych & L Bulletin of the American Academy of Psychiatry and the Law.

Bull Can Wel Law Bulletin of Canadian Welfare Law.

Bull Cr Soc Bulletin of the Copyright Society of the United States of America.

Buller Buller's Nisi Prius Reports (England).

Bull Intl Fiscal Doc Bulletin for International Fiscal Documentation.

Bull JAG Bulletin of the Judge Advocate General (Army).

Bull NP Buller's Nisi Prius Reports (England).

Bull NTA Bulletin of the National Tax Association.

Bull O Weekly Law Bulletin (Ohio).

BU L Rev Boston University Law Review.

Bulst Bulstrode's King's Bench Reports (England).

bun blood urea nitrogen.

Bunb Bunbury's Exchequer Reports (England).

buo bruising (bleeding) of undetermined origin.

buq both upper quadrants.

Bur, BUR, bur Burnett's Reports (Wisconsin); Burnett's King's Bench Reports (England); Burma; buried; bureau.

Bu Rec Bureau of Reclamation.

Burf Burford's Reports (Oklahoma).

Burgess Burgess' Reports (Ohio).

Burlesque Rep Skillman's Police Reports (New York).

Bur M or **Burr t M** Burrow's Reports temp. Mansfield (England).

Burn High Commission Court (England).

Burnett Burnett's Reports (Wisconsin); Burnett's Reports (Oregon).

Burr Burrow's King's Bench Reports (England).

Burrell Burrell's Admiralty Reports (England).

Burr t M or **Bur M** Burrow's Reports temp. Mansfield (England).

Bur SC or **Burr S Cas** Burrow's Settlement Cases (England).

BUS, bus Bank of the United States; business; bushel.

Bus & L Business and Law.

Busb Busbee's Law Reports (North Carolina).

Bus Eq or **Busb Eq** Busbee's Equity Reports (North Carolina).

Bush Bush's Reports (Kentucky).

Bus L Busbee's Law Reports (North Carolina).

Bus Law The Business Lawyer.

Bus L Rev Business Law Review.

Bus Reg L Rep Business Regulation Law Report.

BUSTDS Bureau of Standards.

Buxton Buxton's Reports (North Carolina).

bv book value; balanced voltage; beverage; blood volume; blood vessel.

BVA Bureau of Veterans Appeals.

bvd bovine virus diarrhea.

BVI, bvi British Virgin Islands; blood vessel invasion.

bvl bilateral vas ligation.

BVM, bvm Bureau of Veterinary Medicine; bronchovesicular markings.

bvo brominated vegetable oil.

bvp blood vessel prostheses.

BVRR Bureau of Veterans Reemployment Rights.

BVS Bureau of Vital Statistics.

bvv bovine vaginitis virus.

BW, bw Botswana; bonded warehouse; biweekly; birth weight; body weight; below waist; biological warfare; blood Wassermann.

bwa bed waiting admission.

BWCC Butterworth's Workmen's Compensation Cases (England).

bwd bulk weight density; bacillary white diarrhea.

BWG Birmingham wire gauge; Bland, White, Garland.

BWI, bwi British West Indies; battle wound injury.

BWRL Bureau of War Risk Litigation.

bws battered woman syndrome.

B Wt birth weight.

bx box; base exchange; biopsy.

by budget year.

byp bypass.

BYU L Rev Brigham Young University Law Review.

BZ, Bz Belize; benzoyl.

BZA Board of Zoning Adjustment.

bzd benzidine.

Bzl benzyl.

C, c Cowen's Reports (New York); Cuba; Canada; Chancellor; Congress; copyright; court; cause; canceled; closure; current; confidential; chapter; cousin; child; cost; calorie; celsius; charge; centigrade; centimeter; circumference; cubic; clearance; carbon; carat; chairman; cedi; consultation; the number 12 (in the hexadecimal number system); cathode; cylinder; contraction; cancer; cervical; colon; capillary.

CA, Ca, ca Court of Appeals; Customs Appeals Reports; Recueils de jurisprudence, Cour d'appel (Québec); California; Central America; calcium; cancelled; civil action; capital asset; capital account; current account, credit account; controller of accounts; correct or amplify; claim agent; commercial agent; cooperative agreement; connecting arrangement; chronological age; coronary artery; cardiac arrest; cancer.

C&A Cooke and Alcock's King's Bench and Exchequer Reports (Ireland).

CAA, caa Civil Aeronautics Authority; Community Action Agency; Clean Air Act; constitutional aplastic anemia; crystalline amino acids.

CAAB Contract Administration Advisory Board.

CAA Op Civil Aeronautics Authority Opinions.

caat computer assisted axial tomography.

CAB, cab Civil Aeronautics Board; Contract Appeals Board; Citizens Advice Bureau; cable; cabinet; coronary artery bypass.

Cab & E Cababe and Ellis' Reports Queen's Bench (England).

cabg coronary artery by-pass graft.

cabs coronary artery bypass surgery.

CAC, cac Consumer Advisory Council; circulating anticoagulant; cardiac accelerator center; cardiac arrest code.

cacg computer assisted career guidance.

cacx cancer of the cervix.

CAD, cad Customs Appeals Decisions; Canadian Annual Digest; cadmium; cash against documents; compressed air disease; computer assisted design; computer assisted diagnosis; computer aided diagnosis; coronary artery disease; compressed air disease.

cad/cam computer aided design/computer aided manufacturing.

cadf contract administration data file.

Cadwalader Cadwalader's District Court Cases (Pennsylvania).

cae cellulose acetate electrophoresis; coronary artery embolization.

caf clerical, administrative, fiscal; caucasian adult female; cost, assurance, and freight; cleared as filed; cell adhesion factor.

cag coronary angiography; chronic atrophic gastritis.

cah congenital adrenal hyperplasia; chronic active hepatitis.

Cai, cai Caines' Reports (New York); computer aided instruction; confused artificial insemination.

Cai Cas Caines' Cases in Error (New York).

Caines & LCC Caines and Leigh's Crown Cases (England).

Cai R Caines' Reports (New York).

CAJ Center for Administrative Justice.

Cal, cal California Reports (2d: Second Series) (3d: Third Series); Calthrop's King's Bench Reports (England); Caldecott's King's Bench Reports (England); California; calendar; calibrate; calorie; computer assisted learning; chronic airflow limitation; calculated average life.

Cal App California Appeals Reports (2d: Second Series) (3d: Third Series).

Cal App Dec California Appellate Decisions.

Cal App Supp California Appellate Reports Supplement (2d: Second Series) (3d: Third Series).

Cald, cald Caldwell's Reports (West Virginia); chronic active liver disease.

Cal Dec California Decisions.

Cald SC Caldecott's Settlement Cases (England).

Calif L Rev or **Cal L Rev** California Law Review.

Calif SBJ California State Bar Journal.

Calif West Int LJ California Western International Law Journal.

Calif West L Rev California Western Law Review.

Cal Ind Acct Dec California Industrial Accidents Decisions.

Cal Jur California Jurisprudence (2d ed: Second Edition).

Call Call's Reports (Virginia).

Cal Leg Rec California Legal Record.

Cal L Rev California Law Review.

Cal Prac California Practice.

Cal Rptr West's California Reporter.

Cal St BJ California State Bar Journal.

Cal Sup California Superior Court Reports.

Calth Calthrop's King's Bench Reports (England).

Cal Unrep California Unreported Cases.

Cam, cam Cameron's Reports Upper Canada; caucasian adult male; computer aided manu- facturing; content addressable memory; contralateral axillary metastasis.

Cam & N Cameron and Norwood's Conference Reports (North Carolina).

Camb LJ Cambridge Law Journal.

Cameron Pr Cameron's Practice (Canada).

Camp Campbell's Nisi Prius Reports (England); Campbell's Reports (Nebraska); Camp's Reports (North Dakota).

Campb or **Campbell** See Camp.

Camp LG Campbell's Legal Gazette (Pennsylvania).

Can, can Supreme Court of Canada; canon; child abuse and neglect; cost account number; cancel; cancel char- acter; ceric ammonium nitrate; cancer.

Can App Cas Canadian Appeal Cases.

Can Bar R Canadian Bar Review.

Can BJ Canadian Bar Journal.

canc cancelled.

Can BAJ Canadian Bar Association Journal.

Can BJ Canadian Bar Journal.

Can BR or **Can B Rev** Canadian Bar Review.

Can Bankr Ann Canadian Bankruptcy Reports Annotated (NS: New Series).

Can Bus LJ Canadian Business Law Journal.

Can CC or **Can Cr Cas** Canadian Criminal Cases.

Can Com R Canadian Commercial Law Reports.

Can Crim Criminal Reports (Canada).

Can Crim Cas Canadian Criminal Cases (Ann: Annotated) (NS: New Series).

Can Yearbook Int L Canadian Yearbook of International Law.

C&A Cooke and Alcock's King's Bench and Exchequer Reports (Ireland).

C&C Coleman and Caines' Cases (New York); Case and Comment.

C&D, c&d Corbett & Daniel's Election Cases (England); Crawford and Dix' Abridged Cases (Ireland); collection and delivery; construction and development.

C&DAC Crawford and Dix's Abridged Cases (Ireland).

C&DCC Crawford and Dix's Circuit Cases (Ireland); Crawford & Dix's Criminal Cases (Ireland)

C&E, c&e Cababe and Ellis' Reports Queen's Bench (England); consultation and examination.

C&F, c&f Clark and Finnelly's House of Lords Cases (England); cost and freight.

c&i cost and insurance.

C&J Crompton & Jervis' Exchequer Reports (England).

C&K Carrington and Kirwan's Nisi Prius Reports (England).

C&L Connor and Lawson's Chancery Reports (Ireland).

C&LCC Caines and Leigh's Crown Cases (England).

C&M Crompton and Meeson's Exchequer Reports (England); Carrington and Marshmann's Nisi Prius Reports (England).

C & Marsh Carrington and Marshmann's Nisi Prius Reports (England).

C&N Cameron and Norwood's Conference Reports (North Carolina).

C&P Carrington and Payne's Nisi Prius Reports (England); Craig & Phillips' Chancery Reports (England).

C&R Cockburn and Rowe's Election Cases (England).

C&S Clarke & Scully's Drainage Cases (Ontario).

Can Envir L News Canadian Environmental Law News.

Can Exch Canadian Exchequer Court Reports.

Can Gaz Canadian Gazette.

Can Hum Rts R Canadian Human Rights Reporter.

Can J Corr Canadian Journal of Corrections.

Can J Crim and Corr Canadian Journal of Criminology and Corrections.

Can J Fam L Canadian Journal of Family Law.

Can LJ Canadian Law Journal (NS: New Series).

Can LT Occ N Canadian Law Times Occasional Notes.

Can L Rev Canadian Law Review.

Can L Times Canadian Law Times.

Can Med AJ Canadian Medical Association Journal.

Can Mun J Canadian Municipal Journal.

Can Pub Ad Canadian Public Administration.

Can RAC Canadian Reports, Appeal Cases.

Can R Cas or **Can Ry Cas** Canadian Railway Cases.

Can S Ct Rep Canadian Supreme Court Reports.

Can Stat Statutes of Canada.

Can Tax App Bd Canada Tax Appeal Board Cases.

Can Tax Cas Ann Canada Tax Cases Annotated.

Can Tax J Canadian Tax Journal.

Can USLJ Canada-United States Law Journal.

Can YB Intl L Canadian Yearbook of International Law.

Cane & L Cane and Leigh's Crown Cases Reserved (England).

CAO, cao Consumer Affairs Office; chief administrative officer; coronary artery occlusion; chronic airway obstruction.

CAP, cap Community Action Program; Civil Air Patrol; Cleveland Association of Paralegals; Connecticut Association of Paralegals; collection agency practice; consumer awareness program; capital; cost analysis plan; capacity; capsule; chloramphenicol; chronic alcoholic pancreatitis; community acquired pneumonia.

CAPA California Alliance of Paralegal Associations.

Capital UL Rev or **Cap ULR** Capital University Law Review.

cap moll soft capsule (capsula mollis).

capp clinical appraisal of psychosocial problems.

C App R Criminal Appeal Reports (England).

caps capital letters; capsules.

CAR, car Criminal Appeal Reports (England); Commonwealth Arbitration Reports (Australia); Caribbean; Central African Republic; Commission on Administrative Review; contract authorization request;

computer assisted retrieval; computer assisted research; carrier; cargo; carat; carrier; conditioned avoidance response; chronic articular rheumatism.

Car & Mar Carrington and Marshmann's Nisi Prius Reports (England).

Car & P Carrington and Payne's Nisi Prius Reports (England).

Car & K or **Carr & K** Carrington and Kirwan's Nisi Prius Reports (England).

Cardozo L Rev Cardozo Law Review.

CARE, care Cooperative for American Relief to Everywhere; computer aided reliability estimation.

CARF Commission on Accreditation of Rehabilitation Facilities.

CARG Corporate Accountability Research Group.

Car H&A Carrow, Hamerton and Allen's New Session Cases (England).

Carl Carleton's Reports (New Brunswick).

Car L Rep Carolina Law Repository (North Carolina).

Carolina LJ Carolina Law Journal.

Carp or **Carpenter** Carpenter's Reports (California).

Carp PC Carpmael Patent Cases (England).

Carrib LJ Caribbean Law Journal.

Cart or **Carter** Carter's Reports (Indiana): Carter's Common Pleas Reports (England).

Cart BNA Cartwright's Constitutional Cases (Canada).

Carth Carthew's King's Bench Reports (England).

Cartwr Cas Cartwright's Cases (Canada).

Cary Cary's Chancery Reports (England).

CAS, Cas, cas Center for Alcohol Studies; Casey's Reports (Pennsylvania); casualty; casing; calibrated air speed;

collision avoidance system; column address strobe; cardiac adjustment scale; coronary artery spasm; cold agglutinin syndrome; cerebral arteriosclerosis.

Cas App Cases of Appeal to the House of Lords (England).

Cas Ch Cases in Chancery.

Cas CL Cases in Crown Law (England).

Case & Com Case and Comment.

Cas Eq Cases in Equity, Gilbert's (England).

Case W Res L Rev Case Western Reserve Law Review.

Case W Res J Int L Case Western Reserve Journal of International Law.

Casey or **Cas** Casey's Reports (Pennsylvania).

Cas P Cases in Parliament.

Cas R Casey's Reports (Pennsylvania).

Cass Pr Cas Cassel's Practice Cases (Canada).

Cass SC Cassels' Supreme Court Decisions.

Cas t K Cases in Chancery, temp., King (England).

Cas t T Cases in Chancery, temp., Talbert (England).

cat computer aided teaching; catalog; category; catalyst; clear air turbulence; clerical aptitude test; computerized axial tomography; chronic abdominal tympany; cataract.

Cates Cates' Reports (Tennessee).

Cath, cath Catholic; cathode; catheter.

Cath Law Catholic Lawyer.

CATLINE Catalog On Line.

Cath UL Rev Catholic University of America Law Review.

catscan computerized axial tomography scanner.

catv community antenna television.

caut caution.

cav the court wishes to consider (curia advisari vult); caveat; cavity; constant angular velocity; croup associated virus; congenital adrenal virilism.

CB, Cb, cb Common Bench Reports (Manning, Granger & Scott's) (England); Cumulative Bulletin (IRS); Census Bureau; Bachelor of Surgery (chirurgiae baccalaureus); carbobenzoxy; columbium; currency bond; citizen's band; confirmation of balance; circuit breaker; code blue; code book; chronic bronchitis.

cba cost benefit analysis; chronic bronchitis with asthma.

CBBB Council of Better Business Bureaus.

CBC, cbc Colliers Bankruptcy Cases; Congressional Black Caucus; Canadian Broadcasting System; contraband control; complete blood count; child behavior characteristics.

cbcc conviction by civil court.

cbd cash before delivery; central business district; cannabidiol; common bile duct; closed bladder drainage.

cbf cerebral blood flow.

cbh chronic benign hepatitis.

CBI, cbi Caribbean Based Initiative; Cumulative Book Index; computer aided instruction; continuous bladder irrigation.

cbl commercial bill of lading; circulating blood lymphocyte.

CB NS Common Bench Reports New Series.

CBO Congressional Budget Office.

CBOE Chicago Board Options Exchange.

CBR, cbr Canadian Bankruptcy Reports; Canadian Bar Review; cost benefit ratio; chemical, biological, radiological; chronic bed rest.

cbs consolidated balance sheet; call box station; chronic brain syndrome.

CBT, cbt Chicago Board of Trade;

cabinet; cognitive behavior therapy.

cbu collective bargaining unit.

cbv circulating blood volume; central blood volume.

cbw chemical and biological warfare.

cby carboy.

CC, Cc, cc Coleman's Cases (New York); Cases in Chancery (England); Circuit Court Reports (NS: New Series) (Ohio); Crown Cases; Chamber of Commerce; City Council; civil cases; criminal cases; cirrocumulus; chief counsel; chief clerk; circuit court; county court; cashier's check; continuation clause; civil commotion; common carrier; current cost; certificate of competency; carbon copy; counterclockwise; cubic centimeter; copper chromite; chief complaint; critical condition.

C&C Coleman and Caines' Cases (New York); Case and Comment.

CCA, cca Court of Criminal Appeals; Circuit Court of Appeals; County Court Appeals; colitis colon antigen.

CCALL Central Connecticut Association of Legal Assistants.

CCB Common Carrier Bureau.

ccbv central circulating blood volume.

CCC, ccc Cox's Criminal Cases (England); Central Criminal Court (England); Canadian Criminal Cases; Choyce's Cases in Chancery (England); Commodity Credit Corporation; Civilian Conservation Corps; calcium cyanamide citrated; care cure coordination; chronic calculous cholecystitis.

CC Ct Cas Central Criminal Court Cases (England).

cccr closed chest cardiac resuscitation.

cccu comprehensive cardiovascular care unit.

ccd construction completion date; charge-coupled devise; childhood celiac disease.

ccdw carrying a concealed deadly weapon.

CCE, cce Caine's Cases in Error (New York); chamois contagious ecthyma.

CCF, ccf Federal Contract Cases (Commerce Clearing House); congestive cardiac failure; cancer coagulative factor.

CCG Committee for Constitutional Government.

CCH, cch Commerce Clearing House, Inc.; computerized criminal history; chronic cholestatic hepatitis.

CCH Atom En L Rep Atomic Energy Law Reporter (Commerce Clearing House).

CCH Comm Mkt Rep Common Market Reporter (Commerce Clearing House).

CCH Fed Bank L Rep Federal Banking Law Reporter (Commerce Clearing House).

CCH Fed Sec L Rep Federal Securities Law Reporter (Commerce Clearing House).

CCH Inh Est & Gift Tax Rep Inheritance, Estate, and Gift Tax Reporter (Commerce Clearing House).

CCH Lab Arb Awards Labor Arbitration Awards (Commerce Clearing House).

CCH Lab Cas Labor Cases (Commerce Clearing House).

CCH Lab L Rep Labor Law Reporter (Commerce Clearing House).

CCH Stand Fed Tax Rep Standard Federal Tax Reporter (Commerce Clearing House).

CCH State Tax Cas Rep State Tax Reporter (Commerce Clearing House).

CCH State Tax Rev State Tax Review (Commerce Clearing House).

CCH Tax Ct Mem Tax Court Memorandum Decisions (Commerce Clearing House).

CCH Tax Ct Rep Tax Court Reporter (Commerce Clearing House).

cci consumer confidence index; chronic coronary insufficiency.

CCIA Consumer Credit Insurance Association.

CCITT Comité Consultatif International Téléphonique et Télégraphique.

CCJ Conference of Chief Justices.

ccl conforms to copyright law; carcinoma cell line.

CCLAA Central Coast Legal Assistant Association; Channel Cities Legal Assistants Association.

CCLM Committee on Constitutional and Legal Matters.

C Cls Court of Claims.

C Cls R Court of Claims Reports.

CCLT Canadian Cases on the Law of Torts.

ccm critical care medicine.

CCMS Congress of County Medical Societies.

ccn contract change negotiation; contract completion notice; critical care nursing.

CCNS Circuit Court Reports New Series (Ohio).

CCO Contracts Compliance Regional Office.

CCP, ccp Court of Common Pleas; Compendium of Copyright Office Practices; credit card purchase; cytidine cyclic phosphate; chronic calcifying pancreatitis.

CCPA Court of Customs and Patent Appeals; Consumer Credit Protection Act.

CCR, ccr Crown Cases Reserved (England); County Courts Reports; Circuit Court Reports; Center for Constitutional Rights; Commission on Civil Rights; contract change request.

CCRN Cardiac Care Registered Nurse.

ccs casualty clearing station; cloudy cornea syndrome.

CCSB Credit Card Service Bureau.

CC Supp City Court Reports Supplement (New York).

cct chocolate coated tablet; composite cyclic therapy.

cctv closed circuit television.

ccu cardiac care unit; coronary care unit.

CCUS Chamber of Commerce of the United States.

ccvd chronic cerebrovascular disease.

ccw carrying a concealed weapon; counterclockwise.

CD, Cd, cd Commissioner's Decisions (Patent and Trademark Office); Classification Decision of the United States Customs Court; Circuit Decisions (Ohio); Chancery Division; Congressional District; cadmium; civil defense; certificate of deposit; with dividend; cash discount; code; condemned; could; cystic duct; cadaver donor; cesarean delivery; communicable or convulsive disorder; contagious (communicable) disease; cardiovascular disease; cardiac disease.

C&D, c&d Corbett & Daniel's Election Cases (England); Crawford and Dix' Abridged Cases (Ireland); collection and delivery; construction and development.

CDA, cda Certified Dental Assistant; Community Development Agency; congenital dyserythropoietic anemia.

C&DAC Crawford and Dix' Abridged Cases (Ireland).

c&db cough and deep breathing.

C&DCC Crawford and Dix' Circuit Cases (Ireland); Crawford & Dix' Criminal Cases (Ireland).

CDB Caribbean Development Bank.

cdbg community development block grant.

CDC, cdc Center for Disease Control; Commissioners of the District of Columbia; call direction code; Cryogenic Data Center; cell division cycle.

cdd chronic degenerative disease.

cde common duct exploration.

C de D Les Cahiers de Droit.

CDF, cdf Children's Defense Fund; capital development fund; chronic disease facility.

cdh chronic disease hospital.

cdi cranial diabetes insipidus.

CDL Citizens for Decency Through Law.

cdp chronic destructive periodontitis.

cdh congenital dislocation of hip.

cdr commander; correct delayed reaction.

CdS, cds cadmium sulfide; cash on delivery service; cervicodorsal syndrome.

cdt central daylight time; carbon dioxide therapy.

cdw carrying a concealed weapon.

CE, Ce, ce Council of Europe; Chancellor of the Exchequer (England); Church of England; Corps of Engineers; cerium; chemical engineer; customs and excise; let the buyer beware (caveat emptor); counterespionage; chip enable; cardiac enlargement.

C&E Cababe and Ellis' Queen's Bench (England); consultation and examination.

CEA, cea Council of Economic Advisors; Coal Exporters Association of the United States; cost effectiveness analysis; carcinoembryonic antigen.

CEB Council on Employee Benefits.

CEBA Competitive Equality Banking Act.

CEC, cec Commodity Exchange Commission; Commission of the European Communities; ciliated epithelial cell.

CED, ced Canadian Encyclopedia Digest; Committee for Economic Development; capacitance electronic disc.

ceg chronic erosive gastritis.

CEGJA Coalition to End Grand Jury Abuse.

CE Gr C.E. Green's Equity Reports (New Jersey).

CEIP Carnegie Endowment for International Peace.

CEL, cel Constitutional Education League; Cryogenic Engineering Laboratory; celsius; celluloid.

cem cemetery; cement; channel electron multiplier.

CEMR Contractor Estimating Methods Review.

cent central; century; center; centigrade.

Cent Crim CR Central Criminal Court Reports (England).

Cent Dig Century Digest.

centi hundred.

CENTRANS Center for Transportation.

Centr LJ Central Law Journal.

ceo chief executive officer; customs enforcement officer.

CEP, cep Court Employment Project; circular error probable; continuing education program; counter-electro-phoresis.

ceph floc cephalin flocculation.

CEPR Council on Education in Professional Responsibility.

CEQ Council on Environmental Quality.

cer conditioned emotional response.

CERCLA Comprehensive Environmental Response, Compensation and Liability Act.

CERI Clean Energy Research Institute.

CERN Centre European pour Recherche Nucleaire.

cert certiorari; certification.

cerv cervical.

ces central excitatory state.

CET, cet Central European Time; computerized emission tomogram.

CETA Comprehensive Employment and Training Act.

ceti communication with extraterrestrial intelligence.

ceu continuing education unit.

Cf, cf californium; compare; compensation fee; cost and freight; commerce and finance; carried forward; central files; centrifugal force; control footing; conversion factor; cystic fibrosis; coronary flow; cardiac failure.

C&F, c&f Clark and Finnelly's House of Lords Cases (England); cost and freight.

CFA, cfa Consumer Federation of America; Chartered Financial Analyst; cleared for approach; complement fixing antibody.

CFC, cfc Controlled Foreign Corporation; chlorofluoro-carbon.

CFDA Catalog of Federal Domestic Assistance.

cff cystic fibrosis factor.

cfh cubic feet per hour.

CFI, cfi Certified Flight Instructor; cost, freight, and insurance; cardiac function index.

CFLETC Consolidated Federal Law Enforcement Training Center.

CFM, cfm Council of Foreign Ministers; customer furnished materials; cubic feet per minute; chlorofluoromethane.

cfo chief financial officer; cancel former order.

CFP, cfp Commission on Federal Paperwork; Certified Financial Planner; cystic fibrosis patient.

CFR, cfr Code of Federal Regulations; Council on Foreign Relations; citrovorum factor rescue.

cfs cubic feet per second; call for service.

CFSEB Conference of Funeral Service Examining Boards.

CFTC Commodity Futures Trading Commission.

cfy current fiscal year.

cfz contiguous fisheries zone; capillary free zone.

CG, cg Comptroller General; Coast Guard; Consul General; center of gravity; centigram; convenience of the government; chorionic gonadotropin.

CGA, cga Compressed Gas Association; Certified General Accountant; cargo's proportion of general average; catabolite gene activator.

cgd chronic granulomatous disease.

cge carriage.

CGEN Consul General.

cgh cough.

cgm central gray matter.

cgn chronic glomerulonephritis.

CGO, cgo Comptroller General's Opinions; cargo.

CGR, cgr Coast Guard Reserve; Coast Guard Regulations; crime on governmental reservation.

cgs cardiogenic shock.

cgtt cortisone glucose tolerance test.

Ch Chancery; Law Reports, Chancery (England); chancellor; clearing house; court house; customs house; check; chapter; central heating; chaplain; chairman; child; control heading; chest; choke; chronic.

CHA, cha Community Health Association; congenital hypoplastic anemia; common hepatic artery.

chair chairman.

Chamb Rep Chambers' Chancery Reports (Ontario).

Chan or **Chaney** Chaney's Reports (Michigan).

chanc chancellor.

Chand Chandler's Reports (New Hampshire); Chandler's Reports (Wisconsin).

chap chapter.

Ch App or **Cha App** Law Reports Chancery Appeals (England).

char character; charter; charity

Charl R.M. Charlton's Reports (Georgia); T.U.P Charlton's Reports (Georgia).

Charley Pr Cas Charley's Practice Cases (England).

Chase Chase's United States Circuit Court Decisions.

CHC, chc Community Health Center; chance.

Ch Cal Calendar of Proceedings in Chancery (England).

Ch Cas Cases in Chancery (England).

Ch Ch or **Ch Cham** Chancery Chambers (Upper Canada).

Ch Col Op Chalmer's Colonial Opinions (England).

Ch D, chd Law Reports, Chancery Division (2d: Second Series) (England); coronary heart disease; congenital heart disease; childhood disease.

ChE cholinesterase; chemical engineer.

Chem Ab Chemical Abstracts.

Chest Co Chester County Reports (Pennsylvania).

Chev Cheve's Reports (South Carolina).

Chev Ch or **Chev Eq** Cheve's Equity Reports (South Carolina).

chf chief; congestive heart failure; congenital hepatic fibrosis.

CHGC Committee for Hand Gun Control.

chgd charged.

Chi, chi Chicago; closed head injury.

CHIAA Crop Hail Insurance Actuarial Association.

Chi B Rec Chicago Bar Record.

Chicago LB Chicago Law Bulletin.

Chicago LJ Chicago Law Journal.

Chicago LR Chicago Law Record.

Chicano L Rev Chicano Law Review.

Chic LT Chicago Law Times.

Chi Kent L Rev Chicago-Kent Law Review.

Chi Leg N Chicago Legal News.

Chil Rt Rep Children Rights Reports.

Chin Law & G Chinese Law and Government.

Chip Chipman's Reports (Vermont); Chipman's Reports (New Brunswick).

Chit BC Chitty's Bail Court Reports (England).

Chitty's LJ Chitty's Law Journal.

chk check.

chl, Chl confinement at hard labor; chloroform.

chm chamber; chairman.

CHMA Comprehensive Health Manpower Act.

chn carbon, hydrogen, nitrogen.

cho carbohydrate; chorea.

Cho Cas Ch Choyce's Cases in Chancery (England).

chol cholesterol.

chp child psychiatry; comprehensive health planning.

Ch Pr Precedents in Chancery (England).

Ch R, chr Chitty's King's Bench Reports (England); Chamber's Reports (Upper Canada); constant hazard ratio; chronic.

Ch Rep Chancery Reports.

Ch RM R.M. Charlton's Reports (Georgia).

Ch Rob or **Chr Rob** Christopher Robinson's Admiralty Reports (England).

Chr Rep Chamber's Reports (Upper Canada).

CHRPI Center for Health Resources Planning Information.

CHS, chs Community Health Service; crime on the high seas; contact hypersensitivity; chondroitin sulfate.

Ch Sent Chancery Sentinel (New York).

chtr charter.

Ch TUP T.U.P. Charlton's Reports (Georgia).

chu centigrade heat unit.

Chy Chrs Chancery Chambers Reports (Upper Canada).

CI, ci Cayman Islands; criminal informant; center of impact; commerce and industry; cost and insurance; certificate of insurance; cast iron; cirrus.

c&i cost and insurance.

CIA, cia Central Intelligence Agency; Certified Internal Auditor; Correctional Industries Association; cash in advance; congenital intestinal aganglionosis.

CIAA Coordinator of Inter-American Affairs.

CIB, cib Criminal Intelligence Bureau; food (cibus).

cic circulating immune complexes.

cics customer information control system.

CICU Coronary Intensive Care Unit.

CID, cid Criminal Investigation Department; cubic inch displacement; cytomegalic inclusion disease.

CIF, cif Community Investment Fund; cost, insurance, and freight; cost plus incentive fee.

cifc cost, insurance, freight, and commission.

cifi cost, insurance, freight, and interest.

cig cigarette.

cii criminal identification and investigation.

CIM, cim Cumulated Index Medicus; computer input microfilm; cortical induction of movement.

CIMA Construction Industry Manufacturers Association.

cin contract item number; code identification number; chronic interstitial nephritis; cervical intra-epithelial neoplasia.

Cin BAJ Cincinnati Bar Association Journal.

Cin Law Bull Cincinnati Law Bulletin; Weekly Law Bulletin.

Cin L Rev Cincinnati Law Review.

Cin Mun Dec Cincinnati Municipal Decisions.

Cin R or **Cin Rep** or **Cin SCR** or **Cin Sup Ct R** Cincinnati Superior Court Reporter.

CIO Congress of Industrial Organizations.

ciocs communication input/output control system.

CIP, cip Community Investment Program; capital improvement program; chronic inflammatory polyneuropathy.

CIPA Chartered Institute of Patent Agents (England).

CIR, cir Crime on Indian Reservation; circuit; circumference; circle; about (circa); circumcision.

circ circumcision; circuit; circumference; about (circa).

Cir Ct Dec Circuit Court Decisions (Ohio).

CIS, cis Congressional Information Service; carcinoma in situ.

ciss contract items specification and schedule.

cit citation; citizen; citrate; combined intermittent therapy.

City Ct Rep City Court Reports (Supp: Supplement) (New York).

City Hall Rec City Hall Recorder (New York).

City H Rep or **City Hall Rep** City Hall Reporter (New York).

CIU Congress of Independent Unions.

Civil See Civ.

Civ Lib Dock Civil Liberties Docket.

Civ Lib Rptr Civil Liberties Reporter.

Civ Pr Rep or **Civ Proc R** Civil Procedure Reports (New York).

Civ Rights Dig Civil Rights Digest.

Civ Serv J Civil Service Journal.

CJ Corpus Juris (first edition of CJS); Chief Justice; Chief Judge.

C&J Crompton & Jervis' Exchequer Reports (England).

CJ Ann Corpus Juris Annotations.

CJ Can Corpus Juris Canonici.

CJ Civ Corpus Juris Civilis.

CJI Criminal Justice Index.

CJIS Criminal Justice Information System.

CJS Corpus Juris Secundum.

CK, ck Cook Islands; check; cask; carnal knowledge.

C&K Carrington and Kirwan's Nisi Prius Reports (England).

ckw clockwise.

CL, Cl, cl Common Law Reports; Chile; Ceylon; chlorine; chloride; civil law; civil liberties; carload; cost of living; centiliter; claim; classification; clerk; cash letter; closure; clear; critical list.

C&L Connor and Lawson's Chancery Reports (Ireland).

CLA Certified Legal Assistant; Computer Lawyers Association.

Cl App or **Clark App** Clark's House of Lords Appeal Cases (England).

Clark Clark's House of Lord's Cases (England); Clark's Reports (Pennsylvania).

Clark & F or **Cl & Fin** Clark and Finnelly's House of Lords Cases (NS: New Series) (England).

Clarke Clarke's Reports (Michigan); Clarke's Reports (Iowa).

Clarke & S Dr Cas Clarke & Scully's Drainage Cases (Ontario).

Clarke Ch Clarke's Chancery Reports (New York).

Clay or **Clayt** Clayton's Reports, York Assizes (England).

CLB, clb Bachelor of Civil Law; curvilinear body; chlorambucil.

CLC Cost of Living Council.

C&LCC Caines and Leigh's Crown

Cases (England).

Cl Ch Clark's Chancery Reports (New York).

CL Ch Common Law Chamber Reports (Ontario).

CLD, cld Doctor of Civil Law; cleared; cost laid down; chronic lung disease.

CLE, cle Chicago Livestock Exchange, continuing legal education.

CLEAR National Clearinghouse on Licensure, Enforcement and Regulation.

Clem Clemens' Reports (Kansas).

CLEO Council on Legal Education Opportunity.

CLEPR Council on Legal Education for Professional Responsibility.

Clev BAJ Cleveland Bar Association Journal.

Clev Mar L Rev Cleveland Marshall Law Review.

Clev St LR Cleveland State Law Review.

Clev L Rec or **Clev Law Rec** Cleveland Law Record.

Clev L Reg or **Clev Law Reg** Cleveland Law Register.

Clev L Rep or **Cleve Law R** Cleveland Law Reporter.

Clev Mar L Rev Cleveland Marshall Law Review.

clg ceiling.

CLI, cli Christian Law Institute; cost of living index; corpus luteum insufficiency.

Cliff Clifford's Circuit Court Reports.

Clif South El Cas Clifford's Southwick Election Cases.

clin clinical.

CLIPI Center for Law in the Public Interest.

CLJ Chicago Law Journal; Canada Law Journal (NS: New Series) (OS: Old Series); Central Law Journal.

clk clerk; clock.

Clk Mag Clerk's Magazine (London); Clerk's Magazine (Rhode Island).

clh chronic lobular hepatitis.

cll chronic lymphocytic leukemia.

CLLA Commercial Law League of America.

CLLC Canadian Labour Law Cases.

CLLDF Civil Liberties Legal Defense Fund.

CLN Chicago Legal News.

CLO, clo Community Law Office; cod liver oil.

clp criminal law and procedure; contract laboratory program; cleft lip with cleft palate; clinical pathology.

CLR, clr California Law Review; Common Law Reports (England); Canada Law Reports; Commonwealth Law Reports (Australia); clearance.

CL Rec Cleveland Law Record.

CL Reg Cleveland Law Register.

CL Rep Cleveland Law Reporter.

CLS, cls Canon Law Society of America; Consular Law Society; confused language syndrome.

CLSR Computer Law Service Reporter.

CLT, clt Canadian Law Times; collateral; claimant; chronic lymphocytic thyroiditis; clotting time.

CLUJ Chartered Life Underwriter Journal.

CLW Commercial Laws of the World (Oceana).

CLYB Current Law Year Book (England).

CM, Cm, cm Court Martial Reports (Army); curium; cumulative; on the occasion or by reason of death (causa mortis); circular measure; court martial; centimeter; carboxymethyl; corrective maintenance; congenital malformation; circular muscle.

C&M Crompton and Meeson's Exchequer Reports (England); Carrington and Marshmann's Nisi Prius Reports (England).

CMA, cma Court of Military Appeals; Certified Medical Assistant; current market appraisal.

cmao court martial appointing order.

CMAR Canadian Court Martial Appeal Reports.

CMC, cmc Committee for Modern Courts; carpometacarpal.

cmd command; childhood muscular dystrophy.

cmdty commodity.

cme continuing medical education; cystoid macular edema.

CMET Certified Medical Electroencephalographic Technician.

cmf court martial forfeiture; calcium/magnesium free.

cmg cystometrogram; congenital myasthenia gravis.

CMHCA Community Mental Health Centers Act.

cmi chronic mesenteric ischemia; care management integration.

cml current mode logic; chronic myelocytic leukemia.

CMO, cmo Collateralized Mortgage Obligation; Compilation of Court Martial Orders (Navy); comfort measures only.

CMPA Central Massachusetts Paralegal Association.

CMR, cmr Court of Military Review; Cameroon; court martial report; cerebral metabolic rate.

CMR AF Court Martial Reports, Judge Advocate General (Air Force).

CM&R Crompton, Meeson & Roscoe's Exchequer Reports (England).

cms circulation, motion, sensation.

cmt current medical terminology; cervical motion tenderness.

cmv cytomegalovirus; cool mist vaporizer.

CN, cn China; Code Napoleon; Commonwealth Nation; canon; credit note; cover note; consignment note; carelessness and negligence; consolidated; compass north; charge nurse; tomorrow night (cras nocte); caudate nucleus; cranial nerve.

C&N or **CN Conf** Cameron and Norwood's Conference Reports (North Carolina).

cna calcium nutrient agar.

cnc computer numerical control.

cncl concealed.

cncr concurrent.

cnd cannot determine.

cne chronic nervous exhaustion.

cng compressed natural gas.

cni chronic nerve irritation.

CNJA Chief Naval Judge Advocate.

CNM Certified Nurse Midwife.

CNO Chief of Naval Operations.

cnp continuous negative pressure.

cns central nervous system.

cnt could not test.

CNTU Confederation of National Trade Unions.

cnv contingent negative variation.

cnvt convict.

CO, Co, co Colombia; Colorado; Copyright Office; Coke's Institutes; Coke's King's Bench Reports (England); Crown Office; cobalt; certificate of origin; contracting officer; conscientious objector; care of; carried over; company; county; central office; county; carbon monoxide; complains of; cardiac output.

c/o complains of; care of.

coa change of address; change of assignment; condition on admission.

coag coagulation.

COB, cob Congressional Office of the Budget; close of business; confirmation of balance.

Cobb Cobb's Reports (Alabama); Cobb's Reports (Georgia).

COBOL Common Business Oriented Language.

cobt chronic obstruction of the biliary tract.

COC, coc Chamber of Commerce; contempt of court; change of contract; certificate of competency; code of conduct; cathodal opening contraction.

Coch or **Cochr** Cochran's Reports (Nova Scotia); Cochran's Reports (North Dakota).

cochl spoonful (cochleare).

Cockb & R Cockburn and Rowe's Election Cases (England).

Cocke Cocke's Reports (Florida); Cocke's Reports (Alabama).

Co Ct Ch County Court Chronicle (England).

Co Ct Rep County Court Reports (Pennsylvania).

COCTS County Courts (England).

cod codicil; collect on delivery; cash on delivery; certificate of deposit; cause of death; codex; chemical oxygen demand; condition on discharge.

codasyl conference on data systems languages.

code controller decision evaluation.

codec coder/decoder.

Code Rep Code Reporter (NS: New Series) (New York).

codl codicil.

COE, coe Core of Engineers; cab over engine.

COEDA Corps of Engineers Design Assistance.

coef coefficient.

c of b confirmation of balance.

C of C Chamber of Commerce.

Coff or **Coff Prob** Coffey's Probate Decisions (California).

COG, cog Council of Governments; convenience of the government.

COGEL Council on Governmental Ethics Laws.

COH carbohydrate.

COHO Council of Health Organizations.

Co Inst Coke's Institutes (England).

COK Cook Islands.

Coke Coke's King's Bench Reports (England); see also Co Inst, Co Litt.

Col, col Coleman's Reports (Alabama); Coldwell's Reports (Tennessee); Colombia; cost of living; collective; college; colony; collateral.

cola cost of living allowance; cost of living adjustment.

Col & Cai Cas Coleman and Caines' Cases (New York).

Col App Colorado Appeals Reports.

Col Cas Coleman's Practice Cases (New York).

Col CC or **Coll** Collyer's Chancery Cases (England).

Cold, cold Coldwell's Reports (Tennessee); chronic obstructive lung disease.

Cole Coleman's Reports (Alabama).

Cole Cas or **Colem Cas** Coleman's Cases (New York).

Colem & C or **Col & C Cas** Coleman and Caines' Cases (New York).

Co Litt Coke on Littleton (England).

Coll, coll Collyer's Chancery Cases (England); collateral.

Coll & E Bank Collier and Eaton's American Bankruptcy Reports.

Colles Colles' Cases in Parliament (England).

Coll LB College Law Bulletin.

Col L Rep Colorado Law Reporter.

Col L Rev Columbia Law Review.

Cold or **Coldw** Coldwell's Reports (Tennessee).

Colo Colorado.

Colo App Colorado Appeals Reports.

Colo Law Rep Colorado Law Reporter.

Colo Law Colorado Lawyer.

Colo NP Dec Colorado Nisi Prius Decisions.

COLPA National Jewish Commission on Law and Public Affairs.

Colq Colquit's Modern Reports (England).

Coltm Coltman's Registration Appeal Cases (England).

Colum Hum Rts L Rev Columbia Human Rights Law Review.

Colum J Envt L Columbia Journal of Environmental Law.

Colum J Int Aff Columbia Journal of International Affairs.

Colum JL & Soc Prob Columbia Journal of Law and Social Problems.

Colum J Transnl Law Columbia Journal of Transnational Law.

Colum JWB Columbia Journal of World Business.

Colum L Rev Columbia Law Review.

Colum Soc Intl L Bull Columbia Society of International Law Bulletin.

Colum Surv Hum Rts L Columbia Survey of Human Rights Law Review.

Com, com Commentaries of Blackstone; Comstock's Reports (New York); customer's own material; commitment; computer output on microfilm; chronic otitis media.

Com & L Communications and the Law.

Co Mass Pr Colby's Massachusetts Practice.

Com B or **Comm B** Manning, Granger & Scott's Common Bench Reports (England).

Comb Comberbach's King's Bench Reports (England).

Com Cas Commercial Cases (England).

Com Dec Commissioner's Decisions, Patent.

COMECON Council for Mutual Economic Assistance.

Com L Commercial Law (Canada).

Com LJ Commercial Law Journal.

Com LR Common Law Reports (England).

Comm, comm Commonwealth; commission; committee; commerce; community; common; communication.

COMMBCA Commerce Board of Contract Appeals, Department of.

Comm Mkt LR Common Market Law Reports.

Comm Mkt L Rev Common Market Law Review.

commn commission.

Comm Prop J Community Property Journal.

Commonw Arb Commonwealth Arbitration Reports.

Commonw LR Commonwealth Law Reports.

comp complaint; comptroller; companion; composite; company.

companding compressing expanding.

Comp & Intl LJSA Comparative and International Law Journal of South Africa.

Comp Dec or **Comptr Treas Dec** Comptroller of the Treasury Decisions.

comp fix complement fixation.

Comp Gen Comptroller General Decisions.

Comp Jurid Rev Comparative Juridical Review.

Comp LJ Company Law Journal.

Comp LS Comparative Law Series.

Com P Rptr Common Pleas Reporter (Scranton).

compt comptroller.

Computer LJ Computer Law Journal.

comr commissioner.

Comst Comstock's Reports (New York).

Comyns Comyns' King's Bench Reports (England).

Comyns Dig Comyns' Digest (England).

Con, con Connolly's Criminal Reports (New York); connection; conclusion; controller; against (contra); continued; certificate of need.

cond condition; conduct; condensed.

Condit Sale Chat Mort Rep

Conditional Sale-Chattel Mortgage Reporter (Commerce Clearing House).

Conf, conf Conference Reports (North Carolina); confidential; confederation; conference.

Conf Per Fin LQ Rep Conference on Personal Finance Law Quarterly Report.

cong congenital; congress.

Cong Deb Congressional Debates.

Cong Dig Congressional Digest; Congdon's Digest (Canada).

Cong Q Congressional Quarterly.

Cong R Congressional Record.

conj conjunctiva.

Conn Connecticut Reports.

Conn BJ Connecticut Bar Journal.

Conn L Rev Connecticut Law Review.

Connor & L Connor and Lawson's Chancery Reports (Ireland).

Conn Supp Connecticut Supplement.

Conn Sur Connolly's Surrogate Reports (New York).

con obj conscientious objector.

Conov Conover's Reports (Wisconsin).

cons consignment; constitution; consul; consolidate.

consgt consignment.

const constitution; constant; construction.

constl constitutional.

constr construction.

Const Rep Constitutional Reports, (South Carolina).

Const Rev Constitutional Review.

Con Sur Connolly's Surrogate Reports (New York).

cont contract; continued; contrary; continent.

contbd contraband.

contd continued.

Cont Drug P Contemporary Drug Problems.

contl control.

contrib contributory.

Conv, conv Conveyancer and Property Lawyer (NS: New Series); convict; convention;

convenient; convalescent.

Convey Conveyancer and Property Lawyer (NS: New Series).

cood chronic obstructive outflow disease.

Cooke CP Cooke's Common Pleas Reports (England).

Cooke & A Cooke and Alcock's King's Bench Reports (Ireland).

Cook Vice Adm Cook's Vice Admiralty Reports (Canada).

Cooley Cooley's Reports (Michigan).

Coop, coop Cooper's Reports (Florida); Cooper's Chancery Reports (England); Cooper's Chancery Reports (Tennessee); cooperative.

Coop Ch Cooper's Chancery Reports (Tennessee).

Coop Pr Cas Cooper's Chancery Practice Cases.

Coop t Brough Cooper's Cases, temp. Chancery Broughham (England).

cop copyrighted; copy; change of plaster; copulative; coefficient of performance; colloid osmotic pressure.

COPA Council on Postsecondary Accreditation.

Co PC Coke's Pleas of the Crown (England).

copd chronic obstructive pulmonary disease.

Cope, cope Cope's Reports (California); chronic obstructive pulmonary emphysema.

COPICS Copyright Office Publication and Interactive Cataloging System.

Copp Min Dec Copp's Mining Decisions.

Copy Bull Copyright Bulletin.

copy copyright.

CoQ coenzyme Q.

cor coroner; body (corpus); correspondence; correction; corrosive; cash on receipt; custodian of records; coronary.

Corb & D Corbett & Daniel's Election Cases (England).

CORE Congress of Racial Equality.

Co Rep Coke's King's Bench Reports (England).

Cornell Int LJ Cornell International Law Journal.

Cornell LQ Cornell Law Quarterly.

Cornell L Rev Cornell Law Review.

corp corporation.

Corp J Corporation Journal.

Corp L Rev Corporation Law Review.

Corp Pract Comm Corporate Practice Commentator.

Corp Reorg Corporate Reorganizations.

Corp Reorg & Am Bankr Rev Corporate Reorganization and American Bankruptcy Review.

corr correspondence; correction; corrigendum; corruption.

cos condemned or suppressed; chief of staff; counties; companies; clinically observed seizure.

cot critical off time; content of thought; contralateral optic tectum.

COTA Certified Occupational Therapy Assistant.

coun counsel; council.

Coup Couper's Justiciary Reports (Scotland).

Court & MacL Courtenay & MacLean's Appeals (Scotland).

Cout Coutlee's Unreported Cases (Canada).

Coutlea Coutlea's Supreme Court Cases.

Cow Cowen's Reports (New York).

COWP Council on Wage and Price Stability.

Cow Cr Cowen's Criminal Reports (New York).

Cowp Cowper's King's Bench Reports (England).

Cowp Cas Cowper's Chancery Cases (England).

Cox Cox' Reports (Arkansas).

Cox & Atk Cox and Atkinson's Registration Appeals (England).

Cox Am T Cas Cox' American Trademark Cases.

Cox CC or **Cox Crim Cas** Cox' Criminal Law Cases (England).

Cox Ch Cox' Chancery Cases (England).

Cox Eq Cox' Equity Cases (England).

Cox JS Cas Cox' Joint Stock Cases (England).

Coxe Coxe's Reports (New Jersey).

CP, cp Common Pleas; Court of Probate; code of practice; chapter; civil procedure; civil powers; construction permit; carriage paid; custom of port; compare; coupon; command post; center of pressure; cuticular plate; chemically pure; cerebral palsy; capillary pressure; clinical pathology.

c/p compensation and pension; cholesterol phospholipid ratio.

C&P Carrington and Payne's Nisi Prius Reports (England); Craig & Phillips' Chancery Reports (England).

CPA, cpa Certified Public Accountant; Chartered Public Accountant; Cincinnati Paralegal Association; cardiopulmonary arrest.

cpaf cost plus award fee.

CPAJ Certified Public Accountant Journal.

cpap continuous positive airway pressure.

CPB, cpb Censorship Policy Board; Corporation for Public Broadcasting; competitive protein binding; cardiopulmonary bypass.

CPC, cpc Carswell's Practice Cases; Cooper's Common Pleas Practice Cases (England); Clerk of the Privy Council; copy payments center; chronic passive congestion.

cpcn certificate of public convenience and necessity.

CP Coop C.P. Cooper's Chancery Practice Cases (England).

CPC t BR C.P. Cooper's Chancery Reports temp. Brougham (England).

CPC t Cott C.P. Cooper's Chancery Reports temp. Cottenham (England).

cpcu chartered property and casualty underwriter.

CPD, cpd Law Reports, Common Pleas Division (England); compound; citrate phosphate dextrose; cephalopelvic disproportion; contagious pustular dermatitis.

cpe complete physical examination.

cpf clot promoting factor.

cpff cost plus fixed fee.

cph chronic persistent hepatitis.

cpi consumer price index; customs port investigator; constitutional psychopathic inferiority.

cpif cost plus incentive fee.

CPJ Committee for Public Justice.

cpk creatine phosphokinase.

CPL, cpl Current Property Law (England); complete; corporal.

cplr civil procedure law and rules.

CPM, cpm Certified Property Manager; critical path method; cards per minute; cycles per minute; counts per minute; cost per thousand.

cp/m control program/microcomputer.

CPO, cpo Certified Prosthetist Orthotist; cases per officer; chief petty officer.

cpp card punching printer; cerebral perfusion pressure.

CPPA Central Pennsylvania Paralegal Association.

cppb continuous positive pressure breathing.

CPQ Civil Procedures, Quebec.

CPR, cpr Canadian Patent Reporter; Citizens for Parents

Rights; copper; cardiopulmonary resuscitation; cardiac pulmonary reserve.

CP Rep Common Pleas Reports (Pennsylvania).

CPS, cps Certified Professional Secretary; central power system; constitutional psychopathic state; cycles per second; characters per second.

CPSC Consumer Product Safety Commission.

cpt carotid pulse tracing; cold pressor test.

cpu central processing unit.

CPUC Upper Canada Common Pleas Reports.

cpv canine parovirus.

CQ, cq Congressional Quarterly; commercial quality.

CR, Cr, cr Code Reports; Canadian Reports Appeal Cases; Criminal; Criminal Reports (Canada); Central Reporter; Congressional Record; Costa Rica; Cranch's Supreme Court Reports; chromium; consolidated report; carrier's risk; commodity rate; current rate; change of rate; creditor; center; councillor; civil rights; carriage return; child resistant; clot retraction; condition reflex; complete remission; cardiorespiratory.

C&R Cockburn and Rowe's Election Cases (England).

CRA, cra Community Reinvestment Act; Civil Rights Act; chronic rheumatoid arthritis.

Crabbe Crabbe's District Court Reports.

CRAC Canadian Reports Appeal Cases.

Craig & Ph Craig & Phillips' Chancery Reports (England).

cram card random access memory (method).

Cranch Cranch's Supreme Court Reports; Cranch's District of Columbia Reports.

Cranch CC Cranch's Circuit Court Reports.

Cranch Pat Dec Cranch's Patent Decisions.

Cr & J Crompton and Jervis' Exchequer Reports (England).

Cr & M Crompton and Meeson's Exchequer Reports (England).

Cr & Ph Craig and Phillips' American Chancery Reports (England).

Cr App Criminal Appeals.

Crane Crane's Reports (Montana).

Craw Crawford's Reports (Arkansas).

Crawf & D Abr C Crawford and Dix's Abridged Cases (Ireland).

Crawf & Dix Crawford and Dix's Circuit Cases (Ireland); Crawford & Dix's Criminal Cases (Ireland).

CRB Clemency Review Board.

CRC, crc Canadian Railway Cases; Civil Rights Commission; cyclic redundancy check; cardiovascular reflex conditioning.

Cr Cas Res Crown Cases Reserved (England).

crd childhood rheumatic disease; chronic respiratory disease.

creat creatinine.

Creighton L Rev Creighton Law Review.

CRF, crf Constitutional Rights Foundation; chronic renal failure.

cri chronic renal insufficiency.

crim criminal.

Crim Ab Abstracts on Criminology and Penology.

Crim App Criminal Appeal Reports (England).

Crim App Rep Cohen's Criminal Appeals Reports (England).

crim con criminal conversation.

Crim Delin Crime and Delinquency.

Crim JJ Criminal Justice Journal.

Crim JQ Criminal Justice Quarterly.

Crim Just Criminal Justice.

Crim L Bul Criminal Law Bulletin.

Crim L Mag Criminal Law Magazine (New Jersey).

Crim Law Q Criminal Law Quarterly.

Crim Law Rec Criminal Law Recorder.

Crim Law Rev Criminal Law Review.

Crim Law Rptr Criminal Law Reporter.

Crim Rec Criminal Recorder (Pennsylvania); Criminal Recorder (New York).

Crim Rep Criminal Reports (NS: New Series).

Crime & Delq Crime and Delinquency.

Cripp Ch Cas Cripp's Church and Clergy Cases.

Critch Critchfield's Reports (Ohio State).

CRJ Commission for Racial Justice.

CRLA California Rural Legal Assistance.

Cr M & R Crompton, Meeson & Roscoe's Exchequer Reports (England).

CRNA Certified Registered Nurse Anesthetist.

CR NS Code Reports, New Series (New York).

Cro, CRO, cro Croke's King's Bench Reports (England); Central Records Office; cathode ray oscilloscope.

C Rob Christopher Robinson's Admiralty Reports (England).

Cro Car Croke's King's Bench Reports, temp. Charles I (England).

Crock Crockford's Maritime Law Reports (England).

Cro Eliz Croke's King's Bench Reports, temp. Elizabeth I (England).

Cro Jac Croke's King's Bench Reports, temp. James I, Jacobus (England).

Croke Croke's King's Bench Reports (England).

crom control read only memory.

Cromp Crompton's Star Chamber Cases (England).

Cromp & J or **Cromp & Jerv** Crompton & Jervis' Exchequer Reports (England).

Cromp M & R Crompton, Meeson & Roscoe's Exchequer Reports (England).

Crosw Pat Cas Croswell's Collection of Patent Cases.

Crounse Crounse's Reports (Nebraska).

crp child-resistant packaging; community relations plan; c-reactive protein; creatine phosphate; chronic relapsing pancreatitis.

crr cost reduction report.

CRS, crs Congressional Research Service; Catholic Relief Services; congenital rubella syndrome; colorectal surgery.

crsp criminally receiving stolen property.

CRT, crt Copyright Royalty Tribunal; court; cathode ray tube.

CRTC Canadian Railway and Transport Cases.

CRTR Current Retail Trade Reports.

Crumrine Crumrine's Reports (Pennsylvania).

CRUS Customs Regulations of the United States.

crv conditional release violator; certificate of reasonable value; central retinal vein.

CS, Cs, cs Court of Sessions; Recueils de jurisprudence, Cour supérieure (Quebéc), Supreme Court Reports (Quebec); cesium; cat scratch; capital stock; county seat; case; consul; civil service; cost sharing; capital stock; current strength; certificate of service; chief of staff; chip select; cirrostratus; corticosteroid; conditioned stimulus; congenital syphilis; cesarean section.

C&S, c&s Clark & Scully's Drainage Cases (Ontario);

culture and sensitivity.

CSA, csa Community Services Administration; Confederate States of America; Canadian Standards Association; cognitive skills assessment; chondroitin sulfate A.

CSAB Contract Settlement Appeal Board.

CSAC Credit Standards Advisory Committee.

CSB, csb Civil Service Board; chemical stimulation of the brain; contaminated small bowel.

CSC, csc Civil Service Commission; certificate of security clearance; cosecant; collagen sponge contraceptive.

CSCA Conference of State Court Administrators.

CSCR Cincinnati Superior Court Reporter.

csd combined system disease.

CSDI Center for the Study of Democratic Institutions.

csf cerebrospinal fluid.

CSG Council of State Governments.

csho compliance safety and health officer.

CSI, csi Construction Specification Institute; cholesterol saturation index.

CSJ Civil Service Journal.

CSK, csk Czechoslovakia; cask.

csl computer sensitive language.

csm cerebrospinal meningitis; color, sensation, and motion.

csn contract serial number; cardiac sympathetic nerve.

cso common source outbreak.

csp corporate standard practice; cell surface protein.

CSPA Council of State Planning Agencies.

C-Span Cable Satellite Public Affairs Network.

CSPI Center for Science in the Public Interest.

c-spine cervical spine.

csr contract status report; certified

shorthand reporter; corrected sedimentation rate.

CSRDF Civil Service Retirement and Disability Fund.

CSS, css Commodity Stabilization Service; chewing, sucking, swallowing.

CST, cst Capital Stock Tax Division (Internal Revenue Service); central standard time; convulsive shock therapy.

cstms customs.

csu catheter specimen of urine.

CSUSA Copyright Society of the United States of America.

CSW Certified Social Worker.

CT, ct Carriers Tax Ruling (Internal Revenue Bulletin); Connecticut; county; court; current; central time; carat; cent; circuit; carbon tetrachloride; corneal transplant; connective tissue; continue treatment.

cta cystine trypticase agar.

CTB, ctb Comprehensive Test Ban; ceased to breathe.

CTC, ctc Canada Tax Cases; conditional transfer of control; carbon tetrachloride.

ctci contract technical compliance inspection.

Ct Cl Court of Claims.

Ct Com Pl Court of Common Pleas.

Ct Crim App Court of Criminal Appeals.

Ct Cust App Court of Customs Appeals.

Ct Cust & Pat App Court of Customs and Patent Appeals.

ctd connective tissue disease.

ctf chlorine trifluoride.

ctft counterfeit.

CtK Macnaghten's Chancery Cases temp. King (England).

Ct Just Court of Justiciary.

CTLJ California Trial Lawyers Journal.

ctn caution; computed tomography number.

ctp cytidine triphosphate.

ctr currency transaction report; cardiothoracic ratio.

Ct Rev Court Review.

ct rptr court reporter.

CTS, cts Consolidated Treaty Series; clear to send; carpal tunnel syndrome.

ctsp called to see patient.

ctu centigrade thermal unit.

ctw combined testicular weight.

cty county; city.

CU, Cu, cu Consumers Union; Cuba; copper; cumulative; cubic; credit union; clinical unit.

cuc chronic ulcerative colitis.

cud cause undetermined.

cu ft cubic foot.

cug cystourethrogram.

cu in cubic inch.

cum cumulative.

Cumber Sam L Rev Cumberland Samford Law Review.

Cum Bull Cumulative Bulletin (Internal Revenue Service).

Cum L Rev Cumberland Law Review.

Cum Sam L Rev Cumberland-Samford Law Review.

Cummins Cummins' Reports (Idaho).

CUNA Credit Union National Association.

Cunn Cunningham's King's Bench Reports (England).

CUP, cup Cambridge University Press; copper unit of pressure.

cupfc criminally uttering and publishing a false check.

Cur, cur Curtis' Circuit Court Reports; curative; currency.

CURE Citizens United for Racial Equality.

Cur Leg Thought Current Legal Thought.

curr currency.

Current L & Soc Prob Current Law and Social Problems.

Current LY Current Law Yearbook.

Current Med Current Medicine for Attorneys.

Curr Mun Pro Current Municipal Problems.

Curry Curry's Reports (Louisiana).

Curt Curtis' Circuit Court Reports; Curtis' Edition, United States Supreme Court Reports.

Curt Eccl Curtis' Ecclesiastical (England).

Cush Cushing's Reports (Massachusetts).

Cushman Cushman's Reports (Mississippi).

cust customs; customer; custodian; custody.

Cust App United States Customs Appeals.

Cust Bull Customs Bulletin.

Cust Ct Custom Court Reports.

Cut Pat Cas Cutler's Trademark and Patent Cases.

cuts cassette user tape system.

CV, cv Cape Verde; resume (curriculum vitae); common version; convertible; cerebrovascular; cardiovascular.

cva cerebrovascular accident.

cvat costovertebral angle tenderness.

cvc central venous catheter.

cvf cardiovascular failure.

CVI, cvi Cape Verde Islands; cerebrovascular insufficiency; cholera vaccine immunization.

cvm cardiovascular monitor.

cvp central venous pressure.

cvr cardiovascular respiratory.

cvs current vital signs.

cw clockwise; commercial weight; counterweight; case work; chemical warfare; child welfare; children's ward; chest wall; cold water.

CWA Communications Workers of America; Clean Water Act.

CWAG Conference of Western Attorney Generals.

cwd concealed weapon detector; cell wall defective.

CW Dud C.W. Dudley's Law or Equity Reports (South Carolina).

cwip construction work in progress.

cwl cultaneous water loss.

cwo cash with order; chief warrant officer.

CWPS Council on Wage and Price Stability.

cwt hundred weight; cold water treatment.

cx cervix; convex; chest x-ray.

cxr chest x-ray.

CY, Cy, cy Cyprus; cyanogen; currency; capacity; calendar year; county; cycle.

Cyc Cyclopedia of Law and Procedure.

cyl cylinder.

cyn cyanide.

CYO Catholic Youth Organization.

CYP Cyprus.

cysto cystoscopy.

Cyt cytosine.

CZ, cz Canal Zone; Czechoslovakia; combat zone.

czb carbon zinc battery.

Czech Y Intl L Czechoslovak Yearbook of International Law.

CZMA Coastal Zone Management Act.

CZMP Coastal Zone Management Plan.

CZO Canal Zone Order.

CZ Rep Canal Zone Reports.

D, d December; Denmark; digest; date; dollar; dividend; discharge; delete; deputy; desertion; diameter; delivery; divorce; defense; daughter; department; the number 13 (in the hexadecimal number system); diagnosis; dead; deceased; diameter; deciduous; doctor.

DA, da District Attorney; documents against

acceptance; documents attached; days after acceptance; deposit account; daughter; delayed action; damaged; digital to analog; disability aid; developmental age; degenerative arthritis.

d/a date of accident; date of admission.

daa data access arrangement; deputy assistant administrator.

dab diagnostic achievement battery; display assignment bits; days after birth.

DAC, dac Drug Abuse Council; digital-to-analog converter; disaster assistance center; data acquisition and control system.

dad dispense as directed.

d&d drunk and disorderly.

dai death from accidental injury.

Dak L Rev Dakota Law Review.

Dal Dallas' United States Reports; Dallas' Reports (Pennsylvania).

DALA Dallas Association of Legal Assistants; Dade Association of Legal Assistants.

Dal CP Dalison's Common Pleas Reports (England).

DALE, Dale Drug Abuse Law Enforcement; Dale's Reports (Oklahoma).

Dale Ecc Dale's Ecclesiastical Reports (England).

Dale Leg Rit Dale's Legal Ritual (England).

Dalhousie LJ Dalhousie Law Journal.

Dall Dallas' United States Reports; Dallas' Reports (Pennsylvania); Dallam's Supreme Court Decisions (Texas).

Dall in Keil Dallison's Reports in Keilway's King's Bench Reports (England).

Dalr Dalrymple's Decisions (Scotland).

Daly Daly's Common Pleas Reports (New York).

dam damage; degraded amyloid; dekameter.

Dan Daniell's Exchequer, Equity

Reports (England); Danner's Reports (Alabama).

Dana Dana's Reports (Kentucky).

Dan & L Danson and Lloyd's Mercantile Cases (England).

D&B Dearsley & Bell's Crown Cases (England); Devereux & Battle's Reports (North Carolina).

D&C, d&c Dow & Clark's Parliamentary Cases (England); Deacon & Chitty's Bankruptcy Cases (England); dilation and curettage.

d&d drunk and disorderly.

D&E, d&e Durnford & East's King's Bench Reports, Term Reports (England); diet and elimination.

D&J DeGex and Jones' Chancery Reports (England).

D&L Dowling and Lowndes' Bail Court Reports (England).

D&M Davison and Merivale's Queen's Bench Reports (England).

D&P Dearsley and Pearce's Crown Cases (England).

D&R Dowling and Ryland's King's Bench Reports (England).

D&RNP Dowling and Ryland's Nisi Prius Cases (England).

D&RMC Dowling and Ryland's Magistrate Cases (England).

D&S Drewry and Smale's Chancery Reports (England); Deane and Swabey's Ecclesiastical Reports (England).

D & Sw Deane and Swabey's Ecclesiastical Reports (England).

D&W Drewry and Walsh's Chancery Reports (Ireland); Drewry and Warren's Chancery Reports (Ireland).

d&v ductions and versions; diarrhea and vomiting.

Dane Abr Dane's Abridgment (England).

dang dangerous.

Dann Dann's Reports (California); Dann's Reports (Arizona);

Danner's Reports (Alabama).

Dans & L Danson and Lloyd's Mercantile Cases (England).

Danv Danvers' Abridgment (England).

dap diastolic aortic pressure.

DAR, dar Daughters of the American Revolution; death after resuscitation.

das delivered alongside ship; digital-analog simulator.

dasd direct access storage devise.

Dass Ed Dassler's Edition Reports (Kansas).

dat diet as tolerated; delayed action tablet.

Dauph Co Dauphin County Reports (Pennsylvania).

DAV, Dav, dav Disabled American Veteran; Daveis' District Court Reports; data above voice; see also Davis.

Dav & Mer Davison and Merivale's Queen's Bench Reports (England).

Davis Davis' Reports (Hawaii); Davis' King's Bench Reports (Ireland). See also Dav.

Davys Davys' King's Bench Reports (England).

daw dispense as written.

Day Day's Reports (Connecticut).

Dayton Miscellaneous Decisions (Ohio).

DB, db Domesday Book; debenture, deposit book; data base; decibel.

dba doing business as.

db/dc data base/data communications.

dbd definite brain damage.

dbk data bank; drawback.

dbl double.

DB&M Dunlop, Bell and Murry's Session Cases (Scotland).

dbms data base management system.

dbn of the goods that were not administered by a former executor or administrator (de bonis non).

dbp diastolic blood pressure.

dbr disordered breathing rate.

DBS, dbs Division of Biological Standards; deep brain stimulation.

dbw desirable body weight.

DC, dc District of Columbia; District Court; Treasury Department Circular; Doctor of Chiropractic; defense counsel; disorderly conduct; discharge; from the beginning (da capo); data collection; direct current; decimal classification; diagnostic center; deviation clause; discontinue.

D&C, d&c Dow & Clark's Parliamentary Cases (England); Deacon & Chitty's Bankruptcy Cases (England); dilation and curettage.

DCA, dca Dorion's Queen's Bench Reports (Canada); deoxycholic acid.

D Can L Doctor of Canon Law.

DC App District of Columbia Appeals Reports.

dcb data control block.

DCBJ District of Columbia Bar Journal.

dcc dorsal cell column.

DC Cir District of Columbia Circuit Court of Appeals.

dce data circuit-terminating equipment; data communications equipment.

dcf discounted cash flow.

DCG Decisions of the Comptroller General.

dch delayed cutaneous hypersensitivity.

D Chip D. Chipman's Reports (Vermont).

DCJ Doctor of Criminal Jurisprudence.

DCL Doctor of Canon Law; Doctor of Commercial Law; Doctor of Civil Law.

DCM District Court Martial; Doctor of Comparative Medicine.

dcn delayed conditioned necrosis.

D Cn L Doctor of Canon Law.

dco draft collection only.

D Comp L Doctor of Comparative Law.

D Cr Doctor of Criminology.

dcr direct cortical response.

dcs data control system; diffuse cerebral sclerosis.

D Ct District Court.

DD, dd drunk and disorderly; dishonorable discharge; demand draft; gave as a gift (dono dedit); delivered; due date; dated; data definition; data demand; days after delivery; date delivered; delay driver; decimal display; delayed delivery; digital display; digital data; differential diagnosis.

dda demand deposit accounting; digital display alarm; digital differential analyser.

DDC, ddc United States District Court, District of Columbia; drunk and disorderly conduct; direct digital control.

ddce digital data conversion equipment.

ddcmp digital data communication message protocol.

ddd direct distance dialing; defined daily dose.

ddg digital display generator.

ddgc dishonorable discharge, general court martial.

ddl data definition language; data description language; document description language.

ddp digital data processor; distributed data processing.

ddr daily demand rate; diastolic descent rate.

DDS, dds Doctor of Dental Science; digital display scope; dataphone digital service; disease disability scale.

ddt ductus deferens tumor.

DE, de Delaware; Doctor of Engineering; double entry; date of entry; decision error.

D&E, d&e Durnford (Dwinford) & East's King's Bench Term Reports (England); diet and elimination.

DEA, Dea Drug Enforcement Administration; Deady's

Circuit and District Court Reports.

Dea & Sw Deane and Swabey's Ecclesiastical Reports (England).

Deac Deacon's Bankruptcy Reports (England).

Deac & C Deacon & Chitty's Bankruptcy Cases (England).

Deady See Dea.

Deane Deane's Reports (Vermont).

Deane & S Eccl Deane and Swabey's Ecclesiastical Reports (England).

Deane & Sw Deane and Swabey's Probate and Divorce Reports (England).

Dears & B Dearsley & Bell's Crown Cases (England).

Deas & A Deas & Anderson's Decisions (Scotland).

DEB, deb Dental Examining Board; debenture; debridement.

Dec, dec December; decimeter; decade; declaration; decrease; deceased.

Decalogue Decalogue Journal.

Dec Com Pat Decisions of the Commissioner of Patents.

decd deceased.

Dec Dig Decennial Digest.

decn decision.

Dec O Decisions (Ohio).

Dec Rep Decisions Reprint (Ohio).

Decub lying down (Decubitus).

Dec US Comptr Gen Decisions of the United States Comptroller General.

DEd, ded Doctor of Education; dedicated; date of expected delivery.

def defendant; defense; deficient; definition; deferred; defective; defecation.

Defense LJ Defense Law Journal.

defr defrauding.

deft defendant.

deg degree; degenerating.

DeG & J DeGex and Jones' Chancery Reports (England).

DeG F&J DeGex, Fisher and Jones' Chancery Reports (England).

DeGJ&S DeGex, Jones & Smith's Chancery Reports (England).

DeG M&G DeGex, Macnaghten and Gordon's Chancery Reports (England).

De Gex De Gex' Bankruptcy Reports (England).

DEH dysplasia epiphysealis hemimelica.

Del, del Delaware Reports; delegate; deliver; delete character; delivery.

del acct delinquent account.

Del Ch Delaware Chancery Reports.

Del Co Delaware County Reports (Pennsylvania).

Del Cr Cas Delaware Criminal Cases.

Delehanty Miscellaneous Reports (New York).

Del J Corp Delaware Journal of Corporate Law.

delinq delinquent.

Dem, dem Demarest's Surrogate Reports (New York); democrat; demurrage; diethylmaleate; demerol.

Den, den Denio's Reports (New York); Denis' Reports (Louisiana); Denmark; density; dentistry.

Den & P Denison and Pearce's Crown Cases (England).

Den CC Denison's Crown Cases (England).

Denio Denio's Reports (New York).

Denis Denis' Reports (Louisiana).

Den J Intl L&P Denver Journal of International Law and Policy.

Den LJ Denver Law Journal.

Den LN Denver Legal News.

dent dental.

dep deponent; deposition; deposit; department; dependents.

DePaul L Rev DePaul Law Review.

depl depletion.

depn dependent.

depos depositary.

depr depreciation.

dept department; deponent.

Dept State Bull Department of State Bulletin.

der derivation.

derm dermatitis; dermatology.

Des, des Dessaussure's Equity Reports (South Carolina); desertion; desire; design; diethylstilbestrol; doctor emergency service; dermal epidermal separation.

desc descendant.

desi drug efficacy study implementation.

destn destination.

det determination; detective; diethyltryptamine.

Det CLR Detroit College of Law Review.

Det Law Detroit Lawyer.

Det Leg N Detroit Legal News.

Det LJ Detroit Law Journal.

Det LR Detroit Law Review.

detn detention; determination.

detox detoxification.

dev deviation.

Dev, dev Devereux' Reports (North Carolina); Devereux' Court of Claims Reports; deviation; development.

Dev & B Devereux & Battle's Reports (North Carolina).

Dev Ct Cl Devereux' Court of Claims Reports.

devel development.

Dew Dewey's Reports (Kansas).

De Witt De Witt's Reports (Ohio).

dex dexamethasone.

df damage free; disposition and finding; degrees fahrenheit; dead freight; direction finding; dorsiflexion; degree of freedom; deficiency factor.

DF&J DeGex, Fisher and Jones' Chancery Reports (England).

dfd defined formula diet.

dfg direct forward gaze.

dfi disease free interval.

dfm decreased fetal movement.

dfr dropped from the rolls.

dfs disease free survival.

dft defendant; design feasibility test; draft; defibrillation threshold.

dfu dideoxyfluorouridine; dead fetus in uterus.

dg damages goods; distogingival; degaussing; diastolic gallop; diagnosis.

dgf duct growth factor.

dgi disseminated gonococcal infection.

dgm decigram.

dgr danger.

dgs diabetic glomerulosclerosis.

dgt daughter.

dh disorderly house; dead heat.

dha dehydroascorbic acid.

dhb duct hepatitis b virus.

dhf dengue hemorrhagic fever.

dhp dehydrogenated polymer.

dhr delayed hypersensitivity reaction.

Di, di didymium; double indemnity; date of injury; due in; deterioration index; disability insurance; diabetes insipidus.

d/i date of injury.

DIA, dia Defense Intelligence Agency; diameter; death in action; diabetes.

diam diameter.

dib drug information center; discovery and investigations branch; disability insurance benefits.

dic diffuse (disseminated) intravascular coagulation.

Dice Dice's Reports (Indiana).

Dick Dickinson's Reports (New Jersey); Dickens' Chancery Reports (England).

Dick L Rev Dickerson Law Review.

Dicta Dicta of the Denver Bar Association.

did dead of intercurrent disease.

die died in emergency room.

dif difference; data interchange format; dose increase factor.

diff differential.

dig digest; let it be digested; digitalis.

DIL, dil Digest of International Law; Doctor of International Law; dilute; dilation; daughter in law.

dilat dilation.

dild diffuse interstitial (infiltrative) lung disease.

Dill Dillon's Circuit Court Reports.

dim dosis infectiosis media; diminished.

dip drip infusion pyelogram; distal interphalangeal.

diph diphtheria.

dir directive; direct; disturbed interpersonal relationships.

dird drug induced renal disease.

Dirl Dec Dirleton's Decisions (Scotland).

dis disorderly; discount; discovery; discharge; discontinued; district; disease; disability.

Dis Ab Dissertations Abstracts.

disap disapprove.

disbmt disbursement.

DISC, disc Domestic International Sales Corporation; discovery; discharge; discontinue.

disch discharge.

Disn Disney's Superior Court Reports (Ohio).

disp dispensary; dispense; dispatch.

dispn disposition.

disq disqualification.

disre disregard.

diss dissertation.

dissd dissolved.

dist district; distill.

dist atty district attorney.

District Director District Director of Internal Revenue.

dit diet induced thermogenesis.

div divorce; diversion; dividend.

DJ Doctor of Law (doctor juris); District Judge; Department of Justice; Dow Jones.

D&J DeGex and Jones' Chancery Reports (England).

DJAG Deputy Judge Advocate General.

djd degenerative joint disease.

DJS Doctor of Juridical Science;

Dubin Johnson Syndrome.

DJ&S DeGex, Jones & Smith's Chancery Reports (England).

DJSC Daily Journal of the Supreme Court.

D Jur Doctor of Jurisprudence.

DK, dk Denmark; dock; dark; diseased kidney.

dka didn't keep appointment.

dkb deep knee bends.

dkt docket.

DL, dl Department of Labor; Doctor of Law; demand loan; days lost; daylight; distolingual; deciliter; developmental level; danger list.

d/l date of loss.

D&L Dowling and Lowndes' Bail Court Reports (England).

DLa distolabial.

dlc data link control; dual lumen catheter.

dld delivered.

dle data link escape character; discoid lupus erythematosus.

dlo dispatch loading only; distolinguo occlusal.

dlp developmental learning problems.

DLR Dominion Law Reports (2d: Second Series) (3d: Third Series) (Canada).

DLRB Digest of Decisions of the National Labor Relations Board.

DLS, dls Doctor of Library Science; debt liquidation schedule.

dlv defective leukemia virus.

dlvy delivery.

dly delay; daily; delivery.

DM, dm Dominicia; decision maker; decimeter; deutsche mark; data management; right hand (destra mano); diastolic murmur; diabetes mellitus.

D&M Davison and Merivale's Queen's Bench Reports (England).

DMA, dma Dental Manufacturers of America; Dominica; direct memory access.

dmac direct memory access channel.

DM&G DeGex, Macnaghten and Gordon's Chancery Reports (England).

dmcl device media control language.

DMD, dmd Doctor of Dental Medicine; duchenne muscular dystrophy.

dme drug metabolizing enzyme.

dmft decayed, missing, filled teeth.

dmg damage.

dmi direct migration inhibition.

DMIAA Diamond Manufacturers and Importers Association of America.

DMJ Diploma in Medical Jurisprudence (England).

dml data manipulation language; distal motor latency.

DMMA Direct Mail Marketing Association.

dmp dimethyl phthalate.

dmr discharge monitoring report.

dms deviation from mean standard; digital multiplex switching system; data management system; dermatomyositis.

DMV Department of Motor Vehicles.

dmz demilitarized zone.

dn debit note; down.

DNA, dna does not apply; does not answer; deoxyribonucleic acid.

DNC, dnc Democratic National Committee; direct numerical control; did not come.

dnd died natural death.

dnf did not finish.

DNK, dnk Denmark; did not keep.

dnka did not keep appointment.

dnp did not pay; do not publish.

DNR, dnr Department of Natural Resources; dorsal nerve root; did not respond.

DNS, dns Dow's House of Lords Cases, New Series (England); diaphragm nerve stimulation.

dnt did not test.

dnu do not use.

DO, do Dominican Republic; Doctor of Osteopathy; district office; daughter of; delivery order; drugs only; doctor's orders; diamine oxidase.

doa documents of acceptance; date of arrival; date of admission; dead on arrival.

dob date of birth.

DOC, doc Department of Commerce; document; date of conception.

DOD, Dod, dod Dodson's Admiralty Reports (England); Department of Defense; died of disease; day of delivery.

DOE, doe Department of Energy; dyspnea on exertion; date of examination.

dof direction of flight.

DOI, doi Department of Interior; died of injuries.

DOJ Department of Justice.

DOL Department of Labor.

DOM, dom Dominican Republic; dominant; domestic; dimethoxy methylamphetamine.

Dom LR Dominion Law Reports (Canada).

Dom Rep Dominican Republic.

Donaker Donaker's Reports (Indiana).

Donn Donnelly's Chancery Reports (England); Donnelly's Land Cases (Ireland).

dop documents on payment.

dopa dihydroxyphenylalanine.

dops diffuse obstructive pulmonary syndrome.

dor date of request.

Dorion Dorion's Queen's Bench Reports (Quebec).

DOS, dos Department of State; disk operating system; dosage; day of surgery.

DOT, dot Department of Transportation; date of transfer.

DOTCAB Department of Transportation Contract Appeals Board.

Doug Douglas' Reports (Michigan); Douglas' King's Bench Reports (England).

Doug El Cas Douglas' Election Cases (England).

Dow Dow's House of Lords Cases (England); Dowling's Practice Cases (England).

Dow & C Dow & Clark's Parliamentary Cases (England).

Dow & L Dowling and Lowndes' Bail Court Reports (England).

Dow & Ry Dowling and Ryland's King's Bench Reports (England).

Dow & Ry NP Dowling and Ryland's Nisi Prius Cases (England).

Dow & Ry Dowling and Ryland's King's Magistrate Cases (England).

Dow PC Dowling's Practice Cases (NS: New Series) (England).

doz dozen.

DP, dp Doctor of Podiatry; disorderly person; displaced person; data processing; duty paid; documents for payment; departure point; direct port; donor's plasma.

D&P Dearsley and Pearce's Crown Cases (England).

DPA, dpa Delaware Paralegal Association; dynamic physical activity.

DPB, dpb Disability Policy Board; deposit passbook; days postburn.

dpc direct patient care; delayed primary closure.

dpd diffuse pulmonary disease.

dpg dumping; displacement placentogram.

DPH, DPh, dph Department of Public Health; Doctor of Philosophy; diaphragm.

DPI, dpi Department of Public Information; dots per inch; daily permissible intake.

dpj dementia paralytica juvenilis.

DPL, dpl Decisiones de Puerto Rico; Doctor of Patent Law; diploma; diplomat.

dpm documents per minute; data processing machine; discontinue previous medication.

DPMA Data Processing Management Association.

dpn diphosphopyridine nucleotide.

dpo deputy project officer.

DPP, dpp Director of Public Prosecutions (England); differential pulse polarography.

DPR, dpr District Probate Registry; doctor population ratio.

dpt deponent; department; diphtheria, pertussis, tetanus.

dptp diphtheria, pertussis, tetanus, poliomyelitis.

DPW Department of Public Works; Department of Public Welfare.

dq disqualified; direct question; deterioration quotient.

dqo data quality objectives.

dr doctor; deposit receipt; district registry; delivery room; debtor.

D&R Dowling and Ryland's King's Bench Reports (England).

DRA, Dra, dra De-Rating Appeals (England); Draper's King's Bench Reports (Canada); deputy regional administrator; dextran reactive antibody.

Drake BJ Drake Bar Journal.

Drake L Rev Drake Law Review.

dram direct random access memory.

Draper See Dra.

drc damage risk criteria.

drd dorsal root dilator.

d reg diseased region.

D Rep Decisions Reprint (Ohio).

Drew Drew's Reports (Florida); Drewry's Vice Chancellor's Reports (England).

Drew & Sm Drewry and Smale's Chancery Reports (England).

Drewry Drewry and Walsh's Chancery Reports (Ireland); Drewry and Warren's Chancery Reports (Ireland).

drf dose reduction factor.

drg disease related group.

DRI Defense Research Institute; Discharge Readiness Index.

Drink Drinkwater's Common Pleas Reports (England).

drk drunk.

Dr Jur Doctor of Jurisprudence.

drl dorsal root, lumbar.

Dr LL Doctor of Laws.

drms drug reaction monitoring system.

D&RNP Dowling and Ryland's Nisi Prius Cases (England).

D&RMC Dowling and Ryland's King's Magistrate Cases (England).

dro destructive read out.

drp dorsal root potential; digoxin reduction product.

drq discomfort relief quotient.

DRS, drs Dominican Report Service (Commerce Clearing House) (Canada); drowsiness.

Drug Abuse LR Drug Abuse Law Review.

Drug LJ Drug Law Journal.

Drury Drury's Chancery Reports (Ireland).

DS, ds Department of State; dangerous and suspicious; days after sight; document signed; design specifications; down's syndrome; dilute strength; double strength; disseminated sclerosis.

D&S Drewry and Smale's Chancery Reports (England); Deane and Swabey's Ecclesiastical Reports (England).

dsa disease susceptible antigen.

DSB Department of State Bulletin.

dsbl disabled.

dscb data set control block.

dsd dry sterile dressing.

dse data switching exchange.

dsn data set name.

dsg dry sterile gauze; dressing.

DSL Decalogue Society of Lawyers.

dsm dextrose solution mixture.

dso district sales office.

dsp delayed sleep phase; decreased sensory perception.

dsr distal splenorenal.

dss dependent step son; decision support system; dioctyl sodium sulfosuccinate; docusate sodium.

dst daylight savings time; donor specific transfusion.

dstn destination.

dsuh direct suggestion under hypnosis.

D & Sw Deane and Swabey's Ecclesiastical Reports (England).

dsw device status word.

dswi deep surgical wound infection.

dt delirium tremens; date; daylight time.

d/t date of treatment.

DTC Dominican Tax Cases; day treatment center; d-tubo-curarine.

dte data terminal equipment.

dtn diphtheria toxin normal.

dtp diphtheria, tetanus, pertussis.

dtr daughter; data terminal ready; deep tendon reflex.

dtt diagnostic and therapeutic team.

dtx detoxification.

du dual; diagnosis unknown; duodenal ulcer; diagnosis undetermined.

dua dorsal uterine artery.

dub dysfunctional uterine bleeding.

Dublin Univ LR Dublin University Law Review.

Dud Ch Dudley's Equity Reports (Scotland).

Dudl Dudley's Reports (Georgia).

Dud L Dudley's Law Reports (Scotland).

Duer Duer's Superior Court Reports (New York).

dui driving under the influence.

Duke BAJ Duke Bar Association Journal.

Duke LJ Duke Law Journal.

dul diffuse undifferentiated lymphoma.

DULR Dublin University Law Review.

Dunc Ent Cas Duncan's Entail Cases (Scotland).

Dunc NP Duncombe's Nisi Prius.

Dunl, B&M Dunlop, Bell and Murry's Session Cases (Scotland).

Dunn Dunning's King's Bench Reports (England).

duod duodenum.

dup duplicate.

Duquesne UL Rev Duquesne University Law Review.

dur drug use review.

Durf Durfee's Reports (Rhode Island).

Durie Durie's Session Cases (Scotland).

Durn & E Durnford & East's King's Bench Reports, Term Reports (England).

Dutch Dutcher's Reports (New Jersey).

Duv, duv Duvall's Reports (Kentucky); Duval's Reports (Canada); data under voice; damaging ultraviolet.

dv double vibration; dilute volume; distinguished visitor; distemper virus.

d&v ductions and versions; diarrhea and vomiting.

DVB Department of Veterans Benefits.

dvd double vessel disease.

dve duct virus enteritis.

dvi digital vascular imaging.

dvn dorsal vagal nucleus.

dvr driver; double valve replacement.

dvt deep vein thrombosis.

dw dock warrant; deadweight.

d/w dextrose in water.

d₅w 5% dextrose in water.

D&W Drewry and Walsh's Chancery Reports (Ireland); Drewry and Warren's Chancery Reports (Ireland).

dwc deadweight capacity.

dwd driving while drunk; died with disease.

dwg dwelling.

DWI, dwi Descriptive Word Index; die without issue;

driving while intoxicated.

dwlg dwelling.

dx diagnosis.

dxt dextrose.

Dy, dy Dyer's King's Bench Reports (England); dysprosium; delivery; duty.

dz dozen; drop zone; disease.

E, e East's King's Bench Reports (England); emergency; evidence; estimate; earnings; energy; electric field; English; east; error; edition; the number 14 (in the hexadecimal number system); enema; expired gas; enterococcus; enzyme; elastance; exercise; epinephrine; vitamin E; embryo; esophagus.

e_2 estradiol.

e_3 estriol.

Ea, ea East's King's Bench Reports (England); each; educational age; ethyl acrylate; enzymatic active.

E&A, e&a Spink's Ecclesiastical and Admiralty Reports; Error and Appeal Reports (Upper Canada); evaluate and advise.

eaa extrinsic allergic alveolitis.

EAB Ethics Advisory Board; elective abortion.

EAC, eac European Advisory Commission; external auditory canal; electroacupuncture.

ead extracranial arterial disease.

eae experimental allergic encephalomyelitis.

E Afr LR East African Law Reports.

eag electroantennogram.

Eag & Y Eagle and Young's Tithe Cases (England).

Eag T Eagle's Tithes.

eak ethyl amyl ketone.

eal estimated average life.

eam electrical accounting machine.

ean experimental allergic neuritis.

E&A, e&a Spink's Ecclesiastical and Admiralty Reports; Error and Appeal Reports (Upper Canada); evaluate and advise.

E&B Ellis and Blackburn's Queen's Bench Reports (England).

E&E Ellis and Ellis' Queen's Bench Reports (England).

e&h environment and heredity.

E&I English and Irish Appeals, House of Lords (England).

e&m endocrine and metabolism.

e&oe errors and omissions excepted.

e&p earnings and profits; extraordinary and plenipotentiary.

eaon except as otherwise noted.

eap electroacupuncture.

eaq eudismic affinity quotient.

e&r examination and report.

earom electrically alterable read-only memory.

Earth LJ Earth Law Journal.

EAS Executive Agreement Series.

East East's King's Bench Reports (England); Eastern Law Reporter (Canada).

East L Rep Eastern Law Reporter (Canada).

East PC East's Pleas of the Crown (England).

East Rep Eastern Reporter.

East T Eastern Term (England).

eat electroaerosol therapy.

eav equine abortion virus; extra alveolar vessel.

EB, eb Epstein Barr (virus); elementary body; east bound; estradiol benzoate.

E&B Ellis and Blackburn's Queen's Bench Reports (England).

eba emergency breathing apparatus; epidermolysis bullosa acquisita.

EBALA East Bay Association of Legal Assistants.

EB&E Ellis, Blackburn, and Ellis' Queen's Bench Reports (England).

EB&S Ellis, Best, and Smith's Queen's Bench Reports (England).

ebcdic extended binary coded decimal interchange code.

ebd epidermolysis bullosa dystrophica.

Ebersole Ebersole's Reports (Iowa).

ebf erythroblastosis fetalis.

ebg electroblepharogram.

ebi expanded background investigation; emetine bismuth iodide.

ebk embryonic bovine kidney.

ebl estimated blood loss.

ebp estradiol binding protein; epidural blood patch.

ebr electron beam recording.

EBS, ebs Emergency Broadcast System; emergency bed service; epidermolysis bullosa simplex; electric brain stimulator.

ebt external beam therapy.

ebv effective blood volume.

EC, ec English Chancery; Ecuador; East Caribbean; error corrected; error correcting; economics; eye care; excitation/contraction; epidermal cell; extracellular; enzyme-treated cell.

eca external carotid artery.

ECAB Employee Compensation Appeals Board.

ecbo enteric cytopathogenic bovine orphan.

ecbv effective circulating blood volume.

ECC, ecc Electronic Calibration Center; emergency cardiac care; error correction code; emergency core cooling; electrocorticogram; endocervical curettage.

ecce extra capsular cataract extraction.

eccl ecclesiastical.

Eccl & Adm Spink's Ecclesiastical and Admiralty Reports.

Eccl R Ecclesiastical Reports (England).

ecd estimated completion date; electron capture detector; enzymatic cell dispersion.

ece extended coverage endorsement.

ECF, ecf Employees Compensation Fund; extended care facility; extracellular fluid; effective capillary flow.

ecg electrocardiogram.

echo echocardiography; enteric cytopathogenic human organism.

eci electrocerebral inactivity.

eck extracellular kalium.

ECL, ecl English Common Law; emitter-coupled logic; euglobulin clot lysis.

ECLC Emergency Civil Liberties Committee.

ECM, ecm European Common Market; electronic counter-measures; external cardiac massage.

ECMA European Computer Manufacturing Association.

Ecol LQ Ecology Law Quarterly.

econ economics.

ECOP Extension Committee on Organization and Policy.

ecp endocardial potential; external cardiac pressure.

ecpr external cardiopulmonary resuscitation.

ECR, ecr European Court Reports; error cause removal.

ECRA Excess and Casualty Reinsurance Association.

ECS, ecs Education Commission of the States; elective cosmetic surgery.

ect electroconvulsive therapy.

ECU, ecu Ecuador; European currency unit; extended care unit.

ecv extracellular volume.

ecw extracellular water.

ECWAS Economic Community of West African States.

Ed, ed Eden's Chancery Reports (England); ex dividend; estimated date; extra duty; edu-

cation; edition; error detecting; external device; evidence of disease; erythema dose; ethynodiol; effective dose; electrodialysis; embryonic death; epidural.

EDA, eda Economic Development Administration; estimated date of arrival; electrodermal audiometry.

edb early dry breakfast; extensor digitorum brevis.

edbp erect diastolic blood pressure.

EDC, edc European Defense Community; expected date of confinement; extensor digitorum communis.

Ed Ch or **Ed CR** Edward's Chancery Reports (New York).

edd estimated date of delivery; effective drug duration.

Eden, eden Eden's Chancery Reports (England).

EDF, edf Environmental Defense Fund; extradural fluid.

Edg Edgar's Reports (Scotland).

edh extradural hematoma.

edl extensor digitorum longus.

ed/ld emotionally disturbed/learning disabled.

Ed LJ or **Edin LJ** Edinburgh Law Journal.

edm early diastolic murmur.

Edm Sel Cas Edmond's Select Cases (New York).

edp electronic data processing; end diastolic pressure.

edpm electronic data processing machine.

edps electronic data processing system.

edr estimated date of resumption; effective direct radiation.

eds exchangeable disk store; excessive daytime sleepiness.

E. D. Smith E. D. Smith's Common Pleas Reports (New York).

edst eastern daylight saving time.

edt eastern daylight time.

edta ethylenediamine tetraacetic acid.

educ education.

edv end diastolic volume.

Edw Edwards' Reports (Missouri); Edwards' Chancery Reports (New York); Edwards' Admiralty Reports (England).

Edw Abr Edward's Abridgment Privy Council; Edward's Abridgment Prerogative Court Cases.

Edw Ch Edward's Chancery Reports (New York).

Edw Lead Dec Edward's Leading Decisions in Admiralty.

Edw PC Edward's Prize Cases (England).

Edw Pr Ct Cas Edward's Prerogative Court Cases (England).

EE, ee English Exchequer; errors excepted; envoy extraordinary; eye and ear; energy expenditure; embryo extract.

E&E Ellis and Ellis' Queen's Bench Reports (England).

eea electroencephalic audiometry.

EEC European Economic Community.

eecg electroencephalogram.

EECL Encyclopedia of European Community Law.

eee external eye examination.

eeg electroencephalogram.

eent eyes, ears, nose, throat.

EEO, eeo Equal Employment Officer; equal employment opportunity.

EEOC Equal Employment Opportunity Commission.

eep end expiratory pressure.

EER, eer English Ecclesiastical Reports; energy efficiency ratio; electroencephalographic response.

eerom electrically erasable read-only memory.

EES European Exchange System.

EF, ef Environmental Fund; essential findings; extrinsic factor; exposure factor; endurance factor; embryo fetal.

efa essential fatty acids.

efc endogenous fecal calcium.

eff efficiency; effect; effaced.

effcy efficiency.

Efird Efird's Reports (South Carolina).

efl external fluid loss.

efm external fetal monitor.

efo earnings from operations.

efp endoneural fluid pressure.

efr effective filtration rate.

efs electric foot shock.

eft electronic funds transfer.

EFTA European Free Trade Association.

efv extracellular fluid volume.

efw estimated fetal weight.

efy end of the fiscal year.

EG, eg Egypt; for example (exempli gratia); edge grain; esophagogastrectomy; external genitalia.

ega estimated gestational age.

egc early gastric cancer.

egf epidermal growth factor.

egg electrogastrogram.

EGL, egl Encyclopedia of Georgia Law; eosinophilic granuloma of the lung.

egm electrogram.

eh extra hazardous; environment and heredity; early healed.

e&h environment and heredity.

ehb elevate head of bed.

ehbd extrahepatic bile duct.

ehbf extrahepatic blood flow.

ehc extended health care; enterohepatic clearance.

ehf extremely high frequency; epidermic hemorrhagic fever.

ehl extensor hallucis longus.

eho extrahepatic obstruction.

ehp effective horsepower.

eht essential hypertension.

ehv electric heat vector.

EI, ei East Indies; environmental impact; endorsement irregular; external intervention; electron impact; enzyme inhibitor.

e/i expiration/inspiration.

E&I English and Irish Appeals, House of Lords (England).

EIA, eia Electronic Industries Association; exercise induced asthma.

EIB, eib Export Import Bank; European Investment Bank; exercise induced bronchospasm.

eic equipment identification code.

eid electroimmunodiffusion; electronic induction desorption.

eim excitability inducing material.

eip extensor indicis proprius.

eis environmental impact statement; epidemic intelligence service; endoscopic injection sclerosis.

eiv external iliac vein.

ej elbow jerk.

ejusd of the same (ejusdem).

ek or **ekg** electrocardiogram.

eky electrokymogram.

El, el Elchie's Decisions (Scotland); elections law; electricity; eldest; elevated; exercise limit; early latent; external lamina; elbow.

El & B Ellis and Blackburn's Queen's Bench Reports (England).

EL & Eq English Law and Equity Reports.

ela endotoxin like activity.

ELAP Emergency Legal Assistance Project.

elb early light breakfast; elbow.

El B&E Ellis, Blackburn, and Ellis' Queen's Bench Reports (England).

El Cas Election Cases.

Elchies Elchies' Decisions (Scotland).

ele engine life expectancy.

elec electricity.

elect elective.

Elect Cas Armstrong's Election Cases (New York).

Elect Rep Election Reports (Ontario).

elem elementary.

elev elevate.

elf extremely low frequency; elective low forceps.

ELGB Emergency Loan Guarantee Board.

ELI, eli Environmental Law Institute; exercise lability index.

elix elixir.

elj executive, legislative, judicial.

Ell & B Ellis and Blackburn's Queen's Bench Reports (England).

Ell Bl & E Ellis, Blackburn, and Ellis' Queen's Bench Reports (England).

Ell & El Ellis and Ellis' Queen's Bench Reports (England).

Ell B&S Ellis, Best, and Smith's Queen's Bench Reports (England).

elm element; external limiting membrane.

elp endogenous limbic potential.

ELR Eastern Law Reporter (Canada).

ELS, els Environmental Law Society; electron loss spectroscopy.

El Sal El Salvador.

Els W Bl Elsley's Edition of William Blackstone's King's Bench Reports (England).

elt enforcement of laws and treaties; emergency locator transmitter; euglobulin lysis time.

em emergency message; enlisted man; end-of-medium character; electron microscope; ejection murmur; emphysema; erythromycin; early memory.

e&m endocrine and metabolism.

EMA, ema Envelope Manufacturers Association; Electronics Manufacturers Association; electronic microanalyzer; epithelial membrane antigen.

Em App Emergency Court of Appeals.

emb embassy; embargo; embankment; embryo; explosive mental behavior.

EMBASE Excerpta Medica Database.

embr embryo.

emc encephalomyocarditis.

em con emission control.

emd esophageal mobility disorder.

em dash a dash equal to the width of one em (see em space).

emer emergency.

emf electromagnetic force; erythrocyte maturation factor.

emg eye movement gauge; electromyogram.

emh educable mentally handicapped.

emi electromagnetic interference.

emic emergency maternity and infant care.

eml effective mandibular length.

emma eye movement measuring apparatus.

Emory LJ Emory Law Journal.

emp employment; end of month payment; electromechanical power; external membrane protein; electromagnetic pulse.

Empl Rel LJ Employee Relations Law Journal.

emr eye movement recording; educable mentally retarded.

ems engineering master schedule; early morning specimen; emergency medical system.

em space the letter occupied by the capital letter M in the font being used.

emt emergency medical treatment; emergency medical technician.

Emu, emu European Monetary Unit; electromagnetic unit; early morning urine.

emul emulsion.

en exception noted; enemy; erythema nodosum; electronarcosis; enrolled nurse; enema.

encl enclosure.

Enc Pl & Pr Encyclopedia of Pleading and Practice.

Enc US Sup Ct Rep Encyclopedia Of United States Supreme Court Reports.

end endorsement; elective node dissection.

ENDEX Environmental Data Index.

Energy LJ Energy Law Journal.

Eng, eng English's Reports (Arkansas); England; engineer; engine; electronic news gathering; electronystagmogram.

Eng Adm English Admiralty Reports.

Eng & Ir English and Irish Appeals, House of Lords (England).

Eng CC or **Eng Cr Cas** English Crown Cases.

Eng CL English Common Law Reports.

Eng Ecc R English Ecclesiastical Reports.

Eng Ex English Exchequer.

Eng Hist Rev English Historical Review.

Eng Ir App English Reports, English and Irish Appeals.

Eng Judg English Judges (Scotland).

Eng L & Eq English Law and Equity Reports.

Eng Rep English Reports, Full Reprint.

Eng Rul Cas English Ruling Cases.

Eng Ry & C Cas English Railway and Canal Cases.

Eng Sc Ecc English and Scotch Ecclesiastical Reports.

eni elective neck irradiation.

eniac electronic numerical integrator and calculator.

enl enlistment.

enq enquiry character.

enr en route.

ens enteral nutritional support; enteric nervous system.

en space a fixed space equal to half the width of the type size being used.

ent entrance; entomology; eyes, nose, throat; entranodular tissue.

entom entomology.

env envoy.

Envt Aff Environmental Affairs.

Envt F Environmental Forum.

Envt L Rev Environmental Law Review.

Envt L Rptr Environmental Law Reporter.

envmt environment.

EO, eo Executive Order; errors and omissions; ex officio; eyes open; elbow orthosis.

eoa examination, opinion, and advice; effective orifice area.

EOB, eob Executive Office Building; emergency observation bed.

eod expected occupancy date; end of day; entry on duty.

eoe errors and omissions excepted; equal opportunity employer.

eof end of file.

eofy end of fiscal year.

eog educational opportunity grant; electrooculogram.

eohp except as otherwise herein provided.

eoj extrahepatic obstructive jaundice.

eol end of life.

eom end of message; end of month; error of measurement; extra ocular movements.

EOP, eop Executive Office of the President; Equal Opportunity Program; employee ownership plan; emergency outpatient.

eor end of run.

eos eosinophil.

eot end of transmission; end of tape; effective oxygen transport.

eoy end of year.

EP, ep excess profits; extraordinary and plenipotentiary; electroplate; electric power; extended play; extreme pressure; enzyme product; edible portion; ectopic pregnancy; erythropoietic porphyria.

e&p earnings and profits; extraordinary and plenipotentiary.

EPA, epa Environmental Protection Agency; erect posterior anterior; extrinsic plasminogen activator.

EPALA El Paso Association of Legal Assistants.

EPB Economic Policy Board.

EPC, epc English Prize Cases; editor presentation copy; environmental pollution control; external pneumatic compression.

EPD, epd Employment Practices Decisions (Commerce Clearing House); excess profits duty; effective pressor dose.

epe emergency passenger exit.

epf early pregnancy factor.

epi epinephrine.

epid epidemic.

epil epilogue; epilepsy.

Epis, epis Episcopal; episiotomy.

epl extensor pollicis longus; effective patient life.

epm energy protein malnutrition.

epp excess personal property; equal pressure point.

epr electrophrenic respiration.

EPRI Environmental Protection Research Institute.

eprom erasable programmable read-only memory.

eps earnings per share; emergency power supply; expressed prostatic secretion.

ept excess profits tax; early pregnancy test.

epte existed prior to entry.

epts existed prior to service.

eq equivalent; equilibrium; equal; equitable; equator; educational quotient; environmental quality.

Eq Cas Equity Cases (Modern Reports) (England).

eqp equipment.

Eq Rep Equity Reports (England); Harper's Equity Reports (South Carolina); Gilbert's Equity Reports (England).

equiv equivalency.

ER, Er, er English Reports; East's King's Bench Reports (England); Election Reports (Ontario); erbium; evoked response; erroneous; emergency room; ejection rate; extended release; endoplasmic reticulum; external resistance; esophageal rupture.

e&r examination and report.

ERA, era Equal Rights Amendment; Economic Regulatory Association; expedited response action; estrogen receptor assay; electric response activity.

ERC Environmental Reporter Cases; English Ruling Cases; Eastern Regional Conference.

ercp endoscopic retrograde cholangiopancreatography.

erd evoked response detector; emergency response division.

erg electron radiography.

ERI Environmental Research Institute.

ERIC Educational Resources Information Center.

ERISA Employee Retirement Income Security Act.

erm extended radical mastectomy.

erom erasable read only memory.

erp estrogen receptor protein.

erpf effective renal plasma flow.

err erroneous.

Err & App Errors and Appeals Reports (Upper Canada).

Ersk D Erskine's Decisions (Georgia).

ert environmental response team; estrogen replacement therapy; external radiation therapy.

erv expiratory reserve volume.

Es, es einsteinium; executive secretary; employment striker; enema saponis; electrostatic; electroshock; enzyme substrate; endoscopic sphincterotomy.

ESA Euthanasia Society of America; Employment Standards Association.

esb electrical stimulation of the brain.

esc escape character.

E Sch L Rev Eastern School Law Review.

esd estimated shipping date; environmental services division; emission spectrometric detector.

ESEA Elementary and Secondary Education Act.

esg estrogen.

esi epidural steroid injection.

ESL English as a second language.

esm ejection systolic murmur.

esn essential; educationally subnormal.

eso esophagus.

esop employee stock ownership plan.

Esp, esp Espinasse's Nisi Prius Reports (England); espionage; exchange sale property; especially; extra sensory perception.

espg espionage.

Esq Esquire.

esr erythrocyte sedimentation rate.

ess electronic switching system; essence; excited skin syndrome.

EST, est Eastern Standard Time; Erhard Seminars Training; estate; estuary; estimate; exercise stress test; electroshock therapy.

Est & Tr Estates and Trusts.

este estate.

Estee Estee's District Court Reports (Hawaii).

est wt estimated weight.

esv esophageal valve.

ET, Et, et Estate and Gift Tax Ruling; Egypt; Ethiopia; Eastern Time; ethyl; etiology; environmental test; extraterrestrial; electrical transcription; ephemeris time; elapsed time; eustachian tube; endotracheal tube.

ETA, eta Employment and Training Administration; estimated time of arrival; electron transfer agent; endotracheal airway.

et al and others (et alia).

etb end of transmission block.

etc and so forth (et cetera); estimated time of conception.

etd estimated time of departure; eustachian tube dysfunction.

etf eustachian tube function.

ETH, eth Ethiopia; ethics; ether; ethionamide.

eti extraterrestrial intelligence.

etim elapsed time.

etiol etiology.

etkm every test known to man.

etlt equal to or less than.

eto estimated time of ovulation.

etoh ethyl alcohol.

etox ethylene oxide.

etp eustachian tube pressure; entire treatment period.

ETS, ets Educational Testing Service; expiration of term of service.

et seq and following (et sequens).

etsp entitled to severance pay.

ett exercise tolerance test; endotracheal tube.

etu emergency treatment unit; emergency and trauma unit.

et ux and wife (et uxor).

ETV Educational Television.

etx end of text.

ety etymology.

Eu, eu European; europium; etiology unknown; expected utility; emergency unit.

eua examination under anesthesia.

Euer Euer Doctrina Placitandi (England).

eul expected upper limit.

eum external urethral meatus.

euo emergency use only.

eup experimental use permit; estimated unit price; extrauterine pregnancy.

Eur European.

Eur LD European Law Digest.

Eur Parl Deb European Parliamentary Debates.

Eur TS European Treaty Series.

Eur Y European Yearbook.

euv extreme ultraviolet laser.

ev electron volt; extravehicular; evangelical; extravascular; eversion; evoked; enterovirus.

eval evaluation.

Evans Evans' Reports

(Washington Territory).

evap evaporation.

evd external ventricular drainage.

eve evening.

evg or **evng** evening.

evi endocardial, vascular, interstitial.

evid evidence.

evlw extravascular lung water.

evp executive vice president.

evr evoked visual response.

evs endoscopic variceal sclerosis.

ew elsewhere; enlisted woman; emergency ward; extensive wound.

ewb estrogen withdrawal bleeding.

ewi entered without inspection.

ewl evaporative water loss.

EWLTP Earl Warren Legal Training Program.

ewr early warning radar.

eww extended work week.

Ex, ex Exchequer Reports (England); without; example; exempt; exhibit; export; extra; executive; express; exchange; exposure; extraction; examination; exacerbation.

exam examination.

examr examiner.

exc excellent; excepted; exchange; excuse; excision.

exc bx excisional biopsy.

Exch, exch Exchequer; exchange.

Exch Can Exchequer Court Reports (Canada).

Exch Rep Exchequer Reports, Welsby, Hurlstone and Gordon (England).

excl exclusive.

excpt exception.

Ex CR Exchequer Court Reports (Canada).

exd examined.

Ex Div, ex div Exchequer Division Law Reports (England); ex dividend.

exec executor.

Exec Or Executive Order.

EXIM Export Import Bank.

exmr examiner.

exo exophoria.

EXOP Executive Office of the President.

exor or **exr** executor.

exp expense; experience; expiration; expired; expulsion; export; exposure.

expc experience.

expec, expect expectorant.

expend or **expnt** expenditure.

exper experience; experiment.

expl exploratory.

exp lap exploratory laparotomy.

expt export; expert; expectorant.

expy expressway.

exr executor.

ex rel by the relation of (ex relatione).

exrx or **exx** executrix.

exs expenses; externally supported.

ext exterior; extend; extract; exterior; external; extremity.

extm in accordance with the testament of (ex-testamento).

Extra Ca Extraterritorial Cases, United States Court for China.

extrem extremities.

exu excretory urogram.

exx executrix; examples.

Eyre Eyre's King's Bench Reports (England).

ez eczema.

F, f Federal Reporter (2d: Second Series); February; Friday; France; franc; false; finance; frequency; failure; fire; fixed; final; foot; formula; franchise; the number 15 (in the hexadecimal number system); fahrenheit; fluorine; father; female; filial; fluid; flow; fracture; feces.

F2d Federal Reporter, Second Series.

FA, fa Families Anonymous; felonious assault; free alongside; freight agent; financial advisor; free of all average; food additive; family allowance; first aid; femoral artery; fatty acids; florescent antibody; false aneurysm.

f/a fetus active.

f&a fore and aft.

FAA, faa Federal Aviation Administration; free of all average; folic acid antagonist.

FAAP Fellow of the American Academy of Pediatrics.

FAAR Feminist Alliance Against Rape.

fab fabricated; functional arm brace; formalin ammonium bromide.

fabf femoral artery blood flow.

fabx fire alarm box

FAC, fac Federal Advisory Council; fast as you can; faculty; factor; facsimile.

FACA Federal Advisory Committee Act; Fellow of the American College of Apothecaries; Fellow of the American College of Anesthetists.

FACAl Fellow of the American College of Allergists.

FACAn Fellow of the American College of Anesthesiologists.

FACC Fellow of the American College of Cardiology.

FACD Fellow of the American College of Dentists.

FACFP Fellow of the American College of Family Physicians.

FACFS Fellow of the American College of Foot Surgeons.

FACG Fellow of the American College of Gastroenterology.

Fac L Rev Faculty of Law Review (Toronto).

FACO Fellow of the American College of Otolaryngology.

FACOG Fellow of the American College of Obstetricians and Gynecologists.

FACP Fellow of the American College of Physicians.

FACR Fellow of the American College of Radiology.

FACS, facs Fellow of the American College of Surgeons; facsimile.

FAD, fad Federal Antitrust Decisions; funding authorization document; free air delivered; flavin adenine dinucleotide.

FADA Federal Asset Disposition Association.

faf fatty acid free.

fagt first available government transportation.

FAH, fah Federation of American Hospitals; fahrenheit.

FAHRB Federation of Associations of Health Regulatory Boards.

fai fly as is; first aid instructor; functional aerobic impairment.

FAIA Fellow of the American Institute of Architects.

FAIC Fellow of the American Institute of Criminology.

FAIEE Fellow of the American Institute of Electrical Engineers.

Fair, fair Fairfield's Reports (Maine); fair and impartial random access.

faj fused apophyseal joints.

FALA Fairbanks Association of Legal Assistants.

Falc Falconer's Court of Session Cases (Scotland).

Falc & F Falconer and Fitzherbert's Election Cases (England).

FALJC Federal Administrative Law Judges Conference.

fam family; foreign air mail.

FAMA Fellow of the American Medical Association.

Fam L Comm Family Law Commentator.

Fam LQ Family Law Quarterly.

Fam Law Rep Family Law Reporter.

f&a fore and aft.

f&d freight and demurrage.

F&F, f&f Foster and Finlanson's Nisi Prius Reports (England); furniture and fixtures.

fana fluorescent antinuclear antibody.

FAO Field Audit Office; United Nations Food and Agricultural Organization.

fap Fortran assembly language; femoral artery pressure; familial amyloid polyneuropathy.

FAPA Fellow of the American Psychiatric Association; Fellow of the American Psychological Association; Fellow of the American Psychoanalytic Association.

FAPHA Fellow of the American Public Health Association.

faq fair average quality.

FAR, Far, far Federal Aviation Regulations; Farresley's Holt's King's Bench Reports (England); floor area ratio.

FAS, fas Foreign Agricultural Service; Federation of American Scientists; free alongside ship; firsts and seconds; fetal alcohol syndrome.

FASB Federal Accounting Standards Board.

fast flexible algebraic scientific translator.

fat fluorescent antibody test; family attitudes test.

Fawc Fawcett's Court of References Reports (England).

fax facsimile.

FB, fb Fishery Board; fire brigade; freight bill; foreign body; feedback; fasting blood sugar.

FBA, fba Federal Bar Association; fecal bile acid.

FBC Fonblanque's Bankruptcy Cases (England); Foreign Base Company.

FBCI Foreign Base Company Income.

FBCSI Foreign Base Company Sales Income.

fbd functional bowel disorder.

fbe full blood examination.

fbf forearm blood flow.

FBI, fbi Federal Bureau of Investigation; flossing, brushing, irrigation.

FBILEB Federal Bureau of Investigation Law Enforcement Bulletin.

fbm foot board measure; fetal breathing movement.

fbo for the benefit of.

fbp femoral blood pressure.

fbs fasting blood sugar; fetal bovine serum.

fbt full berth terms.

FC, fc Federal Cases; Faculty Collection of Decisions (Scotland); Federal Court; bequest in trust (fidei commissum); finance charge; full charge; facilities contract; foreign currency; flood control; font change; fuel cell; frontal cortex; foster care.

FCA, fca Federal Code Annotated; Farm Credit Administration; Federal Communications Act; fracture, complete, angulated.

FCAP Fellow of the College of American Pathologists.

F Carr Cas Federal Carrier Cases (Commerce Clearing House).

fc&s free of capture and seizure.

FCBA Federal Communications Bar Association.

FCC, fcc Federal Communications Commission; falsely claiming citizenship; first class certificate; fluid convection cathode; fracture, complete, compound.

f/cc fiber/per cubic centimeter.

FCCA Federal Court Clerks Association.

fccc fracture, complete, compound, comminuted.

fcd focal cytoplasmic degradation.

fcf fetal cardiac frequency.

FCGP Fellow of the College of General Practitioners.

fci food chemical intolerance.

FCIC Federal Crop Insurance Corporation.

fcj foreign criminal jurisdiction.

fdm frequency division multiplexing.

FCO Federal Coordinating Officer.

FCPC Fair Campaign Practices Committee.

FCPS Fellow of the College of Physicians and Surgeons.

fcr fractional catabolic rate.

FCRA Fair Credit Reporting Act.

fcs free of capture and seizure; fecal containment system.

FCSC Foreign Claims Settlement Commission.

fcsrcc free of capture, seizure, riots, and civil commotions.

fcst forecast.

fct function.

FCU, fcu Federal Credit Union; fraud control unit.

Fcx frontal cortex.

Fd, fd ferredoxin; frequency times deviation; freight and demurrage; fire department; free delivery; frequency deviation; forceps delivery; fetal danger; fatal dose; family doctor; freeze dried; follicular diameter.

f&d freight and demurrage.

FDA Food and Drug Administration.

fdbl fecal daily blood loss.

FDCA Food, Drug, and Cosmetic Act.

FD Cosm L Rep Food, Drug, and Cosmetic Law Reporter (Commerce Clearing House).

fde final drug evaluation.

fdf fast death factor.

fdg feeding.

fdi formal documents issued.

FDIA Federal Deposit Insurance Act.

FDIC Federal Deposit Insurance Corporation.

FDIP Foreign Direct Investment Program.

fdiu fetal death in utero.

FDLI Food and Drug Law Institute.

fdlmp first day of last menstrual period.

fdos floppy disk operating system.

fdt frontodextra transversa.

fdv friend disease virus.

fdz fetal danger zone.

Fe, fe iron (ferrum); field engineer; fraudulent enlistment; format effector; freely eating; fatty ester; fetal erythroblastosis; fecal emesis.

FEA Federal Energy Administration; Foreign Economic Administration.

FEAA Federal Employees Appeal Authority.

FEB, Feb, feb Fair Employment Board; February; febris (fever).

FEC, fec Federal Elections Commission; forced expiratory capacity.

FECA Federal Employees Compensation Act.

Fed, fed Federal Reporter, First Series; federal; federation.

Fed BJ Federal Bar Journal.

Fed BAJ Federal Bar Association Journal.

Fed Car Rep Federal Carriers Reporter (Commerce Clearing House).

Fed Cas Federal Cases.

Fed Comm BJ Federal Communications Bar Journal.

Fed Est & Gift Tax Rep Federal Estate and Gift Tax Reporter (Commerce Clearing House).

Fed Ins CQ Federal Insurance Counsel Quarterly.

Fed Jur Federal Juror.

Fed L Rep Federal Law Reports.

Fed L Rev Federal Law Review.

Fedn Ins CQ Federation of Insurance Counsel Quarterly.

Fed Prob Federal Probation.

Fed RD Federal Rules Decisions.

Fed Reg Federal Register.

Fed Rep Federal Reporter.

Fed Rules Serv Federal Rules Service (2d: Second Series).

fed spec federal specification.

Fed Supp Federal Supplement.

fef forced expiratory flow.

FEGLI Federal Employees Group Life Insurance.

FEHBA Federal Employees Health Benefits Act.

fel felony.

felc friend erythroleukemia cell.

fem female; femur; femoral.

FEMA Federal Emergency Management Agency; Farm Equipment Manufacturers Association.

FEP, fep Fair Employment Practice Cases (Bureau of National Affairs); free erythrocyte protoporphyrin.

FEPC Fair Employment Practices Commission.

FEPCA Federal Environmental Pesticide Control Act.

Fer iron (ferrum).

FERA Federal Emergency Relief Administration.

Ferg Cons Fergusson's Consistory, Divorce (Scotland).

Fergusson Fergusson of Kilkeran (Scotland).

fes forced expiratory spirogram.

fet federal excise tax; forced expiratory time; fetus.

FETC Federal Excise Tax Council.

feuo for external use only.

fev1 forced expiratory volume in one second.

FEVA Federal Employees Veterans Association.

ff freight forwarder; fixed fee; furniture and fixtures; fixed focus; form feed; foster father; and the following; fat free.

F&F, f&f Foster and Finlanson's Nisi Prius Reports (England); furniture and fixtures.

FFA, ffa Federal Firearms Act; Future Farmers of America; foreign freight agent; full freight allowed; free fatty acid; free from alongside; free from average.

FFB, ffb Federal Financing Bank; flexible fiberoptic bronchoscopy.

ffc full faith and credit; free from chlorine.

FFCB Federal Farm Credit Board.

FFDA Federated Funeral Directors of America.

FFDCA Federal Food, Drug, and Cosmetic Act.

ffg friendly foreign government.

ffi free from infection.

FFIEC Federal Financial Institutions Examination Council.

ffp fresh frozen plasma.

ffpc firm fixed price contract.

ffs fee for service; focused feasibility study.

fft for further transfer.

ffw fat free weight.

fg fuel gas; flat grain; fine grain; fast glycolytic.

fga foreign general agent; free of general average.

FGAA Federal Government Accountants Association.

fgcm field general court martial.

fgd fatal granulomatous disease.

fgf father's grandfather.

fgm father's grandmother.

fgn foreign.

FGSA Fellow of the Geological Society of America.

fgt freight; fluorescent gonorrhea test; female genital tract.

fh flight hour; family history; fire hydrant; fetal heart.

FHA, fha Federal Highway Administration; Federal Housing Administration; familial hypoplastic anemia.

FHAI Federal Housing Authority Insurance.

FHC Family Health Center.

fhd family history of diabetes.

fhf fulminant hepatic failure.

FHFB Federal Housing Finance Board.

FHL, fhl Fraser's House of Lords Reports (Scotland); functional hearing loss.

FHLB Federal Home Loan Bank.

FHLBB Federal Home Loan Bank Board.

FHLBS Federal Home Loan Bank System.

FHLMC Federal Home Loan Mortgage Corporation.

fhn family history negative.

fhp family history positive.

FHR, fhr Fund for Human Rights; fetal heart rate.

FHSA Federal Hazardous Substances Act.

fht fetal heart tone.

FHWA Federal Highway Administration.

FI, fi Finland; fixed interval; furnished/installed; for instance; flood insurance; forced inspiration.

FI Arb Fellow of the Institute of Arbitrators.

fib fibrosis.

FIC, fic Federation of Insurance Counsel; Federal Information Center; freight, insurance, carriage.

FICA Federal Insurance Contributions Act.

FICD Fellow of the International College of Dentists.

FICO Financing Corporation.

FICS Fellow of the International College of Surgeons.

fid fiduciary.

Fid L Chron Fiduciary Law Chronicle.

fifo first in - first out.

FIFRA Federal Insecticide, Fungicide, and Rodenticide Act.

fih fat induced hyperglycemia.

fil filter; father in law; filial; filament.

filt filter.

Fin, fin Finch's Chancery Reports (England); Finland; finance; finish; fine intestinal needle.

fina following items not available.

fio free in and out.

FIP Fellow of the Institute of Physics.

fips federal information processing standards.

FIPSE Fund for Improvement of Postsecondary Education.

Fire & Casualty Cas Fire and Casualty Cases (Commerce Clearing House).

FIRREA Financial Institutions

Reform, Recovery and Enforcement Act.

fis forced inspiratory spirogram.

FISC, fisc Foreign International Sales Corporation; fiscal.

Fish Pat Cas Fisher's Patent Cases.

Fish Pat Rep Fisher's Patent Reports.

Fish Pr Cas Fisher's Prize Cases.

FISL Federally Insured Student Loan.

fiss fissure.

fit free of income tax; field investigation team; foreign independent travel.

fitw federal income tax withholding.

Fitzg Fitzgibbon's King's Bench Reports (England).

Fitzh Fitzherbert's Abridgment (England).

Fitzh NB Fitzherbert's Natura Brevium (England).

fiuo for internal use only.

FJC Federal Judicial Center.

FK Falkland Islands.

FL, Fl, fl Florida; florentium; full load; flood; fuel; fluid; foot lambert; foreign language; fatty liver; fluorescent; frontal lobe.

FLA, fla Florida Legal Assistants; frontolaeva anterior.

Fla & K Flanagan and Kelly's Rolls (Ireland).

Fla BJ Florida Bar Journal.

flac flaccid.

Fla Jur Florida Jurisprudence.

Fla LJ Florida Law Journal.

Flan & Kel Flanagan and Kelly's Rolls (Ireland).

Fla St ULR Florida State University Law Review.

Fla St UL Rev Florida State University Law Review.

Fla Supp Florida Supplement.

FLBA Federal Land Bank Association.

flc friend leukemia cell; fatty liver cell.

fld fibrotic lung disease; fluid.

FLETC Federal Law Enforcement Training Center.

FLEX, flex Federal Licensing Exam; flexion.

FLI Food Law Institute.

Flip, flip Flippin's Circuit Court Reports; flexible loan insurance plan.

FLJ Fortnightly Law Journal (Canada); Forum Law Journal.

flks fatty liver and kidney syndrome.

FLLS Family Location and Legal Service.

flmb flammable.

fl oz fluid ounce.

FLP Florida Law and Practice.

FLQ Front de Liberation du Quebec.

FLR Family Law Reporter; Federal Law Reports (India).

FLRC Federal Labor Relations Council.

FL Rev Federal Law Review.

fls family location service.

FLSA Fair Labor Standards Act.

fluoro fluoroscopy.

flv friend (or feline) leukemia virus.

FM, Fm, fm Franklin Mint; foreign mission; fermium; forensic medicine; farm; form; from; formerly married; flight mechanic; frequency modulation; full mouth; face mask; fetal movement; fetal monitor.

FMA Food Merchandisers of America; Financial Management Association.

FMB Federal Maritime Board.

FMC, fmc Federal Maritime Commission; Fund for Modern Courts; facilities management contract.

FMCS Federal Mediation and Conciliation Service.

fmd family medical doctor; foot and mouth disease; fibromuscular disease.

fme full mouth extraction.

fmf fetal movement felt; familial Mediterranean fever.

fmg foreign medical graduate; fine mesh gauze.

fmh family medical history; feto-maternal hemorrhage.

FmHA Farmers Home Administration.

FMHC Federation of Mental Health Centers.

FMI Food Marketing Institute.

FMIA Federal Meat Inspection Act.

fmn flavin mononucleotide; first malignant neoplasm.

fmp first menstrual period; fructose monophosphate.

FMPP Federal Merit Promotion Program.

fmv fair market value.

fmvss federal motor vehicle safety standard.

fmx full mouth x-ray.

fn fusion; footnote; false negative.

fnf femoral neck fracture.

F neg false negative.

FNMA Federal National Mortgage Association.

FNP Family Nurse Practitioner.

FNS Food and Nutrition Service.

fo firm offer; free overside; finance officer; fuel oil; foreign office; foot orthosis; fiberoptic.

FOA or FOIA Freedom of Information Act.

foa fugitive, other authorities.

foavf failure of all vital forces.

fob free on board; freight on board; foot of bed; fecal occult blood; foreign object/body.

foc free of charge; frequency of contact.

fod free of damage; free of disease.

FOE Friends of the Earth; Fraternal Order of Eagles.

Fogg Fogg's Reports (New Hampshire).

FOIA Freedom of Information Act.

FOID Freedom of Information Digest.

Fonbl Fonblanque's Bankruptcy Reports (England).

foob feet out of bed.

Food Cosmet Food and Cosmetics Toxicology.

Food Drug Cos L Rep Food,

Drug, and Cosmetics Law Reporter.

foq free on quay.

For, for Forrest's Exchequer Reports (England); forensic; foreign; forest; free on rail.

For Aff Foreign Affairs.

Forbes Forbes' Journal of the Session (Scotland).

for body foreign body.

Fordham Intl LF Fordham International Law Forum.

Fordham L Rev Fordham Law Review.

Fordham Urb LJ Fordham Urban Law Journal.

Form Forman's Reports (Illinois).

For Pol Bul Foreign Policy Bulletin.

Forr Forrest's Exchequer Reports (England); Forrester's Chancery Cases, temp. Talbot (England).

For Sci Forensic Science.

For Tax L Foreign Tax Law.

Fort Fortescue's King's Bench Reports (England).

Fort LJ Fortnightly Law Journal.

FORTRAN FORmula TRANslator.

fos fissura orbitalis superior.

Fost Foster's Reports (New Hampshire); Foster's Reports (Hawaii); Foster's Legal Chronicle Reports (Pennsylvania); Foster's Crown Cases (England).

Fost & Fin Foster and Finlanson's Nisi Prius Reports (England).

fot free on truck.

Fount Dec Fountainhall's Decisions (Scotland).

fouo for official use only.

FOW, fow Friends of the Wilderness; free on wagon.

Fox Fox's Registration Cases (England); Fox's Circuit and District Court Decisions.

Fox & S Fox and Smith's King's Bench Reports (Ireland).

Fox Pat Cas Fox's Patent, Trade Mark, Design, and Copyright Cases (Canada).

FP, fp fixed price; fully paid;

freight and passenger; family planning; foot pound; flavin phosphate; freezing point; frozen plasma; food poisoning; flavoprotein; family practitioner; false positive.

FPA, fpa Foreign Press Association; free of particular average; fluorophenylalanine.

FPB, fpb Federal Petroleum Board; femoral popliteal bypass.

FPC, fpc Federal Power Commission; fixed price contract; for private circulation; family planning clinic; fish protein concentrate; familial polyposis coli.

FPCR Federal Power Commission Reports.

fpd full paid; flame photometric detector.

fpe fixed price with escalation; first pass effect.

fpf fixed price firm; false positive fraction.

FPHC Foreign Personal Holding Company.

FPHCI Foreign Personal Holding Company Income.

FPI Federal Prison Industries.

fpic fixed price incentive contract.

fpl flexor pollicis longus.

FPLA, fpla Fair Packaging and Labeling Act; field programmable logic array.

FPLS Federal Parent Locator Service.

fpm feet per minute.

fpo federal protective order; field post office.

fpoe first port of entry.

FPR Federal Procurement Regulations.

fps federal prison system; feet per second; footpad swelling.

fpv fowl pest (plague) virus.

fpwa further particulars when available.

fqt frequent.

FR, Fr, fr Federal Register; Federal Reserve; France; Friday; francium; freight

release; franc; fruit; fire resistent; fixed ratio; frequent; flow rate; fluid restriction; failure rate.

FRA Federal Railroad Administration; Federal Reserve Act.

frac fracture.

fract fractional.

frag fragile; fragment.

FRAME Fund for the Replacement of Animals in Medical Experiments.

France France's Reports (Colorado).

Fraser Fraser's Court of Session Cases (Scotland).

FRB Federal Reserve Board.

fr bb fracture of both bones.

FRC, frc Federal Records Center; functional residual capacity; functional reserve capacity; frozen red cells.

FRD, frd Federal Rules Decisions; fraud.

Free Freeman's Reports (Illinois).

Free Ch Freeman's Chancery Reports (England); Freeman's Chancery Reports (Mississippi).

Free KB Freeman's King's Bench Reports (England).

Freem Freeman. See Free.

French French's Reports (New Hampshire).

freq frequent; frequency.

FRF FSLIC Resolution Fund.

FRG Federal Republic of Germany.

frjm full range joint motion.

FRLA Federal Regulation of Lobbying Act.

FRN Federal Reserve Note.

frof fire risk on freight.

from full range of motion.

FRS Federal Rules Service; Federal Reserve System.

frt freight; full recovery time.

fru fructose.

fs final settlement; feasibility study; food service; foreign service; please forward (faire suivre); factor of safety; file separator; facsimile; fracture, simple; frozen section; forearm supinated; full strength.

FSA Farm Security Administration; Federal Security Agency; Fellow of the Society of Actuaries.

fsb federal supplemental benefits.

FSC, fsc Federal Safety Council; fracture, simple, complete.

FSEE Federal Service Entrance Examination.

FSF Forensic Science Foundation.

fsg fasting serum glucose.

FSGB Foreign Service Grievance Board.

fsh follicle stimulating hormone.

fshrf follicle stimulating hormone releasing factor.

FSI Foreign Service Institute.

FSIS Food Safety and Inspection Act.

fsk frequency shift keying.

fsl formal semantics language.

FSLIC Federal Savings and Loan Insurance Corporation.

fsm free speech movement.

FSMB Federation of State Medical Boards.

FSP, fsp Food Stamp Program; familial spastic paraplegia.

FSRB Flight Safety Review Board.

F Supp Federal Supplement.

fsw field service worker.

ft foot; feet; fortified; full terms; full time; fibrous tissue; family therapy.

FTA, fta Federation of Tax Administrators; fluorescent treponemal antibody.

fta-abs fluorescent treponemal antibody absorption test.

ftb finger tip blood.

ftbd full term born dead.

FTC, ftc Federal Trade Commission; foreign tax credit.

FTCA Federal Tort Claims Act.

fte full time equivalent.

FTEC Federal Trial Examiners Conference.

fti federal tax included.

ftka failed to keep appointment.

ftlb full term living birth.

ftnd full term normal delivery.

FTR Federal Trade Reports.

FTS Federal Telecommunications System.

ftt failure to thrive; fructose tolerance test.

ftz federal trade zone.

fu fractional urinalysis.

f/u follow up.

fub functional uterine bleeding.

Fuller Fuller's Reports (Michigan).

fum fumigation.

fuo fever of unknown origin.

fuov follow up office visit.

fur furlough.

FUTA Federal Unemployment Tax Act.

fv on the back of the page (folio verso); fluid volume; friend virus; femoral vein.

fva friend virus anemia.

fvc forced vital capacity.

fvl femoral vein ligation.

fvm familial visceral myopathy.

FW, fw Falconer Weddell (syndrome); fresh water.

fwb full weight bearing.

fwd forward; front wheel drive.

fwdd forwarded.

FWPCA Federal Water Pollution Control Act.

FWPO Federal Wildlife Permit Office.

FWQA Federal Water Quality Administration.

fwy freeway.

fx foreign exchange; fracture.

fxd four times daily.

fy full year; fiscal year; ferry.

fyi for your information.

G, g Gale's Exchequer Reports (England); Germany; Greenwich; government; gas;

garage; goal; general; gravity; gram; gross; glycine; gender; gauss; immunoglobulin G; gravida.

GA, Ga, ga Gabon; General Appraisers; General Assembly; Gamblers Anonymous; Georgia; gallium; general average; general accounting; gauge; gestational age; general anesthesia.

GAA Gay Activists Alliance.

gaap generally accepted accounting principles

Ga App Georgia Appeals Reports.

gaas generally accepted auditing standards; generally accepted appraisal standards.

Ga BJ Georgia Bar Journal.

Ga Bus Law Georgia Business Lawyer.

gad glutamic acid decarboxylase.

Ga Dec Georgia Decisions.

gai guaranteed annual income.

Ga J Int & Comp L Georgia Journal of International and Comparative Law.

Gal, gal gallon; galactose.

GALA Georgia Association of Legal Assistants.

Galb Galbraith's Reports (Florida).

Galb & M Galbraith and Meek's Reports (Florida).

Gale Gale's Exchequer Reports (England).

Gale & D Gale and Davison's Queen's Bench Reports (England).

Ga LJ Georgia Law Journal.

Gall Gallison's Circuit Court Reports.

Ga L Rep Georgia Law Reports.

Ga L Rev Georgia Law Review.

G&D Gale and Davison's Queen's Bench Reports (England).

G&G Goldsmith & Guthrie's Reports (Missouri).

G&J Gill and Johnson's Reports (Maryland); Glyn and Jameson's Bankruptcy Reports (England).

G&R Geldert and Russell's Reports (Nova Scotia).

Garden Gardenhire's Reports (Missouri).

Gard NY Rep Gardiner's New York Reporter.

GAO General Accounting Office.

GARP Global Atmospheric Research Program.

gas general adaptation syndrome; generalized arteriosclerosis; gastric acid secretion.

gast gastrocnemius.

Ga St BJ Georgia State Bar Journal.

Ga Supp Georgia Supplement (Lester).

GATT General Agreement on Tariffs and Trade.

Gayarre Gayarre's Reports (Louisiana).

Gaz Weekly Law Gazette.

Gaz LR Gazette Law Reports.

GB, gb Great Britain; gold bond; goofball; gallbladder.

gbd gallbladder disease.

GBH gamma benzene hexachloride.

gbi globulin bound insulin.

gbl government bill of lading.

gbs gallbladder series; gastric bypass surgery.

gc general counsel; general condition; general circular; general circulation; gas chromatography; gonococcus; ganglion cell; gonorrhea.

gca general claims agent; giant cell arteritis; gastric cancerous area.

GCL, gcl Guild of Catholic Lawyers; ground controlled landing.

GCM, gcm General Counsel's Memorandum (Internal Revenue Service); general court martial.

G Coop G. Cooper's Chancery Reports (England).

gcr group conformity rating.

gcs glucocorticosteroid.

gct general care and treatment.

gcu gonococcal urethritis.

gcv gross caloric value; great cardiac vein.

GD, Gd, gd Grenada; gadolinium; good; granddaughter; general duty; gestational day; gastroduodenal; general delivery; general discharge.

G&D Gale and Davison's Queen's Bench Reports (England).

gdh glucose dehydrogenase.

gdm gestational diabetes mellitus.

gdp gross domestic product.

GDPA Greater Dayton Paralegal Association.

GDR German Democratic Republic.

gds goods.

Ge, ge germanium; greater than or equal to; gastroenterology; gastric emptying.

GED General Equivalency Diploma.

gej gaseous ejection.

Geld & M Geldart and Maddock's Chancery Reports (England).

Geld & O Geldert and Oxley's Decisions (Nova Scotia).

Geld & R Geldert and Russell's Reports (Nova Scotia).

gem growing equity mortgage.

gemp genetically engineered microbial pesticide.

gen general; generation; generator; gender; genetics; genitalia.

Gen Dig General Digest.

genit genitalia.

Geo Georgia.

Geo Dec Georgia Decisions.

geog geography.

geol geology.

Geo LJ Georgetown Law Journal.

geom geometric.

George George's Reports (Mississippi).

George Wash L Rev George Washington University Law Review.

Ger Germany.

GERR Government Employees Relations Reports (Bureau of National Affairs).

gest gestational.

gf grandfather; gastric fluid; germ free.

gfa general freight average; good fair average.

gfd government furnished data; gluten free diet.

gfi ground fault interrupter.

gfp gamma fetoprotein; glomerular filtered phosphate.

GFR, gfr West Germany (German Federal Republic); glomerular filtration rate.

gg gamma globulin.

G&G Goldsmith & Guthrie's Reports (Missouri).

G Gr G. Green's Reports (Iowa).

GH, gh Ghana; growth hormone; general hospital; general health; good health.

ghd growth hormone deficiency.

ghl guardhouse lawyer.

ghrf growth hormone releasing factor.

ghrif growth hormone release inhibiting factor.

GI, gi Gibraltar; growth and income; general issue; galvanized iron; gill; glucose intolerance; growth inhibition; gastrointestinal.

gia gastrointestinal anastomosis.

Gibb S Gibbon's Surrogate (New York).

Gibbs Gibbs' Reports (Michigan).

Giff Giffard's Chancery Reports (England).

Giff & H Giffard and Hemming's Chancery Reports (England).

gigo garbage in, garbage out.

gih gastrointestinal hormone.

Gil Gilman's Reports (Illinois).

Gill & J Gill and Johnson's Reports (Maryland).

Gil Gilman's Reports (Illinois); Gilmer's Reports (Virginia); Gilbert's Chancery Reports (England).

Gilb Gilbert's Chancery Reports (England).

Gilb CP Gilbert's Common Pleas Reports (England).

Gilb Cas Gilbert's Cases in Law and Equity (England).

Gild Gildersleeve's Reports (New Mexico).

Gilf Gilfillan's Reports (Minnesota).

Gill Gill's Reports (Maryland).

Gill & John Gill and Johnson's Reports (Maryland).

Gilm Gilmer's Reports (Virginia); Gilman's Reports (Illinois).

Gilm & Falc Gilmour and Falconer's Reports (Scotland).

Gilp Gilpin's Reports.

gip gastric inhibitory polypeptide.

gis gas in stomach.

git gastrointestinal tract.

gj grand jury.

G&J Gill and Johnson's Reports (Maryland); Glyn and Jameson's Bankruptcy Reports (England).

Gk Greek.

GL, gl Greenland; Graduate in Law; grand larceny; general ledger; gill; ground level; glaze; granular layer.

g/l grams per liter.

Gl & J Glyn and Jameson's Bankruptcy Reports (England).

Glanv Glanville's De Legibus et Consuetudinibus Angliae (England).

Glanv El Cas Glanville's Election Cases (England).

Glas Glascock's Reports (Ireland).

glau or **glc** glaucoma.

gld glutamate dehydrogenase.

Glendale L Rev Glendale Law Review.

Glenn Glenn's Reports (Louisiana).

glob globulin.

glp good laboratory practices.

GLR Gazette Law Reports (New Zealand).

Glu, glu glutamic acid; glucose.

gluc glucosidase.

gluc tol glucose tolerance.

glv gross leukemia virus.

Glyn & J Glyn and Jameson's Reports Bankruptcy (England).

GM, gm Greenwich Meridian; Geiger-Muller; General Motors; general mortgage; gram; grandmother; guided missile; general merchandise; general manager; genetic manipulation; gastric mucosa.

gma gross motor activities; glyceral methacrylate.

GMAT Graduate Management Admission Test.

gmb general mortgage bond; gastric mucosal barrier.

gmc general medical clinic.

gm cal gram calorie.

gmcu gracilis myocutaneous unit.

GM Dud Dudley's Reports (Georgia).

gme graduate medical education.

gmh germinal matrix hemorrhage.

gmp good manufacturing practice.

GMT Greenwich Mean Time.

gmw gram molecular weight.

GN, gn Guinea; Graduate Nurse; general; gun; glucagon; Gandy Nanta; gram negative.

gna general nursing assistance.

GNB, gnb Guinea-Bissau; gram negative bacillus.

gnc general nursing care; glandular neck cell.

gni gross national income.

GNMA Government National Mortgage Association.

gnp gross national product.

GnRH gonadotrophin releasing hormone.

go government owned; government obligation; general order; gonorrhea; glucose oxidase; gas and oxygen.

goco government owned, contractor operated.

god glucose oxidase.

Godb Godbolt's King's Bench Reports (England).

goe gas, oxygen, ether.

Goebel Goebel's Probate Reports (Ohio).

gogo government owned, government operated.

gok God only knows.

Gold & G Goldsmith & Guthrie's Reports (Missouri).

Golden Gate L Rev Golden Gate University Law Review.

Gong Gongwer's State Reports (Ohio).

Gonzaga L Rev Gonzaga Law Review.

GOP Republicans (Grand Old Party); government owned property.

goq glucose oxidation quotient.

gor general operating room.

Gordon Gordon's Reports (Colorado).

got goals of treatment.

Gottschall Gottschall's Reports (Ohio).

Gouldsb Gouldsborough's King's Bench Reports (England).

gov or **govt** government.

Govt Con Rep Government Contracts Reporter (Commerce Clearing House).

Gow Gow's Nisi Prius Reports (England).

gox gaseous oxygen.

gp group; general practitioner; government property; geographic position; general purpose; general processor; generalized programming; glucose phosphate; general paralysis; guinea pig; gastroplasty.

gpa general public assistance; general passenger agent; grade point average; guinea pig albumin.

GPB Government Patents Board.

gpc general purpose computer; giant papillary conjunctivitis.

gpd gallons per day.

g6pd glucose-6-phosphate dehydrogenase.

gpf glomerular plasma flow.

gpi general paralysis of the insane.

gpib general purpose interface bus.

gpm graduated payment mortgage; general preventive medicine.

GPO Government Printing Office.

gps general problem solver.

GPSA Gas Processors Suppliers Association.

gpss general purpose simulation system.

gpt glutamic pyruvic transaminase.

gp th group therapy.

Gr, gr See Green; Grant's Chancery Reports (Upper Canada); Greece; government regulation; grain; grade; grammar; gross; gravity; general reserve; general research; gamma rays; good recovery; generalized rash.

G&R Geldert and Russell's Reports (Nova Scotia).

Gra, gra Graham's Reports (Georgia); gated radionuclide angiography.

grad graduate; gradient.

grae generally regarded as effective.

Granger Granger's Reports (Ohio).

Grant Grant's Cases (Pennsylvania); Grant's Chancery Reports (Upper Canada).

Grant Err & App Grant's Error and Appeal (Upper Canada).

gras generally recognized as safe.

Grat Grattan's Reports (Virginia).

grav gravity.

Gray Gray's Reports (North Carolina); Gray's Reports (Massachusetts).

grd gender role definition.

GRE Graduate Record Examination.

Green Green's Reports (Rhode Island); Green's Reports (Oklahoma); Green's Reports (Maine); Green's Reports (New Jersey).

Green Ch Green's Equity Reports (New Jersey).

Green Cr Green's Criminal Law (England).

Greene Greene's Reports (New York); Greene's Reports (Iowa).

Green L Green's Law Reports (New Jersey).

Greenl Greenleaf's Reports (Maine).

Greenl Ov Cas Greenleaf's Overruled Cases.

Grein Pr Greiner's Practice (Louisiana).

grf growth-hormone releasing factor.

grgl groundwater residue guidance level.

GRI, gri Government Reports Index; Gas Research Institute; graduated retirement income.

grid gay related immunodeficiency.

Griffith Griffith's Reports (Indiana).

Grisw Griswold's Reports (Ohio).

grit grantor retained income trust.

grp group.

grs general revenue sharing; generalized retrieval system.

gr tr graphite treatment.

gr wt gross weight.

GS, gs General Schedule; General Sessions; grandson; gold standard; government service; general secretary; group separator; gauss; graft survival; general surgery; gallstone.

g/s gallons per second.

GSA, gsa General Services Administration; Genetics Society of America; Girl Scouts of America; general somatic afferent.

GSA BCA General Services Administration Board of Contract Appeals.

gsb graduated spinal block.

gsd genetically significant close; glycogen storage disease.

GSE Government Sponsored Enterprise.

gsf galactosemic fibroblast.

gsl guaranteed student loan.

gsn giant serotonin neuron.

GSR, gsr Gongwer's State Reports (Ohio); galvanic skin response.

gst graphic stress telethermometry.

gsw gun shot wound.

gswa gun shot wound to the abdomen.

GT, gt Greenwich Time; Guatemala; grand theft; gross ton; greater than; great toe; glucose tolerance; greater trochanter; group therapy; gastrostomy.

g/t granulation time.

gtc good till cancelled.

gtd guaranteed; gestational trophoblastic disease.

gtf glucose tolerance test; glucose tolerance factor.

gtn glomerulotubulonephritis.

gtow gross takeoff weight.

gtr galvanic tetanus ratio.

gts glucose transport system.

gtt glucose tolerance test; drops.

GU, gu Guam; guarantee; guinea; gastric ulcer; glucose uptake; genitourinary.

guar guarantee; guaranty.

GUARD Government Employees United Against Racial Discrimination.

Guat Guatemala.

Guild Prac Guild Practitioner.

Gunby Gunby's District Court Reports (Louisiana).

gus genitourinary system.

Guthrie Guthrie's Reports (Missouri).

GUY Guyana.

gv ground visibility; granulosis virus; gentian violet.

gvh government vehicle; graft versus host.

gvl graft versus leukemia.

gw gross weight; gigawatt; gradual withdrawal; general warning.

g/w glucose in water.

Gwill Gwillim's Tithe Cases (England).

gww guaranteed weekly wage.

GY, gy Guyana; gray.

gyn gynecology.

H, h Howard's Supreme Court Reports; Handy's Reports (Ohio); Hungary; husband; heir; heroin; homosexual; horizontal; harbor; hail; headquarters; height; humidity; heat; hazardous; heart disease; hygiene.

HA, Ha, ha Hatch Act; Hare's Vice Chancellor's Reports (England); hour angle; hazardous area; home address; headache; hearing aid; hospital admission; halothane anesthesia; hepatitis A.

HAA, haa Housing Assistance Administration; hearing aid amplifier.

Ha & Tw Hall and Twell's Chancery Reports (England).

hab habitual; habitat.

hab corp habeas corpus.

Had or **Hadl** Hadley's Reports (New Hampshire).

had hospital administration; hemadsorption.

Hadd Haddington's Manuscript Reports (Scotland).

hae hepatic artery embolization.

haf hepatic arterial flow.

Hagan Hagan's Reports (Utah).

Hagans Hagans' Reports (West Virginia).

Hagg Con Haggard's Consistory Reports (England).

Hagg Adm Haggard's Admiralty Reports (England).

Hagn & M Hagner and Miller's Reports (Maryland).

hai hemagglutination inhibition.

Hailes Dec Hailes' Decisions (Scotland).

hal halothane.

HALA Hawaii Association of Legal Assistants.

Hale Hale's Reports (California); Hale's Common Law (England).

Hale PC Hale's Pleas of the Crown (England).

Hall Hall's Reports (New Hampshire); Hall's Superior Court Reports (New York).

Hall & T Hall and Twell's Chancery Reports (England).

Hal Law Halsted's Law Reports (New Jersey).

Hallet Hallet's Reports (Colorado).

Hals Ch Halsted's Chancery Reports (New Jersey).

Halst or **Hals** Halsted's Law Reports (New Jersey).

Ham, ham Hammond's Reports (Ohio); Hammond's Reports (Georgia); hearing aid microphone; human albumin microsphere.

Ham A&O Hamerton, Allen and Otter's New Session Cases (England).

Hamlin Hamlin's Reports (Maine).

Hamline LR Hamline Law Review.

Hamm & J Hammond and Jackson's Reports (Georgia).

Hammond See Ham.

Han or **Handy** Handy's Reports (Ohio).

H&B Hudson and Brooke's King's Bench Reports (Ireland).

H&C Hurlstone and Coltman's Exchequer Reports (England).

H&D Hill and Denio's Reports, Lalor's Supplement (New York).

H&G Harris and Gill's Reports (Maryland); Hurlstone and Gordon's Reports (England).

H&H Horn and Hurlstone's Exchequer Reports (England); Harrison and Hodgin's Municipal Reports (Upper Canada).

H&J, h&j Harris and Johnson's Reports (Maryland); Hayes and Jones' Exchequer Reports (Ireland); Hammond and Jackson's Reports (Georgia); hyphenation and justification.

H&M Hening and Munford's Reports (Virginia); Hemming and Miller's Vice-Chancellor's Reports (England); Hagner and Miller's Reports (Maryland).

H&Mc Harris and McHenry's Reports (Maryland).

H&N, h&n Hurlstone and Norman's Exchequer Reports (England); head and neck.

h&p history and physical.

H&R Harrison and Rutherford's Common Pleas Reports (England).

H&S Harris & Simrall's Reports (Mississippi).

H&T, h&t Hall and Twell's Chancery Reports (England); hospitalization and treatment.

H&W Harrison and Wollaston's King's Bench Reports (England); Hurlstone and Walmsley's Exchequer Reports (England).

Hand Hand's Reports (New York).

Handy or **Han** Handy's Reports (Ohio).

Han NB Hannay's Reports (New Brunswick).

Hans or **Hansb** Hansbrough's Reports (Virginia).

hap humeral antibody production.

HAPAB Health Aspects of Pesticides Abstract Bulletin.

Har, har Harrington's Reports (Delaware); Harrington's Chancery Reports (Michigan); Harrison's Chancery Reports (Michigan); Harrison (Louisiana); harbor.

Har & Gil Harris and Gill's Reports (Maryland).

Harc Harcarse's Decisions (Scotland).

Har Del Harrington's Reports (Delaware).

Hardes Hardesty's Reports (Delaware).

Hardin Hardin's Reports (Kentucky).

Hardres Hardres' Exchequer Reports (England).

Hare Hare's Vice Chancellor's Reports (England).

Hare & W Hare and Wallace's American Leading Cases.

Harg Hargrove's Reports (North Carolina).

Harm Harmon's Reports (California).

Harp Harper's Conspiracy Cases (Maryland); Harper's Equity Reports (South Carolina);

Harper's Law Reports (South Carolina).

Harr Harrison's Reports (New Jersey); Harrison's Reports (Indiana).

Harr & G Harris and Gill's Reports (Maryland).

Harr & H Harrison and Hodgin's Municipal Reports (Upper Canada).

Harr & John Harris and Johnson's Reports (Maryland).

Harr & Mc Harris and McHenry's Reports (Maryland).

Harr & R Harrison and Rutherford's Common Pleas Reports (England).

Harr & S Harris & Simrall's Reports (Mississippi).

Harr & W Harrison and Wollaston's King's Bench Reports (England).

Harr Ch Harrison's Chancery Reports (Michigan).

Harr Con Harrison's Condensed Reports (Louisiana).

Harring Harrington's Reports (Delaware); Harrington's Chancery Reports (Michigan).

Harris Harris' Reports (Pennsylvania).

Harrison Harrison's Reports (New Jersey); Harrison's Reports (Indiana).

Hart Hartley's Reports (Texas).

Hart and Hart Hartley and Hartley's Reports (Texas)

Harv Bus Rev Harvard Business Review.

Harv Civ Rts-Civ Lib LR Harvard Civil Rights - Civil Liberties Law Review.

Harv Env L Rev Harvard Environmental Law Review.

Harv Int LJ Harvard International Law Journal.

Harv J Leg Harvard Journal on Legislation.

Harv J of L & Pub P Harvard Journal of Law and Public Policy.

Harv L Rev Harvard Law Review.

has hypertensive arteriosclerotic.

Hasb Hasbrouck's Reports (Idaho).

Hask Haskell's Reports (United States Courts in Maine).

Hast Hasting's Reports (Maine).

Hast Con Law Q Hastings Constitutional Law Quarterly.

Hast Int & Comp L Rev Hastings International and Comparative Law Review.

Hast LJ Hastings Law Journal.

hat head, arms, trunk.

hau hemagglutination unit.

HAV hepatitis A virus.

Havil Haviland's Reports (Prince Edward Island).

Hawaii BJ Hawaii Bar Journal.

Hawarde Hawarde's Star Chamber Cases (England).

Hawk Hawkins' Reports (Louisiana Annual).

Hawk PC Hawkins' Pleas of the Crown.

Hawks Hawks' Reports (North Carolina).

Hawl Hawley's Reports (Nevada).

Hay & H Hay and Hazelton's Circuit Court Reports.

Hay & M Hay and Marriott's Admiralty Reports (England).

Hayes & J Hayes and Jones' Exchequer Reports (Ireland).

Hayw Haywood's Reports (North Carolina); Haywood's Reports (Tennessee).

haz hazardous.

Haz Reg Hazard's Register (Pennsylvania).

HB, Hb, hb House Bill; hemoglobin; hand book; house breaking; heart block; hepatitis B; hold breakfast.

H&B Hudson and Brooke's King's Bench Reports (Ireland).

hbd has been drinking.

hbf hemoglobinuric bilious fever.

Hbg hemoglobin.

H Bl H. Blackstone's Common Pleas Reports (England).

HBO, hbo Home Box Office; hyperbaric oxygenation.

hbp high blood pressure.

HBr hydrobromic acid.

HBSAg hepatitis B surface antigen.

hbt human breast tumor.

HBV hepatitis B virus.

HC, hc House of Commons; house of correction; habitual criminal; hard copy; hand control; hydrocarbon; home care; head circumference; hepatic catalase; handicapped; hydrocarbon.

H&C Hurlstone and Coltman's Exchequer Reports (England).

hca hydrocortisone acetate.

hcap handicapped.

HCB, hcb House of Commons Bill; hexachlorobenzene.

hcc history of chief complaint; hepatitis contagiosa canis.

hcd high carbohydrate (caloric) diet.

hce human caused error.

hcee discharge under honorable conditions at the expiration of enlistment.

hcf heredity capillary fragility.

hcg human chorionic gonadotropin.

HCJ High Court of Justice.

HCL, H Cl, hcl hydrogen chloride; hydrochloric acid; hard contact lens; hairy cell leukemia.

hcm health care maintenance.

hcn hydrocyanic acid.

H Con Res House Concurrent Resolution.

hcp high cell passage; handicapped.

hcs hazard communication standard; human cord serum.

hct hundred count; hematocrit; homocytotrophic.

hctz hydrochlorothiazide.

hcu hyperplasia cystica uteri.

hcv human coronary viruses.

hcvd hypertensive cardiovascular disease.

HD, hd House Document; head; high density; honorable discharge; Huntington's disease; Hodgkin's disease; Hansen's disease; hearing disease; heart disease; high dose; hemodialysis.

H&D Hill and Denio's Reports, Lalor's Supplement (New York).

hdac headache.

hdc holder in due course.

hdd high dose depth.

hdh heart disease history.

hdl high density lipoprotein.

hdlc high level data link control.

hdlp high density lipoprotein.

H Doc House Document.

HDP hexose diphosphate.

hdqrs headquarters.

hds herniated disc syndrome.

hdsp hardship.

HDTV High Definition Tele Vision.

HE, He, he Hearing Examiner; helium; high school equivalency; high efficiency; highly explosive; hypophysectomy; heart; heredity/environment.

h&e hematoxylin and eosin.

HEA, hea Higher Education Act; human erythrocyte antigen.

Head Head's Reports (Tennessee).

Heath Heath's Reports (Maine).

hec human endothelial cell.

HED Hazard Evaluation Division.

Hedges Hedges' Reports (Montana).

heent head, ears, eyes, nose, and throat.

heg hemorrhagic erosive gastritis.

Heisk Heiskell's Reports (Tennessee).

hek human embryonic kidney.

hel human embryonic lung.

Helm Helm's Reports (Nevada).

HELP Hemophile Effort for Legal Protection.

hem hemorrhage; hematology.

hemi hemiparalysis.

Hem & M Hemming and Miller's Vice-Chancellor's Reports (England).

Heming Hemingway's Reports (Mississippi).

Hemp Hempstead's Circuit Court Reports.

Hen & Mun Hening and Munford's Reports (Virginia).

Hennepin Law Hennepin Lawyer.

hep human epithelia cell; hydroelectric power; high energy phosphate; high egg passage.

HEPAF High Efficiency Particulate Air Filter

Hepb Hepburn's Reports (California).

her hernia.

HERA Housewives for the Equal Rights Amendment.

hes human embryonic skin.

Het Hetley's Common Pleas Reports (England).

hev human enteric virus.

HEW Department of Health, Education and Welfare.

hex hexagon.

Hf, hf hafnium; half; high frequency; held for; human fibroblast; high fast; heart failure; hard feces.

hfc histamine forming capacity.

hfd high fiber diet.

hfi human fibroblast interferon; hereditary fructose intolerance.

hfm held for money; hemifacial microsomia.

hfo high frequency oscillation.

hfp hypofibrinogenic plasma.

hfr hold for release; high frequency.

hfs hemifacial spasm.

hft high frequency transduction.

Hg, hg mercury (hydrargyrum); hectogram; hypoglycemia; high glucose; herpes gestationis.

H&G Harris and Gill's Reports (Maryland); Hurlstone and Gordon's Reports (England).

hgb hemoglobin.

hgg human gamma globulin; herpetic geniculate ganglionitis.

hgh human growth hormone.

hgm hectogram; human glucose monitoring.

hgo human glucose output.

hgt height.

hgwy highway.

hh hiatal hernia; holistic health; hard of hearing.

H&H, h&h Horn and Hurlstone's Exchequer Reports (England); Harrison and Hodgin's Municipal Reports (Upper Canada); hemoglobin and hematocrit.

hha hereditary hemolytic anemia.

hhc home health care.

hhd hypertensive heart disease.

hhe household effects; health hazard evaluation.

hhf household furniture.

HHFA Housing and Home Finance Agency.

hhg household goods.

HHS Health and Human Services.

hht head halter traction.

HI, hi Hawaii; harassment and interdiction; hospital insurance; humidity index; hearing impaired; hydrogen iodide; histidine; hemagglutination inhibition.

HIA, hia Housing Industry Association; Health Industries Association; held in abeyance; heat infusion agar; hemagglutination inhibition antibody.

HIAA Health Insurance Association of America.

hib hemolytic immune body.

Hibb Hibbard's Reports (New Hampshire).

hid herniated intervertebral disc; headache, insomnia, depression.

hie human intestinal epithelium.

hif house of ill fame; higher intellectual function.

hig human immunoglobulin.

Higgins Higgins' Reports (Tennessee).

Hight Hight's Reports (Iowa).

Hill Hill's Reports (New York); Hill's Reports (South Carolina).

Hill & Den Hill and Denio's Reports, Lalor's Supplement (New York).

Hill Eq Hill's Equity Reports (South Carolina).

Hillyer Hillyer's Reports (California).

Hil T Hilart Term (England).

Hilt Hilton's Common Pleas Reports (New York).

him high impact; hepatitis infectious mononucleosis.

Hines Hines' Reports (Kentucky).

hipo hierarchy of input, processing, and output.

hir high irradiance response.

His, his history; hyperimmune serum; histidine.

hisg human immune serum globulin.

hit histamine inhalation test.

H&J, h&j Harris and Johnson's Reports (Maryland); Hayes and Jones' Exchequer Reports (Ireland); Hammond and Jackson's Reports (Georgia); hyphenation and justification.

HJR or **HJ Res** House Joint Resolution.

HK, hk Hong Kong; human kidney; hexokinase; head to knee.

hkh hyperkinetic heart (syndrome).

HL, hl House of Lords; hectoliter; horizontal line; histiocytic lymphoma; heart and lungs; hearing loss; hearing level; hairline.

hla human leukocyte antigen; heart, lungs, abdomen.

HLBB Home Loan Bank Board.

HLC or **HL Cas** House of Lords Cases (England).

hld herniated lumbar disc.

hlf human lung field.

hlh hypoplastic left heart.

hli human leukocyte interferon.

hln hyperplastic liver nodules; hilar lymph node.

HLR, hlr Harvard Law Review; heart lung resuscitation.

hls holograph letter signed.

hlt human lipotropin.

hlv herpes like virus.

hm homemade; hectometer; health maintenance; human milk; heart murmur; hand movements.

H&M Hening and Munford's Reports (Virginia); Hemming and Miller's Vice-Chancellor's Reports (England); Hagner and Miller's Reports (Maryland)..

H & Mc Harris and McHenry's Reports (Maryland).

HMC, hmc Her Majesty's Customs; heroin, morphine, cocaine.

hmd hyaline membrane disease.

HMDA Home Mortgage Disclosure Act.

hme heat, massage, exercise.

hmg human menopausal gonadotropin.

hmi healed myocardial infarction.

hml human milk lysosome.

HMO Health Maintenance Organization.

hmp hexose monophosphate pathway; hot moist packs; ; hydromotive pressure.

hms hypermobility syndrome.

HMSO Her Majesty's Stationery Office.

hmt hematocrit.

HMTA Hazardous Materials Transportation Act.

hmw high molecular weight.

HN, hn Honduras; head nurse; hilar node; head, neck.

H&N, h&n Hurlstone and Norman's Exchequer Reports (England); head and neck.

hnb human neuroblastoma.

hnd hundred.

HNIS Human Nutrition Information Service.

HNL HUD Newsletter.

hnp herniated nucleus pulposus.

hns head and neck surgery.

Ho, ho holmium; home office; house; history of; high oxygen; hand orthosis.

HOA, hoa Home Owner Association; hip osteoarthritis.

Hob, hob Hobart's King's Bench Reports (England); head of bed.

hoc human ovarian cancer.

Hod, hod Hodges' Common Pleas Reports (England); hospital day.

Hodg El Hodgin's Election Cases (Upper Canada).

hof hepatic outflow.

Hoff Hoffman's Chancery Reports (New York).

Hoff LC Hoffman's Land Cases.

Hofstra L Rev Hofstra Law Review.

Hog Hogan's Rolls Court Reports (Ireland).

Hogue Hogue's Reports (Florida).

hoh hard of hearing.

hoi hospital onset of infection.

HOL House of Lords.

HOLA Home Owners Loan Act.

HOLC Home Owner's Loan Corporation.

Holl Hollingshead's Reports (Minnesota).

Holm Holmes' Reports (Oregon); Holmes' Circuit Court Reports.

Holt Adm Holt's Admiralty Cases, Rule of the Road (England).

Holt Eq Holt's Equity Reports (England).

Holt KB Holt's King's Bench Reports (England).

Holt NP Holt's Nisi Prius Reports (England).

Home Home's Decisions (Scotland).

homeop homeopathy.

homo highest occupied molecular orbital; homosexual.

Hon, hon Honduras; honorable.

Hook Hooker's Reports (Connecticut).

hop high oxygen pressure.

Hope Dec Hope's Decisions (Scotland).

hopi history of present illness.

Hopk Ch Hopkins' Chancery (New York).

Hopk Dec Hopkinson's Admiralty Decisions (Pennsylvania).

Hopw & C Hopwood and Coltman's Registration Appeal Cases (England).

Hopw & P Hopwood and Philbrick's Registration Appeal Cases (England).

hor horizontal.

hor decu at bedtime (hora decubitus).

Horn & Hur Horn and Hurlstone's Exchequer Reports (England).

Horner Horner's Reports (South Dakota).

Horw Y Horwood Yearbook, Edward I.

hos human osteosarcoma.

Hosea Hosea's Reports (Ohio).

Hoskins Hoskins' Reports (North Dakota).

hosp hospital.

hot hyperbaric oxygen therapy.

Houghton Houghton's Reports (Alabama).

Houst Houston's Reports (Delaware).

Houston J Intl L Houston Journal of International Law.

Houston Law Houston Lawyer.

Houston L Rev Houston Law Review.

Hov Hovenden Supplement, Vesey's Chancery Reports (England).

How, how Howard's Reports, United States Supreme Court; Howard's Reports (Mississippi); Howard's Practice Reports (New York); Howell's Reports (Nevada); home owners warranty.

How App Cas Howard's Appeals Cases (New York).

How & Beat Howell and Beatty's Reports (Nevada).

How & N Howell and Norcross' Reports (Nevada).

Howard Howard's Reports, United States Supreme Court.

Howard L J Howard Law Journal.

How Ch Howard's Chancery Reports (Ireland).

How NP Howell's Nisi Prius Cases (Michigan).

How Pr Howard's Practice Reports (NS: New Series) (New York).

How St Tr Howell's State Trials (England).

HP, hp House of Parliament; handicapped person; horsepower; horizontal plane; hot pad; haptoglobin; hydrostatic pressure; high protein; heparin; heat production; high pressure; hypertension and proteinuria.

h&p history and physical.

hpa hemagglutinating penicillin antibody.

HPC, hpc Hale's Pleas of the Crown (England); history of present complaint.

hpd high protein diet.

hpe history and physical examination.

hpf high power field; hepatic plasma flow.

hpg human pituitary gonadotropin.

hpi history of present injury (illness).

HP-IB Hewlett-Packard Interface Bus.

hpl human placental lactogen.

HPM Harding Passey melanoma.

hpn hypertension.

hpns high pressure nervous syndrome.

hpo high pressure oxygen.

hq headquarters; see this (hoc quaere).

hps hypertrophic pyloric stenosis.

hpt human placental thyrotropin; hypothalamic pituitary thyroid.

hpz high pressure zone.

hq headquarters.

HR, Hr, hr House of Representatives; House Document; home rule; heart rate; hour; high resistance; hospital record; hormone responsive.

H&R Harrison and Rutherford's Common Pleas Reports (England).

HRA, hra Human Resources Administration; health risk appraisal; histamine releasing activity.

hre hormone receptor enzyme.

H Res or **HR** House Resolution.

hrp high risk pregnancy.

hrr heart rate range; head rotation to right.

HR Rpt House of Representatives Report.

hrs hours; humeroradial synostosis; hormone receptor site.

hrt heart; heart rate; hormone replacement therapy.

hrv heart rate variability.

HRW Human Rights for Women.

HS, hs high speed; herpes simplex; hour of sleep; at bedtime (hora somni); hypersensitivity; house surgeon; hospital stay; heavy smoker; hysterotomy and sterilization; half strength.

h/s hemorrhage and shock; helper-suppressor.

H&S Harris & Simrall's Reports (Mississippi).

HSA, hsa Health Services Administration; Hazardous Substances Act; human serum albumin.

HSC, hsc Health and Safety Commission; human skin collagenase.

hse house; herpes simplex encephalitis.

hsg housing; herpes simplex genitalis; hysterosalpingogram.

HSIS Highway Safety Information Service.

hsl herpes simplex labialis.

hsm high-speed memory.

hsp high speed printer; human serum protein.

hsr high speed reader.

hss hypertrophic subaortic stenosis.

HST Hawaiian Standard Time.

hsv herpes simplex virus.

HT, ht Haiti; under this title (hoc titulo); horizontal tabulation; height; heart; heat; hypertension; hospital treatment; high tension; high temperature.

H&T, h&t Hall and Twell's Chancery Reports (England); hospitalization and treatment.

hta heavier than air.

htb hot tub bath.

HTF, htf Highway Trust Fund; house tube feeding; heterothyrotropic factor.

htk heel to knee.

htn hypertension.

hto hospital transfer order.

htr high temperature reactor.

hts human thyroid stimulator.

htv herpes type virus.

hu human; heat unit; hydroxyurea.

HUAC House Un-American Activities Committee.

Hub Hubbard's Reports (Maine).

HUD Department of Housing and Urban Development.

Hud & B Hudson and Brooke's King's Bench Reports (Ireland).

Hughes Hughes's Reports, United States Supreme Court; Hughes' Reports (Kentucky).

Hume Hume's Decisions (Scotland).

humint human intelligence.

Humph Humphrey's Reports (Tennessee).

Hum Rts J Human Rights Journal.

Hun, hun Hun's Reports (New York); Hungary; hundred.

Hung L Rev Hungarian Law Review.

Hunt Torrens Hunter's Torrens Cases.

Hurl & Colt Hurlstone and Coltman's Exchequer Reports (England).

Hurl & Gor Hurlstone and Gordon's Reports (England).

Hurl & Nor Hurlstone and Norman's Exchequer Reports (England).

Hurl & Wal Hurlstone and Walmsley's Exchequer Reports (England).

hus hemolytic uremic syndrome.

husb husband.

Hutch Hutcheson's Reports (Alabama).

Hutt Hutton's Common Pleas Reports (England).

hv high voltage; high velocity; heating and ventilation; hospital visit; hyperventilation; hepatic vein; heat volume; this evening (hoc vespere).

hvac heating, ventilation, air conditioning.

hvd hypertensive vascular disease.

hvlp high volume, low pressure.

hvs herpes virus sensitivity.

hw housewife; hot water; healing well.

hwb hot water bottle.

H&W Harrison and Wollaston's King's Bench Reports (England); Hurlstone and Walmsley's Exchequer Reports (England).

HW Gr H.W. Green's Equity Reports (New Jersey).

hwm high water mark; hazard waste management.

hwy highway.

hx history.

hy history; heavy; hysteria.

hyb hybrid.

Hy Bl Henry Blackstone's Common Pleas Reports (England).

hyd hydrostatic; hydration.

hydr hydraulic.

hyg hygiene.

hyp hypnosis.

hyper hyperactive.

hyperten hypertension.

hypo hypodermic.

hys hysterical; hysterectomy.

hz hertz; herpes zoster.

I, i India; Iraq; Iran; Israel; Italy; inventory; interstate; incendiary; intelligence; institution; international; industry; initial; inside; income; inertia; inactive; incomplete; independent; iodine; iron; inhalation; internal.

i&a irrigation and aspiration.

IA, ia Iowa; incorporated accountant; in absentia; impedance angle; infected area; intraarterial; inactive alcoholic.

iaa indoleacetic acid.

IAAI International Association of Arson Investigators.

IAB, iab Industrial Accident Board; Inter-American Bank; intra abdominal.

IABA Inter-American Bar Association.

IABF Inter-American Bar Foundation.

IAC, iac Immigration Appeal Cases; internal auditory canal.

IACA International Association of Corporation Administrators.

IACAC Inter-American Commercial Arbitration Commission.

IACRL Italian-American Civil Rights League.

iad internal absorbed dose; inactivating dose.

IADB Inter-American Development Bank.

IADL International Association of Democratic Lawyers.

IAEA International Atomic Energy Agency.

IAECOSOC Inter-American Economic and Social Council.

IAIC International Association of Insurance Counsel.

ial international algebraic language.

IALA International African Law Association; Idaho Association of Legal Assistants.

IALL International Association of Law Libraries.

Ia L Rev Iowa Law Review.

IALS International Association of Legal Science.

ian intern admit note.

i&a irrigation and aspiration.

i&d incision and drainage.

i&e internal and external.

I&N Dec Immigration and Nationality Decisions.

i&o intake and output.

i&r initiative and referendum.

iao immediately after onset.

iap international airport; intermittent acute porphyria.

iar instruction address register.

IARC International Agency for Research on Cancer.

IAS, ias Institute for Atmospheric Sciences; immunosuppressive acidic substance.

IATA, iata International Air Transport Association; is amended to add.

IATL International Academy of Trial Lawyers.

iatr is amended to read.

IAWL International Association for Water Law.

ib invoice book; in the same place (ibidem); incendiary bomb; in bond; infectious bronchitis; inclusion body; immune body.

IBA, iba Independent Bar Association; International Bar Association; indolebutyric acid.

ibc isobutyl cyanoacrylate.

IBCA Department of Interior Board of Contract Appeals.

ibd inflammatory bowel disease.

IBEW International Brotherhood of Electrical Workers.

ibf immunoglobulin binding factor.

IBFD International Bureau of Fiscal Documentation.

ibg interblock gap; insoluble bone gelatin.

ibi intermittent bladder irrigation.

ibid in the same place (ibidem).

IBL International Brotherhood of Longshoremen.

IBM, ibm International Business Machines; intercontinental ballistic missile.

ibo invoice book outbound.

ibp international balance of payments.

IBPCT International Bureau for the Publication of Customs Tariffs.

IBRD International Bank for Reconstruction and Development.

ibs irritable bowel syndrome.

ibt ink blot test.

ibv infectious bronchitis virus.

IBWM International Bureau of Weights and Measures.

ic in charge; integrated circuit; instruction counter; internal combustion; index correlation; intracerebral; inspiratory center; irritable colon; internal cerebral; intensive care; immune complex.

ICA, ica International Communication Agency; integrated communications adapter; internal carotid artery.

ICAO International Civil Aviation Organization.

icbm intercontinental ballistic missile.

ICC, icc Indian Claims Commission; Interstate Commerce Commission; International Chamber of Commerce; International Computation Center; internal conversion coefficient; immunocompetent cells; intensive coronary care.

icce intracapsular cataract extraction.

ICC Pract J Interstate Commerce Commission Practitioners' Journal.

iccu intensive coronary care unit.

icd immune complex disease.

ICDCD International Classification of Diseases and Causes of Death.

Ice, ice Iceland; internal combustion engine.

icf intensive care facility; intracellular fluid.

ich ichthyology; intracranial hemorrhage.

ici intracisternal.

ICIP International Conference on Information Processing.

ICJ International Court of Justice; International Commission of Jurists.

ICJYB International Court of Justice Yearbook.

ICJC International Criminal Justice Clearinghouse.

ICLQ International and Comparative Law Quarterly.

icm intracytoplasmic membrane; inner cell mass.

icp intracranial pressure; inductively coupled plasma; infectious cell protein.

icr intermittent catheter routine.

ICRC International Committee of the Red Cross.

IC Rep Interstate Commerce Commission Reports.

ics intercostal space; intensive care, surgery.

icsh interstitial cell stimulating hormone.

ICSID International Centre for Settlement of Investment Disputes.

ict interstitial cell tumor; inflammation of connective tissue; insulin coma therapy.

icu intensive care unit.

icw intensive care ward.

icx immune complex.

ID, id Interior Department Decisions; Idaho; Indonesia; the same (idem); identification; immediate delivery; internal diameter; intradermal; incision and drainage; initial dose; infant death; immunodeficiency.

i&d incision and drainage.

IDA, Ida, ida International Development Association; Idaho; iron deficiency anemia.

IDAA Industrial Diamond Association of America.

idb industrial development bond.

IDDJ Interim Decisions of the Department of Justice.

iddm insulin dependent diabetes mellitus.

Idd TR Idding's Term Reports (Dayton, Ohio).

IDL Index to Dental Literature.

Id LJ Idaho Law Journal.

idm idiopathic disease of the myocardium.

idp integrated data processing; international driving permit; inosine diphosphate; initial dose period.

idr international drawing rights; industrial development revenue bond.

ids immune deficiency state.

idu idoxuridine.

IE, ie Ireland; Indo-European; that is (id est); industrial engineer; ingress egress; internal ear; infective endocarditis.

i&e internal and external.

i/e inspiratory/expiratory ratio.

iea immediate early antigen.

IEEE Institute of Electrical and Electronics Engineers.

iei isoelectric interval.

iel internal elastic lamina.

IEPB Interagency Emergency Planning Board.

ies ingressive/egressive sequence.

IESS International Encyclopedia of the Social Sciences.

iet interest equalization tax.

if in full; internal friction; intermediate factor; interferon.

IFATCA International Federation of Air Traffic Control Associations.

IFA, ifa International Fertility Association; immunofluorescent antibody.

ifb invitation for bid.

IFC International Finance Corporation.

iff if and only if; inner fracture, face.

IFIPS International Federation of Information Processing Societies.

ifm internal fetal monitor.

if nec if necessary.

ifo identified flying object.

ifr inspiratory flow rate.

IFWL International Federation of Women Lawyers.

IG, ig Inspector General; immunoglobulin; intragastric.

IgA immunoglobulin A.

IgD immunoglobulin D.

IgE immunoglobulin E.

igf insulin like growth factor.

IGFPIL International Grotius Foundation for the Propagation of International Law.

IgG immunoglobulin G.

IgM immunoglobulin M.

igh immunoreactive growth hormone.

ign ignition.

igr immediate generalized reaction; intergovernmental review.

ih in hospital; infectious hepatitis; inhibiting hormone.

ihc inner hair cell.

ihd ischemic heart disease.

ihh infectious human hepatitis.

ihr intrinsic heart rate.

ihsa iodinated human serum albumin.

II, ii Immigration Inspector; indorsement irregular.

IIAA Independent Insurance Agents of America.

IIC International Review of Industrial Property and Copyright Law.

iif immune interferon.

iip idiopathic interstitial pneumonia.

IISL International Institute of Space Law.

iit ineffective iron turnover.

IJ Irish Jurist.

IJA Institute of Judicial Administration.

ijd inflammatory joint disease.

ijp internal jugular pressure.

ijv internal jugular vein.

ik immobilized knee.

IL, Il, il Illinois; Israel; illinium; interleukin; including loading; inside length; intralumbar; intestinal lymphocyte.

ILA International Law Association; International Longshoremen's Association; Indiana Legal Assistants.

ILAA International Legal Aid Association; Iowa Legal Assistants Association.

ilbw infant, low birth weight.

ILC, ilc International Law Commission; International Legal Center; irrevocable letter of credit.

ild interstitial lung disease.

ILE Indiana Law Encyclopedia.

ILGWU International Ladies Garment Workers' Union.

ILHR International League for Human Rights.

ill illustration.

Ill App Illinois Appellate Court Reports (2d: Second Series) (3d: Third Series).

Ill BJ Illinois Bar Journal.

Ill Cir Illinois Circuit Court.

Ill CLE Illinois Continuing Legal Education.

Ill Ct Cl Illinois Court of Claims.

Ill LB Illinois Law Bulletin.

Ill LQ Illinois Law Quarterly.

Ill L Rev Illinois Law Review.

ILM, ilm International Legal Materials; internal limiting membrane.

ILO, ilo, iLo International Labor Organization; in lieu of; iodine lotion.

ILP Index to Legal Periodicals; Illinois Law and Practice; Independent Labour Party.

ILQ International Law Quarterly.

ILR, ilr International Law Reports; Insurance Law Reporter; irreversible loss rate.

ILS, ils Incorporated Law Society; instrument landing system.

ILT Irish Law Times.

IM, im Index Medicus; Isle of Man; intramural; intermodulation distortion; intramuscular; internal medicine; infectious mononucleosis; inner membrane.

ima inferior mesenteric artery.

imb intermenstrual bleeding.

I Med Index Medicus.

IMF, imf International Monetary Fund; intermaxillary fixation.

img immigration; internal medicine group.

imi impending (or inferior) myocardial infarction; imipramine.

imis integrated management information system.

iml initial microcode (micro- program) load.

IMM International Monetary Market.

immat immature.

Immig B Bull Immigration Bar Bulletin.

immob immobilize.

immun immunity; immunization.

immy immediately.

IMP, imp Index to Maritime Publications; imperfect; important; impersonating; impression; improvement.

impl impulse; implement; initial microcode (microprogram) load.

impr improved.

impx impacted.

imr institution for the mentally retarded; infant mortality rate.

ims international metric system; information management system; incurred in military service.

imv inferior mesenteric vein.

IN, in India; Indiana; immigration and naturalization; incidence; insulin; inch; inlet; initial dose; interstitial nephritis.

ina inferior nasal artery.

inac inactive.

inc incorporated; income; increase; including; inclosure; incomplete; increment; incision; incontinent.

INCB International Narcotics Control Board.

inch inchoative.

INCINC International Copyrights Information Center.

incl including; inclosure.

INCOG, incog Indian Nations Council of Governments; incognito.

incont incontinent.

incr increasing.

Ind, ind Indiana; indecent; indorse; industry; inde- pendent.

Ind & Lab Rel R Industrial and Labour Relations Review.

Ind App Indiana Appellate Court.

Ind Cl Comm Indian Claims Commission.

indef indefinite.

indemy indemnity.

indet indeterminate.

India Crim LJR India, Criminal Law Journal Reports.

Indian LR Indian Law Reports.

Indian L Rev Indian Law Review.

Indian R Indian Rulings.

India S Ct India Supreme Court Reports.

Indian T Indian Territory Reports.

indic indicated.

indig indigestion.

Ind J Intl L Indian Journal of International Law.

Ind Legal F Indiana Legal Forum.

Ind LJ Indiana Law Journal.

Ind L Rev Indiana Law Review.

Ind Med Index Medicus.

Indon Indonesia.

Ind Prop Q Industrial Property Quarterly.

indre indenture.

Ind Rel J Econ & Soc Industrial Relations: Journal of Economy and Society.

Ind SC Indiana Superior Court.

Ind Super Indiana Superior Court Reports.

Ind T or **Indian T** Indian Territory Reports.

ind th individual therapy.

Indus LJ Industrial Law Journal.

Indus Rel LJ Industrial Relations Law Journal.

Indust L Rev Q Industrial Law Review Quarterly.

Ind Y Indian Yearbook of International Affairs.

INF, inf Intermediate Range Nuclear Force; informant; information; inferior; infusion; infantry; infant; infinity; infec- tious; infirmary; infarction.

infl influence; inflammable; inflammation.

info information.

infra infrared.

ing inguinal.

ink injury not known.

inj injection; injury.

injct injunction.

inm international nautical mile.

inoc inoculate.

inp international news photo.

INPADOC International Patent Documentation Center.

inq inquiry; inferior nasal quadrant.

in re in regard to.

INS, ins Immigration and Naturalization Service; inches; inside; insulation; insurance.

Ins Counsel J Insurance Counsel Journal.

insid insidious.

Ins LJ Insurance Law Journal.

Ins L Rep Insurance Law Reporter (Commerce Clearing House).

insol insoluble.

insp inspection; inspiration.

Insp Gen Inspector General.

Inst, inst Institutes; institution; instant; installment.

Inst Estate Plan Institute on Estate Planning.

Inst Min L Institute on Mineral Law.

insuf insufficient.

int interest; interview; interna- tional; intelligence; inter- section; internal; intestinal; intermittent; intern. See also Intl.

Int Aff International Affairs.

Int Com Rep Interstate Commerce Commission Reports.

INTELSAT International Telecommunications Satellite.

inter intermittent; interrogatories; internal.

Inter-Am L Rev Inter-American Law Review.

Interior Dec Interior Department Decisions, United States.

INTERPOL International Criminal Police Organization.

interrog or **intg** interrogation.

intes intestinal.

Int J Offen International Journal of Offender Therapy.

intl international; internal.

Intl Arb J International Arbitration Journal.

Int Law International Lawyer.

Intl BJ International Bar Journal.

Intl Bus Law International Business Lawyer.

Intl JL Lib International Journal of Law Libraries.

Intl J Pol International Journal of Politics.

Intl Jurid Assn B International Juridical Association Bulletin.

Intl LQ International Law Quarterly.

Intl Law International Lawyer.

Intl Leg Mat International Legal Materials.

Intl Tax J International Tax Journal.

Intl Trade LJ International Trade Law Journal.

Intl Woman L International Woman Lawyer.

Intl & Comp LQ International and Comparative Law Quarterly.

intn intention.

intr intermittent.

Intra L Rev Intramural Law Review.

Int Rev Bull Internal Revenue Bulletin.

Int Rev Code Internal Revenue Code.

Int Rev Rec Internal Revenue Record.

intro introduction.

inv invalid; invoice; inventory; investment; involuntary; inferior nasal vein.

invert invertebrate.

invest investigation.

invet inveterate.

invol involuntary.

Io, io ionium; input/output; in order; intestinal obstruction; inside out; incisal opening.

i&o intake and output.

i/o input/output; in and out.

IOC, ioc International Olympic Committee; input/output controller; intern on call.

IOCC Bull Interstate Oil Compact Commission Bulletin.

IOCI Interstate Organized Crime Index.

iocs input/output control system.

iod injured on duty.

iol intraocular lens.

IOM, iom Isle of Man; interoffice memorandum.

iop intraocular pressure.

iops input/output programming system.

iou I owe you; intensive observation unit.

Iowa LB Iowa Law Bulletin.

Iowa L Rev Iowa Law Review.

ip installment paid; ice point; India paper; intermediate pressure; initial pressure; interphalangeal; incubation period; icterus praecox; infection prevention; inpatient.

IPA, ipa International Police Association; Illinois Paralegal Association; Indiana Paralegal Association; indicated pressure altitude; including particular average; isopropyl alcohol.

ipc industrial process control.

ipd incurable problem drinker; inflammatory pelvic disease.

ipe interstitial pulmonary emphysema.

ipf imperfect; idiopathic pulmonary fibrosis.

IPI, ipi International Patent Institute; interpulse interval.

ipl information processing language; initial program load (loader).

ipm inches per minute; integrated pest management.

ipn intern progress note.

IPO, ipo Intellectual Patent

Owners; improved pregnancy outcome.

ipp intermittent positive pressure; independent practice plan.

ippb intermittent positive pressure breathing.

ipr insulin production rate.

ips iron pipe size; impulse per second.

ipt interpersonal psychotherapy.

IPTA International Patent and Trademark Association.

ipts international practical temperature scale.

ipv infectious pustular vaginitis.

iq intelligence quotient; the same as (idem quod).

iqed that which is to be proved (id quod erat demonstrandum).

IR, Ir, ir Internal Revenue Decisions; Law Reports (Ireland); Irish; Iran; iridium; infrared; information retrieval; instruction register; insoluble residue; inversion recovery; inferior rectus; immune response.

i/r initiative and referendum.

IRA, ira Indian Rights Association; Irish Republican Army; individual retirement account.

IRB, irb Internal Revenue Bulletin; Institutional Review Board; industrial revenue bond.

irbbb incomplete right bundle branch block.

irbc infected red blood cell.

IRC, irc Internal Revenue Code; International Red Cross; irregular route carrier.

Ir Ch Irish Chancery.

Ir Cir Irish Circuit Reports.

Ir CL Irish Common Law Reports.

Ir Eccl Irish Ecclesiastical Reports.

Ired Iredell's Reports (North Carolina).

Ir Eq Irish Equity Reports.

irg interrecord gap; immunoreactive glucagon.

irh intraretinal hemorrhage.

iri immunoreactive insulin.

Irish LT Irish Law Times.

Ir Jur Irish Jurist.

irl information retrieval language.

Ir L & Eq Irish Law and Equity.

Ir LTR Irish Law Times Reports.

irp immunoreactive plasma.

irr irregular; irredeemable; irradiation.

Ir R Irish Reports.

Ir RCL Irish Reports Common
Law.

irreg irregular.

Ir R Eq Irish Reports Equity.

irrg irrigation.

IRS, irs Internal Revenue Service;
immunoreactive secretin.

iru international radium unit;
interferon reference unit.

irv inspiratory reserve volume.

Irv Just Irvine's Justiciary Cases
(Scotland).

is interstate; island; information
separator; intraspinal; immune
serum; insulin secretion.

isa irregular spiking activity.

isam indexed sequential access
method.

ISBN International Standard Book
Number.

ISC, isc International Statistical
Classification; interstate commerce; interstitial cell.

ISCN International System for
Human Cytogenetic
Nomenclature.

isd inhibited sexual desire.

ise inhibited sexual excitement.

isf interstitial fluid.

isg immune serum globulin.

ish icteric serum hepatitis.

isi injury severity index.

ISL Institute of Space Law;
International School of Law,
Law Review.

ISLLSL International Society for
Labor Law and Social
Legislation.

ism intersegmental muscles.

ISO, iso International Standards
Organization; incentive stock
option; isotropic.

isol isolation.

isom isometric.

isp intraspinal.

isr information storage and
retrieval; insular secretion rate.

Isr L Rev Israel Law Review.

iss issue; injury severity scale.

ISSN International Standard Serial
Number.

ist insulin shock therapy.

isv international scientific vocabulary.

isw interstitial water.

IT, It, it Income Tax Unit Rulings;
Italy; in transit; internal thread;
immunity test; inhalation
therapy; industrial therapy;
insulin therapy; intratracheal
tube; immunotherapy.

ita individual task authorization;
inferior temporal artery.

ITAL, ital Italian; italics.

ITB, itb International Time
Bureau; invitation to bid.

ITBS Iowa Test of Basic Skills.

ITC; itc International Trade
Commission; International
Trade Center; Interagency
Testing Committee; investment
tax credit.

itd insulin treated diabetic.

ite in the ear.

itf interferon.

ith intrathecal.

ITMA Institute for Training in
Municipal Administration.

ITO International Trade
Organization.

itom interstate transportation of
obscene matter.

itou intensive therapy observation
unit.

itp islet-cell tumor of the pan-
creas; idiopathic thrombocytopenic purpura.

itq inferior temporal quadrant.

ITR, itr Irish Term Reports; intratracheal.

itsc interstate transportation of
stolen cattle.

itsmv interstate transportation of
stolen motor vehicle.

ITT, itt International Telephone
and Telegraph Company;
insulin tolerance test.

ITU, itu International
Telecommunication Union;
income tax unit; intensive
therapy unit.

itv inferior temporal vein.

itwi interstate transportation of
wagering information.

iu immunizing unit; international
unit; in utero; intrauterine.

iuc idiopathic ulcerative colitis.

iucd intrauterine contraceptive
device.

IUD, iud intrauterine device.

iufb intrauterine foreign body.

iugr intrauterine growth retardation.

IULIA International Union of Life
Insurance Agents.

iup intrauterine pregnancy.

IUSTFI Institute on United States
Taxation of Foreign Income.

iut intrauterine transfusion.

iv invoice value; increased value;
iodine value; interventricular;
intravenous.

iva inventory valuation adjustments.

ivag intravaginal.

ivc inferior vena cava; intravascular coagulation.

ivcd intraventricular condition
defect.

ivd intervertebral disc.

ivf intravascular fluid; in vitro fertilization.

ivgtt intravenous glucose tolerance test.

ivh intraventricular hemorrhage.

ivp intravenous push; intravenous
pyelogram; intraventricular
pressure.

ivpb intravenous piggy back.

ivsd intraventricular septal
defect.

ivt intravenous transfusion.

ivu intravenous urography.

IW, iw Isle of Wright; inspector of
works; inside width; interchangeable with; isotopic
weight; inner wall.

IWCT International War Crimes
Tribunal.

iwl insensible water loss.

iwmi inferior wall myocardial infarction.

IWO Institute of World Order.

iws industrial water supply.

IWW, iww Industrial Workers of the World; inland waterway.

iz infarction zone.

J, j Johnson's Reports (New York); Japan; January; July; June; jus; Jewish; judge; justice; junior; joint; journal; juvenile; juice.

JA, ja Judge Advocate; Japan; Jamaica; January; joint agent; joint account; job analysis.

JAA Judge Advocates Association.

J Abn Psych Journal of Abnormal Psychology.

J Account or **J Accy** Journal of Accountancy.

Jac Jacob's Chancery Reports (England).

Jack Jackson's Reports (Georgia); Jackson's Reports (Texas).

Jack & Lum Jackson and Lumpkin Reports (Georgia).

Jackson See Jack.

Jack Tex App Jackson's Texas Court of Appeals Reports.

Jac LD Jacob's Law Dictionary.

Jacob & W Jacob and Walker's Chancery Reports (England).

JAF Judge Advocate of the Fleet.

J Afr L Journal of African Law.

JAG Judge Advocate General.

JAG Bull Judge Advocate General's Bulletin.

JAGJ or **JAJ** Judge Advocate General's Journal.

JAG L Rev Judge Advocate General Law Review.

JAGO Judge Advocate General's Office.

J Air L & Comm Journal of Air Law and Commerce.

JAJ or **JAGJ** Judge Advocate General's Journal.

Jam Jamaica.

JAMA Journal of the American Medical Association.

J Am Dent A Journal of the American Dental Association.

James James' Reports (Nova Scotia).

James & Mont James and Montagu's Bankruptcy Reports (England).

J Am Jud Soc Journal of the American Judicature Society.

J Am Med Ac Journal of the American Medical Association.

JAMS Joint Agency for Municipal Securities Dealers.

J Am Soc CLU Journal of the American Society of Chartered Life Underwriters.

J Am Stat A Journal of the American Statistical Association.

JAN, Jan Joint Army Navy; January.

J&C Jones and Carey's Exchequer Reports (Ireland).

J&H Johnson and Hemming's Chancery Reports (England).

J&L Jones and LaTouche's Chancery Reports (Ireland).

J&S Jones and Spencer's Reports (New York).

J&W Jacob and Walker's Chancery Reports (England).

Jap Ann Int L Japanese Annual of International Law.

jas job analysis schedule.

J Assn L Teach Journal of the Association of Law Teachers.

JB, jb Bachelor of Laws (juris baccalaureus); joint bond; junction box; job.

JBADC or **JB Assn DC** Journal of the Bar Association of the District of Columbia.

JB Assn St Kan Journal of Bar Association of the State of Kansas.

J Bev Hills Ba A Journal of the Beverly Hills Bar Association.

JBL or **J Bus L** Journal of Business Law.

JB Moore J.B. Moore's Common Pleas Reports (England).

J Bridg J. Bridgman's Common Pleas Reports (England).

J Bus L or **JBL** Journal of Business Law.

JC, jc Johnson's Cases (New York); Justiciary Cases (England); juvenile court; justice clerk; junior college; junction; Jesus Christ; joint contracture.

J&C Jones and Carey's Exchequer Reports (Ireland).

jca juvenile chronic arthritis.

JCAH Joint Commission on Accreditation of Hospitals.

J Can B or **JCB** Bachelor of Canon Law (juris canna baccalaureus).

J Can BA Journal of the Canadian Bar Association.

J Can D or **JCD** Doctor of Canon Law (juris canonos doctor).

JC&UL or **J Coll & UL** Journal of College and University Law.

JCB Bachelor of Canon Law (juris canonos baccalaureus); Bachelor of Civil Law (juris civilis baccalaureus).

jcc joint communications center; junior chamber of commerce.

JCCLE Joint Committee on Continuing Legal Education.

JCD Doctor of Canon Law (juris canonos doctor); Doctor of Civil Law (juris civilis doctor).

J Ch Johnson's Chancery Reports (New York).

JCHA Joint Commission on Hospital Accreditation.

J Church & S Journal of Church and State.

JCL, jcl Journal of Comparative Legislation; job control language.

JCM Master of Civil Law (juris civils magister).

J Com Mkt S or **J Comm M Stud** Journal of Common Market Studies.

J Comp Leg & Int L Journal of Comparative Legislation and International Law.

J Conf Res Journal of Conflict Resolution.

J Contemp L Journal of Contemporary Law.

J Corp L Journal of Corporate Law.

J Corp Tax Journal of Corporate Taxation.

jcp juvenile chronic polyarthritis.

JCR Johnson's Chancery Reports (New York); Judicial Council Reports.

J Crim J Journal of Criminal Justice.

J Crim Law Journal of Criminal Law (England).

J Crim LC&PS Journal of Criminal Law, Criminology, and Police Science.

J Crim Law & Crim Journal of Criminal Law and Criminology.

J Crim Sci Journal of Criminal Science.

JCS Joint Chiefs of Staff.

JCSLHG Joint Center for the Study of Law and Human Genetics.

jct junction.

JCUS Joint Center on Urban Studies.

JD, jd Doctor of Jurisprudence (juris doctor); Justice Department; jury duty; juvenile delinquency; job description; juvenile diabetes.

JDA Juvenile Delinquency Act.

JDS Doctor of Juridical Science.

JDYD Juvenile Delinquency and Youth Development Office.

Je, je June; job estimate; Japanese encephalitis.

jea joint export agent.

Jebb Jebb's Crown Cases (Ireland).

Jebb & B Jebb and Bourke's Queen's Bench Reports (Ireland).

Jebb & S Jebb and Symes' Queen's Bench Reports (Ireland).

J Econ H or **JEH** Journal of Economic History.

Jeff Jefferson's Reports (Virginia).

JEH or **J Econ H** Journal of Economic History.

jej jejunum.

Jenk Jenkins' Exchequer Reports (England).

Jenks Jenks' Reports (New Hampshire).

Jenn Jennison's Reports (Michigan).

jett jettison.

J Fam L Journal of Family Law.

J For Med Journal of Forensic Medicine.

J For Sci Journal of Forensic Sciences.

jg junior grade.

J Gen Journal of Genetics.

jgp juvenile general paralysis.

jgtl job grading for trades and labor occupations.

JH Journal of the House of Representatives.

J&H Johnson and Hemming's Chancery Reports (England).

J High Ed Journal of Higher Education.

JHLB Journal of the Federal Home Loan Bank.

jic joint industrial council.

J Infec Dis Journal of Infectious Diseases.

J Int Aff Journal of International Affairs.

J Int Law E Journal of International Law and Economics.

J Intl Comm Jur Journal of the International Commission of Jurists.

J Intl L & Econ Journal of International Law and Economics.

J Intl L & Pol Journal of International Law and Politics.

jj justices; judges; jaw jerk.

JJ Mar J.J. Marshall's Reports (Kentucky).

J Jur Journal of Jurisprudence.

J Juv L Journal of Juvenile Law.

J Kan B Assn Journal of Kansas Bar Association.

J Kel John Kelyng's Crown Cases (England).

JL, Jl, jl Jaffe Lichtenstein syndrome; July; journal.

J&L Jones and LaTouche's Chancery Reports (Ireland).

JL & Educ Journal of Law and Education.

JLA Jacksonville Legal Assistants.

JLAA Juneau Legal Assistants Association.

J Land & PU Econ Journal of Land and Public Utility Economics.

J Law & Econ or **JLE** Journal of Law and Economics.

J Law Ref Journal of Law Reform.

JLE Journal of Law and Economics.

J Leg Ed or **Jour Legal Ed** Journal of Legal Education.

J Legis Journal of Legislation.

J Leg Med Journal of Legal Medicine.

J Leg Prof Journal of the Legal Profession.

J Leg Stud Journal of Legal Studies.

jlp juvenile laryngeal papilloma.

JL Soc Journal of the Law Society of Scotland.

JM Jamaica; Master of Laws (juris magister).

J Mar John Marshall.

J Mar L&C Journal of Maritime Law and Commerce.

J Mo Bar Journal of the Missouri Bar.

jn junction.

jnd just noticeable difference.

jnl journal.

jnr junior.

JO, jo Jordan; job order.

Jo & LaT Jones and LaTouche's Chancery Reports (Ireland).

joc joint operations center.

jodm juvenile onset diabetes mellitus.

John Johnson's Reports (New York); Johnson's Vice-Chancellor's Reports (England).

John Mar J Prac & Proc John Marshall Journal of Practice and Procedure.

John Marshall LJ John Marshall Law Journal.

John Marshall LQ John Marshall Law Quarterly.

Johns Cas Johnson's Cases (New York).

Jon & LaT Jones and LaTouche's Chancery Reports (Ireland).

Jones Ch Joneson's Chancery Decisions (Maryland); Johnson's Chancery Reports (New York).

Johns & H Johnson and Hemming's Chancery Reports (England).

Johns Ct Err Johnson's Court of Errors (New York).

Johns Dec Johnson's Chancery Decisions (Maryland).

Johns Eng Ch Johnson's Chancery Reports (England).

Johns NZ Johnson's Reports (New Zealand).

Johns Rep Johnson's Reports (New York).

Johns US Johnson's Reports (Chase's United States Circuit Court Decisions).

Johns VC Johnson's Vice Chancellor's Reports (England).

Jones Jones' Reports (Pennsylvania); Jones' Reports (Alabama); Jones' Reports (North Carolina); Jones' Reports (Missouri); Jones' King's Bench Reports (England); Jones' Common Pleas Reports (Upper Canada); Jones' Exchequer Reports (Ireland).

Jones & C Jones and Carey's Exchequer Reports (Ireland).

Jones & L Jones and LaTouche's Chancery Reports (Ireland).

Jones & McM Jones and McMurtrie's Reports (Pennsylvania).

Jones & S Jones and Spencer's Reports (New York).

Jones, B&W Jones, Barclay, and Whittelsey's Reports (Missouri).

jop joint operating procedure.

JOR Jordon.

Jos Joseph's Reports (Nevada).

Jo T T. Jones' King's Bench Reports (England).

jour journal.

Jour Am Soc CLU Journal of American Society of Chartered Life Underwriters.

Jour Conf Res Journal of Conflict Resolution.

Jour Crim Law & PS Journal of Criminal Law, Criminology, and Police Science.

Jour Law & Econ Journal of Law and Economic Development.

Jour Legal Ed or **J Leg Ed** Journal of Legal Education.

Jour Pub Law or **J Pub L** Journal of Public Law.

JP, jp Japan; Justice of the Peace; joists and planks; jet power; juvenile periodontitis.

J Pat Of Soc or **JOPS** or **J POS** Journal of the Patent Office Society.

jpb joint planning board.

jpc joint planning committee; junctional premature contraction.

jpd juvenile plantar dermatosis.

J Pharm Journal of Pharmacy and Pharmacology.

JPL Journal of Public Law; Journal of Planning Law.

J Pl L Journal of Planning Law.

J Polic Sci Journal of Police Science and Administration.

JPOS Journal of the Patent Office Society.

J Prod L Journal of Products Liability.

JP Sm J. P. Smith's King's Bench Reports (England).

J Psych & Law Journal of Psychiatry and Law.

J Pub L or **Jour Pub L** Journal of Public Law.

jq job questionnaire.

JR, Jr, jr Joint Resolution; Johnson's Reports (New York); juror; junior; journal.

jra juvenile rheumatoid arthritis.

J Radio L Journal of Radio Law.

J Res Crime Journal of Research in Crime and Delinquency.

J Res Nat Bur Stan or **J Res NBS** Journal of Research of the National Bureau of Standards.

js job specification; joint support.

J&S Jones and Spencer's Reports (New York).

JSB Joint Stock Bank; Bachelor of Judicial Science.

jsc joint stock company.

JSD or **Jur Sc D** Doctor of Judicial Science.

JS Gr J.S. Green's Reports (New Jersey).

JSM Master of Judicial Science.

J Soc Pub TL Journal of the Society of Public Teachers of Law (NS: New Series).

J Soc Welfare L Journal of Social Welfare Law.

J Space L Journal of Space Law.

J St Tax Journal of State Taxation.

jt joint.

jta joint tenancy agreement; job task analysis.

J Tax Journal of Taxation.

jts job training standards.

jtsn jettison.

Ju June.

JUD, jud Doctor of Both Laws - Civil and Canon (juris utriusque doctor); judge; judgment; judicial.

Jud Chr Judicial Chronicle.

Judd Judd's Reports (Hawaii).

Judge Advoc J The Judge Advocate Journal.

Judge's J Judge's Journal.

judgt judgment.

Judg UB Judgments of Upper Bench (England).

Judicature Journal of American Judicature Society.

Jud Rep Judicial Repository (New York).

Jul July.

junc junction.

Jur, jur Jurist (NS: New Series) (England); jurisdiction.
J Urban L Journal of Urban Law.
Jurid R Juridical Review.
Jurimetrics J Jurimetrics Journal.
juris jurisdiction.
Jur M Master of Jurisprudence.
Jur Sc D or **JSD** Doctor of Judicial Science.
jus justice.
Just Cas Justiciary Cases.
Just LR Justice Law Reporter (Pennsylvania).
Just P Justice of the Peace and Local Government Review.
Just Syst J Justice System Journal.
juv juvenile.
Juv & Fam Ct J Juvenile and Family Courts Journal.
Juv Ct J Juvenile Court Journal.
Juv Ct Judges J Juvenile Court Judges Journal.
Juv Just Juvenile Justice.
jv jugular vein.
jvd jugular venous distention.
jvp jugular venous pressure.
JW John Wiley & Sons.
J&W Jacob and Walker's Chancery Reports (England).
jwc junction wire connector.
jwo jettison and washing overboard; job work order.
J World Tr L Journal of World Trade Law.
Jy July.

K, k Keyes' Court of Appeals Reports (New York); potassium (kalium); killed; contract; kink; karat; care; knots; one thousand; 1024 bytes; absolute zero degrees kelvin; kilogram; kilo; kindergarten; kidney; knee.

KA, Ka, ka King-Armstrong units; ketoacidosis; cathode.
kab knowledge, attitude, behavior.
KALA Kansas Association of Legal Assistants
Kames Dec Kames' Decisions (Scotland).
Kames Elucid Kames' Elucidation (Scotland).
Kames Rem Dec Kames' Remarkable Decisions (Scotland).
Kames Sel Dec Kames' Select Decisions (Scotland).
Kan App Kansas Appeals Reports.
Kan B Assn J Kansas Bar Association Journal.
Kan City L Rep Kansas City Law Reporter.
Kan City L Rev Kansas City Law Review.
Kan LJ Kansas Law Journal.
Kan L Rev University of Kansas Law Review.
Kan St LJ Kansas State Law Journal.
K&G or **K&GRC** Keane and Grant's Registration Appeal Cases (England).
K&J Kay and Johnson's Reports (England).
Kay Kay's Chancery Reports (England).
Kay & J Kay and Johnson's Vice Chancellors' Reports (England).
KB, kb Law Reports King's Bench (England); key board; kilobase; kilobit; kilobyte; knee brace; ketone bodies.
kbs one kilobyte per second.
KBUC King's Bench Reports (Upper Canada).
KC, kc King's Counsel (England); Knights of Columbus; kilocycle; knees to chest; cathodal closing.
kcal kilocalorie.
KCALA Kansas City Association of Legal Assistants.

k cell killer cell.
kcf thousand cubic feet.
KCl potassium chloride.
K Counsel King's Counsel.
kcs 1,000 characters per second; kilocycles per second. killed; knocked down; kiln dried.
kda known drug allergies.
kdm kingdom.
KE, ke Keen's Rolls Court Reports (England); Kenya; kinetic energy.
Keane & GRC Keane and Grant's Registration Appeal Cases (England).
Keb Keble's King's Bench Reports (England).
Keen Keen's Rolls Court Reports (England).
Keil Keilway's King's Bench Reports (England).
Keith Ch Pa Keith's Court of Chancery, Registrar's Book (Pennsylvania).
Kel or **Kel CC** John Kelyng's Crown Cases (England).
Kel or **Kelly** Kelly's Reports (Georgia).
Kellen Kellen's Reports (Massachusetts).
Kelly & C Kelly and Cobb's Reports (Georgia).
Kelyng Kelyng's Crown Cases (England).
Kenan Kenan's Reports (North Carolina).
Ken Dec Kentucky Decisions.
Ken LJ Kentucky Law Journal.
Keny Kenyon's King's Bench Reports (England).
Kenya LR Kenya Law Review.
Keny Ch Chancery Cases, Kenyon (England).
Kern Kern's Reports (Maryland); Kernan's Reports (New York).
Kerr Kerr's Reports (Indiana); Kerr's Reports (New York).
Keyes Keyes' Reports (New York).
KFS Klippel Feil syndrome.
kg kingdom; keg; kilogram; kindergarten.

K&G Keane and Grant's Registration Appeal Cases (England).

KGB Soviet State Security Committee.

kg-m kilogram meter.

kgs ketogenic steroid.

khif keeping a house of ill fame.

khz kilohertz.

kia killed in action.

kid kidnapping.

kil kilderkin.

Kilk Kilkerran's Decisions (Scotland).

kilo kilogram; kilometer.

kilo- one thousand.

King King's Reports (Louisiana Annual); King's Civil Practice Cases (Colorado).

King Conf Cas King's Conflicting Cases (Texas).

kips kilo instructions per second.

Kir Kirby's Reports (Connecticut).

kiss keep it simple, sir (stupid).

KJ, kj Knights of Jurisprudence; knee jerk.

kk knee kick.

KKK Ku Klux Klan.

kl kiloliter; kelvin law; kidney lobe.

KLAS Kansas Legal Assistants Society.

klm or **km** kilometer.

kls kidneys, liver, spleen.

km kilometer.

kmps kilometers per second.

kn knot; known; knee.

Kn AC Knapp's Appeal Cases (England).

Knapp Knapp's Privy Council Reports (England).

Knapp & O Knapp & Ombler's Election Cases (England).

Knight's Ind Knight's Industrial Reports.

Knowles Knowles' Reports (Rhode Island).

Knox Knox' Reports (New South Wales, Australia).

Knox & Fitz Knox and Fitzhardinge's Reports (New South Wales, Australia).

Kn PC Knapp's Privy Council Cases (England).

ko killed organism; keep open.

koh potassium hydroxide.

Kor Korea.

Korean J Intl L Korean Journal of International Law.

kp kinetic potential; king's proctor; kitchen police; kidney punch.

kpp keeper of the privy purse.

kpv killed parenteral vaccine.

KR, Kr, kr Republic of Korea; krypton; krona; knowledge of results; key ridge.

Kreider Kreider's Reports (Washington).

Kress Kress' Reports (Pennsylvania).

kro kathode ray oscilloscope.

KS, ks Kansas; keep standing; ketosteroid; Kaposi's sarcoma; kidney sac.

ksam keyed sequential access method.

ksr keyboard send/receive.

kt karat; kinetic theory; knot; kiloton; kidney transplant.

kts kelvin temperature scale.

kub kidneys, ureter, bladder.

Kulp Kulp's Legal Register Reports (Pennsylvania).

kutd keep up to date.

kv kilovolt; kidney valve; killed vaccine.

kva kilovolt ampere.

kvo keep vein open.

kw kilowatt.

kwh kilowatt hour.

kwic key word in context.

Ky Kentucky.

Ky Bench & B Kentucky Bench and Bar.

Ky Comment'r Kentucky Commentator.

Ky Dec Kentucky Decisions.

Ky LJ Kentucky Law Journal.

Ky L Rptr Kentucky Law Reporter.

Ky Op Kentucky Opinions.

Ky St BJ Kentucky State Bar Journal.

L, l Lansing Cases (New York); Luxembourg; lithium; larceny; law; legitimate; liter; latitude; landing; large; liquid; lost; license; low; fifty; left; land; liver; lung; ligament.

LA, La, la Louisiana; Los Angeles; Laos; Latin America; legislative assembly; lanthanum; labial; law agent; local agent; letter of authority; local authority; low altitude; land agent; lighter than air; left auricle; linguoaxial; leukemia antigen; lactic acid.

LAAM Legal Assistants Association of Michigan.

La Ann Louisiana Annual Reports.

LAA/PB Legal Assistants Association/Permian Basin.

La App Louisiana Court of Appeals Reports .

LAAU Legal Assistants Association of Utah.

Lab, lab Labatt's District Court Reports (California); labor; laboratory; lead acid battery; laboratory.

Lab Arb Labor Arbitration Reports (Bureau of National Affairs).

LABB Los Angeles Bar Bulletin.

LABC Legal Assistants of Broome County.

La BJ, LABJ Louisiana Bar Journal; Los Angeles Bar Journal.

Labor LJ Labor Law Journal.

Lab Rel Rep Labor Relations Reporter (Bureau of National Affairs).

LAC, lac Labour Arbitration Cases; Legal Assistants of Colorado; laceration; left atrial contraction.

Lac Jur Lackawanna Jurist (Pennsylvania).

Lac Leg N Lackawanna Legal News (Pennsylvania).

Lac Leg Rec Lackawanna Legal Record (Pennsylvania).

LACO Legal Assistants of Central Ohio.

LACS Los Angeles Copyright Society.

lad language acquisition device; lactic acid dehydrogenase; left anterior descending; left axis deviation.

lada left acromiodorso anterior.

Ladd Ladd's Reports (New Hampshire).

lae left atrial enlargement.

laer lowest achievable emission rate.

laev left (laevus).

LAG Legal Action Group.

lah left atrial hypertrophy.

lais loan accounting information system.

lal limulus amebocyte lysate.

lali lymphocyte antibody lympho-cytolytic interaction.

La LJ Louisiana Law Journal; Labor Law Journal.

Lalor Lalor's Supplement to Hill and Denio's Reports (New York).

La L Rev Louisiana Law Review.

lam laminated; laminectomy; left atrial myxoma.

LAMA Legal Assistant Managers Association.

Lamar Lamar's Reports (Florida).

Lamb Lamb's Reports (Wisconsin).

LAMP Center for the Study of Legal Authority and Mental Patient Status.

L Am Soc Law in American Society.

lan local area network.

Lanc Bar Lancaster Bar (Pennsylvania).

Lanc L Rev Lancaster Law Review (Pennsylvania).

L&B Bull Weekly Law and Bank Bulletin.

L&C Leigh and Cave's Crown Cases (England); Lefroy and Cassels' Practice Cases (Ontario).

l&d loss and damage; loans and discounts; labor and delivery.

Land & Water L Rev Land and Water Law Review.

Land Dec Land Decisions.

L&E English Law and Equity Reports (Boston).

L&E Rep Law and Equity Reporter (New York).

Land Est C Landed Estate Court (England).

l&i liver and iron.

L&M Lowndes and Maxwell's Practice Cases (England).

l&u lower and upper.

Land Use & Env L Rev Land Use and Environmental Law Review.

L&W, l&w Lloyd and Welsby's Mercantile Cases (England); living and well.

Lane Lane's Exchequer Reports (England).

LANL Legal Assistants of Northeast Louisiana.

Lans Lansing's Supreme Court Reports (New York).

Lans Sel Cas Lansing's Select Cases (New York).

LAO, lao Laos; left anterior oblique.

LAP, lap Louisville Association of Paralegals; laparotomy; left atrial pressure.

LAPA Los Angeles Paralegal Association; Lancaster Area Paralegal Association.

lapw left atrial posterior wall.

lar larynx.

larc larceny.

larct last radio contact.

laryn laryngitis; laryngeal.

las left anterior superior.

LASC Legal Assistants of Southeastern Connecticut.

laser light amplification by stimulated emission of radiation.

lash legislative action on smoking and health.

Lat, lat Latch's King's Bench Reports (England); Latvia; latent; lateral; latitude; left anterior thigh.

Lat Am Latin America.

latd latitude.

LATE Legal Assistance for the Elderly.

Lath Lathrop's Reports (Massachusetts).

lat men lateral meniscectomy.

La TR Martin's Louisiana Term Reports.

lats long acting thyroid stimulator.

LAW, law Legal Aid Warranty; lawyer; left atrial wall.

Law Am Lawyer of the Americas.

Law & Bank Lawyer and Banker (New Orleans); Lawyers and Bankers' Quarterly (St. Louis).

Law & Banker Lawyer and Banker and Central Law Journal.

Law & Bk Bull Weekly Law and Bank Bulletin (Ohio).

Law & Contemp Prob Law and Contemporary Problems.

Law & Pol Intl Bus Law and Policy in International Business.

Law & Psych Rev Law and Psychology Review.

Law & Soc Ord Law and Social Order, Arizona State Law Journal.

Law & Socy Rev Law and Society Review.

LAWASIA Law Association for Asia and the Western Pacific.

Law & Cont Prob Law and Contemporary Problems.

Law & LN Lawyer and Law Notes.

Law & Pol Intl Bus Law and Policy in International Business.

Law & Soc Order Law and Social Order.

Law Cases Law Cases, William I - Richard I (England).

Law Chr Law Chronicle.

Law Ed See L Ed.

Law Guild Rev Lawyers Guild Review.

Law Inst J Law Institute Journal.

Law J Lawyers Journal; Law Journal.

Law Lib J Law Library Journal.
Law Libn Law Librarian.
Law Med J Lawyers Medical Journal.
Law Off Econ & Man Law Office Economics and Management.
Law QR Law Quarterly Review.
Lawr Lawrence (Ohio).
Law Reg Law Register.
Lawrence Comp Dec Lawrence's Comptroller Decisions.
Law Rep Law Reports; Law Reporter.
Law Rep NS Law Reports, New Series.
Law Repos Carolina Law Repository.
Law Socy Gaz Law Society Gazette.
Law Socy J Law Society Journal (New South Wales, Australia); Law Society of Massachusetts Journal.
Law Times Law Times (Pennsylvania).
Law T Rep Law Times Reports (OS: Old Series) (NS: New Series) (England).
LAWV Legal Assistants of West Virginia.
Lawyer and Banker Lawyer and Banker and Central Law Journal.
Lawyers' Med J Lawyers' Medical Journal.
lax laxative.
Lay Lay's Chancery Reports (England).
LB, lb Lebanon; local board; landing barge; letter box; pound; lung biopsy; live birth; left buttock; left breast; limpid body; large bowel.
lba left basal artery.
lbb low back bend; left bundle branch.
lbbb left bundle branch block.
L&B Bull Weekly Law and Bank Bulletin.
LBC, lbc London Bankruptcy Court; lidocaine blood concentration
lbd large bile duct.

lbf pound force.
LBH, lbh Local Board of Health; length, breath, and height.
lbm loose bowel movements.
LBN Lebanon.
lbo leveraged buyout.
lbp length between perpendiculars; low birth weight; lower back pain; low blood pressure.
LBR, lbr Lloyd's Bank Review; Liberia; labor; lumber.
lbv lung blood volume; left brachial vein.
lbw low body weight; low birth weight.
LBY Libya.
LC, lc Land Court (England); Lord Chancellor; Library of Congress; Labor Cases; Lower Canada; law court; letter contract; letter of credit; lower case; lance corporal; landing craft; level crossing; living children; liquid capacity; liquid chromatography; load cell; lung cell; lamina cortex; liver cirrhosis; lethal concentration.
L&C Leigh and Cave's Crown Cases (England); Lefroy and Cassels' Practice Cases (Ontario).
lca left coronary artery.
lcat lecithin cholesterol acyltransferase.
lcb left costal border.
LCC, lcc Library of Congress Classification; left coronary cusp.
lcca left common carotid artery.
LCCR Leadership Conference on Civil Rights.
LCD, lcd Lower Court Decisions (Ohio); liquid crystal display; lowest common denominator.
lcf least common factor.
lci labor cost index.
lcis lobular carcinoma in situ.
LC Inf Bul Library of Congress Information Bulletin.
LCJ Lord Chief Justice (England); Lower Canada Jurist.

lcl licentiate of civil law; less than carload; lymphoid cell line.
LCLJ Lower Canada Law Journal.
LCM, lcm Master of Comparative Law; lower of cost or market; lowest common multiple; liquid curling medium; left costal margin.
lcn left caudate nucleus; lateral cervical nucleus.
L Comment'y Law Commentary.
LC Rep S Qu Lower Canada Reports Seigniorial Questions.
lcs low continuous suction; left coronary sinus.
lct latest closing time; local civil time; liver cell tumor.
lcx left circumflex artery.
LD, ld Land Office Decisions; Labor Department; loss and damage; lethal dose; line of duty; learning disability; loan and discount; lord; limited; low density; land; local delivery; long distance; living donor; liver disease; laboratory data.
l&d loss and damage; loan and discount; labor and delivery.
lda left dorso anterior.
LDB Legionnaires' disease bacillus.
Ld Birk Lord Birkenhead's Judgments (England).
ldc less developed countries.
LDCC Less Developed Country Corporation.
lde linear differential equation.
LDF Legal Defense and Educational Fund.
ldg low density gas; landing; lodging.
ldh lactic dehydrogenase.
ldl learned doctor of laws; lower deviation level; low density lipoprotein.
ldm line driver modem; last day of the month.
ldp left dorso posterior.
Ld Raym Lord Raymond's King's Bench Reports (England).
ldri low data rate input.
LDS Latter Day Saints.

ldt logic design translator.

ldv lower dollar value.

le law enforcement; lease; labor exchange; less than or equal to; low efficiency; left eye; left ear; lupus erythematosus; left extremity; lower extremity; late entry.

L&E English Law and Equity Reports (Boston).

L&E Rep Law and Equity Reporter (New York).

Lea Lea's Reports (Tennessee).

LEAA Law Enforcement Assistance Administration.

Le & Ca Leigh and Cave's Crown Cases (England).

Leach Leach's Crown Cases (England).

LEAF Law Enforcement Assistance Foundation.

League of Nations Off J League of Nations Official Journal.

LEAP Legal and Educational Aid to the Poor.

Leb Lebanon.

L Ed Lawyers' Edition, United States Supreme Court Reports (2d: Second Series).

LED, led Law Enforcement Division; ledger; light emitting diode; low energy diffraction; lowest effective dose.

leds law enforcement data system.

Lee Lee's Reports (California).

Lee Eccl Lee's Ecclesiastical.

LEEP Law Enforcement Education Program.

Leese Leese's Reports (Nebraska).

Lee t Hard Lee's Cases, temp. Hardwicke (England).

Lefroy & C Lefroy and Cassels' Practice Cases (Ontario).

leg legal; legislation; legation.

Legal Ad Legal Advertiser (Chicago).

Legal Med Q Legal Medical Quarterly.

Leg & Ins R Legal and Insurance Reporter (Pennsylvania).

Leg Chron Legal Chronicle (Pennsylvania).

leg com legally committed.

Leg Gaz Legal Gazette Reports (Pennsylvania).

Leg Int Legal Intelligencer (Philadelphia).

Leg Op Legal Opinion (Pennsylvania).

Leg Per Index to Legal Periodicals.

Leg Rec Legal Record (Detroit).

Leg Rec Rep Legal Record Reports (Schuylkill County, Pennsylvania).

Leg Rep Legal Reporter (Tennessee).

Leg Rev Legal Review (England).

LEG UN Department of Legal Affairs, United Nations.

Lehigh Co LJ Lehigh County Law Journal (Pennsylvania).

Lehigh Val LR Lehigh Valley Law Reporter (Pennsylvania).

Leigh Leigh's Reports (Virginia).

Leigh & C Leigh and Cave's Crown Cases (England).

LEIU Law Enforcement Intelligence Units.

LEMAR Legalize Marijuana.

Leo or **Leon** Leonard's King's Bench Reports (England).

lep lowest effective power; lethal effective phase; lower esophagus.

LEPC Law Enforcement Planning Commission.

ler lysosomal enzyme release.

les local excitatory state; lesion.

LESL Law Enforcement Standards Laboratory.

Lester Lester's Reports (Georgia).

Lester & B Lester and Butler's Supplement (Georgia).

Lest PL Lester's Public Land Decisions.

LETS Law Enforcement Teletype Service.

leu leucine.

Lev Levinz's King's Bench Reports and Common Pleas Reports (England).

Lev Ent Levinz's Entries (England).

Lew See Lewis.

Lew CC Lewin's Crown Cases (England).

Lewis Lewis' Law Reporter (Kentucky); Lewis' Reports (Missouri); Lewis' Reports (Nevada).

Lex et Sci Lex et Scientia.

l/ext lower extremity.

Ley Ley's King's Bench Reports (England).

lf line feed; low frequency; load factor; linear foot; low frequency; leaflet; ledger folio; left foot; low forceps.

lfa local freight agent; left femoral artery.

lfc low frequency current; low fat and cholesterol.

lfd low frequency disturbance; low forceps delivery; least fatal dose; low fat diet.

lfh left femoral hernia.

LFL, lfl Lesbian Feminist Liberation; left frontolateral.

lfp left frontoposterior.

lfr lymphoid follicular reticulosis.

lft leaflet; left frontotransverse; liver function test.

lfv lassa fever virus.

l fx linear fracture.

LG, lg Law Glossary; Law Gazette; Law Guardian; life guard; long; large; landing ground; liquid gas; lymph glands; linguogingival; lactoglobulin.

lga large for gestational age.

lgb local government board.

lgc left giant cell.

lge large.

lgh lactogenic hormone.

lgl large granular lymphocyte.

LGR, lgr Local Government Reports (England); larger; longer.

lgt light; ligament.

L Guard Law Guardian.

lgv lymphogranuloma venereum; large granular vesicle.

lh labor hour; liquid hydrogen; lower half; left hand; luteinizing hormone; late healed.

LHA, lha Local Health Authority;

local hour angle; left hepatic artery.

lhbv left heart blood volume.

LHC, lhc Lord High Chancellor; liquid hydrogen container.

lhe liquid helium.

lhf left heart failure.

lhl left hepatic lobe.

lhrf luteinizing hormone releasing factor.

lhs left hand side.

lht left hypertropia.

LI, Li, li Legal Intelligencer (Philadelphia); Liechtenstein; lithium; letter of intent; license inquiry; light infantry; low intensity; liter; learning impaired; lactose intolerance.

l&i liver and iron.

lia life insurance agent; liaison.

lib library; liberation.

Lib Ass Liber Assisarum, Year Books (England).

Lib Cong Library Congress.

Lib Cong Inf Bull Library Congress Information Bulletin.

Lib Cong Q J Cur Acq Library Congress Quarterly Journal of Current Acquisitions.

LiBr lithium bromide.

lic license; limiting isorrheic concentration.

LICA, lica Land Improvement Contractors of America; left internal carotid artery.

lid low iodine diet.

lidc low intensity direct current.

LIE Liechtenstein.

lieut lieutenant.

lif left index finger.

Lif Cas Life, Health, and Accident Cases (2d: Second Series) (Commerce Clearing House).

lifo last in, first out.

lig ligament.

lih left inguinal hernia.

LIHDC Low Income Housing Development Corporation.

Lilly Lilly's Reports in Assize (England).

lim limited.

lima left internal mammary artery.

lin liniment; linear; liquid nitrogen.

Lincoln LR Lincoln Law Review.

linft linear foot.

L in Socy Law in Society.

L Inst J Law Institute Journal.

L in Trans Law in Transition.

lio left inferior oblique.

lip life insurance policy.

LIPA Long Island Paralegal Association.

liq liquor; liquid; low inner quadrant.

lir lost item replacement; left inferior rectus.

lis left intercostal space.

LISA Life Insurance Society of America.

lisp list processing.

Lit, lit Littell's Reports (Kentucky); Littleton's Common Pleas Reports (England); liter; literal.

LITE Legal Information Through Electronics.

Lith, lith Lithuanian; lithography.

liv legislative indexing vocabulary; living.

livc left inferior vena cava.

Liv Cas Livingston's Cases in Error (New York).

Liv Jud Op Livingston's Judicial Opinions (New York).

LJ Law Journal; Lord Justice; Larsen-Johansson syndrome.

LJA Lord Justice of Appeal.

LJ Adm Law Journal Reports, Admiralty (England).

LJ Bank Law Journal Reports, Bankruptcy (England).

LJCCR Law Journal Reports, Crown Cases Reserved (England).

LJ Ch Law Journal Chancery Reports (OS: Old Series) (England).

LJCP Law Journal Common Pleas (NS: New Series) (OS: Old Series) (England).

LJ Eccl Law Journal Reports, Ecclesiastical Cases (England).

LJ Exch Law Journal Reports, Exchequer (OS: Old Series) (England).

LJHL Law Journal Reports, House of Lords (England).

LJJ Lord Justices of Appeal.

LJKB Law Journal Reports, King's Bench (England).

ljl lateral joint line.

LJ Mag Law Journal, Magistrates' Cases.

LJMC Law Journal Reports, Magistrates' Cases (OS: Old Series) (England).

LJNC Law Journal Notes of Cases (England).

LJOS Law Journal Old Series (England).

LJP&M Law Journal Probate and Matrimonial (England).

LJPC Law Journal Reports, Privy Council (NS: New Series) (England).

LJPD & Adm Law Journal Reports, Probate, Divorce, and Admiralty (England).

LJQB Law Journal Reports, Queen's Bench (England).

LJR Law Journal Reports (NS: New Series) (England).

LK, lk lichenoid keratosis; left kidney.

lkg leakage.

lks liver, kidneys, spleen.

ll laws; legislative liaison; limited liability; loose leaf; low level; lewd and lascivious; live load; liquor law; lend lease; lysolecithin; lower left; left lung; lymphoid leukemia; large lymphocyte.

Ll & G t Pl Lloyd and Goold's temp. Chancery Reports, Plunkett (Ireland).

Ll & G t S Lloyd and Goold's temp. Chancery Reports, Sugden (Ireland).

Ll & W Lloyd and Welsby's Mercantile Cases (England).

LLB, llb Bachelor of Laws (legum baccalaureus); left lateral border.

llc lliquid-liquid chromatography; long leg cast.

LLCUNAE Law Library of Congress United Association of Employees.

LLD, lld Doctor of Laws (legum

doctor); left lateral decubitus.

lle left lower extremity.

llf left lateral femoral.

lli latitude and longitude indicator.

LLJ or **L Lib J** Law Library Journal.

LLJJ Lord Justices.

LLL, lll Licentiate in Laws; left lower lobe.

Ll L Rep Lloyd's List Law Reports (England).

LLM Master of Laws (legum magister).

LLM CL Master of Laws in Comparative Law.

LLM Com Master of Commercial Law.

LLM Int Master of Laws in International Law.

Lloyd LR Lloyd's Law Reports (England).

Lloyds Mar & Comm LQ Lloyds Maritime and Commercial Law Quarterly.

Lloyd's Rep Lloyd's List Law Reports (England).

LLP Law and Liberty Project.

llq left lower quadrant.

llr line of least resistance; left lateral rectus.

lls long leg splint.

llt left lateral thigh.

llv lymphatic leukemia virus.

llw low level waste.

llwc long leg walking cast.

llx left lower extremity.

lm legal medicine; liquid metal; lumen; land mine; long meter; lethal material; lincomycin; laryngeal muscle; liquid membrane; lactose malabsorption.

lma left mentoanterior.

L Mag & Rev Law Magazine and Review (England).

L&M Lowndes and Maxwell's Practice Cases (England).

LMAC Labor Market Advisory Councils.

LM&P Lowndes, Maxwell, and Pollock's Bail Cases (England).

lmc left main coronary.

lmd local medical doctor.

lmf low and medium frequency.

lmg liquid methane gas.

LMIS Labor Market Information System.

lml left middle lobe.

LMMC Labor Management Maritime Committee.

LMNDF Lesbian Mothers National Defense Fund.

lmp light metal product; last menstrual period; lumbar puncture.

lmr left medial rectus.

LMRA Labor Management Relations Act.

LMRDA Labor Management Reporting and Disclosure Act.

LMRS Labor Management Reporting Service.

LMSA Labor Management Services Administration.

lmt length, mass, time; local mean time; limit; left mentotransverse.

lmw low molecular weight.

lmwd low molecular weight dextran.

LMWP Labor Management Welfare Pension Reports.

LN, Ln, ln League of Nations; lanthanide; lien; loan; liaison; lane; natural logarithm; liquid nitrogen; lymph node.

lng liquified natural gas.

lnmp last normal menstrual period.

LNTS League of Nations Treaty Series.

LO, lo Law Opinion, Solicitor, Internal Revenue; Legal Observer; law officer; letter of offer; liaison office; liquid oxygen.

loa letter of offer and acceptance; leave of absence; left occipitoanterior.

lob line of business; list of bidders.

LOC, loc Library of Congress; letter of credit; line of communication; loss of consciousness.

Loc Govt Local Government and Magisterial Reports.

Loc Govt R Aust Local Government Reports of Australia.

Lock Rev Cas Lockwood's Reversed Cases (New York).

lod line of duty.

lodi list of deleted items.

loe level of effort.

L Off Econ & Manag Law Office Economics and Management.

Lofft Lofft's King's Bench Reports (England).

logo limitation of government obligation; a conversational language for computers.

loi letter of intent; letter of interest; level of incompetence.

Lois Rec Lois Recentes du Canada.

lol left occipitolateral.

lom limitation of motion; left otitis media.

LON, lon London; longitude.

Lond London.

long longitude.

Long & R Long and Russel's Election Cases (Massachusetts).

Longf & T Longfield and Townsend's Exchequer Reports (Ireland).

lop left occipitoposterior.

lops length of patient stay.

loran long range navigation.

los law of the sea; line of sight; length of stay.

LOST Law Of The Sea Treaty.

lot left occiput transverse; lateral olfactory tract.

Louisville L Louisville Lawyer.

Lou LJ Louisville Law Journal.

Lou Leg N Louisiana Legal News.

lov loss of visibility; large opaque vesicle.

Low See Lowell.

Low Can Jur Lower Canada Jurist.

Low Can LJ Lower Canada Law Journal.

Low Can R Lower Canada Reports.

Low C Seign Lower Canada Seigniorial Reports.

Lowell Lowell's District Court Reports.
Lower Ct Dec Lower Court Decisions (Ohio).
Lowndes & M Lowndes and Maxwell's Practice Cases (England).
Lowndes, Max & P Lowndes, Maxwell, and Pollock's Bail Cases (England).
lox liquid oxygen.
Loy Dig Loyola Digest.
Loy Law Loyola Lawyer.
Loy LJ or **Loyola LJ** Loyola Law Journal (Illinois).
Loyola L Rev Loyola Law Review (New Orleans).
Loyola LA L Rev Loyola of Los Angeles Law Review.
Loyola U Chi LJ Loyola University of Chicago Law Journal.
lp loss of pay; low pressure; local purchase; large particle; liquified petroleum; long playing; linear programming; low protein; linguopulpal; lumbar puncture.
lpa left pulmonary artery.
LPB Loan Policy Board.
LPC, lpc Landmarks Preservation Commission; linear predictive coding.
lpd liquid protein diet.
lpf low power field.
lpg liquid propane gas; liquified petroleum gas.
lph left posterior hemiblock.
lpm lines per minute; liters per minute; liver plasma membrane; lateral pterygoid muscle.
LPN Licensed Practical Nurse.
lpo low pressure oxygen; left posterior oblique.
lpr late phase response.
LPS, lps Lord Privy Seal; lines per second.
lpv left pulmonary veins.
lpw lumens per watt; lateral pharyngeal wall.
LQ, lq Law Quarterly; lowest quadrant.

lqd liquid.
LQR or **LQ Rev** Law Quarterly Review (England).
LR, Lr, lr Law Reporter (Ohio); Law Reports (England); Law Recorder (NS: New Series) (Ireland); Labor Review; Lloyd's Register of Shipping; Liberia; lawrencium; larceny and receiving; lock rail; living room; left rear; lab report; lateral rectus; labor room.
LRA, lra Lawyers' Reports Annotated (NS: New Series); low right atrium.
LRAC or **LR App Cas** Law Reports Appeal Cases (England).
LRA&E Law Reports, Admiralty and Ecclesiastical Cases.
LRB Loyalty Review Board.
LRC, lrc Lesbian Resource Center; longitudinal redundancy check; low rib cage.
LRCCR Law Reports, Crown Cases Reserved (England).
LR Ch Law Reports, Chancery Appeal Cases (England).
LRCP Law Reports, Common Pleas (England).
LRCPD Law Reports, Common Pleas Division (England).
lrd living related donor.
LR Eq Law Reports, Equity (England).
LR Exch Law Reports, Exchequer (England).
LR Exch Div Law Reports, Exchequer Division (England).
lrf luteinizing hormone releasing factor.
lrg large.
lrh luteinizing hormone releasing hormone.
LRHL Law Reports, English and Irish Appeals, House of Lords (England).
LRHL Sc Law Reports, Scotch Appeals, House of Lords.
lri lower respiratory tract illness.
LR Indian App Law Reports, Indian Appeals (England).
LR Ir Law Reports (Ireland).

LRKB Law Reports, King's Bench (England).
lrm left radical mastectomy.
lrmp left regular menstrual period.
LRNWS Law Reports (New South Wales, Australia).
lrp long range plan.
LRP&D Law Reports, Probate and Divorce (England).
LRP&M Law Reports, Probate and Matrimonial (England).
LRPC Law Reports, Privy Council (England).
lrq lower right quadrant.
LRQB Law Reports, Queen's Bench (England).
LRQBD Law Reports, Queen's Bench Division (England).
LRR Labor Relations Reporter.
LRRC Labor Relations and Research Center.
LRRM Labor Relations Reference Manual.
LRS, lrs Lawyer Referral Service; Legislative Reference Service; lactated ringer's solution.
LRSA Law Reports (South Australia).
LR Sess Cas Law Reports, Session Cases (England).
lrt lower respiratory tract.
lru least recently used.
LS, ls Lesotho; lump sum; listed securities; legal scroll; place of the seal (locus sigilli); letter signed; low speed; landing site; landing ship; longitudinal section; life support; low sodium; lymphosarcoma; length of stay; lumbosacral; left side; left sacrum.
LSA, lsa Legal Services Assistant; Law and Society Association; Labor Services Agency; lymphosarcoma; left sacro anterior.
LSAT Law School Admission Test.
lsb least significant bit; left sternal border.
LSC, lsc Legal Services Corporation; Law of the Sea Conference; Logistical Support

Center; least significant character; in the place cited above (loco supra citato); lump sum contract.

LSCA Library Services and Construction Act.

L Sc D Doctor of the Science of Law.

LSCRRC Law Students Civil Rights Research Council.

lsd landing ship dock; least significant digit; lysergic acid diethylamide; low sodium diet.

LSE, lse London Stock Exchange; life support equipment.

LSG Law Society Gazette (England).

lsh lutein stimulating hormone.

lsi large scale integration.

lsk liver, spleen, kidney.

LSI, lsi Law of the Sea Institute; large scale integration.

lsl left sacrolateral.

lsn left sympathetic nerve; left substantia nigra.

LSO, lso Lesotho; landing signal officer; lumbosacral orthosis; left superior oblique.

L Soc Gaz Law Society Gazette.

L Soc J Law Society Journal.

L & Soc Order Law and the Social Order.

lsp left sacro posterior.

l-spine lumbar spine.

lsr left superior rectus.

lss life support system.

lst local standard time; local sidereal time; left sacro transverse.

lstl laparoscopic tubal ligation.

lsv lateral subclavian vein.

LT, lt Law Times Reports (NS: New Series) (OS: Old Series) (England); Law Times (Pennsylvania); legal tender; lieutenant; low tension; lead time; long ton; long term; local time; limit; light; less than; lower torso; left thigh; leukotriene.

lta lighter than air.

ltc lieutenant colonel; long term care.

ltcf long term care facility.

ltd limited.

lte long term effect.

LTG, ltg lieutenant general; lightning.

LTGF Lawyers' Title Guaranty Funds.

lth luteotropic hormone.

ltho lighthouse

LTJ Law Times Journal.

lto landing and takeoff.

LTOS Law Times, Old Series (England).

ltp limit on tax preferences.

LTR, ltr Law Times Reports (England); lighter; letter.

LTRA Lands Tribunal Rating Appeals (England).

L in Trans Law in Transition.

ltv lung thermal volume.

LU, Lu, lu Luxembourg; lutetium; lumen; left upper.

l&u lower and upper.

lua left upper arm.

LUAP Land Use Adjustment Program.

lub lubricant.

Luc Lucas' Reports (England).

Ludd Ludden's Reports (Maine).

lue left upper extremity.

lul left upper lobe.

Lump Lumpkin's Reports (Georgia).

luo left ureteral orifice.

LUPAC Life Underwriters Political Action Committee.

luq left upper quadrant.

Lush Lushington's Admiralty Reports (England).

lutt lower urinary tract tumor.

Lutw Reg Cas Lutwyche's Registration Cases (England).

LUX Luxembourg.

Luz Leg Obs Luzerne Legal Observer (Pennsylvania).

Luz Leg Reg Luzerne Legal Register (Pennsylvania).

Luz LJ Luzerne Law Journal (Pennsylvania).

Luz LT Luzerne Law Times (Pennsylvania).

lv leave; live vaccine; lumbar vertebra; legal volt; leukemia

virus; left ventricular.

lva left ventricular aneurysm.

lve left ventricular enlargement.

lvedp left ventricular end diastolic pressure.

lvet left ventricular ejection time.

lvf left visual field.

lvh left ventricular hypertrophy.

LVN Licensed Vocational Nurse.

lvp left ventricular pressure.

LV Rep Lehigh Valley Law Reporter (Pennsylvania).

lvs left ventricular strain.

lvsv left ventricular stroke volume.

lvw left ventricular work.

lw low water; lacerating wound.

l/w living and well.

L&W, l&w Lloyd and Welsby's Mercantile Cases (England); living and well.

lwl load waterline.

lwm low water mark.

lwop leave without pay.

lwp leave with pay.

lwr lower; light weight reactor.

LWUI Longshoremen and Warehousemen Union International.

LWV League of Women Voters.

Lx, lx latex; local irradiation.

LY, ly Libya; lying; linear yard; light year; lymphocyte.

lymph lymphocyte.

Lynd Lyndwoode, Provinciale (England).

Lyne Lyne's Chancery Cases (Ireland).

lyp lymphosarcoma.

lytes electrolytes.

lz loading zone; landing zone.

M, m Miles' Reports (Pennsylvania); Miscellaneous

Reports (New York); March; May; Monday; monthly; morning; mortgage; memorandum; maritime; magistrate; missing; mail; male; masculine; married; one thousand; mil; micro; middle; meridian; median; mean; medium; miles; mechanical; measure; magnetic; molecular; molar; medicine; muscle; musculus; myopia; malignant; minim.

MA, ma Missouri Appeals Reports; Massachusetts; Maritime Administration; my account; multiple access; medical assistance; military attache; military assistance; milliampere; medical audit; menstrual age; mental age; Miller-Abbott (tube).

M&A Montague and Ayrton's Bankruptcy (England).

maa medical assistance for the aged; monarticular arthritis.

MAB Medical Advisory Board.

maba meta aminobenzoic acid.

mabp mean arterial blood pressure.

MAC, Mac, mac Municipal Assistance Corporation; Macnaghten's Chancery Reports (England); multiple access computer; machine aided congition; macerate; maximum allowable concentration; malignancy associated changes. See also Mc.

MacAll McAllister's Circuit Court Reports.

Mac & G or **Manc & G** Macnaghten and Gordon's Chancery Reports (England).

MACAP Major Appliance Consumer Action Panel.

MacAr or **MacArth** MacArthur's Reports (District of Columbia).

MacAr Pat Cas MacArthur's Patent Cases (District of Columbia).

MacAr & M MacArthur and

Mackey's Reports (District of Columbia).

MacFarl MacFarlane's Reports (Scotland).

MacG CC MacGillivray's Copyright Cases (England).

mach machine.

Mackey Mackey's Reports (District of Columbia).

MacL & R MacLean and Robinson's House of Lords (England).

MacLean MacLean's Circuit Court Reports.

Macn Macnaghten's Select Cases.

Macph Macpherson's Court of Session Cases (Scotland).

Macph L&B Macpherson, Lee and Bell (Scotland).

Macph S&L Macpherson, Shireff and Lee (Scotland).

Macq Macqueen's Appeal Cases (Scotland).

Macr Macrory's Patent Cases (England).

Mad, mad Maddock's Reports (Montana); Maddock's Chancery Reports (England); mutual assured destruction; magnetic airborne detector; maximum allowable dose.

Mad & Gel Maddock and Geldart's Chancery Reports.

Madd Maddock's Reports (Montana); Maddock's Chancery Reports (England).

Madd & B Maddock and Back's Reports (Montana).

Mag, mag Magruder's Reports (Maryland); magistrate; magnesium; magnetic; magnitude; magazine.

Mag & Con Magistrate and Constable.

Mag Cas Magisterial Cases (England).

MAHA Metropolitan Association of Handwriting Analysts.

Maine LR Maine Law Review.

maint maintenance.

Mait Maitland's Select Pleas of the Crown.

maj major; majority.

MAL, mal Malayan; malicious; malignant; malfunction; midaxillary line.

MALA Minnesota Association of Legal Assistants; Mississippi Association of Legal Assistants.

MALD Master of Arts in Law and Diplomacy.

malf malfunction.

Mal LJ Malayan Law Journal.

Malloy Malloy's Chancery Reports (Ireland).

Malone Heiskell's Reports (Tennessee).

MALS Master of Arts in Library Science.

MAN, man Manning Reports (Michigan); Manitoba, manufacture; management and administration; manager.

mand mandible.

Man & G Manning and Granger's Common Pleas Reports (England).

Man Gr & S Manning, Granger and Scott's Common Bench Reports (England).

Man & Sc Manning and Scott's Reports (England).

Man B New Manitoba Bar News.

M&A Montague and Ayrton's Bankruptcy (England).

M&B Montague and Bligh's Bankruptcy Reports (England).

M&C Montague and Chitty's Bankruptcy Reports (England); Mylne and Craig's Chancery Reports (England).

M&G Maddock and Geldart's Chancery Reports; Manning and Granger's Common Pleas Reports (England).

M & Gel Maddock and Geldart's Chancery Reports.

M & Gord Macnaghten and Gordon's Chancery Reports (England).

M&H Murphy and Hurlstone's Exchequer Cases (England).

M&K Mylne and Keen's Chancery Reports (England).

M&M Moody and Malkin's Nisi Prius Reports (England).

M & McA Montague and McArthur's Bankruptcy (England).

M&P Moore and Payne's Common Pleas Reports (England).

M&R Maclean and Robinson's Appeal Cases (Scotland); Manning and Ryland's King's Bench Reports (England); Moody and Robinson's Nisi Prius Reports (England); Meeson and Roscoe's Exchequer Reports (England).

M&RMC Manning and Ryland's Magistrates' Cases, King's Bench (England).

M & Rob Moody and Robinson's Nisi Prius Reports (England).

M&S Manning and Scott's Reports (England); Maule and Selwyn's King's Bench Reports (England); Moore and Scott's Common Pleas Reports (England).

M & Scott Moore and Scott's Common Pleas Reports (England).

M&W Meeson and Welsby's Exchequer Reports (England); Moore & Walker's Reports (Texas).

M&W Cas Mining and Water Cases Annotated.

M&Y Martin and Yerger's Reports (Tennessee).

mangt management.

Man LJ Manitoba Law Journal.

Man & Ry Mag Manning and Ryland's Magistrates' Cases, King's Bench (England).

Man & Ry Manning and Ryland's King's Bench Reports (England).

Mann Manning's Reports (Michigan).

Mann & G Manning and Granger's Common Pleas Reports (England).

Man R t Wood Manitoba Reports, temp. Wood.

Mans Mansfield's Reports (Arkansas).

Manson Manson's Bankruptcy Cases (England).

manuf manufacturing.

Manum Cas Bloomfield's Manumission Cases (New Jersey).

Man Unrep Cas Manning's Unreported Cases (Louisiana).

mao monoamine oxidase.

map measurement assurance program; modified American plan; maximum average price; mean arterial pressure; medical aid post.

maps monetary and payments system.

maq measures for air quality.

Mar, mar Martin's Reports (Louisiana); Martin's Reports (North Carolina); March; marine; maritime; market; married; memory address register; microanalytical reagent; main admitting room.

MARAD Maritime Administration.

Mar Cas Maritime Cases (England).

March March's King's Bench Reports (England).

March NC March's New Cases, King's Bench (England).

marg marginal.

Marks & Sayre Marks and Sayre's Reports (Alabama).

Mar LC Maritime Law Cases (NS: New Series) (England).

Mar L Rev Maryland Law Review.

Mar N&Q Maritime Notes and Queries.

Mar Prov Maritime Provinces Reports (Canada).

Marq L Rev Marquette Law Review.

Mar R Maritime Law Reports.

Mars Adm Marsden's Admiralty (England).

Marsh Marshall's Reports (Utah); Marshall's Reports (Kentucky); Marshall's Circuit Court Decisions; Marshall's Common Pleas Reports (England).

Mart Ark Martin's Decisions in Equity (Arkansas).

Mart & Yerg Martin and Yerger's Reports (Tennessee).

Mart Cond La Martin's Condensed Reports (Louisiana).

Mart Dec Martin's Decisions (North Carolina).

Mart Ga Martin's Reports (Georgia).

Martin Martin's Reports (Louisiana); Martin's Reports (Georgia); Martin's Reports (North Carolina).

Mart Ind Martin's Reports (Indiana).

Mart La Martin's Reports (OS: Old Series) (NS: New Series) (Louisiana).

Mart NC Martin's Reports (North Carolina).

Marvel Marvel's Reports (Delaware).

mas masculine; milliampere second.

Mason Mason's Circuit Court Reports.

Mass Acts Acts and Resolves of Massachusetts.

Mass Adv Legis Massachusetts Legislative Service.

Mass Ann Laws Annotated Laws of Massachusetts.

Mass App Dec Massachusetts Appellate Decisions.

Mass App Div Massachusetts Appellate Division Reports; Massachusetts Appellate Division Advance Sheets.

Mass Gen L General Laws of the Commonwealth of Massachusetts.

Mass LQ Massachusetts Law Quarterly.

Mass Reg Massachusetts Register.

Mass Regs Code Code of Massachusetts Regulations.

Mast Master's Reports (Canada).

mat machine available time; Miller analogy test; mechanical aptitude test; material; maternity; multifocal atrial tachycardia; maturity.

MATE Married Americans for Tax Equality.

Math, math Mathieu's Reports (Quebec); mathematics.

Matson Matson's Reports (Connecticut).

Matthews Matthews' Reports (Virginia); Matthews' Reports (West Virginia).

Mau & Sel Maule and Selwyn's King's Bench Reports (England).

MAW Mothers for Adequate Welfare.

max maximum.

MB, Mb, mb Municipal Board; Miscellaneous Branch (Internal Revenue Service); Manitoba; municipal borough; mail box; memory buffer; megabyte; megabit; motor boat; millibar; medical bulletin; methyl bromide; muscle balance; maximum breathing.

M&B Montague and Bligh's Bankruptcy Reports (England).

MBA Mortgage Bankers Association of America; Migratory Bird Act; Master of Business Administration.

mbb mortgage backed bonds.

mbc minimum bactericidal concentration.

MBCC Migratory Bird Conservation Commission.

mbd million barrels per day; minimal brain damage.

MBE, mbe Multistate Bar Examination; minority business enterprise.

mbf muscle blood flow.

mbh maximum benefit from hospitalization.

mbi may be issued.

MBIA Municipal Bond Insurance Association.

mbl mobile; menstrual blood loss.

mbo management by objective.

mbp mean blood pressure; mesiobuccopulpal.

MBR, mbr maximum base rent; member; master bedroom.

MC, mc Magistrates Cases (England); Monthly Catalog; Member of Congress; Maritime Commission; Magistrate Court; Mayor's Court; multiple contact; memorandum of conditions; material code; motor carrier; motorcycle; marginal credit; magnetic course; metric carat; megacycle; machinery certificate; maintenance cycle; metal carbide; methylcellulose; myocarditis; medical center; medical corps; monkey cell. See also Mac.

m/c marginal credit; male, castrated.

M&C Montague and Chitty's Bankruptcy Reports (England); Mylne and Craig's Chancery Reports (England).

MCA, mca Model Cities Administration; Manufacturing Chemists Association; motorcycle accident; monochloroacetic acid; major coronary artery.

MCAA Mechanical Contractors Association of America.

McAll McAllister'a Circuit Court Reports.

M Can L Master of Canon Law.

MCAT Medical College Admission Test.

McBride McBride's Reports (Missouri).

MCBW Amalgamated Meat Cutters and Butcher Workmen of North America.

MCC, mcc Motor Carrier Cases (Interstate Commerce Commission); Mixed Claims Commission; mechanical chemical codes; midcourse correction; master control center.

McCahon McCahon's Reports (Kansas).

McCarter McCarter's Chancery Reports (New Jersey).

McCartney McCartney's Civil Procedure (New York).

McClelland McClelland's Exchequer Reports (England).

McCl & Y or **McClell & Y** McClelland and Younge's Exchequer Reports (England).

McCook McCook's Reports (Ohio).

McCord McCord's Reports (South Carolina).

McCorkle McCorkle's Reports (North Carolina).

McCrary McCrary's Circuit Court Reports.

MCD, mcd Maritime Commission Decisions; Magistrate Court Decisions (New Zealand); Military Contracts Department; Doctor of Comparative Medicine; mean corpuscular diameter.

mcf thousand cubic feet; most comfortable frequency.

mcfche microfiche.

mcflm microfilm.

mcg microgram.

McGill LJ McGill Law Journal.

McGloin McGloin's Reports (Louisiana).

mch mean cell hemoglobin; mean corpuscular hemoglobin.

mchc mean corpuscular hemoglobin concentration.

mcht merchant.

MCI, mci malleable cast iron; materials cost index; mean cardiac index; methicillin.

MCJ Michigan Civil Jurisprudence; Master of Comparative Jurisprudence.

MCL, mcl Master of Comparative Law; Master of Civil Law; maximum contaminant level; mid-clavicular line; maximum confort level.

McLean McLean's Circuit Court Reports.

MCLI Meiklejohn Civil Liberties Institute.

MCM Manual for Courts Martial.

McMullan McMullan's Reports (South Carolina).

MCO, mco Monaco; mill culls out; medical care organization.

M Comp L or **MCL** Master of Comparative Law.

MCP, mcp Model Cities Program; male chauvinist pig; metacarpophalangeal.

MCPL Members of Congress for Peace through Law.

MCPS Mechanical Copyright Protection Society.

mcq multiple choice question.

MCR, mcr Montreal Condensed Reports; Magistrates Court Reports (New Zealand); Marine Corps Reserve; master control room; mother-child relationship.

MCS measurements calibration system; missile control system.

MCSTB Motor Carriers Service Tariff Bureau.

mct mean cell thickness.

MCTA Motor Carriers Tariff Association.

mcv mean cell volume; mean corpuscular volume.

McWillie McWillie's Reports (Mississippi).

MD, Md, md Master's Decisions (patents); Maryland; medical doctor; mendelevium; memorandum of deposit; months after date; management directive; malfunction-defect; married; mean deviation; right hand (main droit); myocardial disease; muscular dystrophy; medical discharge; mentally deficient; main duct; maximum dose; minimum dose; mental defective; mitral disease.

mda mento dextra anterior.

MDAA Mutual Defense Assistance Act.

Md App Maryland Appellate Reports.

mdar minimum daily adult requirement.

Md BJ Maryland Bar Journal.

mdc minimum detectable concentration.

Md Ch Maryland Chancery Reports.

Md Code Ann Annotated Code of Maryland.

mdd major depressive disorder.

MDG Madagascar.

Md L Rec Maryland Law Record.

Md L Rep Maryland Law Reporter.

Md L Rev Maryland Law Review.

mdnt midnight.

mdp malicious destruction of property.

mdr memory data register; minimum daily requirement.

Md Reg Maryland Register.

Md Regs Code Code of Maryland Regulations.

MDS, mds Master of Dental Surgery; multipoint distribution service; milk drinker syndrome.

mdse merchandise.

mdt moderate.

MDT Mountain Daylight Time.

MDTA Manpower Development and Training Act.

MDV, mdv Maldives; mid variant; mucosal disease virus.

mdy month, day, year.

ME, Me, me Maine; Middle East; methyl; mechanical engineer; managing editor; molecular electronics; metabolic energy; middle ear; maximum effort; medical examiner; macular edema.

Me Acts Acts, Resolves and Constitutional Resolutions of Maine.

Means Means' Reports (Kansas).

MEB Medical Examining Board.

mec middle ear canals.

Med, med Mediterranean; medium; median; medial; medicine; minimum effective dose; minimum erythema dose.

Medd Meddaugh's Reports (Michigan).

Med Legal J Medico-Legal Journal.

meds medications.

Med Sci & L Medicine, Science, and the Law.

Med Trial Tech Q Medical Trial Techniques Quarterly.

Mees & Ros Meeson and Roscoe's Exchequer Reports (England).

Mees & Wels Meeson and Welsby's Exchequer Reports (England).

mef maximal expiratory flow.

Meg, meg Megone Company Cases (England); megohm.

mega one million.

megs megasecond.

megw megawatt.

MEI Middle East Institute.

Meigs Meigs's Reports (Tennessee).

mek methyl ethyl ketone.

mEq milliequivalent.

Melanesian LJ Melanesian Law Journal (Papua and New Guinea).

Me Laws Laws of the State of Maine.

Melb UL Rev Melbourne University Law Review.

Me Legis Serv Maine Legislative Service.

Me L Rev Maine Law Review.

MELP Mid-European Law Project.

mem memorandum; memory; membrane; minimal essential medium.

Mem LJ Memphis Law Journal.

memo memorandum.

Mem St UL Rev Memphis State University Law Review.

MEN, men Male Equality Now, Inc.; multiple endocrine neoplasia

Menken Menken's Reports, Civil Procedure (New York).

meo malignant external otitis.

mep mean effective pressure.

Mer, mer Merivale's Chancery Reports (England); meridian; merchant; mercantile.

Mercer BLR Mercer Beasley Law Review.

Mercer Law Rev Mercer Law Review.

Me Rev Stat Ann Maine Revised Statutes Annotated.

Meriv Merivale's Chancery Reports (England).

mes muscles in elongated state.

MESA Mining Enforcement and Safety Administration.

Met, met Metcalf's Reports (Massachusetts); Metcalf's Reports (Rhode Island);

Metcalfe's Reports (Kentucky); methionine; metropolitan; minimum exposure time; manufacturer excise tax; meteorological; metallurgy; metal.

Metc Metcalf's Reports (Massachusetts); Metcalf's Reports (Rhode Island); Metcalfe's Reports (Kentucky).

meteor meteorological.

Meth, meth Methodist; method; methane; methylated.

METO Middle East Treaty Organization.

metro metropolitan.

Mews Mews' Digest of English Case Law.

Mex Mexico.

mf master file; motor freight; machine finish; manufacture; medium frequency; microfiche; male/female; millifarad; mycosis fungoides; mucosal fluid; midcavity forceps.

mfa malicious false alarm.

mfd manufactured; minimum fatal dose.

mfe magnetic field energy.

mfg manufacturing.

mflops million floating-point operations per second.

mfmwws male, female, married, widow, widower, single.

mfn most favored nation.

mfp mean free path.

MFPD Modern Federal Practice Digest.

mfpds myofascial pain-dysfunction syndrome.

mfr manufacturer; malfunction rate.

mfs medical fee schedule.

MFTB Motor Freight Tariff Bureau.

mfv microfilm viewer.

MG, Mg, mg Madagascar; magnesium; major general; miles per gallon; marginal; make good; mixed grain; machine gun; morning; milligram; left hand (main gauche); myasthenia gravis.

M&G Maddock and Geldart's Chancery Reports (England); Manning and Granger's Common Pleas Reports (England).

MGC Midwestern Governors' Conference.

mgm milligram.

mgmt or **mgt** management.

mgr milligram.

MgSO$_4$ magnesium sulfate.

mgt management.

MH, mh man hours; miles per hour; mobile home; maleic hydrazide; murine hepatitis; mental health; medical history; malignant hypothermia.

M&H Murphy and Hurlstone's Exchequer Cases (England).

MHD, mhd Mental Health Digest; minimum hemolytic dose.

MHDNA Mobile Home Dealers National Association.

MHR Member of the House of Representatives.

mht mean high tide.

mhv magnetic heart vector; murine hepatitis virus.

m hx medical history.

MHz megahertz.

MI, mi Michigan; Midway Islands; Marshall Islands; meat inspection; medical inspection; malleable iron; mill; mile; minute; mental illness; metabolic index; master index; myocardial infarction.

MIA, mia Master of International Affairs; missing in action.

Miami LQ Miami Law Quarterly.

MIB Medical Information Bureau.

MIC Meat Importers Council; military industrial complex; minimal (minimum) inhibitory concentration.

MICA Mortgage Insurance Companies of America.

Mich Michigan Reports.

Mich App Michigan Appeals Reports.

Mich Comp Laws Michigan Compiled Laws.

Michie's Jur Michie's Jurisprudence of Virginia and West Virginia.

Mich Jur Michigan Jurisprudence.

Mich Law Rev Michigan Law Review.

Mich Legis Serv Michigan Legislative Service.

Mich NP Michigan Nisi Prius Reports (Brown or Howell).

Mich Pub Acts Public and Local Acts of the Legislature of the State of Michigan.

Mich Reg Michigan Register.

Mich SBJ Michigan State Bar Journal.

Mich Stat Ann Michigan Statutes Annotated.

Mich T Michaelmas Term (England).

micr magnetic ink character recognition.

micro microscopic.

mid middle; midnight; minimal infective dose; mesioincisodistal; midline.

midr mandatory incident/defect reporting.

mifr maximal inspiratory flow rate.

MIG Moody's Investment Guide.

MIIA Mine Inspector's Institute of America.

Mil, mil Miles' Reports (Pennsylvania); million; millileter; military; militia; mileage; mother in law.

Miles Miles' District Court Reports (Philadelphia).

Mill Miller's Reports (Louisiana); Miller's Reports (Maryland).

Mill Const Mill's Constitutional Reports (South Carolina).

Mill Dec Miller's Circuit Court Decisions.

Mil L Rev Military Law Review.

Mills Mills' Reports, Surrogate Court (New York).

Milw Milward's Ecclesiastical Reports (Ireland).

Min, min Minor's Reports (Alabama); minor; minister; minority; mineral; minimum; minimal.

Minn Minnesota Reports.

Minn Cont Leg Ed Minnesota Continuing Legal Education.

Minn L Rev Minnesota Law Review.

Minn R Minnesota Rules.

Minn Reg Minnesota State Register.

Minn Stat Ann Minnesota Statutes Annotated.

Minn Sess Law Serv Minnesota Session Law Service.

Minor Minor's Reports (Alabama).

MIRV Multiple Independently Targetable Reentry Vehicle.

mip mortgage insurance premium; marine insurance policy; mean indicated pressure; maximum inspiratory pressure.

mips million instructions per second.

mis missing; miscellaneous; management information system.

Misc, misc Miscellaneous Reports (New York); miscarriage.

misd misdemeanor.

Misc Dec Miscellaneous Decisions (Ohio).

misg modified immune serum globulin.

Miss Mississippi Reports.

Miss Code Ann Mississippi Code Annotated.

Miss Dec Mississippi Decisions.

Miss Law J Mississippi Law Journal.

Miss Law Rev Mississippi Law Review.

Miss Laws General Laws of Mississippi.

Miss St Cas Mississippi State Cases (Morris).

Mister Mister's Reports (Missouri).

mit male impotence test; master instruction tape; mitomycin; monoiodotyrosine.

mixt mixture.

MJ Military Judge.

MJD Doctor of Medical Jurisprudence.

mk morse key; mark.

M&K Mylne and Keen's Chancery Reports (England).

mkt market.

ML, ml Mali; Master of Laws; mixed lengths; mean level; mother in law; myeloid leukemia; milliliter; malignant lymphoma; middle lobe.

MLA, mla Maritime Law Association; Member of the Legislative Assembly; mentolaeva anterior.

MLB Maritime Labor Board.

MLC, mlc Medical Liability Commission; Major Legislation of Congress; Midwestern Legislative Conference; master labor contract.

mld mold; minimum lethal dose; mild.

ML Dig & R Monthly Law Digest and Reporter (Canada).

MLDU Marriage Law Defense Union.

MLE, mle Maryland Law Encyclopedia; maximum likelihood estimation.

MLEP Minority Legislative Education Program.

mlf multilateral force.

MLJ Memphis Law Journal.

MLI Mali.

MLKCSC Martin Luther King Center for Social Change.

ML Libr Master of Law Librarianship.

mln mesenteric lymph node.

MLP Michigan Law and Practice.

MLR, mlr Modern Law Review (England); Monthly Labor Review; Military Law Reporter; Maryland Law Record; muzzle loading rifle.

MLRQB Montreal Law Reports, Queen's Bench.

MLRSC Montreal Law Reports, Superior Court.

MLRA Marriage Law Reform Association.

MLS, mls Master of Library Science; median life span.

MLT, mlt Master of Law and Taxation; median low tide; median lethal time; medical lab technician.

mlv murine leukemia virus.

MM, mm Merchant Marine; made merchantable; master mechanic; mutatis mutandis (with the necessary changes); millimeter; methyl methacrylate; mismatch; malignant melanoma; mucous membrane; major medical; morbidity and mortality.

M&M Moody and Malkin's Nisi Prius Reports (England).

M'Mullan McMullan's Reports (South Carolina).

M & McA Montague and McArthur's Bankruptcy (England).

MMCB Midwest Motor Carriers Bureau.

mmh maintenance man hours.

mmHg millimeters of mercury.

MMPI Minnesota Multiphasic Personality Inventory.

MMSW International Union of Mine, Mill, and Smelter Workers.

M'Mullan McMullan's Reports (South Carolina).

MN, Mn, mn Minnesota; Mongolia; manganese; magnetic north; midnight; main; myoneural; mucosal neurolysis; a blood group in the MNS group.

mmr measles, mumps, rubella.

mm str muscle strength.

mmt manual muscle test; manganese tricarbonyl.

mnc multinational corporation.

MNI Ministry of National Insurance (England).

mnm minimum.

mntn maintenance.

Mo, mo Missouri Reports; Moore's Common Pleas Reports (England); Macao; molybdenum; month; make offer; modus operandi (method of operation); money order; mail order; mesio occlusal; medical officer; manually operated.

moa memorandum of agreement.

MOAA Mail Order Association of America.

Moak Moak's Reports (England).

Mo & P See Moore and P.

Mo & R See Mood & R.

Mo & S See M & Scott.

Mo Ann Stat Vernon's Annotated Missouri Statutes.

Mo App Missouri Appeals Reports.

Mo AR Missouri Appellate Reporter.

Mo BJ Missouri Bar Journal.

Mo Code Reg Missouri Code of State Regulations.

MOD, Mod, mod Medical Officer of the Day; Modern Reports (England); mail order delivery; modification; modulation; modulus; modern; moderate; modicus; maturity onset diabetes; mesio-occlusodistal.

Mod Cas Modern Cases, Modern Reports (England).

Mo Dec Missouri Decisions.

mod moderate.

modem modulator-demodulator.

modfn or **modif** modification.

Mod Law Soc Modern Law and Society.

Mod L Rev Modern Law Review (England).

Mod Pract Comm Modern Practice Commentator.

Mod Rep Modern Reports (England).

moe measure of effectiveness.

mof multiple organ failure.

moi maximum oxygen intake.

MO JAGA Memorandum Opinions of the Judge Advocate General, Army.

Mo JB J.B. Moore's Common Pleas Reports (England).

Mo Jur Monthly Jurist.

mol molestation; molecule.

Mo Labor R Monthly Labor Review.

Mo Laws Laws of Missouri.

Moll, moll Molloy's Chancery Reports (Ireland); soft (mollis).

Mo L Rev Missouri Law Review.

Mo Legis Serv Missouri Legislative Service.

mol wt molecular weight.

Moly Molyneaux's Reports (England).

mom minutes of the meeting; middle of the month; milk of magnesia.

Mon, mon Monroe's Reports (Kentucky); Monaghan's Unreported Cases (Pennsylvania); Monday; Mongolian; monitor; monument; month; monetary; monocyte; mononucleosis.

Monag Monaghan's Reports (Pennsylvania).

mono mononucleosis.

Mont Montana Reports; Montreal.

Mont Admin R Administrative Rules of Montana.

Mont Admin Reg Montana Administrative Register.

Mont & Ayr Montague and Ayrton's Bankruptcy (England).

Mont & B Montague and Bligh's Bankruptcy Reports (England).

Mont & C Montague and Chitty's Bankruptcy Reports (England).

Mont & McA Montague and McArthur's Bankruptcy (England).

Mont Code Ann Montana Code Annotated.

Mont Co LR Montgomery County Law Reporter (Pennsylvania).

Month Leg Exam Monthly Legal Examiner (New York).

Month LJ Monthly Journal of Law (Washington).

Month L Mag Monthly Law Magazine (England).

Month L Rep Monthly Law Reporter (Massachusetts); Monthly Law Reports (Canada).

Month L Rev Monthly Law Review.

Mont Leg News Montreal Legal News.

Mont L Rev Montana Law Review.

Montr Cond Rep Montreal Condensed Reports.

Montr QB Montreal Queen's Bench Law Reports.

Mont Super Montreal Superior Court Law Reports.

Moo See Moody; Moore.

Moo CC Moody's Crown Cases Reserved (England).

Moo CP See Moore CP.

Mood & M Moody and Mackin's Nisi Prius Reports (England).

Mood & R Moody and Robinson's Nisi Prius Reports (England).

Moody Moody's Crown Cases Reserved (England).

Moon Moon's Reports (Indiana).

Moo PC See Moore PC.

Moore Moore's Reports (Texas); Moore's Reports (Arkansas); Moore's Reports (Alabama).

Moore & P Moore and Payne's Common Pleas Reports (England).

Moore & S Moore and Scott's Common Pleas Reports (England).

Moore & Walk Moore & Walker's Reports (Texas).

Moore CP Moore's Common Pleas Reports (England).

Moore Ind App Moore's Indian Appeals (England).

Moore KB Moore's King's Bench Reports (England).

Moore PC Moore's Privy Council Reports (NS: New Series) (England).

mop memorandum of policy; mustering out pay; medical outpatient.

Mo PC Moore's Privy Council Reports (England).

moq minimum order quantity.

MOR, mor Morocco; morphine; medical officer report.

MORAL Massachusetts Organization for the Repeal of Abortion Laws.

mor dict as directed (more dicto).

Mo Reg Missouri Register.

Mo Rev Stat Missouri Revised Statutes.

Morg Morgan's Chancery Acts and Orders (England).

morph morphine.

Morr Morris' Reports (California); Morris' Reports (Iowa); Morris' Reports (Mississippi); Morris' Reports (Oregon); Morrow's Reports (Oregon); Morrill's Bankruptcy Cases (England).

Morris Morrissett's Reports (Alabama); see also Morr. .

Morr St Cas Morris' State Cases (Mississippi).

Morr Trans Morrison's Transcript, United States Supreme Court Decisions.

Morse Exch Rep Morse's Exchequer Reports (Canada).

mort mortality.

Mos, mos Mosely's Chancery Reports (England); months; metal oxide semiconductor; mosaic; material ordering schedule; medial orbital sulcus; myelofibrosis osteosclerosis.

m0s milliosmole.

mosfet metal oxide semiconductor field effect transistor.

mot mean operating time; motor.

mou memorandum of understanding.

Moult Ch Moulton's Chancery Practice (New York).

Mo W Jur Monthly Western Jurist.

MOZ Mozambique.

MP, mp Member of Parliament; Metropolitan Police; Marine Police; Military Police; minister plenipotentiary; military property; memorandum of partnership; mail payment; manpower; maintenance procedure; melting point; magnetic particle; medium pressure; middle phalanx; medical payment; mycoplasmal pneumonia; mesiopulpal; menstrual period.

M&P Moore and Payne's Common Pleas Reports (England).

MPA, mpa Magazine Publishers Association; Massachusetts Paralegal Association; Metrolina Paralegal Association; Manhattan Paralegal Association; Memphis Paralegal Association; main pulmonary artery.

MPAA Motion Picture Association of America.

mpap mean pulmonary arterial pressure.

MPB Missing Person Bureau.

MPC, mpc Moore's Privy Council Cases (England); maximum permissible concentration.

MPCI Military Police Criminal Investigation.

MPCLP Mental Patient Civil Liberties Project.

mpd minimum permissible dose.

MPEA Meat and Poultry Export Association.

mpel maximum permissible exposure level.

mpf maturation promoting factor.

mpg miles per gallon.

mph miles per hour.

MPI, mpi Max Planck Institute; mean point of impact; maximum permissible intake; myocardial perfusion imaging.

MPL Master of Patent Law.

MPLR Municipal and Planning Law Reports (Canada).

mpm miles per minute; meters per minute; medial pterygoid muscle.

mpp medical personnel pool; metacarpophalangeal profile.

MPR, mpr Maritime Province Reports; Mongolian Peoples Republic; monthly progress report.

mps master planning schedule; miles per second; meters per second.

mpu microprocessor unit.

mpv mean platelet volume.

MQ Martinique.

MR, mr Manitoba Reports (Canada); Mauritania; Master of the Rolls; maintenance/repair; military reserve; military regulation; manual removal; milliroentgen; mental retardation; metabolic rate; menstrual regulation; medical release; mortality rate; may repeat; mitral regurgitation.

M&R Maclean and Robinson's Appeal Cases (Scotland); Manning and Ryland's King's Bench Reports (England); Moody and Robinson's Nisi Prius Reports (England).

mra main renal artery; medical records administrator.

MRAA Marine Retailers Association of America.

mrad mass random access disk; millirad.

MRB Modification Review Board.

mrd minimum reacting dose.

MRI Mass Retailing Institute.

MRID mechanical retrieval identification.

MRIS Maritime Research Information Service.

mrn malignant renal neoplasm.

mro military release order; maintenance, repair, and operation.

mrr medium range radar.

mrs medical receiving station.

MRT, mrt Mauritania; medical records technology.

mrtm maritime.

MS, Ms, ms Montserrat; Mauritius; Mississippi; Master of Science; method of sale; metric system; millisecond; meters per second; mean square; margin of safety; manufacturing standard; master switch; magnetic south; manuscript; miss; left hand (mano sinistra); mitral stenosis; motile sperm; mental status; Marie-Sée syndrome; mass spectrometry; medical supplies; microscope slide; muscle strength; multiple sclerosis; morphine sulphate.

M&S Manning and Scott's Reports (England); Maule and

Selwyn's King's Bench Reports (England); Moore and Scott's Common Pleas Reports (England).

MSA, msa Medical Services Administration; Mutual Security Act; Merchant Shipping Act; most seriously affected; minimum safe altitude; medical short appointment.

MSALA Mid-South Association of Legal Assistants.

MSB, msb Municipal Securities Board; Maritime Subsidy Board; most significant bit; mid small bowel.

msc miscellaneous; millisecond; most significant character.

MSCJ Master of Science in Criminal Justice.

M Sc L Master of Science of Law.

msd most significant digit.

Ms D Manuscript Decisions (Patents) (Comptroller General).

MSDS material safety data sheet.

mse medical support equipment.

msec millisecond.

msf medium standard frequency; muscle shock factor; macrophage spreading factor.

msg monosodium glutamate.

msh melanocyte stimulating hormone.

msl missile; mean sea level; mid-sternal line.

MSLS Master of Science in Library Science.

msmt measurement.

mso military supply officer; multiple systems operator.

msod military service obligation date.

msp die without issue (mortuus sine prole); muscle spasm.

MSR Montserrat.

MSRB Municipal Securities Rulemaking Board.

msrp manufacturer suggested retail price.

mss manuscripts; multiple sclerosis susceptibility.

MSSW Master of Science in Social Work.

MST, mst Mountain Standard Time; mean solar time; mean survival time; measurement.

msu monosodium urate.

msv murine sarcoma virus.

MSW, msw Master of Social Work; multiple stab wounds.

msy maximum sustainable yield.

MT, mt Miscellaneous Tax Ruling; Malta; Montana; Medical Technologist; mandated territory; mechanical (machine) translation; metric ton; motor transport; mountain; meter; mean tide; mean time; metatarsal; muscles and tendons; medical treatment; mammary tumor.

mta medical technical assistant; mammary tumor agent.

mtbe methyl tert butyl ether.

mtbf mean time between failures.

MTC, mtc Multistate Tax Commission; maximum tolerated concentration.

mtd mean temperature difference; maximum tolerated dose.

mtg mortgage; meeting.

mtgd mortgaged.

mtgee mortgagee.

mtgor mortgagor.

MTN, mtn Multilateral Trade Negotiations; mountain; motion.

mtp metatarsophalangeal; maximum tolerated pressure.

MTPA Middle Tennessee Paralegal Association.

MTQ Martinique.

mtr multiple track radar.

MTRB Maritime Transportation Research Board.

MTS Monthly Treasury Statement.

mtst maximal treadmill stress test.

mttr mean time to repair.

mtv mammary tumor virus.

mtx methotrexate.

MU, mu Mauritius; maternal uncle; mobile unit; motor unit; maintenance unit.

mua memorandum of understanding and agreement.

muc maximum urinary concentration.

Mu LJ Municipal Law Journal.

MULR Melbourne University Law Review.

multip multiparous.

mulv murine leukemia virus.

Mun, mun Munford's Reports (Virginia); munitions; municipal.

Mun Atty Municipal Attorney.

Mun Corp Cas Municipal Corporation Cases.

Munf Munford's Reports (Virginia).

Munic & PL Municipal and Parish Law Cases (England).

Mun L Ct Dec Municipal Law Court Decisions.

Mun LJ Municipal Law Journal.

Mun Ord Rev Municipal Ordinance Review.

Mun Rep Municipal Reports (Canada).

muo myocardiopathy of unknown origin.

Mur, mur Murphey's Reports (North Carolina); Murray's Reports (New South Wales, Australia); Murray's Scotch Jury Court Reports; murder.

Mur & Hurl Murphy and Hurlstone's Exchequer Cases (England).

murc measurable undesirable respiratory contaminants.

Murph Murphey's Reports (North Carolina).

Murr Murray's Scotch Jury Court Reports.

Murr Over Cas Murray's Overruled Cases.

MUS Mauritius.

mut mutilation.

MV, Mv, mv Maldives; mendelevium; market value; motor vehicle; methyl violet; million volts; millivolt; mean voltage; mean variation; mitral valve; measles virus.

mva motor vehicle accident; mechanical ventricular assistance.

mvd mitral valve disease.

MVMA Motor Vehicle Manufacturers Association of the United States.

mvo maximum venous oxygen.

mvp mitral valve prolapse.

mvss motor vehicle safety standard.

mvt movement.

mvv maximum voluntary ventilation.

MW, mw Malawi; molecular weight; mixed widths; microwave; megawatt; molecular weight; multiple wounds.

M&W Meeson and Welsby's Exchequer Reports (England).

MWAA Movers and Warehousemen Association of America.

MWD Metropolitan Water District.

MWI Malawi.

mwl mean water level.

mwt myocardial wall thickness; molecular weight.

MX, mx Mexico; maxwell; missile, experimental.

MY, my Malaysia; May; man year; myopia; myelocyte.

M&Y Martin and Yerger's Reports (Tennessee).

myc mycology.

myel myelogram.

Myer Fed Dec Myer's Federal Decisions.

Myl & Cr Mylne and Craig's Chancery Reports (England).

Myl & K Mylne and Keen's Chancery Reports (England).

myg myriagram; myasthenia gravis.

myo myocardial.

Myr Myrick's Probate Reports (California).

Mysore LJ Mysore Law Journal (India).

MZ, mz Mozambique; monozygotic.

N, n Nebraska; Norway; November; national; navigation; number of observations; north; nautical; normal; name; net; nephew; nucleus; neutron; negative; nodules; nicotinamide; neuropathy; nitrogen; a blood group in the MNS blood group.

NA, Na, na Namibia; North America; Native American; sodium (natrium); noise abatement; no advice; not authorized; nonacceptance; no account; not available; not assigned; not applicable; narcotics anonymous; nurse's aide; numerical aperture; nucleic acid; nonalcoholic.

n&a normal and active.

NAA, naa National Academy of Arbitrators; National Association of Accountants; National Aeronautic Association; neutron activation analysis; nonattainment area; no apparent abnormalities.

NAAB National Architectural Accrediting Board; National Association of Animal Breeders.

NAA Bul National Association of Accountants Bulletin.

NAACP National Association for the Advancement of Colored People.

NAAG National Association of Attorneys General.

NAAP National Association for Accreditation in Psychoanalysis.

NAATTFO National Association of Alcohol and Tobacco Tax Field Officers.

NAB, nab National Alliance of Businessmen; National Association of Broadcasters; novarsenobenzene.

NABA National Association of Black Accountants.

NABCA National Alcoholic Beverage Control Association.

NABE National Association of Bar Executives; National Association for Bilingual Education.

NABP National Association of Boards of Pharmacy.

NABS National Association of Black Students.

NABUG National Association of Broadcast Unions and Guilds.

NABW National Association of Black Women.

NAC, nac National Association of Coroners; National Association of Counties; national advisory council.

NACA National Association for Court Administration; National Air Carrier Association.

NACCA National Association of Claimants' Counsel of America; National Association of Claimants' Compensation Attorneys; National Association of Consumer Credit Administrators.

NACCC National Association of Citizen Crime Commissions.

NAAQS National Ambient Air Quality Standards.\

NACDAP National Advisory Council for Drug Abuse Prevention.

NACDL National Association of Criminal Defense Lawyers.

NACEO National Advisory Council on Economic Opportunity.

NACHC National Association of Community Health Centers.

NACHO National Association of County Health Officials.

NaCl sodium chloride.

NACLIS National Commission on Libraries and Information Service.

NACM National Association of Credit Management.

NACO National Association of Consumer Organizations.

NACORE National Association of Corporate Real Estate Executives.

NACPA National Association of County and Prosecuting Attorneys.

NACPD National Association of County Planning Directors.

NACRC National Association of County Recorders and Clerks.

NACS National Association of Convenience Stores; National Association of Cosmetology Schools.

NACSA National Association of Casualty and Surety Agents.

NACSE National Association of Civil Service Employees; National Association of Casualty and Surety Executives.

NACTFO National Association of County Treasurers and Finance Officers.

NACTP National Association of Computerized Tax Processors.

NACU National Association of Colleges and Universities.

NACUA National Association of College and University Attorneys; National Association of Colleges and University Administrators.

NACVE National Advisory Council on Vocational Education.

NACW National Association of College Women.

NACWD National Association of County Welfare Directors.

NAD, nad National Association of the Deaf; no apparent defect; no acute distress; no abnormality detected; nicotinamide adenine dinucleotide.

NADA National Automobile Dealers Association; National Association of Dental Assistants; new animal drug approval.

NADC National Anti-Dumping Committee; National

Association of Demolition Contractors; National Association of Dredging Contractors.

NADE National Association of Disability Examiners.

NADL National Association of Dental Laboratories.

NADLCC National Association of Defense Lawyers in Criminal Cases.

NADUSM National Association of Deputy United States Marshals.

nae net acid excretion.

NAEC National Association of Engineering Companies.

NAEFTA National Association of Enrolled Federal Tax Accountants.

NAEN National Association of Educational Negotiators.

NAEO National Association of Extradition Officers.

NAES National Association of Executive Secretaries.

NAESP National Association of Elementary School Principals.

NAF, NaF, naf National Arts Foundation; sodium fluoride; nonappropriated funds; net acid flux; Negro adult female.

NAFCO National Association of Franchise Companies.

NAFCU National Association of Federal Credit Unions.

NAFEO National Association for Equal Opportunity in Higher Education.

NAFI National Association of Fire Investigators.

NAFM National Association of Furniture Manufacturers.

NAGARA National Association of Government Archives and Records Administrators.

NAGE National Association of Government Employees.

NAGI National Association of Government Inspectors.

NAGS National Association of Government Secretaries.

NAGTC North American Gasoline

Tax Conference.

NAHA National Association of Handwriting Analysts.

NAHB National Association of Home Builders.

NAHC National Association of Housing Cooperatives.

NAHD National Association for Human Development.

NAHHA National Association of Home Health Agencies.

NAHM National Association of Home Manufacturers.

NAHRO National Association of Housing and Redevelopment Officials.

NAHRW National Association of Human Rights Workers.

NAHSE National Association of Health Services Executives.

nai nonaccidental injury; no action indicated.

NAIA North American Indian Association; National Association of Insurance Agents; National Association of Intercollegiate Athletics.

NAIB National Association of Insurance Brokers.

NAIC National Association of Insurance Commissioners; National American Indian Council.

NAICU National Association of Independent Colleges and Universities.

NAIFA National Association of Independent Fee Appraisers.

NAIFR National Association of Independent Food Retailers.

NAII National Association of Independent Insurers.

NAIIA National Association of Independent Insurance Adjusters.

NAIRE National Association of Internal Revenue Employees.

NAIS National Association of Independent Schools.

NAJ National Association for Justice.

NAJA North American Judges Association.

nak negative acknowledge character.

NALA National Association of Legal Assistants; Nebraska Association of Legal Assistants.

NALC National Association of Letter Carriers; National Afro-American Labor Council.

NALDEF Native American Legal Defense and Education Foundation.

NALS National Association of Legal Secretaries.

NALU National Association of Life Underwriters.

NAM, nam National Association of Manufacturers; Namibia; Negro adult male.

NAMC National Association of Minority Contractors.

NAMCC National Association of Mutual Casualty Companies.

NAMH National Association for Mental Health.

NAMIA National Association of Mutual Insurance Agents.

NAMP National Association of Magazine Publishers.

NAMPW National Association of Meat Processors and Wholesalers.

NAMS National Association of Municipal Securities Dealers.

NAMSB National Association of Mutual Savings Banks.

nan unless otherwise noted (nisi aliter notetur).

n&a normal and active.

N&G North and Guthrie's Reports (Missouri).

N&H Nott and Huntington's Reports, United States Court of Claims; Nott and Hopkins' Reports, United States Court of Claims.

N&M, n&m Nevile and Manning's King's Bench Reports (England); nerves and muscles; night and morning.

N & Mc Nott and McCord's Reports (South Carolina).

N & Macn Nevile and Macnamara's Railway and Canal Cases (England).

N&P Nevile and Perry's King's Bench Reports (England).

n&t nose and throat.

n&v nausea and vomiting.

NAO National Association of Optometrists.

NAOO National Association of Optometrists and Opticians.

NAP, nap National Association of Postmasters; National Association of Parliamentarians; not at present; noise abatement procedure; naval aviation pilot.

NAPA National Association of Purchasing Agents.

NAPCA National Association of Professional Contracts Administrators.

NAPENA National Association of Public Employer Negotiators and Administrators.

NAPFE National Alliance of Postal and Federal Employees.

NAPH National Association of the Physically Handicapped.

NAPIA National Association of Public Insurance Adjusters.

NAPL National Association of Police Laboratories.

NAPO National Association of Property Owners.

NAPPH National Association of Private Psychiatric Hospitals.

NAPRR National Association for Puerto Rican Rights.

NAPS National Association of Postal Supervisors.

Napt Napton's Reports (Missouri).

NAPUS National Association of Postmasters of the United States.

nar nasal airway resistance; no answer (action) required.

NARA Narcotics Addict Rehabilitation Act.

NARAL National Abortion Rights Action League.

NARB National Association of Referees in Bankruptcy; National Advertising Review Board.

narc narcotics.

NARCO Narcotics Commission.

Narcotics Control Dig Narcotics Control Digest.

NARD National Association of Retail Druggists.

NAREB National Association of Real Estate Boards; National Association of Real Estate Brokers.

NARELLO National Association of Real Estate License Law Officials.

NARF Native American Rights Fund.

NARFE National Association of Retired Federal Employees.

NARMFD National Association of Retail Meat and Food Dealers.

Narr Mod Narrationes Modernae (England).

NARS National Archives and Records Service.

NARSLL National Association to Reform State Liquor Laws.

NARTC National Association of Railroad Trial Counsel.

NARUC National Association of Regulatory Utility Commissioners.

NAS, nas National Academy of Sciences; National Audubon Society; no added salt; nasal.

NASA National Aeronautics and Space Administration; National Association of Securities Administrators.

NASABCA National Aeronautics and Space Administration Board of Contract Appeals.

NASACT National Association of State Auditors, Comptrollers, and Treasurers.

NASAPR National Aeronautics and Space Administration Procurement Regulations.

NASBA National Association of State Boards of Accountancy.

NASBE National Association of State Boards of Education.

NASBLA National Association of State Boating Law Administrators.

NASBO National Association of State Budget Officers.

NASC National Association of School Counselors.

NASCSA National Association of State Controlled Substances Authorities.

NASD National Association of Securities Dealers.

NASDA National Association of State Departments of Agriculture; National Association of State Development Agencies.

NASDAQ National Association of Securities Dealers Automated Quotations.

NASDLET National Association of State Directors of Law Enforcement Training.

NASIRE National Association of State Information Resource Administrators.

NASIS National Association for State Information Systems.

NASLR National Association of State Land Reclamationists.

NASPE National Association of State Personnel Executives.

NASS National Association of Secretaries of State.

NAST National Association of State Treasurers.

NASULGC National Association of State Universities and Land Grant Colleges.

NASW National Association of Social Workers.

NAT, nat National Arbitration Tribunal; no action taken; natural; native; non-accidental trauma.

NATA National Association of Tax Administrators; North Atlantic Treaty Alliance.

NATB National Automobile Theft Bureau.

Nat Bank Rev National Banking Review.

Nat Bankr Reg National Bankruptcy Register.

Nat Bur Stand National Bureau of Standards.

Nat Civ Rev National Civic Review.

Nat Corp Rep National Corporation Reporter.

natl national.

Natl Legal Mag National Legal Magazine.

Natl LF National Law Forum.

N Atl Reg Bus L Rev North Atlantic Regional Business Law Review.

Nat L Rep National Law Reporter.

Nat L Rev National Law Review.

Natl Mun Rev National Municipal Review.

Natl Prob Assn Yrbk National Probation and Parole Association Yearbook.

Natl Resources J National Resources Journal.

Natl School L Rptr National School Law Reporter.

Natl Tax J National Tax Journal.

NATO North Atlantic Treaty Organization.

natr natrium.

Nat Reg National Register (Mead).

Nat Res Law Natural Resources Lawyer.

Nat Tax J National Tax Journal.

NATTS National Association of Trade and Technical Schools.

Natural LF Natural Law Forum.

Natur Res J Natural Resources Journal.

NAUA National Automobile Underwriters Association.

NAUPA National Association of Unclaimed Property Administrators.

naut nautical.

nav net asset value; navigation; naval.

NAVH National Association for Visually Handicapped.

NAW National Agricultural Workers Union.

NAWCJ National Association of Women in Criminal Justice.

NAWL National Association of Women Lawyers.

NB, Nb, nb Nebraska; New Brunswick; New Benloe

King's Bench Reports (England); niobium; north bound; note well (nota bene); no bid; nervus buccalis; new born; negri bodies.

NBA National Bar Association; National Bankers Association; National Bankruptcy Act; National Basketball Association; National Boxing Association.

NBC National Board for Certification; National Beef Council; National Broadcasting Company.

NBCC National Bituminous Coal Commission.

NBCU National Bureau of Casualty Underwriters.

N Benl New Benloe's King's Bench Reports (England).

NBEO National Board of Examiners in Optometry.

NBEOPS National Board of Examiners for Osteopathic Physicians and Surgeons.

NB Eq New Brunswick Equity Reports.

NBER National Bureau of Economic Research.

nbf not breast fed.

NBFU National Board of Fire Underwriters.

nbi no bones injured.

NBJ National Bar Journal.

NBL National Business League.

nbm nothing by mouth.

NBMDA National Building Material Distributors Association.

NBME National Board of Medical Examiners.

nbp normal boiling point.

NBPDW National Brotherhood of Packinghouse and Dairy Workers.

NBPE National Board of Polygraph Examiners; National Board of Podiatry Examiners.

NBR National Board of Review of Motion Pictures.

NB Rep or **N Bruns** New Brunswick Reports (Canada).

NBRT National Board for Respiratory Therapy.

NBS, nbs National Bureau of Standards; normal bowel sounds.

nbt normal breast tissue.

nbtnf newborn, term, normal, female.

nbtnm newborn, term, normal, male.

nbw normal birth weight.

NC, nc Notes of Cases (England); North Carolina Reports; non-collectable; new charter; no credit; no change; no charge; normal control; neurologic control; neck complaint; no complaints.

n/c numerical control; no complaints; nerves and circulation.

NCA, nca National Commission on Accrediting; National Contractors Association; National Chiropractic Association; National Council on the Arts; National Council on Alcoholism; National Coal Association; National Canners Association; neurocirculatory asthenia.

NCAA National Collegiate Athletic Association.

NCAB Navy Contract Adjustment Board.

NCAC National Consumer Advisory Council; National Coalition Against Censorship.

NCACC National Conference of Appellate Court Clerks.

NCADH National Committee Against Discrimination in Housing.

NC Admin Code North Carolina Administrative Code.

NC Adv Legis Serv Advance Legislative Service to the General Statutes of North Carolina.

NCAE National Council of Agricultural Employers.

NCAI National Congress of American Indians; National Clearinghouse for Alcohol Information.

NCAP Neighborhood Community Action Program.

NCAPA National Capital Area Paralegal Association.

NC App North Carolina Court of Appeals Reports.

NCARB National Council of Architectural Registration Boards.

NCARL National Committee Against Repressive Legislation.

NCATE National Council for Accreditation of Teacher Education.

NCB, ncb Naval Courts and Boards; National Coal Board; National Classification Board; nickel cadmium battery.

NCBE National Conference of Bar Executives; National Conference of Bar Examiners.

NCBFAA National Customs Brokers and Forwarders Association of America.

NCBH National Coalition to Ban Handguns.

NCBL National Conference of Black Lawyers.

NCBP National Conference of Bar Presidents.

NCC, ncc New Chancery Cases (England); National Crime Commission; National Consumer Congress; National Clients Council; nursing care continuity; noncoronary cusp.

NCCA Negligence and Compensation Cases Annotated; National Center for Child Advocacy; National Concrete Contractors Association.

NCCAN National Center on Child Abuse and Neglect.

NCCD National Council on Crime and Delinquency.

NCCE National Commission for Cooperative Education.

NC Cent LJ North Carolina Central Law Journal.

NCCH National Council to Control Handguns.

NCCI National Council on Compensation Insurance.

NCCIJ National Catholic Conference for Interracial Justice.

NCCJ National Conference of Christians and Jews.

NCCLS National Consumer Center for Legal Services.

NC Conf North Carolina Conference Reports.

NCCP National Council on City Planning.

NCCUSL National Conference of Commissioners on Uniform State Laws.

ncd notice of credit due; normal childhood disorder; not considered disabling; no congenital deformities.

NCDA National College of District Attorneys; National Council on Drug Abuse.

NCDC National Center for Disease Control.

NCDH National Committee Against Discrimination in Housing.

NCDS National Center for Dispute Settlement.

nce nonconvulsive epilepsy.

NCEC National Committee for an Effective Congress.

NCEE National Council of Engineering Examiners.

N Cent School L Rev North Central School Law Review.

NCER National Council on Educational Research.

NCF National Cancer Foundation.

NCFA National Consumer Finance Association.

NCFC National Council of Farm Cooperatives.

NC Gen Stat General Statutes of North Carolina.

NCH National Council on the Humanities.

N Chipm North Chipman's Reports (Vermont).

N Ch R Nelson's Chancery Reports (England).

NCI National Cancer Institute.

NCIA National Crop Insurance Association.

NCIAC National Construction Industry Arbitration Center.

NCIC National Crime Information Center; National Construction Industry Council.

NCIS National Credit Information Service.

NCIT National Certified Investigator Training.

NCJC National Conference of Judicial Councils..

NCJCJ National Council of Juvenile Court Judges.

NCJRS National Criminal Justice Reference Service.

NCJSC National Criminal Justice Statistics Center.

NCL National Consumers League.

NC Law Repos North Carolina Law Repository.

NCLC National Council on Legal Clinics.

NCLP National Conference on Law and Poverty.

NC L Rev North Carolina Law Review.

NCLSW National Conference of Lawyers and Social Workers.

NCM Navy Court Martial Reports.

NCMDA National Commission on Marihuana and Drug Abuse.

NCO, nco National Credit Office; noncommissioned officer; no complaints offered.

NCOA National Condominium Owners Association.

NCOC National Council on Organized Crime.

NCOL National Council on Occupational Licensing.

NCOPA National Conference of Police Associations.

NCP National Contingency Plan.

NCPA North Carolina Paralegal Association.

NCPCA National Committee for the Prevention of Child Abuse.

NCPI National Crime Prevention Institute.

NCPLA National Council of Patent Law Associations.

NCPS National Commission on Product Safety.

NCR Not in Compliance Report.

NCRFCL National Commission on Reform of Federal Criminal Laws.

ncs noncoronary sinus.

NCSBCS National Conference of States on Building Codes and Standards.

NCSBEE National Council of State Boards of Engineering Examiners.

NCSC National Center for State Courts; National Child Safety Council.

NC Sess Laws Session Laws of North Carolina.

NCSH National Clearinghouse on Smoking and Health.

NCSL National Conference of State Legislatures.

NCSWCL National Commission on State Workmen's Compensation Laws.

NC T Rep North Carolina Term Reports.

NCUA National Credit Union Administration.

ncup no commission until paid.

NCUSIF National Credit Union Share Insurance Fund.

NCUTLO National Committee on Uniform Traffic Laws and Ordinances.

ncv no commercial value.

Nd, nd North Dakota Reports; Newfoundland; neodymium; no date; not done; nothing done; no defects; next day; national debt; normal delivery; neoplastic disease; no disease; neurotic depression; natural death; normal dose; naso-lacrimal duct.

n&d nodular and diffuse.

NDA, nda National Dental Association; National Defense Act; no data available; new drug application.

NDAA National District Attorneys Association.

ND Admin Code North Dakota Administrative Code.

NDBCA National Department Board of Contract Appeals.

NDC, ndc National Dairy Council; national drug code.

ND Cent Code North Dakota Century Code.

NDEA National Defense Education Act.

ndga nordihydroguaiaretic acid.

ND Laws Laws of North Dakota.

ND L Rev North Dakota Law Review.

ndro nondestructive readout.

nds new drug submission.

ndt noise detection threshold.

NE, Ne, ne North Eastern Reporter; (2d: Second Series); Nebraska; Netherlands; neon; north east; new edition; not exceeding; not equal to; national emergency; neuro-logic examination; not essential; not examined; no effects.

NEA, nea National Education Association; Nuclear Energy Agency; National Endowment for the Arts; no evidence of abnormality.

NEAJ National Education Association Journal.

Neb Nebraska Reports.

Neb Admin R & Regs Nebraska Administrative Rules and Regulations.

Neb Laws Laws of Nebraska.

Neb LB Nebraska Law Bulletin.

Neb L Rev Nebraska Law Review.

Neb Rev Stat Revised Statutes of Nebraska.

Neb St BJ Nebraska State Bar Journal.

Neb Unoff Nebraska Unofficial Reports.

nec necessary; no essential change.

NECLC National Emergency Civil Liberties Committee.

ned no evidence of disease.

neg neglect; negligence; nego-tiable; negative.

Negl & Comp Cas Ann

Negligence and Compensation Cases Annotated (NS: New Series).

Negl Cas Negligence Cases (2d: Second Series) (Commerce Clearing House).

Negro Cas Bloomfield's Manumission Cases (New Jersey).

NEH National Endowment for the Humanities.

NEI National Eye Institute.

NEJM New England Journal of Medicine.

Nel or **Nels** Nelson's Chancery Reports (England).

Nels Abr Nelson's Abridgment.

NELP National Employment Law Project.

nem not elsewhere mentioned.

NEMA National Electrical Manufacturers Association; National Emergency Management Association.

nem diss no one dissenting (nemine dissentiente).

N Eng L Rev New England Law Review.

nep no evidence of pathology.

NEPA National Environmental Policy Act of 1969.

ner no evidence of recurrence.

NESC National Electric Safety Code.

NESHAP National Emission Standards for Hazardous Air Pollutants.

net not earlier than.

NETC National Emergency Transportation Center.

Neth Int L Rev Netherlands International Law Review.

Neth Yearbook Int L Netherlands Yearbook of International Law.

n et m night and morning (nocte et mane).

neuro neurologic.

neut neutralize.

Nev Nevada Reports.

Nev Admin Code Nevada Administrative Code.

Nev & M Nevile and Manning's King's Bench Reports (England).

Nev & Macn Nevile and Macnamara's Railway and Canal Cases (England).

Nev & P Nevile and Perry's King's Bench Reports (England).

Nev Rev Stat Nevada Revised Statutes.

Nev Stat Statutes of Nevada.

Nev St Bar J Nevada State Bar Journal.

New Newell's Reports (Illinois).

Newb Newberry's Admiralty Reports.

New B Eq Ca New Brunswick Equity Cases.

New Br New Brunswick Reports.

New Eng L Rev New England Law Review.

Newfld Newfoundland.

Newf S Ct Newfoundland Supreme Court Decisions.

New LJ New Law Journal.

New Mex L Rev New Mexico Law Review.

New Rep New Reports (England).

New Sess Cas New Session Cases (England).

New York See NY.

NF, nf Newfoundland; Negro female; no funds; nonfundable; noise frequency; nonferrous; normal flow; noise factor; not found.

NFA National Food Administration; National Firearms Act.

NFAA National Federation of Advertising Agencies.

NFAH National Foundation on Arts and Humanities.

NFB National Federation of the Blind.

NFBF National Farm Bureau Federation.

NFBPW National Federation of Business and Professional Women's Clubs.

NFC, nfc National Football Conference; not favorably considered.

nfd no fixed date; no family doctor.

NFDA National Funeral Directors Association.

NFGC National Federation of Grain Cooperatives.

NFI National Fisheries Institute.

NFIB National Federation of Independent Businesses.

NFIU National Federation of Independent Unions.

NFL National Forensic League; National Football League.

Nfld & PEIR Newfoundland and Prince Edward Island Reports.

Nfld LR Newfoundland Law Reports.

NFLPN National Federation of Licensed Practical Nurses.

nfm nonferrous metal.

nfp no family physician.

NFPA National Fire Protection Association; National Federation of Paralegal Associations.

nfs not for sale.

NFTC National Foreign Trade Council.

nftd normal full term delivery.

nfv no further visits.

NFWA National Farm Workers of America.

NG, ng Nigeria; New Guinea; National Guard; not good; no growth; nasogastric; nanogram; nitroglycerin.

NGA National Governors' Association.

ngbri not guilty by reason of insanity.

NGC National Governors Conference.

NGF, ngf National Genetics Foundation; nerve growth factor.

ngi not guilty insanity.

ngl natural gas liquid.

ngr narrow gauze roll.

NGS National Geographic Society.

NGSC National Gay Student Center.

ngt normal glucose tolerance.

NH, nh New Hampshire Reports; New Hebrides; nursing home; nonhygroscopic.

N&H Nott and Huntington's Reports, United States Court of Claims; Nott and Hopkins' Reports, United States Court of Claims.

NHA, nha National Housing Act; National Housing Administration; next higher authority.

NHAIAC National Highway Accident and Injury Analysis Center.

NHBJ New Hampshire Bar Journal.

NHC, nhc National Health Center; National Housing Center; neighborhood health center.

NH Code Admin R New Hampshire Code of Administrative Rules.

NHEDLP National Housing and Economic Development Law Project.

nhi national health insurance.

nhk normal human kidney.

NHL, nhl National Hockey League; nodular histiocytic lymphoma.

NHLA National Health Lawyers Association.

NH Laws Laws of the State of New Hampshire.

NHLPA National Hockey League Players Association.

NH L Rep New Hampshire Law Reporter.

nhp normal human pooled plasma.

NHPRC National Historical Publications and Records Commission.

NHR New Hampshire Reports.

NH Rev Stat Ann New Hampshire Revised Statutes Annotated.

NH Rulemaking Reg New Hampshire Rulemaking Register.

NHS, nsh National Health Service; normal human serum.

NHSA National Highway Safety Administration.

NHTSA National Highway Traffic Safety Administration.

NI, Ni, ni Nicaragua; Northern Ireland; nickel; night; not issued; no information; not interested.

NIA, nia National Institute on Aging; nickel iron alloy; no information available.

NIB National Information Bureau.

NICD National Institute on Crime and Delinquency.

NICJ National Institute for Consumer Justice.

NICPRO National Institute for Crime Prevention and Rehabilitation of Offenders.

NIDA National Independent Dairy Association.

NIE National Institute of Education.

nif negative inspiratory force.

Nigeria LR Nigeria Law Reports.

NIH National Institutes of Health.

nihl noise induced hearing loss.

NIIC National Injury Information Clearinghouse.

NIJ National Institute of Justice.

NILECJ National Institute of Law Enforcement and Criminal Justice.

NIMC National Institute of Municipal Clerks.

NIMH National Institute of Mental Health.

NIMLO National Institute of Municipal Law Officers.

NIOSH National Institute for Occupational Safety and Health.

nip notice of intent to purchase; no infection present; nipple.

NIPH National Institute of Public Health.

ni pr or **ni pri** unless before (Nisi Prius).

NIRA National Industrial Recovery Act.

NIRB National Insurance Rating Bureau.

NIRC National Industrial Relations Court (England).

N Ir LQ Northern Ireland Law Quarterly.

N Ir LR Northern Ireland Law Reports.

NIS, nis National Institute of Science; not in stock; no inflammatory signs.

NISS National Institute of Social Sciences.

NIT, nit National Institute of Technology; negative income tax.

NITA National Institute for Trial Advocacy.

nitro nitroglycerin.

NJ, nj New Jersey Reports; nasojejunal.

NJA National Jail Association.

NJ Admin New Jersey Administrative Reports.

NJ Admin Code New Jersey Administrative Code.

NJ Eq New Jersey Equity Reports.

NJFA National Justice Foundation of America.

NJ L Rev New Jersey Law Review.

NJL or **NJ Law** New Jersey Law Reports.

NJ Laws Laws of New Jersey.

NJLC National Juvenile Law Center.

NJLJ New Jersey Law Journal.

NJ Misc New Jersey Miscellaneous Reports.

NJ Reg New Jersey Register.

NJ Rev Stat New Jersey Revised Statutes.

NJ Sess Law Serv New Jersey Session Law Service.

NJ Stat Ann New Jersey Statutes Annotated.

NJ St BJ New Jersey State Bar Journal.

NJ Super New Jersey Superior Court Reports.

NJ Tax New Jersey Tax Court Reports.

NK, nk North Korea; not known; next of kin; neck; natural killer.

nka no known allergies.

nkda no known drug allergies.

NKF National Kidney Foundation.

N Ky L Rev Northern Kentucky Law Review.

NL, nl Netherlands; no license; it is not permitted (non licet); north latitude; new line.

nla normal lactase activity.

NLADA National Legal Aid and Defender Association.

NLC National League of Cities; National Legislative Council.

NLD, nld National Legion of Decency; not in line of duty.

NLDC National Legal Data Center.

NLGQ National Lawyers Guild Quarterly.

NLM National Library of Medicine.

nlmc nocturnal leg muscle cramp.

nln no longer needed.

NLRB National Labor Relations Board.

NLSP Neighborhood Legal Services Program.

nlt not later than; net long ton; not less than.

NM, nm New Mexico Reports; nautical mile; not measured; not marked; nanometer; non-malignant; nuclear medicine; night and morning.

N&M, n&m Nevile and Manning's King's Bench Reports (England); nerves and muscles; night and morning.

N & Macn Nevile and Macnamara's Railway and Canal Cases (England).

N&Mc Nott and McCord's Reports (South Carolina).

NMB National Metric Board; National Mediation Board.

NMC National Maritime Council.

nmi no mental illness.

NM Laws Laws of New Mexico.

NMLR New Mexico Law Review; Nigerian Monthly Law Reports.

nmn no middle name.

nmp normal menstrual period.

nmr nuclear magnetic resonance.

NM Stat Ann New Mexico Statutes Annotated.

nmt neuromuscular tension; not more than.

nn names; nurse's notes.

NNA National Notary Association.

nnd new and nonofficial drug.

nnr no need to return.

NO, No, no Norway; nobelium; narcotics officer; nitric oxide; name of; no orders; number; none obtained.

NOAA National Oceanic and Atmospheric Administration.

nob new obstetric.

NOBC National Organization of Bar Counsel.

Noble Noble's Current Court Decisions (New York).

No Car L Rev North Carolina Law Review.

no compl no complaints.

noct night (nocte).

noel no observable effect level.

No Ire LQ Northern Ireland Law Quarterly.

nois notice of intent to suspend.

nok next of kin.

Nolan Nolan's Magistrate Cases (England).

NOLPE National Organization of Legal Problems of Education.

nol pros non prosequitur (unwilling to prosecute).

nom nominal.

Nonacq Nonacquiescence.

noncontrib noncontributory.

non obs notwithstanding (non obstante).

non pros non prosequitur (he does not prosecute).

non seq a statement that does not logically follow (non sequitur).

no-op no operation.

nop not otherwise provided.

NOPA New Orleans Paralegal Association.

Nor, nor Norway; normal; notice of readiness.

NORAD North American Air Defense Command.

Norc Norcross' Reports (Nevada).

NORML National Organization for the Reform of Marijuana Laws.

Norris Norris' Reports (Pennsylvania).

North Northington's Chancery Reports.

Northam Northampton County (Pennsylvania).

North & G North and Guthrie's Reports (Missouri).

North Co Northampton County (Pennsylvania).

Northum LJ Northumberland Legal Journal (Pennsylvania).

Northw UL Rev Northwest University Law Review.

nos not otherwise specified; numbers.

not nocturnal oxygen therapy.

Notes of Cas Notes of Cases (England).

Notre Dame Law Notre Dame Lawyer.

Nott & Hop Nott and Hopkins' Reports, United States Court of Claims.

Nott & Hunt Nott and Huntington's Reports, United States Court of Claims.

Nott & Mc Nott and McCord's Reports (South Carolina).

Nov, nov November; notwithstanding the verdict (non obstante veredicto); notice of violation.

Nova LJ Nova Law Journal.

Nov Sc Nova Scotia.

NOW, now National Organization for Women; negotiable order of withdrawal.

Noy Noy's King's Bench Reports (England).

NP, Np, np Nisi Prius (unless before); Nisi Prius Reports (Ohio); Nepal; neptunium; notary public; net proceeds; no protest; nonparticipating; new paragraph; nurse practitioner; nonpaying; normal pressure; new patient; neuropsychiatry.

N&P Nevile and Perry's King's Bench Reports (England).

NPA National Petroleum Association; Nevada Paralegal Association.

NPC, npc New Practice Cases; Nisi Prius Cases; National Patent Council; National Press

Club; near point of convergence; nasopharyngeal carcinoma; nonparenchymal cell.

NPDES National Pollutant Discharge Elimination System.

npf not provided for.

NP&GT Rep Nisi Prius and General Term Reports (Ohio).

npg nonpregnant.

NPI, npi National Paralegal Institute; no present illness.

npl nonpersonal liability; national priority list.

npn nonprotein nitrogen.

npna no protest nonacceptance.

NP NS Nisi Prius Reports New Series (Ohio).

npo nothing by mouth (nulla per os).

NPPA National Probation and Parole Association.

NPR National Public Radio.

NPS National Park Service.

npt normal pressure and temperature.

npv no par value.

NR, nr Bosanquet and Puller's New Reports (England); natural resources; note receivable; net register; no risk; not recorded; do not repeat (non repetatur); nonreactive; no recurrence; normal reaction.

NRA National Rifle Association; National Recovery Act; National Recovery Administration; nitrate reductase.

NRAB National Railroad Adjustment Board Awards.

nrad no risk after discharge.

nrbs non rebreathing system.

NRC, nrc Nuclear Regulatory Commission; National Research Council; National Response Center; nonrecurring costs.

nrd nonrenal death.

NRDC Natural Resources Defense Council.

nri nerve root irritation; nonrespiratory infection.

NRLC National Right to Life Committee.

nrm normal range of motion.

NRMA National Retail Merchants Association.

nrt net register ton; national response team..

NRWLDEF National Right to Work Legal Defense and Education Fund.

NS, Ns, ns Nova Scotia; New Series; nimbostratus; not specified; not sufficient; not significant; near side; nose; nanosecond; no specimen; nervous system; nonsmoker; neurosyphilis.

n/s normal saline.

NSA, nsa National Security Agency; National Secretaries Association; no serious abnormality; no salt added.

NSC, nsc New Sessions Cases (England); National Security Council; no significant change; nonservice connected.

nsd normal spontaneous delivery; normal single dose; no significant deviation.

NS Dec Nova Scotia Decisions.

NSF, nsf National Science Foundation; not sufficient funds.

nsg nursing.

nsgt non self governing territories.

nsi no signs of infection.

NSL National Standards Laboratory.

NSLR Nova Scotia Law Reports.

nsm nonsmoker.

NSPA National State Printing Association.

NSPCA National Society for the Prevention of Cruelty to Animals.

NSPCC National Society for the Prevention of Cruelty to Children.

nsq not sufficient quantity.

NSR, nsr Nova Scotia Reports; normal sinus rhythm; not seen regularly.

N Sc Dec Nova Scotia Decisions.

nss normal size and shape.

NSSAB National Selective Service Appeal Board.

nssc normal size, shape, and consistency.

NSSTTC non specific ST and T wave changes.

nst non stress test.

nsu nonspecific urethritis.

nsv nonspecific vaginitis.

NSW or **NS Wales** New South Wales.

NS Wales LR Eq New South Wales Law Reports Equity.

NSW St R New South Wales State Reports.

NT, nt Northern Territory; Northwest Territories; new terms; net ton; normal temperature; not tested; nasotracheal.

n&t nose and throat.

NTA, nta National Tax Association; nitrilotriacetic acid.

ntfy notify.

ntg nitroglycerin.

NTHP National Trust for Historic Preservation.

nti nonthyroid illness.

NTJ National Tax Journal.

ntm net ton mile.

nto not thrown out (of vehicle).

ntp normal temperature and pressure; national toxicology program.

ntr nutrition; negative therapeutic reaction.

NT Rep New Term Reports, Queen's Bench (England).

nts not to scale.

NTSB National Transportation Safety Board.

nt wt net weight.

nu name unknown.

NUL, nul National Urban League; null character.

nullip nulliparous.

NV, nv Nevada; non voting; new version; nonvenereal; next visit.

n&v nausea and vomiting.

nvd nausea, vomiting, diarrhea.

NW, nw North Western Reporter (2d: Second Series); net weight; northwest; not weighed.

nwb no weight bearing.

NWF National Wildlife Federation.

nwg national wire gauge.

NWPC National Women's Political Caucus.

NWRO National Welfare Rights Organization.

NWT Northwest Territories.

NW Terr Northwest Territories Supreme Court Reports.

NWTLR North West Territories Law Reports.

NW UL Rev Northwestern University Law Review.

NY, ny New York Reports (2d: Second Series); new year; navy yard.

NY Anno Cas New York Annotated Cases.

NY Anno Cas Dig New York Annotated Cases Digest.

NY App Dec New York Court of Appeals Decisions.

NY App Div New York Supreme Court Appellate Division.

NY Cas Err New York Cases in Error (Caines).

NYCBA Bull Bulletin of the Association of the Bar of the City of New York.

NY Ch Sent New York Chancery Sentinel.

NY City Ct Rep New York City Court Reports.

NY City Ct Supp New York City Court Reports Supplement.

NY City H Rec New York City Hall Recorder.

NY Civ Pro R New York Civil Procedure Reports (NS: New Series).

NY Code Reptr New York Code Reporter (NS: New Series).

NY Comp Codes R & Regs Official Compilation of Codes, Rules and Regulations of the State of New York.

NY Cond New York Condensed Reports.

NY Cont L Ed New York Continuing Legal Education.

NY County Law Assn B Bull New York County Lawyers Association Bar Bulletin.

NY Cr R New York Criminal Reports.

nyd not yet diagnosed.

NY Daily L Gaz New York Daily Law Gazette.

NY Daily L Reg New York Daily Law Register.

NY Dept R New York Department Reports.

Nye Nye's Reports (Utah).

NY Elec Cas New York Election Cases.

NYFE New York Futures Exchange.

NY Jud Rep New York Judicial Repository.

NY Jur New York Jurisprudence; New York Jurist.

NY Law For or **NYLF** New York Law Forum.

NY Law Gaz New York Law Gazette.

NY Laws Laws of New York.

NYL Cas New York Leading Cases.

NY Leg N New York Legal News.

NY Leg Obs New York Legal Observer.

NY Leg Reg New York Legal Register.

NYLF New York Law Forum.

NYLJ or **NY Law J** New York Law Journal.

NYL Rec New York Law Record.

NYL Rev or **NY Law Rev** New York Law Review.

NYL Sch Intl L Socy J New York Law School International Law Society Journal.

NYLS Rev New York Law School Review.

NY Misc Miscellaneous Reports (2d: Second Series) (New York).

NY Month L Rep New York Monthly Law Reports.

NY Mun Gaz New York Municipal Gazette.

nyp not yet published.

NYPR or **NY Pr** New York Practice Reports.

nyr not yet returned.

NY Rec New York Record.

NY Rep New York Court of Reports.

NYS New York Supplement (2d: Second Series).

NYSBJ New York State Bar Journal.

NYSE New York Stock Exchange.

NY St New York State Reporter.

NY St BJ New York State Bar Journal.

NY St R New York State Reporter.

NY St Reg New York State Register.

NY Sup Ct New York Supreme Court Reports.

NY Super New York Superior Court.

NY Supp New York Supplement (2d: Second Series).

NYTR New York Term Reports (Caines).

NY Trans New York Transcript (NS: New Series).

NYU Conf Charitable New York University Conference on Charitable Foundation Proceedings.

NYU Conf Lab New York University Conference on Labor.

NYU Inst Fed Tax New York University Institute on Federal Taxation.

NYU Intra L Rev New York University Intramural Law Review.

NYUJ Intl L & Pol New York University Journal of International Law and Politics.

NYUL Center Bull New York University Law Center Bulletin.

NYULQ Rev New York University Law Quarterly Review.

NYUL Rev New York University Law Review.

NYU Rev L & Soc Change New York University Review of Law and Social Change.

NY Wkly Dig New York Weekly Digest.

nz normal zone.

NZLJ New Zealand Law Journal.

NZLR New Zealand Law Reports.

NZU L Rev New Zealand Universities Law Review.

O, o October; Ohio; Oklahoma; Oregon; Ontario; opinion; official; oath; owner; zero; ohm; oxygen; opium; oral; operation; objective; observation; obese; occlusal; eye (oculus); a blood group in the ABO system.

O: objective findings.

OA, oa Ohio Appellate Reports; observation and assessment; open account; on or about; old age; on account; office automation; osteoarthritis; op amps; orotic acid; ocular albinism; oxalic acid; occipito anterior; occipital artery.

OAA, oaa Older Americans Act; old age assistance.

oab old age benefits.

OAC Ontario Appeal Cases.

oad obstructive airway disease.

OAG Opinions of the Attorney General; Official Airline Guide.

o & m operation and maintenance.

o&o owned and operated.

oap old age pension.

OAR Ohio Appellate Reports; Ontario Appeal Reports (Canada); Office of Air and Radiation.

OAS, oas Organization of American States; on active service; osmotically active substance.

OASDI Old Age, Survivors, and Disability Insurance.

OASDHI Old Age, Survivors, Disability, and Health Insurance.

OASI Old Age and Survivors Insurance.

OB, ob Old Bailey (England); obsolete; on board, observation; obstetrics; obese.

OB&FNZ Olliver, Bell and Fitzgerald's New Zealand Reports.

OB&L Oliver, Beavan and Lefroy's Railway and Canal Cases (England).

obd organic brain disease.

obe out of body experience.

O Ben Old Benloe's Common Pleas Reports (England).

obf organ blood flow.

ob-gyn obstetrics-gynecology.

obl obligation; order bill of lading; oblique.

O Bridg Orlando Bridgman's Common Pleas Reports (England)

O'Brien O'Brien's Reports (Upper Canada).

obs observation; obstruction; obstetrics; organic brain syndrome.

OBSP Old Bailey, Sessional Papers (England).

obst obstruction.

oc by aid and counsel (ope et consilio); organized crime; order cancelled; over the counter; ocean; office copy; officer in charge; overcharge; only child; oxygen consumed; oral contraceptive; ovarian cancer; on call.

o&c onset and course.

OCA Ohio Court of Appeals Reports; Office of Consumer Affairs; oral contraceptive agent; oculocutaneous albinism.

OCC, occ Office of the Comptroller of the Currency; Ohio Circuit Court Reports (NS: New Series); occasional; occurrence; occipital; occlusion.

occas occasionally.

occl occlusion.

OCD, ocd Ohio Circuit Court Decisions; ovarian cholesterol depletion; osteochondritis dissecans.

OCDM Office of Civil and Defense Mobilization.

Ocean Dev & Intl LJ Ocean Development and International Law Journal.

ocg oral cholecystogram.

och oral contraceptive hormone.

OCM Office of Compliance Monitoring.

ocp oral contraceptive pill.

OCPA Orange County Paralegal Association.

OCR, ocr Office of Civil Rights; optical character reader.

OCS, ocs Office of Contract Settlement; oral contraceptive steroid; open canalicular system.

Oct, oct October; oxytocin challenge test.

OD, od Office Decisions (Internal Revenue Service); Ohio Decisions (NP: Nisi Prius); Doctor of Optometry; overdrawn; out of date; origin and destination; on demand; on duty; outside diameter; overdose; once a day; every day (omni die); right eye (oculus dexter); open duct; optimal dose; occupational disease.

ODCC Ohio Decisions, Circuit Court.

O Dec Rep Ohio Decisions Reprint.

Odeneal Odeneal's Reports (Oregon).

ODM, odm Office of Defense Mobilization; opthalmodynamometry.

odq on direct questioning.

oe omissions excepted; oersted; on examination.

o&e observation and examination.

OECD Organization for Economic Cooperation and Development.

OED Oxford English Dictionary.

OEM, oem Office of Emergency Management; original equipment manufacturer; opposite ear masked.

OEO Office of Economic Opportunity.

OERR Office of Emergency and Remedial Response.

of occipital frontal; oxidizing flame.

ofc office.

ofcl official.

OFD, ofd Ohio Federal Decisions; oral facial digital; object/film/distance.

OFDI Office of Foreign Direct Investment.

OFEC Office of Federal Employees Compensation.

off official; office.

Off Brev Officina Brevium.

Off Gaz Official Gazette (Patent Office).

Officer Officer's Reports (Minnesota).

OFPP Office of Federal Procurement Policy.

OFR Office of the Federal Register.

OG, og Official Gazette (Patent Office); outside guard; optic ganglion; orogastric; obstetrics/gynecology.

o&g obstetrics and gynecology.

OGC Office of the General Counsel.

Ogd Ogden's Reports (Louisiana).

ogfp obtaining goods by false pretenses.

ogtt oral glucose tolerance test.

Oh, oh Ohio Reports; overhead; on hand; office hours; out of hospital; occupational health; obstructive hypopnea; every hour (omni hora); hydroxyl group; open heart.

Oh A, oha Ohio Court of Appeals; oral hypoglycemic agent.

Oh Cir Ct Ohio Circuit Court Reports (NS: New Series).

Oh Cir Dec Ohio Circuit Decisions.

ohd organic heart disease.

Oh Dec Ohio Decisions.

Oh F Dec Ohio Federal Decisions.

ohi ocular hypertension indicator.

Ohio Ohio Reports.

Ohio Admin Code Ohio Administrative Code.

Ohio App Ohio Appellate Reports (2d: Second Series), (3d: Third Series).

Ohio B Ohio Bar Association Reports.

Ohio CA Ohio Court of Appeals Reports.

Ohio CC or Ohio CCR or Ohio Cir Ct or Ohio Cir Ct R Ohio Circuit Court Reports (NS: New Series).

Ohio Cir Dec Ohio Circuit Decisions.

Ohio Ct App Ohio Court of Appeals Reports.

Ohio Dec Ohio Decisions.

Ohio Dec Reprint Ohio Decisions Reprint.

Ohio Dep't Ohio Department Reports.

Ohio F Dec Ohio Federal Decisions.

Ohio Gov't Ohio Government Reports.

Ohio Jur Ohio Jurisprudence (2d: Second Edition).

Ohio L Abs or Ohio Law Abst Ohio Law Abstract.

Ohio Laws State of Ohio: Legislative Acts Passed and Joint Resolutions Adopted.

Ohio LB or Ohio Law Bull Ohio Weekly Law Bulletin.

Ohio Legis Bull Ohio Legislative Bulletin (Anderson).

Ohio Legis Serv Ohio Legislative Service (Baldwin).

Ohio Leg N Ohio Legal News.

Ohio LJ or Ohio Law J Ohio Law Journal.

Ohio LD Ohio Lower Court Decisions.

Ohio LR or Ohio Law R Ohio Law Reporter.

Ohio Misc Ohio Miscellaneous Reports (2d: Second Series).

Ohio Misc Dec Ohio Miscellaneous Decisions.

Ohio Monthly Rec Ohio Monthly Record (Banks-Baldwin).

Ohio NP Ohio Nisi Prius Reports (NS: New Series).

Ohio NUL Rev Ohio Northern University Law Review.

Ohio Op Ohio Opinions (2d: Second Series), (3d: Third Series).

Ohio Prob Goebel's Ohio Probate Reports.

Ohio R Cond Ohio Reports Condensed.

Ohio Rev Code Ann Ohio Revised Code Annotated.

Ohio S&CP Dec or Ohio Sup & CP Dec Ohio Superior and Common Pleas Decisions.

Ohio SLJ or Ohio St LJ Ohio State Law Journal.

Ohio St Ohio State Reports (2d: Second Series), (3d: Third Series).

Ohio SU Ohio Supreme Court Unreported Cases.

Ohio Supp or O Supp Ohio Supplement.

Ohio Unrep Cas Ohio Unreported Supreme Court Cases.

ohir operating a house of ill repute.

Oh Jur Ohio Jurisprudence (2d: Second Edition).

Oh L Bul Ohio Law Bulletin.

Oh L Ct D Ohio Lower Court Decisions.

Oh LJ Ohio Law Journal.

Oh LN Ohio Legal News.

Oh L Rep Ohio Law Reporter.

Oh NP Ohio Nisi Prius Reports (NS: New Series).

ohp oxygen under high pressure.

Oh Prob Ohio Probate.

Oh S&CP Dec Ohio Superior and Common Pleas Decisions.

Oh SCD Un Ohio Supreme Court

Decisions, Unreported Cases.

Oh St Ohio State Reports.

oi oxygen intake.

Oil & Gas Compact Bull Oil and Gas Compact Bulletin.

Oil & Gas Inst Oil and Gas Institute.

Oil & Gas J Oil and Gas Journal.

Oil & Gas Rptr Oil and Gas Reporter.

Oil & Gas Tax Q Oil and Gas Tax Quarterly.

oint ointment.

OIR Office of Indian Rights.

ois optical image sensor.

OIT Office of International Trade.

OITA Office of International Tax Affairs.

OIWR Office of Indian Water Rights.

oj orange juice.

OJJDP Office of Juvenile Justice and Delinquency Prevention.

OJP Office of Justice Programs.

ojt on the job training.

O Jur Ohio Jurisprudence.

OK Oklahoma; outer keel; approved.

oka otherwise known as.

Okla Oklahoma Reports.

Okla Ap Ct Rep Oklahoma Appellate Court Reporter.

Okla Bar Assn J Oklahoma Bar Association Journal.

Okla City ULR Oklahoma City University Law Review.

Okla Cr or **Okla Crim** Oklahoma Criminal Reports.

Okla LJ Oklahoma Law Journal.

Okla L Rev Oklahoma Law Review.

Okla SBJ Oklahoma State Bar Journal.

Okla Sess Law Oklahoma Session Law Service (West).

Okla Sess Laws Oklahoma Session Laws.

Okla Stat Ann Oklahoma Statutes Annotated.

OL, ol operating license; oleum (oil); left eye (oculus laevus).

OLA, ola Ohio Law Abstract; Office of Legislative Affairs;

occipitolaeva anterior.

OLAA Oregon Legal Assistants Association.

OLB, olb Ohio Law Bulletin; open liver biopsy; olfactory bulb.

OLC, Olc Office of Legal Counsel; Olcott's District Reports.

OLD, Old, old Ohio Lower Court Decisions; Oldright's Reports (Nova Scotia); obstructive lung disease.

OLJ Ohio Law Journal.

Oliv B&L Oliver, Beavan and Lefroy's Railway and Canal Cases (England).

Olliv B&F Olliver, Bell and Fitzgerald's Reports (New Zealand).

OLN Ohio Legal News.

olp occipitolaeva posterior.

OLR, olr Ohio Law Reporter; Ontario Law Reports; otology, laryngology, rhinology.

OLRB Ontario Labor Relations Board.

OL Rep Ohio Law Reporter.

O Leg News Ohio Legal News.

O Lower D Ohio Lower Court Decisions.

olrt on line real time.

olt owners, landlords, tenants.

om outer marker; organization and methods; every morning (omni mane); outer membrane; otitis media; osteomyelitis.

O'M & H El Cas O'Malley and Hardcastle's Election Cases (England).

OMB Office of Management and Budget.

OMBE Office of Minority Business Enterprise.

omn hor every hour (omni hora).

omn man every morning (omni mane).

omp outer membrane protein.

on order, notify; octane number.

ono or nearest offer.

ONP, onp Ohio Nisi Prius Reports (NS: New Series); ortho nitro-phenyl; operating nursing procedure.

Ont Ontario.

Ont App Ontario Appeals Reports.

Ont El Cas Ontario Election Cases.

Ont L Ontario Law Reports.

Ont LJ Ontario Law Journal (NS: New Series).

Ont L Rep Ontario Law Reports.

Ont Pr Ontario Practice Reports.

Ont R Ontario Reports.

Ont Reg Ontario Regulations.

Ont Rev Reg Revised Regulations of Ontario.

Ont Rev Stat Revised Statutes of Ontario.

Ont Stat Statutes of Ontario.

Ont WN Ontario Weekly Notes.

Ont WR Ontario Weekly Reporter.

OO, oo Ohio Opinions; on order; order of; off and on; outer to outer; ordnance officer; oophorectomy.

o/o on account of.

o&c onset and course.

o&e observation and examination.

o&g obstetrics and gynecology.

o&o owned and operated.

oob out of bed.

ooc out of control.

ooj obstruction of justice.

oop out of plaster.

oow out of wedlock.

op original package; out of print; observation post; operation; opposite; opposed; osmotic pressure; outpatient; occiput posterior.

o/p outpatient.

o&p ova and parasites.

OPA Office of the Pardon Attorney; Office of Price Administration.

Op Att Gen or **Ops AG** Opinions of the Attorney General.

opc out patient clinic.

op cit in the work cited (opere citato).

op code operation code.

OPEC Organization of Petroleum Exporting Countries.

opg opening.

oph ophthalmology; obliterative pulmonary hypertension.

OPI Office of Patents and Inventions.

opm other people's money.

opn opinion; operation.

OPP, opp Office of Pesticides Programs; opposed; opposite; opportunity.

OPR Office of Professional Responsibility; Ontario Practice Reports.

OPS, ops Office of Price Stabilization; opinions; outpatient surgery; outpatient service.

Ops AG or **Op Att Gen** Opinions of the Attorney General.

Ops JAG Opinions of the Judge Advocate General.

Op Sol Dept United States Department of Labor, Opinions of the Solicitor.

OPSR Office of Professional Standards Review.

opt option; optician; optimum; outpatient treatment.

opv oral polio vaccine.

OR, Or, or Ontario Reports; Oregon Reports; owner's risk; own recognizance; official referee; on request; original; operations research; operating room; oxidation reduction; orthopedic; oral rehydration; orienting response.

ora occiput right anterior.

Or Admin R Oregon Administrative Rules.

Or Admin R Bull Oregon Administrative Rules Bulletin.

ORC Office of Regional Counsel.

Or App Oregon Court of Appeals Reports.

ORD, ord Office of Research and Development; ordinance; ordnance; order; owner's risk of damage.

Ore St B Bull Oregon State Bar Bulletin.

Or L Rev or **Ore L Rev** Oregon Law Review.

orf owner's risk of fire.

org organization; organ.

orif open reduction with internal fixation.

orig original.

orl owner's risk of leakage.

Or Laws Oregon Laws and Resolutions.

Orl Bridgman Orlando Bridgman's Common Pleas Reports (England).

Orleans App Orleans' Appeals (Louisiana).

Orl TR or **Orleans TR** Orleans' Term Reports (Louisiana).

orm other regulated materials.

ORMA Office of Refugee and Migration Affairs.

Ormond Ormond's Reports (Alabama).

orn operating room nurse.

orom optical read-only memory.

orp occiput right posterior.

ORS, ors Office of Revenue Sharing; orthopaedic surgery; oral surgeon.

Or Tax or **Or Tax Ct** Oregon Tax Reports.

ORUS Official Register of the United States.

OS, Os, os Ohio State Reports; Old Series; osmium; occupational safety; out of stock; on schedule; on sample; on sale; operating system; oxygen saturation; occipitosacral; left eye (oculus sinister); oral surgery; osteosclerosis; Osgood Schlatter (disease); osteogenic sarcoma.

Osaka UL Rev Osaka University Law Review.

osc order to show cause; oscillate; on-site coordinator.

OSCD Ohio Supreme Court Decisions.

osd outside doctor.

OSG Office of the Solicitor General; Office of the Surgeon General.

Osgoode Hall LJ Osgoode Hall Law Journal.

OSHA Occupational Safety and Health Administration.

OSH Rep Occupational Safety and

Health Reporter (Bureau of National Affairs).

osp died without issue (obiit sine prole).

OSS, oss Office of Strategic Services; object sorting scale; osseous.

O St, ost Ohio State Reports; object sorting test; osteopathic.

osteo osteopathy; osteomyelitis; osteoarthritis.

OSTP Office of Science and Technology Policy.

OSU Ohio Supreme Court Decisions, Unreported Cases.

O Supp Ohio Supplement.

ot occupational therapy; old terms; on truck; objective test; overtime; orthopaedic treatment; orotracheal.

OTA Office of Technology Assessment.

Otago L Rev Otago Law Review.

otb off track betting; open to buy.

otc over the counter; oxytetracycline.

otj on the job.

OTS Office of Thrift Supervision; Office of Toxic Substances.

Ottawa L Rev Ottawa Law Review.

Otto Otto's United States Supreme Court Reports.

ou both eyes together (oculi unitas); each eye (oculus uterque).

ouo official use only.

Out Outerbridge's Reports (Pennsylvania).

ov office visit; ovary; ovulating; over ventilation.

ovd overdue.

Over Overton's Reports (Tennessee).

ovhd overhead.

OVP Office of the Vice President.

ovuil operating a vehicle under the influence of liquor.

Ow, ow Owen's King's Bench Reports (England); Owen's Common Pleas Reports (England); out of wedlock; off work; once a week; oil/water; outer wall.

OWCP Office of Workers Compensation Programs.

owf optimum working frequency.

OWM Office of War Mobilization.

OWN Ontario Weekly Notes.

OWR, owr Ontario Weekly Reporter; ovarian wedge resection.

Ox oxygen.

Oxford L Oxford Lawyer.

Oxley Young's Vice Admiralty Decisions (Oxley) (Nova Scotia).

oz ounce.

P, p Pacific Reporter (2d: Second Series); Pickering (Massachusetts); Pennsylvania; Portugal; probate; professional; phosphate group; phosphorus; private; principal; person; page; perimeter; port; primary; percentile; poison; probation; polymyxin; pain; posterior; pulse; pressure; patient; pulmonary; penicillin; psychiatry; protein; premolar; placebo; paternal.

P: plan.

P₂ pulmonic second sound.

P2d Pacific Reporter, Second Series.

PA, Pa, pa Panama; Pennsylvania; Physician's Assistant; public act; prosecuting attorney; power of attorney; purchasing agent; private account; public accountant; public assistance; personal appearance; per annum; preliminary assessment; paper advance; postpartum; pernicious

anemia; peridural artery; pulmonary artery; postanesthetic; posteroanterior.

p&a percussion and auscultation.

PAA Pittsburgh Paralegal Association.

paba para-aminobenzoic acid.

Pa B Assn Q Pennsylvania Bar Association Quarterly.

Pa B Brief Pennsylvania Bar Brief.

pabx private automatic branch exchange.

PAC, Pac, pac Pacific Reporter; Political Action Committee; premature auricular contraction; premature atrial contractions; phenacetin, aspirin, caffeine.

Pa Cas Pennsylvania Supreme Court Cases, Sadler.

PACE Professional and Administrative Career Examination.

Pac Law Reptr Pacific Law Reporter.

Pac Leg N Pacific Legal News.

Pac LJ Pacific Law Journal.

PACNY Paralegal Association of Central New York.

Pa Co Ct Pennsylvania County Court Reports.

Pa Corp Rep Pennsylvania Corporation Reporter.

Pa CP or **Pa C Pl** Pennsylvania Common Pleas Reporter.

PAD, pad Peters' Admiralty Decisions; Phi Alpha Delta; packet assembly/diassembly; psychoaffective disorder; phenacetin, aspirin, desoxyephedrine.

Pa D&C or **Pa Dist & C Rep** Pennsylvania District and County Reporter (2d: Second Series).

Pa Dist R District Reports (Pennsylvania).

p ae equal parts (partes aequales).

Pa Fid Pennsylvania Fiduciary Reporter.

pah para aminohippurate.

Pai or **Paige** Paige's Chancery Reports (New York).

Paine CC Paine's Circuit Court Reports.

Pak Pakistan.

pa key program attention key.

Pak LR Pakistan Law Reports.

Pal, pal Palmer's Reports (Vermont); Palmer's King's Bench Reports (England); prisoner at large.

Pa LJ Pennsylvania Law Journal.

Pa LJR Pennsylvania Law Journal Reports (Clark).

Palmer Palmer's Reports (Vermont); Palmer's King's Bench Reports (England).

palp palpable.

Pa L Rec Pennsylvania Law Record.

PALS Patient Advocacy Legal Service.

pam pamphlet; phenylalanine mustard.

Pa Misc Pennsylvania Miscellaneous Reports.

Pan, pan Panama; peroxyacetyl nitrate.

Pan-Am TS Pan-American Treaty Series.

pand pandering.

P&B Pugsley and Burbridge's Reports (New Brunswick).

P&C, p&c Prideaux and Cole's New Session Cases (England); put and call.

P&D, p&d Perry and Davison's Queen's Bench Reports (England); probate and divorce.

P&F Pike and Fischer's Administrative Law.

P&F Radio Reg Pike and Fischer's Radio Regulation Reporter.

P&H, p&h Patton and Heath's Reports (Virginia); postage and handling.

p&i protection and indemnity.

P&K Perry and Knapp's Election Cases (England).

p&l profit and loss.

P&M Probate and Matrimonial Cases (England).

p&s paracentesis and suction;

physician and surgeon; permanent and stationary.

P&T Pugsley and Trueman's Reports (New Brunswick).

P&W Penrose and Watts's Reports (Pennsylvania).

panh panhandling.

PANP Paralegal Association of Northwestern Pennsylvania.

PAP, pap Philadelphia Association of Paralegals; paper; pulmonary arterial pressure; papanicolaou (stain, smear test).

Papua & NG Papua and New Guinea Law Reports.

Papy Papy's Reports (Florida).

PAR, Par, par Paralegal Association of Rochester; Parker's Criminal Cases (New York); Parker's Exchequer Reports (England); Paraguay; paragraph; precision approach radar; parallel; paraffin; pulmonary arteriolar resistance; perennial allergic rhinitis.

para paragraph.

Par Dec or **Pars Dec** Parsons' Decisions (Massachusetts).

Pa Rep Pennsylvania Reports.

Par Eq Cas or **Pars Eq Cas** Parsons' Select Equity Cases (Pennsylvania).

Park or **Parker** Parker's Reports (New Hampshire); Parker's Criminal Cases (New York); Parker's Exchequer Reports (England).

Parker Cr Cas Parker's Criminal Cases (New York).

Park Ins Parker's Insurance (England).

parl parliament.

Parl Cas Parliamentary Cases, House of Lords (England).

Parl Deb Parliamentary Debates.

Pars Dec or **Par Dec** Parsons' Decisions (Massachusetts).

Pars Eq Cas or **Par Eq Cas** Parsons' Select Equity Cases (Pennsylvania).

part partner; participating.

partn partition.

pas or pasa para-aminosalicylic acid.

Pasc Paschal's Reports (Texas).

PASCC Paralegal Association of Santa Clara County.

pass passenger.

Pa St Pennsylvania State Reports.

Pa Super Pennsylvania Superior Court Reports.

PAT, pat Patent Rolls (England); patent; patrol; patient; paroxysmal atrial tachycardia.

Pat & H Patton and Heath's Reports (Virginia).

Pat & TM Rev Patent and Trade Mark Review.

Pat Cas Reports of Patent, Design and Trade Mark Cases.

Pat Dec Commissioner of Patent Decisions.

Pater App Cas Paterson's Appeal Cases (Scotland).

path pathology.

Pat L Rev Patent Law Review.

Pat Off Gaz Patent Office, Official Gazette.

Pat Off Rep Patent Office Reports.

Pat Off Soc J Patent Office Society Journal.

Paton App Cas Paton's Appeal Cases (Canada).

Pat TM & Copy J Patent, Trademark and Copyright Journal.

PAU Pan American Union.

PAW Paralegal Association of Wisconsin.

paye pay as you enter.

payt payment.

Pb, pb lead (plumbum); privately bonded; passbook; power brake; periodic breathing.

P&B Pugsley and Burbridge's Reports (New Brunswick).

PBA, pba Patrolmen's Benevolent Association; permanent budget account; pressure breathing assist.

pbf pulmonary blood flow.

PBGC Pension Benefit Guaranty Corporation.

pbi protein bound iodine.

pbm permanent bench mark.

pbo placebo.

PBS Public Broadcasting Service.

pbx private branch exchange.

pbz pyribenzamine.

pbv pulmonary blood volume.

PC, pc Patent Cases; Price Control Cases (Commerce Clearing House); Pleas of the Crown; Panama Canal; Peace Corps; Professional Corporation; parliamentary cases; practice cases; privy council; public contract; phone call; private corporation; price current; percent; personal computer; program counter; printed circuit; petty cash; parsec; after meals (post cibum); post coital; parent cell; proximal colon; pulmonary capillary; pelvic cramps; posterior chamber; plasma concentration; poor condition.

P&C, p&c Prideaux and Cole's New Session Cases (England); put and call.

PCA, pca Permanent Court of Arbitration; Acts of the Privy Council (England); Production Credit Association; perchloric acid; patient care area; posterior communicating aneurysms.

PC App Privy Council Appeals, Law Reports (England).

PCB, pcb Patent Compensation Board; polychlorinated biphenyl.

PCC, pcc Poison Control Center; Privy Council Cases (England); Prerogative Court of Canterbury (England); phosphate carrier compound; premature chromosome condensation; postcoronary care.

pcd poly cystic disease.

pce physical capacity evaluation.

pcf peripheral circulatory failure.

pchs purchase.

PCIJ Permanent Court of International Justice.

pcis postcardiac injury syndrome.

pcl printer command language; persistent corpus luteum; posterior cruciate ligament.

PCLJ or **P Coast LJ** Pacific Coast Law Journal.

pcm pulse code modulation; punch card machine.

pcn penicillin; primary care nursing; public convenience and necessity.

pco pest control operator; patient complains of.

pcod polycystic ovarian disease.

pcp pentachlorophenol; primary care physician.

PCR, pcr Planning and Compensation Reports (England); Parker's Criminal Reports (New York); patient contact record; protein catabolic rate.

PC Rep Privy Council Reports (England).

P Cas Prize Cases (England).

pcs principal clerk of session; print contrast signal; proximal coronary sinus.

pct percent; porphyria cutanea tarda; pulmonary care team.

pcv packed cell volume.

pcwp pulmonary capillary wedge pressure.

PCY Prerogative Court of York (England).

PD, Pd, pd Probate, Divorce and Admiralty Division, Law Reports (England); Police Department; Parliamentary Debates; palladium; probate/divorce; paid; per diem; period; postage due; post dated; public domain; property damage; prism diopter; problem drinker; protein diet; patient day; packs per day; pediatrics; plasma defect; postnasal drainage; pulse duration; Parkinson's Disease; Paget's disease; pupillary distance.

p(d+) probability of having the disease.

p(d-) probability of not having the disease.

P&D, p&d Perry and Davison's Queen's Bench Reports (England); probate and divorce.

PDA, pda Probate, Divorce, Admiralty; predicted drift angle; pulmonary disease anemia; patent ductus arteriosus; patient distress alarm.

PDAB Physical Disability Appeal Board.

pdb paradichlorobenzene.

PDD, pdd Public Documents Department; post due date; primary degenerative dementia.

pdh past dental history.

pdi pilot direction indicator.

P Div Probate Division.

pdl page description language.

pdm pulse duration modulation.

pdp program delivery plan.

pdq pretty damn quick.

PDR, pdr Physicians Desk Reference; powder; post delivery room.

PDT Pacific Daylight Time.

PE, pe Peru; Prince Edward Island; petroleum engineer; periodic; price/earnings ratio; post exchange; printer error; photoelectric; polyethylene; physical examination; pelvic examination; pulmonary embolism.

p/e point of entry.

pe··a pelvic examination under anesthesia.

Pea Peake's Nisi Prius Reports (England); phenethyl alcohol.

Peab L Rev Peabody Law Review.

Peake NP Peake's Nisi Prius Reports (England).

Peake NP Add Cas Peake's Nisi Prius Additional Cases (England).

PEAL Publishing, Entertainment, Advertising, and Allied Fields Law Quarterly.

Pearce CC Pearce's Crown Cases (Dearsley) (England).

Pears Pearson's Reports (Pennsylvania).

pec photoelectric cell.

Peck Peck's Reports (Illinois); Peck's Reports (Tennessee).

Peck El Cas Peckwell's Election Cases (England).

ped pedestrian; pediatrics.

peep positive end expiratory pressure.

Peeples Peeples' Reports (Georgia).

Peeples & Stevens Peeples and Stevens' Reports (Georgia).

Peere Wms Peere Williams' Chancery and King's Bench Reports (England).

peg prior endorsement guaranteed.

PEI, pei Haszard and Warburton's Reports (Prince Edwards Island); phosphorus excretion index.

PEI Acts Acts of Prince Edward Island.

PEI Rev Reg Revised Regulations of Prince Edward Island.

PEI Rev Stat Revised Statutes of Prince Edward Island.

pel permissible exposure limit; personal exposure limit.

Pen, PEN, pen Pennington's Reports (New Jersey); International Association of Poets, Playwrights, Editors, Essayists, and Novelists; penis; penicillin.

Pen & W Penrose and Watts's Reports (Pennsylvania).

Penn Pennington's Reports (New Jersey); Pennypacker's Reports (Pennsylvania).

Penn Bar AQ Pennsylvania Bar Association Quarterly.

Penn Co Ct Rep Pennsylvania County Court Reports.

Penn Corp Rep Pennsylvania Corporation Reporter.

Penn Del Pennewill's Reports (Delaware).

Pennewill Pennewill's Reports (Delaware).

Penning Pennington's Reports (New Jersey).

Penn LG Pennsylvania Legal Gazette.

Penny Pennypacker's Reports (Pennsylvania).

Penny Col Cas Pennypacker's Colonial Cases (Pennsylvania).

Penr & W Penrose and Watts' Reports (Pennsylvania).

Pens Rep Pension Reporter (Bureau of National Affairs).

pent pentothal.

pep phosphoenolpyruvate; positive expiratory pressure.

per period; person.

Per & Dav Perry and Davison's Queen's Bench Reports (England).

Per & K Perry and Knapp's Election Cases (England).

Per CS Perrault's Conseil Superior (Canada).

PERI, peri Psychiatric Epidemiology Research Interview; perineal.

perj perjury.

Perrault See Per CS.

perrla pupils equal, round, react to light and accommodation.

Pers Fin LQ Personal Finance Law Quarterly Report.

Pers Inj Comm Personal Injury Commentator.

pert project evaluation and review technique.

Pet, pet Peters' Supreme Court Reports, United States; Peters' Circuit Court Reports; Peters' Admiralty Reports; Peters' Reporter (Prince Edwards Island); petroleum; parent effectiveness training; polyethylene terephthalates.

Pet Ab Petersdorf's Abridgment.

Pet Adm Peters' Admiralty Reports.

Pet Br or **Petit Br** Petit Brooke New Cases.

Pet CC Peters' Circuit Court Reports.

Peters See Pet.

petn petition.

petr petitioner.

Pet SC Peters' Supreme Court

Reports, United States.

peua pelvic examination under anesthesia.

pex physical examination.

pf plantar flexion; preferred; plasma fibronectin; peak flow.

P&F Pike and Fischer's Administrative Law.

P&F Radio Reg Pike and Fischer's Radio Regulation Reporter.

pfd preferred.

pf key program function key.

pfp platelet free plasma.

PFS, pfs P.F. Smith's Reports (Pennsylvania); pulmonary function score.

PF Smith P.F. Smith's Reports (Pennsylvania).

pft pulmonary function test.

PG, pg Papua New Guinea; Portugal; page; postgraduate; picogram; public gaol; paralysie generale; prostaglandin; pressure of gas; pregnant; postgraft.

pgf paternal grandfather.

pgh pituitary growth hormone.

pgr psychogalvanic response.

P-H, Ph, ph Prentice Hall; phenyl; phosphor; phosphate; page heading; pharmacopoeia; pharmacy; persistent hepatitis; punctate hemorrhage; public health; patient history; past history; posterior hypothalamus; parathyroid hormone.

P&H, p&h Patton and Heath's Reports (Virginia); postage and handling.

PHA Public Housing Authority; Public Housing Administration.

P-H Am Lab Arb Awards American Labor Arbitration Awards (Prentice-Hall).

P-H Am Lab Cas American Labor Cases (Prentice-Hall).

phar pharmacy; pharmacopoeia.

PHC, phc Personal Holding Company; primary health care; post hospital care.

P-H Cas American Federal Tax Reports (Prentice-Hall).

P-H Corp Corporation (Prentice-Hall).

phd pulmonary heart disease.

phen phenobarbital.

Pheney Rep Pheney's New Term Reports.

P-H Est Plan Estate Planning (Prentice-Hall).

P-H Fed Taxes Federal Taxes (Prentice-Hall).

P-H Fed Wage & Hour Federal Wage & Hour (Prentice-Hall).

Phil Phillips' Reports (North Carolina); Phillips' Reports (Illinois); Phillips' Chancery Reports (England); Philippines.

Phila Philadelphia Reports (Pennsylvania).

Phila Leg Int Philadelphia Legal Intelligencer (Pennsylvania).

Phil El Cas Phillips' Election Cases (England).

Phil Eq Phillips' Equity Reports (North Carolina).

Philip Int LJ Philippine International Law Journal.

Philip LJ Philippine Law Journal.

Philip Yearbook Int L Philippine Yearbook of International Law.

Phil Law Phillips' Law Reports (North Carolina)

Phillim Phillimore Ecclesiastical Reports (England).

Phil LJ Philippine Law Journal.

Phil St Tr Phillips' State Trials.

P-H Ind Rel Lab Arb Industrial Relations, American Labor Arbitration (Prentice-Hall).

P-H Ind Rel Union Conts Industrial Relations, Union Contracts and Collective Bargaining (Prentice-Hall).

phl public health law.

phn public health nurse.

php prepaid health plan.

PHS, phs Public Health Service; posthypnotic suggestion.

P-H Soc Sec Taxes Social Security Taxes (Prentice-Hall).

P-H State & Local Taxes State and Local Taxes (Prentice-Hall).

P-H Tax Ct Mem Tax Court Memorandum Decisions (Prentice-Hall).

P-H Tax Ct Rep & Mem Dec Tax Court Reported and Memorandum Decisions (Prentice-Hall).

P-H Unrep Tr Cas Unreported Trust Cases (Prentice-Hall).

phv for this occasion (pro hace vice).

phys physician; physical.

PI, pi Philippine Islands; personal injury; programmed instruction; private investigator; primary infarction; present illness; premature infant; poison ivy.

p&i protection and indemnity.

pia peripheral interface adapters.

pica a type size: one sixth of an inch or twelve points.

Pick Pickering's Reports (Massachusetts).

Pickle Pickle's Reports (Tennessee).

pid pelvic inflammatory disease.

Pig & R Pigott and Rodwell's Registration Cases (England).

pik payment in kind.

Pike Pike's Reports (Arkansas).

Pike & F Pike and Fischer's Administrative Law.

Pike & F Radio Reg Pike and Fischer's Radio Regulation Reporter.

pil patient information leaflet.

Pin, pin Pinney's Reports (Wisconsin); private (personal) identification number; personal injury notice.

pins person in need of supervision.

pio public information office; parallel input/output.

pip proximal interphalangeal.

PIRG Public Interest Research Group.

pit pitocin; pituitary.

piti principal, interest, taxes, insurance.

Pitts LJ Pittsburgh Legal Journal (NS: New Series).

Pitts Rep Pittsburgh Reports (Pennsylvania).

pixel pictures element.

PJ, pj Probate Judge; Presiding Judge; pancreatic juice.

P Jr & H Patton, Jr. & Heath's Reports (Virginia).

PK, pk Pakistan; psychokinesis; pericardial knock.

P&K Perry and Knapp's Election Cases (England).

pkg package.

pku phenylketonuria.

PL, pl Poland; Public Law; public liability; picoliter; profit/loss; petty larceny; property line; partial loss; platoon; programming language; problem list; placebo; plastic surgery; preleukemic; placental lactogen; peroneus longus; perception of light.

p&l profit and loss.

PLA, pla Professional Legal Assistants; Pensacola Legal Assistants; programmable logic array.

plac placenta.

plam price level adjusted mortgage.

Plan & Comp Planning and Compensation Reports.

Pl Ang Norm Bigelow's Placita Anglo Normannica Cases.

Plan Zoning & ED Inst Planning, Zoning and Eminent Domain Institute.

plat or **plts** platelets.

plbo placebo.

PLC, Pl C, plc Poor Law Commissioners (England); Pleas of the Crown (England); public limited company; protein lipid complex; primary liver cancer.

PLE, ple Pennsylvania Law Encyclopedia; pleura; protein losing enteropathy; panlobular emphysema.

PLEA Poverty Lawyers for Effective Advocacy.

PLEI Public Law Education Institute.

plen plenipotentiary.

plf plaintiff.

PLG Poor Law Guardian (England).

PLI Practicing Law Institute.

PLO Palestine Liberation Organization; Public Land Order.

plob place of birth.

Plow Plowden's Reports (England).

plpd public liability and property damage.

PLR, plr Pacific Law Reporter; Pennsylvania Law Record; public lending right; pupillary light reflex.

plss portable life support system.

pltf plaintiff.

PM, Pm, pm Police Magistrate; Prime Minister; promethium; post mortem; project manager; probate/matrimonial; purchase money; premium; per month; afternoon/night; phase modulation; plasma membrane; papillary muscle; preventive medicine; preventive maintenance; premolar.

P&M Probate and Matrimonial Cases (England).

pmb postmenopausal bleeding.

PMG Postmaster General.

pmh production per man-hour; past medical history.

pmi private mortgage insurance; post-myocardial infarction; point of maximal impulse; past medical illness; present medical illness.

pmk postmark.

pmn polymorphonuclear neutrophil; premanufacture notification.

pmp previous menstrual period.

pms premenstrual syndrome; postmenopausal syndrome.

pmt payment; premenstrual tension.

PN, pn Practical Nurse; promissory note; position; partition; pneumonia; psychoneurotic; polyneuritis; post nausea.

pna pentosenucleic acid.

pnb perineal needle biopsy.

pnc premature nodal contractions.

pnd paroxysmal nocturnal dyspnea; post nasal drip.

pnfl painful.

PNG, png Papua New Guinea; persona non grata.

pnh paroxysmal nocturnal hemoglobinuria.

pni peripheral nerve injury; postnatal infection.

PNP, pnp Peake's Nisi Prius Cases (England); Pediatric Nurse Practitioner; purine nucleoside phosphorylase; pneumoperitoneum.

pnr prior notice required.

pns position.

PO, Po, po Portugal; Patent Office; Post Office; Passport Office; polonium; probation officer; parole officer; project officer; phone order; purchase order; posterior; period of onset; orally (per os); post operative.

pob post office box.

poc purchase order contract; port of call; post operative care.

pod payable on delivery; port of delivery; postoperative day; place of death.

Pod D Doctor of Podiatry.

poe port of entry; point of entry.

POI Paralegals of Iowa, Inc.

pois poisoning.

Pol, pol Pollexfen's King's Bench Reports (England); Pollack's Unreported Judicial Decisions (Ohio); Poland; political; polish; petroleum, oil, and lubricants.

Police LQ Police Law Quarterly.

polio poliomyelitis.

Pollution Abs Pollution Abstracts.

Pol Sci Q Political Science Quarterly.

Poly, poly polygamy; polymorphonuclear.

Pomeroy Pomeroy's Reports (California).

poo post office order.

Pop, pop Popham's King's Bench Reports (England); point of purchase; population; popular; plaster of paris; popliteal; polycystic ovarian syndrome; pituitary opioid peptide; persistent occiputa posterior.

Poph Popham's King's Bench Reports (England).

por payable on receipt; price on request; purchase order request.

Port, port Porter's Reports (Alabama); Porter's Reports (Indiana); Portugal; portfolio; portable.

Portia LJ Portia Law Journal.

Portland UL Rev Portland University Law Review.

Porto Rico Fed or **Puerto Rico Fed** Puerto Rico Federal Reports; see also PR Dec, PRR, PRSCR, PR Sent.

POS, pos Patent Office Society; period of service; possession; positive; position; periosteal osteosarcoma.

Posey Unrep Cas Posey's Unreported Cases (Texas).

poss possession.

Post, post Post's Reports (Missouri); Post's Reports (Michigan); post mortem; posterior.

pot potentiometer; potassium; potential.

Potter Potter's Reports (Wyoming).

pou placenta, ovaries, uterus.

pov privately owned vehicle.

pow prisoner of war.

Pow Surr Power's Reports, Surrogate Court (New York).

pp pages; pickpocket; personal property; pay period; prepaid; by proxy (per procurationem); public property; parcel post; planned parenthood; posterior pituitary; pinprick; partial pressure; post prandial; post partum; plaster of paris.

ppa per power of attorney.

ppb positive pressure breathing; parts per billion.

ppbs postprandial blood sugar.

PPCAA Parole and Probation Compact Administrators' Association.

ppd postpaid; port protection device; purified protein derivative; permanent partial disability; packs per day.

ppe porcine pancreatic elastase.

ppgp prepaid group practice.

pph pamphlet; postpartum hemorrhage.

ppi packing, postage, and insurance; parcel post insured; policy proof of interest; present pain intensity; partial permanent impairment.

pplo pleuropneumonia-like organism.

ppm parts per million; pulses per minute; posterior papillary muscle.

ppo polypropylene oxide.

PPPA Poison Prevention Packaging Act.

pppi primary private practice income.

ppr prior permission required; patient/physician relationship.

pps pulses per second; postpartum sterilization.

ppt partial prothrombin time; peak to peak threshold.

pptl postpartum tubal ligation.

ppty property.

ppw petition for patent waiver.

PQ, pq Province of Quebec; previous question; personal quality.

PR, Pr, pr Pennsylvania Reports (Penrose and Watts); Price's Exchequer Reports (England); Philippine Islands Reports; Parliamentary Reports; Practice Reports (Ontario); Puerto Rico; Press Release; praseodymium; propyl; proposed regulation; pesticide registration; peer review; protein; prism; proved; pro rata; prior; progress report; punctum remotum; Preyer's reflex; prolonged remission; public relations; private; profit rate; parcel receipt; presbyopia; pulse rate; potency ratio; proctology; phenol red; per rectum; pelvic and rectal; partial remission.

pra progesterone receptor assay; plasma renin activity.

prac practice; practitioner.

Prac Law or **Pract Law** Practical Lawyer.

PR & D El Cas Power, Rodwell and Dew's Election Cases (England).

Pr & Div Probate and Divorce, Law Reports (England).

prbc packed red blood cells.

PRC, prc Postal Rate Commission; People's Republic of China; peer review committee.

PR Ch Practical Register in Chancery (England).

PRCP Practical Register, Common Pleas.

PR Dec Decisiones de Puerto Rico.

Pr Div Probate Division, Law Reports (England).

pre progressive resistive exercises; preliminary.

p rec through the rectum (per rectum).

Prec Ch Precedents in Chancery (England).

Pr Edw Is Prince Edward Islands Reports; see also PEI.

pref preference.

prej prejudice.

prem premium; premature; preliminary.

premie premature infant.

preop preoperative.

prep preparation.

prepd prepaid.

prereq prerequisite.

prev preventive.

Pr Exch Price's Exchequer Reports (England).

prf proof; pulse repetition frequency; patient report form.

PR Fed Puerto Rico Federal Reports.

prh past relevant history; prolactin releasing hormone.

Pri, pri Price's Exchequer Reports (England); Price's Mining Commissioner's Cases (Ontario); primary; private; phosphate reabsorption index; plexus rectales inferiores.

Price See Pri.

Price Pr Cas Price's Practice Cases.

Prickett Prickett's Reports (Idaho).

Prid & C Prideaux and Cole's New Session Cases (England).

primip woman bearing first child (primipara).

pris prisoner.

Prison LR Prison Law Reporter.

priv privilege.

Priv C App Privy Council Appeals (England).

PR Laws Ann Puerto Rico Laws Annotated.

prm premium; preventive medicine.

prn as necessary, as circumstances may require (pro re nata).

PRO, pro Patients Rights Organization; procedure; prophylactic; probate; public relations office; pronation.

prob probate; probation; probable; problem.

Prob & Adm Div Probate and Admiralty Division Law Reports (England).

Prob & Div Probate and Divorce Law Reports (England).

Prob & M Probate and Matrimonial Cases (England).

Prob & Prop Probate and Property.

Prob Ct Rep Probate Court Reports (Ohio).

Prob Div Probate Division, Law Reports (England).

Prob Law Probate Lawyer.

Prob Rep Probate Reports (Ohio).

proc procedure; process; proceeding; proctor; proclamation.

Proc Am Soc Int L Proceedings of the American Society of International Law.

Proc Rules Procedural Rules (Internal Revenue Service).

Prod Liab Intl Products Liability International.

prof profanity; professional.

prog prognosis.

proh prohibition.

prom programmable read-only memory; premature rupture of membranes.

prop property; proprietary.

Prop & Comp Property and Compensation Reports.

proph prophylactic.

Prop Law Property Lawyer.

Proposed Reg Proposed Regulations (Internal Revenue Service).

pro quer for the plaintiff (pro querente).

pros prosecution; prosthesis.

prost prostitute; prostate.

pro tem for now, for the time being (pro tempore).

pro us ext for external use only (pro usu externo).

Prouty Prouty's Reports (Vermont).

Prov Can Stat Statutes of the Province of Canada.

prox proximal.

prp potentially responsible party.

PRR, Pr R, prr Puerto Rico Reports; Practice Reports; pulse repetition rate; protein relaxation rate.

PRR & Regs Commonwealth of Puerto Rico Rules and Regulations.

Pr Reg BC Practice Register, Bail Court (England).

Pr Reg Ch Practice Register Chancery (England).

Pr Reg CP Practice Register Common Pleas (England).

Pr Rep or **Prt Rep** Practice Reports.

PRSCR Puerto Rico Supreme Court Reports.

PR Sent Sentencias del Tribunal Supremo de Puerto Rico.

prtn partition.

PRUC Practice Reports, Upper Canada.

PRY Paraguay.

ps public sale; penal servitude; police sergeant; privy seal; public sale; postal service; post script; picosecond; per second; pathological state; pulmonary stenosis; plastic surgery; paracentesis and suction.

p&s paracentesis and suction.

PSC, psc Public Service Commission; per standard compass; posterior subcapsular cataracts; pulse synchronized contractions; pluripotential stem cell.

PSCUS Peters' Supreme Court Reports, United States.

psd prevention of significant deterioration.

psec picosecond.

psgr passenger.

psi presentence investigation report.

psis posterior superior iliac spine.

psp phenolsulfonphthalein; pseudopregnancy.

PSQ Public Service Quarterly.

PSR, psr Pennsylvania State Reports; pulmonary stretch receptors; pain sensitivity range.

pss progressive systemic sclerosis.

PST Pacific Standard Time.

pstg postage.

psw program status word; processor state word.

psy psychological.

psych psychology; psychiatry.

Psych & MLJ Psychological and Medico-Legal Journal.

PT, Pt, pt Processing Tax Division (Internal Revenue Service); Portugal; Pacific Time; Poll Tax Rolls (England); platinum; phenytoin; petty theft; payment; part time; port; for the time being (pro tempore); permanent and total; premature termination;

parathyroid; patient; physical therapist; permanent and total; pulmonary thrombosis; pronator teres; posterior tibial; prothrombin time.

P&T Pugsley and Trueman's Reports (New Brunswick).

PTA, pta Parent Teachers Association; prior to admission.

ptb prior to birth; pulmonary tuberculosis.

ptc plasma thromboplastin component; prior to conception; patient to call.

PTCJ Patent, Trademark, and Copyright Journal.

ptd prior to delivery; permanent and total disability.

pte pulmonary thromboembolism.

pth parathyroid hormone; prior to hospitalization; pathology.

ptm post traumatic meningitis; post transfusion mononucleosis.

ptn partition.

PTO Patent and Trademark Office.

pts points; patients.

ptt partial thromboplastin time.

ptu propylthiouracil.

pty proprietary; party.

Pu, pu plutonium; paid up; passed urine.

pub public; pubic.

Pub Adm Rev Public Administrative Review.

Pub Con LJ Public Contract Law Journal.

Pub Cont Newsl Public Contract Newsletter.

Pub Emp Rel Rep Public Employee Relations Reports.

Pub L Public Law.

Pub Land & Res L Dig Public Land and Resources Law Digest.

Pub Util Fort Public Utilities Fortnightly.

PUC Public Utilities Commission.

pud planned unit development; pregnancy, uterine, delivered; pulmonary disease; peptic ulcer disease.

Puerto Rico Fed or **Porto Rico Fed** Puerto Rico Federal Reports; see also PR Dec, PRR, PRSCR, PR Sent.

PU Fort Public Utilities Fortnightly.

Pug or **Pugs** Pugsley's Reports (New Brunswick).

Pug & Bur Pugsley and Burbridge's Reports (New Brunswick).

Pug & T Pugsley and Trueman's Reports (New Brunswick).

pulm pulmonary.

Puls or **Pulsifer** Pulsifer's Reports (Maine).

pund pregnancy, uterine, not delivered.

puo pyrexia of unknown origin.

PUR, pur Public Utilities Reports (NS: New Series) (3d: Third Series); purchaser; polyurethane.

PUSH People United to Save Humanity.

pv par value; parole violator; polyvinyl; pipe ventilated; plasma volume; pulmonary vein; portal vein.

pvc premature ventricular contraction.

pvd peripheral vascular disease; patient very disturbed.

pvr peripheral vascular resistance.

pvt private; pressure, volume, and temperature; paroxysmal ventricular tachycardia.

pvw posterior vaginal wall.

PW, Pw, pw Peere Williams' Chancery Reports (England); progesterone withdrawal; public works; packed weight; public welfare; prisoner of war; pulsed wave; pulmonary wedge; pinworms; plantar wart; posterior wall; Parkes Weber.

P&W Penrose and Watts's Reports (Pennsylvania).

PWA Person With AIDS.

pwb partial weight bearing.

P Wms Peere Williams' Chancery Reports (England).

pwp pulmonary wedge pressure.
px private exchange; physical examination; prognosis.
PY, py Paraguay; prior year.
pya psychoanalysis.
Pyke Pyke's Reports (Lower Canada); Pyke's King's Bench Reports (Quebec).
pymt payment.
pzi protamine zinc insulin.

Q, q Quebec; query; quaere; question; quart; quotient; quarterly; quantity; quality; quasi; quinone; quinidine; coenzyme Q; every (quaque).
qa question/answer; quality assurance.
qam quality assurance monitor; quadrature amplitude modulation.
QAPP Quality Assurance Project Plan.
qas quality assurance standards.
QAT Qatar.
QB Queen's Bench (England); Queen's Bench (Canada).
QBD Queen's Bench Division, Law Reports (England).
QBLC Queen's Bench Reports (Lower Canada).
QBR Adolphus and Ellis' Queen's Bench Reports (England).
QBUC Queen's Bench Reports (Upper Canada).
QC, qc Queen's Counsel (England); quality control.
Q Cr Lands LR Crown Lands Law Reports - Queensland.
qd every day (quaque die).
qda quantity discount agreement.
Qd R Queensland Reports.
qds four times a day (quarter die sumendum).

qea qualified export assets.
qed quantum electrodynamics.
qer qualified export receipts.
qh every hour (quaque hora).
qid four times a day (quater in die).
qisam queued indexed sequential access method.
QJPR Queensland Justice of the Peace Reports.
QL, ql Quebec Law; as much as wanted (quantum libet).
Q Land Ct R Queensland Land Court Reports.
Q Law Queensland Lawyer.
Qld Queensland (Australia).
qlfy qualified.
QLJ Queen's Law Journal.
QLJ&R Queensland Law Journal and Reports.
QLR Queen's Law Reports; Queensland Law Reports.
qm quartermaster; every morning (quaque mane).
QN, qn Quarterly Newsletter; quotation; question; every night (quaque nocte).
qns quantity not sufficient.
qoc quality of contact.
qod every other day (quaque altera die).
qp as much as you please (quantum placeat).
qpc quality of patient care.
qqh every four hours (quaque quarta hora).
QR, qr Queensland Reports; quarterly; quadriradial; quantum rectum; quinaldine red.
qrly or **qtr** quarterly.
QRKB Quebec King's Bench Reports.
QRQB Quebec Queen's Bench Reports.
QRSC Queen's Reports, Superior Court.
qs quiet sleep; sufficient quantity (quantum satis); as much as will suffice (quantum sufficit).
qsam queued sequential access method.
QS Ct R or **QSCR** Queensland Supreme Court Reports.

Q St R Queensland State Reports.
qt quantity; quality; quart.
qtam queued telecommunications access method.
qte quote.
QTL Qualified Thrift Lender.
qtr quarterly.
qty quantity.
qu question; quart.
quad quadrant; quadriplegic.
qual quality; qualitative; qualification.
quan quantity.
quant quantitative.
Que Quebec.
Queb Pr Quebec Practice Reports.
Que CA Quebec Court of Appeals.
Queens BB Queens Bar Bulletin.
Queensl Queensland Reports.
Queensl Acts Queensland Acts.
Queensl JP Queensland Justice of the Peace.
Queensl L Queensland Law.
Queen's LJ Queen's Law Journal
Queensl LJ Queensland Law Journal.
Queensl L Soc J Queensland Law Society Journal.
Queensl Pub Acts Public Acts of Queensland (Reprint).
Queensl SCR Queensland Supreme Court Reports.
Queensl St Rep Queensland State Reports.
Queensl Stat Queensland Statutes.
Queensl WN Queensland Weekly Notes.
Que KB Quebec Reports, King's Bench.
Que L Quebec Law.
Que LR Quebec Law Reports.
Que Pr Quebec Practice.
Que QB Quebec Reports, Queen's Bench.
Que Rev Jud Quebec Revised Judicial.
Que Rev Regs Revised Regulations of Quebec.
Que Rev Stat Revised Statutes of Quebec.
Que SC Quebec Superior Court

Reports.
Que Stat Statutes of Quebec.
Que Super Quebec Superior
   Court Reports.
quinq five
Quincy Quincy Reports
   (Massachusetts).
quint fifth
quotid every day (quotidie).
qv as much as you wish
   (quantum vis); which see
   (quod vide).
QWN Queensland Weekly Notes.
qy query.

R, r Rawle's Reports
   (Pennsylvania); The Reports,
   Coke's King's Bench
   (England); respondent;
   reversed; revised; repealed;
   route; residence; received;
   right; radius; ratio; railroad;
   registered; reconnaissance;
   response; restricted; refused;
   routine; race; radiology;
   relapse; remission; residue;
   respiratory; rib; rectum.
R 1 Cro Croke, Elizabeth.
R 2 Cro Croke, James I.
R 3 Cro Croke, Charles I.
Ra, ra radium; robbery, armed;
   rental agreement; random
   access; regional administrator;
   renal artery; room air;
   radioactive; right arm;
   rheumatoid arthritis.
RAC Ramsey's Appeal Cases
   (Canada); racemic; right atrial
   contraction; radial artery
   catheter.
Race Rel L Rep Race Relations
   Law Reporter.
Race Rel L Survey Race Relations
   Law Survey.

rad radius; random access disk;
   radiation absorbed dose; right
   axis deviation.
Rader Rader's Reports (Missouri).
rah right atrial hypertrophy.
rai radioactive iodine.
Rail & Can Cas Railway and
   Canal Cases (England).
ral resorcylic acid lactone.
RALA Richmond Association of
   Legal Assistants.
Ram, ram Ramsey's Quebec
   Appeal Cases; reverse annuity
   mortgage; random access
   memory; right anterior mea-
   surement; rapid alternating
   movement.
Ram & Mor Ramsey and Morin's
   Montreal Law Reporter.
ramps resource allocation in
   multi-project scheduling.
ran resident's admission note;
   random.
Rand Rand's Reports (Ohio);
   Randall's Reports (Ohio);
   Randolph's Reports (Kansas);
   Randolph's Reports (Virginia);
   Randolph's Reports
   (Louisiana).
R&C Russell and Chesley's
   Reports (Nova Scotia).
R & Can Cas Railway and Canal
   Cases (England).
R & Can Tr Cas Railway and
   Canal Traffic Cases (England).
r&d research and development.
R&G Russell and Geldert's
   Reports (Nova Scotia).
R&J Robertson and Jacob's
   Marine Court (New York);
   Robards and Jackson's
   Reports (Texas).
R&M, r&m Russell and Mylne's
   Chancery Reports (England);
   Ryan and Moody's Nisi Prius
   Reports (England); routine
   and microscopic.
R&MCC Ryan and Moody's
   Crown Cases (England).
R&NLR Rhodesia and Nyasaland
   Law Reports.
R&R, r&r Russell and Ryan's
   Crown Cases (England); rest

and recuperation; rate and
   rhythm.
Raney Raney's Reports (Florida).
rao right anterior oblique.
rap regulatory accounting practices; rapid; right atrial
   pressure; recurrent abdominal
   pain.
ras regular analytic services; renal
   artery stenosis.
rat right anterior thigh; repeat
   action tablet.
Raw or **Rawle** Rawle's Reports
   (Pennsylvania).
Rawle, Pen & W Rawle, Penrose
   and Watts' Reports
   (Pennsylvania).
Raym Ent Raymond Entries
   (England).
Raymond Raymond's Reports
   (Iowa).
RB, Rb, rb Renegotiation Board;
   rubidium; rating board; room
   and board; relative bearing;
   Roth-Bernhardt; reticulate
   body; right buttock; respiratory bronchiole.
rba rescue breathing apparatus.
rbb right bundle branch.
rbbb right bundle branch block.
rbc red blood count; red blood
   cell.
rbcm red blood cell mass.
rbcv red blood cell volume.
rbf renal blood flow.
rbw relative body weight.
RC, rc Rolls Court (England);
   Revised Code; Revue Critique
   de Legislation (Canada);
   Register of Copyrights; Roman
   Catholic; Red Cross; release
   clause; reinforced concrete;
   remote control; red cell; rehabilitation center; receptor;
   response conditioned; rib
   cage; root canal; routine chole-
   cystectomy; respiratory care.
R&C Russell and Chesley's
   Reports (Nova Scotia).
rca right coronary artery; renal
   cell carcinoma.
R & Can Cas Railway and Canal
   Cases (England).

R & Can Tr Cas Railway and Canal Traffic Cases (England).

RC&CR Revenue, Civil and Criminal Reporter.

rcc riot and civil commotion; radio common carrier.

rcd record; received.

rcdr recorder.

RCIA Retail Credit Institute of America.

RCJ Royal Courts of Justice (England).

RCL Ruling Case Law.

rcm regimental court martial; red cell mass.

rcn reconnaissance.

RCRA Resource Conservation Recovery Act.

R 1 Cro Croke, Elizabeth.

R 2 Cro Croke, James I.

R 3 Cro Croke, Charles I.

rcpt or **rct** receipt.

rcu respiratory care unit.

rcvy recovery.

RD, rd Registered Dietitian; refer to drawer; remedial design; rod; reduction; respiratory disease; ruptured disk.

r&d research and development.

rda recommended daily allowance.

rdf rapid deployment force.

rdi recommended daily intake.

rdm readmission.

rDNA recombinant DNA; ribosomal deoxyribonucleic acid.

rdp right dorsoposterior.

rds respiratory distress syndrome.

RDT, rdt Revue de Droit du Travail; right dorsotransverse; routine dialysis treatment; retinal damage threshold.

Re, re rhenium; regarding; repayable to either; real estate; rate of exchange; right eye; right ear; rectal examination; readmission.

REA, rea Rural Electrification Administration; renal anastomosis; radio enzymatic assay.

READ Real Estate Asset Division.

Real Est LJ Real Estate Law Journal.

Real Est L Rep Real Estate Law Report.

Real Est Rev Real Estate Review.

Real Prop, Prob & Tr J Real Property, Probate and Trust Journal.

Reap Dec Reappraisement Decision, United States Custom Court.

reas reasonable.

rec record; receipt; recommendation; recovery.

recd received.

Rec Dec Vaux' Recorders Decisions (Pennsylvania).

recip recipient; reciprocity.

Rec Laws Recent Laws in Canada.

Record of NYCBA Record of the Association of the Bar of the City of New York.

recpt receipt.

rect rectal.

RED, red Redington's Reports (Maine); Redfield's Surrogate Court Reports (New York); Russell's Equity Decisions (Nova Scotia); reduction; rapid erythrocyte degeneration; radiation experience data.

Re de D Revue de Droit (Canada).

Re de J Revue de Jurisprudence (Canada).

Re de L Revue de Legislation (Canada).

Redf Redfield's Surrogate Court Reports (New York).

Redf & B Redfield and Bigelow's Leading Cases (England).

Redington Redington's Reports (Maine).

Reese Reese, Heiskell's Reports (Tennessee).

Reeve Eng L Reeve's English Law.

re ex re-examination.

ref referee; refund; reference; release of excess funds.

REFCORP Resolution Funding Corporation.

Ref J Journal of the National Conference of Referees in Bankruptcy.

refr refraction.

Reg, reg Register, regulation; reg-

iment; regular; radioencephalography.

Reg Deb Register of Debates in Congress (Gales and Seaton).

rehab rehabilitation.

REIT Real Estate Investment Trust.

rel religion; related; release; rate of energy loss.

Rel & Pub Order Religion and the Public Order.

rem remainder; remittance; remedial evaluation management; return electrode monitor; rapid eye movement.

Remy Remy's Reports (Indiana).

reo real estate owned.

rep request for proposal; report; repeat; repetendum; represent; roentgen equivalent physical; rest exercise program.

Rep Atty Gen Attorney General's Reports.

Rep Cas Eq Gilbert's Chancery Reports (England).

Rep Ch Reports in Chancery (England).

Rep Const Ct Constitutional Court Reports (South Carolina).

Rep Eq Gilbert's Reports in Equity (England).

repl replacement.

Reports Coke's King's Bench Reports (England).

Rep Pat Cas Reports of Patents, Designs and Trade Mark Cases (England).

repr representative.

Reprints Reports, Full Reprint (England).

rept report; receipt.

Rep t Finch Reports temp. Finch's Chancery (England).

Rep t Hard Reports temp. Hardwick's King's Bench (Lee) (England).

Rep t Holt Reports temp. Holt, Settlement Cases (England).

Rep t QA Reports temp. Queen Ann (Modern Reports) (England).

Rep t Talb Reports temp. Talbot, Chancery (England).

repud repudiate.

req requisition.

reqmt requirement.

res resolution; residual; residence; reserve; research; resistance; resource; remote entry services; respiratory emergency syndrome.

Res & Eq Judg Reserved and Equity Judgments (New South Wales, Australia).

resc rescind.

Res Ipsa Res Ipsa Loquitur.

resp respondent; responsible; respiratory; respiration.

RESPA Real Estate Settlement Procedures Act.

ret return; retainer; retired; retarded; retina.

retd returned.

retic reticulocyte.

retr retract.

Restric Prac Reports of Restrictive Practice Cases.

Rettie Rettie, Crawford and Melville's Session Cases (Scotland).

Rev Belge Droit Int Revue Belge de Droit International.

rev reverse; revenue; revision; review.

Rev C Abo PR Revista del Colegio de Abogados de Puerto Rico.

Rev Crit de Legis et Jur Revue Critique de Legislation et de Jurisprudence (Canada).

Rev de Leg Revue de Legislation (Canada).

Rev Droit Int Revue de Droit International.

Rev Egypt Droit Int Revue Egyptienne de Droit International.

Rev Gen Reg Revised General Regulation (General Accounting Office).

Rev Hell Droit Int Revue Hellenique de Droit International.

Rev Jur Revista Juridica.

Rev Jur UPR Revista Juridica de Universidad de Puerto Rico.

Rev Leg Revue Legale (OS: Old Series) (NS: New Series) (Canada).

Rev Litigation Review of Litigation.

Rev Not Revue de Notariat.

Rev PR Revista de Derecho Puerto Riqueno.

Rev Proc Revenue Procedures (Internal Revenue Service).

Rev R or **Rev Rep** Revised Reports (England).

Rev Rul Revenue Rulings (Internal Revenue Service).

Rev Sec Reg Review of Securities Regulation.

Rev Sel Code Leg Review of Selected Code Legislation.

Rev Sol L Review of Socialist Law.

Rev St or **Rev Stat** Revised Statutes.

Reynolds Reynolds' Reports (Mississippi).

rf refund; radio frequency; rapid fire; rheumatic fever; right front; right foot; renal failure; respiratory failure.

rfb request for bid.

RFC, rfc Reconstruction Finance Corporation; rosette forming cells; right frontal craniotomy.

rfd report for duty; rural free delivery; referred.

RFE Radio Free Europe.

rfp request for proposal; right frontoposterior.

rfv right femoral vein.

rg register; right gluteus.

R&G Russell and Geldert's Reports (Nova Scotia).

rgph registered pharmacist.

rgt regiment.

Rh, rh rhodium; rhesus blood group; rheumatic; relative humidity; report heading; right hand; right hyperphoria; releasing hormone; retinal hemorrhage.

r/h roentgens per hour.

RhA rheumatoid arthritis.

rhd rheumatic heart disease.

rheo rheostat.

rhf right heart failure.

Rhod & NLR Rhodesia and Nyasaland Law Reports.

Rhodes LJ Rhodesian Law Journal.

rhs right hand side.

RI, ri Rhode Island Reports; reinsurance; refractive index; radio interference; remedial investigation; respiratory illness; regional ileitis.

ria radioimmunoassay.

RI Acts & Resolves Acts and Resolves of Rhode Island and Providence Plantations.

rib riboflavin.

RIBJ Rhode Island Bar Journal.

Rice, rice Rice's Reports (South Carolina); rest, ice, compression, and elevation.

Rice Eq Rice's Equity Reports (South Carolina).

Rich Richardson's Law Reports (NS: New Series) (South Carolina); Richardson's Reports (New Hampshire).

Rich & H Richardson and Hook's Street Railway Decisions.

Rich & W Richardson and Woodbury's Reports (New Hampshire).

Rich Ch or **Rich Eq** Richardson's Equity Reports (South Carolina).

Rich CP Richardson's Practice, Common Pleas Reports (England).

Rich Ct Cl Richardson's Court of Claims Reports.

Rich Law Richardson's Law Reports (South Carolina).

RICO Racketeer Influenced and Corrupt Organizations Act.

rid ruptured intervertebral disc.

Ridg Ridgeway's Reports (England).

Ridg Ap Ridgeway's Appeals, Parliament Cases (Ireland).

Ridge t Hard Ridgeway temp. Hardwick, Chancery and King's Bench Reports (England).

rie retirement income endowment.

Ried Riedell's Reports (New Hampshire).

rif reduction in force; right index finger.

Ridg L&S Ridgeway, Lapp and Schoales' King's Bench Reports (Ireland).

RI Gen Laws General Laws of Rhode Island.

rih right inguinal hernia.

rihsa radioactive iodinated human serum albumin.

rik replacement in kind.

Ril See Riley.

Riley Riley's Reports (South Carolina); Riley's Reports (West Virginia).

Rin Riner's Reports (Wyoming).

rinn recommended international nonproprietary name.

rio right inferior oblique.

rip retirement income plan.

RIPA Rhode Island Paralegal Association.

RI Pub Laws Public Laws of Rhode Island and Providence Plantations.

rir right inferior rectus.

risa radioactive iodinated serum albumin.

risc reduced instruction set computing.

riskac risk accepted.

rit realty income trust; refining in transit.

Ritch Ritchie's Equity Reports (Nova Scotia).

riu radioactive iodine uptake.

Riv Diritto Int Rivista di Diritto Internazionale.

rj road junction.

rje remote job entry.

RJQ Rapports Judiciaires (Quebec).

RJRQ Quebec Revised Reports, Mathieu.

rk right kidney.

rkg radiokardiogram.

RL, rl Revue Legale (NS: New Series) (Canada); redline; reduced level; random lengths; reiz limen; reticular lamina; right-left; right lung; right lower.

RL&S Ridgeway, Lapp and Schoales' King's Bench Reports (Ireland).

RL&W Robert, Leaming and Wallis' County Reports (England).

RLB, rlb Railroad Labor Board Decisions; right lateral bending.

rld relocation dictionary; related living donor.

rle or **rlx** right lower extremity.

rlf right lateral femoral; retrolental fibroplasia.

rll right lower lateral.

rlm right lower medial.

rln recurrent laryngeal nerve.

rlq right lower quadrant.

rlr right lateral rectus.

rls release.

RLSC Revue Legale, Supreme Court (Canada).

RLT, rlt Registered Laboratory Technician; right lateral thigh.

rltr realtor.

rlx or **rle** right lower extremity.

rm regional manager; remission; ruptured membranes; respiratory metabolism; range of motion; radical mastectomy.

R&M, r&m Russell and Mylne's Chancery Reports (England); Ryan and Moody's Nisi Prius Reports (England); routine and microscopic.

rma right mentoanterior.

RMCC or **R&MCC** Ryan and Moody's Crown Cases (England).

RM Ch R.M. Charlton's Reports (Georgia).

rmd retromanubrial dullness.

rmf right middle finger.

rml right middle lobe.

RMLAA Rocky Mountain Legal Assistants Association.

rmm read mostly memory.

rms root mean square; respiratory muscle strength.

rmp right mentoposterior.

rmr right medial rectus.

RMT, rmt Registered Medical Technologist; right mento-transverse.

rmv respiratory minute volume.

rmw read-modify-write.

RN, rn Registered Nurse; radon; residual nitrogen.

rna robbery, not armed; ribonucleic acid.

R&NLR Rhodesia and Nyasaland Law Reports.

RNC Republican National Committee.

Ro, RO, ro Rolle's Abridgment; Romania; road; routine order; read only; receive only; rule out; read out; reverse osmosis; reality orientation.

roa return on assets; right occipito anterior.

Rob, rob Robinson's Reports (Louisiana); Robinson's Reports (Upper Canada); Robinson's Reports (Ontario); Robinson's Reports (Virginia); Robinson's Reports (California); Robinson's Reports (Colorado); Robinson's Reports (Nevada); Robinson's Admiralty Reports (England); Robard's Conscript Cases (Texas); Robard's Reports (Missouri); Robert's Reports (Louisiana); Robertson's Marine Court (New York); Robertson's Reports (Hawaii); Robertsonian translocation; return obstetric.

Rob Adm Robinson's Admiralty Reports (England).

Rob & J Robertson and Jacob's Marine Court (New York); Robards and Jackson's Reports (Texas).

Rob L&W Robert, Leaming and Wallis County Reports (England).

Robards Robards' Reports (Missouri); Robards' Conscript Cases (Texas).

Robards & Jack Robards and Jackson's Reports (Texas).

Robb Robbins' Reports (New Jersey).

Robb Pat Cas Robb's Patent Cases.

Rob Cal Robinson's Reports (California).

Rob Cons Cas Robard's Conscript Cases (Texas).

Rob Eccl Robertson's Ecclesiastical Reports (England).

Robert App Robertson's Appeals (Scotland).

Roberts Roberts' Reports (Louisiana).

Robertson Robertson's Reports (Hawaii); Robertson's Reports, Marine Court (New York); Robertson's Ecclesiastical Reports (England).

Rob Haw Robinson's Reports (Hawaii).

Robin App Robinson's Appeals (Scotland).

Robinson See Rob.

Rob La Robinson's Reports (Louisiana).

Rob Mo Robart's Reports (Missouri).

Rob Nev Robinson's Reports (Nevada).

Rob NY Robertson's Reports (New York).

Rob Ont Robinson's Reports (Ontario).

Rob Super Ct Robertson's Superior Court Reports (New York).

Robt Robertson. See Rob.

Rob UC Robinson's Reports (Upper Canada).

Rob Va Robinson's Reports (Virginia).

Rob Wm Adm William Robinson's Admiralty Reports (England).

roc return on capital; resident on call.

Rocky Mt L Rev Rocky Mountain Law Review.

Rocky Mt Min L Inst Rocky Mountain Mineral Law Institute.

Rocky Mt Miner L Rev Rocky Mountain Mineral Law Review.

rod record of decision.

Rodm Rodman's Reports (Kentucky).

roe return on equity; roentgen.

rog receipt of goods.

Rog CHR Rogers' City Hall Recorder (New York).

Rogers Rogers' Reports (Louisiana).

Rog Rec Rogers' New City Hall Recorder (New York).

roi return on investment

rol right occipitolateral.

Roll Rolle's King's Bench Reports (England); Rolle's Abridgment (England).

Roll Rep Rolle's King's Bench Reports (England).

Rolle Abr Rolle's Abridgment (England).

Rolls Ct Rep Rolls Court Reports.

Rom, rom Romania; read only memory; rupture of membrane; range of motion.

Rom Cas Romilly's Notes of Chancery Cases (England).

Root Root's Reports (Connecticut).

rop record of production; right occipitoposterior.

Ror, ror Rorschach test; rate of return; release on own recognizance.

ros read only storage; review of systems.

Rose Rose's Bankruptcy Reports (England).

Rose's Notes Rose's Notes on United States Reports.

Ross Lead Cas Ross' Leading Cases (England).

rot rotation; right occiput transverse.

ROTC Reserve Officers' Training Corps.

Rot Chart Rotulus Chartarum (Charter Roll).

Rot Claus Rotuli Clause (Close Roll).

Rot Parl Rotulae Parliamentarium.

Rot Pat Rotuli Patenes.

Rot Plac Rotuli Placitorum.

Rotuli Curiae Reg Rotuli Curiae Regis (England).

row right of way

Rowe Rowe's Parliament and Military Cases.

Rowe Rowe's Reports (England).

Rowell Rowell's Reports (Vermont).

Rowell El Cas Rowell's Election Cases.

rp real property; rules and procedures; responsible party; repeat; return premium; rust preventative; refractory period; resting pressure; radial pulse; respiratory rate.

rpa right pulmonary artery.

rpar rebuttable presumption against registration.

RPC, rpc Restrictive Practices Court (England); Reports of Patent Cases (England); Regional Planning Commission; relapsing polychondritis.

RP&W Rawle, Penrose and Watts' Reports (Pennsylvania).

rpf renal plasma flow.

rpg report program generator.

RPh Registered Pharmacist.

rpm revolutions per minute; remedial project manager; rate per minute.

rpo regional project officer; right posterior oblique.

rpq request for price quotation.

RPR, rpr Real Property Reports (Canada); retinitis proliferans; rapid plasma reagin.

rps revolutions per second; renal pressor substance.

RPT, rpt Registered Physical Therapist; report; repeat.

rpv right portal vein.

rq reportable quantity; respiratory quotient.

rqmt requirement

rqn requisition.

RR, rr Radio Regulation (2d: Second Series) (Pike and Fischer); Revised Reports

(England); rights reserved; registered representative; railroad; remove and replace; right rear; respiratory rate; recovery room; ruthenium red; rest and recuperation; renin release; radiation response; relative risk.

R&R, r&r Russell and Ryan's Crown Cases (England); rest and recuperation; rate and rhythm.

RRB Railroad Retirement Board.

RRC Regional Response Center.

rrf right ring finger.

rrr regular rate and rhythm.

RRT Regional Response Team; Registered Respiratory Therapist.

RRVLA Red River Valley Legal Assistants.

RS, rs Revised Statutes; Rolls Series; rabbinical supervision; recording secretary; record separator; revenue sharing; radio station; rating schedule; recipient's serum; right subclavian; right side; right sacrum; rhinal sulcus; respiratory syncytial; rectal sinus.

rsa right sacro-anterior.

rsb right sternal border.

RSC Revised Statutes of Canada; Rules of the Supreme Court; right side colon; rested state contraction.

rsg receiving stolen goods.

RSO, rso Resident Surgical Officer; right superior oblique.

rsp receiving stolen property; right sacroposterior.

rsr regular sinus rhythm; right superior rectus.

rst right sacrotransverse.

rsv respiratory syncytial virus.

rsvp please respond.

RT, rt Radiological Technologist; return ticket; release time; real time; route; rate; room temperature; routine; right; rectal temperature; radiotherapy; respiratory therapy.

rta reciprocal trade agreement.

RTC, rtc Resolution Trust Corporation; real time clock; return to clinic.

rte route.

RTECS Registry of Toxic Effects of Chemical Substances.

R t F Reports temp. Finch, Chancery (England).

rtg roentgen.

R t H Ridgway's Chancery and King's Bench Reports temp. Hardwicke (England); Reports temp. Hardwicke (England).

Rt Hon Right Honorable.

R t QA Reports temp. Queen Anne (England).

rtm registered trademark.

rtn registered trade name; return.

rtnr retainer.

rts request to send.

rtv return to vendor.

rtw right to work.

R t W Manitoba Reports temp. Wood.

Ru, ru ruthenium; routine urinalysis; right upper.

Rucker Rucker's Reports (West Virginia).

rue right upper extremity.

Ruff Ruffhead, Statutes at Large (England).

Ruff & H Ruffin and Hawks' Reports (North Carolina).

rul right upper lobe.

Runn Runnel's Reports (Iowa).

ruo right ureteral orifice.

rupt rupture.

ruq right upper quadrant.

Rus, rus Russell's Election Cases (Nova Scotia); recurrent ulcerative stomatitis; radioulnar synostosis.

Rus & C Eq Cas Russell and Chesley's Equity Cases (Nova Scotia).

Russ & C Russell and Chesley's Reports (Nova Scotia).

Russ & G Russell and Geldert's Reports (Nova Scotia).

Russ & M Russell and Mylne's Chancery Reports (England).

Russ & Ry Russell and Ryan's Crown Cases (England).

Russ El Cas Russell's Election Cases (Nova Scotia).

Russ Eq Cas Russell's Equity Cases (Nova Scotia).

Russ NS Russell's Equity Decisions (Nova Scotia).

Russ t Eld Russell temp. Chancery Reports, Eldon (England).

Rutgers Camden LJ Rutgers Camden Law Journal.

Rutgers J Computers & Law Rutgers Journal of Computers and the Law.

Rutgers J Computers Tech & Law Rutgers Journal of Computers, Technology and the Law.

Rutgers L Rev Rutgers Law Review.

rux right upper extremity.

rv rendezvous; recreational vehicle; renal venous; return visit; right ventricle; rectovaginal.

rva right vertebral artery.

rvf renal vascular failure.

rvp right ventricular pressure.

RVPA Roanoke Valley Paralegal Association.

rvse reverse.

rv/tlc residual volume/total lung capacity.

rvh right ventricular hypertrophy.

RW, rw Rwanda; return to work; read/write`; random widths; right of way.

r/w read/write.

rwd rewind.

rwm read-write memory.

rwy or **ry** railway.

Rx prescription.

Ry & M or **Ryan & M** Ryan and Moody's Nisi Prius Reports (England).

Ryde Ryde's Rating Appeals (England).

Ry MCC Ryan and Moody's Crown Cases (England).

ryrqd reply requested.

rz return to zero.

S, s Southern Reporter, First Series; Senate Bill; Shaw's Appeal Cases (Scotland); Shaw, Dunlop and Bell's Reports (Scotland); Sweden; Saturday; September; Sabbath; statute; speed; standard; single; species; south; signature; sentence; small; secretary; surplus; section; sine (without); school; stimulus; sulfur; surgeon; symptom; serine; serum; stimulus; sacrum; senile; spasm; schistosoma; spleen; streptococcus; streptomycin; suture.

S: subjective.

SA, Sa, sa State's Attorney; Saudi Arabia; South Africa; corporation (société anonyme); samarium; subject to approval; semiannual; seasonably adjusted; secondary arrest; supplemental agreement; salt added; sinoatrial; serum albumin; sarcoma; sperm abnormality; salicylic acid.

s/a sugar/acetone; same as above.

saa same as above; serum amyloid.

sab sabotage; science advisory board; significant asymptomatic bacteriuria.

SAC, sac Strategic Air Command; short arm cast; saccharin.

sad source to axis distance; seasonal affective disorder; social avoidance and distress; sugar, acetone, diacetic acid (test).

SADD Standardized Assessment of Depressive Disorders; Students Against Drunk Driving.

Sadler Sadler's Cases (Pennsylvania).

SAE Society of Automotive Engineers.

saf safety.

SAFA School Assistance in Federally Affected Areas.

S Afr LJ South Africa Law Journal.

S Afr LR South Africa Law Reports (App: Appellate).

S Afr Tax Cas South African Tax Cases.

S Afr Yearbook Int L South Africa Yearbook of International Law.

SAG Screen Actors Guild.

sah subarachnoid hemorrhage; subsist at home.

said sexually acquired immunodeficiency.

SAIF Savings Association Insurance Fund.

St John's L Rev St. John's Law Review.

St Louis L Rev St. Louis Law Review.

St Louis ULJ St. Louis University Law Journal.

St Mary's LJ St. Mary's Law Journal.

Sal, sal Salinger's Reports (Iowa); according to the rules of the art (secundum artis legis); salmonella; saline; saliva; sensorineural acuity level.

SALA Sacramento Association of Legal Assistants.

SALJ South African Law Journal.

Salk Salkeld's King's Bench Reports (England).

SALR South Australia Law Reports.

SALT Strategic Arms Limitation Talks.

salv salvage.

sam shared appreciation mortgage; sequential access method; surface to air missile.

San, san Sandford's Reports (Alabama); sanitation; slept all night; sinoatrial node; styrene acrylonitrile.

Sand Sandford's Superior Court Reports (New York).

S&B Smith and Batty's King's Bench Reports (Ireland).

S&C, s&c Saunders and Cole's Bail Court Cases (England); Swan and Critchfield, Revised Statutes (Ohio); shipper and carrier.

Sand Ch Sandford's Chancery Court Reports (New York).

S&D Shaw, Dunlop and Bell's Session Reports (Scotland).

S&G Smale and Giffard's Vice Chancellor's Reports (England); Smith and Guthrie's Reports (Missouri).

s&h sundays and holidays.

San Diego L Rev San Diego Law Review.

Sand I Rep Sandwich Islands Reports (Hawaii).

Sandf Sandford's Superior Court Reports (New York).

Sandf Ch Sandford's Chancery Court Reports (New York).

S&L, s&l Schoales and Lefroy's Chancery Reports (Ireland); savings and loan.

S&M, s&m Smedes and Marshall's Reports (Mississippi); Shaw & Maclean's House of Lords Cases; sadism and masochism.

S&M Ch Smedes and Marshall's Chancery Reports (Mississippi).

S&P Standard and Poor's.

S&R Sergeant and Rawles' Reports (Pennsylvania).

S&S, s&s Sausse and Scully's Rolls Court Reports (Ireland); Simons and Stuart's Vice Chancellor's Reports (England); signs and symptoms.

S & Sm Searl and Smith's Probate and Divorce Reports (England).

S&T Swabey and Tristram's Probate and Divorce Cases (England).

Sanf Sandford's Reports (Alabama).

San Fern VLR San Fernando Valley Law Review.

San Fran LJ San Francisco Law Journal.

sanr subject to approval, no risk.

Santa Clara Law Santa Clara Lawyer.

Santa Clara L Rev Santa Clara Law Review.

sap stock appreciation rights; scientific advisory panel; serum acid phosphatase; soon as possible.

sar sales authorization request.

SARA Superfund Amendments and Reauthorization Act of 1986.

Sar Ch Sen Saratoga Chancery Sentinel.

sas statistical analysis system; special analytic services; sterile aqueous suspension; subaortic stenosis.

Sask B Rev Saskatchewan Bar Review.

Sask L Rep Saskatchewan Law Reports.

Sask L Rev Saskatchewan Law Review.

SA St R South Australia State Reports.

SAT, sat Scholastic Aptitude Test; Saturday; satellite; satisfactory; saturation; saturated.

Sau & Sc Sausse and Scully's Rolls Court Reports (Ireland).

Sauls Saulsbury Reports (Delaware).

Saund Saunders' King's Bench Reports (England).

Saund & C Saunders and Cole's Bail Court Cases (England).

S Aust L South Australia Law.

S Austl South Australia State Reports.

S Austl Acts Acts of the Parliament of South Australia.

S Austl Acts & Ord Acts and Ordinances of South Australia.

S Austl LR South Australian Law Reports.

S Austl Pub Gen Acts Public General Acts of South Australia.

S Austl Stat South Australian Statutes.

Sav, sav Savile's Common Pleas Reports (England); savings; stock at valuation.

Saw Sawyer's Circuit Court Reports.

Sax Saxton's Chancery Reports (New Jersey).

Say Sayer's King's Bench Reports (England).

SB, Sb, sb Senate Bill; Stanford-Binet; stibium; statement of billing; substantive; small business; short bill; sales book; switch board; should be; savings bank; small bowel; shortness of breadth; serum bilirubin; stillbirth.

S&B Smith and Batty's King's Bench Reports (Ireland).

SBA, sba Small Business Administration; stand by assistance; soybean agglutinin.

sbc single board computer; strict bed confinement.

sbd senile brain disease.

sbe subacute bacterial endocarditis; self-examination, breast.

sbft small bowel follow through.

sbic small business investment company.

SBJ Journal of the State Bar of California.

SBLI Savings Bank Life Insurance.

SBN Standard Book Number.

sbo small bowel obstruction.

sbp systolic blood pressure.

sbr styrene butadiene rubber; strict bed rest.

sbt single bredth test.

SC, Sc, sc South Carolina Reports; Session Cases (England); Court of Session Cases (Scotland); Supreme Court; Security Council; Summary Court; Scammon's Reports (Illinois); Seychelles; scandium; schedule change; statement of charges; service charge; salvage charge; science; select cases; same case; subcontractor; supplemental contract; subcutaneous; without correction (sine correctione); surgical cone; suppressor cell; spinal cord; silicone coated; service connected; sugar coated; sex chromatin; stellate cell; sickle cell; sacrococcygeal; Schuller-Christian (disease).

sca sickle cell anemia.

SC Acts Acts and Joint Resolutions, South Carolina.

S&C, s&c Saunders and Cole's Bail Court Cases (England); Swan and Critchfield, Revised Statutes (Ohio); shipper and carrier.

S Cal L Rev Southern California Law Review.

SCALP Students Concerned About Legal Prices.

Scam Scammon's Reports (Illinois).

Scand Studies in L Scandinavian Studies in Law.

S Car South Carolina.

SCBCA Small Claims Board of Contract Appeals.

scc short circuit current.

scca semiclosed circle absorber system.

SC Cas Supreme Court Cases.

SC Code Ann Code of Laws of South Carolina Annotated.

SC Code Regs Code of Laws of South Carolina Annotated, Code of Regulations.

scd schedule; sudden cardiac death.

SCDC Supreme Court Reports (NS: New Series) (District of Columbia).

sce saturated calomel electrode.

SC Eq South Carolina Courts of Equity Reports.

scf standard cubic feet.

sch schedule; school.

Sch & L Schoales and Lefroy's Chancery Reports (Ireland).

Scher Scherer's Miscellaneous Reports (New York).

schiz schizophrenia.

Schm LJ Schmidt's Law Journal (New Orleans).

Schuyl L Rec Schuylkill Legal Record (Pennsylvania).

SCI, sci Science Citation Index; spinal cord injury.

scid severe combined immune deficiency.

scj squamocolumnar junction; sternoclavicular joint.

Sc Jur Scottish Jurist.

SCL, Scl, scl South Carolina Courts of Law Reports; Student of the Civil Law; scanner command language; soft contact lens; symptom check list; spinocervicolemniscal; sclerosis.

SCLC Southern Christian Leadership Conference.

SCLDF Sierra Club Legal Defense Fund.

SCLQ South Carolina Law Quarterly.

SCL Rev South Carolina Law Review.

Sc LT Scots Law Times.

SCM, scm State Certified Midwife; summary court martial; special court martial; streptococcal cell membrane.

scn show cause notice.

Sc NR Scott's New Reports (England).

Sco, sco Scott's Common Pleas Reports (England); subcommissural organ.

Sco NR Scott's New Reports, Common Pleas (England).

S Con Res Senate Concurrent Resolution.

Scot Jur Scottish Jurist.

Scot LJ Scottish Law Journal and Sheriff Court Record.

Scot LM Scottish Law Magazine and Sheriff Court Reporter.

Scot L Rep Scottish Law Reporter.

Scot L Rev Scottish Law Review.

Scot LT Scots Law Times.

Scot LTR Scots Law Times Reports.

Scott Scott's Common Pleas Reports (England); Scott's Reports (New York).

Scott NR Scott's New Reports, Common Pleas (England).

scp single cell protein.

SCR, scr Supreme Court Reports (Canada); scruple; serum creatinine; Schick Conversion Rate; spondylitic caudal radiculopathy; skin conductance response.

SC Reg South Carolina State Register.

Scr LT Scranton Law Times (Pennsylvania).

SCS, scs Soil Conservation Service; systolic click syndrome.

Sc Sess Cas Scotch Court of Session Cases.

S Ct, sct Supreme Court Reporter; sugar coated tablet.

S Ct Rev Supreme Court Review.

scu special care unit.

SCUN Security Council, United Nations.

SCUS Supreme Court of the United States.

scv subclavian vein.

SD, sd South Dakota Reports; Senate Document; Superintendent of Documents; sight draft; without date (sine dato); same day; signed; special delivery; short delivery; sea damage; standard deviation; sudden death; shoulder dislocation; senile dementia; septal defect.

S&D Shaw, Dunlop and Bell's Session Reports (Scotland).

sda sacrodextra anterior.

S Dak South Dakota.

SD Admin R Administrative Rules of South Dakota.

sdbl sight draft, bill of lading attached.

SDBJ South Dakota Bar Journal.

sdc services during construction.

SD Codified Laws Ann South Dakota Codified Laws Annotated.

SDALA San Diego Association of Legal Assistants.

sdd store door delivery; sterile dry dressing.

sdh subdural hematoma.

SDI, sdi Strategic Defense Initiative; state disability insurance; standard deviation interval.

SD Laws Laws of South Dakota.

sdlc synchronous data link control.

SD L Rev South Dakota Law Review; San Diego Law Review.

sdm single, divorced, married.

S Doc Senate Document.

sdp sacrodextra posterior.

SDR, sdr State Department Reports (New York); sender; surgical dressing room.

SD Reg South Dakota Register.

SDS, sds Students for a Democratic Society; sodium dodecyl sulfate; sudden death syndrome.

SD St BJ South Dakota State Bar Journal.

SDWA Safe Drinking Water Act.

SE, Se, se South Eastern Reporter (2d: Second Series); Sweden; selenium; stock exchange; self explanatory; standard error; single entry; sign extend; southeast; starch equivalent; status epilepticus; squamous epithelium; side effect; stage of exhaustion; skeletal/extremities; saline enema.

Sea & Sm Searl and Smith's Probate and Divorce Reports (England).

SEATO Southeast Asia Treaty Organization.

SEC, sec Securities and Exchange Commission; section; second; secondary; security; secant; secretin; soft elastic capsules; series elastic component.

Sec & Ex C Securities and Exchange Commission.

sec leg according to law (secundum legum).

Sec L Rev Securities Law Review.

Sec Reg & Trans Securities Regulation and Transfer Report.

Sec Reg LJ Securities Regulation

Law Journal.

sect section.

Secur RLJ Securities Regulation Law Journal.

secy secretary.

sed sedimentation; skin erythema dose.

seg segmented.

Seign Rep Seigniorial Reports (Lower Canada).

Sel Cas Ch Select Cases in Chancery (England).

Sel Cas NY Yates' Select Cases (New York).

Seld Selden's Reports (New York); Selden's Notes (New York).

Seld Soc Selden Society.

Sel Serv L Rptr Selective Service Law Reporter.

Selw NP Selwyn's Nisi Prius (England).

sem shared equity mortgage; semen; systolic ejection murmur.

semi subendocardial myocardial infarction.

semih half an hour (semihora).

Sen, sen Senate; Senegal; sentence.

Sen Doc Senate Document.

Sen Jo Senate Journal.

Sen Rep Senate Report.

sep simplified employee pension; separation.

sepol soil engineering problem-oriented language.

Sept September.

seq the following (sequitur); sequence; sequela.

ser service; serial; series.

Serg & Lowb Sergeant and Lowbar's Common Law Reports (England).

Serg & Ra Sergeant and Rawles' Reports (Pennsylvania).

SES Senior Executive Service.

Sess Session.

Sess Ca Sessions Cases, King's Bench (England).

Sess Cas Court of Sessions Cases (Scotland); Sessions Cases, King's Bench (England).

Sess Laws Session Laws.

seti search for extraterrestrial intelligence.

Seton Hall Leg J Seton Hall Legislative Journal.

Seton Hall L Rev Seton Hall Law Review.

sev severe.

Sex L Rep Sexual Law Reporter.

Sex Probs Ct Dig Sex Problems Court Digest.

sf standard frequency; square foot; sinking fund; safety factor; spontaneous fracture; seminal fluid; salt free.

sfa superficial femoral artery.

SFALA San Francisco Association of Legal Assistants.

SFAS Statement of Financial Accounting Standards.

SFC Sergeant First Class.

SFLJ San Francisco Law Journal.

sfp straight fixed price.

SG, sg Surgeon General; Solicitor General; Secretary General; Singapore; specific gravity; senior grade; skin graft; serum globulin.

S&G Smale and Giffard's Vice Chancellor's Reports (England).

SGA, sga Southern Governors' Association; small for gestational age.

sgd signed.

SGO, sgo Surgeon General's Office; surgery, gynecology, obstetrics.

sgot serum glutamic oxaloacetic transaminase.

sgpt serum glutamic pyruvic transaminase.

sgt sergeant.

SGUN Secretary General, United Nations.

Sh, sh Shepherd's Reports (Alabama); Shipp's Reports (North Carolina); Shepley's Reports (Maine); Sheldon's Reports (Buffalo, New York); Shaw's Reports (Vermont); Shirley's Reports (New Hampshire); Shand's Reports (South Carolina); sex

harassment; share; shipping and handling; shorthand; semester hour; social history; state hospital; speech and hearing; sex hormone; sinus histiocytosis; somatotrophic hormone; serum hepatitis.

s&h shipping and handling; sundays and holidays.

sha sidereal hour angle.

Shad Shadford's Reports (Victoria).

Shan Shannon's Unreported Reports (Tennessee).

Shand Shand's Reports (South Carolina).

Shand Pr Shand, Practice Court of Sessions (Scotland).

Shaw Shaw's Reports (Vermont); Shaw's Scotch Judiciary Cases; Shaw's Court of Sessions, Scotch Teind Reports; Shaw's Appeal Cases House of Lords from Scotland.

Shaw & D Shaw and Dunlop's Session Reports (Scotland).

Shaw & M Shaw & Maclean's House of Lords Cases.

Shaw D&B or **Shaw Dunl & B** Shaw, Dunlop and Bell's Session Reports (Scotland).

Shaw D&B Supp Shaw, Dunlop and Bell's Supplement House of Lords Decisions (Scotland).

Shaw App Shaw's Appeal Cases House of Lords (Scotland).

Shaw Crim Cas Shaw's Criminal Cases, Justiciary Court (Scotland).

Shaw W&C Shaw, Wilson and Courtnay's House of Lords Scotch Appeals Reports.

Shaw Dec Shaw's Decisions in Scotch Court of Sessions.

SHCT Sheriff's Court (England).

Sheld Sheldon's Reports (Buffalo, New York).

Shep Shepley's Reports (Maine); Shepherd's Reports (Alabama).

Shep Abr Sheppard's Abridgment.

Shepley Shepley's Reports (Maine).

Shep Sel Cas Shepherd's Select

Cases (Alabama).

Sher Ct Rep Sheriff Court Reports (Scotland).

shg shipping.

Shingle Shingle (Philadelphia Bar Association).

Shipp Shipp's Reports (North Carolina).

Shirl LC Shirley's Leading Crown Cases.

Shirley Shirley's Reports (New Hampshire).

shl or **shld** shoulder.

shln shoreline.

Show KB Shower's King's Bench Reports (England).

Show PC Shower's Parliamentary Cases (England).

shpg shipping.

shpmt shipment.

shtg shortage.

shv simian herpes virus.

Si, si silicon; surveillance and inspection; site inspection; short interest; square inch; shift-in character; superimpose; stress incontinence; saline injection; sacroiliac.

SIA Self Insurers Association.

siadh syndrome of inappropriate antidiuretic hormone.

sib self-injurious behavior.

sic standard industrial capacity; standard industrial classification.

Sick Sickel's Reports (New York).

Sick Min Dec Sickels' United States Mining Laws and Decisions.

Sid, sid Siderfin's King's Bench Reports (England); once a day (semel in die); sudden infant death; sudden ionospheric disturbance; systemic inflammatory disease.

sids sudden infant death syndrome.

SIG, sig Special Interest Group; signature; significant; serum immune globulin.

Sil, sil Silver Tax Division (Internal Revenue Bulletin); sister in law.

S Ill ULJ Southern Illinois University Law Journal.

Silv Silvernail's Reports (New York).

Silv A Silvernail's Appeals (New York).

Silv Sup Silvernail's Supreme Court (New York).

Silv Unrep Silvernail's Unreported Cases (New York).

Sim, sim Simmons' Reports (Wisconsin); Simons' Chancery Reports (England); similar; simulated; simultaneous; sucrase isomaltose.

Sim & C Simmons and Conover's Reports (Wisconsin).

Sim & St Simons and Stuart's Vice Chancellor's Reports (England).

Sim NS Simons' Chancery Reports New Series (England).

simul at the same time (simultaneous).

sin left hand (sinistra).

sio serial input/output.

sip standard inspection procedure; state implementation plan.

siq sick in quarters.

Sir JS Sir John Strange's Reports (England).

Sir TJ Sir Thomas Jones' King's Bench and Common Pleas Reports (England).

sit stopping in transit.

siw self inflicted wound.

SJ, sj Solicitors Journal (England); Society of Jesus; under consideration (sub judice); Stevens-Johnson syndrome.

SJA Staff Judge Advocate.

SJC Supreme Judicial Court.

SJD Doctor of Juridical Science.

SJPA South Jersey Paralegal Association.

SJR Social Justice Review.

SJ Res Senate Joint Resolution.

SK, sk Saskatchewan; sick; streptokinase; skin.

Skill Pol Rep Skillman's Police Reports (New York).

Skin Skinner's King's Bench

Reports (England).

Skinker Skinker's Reports (Missouri).

SL, sl Solicitor at Law; Savings and Loan; Sierra Leone; seditious libeler; statutory law; salvage loss; according to law (secundum legem); straight line; standard of living; sea level; sick leave; serious list; sodium lactate; sarcolemma.

S&L, s&l Schoales and Lefroy's Chancery Reports (Ireland); savings and loan.

SLA, sla Symbionese Liberation Army; State Liquor Authority; sacrolaeva anterior.

Slade Slade's Reports (Vermont).

slan slander.

slb short leg brace.

SLC, slc Stuart's Appeal Cases (Lower Canada); Southern Legislative Conference; straight line capacitance; short leg cast; sodium lithium countertransport.

sld sealed.

sle systemic lupus erythematosus.

SLJR Sudan Law Journal and Reports.

SLO streptolysin-O.

Sloan Leg Reg Sloan's Legal Register.

slp without lawful issue (sine legitima prole).

SLR, slr Southern Law Review; Scottish Law Reporter; Saskatchewan Law Reporter; straight leg raising; streptococcus lactis R.

SLRB State Labor Relations Board.

slsi super large scale integration.

SLT, slt Scots Law Times; slight; solid logic technology; sacrolaeva transversa.

sltx sales tax.

slv solvent.

slwc short leg walking cast.

SM, Sm, sm Solicitor's Memorandum (Internal Revenue Service); San Marino; Senior Magistrate; samarium; small; self monitoring; staff memorandum; signalman; left hand (sinistra mano); sado-masochism; synovial membrane; substitute for morphine; simple mastectomy; stapedius muscle; streptomycin.

S&M, s&m Smedes and Marshall's Reports (Mississippi); Shaw & Maclean's House of Lords Cases; sadism and masochism.

sma superior mesenteric artery.

S&M Ch Smedes and Marshall's Chancery Reports (Mississippi).

Sm CCM or **Smith CCM** Smith's Circuit Court Martial Reports (Maine).

Sm Con Smith's Condensed Reports (Alabama).

smg submachine gun; submandibular gland.

Sm & G Smale and Giffard's Vice Chancellor's Reports (England).

Sm & M or **Smed & M** Smedes and Marshall's Reports (Mississippi).

Sm & M Ch Smedes and Marshall's Chancery Reports (Mississippi).

Sm & S Smith and Sager's Drainage Cases (Canada).

Sm ED E.D. Smith's Common Pleas Reports (New York).

Sm Eng Smith's King's Bench Reports (England).

Sm Eq Smith's Principles of Equity.

smh state mental hospital.

smi supplementary medical insurance; statute miles; severely mentally impaired.

Sm Ind Smith's Reports (Indiana).

Smith Smith's Reports (Wisconsin); Smith's Reports (Missouri); Smith's Reports (New Hampshire); Smith's Reports (South Dakota); Smith's Reports (California); Smith's Circuit Court Martial Reports (Maine); Smith's Reports (Maine); Smith's

Reports (Indiana); E.B. Smith's Reports (Illinois); E.P. Smith's Reports (New York); E.H. Smith's Reports (New York); E.D. Smith's Common Pleas Reports (New York); Smith's Reports (England).

Smith & B Smith and Batty's King's Bench Reports (Ireland).

Smith & BRC Smith and Bates' American Railway Cases.

Smith & G Smith and Guthrie's Reports (Missouri).

Smith & H Smith and Heiskell's Reports (Tennessee).

Smith CCM or **Sm CCM** Smith's Circuit Court Martial Reports (Maine).

Smith Cond Smith's Condensed Reports (Alabama).

Smith CP Smith's Common Pleas Reports (New York).

Smith ED E.D. Smith's Reports (New York).

Smith Ind Smith's Reports (Indiana).

Smith JP J.P. Smith's King's Bench Reports (England).

Smith KB Smith's King's Bench Reports (England).

Smith LJ Smith's Law Journal.

Smith Lead Cas Smith's Leading Cases (England).

Smith Me Smith's Reports (Maine).

Smith NH Smith's Reports (New Hampshire).

Smith NY Smith's Reports (New York).

Smith PF P.F. Smith's Reports (Pennsylvania).

Smith Reg Cas Smith's Registration Cases.

Smith Wis Smith's Reports (Wisconsin).

Sm KB Smith's King's Bench Reports (England).

SMJ Society of Medical Jurisprudence.

Sm Me Smith's Reports (Maine).

Sm NH Smith's Reports (New Hampshire).

smp without male issue (sine mascula prole); standard maintenance procedure; standard medical practice.

smr skeletal muscle relaxant.

smug smuggling.

smv slow moving vehicle; superior mesenteric vein.

Smy Smythe's Common Pleas Reports (Ireland).

SN, Sn, sn Session Notes (England); Senegal; tin (stannum); shipping note; stock number; sanitation; without name (sine nomine); serial number; subnormal; scrub nurse.

sna systems network architecture; superior nasal artery.

SNCC Student Nonviolent Coordinating Committee.

Sneed Sneed's Reports (Tennessee); Sneed's Decisions (Kentucky).

Sneed Dec Sneed's Decisions (Kentucky).

sng synthetic natural gas.

snlr services no longer required.

snobol string oriented symbolic language.

Snow Snow's Reports (Utah).

snq superior nasal quadrant.

snr senior.

sns sympathetic nervous system.

So, so Southern Reporter (2d: Second Series); Somalia; sex offender; seller's option; standing order; special order; south; sales order; second offender; shift-out character; superior oblique; shoulder orthosis; salpingo oophorectomy.

soa state of the art.

soap subjective, objective, assessment plan.

SOB, sob Senate Office Building; shortness of breadth.

soc standard of care; state of consciousness; social.

Soc Act & L Social Action and the Law.

So Cal L Rev Southern California

Law Review.

So Car Const South Carolina Constitutional Reports.

So Car LJ South Carolina Law Journal.

Soc Sec Bull Social Security Bulletin.

sod seller's option to double; sodium; sodomy.

So East Rep South Eastern Reporter.

soh start of heading.

So Ill ULJ Southern Illinois University Law Journal.

sol shipowner liability; solicitor; solarium; solution; solenoid; solubilis; soleus; space occupying lesion.

Solar L Rep Solar Law Reports.

So Law Southern Lawyer.

So Law T Southern Law Times.

Sol J Solicitor's Journal.

So LJ Southern Law Journal.

soln solution.

Sol O Solicitor's Opinions (Internal Revenue Bulletin).

So LQ Southern Law Quarterly.

Sol Q Solicitor Quarterly.

So L Rev Southern Law Review (NS: New Series).

solv solvent.

som start of message; sensitivity of method; serous otitis media.

Somerset LJ Somerset Law Journal.

sop standard operating procedure.

sor stimulus organism response.

So Rep Southern Reporter.

sos distress signal; silicon on sapphire; suspend other service; source of supply.

So Tex LJ South Texas Law Journal.

So UL Rev Southern University Law Review.

South Southern Reporter.

Southard Southard's Reports (New Jersey).

South Texas LJ South Texas Law Journal.

Southwestern LJ Southwestern

Law Journal (Texas).

Sov Law Gov or **Soviet L & Govt** Soviet Law and Government.

So West Rep South Western Reporter.

SP, sp Spear's Reports (South Carolina); Spain; stop payment; speed; selling price; starting price; standard practice; subprofessional; supplement; space character; static pressure; species; secretory piece; specimen; spine; spleen; serum protein; speech pathology; symphysis pubis; subliminal perception; suprapubic.

s/p status post.

S&P Standard and Poor's.

SPA, spa State Planning Agency; special public assistance; subject to particular average; salt-poor albumin.

S Pac L Rev South Pacific Law Review.

Spaulding Spaulding's Reports (Maine).

spc salicylamide, phenacetin, caffeine.

SPCA, spca Society for the Prevention of Cruelty to Animals; serum prothrombin conversion accelerator.

SPCC Society for the Prevention of Cruelty to Children; Spill Prevention Control and Countermeasure.

sp cd spinal cord.

sp cm special court martial.

spe sustained physical exercise.

Spear Spear's Reports (South Carolina).

Spear Eq Spear's Equity Reports (South Carolina).

spec specification; specimen; specialist.

Speer See Spear.

Spencer Spencer's Reports (Minnesota); Spencer's Law Reports (New Jersey).

spf sun protection factor.

sp fl spinal fluid.

sp gra specific gravity.

sph spherical.

Spinks or **Spinks Eccl & Adm** Spinks' Ecclesiastical and Admiralty Reports (England).

spl system programming language; spontaneous lesion.

spon spontaneous.

spool simultaneous peripheral operations on-line.

Spoon Spooner's Reports (Wisconsin).

Spottis Spottiswoode's Session Reports (Scotland).

Spottis CL & Eq Spottiswoode's Common Law and Equity Reports.

Spottis Eq Spottiswoode's Equity Reports (Scotland).

Spr, spr Sprague's District Court, Admiralty, Decisions; sprain; solid phase radioimmunoassay; serial probe recognition.

sps symbolic programming systems; status postsurgery.

spss statistical package for the social sciences.

SPUC Society for the Protection of Unborn Children.

sq status quo; subcutaneous.

sqft square foot.

sqin square inch.

SR, Sr, sr Solicitor's Recommendation (Internal Revenue Service); State Reporter (New York); Senate Resolution; Senate Report; State Register; Surinam; strontium; service record; shipping receipt; sentence repetition; supplementary regulation; self-rectifying; storage room; stimulus response; short rate; secretion rate; sedimentation rate; sarcoplasmic reticulum; sinus rhythm; stimulus response; skin resistance; superior rectus; soluble repository; spontaneous rate.

S&R Sergeant and Rawles' Reports (Pennsylvania).

sra supplemental retirement annuity.

SRC, src Stuart's Reports (Lower Canada); sedimented red cells; sensitization response cell.

srcc strikes, riots, civil commotions.

SREA Society of Real Estate Appraisers.

srf somatotropin releasing factor.

srg surgery.

srm superior rectus muscle; spontaneous rupture of membrane.

sro single room occupancy; statutory rules and orders; standing room only.

SR & O & SI Rev Statutory Rules and Orders and Statutory Instruments Revised (England).

S Rept Senate Reports.

S Res Senate Resolution.

srom spontaneous rupture of membranes.

srr surgery recovery room.

SRS, srs Statistical Reporting Service; slow reacting substance.

SS, ss Synopsis Series (United States Treasury Decisions); Silvernail's Superior Court Reports (New York); Social Security; Selective Service; Special Session; Security Service; suspended sentence; social science; sections; one half (semis); standard score; sworn statement; sterile solution; saline solution; sodium salicylate; systemic sclerosis; subaortic stenosis; serum sickness; schizophrenia spectrum; saturated solution.

S&S, s&s Sausse and Scully's Rolls Court Reports (Ireland); Simons and Stuart's Vice Chancellor's Reports (England); signs and symptoms.

SSA, ssa Social Security Administration; subsegmental airway.

SSB Selective Service Board; Social Security Bulletin.

SSC, ssc Solicitor before the Supreme Court; scientific support coordinator; sister strand crossover; standard saline citrate; syngeneic spleen cells.

SSCI Social Sciences Citation Index.

SSI, ssi Supplemental Security Income; small scale integration; symptom-sign inventory.

sski saturated solution of potassium iodine.

ssl suggested state legislation.

ssm subsynaptic membrane.

SSN Social Security Number.

sspe subacute sclerosing panencephalitis.

SSR Social Security Rulings; surgical supply room; steroid resistant rejection.

SSS, sss Selective Service System; specific soluble substance.

SST, sst Social Security Tax Ruling (Internal Revenue Service); supersonic transport; sodium sulfite titration; somatostatin.

SSURO Stop Sale, Use or Removal Order.

ssv simian sarcoma virus.

ST, st State Trials (England); Story's Circuit Court Reports; Sales Tax Division (Internal Revenue Service); statute; shipping ticket; subtotal; straight; street; short ton; standard time; striatum; speech therapy; sterile; serum thrombotic accelerator; systolic time; standard treatment; standardized test; shock therapy; skin test; surface tension; stimulus; sinus tachycardia.

S&T Swabey and Tristram's Probate and Divorce Cases (England).

sta serum thrombotic accelerator.

St Ab Statham's Abridgment.

Stafford Stafford's Reports (Vermont).

Stair Stair's Decisions (Scotland).

STALA Southeast Texas Association of Legal Assistants.

Stan Envt LA Stanford Environmental Law Annual.

Stanford Stanford's Pleas of the Crown.

Stan J Intl Stud Stanford Journal of International Studies.

Stan L Rev Stanford Law Review.

Stan Pa Prac Standard Pennsylvania Practice.

Stant Stanton's Reports (Ohio).

STAP Southern Tier Association of Paralegals.

staph staphylococcus.

Star Starkie's Nisi Prius Reports (England).

Star Ch Cas Star Chamber Cases (England).

Stark NP Starkie's Nisi Prius Reports (England).

START Strategic Arms Reduction Talks.

Stat, stat Statutes at Large; statute; suprathreshold adaptation test; immediately (statim).

Stat at L Statutes at Large.

State Ct J State Court Journal.

State Tr Howell's State Trials (NS: New Series) (England).

Stath Abr Statham's Abridgment.

Stat Realm Statutes of the Realm (England).

Staund Pl Cr Staundford's Pleas of the Crown (England).

stbr starboard.

STC, stc State Tax Cases (Commerce Clearing House); sexually transmitted condition; soft tissue calcification; serum theophylline concentration.

St Ch Cas Star Chamber Cases (England).

STD, std Synopsis Decisions, Treasury Department; standard; sexually transmitted disease; saturated; sodium tetradecyl sulfate.

stdm synchronous time division multiplexing.

stel short-term exposure limit.

ster sterilization.

stet let it stand.

Stetson L Rev Stetson Law Review.

Stev & G Stevens and Graham's Reports (Georgia).

Stew Stewart's Reports (Alabama); Stewart's Admiralty Reports (Nova Scotia); Stewart's Reports (New Jersey); Stewart's Reports (South Dakota).

Stew Adm or **Stew N Sc** Stewart's Admiralty Reports (Nova Scotia).

Stew & P Stewart and Porter's Reports (Alabama).

Stew Eq Stewart's Equity Reports (New Jersey).

Stew VA Stewart's Vice Admiralty Reports (Nova Scotia).

S Tex LJ South Texas Law Journal.

sth somatotropic hormone.

Stiles Stiles' Reports (Iowa).

St Inst Statutory Instruments (England).

Still Eccl Cas Stillingfleet's Ecclesiastical Cases (England).

Stiness Stiness' Reports (Rhode Island).

STJ Special Trial Judge.

St John's L Rev St. John's Law Review.

STLJ South Texas Law Journal.

St Louis L Rev St. Louis Law Review.

St Louis ULJ St. Louis University Law Journal.

stm storm.

St Mary's LJ St. Mary's Law Journal.

Sto Story's Reports (Delaware).

Sto CC Story's Circuit Court Reports.

Stock Stockton's Equity Reports (New Jersey).

Stock Adm Stockton's Admiralty Reports (New Brunswick).

Stockett Stockett's Reports (Maryland).

Stockt Ch Stockton's Equity Reports (New Jersey).

Stockt Vice Adm Stockton's Vice Admiralty Reports (New Brunswick).

Story Story's Circuit Court Reports.

Story Eq Jur Story on Equity Jurisprudence.

stp sewage treatment plant; scientifically treated petroleum; standard temperature and pressure (pulse).

St P State Papers.

St Pl Cr Staundford's Pleas of the Crown (England).

stpp sodium tripolyphosphate.

Str, STR, str Strange's King's Bench Reports (England); Special Trade Representative; striatum; strength; streptococcus.

Strahan Strahan's Reports (Oregon).

Strange Strange's King's Bench Reports (England).

Stratton Stratton's Reports (Oregon).

strep streptococcus.

St Rep State Reporter.

St Rep NSW State New South Wales Reports (Australia).

Stringf Stringfellow's Reports (Missouri).

Strob Strobhardt's Law Reports (South Carolina).

Strob Eq Strobhardt's Equity Reports (South Carolina).

Struve Struve's Reports (Washington Territory).

sts serologic test for syphilis; sodium tetradecyl sulfate.

stsg split thickness skin graft.

St Tr Howell's State Trials.

Stuart Stuart's King's Bench Reports (Lower Canada).

Stuart Vice Adm Stuart's Vice Admiralty (Lower Canada).

Student Law J Student Lawyer Journal.

Stud L & Econ Dev Studies in Law and Economic Development.

sui stress urinary incontinence.

Stu M&P Stuart, Milne and Peddle's Session Court Cases (Scotland).

stv superior temporal vein.

stwy stairway.

stx start of text.

Style Style's King's Bench Reports (England).

SU, su Soviet Union; service unit; standard upkeep; surgery; status uncertain.

sub supplemental unemployment benefits; subcontractor; subsidiary; subordinate; subject; substitute.

substd substandard.

suc successor.

sud sudden unexplained death.

suf sufficient.

Suffolk Transnatl LJ Suffolk Transnational Law Journal.

Suffolk UL Rev Suffolk University Law Review.

SUL Rev Southern University Law Review.

Sum, sum Sumner's Circuit Court Reports; summation; let him take (sumat).

sum cm summary court martial.

Summerfield Summerfield's Reports (Nevada).

Sumn Sumner's Circuit Court Reports.

sup superseded; supplement; superior.

Sup Ct Supreme Court; Superior Court.

Sup Ct Hist Socy YB Supreme Court Historical Society Yearbook.

Super Ct Rep Superior Court Reports (Pennsylvania); Superior Court Reports (New York).

Sup Ct Rev Supreme Court Review.

Super Superior Court.

supp supplement; suppository.

supr superintendent; supervisor.

supsd superseded.

supt superintendent.

sur surcharged; surplus.

surg surgery.

surr surrogate.

susp suspension.

Susq LC Susquehanna Legal Chronicle (Pennsylvania).

sut state unemployment tax.

sux succinylcholine.

sv set value; security violation; stop valve; safety valve; severe; sarcoma virus; sinus venosus; scalp vein.

svc supervisor call; superior vena cava.

svd simple vertex delivery; spontaneous vaginal delivery.

svgs savings.

svt supraventricular tachycardia.

svy survey.

SW, Sw, sw South Western Reporter (2d: Second Series); Swan's Reports (Tennessee); Sweeney's Superior Court Reports (New York); Swabey's Admiralty Reports (England); Swanston's Chancery Reports (England); Swinton's Justiciary Cases (Scotland); Switzerland; Sweden; social worker; software; shipper's weights; semiweekly; salt water; seriously wounded; spherule wall; spiral wound; swelling.

SWA South West Africa.

Swab Swabey's Admiralty Reports (England).

Swan Swan's Reports (Tennessee).

Swan & C Swan and Critchfield's Revised Statutes (Ohio).

Sw & Tr Swabey and Tristram's Probate and Divorce Cases (England).

Swanst Ch Swanston's Chancery Reports (England).

SWAT Special Weapons and Tactics.

swbd switch board.

Sween Sweeney's Superior Court Reports (New York).

swg standard wire gauge.

Swin Swinton's Registration Appeal Cases (Scotland).

SWLJ South Western Law Journal.

Sw L Rev Southwestern Law Review.

swr serum wassermann reaction.

Sw UL Rev Southwestern University Law Review.

SWZ Swaziland.

sx symptoms.

SY, sy Syria; Seychelles; square yard; syphilis.

Sydney L Rev Sydney Law Review.

sysgen system generation.

Syl The Syllabi.

sym symptoms; symmetrical.

Syme Syme's Justiciary Cases (Scotland).

symp or **sx** symptoms.

syn synchronization; synchronous; synagogue.

synd syndicate.

Syn Ser Synopsis Series, Treasury Decisions.

syph syphilis.

Syr, syr Syria; syrup.

Syracuse J Intl L & Com Syracuse Journal of International Law and Commerce.

Syracuse L Rev Syracuse Law Review.

Syr J Int L & Com Syracuse Journal of International Law and Commerce.

sys system.

sysgen system generation.

SZ, sz Swaziland; size; seizure; streptozocin.

szb silver zinc battery.

T, t Tappan's Common Pleas Reports (Ohio); Tuesday; Tobacco; Thursday; tritium; in the time of (tempore); thief; treasurer; territory; transit; ton; true; troy; teaspoon; tablespoonful; terminal; temperature; tumor; tuberculosis; toxoplasma; thyroid; tetracycline.

T_3 triiodothyronine.

T_4 thyroxine.

Ta, ta tantalum; tax agent; traffic accidents; table of allowances; teaching assistant; trading as; tax amortization; truth in advertising; transit authority; tonsils and adenoids; therapeutic abortion.

t&a tonsillectomy and adenoidectomy.

TAA Trade Agreement Act.

TAB, tab Technical Assistance Board; tablet.

TAC, tac Tax Court Reports; total average cost.

tad temporary additional duty.

taf tumor angiogenesis factor.

tah total abdominal hysterectomy.

TAI, Tai International Atomic Time (temps atomique international); Taiwan.

Tait Tait's Manuscript Decisions (Scotland).

Tal, tal Chancery Cases tempore Talbot (England); thymic alymphoplasia; tendon Achilles lengthening.

TALA Tucson Association of Legal Assistants; Tidewater Association of Legal Assistants; Toledo Association of Legal Assistants; Tulsa Association of Legal Assistants.

Tam, tam Tamlyn's Rolls Court Reports (England); teenage mother; thermoacidurans agar modified.

tamp tampering.

Tan, tan Taney's Circuit Court Reports; total ammonia nitrogen; tangent; tonically autoactive neuron.

t&a tonsillectomy and adenoidectomy.

T&C Thompson and Cook's Reports (New York); type and crossmatch.

t&e travel and entertainment; testing and evaluation.

T&G Tyrwhitt and Granger's Exchequer Reports (England).

T&M Temple and Mew's Crown Cases (England).

T&P Turner and Phillips' Chancery Reports (England).

T&R Turner and Russell's Chancery Reports (England).

t&s type and screen.

t&t through and through.

Taney Taney's Circuit Court Reports.

Tann Tanner's Reports (Utah); Tanner's Reports (Indiana).

Tapp Tappan's Common Pleas Reports (Ohio).

Tas LR Tasmania Law Reports.

Tasm or **Tas SR** Tasmania State Reports.

Tasm UL Rev Tasmanian University Law Review.

tat toxin-antitoxin; tetanus antitoxin.

Taun, TAUN Taunton's Common Pleas Reports (England); Technical Assistance, United Nations.

TAUS Tobacco Association of the United States.

Tax ABC Canada Tax Appeal Board Cases.

Tax Adm'rs News Tax Administrators News.

Tax Cas Tax Cases (England).

Tax Coun Q Tax Counselor's Quarterly.

Taxes Taxes, The Tax Magazine.

Tax Exec Tax Executive.

Tax Law Tal Lawyer.

Tax L Rep Tax Law Reporter.

Tax L Rev Tax Law Review.

Tax Mag Tax Magazine.

Tax Mngt Tax Management (Bureau of National Affairs).

Taxn for Law Taxation for Lawyers.

Tax R Taxation Reports.

taw twice a week.

Tay Taylor's Reports (North Carolina); Taylor's King's Bench Reports (Ontario).

Taylor See Tay.

TB, Tb, tb Tariff Bureau; terbium; treasury bill; trial balance; tablespoon; tuberculosis; tracheobronchitis; total body.

tba to be announced; tertiary butyl acetate.

TB&M Tracewell, Bowers and Mitchell's Comptroller's Decisions.

tbc tuberculosis.

tbg thyroid binding globulin.

tbl through bill of lading.

TBM, tbm Tax Board Memorandum (Internal Revenue Service); tubular basement membrane; total body mass; thyroxin binding meningitis.

TB Mon T.B. Monroe's Reports (Kentucky).

TBR Tax Board Recommendation, Advisory (Internal Revenue Service); tumor bearing rabbit.

tbs tablespoon; tribromosalicylanilide.

tbsp tablespoon.

tbt tax benefit transfer.

tbv total blood volume.

tbw total body weight; to be withheld.

TC, Tc, tc Tax Court of the United States; Tax Court Reports; Tax Cases (England); Tariff Commission; technetium; trial counsel; till countermanded; total correction; town councillor; traffic collision; total cost; telephone call; terra cotta; tetracycline; tumor cell; tuberculin contagious; throat culture; tissue culture.

T&C, t&c Thompson and Cook's Reports (New York); type and crossmatch.

tcam telecommunications access method.

tcb task control block.

tcc triclocarban; transitional cell carcinoma.

tcca transitional cell cancer associated.

tce tetrachloroethylene.

TCM, tcm Tax Court Memorandum Decisions (Commerce Clearing House); tissue culture medium.

TC Memo Tax Court Memorandum Decisions (Prentice-Hall).

tcmp taxpayer compliance measurement program.

tcn tetracycline.

TCUS Tax Court of the United States.

TD, td Treasury Decisions; trust deed; total disability; temporary disability; time deposit; three times a day (ter die); treatment discontinued; tardive dyskinesia; thoracic duct; typhoid dysentery; threshold of discomfort; tetanus diphtheria; tocopherol deficient.

tda tax deferred annuity.

tdi temporary disability insurance.

tdm time division multiplexing.

tdn total digestible nutrients.

TDS, tds Treasury Daily Statement; time, distance, speed; take three times a day (ter die sumendum).

tdy temporary duty.

Te, te tellurium; tenancy by the entirety; trade expense; tetanus; tracheoesophageal.

t&e travel and entertainment; testing and evaluation.

tec total estimated cost; technician.

tel telephone; telegram; tetraethyl lead.

Tel-Aviv USL Tel-Aviv University Studies in Law.

telcon telephone conversation.

temp in the time of (tempore); temporary; temperature.

Temp & M Temple and Mew's Crown Cases (England).

Temp Geo II Cases in Chancery temp. George II (England).

Temp LQ Temple Law Quarterly.

Temporary Reg Temporary Regulations (Internal Revenue Service).

Temp Wood Manitoba Reports temp. Wood (Canada).

Tenn Tennessee Reports.

Tenn Admin Reg Tennessee Administrative Register.

Tenn App Tennessee Appeals.

Tenn App Bull Tennessee Appeals Bulletin.

Tenn BJ Tennessee Bar Journal.

Tenn Cas Shannon's Cases (Tennessee).

Tenn CCA Tennessee Court of Civil Appeals.

Tenn Ch Cooper's Tennessee Chancery Reports.

Tenn Ch App Tennessee Chancery Appeal.

Tenn Civ App Tennessee Civil Appeals

Tenn Code Ann Tennessee Code Annotated.

Tenn Comp R & Regs Official Compilation Rules and Regulations of the State of Tennessee.

Tenn Crim App Tennessee Criminal Appeals Reports.

Tenn L Rev Tennessee Law Review.

Tenn Leg Rep Tennessee Legal Reporter.

Tenn Priv Acts Private Acts of the State of Tennessee.

Tenn Pub Acts Public Acts of the State of Tennessee.

TEPD Trademark Examining Procedure Directives.

Term, term Durnford and East's Term Reports (England); termination; terminal.

Term NC Taylor's Term Reports (North Carolina).

Term Rep Durnford and East's Term Reports (England).

Terr, terr Terrell's Reports (Texas); territory.

Terr & Wal Terrell and Walker's Reports (Texas).

Terr LR Territories Law Reports (Canada).

Tet, tet tetanus; treadmill exercise test

tet tox tetanus toxoid.

Tex Texas Reports.

Tex A Civ Cas White and Wilson's Civil Cases (Texas).

Tex A Civ Cas (Wilson) Texas Court of Appeal Civil Cases.

Tex Admin Code Texas Administrative Code.

Tex App Texas Appeals Reports; Texas Court of Appeals Cases.

Tex BJ Texas Bar Journal.

Tex Bus Corp Act Ann Texas Business Corporation Act Annotated.

Tex Civ App Texas Civil Appeals Reports.

Tex Civ Cas White and Wilson's Texas Court of Appeals Decisions, Civil Cases.

Tex Code Ann Texas Code Annotated (Vernon).

Tex Com App Texas Commission Appeals.

Tex Crim Texas Criminal Reports.

Tex Crim App or **Tex Cr R** Texas Court of Criminal Appeals Reports.

Tex Ct App R Texas Court of Appeals Reports.

Tex Dec Texas Decisions.

Tex Gen Laws General and Special Laws of the State of Texas.

Tex Intl L Forum Texas International Law Forum.

Tex Intl LJ Texas International Law Journal.

Tex Jur Texas Jurisprudence (2d: Second Series).

Tex LJ Texas Law Journal.

Tex L Rev Texas Law Review.

Tex R Civ P Ann Texas Rules of Civil Procedure Annotated.

Tex Rev Civ Stat Ann Texas Revised Civil Statutes Annotated.

Tex Reg Texas Register.

Tex S Ct Texas Supreme Court Reporter.

Tex Sess Laws Texas Session Law Service (Vernon).

Tex So UL Rev Texas Southern University Law Review.

Tex Sup Ct J Texas Supreme Court Journal.

Tex Supp Texas Supplement.

Tex Tech L Rev Texas Tech Law Review.

Tex Unrep Cas Posey's Unreported Cases (Texas).

tf total forfeiture; trust fund; territorial force; tuberculin filtrate; to follow.

tfc total fixed cost.

tfn till further notice.

TG, tg Togo; telegram; telegraph; type genus; tendon graft.

T&G Tyrwhitt and Granger's Exchequer Reports (England).

tge transmissible gastroenteritis.

tgp theft of government property.

TH, Th, th Thailand; Thursday; thorium; thyroid hormone; therapy.

THA Taft Hartley Act.

Thai Thailand.

Th & C or **Thompson & C** Thompson and Cook's Supreme Court Reports (New York).

Thayer Thayer's Reports (Oregon).

Th CC or **Thacher Cr** Thacher's Criminal Cases (Massachusetts).

Themis La Revue Juridique Themis.

ther therapy.

The Rep The Reports, Coke's (England); The Reporter (Phi Alpha Delta).

thi temperature humidity index.

Thom Thomas' Reports (Wyoming); Thompson's Reports (Nova Scotia).

Thom & C Thompson and Cook's Supreme Court Reports (New York).

Thom & Fr Thomas and Franklin's Chancery Reports (Maryland).

Thomp or **Thompson** Thompson's Reports (California).

Thompson & C Thompson and Cook's New York Supreme Court Reports.

Thomp Tenn Cas Thompson's Unreported Tennessee Cases.

Thom Rep Thomson's Reports (Nova Scotia).

Thomson Thomson's Reports (Nova Scotia).

Thor, thor Thorington's Reports (Alabama); thoracic; thorax.

Thorpe Thorpe's Reports (Louisiana Annual).

thy thymine.

TI, Ti, ti Tobacco Institute; titanium; tricuspid insufficiency.

tia transient ischemic attack.

TIAA Teachers Insurance and Annuity Association.

TIAS Treaties and Other International Acts Series.

tibc total iron binding capacity.

tid three times a day (ter in die).

TIE Technical Information Exchange.

TIF, tif Treaties in Force; tumor inducing factor.

Tiff, tiff Tiffany's Reports (New York); tag image file format.

Till Tillman's Reports (Alabama).

TILRA Tribal Indian Land Rights Association.

Times LR Times Law Reports (England).

tin taxpayer identification number.

tinct tincture.

Tinw Tinwald's Reports (Scotland).

tip top tape input tape output.

tis time in service; tetracycline induced steatosis.

TJA Trial Judge Advocate.

T Jo or **T Jones** T. Jones' King's Bench Reports (England).

Tl, tl thallium; threat to life; time loan; total loss; truck load; thrift and loans; tubal ligation.

tlc tender loving care; total lung capacity.

TLEICS Treasury Law Enforcement Information and Communications System.

tli total lymphoid irradiation.

TLR, tlr Times Law Reports (England); tonic labyrinthine reflex.

tls typed letter signed.

tlu table look up.

Tm, tm thulium; trademark; true mean; transcendental meditation; tumor; teres major; tympanic membrane.

T&M Temple and Mew's Cases (England).

TMA, tma Tobacco Merchants Association; trimellitic anhydride.

TM Bull Trade Mark Bulletin (NS: New Series).

tmj temporomandibular joint.

tml terminal; three mile limit.

TMM, tmm Tax Management Memorandum (Bureau of National Affairs); tonometer Mackay Marg.

tmo telegraph money order.

tmrc theoretical maximum residue contribution.

TM Rep Trade Mark Reporter.

TMSOG Trademark Section Official Gazette.

TN, tn Tennessee; trade name; tariff number; telephone number; ton; town; translator note; tar and nicotine; temperature normal.

TNEC Temporary National Economic Committee.

tng training.

tnge tonnage.

tns transaction network service.

tnt trinitrotoluene.

tntc too numerous to count.

TO, to Tonga; thrown out (vehicle); turn over; oral; tincture of opium; telephone order.

toa time of arrival; tubo ovarian abscess.

Tobey Tobey's Reports (Rhode Island).

tol tolerate.

toor trans-oral open reduction.

top tax-offset pension; temporarily out of print; termination of pregnancy.

topv trivalent oral polio vaccine.

tos terms of service; temporarily out of stock; tape operating system.

Tot, tot Tothill's Chancery Reports (England); total.

tov trial of voiding.

tow transfer off ward; to other ward.

tp township; telephone; teleprocessing; transaction processing; target practice; tuberculin precipitation; true positive; temperature/ pressure; total protein; threshold potential; trigger point.

T&P Turner and Phillips' Chancery Reports (England).

TPA, tpa Tennessee Paralegal Association; treponema palidum agglutination.

tpc thromboplastic plasma component.

tpd temporary partial disability.

tpk turnpike.

tpn total parenteral nutrition.

tpp thiamine pyrophosphate.

tpr temperature, pulse, respiration.

TPUS Transportation and Public Utilities Service.

TR, tr Durnford and East's Term Reports (England); Caine's Term Reports (New York); Taxation Reports (England); Turkey; tons registered; turnover rate; transmit-receive; tape recorder; transaction; treasurer; transportation; trust receipt; tuberculin residue; temperature, rectal; teaching and research; treatment; tricuspid regurgitation.

T&R Turner and Russell's Chancery Reports (England).

TRA Thoroughbred Racing Association.

Trace & M Tracewell and Mitchell's Comptroller's Decisions (United States).

Trade Cas Trade Cases (Commerce Clearing House).

Trademark Bull Bulletin of the United States Trademark Association (NS: New Series).

Trademark Rptr Trademark Reporter.

Trade Reg Rep Trade Regulation Reporter.

Trade Reg Rev Trade Regulation Review.

Tr & Est Trusts and Estates.

trans transferred; transmitter; transverse; transportation.

Tr & H Pr Troubat and Haly's Practice (Pennsylvania).

Trans & Wit Transvaal and Witswatersrand Reports.

Transit L Rev Transit Law Review.

Tr App or **Trans Ap** or **Transc A** Transcript Appeals (New York).

TRASOP Tax Reduction Act Stock Ownership Plan.

Transp LJ Transportation Law Journal.

T Raym T. Raymond's King's Bench Reports (England).

trbf total renal blood flow.

TRBU Treasury Bulletin.

TRC Trade Relations Council.

trd try repeating dose; tongue retaining device.

Tread Treadway's Constitutional Reports (South Carolina).

treas treasurer.

Treas Dec Treasury Decisions.

Trem or **Trem PC** Tremaine's Pleas of the Crown (England).

Trent LJ Trent Law Journal.

trf tariff; thyrotropin releasing factor.

Trial Law Guide Trial Lawyer's Guide.

Trial Law Q Trial Lawyers Quarterly.

Trin Trinidad.

Trin T Trinity Term (England).

Tripp Tripp's Reports (Dakota).

trit triturate.

Tr Law Guide Trial Lawyer's Guide.

Tr Law Q Trial Lawyers Quarterly.

trm terminal.

TRPB Thoroughbred Racing Protective Bureau.

trs transpose; transfer.

TRT, trt Trade Registration Treaty; treatment.

Tru, tru Trueman's Reports (New Brunswick); trustee; truancy; turbidity reducing unit.

Truem Eq Trueman's Equity Cases (New Brunswick).

Tru Rail Rep Truman's American Railway Reports.

Trust Bull Trust Bulletin.

Trust Terr Trust Territory Reports.

Trusts & Est Trusts and Estates.

TRVB Tables of Redemption Values for United States Savings Bonds.

TS, Ts, ts Treaty Series, United States; transsexual; time sharing; teaspoon; tracking system; technical support; tensile strength; test solution; tricuspid stenosis; total solids; thyroid-serum; toxic substance; tuberous sclerosis; temperature sensitive.

TSCA Toxic Substances Control Act.

tsd time, speed, distance.

tsdf treatment, storage and disposal facility.

TSF Treasury Security Force.

tsh thyroid stimulating hormone.

tso time sharing option.

tsp teaspoonful; trisodium phosphate.

tss toxic shock syndrome.

TSUS Tariff Schedule of the United States.

TT, tt Trinidad and Tobago; total time; tuberculin tested; tetanus toxoid; thymol turbidity.

t&t through and through.

TTAB Trademark Trial and Appeal Board.

ttd total to date; temporary total disability.

ttl transistor transistor logic.

ttnb transthoracic needle biopsy.

ttp total taxable pay; thrombotic thrombocytopenic purpura.

TTPI Trust Territory of the Pacific Islands.

tty teletypewriter.

TU, tu Turkey; Tuesday; trade union; transfer unconditionally; toxic unit; thermal unit.

tuc temporary unemployment compensation.

Tuck Tucker's Reports (Massachusetts); Tucker's Surrogate Reports (New York); Tucker's Reports (District of Columbia).

Tuck & C Tucker and Clephane's Reports (District of Columbia).

Tuck Sel Cas Tucker's Select Cases (Newfoundland).

Tuck Surr Tucker's Surrogate Reports (New York).

Tul L Rev Tulane Law Review.

Tul LJ Tulane Law Journal.

Tulsa LJ Tulsa Law Journal.

Tul Tax Inst Tulane Tax Institute.

Tul Tidelands Inst Tulane Mineral and Tidelands Law Institute.

Tun Tunisia.

TUP Charlt T.U.P. Charlton's Reports (Georgia).

Tup App Tupper's Appeal Reports (Ontario).

tur transurethral resection.

Turn See Turner.

Turn & P Turner and Phillips' Chancery Reports (England).

Turn & R Turner and Russell's Chancery Reports (England).

Turner Turner's Reports (Arkansas); Turner's Reports (Kentucky).

TUS Treasurer of the United States.

Tutt & C Tuttle and Carpenter's Reports (California).

tv transvestite; television; tidal volume; trichomoniasis vaginitis.

TVA, tva Tennessee Valley Authority; tax on value added.

tvc timed vital capacity.

tvd true vertical depth.

tvh total vaginal hysterectomy.

tvu total volume urine.

tw temporary warrant; terawatt; total water.

twa time weighted average.

TWEA Trading with the Enemy Act.

twep terminate with extreme prejudice.

twg total weight gain.

twimc to whom it may concern.

twp township.

twr tool wear rate.

TWU Transport Workers Union.

twx teletypewriter exchange service.

TX, Tx, tx Texas; tax; treatment; transfusion.

ty total yield; territory; temporary.

Tyl Tyler's Reports (Vermont).

Tyng Tyng's Reports (Massachusetts).

typ typical.

Tyrw & G Tyrwhitt and Granger's Exchequer Reports (England).

TZ Tanzania.

U, u Uruguay; Utah; universal; union; unit; use; uniform; uncertain; unknown; unable; unclassified; unsatisfactory; upper; urethra; uvula; uncircumcised; urine; ulcer; umbilicus.

ua under age; unauthorized absence; user area; urinalysis; uronic acid; upper arm.

UAB Unemployment Assistance Board.

UAE United Arab Emirates.

u&l upper and lower.

u&o use and occupancy.

UAR United Arab Republic.

U Ark Little Rock LJ University of Arkansas at Little Rock Law Journal.

UART Universal Asynchronous Receiver Transmitter.

UAW United Automobile, Aerospace and Agricultural Implements Workers of America.

ub undistributed budget.

U Balt L Rev University of Baltimore Law Review.

UBC Legal Notes University of British Columbia Legal Notes.

UBCL Rev University of British Columbia Law Review.

U Bridg LR University of Bridgeport Law Review.

UC, uc Upper Canada; unemployment compensation; usual and customary; unclassified; undercharge; unsatisfactory condition; utility cargo; under construction; unchanged; urethral and cervical; urine culture; urinary catheter; unconscious; umbilical cord; ulcerative colitis.

UC App Upper Canada Appeal Reports.

UCAS Uniform Cost Accounting Standards.

UCC Uniform Commercial Code; Uniform Credit Code; Universal Copyright Convention.

UC Ch Upper Canada Chancery Reports.

UC Cham Upper Canada Chambers Reports.

UC Chan Upper Canada Chancery Reports.

UCCLJ Uniform Commercial Code Law Journal.

UCC Law Letter Uniform Commercial Code Law Letter.

UCCP Upper Canada Common Pleas Reports.

UCCPD Upper Canada Common Pleas Division Reports (Ontario).

UCC Rep Serv Uniform Commercial Code Reporting Service.

ucd usual childhood diseases.

UCDL Rev University of California at Davis Law Review.

UCE&A or UC Err & App Upper Canada Error and Appeal Reports.

ucg urinary chorionic gonadotropin.

uchd usual childhood disease.

U Chi L Rec University of Chicago Law School Record.

U Chi L Rev University of Chicago Law Review.

U Chi LS Conf Series University of Chicago Law School Conference Series.

U Cin L Rev University of Cincinnati Law Review.

UCIS Unemployment Compensation Interpretation Service.

ucj unsatisfied claim and judgment.

UC Jur Upper Canada Jurist.

UCKB Upper Canada King's Bench Reports, Old Series.

UCLA-Alaska L Rev University of California at Los Angeles-Alaska Law Review.

UCLA Intra L Rev University of California at Los Angeles Intramural Law Review.

UCLA L Rev University of California at Los Angeles Law Review.

UCLJ Upper Canada Law Journal (NS: New Series).

UCMJ Uniform Code of Military Justice.

UCMP Union Catalog of Medical Periodicals.

U Colo L Rev University of Colorado Law Review.

UC OS Upper Canada King's Bench Reports, Old Series.

UCPR or UC Pr Upper Canada Practice Reports.

UCQB Upper Canada Queen's Bench Reports (OS: Old Series).

UCR, ucr Uniform Crime Reports; Upper Canada Reports; usual, customary, and reasonable; unconditioned reflex.

UC Rep Upper Canada Reports.

UCS, ucs Union of Concerned Scientists; user control store; unconscious.

ucv uncontrolled variable.

ud unavoidable delay; unlisted drug; as directed (ut dictum); undesirable discharge; ulnar deviation; urethral discharge; uridine diphosphate.

UDAG Urban Development Action Grant.

Udal Udal's Fiji Law Reports.
Uganda LF Uganda Law Focus.
U Dayton L Rev University of Dayton Law Review.
udc undeveloped country; universal decimal classification; usual diseases of childhood.
U Det J Urb L University of Detroit Journal of Urban Law.
U Det LJ University of Detroit Law Journal.
udo undetermined origin.
ue upper extremity.
UEW United Electrical Workers.
uf used for; unknown factor.
ufa until further advised.
ufac unlawful flight to avoid custody.
ufap unlawful flight to avoid prosecution.
ufat unlawful flight to avoid testimony.
UFIRS Uniform Fire Incident Reporting System.
U Fla L Rev University of Florida Law Review.
ufo unidentified flying object.
UFPC United Federation of Postal Clerks.
ufr urine filtration rate.
UFT United Federation of Teachers.
UFW United Farm Workers of America.
UG, ug Uganda; urogenital.
ugi upper gastrointestinal.
ugt urgent; urogenital tuberculosis.
UGW United Garment Workers of America.
uh upper half.
U Hawaii L Rev University of Hawaii Law Review.
uhc under honorable conditions.
ui unemployment insurance.
u/i unidentified.
uibc unsaturated iron binding capacity.
UIBPIP United International Bureau for the Protection of Intellectual Property.
uic underground injection control.
U Ill LF University of Illinois Law Forum.

uip unfair industrial practice.
UK, uk United Kingdom; unknown.
U Kan City L Rev University of Kansas City Law Review.
U Kan L Rev University of Kansas Law Review.
ul unauthorized leave; underwriters laboratories; upper lobe.
u&l upper and lower.
ULA, ula Uniform Law Annotations; undedicated logic array.
uln upper limits of normal.
ulp unfair labor practice.
ULS Union List of Serials.
ult praes last prescribed (ultimum praescriptus).
um unmarried; unable to maintain
U Mary LF University of Maryland Law Forum.
umb umbilicus.
U Miami L Rev University of Miami Law Review.
U Mich JL Ref University of Michigan Journal of Law Reform.
UMKCL Rev University of Missouri at Kansas City Law Review.
U Mo Bull L Ser University of Missouri Bulletin Law Series.
U Mo KCL Rev University of Missouri at Kansas City Law Review.
ums universal military service.
UMTA Urban Mass Transportation Administration.
UMW United Mine Workers.
UN, un United Nations; union; university; unable; undernourished; urinary nitrogen; urea nitrogen; ulnar nerve.
UNBLJ University of New Brunswick Law Journal.
UN Bul United Nations Bulletin.
unc unclassified.
UNCF United Negro College Fund.
UNCLOS United Nations Conference on the Law of the Sea.

UNCOPUOS United Nations Committee on the Peaceful Uses of Outer Space.
UNCTAD United Nations Conference on Trade and Development.
undetd undetermined.
UNDI United Nations Document Index.
UN Doc United Nations Documents.
Unempl Ins Rep Unemployment Insurance Reporter (Commerce Clearing House).
UNESCO United Nations Educational, Scientific and Cultural Organization.
U New So Wales LJ University of New South Wales Law Journal.
U Newark L Rev University of Newark Law Review.
UNFAO United Nations Food and Agriculture Organization.
UNGA United Nations General Assembly.
UNGAOR United Nations General Assembly Official Records.
UNICEF United Nations International Children's Emergency Fund.
Unif L Conf Uniform Law Conference (Canada).
UNIVAC Universal Automatic Computer.
unk unknown.
Univ Chi L Rev University of Chicago Law Review.
Univ Cin L Rev University of Cincinnati Law Review.
Univ ILL Law F University of Illinois Law Forum.
Univ Penn L Rev University of Pennsylvania Law Review.
Univ Toledo L Rev University of Toledo Law Review.
UN Jurid YB United Nations Juridical Yearbook.
UNLL United Nations League of Lawyers.
UNLOS United Nations Law of the Sea.
unm unmarried.
Unof Unofficial Reports.

Un Prac News Unauthorized Practice News.

unrel unreliable.

UNRIAA United Nations Reports of International Arbitral Awards.

UNRISD United Nations Research Institute for Social Development.

UNRWA United Nations Relief and Works Agency.

uns unsymmetrical; unsatisfactory.

unsat unsatisfactory.

UNSC United Nations Security Council.

UNSCOR United Nations Security Council Official Records.

unsgd unsigned.

UNTAA United Nations Technical Assistance Administration.

UNTS United Nations Treaty Series.

UNTT United Nations Trust Territory.

uo under observation; undetermined origin; ureteral orifice.

u&o use and occupancy.

UP, up University Press; uttering and publishing; unit price; upper; ureteropelvic.

U Pa L Rev University of Pennsylvania Law Review.

UPC Universal Product Code.

UPI Universal Press International.

U Pitt L Rev University of Pittsburgh Law Review.

upj ureteropelvic junction.

UP News Unauthorized Practice News.

upp urethral pressure profile.

UPR Uniform Parole Reports.

UPS, ups United Parcel Service; ultraviolet photoelectron spectroscopy.

U Puget Sound L Rev University of Puget Sound Law Review.

U Queens LJ University of Queensland Law Journal.

UR, ur Uruguay; upper right; urine; unconditioned response.

Urban L Ann Urban Law Annual.

Urban Law Urban Lawyer.

urd upper respiratory disease.

uri upper respiratory infection.

U Rich L Rev University of Richmond Law Review.

urol urology.

urs ultrasonic renal scanning.

US, us United States; United States Supreme Court Reports; unserviceable; upper segment; unconditioned stimulus; as above (ut supra); unit separator; ultrasound.

USA United Steelworkers of America; United States Army; United States of America.

USACE United States Army Corps of Engineers.

USAFCMR United States Air Force Court of Military Review.

USALSA United States Army Legal Service Agency.

US & Can Av United States and Canadian Aviation Reports.

U San Fernando VL Rev University of San Fernando Valley Law Review.

U San Fran L Rev or USFL Rev University of San Francisco Law Review.

US App United States Appeals.

US App DC United States Court of Appeals for the District of Columbia.

USASCII United States of America Standard Code for Information Interchange.

USASI United States of America Standards Institute.

US Av R United States Aviation Reports.

USBA United States Brewers Association.

USBS United States Bureau of Standards.

USBTA United States Board of Tax Appeals.

USC, usc United States Code; United States Customs; under separate cover.

USCA United States Code Annotated; United States Court of Appeals.

USCC United States Circuit Court;

United States Court of Claims; United States Customs Court.

USCCA United States Circuit Court of Appeals.

USCC&AN or US Code & Ad News United States Code Congressional and Administrative News.

USCCPA United States Court of Customs and Patent Appeals.

USC Govt Rev University of South Carolina Governmental Review.

USCMA United States Court of Military Appeals.

USCG United States Coast Guard.

USCS United States Code Service.

USC Supp United States Code, Supplement.

US Ct Cl United States Court of Claims Reports.

USDA United States Department of Agriculture.

USDC United States District Court.

usdw underground source of drinking water.

USE United States Embassy.

USFL Rev University of San Francisco Law Review.

USFS United States Foreign Service.

USGS United States Geological Survey.

USHA United States Housing Authority.

USIA United States Information Agency.

USICCVR United States Interstate Commerce Commission Valuation Reports.

US Jur United States Jurist.

US L Ed or US Law Ed United States Supreme Court Reports, Lawyers' Edition.

USLJ United States Law Journal.

USL Mag United States Law Magazine.

USL Rev United States Law Review.

USLW United States Law Week.

USM United States Marines; United States mail.

USMC United States Maritime

Commission; United States Marine Corps.

USN United States Navy.

USO United Service Organizations.

U So Cal Tax Inst University of Southern California Tax Institute.

USPC United States Parole Commission.

USPO United States Patent Office.

USPQ United States Patent Quarterly.

USR United States Reports.

US Rep United States Reports.

USRS United States Revised Statutes.

usrt universal synchronous receiver/transmitter.

USS, uss United States Standard; United States shareholder; ultra sound scanning.

USSB United States Shipping Board.

US Sup Ct Rep United States Supreme Court Reporter.

USSR Union of Soviet Socialist Republics.

UST or **USTIT** United States Treaties and Other International Agreements.

USTA United States Trademark Association.

USTC or **US Tax Cas** United States Tax Cases (Commerce Clearing House).

USTD United States Treaty Development.

US Treas Reg United States Treasury Regulations.

US Treaty Ser United States Treaty Series.

USVAAD United States Veterans Administration Administrator's Decisions.

USVBDD United States Veterans Bureau Directors Decisions.

UT, ut Utah; unit; utility; urinary tract.

Utah Utah Reports (2d: Second Series).

Utah Admin R Administrative Rules of the State of Utah.

Utah B Bull Utah Bar Bulletin.

Utah Bull State of Utah Bulletin.

Utah Code Ann Utah Code Annotated.

Utah L Rev Utah Law Review.

U Tasm L Rev University of Tasmania Law Review.

uti urinary tract infection.

util utility.

Util L Rep Utility Law Reporter.

U Tol L Rev University of Toledo Law Review.

U Tor LJ University of Toronto Law Journal.

U Tor L Rev University of Toronto School of Law Review.

utp uridine triphosphate.

utt uttering.

UTU United Transportation Union.

UTWA United Textile Workers of America.

uv ultraviolet; urine volume; umbilical vein.

uvj ureterovesical junction.

uw underwriter; underwater.

U Wash L Rev University of Washington Law Review.

U West Aust L Rev University of Western Australia Law Review.

U Windsor L Rev University of Windsor Law Review.

UWLAL Rev University of West Los Angeles Law Review.

uwm unwed mother.

ux wife (uxor).

V, v Virginia; Vermont; Vatican; Victoria; venue; vanadium; versus; velocity; viscosity; vector; ventilation; visibility; variable; value; vapor; volume; voltage; visit; vein; visit; vision; valine; virgin; vomit; virus; vaccine; vitamin.

VA, va Virginia Reports; Veterans Administration; Voice of America; vice admiral; volt ampere; ventricular aneurysm; visual acuity; visual aid; vertebral artery; valproic acid; vasodilator agent.

Va Acts Acts of the General Assembly of the Commonwealth of Virginia.

Va App Virginia Court of Appeals Reports.

vab voice answer back.

Va Bar News Virginia Bar News.

vac vacant.

VACAB Veterans Administration Contract Appeals Board.

Va Cas Brockenbrough and Holmes, Virginia Cases.

vacc vaccination.

Va Ch Dec Wythe's Chancery Decisions (Virginia).

Va Code Ann Code of Virginia Annotated.

Va Col Dec Randolph and Barradall's Virginia Colonial Decisions.

VAD, vad Veterans' Affairs Decisions; vitamin A deficiency; virus adjusting diluent.

Va Dec Virginia Decisions.

vag vagrancy; vaginal; vaginitis.

vag hys vaginal hysterectomy.

Va J Intl L Virginia Journal of International Law.

Va J Nat Resources Law Virginia Journal of Natural Resources Law.

val valuation; valve.

VALA Ventura County Association of Legal Assistants.

Va LJ Virginia Law Journal.

Val UL Rev Valparaiso University Law Review.

Va L Reg Virginia Law Register (NS: New Series).

Val Rep ICC Valuation Reports (Interstate Commerce Commission).

Va L Rev Virginia Law Review.

Val UL Rev Valparaiso University Law Review.

vamp vincristine, amethopterin, 6-mercaptopurine, prednisone.

Vand J Transnatl L Vanderbilt Journal of Transnational Law.

Vand L Rev Vanderbilt Law Review.

v&p vagotomy and pyloroplasty.

v&t volume and tension.

v&v vulva and vagina.

Van K Van Koughnet's Common Pleas Reports (Upper Canada).

Van N Van Ness' Prize Cases.

var variable; variation; volt ampere reactive.

Va R Gilmer's Virginia Reports.

Va Reg Regs Virginia Register of Regulations.

vasc vascular.

Vat, vat Vatican; value added tax.

Vaugh Vaughan's Common Pleas Reports (England).

Vaux Vaux's Recorder Decisions (Pennsylvania).

VB, vb Veterans' Bureau; vertical beam; vagina bulbi; viable birth; virus buffer; venous blood.

vb$_1$ voided bladder urine - initial.

vbg venous blood pressure.

vc vendor contract; variable cargo; valuation clause; vinyl chloride; vital capacity.

VCALA Ventura County Association of Legal Assistants.

vcg vectorcardiogram.

vcr videocassette recorder.

VC Rep Vice Chancellor's Reports (England).

vcty vicinity.

vcu voiding cystourethrogram.

vd void; vapor density; venereal disease.

vdg voiding; venereal disease gonorrhea.

vdh valvular disease of the heart.

vdrd venereal disease research laboratory.

vdt visual display terminal.

vdu video display unit.

VE, ve Vesey Chancery Reports (England); Venezuela; vinethene and ether; ventilation; vesicular exanthema;

vaginal examination; viral encephalitis.

Ve & B Vesey and Beames' Chancery Reports (England).

Veazey Veazey's Reports (Vermont).

veep vice president.

veh vehicle.

vel velocity.

Ven Venezuela.

Vent Ventris' King's Bench Reports (England); Ventris' Common Pleas Reports (England); ventilation; ventricle.

Ver, ver Vermont; visual evoked response.

Vern Vernon's Chancery Reports (England).

Vern & S Vernor and Scriven's King's Bench Reports (Ireland).

vert vertebrate.

Ves, ves Vesey, Senior, Chancery Reports (England); vesicle; bladder (vesica).

Ves & Bea Vesey and Beames' Chancery Reports (England).

vesic vesicle.

Ves Jr Vesey, Junior, Chancery Reports (England).

Ves Jun Supp or **Ves Supp** Vesey, Junior, Supplement, Chancery Reports (England).

Ves Sen Vesey, Senior, Chancery Reports (England).

vet veterinarian; veteran.

Vez Vezey's Chancery Reports (England).

vf vertical file; voice frequency; vocal fremitus; visual field.

VFD Volunteer Fire Department.

VFib ventricular fibrillation.

VFW Veterans of Foreign Wars.

vg vertical grain; very good.

vgh very good health.

vh Veterans Hospital; viral hepatitis.

vhd valvular heart disease.

VI, Vi, vi Virgin Islands Reports; virginium; viscosity index; vaginal irrigation; visual impairment; vastus intermedius.

VIBJ Virgin Islands Bar Journal.

VI Code Ann Virgin Islands Code Annotated.

Vict Admr Victorian Admiralty.

Vict Eq Victorian Equity.

Vict L Victorian Law.

Vict L Rep Victorian Law Reports.

Vict LR Min Victorian Law Mining Reports.

Vict LT Victorian Law Times.

Vict R Victorian Review.

Vict St Tr Victorian State Trials.

Vict UL Rev Victoria University Law Review.

Vict U Well Rev Victoria University of Wellington Law Review.

Vil & Br Vilas and Bryant's Edition Reports (Wisconsin).

Vilas Vilas' Reports, Criminal (New York).

Vill L Rev Villanova Law Review.

vin vehicle identification number.

Vin Abr Viner's Abridgment of Law and Equity (England).

Vin Supp Viner's Abridgment of Law and Equity Supplement (England).

VIP, vip Virgin Islands Paralegals; very important person; voluntary interruption of pregnancy; vasoactive intestinal peptide.

Vir, vir Virgin's Reports (Maine); variable interest rate; virulent; viridis; virology.

VI R & Regs Virgin Islands Rules and Regulations.

Virg Virginia Cases.

Virgin Virgin's Reports (Maine).

Virgin Is Virgin Islands.

Virg J Int L Virginia Journal of International Law.

Virg L Rev Virginia Law Review.

vis visibility; viscosity.

VI Sess Laws Virgin Islands Session Laws.

VISTA Volunteers in Service to America.

vit vitamin.

vlf very low frequency.

vlol violating local option law.

VLR, vlr Victoria Law Reports;

violation of a law of the road; vinleurosine.

vlsi very large scale integration.

vm voltmeter.

vma vanillylmandelic acid.

VMD Doctor of Veterinary Medicine.

VN, vn Van Ness Prize Cases; Vietnam; Vocational Nurse; visceral nucleus; virus neutralization.

VNA Visiting Nurse Association.

vo verbal order; very old.

VOA Voice of America.

voc vocational.

vol volunteer; volume.

vom volt ohm milliammeter.

vop valued as in original policy.

vopa verbal order purchase agreement.

vou voucher.

vox voice operated transmitter.

vp voting pool; vice president; vulnerable period; vapor pressure; variable pressure.

v&p vagotomy and pyloroplasty.

vph vehicles per hour.

vpm volts per mil.

Vr, VR, vr Vermont Reports; Valuation Reports (Interstate Commerce Commission); Vroom's Law Reports (New Jersey); vendor rating; vital record; voltage relay; vulcanized rubber; vocal resonance; ventral root; vascular resistance; vocational rehabilitation.

VRA Voting Rights Act.

vrbl variable.

vrc vertical redundancy check.

vrm variable rate mortgage.

Vroom Vroom's Law Reports (New Jersey).

vs versus; volumetric solution; visual signaling; vital signs; voluntary sterilization.

vsam virtual storage access method.

vsb visible.

vsd ventricular septal defect.

vsl very serious list.

Vt, vt Vermont Reports; vehicle

theft; variable time; vertical tabulation; ventricular tachycardia; vacuum tube; voting.

v&t volume and tension.

Vt Admin Proc Bull Vermont Administrative Procedures Bulletin.

Vt Admin Proc Comp Vermont Administrative Procedures Compilation.

vtam virtual telecommunications access method.

vtc voting trust company.

Vt Laws Laws of Vermont.

Vt L Rev Vermont Law Review.

vtoc volume table of contents.

vtr video tape recorder.

Vt Stat Ann Vermont Statutes Annotated.

vtx vertex.

vu volume unit.

vv vice versa; veins; vagina and vulva.

v&v vulva and vagina.

vws voice warning system.

vy various years.

W, w Wheaton's United States Supreme Court Reports; Watt's Reports (Pennsylvania); Wright's Reports (Ohio); Wendell's Reports (New York); Wednesday; withdrawal; warehouse; watt; weight; warrant; warning; west; wife; week; wolframium; white cell; tryptophan.

WA, wa Watts' Reports (Pennsylvania); Washington; Western Australia; warrant of arrest; with average; work authorization; when awake.

wab when authorized by.

W A'B & W Webb, A'Beckett and

Williams' Reports (Victoria).

WAC Women's Army Corps.

WACA West African Court of Appeal Reports, Selected Judgments.

WADE World Association of Document Examiners.

wae when actually employed.

waf with all faults.

W Afr App West African Court of Appeal Reports.

Wage & Hour Cas Wage and Hour Cases (Bureau of National Affairs).

Wage-Price L & Econ Rev Wage-Price Law and Economics Review.

WAIS Wechsler Adult Intelligence Scale.

WAJ World Association of Judges.

Wake Forest Intra L Rev Wake Forest Intramural Law Review.

Wake Forest L Rev Wake Forest Law Review.

Wal by L Wallis' Reports by Lyne (Ireland).

Wal Jr or **Wall Jr** Wallace, Jr., United States Circuit Court Reports.

Walk Walker's Reports (Texas); Walker's Reports (Mississippi); Walker's Reports (Alabama); Walker's Reports (Pennsylvania); Walker's Reports (Michigan).

Walk Ch Walker's Chancery Reports (Michigan).

Walker See Walk.

Wall Wallace's United States Supreme Court Reports; Wallace's United States Circuit Court Reports.

Wall CC Wallace's United States Circuit Court Reports.

Wallis Wallis' Chancery Reports (Ireland).

Wallis by L Wallis' Reports by Lyne (Ireland).

Wall Rep Wallace's United States Supreme Court Reports; Wallace, The Reporters.

Wall SC Wallace's United States Supreme Court Reports.

Walsh Walsh's Registry Cases (Ireland).

Walter Walter's Reports (New Mexico).

wam white adult male; words a minute.

W&C Wilson and Courtenay's Appeal Cases.

w&i weighing and inspection.

W&M Woodbury and Minot's Circuit Court Reports.

W&M L Rev William and Mary Law Review.

W&S Watts and Sergeant's Reports (Pennsylvania); Wilson and Shaw's Appeal Cases (Scotland).

W&W White and Webb's Victorian Reports (Australia); White and Wilson's Civil Cases (Texas).

war warrant.

Ward Warden's Reports (Ohio).

Ward & Sm Warden and Smith's Reports (Ohio).

Warden's Law & Bk Bull Warden's Weekly Law and Bank Bulletin (Ohio).

War Dept BCA War Department Board of Contract Adjustment Decisions.

Ware Ware's United States District Court Reports.

War Trade Reg War Trade Regulations.

Wash Washington Reports (2d: Second Series); Washington's Reports (Virginia); Washington's Reports (Vermont).

Wash Admin Code Washington Administrative Code.

Wash & Haz PEI Washburton and Hazard's Reports (Prince Edward Island).

Wash & Lee L Rev Washington and Lee Law Review.

Wash App Washington Appellate Reports.

Washburn Washburn's Reports (Vermont).

Washburn LJ Washburn Law Journal.

Wash Leg Serv Washington Legislative Service (West).

Wash CC Washington Circuit Court Reports.

Wash Co Washington County Reports (Pennsylvania).

Wash L Rep Washington Law Reporter (District of Columbia).

Wash L Rev Washington Law Review.

Wash Rev Code Revised Code of Washington.

Wash St Reg Washington State Register.

Wash Terr or **Wash Ty** Washington Territory Reports; Washington Territory Opinions.

Wash ULQ Washington University Law Quarterly.

Wash Va Washington Reports (Virginia).

WASP White Anglo-Saxon Protestant.

wats wide area telecommunications (telephone) service.

Watts Watts' Reports (West Virginia); Watts' Reports (Pennsylvania).

Watts & Serg Watts and Sergeant's Reports (Pennsylvania).

W Austl Ind Gaz Western Australia Industrial Gazette.

W Austl JP Western Australia Justice of the Peace.

W Austl LR Western Australia Law Reports.

Wayne L Rev Wayne University Law Review.

WB, wb World Bank; Weather Bureau; warehouse book; waybill; will be; westbound; weight and balance; weight bearing; whole blood.

WBA World Boxing Association.

WBC, wbc World Boxing Council; white blood cell count.

Webb Webb's Reports (Texas); Webb's Reports (Kansas).

Webb A'B & W Webb, A'Beckett and Williams' Reports (Victoria).

Webb & D Webb and Duval's Reports (Texas)

wbf wood burning fireplace.

wbi will be issued.

W Bl William Blackstone's King's Bench Reports (England).

wbs without benefit of salvage; whole body shower.

WC, wc World Court; will call; without charge; working capital; ward clerk; workers compensation; water closet; wheel chair; white cell.

w/c wheel chair.

W&C Wilson and Courtenay's Appeal Cases.

wca worst case analysis.

WCC, wcc Workmen's Compensation Cases (England); Washington's Cases Circuit Court Reports; World Council of Churches; white cell count.

WC&IR Workmen's Compensation and Insurance Reports (England).

WC Ins Rep Workmen's Compensation and Insurance Reports.

WCLJ Workmen's Compensation Law Journal.

W Coast Rep West Coast Reporter.

WC Ops Workmen's Compensation Opinions.

WC Rep Workmen's Compensation Reports.

WCT World Championship Tennis.

wd withdrawn; widow; when discovered; when distributed; wind force; war damage; wound; well developed.

WDALA Western Dakota Association of Legal Assistants.

wds wounds.

wdt width.

wdwn well developed, well nourished.

we week ending; wage earner.

WEAL Women's Equity Action League.

Webs Pat Cas Webster's Patent Cases (England).

Week Cin LB Weekly Cincinnati Law Bulletin (Ohio).

Week Dig Weekly Digest (New York).

Week Jur Weekly Jurist (Illinois).

Week L Gaz or **Week Law Gaz** Weekly Law Gazette (Ohio).

Week L Rec Weekly Law Record.

Week L Bull Weekly Law Bulletin (Ohio).

Week No Weekly Notes of Cases (Pennsylvania); Weekly Notes of Cases (England).

Week Rep Weekly Reporter (England).

Week Trans Rep Weekly Transcript Reports (New York).

Week LR Weekly Law Reports (England).

Weekly Notes Weekly Notes of Law Reports (England).

Welfare L Bull Welfare Law Bulletin.

Welfare L News Welfare Law News.

Welsb H&G Welsby, Hurlstone and Gordon's Exchequer Reports (England).

Welsh Welsh's Registry Cases (Ireland).

Wend Wendell's Reports (New York).

Wenz Wenzell's Reports (Minnesota).

Wes CLJ Westmorland County Law Journal.

West West Publishing Company; Weston's Reports (Vermont); West's Chancery Reports (England).

West Aust Western Australian Reports.

West Ch or **West Chy** West's Chancery Reports (England).

Western Ont L Rev Western Ontario Law Review.

Western Res L Rev Western Reserve Law Review.

West HL West's House of Lords Reports (England).

West Jur Western Jurist (Des Moines, Iowa).

West L Gaz Western Law Gazette (Ohio).

West Law J Western Law Journal.

West LM or **West Law Mo** Western Law Monthly (Ohio).

West Legal Obs Western Legal Observer.

West LR Western Law Reporter (Canada).

West L Rev Western Law Review.

Westm Westminster.

Westm LJ Westmorland (County) Law Journal (Pennsylvania).

West Ont L Rev Western Ontario Law Review.

West R Western Reporter.

West Res L Rev Western Reserve Law Review.

West School L Rev Western School Law Review.

West St UL Rev Western State University Law Review.

West t Hardw West's Chancery Reports temp. Hardwicke (England).

Weston Weston's Reports (Vermont).

West Va West Virginia.

West Week Rep Western Weekly Reports (Canada).

Weth Wethey's Queen's Bench Reports (Upper Canada).

wf white female.

wfp wearout failure period.

WFTU World Federation of Trade Unions.

WG, wg West Germany; wire gauge; weight guaranteed.

WGA Weekly Government Abstracts.

wgt weight.

Wh, WH, wh Wheaton's United States Supreme Court Reports; Wheaton's International Law; Wharton's Reports (Pennsylvania); White House; work hour; watt hour; water heater; withholding; wound healing; walking heel; Werdnig Hoffmann.

WH&G Welsby, Hurlstone and Gordon's Exchequer Reports (England).

Whar Law Dic Wharton's Law Dictionary.

Whart Wharton's Reports (Pennsylvania).

Whart St Tr Wharton's State Trials.

wh av when available.

WH Cas Wage and Hour Cases (Bureau of National Affairs).

Wheat Wheaton's United States Supreme Court Reports.

Wheel Wheeler's Criminal Cases (New York); Wheelock's Reports (Texas).

Wheel Abr Wheeler's Abridgment.

Wheel CC or **Wheel Cr Cas** Wheeler's Criminal Cases (New York).

whf wharf.

whfg wharfage.

White White's Reports (Texas); White's Reports (West Virginia); White's Justiciary Cases (Scotland).

White & T Lead Cas Eq White and Tudor's Leading Cases in Equity (England).

White & W White and Webb's Victorian Reports (Australia); White and Wilson's Civil Cases (Texas).

Whitm Lib Cas Whitman's Libel Cases (Massachusetts).

Whit Pat Cas Whitman's Patent Cases.

Whitt Whittlesey's Reports (Missouri).

Whittier LR Whittier Law Review.

WH Man Wage and Hour Manual (Bureau of National Affairs).

WHO, who World Health Organization; wrist hand orthosis.

whol wholesale.

whp whirlpool.

WHR, whr Wage and Hour Reporter; watt hour.

WHR Man Wage and Hour Reference Manual (Bureau of National Affairs).

whse warehouse.

whsle wholesale.

whsmn warehouseman.

WHTC Western Hemisphere Trade Corporation.

WI, wi Wisconsin; West Indies; when issued; wrought iron; within.

w&i weighing and inspection.

wia wounded in action.

Wight Wight's Cases (Scotland).

Wightw Wightwick's Exchequer Reports (England).

wii work information inventory.

Wilc Cond Wilcox's Condensed Reports (Ohio).

Wilcox Wilcox's Lackawanna Reports (Pennsylvania); Wilcox's Reports (Ohio).

Wilk Wilkinson's Court of Appeals and Civil Appeals (Texas).

Will Williams' Reports (Massachusetts); Wilson's Reports (Texas)..

Willamette LJ Willamette Law Journal.

Willes Willes' Common Pleas Reports (England).

Williams Williams's Reports (Vermont); Williams' Reports (Massachusetts); Williams' Reports (Utah).

Williams & Bruce Ad Pr Williams and Bruce's Admiralty Practice.

Williams P or **Will P** Perre-Williams' Chancery Reports (England).

Will LJ Willamette Law Journal.

Willm W&D Willmore, Wollaston, and Davison's Queen's Bench Reports (England).

Willm W&H Willmore, Wollaston, and Hodges's Queen's Bench Reports (England).

Will Mass Williams' Reports (Massachusetts).

Will P or **Williams P** Perre-Williams' Chancery Reports (England).

Willson Willson's Civil Cases (Texas).

Willson Civ Cas Ct App Willson's Civil Cases (Texas)

Will Vt Williams' Reports (Vermont).

Will W&D Willmore, Wollaston, and Davison's Queen's Bench Reports (England).

Will W&H or **Willm Woll & Hodge** Willmore, Wollaston, and Hodges's Queen's Bench Reports (England).

Wilm Wilmot's Notes (England).

Wils Wilson's King's Bench Reports (England); Wilson's Common Pleas Reports (England). See also Wilson.

Wils & C Wilson and Courtenay's Appeal Cases.

Wils & S Wilson and Shaw's Appeal Cases (Scotland).

Wils Ch Wilson's Chancery Reports (England).

Wils CP Wilson's Common Pleas Reports (England).

Wils Exch Wilson's Exchequer Reports (England).

Wils Ind Wilson's Reports (Indiana).

Wils KB Wilson's King's Bench Reports (England).

Wils Minn Wilson's Reports (Minnesota).

Wilson Wilson's Reports (Indiana); Wilson's Reports (Minnesota); Wilson's Reports (Oregon); Wilson's Reports (England).

Wils Oreg Wilson's Reports (Oregon).

Wils PC Wilson's Privy Council Reports (England).

Win, WIN Winston's Reports (North Carolina); Winer's Unreported Opinions (New York); Winch's Common Pleas Reports (England); Work Incentive Program; Whip Inflation Now.

Winch Winch's Common Pleas Reports (England).

Win Eq Winston's Equity Reports (North Carolina).

Winst Winston's Reports (North Carolina).

wip work in progress.

WIPO World Intellectual Property Organization.

Wis, wis Wisconsin Reports (2d: Second Series); ward initiation scale.

Wis Admin Code Wisconsin Administrative Code.

Wis Admin Reg Wisconsin Administrative Register.

Wis B Bull Wisconsin Bar Bulletin.

Wis BTA Wisconsin Board of Tax Appeals.

Wis LN Wisconsin Legal News.

Wis L Rev Wisconsin Law Review.

Wis Legis Serv Wisconsin Legislative Service.

Wis Stat Ann Wisconsin Statutes Annotated.

Wis Stud BJ Wisconsin Student Bar Journal.

Withrow Withrow's Reports (Iowa).

WJC World Jewish Congress.

W Jo William Jones' King's Bench Reports (England).

wk well known; week.

W Kel William Kelynge's Chancery Reports (England).

wkf well known fact.

Wkly See Weekly.

Wkly Dig Weekly Digest (New York).

wl workload; water line; work load; weight loss; wave length; waiting list.

WLAA Washington Legal Assistants Association.

WLB Weekly Law Bulletin (Ohio).

WLC Western legislative Conference.

WLDF Women's Legal Defense Fund.

WLF, wlf World Law Fund; welfare.

WLG Weekly Law Gazette (Ohio).

WLJ Western Law Journal.

WL Jour Weekly Law Journal.

WLM, wlm Western Law Monthly; work level month.

WLR Wisconsin Law Review; Western Law Reporter; Weekly Law Reports (England);

Washington Law Reporter (District of Columbia).

WLSP World List of Scientific Periodicals.

WLT, wlt Western Law Times; weighing less than; whole lung tomography.

wm watermark; white male; weight/measurement.

W&M Woodbury and Minot's Circuit Court Reports.

Wm & Mary L Rev William and Mary Law Review.

Wm Bl See W Bl.

WMI Wildlife Management Institute.

wmk watermark.

W&M L Rev William and Mary Law Review.

wmm white married male.

Wm Mitchell L Rev William Mitchell Law Review.

Wm Rob William Robinson's Admiralty Reports (England).

Wms Williams.

Wms Mass Williams' Reports (Massachusetts).

Wms Perre Perre-Williams' Chancery Reports (England).

Wms Vt Williams' Reports (Vermont).

WN, wn Weekly Notes (England); work notice; well nourished.

wnd wound.

W New Eng L Rev Western New England Law Review.

wng warning.

wnl within normal limits.

WNYPA Western New York Paralegal Association.

wo write off; warrant officer; work order; women; without; war office; wash out.

w/o without; written order; water in oil.

WOAR Women Organized Against Rape.

wob washed overboard.

woc without compensation.

wog water, oil, gas; with other goods.

Wol, wol Wollaston's Bail Court

Reports (England); Wolcott's Chancery Reports (Vermont); wharf owner's liability.

Wolf & B Wolferstan and Bristow's Election Cases (England).

Wolf & D Wolferstan and Dew's Election Cases (England).

Woll Wollaston's Bail Court Reports (England).

Wol Pr Wallston's Bail Court Reports, Practice Cases (England).

Women Law J Women Lawyer's Journal.

Women's Rights L Rptr Women's Rights Law Reporter.

W Ont L Rev Western Ontario Law Review.

Wood & M Woodbury and Minot's Circuit Court Reports.

Woods Wood's Circuit Court Reports.

Woodw Woodworth's Decisions (Pennsylvania); Woolworth's Reports (Nebraska).

Wool Woolworth's Circuit Court Reports.

wop without penalty; without priority; without passport; without pain.

Work Comp L Rev Workmen's Compensation Law Review.

wow written order of withdrawal.

WP, wp Warsaw Pact; without prejudice; word processing; waterproof; weather permitting; weight penalty; wire payment; whirlpool.

WPA, wpa Works Progress Administration; with particular average.

wpb whirlpool bath.

WPC Women's Political Caucus.

WPFM Wright peak flow meter.

WPI, wpi World Patent Index; wholesale price index.

wpm words per minute.

wpn weapon.

WPPDA Welfare and Pension Plans Disclosure Act.

wps water purification system.

WPTLC World Peace Through Law Center.

WPW Wolff-Parkinson-White (syndrome).

wqi water quality index.

WR, wr Wisconsin Reports; Weekly Reporter; Weekly Reports; with rights; with respect to; war risk; warehouse receipt; washroom; work rate; wrist; weak response; weakly reactive; Wassermann reaction.

W Rep West's Chancery Reports temp. Hardwicke (England).

W Res L Rev Western Reserve Law Review.

wrfg wharfage.

Wright Wright's Reports (Ohio) (NP: Nisi Prius); Wright's Reports (Pennsylvania).

wrn warning.

wrnt warrant.

WRO, wro Water Rights Office; work release order; war risks only.

W Rob William Robinson's Admiralty Reports (England).

wrt with respect to.

WS, ws Western Samoa; work stoppage; withholding statement; working storage; weather station; water soluble.

W&S Watts and Sergeant's Reports (Pennsylvania); Wilson and Shaw's Appeal Cases (Scotland).

WSJ Wall Street Journal.

WSPF Watergate Special Prosecution Force.

W St UL Rev Western State University Law Review.

wt warrant; weight; watertight.

WTALA West Texas Association of Legal Assistants.

WTBR War Trade Board Rulings.

wth width.

wthr weather.

wtn witness.

W Ty Washington Territory Reports.

w/u work up.

WUAR Women United Against Rape.

WV, wv West Virginia; wind velocity; weight, volume.

W Va West Virginia Reports.

W Va Acts Acts of the Legislature of West Virginia.

W Va Crim Just Rev Weat Virginia Criminal Justice Review.

W Va Code West Virginia Code.

W Va LQ Weat Virginia Law Quarterly.

W Va L Rev West Virginia Law Review.

wvd waived.

WVLA Willamette Valley Legal Assistants.

ww with warrants; worldwide; warehouse warrant.

W&W White and Webb's Victorian Reports (Australia); White and Wilson's Civil Cases (Texas).

wwa with the will annexed.

WW&D Willmore, Wollaston, and Davison's Queen's Bench Reports (England).

WW&H Willmore, Wollaston, and Hodges's Queen's Bench Reports (England).

WWF World Wildlife Fund.

WW Harr W.W. Harrington's Reports (Delaware).

WWR Western Weekly Reports (NS: New Series) (Canada).

wwts waste water treatment system.

WxB wax pattern.

WxP wax bite.

Wy Wyoming Reports; Wythe's Chancery Reports (Virginia).

Wyo LJ Wyoming Law Journal.

Wyo T Wyoming Territory.

wysiwyg what you see is what you get.

Wythe Wythe's Chancery Reports (Virginia).

Wy & W Wyatt and Webb's Reports (Victoria).

Wy W & A'Beck Wyatt, Webb and A'Beckett Reports (Victoria).

x extra; exchange; extension; extremity; times; exposure; ten; except; x-ray; female sex chromosome.

Xam examination.

XC, xc ex-coupon; excretory cystogram.

x-d ex (without) dividend.

Xe xenon.

x factor unidentified factor.

xh extra high.

x-i ex (without) interest.

xing crossing.

xip x-ray in plaster.

xl excess lactate; extra large.

xm crossmatch.

Xn Christian.

xo xanthine oxidase.

xop x-ray out of plaster.

xpl explosive.

xpn expansion.

xpr ex (without) privileges.

xps x-ray photoemission spectroscopy.

xr or **xrt** ex (without) rights.

xs extra small; cross section.

xu excretory urogram.

xw ex (without) warrant.

xx double strength female chromosome type.

xy male chromosome type.

Xyl xylose

Y, y Yeates Reports (Pennsylvania); Yearbook; YMCA; Yukon; yttrium; yield; year; yard; male sex chromosome.

ya young adult.

YAD Young's Admiralty Decisions (Nova Scotia).

YAF Young Americans for Freedom.

yag yttrium aluminum garnet.

Y&J Younge & Jervis' Exchequer Reports (England).

Yale J World Pub Order Yale Journal of World Public Order.

Yale LJ Yale Law Journal.

Yale Rev Law & Soc Act Yale Review of Law and Social Action.

Yale Stud World Pub Order Yale Studies in World Public Order.

Y&C or **Y&CCC** Younge & Collyer's Chancery Reports (England).

Y&C Ex Younge & Collyer's Exchequer in Equity Reports (England).

Yates Sel Cas Yates' Select Cases (New York).

YB, Yb Yearbook; ytterbium.

YBASL Yearbook of Air & Space Law.

YB Eur Conv on Hum Rts Yearbook of the European Convention on Human Rights.

YB Intl L Comm Yearbook of the International Law Commission.

YB League Yearbook of the League of Nations.

YB Sch L Yearbook of School Law.

YBUN Yearbook of the United Nations.

yc yacht club.

Y&C or **Y&CCC** Younge & Collyer's Chancery Reports (England).

Y&C Ex Younge & Collyer's Exchequer in Equity Reports (England).

Ychrom male sex chromosome.

YCL Young Communist League.

yd yard.

yd² square yard.

YE, ye Yemen; yeast extract.

Yea or **Yeates** Yeates' Reports (Pennsylvania).

Yearbook of WA Yearbook of World Affairs.

yeg yeast extract glucose.

Yel or **Yelv** Yelverton's King's Bench Reports (England).

yf yellow fever.

J&J Younge & Jervis' Exchequer Reports (England).

yk york.

yl yellow.

YLJ Yale Law Journal.

YLR York Legal Record (Pennsylvania).

YMCA Young Men's Christian Association.

YMHA Young Men's Hebrew Association.

Yo, yo Younge's Exchequer in Equity Reports (England); years old.

yob year of birth.

yod year of death.

yom year of marriage.

York Leg Rec York Legal Record (Pennsylvania).

Yorke Ass Yorke Assizes (Clayton).

You Younge's Exchequer in Equity Reports (England).

You & Jerv Younge & Jervis' Exchequer Reports (England).

Young Young's Reports (Minnesota).

Young Adm Dec Young's Vice Admiralty Decisions (Nova Scotia).

Young Naut Dict Young's Nautical Decisions.

Younge & Coll Younge & Collyer's Chancery Reports (England).

Younge & Coll Ex Younge & Collyer's Exchequer in Equity Reports (England).

Younge Exch Younge's Exchequer in Equity Reports (England).

Younge & Jerv Younge & Jervis' Exchequer Reports (England).

Younge ML Cas Younge Maritime Law Cases (England).

yp yield pressure.

yr year.

Yrbk Sch Law Yearbook of School Law.

yrly yearly.

ys yolk sac.

Yt yttrium.

ytd year to date.

ytm yield to maturity.

Yug Yugoslavia.

Yugos L Yugoslav Law.

yuppie young urban professional.

YWCA Young Women's Christian Association.

YWHA Young Women's Hebrew Association.

ZßQuickKeys

Z, z Zambia; Zimbabwe; Zaire; azimuth angle; zero; zinc; zone; no effect.

Zab Zabriskie Reports (New Jersey).

Zam LJ Zambia Law Journal.

Zane Zane's Reports (Utah).

ZBA Zoning Board of Approval.

zbb zero based budgeting.

zd zenith distance; zero defects; zero discharge.

zdc zinc die casting.

ZE Zollinger-Ellison (syndrome).

zeg zero economic growth.

zf zero frequency.

zip zone improvement plan; zoster immune plasma.

zma zinc metaarsenite.

Zn azimuth; zinc.

zpg zero population growth.

ZnO zinc oxide.

ZPO zinc peroxide.

ZR, zr Zaire; zirconium.

zt zone time.

zzv zero, zero visibility.

I N D E X

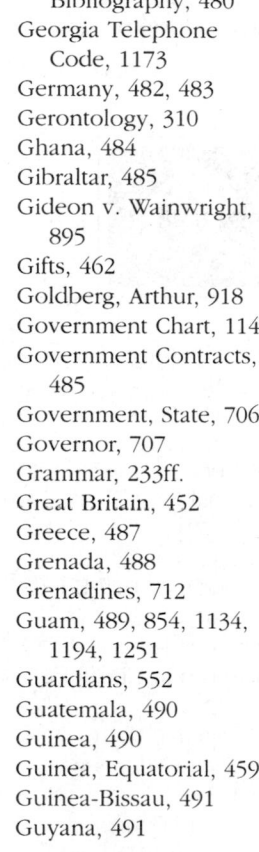